Frommer's®

Europe

11th Edition

D0018348

Wiley Publishing, Inc.

Published by:
WILEY PUBLISHING, INC.
111 River St.
Hoboken, NJ 07030-5774

Copyright © 2010 Wiley Publishing, Inc., Hoboken, New Jersey. All rights reserved. No part of this publication may be reproduced, stored in a retrieval system or transmitted in any form or by any means, electronic, mechanical, photocopying, recording, scanning or otherwise, except as permitted under Sections 107 or 108 of the 1976 United States Copyright Act, without either the prior written permission of the Publisher, or authorization through payment of the appropriate per-copy fee to the Copyright Clearance Center, 222 Rosewood Drive, Danvers, MA 01923, 978/750-8400, fax 978/646-8600. Requests to the Publisher for permission should be addressed to the Permissions Department, John Wiley & Sons, Inc., 111 River Street, Hoboken, NJ 07030, 201/748-6011, fax 201/748-6008, or online at http://www.wiley.com/go/permissions.

Wiley and the Wiley Publishing logo are trademarks or registered trademarks of John Wiley & Sons, Inc. and/or its affiliates. Frommer's is a trademark or registered trademark of Arthur Frommer. Used under license. All other trademarks are the property of their respective owners. Wiley Publishing, Inc. is not associated with any product or vendor mentioned in this book.

ISBN 978-0-470-63232-1 (paper); 978-0-470-90468-8 (ebk); 978-0-470-93120-2 (ebk); 978-0-470-93117-2 (ebk)

Editor: Michael Kelly, with Christine Ryan
Production Editor: Eric T. Schroeder
Cartographer: Elizabeth Puhl
Photo Editor: Richard Fox
Production by Wiley Indianapolis Composition Services
Front cover photo: ©SIME / eStock Photo
Back cover photo: ©Alex Segre / Alamy Images

For information on our other products and services or to obtain technical support, please contact our Customer Care Department within the U.S. at 877/762-2974, outside the U.S. at 317/572-3993 or fax 317/572-4002.

Wiley also publishes its books in a variety of electronic formats. Some content that appears in print may not be available in electronic formats.

Manufactured in the United States of America

5 4 3 2 1

CONTENTS

17 SPAIN 889

18 SWEDEN 968

19 SWITZERLAND 994

Index 1041

LIST OF MAPS

LIST OF MAPS

ABOUT THE AUTHORS

As a team of veteran travel writers, **Darwin Porter** and **Danforth Prince** have produced dozens of previous titles for Frommer's, including many of their guides to Europe, the Caribbean, Bermuda, The Bahamas, and parts of America's Deep South. A film critic, columnist, and radio broadcaster, Porter is also a noted biographer of Hollywood celebrities, garnering critical acclaim for overviews of the life and times of, among others, Marlon Brando, Katharine Hepburn, Howard Hughes, and Michael Jackson. Prince was formerly employed by the Paris bureau of the *New York Times,* and is today the president of www.BloodMoonProductions.com. In 2008, Porter and Prince collaborated on the release of their newest book about Hollywood, sexuality, and sin as filtered through 85 years of celebrity excess, *Hollywood Babylon-It's Back!*

Mark Baker is a long-time American expat who lives in Prague. He's one of the original editors of *The Prague Post* and was for years a correspondent and editor for Radio Free Euorpe/Radio Liberty, based in Prague. He's now a freelance writer and reporter. He's the author of *Frommer's Prague Day by Day,* and coauthor of *Frommer's Eastern Europe* and *Frommer's Poland.*

George McDonald has lived and worked in both Amsterdam and Brussels as deputy editor of the KLM in-flight magazine and as editor-in-chief of the Sabena in-flight magazine. Now a freelance journalist and travel writer, he has written extensively on both the Netherlands and Belgium for magazines and guidebooks. He's the author of *Frommer's Amsterdam, Frommer's Belgium, Holland & Luxembourg,* and a coauthor of *Frommer's Europe by Rail.*

Sherry Marker's love of Greece began when she majored in classical Greek at Harvard. She has studied at the American School of Classical Studies in Athens and ancient history at the University of California at Berkeley. Author or coauthor of a number of Frommer's guides to Greece, she has published articles in the *New York Times, Travel + Leisure,* and *Hampshire Life.*

Dr. Ryan James was born and raised in Long Branch, New Jersey. He earned his doctorate in education from the University of San Francisco, and has taught English at ELTE University in Budapest since 2002. He and his partner own BudaBaB, a bed and breakfast on the Pest side.

Christi Daugherty is an expat American living in London. A former journalist, she's the author of several travel books including *Frommer's Ireland 2007* and *Frommer's Paris Day by Day.* She also co-wrote *Frommer's MTV Ireland* and *Frommer's MTV Europe.* She learned everything she knows about Ireland accidentally, while getting lost repeatedly over the course of many years. She likes to think that she gets lost so you don't have to. On a recent trip, she stumbled across the ruins of the castle her family left behind when they fled Ireland in the 17th century, with the English hot on their trail. There wasn't much left of it. In her spare time she writes unpublished mystery novels.

HOW TO CONTACT US

In researching this book, we discovered many wonderful places—hotels, restaurants, shops, and more. We're sure you'll find others. Please tell us about them, so we can share the information with your fellow travelers in upcoming editions. If you were disappointed with a recommendation, we'd love to know that, too. Please write to:

Frommer's Europe, 11th Edition
Wiley Publishing, Inc. • 111 River St. • Hoboken, NJ 07030-5774

AN ADDITIONAL NOTE

Please be advised that travel information is subject to change at any time—and this is especially true of prices. We therefore suggest that you write or call ahead for confirmation when making your travel plans. The authors, editors, and publisher cannot be held responsible for the experiences of readers while traveling. Your safety is important to us, however, so we encourage you to stay alert and be aware of your surroundings. Keep a close eye on cameras, purses, and wallets, all favorite targets of thieves and pickpockets.

FROMMER'S STAR RATINGS, ICONS & ABBREVIATIONS

Every hotel, restaurant, and attraction listing in this guide has been ranked for quality, value, service, amenities, and special features using a **star-rating system.** In country, state, and regional guides, we also rate towns and regions to help you narrow down your choices and budget your time accordingly. Hotels and restaurants are rated on a scale of zero (recommended) to three stars (exceptional). Attractions, shopping, nightlife, towns, and regions are rated according to the following scale: zero stars (recommended), one star (highly recommended), two stars (very highly recommended), and three stars (must-see).

In addition to the star-rating system, we also use **seven feature icons** that point you to the great deals, in-the-know advice, and unique experiences that separate travelers from tourists. Throughout the book, look for:

Special finds—those places only insiders know about

Fun facts—details that make travelers more informed and their trips more fun

Best bets for kids and advice for the whole family

Special moments—those experiences that memories are made of

Places or experiences not worth your time or money

Insider tips—great ways to save time and money

Great values—where to get the best deals

The following abbreviations are used for credit cards:

AE	American Express	DISC	Discover	V	Visa
DC	Diners Club	MC	MasterCard		

TRAVEL RESOURCES AT FROMMERS.COM

Frommer's travel resources don't end with this guide. Frommer's website, **www.frommers.com**, has travel information on more than 4,000 destinations. We update features regularly, giving you access to the most current trip-planning information and the best airfare, lodging, and car-rental bargains. You can also listen to podcasts, connect with other Frommers.com members through our active-reader forums, share your travel photos, read blogs from guidebook editors and fellow travelers, and much more.

1

PLANNING YOUR TRIP TO EUROPE

by Darwin Porter & Danforth Prince

The goal of a United States of Europe is still a visionary's dream, in spite of the euro, which binds many nations in a common currency. But even the euro can't link all of the countries of the European Union—"holdouts" remain, such as Denmark, which clings to its kroner, and the British Isles, which are still locked into the traditional pound sterling.

Nonetheless, in a continent where neighbors battled neighbors in two world wars, a great renaissance in art, culture, and economic growth is underway. Most of the nations of Western Europe are cooperating as never before, in spite of the inevitable minor squabble.

Of course, you don't visit Europe to fret over their economies and politics. The rich culture and history in each of its myriad countries and regions have always been the lure, and they remain so today. From the splendor of a walled hill town rising above the verdant Tuscan landscape to the majestic snowcapped peaks of the Alps, from the sound of flamenco in a Madrid *tablaos* (flamenco nightclub) to the blasting of a brass band in Munich's Hofbraühaus—no other place exists where you can experience such enormous cultural changes by driving from one mountain valley to the next, where in just a few miles or kilometers you're likely to encounter not only a completely different language but also different food, architecture, and culture.

Europe has seen some of the greatest intellectual and artistic developments the world has ever known, and the landscape is dense with museums, cathedrals, palaces, and monuments serving as repositories for much of this past glory. But artistic and cultural ferment are still very much part of the present, and Europe helps set the trends in fashion, industrial design, cinema, technology, music, literature, and science. The dynamic environment is all about life, innovation, entertainment, and food, which exist side by side with the artistic and cultural grandeur of the past.

Europe

0
150 mi
0
150 km
N
Norwegian Sea
SHETLAND ISLANDS
Bergen
ORKNEY ISLANDS
NORWAY
GRAMPIAN
Aberdeen
TAYSIDE
Perth
Glasgow
North Sea
Edinburgh
Belfast
DENMARK
IRELAND
Dingle Peninsula
Dublin
COUNTY KERRY
Liverpool
U.K.
ATLANTIC OCEAN
COTSWOLDS
Oxford
Bath
Stonehenge
London
Salisbury
THE NETHERLANDS
Hamburg
Amsterdam
GERMANY
Bruges
English Channel
Ghent
Brussels
Bonn
BELGIUM
Liège
Frankfurt am Main
Le Havre
LUX.
Rothenburg ob der Tauber
Paris
Strasbourg
LOIRE VALLEY
Augsburg
Bay of Biscay
FRANCE
Bern
Innsbruck
SWITZERLAND
Geneva
BERNESE OBERLAND
Bordeaux
Milan
Avignon
Bilbao
Arles
PROVENCE
Porto
Marseille
Nice
MONACO
Florence
TUSCANY
Siena
Côte d'Azur
ANDORRA
PORTUGAL
Madrid
Barcelona
Lisbon
SPAIN
CORSICA (France)
Valencia
BALEARIC ISLANDS
ALGARVE
Seville
Córdoba
SARDINIA (Italy)
ANDALUCÍA
Granada
Malaga
Cagliari
Costa del Sol
Mediterranean Sea
Algiers
Oran
Rabat
Tunis
Casablanca
MOROCCO
ALGERIA
TUNISIA

FINLAND
SWEDEN
Gulf of Bothnia
Sundsvall
Tampere
Gävle
Helsinki
St. Petersburg
Oslo
RUSSIA
Tallinn
Stockholm
ESTONIA
Göteborg
Moscow
Riga
LATVIA
Baltic Sea
Copenhagen
LITHUANIA
Vilnius
RUSSIA
Kaliningrad
Minsk
Gdansk
BELARUS
Berlin
Poznan
Warsaw
POLAND
Leipzig
Kiev
Karlovy Vary (Carlsbad)
Prague
Krakow
L'viv
UKRAINE
CZECH REPUBLIC
SLOVAKIA
Munich
Vienna
Bratislava
Danube
MOLDOVA
BAVARIAN ALPS
Salzburg
DANUBE VALLEY
Budapest
Chisinau
Odessa
KITZBÜHEL ALPS
AUSTRIA
HUNGARY
Cluj-Napoca
Lake Balaton
Ljubljana
ROMANIA
SLOVENIA
Zagreb
CROATIA
Venice
Belgrade
Bucharest
Constanta
Black Sea
BOSNIA AND HERZEGOVINA
Sarajevo
Varna
SERBIA
BULGARIA
Assisi
Adriatic Sea
Sofia
MONTENEGRO
ITALY
Skopje
Podgorica
Istanbul
Rome
REPUBLIC OF MACEDONIA
Ankara
Tirana
Naples
Pompeii
ALBANIA
TURKEY
Tyrrhenian Sea
GREECE
Aegean Sea
Izmir
Ionian Sea
Delphi
Athens
CYCLADES
Palermo
SICILY
PELOPONNESE
CYPRUS
RHODES
CRETE
MALTA

Europe is also about people. Europeans have seen the best and the worst of times, and a better-educated, more-sophisticated younger generation is waiting to welcome you. They're as diverse and fascinating as the lands they come from, and throughout this book we've noted places not only where you'll meet other visitors but also where you'll have a chance to meet and chat with the locals.

Irresistible and intriguing, the ever-changing Europe of the 21st century offers you more excitement, experiences, and memories than ever. In compiling this book, we've tried to open the door to Europe's famous cities (their art and architecture, restaurants and theater, hotels and history) and guide you to all the experiences no one would want to miss on even a cursory visit. So though this guide has to point out the highlights, we've also tossed in offbeat destinations and adventurous suggestions leading to surprises and delights around every corner.

This introductory chapter is designed to equip you with what you need to know before you go—the advance-planning tools for an enjoyable and successful trip.

WHEN TO GO

Europe has a Continental climate with distinct seasons, but there are great variations in temperature from one part to another. Northern Norway is plunged into arctic darkness in winter, but in sunny Sicily the climate is usually temperate—though snow can fall even on the Greek Islands in winter, and winter nights are cold anywhere. Europe is north of most of the United States, but along the Mediterranean are weather patterns more along the lines of the U.S. southern states. In general, however, seasonal changes are less extreme than in most of the United States.

The **high season** lasts from mid-May to mid-September, with the most tourists hitting the Continent from mid-June to August. In general, this is the most expensive time to travel, except in Austria and Switzerland, where prices are actually higher in winter during the ski season. And because Scandinavian hotels depend on business clients instead of tourists, you can often find lower prices in the fleeting summer, when business clients vacation and a smaller number of tourists take over.

You'll find smaller crowds, relatively fair weather, and often lower prices at hotels in the **shoulder seasons,** from Easter to mid-May and mid-September to October. **Off season** (except at ski resorts) is from November to Easter, with the exception of December 25 to January 6. Much of Europe, Italy especially, takes August off, and August 15 to August 30 is vacation time for many locals, so expect the cities to be devoid of natives but the beaches packed.

Weather

BRITAIN & IRELAND It rains a lot in Britain and Ireland, but winters are rainier than summers; the sunniest period is from August to mid-October. Summer daytime temperatures average from the low 60s Fahrenheit (mid-teens Celsius) to the mid-60s (upper teens Celsius), dropping to the 40s (single digits Celsius) on winter nights. Ireland, whose shores are bathed by the Gulf Stream, has a milder climate. The Scottish Lowlands have a climate similar to England's, but the Highlands are much colder, with storms and snow in winter.

CENTRAL EUROPE In Vienna and along the Danube Valley the climate is moderate. Summer daytime temperatures average in the low 70s Fahrenheit (low

WHAT TIME IS IT, anyway?

Britain, Ireland, and Portugal are 5 hours ahead of New York City (U.S. Eastern Standard Time); Greece is 7 hours ahead of New York. The rest of the countries in this book are 6 hours ahead of New York. For instance, when it's noon in New York, it's 5pm in London and Lisbon; 6pm in Paris, Copenhagen, and Amsterdam; and 7pm in Athens. The European countries now observe daylight saving time. The time change doesn't usually occur on the same day or during the same month as in North America.

If you plan to travel to Ireland or continental Europe from Britain, keep in mind that the time will be the same in Ireland and Portugal, 2 hours later in Greece, and 1 hour later in the other countries in this guide.

20s Celsius), falling at night to the low 50s (low teens Celsius). Winter temperatures are in the 30s Fahrenheit (btw. –1 and +4 degrees Celsius) and 40s (4–9 degrees Celsius) during the day. In Budapest, temperatures can reach 80°F (27°C) in August and dip to 30°F (–1°C) in January. Winter is damp and chilly, spring is mild, and May and June are usually wet. The best weather is in the late summer through October. In Prague and Bohemia, summer months have an average temperature of 65°F (18°C) but are the rainiest, while January and February are usually sunny and clear, with temperatures around freezing.

FRANCE & GERMANY The weather in Paris is approximately the same as in the U.S. mid-Atlantic states, but as in most of Europe, there's less extreme variation. In summer, the temperature rarely goes above the mid-70s Fahrenheit (mid-20s Celsius). Winters tend to be mild, in the 40s Fahrenheit (4–9 degrees Celsius). It's warmer along the Riviera year-round. Germany's climate ranges from moderate summers and chilly, damp winters in the north to mild summers and very cold, sunny winters in the alpine south.

NORTHERN EUROPE In the Netherlands, the weather is never extreme at any time of year. Summer temperatures average around 67°F (19°C) and the winter average is about 40°F (4°C). The climate is rainy, with the driest months from February to May. From mid-April to mid-May, the tulip fields burst into color. The climate of northern Germany is very similar. Belgium's climate is moderate, varying from an average of 73°F (23°C) in July and August to an average of 40°F (4°C) in December and January. It does rain a lot, but the weather is at its finest in July and August.

SCANDINAVIA Above the Arctic Circle, summer temperatures average around the mid-50s Fahrenheit (low teens Celsius), dropping to around 14°F (–10°C) during the dark winters. In the south, summer temperatures average around 70°F (21°C), dropping to the 20s Fahrenheit (below 0 Celsius) in winter. Fjords and even the ocean are often warm enough for summer swimming, but rain is frequent. The sun shines 24 hours in midsummer above the Arctic Circle; winter brings semipermanent twilight. Denmark's climate is relatively mild by comparison. It has moderate summer temperatures and winters that can be damp and foggy, with temperatures just above the mid-30s Fahrenheit (single digits Celsius).

SOUTHERN EUROPE Summers are hot in Italy, Spain, and Greece, with temperatures around the high 80s Fahrenheit (low 30s Celsius) or even higher in some parts of Spain. Along the Italian Riviera, summer and winter temperatures are mild, and except in the alpine regions, Italian winter temperatures rarely drop below freezing. The area around Madrid is dry and arid, and summers in Spain are coolest along the Atlantic coast, with mild temperatures year-round on the Costa del Sol. Seaside Portugal is very rainy but has temperatures of 50°F to 75°F (10°C–24°C) year-round. In Greece there's sunshine all year, and winters are usually mild, with temperatures around 50°F to 54°F (10°C–12°C). Hot summer temperatures are often helped by cool breezes. The best seasons to visit Greece are from mid-April to June and mid-September to late October, when the wildflowers bloom and the tourists go home.

SWITZERLAND & THE ALPS The alpine climate is shared by Bavaria in southern Germany and the Austrian Tyrols and Italian Dolomites—winters are cold and bright, and spring comes late, with snow flurries well into April. Summers are mild and sunny, though the alpine regions can experience dramatic changes in weather any time of year.

Europe Calendar of Events

For an exhaustive list of events beyond those listed here, check http://events.frommers.com, where you'll find a searchable, up-to-the-minute roster of what's happening in cities all over the world.

JANUARY

Epiphany celebrations, Italy, nationwide. All cities, towns, and villages in Italy stage Roman Catholic Epiphany observances. One of the most festive celebrations is the Epiphany Fair at Rome's Piazza Navona. January 6.

FEBRUARY

Carnevale, Venice, Italy. At this riotous time, theatrical presentations and masked balls take place throughout Venice and on the islands in the lagoon. The balls are by invitation only (except the Doge's Ball), but the street events and fireworks are open to everyone. Contact the **Venice Tourist Office,** Apt Venezia, Castello 5050, 30122 Venezia (✆ **041/5298711;** www.turismovenezia.it). The week before Ash Wednesday, the start of Lent.

February Basler Fasnacht, Basel, Switzerland. Called "the wildest of carnivals," with a parade of "cliques" (clubs and associations). Call ✆ **061/268-68-68** or visit www.fasnacht.ch for more information. First Monday after Ash Wednesday.

MARCH

Holmenkollen Ski Festival, Oslo, Norway. This is one of Europe's largest ski festivals, with World Cup Nordic skiing and biathlons and international ski-jumping competitions, all held at Holmenkollen Ski Jump on the outskirts of Oslo. To participate or request more information, contact **Skiforeningen,** Kongeveien 5, Holmenkollen, N-0390 Oslo 3 (✆ **22-92-32-00;** www.skiforeningen.no). Early March.

St. Patrick's Dublin Festival, Dublin, Ireland. This massive 4-day fest is open, free, and accessible to all. Street theater, carnival acts, music, fireworks, and more culminate in Ireland's grandest parade. Call ✆ **01/676-3205,** or go to www.stpatricksday.ie. March 16 to March 19.

Budapest Spring Festival, Budapest, Hungary. For 2 weeks, performances of everything from opera to ballet, from classical music to drama, are held in all the major halls and theaters of Budapest. Simultaneously, temporary exhibitions open in many of Budapest's museums. Tickets are available at 1053 Budapest, Egyetem tér 5

(✆ **36/1-486-3311;** www.festivalcity.hu), and at the individual venues. Mid-March to early April.

APRIL

Semana Santa (Holy Week), Seville, Spain. Although many of the country's smaller towns stage similar celebrations, the festivities in Seville are by far the most elaborate. From Palm Sunday to Easter Sunday, processions with hooded penitents move to the piercing wail of the *saeta,* a love song to the Virgin or Christ. Contact the **Seville Office of Tourism** for details (✆ **95-423-4465;** www.sevilla.org). Ten days before Easter Sunday.

Holy Week observances, Italy, nationwide. Processions and age-old ceremonies—some from pagan days, some from the Middle Ages—are staged. The most notable procession is led by the pope, passing the Colosseum and the Roman Forum up to Palatine Hill; a torch-lit parade caps the observance. Four days before Easter Sunday.

Pasqua (Easter Sunday), Rome, Italy. In an event broadcast around the world, the pope gives his blessing from the balcony of St. Peter's. Easter Sunday.

Feria de Sevilla (Seville Fair), Seville, Spain. This is the most celebrated week of revelry in all of Spain, with all-night flamenco dancing, entertainment booths, bullfights, flower-decked coaches, and dancing in the streets. Reserve your hotel early. Contact the **Seville Office of Tourism** (✆ **95-423-4465;** www.sevilla.org). Second week after Easter.

MAY

Brighton Festival, Brighton, England. The country's largest arts festival features some 400 cultural events. Call ✆ **01273/709-709,** or go to www.brightonfestival.org. Most of May.

Prague Spring Music Festival, Prague, Czech Republic. This world-famous 3-week series of classical music and dance performances brings some of the world's best talent to Prague. For details, call ✆ **420/25731-2547,** or go to www.festival.cz. Mid-May to early June.

Festival International du Film (Cannes Film Festival), Cannes, France. Movie madness transforms this city into a media circus. Reserve early and make a deposit. Admission to the competition itself is by invitation only; however, many screenings are made available to the public and play round-the-clock. Contact the **Festival de Cannes Association Francaise du Festival International du Film,** 3 rue Amélie, 75007 Paris (✆ **01-53-59-61-00;** www.festival-cannes.org). Mid-May.

International Music Festival, Vienna, Austria. This traditional highlight of Vienna's concert calendar features top-class international orchestras, conductors, and classical greats. The venue and booking address is **Wiener Musikverein,** Lothringerstrasse 20, A-1030 Vienna (✆ **01/5058190;** www.musikverein.at). Early May through first 3 weeks of June.

Fiesta de San Isidro, Madrid, Spain. Madrileños run wild with a 10-day celebration honoring their city's patron saint. Food fairs, street parades, parties, dances, bullfights, and other events mark the occasion. Expect crowds and traffic. For details, contact the **Instituto de Turismo de España-Turespaña,** 6 Jose Lázaro Galdiano 2807, Madrid (✆ **91-343-3500;** www.tourspain.es). Mid-May.

Maggio Musicale Fiorentino (Musical May Florentine), Florence, Italy. Italy's oldest and most prestigious music festival emphasizes music from the 14th century to the 20th century but also presents ballet and opera. For schedules and tickets, contact the **Maggio Musicale Fiorentino/Teatro Comunale,** Corso Italia 16, 50123 Firenze (✆ **055-213-535;** www.maggiofiorentino.com). Late April to early June.

Bergen Festspill (Bergen International Festival), Bergen, Norway. This world-class music event features artists from Norway and around the world. Many styles of music are presented, but classical music—especially the work of Grieg—is emphasized. This is one of the largest annual musical events in Scandinavia. Contact the **Bergen International Festival,** Vågsallmenningen 1, 5804, Bergen (✆ **55-21-06-30;** www.fib.no). Mid-May to early June.

Bath International Music Festival, Bath, England. One of Europe's most prestigious international festivals of music and the arts features as many as 1,000 performers at various venues. Contact the **Bath Festivals Trust,** 5 Broad St., Bath, Somerset BA1 5LJ (✆ **01225/463362;** www.bathmusicfest.org.uk). Late May to early June.

JUNE

Hellenic Festival (Athens, Lycabettus, and Epidaurus festivals), Greece. The three festivals are now organized under the umbrella term of Hellenic Festival. The Athens Festival features superb productions of ancient drama, opera, modern dance, ballet, and more in the Odeum of Herodes Atticus, on the southwest side of the Acropolis. The Lycabettus Festival presents performances at the amphitheater on Mount Lycovitos. The Epidaurus Festival presents classic Greek drama in its famous amphitheater. Call ✆ **210/928-2900** or go to www.greekfestival.gr. June to early October.

Festival di Spoleto, Spoleto, Italy. Dating from 1958, this festival was the artistic creation of maestro and world-class composer Gian Carlo Menotti, who died in 2007. International performers convene for 3 weeks of dance, drama, opera, concerts, and art exhibits in this Umbrian hill town. The main focus is music composed from 1300 to 1799. For tickets and details, contact the **Spoleto Festival,** Piazza del Duomo 8, 06049 Spoleto (✆ **0743/221689;** www.festivaldispoleto.com). Late June to mid-July.

Roskilde Festival, Roskilde, Denmark. Europe's biggest rock festival has been going strong for more than 30 years, now bringing about 90,000 revelers each year to the central Zealand town. Besides major rock concerts, scheduled activities include theater and film presentations. Call ✆ **46-36-66-13** or check www.roskilde-festival.dk. Late June to early July.

Il Palio, Siena, Italy. Palio fever grips this Tuscan hill town for a wild and exciting horse race from the Middle Ages. Pageantry, costumes, and the celebrations of the victorious *contrada* (sort of a neighborhood social club) mark the spectacle. For details, contact the **Azienda di Promozione Turistica,** Piazza del Campo 56, 53100 Siena (✆ **0461-839000;** www.ilpalio.org). Late June to mid-August.

JULY

Tour de France, France. Europe's most hotly contested bicycle race pits crews of wind-tunnel-tested athletes along an itinerary that detours deep into the Massif Central and ranges across the Alps. The race is decided at a finish line drawn across the Champs-Elysées. Call ✆ **01-41-33-15-00,** or check www.letour.fr. Month of July.

Karlovy Vary International Film Festival, Karlovy Vary, Czech Republic. This annual 10-day event predates Communism and has regained its "A" rating from the international body governing film festivals, which puts it in the same league as Cannes and Venice but without the star-drawing power of the more glittery stops. For more information, call ✆ **420/221-411-011,** or check www.kviff.com. Early to mid-July.

Montreux International Jazz Festival, Montreux, Switzerland. More than jazz, this festival features everything from reggae bands to African tribal chanters. Monster dance fests also break out nightly. The 2½-week festival concludes with a 12-hour marathon of world music. Write to the **Montreux Jazz Festival,** Case Postale Box 97, CH-1820 Montreux, call ✆ **021/966-44-44,** or check www.montreuxjazz.com. Early July.

Bastille Day, France, nationwide. Celebrating the birth of modern-day France, the nation's festivities reach their peak in Paris with street fairs, pageants, fireworks, and feasts. In Paris, the day begins with a parade down the Champs-Elysées and ends with fireworks at Montmartre. July 14.

Around Gotland Race, Sandhamn, Sweden, The Gotland Runt. The biggest and most exciting open-water Scandinavian sailing race starts and finishes at Sandhamn in the Stockholm archipelago. About 450 boats, mainly from Nordic countries, take part. Contact the **Stockholm Tourist Center** (✆ **08/508-285-00;** www.stockholmtown.com) for information. Two days in mid-July.

The Proms, London, England. A night at The Proms—the annual Henry Wood promenade concerts at Royal Albert Hall—attracts music aficionados from around the world. Staged almost daily (except for a few Sun), these traditional concerts were launched in 1895 and are the principal summer engagements for the BBC Symphony Orchestra. Cheering and clapping, Union Jacks on parade, banners, and balloons—it's great summer fun. Call ✆ **020/7589-8212,** or go to www.bbc.co.uk/proms. Mid-July to mid-September.

Salzburg Festival, Salzburg, Austria. Since the 1920s, this has been one of the premier cultural events of Europe, sparkling with opera, chamber music, plays, concerts, appearances by world-class artists, and many other cultural presentations. Always count on stagings of Mozart operas. For tickets, write several months in advance to the **Salzburg Festival,** Postfach 140, A-5010 Salzburg (✆ **0662/8045-500;** www.salzburgerfestspiele.at). Late July to late August.

Richard Wagner Festival, Bayreuth Festspielhaus, Germany. One of Europe's two or three major opera events, this festival takes place in the composer's Festspielhaus in Bayreuth, the capital of upper Franconia. ***Note:*** Opera tickets often must be booked years in advance. Contact **Festival Administration,** Bayreuther Festspiele, Am Festspiele, Kartenbüro Postfach 100262, D-95445 Bayreuth (✆ **0921/78-780;** www.festspiele.de). Late July to late August.

Festival d'Avignon, Avignon, France. This world-class festival has a reputation for exposing new talent to critical acclaim. The focus is usually on avant-garde works in theater, dance, and music. Much of the music is presented within the 14th-century courtyard of the Palais de l'Ancien Archevеché (the Old Archbishop's Palace). Make hotel reservations early. For information, call ✆ **04-90-27-66-50,** or go to www.festival-avignon.com. Last 3 weeks of July.

AUGUST

Edinburgh International Festival, Edinburgh, Scotland. Scotland's best-known festival is held for 3 weeks. Called an "arts bonanza," it draws major talent from around the world, with more than a thousand shows presented and a million tickets sold. Book, jazz, and film festivals are also staged at this time. Contact the **Edinburgh International Festival,** The Hub, Castle Hill, Edinburgh EH1 2NE (✆ **0131/473-2099;** www.eif.co.uk). Three weeks in August.

Illuminations' Regatta at Silkeborg, Silkeborg, Denmark. Denmark's oldest and biggest festival features nightly cruises on the lakes, with thousands of candles illuminating the shores. The fireworks display on the last night is the largest and most spectacular in northern Europe. Popular Danish artists provide entertainment at a large funfair. Contact the **Silkeborg Tourist Bureau,** Turbådene Åhavevej 2a, DK-8600 Silkeborg (✆ **86-82-19-11;** www.silkeborg.com). Mid-August.

Festas da Senhora da Agonia, Viana do Castelo, north of Porto, Portugal. The most spectacular festival in northern Portugal honors "Our Lady of Suffering." A replica of the Virgin is carried through the streets over carpets of flowers. Float-filled parades mark the 3-day event as a time of revelry. A blaze of fireworks ends the festival. Call the **tourist office** (✆ **223/393-470**) for exact dates, which vary from year to year. Mid-August.

St. Stephen's Day, Hungary. This is Hungary's national day. The country's patron saint is celebrated with cultural events and a dramatic display of fireworks over the Danube. Hungarians also ceremoniously welcome the first new bread from the crop of July wheat. August 20.

SEPTEMBER

Highland Games & Gathering, Braemar, Scotland. The queen and many members of the royal family often show up for this annual event, with its massed bands, piping and dancing competitions, and performances of great strength by a tribe of gigantic men. Contact the **tourist office** in Braemar, The Mews, Mar Road, Braemar, Aberdeenshire, AB35 5YL (✆ **01339/741-098;** www.braemargathering.org). First Saturday in September.

Oktoberfest, Munich, Germany. Germany's most famous festival happens mainly in September, not October. Millions show up, and hotels are packed. Most activities are at Theresienwiese, where local breweries sponsor gigantic tents that can hold up to 6,000 beer drinkers. Always reserve hotel rooms well in advance. Contact the **Munich Tourist Office** (✆ **089/233-965-00;** www.muenchen.de). Mid-September to the first Sunday in October.

OCTOBER

Autumn Winegrowers' Festival, Lugano, Switzerland. A parade and other festivities mark harvest time. Little girls throw flowers from blossom-covered floats, and oxen pull festooned wagons in a colorful procession. For information call the Lugano Tourist Office (✆ **091/913-32-32**). Three days in early October.

NOVEMBER

All Saints' Day, Spain, nationwide. This public holiday is reverently celebrated, as relatives and friends lay flowers on the graves of the dead. November 1.

DECEMBER

La Scala Opera Season, Teatro alla Scala, Milan. At the most famous opera house of them all, the season opens on December 7, the feast day of Milan's patron St. Ambrogio, and runs into July. Even though opening-night tickets are close to impossible to get, it's worth a try; call ✆ **02/7200-3744** for information, or 02/88-791 for reservations, or go to www.teatroallascala.org. Early December to mid-July.

Nobel Peace Prize Ceremony, Oslo, Norway. This major event on the Oslo calendar attracts world attention. It's held at Oslo City Hall and attendance is by invitation only. For details, contact the **Nobel Institute,** Drammensveien 19, N-0255 Oslo 2 (✆ **08-663-09-20;** http://nobelprize.org). December 10.

ENTRY REQUIREMENTS

Passports

If you don't already have one, you can download a passport application from the websites listed below. Countries covered in this guide do *not* require visas for U.S. or Canadian citizens for stays less than 90 days. Though a valid U.S. state driver's license usually suffices, it's wise to carry an **International Driving Permit** (US$15), which you can obtain from any AAA branch if you bring two passport-size photos.

UNITED STATES Whether you're applying in person or by mail, you can download passport applications from the U.S. State Department website at **http://travel.state.gov**. For general information, call the **National Passport Information Center** (✆ **877/487-2778**). To find your regional passport office, check the U.S. State Department website at http://travel.state.gov.

Savvy Travel Safeguards

Safeguard your passport in an inconspicuous, inaccessible place like a money belt. If you lose it, visit the nearest consulate of your native country as soon as possible for a replacement. Before leaving home, make two photocopy collages of your important documents: the first page of your passport (the page with the photo and identifying info), driver's license, and other ID. Leave one copy at home with a family member or friend and carry the other with you (separate from the originals!).

CANADA Passport applications are available at travel agencies throughout Canada or from the central **Passport Office,** Department of Foreign Affairs and International Trade, Ottawa, ON K1A 0G3 (✆ **800/567-6868;** www.ppt.gc.ca).

UNITED KINGDOM To pick up an application for a standard 10-year passport (5-year passport for children 15 and under), visit your nearest passport office, major post office, or travel agency or contact the **United Kingdom Passport Service** at ✆ **0300/222-0000** or go to www.ips.gov.uk.

IRELAND You can apply for a 10-year passport at the **Passport Office,** 80 St. Stephen's Green, Dublin 2 (✆ **01/478-0822;** www.foreignaffairs.gov.ie). Those under age 18 and over 65 must apply for a €12 3-year passport. You can also apply at 1A South Mall, Cork (✆ **021/484-4700**), or at most main post offices.

AUSTRALIA You can pick up an application from your local post office or Australian Passport Information Service, but you must schedule an interview at the passport office to present your application materials. Call the **Australian Passport Information Service** at ✆ **131-232,** or visit the government website at www.passports.gov.au.

NEW ZEALAND You can pick up a passport application at any New Zealand Passports Office or download it from their website. Contact the **Passports Office** at ✆ **0800/225-050** in New Zealand or 04/474-8100, or log on to www.passports.govt.nz.

Customs

U.S. CITIZENS Returning **U.S. citizens** who have been away for at least 48 hours are allowed to bring back, once every 30 days, US$800 worth of merchandise duty-free. You'll be charged a flat rate of 10% duty on the next US$1,000 worth of purchases. Be sure to have your receipts handy. On mailed gifts, the duty-free limit is US$200. You cannot bring fresh foodstuffs into the United States; some tinned foods, however, are allowed. For specifics on what you can bring back and the corresponding fees, download the invaluable free pamphlet *Know Before You Go* online at **www.cbp.gov**. (Click on "Travel," and then click on "Know Before You Go.") Or contact the **U.S. Customs & Border Protection (CBP),** 1300 Pennsylvania Ave., NW, Washington, DC 20229 (✆ **877/227-5511**), and request the pamphlet.

U.K. CITIZENS If you are **returning from a European Union (E.U.) country,** you will go through a separate Customs exit (called the Blue Exit) especially for E.U. travelers. In essence, there is no limit on what you can bring back from an E.U.

country, provided the items are for personal use (this includes gifts), and you have already paid the necessary duty and tax. Customs law, however, sets out guidance levels. If you bring in more than these levels, you may be asked to prove that the goods are for your own use. Guidance levels on goods bought in the E.U. for personal use are 3,200 cigarettes, 200 cigars, 400 cigarillos, 3 kilograms of smoking tobacco, 10 liters of spirits, 90 liters of wine, 20 liters of fortified wine (such as port or sherry), and 110 liters of beer.

U.K. citizens returning from a non-E.U. country have a Customs allowance of 200 cigarettes; 50 cigars; 250 grams of smoking tobacco; 2 liters of still table wine; 1 liter of spirits or strong liqueurs (over 22% volume); 2 liters of fortified wine, sparkling wine, or other liqueurs; 60cc (mL) of perfume; 250cc (mL) of toilet water; and £145 worth of all other goods, including gifts and souvenirs. People 16 and under cannot have the tobacco or alcohol allowance. For information, contact **HM Revenue & Customs & Excise** at ✆ **0845/010-9000,** or 02920/501-261 from outside the U.K., or consult their website at **www.hmrc.gov.uk**.

AUSTRALIAN CITIZENS The duty-free allowance in **Australia** is A$900 or, for those 17 and under, A$450. Citizens can bring in 250 cigarettes or 250 grams of loose tobacco, and 2.25 liters of alcohol. If you're returning with valuables you already own, such as foreign-made cameras, you should file form B263. A helpful brochure available from Australian consulates or Customs offices is *Know Before You Go*. For more information, call the **Australian Customs Service** at ✆ **1300/363-263,** or log on to **www.customs.gov.au**.

NEW ZEALAND CITIZENS The duty-free allowance for **New Zealand** is NZ$700. Citizens 18 and over can bring in 200 cigarettes, 50 cigars, or 250 grams of tobacco (or a mixture of all three if their combined weight doesn't exceed 250g); plus 4.5 liters of wine and beer, or 1.125 liters of liquor. New Zealand currency does not carry import or export restrictions. Fill out a certificate of export, listing the valuables you are taking out of the country; that way, you can bring them back without paying duty. Most questions are answered in a free pamphlet available at New Zealand consulates and Customs offices: *New Zealand Customs Guide for Travellers, Notice no. 4*. For more information, contact **New Zealand Customs,** The Customhouse, 17–21 Whitmore St., Box 2218, Wellington (✆ **04/473-6099** or 0800/428-786; **www.customs.govt.nz**).

CANADIAN CITIZENS For a clear summary of **Canadian** rules, write for the booklet *I Declare,* issued by the **Canada Border Services Agency** (✆ **800/461-9999,** or 204/983-3500 in Canada; **www.cbsa-asfc.gc.ca**). Canada allows its citizens a C$750 exemption, and you're allowed to bring back duty-free one carton of cigarettes, one can of tobacco, 40 imperial ounces of liquor, and 50 cigars. In addition, you're allowed to mail gifts to Canada valued at less than C$60 a day, provided they're unsolicited and don't contain alcohol or tobacco (write on the package "Unsolicited gift, under C$60 value"). All valuables should be declared on the Y-38 form before departure from Canada, including serial numbers of valuables you already own, such as expensive foreign cameras. ***Note:*** The C$750 exemption can be used only once a year and only after an absence of 7 days.

Visitor Information

TOURIST OFFICES

Start with the **European tourist offices** in your own country; for a complete list, see below. If you aren't sure which countries you want to visit, send for an information-packed free booklet called ***Planning Your Trip to Europe,*** revised annually by the 31-nation **European Travel Commission** (www.visiteurope.com).

Austrian Tourist Office, Inc.

www.austriatourism.com or www.austria.info

IN THE U.S. 500 5th Ave., New York, NY 10110 (✆ **212/944-6880;** fax 212/730-4568).

IN CANADA Call ✆ **416/967-3381.**

IN THE U.K. 9–11 Richmond Buildings, London W1D 3HF (✆ **0845/101-1818;** fax 0845/101-1819).

IN AUSTRALIA Call ✆ **02-9299-3621.**

Belgian Tourist Office

www.visitbelgium.com or www.belgiumtheplaceto.be

IN THE U.S. 220 E. 42nd St., Ste. 3402, New York, NY 10017 (✆ **212/758-8130;** fax 212/355-7675).

IN CANADA P.O. Box 760 NDG, Montreal, QC, H4A 342 (✆ **514/457-2888;** fax 212/355-7675).

IN THE U.K. 217 Marsh Wall, London E14 9FJ (✆ **020/7537-1132;** fax 020/7531-0393).

Visit Britain

www.visitbritain.com

IN THE U.S. Call (✆ **800/462-2748**) for information.

IN CANADA 160 Bloor St. E., Ste. 905, Toronto, ON M4W 1B9. ***Note:*** Office not open to visitors.

IN AUSTRALIA GPO Box 2721, Sydney, Australia, NSW 1006 (✆ **22-9331-6469;** www.tourismaustralia.com).

IN NEW ZEALAND P.O. Box 91893, Auckland Mail Centre, Auckland, New Zealand (✆ **9914-4780;** www.tourismnewzealand.com).

Czech Tourist Authority

www.czechtourism.com

IN THE U.S. 1109 Madison Ave., New York, NY 10028 (✆ **212/288-0830;** fax 212/288-0971).

IN CANADA 2 Bloor St. W., Ste. 1300, Toronto, ON M4W 3E2 (✆ **416/363-9928;** fax 416/972-6991).

IN THE U.K. 13 Harley St., London W1G 9QG (✆ **020/7631-0427;** fax 020/7631-0419).

French Government Tourist Office

www.franceguide.com

IN THE U.S. 825 Third Ave., 29th Floor, New York, NY 10022 (✆ **212/838-7800;** fax 212/838-7855).

IN CANADA Maison de la France/French Government Tourist Office, 1800 av. McGill College, Ste. 1010, Montreal, QC H3A 3J6 (✆ **514/288-2026;** fax 514/845-4868).

IN THE U.K. Maison de la France/French Government Tourist Office, 300 High Holborn, London WC1V 7JH (✆ **09068/244-123,** costs 60p per minute; fax 020/7493-6594).

IN AUSTRALIA French Tourist Bureau, 25 Bligh St., Sydney, NSW 2000 (✆ **02/9231-5244;** fax 02/9221-8682).

German National Tourist Office

www.cometogermany.com

IN THE U.S. 122 E. 42nd St., 52nd Floor, New York, NY 10168-0072 (✆ **212/661-7200;** fax 212/661-7174).

IN CANADA 480 University Ave., Ste. 1500, Toronto, ON M53 1V2 (✆ **416/968-1685;** fax 416/921-1353; www.gaccom.org).

IN THE U.K. P.O. Box 2695, London W1A 3TN (✆ **020/7317-0908** or 020/7317-0917; www.germany-tourism.co.uk).

IN AUSTRALIA P.O. Box A980, Sydney, NSW 1235 (✆ **02/8296-0488;** fax 02/8296-0487).

Greek National Tourist Organization

www.gnto.gr or www.greektourism.com

IN THE U.S. 645 Fifth Ave., Ste. 903, New York, NY 10022 (✆ **212/421-5777;** fax 212/826-6940).

IN CANADA 1300 Bay St., Toronto, ON M5R 3K8 (✆ **416/968-2220;** fax 416/968-6533).

IN THE U.K. 4 Conduit St., London W1S 2DJ (✆ **020/7495-9300;** fax 020/7495-4057; www.gnto.co.uk).

IN AUSTRALIA 51–57 Pitt St., Sydney, NWS 2000 (✆ **02/9241-1663;** fax 02/9252-1441).

Hungarian National Tourist Office

www.gotohungary.com

IN THE U.S. & CANADA 350 Fifth Ave., Ste. 7107, New York, NY 10118 (✆ **212/695-1221**).

IN THE U.K. 46 Eaton Place, London, SW1X 8AL (✆ **020/7823-1032;** fax 020/7823-1459).

Irish Tourist Board

www.discoverireland.ie

IN THE U.S. 345 Park Ave., New York, NY 10154 (✆ **800/223-6470** or 212/418-0800; fax 212/371-9052).

IN THE U.K. Nations House, 103 Wigmore St., London W1U 1QS (✆ **020/7518-0800;** fax 020/7493-9065).

IN AUSTRALIA 36 Carrington St., 5th Floor, Sydney, NSW 2000 (✆ **02/9299-6177;** fax 02/9299-6323).

Italian Government Tourist Board

www.enit.it or www.italiantourism.com

IN THE U.S. 630 Fifth Ave., Ste. 1565, New York, NY 10111 (✆ **212/245-5618;** fax 212/586-9249); 500 N. Michigan Ave., Ste. 2240, Chicago, IL 60611 (✆ **312/644-0996;** fax 312/644-3019); 12400 Wilshire Blvd., Ste. 550, Los Angeles, CA 90025 (✆ **310/820-1898;** fax 310/820-6357).

IN CANADA 175 Bloor St. E., South Tower, Ste. 907, Toronto, ON M4W 3R8 (✆ **416/925-4882;** fax 416/925-4799).

IN THE U.K. 1 Princes St., London W1B 2AY (✆ **020/7399-3562;** fax 020/7399-3567).

Monaco Government Tourist Office

www.monaco-tourism.com

IN THE U.S. & CANADA 565 Fifth Ave., New York, NY 10017 (✆ **212/286-3330;** fax 212/286-9890).

IN THE U.K. 7 Upper Grosvenor St., London, W1K 2LX (✆ **020/7491-4264;** fax 020/7408-2487).

Netherlands Board of Tourism

www.goholland.com

IN THE U.S. & CANADA 355 Lexington Ave., 19th Floor, New York, NY 10017 (✆ **888/464-6552** or 212/370-7360; fax 212/370-9507).

IN THE U.K. Imperial House, 7th Floor, 15–19 Kingsway, London, WC2B 6DH (✆ **020/7539-7950;** fax 020/7539-7953).

Portuguese Trade & Tourism Office

www.portugalglobal.pt

IN THE U.S. 590 Fifth Ave., 3rd Floor, New York, NY 10036 (✆ **646/723-0200;** fax 212/764-6137).

IN CANADA 60 Bloor St. W., Ste. 1005, Toronto, ON M4W 3B8 (✆ **416/921-7376;** fax 416/921-1353).

IN THE U.K. 11 Belgrave Sq., London, SW1X 8PP (✆ **0845/355-1212;** fax 020/7201-6633; www.visitportugal.com).

Scandinavian Tourist Boards (Denmark, Norway & Sweden)

www.goscandinavia.com, www.visitdenmark.com, www.visitnorway.com, or www.visitsweden.com

IN THE U.S. & CANADA Call ✆ **212/885-9700;** fax 212/885-9710. ***Note:*** Office not open to visitors.

IN THE U.K. Danish Tourist Board, 55 Sloane St., London SW1X 9SY (✆ **020/7259-5959;** fax 020/7259-5955); Norwegian Tourist Board, 5 Lower Regent St.,

London, SW1Y 4LR (✆ **020/7389-8800;** fax 020/7839-6014); Swedish Travel & Tourism Council, 11 Upper Montagu Place, London W1H 2AL (✆ **020/7108-6168;** fax 020/7724-5872).

Tourist Office of Spain

www.spain.info

IN THE U.S. 666 Fifth Ave., 35th Floor, New York, NY 10103 (✆ **212/265-8822;** fax 212/265-8864); 845 N. Michigan Ave., Ste. 915E, Chicago, IL 60611 (✆ **312/642-1992;** fax 312/642-9817); 8383 Wilshire Blvd., Ste. 960, Los Angeles, CA 90211 (✆ **323/658-7195;** fax 323/658-1061); 1395 Brickell Ave., Ste. 1130, Miami, FL 33131 (✆ **305/358-1992;** fax 305/358-8223).

IN CANADA 2 Bloor St. W., Ste. 3402, Toronto, ON M4W 3E2 (✆ **416/961-3131;** fax 416/961-1992).

IN THE U.K. 79 New Cavendish St., London W1W 6XB (✆ **020/7486-8077;** fax 020/7486-8034).

Switzerland Tourism

www.myswitzerland.com

IN THE U.S. 608 Fifth Ave., New York, NY 10020 (✆ **877/794-8037** or 212/757-5944; fax 212/262-6116).

IN CANADA 926 The East Mall, Toronto, ON M9B 6K1 (✆ **416/695-3375;** fax 416/695-2775). ***Note:*** Office not open to visitors.

IN THE U.K. Switzerland Tourism, 30 Bedford St., London WC2E 9ED (✆ **020/7845-7681**).

Travel Agents

Travel agents can save you plenty of time and money by hunting down the best airfare for your route and arranging for rail passes and rental cars. For now, most travel agents still charge you nothing for their services—they're paid through commissions from the airlines and other agencies they book for you. However, a number of airlines have begun cutting commissions, and increasingly, agents are finding they have to charge you a fee to hold the bottom line (or else unscrupulous agents will offer you only the travel options that bag them the juiciest commissions). Shop around and ask hard questions.

If you decide to use a travel agent, make sure the agent is a member of the **American Society of Travel Agents (ASTA),** 1101 King St., Alexandria, VA 22314 (www.asta.org), or the equivalent oversight agency in your country. If you send them a self-addressed stamped envelope, ASTA will mail you the booklet *Avoiding Travel Problems* for free.

GETTING THERE & GETTING AROUND

Flying from North America

Most major airlines charge competitive fares to European cities, but price wars break out regularly and fares can change overnight. Tickets tend to be cheaper if you fly midweek or off season. **High season** on most routes is usually from June to mid-September—the most expensive and most crowded time to travel. **Shoulder season** is from April to May, mid-September to October, and December 15 to December 24. **Low season**—with the cheapest fares—is from November to December 14 and December 25 to March.

MAJOR NORTH AMERICAN AIRLINES North American carriers with frequent service and flights to Europe are **Air Canada** (✆ 888/247-2262; www.aircanada.ca), **American Airlines** (✆ 800/433-7300; www.aa.com), **Continental Airlines** (✆ 800/231-0856; www.continental.com), **Delta Airlines** (✆ 800/221-1212; www.delta.com), **Northwest KLM Airlines** (✆ 800/225-2525; www.nwa.com), and **US Airways/America West** (✆ 800/622-1015; www.usairways.com).

EUROPEAN NATIONAL AIRLINES Not only will the national carriers of European countries offer the greatest number of direct flights from the United States (and can easily book you through to cities beyond the major hubs), but because their entire U.S. market is to fly you to their home country, they often run more competitive deals than most North American carriers. Major national and country-affiliated European airlines include the following:

- **Austria: Austrian Airlines** (✆ **800/843-0002** in the U.S. and Canada; ✆ 020/7766-0300 in the U.K.; www.aua.com).
- **Belgium: Brussels Airlines** (✆ **866/308-2230** in the U.S. and Canada; ✆ 0121/767-8712 in the U.K.; www.brusselsairlines.com).
- **Czech Republic: CSA Czech Airlines** (✆ **800/223-2365** in the U.S.; ✆ 866/293-8702 in Canada; ✆ 0871/663-3747 in the U.K.; ✆ 02/8248-0000 in Australia; www.csa.cz).
- **France: Air France** (✆ **800/237-2747** in the U.S.; ✆ 800/667-2747 in Canada; ✆ 0870/242-9242 in the U.K.; www.airfrance.com).
- **Germany: Lufthansa** (✆ **800/645-3880** in the U.S.; ✆ 800/563-5954 in Canada; ✆ 0871/945-9747 in the U.K.; ✆ 1300-655-727 in Australia; ✆ 0800/945220 in New Zealand; www.lufthansa.com).
- **Greece: Olympic Air** (✆ **800/223-1226** in the U.S. and Canada; ✆ 0870/606-0460 in the U.K.; www.olympicair.com).
- **Hungary: Malev Hungarian Airlines** (✆ **800/223-6884** in the U.S.; ✆ 866/379-7313 in Canada; ✆ 0870/909-0577 in the U.K.; www.malev.hu).
- **Ireland: Aer Lingus** (✆ **800/IRISH-AIR** [474-7424] in the U.S. and Canada; ✆ 0870/876-5555 in the U.K.; www.aerlingus.com).
- **Italy: Alitalia** (✆ **800/223-5730** in the U.S. and Canada; ✆ 0871/424-1424 in the U.K.; www.alitalia.com).
- **The Netherlands: Northwest KLM** (✆ **800/225-2525** in the U.S. and Canada; ✆ 0870/507-4074 in the U.K.; www.klm.com).
- **Portugal: TAP Portugal** (✆ **800/221-7370** in the U.S. and Canada; ✆ 0845/601-0932 in the U.K.; www.flytap.com).
- **Scandinavia (Denmark, Norway, Sweden): SAS Scandinavian Airlines** (✆ **800/221-2350** in the U.S. and Canada; ✆ 0871/521-2772 in the U.K.; ✆ 1300/727-707 in Australia; www.flysas.com).
- **Spain: Iberia** (✆ **800/772-4642** in the U.S. and Canada; ✆ 0870/609-0500 in the U.K.; www.iberia.com).

Don't Stow It—Ship It

Though pricey, it's sometimes worthwhile to travel luggage-free. Specialists in door-to-door luggage delivery include **Virtual Bellhop** (✆ **877/235-5467; www.virtualbellhop.com**), **SkyCap International** (✆ **877/775-9227; www.skycapinternational.com**), and **Luggage Express** (✆ **866/744-7224; www.myluggageexpress.com**).

- **Switzerland: Swiss International Air Lines** (✆ **877/359-7947** in the U.S. and Canada; ✆ 0845/601-0956 in the U.K.; www.swiss.com).
- **United Kingdom: British Airways** (✆ **800/247-9297** in the U.S. and Canada; ✆ 0870/850-9850 in the U.K.; ✆ 1300/767-177 in Australia; www.britishairways.com) and **Virgin Atlantic Airways** (✆ **800/821-5438** in the U.S. and Canada; ✆ 0870/574-7747 in the U.K.; ✆ 1300/727-340 in Australia; www.virgin-atlantic.com).

Getting to the Continent from the United Kingdom

BY TRAIN Many rail passes and discounts are available in the United Kingdom for travel in continental Europe. One of the most complete overviews is available from **Rail Europe Special Services Department,** 10 Leake St., London SE1 7NN (✆ **08448/484-088**). This organization is particularly well versed in information about discount travel as it applies to persons 25 and under, full-time or part-time students, and seniors.

The most prevalent option for younger travelers, the **EuroYouth passes,** are available only to travelers 25 and under and entitle the pass holder to unlimited second-class rail travel in 26 European countries.

BY CHUNNEL The Eurostar train shuttles between London and both Paris and Brussels; trip time is under 3 hours (compared to 10 hr. on the traditional train-ferry-train route). **Rail Europe** (✆ **877/272-RAIL** [272-7245]; www.raileurope.com) sells tickets on the Eurostar between London and Paris or Brussels (both US$421 one-way).

For Eurostar reservations, call ✆ **800/EUROSTAR** (387-6782) in the U.S., 0870/5186-186 in the U.K., or 08-92-35-35-39 in France; or go to www.eurostar.com. Eurostar trains arrive at and depart from Waterloo Station in London, Gare du Nord in Paris, and Central Station in Brussels.

BY FERRY & HOVERCRAFT **Brittany Ferries** (✆ **0870/907-6103;** www.brittanyferries.com) is the largest British ferry/drive outfit, sailing from the southern coast of England to five destinations in Spain and France. From Portsmouth, sailings reach St-Malo, Cherbourg, and Caen in France, and Santander in Spain. From Poole, you can ferry to Cherbourg in France. From Plymouth, sailings go to Roscoff in France and Santander in Spain. **P&O Ferries** (✆ **0871/664-5645;** www.poferries.com) operates car and passenger ferries between Dover and Calais, France (25 sailings a day; 1¼ hr.).

BY CAR Many car-rental companies won't let you rent a car in Britain and take it to the Continent, so always check ahead. There are many "drive-on/drive-off" car-ferry services across the Channel; see "By Ferry & Hovercraft," above. There are also Chunnel trains that run a drive-on/drive-off service every 15 minutes (once an hour at night) for the 35-minute ride between Ashford and Calais.

BY COACH Though travel by coach is considerably slower and less comfortable than travel by train, if you're on a budget you might opt for one of Eurolines' regular departures from London's Victoria Coach Station to destinations throughout Europe. Contact **Eurolines** at 52 Grosvenor Gardens, Victoria, London SW1W OAU (✆ **0870/514-3219;** www.eurolines.com).

Getting Around Europe by Train

In Europe, the shortest—and cheapest—distance between two points is lined with rail tracks. European trains are less expensive than those in the United States, far more advanced in many ways, and certainly more extensive. Modern high-speed trains (209kmph/130 mph) make the rails faster than the plane for short journeys, and overnight trains get you where you're going without wasting valuable daylight hours—and you save money on lodging to boot.

SOME TRAIN NOTES

Many European high-speed trains, including the popular EC (EuroCity), IC (Inter-City), and EN (EuroNight), require you to pay a **supplement** in addition to the regular ticket fare. It's included when you buy tickets but not in any rail pass, so check at the ticket window before boarding; otherwise, the conductor will sell you the supplement on the train—along with a fine. **Seat reservations** (US$20–US$50, or more when a meal is included) are required on some high-speed runs—any marked with an R on a printed train schedule. You can usually reserve a seat within a few hours of departure, but be on the safe side and book your seat a few days in advance. You need to reserve any sleeping couchette or sleeping berth too.

With two exceptions, there's no need to buy individual train tickets or make seat reservations **before you leave the United States.** First, on the high-speed Artesia run (Paris to Turin and Milan), you must buy a supplement, on which you can get a substantial discount if you have a rail pass, but only if you buy the supplement in the United States along with the pass. It's also wise to reserve a seat on the Eurostar, as England's frequent **bank holidays** (long weekends) book the train solid with Londoners taking a short vacation to Paris.

The difference between **first class** and **second class** on European trains is minor—a matter of 1 or 2 inches of extra padding and maybe a bit more elbowroom. European **train stations** are usually as clean and efficient as the trains, if a bit chaotic at times. In stations you'll find posters showing the track number and timetables for regularly scheduled runs (departures are often on the yellow poster). Many stations also have tourist offices and hotel reservations desks, banks with ATMs, and newsstands where you can buy phone cards, bus and metro tickets, maps, and local English-language event magazines.

You can get many more details about train travel in Europe and automated schedule information by fax by contacting **Rail Europe** (✆ **877/272-RAIL** [7245]; www.raileurope.com). If you plan to travel a great deal on the European railroads, it's worth buying a copy of the ***Thomas Cook Timetable of European Passenger Railroads.*** It's available exclusively online at www.thomascookpublishing.com.

RAIL PASSES

The greatest value in European travel has always been the **rail pass,** a single ticket allowing you unlimited travel (or travel on a certain number of days) within a set time period. If you plan on going all over Europe by train, buying a rail pass will end up being much less expensive than buying individual tickets. Plus, a rail pass gives you the freedom to hop on a train whenever you feel like it, and there's no waiting in ticket lines. For more focused trips, you might want to look into national or regional passes or just buy individual tickets as you go.

PASSES AVAILABLE IN THE UNITED STATES The granddaddy of passes is the **Eurail Global Pass,** covering some 25 countries (most of western Europe except Britain).

It's best to buy these passes in the United States; they're available from some major European train stations but are up to 10% more expensive. You can get them from most travel agents, but the biggest supplier is **Rail Europe** (**© 877/272-RAIL** [272-7245]; www.raileurope.com), which also sells most national passes, except for a few minor British ones. The company also publishes a free annual brochure, "Europe on Track," outlining a traveler's various pass and rail options.

The most popular pass is the **Eurail Global Pass,** which offers first-class travel for adults 26 and older. Options are US$799 for 15 days, US$1,035 for 21 days, US$1,285 for 1 month, US$1,815 for 2 months, or US$2,239 for 3 months. Substantial reductions are granted on the **First Class Saver Pass** for two or more people traveling together or for **Second Class Youth Travel** for those 25 and younger. Children, ages 4 to 11, on their first day of travel, receive a 50% discount on the first-class adult fare, and those 3 and under travel free.

You can also consider a **Eurail Select Pass,** allowing travel in three, four, or five bordering European countries. With this pass, you can customize your own trip, traveling by train from 6 to 10 days within a 2-month period. For five countries, there is also a 15-day travel option.

A **Eurail Regional Pass** is for those who want to see only a small part of Europe in a short time frame. A total of 25 regional passes are offered, granting train travel for 3 to 10 days within 2 months. You're allowed unlimited travel within one of the 25 available country combinations. Such a pass, for example, would grant you unlimited travel in both France and Switzerland, plus various other combinations such as Greece and Italy, or even a Scandinavia Pass granting travel in four countries. Seventeen countries, including Austria and Italy, participate in the **Eurail One Country Pass.** This pass grants unlimited train travel from 3 to 8 days within a 1-month period.

Countries Honoring Train Passes

Eurail Countries: Austria, Belgium, Bulgaria, Croatia, Czech Republic, Denmark, Finland, France, Germany, Greece, Hungary, Ireland, Italy, Luxembourg, Montenegro, Netherlands, Norway, Poland, Portugal, Romania, Serbia, Slovenia, Spain, Sweden, Switzerland.

TRAIN TRIP tips

To make your train travels as pleasant as possible, remember a few general rules:

- **Hold on to your train ticket** after it's been marked or punched by the conductor. Some European railroad systems require that you present your ticket when you leave the station platform at your destination.
- While you sleep—or even nap—**be sure your valuables are in a safe place.** You might temporarily attach a small bell to each bag to warn you if someone attempts to take it. If you've left bags on a rack in the front or back of the car, consider securing them with a small bicycle chain and lock to deter thieves, who consider trains happy hunting grounds.
- Few European trains have drinking fountains, and the dining car may be closed just when you're at your thirstiest, so **take along a bottle of mineral water.** As you'll soon discover, the experienced European traveler comes loaded with hampers of food and drink and munches away throughout the trip.
- If you want to leave bags in a train station locker, **don't let anyone help you store them in it.** A favorite trick among thieves is feigned helpfulness, and then pocketing the key to your locker while passing you the key to an empty one.

You have to study these passes carefully to see which one would be ideal for you. You can check online or call for the latest prices and offerings, which are subject to change in the lifetime of this edition.

If you plan on traveling in Great Britain, then **BritRail** (✆ **877/677-1066;** fax 877/477-1066; www.britrail.com), which specializes in rail passes for use in Great Britain, is your best bet.

PASSES AVAILABLE IN THE UNITED KINGDOM Many rail passes are available in the United Kingdom for travel in Britain and Europe. The most popular ticket is the **Interrail Card,** which is offered for persons who have lived in Europe at least 6 months. It offers unlimited travel in most European countries within 5 days, 10 days, 22 days, or 1 month and is valid on all normal trains; the card is valid on high-speed trains such as TGV if you pay a supplement. The price depends on the trip duration and how many of the eight different zones you plan to travel in. Typical zones include Britain or Ireland; Finland, Norway, and Sweden; or combos such as Austria, Denmark, Germany, and Switzerland. A typical fare for 5 days of travel within 10 days is 316€ in first class, 240€ in second class, and 158€ for a youth fare.

For help in determining the best option for your trip and to buy tickets, stop in London at the **International Rail Centre** in Victoria Station (✆ **0871/231-0790**).

Getting Around Europe by Car

Many rental companies grant discounts if you **reserve in advance** (usually 48 hr.) from your home country. Weekly rentals are almost always less expensive than day

THE RULES OF THE ROAD: driving IN EUROPE

- First, know that European drivers tend to be more aggressive than their North American counterparts.
- Drive on the right except in England, Scotland, and Ireland, where you drive on the left. And *do not drive* in the left lane on a four-lane highway; it is truly only for passing.
- If someone comes up from behind and flashes his lights at you, it's a signal for you to slow down and drive more on the shoulder so that he can pass you more easily (two-lane roads here routinely become three cars wide).
- Except for the German Autobahn, most highways do indeed have speed limits of around 100 to 135kmph (62–84 mph).
- Remember that everything's measured in kilometers here (mileage and speed limits). For a rough conversion, 1km = 0.6 miles.
- Be aware that although gas may look reasonably priced, the price is per liter, and 3.8 liters equals 1 gallon—so multiply by 4 to estimate the equivalent per-gallon price.
- Never leave anything of value in the car overnight, and don't leave anything visible when you leave the car (this goes double in Italy, triple in Naples).

rentals. Three or more people traveling together can usually get around cheaper by car than by train (even with rail passes).

When you reserve a car, be sure to ask if the price includes the E.U. value-added tax (VAT), personal accident insurance (PAI), collision-damage waiver (CDW), and any other insurance options. If not, ask what these extras cost, because at the end of your rental, they can make a big difference in your bottom line. The CDW and other insurance might be covered by your credit card if you use the card to pay for the rental; check with the card issuer to be sure.

If your credit card doesn't cover the CDW (and it probably won't in Ireland), try **Travel Guard International,** 1145 Clark St., Stevens Point, WI 54481 (✆ **800/826-4919** or 715/345-0505; www.travelguard.com), which will insure you. Avis and Hertz, among other companies, require that you purchase a theft-protection policy in Italy.

The main car-rental companies are **Avis** (✆ **800/331-1212;** www.avis.com), **Budget** (✆ **800/472-3325;** www.budget.com), **Dollar** (✆ **800/800-3665;** www.dollar.com), **Hertz** (✆ **800/654-3001;** www.hertz.com), and **National** (✆ **800/227-7368;** www.nationalcar.com). U.S.-based companies specializing in European rentals are **Auto Europe** (✆ **800/223-5555;** www.autoeurope.com), **Europe by Car** (✆ **800/223-1516,** or 212/581-3040 in New York; www.europebycar.com), and **Kemwel Drive Europe** (✆ **877/820-0668;** www.kemwel.com). Europe by Car, Kemwel, and **Renault USA** (✆ **800/221-1052** or 212/730-0676; www.renaultusa.com) also offer a low-cost alternative to renting for longer than 15 days: **short-term leases** in which you technically buy a fresh-from-the-factory car and then sell it back when you return it. All insurance is included, from liability and theft to personal injury and CDW, with no deductible. And unlike at many rental agencies, who won't rent to anyone 24 and under, the minimum age for a lease is 18.

The **AAA** supplies good maps to its members. **Michelin maps** (✆ **800/423-0485;** www.viamichelin.co.uk) are made for the tourist. The maps rate cities as "uninteresting" (as a tourist destination); "interesting"; "worth a detour"; or "worth an entire journey." They also highlight particularly scenic stretches of road in green, and have symbols pointing out scenic overlooks, ruins, and other sights along the way.

Getting Around Europe by Plane

Though trains remain the cheapest and easiest way to get around in Europe, air transport options have improved drastically in the past few years. Intense competition with rail and ferry companies has slowly forced airfares into the bargain basement. **British Airways** (✆ **800/AIRWAYS** [247-9297] in the U.S., or 0870/850-9850 in the U.K.; www.britishairways.com) and other scheduled airlines fly regularly from London to Paris for only £100 round-trip, depending on the season. Lower fares usually apply to midweek flights and carry advance-purchase requirements of 2 weeks or so.

The biggest airline news in Europe is the rise of the **no-frills airline** modeled on American upstarts like Southwest. By keeping their overhead down through electronic ticketing, forgoing meal service, and flying from less popular airports, these airlines are able to offer low fares. Most round-trip tickets are US$40 to US$170. This means now you can save lots of time, and even money, over long train hauls, especially from, say, London to Venice or from central Europe out to peripheral countries like Greece and Spain. Budget airlines include **EasyJet** in England (✆ **0871/244-2366;** www.easyjet.com); **Ryanair** in England (✆ **0871/246-0000;** www.ryanair.com) and in Ireland (✆ **1530-787-787**); and **Brussels Airlines** in Belgium (✆ **0902/51-600;** www.brusselsairlines.com). Be aware, though, that the names might change because these small airlines are often economically vulnerable and can fail or merge with a big airline. Still, as quickly as one disappears, another will take off.

Lower airfares are also available throughout Europe on **charter flights** rather than regularly scheduled ones. Look in local newspapers to find out about them. Consolidators cluster in cities like London and Athens.

Flying across Europe on regularly scheduled airlines can destroy a budget and be super expensive. Whenever possible, book your total flight on one ticket before leaving. For example, if you're flying from New York to Rome, but also plan to visit Palermo, Florence, and Turin, have the total trip written up on one ticket. Don't arrive in Rome and book separate legs of the journey, which costs far more when it's done piecemeal.

American citizens can contact **Europe by Air** (✆ **888/321-4737;** www.europebyair.com) for their Europe flight pass serving 30 countries, 30 airlines, and 150 European cities. It costs from US$99 to US$129 to travel one-way between these cities.

Getting Around Europe by Bus

Bus transportation is readily available throughout Europe; it sometimes is less expensive than train travel and covers a more extensive area but can be slower and much less comfortable. European buses, like the trains, outshine their American counterparts, but they're perhaps best used only to pick up where the extensive train network leaves off. One major bus company serves all the countries of western Europe (no service to Greece): **Eurolines** in London (✆ **0870/514-3219;** www.eurolines.com). The staff at Eurolines can check schedules, make reservations, and quote prices.

MONEY

Currency

On March 1, 2002, the euro officially replaced the legacy currencies as legal tender in the **euro zone,** including the countries of Austria, Belgium, Finland, France, Germany, Greece, Ireland, Italy, Luxembourg, the Netherlands, Portugal, and Spain. Britain, the Czech Republic, Denmark, Hungary, and Sweden do not fall under the euro umbrella, even though they are members of the E.U. Norway and Switzerland are not part of the E.U. See the "Fast Facts" section in each destination chapter for the currency used in that country and the exchange rate at the time this book went to press.

Euros come in note denominations of 5, 10, 20, 50, 100, 200, and 500, and coin denominations of 1 and 2 euros and 1, 2, 5, 10, 20, and 50 cents. Coins have a common face on one side. The opposite face has a design chosen by the issuing country. As this book went to press, 1€ was worth approximately US$1.40 and gaining in strength, so your dollars might not go as far as you'd expect. For up-to-the-minute exchange rates between the euro and the dollar, check the currency-converter website **www.xe.com**.

ATMs

The easiest and best way to get cash away from home is from an **ATM,** sometimes referred to as a **cash machine** or **cashpoint.** The **Cirrus** (✆ **800/424-7787;** www.mastercard.com) and **PLUS** (✆ **800/843-7587;** www.visa.com) networks span the globe; look at the back of your bank card to see which network you're on, and then call or check online for ATM locations at your destination. Be sure you know your personal identification number (PIN) and daily withdrawal limit before you depart. ***Note:*** Remember that many banks impose a fee every time you use a card at another bank's ATM, and that fee can be higher for international transactions (up to US$5 or more) than for domestic ones (where they're rarely more than US$2). In addition, the bank from which you withdraw cash may charge its own fee. For international withdrawal fees, ask your bank.

Credit Cards

Credit cards are another safe way to carry money. They also provide a convenient record of all your expenses, and they generally offer relatively good exchange rates. You can withdraw cash advances from your credit cards at banks or ATMs, provided you know your PIN. Remember that you'll pay interest from the moment of your withdrawal, even if you pay your monthly bills on time. Also, note that many banks now assess a 1% to 3% "transaction fee" on **all** charges you incur abroad (whether you're using the local currency or your native currency).

Easy Money

You'll avoid lines at airport ATMs by exchanging at least some money—just enough to cover airport incidentals and transportation to your hotel—before you leave home.

When you change money, ask for some small bills or loose change. Petty cash will come in handy for tipping and public transportation. Consider keeping the change separate from your larger bills so that it's readily accessible and you'll be less of a target for theft.

Most middle-bracket and virtually all first-class and deluxe hotels, restaurants, and shops in Europe accept major credit cards—American Express, Diners Club, MasterCard, and Visa (but not Discover). Some budget establishments accept plastic; others don't. The most widely accepted cards these days are Visa and MasterCard, but it pays to carry American Express too. Note that you can now often choose to charge credit card purchases at the price in euros or in the local currency; because most European currencies are now locked together, the dollar amount always comes out the same, but it could help you comparison shop. If you do choose to stick with plastic, keep in mind that most banks assess a 2% fee for currency conversion on credit charges.

Traveler's Checks

Traveler's checks are something of an anachronism from the days before the ATM made cash accessible at any time. Given the fees you'll pay for ATM use at banks other than your own, however, you might be better off with traveler's checks if you're withdrawing money often.

The most popular traveler's checks are offered by **American Express** (✆ **800/528-4800** for cardholders—this number accepts collect calls, offers service in several foreign languages, and exempts Amex gold and platinum cardholders from the 1% fee); **Visa** (✆ **800/222-4357**)—AAA members can obtain Visa checks for a US$9.95 fee (for checks up to US$1,500) at most AAA offices or by calling ✆ **866/339-3378;** and **MasterCard** (✆ **800/223-9920**).

American Express, Thomas Cook, Visa, and **MasterCard** offer **foreign currency traveler's checks,** which are useful if you're traveling to one country, or to the euro zone; they're accepted at locations where dollar checks may not be.

If you do carry traveler's checks, keep a record of their serial numbers separate from your checks in the event that they are stolen or lost. You'll get a refund faster if you know the numbers.

Value-Added Tax (VAT)

All European countries charge a **value-added tax (VAT)** of 15% to 25% on goods and services—it's like a sales tax that's already included in the price. Rates vary from country to country (as does the name—it's called the IVA in Italy and Spain, the TVA in France, and so on), though the goal in E.U. countries is to arrive at a uniform rate of about 15%. Citizens of non-E.U. countries can, as they leave the country, get back most of the tax on purchases (not services) if they spend above a designated amount (usually US$80–US$200) in a single store.

Regulations vary from country to country, so inquire at the tourist office when you arrive to find out the procedure; ask what percentage of the tax is refunded, and whether the refund is given to you at the airport or mailed to you later. Look for a **tax free shopping for tourists** sign posted in participating stores. Ask the storekeeper for the necessary forms, and, if possible, keep the purchases in their original packages. Save all your receipts and VAT forms from each E.U. country to process all of them at the **"Tax Refund"** desk in the airport of the last country you visit before flying home (allow an extra 30 min. or so at the airport to process forms).

To avoid VAT refund hassles, ask for a Global Refund form ("Shopping Cheque") at a store where you make a purchase. When leaving an E.U. country, have it stamped by Customs, after which you take it to the Global Refund counter at more than 700 airports and border crossings in Europe. Your money is refunded on the spot. For information, contact **Global Refund** (✆ **866/706-6090;** www.globalrefund.com).

HEALTH

Staying Healthy

In most of Europe the tap water is generally safe to drink (except on trains and wherever it's marked as nondrinking water), the milk is pasteurized, and health services are good. You will, however, be eating foods and spices your body isn't used to, so you might want to bring along Pepto-Bismol or Imodium tablets in case indigestion or diarrhea strikes.

GENERAL AVAILABILITY OF HEALTHCARE

Contact the **International Association for Medical Assistance to Travelers** (**IAMAT;** ✆ **716/754-4883,** or 416/652-0137 in Canada; www.iamat.org) for tips on travel and health concerns in the countries you're visiting, and for lists of local, English-speaking doctors. The United States **Centers for Disease Control and Prevention** (✆ **800/CDC-INFO** [232-4636]; www.cdc.gov) provides up-to-date information on health hazards by region or country and offers tips on food safety. The website **Travel Health Online** (**www.tripprep.com**), sponsored by a consortium of travel medicine practitioners, may also offer helpful advice on traveling abroad. You can find listings of reliable clinics overseas at the **International Society of Travel Medicine** (✆ **404/373-8282;** www.istm.org).

If anything, pharmacies in European cities are better stocked than some American drugstores, in that certain drugs might be available in Europe and not yet in the United States. There is no need to stock up on over-the-counter medications. Generic equivalents of your common prescription drugs are likely to be available at your destination.

WHAT TO DO IF YOU GET SICK AWAY FROM HOME

Any foreign consulate can provide a list of area doctors who speak English. If you get sick, consider asking your hotel concierge to recommend a local doctor—even his or her own. You can also try the emergency room at a local hospital. Many hospitals also have walk-in clinics for emergency cases that are not life-threatening; you may not get immediate attention, but you won't pay the high price of an emergency room visit.

We list **hospitals** and **emergency numbers** under "Fast Facts" in each destination chapter.

If you suffer from a chronic illness, consult your doctor before your departure. Pack **prescription medications** in your carry-on luggage, and carry them in their original containers, with pharmacy labels—otherwise they won't make it through airport security. Carry the generic name of prescription medicines, in case a local pharmacist is unfamiliar with the brand name.

You may have to pay all medical costs upfront and be reimbursed later.

SPECIALIZED TRAVEL RESOURCES

Travelers with Disabilities

Europe won't win any medals for accessibility for travelers with disabilities, but in the past few years its big cities have made an effort to accommodate them.

Many travel agencies offer customized tours and itineraries for travelers with disabilities. Among them are **Flying Wheels Travel** (✆ **507/451-5005;** www.flyingwheelstravel.com); **Access-Able Travel Source** (www.access-able.com); and **Accessible Journeys** (✆ **800/846-4537** or 610/521-0339; www.disabilitytravel.com).

Organizations that offer assistance to travelers with disabilities include **Moss-Rehab** (✆ **800/CALL-MOSS** [225-5667]; www.mossresourcenet.org); the **American Foundation for the Blind** (**AFB;** ✆ **800/232-5463;** www.afb.org); and **SATH** (Society for Accessible Travel & Hospitality; ✆ **212/447-7284;** www.sath.org). **AirAmbulanceCard.com** (✆ **877/424-7633**) is now partnered with SATH and allows you to preselect top-notch hospitals in case of an emergency.

For U.K. citizens, the **Royal Association for Disability and Rehabilitation (RADAR),** Unit 12, 250 City Rd., London EC1V 8AF (✆ **020/7250-3222;** www.radar.org.uk), provides general info, including planning and booking a holiday, insurance, finances, useful organizations, holiday providers, transportation and rental equipment options, and specialized accommodations. Another good service is the **Holiday Care Service,** Sunley House, 7th Floor, 4 Bedford Park, Croydon, Surrey CR0 2AP (✆ **0845/124-9971;** www.holidaycare.org), a national charity that advises on accessible accommodations for seniors and persons with disabilities.

Gay & Lesbian Travelers

Much of Europe has grown to accept same-sex couples over the past few decades, and in most countries homosexual sex acts are legal. To be on the safe side, do a bit of research and test the waters for acceptability in any one city or area. As you might expect, smaller towns tend to be less accepting than cities. Gay centers include London, Paris, Amsterdam, Berlin, Milan, Ibiza, Sitges, and the Greek Islands (Mykonos).

The **International Gay and Lesbian Travel Association** (**IGLTA;** ✆ **800/448-8550** or 954/630-1637; www.iglta.org) is the trade association for the gay and lesbian travel industry, and offers an online directory of gay- and lesbian-friendly travel businesses; go to their website and click on "Destinations."

Many agencies offer tours and travel itineraries specifically for gay and lesbian travelers. Among them are **Above and Beyond Tours** (✆ **800/397-2681;** www.abovebeyondtours.com); **Now, Voyager** (✆ **800/255-6951;** www.nowvoyager.com); and **Olivia Cruises & Resorts** (✆ **800/631-6277;** www.olivia.com).

Gay.com Travel (✆ **415/834-6500;** www.gay.com) is an excellent online source for travel. It provides regularly updated information about gay-owned, gay-oriented, and gay-friendly lodging, dining, sightseeing, nightlife, and shopping establishments in every important destination worldwide.

The following travel guides are available at many bookstores, or you can order them from any online bookseller: ***Spartacus International Gay Guide*** (Bruno Gmünder Verlag; www.spartacusworld.com/gayguide) and the ***Damron*** guides (www.damron.com), with separate, annual books for gay men and lesbians.

Senior Travel

Don't be shy about asking for discounts, but always carry some kind of ID, such as a driver's license, showing your date of birth. Also mention that you're a senior when you first make your travel reservations. Many hotels offer seniors discounts, and in most cities people 60 and over qualify for reduced admission to theaters, museums, and other attractions, as well as discounted fares on public transportation.

Members of **AARP,** 601 E St. NW, Washington, DC 20049 (✆ **888/687-2277;** www.aarp.org), get discounts on hotels, airfares, and car rentals. AARP offers members a wide range of benefits, including *AARP The Magazine* and a monthly newsletter. Anyone 50 and over can join.

Many reliable agencies and organizations target the 50-plus market. **Road Scholar,** formerly known as Elderhostel (✆ **800/454-5768;** www.roadscholar.org), arranges study programs for those age 55 and over.

Recommended publications offering travel resources and discounts for seniors include the quarterly magazine ***Travel 50 & Beyond*** (www.travel50andbeyond.com); ***Travel Unlimited: Uncommon Adventures for the Mature Traveler*** (Avalon); and ***Unbelievably Good Deals and Great Adventures That You Absolutely Can't Get Unless You're Over 50*** (McGraw-Hill), by Joan Rattner Heilman.

Family Travel

Europeans expect to see families traveling together. It's a multigenerational continent, and you'll sometimes see the whole clan traveling around. And Europeans tend to love kids. You'll often find that a child guarantees you an even warmer reception at hotels and restaurants.

At **restaurants,** ask waiters for a half portion to fit junior's appetite. If you're traveling with small children, three- and four-star hotels may be your best bet—**babysitters** are on call so that you can take the occasional romantic dinner, and such hotels have a better general ability to help you access the city and its services. But even cheaper hotels can usually find you a sitter. Traveling with a pint-size person usually means pint-size rates. An **extra cot** in the room won't cost more than 30% extra (if anything), and most museums and sights offer **reduced or free admission** for children under a certain age (which can range from 6–18). And kids almost always get discounts on plane and train tickets.

To locate accommodations, restaurants, and attractions that are particularly kid-friendly, refer to the "Kids" icon throughout this guide.

Recommended family travel websites include **Family Travel Forum** (www.familytravelforum.com); **Family Travel Network** (www.familytravelnetwork.com); **Traveling Internationally with Your Kids** (www.travelwithyourkids.com); and **Family Travel Files** (www.thefamilytravelfiles.com).

Student Travel

The **International Student Travel Confederation (ISTC)** (www.istc.org) was formed in 1949 to make travel around the world more affordable for students. Check out its website for comprehensive travel services information and details on how to get an **International Student Identity Card (ISIC),** which qualifies students for substantial savings on rail passes, plane tickets, entrance fees, and more. It also provides students with basic health and life insurance and a 24-hour help line. The card is valid for a maximum of 18 months. You can apply for the card online or in person at **STA Travel** (✆ **800/781-4040** in North America; www.statravel.com), the biggest student travel agency in the world; check out the website to locate STA Travel offices worldwide. If you're no longer a student but are still 25 and younger, you can get an **International Youth Travel Card (IYTC)** from the same people, which entitles you to some discounts. **Travel CUTS** (✆ **800/592-2887;** www.travelcuts.com) offers similar services for both Canadians and U.S. residents. Irish students may prefer to turn to **USIT** (✆ **01/602-1906;** www.usit.ie), an Ireland-based specialist in student, youth, and independent travel.

SUSTAINABLE TOURISM

The following websites provide valuable wide-ranging information on sustainable travel. For a list of even more sustainable resources, as well as tips and explanations on how to travel greener, visit www.frommers.com/planning.

- **Responsible Travel** (www.responsibletravel.com) is a great source of sustainable travel ideas; the site is run by a spokesperson for ethical tourism in the travel industry. **Sustainable Travel International** (www.sustainabletravelinternational.org) promotes ethical tourism practices, and manages an extensive directory of sustainable properties and tour operators around the world.
- In the U.K., **Tourism Concern** (www.tourismconcern.org.uk) works to reduce social and environmental problems connected to tourism. The **Association of Independent Tour Operators** (**AITO;** www.aito.co.uk) is a group of specialist operators leading the field in making holidays sustainable.
- In Canada, **Green Living** (www.greenlivingonline.com) offers extensive content on how to travel sustainably, including a travel and transport section and profiles of the best green shops and services in major Canadian cities.
- In Australia, the national body that sets guidelines and standards for eco-tourism is **Ecotourism Australia** (www.ecotourism.org.au). **The Green Directory** (www.thegreendirectory.com.au), **Green Pages** (www.thegreenpages.com.au), and **EcoDirectory** (www.ecodirectory.com.au) offer sustainable travel tips and directories of green businesses.

- **Carbonfund** (www.carbonfund.org), **TerraPass** (www.terrapass.org), and **Carbon Neutral** (www.carbonneutral.org) provide info on "carbon offsetting," or offsetting the greenhouse gas emitted during flights.
- **Greenhotels** (www.greenhotels.com) recommends green-rated member hotels around the world that fulfill the company's stringent environmental requirements. **Environmentally Friendly Hotels** (www.environmentallyfriendlyhotels.com) offers more green accommodations ratings.
- For information on animal-friendly issues throughout the world, visit **Tread Lightly** (www.treadlightly.org). For information about the ethics of swimming with dolphins, visit the **Whale and Dolphin Conservation Society** (www.wdcs.org).
- **Volunteer International** (www.volunteerinternational.org) has a list of questions to help you determine the intentions and the nature of a volunteer program. For general info on volunteer travel, visit **www.volunteerabroad.org** and **www.idealist.org**.

SPECIAL-INTEREST TRIPS & ESCORTED TOURS

Special-Interest Trips

CYCLING

Cycling tours are a great way to see Europe at your own pace. Some of the best are conducted by the **CTC** (Cyclists' Tourist Club), Parklands, Railton Road, Guildford, Surrey, England GU2 9JX (✆ **0870/873-0060;** www.ctc.org.uk). **Hindriks European Bicycle Tours, Inc.,** P.O. Box 7010, Citrus Heights, CA 95621 (✆ **800/852-3258;** www.hindrikstours.com), leads 8-day bicycle tours throughout Europe. **ExperiencePlus!,** 415 Mason Court, Number 1, Fort Collins, CO 80524 (✆ **800/685-4565** or 970/484-8489; www.experienceplus.com), runs bike and walking tours across Europe. **Ciclismo Classico,** 30 Marathon St., Arlington, MA 02474 (✆ **800/866-7314** or 781/646-3377; www.ciclismoclassico.com), is an excellent outfit running tours of Italy. Florence-based **I Bike Italy, Inc.** ★, P.O. Box 64-3824, Vero Beach, FL (✆ **772/321-0267;** www.ibikeitaly.com), offers guided single-day rides in the Tuscan countryside.

HIKING

Wilderness Travel, 1102 9th St., Berkeley, CA 94710 (✆ **800/368-2794** or 510/558-2488; www.wildernesstravel.com), specializes in walking tours, treks, and inn-to-inn hiking tours of Europe, as well as less strenuous walking tours. **Sherpa Expeditions,** 131A Heston Rd., Hounslow, Middlesex, England TW5 0RF (✆ **020/8577-2717;** www.sherpaexpeditions.com), offers both self-guided and group treks through off-the-beaten-track regions. Two somewhat upscale walking-tour companies are **Butterfield & Robinson,** 70 Bond St., Ste. 300, Toronto, ON M5B 1X3 (✆ **866/551-9090** or 800/67-81-14-77 outside North America; www.butterfield.com); and **Country Walkers,** P.O. Box 180, Waterbury, VT 05676 (✆ **800/464-9255** or 802/244-1387; www.countrywalkers.com).

Most European countries have associations geared toward aiding hikers and walkers. In England, it's the **Ramblers Association,** 87–90 Albert Embankment, London

SE1 7TW, 2nd Floor, Camelford House (✆ **020/7339-8500;** www.ramblers.org.uk). In Italy, contact the **Club Alpino Italiano,** 6 Via Silvo Pellico, Milan 20121 (✆ **02/8646-3516;** www.caimilano.it). For Austria, try the **Österreichischer Alpenverein (Austrian Alpine Club),** Wilhelm-Greil-Strasse 15, A-6010 Innsbruck (✆ **0512/59547;** www.alpenverein.at). In Norway, it's **Den Norske Turistforening (Norwegian Trekking Association),** Storgata 3, Box 7 Sentrum, 0101 Oslo (✆ **40-00-18-68;** www.turistforeningen.no).

HORSEBACK RIDING

One of the best companies is **Equitour,** P.O. Box 807, Dubois, WY 82513 (✆ **800/545-0019** or 307/455-3363; www.ridingtours.com), which offers 5- to 7-day rides through many of Europe's most popular areas, such as Tuscany and the Loire Valley.

EDUCATIONAL TRAVEL

The best (and one of the most expensive) of the escorted tour operators is **Group IST (International Specialty Travel;** ✆ **212/594-8787;** www.groupist.com), whose tours are first class all the way and accompanied by a certified expert in whatever field the trip focuses on. If you missed out on study abroad in college, the brainy **Smithsonian Journeys** (✆ **877/338-8687;** www.smithsonianjourneys.org) may be just the ticket, albeit a pricey one. Study leaders are often world-renowned experts in their field. Journeys are carefully crafted and go to some of the most compelling places in Europe, avoiding tourist traps. Also contact your alma mater or local university to find out whether it offers summer tours open to the public and guided by a professor specialist.

The **National Registration Center for Studies Abroad (NRCSA),** P.O. Box 1393, Milwaukee, WI 53201 (✆ **414/278-0631;** www.nrcsa.com), and the **American Institute for Foreign Study (AIFS),** River Plaza, 9 W. Broad St., Stamford, CT 06902 (✆ **866/906-2437** or 203/399-5000; www.aifs.com), can both help you arrange study programs and summer programs abroad.

The biggest organization dealing with higher education in Europe is the **Institute of International Education (IIE),** with headquarters at 809 United Nations Plaza, New York, NY 10017-3500 (✆ **212/883-8200;** www.iie.org). A few of its booklets are free, but for US$50, plus US$6 postage, you can buy the more definitive *Short Term Study Abroad.* To order publications, check out the IIE's online bookstore at www.iiebooks.org.

A clearinghouse for information on European-based language schools is **Lingua Service Worldwide,** 42 Artillery Rd., Woodbury, CT 06798 (✆ **800/394-LEARN** [394-5327] or 203/263-6294; www.linguaserviceworldwide.com).

CULINARY SCHOOLS

Apicius, Via Guelfa 85, 50129 Florence, Italy (✆ **055/2658135;** www.apicius.it), is the finest cooking school in Florence, an expert on Tuscan culinary arts. Its monthly programs are taught by local chefs and food experts, with an emphasis on wine appreciation. From May to October, the **International Cooking School of Italian Food and Wine,** 201 E. 28th St., Ste. 15B, New York, NY 10016-8538 (✆ **212/779-1921;** www.internationalcookingschool.com), offers courses in Bologna, the "gastronomic capital of Italy." **Le Cordon Bleu,** 8 rue Léon-Delhomme,

ASK before YOU GO

Before you invest in a package deal or an escorted tour:

- Always ask about the **cancellation policy.** Can you get your money back? Is a deposit required?
- Ask about the **accommodations choices and prices** for each. Then look up the hotels' reviews in a Frommer's guide and check their rates online for your specific dates of travel. Also find out what types of rooms are offered.
- Request a complete **schedule** (escorted tours only).
- Ask about the **size** and demographics of the group (escorted tours only).
- Discuss what is included in the **price** (transportation, meals, tips, airport transfers, and so on; escorted tours only).
- Finally, look for **hidden expenses.** Ask whether airport departure fees and taxes, for example, are included in the total cost—they rarely are.

75015 Paris (✆ **800/457-2433** in the U.S. and Canada, or 01-53-68-22-50; www.cordonbleu.edu), was established in 1895 as a means of spreading the tenets of French cuisine to the world at large. It offers many programs outside its flagship Paris school.

Escorted General-Interest Tours

Escorted tours are structured group tours, with a group leader. The price usually includes everything from airfare to hotels, meals, tours, admission costs, and local transportation.

The two largest tour operators conducting escorted tours of Europe are **Globus/Cosmos** (✆ **866/755-8581;** www.globusandcosmos.com) and **Trafalgar** (✆ **866/544-4434;** www.trafalgartours.com). Both companies have first-class tours that vary in prices. The differences are mainly in hotel location and the number of activities. There's little difference in the companies' services, so choose your tour based on the itinerary and preferred date of departure. Brochures are available at travel agencies, and all tours must be booked through travel agents.

Despite the fact that escorted tours require big deposits and predetermine hotels, restaurants, and itineraries, many people derive security and peace of mind from the structure they offer. Escorted tours—whether they're navigated by bus, motorcoach, train, or boat—let travelers sit back and enjoy the trip without having to drive or worry about details. They take you to the maximum number of sights in the minimum amount of time with the least amount of hassle. They're particularly convenient for people with limited mobility and they can be a great way to make new friends.

On the downside, you'll have little opportunity for serendipitous interactions with locals. The tours can be jampacked with activities, leaving little room for individual sightseeing, whim, or adventure—plus they often focus on the heavily touristed sites, so you miss out on many a lesser-known gem.

Packages for Independent Travelers

Package tours are simply a way to buy the airfare, accommodations, and other elements of your trip (such as car rentals, airport transfers, and sometimes even activities) at the same time and often at discounted prices.

All major airlines flying to Europe sell vacation packages, including **American Airlines Vacations** (✆ **800/321-2121;** www.aavacations.com), **Delta Vacations** (✆ **800/654-6559;** www.deltavacations.com), **Continental Airlines Vacations** (✆ **800/301-3800;** www.covacations.com), and **United Vacations** (✆ **888/854-3899;** www.unitedvacations.com). Several big **online travel agencies**—Expedia, Travelocity, Orbitz, and Lastminute.com—also do a brisk business in packages.

A leading packager offering European vacations is **EuroVacations** (www.eurovacations.com), an affiliate of Rail Europe, featuring highlights of such countries as England, France, Germany, Italy, and Spain, but also dealing in eastern Europe. For more information, call ✆ **877/471-3876** or write EuroVacations at 851 SW Sixth, Ste. 900, Portland, OR 97204. More great deals are offered by **Sherman's Travel** (www.shermanstravel.com), which features bargains on airfare and hotel deals, such as 10 days in the south of Spain or a Paris-and-Madrid combo. One of its most popular offerings is a trio of London, Paris, and Rome, including airfare and 2 nights in each capital. A 7-day Greek Islands tour, including Athens, is also featured. You can reach the outfit via e-mail at info@shermanstravel.com. Another worthy contender is **I Travel to Europe** (www.itraveltoeurope.com), which puts together some hot package deals, including special-interest trips such as a 9-day escorted Tuscan Food and Wine festival, taking in Florence, Siena, and other trendy spots. One of its best deals is 2 weeks in southern Spain in winter, featuring airfare and hotels starting at US$899 per person. For more information, write to I Travel to Europe, 2300 Corporate Blvd., Ste. 214, Boca Raton, FL 33431.

Travel packages are also listed in the travel section of your local Sunday newspaper. Or check ads in the national travel magazines such as *Arthur Frommer's Budget Travel Magazine, Travel + Leisure, National Geographic Traveler,* and *Condé Nast Traveler.*

STAYING CONNECTED

Mobile Phones

The three letters that define much of the world's wireless capabilities are **GSM** (Global System for Mobile Communications), a big, seamless network that makes for easy cross-border cellphone use throughout Europe and dozens of other countries worldwide. In the U.S., T-Mobile and AT&T Wireless use this quasi-universal system; in Canada, some Fido and Rogers customers use GSM; and all Europeans and most Australians use GSM. GSM phones function with a removable plastic SIM card, encoded with your phone number and account information. If your cellphone is on a GSM system, and you have a world-capable multiband phone such as many Sony Ericsson, Motorola, or Samsung models, you can make and receive calls across civilized areas around much of the globe. Just call your wireless operator and ask for international roaming to be activated on your account. Unfortunately, per-minute charges can be high—usually US$1 to US$1.50 in western Europe.

NUMBER, PLEASE: calling EUROPE

To make a phone call **from the United States to Europe,** dial the international access code, **011,** then the **country code** for the country you're calling, then the **city code** for the city you're calling, and then the regular phone number. For an operator-assisted call, dial **01,** then the country code, then the city code, and then the regular phone number; an operator then comes on the line.

The following are the codes for the countries and major cities in this guide. These are the codes you use to call from overseas or from another European country. If you're calling from within the country or within the city, see "Telephone" in the "Fast Facts" section for each city.

European phone systems are undergoing a prolonged change. **Italy, France, Spain, Monaco, Copenhagen, and Portugal no longer use separate city codes.** The code is now built into all phone numbers, and you must always dial the initial 0 or 9 (which was previously—and still is in most other countries—added before a city code only when dialing from another city within the country). Also, be aware of these two recent changes: (1) The city codes for London (171 and 181) have been replaced by a new single code, 20, which is then followed by an eight-digit number beginning with either 7 or 8; and (2) the city code for Lisbon has changed from 1 to 21.

Austria	43
Innsbruck	512
Salzburg	662
Vienna	1
Belgium	32
Bruges	50
Brussels	2
Ghent	9
Czech Republic	420
Prague	2
Denmark	45
Copenhagen	31–39
England	44
Bath	1225
London	207–208
Oxford	1865
Stratford-upon-Avon	1789
France	33
Germany	49
Berlin	30
Frankfurt	69
Munich	89
Greece	30
Athens	210
Delphi	265

For many, **renting** a phone is a good idea. While you can rent a phone from any number of overseas sites, including kiosks at airports and at car-rental agencies, we suggest renting the phone before you leave home. North Americans can rent one before leaving home from **InTouch USA** (© 800/872-7626; www.intouchglobal.com) or **RoadPost** (© 888/290-1616 or 905/272-5665; www.roadpost.com). InTouch will also, for free, advise you on whether your existing phone will work overseas.

Buying a phone can be economically attractive, as many nations have cheap prepaid phone systems. Once you arrive at your destination, stop by a local cellphone shop and get the cheapest package; you'll probably pay less than US$100 for a phone and a starter calling card. Local calls may be as low as 10¢ per minute, and in many countries incoming calls are free.

Hungary	36
Budapest	1
Ireland	353
Dublin	1
Italy	39
Milan	2
Rome	6
Venice	41
Monaco	377
Netherlands	31
Amsterdam	20
Norway	47
Oslo	22
Portugal	351
Lisbon	21
Scotland	44
Edinburgh	131
Spain	34
Barcelona	93
Madrid	91
Seville	95
Sweden	46
Stockholm	8
Switzerland	41
Bern	31
Geneva	22
Zurich	1

The easiest and cheapest way to call home from abroad is with a calling card. On the road, you just dial a local access code (almost always free) and then punch in the number you're calling as well as the calling card number. If you're in a country without touch-tone, just wait for an English-speaking operator to put your call through. The "Telephone" entry in the "Fast Facts" in each destination chapter gives the AT&T, MCI, and Sprint access codes for that country (your calling card will probably come with a wallet-size list of local access numbers). You can also call any one of those companies' numbers to make a collect call as well; just dial it and wait for the operator.

When it comes to dialing direct, calling from the United States to Europe is much cheaper than the other way around, so whenever possible, have friends and family call you at your hotel rather than calling them yourself. To dial direct back to the **United States** and **Canada** from Europe, the international access code is often, but not always, **00;** the country code is **1,** and then you punch in the area code and number. For **Australia** and **New Zealand,** the access code is also **00;** the country codes are **61** and **64,** respectively.

Voice over Internet Protocol (VoIP)

If you have Web access while traveling, you might consider a broadband-based telephone service (in technical terms, **Voice over Internet Protocol,** or **VoIP**) such as Skype (www.skype.com) or Vonage (www.vonage.com), which allows you to make free international calls if you use their services from your laptop or in a cybercafe. Check the sites for details.

Internet/E-Mail

WITHOUT YOUR OWN COMPUTER

To find cybercafes in your destination check **www.cybercaptive.com** and **www.cybercafe.com**.

Most major airports have **Internet kiosks** that provide basic Web access for a per-minute fee that's usually higher than cybercafe prices. Check out copy shops like **FedEx Office** (formerly FedEx Kinko's), which offers computer stations with fully loaded software (as well as Wi-Fi).

WITH YOUR OWN COMPUTER

More and more hotels, resorts, airports, cafes, and retailers are going **Wi-Fi** (wireless fidelity), becoming "hot spots" that offer free high-speed Wi-Fi access or charge a small fee for usage. Most laptops sold today have built-in wireless capability. To find public Wi-Fi hot spots at your destination, go to **www.jiwire.com**; its Hotspot Finder holds the world's largest directory of public wireless hot spots.

For dial-up access, most business-class hotels throughout the world offer dataports for laptop modems, and a few thousand hotels in Europe now offer free high-speed Internet access.

Wherever you go, bring a **connection kit** of the right power and phone adapters, a spare phone cord, and a spare Ethernet network cable—or find out whether your hotel supplies them to guests.

TIPS ON ACCOMMODATIONS

Traditional European hotels tend to be simpler than American ones and emphasize cleanliness and friendliness over amenities. For example, even in the cheapest American chain motel, free cable is as standard as indoor plumbing. In Europe, however, few hotels below the moderate level even have in-room TVs.

Most European countries rate hotels by stars, ranging from five stars (grand luxe) to one star (modest). A four-star hotel offers first-class accommodations, a three-star hotel is moderately priced, and a one- or two-star hotel is inexpensively priced. Governments grant stars based on a rigid criterion, evaluating such amenities as elevators, private bathrooms, pools, and air-conditioning. The hotel with the most stars is

ONLINE TRAVELER'S toolbox

Veteran travelers usually carry some essential items to make their trips easier. Following is a selection of handy online tools to bookmark and use.

- **Airplane Food** (www.airlinemeals.net)
- **Airplane Seating** (www.seatguru.com; www.airlinequality.com)
- **Foreign Languages for Travelers** (www.travlang.com)
- **Maps** (www.mapquest.com)
- **Subway Navigator** (http://gridskipper.com/55950/subwaynavigator)
- **Time and Date** (www.timeanddate.com)
- **Travel Warnings** (http://travel.state.gov, www.fco.gov.uk/travel, www.voyage.gc.ca, or www.smarttraveller.gov.au)
- **Universal Currency Converter** (www.xe.com/ucc)
- **Visa ATM Locator** (www.visa.com), **MasterCard ATM Locator** (www.mastercard.com)
- **Weather** (www.intellicast.com; www.weather.com)

FROMMERS.COM: THE complete TRAVEL RESOURCE

It should go without saying, but we highly recommend **Frommers.com,** voted Best Travel Site by *PC Magazine.* We think you'll find our expert advice and tips; independent reviews of hotels, restaurants, attractions, and preferred shopping and nightlife venues; vacation giveaways; and an online booking tool indispensable before, during, and after your travels. We publish the complete contents of more than 128 travel guides in our **Destinations** section covering nearly 3,800 places worldwide to help you plan your trip. Each weekday, we publish original articles reporting on **Deals and News** via our free **Frommers.com Newsletter** to help you save time and money and travel smarter. We're betting you'll find our new **Events** listings (http://events.frommers.com) an invaluable resource; it's an up-to-the-minute roster of what's happening in cities everywhere—including concerts, festivals, lectures, and more. We've also added weekly **podcasts, interactive maps,** and hundreds of new images across the site. Check out our **Travel Talk** area featuring **Message Boards** where you can join in conversations with thousands of fellow Frommer's travelers and post your trip report once you return.

not necessarily the most elegant or charming. For example, a five-star hotel might be an ugly, modern building, whereas a one-star hotel might be a town mansion but with no elevator, bar, or restaurant.

Unless otherwise noted, all hotel rooms in this book have **private en suite bathrooms.** However, the standard European hotel bathroom might not look like what you're used to. For example, the European concept of a shower is to stick a nozzle in the bathroom wall and a drain in the floor. Shower curtains are optional. In some cramped private bathrooms, you'll have to relocate the toilet paper outside the bathroom before turning on the shower and drenching the whole room. Another interesting fixture is the "half tub," in which there's only room to sit, rather than lie down. The half tub usually sports a shower nozzle that has nowhere to hang—so your knees get very clean and the floor gets very wet. Hot water may be available only once a day and not on demand—this is especially true with shared bathrooms. Heating water is costly, and many smaller hotels do it only once daily, in the morning.

In addition to the hotel recommendations listed in the destination chapters, **Untours** (**888/868-6871;** www.untours.com) provides exceptional apartment, farmhouse, or cottage stays of 2 weeks or more in many European destinations for a reasonable price. The price includes air/ground transportation, cooking facilities, and on-call support from a local resident. Best of all, Untours—named the "Most Generous Company in America" by Newman's Own—donates most profits to provide low-interest loans to underprivileged entrepreneurs around the world (see website for details).

2

AUSTRIA

by Darwin Porter & Danforth Prince

Austria stands at the crossroads of Europe, as it did in the heyday of the Austro-Hungarian Empire. Its capital, Vienna, stranded during the postwar years on the edge of western Europe, is taking its place again as an important international city.

The country offers plenty to do, from exploring historic castles and palaces to skiing on some of the world's finest alpine slopes.

VIENNA ★★★

Vienna still retains much of the glory and grandeur of the empire's heady days. Museum treasures from all over Europe, baroque palaces through which Maria Theresa and her brood wandered, Johann Strauss's lively music, Gustav Klimt's paintings, the concert halls, the unparalleled opera—it's all still here, as if the empire were still flourishing.

Tourism is growing as thousands arrive every year to view Vienna's great art and architecture; to feast on lavish Viennese pastries; to explore the Vienna Woods; to sail down the Danube; to attend Vienna's balls, operas, and festivals; and to listen to the "music that never stops."

Visitors today face a newer and brighter Vienna, a city with more *joie de vivre* and punch than it's had since before the war. There's also a downside: Prices are on the rise—they haven't reached the height of the Ferris wheel at the Prater, but they're climbing there.

Essentials

GETTING THERE

BY PLANE **Vienna International Airport** (**VIE; ✆ 01/7007-22233;** www.viennaairport.at) is about 19km (12 miles) southeast of the city center. There's regular bus service between the airport and the **City Air Terminal,** adjacent to the Vienna Hilton and directly across from the **Wien Mitte/Landstrasse** rail station, where you can easily connect with subway and tram lines. Buses run every 20 minutes from 5am to midnight and hourly from midnight to 5am. The trip takes about 20 minutes and costs 6€ per person. Tickets are sold on the bus and must be purchased with euros. There's also bus service between the airport and two railroad stations, the Westbahnhof and the Südbahnhof, leaving every 30 minutes to an hour. Fares are also 6€. There is also a direct city/airport train from Wien Mitte to the airport that takes 16 minutes and costs 9€.

Austria

The official **Vienna Tourist Information Office** in the arrival hall of the airport is open daily from 8:30am to 9pm.

BY TRAIN Vienna has four principal rail stations, with frequent connections from all Austrian cities and towns and from all major European cities. For train information for all stations, call ✆ **05/1717.**

Westbahnhof (West Railway Station), on Europaplatz, is for trains arriving from western Austria, France, Germany, Switzerland, and some eastern European countries. It has frequent links to major Austrian cities such as Salzburg, which is a 3-hour train ride from Vienna. The Westbahnhof connects with local trains, the U3 and U6 underground lines, and several tram and bus routes.

Südbahnhof (South Railway Station), on Südtirolerplatz, has train service to southern and eastern Austria, Italy, Hungary, Slovenia, and Croatia. It is linked with local rail service and tram and bus routes.

Both of these stations house useful travel agencies **(Österreichisches Verkehrsbüro)** that provide tourist information and help with hotel reservations. In the Westbahnhof, the agency is in the upper hall; at the Südbahnhof, it's in the lower hall.

Other stations in Vienna include **Franz-Josef Bahnhof,** on Franz-Josef-Platz, used mainly by local trains, although connections are made here to Prague and Berlin. You can take the D-tram line to the city's Ringstrasse from here. **Wien Mitte,** at Landstrasser Hauptstrasse 1, is also a terminus for local trains, plus a depot for trains to the Czech Republic and to Vienna International Airport.

BY BUS The **City Bus Terminal** is at the Wien Mitte rail station, Landstrasser Hauptstrasse 1. This is the arrival depot for Post buses and Bundesbuses from points all over the country, and also the arrival point for private buses from various European cities. The terminal has lockers, currency-exchange kiosks, and a ticket counter

Vienna

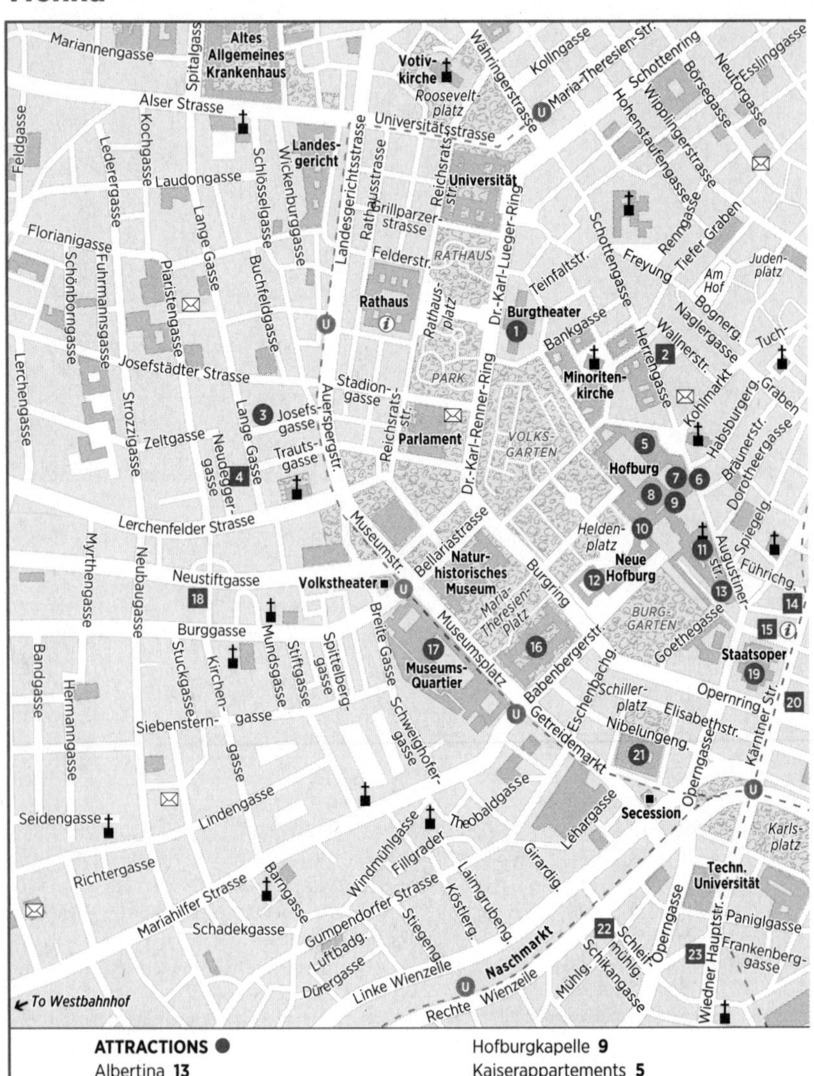

ATTRACTIONS ●

Albertina **13**
Augustinerkirche **11**
Burgtheater **1**
Die Burgkapelle **7**
Domkirche St. Stephan **26**
Gemäldegalerie der Akademie der Bildenden Kunste **21**
Haus der Musik **29**
Hofburg Palace Complex **10**
Hofburgkapelle **9**
Kaiserappartements **5**
Kunsthistorisches Museum **16**
Lipizzaner Museum **7**
MuseumsQuartier **17**
Neue Hofburg **12**
Schatzkammer **8**
Spanische Reitschule **6**
Vienna's English Theatre **3**
Wiener Staatsoper **19**

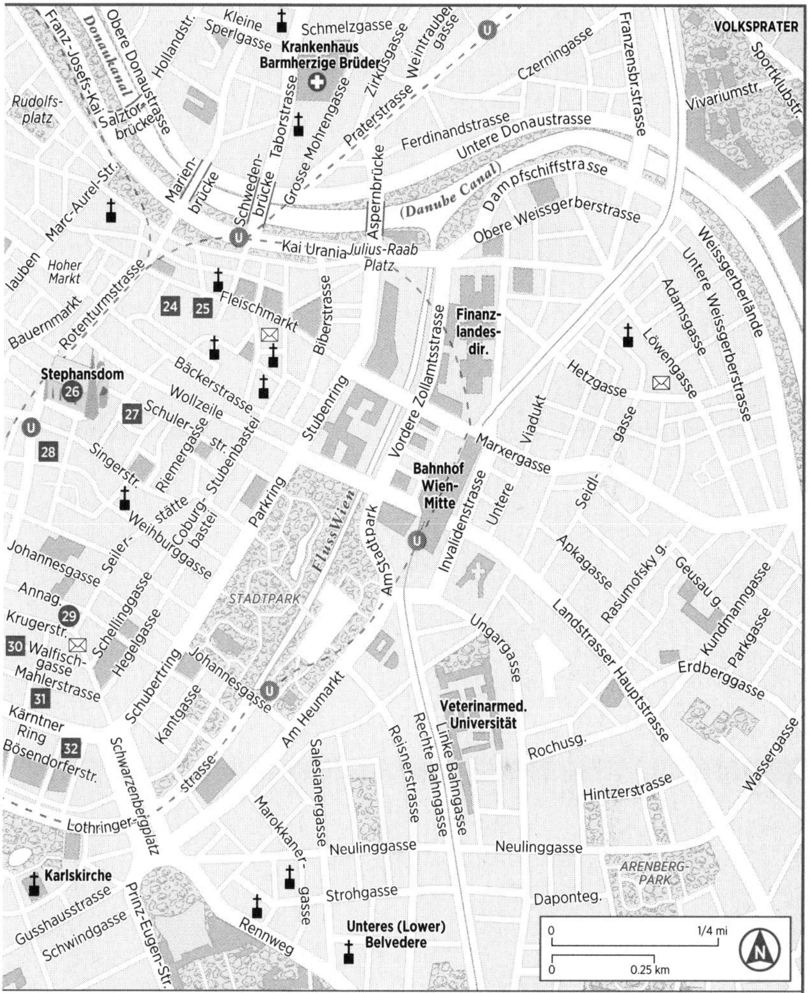

ACCOMMODATIONS ■

Drei Kronen **22**
Falkensteiner Hotel Am Schottenfeld **18**
Grand Hotel Wien **31**
Hollmann Beletage—Design & Boutique **25**
Hotel Astoria **14**
Hotel Bristol **20**
Hotel Das Triest **23**
Hotel Imperial **32**
Hotel Kaiserin Elisabeth **28**
Hotel Kärntnerhof **24**
Hotel König von Ungarn **27**
Hotel-Pension Suzanne **30**
Hotel Rathaus Wine & Design **4**
Hotel Sacher Wien **15**
Steigenberger Hotel Herrenhof **2**

✉ Post Office
ⓘ Information
Railway
U-Bahn

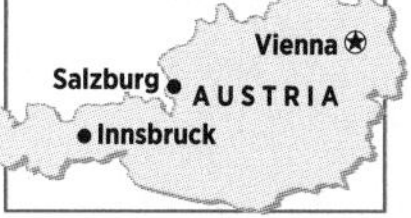

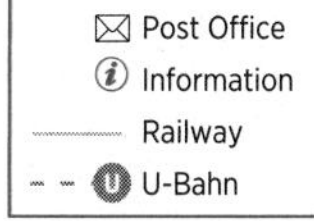

NATIVE behavior

Get accustomed to hearing *"Grüss Gott"* ("God bless you") when Austrians greet you and *"Auf Wiedersehen"* when they leave. These greetings are practiced by everybody from your hotel manager to the shoeshine man.

Although no one will kick you off the premises, it is a local custom to dress up for a night at the opera or ballet. You can show up in a jogging suit or jeans, but you might feel out of place.

Austria is perhaps the most formal of the countries reviewed in this guide. Yes, some gents nostalgic for the old Austro-Hungarian Empire still bow and click their heels when introduced to a lady. Prepare to shake hands on both meeting and parting. The Austrians are great sticklers for titles, however minor or honorific, including *Doktor* or *Professor.*

If you've never hung out in coffee-houses before, making one your second living room, Austria provides a wonderful introduction to this custom. The Viennese especially can sit for hour after hour over a single cup of coffee, reading magazines and newspapers or else watching the world parade by.

open daily from 6:15am to 6pm. For bus information, call ✆ **05/1717** daily from 6:15am to 6pm.

BY CAR You can reach Vienna from all directions via major highways *(Autobahnen)* or by secondary highways. The main artery from the west is Autobahn A1, coming in from Munich 468km (291 miles), Salzburg 336km (209 miles), and Linz 187km (116 miles). Autobahn A2 arrives from the south, from Graz 200km (124 miles) and Klagenfurt 309km (192 miles). Autobahn A4 comes in from the east, connecting with Route E58, which runs to Bratislava and Prague. Autobahn A22 takes traffic from the northwest, and Route E10 connects to the cities and towns of southeastern Austria and Hungary.

VISITOR INFORMATION **Tourist Office** The official **Wien Tourist-Information,** Albertinaplatz 7 (✆ **01/24-555;** www.wien.info), is open daily from 9am to 7pm. You can make room reservations here.

Websites Besides **Wien Tourist-Information** (www.wien.info), go to the **Austrian National Tourist Office** (www.austria.info/us) for current information on culture and events.

CITY LAYOUT Vienna has evolved into one of the largest metropolises of central Europe, with a surface area covering 415 sq. km (160 sq. miles). It's divided into 23 districts *(Bezirke),* each identified by a numeral.

The size and shape of the **First District,** known as the **Innere Stadt (Inner City),** roughly corresponds to the original borders of the medieval city. Other than St. Stephan's Cathedral, very few Gothic or medieval buildings remain—many were reconstructed in the baroque or neoclassical style, whereas others are modern replacements of buildings bombed during World War II. As Austria's commercial and cultural nerve center, the central district contains dozens of streets devoted exclusively to pedestrian traffic. The most famous of these is **Kärntnerstrasse,** which bypasses the Vienna State Opera House during its southward trajectory toward the province of Carinthia (Kärnten).

Ringstrasse is a circular boulevard about 4km (2½ miles) long whose construction between 1859 and 1888 was one of the most ambitious (and controversial) examples of urban restoration in the history of central Europe. The boulevard surrounds the Inner City. Confusingly, the name of this boulevard changes many times during its encirclement of the Inner City. Names that apply to it carry the suffix *-ring:* for example, Opernring, Schottenring, Burgring, Dr.-Karl-Lueger-Ring, Stubenring, Parkring, Schubertring, and Kärntner Ring.

Surrounding Ringstrasse and the Inner City, in a more or less clockwise direction, are the inner suburban districts (2–9), which contain many hotels and restaurants popular for their close proximity to the city center. The outer districts (10–23) form another concentric ring of suburbs, comprising a variety of neighborhoods from industrial parks to rural villages.

Northeast of the Inner City, beyond the Danube Canal, is the **2nd District,** home to the Prater, the famous amusement park. East of the center, in the **3rd District,** you'll find the art treasures and baroque setting of the Belvedere Palace. West of the center is Schönbrunn Palace, located in the **13th District.**

GETTING AROUND **By Public Transportation** **Wiener Verkehrsbetriebe (Vienna Transport),** with its network of facilities covering hundreds of miles, can take you where you want to go—by U-Bahn (subway), tram (streetcar), or bus. **Informationdienst der Wiener Verkehrsbetriebe (Vienna Public Transport Information Center)** has five locations: Opernpassage (an underground passageway adjacent to the Wiener Staatsoper [State Opera]), Karlsplatz, Stephansplatz (near Vienna's cathedral), Westbahnhof, and Praterstern. For information about any of these outlets, call ✆ **01/790-9105.**

Vienna maintains a uniform fare that applies to all forms of public transport. A ticket for the bus, subway, or tram will cost 1.70€ if you buy it in advance or 2.20€ if you buy it onboard. Smart Viennese buy their tickets in advance, usually in blocks of at least five at a time, from any of the city's thousands of Tabac-Trafiks (a store or kiosk selling tobacco products and newspapers) or at any of the public transport

The Vienna Card

The **Vienna Card** gives you access to all public modes of transportation (subway, bus, and tram) within Vienna—as well as discounts in city museums, shops, and restaurants—for a single discounted price. A 24-hour network pass costs 5.70€ and is good for a full day of public transport. A 72-hour network pass sells for 19€. There's also an 8-day ticket, priced at 28€, which contains eight individual partitions. Each of these, when stamped, is good for 1 day of unlimited travel. An individual can opt to reserve all eight of the partitions for his or her own use, thereby gaining 8 days of cost-effective travel on the city's transport system. Or the partitions can be subdivided among a group of several riders, allowing, for example, two persons 4 days each of unlimited rides. Vienna Cards are easy to find throughout the capital, or you can buy one outside Vienna with a credit card by calling ✆ **01/7984-400148.**

centers noted above. No matter what vehicle you decide to ride within Vienna, remember that once a ticket has been stamped (validated) by either a machine or a railway attendant, it's valid for one trip in one direction, anywhere in the city, including transfers.

BY U-BAHN (SUBWAY) The U-Bahn consists of five lines labeled as U1, U2, U3, U4, and U6 (there is no U5). Karlsplatz, in the heart of the Inner City, is the most important underground station for visitors, as the U1, U2, and U4 converge here. The U2 traces part of the Ring, the U4 goes to Schönbrunn, and the U1 stops in Stephansplatz. The U3 also stops in Stephansplatz and connects with the Westbahnhof. The U-Bahn runs daily from 6am to midnight.

BY BUS Buses traverse Vienna in all directions and operate Monday through Saturday from 6am to 10pm and Sunday from 6am to 8pm. Bus nos. 1A, 2A, and 3A will get you around the Inner City. Convenient night buses are available on weekends and holidays starting at 12:15am. They go from Schwedenplatz to the outer suburbs (including Grinzing). Normal tickets are not valid on these late "N" buses. Instead, you pay a special fare of 1.70€ onboard.

BY TRAM Riding the red-and-white trams (*Strassenbahn*) is not only a practical way to get around, but a great way to see the city. Tram stops are well marked and lines are labeled as numbers or letters. Lines 1 and 2 will bring you to all the major sights on the Ringstrasse. Line D skirts the outer Ring and goes to the Südbahnhof, whereas line 18 goes between the Westbahnhof and the Südbahnhof.

BY TAXI Taxi stands are marked by signs, or you can call for a radio cab by phoning © **31300,** 81400, 44444, 60160, or 40100. Fares are indicated on an officially calibrated taximeter. The basic fare is 2.50€, plus 1.10€ per kilometer. For rides after 11pm, and for trips on Sunday and holidays, there's a surcharge of 1€. There is an additional charge of 2€ if the taxi is ordered by phone.

BY CAR Major car-rental companies operating in Vienna include **Avis,** Opernring 3–5 (© **800/331-1212** in the U.S. and Canada, or 01/587-62-41 at the Vienna airport; U-Bahn: Karlsplatz); **Budget Rent-a-Car** (© **800/527-0700** in the U.S., or 01/70-0732711 at the Vienna Airport; U-Bahn: Landstrasse/Wien Mitte); and **Hertz,** at the airport (© **800/654-3001** in the U.S., or 01/70-0732661).

BY BICYCLE Vienna has more than 250km (155 miles) of marked bicycle paths within the city limits. In the summer, many Viennese leave their cars in the garage and ride bikes. You can take bicycles on specially marked U-Bahn cars free, but only Monday to Friday from 9am to 3pm and 6:30pm to midnight; on weekends in July and August, bicycles are carried free from 9am to midnight.

Rental stores abound at the Prater and along the banks of the Danube Canal, which is the favorite bike route for most Viennese. One of the best of the many sites specializing in bike rentals is **Pedalpower,** Ausstellungsstrasse 3 (© **01/729-7234;** www.pedalpower.at), which is open March to October from 9am to 7pm. The Vienna Tourist Board can also supply a list of rental shops and more information about bike paths. Bike rentals begin at about 28€ per day. You are supplied with a map for a self-guided tour.

[FastFACTS] VIENNA

American Express The office at Kärntnerstrasse 21–23 (✆ **01/5125-110**), near Stock-im-Eisenplatz, is open Monday to Friday 9am to 5:30pm and Saturday 9am to noon.

Business Hours Most shops are open Monday to Friday 9am to 6pm and Saturday 9am to noon, 12:30pm, or 1pm, depending on the store. On the first Saturday of every month, shops customarily remain open until 4:30 or 5pm. The tradition is called *langer Samstag.*

Currency Austria uses the **euro** (€). At press time, 1€ = US$1.40.

Currency Exchange During off-hours you can exchange money at *bureaux de change* (exchange bureaus) throughout the Inner City (there's one at the intersection of Kohlmarkt and the Graben), as well as at travel agencies, train stations, and the airport. There's also a 24-hour exchange service at the post office (Hauptpostamt) at Fleischmarkt 19.

Dentists & Doctors For dental problems, call ✆ **01/512-2078.** A list of physicians can be found in the telephone directory under *Arzte.* If you have a medical emergency at night, call ✆ **141** daily 7pm to 7am.

Drugstores Called *Apotheke,* they're open Monday to Friday 8am to noon and 2 to 6pm and Saturday from 8am to noon. Each Apotheke posts in its window a list of shops that take turns staying open at night and on Sunday.

Embassies & Consulates The embassy of the **United States** is at Boltzmanngasse 16, A-1090 Vienna (✆ **01/31339-0;** http://vienna.usembassy.gov; U-Bahn: Stadtpark). The consular section, Parkring 12, A-1010 Vienna (✆ **01/31339-0**), handles lost passports, tourist emergencies, and other matters. Both are open Monday to Friday 8:30am to noon and 1 to 2pm.

The embassy of **Canada,** Laurenzerberg 2 (✆ **01/531-38-3000;** www.canadainternational.gc.ca/austria-autriche; U-Bahn: Schwedenplatz), is open Monday to Friday 8:30am to 12:30pm and 1:30 to 3:30pm. The embassy of the **United Kingdom,** Jauresgasse 12 (✆ **01/71613-0;** http://ukinaustria.fco.gov.uk/en; U-Bahn: Stadtpark), is open Monday to Friday 10am to noon and 2 to 4pm. The embassy of **Australia,** Mattiellistrasse 2–4 (✆ **01/50674-0;** www.austria.embassy.gov.au; U-Bahn: Karlsplatz), is open Monday to Friday 8:30am to 4:30pm. The **New Zealand** Consulate General's office, Salesianergasse 15/3 (✆ **01/318-8505;** http://new-zealand.visahq.com; U-Bahn: Stadtpark), is open Monday to Friday 8:30am to 5pm, but it's best to call to see if it's actually open. The embassy of **Ireland,** Rotenturmstrasse 16–18 (✆ **01/715-4246;** www.embassyofireland.at; U-Bahn: Schwedenplatz), is open Monday to Friday 9:30 to 11:30am and 1:30 to 4pm.

Emergencies Call ✆ **122** to report a fire, ✆ **133** for the police, or ✆ **144** for an ambulance.

Internet Access **Café Stein,** Währingerstrasse 6–8 (✆ **01/319-72-419**), offers Internet access and is open Monday to Saturday 7am to 1am, and Sunday 9 to 1am. The service is free but you have to bring your own laptop.

Police The emergency number is ✆ **133.**

Post Office Post offices in Vienna can be found in the heart of every district. Addresses for these can be found in the telephone directory under "Post." Post offices are generally open for mail services Monday to Friday from 7am to noon and 2 to 6pm. The central post office (Hauptpostamt), Barbaragasse 2 (✆ **01/51570**), and most general post offices are open 24 hours a day, 7 days a week.

Safety In recent years, Vienna has been plagued by purse snatchers. Small foreign children often approach sympathetic adults and ask for money. As the adult goes for his wallet or her purse, full-grown thieves rush in and grab the money, fleeing with it. Unaccompanied women should hold on to their purses tightly, and never open them in public.

Telephone The **country code** for Austria is **43.** The **city code** for Vienna is **1;** use this code when you're calling from outside Austria. If you're within Austria, use **01** before the local number (**01** is included in all telephone numbers in this chapter, so it is not necessary to add any other numbers when calling these telephone numbers within Austria).

Hotels add huge surcharges to long-distance calls; go to the post office instead. Consider purchasing a **phone card** at any post office.

Tipping A service charge of 10% to 15% is included on hotel and restaurant bills, but it's a good policy to leave something extra for waiters and 2€ per day for your hotel maid. Railroad station, airport, and hotel porters get 1.50€ per piece of luggage, plus a 1€ tip. Tip your hairdresser 10% of the bill, and give the shampoo person a 1.50€ gratuity. Toilet attendants are usually given .50€, and coat-check attendants expect .50€ to 1.25€.

Where to Stay

VERY EXPENSIVE

Grand Hotel Wien ★★★ Some of the most discerning hotel guests in Europe, often music lovers, prefer this seven-story deluxe hotel to the more traditional and famous Imperial or Bristol. Only a block from the Staatsoper, it's a honey, and has been at the hub of Viennese social life since the turn of the 20th century. You enter a world of beveled mirrors, crystal chandeliers, and a grand staircase. The spacious accommodations are posh, with all the modern extras such as heated floors, phones in the marble bathrooms, and even antifog mirrors. The more expensive units have more elaborate furnishings and decoration, including delicate stuccowork.

Kärntner Ring 9, A-1010 Vienna. ✆ **01/515-800.** Fax 01/515-13-10. www.grandhotelwien.com. 205 units. 119€–510€ double; 595€–850€ junior suite; from 980€ suite. AE, DC, MC, V. Parking 30€. U-Bahn: Karlsplatz. **Amenities:** 4 restaurants; bar; lounge; babysitting; exercise room; room service. *In room:* A/C, TV/DVD, hair dryer, minibar, Wi-Fi (free).

Hotel Astoria ★ This landmark is for nostalgia buffs who want to recall the grand life of the closing days of the Austro-Hungarian Empire. A first-class hotel, the Astoria has a desirable location on the shopping mall close to St. Stephan's Cathedral and the State Opera. Decorated in a slightly frayed late-19th-century style, the hotel offers well-appointed and traditionally decorated rooms. The interior rooms tend to be too dark, and singles are just too cramped. Bathrooms are luxurious with dual basins and heated towel racks.

Kärntnerstrasse 32–34, A-1015 Vienna. ✆ **01/515-77.** Fax 01/515-77-582. www.austria-trend.at/Hotel-Astoria. 128 units. 450€–550€ double; 650€ junior suite. Rates include breakfast. AE, DC, MC, V. Parking 30€. U-Bahn: Stephansplatz. Tram: 1, 2, or D. **Amenities:** Restaurant; bar; babysitting. *In room:* TV, hair dryer, minibar, Wi-Fi (free).

Hotel Bristol ★★★ This six-story landmark is a superb choice—only the Imperial is grander. When it was constructed in 1894 across the street from the

Staatsoper, it was the ultimate in luxury style, but it's been updated to give guests the benefit of black-tiled bathrooms equipped with modern conveniences. Rooms are sumptuously appointed. The club floor offers luxurious comfort, enhanced by period furnishings. Corkscrew columns of rare marble grace the **Korso,** Bristol's fine-dining restaurant (p. 50), which is one of the best in Vienna.

Kärntner Ring 1, A-1015 Vienna. ✆ **888/625-5144** in the U.S., or 01/515-160. Fax 01/515-16-550. www.bristolvienna.com. 140 units. 265€–429€ double; 849€–1,710€ suite. AE, DC, MC, V. Parking 30€. U-Bahn: Karlsplatz. Tram: 1 or 2. **Amenities:** 3 restaurants (1 seasonal); bar; babysitting; exercise room; Jacuzzi; room service. *In room:* A/C, TV, CD player, hair dryer, minibar, Wi-Fi (free).

Hotel Imperial ★★★ This hotel is Vienna's grandest and the most "imperial" looking in Austria, 2 blocks from the Staatsoper and 1 block from the Musikverein. The hotel was built in 1869 as a private residence and was converted into a private hotel in 1873. Everything is outlined against a background of polished marble, crystal chandeliers, Gobelin tapestries, and fine rugs. Some of the royal suites are palatial, but all rooms are soundproof and generally spacious, with deluxe full bathrooms. The **Hotel Imperial Restaurant** is a fabled turn-of-the-20th-century restaurant.

Kärntner Ring 16, A-1015 Vienna. ✆ **800/325-3589** in the U.S., or 01/501100. Fax 01/5011-0410. www.hotelimperialvienna.com. 138 units. 360€–569€ double; from 710€ suite. AE, DC, MC, V. Parking 30€. U-Bahn: Karlsplatz. **Amenities:** 2 restaurants; bar; babysitting; exercise room; room service. *In room:* A/C, TV/DVD, hair dryer, minibar, Wi-Fi (free).

Hotel Sacher Wien ★★★ Much of the glory of the Hapsburgs is still evoked by the public rooms here, although the hotel, founded in 1876, is no longer the grandest in Vienna, having lost out to the Bristol or Imperial. The red velvet, crystal chandeliers, and brocaded curtains are reminiscent of Old Vienna. The reception desk is fairly flexible about making arrangements for salons or apartments, or joining two rooms together. Most accommodations are generous in size and often have sitting areas plus midsize marble bathrooms. The hotel added two additional upper floors, creating 42 more accommodations, opening onto some of the most panoramic views of any hotel in Vienna. We prefer these rooms to the ones down below because of their greater amenities, such as illuminated mirrors, plasma TVs, and marble bathrooms, and, of course, those room terraces. The hotel also launched one of the most sophisticated spas of any hotel in Vienna.

Philharmonikerstrasse 4, A-1010 Vienna. ✆ **01/514560.** Fax 01/512-56-810. www.sacher.com. 152 units. 395€–598€ double; 828€ junior suite; from 1,338€ suite. AE, DC, MC, V. Parking 30€. U-Bahn: Karlsplatz/Oper. Tram: 1, 2, 62, 65, D, or J. Bus: 4A. **Amenities:** 2 restaurants; cafe; bar; babysitting; health club and spa; room service. *In room:* A/C, TV/DVD, hair dryer, minibar, Wi-Fi (free).

EXPENSIVE

Hotel Das Triest ★★ Sir Terence Conran, the famous English architect and designer, has created the interior decoration for this contemporary hotel in the center of Vienna, a 5-minute walk from St. Stephan's Cathedral. Conran has done for Das Triest what Philippe Starck did for New York's Paramount Hotel—created a stylish address in the heart of one of the world's most important cities. An emerging favorite with artists and musicians, this hip hotel has such grace notes as a courtyard garden and cozy fireplace. Its cross-vaulted rooms, which give the structure a distinctive flair, have been transformed into lounges and suites. Guest rooms are midsize to spacious, tastefully furnished, and comfortable.

Wiedner Hauptstrasse 12, A-1040 Vienna. ✆ **01/589-18.** Fax 01/589-18-80. www.dastriest.at. 72 units. 289€ double; 358€ junior suite; 442€–589€ suite. Rates include buffet breakfast. AE, DC, MC, V. Parking 27€. U-Bahn: Karlsplatz. **Amenities:** Restaurant; bar; babysitting; exercise room; room service. *In room:* A/C, TV, hair dryer, minibar, Wi-Fi (free).

Hotel König von Ungarn ★ In a choice site on a narrow street near the cathedral, this hotel has been in the business for more than 4 centuries and is Vienna's oldest continuously operated accommodations. It's an evocative, intimate, and cozy retreat in an early-17th-century building. Everywhere you look you'll find low-key luxury, tradition, and modern convenience. Guest rooms have been remodeled with Biedermeier accents and traditional furnishings. Most bathrooms are generous in size and have dual basins, tub/shower combinations, and tiled walls. The professional staff is highly efficient, keeping the hotel spotless. The hotel restaurant is one of Vienna's finest.

Schulerstrasse 10, A-1010 Vienna. ✆ **01/515-84-0.** Fax 01/515-848. www.kvu.at. 33 units. 219€ double; 300€–360€ apt. Rates include breakfast. AE, DC, MC, V. Nearby parking 18€. U-Bahn: Stephansplatz. **Amenities:** Restaurant; bar; babysitting; room service. *In room:* A/C, TV, hair dryer, Internet (free), minibar.

MODERATE

Falkensteiner Hotel Am Schottenfeld ★ Modern, innovative, and young at heart, this designer hotel is alluring, attracting a young clientele. The lighting seems to set the stage for every room in the hotel, from the colored lights in the lounge to the natural light in other public rooms. The bedrooms are furnished in a sleek, contemporary, and rather chic style, with marble-floored bathrooms. The neighborhood surrounding the hotel is part of its allure, as it's filled with junk shops, trendy boutiques, small bars, good restaurants, antiquarian bookshops, and Internet cafes.

Schottenfeldgasse 74, A-1070 Vienna. ✆ **01/526-5181.** Fax 01/526-81-160. www.falkensteiner.com. 91 units. 85€–240€ double. AE, DC, MC, V. Parking 13€. U-Bahn: Mariahilferstrasse. **Amenities:** Restaurant; bar; room service; sauna. *In room:* TV, hair dryer, Internet (free), minibar.

Hollmann Beletage—Design & Boutique ★★ This small boutique hotel was the house of a nobleman in the 1800s. It has been skillfully converted to receive a few guests and is one of the special discoveries of Vienna, featuring a lobby with a fireplace, a small and elegant spa, and live piano music in the lounge at night. Within a 2-minute walk of St. Stephan's, it lies in the heart of historic Vienna. Bedrooms are generally spacious and bright, with a chic modern design plus a "closet without limits." In addition to modern amenities, some of the best in town, the rooms are filled with little extras like fresh fruit, slippers, and even a kimono.

Köllnerhofgasse 6, 1010 Vienna. ✆ **01/961-1960.** Fax 01/961-196-033. www.hollmann-beletage.at. 25 units. 160€–250€ double. Rates include breakfast. AE, DC, MC, V. Parking 23€. U-Bahn: Stephansplatz. **Amenities:** Breakfast room; bar; airport transfer 34€; room service; spa. *In room:* A/C, TV/DVD, hair dryer, minibar, MP3 docking station, Wi-Fi (free).

Hotel Kaiserin Elisabeth ★ This yellow-stoned hotel is conveniently located near the cathedral. The interior is decorated with Oriental rugs on well-maintained marble and wood floors. The small, quiet rooms have been considerably updated since Wolfgang Mozart, Richard Wagner, Franz Liszt, and Edvard Grieg stayed here, and their musical descendants continue to patronize the place. Polished wood, clean linen, and perhaps another Oriental rug grace each guest room. Bathrooms are a bit cramped, but they are tiled and well equipped.

Weihburggasse 3, A-1010 Vienna. ✆ **01/515-260.** Fax 01/515-267. www.kaiserinelisabeth.at. 63 units. 216€ double; 245€ suite. Rates include buffet breakfast. AE, DC, MC, V. Parking 20€. U-Bahn: Stephansplatz. **Amenities:** Restaurant; bar; room service. *In room:* A/C (in some), TV, hair dryer, minibar, Wi-Fi (free).

Hotel Rathaus Wine & Design ★★ This is one of the most unusual hotels in Austria, lying just outside the city center. Here everything focuses on the subject of wine, and each of the individually designed double rooms is dedicated to a top Austrian winegrower. There are even "wine cosmetics" in the bedrooms, and the manager organizes wine tastings for his guests. The owners, the Fleischhaker family, are imbued with a vinophile philosophy. There is wine cheese on the breakfast buffet, and wine Guglhupf comes with your coffee. In the bedroom noble wines are provided in the "somewhat different" minibar. The modern bedrooms are spread across four floors in a restored town house. In the on-site wine lounge, conversation centers on . . . guess what? The staff can help wine devotees take 1-day excursions to wine regions in eastern Austria.

Lange Gasse 13, A-1080 Vienna. ✆ **01/400-1122.** Fax 01/400-112288. www.hotel-rathaus-wien.at. 39 units. 148€–198€ double; 398€ suite. AE, MC, V. Parking 15€. U-Bahn: Herrengasse. **Amenities:** Wine lounge; concierge; room service. *In room:* TV, hair dryer, Internet (free), minibar.

Steigenberger Hotel Herrenhof ★★ In the center of Vienna, behind a well-preserved neoclassical facade, a deluxe hotel has been installed in a restored building dating from 1913. Inside, the hotel has been completely modernized with up-to-date amenities throughout. The location is idyllic for exploring Old Town Vienna, including St. Stephan's Cathedral and the Spanish Riding School. Much of the design inside reflects the Belle Epoque era at the turn of the 20th century and through to the 1920s. Rooms are soundproof, and both regional and international cuisine is served. The personal service here is among the finest in Vienna.

Herrengasse 10, 1010 Vienna. ✆ **01/534-040.** Fax 01/534-041-00. www.steigenberger.com. 196 units. 169€–199€ double; 570€ suite. AE, MC, V. Parking 32€. U-Bahn: Stephansplatz. **Amenities:** Restaurant; bar; babysitting; concierge; exercise room; room service. *In room:* A/C, TV/DVD, hair dryer, minibar, Wi-Fi (free).

INEXPENSIVE

Drei Kronen ★ The celebrated architect Ignaz Drapala designed this splendid Art Nouveau building in a charming section of Vienna close to the famous Naschmarkt. The hotel enjoys one of Vienna's best locations, close to such monuments as the Vienna State Opera and St. Stephan's Cathedral. The midsize-to-spacious guest rooms are fresh and bright, with comfortable furnishings along with immaculate bathrooms with shower. Some of the rooms are large enough to contain three beds.

Schleifmühlgasse 25, A-1040 Vienna. ✆ **01/587-32-89.** Fax 01/587-32-89-11. www.hotel3kronen.at. 41 units. 49€–159€ double; 99€–179€ triple. Rates include breakfast buffet. AE, DC, MC, V. Parking 15€. U-Bahn: Karlsplatz. **Amenities:** Breakfast room. *In room:* TV, Internet (free).

Hotel Kärntnerhof ★ ☺ A 4-minute walk from the cathedral, the Kärntnerhof advertises itself as a family-oriented hotel because there are many triples and the suites sleep four to six guests. The decor of the public areas is tastefully arranged around Oriental rugs, well-upholstered chairs and couches with cabriole legs, and an occasional 19th-century portrait. The midsize rooms are more up to date, usually with the original parquet floors and striped or patterned wallpaper set off by curtains. The small private bathrooms glisten with tile walls and floors.

Grashofgasse 4, A-1011 Vienna. ✆ **01/512-19-23.** Fax 01/513-22-28-33. www.karntnerhof.com. 44 units. 90€–175€ double; 180€–280€ suite. Rates include buffet breakfast. AE, DC, MC, V. Parking 16€. U-Bahn: Stephansplatz. **Amenities:** Room service. *In room:* TV, Wi-Fi (free).

Hotel-Pension Suzanne ★ ☺ Only a 45-second walk from the opera house, this is a real discovery. Once you get past its postwar facade, the interior warms considerably, brightly decorated in a comfortable, traditional style, with antique beds, plush chairs, and the original molded ceilings. Rooms are midsize and exceedingly well maintained, facing either the busy street or a courtyard. Families often stay here because some accommodations contain three beds. A number of guest rooms are like small apartments with kitchenettes.

Walfischgasse 4, A-1010 Vienna. ✆ **01/513-25-07.** Fax 01/513-25-00. www.pension-suzanne.at. 25 units. 103€–118€ double; 124€–127€ apt. Rates include continental breakfast. AE, DC, MC, V. No parking. U-Bahn: Karlsplatz. **Amenities:** Breakfast room; babysitting; Wi-Fi (free). *In room:* TV, hair dryer.

Where to Dine

VERY EXPENSIVE

Drei Husaren ★★★ VIENNESE/INTERNATIONAL Just off Kärntnerstrasse, this enduring favorite—a Viennese landmark since 1935—serves an inventive and classic Viennese cuisine. To the music of Gypsy melodies, you'll dine on such stellar dishes as freshwater salmon with pike soufflé, mussel soup, breast of guinea fowl, an array of sole dishes, and longtime favorites such as *Tafelspitz* (savory boiled beef). The chef specializes in veal, including his deliciously flavored Kalbsbrücken Metternich. The place is justifiably celebrated for its repertoire of more than 35 hors d'oeuvres, which waitstaff roll around the dining room on four separate carts.

Weihburggasse 4. ✆ **01/512-10-92-0.** www.drei-husaren.at. Reservations required. Main courses 29€–39€; *menu dégustation* (6 courses) 89€; 4-course fixed-price business lunch 43€. AE, DC, MC, V. Daily noon–3pm and 6pm–1am. U-Bahn: Stephansplatz.

Korso bei der Oper ★★★ VIENNESE/INTERNATIONAL This chic and glittering choice is decorated with tasteful paneling, sparkling chandeliers, and, flanking either side of a baronial fireplace, two of the most breathtaking baroque columns in Vienna. The kitchen concocts an alluring mixture of traditional and modern cuisine. Your meal may feature filet of char with a sorrel sauce, saddle of veal with cèpe mushrooms and homemade noodles, or the inevitable Tafelspitz. The rack of lamb is excellent, as are the medallions of beef with a shallot-infused butter sauce and Roquefort-flavored noodles. The wine list is extensive.

In the Hotel Bristol, Kärntneering 1. ✆ **01/515-16-546.** Reservations required. Main courses 36€–38€; fixed-price menu 38€–45€. AE, DC, MC, V. Daily 6pm–1am. U-Bahn: Karlsplatz. Tram: 1 or 2.

Sacher Hotel Restaurant ★ AUSTRIAN/INTERNATIONAL This is a long-enduring favorite for pre- or postopera dining. It seems as if all celebrities who come to Vienna eventually are seen either in the **Red Bar,** with its adjacent dining room, where live piano music is presented every evening from 7pm to midnight, or in the brown-and-white **Anna Sacher Room,** the site of many a high-powered meal. There's no better place in Vienna to sample the restaurant's most famous dish, Tafelspitz, which is fit for an emperor. The chef serves it with a savory herb-flavored sauce. Other delectable dishes include fish terrine and veal steak with morels. For dessert, the Sacher torte enjoys world renown. It's primarily a chocolate sponge cake that's sliced in half and filled with apricot jam. This most famous of pastries in Vienna was supposedly created in 1832 by Franz Sacher when he served as Prince Metternich's apprentice.

Philharmonikerstrasse 4. ✆ **01/514-560.** Reservations required. Main courses 28€–36€; fixed-price menus 62€–84€. AE, DC, MC, V. Daily noon–3pm and 6–11:30pm. U-Bahn: Karlsplatz.

Steirereck ★★★ VIENNESE/AUSTRIAN/INTERNATIONAL *Steirereck* means "corner of Styria," which is exactly what Heinz and Margarethe Reitbauer have created in the rustic decor of this intimate restaurant. It has been acclaimed by some Viennese as the best restaurant in the city. The Reitbauers offer both traditional Viennese dishes and "New Austrian" selections. You might begin with a caviar-semolina dumpling, roasted turbot with fennel (served as an appetizer), or the most elegant and expensive item of all, gooseliver Steirereck. The menu is wisely limited and well prepared, changing daily depending on the fresh produce available at the market. The restaurant is popular with after-theater diners. The large wine cellar holds some 35,000 bottles. In addition to the fabled restaurant, there is also Ess. Bar, plus a Light-Restaurant for gourmet-level food during the day, and Meierei, which is all about dairy products with, among other offerings, 150 kinds of cheese.

Steirereck im Stadtpark. ✆ **01/713-31-68.** http://steirereck.at. Reservations required. Main courses 24€–44€; 5-course fixed-price dinner 95€. AE, DC, MC, V. Steirereck-Restaurant Mon–Fri from 7pm; Light-Restaurant Mon–Fri 11am–5pm; Meierei Mon–Fri 2pm–midnight; Ess. Bar 5pm–midnight. Closed holidays. U-Bahn: Stadtpark.

EXPENSIVE

Artner am Franziskanerplatz ★★ AUSTRIAN A former printing workshop has been converted into a culinary showcase for a Michelin-starred head chef, Maximilian Aichinger. He specializes in traditional Austrian dishes, giving them an original modern twist limited only by his imagination. Inspired by the bounty of the alpine country in which he lives, his dishes are creative and wonderfully delicate. You'll be impressed with his selection of appetizers, likely to include such curiosities as gooseliver and smoked eel with Granny Smith sorbet. How many kitchens turn out a consommé of pumpkin? Try such mains as braised deer with cranberries and black chanterelles or a codfish bouillabaisse with eggplant (aubergine) and a green sauce. For dessert, his plum dumpling comes with sour cream ice and grapefruit honey, or you might opt for a goat-cheese soufflé with a ragout of dark elderberries and walnut ice.

Franziskanerplatz 5. ✆ **01/503-5034.** www.artner.co.at. Reservations required. Main courses 25€–29€; 3-course menu 38€; 4-course menu 48€; 6-course menu 68€. AE, MC, V. Mon–Fri noon–midnight; Sat–Sun 6pm–midnight. U-Bahn: Stephansplatz or Karlsplatz.

Dö & Co ★ CONTINENTAL/INTERNATIONAL Stylish, upscale, and rather expensive, this restaurant is owned by one of Austria's most esoteric food stores. Its location is on the seventh floor of the aggressively ultramodern Haas Haus, which stands in jarring proximity to Vienna's cathedral. Menu items change with the season, but considering the rarefied nature of the organization presenting it, each is appropriately rare, and unusual. Examples include Uruguayan beef, Austrian venison, grilled baby turbot from the coast of Norway, deep-fried monkfish, and carpaccio "Parmigiana," as well as traditional Austrian specialties. There's also a repertoire of Thai dishes, including crispy pork salad, red curried chicken, and sweet-and-sour red snapper. And there's a "wok buffet," wherein you assemble the ingredients for your meal on a plate, and then deliver it to a uniformed chef who will quick-sear it for you with whatever sauces you want.

In the Haas Haus, Stephansplatz 12. ✆ **01/535-39-69.** www.doco.com. Reservations recommended. Main courses 18€–36€; set menus 45€–65€. V. Daily noon–3pm and 6pm–midnight. U-Bahn: Stephansplatz.

König von Ungarn (King of Hungary) ★ VIENNESE/INTERNATIONAL This beautifully decorated restaurant is inside the famous hotel of the same name. Food is well prepared but traditional—not at all experimental. You dine under a vaulted ceiling in an atmosphere of crystal, chandeliers, antiques, and marble columns. If you're in doubt about what to order, try the Tafelspitz. Other seasonal choices include a ragout of seafood with fresh mushrooms, tournedos of beef with a mustard-and-horseradish sauce, and appetizers such as scampi in caviar sauce. The service is superb.

Schulerstrasse 10. ✆ **01/515-840.** www.kvu.at. Reservations required. Main courses 13€–20€; fixed-price menu 29€–40€ dinner. AE, DC, MC, V. Daily 6–10:30pm. U-Bahn: Stephansplatz. Bus: 1A.

Plachutta ★ VIENNESE Few restaurants have built such a culinary shrine around one dish: Tafelspitz, the boiled beef dish that was the favorite of Emperor Franz Josef throughout his prolonged reign. Whichever of the 10 versions you order, it will invariably come with sauces and garnishes that perk up what sounds like a dull dish into a delectable culinary traipse through the tastes of yesteryear. The differences between the versions are a function of the cut of beef you request as part of your meal. Regardless of the cut you specify, your meal will be accompanied by hash brown potatoes, chives, and an appealing mixture of horseradish and chopped apples.

Wollzeile 38. ✆ **01/512-1577.** www.plachutta.at. Reservations recommended. Main courses 15€–35€. AE, DC, MC, V. Daily 11:30am–midnight. U-Bahn: Stubentor.

Wiener Rathauskeller ★★ VIENNESE/INTERNATIONAL City halls throughout the Teutonic world have traditionally maintained restaurants in their basements, and Vienna is no exception. In half a dozen richly atmospheric dining rooms, with high vaulted ceilings and stained-glass windows, you can enjoy good and reasonably priced food. The chef's specialty is a Rathauskellerplatte for two, consisting of various cuts of meat, including a veal schnitzel, lamb cutlets, and pork medallions. Beginning at 8pm, live musicians ramble through the world of operetta, waltz, and *Schrammel* (traditional Viennese music), as you dine.

Rathausplatz 1. ✆ **01/405-12-10.** www.wiener-rathauskeller.at. Reservations required. Main courses 11€–23€. AE, DC, MC, V. Mon–Sat 11:30am–3pm and 6–11pm. U-Bahn: Rathaus.

MODERATE

Griechenbeisl AUSTRIAN This local favorite opened in 1450 and is still one of Vienna's leading restaurants. It has a labyrinthine collection of dining areas on three floors, all with low vaulted ceilings, smoky paneling, and wrought-iron chandeliers. As you go in, be sure to see the so-called inner sanctum, with signatures of such former patrons as Mozart, Beethoven, and Mark Twain. The food is hearty, ample, and solidly bourgeois. Menu items include deer stew, both Hungarian and Viennese goulash, sauerkraut garni, Wiener schnitzel, and venison steak—in other words, all

COFFEEHOUSES & cafes

One of the best-known cafes in Vienna also pays more attention to its window displays than any of its competitors. The windows of the **Café Demel,** Kohlmarkt 14 (✆ **01/535-17-17-0;** www.demel.at; U-Bahn: Stephansplatz or Herrengasse), are filled with fanciful tributes to a changing array of themes, some of which have made, in a small-scale way, local history. Depending on the season, you might see spun-sugar and marzipan depictions of Christmas or *A Midsummer Night's Dream* characters; depictions of famous Austrian emperors or composers; autumn or spring foliage in the city's parks; even effigies of famous visitors to the city. Inside is a splendidly baroque Viennese landmark with black marble tables, cream-colored embellished plaster walls, and crystal chandeliers covered with white milk-glass globes. Dozens of pastries are offered every day, including cream-filled horns *(Gugelhupfs).* It's open daily 10am to 7pm.

Café Dommayer, Auhofstrasse 2 (✆ **01/877-54-60;** www.oberlaa-wien.at; U-Bahn: Schönbrunn), boasts a reputation for courtliness that dates from 1787. In 1844, Johann Strauss, Jr., made his musical debut here, and beginning in 1924, the site became known as *the* place in Vienna for tea dancing. During clement weather, a garden with seats for 300 opens in back. The rest of the year, the venue is restricted to a high-ceilinged black-and-white old-world room. Every Saturday from 2 to 4pm, a pianist and violinist perform; and on the first Saturday of every month, an all-woman orchestra plays mostly Strauss from 2 to 4pm. It's open daily 7am to 10pm.

One of the Ring's great cafes, **Café Landtmann,** Dr.-Karl-Lueger-Ring 4 (✆ **01/24-100-100;** www.landtmann.at; tram: 1, 2, or D), dates from the 1880s. Overlooking the Burgtheater and the Rathaus, it has traditionally drawn a mix of politicians, journalists, and actors, and was Freud's favorite. The original chandeliers and the prewar chairs have been refurbished. We highly suggest spending an hour or so here, whether perusing the newspapers, sipping on coffee, or planning the day's itinerary. The cafe is open daily 7:30am to midnight (meals are served 11am–11:30pm).

those favorite recipes from Grandmother's kitchen. As an added treat, the restaurant features nighttime accordion and zither music.

Fleischmarkt 11. ✆ **01/533-19-77.** www.griechenbeisl.at. Reservations required. Main courses 16€–24€. AE, DC, MC, V. Daily 11:30am–1am (last orders at 11:30pm). Tram: 1, 2, 21, or N.

INEXPENSIVE

Augustinerkeller AUSTRIAN The beer and wine flow at this Viennese legend. Augustinerkeller, in the basement of the part of the Hofburg complex that shelters the Albertina Collection, has served wine, beer, and food since 1857, although the vaulted ceilings and sense of timelessness evoke an establishment even older than that. It attracts a lively group of patrons from all walks of life, and sometimes they get boisterous, especially when the Schrammel music goes late into the night. It's one of the best values for wine tasting in Vienna. Aside from the wine and beer, the establishment serves simple food, including roast chicken on a spit, schnitzel, and Tafelspitz. Most dishes are at the low end of the price scale.

Augustinerstrasse 1. ✆ **01/533-1026.** www.bitzinger.at. Reservations not necessary. Main courses 9€–25€. AE, DC, MC, V. Daily 11am–midnight. U-Bahn: Herrengasse.

Buffet Trześniewski ★ SANDWICHES Everyone in Vienna knows about this place, from the most hurried office workers to the city's elite hostesses. Its current incarnation is unlike any buffet you may have seen, with six or seven cramped tables and a rapidly moving queue of clients who jostle for space next to the glass countertops. You'll indicate to the waitress the kind of sandwich you want, and if you can't read German signs, just point. Most people come here for the delicious finger sandwiches, which include 18 combinations of cream cheese, egg, onion, salami, mushrooms, herring, green and red peppers, tomatoes, lobster, and many more items. If you order a drink, the cashier will give you a rubber token, which you'll present to the person at the far end of the counter.

Dorotheergasse 1. ✆ **01/512-3291.** www.trzesniewski.at. Reservations not accepted. Sandwiches 1€–2.80€. No credit cards. Mon–Fri 8:30am–7:30pm; Sat 9am–5pm. U-Bahn: Stephansplatz.

Café Leopold ★ INTERNATIONAL Critics have defined this restaurant as a postmodern version, in architectural form, of the Viennese expressionist paintings (including many by Egon Schiele) that are exhibited within the museum that contains it. During the day, the place functions as a conventional cafe and restaurant, serving a postmodern blend of *Mitteleuropaïsche* (central European) and Asian food. Three nights a week, however, from around 10pm until at least 2am, any hints of kitsch and coziness are banished as soon as a DJ begins cranking out dance tunes for a hard-drinking denizens-of-the-night crowd.

In the Leopold Museum, Museumsplatz 1. ✆ **01/523-67-32.** www.cafe-leopold.at. Reservations not necessary. Main courses 3€–10€; 2-course set-price menu 10€. AE, DC, MC, V. Daily 10am–2am. U-Bahn: Volkstheater or Babenbergstrasse/MuseumsQuartier.

Café Restaurant Halle INTERNATIONAL Set within the Kunsthalle, this is the direct competitor of the also-recommended Café Leopold. Larger, and with a more sophisticated menu than the Café Leopold's, it's a postmodern, airy, big-windowed quartet of wood-trimmed, cream-colored rooms. The menu will always contain a half-dozen meal-size salads, many garnished with strips of steak, chicken, or shrimp; two daily homemade soups; and a rotating series of platters.

In the Kunsthalle Wien, Museumsplatz 1, in the MuseumsQuartier. ✆ **01/523-70-01.** www.motto.at. Reservations not necessary. Main courses 8€–16€. MC, V. Daily 10am–2am. U-Bahn: MuseumsQuartier.

Gulaschmuseum ★ AUSTRIAN/HUNGARIAN If you thought that *Gulasch* (goulash) was available in only one form, think again. This restaurant celebrates at least 15 varieties of it, each of them an authentic survivor of the culinary traditions of Hungary, and each redolent with the taste of that country's most distinctive spice, paprika. You can order versions of goulash based on roast beef, veal, pork, and fried chicken livers. Vegetarians rejoice: Versions made with potatoes, beans, or mushrooms are also available. Boiled potatoes and rough-textured brown or black bread will usually accompany your choice. An excellent beginning is a dish so firmly associated with Hungary that it's been referred to as the Magyar national crepe, *Hortobágyi Palatschinken,* stuffed with minced beef and paprika-flavored cream sauce.

Schulerstrasse 20. ✆ **01/512-10-17.** www.gulasch.at. Reservations recommended. Main courses 7€–14€. MC, V. Mon–Fri 11:30am–11pm; Sat–Sun 10am–11pm. U-Bahn: Wollzeile or Stephansplatz.

Hansen ★ MEDITERRANEAN/INTERNATIONAL Part of the charm of this intriguing and stylish restaurant involves trekking through masses of plants and elaborate garden ornaments on your way to your dining table. Choose from a small but savory menu that changes every week. Excellent examples include a spicy bean salad with strips of chicken breast served in a summer broth; risotto with cheese and sour cherries; and poached *Saibling* (something akin to trout from the cold-water streams of the Austrian Alps) with a potato-and-celery purée and watercress.

In the cellar of the Börsegebäude (Vienna Stock Exchange), Wipplingerstrasse 34 at the Schottenring. ✆ **01/532-05-42.** www.hansen.co.at. Reservations recommended. Main courses 9.50€–24€. AE, DC, MC, V. Mon–Fri 9am–11pm (last order 8pm); Sat 9am–5pm (last order 3pm). U-Bahn: Schottenring.

Palmenhaus AUSTRIAN Architectural grace and marvelous food combine for a happy marriage here. Many architectural critics consider the Jugendstil glass canopy of this greenhouse the most beautiful in Austria. A sophisticated menu changes monthly, and might include perfectly prepared fresh Austrian goat cheese with stewed peppers and zucchini salad; young herring with sour cream, horseradish, and deep-fried beignets stuffed with apples and cabbage; or breast of chicken layered with gooseliver. If you've already eaten, no one will mind if you drop in just for a drink and one of the voluptuous pastries.

In the Burggarten. ✆ **01/533-1033.** www.palmenhaus.at. Reservations recommended for dinner. Main courses 14€–25€; pastries 3.50€–7.80€. AE, DC, MC, V. Daily 10am–2am (closed Sun–Mon Nov–Mar). U-Bahn: Opera.

Zu den 3 Hacken ★ AUSTRIAN Cozy, small-scale, and charming, this restaurant was established 350 years ago and today bears the reputation as the oldest *Gasthaus* (tavern) in Vienna. In 1827, Franz Schubert had an ongoing claim to one of the establishment's tables as a site for entertaining his cronies. There are three dining rooms, each paneled and each evocative of an inn high in the Austrian Alps. Expect an old-fashioned menu replete with the kind of dishes that fueled the Austro-Hungarian Empire. The best examples are Tafelspitz, beef goulash, mixed grills piled high with chops and sausages, and desserts that include Hungarian-inspired *Palatschinken* (crepes) with chocolate-hazelnut sauce.

Singerstrasse 28. ✆ **01/5125895.** www.vinum-wien.at. Reservations recommended. Main courses 8€–20€. DC, MC, V. Mon–Sat 11:30am–midnight. U-Bahn: Stephansplatz.

Zwölf-Zwölf-Apostelkeller VIENNESE For those seeking a taste of Old Vienna, this is the place. Sections of this old wine tavern's walls predate 1561. Rows of wooden tables stand under vaulted ceilings, with lighting provided partially by streetlights set into the masonry floor. This place is popular with students, partly because of its low prices and because of its proximity to St. Stephan's. In addition to beer and wine, the establishment serves hearty Austrian fare. Specialties include roast pork with dumplings, Hungarian goulash soup, a limited number of vegetarian dishes, and a *Schlachtplatte* (hot black pudding, liverwurst, pork, and pork sausage with a hot bacon-and-cabbage salad).

Sonnenfelsgasse 3. ✆ **01/512-67-77.** www.zwoelf-apostelkeller.at. Reservations recommended. Main courses 6€–22€. AE, DC, MC, V. Daily 11am–midnight. U-Bahn: Stephansplatz. Tram: 1, 2, 21, D, or N. Bus: 1A.

Seeing the Sights of Vienna

The Inner City (Innere Stadt) is the tangle of streets from which Vienna grew in the Middle Ages. Much of your exploration will be confined to this area, encircled by the boulevards of "The Ring" and the Danube Canal. The main street of the Inner City is **Kärntnerstrasse,** most of which is a pedestrian mall. The heart of Vienna is **Stephansplatz,** the square on which St. Stephan's Cathedral sits.

EXPLORING THE HOFBURG PALACE COMPLEX ★★★

The winter palace of the Hapsburgs, known for its vast, impressive courtyards, the Hofburg sits in the heart of Vienna. To reach it (you can hardly miss it), head up Kohlmarkt to Michaelerplatz 1, Burgring (✆ **01/533-75-70;** www.hofburg-wien.at). You can take the U-Bahn to Stephansplatz, Herrengasse, or Mariahilferstrasse, or tram no. 1, 2, D, or J to Burgring.

This complex of imperial edifices, the first of which was constructed in 1279, grew and grew as the empire did, so that today the Hofburg Palace is virtually a city within a city. The palace, which has withstood three major sieges and a great fire, is called simply *die Burg,* or "the palace," by Viennese. Of its more than 2,600 rooms, fewer than two dozen are open to the public.

Schatzkammer (Imperial Treasury) ★★★ This is the greatest treasury in the world. It's divided into two sections: the Imperial Profane and the Sacerdotal Treasuries. One part displays the crown jewels and an assortment of imperial riches; the other exhibits ecclesiastical treasures. The most outstanding exhibit is the imperial crown, dating from 962. It's so big that even though padded, it probably slipped down over the ears of many a Hapsburg at his coronation. Studded with emeralds, sapphires, diamonds, and rubies, this 1,000-year-old symbol of sovereignty is a priceless treasure. Also on display is the imperial crown worn by the Hapsburg rulers from 1804 to the end of the empire. You'll see the saber of Charlemagne and the holy lance. Among great Schatzkammer prizes is the Burgundian Treasure seized in the 15th century, rich in vestments, oil paintings, gems, and robes.

Hofburg, Schweizerhof. ✆ **01/525-240.** Admission 12€ adults, free for students and children 18 and under. Wed–Mon 10am–6pm.

Kaiserappartements (Imperial Apartments) ★★ The Hofburg complex includes the Kaiserappartements on the first floor, where the emperors and their wives and children lived. To reach these apartments, enter via the rotunda of Michaelerplatz. The apartments are richly decorated with tapestries, many from Aubusson. The Imperial Silver and Porcelain Collection provides an insight into Hapsburg court etiquette. Most of these pieces are from the 18th and 19th centuries. Leopoldinischer Trakt (Leopold's Apartments) dates from the 17th century. These Imperial Apartments are more closely associated with Franz Josef than with any other emperor.

Michaeler Platz 1 (inside the Ring, about a 4-min. walk from Herrengasse; entrance via the Kasertor in the Inneren Burghof). ✆ **01/533-75-70.** Admission 9.90€ adults, 8.90€ students 25 and under, 4.90€ children 6–15, free for children 5 and under. Daily 9am–5pm (July–Aug to 5:30pm). U-Bahn: U-1 or U-3 to Herrengasse.

Die Burgkapelle (Home of the Vienna Boys' Choir) Construction of this Gothic chapel began in 1447 during the reign of Emperor Frederick III, but the

The Vienna Boys' Choir

In 1498, the emperor Maximilian I decreed that 12 boys should be included among the official court musicians. Over the next 500 years, this group evolved into the world-renowned Vienna Boys' Choir *(Wiener Sängerknaben).* They perform in Vienna at various venues, including the Staatsoper, the Volksoper, and Schönbrunn Palace. The choir also performs at Sunday and Christmas Masses with the Hofmusikkapelle (Court Musicians) at the Burgkapelle (see above review for details). The choir's boarding school is at Augartenpalais, Obere Augartenstrasse. For more information on where they are performing and how to get tickets, go to the choir's website (www.wsk.at).

building was subsequently massively renovated. From 1449, it was the private chapel of the royal family. Today the Burgkapelle is the home of the **Hofmusikkapelle (Court Musicians) ★★**, an ensemble consisting of the Vienna Boys' Choir and members of the Vienna State Opera chorus and orchestra. Written applications for reserved seats should be sent at least 8 weeks in advance. Use a credit card; do not send cash or checks. For reservations, write to Verwaltung der Hofmusikkapelle, Hofburg, A-1010 Vienna. If you fail to reserve in advance, you might be lucky enough to secure tickets from a block sold at the Burgkapelle box office every Friday from 11am to 1pm or 3 to 5pm. The line starts forming at least half an hour before that. If you're willing to settle for standing room, it's free.

Hofburg (entrance on Schweizerhof). ✆ **01/533-9927.** www.hofburgkapelle.at. Mass: Seats 5€–45€; standing room free. Masses (performances) held only Jan–June and mid-Sept to Dec, Sun and holidays 9:15am. U-Bahn: Stephansplatz.

Neue Hofburg The last addition to the Hofburg complex was the Neue Hofburg (New Château). Construction started in 1881 and continued until work was halted in 1913. The palace was the residence of Archduke Franz Ferdinand, the nephew and heir apparent of Franz Josef, whose assassination at Sarajevo set off the chain of events that led to World War I. The **arms and armor collection ★★** is second only to that of the Metropolitan Museum of Art in New York. It's in the **Hofjagd and Rüstkammer,** on the second floor of the New Château. On display are crossbows, swords, helmets, pistols, and armor. Another section, the **Musikinstrumentensammlung ★** (✆ **01/525-244-471**), is devoted to musical instruments, mainly from the 17th and 18th centuries. In the **Ephesos-Museum** (**Museum of Ephesian Sculpture;** ✆ **01/525-24-476**), with an entrance behind the Prince Eugene monument, you'll see high-quality finds from Ephesus in Turkey and the Greek island of Samothrace.

Heldenplatz. ✆ **01/525-24-0.** www.khm.at. Admission 12€ adults, free for students 19 and under. Wed–Mon 10am–6pm. U-Bahn: Mariahilferstrasse.

Albertina ★★ Housing one of the greatest graphics collections in the world, the Albertina offers more exhibition space than before, a restaurant, and a four-story graphic-arts collection ranging from the late Gothic era through the present day. It's housed in the neoclassical Albertina Palace, the largest residential palace in Vienna, and it's named for Albert, duke of Saxony-Teschen (1738–1822), who launched the collection. Today it comprises some 65,000 drawings and a million prints that include such Old Masters as Leonardo da Vinci, Michelangelo, Manet, and Rubens. Its most important collection is the Dürer exhibition; unfortunately, much of the art you see from that master is a copy; the originals, such as *Praying Hands,* are shown only during special exhibitions.

For the first time, visitors can walk through the historic staterooms designed for Archduke Charles (1771–1847), who defeated Napoleon at the Battle of Aspern in 1809. Unknown to many of the Viennese themselves, the Albertina contains a wealth of 20th-century art from Jackson Pollock to Robert Rauschenberg.

The graphic arts on parade here go back to the 14th century. Yes, Poussin; yes, Fragonard; yes, Rembrandt—the list of artists on exhibit seems limitless. Allow at least 3 hours just to skim the surface.

Albertinaplatz 1. ✆ **01/534-83-0.** www.albertina.at. Admission 9.50€ adults, 8€ seniors, 7€ students, free for children 5 and under. Daily 10am–6pm (Wed to 9pm). U-Bahn: Stephansplatz.

Augustinerkirche This church was constructed in the 14th century as part of the Hofburg complex to serve as the parish church of the imperial court. In the latter part of the 18th century, it was stripped of its baroque embellishments and returned to the original Gothic features. The Chapel of St. George, dating from 1337, is entered from the right aisle. The **Tomb of Maria Christina ★**, the favorite daughter of Maria Theresa, is housed in the main nave near the rear entrance, but there's no body in it. (The princess was actually buried in the Imperial Crypt at Katuzinerkirche.) This richly ornamented empty tomb is one of Canova's masterpieces. The royal weddings of Maria Theresa and François of Lorraine (1736), Marie Antoinette and Louis XVI of France (1770), Marie-Louise of Austria and Napoleon (1810, but by proxy—he didn't show up), and Franz Josef and Elizabeth of Bavaria (1854) were all held in the church. The most convenient, and dramatic, time to visit is Sunday at 11am, when a High Mass is celebrated with choir, soloists, and orchestra.

Augustinerstrasse 1. ✆ **01/533-70-99.** www.augustinerkirche.at. Free admission. Daily 6:30am–6pm. U-Bahn: Stephansplatz.

Spanische Reitschule (Spanish Riding School) ★ The Spanish Riding School is in the crystal-chandeliered white ballroom in an 18th-century building of the Hofburg complex. We always marvel at the skill and beauty of the sleek Lipizzaner stallions as their adept trainers put them through their paces in a show that hasn't changed in 4 centuries. These are the world's most famous, classically styled equine performers. Reservations for performances must be made in advance, as early as possible. Order your tickets for the Sunday and Wednesday shows by writing to **Spanische Reitschule,** Hofburg, A-1010 Vienna (fax 01/533-903-240), through a travel agency in Vienna (tickets for Sat shows can be ordered only through a travel agency), or online at the website listed below. Tickets for training sessions with no advance reservations can be purchased at the entrance.

Michaelerplatz 1, Hofburg. ✆ **01/533-9032.** www.srs.at. Regular performances 38€–130€ seats, 20€–25€ standing room; children 2 and under not admitted to performances. Morning exercise with music 12€ adults, 9€ seniors, 6€ children 7 and over, free for children 6 and under. Training session with music and guided tour 19€ adults, 16€ seniors, 12€ children 7 and over, free for children 6 and under. Regular shows Mar–June and Sept to mid-Dec, most Sun at 11am and some Fri at 6pm. Classical dressage with music performances Apr–June and Sept, most Sun at 11am. Training session months vary, but are held Tues–Sat 10–11am. Call ahead for open dates. U-Bahn: Stephansplatz.

EXPLORING THE MUSEUMSQUARTIER COMPLEX ★★★

With the opening of this long-awaited giant modern-art complex, critics claim that the assemblage of art installed in 18th-century royal stables has tipped the city's cultural center of gravity from Hapsburgian pomp into the new millennium. This massive structure, one of the 10 largest cultural complexes in the world, has been likened to a combination of the Guggenheim Museum and New York's Museum of Modern Art, with the Brooklyn Academy of Music, a children's museum, an architecture and design center, theaters, art galleries, video workshops, and much more thrown in for good measure. There is even an ecology center and a tobacco museum. For more information, go the MuseumsQuartier website at **www.mqw.at**.

Kunsthalle Wien ★ Cutting-edge contemporary and classic modern art are showcased here. Exhibits focus on specific subjects and seek to establish a link between modern art and current trends. You'll find works by everyone from Picasso and Juan Miró to Jackson Pollock and Paul Klee, from Wassily Kandinsky to Andy Warhol and, surprise, Yoko Ono. From expressionism to cubism to abstractionism, exhibits reveal the major movements in contemporary art since the mid–20th century. The five floors can be explored in 1 to 2 hours, depending on what interests you.

Museumsplatz 1. ✆ **01/521-890.** www.kunsthallewien.at. Admission 6€–8.50€ adults; 5€–6€ seniors, students, and children. Thurs–Tues 10am–7pm (Thurs to 9pm).

Leopold Museum ★★ This extensive collection of Austrian art includes the world's largest treasure-trove of the works of Egon Schiele (1890–1918), who was once forgotten in art history but now takes his place alongside van Gogh and Modigliani in the ranks of great doomed artists, dying before he was 28. His collection of art at the Leopold includes more than 2,500 drawings and watercolors and 330 oil canvases. Other Austrian modernist masterpieces include paintings by Oskar Kokoschka, the great Gustav Klimt, Anton Romaki, and Richard Gerstl. Major statements in Arts and Crafts from the late 19th and 20th centuries include works by Josef Hoffmann, Kolo Moser, Adolf Loos, and Franz Hagenauer.

Museumsplatz 1. ✆ **01/525-70-0.** www.leopoldmuseum.org. Admission 10€ adults, 7.50€ seniors, 6.50€ students and children 8 and over. Mon–Wed and Fri–Sun 10am–6pm; Thurs 10am–9pm.

MUMOK (Museum of Modern Art Ludwig Foundation) ★ This gallery presents one of the most outstanding collections of contemporary art in central Europe. It comprises mainly works from American Pop Art mixed with concurrent Continental movements such as the hyperrealism of the 1960s and 1970s. The museum features five exhibition levels (three of them aboveground and two underground). So that it will be easier to cross and compare a single art movement such as cubism or surrealism, paintings "in the same family" are grouped together. Expect to encounter works by all the fabled names such as Robert Indiana, Jasper Johns, Roy Lichtenstein, Robert Rauschenberg, George Segal, and, of course, Andy Warhol.

Museumsplatz 1. ✆ **01/525-00.** www.mumok.at. Admission 9€. Tues–Sun 10am–6pm (Thurs to 9pm).

OTHER TOP ATTRACTIONS IN THE INNER CITY

Domkirche St. Stephan (St. Stephan's Cathedral) ★★★ The cathedral was founded in the 12th century in what was the town's center. Stephansdom was virtually destroyed in a 1258 fire, and in the early 14th century the ruins of the Romanesque basilica gave way to a Gothic building. It suffered terribly in the

Turkish siege of 1683 and from the Russian bombardments of 1945. Reopened in 1948, the cathedral is today one of the greatest Gothic structures in Europe, rich in woodcarvings, altars, sculptures, and paintings. The chief treasure of the cathedral is the carved, wooden **Wiener Neustadt altarpiece ★★** that dates from 1447. Richly painted and gilded, the altar was discovered in the Virgin's Choir. In the Apostles' Choir look for the curious **Tomb of Emperor Frederick III ★★**. Made of a pinkish Salzburg marble, the carved 17th-century tomb depicts hideous little hobgoblins trying to enter and wake the emperor from his eternal sleep. The steeple, rising some 135m (443 ft.), has come to symbolize the very spirit of Vienna. You can climb the 343-step South Tower, which dominates the Viennese skyline and offers a view of the Vienna Woods. Called Alter Steffl (Old Steve), the tower with its needle-like spire was built between 1350 and 1433. The North Tower (Nordturm), reached by elevator, was never finished, but was crowned in the Renaissance style in 1579. From here you get a panoramic sweep of the city and the Danube.

Stephansplatz 3. ✆ **01/515-52-3526.** www.stephanskirche.at. Cathedral free admission; tour of catacombs 4.50€ adults, 1.50€ children 14 and under. Guided tour of cathedral 4.50€ adults, 1.50€ children 14 and under. North Tower 4.50€ adults, 1.50€ children 14 and under; South Tower 4.50€ adults, 2.50€ students, 1.50€ children 14 and under. Evening tours June–Sept, including tour of the roof, 10€ adults, 4€ children 14 and under. Cathedral daily 6am–10pm except times of service. Tour of catacombs Mon–Sat 10, 11, and 11:30am, 12:30, 1:30, 2, 2:30, 3:30, 4, and 4:30pm; Sun 2, 2:30, 3, 3:30, 4, and 4:30pm. Guided tour of cathedral Mon–Sat 9am and 1pm; Sun 3pm. Special evening tour Sat 7pm (June–Sept). North Tower Oct–Mar daily 8am–5pm; Apr–Sept daily 6am–10pm. South Tower daily 6am–10pm. U-Bahn: Stephansplatz. Bus: 1A, 2A, or 3A.

Gemäldegalerie der Akademie der Bildenden Kunste (Gallery of Painting and Fine Arts) ★ Visit this painting gallery to see the *Last Judgment* by the incomparable Hieronymus Bosch. In this work, the artist conjured up all the demons of the nether regions for a terrifying view of the suffering and sins of humankind. The gallery also houses many 15th-century Dutch and Flemish paintings and several works by Lucas Cranach the Elder. The academy is noted for its 17th-century art by Van Dyck, Rembrandt, Botticelli, and a host of others. Rubens is represented here by more than a dozen oil sketches. You can see Rembrandt's *Portrait of a Woman* and scrutinize Guardi's scenes of 18th-century Venice.

Schillerplatz 3. ✆ **01/588-16-225.** www.akademiegalerie.at. Admission 6€ adults; 3.50€ seniors, students, and children. Tues–Sun 10am–4pm. U-Bahn: Karlsplatz.

Haus der Musik ★ Mozart is long gone, but Vienna finally got around to opening a full-scale museum devoted to music. This hands-on museum is high-tech. You can take to the podium and conduct the Vienna Philharmonic. Wandering the halls and niches of this museum, you encounter nostalgic reminders of the great composers who have lived in Vienna, not only Mozart but also Beethoven, Schubert, Brahms, and others. In the rooms you can listen to your favorite renditions of their works and explore their memorabilia. A memorial, *Exodus,* pays tribute to the Viennese musicians driven into exile or murdered by the Nazis. At the **Musicantino Restaurant** on the top floor, you can enjoy a panoramic view of the city.

Seilerstätte 30. ✆ **01/516-48-50.** www.hdm.at. Admission 10€ adults, 8.50€ students and seniors, 5.50€ children 3–11, free for children 2 and under. Daily 10am–10pm. U-Bahn: Stephansplatz.

Kunsthistorisches Museum (Museum of Art History) ★★★ Across from the Hofburg, this huge building houses the fabulous art collections gathered by the

Hapsburgs. A highlight is the fine collection of ancient Egyptian and Greek art. The museum also has works by many of the greatest European masters, such as Velázquez, Titian, Brueghel the Elder, Van Dyck, Ruben, Rembrandt, and Dürer. ***Warning:*** Because of ongoing restoration, not all of the rooms may be open when you visit.

Maria-Theresien-Platz, Burgring 5. ✆ **01/525-24-4025.** www.khm.at. Admission 12€ adults, free for ages 19 and under. Tues–Sun 10am–6pm (Thurs to 9pm). U-Bahn: Mariahilferstrasse. Tram: 1, 2, D, or J.

Liechtenstein Museum ★★★ This collection of art treasures from the Liechtenstein's princely collections is installed in the royal family palace in the Rossau district. For the first time visitors can see this fabled collection of Raphaels, Rubens, and Rembrandts, one of the world's greatest private art collections. The palace itself is a work of art, dating from the late 17th and early 18th centuries. Art, such as works by Frans Hals and Van Dyck, is displayed in the neoclassical Garden Palace, which became Vienna's first museum when it opened its doors in 1807. There are some 1,700 works of art in the collection, although not all of them can be displayed at once, of course. There are some 200 works of art spread over eight galleries. Works range from the 13th to the 19th century, and include *Venus in Front of the Mirror* (ca. 1613) by Peter Paul Rubens, who is clearly the star of the museum. The galleries also present sculptures, antiques, and rare porcelain. Of spectacular beauty is the splendid **Hercules Hall ★**, the largest secular baroque room in Vienna. Frescoes were painted between 1704 and 1708 by Andrea Pozzo.

Lichtenstein Garden Palace, Fürstengasse 1. ✆ **01/31957670.** www.liechtensteinmuseum.at. Admission 10€ adults, 8€ seniors, 5€ students, free for children 15 and under, 20€ family ticket. Fri–Mon 10am–5pm. U-Bahn: Rossauer Lände. Tram: D to Porzellangasse.

ATTRACTIONS OUTSIDE THE INNER CITY

Schönbrunn Palace ★★★ A Hapsburg palace of 1,441 rooms, Schönbrunn was designed and built between 1696 and 1712 in a grand baroque style meant to surpass that of Versailles. When Maria Theresa became empress in 1740, she changed the original plans, and the Schönbrunn we see today, with its delicate rococo touches, is her conception. It was the imperial summer palace during Maria Theresa's 40-year reign, the scene of great ceremonial balls, lavish banquets, and the fabulous receptions during the Congress of Vienna in 1815. The State Apartments are the most stunning. Much of the interior ornamentation is in 23½-karat gold, and many porcelain tile stoves are in evidence. Of the 40 rooms that you can visit, particularly fascinating is the "Room of Millions" decorated with Indian and Persian miniatures, the grandest rococo salon in the world.

Schönbrunner Schlossstrasse. ✆ **01/811-13-239.** www.schoenbrunn.at. Admission 9.50€–15€ adults, 8.50€–13€ students, 4.70€–7.90€ children 6–15, free for children 5 and under. ***Note:*** Tickets have a price range because admission is based on how many areas you wish to view. Apr–Oct daily 8:30am–5pm (until 6pm July–Aug); Nov–Mar daily 8:30am–4:30pm. U-Bahn: Schönbrunn.

Österreichische Galerie Belvedere ★★ The Belvedere Palace was built as a summer home for Prince Eugene of Savoy and consists of two palatial buildings. The pond reflects the sky and palace buildings, which are made up of a series of interlocking cubes, and the interior is dominated by two great, flowing staircases. The Unteres Belvedere (Lower Belvedere), with its entrance at Rennweg 6A, was constructed from 1714 to 1716 and contains the Gold Salon, one of the palace's most beautiful rooms. It also houses the Barockmuseum (Museum of Baroque Art). The original sculptures from the Neuermarkt fountain, the work of Georg Raphael Donner, are displayed here. The Oberes Belvedere (Upper Belvedere) was started in 1721 and completed in 1723. It contains the Gallery of 19th- and 20th-Century Art, with an outstanding collection of the works of Gustav Klimt, including his extraordinary *Judith*. The Museum of Medieval Austrian Art is in the Orangery.

Prinz-Eugen-Strasse 27. ✆ **01/79557-0.** www.belvedere.at. Admission 9.50€ adults, 7.50€ seniors, 6€ students, free for children 5 and under. Tues–Sun 10am–6pm (last entrance 5:30pm). Tram: D to Schloss Belvedere.

ORGANIZED TOURS

Wiener Rundfahrten (Vienna Sightseeing Tours), Graf Starhemberggasse 25 (✆ **01/712-46-83-0;** www.viennasightseeingtours.com; U-Bahn: Landstrasse Wien Mitte), offers some of the best-organized tours of Vienna and its surroundings (several are noted below). Tours depart from a signposted area in front of the State Opera (U-Bahn: Karlsplatz) and include running commentary in both German and English.

CITY TOURS A **"Historical City Tour,"** which includes visits to Schönbrunn and Belvedere palaces, leaves the Staatsoper daily at 9:45am and 2pm (in summer also at 10:30am; U-Bahn: Karlsplatz). It lasts about 3½ hours and costs 37€ adults and 15€ children. It's ideal for visitors who are pressed for time and yet want to be shown the major (and most frequently photographed) monuments of Vienna. It takes you past the historic buildings of Ringstrasse—the State Opera, Hofburg Palace, museums, Parliament, City Hall, the Burgtheater, the University, and the Votive Church—into the heart of Vienna.

Another tour, **"Following Sisi's Footsteps,"** is the same as the "Historical City Tour" except that you also watch the Lipizzaner horses being trained at the Spanish Riding School. These tours leave at 9:45am Tuesday to Saturday. They cost 39€ adults and 15€ children, with the entrance fee to the Spanish Riding School (see above) to be paid separately.

TOURS OUTSIDE THE CITY **"Vienna Woods—Mayerling,"** another popular excursion, lasting about 4 hours, leaves from the Staatsoper and takes you to the towns of Perchtoldsdorf and Modling, and also to the Abbey of Heiligenkreuz, a center of Christian culture since medieval times. The tour also takes you for a short walk through Baden, the spa that was once a favorite summer resort of the aristocracy. This tour costs 43€ adults and 15€ children.

The Shopping Scene

Vienna is known for the excellent quality of its works, including petit point, hand-painted porcelain, work by goldsmiths and silversmiths, handmade dolls, ceramics, enamel jewelry, wrought-iron articles, and leather goods. Also popular is loden, a boiled and rolled wool fabric made into overcoats, suits, and hats, as well as knitted sweaters. Popular destinations can be found on **Kärntnerstrasse,** between the Staatsoper and Stock-im-Eisen-Platz; the **Graben,** between Stock-im-Eisen-Platz and Kohlmarkt; **Kohlmarkt,** between the Graben and Michaelplatz; and **Rotenturmstrasse,** between Stephansplatz and Kai. You can also shop on **Mariahilferstrasse,** between Babenbergerstrasse and Schönbrunn, one of the longest streets in Vienna; **Favoritenstrasse,** between Südtirolerplatz and Reumannplatz; and **Landstrasser Hauptstrasse.**

The **Naschmarkt** is a vegetable-and-fruit market with a lively scene every day. It's at Linke and Rechte Wienzeile, south of the opera district.

Albin Denk, Graben 13 (✆ **01/512-44-39;** U-Bahn: Stephansplatz), is the oldest continuously operating porcelain store in Vienna, in business since 1702. You'll see thousands of objects from Meissen, Dresden, and other regions.

Opened in 1830 by the Plankl family, **Loden Plankl,** Michaelerplatz 6 (✆ **01/533-80-32;** www.loden-plankl.at; U-Bahn: Stephansplatz), is the oldest and most reputable outlet in Vienna for traditional Austrian clothing. You'll find Austrian loden coats, shoes, trousers, dirndls, jackets, lederhosen, and suits for men, women, and children. The building, opposite the Hofburg, dates from the 17th century. The three-floor **Ö. W. (Österreichische Werkstatten),** Kärntnerstrasse 6 (✆ **01/512-24-18;** U-Bahn: Stephansplatz), sells hundreds of handmade art objects from Austria. Some 200 leading artists and craftspeople throughout the country organized this cooperative to showcase their wares. It's easy to find, only half a minute's walk from St. Stephan's Cathedral.

Vienna After Dark

The best source of information about what's happening on the cultural scene is ***Wien Monatsprogramm,*** distributed free at tourist information offices and at many hotel reception desks. ***Die Presse,*** the Viennese daily, publishes a special magazine in its Thursday edition outlining the major cultural events for the coming week. It's in German but might still be helpful.

THE PERFORMING ARTS

OPERA & CLASSICAL MUSIC Music is at the heart of cultural life in Vienna. This has been true for a couple of centuries or so, and the city continues to lure composers, musicians, and music lovers.

The **Wiener Staatsoper (State Opera),** Opernring 2 (✆ **01/5144-42250;** www.staatsoper.at; U-Bahn: Karlsplatz), is one of the three most important opera houses in the world. With the Vienna Philharmonic in the pit, some of the leading opera stars of the world perform here. In their day, Richard Strauss and Gustav Mahler worked as directors. Daily performances are given September through June. Tickets range from 3.50€ to 280€. Tours are offered two to five times daily, for 6.50€ per adult, 5.50€ seniors, and 3.50€ students and children; times are posted on a board outside the entrance.

Count yourself fortunate if you get to hear a concert at **Musikverein,** Dumbastrasse 3 (✆ **01/505-8190;** www.musikverein.at; U-Bahn: Karlsplatz). The Golden Hall is regarded as one of the four acoustically best concert halls in the world. Some 500 concerts per season (Sept–June) are presented here. Only 10 to 12 of these are played by the Vienna Philharmonic, and those are subscription concerts, which are always sold out long in advance. Standing room is available at almost any performance, but you must line up hours before the show. Tickets for standing room are 6€ to 7€; 10€ to 80€ for seats. The box office is open Monday to Friday 9am to 8pm, Saturday from 9am to 1pm.

Vienna is the home of four major symphony orchestras, including the world-acclaimed Vienna Symphony and the Vienna Philharmonic. In addition to the ÖRF Symphony Orchestra and the Niederösterreichische Tonkünstler, there are dozens of others, ranging from smaller orchestras to chamber orchestras. The orchestras

WINE TASTING IN THE heurigen

Heurigen are Viennese wine taverns, celebrated in operettas, films, and song. They are found on the outskirts of Vienna, principally in Grinzing (the most popular district) and in Sievering, Neustift, Nussdorf, or Heiligenstadt. **Grinzing** (tram: 38) lies at the edge of the Vienna Woods, a 15-minute drive northwest of the center.

Only 20 minutes from Vienna, **Weingut Wolff,** Rathstrasse 50, Neustift (✆ **01/440-37-27;** www.wienerheuriger.at; bus: 35), is one of the most durable of Heurigen. Although aficionados claim the best are "deep in the countryside" of Lower Austria, this one comes closest on the borderline of Vienna to offering an authentic experience. In summer, you're welcomed to a flower-decked garden set against a backdrop of ancient vineyards. You can really fill up your platter here, with some of the best *wursts* (sausages) and roast meats (especially the delectable pork), as well as fresh salads. Find a table under a cluster of grapes and sample the fruity young wines, especially the chardonnay, Sylvaner, and Gruner Veltliner. The tavern is open daily from 11am to 1am with main courses ranging from 8€ to 15€.

Altes Presshaus, Cobenzlgasse 15 (✆ **01/320-02-03**), was established in 1527, the oldest continuously operating *Heurige* in Grinzing, with an authentic cellar you might ask to visit. The place has an authentic, smoke-stained character with wood paneling and antique furniture. The garden terrace blossoms throughout the summer. Live music is also a part of your meal. Try such Heurigen-inspired fare as smoked pork shoulder, roast pork shank, sauerkraut, potatoes, and dumplings. Meals cost 10€ to 18€; special featured menus are 21€ to 26€; themed menus (Wiener menu, chicken menu, Hauer menu, low-fat menu, and steak menu) run 17€ to 25€; drinks begin at 2€. Wine packages can be added for 6€ to 20€. It's open March to October daily from 4 to 11pm.

sometimes perform at the **Konzerthaus,** Lothringerstrasse 20 (✆ **01/242-00-100;** www.konzerthaus.at; U-Bahn: Stadtpark), a major concert hall with three auditoriums, and also the venue for chamber music and other programs.

THEATER For performances in English, head to **Vienna's English Theatre,** Josefsgasse 12 (✆ **01/402-12-60-0;** www.englishtheatre.at; U-Bahn: Rathaus). The **Burgtheater (National Theater),** Dr.-Karl-Lueger-Ring 2 (✆ **01/5144-41-40;** www.burgtheater.at; tram: 1, 2, D, or J to Burgtheater), produces classical and modern plays. Even if you don't understand German, you might want to attend a performance here, especially if a familiar Shakespeare play is being staged. This is one of Europe's premier repertory theaters. Tickets are 5€ to 65€ for seats, 1€ to 9€ for standing room.

NIGHTCLUBS, CABARETS & BARS

The noteworthy architect Adolf Loos designed the very dark, sometimes mysterious **Loos American Bar,** Kärntnerdurchgang 10 (✆ **01/512-32-83;** www.loosbar.at; U-Bahn: Stephansplatz), in 1908. Today it welcomes singles, couples who tend to be bilingual and very hip, and all manner of clients from the arts and media scenes of Vienna. The mixologist's specialties include six kinds of martinis, plus five kinds of Manhattans. It's open Sunday to Wednesday noon to 4am, and Thursday to Saturday noon to 5am.

The most famous jazz pub in Austria, **Jazzland,** Franz-Josefs-Kai 29 (✆ **01/533-25-75;** U-Bahn: Schwedenplatz), is noted for the quality of its U.S.- and central European–based performers. It's in a deep, 200-year-old cellar, of the type the Viennese used to store staples during the city's many sieges. Amid exposed brick walls and dim lighting, you can order drinks or dinner. The place is open Monday to Saturday from 7pm to 1am. Music begins at 9pm, and three sets are performed.

In a surprising location in the Leopold Museum, **Café Leopold,** Museumsplatz 1 (✆ **01/523-67-32**), is all the rage. It has a revolving cycle of DJs, each vying for local fame, and a wide selection of party-colored cocktails, priced from 7€. The cafe-and-restaurant section of this place is open Sunday to Wednesday 10am to 2am, and Thursday and Friday 10am to 4am. The disco operates Thursday to Saturday 10pm to between 2 and 4am, depending on business.

Alfi's Goldener Spiegel, Linke Wienzeile 46 (entrance on Stiegengasse; ✆ **01/586-6608;** U-Bahn: Kettenbrückengasse), is the most enduring gay restaurant in Vienna and also its most popular gay bar, attracting mostly male clients to its position near Vienna's Naschmarkt. The place is very cruisy. The bar is open Wednesday to Monday 7pm to 2am.

Frauencafé, Lange Gasse 11 (✆ **01/406-37-54;** U-Bahn: Volkstheater), is exactly what a translation of its name would imply: a politically conscious cafe for lesbians and (to a lesser degree) heterosexual women who appreciate the company of other women.

SALZBURG ★★★

A baroque city on the banks of the Salzach River, set against a mountain backdrop, Salzburg is the beautiful capital of the state of Salzburg. The city and the river were named after its early residents who earned their living in the salt mines. In this "heart of the heart of Europe," Mozart was born in 1756, and the composer's association with the city beefs up tourism.

The **Old Town** lies on the left bank of the river, where a monastery and bishopric were founded in 700. From that start, Salzburg grew in power and prestige, becoming an archbishopric in 798. In the heyday of the prince-archbishops, the city became known as the "German Rome." Responsible for much of its architectural grandeur are those masters of the baroque, Fischer von Erlach and Lukas von Hildebrandt.

The City of Mozart, "Silent Night," and *The Sound of Music*—Salzburg lives essentially off its rich past. It is a front-ranking cultural mecca for classical music year-round. The city is the setting for the Salzburg Festival, a world-renowned annual event that attracts music lovers, especially Mozart fans, from all over the globe. Salzburg's natural setting among alpine peaks on both banks of the Salzach River gives it the backdrop perpetuating its romantic image.

As one of Europe's greatest tourist capitals, most of Salzburg's day-to-day life spins around promoting its music and its other connections. Although *The Sound of Music* was filmed in 1964, this Julie Andrews blockbuster has become a cult attraction and is definitely alive and well in Salzburg. Ironically, Austria was the only country in the world where the musical failed when it first opened. It played for only a single week in Vienna, closing after audiences dwindled.

Salzburg is only a short distance from the Austrian-German frontier, so it's convenient for exploring many of the attractions of Bavaria (see chapter 8). Situated on the northern slopes of the Alps, the city lies at the intersection of traditional European trade routes and is well served by air, Autobahn, and rail.

Essentials

GETTING THERE

BY PLANE The **Salzburg Airport–W.A. Mozart,** Innsbrucker Bundesstrasse 95 (✆ **0662/8580-7911;** www.salzburg-airport.com), lies 3km (1¾ miles) southwest of the city center. It has regularly scheduled air service to all Austrian airports, as well as to Frankfurt, Amsterdam, Brussels, Berlin, Dresden, Düsseldorf, Hamburg, London, Paris, and Zurich. Major airlines serving the Salzburg airport are **Austrian Airlines** (✆ **800/843-0002** in the U.S., or 888/817-4444 in Canada) and **Lufthansa** (✆ **800/399-5838** in the U.S.).

Bus no. 2 runs between the airport and Salzburg's main rail station. Departures are frequent, and the 20-minute trip costs 2€ one-way for adults, 1€ for children. By taxi it's only about 15 minutes, but you'll pay at least 20€ to 30€.

BY TRAIN Salzburg's main rail station, the **Salzburg Hauptbahnhof,** Südtirolerplatz (✆ **05/1717**), is on the major rail lines of Europe, with frequent arrivals from all the main cities of Austria and from European cities such as Munich. Between 5:05am and 8:05pm, trains arrive every 30 minutes from Vienna (trip time: 3½ hr.); a one-way fare is 23€ to 83€. There are eight daily trains from Innsbruck (2 hr.); a one-way fare is 18€ to 65€. Trains also arrive every 30 minutes from Munich (2½ hr.), with a one-way ticket costing 28€ to 61€.

From the train station, buses depart to various parts of the city, including the Altstadt. Or you can walk to the Altstadt in about 20 minutes. Taxis are also available. The rail station has a currency exchange and storage lockers.

BY CAR Salzburg is 334km (208 miles) southwest of Vienna and 152km (94 miles) east of Munich. It's reached from all directions by good roads, including Autobahn A8 from the west (Munich), A1 from the east (Vienna), and A10 from the

The Salzburg Card

The **Salzburg Card** (www.salzburg.info) not only lets you use **unlimited public transportation,** but acts as an admission ticket to the city's most important **cultural sights.** With the card you can visit Mozart's birthplace, the Hohensalzburg fortress, the Residenz gallery, the world-famous water fountain gardens at Hellbrunn, the Baroque Museum in the Mirabell Gardens, and the gala rooms in the Archbishop's Residence. The card is also good for sights outside of town, including the Hellbrunn Zoo, the open-air museum in Grossingmain, the salt mines of the Dürnberg, and the gondola trip at Untersberg. The card, approximately the size of a credit card, comes with a brochure with maps and sightseeing hints.

A card costs 22€ for 24 hours, 30€ for 48 hours, and 35€ for 72 hours. Children from 6 to 15 years of age receive a 50% discount. You can buy the pass from Salzburg travel agencies, the airport, hotels, tobacconists, and municipal offices.

Salzburg

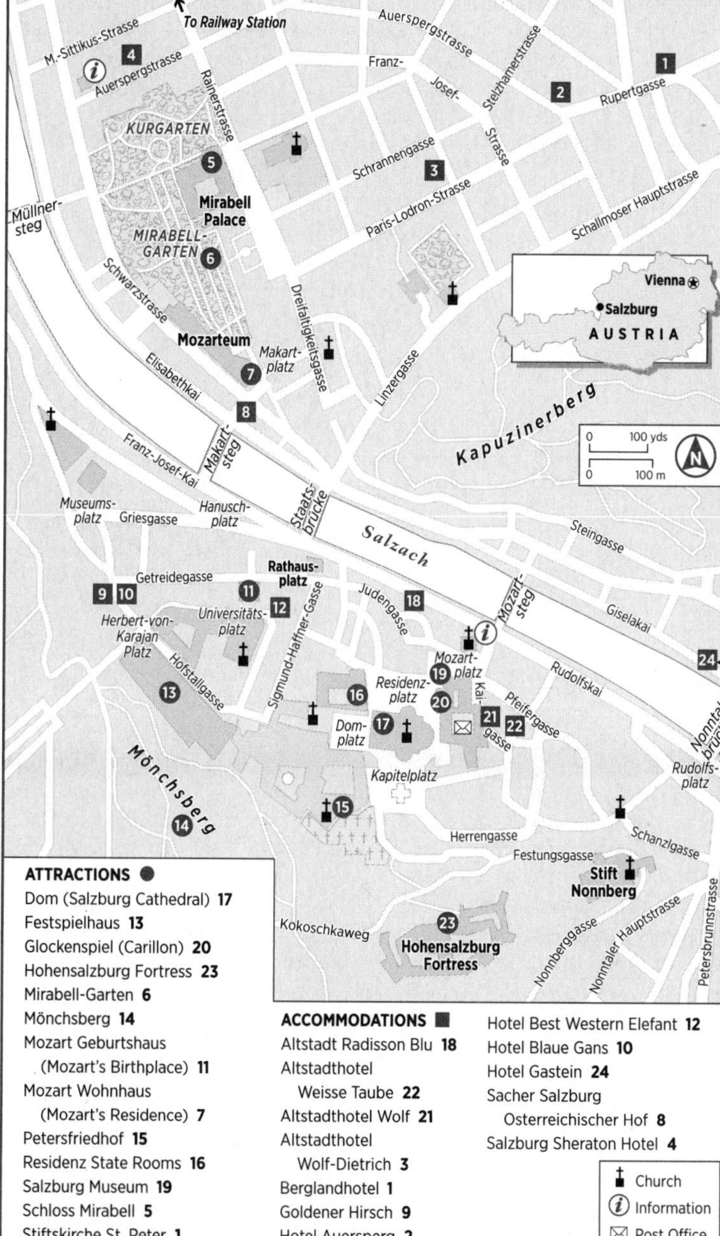
To Railway Station
M.-Sittikus-Strasse
Auerspergstrasse
Rainerstrasse
KURGARTEN
Mirabell Palace
MIRABELL-GARTEN
Müllner-steg
Schwarzstrasse
Mozarteum
Makart-platz
Dreifaltigkeitsgasse
Franz-Josef-Strasse
Stelzhamerstrasse
Rupertgasse
Schrannengasse
Paris-Lodron-Strasse
Schallmoser Hauptstrasse
Linzergasse
Vienna
Salzburg
AUSTRIA
Kapuzinerberg
0 100 yds
0 100 m
N
Elisabethkai
Makart-steg
Franz-Josef-Kai
Museums-platz
Griesgasse
Hanusch-platz
Staats-brücke
Salzach
Steingasse
Rathaus-platz
Getreidegasse
Universitäts-platz
Herbert-von-Karajan Platz
Hofstallgasse
Sigmund-Haffner-Gasse
Judengasse
Mozart-steg
Giselakai
Mozart-platz
Residenz-platz
Dom-platz
Kai-gasse
Pfeifergasse
Rudolfskai
Nonntaler-brücke
Rudolfs-platz
Kapitelplatz
Mönchsberg
Herrengasse
Festungsgasse
Schanzlgasse
Stift Nonnberg
Kokoschkaweg
Hohensalzburg Fortress
Nonnberggasse
Nonntaler Hauptstrasse
Petersbrunnstrasse
ATTRACTIONS ●
Dom (Salzburg Cathedral) 17
Festspielhaus 13
Glockenspiel (Carillon) 20
Hohensalzburg Fortress 23
Mirabell-Garten 6
Mönchsberg 14
Mozart Geburtshaus (Mozart's Birthplace) 11
Mozart Wohnhaus (Mozart's Residence) 7
Petersfriedhof 15
Residenz State Rooms 16
Salzburg Museum 19
Schloss Mirabell 5
Stiftskirche St. Peter 1
ACCOMMODATIONS ■
Altstadt Radisson Blu 18
Altstadthotel Weisse Taube 22
Altstadthotel Wolf 21
Altstadthotel Wolf-Dietrich 3
Berglandhotel 1
Goldener Hirsch 9
Hotel Auersperg 2
Hotel Best Western Elefant 12
Hotel Blaue Gans 10
Hotel Gastein 24
Sacher Salzburg Osterreichischer Hof 8
Salzburg Sheraton Hotel 4
Church
Information
Post Office

south. Route 20 comes into Salzburg from points north and west, and Route 159 serves towns and cities from the southeast.

VISITOR INFORMATION The **Salzburg Information Office,** Auerspergstrasse 6 (✆ **0662/88987-0;** www.salzburg.info; bus: 5, 6, or 51), is open July to August, daily from 9am to 7pm, and September, Monday to Saturday from 9am to 6pm. The office makes hotel reservations for a 10% deposit (which will be credited to your hotel bill), plus a 2.20€ booking fee. There's also a **tourist information office** on Platform 2A of the Hauptbahnhof, Südtirolerplatz (✆ **0662/88987-340**).

CITY LAYOUT Most of what visitors come to see lies on the left bank of the Salzach River in the **Altstadt (Old Town).** If you're driving, you must leave your car in the modern part of town—the right bank of the Salzach—and enter the Old Town on foot, as most of it is for pedestrians only.

The heart of the inner city is **Residenzplatz,** which has the largest and finest baroque fountain this side of the Alps. On the western side of the square stands the **Residenz,** palace of the prince-archbishops, and on the southern side of the square is the **Salzburg Cathedral** (or Dom). To the west of the Dom lies **Domplatz,** linked by archways dating from 1658. Squares to the north and south appear totally enclosed. On the southern side of Max-Reinhardt-Platz and Hofstallgasse, edging toward **Mönchsberg,** stands the **Festspielhaus (Festival Theater),** built on the foundations of the 17th-century court stables.

GETTING AROUND **By Bus/Tram** The city buses and trams provide quick, comfortable service through the city center from the Nonntal parking lot (located just next to the old city center) to Sigsmundsplatz, the city-center parking lot. The one-ride fare is 2€ adults, 1€ children 6 to 15; those 5 and under travel free. Note that buses stop running at 11pm.

BY TAXI You'll find taxi stands scattered at key points all over the city center and in the suburbs. The **Salzburg Funktaxi–Vereinigung** (radio taxis) office is at Rainerstrasse 27 (✆ **0662/8111** to order a taxi in advance). Fares start at 3€.

BY CAR Driving a car in Salzburg isn't recommended. However, you'll probably want a car for touring the areas outside the city (such as Land Salzburg), as using public transportation can be time-consuming. Arrangements for car rentals are always best if made in advance. Try **Avis** (✆ **0662/877278**) or **Hertz** (✆ **0662/876674**), both at Ferdinand-Porsche-Strasse 7 and open Monday to Friday 8:30am to 6pm and Saturday 8am to 1pm.

BY HORSE-DRAWN CAB You rent a horse-drawn cab (called a *Fiaker* in German) at Residenzplatz (✆ **0664/3081765;** www.fiaker-salzburg.at). Four people usually pay 40€ for 20 to 25 minutes, 70€ for 50 minutes, and 100€ for 1 hour and 15 minutes. But all fares are subject to negotiation.

BY BICYCLE City officials have developed a network of bicycle paths, which are indicated on city maps. May through September, you can rent bicycles at **Topbike,** at the Staatsbrücke or Main Bridge (✆ **0627/24656;** www.topbike.at), daily from 9am to 7pm. Rentals cost about 15€ per day, with a 20% discount for Salzburg Card holders.

[FastFACTS] SALZBURG

American Express The office at Mozartplatz 5–7, adjacent to Residenzplatz (✆ **0662/8080-544;** bus: 5 or 6), is open Monday to Friday 9am to 5:30pm and Saturday 9am to noon.

Business Hours Most shops and stores are open Monday to Friday 9am to 6pm and Saturday usually 9am to noon. Some of the smaller shops shut down at noon for a lunch break. Salzburg observes *langer Samstag,* which means that most stores stay open until 5pm on selected Saturdays. Banks are open Monday to Friday 8am to noon and 2 to 4:30pm.

Currency Exchange You can exchange money at the Hauptbahnhof on Südtirolerplatz daily 7am to 10pm, and at the airport daily 9am to 4pm.

Dentists For an English-speaking dentist, call **Dentistenkammer,** Faberstrasse 2 (✆ **0662/87-34-66**).

Doctors If you suddenly fall ill, your best source of information for finding a doctor is the reception desk of your hotel. If you want a comprehensive list of doctors and their respective specialties, which you can acquire in Salzburg or even before your arrival, contact **Ärztekammer für Salzburg,** Bergstrasse 14, A-5020 Salzburg (✆ **0662/87-13-27**). And if your troubles flare up over a weekend, the **Medical Emergency Center of the Austrian Red Cross** maintains a hot line (✆ **141**), which you can use to describe your problem. A staff member there will either ask you to visit their headquarters at Karl Renner Strasse 7, or send a medical expert to wherever you're staying. This service is available from 5pm on Friday to 8am on Monday, and on public holidays.

Drugstores (Apotheke) Larger pharmacies, especially those in the city center, tend to remain open without a break Monday to Friday 8am to 6pm and Saturday 8am to noon. For night service, and service on Saturday afternoon and Sunday, pharmacies display a sign giving the address of the nearest pharmacy that has agreed to remain open over the weekend or throughout the night. A pharmacy that's particularly convenient to Salzburg's commercial center is **Elisabeth-Apotheke,** Elisabethstrasse 1 (✆ **0662/87-14-84**), north of Rainerstrasse toward the train station.

Embassies & Consulates The consular agency of the **United States,** at Alter Markt 1 (✆ **0662/84-87-76**), is open Monday, Wednesday, and Thursday from 9am to noon to assist U.S. citizens with emergencies. The consulate of **Great Britain,** at Alter Markt 4 (✆ **0662/84-81-33**), is open Monday through Friday from 9am to noon.

Emergencies Call ✆ **133** for police, ✆ **122** to report a fire, and ✆ **144** for an ambulance.

Internet Access The most convenient cafe with Internet capability is the **Internet Café,** Mozartplatz (✆ **0662/84-48-22;** bus: 5 or 6), across from the tourist office. It's open daily 9am to 11pm and charges 9€ per hour of Internet access.

Post Office The main post office is at Residenzplatz 9 (✆ **0662/844-12-10;** bus: 5 or 6). The post office at the main railway station is open Monday to Friday 7am to 9:30pm, Saturday 7am to 2pm, and Sunday 7am to 6pm.

Telephone The **country code** for Austria is **43.** The **city code** for Salzburg is **662;** use this code when you're calling from outside Austria. If you're within Austria, use **0662.**

Where to Stay

ON THE LEFT BANK (ALTSTADT)

Very Expensive

Altstadt Radisson Blu ★★ This is not your typical Radisson property—in fact, it's a radical departure for the chain in style and charm. Dating from 1377, it's a luxuriously and elegantly converted Altstadt hostelry. Its closest rivals in town are the old-world Goldener Hirsch and the Sacher Salzburg Österreichischer Hof, to which it comes in third. The old and new are blended in perfect harmony here, and the historic facade conceals top-rate comforts and amenities. In a structure this large, rooms naturally vary greatly in size, but all have a certain charm and sparkle and are exceedingly comfortable with some of the city's best beds, plus luxurious bathrooms with showers.

Rudolfskai 28/Judengasse 15, A-5020 Salzburg. ✆ **0662/848-571.** Fax 0662/848-571-6. www.austria-trend.at. 62 units. 424€–545€ double; 650€ suite. Rates include buffet breakfast. AE, DC, MC, V. Parking 25€. Bus: 55 or 77. **Amenities:** Restaurant; bar; babysitting; room service; Wi-Fi (free). *In room:* TV, hair dryer, minibar.

Goldener Hirsch ★★★ The award for the finest hotel in Salzburg goes to this place, steeped in legend and with a history dating from 1407. The hotel is built on a small scale yet it absolutely exudes aristocratic elegance, which is enhanced by the superb staff. Near Mozart's birthplace, the hotel is composed of four medieval town houses, three of which are joined together in a labyrinth of rustic hallways and staircases. The fourth, called "The Coppersmith's House," is across the street and contains 17 charming, spacious rooms. All rooms in the complex are beautifully furnished and maintained, with luxurious full-size bathrooms.

Getreidegasse 37, A-5020 Salzburg. ✆ **800/325-3589** in the U.S. and Canada, or 0662/8084-0. Fax 0662/843349. www.goldenerhirschsalzburg.com. 69 units. 155€–640€ double; 485€–950€ suite. Higher rates at festival time (the 1st week of Apr and mid-July to Aug). AE, DC, MC, V. You can double-park in front of the Getreidegasse entrance or at the Karajanplatz entrance, and a staff member will take your vehicle to the hotel's garage for 28€. Bus: 55. **Amenities:** 2 restaurants; bar; babysitting; room service. *In room:* A/C, TV, hair dryer, minibar, Wi-Fi (18€ per day).

Moderate

Altstadthotel Weisse Taube This hotel is in the pedestrian area of the Old Town a few steps from Mozartplatz, but you can drive up to it to unload baggage. Constructed in 1365, the Weisse Taube has been owned by the Haubner family since 1904. Rooms are, for the most part, renovated and comfortably streamlined, with traditional furnishings, frequently renewed beds, and small but efficiently laid-out bathrooms. The whole place is kept up with spotless housekeeping.

Kaigasse 9, A-5020 Salzburg. ✆ **0662/84-24-04.** Fax 0662/84-17-83. www.weissetaube.at. 31 units. 98€–185€ double. Rates include breakfast. AE, MC, V. Parking 7€–9€. Bus: 3, 5, 6, or 25. **Amenities:** Breakfast room. *In room:* TV, hair dryer, minibar, Wi-Fi (18€ per day).

Altstadthotel Wolf Ideally located near Mozartplatz, this place dates from 1429. A stucco exterior with big shutters hides the rustic and inviting interior that is decorated with a few baroque touches and often sunny rooms. Many new bathrooms have been installed, making this a more inviting choice than ever. The rooms are a bit cramped, as are the shower-only bathrooms. Still, this pension represents very good value for high-priced Salzburg. Since the hotel is usually full, reservations are imperative.

Kaigasse 7, A-5020 Salzburg. ✆ **0662/8434530.** Fax 0662/8424234. www.hotelwolf.com. 15 units. 108€–214€ double; 188€–248€ junior suite. Rates include buffet breakfast. V. No parking. Tram: 3, 5, or 6. **Amenities:** Breakfast room; babysitting. *In room:* TV, Internet (free).

Hotel Best Western Elefant Near the Old Town Rathaus, in a quiet alley off Getreidegasse, is this well-established, family-run hotel in one of Salzburg's most ancient buildings—more than 700 years old. The well-furnished and high-ceilinged rooms have small bathrooms with tub/shower combinations. Inside the hotel are two restaurants serving Austrian and international cuisine: the vaulted Bürgerstüberl, where high wooden banquettes separate the tables, and the historic Ratsherrnkeller, known as the wine cellar of Salzburg in the 17th century.

Sigmund-Haffner-Gasse 4, A-5020 Salzburg. ✆ **800/780-7234** in the U.S. and Canada, or 0662/84-33-97. Fax 0662/84-01-0928. www.elefant.at. 31 units. 102€–200€ double. Rates include buffet breakfast. AE, DC, MC, V. Nearby parking 10€. Bus: 1, 3, 5, or 6. **Amenities:** 2 restaurants; bar; babysitting; room service. *In room:* A/C (in some), TV, hair dryer, Internet (free), minibar.

Hotel Blaue Gans Only a short walk from the much more expensive Goldener Hirsch, the much-renovated "Blue Goose" has been functioning as an inn for more than 400 years. The building that houses the inn is probably 700 years old, but the rooms have been renovated. All have good beds with firm mattresses and full bathrooms. Those facing the courtyard are quieter and much more desirable. Room nos. 332 and 336 are the most spacious.

Getreidegasse 41–43, A-5020 Salzburg. ✆ **0662/84-24-910.** Fax 0662/84-24-91-9. www.hotel-blaue-gans-salzburg.at. 37 units. 119€–259€ double; 259€–420€ junior suite. Rates include buffet breakfast. AE, DC, MC, V. Parking 15€. Bus: 1 or 2. **Amenities:** Restaurant; bar; babysitting. *In room:* TV, hair dryer, Wi-Fi (free).

ON THE RIGHT BANK

Expensive

Sacher Salzburg Österreichischer Hof ★★★ Only the Goldener Hirsch rivals this charmer. Built as the Hotel d'Autriche in 1866, this hotel has survived the ravages of war and been renovated countless times. A new era began when the owners of the Hotel Sacher in Vienna took over in 1988, turning the hotel into a jewel amid the villas on the riverbank. The cheerful rooms are well furnished, quite spacious, and individually decorated; each has a luxurious bathroom. Try to reserve one overlooking the river. The cafe serves Austria's most fabled pastry, the original Sacher torte.

Schwarzstrasse 5–7, A-5020 Salzburg. ✆ **800/745-8883** in the U.S. and Canada, or 0662/88-977. Fax 0662/889-77-551. www.sacher.com. 113 units. 225€–391€ double; 471€–910€ junior suite; from 910€ suite. AE, DC, MC, V. Parking 25€. Bus: 1, 5, 6, 29, or 51. **Amenities:** 2 restaurants; 2 bars; cafe; lounge; exercise room; room service; sauna. *In room:* TV, hair dryer, minibar, Wi-Fi (free).

Salzburg Sheraton Hotel ★★ One of the crown jewels of the Sheraton chain, this government-rated five-star seven-story hotel opened in 1984 in a desirable location about a 10-minute walk from Mozartplatz. The Austrian architect who designed this place took great pains to incorporate it into its 19th-century neighborhood. Rooms have thick wall-to-wall carpeting and contain beds with built-in headboards. Bathrooms have makeup mirrors and hair dryers. The exclusive junior, queen, and presidential suites are filled with elegant Biedermeier furniture. Half the rooms overlook the Mirabell Gardens.

Auerspergstrasse 4, A-5020 Salzburg. ✆ **800/325-3535** in the U.S., or 0662/88-99-90. Fax 0662/88-17-76. www.sheratonsalzburg.com. 166 units. 140€–255€ double; 365€–440€ junior suite; 580€ suite. AE, DC, MC, V. Parking 15€. Bus: 1. **Amenities:** 2 restaurants; bar; babysitting; indoor pool; room service; sauna. *In room:* A/C, TV, hair dryer, minibar, Wi-Fi (18€ per day).

Moderate

Altstadthotel Wolf-Dietrich ★ Two 19th-century town houses were joined to make this select little hotel. The lobby and ground-floor reception area have a friendly and elegant atmosphere and bright, classical furnishings. The smallish rooms are appealing and comfortably furnished, with tiny bathrooms with tub/shower combinations. Most rooms are at the lower end of the price scale. The **Ärlich Restaurant** is Austria's first licensed organic restaurant. The ground-floor cafe, **Weiner Kaffeehaus,** is reminiscent of the extravagant coffeehouses built in the 19th century in Vienna, Budapest, and Prague.

Wolf-Dietrich-Strasse 7, A-5020 Salzburg. ✆ **0662/87-12-75.** Fax 0662/871-2759. www.salzburg-hotel.at. 27 units. 114€–204€ double; 164€–235€ suite. Rates include breakfast. AE, DC, MC, V. Parking 12€. Restaurant closed Feb–Mar 15. Bus: 1, 2, 5, 6, or 51. **Amenities:** 2 restaurants; bar, cafe; babysitting; indoor pool; room service; sauna; spa. *In room:* TV/DVD, hair dryer, Internet (free), minibar.

Hotel Auersperg ★ With its own sunny gardens, this traditional family-run hotel consists of two buildings: a main structure and a less expensive and less desirable annex. There's an old-fashioned look of charm wherever you go, from the reception hall with its molded ceilings to the antiques-filled drawing room to the convivial and informal library bar. The warm, cozy, and large guest rooms are especially inviting, with excellent beds and well-equipped bathrooms with tubs and showers.

Auerspergstrasse 61, A-5027 Salzburg. ✆ **0662/889-44-0.** Fax 0662/88-944-55. www.hotel-salzburg.net/en. 55 units. 145€–215€ double; 205€–275€ suite. Rates include breakfast. AE, DC, MC, V. Parking 10€. Bus: 15 from the train station. **Amenities:** Breakfast room; bar; exercise room; sauna. *In room:* TV, hair dryer, Wi-Fi (free).

Hotel Mozart ☺ The six-story Hotel Mozart, known for its unpretentious charm and welcoming hospitality, is a comfortable family-run hotel located in the city center. Everything is homey and traditional, with Oriental rugs, local paintings, and an attractive TV lounge. It's a 10-minute walk from the train station and only 5 minutes from the pedestrian area of Linzergasse and the famous Mirabell Gardens. Rooms are often sunny and come with all the standard extras. Most are quite spacious, with built-in furniture and twin beds. Some of the guest rooms are big enough to sleep four comfortably.

Franz-Josef-Strasse 27, A-5020 Salzburg. ✆ **0662/872274.** Fax 0662/870079. www.hotel-mozart.at. 33 units. 90€–155€ double; 110€–175€ triple. AE, MC, V. Parking 10€. Closed Nov 9–26. **Amenities:** Breakfast room; babysitting; room service; smoke-free rooms. *In room:* TV, minibar, hair dryer.

Inexpensive

Berglandhotel ★ Cozy, personalized, and substantial, this guesthouse sits in a quiet residential neighborhood. It welcomes visitors in a "music room" where there's a bar serving beer, wine, and coffee, and a collection of guitars and lutes displayed on the walls. Guest rooms are comfortable, minimalist, and modern looking, with larger-than-expected bathrooms containing tub/shower combinations. The pension will rent you a bike and dispense information about where to ride.

Rupertsgasse 15, A-5020 Salzburg. ✆ **0662/872318.** Fax 0662/872318-8. www.berglandhotel.at. 17 units. 83€–150€ double. Rates include buffet breakfast. AE, DC, MC, V. Free parking. Closed mid-Nov to mid-Dec. Bus: 27 or 29. **Amenities:** Breakfast room; lounge; bikes. *In room:* TV, hair dryer, Wi-Fi (free).

Where to Dine

Two special desserts you'll want to sample while here are the famous ***Salzburger Nockerln,*** a light mixture of stiff egg whites, as well as the elaborate confection known as the ***Mozart-Kugeln,*** with bittersweet chocolate, hazelnut nougat, and marzipan. You'll also want to taste the beer in one of the numerous Salzburg breweries.

ON THE LEFT BANK (ALTSTADT)

Very Expensive

Goldener Hirsch ★★★ AUSTRIAN/VIENNESE The best restaurant in Salzburg's best hotel attracts the brightest luminaries of the international music and business community. The venue is chic, top-notch, impeccable, and charming, richly sought after during peak season. It's staffed with a superb team of chefs and waiters who preside over an atmosphere of elegant simplicity. The food is so tasty and beautifully served that the kitchen ranks among the top two or three in Salzburg. Specialties include saddle of farm-raised venison with red cabbage, king prawns in an okra-curry ragout served with perfumed Thai rice, and tenderloin of beef and veal on morel cream sauce with cream potatoes. In season, expect a dish devoted to game.

Getreidegasse 37. ✆ **0662/80-84-0.** Reservations required. Main courses 25€–45€; 3-course fixed-price lunch or dinner 40€; 5-course fixed-price dinner 65€. AE, MC, V. Daily noon–2:30pm and 6:30–9:30pm. Bus: 55.

Expensive

Purzelbaum ★ AUSTRIAN/FRENCH In a residential neighborhood, this restaurant is near a duck pond at the bottom of a steep incline leading up to Salzburg Castle. During the Salzburg Festival you're likely to see the most dedicated music lovers in Europe hanging out here. Menu items change according to the whim of the chef and include such well-prepared dishes as turbot-and-olive casserole; lamb in white-wine sauce with beans and polenta; and the house specialty, scampi Grüstl, composed of fresh shrimp with sliced potatoes baked with herbs in a casserole.

Zugallistrasse 7. ✆ **0662/84-88-43.** www.purzelbaum.at. Reservations required. Main courses 10€–21€; 5-course fixed-price menu 46€. AE, DC, MC, V. Mon–Sat noon–2pm and 6–11pm. Also open Sun in Aug. Closed July 1–14. Bus: 55.

Moderate

Herzl Tavern ★★ AUSTRIAN/VIENNESE With an entrance on the landmark Karajanplatz, Herzl Tavern lies next door to the glamorous Goldener Hirsch, of which it's a part. Good value attracts both visitors and locals to its pair of cozy rooms, one paneled and timbered. Waitresses in dirndls serve appetizing entrees, which are likely to include roast pork with dumplings, various grills, game stew (in season), and, for the heartiest eaters, a farmer's plate of boiled pork, roast pork, grilled sausages, dumplings, and sauerkraut.

Karajanplatz 7. ✆ **0662/808-4889.** Reservations recommended. Main courses 10€–21€. AE, DC, MC, V. Daily 11:30am–10pm. Bus: 55.

Krimpelstätter SALZBURGER/AUSTRIAN This is an enduring Salzburg favorite dating from 1548. In summer, the beer garden, full of roses and trellises, attracts

CAFE society

Café-Restaurant Glockenspiel, Mozartplatz 2 (✆ **0662/84-14-03-0;** bus: 5, 6, 49, 51, 55, or 95), is the city's most popular cafe, with about 100 tables with armchairs out front. You might want to spend an afternoon here, particularly when there's live chamber music. Upon entering, you can't miss a glass case filled with every caloric delight west of Vienna. For dinner, you can sit on the balcony and look over Salzburg's famous buildings while enjoying regional and international specialties. Many people, however, come just for the drinks and pastries. Try the Maria Theresia, which contains orange liqueur. In summer, the cafe is open daily from 9am to between 10pm and midnight, and in winter, it's open daily from 9am to between 7 and 8pm, depending on business and the season. Although snacks are available throughout opening hours, warm food is usually available until around 2 hours prior to closing. It's closed the 2nd and 3rd weeks of November and January.

Established in 1705, **Café Tomaselli ★**, Alter Markt 9 (✆ **0662/84-44-88;** www.tomaselli.at; bus: 5, 6, 51, 55, or 95), opens onto one of the most charming cobblestone squares of the Altstadt. Aside from the summer chairs placed outdoors, you'll find a high-ceilinged room with many tables. It's a great place to just sit and talk. Another, more formal room to the right of the entrance with oil portraits of well-known 19th-century Salzburgers attracts a haute bourgeois crowd. A waiter will show you a pastry tray filled with 40 kinds of cakes, which you're free to order or wave away. Other menu items include omelets, wursts, ice cream, and a wide range of drinks. Of course, the pastries and ice cream are all homemade. The cafe is open Monday to Saturday 7am to 9pm and Sunday 8am to 9pm.

up to 300 visitors at a time. If you want a snack, a beer, or a glass of wine, head for the paneled door marked GASTEZIMMER in the entry corridor. If you're looking for a more formal, less visited area, three cozy antique dining rooms sit atop a flight of narrow stone steps. You'll find tasty and high-quality Land Salzburg regional cuisine featuring wild game dishes. Start with the cream of goose soup or homemade chamois sausage. Traditional main courses include roast pork with dumplings, schnitzel, and fried sausages with sauerkraut and potatoes. Spinach dumplings are topped with a cheese sauce, and marinated beef stew comes with noodles in butter.

Müllner Hauptstrasse 31. ✆ **0662/432-2740.** www.krimpelstaetter.at. Reservations recommended. Main courses 6€–12€. No credit cards. Tues–Sat 11am–midnight (also Mon May–Sept); Sun 11am–2pm. Closed 3 weeks in Jan. Bus: 27, 49, or 95.

Sternbräu AUSTRIAN This place seems big enough to have fed half the Austro-Hungarian army, with a series of rooms that follow one after the other in varying degrees of formality. The Hofbräustübl is a rustic fantasy. You can also eat in the chestnut-tree-shaded beer garden, usually packed on a summer's night, or under the weathered arcades of an inner courtyard. Daily specials include typical Austrian dishes such as Wiener and chicken schnitzels, trout recipes, cold marinated herring, Hungarian goulash, hearty regional soups, and lots of other *gutbürgerlich* selections. You come here for hearty portions—not for refined cuisine.

Griesgasse 23. ✆ **0662/84-21-40.** www.sternbraeu.com. Reservations not accepted. Main courses 6€–17€. AE, MC, V. Daily 9am–11pm. Bus: 2, 5, 12, 49, or 51.

Stiftskeller St. Peter (Peterskeller) ★ AUSTRIAN/VIENNESE Legend has it that Mephistopheles met with Faust in this tavern, which isn't that far-fetched, considering it was established by Benedictine monks in A.D. 803. In fact, it's the oldest restaurant in Europe and is housed in the abbey of the church that supposedly brought Christianity to Austria. Aside from a collection of baroque banquet rooms, there's an inner courtyard with rock-cut vaults, a handful of dignified wood-paneled rooms, and a brick-vaulted cellar. In addition to wine from the abbey's own vineyards, the tavern serves good home-style Austrian cooking, including roast pork in gravy with sauerkraut and bread dumplings, and loin of lamb with asparagus. Vegetarian dishes, such as semolina dumplings on noodles in a parsley sauce, are also featured. They are especially known here for their desserts. Try the apple strudel or sweet curd strudel with vanilla sauce or ice cream, and most definitely the famed Salzburger Nockerln.

St.-Peter-Bezirk 1–4. ✆ **0662/84-12-680.** www.haslauer.at. Reservations recommended. Main courses 10€–27€; fixed-price menus 20€–38€. AE, MC, V. Mon–Sat 11am–midnight; Sun 10am–midnight. Closed Dec. Bus: 1, 2, 15, 27, 29, 49, or 95.

Zum Eulenspiegel ★ AUSTRIAN/VIENNESE Opposite Mozart's birthplace, this restaurant sits at one end of a quiet cobblestone square in the Old Town. Inside, guests have a choice of five rooms on three different levels, all rustically but elegantly decorated. Traditional Austrian cuisine is meticulously adhered to here. The menu features such classic dishes as Tafelspitz (boiled beef), the famous Wiener schnitzel, saddle of venison with cherry sauce, and crème brûlée with stewed berries for dessert.

Hagenauerplatz 2. ✆ **0662/84-31-80.** www.zum-eulenspiegel.at. Reservations required. Main courses 13€–23€. AE, MC, V. Mon–Sat 11am–2pm and 6–10:30pm. Tram: 2. Bus: 2.

Inexpensive

Festungsrestaurant ★ SALZBURG/AUSTRIAN Come here and you'll be dining at the former stronghold of the prince-archbishops of Salzburg. The restaurants and gardens are actually in the castle, perched on a huge rock 122m (400 ft.) above the Old Town and the Salzach. The restaurant commands a panoramic view of the city and the surrounding countryside. From Easter to October classical concerts are held nightly in the *Fürstenzimmer,* often featuring the work of Mozart. You can begin with one of the appetizers such as arugula salad with king prawns or else a freshly made soup, perhaps tomato cream with mozzarella-coated crostini. For a main course, try the Wiener schnitzel with cranberries or beef goulash with bread dumplings. In winter, when the restaurant is closed, the *Burgtaverne* inside the castle serves food and drink.

Hohensalzburg, Mönchsberg 34. ✆ **0662/84-17-80.** www.festungsrestaurant.at. Reservations required July–Aug. Main courses 8€–15€. MC, V. Apr–Oct daily 10am–9pm; Dec–Mar daily 10am–5pm. Closed Nov. Funicular from the Old Town.

ON THE RIGHT BANK

Expensive

Restaurant Bristol CONTINENTAL This is the dining counterpart to the upscale restaurant in Salzburg's other top-notch hotel, the Goldener Hirsch. In this case, the venue is a stately, baronial-looking area outfitted in tones of pale orange and accented with large-scale oil paintings. A well-trained staff organizes meals, the best of which include scampi with arugula salad and tomatoes; carpaccio of beef or (in season) venison; arctic char served with homemade noodles, saffron sauce, and gooseliver; roasted lamb served with a gratin of polenta and spinach; and all-vegetarian casseroles.

In the Hotel Bristol, Makartplatz 4. © **0662/873-5577.** www.bristol-salzburg.at. Reservations recommended. Main courses 18€–32€. AE, DC, MC, V. Mon–Sat 11am–2pm and 6–10pm. Bus: 1, 5, 6, 15, 27, 29, 51, or 55.

Inexpensive

BIO Wirtshaus Hirschenwirt ★ AUSTRIAN This is a hotel dining room, but a hotel dining room with a difference: All of the ingredients used in its cuisine derive from organically grown ingredients, raised in Austria without chemical fertilizers or insecticides. The setting is a quartet of cozy and traditional-looking dining rooms. Menu items change with the season, but might include a creamy pumpkin soup, carpaccio of Austrian beef, Tafelspitz, several versions of Wiener schnitzel, and about five different vegetarian dishes, the best of which is small spaetzle in a cheese-flavored onion sauce.

In the Hotel zum Hirschen, St. Julien Strasse 23. © **0662/88-13-35.** www.biowirtshaus.at. Reservations recommended. Main courses 8.50€–16€. AE, DC, MC, V. Mon–Sat 11am–2pm and 5pm–midnight. Bus: 3 or 6.

Hotel Stadtkrug Restaurant AUSTRIAN/INTERNATIONAL Across the river from the Altstadt, on the site of a 14th-century farm, this restaurant occupies a structure rebuilt from an older core in 1458. In the 1960s, a modern hotel was added in back. In an antique and artfully rustic setting, you can enjoy hearty, traditional Austrian cuisine, such as cream of potato soup "Old Vienna" style; braised beef with burgundy sauce; or glazed cutlet of pork with caraway seeds, deep-fried potatoes, and French beans with bacon. A dessert specialty is apple strudel.

Linzer Gasse 20. © **0662/87-35-45-0.** www.stadtkrug.at. Reservations recommended. Main courses 15€–23€. AE, DC, MC, V. Wed–Mon noon–2pm and 6–10:30pm. Bus: 27 or 29.

Zum Fidelen Affen AUSTRIAN On the eastern edge of the river near the Staatsbrücke, this is the closest thing in Salzburg to a loud, animated, and jovial pub with food service. It's in one of the city's oldest buildings, dating from 1407. Management's policy is to allow only three reserved tables on any particular evening; the remainder are given to whoever happens to show up. It's best to give your name to the *maître d'hôtel,* and then wait at the bar. Menu items are simple, inexpensive, and based on regional culinary traditions. A house specialty is a gratin of green (spinach) noodles in cream sauce with strips of ham. Also popular are Wiener schnitzels, ham goulash with dumplings, and at least three kinds of main-course dumplings flavored with meats, cheeses, herbs, and various sauces.

Priesterhausgasse 8. © **0662/87-73-61.** Very limited reservations accepted. Main courses 10€–17€. DC, MC, V. Mon–Sat 5pm–midnight.

Seeing the Sights in the City of Mozart

The Old Town lies between the left bank of the Salzach River and the ridge known as the **Mönchsberg,** which rises to a height of 500m (1,640 ft.) and is the site of Salzburg's gambling casino. The main street of the Altstadt is **Getreidegasse,** a narrow little thoroughfare lined with five- and six-story burghers' buildings. Most of the houses along the street are from the 17th and 18th centuries. Mozart was born at no. 9 (see below). Many lacy-looking wrought-iron signs are displayed, and a lot of the houses have carved windows.

You might begin your tour at **Mozartplatz,** with its outdoor cafes. From here you can walk to the even more expansive Residenzplatz, where torchlight dancing is staged every year, along with outdoor performances.

THE TOP ATTRACTIONS

Dom (Salzburg Cathedral) ★ Located where Residenzplatz flows into Domplatz, this cathedral is world renowned for its 4,000-pipe organ. Hailed by some critics as the "most perfect" northern Renaissance building, the cathedral has a marble facade and twin symmetrical towers. The mighty bronze doors were created in 1959. The themes are Faith, Hope, and Love. The interior has a rich baroque style with elaborate frescoes, the most important of which, along with the altarpieces, were designed by Mascagni of Florence. In the crypt, traces of the old Romanesque cathedral have been unearthed.

The treasure of the cathedral and the "arts and wonders" the archbishops collected in the 17th century are displayed in the **Dom Museum** entered through the cathedral. The **cathedral excavations** around the corner (left of the Dom entrance) show the ruins of the original foundation.

South side of Residenzplatz. ✆ **0662/84-41-89.** Free admission to cathedral; excavations 2€ adults, 1€ children 6–15, free for children 5 and under; museum 5€ adults, 2€ children. Cathedral daily 8am–7pm (to 6pm in winter); excavations May–Sept Tues–Sun 9am–5pm (closed mid-Oct to Easter); museum Wed–Sun 10am–5pm, Sun 1–6pm. Closed Nov–Apr. Bus: 1, 3, or 5.

Glockenspiel (Carillon) The celebrated Glockenspiel with its 35 bells stands across from the Residenz. You can hear this 18th-century carillon at 7am, 11am, and 6pm. Actual visitation of the interior is not allowed. The ideal way to hear the chimes is from one of the cafes lining the edges of the Mozartplatz while sipping your favorite coffee or drink.

Mozartplatz 1. ✆ **0662/80-42-27-84.** Bus: 1, 5, 6, or 51.

Hohensalzburg Fortress ★★ ☺ The stronghold of the ruling prince-archbishops before they moved "downtown" to the Residenz, this fortress towers 120m (394 ft.) above the Salzach River on a rocky dolomite ledge. The massive fortress crowns the Festungsberg and literally dominates Salzburg. Work on Hohensalzburg began in 1077 and wasn't finished until 1681. This is the largest completely preserved castle in central Europe. The elegant state apartments, once the courts of the prince-archbishops, are on display. The **Burgmuseum** contains a collection of medieval art. Plans and prints tracing the growth of Salzburg are on exhibit, as well as instruments of torture and many Gothic artifacts. The **Rainermuseum** has displays of arms and armor. The beautiful late-Gothic **St. George's Chapel** (1501) is adorned with marble reliefs of the apostles. If you're athletic you can reach the fortress on foot from Kapitelplatz by way of Festungsgasse or from the Mönchsberg via the Scharten-tor; otherwise, you can take the funicular.

Visit Hohensalzburg even if you're not interested in the fortress, just for the view from the terrace. From the Reck watchtower you get a panoramic sweep of the Alps. The Kuenberg bastion has a fine view of Salzburg's domes and towers.

You can see the fortress grounds on your own or take a tour of the interior. Conducted 40- to 50-minute tours go through the fortress daily, but hours and departure times depend on the season.

Mönchsberg 34. ✆ **0662/84-24-30-11.** www.salzburg-burgen.at. Admission (combination Fortress Card includes funicular, museums, fortress, and multimedia show) 11€ adults, 9.60€ seniors, 6€ children 6–19, free for children 5 and under, 24€–30€ family ticket. Fortress and museums daily Jan–Apr 10:30am–6pm; May–June and Sept 10am–6pm; July–Aug 9am–7pm; Oct–Dec 9:30am–5pm.

Petersfriedhof (St. Peter's Cemetery) ★★ This cemetery lies at the stone wall that merges into the Mönchsberg. Many of the aristocratic families of Salzburg lie buried here, as do many other noted persons, including Nannerl Mozart, sister of Wolfgang Amadeus (4 years older than her better-known brother, Nannerl was also an exceptionally gifted musician). You can see the Romanesque Chapel of the Holy Cross and St. Margaret's Chapel, dating from the 15th century. You can also take a self-guided tour through the early Christian catacombs in the rock above the church cemetery.

St.-Peter-Bezirk. ✆ **0662/84-45-78-0.** Free admission to cemetery. Catacombs 1€ adults, .60€ children 5–12. May–Sept daily 10:30am–5pm; Oct–Apr Wed–Thurs 10:30am–3:30pm, Fri–Sun 10:30am–4pm. Bus: 1.

Residenz zu Salzburg/Residenzgalerie Salzburg ★★ This opulent palace, just north of Domplatz in the pedestrian zone, was the seat of the Salzburg prince-archbishops after they no longer needed the protection of the gloomy Hohensalzburg Fortress of Mönchsberg. The Residenz dates from 1120, but work on its series of palaces, which comprised the ecclesiastical complex of the ruling church princes, began in the late 1500s and continued until about 1796. The 17th-century Residenz fountain is one of the largest and most impressive baroque fountains north of the Alps. More than a dozen staterooms, each richly decorated, are open to the public via guided tour. On the second floor you can visit the **Residenzgalerie Salzburg** (✆ **0662/84-04-51,** ext. 24), an art gallery containing European paintings from the 16th century to the 19th century.

Residenzplatz 1. ✆ **0662/80-42-26-90.** www.salzburg-burgen.at. Combined ticket to staterooms and gallery 8.50€ adults, 6.50€ seniors, 2.70€ children 6–15, 19€ family. Tues–Sun 10am–5pm. Bus: 5 or 6.

Stiftskirche St. Peter ★★ Founded in A.D. 696 by St. Rupert, whose tomb is here, this is the church of St. Peter's Abbey and Benedictine Monastery. Once a Romanesque basilica with three aisles, it was completely overhauled in the 17th and 18th centuries in elegant baroque style. The west door dates from 1240. The church is richly adorned with art treasures that include altar paintings by Kremser Schmidt.

St.-Peter-Bezirk. ✆ **0662/844-578-0.** Free admission. Daily 9am–5pm. Bus: 5, 6, or 55.

MORE ATTRACTIONS

Mirabell-Garten (Mirabell Gardens) ★ Laid out by Fischer von Erlach on the right bank of the river off Makartplatz, these baroque gardens are studded with statuary and reflecting pools, making them a virtual open-air museum. Be sure to visit the bastion with fantastic marble baroque dwarfs and other figures, by the Pegasus Fountains in the lavish garden west of Schloss Mirabell. You'll also find a natural theater. In summer, free brass band concerts are held Wednesday at 8:30pm and Sunday at 10:30am. From the gardens, you have an excellent view of the Hohensalzburg Fortress.

Free admission. Daily 7am–8pm. Bus: 1, 5, 6, or 51.

Mönchsberg ★★ This heavily forested ridge extends for some 2km (1¼ miles) above the Altstadt and has fortifications dating from the 15th century. A panoramic view of Salzburg is possible from Mönchsberg Terrace just in front of the Grand Café Winkler.

West of the Hohensalzburg Fortress. ✆ **0662/448-06-285.** The elevators leave daily 9am–11pm; round-trip fare is 4€ adults, 2.50€ children 6–15, free for children 5 and under. Bus: 2, 15, or 29.

Mozart Geburtshaus (Mozart's Birthplace) ★ The house where Wolfgang Amadeus Mozart was born on January 27, 1756, contains exhibition rooms and the apartment of the Mozart family. The main treasures are the valuable paintings (such as the well-known *Mozart and the Piano,* by Joseph Lange) and the violin Mozart used as a child; his concert violin; and his viola, fortepiano, and clavichord.

Getreidegasse 9. ✆ **0662/84-43-13.** www.mozarteum.at. Admission 7€ adults, 6€ seniors, 3€ students 15–18, 2.50€ children 6–14, 17€ family ticket. Combined admission with Mozart Wohnhaus 12€ adults, 10€ seniors, 4.50€ students 15–18, 3.50€ children 6–14, 26€ family ticket. Daily 9am–6pm (until 7pm July–Aug).

Mozart Wohnhaus (Mozart Residence) ★ In 1773, the Mozart family vacated the cramped quarters of Mozart's birthplace, and the young Mozart lived here with his family until 1780. In the rooms of the former Mozart family apartments, a museum documents the history of the house and the life and work of Wolfgang Amadeus. The original house was destroyed by bombing in 1944, was rebuilt, and reopened on the eve of Mozart's birthday in 1996. A mechanized 30-minute audio tour in six languages with relevant musical samples accompanies the visitor through the museum.

Makartplatz 8. ✆ **0662/87-42-27-40.** www.mozarteum.at. Admission 7€ adults, 6€ seniors, 3€ students 15–18, 2.50€ children 6–14, 17€ family ticket. Combined admission with Mozart Geburtshaus 12€ adults, 10€ seniors, 4.50€ students 15–18, 3.50€ children 6–14, 26€ family ticket. Daily 9am–6pm (until 7pm July–Aug).

Salzburg Museum Devoted to the cultural history of Salzburg, this newly reorganized museum, formerly the Carolino Augusteum, has a new home. The first part opened early in 2006, the second floor in 2007. The archaeological collections contain the well-known Dürnberg beaked pitcher, as well as Roman mosaics. Some 15th-century Salzburg art is on view, and there are many paintings from the romantic period, as well as works by Hans Makart, born in Salzburg in 1840. The second floor displays Salzburg's history of music and visual arts. On-site is Mozart's, a cafe with an outdoor terrace.

Mozartplatz 1. ✆ **0662/6208-08-700.** www.salzburgmuseum.at. Admission 8€ adults, 6.60€ seniors and adults up to age 26, 3.30€ children 6–15, free for children 5 and under, 16€ family. Daily 9am–6pm (until 8pm Thurs). Bus: 5 or 6.

Schloss Mirabell (Mirabell Palace) ★ This palace and its gardens were built as a luxurious private residence called Altenau. Prince-Archbishop Wolf Dietrich had it constructed in 1606 for his mistress and the mother of his children, Salome Alt. Not much remains of the original grand structure. Lukas von Hildebrandt rebuilt the palace in the first quarter of the 18th century, and it was modified after a great fire in 1818. The palace, which is a smaller version of the Tuileries in Paris, today serves as the official residence of the mayor of Salzburg. The ceremonial marble "angel staircase," with its sculptured cherubs, carved by Raphael Doner in 1726, is a stunning piece of architectural fantasy.

Rainerstrasse. ✆ **0662/8072-0.** Free admission. Staircase daily 9am–6pm. Bus: 1, 5, 6, or 51.

ORGANIZED TOURS

The best-organized tours are offered by **Salzburg Panorama Tours,** Mirabellplatz (✆ **0662/88-32-11-0;** www.panoramatours.at), which is the Gray Line company for Salzburg.

The original **"*Sound of Music* Tour"** combines the Salzburg city tour with an excursion to the lake district and other places where the 1965 film with Julie Andrews was shot. The English-speaking guide shows you not only the highlights from the film but also historical and architectural landmarks in Salzburg and parts of the Salzkammergut countryside. The 4-hour tour departs daily at 9:30am and 2pm and costs 37€ for adults, 18€ children 4 to 12.

You must take your passport along for any of the trips into **Bavaria** in Germany. One of these—called the **"Eagle's Nest Tour"**—takes visitors to Berchtesgaden and on to Obersalzburg, where Hitler and his inner circle had a vacation retreat. The 4½-hour tour departs daily at 9am, May 15 to October 31, and costs 50€ for adults, 35€ children 4 to 12. **"The City & Country Highlights"** tour takes in historic castles and the surrounding Land Salzburg landscape. This 5-hour tour departs daily at 2pm, and costs 50€ adults, 35€ children 4 to 12. Coffee and pastry at the Castle Fuschl are an added treat.

The Shopping Scene

Good buys in Salzburg include dirndls, lederhosen, petit point, and all types of sports gear. **Getreidegasse** is a main shopping thoroughfare, but you'll also find some intriguing little shops on **Residenzplatz.**

Opened in 1871, **Gertraud Lackner,** Badergasse 2 (✆ **0662/84-23-85;** bus: 68 or 81), offers both antique and modern country wood furniture. Among the new items are chests, chessboards, angels, cupboards, crèches, candlesticks, and especially chairs. **Musikhaus Pühringer,** Getreidegasse 13 (✆ **0662/84-32-67;** bus: 1, 2, 29, or 49), established in 1910, sells all kinds of classical musical instruments, especially those popular in central Europe, as well as a large selection of electronic instruments (including synthesizers and amplifiers). You'll find classical and folk music CDs and tapes, plus many classical recordings, especially those by Mozart.

Salzburger Heimatwerk, Am Residenzplatz 9 (✆ **0662/84-41-10;** bus: 5, 6, 49, 51, 55, or 95), is one of the best places in town to buy local Austrian handicrafts and original regional clothing.

Wiener Porzellanmanufaktur Augarten Gesellschaft, Alter Markt 11 (✆ **0662/84-07-14;** bus: 2), might very well tempt you to begin a porcelain collection. The origins of this world-class manufacturer go back 275 years. Today, its product is legendary and its patterns, such as *Wiener Rose, Maria Theresia,* and the highly distinctive *Biedermeier,* are well known. The company also produces such historical pieces as the black-and-white demitasse set created by architect/designer Josef Hoffman.

Getting Tickets to the Salzburg Festival

One of the premier music attractions of Europe, the Salzburg Festival celebrated its 87th season in 2007. Details on the festival are available by contacting Salzburg Festival, Hofstallgasse 1, A-5010 Salzburg, Austria (✆ 0662/8045-500; www.salzburgerfestspiele.at).

Salzburg After Dark

THE PERFORMING ARTS

It's said there's a musical event—often a Mozart concert—staged virtually every night in Salzburg. To find the venue, visit the **Salzburg tourist office,** Auerspergstrasse 6 (✆ **0662/88987-0**). Here you'll be given a free copy of ***Offizieller Wochenspiegel,*** a monthly pamphlet listing all major and many minor local cultural events. The annual Mozart Week is in January.

The major ticket agency affiliated with the city of Salzburg is located adjacent to Salzburg's main tourist office, at Mozartplatz 5. The **Salzburger Ticket Office** (✆ **0662/84-03-10**) is open Monday to Friday 9am to 6pm (to 7pm in midsummer) and Saturday 9am to noon.

If you don't want to pay a ticket agent's commission, you can go directly to the box office of a theater or concert hall. However, many of the best seats may have already been sold, especially those at the Salzburg Festival.

CONCERTS & OTHER ENTERTAINMENT

The rich collection of concerts that combine every summer to form the Salzburg Festival's program is presented in several concert halls scattered throughout Salzburg. The largest is the **Festspielhaus,** Hofstallgasse 1 (✆ **0662/8045;** bus: 1, 5, or 6). Within the Festspielhaus complex you'll find the **Felsenreitschule,** an outdoor auditorium with a makeshift roof. Originally built in 1800 as a riding rink, it's famous as the site where scenes from *The Sound of Music* were filmed. Tickets cost from 15€ to 360€, with the more expensive representing the higher cost for the best seats at the Salzburg Festival; average but good seats run 35€ to 105€. Instead of going directly to the Festspielhaus, you can purchase tickets in advance at the box office at Waagplatz 1A (✆ **0662/84-53-46**), close to the tourist office, Monday to Friday 8am to 6pm.

On the right bank of the Salzach River, near the Mirabell Gardens, is the **Mozarteum,** Schwarzstrasse 26 and Mirabellplatz 1 (✆ **0662/87-31-54;** bus: 1, 5, 6, or 51), the major music and concert hall of Salzburg. All the big orchestra concerts, as well as organ recitals and chamber-music evenings, are offered here. It's also a music school, and you can ask about free events staged by the students. The box office is open Monday to Thursday 9am to 2pm and Friday 9am to 4pm with some exceptions. Performances are usually at 11am or 7:30pm. Tickets cost 8€ to 220€.

Besides the venues above, you can attend a concert in dramatic surroundings in the Fürstenzimmer (Prince's Chamber) of the **Hohensalzburg Fortress.** You're likely to hear heavy doses of Mozart and, to a lesser degree, works by Schubert, Brahms, and Beethoven. From mid-May to mid-October, performances are generally held at 9am or 8:30pm every night of the week. The rest of the year, they're presented most (but not all) nights, with occasional weeklong breaks, usually at 7:30pm. The box office for the events is at Adlgasser Weg 22 (✆ **0662/82-58-58**). To reach the fortress, take the funicular from Festungsgasse.

BEER GARDENS

Regardless of the season, you'll have one of your most enjoyable and authentic evenings in Salzburg at **Augustiner Bräustübl,** Augustinergasse 4 (✆ **0662/43-12-46-0;** bus: 27, 49, 60, 80, or 95). This Bierstube and Biergarten has been dispensing oceans of beer since it was established in 1622. Depending on the weather, the city's beer-drinking fraternity gathers either within the cavernous interior, where three separate rooms each hold up to 400 people, or in the chestnut-shaded courtyard. You'll find about a dozen kiosks, where you can buy takeout portions of wursts, sandwiches, and pretzels. Farther on, choose a thick stoneware mug from the racks and carry it to the beer tap, paying the cashier as you go. A full liter begins at 6€; a half liter costs 4€ depending on the type of beer. The place is open Monday to Friday 3 to 11pm and Saturday and Sunday 2:30 to 11pm.

Immediately below the Hohensalzburg Fortress and established in the early 1800s is the **Restaurant StieglKeller,** Festungsgasse 10 (✆ **0662/84-26-81;** bus: 5, 6, or 55), part of which is carved into the rocks of Mönchsberg. To get here, you'll have to negotiate a steep cobblestone street that drops off on one side to reveal a panoramic view of Salzburg. The cavernous interior is open only in summer, when you can join hundreds of others in drinking beer and eating sausages, schnitzels, and other Bierkeller food.

The **Sternbräu,** Getreidegasse 34, in the heart of historic Salzburg has a Biergarten atmosphere and serves traditional Austrian cuisine. The Sternbräu is also home to the **Sound of Salzburg Dinner Show** (✆ **0662/82-66-17;** www.soundofsalzburgshow.com), featuring the music of Mozart, traditional Salzburg folk music, and, of course, songs from *The Sound of Music*. The show takes place from May 15 to October 15, daily at 7:30pm. A three-course meal, including your choice of chicken and noodles or roast pork, and the show cost 46€. If you want to skip the meal, you can arrive at 8:15pm to see the show for 32€.

No one in Salzburg is really sure whether to classify **Salzburger Altstadtkeller,** Rudolfskai 27 (✆ **0662/849688**), as a restaurant, an inn, a pub, or a nightclub, because it combines so gracefully elements of all of them. The result is fun and convivial. The setting is a medieval cellar beneath the Altstadt Radisson Hotel, immediately adjacent to the banks of the river. Don't come here expecting fine dining: What you'll get is a short list of Austrian-style platters, and a reverberating roster of musical acts that include swing, Latino, jazz, and blues. Every Thursday, the acts get more nostalgic and folkloric, as the stage is turned over to bands specializing in Austrian or Bavarian "evergreen" music. Music plays from around 9:15pm to 1am, with guests then lingering over their drinks for at least another hour. There's no cover charge, but a half-liter mug of beer costs 5€. Main courses cost from 9€ to 17€. Service is Tuesday to Saturday from 7pm to 2:30am.

INNSBRUCK ★ & TYROL

Land of ice and mountains, dark forests and alpine meadows full of spring wildflowers, summer holidays and winter sports—that's Tyrol. Those intrepid tourists, the

Innsbruck

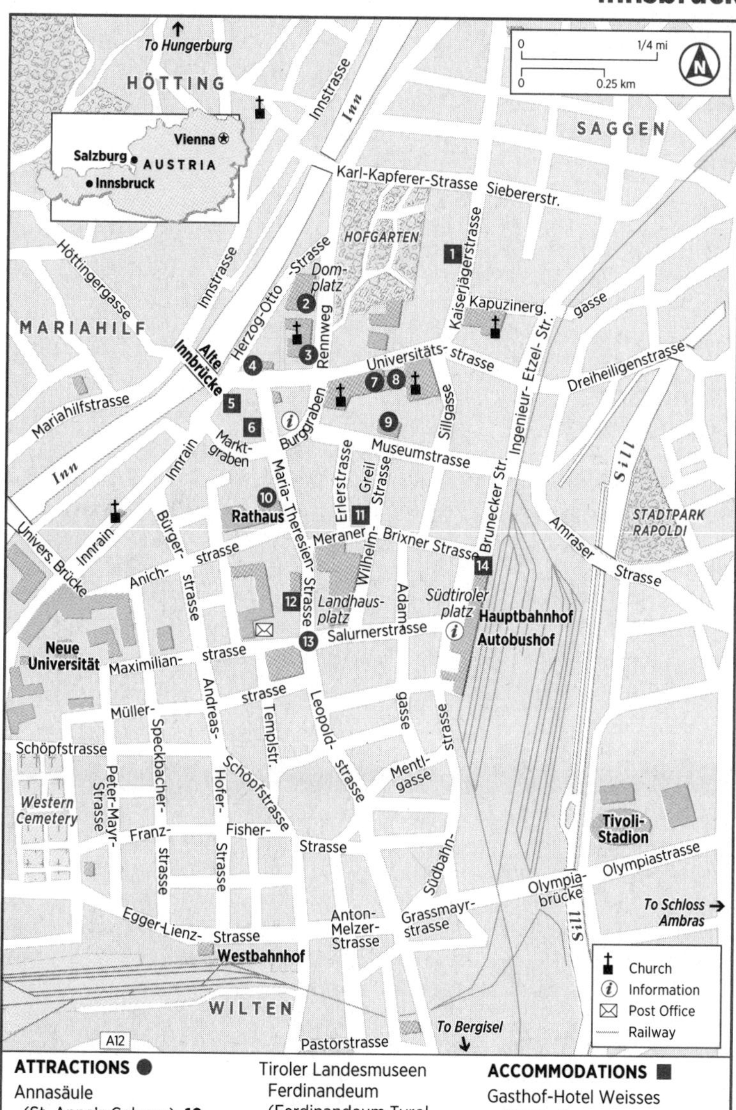

ATTRACTIONS ●

Annasäule (St. Anna's Column) **10**
Dom zu St. Jakob (Cathedral of St. James) **2**
Goldenes Dachl (Golden Roof) & Maximilianeum **4**
Hofburg **3**
Hofkirche **7**
Tiroler Landesmuseen Ferdinandeum (Ferdinandeum Tyrol Museum) **9**
Tiroler Volkskunst-Museum (Tyrol Museum of Folk Art) **8**
Triumphpforte (Triumphal Arch) **13**

ACCOMMODATIONS ■

Gasthof-Hotel Weisses Kreuz **5**
Goldene Krone **12**
Grand Hotel Europa **14**
Hotel Central **11**
Hotel Goldener Adler **6**
Romantik Hotel-Restaurant Schwarzer Adler **1**

British, discovered its vacation delights and made it a fashionable destination in the last century. Tyrol is now the most frequented winter playground in Austria, and in summer, the extensive network of mountain paths lures visitors.

Skiers flock here in winter for a ski season that runs from mid-December to the end of March. Many prefer its ski slopes to those of Switzerland. It's been a long time since the eyes of the world focused on Innsbruck at the Winter Olympics in 1964 and 1976, but the legacy lives on in the ski conditions and facilities on some of the world's choicest slopes.

Innsbruck

Innsbruck has a particularly lovely medieval town center, and town planners have protected this historic Altstadt. Visitors can take countless excursions in the environs; at Innsbruck's doorstep lie some of the most beautiful drives in Europe. Just take your pick: Head in any direction, up any valley, and you'll be treated to mountains and alpine beauty almost unmatched anywhere else, including Switzerland.

ESSENTIALS

Getting There

BY PLANE Innsbruck's airport, **Flughafen Innsbruck-Kranebitten,** Fürstenweg 180 (✆ **0512/22525-0;** www.innsbruck-airport.com), is 3km (1¾ miles) west of the city. It offers regularly scheduled air service from the major airports of Austria and of Europe's major cities.

BY TRAIN Innsbruck is connected with all parts of Europe by international railway links. Trains arrive at the main railway station, the **Hauptbahnhof,** Südtiroler Platz (✆ **05/1717** for all rail information). There are at least five daily trains from Munich (trip time: 3 hr.) and eight daily trains from Salzburg (1 hr.).

BY CAR If you're **driving** down from Salzburg in the northeast, take Autobahn A8 west, which joins Autobahn A93 (later it becomes the A12), heading southwest to Innsbruck. This latter Autobahn (A93/A12) is the main artery from Munich. From the south, you can take the Brenner toll motorway.

VISITOR INFORMATION The **tourist office,** Burggraben 3 (✆ **0512/59-850;** www.innsbruck.info), is open Monday to Saturday 8am to 6pm and Sunday 9am to 6pm. It will supply you with a wealth of information, as well as a list of inexpensive private rooms for rent in Innsbruck. The office can also book bus or walking tours of the city.

CITY LAYOUT This historic city is divided by the Inn River into left- and right-bank districts. Two major bridges cross the Inn, the **Universittssbrücke** and the **Alte Innsbrücke (Old Inn Bridge).** Many of the attractions, including the Hofkirche and the Goldenes Dachl, are on the right bank. If you arrive at the Hauptbahnhof, take Salurner Strasse and Brixner Strasse to Maria-Theresien-Strasse, which will put you into the very heart of Innsbruck.

The **Altstadt** is bounded on the north by the Inn River and on the south by Burggraben and Marktgraben. The main street of this historic district is **Herzog-Friedrich-Strasse,** which becomes **Maria-Theresien-Strasse,** the axis of the postmedieval new part of town. The Altstadt becomes a pedestrian zone after 10:30am (wear good shoes on the cobblestone streets).

GETTING AROUND A network of 3 **tram** and 25 **bus lines** covers all of Innsbruck and its close environs, and buses and trams use the same tickets. Single tickets in the central area cost 1.70€, and a booklet of four tickets goes for 5.70€. The tram is called either *Strassenbahn* or *Trambahn*. On the left bank of the Inn River, the main tram and bus arteries are Museumstrasse and Mariahilferstrasse. On the right bank, trams and buses aren't routed into the pedestrian zone but to their main stop in Marktgraben. For information about various routes, call the **Innsbrucker Verkehrsbetriebe** (✆ **0512/530-70**). Most tickets can be purchased at the Innsbruck tourist office, tobacco shops, and automated vending machines. A ***Tageskarte* (day pass),** costing 3.80€ for 24 hours, is available only from the tourist information office, tobacco shops, and cafes. It allows you to ride on all trains and buses. If you plan to move about the Innsbruck area extensively, ask about the **Innsbruck Card,** which offers unlimited transportation and other advantages. A 24-hour pass sells for 25€, a 48-hour pass for 30€, and a 72-hour pass for 35€.

Austria Postal Service buses (one of two different bus networks maintained by the Austrian government) leave from the Autobushof (Central Bus Station), adjacent to the Hauptbahnhof on Sterzinger Strasse. Here buses head for all parts of Tyrol. The station is open Monday to Friday 7:30am to 6pm and Saturday 7am to 1pm. For information about bus schedules, call ✆ **0512/500-53-07.**

Taxi stands are scattered at strategic points throughout the city, or you can call a radio car (✆ **0512/5311** or 1718). For a nostalgic ride, you can hire a horse-drawn carriage *(Fiaker)* from a spot adjacent to the **Tiroler Landestheater,** Rennweg.

If neither the tram nor the carriage option appeals to you, consider renting a **bike** at the Hauptbahnhof. Rentals cost 22€ per day or 18€ for 5 hours. You can return these bikes to any rail station in Austria if you don't plan to return to Innsbruck. Rentals are available April to early November only. For more information, call **Sport Neuner** (✆ **0512/561-501**).

Although you can make a better deal renting a car before you leave North America, it's possible to rent cars in Innsbruck. You might try **Avis,** Salurner Strasse 15 (✆ **0512/57-17-54**); or **Hertz,** Südtirolerplatz 1 (✆ **0512/58-09-01**), across from the Hauptbahnhof. Although paperwork and billing errors are harder to resolve whenever you rent from a non-U.S.-based car-rental outfit, you might also check the rates at a local car outfitter, **Ajax,** Amrasserstrasse 6 (✆ **0512/583-232**).

[FastFACTS] INNSBRUCK

Currency Exchange Banks are usually open Monday to Thursday 7:45am to 12:30pm and 2:30 to 4pm, and Friday 7:45am to 3pm. There are also exchange facilities at Innsbruck's tourist office (see above). The automated currency exchange facilities at the Hauptbahnhof are available 24 hours a day.

Dentists & Doctors Check with the tourist office for a list of private English-speaking dentists and doctors; or contact the **University Clinic,** Anichstrasse 35 (✆ **0512/504**).

Drugstores In the heart of Innsbruck, **St.-Anna Apotheke,** Maria-Theresien-Strasse 4 (✆ **0512/58-58-47**), is open Monday to Saturday 8am to 6pm. The pharmacy posts addresses of other pharmacies open on weekends or at night.

Emergencies In case of trouble, call ✆ **133** for the police, ✆ **122** for a fire, or ✆ **144** for an ambulance.

Internet Access You can check e-mail or access the Internet free with your own laptop at the **Picasso Internet Café,** Maria-Theresien-Strasse 16 (✆ **0512/58-48-48;** tram: 3). It's open Monday to Saturday from 6:30am to 1am.

Post Office The **Hauptpostamt (Central Post Office),** Maximilianstrasse 2 (✆ **0512/5000**), is open daily from 8am to 9pm. The post office at the **Hauptbahnhof,** Bruneckstrasse 1–3 (✆ **0512/5000**), is open Monday to Saturday 6:30am to 9pm.

Telephone The **country code** for Austria is **43.** The **city code** for Innsbruck is **512;** use this code when you're calling from outside Austria. If you're within Austria, use **0512.**

WHERE TO STAY

Expensive

Grand Hotel Europa ★★ The town's finest and most elegant hotel stands opposite the rail station, inviting you inside its formal lobby. The spacious rooms and suites are handsomely furnished, with all the modern conveniences and Tyrolean or Biedermeier-style decorations. Each tasteful unit offers a well-equipped bathroom. The restaurant, **Europa Stüberl** (below), is the finest in Tyrol.

Südtirolerplatz 2, A-6020 Innsbruck. ✆ **0512/5931.** Fax 0512/58-78-00. www.grandhoteleuropa.at. 122 units. 149€–372€ double; 369€–584€ suite. Rates include breakfast. AE, DC, MC, V. Parking 15€. **Amenities:** Restaurant; bar; babysitting; room service; sauna. *In room:* A/C, TV, hair dryer, Wi-Fi (free).

Romantik Hotel-Restaurant Schwarzer Adler ★★ This is it for those who like authentic Austrian charm. The hotel's owners, the Ultsch family, have furnished the charming interior with hand-painted regional furniture, antiques, and lots of homey clutter, making for a cozy and inviting ambience. The midsize rooms are virtually one of a kind, each with its special character. Beds are exceedingly comfortable, with some of the thickest mattresses in town and well-stuffed duvets. We prefer the older accommodations, which are more spacious and have more Tyrolean character.

Kaiserjägerstrasse 2, A-6020 Innsbruck. ✆ **0512/58-71-09.** Fax 0512/56-16-97. www.deradler.com. 39 units. 124€–270€ double; 360€–480€ suite. Additional person 46€–50€. Rates include breakfast. AE, DC, MC, V. Parking 10€. Tram: 1 or 3. **Amenities:** Restaurant; bar; room service; spa. *In room:* A/C, TV, hair dryer, Internet (free), minibar.

Moderate

Hotel Central One of the most unusual hotels in Innsbruck, Hotel Central was originally built in the 1860s, but from its very modern exterior you might not realize it. The comfortable rooms have an Art Deco design that evokes an almost Japanese simplicity. Most rooms are quite spacious with excellent beds. Bathrooms are small, with shower units. In total contrast to the simplicity of the rest of the hotel, the ground floor contains a grand Viennese cafe with marble columns, sculpted ceilings, and large gilt-and-crystal chandeliers.

Gilmstrasse 5, A-6020 Innsbruck. ✆ **0512/59-20.** Fax 0512/58-03-10. www.central.co.at. 85 units. 125€–170€ double. Rates include breakfast. AE, DC, MC, V. Parking 12€. Tram: 1 or 3. **Amenities:** Restaurant; bar; exercise room; room service; sauna. *In room:* TV, hair dryer, Internet (4€ per hour), minibar.

Hotel Goldener Adler ★★ Even the phone booth near the reception desk of this 600-year-old family-run hotel is outfitted in antique style. Famous guests have included Goethe, Mozart, and the violinist Paganini, who cut his name into the windowpane of his room. Rooms are handsomely furnished, and vary in size and decor. Some have decorative Tyrolean architectural features such as beamed ceilings. Others are furnished in a more modern style. The bathroom's size depends on your room assignment; bathrooms can be everything from spacious combination models to cramped rooms with shower stalls. This is now a Best Western–affiliated property.

Herzog-Friedrich-Strasse 6, A-6020 Innsbruck. ✆ **800/780-7234** in the U.S. and Canada, or 0512/57-11-11. Fax 0512/58-44-09. www.goldeneradler.com. 31 units. 126€–210€ double; from 250€ suite. Rates include breakfast. AE, DC, MC, V. Parking 11€. Tram: 1 or 3. **Amenities:** Restaurant; bar; babysitting; room service. *In room:* TV, hair dryer, minibar, Wi-Fi (free).

Inexpensive

Gasthof-Hotel Weisses Kreuz ★ This atmospheric inn, located in the center of Innsbruck, has not changed much during its lifetime. Rooms are cozy and atmospheric, either small or medium size, with comfortable furnishings. Double rooms have private bathrooms with neatly kept shower units. Hallway bathrooms for single rooms are adequate and well maintained. In 1769, 13-year-old Wolfgang Mozart and his father, Leopold, stayed here.

Herzog-Friedrich-Strasse 31, A-6020 Innsbruck. ✆ **0512/594790.** Fax 0512/59-47-990. www.weisseskreuz.at. 40 units, 31 with bathroom. 68€–72€ double without bathroom; 99€–128€ double with bathroom. Rates include breakfast. AE, MC, V. Parking 11€. Tram: 3. **Amenities:** Restaurant; bar; room service; Wi-Fi (free). *In room:* TV.

Goldene Krone Near the Triumphal Arch on Innsbruck's main street, this baroque house is one of the city's best budget bets. All rooms are modern, comfortable, well maintained, and, for the most part, spacious with plenty of light. The duvet-covered beds are comfortable, and bathrooms are small but spotless, with shower stalls. The hotel offers a Viennese-inspired coffeehouse/restaurant, the **Art Gallery-Café.**

Maria-Theresien-Strasse 46, A-6020 Innsbruck. ✆ **0512/58-61-60.** Fax 0512/580-18-96. www.goldenekrone.at. 36 units. 79€–118€ double; 120€–176€ suite. Rates include breakfast. AE, MC, V. Parking 10€. Tram: 1. Bus: A, H, K, or N. **Amenities:** Restaurant; bar; cafe. *In room:* TV.

WHERE TO DINE

Expensive

Europa Stüberl ★★ AUSTRIAN/INTERNATIONAL This distinguished restaurant, with a delightful Tyrolean ambience, is in a hotel that's the finest address in Innsbruck. The chef succeeds beautifully in fashioning creative takes on traditional regional cooking. Diners can choose from both warm and cold appetizers, ranging from iced angler fish with Chinese tree morels to a small ragout of crayfish in a spicy biscuit with kohlrabi. Some dishes are served only for two people, such as Bresse guinea hen roasted and presented with an herb sauce. Fresh Tyrolean trout almost always appears on the menu, or you may prefer one of the many meat dishes, including red deer ragout and saddle of venison.

In the Grand Hotel Europa, Brixnerstrasse 6. ✆ **0512/5931.** Reservations required. Main courses 12€–34€; fixed-price 4-course menu 48€; fixed-price 6-course menu 64€; fixed-price 7-course menu 69€. AE, DC, MC, V. Daily noon–2pm and 6:30–10pm.

Restaurant Goldener Adler ★ AUSTRIAN/TYROLEAN/INTERNATIONAL Richly Teutonic and steeped in the decorative traditions of alpine Tyrol, this beautifully decorated restaurant has a deeply entrenched reputation and a loyal following among local residents. The menu includes good, hearty fare inspired by cold-weather outdoor life—the chefs aren't into delicate subtleties. Examples of the cuisine are Tyrolean bacon served with horseradish and farmer's bread; cream of cheese soup with croutons; and Tyroler *Zopfebraten,* a flavorful age-old specialty consisting of strips of veal steak served with herb-enriched cream sauce and spinach dumplings. A well-regarded specialty is a platter known as *Adler Tres.* It contains spinach dumplings, stuffed noodles, and cheese dumplings, all flavorfully tied together with a brown butter sauce and a gratin of mountain cheese.

Herzog-Friedrich-Strasse 6. ✆ **0512/57-11-11.** Reservations recommended. Main courses 15€–27€; set menus 18€–50€. AE, DC, MC, V. Daily 11:30am–10:30pm. Tram: 1 or 3.

Restaurant Schwarzer Adler ★★ AUSTRIAN Even if you're not a guest at the richly atmospheric Romantik Hotel, you might appreciate a meal within its historic premises. Among the finest examples of the elaborate cuisine is a salad of wild quail served with lentils, strips of braised gooseliver, and a sauce that's enhanced with apple liqueur. The wine list is long, broad, and impressive, with lots of wines from relatively obscure regions of Austria.

In the Romantik Hotel, Kaiserjägerstrasse 2. ✆ **0512/587-109.** www.deradler.com. Reservations recommended. Main courses 20€–32€. AE, DC, MC, V. Mon–Sat 11:30am–2pm and 6–10:30pm. Tram: 1 or 3.

Moderate

Hirschenstuben INTERNATIONAL Beneath a vaulted ceiling in a house built in 1631, this well-established restaurant is charming and welcoming. By its own admission, the establishment is at its best in spring, autumn, and winter, as it lacks a garden or an outdoor terrace for alfresco summer dining. Menu items include steaming platters of pasta, fish soup, trout meunière, sliced veal in cream sauce Zurich-style, beef stroganoff, pepper steak, stewed deer with vegetables, and filet of flounder with parsley and potatoes. The kitchen staff is equally familiar with the cuisines of both Austria and Italy.

Kiebachgasse 5. ✆ **0512/58-29-79.** Reservations recommended. Main courses 9€–22€. DC, MC, V. Mon–Sat 6–11pm; Tues–Sat noon–2pm and 6–11pm. Tram: 1 or 3.

Restaurant Ottoburg ★ AUSTRIAN/INTERNATIONAL This historic restaurant, established around 1745, occupies a 13th-century building that some historians say is the oldest in Innsbruck. Inside, four intimate and atmospheric dining rooms—with a decor that is best described as "19th-century neo-Gothic"—lie scattered over two different floors. Hearty dishes include venison stew, "grandmother's mixed grill," and fried trout. In summer, a beer garden operates in the rear, open April to October, Tuesday to Sunday from 11am to midnight.

Herzog-Friedrich-Strasse 1. ✆ **0512/58-43-38.** www.ottoburg.at. Reservations recommended. Main courses 10€–25€. AE, DC, MC, V. Daily 11am–2:30pm and 6pm–midnight. Closed 3 weeks in Jan and 2 weeks in late May and early June. Tram: 1 or 3.

Inexpensive

Weisses Rössl ★ AUSTRIAN/TYROLEAN You'll enter this time-honored place through a stone archway set on one of the Old Town's most famous streets. At the end of a flight of stairs, marked with a very old crucifix, you'll find a trio of dining rooms with red-tile floors and a history of welcoming guests since 1590. The menu has simple "down-home" cooking, listing such dishes as a Tyroler *Grüstl* (a kind of hash composed of sautéed onions, sliced beef, alpine herbs, and potatoes cooked and served in a frying pan), *Saftgoulash* with polenta, several kinds of schnitzels, and a grilled platter *(Alt Insprugg)* for two diners.

Kiebachgasse 8. ✆ **0512/58-30-57.** Reservations recommended. Main courses 8€–20€; 3-course lunch 8€–12€; 3-course dinner 18€–23€. AE, DC, MC, V. Daily 9am–3pm and 5pm–midnight. Closed Nov. Tram: 1 or 3.

EXPLORING THE TOWN

The Altstadt and the surrounding alpine countryside are Innsbruck's main attractions. Often it's fascinating just to watch the passersby, who are occasionally attired in Tyrolean regional dress.

Maria-Theresien-Strasse ★, which cuts through the heart of the city from north to south, is the main street and a good place to begin exploring the city. Many 17th- and 18th-century houses line this wide street. On the south end of the street, there's a **Triumphpforte (Triumphal Arch),** modeled after those in Rome. Maria Theresa ordered it built in 1765 to honor her son's marriage and to commemorate the death of her beloved husband, Emperor Franz I. From this arch southward the street is called Leopoldstrasse.

Going north from the arch along Maria-Theresien-Strasse, you'll see **Annasäule (St. Anna's Column)** in front of the 19th-century Rathaus (town hall). The column was erected in 1706 to celebrate the withdrawal in 1703 of invading Bavarian armies during the War of the Spanish Succession. Not far north of the Annasäule, the wide street narrows and becomes **Herzog-Friedrich-Strasse,** running through the heart of the medieval quarter. This street is arcaded and flanked by a number of well-maintained burghers' houses with their jumble of turrets and gables; look for the multitude of dormer windows and oriels.

Dom zu St. Jakob (Cathedral of St. James) Designed and rebuilt from 1717 to 1724 by Johann Jakob Herkommer, the Dom has a lavishly embellished baroque interior. A chief treasure is Lucas Cranach the Elder's *Maria Hilf (St. Mary of Succor).*

Domplatz 6. ✆ **0512/58-39-02.** Free admission. Winter daily 6:30am–6pm; summer daily 7am–7pm. Closed Fri noon–3pm. Tram: 1 or 3.

Goldenes Dachl (Golden Roof) & Maximilianeum ★ "The Golden Roof," Innsbruck's greatest tourist attraction and its most characteristic landmark, is a three-story balcony on a house in the Altstadt; the late-Gothic oriels are capped with 2,657 gold-plated tiles. It was constructed for Emperor Maximilian I in the beginning of the 16th century to serve as a royal box where he could sit in luxury and enjoy tournaments in the square below.

A small museum, the **Maximilianeum,** is on the second floor of the municipal building attached to the Goldenes Dachl. Inside are exhibits celebrating the life and accomplishments of the Innsbruck-based Hapsburg emperor, Maximilian I, who bridged the gap between the Middle Ages and the German Renaissance.

Herzog-Friedrich-Strasse 15. ✆ **0512/581-111.** www.goldenes-dachl.at. Admission to the Maximilianeum 4€ adults; 3€ seniors, students, and children 17 and under. No charge for views of the Goldenes Dachl, and no restrictions as to when it can be viewed. Maximilianeum May–Oct daily 10am–6pm; Nov–Apr Tues–Sun 10am–5pm. Tram: 1 or 3.

Hofburg ★ The 15th-century imperial palace of Emperor Maximilian I, flanked by a set of domed towers, was rebuilt in the baroque style (with rococo detailing) during the 18th century on orders of Maria Theresa. It's a fine example of baroque secular architecture, with four wings and a two-story *Riesensaal* (Giant's Hall), painted in white and gold and filled with portraits of the Hapsburgs. Also of compelling interest are the State Rooms, the chapel, and a scattering of private apartments. You can wander at will through the rooms, but if you want to participate in a guided tour, management conducts two a day, at 11am and 2pm, in a multilingual format that includes English. Each tour lasts 30 to 45 minutes and costs 2.20€.

Rennweg 1. ✆ **0512/58-71-86-12.** www.hofburg-innsbruck.at. Admission 5.50€ adults, 4€ seniors and students 19–27, 2.50€ students 15–18, 1.10€ children 6–14. Daily 9am–5pm. Tram: 1 or 3.

Hofkirche The most important treasure in the Hofkirche is the cenotaph of Maximilian I, a great example of German Renaissance style. It has 28 bronze 16th-century statues of Maximilian's real and legendary ancestors surrounding the kneeling emperor.

Universitätsstrasse 2. ✆ **0512/58-43-02.** www.hofkirche.at. Admission 8€ adults, 2€ students, 4€ seniors, free for children 5 and under. Mon–Sat 9am–5pm. Tram: 1 or 3.

Swarovski Kristallwelten (Crystal Worlds) ★★★ ☺ Designed by the Viennese multimedia artist Andrew Heller, this attraction some 15km (9⅓ miles) from Innsbruck is dedicated to the vision of Daniel Swarovski, founder of the world's leading producer of full crystal.

After entering the giant head with its glittering eyes and waterfall, you'll immediately see a long wall of crystal with 12 tons of the finest cut stones in the world. In other chambers you can wander into the "Planet of the Crystals," with a 3-D light show. Crystalline works of art on display were designed by everybody from Andy Warhol to Salvador Dalí. In the Crystal Dome you get an idea of what it's like being inside a giant crystal, and in the Crystal Theater a fairy tale world of color, mystery, and graceful movement unfolds. You can easily spend 2 hours here.

Kristallweltenstrasse 1. ✆ **05224/51080.** http://kristallwelten.swarovski.com. Admission 9.50€, free for children 11 and under. Daily 8am–6:30pm (last entrance 5:30pm). Take the Wattens motorway exit (A12) and follow signs to Kristallwelten, or take the Wattens bus from the Busbahnhof, next to the Hauptbahnhof.

Tiroler Landesmuseen Ferdinandeum (Ferdinandeum Tyrol Museum) ★ This celebrated gallery of Flemish and Dutch masters also traces the development of popular art in Tyrol, with highlights from the Gothic period. You'll see the original bas-reliefs used in designing the Goldenes Dachl.

Museumstrasse 15. ✆ **0512/59-489-510.** www.tiroler-landesmuseum.at. Admission 8€ adults, 4€ students, 4€ children 6 and under. June–Sept daily 10am–6pm; Oct–May Tues–Sat 10am–5pm, Sun 10am–1pm. Tram: 1 or 3.

Tiroler Volkskunst-Museum (Tyrol Museum of Folk Art) ★★ This popular art museum is in the Neues Stift (New Abbey) adjoining the Hofkirche on its eastern side. It contains one of the largest and most impressive collections of Tyrolean artifacts, ranging from handicrafts, furniture, Christmas cribs, and national costumes to religious and secular popular art. You'll also find a collection of models of typical Tyrolean houses.

Universitätsstrasse 2. ✆ **0512/594-89-510.** www.tiroler-volkskunstmuseum.at. Admission 8€ adults, 4€ seniors, 4€ children 6 and under. Mon–Sat 9am–5pm; Sun 10am–5pm. Tram: 1 or 3.

ENJOYING THE GREAT OUTDOORS

Five sunny, snow-covered, avalanche-free **ski areas** around the Tyrol are served by five cableways, 44 chairlifts, and ski hoists. The area is also known for bobsled and toboggan runs and ice-skating rinks.

In summer you can play tennis at a number of courts, and golf on either a 9- or an 18-hole course; or you can go horseback riding, mountaineering, gliding, swimming, hiking, or shooting.

The **Hofgarten,** a public park containing lakes and many shade trees, lies north of Rennweg. Concerts are often presented in the garden during the summer.

THE SHOPPING SCENE

You'll find a large selection of Tyrolean specialties and all sorts of skiing and mountain-climbing equipment for sale in Innsbruck. Stroll around **Maria-Theresien-Strasse, Herzog-Friedrich-Strasse,** and **Museumstrasse,** ducking in and making discoveries of your own. Here are some suggestions.

Lodenbaur, Brixner Strasse 4 (✆ **0512/58-09-11**), is devoted to regional Tyrolean dress, most of which is made in Austria. There's a full array for men, women, and children. **Tiroler Heimatwerk,** Meraner Strasse 2 (✆ **0512/58-23-20**), is one of the best stores in Innsbruck for handcrafted sculpture and pewter, carved chests, furniture, and lace. Do-it-yourselfers can buy regionally inspired fabrics and dress patterns, and whip up a dirndl (or whatever).

Using old molds discovered in abandoned Tyrolean factories, **Zinnreproduktionen U,** Kiebachgasse 8 (✆ **0512/58-92-24**), offers fine reproductions of century-old regional pewter at reasonable prices. The owner also reproduces rare pewter objects acquired from auctions throughout Europe. Look for a copy of the 18th-century pewter barometer emblazoned with representations of the sun and the four winds.

INNSBRUCK AFTER DARK

THE PERFORMING ARTS The major venue for the performing arts is the 150-year-old **Landestheater,** Rennweg 2 (✆ **0512/52-074-4;** www.landestheater.at). The box office is open daily from 9:30am to 7pm, and performances usually begin at 7:30 or 8pm. Ticket prices are 4€ to 47€ for most operas or operettas, 5€ to 65€ for theater seats. It's also the showcase for musicals and light operetta. For tickets, call ✆ **0512/52-074-4.** Concerts are presented in the Hofgarten in summer.

BARS, CLUBS & FOLK MUSIC One of Innsbruck's most whimsical discos is **Blue Chip,** Wilhelm-Greil-Strasse 17 (✆ **0512/56-50-50;** www.chip-ibk.com), situated in a modern building in the center of town. The busy dance floor attracts a clientele in the 25-to-40 age range, and music includes an appealing mixture of funk, soul, and "black beat" (their term). Entrance is free, and hours are Tuesday to Saturday from 11pm to 4am. One flight up in the same building is **Jimmy's Bar** (✆ **0512/570-473**). There's no dance floor and no live music, but it's something of an Innsbruck cliché that you should begin your evening at Jimmy's with a drink or two before proceeding downstairs to Blue Chip. Jimmy's is open daily 11am to 2am.

If you're looking for the biggest and the best in Innsbruck, head for the **Hofgartencafé,** Rennweg 6 (✆ **0512/58-88-71;** www.der-hofgarten.at), where a lively crowd of young people, mostly in their 20s and 30s, grace the largest beer garden in town. With three massive outdoor bars and a modern indoor decor, this hot spot is the place to be seen. You'll find live music here during the summer. It's open daily 11am to 3am.

Young people hang out at **Treibhaus,** Angerzellgasse 8 (✆ **0512/57-20-00;** www.treibhaus.at), a combination cafe, bar, and social club. Within its battered walls, you can attend a changing roster of art exhibitions, cabaret shows, and protest rallies, Monday to Saturday 10am to 1am, with live music presented at erratic intervals. Cover for live performances is 10€ to 25€.

Limerick Bill's Irish Pub, Maria-Theresia-Strasse 9 (✆ **0512/582-0111**), is dark and cavelike because of its location in a building without windows, a short walk north of Old Town. It's a genuine Irish pub for Celtic wannabes, and the cellar attracts a dancing crowd on Friday and Saturday nights, especially between December and March, when there's live music from 9pm to midnight. It's open daily from 3:30pm to 2am.

Fischerhausel Bar, Herrengasse 8 (✆ **0512/58-35-35**), is a rustic second-floor restaurant and street-level bar open Monday to Saturday from 10am to 2am, Sunday from 6pm to 2am. In the Tyrolean style, it's a good, friendly joint for quaffing schnapps or suds. In warm weather, drinkers move out to the garden in back.

St. Anton am Arlberg ★★★

A modern resort has grown out of this old village on the Arlberg Pass, 99km (62 miles) west of Innsbruck. At St. Anton (1,288m/4,226 ft.), Hannes Schneider developed modern skiing techniques and began teaching tourists how to ski in 1907. Before his death in 1955, Schneider saw his ski school rated as the world's finest. Today the school is still one of the world's largest and best, with about 300 instructors (most of whom speak English). St. Anton am Arlberg in winter is popular with the wealthy and occasional royalty—a more conservative segment of the rich and famous than you'll see at other posh ski resorts.

There's so much emphasis on skiing here that few seem to talk of the summertime attractions. In warm weather, St. Anton is tranquil and bucolic, surrounded by meadowland. A riot of wildflowers blooming in the fields announces the beginning of spring.

ESSENTIALS

Getting There

BY TRAIN Because of St. Anton's good rail connections to eastern and western Austria, most visitors arrive by train. St. Anton is an express stop on the main lines crossing the Arlberg Pass between Innsbruck and Bregenz. About one train per hour arrives in St. Anton from each direction. Trip time from Innsbruck is 75 to 85 minutes; from Bregenz, around 85 minutes. For rail information, call ✆ **05/1717.**

BY CAR Motorists should take Route 171 west from Innsbruck.

VISITOR INFORMATION The **tourist office** in the **Arlberghaus** in the town center (✆ **05446/22-690;** www.stantonamarlberg.com) is open Monday to Friday 8am to 7pm, Saturday 9am to noon and 2 to 6pm, and Sunday 10am to noon.

WHERE TO STAY

Hotel Schwarzer Adler ★★ Owned and operated by the Tschol family since 1885, this beautiful building in the center of St. Anton was constructed as an inn in

1570. The interior is rustic yet elegant, with blazing fireplaces, painted Tyrolean baroque armoires, and Oriental rugs. There are handsomely furnished and well-equipped guest rooms in the main hotel, plus 13 slightly less well-furnished (but less expensive) rooms in the annex across the street.

A-6580 St. Anton am Arlberg. ✆ **05446/22-440.** Fax 05446/22-44-0-62. www.schwarzeradler.com. 72 units. Winter 210€–772€ double; summer 120€–240€ double. Rates include half board. MC, V. Closed May–June and Sept–Dec 5. **Amenities:** Restaurant (see below); bar; babysitting; exercise room; room service; sauna. *In room:* TV, hair dryer, Internet (5€ per day).

WHERE TO DINE

If you're not able to secure a reservation at Raffl-Stube (see below), don't despair. You can get classic Austrian dishes at the historic **Hotel Alte Post Restaurant,** A-6580 St. Anton am Arlberg (✆ **05446/25530**); and at the first-rate **Hotel Kertess Restaurant,** A-6580 St. Anton am Arlberg (✆ **05446/2005**), located high on a slope in the suburb of Oberdorf. For superb international cuisine, head to the medieval **Hotel Schwarzer Adler Restaurant,** A-6580 St. Anton am Arlberg (✆ **05446/22440**).

Raffl-Stube ★ AUSTRIAN This place contains only eight tables, and in the peak of the season, reservations are imperative. Overflow diners are offered a seat in a spacious but less special dining room across the hall. Quality ingredients are always used, and the kitchen prepares such tempting specialties as roast gooseliver with salad, cream of parsley soup with sautéed quail eggs, filet of salmon with wild rice, and roast filet of pork, along with the ever-popular fondue bourguignon.

In the Hotel St. Antoner Hof, St. Anton am Arlberg. ✆ **05446/29-10.** Reservations required. Main courses 17€–42€. AE, DC, MC, V. Daily 11:30am–2pm and 7–9:30pm. Closed May–Nov.

HITTING THE SLOPES IN ST. ANTON

The snow in this area is perfect for skiers, and the total lack of trees on the slopes makes the situation ideal. The ski fields of St. Anton stretch over some 16 sq. km (6¼ sq. miles). Beginners stick to the slopes down below, and more experienced skiers head to the runs from the peaks of **Galzig** (2,092m/6,864 ft.) and **Valluga** (2,812m/9,226 ft.), both reached by cableway.

Other major ski areas include the **Gampen/Kapall,** an advanced-intermediate network of slopes, whose lifts start just behind St. Anton's railway station; and the **Rendl,** a relatively new labyrinth of runs to the south of St. Anton that offers many novice and intermediate slopes.

You'll find many other cold-weather pursuits in St. Anton, including ski jumping, mountain tours, curling, skating, tobogganing, and sleigh rides, plus après-ski relaxing.

The Kitzbühel Alps ★★★

Hard-core skiers and the rich and famous are attracted to this ski region. The Kitzbühel Alps are covered with such a dense network of lifts that they now form the largest skiing complex in the country, with a series of superlative runs. The action centers on the town of Kitzbühel, but there are many satellite resorts that are much less expensive, including St. Johann in Tyrol. Kitzbühel is, in a sense, a neighbor of Munich, which lies 130km (81 miles) to the northeast: Most visitors to the Kitzbühel Alps use Munich's international airport.

ESSENTIALS

Arriving

BY TRAIN Two and three **trains** per hour (many express) arrive in Kitzbühel from Innsbruck (trip time: 60 min.) and Salzburg (2½ hr.), respectively.

BY BUS The most useful of these bus lines runs every 30 to 60 minutes between Kitzbühel and St. Johann in Tyrol (25 min.). In addition, about half a dozen buses travel every day from Salzburg's main railway station to Kitzbühel (2¼ hr.). For regional bus information, call ✆ **05356/627-15.**

BY CAR Kitzbühel is 449km (279 miles) southwest of Vienna and 100km (62 miles) east of Innsbruck. If you're driving from Innsbruck, take Autobahn A12 east to the junction with Route 312 heading to Ellmau. After bypassing Ellmau, continue east to the junction with Route 342, which you take south to Kitzbühel.

VISITOR INFORMATION The **tourist office,** Hinterstadt 18 (✆ **05356/66660;** www.kitzbuehel.com), is open Monday to Friday 8:30am to 6pm, Saturday 9am to 6pm, and Sunday 10am to noon and 4 to 6pm.

WHERE TO STAY

Hotel Bruggerhof ★ About 1.6km (1 mile) west of the town center, near the Schwarzsee, is this countryside chalet with a sun terrace. Originally built as a farmhouse in the 1920s, it later gained local fame as a restaurant. Rooms are comfortable and cozy and decorated in an alpine style. All have a well-lived-in look, although housekeeping is attentive. Bathrooms can be a bit cramped.

Reitherstrasse 24, A-6370 Kitzbühel. ✆ **05356/628-06.** Fax 05356/64-47-930. www.bruggerhof-camping.at. 28 units. Winter 160€–265€ double; summer 120€–190€ double. Rates include half board. AE, DC, MC, V. Free parking. Closed Apr and Oct 15–Dec 15. **Amenities:** Restaurant; bar; babysitting; exercise room; Jacuzzi; room service; sauna; Wi-Fi (free). *In room:* TV, hair dryer, minibar.

Hotel Zur Tenne ★ This hotel combines Tyrolean congeniality with urban style and panache, and the staff shows genuine concern for its clientele. The hotel was created in the 1950s by joining a trio of 700-year-old houses. Rooms are as glamorous as anything in Kitzbühel: wood trim, comfortable beds, eiderdowns, and copies of Tyrolean antiques. Many have working fireplaces and canopied beds for a romantic touch. In addition to intimate lounges, niches, and nooks, the hotel sports the most luxurious health complex in town, complete with a tropical fountain, two hot tubs, and a hot-and-cold foot bath.

Vorderstadt 8–10, A-6370 Kitzbühel. ✆ **05356/64-44-40.** Fax 05356/648-03-56. www.hotelzurtenne.com. 51 units. 154€–409€ double; 239€–492€ junior suite; 324€–749€ suite. Rates include breakfast. Half board 38€ per person. AE, DC, MC, V. Free parking outdoors; 14€ in covered garage nearby. **Amenities:** 3 restaurants; bar; babysitting; exercise room; Internet (free); 2 Jacuzzis; room service; sauna. *In room:* TV, hair dryer, minibar.

WHERE TO DINE

The Dining Rooms in the Schloss Lebenberg ★ AUSTRIAN/INTERNATIONAL Although the Schloss Lebenberg hotel offers comfortable rooms, we actually prefer it for its well-managed restaurant and its sense of history. Originally built in 1548, it was transformed in 1885 into Kitzbühel's first family-run hotel. Always-reliable specialties include cream of tomato soup with gin, Tyrolean-style calves' liver, Wiener schnitzel, roulade of beef, and many desserts.

Lebenbergstrasse 17. ✆ **05356/690-10.** Reservations required. Main courses 14€–32€. AE, DC, MC, V. Daily 7–10am and 6:45–9pm.

Restaurant Goldener Greif ★★ TYROLEAN The setting is cozy and warm, and the cuisine is some of the resort's best. The dining room features vaulted ceilings, intricate paneling, and, in some cases, views out over the base of some of Kitzbühel's busy cable cars. Menu items are savory and designed to satisfy appetites heightened by the bracing alpine climate. You might order veal steak with fresh vegetables, pepper steak Madagascar, or venison. Many kinds of grilled steaks are regularly featured. A "Vienna pot" is one of the chef's specials, and fresh Tyrolean trout is offered daily.

Hinterstadt 24. ✆ **05356/643-11.** Reservations recommended. Main courses 10€–30€; fixed-price menus 20€–35€. AE, DC, MC, V. June to mid-Oct daily 10am–2pm and 7–10pm; mid-Dec to mid-Apr daily 6–10pm. Closed mid-Apr to late May and mid-Oct to mid-Dec.

SEEING THE SIGHTS IN TOWN

The town has two main streets, both pedestrian walkways: **Vorderstadt** and **Hinterstadt.** Along these streets Kitzbühel has preserved its traditional architectural style. You'll see three-story stone houses with oriels and scrollwork around the doors and windows, heavy overhanging eaves, and Gothic gables.

The **Pfarrkirche (Parish Church)** was built from 1435 to 1506 and renovated in the baroque style during the 18th century. The lower part of the **Liebfrauenkirche (Church of Our Lady)** dates from the 13th century, the upper part from 1570. Between these two churches stands the **Ölbergkapelle (Ölberg Chapel)** with a 1450 "lantern of the dead" and frescoes from the latter part of the 16th century.

In the **Heimatmuseum,** Hinterstadt 34 (✆ **05356/645-88**), you'll see artifacts from prehistoric European mining eras and the north alpine Bronze Age, a winter-sports section with trophies of Kitzbüheler skiing greats, and exhibits detailing the town's history. The museum is open year-round Monday through Saturday from 10am to 1pm. Admission is 6.50€ adults, 3€ persons 17 and under.

HITTING THE SLOPES & OTHER OUTDOOR ACTIVITIES

SKIING In winter the emphasis in Kitzbühel, 702m (2,300 ft.) above sea level, is on skiing, and facilities are offered for everyone from novices to experts. The ski season starts just before Christmas and lasts until late March. With more than 62 lifts, gondolas (cable cars), and mountain railroads on five different mountains, Kitzbühel has two main ski areas, the **Hahnenkamm** (renovated in 1995) and the **Kitzbüheler Horn ★★**. Cable cars (Hahnenkammbahn) are within easy walking distance, even for those in ski boots.

The linking of the lift systems on the Hahnenkamm has created the celebrated **Kitzbühel Ski Circus ★★★**, which makes it possible to ski downhill for more than 80km (50 miles), with runs that suit every stage of proficiency. Numerous championship ski events are held here. The toughest, fastest downhill course in the world, a stretch of the Hahnenkamm especially designed for maximum speed called Die Streif, is both feared and respected among skiers.

OTHER WINTER ACTIVITIES There's also curling, ski-bobbing, ski jumping, ice-skating, tobogganing, hiking on cleared trails, and hang gliding, as well as indoor activities such as tennis, bowling, and swimming. The children's ski school, **Schischule Rote Teufel,** Museumkeller, Hinterstadt (✆ **05356/625-00;** www.roteteufel.at), provides training for the very young skier. And don't forget the après-ski, with bars, nightclubs, and dance clubs rocking from teatime to the wee hours.

SUMMER ACTIVITIES Kitzbühel has summer pastimes, too, such as walking tours, visits to the **Wild Life Park at Aurach** (about 3km/1¾ miles from Kitzbühel), tennis, horseback riding, golf, squash, brass-band concerts in the town center, cycling, and swimming. For the last, there's an indoor swimming pool, but we recommend going to the **Schwarzsee (Black Lake).** This *See,* about a 15-minute walk northwest of the center of town, is an alpine lake with a peat bottom that keeps the water relatively murky. Covering an area of 6.4 hectares (16 acres), it's the site of beaches and **Seiwald Bootsverleih,** Schwarzsee (✆ **05356/623-81**), an outfit that rents rowboats and putt-putt electric-driven engines in case you want to fish or sunbathe from a boat.

One of the region's most exotic collections of alpine flora is clustered into the jagged and rocky confines of the **Alpine Flower Garden Kitzbühel,** where various species of gentian, gorse, heather, and lichens are found on the sunny slopes of the Kitzbüheler Horn. Set at a height of around 1,830m (6,000 ft.) above sea level, the garden is open from late May to early September, daily 8:30am to 5:30pm, and is most impressive in June, July, and August. Admission is free. Many visitors see the garden by taking the Seilbahn Kitzbüheler cable car to its uppermost station and then descending on foot via the garden's labyrinth of footpaths to the gondola's middle station. The **Seilbahn Kitzbüheler cable car** (✆ **05356/69-51**), 25€ round-trip, departs from Kitzbühel at half-hour intervals daily throughout the summer and winter. In spring and autumn, it operates Saturday and Sunday only.

BELGIUM

by George McDonald

Modest little Belgium has never been known to boast of its charms, yet its variety of languages, cultures, history, and cuisines would do credit to a country many times its size. Belgium's diversity stems from its location at a cultural crossroads. The boundary between Europe's Germanic north and Latin south cuts clear across the nation's middle, leaving Belgium divided into two major ethnic regions: Dutch-speaking Flanders and French-speaking Wallonia.

3

International attention generally focuses on Brussels as the "capital of Europe," and the city has been upping its cultural game in recent years to meet the expectations that go along with this label. Yet another Belgium waits in the wings—a place of Gothic cathedrals, medieval castles, cobblestone streets, and tranquil canals. In a country you can drive clear across in little more than 2 hours, the timeless beauty of Bruges and Ghent are accessible even to the most hurried visitor. Both of these Flemish cities are showcases of medieval art and architecture. Some of the northern Renaissance's most outstanding paintings hang in their museums and churches. Yet each has a distinctive character that makes visiting them complementary. You can easily visit both in day trips from Brussels, but for a more thorough inspection you'll want to stay overnight.

BRUSSELS ★★★

As the headquarters city of the European Union, Brussels both symbolizes the Continent's vision of unity and is a bastion of officialdom, a breeding ground for the regulations that govern and often exasperate the rest of Europe.

Bruxellois have ambivalent feelings about their city's transformation into a power center. The armies of well-heeled Eurocrats, and their many hangers-on in business, lobbying, and the media, have brought a cosmopolitan air, but with entire old neighborhoods leveled to make way for massive office complexes, people wondered whether Brussels was losing its soul. After all, this is the city that inspired surrealism and Art Nouveau, worships comic strips, prides itself on handmade lace and chocolate, and serves each one of its craft beers in its own unique glass.

Belgium

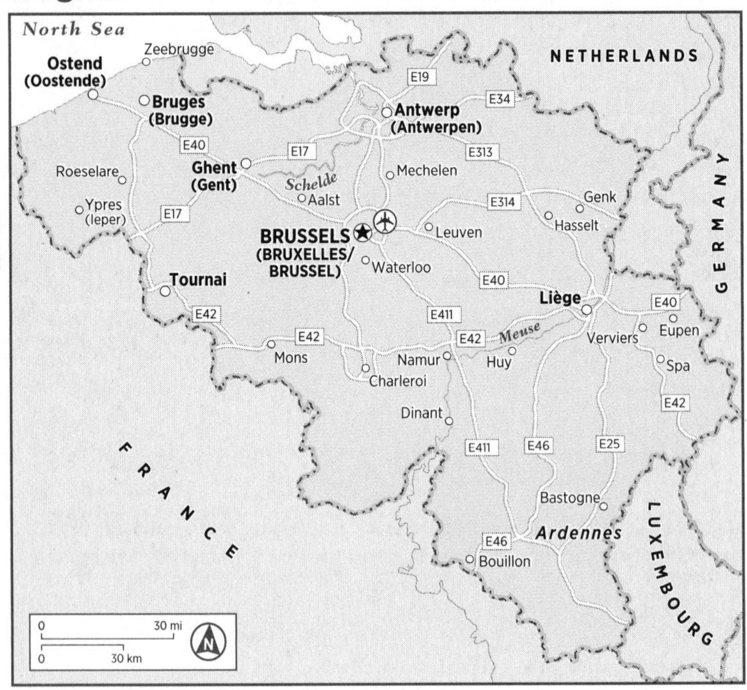

Fortunately, not all of Brussels's individuality has been lost. The city's spirit survives in traditional bars, bistros, and restaurants. Whether elegantly Art Nouveau or eccentrically festooned with posters, curios, and knickknacks, such centuries-old establishments provide a warm, convivial ambience that is peculiarly Belgian.

Essentials

GETTING THERE

BY PLANE Modern, efficient **Brussels Airport** (✆ **0900/70-000** in Belgium, or 02/753-77-53 from abroad; www.brusselsairport.be), 11km (6¾ miles) northeast of the center city, is Belgium's principal airport and handles virtually all of the country's international flights. In the arrival hall are currency-exchange offices, ATMs, a tourist information office, car-rental desks from the major international rental companies, bars, restaurants, and shops.

Brussels Airport Express trains connect the airport with Brussels's three major rail stations (see below) up to four times an hour daily from 5:30am to 11:30pm; a one-way ride is 6.75€ in first class, and 5.05€ in second class; trip time to Gare Centrale is around 15 minutes (other city stops are just minutes away). The **Airport Line bus** no. 12 or 21 departs from the airport about every half-hour to the European District in the city; the fare is 3€ for a one-way ticket purchased before boarding the bus, and 5€ for one purchased onboard. **De Lijn bus** no. 272 or 471 departs from the airport hourly to Gare du Nord rail station; the fare is 2€ for a one-way ticket purchased before boarding the bus, and 3€ for one purchased onboard. A **taxi** from the airport to the center city is around 35€; be sure to use only licensed cabs, which you can find at the stand outside the terminal.

BY TRAIN High-speed trains—Eurostar from London; Thalys from Paris, Amsterdam, and Cologne; TGV from France (not Paris); and ICE from Frankfurt—zip into town from all points of the compass, and arrive at Gare du Midi, south of the city center. Other international trains also arrive at Gare du Midi, as well as at Gare Centrale, downtown, a few blocks from the Grand-Place, and Gare du Nord, north of the city center. For train information, call ✆ **02/528-28-28** or visit **www.b-rail.be**.

All three stations have currency exchange offices, luggage storage, waiting rooms, fast-food restaurants, bars, cafes, snack kiosks, and stores, with Gare du Midi being outfitted the best in all these services. Both Gare du Midi and Gare du Nord also have a bus station and stops for tram (streetcar) lines; Gare Centrale has an adjacent Métro (subway) station and multiple bus stops outside. All three have taxi stands outside.

Warning: Attracted by rich pickings from international travelers, bag snatchers roam the environs of Gare du Midi, and pickpockets work the interior. Do not travel to or depart from the station on foot if you can avoid it. Take a taxi or use public transportation, and once inside, keep a close eye on your possessions. This seems to be less of a problem than it once was, but why take a chance?

BY BUS **Eurolines** (✆ **02/274-13-50;** www.eurolines.com) buses from London, Paris, Amsterdam, and other cities arrive at the bus station below Gare du Nord.

BY CAR Major expressways to Brussels are E19 from Amsterdam and Paris, and E40 from Bruges and Cologne. Avoid if possible driving the "hell on wheels" R0 Brussels ring road. After you arrive in Brussels, do yourself a favor: Leave the car at a parking garage.

VISITOR INFORMATION **Tourist Offices** **Brussels International Tourism & Congress** has several tourist offices around the city, along with desks in the Arrivals hall at Brussels Airport and in the main hall at Gare du Midi rail station. The most central city office is at the Hôtel de Ville (Town Hall), on the Grand-Place (✆ **02/513-89-40;** fax 02/513-83-20; www.brusselsinternational.be; Métro: Gare Centrale; Apr–Oct daily 9am–6pm; Nov–Dec Mon–Sat 9am–6pm, Sun 10am–2pm; Jan–Mar Mon–Sat 9am–6pm). Other offices are at rue Royale 2 (tram: 92 or 94; daily 10am–6pm) and at rue Wiertz 43, in the European District (bus: 22 or 54; Mon 1–5pm, Tues–Thurs 9am–5pm, Fri 9am–noon).

PRESS For English-speaking visitors, the most useful publication is the weekly magazine ***The Bulletin,*** published on Thursdays and filled with local news, articles, shopping, and information on cultural events.

WEBSITES A good starting point for exploring Brussels and the Wallonia and Flanders regions of Belgium on the Web is at the official tourist-office websites **www.brusselsinternational.be**, **www.visitbelgium.com**, **www.opt.be**, and **www.visitflanders.com**. You might also want to check out the independent **www.trabel.com**. A website in English that covers Belgian news, weather, tourism, and more is

Brussels

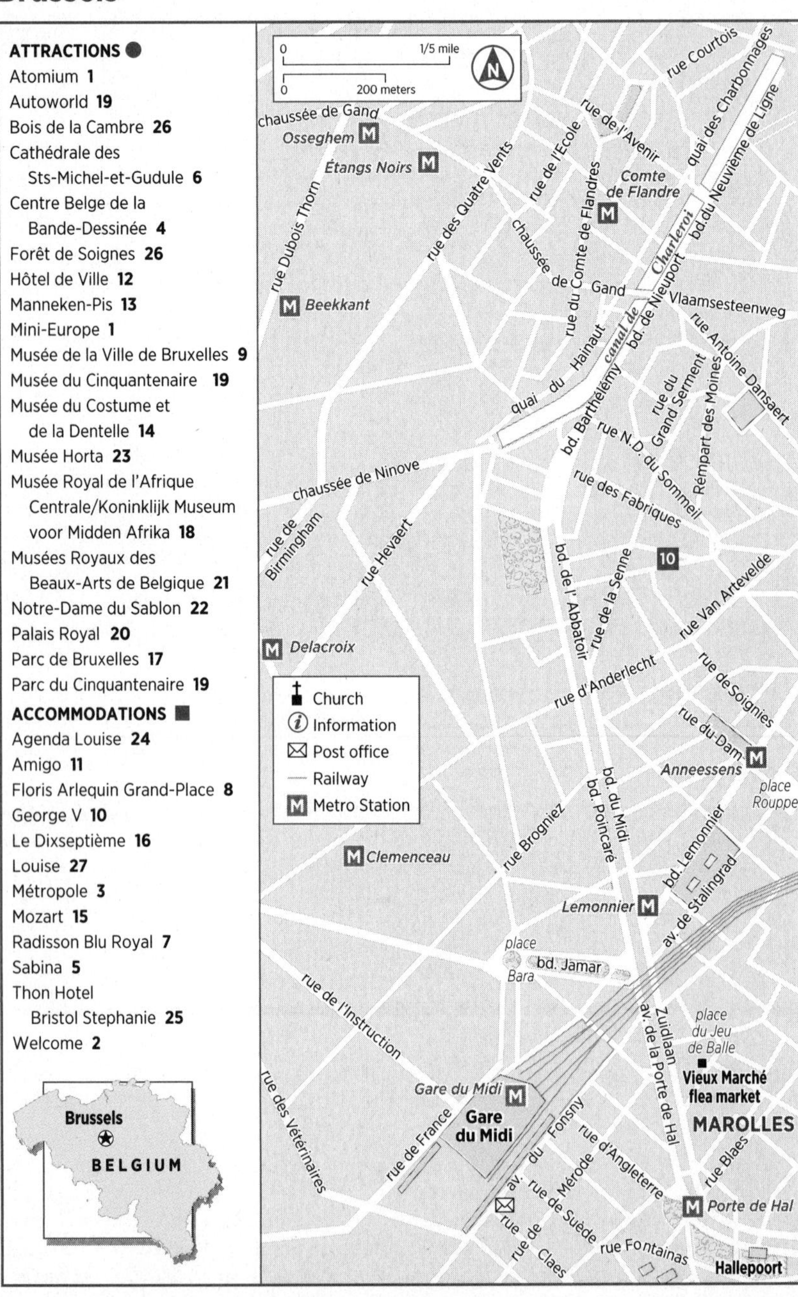
ATTRACTIONS ●
Atomium 1
Autoworld 19
Bois de la Cambre 26
Cathédrale des Sts-Michel-et-Gudule 6
Centre Belge de la Bande-Dessinée 4
Forêt de Soignes 26
Hôtel de Ville 12
Manneken-Pis 13
Mini-Europe 1
Musée de la Ville de Bruxelles 9
Musée du Cinquantenaire 19
Musée du Costume et de la Dentelle 14
Musée Horta 23
Musée Royal de l'Afrique Centrale/Koninklijk Museum voor Midden Afrika 18
Musées Royaux des Beaux-Arts de Belgique 21
Notre-Dame du Sablon 22
Palais Royal 20
Parc de Bruxelles 17
Parc du Cinquantenaire 19
ACCOMMODATIONS ■
Agenda Louise 24
Amigo 11
Floris Arlequin Grand-Place 8
George V 10
Le Dixseptième 16
Louise 27
Métropole 3
Mozart 15
Radisson Blu Royal 7
Sabina 5
Thon Hotel Bristol Stephanie 25
Welcome 2
Brussels
BELGIUM
0 1/5 mile
0 200 meters
N
Church
Information
Post office
Railway
Metro Station
chaussée de Gand
Osseghem
Étangs Noirs
rue Dubois Thorn
Beekkant
rue des Quatre Vents
rue de l'Ecole
rue de l'Avenir
rue Courtois
quai des Charbonnages
bd. du Neuvième de Ligne
Comte de Flandre
rue du Comte de Flandres
chaussée de Gand
canal de Charleroi
bd. de Nieuport
Vlaamsesteenweg
rue Antoine Dansaert
quai du Hainaut
bd. Barthélémy
rue du Grand Serment
Rempart des Moines
rue N.D. du Sommeil
rue des Fabriques
chaussée de Ninove
rue de Birmingham
rue Hevaert
bd. de l' Abbatoir
rue de la Senne
10
rue Van Artevelde
Delacroix
rue d'Anderlecht
rue de Soignies
rue du Dam
Anneessens
place Rouppe
bd. du Midi
bd. Poincaré
rue Brogniez
Clemenceau
bd. Lemonnier
Lemonnier
av. de Stalingrad
place Bara
bd. Jamar
rue de l'Instruction
av. de la Porte de Hal
Zuidlaan
place du Jeu de Balle
Vieux Marché flea market
MAROLLES
Gare du Midi
Gare du Midi
rue de France
rue des Vétérinaires
av. du Fonsny
rue Mérode
rue d'Angleterre
rue Blaes
Porte de Hal
rue de Suède
rue de Claes
rue Fontainas
Hallepoort

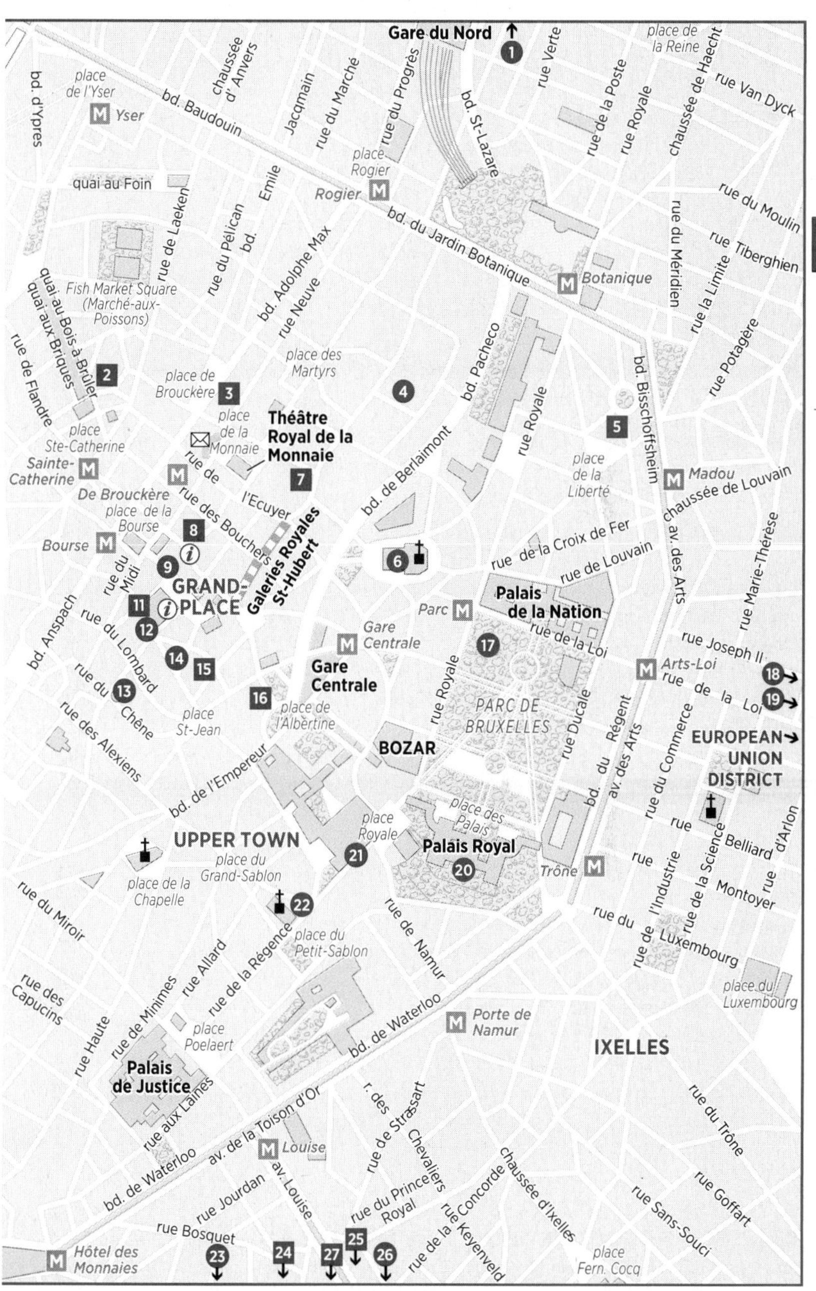

3 BELGIUM | Brussels

NATIVE behavior

Bruxellois are never happier than when they're setting forks and spoons to work on one of their country's proud regional cuisine specialties, and easing its assimilation with a carefully crafted artisanal Belgian beer—or three. If this can be done over an extended lunch, on the boss's time, and at the boss's expense, so much the better. You can join them in spirit, if not on expenses, by making lunch an important part of the day's proceedings.

Then, to really feel like a local, start grousing about the overpaid, underworked, arrogant, dimwitted, probably corrupt, expense-account-toting, comfortably pensioned "Eurocrats" who run the bureaucracy—and boy, is that some bureaucracy—of the gravy train that goes by the name of the European Union and is ensconced like a bloated alien body in their midst. See, it's easy!

www.xpats.com. A good website for hotel research, where you can compare prices and see pictures of the rooms, is **www.hotels-belgium.com**. For dining-out pointers, go to **www.resto.be**.

CITY LAYOUT The center city's small, cobbled streets are clustered around the magnificent **Grand-Place.** Two of the most traveled lanes nearby are restaurant-lined **rue des Bouchers** and **Petite rue des Bouchers,** part of an area known as the **Ilot Sacré.** A block from the Grand-Place is the classical colonnaded Bourse (Stock Exchange). A few blocks north, on **place de la Monnaie,** is the Monnaie opera house and ballet theater, named after the coin mint that once stood here. Brussels's busiest shopping street, pedestrianized **rue Neuve,** starts from place de la Monnaie and runs north for several blocks.

The Upper Town is spread along an escarpment southeast of the center city, where you find the second great square, **place du Grand Sablon,** the Royal Fine Arts Museums, and the Royal Palace. If you head southwest and cross the broad **boulevard de Waterloo,** where you find the most exclusive designer stores, you come to **place Louise.** From here, Brussels's most fashionable thoroughfare, **avenue Louise,** runs south all the way to a large wooded park called the **Bois de la Cambre.** Both main streets are flanked by attractive residential side streets.

Between the Palais de Justice and Gare du Midi, the unpretentious working-class **Marolles** area has cozy cafes, drinking-man's bars, and inexpensive restaurants; its denizens even speak their own dialect.

East of this zone, the **Ixelles** district, near the Free University, has many casual, inexpensive restaurants, bars, and cafes. North of Ixelles, the modern European Union district surrounds **place Schuman.**

In this bilingual city, called *Bruxelles* in French and *Brussel* in Dutch, street names and places are in both languages. Grand-Place is *Grote Markt* in Dutch; Gare Centrale is *Centraal Station;* Théatre Royal de la Monnaie is *Koninklijke Muntthe-ater.* For convenience and to save space, I use only the French names in this chapter.

GETTING AROUND **By Métro, Tram & Bus** Public transportation begins at around 6am and the regular service ends around midnight. After that, there are infrequent night buses. The Métro (subway) network is good for getting to major destinations around and on the edge of town. Métro stations are indicated by signs showing a large white M on a blue background. Trams (streetcars) and buses are colored silver and bronze; stop them by extending your arm as they approach. Stops are marked with red-and-white signs. Though not as fast as the Métro, trams are generally faster than buses and are a great way to get around, because you can view the cityscape while you ride—lines 92 and 94 cover a bunch of key sights along rue Royale, rue de la Régence, and as far as avenue Louise.

Free pocket maps of the public transportation network are available from the tourist office, the main Métro stations, and the **STIB** transit authority, Galerie de la Toison d'Or 20 (✆ **070/23-20-00;** www.stib.be; Métro: Louise). Maps of the network are posted at all Métro stations and on many bus and tram shelters.

A one-ride ticket costs 2€ when purchased from tram and bus drivers, and 1.70€ when purchased before boarding. It costs 7.30€ for a 5-ride ticket, 12.30€ for a 10-ride ticket, 4.50€ for a 1-day ticket, and 9.50€ for a 3-day ticket. The 5-ride, 10-ride, and 1-day tickets cannot be purchased on board trams or buses of the STIB city transit authority, but only from sales points and ticket machines; they can, however, be purchased on board buses of the regional transit companies De Lijn and TEC that have stops inside the city limits; the 3-day ticket can be used only with STIB and must be purchased before boarding. Finally, whatever ticket you want, if you plan to use it on Métro trains you must purchase it before boarding.

You validate your ticket by inserting it into the orange electronic machines that stand inside buses and trams and at the access to Métro platforms. Though the ticket must be revalidated each time you board, you are allowed multiple transfers within a 1-hour period of the initial validation, so you can hop on and off Métro trains, trams, and buses during that time and only one journey will be canceled by the electronic scanner. If more than one person is traveling on one ticket, the ticket must be validated each time for each traveler. Up to four children age 5 and under per paying adult ride free.

STIB has introduced an electronic stored-value card, the **MOBIB,** available from KIOSK and BOOTIK sales points at some rail and Métro stations. It is more complicated to purchase and use this card compared with the ordinary tickets detailed above, and for short-stay visitors may currently not be worth the extra hassle. Still, there's a saving of around 10% over the price of ordinary tickets.

BY TAXI The fare starts at 2.40€ from 6am to 10pm, and at 4.40€ between 10pm and 6am, increasing by 1.35€ a kilometer inside the city (tariff 1) and 2.70€ a kilometer outside (tariff 2)—make sure the meter is set to the correct tariff. Taxis cannot be hailed on the street, but there are stands at prominent locations around town. Call **Taxis Bleus** (✆ **02/268-00-00**), **Taxi Orange** (✆ **02/349-43-43**), or **Taxis Verts** (✆ **02/349-49-49**).

BY CAR Driving in Brussels is akin to life during the Stone Age: nasty and brutish—though it's rarely short. In some cases (but not always), traffic from the right has the right of way, even if it is coming from a minor street onto a more important one. You can imagine how this plays at multistreet intersections, particularly since Belgian drivers will relinquish their *priorité à droite* under no known circumstances, cost what it might. If you must drive, rental cars are available from **Hertz** (✆ **800/654-3001** in the U.S., or 02/717-32-01 in Belgium; www.hertz.be); **Avis**

(✆ **800/331-2112** in the U.S., or 070/22-30-01 in Belgium; www.avis.be); **Budget** (✆ **02/712-08-40;** www.budget.be); and **Europcar** (✆ **02/522-95-37;** www.europcar.be). All of these firms have city offices and desks at the airport. Rates begin at around 60€ for a small car with unlimited mileage.

Remember: You get the best deal if you arrange the rental before you leave home.

BY FOOT There's no better way to explore the historic core of the town than walking, especially around Grand-Place. You'll also enjoy strolling uptown around place du Grand Sablon. Beyond these areas, you'll want to use public transportation. Don't expect cars to stop for you just because you're crossing at a black-and-white "pedestrian crossing."

[FastFACTS] BRUSSELS

American Express Brussels no longer has an American Express office that's open to the general public. For card services, call ✆ **02/676-21-21.**

Business Hours **Banks** are open Monday to Friday from 9am to 1pm and 2 to 4:30 or 5pm. Open hours for **offices** are Monday to Friday from 9 or 10am to 4 or 5pm. Most **stores** are open Monday to Saturday from 9 or 10am to 6 or 7pm; some stay open on Friday to 8 or 9pm.

Currency Belgium's currency is the **euro** (€). At press time, 1€ equals US$1.40.

Currency Exchange Banks give the best rates, and currency-exchange offices in rail stations come close. Hotels and *bureaux de change* (currency-exchange offices), open regular hours plus evenings and weekends, charge a low commission (or none at all) but give a low rate. **Travelex,** with offices at both Gare du Midi (✆ **02/556-36-00**) and Gare du Nord (✆ **02/203-89-00**), has fair rates. You'll find many **ATMs** around town, identified by BANCONTACT and MISTER CASH signs. A convenient bank with ATMs, inside and outside, is **CBC,** Grand-Place 5 (✆ **02/547-12-11;** Métro: Gare Centrale).

Doctors & Dentists For doctors, call **Médi-Garde** at ✆ **02/479-18-18** or **SOS Médecins** at ✆ **02/513-02-02,** and ask for an English-speaking doctor. For emergency dental care, call ✆ **02/426-10-26.**

Drugstores & Pharmacies For both prescription and nonprescription medicines, go to a pharmacy (*pharmacie* in French; *apotheek* in Dutch). Regular pharmacy hours are Monday to Saturday from 9am to 6pm (some close earlier on Sat). Try the centrally located **Grande Pharmacie de Brouckère,** Passage du Nord 10–12 (✆ **02/218-05-07;** Métro: De Brouckère). All pharmacies post locations of nearby all-night and Sunday pharmacies on the door.

Embassies **United States,** bd. du Régent 25–27 (✆ **02/508-21-11;** www.usembassy.be; Métro: Arts-Loi), open Monday to Friday 9am to noon for visas and 1:30 to 4:30pm for assistance. **Canada,** av. de Tervueren 2 (✆ **02/741-06-11;** www.ambassade-canada.be; Métro: Mérode), open Monday to Friday 9am to noon. **United Kingdom,** av. d'Auderghem 10 (✆ **02/287-62-11;** http://ukinbelgium.fco.gov.uk/en; Métro: Schuman), open Monday to Friday 9:30am to 12:30pm and 2:15 to 4pm. **Ireland,** chaussée d'Etterbeek 180 (✆ **02/282-34-00;** www.embassyofireland.be; bus: 59), open Monday to Friday 10am to 1pm. **Australia,** rue Guimard 6–8 (✆ **02/286-05-00;** www.belgium.embassy.gov.au; Métro: Arts-Loi), open Monday to Friday 9am to 12:30pm and 2 to 4pm. **New Zealand,** av. des Nerviens 9–31

(✆ **02/512-10-40;** www.nzembassy.com/belgium; bus: 22 or 27), open Monday to Friday 9am to 1pm and 2 to 3:30pm.

Emergencies For police assistance, call ✆ **101.** For an ambulance or the fire department, call ✆ **100.**

Hospital **Cliniques Universitaires St-Luc,** av. Hippocrate 10 (✆ **02/764-11-11;** Métro: Alma), has an emergency department.

Internet Access **Dotspot,** rue du Lombard 83 (✆ **02/513-61-03;** Métro: Bourse), is open daily from 11am to 9pm; access is 4€ an hour.

Mail Most post offices are open Monday to Friday from 9am to 5pm. The office at Centre Monnaie, place de la Monnaie (✆ **022/012345;** Métro: De Brouckère), is open Monday to Friday from 8am to 6pm, and Saturday from 10:30am to 4:30pm.

Police In an emergency, call ✆ **101.** In nonurgent situations, go to the **Brussels Central Police Station,** rue du Marché au Charbon 30 (✆ **02/279-79-79**), just off the Grand-Place.

Safety Brussels is generally safe so far as the threat of violent crime goes, but there's a risk of bag snatching, pickpocketing, and robbery in deserted places at night and in Métro station foot tunnels. There's no need to overestimate the risk, only to take sensible precautions, particularly in obvious circumstances such as on crowded Métro trains and when taking cash from an ATM at night.

Taxes There's a **value-added tax (TVA)** of 6% on hotel bills and 21% on restaurant bills and on many purchases. For information on how to recover some of the tax on purchases, see "The Shopping Scene," later in this chapter.

Telephone Belgium's **country code** is **32.** Brussels's **city code** is **2;** use the **32-2** code when calling from the United States or any other country outside Belgium. In Belgium, use the **area code 02.** You need to dial the **02** area code both from inside Brussels and from elsewhere in Belgium.

You can use pay phones in booths all around town with a Belgacom *telecard* (phone card), selling for 5€, 10€, and 20€, from post offices, train ticket counters, and newsstands. Some pay phones take coins of .10€, .20€, .50€, and 1€. On both card and coin phones, watch the digital reading, which tracks your decreasing deposit, so that you know when to add another card or more coins. For information inside the country, call ✆ **1207** or 1307; for international information in English, call ✆ **1405.**

To charge a call to your calling card, dial **AT&T** (✆ 0800/100-10); **MCI** (✆ 0800/100-12); **Sprint** (✆ 0800/100-14); **Canada Direct** (✆ 0800/100-19); **British Telecom** (✆ 0800/100-24); **Australia Direct** (✆ 0800/100-61); or **Telecom New Zealand** (✆ 0800/756-74).

Tipping The prices on most restaurant menus already include a service charge of 16%, so it's unnecessary to tip. However, if the service is good, it's usual to show appreciation with a tip (5%–10%). Service is included in your hotel bill as well. For taxi drivers, round up the fare if you like, but you need not add a tip unless you have received an extra service such as help with luggage.

Toilets Be sure to *pay the person* who sits at the entrance to a *toilette.* He or she has a saucer in which you put your money. Toilet use is usually only about .50€.

Where to Stay

If you arrive in Brussels without a reservation, you should stop by one of the **Brussels International Tourism & Congress** tourist offices or information desks (see "Visitor Information," earlier in this chapter). The staff in these offices can make same-day reservations, if you go in person, for a small fee (deducted by the hotel from its rate).

AROUND THE GRAND-PLACE

Very Expensive

Amigo ★★★ In Brussels slang, an *amigo* is a prison, and indeed a prison once stood here. But any resemblance to the former accommodations is purely nominal, as this Rocco Forte Collection hotel is among the city's finest lodgings. Its Spanish Renaissance architecture, stately corridors, and flagstone lobby are right at home in this ancient neighborhood. The rooms are spacious and traditionally elegant, but with touches of modern Belgian design to brighten things up—and motifs from the classic comic *Tintin* in the bathrooms to add an element of whimsy. Ask for a room with a view of the Town Hall's Gothic spire.

Rue de l'Amigo 1-3 (off Grand-Place), 1000 Bruxelles. ✆ **02/547-47-47.** Fax 02/513-52-77. www.hotelamigo.com. 173 units. 199€-640€ double; from 800€ suite. AE, DC, MC, V. Valet parking 30€. Métro: Bourse. **Amenities:** Restaurant; bar; lounge; babysitting; concierge; executive rooms; exercise room; room service; smoke-free rooms. *In room:* A/C, TV, hair dryer, minibar, Wi-Fi (20€ per 24 hr.).

Expensive

Métropole ★★★ Even if you're not staying here, the hotel is worth a visit. An ornate, marble-and-gilt interior distinguishes this late-19th-century hotel several blocks from the Grand-Place. Soaring ceilings, potted palms, and lavishly decorated public rooms add to the Belle Epoque allure. Spacious rooms have classic furnishings and some modern luxuries, including heated towel racks, hair dryers, and trouser presses.

Place de Brouckère 31 (close to Centre Monnaie), 1000 Bruxelles. ✆ **02/217-23-00.** Fax 02/218-02-20. www.metropolehotel.be. 298 units. 275€-450€ double; from 650€ suite. AE, DC, MC, V. Valet parking 21€. Métro: De Brouckère. **Amenities:** Restaurant; lounge; sidewalk cafe; babysitting; concierge; exercise room; room service; smoke-free rooms. *In room:* TV, hair dryer, minibar, Wi-Fi (free).

Radisson Blu Royal ★★ Modern, yet in harmony with its neighborhood a few blocks from the Grand-Place, this highly regarded hotel incorporates part of the medieval city wall. The large rooms are decorated in a variety of styles, including Scandinavian, Asian, and Italian, and the Royal Club rooms are plushly upholstered. There's a huge atrium with cafe terraces and fountains; some rooms look out on this atrium rather than the outside world.

Rue du Fossé aux Loups 47 (close to Galeries Royales St-Hubert), 1000 Bruxelles. ✆ **800/333-3333** in the U.S. and Canada, or 02/219-28-28. Fax 02/219-62-62. www.radissonblu.com. 281 units. 220€-405€ double; 590€-890€ suite. AE, DC, MC, V. Valet parking 25€. Métro: Gare Centrale. **Amenities:** 2 restaurants; bar; lounge; babysitting; concierge; health club; Jacuzzi; room service; sauna; smoke-free rooms. *In room:* A/C, TV, hair dryer, minibar, Wi-Fi (free).

Moderate

Floris Arlequin Grand Place You can't get closer to the heart of the city than this, with the restaurant-lined rue des Bouchers right outside the hotel's back entrance. Then there's the fine view, from some rooms, of the Town Hall spire on the neighboring Grand-Place (which is spectacular when lit at night), and of the Old City's rooftops and narrow medieval streets from the top-floor breakfast room. The guest rooms are not quite so spectacular, but all have contemporary, comfortable furnishings, and most have lots of natural light. The more expensive rooms have air-conditioning.

Rue de la Fourche 17-19 (off rue des Bouchers), 1000 Bruxelles. ✆ **02/514-16-15.** Fax 02/514-22-02. www.florishotels.com. 92 units. 100€–230€ double. Rates include buffet breakfast. AE, DC, MC, V. No parking. Métro: Bourse. **Amenities:** Bar; lounge; exercise room; room service. *In room:* A/C, TV, hair dryer, Wi-Fi (15€ per 24 hr.).

Le Dixseptième ★★ This graceful 17th-century house, once the official residence of the Spanish ambassador, stands close to the Grand-Place in a neighborhood of restored dwellings. Guest rooms have wood paneling and marble chimneys, and are as big as the suites in many hotels; some have balconies, and most overlook a tranquil courtyard patio. All are in 18th-century style and are named after Belgian painters from Brueghel to Magritte. Both the bar and the lounge are decorated with carved wooden medallions and 18th-century paintings.

Rue de la Madeleine 25 (off place de l'Albertine), 1000 Bruxelles. ✆ **02/517-17-17.** Fax 02/502-64-24. www.ledixseptieme.be. 24 units. 100€–200€ double; from 170€ suite. Rates include buffet breakfast. AE, DC, MC, V. Very limited street parking. Métro: Gare Centrale. **Amenities:** Bar; lounge. *In room:* A/C, TV, hair dryer, minibar, Wi-Fi (15€ per 24 hr.).

Inexpensive

Mozart ★ Go up a flight from the busy, cheap-eats street level, and guess which famous composer's music wafts through the lobby? Salmon-colored walls, plants, and old paintings create a warm, intimate ambience that's carried over into the guest rooms. Furnishings are in Louis XV style, and exposed beams lend each room a cozy originality. Several are duplexes with a sitting room underneath the loft bedroom. Top-floor rooms have a great view.

Rue du Marché aux Fromages 23 (close to the Grand-Place), 1000 Bruxelles. ✆ **02/502-66-61.** Fax 02/502-77-58. www.hotel-mozart.be. 50 units. 100€–150€ double. Rates include buffet breakfast. AE, DC, MC, V. No parking. Métro: Gare Centrale. *In room:* TV, hair dryer.

Sabina This small hostelry is like a private residence, presided over by hospitable owners. A grandfather clock in the reception area and polished wood along the restaurant walls give it a warm, homey atmosphere. Rooms vary in size, but all are comfortable and simply yet tastefully done in modern style with twin beds. Three rooms have kitchenettes.

Rue du Nord 78 (at place des Barricades), 1000 Bruxelles. ✆ **02/218-26-37.** Fax 02/219-32-39. www.hotelsabina.be. 24 units. 60€–90€ double. Rates include buffet breakfast. AE, DC, MC, V. Limited street parking. Métro: Madou. *In room:* TV, hair dryer.

THE LOWER CITY

Moderate

Welcome ★★ The name of this gem of a hotel, overlooking the Fish Market, couldn't be more accurate, thanks to the untiring efforts of the husband-and-wife proprietors. You can think of it as a country *auberge* (inn) right in the heart of town. Rooms are furnished and styled on individual, unrelated themes, such as Provence, Africa, and Laura Ashley, all to a high standard. The hotel provides a free airport shuttle to and from Brussels National Airport. Book ahead.

Quai au Bois à Brûler 23 (at the Marché aux Poissons), 1000 Bruxelles. ✆ **02/219-95-46.** Fax 02/217-18-87. www.hotelwelcome.com. 15 units. 95€–155€ double; 160€–240€ suite. Rates include buffet breakfast. AE, DC, MC, V. Parking 13€. Métro: Ste-Catherine. **Amenities:** Lounge; airport transfers (some free, others 45€); Internet in lobby (free). *In room:* A/C (some units), TV, hair dryer, minibar, Wi-Fi (free).

Inexpensive

George V This agreeable little hotel is tucked away on a corner of the center city that is being reborn as a trendy shopping-and-eating area. Situated in a renovated town house from 1859 within easy walking distance of the Grand-Place, the rooms are plain but clean and have new furnishings.

Rue T'Kint 23 (off place du Jardin aux Fleurs), 1000 Bruxelles. ✆ **02/513-50-93.** Fax 02/513-44-93. www.hotelgeorge5.be. 17 units. 80€–100€ double. Rates include buffet breakfast. AE, MC, V. Limited street parking. Métro: Bourse. **Amenities:** Bar; room service. *In room:* TV, hair dryer, minibar, Wi-Fi (free).

AROUND AVENUE LOUISE

Expensive

Thon Hotel Bristol Stephanie ★★ From its lobby fittings to furnishings in the kitchenette suites, every feature of this sleek Norwegian-owned hotel, set on one of the city's toniest shopping streets, is streamlined, functional, and representative of the best in Nordic design. Some rooms have four-poster beds and "antiallergy" hardwood floors; all are quite large, and furnished to a high level of modern style and comfort (though the standard rooms could use a little more Nordic drawer space). The French restaurant **Le Chalet d'Odin** has a refined Continental menu.

Av. Louise 91–93, 1050 Bruxelles. ✆ **02/543-33-11.** Fax 02/538-03-07. www.bristol.be. 142 units. 120€–280€ double; from 600€ suite. AE, DC, MC, V. Parking 25€. Métro: Louise. **Amenities:** Restaurant; lounge; bar; babysitting; concierge; exercise room; Jacuzzi; heated indoor pool; room service; sauna; smoke-free rooms. *In room:* A/C, TV, hair dryer, minibar, Wi-Fi (18€ per 24 hr.).

Moderate

Agenda Louise This fine, small, middle-of-the-road hotel affords a good balance of advantages for both leisure visitors and business visitors on a budget. The rooms are pleasantly decorated with light-colored wood furniture and gold-and-orange curtains, and have enough room to swing a cat, as long as it's not an overly big one. The bathrooms have tiled walls and floors and just about break out of the shoehorned-in syndrome that afflicts many moderately priced city hotels. Ask for a room that overlooks the inner courtyard for the best view.

Rue de Florence 6–8 (off av. Louise), 1000 Bruxelles. ✆ **02/539-00-31.** Fax 02/539-00-63. www.hotel-agenda.com. 37 units. 160€ double. Rates include buffet breakfast. AE, DC, MC, V. Parking 17€. Métro: Louise. **Amenities:** Lounge; smoke-free rooms. *In room:* A/C, TV, hair dryer, minibar, Wi-Fi (free).

Louise ★ In a quiet, well-maintained 19th-century town house, this graceful hotel has some unusually spacious rooms and some so small you'll need to shoehorn yourself and your luggage into them. If you need one of the larger rooms, you'll want to check it out first, if possible, or confirm how large it is when you reserve. No rooms measure up to the Victorian elegance of the public spaces, but they are adequately furnished, with comfortable beds, soft carpeting, and floral-patterned curtains.

Rue Veydt 40 (off chaussée de Charleroi), 1050 Bruxelles. ✆ **02/537-40-33.** Fax 02/534-40-37. www.louisehotel.com. 49 units. 140€–180€ double. AE, DC, MC, V. Limited street parking. Métro: Louise. **Amenities:** Bar. *In room:* A/C (some units), TV, hair dryer, minibar (some units), Wi-Fi (free).

Where to Dine

The city's French- and Dutch-speaking residents may have their differences, but they both value a good meal. Throw in the city's many prosperous expats, and its ethnic minorities (not so prosperous, but possessing considerable culinary wealth), and you have both an ample supply of and a demand for good food.

On Your Guard in the Ilot Sacré

A few restaurants (not reviewed here) in this colorful district just off the Grand-Place take advantage of tourists. If you don't want to get fleeced, be sure to ask the price of everything *before* you order it. Most visitors leave the Ilot Sacré with no more serious complaint than an expanded waistline, but a little caution is in order.

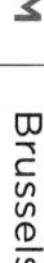

Among the sturdy regional dishes you find on menus around town are *waterzooï,* fish or chicken stew with a parsley-and-cream sauce; *stoemp,* a purée of vegetables and potatoes with sausage, steak, or chops; *paling in 't groen,* eel in a grass-green sauce; *ballekes,* spicy meatballs; *hochepot,* stew; *lapin à la gueuze,* rabbit with a Brussels beer sauce; and *carbonnades à la flamande,* beef stew with a beer sauce. While most of the city's favorite dishes are based on local products, the famous *moules* (mussels)—prepared in countless ingenious variations and served in tureens—come from Zeeland in neighboring Holland. A selection from Belgium's 300 craft cheeses is a good way to finish off.

Finally, don't fret if the service is slow: People take their time dining out here.

AROUND THE GRAND-PLACE

Very Expensive

La Maison du Cygne ★ CLASSIC FRENCH This grande dame of Brussels's internationally recognized restaurants overlooks the Grand-Place from the former guild house of the Butchers Guild—where Karl Marx and Friedrich Engels cooked up *The Communist Manifesto*. The service, though a tad stuffy, is as elegant as the polished walnut walls and bronze wall sconces. The menu has haute cuisine Belgian and French classics. Because of its location, the restaurant is usually crowded at lunchtime than at dinner.

Grand-Place 9 (entrance at rue Charles Buls 2). ✆ **02/511-82-44.** www.lamaisonducygne.be. Reservations recommended. Main courses 36€–45€; fixed-price menu 65€. AE, DC, MC, V. Mon–Fri noon–2pm and 7pm–midnight; Sat 7pm–midnight. Métro: Gare Centrale.

Expensive

De l'Ogenblik ★★ FRENCH/BELGIAN In the elegant surrounds of the Galeries Royales St-Hubert, this restaurant supplies good taste in a Parisian bistro–style setting that's popular with off-duty actors and audiences from the nearby Gallery theater, among others. It often gets busy, but the ambience in the split-level, wood-and-brass-outfitted dining room, with a sand-strewn floor, is convivial, though a little too tightly packed when it's full. Look for garlicky meat and seafood dishes, and expect to pay a smidgen more for atmosphere than might be strictly justified by results on the plate.

Galerie des Princes 1 (in the Galeries Royales St-Hubert). ✆ **02/511-61-51.** www.ogenblik.be. Reservations recommended. Main courses 23€–32€; *plat du jour* (lunch only) 11€. AE, DC, MC, V. Mon–Thurs noon–2:30pm and 7pm–midnight; Fri–Sat noon–2:30pm and 7pm–12:30am. Métro: Gare Centrale.

Moderate

La Roue d'Or ★ TRADITIONAL BELGIAN This welcoming Art Nouveau brasserie, with lots of dark wood, mirrors, a high frescoed ceiling, and marble-topped tables, has a loyal local following. An extensive menu, ranging from grilled meats to seafood, and old Belgian favorites like stoemp, caters to just about any appetite. The beer, wine, and spirits list is long.

Rue des Chapeliers 26 (off the Grand-Place). ✆ **02/514-25-54.** Main courses 14€–24€; *menus de jour* 23€–28€. AE, DC, MC, V. Daily noon–12:30am. Métro: Gare Centrale.

Inexpensive

L'Auberge des Chapeliers ★ TRADITIONAL BELGIAN Behind a beautiful brick facade, in a 17th-century building that was once the headquarters of the hat-makers' guild, these dining rooms are graced with timber beams and paneling and connected by a narrow wooden staircase. Popular with both locals and visitors for its historical charm, fine food, and modest prices, it can get crowded at the height of lunch hour, so a good idea is to come before noon or after 2pm. The food is typical hearty Belgian fare, with an accent on mussels in season and dishes cooked in beer.

Rue des Chapeliers 3 (off the Grand-Place). ✆ **02/513-73-38.** Reservations recommended on weekends. Main courses 10€–18€; fixed-price menus 15€–22€. AE, DC, MC, V. Mon–Thurs noon–2pm and 6–11pm; Fri noon–2pm and 6pm–midnight; Sat noon–3pm and 6pm–midnight; Sun noon–3pm and 6–11pm. Métro: Gare Centrale.

't Kelderke ★★ TRADITIONAL BELGIAN The Little Cellar is one of the Grand-Place's most delightful surprises, even if it has little in the way of frills. Hidden beneath an ornate guild house, the entrance isn't easy to spot. But when you descend the steps, you'll find a crowded, lively restaurant in the 17th-century brick-vaulted room at the bottom. As many locals as tourists throng the long wooden tables. The menu features Belgian favorites like stoemp, served with a pork chop; Flemish beef stew; rabbit in beer; and Zeeland mussels in season, served from an open kitchen.

Grand-Place 15. ✆ **02/513-73-44.** Main courses 9€–27€; *plat du jour* 9€. AE, DC, MC, V. Daily noon–2am. Métro: Gare Centrale.

THE LOWER CITY

Very Expensive

Comme Chez Soi ★★★ CLASSIC FRENCH A visit to the revered, Art Nouveau "Just Like Home," which sports two Michelin stars, will surely be the culinary highlight of your trip—though the food is a long way from being what most people actually eat at home. Under the influence of Chef Lionel Rigolet, the dishes have been looking lighter in recent times—even the Burgundian Bruxellois are having to conform to a faster, slimmer world. Ask for a table in the kitchen, where you can watch the masters at work. Book for dinner as far ahead as possible; getting a table at short notice is more likely at lunchtime.

Place Rouppe 23 (at av. de Stalingrad). ✆ **02/512-29-21.** www.commechezsoi.be. Reservations required. Main courses 43€–173€; fixed-price menus 84€–191€. AE, DC, MC, V. Tues–Sat noon–1:30pm and 7–9:30pm. Métro: Anneessens.

Expensive

Aux Armes de Bruxelles ★★ TRADITIONAL BELGIAN In business since 1921, this large, family-run Art Deco restaurant commands universal respect. It has hosted countless celebrities over the years, from Laurel and Hardy to Danny DeVito to Belgian favorites like singer Jacques Brel. The service is gracious and rather formal, but the ambience is totally relaxed. The vast menu—a Belgian cuisine primer in itself—includes local specialties like beef stewed in beer, mussels in a variety of guises, a delicious waterzooï, and shrimp croquettes, all at quite reasonable prices.

Rue des Bouchers 13 (a block from Grand-Place). ✆ **02/511-55-98.** Reservations recommended. Main courses 15€-44€; fixed-price menus 25€-49€. AE, DC, MC, V. Tues-Sun noon-11:15pm. Métro: Gare Centrale.

François ★★ SEAFOOD A bright and cheerful ambience complements fine cuisine at this restaurant on the ground floor of a 19th-century *maison de maître* (town house) that has housed a fishmongers since 1922, and the tradition is taken seriously. The presentation is professional yet relaxed. In fine weather, you can dine on a sidewalk terrace across the street on the old Fish Market square. If you're dining indoors, try to get one a table with a view on the square.

Quai aux Briques 2 (at the Marché aux Poissons). ✆ **02/511-60-89.** Reservations recommended. Main courses 23€-58€; fixed-price menus 25€-55€. AE, DC, MC, V. Tues-Sat noon-2:30pm and 7-11:30pm. Métro: Ste-Catherine.

Moderate

In 't Spinnekopke ★ 🎁 TRADITIONAL BELGIAN This restaurant, translated "In the Spider's Web" occupies a coach inn from 1762, just far enough off the beaten track downtown to be frequented mainly by those in the know. You dine in a tilting, tiled-floor building, at plain tables, and more likely than not squeezed into a tight space. This is one of Brussels's most traditional restaurants—so much so that the menu lists its hardy regional standbys in the old Bruxellois dialect. *Stoemp mi sossisse* is stew with sausage, and *toung ave mei* is sole. The bar stocks a large selection of Belgian beers.

Place du Jardin aux Fleurs 1 (off rue Van Artevelde). ✆ **02/511-86-95.** Reservations recommended. Main courses 13€-30€. AE, DC, MC, V. Mon-Fri noon-3pm and 6-11pm; Sat 6pm-midnight. Métro: Bourse.

La Manufacture ★ FRENCH/INTERNATIONAL This was formerly the factory of chic leather-goods maker Delvaux, and even in its former industrial incarnation, style was a primary concern—though the neighborhood is unprepossessing. Fully refurbished, with parquet floors, polished wood, leather banquettes, and stone tables set amid iron pillars and exposed air ducts, it produces trendy world cuisine with a French foundation for a mostly youthful public. It might at first seem disconcerting to find dim sum, sushi, Moroccan couscous, Lyon sausage, and Belgian waterzooï on the same menu, but don't worry—everything is tasty. There's piano music some evenings.

Rue Notre-Dame du Sommeil 12-20 (off place du Jardin aux Fleurs). ✆ **02/502-25-25.** www.lamanufacture.be. Reservations recommended. Main courses 12€-31€; *menu du jour* (lunch only) 15€; fixed-price menus 35€-50€. AE, DC, MC, V. Mon-Fri noon-2pm and 6-11pm; Sat 6pm-midnight. Métro: Bourse.

AROUND AVENUE LOUISE

Expensive

La Quincaillerie ★★ MODERN FRENCH/OYSTER BAR In the Ixelles district, where fine restaurants are as common as streetlights, this spot stands out, even though it may be a little too aware of its own modish good looks and is a shade pricey. The setting is a traditional former hardware store from 1903, with a giant rail-station clock, wood paneling, and masses of wooden drawers, designed by students of Art Nouveau master Victor Horta. It's busy enough to get the waitstaff harassed and absent-minded, yet they're always friendly. Seafood dishes predominate on the menu. Rue du Page 45 (at rue Américaine). ✆ **02/533-98-33.** www.quincaillerie.be. Reservations recommended. Main courses 15€–29€; fixed-price menus 13€–29€. AE, DC, MC, V. Mon–Sat noon–2:30pm and 7pm–midnight; Sun 7pm–midnight. Tram: 81 to Trinité.

Moderate

Au Vieux Bruxelles ★ BELGIAN/SEAFOOD This convivial, brasserie-style restaurant from 1882 specializes in mussels, which it serves in a wide variety of ways. In Belgium, the personality of the humble but tasty mussel is a staple of conversation as much as of diet, and people assess the quality of each year's crop with the same critical eye that other countries reserve for fine wines. Au Vieux Bruxelles, a kind of temple to the Belgian obsession with mussels, serves the shellfish in 15 different ways. Should you not wish to work on the mussels, you can get great steaks like *steak au poivre flambé* (flamed pepper steak), *escargots* (snails), and crepes. Rue St-Boniface 35 (close to Porte Namur). ✆ **02/503-31-11.** www.auvieuxbruxelles.com. Reservations not accepted. Main courses 15€–21€. AE, MC, V. Mon–Thurs 6:30–11:30pm; Fri–Sat 6:30pm–midnight; Sun noon–3pm and 6:30–11:30pm. Métro: Porte de Namur.

Seeing the Sights

Brussels has such a wide variety of things to see and do. There are more than 75 museums dedicated to just about every special interest under the sun (from cartoons to cars), in addition to impressive public buildings, leafy parks, and interesting squares. History is just around every corner. Fortunately, numerous sidewalk cafes offer respite for weary feet, and there's good public transportation to those attractions beyond walking distance of the compact, heart-shaped center city, which contains many of Brussels's most popular attractions.

THE GRAND-PLACE ★★★

Ornamental gables, medieval banners, gilded facades, sunlight flashing off gold-filigreed rooftop sculptures, a general impression of harmony and timelessness—there's a lot to take in all at once when you first enter the historic **Grand-Place** (Métro: Gare Centrale). The city's central square has always been the very heart of Brussels. Characterized by French playwright Jean Cocteau as "a splendid stage," it's the city's theater of life. Some call it the world's most beautiful square.

The Grand-Place has been the center of the city's commercial life and public celebrations since the 12th century. Most of it was destroyed in 1695 by the army of France's Louis XIV and then rebuilt over the next few years. Thanks to the town's close monitoring of later alterations, each building preserves its baroque splendor. Important guilds owned most of these buildings, and each competed to outdo the others with highly ornate facades of gold leaf and statuary, often with emblems of their guilds. The illuminated square is even more beautiful at night than during the day.

Top honors go to the Gothic **Hôtel de Ville** and the neo-Gothic **Maison du Roi.** You'll also want to admire no. 9, **Le Cygne,** former headquarters of the butchers' guild and now a tony restaurant of the same name; no. 10, **L'Arbre d'Or,** headquarters of the brewers' guild and location of the Brewing Museum; and nos. 13 to 19, an ensemble of seven mansions known as the **Maison des Ducs de Brabant,** adorned with busts of 19 dukes.

A COOL LITTLE guy

Two blocks south of the Grand-Place, at the intersection of rue de l'Etuve and rue du Chêne, is the ***Manneken-Pis*** ★ (Métro: Bourse). A small bronze statue of a urinating child, Brussels's favorite character gleefully does what a little boy's gotta do, generally ogled by a throng of admirers. Children especially enjoy his bravura performance.

No one knows when this child first came into being, but he dates from quite a few centuries ago—the 8th century, according to one legend. Thieves have made off with the tyke several times in history. One criminal who stole and shattered the statue in 1817 was sentenced to a life of hard labor. The pieces were used to recast another version and that "original" was removed for safekeeping.

King Louis XV of France began the tradition of presenting colorful costumes to "Little Julian," which he wears on special occasions (during Christmas season he dons a Santa suit, complete with white beard), to make amends for Frenchmen having kidnapped the statue in 1747. The vast wardrobe is housed in the Musée de la Ville de Bruxelles on the Grand-Place (see below).

Hôtel de Ville ★★ The facade of the dazzling Town Hall, from 1402, shows off Gothic intricacy at its best, complete with dozens of arched windows and sculptures—some, like the drunken monks, a sleeping Moor and his harem, and St. Michael slaying a female devil, displaying a sense of humor. A 66m (217-ft.) tower sprouts from the middle, yet it's not placed directly in the center. A colorful but untrue legend has it that when the architect realized his "error," he jumped from the tower's summit.

The building is still the seat of the civic government, and its wedding room is a popular place to tie the knot. You can visit the interior on 40-minute tours, which start in a room full of paintings of the past foreign rulers of Brussels, who have included the Spanish, Austrians, French, and Dutch. In the spectacular Gothic Hall, open for visits when the city's aldermen are not in session—and surrounded by mirrors, presumably so each party can see what underhanded maneuvers the others are up to—you can see baroque decoration. In other chambers are 16th- to 18th-century tapestries.

Grand-Place. ✆ **02/548-04-47.** Admission (guided tours only) 3€ adults, 2.50€ seniors and students, 1.50€ children 6–15, free for children 5 and under. Guided tours in English: Apr–Sept Tues–Wed 3:15pm, Sun 10:45am and 12:15pm; Oct–Mar Tues–Wed 3:15pm; tours at other times in French and Dutch. Closed Jan 1, May 1, Nov 1 and 11, and Dec 25. Métro: Gare Centrale.

Musée de la Ville de Bruxelles (Museum of the City of Brussels) ★ Housed in the 19th-century neo-Gothic Maison du Roi (King's House)—though no king ever lived here—the museum displays a mixed collection associated with the art and history of Brussels. On the ground floor you can admire detailed tapestries from the 16th and 17th centuries, and porcelain, silver, and stone statuary. After climbing a beautiful wooden staircase, you can trace the history of Brussels in old maps, prints, photos, and models. Among the most fascinating exhibits are old paintings and scaled reconstructions of the historic center city, particularly those showing the riverside ambience along the now-vanished River Senne. On the third floor are more than 780 costumes that have been donated to *Manneken-Pis* (see "A Cool Little Guy" box above), including an Elvis costume.

Grand-Place. ✆ **02/279-43-50.** www.brusselsmuseums.be. Admission 3€ adults, 2.50€ seniors and students, 1.50€ travelers with limited mobility and children 6–15, free for children 5 and under. Tues–Sun 10am–5pm. Closed Jan 1, May 1, Nov 1 and 11, and Dec 25. Métro: Gare Centrale.

SOME MEMORABLE MUSEUMS

Centre Belge de la Bande-Dessinée (Belgian Comic-Strip Center) ★★ ☺ As you'll soon find out, Belgians are crazy for cartoons. The unique "CéBéBéDé" focuses on Belgium's own popular cartoon characters, like Lucky Luke, Thorgal, and, of course, Tintin, complete with red-and-white-checkered moon rocket, yet it doesn't neglect the likes of Superman, Batman, and the Green Lantern. The building, the Maisons des Waucquez, designed by Art Nouveau architect Victor Horta, is an attraction in itself.

Rue des Sables 20 (off bd. de Berlaimont). ✆ **02/219-19-80.** www.comicscenter.net. Admission 7.50€ adults, 6€ students and seniors, 3€ children 5–12, free for children 4 and under. Tues–Sun 10am–6pm. Closed Jan 1 and Dec 25. Métro: Gare Centrale.

Musée du Costume et de la Dentelle Honoring a once-vital industry—10,000 Bruxellois produced lace in the 18th century—that now operates in a reduced but still notable fashion, this recently expanded museum shows off particularly fine costumes and lace from 1599 to the present, and mounts frequently changing exhibitions.

Rue de la Violette 12 (near Grand-Place). ✆ **02/213-44-50.** Admission 3€ adults, 1.50€ children 6–16, free for children 5 and under. Mon–Tues and Thurs–Fri 10am–12:30pm and 1:30–5pm (until 4pm Oct–Mar); Sat–Sun 2–4:30pm. Closed Jan 1, May 1, Nov 1 and 11, and Dec 25. Métro: Gare Centrale.

Musée Horta 🎁 Brussels owes much of its rich Art Nouveau heritage to Victor Horta (1861–1947), a resident architect who led the development of the style. His home and studio in St-Gilles, restored to their original condition, showcase his use of flowing, sinuous shapes and colors, in both interior decoration and architecture.

Rue Américaine 25 (off chaussée de Charleroi). ✆ **02/543-04-90.** www.hortamuseum.be. Admission 7€ adults, 3.50€ seniors and students, 2.50€ children 5–18, free for children 4 and under. Tues–Sun 2–5:30pm. Closed national holidays. Tram: 81, 82, 91, or 92.

Musée Royal de l'Afrique Centrale (Royal Museum for Central Africa) ★★ Originally founded to celebrate Belgium's colonial empire in the Belgian Congo (now the Democratic Republic of Congo), this museum has moved beyond imperialism to feature exhibits on ethnography and environment, mostly in Africa, but also in Asia and South America. The beautiful grounds of this impressive museum are as much a draw as the exhibits inside. The collection includes some excellent animal dioramas, African sculpture, and other artwork, and even some of the colonial-era guns and artillery pieces that no doubt helped make Belgium's claim to its African colonies more persuasive. A modern perspective is added by environmental displays that explain desertification, the loss of rainforests, and the destruction of habitats.

Leuvensesteenweg 13, Tervuren (a suburban Flemish *gemeente*/district just east of Brussels). ✆ **02/769-52-11.** www.africamuseum.be. Admission 4€ adults, 1.50€ children 12–18, free for children 11 and under. Tues–Fri 10am–5pm; Sat–Sun 10am–6pm. Closed Jan 1, May 1, and Dec 25. Tram: 44 from Montgomery Métro station to Tervuren terminus.

Passport to Brussels

One of the best discounts is the **Brussels Card,** available from the Brussels International tourist office on the Grand-Place, and from hotels, museums, and offices of the STIB city transit authority. Valid for 1, 2, or 3 days, the card costs 24€, 34€, and 40€, respectively. It allows free use of public transportation; free and discounted admission to around 30 of the city's museums and attractions; and discounts at some restaurants and other venues, and on some guided tours.

Musées Royaux des Beaux-Arts de Belgique (Royal Museums of Fine Arts of Belgium) ★★★ In a vast museum of several buildings, this complex combines the **Musée d'Art Ancien** and the **Musée d'Art Moderne** under one roof, connected by a passage. The collection displays mostly Belgian works, from the 14th century to the 20th century. Included in the historical collection are Hans Memling's portraits from the late 15th century, which are marked by sharp lifelike details; works by Hieronymus Bosch; and Lucas Cranach's *Adam and Eve.* Be sure to see the works of Pieter Brueghel, including his *Adoration of the Magi,* and his unusual *Fall of the Rebel Angels,* with grotesque faces and beasts. Later artists represented include Rubens, Van Dyck, Frans Hals, and Rembrandt.

Next door, in a circular building connected to the main entrance, the modern art section has an emphasis on underground works—if only because the museum's eight floors are all below ground level. The overwhelming collection includes works by van Gogh, Matisse, Dalí, Ernst, Chagall, Miró, and local heroes Magritte, Delvaux, de Braekeleer, and Permeke.

Rue de la Régence 3 (at place Royale). ✆ **02/508-32-11.** www.fine-arts-museum.be. Admission 8€ adults, 5€ seniors, 2€ students, free for children 12 and under, free for everyone 1st Wed afternoon of the month (except during special exhibits). Tues–Sun 10am–5pm. Closed Jan 1, May 1, Nov 1 and 11, and Dec 25. Métro: Parc.

ROYAL BRUSSELS

Palais Royal (Royal Palace) ★ The King's Palace, which overlooks the Parc de Bruxelles, was begun in 1820 and had a grandiose Louis XVI–style face-lift in 1904. The older side wings date from the 18th century and are flanked by two pavilions, one of which sheltered numerous notables during the 1800s. Today the palace is used for state receptions. It contains the offices of King Albert II, though he and Queen Paola do not live there—their *pied-à-terre* is the Royal Palace at Laeken. The national flag flies when the sovereign is in Belgium.

Place des Palais. ✆ **02/551-20-20.** www.monarchie.be. Free admission. From 3rd week of July to late Sept (exact dates announced yearly). Tues–Sun 10:30am–4:30pm. Métro: Parc.

PARC DU CINQUANTENAIRE

Designed to celebrate the half centenary of Belgium's 1830 independence, the Cinquantenaire Park was a work in progress from the 1870s until well into the 20th century. Extensive gardens have at their heart a triumphal arch topped by a bronze four-horse chariot sculpture, representing *Brabant Raising the National Flag,* flanked by several fine museums.

Autoworld ☺ Even if you're not a car enthusiast, you'll find this display of 500 historic cars set in the hangar-like Palais Mondial fascinating. The collection starts with early motorized tricycles from 1899 and moves on to a 1911 Model T Ford, a 1924 Renault, a 1938 Cadillac that was the official White House car for FDR and Truman, a 1956 Cadillac used by Kennedy during his June 1963 visit to Berlin, and more.

Parc du Cinquantenaire 11. ✆ **02/736-41-65.** www.autoworld.be. Admission 6€ adults, 4.70€ students and seniors, 3€ children 6-13, free for children 5 and under. Apr-Sept daily 10am-6pm; Oct-Mar daily 10am-5pm. Closed Jan 1 and Dec 25. Métro: Mérode.

Musée du Cinquantenaire ★ This vast museum shows off an eclectic collection of antiques, decorative arts (tapestries, porcelain, silver, and sculptures), and archaeology. Some highlights are an Assyrian relief from the 9th century B.C., a Greek vase from the 6th century B.C., a tabletop model of imperial Rome in the 4th century A.D., the A.D. 1145 reliquary of Pope Alexander, some exceptional tapestries, and colossal statues from Easter Island.

Parc du Cinquantenaire 10. ✆ **02/741-72-11.** www.kmkg-mrah.be. Admission 5€ adults; 4€ seniors, students, and children 13-17; free for children 12 and under; free for everyone 1st Wed afternoon of the month (except during special exhibits) from 1pm. Tues-Fri 9:30am-5pm; Sat-Sun and holidays 10am-5pm. Closed Jan 1, May 1, Nov 1 and 11, and Dec 25. Métro: Mérode.

BRUPARCK

Built on the site of the 1958 Brussels World's Fair, this park (Métro: Heysel) is home to the **Atomium** and **Mini-Europe** (see below); the **Village,** a collection of restaurants and cafes; **Océade,** an indoor/outdoor watersports pavilion with water slides, pools, and saunas; a **planetarium;** and **Kinepolis,** a 26-screen movie multiplex. Ask about combination tickets if you plan to visit more than one Bruparck attraction.

Atomium ★ As the Eiffel Tower is the symbol of Paris, the Atomium is the symbol of Brussels, and, like Paris's landmark, it was built for a world's fair, the 1958 Brussels World's Fair. Rising 102m (335 ft.) like a giant plaything of the gods that's fallen to earth, the Atomium is an iron crystal magnified 165 billion times. Its metal-clad spheres, representing individual atoms, are connected by enclosed escalators and elevators. It's the topmost atom that attracts most people: a restaurant/observation deck that provides a sweeping panorama of the metropolitan area.

Bd. du Centenaire, Heysel. ✆ **02/475-47-77.** www.atomium.be. Admission 11€ adults; 8€ students, seniors, and children 12-18; 4€ children 6-11; free for children 5 and under. Daily 10am-6pm. Métro: Heysel.

Mini-Europe ★★ ☺ Because Brussels is the "capital of Europe," it's fitting that the city is home to a miniature rendering of all the Continent's most notable architectural sights. Even a few natural wonders and technological developments are represented. Built on a scale of 1/25 of the originals, Big Ben, the Leaning Tower of Pisa, the Seville bullring, the Channel Tunnel, the Brandenburg Gate, and more exhibit remarkable detail. Although children like Mini-Europe the best, adults certainly find it fun.

Bruparck, Heysel. ✆ **02/478-05-50.** www.minieurope.com. Admission 13€ adults, 9.80€ children 12 and under, free for children under 1.2m (4 ft.) accompanied by parent. Late Mar to June and Sept daily 9:30am-6pm; July-Aug daily 9:30am-8pm (except Aug Sat-Sun 9:30am-midnight); Oct-Dec and 1st week Jan 10am-6pm. Closed rest of Jan to late Mar. Métro: Heysel.

HISTORIC CHURCHES

Cathédrale des Sts-Michel-et-Gudule ★ Victor Hugo considered this magnificent church, dedicated to the city's patron St. Michael and to St. Gudula, to be the "purest flowering of the Gothic style." Begun in 1226, it was officially consecrated as a cathedral only in 1961. The 16th-century Hapsburg Emperor Charles V donated the superb stained-glass windows. Apart from these, the spare interior decoration focuses attention on its soaring columns and arches. The bright exterior stonework makes a fine sight. In the crypt and an associated archaeological zone are foundations and other construction elements from an earlier church dating from the 11th century. The Trésor (Treasury) is also worth visiting, for its religious vessels in gold, silver, and precious stones, and ecclesiastical vestments.

Parvis Ste-Gudule (off bd. de l'Impératrice 2 blocks west of Gare Centrale). ✆ **02/217-83-45.** www.cathedralestmichel.be. Cathedral free admission; crypt 1€; treasury 1€; archaeological zone 2.50€ (in all cases, free for children age 13 and under). Mon–Fri 7am–7pm (Oct–Mar 6pm); Sat–Sun 8:30am–7pm (Oct–Mar 6pm); tourist visits not permitted during services Sat from 3:30pm, Sun until 2pm. Métro: Gare Centrale.

Notre-Dame du Sablon This late-Gothic 15th- to 16th-century structure is noted for its fourfold gallery with brightly colored stained-glass windows, illuminated from the inside at night, in striking contrast with the gray-white Gothic arches and walls. Also worth seeing are the two baroque chapels, which are decorated with funeral symbols in white marble.

Rue Bodenbroeck 6 (at place du Grand Sablon). ✆ **02/511-57-41.** Free admission. Mon–Fri 9am–5pm; Sat–Sun 10am–6:30pm. Tram: 92, 93, or 94.

OTHER HISTORIC SQUARES

Considered classier than the Grand-Place (see earlier in this chapter) by the locals, though busy traffic diminishes your enjoyment of its cafe-terraces, **place du Grand Sablon ★★** (tram: 92, 93, or 94) is lined with gabled mansions. This is antiques territory, and many of those mansions house antiques stores or private art galleries, with pricey merchandise on display. On Saturday and Sunday an excellent antiques market sets up its stalls in front of Notre-Dame du Sablon Church (see above).

Across rue de la Régence, the Grand Sablon's little cousin, **place du Petit Sablon ★** (tram: 92, 93, or 94), has a small sculptured garden with a fountain and pool at its center. This magical little retreat from the city bustle is surrounded by wrought-iron railings, atop which stand 48 small statues of medieval guildsmen.

At the meeting point of rue de la Régence and rue Royale (streets on which stand many of the city's premier attractions), **place Royale ★** (tram: 92, 93, or 94) is graced by an equestrian statue of Duke Godefroid de Bouillon, leader of the First Crusade. Also on place Royale is the neoclassical St-Jacques-sur-Coudenberg Church.

PARKS

The most attractive park in town is the **Parc de Bruxelles ★★** (Métro: Parc), extending in front of the Palais Royal. Once the property of the dukes of Brabant, this well-designed park with geometrically divided paths running through it—which form the outline of Masonic symbols—became public in 1776. The many benches make it a fine place to stop for a picnic. It's also historic: The first shots in Belgium's 1830 war of independence were fired here. The park has been restored as close as possible to its 18th-century look, and the refurbished 1840s bandstand hosts regular summer concerts.

The large public park called the **Bois de la Cambre ★** begins at the top of avenue Louise in the southern section of Brussels (tram: 23, 90, 93, or 94). It gets busy on sunny weekends. Its centerpiece is a small lake with an island in its center that you can reach via an electrically operated pontoon. ***Note:*** Some busy roads run through the park and traffic moves fast on them, so be careful with children at these points.

Continuing south from the Bois, the **Forêt de Soignes ★** is no longer a park with playing areas and regularly mown grass, but a forest stretching almost to Waterloo; this is a great place for getting away from it all, particularly in the fall, when the colors are dazzling.

ORGANIZED TOURS

A guided 2¾-hour "Brussels City Tour" by bus is available from **Brussels City Tours,** rue de la Colline 8, off Grand-Place (✆ **02/513-77-44;** www.brussels-city-tours.com; Métro: Gare Centrale). Tours cost 27€ for adults; 24€ for students, seniors, and children ages 13 to 18; 14€ for children ages 6 to 12; and free for children 5 and under. You can book tours at most hotels, and arrangements can be made for hotel pickup.

From June 15 to September 15, **Le Bus Bavard,** rue des Thuyas 12 (✆ **02/673-18-35;** www.busbavard.be), operates a variety of fascinating city walking and bus tours through the historic center city, and parts of the city that the average visitor never sees. You hear about life in Brussels and get a real feel for the city. Most tours cost around 8€.

ARAU, bd. Adolphe Max 55 (✆ **02/219-33-45;** www.arau.org; Métro: De Brouckère), organizes tours that help you discover not only Brussels's countless treasures but also problems the city faces. It runs 3-hour themed coach tours: "Grand-Place and Its Surroundings," "Brussels 1900—Art Nouveau," "Brussels 1930—Art Deco," "Surprising Parks and Squares," and "Alternative Brussels." You are advised to book ahead. Tours by bus are 17€, and 32€ for those 25 and under; tours by foot are 10€; in both cases, children 11 and under are free. Tours take place on Saturday mornings from March to November; private group tours can be arranged year-round.

The Shopping Scene

Lace is the overwhelming favorite purchase, followed by crystal, jewelry, antiques, and pewter. Chocolate, beer, and other foods are more economical. And in souvenir stores you find replicas of *Manneken-Pis,* so you can bring the little guy home with you.

Don't look for many bargains. As a general rule, Upper Town around avenue Louise and Porte de Namur is more expensive than Lower Town around rue Neuve. You can enjoy a stroll along modern shopping promenades, the busiest of which is the pedestrians-only rue Neuve, starting at place de la Monnaie and running north to place Rogier: It's home to boutiques; big department stores, such as Inno and H&M; and several malls.

Some of the trendiest boutiques are on rue Antoine Dansaert, across from the Bourse. An interesting street for window-shopping, rue des Eperonniers, near the Grand-Place, hosts many small stores selling antiques, toys, old books, and clothing.

Tax Saver

If you spend over 125€ in some stores, and you are not a resident of the European Union, you can get a tax refund when you leave the E.U. Stores that display a TAX-FREE SHOPPING sign provide visitors who are not resident in the E.U. the form they need for recovering some of the 21% value-added tax (TVA) on purchases. At the airport, show the Customs officials your purchase and receipt and they'll stamp the form. Mail this form back to the Belgian Tax Bureau (the address is on the form) or bring it in directly to the Best Change office at the airport, which charges a small commission but gives you an on-the-spot refund.

STORES WORTH A VISIT

The **Galeries Royales St-Hubert** (Métro: Gare Centrale) is an airy arcade hosting expensive boutiques, cafes with outdoor terraces, and buskers playing classical music. Opened in 1847, architect Pierre Cluysenaer's Italian neo-Renaissance gallery has a touch of class and is well worth a stroll through, even if you have no intention of shopping. The elegant gallery is near the Grand-Place, between rue du Marché aux Herbes and rue de l'Ecuyer, and is split by rue des Bouchers.

In a former guild house, **Maison Antoine,** Grand-Place 26 (✆ **02/512-48-59;** Métro: Gare Centrale), is one of the best places in town to buy lace. The quality is superb, the service is friendly, and the prices aren't unreasonable.

Visit **De Boe,** rue de Flandre 36 (✆ **02/511-13-73;** Métro: Ste-Catherine), a small store near the Marché aux Poissons, for the heavenly aromas of roasted and blended coffee, a superb selection of wines in all price categories, and an array of specialty teas, spices, and epicurean snacks. **Dandoy,** rue au Beurre 31 (✆ **02/511-03-26;** Métro: Bourse), is where cookie and cake fans can try traditional Belgian specialties like spicy *speculoos* (traditional Belgian cookies made with brown sugar and cinnamon and baked in wooden molds) and *pain à la grecque* (caramelized, sugary, flaky pastries).

If you have a sweet tooth, you'll feel you're in heaven when you see Brussels's famous chocolate stores, filled with sumptuous soft-centered pralines, from around 12€ a kilogram (2¼ lb.). You find some of the best confections at **Chocolatier Mary,** rue Royale 73 (✆ **02/217-45-00;** Métro: Parc), supplier to the royal court; **Neuhaus,** Galerie de la Reine 25 (✆ **02/502-59-14;** Métro: Gare Centrale); **Wittamer,** place du Grand Sablon 12 (✆ **02/512-37-42;** tram: 92, 93, or 94); and **Léonidas,** bd. Anspach 46 (✆ **02/218-03-63;** Métro: Bourse).

For kids, pick up some Tintin mementos from **Boutique de Tintin,** rue de la Colline 13 (✆ **02/514-51-52;** Métro: Gare Centrale). **Waterstone's,** boulevard Adolphe Max 71–75 (✆ **02/219-27-08;** Métro: Rogier), has English-language books, newspapers, and magazines.

OUTDOOR MARKETS

The city's favorite *marché aux puces* (flea market) is the **Vieux Marché** (**Old Market;** Métro: Porte de Hal), on place du Jeu de Balle, a large cobblestone square in the Marolles district, open daily from 7am to 2pm. Every Sunday from 7am to 2pm, hundreds of merchants assemble their wares in a **street market** outside Gare du Midi (Métro: Gare du Midi), and because many of the merchants are of Arab origin, the scene resembles a casbah. It has many excellent food bargains, making it a perfect place to gather provisions for a few days. You can also find household items and odds and ends at low cost. Hold on to your wallet, though: The market attracts pickpockets.

Brussels After Dark

Although the city isn't as noted for its nightlife as some other European capitals, it has a full array of things to do. And if the range is narrower than in bigger cities like London and Paris, the quality is not. A listing of upcoming events—opera, classical music, dance, theater, live music, film, and other events—is in the *What's On* guide in the weekly English-language magazine ***The Bulletin.***

THE PERFORMING ARTS

An opera house in the grand style, the **Théâtre Royal de la Monnaie ★★**, place de la Monnaie (✆ **070/23-39-39;** www.lamonnaie.be; Métro: De Brouckère), is home to the Opéra Royal de la Monnaie, which has been called the best in the French-speaking world, and to the Orchestre Symphonique de la Monnaie. The resident modern dance company, Anne Theresa de Keersmaeker's Group Rosas, is noted for its original moves. The box office is open Tuesday to Saturday from 11am to 6pm. Tickets run 10€ to 150€.

The **BOZAR,** rue Ravenstein 23 (✆ **02/507-82-00;** www.bozar.be; Métro: Gare Centrale)—formerly the Palais des Beaux-Arts—is home to the Belgian National Orchestra. The box office is open Monday to Saturday from 11am to 6pm, with tickets running 10€ to 80€. The **Cirque Royal,** rue de l'Enseignement 81 (✆ **02/218-37-32;** www.botanique.be; Métro: Parc), formerly a real circus, now hosts music, opera, and ballet. The box office is open Tuesday to Saturday from 11am to 6pm, with tickets for 10€ to 75€.

LIVE-MUSIC CLUBS

Jazz is a popular but ever-changing scene. **L'Archiduc,** rue Antoine Dansaert 6 (✆ **02/512-06-52**), puts on jazz concerts on Saturday and Sunday. **Le Sounds,** rue de la Tulipe 28 (✆ **02/512-92-50**), has daily jazz concerts, and a workshop on Mondays at 7:30pm. For those who like their licks a tad restrained, there's a jazz brunch at the **Airport Sheraton Hotel,** facing the terminal building (✆ **02/725-10-00**), every Sunday from noon to 3pm.

DANCE CLUBS

Top clubs include the always popular **You,** rue Duquesnoy 18 (✆ **02/639-14-00;** Métro: Gare Centrale); **Le Fuse,** rue Blaes 208 (✆ **02/511-97-89;** bus: 20 or 48), for techno; and **Duke's Club,** in the Royal Windsor Hotel, rue Duquesnoy 5 (✆ **02/505-55-55;** Métro: Gare Centrale), fashionable for older hoofers.

GAY & LESBIAN CLUBS

Rue des Riches-Claires and **rue du Marché au Charbon** host gay and lesbian bars. **Macho 2,** rue du Marché au Charbon 108 (✆ **02/512-45-87;** Métro: Bourse), a block from rue des Riches-Claires, has a gay men's sauna, pool, steam room, and cafe. **Le Fuse** and **You** (see above) have gay nights.

Puppet Theater

Traditional Brussels marionette theater is performed at **Théâtre Royal de Toone,** impasse Schuddeveld 6, Petite rue des Bouchers 21 (✆ **02/217-27-23;** www.toone.be; Métro: Gare Centrale). In a tiny theater in the old **Toone VII** cafe, puppet master José Géal presents adaptations of classic tales like *Faust* and *The Three Musketeers.* Some performances are in English, others are in French, Dutch, German, or Bruxellois, but the plots and characters are so familiar that even if you don't understand a word, you'll be able to follow the action. Performances are Tuesday to Saturday at 8:30pm; tickets are 10€ for adults, and 7€ for seniors, students, and children (except Fri–Sat, when all pay full price).

For more information about clubs and gay life in Brussels, stop by the gay and lesbian community center, **Tels Quels,** rue du Marché au Charbon 81 (✆ **02/512-45-87;** Métro: Bourse), open Saturday to Thursday 5pm to 2am, Friday 5pm to 4am.

CAFES & BARS

The city's many watering holes run the gamut from Art Nouveau palaces to plain and convivial. You should linger a few hours in one, preferably savoring one of the incredible beers for which Belgium is famous. It's always satisfying to sit at a sidewalk cafe on the Grand-Place and drink in the beauty of the floodlit golden buildings ringing the square. Drinks on a Grand-Place terrace are more expensive than those in ordinary cafes, but once you've ordered one you can nurse it for hours—or until the waiter's patience wears out and he grabs the glass from you, empty or not.

The city's oldest cafe, in a 1690 building, **Le Roy d'Espagne,** Grand-Place 1 (✆ **02/513-08-07;** Métro: Gare Centrale), accommodates patrons in several areas. In addition to the outdoor tables, you can drink in a room preserving a 17th-century Flemish interior—a masterpiece of wooden architecture with a wooden walkway, wooden beams above, and a fireplace covered by a black metal hood. The fourth-floor view of the Grand-Place is spectacular. It's open daily from 10am to 1am.

Although its name means "Sudden Death," you'll likely survive **A la Mort Subite,** rue Montagne aux Herbes Potagères 7 (✆ **02/513-13-18;** Métro: Gare Centrale), a 1911 cafe with stained-glass mirrors, old photographs, paintings, and prints. A good place to enjoy an afternoon coffee or an evening beer, it's open daily from 10am to 1am. A block from the Grand-Place, in a 1642 house, **A l'Imaige de Nostre-Dame,** rue du Marché aux Herbes 6–8 (✆ **02/219-42-49;** Métro: Gare Centrale), is often filled with people of all ages enjoying reasonably priced beer amid wooden ceiling beams and old wooden tables. It's open daily from noon to midnight.

You can still enjoy a drink in the stunning setting of legendary Art Nouveau tavern **Le Falstaff,** rue Henri Maus 19 (✆ **02/511-87-99;** Métro: Bourse), though its cool image has suffered under new owners. It's open daily from 8am to around 3am (4am on weekends). Across the way, at **Le Cirio,** rue de la Bourse 18 (✆ **02/512-13-95;** Métro: Bourse), you sip your drink in quiet, refined surroundings that make the exercise seem worthwhile. It's open daily from 10am to 1am.

In a 17th-century building, **La Fleur en Papier Doré,** rue des Alexiens 53, off place de la Chapelle (✆ **02/511-16-59;** Métro: Bourse), calls itself a "temple of

Belgian Brews Pack a Punch

Be warned: Belgian beers are stronger than their American counterparts—alcohol content can be as high as 12%. Try a rich, dark Trappist ale brewed by monks from Chimay, Orval, Rochefort, Sint-Benedictus, Westmalle, and Westvleteren monasteries. Brussels is well known for its *lambic* beers, which use naturally occurring yeast for fermentation; they are often flavored with fruit, and come in bottles with champagne-type corks. Unlike any other beer, they're more akin to a sweet sparkling wine. *Gueuze,* a blend of young and aged lambic beers, is one of the least sweet. If you prefer something sweeter, try raspberry-flavored *framboise* or cherry-flavored *kriek. Faro* is a low-alcohol beer, sometimes sweetened or lightly spiced.

surrealism" because Magritte used to relax here. Despite the grandmotherly decor, the cafe attracts a wide assortment of arty types. On Friday and Saturday from 9 or 10pm, an accordion player pumps out some tunes, and there are occasional poetry readings upstairs. The cafe is open daily from 11am to 11pm.

In an early-1900s town house on the edge of the center city, **De Ultieme Hallucinatie,** rue Royale 316 (✆ **02/217-06-14;** Métro: Botanique), has rocky walls and plants along one side, a long marble-top bar along the other, and a small outdoor cafe area in back. You can choose from beers and wines (a wide selection), coffee, and a few snacks. Downstairs, a futuristic dance club has abstract outer-space art. The bar is open Monday to Friday from 11am to 3am, Saturday and Sunday from 4pm to 3am.

A Side Trip to Waterloo ★

Europe's Gettysburg, the battle that ended Napoleon's empire, was fought on rolling farmland near **Waterloo,** just south of Brussels. On June 18, 1815, 72,000 British, Dutch, Belgian, and German troops, aided before the day's end by around 40,000 Prussians, defeated the mighty Napoleon Bonaparte and his 76,000 French, leaving 40,000 dead and wounded on the field. Napoleon survived, but his attempt to rebuild his empire was crushed; he was exiled to the island of St. Helena, where he died 6 years later.

From Brussels, the TEC bus W departs twice hourly for Waterloo from Gare du Midi (Métro: Gare du Midi). The 18km (11-mile) ride takes 55 minutes and costs 3.25€. The bus stops at both the Wellington Museum in Waterloo itself and the battlefield visitor center, south of the town. By **car** from Brussels, take the ring road (R0) to exit 27 for Waterloo, and N5 south to the battlefield.

The battlefield remains much as it was on that fateful day. Before touring it, you should study a 360-degree **Panoramic Mural** and see a short audiovisual presentation of the battle, including scenes from Sergei Bondarchuk's epic movie *Waterloo,* at the **Centre du Visiteur,** route du Lion 252–254, Braine l'Alleud (✆ **02/385-19-12;** www.waterloo1815.be). To survey the battlefield, climb the nearby **Butte du Lion (Lion Mound),** a conical hill surmounted by a bronze lion, behind the visitor center. Across the road from the visitor center is the **Musée des Cires (Waxworks Museum),** where Napoleon, Wellington, Blücher, and other key participants appear as rather tatty wax figures.

These four sites are open daily April to October from 9:30am to 6:30pm and November to March from 10am to 5pm; closed January 1 and December 25. Admission to the visitor center is free. Admission to its audiovisual presentation and the four on-site attractions is 12€ for adults, 9€ for seniors and students, 7.50€ for children ages 6 to 17, and free for children 5 and under.

In Waterloo itself, you can fill in details of the battle at the **Musée Wellington,** chaussée de Bruxelles 147 (✆ **02/354-78-06;** www.museewellington.com), a former inn that served as Wellington's headquarters. It's open daily, April to September from 9:30am to 6:30pm and October to March from 10:30am to 5pm. Admission, which includes an audio guide (except for children 5 and under), is 5€ for adults, 4€ for seniors and students, 2€ for children ages 6 to 12, and free for children 5 and under.

BRUGES ★★★

Walking around the almost perfectly preserved city of Bruges is like taking a step back in time. From its 13th-century origins as a cloth-manufacturing town to its current incarnation as a tourism mecca, Bruges (its name is Brugge in Dutch) seems to have changed little. As in a fairy tale, swans glide down the winding canals and the stone houses look like they're made of gingerbread. Even though glass-fronted stores have taken over the ground floors of ancient buildings, and the swans scatter before tour boats chugging along the canals, Bruges has made the transition from medieval to modern with remarkable grace. The town seems revitalized rather than crushed by the tremendous influx of tourists.

Essentials

GETTING THERE

BY TRAIN Bruges is a 1-hour train ride from Brussels. Trains depart every hour; a one-way ticket is 20€ in first class, 13€ in second class. Bruges has good rail connections to Ghent, Antwerp, and the North Sea ferry ports of Oostende (Ostend) and Zeebrugge. For train schedule and fare information, call ✆ **02/528-28-28,** or visit **www.b-rail.be**. Bruges station (look out for BRUGGE, the town's Dutch name, on the destination boards) is on Stationsplein, 1.5km (1 mile) by foot from the center of town; to get there by bus, take any **De Lijn** (✆ **070/220-200;** www.delijn.be) bus for CENTRUM from outside the rail station and get out at the Markt.

BY BUS **Eurolines** (✆ **02/274-13-50;** www.eurolines.com) buses from Brussels, London, Paris, Amsterdam, and other cities arrive at the bus station adjoining Bruges rail station.

BY CAR If you're driving from Brussels or Ghent, take A10/E40. Drop off your car at a parking lot or garage (see "Getting Around," below). The network of one-way streets in the center city makes driving a trial.

VISITOR INFORMATION The tourist information office, **In & Uit Brugge,** Concertgebouw, 't Zand 34, 8000 Brugge (✆ **050/44-86-86;** fax 050/44-86-00; www.brugge.be), is open daily from 10am to 6pm (Thurs until 8pm). This friendly, efficient office has brochures that outline walking, coach, canal, and horse-drawn carriage tours, as well as detailed information on many sightseeing attractions. Ask for the complimentary annual ***events@brugge*** brochure and monthly ***Exit*** newsletter, both of them excellent directories of current goings-on.

A Card for Bruges

Should you plan to do a lot of sightseeing in Bruges, consider purchasing a **Brugge City Card** (www.bruggecity card.be). This card affords free admission to many city museums and attractions, a free canalboat tour or bus tour, a 60% reduction on the price of a 3-day public transportation pass, and more. The card costs 33€ for 48 hours and 38€ for 72 hours. In addition to purchasing the card online, you can buy one at locations around the city, including the Concertgebouw on 't Zand (see later in this chapter) and the railway station on Stationsplein (see above).

CITY LAYOUT Narrow streets fan out from two central squares, the **Markt** and the **Burg.** A network of canals threads its way to every section of the small city, and the center city is almost encircled by a canal that opens at its southern end to become a swan-filled lake, the **Minnewater**—this translates as Lake of Love, though the name actually comes from the Dutch *Binnen Water,* meaning Inner Water, or Harbor—bordered by the Begijnhof and a fine park.

GETTING AROUND Walking is by far the best way to see Bruges, since much of the center city is traffic free (but wear good walking shoes, as those charming cobblestones can be hard going).

BY BICYCLE Biking is a terrific way to get around town. You can rent a bike from the rail station for 10€ a day, plus a deposit. Some hotels and stores rent bikes, for 8€ to 10€ a day.

BY BUS **De Lijn** city buses (✆ **070/22-02-00;** www.delijn.be) depart from the bus station outside the rail station, and from the big square called 't Zand, west of the Markt. Several bus routes pass through the Markt.

BY TAXI There's a taxi stand outside the rail station (✆ **050/38-46-60**), and another at the Markt (✆ **050/33-44-44**).

BY CAR Movement by car through the center city is tightly restricted. Leave your car in your hotel's parking garage, if it has one. You can use one of the large, prominently signposted underground parking garages around the center city—these get expensive for long stays—or the inexpensive parking lot at the rail station, from where you can take a bus or walk into the heart of the city.

Where to Stay

Bruges's hotels fill up fast. Don't arrive without a reservation, particularly in summer.

EXPENSIVE

Die Swaene ★★★ This small hotel on the beautiful center-city Groenerei canal has been called one of the most romantic in Europe, thanks in part to the care lavished on it by the Hessels family. The comfortable rooms are elegantly and individually furnished, and the lounge, from 1779, was once the Guild Hall of the Tailors. You might be expected to lodge in an annex across the canal, where the rooms are luxurious enough but not so convenient—you have to recross the canal to take advantage of the main building's amenities, for instance. The in-house **Pergola**

Bruges

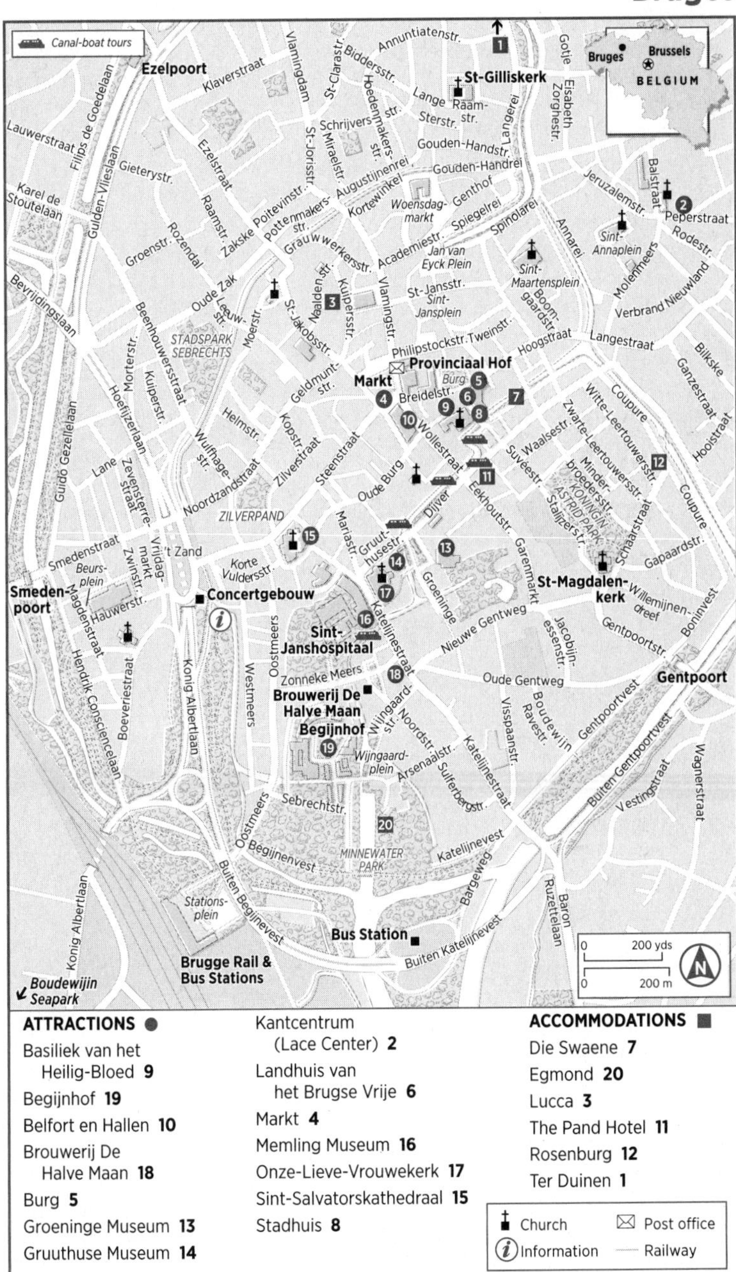
Canal-boat tours
Ezelpoort
St-Gilliskerk
Bruges
Brussels
BELGIUM
Provinciaal Hof
Markt
Burg
STADSPARK SEBRECHTS
ZILVERPAND
't Zand
Concertgebouw
Smedenpoort
Sint-Janshospitaal
Brouwerij De Halve Maan
Begijnhof
St-Magdalenkerk
Gentpoort
KONINGIN ASTRIDPARK
MINNEWATER PARK
Stationsplein
Bus Station
Brugge Rail & Bus Stations
Boudewijn Seapark
0 200 yds
0 200 m
N
ATTRACTIONS
Basiliek van het Heilig-Bloed 9
Begijnhof 19
Belfort en Hallen 10
Brouwerij De Halve Maan 18
Burg 5
Groeninge Museum 13
Gruuthuse Museum 14
Kantcentrum (Lace Center) 2
Landhuis van het Brugse Vrije 6
Markt 4
Memling Museum 16
Onze-Lieve-Vrouwekerk 17
Sint-Salvatorskathedraal 15
Stadhuis 8
ACCOMMODATIONS
Die Swaene 7
Egmond 20
Lucca 3
The Pand Hotel 11
Rosenburg 12
Ter Duinen 1
Church
Post office
Information
Railway

Kaffee restaurant has deservedly earned great reviews from guests and food critics alike.

Steenhouwersdijk 1 (across the canal from the Burg), 8000 Brugge. ✆ **050/34-27-98.** Fax 050/33-66-74. www.dieswaene-hotel.com. 32 units. 195€–295€ double; 360€–460€ suite. AE, DC, MC, V. Parking 15€. Bus: 1 or 6. **Amenities:** Restaurant; lounge; bar; babysitting; concierge; exercise room; heated indoor pool; room service; sauna; Wi-Fi in lobby (5€ per hour). *In room:* A/C (some units), TV, hair dryer, minibar.

The Pand Hotel ★★ On a side street just off of Bruges's handsome central canal, this hotel in a restored 18th-century mansion surrounded by plane trees is an oasis of tranquillity. Although it provides modern conveniences, its exquisite, old-fashioned furnishings lend special grace to comfortable rooms that (except for the suites) may be a little small for some tastes, though that's not unusual for old buildings in Bruges. Guests praise Mrs. Chris Vanhaecke-Dewaele for her hospitality and attention to detail.

Pandreitje 16 (off Rozenhoedkaai), 8000 Brugge. ✆ **050/34-06-66.** Fax 050/34-05-56. www.pandhotel.com. 24 units. 185€–362€ double; 279€–443€ suite. AE, DC, MC, V. Parking 24€. Bus: 1 or 6. **Amenities:** Bar; babysitting; concierge; Internet in lobby (free); room service; sauna; smoke-free rooms. *In room:* A/C, TV/DVD, hair dryer, minibar.

MODERATE

Egmond ★★ In a rambling mansion next to Minnewater Park, the Egmond has just eight rooms, but the lucky few who stay here will find ample space, plenty of family ambience, abundant local color, and lots of peace and tranquillity. All guest rooms are furnished in an individual style with views of the garden and Minnewater Park. Every afternoon, free coffee and tea are served in the new garden terrace or in the lounge, which has an 18th-century fireplace. At the "honesty bar" you can help yourself to a drink and leave the payment.

Minnewater 15 (at Minnewater Park), 8000 Brugge. ✆ **050/34-14-45.** Fax 050/34-29-40. www.egmond.be. 8 units. 98€–140€ double. Rates include buffet breakfast. MC, V. Parking 10€. Bus: 1 or 11. **Amenities:** Smoke-free rooms. *In room:* TV, hair dryer, Wi-Fi (free).

Rosenburg ★ This ultramodern brick hotel is set alongside a lovely canal, a short walk west from the center of Bruges. The hotel is an artful marriage of old Bruges style and modern amenities and fittings. Its spacious guest rooms are restfully decorated in warm colors (such as peach) and furnished with bamboo and rattan beds. Most have a view of the canal at Coupure.

Coupure 30 (close to Gentpoort), 8000 Brugge. ✆ **050/34-01-94.** Fax 050/34-35-39. www.rosenburg.be. 27 units. 100€–170€ double; 140€–350€ suite. AE, DC, MC, V. Limited street parking. Bus: 6. **Amenities:** Lounge; room service; smoke-free rooms. *In room:* TV, hair dryer, minibar.

Ter Duinen ★ This charming hotel is an ideal blend of classical style and modern conveniences. Guest rooms are ample in size and brightly decorated, and have modern furnishings. Some rooms have wooden ceiling beams, and some have a great view overlooking the tranquil Langerei canal, just north of the center city and within easy walking distance. Proprietors Marc and Lieve Bossu-Van Den Heuvel take a justified pride in their hotel.

Langerei 52 (at Kleine Nieuwstraat), 8000 Brugge. ✆ **050/33-04-37.** Fax 050/34-42-16. www.terduinenhotel.be. 20 units. 130€–167€ double. Rates include buffet breakfast. AE, DC, MC, V. Limited street parking. Bus: 4 or 8. **Amenities:** Lounge; room service. *In room:* A/C, TV, hair dryer.

INEXPENSIVE

Lucca ★ This mansion right in the heart of romantic Bruges was built in the 14th century by a wealthy merchant from Lucca, Italy. The high ceilings and wide halls convey a sense of luxury—not that this is entirely backed up in reality, though the guest rooms are in reasonable condition and sport pine furnishings. Units with bathrooms also have TVs. Breakfast is served in a cozy medieval cellar decorated with antiques.

Naaldenstraat 30 (off Sint-Jakobsstraat), 8000 Brugge. ✆ **050/34-20-67.** Fax 050/33-34-64. www.hotellucca.be. 19 units, 14 with bathroom. 53€ double without bathroom; 68€–88€ double with bathroom. Rates include buffet breakfast. AE, DC, MC, V. Limited street parking. Bus: 3 or 13. *In room:* TV (some units).

Where to Dine

VERY EXPENSIVE

De Karmeliet ★★★ BELGIAN/FRENCH In 1996, chef Geert Van Hecke became the first Flemish chef to be awarded three Michelin stars. He has described his award-winning menu as "international cuisine made with local products" that aims to merge French quality with Flemish quantity. Menu items might include lamb shoulder with local vegetables, or sea bass with a hazelnut, pistachio, and Parmesan crust. The result is outstanding, and the decor in the 1833 town house is as elegant as the cuisine deserves.

Langestraat 19 (off Hoogstraat). ✆ **050/33-82-59.** www.dekarmeliet.be. Reservations required. Main courses 55€–110€; fixed-price menus 80€–180€. AE, DC, MC, V. Tues–Sat noon–2pm and 7–9:30pm; Sun 7–9:30pm (except June–Sept). Bus: 6 or 16.

EXPENSIVE

't Pandreitje ★★ FRENCH/BELGIAN This restaurant is one of the nicest spots in town. It's in the shade of the medieval Market Hall's bell tower, just off Rozenhoedkaai, one of the most beautiful canal sides in Bruges. The interior of this Renaissance-era private home has been turned into an elegant Louis XVI setting from 1740 for a menu of classic dishes, such as roasted squab and grilled lamb ribs.

Pandreitje 6 (off Rozenhoedkaai). ✆ **050/33-11-90.** www.pandreitje.be. Reservations required. Main courses 30€–45€; fixed-price menus 50€–95€. AE, DC, MC, V. Mon–Tues and Thurs–Sat noon–2pm and 7–9:30pm. Bus: 1, 6, 11, or 16.

MODERATE

Bhavani ★ INDIAN For a change from traditional Belgian food, try the better of Bruges's pair of traditional Indian restaurants. It's a consistently fine performer across a wide range of Subcontinental cuisine—thali, tandoori, curry, vegetarian, and seafood—without being exactly outstanding in any category. The chicken tikka Maharaja is a good bet, as is the vegetarian thali. A mix of coziness, colonial atmosphere, Indian music, and exotic charm marks a setting that gives traditional Indian motifs a modern slant.

Simon Stevinplein 5 (off Oude Burg). ✆ **050/33-90-25.** Reservations recommended. Main courses 16€–25€; fixed-price menus 19€–27€. AE, DC, MC, V. Daily 4:30pm–12:30am. Bus: 6, 12, or 14.

Brasserie Erasmus ★ FLEMISH Small but popular, this is a great stop after viewing the cathedral and nearby museums. It serves a large variety of dishes, including a very good waterzooï with fish and rabbit in a beer sauce, and has around 150 brands of beer.

In the Hotel Erasmus, Wollestraat 35 (close to the Markt). ✆ **050/33-57-81.** Reservations recommended. Main courses 15€–25€; fixed-price menus 40€. MC, V. Tues–Sun noon–4pm (summer also Mon) and 6–11pm. Bus: All buses to Markt.

INEXPENSIVE

Lotus ★ VEGETARIAN Even nonvegetarians will likely enjoy the delicious lunch here. There are just two menu options—but you can choose from small, medium, or large servings—each with a hearty assortment of imaginatively prepared vegetables, served in a tranquil but cheery Scandinavian-style dining room.

Wapenmakersstraat 5 (off the Burg). ✆ **050/33-10-78.** Fixed-price lunch menus 9€–12€. No credit cards. Mon–Sat 11:30am–2pm. Bus: All buses to Markt.

Exploring Historic Bruges

THE MARKT ★★

Begin at this historic market square, where a **sculpture group** in the middle depicts two Flemish heroes, butcher Jan Breydel and weaver Pieter de Coninck. They led a bloody 1302 uprising against pro-French merchants and nobles who dominated the city, and then went on to an against-all-odds victory over French knights later the same year at the Battle of the Golden Spurs. The large neo-Gothic **Provinciaal Hof,** which was constructed in 1887, houses the government of West Flanders province.

Belfort en Hallen (Belfry and Market Halls) ★★ The 13th-to-16th-century belfry's octagonal tower soars 84m (276 ft.) and has a magnificent 47-bell carillon. If you have enough energy, climb the 366 steps to the summit for a panoramic view of the old town—you can pause for breath at the second-floor Treasury, where the town seal and charters were kept behind multiple wrought-iron grilles. Much of the city's cloth trade and other commerce was conducted in the Hallen in centuries past. Local art dealers now use the building for exhibits.

Markt. ✆ **050/44-87-11.** Admission 5€ adults, 4€ seniors and ages 13–25, free for children 12 and under. Daily 9:30am–5pm. Closed Jan 1, Ascension Day afternoon, and Dec 25. Bus: All buses to Markt.

THE BURG ★★★

An array of beautiful buildings, which adds up to a trip through the history of Bruges architecture, stands on this beautiful square just steps away from the Markt. During the 9th century, Count Baldwin "Iron Arm" of Flanders built a castle here at a then-tiny riverside settlement that would grow into Bruges.

Basiliek van het Heilig Bloed (Basilica of the Holy Blood) ★★ Since 1150, this basilica next to the Town Hall has been the repository of a fragment of cloth stained with what's said to be Christ's holy blood, brought to Bruges after the Second Crusade by the count of Flanders. On the ground floor is the original Romanesque St. Basil's Chapel. The relic is housed upstairs, in the basilica museum next door to the later, richly decorated Gothic Relic Chapel. It's kept inside a rock-crystal vial that's stored in a magnificent gold-and-silver reliquary, and is exposed frequently for the faithful to kiss. Every Ascension Day, in the Procession of the Holy Blood, the relic is carried through the streets, accompanied by costumed residents acting out biblical scenes.

Burg 10. ✆ **050/33-67-92.** www.holyblood.org. Basilica free admission; museum 1.50€ adults, 1€ students, free for children 12 and under. Apr–Sept daily 9:30am–noon and 2–6pm; Oct–Mar Thurs–Tues 10am–noon and 2–4pm, Wed 10am–noon. Closed Jan 1, Nov 1, and Dec 25. Bus: All buses to Markt.

Bruggemuseum-Brugse Vrije (Bruges Museum-Liberty of Bruges) This palace dates mostly from 1722 to 1727, when it replaced a 16th-century building as the seat of the Liberty of Bruges—the Liberty being the district around Bruges in the Middle Ages. The palace later became a courthouse and now houses the city council's administration. Inside, at no. 11A, is the **Renaissancezaal (Renaissance Hall) ★★**, the Liberty's council chamber, which has been restored to its original 16th-century condition. The hall has a superb black-marble fireplace decorated with an alabaster frieze and topped by an oak chimney piece carved with statues of Emperor Charles V, who visited Bruges in 1515, and his grandparents: Emperor Maximilian of Austria, Duchess Mary of Burgundy, King Ferdinand II of Aragon, and Queen Isabella I of Castile.

Burg 11. ✆ **050/44-87-11.** Courtyard free admission; Renaissance Hall (includes admission to Town Hall's Gothic Room; see below) 2€ adults, 1€ seniors, free for visitors 25 and under. Tues–Sun (also Easter Monday, Pentecost Monday) 9:30am–12:30pm and 1:30–5pm. Closed Jan 1, Ascension Day afternoon, and Dec 25. Bus: All buses to Markt.

Stadhuis (Town Hall) ★ This beautiful Gothic building, from the late 1300s, is Belgium's oldest. Don't miss the upstairs **Gotische Zaal (Gothic Room) ★★**, with an ornate, oak-carved vaulted ceiling and murals depicting biblical scenes and highlights of the town's history. The statues in the niches on the Town Hall facade are 1980s replacements for the originals, which had been painted by Jan van Eyck and were destroyed by the French in the 1790s.

Burg 12. ✆ **050/44-87-11.** Admission (includes admission to Renaissance Hall in the Palace of the Liberty of Bruges; see above) 2€ adults, 1€ seniors, free for visitors 25 and under. Tues–Sun (also Easter Monday, Pentecost Monday) 9:30am–5pm. Closed Jan 1, Ascension Day afternoon, and Dec 25. Bus: All buses to Markt.

TOP MUSEUMS & ATTRACTIONS

Groeninge Museum ★★★ This is one of Belgium's leading traditional museums of fine arts, with a collection that covers Low Countries painting from the 15th century to the 20th century. The Flemish Primitives Gallery has 30 works—which seem far from primitive—by such painters as Jan van Eyck (portrait of his wife, Margareta van Eyck), Rogier van der Weyden, Hieronymus Bosch (*The Last Judgment*), and Hans Memling. Works by Magritte and Delvaux are also on display.

Dijver 12. ✆ **050/44-87-11.** Admission (combined ticket with neighboring Arentshuis) 8€ adults, 6€ seniors, 1€ visitors 25 and under. Tues–Sun 9:30am–5pm (also Easter Monday, Pentecost Monday). Closed Jan 1, Ascension Day afternoon, and Dec 25. Bus: 1 or 11.

Gruuthuse Museum ★ In a courtyard next to the Groeninge Museum is the ornate mansion where Flemish nobleman Lodewijk van Gruuthuse lived in the 1400s. It contains thousands of antiques and antiquities, including paintings, sculptures, tapestries, lace, weapons, glassware, and richly carved furniture.

Dijver 17 (in a courtyard next to the Groeninge Museum). ✆ **050/44-87-11.** Admission 6€ adults, 5€ seniors, free for visitors 25 and under. Tues–Sun 9:30am–5pm (also Easter Monday, Pentecost Monday). Closed Jan 1, Ascension Day afternoon, and Dec 25. Bus: 1.

Kantcentrum (Lace Center) ★ Bruges lace is famous the world over, and there's no lack of stores to tempt you with the opportunity to take some home. The Lace Center, in the 15th-century Jerusalem Almshouse founded by the Adornes family of Genoese merchants, is where the ancient art of lace making is passed on to the next generation. In the afternoon, you get a firsthand look at craftspeople making items for future sale in the town's lace stores (handmade lace is the best, but it's more expensive than machine made).

Peperstraat 3A. ✆ **050/33-00-72.** www.kantcentrum.com. Admission 2.50€ adults, 1.50€ seniors and children 7–12, free for children 6 and under. Mon–Sat 10am–5pm. Closed holidays. Bus: 6 or 16.

Memling in Sint-Jan ★★ The former Sint-Janshospitaal (Hospital of St. John), where the earliest wards date from the 13th century, houses a magnificent collection of paintings by the German-born artist Hans Memling (ca. 1440–94), who moved to Bruges in 1465. You can view masterpieces like his triptych altarpiece of St. John the Baptist and St. John the Evangelist, which consists of the paintings *The Mystic Marriage of St. Catherine,* the *Shrine of St. Ursula,* and the *Virgin with Child and Apple.* A 17th-century apothecary in the cloisters near the hospital entrance is furnished as it was when the building's main function was to care for the sick.

Mariastraat. ✆ **050/44-87-11.** Admission 8€ adults, 6€ seniors, free for visitors 25 and under. Tues–Sun 9:30am–5pm (also Easter Monday, Pentecost Monday). Closed Jan 1, Ascension Day afternoon, and Dec 25. Bus: 1.

SIGHTS OF RELIGIOUS INTEREST

One of the most tranquil spots in Bruges is the **Begijnhof ★★**, Wijngaardstraat (✆ **050/33-00-11;** bus: 1). Begijns were religious women, similar to nuns, who accepted vows of chastity and obedience but drew the line at poverty. Today, the begijns are no more, and the Begijnhof is occupied by Benedictine nuns who try to keep the begijn traditions alive. Little whitewashed houses surrounding a lawn with trees make a marvelous place of escape. One of the begijns' houses has been set up as a museum. The house is open March and October to November, daily 10:30am to noon and 1:45 to 5pm; April to September, daily 10am to noon and 1:45 to 5:30pm (6pm Sun); December to February, Wednesday, Thursday, Saturday, Sunday 2:45 to 4:15pm, and Friday 1:45 to 6pm. Admission is 2€ adults, 1€ children ages 5 to 18, and free for children 4 and under. The Begijnhof itself is permanently open, and admission is free.

Onze-Lieve-Vrouwekerk (Church of Our Lady) ★★ It took 2 centuries (13th–15th) to build the magnificent Church of Our Lady, and its soaring spire, 122m (400 ft.) high, is visible from a wide area around Bruges. Among its many art treasures are a marvelous marble ***Madonna and Child*** **★★★** by Michelangelo (one of his few works outside Italy); the *Crucifixion,* a painting by Anthony Van Dyck; and inside the church sanctuary the impressive side-by-side bronze **tomb sculptures ★** of Charles the Bold of Burgundy (d. 1477) and his daughter Mary of Burgundy (d. 1482).

Onze-Lieve-Vrouwekerkhof-Zuid (at Mariastraat). ✆ **050/34-53-14.** Church and *Madonna and Child* altar free admission; sanctuary of Charles and Mary and museum 2€ adults, 1€ seniors, free for visitors 25 and under. Mon–Fri 9:30am–5pm; Sat 9:30am–4:45pm; Sun 1:30–5pm. Bus: 1.

Sint-Salvatorskathedraal (Holy Savior's Cathedral) This mainly Gothic church with a 100m (328-ft.) belfry has been Bruges's cathedral since 1834. The 15th-century wooden choir stalls flanking the altar bear a complete set of escutcheons of the Knights of the Golden Fleece, who held a chapter meeting here in 1478. In the Cathedral Museum (Mon–Fri 2–5pm; Sun 3–5pm) is the *Martyrdom of St. Hippolytus* altarpiece by Dirk Bouts with a side panel by Hugo van der Goes, and the Cathedral Treasury of gold and silver religious vessels, reliquaries, and Episcopal vestments.

Sint-Salvatorskerkhof (off Steenstraat). ✆ **050/33-68-41.** www.sintsalvator.be. Cathedral free admission; treasury 2€ adults, 1€ seniors, free for visitors 25 and under. Museum: Mon 2–5:45pm; Tues–Fri 8:30–11:45am and 2–5:45pm; Sat 8:30–11:45am and 2–3:30pm; Sun 9–10:15am and 2–5:45pm; closed to casual visitors during services. Treasury: Sun–Fri 2–5pm. Bus: most center-city buses.

A BRUGES BREWERY

Brouwerij De Halve Maan (Half-Moon Brewery) ★ The brewery here was turning out ale at least as long ago as 1546. Today it produces Bruges's famous Straffe Hendrik beer, a strapping blond ale that can be sampled in the brewery's own brasserie, after a perusal of the facility.

Walplein 26. ✆ **050/33-26-97.** www.halvemaan.be. Admission 5.50€. Guided visits Apr–Oct Mon–Fri on the hour 11am–4pm, Sat–Sun on the hour 11am–5pm; Nov–Mar Mon–Fri on the hour 11am–3pm, Sat–Sun on the hour 11am–4pm. Bus: 1.

ESPECIALLY FOR KIDS

The **Boudewijn Seapark ★**, De Baeckestraat 12 (✆ **050/38-38-38;** www.boudewijnpark.be; bus: 7 or 17), in the southern suburb of Sint-Michiels, is a big favorite with children. For some unfathomable reason, they seem to prefer its rides, paddle boats, and dolphins over Bruges's many historic treasures. Strange but true! The park is open Easter holidays, daily 11am to 5pm; May to June, daily 10:30am to 5pm (6pm Sun and holidays); July to August, daily 10am to 6pm; September, Wednesday and Saturday 10:30am to 5pm, and Sunday 10:30am to 6pm. Admission is 24€ for adults; 20€ for seniors, people of reduced mobility, and children over 1m (39 in.) and 11 and under; and free for children under 1m (39 in.).

Boat Trips & Other Organized Tours

Be sure to take a **boat trip ★★★** on the canals, on board one of the open-top tour boats that cruise year-round from five departure points around the center city, all marked with an anchor icon on maps available from the tourist office. The boats operate March to November, daily from 10am to 6pm; and December to February, Saturday, Sunday, and school holidays from 10am to 6pm (except if the canals are frozen). A half-hour cruise is 6.90€ for adults, 3.20€ for children ages 4 to 11 accompanied by an adult, and free for children 3 and under.

Another lovely way to tour Bruges is by **horse-drawn carriage.** From March to November, carriages are stationed on the Burg (Wed on the Markt); a 30-minute ride is 36€ for a carriage, which holds up to five people.

Minivan tours by **City Tour Brugge** (✆ **050/35-50-24;** www.citytour.be) last 50 minutes and depart hourly every day from the Markt. The first tour departs at 10am; the last tour departs at 8pm July to September, at 7pm April to June, at 6pm October, at 5pm March, and at 4pm November to February. Fares are 15€ for adults, 8.50€ children ages 6 to 11, free for children 5 and under, and 30€ for a family of two adults and two children.

If you'd like a qualified guide to accompany you, the tourist office can provide one for 50€ for the first 2 hours, and 25€ for each additional hour. In July and August, join a daily guided **walking tour** at 3pm from the tourist office for 8€, and free for children 11 and under.

You can ride through Bruges, and get out of town into the West Flanders countryside, on a bicycling tour with **QuasiMundo Biketours Brugge** (© **050/33-07-75;** www.quasimundo.eu). Call ahead to book; meeting and departure point is the Burg. Tours cost 24€ for adults, 20€ for students 25 and under, and free for children 7 and under.

Bruges After Dark

For information on what's on and where, pick up a copy of the free monthly ***Exit*** brochure from the tourist office.

THE PERFORMING ARTS Classical music, opera, and ballet are performed at the ultramodern **Concertgebouw,** 't Zand 34 (© **050/47-69-99;** www.concertgebouw.be). The **Koninklijke Stadsschouwburg,** Vlamingstraat 29 (© **050/44-30-60;** www.cultuurcentrumbrugge.be), from 1869, features theater (mostly in Dutch) and dance.

PERIOD THEATER Step back in time to medieval Bruges, at Brugge Anno 1468, Vlamingstraat 84–86 (© **050/34-75-72;** www.celebrations-entertainment.be), in a former Jesuit church. Players re-create the wedding of Duke Charles the Bold of Burgundy to Duchess Margaret of York while the audience piles into a period banquet. Performances take place April to October, Friday and Saturday from 7:30 to 10:30pm; and November to March, Saturday from 7:30 to 10:30pm. Tickets are 30€ to 73€ for adults, 50% of the adult price for children ages 11 to 14, 13€ for children ages 6 to 10, and free for children 5 and under.

BARS & TAVERNS Traditional cafe **'t Brugs Beertje,** Kemelstraat 5 (© **050/33-96-16**), serves more than 300 kinds of beer. **'t Dreupelhuisje,** Kemelstraat 9 (© **050/34-24-21**), does something similar with *jenever* (a ginlike spirit), serving dozens of craft-produced examples of this deadly art. **Gran Kaffee De Passage,** Dweersstraat 26 (© **050/34-02-32**), is a quiet and elegant spot to sip a drink.

GHENT ★★

Austere but more authentic than Bruges, Ghent (it is written *Gent* in Dutch, and you may see it as *Gand* in French) has been spruced up and has never looked so good. This historic seat of the powerful counts of Flanders, at the confluence of the Scheldt and Leie rivers, has plenty of cobblestone streets, meandering canals, and antique Flemish architecture.

Essentials

GETTING THERE

BY TRAIN Ghent is a 35-minute train ride from Brussels. Trains depart every 20 minutes or so; tickets cost 13€ in first class, 8.10€ in second class. For schedule and fare information, call © **02/528-28-28,** or visit **www.b-rail.be**. The city's main rail station, **Gent-Sint-Pieters,** is 1.5km (1 mile) south of the center city, on Maria Hendrikaplein. To get quickly and easily to the heart of town, take tram no. 1 from the first platform under the bridge to your left as you exit the station, and get out at Korenmarkt.

BY CAR Take A10/E40 from both Brussels and Bruges.

VISITOR INFORMATION The excellent **Toerisme Gent Infokantoor (Ghent Tourist Information Office),** Raadskelder (Council Cellar), Botermarkt 17A, 9000 Gent (© **09/266-56-60;** fax 09/266-56-73; www.visitgent.be), in the

Ghent

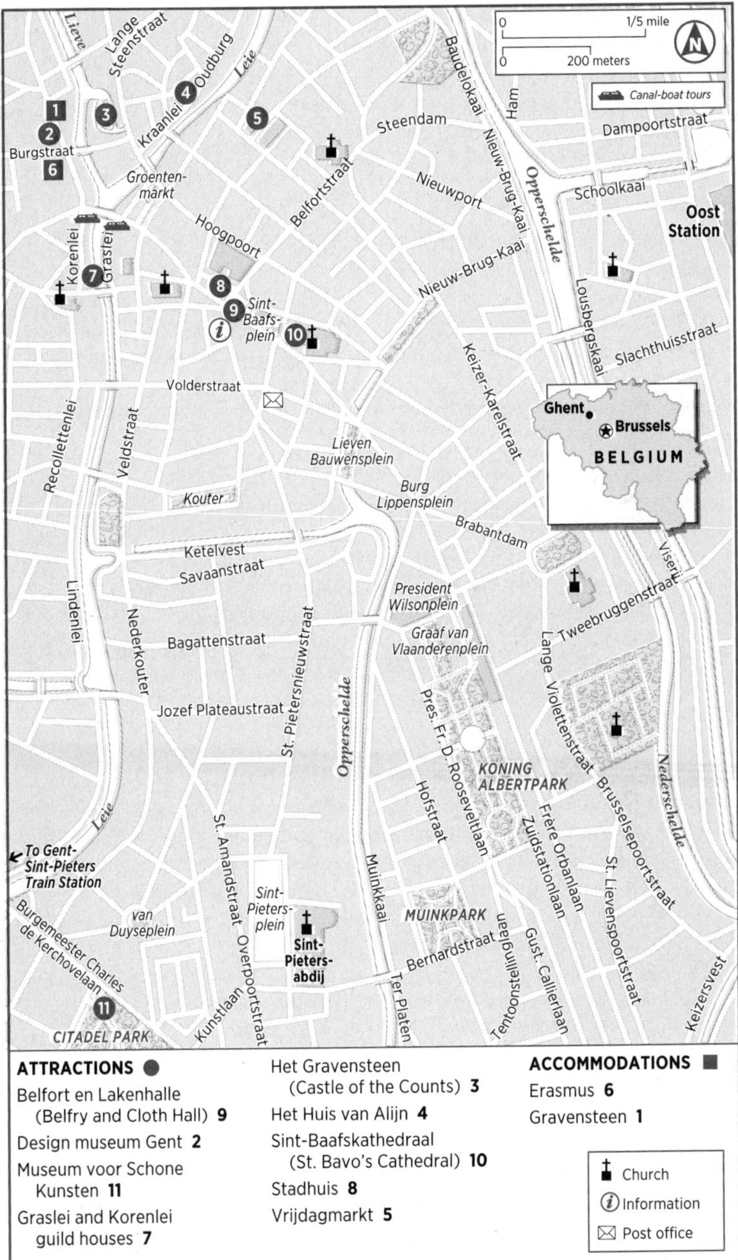
0 1/5 mile
0 200 meters
N
Canal-boat tours
Lieve
Lange Steenstraat
Oudburg
Leie
Kraanlei
Burgstraat
Groenten-markt
Steendam
Baudelokaai
Ham
Dampoortstraat
Nieuw-Brug-Kaai
Oppersschelde
Schoolkaai
Oost Station
Nieuwport
Belfortstraat
Hoogpoort
Korenlei
Graslei
Sint-Baafs-plein
Lousbergskaai
Slachthuisstraat
Keizer-Karelstraat
Volderstraat
Ghent
Brussels
BELGIUM
Lieven Bauwensplein
Recollettenlei
Veldstraat
Kouter
Burg Lippensplein
Brabantdam
Ketelvest
Savaanstraat
President Wilsonplein
Graaf van Vlaanderenplein
Tweebruggenstraat
Visserij
Lindenlei
Nederkouter
Bagattenstraat
St. Pietersnieuwstraat
Lange Violettenstraat
Jozef Plateaustraat
Pres. Fr. D. Rooseveltlaan
KONING ALBERTPARK
Nederschelde
Hofstraat
Zuidstationlaan
Frère Orbanlaan
Brusselsepoortstraat
St. Amandstraat
To Gent-Sint-Pieters Train Station
Sint-Pieters-plein
Sint-Pieters-abdij
Muinkkaai
MUINKPARK
St. Lievenspoortstraat
Burgemeester Charles de Kerchovelaan
van Duyseplein
Overpoortstraat
Bernardstraat
Tentoonstellingslaan
Gust. Callierlaan
Keizersvest
Kunstlaan
Ter Platen
CITADEL PARK
ATTRACTIONS
Belfort en Lakenhalle (Belfry and Cloth Hall) 9
Design museum Gent 2
Museum voor Schone Kunsten 11
Graslei and Korenlei guild houses 7
Het Gravensteen (Castle of the Counts) 3
Het Huis van Alijn 4
Sint-Baafskathedraal (St. Bavo's Cathedral) 10
Stadhuis 8
Vrijdagmarkt 5
ACCOMMODATIONS
Erasmus 6
Gravensteen 1
Church
Information
Post office

Belfort (Belfry), is open April to October daily from 9:30am to 6:30pm, and November to March daily from 9:30am to 4:30pm.

GETTING AROUND Ghent has a fine public transportation network (✆ **09/210-94-91**) of **trams** and **buses**—and a single **trolleybus** line, no. 3. Many lines converge at central Korenmarkt and at Gent-Sint-Pieters rail station in the south of the city. Walking is the best way to view the heart of town and experience its combination of history and modernity at a human pace. Beyond the center city, use public transportation. For a **taxi,** call **V-Tax** (✆ **09/222-22-22**).

Where to Stay

Erasmus ★ Each room is different in this converted 16th-century house, and all are plush, furnished with antiques and knickknacks. Rooms have high oak-beam ceilings, and bathrooms are modern. Some rooms have leaded-glass windows, some overlook a carefully manicured inner garden, and some have elaborate marble fireplaces. Breakfast is served in an impressive room that would have pleased the counts of Flanders.

Poel 25 (off Sint-Michielsstraat), 9000 Gent. ✆ **09/224-21-95.** Fax 09/233-42-41. www.erasmushotel.be. 11 units. 99€–150€ double. Rates include buffet breakfast. AE, MC, V. Limited street parking. **Amenities:** Bar. *In room:* TV, hair dryer.

Gravensteen ★★ You enter this lovely mansion, built in 1865 as the home of a Ghent textile baron, through the old carriageway (made up of ornamented pillars and an impressive wall niche occupied by a marble statue), which sets the tone for what you find inside. The elegant, high-ceilinged parlor is a sophisticated blend of pastels, gracious modern furnishings, and antiques, with a small bar tucked into one corner. The rooms are attractive and comfortably furnished.

Jan Breydelstraat 35 (close to the Castle of the Counts), 9000 Gent. ✆ **09/225-11-50.** Fax 09/225-18-50. www.gravensteen.be. 49 units. 150€–210€ double. AE, DC, MC, V. Parking 10€. Tram: 1 or 4 to Sint-Veerleplein. **Amenities:** Bar; lounge; exercise room; sauna. *In room:* A/C (some units), TV, hair dryer, minibar, Wi-Fi (20€ per 24 hr.).

Where to Dine

Brasserie Pakhuis ★ FLEMISH/CONTINENTAL In a town where the Middle Ages are *big,* this brasserie is almost modern and certainly hip. In fact, Pakhuis (which means "warehouse" in Dutch) may be a little too conscious of its own sense of style. The oyster and seafood platters are notable, and you won't go wrong with meat-based offerings like baked ham in a mustard sauce, or Flemish favorites like waterzooï and *garnaalkroketten* (shrimp croquettes).

Schuurkenstraat 4 (off Veldstraat). ✆ **09/223-55-55.** www.pakhuis.be. Reservations accepted. Main courses 11€–21€; fixed-price menus 25€–41€. AE, DC, MC, V. Mon–Thurs 11:30am–1am; Fri–Sat 11:30am–2am (full meals at lunch and dinner only).

Keizershof ★★ BELGIAN/CONTINENTAL Convivial and trendy, this place on the garish market square has an attractively informal ambience. Behind its narrow, 17th-century baroque facade, even a capacity crowd of 150 diners can seem sparsely dispersed at the plain wood tables on multiple floors around a central stairwell. The decor beneath the timber ceiling beams is spare, tastefully tattered, and speckled with paintings by local artists. Service for office workers doing lunch is fast but not furious; in the evenings you're expected to linger. In summer, you can dine alfresco in a courtyard at the rear.

Vrijdagmarkt 47. ✆**09/223-44-46.** Reservations accepted. Main courses 15€–21€. AE, MC, V. Tues–Sat noon–2:30pm and 6–11pm. Tram: 1 or 4 to Geldmunt.

Exploring Historic Ghent

Belfort en Lakenhalle (Belfry and Cloth Hall) ★★ These form a glorious medieval ensemble. From the 14th-century Belfry, great bells have rung out Ghent's civic pride down through the centuries, and a 54-bell carillon does so today. You can get high in the belfry with a guide and the aid of an elevator. The Cloth Hall of 1425 was the gathering place of medieval wool and cloth merchants.

Emile Braunplein. ✆**09/223-99-22.** Admission 3€ adults, 2.50€ seniors and students, free for children 12 and under. Mid-Mar to mid-Nov daily 10am–12:30pm and 2–6pm. Free guided tours of Belfry May–Sept 2:10, 3:10, and 4:10pm. Tram: 1 or 4 to Sint-Baafsplein.

Design museum Gent ★ Something of a split personality, this worthwhile museum is housed in the Hotel de Coninck, an elegant baroque mansion dating from 1755 that's been joined by an ultramodern extension at the rear. Its collection ranges through a series of period rooms furnished and decorated in 18th- and 19th-century style, in the old place, and modern design in the new. Tapestries and a collection of Chinese porcelain are among the stellar items in the former setting. The new wing is strong on Art Nouveau—from Belgian masters of the genre Victor Horta, Henry van de Velde, and Paul Hankar, among others—and Art Deco design.

Jan Breydelstraat 5 (off Korenlei). ✆ **09/267-99-99.** http://design.museum.gent.be. Admission 5€ adults, 3.75€ seniors, free for visitors 18 and under. Tues–Sun 10am–6pm. Closed Jan 1 and Dec 25–26 and 31. Tram: 1 or 4 to Sint-Veerleplein.

Het Gravensteen (Castle of the Counts) ★ Formidable and forbidding, the castle was designed by the counts of Flanders to send a clear message to rebellion-inclined Gentenaars. Surrounded by the waters of the Leie River, the castle begun by Count Philip of Alsace in 1180 has walls 2m (6½ ft.) thick, and battlements and turrets. If these failed to intimidate the populace, the counts could always turn to a well-equipped torture chamber; some of its accouterments are on display in a small museum.

Sint-Veerleplein. ✆**09/225-93-06.** Admission 8€ adults, 6€ seniors and visitors 19–26, free for visitors 18 and under. Apr–Sept daily 9am–6pm; Oct–Mar daily 9am–5pm. Closed Jan 1 and Dec 24–25 and 31. Tram: 1 or 4 to Sint-Veerleplein.

Museum voor Schone Kunsten (Museum of Fine Arts) ★ In a park close to Sint-Pieters rail station, this museum is home to old and new masterpieces, including works by Van der Weyden, Brueghel, Rubens, Van Dyck, and Bosch, along with moderns like James Ensor and Constant Permeke.

Citadelpark. ✆**09/240-07-00.** www.mskgent.be. Admission 5€ adults, 3.75€ seniors and ages 19–26, free for visitors 18 and under. Tues–Sun 10am–6pm. Closed Jan 1 and Dec 25–26. Bus: 8, 55, or 58.

Sint-Baafskathedraal (St. Bavo's Cathedral) ★★★ The 14th-century cathedral's plain Gothic exterior belies a splendid baroque interior and some priceless art. A 24-panel altarpiece, *The Adoration of the Mystic Lamb,* completed by Jan van Eyck in 1432, is St. Bavo's showpiece. Other treasures include Rubens's *The Conversion of St. Bavo* (1624), in the Rubens Chapel off the semicircular ambulatory behind the high altar.

Sint-Baafsplein. ✆ **09/269-20-45.** Cathedral free admission; *Mystic Lamb* chapel and crypt 2.50€ adults (includes audio guide in English), 1.50€ children 6–12, free for children 5 and under. Cathedral

Apr–Oct Mon–Sat 8:30am–6pm, Sun 1–6pm; Nov–Mar Mon–Sat 8:30am–5pm, Sun 1–5pm; chapel and crypt Apr–Oct Mon–Sat 9:30am–5pm, Sun 1–5pm; Nov–Mar Mon–Sat 10:30am–4pm, Sun 1–4pm. Tram: 1 or 4 to Sint-Baafsplein.

MORE PLACES OF INTEREST

A row of gabled **guild houses** ★ built along **Graslei** between the 1200s and 1600s, when the waterway was Ghent's harbor, forms an ensemble of colored facades reflected on the Leie River. To view them as a whole, cross the bridge over the Leie to **Korenlei,** and stroll along the bank. These buildings were once the headquarters of the craftsmen, tradespeople, and merchants who formed the city's commercial core.

In the **Vrijdagmarkt,** a statue of Jacob Van Arteveld pays tribute to a rebel hero of the 1300s. This large, lively square hosts a street market every Friday.

The mixed Renaissance and Gothic style of the **Stadhuis (Town Hall),** Botermarkt 1, reflects a construction period that ran from 1518 until the 18th century. In an upstairs chamber called the **Pacificatiezaal** was signed the 1567 Pacification of Ghent, by which the Low Countries repudiated Spanish rule and declared religious freedom. The building can be visited only by guided tour from the tourist office (see above).

Boat Trips & Other Organized Tours

A **boat trip** ★ on the canals with **Rederij Dewaele** (✆ **09/223-88-53;** www.debootjesvangent.be) is a good way to view the city's highlights. Tour boats sail from Graslei and Korenlei April to October, daily from 10am to 6pm; November to March, on weekends from 11am to 4pm. Forty-minute cruises cost 6€ for adults, 5.50€ for seniors, 3.50€ for children ages 3 to 12, and free for children 2 and under; longer tours are available.

If you'd like a qualified guide to accompany you, the tourist office can provide one for 65€ for 2 hours, 80€ for 3 hours, and 30€ for each subsequent hour. May to November, you can join a daily guided **walking tour** at 2:30pm (Apr, weekends only) from the tourist office for 7€, and free for children 11 and under.

Easter to October, tours by **horse-drawn carriage** (✆ **09/227-62-46**) depart from Sint-Baafsplein daily from 10am to 6pm. A half-hour ride is 25€ for a four- or five-seat carriage.

Ghent After Dark

THE PERFORMING ARTS Opera is performed at the 19th-century **Vlaamse Opera,** Schouwburgstraat 3 (✆ **09/225-24-25;** www.vlaamseopera.be).

BARS & TAVERNS You should have a memorable evening in any one of Ghent's atmospheric cafes. **De Witte Leeuw,** Graslei 6 (✆ **09/233-37-33**), has a 17th-century setting and more than 300 varieties of beer. At **Dulle Griet,** Vrijdagmarkt 50 (✆ **09/224-24-55**), also known as Bier Academie, you'll be asked to deposit one of your shoes before being given a potent Kwak beer in a too-collectible glass with a wood frame that allows the glass to stand up.

Het Waterhuis aan de Bierkant, Groentenmarkt 9 (✆ **09/225-06-80**), has more than 100 different Belgian beers, including locally made Stopken. A couple of doors along, **'t Dreupelkot,** Groentenmarkt 12 (✆ **09/224-21-20**), specializes in deadly little glasses of *jenever* (a stiff spirit similar to gin), of which it has 100 varieties. Across the tram lines, the tiny **'t Galgenhuisje,** Groentenmarkt 5 (✆ **09/233-42-51**), is popular with students.

THE CZECH REPUBLIC

by Mark Baker

The Czech Republic, comprising the ancient kingdoms of Bohemia, Moravia, and Silesia, is the westernmost of the former Soviet satellite countries and the best place to explore what used to be the other side of the iron curtain. It's certainly one of the most progressive. In May 2004, nearly 15 years after 1989's bloodless "Velvet Revolution" over Communism and over a decade after the peaceful split with the Slovak part of the former Czechoslovakia, the Czechs topped the list of new states admitted to the European Union.

If you have time to visit only one eastern European city, it should be Prague—widely regarded as one of the most beautiful cities in Europe, if not the world. The quirky and compact heart of Bohemia is a jumble of architecture. Gothic bestrides baroque, Renaissance adjoins cubist, with a splash of socialist realism and postmodern kitsch thrown in for good measure. On the hills and plains fronting the River Vltava you will glimpse the triumphs and tragedies of the past 10 centuries spiked with the peculiarity of the post-Communist reconstruction.

But Prague isn't the Czech Republic's only draw. Visitors are flocking to west Bohemia's world-renowned spas, which have been restored to their Victorian-era splendor, and to its many historic castles.

PRAGUE

In retrospect, the first years after the 1989 Velvet Revolution that overthrew the Communist government in power were a little rocky. The city suffered from a chronic shortage of hotel rooms, restaurant food was mediocre, and everything from the quality of the service to the state of the trains was second-rate.

The good news is that Prague has *finally* arrived. The years 2008 and 2009 saw the opening of no fewer than three five-star hotels to add to an already impressive list of deluxe properties. Looking over the lodging choices in Malá Strana alone, many in restored Renaissance and baroque palaces, it's hard to find a more stylish bunch anywhere in Europe.

All this progress has come at a price—literally. Prague is no longer that bargain-basement tourist outlet of yesteryear, where a meal on the town would set you back a couple of dollars and a glass of beer 25¢. But that's okay. Today's city is cleaner, livelier, more fun, and simply better than it was. Prague is worth the splurge.

Essentials

GETTING THERE

BY PLANE **Prague Airport** (code PRG; ✆ **220-113-314;** www.prg.aero) is the main international air gateway to the Czech Republic. The airport lies in the suburb of Ruzyně about 18km (11 miles) northwest of the center. The airport has two passenger terminals: North 1 and North 2 (in Czech: *Severin 1* and *Severin 2*). North 1 handles destinations outside the European Union, including overseas flights to and from the U.S. as well as flights from the U.K. (which is outside the E.U.'s Schengen common border zone). North 2 handles what are considered to be internal flights within the European Union, including flights to and from France, Germany, Italy, and Switzerland.

Prague is well served by the major European and international carriers, including several budget airlines. The Czech national carrier, **CSA** (www.czechairlines.com), operates regular direct service to New York's JFK airport, as well as Toronto. **Delta Airlines** (www.delta.com) offers regular direct service between Prague and both New York JFK and Atlanta.

To get to Prague from the airport, taxis are the quickest but most expensive option. Two cab companies are licensed to operate at the airport. The more reliable of the two is **AAA Radiotaxi** (✆ **222-333-222;** www.aaa-taxi.cz); look for the yellow cabs lined up outside both main terminals, North 1 and North 2. Fares with AAA average about 600Kč to the center. The trip normally takes about 25 minutes, but the drive can run as long as an hour during rush hour.

If you're staying in the center of town, a cheaper alternative is to share a minibus operated by **CEDAZ** (✆ **221-111-111;** www.cedaz.cz). Minibuses run regularly between the airport and the center for a flat fee of 480Kč for groups of one to four persons. CEDAZ also takes individual passengers from the airport to V Celnici street in central Prague (near Náměstí Republiky) for 120Kč per person.

The most affordable option is public transportation. City bus no. 119 stops at both terminals and runs regularly from the airport to the Dejvická metro station (on line A), from where the center is just three metro stops away. Bus no. 100 runs south from the airport to the area of Zličín and connects to metro line B. Travel on both requires a 26Kč ticket purchased from yellow ticketing machines at the bus stop (note that the machines accept only change), or 30Kč if bought from the driver (exact change appreciated). Buy two tickets if you're carrying large luggage. A special **Airport Express** (designated AE on buses) runs to and from Prague's main train station and costs 50Kč per person each way. This is convenient if you are connecting directly to an international train.

BY CAR Prague is easily accessible by major highway from around Europe. The main four-lane highways leading into and out of the city include the D1 motorway running south and east to Brno (2 hr.) and Bratislava (3 hr.), and with connections to Kraków (8 hr.) and Budapest (6 hr.); the D5 running southwest to Plzeň (Pilsen; 1 hr.) and Nuremberg (3 hr.), with connections to Italy and points in southern and western Europe; and the D8 running north to Dresden (2 hr.) and eventually Berlin

The Czech Republic

(5 hr.). Vienna is about 5 hours by car, most of the way along crowded two-lane highway.

BY TRAIN Prague lies on major European rail lines, with good connections to Dresden (2 hr.) and Berlin (5 hr.) to the north, and Brno (2–3 hr.), Vienna (4–5 hr.), Bratislava (3 hr.), and Budapest (7 hr.) to the south and east. New high-speed rail service, the Pendolino, has been introduced on the Prague-Vienna run, shortening the travel time on some trains to as little as 4 hours. More high-speed rail links are on the drawing board.

Prague has two international train stations, so make sure to ask which station your train is using when you buy your ticket. Most international trains arrive at the main station, **Hlavní nádraží** (Wilsonova 80, Prague 1; ✆ **224-614-071;** www.cd.cz; metro: Hlavní nádraží, line C). Trains to and from Berlin, Vienna, and Budapest, however, often stop at the northern suburban station, **Nádraží Holešovice** (Vrbenského ul., Prague 7; ✆ **224-615-865;** www.cd.cz; metro: Nádraží Holešovice, line C). Train information is available at ✆ **840-112-113** or on the Web at http://jizdnirady.idnes.cz.

Of the two main stations, Hlavní nádraží is the larger and more popular, but it's also seedier. Built in 1909, this once-beautiful four-story Art Nouveau structure was one of the city's beloved architectural gems before it was connected to a darkly modern dispatch hall in the mid-1970s. It has been neglected for years, but at this writing a massive reconstruction of the building complex and its surroundings is underway. From the train platform, you'll walk down a flight of stairs and through a tunnel before arriving in the ground-level main hall, which contains ticket windows, a useful **Prague Information Service** office that sells city maps and dispenses information, and restrooms. Also useful is the **ČD center** (✆ **840-112-113;** www.cd.cz) run by the Czech Railways. It provides domestic and international train

Prague

ATTRACTIONS ●

Bazilika sv. Jiří (St. George's Basilica) **7**
Chrám sv. Víta (St. Vitus Cathedral) **6**
Estates' Theater **29**
Havelský trh (Havel's Market) **28**
Jewish Museum **17**
Karlův most (Charles Bridge) **20**
Klášter sv. Anežky České (St. Agnes Convent) **15**
Klášter sv. Jiří (St. George's Convent) **7**
Královská zahrada (Royal Garden) **4**
Královský palác (Royal Palace) **8**
Maisel Synagogue **23**
Old Town Hall & Astronomical Clock **24**
Petřínské sady (Petřín Hill) **13**
Pinkas Synagogue **18**
Prašná věž (Powder Tower) **31**
Pražský Hrad (Prague Castle) **5**
Staroměstské náměstí (Old Town Square) **25**
Staronová synagoga (Old-New Synagogue) **17**
Starý židovský hřbitov (Old Jewish Cemetery) **18**
Šternberský palace (Šternberk Palace) **3**
Václavské náměstí (Wenceslas Square) **32**
Veletržní Palace **14**
Vyšehrad Park **38**
Valdštejnská zahrada (Wallenstein Garden) **10**
Zahrada na Valech (Garden on the Ramparts) **9**

INFORMATION ●

Castle Information Office **5**
Čedok Office **30**

ACCOMMODATIONS ■

Andante **37**
Betlem Club **22**
Four Seasons Hotel **19**
Hotel Aria **11**
Hotel Cloister Inn **21**
Hotel Evropa **33**
Hotel Inter-Continental Prague **16**
Hotel Jalta **35**
Hotel Josef **27**
Hotel Meran **34**
Hotel Savoy **1**
Hotel Ungelt **26**
Hotel U páva **12**
Pension Museum **36**
Romantik Hotel U raka **2**

0 — 1/5 mi
0 — 0.2 km

Metro
Royal Route
Pedestrian passage
Steps

BUBENEČ
HRADČANY
PRAGUE CASTLE
MALÁ STRANA
PETŘÍN HILL
SMÍCHOV
Strahov Monastery
Loreto
Černín Palace
Wallenstein Palace
Nostitz Palace
Museum Kampa
Petřín Observation Tower
Velký Strahovský Stadium

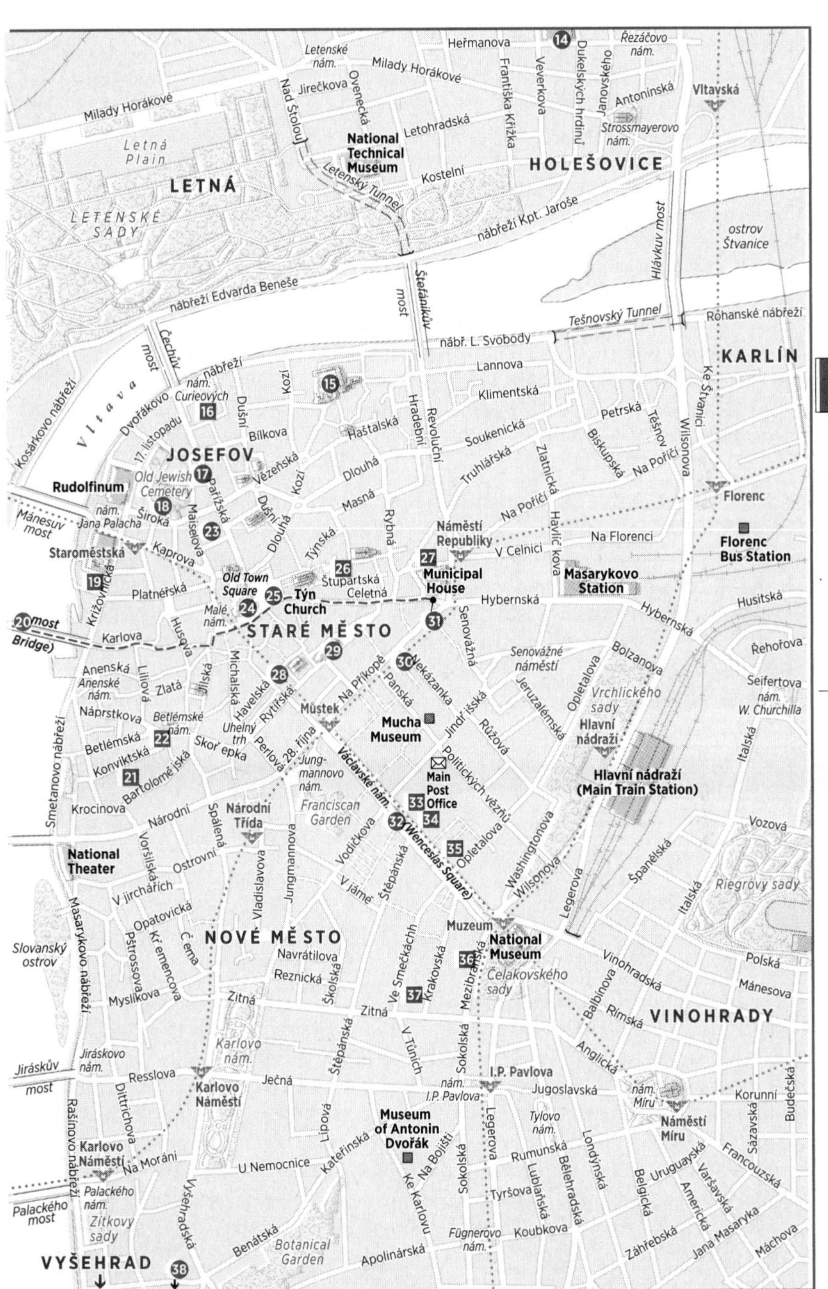
LETNÁ
Letná Plain
LETENSKÉ SADY
HOLEŠOVICE
KARLÍN
JOSEFOV
STARÉ MĚSTO
NOVÉ MĚSTO
VINOHRADY
VYŠEHRAD
Vltava
National Technical Museum
Letenský Tunnel
Letenské nám.
Milady Horákové
Heřmanova
Jirečkova
Ovenecká
Nad Štolou
Letohradská
Kostelní
Františka Křížka
Veverkova
Dukelských hrdinů
Janovského
Řezáčovo nám.
Antonínská
Strossmayerovo nám.
Vltavská
nábřeží Kpt. Jaroše
Hlávkuv most
ostrov Štvanice
nábřeží Edvarda Beneše
Štefánikův most
Těšnovský Tunnel
Rohanské nábřeží
nábř. L. Svobody
Čechův most
Kosárkovo nábřeží
Dvořákovo nábřeží
nám. Curieových
Lannova
Klimentská
Kozí
Hradební
Revoluční
Dušní
Bílkova
Haštalská
Soukenická
Petrská
Těšnov
Ke Štvanici
Wilsonova
Biskupská
Na Poříčí
Zlatnická
Truhlářská
17. listopadu
Vězeňská
Dlouhá
Rudolfinum
Old Jewish Cemetery
Pařížská
Široká
nám. Jana Palacha
Mánesův most
Maiselova
Masná
Rybná
Náměstí Republiky
V Celnici
Havlíčkova
Na Florenci
Florenc
Florenc Bus Station
Staroměstská
Kaprova
Týnská
Old Town Square
Týn Church
Štupartská
Celetná
Municipal House
Masarykovo Station
Hybernská
Husitská
Křižovnická
Platnéřská
Malé nám.
Karlova
most (Charles Bridge)
Husova
Senovážná
Senovážné náměstí
Bolzanova
Řehořova
Anenská
Anenské nám.
Liliová
Zlatá
Jilská
Michalská
Na Příkopě
Panská
Nekázanka
Jeruzalémská
Opletalova
Vrchlického sady
Seifertova
nám. W. Churchilla
Náprstkova
Betlémské nám.
Havelská
Rytířská
Můstek
Mucha Museum
Jindřišská
Růžová
Hlavní nádraží
Hlavní nádraží (Main Train Station)
Italská
Betlémská
Konviktská
Skořepka
Uhelný trh
Perlova
28. října
Václavské nám.
Jungmannovo nám.
Main Post Office
Politických vězňů
Bartolomějská
Smetanovo nábřeží
Krocínova
Národní
Spálená
Národní Třída
Franciscan Garden
Vodičkova
(Wenceslas Square)
Washingtonova
Vozová
National Theater
Voršilská
Ostrovní
Vladislavova
Jungmannova
Štěpánská
V jámě
Španělská
Riegrovy sady
V jirchářích
Opatovická
Pštrossova
Křemencova
Černá
Muzeum
National Museum
Legerova
Masarykovo nábřeží
Slovanský ostrov
Navrátilova
Reznická
Školská
Ve Smečkách
Krakovská
Mezibranská
Čelakovského sady
Vinohradská
Polská
Mánesova
Myslíkova
Žitná
Balbínova
Římská
Karlovo nám.
Štěpánská
V Tůních
Sokolská
Anglická
Jiráskovo nám.
Jiráskův most
Resslova
Karlovo Náměstí
Ječná
I.P. Pavlova
nám. I.P. Pavlova
Jugoslávská
nám. Míru
Náměstí Míru
Korunní
Sázavská
Budečská
Dittrichova
Rašínovo nábřeží
Lípová
Museum of Antonín Dvořák
Tylovo nám.
Londýnská
Na Moráni
U Nemocnice
Kateřinská
Na Bojišti
Rumunská
Bělehradská
Belgická
Uruguayská
Varšavská
Francouzská
Palackého nám.
Palackého most
Vyšehradská
Ke Karlovu
Tyršova
Lublaňská
Americká
Zítkovy sady
Benátská
Botanical Garden
Apolinářská
Fügnerovo nám.
Koubkova
Záhřebská
Jana Masaryka
Máchova
14
15
16
17
18
19
20
21
22
23
24
25
26
27
28
29
30
31
32
33
34
35
36
37
38

information as well as currency exchange and accommodations services. It is open daily 7 to 11am, 11:30am to 2pm, and 2:30 to 5:45pm. Visa and MasterCard are accepted. The station's basement has luggage lockers, but they aren't secure and should be avoided.

After you leave the modern terminal hall, a 5- to 10-minute walk to the left puts you at the top of Wenceslas Square and 15 minutes by foot from Old Town Square. Metro line C connects the station easily to the other two subway lines and the rest of the city. Metro trains depart from the lower level, and tickets are available from the newsstand near the metro entrance. Gouging taxi drivers line up outside the station and are plentiful throughout the day and night but are not recommended.

Prague has two smaller train stations. **Masaryk Station,** Hybernská ul., Prague 1 (✆ **221-111-122**), is primarily for travelers arriving on trains originating from other Bohemian cities. Situated about 10 minutes by foot from the main train station, Masaryk is near Staré Město, just a stone's throw from Náměstí Republiky metro station. **Smíchov Station,** Nádražní ul. at Rozkošného, Prague 5 (✆ **224-617-686**), is the terminus for commuter trains from western and southern Bohemia, though it's a convenient station for getting to popular day-trip destinations like Karlštejn and Plzeň. The station has a 24-hour baggage check and is serviced by metro line B.

BY BUS The **Central Bus Station–Florenc,** Křižíkova 4–6, Prague 8 (✆ **900-144-444;** www.florenc.cz for timetable info), is a few blocks north of the main train station. Most local and long-distance buses arrive here. The adjacent Florenc metro station is on both lines B (yellow) and C (red). Florenc station is relatively small and doesn't have many visitor services. There are even smaller bus depots at **Želivského** (metro line A), **Smíchovské nádraží** (metro line B), and **Nádraží Holešovice** (metro line C).

VISITOR INFORMATION **Tourist Offices** The official tourist information service for the Czech Republic is the **Czech Tourist Authority,** known as CzechTourism (www.czechtourism.com). They have offices in several countries abroad and can help make basic travel arrangements and answer questions.

- **In the U.S.**, the CzechTourism office is at 1109 Madison Ave., New York, NY 10028 (✆ 212/288-0830, ext. 101).
- **In Canada:** CzechTourism is at 2 Bloor St. W., Ste. 1500, Toronto, M4W 3E2 (✆ 416/363-9928).
- **In the U.K.,** contact CzechTourism at 13 Harley St., London W1G 9QG (✆ 0207-631-0427).

If you want to arrange accommodations before you come, Prague-based **E-travel.cz** offers handy English websites. Its general site at www.travel.cz provides booking for hotels and practical touring information, while at www.apartments.cz, you can book a private apartment in a wide range of prices and areas. Once in the city, you can find E-travel.cz near the National Theater at Divadelní 24; or call its 24-hour call center (✆ **224-990-990;** fax 224-990-999; www.travel.cz). Especially for those arriving by train or air, **AVE Travel** (✆ **251-551-011;** www.avetravel.cz) arranges accommodations or transfers inside these terminals. It has outlets at the airport, open daily from 7am to 10pm; and at the Nádraží Holešovice, open daily from 7am to 9pm.

The **Prague Information Service (PIS),** Rytířská 31, Prague 1 (✆ **12-444;** fax 222-221-721; www.pis.cz), near Můstek metro station, provides tips and tickets for upcoming cultural events and tours. It can also help you find a room. From April to October, it's open daily 9am to 7pm. During the rest of the year, it's open daily 9am to 6pm. There are also PIS offices inside Old Town Hall and the main train station.

The Prague Post (www.praguepost.com), a weekly newspaper, has a fairly beefy culture section and a special supplement to help visitors. It can be found at most central newsstands.

Čedok, at Na Příkopě 18, Prague 1 (✆ **800-112-112** or 224-197-111; fax 224-216-324; www.cedok.cz), once the state travel bureau, has access to tickets and information about domestic events, and the staff can book rail and bus tickets and hotel rooms. Čedok accepts major credit cards and is open Monday to Friday from 9am to 7pm, Saturday 9:30am to 1pm.

WEBSITES Helpful websites include **www.mapy.cz**, an online map and journey planner that covers Prague and the entire Czech Republic. For the ins and outs of the public transportation system, go to **www.dp-praha.cz/en**.

The site **www.idos.cz** provides an online timetable for trains and buses, including international destinations. Just type in the city (using the Czech spellings, such as "Praha" for Prague, but note that the diacritical marks are not required) and you'll get a complete listing of train and bus connections.

CITY LAYOUT The **River Vltava** bisects Prague and provides the best line of orientation; you can use **Charles Bridge** as your central point. From the bridge, turn toward **Prague Castle,** the massive complex on the hill with the cathedral thrusting out. Now you're facing west.

Up on the hill is the Castle District known as **Hradčany.** Running up the hill between the bridge and the castle is the district known as **Malá Strana** (literally the "Small Side," but known as Lesser Town in English). Turn around, and behind you on the right (east) bank is **Staré Město (Old Town),** and farther to the south and east **Nové Město (New Town).** The highlands even farther east used to be the royal vineyards, **Vinohrady,** now a popular neighborhood for expatriates with a growing array of accommodations and restaurants.

On the left bank coming off Charles Bridge is **Mostecká Street,** and at the end of it sits the cozy square under the castle hill, **Malostranské náměstí.** On the hill outside the main castle gate is the motorcade-worn **Hradčanské náměstí,** on the city side of which you'll find a spectacular view of spires and red roofs below.

On the east side of Charles Bridge, the tourist-packed route through Old Town is **Karlova Street.** Like Karlova, almost any other route in Old Town will eventually lead you to **Staroměstské náměstí (Old Town Square),** the breathtaking heart of Staré Město. A black monument to Jan Hus, the martyred Czech Protestant leader, dominates the square. The tree-lined boulevard to the right behind Hus is **Pařížská (Parisian Blvd.),** with boutiques and restaurants; it forms the edge of the Jewish Quarter. Over Hus's left shoulder is **Dlouhá Street,** and in front of him to his left is the kitschy shopping zone on **Celetná.** Across the square to Hus's right, past the clock tower of Old Town Hall (Staroměstská radnice), is **Železná Street,** which leads to Mozart's Prague venue, the Estates' Theater. Farther to Hus's right is the narrow alley **Melantrichova,** which winds southeast to **Václavské náměstí (Wenceslas Square),** site of pro-democracy demonstrations in 1968 and 1989.

GETTING AROUND **On Foot** Prepare to do plenty of walking. Most of the center of the city is closed to vehicles, including taxis, meaning you'll have to walk pretty much everywhere. Distances are relatively close, but always wear comfortable shoes since many of the streets are *paved* (if that's the right word) with cobblestones.

BY PUBLIC TRANSPORTATION Prague's highly efficient public transportation network of metros (subways), trams, and buses (www.dpp.cz/en) is one of the few sound Communist-era legacies. In central Prague, metro stations abound. Trams and buses offer a cheap sightseeing experience but also require a strong stomach for jostling with fellow passengers in close quarters.

For single-use **tickets,** there are two choices. The first is a discount ticket, which costs 18Kč, or 9Kč for 6- to 15-year-olds (children 5 and under ride free), and this allows travel to up to five stations on the metro (not including the station of validation) or 20 minutes on a tram or bus. A full-price ticket costs 26Kč and allows for unlimited travel on metros, trams, and buses for up to 75 minutes (90 min. on Sat–Sun, public holidays, and after 8pm on workdays). The cheaper ticket is usually sufficient for short hops within the center, but note that you can't use it to transfer from metros to trams or between trams.

A **1-day pass** good for unlimited travel is 100Kč, a **3-day pass** is 330Kč, and a **5-day pass** is 500Kč. The 3- and 5-day passes include travel with one child from 6 to 15 years of age and make sense only if you are traveling with a child.

You can buy tickets from yellow coin-operated machines in metro stations or at most newsstands marked TABÁK or TRAFIKA. The machines have English instructions but are a little clunky to operate. First push the button for the ticket you want (either 18Kč or 26Kč) and then insert the money in the slot. Validate your ticket in the little stamping machine before you descend the escalator in the metro or as you enter the tram or bus. Hold on to your validated ticket throughout your ride—you'll need to show it if a ticket collector (be sure to check for his or her badge) asks you. If you're caught without a valid ticket, you'll be asked, and not so kindly, to pay a fine on the spot while all the locals look on, shaking their heads in disgust. The fine is 700Kč if paid on the spot and 950Kč if paid later.

Metro trains operate daily from 5am to midnight and run every 2 to 10 minutes depending on the time of day. The three lines are identified by both letter and color: A (green), B (yellow), and C (red). The most convenient central stations are Muzeum, on both the A and C lines at the top of Václavské náměstí (Wenceslas Sq.); Můstek, on both the A and B lines at the foot of Václavské náměstí; Staroměstská, on the A line, for Old Town Square and the Charles Bridge; and Malostranská, on the A line, serving Malá Strana and the Castle District.

The city's 24 **tram** lines run practically everywhere, and there's always another tram with the same number traveling back. You never have to hail trams; they make every stop. The most popular tram, no. 22 (aka the "tourist tram" or the "pickpocket express"), runs past top sights like the National Theater and Prague Castle. Regular bus and tram service stops at midnight, after which selected routes run reduced night schedules, usually only once per hour. Schedules are posted at stops. If you miss a night connection, expect a long wait for the next.

Buses tend to be used only outside the older districts of Prague and have three-digit numbers. Both the buses and tram lines begin their morning runs around 4:30am.

BY FUNICULAR The funicular (cog railway) makes the scenic run up and down Petřín Hill every 10 minutes (15 min. in winter season) daily from 9am to 11:30pm with an intermediate stop at the Nebozízek restaurant halfway up the hill, which overlooks the city. It requires the 26Kč ticket or any of the same transport passes as other modes of public transport and departs from a small house in the park near the Újezd tram stop (tram: 12, 20, or 22) in Malá Strana.

BY TAXI While the situation has gotten marginally better in recent years, you still run the risk of getting ripped off by a taxi driver if you hail a taxi off the street in a heavily touristy area like Václavské náměstí or take one of the cabs parked at the main train station or at major hotels. A better idea is to call a taxi by phone or have your hotel or restaurant call one for you. Reputable companies with English-speaking dispatchers include **AAA Radiotaxi** (✆ **14014** or 222-333-222; www.aaa-taxi.cz); **ProfiTaxi** (✆ **844-700-800;** www.profitaxi.cz); or **SEDOP** (✆ **841-666-333;** www.sedop.cz). AAA operates a few dedicated taxi stands around town, including ones conveniently located on Václavské náměstí and Malostranské náměstí, where you will find honest drivers.

The meter in an honest cab starts at 40Kč, 30Kč if you've ordered by phone, and it increases by 28Kč per kilometer. Fares around the center typically run from 100Kč to 200Kč, depending on the journey. A taxi from the center to the airport will cost around 600Kč.

To avoid being ripped off, never get into an unmarked cab; ask the driver on entering what the approximate fare will be to your destination (he may not know exactly, but should have some idea); make sure the driver has switched on the meter; and tell the driver you will need a receipt at the end of the ride. If you do get ripped off, it's better to pay the fare and learn a lesson than argue and end up with a bloody nose.

BY CAR Driving in Prague isn't worth the money or effort. The roads are crowded and the high number of one-way streets can be incredibly frustrating. Parking in the center is often restricted and available only to residents with prepaid parking stickers. The only time you *might* want a car is if you have only a few days and plan to explore other parts of the Czech Republic. If you want to rent a car, try **Europcar,** Elišky Krásnohorské 9, Prague 1 (✆ **224-811-290;** www.europcar.cz). There's also **Hertz,** Karlovo nám. 15, Prague 2 (✆ **225-345-031;** www.hertz.cz). **Budget** is at Prague Airport (✆ **220-560-443;** www.budget.cz) and in the Hotel InterContinental, náměstí Curieových 5, Prague 1 (✆ **222-319-595**).

Local car-rental companies sometimes offer lower rates than the big international firms. Compare **CS Czechocar,** Kongresové centrum (Congress Center at Vyšehrad metro stop on the C line), Prague 4 (✆ **261-222-079** or 261-222-143; www.czechocar.cz), or at Prague Airport, Prague 6 (✆ **220-113-454**); or try **SeccoCar,** Přístavní 39, Prague 7 (✆ **220-800-647;** www.seccocar.cz).

Car rates can be negotiable. Try to obtain the best possible deal with the rental company by asking about discounts. Special deals are often offered for keeping the car for an extended period, for unlimited mileage (or at least getting some miles thrown in free), or for a bigger car at a lower price. You can usually get some sort of discount for a company or an association affiliation. Check before you leave home and take a member ID card with you.

[FastFACTS] PRAGUE

Area Codes There are no area or city codes in the Czech Republic. Each telephone number is a unique nine-digit number, usually written xxx-xxx-xxx. Numbers that begin with a "6" or "7" indicate a mobile phone.

Business Hours Normal business and banking hours run from 9am to 5pm Monday to Friday. Stores in central Prague are typically open weekdays from 9am to 7pm and on Saturday from 9am to at least 1pm; larger stores and shopping centers are likely to be open on Sundays and holidays as well. Post offices are open from 8am to 7pm Monday to Friday. Some larger post offices have limited Saturday hours. Museums are almost always closed on Mondays. Tourist attractions may have shorter hours or shut down altogether during the winter (Nov–Apr).

Currency The Czech currency is the **koruna (crown).** It is usually noted as "Kč" in shops or "CZK" in banks. At press time US$1 = 18Kč.

Currency Exchange Banks and ATMs generally offer the best rates and lowest commissions. Changing money is not a problem in the Czech Republic. If you're arriving at Prague Airport, skip the currency-exchange booths in the arrivals hall and instead use the ATMs that are lined up just as you enter the main airport hall from Customs clearance.

Komerční banka has three convenient Prague 1 locations with ATMs that accept Visa, MasterCard, and American Express: Na Příkopě 33, Spálená 51, and Václavské nám. 42 (✆ **800-111-055,** central switchboard for all branches; www.kb.cz). The exchange offices are open Monday to Friday 8am to 5pm.

Doctors & Dentists If you are seeking nonurgent medical attention, practitioners in many fields can be found at the Canadian Medical Care center at Veleslavínská 1, Prague 6, Dejvice (✆ **235-360-133;** www.cmcpraha.cz).

Embassies & Consulates All foreign embassies are located in the capital, Prague. The embassy of the **United States** is located at Tržiště 15, Prague 1, Malá Strana (✆ **257-022-000;** http://prague.usembassy.gov). The embassy of **Canada** is at Muchova 6, Prague 6, Dejvice (✆ **272-101-800;** www.canada.cz). The embassy of the **United Kingdom** is at Thunovská 14, Prague 1, Malá Strana (✆ **257-402-111;** www.britain.cz). The local consular office of **Australia** is at Klimentská 10, Prague 1, Nové Město (✆ **296-578-350**).

Emergencies Dial the following numbers in an emergency: ✆ **112** (general emergency, equivalent to U.S. 911); ✆ **155** (ambulance); ✆ **158** (police); ✆ **150** (fire); and ✆ **1230** or 1240 (emergency road service).

Hospitals For emergency medical treatment, go to **Nemocnice Na Homolce (Hospital Na Homolce)** at Roentgenova 2, Prague 5, Smíchov (✆ **257-271-111;** www.homolka.cz). If you need nonurgent medical attention, practitioners in many fields can be found at the **Canadian Medical Care** center at Veleslavínská 1, Prague 6, Dejvice (✆ **235-360-133;** www.cmcpraha.cz). For dental service, call **American Dental Associates** at V Celnici 4, Prague 1, Nové Město (✆ **221-181-121;** www.americandental.cz), open 8am to 8pm Monday to Friday.

Internet Access Central Prague has several Internet cafes. Rates typically run from 1Kč to 2Kč per minute. Near Old Town Square, try **Bohemia Bagel** at Masná 2, Prague 1, Staré Město (✆ **224-812-560;** www.bohemiabagel.cz). They have a dozen PCs in a pleasant setting for 2Kč per minute; open daily from 8am to 11pm. **Spika** at Dlážděná 4, Prague 1, Nové Město (✆ **224-211-521;** http://netcafe.spika.cz), is open Monday to Friday 8am to midnight and Saturday and Sunday 10am to 11pm, and charges 20Kč for 15 minutes.

Mail Most post offices are open Monday through Friday from 8am to 7pm. The main post office (Hlavní pošta), at Jindřišská 14, Prague 1 (✆ **221-131-111**), is open 24 hours a day. You can receive mail, marked POSTE RESTANTE and addressed to you, in care of this post office.

Postcards to the U.S. cost 19Kč; to any E.U. country, 18Kč. Rates for letters vary by weight and letters should be weighed at the post office to ensure proper postage. Mail service within Europe takes 3 to 5 days, and to the U.S. 7 to 10 days.

Police Dial the European Emergency Number ✆ **112** from any phone in an emergency. For Czech police dial ✆ **158.**

Safety In Prague's center you'll feel generally safer than in most big cities, but always take common-sense precautions. Be aware of your immediate surroundings. Don't walk alone at night around Wenceslas Square—one of the main areas for prostitution and where a lot of unexplainable loitering takes place. All visitors should be watchful of pickpockets in heavily touristed areas, especially on Charles Bridge, in Old Town Square, and in front of the main train station.

Smoking Smoking is generally permitted in restaurants, bars, and cafes, though there has been discussion of imposing a blanket indoor smoking ban that may or may not be in force by the time of your visit. Restaurants are required to offer nonsmoking seating, though this may not always be in the most desirable section of the restaurant. Note that it's illegal to smoke outdoors near bus and tram stops. This rule is rarely enforced, but the fine, 1,000Kč, is steep. Smoking is banned on all trains and public transportation.

Taxes All goods and services in the Czech Republic are levied a value-added tax (VAT, or *DPH* in Czech), ranging from 9% to 19% depending on the item. This tax is normally included in the price.

Telephones There are a few surviving coin-operated pay phones around town, but most public phones require a prepaid magnetic card. Find the cards at tobacco and magazine kiosks (cards are available for 200Kč–500Kč). Simply insert the card, listen for the dial tone, and dial. You can use pay phones with prepaid cards to dial abroad.

You can also dial abroad from the main post office (see "Mail," above) or, more cheaply, over the Internet at many Internet cafes (see "Internet Access," above).

The country code for the Czech Republic is 420. To dial the Czech Republic from abroad, dial your country's international access code (011 in the United States) plus the unique nine-digit local number. Once you are here, to dial any number anywhere in the Czech Republic, simply dial the nine-digit number.

To make a direct international call from the Czech Republic, dial 00 plus the country code of the country you are calling and then the area code and number.

For directory inquiries regarding phone numbers within the Czech Republic, dial ✆ **1180.** For information about services and rates abroad, call ✆ **1181.**

Tipping In hotels, tip **bellhops** 20Kč per bag (more if you have a lot of luggage), and though it's not expected, it's a nice gesture to leave the **chamber staff** 20Kč per night (depending on the level of service). Tip the **doorman** or **concierge** only if he or she has provided a specific service (for example, calling a cab for you or obtaining difficult-to-get theater tickets).

In restaurants, bars, and nightclubs, tip **service staff or bartenders** 10% of the check to reward good service. On smaller tabs it's easiest just to round up to the next highest multiple of 10. For example, if the bill comes to 72Kč, hand the waiter 80Kč and tell him to keep the change.

Tip **cabdrivers** 5% to 10% of the fare (provided they haven't already overcharged you).

Toilets Acceptably clean public pay toilets are scattered around tourist areas and can be found in every metro station. Expect to pay 5Kč to 10Kč for the privilege. You'll find generally cleaner free toilets in restaurants, hotels, and fast-food outlets, but these are usually reserved for customers.

Where to Stay

Hotel construction became a boom industry during the past decade, and if anything, the city now has too many beds, not too few. The combination of new hotels plus the worldwide economic recession in 2009 succeeded in driving down prices somewhat, meaning that, depending on the night, it was possible to snag a good place in the center for under $100 for the first time in many years. It's not clear what the future will bring, but it always pays to shop around. Bargains are out there.

HRADČANY

Very Expensive

Hotel Savoy ★ One of Prague's finest hotels, the Savoy occupies a quiet spot behind the Foreign Ministry and Černín Palace, and is just a few blocks from the castle. The guest rooms are richly decorated and boast every amenity as well as spacious marble bathrooms. The beds are huge, which contrasts with the customary central European style of two twin beds shoved together. The pleasant staff provides an attention to detail that's a cut above that at most hotels in Prague. The Hradčany restaurant is excellent.

Keplerova 6, Prague 1. ✆ **224-302-430.** Fax 224-302-128. www.savoyhotel.cz. 61 units. From 4,500Kč double; from 8,000Kč suite. Rates include breakfast. AE, DC, MC, V. Tram: 22. **Amenities:** Restaurant; bar; concierge; Jacuzzi; room service; sauna; spa w/small set of exercise machines; Wi-Fi (free in lobby). *In room:* A/C, TV/DVD, hair dryer, minibar.

Expensive

Romantik Hotel U raka ★ Hidden among the stucco houses and cobblestone streets of a pristine medieval neighborhood below Prague Castle is this pleasant surprise. The Romantik Hotel U raka (At the Crayfish) has been lovingly reconstructed as an old-world farmhouse. It is the quietest getaway in this tightly packed city. The rustic rooms have heavy wooden furniture, open-beamed ceilings, and stone walls. The suite has a fireplace and adjoins a private manicured garden, making it a favorite with honeymooners. Water trickles through the Japanese garden that surrounds the hotel.

The owners are relaxed but attentive. Prague Castle is a 10-minute walk away, and you can catch a tram into the city center by walking up ancient steps at the side of the hotel. Make reservations well in advance.

Černínská 10, Prague 1. ✆ **220-511-100.** Fax 233-358-041. www.romantikhotel-uraka.cz. 6 units (5 with shower only). From 3,800Kč double; from 7,000Kč suite. Rates include breakfast. AE, MC, V. Tram: 22. *In room:* A/C, TV, hair dryer, minibar.

MALÁ STRANA (LESSER TOWN)

Very Expensive

Hotel Aria ★ This music-themed hotel occupies a luxuriously reconstructed town house in the heart of Malá Strana, just around the corner from the St. Nicholas Cathedral. Each of its four floors is tastefully decorated to evoke a different genre of music, famous composer, or musician. The rooms and bathrooms vary in their size and layout, and all are kept to the same exceptionally high standard. There is an impressive library of CDs, DVDs, and books about music off the lobby, and a full-time resident musicologist is available to help you choose a concert in the city. The Aria will delight newlyweds or any romantic soul with its luxurious but cozy atmosphere, and the extensive list of amenities, which includes a roof terrace garden with spectacular views of Malá Strana, a screening room, and music salon.

Tržiště 9, Prague 1. ✆ **225-334-111.** Fax 225-334-666. www.aria.cz. 52 units. From 5,800Kč double; 9,500Kč suite. Rates include breakfast. AE, MC, V. Metro: Malostranská and then tram no. 12, 20, or 22 to Malostranské nám. **Amenities:** Restaurant; bar; free airport transfers; exercise room; room service. *In room:* A/C, DVD/CD player, hair dryer, Internet, minibar, MP3 docking station.

Expensive

Hotel U páva ★ The "Peacock" is a fine B&B in Malá Strana, a stone's throw from Charles Bridge. This family-run hotel has the intimacy of a farmhouse and offers room service from its decent kitchen. Original wooden ceilings, antique chairs, and comfortable beds accent the reasonably spacious rooms. The best rooms on the top floor facing the front have a fantastic low-angle view of Prague Castle. The fully tiled bathrooms of adequate size have tub/shower combinations.

U Lužického semináře 32, Prague 1. ✆ **257-533-360.** Fax 257-530-919. www.romantichotels.cz. 27 units (tub/shower combination in bathrooms). From 4,000Kč double. Rates include breakfast. AE, MC, V. Metro: Malostranská. **Amenities:** Restaurant; cafe; bar; babysitting; room service; sauna. *In room:* TV, hair dryer, minibar.

STARÉ MĚSTO (OLD TOWN) & JOSEFOV

Very Expensive

Four Seasons Hotel ★★★ Located in an imposing position on the banks of the Vltava River right next to Charles Bridge, the Four Seasons provides an elegant base for exploring Old Town and has a wonderful panoramic view of Prague Castle across the river.

The property actually melds three historic buildings from the city's most important architectural periods—baroque, Renaissance, and Art Nouveau. The most impressive wing, the 17th-century baroque villa, houses the Presidential Suite as well as some smaller (but still nicely appointed) executive suites and guest rooms. The best have sweeping views and sunken marble tubs. The Art Nouveau wing is less expensive but the street-side views are less impressive. All rooms are fitted with fine solid-wood furniture: some with antique pieces, others with more modern avant-garde accents. The house restaurant, **Allegro** (p. 155), is a two-time Michelin star winner.

Veleslavínova 2a, Prague 1. ✆ **221-427-000.** Fax 221-426-000. www.fourseasons.com/prague. 161 units. From 9,600Kč double; from 20,000Kč suite. AE, DC, MC, V. Metro: Staroměstská. **Amenities:** Restaurant; bar; concierge; health club; room service. *In room:* A/C, TV/DVD, CD player, hair dryer, minibar.

Expensive

Hotel InterContinental Prague The upper suites of this hotel have hosted luminaries including former U.S. secretary of state Madeleine Albright, and legend has it global terrorist Carlos the Jackal. Secretary Albright came for the comfortably reconstructed rooms; the Jackal apparently came because during the Communist era the hotel was a safe house with decent room and board. The 1970s facade is unappealing, but the interior has been updated with modern rooms, a glittering fitness center, and an atrium restaurant. The standard guest rooms aren't very large but are comfortable, with decent but not exceptional upholstered furniture, computer ports, and marble bathrooms. A riverside window might give you a glimpse of the castle or at least the metronome at the top of Letná Park across the river, where a massive statue of Joseph Stalin once stood in the late 1950s and early 1960s.

Pařížská 30, Prague 1. ✆ **296-631-111.** Fax 224-811-216. www.icprague.com. 364 units. From 4,161Kč double; from 7,605Kč suite. Rates include buffet breakfast. AE, DC, MC, V. Metro: Staroměstská. **Amenities:** 2 restaurants; cafe; concierge; health club; indoor pool; room service. *In room:* TV, hair dryer, Internet, minibar, MP3 docking station.

Hotel Josef ★★ The Josef is the hippest of Prague's hip hotels. British-based Czech architect Eva Jiřičná brings a new study on the interior use of glass to her native land with its own long history of the glazier's craft. Every piece of space breathes with life and light, breaking the stuffy mold of most high-end hotels. She uses modern glass walls, tables, and chairs bathed with the light of modern lighting fixtures to offset funky yellows and greens, and even rust-colored bedspreads are thrown in. There is a daring and dramatic effect in every room. Superior rooms are so bold as to offer transparent bath nooks, shower stalls, and washrooms with a full view of grooming activities for your partner to absorb in the main sleeping chamber. Room no. 801, a penthouse suite with a magnificent vista of the Prague skyline, is highly sought after for those who want to absorb the Golden City in its full glory.

Rybná 20, Prague 1. ✆ **221-700-111.** Fax 221-700-999. www.hoteljosef.com. 109 units. From 4,300Kč double. AE, DC, MC, V. Metro: Náměstí Republiky. **Amenities:** Restaurant; babysitting; concierge; health club; room service; Wi-Fi. *In room:* A/C, TV/DVD, CD player, hair dryer, Internet, minibar.

Hotel Ungelt ★★ In the afternoon shadow of the Týn Church, just off Old Town Square, you'll find a place not as opulent as other nearby accommodations, but still a good value. The three-story Ungelt offers full apartments that are airy, spacious, and very comfortable for families. Each unit contains a bedroom, living room, full kitchen, and bathroom. The bedrooms have standard-issue beds and not-too-attractive upholstered couches, but do boast luxurious accents such as huge chandeliers and antique dressers. Some have magnificent hand-painted ceilings. Because the Ungelt is in a tightly constructed neighborhood behind the church, there are no great exterior views. However, the back rooms overlook a quaint courtyard.

Štupartská 7, Prague 1. ✆ **222-745-900.** Fax 222-745-901. www.ungelt.cz. 6 units. From 2,700Kč 1-bedroom suite; from 3,600Kč 2-bedroom suite. Rates include breakfast. AE, MC, V. Metro: Staroměstská or line B to Náměstí Republiky. **Amenities:** Bar; Internet. *In room:* TV, hair dryer, minibar.

Moderate

Betlem Club Protestant firebrand Jan Hus launched his reformation drive at the reconstructed chapel across the street, but other than the vaulted medieval cellar where breakfast is served, little about the Betlem Club recalls those heady

15th-century days. Still, this small hotel has a great location on a cobblestone square. The rooms are unimaginatively decorated with bland modern pieces but are comfortable and fairly priced. The bathrooms are small but clean.

Betlémské nám. 9, Prague 1. ✆ **222-221-575.** Fax 222-220-580. www.betlemclub.cz. 22 units (tub/shower combination). From 2,600Kč double; from 3,100Kč suite. Rates include breakfast. AE, MC, V. Metro: Národní třída. **Amenities:** Babysitting; Internet. *In room:* TV, hair dryer, minibar.

Hotel Cloister Inn ★★ Between Old Town Square and the National Theater, this property has been renovated into a good-value, midrange hotel. The original rooms of this unique spot were developed from holding cells used by the Communist secret police, the StB; the cells themselves were converted from a convent. It sounds ominous, but the Cloister Inn rooms are actually very inviting. A new proprietor has taken over management from the secret police and has refurbished and expanded the hotel with smart colors and comfortable Nordic furniture. The rooms offer enough space, beds with firm mattresses, and reasonably sized bathrooms with showers only. It is just a short walk from both Charles Bridge and Old Town Square.

Konviktská 14, Prague 1. ✆ **224-211-020.** Fax 224-210-800. www.cloister-inn.cz. 73 units (showers only). From 2,100Kč double. Rates include breakfast. AE, DC, MC, V. Metro: Národní třída. **Amenities:** Concierge; Internet. *In room:* A/C, TV, hair dryer, minibar.

NOVÉ MĚSTO (NEW TOWN)

Expensive

Hotel Jalta ★ Recently reconstructed, the Jalta has put on a fresh face and a new attitude. The lobby is pretty cold and unwelcoming, but the rooms have high ceilings and decent upholstered chairs. An infusion of Japanese money has improved the hotel furnishings, which were formerly depressing Communist-issue pieces. The Jalta is just below the statue of St. Wenceslas, where the masses gathered to ring out the Communist government in 1989. The rooms facing the square have balconies, allowing a broad view of the busy square.

Václavské nám. 45, Prague 1. ✆ **222-822-111.** Fax 222-822-833. www.hoteljalta.com. 94 units. From 3,500Kč double; from 5,000Kč suite. Rates include breakfast. AE, DC, MC, V. Metro: Muzeum. **Amenities:** 2 restaurants; casino; concierge; fitness center; room service. *In room:* A/C, TV, hair dryer, minibar, Wi-Fi.

Moderate

Andante This best-value choice near Wenceslas Square is tucked away on a dark side street, about 2 blocks off the top of the square. Despite the unappealing neighborhood, this is the most comfortable property at this price. With modern beds and good firm mattresses, as well as high-grade Scandinavian furniture and colorful decorations, the rooms are extremely comfortable. They offer plenty of space and white, well-kept bathrooms with tub/shower combinations, some with shower only.

Ve Smečkách 4, Prague 1. ✆ **222-210-021.** Fax 222-210-591. www.andante.cz. 32 units (some with shower only, some with tub only). From 2,700Kč double; from 3,600Kč suite. Rates include breakfast. AE, MC, V. Metro: Muzeum. **Amenities:** Restaurant; room service. *In room:* TV, hair dryer, minibar.

Hotel Meran This used to be part of the Hotel Evropa next door (see below), but the Meran is a bit brighter and more inviting than its bigger Art Nouveau neighbor, which draws so much attention to its gilded facade. The Meran has had a face-lift to make it a fair but not spectacular midrange choice on Wenceslas Square, a walkable distance to the main train station. The lobby interior has retained some original

Art Nouveau accents, although the rooms have few. They are unimaginatively decorated and seem cramped. The tiny bathrooms have tub/shower combinations or shower only. Front windows overlook the place where hundreds of thousands demonstrated until the Communist government fell in a peaceful coup in 1989.

Václavské nám. 27, Prague 1. ✆ **224-238-440.** Fax 224-230-411. www.hotelmeran.cz. 20 units with bathroom (tub or shower). From 2,400Kč double. Rates include breakfast. AE, DC, MC, V. Metro: Muzeum or Můstek. **Amenities:** Concierge. *In room:* TV, Wi-Fi.

INEXPENSIVE

Hotel Evropa Established in 1889 as the Hotel Archduke Stephan, the Evropa was recast in the early 1900s as a gleaming Art Nouveau hotel. However, this is yet another classic that has seen much better days. Though the statue-studded exterior, still one of the most striking landmarks on Wenceslas Square, has recently been polished, the rooms are aging; most don't have bathrooms and some are just plain shabby. The best choice is a room facing the square with a balcony. The hotel's famous cafe, a wood-encased former masterpiece that no longer glows, furthers the theme. Still, this is an affordable way to stay in one of Wenceslas Square's once grand addresses.

Václavské nám. 25, Prague 1. ✆ **224-215-387.** www.evropahotel.cz. 90 units, 20 with bathroom (tub only). 1,600Kč double without bathroom; 2,500Kč double with bathroom. Rates include continental breakfast. AE, MC, V. Metro: Můstek or Muzeum. **Amenities:** Restaurant; cafe; concierge.

Pension Museum ★ This is yet another example of a successful renovation of a 19th-century building in the very center of the city. Located just across the National Museum, the Pension offers clean and comfortable rooms with modern furniture. Do not be put off by the busy road in front, however. There are actually only two rooms facing it, and their new double-glazed windows block the noise very well. The private, cozy courtyard garden serves as an oasis for relaxation.

Mezibranská 15, Prague 1. ✆ **296-325-186.** Fax 296-325-188. www.pension-museum.cz. 12 units with bathroom (shower only). From 1,970Kč double; 2,440Kč suite. Rates include breakfast. AE, MC, V. Metro: Muzeum. **Amenities:** Concierge; Internet. *In room:* A/C, TV, fridge, hair dryer.

Where to Dine

Prague still has a long way to go before people travel here just for the food, but the quality and variety of restaurants have improved tremendously in the past decade. Not that long ago, dining out meant choosing between a pizza covered in ketchup, listless pub grub, or a handful of overpriced "luxury" restaurants—the kind where stiff waiters wheel around tired appetizers on a little cart. Today, thanks to a massive influx of tourist dollars as well as rising incomes of ordinary Czechs, Prague now supports many very good restaurants, with traditional Czech places supplemented by French, Italian, Japanese, Chinese, and Indian restaurants. The country has also seen its first Michelin star, awarded to **Allegro,** the house restaurant of the Four Seasons Hotel (p. 149).

HRADČANY

Very Expensive

Villa Richter ★ CONTINENTAL/CZECH A relatively recent entry into Prague's top echelon is this luxury restaurant in a hilltop vineyard just as you exit the Prague Castle complex on the eastern end. There are actually three restaurants here, including a relatively inexpensive option that serves burgers and has wine tastings

A FEW DINING warnings

Though the practice is declining, in the past some Czech restaurants have tried to raise a little extra revenue by placing seemingly free bowls of nuts or olives on the table or offering platters of appetizers or aperitifs that appeared to be on the house. Needless to say, they were not and diners were often surprised to find they were paying the equivalent of $5 or more for a bowl of stale cashews.

These days it's more common for dining establishments to simply charge a cover, labeled *couvert* on the menu, of anywhere from 30Kč to 50Kč per person to cover things like the bread basket, spreads, and condiments. Regardless, it's good to be aware of the practice and if in doubt ask the waiter before touching any food on the table.

Many restaurants now accept credit cards, but waiters may not be adept at tricks like dividing a bill between two or three cards. It's best to keep it simple. Leave tips in cash on the table rather than charging them to the card; otherwise, the server may never get them. Stories of credit card fraud by waiters are rare, but still it's always a good idea to keep a close watch on credit card statements.

for 45Kč a glass, but the big culinary draw is the "Piano Nobile," a gourmet restaurant offering the best of Czech and international cooking and a wine vault with some 2,000 bottles. There's a five-course tasting menu for 1,690Kč. In winter, dress up for the fancy dining room; in summer, it's more relaxed, with dining on the terrace overlooking Malá Strana to your right and the Old Town across the river.

Staré zámecké schody 6, Prague 1. ✆ **257-219-079.** www.villarichter.cz. Reservations recommended. Main courses 610Kč–690Kč; 5-course tasting menu 1,690Kč. AE, DC, MC, V. Daily 11am–1am. Metro: Malostranská plus a walk up the stairs.

Moderate

Vikárka ★ ☺ CZECH Decent places to eat in Hradčany are rare. Not only does this restored Romanesque and Gothic cellar restaurant within the castle walls offer good Czech and international dishes at decent prices, but you also get to eat amid more than 600 years of history. The staff gets into the mood with period costumes, but this is no tourist trap. For a real Czech treat, try the pork knee baked on dark beer served in the traditional style with slices of brown bread, horseradish, and mustard.

Vikářská 39, inside the Prague Castle complex, Prague 1. ✆ **233-311-962.** http://vikarka.cz. Reservations accepted. Main courses 180Kč–250Kč. AE, DC, MC, V. Daily 11am–9pm. Tram: 22 to Prague Castle.

MALÁ STRANA (LESSER TOWN)

Very Expensive

Kampa Park ★ CONTINENTAL This restaurant is worth the considerable splurge, but only if you can snag one of the highly coveted riverside tables. If you can't, move on and try for the terrace at Hergetova Cihelna (see below). For years, Kampa Park was considered Prague's premier restaurant and lured its fair share of visiting celebs (check out the photos on the wall). These days, there's lots more competition, but the setting on the Vltava is still arguably the best in town. The menu, with items like seared monkfish and roast saddle of lamb, looks relatively tame, but the quality of the food is excellent.

Na Kampě 8b, Prague 1. ✆ **296-826-112.** www.kampagroup.com. Reservations recommended. Main courses 495Kč–895Kč. AE, DC, MC, V. Daily 11:30am–1am. Metro: Malostranská.

U Malířů FRENCH This is arguably the most romantic setting in one of the loveliest parts of Malá Strana. Surrounded by Romance-age murals and gorgeously appointed tables in three intimate dining rooms, you're faced with some tough choices, including a delicious baked duck breast and tuna served on roast noodles in a tomato mousse. Three-course set menus and a bottle of Czech wine, instead of French, can help keep the costs manageable, but if you want a truly old-world evening of elegant romance and French specialties, U Malířů may be worth it.

Maltézské nám. 11, Prague 1. ✆ **257-530-318.** www.umaliru.cz. Reservations recommended. Main courses 480Kč–690Kč; 3-course rotating summer menu 490Kč. AE, DC, MC, V. Daily 6–11pm. Metro: Malostranská.

Expensive

Hergetova Cihelna ★ INTERNATIONAL/CZECH The main draw here is the riverside terrace with an unparalleled view of the Charles Bridge—plus the very good food (from the same people who run the more expensive Kampa Park; see above). The building, dating from the 18th century, once served as a brick factory (*cihelna*) before it was renovated into this stylish modern restaurant around a decade ago. The first dining concept here was burgers and pizza, which the owners quickly ditched for more expensive items like rib-eye steaks with maple-glazed carrots. Still, it's possible to eat cheaply if you stick to the Czech specialties and pasta dishes. Reserve several days in advance for the terrace.

Cihelná 2b, Prague 1. ✆ **296-826-103.** www.kampagroup.com. Reservations recommended. Main courses 215Kč–695Kč. AE, MC, V. Daily 11:30am–1am. Metro: Malostranská.

U modré kachničky ★ CZECH/WILD GAME The "Blue Duckling," on a narrow Malá Strana street, comes close to refining standard Czech dishes into true Bohemian haute cuisine. This series of small dining rooms with vaulted ceilings and playfully frescoed walls is packed with antique furniture and pastel-flowered linen upholstery. The menu is loaded with an array of wild game and quirky spins on Czech village favorites. Starters include lightly spiced venison pâté and duck liver on toast. You can choose from six duck main courses. Finally, the ubiquitous *palačinky* crepes are thin and tender and filled with fruit, nuts, and chocolate. There is an even more popular sister to the first "kachnička," at Michalská 16, Prague 1 (✆ **224-213-418**), with a similar menu and prices. Reservations are recommended (daily 11:30am–11:30pm; metro: Můstek).

Nebovidská 6, Prague 1. ✆ **257-320-308.** www.umodrekachnicky.cz. Reservations recommended for lunch, required for dinner. Main courses 290Kč–690Kč. AE, MC, V. Daily noon–4pm and 6:30pm–midnight. Metro: Malostranská.

Moderate

Vinárna U Maltézských rytířů (At Knights of Malta) ★ CZECH This restaurant on the ground floor and in the cellar of a charming house provides one of the friendliest and most reasonable home-cooked Czech meals in central Prague. The atmosphere makes you feel as if you've been invited into the family's home for a cozy candlelit dinner. The menu offers a fine and affordable chateaubriand for two and a breast of duck with saffron apples. Save room for the flaky strudel served with egg cognac.

Prokopská 10, Prague 1. ✆ **257-530-075.** www.umaltezskychrytiru.cz. Reservations recommended. Main courses 325Kč–600Kč. AE, MC, V. Daily 1–11pm. Metro: Malostranská plus tram no. 12, 20, or 22 to Malostranské náměstí.

Inexpensive

Bohemia Bagel ☺ BAGELS/SANDWICHES The local Bohemia Bagel chain is a solid choice for breakfast or lunch, with several outlets scattered around town. Breakfast offerings include the standard bagel with cream cheese as well as more items like bacon and eggs. The lunch menu is filled with soups and fresh sandwiches, served on a bagel or French bread. Another branch is located just off Old Town Square at Masná 2 (Staré Město; ✆ **224-812-560;** daily 8am–11pm; metro: Staroměstská), which includes an Internet cafe with 15 terminals, a small garden with outside seating, and a playroom for children.

Lázeňská 19, Prague 1 (Malá Strana). ✆ **257-218-192.** www.bohemiabagel.cz. Bagels and sandwiches 60Kč–175Kč. No credit cards. Daily 7:30am–7pm. Metro: Malostranská plus tram no. 12, 20, or 22 to Malostranské náměstí.

STARÉ MĚSTO (OLD TOWN)

Very Expensive

Allegro ★★ ITALIAN/INTERNATIONAL The house restaurant of the Four Seasons Hotel has been at the forefront of Prague dining since opening its doors a few years ago. It was the first recipient of a Michelin star in central Europe and has now grabbed the prize 2 years running. Chef Andrea Accordi's cooking mixes northern Italian influences with international trends and even a few local influences. Dinners can be prohibitively expensive for anyone not traveling on the company's dime, though the daily prix-fixe lunch menus help bring the food within reach of mere mortals.

Veleslavínova 2a, Prague 1. ✆ **221-427-000.** www.fourseasons.com. Reservations recommended. Main courses 750Kc–1,250Kc; 2-course fixed-price lunch 750Kč, 3-course fixed-price lunch 950Kč. AE, DC, MC, V. Daily 11:30am–5pm and 5:30–10:30pm; Sun brunch 11:30am–3pm. Metro: Staroměstská.

Bellevue ★★ INTERNATIONAL With its excellent views of Prague Castle, the Bellevue is a perennial top choice. The ambitious owners have put all their energy into the intelligent menu: beef, nouvelle sauces, well-dressed fish and duck, delicate pastas, and artistic desserts. For a tamer but extraordinary treat, try the roasted veal cheek with potato purée. Desserts feature a vanilla-bean crème brûlée. Reserve in advance to snag a coveted table with a castle view.

Smetanovo nábřeží 18, Prague 1. ✆ **222-221-443.** www.bellevuerestaurant.cz. Reservations recommended. Set meals from 990Kč (2-course) to 1,390Kč (5-course), excluding wine. AE, DC, MC, V. Daily noon–3pm and 5:30–11pm; Sun brunch 11am–3pm. Metro: Staroměstská.

La Degustation ★★★ CONTINENTAL/CZECH Without a doubt, this is one of the city's best dining spots. It is housed in an Old Town corner building and has a minimalist interior. Two different prix-fixe, seven-course menus are served, as diners are invited to sample a wide array of food and wine. The Bohême Bourgeois menu finds inspiration in old Czech cookbooks and raises by miles the level of Czech cuisine usually served in restaurants here. The Chef's Menu adds more exotic items such as Kobe beef. Each dish is accompanied by an excellent selection of wines served by experienced sommeliers. Daily lunch specials can bring the price down to a more manageable 600Kč per meal.

Haštalská 18, Prague 1. ✆ **222-311-234.** www.ladegustation.cz. Reservations recommended. Fixed-price menu 2,250Kč–2,750Kč. AE, MC, V. Mon–Sat 6pm–midnight; Tues–Thurs noon–2:30pm. Metro: Staroměstská.

Expensive

King Solomon Restaurant ★KOSHER Under the supervision of the Orthodox Council of Kashrut, the King Solomon has brought to Prague a truly kosher restaurant, across from the Pinkas Synagogue. The restaurant's dozen booths are camped under an industrial-looking atrium. During dining hours, which strictly adhere to the Sabbath, you can choose from a variety of fresh vegetable and meat dishes following kosher dietary rules. The broad menu ranges from vegetable béchamel to stuffed roast quail. Selections of Israeli, American, and Moravian kosher wine include the restaurant's pride: a Frankovka red from the Baron Aaron Günsberger Moravian cellars.

Široká 8, Prague 1. ✆ **224-818-752.** www.kosher.cz. Reservations recommended. Main courses 250Kč–1,600Kč. AE, MC, V. Sun–Thurs noon–11pm; Fri dinner and Sat lunch by arrangement only. Metro: Staroměstská.

Moderate

Kogo ★ITALIAN This modern, upscale trattoria for years has been a local favorite for brokers and bankers who work nearby. Tucked away on a side street just opposite the Havel Market, Kogo manages to combine the warmth and boisterousness of a family restaurant with a high culinary standard in its pastas, meaty entrees, and desserts. Try the fresh, zesty mussels in white wine and garlic (*cozze al vino bianco e aglio*) or the tangy grilled salmon. The wine list is extensive, and the tiramisu is light and sweet without being soggy.

Kogo has a second, even more popular, location in the atrium of the Slovanský Dům shopping center at Na Příkopě 22 (✆ **221-451-259**). The prices are higher here but the location makes it a logical choice for a meal before or after taking in a movie at the multiplex cinema.

Havelská 27, Prague 1. ✆ **224-214-543.** www.kogo.cz. Reservations recommended. Main courses 210Kč–480Kč. AE, MC, V. Daily 9am–midnight. Metro: Můstek.

Inexpensive

Bakeshop ★★AMERICAN/DELI Prague's lucky enough to have an American-style bakery and sandwich shop that would be the envy of many an American town or city. Bakeshop is simply the best bakery for miles. Come here for soups, salads, ready-made sandwiches, yogurt cups, and, naturally, bread, cakes, brownies, and cookies. It's one-stop shopping for a picnic lunch. You can eat in at the counter or get it to go.

Kozí 1, Prague 1. ✆**222-316-823.** www.bakeshop.cz. Sandwiches 90Kc–145Kč. AE, MC, V. Daily 7am–7pm. Metro: Staroměstská.

Pizzeria Rugantino ★★ ☺PIZZA Pizzeria Rugantino serves generous salads and the best selection of individual pizzas in Prague. Wood-fired stoves and handmade dough result in a crisp and delicate crust. The pizza "calabrese," with hot chili peppers and spicy pepperoni, is as close as you'll find to American-style pepperoni pizza in this part of Europe. A more spacious Rugantino II is located at Klimentská 40, Prague 1 (✆ **224-815-192;** metro: Florenc or Náměstí Republiky), with a children's corner and plasma TV. The constant buzz, nonsmoking area, heavy child-proof wooden tables, and lots of baby chairs make this a family favorite.

Dušní 4, Prague 1. ✆ **222-318-172.** www.rugantino.cz. Individual pizzas 120Kč–220Kč. AE, MC, V. Mon–Sat 11am–11pm; Sun noon–11pm. Metro: Staroměstská.

NOVÉ MĚSTO (NEW TOWN)

Moderate

Zahrada v Opeře (Garden at the Opera) ★★ INTERNATIONAL Czech designer Bořek Šípek, the man who remodeled former president Havel's offices in Prague Castle, has created a restaurant with a pleasant earthy interior mixing dark and light wood, rattan chairs, and intricate floral arrangements. In this calm oasis, you can relax and enjoy a truly excellent meal (and possibly the best price/quality ratio in town). Highly recommended among the light (but lively) salads and fish and vegetarian dishes is the filet of salmon boiled in champagne with an egg yolk tarragon sauce and served with ginger rice and sautéed vegetables.

Legerova 75, Prague 1 (beside National Museum). ✆ **224-239-685.** www.zahradavopere.cz. Main courses 150Kč–530Kč. AE, MC, V. Daily 11:30am–1am (kitchen open until midnight). Metro: Muzeum.

Inexpensive

Pivovarský dům ★★ CZECH Good Czech beer is not made only by the big brewers. This very popular microbrewery produces its own excellent lager as well as harder-to-find varieties like dark beer and wheat beer. The "Brewery House" also dabbles in borderline-blasphemous (but still pretty good) concoctions such as coffee-, cherry-, and banana-flavored beer. Sharing the spotlight with the beer is excellent traditional Czech food including pork, dumplings, rabbit, goulash, and schnitzel, served in an upscale publike setting. The dining areas are all nonsmoking. You'll need reservations to walk in the door—it's that popular.

Lípová 15 (corner of Ječná), Prague 2. ✆ 296-216-666. www.gastroinfo.cz/pivodum. Reservations recommended. Main courses 135Kč–275Kč. AE, MC, V. Daily 11am–11:30pm. Metro: I. P. Pavlova plus tram no. 4, 6, 10, or 22, one stop to Štěpánská.

VINOHRADY

Very Expensive

Aromi ★★ ITALIAN Definitely worth the splurge and trip out to residential Vinohrady for easily the best Italian cooking and possibly the best seafood in Prague. The swank interior manages to be both fancy and inviting at the same time, lending any meal the feeling of an occasion. The waitstaff is professional yet surprisingly unpretentious for a restaurant of this caliber. My favorite is the homemade ravioli stuffed with potatoes and sea bass, but everything is delicious. Sticking to the pastas can keep the bill manageable. The daily lunch special is a steal at around 200Kč.

Mánesova 78, Prague 2. ✆ **222-713-222.** www.aromi.cz. Reservations recommended. Pastas and main courses 345Kč–600Kč. AE, MC, V. Daily noon–11pm. Metro: Jiřího z Poděbrad or Muzeum plus tram no. 11.

Moderate

Masala ★★ INDIAN This Indian mom-and-pop place is just what the doctor ordered if you have a taste for a well-made curry. Be sure to reserve, especially on a Friday or Saturday night, as there's only a handful of tables and they fill up quickly. The engaging staff will ask you how much spice you want—go for broke, since even "very spicy" would only qualify as "medium" in the U.S. or England, let alone back home in India. All of the classics are offered, including crispy nan bread and flavored yogurt drinks to start.

Mánesova 13, Prague 2 (behind the National Museum). ✆ **222-251-601.** www.masala.cz. Reservations recommended. Main courses 175Kč–395Kč. AE, MC, V. Mon–Fri 11:30am–10:30pm; Sat–Sun 12:30–10:30pm. Metro: Muzeum.

Inexpensive

Radost FX VEGETARIAN Radost has been coasting for years on a menu that was considered daring when it was introduced in 1993, but it's still one of the few—and best—vegetarian options in Prague. The veggie burger served on a grain bun is well seasoned and substantial, and the soups, like lentil and onion, are light and full of flavor. Sautéed vegetable dishes, tofu, and huge Greek salads round out the health-conscious menu. The hipster interior draws a stylish clientele.

Bělehradská 120, Prague 2. ✆ **603-181-500.** www.radostfx.cz. Main courses 80Kč–285Kč. AE, MC, V. Daily 11:30am–5am. Metro: I. P. Pavlova.

Seeing the Sights

Prague's most intriguing aspects are its architecture and atmosphere, best enjoyed while slowly wandering through the city's heart. So, with that in mind, your itinerary should be a loose one. If you have the time and energy, go to Charles Bridge at sunrise and then at sunset to view the grand architecture of Prague Castle and the Old Town skyline. You'll see two completely different cities.

PRAŽSKÝ HRAD (PRAGUE CASTLE) & KARLŮV MOST (CHARLES BRIDGE)

Dating from the 14th century, **Charles Bridge (Karlův most)** ★★★, Prague's most celebrated statue-studded structure, links Staré Město and Malá Strana. For most of its 600 years, the 510m-long (1,673-ft.) span has been a pedestrian promenade, though for centuries walkers had to share the concourse with horse-drawn vehicles and trolleys. These days, the bridge is filled to brimming with tourists, souvenir hawkers, portraitists, and the occasional busking musician. In 2009, the crowding was made all the worse by the presence of scaffolding, as city authorities began a long-term project to clean and revitalize the bridge. The bridge is still fully accessible, though the presence of modern construction equipment does mar the views somewhat.

The best times to stroll across the bridge are early morning and around sunset, when the crowds have thinned and the shadows are more mysterious.

Pražský Hrad (Prague Castle) ★★★ This huge hilltop complex on Hradčanské náměstí encompasses dozens of houses, towers, churches, courtyards, and monuments. A visit to the castle can easily take an entire day, depending on how thoroughly you explore it. Still, you can see the top sights—St. Vitus Cathedral, the Royal Palace, St. George's Basilica, the Powder Tower, and Golden Lane—in the space of a morning or an afternoon.

Chrám sv. Víta (St. Vitus Cathedral), named for a wealthy 4th-century Sicilian martyr, isn't just the dominant part of the castle, it's the most important section historically. Built over various phases, beginning in A.D. 926 as the court church of the Přemyslid princes, the cathedral has long been the center of Prague's religious and political life. Of the massive Gothic cathedral's 21 chapels, the **Svatováclavská kaple (St. Wenceslas Chapel)** ★★ is one of Prague's few must-see indoor sights.

For more than 700 years, beginning in the 9th century, Bohemian kings and princes resided in the **Starý královský palác (Old Royal Palace)** ★★, located in the third courtyard of the castle grounds. Vaulted **Vladislavský sál (Vladislav Hall),** the interior's centerpiece, hosted coronations and is still used for special occasions of state such as inaugurations of presidents.

Bazilika sv. Jiří (St. George's Basilica) ★, adjacent to the Old Royal Palace, is Prague's oldest Romanesque structure, dating from the 10th century. It also houses Bohemia's first convent. No longer serving a religious function, the convent now contains the National Gallery's collection of 19th-century Czech art.

Zlatá ulička (Golden Lane) and Daliborka Tower is a picturesque street of tiny 16th-century houses built into the castle fortifications. Once home to castle sharpshooters, the houses now contain small shops, galleries, and refreshment bars. In 1917, Franz Kafka is said to have lived briefly at no. 22; however, the debate continues as to whether Kafka actually took up residence or just worked in a small office there.

The **Prašná věž (Powder Tower, aka Mihulka)** forms part of the northern bastion of the castle complex just off the Golden Lane. Originally a gunpowder storehouse and a cannon tower, it was turned into a laboratory for the 17th-century alchemists serving the court of Emperor Rudolf II.

Hradčanské náměstí, Hradčany, Prague 1. ✆ **224-373-368.** Fax 224-310-896. www.hrad.cz. Grounds free. Combination ticket for permanent exhibition, St. George's Basilica, Powder Tower, Golden Lane, Daliborka Tower, the Prague Castle Picture Gallery, without guide, 350Kč adults, 175Kč students; short tour (Royal Palace, St. George's Basilica, Golden Lane, and Daliborka Tower) 250Kč adults, 125Kč students. Tickets valid 2 days. Daily 9am–6pm (to 4pm Nov–Mar). Metro: Malostranská, then tram no. 22 or 23, up the hill 2 stops.

THE JEWISH MUSEUM

The **Jewish Museum in Prague** (✆ **221-711-511;** www.jewishmuseum.cz) doesn't refer to one building, but rather the organization that manages the main sites of the former Jewish quarter. These include the **Old Jewish Cemetery,** the **Pinkas Synagogue,** the **Klaus Synagogue,** the **Maisel Synagogue,** the **Ceremonial Hall,** and the **Spanish Synagogue.** Each synagogue features a different exhibition on various aspects of Jewish customs and history. It's not possible to visit the sites individually; instead, you have to purchase a combined-entry ticket that allows access to all the main buildings. You'll find ticket counters selling the tickets inside the synagogues and at ticket windows around the quarter. Admission is 300Kč for adults, 200Kč for students, and free for children 5 and under. The museum's sites are open from April to October Sunday to Friday 9am to 6pm, and November to March Sunday to Friday 9am to 4:30pm. Note that the museum is closed on Saturdays and Jewish holidays. Another synagogue, the **Old-New Synagogue** (see below), is considered separate from the Jewish Museum's main holdings and requires an additional admission ticket.

Staronová synagóga (Old-New Synagogue) ★ First called the New Synagogue to distinguish it from an even older one that no longer exists, the Old-New Synagogue, built around 1270, is Europe's oldest remaining Jewish house of worship. The faithful have prayed here continuously for more than 700 years, carrying on even after a massive 1389 pogrom in Josefov that killed more than 3,000 Jews. Its use as a house of worship was interrupted only between 1941 and 1945 because of the Nazi occupation. The synagogue is also one of Prague's great Gothic buildings, built with vaulted ceilings and retrofitted with Renaissance-era columns. It is not part of the Jewish Museum and requires a separate admission ticket.

Červená 2. ✆ **224-800-812.** www.synagogue.cz. Admission 200Kč adults, 140Kč students (if part of the package for Jewish Museum, 490Kč adults, 330Kč students), free for children 5 and under. Jan–Mar Sun–Thurs 9:30am–4:30pm, Fri 9am–2pm; Apr–Oct Sun–Fri 9:30am–6pm; Nov–Dec Sun–Thurs 9:30am–5pm, Fri 9am–2pm. Closed Sat and Jewish holidays. Metro: Line A to Staroměstská.

Starý židovský hřbitov (Old Jewish Cemetery) ★★ One block from the Old-New Synagogue, this is one of Europe's oldest Jewish burial grounds, dating from the mid–15th century. Because the local government of the time didn't allow Jews to bury their dead elsewhere, graves were dug deep enough to hold 12 bodies vertically, with each tombstone placed in front of the last. The result is one of the world's most crowded cemeteries: a 1-block area filled with tens of thousands of graves. Among those buried here are the celebrated Rabbi Loew (Löw; 1520–1609), who created the legend of Golem (a giant clay "monster" to protect Prague's Jews); and banker Markus Mordechai Maisel (1528–1601), then the richest man in Prague and protector of the city's Jewish community during the reign of Rudolf II.

U Starého hřbitova; the entrance is from Široká 3. ✆ **221-711-511.** www.jewishmuseum.cz. Admission (combined entry to all of the Jewish Museum sites) 300Kč adults, 200Kč students, free for children 5 and under. Apr–Oct Sun–Fri 9am–6pm; Nov–Mar Sun–Fri 9am–4:30pm. Closed Sat and Jewish holidays. Metro: Line A to Staroměstská.

THE NATIONAL GALLERY SITES

The national collection of fine art is grouped for display in a series of venues known collectively as the **Národní Galerie (National Gallery).** Remember that this term refers to several locations, not just one gallery.

The National Gallery's holdings are eclectic and range from classic European masters at the **Šternberský palác** across from the main gate to Prague Castle to modern Czech and European works from the 20th and 21st centuries at the **Veletržní palác** in the neighborhood of Holešovice in Prague 7. Other important museums include a collection of 19th-century Czech art at **St. George's Convent** in the Prague Castle complex and the extensive holdings of medieval and Gothic art at **St. Agnes Convent** near the river in Old Town.

The key Prague sites within the national gallery system are listed below.

Klášter sv. Anežky České (St. Agnes Convent) ★★ A complex of early Gothic buildings and churches dating from the 13th century, the convent, tucked in a quiet corner of Staré Město, began exhibiting much of the National Gallery's collection of medieval art in 2000. Once home to the Order of the Poor Clares, it was established in 1234 by St. Agnes of Bohemia, sister of Wenceslas I. The Blessed Agnes became St. Agnes when Pope John Paul II paid his first visit to Prague in 1990 for her canonization. The most famous among the unique collection of Czech Gothic panel paintings are those by the Master of the Hohenfurth Altarpiece and the Master Theodoricus. The convent is at the end of Anežka, off Haštalské náměstí.

U Milosrdných 17, Prague 1. ✆ **224-810-628.** www.ngprague.cz. Admission 150Kč adults, 80Kč children. Tues–Sun 10am–6pm. Metro: Line A to Staroměstská.

Klášter sv. Jiří na Pražském hradě (St. George's Convent at Prague Castle) ★ The former convent at St. George's houses a fascinating collection of 19th-century Czech painting and sculpture that is especially strong on landscapes and pieces from the Czech national revival period. The collection shows the progression of the Czech lands from a largely agrarian province at the start of the century to a highly developed cultural and industrial space by the end.

Jiřské nám. 33. ✆ **257-531-644.** www.ngprague.cz. Admission 150Kč adults, 80Kč students, free for children 5 and under. Daily 10am–6pm. Metro: Line A to Malostranská plus tram no. 22.

Šternberský palác (Sternberg Palace) ★★ The jewel in the National Gallery crown, the gallery at Sternberg Palace, adjacent to the main gate of Prague Castle, displays a wide menu of European art throughout the ages. It features 5 centuries of everything from Orthodox icons to Renaissance oils by Dutch masters. Pieces by Rembrandt, El Greco, Goya, and Van Dyck are mixed among numerous pieces from Austrian imperial court painters. Exhibits rotate throughout the seasons.

Hradčanské nám. 15, Prague 1. ✆ **233-090-570.** www.ngprague.cz. Admission 150Kč adults, 80Kč students, free for children 5 and under. Tues–Sun 10am–6pm. Metro: Line A to Malostranská plus tram no. 22.

Veletržní palác (Museum of 20th- and 21st-Century Art) ★★ This 1928 Functionalist (Bauhaus-style) palace, built for trade fairs, was remodeled and reopened in 1995 to hold the bulk of the National Gallery's collection of 20th- and 21st-century works by Czech and other European artists. The highlights on three floors of exhibition space include paintings by Klimt, Munch, Schiele, and Picasso, among other modern European masters, as well as a riveting display of Czech constructivist and surrealist works from the 1920s and 1930s. The first floor features temporary exhibits from traveling shows. There's also a good gift shop on the ground floor.

Veletržní at Dukelských hrdinů 47, Prague 7. ✆ **224-301-111.** www.ngprague.cz. Admission 200Kč adults, 100Kč students, free for children 5 and under. Tues–Sun 10am–6pm. Metro: Line C to Vltavská. Tram: 12, 14, or 17 to Strossmayerovo nám.

HISTORIC SQUARES

The most celebrated square in the city, **Staroměstské Náměstí (Old Town Square) ★★★**, is surrounded by baroque buildings and packed with colorful craftspeople, cafes, and entertainers. In ancient days, the site was a major crossroads on central European merchant routes. In its center stands a memorial to Jan Hus, the 15th-century martyr who crusaded against Prague's German-dominated religious and political establishment. It was unveiled in 1915, on the 500th anniversary of Hus's execution. Its most compelling features are the dark asymmetry and fluidity of the figures. It has been in reconstruction since 2007. Take metro line A to Staroměstská.

One of the city's most historic squares, **Václavské Náměstí (Wenceslas Square) ★★**, was formerly the horse market (Koňský trh). The once muddy swath between the buildings played host to the country's equine auctioneers. The top of the square, where the National Museum now stands, was the outer wall of the New Town fortifications, bordering the Royal Vineyards. Unfortunately, the city's busiest highway now cuts the museum off from the rest of the square it dominates. Trolleys streamed up and down the square until the early 1980s. Today the 1km-long (⅔-mile) boulevard is lined with cinemas, shops, hotels, restaurants, and casinos.

The square was given its present name in 1848. The giant equestrian statue of St. Wenceslas on horseback surrounded by four other saints has become a popular platform for speakers. Actually, the square has thrice been the site of riots and revolutions—in 1848, 1968, and 1989. Take metro line A or B to Můstek.

PARKS & GARDENS

A favorite getaway is **Vyšehrad Park ★** above the Vltava south of the city center. This 1,000-year-old citadel encloses a peaceful set of gardens, playgrounds, footpaths, and the national cemetery next to the twin-towered Church of Sts. Peter and Paul, reconstructed from 1885 to 1887. The park provides a fantastic wide-angle view of the whole city. Take metro line C to Vyšehrad or tram no. 3 or 16 to Výtoň. The park is open at all times.

The **Královská zahrada (Royal Garden) ★** at Prague Castle, Prague 1, once the site of the sovereigns' vineyards, was founded in 1534. Dotted with lemon trees and surrounded by 16th-, 17th-, and 18th-century buildings, the park is consciously and conservatively laid out with abundant shrubbery and fountains. Entered from U Prašného mostu street, north of the castle complex, it's open daily from 10am to 6pm in the summer season.

The castle's **Zahrada na Valech (Garden on the Ramparts) ★** is on the cityside hill below the castle. Beyond beautifully groomed lawns and sparse shrubbery is a tranquil low-angle view of the castle above and the city below. Enter the garden from the south side of the castle complex, below Hradčanské náměstí. The garden is open daily from 10am to 6pm in the summer season.

Looming over Malá Strana, adjacent to Prague Castle, lush green **Petřínské sady (Petřín Hill)** is easily recognizable by the miniature replica of the Eiffel Tower that tops it. Gardens and orchards bloom in spring and summer. Throughout the myriad monuments and churches are a mirror maze and an observatory. The Hunger Wall, a decaying 6m-high (20-ft.) stone wall that runs up through Petřín to the grounds of Prague Castle, was commissioned by Charles IV in the 1360s as a medieval welfare project designed to provide jobs for Prague's starving poor. Take tram no. 12, 20, or 22 to Újezd and ride the funicular or start climbing.

Part of the excitement of **Valdštejnská zahrada (Waldstein [Wallenstein] Gardens) ★** at Letenská, Prague 1 (✆ **257-071-111**), is its location, behind a 9m (30-ft.) wall on the back streets of Malá Strana. Inside, elegant gravel paths dotted with classical bronze statues and gurgling fountains fan out in every direction. Laid out in the 17th century, the baroque park was the garden of Gen. Albrecht Waldstein (or Wallenstein; 1581–1634), commander of the Roman Catholic armies during the Thirty Years' War. These gardens are the backyards of Waldstein's Palace—Prague's largest—which replaced 23 houses, three gardens, and the municipal brick kiln. It's now home to the Czech Senate. The gardens are open March to October, daily from 10am to 6pm.

The Shopping Scene

The rapid influx of visitors, wage growth, and a new consumer economy fueled by the shopping habits of the Czech nouveau riche have resulted in expensive boutiques and specialty shops burgeoning in Prague. Shopping malls now offer everything from designer baby clothes to Bruno Magli shoes. The selection of world-renowned labels is beginning to rival that of many western European cities, though shops tend to have a tiny inventory compared with the same outlets in Paris or London. Still, since labor and rent make operations cheaper here, you might find a bargain—particularly at sale time—for the same items offered at points farther west.

For those looking for a piece of Czech handiwork, you can find some of the world's best **crystal** and **glass.** Antiques shops and booksellers abound, and the selection of classical, trendy, and offbeat art is immense at the numerous private galleries. Because beer is a little heavy to carry home and the local wine isn't worth it, take home a bottle of **Becherovka,** the nation's popular herbal liqueur from Karlovy Vary.

The L-shaped half-mile running from the middle of **Wenceslas Square** around the corner to the right on **Na Příkopě** and to the **Palladium Shopping Center** on **Náměstí Republiky** has become Prague's principal shopping hub. In this short distance you'll find several multilevel shopping gallerias, with foreign chains like **H&M, Next, Kenvelo, Pierre Cardin, Adidas,** and **Zara.** Between the centers is a wide array of boutiques and antiques shops.

For glass and crystal, try **Moser ★★★**, Na Příkopě 12, Prague 1 (✆ **224-211-293;** www.moser-glass.com; metro: Náměstí Republiky). The Moser family began selling Bohemia's finest crystal in central Prague in 1857, drawing customers from around the world.

Celetná Crystal ★, Celetná 15, Prague 1 (✆ **222-324-022;** metro: Náměstí Republiky), has a wide selection of world-renowned Czech crystal, china, arts and crafts, garnets, and jewelry displayed in a spacious three-floor showroom right in the heart of Prague.

Czechs swear by **Halada ★**, Na Příkopě 16, Prague 1 (✆ **224-218-643;** www.halada.cz; metro: Můstek), which boasts one of the best arrays of market-priced gold, silver, platinum, and fine gems in this city.

On the short, wide street perpendicular to Melantrichova, between Staroměstské náměstí and Václavské náměstí, **Havel's Market** (Havelský trh; not named after former president Václav Havel), Havelská ulice, Prague 1, features dozens of vendors selling seasonal homegrown fruit and vegetables at decent prices for the city center. Other goods, including detergent, flowers, and cheap souvenirs, are also for sale. Open Monday to Friday from 8am to 6pm. Take metro line A or B to Můstek.

Prague After Dark

For many Czechs, the best way to spend an evening is at the neighborhood pub, enjoying world-class beer and some boisterous conversation. These types of evenings are always open to visitors, of course, though the language may occasionally be an issue (at least at the start of the night before the beer kicks in).

If raucous beer nights are not your thing, Prague for decades has enjoyed a vibrant drama scene. In addition, Prague has at least two premier opera venues: the State Opera at the top of Wenceslas Square (Václavské nám.) and the National Theater.

Prague's longest-running entertainment tradition, of course, is classical music. Serious music lovers are best advised to take in a performance of the **Czech Philharmonic** at the Rudolfinum in Staré Město or the **Prague Symphony Orchestra** at the Obecní dům, near Náměstí Republiky. Another option is to see one of the many **chamber concerts** offered at churches and palaces around town. These can be very good, though ticket prices are often higher than for the Philharmonic and the quality may not be nearly as good.

Once in Prague, you can buy tickets at the venue box office or at one of the many local ticket agency offices throughout the city center. **Ticketpro** has several offices around town, including at **Prague Information Services** (✆ **221-714-444;**

www.pis.cz) offices at the Old Town Hall and at Rytířská 31. Ticketpro also sells tickets at Václavské nám. 38, Prague 1 (✆ **296-329-999**), and through the helpful **Prague Tourist Center,** near the Můstek metro stop at Rytířská 12, Prague 1 (✆ **296-333-333**), open daily from 9am to 8pm. **Bohemia Ticket** has offices at Na Příkopě 16, Prague 1 (✆ **224-215-031;** www.bohemiaticket.cz), and is open Monday to Friday 10am to 7pm, Saturday 10am to 5pm, and Sunday 10am to 7pm.

THE PERFORMING ARTS

Although there's plenty of music year-round, the city's orchestras all come to life during the international **Prague Spring Festival,** an annual 3-week series of classical music events that runs from mid-May to early June; the events began as a rallying point for Czech culture in the aftermath of World War II. The country's top performers usually participate in the festival, as well as some noted international stars. Tickets for concerts range from 250Kč to 2,000Kč and are available in advance from Hellichova 18, Prague 1 (✆ **257-312-547;** www.festival.cz).

The Czech Philharmonic Orchestra performs at the **Rudolfinum,** Alšovo nábřeží 12, Prague 1 (✆ **227-059-352;** www.ceskafilharmonie.cz; metro: Staroměstská). It's the traditional voice of the country's national pride, often playing works by Dvořak and Smetana. The **Prague Symphony** performs at the Art Nouveau **Smetana Hall ★★**, naměstí Republiky 5, Prague 1 (✆ **222-002-336;** metro: Naměstí Republiky). It focuses more on 20th-century music with occasional forays into Bach.

Lavishly constructed in the late-Renaissance style of northern Italy, the gold-crowned **Národní divadlo (National Theater),** Národní 2, Prague 1 (✆ **224-901-448;** www.narodni-divadlo.cz; metro: Národní třída), overlooking the Vltava River, is one of Prague's most recognizable landmarks. Completed in 1881, the theater was built to nurture the Czech National Revival—a grass-roots movement to replace the dominant German culture with that of native Czechs. Today, classic productions are staged here.

THE CLUB & MUSIC SCENE

The Velvet Revolution had its roots in the underground rock clubs that kept the youth tuned into something more than the monotones of the Communist Party during the gray 1970s and 1980s period known as "normalization." The Communists' persecution of the Czech garage band Plastic People of the Universe, named for a Frank Zappa refrain, motivated playwright Václav Havel and his friends to keep the human rights heat on the Politburo. As president, Havel paid homage to rock's part in the revolution and kept company with the likes of Zappa, Springsteen, Dylan, and the Stones—all of whom paid tribute to him as "the rock-'n'-roll president."

Almost universally, the amps in clubs are turned up to absurd distortion. But while most bands playing Prague today lack the political edge of the prerevolution days, some have kept their unique Slavic passion without slavishly copying international trends. Some bands to watch out for include hard rockers Kabát, the trendy folk band Čechomor, and pop acts like Kryštof, Chinaski, and Support Lesbiens.

JAZZ & BLUES CLUBS Upscale by Czech standards, the AghaRTA Jazz Centrum ★, Železná 16, Prague 1 (✆ **222-211-275;** www.agharta.cz; metro: Můstek), regularly features some of the best music in town, from standard acoustic trios and quartets to Dixieland, funk, and fusion. Bands usually begin at 9pm, but try to come much earlier to snag one of the few places to sit. Open daily from 7pm to midnight. **Blues Sklep,** Liliová 10, Prague 1 (✆ **221-466-138;** www.bluessklep.cz; metro: Staroměstská), is a relative and welcome newcomer to Prague's jazz scene. The "Blues Cellar" focuses not surprisingly on the blues, bringing in bands and singers from around central Europe. Open daily from 7pm to 2:30am. **JazzDock ★★**, Janáčkova nábřeží 2, Praha 5 (✆ **774-058-838;** www.jazzdock.cz; metro: Anděl), one of the hottest openings of late, is a riverside jazz club bringing together a lineup of some of central Europe's best jazz, blues, and soul singers, along with good food and beautiful views out over the river. The club is big enough to give at least some of the tables good sightlines to the stage (unlike lots of other clubs in Prague); at the same time, it's small enough to be intimate. Concerts begin around 9pm. Open daily from 11am to 4am. **Reduta Jazz Club ★**, Národní 20, Prague 1 (✆ **224-933-487;** www.redutajazzclub.cz; metro: Národní třída), has been around since the 1950s and still has a kind of welcoming retro feel, as if Charlie Parker or Miles himself might walk in at some point during the night. The music usually starts around 9:30pm. Open daily from 9pm to midnight.

PUBS & BARS

Good pub brews and conversations are Prague's preferred late-evening entertainment. Unlike British, Irish, or German beer halls, a true Czech pub ignores accouterments like cushy chairs and warm wooden paneling, and cuts straight to the chase—beer. While some Czech pubs do serve a hearty plate of food alongside the suds, it's the brew, uncommonly cheap at usually less than 35Kč a pint, that keeps people sitting for hours.

Foreign-theme pubs are popping up all over Prague, offering tastes ranging from Irish to Mexican. Still, it feels a bit like trying to sell Indian tea in China. One of the most Czech of the central city pubs, **U zlatého tygra (At the Golden Tiger),** Husova 17, Prague 1 (✆ **222-221-111;** www.uzlatehotygra.cz; metro: Staroměstská or Můstek), was once the favorite watering hole of Václav Havel and one of his mentors, writer Bohumil Hrabal, who died in 1997. Particularly smoky and not especially visitor-friendly, this is a one-stop education in Czech pub culture. Pilsner Urquell is the house brew. Havel and former U.S. president Bill Clinton joined Hrabal for a traditional Czech pub evening here during Clinton's visit in 1994, much to the chagrin of the regulars. Open daily from 3 to 11pm; try to arrive before 3pm to secure a table.

Day Trips from Prague

KARLŠTEJN CASTLE

By far the most popular destination in the Czech Republic after Prague, **Karlštejn Castle ★★** is an easy day trip for those interested in getting out of the city. Charles IV built this medieval castle from 1348 to 1357 to safeguard the crown jewels of the Holy Roman Empire. Although the castle had been changed over the years, with such additions as late Gothic staircases and bridges, renovators have removed these additions, restoring the castle to its original medieval state.

As you approach, little can prepare you for your first view: a spectacular Disney-like castle perched on a hill, surrounded by lush forests and vineyards. In its early days, the king's jewels housed within enhanced the castle's importance and reputation. Vandalism having forced several of its finest rooms to close, these days the castle is most spectacular from the outside. Unfortunately, many of the more interesting restored rooms are kept off-limits and open only for special guests.

GETTING THERE The best way to get to Karlštejn is by **train** (there's no bus service). Trains leave regularly from either Prague's Main Station (at the Hlavní nádraží metro stop on line C) or Smíchovské nádraží, metro line B, and take about 40 minutes to reach Karlštejn. The one-way, second-class fare is 49Kč. It's a short, relaxing trip along the Berounka River. On the way you pass through Řevnice, Martina Navrátilová's birthplace. Keep your eyes open for your first glimpse of the majestic castle. Once you arrive at Karlštejn train station, it's a 20- to 30-minute hike up the road to the castle. While you're at the station, mark down the return times for trains to Prague to better plan your trip back.

You can also **drive** along one of two routes, both of which take 30 minutes. Here's the more scenic one: Leave Prague from the southwest along Hwy. 4 in the direction of Strakonice and take the Karlštejn cutoff, following the signs (and traffic!). The second, much less scenic route follows the main highway leading out of Prague from the west as if you were going to Plzeň. About 20 minutes down the road is the well-marked cutoff for Karlštejn. (You can tell you have missed the cutoff if you get to the town of Beroun. If that happens, take any exit and head back the other way; the signs to Karlštejn are also marked heading toward Prague.)

TEREZÍN (THERESIENSTADT)

Noticing that northwest Bohemia was susceptible to Prussian attacks, Joseph II, the son of Austrian Empress Maria Teresa, decided to build **Terezín** ★★ to ward off further offensives. Two fortresses were built, but the Prussian army bypassed the area during the last Austro-Prussian conflict and in 1866 attacked Prague anyway. That spelled the end of Terezín's fortress charter, which was repealed in 1888. More than 50 years later, the fortifications were just what occupying Nazi forces needed.

When people around the world talk of Nazi atrocities during World War II, the name Terezín (*Theresienstadt* in German) rarely comes up. At the so-called Paradise Ghetto, there were no gas chambers, no mass machine-gun executions, and no medical testing rooms. Terezín wasn't used to exterminate the Jews, Gypsies, homosexuals, and political prisoners it held. Rather, the occupying Nazi forces used it as a transit camp. About 140,000 people passed though Terezín's gates; more than half ended up at the death camps of Auschwitz and Treblinka.

Instead, Terezín will live in infamy for the cruel trick that SS chief Heinrich Himmler played on the world within its walls. On June 23, 1944, three foreign observers—two from the Red Cross—came to Terezín to find out if the rumors of Nazi atrocities were true. They left with the impression that all was well, duped by a well-planned "beautification" of the camp. The Germans carefully choreographed every detail of the visit. The observers saw children studying at staged schools that didn't exist, and store shelves, which had been specially set up, stocked with goods. So that the observers wouldn't think the camp was overcrowded, the Nazis transported some 7,500 of the camp's sick and elderly prisoners to Auschwitz. Children even ran up to an SS commandant just as the observers passed; the commandant handed the children cans of sardines to shouts of "What? Sardines again?" The trick worked so well that the Nazis made a film of the camp, *A Town Presented to the Jews from the Führer,* while it was still "self-governing."

Russian forces liberated Terezín on May 10, 1945, several days after Berlin had fallen to the Allies. Today, the camp stands as a memorial to the dead and a monument to human depravity.

GETTING THERE If you're **driving,** Terezín lies just off the D-8 motorway that leads north out of Prague in the direction of Dresden and Berlin. Watch for the turnoff signs. It's a 45-minute drive. Several **buses** leave daily from the small bus station above the **Nádraží Holešovice metro stop** (line C, red). The ride takes about an hour and costs 75Kč.

WEST BOHEMIA & THE SPAS

Of the two regions that make up the Czech Republic, the better known is the westernmost one, Bohemia. It is the land that gave Europe its favorite catchall term for free spirit: "Bohemian." Despite being beaten into submission by successive Austrian, German, and Soviet hegemony, that spirit has lived on. In the 14th century, the region's capital, Prague, was the seat of the Holy Roman Empire under Charles IV. So Bohemians maintain their collective historical memory that they too, at least briefly, ruled the world. Even under the domination of the Austrians, Bohemia's industrial base was world-class, and in the peace between the two world wars of the 20th century, independent Bohemia, especially Prague, created some of the greatest wealth on earth.

Much was lost in the destruction of World War II and the 4 decades of Communism that followed. The good news is that Bohemia is slowly returning to its earlier prominence, leaving behind its reputation as a satellite in the former Eastern Bloc and forging a more familiar role as a crossroads at the heart of Europe.

Karlovy Vary (Carlsbad) ★

The discovery of Karlovy Vary (Carlsbad) by Charles IV reads like a 14th-century episode of the old hit TV show *The Beverly Hillbillies.* According to local lore, the king was out huntin' for some food when up from the ground came a-bubblin' *water* (though discovered by his dogs and not an errant gunshot). Knowing a good thing when he saw it, Charles immediately set to work building a small castle in the area, naming the town that evolved around it Karlovy Vary, which translates as "Charles's Boiling Place." The first spa buildings were built in 1522, and before long, notables like Albrecht of Wallenstein, Peter the Great, and later Bach, Beethoven, Freud, and Marx all came to Karlovy Vary for a holiday retreat.

After World War II, Eastern Bloc travelers (following in the footsteps of Marx, no doubt) discovered the town, and Karlovy Vary became a destination for the proletariat. On doctors' orders, most workers would enjoy regular stays of 2 or 3 weeks, letting the mineral waters ranging from 110°F to 162°F (43°C–72°C) from the town's 12 springs heal their tired and broken bodies. Even now, a large number of spa guests are here on doctor's orders and many of the "resorts" you see, in fact, are upscale hospitals.

Most of the 40-plus years of Communist neglect have been erased as a barrage of renovations continues to restore the spa's former glory. Gone is the statue of Russian cosmonaut Yuri Gagarin. Gone are almost all the fading, crumbling building facades

SPA CURES & treatments IN KARLOVY VARY

Most visitors come for a spa treatment, a therapy that lasts 1 to 3 weeks. After consulting with a spa physician, you're given a specific regimen of activities that may include mineral baths, massages, waxings, mudpacks, electrotherapy, and pure oxygen inhalation. After spending the morning at a spa or sanatorium, you're usually directed to walk the paths of the town's surrounding forest.

The common denominator of all the cures is an ample daily dose of hot mineral water, which bubbles up from 12 springs. This water definitely has a distinct odor and taste. You'll see people chugging it down, but it doesn't necessarily taste very good. Some thermal springs actually taste and smell like rotten eggs. You may want to take a small sip at first. Do keep in mind that the waters are used to treat internal disorders, so the minerals may cleanse the body thoroughly—in other words, they can cause diarrhea.

You'll also notice that almost everyone in town seems to be carrying "the cup." This funny-looking cup is basically a mug with a built-in straw running through the handle. Young and old alike parade around with their mugs, filling and refilling them at each thermal water tap. You can buy these mugs everywhere for as little as 60Kč or as much as 230Kč; they make a quirky souvenir. ***But be warned:*** None of the mugs can make the warmer hot springs taste any better.

The minimum spa treatment lasts 1 week and must be arranged in advance. A spa treatment package traditionally

that used to line both sides of the river. In their places stand restored buildings, cherubs, caryatids, and more.

Today, some 150,000 people travel to the spa resort every year to sip, bathe, and frolic, though most enjoy the "13th spring" (actually a hearty herb-and-mineral liqueur called Becherovka) as much as—if not more than—the 12 nonalcoholic versions. Czechs will tell you that all have medical benefits. In a historical irony, the Russians have rediscovered Karlovy Vary in droves, so don't be surprised to hear Russian on the streets much more frequently than English, German, or Czech.

ESSENTIALS

GETTING THERE At all costs, **avoid the train from Prague,** which takes more than 4 hours on a circuitous route. If you're arriving from another direction, Karlovy Vary's main train station is connected to the town center by bus no. 12 or 13.

Taking a bus to Karlovy Vary is much more convenient. Frequent express **buses** travel from Prague's Florenc bus station in 2¼ hours at a cost of about 140Kč. One of the best bus lines offering the trip is **Student Agency** (**© 800-100-300;** www.studentagency.cz), which runs hourly buses to Karlovy Vary from Florenc bus station, and even shows a film during the trip. For information on train and bus timetables, go to www.jizdnirady.cz.

From Karlovy Vary's Dolní nádraží (bus station) take a 10-minute walk or the local bus no. 4 into Karlovy Vary's spa center. Note that you must have a ticket to board local transport. You can buy tickets for 16Kč at the bus station stop, or from the bus driver, which will then cost you 20Kč.

includes room, full board, and complete therapy regimen; the cost varies from about 900Kč to 2,500Kč per person per day, depending on season and facilities. Rates are highest from May to September and lowest from November to February. Nearly all of the hotels in town will provide spa and health treatments, so ask when you book your room. Most will happily arrange a treatment if they don't provide them directly.

If you're coming for just a day or two, you can experience the waters on an "outpatient" basis. The largest therapeutic complex in town (and in the Czech Republic) is the **Alžbětiny Lázně-Lázně V,** Smetanovy sady 1145/1 (✆ **353-304-211;** www.spa5.cz). On its menu are more than 60 kinds of treatments, including water cures, massages, a hot-air bath, a steam bath, a whirlpool, and a pearl bath, as well as use of their swimming pool. You can choose packages of different procedures that run between 340Kč for an anticellulite beer bath to 980Kč for a hot stone massage. It's open Monday to Friday 8am to 3pm for spa treatments; the pool is open Monday to Friday 9am to noon and 1 to 9pm, Saturday 9am to 9pm, and Sunday 9am to 6pm.

The **Sanatorium Baths III,** Mlýnské nábřeží 7 (✆ **353-225-641**), welcomes day-trippers with mineral baths, massages, saunas, and a cold pool. It's open Monday to Friday 7am to 2pm for spa treatments; the swimming pool and sauna are open Monday to Friday 3 to 6pm and Saturday 1 to 5pm.

The nearly 2-hour **drive** from Prague to Karlovy Vary can be very busy and dangerous due to undisciplined Czech drivers. If you're going by car, take Hwy. E48 from the western end of Prague and follow it straight through to Karlovy Vary. This two-lane highway widens in a few spots to let cars pass slow-moving vehicles on hills. The spa area is closed to private vehicles, so you'll have to leave the car in one of several parking lots surrounding the area and walk from there.

VISITOR INFORMATION **Infocentrum města Karlovy Vary** is located near the main Mlýnská Kolonáda, at Mlýnské nabřeží 5 (✆ **355-321-176**). It's open Monday to Friday from 9am to 7pm and Saturday and Sunday from 10am to 6pm. It has a window at the terminal of the **Dolní (lower) nádraží** bus and train station, Západní ulice (✆ **353-232-838**). These are the official town's information centers, which will answer your questions and help you with accommodations, getting tickets for entertainment in the city, and so on. Be sure to pick up *Promenáda* magazine, a comprehensive collection of events with a small map of the town center. Alternatively, you'll find information on www.karlovyvary.cz.

WHERE TO STAY

Private rooms used to be the best places to stay in Karlovy Vary with regard to quality and price. But this is changing as more and more hotels renovate and raise standards—as well as prices. Private accommodations can still provide better value, but they take a little extra work. If you want to arrange a room, try the **Infocentrum** (see above). Expect to pay about 1,500Kč for a double.

Some of the town's major spa hotels accommodate only those who are paying for complete treatment, unless for some reason their occupancy rates are particularly low. The hotels I've listed below accept guests for stays of any length.

Grandhotel Pupp ★ The Pupp, built in 1701, is one of Europe's oldest grand hotels. Its public areas boast the expected splendor and charm, as do the renovated guest rooms. The best ones tend to be those facing the town center and are located on the upper floors; these have good views and sturdy wooden furniture. Some rooms have amenities such as air-conditioning, television, minibar, and safe, though not all do. The Grand has as grand a dining room as you'll find, with the food to match (see "Where to Dine," below). The hotel also has a stylish casino (open midnight–4am). The rack rates are high, but check the website for occasional deals.

Mírové nám. 2, 360 91, Karlovy Vary. ✆ **353-109-111.** Fax 353-226-032. www.pupp.cz. 111 units. From 7,750Kč double deluxe; from 11,250Kč suite. Rates include breakfast. AE, DC, MC, V. Valet parking. **Amenities:** 4 restaurants; bar; cafe; casino; golf course; health club; room service; tennis courts. *In room:* TV, hair dryer, minibar.

Hotel Dvořák ★ As part of the Vienna International hotel chain, the Dvořák has improved immensely over the past several years, especially in terms of service. This hotel is within sight of the Pupp, but it's less expensive. The Pupp may have the history and elegance, but the Dvořák has the facilities. The rooms are spacious, with elegant decor and medium-size bathrooms with lots of marble. The staff is very attentive. Business travelers will appreciate the hotel's business facilities.

Nová Louka 11, 360 21 Karlovy Vary. ✆ **353-102-111.** Fax 353-102-119. www.hotel-dvorak.cz. 126 units. From 3,375Kč double. AE, DC, MC, V. **Amenities:** Restaurant; fitness center; indoor pool; sauna. *In room:* TV, hair dryer, minibar.

Hotel Embassy ★ On the riverbank across from the Pupp, the Embassy has well-appointed rooms, many with an early-20th-century motif. Set in a historic house, the rooms are medium size with medium-size bathrooms. The staff here really helps make this hotel worthy of consideration, as does the proximity to the pub, which serves some of the best goulash and beer in the city.

Nová Louka 21, 360 01 Karlovy Vary. ✆ **353-221-161.** Fax 353-223-146. www.embassy.cz. 20 units. From 3,130Kč double; from 3,990Kč suite. AE, MC, V. **Amenities:** Pub; lobby bar; indoor golf. *In room:* TV, minibar.

Hotel Palacký This is one of the better deals in town. The hotel is ideally situated on the west side of the river so it gets sun almost all day. The rooms, with their mostly bare walls and low beds, seem huge, especially the ones with a river view. The staff can seem more like furniture than people who help guests, but that's a small price to pay for the relatively good value.

Stará Louka 40, 360 01 Karlovy Vary. ✆ **353-222-544.** Fax 353-223-561. www.hotelpalacky.cz. 21 units. From 2,000Kč double; from 3,000Kč suite. AE, MC, V. **Amenities:** 2 restaurants; Wi-Fi. *In room:* TV, fridge, hair dryer.

WHERE TO DINE

Embassy Restaurant ★★ CZECH/CONTINENTAL On the ground floor of the Embassy Hotel, this is one of the oldest and best restaurants in town. It offers an intimate dining room with historic interior. If you visit in winter, get a table next to the original hearth. In summer, sit on the bridge outside the front door. Here you'll find many traditional Czech dishes with slight twists that make them interesting. The grilled loin of pork covered with a light, creamy green-pepper sauce makes a nice change from the regular roast pork served by most Czech restaurants. The spicy goulash is more reminiscent of Hungary's piquant flavors than blander Czech fare. The warm strawberries and peppercorns dessert is much better than it sounds.

Nová Louka 21. ✆ **353-221-161.** Reservations recommended. Soups 70Kč; main courses 220Kč–600Kč. AE, MC, V. Daily 11am–11pm.

Grand Restaurant CONTINENTAL It's no surprise that the Grandhotel Pupp has the nicest dining room in town: an elegant space with tall ceilings, huge mirrors, and glistening chandeliers. A large menu features equally large portions of salmon, chicken, veal, pork, turkey, and beef in a variety of heavy and heavier sauces. Even the mouthwatering trout with mushrooms is smothered in butter sauce.

In the Grandhotel Pupp, Mírové nám. 2. ✆ **353-109-646.** Reservations recommended. Soups 80Kč; main courses 290Kč–750Kč. AE, MC, V. Daily noon–3pm and 6–11pm.

Hospoda U Švejka CZECH This addition to the pub scene plays on the tried-and-true touristy *Good Soldier Švejk* theme. Luckily, the tourist trap goes no further, and once inside, you find a refreshingly nonsmoky though thoroughly Czech atmosphere. Locals and tourists alike rub elbows while throwing back some fine lager for 69Kč per half liter, and standard pub favorites such as goulash and beef tenderloin in cream sauce.

Stará Louka 10. ✆ **353-232-276.** Soups 55Kč; appetizers 69Kč–109Kč; main courses 159Kč–319Kč. AE, MC, V. Daily 11am–10pm.

Promenáda ★ CZECH/CONTINENTAL This cozy, intimate spot may not be as elegant as the Grand Restaurant, but the cooking is more adventurous. Across from the Vřídelní Kolonáda, the Promenáda offers a wide menu with generous portions. The daily menu usually includes well-prepared wild game, but the mixed grill for two and the chateaubriand, both flambéed at the table, are the chef's best dishes. The wine list features a large selection of wines from around Europe, but don't neglect the Czech wines. An order of crêpes suzette, big enough to satisfy two, tops off a wonderful meal.

Tržiště 31. ✆ **353-225-648.** Reservations highly recommended. Soups 70Kč; appetizers 90Kč–320Kč; main courses 290Kč–750Kč. AE, MC, V. Daily noon–11pm.

EXPLORING KARLOVY VARY

The town's slow pace and pedestrian promenades, lined with turn-of-the-20th-century Art Nouveau buildings, turn strolling into an art form. Nighttime walks take on an even more mystical feel as the sewers, the river, and the many major cracks in the roads emit steam from the hot springs running underneath.

If you're traveling here by train or bus, a good place to start your exploration is the **Hotel Thermal,** I. P. Pavlova 11 (✆ **359-001-111**), at the northern end of the Old Town's center. Built in the 1970s, it exemplifies how obtrusive Communist architecture could be. Nestled between the town's eastern hills and the Ohře River, the glass, steel, and concrete Thermal sticks out like a sore thumb amid the rest of the town's 19th-century architecture. Nonetheless, you'll find three important places at the Thermal: the only centrally located outdoor public pool; an upper terrace boasting a truly spectacular view of the town; and Karlovy Vary's largest theater, which holds many of the town's film festival's premier events. Take it all in. But because the Hotel Thermal is not that pleasing to the eye, it's best to keep walking.

As you enter the heart of the town on the river's west side, you'll see the ornate white wrought-iron gazebo named **Sadová Kolonáda** adorning the beautifully manicured park, **Dvořákovy Sady.** Continue to follow the river, and about 100m (328 ft.) later you'll encounter the **Mlýnská Kolonáda.** This long, covered walkway houses several Karlovy Vary springs, which you can sample free 24 hours a day. Each spring has a plaque beside it describing its mineral elements and temperature. Bring your own cup or buy one just about anywhere (see the box "Spa Cures & Treatments in Karlovy Vary," above) to sip the waters, as most are too hot to drink from with your hands. When you hit the river bend, you'll see the majestic **Church of St. Mary Magdalene** perched atop a hill, overlooking the **Vřídlo,** the hottest spring. Built in 1736, the church is the work of Kilián Ignác Dientzenhofer, who also created two of Prague's more notable churches—both named St. Nicholas.

Housing Vřídlo, which blasts water some 15m (49 ft.) into the air, is the glass building where a statue of Soviet cosmonaut Yuri Gagarin once stood. (Gagarin's statue has since made a safe landing at the Karlovy Vary Airport, where it greets the waves of Russian visitors who flood the town.) Now called the **Vřídelní Kolonáda,** the structure, built in 1974, houses several hot springs that you can sample for free daily from 6am to 7pm. There are also public restrooms, open daily 6am to 6pm and costing 10Kč.

Heading away from the Vřídelní Kolonáda are Stará and Nová Louka streets, which line either side of the river. Along **Stará (Old) Louka** are several fine cafes and glass and crystal shops. **Nová (New) Louka** is lined with many hotels and the historic town's main theater, built in 1886, which houses paintings by notable artists like Klimt and has just finished a major renovation project that has restored the theater to its original splendor.

Both streets lead eventually to the **Grandhotel Pupp,** Mírové nám. 2 (**© 353-109-111**). The Pupp's main entrance and building several years ago underwent extensive renovations that more or less erased the effects of 40 years of state ownership under Communism (under the former regime, the hotel's name was actually "Moskva-Pupp" just to remind everyone who was actually calling the shots). Regardless of capitalism or Communism, the Pupp remains what it always was: the grande dame of hotels in central Europe. Once catering to nobility from all over Europe, the Pupp still houses one of the town's finest restaurants, the Grand (see above), while its grounds are a favorite with the hiking crowd.

If you still have the energy, atop the hill behind the Pupp stands the **Diana Lookout Tower** (**© 353-222-872**). Footpaths lead to the tower through the forests and eventually spit you out at the base of the tower, as if to say, "Ha, the trip is only half over." The five-story climb up the tower tests your stamina, but the view of the town is more than worth it. For those who aren't up to the climb up the hill, a cable car runs up the hill every 15 minutes June to September daily from 9:15am to 6:45pm; February, March, November, and December 9:15am to 4:45pm; April, May, and October 9:15am to 5:45pm (closed Jan); cost is 40Kč one-way, 70Kč round-trip.

And if you have some time left at the end of your stay, visit the **Jan Becher Museum,** T. G. Masaryka 57 (**© 359-578-142;** www.becherovka.cz), to find out about the history of the town's secret: the formula for Becherovka. This herbal liquor is a sought-after souvenir, and you will get to taste it here. The museum is open daily 9am to 5pm; admission is 100Kč adults, 50Kč students.

THE SHOPPING SCENE

Crystal and porcelain are Karlovy Vary's other claims to fame. Dozens of shops throughout town sell everything from plates to chandeliers.

Ludvík Moser founded his first glassware shop in 1857 and became one of this country's foremost names in glass. You can visit and take a 30-minute tour of the **Moser Factory,** kapitána Jaroše 19 (✆ **353-416-132;** www.moser-glass.com; bus: 1, 10, or 22), just west of the town center. Its glass museum is open daily 9am to 5pm, and tours run daily 9am to 3pm. There's also a **Moser Store,** on Tržiště 7 (✆ **353-235-303**), right in the heart of New Town; it's open daily from 10am to 7pm (Sat–Sun until 6pm). Dozens of other smaller shops also sell the famed glass and are as easy to find in the Old Town as spring water.

If you're looking for something a little cheaper, try a box of *Oplatky,* thin round wafer cookies on sale throughout the area. The fillings range from vanilla to chocolate to nut and coffee—just don't try to wash them down with a mug of spa water!

České Budějovice

This fortress town was born in 1265, when Otakar II decided that the intersection of the Vltava and Malše rivers would be the site of a bastion to protect the approaches to southern Bohemia. Although Otakar was killed at the battle of the Moravian Field in 1278 and the town was subsequently ravaged by the rival Vítkovic family, the construction of České Budějovice continued, eventually taking the shape originally envisaged.

Today, České Budějovice, the hometown of the original Budweiser-brand beer, is now more a bastion for the beer drinker than a protector of Bohemia. But its slow pace, relaxed atmosphere, and interesting architecture make it a worthy stop, especially as a base for exploring southern Bohemia or for those heading on to Austria.

ESSENTIALS

GETTING THERE If you're **driving,** leave Prague to the south via the main D1 expressway and take the cutoff for Hwy. E55, which runs straight to České Budějovice. The trip takes about 1½ hours.

Daily express **trains** from Prague make the trip to České Budějovice in about 2½ hours. The fare is 320Kč first class or 213Kč second class. Several express **buses** run from Prague's Roztyly station (on the metro's C line) each day and take 3 hours; tickets cost 152Kč.

VISITOR INFORMATION **Tourist Infocentrum,** náměstí Přemysla Otakara II. 2 (✆ **386-801-413;** www.c-budejovice.cz), provides maps and guidebooks and finds lodging. It is open Monday to Friday 8:30am to 6pm, Saturday until 5pm, and Sunday 10am to 4pm. In winter it is open Monday and Wednesday 9am to 5pm; Tuesday, Thursday, Friday 9am to 4pm; and Saturday 9am to 1pm.

SPECIAL EVENTS Each August, České Budějovice hosts the largest **International Agricultural Show** in the country (www.vcb.cz).

WHERE TO STAY

Several agencies can locate reasonably priced private rooms. Expect to pay about 700Kč per person, in cash. The **Tourist Infocentrum,** náměstí Přemysla Otakara II. 2 (✆ **386-801-413**), can point you toward a wide selection of conveniently located rooms and pensions.

Grandhotel Zvon Location is everything to the city's most elegant hotel, which occupies several historic buildings on the main square. In fact, pretty soon the hotel and its accompanying businesses will occupy nearly a quarter of the addresses in the area. The upper-floor rooms have been thoroughly renovated and tend to be more expensive, though the views from all the front rooms can't be topped. Try to avoid the smaller rooms, usually reserved for tour groups. In recent years, the staff appears to have learned that guests deserve respect and quality treatment.

Náměstí Přemysla Otakara II. 28, 370 01 České Budějovice. ✆ **381-601-601.** Fax 381-601-605. www.hotel-zvon.cz. 75 units. 2,800Kč–5,000Kč double. AE, DC, MC, V. **Amenities:** Restaurant; cafe; bar; Internet. *In room:* TV, minibar.

Hotel Malý Pivovar (Small Brewery) ★★ Around the corner from the Zvon, this renovated 16th-century microbrewery combines the charms of a B&B with the amenities of a modern hotel. The kind of management found here is a rarity in the Czech tourism industry: They work hard to help out. The rooms are bright and cheery, with antique-style wooden furniture and exposed wooden ceiling beams providing a farmhouse feeling in the center of town. It's definitely worth consideration if being directly on the square (you're only 30m/98 ft. from it) isn't a priority. This is also one of the best places to arrange a trip to the brewery.

Ulice Karla IV. 8–10, 370 01 České Budějovice. ✆ **386-360-471.** Fax 386-360-474. www.malypivovar.cz. 29 units. From 2,760Kč double; from 3,200Kč suite. Rates include breakfast. AE, DC, MC, V. **Amenities:** Restaurant/pub; wine bar. *In room:* TV, minibar.

WHERE TO DINE

Potrefená husa CZECH/INTERNATIONAL This addition to the list of local restaurants is owned by Budvar's competitor, the Prague brewery Staropramen. In its modern interior, which is divided into a bar, restaurant, and large terrace with a pleasant view of the river, there is a good selection of pasta, meat dishes, and salads at reasonable prices. The barbecue ribs are very popular, and so is the Czech potato soup served in a bread bowl.

Česká 66. ✆ **387-420-560.** Main courses 89Kč–295Kč. AE, MC, V. Mon 11am–midnight; Tues–Thurs 11am–1am; Fri 11am–1:30am; Sat noon–1:30am; Sun noon–midnight.

U královské pečeti (At the Royal Seal) ★ CZECH This typical Czech-style pub serves up hearty food at reasonable prices. It offers a tasty goulash as well as *svíčková* or game dishes. Located in the popular Hotel Malý Pivovar, this is a very good choice for authentic Czech food.

In the Hotel Malý Pivovar, ulice Karla IV. 8–10. ✆ **386-360-471.** Soups 40Kč; main courses 80Kč–290Kč. AE, DC, MC, V. Daily 10am–11pm.

EXPLORING ČESKÉ BUDĚJOVICE

You can comfortably see České Budějovice in a day. At its center is one of central Europe's largest squares, the cobblestone **náměstí Přemysla Otakara II.**—it may actually be too large, as many of the buildings tend to get lost in all the open space.

The square contains the ornate **Fountain of Sampson,** an 18th-century water well that was once the town's principal water supply, plus a mishmash of baroque and Renaissance buildings. On the southwest corner is the **Town Hall,** an elegant baroque structure built by Martinelli between 1727 and 1730. On top of the Town Hall, the larger-than-life statues by Dietrich represent the civic virtues: justice, bravery, wisdom, and diligence.

One block northwest of the square is **Černá věž (Black Tower),** which you can see from almost every point in the city. Its 360 steps are worth the climb to get a bird's-eye view in all directions. The most famous symbol of České Budějovice, this 70m-tall (230-ft.) 16th-century tower was built as a belfry for the adjacent **St. Nicholas Church.** This 13th-century church, one of the town's most important sights, was a bastion of Roman Catholicism during the 15th-century Hussite rebellion. You shouldn't miss the church's flamboyant, white-and-cream, 17th-century baroque interior. The tower is open Tuesday to Sunday (daily July–Aug) from 10am to 6pm; admission is 20Kč. The church is open daily from 9am to 6pm.

TOURING A BEER SHRINE

On the town's northern edge sits a shrine to those who pray to the gods of the amber nectar. This is where **Budějovický Budvar,** Karolíny Světlé 4 (✆ **387-705-111**), the original brewer of Budweiser beer, has its one and only factory. Established in 1895, Budvar draws on more than 700 years of the area's brewing tradition to produce one of the world's best beers.

One trolley bus—no. 2—and bus no. 8 stop by the brewery; this is how the brewery ensures that its workers and visitors reach the plant safely each day. You can also hop a cab from the town square for about 150Kč.

The brewery offers 1-hour guided tours in Czech, English, and German at 2pm from Monday to Friday in season (Apr–Oct) and Tuesday to Friday at 2pm during the rest of the year. Normally, it's okay just to show up, but be sure to call ahead to the **Budvar Visitors' Centre** at the brewery (✆ **387-705-341;** http://budweiser-budvar.cz) to reserve a place. Tours cost 100Kč.

Český Krumlov ★★★

If you have time on your visit to the Czech Republic for only one excursion, seriously consider making it **Český Krumlov.** One of Bohemia's prettiest towns, Krumlov is a living gallery of elegant Renaissance-era buildings housing charming cafes, pubs, restaurants, shops, and galleries. In 1992, UNESCO named Český Krumlov a World Heritage Site for its historical importance and physical beauty.

Bustling since medieval times, the town, after centuries of embellishment, is exquisitely beautiful. In 1302, the Rožmberk family inherited the castle and moved in, using it as their main residence for nearly 300 years. You'll feel that time has stopped as you look from the Lazebnický Bridge and see the waters of the Vltava below snaking past the castle's gray stone. At night, by the castle lights, the view becomes even more dramatic.

Few dared change the appearance of Český Krumlov over the years, not even the Schwarzenbergs, who had a flair for opulence. At the turn of the 19th century, several facades of houses in the town's outer section were built, as were inner courtyards. Thankfully, economic stagnation in the area under Communism meant little money for "development," so no glass-and-steel edifices (the Hotel Thermal in Karlovy

Vary comes to mind) jut out to spoil the architectural beauty. Instead, a medieval sense reigns supreme, now augmented by the many festivals and renovations that keep the town's spirit alive.

ESSENTIALS

GETTING THERE From České Budějovice, it's about a 45-minute **drive** to Krumlov, depending on traffic. Take Hwy. 3 from the south of České Budějovice and turn onto Hwy. 159. The roads are clearly marked, with several signs directing traffic to the town. From Prague, it's a 2- to 3-hour drive down Hwy. 3 through Tábor. At Krumlov, you'll have to stow the car in one of several numbered paid parking lots around town. Choose **parking lot no. 2,** and follow the road all the way to the end; this puts you within 5 to 10 minutes' walk of the historic square.

The only way to reach Český Krumlov **by train** from Prague is via České Buděá jovice, a slow ride that deposits you at a station relatively far from the town center (trip time: 3 hr. 50 min.). Several trains leave daily from Prague's Hlavní nádraží; the fare is 250Kč. If you are already in České Budějovice and you want to make a trip to Krumlov, several trains connect these two cities throughout the day. The trip takes about an hour and costs 50Kč. For timetables, go to **www.jizdnirady.cz**.

The nearly 3-hour **bus** ride from Prague sometimes involves a transfer in České Budějovice. The fare is 136Kč, and the bus station in Český Krumlov is a 10-minute walk from the town's main square.

VISITOR INFORMATION Right on the main square, the **Information Centrum,** náměstí Svornosti 2, 381 01 Český Krumlov (✆ **380-704-622;** fax 380-704-619; www.ckrumlov.info), provides a complete array of services, from booking accommodations to reserving tickets for events, as well as a phone and Internet service. It's open daily June through September from 9am to 7pm; in April, May, and October from 9am to 6pm; and from November to March from 9am to 5pm.

Be warned that the municipal hall is in the same building, and it's crowded with weddings on weekends. If someone holds out a hat, throw some change into it, take a traditional shot of liquor from them, and say *"Blahopřeji!"* ("Congratulations!") to everyone in the room.

SPECIAL EVENTS After being banned during Communism, the **Slavnosti pětilisté růže (Festival of the Five-Petaled Rose)** has made a triumphant comeback. It's held each year during the summer solstice. Residents of Český Krumlov dress up in Renaissance costume and parade through the streets. Afterward, the streets become a stage for chess games with people dressed as pieces, music, plays, and even duels "to the death."

Český Krumlov also plays host to the **International Music Festival** every July and August, attracting performers from all over the world. Performances are held in nine spectacular venues. Tickets and details are available over the festival website (www.festivalkrumlov.cz) or through **Ticketstream** (www.ticketstream.cz) or the event organizer in Prague: **Auviex,** at Perlitová 1820, Prague 4 (✆ **241-445-404;** www.auviex.cz).

WHERE TO STAY

With the rise of free enterprise after the fall of Communism, many hotels have sprouted up or are getting a "new" old look. PENSION and ZIMMER FREI signs line the streets and offer some of the best values in town. For a comprehensive list of area

Český Krumlov

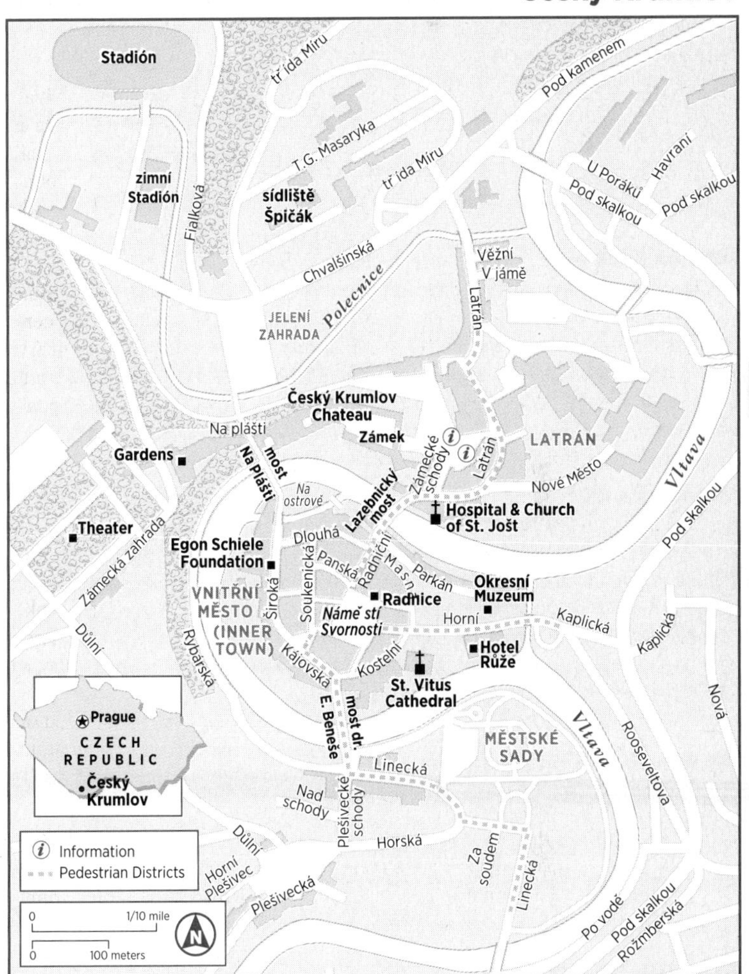

hotels and help with bookings, call or write to the Information Centrum listed above in "Visitor Information."

Hotel Konvice ★★ The rooms at the Konvice are on the small side and have rustic furniture. The real lure here is the view. Ask for a room with a view out the back—as you gaze at the river and the castle on the opposite bank, you'll wonder why anyone would choose to stay anywhere else.

Horní ul. 144. 381 01 Český Krumlov. ✆ **380-711-611.** Fax 380-711-327. www.boehmerwaldhotels.de. 10 units. From 1,500Kč double; from 3,500Kč suite with castle view. Rates include breakfast. AE, MC, V. **Amenities:** Restaurant. *In room:* TV.

Hotel Růže (Rose Hotel) Once a Jesuit seminary, this stunning Italian Renaissance building has been converted into a well-appointed hotel. Comfortable in a big-city kind of way, it's packed with amenities and is one of the top places to stay in Český Krumlov (though prices have risen considerably in recent years and it's not clear it's still really worth this much money). For families or large groups, the larger suites (while still *very* expensive for what you get) have eight beds and at least provide better value.

Horní 154, 381 01 Český Krumlov. ✆ **380-772-100.** Fax 380-713-146. www.hotelruze.cz. 71 units. From 5,800Kč double; from 7,300Kč suite. Rates include breakfast. AE, MC, V. **Amenities:** Restaurant; bar; health club; pool. *In room:* TV, hair dryer, minibar.

Pension Anna ★ ☺ Along "pension alley," this comfortable and rustic place is a favorite, known for its friendly management and the homey feeling you get as you walk up to your room. Forget hotels—this is the kind of place where you can relax. You can even buy drinks and snacks at the bar downstairs and take them to your room. The suites, with four beds and a living room, are great for families and groups.

Rooseveltova 41, 381 01 Český Krumlov. ✆/fax **380-711-692.** www.pensionanna.euweb.cz. 8 units. From 1,250Kč double; from 1,550Kč suite. Rates include breakfast. No credit cards. **Amenities:** Bar. *In room:* TV.

Pension Na louži ★ Smack-dab in the heart of the Inner Town, the small Na louži, decorated with early-20th-century wooden furniture, is a charming change from many of the bigger, bland rooms found in nearby hotels. If the person at reception starts mentioning names without apparent reason, don't worry; it's not a language problem. Management has given the rooms human names instead of numbers. The only drawback is that the beds (maybe the people for whom the rooms were named were all short) can be a little on the short side.

Kájovská 66, 381 01 Český Krumlov. ✆/fax **380-711-280.** www.nalouzi.cz. 7 units. From 1,500Kč double; from 2,300Kč suite. No credit cards. **Amenities:** Restaurant/bar.

Pension Ve věži (In the Tower) ★ 🎁 A private pension in a renovated medieval tower just a 5-minute walk from the castle, Ve Věži is one of the most magnificent places to stay in town. It's not the accommodations themselves that are so grand; none has a bathroom and all are sparsely decorated. What's wonderful is the ancient ambience. Reservations are recommended.

Pivovarská 28, 381 01 Český Krumlov. ✆ **721-523-030.** www.pensionvevezi.cz. 4 units (all with shared bathroom). From 1,200Kč double. Rates include breakfast. No credit cards.

WHERE TO DINE

Krumlovský mlýn CZECH This restored mill house, whose history dates from the 16th century, is a restaurant, antiques shop, and exhibition in one. Large wooden tables and benches are part of the thematic restaurant on the ground floor, where a traditional Czech menu is served. The terrace on the bank of the Vltava River above the water channel here is a terrific place to sit in the summer.

Široká 80. ✆ **736-634-461.** www.krumlovskymlyn.cz. Main courses 180Kč–425Kč. No credit cards. Daily 10am–10pm.

Restaurace Na Ostrově (On the Island) CZECH In the shadow of the castle and, as the name implies, on an island, this restaurant is best on a sunny day when the terrace overflows with flowers, hearty Czech food (including plenty of chicken and fish), and lots of beer. The staff is very friendly, which helps with your patience since usually only two waiters work each shift, making service on the slow side. A great place to relax and enjoy the view.

Na ostrově 171. ✆ **380-711-326.** Main courses 139Kč–399Kč. No credit cards. Daily 10am–10pm.

Hospoda Na louži CZECH The large wooden tables encourage you to get to know your neighbors at this Inner Town pub, located in a 15th-century house. The atmosphere is fun and the food above average. If no table is available, stand and have a drink; tables turn over pretty quickly, and the staff is accommodating. In summer, the terrace seats only six, so dash over if a seat empties. Be sure to save space for homemade fruit dumplings for dessert.

Kájovská 66. ✆ **380-711-280.** Main courses about 100Kč. No credit cards. Mon–Sat 10am–11pm; Sun 10am–10pm.

EXPLORING ČESKÝ KRUMLOV

Bring a good pair of walking shoes and be prepared to wear them out. Český Krumlov's hills and alleyways cry out for hours of exploration, but if you push the pace you can see everything in 1 day. No cars, thank goodness, are allowed in the historic town, and the cobblestones keep most other vehicles at bay. The town is split into two parts—the **Inner Town** and **Latrán,** which houses the castle. They're best tackled separately, so you won't have to crisscross the bridges several times.

Begin your walk at the **Okresní Muzeum** (**Regional Museum;** ✆ **380-711-674**) at the top of Horní ulice 152. Once a Jesuit seminary, the three-story museum now contains artifacts and displays relating to Český Krumlov's 1,000-year history. The highlight of this mass of folk art, clothing, furniture, and statues is a giant model of the town that offers a bird's-eye view of the buildings. Admission is 60Kč. The museum is open May to September, daily 10am to 5pm (until 6pm July–Aug); in October to December and March to April, it's open Tuesday to Friday 9am to 4pm, and Saturday and Sunday 1 to 4pm.

Across the street is the **Hotel Růže (Rose),** Horní 154 (✆ **380-772-100;** www.hotelruze.cz), which was once a Jesuit student house. Built in the late 16th century, the hotel and the prelature next to it show the development of architecture—Gothic, Renaissance, and rococo influences are all present. If you're not staying at the hotel, don't be afraid to walk around and even ask questions at the reception desk.

Continue down the street to the impressive late-Gothic **St. Vitus Cathedral.** The church is open daily from 9am to 5pm.

As you continue down the street, you'll come to **náměstí Svornosti.** Few buildings here show any character, making the main square of such an impressive town a little disappointing. The **Radnice (Town Hall),** at náměstí Svornosti 1, is one of the few exceptions. Open daily from 9am to 6pm, its Gothic arcades and Renaissance vault inside are exceptionally beautiful in this otherwise run-down area. From the square, streets fan out in all directions. Take some time to wander through them.

When you get closer to the river, you still can see the high-water marks on some of the quirky bankside houses, which were devastated by the floods of 2002. Most of the places have taken the opportunity to make a fresh start after massive reconstruction. **Krumlovský Mlýn (Krumlov Mill),** Široká 80 (✆ **736-634-460;** www.krumlovskymlyn.cz), is a combination restaurant, gallery, antiques shop, and exhibition space. For an additional treat, stroll through the exhibition of historical motorcycles. Open daily 10am to 10pm.

One of Český Krumlov's most famous residents was Austrian-born artist Egon Schiele. He was a bit of an eccentric who on more than one occasion raised the ire of the town's residents (many found his use of young women as nude models distressing), and his stay was cut short when the locals' patience ran out. But the town readopted the artist in 1993, setting up the **Egon Schiele Art Centrum** in Inner Town, Široká 70–72, 381 01 Český Krumlov (✆ **380-704-011;** www.schieleart centrum.cz). It documents his life and work, housing a permanent selection of his paintings as well as exhibitions of other 20th-century artists. Admission is 120Kč; hours are daily from 10am to 6pm.

After you see the museum, cut down Panenská ulice to Soukenická 39 and stop in at **Galerie u rytíře Kryštofa,** Panenská 6, where you can try on the latest in body armor! This place is like the wardrobe room at a theater, and almost everything is for sale. It's open Monday to Saturday from 10am to 6pm, Sunday from 1 to 6pm.

For a different perspective on the town, take the stairs from the **Městské divadlo (Town Theater)** on Horní ulice down to the riverfront and rent a rowboat from **Maleček Boat Rentals** (✆ **380-712-508;** www.malecek.cz) at 400Kč for an hour-long trip.

You might want to grab a light lunch at one of the many cafes in Inner Town before crossing the river. As you cross the bridge and head toward the castle, you'll see immediately to your right the former **hospital and church of St. Jošt.** Founded at the beginning of the 14th century, it has since been turned into apartments. Feel free to snoop around, but don't enter the building.

EXPLORING THE CHÂTEAU

Reputedly the second-largest castle in Bohemia (after Prague Castle), **Český Krumlov Château** was constructed in the 13th century as part of a private estate. Throughout the ages, it has been passed on to a variety of private owners, including the Rožmberk family, Bohemia's largest landholders, and the Schwarzenbergs, the Bohemian equivalent of the Hilton family. Perched high atop a rocky hill, the château is open only from April to October, exclusively by guided tours.

Follow the path for the long climb up to the **castle.** Greeting you is a round 12th-century **tower**—painstakingly renovated, with its Renaissance balcony. You'll pass over the moat, now occupied by two brown bears. Next is the **Dolní Hrad (Lower Castle)** and then the **Horní Hrad (Upper Castle).**

There are three main guided tours, plus separate entries to the Castle Tower and the Lapidarium. If you don't have the money or time for one of the tours, you're free to walk around the grounds, though most of the interiors will be inaccessible. Tour 1 begins in the rococo **Chapel of St. George,** and continues through the portrait-packed **Renaissance Rooms,** and the **Schwarzenberg Baroque Suite,** outfitted with ornate furnishings that include Flemish wall tapestries, European paintings, and also the extravagant 17th-century **Golden Carriage.** Tour 2 includes the **Schwarzenberg portrait gallery** as well as their 19th-century suite. Tour 3 presents the Castle's fascinating **Baroque Theater,** though with the more expensive tickets, sadly, this is priced more for real theater aficionados than the general public. Tours last about 1 hour and depart frequently. Most are in Czech or German, however.

If you want an English-language tour, arrange it ahead of time (© **380-704-711;** www.castle.ckrumlov.cz). The guided tours in English cost 240Kč adults, 140Kč students (Tour 1); 180Kč adults, 100Kč students (Tour 2); and 380Kč adults, 220Kč students (Tour 3). The tickets are sold separately. The castle hours are from Tuesday to Sunday: June to August 9am to 6pm; April, May, September, and October 9am to 5pm. The last entrance is 1 hour before closing.

Past the main castle building is one of the more stunning views of Český Krumlov from **Most Na Plášti,** a walkway that doubles as a belvedere to the Inner Town. Farther up the hill lie the castle's riding school and gardens.

DENMARK

by Darwin Porter & Danforth Prince

In this chapter, we focus on Copenhagen, Denmark's capital, adding a few tantalizing side trips you can take in a day or two. Copenhagen got its name from the word *københavn,* meaning "merchants' harbor." This city grew in size and importance because of its position on the Øresund (the Sound) between Denmark and Sweden, guarding the entrance to the Baltic. From its humble beginnings, Copenhagen has become the largest city in Scandinavia, home to 1.7 million people.

If you'd like to tie in a visit to Copenhagen with the château country of Sweden, it's as easy as crossing a bridge: In 2000, Denmark was linked to Sweden by the 16km (10-mile) Øresund Bridge. The two cities of Copenhagen and Malmö, Sweden, are the hubs of the Øresund Region, northern Europe's largest domestic market, larger than Stockholm and equal in size to Berlin, Hamburg, and Amsterdam. The bridge is the longest combined rail-and-road bridge in the world.

COPENHAGEN

Copenhagen is a city with much charm, as reflected in its canals, narrow streets, and old houses. Its most famous resident was the writer Hans Christian Andersen, whose memory still lives on here. Another of Copenhagen's world-renowned inhabitants was Søren Kierkegaard, who used to take long morning strolls in the city, planning his next essay; his completed writings eventually earned him the title "father of existentialism."

But few modern Copenhageners are reading Kierkegaard today, and neither are they as melancholy as Hamlet. Most of them are out having too much fun. Copenhagen epitomizes the Nordic *joie de vivre,* and the city is filled with a lively atmosphere, good times (none better than at the Tivoli Gardens), sex shows, countless outdoor cafes, and all-night dance clubs. Of course, if you come in winter, the fierce realities of living above the 55th parallel set in. That's when Copenhageners retreat inside their smoky jazz clubs and beer taverns.

Modern Copenhagen still retains some of the characteristics of a village. If you forget the suburbs, you can cover most of the central belt on foot, which makes it a great tourist spot. It's almost as if the city were

Denmark

designed for pedestrians, as reflected by its **Strøget** (strolling street), Europe's longest and oldest walking street.

Essentials

GETTING THERE

BY PLANE **SAS** (✆ **800/221-2350;** www.flysas.com) is the major carrier to Copenhagen. **Finnair** (✆ **800/950-5000;** www.finnair.com) offers flights through Helsinki from New York and Miami. **Icelandair** (✆ **800/223-5500;** www.icelandair.com) has service through Reykjavik from several North American cities.

You arrive at **Kastrup Airport** (✆ **45/3231-3231;** www.cph.dk), 12km (7½ miles) from the center of Copenhagen. Since 1998, air-rail trains have linked the airport with Copenhagen's Central Railway Station, in the center of the hotel zone, and the whole affair now takes a mere 11 minutes and costs 25DKK. The Air Rail Terminal is underneath the airport's arrivals and departure halls, just a short escalator ride from the gates. You can also take an SAS bus to the city terminal; the fare is 25DKK. A taxi to the city center costs around 200DKK. Yet another option is a local

Copenhagen

ATTRACTIONS ●

Amalienborg Palace **15**
Botanisk Have **12**
Christiansborg Palace **24**
Frederikskirke **14**
Frihedsmuseet **9**
Frilandsmuseet (Open Air Museum) **1**
Den Hirschsprungske Samling **10**
Little Mermaid **8**
Nationalmuseet **25**
Ny Carlsberg Glyptotek **28**
Rådhus and World Clock **26**
Rosenborg Castle **13**
Rundetårn **19**
Statens Museum for Kunst **11**
Tivoli Gardens **27**
Tøjhusmuseet **29**
Vor Frue Kirke **21**

ACCOMMODATIONS ■

Absalon Hotel **7**
Ascot Hotel **20**
Christian IV **17**
Copenhagen Strand **23**
Hotel Alexandra **3**
Hotel d'Angleterre **18**
Hotel Selandia **6**
Kong Arthur **2**
Nimb Hotel **5**
Phoenix Copenhagen **16**
Profil Copenhagen Plaza **4**
71 Nyhavn **22**

0 1/4 mi
0 0.25 km
N
To Helsingør and Lyngby
Blegdamsvej
Fredensgade
Nørre Allé
Møllegade
Nørrebrogade
ASSISTENS KIRKEGÅRD
MOSAISK KIRKEGÅRD
Skt. Hans Tørv
Ryesgade
Sortedam Dossering
Sortedams
Øster
Faelledvej
Kapeivej
Griffenfeldsgade
Dronning Louises Bro
Rantzausgade
Korsgade
Blågårdsgade
Frederiksborg-
Vendersgade
Ågade
Aboulevarden
Peblinge Dossering
Peblinge Sø
Nørreport Station
Rosenørns Allé
Nørre Søgade
Nansensgade
Gyldenløvesgade
Nørre Farimagsgade
ØRSTEDS PARKEN
Sankt Jørgens Sø
Vester Søgade
Nyropsgade
Jarmers Plads
Danasvej
Vodroffsvej
Kampmannsgade
Vester Farimagsgade
Hammerichsgade
Skt. Knuds Vej
Svineryggen
Gammel Kongevej
Vesterport
TIVOLI
Bernstorffsgade
Vesterbrogade
Reventlowsgade
Central Railway Station
Viktoriagade
Gasvaerksvej
Istedgade
VESTERBRO
Dannebrogsgade
Absalonsgade
Tietgensgade
Ingerslevsgade
Matthaeusgade

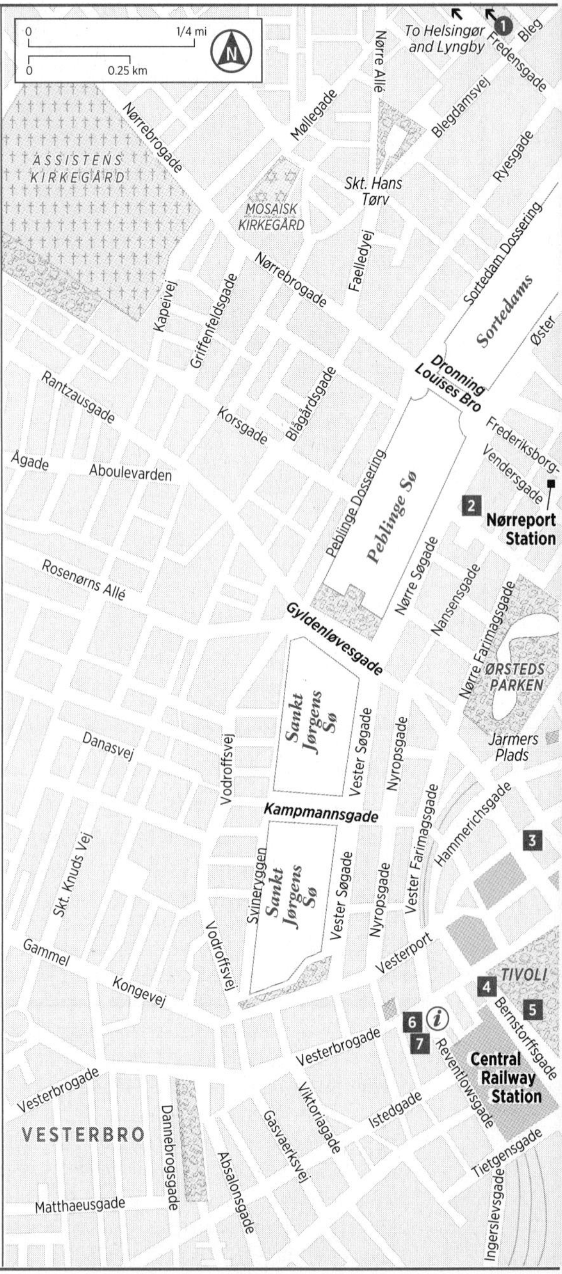

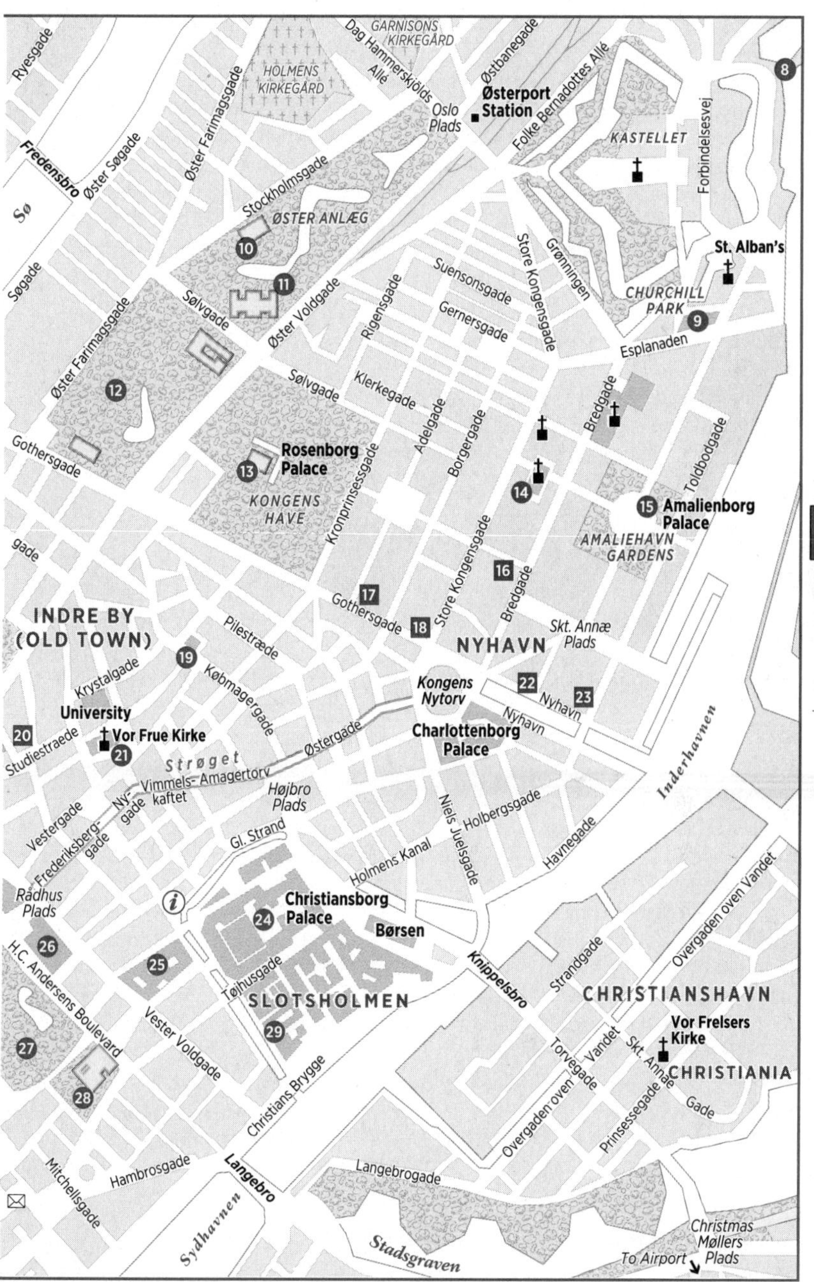

5 DENMARK | Copenhagen

bus, no. 250S, which leaves from the international arrivals terminal every 15 or 20 minutes for Town Hall Square in central Copenhagen and costs 25DKK.

BY TRAIN Trains from the Continent arrive at the **Hoved Banegård (Central Railroad Station),** in the very center of Copenhagen, near the Tivoli and the Rådhuspladsen. For **rail information,** call ✆ **33-14-17-01.** The station operates a luggage-checking service, but room bookings are available only at the tourist office (see "Visitor Information," below). You can also exchange money at the **Den Danske Bank** branch on-site, open daily from 7am to 8pm.

From the Central Railroad Station, you can connect with **S-tog,** the local subway, with trains leaving from platforms in the terminus itself. To find out which train you should board to reach your destination, inquire at the information desk near tracks 9 and 12.

BY CAR If you're driving from Germany, a car-ferry will take you from Travemünde to Gedser in southern Denmark. From Gedser, get on E-55 north, an express highway that will deliver you to the southern outskirts of Copenhagen. If you're coming from Sweden and crossing at Helsingborg, you'll land on the Danish side at Helsingør. Take express highway E-55 south to the northern outskirts of Copenhagen. If you're coming from Malmö, Sweden, you can cross on the Øresund Bridge.

VISITOR INFORMATION

TOURIST OFFICE **Wonderful Copenhagen Tourist Information Center,** Gammel Kongevej 1 (✆ **33-25-74-00;** see website below), is open September to October, Monday to Saturday 9am to 4pm; November to April, Saturday 9am to 2pm; May and June, daily 9am to 8pm; July and August, daily 8am to 11pm.

WEBSITES At the Wonderful Copenhagen Tourist Information Center website (**www.visitcopenhagen.dk**), you'll find all the basics on dining, lodging, and attractions. The **Danish Tourist Board** (**www.visitdenmark.com**) offers a wide-ranging website where you'll find late news and transportation tips; the accommodations choices range from castles and manor houses to farm vacations.

CITY LAYOUT The heart of **Old Copenhagen** is a maze of pedestrian streets, formed by Nørreport Station to the north, Town Hall Square (Rådhuspladsen) to the west, Kongens Nytorv to the east, and the Inderhavnen (Inner Harbor) to the south. One continuous route, **Strøget,** the world's longest pedestrian street, goes east from Town Hall Square to Kongens Nytorv and is made up of five streets: Frederiksberggade, Nygade, Vimmelskaftet, Amagertorv, and Østergade. Strøget is lined with shops, bars, restaurants, and sidewalk cafes in summer. **Pistolstræde,** a narrow street a 3-minute walk west of Kongens Nytorv, is a maze of galleries, restaurants, and boutiques, all housed in restored 18th-century buildings.

Fiolstræde (Violet St.), a dignified street with antiques shops and bookshops, cuts through the university (Latin Quarter). If you turn into Rosengaarden at the top of Fiolstræde, you'll come to **Kultorvet (Coal Sq.)** just before you reach Nørreport Station. Here you join the third main pedestrian street, **Købmagergade (Butcher St.),** which winds around and finally meets Strøget on Amagertorv.

At the end of Strøget you approach **Kongens Nytorv (King's Sq.),** the site of the Royal Theater and Magasin, the largest department store. This will put you at the beginning of **Nyhavn,** the former seamen's quarter that has been gentrified into an upmarket area of expensive restaurants, apartments, cafes, and boutiques. The

Traveling for Less

The **Copenhagen Card** entitles you to free and unlimited travel by bus and rail throughout the metropolitan area (including North Zealand), 25% to 50% discounts on crossings to and from Sweden, and free admission on more than 60 sights and museums. The card is available for 1 or 3 days. The 1-day card costs 225DKK adults, 115DKK children between 10 and 15 years old; 3-day card, 450DKK adults, 225DKK children. Up to two children age 9 and under are allowed free entrance with each adult card. For more information, contact the Copenhagen Tourist Information Center (see above) or www.visitcopenhagen.com.

government of Denmark is centered on the small island of **Slotsholmen,** connected to the center by eight bridges. Several museums, notably Christiansborg Castle, are found here.

The center of Copenhagen is **Rådhuspladsen (Town Hall Sq.).** From here it's a short walk to the Tivoli Gardens, the major attraction, and to the Central Railroad Station, the main railroad and subway terminus. The wide boulevard, **Vesterbrogade,** passes by Tivoli until it reaches the Central Railroad Station. Another major street is named after Denmark's most famous writer; **H. C. Andersens Boulevard** runs along Rådhuspladsen and the Tivoli Gardens.

Copenhagen lies in the northern part of the island of Zealand. In spite of Copenhagen, most of North Zealand is rather rural and enjoys many associations with Danish royalty. It is, in fact, the site of Helsing (Hamlet's castle) and many seashores, lakes, fishing villages, and woodlands.

GETTING AROUND A joint zone-fare system includes Copenhagen Transport buses and State Railway and S-tog trains in Copenhagen and North Zealand, plus some private rail routes within a 40km (25-mile) radius of the capital, enabling you to transfer from train to bus and vice versa with the same ticket.

A *grundbillet* (basic ticket) for both buses and trains costs 21DKK. You can buy 10 tickets for 130DKK. Children 11 and under ride for half fare; those 4 and under travel free on local trains, and those 6 and under ride free on buses. You can purchase a ticket allowing 24-hour bus and train travel through nearly half of Zealand for 120DKK; half price for children 7 to 11; free for children 6 and under.

Eurailpasses and Nordturist Pass tickets are accepted on local trains.

BY BUS Copenhagen's well-maintained buses are the least expensive method of getting around. Most buses leave from Rådhuspladsen. A basic ticket costing 21DKK allows 1 hour of travel and unlimited transfers within two zones. For information, call ✆ **36-13-14-15.**

BY S-TOG (SUBWAY) The S-tog connects heartland Copenhagen with its suburbs. Use of the tickets is the same as on buses (above). You can transfer from a bus line to an S-train on the same ticket. Eurailpass holders generally ride free. For more information, call ✆ **33-14-17-01** anytime.

BY METRO In 2001 Copenhagen launched its first Metro line, taking passengers from east to west across the city and vice versa. Operating round-the-clock, the

Metro runs as far west as Vanløse and as far south as Vestamager. Nørreport is the transfer station to the S-tog system, the commuter rail link to the suburbs. Metro trains run every 2 minutes during rush hours and every 15 minutes at night. Fares are integrated into the existing zone system (see "By Bus," above). For information, call ✆ **33-11-17-00.**

BY CAR It's best to park your car in any of the dozens of city parking lots, and then retrieve it when you're ready to explore the capital's environs. Many parking lots are open 24 hours; a few others tend to close between 1 and 7am. Some close on Saturday afternoon and on Sunday during nonpeak business hours when traffic is presumably lighter. Costs tend to be about 25DKK to 30DKK per hour or 250DKK per 24 hours. One of the most central parking lots is **Industriens Hus,** H. C. Andersens Blvd. 18 (✆ **33-91-21-75**), open Monday to Friday 7am to 1:30am and Saturday and Sunday from 9am to 12:45am.

BY TAXI Watch for the FRI (free) sign or green light to hail a taxi. Be sure the taxis are metered. **Hovedstadens Taxi** (✆ **38-77-77-77**) operates one of the most central taxi companies. ***Note:*** Tips are included in the meter price: 24DKK at the drop of the flag and 11.50DKK per kilometer thereafter, Monday to Friday from 7am to 4pm. From 4pm to 7am, the fare is 12.50DKK. On Saturday and Sunday between 11pm and 7am, the cost is 15.80DKK per kilometer. Basic drop-of-the-flag costs remain the same, however. Many drivers speak English.

BY BICYCLE To reduce pollution from cars, Copenhageners ride bicycles. For 60DKK to 130DKK per 6-hour rental, plus a 200DKK to 500DKK deposit, you can rent a bike at **Københavns Cyklebors,** Reventlowsgade 11 (✆ **33-14-07-17**). Hours are Monday to Friday 8:30am to 5:30pm, Saturday 10am to 1:30pm, and Sunday by appointment.

[Fast FACTS] COPENHAGEN

Business Hours Most **banks** are open from Monday to Friday 9:30am to 4pm (Thurs to 6pm). **Stores** are generally open Monday to Thursday 9am to 6pm, Friday 9am to 7 or 8pm, and Saturday 9am to 3pm; most are closed Sunday.

Currency The Danish currency is the **krone (crown),** or DKK, made up of 100 øre. The rate of exchange as of this writing is $1 = 5.25DKK, or 1DKK = 19¢. Note that in contrast to the fiscal policies of most of western Europe, Denmark opted not to convert its monetary system to the euro in January 2001, despite its membership in the E.U. Therefore, at least as of press time, the euro is not the legal tender of Denmark.

Currency Exchange Banks are generally your best bet to exchange currency. When banks are closed, you can exchange money at **Forex** (✆ **33-11-22-20;** S-tog: Central Station) in the Central Railroad Station, open daily from 8am to 9pm, or at the **Change Group** (✆ **33-93-04-55;** bus: 1, 6, or 9; Metro: Kongens Nytorv), Østergade 61, open Monday to Saturday from 8:30am to 10pm and Sunday from 10am to 6pm.

Dentists & Doctors For emergency dental treatment, go to **Tandlægevagten,** Oslo Plads 14 (✆ **35-38-02-51;** S-tog: Østerport), near Østerport Station and the U.S. Embassy. It's open Monday to Friday 8am to 9:30pm and Saturday, Sunday, and holidays 10am to noon. Be prepared to pay in cash. To reach a doctor, dial ✆ **33-93-63-00** Monday to Friday 8am to 4pm or ✆ **38-88-60-41** after hours. The doctor's fee is payable in cash. Virtually every doctor speaks English.

Drugstores An *apotek* (pharmacy) open 24 hours a day in central Copenhagen is **Steno Apotek,** Vesterbrogade 6C (✆ **33-14-82-66;** bus: 6).

Embassies All embassies are in Copenhagen. The embassy of the **United States** is at Dag Hammärskjölds Allé 24, DK-2100 København 0 (✆ 33-41-71-00; http://denmark.usembassy.gov). Other embassies are the **United Kingdom,** Kastelsvej 36–40, DK-2100 København (✆ 35-44-52-00; http://ukindenmark.fco.gov.uk); **Canada,** Kristen Berniskowsgade 1, DK-1105 København (✆ 33-48-32-00; http://denmark.gc.ca); **Australia,** Dampfærgevej 26, DK-2100 København (✆ 70-26-36-76; www.denmark.embassy.gov.au); and **Ireland,** Østbanegade 21, DK-2100 København (✆ 35-42-32-33; www.embassyofireland.dk).

Emergencies Dial ✆ **112** for the fire department, the police, or an ambulance, or to report a sea or air accident.

Internet Access
Across from the entrance to the Tivoli, **Boomtown,** Axeltorv 1-3 (✆ **33-32-10-32**), is open 24 hours, charging 30DKK for use of one of its computers.

Post Office For information about the Copenhagen post office, call ✆ **33-41-56-00.** The main post office is at Tietgensgade 35–39, DK-1570 København (✆ **31-41-56-00;** S-tog: Central Station), open Monday to Friday 9am to 5pm, Saturday 9am to noon. The post office at the Central Railroad Station is open Monday to Friday 8am to 10pm, Saturday 9am to 4pm, and Sunday 10am to 4pm.

Taxes The 25% VAT (value-added tax) on goods and services is known in Denmark as *moms* (pronounced "mumps") and is normally included in the price. Special tax-free exports are possible, and many stores will mail goods home to you, circumventing *moms.* If you want to take your purchases with you, look for shops displaying Danish tax-free shopping notices. Such shops offer tourists' tax refunds for personal export. This refund applies to purchases of at least 300DKK for U.S. and Canadian visitors. Your tax-free invoice must be stamped by Danish Customs when you leave the country. You can receive your refund at Copenhagen's Kastrup International Airport when you depart. If you go by land or sea, you can receive your refund by mail. Mail requests for refunds to Danish Tax-Free Shopping A/S, H. J. Holstvej 5A, DK-2605 Brøndby, Denmark. You'll be reimbursed by check, cash, or credit or charge card in the currency you want. Service and handling fees are deducted from the total, so actual refunds come to about 18%.

A 25% *moms* is included in hotel and restaurant bills, service charges, entrance fees, and repair bills for foreign-registered cars. No refunds are possible on these items.

Telephone The country code for Denmark is **45.** It should precede any call made to Denmark from another country.

Danish phones are fully automatic. Dial the eight-digit number; there are no city area codes. At public telephone booths, don't insert any coins until your party answers. Use two 50-øre coins or a 1-krone or 5-krone coin only. You can make more than one call on the same payment if your time hasn't run out. Remember that calling direct from your hotel room can be expensive. Emergency calls are free.

Tipping Tips are seldom expected, but when they are, you should give only

1DKK or 2DKK. Porters charge fixed prices, and tipping is not customary for hairdressers or barbers. Service is built into the system, and hotels, restaurants, and even taxis include a 15% service charge in their rates. Because of the service charge, plus the 25% *moms,* you'll probably have to pay an additional 40% for some services!

Consider tipping only for special services—some Danes would feel insulted if you offered them a tip.

Where to Stay

NEAR KONGENS NYTORV & NYHAVN

Very Expensive

Hotel D'Angleterre ★★★ If you've made it, stay here. At the top of Nyhavn, this seven-story hotel, built in 1755 and extensively renovated, is the premier choice for Denmark (though it's a bit staid and stodgy). The rooms are beautifully furnished with art objects and the occasional antique. They vary in size, but each has a grand bed that has sheltered notables ranging from Hans Christian Andersen to Madonna and Ricky Martin. The bathrooms come with phones and scales.

Kongens Nytorv 34, DK-1021 København. ✆ **33-12-00-95.** Fax 33-12-11-18. www.dangleterre.com. 123 units. 3,300DKK–4,195DKK double; from 5,488DKK junior suite; from 9,950DKK suite. AE, DC, MC, V. Parking 400DKK. Bus: 1A, 5, 15, or 18. **Amenities:** Restaurant; bar; babysitting; exercise room; indoor pool; room service; sauna; spa. *In room:* A/C, TV, hair dryer, minibar, Wi-Fi (free).

Nimb Hotel ★★★ This boutique hotel has only a dozen or so rooms, but its devotees hailed it as the best place to stay in all of Copenhagen. This small Moorish-style palace with a striking Venetian facade faces the Tivoli Gardens. The restored hotel fills its rooms with antiques, and the interiors are in wood and stone. All rooms overlook the Tivoli except no. 14, which faces the rail station. Each room is individually designed, with fireplaces and spacious bathrooms. There is the aura of a private home about this pocket of posh. Four-poster beds add more grace notes. One bar was created from a former ballroom with chandeliers, paintings, a grand piano, and a blazing fireplace. Even if you don't stay here, consider a meal in one of its first-class restaurants. There's a deli, even a dairy (the hotel churns its own butter and cream). There's also a gourmet sausage stand adjacent to the Tivoli.

Bernstorffsgade 5, DK-1577 København. ✆ **88-70-00-00.** Fax 88-70-00-99. www.nimb.dk. 13 units. 2,500DKK–4,500DKK double; 5,500DKK–6,500DKK junior suite; 8,500DKK suite. AE, DC, MC, V. Parking nearby 350DKK. Bus: 1 or 16. **Amenities:** 2 restaurants; 2 bars; babysitting; concierge; access to health club; room service. *In room:* A/C, TV/DVD, hair dryer, minibar, Wi-Fi (free).

Expensive

Phoenix Copenhagen ★★ More than any other hotel, this top-of-the-line lodging poses a challenge to the discreet grandeur of the nearby D'Angleterre. Opened in 1991, the Phoenix was a royal guesthouse, originally built in 1780 to accommodate the aristocratic courtiers of Amalienborg Palace. The spacious rooms are tastefully elegant and decorated with discreet Louis XVI reproductions. The large beds sport fine linens, and the bathrooms are state of the art. The very best units also have faxes, bathrobes, and phones in the bathrooms.

Bredgade 37, DK-1260 København. ✆ **33-95-95-00.** Fax 33-33-98-33. www.phoenixcopenhagen.com. 213 units. 1,120DKK–1,520DKK double; 2,120DKK junior suite; 4,120DKK suite. AE, DC, MC, V. Parking 225DKK. Bus: 1, 6A, 15, or 19. **Amenities:** Restaurant; bar; babysitting; room service. *In room:* A/C, TV, hair dryer, minibar, Wi-Fi (free).

71 Nyhavn ★★ On the corner between Copenhagen harbor and Nyhavn Canal, this hotel is housed in a restored old warehouse from 1804, and was thoroughly renovated in 1997. Most of the rooms have a harbor and canal view. The rooms have a nautical decor, with exposed brick, dark woods, and crisscrossing timbers. Bathrooms are rather small; most have a stall shower. The best rooms are equipped with bathrobes and faxes.

Nyhavn 71, DK-1051 København. ✆ **33-43-62-00.** Fax 33-43-62-01. www.71nyhavnhotel.com. 150 units. 1,320DKK–1,820DKK double; 2,270DKK junior suite; 4,270DKK suite. AE, DC, MC, V. Free parking. Bus: 1A, 6A, 29, or 650-S. Metro: Kongens Nytorv. **Amenities:** Restaurant; bar; babysitting; room service. *In room:* A/C (in some), TV, hair dryer, minibar, Wi-Fi (free).

Moderate

Christian IV This small, cozy hotel enjoys one of the most desirable locations in Copenhagen. Dating from 1958, the hotel takes its name from Christian IV, who constructed Rosenborg Castle lying adjacent to the hotel. The hotel provides a "bridge" linking King's Garden, the castle, and the more modern structures in the neighborhood. Enjoying a lot of repeat business, it offers attractively decorated bedrooms with a modern Danish design, along with immaculately kept private bathrooms with tub and shower.

Dronningens Tværgade 45, DK-1302 København. ✆ **33-32-10-44.** Fax 33-32-07-06. www.hotelchristianiv.dk. 42 units. 995DKK–1,295DKK double. Rates include breakfast. MC, V. Parking 195DKK. Bus: 26. **Amenities:** Breakfast room; bar; access to nearby health club. *In room:* TV, minibar (in some), Wi-Fi (free).

Copenhagen Strand ★ One of the city's most modern hotels, opened in 2000, lies within a pair of former brick-and-timber factories. The savvy architects retained as many of the old-fashioned details as they could. The medium-size rooms are filled with comfortable, contemporary-looking furnishings. The hotel is rated three stars by the Danish government, but frankly, all that it lacks for elevation into four-star status is a full-fledged restaurant.

Havnegade 37, DK-1058 København K. ✆ **33-48-99-00.** Fax 33-48-99-01. www.copenhagenstrand.dk. 174 units. 770DKK–1,220DKK double; 1,170DKK–1,420DKK suite. AE, DC, MC, V. Parking 125DKK. Metro: Kongens Nytorv. **Amenities:** Bar; babysitting; room service. *In room:* TV, hair dryer, Internet (free), minibar.

NEAR RÅDHUSPLADSEN & TIVOLI

Expensive

Profil Copenhagen Plaza ★ This successful overhaul of an older hotel near the rail station combines first-class comfort and antique furnishings. Opposite the Tivoli Gardens, the hotel was commissioned by King Frederik VIII in 1913 and has entertained its share of celebrities and royalty. Rooms vary greatly in size and resemble what you might find in an English country house—but with all the modern amenities. The antiques, double-glazed windows, and views from many rooms make this a good choice. Bathrooms are generous in size. The **Library Bar** is one of Copenhagen's most charming.

Bernstorffsgade 4, DK-1577 København. ✆ **800-SOFITEL** (763-4835) or 33-14-92-62. Fax 33-93-93-62. www.profilhotels.dk. 93 units. 1,150DKK–2,640DKK double; from 3,140DKK suite. AE, DC, MC, V. Parking 225DKK. Bus: 2A, 5A, 46, or 150S. Metro: Nørreport. **Amenities:** Restaurant; bar; babysitting; exercise room; room service. *In room:* A/C, TV, hair dryer, minibar, Wi-Fi (free).

Moderate

Absalon Hotel ★ Since 1938 the Nedergaard family has been welcoming guests to its hotel, which has grown and expanded over the years in the neighborhood near the rail station. Today the hotel comprises a government-rated three-star hotel with private bathrooms, and a one-star annex without private bathrooms, the two facilities sharing the same entrance and reception. You can stay here in comparative luxury or at budget prices, depending on your choice of accommodations. Most bedrooms are medium in size or even somewhat cramped, but all are comfortably furnished and well maintained. If you want to stay here luxuriously, opt for one of the large and elegantly furnished top-floor rooms in a classical English or French Louis XIV style.

Helgolandsgade 15, DK-1653 København. ✆ **33-24-22-11.** Fax 33-24-34-11. www.absalon-hotel.dk. 165 units. Absalon Hotel (with private bathroom) 835DKK–1,290DKK double; annex (without private bathroom) 750DKK double. Rates include breakfast. MC, V. Parking 244DKK. Closed Dec 19–Jan 2. Bus: 6, 10, 16, 27, or 28. **Amenities:** Breakfast room; lounge. *In room:* TV, fridge (in some), hair dryer (in some), Wi-Fi (free).

Ascot Hotel ★ On a side street, 180m (591 ft.) from the Tivoli and a 2-minute walk from Town Hall Square, sits one of Copenhagen's best small hotels. The Ascot was built in 1902 and enlarged and modernized in 2007. The furniture is tasteful and very comfortable, and a few of the units are rented as apartments. The finest rooms open onto the street, though the accommodations in the rear get better air circulation and more light.

Studiestræde 61, DK-1554 København. ✆ **33-12-60-00.** Fax 33-14-60-40. www.ascot-hotel.dk. 165 units. 1,490DKK–1,590DKK double; 1,790DKK–2,590DKK apt. Rates include buffet breakfast. Winter discounts available. AE, DC, MC, V. Parking 125DKK. Bus: 2, 6, 8, 11, 14, 28, 29, 30, 34, 67, 68, 69, 150S, or 250S. Metro: Nørreport. **Amenities:** Breakfast room; bar; babysitting; exercise room; room service. *In room:* TV, hair dryer, kitchenette (in some), Wi-Fi (free).

Hotel Alexandra ★ This conveniently located address is a designer hotel with period furniture from Danish modern masters Arne Jacobsen and Ole Wanscher, with avant-garde lighting by Paul Henningsen. Each room is uniquely decorated, and 13 units are "special design rooms." Danish furniture classics are enhanced by Danish art on the walls. Guests meet fellow guests in the hotel's restaurant, Bistroen KBH, which serves a large Danish buffet in the morning.

H. C. Andersens Blvd. 8, D-1553 København. ✆ **33-74-44-44.** Fax 33-74-44-88. www.hotelalexandra.dk. 61 units. 1,745DKK–2,545DKK double. Rates include breakfast. AE, DC, MC, V. Bus: 1, 6, or 8. **Amenities:** Restaurant; bar; room service. *In room:* TV, hair dryer, spa next door, Wi-Fi (free).

Hotel Selandia One of the better hotels behind the railroad station, this solidly built structure has been receiving guests since 1928, and has been renovated many times over the years. A longtime favorite of budget-conscious travelers, it is well maintained, with comfortable, immaculately kept bedrooms. The furnishings in the midsize rooms are contemporary Scandinavian modern. A good Danish breakfast is served in a ground-floor room.

Helgolandsgade 12, DK-1653 København. ✆ **33-31-46-10.** Fax 33-31-46-09. www.hotel-selandia.dk. 87 units, 57 with bathroom. 675DKK–803DKK double without bathroom; 875DKK–1,360DKK double with bathroom. Rates include breakfast. AE, DC, MC, V. Parking 222DKK. Closed Dec 15–Jan 5. Bus: 10 or 26. **Amenities:** Breakfast room; babysitting. *In room:* TV, hair dryer (in some), Internet (free).

Kong Arthur ★ An orphanage when it was built in 1882, this hotel sits behind a private courtyard next to the tree-lined Peblinge Lake. Today, it's an antiques-filled mansion of old-world charm. It's been completely renovated into a contemporary hostelry, and a recent expansion offers more spacious rooms, including 30 for nonsmokers.

Nørre Søgade 11, DK-1370 København. ✆ **33-11-12-12.** Fax 33-32-61-30. www.kongarthur.dk. 117 units. 1,460DKK–1,560DKK double; 2,060DKK junior suite; 3,560DKK suite. Rates include buffet breakfast. AE, DC, MC, V. Free parking. Bus: 5, 8, 14, 42, or 43. **Amenities:** 3 restaurants; bar; babysitting; room service; sauna. *In room:* TV, hair dryer, minibar, Wi-Fi (free).

Where to Dine

That national institution, the smørrebrød (open-faced sandwich), is introduced at lunch. Literally, this means "bread and butter," but the Danes stack this sandwich as if it were the Leaning Tower of Pisa—then they throw in a slice of curled cucumber and bits of parsley or perhaps sliced peaches or a mushroom for added color.

NEAR KONGENS NYTORV & NYHAVN

Very Expensive

Era Ora ★★★ ITALIAN This reminder of the "Golden Age" is on virtually everyone's list as the best Italian restaurant in Denmark, and is one of the consistently best restaurants of any kind within Copenhagen. Established in 1982 by Tuscan-born partners Alessandro and Elvio, it offers an antique-looking dining room. Enjoy a cuisine based on Tuscan and Umbrian models, with sophisticated variations inspired by Denmark's superb array of fresh seafood and produce. Traditional favorites include a platter of 10 types of antipastos. All pastas are freshly made every day. Depending on the season and the inspiration of the chef, main courses include succulent veal dishes, rack of venison with balsamic vinegar and chanterelles, and ultrafresh fish.

Overgaden Neden Vandet 33B. ✆ **32-54-06-93.** www.era-ora.dk. Reservations required. Main courses 1,350DKK–1,950DKK; fixed-price lunch (4–7 courses) 325DKK–495DKK; fixed-price dinner (12–17 small dishes) 680DKK–980DKK. AE, DC, MC, V. Mon–Sat 7pm–1am. Bus: 2, 8, or 48.

Expensive

Godt ★★★ INTERNATIONAL This small-scale favorite is known to everyone in the neighborhood, including the queen of Denmark. Despite its fame, there's an appealing lack of pretentiousness here. Food is prepared fresh every day, based on ingredients that are the best at the market. The repertoire served here is splendid and the atmosphere so special it is worth reserving for your final night in Copenhagen. Some exciting dishes on the menu include quail stuffed with foie gras served with a salad of apple and celery; venison with a sauce of wild mushrooms; or fresh fish served with a sauce of almonds, vanilla, and fresh berries.

Gothersgade 38. ✆ **33-15-21-22.** www.restaurant-godt.dk. Reservations required. Fixed-price menus 495DKK–660DKK. DC, MC, V. Tues–Sat 6pm–midnight. Closed July and Dec 23–Jan 3. Bus: 6, 10, or 14.

Kommandanten ★★ DANISH/FRENCH Built in 1698 as the residence of the city's military commander, this deluxe restaurant is the epitome of Danish chic and charm. The menu offers a mouthwatering array of classical dishes mixed with innovative selections, a medley of strong yet subtle flavors. The finest seasonal ingredients are used, and the menu changes every 2 weeks. You might be offered the grilled catch of the day, fried veal tenderloin, grilled turbot with langoustines, or scallops and smoked quail. The service is the best in Copenhagen.

Ny Adelgade 7. ✆ **33-12-09-90.** Reservations required. Main courses 330DKK–450DKK; 3-course menu 800DKK. AE, DC, MC, V. Mon–Sat 5:30–10pm. Bus: 1, 2, 5, or 6.

Kong Hans Kælder ★★★ MODERN DANISH/INTERNATIONAL Housed in the oldest building in the city that's still in commercial use, this vaulted Gothic cellar may be the best restaurant in Denmark. Its most serious competition comes from Kommandanten, which many discriminating palates hail as the best. On "the oldest corner of Copenhagen," the restaurant has been carefully restored and is now a Relais Gourmand. A typical three-course dinner would include smoked salmon from the restaurant's smokehouse, breast of duck with *bigarade* (sour orange) sauce, and plum ice cream with Armagnac. If you dine here, prepare for innovation and delightful taste sensations, as evoked by slightly smoked scallops with a side of Sevruga caviar. Another signature dish is sautéed lobster with Jerusalem artichokes in a soy-ginger butter. These dishes can be served as either a starter or a main course.

Vingårdsstræde 6. ✆ **33-11-68-68.** www.konghans.dk. Reservations required. Main courses 450DKK; fixed-price menu 1,100DKK. AE, DC, DISC, MC, V. Mon–Sat 6–10pm. Closed July 20–Aug 4 and Dec 24–26. Bus: 1, 6, or 9.

Moderate

Café Lumskebugten ★ DANISH This restaurant is a well-managed bastion of Danish charm, with an unpretentious elegance. Now-legendary matriarch Karen Marguerita Krog established it in 1854 as a rowdy tavern for sailors. A tastefully gentrified version of the original beef hash is still served. Two glistening-white dining rooms are decorated with antique ships' models and oil paintings. The food and service are excellent. Specialties include tartar of salmon with herbs, Danish fish cakes with mustard sauce and minced beet root, sugar-marinated salmon with mustard-cream sauce, and a symphony of fish with saffron sauce and new potatoes. A filling lunch platter of assorted house specialties is offered for 275DKK.

Esplanaden 21. ✆ **33-15-60-29.** Reservations recommended. Main courses 175DKK–280DKK; 3-course fixed-price lunch 275DKK; 5-course fixed-price dinner 555DKK. AE, DC, MC, V. Mon–Fri 11am–10:30pm; Sat 5–10pm. Bus: 1, 6, or 9.

Custom House ★★ DANISH/JAPANESE/ITALIAN The Terence Conran group from England has moved into Copenhagen opening a restaurant complex, including bars, in a renovated ferry terminal overlooking the harbor. It's a unique dining adventure. **Bacino** serves some of the best specialties from the Italian kitchen, including a range of antipastos, succulent pastas, and risottos, as well as freshly caught fish and various meat dishes, especially tender veal such as a braised shank in Barolo wine sauce and truffles, artichokes, and polenta. The **Custom House Bar & Grill** specializes in a flavor-filled Danish and Continental cuisine, everything from lobster to roast pork. Specialties are rack of lamb and filet of salmon in a choice of sauces including roasted garlic butter. In a minimalist but elegant atmosphere, **Ebisu** serves a traditional Japanese cuisine with specialties often turned out on a large charcoal grill. The grilled duck breast teriyaki with a pear sauce is one of the best dishes in this complex.

Havnegade 44. ✆ **33-31-01-30.** www.customhouse.dk. Reservations recommended. Bacino main courses 125DKK-315DKK, fixed-price 7-course menus 465DKK-675DKK; the Custom House Bar & Grill main courses 135DKK-255DKK; Ebisu main courses 295DKK, fixed-price menus 395DKK-495DKK. AE, DC, MC, V. Bacino Mon-Sat 11:30am-2pm and 5:30-11pm; the Custom House Bar & Grill daily 11am-midnight; Ebisu Tues-Sat 5:30-11pm. Bus: 1A, 6A, or 29.

Restaurant Els DANISH/FRENCH With its original 1854 decor and murals by the famous 19th-century Danish artist, Christian Hitsch, this is one of the most respected and traditional restaurants of Copenhagen, attracting such clients as Hans Christian Andersen. If you're dropping in for lunch, you might make an entire meal out of those delectable open-faced Danish sandwiches, but in the evening the market-fresh menu is based on an expanded, mainly French-inspired repertoire. You'll feast on dishes made with prime ingredients, including breast of wild duck with blackberry sauce and other tasty delights.

Store Strandstræde 3, off Kongens Nytorv. ✆ **33-14-13-41.** www.restaurant-els.dk. Reservations recommended. Main courses 85DKK-145DKK lunch, 198DKK-295DKK dinner; 4-course menu 448DKK. AE, DC, MC, V. Mon-Sat 11am-5pm; daily 5pm-midnight. Bus: 1, 6, or 10.

Inexpensive

Ida Davidsen ★ ☺ SANDWICHES This restaurant has flourished since 1888, when the forebears of its present owner, Ida Davidsen, established a sandwich shop. Today, five generations later, the matriarch and namesake is known as the "smørrebrød queen of Copenhagen." Her restaurant sells a greater variety of open-faced sandwiches (250 kinds) than any other in Denmark. The fare has even been featured at royal buffets at Amalienborg Castle. You select by pointing to your choice in a glass-fronted display case; a staff member carries it to your table. The vast selection includes salmon, lobster, smoked duck with braised cabbage and horseradish, liver pâté, ham, and boiled egg. Two of them, perhaps with a slice of cheese, make a worthy lunch. If you are in doubt, a member of the service team, or perhaps Ida's charming husband, Adam Siesbye, will offer suggestions.

Store Kongensgade 70. ✆ **33-91-36-55.** www.idadavidsen.dk. Reservations recommended. Sandwiches 50DKK-135DKK. AE, DC, MC, V. Mon-Fri 10:30am-4pm. Bus: 6, 9, or 15.

NEAR RÅDHUSPLADSEN & TIVOLI

Moderate

Copenhagen Corner ☺ SCANDINAVIAN In the very heart of Copenhagen, this restaurant opens onto Rådhuspladsen, around the corner from the Tivoli Gardens. It offers well-prepared, unpretentious, and reasonably priced meals. The menu features the Danes' favorite dishes, beginning with three kinds of herring or freshly peeled shrimp with dill and lemon. The fish is fresh and beautifully prepared, especially the steamed Norwegian salmon with a "lasagna" of potatoes, and baked halibut with artichokes. Meat and poultry courses, although not always equal to the fish, are tasty and tender, especially the veal liver Provençal.

H. C. Andersens Blvd. 1A. ✆ **33-91-45-45.** Reservations recommended. Main courses 145DKK-275DKK; 3-course fixed-price menu 385DKK. AE, DC, MC, V. Daily 11:30am-11pm. Bus: 1, 6, or 8.

Søren K ★ MODERN/EUROPEAN Named after Denmark's most celebrated philosopher, this is an artfully minimalist dining room that's on the ground floor of the latest addition to the Royal Library. Opened in 1999, it has big-windowed views that stretch out over the sea. Menu items change frequently but might include carpaccio of veal, foie gras, oyster soup, and main courses such as veal chops served with lobster sauce and a half-lobster, and venison roasted with nuts and seasonal berries and a marinade of green tomatoes. The restaurant virtually never cooks with butter, cream, or high-cholesterol cheeses, making a meal here a dietetic as well as a savory experience.

On the ground floor of the Royal Library's Black Diamond Wing, 1 Søren Kierkegaards Plads. ✆ **33-47-49-49.** www.soerenk.dk. Reservations recommended. Main courses 75DKK-195DKK lunch, 235DKK-275DKK dinner; 3-course fixed-price dinner 365DKK-550DKK. AE, DC, MC, V. Mon-Sat noon-midnight. Bus: 1, 2, 5, 6, or 8.

Inexpensive

Axelborg Bodega DANISH Across from the Benneweis Circus and near Scala and the Tivoli, this 1912 cafe has outdoor tables where you can enjoy a brisk Scandinavian evening. Order the *dagens ret* (daily special); typical Danish dishes are featured, including *frikadeller* (meatballs) and pork chops. A wide selection of club sandwiches is also available. Although the atmosphere is somewhat impersonal, this is a local favorite; diners enjoy recipes that seem drawn from Grandma's kitchen.

Axeltorv 1. ✆ **33-11-06-38.** www.axelborgbodega.dk. Reservations recommended. Main courses 99DKK-179DKK. DC, MC, V. Daily 11am-9pm. Bar daily 11am-2am (Fri-Sat to 4am). Bus: 1 or 6.

Domhus Kælderen DANISH/INTERNATIONAL The good food at this bustling, old-fashioned emporium of Danish cuisine draws a mixed crowd from City Hall's courtrooms across the square as well as visiting foreigners. The half-cellar room holds memorabilia from its 50 years as a restaurant (before that, it was a butcher shop). Lunch tends to be more conservative and more Danish than dinner. It might include frikadeller and heaping platters of herring, cheeses, smoked meats and fish, and salads. Dinner could be pickled salmon; prime rib of beef with horseradish; and fine cuts of beef, served with béarnaise or pepper sauce. Also look for the catch of the day, prepared just about any way you like. You get no culinary surprises here, but you're rarely disappointed.

Nytorv 5. ✆ **33-14-84-55.** Reservations recommended. Main courses 70DKK-160DKK lunch, 130DKK-205DKK dinner; fixed-price menus 225DKK-275DKK. AE, DC, MC, V. Daily 11am-4pm and 5-10pm. Bus: 5.

NEAR ROSENBORG SLOT

Expensive

Sankt Gertruds Kloster ★ INTERNATIONAL Near Nørreport Station and south of Rosenborg Castle, this is the most romantic restaurant in town. There's no electricity in the labyrinth of 14th-century underground vaults, and the 1,500 flickering candles, open grill, iron sconces, and rough-hewn furniture create an elegant medieval ambience. The food is equally impressive. Try the fresh homemade foie gras with black truffles; lobster served in turbot bouillon; scallops sautéed with herbs in sauterne; venison with green asparagus and truffle sauce; or fish and shellfish terrine studded with chunks of lobster and salmon.

Hauser Plads 32. ✆ **33-14-66-30.** www.sgk.as. Reservations required. Main courses 338DKK-380DKK; fixed-price menus 398DKK-758DKK. AE, DC, MC, V. Daily 4pm-midnight (until 11pm Sun). Closed Dec 25-Jan 1. Bus: 4E, 7E, 14, or 16. Metro: Nørreport.

AT GRÅBRØDRETORV

Moderate

Bøf & Ost DANISH/FRENCH "Beef & Cheese" is housed in a 1728 building, and its cellars come from a medieval monastery. In summer, a pleasant outdoor terrace overlooks Gray Friars Square. Although the menu changes monthly, specialties can include lobster soup, fresh Danish bay strips, a cheese plate with six selections, and some of the best grilled tenderloin in town. One local diner confided: "The food is not worthy of God's own table, but it's so good I come here once a week."

Gråbrødretorv 13. ✆ **33-11-99-11.** www.boef-ost.dk. Reservations required. Main courses 139DKK-225DKK; fixed-price lunch 109DKK-138DKK. DC, MC, V. Mon-Sat 11:30am-10:30pm. Closed Jan 1 and Dec 24-25. Bus: 5.

Peder Oxe's Restaurant/Vinkælder Wine Bar DANISH/ASIAN This romantic building dates from the 1700s, with its original wooden floors and Portuguese tiles, and the crowd is young, fun, and value-conscious. The salad bar is 32DKK when accompanied by a main course. It's so tempting that many prefer to enjoy it alone for 78DKK per person. Dishes include lobster soup, Danish bay shrimp, fresh asparagus, open-faced sandwiches, hamburgers, and fresh fish. Specialties influenced by Asia have been added to the menu, including such delights as tuna tartare with avocado and mango.

Gråbrødretorv 11. ✆ **33-11-00-77.** www.pederoxe.dk. Reservations recommended. Main courses 115DKK-198DKK; fixed-price lunch 138DKK-148DKK. DC, MC, V. Daily 11:30am-midnight. Bus: 5.

Inexpensive

Pasta Basta ITALIAN/INTERNATIONAL This restaurant's main attraction is an enormous buffet (sometimes called the "Pasta Basta Table") loaded with cold antipastos and salads. With more than nine selections, it's one of the best deals in town at 89DKK. The restaurant is divided into half a dozen cozy dining rooms decorated in the style of ancient Pompeii, with faded frescoes patterned after originals from Italy. It's on a historic cobblestone street off the main shopping street, Strøget. Menu choices include at least 15 kinds of pasta (all made fresh on the premises); a platter with three kinds of Danish caviar (whitefish, speckled trout, and vendace, served with chopped onions, lemon, toast, and butter); fresh mussels cooked in dry white wine with pasta and creamy saffron sauce; thinly sliced salmon with a cream-based sauce of salmon roe; and sliced Danish suckling lamb with fried spring onions and tarragon.

Valkendorfsgade 22. ✆ **33-11-21-31.** www.pastabasta.dk. Reservations recommended. Lunch main courses 79DKK-89DKK; dinner main courses 98DKK-185DKK; 2- to 3-course fixed-price menus 198DKK-298DKK. DC, MC, V. Sun-Thurs 11:30am-3am; Fri-Sat 11:30am-5am. Bus: 5.

AT CHRISTIANSBORG

Expensive

Krogs Fiskerestaurant ★ SEAFOOD A short walk from Christiansborg Castle, the most famous restaurant in the district was built in 1789 as a fish shop. The canalside plaza where fishers once moored their boats is now the site of the restaurant's outdoor dining terrace. The restaurant serves fresh seafood in a single large room decorated in antique style, with old oil paintings. The well-chosen menu includes lobster soup, bouillabaisse, oysters, mussels steamed in white wine, and poached salmon trout with saffron sauce. Each dish is impeccably prepared and flavorful. A selection of meat dishes is available, but the fish is better.

Gammel Strand 38. ✆ **33-15-89-15.** www.krogs.dk. Reservations required. Main courses 310DKK-475DKK; 5-course fixed-price menu 575DKK-825DKK. AE, DC, MC, V. Mon-Sat noon-4pm and 5:30-10:30pm. Bus: 1, 2, 10, 16, or 29.

Moderate

Cafeen Nikolaj DANISH This place makes no pretense of being more than it is: a simple cafe that prepares good-tasting food with fresh ingredients at fair prices. The cafe, which evokes Greenwich Village in the 1950s, lies on the site where Hans Tausen, a father of the Danish Reformation, delivered thundering sermons in the 16th century. No one is thundering now—they're ordering an array of typical Danish lunches, including a tasty variety of open-faced sandwiches and homemade soups. You can always count on various types of herring. Danish sliced ham on good homemade bread is a perennial favorite, and there is also a selection of Danish cheeses.

Nikolaj Plads 12. ✆ **33-11-63-13.** Main courses 98DKK-158DKK; 3-course fixed-price menu 348DKK-448DKK. AE, DC, MC, V. Mon-Sat 11:30am-4pm. Bus: 2, 6, 8, or 10.

IN VESTERBRO

Copenhagen Food Consulting Company ("Cofoco") ★★ DANISH/FRENCH In the trendy Vesterbro area, this haven of haute cuisine is in a minimalist Danish style and offers one of the best value fixed-price menus in town. Each day brings something new and market-fresh to the menu. The cuisine is based on fresh seafood and local farm products from the Danish countryside, which are skillfully handled by well-trained Danish and continental chefs. You're likely to revel in such dishes as cod with apple and mint or else duck cooked in yogurt served with beets and horseradish. Their soups are among the best in town, and they serve tender veal dishes accompanied by fresh spinach. For dessert, savor their crème brûlée.

Abel Cathrines gade 7. ✆ **33-31-70-55.** www.cofoco.dk. Reservations required. Fixed-price menu 275DKK-650DKK. AE, MC, V. Mon-Sat 5:30pm-midnight. Bus: 6A.

IN KØDBYEN

BioMio ★ In the increasingly trendy meatpacking district known as Kødbyen, this is the greenest of the green restaurants of Denmark. Even the waitstaff's cotton uniforms are organic. The menu is changed seasonally to keep the produce as regional as possible. Salads are a specialty, and one features a medley of greens in a trio of dips, hummus of butter beans, taatiki, and olive tapenade. Spicy beef noodles are flavored with ginger and soya and served with fresh herbs and restaurant almonds. The red chocolate cake is made from beet root. A green-colored cocktail is made from organic gin, green-apple liqueur, freshly squeezed apples, and cucumber.

Halmtorvet 19. ✆ **33-311-20-00.** www.biomio.dk. Reservations required. Main courses 955DKK-165DKK. AE, DC, MC, V. Sun-Thurs noon-9pm; Fri-Sat noon-10pm. Closed 2 weeks around Christmas. Metro: Hovedbanegard (Central Station).

IN TIVOLI

Food prices inside Tivoli are about 30% higher than elsewhere. Try skipping dessert at a restaurant and picking up a less expensive treat at one of the many stands. Take

COPENHAGEN'S little mermaid

The one statue *everybody* wants to see is the life-size bronze of ***Den Lille Havfrue*** ★, inspired by Hans Christian Andersen's "The Little Mermaid," one of the world's most famous fairy tales. The statue, unveiled in 1913, was sculpted by Edvard Eriksen and rests on rocks right off the shore. The mermaid has been attacked more than once, losing an arm in one misadventure, decapitated as recently as January 6, 1998. The latest attack occurred in the early-morning hours in September 2003 when explosives may have been used to topple the statue from its stone base. The much-abused statue is based on a mythical sea king's mermaid daughter who, according to the Hans Christian Andersen tale, falls in love with a prince and must wait 300 years to become human.

All year, a 2½-hour **City and Harbor Tour** of Copenhagen makes a significant stop at the *Little Mermaid* and costs 220DKK adults, 90DKK children 11 and under. For more information, call Copenhagen Excursions at ✆ **32-54-06-06;** www.cex.dk. In summer, a special "Mermaid Bus" leaves from Rådhuspladsen (Vester Voldgade) at 9am and then at half-hour intervals until 5:30pm. On the "Langelinie" bus there's a 20-minute stop at *The Little Mermaid.* If you want more time, take bus no. 1, 6, or 9.

bus no. 1, 6, 8, 16, 29, 30, 32, or 33 to reach the park and either of the following restaurants. ***Note:*** These restaurants are open only May to mid-September.

Divan II ★★ DANISH/FRENCH This landmark restaurant, established in 1843 in a garden setting, is one of the finest in Tivoli. Expect flowered garden terraces, splashing fountains, and an interior decor inspired by a lattice-ringed greenhouse. The service is uniformly impeccable, and the cuisine is among the most sophisticated in Copenhagen. Try the breast of free-range cockerel from Bornholm; it's braised in white wine and served with morels and fresh shallots. Roasted rack of Danish veal with new peas and morels, or *tournedos* Rossini, are always appealing. An ongoing staple is the "Madame Waleska," steamed filets of sole that are elaborately presented with truffles and a lobster-studded Morney sauce. Strawberries Romanoff finishes off the meal delightfully.

Tivoli. ✆ **33-75-07-50.** www.divan2.dk. Reservations recommended. Main courses 320DKK–350DKK. AE, DC, MC, V. Apr 15–Sept 23 daily noon–10pm.

Færgekroen DANISH In a cluster of trees at the edge of the lake, this restaurant resembles a pink half-timbered Danish cottage. In warm weather, try to snag a table on the outside terrace. The menu offers drinks, snacks, and full meals. Meals might include omelets, beef with horseradish, fried plaice (a flounder-like fish) with melted butter, pork chops with red cabbage, curried chicken, or fried meatballs. If you like honest and straightforward fare, without fancy trimmings, and don't like to spend a lot of money, this is the place for you. A pianist provides singalong music every evening starting at 8pm.

Vesterbrogade 3, Tivoli. ✆ **33-75-06-80.** Main courses 175DKK–250DKK; fixed-price lunch 150DKK-195DKK. AE, DC, MC, V. Daily 11am–midnight (hot food until 9:45pm).

Seeing the Sights in Copenhagen

THE TIVOLI GARDENS

Tivoli Gardens ★★ ☺ Since it opened in 1843, this 8-hectare (20-acre) garden and amusement park in the center of Copenhagen has been a resounding success, with its thousands of flowers, a merry-go-round of tiny Viking ships, games of chance and skill (pinball arcades, slot machines, shooting galleries), and a Ferris wheel of hot-air balloons and cabin seats. There's even a playground.

An Arabian-style fantasy palace, with towers and arches, houses more than two dozen restaurants in all price ranges, from a lakeside inn to a beer garden. Take a walk around the edge of the tiny lake, with its ducks, swans, and boats.

A parade of the red-uniformed Tivoli Boys Guard takes place on weekends at 5:30 and 7:30pm, and their regimental band gives concerts Saturday at 3pm on the open-air stage. The oldest building at Tivoli, the Chinese-style Pantomime Theater, with its peacock curtain, stages pantomimes in the evening.

Vesterbrogade 3. ✆ **33-15-10-01.** www.tivoli.dk. Admission 95DKK, 50DKK children 3–11; multiride ticket 205DKK, 170DKK children 3–11. Apr 15 to mid-Sept daily 11am–midnight. Partial Christmastime opening from mid-Nov to Christmas Eve (reduced admission). Closed mid-Sept to Apr 14. Bus: 1 or 16.

THE TOP MUSEUMS

Don't worry about not understanding the explanations in the museums; virtually all have write-ups in English.

Amalienborg Palace ★★ These four 18th-century French-inspired rococo mansions are the home of the Danish royal family, a position they have held since 1794, when the original royal palace burned. Visitors flock to witness the changing of the guard at noon when the royal family is in residence. A swallowtail flag at mast signifies that the queen is in Copenhagen. The Royal Life Guard in black bearskin busbies leaves Rosenborg Castle at 11:30am and marches to Amalienborg. After the event, the guard, still accompanied by the band, returns to Rosenborg Castle.

In 1994, some of the official and private rooms in Amalienborg were opened to the public for the first time. The rooms, reconstructed to reflect the period 1863 to 1947, belonged to members of the reigning royal family, the Glücksborgs, who ascended the throne in 1863. The highlight is the period devoted to the long reign (1863–1906) of King Christian IX and Queen Louise.

Christian VIII's Palace. ✆ **33-12-21-86.** www.amalienborgmuseet.dk. Admission 60DKK adults, 35DKK students, 40DKK seniors, free for children 17 and under. Oct–May Tues–Sun 11am–4pm; June–Aug daily 7am–4pm; Sept daily 11am–4pm. Closed Dec 14–25. Bus: 1, 6, 9, or 10.

Christiansborg Palace ★ This granite-and-copper palace on the Slotsholmen—a small island that has been the center of political power in Denmark for more than 800 years—houses the Danish parliament, the Supreme Court, the prime minister's offices, and the Royal Reception Rooms. A guide will lead you through richly decorated rooms, including the Throne Room, banqueting hall, and Queen's Library. Before entering, you'll be asked to put on soft overshoes to protect the floors. Under the palace, visit the well-preserved ruins of the 1167 castle of Bishop Absalon, founder of Copenhagen.

Christiansborg Slotsplads. ✆ **33-92-64-92.** www.ses.dk. Royal Reception Rooms 70DKK adults, 60DKK students and seniors, 35DKK children 7–14; parliament free; castle ruins 40DKK adults, 30DKK students, 20DKK children 7–14. Reception rooms guided tours May–Sept daily at 11am, 1pm, and 3pm; Oct–Apr Tues–Sun at 3pm. Parliament English-language tours daily—call for appointment. Ruins May–Sept daily 10am–4pm; Oct–Apr Tues–Sun 10am–4pm.

Den Hirschsprungske Samling (The Hirschsprung Collection) This collection of 19th- and early-20th-century Danish art is in Ostre Anlæg, a park in the city center. Tobacco merchant Heinrich Hirschsprung (1836–1908) created the collection, and it has been growing ever since. The emphasis is on the Danish golden age, with such artists as Eckersberg, Købke, and Lundbye, and on the Skagen painters, P. S. Krøyer, and Anna and Michael Ancher. Some furnishings from the artists' homes are exhibited.

Stockholmsgade 20. ✆ **35-42-03-36.** www.hirschsprung.dk. Admission 50DKK adults, 40DKK students and seniors, free for children 17 and under. Wed–Mon 11am–4pm. Bus: 6A, 14, 40, 42, 43, 150S, 184, or 185.

Frihedsmuseet (Museum of Danish Resistance, 1940–45) The horrors of the Nazi occupation of Denmark live on here. On display are relics of torture and concentration camps, the equipment used by the Danish resistance for forbidden wireless communications and the production of illegal propaganda films, British propaganda leaflets, satirical caricatures of Hitler, information about both Danish Jews and Danish Nazis, and the paralyzing nationwide strikes. Also look for an armed car used for drive-by shootings of Danish Nazi informers and collaborators.

Churchillparken. ✆ **33-47-39-21.** www.nationalmuseet.dk. Free admission. May–Sept Tues–Sun 10am–5pm; Oct–Apr Tues–Sun 10am–3pm. Bus: 1 or 6.

Frilandsmuseet (Open-Air Museum) ★ This reconstructed village in Lyngby, on the fringe of Copenhagen, captures Denmark's one-time rural character. The "museum" is nearly 36 hectares (89 acres); a 3.2km (2-mile) walk around the compound reveals a dozen authentic buildings—farmsteads, windmills, fishermen's cottages. Exhibits include a half-timbered 18th-century farmstead from one of the tiny wind-swept Danish islands, a primitive longhouse from the remote Faroe Islands, thatched fishers' huts from Jutland, tower windmills, and a mid-19th-century potter's workshop.

Kongevejen 100. ✆ **33-13-44-11.** www.nationalmuseet.dk. Free admission. Easter to late Oct Tues–Sun 10am–5pm. Closed late Oct to Easter. S-tog: Copenhagen Central Station to Sorgenfri (trains leave every 20 min.). Bus: 184 or 194.

Nationalmuseet (National Museum) ★★★ A gigantic repository of anthropological artifacts, this museum features objects from prehistory, the Middle Ages, and the Renaissance in Denmark, including Viking stones, helmets, and fragments of battle gear. Especially interesting are the "lur" horn, a Bronze Age musical instrument among the oldest in Europe, and the world-famous Sun Chariot, an elegant Bronze Age piece of pagan art. The Royal Collection of Coins and Medals contains various coins from antiquity. There are also outstanding collections of Egyptian and classical antiquities.

Ny Vestergade 10. ✆ **33-13-44-11.** www.nationalmuseet.dk. Free admission. Tues–Sun 10am–5pm. Wed free entry to permanent exhibitions. Closed Dec 24, 25, and 31. Bus: 1, 5, 6, 8, or 10.

Ny Carlsberg Glyptotek ★★★ The Glyptotek, behind the Tivoli, is one of Scandinavia's most important art museums. Founded by 19th-century art collector Carl Jacobsen, the museum holds modern art and antiquities. The modern section has both French and Danish art, mainly from the 19th century; sculpture, including works by Rodin; and works of the Impressionists and related artists, including van Gogh's *Landscape from St-Rémy.* Antiquities include Egyptian, Greek, Roman, and Etruscan works. The Egyptian collection is outstanding; the prize is a prehistoric rendering of a hippopotamus. A favorite of ours is the Etruscan art display. In 1996, the Ny Glyptotek added a French Masters' wing, where you'll find an extensive collection of masterpieces.

Dantes Plads 7. ✆ **33-41-81-41.** www.glyptoteket.dk. Admission 60DKK adults, free for children 17 and under, free for all Wed and Sun. Tues–Sun 11am–5pm. Bus: 1, 2, 5, 6, 8, or 10.

Rosenborg Castle ★★★ This red-brick Renaissance-style castle houses everything from narwhal-tusk and ivory coronation chairs to Frederik VII's baby shoes—all from the Danish royal family. Its biggest draws are the dazzling crown jewels and regalia in the basement Treasury, where a lavishly decorated coronation saddle from 1596 is also shown. Try to see the Knights Hall (room no. 21), with its coronation seat, three silver lions, and relics from the 1700s. Room no. 3 was used by founding father Christian IV, who died in this bedroom decorated with Asian lacquer art and a stucco ceiling.

Øster Voldgade 4A. ✆ **33-15-32-86.** www.rosenborgslot.dk. Admission 75DKK adults, 45DKK students and seniors, free for children 17 and under. Palace and treasury (royal jewels) Jan–Apr Tues–Sun 11am–4pm; May–Oct daily 10am–4pm; Nov–Dec 18 Tues–Sun 11am–4pm; Dec 27–30 daily 11am–4pm. Closed Jan 1, Dec 19–26, and Dec 31. S-tog: Nørreport. Bus: 5, 10, 14, 16, 31, 42, 43, 184, or 185. Metro: Nørreport.

Statens Museum for Kunst (Royal Museum of Fine Arts) ★★ This well-stocked museum, one of the best in Scandinavia, houses painting and sculpture from the 13th century to the present. There are Dutch golden-age landscapes and marine paintings by Rubens, plus portraits by Frans Hals and Rembrandt. Eckersberg, Købke, and Hansen represent the Danish golden age. French 20th-century art

Native Behavior

If you want to be taken for a real Copenhagener, rent a bike and pedal your way around the city, up and down its streets and along its canals. It's estimated that half the population does the same.

After all that exercise, do as the Danes do and order your fill of smørrebrød for lunch. Sold all over the city, these are open-faced sandwiches on which Danes are known to pile almost anything edible. Our favorite is a mound of baby shrimp, although roast beef topped with pickle is another tasty offering. And to top off the native experience, order aquavit (also called snaps in Denmark) with your lunch, though less reliable stomachs may opt instead for a Carlsberg or Tuborg beer.

Whatever you do, though, don't tell any Dane that you eat pancakes for breakfast. In Denmark, a pancake is strictly a dessert.

And finally, greet everyone you encounter with a *"God dag"* ("Good day"). If you do, you'll no doubt end up having one yourself.

includes 20 works by Matisse. In the Royal Print Room are 300,000 drawings, prints, lithographs, and other works by such artists as Dürer, Rembrandt, Matisse, and Picasso.

A major expansion in 1998 added a concert hall, a Children's Art Museum, and a glass wing designed for temporary exhibits.

Sølvgade 48-50. ✆ **33-74-84-94.** www.smk.dk. Admission 80DKK adults, 60DKK seniors, 50DKK students, free for children 17 and under. Higher admission for special exhibitions only. Tues-Sun 10am-5pm (until 8pm Wed). Bus: 6A, 14, 40, 42, 43, 150S, 184, or 185.

Tøjhusmuseet (Royal Arsenal Museum) This museum features a fantastic display of weapons used for hunting and warfare. On the ground floor is the Canon Hall, the longest vaulted Renaissance hall in Europe, stocked with artillery equipment dating from 1500 up to the present day. Above the Canon Hall is the impressive Armory Hall, which houses one of the world's finest collections of small arms, colors, and armor.

Tøjhusgade 3. ✆ **33-11-60-37.** www.thm.dk. Admission 30DKK adults, 15DKK students and seniors, free for children 17 and under. Tues-Sun noon-4pm. Closed Jan 1 and Dec 23-26 and 31. Bus: 1, 2, 5, 6, 8, 10, 28, 29, 30, 32, 33, or 42.

CHURCHES & OTHER ATTRACTIONS

Botanisk Have (Botanical Gardens) Planted from 1871 to 1874, the Botanical Gardens, across from Rosenborg Castle, are on a lake that was once part of the city's defensive moat. Special features include a cactus house and a palm house, all of which appear even more exotic in the far northern country of Denmark. An alpine garden contains mountain plants from all over the world.

Gothersgade 140. ✆ **35-32-22-40.** Free admission. May-Sept daily 8:30am-6pm; Oct-Apr Tues-Sun 8:30am-4pm. S-tog: Nørreport. Bus: 5A, 14, 40, 42, or 43.

Frederikskirke This 2-centuries-old church, with its green copper dome—one of the largest in the world—is a short walk from Amalienborg Palace. After an unsuccessful start during the neoclassical revival of the 1750s in Denmark, the church was finally completed in Roman baroque style in 1894. In many ways, it's more impressive than Copenhagen's cathedral.

Frederiksgade 4. ✆ **33-15-01-44.** Free admission to church; dome 40DKK adults, 10DKK children. Church Mon-Tues and Thurs 10am-5pm; Wed 10am-6pm; Fri-Sun noon-5pm. Dome June-Sept 1 daily 1-3pm; Sept 2-May Sat-Sun 1-3pm. Bus: 1, 6, or 9.

Rådhus (Town Hall) and World Clock ★ Built in 1905, the Town Hall has impressive statues of H. C. Andersen and Niels Bohr, the Nobel prize–winning physicist. Jens Olsen's famous **World Clock** is open for viewing Monday to Friday 8:30am to 4:30pm and Saturday 10am to 1pm. The clockwork is so exact that the variation over 300 years is 0.4 second. Climb the tower for an impressive view.

Rådhuspladsen. ✆ **33-66-25-82.** Rådhus 25DKK; clock 15DKK adults, 5DKK children. Guided tour 30DKK adults and children. Rådhus Mon-Fri 3pm, Sat 10 and 11am; tower Mon-Sat noon. Bus: 1, 6, or 8.

Rundetårn (Round Tower) ★ This 17th-century public observatory, attached to a church, is visited by thousands who climb the spiral ramp (no steps) for a panoramic view of Copenhagen. The tower is one of the crowning architectural achievements of the Christian IV era. Peter the Great, in Denmark on a state visit, galloped up the ramp on horseback.

Købmagergade 52A. ✆ **33-73-03-73.** www.rundetaarn.dk. Admission 25DKK adults, 5DKK children 5–15. May 21–Sept 20 daily 10am–8pm, Sept 21–May 20 daily 10am–5pm; closed Dec 24–25 and Jan 1. Bus: 5, 7E,14, 16, or 42. Metro: Nørreport.

Vor Frue Kirke (Copenhagen Cathedral) This early-19th-century Greek Revival–style church, near Copenhagen University, features Bertel Thorvaldsen's white marble neoclassical works, including *Christ and the Apostles.* The funeral of H. C. Andersen took place here in 1875, and that of Søren Kierkegaard in 1855.

Nørregade 8. ✆ **33-14-21-28.** Free admission. Mon–Fri 9am–5pm; Sat 8:30am–5pm; Sun noon–4:30pm. Bus: 5.

ORGANIZED TOURS

Bus & Boat Tours For orientation, try the 1½-hour **City Tour** (2½ hr. with a visit to a brewery) that covers major scenic highlights like *The Little Mermaid,* Rosenborg Castle, and Amalienborg Palace. On workdays, tours also visit the Carlsberg brewery. Tours depart daily April 8 to May 14 at 11:30am; May 15 to September 30 at 9:30am, 11:30am, and 1:30pm; October 1 to October 15 at 11:30am; and they cost 140DKK adults and 70DKK children.

The **City and Harbor Tour,** a 2-hour-and-15-minute trip by launch and bus, departs from Town Hall Square. The boat tours the city's main canals, passing *The Little Mermaid* and the Old Fish Market. It operates from April 8 to December 17. Tours cost 175DKK adults and 80DKK children 11 and under.

Shakespeare buffs will be interested in an afternoon excursion to the castles of North Zealand. The 7-hour English-language tour explores the area north of Copenhagen, including a visit to Kronborg (Hamlet's Castle); a brief trip to Fredensborg, the queen's residence; and a stopover at Frederiksborg Castle and the National Historical Museum. Tours depart from the Town Hall Square May 2 to October 16, Wednesday, Saturday, and Sunday at 9:30am; November to April, Wednesday to Sunday at 9:30am. The cost is 480DKK adults, 230DKK for children.

For more information about these tours, contact **Sightseeing DK** (✆ **32-66-00-00;** www.sightseeing.dk).

Guided Walks Through Copenhagen Licensed Danish tour guides conduct 2-hour guided walking tours of the city Monday to Saturday at 10:30am, between May and September. The price is 100DKK for adults, 30DKK for children. For information, contact **Copenhagen Walking Tours** (✆ **40-81-12-17;** www.copenhagen-walkingtours.dk).

The Shopping Scene

Royal Copenhagen, Amagertorv 6 (✆ **33-13-71-81;** www.royalcopenhagen.com; bus: 1, 2, 6, 8, 28, 29, or 41 for the retail outlet, 1 or 15 for the factory), was founded in 1775. Royal Copenhagen's trademark, three wavy blue lines, has come to symbolize quality in porcelain throughout the world.

In the Royal Copenhagen retail center, legendary **Georg Jensen,** Amagertorv 6 (✆ **33-11-40-80;** www.georgjensen.com; bus: 1, 6, 8, 9, or 10), is known for its fine silver. For the connoisseur, there's no better address—this is the largest and best collection of Jensen holloware in Europe. Jewelry in traditional and modern design is also featured. One department specializes in seconds produced by various porcelain and glassware manufacturers.

Customers refer to the two owners of the **Amber Specialist,** Frederiksberggade 28 (© **33-11-88-03;** bus: 28, 29, or 41), as "The Amber Twins." These blonde-haired ladies specialize in "the gold of the north." This stone—really petrified resin—originated in the large coniferous forests that covered Denmark some 35 million years ago.

The elegant **Magasin,** Kongens Nytorv 13 (© **33-11-44-33;** http://shop.magasin.dk; bus: 1, 6, 9, or 10), is the biggest department store in Scandinavia. It offers an assortment of Danish designer fashion, glass and porcelain, and souvenirs. Goods are shipped abroad tax-free.

Copenhagen After Dark

In Copenhagen, a good night means a late night. On warm weekends hundreds of rowdy revelers crowd Strøget until sunrise, and jazz clubs, traditional beer houses, and wine cellars are routinely packed. The city has a more serious cultural side as well, exemplified by excellent theaters, operas, and ballets. **Half-price tickets** for some concerts and theater productions are available the day of the performance from the ticket kiosk opposite the Nørreport rail station, at Nørrevoldgade and Fiolstræde; it's open Monday to Friday from noon to 7pm and Saturday from noon to 3pm. On summer evenings outdoor concerts are held in Fælled Park near the entrance, near Frederik V's Vej; inquire about dates and times at the Copenhagen tourist office.

THE PERFORMING ARTS

Opened by Queen Margrethe, this $441-million 1,700-seat **Copenhagen Opera House ★★★**, Ekuipagemesteruej 10 (© **33-69-69-33**), is the luxurious home of the Royal Danish Opera. Designed by Danish architect Henning Larsen, the opera house uses precious stones and metals, including 105,000 sheets of gold leaf, and chandeliers which outsparkle and outshine anything in Las Vegas. In addition to the international artists, the opera house also showcases the works of such Danish composers as Carl Nielsen and Poul Ruders. You can dine at the on-site **Restauranten** before curtain time, with a three-course menu costing 465DKK. In addition, there is an **Opera Café,** serving sandwiches, salads, and light Danish specialties. The season runs from mid-August to the beginning of June. During performance season, tours of the building are offered daily on a frequently changing schedule, which usually requires a phone call as a means of hammering out the schedule. Tickets are 100DKK each. The box office (© **33-69-69-69;** www.kglteater.dk) is open Monday to Saturday from noon to 6pm.

Det Kongelige Teater (Royal Theater), Kongens Nytorv (© **33-69-69-69;** www.kglteater.dk; bus: 1, 6, 9, or 10), dates from 1748 and is a venue for cultural events. Because the arts are state subsidized in Denmark, ticket prices are comparatively low, and some seats may be available at the box office the day before a performance. We recommend making reservations in advance. The season runs from August to May. Tickets are 90DKK to 650DKK, half price for seniors 67 and over and those 25 and under (1 week before a show begins). The box office is open Monday to Saturday 1 to 8pm; phone hours are Monday to Friday 1 to 8pm, Saturday 10am to 8pm, and Sunday 3 hours before a performance (performances are usually at 3pm).

LIVE-MUSIC CLUBS

Copenhagen JazzHouse, Niels Hammingsensgade 10 (✆ **33-15-26-00;** S-tog: Nørreport), plays host to more non-Danish jazz artists than just about any other jazz bar in town. Live music tends to begin around 8:30pm and usually finishes reasonably early. Around midnight on Thursday, Friday, and Saturday, the venue shifts from a live concert hall into a dance club. Cover is 75DKK to 300DKK; closed Monday.

Mojo Blues Bar, Løngangsstræde 21C (✆ **33-11-64-53;** bus: 2, 8, or 30), is a candlelit drinking spot that offers blues music, mostly performed by Scandinavian groups. It's open daily from 8pm to 5am. There's no cover from Sunday to Thursday, a cover of 55DKK to 70DKK Friday and Saturday.

In the trendy western neighborhood of Vesterbro, **Boutique Lize,** Enghave Plads 6 (✆ **33-31-15-60**), is a bar with music that ranges from punk to electro to hip-hop. Drawing an artsy crowd under 35, the bar is in the Danish minimalism style of wood plank floors and exposed bricks. Open daily from 11am to midnight; take bus no. 10 to this western part of the city.

BARS & CELLARS

Det Lille Apotek, Stor Kannikestræde 15 (✆ **33-12-56-06;** www.detlilleapotek.dk; bus: 2, 5, 8, or 30), is a good spot for English-speaking foreign students to meet their Danish contemporaries. Though the menu varies, keep an eye out for the prawn cocktail and tenderloin. The main courses run about 95DKK to 188DKK at dinner. It's open daily 11am to midnight.

Frequented by celebrities and royalty, the **Library Bar,** in the Profil Copenhagen Plaza Hotel, Bernstorffsgade 4 (✆ **33-14-92-62;** bus: 6), was rated by the late Malcolm Forbes as one of the top five bars in the world. In a setting of antique books and works of art, you can order everything from a cappuccino to a cocktail. It's open daily 4pm to midnight.

Nyhavn 17, Nyhavn 17 (✆ **33-12-54-19;** bus: 1, 6, 27, or 29; Metro: Kongens Nytorv), is the last of the honky-tonks that used to make up the former sailors' quarter. This cafe is a short walk from the Kongens Nytorv and d'Angleterre hotels. In summer you can sit outside. In the evening there's free entertainment from a solo guitarist or guitar duet. The cafe is open Sunday to Thursday 10am to 2am and Friday and Saturday 10am until 3am. Built in 1670, **Hviids Vinstue,** Kongens Nytorv 19 (✆ **33-15-10-64;** www.hviidsvinstue.dk; bus: 1, 6, 9, or 10), is a wine cellar that's a dimly lit safe haven for an eclectic crowd, many patrons—both theatergoers and actors and dancers—drawn from the Royal Theater across the way. It's open Sunday to Thursday 10am to 1am, Friday and Saturday 10am to 2pm.

A leading nightlife venue, popular with gay men and women, is **Oscar Bar & Café,** 77 Rådhuspladsen (✆ **33-12-09-99;** www.oscarbarcafe.dk), which operates a good restaurant serving an international cuisine and also has a cruisy bar. It's an all-around rendezvous point for many of the capital's gay men and women, also attracting foreign visitors looking for action. The crowd is trendy and hip, and the bar is also frequented by straight people for its music and atmosphere. The bar/cafe is open daily from noon to 2am, the restaurant daily from noon to 10pm. Happy hour is 5 to 9pm.

DAY TRIPS FROM COPENHAGEN

Dragør ★★

Visit the past in this old seafaring town on the island of Amager, 5km (3 miles) south of Copenhagen's Kastrup Airport. It's filled with well-preserved, half-timbered, ocher-and-pink 18th-century cottages with steep red-tile or thatch roofs, many of them under the protection of the National Trust.

Dragør (pronounced *Drah*-wer) was a busy port on the herring-rich Baltic Sea in the early Middle Ages, but when fishing fell off, it became just another sleepy waterfront village. After 1520, Amager Island and its villages—Dragør and Store Magleby—were inhabited by the Dutch, who brought their own customs, Low-German language, and agricultural expertise, especially their love of bulb flowers. In Copenhagen, you still see wooden-shoed Amager islanders selling their hyacinths, tulips, daffodils, and lilies in the streets.

A rich trove of historic treasures is in the **Amager Museum,** Hovedgaden 4–12, Store Magleby (✆ **32-53-93-07;** www.museumamager.dk; bus: 30, 33, or 350S), outside Dragør. The exhibits reveal the affluence achieved by the Amager Dutch, with rich textiles, fine embroidery, and amenities like carved silver buckles and buttons. The interiors of a Dutch house are especially interesting. Admission is 30DKK adults, free for ages 17 and under. The museum is open May 1 to September 30, Tuesday daily noon to 4pm; October to April 30, Wednesday and Sunday noon to 4pm.

The exhibits at the harborfront **Dragør Museum,** Havnepladsen 2–4 (✆ **32-53-41-06;** www.museumamager.dk; bus: 30, 36, 73E, or 350S), show how the Amager Dutch lived from prehistoric times to the 20th century. Farming, goose breeding, seafaring, fishing, ship piloting, and ship salvage are delineated through pictures and artifacts. Admission is 20DKK adults, free for ages 18 and under. It's open May to September, Tuesday to Sunday noon to 4pm; closed October to April.

Louisiana

Established in 1958, the **Louisiana Museum of Modern Art ★★★**, Gl. Strandvej 13 (✆ **49-19-07-19;** www.louisiana.dk), is idyllically situated in a 19th-century mansion on the Danish Riviera, surrounded by a sculpture park opening directly onto the Øresund. Paintings and sculptures by modern masters, such as Giacometti and Henry Moore, as well as the best and most controversial works of modern art, are displayed. The museum's name came from the estate's first owner, Alexander Brun, who had three wives, each named Louise. Admission is 95DKK adults, 85DKK students and seniors, free for those 18 and under. It's open Thursday to Tuesday 10am to 5pm, Wednesday 10am to 10pm; closed December 24, 25, and 31.

GETTING THERE **Humlebæk,** the nearest town to Louisiana, may be reached by train from Copenhagen (København-Helsingør). Two trains an hour leave from the main station in Copenhagen (trip time: 40 min.). Once you're at Humlebæk, follow signs to the museum, a 15-minute walk.

Helsingør (Elsinore) ★

Helsingør is visited chiefly for "Hamlet's Castle." Aside from its literary associations, the town has a certain charm: a quiet market square, medieval lanes, and old half-timbered and brick buildings, remains of its once-prosperous shipping industry. The **Tourist Office,** Havnepladsen 3 (✆ **49-21-13-33;** www.visithelsingor.dk), is open September to June 19, Monday to Friday from 10am to 4pm and Saturday from 10am to 1pm; June 20 to August 31, Monday to Thursday 10am to 5pm, Friday 10am to 6pm, and Saturday 10am to 3pm.

There's no evidence Shakespeare ever saw this sandstone-and-copper Dutch Renaissance–style castle, full of intriguing secret passages and casemates, but he made **Kronborg Slot ★★★**, Kronborg (✆ **49-21-30-78;** www.ses.dk), famous in *Hamlet.* According to 12th-century historian Saxo Grammaticus, though, if Hamlet had really existed, he would have lived centuries before Kronborg was erected (1574–85). Over the years, some famous productions of *Hamlet* have been staged here, the castle's bleak atmosphere providing a good foil to the drama.

During its history, the castle has been looted, bombarded, gutted by fire, and used as a barracks (1785–1922). The starkly furnished Great Hall is the largest in northern Europe. The church, with its original oak furnishings, and the royal chambers are also worth exploring. Admission to the castle is 50DKK adults, 15DKK children 6 to 14. May to September, it's open daily 10:30am to 5:30pm; October and April, hours are Tuesday to Sunday 10:30am to 5pm; November to March, it's open Tuesday to Sunday 11am to 4pm (closed Christmas). The castle is 1km (⅔ mile) from the rail station.

GETTING THERE Once you reach Helsingør, 40km (25 miles) north of Copenhagen, you'll be deposited in the center of town and can cover all the major attractions on foot. There are frequent trains from Copenhagen, taking about 1 hour. A one-way ticket is 104DKK. Buses leave Copenhagen daily via the town of Klampeborg for the 90-minute trip to Helsingør.

ENGLAND

by Darwin Porter & Danforth Prince

London is Europe's largest and most happening city—like a great wheel, with Piccadilly Circus at the hub and dozens of communities branching out from it. In Britspeak, Circus means a circular area at an intersection of streets, not a Barnum & Bailey spectacular under the tent. London is more eclectic and electric than it's been in years. Some even think it has surpassed New York for sheer energy, outrageous fashion, trendy restaurants, and a nightlife that's second to none. It's still a city of fascinating contradictions, a jumble of antiquity and a world leader in fashion and food. As stimulating as the city is, however, you'll want to tear yourself away to visit legendary Stonehenge, Oxford University, and the classic city of Bath.

LONDON

Samuel Johnson said, "When a man is tired of London, he is tired of life; for there's in London all that life can afford." We'll survey a segment of that life: ancient monuments, literary shrines, museums, walking tours, Parliament debates, royal castles, palaces, cathedrals, and parks.

Essentials

GETTING THERE

BY PLANE The major airport for arrivals from North America is **London Heathrow Airport,** west of London in Hounslow (✆ **0844/335-1801;** www.heathrowairport.com). Heathrow is one of the world's busiest airports. It has four terminals, each relatively self-contained. Terminal 4, the most modern, handles the long-haul and transatlantic operations of British Airways. Most transatlantic flights on U.S.-based airlines arrive at Terminal 3. Terminals 1 and 2 receive the intra-European flights of several European airlines.

The British Airport Authority now operates **Heathrow Express** (✆ **0845/600-1515;** www.heathrowexpress.com), a 161kmph (100-mph) train service running every 15 minutes daily from 5:10am to 11:40pm between Heathrow and Paddington Station in the center of London. Trips cost £18 each way in economy class (£32 round-trip), rising to £26 one-way in first class (£50 round-trip). Children ages 5 to 15 pay £9 in economy, £13 in first class (£16 and £25 round-trip, respectively). Kids 4 and under travel free. The trip takes 15 minutes each way between Paddington and terminals 1, 2, and 3, and 23 minutes from Terminal 4. The trains have special areas for wheelchairs. From Paddington, passengers can connect to other trains and the Underground, or you can hail a taxi. You can buy tickets on the train with a £1.50 surcharge, or at self-service machines at Heathrow Airport. Tickets are also available from travel agents.

While Heathrow still dominates, more and more scheduled flights land at relatively remote **Gatwick** (✆ **0844/335-1802;** www.gatwickairport.com), located some 40km (25 miles) south of London in West Sussex but only a 30-minute train ride away. From Gatwick, the fastest way to get to London is via the **Gatwick Express trains** (✆ **0845/850-1530;** www.gatwickexpress.com), which depart approximately every 15 minutes, daily between 4:35am and 1:35am. Trips cost £15 each way in economy class (£26 round-trip), rising to £22 one-way in first class (£43 round-trip). Children ages 5 to 15 pay £7.60 in economy, £11 in first class (£13 and £22 round-trip, respectively). Children 4 and under ride free. The travel time each way is 30 minutes Monday to Saturday, and 35 minutes on Sunday.

A **taxi** from Gatwick Airport to central London costs from £77 to £100. Fares vary according to a printed price list that defines the fare from Gatwick to whichever neighborhood of London you're traveling to. Meters in this case don't apply because Gatwick lies outside the Metropolitan Police District. For further transportation information, call ✆ **020/7222-1234.**

BY TRAIN Each of London's train stations is connected to the city's vast bus and Underground network, and each has phones, restaurants, pubs, luggage storage areas, and Transport for London Information Centres.

St. Pancras International (www.stpancras.com) is the London hub for Eurostar, replacing Waterloo Station as the arrival point from the Continent. Restored and opened in 2007, it is the point where the high-speed Eurostar pulls into London, connecting England with Belgium and France through the Channel Tunnel.

The station boasts Europe's longest champagne bar, a daily farmers' market, all the Wi-Fi you'll ever need, plus dozens of boutiques—and some of the world's fastest trains. It is also served by six underground Tubes, including Victoria, Northern, Piccadilly, Circle, Hammersmith & City, and Metropolitan, as well as seven other rail companies. With such a vast network of transport, you can head virtually anywhere in greater London.

BY CAR Once you arrive on the English side of the Channel, the M20 takes you directly into London. *Remember to drive on the left.* Two roadways encircle London: The A406 and A205 form the inner beltway; the M25 rings the city farther out. Determine which part of the city you want to enter and follow signposts.

We suggest you confine driving in London to the bare minimum, which means arriving and parking. Because of parking problems and heavy traffic, getting around London by car is not a viable option. Once there, leave your car in a garage and rely on public transportation or taxis. Before arrival in London, call your hotel and inquire if it has a garage (and what the charges are), or ask the staff to give you the name and address of a garage nearby.

England

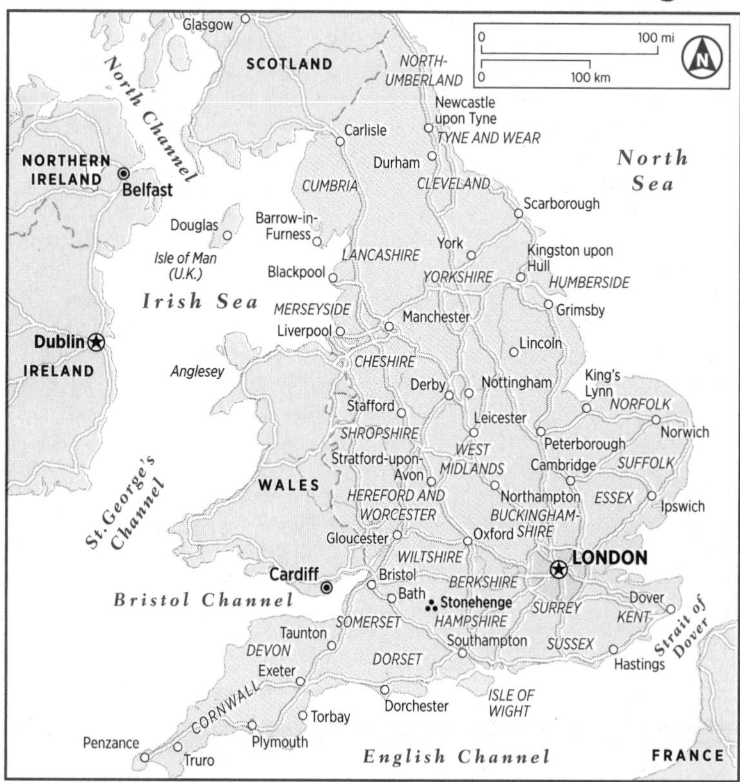

VISITOR INFORMATION **Tourist Offices** The London Tourist Board's **London Visitor Centre,** 1 Lower Regent St., London SW1Y 4XT (✆ **8701/566-366;** www.visitlondon.com; Tube: Piccadilly Circus), can help you with almost anything, from the most superficial to the most serious. Located within a 10-minute walk from Piccadilly Circus, it deals chiefly with procuring accommodations in all price categories through an on-site travel agency (www.lastminute.com), which can also book transit on British Rail or with bus carriers throughout the U.K. There's a kiosk for procuring theater or group tour tickets, a bookshop loaded with titles dealing with travel in the British Isles, a souvenir shop, and a staff that's pleasant, helpful, and friendly. It's open year-round Monday 9:30am to 6:30pm, Tuesday to Friday 9am to 6:30pm, and Sunday 9am to 5pm. Between October and May, Saturday hours are 10am to 4pm, and between June and September, Saturday hours are 9am to 5pm.

A roughly equivalent organization that was conceived to help foreign visitors with their inquiries and confusion about London is the **London Information Centre,** at Leicester Square, W1 (✆ **020/7292-2333;** www.londoninformationcentre.com;

Tube: Leicester Sq.). The London Information Centre is a privately owned, commercially driven organization that may have a vested interest in steering you toward a particular venue.

An option that might help you navigate your way through the logistics of one of the world's biggest cities involves your call to ✆ **0800/LONDON** (566366) for city information and to book sometimes discounted rates for London hotels, theaters, sightseeing tours, and airport transfers. A sales staff is available daily from 8am to midnight.

CITY LAYOUT For our purposes, London begins at Chelsea, on the north bank of the Thames, and stretches north through Kensington to Hampstead, and then east and south to Tower Bridge. Within this area, you'll find all the hotels and restaurants and nearly all the sights that are usually of interest to visitors.

The logical, though not geographical, center of this area is Trafalgar Square. Stand here facing the steps of the imposing National Gallery; you're looking northwest. That's the direction of Piccadilly Circus—the real core of tourist London—and the maze of streets that makes up Soho. Farther north runs Oxford Street, London's gift to moderately priced shopping, and still farther northwest lie Regent's Park and the zoo.

At your back (south from Trafalgar Sq.) runs Whitehall, which houses or skirts nearly every British government building, including the official residence of the prime minister at 10 Downing St. A bit farther south stand the Houses of Parliament and Westminster Abbey. Flowing southwest from Trafalgar Square is the table-smooth Mall, flanked by parks and mansions and leading to Buckingham Palace, the queen's residence. Farther along in the same direction lie Belgravia and Knightsbridge, the city's plushest residential areas; and south of them are chic Chelsea and King's Road (an upscale boulevard for shopping).

Due west from Trafalgar Square stretches the superb and high-priced shopping area bordered by Regent Street and Piccadilly. Farther west lie the equally elegant shops and even more elegant homes of Mayfair. Then comes Park Lane, with its deluxe hotels. Beyond is Hyde Park, the biggest park in central London and one of the largest in the world.

Charing Cross Road runs north from Trafalgar Square, past Leicester Square, and intersects with Shaftesbury Avenue. This is London's Theaterland. A bit farther along, Charing Cross Road turns into a browser's paradise, lined with shops selling new and secondhand books. At last, it funnels into St. Giles Circus. Beyond is Bloomsbury, site of the University of London, the British Museum, and erstwhile stamping ground of the famed "Bloomsbury group," led by Virginia Woolf. Northeast from Trafalgar Square lies Covent Garden, known for its Royal Opera House; today it's a major shopping, restaurant, and cafe district.

Follow The Strand eastward from Trafalgar Square and you'll come to Fleet Street. From the 19th century through most of the 20th century, this area was the most concentrated newspaper district in the world. Temple Bar stands where The Strand becomes Fleet Street, and only here do you enter the actual City of London, or "the City." Its focal point and shrine is the Bank of England on Threadneedle Street, with the Stock Exchange next door and the Royal Exchange across the street. In the midst of all the hustle and bustle rises St. Paul's Cathedral, Sir Christopher Wren's monument to beauty and tranquillity. At the far eastern fringe of the City looms the Tower of London, shrouded in legend, blood, and history and permanently besieged by battalions of visitors.

GETTING AROUND The London Underground and the city's buses operate on the same system of six fare zones. The fare zones radiate in rings from the central zone 1, which is where most visitors spend the majority of their time. Zone 1 covers the area from Liverpool Street in the east to Notting Hill in the west, and from Waterloo in the south to Baker Street, Euston, and Kings Cross in the north. To travel beyond zone 1, you need a multizone ticket; for example, an adult Day Travelcard for zones 1 and 2 costs £5.60 for off-peak hours (after 9:30am Mon–Fri and all day Sat–Sun and holidays) and £7.20 for anytime travel. Note that all single one-way, round-trip, and 1-day pass tickets are valid only on the day of purchase. Seven-day Travelcards start at £26 for adults traveling in zones 1 and 2. Tube and bus maps should be available at any Underground station. You can download them before your trip from the excellent **Transport for London (TFL)** website **www.tfl.gov.uk**, where you can also find the complete menu of fares and Travelcards available.

There are **TFL Information Centres** at several major Tube stations: Euston, Kings Cross, Oxford Circus, St. James's Park, Liverpool Street Station, and Piccadilly Circus, as well as in the British Rail stations at Euston and Victoria and in each of the terminals at Heathrow Airport. Most of them are open daily (some close Sun) from at least 9am to 6pm. A 24-hour public-transportation information service is also available at ✆ **020/7222-1234.**

The comparably priced bus system is almost as good as the Underground and gives you better views of the city. To find out about current routes, pick up a free bus map at one of the Transport for London Information Centres, listed above. The map is available in person only, not by mail. You can also obtain a map at **www.tfl.gov.uk**.

As with the Underground, fares vary according to distance traveled. Generally, bus fares are £1.20 to £3.80. If you want your stop called out, simply ask the conductor or driver. To speed up bus travel, passengers have to purchase tickets before boarding. Drivers no longer collect fares onboard. Some 300 roadside ticket machines serve stops in central London—in other words, it's "pay as you board." You'll need the exact fare, however, as ticket machines don't make change.

Buses generally run 24 hours a day. A few night buses have special routes, running once an hour or so; most pass through Trafalgar Square. Keep in mind that night buses are often so crowded (especially on weekends) that they are unable to pick up passengers after a few stops. You may find yourself waiting a long time. Consider taking a taxi. Call the 24-hour **hot line** (✆ **020/7222-1234**) for schedule and fare information.

BY TAXI London cabs are among the most comfortable in the world. You can pick one up either by heading for a cab rank or by hailing one in the street. (The taxi is available if the yellow taxi sign on the roof is lit.) To **call a cab,** phone ✆ **0871/871-8710.**

The meter starts at £2.20, with increments of £2 per mile thereafter, based on distance or time. Surcharges are imposed after 8pm and on weekends and public holidays. All these tariffs include VAT; plan to tip 10% to 15%.

If you call for a cab, the meter starts running when the taxi receives instructions from the dispatcher, so you could find that the meter already reads a few pounds more than the initial drop of £2.20 when you step inside.

Minicabs are also available, and they're often useful when regular taxis are scarce or when the Tube stops running. These cabs are meterless, so you must negotiate the fare in advance. Unlike regular cabs, minicabs are forbidden by law to cruise for fares. They operate from sidewalk kiosks, such as those around Leicester Square. If you need to call one, try **Brunswick Chauffeurs/Abbey Cars** (✆ **020/8969-2555**) in west London or **Newham Minicars** (✆ **020/8472-1400**) in south London. Minicab kiosks can be found near many Tube or BritRail stops, especially in outlying areas.

If you have a complaint about taxi service or if you leave something in a cab, contact the **Public Carriage Office,** 15 Penton St., N1 9PU (✆ **0845/602-7000** or 020/7222-1234; Tube: Angel Station). If it's a complaint, you must have the cab number, which is displayed in the passenger compartment.

BY CAR Don't drive in congested London. It is easy to get around without a car; traffic and parking are nightmares; and, to top it off, you'd have to drive from what you normally consider the passenger seat on the wrong side of the road. Rent a car only if you plan to take excursions.

BY BICYCLE One of the most popular bike-rental shops is **On Your Bike,** 52–54 Tooley St., London Bridge, SE1 (✆ **020/7378-6669;** www.onyourbike.com; Tube: London Bridge), open Monday to Friday 7:30am to 7pm, Saturday 10am to 6pm, and Sunday 11am to 5pm. The first-class mountain bikes, with high seats and low-slung handlebars, cost £12 for the first day and £8 for each day thereafter, or £35 per week, and require a 1p deposit on a credit card, so they will have your credit card number.

[FastFACTS] LONDON

American Express The main office is at the American Express Travel Service at 78 Brompton Rd., Knightsbridge SW (✆ **020/7761-7905;** Tube: Knightsbridge).

Area Code London's area code is **020.** Within the city limits, you don't need to dial it; use only the eight-digit number. If you're calling London from home before your trip, the country code for England is **44.** It must precede the London area code. When you're calling London from outside Britain, drop the "0" in front of the local area code.

Business Hours With many, many exceptions, business hours are Monday to Friday 9am to 5pm. In general, stores are open Monday to Saturday 9am to 5:30pm. In country towns, there is usually an early closing day (often Wed or Thurs) when the shops close at 1pm.

Currency The basic unit of currency is the pound sterling (£), which is divided into 100 pence (p). At press time, £1 equals about $1.60.

Dentist For dental emergencies, call **Eastman Dental Hospital** (✆ **020/7915-1000;** www.ucl.ac.uk/eastman; Tube: Kings Cross).

Doctor Call ✆ **999** in a medical emergency. Some hotels have physicians on call for emergencies. For nonemergencies, try **Medical Express,** 117A Harley St., W1 (✆ **020/7499-1991;** www.medicalexpressclinic.com; Tube: Regent's Park). A private British clinic, it's not part of the free British medical establishment. The clinic is open Monday to Friday 9am to

6pm and Saturday 10am to 2pm.

Drugstores In Britain, they're called "chemists." Ask at your hotel for the nearest location. For an emergency chemist, dial "0" (zero) and ask the operator for the local police, who will give you the name of one nearest you.

Embassies The **U.S. Embassy** is at 24 Grosvenor Sq., London, W1 (✆ **020/7499-9000;** www.usembassy.org.uk; Tube: Bond St.). Hours are Monday to Friday 8:30am to 5:30pm. However, for passport and visa information, go to the **U.S. Passport and Citizenship Unit,** 55–56 Upper Brook St., London, W1 (✆ **020/7894-0563;** Tube: Marble Arch or Bond St.). Passport and Citizenship Unit hours are Monday to Friday 8:30am to 12:30pm.

The **Canadian High Commission,** Macdonald House, 38 Grosvenor St., London, W1 (✆ **020/7258-6600;** www.canadainternational.gc.ca; Tube: Bond St.), handles visas for Canada. Hours are Monday to Friday 8 to 11am for immigration services, and 9:30am to 1:30pm for passports.

The **Australian High Commission** is at Australia House, the Strand, London, WC2 (✆ **020/7379-4334;** www.australia.org.uk; Tube: Charing Cross or Aldwych). Hours are Monday to Friday 9am to 5pm. For immigration services, hours are 9 to 11am; for passports, hours are 9:30am to 3:30pm.

The **New Zealand High Commission** is at New Zealand House, 80 Haymarket at Pall Mall, London, SW1 (✆ **020/7930-8422;** www.nzembassy.com; Tube: Charing Cross or Piccadilly Circus). Hours are Monday to Friday 10am to 4pm.

The **Irish Embassy** is at 17 Grosvenor Place, London, SW1 (✆ **020/7235-2171;** www.embassyofireland.co.uk; Tube: Hyde Park Corner). Hours are Monday to Friday 9:30am to 5:30pm.

Emergencies In London, for police, fire, or an ambulance, dial ✆ **999.**

Hospitals The following offer emergency care in London, 24 hours a day, with the first treatment free under the National Health Service: **Royal Free Hospital,** Pond Street (✆ **020/7794-0500;** Tube: Belsize Park), and **University College Hospital,** 235–250 Euston Rd., NW1 (✆ **0845/46-47;** Tube: Great Portland St.). Many other London hospitals also have accident and emergency departments.

Internet Access If you've brought your laptop, the quest for access will be easier, as many hotels are wired; rates run from £10 to £20 a day, although £12 is probably the average. Countless Internet cafes and coin-operated kiosks can be found around town. Libraries are reserved for residents, so you can't rely on them. The most common Internet cafe chain is **easyInternetcafe** (www.easyinternetcafe.com). Fifteen locations are around town, with West End locations in the basement of the following Burger Kings: Piccadilly Circus (46 Regent St., W1, Tube: Piccadilly Circus; 358 Oxford St., W1, Tube: Bond St.; 9–16 Tottenham Court Rd., W1, Tube: Tottenham Court Rd.; and east of Trafalgar Sq., 456–459 Strand, WC2, Tube: Charing Cross).

Mail An airmail letter to North America costs 56p for 10 grams; postcards also require a 56p stamp; letters generally take 7 to 10 days to arrive in the United States.

Maps If you plan to explore London in any depth, you'll need a detailed street map with an index, not one of those superficial overviews given away at many hotels and tourist offices. The best ones are published by Falk, and they're available at most newsstands and nearly all bookstores. And no Londoner is without a ***London A to Z*** *(www.a-zmaps.co.uk),* the ultimate street-by-street reference, available at bookstores and newsstands everywhere.

Police In an emergency, dial ✆ **999** (no coins are needed).

Post Office The main post office is at 24–28 William IV St., WC2 (✆ **020/7484-9307;** Tube: Charing Cross). Hours for stamps and postal services are Monday to Friday 8:30am to 6:30pm and Saturday 9am to 5:30pm. Other post office branches are open Monday to Friday 9am to 5:30pm and Saturday 9am to 12:30pm. Many post office branches are closed for an hour at lunch.

Taxes To encourage energy conservation, the British government levies a 25% tax on gasoline (petrol). There is also a 19.5% national value-added tax (VAT) that is added to all hotel and restaurant bills and is included in the price of many items you purchase. This can be refunded if you shop at stores that participate in the Retail Export Scheme (signs are posted in the window).

Telephone For **directory assistance** for London, dial ✆ **118212** for a full range of services; for the rest of Britain, dial ✆ **118118.** See also "Area Code," above.

Tipping For cabdrivers, add about 10% to 15% to the fare on the meter. However, if the driver loads or unloads your luggage, add something extra.

In hotels, porters receive 75p per bag, even if you have only one small suitcase. Hall porters are tipped only for special services. Maids receive £1 per day. In top-ranking hotels, the concierge will often submit a separate bill showing charges for newspapers and other items; if he or she has been particularly helpful, tip extra.

In both restaurants and nightclubs, a 15% service charge is added to the bill. To that, add another 3% to 5%, depending on the service. Tipping in pubs isn't common.

Tour guides expect £2, though it's not mandatory. Theater ushers don't expect tips.

Toilets They're marked by PUBLIC TOILETS signs in streets, parks, and Tube stations; many are automatically sterilized after each use. The English often call toilets "loos."

Where to Stay

MAYFAIR

Very Expensive

Brown's Hotel ★★ This quintessential town-house hotel was founded by James Brown, a former manservant to Lord Byron, who knew the tastes of well-bred gentlemen and wanted to create a dignified, clublike place for them. He opened its doors in 1837, the same year Queen Victoria took the throne.

Brown's occupies 14 historic houses just off Berkeley Square. Its guest rooms, completely renovated, vary considerably in decor, but all show restrained taste in decoration and appointments; even the wash basins are antiques. Accommodations range in size from small to extraspacious; some suites have four-poster beds.

30 Albemarle St., London W1S 4BP. ✆ **020/7493-6020.** Fax 020/7493-9381. www.brownshotel.com. 117 units. £475–£645 double; £885–£3,200 suite. AE, DC, MC, V. Tube: Green Park. **Amenities:** Restaurant; bar; concierge; health club & spa; room service. *In room:* A/C, TV/DVD, hair dryer, Internet (£15), minibar, MP3 docking station.

Expensive

Sheraton Park Lane Hotel ★★ Since 1924, this has been the most traditional of the Park Lane mansions. The hotel was sold in 1996 to the Sheraton Corporation, which continues to upgrade it but maintains its quintessential British style. Its Silver Entrance remains an Art Deco marvel that has been used as a backdrop in many film and television productions, including the classic BBC miniseries *Brideshead Revisited.*

Overlooking Green Park, the hotel offers luxurious accommodations that are a good deal—at least for pricey Park Lane. Many suites have marble fireplaces and original marble bathrooms. The rooms have all benefited from impressive refurbishment. The most tranquil rooms open onto a street in the rear. Rooms opening onto the court are dark. In the more deluxe rooms, you get better views.

Piccadilly, London W1J 7BX. ✆ **800/325-3535** in the U.S., or 020/7499-6321. Fax 020/7499-1965. www.sheratonparklane.com. 302 units. £189–£299 double; £264–£349 suite. AE, DC, MC, V. Tube: Hyde Park Corner or Green Park. **Amenities:** 2 restaurants; bar; concierge; state-of-the-art health club; room service. *In room:* A/C (in some), TV/DVD, movie library, hair dryer, Wi-Fi (£18).

MARYLEBONE

Moderate

Hart House Hotel ★ ☺ Hart House is a long-enduring favorite with Frommer's readers. In the heart of the West End, this well-preserved historic building (one of a group of Georgian mansions occupied by exiled French nobles during the French Revolution) lies within easy walking distance of many theaters. The rooms—done in a combination of furnishings, ranging from Portobello antique to modern—are comfortably appointed and spick-and-span, each one with a different character. Favorites include no. 7, a triple with a big bathroom and shower. Ask for no. 11, on the top floor, if you'd like a brightly lit aerie. Hart House has long been known as a good, safe place for traveling families. Many of its rooms are triples. Larger families can avail themselves of special family accommodations with connecting rooms.

51 Gloucester Place, Portman Sq., London W1U 8JF. ✆ **020/7935-2288.** Fax 020/7935-8516. www.harthouse.co.uk. 15 units. £110–£150 double; £130–£175 triple; £155–£185 quad. Rates include English breakfast. MC, V. Tube: Marble Arch or Baker St. **Amenities:** Babysitting. *In room:* TV, hair dryer, Wi-Fi (£5).

Inexpensive

Edward Lear Hotel This popular hotel, situated 1 block from Marble Arch, occupies a pair of brick town houses dating from 1780. The western house was the London home of 19th-century artist and poet Edward Lear, famous for his nonsense verse, and his illustrated limericks adorn the walls of one of the sitting rooms. Steep stairs lead up to cozy rooms, which range from spacious to broom-closet size. Bedrooms are looking better than ever following a wholesale renovation in 2007. One major drawback to the hotel: This is a very noisy part of town. Rear rooms are quieter.

28–30 Seymour St., London W1H 7JB. ✆ **020/7402-5401.** Fax 020/7706-3766. www.edlear.com. 32 units, 18 with bathroom. £68–£85 double without bathroom; £94–£117 double with bathroom; £94–£117 triple without bathroom; £124–£150 triple with shower only. Rates include English breakfast and tax. AE, MC, V. Tube: Marble Arch. *In room:* TV, Wi-Fi (free).

ST. JAMES'S

Very Expensive

Dukes Hotel ★★★ Dukes provides elegance without ostentation in what was presumably someone's *Upstairs, Downstairs* town house. It caters to those looking for charm, style, and tradition in a hotel. It stands in a quiet courtyard off St. James's Place; turn-of-the-20th-century gas lamps help put you into the proper mood before entering the front door. Each well-furnished guest room is decorated in the style of a particular English period, ranging from Regency to Edwardian. It's cozy, intimate, and clubbish; Dukes feels even more tranquil because it's set in its own gaslit alley.

London Accommodations

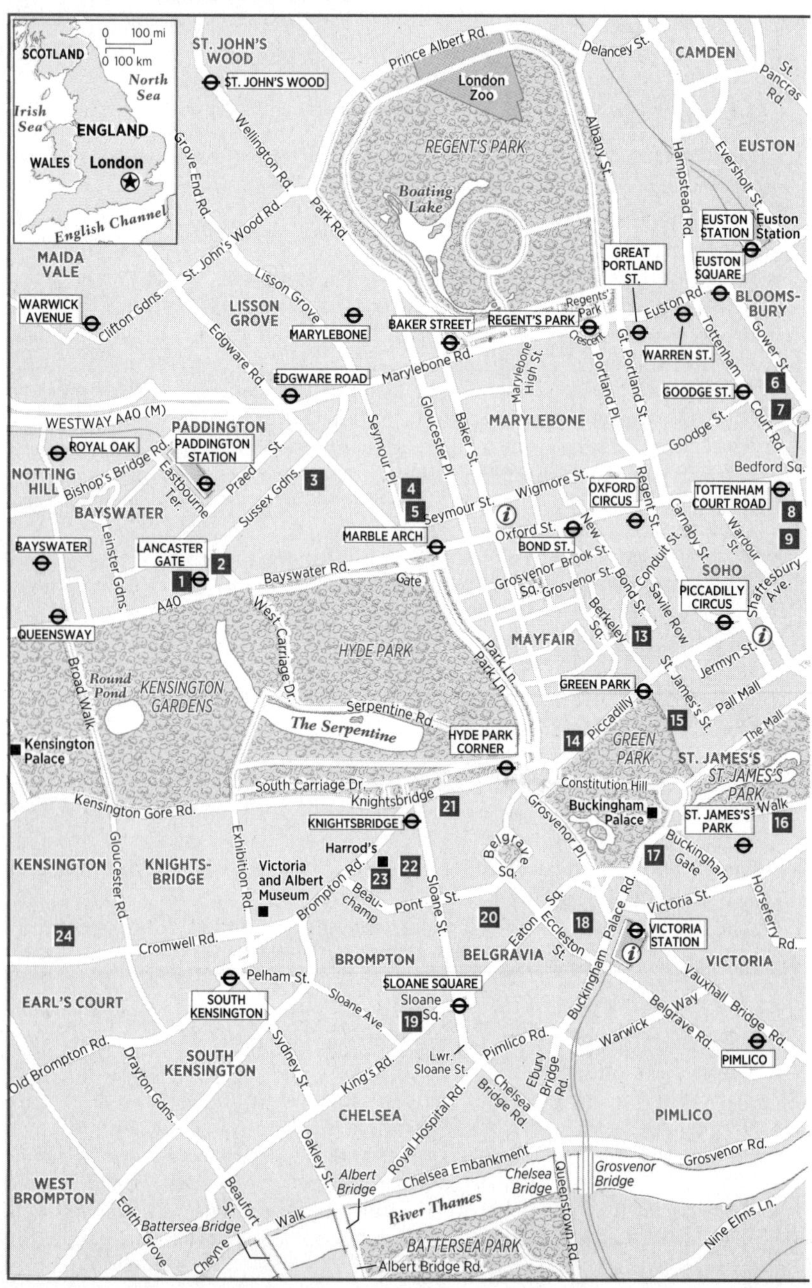

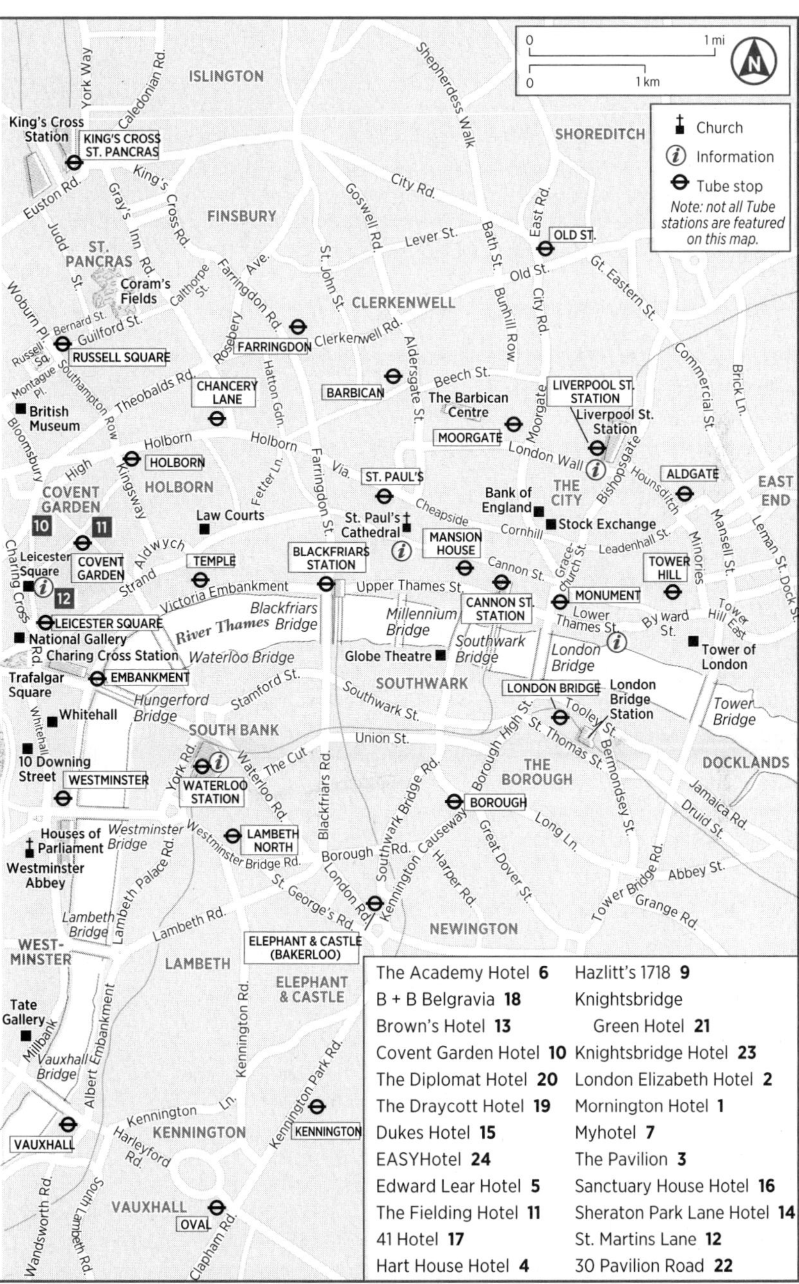
0 1 mi
0 1 km
N
Church
Information
Tube stop
Note: not all Tube stations are featured on this map.
ISLINGTON
SHOREDITCH
FINSBURY
ST. PANCRAS
CLERKENWELL
HOLBORN
COVENT GARDEN
THE CITY
EAST END
SOUTHWARK
SOUTH BANK
THE BOROUGH
DOCKLANDS
NEWINGTON
WEST-MINSTER
LAMBETH
ELEPHANT & CASTLE
KENNINGTON
VAUXHALL
King's Cross Station
KING'S CROSS ST. PANCRAS
OLD ST.
RUSSELL SQUARE
FARRINGDON
CHANCERY LANE
BARBICAN
LIVERPOOL ST. STATION
Liverpool St. Station
MOORGATE
HOLBORN
ST. PAUL'S
ALDGATE
MANSION HOUSE
BLACKFRIARS STATION
TEMPLE
COVENT GARDEN
TOWER HILL
MONUMENT
CANNON ST. STATION
LEICESTER SQUARE
EMBANKMENT
LONDON BRIDGE
London Bridge Station
WESTMINSTER
WATERLOO STATION
LAMBETH NORTH
BOROUGH
ELEPHANT & CASTLE (BAKERLOO)
KENNINGTON
VAUXHALL
OVAL
Coram's Fields
British Museum
The Barbican Centre
Bank of England
Stock Exchange
Law Courts
St. Paul's Cathedral
Leicester Square
National Gallery
Charing Cross Station
Trafalgar Square
Whitehall
10 Downing Street
Houses of Parliament
Westminster Abbey
Tate Gallery
Globe Theatre
Tower of London
Tower Bridge
River Thames
Blackfriars Bridge
Millennium Bridge
Southwark Bridge
London Bridge
Waterloo Bridge
Hungerford Bridge
Westminster Bridge
Lambeth Bridge
Vauxhall Bridge
York Way
Caledonian Rd.
Shepherdess Walk
City Rd.
Euston Rd.
King's Cross Rd.
Gray's Inn Rd.
Judd St.
Goswell Rd.
Lever St.
Bath St.
East Rd.
Old St.
Gt. Eastern St.
St. John St.
Bunhill Row
City Rd.
Woburn Pl.
Bernard St.
Guilford St.
Calthorpe St.
Farringdon Rd.
Ave.
Rosebery
Clerkenwell Rd.
Aldersgate St.
Russell Sq.
Montague Pl.
Southampton Row
Theobalds Rd.
Hatton Gdn.
Beech St.
Moorgate
Commercial St.
Brick Ln.
Bloomsbury
High
Holborn
Kingsway
Fetter Ln.
Farringdon St.
Via.
London Wall
Bishopsgate
Houndsditch
Cheapside
Cornhill
Leadenhall St.
Mansell St.
Leman St.
Dock St.
Minories
Aldwych
Strand
Charing Cross Rd.
Victoria Embankment
Upper Thames St.
Cannon St.
Gracechurch St.
Lower Thames St.
By ward St.
Tower Hill East
Stamford St.
Southwark St.
Borough High St.
Tooley St.
St. Thomas St.
Union St.
Whitehall
York Rd.
The Cut
Waterloo Rd.
Blackfriars Rd.
Southwark Bridge Rd.
Bermondsey St.
Jamaica Rd.
Druid St.
Westminster Bridge Rd.
Borough Rd.
Kennington Causeway
Great Dover St.
Long Ln.
Lambeth Palace Rd.
London Rd.
St. George's Rd.
Harper Rd.
Tower Bridge Rd.
Abbey St.
Grange Rd.
Lambeth Rd.
Millbank
Albert Embankment
Kennington Rd.
Kennington Park Rd.
Kennington Ln.
Harleyford Rd.
Wandsworth Rd.
South Lambeth Rd.
Clapham Rd.
10
11
12
The Academy Hotel 6
B + B Belgravia 18
Brown's Hotel 13
Covent Garden Hotel 10
The Diplomat Hotel 20
The Draycott Hotel 19
Dukes Hotel 15
EASYHotel 24
Edward Lear Hotel 5
The Fielding Hotel 11
41 Hotel 17
Hart House Hotel 4
Hazlitt's 1718 9
Knightsbridge Green Hotel 21
Knightsbridge Hotel 23
London Elizabeth Hotel 2
Mornington Hotel 1
Myhotel 7
The Pavilion 3
Sanctuary House Hotel 16
Sheraton Park Lane Hotel 14
St. Martins Lane 12
30 Pavilion Road 22

35 St. James's Place, London SW1A 1NY. ✆ **800/381-4702** in the U.S., or 020/7491-4840. Fax 020/7493-1264. www.campbellgrayhotels.com. 90 units. £235–£365 double; £450–£1,125 suite. AE, DC, MC, V. Tube: Green Park. **Amenities:** Restaurant; bar; babysitting; concierge; health club & spa; room service. *In room:* A/C, TV/DVD, hair dryer, minibar, MP3 docking station, Wi-Fi (free).

SOHO

Very Expensive

The Soho Hotel ★★★ A former parking garage in the heart of bustling Soho has become our favorite nest in London. When it's time to check out, we never want to leave. British hoteliers Kit and Tim Kemp have come up with a stunner here. At night, we have a cocoon-like feeling entering this luxury lair in a cul-de-sac off Dean Street. The theaters of Shaftesbury are only a block or two away, as is the Ivy restaurant (p. 227).

All the extremely spacious bedrooms are individually designed in granite and oak. There are four penthouses on the fifth floor, with tree-lined terraces opening onto panoramic sweeps of London. All the famous Kemp touches can be found, from boldly striped furnishings to deep bathtubs for a late-night soak. The glitterati, mostly actors and filmmakers, can be seen hanging out at the bar.

4 Richmond Mews, London W1D 3DH. ✆ **020/7559-3000.** Fax 020/7559-3003. www.firmdale.com. 91 units. £290–£360 double; £400–£2,750 suite. AE, MC, V. Tube: Oxford Circus or Piccadilly Circus. **Amenities:** Restaurant; bar; concierge; exercise room; room service. *In room:* A/C, TV/DVD, CD player, hair dryer, Wi-Fi (£20).

Expensive

Hazlitt's 1718 ★★ 🎁 This gem, housed in three historic homes on Soho Square, is one of London's best small hotels. Built in 1718, the hotel is named for William Hazlitt, who founded the Unitarian Church in Boston and wrote four volumes on the life of his hero, Napoleon.

Hazlitt's is a favorite with artists, actors, and models. It's eclectic and filled with odds and ends picked up around the country at estate auctions. Some find its Georgian decor a bit spartan, but the 2,000 original prints hanging on the walls brighten it considerably. Many bedrooms have four-poster beds; some of the floors dip and sway, and there's no elevator, but it's all part of the charm. It has just as much character as the Fielding Hotel (see below) but is a lot more comfortable. Some rooms are a bit small, but most are spacious, all with state-of-the-art appointments. Accommodations in the back are quieter but perhaps too dark.

6 Frith St., London W1D 3JA. ✆ **020/7434-1771.** Fax 020/7439-1524. www.hazlittshotel.com. 23 units. £159–£295 double; £450–£700 suite. AE, DC, MC, V. Tube: Leicester Sq. or Tottenham Court Rd. **Amenities:** Babysitting; concierge; room service. *In room:* A/C, TV, hair dryer, minibar, Wi-Fi (free).

BLOOMSBURY

Expensive

The Academy Hotel ★ The Academy is in the heart of London's publishing district. If you look out your window, you see where Virginia Woolf and other literary members of the Bloomsbury Group passed by every day. Many original architectural details were preserved when these three 1776 Georgian row houses were joined. The hotel was substantially upgraded in the 1990s, with a bathroom added to every bedroom (whether there was space or not). Grace notes include glass panels, colonnades, and intricate plasterwork on the facade. With overstuffed armchairs and half-canopied beds, rooms sometimes evoke English-country-house living, but that of the poorer relations. Guests who have been here before always request rooms opening on the garden in back and not those in front with ducted fresh air, though the front units have double-glazing to cut down on the noise. ***Warning:*** If you have a problem with stairs, know that no elevators rise to the four floors.

21 Gower St., London WC1E 6HG. ✆ **020/7631-4115.** Fax 020/7636-3442. www.theetoncollection.com. 49 units. £235 double; £353 suite. AE, DC, MC, V. Tube: Tottenham Court Rd., Goodge St., or Russell Sq. **Amenities:** Bar; room service. *In room:* A/C, TV, CD player, hair dryer, minibar, Wi-Fi (free).

Myhotel ★ Creating shock waves among staid Bloomsbury hoteliers, Myhotel is a London row house on the outside with an Asian *moderne*–style interior. It is designed according to feng shui principles—the ancient Chinese art of placement that utilizes the flow of energy in a space. The rooms have mirrors, but they're positioned so that you don't see yourself when you first wake up—feng shui rule number one (probably a good rule, feng shui or no feng shui). Rooms are havens of comfort, taste, and tranquillity. Excellent sleep-inducing beds are found in all rooms. Tipping is discouraged, and each guest is assigned a personal assistant responsible for his or her happiness. Aimed at today's young, hip traveler, Myhotel lies within a short walk of Covent Garden and the British Museum.

11-13 Bayley St., Bedford Sq., London WC1B 3HD. ✆ **020/7667-6000.** Fax 020/7667-6044. www.myhotels.co.uk. 78 units. £148–£279 double; £566–£805 suite. AE, DC, MC, V. Tube: Tottenham Court Rd. or Goodge St. **Amenities:** Restaurant; bar; babysitting; exercise room; room service. *In room:* A/C, TV, hair dryer, Wi-Fi (free).

COVENT GARDEN

Very Expensive

Covent Garden Hotel ★★★ This former hospital building lay neglected for years until it was reconfigured in 1996 by hot hoteliers Tim and Kit Kemp—whose flair for interior design is legendary—into one of London's most charming boutique hotels, in one of the West End's hippest shopping neighborhoods. *Travel + Leisure* called this hotel one of the 25 hottest places to stay in the *world*. It remains so. Behind a bottle-green facade reminiscent of a 19th-century storefront, the hotel has a welcoming lobby outfitted with elaborate inlaid furniture and elegant draperies, plus a charming restaurant. Upstairs, accessible via a dramatic stone staircase, soundproof bedrooms are furnished in English style with Asian fabrics, many adorned with hand-embroidered designs. The hotel has a decorative trademark—each room has a clothier's mannequin.

10 Monmouth St., London WC2H 9HB. ✆ **800/553-6674** in the U.S., or 020/7806-1000. Fax 020/7806-1100. www.firmdale.com. 58 units. £240–£340 double; £395–£1,195 suite. AE, DC, MC, V. Tube: Covent Garden or Leicester Sq. **Amenities:** Restaurant; bar; babysitting; concierge; exercise room; room service. *In room:* A/C, TV/DVD, movie library, CD player, hair dryer, minibar, Wi-Fi (£20).

St. Martins Lane ★★★ "Eccentric and irreverent, with a sense of humor" is how Ian Schrager describes his cutting-edge Covent Garden hotel, which he transformed from a 1960s office building into a chic enclave. This was the first hotel that Schrager designed outside the United States, after a string of successes from New York to West Hollywood. The mix of hip design and a sense of cool have been imported across the pond. Whimsical touches abound. For example, a string of daisies replaces DO NOT DISTURB signs. Rooms are all white, but you can use the full-spectrum lighting to make them any color. Floor-to-ceiling windows in every room offer a panoramic view of London.

45 St. Martins Lane, London WC2N 4HX. ✆ **800/697-1791** in the U.S., or 020/7300-5500. Fax 020/7300-5501. www.stmartinslane.com. 204 units. £215–£330 double; £380–£550 suite. AE, DC, MC, V. Tube: Covent Garden or Leicester Sq. **Amenities:** Restaurant; 2 bars; babysitting; concierge; exercise room; room service. *In room:* A/C, TV/DVD, movie library, hair dryer, minibar, Wi-Fi (£15).

Moderate

The Fielding Hotel ★ One of London's more eccentric hotels, this rickety walk-up is cramped, quirky, and quaint, and an enduring favorite of some. Luring media types, the hotel is named after novelist Henry Fielding of *Tom Jones* fame, who lived in Broad Court. It lies on a pedestrian street still lined with 19th-century gas lamps. The Royal Opera House is across the street, and the pubs, shops, and restaurants of lively Covent Garden are just beyond the front door. Rooms are small but charmingly old-fashioned and traditional. Some units are redecorated or at least "touched up" every year, though floors dip and sway, and the furnishings and fabrics, though clean, have known better times. With a location like this, in the heart of London, the Fielding keeps guests coming back; in fact, some love the hotel's claustrophobic charm. Children 12 and younger are not welcome; occasionally the staff makes adult patrons feel the same.

4 Broad Court, Bow St., London WC2B 5QZ. ✆ **020/7836-8305.** Fax 020/7497-0064. www.thefielding hotel.co.uk. 24 units. £115–£170 double. AE, DC, MC, V. Tube: Covent Garden. *In room:* TV, Wi-Fi (free).

WESTMINSTER/VICTORIA

Expensive

41 Hotel ★★★ This relatively unknown but well-placed gem offers the intimate atmosphere of a private club combined with a high level of personal service. Completely self-contained, it occupies the fifth (top) floor of the building whose lower floors contain another oft-recommended hotel, the Rubens at the Palace Hotel. 41 Hotel is best suited to couples or those traveling alone—especially women. Public areas feature an abundance of mahogany, antiques, fresh flowers, and rich fabrics. Read, relax, or watch TV in the library-style lounge, where a complimentary continental breakfast and afternoon snacks are served each day. Guest rooms are individually sized, but all feature elegant black-and-white color schemes and magnificent beds with Egyptian-cotton linens.

41 Buckingham Palace Rd., London SW1W OPS. ✆ **877/955-1515** in the U.S. and Canada, or 020/7300-0041. Fax 020/7300-0141. www.41hotel.com. 30 units. £275–£295 double; £525–£725 suite. Rates include continental breakfast, afternoon snacks, and evening canapés. AE, DC, MC, V. Tube: Victoria. **Amenities:** Bar; babysitting; concierge; room service. *In room:* A/C, TV/DVD, CD player, hair dryer, Internet (free), MP3 docking station.

Moderate

Sanctuary House Hotel ★ Only in the new London, where hotels are bursting into bloom like daffodils, would you find a hotel so close to Westminster Abbey. And a pub hotel, no less, with rooms on the upper floors above the tavern. The building was converted by Fuller Smith and Turner, a traditional brewery in Britain. Accommodations have a rustic feel, but they have first-rate beds. Downstairs, a pub/restaurant, part of the Sanctuary, offers old-style British meals that have ignored changing culinary fashions. "We like tradition," one of the perky staff members told us. "Why must everything be trendy? Some people come to England nostalgic for the old. Let others be trendy." Actually, the food is excellent if you appreciate the roast beef,

Welsh lamb, and Dover sole that pleased the palates of Churchill and his contemporaries. Naturally, there's always plenty of brew on tap.

33 Tothill St., London SW1H 9LA. ✆ **020/7799-4044.** Fax 020/7799-3657. www.fullershotels.com. 34 units. £139–£195 double. AE, DC, MC, V. Tube: St. James's Park. **Amenities:** Restaurant; pub; room service. *In room:* A/C, TV, hair dryer, Wi-Fi (£11 per day).

IN & AROUND KNIGHTSBRIDGE

Expensive

Knightsbridge Green Hotel ★ Repeat guests from around the world view this dignified 1890s structure as their home away from home. In 1966, when it was converted into a hotel, the developers kept its wide baseboards, cove moldings, high ceilings, and spacious proportions. Even without kitchens, the well-furnished suites come close to apartment-style living. Most rooms are spacious, with adequate storage space. Bedrooms are decorated with custom-made colors and are often individualized—one has a romantic sleigh bed. This is a solid choice for lodging, just around the corner from Harrods.

159 Knightsbridge, London SW1X 7PD. ✆ **020/7584-6274.** Fax 020/7225-1635. www.thekghotel.co.uk. 28 units. £225 double; £300–£350 suite. AE, DC, MC, V. Tube: Knightsbridge. **Amenities:** Room service. *In room:* A/C, TV, hair dryer, Wi-Fi (free).

Knightsbridge Hotel ★★ The Knightsbridge Hotel attracts visitors from all over the world seeking a small, comfortable hotel in a high-rent district. It's fabulously located, sandwiched between fashionable Beauchamp Place and Harrods, with many of the city's top theaters and museums close at hand. Built in the early 1800s as a private town house, this place sits on a tranquil, tree-lined square, free from traffic. Two of London's premier hoteliers, Kit and Tim Kemp, who have been celebrated for their upmarket boutique hotels, have gone more affordable with a revamp of this hotel in the heart of the shopping district. All the Kemp "cult classics" are found here, including such luxe touches as granite-and-oak bathrooms, the Kemps' famed honor bar, and Frette linens. The hotel has become an instant hit. Most bedrooms are spacious and furnished with traditional English fabrics. The best rooms are nos. 311 and 312 at the rear, each with a pitched ceiling and a small sitting area.

10 Beaufort Gardens, London SW3 1PT. ✆ **020/7584-6300.** Fax 020/7584-6355. www.firmdale.com. 44 units. £220–£310 double; £360–£625 suite. AE, DC, MC, V. Tube: Knightsbridge. **Amenities:** Self-service bar; babysitting; room service. *In room:* TV/DVD, CD player, hair dryer, minibar, Wi-Fi (£20).

Moderate

30 Pavilion Road ★ Searcy, one of London's best catering firms, operates this recycled surprise: an old pumping station that has been turned into a hotel that's only a hop, skip, and a jump from Harrods and the boutiques of Sloane Street. At this Knightsbridge oasis, you press a buzzer and are admitted to a freight elevator that carries you to the third floor. Upstairs, you'll encounter handsomely furnished rooms with antiques, tasteful fabrics, comfortable beds (some with canopies), and often a sitting alcove. Some of the tubs are placed right in the room instead of in a separate unit. Check out the rooftop garden.

30 Pavilion Rd., London SW1X 0HJ. ✆ **020/7584-4921.** Fax 020/7823-8694. www.30pavilionroad.co.uk. 10 units. £180 double; £200 suite. Rates include continental breakfast. AE, DC, MC, V. Tube: Knightsbridge. **Amenities:** Babysitting; room service. *In room:* A/C, TV, Wi-Fi (free).

CHELSEA

Expensive

The Draycott Hotel ★★★ Everything about this place, radically upgraded into a government five-star rating, reeks of British gentility, style, and charm. So attentive is the staff that past clients, who have included John Malkovich, Pierce Brosnan, and Gérard Depardieu, are greeted like old friends by a staff that manages to be both hip and cordial. The hotel took its present-day form when a third brick-fronted town house was added to a pair of interconnected town houses that had been functioning as a five-star hotel since the 1980s. That, coupled with tons of money spent on English antiques, rich draperies, and an upgrade of those expensive infrastructures you'll never see, including security, have transformed this place into a gem. Bedrooms are each outfitted differently, each with haute English style and plenty of fashion chic. As a special feature, the hotel serves complimentary drinks—tea at 4pm daily, champagne at 6pm, and hot chocolate at 9:30pm.

26 Cadogan Gardens, London SW3 2RP. ✆ **800/747-4942** or 020/7730-6466. Fax 020/7730-0236. www.draycotthotel.com. 35 units. £260–£315 double; £385 suite. AE, DC, MC, V. Tube: Sloane Sq. **Amenities:** Bar; access to nearby health club & spa; room service. *In room:* A/C, TV/DVD, CD player, minibar, Wi-Fi (free).

BELGRAVIA

Moderate

The Diplomat Hotel ★ Part of the Diplomat's charm is that it is a small and reasonably priced hotel located in an otherwise prohibitively expensive neighborhood. Only minutes from Harrods Department Store, it was built in 1882 as a private residence by noted architect Thomas Cubbitt. The registration desk is framed by the sweep of a partially gilded circular staircase; above it, cherubs gaze down from a Regency-era chandelier. The staff is helpful, well mannered, and discreet. The high-ceilinged guest rooms are tastefully done in Victorian style. You get good—not grand—comfort here. Rooms are a bit small and usually furnished with twin beds.

2 Chesham St., London SW1X 8DT. ✆ **020/7235-1544.** Fax 020/7259-6153. www.thediplomathotel.co.uk. 26 units. £115–£170 double. Rates include English buffet breakfast. AE, DC, MC, V. Tube: Sloane Sq. or Knightsbridge. **Amenities:** Snack bar; babysitting. *In room:* TV, hair dryer, Wi-Fi (free).

Inexpensive

B + B Belgravia ★★ ☺ In its first year of operation (2005), this elegant town house won a top Gold Award as "the best B&B in London." It richly deserves it. Design, service, quality, and comfort paid off. The prices are also reasonable, the atmosphere in this massively renovated building is stylish, and the location is grand: just a 5-minute walk from Victoria Station. The good-size bedrooms are luxuriously furnished. In the guest lounge with its comfy sofas, an open fire burns on nippy nights. There is also a DVD library, and tea and coffee are served 24 hours a day. The full English breakfast in the morning is one of the finest in the area.

64–66 Ebury St., Belgravia, London SW1W 9QD. ✆ **020/7259-8570.** Fax 020/7259-8591. www.bb-belgravia.com. 17 units. £120–£130 double; £150–£160 family room. Rates include a full English breakfast. AE, MC, V. Tube: Victoria Station. **Amenities:** Breakfast room. *In room:* TV, Wi-Fi (free).

KENSINGTON

Inexpensive

EASYHotel This hotel runs on the principle that guests would rather have smaller hotel rooms and pay less. If you're claustrophobic, this hotel is definitely not for you. The rooms are 6 to 7 sq. m (65–75 sq. ft.), with most of the space taken up by standard double beds. If you can get a room with a window, do so because it makes a big difference. Just off Cromwell Road between South Kensington and Earls Court, EASY offers all doubles with cramped bathrooms containing a shower. There are flatscreen TVs in every unit, but a £5 fee is assessed to use the set. One staff member is permanently on-site, but no services are offered. Housekeeping service costs an optional £10 per day, there is no elevator, and checkout time is 10am. Instead of phoning the hotel, all EASYHotel bookings are taken and confirmed by credit card through its website.

14 Lexham Gardens, Kensington, London W8 5JE. ✆ **020/7706-9911.** www.easyhotel.com. 34 units. £30–£50 double. MC, V. Tube: South Kensington or Earls Court. *In room:* A/C, TV, Wi-Fi (£10).

PADDINGTON

Moderate

London Elizabeth Hotel ★ This elegant Victorian town house is ideally situated, overlooking Hyde Park. Amid the buzz and excitement of central London, the hotel's atmosphere is an oasis of charm and refinement. Even before the hotel's recent £3-million restoration, it oozed character. Individually decorated rooms range from executive to deluxe and remind us of staying in an English country house. Deluxe rooms are fully air-conditioned, and some contain four-poster beds. Executive units usually contain one double or twin bed. Some rooms have special features such as Victorian antique fireplaces. Suites are pictures of grand comfort and luxury—the Conservatory Suite boasts its own veranda, part of the house's original 1850 conservatory.

Lancaster Terrace, Hyde Park, London W2 3PF. ✆ **800/721-5566** in the U.S., or 020/7402-6641. Fax 020/7224-8900. www.londonelizabethhotel.co.uk. 49 units. £165–£190 double; £275 suite. AE, DC, MC, V. Tube: Lancaster Gate or Paddington. **Amenities:** Restaurant; bar; room service. *In room:* A/C (in some), TV, hair dryer, minibar, Wi-Fi (free).

Inexpensive

Mornington Hotel ★ Affiliated with Best Western, the Mornington brings a touch of northern European hospitality to the center of London. Just north of Hyde Park and Kensington Gardens, the hotel has a Victorian exterior and a Scandinavian-inspired decor. The area isn't London's most fashionable, but it's close to Hyde Park and convenient to Marble Arch, Oxford Street shopping, and the ethnic restaurants of Queensway. Renovated guest rooms are tasteful and comfortable. Every year we get our annual Christmas card from "the gang," as we refer to the hotel staff—and what a helpful crew they are.

12 Lancaster Gate, London W2 3LG. ✆ **800/633-6548** in the U.S., or 020/7262-7361. Fax 020/7706-1028. www.bw-morningtonhotel.co.uk. 66 units. £89–£145 double. Rates include Scandinavian and English breakfast. AE, DC, MC, V. Tube: Lancaster Gate. **Amenities:** Bar. *In room:* TV, Wi-Fi (free).

The Pavilion ★ Until the early 1990s, this was a rather ordinary-looking B&B. Then a team of entrepreneurs with ties to the fashion industry took over and redecorated the rooms with sometimes wacky themes, turning it into an idiosyncratic little hotel. The result is a theatrical and often outrageous decor that's appreciated by the many fashion models and music-industry folks who regularly make this their temporary home in London. Rooms are, regrettably, rather small, but each has a distinctive style. Examples include a kitschy 1970s room ("Honky-Tonk Afro"), an Asian bordello–themed room ("Enter the Dragon"), and even rooms with

19th-century ancestral themes. One Edwardian-style room, a gem of emerald brocade and velvet, is called "Green with Envy."

34-36 Sussex Gardens, London W2 1UL. ✆ **020/7262-0905.** Fax 020/7262-1324. www.pavilionhoteluk.com. 30 units. £100 double; £120 triple. Rates include continental breakfast. AE, MC, V. Tube: Edgeware Rd. *In room:* TV, Wi-Fi (free).

Where to Dine

MAYFAIR

Very Expensive

Alain Ducasse at the Dorchester ★★ FRENCH In 2007, the maestro of upper-strata French cuisine reached across the Channel and planted a bulkhead in England with the establishment of this ultrachic corner of gastronomy. Outfitted in tones of pastels and grays, it's rather startlingly arranged around a circular central table for six, which is surrounded with a translucent silk curtain and illuminated with a "waterfall" of illuminated fiber-optic cables. Collectively, it seems to conceal the patrons in a gauzy cloud. What, pray, does someone order in an environment this rarefied? Consider prawns wrapped in a hot and spicy cocoon of seaweed; steamed crayfish with hearts of artichoke, served in a potato and truffle shell; steamed halibut with yogurt, spicy condiments, and beans; or a filet of beef Rossini-style, with seared foie gras, root veggies, and Perigueux sauce. Can you expect to see the maestro himself whipping up sauces in the kitchen? It's unlikely, since he's farmed many of the day-to-day operations to his long-term disciple, Jocelyn Herland. Nonetheless, he keeps a tight rein on the place from other parts of his empire.

On the lobby level of the Dorchester Hotel, Park Lane. ✆ **020/7629-8866.** www.alainducasse-dorchester.com. Reservations required 2 weeks in advance. Set-price menus £75 for 3 courses, £95 for 4 courses, £115 for 7 courses. AE, DC, MC, V. Tues–Fri noon–2pm; Tues–Sat 6:30–10pm. Tube: Green Park, Hyde Park Corner, or Marble Arch.

Le Gavroche ★★★ FRENCH Although challengers come and go, this luxurious "gastro-temple" remains the number-one choice in London for classical French cuisine. It may have fallen off briefly in the early 1990s, but it's fighting its way back to stellar ranks. There's always something special coming out of the kitchen of Michel Roux, Jr., the son of the chef who founded the restaurant in 1966. The service is faultless, and the ambience formally chic without being stuffy. The menu changes constantly, depending on the fresh produce that's available and the current inspiration of the chef. But it always remains classically French, though not of the "essentially old-fashioned bourgeois repertoire" that some critics suggest. Signature dishes honed over years of unswerving practice include the town's grandest cheese soufflé (Soufflé Suissesse); warm foie gras with crispy, cinnamon-flavored crepes; and Scottish filet of beef with port-wine sauce and truffled macaroni. Depending on availability, game is often served as well. A truly Gallic dish is the cassoulet of snails with frog thighs or the mousseline of lobster in a champagne sauce.

43 Upper Brook St., W1. ✆ **020/7408-0881.** Fax 020/7491-4387. www.le-gavroche.co.uk. Reservations required as far in advance as possible. Main courses £30–£60; fixed-price lunch £48; *Le Menu Exceptionnel* £95 without wine, £150 with wine. AE, MC, V. Mon–Fri noon–2pm; Mon–Sat 6:30–11pm. Tube: Marble Arch.

The Square ★★★ FRENCH Hip, chic, casual, sleek, and modern, the Square still doesn't scare Le Gavroche as a competitor for first place on London's dining circuit, but it is certainly a restaurant to visit on a serious London gastronomic tour. Chef Philip Howard delivers the goods at this excellent restaurant. You get creative, personalized cuisine in a cosseting atmosphere with abstract modern art on the walls. The chef has a magic touch, with such concoctions as a starter of terrine of partridge with smoked foie gras and pear with cider jelly, or else a lasagna of Cornish crab with a champagne foam. For a main course we urge you to try the peppered aged rib-eye of Ayrshire beef with smoked shallots, Tuscan snails, and a red-wine sauce, or else the roast saddle of hare with port-glazed endive. The fish dishes, such as steamed turbot with buttered langoustine claws and poached oysters, are always fresh, and Bresse pigeon is as good as it is in its hometown in France.

6–10 Bruton St., W1. ✆ **020/7495-7100.** www.squarerestaurant.org. Reservations required. Fixed-price lunch £60–£75, dinner £100. AE, DC, MC, V. Mon–Fri noon–3pm; Mon–Sat 6:30–10:45pm; Sun 6:30–10pm. Tube: Bond St. or Green Park.

Expensive

Nobu ★★ JAPANESE/SOUTH AMERICAN London's innovative restaurant, a celebrity haunt, owes much to its founders, actor Robert De Niro and Chef Nobu Matsuhisa. The kitchen staff is brilliant and as finely tuned as their New York counterparts. The sushi chefs create gastronomic pyrotechnics. Those on the see-and-be-seen circuit don't seem to mind the high prices that go with these incredibly fresh dishes. Elaborate preparations lead to perfectly balanced flavors. Where else can you find an excellent sea urchin tempura? Salmon tartare with caviar is a brilliant appetizer. Follow with a perfectly done filet of sea bass in a sour bean paste or soft-shell crab rolls. The squid pasta is sublime, as is the incredibly popular sukiyaki. Cold sake arrives in a green bamboo pitcher.

In the Metropolitan Hotel, 19 Old Park Lane, W1. ✆ **020/7447-4747.** www.noburestaurants.com. Reservations required 1 month in advance. Main courses £11–£33; sushi and sashimi £3–£8.25 per piece; fixed-price lunch £26, dinner £11–£33. AE, DC, MC, V. Mon–Fri noon–2:15pm and 6–10:15pm; Sat–Sun 12:30–2:30pm; Sat 6–11pm; Sun 6–9:30pm. Tube: Hyde Park Corner.

PICCADILLY CIRCUS & LEICESTER SQUARE

Expensive

The Ivy ★★ MODERN ENGLISH/INTERNATIONAL Effervescent and sophisticated, the Ivy is the dining choice of visiting theatrical luminaries and has been intimately associated with the theater district ever since it opened in 1911. With its ersatz 1930s look and tiny bar near the entrance, this place is fun and hums with the energy of London's glamour scene. The kitchen has a solid appreciation for fresh ingredients and a talent for preparation. Some appetizers may be a bit much, like wild rabbit salad with black pudding, whereas others are more appealing, such as Bang Bang chicken. The crispy duck and watercress salad is another favorite. For years, the 14-ounce Dover sole has been enjoyed by celebrities and wannabes alike. Mains feature a chargrilled fish of the day, and carnivores take to the sautéed veal kidneys or the escalope of veal Holstein. The Ivy Hamburger continues to appear on the menu. Desserts are familiar, including chocolate pudding soufflé or rhubarb sponge pudding with custard.

1–5 West St., WC2. ✆ **020/7836-4751.** www.the-ivy.co.uk. Reservations required. Main courses £8–£40; Sat–Sun fixed-price lunch £29. AE, DC, MC, V. Mon–Sat noon–3pm; Sun noon–3:30pm; daily 5:30pm–midnight (last order). Tube: Leicester Sq.

Moderate

Cork & Bottle Wine Bar ★★ INTERNATIONAL Don Hewitson, a connoisseur of fine wines for more than 30 years, presides over this trove of blissful fermentation. The ever-changing wine list features an excellent selection of Beaujolais Crus from Alsace, 30 selections from Australia, 30 champagnes, and a good selection of California labels. If you want something to wash down, the most successful dish is a raised cheese-and-ham pie, with a cream cheese–like filling and crisp, well-buttered pastry—not your typical quiche. There's also chicken-and-apple salad, black pudding, Mediterranean prawns with garlic and asparagus, lamb in ale, and a Thai chicken-wings platter.

44–46 Cranbourn St., WC2. ✆ **020/7734-7807.** www.corkandbottle.net. Reservations not accepted after 6:30pm. Fixed-price menu £11–£14; main courses £8–£16. AE, DC, MC, V. Mon–Sat 11am–midnight; Sun noon–11pm. Tube: Leicester Sq.

SOHO

Moderate

Arbutus Restaurant ★ BRITISH/CONTINENTAL This Soho eatery was the brainchild of Anthony Demetre and Will Smith, who have operated Michelin-starred restaurants elsewhere. They now bring their quality cooking and service to the heart of Soho in rather unpretentious surroundings. They don't please all diners, but not for lack of effort. Sometimes they use parts of the pig not seen since the days of Henry VIII—pig's head, for example, which may be too rich for some diners who'd prefer the wintery beef daube in a dark but flavorful sauce. Ever had a squid-and-mackerel burger? It's an oddity but won't put McDonald's out of business. Other winning dishes include smoked eel risotto, Welsh breast of lamb, or pork rillettes with a celeriac rémoulade. A traditional bouillabaisse also scores points (it's made with regular fish, not shellfish).

63–64 Frith St., W1. ✆ **020/7734-4545.** www.arbutusrestaurant.co.uk. Reservations required. Main courses £15–£20; 3-course lunch £17; pre- and post-theater fixed-price menu £19. AE, DC, MC, V. Mon–Sat noon–2:30pm and 5–11pm; Sun noon–3pm and 5:30–10:30pm. Tube: Tottenham Court Rd.

The Criterion Brasserie ★ FRENCH/MODERN ENGLISH Designed by Thomas Verity in the 1870s, this palatial neo-Byzantine mirrored marble hall is a glamorous backdrop for a superb cuisine, served under a golden ceiling, with theatrical peacock-blue draperies. The menu is wide ranging, offering everything from Paris brasserie food to "nouvelle-classical," a combination of classic French cooking techniques with some of the lighter, more experimental leanings of modern French cuisine. The food is excellent but falls short of sublime. Start with beef carpaccio in a mustard dressing or else spaghetti with clams and chili peppers, to be followed by such fish as wild sea bass with a shellfish fondue or else roast suckling pig in applesauce.

224 Piccadilly, W1. ✆ **020/7930-0488.** www.criterionrestaurant.com. Main courses £16–£26; 2- to 3-course set menu £17–£20. AE, MC, V. Mon–Sat noon–2:30pm and 5:30–11:30pm; Sun noon–3:30pm and 5:30–10:30pm. Tube: Piccadilly Circus.

Hakkasan ★ CHINESE Asian mystique and pastiche are found in this offbeat restaurant in a seedy alley off Tottenham Court Road. This is another London venture created by Alan Yau, who became a citywide dining legend because of his Wagamama noodle bars (see below). Come here for great dim sum and tantalizing cocktails. Feast on such dishes as *har gau* (steamed prawn dumplings) and strips of tender barbecued pork. The spring roll is refreshing with the addition of fried mango and a delicate prawn-and-scallop filling. Steamed scallop *shumai* (dumplings) with *tobiko* caviar are fresh and meltingly soft. Desserts in most of London's Chinese restaurants are hardly memorable, but the offerings here are an exception to that rule, especially the layered banana sponge with chocolate cream.

8 Hanway Place. ✆ **020/7927-7000.** www.hakkasan.com. Reservations recommended. Main courses £10–£68. AE, MC, V. Lunch Mon–Fri noon–3pm, Sat noon–5pm; dinner Mon–Wed 6–11:30pm, Thurs–Sat 6–11:30pm, Sun 6–11pm. Tube: Tottenham Court Rd.

Randall & Aubin ★ SEAFOOD Past the sex boutiques of Soho you stumble upon this real discovery, whose consultant is TV chef Ed Baines, an ex-Armani model who turned this butcher shop into a cool, hip champagne-and-oyster bar. The impressive shellfish display of the night's goodies is the "bait" used to lure you inside. Chances are you won't be disappointed. Loch Fyne oysters, lobster with chips, pan-fried fresh scallops—the parade of seafood we've sampled here, in each case, has been genuinely excellent. The *soupe de poisson* (fish soup) is the best in Soho, or else you might want one of the hors d'oeuvres such as delightful Japanese-style fish cakes or fresh Cornish crab. Yes, they still have Sevruga caviar for lotto winners. For the rare meat-only eater, there is a limited array of dishes such as a perfectly roasted chicken on the spit that has been flavored with fresh herbs. The lemon tart with crème fraîche rounds out a perfect meal.

16 Brewer St., W1. ✆ **020/7287-4447.** www.randallandaubin.com. Reservations not accepted. Main courses £10–£29. AE, DC, MC, V. Mon–Sat noon–11pm; Sun 4–10pm. Tube: Piccadilly Circus or Leicester Sq.

BLOOMSBURY

Expensive

Pied-à-Terre ★★★ FRENCH A meticulously rendered French cuisine is served at the most acclaimed restaurant in Bloomsbury. The interior is stylish, with intimate tables; we prefer those in the rear. Chef Shane Osborn cleverly combines a classical technique with his own modern inventiveness in the kitchen. He demonstrates a flair for flavorful "marriage" of ingredients. Try his seared and poached foie gras with borlotti beans or his steamed halibut with a tomato fondue. Blackleg chicken breast from Landes arrives with a garlic purée, or else you can order kid goat with caramelized endive and roasted shallots, certainly the roasted Devonshire loin of venison with a quince purée and walnuts. New World/Old World wines are on the *carte*.

34 Charlotte St., W1. ✆ **020/7636-1178.** www.pied-a-terre.co.uk. Reservations recommended. Fixed-price lunch £24; fixed-price dinner £58; 10-course tasting menu £87. AE, MC, V. Mon–Fri 12:15–2:30pm; Mon–Sat 6:15–11pm. Tube: Goodge St.

Inexpensive

Wagamama JAPANESE This noodle joint, in a basement just off New Oxford Street, is noisy and overcrowded, and you'll have to wait in line for a table. It calls itself a "nondestination food station" and caters to some 1,200 customers a day. Many dishes are built around ramen noodles paired with your choice of chicken, beef, or salmon. Try the tasty *gyoza,* light dumplings filled with vegetables or chicken. Vegetarian dishes are available, but skip the so-called Korean-style dishes. Check the website to find other locations throughout London.

4 Streatham St., WC1. ✆ **020/7323-9223.** www.wagamama.com. Reservations not accepted. Main courses £7–£11. AE, MC, V. Mon–Sat noon–11pm; Sun noon–10pm. Tube: Tottenham Court Rd.

COVENT GARDEN & THE STRAND

Expensive

Rules ★ TRADITIONAL ENGLISH If you're looking for London's most quintessentially British restaurant, eat here. London's oldest restaurant was established in 1798 as an oyster bar; today, the antler-filled Edwardian dining rooms exude nostalgia. You can order such classic dishes as Irish or Scottish oysters, jugged hare, and mussels. Game and fish dishes are offered from mid-August to February or March, including wild Scottish salmon; wild sea trout; wild Highland red deer; and game birds such as grouse, snipe, partridge, pheasant, and woodcock. As a finale, the "great puddings" continue to impress.

35 Maiden Lane, WC2. ✆ **020/7836-5314.** www.rules.co.uk. Reservations recommended. Main courses £17–£28. AE, DC, MC, V. Mon–Sat noon–11:30pm; Sun noon–10:30pm. Tube: Covent Garden.

Moderate

Belgo Centraal BELGIAN Chaos reigns supreme in this cavernous basement, where mussels *marinières* with fries, plus 100 Belgian beers, are the raison d'être. Take a freight elevator past the busy kitchen and into a converted cellar, divided into two large eating areas. One section is a beer hall seating about 250; the menu here is the same as in the restaurant, but you don't need reservations. The restaurant side has three nightly seatings: 5:30, 7:30, and 10pm. Although heaps of fresh mussels are the big attraction, you can opt for fresh Scottish salmon, roast chicken, a perfectly done steak, or one of the vegetarian specialties. Gargantuan plates of wild boar sausages arrive with *stoemp*—Belgian mashed spuds and cabbage. Belgian stews, called *waterzooï*, are also served.

50 Earlham St., WC2. ✆ **020/7813-2233.** www.belgo-restaurants.co.uk. Reservations required for the restaurant. Main courses £11–£13. AE, DC, MC, V. Mon–Thurs noon–11pm; Fri–Sat noon–11:30pm; Sun noon–10:30pm. Closed Christmas. Tube: Covent Garden.

Porters English Restaurant ★★ ☺ TRADITIONAL ENGLISH The seventh earl of Bradford serves "real English food at affordable prices." He succeeds notably—and not just because Lady Bradford turned over her carefully guarded recipe for banana-and-ginger steamed pudding. This comfortable, two-storied restaurant is family-friendly, informal, and lively. Porters specializes in classic English pies, including Old English fish pie, lamb and apricot, and, of course, bangers and mash. The overwhelming favorite is steak, Guinness, and mushroom pie. Main courses are so generous—and accompanied by vegetables and side dishes—that you hardly need appetizers. They have also added grilled English fare to the menu, including sirloin and lamb steaks and marinated chicken. Porters is famous for its mouthwatering puddings. Where can you find a good spotted dick these days? It's a steamed syrup sponge cake with sultanas (raisins). Another favorite is a dark-chocolate-chip pudding made with steamed chocolate sponge, chocolate chips, and chocolate custard. Even the ice cream is homemade. The bar does quite a few exotic cocktails, as well as beer, wine, or English mead. A traditional English tea is served from 2:30 to 5:30pm.

17 Henrietta St., WC2. ✆ **020/7836-6466.** www.porters.uk.com. Reservations recommended. Main courses £11–£19; fixed-price lunch and pre-theater menu £12; fixed-price dinner menu £23. AE, MC, V. Mon–Sat noon–11:30pm; Sun noon–10:30pm. Tube: Covent Garden or Leicester Sq.

WESTMINSTER/VICTORIA

Moderate

Rex Whistler ★★ MODERN ENGLISH The Tate Britain's restaurant is particularly attractive to wine fanciers. It offers what may be the best bargains for superior wines anywhere in Britain. Bordeaux and burgundies are in abundance, and the management keeps the markup between 40% and 65%, rather than the 100% to 200% added in most restaurants. In fact, the prices here are lower than they are in most wine shops. Wine begins at £15 per bottle or £4 per glass. Oenophiles frequently come for lunch. The restaurant offers an English menu that changes about every month. Dishes might include fresh fish of the day fresh from the Newlyn boats in Cornwall, roast red-leg partridge with bread sauce, and Welsh lamb with caramelized sweetbreads. One critic found the staff and diners as traditional "as a Gainsborough landscape." Access to the restaurant is through the museum's main entrance on Millbank.

Tate Britain, Millbank, SW1. ✆ **020/7887-8825.** www.tate.org.uk. Reservations recommended. 2-course fixed-price menu £16; 3-course fixed-price menu £20; breakfast from £3.95; afternoon tea £7.25. AE, DC, MC, V. Mon–Fri 11:30am–3pm; Sat–Sun 10am–3pm; daily 3:30–5pm for afternoon tea. Tube: Pimlico. Bus: 77 or 88.

KNIGHTSBRIDGE

Expensive

Amaya ★ INDIAN This chic restaurant, a hot dining ticket, is credited with introducing the small-plates concept to Indian food. Dishes are shared, hopefully with a party of friends. This is no mere curry house, but an ambitious restaurant with skilled chefs standing over grills and tandoor ovens, in the eye-catching open kitchen. After devouring the rock oysters in a ginger-studded coconut sauce, we knew we were in for a special meal. Our table shared grilled baby eggplant sprinkled with mango powder. Chicken tikka is one of the signature dishes, the lamb chops are fork tender, and the lobster is beautifully spiced. Vegetarians delight in the tandoor-cooked broccoli in a yogurt sauce or artichoke *biryani* (basmati rice cooked with spices) baked in a pastry-sealed pot. For dessert, try the fresh pomegranate granita, which is sugar free.

Halkin Arcade, Motcomb St., Knightsbridge SW1. ✆ **020/7823-1166.** www.amaya.biz. Reservations required. Main courses £9.50–£36; set-price lunch £16–£25; set-price dinner £45. AE, DC, MC, V. Mon–Sat 12:30–2:15pm and 6:30–11:30pm; Sun 12:45–2:45pm and 6–10:30pm. Tube: Knightsbridge.

Black & Blue ★ STEAK/ENGLISH The atmosphere is marvelously informal, the prices are affordable, and the steaks are of high quality, each from a traditionally reared, grass-fed Scottish cow. Take your pick—Scottish sirloin, rib-eye, T-bone. We especially like the *cote de boeuf*, a hefty rib of beef for two to share. The sauces served with the steaks are divine. Burgers, chargrilled chicken, and fish dishes are also on offer on the changing menu, even freshly made salads and platters for the vegetarian.

215–217 Kensington Church St., W8. ✆ **020/7727-0004.** www.blackandbluerestaurants.com. Reservations required. Main courses £9–£26. MC, V. Sun–Thurs noon–11pm; Fri–Sat noon–11:30pm. Tube: Notting Hill Gate.

CHELSEA

Expensive

Le Cercle ★★ FRENCH At last, in this chic subterranean dining room, a sort of Chelsea speak-easy, Sloane Street has a restaurant that is to food what the boulevard has long been to fashion. Service may not be the most efficient, and the noise level is at times deafening, but the food is amazing. You make your menu selection among an occasional famous face and a lot of lesser mortals.

For us, the best dish was tuna carpaccio with crispy pork cubes. The French-styled dishes are served as tapas-size portions. The menu is divided into seven sections according to principal ingredients. The waitstaff suggests three portions of these small plates before choosing one of the delectable desserts. The milk-fed Pyrenean lamb is meltingly tender. The chefs turn out one of the most succulent cuts of beef in London—it appears as *onglet* on the menu. Particularly memorable was the duck and fig combo and the chestnut risotto. For dessert, the chocolate fondant may arguably be the best served in London. It's served with vanilla and pepper (you heard right) ice cream. As for the cheese selection, one habitué described the options to us as "top dog."

1 Wilbraham Place, SW1. ✆ **020/7901-9999.** www.lecercle.co.uk. Reservations required. Fixed-price lunch £15–£20; French tapas £5–£25. AE, MC, V. Tues–Sat noon–3pm and 6–11pm. Tube: Sloane Sq.

Tom's Kitchen ★ BRITISH A former pub has been stylishly converted into this chic restaurant, which, from the moment of its opening, has attracted a loyal following of the local smart set. Today a bright, bustling brasserie, with an open kitchen in back, it's the dream come true for Tom Aikens, who is assisted by his twin brother, Rob. Stop in for breakfast if you crave brioche French toast with caramelized apples, cinnamon ice cream, and maple syrup. Or else make a rendezvous to tuck into Tom's seductive fish and chips.

27 Cale St., SW3. ✆ **020/7349-0202.** www.tomskitchen.co.uk. Reservations required. Main courses £14–£30. AE, MC, V. Mon–Fri 7–10am, noon–3pm, and 6–11pm; Sat–Sun 10am–4pm and 6–11pm. Tube: Fulham Broadway.

Inexpensive

The Pig's Ear ★ 🎁 ENGLISH The staff are still talking about the surprise visit of Prince William; he may be heir to one of the world's most fabled fortunes, but at the end of the evening here, he split the bill among his friends, paying only his fair share at this, one of the best gastropubs in Chelsea. It might be called the Pig's Ear, but it's really the silk purse when it comes to food. Start with such dishes as Jerusalem artichoke soup with truffle oil, or chicken livers flavored with sherry vinegar. Other dishes include seared tuna with black olives and chicory or else foie gras ballantine with onion marmalade. In honor of its namesake, the chefs deep-fry pigs' ears. Filet of sea bass appears with beet and baby leeks, and a roast wood pigeon is stuffed with garlic-laced portobello mushrooms. The atmosphere is friendly and unpretentious in either the ground-floor pub area or the wood-paneled restaurant upstairs.

35 Old Church St. ✆ **020/7352-2908.** www.thepigsear.info. Reservations required in restaurant. Main courses £12–£16. AE, DC, MC, V. Mon–Sat noon–11pm; Sun noon–10:30pm. Tube: Sloane Sq.

WHERE TO HAVE A cuppa

The pair of tea salons known as **St. James Restaurant** and the **Fountain Restaurant** (181 Piccadilly, W1; the Fountain ✆ **020/7973-4140;** www.fortnumandmason.com; St. James **020/7734-8040,** ext. 2241) functions as a culinary showplace for London's most prestigious grocery store, Fortnum & Mason. The more formal of the two, the St. James, on the store's fourth floor, is a pale green-and-beige homage to formal Edwardian taste. More rapid and less formal is the Fountain Restaurant, on the street level, where a sense of tradition and manners is very much a part of the dining experience, but in a less opulent setting. There is no longer an "official" afternoon tea at the Fountain, but you can order pots of tea plus food from an a la carte menu that includes sandwiches, scones, and the like.

Visitors herd gracefully into the high-volume but nevertheless elegant **Georgian Restaurant,** on the fourth floor of Harrods, 87–135 Brompton Rd., SW1 (✆ **020/7255-6800;** www.harrods.com; Tube: Knightsbridge), in a room so long its staff refers to its shape and size as the "Mississippi River." The list of teas available—at least 50—is sometimes so esoteric the experience might remind you of choosing among vintages in a sophisticated wine cellar. Served Monday through Saturday from 3:30 to 5:30pm (last order), high tea runs £25 per person; reservations are recommended.

The **Orangery,** in the gardens just north of Kensington Palace, W8 (✆ **020/7376-0239;** Tube: High St. Kensington or Queensway), occupies a long and narrow garden pavilion built in 1704 by Queen Anne as a site for her tea parties. Tea is still served (daily 3–5pm) amid rows of potted orange trees basking in sunlight from soaring windows. Reservations are not accepted. A pot of tea costs £1.95 to £5, summer cakes and puddings run £3.50 to £8.75, and afternoon tea costs £13 to £35.

KENSINGTON & SOUTH KENSINGTON

Very Expensive

Tom Aikens ★★★ CONTINENTAL The amazingly skilled Tom Aikens is one of the truly top-flight Gallic chefs of London. Aikens certainly was trained well, working in Paris under Joël Robuchon during the time he was proclaimed as France's greatest chef. Aikens also ran the prestigious Pied-à-Terre in London. In elegant surroundings in chic Knightsbridge, the food is basically a modern interpretation of high French cuisine, with a great deal of flourish and some very elaborately worked dishes.

Regardless of the contrast in ingredients, main courses show harmony and cohesion, as exemplified by the poached sea bass with saffron risotto and a bouillabaisse sauce. Everything sounds like an unlikely combination, but the end result is most satisfying. The menu's most voluptuous side is evoked by braised suckling pig with roasted fresh almonds, apple purée, and pork lasagna.

43 Elystan St., Knightsbridge, SW3. ✆ **020/7584-2003.** www.tomaikens.co.uk. Reservations required. Fixed-price 2-course lunch £23, 3-course lunch £29; dinner main courses £25–£40; tasting menu £80, or £140 with wine pairings. AE, DC, MC, V. Tues–Fri noon–2:30pm; Mon–Sat 6:45–11pm. Tube: South Kensington.

Expensive

Bibendum/The Oyster Bar ★ FRENCH/MEDITERRANEAN In trendy Brompton Cross, this still-fashionable restaurant occupies two floors of a garage that's now an Art Deco masterpiece. Though its heyday came in the early 1990s, the white-tiled room with stained-glass windows, lots of sunlight, and a chic clientele is still an extremely pleasant place. The eclectic cuisine, known for its freshness and simplicity, is based on what's available seasonally. Dishes might include roast pigeon with celeriac purée and apple sauté, rabbit with artichoke and parsley sauce, or grilled lamb cutlets with a delicate sauce. Some of the best dishes are for splitting between two people, including Bresse chicken flavored with fresh tarragon and grilled veal chops with truffle butter. Simpler meals and cocktails are available in the **Oyster Bar** on the building's street level. The bar-style menu stresses fresh shellfish presented in the traditional French style, on ice-covered platters adorned with strands of seaweed.

81 Fulham Rd., SW3. ✆ **020/7581-5817.** www.bibendum.co.uk. Reservations required in Bibendum, not accepted in Oyster Bar. Main courses £17–£46; fixed-price 2-course lunch £25; fixed-price 3-course lunch £30; cold seafood platter in Oyster Bar £30. AE, DC, MC, V. Bibendum Mon–Fri noon–2:30pm and 7–11pm; Sat 12:30–3pm and 7–11pm; Sun 12:30–3pm and 7–10:30pm. Oyster Bar daily noon–11pm. Tube: South Kensington.

MARYLEBONE

Expensive

Orrery ★★ FRENCH/INTERNATIONAL With ingredients imported from France, this is one of London's classic French restaurants. Sea bass from the shores of Montpellier, olive oil from Maussane-les-Alpilles, mushrooms from the fields of Calais, and poultry from Bresse—they all turn up on a highly refined menu, the creation of Chef Andre Garret. On the second floor of the Conran Shop in Marylebone, Orrey changes its menu seasonally to take advantage of the best produce. Garret is a purist in terms of ingredients. Our favorites among his first-rate dishes are Bresse pigeon with savoy cabbage and mushroom ravioli, or duckling with an endive tatin and cèpe (flap mushrooms) sauce. Everything has a brilliant, often whimsical touch, as evoked by the sautéed leeks in pumpkin oil. We ended with a cheese plate featuring a Banton goat cheese so fresh that it oozed onto the plate. Enjoy summer evenings on a fourth-floor terrace while drinking and ordering light fare from the bar menu.

55 Marylebone High St., W1. ✆ **020/7616-8000.** www.orreryrestaurant.co.uk. Reservations required. Fixed-price 3-course lunch £29; fixed-price 2-course dinner £44; fixed-price 3-course dinner £50. AE, DC, MC, V. Daily noon–2:30pm and 6:30–10pm. Tube: Baker St.

Moderate

Assaggi ★ 🎁 ITALIAN You wouldn't think of heading to the second floor of a very ordinary pub in Bayswater for fine Italian cuisine, but we urge you to do so in this case to sample Chef Nino Sassu's take on Italian classics, especially those from the south. Serious London foodies have discovered its low-key venue, and flock here for food prepared with flair and passion, using market-fresh and top-quality ingredients.

The chef sets out to prove that straightforward dishes can often be the best when simply handled. Grilled Mediterranean vegetables in virgin olive oil and fresh herbs are always a winning appetizer, followed by such mains as grilled sea bass or filet of pork with black truffles. The menu is short but long on flavor, if you try such dishes as butter-and-sage ravioli, tender calves' liver, or panna cotta.

39 Chepstow Place, W2. ✆ **020/7792-9033.** Reservations required. Main courses £19–£28. AE, MC, V. Mon–Sat 12:30–2:30pm and 7:30–11pm. Tube: Bayswater.

NOTTING HILL GATE

Moderate

The Cow ★ MODERN ENGLISH You don't have to be a young fashion victim to enjoy the superb cuisine served here (although many of the diners are). This increasingly hip Notting Hill watering hole looks like an Irish pub, but the accents you'll hear are "trustafarian" rather than street-smart Dublin. With a pint of Fuller's or London Pride, you can linger over the modern European menu, which changes daily but is likely to include ox tongue poached in milk; mussels in curry and cream; or a mixed grill of lamb chops, calves' liver, and sweetbreads. The seafood selections are delectable. The Cow Special—a half-dozen Irish rock oysters with a pint of Guinness or a glass of wine for £11—is the star of the show. A raw bar downstairs serves other fresh seafood choices.

89 Westbourne Park Rd., W2. ✆ **020/7221-5400.** www.thecowlondon.co.uk. Reservations required. Main courses £9.50–£19. MC, V. Daily noon–midnight. Tube: Westbourne Grove.

THE CITY

Expensive

Prism ★★ MODERN ENGLISH This restaurant attracts London's movers and shakers, at least those with demanding palates. In the former Bank of New York, Harvey Nichols—known for his chic department store in Knightsbridge—took this 1920s neo-Grecian hall and installed Mies van der Rohe chairs in chrome and lipstick-red leather. In this setting, traditional English dishes from the north are given a light touch—try the tempura of Whitby cod or cream of Jerusalem artichoke soup with roasted scallops and truffle oil. For a first course, try a salad composed of flecks of Parmesan cheese seasoning savoy cabbage and Parma ham. The menu reveals the chef has traveled a bit—note such dishes as Moroccan-spiced chicken livers served with a lemon-and-parsley couscous.

147 Leadenhall St., EC3. ✆ **020/7256-3875.** www.harveynichols.com. Reservations required. Main courses £13–£37. AE, DC, MC, V. Mon–Fri 11:30am–3pm and 6–10pm. Tube: Bank or Monument.

Inexpensive

Ye Olde Cheshire Cheese ☺ TRADITIONAL ENGLISH The foundation of this carefully preserved building was laid in the 13th century, and it holds the most famous of the old City chophouses and pubs. Established in 1667, it claims to be the spot where Dr. Samuel Johnson (who lived nearby) entertained admirers with his acerbic wit. Charles Dickens and other literary lions also patronized the place. Later, many of the ink-stained journalists and scandalmongers of 19th- and early-20th-century Fleet Street made it their watering hole. You'll find five bars and two dining rooms here. The house specialties include Ye Famous Pudding (steak, kidney, mushrooms, and game) and Scottish roast beef with Yorkshire pudding and horseradish sauce. Sandwiches, salads, and standby favorites such as steak-and-kidney pie are also available, as are dishes such as Dover sole. The Cheshire is the best and safest venue to introduce your children to an English pub.

Wine Office Court, 145 Fleet St., EC4. ✆ **020/7353-6170.** Reservations not accepted. Main courses £8–£12. AE, DC, MC, V. Meals Mon–Fri noon–10pm; Sat noon–2:30pm and 6–9:30pm; Sun noon–2:30pm. Drinks and bar snacks Mon–Sat 11am–11pm; Sun noon–6pm. Tube: St. Paul's or Blackfriars.

Seeing the Sights

London isn't a city to visit hurriedly. It is so vast, so stocked with treasures, that it would take a lifetime to explore it thoroughly. But even a quick visit will give you a chance to see what's creating the hottest buzz in shopping and nightlife as well as the city's time-tested treasures.

THE TOP ATTRACTIONS

Tower of London ★★★ ☺ This ancient fortress continues to pack in the crowds with its macabre associations with the legendary figures imprisoned and/or executed here (Sir Walter Raleigh, Anne Boleyn, Lady Jane Grey). The Tower is actually an intricately patterned compound of structures built throughout the ages for varying purposes, mostly as expressions of royal power. The oldest is the **White Tower,** begun by William the Conqueror in 1078. Here you can view the **Armouries,** which date from the reign of Henry VIII, as well as a display of instruments of torture and execution that recall some of the most ghastly moments in the Tower's history. In the Jewel House, you'll find the Tower's greatest attraction, the **Crown Jewels.** Here, some of the world's most precious stones are set into robes, swords, scepters, and crowns.

With the opening of a visitor center and the restoration of the Tower's 13th-century wharf, the attraction is more user-friendly than ever before. To the west of the Tower is Tower Hill Square, designed by Stanton Williams, with a series of pavilions housing ticketing facilities, a gift shop, and a cafeteria.

One-hour guided tours of the entire compound are given by the Yeoman Warders (also known as beefeaters) every half-hour daily, starting at 9:30am, from the Middle Tower near the main entrance. The last guided walk starts about 3:30pm in summer, 2:30pm in winter—weather permitting, of course.

Tower Hill, EC3. ✆ **0844/482-7777.** www.hrp.org.uk. Admission £17 adults, £14.50 students and seniors, £9.50 children 5–15, family ticket £47, free for children 4 and under. Mar–Oct Tues–Sat 9am–5:30pm, Sun–Mon 10am–5:30pm; Nov–Feb Tues–Sat 9am–4:30pm, Sun–Mon 10am–4:30pm. Tube: Tower Hill.

Westminster Abbey ★★★ In 1605, the Saxon King, Edward the Confessor, founded the Benedictine abbey on this spot overlooking Parliament Square. The first king crowned in the abbey may have been Harold, in January 1066. The coronation tradition has continued to the present day, although Edward V and Edward VIII were never crowned. The essentially Early English Gothic structure existing today owes more to Henry III's plans than to those of any other sovereign, although many architects, including Wren, have contributed to the abbey.

Henry VIII Chapel is one of the loveliest in Europe, with its fan vaulting, Knights of Bath banners, and Torrigiani-designed tomb for the king himself. You can also visit the most hallowed spot in the abbey, the **Shrine of Edward the Confessor** (canonized in the 12th c.). Near the tomb of Henry V is the Coronation Chair, made at the command of Edward I in 1300 to display the mystical Stone of Scone (which some think is the sacred stone mentioned in Genesis and known as Jacob's Pillar). Another noted spot is **Poets' Corner,** to the right of the entrance to the Royal Chapel, with monuments to Chaucer, Samuel Johnson, Tennyson, Browning, and Dickens; there's even an American, Henry Wadsworth Longfellow.

On Sundays, the abbey is open for services only and all are welcome. The rest of the church is open unless a service is being conducted. For times of services, phone the **Chapter Office** (✆ **020/7222-5152**).

Broad Sanctuary, SW1. ✆ **020/7222-5152.** www.westminster-abbey.org. Admission £15 adults, £12 students 19 and over and seniors, £6 children 11–18, £32 family ticket, free for children 10 and under. Mon–Tues and Thurs–Fri 9:30am–4:30pm; Wed 9:30am–6pm; Sat 9:30am–2:30pm. Tube: Westminster or St. James's Park.

Palaces of Westminster (Houses of Parliament) & Big Ben ★★ The Houses of Parliament, along with their trademark clock tower, are the strongholds of Britain's democracy. Both the House of Commons and the House of Lords are in the former royal Palace of Westminster, which was the king's residence until Henry VIII moved to Whitehall. The current Gothic Revival buildings date from 1840 and were designed by Charles Barry. (The earlier buildings were destroyed by fire in 1834.) The clock tower at the eastern end houses the world's most famous timepiece. **"Big Ben"** refers not to the clock tower itself, but to the largest bell in the chime, which weighs close to 14 tons and is named for the first commissioner of works, Sir Benjamin Hall.

You may observe debates for free from the **Stranger's Galleries** in both houses. Sessions usually begin in mid-October and run to the end of July, with recesses at Christmas and Easter. The chances of getting into the House of Lords when it's in session are generally better than for the more popular House of Commons. Although we can't promise you the oratory of a Charles James Fox or a William Pitt the Elder, the debates in the House of Commons are often lively and controversial (seats are at a premium during crises).

Those who'd like to book a tour can do so, but it takes a bit of work. Both houses are open to the general public for guided tours only for a limited season in July and August. The palace is open Monday, Tuesday, Friday, and Saturday from 9:15am to 4:30pm during those times. All tour tickets cost £15 adults; £10 for seniors, students, and children 15 and younger; and £32 family ticket. Children 3 years old and younger may enter free. For advance tickets, call ✆ **0844/847-1672** (www.parliament.uk/visiting/visiting.cfm).

Westminster Palace, Old Palace Yard, SW1. House of Commons ✆ **020/7219-4272;** House of Lords ✆ **020/7219-3107.** www.parliament.uk. Free admission. Mid-Oct to Aug Mon–Tues 9am–noon; Wed 9–9:55am and 10am–noon; Fri 3:30–5pm. Both houses are open for tours (see above). Join line at St. Stephen's entrance. Tube: Westminster.

British Museum ★★★ This immense museum is one of the most comprehensive collections of art and artifacts in the world. It's impossible to take in this museum in a day. Even on a cursory first visit, be sure to see the Asian collections (the finest assembly of Islamic pottery outside the Islamic world), the Chinese porcelain, the Indian sculpture, and the prehistoric and Romano-British collections. The overall storehouse splits basically into the national collections of antiquities; prints and drawings; coins, medals, and bank notes; and ethnography. Special treasures you might want to seek out on your first visit include the **Rosetta Stone,** in the Egyptian Room, whose discovery led to the deciphering of hieroglyphics; the **Elgin Marbles,** a series of pediments, metopes, and friezes from the Parthenon in Athens, in the Duveen Gallery; and the legendary **Black Obelisk,** dating from around 860 B.C., in the Nimrud Gallery. Other treasures include the contents of

London Attractions

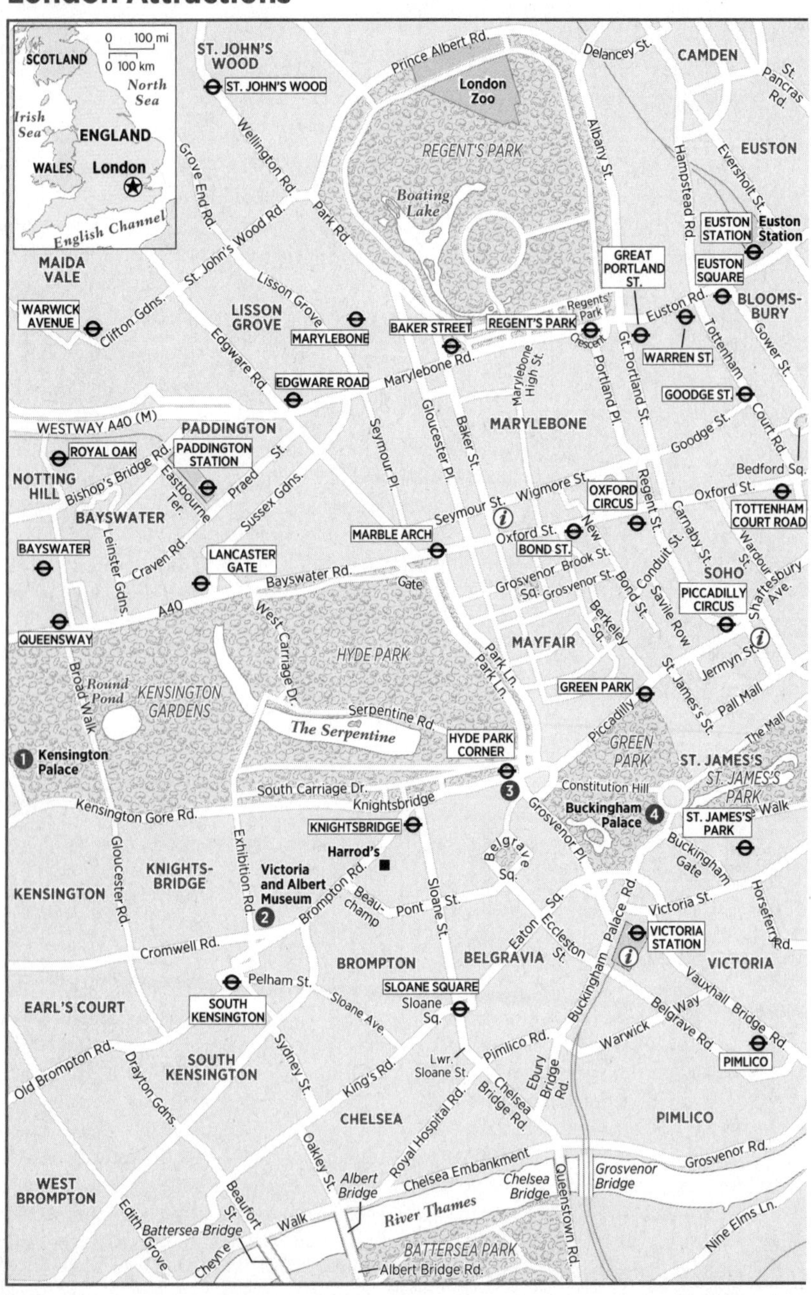

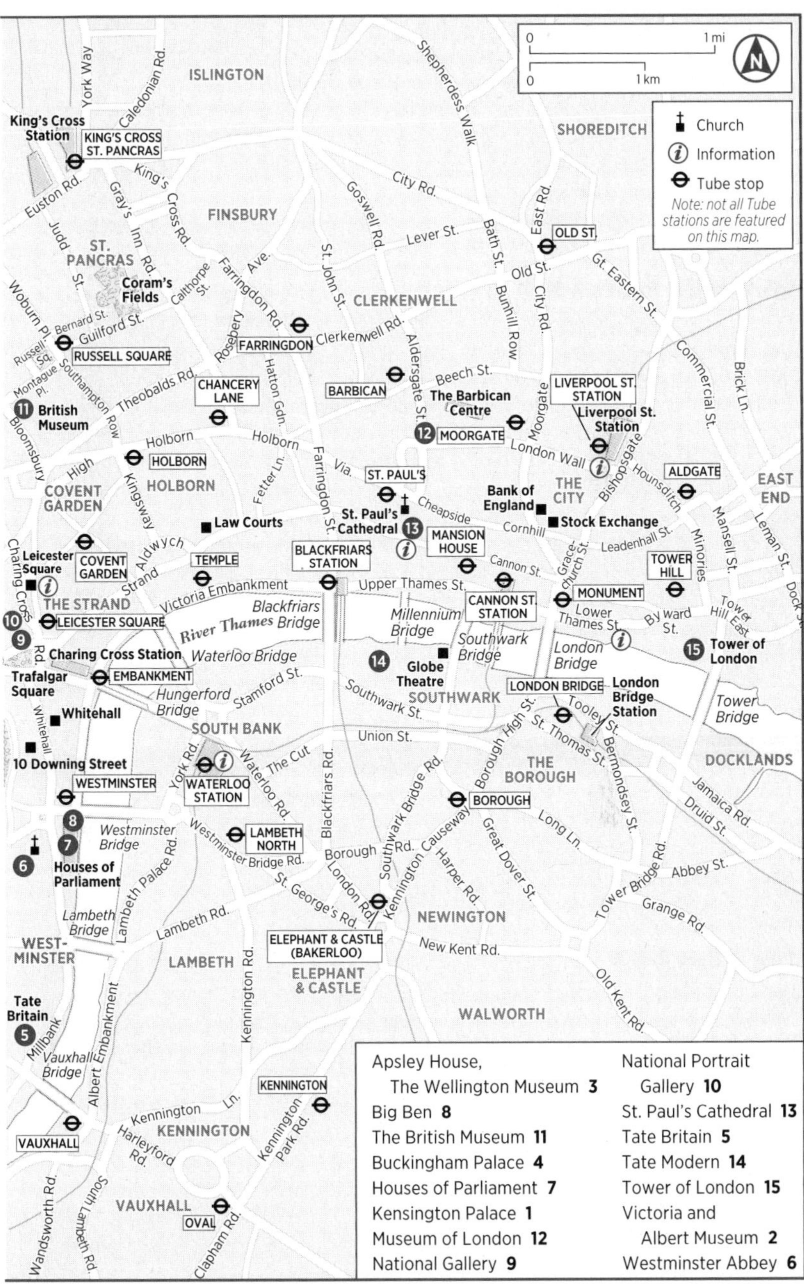
0 1 mi
0 1 km
N
Church
Information
Tube stop
Note: not all Tube stations are featured on this map.
ISLINGTON
SHOREDITCH
FINSBURY
ST. PANCRAS
CLERKENWELL
COVENT GARDEN
HOLBORN
THE CITY
EAST END
THE STRAND
SOUTHWARK
SOUTH BANK
THE BOROUGH
DOCKLANDS
NEWINGTON
LAMBETH
ELEPHANT & CASTLE
WEST-MINSTER
WALWORTH
KENNINGTON
VAUXHALL
King's Cross Station
KING'S CROSS ST. PANCRAS
RUSSELL SQUARE
FARRINGDON
BARBICAN
CHANCERY LANE
HOLBORN
MOORGATE
LIVERPOOL ST. STATION
Liverpool St. Station
OLD ST.
ST. PAUL'S
ALDGATE
TEMPLE
BLACKFRIARS STATION
MANSION HOUSE
CANNON ST. STATION
MONUMENT
TOWER HILL
COVENT GARDEN
LEICESTER SQUARE
EMBANKMENT
LONDON BRIDGE
London Bridge Station
WESTMINSTER
WATERLOO STATION
LAMBETH NORTH
BOROUGH
ELEPHANT & CASTLE (BAKERLOO)
KENNINGTON
VAUXHALL
OVAL
Coram's Fields
British Museum
Law Courts
The Barbican Centre
St. Paul's Cathedral
Bank of England
Stock Exchange
Leicester Square
Charing Cross Station
Trafalgar Square
Whitehall
10 Downing Street
Houses of Parliament
Globe Theatre
Tower of London
Tate Britain
River Thames
Blackfriars Bridge
Millennium Bridge
Southwark Bridge
London Bridge
Tower Bridge
Waterloo Bridge
Hungerford Bridge
Westminster Bridge
Lambeth Bridge
Vauxhall Bridge
York Way
Caledonian Rd.
Shepherdess Walk
City Rd.
Goswell Rd.
Lever St.
Bath St.
East Rd.
Old St.
Gt. Eastern St.
Bunhill Row
King's Cross Rd.
Gray's Inn Rd.
Euston Rd.
Judd St.
Calthorpe St.
Farringdon Rd.
Rosebery Ave.
St. John St.
Clerkenwell Rd.
Aldersgate St.
Beech St.
Commercial St.
Brick Ln.
Woburn Pl.
Bernard St.
Guilford St.
Russell Sq.
Montague Pl.
Southampton Row
Theobalds Rd.
Hatton Gdn.
Bloomsbury
High Holborn
Holborn
Holborn Via.
Fetter Ln.
Farringdon St.
London Wall
Bishopsgate
Houndsditch
Kingsway
Aldwych
Cheapside
Cornhill
Leadenhall St.
Minories
Mansell St.
Leman St.
Dock St.
Charing Cross Rd.
Strand
Victoria Embankment
Upper Thames St.
Cannon St.
Gracechurch St.
Lower Thames St.
Byward St.
Tower Hill East
Stamford St.
Southwark St.
Union St.
Borough High St.
Tooley St.
St. Thomas St.
Bermondsey St.
Jamaica Rd.
Druid St.
Whitehall
York Rd.
Waterloo Rd.
The Cut
Blackfriars Rd.
Southwark Bridge Rd.
Westminster Bridge Rd.
Borough Rd.
Kennington Causeway
Harper Rd.
Great Dover St.
Long Ln.
Lambeth Palace Rd.
St. George's Rd.
London Rd.
Tower Bridge Rd.
Abbey St.
Grange Rd.
Lambeth Rd.
New Kent Rd.
Old Kent Rd.
Kennington Rd.
Millbank
Albert Embankment
Kennington Ln.
Kennington Park Rd.
Harleyford Rd.
Wandsworth Rd.
South Lambeth Rd.
Clapham Rd.
Apsley House, The Wellington Museum 3
Big Ben 8
The British Museum 11
Buckingham Palace 4
Houses of Parliament 7
Kensington Palace 1
Museum of London 12
National Gallery 9
National Portrait Gallery 10
St. Paul's Cathedral 13
Tate Britain 5
Tate Modern 14
Tower of London 15
Victoria and Albert Museum 2
Westminster Abbey 6

Egyptian royal tombs (including mummies); fabulous arrays of 2,000-year-old jewelry, cosmetics, weapons, furniture, and tools; Babylonian astronomical instruments; and winged lion statues (in the Assyrian Transept) that guarded Ashurnasirpal's palace at Nimrud. The exhibits change throughout the year, so if your heart is set on seeing a specific treasure, call to make sure it's on display.

The museum's inner courtyard, hidden for 150 years, has been transformed into the Great Court, a 2-acre square spanned by a spectacular glass roof. Following the removal of the British Library to St. Pancras, the Reading Room has been restored as a public reference library.

Great Russell St., WC1. ✆ **020/7323-8299.** www.britishmuseum.org. Free admission. Sat–Wed 10am–5:30pm; Thurs–Fri 10am–8:30pm. Tube: Holborn, Tottenham Court Rd., Goodge St., or Russell Sq.

Buckingham Palace ★★ ☺ This massive, graceful building is the official residence of the queen. You can tell whether the queen is at home by checking to see if the Royal Standard is flying from the mast outside. For most of the year, you can't visit the palace without an official invitation. Since 1993, though, much of it has been open for tours during an 8-week period in August and September, when the royal family is usually vacationing outside London. Elizabeth II agreed to allow visitors to tour the State Room, the Grand Staircase, the Throne Room, and other areas designed by John Nash for George IV, as well as the Picture Gallery, which displays masterpieces by Van Dyck, Rembrandt, Rubens, and others.

Buckingham Palace's most famous spectacle is the vastly overrated **Changing of the Guard** (daily Apr–July and on alternating days for the rest of the year). The new guard, marching behind a band, comes from either the Wellington or Chelsea barracks and takes over from the old guard in the forecourt of the palace. The ceremony begins at 11:30am, although it's frequently canceled because of bad weather, state events, and other harder-to-fathom reasons. We think the ceremony is overrated; however, few first-time visitors can resist it. If that's you, arrive as early as 10:30am and claim territorial rights to a space in front of the palace. If you're not firmly anchored here, you'll miss much of the ceremony.

At end of the Mall (on the road running from Trafalgar Sq.). ✆ **020/7766-7300.** www.royalcollection.org.uk. Palace tours £17 adults, £15.50 seniors 61 and over and students, £9.75 children 16 and under, £45 family ticket, free for children 4 and under; Changing of the Guard free. Aug 1–Sept 27 (dates can vary), and additional dates may be added. Daily 9:45am–6pm. Changing of the Guard daily Apr–July at 11:30am and alternating days for the rest of the year at 11am. Tube: St. James's Park, Green Park, or Victoria.

Tate Britain ★★★ What's now known as the Tate Britain used to be known as the Tate Gallery before the modern works in its collection were moved to the Tate Modern (see below). Fronting the Thames near Vauxhall Bridge in Pimlico, it houses the national collections, covering British art from the 16th century to the present day, as well as an array of international works.

The works include some of the best of Gainsborough, Reynolds, Stubbs, Blake, and Constable. William Hogarth is well represented, particularly by his satirical *O the Roast Beef of Old England* (known as *The Gate of Calais*). You'll find the illustrations of William Blake, the incomparable mystical poet, including such works as *The Book of Job, The Divine Comedy,* and *Paradise Lost.* The collection of works by J. M. W. Turner is the Tate's largest collection of works by a single artist—Turner himself willed most of his paintings and watercolors to the nation.

Also on display are the works of many major 19th- and 20th-century painters, including Paul Nash.

Millbank, SW1. ✆ **020/7887-8008.** www.tate.org.uk. Free admission; special exhibitions sometimes incur a charge of £5–£15. Daily 10:30am–5:50pm. Tube: Pimlico.

Tate Modern ★★★ In a transformed Bankside Power Station in Southwark, this museum draws some two million visitors a year to see the greatest collection of international 20th-century art in Britain. As such, it is one of the three or four most important art galleries in the world. Tate Modern is also viewer-friendly, with eye-level hangings. All the big painting stars are here, a whole galaxy ranging from Dalí to Matisse to Rothko. The Modern is also a gallery of 21st-century art, displaying new and exciting art. Instead of exhibiting art chronologically and by school, the Tate Modern, in a radical break from tradition, takes a thematic approach. This allows displays to cut across movements.

The Tate Modern unveiled plans for a £400-million extension to be completed in time for the London Olympics of 2012. The extension will resemble glass boxes stacked up arbitrarily to form a 67m (220-ft.) pyramid.

You can cross the Millennium Bridge, a pedestrian-only walk from the steps of St. Paul's, over the Thames to the new gallery.

Bankside, SE1. ✆ **020/7887-8888.** www.tate.org.uk. Free admission. Sun–Thurs 10am–6pm; Fri–Sat 10am–10pm. Tube: Southwark or Blackfriars.

National Gallery ★★★ This stately neoclassical building contains an unrivaled collection of Western art, representing all the major schools from the late 13th to the early 20th century. Of the early Gothic works, the Wilton Diptych (French or English school, late 14th c.) is the rarest treasure; it depicts Richard II being introduced to the Madonna and Child by John the Baptist and the Saxon kings, Edmund and Edward the Confessor. There's also an immense French Impressionist and post-Impressionist collection that includes works by Manet, Monet, Degas, Renoir, and Cézanne. Particularly charming is the peep-show cabinet by Hoogstraten in one of the Dutch rooms: It's like spying through a keyhole.

North side of Trafalgar Sq., WC2. ✆ **020/7747-2885.** www.nationalgallery.org.uk. Free admission. Thurs–Tues 10am–6pm; Wed 10am–9pm. Tube: Charing Cross or Leicester Sq.

Kensington Palace ★ ☺ Once the residence of British monarchs, Kensington dates from 1609 but was redesigned in 1689. Since the end of the 18th century, the palace has housed various members of the royal family, and the State Apartments are open for tours. The Palace was the London home of the late Princess Margaret and is the current home of the duke and duchess of Kent. The palace was also the home of Diana, Princess of Wales, and her two sons.

In the apartments of Queen Mary II is a striking 17th-century writing cabinet inlaid with tortoiseshell. Paintings from the Royal Collection line the walls. A rare 1750 lady's court dress and splendid examples of male court dress from the 18th century are on display in rooms adjacent to the State Apartments, as part of the Royal Ceremonial Dress Collection, which features royal costumes dating as far back as 200 years.

The **Kensington Gardens** are open to the public for leisurely strolls through the manicured grounds and around the Round Pond. One of the most famous sights is the controversial Albert Memorial, a lasting tribute not only to Victoria's consort, but also to the questionable taste of the Victorian era. There's a wonderful afternoon tea offered in the Orangery (p. 233).

The Broad Walk, Kensington Gardens, W8. ✆ **0844/482-7777.** www.hrp.org.uk. Admission £12.50 adults, £11 seniors and students, £6.25 children 5–15, £34 family ticket. Mar–Oct daily 10am–6pm; Nov–Feb daily 10am–5pm. Tube: Queensway or Notting Hill Gate; High St. Kensington on south side.

St. Paul's Cathedral ★★★ St. Paul's was razed during the Great Fire of 1666, making way for a new structure designed by Sir Christopher Wren and built between 1675 and 1710. The classical dome of St. Paul's dominates the City's square mile. In the interior of the dome is the Whispering Gallery, an acoustic marvel in which the faintest whisper can be heard clearly on the opposite side. You can climb to the top of the dome for a 360-degree view of London. From the Whispering Gallery a second steep climb leads to the **Stone Gallery,** opening onto a panoramic view of London. Wren lies in the crypt, along with the duke of Wellington. This was where Prince Charles married Lady Diana Spencer in 1981.

St. Paul's Churchyard, EC4. ✆ **020/7246-8350.** www.stpauls.co.uk. Cathedral and galleries £12.50 adults, £11.50 seniors and students, £4.50 children 6–16, £29.50 family ticket, free for children 5 and under; guided tours £3 adults, £2.50 students and seniors, £1 children; recorded tours £4, free for children 5 and under. Cathedral (excluding galleries) Mon–Sat 8:30am–4pm; galleries Mon–Sat 9:30am–4pm. No sightseeing Sun (services only). Tube: St. Paul's, Mansion House, Cannon St., or Blackfriars.

Victoria and Albert Museum ★★★ The Victoria and Albert is the greatest decorative-arts museum in the world. The medieval holdings include such treasures as the Early English Gloucester Candlestick; the Byzantine Veroli Casket, with its ivory panels based on Greek plays; and the Syon Cope, a unique embroidery made in England in the early 14th century. An area devoted to Islamic art houses the Ardabil Carpet from 16th-century Persia. The V&A boasts the largest collection of Renaissance sculpture outside Italy. A highlight of the 16th-century collection is the marble group *Neptune with Triton* by Bernini. The cartoons by Raphael, which were conceived as designs for tapestries for the Sistine Chapel, are owned by the queen and are on display here.

The story of British design from 1500 to 1900 unfolds in the **British Galleries ★★★**. From Chippendale to Morris, all of the top British designers are featured. Star exhibits range from the 5m-high (16-ft.) Melville Bed (1697), to the wedding suite of James II and one of the most prized possessions, the "Great Bed of Ware," mentioned in Shakespeare's *Twelfth Night.*

On view is a suite of five painting galleries that were originally built in 1850. A trio of these galleries focuses on British landscapes as seen through the eyes of Turner, Constable, and others. Another gallery showcases masters such as Botticelli, Delacroix, Degas, Tintoretto, and Ingres.

In 2009, the **Gilbert Collection ★★★**, one of the most important bequests of the decorative arts ever made in England that includes gold, silver, mosaics, and gold snuffboxes, was moved to a suite of galleries in the V&A.

Cromwell Rd., SW7. ✆ **020/7942-2000.** www.vam.ac.uk. Free admission. Temporary exhibitions often £12. Daily 10am–5:45pm (until 10pm every Wed and the last Fri of each month). Tube: South Kensington.

MUSEUMS

Apsley House, the Wellington Museum ★ This former town house of Arthur Wellesley, the "Iron Duke" of Wellington, who defeated Napoleon at the Battle of

Waterloo and later became prime minister, was opened as a public museum in 1952. The building was designed by Robert Adam, who pioneered the neoclassical style in Britain, with light, elegant lines unbound by strict classical proportion. The collection contains some of the finest silver and porcelain pieces in Europe.

149 Piccadilly, Hyde Park Corner, W1. ✆ **020/7499-5676.** www.english-heritage.org.uk/apsleyhouse. Admission £6 adults, £5.10 seniors and students, £3 children 15 and under. Apr–Oct Tues–Sun 11am–5pm; Nov–Mar Tues–Sun 11am–4pm. Tube: Hyde Park Corner.

Museum of London ★★ In the Barbican District near St. Paul's Cathedral, the Museum of London allows visitors to trace the city's history from prehistoric times to the postmodern era through relics, costumes, household effects, maps, and models. Anglo-Saxons, Vikings, Normans—they're all here, displayed on two floors around a central courtyard.

150 London Wall, EC2. ✆ **020/7001-9844.** www.museumoflondon.org.uk. Free admission. Daily 10am–6pm. Tube: St. Paul's or Barbican.

National Portrait Gallery ★★ In a gallery of remarkable and unremarkable portraits (they're collected for their subjects rather than their artistic quality), a few paintings tower over the rest, including Sir Joshua Reynolds's first portrait of Samuel Johnson ("a man of most dreadful appearance"). There's also a portrait of William Shakespeare (with a gold earring) by an unknown artist that bears the claim of being the "most authentic contemporary likeness" of its subject. One of the most famous pictures in the gallery is the group portrait of the Brontë sisters (Charlotte, Emily, and Anne) by their brother, Bramwell.

In 2000, Queen Elizabeth opened the Ondaatje Wing of the gallery, increasing the gallery's exhibition space by more than 50%. The splendid Tudor Gallery features portraits of Richard III and Henry VII, Richard's conqueror in the Battle of Bosworth in 1485. There's also a portrait of Shakespeare that the gallery acquired in 1856.

St. Martin's Place, WC2. ✆ **020/7306-0055.** www.npg.org.uk. Free admission; fee charged for certain temporary exhibitions. Sat–Wed 10am–6pm; Thurs–Fri 10am–9pm. Tube: Charing Cross or Leicester Sq.

LONDON'S PARKS

London has the greatest system of parklands of any large city on the globe. The largest—and one of the world's biggest—is **Hyde Park ★**, W2. With the adjoining Kensington Gardens, it covers 252 hectares (623 acres) of central London with velvety lawn interspersed with ponds, flower beds, and trees. **Kensington Gardens** are home to the celebrated statue of Peter Pan, with the bronze rabbits that toddlers are always trying to kidnap. The Albert Memorial is also here, and you'll recall the sea of flowers and tributes left here after the death of Diana, Princess of Wales.

East of Hyde Park, across Piccadilly, stretch **Green Park ★** and **St. James's Park ★**, forming an almost-unbroken chain of landscaped beauty. This is an ideal area for picnics, and one that you'll find hard to believe was once a festering piece of swamp near a leper hospital. The classically beautiful **Regent's Park ★★★**, north of Baker Street and Marylebone Road, was designed by 18th-century genius John Nash to surround a palace of the prince regent that never materialized; it's home to an open-air theater and the **London Zoo ★★**.

ORGANIZED TOURS

For the first-timer, the quickest and most economical way to bring the big city into focus is to take a bus tour. One of the most popular is the **Original London**

Sightseeing Tour, which passes by all the major sights in just about 1½ hours. The tour—which uses a traditional double-decker bus with live commentary by a guide—costs £24 for adults, £12 for children 15 and younger, free for those 4 and younger. A family ticket costs £84. The tour, valid for 48 hours, allows you to hop on or off the bus at any point in the tour at no extra charge.

Departures are from convenient points within the city; you can choose your departure point when you buy your ticket. Tickets can be purchased on the bus or at a discount from any London Transport or London Tourist Board Information Centre. Most hotel concierges also sell tickets. For information or phone purchases, call ✆ **020/8877-1722.** It's also possible to book online at **www.theoriginaltour.com**.

The **Original London Walks,** 87 Messina Ave., P.O. Box 1708, London NW6 4LW (✆ **020/7624-3978;** www.walks.com), the oldest established walking-tour company in London, is run by an Anglo-American journalist/actor couple, David and Mary Tucker. Their hallmarks are variety, reliability, reasonably sized groups, and—above all—superb guides. The renowned crime historian Donald Rumbelow, the leading authority on Jack the Ripper and author of the classic guidebook *London Walks,* is a regular guide, as are several prominent actors (including classical actor Edward Petherbridge). Walks are regularly scheduled daily and cost £7 for adults, £5 for students and seniors; children 14 and younger go free. Call for a schedule; no reservations are needed.

A trip up or down the river gives you an entirely different view of London from the one you get from land. You see how the city grew along and around the Thames and how many of its landmarks turn their faces toward the water. Several companies operate motor launches from the Westminster piers (Tube: Westminster), offering panoramic views of one of Europe's most historic waterways en route. For information and reservations, contact **Thames River Services,** Westminster Pier, Victoria Embankment, SW1 (✆ **020/7930-4097;** www.westminsterpier.co.uk), or **Westminster Passenger Association (Upriver) Ltd.,** Westminster Pier, Victoria Embankment, SW1 (✆ **020/7930-2062** or 020/7930-4721; www.wpsa.co.uk), for upriver trips.

The Shopping Scene

THE TOP SHOPPING STREETS & NEIGHBORHOODS

THE WEST END The West End includes the Mayfair district and is home to the core of London's big-name shopping. Most of the department stores, designer shops, and multiples (chain stores) have their flagships in this area.

The key streets are **Oxford Street** for affordable shopping (start at Marble Arch Tube station if you're ambitious, or Bond St. station if you just want to see some of it) and **Regent Street,** which intersects Oxford Street at Oxford Circus (Tube: Oxford Circus).

While there are several branches of the private-label department store **Marks & Spencer,** their Marble Arch store (on Oxford St.) is the flagship and worth shopping at for their high-quality goods. There's a grocery store in the basement and a home-furnishings department upstairs.

Regent Street has fancier shops—more upscale department stores (including the famed **Liberty of London**), and specialty dealers—and leads all the way to Piccadilly.

In between the two, parallel to Regent Street, is **Bond Street.** Divided into New and Old, Bond Street (Tube: Bond St.) also connects Piccadilly with Oxford Street and is synonymous with the luxury trade. Bond Street has had a revival and is the hot address for international designers; **Donna Karan** has not one, but two shops here. Many international hotshots have digs surrounding hers, from **Chanel** and **Ferragamo** to **Versace.**

Burlington Arcade (Tube: Piccadilly Circus), the famous glass-roofed, Regency-style passage leading off Piccadilly, looks like a period exhibition and is lined with intriguing shops and boutiques. The small, smart stores specialize in fashion, jewelry, Irish linen, cashmere, and more. If you linger in the arcade until 5:30pm, you can watch the beadles in their black-and-yellow livery and top hats ceremoniously put in place the iron grills that block off the arcade until 9am the next morning, at which time they just as ceremoniously remove them to mark the start of a new business day. Also at 5:30pm, a hand bell, called the Burlington Bell, is sounded, signaling the end of trading.

Just off Regent Street (actually tucked right behind it) is **Carnaby Street** (Tube: Oxford Circus), which is also having a comeback. While it no longer dominates the world of pace-setting fashion as it did in the 1960s, it's still fun for teens who may need cheap souvenirs, a purple wig, or a little something in leather. A convenient branch of **Boots the Chemists** is also here.

For a total contrast, check out **Jermyn Street,** on the far side of Piccadilly, a tiny 2-block-long street devoted to high-end men's haberdashers and toiletries shops; many have been doing business for centuries. Several hold royal warrants, including **Turnbull & Asser,** where HRH Prince Charles has his pj's made.

The West End leads to the theater district and to two more shopping areas: the still-not-ready-for-prime-time **Soho,** where the sex shops are slowly being turned into cutting-edge designer shops, and **Covent Garden,** which is a masterpiece unto itself. The marketplace has eaten up the surrounding neighborhood so that even though the streets run a little higgledy-piggledy and you can easily get lost, it's fun to just wander and shop.

KNIGHTSBRIDGE & CHELSEA This is the second-most famous of London's retail districts and the home of **Harrods** (Tube: Knightsbridge). A small street nearby, **Sloane Street,** is chockablock with designer shops; **Cheval Place,** in the opposite direction, is also lined with designer resale shops.

Walk toward Museum Row, and you'll soon find **Beauchamp Place** (pronounced *Beech*-am; Tube: Knightsbridge). The street is only a block long, but it features the kinds of shops where young British aristos buy their clothing.

Head out at the **Harvey Nichols** end of Knightsbridge, away from Harrods, and shop your way through the designer stores on Sloane Street (**Hermès, Armani, Prada,** and the like). Walk past Sloane Square and you're in an altogether different neighborhood: Chelsea.

King's Road (Tube: Sloane Sq.), the main street of Chelsea, which starts at Sloane Square, will forever remain a symbol of London in the swinging '60s. Today, the street is still frequented by young people, but with fewer Mohawks, "Bovver boots," and Edwardian ball gowns than before. More and more, King's Road is a lineup of markets and "multistores," large or small conglomerations of indoor stands, stalls, and booths in one building or enclosure.

Chelsea doesn't begin and end with King's Road. If you choose to walk the other direction from Harrods, you connect to a part of Chelsea called **Brompton Cross,** another hip and hot area for designer shops, made popular when Michelin House was rehabbed by Sir Terence Conran for the **Conran Shop.**

Also seek out **Walton Street,** a tiny little snake of a street running from Brompton Cross back toward the museums. About 2 blocks of this 3-block street are devoted to fairy-tale shops for m'lady, where you can buy aromatherapy from **Jo Malone,** needlepoint, or costume jewelry, or meet with your interior designer who runs a small shop of objets d'art.

Finally, don't forget all those museums right there in the corner of the shopping streets. They all have great gift shops.

KENSINGTON & NOTTING HILL **Kensington High Street** is the new hangout of the classier breed of teen who has graduated from Carnaby Street and is ready for street chic. While a few staples of basic British fashion are on this strip, most of the stores feature items that stretch; are very, very short; or are very, very tight. The Tube station here is High Street Kensington.

From Kensington High Street, you can walk up **Kensington Church Street,** which, like Portobello Road, is one of the city's main shopping avenues for antiques. Kensington Church Street dead-ends into the Notting Hill Gate Tube station, which is where you would arrive for shopping on **Portobello Road.** The dealers and the weekend market are 2 blocks beyond.

THE TOP MARKETS

THE WEST END **Covent Garden Market** ★ (**© 020/7836-9136;** www.coventgardenlondonuk.com; Tube: Covent Garden), the most famous market in all of England, offers several markets Monday to Saturday 10am to 6pm, but we think it's most fun to come on Sunday 11am to 6pm when more vendors are set up and street entertainment is at its peak. It can be a little confusing until you dive in and explore. **Apple Market** is the bustling market in the courtyard, where traders sell—well, everything. Many of the items are what the English call collectible nostalgia: a wide array of glassware and ceramics, leather goods, toys, clothes, hats, and jewelry. Some of the merchandise is truly unusual. Many items are handmade, with some of the craftspeople selling their own wares—except on Monday, when antiques dealers take over. Some goods are new, some are very old. Out back is **Jubilee Market** (**© 020/7836-2139**), also an antiques market, which takes place on Monday, but Tuesday to Sunday, it's sort of a fancy hippie market with cheap clothes and books. Out front there are a few tents of cheap stuff, except on Monday.

St. Martin–in-the-Fields Market (Tube: Charing Cross) is good for teens and hipsters who are interested in imports from India and South America, crafts, and local football (soccer) souvenirs. It's located near Trafalgar Square and Covent Garden; hours are Monday to Saturday from 11am to 5pm and Sunday from noon to 5pm.

NOTTING HILL **Portobello Market** (Tube: Notting Hill Gate) is a magnet for collectors of virtually anything. It's mainly a Saturday happening, from 6am to 5pm. You needn't be here at the crack of dawn; 9am is fine. Once known mainly for fruit and vegetables (still sold here throughout the week), in the past 4 decades Portobello has become synonymous with antiques. But don't take the stall holder's word for it that the fiddle he's holding is a genuine Stradivarius left to him in the will of his Italian great-uncle; it might just as well have been "nicked" from an East End pawnshop.

The market is divided into three major sections. The most crowded is the antiques section, running between Colville Road and Chepstow Villas to the south. (***Warning:*** There's a great concentration of pickpockets in this area.) The second section (and the oldest part) is the "fruit and veg" market, lying between Westway and Colville Road. In the third and final section is a flea market, where Londoners sell bric-a-brac and lots of secondhand goods they didn't really want in the first place. But looking around still makes for interesting fun.

London After Dark

Weekly publications such as *Time Out* and *Where* carry full entertainment listings, including information on restaurants and nightclubs. You'll also find listings in daily newspapers, notably the *Times* and the *Telegraph.*

THE PERFORMING ARTS

To see specific shows, especially hits, purchase your tickets in advance. The best method is to buy your tickets from the theater's box office, which you can do over the phone using a credit card. You'll pay the theater price and pick up the tickets the day of the show. You can also go to a ticket agent, especially for discount tickets such as those sold by the **Society of London Theatre** (✆ **020/7557-6700;** www.officiallondontheatre.co.uk) on the southwest corner of Leicester Square, open Monday to Saturday 10am to 7pm and Sunday noon to 3pm. A £2 service fee is charged. You can purchase all tickets here, although the booth specializes in half-price sales for shows that are undersold. These tickets must be purchased in person—not over the phone. For phone orders, you have to call **Ticketmaster** at ✆ **0870/060-2340.**

For tickets and information before you go, try **Keith Prowse,** 234 W. 44th St., Ste. 1000, New York, NY 10036 (✆ **800/669-8687** or 212/398-4175; www.keithprowse.com). Their London office (which operates under the name of both Global Tickets and First Call Tickets) is at the British Visitors Center, 1 Regent St., SW1 Y4XT (✆ **0870/906-3860**). They'll mail your tickets, fax a confirmation, or leave your tickets at the appropriate production's box office. Instant confirmations are available for most shows. A booking and handling fee of up to 20% is added to the price of all tickets.

THEATER One of the world's finest theater companies, the **Royal Shakespeare Company ★★★** performs at various theaters throughout London. Check its website at **www.rsc.org.uk** for current shows and venues, or call ✆ **0844/800-1110** Monday to Saturday 9am to 8pm. The theater troupe performs in London during the winter months, naturally specializing in the plays of the Bard. In summer, it tours England and abroad.

Occupying a prime site on the South Bank of the River Thames is one of the world's greatest stage companies, the **Royal National Theatre,** South Bank, SE1 (✆ **020/7452-3000;** www.nationaltheatre.org.uk; Tube: Waterloo, Embankment, or Charing Cross). The National Theatre houses three theaters. Tickets range from £10 to £50.

At the replica of **Shakespeare's Globe Theatre,** New Globe Walk, Bankside, SE1 (© **020/7902-1400** for box office; www.shakespeares-globe.org; Tube: Mansion House or Blackfriars), productions vary in style and setting; not all are performed in Elizabethan costume. In keeping with the historic setting, no lighting is focused just on the stage, but floodlighting is used during evening performances to replicate daylight in the theater—Elizabethan performances took place in the afternoon. From May to September, the company holds performances Tuesday to Saturday at 2 and 7pm. There is a limited winter schedule. In any season, the schedule may be affected by weather because this is an outdoor theater. Tickets are £5 for groundlings (patrons who stand in the uncovered area around the stage), £15 to £35 for gallery seats.

Sadler's Wells Theatre, Rosebery Avenue, EC1 (© **020/7863-8198;** www.sadlerswells.com; Tube: Northern Line to Angel), is London's premier venue for dance and opera. It occupies the site of a series of theaters, the first built in 1683. In the early 1990s, the turn-of-the-20th-century theater was mostly demolished, and construction began on an innovative new design completed at the end of 1998, which can change its interior shape, size, and mood for almost any performance. The theater offers classical ballet, modern dance of all degrees of "avant-garde-ness," and children's theatrical productions, including a Christmas ballet. Performances are usually at 7:30pm. The box office is open Monday to Saturday from 9am to 8:30pm. Tickets range from £10 to £70.

CLASSICAL MUSIC & OPERA The Royal Ballet and the Royal Opera perform at the **Royal Opera House,** Bow Street, Covent Garden, WC2 (© **0871/663-2587;** www.royalopera.org; Tube: Covent Garden). Performances of the Royal Opera are usually sung in the original language, but supertitles are projected. The Royal Ballet, which ranks with top companies such as the Kirov and the Paris Opera Ballet, performs a repertory with a tilt toward the classics, including works by its earlier choreographer-directors Sir Frederick Ashton and Sir Kenneth MacMillan. Tickets are £6 to £200.

London Coliseum, St. Martin's Lane, WC2 (© **0871/911-0200;** www.eno.org; Tube: Charing Cross or Leicester Sq.), is the city's largest and most splendid theater. The English National Opera performs a range of works here, from classics to Gilbert and Sullivan to new experimental works. Tickets range from £10 on the balcony to £26 to £110 for upper or dress circle or stalls; about 100 discount balcony tickets are sold on the day of performance from 10am.

Royal Albert Hall, Kensington Gore, SW7 2AP (© **020/7589-8212;** www.royalalberthall.com; Tube: South Kensington), is the annual setting for the BBC Henry Wood Promenade Concerts, known as "the Proms," an annual series that lasts for 8 weeks between mid-July and mid-September. The Proms, incorporating a medley of rousing, mostly British orchestral music, have been a British tradition since 1895. Although most of the audience occupies reserved seats, true aficionados usually opt for standing room in the orchestra pit, with close-up views of the musicians on stage. Newly commissioned works are often premièred here. Tickets range from £5 to £150, depending on the event.

Across Waterloo Bridge rises the **Royal Festival Hall,** on the South Bank, SE1 (© **0871/663-2500,** box office; www.southbankcentre.co.uk; Tube: Waterloo or Embankment). Here are three of the most comfortable and acoustically perfect concert halls in the world: Royal Festival Hall, Queen Elizabeth Hall, and the Purcell Room. Together they host more than 1,200 concerts per year. Tickets are £8 to £80.

THE CLUB & MUSIC SCENE

JAZZ & BLUES Although less plush and expensive than some jazz clubs, **100 Club,** 100 Oxford St., W1 (✆ **020/7636-0933;** www.the100club.co.uk; Tube: Tottenham Court Rd. or Oxford Circus), is a serious contender on the music front, with presentations of some remarkably good jazz. Its cavalcade of bands includes the best British jazz musicians and some of their Yankee brethren. Rock, R & B, and blues are also on tap. Open Monday to Thursday and Sunday 7:30 to 11:30pm; Friday noon to 3pm and 8:30pm to 2am; and Saturday 7:30pm to 1am. The cover ranges from £6 to £30.

Inquire about jazz in London, and people immediately think of **Ronnie Scott's Jazz Club,** 47 Frith St., W1 (✆ **020/7439-0747;** www.ronniescotts.co.uk; Tube: Leicester Sq. or Piccadilly Circus), the European vanguard for modern jazz. Only the best English and American combos, often fronted by top-notch vocalists, are booked here. In the main room, you can watch the show from the bar or sit at a table, at which you can order dinner. The downstairs bar is more intimate; among the regulars at your elbow may be some of the world's most talented musicians. The club is open Monday to Saturday 6pm to 3am, Sunday 6pm to midnight. Reservations are recommended. Tickets run from £5 to £50, depending on the event.

DANCE CLUBS **Bar Rumba,** 36 Shaftesbury Ave., W1 (✆ **020/7287-6933;** www.barrumba.co.uk; Tube: Piccadilly Circus), is a Latin bar and music club that could be featured in a book of underground London, despite its location on Shaftesbury Avenue. It leans toward radical jazz-fusion on some nights and phat funk on other occasions. It boasts two full bars and a different musical theme every night. On weeknights, you have to be 18 or older; on Saturday and Sunday, you have to be 21 and over to be allowed in. Cover ranges from £4 to £20 (free Sat before 10pm).

THE GAY & LESBIAN SCENE

Time Out also carries listings on gay and lesbian clubs.

Adjacent to one of Covent Garden's best-known junctions, the **Box,** 32–34 Monmouth St. (at Seven Dials), WC2 (✆ **020/7240-5828;** www.boxbar.com; Tube: Leicester Sq.), is a sophisticated Mediterranean-style bar that attracts all kinds of men. In the afternoon, it is primarily a restaurant, serving meal-size salads, club sandwiches, and soups. Food service ends abruptly at 5pm, after which the place reveals its core: a cheerful, popular rendezvous for London's gay and counterculture crowds. The Box considers itself a "summer bar," throwing open doors and windows to a cluster of outdoor tables at the slightest hint of sunshine. Open Monday to Saturday 11am to 11:30pm and Sunday 11am to 11pm.

First Out Café Bar, 52 St. Giles High St., W1 (✆ **020/7240-8042;** www.firstoutcafebar.com; Tube: Tottenham Court Rd.), prides itself on being London's first (est. 1986) all-gay coffee shop. Set in a 19th-century building whose wood panels have been painted the colors of the gay-liberation rainbow, the bar and cafe are not particularly cruisy. Menu items are exclusively vegetarian. Don't expect a raucous atmosphere—some clients come here with their grandmothers. First Out is open Monday to Saturday 10am to 11pm and Sunday 11am to 10:30pm.

THE pub-crawl, LONDON STYLE

Dropping into the local pub for a pint of real ale or bitter is the best way to soak up the character of the different villages that make up London. You'll hear the accents and slang and see firsthand how far removed upper-crust Kensington is from blue-collar Wapping. Catch the local gossip or football talk and, of course, enjoy some of the finest ales, stouts, ciders, and malt whiskeys in the world.

Central London is awash with wonderful historic pubs as rich and varied as the city itself. The **Cittie of Yorke,** 22 High Holborn, WC1 (✆ **020/7242-7670;** Tube: Holborn or Chancery Lane), boasts the longest bar in Britain, rafters ascending to the heavens, and a long row of immense wine vats, all of which give it the air of a great medieval hall—appropriate since a pub has existed at this location since 1430. Samuel Smiths is on tap, and the bar offers novelties such as chocolate-orange-flavored vodka.

Dickens once hung out in the **Lamb & Flag,** 33 Rose St., off Garrick Street, WC2 (✆ **020/7497-9504;** Tube: Leicester Sq.), and the room itself is little changed from the days when he prowled this neighborhood. The pub has an amazing and somewhat scandalous history. John Dryden was almost killed by a band of thugs outside its doors in December 1679; the pub gained the nickname the "Bucket of Blood" during the Regency era (1811–20) because of the routine bare-knuckled prizefights that broke out. Tap beers include Courage Best, Courage Directors, Old Speckled Hen, John Smith's, and Wadworth 6X.

The **Nags Head,** 10 James St., WC2 (✆ **020/7836-4678;** Tube: Covent Garden), is one of London's most famous Edwardian pubs. In days of yore, patrons had to make their way through lorries of fruit and flowers to drink here. Today, the pub is patronized mainly by young people. The draft Guinness is very good. Lunch is typical pub grub: sandwiches, salads, pork cooked in cider, and garlic prawns. Snacks are available in the afternoon.

The snug little **Dog & Duck,** 18 Bateman St., corner of Frith Street, W1 (✆ **020/7494-0697;** Tube: Tottenham Court Rd. or Leicester Sq.), a Soho landmark, is the most intimate pub in London. One former patron was author George Orwell, who came here to celebrate his sales of *Animal Farm* in the United States. A wide mixture of patrons of all ages and persuasions flock here, chatting amiably while ordering the delights of Tetleys or Timothy Taylor Landlord. If business warrants it, the cozy upstairs bar is opened.

THE BAR SCENE

Bartok, 78–79 Chalk Farm Rd. (opposite the Roundhouse), NW1 (✆ **020/7916-0595;** Tube: Chalk Farm), has been around for about a decade, but still isn't very well known—and it should be. It's the hippest bar in Camden, specializing in classical music (of all things) and named for the Hungarian composer Béla Bartók. It's been called the ultimate chill-out bar in London, ideal for a romantic evening regardless of your sexual persuasion. Crystal chandeliers and the flicker of candles set the rather decadent, hedonistic mood. Visitors sprawl out on tapestry-covered couches, enjoying actual conversation, the music, the food, the drink, and each other. Open Monday to Thursday 5pm to 3am, Friday 5pm to 4am, Saturday 1pm to 4am, and Sunday 1pm to 3am.

If you're looking for a hot singles bar that attracts a crowd in their 20s and 30s, it's hard to beat the Portobello joint, **Beach Blanket Babylon,** 45 Ledbury Rd., W11 (✆ **020/7229-2907;** www.beachblanket.co.uk; Tube: Notting Hill Gate). The decor is a bit wacky, no doubt designed by an aspiring Salvador Dalí who decided to make it a fairy-tale grotto (or was he going for a medieval dungeon look?). It's close to the Portobello Market. Friday and Saturday nights are the hot, crowded times for bacchanalian revelry. Open daily noon to midnight.

Perhaps the best mixologists in London are found right in the heart of the city at **Lab,** 12 Old Compton St., W1 (✆ **020/7437-7820;** www.lab-townhouse.com; Tube: Leicester Sq.), a '70s kitsch-inspired cocktail bar. Come here for the ultimate in intoxication, hanging out in an interior of leather and Formica spread over two floors. A thick cocktail book lies on every table; if you're in London long enough you may want to work your way through all the drinks from the classic to house specialties. In a glam, glossy setting, DJs keep the mood relaxed. Open Monday to Saturday 4pm to midnight and Sunday 4 to 10:30pm.

Day Trips from London

HAMPTON COURT PALACE ★★★ On the north side of the Thames, 21km (13 miles) west of London in East Molesey, Surrey, this 16th-century palace of Cardinal Wolsey can teach us a lesson: Don't try to outdo your boss, particularly if he happens to be Henry VIII. The rich cardinal did just that. He eventually lost his fortune, power, and prestige—and he ended up giving his lavish palace to the Tudor monarch. Although the palace enjoyed prestige and pomp in Elizabethan days, it owes much of its present look to William and Mary—or rather to Christopher Wren, who designed and built the Northern or Lion Gates. You can parade through the apartments today, filled as they are with porcelain, furniture, paintings, and tapestries. The Renaissance Gallery is graced with paintings by Old Masters on loan from Queen Elizabeth II.

Hampton Court (✆ **0844/752-7777;** www.hrp.org.uk) is easily accessible. Frequent trains run from Waterloo Station (Network Southeast) to Hampton Court Station (✆ **0845/748-4950**). Once at the station, buses will take you the rest of the way to the palace. If you're driving from London, take the A308 to the junction with the A309 on the north side of Kingston Bridge over the Thames.

Admission to Hampton Court is £14 adults, £11.50 students and seniors, £7 children 5 to 15, free for children 4 and under, £38 family. Gardens are open year-round daily from 7am to dusk (no later than 9pm); admission is free to all except Privy Garden (admission £4.60 adults, free for children 14 and under) without a palace ticket during summer months. Cloisters, courtyards, state apartments, great kitchen, cellar, and Hampton Court exhibition are open March to October daily from 10am to 6pm; November to February daily from 10am to 4:30pm.

WINDSOR CASTLE ★★★ William the Conqueror first ordered a castle built on this location, and, since his day, it has been a fateful spot for English sovereigns: King John cooled his heels at Windsor while waiting to put his signature on the Magna Carta at nearby Runnymede; Charles I was imprisoned here before losing his head; Queen Bess did some renovations; Victoria mourned her beloved Albert, who died at the castle in 1861; the royal family rode out much of World War II behind its sheltering walls; and when Queen Elizabeth II is in residence, the Royal Standard flies. With 1,000 rooms, Windsor is the world's largest inhabited castle.

The apartments display many works of art, armor, three Verrio ceilings, and several 17th-century Gibbons carvings. Several works by Rubens adorn the King's Drawing Room. In the relatively small King's Dressing Room is a Dürer, along with Rembrandt's portrait of his mother and Van Dyck's triple portrait of Charles I. Of the apartments, the grand reception room, with its Gobelin tapestries, is the most spectacular.

Queen Mary's Dolls' House is a palace in perfect miniature. The Dolls' House was given to Queen Mary in 1923. It was a gift of members of the royal family, including the king, along with contributions made by some 1,500 tradesmen, artists, and authors.

St. George's Chapel is a gem of the Perpendicular style; this chapel shares the distinction with Westminster Abbey of being a pantheon of English monarchs (Victoria is a notable exception). The present St. George's was founded in the late 15th century by Edward IV on the site of the original Chapel of the Order of the Garter (Edward III, 1348).

It is recommended that you take a free guided tour of the castle grounds, including the Jubilee Gardens. Guides are very well informed and recapture the rich historical background of the castle.

Windsor Castle (✆ **01753/83118;** www.royalcollection.org.uk) lies 34km (21 miles) west of London; you can reach it in 50 minutes by train from Paddington Station. Admission is £16 adults, £14.50 students and seniors, £9.50 children 16 and younger, £42 family. Except for periods in April, June, and December when the royal family is in residence, the castle is open daily March to October 9:45am to 5:15pm and November to February 9:45am to 4:15pm.

OXFORD & STRATFORD-UPON-AVON

Town & Gown: Oxford ★★

A walk down the long sweep of the High, one of the most striking streets in England; a mug of cider in one of the old student pubs; students in traditional gowns whizzing past on rickety bikes; towers and spires rising majestically; nude swimming at Parson's Pleasure; the roar of a cannon launching the bumping races; a tiny, dusty bookstall, where you can pick up a valuable first edition—romantic Oxford is still here, but to get to it, you have to experience the bustling and crowded city that is also Oxford. You may be surprised by a never-ending stream of buses and the fast-flowing pedestrian traffic. Surrounding the university are suburbs that keep growing, and not in a particularly attractive manner.

At any time of the year, you can enjoy a tour of the colleges. The Oxford Tourist Information Centre (see below) offers guided walking tours daily throughout the year. Just don't mention the other place (Cambridge), and you shouldn't have any trouble.

The city predates the university—in fact, it was a Saxon town in the early part of the 10th century. By the 12th century, Oxford was growing in reputation as a seat of learning, at the expense of Paris, and the first colleges were founded in the 13th century. The story of Oxford is filled with conflicts too complex and detailed to elaborate upon here. Suffice it to say, the relationship between town and gown wasn't as peaceful as it is today.

Ultimately, the test of a great university lies in the caliber of the people it turns out. Oxford can name-drop a mouthful: Roger Bacon, Sir Walter Raleigh, John Donne, Sir Christopher Wren, Samuel Johnson, William Penn, John Wesley, William Pitt, Matthew Arnold, Lewis Carroll, Harold Macmillan, Graham Greene, A. E. Housman, T. E. Lawrence, and many others. Women were not allowed until 1920, but since then many have graduated from Oxford and gone on to fame—Indira Gandhi and Margaret Thatcher both graduated from Somerville College.

ESSENTIALS

GETTING THERE Trains from Paddington Station reach Oxford in 1½ hours. Five trains run every hour. A cheap, same-day round-trip ticket costs £28. For more information, call ✆ **0845/748-4950** or visit **www.nationalrail.co.uk**.

Stagecoach (✆ **01865/772250;** www.stagecoachbus.com) operates the Oxford Tube, with buses leaving London at the rate of three to five per hour, costing £14 one-way or £11 if you're a student.

If you're driving, take the M40 west from London and just follow the signs. Traffic and parking are a disaster in Oxford. However, there are four large park-and-ride parking lots on the north, south, east, and west of the city's ring road, all well marked. Parking is £2 to £2.50 per hour. From 9:30am on and all day Saturday, you pay £2 for a round-trip ticket for a bus ride into the city, which drops you off at St. Aldate's Cornmarket or Queen Street to see the city center. The buses run every 8 to 10 minutes in each direction. There is no service on Sunday. The parking lots are on the Woodstock road near the Peartree traffic circle, on the Botley road toward Farringdon, on the Abingdon road in the southeast, and on the A40 toward London.

VISITOR INFORMATION The **Oxford Tourist Information Centre** is at 15–16 Broad St. (✆ **01865/252200;** www.visitoxford.org). Guided walking tours leave from the center daily (see "Walking Around the Colleges," below). The center is open Monday to Saturday 9:30am to 5pm, and Sunday and bank holidays 10am to 4pm.

GETTING AROUND The **Oxford Bus Company,** 395 Cowley Rd. (✆ **01865/785400;** www.oxfordbus.co.uk), has green Park-and-Ride buses that leave from four parking lots in the city using the north-south or east-west routes. A round-trip ticket costs £2 to £2.50. Their Airline buses are blue and travel to Heathrow and Gatwick. A one-way ticket from Oxford to Heathrow costs £20 for adults, £10 for children ages 5 to 15. A one-way ticket from Oxford to Gatwick costs £25 for adults, £13 for children ages 5 to 15. The company's red local buses cover 15 routes in all suburbs, with a day pass allowing unlimited travel for £6. Weekly and monthly passes are available.

The competition, **Stagecoach,** Unit 4, Horsepath, Cowley (✆ **01865/772250;** www.stagecoachbus.com), uses blue-and-cream minibuses and coaches colored red, blue, and orange. City buses leave from Queen Street in Oxford's city center. A 1-day ticket that allows unlimited travel within Oxford city (called Dayrider) costs £3.50.

WHERE TO STAY

The **Oxford Tourist Information Centre** (✆ **01865/252200;** www.visitoxford.org) operates a year-round room-booking service for a £5 fee, plus a 10% refundable deposit. If you'd like to seek lodgings on your own, the center has a list of accommodations, maps, and guidebooks.

Expensive

Malmaison Oxford Castle ★★ In a TripAdvisor poll of the top 10 quirkiest hotels in the world, the Malmaison in Oxford made the list. Formerly it was for inmates detained at Her Majesty's pleasure, and many aspects of prison life, including barred windows, have been retained. In a converted Victorian building, guest rooms are remodeled "cells" that flank two sides of a large central atrium, a space that rises three stories and is crisscrossed by narrow walkways like in one of those George Raft prison movies of the '30s. The former inmates never had it so good—great beds, mood lighting, power showers, satellite TV, and serious wines. In spite of its former origins, this is a stylish and comfortable place to stay.

3 Oxford Castle, Oxford OXI 1AY. ✆ **01865/268400.** Fax 01845/3654247. www.malmaison.com. 94 units. £170–£240 double; £255–£505 suite. AE, DC, MC, V. Parking (prebooking required) £20. **Amenities:** Restaurant; bar; exercise room; room service. *In room:* TV/DVD, CD player, minibar, Wi-Fi (£10 per 24 hr.).

Old Bank Hotel ★★ The first hotel created in the center of Oxford in 135 years, the Old Bank opened late in 1999 and immediately surpassed the traditional favorite, the Randolph (not reviewed), in style and amenities. Located on Oxford's main street and surrounded by some of its oldest colleges and sights, the building dates back to the 18th century and was indeed once a bank. The hotel currently features a collection of 20th-century British art. The bedrooms are comfortably and elegantly appointed, often opening onto views. A combination of velvet and shantung silk-trimmed linen bedcovers gives the accommodations added style.

92–94 High St., Oxford OX1 4BN. ✆ **01865/799599.** Fax 01865/799598. www.oldbank-hotel.co.uk. 42 units. £230–£270 double; £370 suite. AE, DC, MC, V. Free parking. Bus: 7. **Amenities:** Restaurant; bar; babysitting; room service. *In room:* A/C, TV, CD player, hair dryer, Internet (free).

Old Parsonage Hotel ★★ This extensively renovated hotel, near St. Giles Church and Keble College, looks like an extension of one of the ancient colleges. Originally a 13th-century hospital, it was restored in the early 17th century. In the 20th century, a modern wing was added, and in 1991 it was completely renovated and made into a first-rate hotel. This intimate old hotel is filled with hidden charms such as tiny gardens in its courtyard and on its roof terrace. In this tranquil area of Oxford, you feel like you're living at one of the colleges yourself. The rooms are individually designed but not large; each of them opens onto the private gardens.

1 Banbury Rd., Oxford OX2 6NN. ✆ **01865/310210.** Fax 01865/311262. www.oldparsonage-hotel.co.uk. 30 units. £175–£230 double; £240–£260 suite. AE, DC, MC, V. Free parking. Bus: 7. **Amenities:** Restaurant; bar; room service. *In room:* A/C, TV, hair dryer, Internet (free).

Moderate

Bath Place Hotel ★★ Its owners took these 17th-century weavers' cottages and converted them into a small inn of charm and grace, one of the "secret addresses" of Oxford. Bath Place lies on a cobbled alleyway off Holywell Street in the center of Oxford between New College and Hertford College. Flemish weavers built the cottages around a tiny flagstone courtyard. The Turf Tavern, adjacent to the hotel, is the oldest in Oxford. The site has had a notorious history, especially when it was known as the Spotted Cow, as a center for illicit gambling, bearbaiting, and cockfighting. Thomas Hardy mentioned the cottages in his novel *Jude the Obscure.* The address became a secret hideaway for the married Richard Burton and his mistress, Elizabeth Taylor. Completely refurbished to a high standard, the inn today offers comfortable and well-appointed bedrooms.

4-5 Bath Place, Oxford OX1 3SU. ✆ **01865/791812.** Fax 01865/791834. www.bathplace.co.uk. 13 units. £99–£160 double; £165–£200 family suite. Rates include continental buffet or room-service breakfast. AE, DC, MC, V. Free parking. **Amenities:** Room service. *In room:* TV, minibar, Wi-Fi (free).

Inexpensive

Dial House Three kilometers (1¾ miles) east of the heart of Oxford, beside the main highway leading to London, is this country-style house originally built between 1924 and 1927. Graced with mock Tudor half-timbering and a prominent blue-faced sundial (from which it derives its name), it has cozy and recently renovated rooms. The owners, the Morris family, serve only breakfast in their bright dining room.

25 London Rd., Headington, Oxford, Oxfordshire OX3 7RE. ✆ **01865/425100.** Fax 01865/427388. www.dialhouseoxford.co.uk. 8 units. £80–£85 double; £90–£125 family room. Rates include English breakfast. AE, MC, V. Free parking. Bus: 2, 7, 7A, 7B, or 22. *In room:* TV, hair dryer, no phone, Wi-Fi (free).

WHERE TO DINE

Very Expensive

Le Manoir aux Quat' Saisons ★★★ MODERN FRENCH Some 19km (12 miles) southeast of Oxford, Le Manoir aux Quat' Saisons offers the finest cuisine in the Midlands. The gray-and-honey-colored stone manor house, originally built by a Norman nobleman in the early 1300s, has attracted many famous visitors. Today, the restaurant's connection with France has been masterfully revived by the Gallic owner and chef, Raymond Blanc. The menu is adjusted to take advantage of the best produce in any season. The best-loved dishes at Le Manoir are smoked haddock soup with sea bass tartare and caviar as a starter, followed by Cornish red mullet with a fricassee of squid. Other options include the slow-roasted aromatic Cornish turbot; the roast Gressingham duck breast with a confit of yuzu fruit; and the braised Cornish brill with scallops and wild asparagus.

Accommodations are also available. Each very pricey room—rates are £460 to £670 for a double, £815 to £970 for a suite—is decorated with luxurious beds and linens, ruffled canopies, and antiques reproductions.

Church Rd., Great Milton, Oxfordshire. ✆ **800/237-1236** in the U.S., or 01844/278881. Fax 01844/278847. www.manoir.com. Reservations required. All main courses £41; lunch *menu du jour* £53. AE, DC, MC, V. Daily noon–2:30pm and 7–10pm. Take exit 7 off M40 and head along A329 toward Wallingford; look for signs for Great American Milton Manor about 1.6km (1 mile) after.

Expensive

Cherwell Boathouse Restaurant ★ FRENCH/MODERN ENGLISH An Oxford landmark on the River Cherwell, this restaurant is owned by Anthony Verdin, who is assisted by a young crew. With an intriguing fixed-price menu, the cooks change the fare every 2 weeks to take advantage of the availability of fresh vegetables, fish, and meat. There is a very reasonable, even exciting, wine list. The success of the main dishes is founded on savory treats such as pork belly with a foie gras terrine, crispy pork cutlets with a Provençal sauce, or perhaps confit of duck in a port sauce. A special treat is the grilled gray mullet with ratatouille accompanied by a basil-and-chili sauce. For dessert, indulge in the lemon-and-almond roulade. The style is sophisticated yet understated, with a heavy reliance on quality ingredients that are cooked in such a way that natural flavors are always preserved.

Bardwell Rd. ✆ **01865/552746.** www.cherwellboathouse.co.uk. Reservations recommended. Main courses £15–£22; fixed-price dinner from £15; Mon–Fri set lunch £19. AE, MC, V. Daily noon–2:30pm and 6–9:30pm. Closed Dec 24–30. Bus: Banbury Rd.

Fishers ★★ SEAFOOD Oxford's best fish restaurant has a predictable interior decorated with a nautical theme, with "porthole" windows and red sails fluttering in the breeze. The fish always tastes remarkably fresh, even though Oxford is inland. A long list of starters includes everything from a seafood bouillabaisse to deep-fried whitebait. You can also both hot and cold shellfish platters (including Irish rock oysters served over ice). Canadian lobster is flown in, but the traditional favorite of students is haddock and chips. Black mussels from the Scottish Highlands, succulent turbot from Wales, and red mullet caught by Cornish fishermen round out the menu.

36–37 St. Clement's St. ✆ **01865/243003.** www.fishers-restaurant.com. Reservations required. Main courses £14–£22. MC, V. Mon–Sat noon–2:30pm and 6–10:30pm; Sun 12:30–3pm and 6–10pm.

Moderate

Gee's Restaurant ★ MEDITERRANEAN/INTERNATIONAL This restaurant, in a spacious Victorian glass conservatory, was converted from what, for 80 years, was the leading florist of Oxford. Its original features were retained by the owners, who also run both the Old Bank and the Old Parsonage hotels (see above), who have turned it into one of the most nostalgic and delightful places to dine in the city. Based on fine ingredients and a skilled preparation, the meals are likely to include smoked eel with horseradish potatoes or lamb sweetbreads with pearl barley, perhaps deep-fried haddock and chips with a warm caper sauce. A good dessert choice is the lemon tart with blackberries.

61 Banbury Rd. ✆ **01865/553540.** www.gees-restaurant.co.uk. Reservations recommended. Main courses £15–£22; fixed-price 2-course menu £22; fixed-price 3-course menu £25; set lunch and pre-theater menu £14–£17. AE, MC, V. Mon–Sat noon–2:30pm; Sun noon–3:30pm; daily 6–10:30pm.

Inexpensive

Al-Shami LEBANESE Expect a clientele of local residents at this Lebanese restaurant, and a formally dressed Arabic- and English-speaking staff wearing black trousers, bow ties, and white vests. Many diners don't go beyond the appetizers because they comprise more than 40 delectable hot and cold selections—everything from falafel to a salad made with lamb's brains. Chargrilled chopped lamb, chicken, or fish constitute most of the main-dish selections. Vegetarian meals are also available.

25 Walton Crescent. ✆ **01865/310066.** www.al-shami.co.uk. Reservations recommended. Main courses £6.20–£12. MC, V. Daily noon–midnight.

WALKING AROUND THE COLLEGES

The best way to get a running commentary on the important sights is to take a 2-hour **walking tour** through the city and the major colleges. The tours leave daily from the Oxford Tourist Information Centre, 15–16 Broad St. (✆ **01865/252200;** www.visitoxford.org), at 11am, 1pm, and 2pm. Tours costs £7 for adults and £3.75 for children 15 and younger; the tours do not include New College or Christ Church.

AN OVERVIEW For a bird's-eye view of the city and colleges, climb **Carfax Tower ★**, located in the center of the city. This structure is distinguished by its clock and figures that strike on the quarter-hour. Carfax Tower is all that remains from St. Martin's Church, where William Shakespeare once stood as godfather for William Davenant, who also became a successful playwright. A church stood on this site from 1032 to 1896. The tower used to be higher, but after 1340 it was lowered, following complaints from the university to Edward III that townspeople threw stones and fired arrows at students during town-and-gown disputes. Admission is £2.10 for adults, £1 for children. The tower is open year-round, except from Christmas Eve to January 1. April to October, hours are 10am to 5:30pm daily. Off-season hours are Monday to Saturday 10am to 3pm. Children 4 and younger are not admitted. For information, call ✆ **01865/792653.**

CHRIST CHURCH ★★ ☺ Begun by Cardinal Wolsey as Cardinal College in 1525, Christ Church (✆ **01865/276492;** www.chch.ox.ac.uk), known as the House, was founded by Henry VIII in 1546. Facing St. Aldate's Street, Christ Church has the largest quadrangle of any college in Oxford. Tom Tower houses Great Tom, an 18,000-pound bell. It rings at 9:05pm nightly, signaling the closing of the college gates. The 101 times it peals originally signified the number of students in residence at the time the college was founded. There are some portraits in the 16th-century Great Hall, including works by Gainsborough and Reynolds. There's also a separate portrait gallery.

The college chapel was constructed over a period of centuries, beginning in the 12th century. (Incidentally, it's not only the college chapel but also the cathedral of the diocese of Oxford.) The cathedral's most distinguishing features are its Norman pillars and the vaulting of the choir, dating from the 15th century. In the center of the great quadrangle is a statue of Mercury mounted in the center of a fishpond. Many of the Hogwarts scenes from the Harry Potter films have been shot here, making this a popular stop for kids of all ages. The college is open Monday to Saturday 9am to 5pm, Sunday 1 to 5pm, charging £6 for adults or £4.50 for students and seniors; free for children 4 and under.

MAGDALEN COLLEGE Pronounced *Maud*-lin, Magdalen College, High Street (✆ **01865/276000;** www.magd.ox.ac.uk), was founded in 1458 by William of Waynflete, bishop of Winchester and later chancellor of England. Its alumni range from Wolsey to Wilde. Opposite the botanic garden, the oldest in England, is the bell tower, where the choristers sing in Latin at dawn on May Day. Charles I, his days numbered, watched the oncoming Roundheads from this tower. Visit the 15th-century chapel, in spite of many of its latter-day trappings. Ask when the hall and other places of special interest are open. The grounds of Magdalen are the most extensive of any Oxford college; there's even a deer park. From July to September it is open daily noon to 6pm; from October to June daily 1 to 6pm. Admission is £4 adults; £3 seniors, students, and children.

MERTON COLLEGE ★★ Founded in 1264, Merton College, Merton Street (✆ **01865/276310;** www.merton.ox.ac.uk), is among the three oldest colleges at the university. It stands near Corpus Christi College on Merton Street, the sole survivor of Oxford's medieval cobbled streets. Merton College is noted for its library, built between 1371 and 1379, which is said to be the oldest college library in England. Though a tradition once kept some of its most valuable books chained, now only one book is secured in that manner to illustrate that historical custom. One of the library's treasures is an astrolabe (an astronomical instrument used for measuring

CALLING ON CHURCHILL AT blenheim palace

Just 13km (8 miles) northwest of Oxford stands the extravagantly baroque **Blenheim Palace** ★★★ (✆ **08700/602080;** www.blenheimpalace.com), England's answer to Versailles. Blenheim is the home of the 11th duke of Marlborough, descendant of the first duke John Churchill, once an on-again, off-again favorite of Queen Anne's. In his day (1650–1722), the first duke became the supreme military figure in Europe. Fighting on the Danube near a village named Blenheim, Churchill defeated the forces of Louis XIV, and the lavish palace of Blenheim was built for the duke as a gift from the queen. It was designed by Sir John Vanbrugh, who was also the architect of Castle Howard; the landscaping was created by Capability Brown.

The palace is loaded with riches: antiques, porcelain, oil paintings, tapestries, and chinoiserie. North Americans know Blenheim as the birthplace of Sir Winston Churchill. The room in which he was born is included in the palace tour, as is the Churchill exhibition: four rooms of letters, books, photographs, and other relics. Today, the former prime minister lies buried in Bladon Churchyard, near the palace. Blenheim Palace is open from 10:30am to 5:30pm; last admission is at 4:45pm. Admission is £18 adults, £14.50 students and seniors, £10 children 5–15, £48 family ticket, free for children 4 and younger. If you're driving, take the A-44 from Oxford; otherwise, the S3 bus (✆ **01865/772250;** www.stagecoachbus.com) leaves Oxford about every 30 minutes during the day for the half-hour trip.

the altitude of the sun and stars) thought to have belonged to Chaucer. You pay £2 to visit the ancient library as well as the Max Beerbohm Room (the satirical English caricaturist who died in 1956). Call ahead for information. The library and college are open Monday to Friday 2 to 4pm, and Saturday and Sunday 10am to 4pm. It's closed for 1 week at Easter and Christmas and on weekends during the winter.

THE SHOPPING SCENE

In its way, **Alice's Shop,** 83 St. Aldate's (✆ **01865/723793;** www.aliceinwonderlandshop.co.uk), played an important role in English literature. Set within a 15th-century building that has housed some kind of shop since 1820, it functioned as a general store (selling brooms, hardware, and the like) during the period that Lewis Carroll, at the time a professor of mathematics at Christ Church College, was composing *Alice in Wonderland.* It is believed to have been the model for important settings within the book. Today, the place is a favorite stopover of Lewis Carroll fans from as far away as Japan, who gobble up commemorative pencils, chess sets, party favors, bookmarks, and, in rare cases, original editions of some of Carroll's works.

The **Bodleian Library Shop,** Old School's Quadrangle, Radcliffe Square, Broad Street (✆ **01865/277091;** www.shop.bodley.ox.ac.uk), specializes in Oxford souvenirs, from books and paperweights to Oxford banners and coffee mugs.

Castell & Son (The Varsity Shop), 13 Broad St. (✆ **01865/244000;** www.varsityshop.co.uk), is the best outlet in Oxford for clothing emblazoned with the

Oxford logo or heraldic symbol. Choices include both whimsical and dead-on-serious neckties, hats, T-shirts, pens, beer and coffee mugs, and cuff links. It's commercialized Oxford, but it's still got a sense of relative dignity and style. A second location is at 109–114 High St. (✆ **01865/249491**).

Stratford-upon-Avon ★★

Crowds of tourists overrun this market town on the River Avon during the summer. In fact, today, Stratford aggressively hustles its Shakespeare connection—everybody seems to be in business to make a buck off the Bard. However, the throngs dwindle in winter, when you can at least walk on the streets and seek out the places of genuine historical interest.

Aside from the historic sites, the major draw for visitors is the **Royal Shakespeare Theatre,** where Britain's foremost actors perform during a long season that lasts from April to November. Other than the theater, Stratford is rather devoid of any rich cultural life, and you may want to rush back to London after you've seen the literary pilgrimage sights and watched a production of *Hamlet*. But Stratford-upon-Avon is also a good center for side trip to Warwick Castle (see "A Visit to Warwick Castle," later in this chapter).

ESSENTIALS

GETTING THERE The journey from London to Stratford-upon-Avon takes about 2¼ hours, and a round-trip ticket costs £28 to £69 depending on the train. For schedules and information, call ✆ **0845/748-4950,** or go to **www.nationalrail.co.uk**. The train station at Stratford is on Alcester Road.

Four **National Express** buses a day leave from London's Victoria Station, with a trip time of 3¼ hours. A single-day round-trip ticket costs £19. For schedules and information, call ✆ **0871/781-81-81** (www.nationalexpress.co.uk).

If you're driving from London, take the M40 toward Oxford and continue to Stratford-upon-Avon on the A34.

VISITOR INFORMATION The **Tourist Information Centre,** Bridgefoot, Stratford-upon-Avon, Warwickshire CV37 6GW (✆ **0870/160-7930;** www.shakespeare-country.co.uk), provides any details you may wish to know about the Shakespeare houses and properties, and will assist in booking rooms. They also operate a Thomas Cook currency-exchange office (✆ **01789/269750**). It's open April to September Monday to Saturday 9am to 5:30pm and Sunday 10am to 4pm, and October to March Monday to Saturday 9am to 5pm and Sunday 10am to 3pm.

To contact **Shakespeare Birthplace Trust,** which administrates many of the attractions, call the Shakespeare Centre (✆ **01789/204016;** www.shakespeare.org.uk).

WHERE TO STAY

Very Expensive

Menzies Welcombe Hotel Spa & Golf Club ★★★ For a formal, historic hotel in Stratford, there's nothing better than the Welcombe. One of England's great Jacobean country houses, this hotel is a 10-minute ride from the heart of Stratford-upon-Avon. Its key feature is an 18-hole golf course. It's surrounded by 63 hectares (156 acres) of grounds and has a formal entrance on Warwick Road, a winding driveway leading to the main hall. Bedrooms are luxuriously furnished in traditional

Jacobean style, with fine antiques and elegant fabrics. Most bedrooms are seemingly big enough for tennis matches, but those in the garden wing, although comfortable, are small. Some of the bedrooms are sumptuously furnished with elegant four-posters.

Warwick Rd., Stratford-upon-Avon, Warwickshire CV37 0NR. ✆ **01789/295252.** Fax 01789/414666. www.menzies-hotels.co.uk. 78 units. £161–£270 double; £250–£6,000 suite. Rates include English breakfast. AE, DC, MC, V. Free parking. Take A439 2km (1¼ miles) northeast of the town center. **Amenities:** 2 restaurants; bar; golf course; gym w/aerobics studio; indoor heated pool; room service; spa; tennis court. *In room:* TV, hair dryer, Wi-Fi (£10).

Expensive

Macdonald Alveston Manor Hotel ★★ This Tudor manor is perfect for theatergoers—it's just a 5-minute walk from the theaters. The hotel has a wealth of chimneys and gables, and everything from an Elizabethan gazebo to Queen Anne windows. Mentioned in the Domesday Book, the building predates the arrival of William the Conqueror. The rooms in the manor will appeal to those who appreciate the old-world charm of slanted floors, overhead beams, and antique furnishings. Some triples or quads are available in the modern section, connected by a covered walk through the rear garden. Most rooms here are original and have built-in walnut furniture and a color-coordinated decor. You can live in luxury in the original rooms with their walnut furniture or be assigned a rather routine standard twin that, though comfortable, will lack romance.

Clopton Bridge (off B4066), Stratford-upon-Avon, Warwickshire CV37 7HP. ✆ **0844/879-9138.** Fax 01789/414095. www.macdonaldhotels.co.uk. 113 units. £137–£153 double; £179–£239 suite. Rates include breakfast. AE, MC, V. Free parking. **Amenities:** Restaurant; bar; babysitting; exercise room; indoor heated pool; room service; sauna; spa. *In room:* TV, hair dryer, minibar, Wi-Fi (£12 per day).

Moderate

Legacy Falcon This inn blends the very old and the very new. The black-and-white timbered inn was licensed a quarter of a century after Shakespeare's death; connected to its rear by a glass passageway is a more sterile bedroom extension added in 1970. In the heart of Stratford, the inn faces the Guild Chapel and the New Place Gardens. The recently upgraded rooms in the older section have oak beams, diamond leaded-glass windows, antiques, and good reproductions. In the inn's intimate Merlin Lounge, you'll find an open copper-hooded fireplace where fires are stoked under beams salvaged from old ships.

Chapel St., Stratford-upon-Avon, Warwickshire CV37 6HA. ✆ **0844/411-9005.** Fax 0844/411-9006. www.legacy-hotels.co.uk. 83 units. £75–£150 double; from £165 suite. AE, DC, MC, V. Free parking. **Amenities:** 2 restaurants; 2 bars; room service; Wi-Fi (free). *In room:* TV, hair dryer, Internet (free).

Mercure Shakespeare Hotel ★★ Filled with historical associations, the original core of this hotel, dating from the 1400s, has seen many additions in its long life. Quieter and plusher than the Falcon (see above), it is equaled in the central core of Stratford only by the Macdonald Alveston Manor (see above). Residents relax in the post-and-timber-studded public rooms, within sight of fireplaces and playbills from 19th-century productions of Shakespeare's plays. Bedrooms are named in honor of noteworthy actors, Shakespeare's plays, or Shakespearean characters. The oldest are capped with hewn timbers, and all have modern comforts. Even the newer accommodations are at least 40 to 50 years old and have rose-and-thistle patterns carved into many of their exposed timbers. Bathrooms range in size.

Stratford-upon-Avon

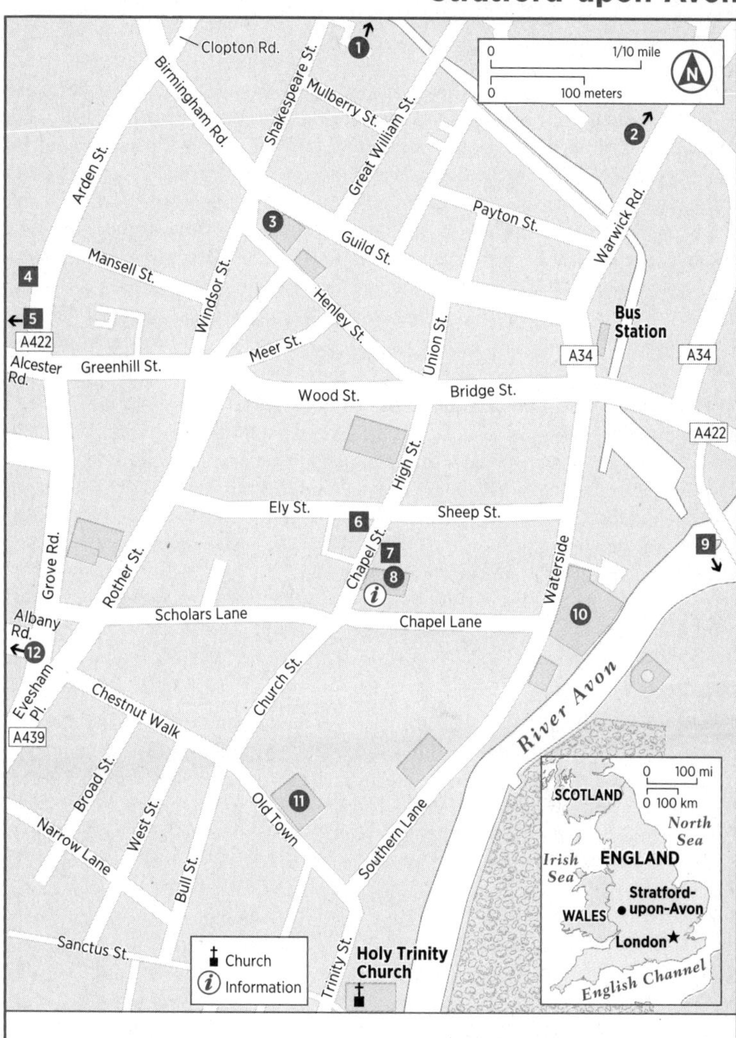

ATTRACTIONS ●

Anne Hathaway's Cottage **12**
Hall's Croft **11**
Mary Arden's House (Glebe Farm)/Palmer's Farm **1**
New Place/Nash's House **8**
Royal Shakespeare Theatre **10**
Shakespeare's Birthplace **3**

ACCOMMODATIONS ■

Heron Lodge **5**
Legacy Falcon **6**
Macdonald Alveston Manor Hotel **9**
Menzies Welcombe Hotel Spa & Golf Club **2**
Mercure Shakespeare Hotel **7**
The Stratford **4**

Chapel St., Stratford-upon-Avon, Warwickshire CV37 6ER. © **01789/294997.** Fax 01789/415411. www.mercure.com. 74 units. £100–£217 double; from £150 suite. Rates include buffet breakfast. Children 12 and under stay free in parent's room. AE, DC, MC, V. Parking £10. **Amenities:** Restaurant; bar; room service. *In room:* A/C, TV, hair dryer, minibar (in some), Wi-Fi (£7 for 2 hr.).

The Stratford ★ This is definitely not one of the atmospheric inns of Stratford-upon-Avon. But if you prefer a modern hotel with up-to-date conveniences, when paying your call on the Bard, the Stratford is for you. It lacks personality but has about everything else. The bedrooms are spaciously and elegantly appointed. Some of the units come with four-poster beds, as in Tudor days, but others are more geared to commercial travelers seeking streamlined conveniences—not romance. The hotel lies only a short walk from the banks of the River Avon. Market-fresh dishes deftly prepared change with the seasons in the on-site Quills Restaurant.

Arden St., Stratford-upon-Avon, Warwickshire CV37 6QQ. © **01789/271000.** Fax 01789/271001. www.qhotels.co.uk. £79–£114 double. AE, DC, MC, V. Free parking. **Amenities:** Restaurant; bar; small exercise room; room service. *In room:* TV, hair dryer, Wi-Fi (2 free hr., £12 per 24 hr.).

Inexpensive

Heron Lodge ★ Bob and Chris Heaps run one of the better B&Bs in Stratford, their lodge lying a kilometer (over half a mile) outside the heart of town. Their midsize bedrooms have individual character, and the furnishings are both tasteful and comfortable. They still practice the old-fashioned custom of an afternoon "cuppa" served in their conservatory. The Heapses serve one of the town's best breakfasts, using local products when available.

260 Alcester Rd., Stratford-upon-Avon, Warwickshire CV37 9JQ. © **01789/299169.** www.heronlodge.com. 5 units. £58–£88 double. Rates include English breakfast. MC, V. Free parking. *In room:* TV, hair dryer, Internet (free), no phone.

WHERE TO DINE

Lambs ★ CONTINENTAL/ENGLISH A stone's throw from the Royal Shakespeare Theatre, this cafe-bistro is housed in a building dating from 1547 (and with connections to Lewis Carroll). For a quick, light meal or pre-theater dinner, it's ideal. The menu changes monthly. Begin with such starters as an English muffin with smoked haddock and creamed leeks, or else Serrano ham with fresh figs and a basil salad. Then you can tuck into such mains as filet of Scottish beef with portobello mushrooms, rack of Cornish lamb with dauphinoise potatoes, or perhaps roast Gressingham duck with Puy lentils. For dessert, why not the dark-chocolate truffle cake with white-chocolate ice cream? Look to the blackboard for daily specials. The chef takes chances (no doubt inspired by trips to the Continent), and it's a nice departure from the bland tearoom food served for decades in Stratford.

12 Sheep St. © **01789/292554.** www.lambsrestaurant.co.uk. Reservations required for dinner Fri–Sat. Main courses £10–£16; fixed-price menu £17 for 2 courses, £20 for 3 courses. MC, V. Mon 5:30–10pm; Tues–Sat noon–2pm and 5–10pm; Sun noon–2:30pm.

Malbec Petit Bistro ★★ BRITISH/FRENCH Many savvy local foodies cite this as the best restaurant in Stratford-upon-Avon, and we're inclined to agree. The chef and owner, Simon Malin, offers market-fresh and unpretentious cuisine in fashionable surroundings. His produce is fresh, his seasonings are on target, and his imagination is active. On the ground floor is an intimate restaurant of character, and on the lower level is a charming cellar with vaulted ceilings and flagstone floors.

You'll be impressed with such starters as sautéed lamb's kidneys with thyme-roasted onions, or crispy fried squid with almond and a roasted-pepper dipping sauce. You might also savor such mains as rump of local lamb with a butternut-squash gnocchi or free-range pork belly with chorizo sausages and butter beans. Desserts are made fresh daily. How about champagne-laced rhubarb with whipped vanilla shortcake?

6 Union St. ✆ **01789/269106.** www.malbecrestaurant.co.uk. Reservations required. Main courses £10–£17. AE, MC, V. Daily noon–2pm; Mon–Sat 7–9:30pm.

Thai Boathouse ★ THAI The only restaurant set on the Avon, this charming choice is reached by crossing Clopton Bridge toward Oxford and Banbury. The second-floor dining room opens onto vistas of the river. This restaurant, originally established 4 decades ago in Bangkok, has brought spice and zest to Stratford's lazy restaurant scene. The decor comes from Thailand itself, with elephants, woodcarvings, and Buddhas adorning the restaurant. Seasonal specialties, such as wild duck and pheasant, are a special feature of the menu. Fresh produce, great skill in the kitchen, and exquisite presentations are the hallmarks of this restaurant. Sample a selection of authentic Thai appetizers before going on to the delectable main courses, which include stir-fried mixed seafood with fresh chili and sweet Thai basil, or else chicken stir-fried with sweet peppers, pineapple, and onion in a sweet-and-sour sauce.

Swan's Nest Lane. ✆ **01789/297733.** www.thaigroup.co.uk/restaurants/boathouse.html. Reservations recommended. Main courses £3–£16; fixed-price menus £21–£26. MC, V. Daily 5:30–10:30pm; Sun–Fri noon–2:30pm.

PUBS

The Black Swan ("The Dirty Duck") ★★ ENGLISH Affectionately known as the Dirty Duck, this has been a popular hangout for Stratford players since the 18th century. The wall is lined with autographed photos of its many famous patrons. Typical English grills, among other dishes, are featured in the Dirty Duck Grill Room, though no one has ever accused it of serving the best food in Stratford. You'll have a choice of a dozen appetizers, most of which would make a meal themselves. In fair weather, you can have drinks in the front garden and watch the swans glide by on the Avon.

Waterside. ✆ **01789/297312.** Reservations required for dining. Main courses £7–£11; bar snacks £4–£10. AE, DC, MC, V (in restaurant only). Restaurant daily noon–10pm. Bar daily 11am–1am.

The Garrick Inn ENGLISH Near Harvard House, this black-and-white timbered Elizabethan pub has an unpretentious charm. The front bar is decorated with tapestry-covered settles, an old oak refectory table, and an open fireplace that attracts the locals. The back bar has a circular fireplace with a copper hood and mementos of the triumphs of the English stage. The specialty is homemade pies such as steak and kidney or chicken and mushroom. Wild boar and venison are other specialties.

25 High St. ✆ **01789/292186.** Main courses £7–£11. MC, V. Meals Mon–Sat noon–10pm; Sun noon–9:30pm. Pub Mon–Sat 11am–11pm; Sun 11am–10:30pm.

THEATER

On the banks of the Avon, the **Royal Shakespeare Theatre (RST),** Waterside, Stratford-upon-Avon CV37 6BB (✆ **01789/403444;** www.rsc.org.uk), is a major showcase for the Royal Shakespeare Company and seats 1,500 patrons. The theater's season runs from April to November and typically features five Shakespearean plays. The company has some of the finest actors on the British stage.

You usually need **ticket reservations,** with two successive booking periods, each one opening about 2 months in advance. You can pick these up from a North American or English travel agent. A small number of tickets are always held for sale on the day of a performance, but it may be too late to get a good seat if you wait until you arrive in Stratford. Tickets can be booked through **Keith Prowse** (✆ **800/669-8687** in North America, or 0870/840-1111 in England; www.keithprowse.com).

You can also call the **theater box office** directly (✆ **0844/800-1110**) and charge your tickets. The box office is open Monday to Saturday 9am to 8pm, although it closes at 6pm on days when there are no performances. Seat prices range from £5 to £45. You can make a credit card reservation and pick up your tickets on the performance day, but you must cancel at least 1 full week in advance to get a refund.

SHAKESPEARE PILGRIMAGE SIGHTS

Besides the attractions on the periphery of Stratford, many Elizabethan and Jacobean buildings are in town, a number of them administrated by the **Shakespeare Birthplace Trust** (✆ **01789/204016;** www.shakespeare.org.uk). One ticket—costing £17 adults, £15 for seniors and students, and £10.50 for children—lets you visit the five most important sights. You can also buy a family ticket to all five sights (good for two adults and three children) for £45—a good deal. Pick up the ticket if you're planning to do much sightseeing (obtainable at your first stopover at any one of the Trust properties).

Anne Hathaway's Cottage ★ Before she married Shakespeare, Anne Hathaway lived in this thatched, wattle-and-daub cottage in the hamlet of Shottery, 1.6km (1 mile) from Stratford. It's the most interesting and the most photographed of the Trust properties. The Hathaways were yeoman farmers, and their descendants lived in the cottage until 1892. As a result, it was never renovated and provides a rare insight into the life of a family in Shakespearean times. The Bard was only 18 when he married Anne, who was much older. Many original furnishings, including the courting settle (the bench on which Shakespeare is said to have wooed Anne) and various kitchen utensils, are preserved inside the house. After visiting the house, take time to linger in the garden and orchard.

Cottage Lane, Shottery. ✆ **01789/292100.** www.shakespeare.org.uk. Admission £7.50 adults, £6.50 seniors and students, £4.50 children, £19.50 family ticket (2 adults, 3 children). Mar–Oct daily 9am–5pm. Call for winter hours. Take a bus from Bridge St. or walk via a marked pathway from Evesham Place in Stratford across the meadow to Shottery.

Hall's Croft This house is on Old Town Street, not far from the parish church, Holy Trinity. It was here that Shakespeare's daughter Susanna probably lived with her husband, Dr. John Hall. Hall's Croft is an outstanding Tudor house with a walled garden, furnished in the style of a middle-class home of the time. Dr. Hall was widely respected and built up a large medical practice in the area. Fascinating exhibits illustrate the theory and practice of medicine in Dr. Hall's time.

Old Town St. (near Holy Trinity Church). ✆ **01789/292107.** www.shakespeare.org.uk. Admission £12.50 adults, £11.50 seniors and students, £8 children, £33.50 family ticket (2 adults, 3 children). Mar–Oct daily 10am–5pm. Call for winter hours. To reach Hall's Croft, walk west from High St., which becomes Chapel St. and Church St. At the intersection with Old Town St., go left.

Mary Arden's House (Glebe Farm)/Palmer's Farm ★ So what if millions of visitors have been tricked into thinking this timber-framed farmhouse with its old stone dovecote and various outbuildings was the girlhood home of Shakespeare's mother, Mary Arden? It's still one of the most intriguing sights outside Stratford, even if local historian Dr. Nat Alcock discovered in 2000 that the actual childhood home of Arden was the dull-looking brick-built farmhouse, Glebe Farm, next door. Glebe Farm has now been properly renamed Mary Arden's House. It was all the trick of an 18th-century tour guide, John Jordan, who decided Glebe Farm was too unimpressive to be the home of the Bard's mother, so he told tourists it was this farmstead instead. What was known for years as "Mary Arden's House" has been renamed Palmer's Farm. Actually, this farm wasn't constructed until the late 16th century, a little late to be Mary Arden's home. After the name confusion, local authorities have converted Palmer's Farm into a working farm. Visitors can tour the property and see firsthand how a farming household functioned in the 1570s—yes, cows to be milked, bread to be baked, and vegetables cultivated in an authentic 16th-century manner. In the barns, stable, cowshed, and farmyard is an extensive collection of farming implements illustrating life and work in the local countryside from Shakespeare's time to the present.

Wilmcote. ✆ **01789/293455.** www.shakespeare.org.uk. Admission £8.50 adults, £7.50 students and seniors, £5.50 children, £22.50 family ticket. Mar–Oct daily 10am–5pm. Closed Nov–Feb. Take A3400 (Birmingham) for 5.5km (3½ miles).

New Place/Nash's House Shakespeare retired to New Place in 1610 (a prosperous man by the standards of his day) and died here 6 years later. Regrettably, the house was torn down, so only the garden remains. A mulberry tree planted by the Bard was so popular with latter-day visitors to Stratford that the garden's owner chopped it down. It is said that the mulberry tree that grows here today was planted from a cutting of the original tree. You enter the gardens through Nash's House (Thomas Nash married Elizabeth Hall, a granddaughter of the poet). Nash's House has 16th-century period rooms and an exhibition illustrating the history of Stratford. The popular Knott Garden adjoins the site and represents the style of a fashionable Elizabethan garden.

Chapel St. ✆ **01789/292325.** www.shakespeare.org.uk. Admission £12.50 adults, £11.50 seniors and students, £8 children, £33.50 family ticket (2 adults, 3 children). Sept–June daily 9am–5pm; July–Aug daily 9am–6pm. Closed Dec 23–26. Walk west down High St.; Chapel St. is a continuation of High St.

Shakespeare's Birthplace ★ The son of a glover and whittawer (leather worker), the Bard was born on St. George's Day, April 23, 1564, and died on the same date 52 years later. Filled with Shakespeare memorabilia, including a portrait and furnishings of the writer's time, the Trust property is a half-timbered structure, dating from the early 16th century. The house was bought by public donors in 1847 and preserved as a national shrine. You can visit the living room, the bedroom where Shakespeare was probably born, a fully equipped kitchen of the period (look for the "babyminder"), and a Shakespeare museum, illustrating his life and times. Later, you can walk through the garden. You won't be alone: It's estimated that some 660,000 visitors pass through the house annually.

Built next door to commemorate the 400th anniversary of the Bard's birth, the modern **Shakespeare Centre** serves both as the administrative headquarters of the

A VISIT TO WARWICK castle

Perched on a rocky cliff above the River Avon in the town center, **Warwick Castle** ★★★, a stately late-17th-century mansion, is surrounded by a magnificent 14th-century fortress, the finest medieval castle in England. Even 3 hours may not be enough time to see everything. Surrounded by gardens, lawns, and woodland, where peacocks roam freely, and skirted by the Avon, Warwick Castle was described by Sir Walter Scott in 1828 as "that fairest monument of ancient and chivalrous splendor which yet remains uninjured by time."

Ethelfleda, daughter of Alfred the Great, built the first significant fortifications here in 914. William the Conqueror ordered the construction of a motte-and-bailey castle in 1068, 2 years after the Norman Conquest. The mound is all that remains today of the Norman castle, which Simon de Montfort sacked in the Barons' War of 1264.

The Beauchamp family, the most illustrious medieval earls of Warwick, is responsible for the appearance of the castle today; much of the external structure remains unchanged from the mid-14th century. When the castle was granted to Sir Fulke Greville by James I in 1604, he spent £20,000 (an enormous sum in those days) converting the existing castle buildings into a luxurious mansion. The Grevilles have held the earl of Warwick title since 1759.

You can also see the Victorian rose garden, a re-creation of an original design from 1868 by Robert Marnock. Near the rose garden is a Victorian alpine rockery and water garden. Warwick Castle (✆ **0870/442-2000;** www.warwick-castle.co.uk) is open April through September daily from 10am to 6pm; October through March daily from 10am to 5pm. Closed December 25. Admission is £18 adults, £12 seniors, £13 students, £10 children ages 4 to 16, £50 family ticket, free for children 3 and younger.

Trains run frequently between Stratford-upon-Avon and Warwick. A one-way ticket costs around £4.50. Call ✆ **0845/748-4950** for schedules and information. One **Stagecoach** bus, no. 16, departs Stratford-upon-Avon every hour during the day (✆ **01865/772250;** www.stagecoachbus.com). The trip takes roughly half an hour. Call the **tourist office** (✆ **0870/160-7930**) for schedules. **National Express** (✆ **0871/781-81-81;** www.nationalexpress.com) runs four buses daily from the Riverside bus station in Stratford-upon-Avon to Puckerings Lane in Warwick for £1.50. Take the A46 if you're driving from Stratford-upon-Avon.

Birthplace Trust and as a library and study center. An extension houses a visitor center, which acts as a reception area for those coming to the birthplace.

Henley St. (in the town center near the post office, close to Union St.). ✆ **01789/204016.** www.shakespeare.org.uk. Admission £12.50 adults, £11.50 students and seniors, £8 children, £33.50 family ticket (2 adults, 3 children). Sept–June daily 9am–5pm; July–Aug daily 9am–6pm. Closed Dec 23–26.

ORGANIZED TOURS

Guided tours of Stratford-upon-Avon are conducted by **City Sightseeing** (✆ **01789/412680;** www.citysightseeing-stratford.com), Civic Hall, Rother Street. In summer, open-top double-decker buses depart every 15 minutes daily from 9:30am to 6pm. You can take a 1-hour ride without stops, or you can get off at any or all of the town's five Shakespeare properties. Though the bus stops are clearly marked along the historic route, the most logical starting point is the sidewalk in front of the Pen & Parchment Pub, at the bottom of Bridge Street. Tour tickets are valid all day, so you can hop on and off the buses as many times as you want. The tours cost £11 for adults, £9 for seniors or students, and £6 for children 5 to 15 (children 4 and younger ride free). A family ticket sells for £28. Tour frequency depends on the time of the year; call for information.

THE SHOPPING SCENE

Among the many tacky tourist traps are some quality shops, including the ones described below.

Set within an antique house with ceiling beams, the **Shakespeare Bookshop,** 39 Henley St. (✆ **01789/292176;** www.shakespeare.org.uk), across from the Shakespeare Birthplace Centre, is the region's premier source for textbooks and academic treatises on the Bard and his works. It specializes in books for every level of expertise on Shakespearean studies, from picture books for junior high school students to weighty tomes geared to anyone pursuing a Ph.D. in literature.

Everything in the **Pickwick Gallery,** 32 Henley St. (✆ **01789/294861**), is a well-crafted work of art produced by copper or steel engraving plates, or printed by means of a carved wooden block. Hundreds of botanical prints, landscapes, and renderings of artfully arranged ruins, each suitable for framing, can be purchased. Topographical maps of regions of the United Kingdom are also available if you're planning on doing any serious hiking.

Other shopping bets include the **Antique Market** along Ely Street, with some 50 or more stalls selling porcelain, silver, jewelry, and Shakespeare memorabilia. **Antique Arms & Armour,** Poet's Arbour on Sheep Street (✆ **01789/293453**), has the best collection of antique swords and armor, some of it looking like old props from previous Shakespeare productions.

STONEHENGE & BATH

Many visitors with very limited time head for the West Country, where they explore its two major attractions: Stonehenge—the most important prehistoric monument in Britain—and Bath, England's most elegant city, famed for its architecture and its hot springs. If you have the time, you may also want to visit Salisbury Cathedral and the other prehistoric sites in the area, at Avebury and Old Sarum.

Stonehenge ★★★

At the junction of A-303 and A-344/A-360, 3km (1¾ miles) west of Amesbury and about 15km (9⅓ miles) north of Salisbury, stands the renowned monument of Stonehenge, a stone circle believed to be approximately 5,000 years old. This circle of lintels and megalithic pillars is the most important prehistoric monument in Britain.

ESSENTIALS

Getting There

BY CAR To reach Stonehenge from London, head in the direction of Salisbury (see below), 145km (90 miles) to the southwest. Take the M-3 to the end of the run, continuing the rest of the way on A-30. Once at Salisbury, after stopping to view its cathedral (see below), head north on Castle Road. At the first roundabout (traffic circle), take the exit toward Amesbury (A-345) and Old Sarum. Continue along this route for 13km (8 miles) and then turn left onto A-303 in the direction of Exeter. Stonehenge is signposted, leading you up the A-344 to the right. In all, it's about 19km (12 miles) from Salisbury.

BY BUS Once in Salisbury (see below), you can catch a bus to Stonehenge. **Wilts & Dorset** (✆ **01722/336855;** www.wdbus.co.uk) runs several buses daily (depending on demand) from Salisbury to Stonehenge, as well as buses from the Salisbury train station to Stonehenge. The bus trip to Stonehenge takes 40 minutes, and a round-trip ticket costs £11 for adults, £5 for children ages 5 to 15 (4 and younger ride free), £6 seniors, and £15 family ticket.

EXPLORING STONEHENGE

Some visitors are disappointed when they see that Stonehenge is nothing more than concentric circles of stones. But perhaps they don't understand that Stonehenge represents an amazing engineering feat because many of the boulders, the bluestones in particular, were moved many miles (perhaps from southern Wales) to this site.

The widely held view of 18th- and 19th-century Romantics that Stonehenge was the work of the Druids is without foundation. The boulders, many weighing several tons, are believed to have predated the arrival in Britain of the Celtic culture. Controversy surrounds the prehistoric site, especially since the publication of *Stonehenge Decoded,* by Gerald S. Hawkins and John B. White, which maintains that Stonehenge was an astronomical observatory—that is, a Neolithic "computing machine" capable of predicting eclipses.

In 2008, Stonehenge made world headlines when part of its eternal mystery may have been solved. From the beginning, it was a monument to the dead, as revealed by radiocarbon dating from human cremation burials around the brooding stones. The site was used as a cemetery from 3000 B.C. until after the monuments were erected in 2500 B.C. In yet another development, archaeologists uncovered hearths, timbers, and other remains of what was probably the village of workers who erected the monoliths on the Salisbury Plain. These ancient ruins appear to form the largest Neolithic village ever found in Britain. The trenches of this discovery, Durrington Walls, lie 2 miles from Stonehenge.

Your ticket permits you to go inside the fence surrounding the site that protects the stones from vandals and souvenir hunters. You can go all the way up to a short rope barrier, about 15m (50 ft.) from the stones. You can make a full circular tour around Stonehenge. A modular walkway was introduced to cross the archaeologically important avenue, the area that runs between the Heel Stone and the main circle of stones. This enables visitors to complete a full circuit of the stones and to see one of the best views of a completed section of Stonehenge as they pass by, an excellent addition to the informative audio tour.

Admission to Stonehenge (✆ **01980/623108** for information; www.stonehenge.co.uk) is £6.90 adults, £5.90 students and seniors, £3.50 children 5 to 15, £17.30 family. It's open daily June to August from 9am to 7pm, March 16 to May 31 and September to October 15 from 9:30am to 6pm, and October 16 to March 15 from 9:30am to 4pm.

Avebury ★★

Avebury (✆ **01672/539250;** www.english-heritage.org.uk/avebury), one of the largest prehistoric sites in Europe, lies on the Kennet River, 11km (6¾ miles) west of Marlborough and 32km (20 miles) north of Stonehenge. Some say visiting Avebury, in contrast to Stonehenge, is a more organic experience—you can walk right up and around the stones, as no fence keeps you away. Also, the site isn't mobbed with tour buses.

Visitors can walk around the 11-hectare (27-acre) site at Avebury, winding in and out of the circle of more than 100 stones, some weighing up to 50 tons. The stones are made of sarsen, a sandstone found in Wiltshire. Inside this large circle are two smaller ones, each with about 30 stones standing upright. Native Neolithic tribes are believed to have built these circles.

Also here is the **Alexander Keiller Museum,** which houses one of Britain's most important archaeological collections, including material from excavations at Windmill Hill and Avebury, and artifacts from other prehistoric digs at West Kennet, Long Barrow, Silbury Hill, West Kennet Avenue, and the Sanctuary.

Admission to Avebury is free; Alexander Keiller Museum is £4.20 adults, £2.10 children ages 5 to 14, free for children 4 and under, £11 family. Both are open daily April to October 10am to 6pm, and November to March 10am to 4pm.

GETTING THERE Avebury is on A-361, between Swindon and Devizes and 1.5km (1 mile) from the A4 London-Bath road. The closest rail station is at Swindon, 19km (12 miles) away, which is served by the main rail line from London to Bath. For rail information, call ✆ **0845/748-4950** or visit www.nationalrail.co.uk. A limited bus service (no. 49) runs from Swindon to Devizes through Avebury.

Wilts & Dorset (✆ **01722/336855;** www.wdbus.co.uk) has two buses (nos. 5 and 6) that run between the Salisbury bus station and Avebury five times a day Monday through Saturday and three times a day on Sunday. The one-way trip takes 1 hour and 40 minutes. Round-trip tickets are £9 for adults, £7 seniors, £15 family ticket, and £6 for children ages 5 to 14 (4 and younger ride free).

Salisbury ★★

Long before you enter Salisbury, the spire of its cathedral comes into view—just as John Constable captured it on canvas. The 121m (404-ft.) pinnacle of the Early English and Gothic cathedral is the tallest in England.

Salisbury, or New Sarum, lies in the valley of the River Avon. Filled with Tudor inns and tearooms, it is the only true city in Wiltshire. It's an excellent base for visitors anxious to explore Stonehenge or Avebury, who, unfortunately, tend to visit the cathedral and then rush on their way. But the old market town is an interesting destination on its own, and if you choose to linger here for a day or two, you find that its pub-to-citizen ratio is perhaps the highest in the country.

ESSENTIALS

GETTING THERE **Trains** depart for Salisbury hourly from Waterloo Station in London; the trip takes 1½ hours. Sprinter trains offer fast, efficient service every hour from Portsmouth, Bristol, and South Wales. Also, direct rail service is available from Exeter, Plymouth, Brighton, and Reading. For rail information, call ✆ **0845/748-4950** or visit **www.nationalrail.co.uk**.

Three **National Express buses** (✆ **0871/781-8178;** www.nationalexpress.com) make a 3-hour run daily from London, costing £16 for a one-way ticket.

If you're driving from London, head west on the M3 to the end of the run, continuing the rest of the way on the A30.

VISITOR INFORMATION The **Tourist Information Centre** is at Fish Row (✆ **01722/334956;** www.visitsalisbury.com) and is open October to April Monday to Saturday 9:30am to 5pm; May Monday to Saturday 9:30am to 5pm and Sunday 10am to 4pm; and June to September Monday to Saturday 9:30am to 6pm and Sunday 10am to 4pm.

WHERE TO STAY

The Beadles ★★ A traditional modern Georgian house with antique furnishings and a view of the cathedral, the Beadles offers unobstructed views of the beautiful Wiltshire countryside from its .4-hectare (1-acre) gardens. It's situated in a small, unspoiled English village, 11km (6¾ miles) from Salisbury, that offers excellent access to Stonehenge, Wilton House, the New Forest, and the rambling moors of Thomas Hardy country. Even the road to Winchester is an ancient Roman byway. Furnished tastefully, this household contains rooms with twins or doubles. Owners David and Anne-Marie Yuille-Baddeley delight in providing information on the area.

Middleton, Middle Winterslow, near Salisbury, Wiltshire SP5 1QS. ✆ **01980/862922.** Fax 01980/863565. www.staywiththebeadles.com. 3 units. £80–£95 double. Rates include English breakfast. MC, V. Turn off A30 at Pheasant Inn to Middle Winterslow. Enter the village, make the 1st right, turn right again, and it's the 1st right after Trevano. Free parking. *In room:* TV, hair dryer.

The Legacy Rose and Crown Hotel ★★★ This half-timbered, 13th-century gem stands with its feet almost in the River Avon; beyond the water, you can see the tall spire of the cathedral. Because of its tranquil location, it's our top choice. From here, you can easily walk over the arched stone bridge to the center of Salisbury in 10 minutes. Old trees shade the lawns and gardens between the inn and the river, and chairs are set out so that you can enjoy the view and count the swans. The inn has both a new and an old wing. The new wing is modern, but the old wing is more appealing, with its sloping ceilings and antique fireplaces and furniture. Bedrooms in the main house range from small to medium in size, though those in the new wing are more spacious and better designed.

Harnham Rd., Salisbury, Wiltshire SP2 8JQ. ✆ **0870/832-9946.** Fax 0870/832-9947. www.legacy-hotels.co.uk. 29 units. £105–£160 double. Rates include continental breakfast. AE, DC, MC, V. Take A3094 2.5km (1½ miles) from the center of town. **Amenities:** Restaurant; 2 bars; room service; Wi-Fi (free, in lobby). *In room:* TV, hair dryer.

WHERE TO DINE

The Gastrobistro at the Pheasant Inn ★★ FRENCH With its ancient beams and cozy inglenooks, this black-and-white timbered pub in the center of Salisbury is arguably the city's finest dining spot. Owner Arnaud Rochette delivers a Gallic-inspired menu that can be served on a summer terrace. A wide range of tastes is catered to here, from the diner seeking such comfort food as a burger or a fresh salad, to the vegetarian, to those wanting to sample delectable French dishes such as cassoulet or bouillabaisse.

You can start with old favorites such as French onion soup or snails from burgundy in garlic butter, following with stuffed peppers with zucchini and artichoke hearts, or pan-fried sea bass flavored with a saffron sauce. Desserts are especially recommendable, including the prune and Armagnac crème brûlée.

19 Salt Lane. ✆ **01722/414926.** www.restaurant-salisbury.com. Reservations required. Main courses £7–£15; fixed-price menu £17. AE, MC, V. Daily noon–2:30pm; Mon–Sat 6–9:30pm.

Howard's House Hotel-Restaurant ★ INTERNATIONAL If you'd like to dine in one of the loveliest places in the area and enjoy a refined cuisine at the same time, leave Salisbury and head for this hotel-restaurant. It's a 14km (8⅔-mile) drive to Teffont Evias, but well worth the trip. The village itself is one of the most beautiful in Wiltshire.

The elegantly appointed restaurant showcases a finely honed cuisine prepared with first-class ingredients. The menu changes daily but is likely to feature such starters as Cornish scallop risotto with deep-fried basil or maple-glazed pork belly. Main courses are very appealing with well-balanced flavors, as exemplified by seared Scottish scallops with a sweet carrot purée and black pudding, or filet of wild turbot with a goat-cheese gnocchi and a beet salad.

Teffont Evias, near Salisbury. ✆ **01722/716392.** www.howardshousehotel.co.uk. Reservations required. Fixed-price 2-course lunch £23, fixed-price 3-course lunch £27; fixed-price 2-course dinner £35, fixed-price 3-course dinner £45. AE, MC, V. Sun–Wed 12:30–1:30pm; daily 7:30–9pm. Leave Salisbury heading east on the A36 until you reach a roundabout. Take the 1st left leading to the A30. On the A30, continue for 5km (3 miles), coming to the turnoff (B3089) for Barford Saint-Martin. Continue for 6.5km (4 miles) on this secondary road to the town of Teffont Evias, where the hotel-restaurant is signposted.

Salisbury Haunch of Venison ENGLISH Right in the heart of Salisbury, this creaky-timbered chophouse (dating from 1320) serves excellent dishes, especially English roasts and grills. Stick to its specialties and you'll rarely go wrong. Begin with a tasty warm salad of venison sausages with garlic croutons, and then follow with the time-honored roast haunch of venison with parsnips and juniper berries. Other dishes likely to tempt you include pan-fried orange-glazed duck breast with a beet salsa, and smoked mackerel salad with roasted cherry tomatoes and a sweet chili dressing.

1 Minster St. ✆ **01722/411313.** www.haunchofvenison.uk.com. Main courses £12–£17. MC, V. Mon–Sat 11:30am–11pm; Sun noon–10:30pm.

SEEING THE SIGHTS IN & AROUND SALISBURY

Old Sarum ★ Believed to have been an Iron Age fortification, Old Sarum was used again by the Saxons and flourished as a walled town into the Middle Ages. The Normans built a cathedral and a castle here; parts of the old cathedral were taken down to build the city of New Sarum (Salisbury).

3km (1¾ miles) north of Salisbury off A345 on Castle Rd. ✆ **01722/335398.** www.english-heritage.org.uk/oldsarum. Admission £3.50 adults, £3 seniors, £1.80 children. Apr–June and Sept daily 10am–5pm; July–Aug daily 9am–6pm; Mar and Oct daily 10am–4pm; Nov–Feb daily 11am–3pm. Bus: 5, 6, 7, 8, or 9, every 30 min. during the day, from the Salisbury bus station.

Salisbury Cathedral ★★★ You'll find no better example of the Early English pointed architectural style than Salisbury Cathedral. Construction on this magnificent building began as early as 1220 and took only 45 years to complete. (Most of Europe's grandest cathedrals took 300 years to build.) Salisbury Cathedral is one of the most homogenous of all the great European cathedrals.

The cathedral's 13th-century octagonal chapter house possesses one of the four surviving original texts of the Magna Carta, along with treasures from the diocese of Salisbury and manuscripts and artifacts belonging to the cathedral. The cloisters enhance the cathedral's beauty, along with an exceptionally large close. At least 75 buildings are in the compound, some from the early 18th century and others from much earlier.

The Close, Salisbury. © **01722/555120.** www.salisburycathedral.org.uk. Suggested donation £6, £4.50 students and seniors, £4 children, £13 family. Sept to mid-June Mon–Sat 7:15am–6:15pm; mid-June to Aug Mon–Sat 7:15am–7:15pm; year-round Sun 7:15am–6:15pm.

Wilton House ★★ This home of the earls of Pembroke is in the town of Wilton. It dates from the 16th century but has undergone numerous alterations, most recently in Victoria's day, and is noted for its 17th-century staterooms, designed by celebrated architect Inigo Jones. Shakespeare's troupe is said to have entertained here, and Eisenhower and his advisers prepared here for the D-day landings at Normandy, with only the Van Dyck paintings as silent witnesses.

The house is filled with beautifully maintained furnishings and world-class art, including paintings by Rubens, Brueghel, and Reynolds. You can visit a reconstructed Tudor kitchen and Victorian laundry.

On the 8.4-hectare (21-acre) estate are giant cedars of Lebanon trees, the oldest of which were planted in 1630, as well as rose and water gardens, riverside and woodland walks, and a huge adventure playground for children.

5km (3 miles) west of Salisbury on A36. © **01722/746714.** www.wiltonhouse.co.uk. Admission (including grounds) £12 adults, £9.75 seniors, £6.50 children 5–15, £30 family ticket, free for children 4 and under. Easter–Sept Sun–Fri 10:30am–5:30pm (last entrance at 4:30pm); grounds Sat only. Closed Oct to Easter Sat.

Bath ★★★

Even before its Queen Anne, Georgian, and Victorian popularity, Bath was known to the Romans as Aquae Sulis. The foreign legions founded the baths here (which you can visit today) to ease rheumatism in their curative mineral springs. In 1702, Queen Anne made the trek from London to the mineral springs of **Bath,** launching a fad that was to make the city the most celebrated spa in England.

The most famous name connected with Bath was the 18th-century dandy Beau Nash, who cut a striking figure as he made his way across the city, with all the plumage of a bird of paradise. This polished arbiter of taste and manners made dueling déclassé. The 18th-century architects John Wood the Elder and his son provided a proper backdrop for Nash's considerable social talents. These architects designed a city of stone from the nearby hills, a feat so substantial and lasting that Bath today is the most harmoniously laid-out city in England. The city attracted leading political and literary figures, such as Dickens, Thackeray, Nelson, and Pitt. Canadians may already know that General Wolfe lived on Trim Street, and Australians may want to visit the house at 19 Bennett St., where their founding father, Admiral Phillip, lived.

Remarkable restoration and careful planning have ensured that Bath retains its handsome look today. Its parks, museums, and architecture continue to draw hordes of visitors, and because of this massive tourist invasion, prices remain high. However, it's one of the high points of the West Country.

Bath

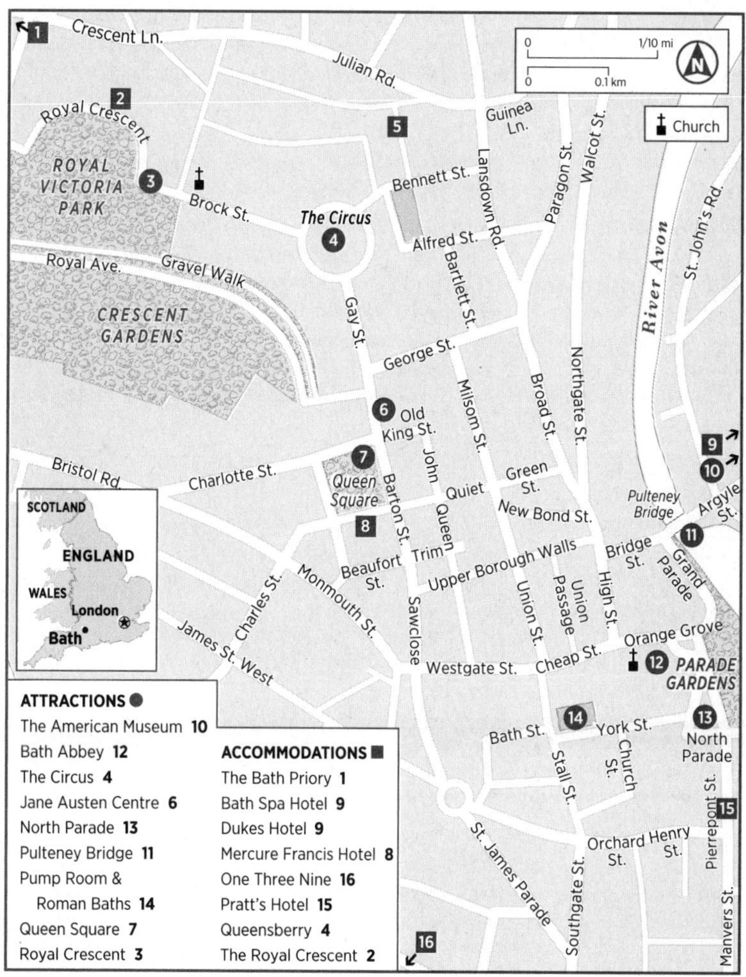

ESSENTIALS

GETTING THERE Trains leave London's Paddington Station bound for Bath once every half-hour during the day. The trip takes about 1½ hours. For rail information, call ✆ **0845/748-4950** or visit **www.nationalrail.co.uk**.

A **National Express** coach leaves London's Victoria Coach Station every 90 minutes during the day. The trip takes 3½ hours. Coaches also leave Bristol bound for Bath and make the trip in 40 minutes. For schedules and information, call ✆ **0871/781-81-78** or visit **www.nationalexpress.com**.

Drive west on the M4 to the junction with the A4, and then continue west to Bath.

VISITOR INFORMATION The **Bath Tourist Information Centre** is at Abbey Chambers, Abbey Church Yard (✆ **0844/847-5257,** or 09067/112000 within the U.K. [toll call, 50p per minute]; www.visitbath.co.uk), next to Bath Abbey. It's open June to September, Monday to Saturday 9:30am to 6pm, Sunday 10am to 4pm; off season, Monday to Saturday 9:30am to 5pm and Sunday 10am to 4pm. It is closed Christmas Day and New Year's Day.

GETTING AROUND One of the best ways to explore Bath is by bike. Rentals are available at the **Bath & Dundas Canal Company,** Brass Knocker Basin at Monkton Combe (✆ **01225/722292;** www.bathcanal.com). Daily rentals go for £14.

SPECIAL EVENTS Bath's graceful Georgian architecture provides the setting for one of Europe's most prestigious international festivals of music and the arts, the **Bath International Music Festival.** For 15 days in late May and early June each year, the city is filled with more than 1,000 performers. The festival focuses on classical music, jazz, new music, and the contemporary visual arts, with orchestras, soloists, and artists from all over the world. For information, contact the **Bath Festivals Box Office,** 2 Church St., Abbey Green, Bath BA1 1NL (✆ **01225/463362;** www.bathmusicfest.org.uk).

WHERE TO STAY

Very Expensive

The Bath Priory ★★★ Converted from one of Bath's Georgian houses in 1969, the Priory is situated on .8 hectares (2 acres) of formal and award-winning gardens with manicured lawns and flower beds. The rooms are furnished with antiques; our personal favorite is Clivia (all rooms are named after flowers or shrubs), a nicely appointed duplex in a circular turret. Rooms range from medium in size to spacious deluxe units, the latter with views, large sitting areas, and generous dressing areas. Each has a lovely old English bed, often a half tester.

Weston Rd., Bath, Somerset BA1 2XT. ✆ **01225/331922.** Fax 01225/448276. www.thebathpriory.co.uk. 27 units. £185–£380 standard double; from £330 junior suite; from £495 family room. Rates include English breakfast. AE, DC, MC, V. Free parking. **Amenities:** Restaurant; bar; babysitting; exercise room; 2 pools (1 heated indoor, 1 outdoor); room service; spa. *In room:* A/C, TV, hair dryer, Internet, minibar.

Bath Spa Hotel ★★★ This stunning restored 19th-century mansion is a 10-minute walk from the center of Bath. Behind a facade of Bath stone, it lies at the end of a tree-lined drive on 2.8 hectares (7 acres) of landscaped grounds, with a Victorian grotto and a Grecian temple. In its long history, it served many purposes (once as a hostel for nurses) before being returned to its original grandeur. The hotel uses log fireplaces, elaborate moldings, and oak paneling to create country-house charm. The rooms are handsomely furnished, and most of them are spacious. Most beds are doubles, and some even offer an old-fashioned four-poster.

Sydney Rd. (east of the city, off A36), Bath, Somerset BA2 6JF. ✆ **0844/8799106.** Fax 01225/444006. www.macdonaldhotels.co.uk/bathspa. 129 units. £178–£515 double; £223–£645 suite. Rates include English breakfast. AE, MC, V. Free parking. **Amenities:** 2 restaurants; bar; exercise room; indoor heated pool; room service; spa. *In room:* A/C, TV, hair dryer, minibar, Wi-Fi (£5 per hour).

The Royal Crescent ★★★ This special place stands proudly in the center of the famed Royal Crescent. Long regarded as Bath's premier hotel (before the arrival of the even better Bath Spa), it has attracted the rich and famous. The bedrooms, including the Jane Austen Suite, are lavishly furnished with such amenities as four-poster beds and marble tubs. Each room is individually designed and offers such comforts as bottled mineral water, fruit plates, and other special touches. Bedrooms, generally quite spacious, are elaborately decked out with thick wool carpeting, silk wallcoverings, and antiques, each with a superb and rather sumptuous bed.

15–16 Royal Crescent, Bath, Somerset BA1 2LS. ✆ **01225/823333.** Fax 01225/339401. www.royalcrescent.co.uk. 45 units. £195–£430 double; £440–£875 suite. Rates include English breakfast. AE, DC, MC, V. Parking £5. **Amenities:** Restaurant; bar; babysitting; exercise room; indoor heated pool; room service; sauna. *In room:* TV/DVD, hair dryer, minibar (in some), Wi-Fi (free).

Expensive

Mercure Francis Hotel ★ An integral part of Queen Square, the Francis is an example of 18th-century taste and style, but we find it too commercial and touristy. Originally consisting of six private residences dating from 1729, the Francis was opened as a private hotel by Emily Francis in 1884 and has offered guests first-class service for more than 100 years. Many of the well-furnished and traditionally styled bedrooms overlook Queen Square, named in honor of George II's consort, Caroline. Rooms range in size from rather small to medium, with either twin or double beds. Accommodations in the older building have more charm, especially on the upper floor.

Queen Sq., Bath, Somerset BA1 2HH. ✆ **888/221-4542** in the U.S. and Canada, or 01225/424105. Fax 01225/319715. www.mercure.com. 95 units. £140–£170 double; £200 suite. Rates include English breakfast. AE, DC, MC, V. Parking £12. **Amenities:** Restaurant; bar; babysitting; room service. *In room:* A/C in some, TV, fridge, hair dryer, Wi-Fi.

Pratt's Hotel ★ Once the home of Sir Walter Scott, Pratt's dates from the heady days of Beau Nash. Functioning as a hotel since 1791, it has become part of the legend and lore of Bath. Several elegant terraced Georgian town houses were joined together to form this complex with a very traditional British atmosphere. Rooms are individually designed, and as is typical of a converted private home, bedrooms range from small to spacious (the larger ones are on the lower floors). Regardless of their dimensions, the rooms are furnished in a comfortable though utilitarian style.

S. Parade, Bath, Somerset BA2 4AB. ✆ **01225/460441.** Fax 01225/448807. www.prattshotel.com. 46 units. £139–£149 double. Rates include English breakfast. Children 13 and under sharing a room with 2 adults stay free. AE, DC, MC, V. Parking £12. **Amenities:** Restaurant; bar; room service; Wi-Fi (£6 per hour, in lobby). *In room:* TV, hair dryer.

Queensberry ★ A gem of a hotel, this early-Georgian-era town house has been beautifully restored. In our view, it is now among the finest places to stay in a city where the competition for restored town-house hotels is fierce. The Marquis of Queensberry commissioned John Wood the Younger to build this house in 1772. Rooms—often spacious but sometimes medium in size—are delightful, each tastefully decorated with antique furniture and such thoughtful extras as fresh flowers.

Russell St., Bath, Somerset BA1 2QF. ✆ **01225/447928.** Fax 01225/446065. www.thequeensberry.co.uk. 29 units. £125–£240 double; £240–£435 suite. AE, MC, V. Free parking. **Amenities:** The Olive Tree restaurant (p. 277); bar; babysitting; room service; Wi-Fi (free, in lobby). *In room:* TV, CD player, hair dryer.

Moderate

Apsley House Hotel ★★ This charming and stately building, just 1.5km (1 mile) west of the center of Bath, dates from 1830, during the reign of William IV. In 1994, new owners refurbished the hotel, filling it with country-house chintzes and a collection of antiques borrowed from the showrooms of an antiques store they own. (Some furniture in the hotel is for sale.) Style and comfort are the keynote here, and all the relatively spacious bedrooms are inviting, appointed with plush beds.

141 Newbridge Hill, Bath, Somerset BA1 3PT. ✆ **01225/336966.** Fax 01225/425462. www.apsley-house.co.uk. 11 units. £70–£170 double; £90–£200 suite. Rates include English breakfast. AE, MC, V. Free parking. Take A4 to Upper Bristol Rd., fork right at the traffic signals into Newbridge Hill, and turn left at Apsley Rd. **Amenities:** Bar; room service. *In room:* TV, hair dryer.

Dukes Hotel A short walk from the heart of Bath, this 1780 building is fresher than ever following a complete restoration. Many of the original Georgian features, including cornices and moldings, have been retained. Rooms, ranging from small to medium, are exceedingly comfortable. All of the bathrooms are small but efficiently arranged and sport tub/shower combinations or just showers. Guests can relax in a refined drawing room or patronize the cozy bar overlooking a garden. The entire setting has been called a "perfect *Masterpiece Theatre* take on Britain," with a fire burning in the grate.

53–54 Great Pulteney St., Bath, Somerset BA2 4DN. ✆ **01225/787960.** Fax 01225/787961. www.dukesbath.co.uk. 17 units. £131–£189 double; £194–£232 four-poster room; £176–£214 suite. Rates include continental breakfast. 2-night minimum stay Sat–Sun. AE, MC, V. Bus: 18. **Amenities:** Restaurant; bar; room service. *In room:* TV, hair dryer, minibar (in some).

Inexpensive

One Three Nine ★ At the southern side of the city on the A367 road to Exeter (Devon), this Victorian residence from the 1870s is a 10-minute walk from the center of Bath, and minibuses pass by frequently. David and Annie Lanz offer one of the best-value accommodations in the area. The hotel rents elegant and spacious bedrooms, individually furnished and decorated.

139 Wells Rd., Bath, Somerset BA2 3AL. ✆ **01225/314769.** Fax 01225/443079. www.139bath.co.uk. 8 units. £65–£175 double; £85–£200 family room. Rates include English breakfast. 2-night minimum stay Sat–Sun. AE, MC, V. Free parking. On approaching Bath, follow A367 Exeter signs but ignore the LIGHT VEHICLES ONLY sign; turn left onto A37/A367 (the Wells Rd.) and follow the black railings. *In room:* A/C, TV/DVD, Wi-Fi.

WHERE TO DINE

Expensive

The Moody Goose ★★★ ENGLISH For some of the finest food in greater Bath, you have to go outside the center to Midsomer Norton. The kitchen has an absolute passion for fresh ingredients—the chefs use produce grown as near home as possible, though the Angus beef comes in from Scotland and the fresh fish from the coasts of Cornwall and Devon. The breads, ice creams, and petits fours are homemade. The kitchen team is expert at chargrilling.

Some of the best-tasting starters include crab salad with tarragon mayonnaise and tomato sorbet, or else a terrine of wood pigeon. Main courses that we highly recommend include local saddle of venison with a golden beet and Jerusalem artichoke purée; steamed sea bass with River Exe mussels and a caviar butter sauce; or roast filet of beef with wild mushrooms in a Madeira sauce with roasted salsify.

In the Old Priory Hotel, Church Sq., Midsomer Norton, outside Bath. ✆ **01761/416784.** www.moodygoose.co.uk. Reservations required. Main courses £18–£22; fixed-price 2-course lunch £23; fixed-price 3-course lunch £29; table d'hôte dinner menu £33. MC, V. Mon–Sat noon–1:30pm and 7–9:30pm.

The Olive Tree ★ MODERN ENGLISH/MEDITERRANEAN This is one of the most sophisticated little restaurants in Bath. Head Chef Marc Salmon uses the best local produce, with an emphasis on freshness. The menu is changed to reflect the season, with game and fish being the specialties. You might begin with a tomato tart with goat-cheese fritters or a galatine of wood pigeon, duck, and rainbow chard set off with spiced gooseberry chutney. Main courses might include pan-fried potato gnocchi with ironbark squash, Parmesan, and pumpkinseeds, or filet of wild sea bass with confit fennel, or carved duck leg with bubble and squeak (cabbage and potatoes).

In the Queensberry Hotel, Russel St. ✆ **01225/447928.** www.thequeensberry.co.uk. Reservations highly recommended. Main courses £15–£25. AE, MC, V. Mon–Sat noon–2pm and 7–10pm; Sun noon–2pm and 7–9:30pm.

Moderate

The Moon and Sixpence BRITISH This popular restaurant with affordable prices has devotees who come here to feed on West Country lamb, sea bass, and calves' liver, along with rib-eye steaks. There is an enclosed outside dining area. The bar offers an extensive choice of wines from around the world, as well as premium beers and lagers on tap.

27 Milsom Place. ✆ **01225/320088.** www.moonandsixpence.co.uk. Reservations recommended. Main courses £11–£19. AE, MC, V. Mon–Sat noon–2:30pm and 6–10pm; Sun noon–2:30pm and 6–10pm.

Woods MODERN ENGLISH/FRENCH/ASIAN This restaurant, named after John Wood the Younger, architect of Bath's famous Assembly Room, offers a fixed-price menu plus a seasonal array of frequently changing a la carte items. Good bets include filet of cod with capers, anchovies, and olive butter; seared filet steak with oyster mushrooms and a Marsala cream sauce; or roast loin of pork chop with fresh tarragon and garlic butter.

9–13 Alfred St. ✆ **01225/314812.** www.woodsrestaurant.com. Reservations recommended. Main courses £12–£20; 2-course fixed-price lunch £15; 2-course fixed-price dinner £15. MC, V. Mon–Sat noon–2:30pm and 6–10:30pm; Sun noon–2pm.

EXPLORING BATH

Stroll around to see some of the buildings, crescents, and squares in town. John Wood the Elder (1704–54) laid out many of the most famous streets and buildings of Bath, including **North and South Parades** and **Queen Square.** His masterpiece is the **Circus** ★★★, built on Barton Fields outside the old city walls. He showed how a row of town houses could be made to look palatial. Fellow architects have praised his "uniform facades and rhythmic proportions." Also of interest is the shop-lined **Pulteney Bridge,** designed by Robert Adam and often compared to the Ponte Vecchio of Florence.

The younger John Wood designed the **Royal Crescent ★★★**, an elegant half-moon row of town houses (copied by Astor architects for their colonnade in New York City in the 1830s). At **No. 1 Royal Crescent** (**✆ 01225/428126;** www.bath-preservation-trust.org.uk), the interior has been redecorated and furnished by the Bath Preservation Trust to look as it might have toward the end of the 18th century. The house lies at one end of Bath's most magnificent crescents, west of the Circus. Admission is £6 for adults, £5 for students and seniors, and £2.50 for children ages 5 to 16; a family ticket is £12. The house is open from mid-March to October Tuesday to Sunday 10:30am to 5pm, and November Tuesday to Sunday from 10:30am to 4pm (last admission 30 min. before closing); it is closed Good Friday and December to mid-February.

The **Jane Austen Centre,** 40 Gay St. (**✆ 01225/443000;** www.janeausten.co.uk), is located in a Georgian town house on an elegant street where Miss Austen once lived. Exhibits and a video convey a sense of what life was like in Bath during the Regency period. The center is open mid-February to October daily from 9:45am to 5:30pm, and November to mid-February Sunday to Friday 11am to 4:30pm, Saturday 10am to 5:30pm. Admission is £7 for adults, £5.50 students and seniors, £4 children 6 to 15, and £18 family ticket.

The American Museum ★★ Some 4km (2½ miles) outside Bath, get an idea of what life was like in America prior to the mid-1800s. The first American museum established outside the U.S., it sits proudly on extensive grounds high above the Somerset Valley. Among the authentic exhibits shipped over from the States are a Conestoga wagon, the dining room of a New York town house of the early 19th century, and (on the grounds) a copy of Washington's flower garden at Mount Vernon. Throughout the summer, the museum hosts various special events, from displays of Native American dancing to reenactments of the Civil War.

Claverton Manor, Bathwick Hill. **✆ 01225/460503.** www.americanmuseum.org. Admission £8 adults, £7 students and seniors, £4.50 children 5–16, £22 family ticket, free for children 4 and under. Late Mar to Oct Tues–Sun noon–5pm. Closed Nov to late Mar. Bus: 18.

Bath Abbey ★ Built on the site of a much larger Norman cathedral, the present-day abbey is a fine example of the late Perpendicular style. When Queen Elizabeth I came to Bath in 1574, she ordered a national fund to be set up to restore the abbey. The west front is the sculptural embodiment of a Jacob's ladder dream of a 15th-century bishop. When you go inside and see its many windows, you'll understand why the abbey is called the "Lantern of the West." Note the superb fan vaulting with its scalloped effect. Beau Nash was buried in the nave and is honored by a simple monument totally out of keeping with his flamboyant character. The Bath Abbey Heritage Vaults opened in 1994 on the south side of the abbey. This subterranean exhibition traces the history of Christianity at the abbey site since Saxon times.

Orange Grove. **✆ 01225/422462.** www.bathabbey.org. £3 donation requested, free for children 15 and under. Abbey Apr–Oct Mon–Sat 9am–6pm; Nov–Mar Mon–Sat 9am–4:30pm; year-round Sun 1–2:30pm (Apr–Oct also 4:30–5:30pm). The Heritage Vaults Mon–Sat 10am–3:30pm (last entrance).

The Pump Room ★ & Roman Baths ★★ Founded in A.D. 75 by the Romans, the baths were dedicated to the goddess Sulis Minerva; in their day, they were an engineering feat. Even today, they're among the finest Roman remains in the country, and they are still fed by Britain's most famous hot-spring water. After centuries of decay, the original baths were rediscovered during Queen Victoria's reign. The site of the Temple of Sulis Minerva has been excavated and is now open to view. The museum displays many interesting objects from Victorian and recent digs (look for the head of Minerva).

Coffee, lunch, and tea, usually with music from the Pump Room Trio, can be enjoyed in the 18th-century pump room, overlooking the hot springs. You can also find a drinking fountain with hot mineral water that tastes horrible.

In the Bath Abbey churchyard, Stall St. ✆ **01225/477785.** www.romanbaths.co.uk. Admission £11.50 adults, £10 seniors, £7.50 children 6–16, £33 family ticket; adult admission £12.25 July–Aug only (all other entry fees remain the same). Apr–June and Sept daily 9am–6pm; July–Aug daily 8am–10pm; Oct–Mar Mon–Sat 9:30am–5:30pm.

SHOPPING

Bath is loaded with markets and fairs, antiques centers, and small shops, with literally hundreds of opportunities to buy just about anything, including the famous spa waters, for sale by the bottle. Prices are comparable to London's.

The whole city is basically one long, slightly undulating shopping area, including a newly opened SouthGate Bath shopping center complex next to the train station (✆ **01225/469061;** www.southgatebath.com). The single best day to visit, if you are a serious shopper intent on hitting the flea markets, is Wednesday.

The **Bartlett Street Antiques Centre,** Bartlett Street, encompasses 20 dealers and 50 showcases displaying furniture, silver, antique jewelry, paintings, toys, military items, and collectibles.

Near Bath Abbey, the **Beaux Arts Gallery,** 12–13 York St. (✆ **01225/464850;** www.beauxartsbath.co.uk), is the largest and most important gallery of contemporary art in Bath, specializing in well-known British artists including Ray Richardson, John Bellany, and Nicola Bealing. Closely linked to the London art scene, the gallery occupies a pair of interconnected, stone-fronted Georgian houses. Its half-dozen showrooms exhibit objects beginning at £30.

The very upscale **Rossiter's,** 38–41 Broad St. (✆ **01225/462227;** www.rossitersofbath.com), sells very traditional English tableware and home decor items. They'll ship anywhere in the world. Look especially for the display of Moorcraft ginger jars, vases, and clocks, as well as the Floris perfumes.

BATH AFTER DARK

To gain a very different perspective of Bath, you may want to take the **Bizarre Bath Walking Tour** (✆ **01225/335124;** www.bizarrebath.co.uk), a 1½-hour improvisational tour of the streets during which the tour guides pull pranks, tell jokes, and behave in a humorously annoying manner toward tourgoers and unsuspecting residents. The tour runs nightly at 8pm from Easter to October, no reservations necessary; just show up, ready for anything, at the Huntsman Inn at North Parade Passage. Cost is £8 for adults, £5 for students and children.

For a more traditional night out, visit the **Bell Inn,** 103 Walcot St. (✆ **01225/460426;** www.walcotstreet.com), where music ranges from jazz and country to reggae and blues on Monday and Wednesday nights and Sunday at lunch and dinner.

7

FRANCE

by Darwin Porter & Danforth Prince

Though France is slightly smaller than Texas, no other country has such a diversity of sights and scenery in such a compact area. A visitor can travel to Paris, one of the world's great cities; drive among the Loire Valley's green hills; or head south to sunny Provence and the French Riviera. Discover the attractions (and transport, lodging, and dining offerings) in each of these regions in this chapter.

PARIS ★★★

The City of Light always lives up to its reputation as one of the world's most romantic cities. Ernest Hemingway referred to the splendors of Paris as a "moveable feast" and wrote, "There is never any ending to Paris, and the memory of each person who has lived in it differs from that of any other."

Here you can stroll along the Seine and the broad tree-lined boulevards; browse the chic shops and relax over coffee or wine at a cafe; visit the museums, monuments, and cathedrals; and savor the cuisine.

Essentials

GETTING THERE **By Plane** Paris has two international airports: **Aéroport d'Orly,** 13km (8 miles) south of the city, and **Aéroport Roissy–Charles de Gaulle,** 22km (14 miles) northeast. A shuttle (19€) makes the 50- to 75-minute journey between the two airports about every 30 minutes.

At Charles de Gaulle Airport (✆ **01-48-62-12-12,** or 39-50 from France only), foreign carriers use Aérogare 1, while Air France uses Aérogare 2. From Aérogare 1, you take a moving walkway to the passport checkpoint and the Customs area. A *navette* (shuttle bus) links the two terminals.

The free shuttle buses also transport you to the **Roissy rail station,** from which fast RER (Réseau Express Régional) trains leave every 10 minutes between 5am and midnight for Métro stations including Gare du Nord, Châtelet, Luxembourg, Port-Royal, and Denfert-Rochereau. A typical fare from Roissy to any point in central Paris is 8.20€ per person (5.60€ children 4–10). Travel time from the airport to central Paris is around 35 to 40 minutes.

France

You can also take an **Air France shuttle bus** (✆ **08-92-35-08-20** or 01-48-64-14-24; www.cars-airfrance.com) to central Paris for 15€ one-way. It stops at the Palais des Congrès (Port Maillot) and continues to place Charles-de-Gaulle–Etoile, where subway lines can carry you to any point in Paris. That ride, depending on traffic, takes 45 to 55 minutes. The shuttle departs about every 20 minutes between 5:40am and 11pm.

The **Roissybus** (✆ **01-58-76-16-16**), operated by the RATP, departs from the airport daily 6am to 11:45pm and costs 8.60€ for the 45- to 50-minute ride. Departures are about every 15 minutes, and the bus leaves you near the corner of rue Scribe and place de l'Opéra in the heart of Paris.

A **taxi** from Roissy into the city will cost about 47€ to 60€; from 8pm to 7am the fare is 40% higher. Long orderly lines for taxis form outside each of the airport's terminals.

Orly Airport (✆ **01-49-75-52-52,** or 39-50 from France only) has two terminals—Orly Sud (south) for international flights and Orly Ouest (west) for domestic flights. A free shuttle bus connects them in 3 minutes.

Air France buses leave from Exit E of Orly Sud and from Exit F of Orly Ouest every 12 minutes between 6am and 11:30pm for Gare des Invalides; the fare is 9€ one-way, 14€ round-trip. Returning to the airport (about 30 min.), buses leave both the Montparnasse and the Invalides terminal for Orly Sud or Orly Ouest every 15 minutes.

Another way to get to central Paris is to take the RER from points throughout central Paris to the station at Pont-de-Rungis/Aéroport d'Orly for a per-person one-way fare of 6€, and from here, take the free shuttle bus that departs every 15 minutes from Pont-de-Rungis to both of Orly's terminals. Combined travel time is about 45 to 55 minutes.

A **taxi** from Orly to central Paris costs about 30€ to 50€, more at night. Don't take a meterless taxi from Orly; it's much safer (and usually cheaper) to hire one of the metered cabs, which are under the scrutiny of a police officer.

BY TRAIN Paris has six major stations: **Gare d'Austerlitz,** 55 quai d'Austerlitz, 13e (serving the southwest, with trains to and from the Loire Valley, Bordeaux, the Pyrénées, and Spain); **Gare de l'Est,** place du 11-Novembre-1918, 10e (serving the east, with trains to and from Strasbourg, Reims, and beyond, to Zurich and Austria); **Gare de Lyon,** 20 bd. Diderot, 12e (serving the southeast, with trains to and from the Côte d'Azur [Nice, Cannes, St-Tropez], Provence, and beyond, to Geneva and Italy); **Gare Montparnasse,** 17 bd. Vaugirard, 15e (serving the west, with trains to and from Brittany); **Gare du Nord,** 18 rue de Dunkerque, 15e (serving the north, with trains to and from London, Holland, Denmark, and northern Germany); and **Gare St-Lazare,** 13 rue d'Amsterdam, 8e (serving the northwest, with trains to and from Normandy). Buses operate between the stations, and each station has a Métro stop. For train information and to make reservations, call ✆ **08-92-35-35-35** from abroad, **36-35** from France between 8am and 8pm daily. From Paris, one-way rail passage to Tours costs 30€ to 51€; one-way to Strasbourg costs 55€ or 80€, depending on the routing.

Warning: The stations and surrounding areas are usually seedy and frequented by pickpockets, hustlers, hookers, and addicts. Be alert, especially at night.

BY BUS Most buses arrive at the **Eurolines France** station, 28 av. du Général-de-Gaulle, Bagnolet (✆ **08-92-89-90-91;** www.eurolines.fr; Métro: Gallieni).

BY CAR Driving in Paris is *not* recommended. Parking is difficult and traffic dense. If you drive, remember that Paris is encircled by a ring road, the *périphérique*. Always get detailed directions to your destination, including the name of the exit on the *périphérique* (exits aren't numbered). Avoid rush hours.

The major highways into Paris are A1 from the north; A13 from Rouen, Normandy, and other points northwest; A10 from Spain and the southwest; A6 and A7 from the French Alps, the Riviera, and Italy; and A4 from eastern France.

VISITOR INFORMATION The **Paris Convention and Visitors Bureau** (✆ **08-92-68-30-00** [.35€ per minute]; http://en.parisinfo.com) has offices throughout the city, with the main headquarters at 25–27 rue des Pyramides, 1er (Métro: Pyramides). It's open Monday through Saturday 10am to 7pm (June–Oct from 9am), Sunday and holidays from 11am to 7pm. Less comprehensive branch offices include Clémenceau Welcome Center, corner of avenue Champs-Elysées and avenue Marigny (8e; Métro: Champs-Elysées), open April 6 to October 20 daily 9am to 7pm. **Espace Tourisme Ile-de-France,** in the Carrousel du Louvre, 99 rue de Rivoli, 1er (Métro: Palais-Royal–Louvre), open daily 10am to 6pm; in the **Gare de Lyon,** 20 bd. Diderot, Paris 12e (Métro: Gare de Lyon), open Monday through Saturday 8am to 6pm; in the **Gare du Nord,** 18 rue de Dunkerque, 10e (Métro: Gare du Nord), open daily 8am to 6pm; and in **Montmartre,** 21 place du Tertre, 18e (Métro: Abbesses or Lamarck-Caulaincourt), open daily 10am to 7pm. You can walk in at any branch to make a hotel reservation; the service is free. The offices are extremely busy year-round, especially in midsummer, so be prepared to wait in line.

CITY LAYOUT Paris is surprisingly compact. Occupying 2,723 sq. km (1,051 sq. miles), its urban area is home to more than 11 million people. The river Seine divides Paris into the **Rive Droite (Right Bank)** to the north and the **Rive Gauche (Left Bank)** to the south. These designations make sense when you stand on a bridge and face downstream (west)—to your right is the north bank, to your left the south. A total of 32 bridges link the Right Bank and the Left Bank. Some provide access to the two islands at the heart of the city: **Ile de la Cité,** the city's birthplace and site of Notre-Dame; and **Ile St-Louis,** a moat-guarded oasis of 17th-century mansions.

The "main street" on the Right Bank is **avenue des Champs-Elysées,** beginning at the Arc de Triomphe and running to place de la Concorde. Avenue des Champs-Elysées and 11 other avenues radiate like the arms of an asterisk from the Arc de Triomphe, giving it its original name, place de l'Etoile (*étoile* means "star"). It was renamed place Charles-de-Gaulle following the general's death; today, it's often referred to as place Charles-de-Gaulle–Etoile.

If you're staying more than 2 or 3 days, purchase an inexpensive pocket-size book called *Paris par arrondissement,* available at newsstands and bookshops; prices start at 6.50€. This guide has a Métro map, a foldout map of the city, and maps of each arrondissement, with all streets listed and keyed.

ARRONDISSEMENTS IN BRIEF The heart of medieval Paris was the **Ile de la Cité** and the areas immediately surrounding it. As Paris grew, it absorbed many of the once-distant villages, and today each of these ***arrondissements*** (districts) retains a distinct character. They're numbered 1 to 20 starting at the center and progressing in a clockwise spiral. The key to finding any address in Paris is to look for the arrondissement number, rendered as a number followed by "er" or "e" (1er, 2e, and so on). If the address is written out more formally, you can tell what arrondissement it's in by looking at the postal code. For example, the address may be written with the street name, and then "75014 Paris." The last two digits, "14," indicate that the address is in the 14th arrondissement, Montparnasse.

On the Right Bank, the **1er** is home to the Louvre, place Vendôme, rues de Rivoli and St-Honoré, Palais Royal, and Comédie-Française—an area filled with grand institutions and grand stores. At the center of the **2e,** the city's financial center, is the Bourse (Stock Exchange). Most of the **3e** and the **4e** is referred to as the Marais, the old Jewish quarter that in the 17th century was home to the aristocracy. Today it's a trendy area of boutiques and restored mansions as well as the center of Paris's gay and lesbian community. On the Left Bank, the **5e** is known as the Latin Quarter, home to the Sorbonne and associated with the intellectual life that thrived in the 1920s and 1930s. Today it is Paris's intellectual soul, featuring bookstores, schools, churches, jazz clubs, student dives, Roman ruins, and boutiques. The **6e,** known as St-Germain-des-Prés, stretches from the Seine to boulevard du Montparnasse. It is associated with the 1920s and 1930s and known as a center for art and antiques; it boasts the Palais and Jardin du Luxembourg. The **7e,** containing both the Eiffel Tower and Hôtel des Invalides, is a residential district for the well-heeled.

Back on the Right Bank, the **8e** epitomizes monumental Paris, with the triumphal avenue des Champs-Elysées, the Elysées Palace, and the fashion houses along avenue Montaigne and the Faubourg St-Honoré. The **18e** is home to Sacré-Coeur and Montmartre and all that the name conjures of the bohemian life painted most notably by Toulouse-Lautrec. The **14e** incorporates most of Montparnasse, including its cemetery. The **20e** is where the city's famous lie buried in Père-Lachaise and is home to Muslims and members of Paris's Sephardic Jewish community, many of whom fled Algeria or Tunisia. Beyond the arrondissements stretch the vast *banlieue,* or suburbs, of Greater Paris, where the majority of Parisians live.

GETTING AROUND Paris is a city for strollers, whose greatest joy is rambling through unexpected alleys and squares. Given a choice of conveyance, try to make it on your own two feet whenever possible.

BY MÉTRO (SUBWAY) The Métro (✆ **32-46** in France, or 08-92-69-32-46 from abroad; www.ratp.fr) is the most efficient and fastest way to get around Paris. All lines are numbered, and the final destination of each line is clearly marked on subway maps, in the system's underground passageways, and on the train cars. The Métro runs daily from 5:30am to 1:15am (last departure at 2am on Sat). It's reasonably safe at any hour, but beware of pickpockets.

To familiarize yourself with the Métro, see the color map on the inside front cover of this book. Most stations display a map of the Métro at the entrance. To locate your correct train on a map, find your destination, follow the line to the end of its route, and note the name of the final stop, which is that line's direction. In the station, follow the signs for your direction in the passageways until you see the label on a train. Many larger stations have maps with push-button indicators that light up your route when you press the button for your destination.

Transfer stations are *correspondances,* and some require long walks; Châtelet is the most difficult—but most trips require only one transfer. When transferring, follow the orange CORRESPONDANCE signs to the proper platform. Don't follow a SORTIE (exit) sign, or you'll have to pay again to get back on the train.

On the urban lines, one ticket for 1.60€ lets you travel to any point. On the Sceaux, Boissy-St-Léger, and St-Germain-en-Laye lines to the suburbs, fares are based on distance. A *carnet* is the best buy—10 tickets for about 12€.

At the turnstile entrances to the station, insert your ticket and pass through. At some exits, tickets are also checked, so hold onto yours. There are occasional ticket checks on trains and platforms and in passageways too.

BY RER TRAINS A suburban train system, RER (Réseau Express Regional), passes through the heart of Paris, traveling faster than the Métro and running daily from 5:30am to 1am. This system works like the Métro and requires the same tickets. The major stops within central Paris, linking the RER to the Métro, are Nation, Gare de Lyon, Charles de Gaulle–Etoile, Gare-Etoile, and Gare du Nord, as well as Châtelet-Les-Halles. All of these stops are on the Right Bank. On the Left Bank, RER stops include Denfert-Rochereau and St-Michel. The five RER lines are marked A through E. Different branches are labeled by a number, the C5 Line serving Versailles–Rive Gauche, for example. Electric signboards next to each track

DISCOUNT TRANSIT passes

The **Paris-Visite pass** (✆ **32-46**) is valid for 1, 2, 3, or 5 days on public transport, including the Métro, buses, the funicular ride to Montmartre, and RER trains. For access to zones 1 to 3, which includes central Paris and its nearby suburbs, its cost ranges from 8.80€ for 1 day to 28.30€ for 5 days. Get it at RATP (Régie Autonome des Transports Parisiens) offices, the tourist office, and Métro stations.

outline all the possible stops along the way. Make sure that the little square next to your intended stop is lit.

BY BUS Buses are much slower than the Métro. The majority run Monday through Saturday from 6:30am to 9:30pm (a few operate until 12:30am, and 10 operate during early-morning hours). Service is limited on Sundays and holidays. Bus and Métro fares are the same; you can use the same tickets on both. Most bus rides require one ticket, but some destinations require two (never more than two within the city limits).

At certain stops, signs list destinations and bus numbers serving that point. Destinations are usually listed north to south and east to west. Most stops are also posted on the sides of the buses. During rush hours, you may have to take a ticket from a dispensing machine, indicating your position in the line at the stop.

If you intend to use the buses a lot, pick up an RATP bus map at the office on place de la Madeleine, 8e, or at the tourist offices at RATP headquarters, 54 quai de La Rapée, 12e. For detailed recorded information (in English) on bus and Métro routes, call ✆ **32-46,** open Monday to Friday 7am to 9pm.

The RATP also operates the **Balabus,** big-windowed orange-and-white motorcoaches that run only during limited hours: Sunday and national holidays from noon to 8:30pm, from April 15 to the end of September. Itineraries run in both directions between Gare de Lyon and the Grande Arche de La Défense, encompassing some of the city's most beautiful vistas. It's a great deal—three Métro tickets, for 1.60€ each, will carry you the entire route. You'll recognize the bus and the route it follows by the BB symbol emblazoned on each bus's side and on signs posted beside the route it follows.

BY TAXI It's virtually impossible to get a taxi at rush hour, so don't even try. Taxi drivers are organized into a lobby that limits their number to 15,000.

Watch out for common rip-offs: Always check the meter to make sure you're not paying the previous passenger's fare; beware of cabs without meters, which often wait outside nightclubs for tipsy patrons; and settle the tab in advance.

You can hail regular cabs on the street when their signs read LIBRE. Taxis are easier to find at the many stands near Métro stations. The flag drops at 5.50€, and from 10am to 5pm, you pay .90€ per kilometer. From 5pm to 10am, you pay 1.15€ per kilometer. On airport trips, you're not required to pay for the driver's empty return ride.

You're allowed several pieces of luggage free if they're transported inside and are less than 5 kilograms (11 lb.). Heavier suitcases carried in the trunk cost 1€ to 1.50€

apiece. Tip 12% to 15%—the latter usually elicits a *merci.* For radio cabs, call **Les Taxis Bleus** (✆ **08-25-16-10-10**) or **Taxi G7** (✆ **01-47-39-47-39**)—but note that you'll be charged from the point where the taxi begins the drive to pick you up.

BY BOAT The **Batobus** (✆ **08-25-05-01-01;** www.batobus.com) is a 150-passenger ferry with big windows. The boats operate along the Seine, stopping at such points of interest as the **Eiffel Tower, Musée d'Orsay,** the **Louvre, Notre-Dame,** and the **Hôtel de Ville.** The Batobus does not provide recorded commentary. The only fare option available is a day pass valid for either 1, 2, or 5 days, each allowing as many entrances and exits as you want. A 1-day pass costs 12€ for adults, 6€ for children 15 and under; a 2-day pass costs 16€ for adults, 8€ for children 15 and under; a 5-day pass costs 19€ for adults, 9€ for children 15 and under. Boats operate daily (closed most of Jan) every 15 to 30 minutes, starting between 10 and 10:30am and ending between 4:30 and 10:30pm, depending on the season of the year.

[Fast FACTS] PARIS

American Express The office at 11 rue Scribe (✆ **01-53-30-99-00**) is open Monday to Saturday from 9am to 6:30pm.

Currency France fell under the **euro** (€) umbrella in 2002. At press time, 1€ = US$1.40.

Currency Exchange American Express can fill most banking needs. Most banks in Paris are open Monday through Friday from 9am to 4:30pm; ask at your hotel for the location of the one nearest you. For the best exchange rate, cash your traveler's checks at banks or foreign-exchange offices, not at shops and hotels. Most post offices will change traveler's checks or convert currency. Currency exchanges are also at Paris airports and train stations and along most of the major boulevards. They charge a small commission.

Some exchange places charge favorable rates to lure you into their stores. For example, **Paris Vision,** 214 rue de Rivoli, 1er (✆ **01-42-60-30-01;** Métro: Tuileries), maintains a minibank in the back of a travel agency, open daily 6:30am to 9pm. Its rates are a fraction less favorable than those offered for large blocks of money as listed by the Paris stock exchange.

Dentists For emergency dental service, call **S.O.S. Dentaire,** 87 bd. du Port-Royal, 13e (✆ **01-43-37-51-00** or 01-43-36-36-00; Métro: Gobelins), Monday through Friday from 6 to 11:30pm and Saturday and Sunday from 9am to midnight. Staff members will arrange an appointment with a qualified dentist either on the day of your call or for early in the morning of the following day. You can also call or visit the **American Hospital** (see "Doctors," below).

Doctors Some large hotels have a doctor on staff. You can also try the **American Hospital,** 63 bd. Victor-Hugo, in the suburb of Neuilly-sur-Seine (✆ **01-46-41-25-25;** www.american-hospital.org; Métro: Pont-de-Levallois or Pont-de-Neuilly; bus: 82), which operates a 24-hour emergency service. The bilingual staff accepts Blue Cross and other American insurance plans.

Drugstores After hours, have your concierge contact the Commissariat de Police for the nearest 24-hour pharmacy. French law requires one pharmacy in any given neighborhood to stay open 24 hours. You'll find the address posted on the doors or windows of all other drugstores. One of the most central all-nighters is **Pharmacie Les Champs "Derhy,"** 84 av. des Champs-Elysées, 8e (✆ **01-45-62-02-41;** Métro: George V).

Embassies & Consulates If you have a passport, immigration, legal, or other problem, contact your consulate. Call *before* you go—they often keep odd hours and observe both French and home-country holidays. The Embassy of the **United States,** 2 av. Gabriel, 8e (✆ **01-43-12-22-22;** http://france.usembassy.gov; Métro: Concorde), is open Monday to Friday 9am to 6pm. The Embassy of **Canada,** 35 av. Montaigne, 8e (✆ **01-44-43-29-00;** www.canadainternational.gc.ca/france/index.aspx; Métro: Franklin-D-Roosevelt or Alma-Marceau), is open Monday to Friday 9am to noon and 2 to 5pm. The Embassy of the **United Kingdom,** 35 rue du Faubourg St-Honoré, 8e (✆ **01-44-51-31-00;** http://ukinfrance.fco.gov.uk/en; Métro: Concorde or Madeleine), is open Monday to Friday 9:30am to 1pm and 2:30 to 5pm. The Embassy of **Ireland,** 4 rue Rude, 16e (✆ **01-44-17-67-00;** www.embassyofireland.fr; Métro: Etoile), is open Monday to Friday 9:30am to 1pm and 2:30 to 5:30pm. The Embassy of **Australia,** 4 rue Jean-Rey, 15e (✆ **01-40-59-33-00;** www.france.embassy.gov.au; Métro: Bir Hakeim), is open Monday to Friday 9:15am to noon and 2:30 to 4:30pm. The Embassy of **New Zealand,** 7 ter rue Léonard-de-Vinci, 16e (✆ **01-45-01-43-43;** www.nzembassy.com/france; Métro: Victor Hugo), is open Monday to Friday 9am to 1pm and 2:30 to 6pm. The Embassy of **South Africa,** 59 quai d'Orsay, 7e (✆ **01-53-59-23-23;** www.afriquesud.net; Métro: Invalides), is open Monday to Friday 9am to noon.

Emergencies For the police, call ✆ **17;** to report a fire, call ✆ **18.** For an ambulance, call ✆ **15** or 01-45-67-50-50.

Police In an emergency, call ✆ **17.** For nonemergency situations, the principal *préfecture* is at 9 bd. du Palais, 4e (✆ **01-53-73-53-73;** Métro: Cité).

Post Offices Most post offices in Paris are open Monday through Friday from 8am to 7pm and every Saturday from 8am to noon. One of the biggest and most central is the main post office for the 1st arrondissement, at 52 rue du Louvre (✆ **01-40-28-76-00;** Métro: Musée du Louvre). It maintains the hours noted above for services that include sale of postal money orders, mail collection and distribution, and expedition of faxes. For buying stamps and accepting packages, it's open on a limited basis 24 hours a day. If you find it inconvenient to go to the post office just to buy stamps, they're sold at the reception desks of many hotels and at cafes designated with red TABAC signs.

Safety Beware of child pickpockets, who prey on visitors around sites such as the Louvre, Eiffel Tower, Notre-Dame, and Montmartre, and who like to pick pockets in the Métro, often blocking the entrances and exits to the escalator. Women should hang on to their purses.

Taxes As a member of the European Union (E.U.), France routinely imposes a value-added tax (VAT in English; TVA in French) on many goods and services. The standard VAT is 19.6% on merchandise, including clothing, appliances, liquor, leather goods, shoes, furs, jewelry, perfumes, cameras, and even caviar. Refunds are made for the tax on certain goods and merchandise, but not on services. The minimum purchase is 184€ at one time for nationals or residents of countries outside the E.U.

Telephones The country code for France is **33.** All phone numbers in France have 10 digits, including the **area code** (or regional prefix). For example, the phone number for the Paris police, 01-53-73-53-73, contains the area code for Paris and the Ile de France **(01).** To make a **long-distance call within France,** dial the 10-digit number. **When calling from outside France,** dial the international prefix for your country (**011** for the U.S. and Canada), the country code for France, and then the last nine digits of the number, dropping the 0 (zero) from the regional prefix.

Public phones are found everywhere in France. The most widely accepted method of payment is the ***télécarte,*** a prepaid calling card available at kiosks, post offices, and Métro stations. Sold in two versions, they cost 11€ and 16€ for 50 and 120 units, respectively. A local call costs one unit, or 6 to 18 minutes of conversation, depending on the rate at the time you make the call. Avoid making calls from your hotel, which may double or triple the charges.

Tipping The law requires all bills to say *service compris,* which means the total includes the tip. But French diners often leave some small change as an additional tip, especially if service has been exceptional.

Some general guidelines: For hotel staff, tip 1.05€ to 1.50€ for every item of baggage the porter carries on arrival and departure, and 1.50€ for the maid. Tip taxi drivers 10% to 15% of the amount on the meter. For guides for group visits to museums and monuments, 1.50€ is a reasonable tip.

Where to Stay

Although Paris hotels are quite expensive, there is some good news. Scores of lackluster lodgings, where the wallpaper dated from the Napoleonic era, have been renovated and offer much better value in the moderate-to-inexpensive price range. The most outstanding examples are in the **7th arrondissement,** where several good-value hotels have blossomed from dives.

By now, the "season" has almost ceased to exist. Most visitors, at least from North America, visit in July and August. Because many French are on vacation, and trade fairs and conventions come to a halt, there are usually plenty of rooms, even though these months have traditionally been the peak season for European travel. In most hotels, February is just as busy as April or September because of the volume of business travelers and the increasing number of tourists who've learned to take advantage of off-season discount airfares.

Hot weather doesn't last long in Paris, so most hotels, except the deluxe ones, don't provide air-conditioning. To avoid the noise problem when you have to open windows, request a room in the back when making a reservation.

Some hotels offer a continental breakfast of coffee, tea, or hot chocolate; a freshly baked croissant and roll; and butter and jam or jelly. Though nowhere near as filling as a traditional English or American breakfast, it is quick to prepare—it'll be at your door moments after you request it—and can be served at almost any hour. The word "breakfast" in these entries refers to this version.

Rates quoted include service and value-added tax unless otherwise specified. Unless otherwise noted, all hotel rooms have private bathrooms.

RIGHT BANK: 1ST ARRONDISSEMENT

Very Expensive

Hôtel Meurice ★★★ This landmark lies between the place de la Concorde and the Grand Louvre, facing the Tuileries Gardens. Since the 1800s, it has welcomed the royal, the rich, and even the radical. The mad genius Salvador Dalí made the

Meurice his headquarters. The mosaic floors, plaster ceilings, hand-carved moldings, and Art Nouveau glass roof atop the Winter Garden look new. Each room is individually decorated with period pieces, fine carpets, Italian and French fabrics, marble bathrooms, and modern features such as fax and Internet access. Suites are among the most lavish in France.

228 rue de Rivoli, 75001 Paris. ✆ **01-44-58-10-10.** Fax 01-44-58-10-15. www.meuricehotel.com. 160 units. 640€–980€ double; from 1,050€ junior suite; from 1,700€ suite. AE, DC, MC, V. Parking 27€. Métro: Tuileries or Concorde. **Amenities:** 2 restaurants; bar; babysitting; room service; full-service spa. *In room:* A/C, TV, hair dryer, minibar, Wi-Fi (20€ per day).

Hôtel Ritz ★★★ The Ritz is Europe's greatest hotel, an enduring symbol of elegance on one of Paris's most beautiful and historic squares. César Ritz, the "little shepherd boy from Niederwald," converted the Hôtel de Lazun into a luxury hotel in 1898. With the help of the culinary master Escoffier, he made the Ritz a miracle of luxury. In 1979, the Ritz family sold the hotel to Mohammed al Fayed, who refurbished it and added a cooking school. The hotel annexed two town houses, joined by an arcade lined with display cases representing 125 of Paris's leading boutiques. The public salons are furnished with museum-caliber antiques. Each guest room is uniquely decorated, most with Louis XIV or XV reproductions; all have fine rugs, marble fireplaces, tapestries, brass beds, and more. Ever since Edward VII got stuck in a too-narrow bathtub with his lover, the tubs at the Ritz have been deep and big.

15 place Vendôme, 75001 Paris. ✆ **800/223-6800** in the U.S. and Canada, or 01-43-16-30-30. Fax 01-43-16-31-78. www.ritzparis.com. 159 units. 770€–870€ double; from 1,020€ suite. AE, DC, MC, V. Parking 48€. Métro: Opéra, Concorde, or Madeleine. **Amenities:** Restaurant; 4 bars; nightclub; babysitting; health club; indoor pool; room service; sauna. *In room:* A/C, TV, hair dryer, minibar, Wi-Fi (25€ per day).

Expensive

Westin Paris ★ ☺ It's location, location, location. You're 30 seconds from the Tuileries Gardens, 3 minutes from the place Vendôme, 5 minutes from the place de la Concorde, and 7 minutes from the Louvre. Renovations have breathed new life into most of the rooms, which are a bit small but comfortably furnished and well maintained. Two connecting rooms can be blocked off for families, and family rates are available. Many units overlook an inner courtyard.

3 rue de Castiglione, 75001 Paris. ✆ **800/454-6835** in the U.S., or 01-44-77-11-11. Fax 01-44-77-14-60. www.thewestinparis.com. 440 units. 350€–410€ double; from 630€ suite. AE, DC, MC, V. Métro: Tuileries. **Amenities:** 2 restaurants; bar; babysitting; health club; room service. *In room:* A/C, TV, hair dryer, minibar, Wi-Fi (25€ per day).

Moderate

Hôtel Britannique Conservatively modern and plush, this is a much-renovated 19th-century hotel near Les Halles and Notre-Dame. The place not only is British in name, but also seems to cultivate English graciousness. The guest rooms are small, but immaculate and soundproof, with comfortable beds. The reading room is a cozy retreat.

20 av. Victoria, 75001 Paris. ✆ **01-42-33-74-59.** Fax 01-42-33-82-65. www.hotel-britannique.fr. 39 units. 190€–221€ double; 279€–325€ suite. AE, DC, MC, V. Métro: Châtelet. **Amenities:** Bar; room service. *In room:* A/C, TV, hair dryer, minibar, Wi-Fi (free).

Paris Accommodations

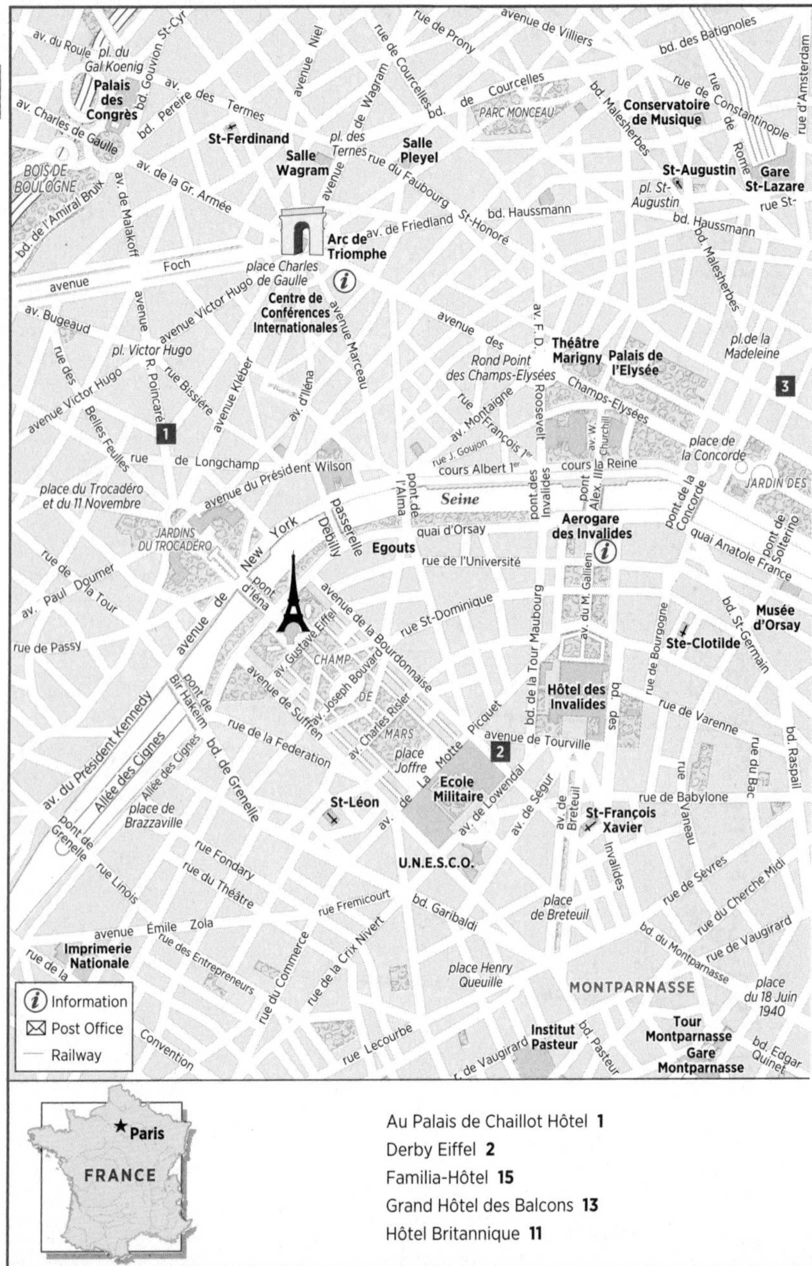

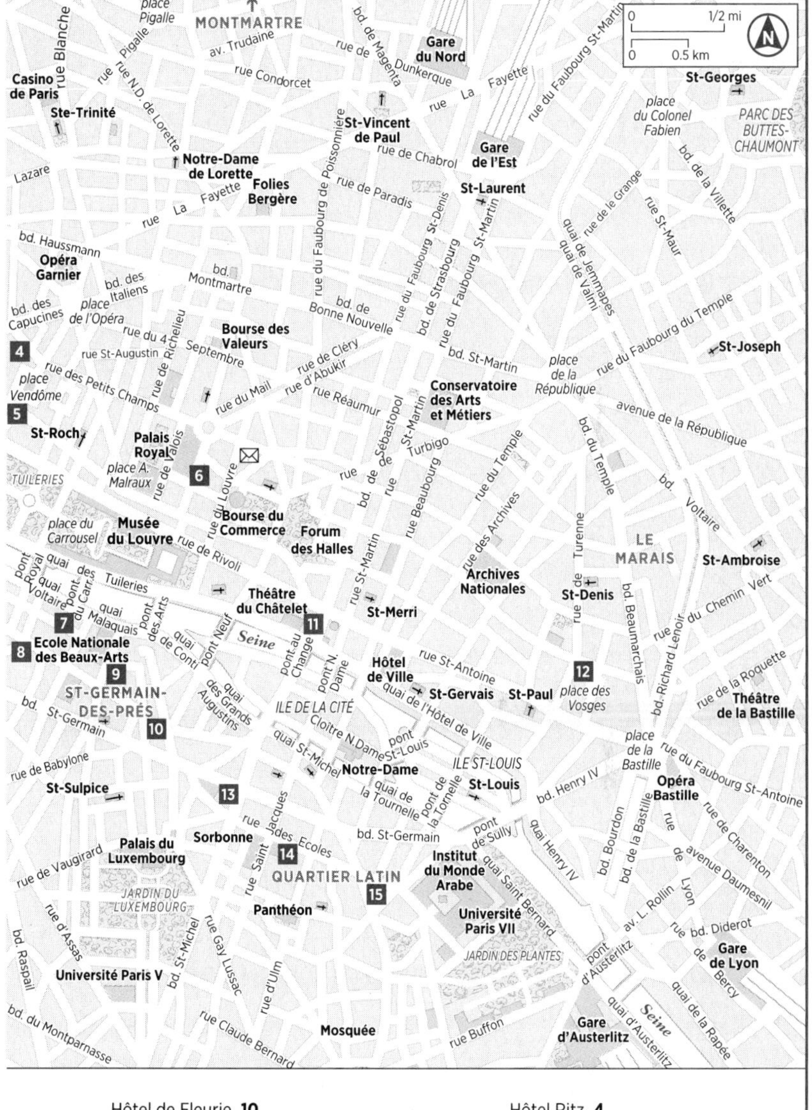

Hôtel de Fleurie **10**
Hôtel du Quai Voltaire **7**
Hôtel Meurice **3**
Hôtel Moderne Saint-Germain **14**
Hôtel Montalembert **8**
Hôtel Ritz **4**
L'Hôtel **9**
Pavillon de la Reine **12**
Timhôtel le Louvre **6**
Westin Paris **5**

Inexpensive

Timhôtel Le Louvre ☺ This hotel and its sibling in the 2nd arrondissement, the Timhôtel Palais-Royal, are part of a new breed of government-rated, two-star, family-friendly hotels cropping up in France. These Timhôtels share the same manager and temperament. Though the rooms at the Palais-Royal branch are a bit larger than the ones here, this branch is so close to the Louvre that it's almost irresistible. The ambience is modern, with monochromatic rooms and wall-to-wall carpeting.

Timhôtel Le Louvre: 4 rue Croix des Petits-Champs, 75001 Paris. ✆ **01-42-60-34-86;** fax 01-42-60-10-39; www.timhotel.fr; 56 units; Métro: Palais-Royal. Timhôtel Palais-Royal: 3 rue de la Banque, 75002 Paris; ✆ **01-42-61-53-90;** fax 01-42-60-05-39; 46 units; Métro: Bourse. 119€–170€ double. AE, DC, MC, V. **Amenities** (at both branches): Restaurant (breakfast only); smoke-free rooms. *In room:* A/C, TV, Wi-Fi (free).

RIGHT BANK: 3RD ARRONDISSEMENT (LE MARAIS)

Expensive

Pavillon de la Reine ★★ This is the kind of hidden gem that Frommer's readers love, opening as it does onto the most romantic square in Paris. In days of yore the 1612 mansion was a gathering place for the likes of Racine, La Fontaine, Molière, and Madame de Sévigné. You enter through an arcade that opens onto a small formal garden. The Louis XIII decor evokes the heyday of the square itself, and iron-banded Spanish antiques create a rustic aura. Each guest room is individually furnished in a historical or modern style—take your pick. Some units are duplexes with sleeping lofts above cozy salons.

28 place des Vosges, 75003 Paris. ✆ **01-40-29-19-19.** Fax 01-40-29-19-20. www.pavillon-de-la-reine.com. 56 units. 380€–490€ double; 610€–710€ duplex; 610€ junior suite; 710€–950€ suite. AE, MC, V. Métro: Bastille. **Amenities:** Bar; babysitting; room service. *In room:* A/C, TV, minibar, Wi-Fi (free).

RIGHT BANK: 16TH ARRONDISSEMENT (TROCADÉRO/ BOIS DE BOULOGNE)

Inexpensive

Au Palais de Chaillot Hôtel Located between the Champs-Elysées and Trocadéro, this restored town house is a contemporary yet informal variation on Parisian chic. The guest rooms come in various shapes and sizes, and are furnished with a light touch, with bright colors and wicker. Room nos. 61, 62, and 63 afford partial views of the Eiffel Tower.

35 av. Raymond-Poincaré, 75116 Paris. ✆ **01-53-70-09-09.** Fax 01-53-70-09-08. www.hotelpalaisdechaillot.com. 28 units. 134€–154€ double; 179€ junior suite. 20€ extra bed. AE, DC, MC, V. Métro: Victor Hugo or Trocadéro. **Amenities:** Room service. *In room:* A/C, TV, hair dryer, Wi-Fi (free).

LEFT BANK: 5TH ARRONDISSEMENT (LATIN QUARTER)

Inexpensive

Familia-Hôtel As the name implies, this hotel has been family run for decades. Many personal touches make the place unique. Finely executed sepia-colored frescoes of Parisian scenes grace the walls of 14 rooms. Eight units have restored stone walls, and seven have balconies with delightful views over the Latin Quarter. The dynamic owners renovate the rooms as often as needed to maintain the highest level of comfort.

11 rue des Ecoles, 75005 Paris. ✆ **01-43-54-55-27.** Fax 01-43-29-61-77. www.hotel-paris-familia.com. 30 units. 99€–122€ double; 167€ triple; 179€ quad. Rates include breakfast. AE, DC, MC, V. Parking 20€. Métro: Jussieu or Maubert-Mutualité. *In room:* TV, hair dryer, minibar, Wi-Fi (free).

Hôtel Moderne Saint-Germain ★ In the heart of the Latin Quarter, between the Pantheon and Saint-Michel, the Hôtel Moderne is better than ever since it ended the 20th century with a complete overhaul. Though the rooms are small, this is still one of the neighborhood's better three-star hotels, offering spotless accommodations. In the units fronting rue des Ecoles, double-glazed windows hush the traffic.

33 rue des Ecoles, 75005 Paris. ✆ **01-43-54-37-78.** Fax 01-43-29-91-31. www.hotel-paris-stgermain.com. 45 units. 150€ double; 180€ triple. AE, DC, MC, V. Parking 26€. Métro: Maubert-Mutualité. **Amenities:** Exercise room; room service. *In room:* A/C, TV, hair dryer, Wi-Fi (free).

LEFT BANK: 6TH ARRONDISSEMENT (ST-GERMAIN/LUXEMBOURG)

Very Expensive

L'Hôtel ★ This is one of the Left Bank's most charming boutique hotels. It was once a 19th-century fleabag whose major distinction was that Oscar Wilde died in one of its bedrooms, but today's guests aren't anywhere near destitution. Guest rooms vary in size, style, and price; all have decorative fireplaces and fabric-covered walls. All the sumptuous beds have tasteful fabrics and crisp linens. About half the bathrooms are small, tubless nooks. Room themes reflect China, Russia, Japan, India, or high-camp Victorian. The Cardinal room is all scarlet, the Viollet-le-Duc room is neo-Gothic, and the room where Wilde died is Victorian.

13 rue des Beaux-Arts, 75006 Paris. ✆ **01-44-41-99-00.** Fax 01-43-25-64-81. www.l-hotel.com. 20 units. 280€–740€ double; 640€–740€ suite. AE, DC, MC, V. Métro: St-Germain-des-Prés. **Amenities:** Restaurant; bar; babysitting; indoor pool; room service; steam room. *In room:* A/C, TV, hair dryer, minibar, Wi-Fi (free).

Moderate

Hôtel de Fleurie ★ ☺ Off the boulevard St-Germain on a colorful little street, the Fleurie is one of the best of the city's "new" old hotels; its statuary-studded facade recaptures 17th-century elegance, and the stone walls in the salon have been exposed. Many of the guest rooms have elaborate draperies and antique reproductions. All of the bedrooms were renovated early in the millennium. Because some rooms are larger than others and contain an extra bed for one or two children, the hotel has long been a family favorite.

32–34 rue Grégoire-de-Tours, 75006 Paris. ✆ **01-53-73-70-00.** Fax 01-53-73-70-20. www.fleurie-hotel-paris.com. 29 units. 250€–320€ double; 465€ family room. Children 12 and under stay free in parent's room. AE, DC, MC, V. Métro: Odéon or Mabillon. **Amenities:** Bar; babysitting; room service; rooms for those with limited mobility. *In room:* A/C, TV, hair dryer, minibar, Wi-Fi (free).

Inexpensive

Grand Hôtel des Balcons ★ The Corroyer-André family welcomes you to this restored 19th-century building, once patronized by Baudelaire and the poets Henri Michaux and Endré Ady. You enter an Art Nouveau setting with stained-glass windows and tulip-shaped molten glass lamps and chandeliers. The hotel lies close to the gardens of Luxembourg, behind a restored facade studded with small balconies—hence its name. Rooms are affordable, harmonious in decor, big on comfort and good maintenance, and, while not large, offer big closets and full-length dressing mirrors.

3 Casimir Delavigne, 75006 Paris. ✆ **01-46-34-78-50.** Fax 01-46-34-06-27. www.balcons.com. 50 units. 125€ double; 220€ triple or quad. AE, MC, V. Métro: Odéon. RER: Luxembourg. **Amenities:** Breakfast room. *In room:* TV, hair dryer, Wi-Fi (5€ per day).

LEFT BANK: 7TH ARRONDISSEMENT

Very Expensive

Hôtel Montalembert ★★ Unusually elegant for the Left Bank, the Montalembert dates from 1926, when it was built in the Beaux Arts style. Its beige, cream, and gold decor borrows elements of Bauhaus and postmodern design. The guest rooms are spacious except for some standard doubles that are small unless you're a very thin model. Frette linens decorate roomy beds topped with cabana-stripe duvets that crown deluxe French mattresses.

3 rue de Montalembert, Paris 75007. ✆ **800/786-6397** in the U.S. and Canada, or 01-45-49-68-68. Fax 01-45-49-69-49. www.montalembert.com. 56 units. 410€–520€ double; 650€–900€ suite. AE, DC, MC, V. Parking 33€. Métro: Rue du Bac. **Amenities:** Restaurant; bar; access to nearby health club; room service. *In room:* A/C, TV, hair dryer, minibar, Wi-Fi (29€ per day).

Inexpensive

Derby Eiffel This hotel faces the Ecole Militaire and contains airy public areas. Our favorite is a glass-roofed conservatory in back, filled year-round with plants and used as a breakfast area. The soundproof and modern guest rooms employ thick fabrics and soothing neutral colors. Most front-facing rooms have views of the Eiffel Tower. In 1998, enormous sums were spent upgrading the rooms and bathrooms and improving the hotel's interior aesthetics, and renovations have been going on ever since. All bathrooms have showers and half tubs.

5 av. Duquesne, Paris 75007. ✆ **01-47-05-12-05.** www.hotelsderby.com. Fax 01-47-05-43-43. 43 units. 135€–155€ double; 196€ triple. AE, DC, MC, V. Métro: Ecole Militaire. **Amenities:** Bar; babysitting; room service. *In room:* A/C, TV, hair dryer, minibar, Wi-Fi (5€ per day).

Hôtel du Quai Voltaire Built in the 1600s as an abbey and transformed into a hotel in 1856, the Quai Voltaire is best known for such illustrious guests as Wilde, Richard Wagner, and Baudelaire, who occupied room nos. 47, 55, and 56, respectively. Camille Pissarro painted *Le Pont Royal* from the window of his fourth-floor room. Guest rooms in this modest inn were renovated in 2008; most overlook the bookstalls and boats of the Seine.

19 quai Voltaire, Paris 75007. ✆ **01-42-61-50-91.** Fax 01-42-61-62-26. www.quaivoltaire.fr. 33 units. 150€–160€ double; 180€ triple. AE, DC, MC, V. Parking 14€. Métro: Musée d'Orsay or Rue du Bac. **Amenities:** Bar; room service. *In room:* Hair dryer, Wi-Fi (free).

Where to Dine

Our best piece of advice—even if your budget is lean—is to splurge on one grand French meal (and to make reservations well in advance). A meal at a place such as **Taillevent, Alain Ducasse,** or **Carré des Feuillants** is something you'll always remember.

Three-star dining remains quite expensive. The 100€ main course (*entrée* means "appetizer" in French; don't confuse *entrées* with main courses) is no longer a novelty, and first courses can exceed 50€; in the top dining rooms, the total bill easily surpasses 175€ to 200€ per person. You can get around that high price tag in many places by ordering a fixed-price menu, perhaps for a "mere" 90€, or by heading for one of the not-so-celebrated but equally stellar dining rooms—**Pierre Gagnaire,** for example, instead of Alain Ducasse.

In the past, suits and ties were a given, and women always wore smart dresses or suits. Well, you can kiss your suits au revoir. Except in first-class and deluxe places, attire is more relaxed, but that doesn't mean sloppy jeans and workout clothes. Parisians still value style, even when dressing informally.

Restaurants are required by law to post their menus outside, so peruse them carefully. The fixed-price menu remains a solid choice if you want to have some idea of what your bill will be when it's presented by the waiter (whom you call *monsieur,* never *garçon*).

RIGHT BANK: 1ST ARRONDISSEMENT

Very Expensive

Carré des Feuillants ★★★ MODERN FRENCH This is a bastion of perfection, an enclave of haute gastronomy. When chef Alain Dutournier turned this 17th-century convent between the place Vendôme and the Tuileries into a restaurant, it was an overnight success. The interior is artfully simple and even, in the eyes of some diners, spartan-looking. It has a vaguely Asian feel, shared by a series of small, monochromatic dining rooms that are mostly outfitted in tones of off-white, black, and beige, and that overlook a flowering courtyard and a glass-enclosed kitchen. You'll find a sophisticated reinterpretation of cuisine from France's southwest, using seasonal ingredients and lots of know-how. Some of the best dishes include roasted rack of milk-fed Pyrénées lamb cooked in a clay pot, or slices of John Dory with potatoes and a tender cabbage lasagna. Milk-fed veal with flap mushrooms and purple artichokes is yet another specialty. For dessert try the mango and passion fruit ravioli.

14 rue de Castiglione (near place Vendôme and the Tuileries), 1er. ✆ **01-42-86-82-82.** Fax 01-42-86-07-71. www.carredesfeuillants.fr. Reservations required far in advance. Main courses 62€–85€; fixed-price lunch 85€–175€, dinner 175€. AE, DC, MC, V. Mon–Fri noon–2:30pm and 7:30–10pm. Closed Aug. Métro: Tuileries, Concorde, Opéra, or Madeleine.

Expensive

Goumard ★★★ SEAFOOD Opened in 1872, this landmark is one of Paris's leading seafood restaurants. It's so devoted to the fine art of preparing fish that other food is banned from the menu (the staff will verbally present a limited roster of meat dishes). The decor consists of a collection of Lalique crystal fish in artificial aquariums. Even more unusual are the restrooms, classified as historic monuments; the Art Nouveau master cabinetmaker Majorelle designed the commodes in the early 1900s. Much of the seafood is flown in from Brittany daily. Examples include flaky crab cakes, flash-fried scallops with black truffles, sautéed wild squid, and grilled John Dory. Nothing (no excess butter, spices, or salt) interferes with the natural flavor of the sea.

9 rue Duphot, 1er. ✆ **01-42-60-36-07.** Fax 01-42-60-04-54. www.goumard.com. Reservations required far in advance. Main courses 19€–79€; fixed-price menu 59€. AE, DC, MC, V. Daily 11:30am–12:30am. Métro: Madeleine or Concorde.

Moderate

Au Pied de Cochon ★★ LATE NIGHT/TRADITIONAL FRENCH Their famous onion soup and namesake specialty (grilled pigs' feet with béarnaise sauce) still lure visitors, and where else in Paris can you get such a good meal at 3am? Other specialties include a platter named after the medieval patron saint of sausage makers, *la temptation de St-Antoine,* which includes grilled pig's tail, pig's snout, and half a pig's foot, all served with béarnaise and *pommes frites;* and *andouillettes* (chitterling sausages) with béarnaise. Two flavorful but less unusual dishes: a *jarret* (shin) of pork, caramelized in honey and served on a bed of sauerkraut, and grilled pork ribs with sage sauce. On the street outside, you can buy some of the freshest oysters in town.

6 rue Coquillière, 1er. ✆ 01-40-13-77-00. www.pieddecochon.com. Reservations recommended for lunch and dinner hours. Main courses 17€–48€. AE, DC, MC, V. Daily 24 hr. Métro: Les Halles or Louvre.

Inexpensive

Angélina ★★ TEA/TRADITIONAL FRENCH In the high-rent area near the InterContinental, this *salon de thé* (tea salon) combines fashion-industry glitter and bourgeois respectability. The carpets are plush, the ceilings are high, and the accessories have the right amount of patina. This place has no equal when it comes to viewing the lionesses of haute couture over tea and sandwiches. The waitresses bear silver trays with pastries, drinks, and tea or coffee to marble-topped tables. Lunch usually offers a salad and a *plat du jour* (dish of the day) such as *salade gourmande* (gourmet salad) with foie gras and smoked breast of duck on a bed of fresh salad greens. An enduring specialty is hot chocolate, as well as Mont Blanc, a combination of chestnut cream and meringue.

226 rue de Rivoli, 1er. ✆ **01-42-60-82-00.** Reservations not accepted for tea. Pot of tea (for 1) 7€; sandwiches and salads 10€–15€; main courses 16€–30€. AE, MC, V. Mon–Fri 8am–7pm; Sun 9am–7pm. Métro: Tuileries or Concorde.

RIGHT BANK: 3RD ARRONDISSEMENT (LE MARAIS)

Inexpensive

L'Ambassade d'Auvergne ★ AUVERGNAT/TRADITIONAL FRENCH You enter this rustic tavern through a bar with heavy oak beams, hanging hams, and ceramic plates. It showcases the culinary bounty of France's most isolated region, the Auvergne, whose pork products are widely celebrated. Try chicory salad with apples and pieces of country ham; pork braised with cabbage, turnips, and white beans; or grilled tripe sausages with mashed potatoes and Cantal cheese with garlic. Nonpork specialties are pan-fried duck liver with gingerbread, perch steamed in verbena tea, and roasted rack of lamb with wild mushrooms.

22 rue de Grenier St-Lazare, 3e. ✆ **01-42-72-31-22.** www.ambassade-auvergne.com. Reservations recommended. Main courses 14€–23€; fixed-price menu 28€. AE, MC, V. Daily noon–2pm and 7:30–10:30pm. Métro: Rambuteau.

RIGHT BANK: 4TH ARRONDISSEMENT

Moderate

Le Georges ★ INTERNATIONAL The Centre Pompidou is again in the spotlight; all of artsy Paris has been talking about this place. Georges is in a large space on the top floor of Paris's most comprehensive arts complex, with views through bay windows over most of the city. The decor is minimalist and postmodern, with lots of brushed aluminum and stainless steel. Tables are made from sandblasted glass, lit from below, and accessorized with hypermodern cutlery. Menu items are mostly Continental, with hints of Asia. Some combinations surprise—macaroni with lobster, for example. Others seem exotic, including roasted ostrich steak. Aside from these dishes, some of the best items on the menu are king crab with coconut milk and curry. To get here, go to the exterior elevator to the left of the Centre Pompidou's main entrance. Tell the guard you have a reservation; otherwise, you may not be allowed up.

Centre Pompidou, 6th Floor, 19 rue Beaubourg, 4e. ✆ **01-44-78-47-99.** www.centrepompidou.fr. Reservations required for dinner, recommended for lunch. Main courses 37€–47€. AE, DC, MC, V. Wed–Mon noon–2am. Métro: Rambuteau.

RIGHT BANK: 8TH ARRONDISSEMENT

Very Expensive

Pierre Gagnaire ★★★ MODERN FRENCH If you're able to get a reservation, it's worth the effort. The menus are seasonal to take advantage of France's rich bounty; owner Pierre Gagnaire demands perfection, and the chef has a dazzling way with flavors and textures. Stellar examples are roast duck, and turbot cooked in a bag and served with fennel and Provençal lemons. Chicken with truffles comes in two stages—first the breast in wine-based aspic and then the thighs, chopped into roughly textured pieces.

6 rue Balzac, 8e. ✆ **01-58-36-12-50.** Fax 01-58-36-12-51. www.pierre-gagnaire.com. Reservations required. Main courses 65€–165€; fixed-price menu 105€ lunch, 255€ dinner. AE, DC, MC, V. Mon–Fri noon–1:30pm; Sun–Fri 7:30–10pm. Métro: George V.

Restaurant Plaza Athénée (Alain Ducasse) ★★★ FRENCH Few other chefs have been catapulted to international fame as quickly as Alain Ducasse. The six-star chef, who supervises the kitchens here, divides his time among Paris, Monaco, Las Vegas, New York, and Tokyo. In this, his Parisian stronghold, he places a special emphasis on "rare and precious ingredients," whipping up flavorful and very expensive combinations of caviar, lobster, crayfish, truffles (both black and white), and shellfish. Cuisine is vaguely Mediterranean and decidedly contemporary, yet based on traditional models. Some of the best examples include smoked, tea-glazed pigeon or line-caught sea bass with flap mushroom. For appetizers, try the creamy pasta with truffles and giblets. Desserts are perhaps the finest in all of Paris's luxe restaurants. The wine list is superb, with some selections deriving from the best vintages of France, Germany, Switzerland, Spain, California, and Italy.

In the Hôtel Plaza Athénée, 25 av. Montaigne, 8e. ✆ **01-53-67-65-00.** Fax 01-53-67-65-12. www.alain-ducasse.com. Reservations required 3–4 weeks in advance. Main courses 70€–175€; fixed-price menus 260€–360€. AE, DC, MC, V. Thurs–Fri 12:45–2:15pm; Mon–Fri 7:45–10:15pm. Closed mid-July to Aug 25 and 10 days in late Dec. Métro: Alma-Marceau or FDR.

Taillevent ★★★ FRENCH This is the Parisian ne plus ultra of gastronomy. Taillevent opened in 1946 and has climbed steadily in excellence; today it ranks among Paris's most outstanding all-around restaurants. It's in a grand 19th-century town house off the Champs-Elysées, with paneled rooms and crystal chandeliers. The place is small, which permits the owner to give personal attention to every facet of the operation and maintain a discreet atmosphere. Each dish is supreme in flavor, including John Dory with olives or lamb saddle seasoned with wild herbs. A cassoulet of crayfish, if featured, is also divine. Chefs dare serve that old standard, *baba au rhum,* but it's perhaps the best you'll ever taste. The wine list is among the best in Paris.

15 rue Lamennais, 8e. ✆ **01-44-95-15-01.** Fax 01-42-25-95-18. www.taillevent.com. Reservations required 3–4 weeks in advance. Main courses 34€–90€; fixed-price lunch 80€; *dégustation* 190€. AE, DC, MC, V. Mon–Fri 12:15–2:30pm and 7:15–10pm. Closed Aug. Métro: George V.

Expensive

L'Angle du Faubourg ★★ TRADITIONAL FRENCH Throughout the 1980s and early 1990s, a reservation at the ultra-upscale Taillevent (above) was sought after by diplomats, billionaires, and *demi-mondains* from around Europe. In 2001, Taillevent's owner, M. Vrinat, opened a cost-conscious bistro that capitalizes on Taillevent's reputation, but at much lower prices. Lunches here tend to be efficient, relatively quick, and businesslike; dinners are more leisurely, even romantic. The restaurant has an ultramodern dining room, additional seating in the cellar, and a menu that simplifies Taillevent's lofty culinary ideas. The best examples include braised lamb with the juice of black olives; risotto with ingredients that change weekly (during our visit, it was studded with braised radicchio); and a grilled, low-fat version of *daurade* (bream), served with artichokes and a reduction of mushrooms, appreciated by the many diet-conscious *photo-modèles* who stop in.

195 rue du Faubourg St-Honoré, 8e. ✆ **01-40-74-20-20.** www.taillevent.com. Reservations required. Main courses 25€–47€; fixed-price menu 38€–75€. AE, DC, MC, V. Mon–Fri noon–2:30pm and 7–10:30pm. Closed Aug. Métro: Terme or Etoile.

Spoon, Food & Wine ★ INTERNATIONAL This hypermodern venture by star chef Alain Ducasse is both hailed as a "restaurant for the millennium" and condemned as surreal and a bit absurd. Despite that, there can be a 2-week wait for a dinner reservation. This upscale but affordable restaurant may be the least pretentious and most hip of Ducasse's ventures. The somewhat claustrophobic dining room blends Parisian and Californian references, and the menu (which changes every 2 months) roams the world. Examples include deliberately undercooked grilled squid (part of it evokes sushi) with curry sauce; grilled lamb cutlets; and spareribs with a devil's marmalade. Vegetarians appreciate stir-fried dishes in which you can mix and match up to 15 ingredients.

In the Hôtel Marignan-Elysée, 14 rue Marignan, 8e. ✆ **01-40-76-34-44.** www.spoon.tm.fr. Reservations recommended 1–2 weeks in advance. Main courses 29€–47€; fixed-price lunch 36€. AE, DC, MC, V. Mon–Fri 12:15–2:30pm and 7:30–10:30pm. Closed Aug and last week of Dec. Métro: Franklin-D-Roosevelt.

RIGHT BANK: 9TH, 10TH & 12TH ARRONDISSEMENTS

Expensive

Chez Jean ★ TRADITIONAL FRENCH The crowd is young, the food is sophisticated, and the vintage 1950s aura makes you think that American expatriate novelist James Baldwin will arrive any minute. Surrounded by well-oiled pine panels and polished copper, you can choose from some of Grandmother's favorites as well as more modern dishes. Owner Jean-Frederic Guidoni worked for more than 20 years at Taillevent (above), but within his own milieu, he demonstrates his own innovative touch at prices that are much more reasonable. For starters, consider a chicken consommé with endives and chorizo; a savory version of a cheesy alpine staple, *raclette,* made with mustard sauce and *Curé Nantais* cheese; and slow-braised pork cooked for 7 hours and served on a bed of carrots, apricots, and confit of lemon.

8 rue St-Lazare, 9e. ✆ **01-48-78-62-73.** www.restaurantjean.fr. Reservations recommended far in advance. Main courses 27€–38€; fixed-price menu 70€–95€; fixed-price lunch 46€. AE, DC, MC, V. Mon–Fri noon–2:30pm and 7:30–10:30pm. Métro: Notre-Dame de Lorette or Saint-Georges.

Moderate

Brasserie Flo ★ ALSATIAN This remote restaurant is hard to find, but once you arrive (after walking through passageway after passageway), you'll see that *fin de siècle* Paris lives on. The restaurant opened in 1860 and has changed its decor very little. The specialty is *la formidable choucroute* (a mound of sauerkraut with boiled ham, bacon, and sausage) for two. Onion soup and sole meunière are always good, as are warm foie gras and guinea hen with lentils. Look for the *plats du jour,* ranging from roast pigeon to tuna steak with hot peppers.

7 cour des Petites-Ecuries, 10e. ✆ **01-47-70-13-59.** Reservations recommended. Main courses 18€-36€; fixed-price dinner 28€; fixed-price lunch 19€. AE, DC, MC, V. Daily noon-3pm and 7pm-1am. Métro: Château d'Eau or Strasbourg-St-Denis.

LEFT BANK: 5TH ARRONDISSEMENT (LATIN QUARTER)

Moderate

Les Papilles ★ One of the most exciting additions to Paris's culinary scene is **Les Papilles,** a deli, bistro, and wine shop all at one address. It features an appetizer (called *entrée* in French), a plat du jour, and dessert for an affordable price. Wine is available by the glass, but patrons are encouraged to order by the bottle since these bottles have some of the cheapest retail prices in France. Near Jardin du Luxembourg, Les Papilles offers superb food, including a four-course *dégustation* menu at night that blends the cookery of the Garonne with the chef's imagination of the day.

30 rue Gay-Lussac, 5e. ✆ **01-43-25-20-79.** Reservations not needed. Market menu 31€; fixed-price dinner 80€. AE, MC, V. Mon-Sat noon-3pm and 7-11pm. Métro: Luxembourg.

Marty ★ MODERN FRENCH Charming, with a stone-trimmed decor that's authentic to the era (1913) when it was established, this restaurant has been "discovered" by new generations of restaurantgoers. Service is attentive, and lots of Jazz Age murals grace the walls. Food is savory, satisfying, and unfussy. Views from the hideaway tables on the mezzanine sweep over the entire human comedy, which is loud, large, and animated, unfolding above and below you. Begin a meal with duckling terrine or Andalusian gazpacho. Continue with *suprême* of guinea fowl with vegetable moussaka, a rump steak in black-pepper sauce, or perhaps fried scallops sautéed in the Provençal style.

20 av. des Gobelins, 5e. ✆ **01-43-31-39-51.** www.marty-restaurant.com. Main courses 21€-35€; fixed-price menu 35€. AE, DC, MC, V. Daily noon-midnight. Métro: Gobelins.

Inexpensive

Coco de Mer ★ SEYCHELLE ISLANDS The theme of this restaurant tugs at the emotions of Parisians who have spent their holidays on the beaches of the Seychelles, in the Indian Ocean. It contains several dining rooms, one of which is outfitted like a beach, with a sand-covered floor, replicas of palm trees, and a scattering of conch shells. Menu items feature such exotic dishes as tartare of tuna flavored with ginger, olive oil, salt, and pepper; and smoked swordfish, served as carpaccio or in thin slices with mango mousse and spicy sauce. Main courses focus on fish, including a species of red snapper *(boirzoes)* imported from the Seychelles.

34 bd. St-Marcel, 5e. ✆ **01-47-07-06-64.** Reservations recommended. Main courses 14€-17€; fixed-price menus 23€-30€. AE, DC, MC, V. Tues-Sat noon-3pm; Mon-Sat 7:30pm-midnight. Métro: Les Gobelins or St-Marcel.

LEFT BANK: 6TH ARRONDISSEMENT

Moderate

Alcazar Restaurant ★ MODERN FRENCH Paris's highest-profile *brasserie de luxe* is this high-tech place funded by British restaurateur Sir Terence Conran. It features a red-and-white futuristic decor in a street-level dining room and a busy upstairs bar (La Mezzanine de l'Alcazar). The menu includes rack of veal sautéed with wild mushrooms, roasted rack of lamb with thyme, and shellfish and oysters from the waters of Brittany. The wines are as stylish and diverse as you'd expect.

62 rue Mazarine, 6e. ✆ **01-53-10-19-99.** Reservations recommended. Main courses 17€–33€; fixed-price lunch 20€–32€, dinner 43€; Sun brunch 32€. AE, DC, MC, V. Daily noon–2:30pm and 7pm–1am. Métro: Odéon.

Ze Kitchen Galerie ★ 🎁 INTERNATIONAL/MODERN FRENCH The setting here is a colorful loft space in an antique building, with an open-to-view showcase kitchen. Menu items change about every 5 weeks; appetizers are subdivided into pastas, soups, and fish; and main courses are divided into meats and fish that are usually *à la plancha* (grilled). For starters, ever had beet gazpacho with candied ginger, cucumber, and fresh shrimp? The grilled chicken and veal sweetbreads with a carrot-and-mustard *jus* (flavored with ginger) is heavenly, as are platters of oysters, mussels, and sea urchins. Sometimes grilled shoulder of wild boar with tamarind sauce is featured. A meal might also be followed with the restaurant's "cappuccino of the month," a frothy dessert concoction with changing ingredients.

4 rue des Grands-Augustins, 6e. ✆ **01-44-32-00-32.** www.zekitchengalerie.fr. Reservations recommended. Main courses 30€–35€; fixed-price lunch with wine 24€–39€; fixed-price dinner 76€. AE, DC, MC, V. Mon–Fri noon–2:30pm; Mon–Sat 7–11pm. Métro: St-Michel or Pont-Neuf.

Inexpensive

Crémerie-Restaurant Polidor ★ ☺ TRADITIONAL FRENCH Crémerie Polidor is the most traditional bistro in the Odéon area, serving *cuisine familiale.* Its name dates from the early 1900s, when it specialized in frosted cream desserts, but the restaurant can trace its history from 1845. The Crémerie was André Gide's favorite, and Joyce, Hemingway, Valéry, Artaud, and Kerouac also dined here. Peer beyond the lace curtains and brass hatracks to see drawers where, in olden days, regular customers used to lock up their cloth napkins. Try the day's soup followed by kidneys in Madeira sauce, boeuf bourguignon, *confit de canard,* or *blanquette de veau.* For dessert, order a chocolate, raspberry, or lemon tart.

39 rue Monsieur-le-Prince, 6e. ✆ **01-43-26-95-34.** www.polidor.com. Main courses 11€–48€; fixed-price menus 22€–32€. No credit cards. Daily noon–2:30pm; Mon–Sat 7pm–12:30am; Sun 7–11pm. Métro: Odéon.

LEFT BANK: 7TH & 14TH ARRONDISSEMENTS

Very Expensive

L'Arpège ★★★ MODERN FRENCH L'Arpège is best known for Alain Passard's specialties—no restaurant in the 7th serves better food. Surrounded by etched glass, burnished steel, and pear-wood paneling, you can enjoy such specialties as couscous of vegetables and shellfish, lobster braised in the yellow wine of the Jura, braised monkfish in an Orléans mustard sauce, pigeon roasted with almonds and honey-flavored mead, and carpaccio of crayfish with caviar-flavored cream sauce. Although Passard is loath to include red meat on his menus, Kobe beef and venison

THE TOP cafes

Whatever your pleasure—reading, meeting a lover, writing your memoirs, nibbling a hard-boiled egg, or drinking yourself into oblivion—you can do it at a French cafe.

Jean-Paul Sartre came to **Café de Flore,** 172 bd. St-Germain, 6e (✆ **01-45-48-55-26;** www.cafe-de-flore.com; Métro: St-Germain-des-Prés), where it's said he wrote his trilogy *Les Chemins de la Liberté (The Roads to Freedom).* The cafe is still going strong, though celebrities have moved on. Open daily from 7:30am to 1:30am.

Next door, the legendary **Deux Magots,** 6 place St-Germain-des-Prés, 6e (✆ **01-45-48-55-25;** Métro: St-Germain-des-Prés), is still the hangout for sophisticated residents and a tourist favorite in summer. Inside are two Asian statues that give the cafe its name. It's open daily from 7:30am to 1am.

Fouquet's, 99 av. des Champs-Elysées, 8e (✆ **01-47-23-50-00;** www.lesdeuxmagots.fr; Métro: George V), is the premier cafe on the Champs-Elysées. Outside, a barricade of potted flowers separates cafe tables from the sidewalk. Inside are a grillroom, private rooms, and a restaurant. The cafe and grillroom are open daily from 8am to 2am; the restaurant and the slightly less formal grill are open daily noon to 3pm and 7pm to 1am.

At **La Coupole,** 102 bd. Montparnasse, 14e (✆ **01-43-20-14-20;** Métro: Vavin), the crowd ranges from artists' models to young men dressed like Rasputin. People come here to see and be seen. Perhaps order a coffee or cognac VSOP at a sidewalk table, repeating a ritual that has continued since the place was established in 1927. The dining room serves food that is sometimes good, sometimes indifferent. It serves a buffet breakfast Monday through Friday from 8:30 to 10:30am. Open 8am to 1am (until 1:30am Fri–Sat).

Café de la Musique, in the Cité de la Musique, place Fontaine Aux Lions, 213 av. Jean-Jaurès, 19e (✆ **01-48-03-15-91;** Métro: Porte de Pantin), attracts a crowd devoted to music. The recorded sounds in the background are likely to be more diverse and eclectic than in any other cafe in Paris. The red-and-green-velour setting may remind you of a modern opera house. On the menu you'll find pasta with shellfish, pork in cider sauce, and stingray in black-butter sauce. Open 8am to 2am (until 1am only Sun–Mon).

In the Marais, **La Belle Hortense,** 31 rue Vieille du Temple, 4e (✆ **01-48-04-71-60;** Métro: Hôtel de Ville or St-Paul), is the most literary cafe in a legendary literary neighborhood. It offers an erudite and accessible staff; an inventory of French literary classics as well as modern tomes about art, psychoanalysis, history, and culture; and two high-ceilinged, 19th-century rooms little changed since the days of Baudelaire and Balzac. The zinc-covered bar serves wine for 3€ to 9€ a glass. Open daily as a cafe and bookstore from 5pm to 2am.

sometimes appear. He focuses on fish, shellfish, poultry, and—his passion—vegetables. These he elevates to levels unequaled by any other chef in Paris.

84 rue de Varenne, 7e. ✆ **01-47-05-09-06.** Fax 01-44-18-98-39. www.alain-passard.com. Reservations required 2 weeks in advance. Main courses 48€–180€; fixed-price lunch 135€; fixed-price dinner 420€. AE, DC, MC, V. Mon–Fri 12:30–2:30pm and 8–10:30pm. Métro: Varenne.

Paris Attractions

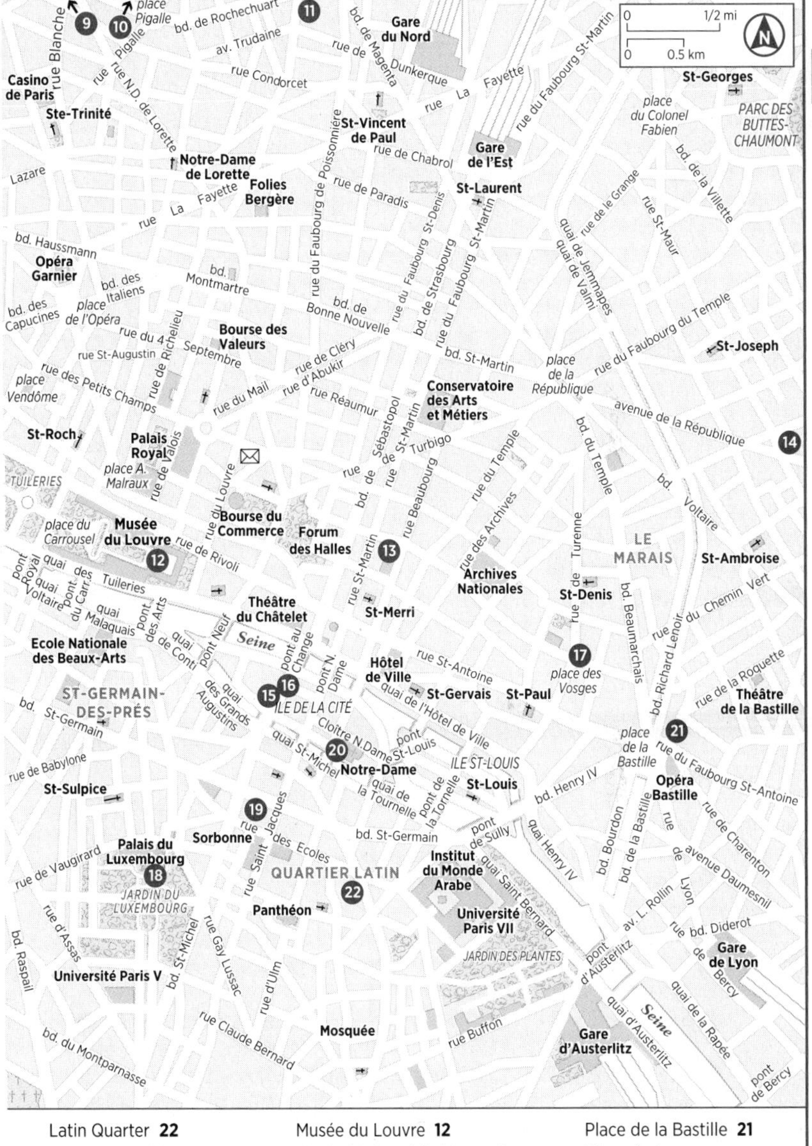

Latin Quarter **22**	Musée du Louvre **12**	Place de la Bastille **21**
Montmartre **11**	Musée National du Moyen Age (Thermes de Cluny) **19**	Place de la Concorde **8**
Musée National d'Art Moderne **13**	Notre-Dame **20**	Place des Vosges **17**
Musée d'Orsay **6**	Parc Monceau **3**	Ste-Chapelle **15**

Expensive

Le Violon d'Ingres ★★★ MODERN FRENCH This restaurant is Paris's *pièce de résistance*. Chef-owner Christian Constant is "the new Robuchon." Those fortunate enough to dine in Violon's warm atmosphere rave about the artistic dishes. They range from wood pigeon cooked on the grill and served with a fricassee of mushrooms to such hearty fare as veal's head with the tongue and brain poached in a sauce of capers and hard-boiled eggs. If you're not steely enough for that, you can opt for the sea bass under a crust of almonds. The service is charming and discreet; the wine selection, well chosen. The Constant family has tied up the dining rituals along this street, with less expensive, less formal restaurants flanking Le Violon d'Ingres.

135 rue St-Dominique, 7e. ✆ **01-45-55-15-05.** Fax 01-45-55-48-42. www.leviolondingres.com. Reservations required at least 2 days in advance. All main courses 27€; fixed-price menu 49€. AE, DC, MC, V. Tues–Sat noon–2:30pm and 7–10:30pm. Métro: Invalides or Ecole-Militaire.

Seeing the Sights in the City of Light

The best way to discover Paris is on foot. Walk along the avenue des Champs-Elysées, tour the quays of the Seine, wander the Ile de la Cité and Ile St-Louis, browse the shops and stalls, and stroll the squares and parks. A walk at dawn can be enthralling as you see the city come to life: Merchants wash shop fronts, cafes begin serving coffee and croissants, and vegetable and fruit vendors start setting up their stalls and arranging their produce.

THE TOP MUSEUMS

Musée du Louvre ★★★ The Louvre is one of the world's largest and greatest museums—and now more beautiful than ever since the facade has been thoroughly cleaned. The $1.2-billion Grand Louvre Project, a 15-year undertaking, is officially complete, but refurbishment of individual galleries and paintings continues. For up-to-the-minute data on what is open and about to open, check out the museum's website (www.louvre.fr).

The collection is staggering. You'll have to resign yourself to missing some masterpieces; you simply can't see everything. People on one of those Paris-in-a-day tours race to glimpse the *Mona Lisa* (in her own special room) and the *Venus de Milo*. Those with an extra 5 minutes go in pursuit of *Winged Victory*, the headless statue discovered at Samothrace that dates from about 200 B.C.

Pressed for time? Take a **guided tour** (in English), which lasts about 90 minutes. The short tour, which is your only option if you visit on Monday, covers the "highlights of the highlights." Tours start under the pyramid at the station marked ACCUEIL DES GROUPES.

The collections are divided into eight departments: Asian antiquities; Egyptian antiquities; Greek, Etruscan, and Roman antiquities; Islamic art; sculpture; paintings; prints and drawings; and objets d'art. The **Grand Galerie,** a 180m (591-ft.) hall opening onto the Seine, is dedicated to mostly Italian paintings from the 1400s to the 1700s, including works by Raphael and Leonardo da Vinci.

The **Richelieu Wing** houses the collection of northern European and French paintings, decorative arts, French sculpture, Oriental antiquities (a rich collection of Islamic art), and the grand salons of Napoleon III. Originally constructed from 1852 to 1857, this wing has been virtually rebuilt. In its 165 rooms, plus three covered courtyards, some 12,000 works of art are displayed. Of the Greek and Roman antiquities, the most notable (aside from *Venus* and *Winged Victory*) are fragments of the Parthenon's frieze.

34-36 quai du Louvre, 1er. Main entrance in the glass pyramid, Cour Napoleon. ✆ **01-40-20-53-17,** 01-40-20-50-50 for operator, or 08-92-68-46-94 for advance credit card sales. www.louvre.fr. Admission 9€, free for children 17 and under, free to all 1st Sun of every month. Sat–Mon and Thurs 9am–6pm; Wed and Fri 9am–10pm. 1½-hr. English-language tours (Mon and Wed–Sun) 6€, free for children 12 and under with museum ticket. Métro: Palais-Royal–Musée du Louvre.

Musée d'Orsay ★★★ The neoclassical Gare d'Orsay train station has been transformed into one of the world's great museums. It contains an important collection devoted to the pivotal years from 1848 to 1914. Across the Seine from the Louvre and the Tuileries, it is a repository of works by the Impressionists, symbolists, pointillists, realists, and late Romantics. Artists represented include van Gogh, Manet, Monet, Degas, and Renoir. It houses thousands of sculptures and paintings across 80 galleries, plus Belle Epoque furniture, photographs, objets d'art, architectural models, and a cinema.

One of Renoir's most joyous paintings is here: *Moulin de la Galette* (1876). Another celebrated work is by the American James McNeill Whistler—*Arrangement in Gray and Black: Portrait of the Painter's Mother.* The most famous piece in the museum is Manet's 1863 *Déjeuner sur l'herbe* (Picnic on the Grass), which created a scandal when it was first exhibited; it depicts a nude woman picnicking with two fully clothed men in a forest. Two years later, his *Olympia,* lounging on her bed wearing nothing but a flower in her hair and high-heeled shoes, met with the same response.

1 rue de Bellechasse or 62 rue de Lille, 7e. ✆ **01-40-49-48-14.** www.musee-orsay.fr. Admission 8€ adults, 5.50€ ages 18–24, free for children 17 and under. Tues–Wed and Fri–Sun 9:30am–6pm; Thurs 9:30am–9:45pm. Closed Dec 25 and Jan 1. Métro: Solférino. RER: Musée d'Orsay.

Centre Pompidou ★★★ This center for 20th-century art opened in 1977 and became a focus of controversy. Its bold exoskeletal architecture and the brightly painted pipes and ducts crisscrossing its transparent facade (green for water, red for heat, blue for air, and yellow for electricity) were jarring. Perhaps the detractors were right all along—within 20 years, the building began to deteriorate so badly that a major restoration was called for. The center was relaunched in 2000.

The Centre Pompidou encompasses four separate attractions. The **Musée National d'Art Moderne (National Museum of Modern Art)** displays a large collection of 20th-century art. With some 40,000 works, this is the big draw, although it can show only about 850 works at one time. If you want to view some real charmers, see Alexander Calder's 1926 *Josephine Baker,* one of his earlier versions of the mobile, an art form he invented. Marcel Duchamp's *Valise* is a collection of miniature reproductions of his fabled dada sculptures and drawings; they're displayed in a carrying case. Every time we visit we have to see Salvador Dalí's *Portrait of Lenin Dancing on Piano Keys.*

Place Georges-Pompidou, 4e. ✆ **01-44-78-12-33.** www.centrepompidou.fr. Admission 12€ adults, 9€ students, free for children 17 and under. Wed–Mon 11am–10pm. Métro: Rambuteau, Hôtel de Ville, or Châtelet–Les Halles.

ON THE CHAMPS-ELYSÉES

Arc de Triomphe ★★★ At the western end of the Champs-Elysées, the Arc de Triomphe is the largest triumphal arch in the world, about 49m (161 ft.) high and 44m (144 ft.) wide. Don't cross the square to reach it! With a dozen streets radiating from the "Star," the traffic circle is vehicular roulette. It's the busiest traffic hub in Paris. Instead, take the underground passage.

Commissioned by Napoleon in 1806 to commemorate his Grande Armée's victories, the arch wasn't completed until 1836, under Louis-Philippe. Four years later, Napoleon's remains—brought from his grave on St. Helena—passed under the arch en route to his tomb at the Hôtel des Invalides. Since then it has become the focal point for state funerals. It's also the site of the Tomb of the Unknown Soldier, where an eternal flame burns.

Of the sculptures decorating the monument, the best known is Rude's *Marseillaise,* also called *The Departure of the Volunteers.* J. P. Cortot's *Triumph of Napoleon in 1810,* along with the *Resistance of 1814* and *Peace of 1815,* both by Etex, also adorn the facade. The arch is engraved with the names of hundreds of generals who commanded troops in Napoleonic victories.

You can take an elevator or climb the stairway to the top, where there's an exhibition hall with lithographs and photos depicting the arch throughout its history. From the observation deck, you have a panoramic view of the Champs-Elysées as well as the Louvre, Eiffel Tower, and Sacré-Coeur.

Place Charles-de-Gaulle-Etoile, 8e. ✆ **01-55-37-73-77.** www.monum.fr. Admission 9€ adults, 5.50€ for those 18–24, free for children 17 and under. Apr–Sept daily 10am–11pm; Oct–Mar daily 10am–10:30pm. Métro: Charles-de-Gaulle-Etoile. Bus: 22, 30, 31, 52, 73, or 92.

ILE DE LA CITE: WHERE PARIS WAS BORN

Medieval Paris, that architectural blending of grotesquerie and Gothic beauty, began on this island in the Seine. Explore as much of it as you can, but at least visit **Notre-Dame,** the Ste-Chapelle, and the Conciergerie. The 4th arrondissement is on the Right Bank, opposite the island.

Notre-Dame ★★★ For 6 centuries, it has stood as a Gothic masterpiece of the Middle Ages. We actually feel that Notre-Dame is more interesting outside than in. You'll have to walk around the entire structure to appreciate this "vast symphony of stone" with its classic flying buttresses. Better yet, cross the bridge to the Left Bank and view it from the quay.

From the square parvis (the courtyard in front), you can view the trio of 13th-century sculpted portals. On the left, the Portal of the Virgin depicts the signs of the zodiac and the Virgin's coronation. The central Portal of the Last Judgment is in three levels: The first shows Vices and Virtues; the second, Christ and his Apostles; and the third, Christ in triumph after the Resurrection. On the right is the Portal of Ste-Anne, depicting such scenes as the Virgin enthroned with Child. Over the central portal is a remarkable rose window, 9m (30 ft.) in diameter, forming a showcase for a statue of the Virgin and Child. Equally interesting is the Cloister Portal (around on the left), with its 13th-century Virgin, a unique survivor of many that originally adorned the facade. (Unfortunately, the Child she's holding is decapitated.)

If possible, view the interior at sunset. Of the three giant medallions that warm the austere cathedral, the north rose window in the transept, from the mid–13th century, is best. The interior is typical Gothic, with slender, graceful columns. The carved-stone choir screen from the early 14th century depicts biblical scenes. Near the altar stands the 14th-century Virgin and Child. Behind glass in the treasury is a display of vestments and gold objects, including crowns. Notre-Dame is especially proud of its relic of the True Cross and the Crown of Thorns.

To visit the gargoyles immortalized by Victor Hugo (where Quasimodo lurked), you have to scale steps leading to the twin square towers, rising to a height of 68m (223 ft.). Once here, you can inspect those devils (some sticking out their tongues), hobgoblins, and birds of prey.

Approached through a garden behind Notre-Dame is the **Memorial des Martyrs Français de la Déportation** (✆ **01-46-33-87-56**), jutting out on the tip of the Ile de la Cité. This memorial honors the French martyrs of World War II, who were deported to camps such as Auschwitz and Buchenwald. In blood red are these words (in French): FORGIVE, BUT DON'T FORGET. It's open June to September daily from 10am to noon and from 2 to 7pm, and off season daily from 10am to noon and 2 to 5pm; admission is free.

6 place du parvis Notre-Dame, 4e. ✆ **01-53-10-07-02.** www.notredamedeparis.fr. Free admission to the cathedral. Towers 8€ adults, 5€ seniors and ages 13–25, free for children 17 and under. Treasury 3€ adults, 2€ ages 13–25, 1€ ages 6–12, free for children 5 and under. Cathedral year-round daily 8am-6:45pm (until 7:15pm Sat-Sun). Towers and crypt year-round Tues–Sun 10am–6pm (until 11pm Sat–Sun June–Aug). Museum Wed and Sat-Sun 2-5pm. Treasury Mon–Fri 9:30am–6pm; Sat 9:30am–6:30pm; Sun 1:30–6:30pm. Métro: Cité or St-Michel. RER: St-Michel.

Ste-Chapelle ★★★ Come here to see one of the world's greatest examples of Flamboyant Gothic architecture—"the pearl among them all," as Proust called it—and brilliant stained-glass windows with a lacelike delicacy. The reds are so red that Parisians have been known to use the phrase "wine the color of Ste-Chapelle's windows." Ste-Chapelle was erected to enshrine relics from the First Crusade, including the Crown of Thorns, two pieces from the True Cross, and the Roman lance that pierced the side of Christ. St. Louis (Louis IX) acquired the relics from the emperor of Constantinople and is said to have paid heavily for them, raising money through unscrupulous means.

Viewed on a bright day, the 15 stained-glass windows depicting Bible scenes seem to glow ruby red and Chartres blue. The walls consist almost entirely of the glass. Built in only 5 years, beginning in 1246, the chapel has two levels. You enter through the lower chapel, supported by flying buttresses and ornamented with fleurs-de-lis. The servants of the palace used the lower chapel, and the upper chamber was for the king and his courtiers; the latter is reached by ascending a narrow spiral staircase.

Ste-Chapelle stages **concerts** in March to November (daily at 7 and 8:30pm); tickets cost 19€ to 25€. Call ✆ **01-44-07-12-38** from 11am to 6pm daily for details.

Ste. Chapelle, 6 bd. du Palais, 1e. ✆ **01-53-40-60-80.** www.monum.fr. 8€ adults, 5€ ages 18–25, free for children 17 and under. Mar-Oct daily 9:30am–6pm; Nov–Feb daily 9am–5pm. Métro: Cité, St-Michel, or Châtelet–Les Halles. RER: St-Michel.

THE EIFFEL TOWER & ENVIRONS ★★★

From place du Trocadéro, you can stand between the two curved wings of the Palais de Chaillot and gaze out on a panoramic view. At your feet are the Jardins du Trocadéro, centered by fountains. Directly in front, Pont d'Iéna spans the Seine, leading to the **Eiffel Tower.** Beyond, stretching as far as your eye can see, is the **Champ-de-Mars,** once a military parade ground and now a garden with arches, grottoes, and cascades.

Eiffel Tower ★★★ This may be the single-most-recognizable structure in the world—it's the symbol of Paris. Weighing 7,000 tons but exerting about the same pressure on the ground as a person sitting in a chair, the tower was not meant to be permanent. Gustave-Alexandre Eiffel, the engineer whose fame rested mainly on his iron bridges, built it for the Universal Exhibition of 1889. (He also designed the framework for the Statue of Liberty.)

The tower, including its 17m (56-ft.) TV antenna, is 317m (1,040 ft.) tall. On a clear day you can see it from 64km (40 miles) away. Its open-framework construction ushered in the almost-unlimited possibilities of steel construction, paving the way for skyscrapers.

You can visit the tower in three stages: Taking the elevator to the first landing, you'll have a view over the rooftops of Paris. A cinema, museum, restaurants, and bar are open year-round. The second landing provides a panoramic look at the city (on this level is Le Jules Verne restaurant, a great place for lunch or dinner). The third landing offers the best view, allowing you to identify monuments and buildings.

To get to **Le Jules Verne** (✆ **01-45-55-61-44**), take the private south foundation elevator. You can enjoy an aperitif in the piano bar and then take a seat at one of the dining room's tables, all of which provide an inspiring view. The menu changes seasonally, offering fish and meat dishes that range from filet of turbot with seaweed and buttered sea urchins to veal chops with truffled vegetables. Reservations are recommended and a fixed-price luncheon menu goes for 85€, set dinners for 200€.

You can ice-skate inside the Eiffel Tower, doing figure eights while taking in views of the rooftops of Paris. Skating takes place on an observation deck 57m (187 ft.) aboveground. The rectangular rink is a bit larger than an average tennis court, holding 80 skaters at once—half the capacity of New York City's Rockefeller Center rink. Admission to the rink and skate rentals is free once you pay the initial entry fee below. The rink is open for 6 weeks during December and January.

Insider tip: The least expensive way to visit the tower is to walk up the first two floors for 4€ adults or 3.10€ ages 25 and under. With this route, you also bypass the long lines for the elevator.

Champ de Mars, 7e. ✆ **01-44-11-23-23.** www.tour-eiffel.fr. Admission to 2nd landing 8€, 3rd landing 13€. Stairs to 2nd floor 4.50€. Sept–May daily 9:30am–11:45pm; June–Aug daily 9am–12:45am. Oct–June stairs open only to 6:30pm. Métro: Trocadéro, Ecole Militaire, or Bir Hakeim. RER: Champ de Mars–Tour Eiffel.

Hôtel des Invalides (Napoleon's Tomb) ★★★ The glory of the French military lives on in the Musée de l'Armée. Louis XIV decided to build the "hotel" to house soldiers with disabilities. It wasn't entirely a benevolent gesture, because the veterans had been injured, crippled, or blinded while fighting Louis's battles. Included in the collections (begun in 1794) are Viking swords, Burgundian basinets, 14th-century blunderbusses, Balkan khanjars, American Browning machine guns, war pitchforks, salamander-engraved Renaissance serpentines, musketoons, and grenadiers. There are suits of armor worn by kings and dignitaries, including the famous "armor suit of the lion" that was made for François I. The displays of swords are among the world's finest.

Crossing the Cour d'Honneur (Court of Honor), you'll come to **Eglise du Dôme,** designed by Hardouin-Mansart for Louis XIV. He began work on the church in 1677, though he died before its completion. In the Napoleon Chapel is the hearse used at the emperor's funeral on May 9, 1821.

To accommodate the Tomb of Napoleon—made of red porphyry, with a green granite base—architect Visconti had to redesign the high altar. First buried at St. Helena, Napoleon's remains were returned to Paris in 1840.

Place des Invalides, 7e. ✆ **01-44-42-37-72.** www.invalides.org. Admission to Musée de l'Armée, Napoleon's Tomb, and Musée des Plans-Reliefs 8.50€ adults, 6.50€ students, free for children 17 and under. Oct–Mar daily 10am–5pm; Dome Apr–Sept daily 10am–6pm. Closed Jan 1, May 1, Nov 1, and Dec 25. Métro: Latour-Maubourg, Varenne, Invalides, or St-Francois-Xavier.

MONTMARTRE ★★★

From the 1880s to just before World War I, Montmartre enjoyed its golden age as the world's best-known art colony, where *la vie de bohème* reigned supreme. Following World War I, pseudoartists flocked here, with tourists hot on their heels. The real artists had long gone to such places as Montparnasse.

Before its discovery, Montmartre was a sleepy farming community, with windmills dotting the landscape. Those who find the trek up to Paris's highest elevations too much of a climb may prefer to ride **Le Petit Train de Montmartre,** which passes all the major landmarks; it seats 55 passengers and offers English commentary. Board at place Blanche (near the Moulin Rouge); the fare is 6€ adults, 3.50€ children 4 to 10, free for children 3 and under. Trains run daily 10am to 6pm, until midnight in July and August. For information, contact **Promotrain,** 131 rue de Clignancourt, 18e (✆ **01-42-62-24-00**).

The simplest way to reach Montmartre is to take the Métro to Anvers and then walk up rue du Steinkerque to the **funicular,** which runs to the precincts of Sacré-Coeur every day 6:15am to 12:45am. The fare is one Métro ticket. Except for Sacré-Coeur (see below), Montmartre has only minor attractions; it's the historic architecture and the atmosphere that are compelling.

Specific attractions to look for include the **Bateau-Lavoir (Boat Warehouse),** on place Emile-Goudeau. Gutted by fire in 1970, it has been reconstructed. Picasso once lived here and, in the winter of 1905 and 1906, painted one of the world's most famous portraits, *The Third Rose* (Gertrude Stein).

L'Espace Montmartre Salvador-Dalí, 11 rue Poulbot, 18e (✆ **01-42-64-40-10;** www.daliparis.com), presents Dalí's phantasmagorical world with 330 original works, including his 1956 *Don Quixote* lithograph. It's open daily from 10am to 6pm (July–Aug until 8pm); admission is 10€ for adults, 7€ seniors, 6€ for ages 8 to 18 and students, and free for children 7 and under.

Basilique du Sacré-Coeur ★★★ Montmartre's crowning achievement is Sacré-Coeur, with its gleaming white domes and campanile (bell tower), though its view of Paris takes precedence over the basilica itself. On a clear day, the vista from the dome can extend for 56km (35 miles). You can also walk around the inner dome of the church, peering down like a pigeon (a few of which will likely be there to keep you company).

After France's defeat by the Prussians in 1870, the basilica was planned as an offering to cure the country's misfortunes; rich and poor alike contributed. Construction began in 1873, but the church wasn't consecrated until 1919. The interior is decorated with mosaics, the most striking of which are the ceiling depiction of Christ and the mural of the Passion at the back of the altar. The crypt contains what some believe is a piece of the sacred heart of Christ—hence the church's name.

Place St-Pierre, 18e. ✆ **01-53-41-89-00.** www.sacre-coeur-montmartre.com. Free admission to basilica; joint ticket to dome and crypt 5€ adults. Basilica daily 6am–11pm; dome and crypt daily 9am–6pm. Métro: Abbesses; take elevator to surface and follow signs to funicular.

Cimetière de Montmartre ★ Novelist Alexandre Dumas and Russian dancer Vaslav Nijinsky are just a few of the famous composers, writers, and artists interred here. The remains of the great Stendhal are here, as are Hector Berlioz, Heinrich Heine, Edgar Degas, Jacques Offenbach, and even François Truffaut. We like to pay our respects at the tomb of Alphonsine Plessis, the courtesan on whom Dumas based his Marguerite Gautier in *La Dame aux Camélias.*

20 av. Rachel (west of the Butte Montmartre and north of bd. de Clichy), 18e. ✆ **01-53-42-36-30.** Mon–Fri 8am–6pm; Sat 8:30am–6pm; Sun 9am–6pm (until 5:30pm in winter). Métro: La Fourche.

IN THE LATIN QUARTER ★★

This is the precinct of the **University of Paris (the Sorbonne),** where students meet and fall in love over coffee and croissants. Rabelais called it the Quartier Latin because the students and professors spoke Latin in the classrooms and on the streets. The sector teems with belly dancers, restaurants from Vietnamese to Balkan, cafes, bookstalls, and *caveaux* (basement clubs).

A good starting point is **place St-Michel** (Métro: St-Michel), where Balzac used to get water from the fountain when he was a youth. This center was the scene of much Resistance fighting in the summer of 1944. The quarter centers on **boulevard St-Michel** (known as "Boul' Mich") to the south.

Musée National du Moyen Age (Thermes de Cluny) ★★ This museum has two draws: the world's finest collection of art from the Middle Ages, including jewelry and tapestries; and the well-preserved manor house, built atop Roman baths, that holds the collection. The Cluny was the mansion of a 15th-century abbot. By 1515, it was the home of Mary Tudor, the widow of Louis XII and daughter of Henry VII of England and Elizabeth of York. Seized during the Revolution, it was rented in 1833 to Alexandre du Sommerard, who adorned it with medieval works of art. After his death in 1842, the government bought the building and the collection.

Most people come to see the **Unicorn Tapestries ★★★**, the world's most outstanding tapestries. They were discovered a century ago in the Château de Boussac in the Auvergne. Five of the six tapestries seem to deal with the senses (one depicts a unicorn looking into a mirror held by a maiden). The sixth shows a woman under an elaborate tent, her pet dog resting on an embroidered cushion beside her. The lovable unicorn and its friendly companion, a lion, hold back the flaps. The red-and-green background forms a rich carpet of spring flowers, fruit-laden trees, birds, rabbits, donkeys, dogs, goats, lambs, and monkeys.

Downstairs are the ruins of the Roman baths, dating from around A.D. 200. You can wander through a display of Gallic and Roman sculptures and an interesting marble bathtub engraved with lions.

Insider tip: The garden represents a return to the Middle Ages. It was inspired by the luxuriant detail of the museum's most fabled treasure, the 15th-century tapestry of *The Lady of the Unicorn.* It's small but richly planted.

In the Hôtel de Cluny, 6 place Paul-Painlevé, 5e. ✆ **01-53-73-78-00** or 01-53-73-78-16. www.musee-moyenage.fr. Admission 8€ adults, free for ages 25 and under. Wed–Mon 9:15am–5:45pm. Métro: Cluny–La Sorbonne, Saint-Michel, or Odéon.

HISTORIC GARDENS & SQUARES

GARDENS Bordering place de la Concorde, the statue-studded **Jardin des Tuileries ★★**, 1er (✆ **01-40-20-90-43;** Métro: Tuileries), are as much a part of Paris as the Seine. Le Nôtre, Louis XIV's gardener and planner of the Versailles grounds, designed them.

Jardin du Luxembourg ★★, 6e (✆ **01-42-34-23-62** [garden]; Métro: Odéon; RER: Luxembourg) has always been associated with struggling artists; students from the Sorbonne and children predominate nowadays. The gardens are the best on the Left Bank (if not in all of Paris).

SQUARES In **place de la Bastille ★**, on July 14, 1789, a mob attacked the Bastille and sparked the French Revolution. Nothing remains of the Bastille, built in 1369. Many prisoners—some sentenced by Louis XIV for "witchcraft"—were kept within. Bastille Day is celebrated every July 14. In the center of the square is the **Colonne de Juillet (July Column),** honoring the victims of the 1830 July Revolution, which put Louis-Philippe on the throne.

Not far away, **place des Vosges ★★★**, 4e (Métro: St-Paul or Chemin Vert), is Paris's oldest square and once its most fashionable. It was called the Palais Royal in the days of Henri IV, who planned to live here—but his assassin, Ravaillac, had other ideas. Henri II was killed while jousting on the square in 1559, in the shadow of the Hôtel des Tournelles. His widow, Catherine de Médicis, had the place torn down. Place des Vosges, once a dueling ground, was one of Europe's first planned squares. Its *grand siècle* red-brick houses are ornamented with white stone, and its covered arcades allowed people to shop even in the rain—an innovation at the time.

The eastern end of the Champs-Elysées is one of the world's grand squares, **place de la Concorde ★★★**, an octagonal traffic hub built in 1757 to honor Louis XV. The statue of the king was torn down in 1792 and the name changed to place de la Révolution. It's dominated by an **Egyptian obelisk** from Luxor, the oldest man-made object in Paris; it was carved around 1200 B.C. and given to France in 1829 by the viceroy of Egypt. During the Reign of Terror, Dr. Guillotin's invention was erected on this spot, where it claimed thousands of lives—from Louis XVI, who died bravely, to Mme. du Barry, who went kicking and screaming. Before the leering crowds, Marie Antoinette, Robespierre, Danton, Mlle. Roland, and Charlotte Corday lost their heads.

For a spectacular sight, look down the Champs-Elysées—the view is framed by Coustou's Marly horses, which once graced the gardens at Louis XIV's Château de Marly. (These are copies; the originals are in the Louvre.)

HISTORIC PARKS & A CEMETERY

PARKS One of the most spectacular parks in Europe is **Bois de Boulogne ★★**, Porte-Dauphine, 16e (✆ **01-40-67-97-00;** Métro: Les-Sablons, Porte-Maillot, or Porte-Dauphine). Spend your time strolling along the many hidden pathways or traversing the park in a horse-drawn carriage. The park was once a forest for royal hunts. When Napoleon III gave the grounds to the city in 1852, Baron Haussmann developed them. Separating Lac Inférieur from Lac Supérieur is the Carrefour des

Cascades (you can stroll under its waterfall). The Lower Lake contains two islands connected by a footbridge.

Parc Monceau, 8e (✆ **01-42-27-39-56;** www.parcmonceau.org; Métro: Monceau or Villiers), is ringed by 18th- and 19th-century mansions, some evoking Proust's *Remembrance of Things Past.* Parc Monceau originally held an Egyptian-style obelisk, a medieval dungeon, an alpine farmhouse, a Chinese pagoda, a Roman temple, an enchanted grotto, various chinoiseries, and a waterfall. The park opened to the public during Napoleon III's Second Empire.

A CEMETERY Cimetière du Père-Lachaise ★★, 16 rue de Repos, 20e (✆ **01-55-25-82-10;** www.pere-lachaise.com; Métro: Père-Lachaise or Philippe Auguste), has been called the "grandest address in Paris." Everybody from Sarah Bernhardt to Oscar Wilde (his tomb is by Epstein) is buried here. So are Balzac, Delacroix, and Bizet, as well as Chopin and Molière. Rock star Jim Morrison's tombstone usually draws the most visitors—and causes the most disruption. If you search hard enough, you can find the tombs of Abélard and Héloïse, the ill-fated lovers of the 12th century. The cemetery is open Monday through Friday from 8am to 6pm, and Sunday from 9am to 6pm (until 5pm Nov to early Mar).

ORGANIZED TOURS

BY BUS Cityrama, 149 rue St-Honoré, 1er (✆ **01-44-55-61-00;** www.pariscityrama.com; Métro: Louvre-Rivoli), offers a 1½-hour ride through the city on a double-decker bus with enough windows for Versailles. While you don't go inside any attractions, you get a look at the outside of Notre-Dame and the Eiffel Tower, among other sites, and a good feel for the city. Earphones provide commentary in 16 languages. Tours depart daily at 10am, 11:30am, 1pm, and 2:30pm, and cost 22€ adults and 10€ children. A morning tour with interior visits to the Louvre costs 44€. Half-day tours to Versailles are 64€, or 63€ to Chartres. A joint ticket that includes Versailles and Chartres costs 110€. A tour of the nighttime illuminations leaves daily at 10pm in summer, 7pm in winter, and costs 30€; it tends to be tame and touristy.

The **RATP** (✆ **08-92-68-77-14;** www.ratp.fr), which runs regular public transportation, also offers tours on the **Balabus,** a fleet of orange-and-white big-windowed motorcoaches. For information, see "Getting Around," earlier in this chapter.

BY BOAT Bateaux-Mouche (✆ **01-42-25-96-10;** www.bateaux-mouches.fr; Métro: Alma-Marceau) cruises depart from the Right Bank of the Seine, adjacent to Pont de l'Alma, and last about 75 minutes. Tours leave daily at 20-minute intervals from 10:15am to 11pm between April and September. Between October and March, there are at least five departures daily between 11am and 9pm, with a schedule that changes according to demand and the weather. Fares are 10€ for adults and 5€ for children 4 to 13. Dinner cruises depart daily at 8:30pm, last 2 hours, and cost 95€ to 135€. On dinner cruises, jackets and ties are required for men. There are also lunch cruises Saturday and Sunday departing at 1pm, costing 50€ for adults, 25€ for kids 11 and under.

Batobus (✆ **08-25-05-01-01;** www.batobus.com) operates 150-passenger ferries with big windows. See "Getting Around," earlier in this chapter, for information.

The Shopping Scene

Shopping is the local pastime. The City of Light is one of the rare places in the world where shopping surrounds you on almost every street. The windows, stores, and people (and even their dogs) brim with energy, creativity, and a sense of expression. You don't have to buy anything, just peer in the vitrines (display windows), absorb cutting-edge ideas, witness new trends, and take home an education in style.

Shops are usually open Monday to Saturday from 9:30 or 10am to 8pm, but hours vary, and Paris doesn't run at full throttle on Monday morning. Small shops sometimes take a 2-hour lunch break and may not open until after lunch on Monday. While most stores open at 10am, some open at 9:30am or even 11am. Thursday is the best day for late-night shopping, with stores open until 9 or 10pm.

THE BEST BUYS

Perfumes and **cosmetics,** including such famous brands as Guerlain, Chanel, Schiaparelli, and Jean Patou, are almost always cheaper in Paris than in the United States. Paris is also a good place to buy Lalique and Baccarat **crystal.** They're expensive but still priced below international market value.

From Chanel to Yves Saint Laurent, Nina Ricci to Sonia Rykiel, the city overflows with **fashion** boutiques, ranging from haute couture to the truly outlandish. Accessories, such as those by Louis Vuitton and Céline, are among the finest in the world. Smart Parisians know how to dress in style without mortgaging their condos: They head for discount and resale shops. **Anna Lowe,** 104 rue du Faubourg St-Honoré, 8e (✆ **01-42-66-11-32;** www.annalowe.com; Métro: Miromesnil), is one of the top boutiques for women who wish to purchase a Chanel or a Versace at a discount, *bien sur.* Many clothes are runway samples; some have been gently worn. French film stars often shop at **Défilé des Marques,** 171 rue de Grenelles, 7e (✆ **01-45-55-63-47;** Métro: Latour-Maubourg), but anyone can pick up discounted Laurent, Dior, Lacroix, Prada, Chanel, Versace, Hermès, and others.

Lingerie is another great French export. All the top lingerie designers are represented in boutiques as well as in the major department stores, Galeries Lafayette and Le Printemps.

Chocolate lovers will find much to tempt them in Paris. **Christian Constant,** 37 rue d'Assas, 6e (✆ **01-53-63-15-15;** www.christianconstant.com; Métro: St-Placide), produces some of Paris's most sinfully delicious chocolates. Racks and racks of chocolates are priced individually or by the kilo at **Maison du Chocolat,** 225 rue du Faubourg St-Honoré, 8e (✆ **01-42-27-39-44;** www.lamaisonduchocolat.com; Métro: Ternes), though it'll cost you about 100€ for a kilo (2.2 lb.). There are five other branches around Paris.

GREAT SHOPPING AREAS

1ER & 8E These two *quartiers* adjoin each other and form the heart of Paris's best Right Bank shopping neighborhood. This area includes the famed **rue du Faubourg St-Honoré,** with the big designer houses, and **avenue des Champs-Elysées,** where the mass-market and teen scenes are hot. At one end of the 1er is the **Palais Royal**—one of the city's best-kept shopping secrets, where an arcade of boutiques flanks the garden of the former palace.

On the other side of town, at the end of the 8e, is **avenue Montaigne,** 2 blocks of the fanciest shops in the world, where you float from one big name to another.

2E Behind the Palais Royal lies the **Garment District (Sentier)** and a few upscale shopping secrets such as **place des Victoires.** This area also holds a few *passages,* alleys filled with tiny stores such as **Galerie Vivienne** on rue Vivienne.

3E & 4E The difference between these two arrondissements gets fuzzy, especially around **place des Vosges,** center stage of the Marais. Even so, they offer several dramatically different shopping experiences.

On the surface, the shopping includes the real-people stretch of **rue de Rivoli** (which becomes **rue St-Antoine**). **BHV** (Bazar de l'Hôtel de Ville), which opened in 1856, is the major department store in this area; it has seven floors and lies adjacent to Paris's City Hall at 52–64 rue de Rivoli (✆ **01-42-74-90-00;** www.bhv.fr). Many shoppers will also be looking for **La Samaritaine,** 19 rue de la Monnaie, once the most famous department store in France. It occupied four noteworthy buildings erected between 1870 and 1927. These buildings have been sold and are undergoing renovation to be completed in 2012. The new owner has not made his intentions clear about the future of this Parisian landmark.

Hidden in the **Marais** is a medieval warren of tiny, twisting streets chockablock with cutting-edge designers and up-to-the-minute fashions and trends. Start by walking around place des Vosges to see galleries, designer shops, and fabulous finds.

Finally, the 4e is also home of **place de la Bastille,** an up-and-coming area for artists and galleries where you'll find the newest entry on the retail scene, the **Viaduc des Arts** (which stretches into the 12e).

6E & 7E Whereas the 6e is one of the most famous shopping districts in Paris—it's the soul of the Left Bank—much of the good stuff is hidden in the zone that becomes the wealthy residential 7e. **Rue du Bac,** stretching from the 6e to the 7e in a few blocks, stands for all that wealth and glamour can buy. The street is jammed with art galleries, home-decor stores, and gourmet food shops.

9E To add to the fun of shopping the Right Bank, the 9e sneaks in behind the 1er, so if you choose not to walk toward the Champs-Elysées and the 8e, you can head to the big department stores in a row along **boulevard Haussmann** in the 9e. Here you'll find the two big French icons, **Au Printemps** and **Galeries Lafayette,** and a large branch of Britain's **Marks & Spencer.**

Paris After Dark

THE PERFORMING ARTS

Announcements of shows, concerts, and operas are on kiosks all over town. You can find listings in *Pariscope,* a weekly entertainment guide, and in the English-language *Boulevard,* a bimonthly magazine.

There are many ticket agencies in Paris, mostly near the Right Bank hotels. *Avoid them if possible.* You can buy the cheapest tickets at the theater box office. Tip the usher who shows you to your seat in a theater or movie house.

Several agencies sell tickets for cultural events and plays at discounts of up to 50%. One is the **Kiosque Théâtre,** 15 place de la Madeleine, 8e (no phone; www.kiosquetheatre.com; Métro: Madeleine), offering day-of-performance tickets for about half price (average price is 20€). Tickets for evening performances and matinees are sold Tuesday to Saturday 12:30 to 8pm, Sunday 12:30 to 4pm.

For easy access to tickets for festivals, concerts, and the theater, try one of two locations of the **FNAC** electronics-store chain: 136 rue de Rennes, 6e (✆ **08-25-02-00-20;** Métro: St. Placide); or 1–7 rue Pierre-Lescot, in the Forum des Halles, 1er (✆ **08-25-02-00-20;** Métro: Châtelet–Les Halles).

Even those with only a modest understanding of French can delight in a sparkling production of Molière at the **Comédie-Française,** 2 rue de Richelieu, 1er (✆ **08-25-10-16-80;** www.comedie-francaise.fr; Métro: Palais-Royal–Musée du Louvre), established to keep the classics alive and to promote important contemporary authors. The box office is open daily from 11am to 6pm; the hall is dark from July 21 to September 5. The Left Bank annex is the **Comédie-Française-Théâtre du Vieux-Colombier,** 21 rue du Vieux-Colombier, 4e (✆ **01-44-39-87-00;** Métro: Sèvres-Babylone or Saint-Sulpice). Although its repertoire can vary, it's known for presenting some of the most serious French dramas in town.

The controversial building known as the **Opéra Bastille ★★★**, place de la Bastille, 120 rue de Lyon (✆ **08-92-89-90-90** or 01-40-01-17-89; www.operadeparis.fr; Métro: Bastille), was inaugurated in July 1989 (for the Revolution's bicentennial), and on March 17, 1990, the curtain rose on Hector Berlioz's *Les Troyens.* Since its much-publicized opening, the opera house has presented works such as Mozart's *Marriage of Figaro* and Tchaikovsky's *Queen of Spades.* The main hall is the largest French opera house, with 2,700 seats, but music critics have lambasted the acoustics. The building contains two additional concert halls, including an intimate room seating 250, usually used for chamber music. Both traditional opera performances and symphony concerts are presented here. Call to find out about occasional free concerts on French holidays.

Opéra Garnier ★★★, place de l'Opéra, 9e (✆ **08-92-89-90-90;** www.operadeparis.fr; Métro: Opéra), is the premier stage for dance and opera. Because of competition from the Opéra Bastille, the original opera has made great efforts to present more up-to-date works, including choreography by Jerome Robbins, Twyla Tharp, and George Balanchine. The architect Charles Garnier designed this rococo wonder in the heyday of the empire. The facade is adorned with marble and sculpture, including *The Dance* by Carpeaux. Restoration has returned the Garnier to its former glory: Its boxes and walls are lined with flowing red and blue damask, the ceiling (painted by Marc Chagall) has been cleaned, and air-conditioning has been added. The box office is open Monday to Saturday 10:30am to 6:30pm.

At the city's northeastern edge in what used to be a run-down neighborhood, **Cité de la Musique ★★★**, 221 av. Jean-Jaurès, 19e (✆ **01-44-84-45-00,** or 01-44-84-44-84 for tickets and information; www.cite-musique.fr; Métro: Porte-de-Pantin), has been widely applauded. The $120-million stone-and-glass structure, designed by Christian de Portzamparc, incorporates a network of concert halls, a library and research center, and a museum. The complex stages a variety of concerts, ranging from Renaissance to 20th-century programs.

New York has its Carnegie Hall, but for years Paris lacked a permanent home for its orchestra. That is, until 2006, when the restored **Salle Pleyel ★★★**, 252 rue du Faubourg-St-Honoré, 8e (✆ **01-42-56-13-13;** www.sallepleyel.fr; Métro: Miromesnil), opened once again. Built in 1927 by the piano-making firm of the same name, Pleyel was the world's first concert hall designed exclusively for a symphony orchestra. Ravel, Debussy, and Stravinsky performed their masterpieces here, only to see the hall devastated by fire less than 9 months after its opening. The original sound quality was never recovered because of an economic downturn. In 1998, real estate developer Hubert Martigny purchased the concert hall, restoring the Art Deco spirit of the original and also refining the acoustics it once knew. Nearly 500 seats were removed to make those that remained more comfortable. The Orchestre Philarmonique de Radio France and the Orchestre de Paris now have a home worthy of their reputations, and the London Symphony Orchestra makes Pleyel its venue in Paris. Tickets range from 10€ to 145€, and seniors and young people 26 and under can arrive an hour before a concert and fill any available seat for just 10€. Reservations are made by phone Monday to Saturday 11am to 7pm.

NIGHTCLUBS & CABARETS

The **Folies-Bergère,** 32 rue Richer, 9e (✆ **01-44-79-98-60** or 08-92-68-16-50; www.foliesbergere.com; Métro: Grands Boulevards or Cadet), has been an institution since 1869. Josephine Baker, the African-American singer who danced in a banana skirt and threw bananas into the audience, became "the toast of Paris" here. According to legend, the first GI to reach Paris at the 1944 Liberation asked for directions to the club. Don't expect the naughty and slyly permissive, skin-and-glitter revue that used to be the trademark of this place. In 1993, that all ended with a radical restoration of the theater and a reopening under new management. Today, it's a conventional 1,600-seat theater devoted to a frequently changing roster of big-stage performances in French, many of which are adaptations of Broadway blockbusters. Shows are usually given Tuesday to Saturday at 9pm and Sunday at 3pm. Tickets cost 25€ to 84€.

The **Moulin Rouge,** 82 bd. Clichy, place Blanche, 18e (✆ **01-53-09-82-82;** www.moulinrouge.fr; Métro: Blanche), is a camp classic. The establishment that Toulouse-Lautrec immortalized is still here, but the artist would probably have a hard time recognizing it. Try to get a table; the view is much better on the main floor than from the bar. What's the theme? Strip routines and the saucy sexiness of *la Belle Epoque*. Handsome men and girls, girls, girls, virtually all topless, keep the place going. Revues begin nightly at 9 and 11pm. Cover including champagne runs 92€ to 102€; a 7pm dinner and show costs 150€ to 180€.

LIVE MUSIC & DANCING

JAZZ The great jazz revival that long ago swept America is still going strong here, with Dixieland or Chicago rhythms pounding out in dozens of jazz cellars, mostly called *caveaux*. Most clubs are on the Left Bank near the Seine, between rue Bonaparte and rue St-Jacques.

It's hard to say which is more intriguing at **Caveau des Oubliettes ★**, 52 rue Galande, 5e (✆ **01-46-34-23-09;** www.caveaudesoubliettes.fr; Métro: St-Michel)—the entertainment and drinking or the setting. An *oubliette* is a dungeon with a trapdoor at the top as its only opening, and the name is accurate. Located in the Latin Quarter, just across the river from Notre-Dame, this nightspot is housed in a genuine 12th-century prison, complete with dungeons, spine-tingling passages, and scattered skulls, where prisoners were tortured and sometimes pushed through portholes to drown in the Seine. Today patrons laugh, drink, talk, and flirt in the narrow *caveau,* or else retreat to the smoke-filled jazz lounge. There's a free jam session every night, perhaps Latin jazz or rock. At some point on Friday and Saturday nights concerts are staged and a 15€ cover is charged. It's open daily 5pm to 2am.

DANCE CLUBS The area around the Eglise St-Germain-des-Prés is full of dance clubs. **Batofar ★**, facing 11 quai François Mauriac, 13e (✆ **01-53-14-76-59;** www.batofar.org; Métro: Quai de la Gare), sits on a converted barge that floats on the Seine, sometimes attracting hundreds of dancers, most of whom are in their 20s and 30s, gyrating to house, garage, techno, and live jazz by groups that hail from (among other places) Morocco, Senegal, and Germany. The cover ranges from 10€ to 14€. It's open Tuesday to Saturday 10pm to 6am; closed November to March.

ROCK **Bus Palladium,** 6 rue Fontaine, 9e (✆ **01-45-26-80-55;** www.lebuspalladiumparis.com; Métro: Blanche or Pigalle), is a single room with a very long bar. This rock-'n'-roll temple has varnished hardwoods and fabric-covered walls that barely absorb the reverberations of nonstop recorded music. It's open Tuesday to Saturday 11pm to 5am (sometimes Mon or Sun for special events).

GAY & LESBIAN BARS Gay life is centered on **Les Halles** and **Le Marais,** with the greatest concentration of gay and lesbian clubs, restaurants, bars, and shops between the Hôtel de Ville and Rambuteau Métro stops. Gay dance clubs come and go so fast that even the magazines devoted to them, such as ***Illico***—distributed free in the gay bars and bookstores—have a hard time keeping up. For lesbians, there is *Lesbian Magazine.* Also look for Gai Pied's ***Guide Gai*** and ***Pariscope***'s regularly featured English-language section, "A Week of Gay Outings." Also important for both men and women is ***Têtu Magazine,*** sold at most newsstands.

Although **Open Café/Café Cox,** 15 rue des Archives, 4e (✆ **01-42-72-26-18** or 01-42-72-08-00; Métro: Hôtel de Ville), are independent, the clientele of these side-by-side gay men's bars is so interconnected, and there's such traffic between them, that we—like many other residents of this neighborhood—usually jumble them together. Both define themselves as bars rather than dance clubs, but on particularly busy nights, one or another couple might actually begin to dance. Open Sunday to Thursday 11am to 2am, Friday and Saturday to 4am

With dim lighting, background music, and comfortable banquettes, **La Champmeslé,** 4 rue Chabanais, 2e (✆ **01-42-96-85-20;** www.lachampmesle.com; Métro: Pyramides or Bourse), provides a cozy meeting place for women and a few (about 5%) "well-behaved" men. Thursday night, one of the premier lesbian events in Paris, a cabaret, begins at 10pm. Open daily 4pm to 6am.

Day Trips from Paris: The Ile de France

VERSAILLES ★★★

Within 50 years, the **Château de Versailles** (✆ **01-30-83-78-00;** www.chateauversailles.fr) was transformed from Louis XIII's hunting lodge into an extravagant palace. Begun in 1661, its construction involved 32,000 to 45,000 workmen, some of whom had to drain marshes and move forests. Louis XIV set out to build a palace that would be the envy of Europe and created a symbol of opulence often copied, yet never duplicated, the world over.

The six magnificent **Grands Appartements ★★★** are in the Louis XIV style; each bears the name of the allegorical painting on the ceiling. The best known and largest is the **Hercules Salon ★★**, with a ceiling painted by François Lemoine, depicting the Apotheosis of Hercules. In the **Mercury Salon** (with a ceiling by Jean-Baptiste Champaigne), the body of Louis XIV was put on display in 1715; his 72-year reign was one of the longest in history.

The most famous room at Versailles is the 71m-long (233-ft.) **Hall of Mirrors ★★★**. Begun by Mansart in 1678 in the Louis XIV style, it was decorated by Le Brun with 17 arched windows faced by beveled mirrors in simulated arcades.

Spread across 100 hectares (247 acres), the **Gardens of Versailles ★★★** were laid out by landscape artist André Le Nôtre. A walk across the park takes you to the pink-and-white-marble **Grand Trianon ★★**, designed by Hardouin-Mansart for Louis XIV in 1687. Traditionally it has been lodging for important guests. Gabriel, the designer of place de la Concorde in Paris, built the **Petit Trianon ★★** in 1768 for Louis XV. Louis used it for his trysts with Mme. du Barry. In time, Marie Antoinette adopted it as her favorite residence, a place to escape the rigid life at the main palace.

In 2005, a previously off-limits section of the vast palace was opened to the public for the first time by an act of the Parliament. The decision adds some 25,085 sq. m (270,000 sq. ft.) of the south wing to public access. Up to now, the area had been reserved for use by Parliament itself. Among the rooms opened up is the mammoth **Battle Gallery,** which at 119m (390 ft.) is the longest hall at Versailles. The gallery displays monumental paintings depicting all of France's great battles, ranging from the founding of the monarchy by Clovis, who reigned in the 5th and 6th centuries, through the Napoleonic wars in the early 19th century.

The château is open from April to October, Tuesday through Sunday from 9am to 6pm (5pm the rest of the year). Call or visit the website for a complete schedule of fees, which vary depending on which attractions you visit. The grounds are open daily from dawn to dusk; the individual attractions may have earlier opening and closing times.

GETTING THERE To get to Versailles, catch the **RER** line C1 to Versailles–Rive Gauche at the Gare d'Austerlitz, St-Michel, Musée d'Orsay, Invalides, Ponte de l'Alma, Champ de Mars, or Javel stop, and take it to the Versailles/Rive Gauche station. The trip takes 35 to 40 minutes. Do not get off at Versailles Chantier, which will leave you on the other end of town, a long walk from the château. The round-trip fare is 5.60€; Eurailpass holders travel free on the RER but need to show the pass at the ticket kiosk to receive an RER ticket. **SNCF trains** make frequent runs from Gare St-Lazare and Gare Montparnasse in Paris to Versailles. Trains departing from Gare St-Lazare arrive at the Versailles/Rive Droite railway station; trains departing from Gare Montparnasse arrive at Versailles/Chantiers station, a long walk as mentioned.

Both Versailles stations are within a 10-minute walk of the château, and we recommend the walk as a means of orienting yourself to the town, its geography, its scale, and its architecture. If you can't or don't want to walk, you can take bus B, or (in midsummer) a shuttle bus marked CHATEAU from either station to the château for either a cash payment of around 2€ (drop the coins directly into the coin box near the driver) or the insertion of a valid ticket for the Paris Métro. Because of the vagaries of the bus schedules, we highly recommend the walk. Directions to the château are clearly signposted from each railway station.

If you're **driving,** exit the *périphérique* (the ring road around Paris) on N10 (av. du Général-Leclerc), which will take you to Versailles; park on place d'Armes in front of the château.

VISITOR INFORMATION The **Office de Tourisme** is at 2 bis av. de Paris (✆ **01-39-24-88-88;** fax 01-39-24-88-89; www.versailles-tourisme.com). The office is closed Sunday and Monday.

CHARTRES ★★★

The architectural aspirations of the Middle Ages reached their highest expression in the **Cathédrale Notre-Dame de Chartres,** 16 Cloître Notre-Dame (✆ **02-37-21-22-07;** www.monum.fr), where visitors are transfixed by the light from the **stained glass ★★★**. Covering an expanse of more than 2,500 sq. m (26,900 sq. ft.), the peerless glass is truly mystical. It was spared in both world wars because of a decision to remove it piece by piece. Most of it dates from the 12th and 13th centuries. It's difficult to single out one panel or window—depending on the position of the sun, the images change constantly; however, an exceptional one is the 12th-century *Vierge de la Belle Verrière (Virgin of the Beautiful Window)* on the south side. Of course, there are three fiery rose windows, but you couldn't miss those even if you tried.

The cathedral you see today dates principally from the 13th century, when it was rebuilt with the efforts of kings, princes, churchmen, and pilgrims from all over Europe. One of the world's greatest High Gothic cathedrals, it was the first to use flying buttresses. French sculpture in the 12th century broke into full bloom when the **Royal Portal ★★★** was added. The portal is a landmark in Romanesque art. The sculptured bodies are elongated, often formalized beyond reality, in long, flowing robes. But the faces are amazingly (for the time) lifelike, occasionally betraying Mona Lisa smiles. Admission is free; the cathedral is open daily from 8:30am to 7:30pm.

If you're fit enough, don't miss the opportunity to climb to the top of the tower. You can visit the crypt, gloomy and somber but rich with medieval history, only as part of a French-language tour. The cost is 2.70€ per person.

GETTING THERE From Paris's Gare Montparnasse, **trains** run directly to Chartres, taking less than an hour. Tickets cost 27€ round-trip. Call ✆ **08-92-35-35-35.** If **driving,** take A10/A11 southwest from the *périphérique,* and follow signs to Le Mans and Chartres. (The Chartres exit is clearly marked.)

VISITOR INFORMATION The **Office de Tourisme** is on place de la Cathédrale (✆ **02-37-18-26-26;** fax 02-37-21-51-91; www.chartres-tourisme.com).

THE LOIRE VALLEY CHÂTEAUX ★★★

Bordered by vineyards, the winding Loire Valley cuts through the land of castles deep in France's heart. Medieval crusaders returning here brought news of the opulence of the East, and soon they began rethinking their surroundings. Later, word came from Italy of an artistic flowering led by Leonardo and Michelangelo. Royalty and nobility built châteaux in this valley during the French Renaissance, and an era of pomp reigned until Henri IV moved his court to Paris, marking the Loire's decline.

The Loire is blessed with attractions, including medieval, Renaissance, and classical châteaux, Romanesque and Gothic churches, and treasures such as the Apocalypse Tapestries. There's even the castle that inspired *Sleeping Beauty.* Trains serve some towns, but the best way to see this region is by car.

Tours ★

Though it doesn't have a major château, Tours (pop. 138,000), at the junction of the Loire and Cher rivers, is known for its food and wine. Many of its buildings were bombed in World War II, and 20th-century apartment towers have taken the place of châteaux. However, because Tours is at the doorstep of some of the most magnificent châteaux in France, it makes a good base from which to explore. Pilgrims en route to Santiago de Compostela in northwest Spain once stopped here to pay homage at the tomb of St-Martin, the "Apostle of Gaul," who was bishop of Tours in the 4th century.

Most Loire Valley towns are rather sleepy, and Tours is where the action is, with busy streets and cafes. A quarter of the residents are students, who add a vibrant touch to a soulless commercial enclave. Allow a morning or an afternoon to see Tours.

ESSENTIALS

GETTING THERE Most of the trains bound for Tours, including all TGVs (as many as 14 per day), depart from Paris's Gare Montparnasse, although a very limited number of trains, including some of the slow and conventional commuter trains, depart from Gare d'Austerlitz. One-way fares range from 29€ to 49€. Many, but not all, of the conventional (non-TGV) trains pull into the center of Tours, at the **Gare Tours Centre Ville,** place du Maréchal-Leclerc, 3 rue Edouard-Vaillant. Some conventional trains and virtually all the TGV trains, however, arrive at the isolated railway station of **Tours/St-Pierre-des-Corps,** about 6km (3¾ miles) east of the center of Tours. If your train drops you off here, know that at least one (and during peak hours, several) *navettes* (buses) await every TGV train for free transport to the center of Tours.

If you're **driving,** take highway A10 to Tours.

GETTING AROUND It's easy to walk from one end of central Tours to the other, and most of the good hotels are near the train station. For taxi service, call **Taxi Radio** (✆ **02-47-20-30-40**). Car-rental offices in or near the train station include **Avis,** inside the station (✆ **02-47-20-53-27**), open Monday to Friday 8am to 12:30pm and 1:30 to 6pm, and Saturday 8am to noon and 2 to 6pm; and **Europcar,** 194 av. Maginot (✆ **02-47-85-85-85**), open Monday to Saturday 8am to noon and 2 to 6:30pm. You can rent a bike at **Detours de Loire,** 35 rue Charles Gilles (✆ **02-47-61-22-23;** www.locationdevelos.com), at a cost of 14€ per day. A passport deposit is required. It's open Monday to Saturday 9am to 1pm and 2 to 7pm, and Sunday 9:30am to 12:30pm and 6 to 7pm.

VISITOR INFORMATION The **Office de Tourisme** is at 78–82 rue Bernard-Palissy (✆ **02-47-70-37-37;** www.ligeris.com).

WHERE TO STAY

Hôtel de l'Univers This hotel was erected in 1853, making it the oldest in town. Upgraded to government-rated four-star status, it's the best in the town center. Its midsize rooms, outfitted in a conservative contemporary style, have monochromatic and tasteful soft-color schemes. The bathrooms, with shower and tub, have also been renewed. On weekdays, the hotel fills with business travelers; on weekends, it hosts many area brides and grooms.

5 bd. Heurteloup, Tours 37000. ✆ **02-47-05-37-12.** Fax 02-47-61-51-80. www.hotel-univers.fr. 85 units. 125€–270€ double; 344€–398€ suite. AE, DC, MC, V. Parking 15€. Bus: 1, 4, or 5. **Amenities:** Room service. *In room:* A/C, TV, hair dryer, minibar, Wi-Fi (free).

The Loire Valley

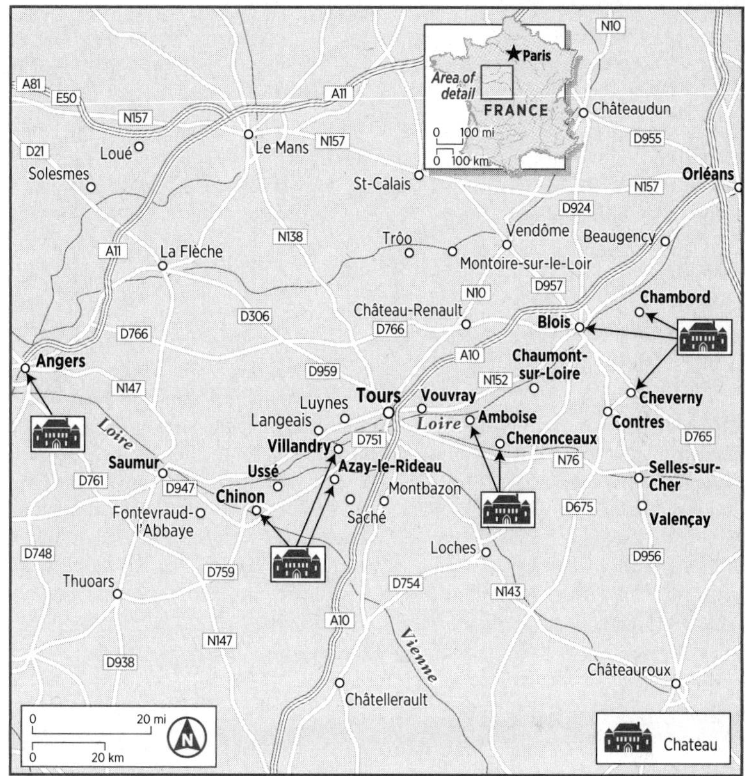

Hôtel du Manoir On a quiet street near the train station, this 19th-century residence is a comfortable place to stay. The cheerful reception area reflects the quality of the rooms. Though small to average in size, all units have windows that let in lots of light and afford views of the neighborhood or the hotel courtyard. Most are furnished simply. About half the rooms have tub/shower combos; the rest have only showers.

2 rue Traversière, Tours 37000. ✆ **02-47-05-37-37.** Fax 02-47-05-16-00. www.hotel-manoir-tours.federal-hotel.com. 20 units. 56€–70€ double. AE, DC, MC, V. Parking 6€. Bus: 3 or 70. *In room:* A/C, TV, Wi-Fi (free).

WHERE TO DINE

La Roche le Roy ★★ MODERN FRENCH Alain Couturier, one of the hottest chefs in town, blends new and old techniques in a gabled 15th-century manor south of the town center. Couturier's repertoire includes scalloped foie gras with lentils, cod with saffron cream sauce, pan-fried scallops with truffle vinaigrette, and *matelote* (stew) of eel with Chinon or Bourgueil wine. His masterpiece is suprême of pigeon with "roughly textured" sauce. For dessert, try a slice of warm orange-flavored chocolate served with coffee-flavored sherbet.

55 rte. St-Avertin. ✆ **02-47-27-22-00.** Reservations recommended. Main courses 28€–32€. AE, MC, V. Tues–Sat noon–1:30pm and 7:30–9:30pm. Closed 1 week in Feb and 3 weeks in Aug. From the center of town, take av. Grammont south (follow signs to St-Avertin-Vierzon). The road crosses a bridge but doesn't change names. The restaurant is beside that road, on the southern periphery of Tours.

Les Tuffeaux TRADITIONAL FRENCH This restaurant in an 18th-century house is one of the best in Tours. Menu items change three times a year, depending on the inspiration of chef Gildas Marsollier. He prepares classics but also experiments, with offerings such as noisettes of roasted rabbit with bacon and almonds, crisp grilled crayfish with partridge-stuffed ravioli, and braised turbot with gratinéed *viennoise* of Comté cheese. Roasted filet of pigeon with pink grapefruit is an enduring favorite.

19 rue Lavoisier. ✆ **02-47-47-19-89.** Reservations required. Main courses 20€–26€. AE, DC, MC, V. Mon–Tues and Thurs–Sat noon–1:30pm; Mon–Sat 7:30–9:30pm. Bus: 1, 4, or 5.

Rive Gauche TRADITIONAL FRENCH Under another name, this has been a local favorite since shortly after World War II. In the commercial heart of Tours, it has two dining rooms and an outdoor terrace for warm-weather dining. The ever-changing menu may include homemade foie gras and whitefish caught in the Loire and served with beurre blanc. Regional ingredients mix well with the local wines, as exemplified by pikeperch with sabayon; a *beuchelle Tourangelle,* a ragout composed of local red wine from the Loire Valley mixed with veal sweetbreads and kidneys; and *magret de canard* (duckling) served with a "jam" of red Chinon wine. In summer, strawberry parfait with raspberry coulis is a perfect finish.

23 rue du Commerce. ✆ **02-47-05-71-21.** Reservations required. Main courses 30€–50€; fixed-price menu 30€–70€. MC, V. Daily 10:30am–4pm and 7:30pm–1am. Bus: 1, 4, or 5.

EXPLORING THE CITY

The heart of town is **place Jean-Jaurès.** The principal street is **rue Nationale,** running north to the Loire River. Head west along rue du Commerce and rue du Grand-Marché to Vieux Tours/Vieille Ville (old town).

Cathédrale St-Gatien This cathedral honors a 3rd-century evangelist and has a Flamboyant Gothic facade flanked by towers with bases from the 12th century. The lanterns date from the Renaissance. The choir is from the 13th century, with new additions built in each century through the 16th. Sheltered inside is the handsome 16th-century tomb of Charles VIII and Anne de Bretagne's two children. Some of the glorious stained-glass windows are from the 13th century.

5 place de la Cathédrale. ✆ **02-47-70-21-00.** Free admission. Daily 9am–7pm (until 8pm July–Aug).

Musée des Beaux-Arts This fine provincial museum in the Palais des Archevêques is worth a visit just to see its lovely rooms and gardens. There are Old Masters here as well, including works by Degas, Delacroix, Rembrandt, and Boucher. The sculpture collection includes works by Houdon and Bourdelle. You can tour the gardens free, daily from 7am to 8:30pm.

18 place François-Sicard. ✆ **02-47-05-68-73.** Admission 4€ adults, 2€ seniors and students, free for children 12 and under. Wed–Mon 9am–12:45pm and 2–6pm. Bus: 3.

Villandry ★★★

The 16th-century-style gardens of the Renaissance **Château de Villandry ★★★**, 3 rue Principale, 37510 Villandry (✆ **02-47-50-02-09;** www.chateauvillandry.com), are celebrated throughout the Touraine. A trio of superimposed cloisters with a water garden on the highest level, they were restored by the Spanish doctor and scientist Joachim Carvallo, grandfather of the present owner.

The grounds contain 17km (11 miles) of boxwood sculpture, which the gardeners cut to style in only 2 weeks each September. Every square of the gardens is like a geometric mosaic. The borders symbolize the faces of love: tender, tragic (represented by daggers), and crazy (with a labyrinth that doesn't get you anywhere).

A feudal castle once stood at Villandry. In 1536, Jean Lebreton, François I's chancellor, built the present château, whose buildings form a U and are surrounded by a moat. Near the gardens is a terrace from which you can see the small village and its 12th-century church. A tearoom on-site, **La Doulce Terrasse,** serves traditional Loire cooking, including hot dishes, freshly baked bread, homemade ice cream, and cocktails made from fresh fruit.

Admission to the gardens, including a guided tour of the château, costs 9€ for adults, 5€ for children 8 to 18, and is free for children 7 and under. Visiting the gardens separately, without a guide, costs 6€ for adults and 3.50€ for children 8 to 18. The gardens are open daily 9am to between 5 and 7:30pm, depending on the hour of sunset; the château is open daily from 9am to between 4:30 and 6:30pm, depending on a complicated seasonal schedule. Tours are conducted in French; leaflets are available in English.

ESSENTIALS

GETTING THERE Villandry has no train service. The nearest connection from Tours is at the town of Savonnières. From Savonnières, you can walk along the Loire for 4km (2½ miles) to reach Villandry, rent a **bike** at the station, or take a **taxi.** You can also **drive,** following D7 from Tours. Allow 1½ hours to see Villandry.

WHERE TO STAY & DINE

Le Cheval Rouge MODERN FRENCH The well-known dining stopover near the château extends a congenial welcome. The conservatively decorated dining room lies about 91m (300 ft.) from the banks of the Cher. Specialties include Quiche Tourangel (made with pork byproducts including chitterling sausages), a flavorful version of eel stew, medallions of veal with morels, and turbot with hollandaise sauce. The inn also rents 41 rooms, all with private bathroom and free in-room Wi-Fi. A double is 58€ to 62€.

9 rue Principale, Villandry 37510. ✆ **02-47-50-02-07.** Fax 02-47-50-08-77. www.lecheval-rouge.com. Reservations recommended. Main courses 15€–17€; fixed-price menu 20€–39€. AE, DC, MC, V. Daily noon–2:30pm and 7–9pm.

Azay-le-Rideau ★★

Its machicolated towers and blue-slate roof pierced with dormers shimmer in the moat, creating a reflection like a Monet painting. The defensive medieval look is all for show: The Renaissance **Château d'Azay-le-Rideau ★★**, 19 rue Balzac, Azay-le-Rideau 37190 (✆ **02-47-45-42-04;** www.monum.fr), was created as a residence at an idyllic spot on the Indre River. Gilles Berthelot, François I's finance minister, commissioned the castle, and his spendthrift wife, Philippa, supervised its construction. So elegant was the creation that the Chevalier King grew jealous. Berthelot was accused of misappropriation of funds and forced to flee, and the château reverted to the king.

Before you enter, circle the château and note the perfect proportions of the crowning achievement of the Renaissance in the Touraine. Check out its most fancifully ornate feature, the bay enclosing a grand stairway with a straight flight of steps. The Renaissance interior is a virtual museum.

From the second-floor Royal Chamber, look out at the gardens. This bedroom, also known as the Green Room, is believed to have housed Louis XIII. The adjoining Red Chamber contains a portrait gallery that includes *Lady in Red* and Diane de Poitiers (Henri II's favorite) in her bath.

The château is open daily in July and August 9:30am to 7pm; April to June and September 9:30am to 6pm; and October to March 10am to 12:30pm and 2 to 5:30pm. Admission is 8€ for adults, 5€ for ages 18 to 25, and free for children 17 and under. Allow 2 hours for a visit.

In warm weather, *son-et-lumière* performances feature recorded music and lights beaming on the exterior of the château. The shows, which last about 1½ hours, begin at 9:30pm from May to September. Tickets are 9€ for adults, 5€ for ages 12 to 25, and free for children 11 and under.

ESSENTIALS

GETTING THERE To reach Azay-le-Rideau, take the **train** from Tours or Chinon. From either starting point, the trip time is about 30 minutes, and the one-way fare is 4.40€ from Chinon, 4.90€ from Tours. Both Tours and Chinon have express service to Paris. For SNCF bus and rail schedules to Azay-le-Rideau, call ✆ **36-35** or 08-91-35-35-35. If you're **driving** from Tours, take D759 southwest to Azay-le-Rideau.

Because trains arrive at Azay-le-Rideau's railway station in relatively small numbers, some visitors prefer to travel to the railway station at nearby Tours, switching to any of the frequent buses between Tours's railway station and Azay. TER, a subsidiary of the SNCF, operates the route and charges 4.50€ each way. For more information, call ✆ **08-92-35-35-35.**

VISITOR INFORMATION The **Office de Tourisme** is on place de L'Europe (✆ **02-47-45-44-40;** www.ot-paysazaylerideau.com).

WHERE TO STAY

Le Grand Monarque The ivy that covers the exterior of this hotel—less than 150m (492 ft.) from the château—seems to protect it from the modern world. As you enter the manor house, with its dark ceiling beams, you'll be transported to a different era. The large guest rooms are outfitted with antiques. Units in the annex aren't as well decorated but are more tranquil. Half the well-maintained bathrooms hold tub/shower combinations. You can enjoy a casual evening in the lounge area or in the dining room. During warmer months, you can dine out on the courtyard terrace.

3 place de la République, Azay-le-Rideau 37190. ✆ **02-47-45-40-08.** Fax 02-47-45-46-25. www.legrandmonarque.com. 24 units. 60€–140€ double. AE, MC, V. Parking 10€. Closed Dec to mid-Jan. **Amenities:** Restaurant; bar; babysitting; room service. *In room:* TV, hair dryer, Wi-Fi (free).

WHERE TO DINE

L'Aigle d'Or ★ TRADITIONAL FRENCH Owners Jean-Luc and Ghislaine Fèvre work in the kitchens and dining room of this century-old house, which has been the best restaurant in town for nearly 2 decades. The restaurant is in the village center, about .3km (¼ mile) from the château. The service is professional, the welcome charming, and the food the best in Azay. In a dining room accented with ceiling beams, a fireplace, and pastel colors, you can savor dishes including crayfish with foie gras and *blanquette* (stew) of Loire Valley whitefish prepared with one of the region's white wines. Desserts are made fresh daily. In summer, the party expands onto an outdoor terrace.

10 av. Adélaïde-Riché. ✆ **02-47-45-24-58.** Reservations recommended. Main courses 16€–28€. V. Wed–Mon noon–1:30pm; Thurs–Mon 7:30–9pm.

Amboise ★★★

Amboise is on the banks of the Loire in the center of vineyards known as Touraine-Amboise. Leonardo da Vinci spent his last years here. Dominating the town is the **Château d'Amboise ★★** (✆ **02-47-57-00-98;** www.chateau-amboise.com), the first in France to reflect the Italian Renaissance.

You enter on a ramp that opens onto a panoramic terrace fronting the river. At one time, buildings surrounded this terrace, and fetes took place in the enclosed courtyard. The castle fell into decline during the Revolution, and today only about a quarter of the once-sprawling edifice remains. You first come to the Flamboyant Gothic **Chapelle de St-Hubert,** distinguished by its lacelike tracery. Today, tapestries cover the walls of the château's grandly furnished rooms. The **Logis du Roi (King's Apartment)** is open to visitors. The château opens daily at 9am. From April to November, closing time is between 5:30 and 7pm. During the winter, closing time is earlier, and the château also closes for a few hours midday. Admission is 9.70€ adults, 8.30€ students, 6.30€ for children ages 7 to 14, free for children 7 and under.

You can also visit **Château du Clos-Lucé ★**, 2 rue de Clos-Lucé (✆ **02-47-57-00-73;** www.vinci-closluce.com), a 15th-century manor that contains a museum devoted to Leonardo da Vinci. In what had been a retreat for Anne de Bretagne, François I installed "the great master in all forms of art and science," Leonardo himself. Da Vinci lived here for 3 years, until his death in 1519. (The paintings of Leonardo dying in François's arms are probably symbolic; the king was supposedly out of town at the time.) Today, the site functions as a small museum, offering insights into Leonardo's life and a sense of the decorative arts of the era. The manor contains furniture from his era; examples of his sketches; models for his flying machines, bridges, and cannon; and even a primitive example of a machine gun. Clos-Luce is open daily, January from 10am to 6pm; February to June and September to October 9am to 7pm; November and December 9am to 6pm; July and August 9am to 8pm. Admission is 12.50€ adults, 9.50€ students and seniors, 7€ children 6 to 15, 32€ family ticket (2 adults, 2 children), free for children 5 and under.

ESSENTIALS

GETTING THERE Amboise is on the Paris-Blois-Tours rail line, with about a dozen **trains** per day from both Tours and Blois. The trip from Tours takes 20 minutes and costs 4.80€ one-way; from Blois, it takes 20 minutes and costs 6€ one-way. About five conventional trains a day leave from Paris's Gare d'Austerlitz (trip time:

3 hr.), and several TGVs (trip time: 2 hr. 15 min.) depart from the Gare Montparnasse for St-Pierre-des-Corps, less than a kilometer (½ mile) from Tours. From St-Pierre-des-Corps, you can transfer to a conventional train to Amboise. Fares from Paris to Amboise start at 27€. For information, call ✆ **36-35** or 08-92-35-35-35.

If you prefer to travel by bus, **Fil Vert Buses** (www.touraine-filvert.com), which operates out of the Gare Routière in Tours, just across from the railway station, runs about 8 to 11 **buses** every day between Tours and Amboise. The one-way trip takes about 35 minutes and costs 3.20€.

If you're **driving** from Tours, take N152 east to D32 and then turn south, following signs to Amboise.

VISITOR INFORMATION The **Office de Tourisme** is on quai du Général-de-Gaulle (✆ **02-47-57-09-28;** www.amboise-valdeloire.com).

WHERE TO STAY & DINE

Le Choiseul ★★★ This 18th-century hotel, in the valley between a hillside and the Loire, is the best address in Amboise and serves the best cuisine. Guest rooms, 25 of which are air-conditioned, are luxurious; though modernized, they retain their old-world charm. The small bathrooms contain combination tub/showers. The formal dining room has a view of the Loire and welcomes nonguests who phone ahead. The cuisine is better than that in Tours or the surrounding area: deluxe, international, classic French, and regional, utilizing the freshest ingredients. Lunch ranges from 27€ to 41€, with dinner going for 45€ to 80€. The grounds showcase a garden with flowering terraces.

36 quai Charles-Guinot, Amboise 37400. ✆ **02-47-30-45-45.** Fax 02-47-30-46-10. www.le-choiseul.com. 32 units. 152€–295€ double; 355€ suite. AE, DC, MC, V. **Amenities:** Restaurant; bar; babysitting; bikes; outdoor pool; room service. *In room:* A/C, TV, hair dryer, minibar, Wi-Fi (free).

Blois ★

This town of 55,000 receives half a million visitors yearly. The town is a piece of living history, with cobblestone streets and restored white houses with slate roofs and red-brick chimneys. Some of its "streets" are mere alleyways originally laid out in the Middle Ages, or lanes linked by a series of stairs. Allow 1½ hours to see Blois.

The murder of the duc de Guise is only one of the events associated with the **Château de Blois ★★★** (✆ **02-54-90-33-33;** www.chateaudeblois.fr), begun in the 13th century by the *comte* de Blois. Blois reached the apex of its power in 1515, when François I moved to the château. For that reason, Blois is often called the "Versailles of the Renaissance," the second capital of France, and the "city of kings." Blois soon became a palace of exile. Louis XIII banished his mother, Marie de Médicis, to the château, but she escaped by sliding into the moat down a mound of dirt left by the builders.

If you stand in the courtyard, you'll find that the château is like an illustrated storybook of French architecture. The Hall of the Estates-General is a beautiful 13th-century work; Louis XII built the Charles d'Orléans gallery and the Louis XII wing from 1498 to 1501. Mansart constructed the Gaston d'Orléans wing between 1635 and 1637. Most remarkable is the François I wing, a French Renaissance masterpiece, containing a spiral staircase with ornamented balustrades and the king's symbol, the salamander.

The château is open daily, July and August 9am to 7pm, April through June and September 9am to 5:30pm, October through March from 9am to 12:30pm and 1:30 to 5:30pm. Admission is 8€ adults, 6.50€ seniors and students, 4€ children 6 to 17, free for children 5 and under. The château presents a *son-et-lumière* show in French from May to September, usually beginning at 10:30pm (but sometimes earlier, depending on the school calendar). As a taped lecture plays, colored lights, and readings evoke the age in which the château was built. The show costs 7€ for adults, 3€ for children 7 to 15, and is free for children 6 and under.

ESSENTIALS

GETTING THERE The Paris-Austerlitz line via Orléans runs six **trains** per day from Paris (trip time: 1½ hr. plus transfer waiting time at Orléans), costing 24€ one-way; from Tours, 8 to 13 trains arrive per day (trip time: 40 min.) at a cost of 10€ one-way. For information and schedules, call ✆ **08-92-35-35-35.** The train station is at place de la Gare. From June to September, you can take a **bus** (✆ **02-54-58-55-44**) from the Blois train station to tour châteaux in the area, including Chambord, Chaumont, Chenonceau, and Amboise. If you're **driving** from Tours, take RN152 east to Blois. If you'd like to explore the area by **bike,** check out **Traineurs de Loire,** place St-Louis L'Embarcadaire (✆ **02-54-33-37-54;** www.traineursde loire.com). Rentals start at 13€ per day.

VISITOR INFORMATION The **Office de Tourisme** is at 23 place du Château (✆ **02-54-90-41-41;** www.bloispaysdechambord.com).

WHERE TO STAY

Hôtel le Savoie This modern 1930s-era hotel is both inviting and livable, from its courteous staff to its guest rooms, which are small but quiet and cozy. Bathrooms are small but have sufficient shelf space; each has a shower. In the morning, a breakfast buffet is set up in the bright dining room.

6–8 rue du Docteur-Ducoux, Blois 41000. ✆ **02-54-74-32-21.** Fax 02-54-74-29-58. www.hotel-blois.com. 24 units. 49€–55€ double. MC, V. **Amenities:** Bar; babysitting; room service. *In room:* TV, minibar, Wi-Fi (free).

Mercure Centre ★ This is one of the best-located hotels in Blois—three stories of reinforced concrete and big windows beside the quays of the Loire, a 5-minute walk from the château. Rooms never rise above the chain format and roadside-motel look, but they are roomy and soundproof.

28 quai St-Jean, Blois 41000. ✆ **02-54-56-66-66.** Fax 02-54-56-67-00. www.mercure.com. 96 units. 95€–240€ double. AE, DC, MC, V. Parking 7€. Bus: Quayside marked PISCINE. **Amenities:** Restaurant; bar; babysitting; Jacuzzi; indoor pool; room service; sauna. *In room:* A/C, TV, hair dryer, minibar, Wi-Fi (10€ per 3 hr.).

WHERE TO DINE

Au Rendez-vous des Pêcheurs ★★ TOURAINE/SEAFOOD This restaurant occupies a 16th-century house and old grocery a short walk from the château. Chef Christophe Cosme enjoys a reputation for quality, generous portions, and creativity. He prepares two or three meat dishes, including roasted Sologne pigeon on a caramelized cauliflower pancake, and succulent line-caught whitefish in puff pastry. These appear alongside a longer roster of seafood dishes, such as poached filet of *sandre* (a freshwater fish; "zander" in English) served with fresh oysters, and freshwater eel in puff pastry with figs.

27 rue du Foix. ✆ **02-54-74-67-48.** www.rendezvousdespecheurs.com. Reservations required. Main courses 29€–35€; fixed-price menu 30€–69€. AE, MC, V. Tues–Sat noon–2:30pm; Mon–Sat 7–10pm. Closed 2 weeks in Jan and 3 weeks in Aug.

L'Orangerie du Château ★★★ ☺ TOURAINE Next to the château, one of the castle's former outbuildings holds the grandest and best restaurant in the area. Chef Jean-Marc Molveaux presides over a floral-themed dining room. Faithful customers and the most discerning foodies visiting Blois delight in his filet mignon with truffles. You can also sample his lovely waffle of potatoes with marinated salmon, or perfectly roasted monkfish flavored with fresh thyme. Everything tastes better with a Sauvignon de Touraine. For dessert, our favorite is melted chocolate and pistachio with crème fraîche.

1 av. Jean-Laigret. ✆ **02-54-78-05-36.** www.orangerie-du-chateau.fr. Reservations required. Main courses 23€–37€; fixed-price menu 33€–77€; children's menu 15€. AE, MC, V. Thurs–Tues noon–1:45pm; Thurs–Sat and Mon–Tues 7:15–9:15pm. Closed mid-Feb to mid-Mar.

Chambord

When François I said, "Come on up to my place," he meant the **Château de Chambord** ★★★ (✆ **02-54-50-40-00;** www.chambord.org). Some 2,000 workers began "the pile" in 1519. What emerged after 20 years was the pinnacle of the French Renaissance, the largest château in the Loire Valley. It was ready for the visit of Charles V of Germany, who was welcomed by nymphets in transparent veils tossing wildflowers in his path. Monarchs such as Henri II and Catherine de Médicis, Louis XIII, and Henri III came and went from Chambord, but none loved it like François I.

The château is in a park of more than 5,260 hectares (13,000 acres), enclosed by a wall stretching some 32km (20 miles). Four monumental towers dominate Chambord's facade. The three-story keep has a spectacular terrace from which the ladies of the court used to watch the return of their men from the hunt. The keep also encloses a corkscrew staircase, superimposed upon itself so that one person may descend and a second ascend without ever meeting. The apartments of Louis XIV, including his redecorated bedchamber, are also in the keep.

The château is open daily April to September 9am to 6:15pm, and October to March 9am to 5:15pm (until 7pm July–Aug). Admission is 9.50€ for adults and free for ages 25 and under. At the tourist office, you can pick up tickets for the summer *son-et-lumière* presentation, "Jours et Siècles" ("Days and Centuries"). The price is 10€. Allow 1½ hours to visit the château.

ESSENTIALS

GETTING THERE It's best to **drive** to Chambord. Take D951 northeast from Blois to Ménars, turning onto the rural road to Chambord. You can also rent a **bicycle** in Blois and ride the 18km (11 miles) to Chambord, or take a **tour** to Chambord from Blois in summer. From June 15 to September 2, **Transports du Loir et Cher** (✆ **02-54-58-55-44**) operates bus service to Chambord, leaving Blois at 9am and 1:30pm with return trips at 1 and 6pm.

VISITOR INFORMATION The **Office de Tourisme** on place St-Michel (✆ **02-54-33-39-16**) is open mid-June to October.

WHERE TO STAY & DINE

Hôtel du Grand-St-Michel Across from the château, and originally built as a kennel for the royal hounds, this inn is the only one of any substance in town. Try for a front room overlooking the château, which is dramatically floodlighted at night. Accommodations are plain but comfortable with provincial decor. Most visitors arrive for lunch, which in summer is served on a terrace. The marvelous collection of Loire wines is so good that it almost overshadows the regional cooking. High points from the menu include stew of wild boar (in late autumn and winter), breast of duckling in green-peppercorn sauce, and several local pâtés and terrines.

103 place St-Louis, Chambord 41250, near Bracieux. ✆ **02-54-20-31-31.** Fax 02-54-20-36-40. www.saintmichel-chambord.com. 40 units. 54€–90€ double. MC, V. Free parking. Closed mid-Nov to mid-Dec. **Amenities:** Restaurant; Internet; tennis court. *In room:* TV.

Cheverny

The upper crust heads to the Sologne area for the hunt as if the 17th century had never ended. However, 21st-century realities—like formidable taxes—can't be entirely avoided, so the **Château de Cheverny ★★★** (✆ **02-54-79-96-29;** www.chateau-cheverny.fr) must open some of its rooms to visitors.

Unlike most of the Loire châteaux, Cheverny is the residence of the original owner's descendants. The family of the *vicomte* de Sigalas can trace its lineage from Henri Hurault, the son of the chancellor of Henri III and Henri IV, who built the first château in 1634. Upon finding his wife carrying on with a page, he killed the page and offered his spouse a choice: She could swallow poison or have his sword plunged into her heart. She elected the poison. Then he had the castle torn down and the present one built for his second wife. Designed in classic Louis XIII style, it has square pavilions flanking the central pile.

You'll be impressed by the antique furnishings, tapestries, and objets d'art. A 17th-century French artist, Jean Mosnier, decorated the fireplace with motifs from the legend of Adonis. The Guards' Room contains a collection of medieval armor; also on display is a Gobelin tapestry depicting the abduction of Helen of Troy. In the king's bedchamber, another Gobelin traces the trials of Ulysses. Most impressive is the stone stairway of carved fruit and flowers.

The château is open daily November to March 9:45am to 5pm, April to June and September 9:15am to 6:15pm, July and August 9:15am to 6:45pm, and October 9:45am to 5:30pm. Admission is 7.50€ for adults, 5.40€ for students, 3.60€ for children 7 to 14, and free for children 6 and under. Allow 2 hours for your visit.

ESSENTIALS

GETTING THERE Cheverny is 19km (12 miles) south of Blois, along D765. It's best reached by **car** or on a **bus tour** from Blois with **Transports du Loir et Cher** (✆ **02-54-58-55-55**). From the railway station at Blois, a bus departs for Cheverny once a day at noon, returning to Blois 4 hours later, according to an oft-changing schedule. Most visitors find it a lot easier to take their own car or a **taxi** from the railway station at Blois.

WHERE TO STAY & DINE

Les Trois Marchands TRADITIONAL FRENCH This coaching inn, more comfortable than St-Hubert (see below), has been handed down for many generations. Jean-Jacques Bricault owns the three-story building, which has awnings, a mansard roof, a glassed-in courtyard, and sidewalk tables under umbrellas. In the tavern-style main dining room, the menu may include foie gras, lobster salad, frogs' legs, fresh asparagus in mousseline sauce, game dishes, or fish cooked in a salt crust. The inn rents 24 well-furnished, comfortable rooms with TVs for 42€ to 55€ for a double.

60 place de l'Eglise, Cour-Cheverny 41700. ✆ **02-54-79-96-44.** Fax 02-54-79-25-60. www.hoteldes3marchands.com. Dining room main courses 17€–40€; fixed-price menu 26€–45€. AE, DC, MC, V. Tues–Sun 7am–11pm. Closed mid-Feb to mid-Mar.

St-Hubert TRADITIONAL FRENCH About 457m (1,500 ft.) from the château, this inn was built in the 1950s in the provincial style. The least expensive menu may include terrine of quail, pikeperch with beurre blanc, cheeses, and a fruit tart. The most expensive menu may list lobster; an aiguillette of duckling prepared with grapes; casserole of seafood with shellfish sauce; and, in season, thigh of roebuck in pepper sauce. The St-Hubert offers 20 conservatively decorated rooms with TVs for 55€ to 90€ for a double. Each of the accommodations comes with free Wi-Fi.

122 rte. Nationale, Cour-Cheverny 41700. ✆ **02-54-79-96-60.** Fax 02-54-79-21-17. www.hotel-sthubert.com. Main courses 16€–22€; fixed-price menu 17€–29€. AE, MC, V. Daily noon–2pm and 7–9pm. Closed Sun night off season.

Chenonceaux

A Renaissance masterpiece, the **Château de Chenonceau ★★★** (✆ **02-47-23-90-07;** www.chenonceau.com) is best known for the dames de Chenonceau, who once occupied it. (The village, whose year-round population is less than 300, is spelled with a final "x," but the château isn't.)

In 1547, Henri II gave Chenonceau to his mistress, Diane de Poitiers. For a time this remarkable woman was virtually queen of France, infuriating Henri's dour wife, Catherine de Médicis. Diane's critics accused her of using magic to preserve her celebrated beauty and to keep Henri's attentions from waning. Apparently Henri's love for Diane continued unabated, and she was in her 60s when he died in a jousting tournament in 1559.

When Henri died, Catherine became regent (her eldest son was still a child) and forced Diane to return the jewelry Henri had given her and to abandon her beloved home. Catherine added her own touches, building a two-story gallery across the bridge—obviously inspired by her native Florence.

Gobelin tapestries, including one depicting a woman pouring water over the back of an angry dragon, cover many of the château's walls. The chapel contains a marble *Virgin and Child* by Murillo as well as portraits of Catherine de Médicis in black and white. There's even a portrait of the stern Catherine in the former bedroom of her rival, Diane de Poitiers. In François I's Renaissance bedchamber, the most interesting portrait is that of Diane as the huntress Diana.

The history of Chenonceau is related in 15 tableaux in the **Musée de Cire (Wax Museum),** located in a Renaissance-era annex near the château. Open the same hours as the château, it charges 12.50€ for adults, 10€ for ages 7 to 18, free for children 6 and under. Diane de Poitiers, who, among other accomplishments, introduced the artichoke to France, is depicted in three tableaux. One portrays Catherine de Medicis tossing out her husband's mistress.

The château is open daily 9am to 8pm July and August; 9am to 7pm mid-March to June; 9am to 6:30pm September and October; 9am to 5pm the rest of the year.

Admission is 10.50€ for adults, and 8€ for students and children 7 to 15. A *son-et-lumière* show, "The Era of the Ladies of Chenonceau," starts at 10:15pm daily in July and August; admission is 6€ and free for children 6 and under. Allow 2 hours to see this château.

ESSENTIALS

GETTING THERE Four daily **trains** run from Tours to Chenonceaux (trip time: 30 min.), costing 5.80€ one-way. The train deposits you at the base of the château; from there, you can walk or take a taxi. If you're **driving,** from the center of Tours, follow the directions east until you reach the N76, which will take you to the signposted turnoff for Chenonceaux.

VISITOR INFORMATION The **Syndicat d'Initiative** (tourist office), 1 rue du Dr. Bretonneau (✆ **02-47-23-94-45**), is open year-round.

WHERE TO STAY & DINE

Auberge du Bon-Laboureur ★★ This inn, within walking distance of the château, is your best bet for a comfortable night's sleep and some of the best cuisine in the Loire Valley. Founded in 1786, the hotel maintains the flavor of that era, thanks to thick walls, solid masonry, and a scattering of antiques. The author Henry James stopped here in 1882, and the inn won his praise. Most guest rooms are small, especially on the upper floors; each comes with a private bathroom with shower or tub. The rear garden has a guesthouse and formally planted roses. The place is noted for its restaurant. In fair weather, tables are set up in the courtyard, amid trees and flowering shrubs.

6 rue du Dr. Bretonneau, Chenonceaux, Bléré 37150. ✆ **02-47-23-90-02.** Fax 02-47-23-82-01. www.amboise.com/laboureur. 25 units. 120€–155€ double; 190€–260€ suite. AE, DC, MC, V. Closed Nov 11–Dec 20 and Jan 7–Feb 14. **Amenities:** Restaurant; bar; babysitting; outdoor pool; room service. *In room:* A/C, TV, hair dryer, Wi-Fi (free).

La Roseraie ★ La Roseraie is the most charming hotel in Chenonceaux, with individually decorated rooms and well-kept gardens. Each unit contains a small bathroom with shower. During World War II, the innkeeper gained fame with the Allies because of his role in smuggling Churchill's nephew out of Vichy-occupied France. The English-speaking innkeepers are the exceptionally charming Laurent and Sophie Fiorito. Their restaurant is open to the public for lunch and dinner. Our favorite dishes include house-style foie gras, *magret* of duckling with pears and cherries, and an unusual and delicious invention—*emincée* (a dish made with braised meat) of rump steak with wine-marinated pears.

7 rue du Dr. Bretonneau, Chenonceaux, Bléré 37150. ✆ **02-47-23-90-09.** Fax 02-47-23-91-59. 18 units. 65€–129€ double; 80€–112€ quad. AE, DC, MC, V. Free parking. Closed mid-Nov to late Mar. **Amenities:** Restaurant; bar; outdoor pool. *In room:* A/C, TV, Wi-Fi (free).

Chinon ★★

In the film *Joan of Arc,* Ingrid Bergman sought out the dauphin as he tried to conceal himself among his courtiers. This took place in real life at the Château de Chinon, one of the oldest fortress-châteaux in France. Charles VII centered his government at Chinon from 1429 to 1450. In 1429, with the English besieging Orléans, the Maid of Orléans prevailed upon the dauphin to give her an army. The rest is history. The seat of French power stayed at Chinon until the end of the Hundred Years' War.

On the banks of the Vienne, the town of Chinon retains a medieval atmosphere—it consists of winding streets and turreted houses, many built in the 15th and 16th centuries in the heyday of the court. For the best view, drive across the river and turn right onto quai Danton. From this vantage point, you'll be able to see the castle in relation to the village and the river. The most typical street is **rue Voltaire,** lined with 15th- and 16th-century town houses. At no. 44, Richard the Lion-Hearted died on April 6, 1199, from a wound suffered during the siege of Chalus in Limousin. The **Grand Carroi,** in the heart of Chinon, served as the crossroads of the Middle Ages.

The most famous son of Chinon, François Rabelais, the earthy and often bawdy Renaissance writer, lived on rue de la Lamproie; today, a plaque marks the spot where his father practiced law and maintained a home and office. The cottage, 5.5km (3½ miles) west of Chinon where he was born is the site of the **Maison de la Devinière** (✆ **02-47-95-91-18;** www.musee-rabelais.fr). It's open daily in July and August from 10am to 7pm, April to June and September daily from 10am to 12:30pm and 2 to 6pm, October to March Wednesday to Sunday from 10am to 12:30pm and 2 to 5pm. Admission is 4.50€ adults, 3€ students, free for children 12 and under.

Château de Chinon ★★ (✆ **02-47-93-13-45**) consists of three buildings, two of which have been partially restored (they're still missing roofs). One of the restored buildings, Château du Milieu, dates from the 11th to the 15th century and contains the keep and clock tower, which houses a museum of Joan of Arc. A moat separates Château du Milieu from the other, Château du Coudray, which contains the Tour du Coudray, where Joan of Arc once stayed. In the 14th century, the Knights Templar were imprisoned here (they're responsible for the graffiti) before meeting violent deaths. The château is open daily April to September from 9am to 7pm, and October to March from 9:30am to 5pm. Admission is 7€ adults, free for children 12 and under.

ESSENTIALS

GETTING THERE The SNCF runs about 7 **trains** and four **buses** every day to Chinon from Tours (trip time: about 1 hr.). Call ✆ **36-35** or 08-92-35-35-35 for information and schedules. Both buses and trains arrive at the train station, which lies at the edge of the very small town. If you're **driving** from Tours, take D759 southwest through Azay-le-Rideau to Chinon.

VISITOR INFORMATION The **Office de Tourisme** is at place Hofheim (✆ **02-47-93-17-85;** www.chinon.com).

WHERE TO STAY

Hostellerie Gargantua ★ This 15th-century mansion has a terrace with a château view. The grand building was once a courthouse where the father of François Rabelais worked as a lawyer in the 15th century. Art historians admire the building's early Renaissance staircase and its chiseled-stone details. The traditional guest rooms have been renovated and are comfortably furnished and well kept. Half of the old-fashioned bathrooms contain tubs. Try to stop here for a meal, served in a medieval hall. You can sample Loire *sandre* prepared with Chinon wine or duckling with dried pears and smoked lard, followed by a medley of seasonal red fruit in puff pastry.

73 rue Haute St. Maurice, Chinon 37500. ✆ **02-47-93-04-71.** Fax 02-47-93-08-02. www.hotel-gargantua.com. 7 units. 53€–79€ double. AE, DC, MC, V. **Amenities:** Restaurant; bar; babysitting; room service. *In room:* TV, Wi-Fi (free).

WHERE TO DINE

Au Plaisir Gourmand ★★ TRADITIONAL FRENCH This is the premier restaurant in the area. Owner Jean-Claude Rigollet used to direct the chefs at the fabled Les Templiers in Les Bézards. The 18th-century building contains an intimate dining room. Menu items are likely to include roasted duck with foie gras sauce, oxtail in Chinon red-wine sauce, and sautéed crayfish with a spicy salad. For dessert, try prunes stuffed in puff pastry.

2 rue Parmentier. ✆ **02-47-93-20-48.** Reservations required. Main courses 18€–42€; tasting menu 28€–59€. AE, V. Wed–Sun noon–1:30pm; Tues–Sat 7:30–9pm. Closed mid-Feb to mid-Mar.

Angers ★★★

Once the capital of Anjou, Angers straddles the Maine River at the western end of the Loire Valley. Though it suffered extensive damage in World War II, it has been restored, blending provincial charm with a suggestion of sophistication. The bustling regional center is often used as a base for exploring the château district to the west.

The moated 9th-century **Château d'Angers ★★★** (✆ **02-41-86-48-77;** www.monum.fr) was the home of the *comtes* d'Anjou. The notorious Black Falcon lived here, and in time, the Plantagenets took up residence. From 1230 to 1238, the outer walls and 17 towers were built, creating a fortress. King René favored the château, and during his reign a brilliant court life flourished until he was forced to surrender to Louis XI. Louis XIV turned the château into a prison. In World War II, the Nazis used it as a munitions depot, and the Allies bombed it in 1944.

Visit the castle to see the **Apocalypse Tapestries ★★★**. They weren't always so highly regarded—they once served as a canopy to protect orange trees and were also used to cover the damaged walls of a church. Woven in Paris by Nicolas Bataille from cartoons by Jean de Bruges around 1375 for Louis I of Anjou, they were purchased for a nominal sum in the 19th century. The series of 77 pieces, illustrating the Book of St. John, stretch 100m (328 ft.).

After seeing the tapestries, you can tour the fortress, including the courtyard, prison, ramparts, windmill tower, 15th-century chapel, and royal apartments. Once you've paid the entrance fee, you can take a guided tour focusing on the architecture and history of the château. Throughout most of the year, guided tours depart daily at 10am, 11:30am, 1:15pm, 2:30pm, and 3:30pm, but between September and April, departures are usually (depending on business) at 10:15am and 2:15pm. Each tour lasts 90 minutes, and it can be conducted in four different languages—French, English, German, and Italian. The château and its tapestries can be visited daily May to August 9:30am to 6:30pm and September to April 10am to 5:30pm. Admission is 6€ adults, 5€ seniors and students, free for children 16 and under.

ESSENTIALS

GETTING THERE Fifteen **trains** per day make the 1- to 2-hour trip from Paris's Gare de Montparnasse; the cost is 40€ to 59€ one-way. From Tours, 10 trains per day make the 1-hour trip; a one-way ticket is 20€. The Angers train station, at place de la Gare, is a convenient walk from the château. For train information, call ✆ **08-92-35-35-35.** From Saumur, there are three **bus** connections a day Monday to Saturday (1½ hr.). Buses arrive at place de la République. If you're **driving** from Tours, take N152 southwest to Saumur, turning west on D952.

VISITOR INFORMATION The **Office de Tourisme,** 7 place du Président-Kennedy (© **02-41-23-50-00;** www.angersloiretourisme.com), is opposite the entrance to the château.

WHERE TO STAY

Hôtel d'Anjou Beside a park, this hotel, built in 1846, is the best choice for overnighting in the area. Although comparable in price to the Quality Hôtel de France, it has more upscale appointments and amenities, along with a better restaurant, Le Salamandre (see "Where to Dine," below). The guest rooms closer to the ground have higher ceilings and are more spacious.

1 bd. Foch, Angers 49100. © **800/528-1234** in the U.S. and Canada, or 02-41-21-12-11. Fax 02-41-87-22-21. www.hoteldanjou.fr. 53 units. 121€–176€ double; extra bed 30€. AE, DC, MC, V. Parking 8.50€. **Amenities:** Restaurant; bar. *In room:* TV, minibar, Wi-Fi (free).

L'Hôtel de France This 19th-century hotel, one of the most respected in town, has been run by the Bouyers since 1893. It's the best choice near the railway station. Rooms are soundproof; each is comfortably furnished and well maintained. Bathrooms are very small and hold tubs.

8 place de la Gare, Angers 49100. © **02-41-88-49-42.** Fax 02-41-87-19-50. www.destination-anjou.com/hoteldefrance. 55 units. 100€–140€ double. AE, DC, MC, V. Parking 7€. **Amenities:** 2 restaurants; bar; room service. *In room:* A/C, TV, hair dryer, minibar, Wi-Fi (free).

WHERE TO DINE

Le Salamandre ★ CLASSIC FRENCH The salamander was the symbol of Renaissance king François I. In this formal, elegant restaurant, you'll see portraits of and references to that cunning strategist everywhere. Beneath massive sculpted ceiling beams, beside a large wooden fireplace, you'll enjoy the most impeccable service and best food in town. Shining examples include filet of red snapper in lime-flavored cream sauce, crayfish in various presentations, scallops in mushroom cream sauce, roasted turbot with béarnaise sauce, and squid stuffed with crayfish and served with shellfish-flavored cream sauce. The restaurant is in a hotel but not owned by the hostelry.

In the Hotel d'Anjou, 1 bd. Foch. © **02-41-88-99-55.** www.restaurant-lasalamandre.fr. Reservations recommended. Main courses 21€–38€; fixed-price menu 28€–75€. AE, DC, MC, V. Mon–Sat noon–2pm and 7:30–9pm; Sun 11:30am–2pm. Main courses 15€; fixed-price menu 18€–32€. MC, V. Tues–Sat noon–2pm and 7–10pm.

PROVENCE & THE CÔTE D'AZUR

Provence has been called a bridge between the past and the present, which blend in a quiet, often melancholy way. Peter Mayle's *A Year in Provence* and its sequels have played a large role in the popularity of this sunny corner of southern France.

The Greeks and Romans filled the landscape with cities boasting baths, theaters, and arches. Romanesque fortresses and Gothic cathedrals followed. In the 19th century, the light and landscapes attracted painters such as Cézanne and van Gogh.

Provence has its own language and its own customs. The region is bounded on the north by the Dauphine, on the west by the Rhône, on the east by the Alps, and

Provence

on the south by the Mediterranean. Each resort on the Riviera, known as the Côte d'Azur (Azure Coast), offers its own unique flavor and charms. This narrow strip of fabled real estate, less than 201km (125 miles) long and located between the Mediterranean and a trio of mountain ranges, has always attracted the jet set with its clear skies, blue waters, and orange groves.

A trail of modern artists captivated by the light and setting has left a rich heritage: Matisse at Vence, Cocteau at Menton and Villefranche, Picasso at Antibes and seemingly everywhere else, Léger at Biot, Renoir at Cagnes, and Bonnard at Le Cannet. The best collection is at the Foundation Maeght in St-Paul-de-Vence.

The Riviera's high season used to be winter and spring only. In recent years, July and August have become the most crowded, and reservations are imperative. The average summer temperature is 75°F (24°C); in winter it's 49°F (9°C).

The corniches of the Riviera, depicted in countless films, stretch from Nice to Menton. The Alps drop into the Mediterranean here, and roads were carved along the way. The lower road, 32km (20 miles) long, is the Corniche Inférieure. Along this road are the ports of Villefranche, Cap-Ferrat, Beaulieu, and Cap-Martin. The

31km (19-mile) Moyenne Corniche (Middle Road), built between World War I and World War II, runs from Nice to Menton, winding in and out of tunnels and through mountains. The highlight is at Eze. Napoleon built the Grande Corniche—the most panoramic—in 1806. La Turbie and Le Vistaero are the principal towns along the 32km (20-mile) stretch, which reaches more than 480m (1,575 ft.) high at Col d'Eze.

Avignon ★★★

In the 14th century, Avignon was the capital of Christendom. The pope lived here during what the Romans called the Babylonian Captivity. The legacy left by that court makes Avignon one of the most beautiful of Europe's medieval cities. Today, this walled city is a major stop on the route from Paris to the Mediterranean. It is increasingly known as a cultural center. Artists and painters have been moving here. Experimental theaters, galleries, and cinemas have brought diversity to the inner city.

ESSENTIALS

GETTING THERE The fastest and easiest way to get here is to **fly** from Paris's Orly Airport to **Aéroport Avignon-Caumont** (✆ **04-90-81-51-51**), 8km (5 miles) southeast of Avignon (trip time: 1 hr.). Taxis from the airport to the center cost 21€. Call ✆ **04-90-82-20-20.** From Paris, TGV **trains** from Gare de Lyon take 3 hours and 30 minutes. The one-way fare is 78€. Trains arrive frequently from Marseille (70 min.; 23€) and from Arles (20 min.; 6€). For train information, call ✆ **36-35** or visit www.voyages-sncf.com.

If you're **driving** from Paris, take A6 south to Lyon, and then A7 south to Avignon. If you'd like to explore the area by **bike,** go to **Provence Bike,** 52 bd. St-Roch (✆ **04-90-27-92-61;** www.provence-bike.com), which rents all sorts of bikes for around 15€ to 25€ per day. A deposit of 150€ to 450€, in cash or a credit card imprint, is required.

VISITOR INFORMATION The **Office de Tourisme** is at 41 cours Jean-Jaurès (✆ **04-32-74-32-74;** fax 04-90-82-95-03; www.ot-avignon.fr).

WHERE TO STAY

Hôtel Clarion Cloître St-Louis ★ This hotel is in a former Jesuit school built in the 1580s. Much of the original premises remain, including the baroque facade, the wraparound arcades, and the soaring ceiling vaults. Guest rooms are more functional; in fact, they're rather dull as a result of renovations. Rooms range from medium size to spacious, and some have sliding glass doors overlooking the patio. Each unit has modern decor without a lot of extras.

20 rue du Portail Boquier, Avignon 84000. ✆ **800/CLARION** (252-7466) in the U.S., or 04-90-27-55-55. Fax 04-90-82-24-01. www.cloitre-saint-louis.com. 80 units. 100€–210€ double; 250€–350€ suite. AE, DC, MC, V. Parking 12€–15€. **Amenities:** Restaurant; bar; outdoor pool; room service. *In room:* A/C, TV, hair dryer, minibar, Wi-Fi (free).

La Mirande ★★★ In the heart of Avignon behind the Palais des Papes, this 700-year-old town house is one of France's grand little luxuries. In 1987, Achim and Hannelore Stein transformed it into a citadel of opulence. The hotel displays 2 centuries of decorative art, from the 1700s Salon Chinois to the Salon Rouge, with striped walls in Rothschild red. Room no. 20 is the most sought after—its lavish premises open onto the garden. All rooms are stunning, with exquisite decor, hand-printed fabrics on the walls, antiques, bedside controls, and huge bathtubs. The restaurant, among the finest in Avignon, deserves its one Michelin star.

4 place de la Mirande, Avignon 84000. ✆ **04-90-85-93-93.** Fax 04-90-86-26-85. www.la-mirande.fr. 19 units. 390€–540€ double; 660€–850€ suite. AE, DC, MC, V. Parking 25€. **Amenities:** Restaurant; bar; babysitting; room service. *In room:* A/C, TV, hair dryer, minibar, Wi-Fi (free).

WHERE TO DINE

Christian Etienne ★★★ PROVENÇAL The stone house containing this restaurant was built in 1180, around the same time as the Palais des Papes (next door). Owner Christian Etienne reaches new culinary heights. His dining room contains early-16th-century frescoes honoring the marriage of Anne de Bretagne to the French king in 1491. Several of the fixed-price menus feature themes: Two present seasonal tomatoes, mushrooms, or other vegetables; one offers preparations of lobster; and the priciest relies on the chef's imagination (*menu confiance*) for unique combinations. In summer, look for the vegetable menu entirely based on ripe tomatoes; the main course is a mousse of lamb, eggplants, tomatoes, and herbs. The vegetable menus aren't completely vegetarian; they're flavored with meat, fish, or meat drippings. A la carte specialties include filet of perch with Châteauneuf-du-Pape, rack of lamb with fresh thyme-and-garlic essence, filet of venison with foie gras, and a dessert of fennel sorbet with saffron-flavored English cream sauce.

10 rue Mons. ✆ **04-90-86-16-50.** www.christian-etienne.fr. Reservations required. Main courses 28€–45€; fixed-price lunch 32€–120€, dinner 65€–120€. AE, DC, MC, V. Tues–Sat noon–1:15pm and 7:30–9:15pm.

La Fourchette FRENCH This bistro creates innovative cuisine at a moderate price, but be aware that it closes on weekends. Its two airy dining rooms have large bay windows that flood the inside with light. You may begin with fresh sardines flavored with citrus, ravioli filled with haddock, or parfait of chicken livers with spinach flan and comfit of onions. For a main course, try monkfish stew with endive, or daube of beef with gratin of macaroni.

17 rue Racine. ✆ **04-90-85-20-93.** Fixed-price lunch 25€–31€; fixed-price dinner 31€. MC, V. Mon–Fri 12:15–1:45pm and 7:15–9:45pm. Closed 3 weeks in Aug. Bus: 11.

EXPLORING THE TOWN

Even more famous than the papal residency is the ditty *"Sur le pont d'Avignon, l'on y danse, l'on y danse"* ("On the bridge of Avignon, we dance, we dance"). **Pont St-Bénézet** ★★ (✆ **04-90-27-51-16**) was far too narrow for the *danse* of the rhyme, however. Spanning the Rhône and connecting Avignon with Villeneuve-lèz-Avignon, the bridge is now a ruin, with only 4 of its original 22 arches. According to legend, it was inspired by a vision that a shepherd named Bénézet had while tending his flock. The bridge was built between 1177 and 1185 and suffered various disasters. (In 1669, half of it fell into the river.) On one of the piers is the two-story **Chapelle St-Nicolas**—one story in Romanesque style, the other in Gothic. The remains of the bridge are open November through March daily 9:30am to 5:45pm, April to June and October daily 9am to 7pm, July and September daily 9am to 8pm, and August daily 9am to 9pm. Admission is 4.50€ for adults, 3.50€ for seniors and students, and free for children 7 and under. Once you pay to walk on the bridge, the small chapel on the bridge can be visited as part of the overall admission fee.

Dominating Avignon from a hilltop is **Palais des Papes ★★★** (✆ **04-90-27-50-00;** www.palais-des-papes.com), one of the most famous, or notorious, palaces in the Christian world. The guided tour (usually lasting 50 min.) can be monotonous, because most of the rooms have been stripped of their finery. The exception is the **Chapelle St-Jean,** known for its frescoes of scenes from the life of John the Baptist and John the Evangelist.

The **Grand Tinel (Banquet Hall)** is about 41m (135 ft.) long and 9m (30 ft.) wide; the pope's table stood on the south side. The **Pope's Bedroom** is on the first floor of the Tour des Anges. It's open daily November to March 9:30am to 5:45pm, April to June and August to October 9am to 7pm, and July 9am to 8pm. Admission (including tour with guide or recording) is 10.50€ adults, 8.50€ seniors and students, free for children 7 and under.

Near the Palais des Papes is the 12th-century **Cathédrale Notre-Dame des Doms,** Place du Palais (✆ **04-90-86-81-01**), containing the Flamboyant Gothic tomb of some of the apostate popes. Crowning the top is a statue of the Virgin from the 19th century. From the cathedral, enter the **promenade du Rocher-des-Doms** (✆ **04-90-82-27-96**) to stroll its garden and enjoy the view across the Rhône to Villeneuve-lèz-Avignon.

St-Rémy-de-Provence ★

Nostradamus, the physician and astrologer, was born here in 1503. However, St-Rémy is more closely associated with van Gogh. He committed himself to an asylum here in 1889 after cutting off his left ear. Between moods of despair, he painted such works as *Olive Trees* and *Cypresses.*

Come to sleepy St-Rémy not only for its memories and sights but also for a glimpse of small-town Provençal life. It's a market town of considerable charm that draws the occasional visiting celebrity trying to escape the spotlight.

ESSENTIALS

GETTING THERE Local **buses** from Avignon (four to nine per day) take 40 minutes and cost around 4€ one-way. In St-Rémy, buses pull into the place de la République, in the town center. For bus information, call ✆ **04-90-82-07-35.** If you're **driving,** head south from Avignon along D571.

VISITOR INFORMATION The **Office de Tourisme** is on place Jean-Jaurès (✆ **04-90-92-05-22;** fax 04-90-92-38-52; www.saintremy-de-provence.com).

WHERE TO STAY

Château des Alpilles ★★★ For luxury and refinement, this is the only château in the area that can equal Vallon de Valrugues (see below). It sits in the center of a tree-studded park 2km (1¼ miles) from the center of St-Rémy. The rooms combine an antique setting with plush upholstery, rich carpeting, and vibrant colors with a garden graced with majestic magnolias. Each guest room is appointed with whimsical accessories, like a pair of porcelain panthers flanking one of the mantels, and travertine-trimmed bathtubs. Units in the 19th-century annex are as comfortable as those in the main house. The midsize bathrooms have tub/showers.

Ancienne Route du Grès, St-Rémy-de-Provence 13210. ✆ **04-90-92-03-33.** Fax 04-90-92-45-17. www.chateaudesalpilles.com. 21 units. 180€–320€ double; 260€–337€ suite. AE, DC, MC, V. Closed early Jan to mid-Mar. **Amenities:** Restaurant; bar; outdoor pool; room service; sauna; 2 tennis courts. *In room:* A/C, TV, hair dryer, minibar, Wi-Fi (free).

Hostellerie du Vallon de Valrugues ★★★ Surrounded by a park, this hotel has the best accommodations and restaurant in town. Constructed in the 1970s, it resembles a fantasy version of an ancient Roman villa. The beautiful rooms and suites all have marble bathrooms with tub/showers. The property has a putting green, and guests have access to horseback riding. The restaurant's terrace is as appealing as its cuisine, which wins praise for innovative light dishes, such as John Dory with truffles, and frozen nougat with comfit of fruit.

Chemin Canto-Cigalo, St-Rémy-de-Provence 13210. ✆ **04-90-92-04-40.** Fax 04-90-92-44-01. www.vallondevalrugues.com. 52 units. 190€–310€ double; 310€–1,310€ suite. AE, MC, V. Closed mid-Jan to mid-Feb. **Amenities:** Restaurant; bar; babysitting; exercise room; outdoor pool; room service; sauna; tennis court. *In room:* A/C, TV, hair dryer, minibar, Wi-Fi (free).

WHERE TO DINE

La Maison Jaune ★★ FRENCH/PROVENÇAL One of the most enduringly popular restaurants in St-Rémy is in the former residence of an 18th-century merchant. Today, in a pair of dining rooms occupying two floors, you'll appreciate cuisine prepared and served with flair by François and Catherine Perraud. In nice weather, additional seats are on a terrace overlooking the Hôtel de Sade. Menu items include pigeon roasted in wine from Les Baux; grilled sardines served with candied lemon and raw fennel; artichoke hearts marinated in white wine and served with tomatoes; and succulent roasted rack of lamb served with tapenade of black olives and anchovies.

15 rue Carnot. ✆ **04-90-92-56-14.** www.lamaisonjaune.info. Reservations required. Fixed-price menu 36€–66€. MC, V. Tues–Sun noon–1:30pm; Tues–Sat 7:30–9pm. Closed Dec–Jan.

EXPLORING ST-REMY & ENVIRONS

Visitors can see the 12th-century cloisters of the asylum that van Gogh made famous in his paintings at the **Monastère St-Paul-de-Mausolée ★★** (✆ **04-90-92-77-00**). Now a psychiatric hospital for women, the former monastery is east of D5, a short drive north of Glanum (see below). You can't visit the cell where the artist was confined from 1889 to 1890, but it's worth visiting to explore the Romanesque chapel and cloisters. The circular arches and columns have beautifully carved capitals. On your way to the church, you'll see a bust of van Gogh. The cloisters are open daily April to October 9:30am to 7pm, November to March 10:15am to 4:45pm. Admission is 4€ adults, 3€ students and children 12 to 16, free for children 11 and under.

Just south of St-Remy on D5 is **Ruines de Glanum ★** (✆ **04-90-92-23-79**), a Gallo-Roman city. Its monuments include a triumphal arch from the time of Julius Caesar, along with a cenotaph called the Mausolée des Jules. Garlanded with sculptured fruit and flowers, the arch dates from 20 B.C. and is the oldest in Provence. The mausoleum was raised to honor the grandsons of Augustus and is the only extant monument of its type. In the area are entire streets and foundations of private residences from the 1st-century town, plus some remains from a Gallo-Greek town of the 2nd century B.C. The excavations are open April to August daily 10am to 6:30pm, and September to March Tuesday to Sunday 10:30am to 5pm. Admission is 7€ adults, 5.50€ students 18 to 25, free for children 17 and under. From the town center, follow the signs to Les Antiques.

Les Baux ★★★

Cardinal Richelieu called Les Baux "a nesting place for eagles." On a wind-swept plateau overlooking the southern Alpilles, Les Baux is a ghost of its former self, though still very dramatic. It was once the citadel of seigneurs who ruled with an iron fist and sent their armies as far as Albania. Today, the castle and ramparts are mere shells, though you can see remains of Renaissance mansions. The dry, foreboding countryside around Les Baux, which nestles in a valley surrounded by shadowy rock formations, offers its own fascination. Vertical ravines lie on either side of the town. Vineyards—officially classified as Coteaux d'Aix-en-Provence—surround Les Baux, facing the Alpilles. If you follow the signposted *route des vin,* you can motor through the vineyards in an afternoon, perhaps stopping off at growers' estates.

Now the bad news: Because of the beauty and drama of the area, Les Baux is virtually overrun with visitors; it's not unlike Mont-St-Michel in that respect.

ESSENTIALS

GETTING THERE Les Baux is best reached by car; there is no rail service. From Arles, take the express highway N570 northeast until you reach the turnoff for a secondary road (D17), which will lead you northeast to Fontvieille. From here, just follow the signs east into Les Baux. By **train,** most passengers get off at Arles. Taxis in Arles (✆ **06-80-27-60-92**) will take you to Les Baux for around 30€ to 40€; be sure to agree on the fare in advance.

VISITOR INFORMATION The **Office de Tourisme** (✆ **04-90-54-34-39;** fax 04-90-54-51-15; www.lesbauxdeprovence.com) is on Maison du Roy, near the northern entrance to the old city.

WHERE TO STAY & DINE

Oustau de Baumanière ★★★ This Relais & Châteaux member is one of southern France's legendary hotels. Raymond Thuilier bought the 14th-century farmhouse in 1945, and by the 1950s, it was a rendezvous for the glitterati. Today, managed by its founder's grandson, it's not as glitzy, but the three stone houses draped in flowering vines are still charming. The plush rooms evoke the 16th and 17th centuries. All units contain large sitting areas, and no two are alike. If there's no vacancy in the main building, the hotel will assign you to one of the annexes. Request Le Manoir, the most appealing. The spacious bathrooms contain tub/shower combinations. In the stone-vaulted dining room, the chef serves specialties such as ravioli of truffles with leeks, *rossini* (stuffed with foie gras) of veal with fresh truffles, and roast duckling with olives. The award-winning *gigot d'agneau* (lamb) *en croûte* has become this place's trademark. Fixed-price menus cost 120€ to 175€.

Les Baux, Maussane-les-Alpilles 13520. ✆ **04-90-54-33-07.** Fax 04-90-54-40-46. www.oustaudebaumaniere.com. 30 units. 230€–410€ double; 380€–555€ suite. AE, DC, MC, V. Closed Jan 4–Feb 5. Restaurant closed Wed all day and Thurs at lunch Oct–Mar. **Amenities:** Restaurant; babysitting; outdoor pool; room service. *In room:* A/C, TV, hair dryer, minibar, Wi-Fi (free).

EXPLORING LES BAUX

Les Baux is one of the most dramatic towns in Provence. You can wander through feudal ruins, called **La Ville Morte (Ghost Village) ★★★**, at the northern end of town. The **Château des Baux** (✆ **04-90-54-55-56**) is carved out of the rocky mountain peak; the site of the castle covers an area at least five times that of Les

Baus itself. As you stand at the ruins, you can look out over the Val d'Enfer (Valley of Hell) and even see the Mediterranean in the distance.

At the castle you can enjoy the panorama from the **Tour Sarrazin (Saracen Tower).** Admission to the castle, including the museum and access to the ruins, is 7.80€ for adults, 5.80€ for students, and free for children 17 and under. The site is open in July and August daily 9am to 7:30pm, March to June and in September and October daily 9am to 6:30pm, and November to February daily 9:30am to 5pm.

Arles ★★★

Often called the soul of Provence, this town on the Rhône attracts art lovers, archaeologists, and historians. To the delight of visitors, many of the vistas van Gogh painted so luminously remain. The painter left Paris for Arles in 1888, the same year he cut off part of his left ear. He painted some of his most celebrated works here, including *The Starry Night, The Bridge at Arles, Sunflowers,* and *L'Arlésienne.*

Though Arles doesn't possess as much charm as Aix-en-Provence, it's still rewarding to visit, with first-rate museums, excellent restaurants, and summer festivals. The city today isn't quite as lovely as it was, but it has enough of the antique charm of Provence to keep its appeal alive.

ESSENTIALS

GETTING THERE There are hourly rail connections between Arles and Avignon (20 min.; 6€–8€), Marseille (50 min.; 13€), and Nîmes (20 min.; 7.30€). For rail schedules and information, call ✆ **36-35.** There are about four **buses** per day from Aix-en-Provence (trip time: 1 hr. 45 min.). For bus information, call ✆ **08-10-00-08-16.** If **driving,** head south along D570 from Avignon.

If you'd like to get around by bicycle, head for **Cycles Peugeot,** 15 rue du Pont (✆ **04-90-96-03-77**), which rents bikes at 15€ per day.

VISITOR INFORMATION The **Office de Tourisme** is on esplanade Charles-de-Gaulle (✆ **04-90-18-41-20;** fax 04-90-18-41-29; www.arlestourisme.com).

WHERE TO STAY & DINE

Hôtel Jules César ★★★ This 17th-century Carmelite convent is now a stately country hotel with one of the best restaurants in town. Although it's in a noisy neighborhood, most rooms face the unspoiled cloister. You'll wake to the scent of roses and the sounds of birds singing. Throughout, you'll find a blend of neoclassical architecture and modern amenities. The decor is luxurious, with antique Provençal furnishings found at auctions in the countryside. The interior rooms are the most tranquil and the darkest, though enlivened by bright fabrics. Most of the downstairs units are spacious; the upstairs rooms are small but have a certain old-world charm. The rooms in the modern extensions are comfortable but lack character. Each bathroom comes with a combination tub/shower. The excellent **Restaurant Lou Marquès** serves creative twists on Provençal specialties. Fixed-price menus run from 21€ to 60€.

9 bd. des Lices, Arles Cedex 13631. ✆ **04-90-52-52-52.** Fax 04-90-52-52-53. www.hotel-julescesar.fr. 58 units. 160€–250€ double; 300€–385€ suite. AE, DC, MC, V. Parking 13€. Closed Nov–Mar. **Amenities:** Restaurant; bar; babysitting; room service. *In room:* TV, hair dryer, minibar, Wi-Fi (10€ per hour).

EXPLORING ARLES

Arles is full of Roman monuments. **Place du Forum,** shaded by plane trees, is around the old Roman forum. The Café de Nuit, immortalized by van Gogh, once stood on this square. You can see two Corinthian columns and fragments from a temple at the corner of the Hôtel Nord-Pinus. Three blocks south of here is **place de la République,** dominated by a 15m-tall (49-ft.) blue porphyry obelisk. On the north is the **Hôtel de Ville** (town hall) from 1673, built to Mansart's plans and surmounted by a Renaissance belfry.

One of the city's great classical monuments is the Roman **Théâtre Antique ★★**, rue du Cloître (✆ **04-90-49-38-20**). Augustus began the theater in the 1st century; only two Corinthian columns remain. The *Venus of Arles* was discovered here in 1651. Take rue de la Calade from city hall. The theater is open daily May to September 9am to 6:30pm; March, April, and October 9 to 11:30am and 2 to 6pm; and November to February 10 to 11:30am and 2 to 4:30pm. Admission is 3€ for adults, 2.20€ for students and children 12 to 18, and free for children 11 and under. Nearby is the **Amphitheater (Les Arènes) ★★**, rond-pont des Arènes (✆ **04-90-49-36-86**), also built in the 1st century. Sometimes called Le Cirque Romain, it seats almost 25,000 and still hosts bullfights in summer. Visit at your own risk: The stone steps are uneven, and much of the masonry is worn. For a good view, you can climb the three towers that remain from medieval times, when the amphitheater was turned into a fortress. Hours are daily May to September 9am to 6pm; March, April, and October 9am to 6pm; and November to February 10am to 5pm. Admission costs 6€ for adults, 4.50€ for students and children 18 and under.

Perhaps the most memorable sight in Arles, **Les Alyscamps ★** (✆ **04-90-49-36-87**), once a necropolis established by the Romans, was converted into a Christian burial ground in the 4th century. It became a setting for legends and was even mentioned in Dante's *Inferno*. Today, it's lined with poplars and studded with ancient sarcophagi. Arlesiens escape here to enjoy a respite from the heat. Hours are the same as for the Théâtre Antique (see above). Admission is 3.50€ adults, 2.60€ children 12 to 18, free for children 11 and under.

Aix-en-Provence ★★

This faded university town is the most charming center in Provence. Founded in 122 B.C. by Roman general Caius Sextius Calvinus, who named the town Aquae Sextiae after himself, Aix (pronounced *Ex*) originated as a military outpost. It became a civilian colony, the administrative capital of a province of the late Roman Empire, the seat of an archbishop, and official residence of the medieval *comtes* de Provence. After the union of Provence with France, Aix remained a judicial and administrative center until the Revolution. Today, the city is quiet in winter but active and bustling when the summer hordes pour in for frequent cultural events, ranging from opera to jazz.

Paul Cézanne, the celebrated son of this old capital of Provence, immortalized the countryside in his paintings. Just as he saw it, Montagne Ste-Victoire looms over the town today, though a string of high-rises now interrupts the landscape.

ESSENTIALS

GETTING THERE The city is easily accessible. Twenty-seven **trains** arrive daily from Marseille; the trip takes 45 minutes and costs 7€ one-way. Twenty-five trains arrive from Nice; the trip takes 3 to 4 hours and costs 36€ one-way. There are also 25 trains per day from Cannes (3½ hr.), costing 35€ one-way. High-speed TGV trains arrive at Vitroll, 5.5km (3⅓ miles) west of Aix. Bus links to the center of Aix cost 4.10€ one-way. For more information, call ✆ **36-35. Buses** from Marseille arrive every 10 minutes; from Avignon, five times a day; and twice a day from Nice. For more information, call ✆ **08-91-02-40-25.** If you're **driving** from Avignon or other points north, take A7 south to RN7 and follow it into town. From Marseille or other points south, take A51 north into town.

To explore the region by bike, head for **La Rotondo,** 2 av. Des Belges (✆ **04-42-26-78-92**), a short walk northeast of the cours Mirabeau. Here you can rent 10-speed racing bikes or more durable mountain bikes for 20€ per day. You must leave a deposit—your passport or driver's license, or cash or monetary objects worth the value of the bike, usually 250€.

VISITOR INFORMATION The **Office de Tourisme** is at 2 place du Général-de-Gaulle (✆ **04-42-16-11-61;** fax 04-42-16-11-62; www.aixenprovencetourism.com).

WHERE TO STAY

Hôtel Cézanne ★★ Named in honor of the painter, this is the first boutique hotel to open in Aix-en-Provence. Bathed in light, the rooms and suites pay homage to Provence and the paintings of Cézanne. The bedrooms are spacious and modern, from the "tropical" showers to free cold drinks in the minibar. Breakfast, served until noon, might include smoked salmon and champagne. The hotel is not only up to date, but innovative and colorful with a strong sense of design. What we like most is how the sunlight seems to caress the mother-of-pearl inlaid walls, on which the light almost dances, as in a Cézanne painting.

40 av. Victor Hugo, Aix-en-Provence 13100. ✆ **04-42-91-11-11.** Fax 04-42-91-11-10. www.hotelaix.com/cezanne. 55 units. 179€ double; 249€ junior suite; 310€ suite. AE, MC, V. **Amenities:** Bar; room service. *In room:* A/C, TV, hair dryer, minibar, Wi-Fi (free).

La Villa Gallici ★★★ This elegant, relentlessly chic inn, which originated in the 18th century as a private home, is the most stylish hotel in town. The rooms, richly infused with the decorative traditions of Aix, are subtle and charming. Some rooms have a private terrace or garden, and each comes with a combination tub/shower. The villa sits in a large enclosed garden in the heart of Aix, close to one of the best restaurants, Le Clos de la Violette (see "Where to Dine," below). It's a 5-minute walk to the town center.

Av. de la Violette, Aix-en-Provence 13100. ✆ **04-42-23-29-23.** Fax 04-42-96-30-45. www.villagallici.com. 22 units. 230€–780€ double; 440€–945€ suite. AE, DC, MC, V. Closed Jan. **Amenities:** Restaurant; bar; babysitting; outdoor pool; room service. *In room:* A/C, TV, hair dryer, minibar, Wi-Fi (free).

WHERE TO DINE

Le Bistro Latin ★★ PROVENÇAL This is the best little bistro in Aix-en-Provence for the price. Guests dine in two intimate rooms: a street-level space and a cellar decorated in Greco-Latin style. The staff is young and enthusiastic, taking special pride in their fixed-price menus. Try chartreuse of mussels, a meat dish with spinach-and-saffron cream sauce, scampi risotto, or rack of lamb in an herbed crust.

18 rue de la Couronne. ✆ **04-42-38-22-88.** Reservations recommended. Main courses 16€–20€; fixed-price lunch 23€, dinner 23€–45€. MC, V. Thurs–Tues noon–2pm and 7–10:30pm.

Le Clos de la Violette ★★★ MODERN FRENCH This innovative restaurant is in an elegant neighborhood that most visitors reach by taxi. The Provençal villa has an octagonal reception area and several dining rooms. The stylish, seasonal dishes highlight the flavors of Provence. A stellar example of the innovative cuisine is an appetizer of mousseline of potatoes with sea urchins and fish roe. An elegant dish is braised sea wolf with crisp fried shallots and spicy Spanish sausages. Delightful rack of suckling lamb is stuffed with carrots and chickpeas and served under an herb-flavored pastry crust. For dessert, try multilayered sugar cookies with hazelnut- and vanilla-flavored cream sauce and thin slices of white chocolate, or a "celebration" of Provençal figs—an artfully arranged platter containing a galette, tart, parfait, and sorbet.

10 av. de la Violette. ✆ **04-42-23-30-71.** www.closdelaviolette.fr. Reservations required. Main courses 46€–49€; fixed-price lunch 50€; tasting menu 130€. AE, MC, V. Tues–Sat noon–1:30pm and 7:30–9:30pm.

EXPLORING THE CITY

Aix's main street, **cours Mirabeau ★**, is one of Europe's most beautiful. Plane trees stretch across the street like umbrellas, shading it from the hot Provençal sun and filtering the light into shadows that play on the rococo fountains below. Shops and sidewalk cafes line one side of the street; sandstone *hôtels particuliers* (mansions) from the 17th and 18th centuries fill the other. The street begins at the 1860 fountain on place de la Libération.

Outside of town, on 9 av. Paul-Cézanne, is the **Atelier de Cézanne** (✆ **04-42-21-06-53;** www.atelier-cezanne.com), the studio of the painter who was the major forerunner of cubism. The house, restored by American admirers, remains much as Cézanne left it in 1906, "his coat hanging on the wall, his easel with an unfinished picture waiting for a touch of the master's brush," as Thomas R. Parker wrote. Open daily April to June 10am to noon and 2 to 6pm, July and August 10am to 6pm, and October to March 10am to noon and 2 to 5pm. Admission is 5.50€ adults, 2€ students and children 12 and under.

St-Tropez ★★

An air of hedonism runs rampant in this sun-kissed town, but the true Tropezian resents the fact that the port has such a bad reputation. "We can be classy, too," one native insists. Creative people along with ordinary folk create a varied atmosphere. St-Tropez attracts artists, composers, novelists, and the film colony in the summer. Trailing behind is a flamboyant parade of humanity. Some of the most fashionable yachts, bearing some of the most chic people, anchor here in summer. Colette lived here for years, and the diarist Anaïs Nin, confidante of Henry Miller, posed for a little cheesecake on the beach in 1939 in a Dorothy Lamour–style bathing suit.

ESSENTIALS

GETTING THERE The nearest rail station is in St-Raphaël, a neighboring resort. At St-Raphaël's Vieux Port, **boats** leave the Gare Maritime de St-Raphaël, rue Pierre-Auble (✆ **04-94-95-17-46**), for St-Tropez (trip time: 50 min.). Sailings are Tuesday and Saturday. The one-way fare is 14€. Year-round, 10 to 15 Sodetrav **buses** per day leave from the Gare Routière in St-Raphaël (✆ **04-94-97-88-51**) for St-Tropez. The trip takes 1½ to 2½ hours, depending on the bus and the traffic, which during midsummer is usually horrendous. A one-way ticket costs 12€. Buses run directly to St-Tropez from Toulon and Hyères and from the nearest airport, at Toulon-Hyères, 56km (35 miles) away.

If you **drive,** note that parking in St-Tropez is very difficult, especially in summer. You can park in the **Parking des Lices** (✆ **04-94-97-34-46**), beneath place des

The French Riviera

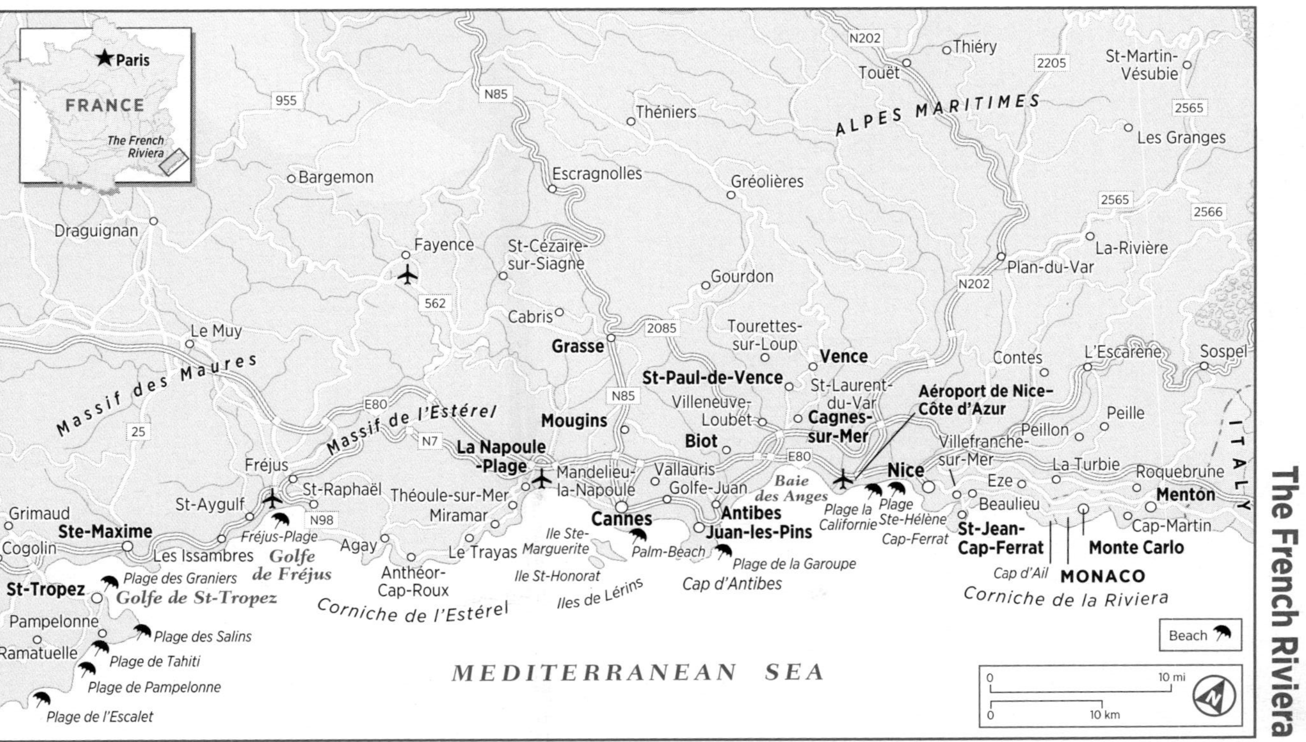

Lices; enter on avenue Paul-Roussel. Designed for 300 cars, this lot charges 2.20€ per hour. Many visitors with expensive cars prefer this lot because it's more secure than any other. Charging the same rates, a new garage, **Parking du Nouveau Port,** avenue Charles de Gaulle (✆ **04-94-97-74-99**), stands at the waterfront. To get here from **Cannes,** drive southwest along the coastal highway (RD98), turning east when you see signs pointing to St-Tropez.

VISITOR INFORMATION The **Office de Tourisme** is on quai Jean-Jaurès (✆ **04-94-97-45-21;** fax 04-94-97-82-66; www.ot-saint-tropez.com).

WHERE TO STAY

Hôtel Byblos ★★★ The builder said he created "an anti-hotel, a place like home." That's true if your home resembles a palace in Beirut and has salons decorated with Phoenician gold statues from 3000 B.C. On a hill above the harbor, this complex encompasses intimate patios and courtyards. It's filled with antiques and rare objects such as polychrome carved woodwork, marquetry floors, and a Persian-rug ceiling. Every room is unique, and all have elegant beds. Unusual features might include a fireplace on a raised hearth or a bed recessed on a dais. The rooms range in size from medium to spacious, often with high ceilings and antiques or reproductions. Some units have such special features as four-posters with furry spreads or sunken whirlpool tubs. Le Hameau, a stylish annex, contains 10 duplex suites built around a small courtyard with an outdoor spa. Some rooms have balconies overlooking an inner courtyard; others open onto a flowery terrace.

Av. Paul Signac, St-Tropez 83990. ✆ **04-94-56-68-00.** Fax 04-94-56-68-01. www.byblos.com. 94 units. 360€–900€ double; from 640€ suite. AE, DC, MC, V. Parking 30€. Closed Nov–Mar. **Amenities:** 2 restaurants; 2 bars; nightclub; babysitting; exercise room; massage; outdoor pool; room service; sauna; spa. *In room:* A/C, TV, hair dryer, minibar, Wi-Fi (free).

Hôtel La Ponche ★★ This cozy nest has long been a favorite of ours, as it's the most discreet, most charming, and least celebrity-flashy establishment in town, making Byblos (see above) look nouveau riche and a bit strident. The redecorated rooms are well equipped and open onto sea views. Each floor holds two or three rooms. Sun-colored walls with subtle lighting lend a homey feeling. The beds are elegantly appointed with linen and quality mattresses.

Port des Pécheurs, St-Tropez 83990. ✆ **04-94-97-02-53.** Fax 04-94-97-78-61. www.laponche.com. 18 units. 195€–460€ double; 225€–630€ suite. AE, MC, V. Parking 21€. Closed Nov–Mar. **Amenities:** Restaurant; bar; babysitting; room service. *In room:* A/C, TV, hair dryer, minibar, Wi-Fi (free).

WHERE TO DINE

Auberge des Maures ★ PROVENÇAL One of our favorite cost-conscious restaurants in an otherwise very expensive town lies close to one end of the all-pedestrian rue Allard. The stone-sided building has a rollaway roof and garden seating (both experienced during nice weather). The open kitchen affords views of the staff preparing items such as grilled versions of many kinds of fresh fish and meat; *panache Provençal,* on which are piled deep-fried zucchini blossoms; hearts of artichoke *barigoule;* and a medley of *petits farcis* (stuffed vegetables).

4 rue du Docteur Boutin. ✆ **04-94-97-01-50.** www.aubergedesmaures.com. Reservations recommended. Main courses 40€–60€; fixed-price menu 47€. AE, DC, MC, V. Daily 7:30pm–1am. Closed Nov–Mar.

Spoon Byblos ★★ FRENCH/INTERNATIONAL Originally launched in Paris, Spoon has traveled everywhere from London to the Riviera. Here it serves the cuisines of many cultures with produce mainly from the Mediterranean. It draws special inspiration from the food of Catalonia, Andalusia, and Morocco, and offers more than 300 wines from around the world. Dig into shrimp and squid consommé with a hint of jasmine and orange; spicy king prawns on a skewer; delectable lamb couscous; or spit-roasted John Dory. You may top off a meal with the chef's favorite cheesecake or a slice of Neapolitan with the taste of strawberry, vanilla, and pistachio.

In the Hôtel Byblos, av. Paul-Signac. ✆ **04-94-56-68-20.** Reservations required. Main courses 32€–49€; fixed-price menu 89€. AE, DC, MC, V. Mid-Apr to Oct daily 8–11pm.

EXPLORING ST-TROPEZ & ENVIRONS

Musée de l'Annonciade (Musée St-Tropez) ★★ Near the harbor, this museum occupies the former chapel of the Annonciade. It showcases one of the Riviera's finest modern-art collections of post-Impressionist masters. Many of the artists, including Paul Signac, depicted the port of St-Tropez. The collection includes such works as Van Dongen's *Women of the Balustrade* and paintings and sculpture by Bonnard, Matisse, Braque, Dufy, Utrillo, Seurat, and Maillol.

Quai de l'Epi le Port. ✆ **04-94-17-84-10.** Admission 6€ adults, 4€ children 11 and under. June–Sept Wed–Mon 10am–noon and 3–7pm; Oct and Dec–May Wed–Mon 10am–noon and 2–6pm. Closed Nov.

HITTING THE BEACH & OTHER OUTDOOR ACTIVITIES

BEACHES The hottest Riviera beaches are at St-Tropez. The best for families are closest to the center, including the **Plage de la Bouillabaisse** and **Plage des Graniers.** More daring are the 9.5km (6-mile) crescents at **Plage des Salins** and **Plage de Pampelonne,** some 3km (1¾ miles) from the town center, best reached by bike if you're not driving

BOATING The highly recommended **Suncap Company,** 15 quai de Suffren (✆ **04-94-97-11-23**), rents boats 5.4 to 12m (18–39 ft.) long. Larger ones come with a captain at the helm. Prices begin at 1,500€ per day.

TENNIS Anyone who phones in advance can use the eight courts (artificial grass or "Quick," a form of concrete) at the **Tennis-Club de St-Tropez,** route des Plages, St-Claude (✆ **04-94-97-15-52**), about 1km (⅔ mile) from the resort's center. Open year-round, the courts rent for 20€ per hour for green set, 25€ per hour for clay set, from 9am to 8pm. there's an extra charge of 4€ for nighttime lighting.

ST-TROPEZ AFTER DARK

On the lobby level of the Hôtel Byblos, **Les Caves du Roy,** avenue Paul-Signac (✆ **04-94-97-16-02**), is the most self-consciously chic nightclub in St-Tropez and the most famous in France. Entrance is free, but drink prices begin at a whopping 18€. It's open nightly from May to late September from 11:30pm to dawn. **Le Papagayo,** in the Résidence du Nouveau-Port, rue Gambetta (✆ **04-94-97-95-95**), is one of the largest nightclubs in town. The decor was inspired by the psychedelic 1960s. Entrance is between 15€ and 18€, and includes one drink.

Adjacent to Le Papagayo is **Le VIP Room,** in the Résidence du Nouveau-Port (✆ **04-94-97-14-70**), whose upscale patrons may be equally at home in Les Caves du Roy. Cocktails run between 14€ and 15€. Expect an active bar area, dance floor, and the kind of social posturing and preening that can be amusing—or not. **Le**

Pigeonnier, 13 rue de la Ponche (✆ **04-94-97-84-26**), rocks, rolls, and welcomes a crowd that's mostly gay or lesbian and between 20 and 50. Most of the socializing revolves around the long, narrow bar, where patrons from all over Europe enjoy chitchat.

Cannes ★★★

When Coco Chanel came here and got a suntan, returning to Paris bronzed, she startled the milk-white society ladies, who quickly began copying her. Today the bronzed bodies—clad in nearly nonexistent swimsuits—that line the beaches of this chic resort continue the late fashion designer's example.

Something is always happening at Cannes, except in November, traditionally a dead month. Popular with celebrities, Cannes is at its most frenzied in late May during the **International Film Festival** at the Palais des Festivals on promenade de la Croisette.

Cannes, sheltered by hills, lies 26km (16 miles) southwest of Nice. For many it consists of only one street, **promenade de la Croisette,** curving along the coast and split by islands of palms and flowers. Hotels, apartment houses, and boutiques line the seafront. Many of the bigger hotels claim parts of the beaches for guests' private use; there are also public areas.

ESSENTIALS

GETTING THERE **Trains** from the other Mediterranean resorts, Paris, and the rest of France arrive throughout the day. By train, Cannes is 15 minutes from Antibes and 35 minutes from Nice. The TGV from Paris via Marseille reaches Cannes in about 5½ to 6 breathless hours. The one-way fare from Paris is 50€ to 95€. For rail information, call ✆ **08-92-35-35-35,** or visit www.voyages-sncf.com. **Rapide Côte d'Azur,** place de l'Hôtel de Ville, Cannes (✆ **04-93-85-64-44**), provides bus service to Nice and back every 20 minutes during the day (trip time: 1½ hr.). The one-way fare is 1€.

The Nice **international airport** (✆ **08-20-42-33-33;** www.rca.tm.fr) is a 30-minute drive northeast. **Buses** pick up passengers at the airport every 40 minutes during the day and drop them at the Gare Routière, place de l'Hôtel de Ville (✆ **04-93-45-20-08**). Bus service from Antibes operates every half-hour.

By **car** from Marseille, take A51 north to Aix-en-Provence, continuing along A8 east to Cannes. From Nice, follow A8 southwest to Cannes.

VISITOR INFORMATION The **Office de Tourisme** is at 1 bd. de la Croisette (✆ **04-92-99-84-22;** fax 04-92-99-84-23; www.cannes.travel).

WHERE TO STAY

Hôtel Le Fouquet's ★ 🎁 This intimate lodging draws a discreet clientele, often from Paris, who'd never think of patronizing the grand hotels. Riviera French in design and decor, the hotel is several blocks from the beach. Each of the cozy guest rooms is outfitted just a bit differently from its neighbor. They're decorated in bold Provençal colors of ocher and blue, and have contemporary, vaguely regional furniture.

2 rond-point Duboys-d'Angers, Cannes 06400. ✆ **04-92-59-25-00.** Fax 04-92-98-03-39. www.le-fouquets.com. 12 units. 110€–280€ double; 280€–320€ suite. AE, DC, MC, V. Closed Nov 1–Apr 12. Bus: 1. **Amenities:** Babysitting; room service. *In room:* A/C, TV, hair dryer, minibar, Wi-Fi (free).

Hôtel Splendid ★ Opened in 1871, and widely renovated, this is a favorite of scholars, politicians, actors, and musicians. The ornate white building with wrought-iron accents looks out onto the sea, the old port, and a park. The rooms are appointed with antique furniture and paintings; about 15 have kitchenettes. Each comes with a good bed and a small but efficient bathroom. The more expensive rooms have sea views.

4-6 rue Félix-Faure, Cannes 06400. ✆ **04-97-06-22-22.** Fax 04-93-99-55-02. www.splendid-hotel-cannes.fr. 62 units. 131€–264€ double. Rates include breakfast. AE, MC, V. **Amenities:** Babysitting; room service. *In room:* A/C, TV, hair dryer, Internet (free).

InterContinental Carlton Cannes ★★★ Here you'll see vehicles of every description dropping off huge amounts of baggage and numbers of fashionable (and sometimes not-so-fashionable) guests. Built in 1912, the Carlton once attracted the most prominent members of Europe's *haut monde*. Today the hotel is more democratic, booking lots of conventions and motorcoach tour groups; however, in summer (especially during the film festival) the public rooms still fill with all the voyeuristic and exhibitionistic fervor that seems so much a part of the Riviera. Guest rooms are plush; the most spacious are in the west wing; and many upper-floor rooms open onto waterfront balconies.

58 bd. de la Croisette, Cannes 06400. ✆ **04-93-06-40-06.** Fax 04-93-06-40-25. www.intercontinental.com. 343 units. 250€–1,050€ double; from 615€ suite. AE, DC, MC, V. Parking 37€. **Amenities:** 3 summer restaurants, 1 winter restaurant; 2 bars; health club; room service. *In room:* A/C, TV, hair dryer, Internet (24€ per day), minibar.

WHERE TO DINE

La Palme d'Or ★★★ MODERN FRENCH Movie stars on the see-and-be-seen circuit head here during the film festival. It's a sophisticated rendezvous that serves some of the Riviera's finest hotel cuisine. The decor is a tawny-colored Art Deco marvel with bay windows, a winter-garden theme, and outdoor and enclosed terraces overlooking the pool, the sea, and La Croisette. Menu items change with the seasons but are likely to include warm foie gras with fondue of rhubarb; filets of fried red mullet with a beignet of potatoes, zucchini, and olive-cream sauce; or crayfish, clams, and squid marinated in peppered citrus sauce. A modernized version of a Niçoise staple includes three parts of a rabbit with rosemary sauce, fresh vegetables, and chickpea rosettes. The most appealing dessert is wild strawberries from Carros with Grand Marnier–flavored *nage* and "cream sauce of frozen milk."

In the Hôtel Martinez, 73 bd. de la Croisette. ✆ **04-92-98-74-14.** www.hotelmartinez.com. Reservations required. Main courses 65€–180€; fixed-price lunch 64€–155€, dinner 79€–180€. AE, DC, MC, V. Wed–Sat 12:30–2pm and 8–10pm. Closed Jan–Feb.

EXPLORING CANNES

Above the harbor, the old town of Cannes sits on Suquet Hill, where you'll see the 14th-century **Tour de Suquet,** which the English dubbed the Lord's Tower.

Nearby is the **Musée de la Castre** ★, in the Château de la Castre, Le Suquet (✆ **04-93-38-55-26**). It displays paintings, sculpture, and works of decorative art. The ethnography section includes objects from all over, including Peruvian and Maya pottery. There's also a gallery devoted to relics of Mediterranean civilizations, from the Greeks to the Romans, from the Cypriots to the Egyptians. Five rooms hold 19th-century paintings. The museum is open daily in July and August 10am to 7pm,

September to March Tuesday to Sunday 10am to 1pm and 2 to 5pm, and April to June Tuesday to Sunday 10am to 1pm and 2 to 6pm. Admission is 3.20€ adults, 2€ ages 18 to 25, free for children 17 and under.

HITTING THE BEACH & OTHER OUTDOOR PURSUITS

BEACHES Looking for a free public beach where you'll have to survive without renting chaises or parasols? Head for **Plage du Midi,** sometimes called Midi Plage, just west of the Vieux Port (no phone), or **Plage Gazagnaire,** just east of the Port Canto (no phone). Here you'll find families with children and lots of caravan-type vehicles parked nearby. Between these two public beaches are many private ones where you can gain entrance by paying a fee that includes a mattress and parasol.

BICYCLING & MOTOR SCOOTERING Despite the roaring traffic, the flat landscapes between Cannes and satellite resorts such as La Napoule are well suited for riding a bike or motor scooter. At **Daniel Location,** 7 rue Suffern (✆ **04-93-99-90-30**), *vélos tout terrain* (mountain bikes) cost 16€ a day. Motorized bikes and scooters cost 36€ per day; renters must be at least 14 years old. For larger scooters, you must present a valid driver's license. Another purveyor of bikes is **Mistral Location,** 4 rue Georges Clemenceau (✆ **04-93-39-08-53**), which charges 14€ per day.

BOATING Several companies rent boats of any size, with or without a crew, for a day, a week, or a month. An outfit known for short-term rentals of small craft, including motorboats, sailboats, and canoes, is **Elco Marine,** 110 bd. du Midi (✆ **04-93-47-12-62;** www.elcomarine.fr).

CANNES AFTER DARK

Cannes has a pair of world-class casinos, each loaded with addicts, voyeurs, and everyone in between. The better established is the **Casino Croisette,** in the Palais des Festivals, Esplanade Lucien Barrière (✆ **04-92-98-78-00**). Run by the Lucien Barrière group, and a well-respected fixture in town since the 1950s, it's a competitor of the newer **Palm Beach Casino,** place F-D-Roosevelt, Pointe de la Croisette (✆ **04-97-06-36-90**), on the southeast edge of La Croisette. With three restaurants and an Art Deco decor, it's glossier, newer, and a bit hungrier for new business. Both casinos maintain slot machines that operate daily 10am to 5am. Suites of rooms devoted to *les grands jeux* (blackjack, roulette, and chemin de fer) open nightly 8pm to 4am.

Antibes & Cap d'Antibes ★★

On the other side of the Baie des Anges (Bay of Angels) from Nice is the port of Antibes. The town has a quiet charm unique on the Côte d'Azur. Its harbor is filled with fishing boats and yachts, and in recent years it has emerged as a hot spot. The marketplaces are full of flowers. If you're in Antibes in the evening, you can watch fishers playing a game of *boule* (similar to boccie).

Spiritually, Antibes is totally divorced from Cap d'Antibes, a peninsula studded with the villas of the superrich. In *Tender Is the Night,* Fitzgerald described it as a place where "old villas rotted like water lilies among the massed pines."

ESSENTIALS

GETTING THERE **Trains** from Cannes arrive at the rail station, place Pierre-Semard, every 20 minutes (trip time: 15 min.); the one-way fare is 2.50€. Trains from Nice arrive at the rate of 25 per day (trip time: 18 min.); the one-way fare is 4.40€. For rail information, call ✆ **36-35,** or visit www.voyages-sncf.com. The **bus** station, La Gare Routière, place Guynemer (✆ **04-93-34-37-60**), receives buses from throughout Provence. Partially subsidized by the government, bus fares between Nice and Antibes or Cannes and Antibes cost only 1€ one-way.

If you're **driving,** follow E1 east from Cannes and take the turnoff to the south for Antibes, which will lead to the historic core of the old city. From Nice, take E1 west until you come to the turnoff for Antibes. From the center of Antibes, follow the coastal road, boulevard Leclerc, south to Cap d'Antibes.

VISITOR INFORMATION The **Office de Tourisme** is at 11 place du Général-de-Gaulle (✆ **04-97-23-11-11;** fax 04-97-23-11-12; www.antibesjuanlespins.com).

WHERE TO STAY

Castel Garoupe We highly recommend this Mediterranean villa, which was built in 1968 on a private lane in the center of the cape. It offers tastefully furnished, spacious rooms with fine beds and compact bathrooms with showers and tubs. Many rooms have private balconies, and each has shuttered windows. There's a tranquil garden on the premises.

959 bd. de la Garoupe, Cap d'Antibes 06160. ✆ **04-93-61-36-51.** Fax 04-93-67-74-88. www.castel-garoupe.com. 28 units. 128€–168€ double; 147€–235€ studio apt with kitchenette. AE, MC, V. Closed Nov to mid-Mar. Bus: A2. **Amenities:** 2 bars; babysitting; exercise room; outdoor pool; room service; tennis court. *In room:* A/C (in some), TV (in some), hair dryer, kitchenette, minibar, Wi-Fi (free).

Hôtel du Cap-Eden Roc ★★★ Legendary for the glamour of its setting and its clientele, this hotel, opened in 1870, is surrounded by masses of gardens. It's like a country estate, with spacious public rooms, marble fireplaces, paneling, chandeliers, and upholstered armchairs. The guest rooms are among the most sumptuous on the Riviera, with deluxe beds. Bathrooms are spacious, with brass fittings and tub/shower combinations. Even though the guests snoozing by the pool—blasted out of the cliff side at enormous expense—appear artfully undraped during the day, evenings are upscale, with lots of emphasis on clothing and style. The world-famous Pavillon Eden Roc, near a rock garden apart from the hotel, has a panoramic sea view. Venetian chandeliers, Louis XV chairs, and elegant draperies add to the drama. Lunch is served on a terrace, under umbrellas and an arbor.

Bd. J.-F.-Kennedy, Cap d'Antibes 06600. ✆ **04-93-61-39-01.** Fax 04-93-67-13-83. www.edenroc-hotel.fr. 130 units. 460€–880€ double; 970€–1,600€ suite. No credit cards. Closed mid-Oct to mid-Apr. Bus: A2. **Amenities:** 2 restaurants; bar; babysitting; exercise room; massage; outdoor pool; room service; sauna. *In room:* A/C, TV (on request), hair dryer, Wi-Fi (free).

WHERE TO DINE

La Taverne du Saffranier PROVENÇAL Earthy and irreverent, this brasserie in a century-old building serves a changing roster of savory local specialties. Portions are generous. Examples are a platter of *petits farcis* (stuffed vegetables); a bouillabaisse sized for single diners; savory fish soup; and an assortment of grilled fish (including sardines) that's served only with a dash of fresh lemon.

Place du Saffranier. ✆ **04-93-34-80-50.** Reservations recommended. Main courses 18€–26€; fixed-price menu 25€. MC, V. Tues–Sun noon–2pm; Tues–Sat 7–10:30pm. Closed mid-Nov to early Feb.

Restaurant de Bacon ★★★ SEAFOOD The Eden Roc restaurant at the Hôtel du Cap is more elegant, but Bacon serves the best seafood around. Surrounded by ultraexpensive residences, this restaurant on a rocky peninsula offers a panoramic coast view. Bouillabaisse aficionados claim that Bacon offers the best in France. In its deluxe version, saltwater crayfish float atop the savory brew; we prefer the simple version—a waiter adds the finishing touches at your table. If bouillabaisse isn't to your liking, try fish soup with garlic-laden rouille sauce; fish terrine; sea bass; John Dory; or something from a collection of fish unknown in North America—for example, sar, pageot, or denti.

Bd. de Bacon. ✆ **04-93-61-50-02.** www.restaurantdebacon.com. Reservations required. Main courses 40€–145€; fixed-price lunch 49€–79€; fixed-price dinner 79€. AE, DC, MC, V. Tues–Sun noon–2pm; Tues–Sun 8–10pm. Closed Nov–Mar.

A MUSEUM WORTH VISITING

On the ramparts above the port is the Château Grimaldi, once the home of the princes of Antibes of the Grimaldi family, who ruled the city from 1385 to 1608. Today it houses **Musée Picasso ★★**, place du Mariejol (✆ **04-92-90-54-20**). Picasso came to town after the war and stayed in a small hotel at Golfe-Juan until the museum director at Antibes invited him to work and live at the museum. Picasso spent 1946 painting here. When he departed, he gave the museum all the work he'd done: 23 paintings, 80 pieces of ceramics, 44 drawings, 32 lithographs, 11 oils on paper, 2 sculptures, and 5 tapestries. In addition, a gallery of contemporary art exhibits Léger, Miró, Ernst, and Calder, among others. Admission is 3€ students and seniors, free for ages 18 and under. The museum is open year-round, Tuesday to Sunday 10am to 6pm (closed noon–2pm Oct–May).

Nice ★★★

Nice is the capital of the Riviera, the largest city between Genoa and Marseille. It was founded by the Greeks, who called it Nike (Victory). By the 19th century, the Victorian upper class and tsarist aristocrats were flocking here. But these days it's not as chichi and expensive, especially compared to Cannes. In fact, of all the major French resorts, from Deauville to Biarritz to Cannes, Nice is the most affordable. It's also the best place to base yourself on the Riviera, especially if you're dependent on public transportation. From the Nice airport, the second largest in France, you can travel by train or bus along the entire coast to resorts such as Juan-les-Pins and Cannes.

ESSENTIALS

GETTING THERE **Trains** arrive at Gare Nice-Ville, avenue Thiers (✆ **08-92-35-35-35;** www.voyages-sncf.com). From there you can take trains to Cannes for 5.80€, Monaco 2.80€, and Antibes 3.90€, with easy connections to anywhere else along the Mediterranean coast. There's a small tourist center at the station, open Monday to Saturday 8am to 7pm and Sunday 9am to 6pm.

Buses to and from Monaco, Cannes, St-Tropez, and other parts of France and Europe serve the main bus station, or **Gare Routière,** 5 bd. Jean-Jaurès (✆ **08-92-70-12-06**).

Transatlantic and intercontinental flights land at **Aéroport Nice–Côte d'Azur** (✆ **08-20-42-33-33**). From there, municipal bus no. 98 departs at 30-minute intervals for the Gare Routière (see above); the one-way fare is 4€. Bus nos. 23 and 99 go to Gare SNCF. A **taxi** from the airport into the city center will cost at least 30€ to 40€ each way. Trip time is about 30 minutes.

VISITOR INFORMATION Nice maintains three **tourist offices,** the largest and most central of which is at 5 promenade des Anglais, near place Masséna (✆ **08-92-70-74-07;** fax 04-92-14-46-49; www.nicetourisme.com). Additional offices are in the arrivals hall of the Aéroport Nice–Côte d'Azur and the railway station on avenue Thiers. Any office can make a hotel reservation (but only for the night of the day you show up) for a modest fee that varies according to the classification of the hotel.

GETTING AROUND Most local buses serve the **Station Central SNCF,** 10 av. Félix-Faure (✆ **04-93-13-53-13;** www.voyages-sncf.com), a very short walk from the place Masséna. Municipal buses charge 1€ for a ride within Greater Nice. Bus nos. 2 and 12 make frequent trips to the beach.

No point within downtown Nice is more than about a 10-minute walk from the sea-fronting promenade, site of such well-known quays as the promenade des Anglais and the promenade des Etats-Unis. Bus nos. 2 and 12 run along its length, dropping passengers off at any of the beaches and concessions that front the edge of the sea.

The best place to rent bikes and mopeds is **Energy Scoot,** promenade des Anglais (✆ **04-97-07-12-64**), just behind the place Grimaldi. Open Monday to Saturday 9am to noon and 2 to 7pm, it charges 15€ per day for a bike or moped and requires a deposit of at least 55€, depending on the value of the machine you rent. To rent a scooter is 39€ per day. Somewhat less appealing, but useful when Energy Scoot is closed, is **Nicea Rent,** 12 rue de Belgique (✆ **04-93-82-42-71**). It charges about the same rates, but the staff isn't always on the premises.

WHERE TO STAY

Hôtel de la Mer In the center of Old Nice, this ocher-colored government-rated two-star hotel was built around 1910 and transformed into a hotel in 1947. Most rooms are of good size, and all have small bathrooms with showers. Some contain minibars. It's a 2-minute walk to the promenade des Anglais and the seafront. Breakfast is served in one of the public salons or in your room.

4 place Masséna, Nice 06000. ✆ **04-93-92-09-10.** Fax 04-93-85-00-64. www.hoteldelamernice.com. 12 units. 65€–95€ double. AE, MC, V. Parking 15€ in nearby lot. Bus: 3, 9, 10, or 12. **Amenities:** Room service. *In room:* A/C, TV, Wi-Fi (free).

Hôtel Gounod ★ A winning choice in the city center, this hotel is a 5-minute walk from the sea. It was built around 1910 in a neighborhood where the street names honor composers. Ornate balconies, a domed roof, and an elaborate canopy of wrought iron and glass embellish the Gounod. The attractive lobby and adjoining lounge are festive and stylish, with old prints, copper flowerpots, and antiques. The high-ceilinged guest rooms are quiet; most overlook the gardens of private homes. The tiled bathrooms are small but efficiently organized, mainly with shower units. Suites have safes. Guests have free unlimited use of the pool and Jacuzzi at the Hôtel Splendid, next door.

3 rue Gounod, Nice 06000. ✆ **04-93-16-42-00.** Fax 04-93-88-23-84. www.gounod-nice.com. 45 units. 110€–160€ double; 150€–260€ suite. AE, DC, MC, V. Parking 17€. Closed Nov 20–Dec 20. Bus: 98. **Amenities:** Babysitting; Internet (free); Jacuzzi; outdoor pool; room service; spa. *In room:* A/C, TV, hair dryer, minibar.

Hôtel Negresco ★★★ The Negresco, on the seafront in the heart of Nice, is one of the Riviera's superglamorous hotels. The Victorian wedding-cake hotel is named after its founder, Henry Negresco, a Romanian who died a pauper in Paris in 1920. The country's châteaux inspired both the interior and the exterior, with its mansard roof and domed tower. The hotel's decorators scoured Europe to gather antiques, tapestries, and art. Some of the accommodations, such as the Coco Chanel room, are outfitted in homage to the personalities who stayed here. Others are modeled on literary or musical themes, such as *La Traviata.* Suites and public areas include the Louis XIV salon, reminiscent of the Sun King, and the Napoleon III suite. The most expensive rooms with balconies face the Mediterranean and the private beach.

37 promenade des Anglais, Nice Cedex 06007. ✆ **04-93-16-64-00.** Fax 04-93-88-35-68. www.hotel-negresco-nice.com. 146 units. 290€–590€ double; from 680€ suite. AE, DC, MC, V. Free parking. **Amenities:** 2 restaurants; bar; babysitting; exercise room; massage; room service. *In room:* A/C, TV, hair dryer, Internet (free), minibar.

La Pérouse ★★ Once a prison, La Pérouse has been reconstructed and is now a unique Riviera hotel. Set on a cliff, it's built right in the gardens of an ancient château-fort. No hotel affords a better view over both the old city and the Baie des Anges. In fact, many people stay here just for the view. The hotel resembles an old Provençal home, with low ceilings, white walls, and antique furnishings. The lovely, spacious rooms are beautifully furnished, often with Provençal fabrics. Most have loggias overlooking the bay. The bathrooms are large, clad in Boticino marble, and hold tubs and showers.

11 quai Rauba-Capéu, Nice 06300. ✆ **04-93-62-34-63.** Fax 04-93-62-59-41. www.hotel-la-perouse.com. 65 units. 270€–750€ double; 650€–1,500€ suite. AE, DC, MC, V. Parking 19€. **Amenities:** Restaurant (mid-May to mid-Sept); bar; babysitting; exercise room; Jacuzzi; outdoor pool; room service; sauna. *In room:* A/C, TV, hair dryer, minibar, Wi-Fi (free).

WHERE TO DINE

La Merenda ★★ NIÇOISE Because there's no phone, you have to go by this place twice—once to make a reservation and once to dine—but it's worth the effort. Though chef Dominique Le Stanc was born in Alsace, his heart and soul belong to the Mediterranean, the land of black truffles, wild morels, sea bass, and asparagus. His food is a lullaby of gastronomic unity, with texture, crunch, richness, and balance. Le Stanc never knows what he's going to serve until he goes to the market. Look for specials on a chalkboard. Perhaps you'll find stuffed cabbage, fried zucchini flowers, or oxtail flavored with fresh oranges. Lamb from the Sisteron is cooked until it practically falls from the bone. Raw artichokes are paired with a salad of mâche.

4 rue Raoul Bosio. No phone. Reservations required. Main courses 38€–55€. No credit cards. Mon–Fri seatings at 7:15 and 9:15pm. Closed Feb 5–13 and Aug 1–15. Bus: 8.

La Zucca Magica ★ VEGETARIAN/ITALIAN The chef at this popular harborside restaurant has been named the best Italian chef in Nice. That this honor should go to a vegetarian restaurant was the most startling part of the news. Chef Marco serves refined cuisine at reasonable prices, using recipes from Italy's Piedmont region and updating them with no meat or fish. The red-and-green decor (the colors of Italy) will put you in the mood for the creative cuisine. You'll have to trust Marco, though, because everyone is served the same meal. You can count on savory cuisine using lots of herbs, Italian cheeses, beans, and pasta.

4 bis quai Papacino. ✆ **04-93-56-25-27.** Reservations recommended. Fixed-price lunch 17€, dinner 29€. No credit cards. Tues–Sat 12:30–2pm and 7–9:30pm.

Le Chantecler ★★★ TRADITIONAL/MODERN FRENCH This is Nice's most prestigious and best restaurant. Panels removed from a château in Pouilly-Fuissé cover the walls, and before- or after-dinner drinks are served in a Regency-style salon. A much-respected chef, Jean-Denis Rieubland, creates the most sophisticated and creative dishes in Nice. They change almost weekly but may include turbot filet served with purée of broad beans, sun-dried tomatoes, and asparagus; roasted suckling lamb served with beignets of fresh vegetables and ricotta-stuffed ravioli; and a melt-in-your-mouth fantasy of marbled hot chocolate drenched in almond-flavored cream sauce.

In the Hôtel Negresco, 37 promenade des Anglais. ✆ **04-93-16-64-00.** Reservations required. Main courses 48€–80€; fixed-price lunch 50€–130€, dinner 90€–130€. AE, MC, V. Wed–Sun 12:30–1:45pm and 7:30–10pm. Closed Jan–Feb 7. Bus: 8, 9, 10, or 11.

IN & AROUND NICE

The wide **promenade des Anglais ★★**, a wide boulevard fronting the bay, is split by "islands" of palms and flowers and stretching for about 7km (4⅓ miles). Along the beach are rows of grand cafes, the Musée Masséna, villas, and hotels—some good, others decaying.

In the east, the promenade becomes **quai des Etats-Unis,** lined with some of the best restaurants in Nice, most offering their own versions of bouillabaisse. Rising sharply on a rock is the site known as **Le Château,** where the ducs de Savoie built their castle, which was torn down in 1706. The hill has been turned into a garden of pines and exotic flowers. To reach the site and take in the view, board an elevator; many people take the elevator up, and then walk down. The park is open daily from 8am to dusk.

Nice's commercial centerpiece is **place Masséna,** with pink buildings in the 17th-century Genoese style and fountains with water jets. Stretching from the main square to the promenade is the **Jardin Albert-1er,** with an open-air terrace and a Triton Fountain. With palms and exotic flowers, it's the most relaxing oasis in town.

A PAIR OF MUSEUMS WORTH A LOOK

Musée des Beaux-Arts ★★ This collection, in the former residence of the Ukrainian Princess Kotchubey, has an important gallery devoted to the masters of the Second Empire and the Belle Epoque. The gallery of sculptures includes works by J. B. Carpeaux, Rude, and Rodin. Note the important collection by a dynasty of painters, the Dutch Vanloo family. One of its best-known members, Carle Vanloo, born in Nice in 1705, was Louis XV's premier *peintre*. A fine collection of 19th- and 20th-century art includes works by Ziem, Raffaelli, Boudin, Monet, Guillaumin, and Sisley.

33 av. des Baumettes. ✆ **04-92-15-28-28.** www.musee-beaux-arts-nice.org. Free admission. Tues–Sun 10am–6pm. Bus: 3, 9, 12, 22, 24, 38, 60, or 62.

Musée International d'Art Naïf Anatole-Jakovsky (Museum of Naive Art) ★ This museum is in the beautifully restored Château Ste-Hélène in the Fabron district. The museum's namesake, for years one of the world's leading art critics, once owned the collection. His 600 drawings and canvases were turned over to the institution and opened to the public. Artists from more than two dozen countries are represented by everything from primitive painting to 20th-century works.

Château St-Hélène, av. de Fabron. ✆ **04-93-71-78-33.** Free admission. Wed–Mon 10am–6pm. Bus: 9, 10, or 23; 10-min. walk. Closed Dec 25, Jan 1, and May 1.

A MUSEUM IN NEARBY CIMIEZ ★★

Founded by the Romans, who called it Cemenelum, Cimiez was the capital of the Maritime Alps province. Excavations have uncovered the ruins of a Roman town, and you can wander the dig sites. To reach this suburb and its attractions, take bus no. 15 or 17 from place Masséna.

Musée Matisse ★ This museum honors the artist, who died in Nice in 1954. Seeing his nude sketches today, you'll wonder how early critics could have denounced them as "the female animal in all her shame and horror." Most of the pieces in the museum's permanent collection were painted in Nice, and many were donated by Matisse and his heirs. These include *Nude in an Armchair with a Green Plant* (1937), *Nymph in the Forest* (1935–42), and a chronologically arranged series of paintings from 1890 to 1919. The most famous of these is *Portrait of Madame Matisse* (1905), usually displayed near a portrait of the artist's wife by Marquet, painted in 1900. There's also an assemblage of designs he prepared as practice sketches for the Matisse Chapel at Vence. Also here are *The Créole Dancer* (1951), *Blue Nude IV* (1952), and around 50 dance-related sketches he did between 1930 and 1931. The artist's last work, *Flowers and Fruit* (1953), is made of cutout gouache.

In the Villa des Arènes-de-Cimiez, 164 av. des Arènes-de-Cimiez. ✆ **04-93-81-08-08.** www.musee-matisse-nice.org. Free admission. Wed–Mon 10am–6pm. Closed Jan 1, May 1, and Dec 25.

HITTING THE BEACH AND OUTDOOR PURSUITS

BEACHES Along Nice's seafront, beaches extend uninterrupted for more than 7km (4⅓ miles), going from the edge of Vieux-Port (the old port) to the international airport, with most of the best bathing spots subdivided into public beaches and private concessionaires. None has sand; they're covered with gravel (often the size of golf balls). The rocks are smooth but can be mettlesome to people with poor balance or tender feet. Most of the public beaches consist of two sections: a free area, and one where you can rent chaise longues, mattresses, and parasols; use changing rooms; and take freshwater showers. For that, you'll pay 10€ to 12€ for a half-day, 12€ to 20€ for a full day. Nude sunbathing is prohibited, but toplessness is common. Take bus no. 9, 10, 12, or 23 to get to the beach.

SCUBA DIVING The best outfit is the **Centre International de Plongée (CIP) de Nice,** 14 quai des Dock (✆ **04-93-89-42-44**). A *baptême* (dive for first-timers) costs 45€. A two-tank dive for experienced divers, equipment included, is 140€; appropriate diver's certification is required.

NICE AFTER DARK

Nice has some of the most active nightlife along the Riviera. Evenings usually begin at a cafe. At kiosks around town you can pick up a copy of *La Semaine des Spectacles,* which outlines the week's diversions.

The major cultural center on the Riviera is the **Opéra de Nice,** 4 rue St-François-de-Paule (✆ **04-92-17-40-00**), built in 1885 by Charles Garnier, fabled architect of the Paris Opéra. It presents a full repertoire, with emphasis on serious, often large-scale operas. In one season you might see *Tosca, Les Contes de Hoffmann,* Verdi's *Macbeth,* Beethoven's *Fidelio,* and *Carmen,* as well as a *saison symphonique,* dominated by the Orchestre Philharmonique de Nice. The opera hall is also the major venue for concerts and recitals. Tickets are available (to concerts, recitals, and full-blown operas) a day or two before any performance. You can show up at the box office (Mon–Sat 10am–5:30pm; Sun 10am–6pm), or buy tickets in advance with a major credit card by phoning ✆ **04-92-17-40-47.** Tickets run from 10€ for nosebleed seats (and we mean it) to 100€ for front-and-center seats on opening night.

Monaco ★★★

Monaco, or more precisely its capital of Monte Carlo, has for a century been a symbol of glamour. The 1956 marriage of Prince Rainier III to American actress Grace Kelly enhanced its status. Though not always happy in her role, Princess Grace won the respect and admiration of her people. The Monégasques still mourn her death in a 1982 car accident.

Monaco became the property of the Grimaldi clan as early as 1297. It has maintained something resembling independence since. In a fit of impatience, the French annexed it in 1793, but the ruling family recovered it in 1814.

ESSENTIALS

GETTING THERE Monaco has rail, bus, and highway connections from other coastal cities, especially Nice. **Trains** arrive every 30 minutes from Cannes, Nice, Menton, and Antibes. For rail information, call ✆ **36-35,** or visit www.voyages-sncf.com. Monaco's underground railway station (Gare SNCF) is on place St. Devote. It's a long walk uphill from the train station to Monte Carlo. If you'd rather take a **taxi** but can't find one at the station, call ✆ **08-20-20-98-98.** There are no border formalities when entering Monaco from France. Monaco is a lengthy **drive** from Paris. Take A6 south to Lyon. At Lyon, connect with A7 south to Aix-en-Provence and take A6 south directly to Monaco. If you're already on the Riviera, drive from Nice along N7 northeast. It's only 19km (12 miles), but with traffic, the drive can take 30 minutes.

VISITOR INFORMATION The **Direction du Tourisme et des Congrés** office is at 2A bd. des Moulins (✆ **92-16-61-16;** fax 92-16-60-00; www.visitmonaco.com).

WHERE TO STAY

Columbus Monaco Hotel ★★ In the modern Fontvieille section of Monaco, this stylish, contemporary hotel faces Princess Grace's rose garden and the sea. Guest rooms are appointed in what's called "hybrid hip," a style that evokes both Miami and London. Elegant touches include Lartigue photos of the Riviera, high-tech cabinets filled with video games, and chocolate-leather furnishings; deluxe linens and Frette bathrobes round out the comforts. Note that the hotel is in a condo complex whose residents share the pool. However, a boat carries guests to a tranquil sandy beach nearby.

23 av. des Papalins, Monaco 98000. ✆ **92-05-90-00.** Fax 92-05-23-86. www.columbushotels.com. 181 units. 310€–345€ double; 610€–920€ suite. AE, MC, V. Parking 23€. **Amenities:** Restaurant (brasserie with antipasto buffet); bar; babysitting; exercise room; outdoor pool; room service; Wi-Fi (12€–48€ per day). *In room:* A/C, TV, hair dryer, minibar.

Hôtel de France Not all Monégasques are rich, as a stroll along rue de la Turbie will convince you. Here you'll find some of the cheapest accommodations and eateries in the high-priced principality. This 19th-century hotel, 3 minutes from the rail station, has modest furnishings but is well kept and comfortable. Guest rooms and bathrooms are small; each unit has a shower.

6 rue de la Turbie, Monaco 98000. ✆ **93-30-24-64.** Fax 92-16-13-34. www.monte-carlo.mc/france. 27 units. 94€–112€ double. Rates include breakfast. MC, V. Parking 7.50€. **Amenities:** Bar; room service. *In room:* TV, hair dryer, Wi-Fi (free).

Hôtel de Paris ★★★ On the resort's main plaza, opposite the casino, this is one of the world's most famous hotels. The decor includes marble pillars, statues, crystal chandeliers, sumptuous carpets, Louis XVI chairs, and a wall-size mural. Elegant fabrics, rich carpeting, classic accessories, and an excellent restaurant make this hotel a favorite of the world's most discerning travelers. The guest rooms come in a variety of styles, with period or contemporary furnishings. Some units are enormous. ***Note:*** The rooms opening onto the sea aren't as spacious as those in the rear.

Place du Casino, Monaco 98007. ✆ **98-06-30-16.** Fax 98-06-59-13. www.montecarloresort.com. 182 units. 420€–960€ double; from 760€ suite. AE, DC, MC, V. Valet parking 32€. **Amenities:** 3 restaurants (see "Where to Dine," below); bar; babysitting; concierge; exercise room; large indoor pool; room service; 2 saunas; smoke-free rooms; Thermes Marins spa offering thalassotherapy under medical supervision. *In room:* A/C, TV, hair dryer, minibar, Wi-Fi (25€ per day).

Monte Carlo Bay Hotel & Resort ★★★ Built on the seashore, this Societé des Bains de Mer hotel aims to recapture some of the chic and splendor of the 1920s. Its neoclassical architecture, with arcades and colonnades, has created a new landmark in Monaco. The sumptuous nature of the resort is reflected in its waterfalls, terraces, spacious bedrooms, exotic woods, lavish marble, and even an indoor pool covered with a monumental glass dome. Of the beautifully furnished bedrooms, more than three-quarters of them open onto sea views. Rooms are decorated with white-oak furnishings, often sandstone floors, and soft Mediterranean pastels.

40 av. Princesse Grace, Monaco 98000. ✆ **98-06-02-00.** Fax 98-06-00-03. www.montecarlobay.com. 334 units. 270€–800€ double; 750€–2,300€ suite. AE, DC, MC, V. Parking 15€. **Amenities:** 4 restaurants; 2 bars; nightclub; casino; disco; babysitting; concierge; exercise rooms; 3 pools (indoor, outdoor, and children's); spa. *In room:* A/C, TV, hair dryer, minibar, Wi-Fi (20€ per day).

WHERE TO DINE

Le Louis XV ★★★ MEDITERRANEAN In the Hôtel de Paris, the Louis XV offers what one critic called "down-home Riviera cooking within a Fabergé egg." Star chef Alain Ducasse creates refined but not overly adorned cuisine, served by the finest staff in Monaco. Everything is light and attuned to the seasons, with intelligent, modern interpretations of Provençal and northern Italian dishes. You'll find chargrilled breast of baby pigeon with sautéed duck liver, a specialty known as "Provençal vegetables with crushed truffles," and everything from truffles and caviar to the best stewed salt cod on the coast.

In the Hôtel de Paris, place du Casino. ✆ **98-06-88-64.** Reservations recommended. Jacket and tie required for men. Main courses 80€–120€; fixed-price lunch 140€, dinner 210€–280€. AE, MC, V. Thurs–Mon 12:15–1:45pm and 8–9:45pm; also June–Sept Wed 12:15–1:45pm. Closed Feb 9–24.

Le Café de Paris ★ TRADITIONAL FRENCH Its *plats du jour* are well prepared, and its location, the plaza adjacent to the casino and the Hôtel de Paris,

Monaco

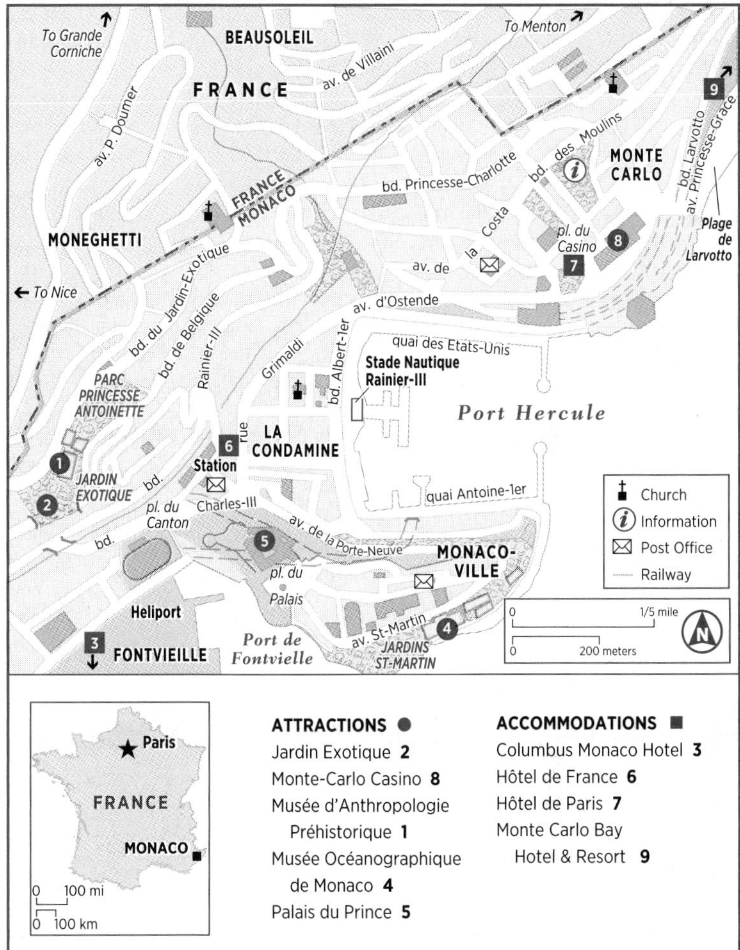

allows a front-row view of the comings and goings of the nerve center of Monte Carlo. Menu items change frequently. Local office workers appreciate the platters, especially at lunchtime, because they can be served and consumed quickly. They range from fresh grilled sea bass to steak tartare with matchstick frites. Adjacent to the restaurant, you'll find (and hear) a jangling collection of slot machines and a predictable cluster of boutiques.

Place du Casino. ✆ **92-16-20-20.** Reservations recommended. Main courses 30€–50€; fixed-price menu 35€. AE, DC, MC, V. Daily 8am–3am.

EXPLORING MONACO

The second-smallest state in Europe (Vatican City is the tiniest), Monaco consists of four parts. The old town, **Monaco-Ville,** on a promontory, "the Rock," 60m (197 ft.) high, is the seat of the royal palace and the government building, as well as the Oceanographic Museum. To the west, **La Condamine,** the home of the Monégasques, is at the foot of the old town, forming its harbor and port sector. Up from the port (Monaco is steep) is **Monte Carlo,** once the playground of royalty and still the center for the wintering wealthy, the setting for the casino and its gardens and deluxe hotels. The fourth part, **Fontvieille,** is a neat industrial suburb. **Monte-Carlo Beach,** at the far frontier, is on French soil. It attracts a chic crowd.

Most summer day-trippers from Nice want to see the home of Monaco's royal family, **Les Grands Appartements du Palais ★**, place du Palais (✆ **93-25-18-31;** www.palais.mc). A tour of the Grands Appartements allows you a glimpse of the Throne Room and some of the art, including works by Brueghel and Holbein, as well as Princess Grace's state portrait. The palace was built in the 13th century, and part dates from the Renaissance. The ideal time to arrive is 11:55am for the 10-minute **Relève de la Garde (Changing of the Guard).**

A combination ticket including admission to the **Musée du Palais du Prince (Souvenirs Napoleoniens et Collection d'Archives)** is 4€ adults, 2€ children 8 to 14; it's free for children 7 and under. The Palace and museum are open daily January to March and December from 10:30am to 5pm, April from 10:30am to 6pm, May to September from 9:30am to 6:30pm, October from 10am to 5:30pm (closed Nov).

Jardin Exotique ★★, boulevard du Jardin-Exotique (✆ **93-15-29-80;** www.jardin-exotique.mc), built on the side of a rock, are gardens known for their cactus collection. They were begun by Prince Albert I, who was a naturalist and scientist. He spotted some succulents growing in the palace gardens and created this garden from them. You can also explore the grottoes here, as well as the **Musée d'Anthropologie Préhistorique** (✆ **93-15-29-80**). The view of the principality is splendid. Admission to the complex is 6.90€ adults, 3.60€ children 6 to 18, and free for children 5 and under. The gardens and museum are open daily mid-May to mid-September 9am to 7pm, and mid-September to mid-May 9am to 6pm (closed Nov 19–Dec 25).

Musée Océanographique de Monaco ★★, avenue St-Martin (✆ **93-15-36-00;** www.oceano.mc), was founded in 1910 by Albert I, great-grandfather of the present prince. In the main rotunda is a statue of Albert in his favorite costume, that of a sea captain. Displayed are specimens he collected during 30 years of expeditions. The aquarium, one of the finest in Europe, contains more than 90 tanks. There is also a shark lagoon. Hours are daily April to June and September 9:30am to 7pm, July and August 9:30am to 7:30pm, and October to March 10am to 6pm. Admission is 13€ adults, 6€ children 6 to 18, and free for children 5 and under.

HITTING THE BEACH & OTHER OUTDOOR ACTIVITIES

BEACHES Just outside the border, on French soil, the **Monte-Carlo Beach Club** adjoins the Monte-Carlo Beach Hotel, 22 av. Princesse-Grace (✆ **98-06-50-00**). The beach club has thrived for years; it's an integral part of Monaco's social life. Princess Grace used to come here in flowery swimsuits, greeting her friends and subjects with humor and style. You'll find two large pools (one for children), cabanas, a restaurant, a cafe, and a bar. As the temperature drops in late August, the beach closes for the winter. The admission charge of 50€ to 90€, depending on the season, grants you access to the changing rooms, toilets, restaurants, and bar, and use of a mattress for sunbathing. A day's use of a cubicle, where you can lock up your street clothes, costs an extra 20€ to 27€. A fee of 35€ to 90€ will get you a day's use of a private cabana. As usual, topless is de rigueur, but bottomless isn't.

Swimming and sunbathing are also offered at the **Plage du Larvotto,** off avenue Princesse-Grace (✆ **93-30-63-84**). There's a charge of 2.20€ to enter this strip of beach, whose surface is frequently replenished with sand hauled in by barge. Part of it is open; other sections are private.

SWIMMING Overlooking the yacht-clogged harbor, the **Stade Nautique Rainier-III,** quai Albert-1er, at La Condamine (✆ **93-30-64-83**), a pool frequented by the Monégasques, was a gift from Prince Rainier to his subjects. It's open May to October daily 9am to 6pm (until midnight July–Aug). Admission for a one-time visit costs 4.70€ per person; discounts are available if you plan to visit 10 times or more. Between November and April, it's an ice-skating rink. If you want to swim in winter, try the indoor **Piscine du Prince Héréditaire Albert,** in the Stade Louis II, 7 av. de Castellane (✆ **92-05-42-13**). It's open Monday, Tuesday, Thursday, and Friday 7:30am to 2:30pm; Saturday 1 to 6pm; and Sunday 8am to 1pm. Admission is 2.30€.

TENNIS & SQUASH The **Monte Carlo Country Club,** 155 av. Princesse-Grace, Roquebrune-Cap Martin, France (✆ **04-93-41-30-15;** www.mccc.mc), has 21 clay and 2 concrete tennis courts. The 41€ fee provides access to a restaurant, health club with Jacuzzi and sauna, putting green, beach, squash courts, and the well-maintained tennis courts. Guests of the hotels administered by the Société des Bains de Mer (Hôtel de Paris, Hermitage, Mirabeau, and Monte Carlo Beach Club) pay half price. Plan to spend at least half a day, ending a round of tennis with use of any of the other facilities. It's open daily 8am to 8 or 9pm, depending on the season.

GAMBLING & OTHER AFTER-DARK DIVERSIONS

CASINOS **Sun Casino,** in the Fairmont Monte Carlo, 12 av. des Spélugues (✆ **98-06-12-12**), is a huge room filled with one-armed bandits. It also features blackjack, craps, and American roulette. Additional slot machines are on the roof, with a wide view of the sea. Slot machines operate daily 11am to 4am, and gaming tables are open daily 10am to 4am. Admission is free.

François Blanc developed the **Monte-Carlo Casino,** place du Casino (✆ **98-06-20-00**), into the most famous in the world, attracting the exiled aristocracy of Russia, Sarah Bernhardt, Mata Hari, King Farouk, and Aly Khan. The architect of Paris's Opéra Garnier, Charles Garnier, built the oldest part of the casino, and it remains an example of the 19th century's most opulent architecture. The building encompasses the casino and other areas for different kinds of entertainment, including a theater (Opéra de Monte-Carlo; see below) presenting opera and ballet. Baccarat, roulette, and chemin de fer are the most popular games, though you can play *le craps* and blackjack as well.

The casino's **Salle Américaine,** containing only slot machines, opens at 2pm Monday to Friday, noon on weekends. Doors for roulette and *trente et quarante* open at the same time. A section for roulette and chemin de fer opens at 3pm. Additional rooms open at 4pm with more roulette, craps, and blackjack. The gambling continues until very late or early, depending on the crowd. The casino classifies its "private rooms" as the more demure, nonelectronic areas without slots. To enter the casino, you must show a passport or other photo ID, and be at least 18. After 9pm, the staff will insist that men wear jackets and neckties for entrance to the private rooms.

The **Opéra de Monte-Carlo** is headquartered in the lavish, recently renovated Belle Epoque **Salle Garnier** of the casino. Tickets to the operas and other events scheduled inside range from 35€ to 120€. Tickets to events within the Salle Garnier are available from a kiosk in the Atrium du Casino (✆ **98-06-28-28**), located within the casino; tickets can be purchased Tuesday to Saturday from 10am to 5:30pm.

GERMANY

by Darwin Porter & Danforth Prince

As Berlin has moved deep into the 21st century, rebuilding continues, especially in the dreary old "Cold War sector" East Berlin. Even so, Berlin has now solidly established itself as the capital of a unified Germany. What was once the city's biggest tourist attraction, the Berlin Wall, is now a bicycle path where Berliners push baby strollers. Restored baroque Munich, in the south, known as Germany's "secret capital," is the gateway to the Bavarian Alps and colorful alpine villages. For a taste of medieval Germany, explore the untouched towns of the Romantic Road and Ludwig II's fairy-tale castle of Neuschwanstein.

BERLIN ★★★

When Heinrich Heine arrived in Berlin in 1819, he exclaimed, "Isn't the present splendid!" Were he to arrive today, he might make the same remark. Visitors who come by plane to Berlin see a splendid panorama. Few metropolitan areas are blessed with as many lakes, woodlands, and parks—these cover one-third of the city's area, and small farms with fields and meadows still exist in the city limits.

Berlin today is an almost completely modern city. Regrettably, Berlin is hardly the architectural gem that old-time visitors remember from the pre-Nazi era; it wasn't rebuilt with the same kind of care lavished on Munich and Cologne. But in spite of its decades-long "quadripartite status," it's a vibrant city, always receptive to new ideas, a major economic and cultural center, and a leader in development and research. Because of its excellent facilities, it is a favored site for trade fairs, congresses, and conventions.

Berlin today is shedding its dark history and reinventing itself as Europe's "capital of cool." Suddenly, it's hip to claim, "Ich bin ein Berliner." Nothing dramatizes the change more than the once dreary Potsdamer Platz, the so-called Times Square of Berlin. No longer a Cold War relic, it has blossomed into a showcase of modern architecture, dominated by the 25-story DaimlerChrysler building, whose viewing platform can be reached in only 20 seconds from the ground.

"No city on earth has gone through such a roller coaster ride—from villain to victim, from horrors to heroics," said Richard Holbrooke, former U.S. ambassador to Germany. Today Berlin is the fourth-most-popular tourist destination in Europe, having surged past Madrid.

Essentials

Getting There

BY PLANE **Tegel Airport** is the city's busiest, serving most flights from the west. **Tempelhof Airport** in Berlin, famous as the symbol of the Berlin Airlift, has closed. With its passing, one of the few examples of Nazi-era architecture fades. Its closing will make way for the expansion of the **Berlin-Schönefeld International Airport,** a former military base, which will be turned into the vastly enlarged **Berlin-Brandenburg International Airport.** Private bus shuttles among the three airports operate constantly, so you can make connecting flights at different airports. Buses from each airport will also take you into the city center. For information on all airports, call ✆ **0180/500-01-86** or visit www.berlin-airport.de.

BY TRAIN Frankfurt and Hamburg, among other cities, have good rail connections to Berlin. From Frankfurt to Berlin takes about 4 hours. Hamburg is now closer than ever, thanks to a high-speed InterCity Express train running between the two cities nonstop in 2 hours and 8 minutes. Eurailpass and GermanRail passes are valid. Most arrivals from western European and western German cities are at the **Bahnhof Zoologischer Garten** (✆ **030/250-025;** www.s-bahn-berlin.de for tourist information), the main train station, called "Bahnhof Zoo," in western Berlin. In the center of the city, close to the Kurfürstendamm, it's well connected for public transportation. Facilities include a tourist information counter dispensing free maps and tourist brochures, open daily from 10am to 7pm. The staff will make same-day hotel reservations for 4€.

Berlin has four other train stations, the **Berlin Hauptbahnhof, Berlin Lichtenberg Lehrterbahnhof,** and **Berlin Spandaubahnhof.** Call the railway information number at ✆ **0800/150-70-90** or visit http://reiseauskunft.bahn.de for information.

BY BUS The operations center for several independent bus operators is headquartered within a central arrivals and departures point, the **ZOB Omnibusbahnhof am Funkturm,** Messedamm 6 (✆ **030/302-53-61;** www.iob-berlin.de). Call for departure times and fare information for routes to and from other parts of Europe.

BY CAR From Frankfurt, take A-66 to Bad Herzfeld, and either go east on A-4 to pick up A-9 to Berlin, or continue on A-7 to Braunschweig and east on A-2 toward Berlin. North of Nürnberg, A-9 leads to Berlin. From Leipzig, take A-14 in the direction of Halle; at the intersection of A-9, head northeast into Berlin. From Dresden, head northeast on A-13 into Berlin. Expect heavy traffic delays on *Autobahnen,* especially on weekends and sunny days when everyone is out touring.

VISITOR INFORMATION **Tourist Office** For tourist information and hotel bookings, head for the **Berlin Tourist Information Center,** in the Europa-Center near the Memorial Church, entrance on the Budapesterstrasse side (✆ **030/25-00-24;** www.visitberlin.de), open Monday to Saturday from 10am to 7pm and Sunday from 10am to 6pm.

Germany

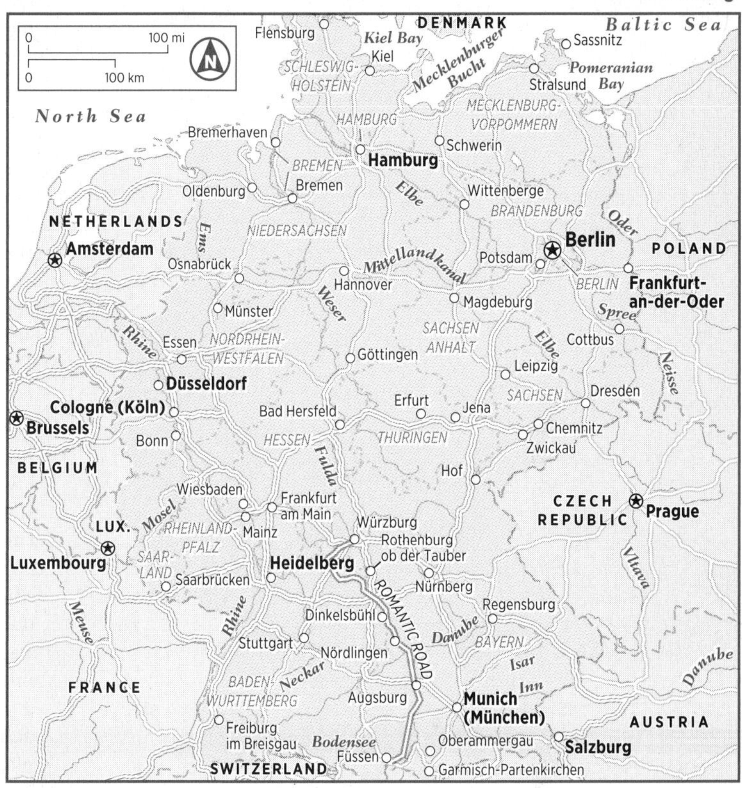

WEBSITES Visit **www.berlin-info.de** for a virtual tour of Berlin's sights, but be aware that some of the links go to German-only pages. The site **www.hotelstravel.com/germany.html** not only provides detailed listings for hotels in Germany but also has links to related sites, like Ritz-Carlton and Relais & Châteaux, that offer lodging and general travel info.

CITY LAYOUT The center of activity in the western part of Berlin is the 3km-long (1¾-mile) **Kurfürstendamm,** called the Ku'damm by Berliners. Along this wide boulevard you'll find the best hotels, restaurants, theaters, cafes, nightclubs, shops, and department stores. The huge **Tiergarten,** the city's largest park, is crossed by Strasse des 17 Juni, which leads to the famed **Brandenburg Gate (Brandenburger Tor);** just north is the Reichstag. On the southwestern fringe of the Tiergarten is the **Zoologischer Garten (Berlin Zoo).** From the Ku'damm you can take Hardenbergstrasse, crossing Bismarckstrasse and traversing Otto-Suhr-Allee, which leads to **Schloss Charlottenburg,** one of your major sightseeing goals. The **Dahlem Museums** are on the southwestern fringe, often reached by going along Hohenzollerndamm.

Western Berlin

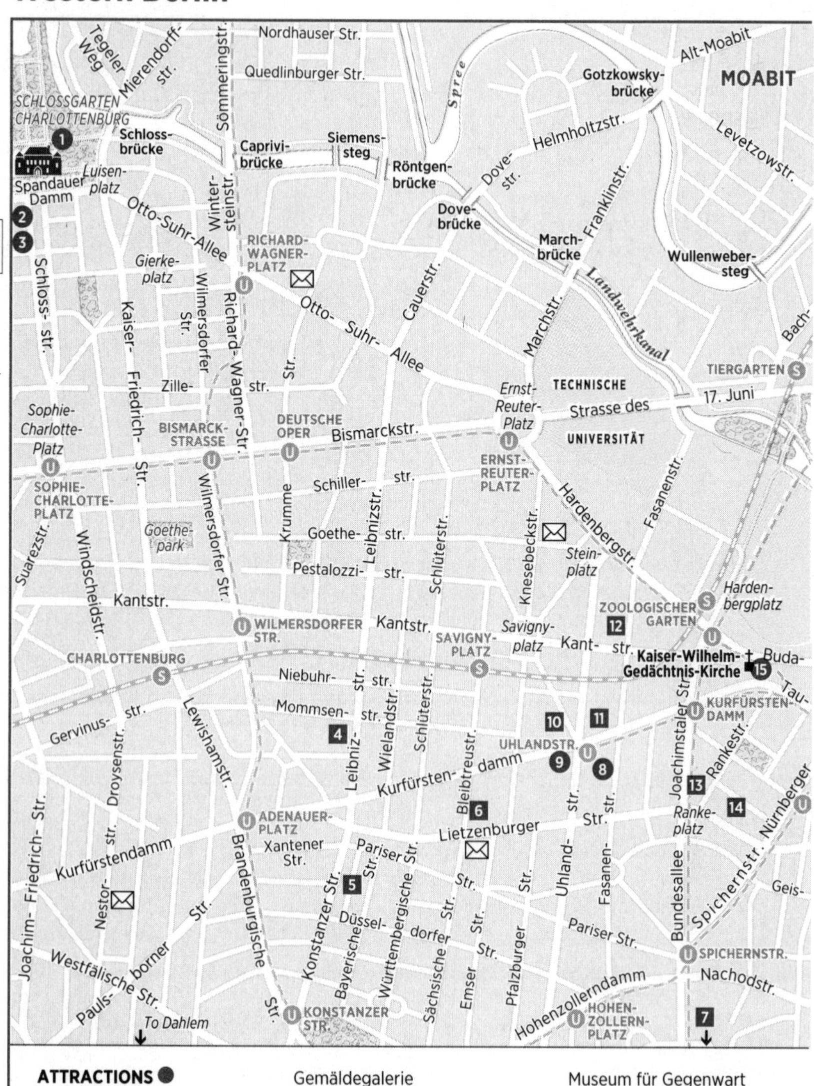

ATTRACTIONS ●

Brandenburger Tor (Brandenburg Gate) **23**

Bröhan Museum **3**

Die Sammlung Berggruen: Picasso und Seine Zeit (The Berggruen Collection: Picasso and his Era) **2**

Gemäldegalerie (Picture Gallery) **21**

Jüdisches Museum Berlin **19**

Kaiser Wilhelm Memorial Church **15**

Käthe-Kollwitz Museum **8**

Kunstgewerbe Museum (Museum of Applied Arts) **22**

Museum für Gegenwart Hamburger Bahnhof **25**

Neue Nationalgalerie (New National Gallery) **20**

Reichstag **24**

Schloss Charlottenburg (Charlottenburg Palace) **1**

Story of Berlin **9**

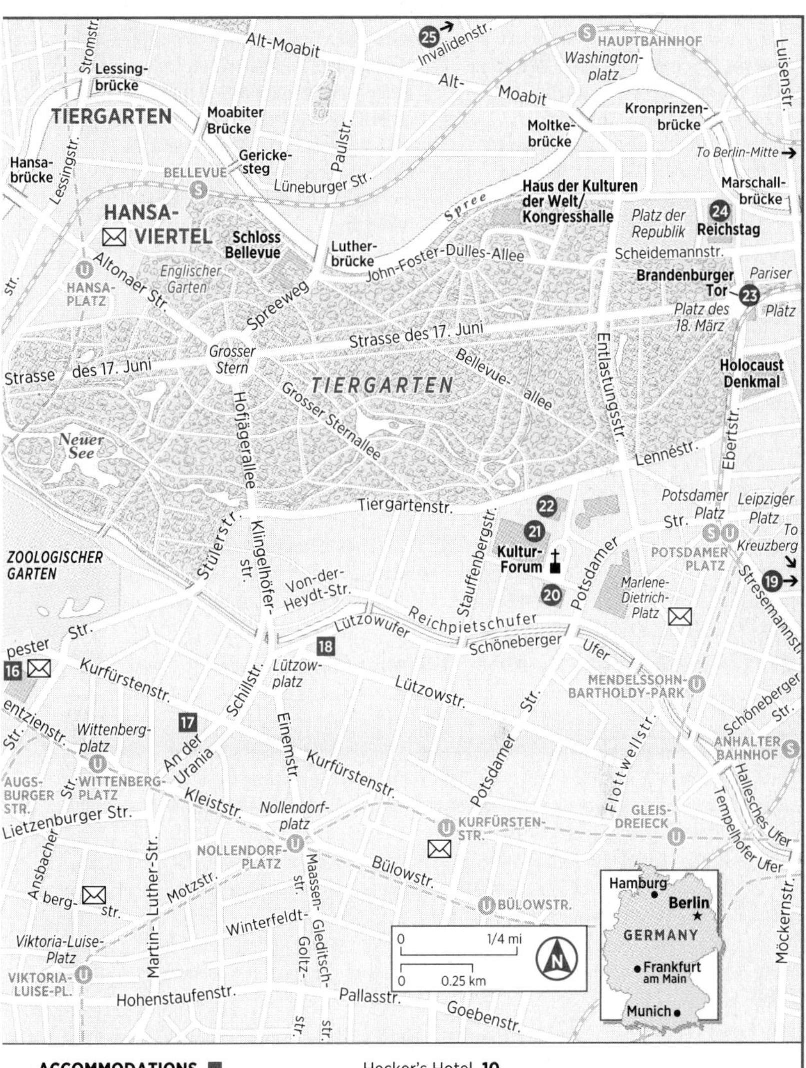

ACCOMMODATIONS ■

Art Nouveau **4**

Art'otel Berlin Kudamm, by Park Plaza **13**

Bleibtreu Hotel **6**

Brandenburger Hof Relais & Châteaux **14**

Grand Hotel Esplanade **18**

Hecker's Hotel **10**

Hotel-Pension Bregenz **5**

Hotel Sylter Hof Berlin **17**

Kempinski Hotel Bristol Berlin **11**

Palace Berlin **16**

Pension München **7**

Savoy **12**

Post office

S-Bahn

U-Bahn

The Welcome Card

If you're going to be in Berlin for a while, you can purchase a **Welcome-Card** granting holders certain discounts, especially on public transportation. A card valid for 48 hours costs 17€ or else 23€ for a 72-hour card. A 5-day card sells for 30€. You also get free admission or price reductions up to 50% on sightseeing tours, museums, and other attractions. Reductions of 25% are granted at 10 of the city's theaters as well. It's valid for one adult and up to three children 14 and younger. For more information, search www.visitberlin.de.

The Brandenburg Gate is the start of Berlin's most celebrated street, **Unter den Linden,** the cultural heart of Berlin before World War II. The famous street runs from west to east, cutting a path through the city. It leads to **Museumsinsel (Museum Island),** where the most outstanding museums of eastern Berlin, including the Pergamon, are situated. As it courses along, Unter den Linden crosses another major Berlin artery, **Friedrichstrasse.** If you continue south along Friedrichstrasse, you'll reach the former location of **Checkpoint Charlie,** the famous border-crossing site of the Cold War days.

Unter den Linden continues east until it reaches **Alexanderplatz,** the center of eastern Berlin, with its Fernsehturm (TV tower). A short walk away is the restored **Nikolaiviertel (Nikolai Quarter),** a neighborhood of bars, restaurants, and shops that evoke life in the prewar days.

GETTING AROUND **By Public Transportation** The Berlin transport system consists of buses, trams, and U-Bahn and S-Bahn trains. The network is run by the **BVG** (✆ **030/1-94-49;** www.bvg.de), which operates an information booth outside the Bahnhof Zoo on Hardenbergplatz, open daily from 6am to 10pm. The staff will provide details about which U-Bahn (underground) or S-Bahn (elevated railway) line to take to various locations and the ticket options. You can also purchase tickets, including discount cards.

The **BVG standard ticket** (*Einzelfahrschein*) costs 2.10€ to 2.80€ and is valid for 2 hours of transportation in all directions, transfers included. Also available at counters and vending machines is a 24-hour ticket; the price is 6.10€ to 19€. On buses, only standard tickets can be purchased, and tram tickets must be purchased in advance. Tickets should be kept until the end of the journey; otherwise, you'll be liable for a fine of 50€.

BY TAXI Taxis are available throughout Berlin. The meter starts at 3€, plus 1.60€ per kilometer (½ mile) after that. After 7km (4⅓ miles), the fare is 1€ per kilometer. Visitors can flag down taxis that have a T-sign illuminated. For a taxi, call ✆ **21-02-02,** 26-10-26, or 44-33-22.

BY CAR Touring Berlin by car isn't recommended. Free parking places are difficult to come by.

BY BICYCLE Berlin marks biking trails along major streets, especially in the leafy neighborhoods of the former West Berlin. A bike is also ideal for exploring old East

Berlin, a city still in redevelopment. One of the best companies for rentals is **Bikes & Jeans** in Mitte at Friedrichstrasse 129 (✆ **030/447-6666**), renting bikes for 10€ for 24 hours.

[FastFACTS] BERLIN

American Express Reiseland American Express offices are at Bayreuther Strasse 37 (✆ **030/21-49-830;** U-Bahn: Wittenbergplatz), open Monday to Friday 9am to 7pm and Saturday 10am to 1pm; and at Friedrichstrasse 172 (✆ **030/ 20-17-400;** U-Bahn: Friedrichstrasse or Stadtmitte), open Monday to Friday 9am to 6pm and Saturday 10am to 1pm.

Business Hours Most **banks** are open Monday to Friday 9am to 1 or 3pm. Most other **businesses** and **stores** are open Monday to Friday 9 or 10am to 6:30pm and Saturday 9am to 4pm. On *langer Samstag,* the first Saturday of the month, shops stay open until 4 or 6pm. Some stores observe late closing on Thursday, usually at 8:30pm.

Currency The long-standing German mark faded into history on January 1, 2002, giving way to the euro. Currently, the U.S. dollar and the European euro are trading at 1€ = $1.40, with slight daily fluctuations.

Currency Exchange You can exchange money at all airports, major department stores, any bank, and the American Express offices (see above).

Dentists & Doctors The Berlin tourist office in the Europa-Center (see "Visitor Information," above) keeps a list of English-speaking dentists and doctors in Berlin. In case of a medical emergency, call ✆ **030/31-00-31** or Dental Emergency Service at ✆ **030/8900-4333.**

Drugstores If you need a pharmacy *(Apotheke)* at night, go to one on any corner. There you'll find a sign in the window giving the address of the nearest drugstore open at night. A central pharmacy is **Europa-Apotheke,** Osnabrücker Strasse 4 (✆ **030/3-44-56-56;** U-Bahn: Kurfürstendamm). It's open Monday to Friday 9am to 8pm and Saturday to 6pm.

Embassies & Consulates The **American Consulate,** Clayallee 170 (U-Bahn: Oskar-Heleme-Heim), is the office that addresses most mundane passport issues and problems. Americans in need of nonemergency services can call ✆ **030/832-9233** Monday to Friday 2 to 4pm. Persons with very important business or with emergencies can call the general switchboard at 030/83050. The **U.S. Embassy,** Pariser Platz 2 at the Brandenburg Gate (http://germany.usembassy.gov), is a "closed building," not open to anyone except high diplomatic missions of major military, diplomatic, or economic concerns to the U.S. Hours are Monday to Friday 8:30am to 4pm. **Canada** maintains an embassy at Leipziger Platz 17 (✆ **030/ 20-31-20;** U-Bahn: Potsdamer Platz). Hours are Monday to Friday 9 to 11am. The **British Embassy** is at Wilhelmstrasse 70–71 (✆ **030-20457-0;** U-Bahn: Friedrichstrasse; http://ukingermany.fco.gov.uk), open Monday to Friday 9am to noon and 2 to 4pm. The embassy of **Australia** is at Wallstrasse 76–79 (✆ **030/8-80-08-80;** U-Bahn: Märkisches Museum; www.germany.embassy.gov.au). Hours are Monday to Thursday 8:30am to 5:30pm, Friday 8:30am to 4:15pm. The embassy of **New Zealand** is at Friedrichstrasse 60 (✆ **030/20-62-10;** U-Bahn: Friedrichstrasse; www.nzembassy.com/germany). Hours are Monday to Friday 9am to 1pm and 2 to 5:30pm. The embassy of **Ireland** is at

Jägerstrasse 51 (✆ **030/22-07-20;** U-Bahn: Taubenstrasse; www.embassyofireland.de). Hours are Monday to Friday 9:30am to 12:30pm and 2:30 to 4:45pm.

Emergencies Call the police at ✆ **110;** dial ✆ **112** to report a fire or to call an ambulance.

Internet Access If you're feeling out of touch, visit **Easy Internet Café,** Kurfürstendamm 224 (✆ **030/88-70-79-70;** U-Bahn: Kurfürstendamm, and then bus no. 109 or 129). Open 24 hours daily.

Post Office You'll find post offices scattered throughout Berlin, with particularly large branches positioned at Bahnhof Zoo, Hardenbergplatz (U-Bahn: Zoologischer Garten); at both Tegel and Schönefeld airports; at the main railway station (Hauptbahnhof); and in the town center at Joachimstalerstrasse 10. With a limited number of exceptions, most post offices in Germany are open Monday to Friday from 8am to 6pm and Saturday from 8am to 1pm. None of them receives direct telephone calls from the public, but if you're interested in postal rates and procedures, go to www.deutschepost.de or call ✆ **0180/23-333** for information about postal procedures throughout Germany. Unlike the old days, German post offices no longer offer the use of pay telephones for long-distance calls, and no longer send international telegrams. (A limited number, however, offer telegram service for destinations within Germany.) When you enter a German post office, know in advance that the yellow-painted windows are for issues about the mail, and that the blue-painted windows are for issues associated with money orders and banking rituals. If you just want to buy a stamp for mailing a letter, it's usually more convenient to buy it at any of thousands of small stores, newsstands, or tobacco shops throughout the country that stock them.

Safety Germany is a reasonably safe country in which to travel, although neo-Nazi skinheads have sometimes attacked black or Asian travelers, especially in the eastern part of the country. One of the most dangerous places, especially at night, is around the large railway stations of large cities, such as Berlin. Some beer halls get rowdy late at night.

Taxes As a member of the European Union, Germany imposes a tax on most goods and services known as the **value-added tax (VAT)** or, in German, ***Mehrwertsteuer.*** Nearly everything is taxed at 19%, including vital necessities such as gas or luxury items like jewelry. VAT is included in the price of restaurants and hotels. Note that goods for sale, such as cameras, also have the 19% tax already factored into the price; but the listed prices of services, such as having a mechanic fix your car, don't include VAT, so an extra 19% will be tacked on to your bill. Stores that display a TAX FREE sticker will issue you a Tax-Free Shopping Check at the time of purchase. You can then get a refund at one of the Tax-Free Shopping Service offices in the major airports and many train stations (and some of the bigger ferry terminals). Otherwise, send checks to Tax-Free Shopping Service, Mengstrasse 19, 23552 Lübeck, Germany.

Telephone The **country code** for Germany is **49;** the **city code** for Berlin is **30** for calls from outside Germany or **030** if you're calling within the country.

If you're going to make a lot of phone calls or wish to make an international call from a phone booth, you'll probably want to purchase a **phone card.** Phone cards are sold at post offices and newsstands. The 6.30€ card offers about 40 minutes, and the 28€ card is useful for long-distance calls. Simply insert them into the telephone slot. Phone cards are becoming so popular in Germany that many public phones no longer accept coins.

Tipping If a restaurant bill says *Bedienung,* that means a service charge has already been added, so just round up to the nearest euro. If not, add 10% to 15%. Round up to the nearest euro for taxis. Bellhops get 1€ per bag, as does the doorperson at your hotel, restaurant, or nightclub. Room cleaning staffs get small tips in Germany, as do concierges who perform some special favors such as obtaining hard-to-get theater or opera tickets. Tip hairdressers or barbers 5% to 10%.

Where to Stay

ON OR NEAR THE KURFÜRSTENDAMM

Very Expensive

Brandenburger Hof Relais & Châteaux ★★★ Rooms at this white-fronted classic, though perhaps too severe and minimalist for some tastes, are among the most stylish in the city. This is authentic Bauhaus—torchiere lamps, black leather upholstery, and platform beds. French doors open to small balconies, but not on the top floors, and bathrooms are spacious. Housekeeping is among the finest in Berlin, and there's state-of-the-art security.

Eislebener Strasse 14, 10789 Berlin. ✆ **030/21-40-50.** Fax 030/21-40-51-00. www.brandenburger-hof.com. 72 units. 295€–345€ double; 425€–595€ suite. Rates include breakfast buffet. AE, DC, MC, V. Parking 24€. U-Bahn: Kurfürstendamm or Augsburger Strasse. S-Bahn: Zoologischer Garten. **Amenities:** 2 restaurants; piano bar; babysitting; room service. *In room:* TV, hair dryer, minibar, Wi-Fi (24€ per day).

Kempinski Hotel Bristol Berlin ★★★ The legendary Kempinski, or "Kempi," is matched in style only by the Grand Hotel Esplanade. Rooms range in size from medium to spacious. Furnishings are elegant and the mattresses firm. The cheapest (and smallest) rooms are called the Berlin rooms. The high-category Bristol rooms are larger and better appointed, and the finest accommodations of all are refined Kempinski rooms. Each room has a spacious bathroom, dual basins, scales, shoehorns, and deluxe toiletries.

Kurfürstendamm 27, 10719 Berlin. ✆ **800/426-3135** in the U.S., or 030/88-43-40. Fax 030/88-360-75. www.kempinskiberlin.de. 301 units. 119€–270€ double; 199€–1,095€ suite. AE, DC, MC, V. Parking 18€–21€. U-Bahn: Kurfürstendamm. **Amenities:** 2 restaurants; bar; babysitting; exercise room; indoor pool; room service; sauna. *In room:* A/C, TV, hair dryer, minibar, Wi-Fi (25€ per day).

Expensive

Savoy ★ If you don't demand the full-service facilities of the grander choices, this is the hotel for you. In general, rooms are a bit small but they are comfortable nonetheless, with such features as double-glazed windows and fine furnishings. Bathrooms are decent sizes and maintained spotlessly. For a nightcap, try the cozy **Times Bar.**

Fasanenstrasse 9–10, 10623 Berlin. ✆ **800/223-5652** in the U.S. and Canada, or 030/3-11-0-30. Fax 030/3-11-03-333. www.hotel-savoy.com. 125 units. 146€–277€ double; 178€–317€ suite. Children 11 and under stay free in parent's room. AE, DC, MC, V. Parking 15€. U-Bahn: Kurfürstendamm. **Amenities:** Restaurant; bar; babysitting; room service; sauna. *In room:* A/C (in some), TV, hair dryer, Internet (5 hr. for 10€), minibar.

Moderate

Art Nouveau ★ On the fourth floor of an Art Nouveau apartment house, this little-known hotel is an atmospheric choice. Even the elevator is a historic gem of the upmarket and desirable neighborhood. Art Nouveau was fully renovated in 1998.

The comfortable midsize rooms are pleasantly decorated and high ceilinged, with excellent beds and immaculate bathrooms. Rooms in the rear are more tranquil except when the schoolyard is full of children. There's an honor bar in the lobby where guests keep track of their own drinks. A generous breakfast is the only meal served.

Leibnizstrasse 59, 10629 Berlin. ✆ **030/3-27-74-40.** Fax 030/327-744-40. www.hotelartnouveau.de. 20 units. 126€–176€ double; 176€–236€ suite. Rates include breakfast. AE, MC, V. Parking 4€. U-Bahn: Adenauerplatz. **Amenities:** Honor bar. *In room:* TV, hair dryer, Internet (free).

Bleibtreu Hotel ★ Hidden away from the bustle of Berlin, this is a trend-conscious choice. Its tiny lobby is accessible via an alleyway that leads past a garden and a big-windowed set of dining and drinking facilities. The setting is the labyrinthine premises of what was built long ago as a Jugendstil-era apartment house. Rooms are small, minimalist, and furnished in carefully chosen natural materials. Bathrooms are cramped but well designed.

Bleibtreustrasse 31, 10707 Berlin (1 block south of the Kurfürstendamm). ✆ **030/88474-0.** Fax 030/88474-444. www.bleibtreu.com. 60 units. 118€–198€ double. AE, DC, MC, V. No parking. U-Bahn: Uhlandstrasse. **Amenities:** 2 restaurants; bar; room service; steam bath. *In room:* TV, hair dryer, minibar, Wi-Fi (free).

Grand Hotel Esplanade ★★★ The Esplanade rivals the Kempinski for supremacy in Berlin. Rooms are spacious, bright, and cheerfully decorated, with sound insulation. Beds are large with quality linens and duvets. Bathrooms, which contain tub/shower combos, are among the city's most luxurious. When reserving, ask for one of the corner rooms, as they're the biggest and have the best views. Even if you don't stay here, stop in for a drink at the elegant **Harry's New York Bar,** or go native at the traditional German **EckKneipe.**

Lützowufer 15, 10785 Berlin. ✆ **866/597-8341** in the U.S. and Canada, or 030/25-47-80. Fax 030/254-78-82-22. www.esplanadeberlin.com. 386 units. 129€–144€ double; from 209€ suite. AE, DC, MC, V. Parking 23€. U-Bahn: Kurfürstenstrasse, Nollendorfplatz, or Wittenbergplatz. **Amenities:** 3 restaurants; 2 bars; babysitting; indoor pool; room service; sauna. *In room:* A/C, TV, hair dryer, kitchenettes (in some), minibar, safe, Wi-Fi (free).

Inexpensive

Hotel-Pension Bregenz This dignified pension occupies the fourth and sunniest floor of a four-story apartment building, accessible by elevator. The owner, Mr. Zimmermann, works hard to maintain the cleanliness and charm of his comfortably furnished, relatively large rooms. Double doors help minimize noise from the public corridors outside. A continental breakfast is served each morning in a small dining area. The staff assists guests in reserving tickets for shows and tours.

Bregenzer Strasse 5, 10707 Berlin. ✆ **030/8-81-43-07.** Fax 030/8-82-40-09. www.hotelbregenz-berlin.de. 14 units, 11 with bathroom (shower only). 62€ double without bathroom; 70€–90€ double with bathroom. Rates include breakfast. MC, V. Parking 4€. S-Bahn: Savignyplatz. U-Bahn: Adenauerplatz. **Amenities:** Breakfast room; Wi-Fi (free). *In room:* TV, hair dryer, minibar.

Pension München This pension occupies only part of the third floor of a massive four-story building (with an elevator) erected as an apartment house in 1908. It offers a simple but tasteful decor of modern furnishings accented with fresh flowers. The small rooms are clean and color-coordinated, with bathrooms containing shower stalls, contemporary furnishings, and prints and engravings by local artists. Look for sculptures by the owner, an artist, in some of the public areas as well. Note that if no rooms are available at this place, you're likely to be recommended to a similar pension.

Guntzelstrasse 62 (close to Bayerischer Platz), 10717 Berlin. ✆ **030/8-57-91-20.** Fax 030/85-79-12-22. www.hotel-pension-muenchen-in-berlin.de. 8 units. 78€–98€ double. AE, DC, MC, V. Parking 6€. U-Bahn: Guntzelstrasse. *In room:* TV, Wi-Fi (free).

NEAR THE MEMORIAL CHURCH & ZOO

Expensive

Hecker's Hotel This hotel is near the Ku'damm and the many bars, cafes, and restaurants around the Savignyplatz. Rooms range from small to medium, but are fairly routine despite good beds. There's a sterility here but also up-to-date comfort and top-notch maintenance. Bathrooms are small.

Grolmanstrasse 35, 10623 Berlin. ✆ **030/8-89-00.** Fax 030/8-89-02-60. www.heckers-hotel.de. 69 units. 180€–220€ double; 280€ suite. AE, DC, MC, V. Parking 12€–18€. U-Bahn: Uhlandstrasse. Bus: 109 from Tegel Airport to Uhlandstrasse or 119 from Tempelhof Airport. **Amenities:** Restaurant; bar (roof dining in summer); room service. *In room:* TV/DVD, hair dryer, minibar, Wi-Fi (free).

Palace Berlin ★ The stylish and comfortable Palace is much improved over recent years. However, in some rooms, the double-glazing on the windows is unable to deafen the noise from the adjacent Europa-Center. Rooms range from medium to spacious, each with deluxe bed. The best are in the Casino Wing. Bathrooms are medium size, most often with tub/shower combo (sometimes with shower only).

In the Europa-Center, Budapesterstrasse 45, 10787 Berlin. ✆ **800/457-4000** in the U.S., or 030/2-50-20. Fax 030/2502-1161. www.palace.de. 282 units. 144€–245€ double; 314€–835€ suite. AE, DC, MC, V. Parking 22€. U-Bahn: Zoologischer Garten. **Amenities:** 2 restaurants; 2 bars; health club; indoor pool; room service; sauna. *In room:* A/C, TV, hair dryer, minibar, Wi-Fi (22€ per day).

Moderate

Hotel Sylter Hof Berlin This hotel offers rich trappings at good prices. The main lounges are warmly decorated in old-world style. The well-maintained rooms, most of which are singles, may be too small for most tastes, but the staff pay special attention to your comfort. Bathrooms are cramped but efficiently arranged.

Kurfürstenstrasse 116, 10787 Berlin. ✆ **030/21-20-0.** Fax 030/21-20-200. www.sylterhof-berlin.de. 161 units. 134€ double; 164€–184€ suite. Rates include buffet breakfast. AE, DC, MC, V. Parking 10€–50€. U-Bahn: Wittenbergplatz. Bus: 119, 129, 146, or 185. **Amenities:** Restaurant; bar; coffee bar. *In room:* TV, hair dryer, minibar, Wi-Fi (free).

Inexpensive

Art'otel Berlin Kudamm, by Park Plaza ★ Those partial to the more famous and highly regarded Brandenburger Hof (see above) also like this tasteful, discreet hotel. Chic and avant-garde, the Park Plaza is unlike any other hotel in Berlin. Rooms, all medium size, are minimalist, with a touch of industrial design. Although they will not please clients seeking a traditional Berlin hotel, modernists will be at home with the pedestal tables evoking cable spools and chrome-legged furnishings, and everyone will appreciate the large beds. Bathrooms are generously proportioned, with showers.

Joachimstalerstrasse 29, 10719 Berlin. ✆ **800/791-9161** in the U.S. and Canada, or 030/88-44-70. Fax 030/88-44-77-00. www.parkplaza.com/hotels/gerkuber. 133 units. 84€–139€ double. Rates include buffet breakfast with champagne. AE, DC, MC, V. Parking 15€. U-Bahn: Kurfürstendamm. **Amenities:** Breakfast room; Wi-Fi (free). *In room:* TV, hair dryer, minibar.

IN BERLIN-MITTE

Very Expensive

Hotel Adlon Kempinski ★★★ Only steps from the Brandenburg Gate, this hotel is one of Berlin's premier addresses and is famous among celebrities. The large, beautifully appointed rooms contain king-size or twin beds. Bathrooms are spacious with deluxe toiletries and a phone.

Unter den Linden 77, 10117 Berlin. ✆ **800/426-3135** in the U.S., or 030/22-61-0. Fax 030/22-61-22-22. www.kempinski.com/berlinadlon. 394 units. 310€–360€ double; 650€–880€ junior suite. AE, DC, MC, V. Parking 32€. S-Bahn: Unter den Linden. **Amenities:** 3 restaurants; bar; babysitting; health club; indoor pool; room service; spa. *In room:* A/C, TV, hair dryer, minibar, Wi-Fi (27€ per day).

The Ritz-Carlton ★★★ One of Berlin's most glamorous and prestigious hotels opened in January 2004 at the Potsdamer Platz. The building evokes the Art Nouveau heyday of the New York City skyscrapers constructed in the 1920s. The club-level rooms and the suites are, of course, the most luxurious way to stay here, but even the standard guest rooms are luxuriously furnished and decorated. The hotel is full of grace notes, such as afternoon tea in the lobby lounge by an open fireplace, live jazz or blues in the hotel bar, the Curtain Club, and an indoor pool. The dining facilities are among the finest in town.

Potsdamer Platz 3, 10785 Berlin. ✆ **800/241-3333** in the U.S. and Canada, or 030/33-77-77. Fax 030/777-55-55. www.ritzcarlton.com. 303 rooms. 154€–285€ double; 295€–305€ junior suite; 345€–995€ suite. AE, DC, MC, V. Parking 19€. U-Bahn: Potsdamer Platz. **Amenities:** 3 restaurants; bar; exercise room; Jacuzzi; indoor pool; room service; sauna. *In room:* A/C, TV, hair dryer, minibar, Wi-Fi (19€ per day).

Westin Grand ★★★ Many hotels call themselves grand—this one truly is, rivaled only by the Kempinski. Since taking over, Westin has spent a fortune in making the rooms among the finest in the city. All are spacious and tastefully decorated. Bathrooms are also large and state of the art with deluxe toiletries.

Friedrichstrasse 158–164, 10117 Berlin. ✆ **888/625-5144** in the U.S., or 030/2-02-70. Fax 030/20-27-33-62. www.westin-grand.com. 400 units. 159€–299€ double; 359€–560€ junior suite; 509€–710€ suite. AE, DC, MC, V. Parking 22€. U-Bahn: Französische Strasse. S-Bahn: Friedrichstrasse. **Amenities:** 3 restaurants; bar; babysitting; exercise room; Jacuzzi; indoor pool; room service. *In room:* A/C, TV, hair dryer, minibar, Wi-Fi (24€ per day).

Moderate

Arte Luise Künsthotel ★ 🎁 Its name translates as "home for artists." No, it's not a communal crash pad for the bohemian fringe, but a choice and select boutique hotel where a different German artist designed and individually furnished each of the guest rooms. Under historic preservation, the hotel is in a restored 1825 city palace. Clients from the arts, media, and even the political or business world are drawn to this unusual hostelry. Each room comes as a total surprise, and, of course, you're treated to some of each artist's work, which runs the gamut from pop to classicism. Some units evoke modern minimalism, whereas others are much more quirky.

Luisenstrasse 19, 10119 Berlin. ✆ **030/28448-0.** Fax 030/28448-448. www.luise-berlin.com. 50 units, 30 with bathroom. 79€–110€ double without bathroom; 99€–210€ double with shower; 130€–240€ double with bathroom. AE, DC, MC. Parking 12€. U-Bahn: Friedrichstrasse. **Amenities:** Restaurant/bar next door. *In room:* A/C (in some), TV, Wi-Fi (free).

Hotel Luisenhof ★ One of the most desirable small hotels in Berlin's eastern district, the Luisenhof occupies a dignified 1822 house. Five floors of high-ceilinged rooms will appeal to those desiring to escape modern Berlin's sterility. Rooms range greatly in size, but each is equipped with good queen-size or twin beds. Bathrooms, though small, are beautifully appointed, with shower stalls (often with a large tub).

Köpenicker Strasse 92, 10179 Berlin. ✆ **030/246-28-10.** Fax 030/246-28-160. www.luisenhof.de. 27 units. 119€–299€ double; 249€–399€ suite. Rates include breakfast. AE, DC, MC, V. Parking 8€. U-Bahn: Märkisches Museum. **Amenities:** Restaurant; bar; room service. *In room:* TV, hair dryer, minibar, Wi-Fi (free).

Lux 11 ★ In the hip central *Mitte* district, among fashionable art galleries and trendy media firms, this is an oasis of charm, comfort, and style. Outfitted in a chic minimalist style, its bedrooms have modern, glamorous decors. The open-to-view bathrooms are furnished in honey-colored wood and concrete. Lux 11 is the latest creation from a well-known duo, Claudio Silvestrin and his wife, Giuliana Salmaso, known for their minimalist designs. In the basement is the **Aveda Spa,** and adjacent to the lobby, there's a "micro" department store operated by a former buyer for Quartier 206, a posh fashion emporium in Berlin. An on-site restaurant and chill-out bar serves Italian and Asian fusion cuisine. Guests get acquainted in the cozy cafe/ lounge.

Rosa-Luxemburg-Strasse 9–13, 10178 Berlin. ✆ **030/93-62-80-0.** Fax 030/93-62-80-80. www.lux-eleven.com. 72 units. 165€–205€ double; 255€–295€ suite. AE, DC, MC, V. Parking 18€. U-Bahn: Weinmeisterstrasse. **Amenities:** Restaurant; cafe; bar; health club; room service; sauna; spa. *In room:* A/C, TV, hair dryer, kitchenette, Wi-Fi (free).

Inexpensive

Arcotel John F. ★ This privately owned "new design" hotel was inspired by the era of the popular U.S. president John F. Kennedy. It lies in the government quarter within view of the Berlin Cathedral. Kennedy, of course, won the hearts of Berliners with his famous 1963 "Ich bin ein Berliner" speech. The increasingly rare dark zebrawood is used throughout, and the delicate lamps were based on a widely publicized dress once wore by Mrs. Kennedy. As a token to JFK, a rocking chair is found in every room. For a true "West Wing" aura, the Kennedy Room presents Oval Office window drapings, U.S. flags, American bathroom fixtures, and a light blue draped bed like the former First Lady once had. The hotel bar claims to have the largest selection of high-quality bourbons in Berlin, including the 25-year-old Bitter Truth Bourbon.

Werderscher Markt 11, 10117 Berlin. ✆ **030/405-0460.** Fax 030/405-046-100. www.arcotel.at. 190 units. 95€–133€ double. AE, MC, V. U-Bahn: Hausvogteiplatz. **Amenities:** Restaurant; bar; room service. *In room:* A/C, TV/DVD, CD player, hair dryer, minibar, Wi-Fi (free).

IN KREUZBERG

Inexpensive

Michelberger Hotel This hotel, opening in the autumn of 2009, immediately became a hangout for hipsters. The modest bedrooms have been installed in a converted old factory building. Management claims their establishment hopes to bring Berlin's vibrant lifestyle and historical patina inside its doors. Their self-described clientele is for Austrian carpenters, Swedish models, English rock stars, Japanese businessmen, German racing-car drivers, and American dudes. The Michelberger is a cosmopolitan, yet street-savvy hangout. Many of the rooms are quite small.

Management will rent a single to a budget-conscious couple at a cost of 60€ to 80€ a night, but with the understanding the space will be very cramped.

Warschauer Strasse 39–40, 10243 Berlin. ✆ **030/297-785-90.** Fax 030/297-785-929. www.michelbergerhotel.com. 119 units. 70€–90€ double; 150€ suite. AE, DC, MC, V. U-Bahn/S-Bahn: Warschauer Strasse. **Amenities:** Restaurant (lunch); bar. *In room:* TV, Wi-Fi (free).

Where to Dine

For food on the run, try one of the dozens of kabob stalls (*Imbisse*) that dot the streets. Some 200,000 Turks live in Berlin, and the food that they've introduced—meat- or *Scharfskäse-* (sheep's cheese, virtually identical to feta) stuffed pitas—makes a filling, cheap meal, but watch out for the cascades of cabbage. Good sit-down Turkish restaurants are harder to find, but one of the best is **Hitit,** Knobelsdorffstrasse 35 (✆ **030/322-45-57**), near Charlottenburg Schloss, with a full array of Turkish specialties, some 150 dishes in all. It's open daily 8am to midnight.

ON OR NEAR THE KURFÜRSTENDAMM

Expensive

Paris Bar ★ FRENCH This French bistro has been a local favorite since the postwar years, when two Frenchmen established the restaurant to bring a little Parisian cheer to the dismal gray of bombed-out Berlin. The place is just as crowded with elbow-to-elbow tables as a Montmartre tourist trap, but you'll find it a genuinely pleasing little eatery. It's a true restaurant on the see-and-be-seen circuit between Savignyplatz and Gedächtniskiche. The food is invariably fresh and well prepared but not particularly innovative.

Kantstrasse 152. ✆ **030/313-80-52.** Reservations recommended. Main courses 15€–42€. AE. Daily noon–2am. U-Bahn: Uhlandstrasse.

Moderate

Marjellchen ★ EAST PRUSSIAN This is the only restaurant in Berlin specializing in the cuisine of Germany's long-lost province of East Prussia, along with the cuisines of Pomerania and Silesia. Amid a Bismarckian ambience of still lifes, vested waiters, and oil lamps, you can enjoy a savory version of red-beet soup with strips of beef, East Prussian potato soup with crabmeat and bacon, *falscher Gänsebraten* (pork spareribs stuffed with prunes and bread crumbs), and *mecklenburger Kümmelfleisch* (lamb with chives and onions).

Mommsenstrasse 9. ✆ **030/883-26-76.** www.marjellchen-berlin.de. Reservations recommended. Main courses 10€–20€. AE, DC, MC, V. Mon–Sat 5pm–midnight. Closed Dec 23–24 and 31. U-Bahn: Adenauerplatz or Uhlandstrasse. Bus: 109, 119, or 129.

YVA Suite ★ INTERNATIONAL There's an excellent restaurant associated with this club, a meeting place for the hip denizens of Berlin's inner sanctum of writers, artists, and cultural icons. The setting is on the ground floor of a building near the Savignyplatz, within a decor that's high-ceilinged, stylish, and almost surgically minimalist. Expect walls almost entirely sheathed in slabs of volcanic lava rock, elegant table settings, well-prepared food that includes selections for both hearty and delicate appetites, and a formidable tradition of welcoming stars and starlets from Germany's world of high fashion, sports, and the arts. Menu items vary with the season and the inspiration of the chefs, but are likely to include lemon-coconut soup with chicken satay; terrine of gooseliver; various forms of carpaccio; curried breast of duck with chorizo sausages; and Thai-style bouillabaisse.

Cafe Society

The family-owned **Café/Bistro Leysieffer**, Friedrichstrasse 68 (✆ **030/2064-9715**; www.leysieffer.de; U-Bahn: Stadtmitte), opened in the early 1980s. The breakfast menu is one of the most elegant in town: Parma ham, smoked salmon, a fresh baguette, French butter, and—to round it off—champagne. Main courses cost 9€ to 15€. Hours are daily 10am to 8pm.

Schlüterstrasse 52. ✆ **030/88-72-55-73.** Reservations recommended. Main courses 16€–28€. AE, MC, V. Bar and full menu daily 6pm–midnight; bar and limited menu daily midnight–3am. S-Bahn: Savignyplatz.

Inexpensive

Hard Rock Cafe ☺ AMERICAN This is the local branch of the familiar worldwide chain that mingles rock-'n'-roll nostalgia with American food. Menu choices range from a veggie burger to a "pig" sandwich (hickory-smoked pork barbecue) that you might find in rural Georgia. The food is unexceptional, but service is friendly.

Meinekestrasse 21. ✆ **030/88-46-20.** www.hardrock.com. Reservations accepted for groups of 10 or more. Main courses 10€–25€. AE, MC, V. Sun–Thurs noon–11pm; Fri–Sat noon–1am. U-Bahn: Kurfürstendamm.

Lubitsch CONTINENTAL Its conservative chic reputation was enhanced in 1999 when Chancellor Schröder dropped in for lunch and a photo op, causing ripples of energy to reverberate through the neighborhood. Menu items include lots of cafe drinks and steaming pots of afternoon tea, but if you drop in for a meal, expect platters of chicken curry salad with roasted potatoes; Berlin-style potato soup; braised chicken with salad and fresh vegetables; a roulade of suckling pig; and Nürnberger-style wursts. Expect brusque service, a black-and-white decor with Thonet-style chairs, and a somewhat arrogant environment that, despite its drawbacks, is very, very *Berliner.*

Bleibtreustrasse 47. ✆ **030/88-72-84-99.** www.restaurant-lubitsch.de. Main courses 8€–22€; business lunch 13€. AE, DC, MC, V. Mon–Sat 10am–midnight; Sun 6pm–1am. U-Bahn: Kurfürstendamm.

NEAR THE MEMORIAL CHURCH & ZOO

Very Expensive

First Floor ★★ REGIONAL GERMAN/FRENCH This is the showcase restaurant within one of the most spectacular hotels ever built near the Tiergarten. Set one floor above street level, it features a perfectly orchestrated service and setting that revolve around the cuisine of a master chef. Winning our praise are such dishes as a terrine of veal with arugula-flavored butter; sophisticated variations of Bresse chicken; guinea fowl stuffed with foie gras and served with a truffle vinaigrette sauce; a cassoulet of lobster and broad beans in a style vaguely influenced by the culinary precepts of southwestern France; filet of sole with champagne sauce; and a mascarpone mousse with lavender-scented honey.

In the Palace Berlin, Budapesterstrasse 42. ✆ **030/25-02-10-20.** Reservations recommended. Main courses 22€–42€; set menus 45€ at lunch only, 92€–112€ at lunch and dinner. AE, DC, MC, V. Mon–Fri noon–3pm; daily 6:30–11pm. U-Bahn: Zoologischer Garten.

IN THE TIERGARTEN

Expensive

Paris-Moskau INTERNATIONAL The grand days of the 19th century are alive and well at this restaurant in the beautiful Tiergarten area, where good dining spots are scarce. Menu items are both classic and more cutting edge. The fresh tomato soup is excellent. Some of the dishes are mundane—the grilled filet of beef in mushroom sauce comes to mind—but other, lighter dishes with delicate seasonings are delightful. We recommend the grilled North Sea salmon with herbs accompanied by basil-flavored noodles. The chef should market his recipe for saffron sauce, which accompanies several dishes. You'll receive attentive service from the formally dressed staff.

Alt-Moabit 141. ✆ **030/3-94-20-81.** www.paris-moskau.de. Reservations recommended. Main courses 25€–28€; fixed-price menus 56€–81€. AE, DC, MC, V. Mon–Fri noon–3pm; daily 6–11:30pm. S-Bahn: Auhalter Bahnhof.

IN & AROUND CHARLOTTENBURG

Expensive

Alt-Luxemburg ★★ CONTINENTAL/FRENCH/GERMAN Alt-Luxemburg's Chef Karl Wannemacher is one of the most outstanding chefs in eastern Germany. Known for his quality and market-fresh ingredients, he prepares a seductively sensual plate. Everything shows his flawless technique, especially the stuffed veal or the saddle of venison with juniper sauce. Taste his excellent lacquered duck breast with honey sauce or saddle of lamb with stewed peppers. Alt-Luxemburg offers a finely balanced wine list, and service is both unpretentious and gracious.

Windscheidstrasse 31. ✆ **030/323-87-30.** www.alt-luxemburg.de. Reservations required. Main courses 27€–32€. Fixed-price 4-course menu 64€; fixed-price 5-course menu 70€. AE, DC, MC, V. Mon–Sat 5–11pm. U-Bahn: Sophie-Charlotte-Platz.

Inexpensive

Rogacki ★ GERMAN/DELI Since 1928, this deluxe deli has been installed in a former stable. Every day it feeds some 1,500 people, many eating at stand-up tables. Separate counters contain the various food groups—more than 200 varieties of cured and fresh meats, some 150 kinds of cheese. It is estimated that Rogacki makes two tons of potato salad in any given week. In the basement workers stay busy all day filleting herring. The freshly baked breads, fresh salads, and other specialties from throughout the world make this a culinary adventure. The fish soup is perhaps the finest in Berlin. You can order smoked salmon, vegetable dishes, lobster, various pastas including spaghetti with the "fruits of the sea," even chili con carne.

Wilmersdorfer Strasse 145–146. ✆ **030/343-8250.** www.rogacki.de. Reservations required. Main courses 5€–15€. MC, V. Mon–Wed 9am–6pm; Thurs–Fri 9am–7pm; Sat 8am–4pm. U-Bahn: Sophie-Charlotte-Platz.

IN BERLIN-MITTE

Expensive

Grill Royal ★★★ STEAK This fashionable place serves the best cuts of steak in Berlin Mitte, lying on the banks of the River Spree. It also specializes in *fine de Claire* oysters to get you started. Many of their select cuts of beef are imported from Ireland, Argentina, and Australia. The chefs also made a rich beef stroganoff and serve delectable lamb chops. For the non–meat eater, there is a selection of fresh fish, including lobster and halibut. American film stars, Swedish novelists, and German politicos feast here, along with artists, business tyros, curators, dealers, and fat burghers. The large, airy dining room is set under low ceilings.

Friedrichstrasse 105B. ✆ **030/2887-9288.** www.grillroyal.com. Main courses 25€–56€. AE, DC, MC, V. Tues–Sun 6pm–midnight. U-Bahn: Friedrichstrasse.

Guy ★ INTERNATIONAL At this top-notch restaurant, anticipate a strong sense of gastronomy as theater. Proceed to any of three separate balconies, each supporting at least one row of artfully decorated tables. The overall effect can be compared to the balconies and private boxes of an old-fashioned opera house. The cuisine is very haute, even to the point of seeming experimental. Examples change frequently, but might include a medley of marinated quail and gooseliver; mussels served on a purée of arugula; lobster and sweetbreads cooked in puff pastry with tarragon-flavored cream sauce; and braised breast of goose with a roulade of potatoes and herbs.

Jägerstrasse 59–60. ✆ **030/20-94-26-00.** www.guy-restaurant.de. Reservations recommended. Main courses 27€–30€; set-price lunches 17€–22€; set-price dinners 59€–79€. AE, MC, V. Mon–Fri noon–3pm and 6pm–1am; Sat 6pm–1am. U-Bahn: Stadtmitte or Französischer Strasse.

Margaux ★★★ CONTINENTAL Chef Michael Hoffmann will dazzle your palate with his seductive, inventive dishes and his brilliant wine cellar. Several 21st-century food magazines have named his the best gourmet restaurant in Berlin. Only a few steps from the Brandenburg Gate, the restaurant has a stunning modern interior, designed by the noted architect Johanne Nalbach. The exceptional food is made from only the highest-quality ingredients. Our party of four launched our repast with such perfectly prepared starters as marinated duck liver and Breton lobster, which appears with curry and, surprisingly, watermelon. Hoffmann's star shines brightest with his fish, such as John Dory with a Mediterranean "aroma" that turned out to be anchovies, olives, tomatoes, and pepper. Frogs' legs are delectably perfumed with parsley and garlic.

Unter den Linden 78. ✆ **030/22-65-26-11.** www.margaux-berlin.de. Reservations required. Main courses 24€–46€; fixed-price lunch 80€–140€; fixed-price dinner 95€–165€. AE, DC, MC, V. Mon–Sat noon–2pm and 7–11pm. S-Bahn: Unter den Linden.

Restaurant VAU ★★ INTERNATIONAL This restaurant is the culinary showcase of master chef Kolja Kleeberg. Choices include terrine of salmon and morels with rocket salad; aspic of suckling pig with sauerkraut; salad with marinated red mullet, mint, and almonds; crisp-fried duck with marjoram; ribs of suckling lamb with thyme-flavored polenta; and desserts such as woodruff soup with champagne-flavored ice cream. The wine list is international and well chosen.

Jägerstrasse 54–55 (near the Four Seasons Hotel and the Gendamenmarkt). ✆ **030/202-9730.** www.vau-berlin.de. Reservations recommended. Main courses 28€–38€; set-price lunches 65€–100€; set-price dinners 120€. AE, DC, MC, V. Mon–Sat noon–2:30pm and 7–10:30pm. U-Bahn: Hausvoigteiplatz.

Moderate

Dressler CONTINENTAL No other bistro along Unter den Linden so successfully re-creates Berlin's prewar decor and style. Designed to resemble an arts-conscious bistro of the sort that might have amused and entertained tuxedo-clad clients in the 1920s, it's outfitted with leather banquettes, tile floors, mirrors, and film memorabilia from the great days of early German cinema. Waiters scurry around, carrying trays of everything from caviar to strudel, as well as three kinds of oysters and hefty portions of lobster salad. Substantial menu items include perfectly prepared turbot with champagne vinaigrette; pheasant breast with Riesling sauce; local salmon trout with white-wine sauce and braised endive; stuffed breast of veal; and calves' liver with apples.

Unter den Linden 39. ✆ **030/204-44-22.** www.restaurant-dressler.de. Reservations recommended. Main courses 12€–28€. AE, DC, MC, V. Daily 8am–1am. S-Bahn: Unter den Linden.

Kaefer's Restaurant Dachgarten CONTINENTAL When a team of cutting-edge architects redesigned the most famous building in Berlin, the Reichstag (Parliament House), they added a restaurant on the uppermost floor. The setting is metallic looking and edgy. Lines to get in can be overwhelming, mingling sightseers and diners in the same queues. Included in the price of your meal will be a close-up view of the dome and the rest of the building's interior. Frankly, a visit here for breakfast may be your best bet, when there's a businesslike aura that's consistent with this building's august role as a Teutonic icon. The lunch menu is more "Berliner" than the Continental/Asian evening menu. Lunchtime menus include house-style meatballs with coleslaw and potato salad and grilled steaks and wursts. Dinners are a bit more exotic, focusing on such dishes as fried filet of duck with Austrian-style scalloped potatoes, Asian asparagus, and water chestnuts; and filet of turbot with a purée of truffles and herb-flavored risotto.

In the Reichstag, Platz der Republik. ✆ **030/22-62-99-0.** www.feinkost-kaefer.de. Reservations necessary. Breakfast 12€–27€; lunch main courses 14€–23€; dinner main courses 24€–30€; fixed-price dinners 98€–117€. AE, DC, MC, V. Daily 9–10:15am, noon–2:30pm, and 6:30pm–midnight. S-Bahn: Unter den Linden.

Malatesta ITALIAN Flavorful Italian food, served within an all-black-and-white venue whose rectilinear simplicity might remind you of a spartan version of a sushi bar, is the heartbeat of this likable Italian restaurant. The aura is high style rather than cozy, with an emphasis on the kind of offhanded hip you might have expected in Milan or Rome. The menu reflects whatever is fresh and succulent at the time, with dishes crafted anew almost every day. Three enduring specialties, however, include tagliatelle with asparagus, fried squid (calamari), and fresh tomatoes; filet of beef with black truffles; and pasta made with ricotta cheese, pesto, and balsamic vinegar. Specialties from throughout Italy are the draw here, with no particular emphasis on northern, southern, or central Italian cuisine over any of the country's other regions.

Charlottenstrasse 59. ✆ **030/20-94-50-71.** www.ristorante-malatesta.de. Reservations recommended. Main courses 9€–25€; pizza 8€–12€; set menus 17€–19€. AE, MC, V. Mon–Sat noon–midnight. U-Bahn: Stadmitte.

Restaurant Borchardt INTERNATIONAL This restaurant is elegant, lighthearted, and fashionable among the city's artistic movers and shakers. You can order anything from a simple salad (as supermodel Claudia Schiffer often does) to the more substantial cream-of-potato soup with bacon and croutons; filet of carp prepared with Riesling and herbs and finished with champagne; foie gras served with caramelized apples; chicken stuffed with morels and served with cream-and-herb sauce; and a pistachio mousse garnished with essence of fresh fruit.

Französische Strasse 47. ✆ **030/8188-6230.** www.borchardt-catering.de. Reservations recommended. Daily special menu 10€; main courses 9.50€–58€. AE, V. Daily 11:30am–2am (kitchen closes at midnight). U-Bahn: Französische Strasse.

NATIVE behavior

Traditional Germans enjoy their big meal at noon and, in the evening, satisfy hunger with deli cold cuts, open-faced sandwiches, sour pickles, and liver sausage, among other food. To be truly native, you'll begin your *Mittagessen* (main noonday meal) with *Leberknodelsuppe* (liver dumpling).

Germany is a land that welcomes all serious beer drinkers. The country is home to about 40% of the world's breweries, with the largest concentration found in Bavaria. The best and most plentiful beer gardens and beer halls are in Munich (see the box "What's Brewing at the Beer Halls?" on p. 417).

In general, the German people are rather candid, especially if they don't agree with something. Whereas this might appear argumentative to foreigners, locals might counterclaim that they are "merely being honest, not hypocritical."

Many young Germans seem obsessed with all things Yankee; yet, almost in contradiction, they possess deeply felt anti-American sentiments. You must wander carefully through the maze of politics, if the subject comes up at all.

As a rule, expect more formality in Germany than in America or even Britain. By all means, if you have an appointment, show up on time!

Inexpensive

La Gaiola CONTINENTAL It's crowded, it's hip, and its decor evokes the 1930s allure of what might have been a coffee plantation in the highlands of Africa. Many clients come here just for its bar scene, but if you're hungry, the food is firmly based on what's cooking in the area that stretches between North Germany and southern Austria, and is served in generous portions. Come here for a chance to meet unattached residents of the surrounding neighborhood, a dialogue with a hip Berliner or two, and good-tasting food items that include beef filet with braised arugula; all manner of fresh fish; homemade salmon with apples, roasted potatoes, and horseradish; and drinks that include raspberry daiquiris.

Monbijouplatz 11-12. ✆ **030/28-53-98-90.** Reservations recommended. Main courses 10€-20€. AE, MC, V. Mon-Sat 6pm-midnight. U-Bahn: Hackescher Markt.

Mutter Hoppe GERMAN This cozy, wood-paneled restaurant still serves the solid Teutonic cuisine favored by a quasi-legendary matriarch (Mother Hoppe) who used to churn out vast amounts of traditional cuisine to members of her extended family and entourage. Within a quartet of old-fashioned dining rooms, you'll enjoy heaping portions of such rib-sticking fare as sauerbraten with roasted potatoes; creamy goulash with wild mushrooms; filets of zander with dill-flavored cream sauce; and braised filets of pork in mushroom-flavored cream sauce. Wine is available, but most guests opt for at least one foaming mug of beer.

Rathausstrasse 21, Nikolaiviertel. ✆ **030/241-56-25.** www.prostmahlzeit.de/mutterhoppe. Reservations recommended. Main courses 8€-27€. DC, MC, V. Daily 11:30am-11:30pm. U- and S-Bahn: Alexanderplatz.

Stäv ★ RHENISH For years, this upscale tavern entertained the politicians and journalists whose business involved the day-to-day running of the German government from Germany's former capital of Bonn. Although its owners at first opposed the reinauguration of Berlin as the German capital, when the switch was made, they valiantly pulled out of the Rhineland and followed their clientele to new digs within a 5-minute walk of the Brandenburg Gate near the Friedrichstrasse Bahnhof. The only beer served is Kölsch, a brew more closely associated with the Rhineland than any other beer. Rhenish food items include a mass of apples, onions, and blood sausage known as *Himmel und Ärd* ("heaven and hell"); braised beef with pumpernickel and raisin sauce; and Rhineland sauerbraten with noodles. Other items, many influenced by the culinary traditions of Berlin, include braised liver with bacon and onions; a crisp version of Alsatian pizza known as *Flammenküche;* and a potato cake topped with apples and shredded beets or with smoked salmon and sour cream.

Schiffbauerdamm 8. ✆ **030/282-3965.** Reservations recommended. Main courses 10€–20€. AE, DC, MC, V. Daily 10am–1am. U-Bahn: Friedrichstrasse.

IN KREUZBERG

Expensive

Horváth INTERNATIONAL In the Kreuzberg district, this restaurant is installed in a 19th-century front room, a showcase for the savory viands of Chef Wolfgang Müller. Celebrities, including the mayor of Berlin, continue to frequent these airy, hyper avant-garde dining rooms, enjoying dishes that are inspired by recipes from Bavaria to Bangkok. Over chilled elderberry soup, you can decide on your next course—perhaps stuffed shoulder of veal with artichoke hearts, olives, pine nuts, and a mushroom-flavored risotto. Finish off with, perhaps, the passion-fruit tart with marinated fruit and a coconut-flavored lime sauce.

Paul-Lincke-Ufer 44A. ✆ **030/6128-9992.** www.restaurant-horvath.de. Reservations recommended. Main courses 32€–46€; fixed-price menu 45€ for 3 courses, 73€ for 10 courses. No credit cards. Tues–Sun 6pm–midnight. U-Bahn: Kottbusser Tor.

Seeing the Sights

THE TOP MUSEUMS

In the Tiergarten

Gemäldegalerie ★★★ This is one of Germany's greatest painting galleries. Several rooms are devoted to early German masters, with altarpieces dating from the 13th to the 15th century. Note the panel of *The Virgin Enthroned with Child* (1350), surrounded by angels that resemble the demons so popular in the later works of Hieronymus Bosch. Eight paintings make up the Dürer collection in adjacent rooms.

Another gallery is given over to Italian painting. Here are five Raphael Madonnas, and works by Titian *(The Girl with a Bowl of Fruit),* Fra Filippo Lippi, Botticelli, and Correggio *(Leda with the Swan).* There are also early Netherlandish paintings from the 15th and 16th centuries (van Eyck, Van der Weyden, Bosch, and Brueghel). Several galleries are devoted to Flemish and Dutch masters of the 17th century, with no fewer than 20 works by Rembrandt, including the *Head of Christ*.

Stauffenbergstrasse (entrance is at Matthäiskirchplatz 4). ✆ **030/266-42-30-40.** www.smb.spk-berlin.de. Admission 8€ adults, 4€ children. Tues–Sun 10am–6pm (Thurs to 10pm). U-Bahn: Potsdamer Platz, then bus 148. Bus: 129 from Ku'damm (plus a 4-min. walk).

Neue Nationalgalerie (New National Gallery) ★ In its modern glass-and-steel home designed by Ludwig Mies van der Rohe, the Neue Nationalgalerie contains a continually growing collection of modern European and American art. Here you'll

Preserving What's Left of a Painful Memory

City officials have allocated $51 million to save what remains of the Berlin Wall. Only a few strips are still left. In the euphoria that accompanied the collapse of the wall in 1989, few bothered to think about it as a monument to history—or even as a tourist attraction. Most Berliners wanted to get rid of it as soon as possible. But now an attempt will be made to preserve what's left so that future generations can see how the superpowers in the Cold War stood nose-to-nose for 4 decades.

find works of 19th-century artists, with a stellar concentration on French Impressionists. German art starts with Adolph von Menzel's paintings from about 1850. The 20th-century collection includes works by Max Beckmann, Edvard Munch, and E. L. Kirchner (*Brandenburger Tor*), as well as a few paintings by "the usual suspects," Bacon, Picasso, Ernst, Klee, and American artists such as Barnett Newman. There's food service in the cafe on the ground floor. Hot meals are served from 11am to 5pm.

Potsdamer Strasse 50 (just south of the Tiergarten). ✆ **030/2-66-42-30-40.** www.smb.spk.berlin.de. Permanent collection 8€ adults, 4€ children. Tues–Wed 10am–6pm; Thurs 10am–10pm; Fri–Sun 10am–8pm. U-Bahn: Mendelssohn-Bartholdy-Park. S-Bahn: Potsdamer Platz.

Museumsinsel (Museum Island)

Alte Nationalgalerie ★ This museum is known for its collection of 19th-century German art as well as for its French Impressionists. A feature of the museum is the world's largest collection of the works of one of the best known of all Berlin artists, Adolph von Menzel (1815–1905). We especially like his *Das Balkonzimmer.* Other paintings include a galaxy of art representing the romantic and classical movements as well as the Biedermeier era. Allow at least an hour and a half to take in canvasses by everybody from Pissarro to Cézanne, from Delacroix to Degas, and from van Gogh to Monet. The collection would have been far greater than it is had not the Nazis either sold or destroyed so many early-20th-century works they viewed as "degenerate."

Bodestrasse 1–3. ✆ **030/2090-5577.** www.smb.spk-berlin.de. Admission 8€ adults, 4€ children. Tues–Sun 10am–6pm (Thurs to 10pm). S-Bahn: Hackescher Markt. Tram: 3, 4, 5, 12, 13, 15, or 53. Bus: 100, 157, or 378.

Altes Museum ★ Karl Friedrich Schinkel, the city's greatest architect, designed this structure, which resembles a Greek Corinthian temple, in 1822. On its main floor is the **Antikensammlung,** or Museum of Greek and Roman Antiquities. This great collection of world-famous works of antique decorative art was inaugurated in 1960. It's rich in pottery; Greek, Etruscan, and Roman bronze statuettes and implements; ivory carvings, glassware, objects in precious stone, and jewelry of the Mediterranean region, as well as gold and silver treasures; mummy portraits from Roman Egypt; wood and stone sarcophagi; and a few marble sculptures. The collection includes some of the finest Greek vases of the black- and red-figures style dating from the 6th century to the 4th century B.C. The best known is a large Athenian wine jar (amphora) found in Vulci, Etruria, dating from 490 B.C., which shows a satyr with a lyre and the god Hermes.

Museumsinsel am Lustgarten. ✆ **030/20-90-55-77.** www.smb.spk-berlin.de. Admission 8€ adults, 4€ children. Tues–Sun 10am–6pm (Thurs to 10pm). U-Bahn/S-Bahn: Friedrichstrasse. Bus: 100 to Lustgarten, 147, 157, or 358.

Bode Museum ★★★ One of the great museums of Germany, long closed for restoration, is now open with enlarged exhibits, better lighting, and more viewer-friendly exhibitions. It contains a vast array of museums, including the Museum of Late Ancient and Byzantine Art, the Sculpture Collection, the **Picture Gallery ★★**, the Museum of Prehistory, the Children's Gallery, and the extensive Cabinet of Coins and Medals.

The Museum of Late Ancient and Byzantine Art has displays of early Christian sarcophagi, Coptic and Byzantine sculpture, icons, and even gravestones dating from the 3rd through the 18th century. The rich Sculpture Collection exhibits magnificent pieces from ancient churches and monasteries, including a sandstone pulpit support by Anton Pilgram (1490) carved in the shape of a medieval craftsman.

The Picture Gallery is devoted in part to masterpieces from the Dutch and German schools of the 15th and 16th centuries, as well as great works by Italian, Flemish, Dutch, French, and British painters from the 14th to the 18th century.

Monbijoubrücke, Bodestrassel 1–3 Museumsinel. ✆ **030/2090-5577.** www.smb.spk-berlin.de. Admission 8€ adults, 4€ students and children. Daily 10am–6pm (Thurs to 10pm). U-Bahn: Friedrichstrasse.

Neues Museum ★★★ When the doors of this museum opened in 2009, it was the first time in 70 years that all five museums on Museum Island could be visited. Severely damaged in World War II, it was left in ruins for decades. The museum now contains the collections of the **Egyptian Museum ★★★** and the Papyrus Collection as well as a part of the collection of the Museum of Prehistory and Early History and the Antiquities Collection.

The famous artifact of Berlin is the bust of **Queen Nefertiti ★★★**, which rests in the North Cupola. She gazes through the Niobe Room, the Bacchus Room, and the Roman Room into the South Cupola. Here, her gaze is returned by two monumental statues that stood in the Egyptian city of Alexandra during the late Roman Empire.

The Egyptian collection ranges from the huge sphinx of Hatsheput (1490 B.C.) to fragments of reliefs from Egyptian temples. Of special interest is the **Burial Cult Room ★★**, where coffins, mummies, and grave objects are displayed along with life-size X-ray photographs of the mummies of humans and animals.

The **Papyrus Collection ★★** displays about 25,000 documents of papyrus, ostraca, parchment, limestone, wax, and wood in eight languages.

Museuminsel. ✆ **030/266-424-242.** www.neues-museum.de. Admission 10€ adults, 5€ students and children. Sun–Wed 10am–6pm; Thurs–Sat 10am–8pm. U-Bahn: Friedrichstrasse.

Pergamon Museum ★★★ The Pergamon Museum houses several departments, but if you have time for only one exhibit, go to the central hall of the U-shaped building to see the **Pergamon Altar ★★★**. This Greek altar (180–160 B.C.) has a huge room all to itself. Some 27 steps lead up to the colonnade. Most fascinating is the frieze around the base, tediously pieced together over a 20-year period. Depicting the struggle of the Olympian gods against the Titans as told in Hesiod's *Theogony,* the relief is strikingly alive, with figures projecting as much as a foot from the background. This, however, is only part of the collection of Greek and Roman antiquities, housed in the north and east wings. You'll also find sculptures from many Greek and Roman cities, including a statue of a goddess holding a pomegranate (575 B.C.), found in southern Attica. If your guidebook is old and you're looking to see the famed Market Gate of Miletus, you're out of luck. This towering Roman gate, built around A.D. 120 at the entrance to the market square in the Aegean coastal city of Miletus (now Turkey) has been dismantled. Museum experts will spend 10 years restoring it, perhaps putting it on display once again in 2015. The **Near East Museum ★**, in the south wing, contains one of the largest collections anywhere of antiquities discovered in the lands of ancient Babylonia, Persia, and Assyria. Among the exhibits is the Processional Way of Babylon with the Ishtar Gate (580 B.C.).

Bodestrasse 1-3. ✆ **030/2090-55-77.** www.smb.spk-berlin.de. Admission 10€ adults, 5€ children, free the 1st Sun of the month. Daily 10am–6pm (Thurs to 10pm). U-Bahn/S-Bahn: Friedrichstrasse. Tram: 1, 2, 3, 4, 5, 13, 15, or 53.

In Charlottenburg

Charlottenburg is the quarter of Berlin just west of the Tiergarten. In addition to viewing the exhaustive collections in Charlottenburg Palace, you can enjoy a relaxing ramble through Schlossgarten Charlottenburg. The gardens have been restored and landscaped much as they were in the days of Friedrich Wilhelm II.

Bröhan Museum This wonderful museum specializes in decorative objects of the Art Nouveau (*Jugendstil* in German) and Art Deco periods (1889–1939), with exquisite vases, glass, furniture, silver, paintings of artists belonging to the Berlin Secession, and other works of art arranged in drawing-room fashion, including an outstanding porcelain collection.

Schlossstrasse 1a. ✆ **030/3269-0600.** www.broehan-museum.de. Admission 6€ adults, 4€ students and children. Tues–Sun 10am–6pm. U-Bahn: Sophie-Charlotte-Platz. Bus: 109 or 145 to Luisenplatz/Schloss Charlottenburg.

Die Sammlung Berggruen: Picasso und Seine Zeit (The Berggruen Collection: Picasso and His Era) ★ One of the most unusual private museums in Berlin has accumulated the awesome collection of respected art and antiques dealer Heinz Berggruen. A native of Berlin who fled the Nazis in 1936, he later established antiques dealerships in Paris and California before returning, with his collection, to his native home in 1996. The setting is a renovated former army barracks designed by noted architect August Stüler in 1859. Although most of the collection is devoted to Picasso, there are also works by Cézanne, Braque, Klee, and van Gogh. Some 60 or more works in all, the Picasso collection alone is worth the trip, ranging from his teenage efforts to all of his major periods.

Schlossstrasse 70. ✆ **030/2090-5577.** www.smb.spk-berlin.de. Admission 8€ adults, 4€ students and children. Tues–Sun 10am–6pm. U-Bahn: Richard-Wagner-Platz, followed by a 10-min. walk. Bus: 129, 145, or 210.

Schloss Charlottenburg (Charlottenburg Palace) ★★ Napoleon exaggerated a bit in comparing Schloss Charlottenburg to Versailles when he invaded Berlin in 1806, but in its heyday this palace was the most elegant residence for Prussian rulers outside the castle in Potsdam. Begun in 1695 as a summer palace for the

Electress Sophie Charlotte, patron of philosophy and the arts and wife of King Frederick I (Elector Frederick III), the little residence got out of hand until it grew into the massive structure you see today. The main wing contains the apartments of Frederick I and his "philosopher queen." The **new wing,** known as the Knobelsdorff-Flügel and built from 1740 to 1746, shelters the apartments of Frederick the Great, which now houses a collection of paintings, many of which were either collected or commissioned by the king.

Luisenplatz. ✆ **030/320-91.** www.smb.spk-berlin.de. Combined ticket for all buildings and historical rooms 16€ adults, 12€ children 13 and under and students. Palace Tues–Fri 9am–4pm, Sat–Sun 10am–4pm; museum Tues–Fri 10am–6pm; gardens (free admission) daily 6:30am–8pm (close at 6pm Nov–Feb). U-Bahn: Richard-Wagner-Platz. Bus: 145 or 204.

OTHER MUSEUMS

Deutsche Guggenheim Berlin ★ This state-of-the-art museum is devoted to organizing and presenting exhibitions of modern and contemporary art. The Guggenheim Foundation conceives, organizes, and installs several exhibitions annually, and also presents exhibitions of newly commissioned works created specifically for this space by world-renowned artists. In addition to contemporary artists, exhibition subjects in the past have ranged from Picasso and Cézanne to Andy Warhol.

Unter den Linden 13-15. ✆ **030/2020-930.** www.deutsche-guggenheim.de. Admission 4€ adults, 3€ students and seniors, free for children 11 and under, free on Mon. Daily 11am–8pm. S-Bahn: Unter den Linden.

Judisches Museum Berlin ★★ The Jewish Museum is the most talked-about museum in Berlin, housed in a building that is one of the most spectacular in the city. Called "the silver lightning bolt," it was designed by architect Daniel Libeskind. To some viewers, the building suggests a shattered Star of David by its building plan and the scarring in the zinc-plated facade.

Inside, the spaces are designed to make the visitor uneasy and disoriented, simulating the feeling of those who were exiled. A vast hollow cuts through the museum to mark what is gone. When the exhibits reach the rise of the Third Reich, the hall's walls, ceiling, and floor close in as the visitor proceeds. A chillingly hollow Holocaust Void, a dark, windowless chamber, evokes much that was lost.

The exhibits concentrate on three themes: Judaism and Jewish life, the devastating effects of the Holocaust, and the post–World War II rebuilding of Jewish life in Germany. The on-site Liebermanns Restaurant features world cuisine, with an emphasis on Jewish recipes—all strictly kosher.

Lindenstrasse 9-14. ✆ **030/259-93-300.** www.jmberlin.de. Admission 5€ adults, 2.50€ students and seniors, free for children 6 and under, 10€ family ticket for 2 adults and up to 4 children. Mon 10am–10pm; Tues–Sun 10am–8pm. U-Bahn: Hallesches Tor or Kochstrasse. Bus: M29, M41, or 248.

Käthe-Kollwitz Museum ★ More than any other museum in Germany, this one reflects the individual sorrow of the artist whose work it contains. Some visitors call it a personalized revolt against the agonies of war, as well as a welcome change from the commercialism of the nearby Ku'damm. Established in 1986, it was inspired by Berlin-born Käthe Kollwitz, an ardent socialist, feminist, and pacifist whose stormy social commentary led to the eventual banning of her works by the Nazis. Many Kollwitz works show the agonies of wartime separation of mother and child, inspired

Charlottenburg

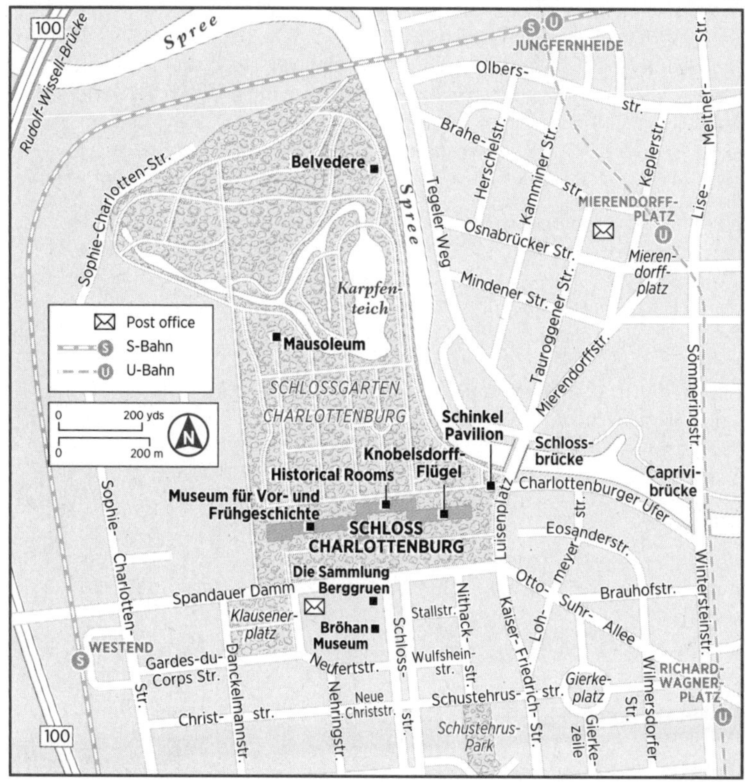

in part by her loss of a son in Flanders during World War I and a grandson during World War II.

Fasanenstrasse 24. ✆ **030/882-52-10.** www.kaethe-kollwitz.de. Admission 6€ adults, 3€ children and students. Wed–Mon 11am–6pm. U-Bahn: Uhlandstrasse or Kurfürstendamm. Bus: 109, 119, 129, or 219.

Kunstgewerbe Museum (Museum of Applied Arts) This museum, next to the Gemäldegalerie in a modern red-brick edifice built for the collection, is devoted to European applied arts from the early Middle Ages to the present, including the Renaissance, baroque, rococo, Jugendstil (German Art Nouveau), and Art Deco periods. Displayed are glassware, porcelain, silver, furniture, jewelry, and clothing. The collection of medieval goldsmiths' works is outstanding, as are the displays of Venetian glass, early Meissen and KPM porcelain, and Jugendstil vases, porcelain, furniture, and objects.

Matthäiskirchplatz. ✆ **030/266-2902.** www.smb.spk.berlin.de. Admission 6€ adults, 3€ students and children. Tues–Fri 10am–6pm; Sat–Sun 11am–6pm. U-Bahn/S-Bahn: Potsdamer Platz. Bus: 129 from Ku'damm to Potsdamer Brücke, also bus 142, 148, 248, 346, or 348.

Märkisches Museum The full cultural history of Berlin is displayed in one of the most prominent buildings on the banks of the Spree; 42 rooms contain collections of artifacts from excavations, plus such art treasures as Slav silver items and Bronze Age finds. You can learn about Berlin's theaters and literature, the arts in Berlin and Brandenburg, and the life and work of Berlin artists. Most visitors like the array of mechanical musical instruments that can be played Sunday from 11am to 2pm, for an extra euro.

Am Köllnischen Park 5. ✆ **030/30-86-215.** www.stadtmuseum.de. Admission 5€ adults, 3€ children. Tues–Sun 9am–5pm. U-Bahn: Märkisches Museum. Bus: 147, 240, or 265.

Museum für Gegenwart Hamburger Bahnhof This Museum of Contemporary Art opened in 1996 north of the Spree in the old Hamburger Bahnhof. The structure was the terminus for trains from Hamburg. Today, the station no longer receives trains but is a premier storehouse of postwar art, a sort of Musée d'Orsay of Berlin. Traces of its former function are still evident in the building, including the high roof designed for steam engines. The modern art on display is some of the finest in Germany, the nucleus of the collection, a donation from the Berlin collector Erich Marx (no relation to Karl Marx). At this multimedia event, you can view everything from Andy Warhol's now-legendary *Mao* to an audiovisual Joseph Beuys archive. The museum houses one of the best collections of Cy Twombly. Other works on display are by Rauschenberg, Lichtenstein, and Dan Flavin. The conceptual artist Beuys is also represented by 450 drawings.

Invalidenstrasse 50–51. ✆ **030/397-834-11.** www.hamburgerbahnhof.de. Admission 12€ adults, 6€ students, free for children 16 and under. Tues–Fri 10am–6pm; Sat 11am–8pm; Sun 11am–6pm. U-Bahn: Zinnowitzer Strasse.

Museum Haus am Checkpoint Charlie This small building houses exhibits depicting the tragic events leading up to and following the erection of the former Berlin Wall. You can see some of the instruments of escape used by East Germans. Photos document the construction of the wall, escape tunnels, and the postwar history of both parts of Berlin from 1945 until today, including the airlift of 1948 and 1949. One of the most moving exhibits is the display on the staircase of drawings by schoolchildren who, in 1961 and 1962, were asked to depict both halves of Germany in one picture.

Friedrichstrasse 43–45. ✆ **030/253-72-50.** www.mauermuseum.de. Admission 12.50€ adults, 5.50€ children. Daily 9am–10pm. U-Bahn: Kochstrasse or Stadtmitte. Bus: 129.

The Story of Berlin This multimedia extravaganza portrays 8 centuries of the city's history through photos, films, sounds, and colorful displays. Beginning with the founding of Berlin in 1237, it chronicles the plague, the Thirty Years' War, Frederick the Great's reign, military life, the Industrial Revolution and the working poor, the golden 1920s, World War II, divided Berlin during the Cold War, and the fall of the Wall. Lights flash in a media blitz as you enter the display on the fall of the Wall, making you feel like one of the first East Berliners to wonderingly cross to the West. Conclude your tour on the 14th floor with a panoramic view over today's Berlin. Though the displays are a bit jarring and the historical information is too jumbled to be truly educational, the museum does leave a lasting impression. Allow at least 2 hours.

Ku'damm-Karree, Kurfürstendamm 207–208 (at the corner of Uhlandstrasse). ✆ **030/887-201-00.** www.story-of-berlin.de. Admission 10€ adults, 8€ students and seniors, 5€ children, 23€ families. Daily 10am–8pm (you must enter by 6pm). U-Bahn: Uhlandstrasse.

HIGHLIGHTS OF BERLIN-MITTE

Brandenburger Tor (Brandenburg Gate) ★★ This triumphal arch stood for many years next to the Wall, symbolizing the divided city. Today it represents the reunited German capital. Six Doric columns hold up an entablature inspired by the Propylaea of the Parthenon at Athens. Surrounded by the famous and much-photographed Quadriga of Gottfried Schadow from 1793, the gate was designed by Carl Gotthard Langhans in 1789. Napoleon liked the original Quadriga so much he ordered them taken down and shipped to Paris, but they were returned to Berlin in 1814. In Berlin's heyday before World War II, the gate marked the grand western extremity of the "main street," Unter den Linden. In the Room of Silence, visitors still gather to meditate and reflect on Germany's past.

Pariser Platz. Free admission. Room of Silence daily 10am–6pm. S-Bahn: Unter den Linden. Bus: 100.

Reichstag (Parliament) On the night of February 17, 1933, a fire broke out in the seat of the German parliament, the Reichstag. It was obviously set by the Nazis, but the German Communist Party was blamed. That was all the excuse Hitler's troops needed to begin mass arrests of "dissidents and enemies of the lawful government." During World War II, the Reichstag faced massive Allied bombardment. Today it's once again the home of Germany's parliament. A glass dome, designed by English architect Sir Norman Foster, now crowns the neo-Renaissance structure originally built in 1894. You can go through the west gate for an elevator ride up to the dome, where a sweeping vista of Berlin opens before you. There's both an observation platform and a rooftop restaurant (the view is better than the food).

Platz der Republik 1. ✆ **030/2273-2152.** Free admission. Daily 8am–midnight (last entrance at 10pm). S-Bahn: Unter den Linden. Bus: 100.

A PARK & A ZOO

Tiergarten ★ Tiergarten, the largest green space in central Berlin, covers just under 2.5 sq. km (1 sq. mile), with more than 23km (14 miles) of meandering walkways. Late in the 19th century, partially to placate growing civic unrest, it was opened to the public, with a layout formalized by one of the leading landscape architects of the era, Peter Josef Lenné. The park was devastated during World War II, and the few trees that remained were chopped down for fuel as Berlin shuddered through the winter of 1945 and 1946. Beginning in 1955, trees were replanted and alleyways, canals, ponds, and flower beds rearranged in their original patterns through the cooperative efforts of many landscape architects.

The park's largest monuments include the Berlin Zoo, described below, and the **Siegessäule (Victory Column),** which perches atop a soaring red-granite pedestal from a position in the center of the wide boulevard (Strasse des 17 Juni) that neatly bisects the Tiergarten into roughly equivalent sections.

From the Bahnhof Zoo to the Brandenburger Tor. Bus: 100, 141, or 341 to Grosser Stern.

Zoologischer Garten Berlin (Berlin Zoo) ★ ☺ Occupying most of the southwest corner of Tiergarten is Germany's oldest and finest zoo. Founded in 1844, it's a short walk north from the Ku'damm. Until World War II, the zoo boasted thousands of animals of every imaginable species and description—many familiar to Berliners by nicknames. The tragedy of the war struck here as well, and by the end of 1945, only 91 animals remained. Since the war, the city has been rebuilding its large and unique collection; today more than 13,000 animals are housed here. The zoo has Europe's most modern birdhouse, with more than 550 species. The most valuable inhabitants here are giant pandas.

Hardenbergplatz 8. © **030/25-40-10.** www.zoo-berlin.de. Zoo 12€ adults, 9€ seniors, 6€ children. Zoo and aquarium 18€ adults, 14€ seniors, 9€ children. Zoo Nov–Feb daily 9am–5pm; Mar daily 9am–5:30pm; Apr–Sept daily 9am–6:30pm; Oct daily 9am–6pm. Aquarium year-round daily 9am–6pm. S-Bahn/U-Bahn: Zoologischer Garten.

ORGANIZED TOURS

BUS & BOAT TOURS Some of the best tours are operated by **Severin+Kühn,** Kurfürstendamm 216 (© **030/880-41-90;** www.berlinerstadtrundfahrten.de), which offers half a dozen tours of Berlin and its environs. Their 3-hour **"Berlin Classic Live Tour"** departs at 30-minute intervals April to October daily from 10am to 6pm. Priced at 19€ per person, 9.50€ ages 6 to 14, the tour passes most of the important attractions using buses equipped with taped commentaries in eight languages. Among the attractions visited are the Europa-Center, the Brandenburg Gate, and Unter den Linden.

You can supplement this bus tour with a 1-hour boat ride on the Spree, which will carry you past the riverbanks and among some of the backwater harbors that are difficult to access except by water. The boat-tour supplement is available only April to October, with departures at 10:30am Wednesday, Friday, and Sunday for 29€ per person. The Severin+Kühn drivers and staff, at the end of the bus-tour portion of the experience, will deposit you at the appropriate quays (either adjacent to the Berliner Dom or in the Nikolaiviertel, depending on the day of your visit) in time for the boat's departure.

One interesting tour lasts 4 hours and visits Potsdam and Sans Souci Palace, former residence of Frederick the Great. The price is 39€ per person. Departures are Tuesday, Thursday, Saturday, and Sunday at 10am; May and October, there are additional departures Friday, Saturday, and Sunday at 2:15pm.

The Shopping Scene

The central shopping destinations are **Kurfürstendamm, Tauentzienstrasse, Am Zoo,** and **Kantstrasse.** You might also want to walk up streets that intersect with Tauentzienstrasse: Marburger, Ranke, and Nürnberger. Most stores are open Monday through Friday from 9 or 10am to 6 or 6:30pm. Many stores stay open late on Thursday evening, usually until about 8:30pm. Saturday hours for most stores are from 9 or 10am to 2pm.

One of Berlin's largest indoor shopping centers, topped by the Mercedes-Benz logo, is the **Europa-Center,** Breitscheidplatz Tauentzienstrasse (© **030/264-97-940;** U-Bahn: Kurfürstendamm), in the heart of the western city. You'll find a number of restaurants and cafes, in addition to an array of shops offering wide-ranging merchandise.

The city's largest shopping and entertainment complex is the **Potsdamer Platz Arkaden,** Alte Potsdamer Strasse 7 (© **030/25-59-27-0**), where you'll find nearly 150 shops, cafes, and restaurants on three different levels. The square is also home to the Grand Hyatt Berlin and a movie complex as well as the Berlin casino.

Berlin-Mitte

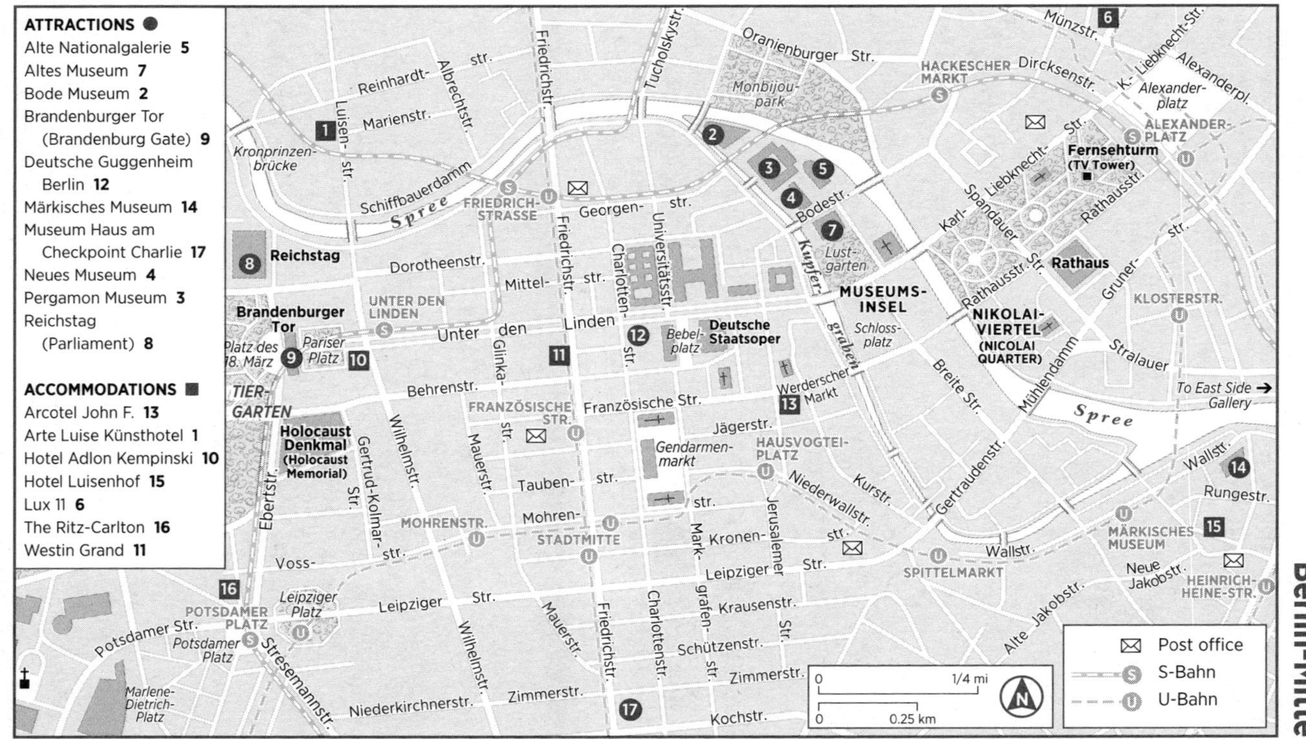

TWO STORES WORTH A LOOK

Known popularly as KaDeWe (pronounced Kah-*Day*-Vay), **Kaufhaus des Westens,** Wittenbergplatz (✆ **030/21-21-0;** www.kadewe.de; U-Bahn: Wittenbergplatz), is about 2 blocks from the Kurfürstendamm. The huge luxury store, whose name means "department store of the west," was established some 75 years ago. Displaying extravagant items, it's known mainly for its sixth-floor food department. It's been called the greatest food emporium in the world. More than 1,000 varieties of German sausages are displayed, and delicacies from all over the world are shipped in.

KPM, Wegelystrasse 1 (✆ **030/39-009-0;** http://en.kpm-berlin.com; S-Bahn: Tiergarten), is one of Europe's most prestigious emporiums of luxury dinnerware. Königliche Porzellan Manufaktur was founded in 1763 when Frederick the Great invested his personal funds in a lackluster porcelain factory and elevated it to royal status. Each item is hand-painted, hand-decorated, and hand-packed in almost unbreakable formats that can be shipped virtually anywhere.

Berlin After Dark

The German *Zitty* and *Tip* include some listings in English, and keep you informed about various nightlife and cultural venues. Both *Berlin Programm* and *Kultur!news* also contain theater listings and other diversions. Performance arts are also covered in *Berlin,* a quarterly published in both English and German. These pamphlets and magazines are available at news kiosks.

THE PERFORMING ARTS

The **Berliner Philharmonisches Orchester (Berlin Philharmonic)** is one of the world's premier orchestras. Its home, the **Philharmonie,** in the Kulturforum, Herbert-von-Karajan Strasse 1 (✆ **030/254-88-999;** www.berliner-philharmoniker.de; U-Bahn: Potsdamer Platz), is a significant piece of modern architecture; you may want to visit even if you don't attend a performance. None of the 2,218 seats is more than 30m (100 ft.) from the rostrum. The box office is open Monday to Friday 3 to 6pm and Saturday and Sunday 11am to 2pm. You can place orders by phone at ✆ **030/25-48-89-99.** If you're staying in a first-class or deluxe hotel, you can usually get the concierge to obtain seats for you. Tickets are 20€ to 85€, special concerts 40€ to 120€.

The famed **Deutsche Oper Berlin (Berlin Opera),** Bismarckstrasse 35 (✆ **030/34-384-343;** www.deutscheoperberlin.de; U-Bahn: Deutsche Oper; S-Bahn: Charlottenburg), performs in one of the world's great opera houses, built on the site of the prewar opera house in Charlottenburg. A ballet company performs once a week. Concerts, including *Lieder* evenings, are also presented on the opera stage. Tickets are 12€ to 125€.

Deutsche Staatsoper (German State Opera), Unter den Linden 7 (✆ **030/20-35-44-38;** www.staatsoperberlin.de; U-Bahn: Französische Strasse), presents some of the finest opera in the world, along with a regular repertoire of ballet and concerts. Its home was rebuilt within the walls of the original 1740s Staatsoper, destroyed in World War II. The box office generally is open Monday to Friday 11am to 7pm and Saturday and Sunday 2 to 7pm. Concert tickets are 15€ to 56€; opera tickets are 5€ to 160€. The opera closes from late June to the end of August.

Komische Oper Berlin, Behrensstrasse 55–57 (✆ **030/20-26-00;** www.komische-oper-berlin.de; U-Bahn: Französische Strasse; S-Bahn: Friedrichstrasse or Unter den Linden), lies in the middle of the city near Brandenburger Tor. Over the

COME TO THE cabaret!

If you know how to sing "Life is a cabaret, old chum," in German no less, you may enjoy an evening in this postwar "Porcupine." Like its namesake, **Die Stachelschweine,** Tauentzienstrasse and Budapester Strasse (in the basement of the Europa-Center; ✆ **030/261-47-95;** www.stachelschweine-berlin.de; U-Bahn: Kurfürstendamm), pokes prickly fun at German, and often American, politicians. Get a ticket early, because the Berliners love this one. The box office is open Tuesday to Friday 11am to 2pm and 3 to 7:30pm, and Saturday 10am to 2pm and 3 to 8:45pm. Shows are presented Tuesday to Friday at 8pm and Saturday at 6 and 9pm. Cover is 13€ to 28€. The cabaret is closed during July.

Opened in 1893 as one of the most popular purveyors of vaudeville in Europe, the **Wintergarten,** Potsdamer Strasse 96 (✆ **030/588-43-40;** www.wintergarten-berlin.de; U-Bahn: Kurfürstenstrasse), was operated in fits and starts throughout the war years, until it was demolished in 1944 by Allied bombers. In 1992, a modernized design reopened. Today, it's the largest and most nostalgic Berlin cabaret, laden with schmaltzy reminders of yesteryear and staffed with chorus girls; magicians from America, Britain, and countries of the former Soviet bloc; circus acrobats; political satirists; and musician/dancer combos. Shows begin at 8pm Monday to Friday, at 6 and 10pm Saturday, and at 6pm Sunday. Shows last around 2¼ hours. The box office is open Monday to Saturday 10am to 6pm and Sunday 2 to 6pm. Cover Friday and Saturday is 25€ to 55€, Sunday to Thursday 15€ to 45€, depending on the seat. The price including a two-course meal is 82€. On Friday and Saturday, the price including a two-course meal is 87€. The price includes your first drink.

years, it has become one of the most innovative theater ensembles in Europe, presenting many avant-garde productions. The box office is open Monday to Saturday 11am to 7pm and Sunday 1pm until 1½ hours before the performance. Tickets are 8€ to 110€.

LIVE-MUSIC CLUBS

A-Trane, Bleibtreustrasse 105 (✆ **030/313-25-50;** www.a-trane.de; S-Bahn: Savignyplatz), is a small and smoky jazz house where virtually everyone seems to have a working familiarity with great names from the jazz world's past and present. The name is a hybrid of the old Duke Ellington standard "Take the 'A' Train," with the "ane" in "Trane" derived from the legendary John Coltrane's name. It's open daily at 8pm; music begins around 10pm. Closing hours vary. Cover is 10€ to 30€, depending on who's playing.

With its kitschy knickknacks, colored lights, and wine-red walls, **Wild at Heart,** Wienerstrasse 20 (✆ **030-6-11-92-31;** www.wildatheartberlin.de; U-Bahn: Görlitzer Bahnhof), is dedicated to the rowdier side of rock. Hard-core punk, rock, and rockabilly bands from Germany and elsewhere are featured. Live performances take place Wednesday to Saturday nights. It's open Monday to Friday 8pm to 3am, and Saturday and Sunday 8pm to 10am (yes, you may miss breakfast). Cover is 10€ to 20€.

Hypertrendy **Oxymoron,** in the courtyard at Rosenthaler Strasse 40–41 (✆ **030/283-91-88-6;** www.oxymoron-berlin.de; S-Bahn: Hackenschen Höfe), is a lot of fun on most nights. The setting is a high-ceilinged room with old-fashioned proportions and enough battered kitsch to remind you of a century-old coffeehouse in Franz-Josef's Vienna. Local wits refer to it as a Gesamtkunstwerk—a self-obsessed, self-sustaining work of art that might have been appreciated by Wagner. On Friday and Saturday after around 11pm, a slightly claustrophobic, much-used annex room—all black with ghostly flares of neon—opens as a disco, usually with a clientele that's about 75% hetero and 100% iconoclastic. If live bands appear at all, it will usually be on Thursday. The restaurant is open daily from 11am to 2am. Cover is 8€ to 15€.

Knaack-Klub, Greifswalderstrasse 224 (✆ **030/442-7060;** www.knaack-berlin.de; S-Bahn: Alexanderplatz), is a household name to an army of young clubgoers in Berlin, thanks partly to the fact that its prices are cheaper than those of any other club in the city, and because of its sprawling premises that incorporate four floors, seven bars, a roiling mass of clients, and a huge variety of musical styles. Painted a strident shade of red, it was originally built as a slaughterhouse in the 19th century, with a small part of its echoing interior transformed into a nightclub in 1952. Expect a very loud medley of, among others, "alternative hard-core punk," heavy metal, indie, rock, and disco from the '70s and '80s. There's even a karaoke bar. Some of the bars within this place open nightly at 7pm; and by 9pm, the whole place is usually in full swing, staying open until at least 2am, and sometimes later. Performances by live bands are interspersed with the recorded tunes every Monday, Wednesday, Friday, and Saturday. Depending on what time of night you arrive, the cover charge ranges from 12€ to 20€.

The premises that contain **Opernschänke,** in the Opernpalais, Unter den Linden 5 (✆ **030/202-683;** U-Bahn: Friedrichstrasse), were built in 1762, a fact that seems to add a certain importance to a setting that's undeniably historic, and to the artists who perform their music live. For the most part, this is a restaurant serving Continental food every day from noon to midnight, with the last order accepted at 11:30pm. Main courses cost 15€ to 25€. The food is augmented with live music, usually jazz, Thursday, Friday, and Saturday nights from 6pm to 1am, as well as Sunday afternoon from 11am to 2pm, as part of set-price "Jazz Brunch" costing 28€. After the end of the jazz brunch, the restaurant remains open until 7pm for food and drink.

DANCE CLUBS

Gays, straights, and everybody in between show up at **SO 36,** Oranienstrasse 190 (✆ **030/61-401-308;** www.so36.de; U-Bahn: Görlitzer Bahnhof), for wild action and frantic dancing into the wee hours. A young, vibrant Kreuzberg crowd is attracted to this joint where the scene changes nightly. On Wednesday and Sunday it's strictly gay and lesbian disco. On Friday and Saturday the parties "get really wild, man," as the bartender accurately promised. Some nights are devoted to themes such as James Bond where you can show up looking like a Cold War spy. Hours are Wednesday through Saturday from 10pm until "we feel like closing," and Sunday from 5pm to 1am. Cover ranges from 6€ to 25€, depending on the venue.

First opened almost 100 years ago, **Clärchens Ballhaus,** Augustrasse 24 (✆ **030/282-9295;** www.ballhaus.de; S-Bahn: Oranienburger Strasse), has reemerged as a landmark in old East Berlin. The legendary dance hall opened in the autumn of 1913 right before the Great War. The club thrived until the end of World War II. A hot DJ and live bands rage through the night, with occasional tango dancers or whatever, even Johann Strauss music. Gypsy street musicians are a favorite. Everybody from wild Turks out for a night on the town to elderly East Berlin couples fill the joint. Nazi officers once used the top floor as a private club. It's usually open from 7 to 11pm but not every night, so call before heading here.

Club der Visionaere, Am Flutgraben 1 (✆ **030/6951-8942;** www.clubdervisionaere.de; U-Bahn: Schlesischestor), is a riverside bar in Kreuzberg that, on any busy night, looks like a shipwreck. A hip 20-something crowd rocks here until the sun rises. Outside look for the concrete watchtower across the street, one of the last surviving that were built by East German police to guard the wall. In summer, the outdoor deck is the site of late-night dance parties, including one that begins on Sunday and lasts until the wee hours of Monday. The cost of a beer and cover is only 6€. DJ of the night plays house music. Open Monday to Friday 2pm to 4am, Saturday and Sunday until dawn.

Watergate Club, Falckensteinstrasse 49 (✆ **030/612-803-94;** www.water-gate.de; U-Bahn: Schlesischestor), is one of Berlin's coolest bars along the Spree River. During the Cold War, Berlin turned its back to the river, which was divided with East Germany. But today riverfront nightlife is flourishing, none more so than at the Watergate, sprawling across two floors, with rotating DJs. Take in the view of the river from the Water Floor Lounge. Cover is 6€, rising to 10€ on Friday and Saturday. Open Wednesday and Friday 11pm to around 4am, Saturday midnight to dawn.

Day Trip from Berlin

POTSDAM ★★★

Of all the tours possible from Berlin, the best attraction is the baroque town of Potsdam, 24km (15 miles) southwest of Berlin on the Havel River, often called Germany's Versailles. From the beginning of the 18th century it was the residence and garrison town of the Prussian kings. World attention focused on Potsdam from July 17 to August 2, 1945, when the Potsdam Conference shaped postwar Europe.

West of the historic core lies **Sans Souci Park,** with its palaces and gardens. Northwest of Sans Souci are the New Garden and the Cecilienhof Palace, on the Heiliger See.

GETTING THERE There are 29 daily connections by rail from Bahnhof Zoo (trip time: 23 min.) and Berliner Hauptbahnhof (54 min.). For rail information in Potsdam, call ✆ **018/05-99-66-33.** Potsdam can also be reached by S-Bahn (30 min.). Car access is via the E-30 Autobahn east and west or the E-53 north and south.

VISITOR INFORMATION The organization known as **Tourist-Information der Stadt Potsdam** maintains two offices in Potsdam, one at Brandenburger-Strasse 3 and another at the **Neuer Markt** (both branches can be reached at ✆ **0331/275-58-50;** www.potsdam-tourism.com). Both branches are open April to October, Monday to Friday 9am to 7pm, Saturday and Sunday 9am to 4pm; November to March, Monday to Friday 10am to 6pm, Saturday and Sunday 10am to 4pm.

EXPLORING POTSDAM In the 18th century, Prussia's answer to Paris's Château de Versailles was clustered within the **Sans Souci Park ★★★**, whose gardens and fountains represented the finest and most elegant aspect of north Germany during the Age of Enlightenment. Covering about a square mile of terraced, statue-dotted grounds, a very short walk west of Potsdam's center, it's the destination of many locals, who stroll around its precincts, perhaps reflecting on another era of

German history. You can enter from many points around the perimeter of the park, but the main entrance, and the one closest to the park's major monument, is in **Zur Historisches Mühle,** inside of which you'll find the Besucher Zentrum (Welcome Station; © **0331/96-94-200;** www.historische-muehle-potsdam.de). Whereas you can visit the park's buildings only during the hours noted below, you can stroll within most areas of the park at any hour.

Frederick II ("the Great") chose Potsdam rather than Berlin as his permanent residence. The style of the buildings he ordered erected is called Potsdam rococo, an achievement primarily of Georg Wenzeslaus von Knobelsdorff. Knobelsdorff built **Sans Souci Palace ★★★**, with its terraces and gardens, as a summer residence for Frederick II. The palace, inaugurated in 1747, is a long one-story building crowned by a dome and flanked by round pavilions. The music salon is the supreme example of the rococo style, and the elliptical Marble Hall is the largest in the palace. As a guest of the king, Voltaire visited in 1750.

The Palace of Sans Souci is open April to October, daily 9am to 5pm; November to March, Tuesday to Sunday 9am to 4pm. You'll have to visit its interior as part of a guided, 40-minute tour that's conducted mostly in German, and which costs 8€ for adults and 5€ for children 17 and under. Entrance is free for children 5 and under.

Schloss Charlottenhof ★, south of Okonomieweg (© **0331/969-42-28;** tram: 1 or 4), was designed by Karl Friedrich Schinkel, the great neoclassical master, and built between 1826 and 1829. He erected the palace in the style of a villa and designed most of the furniture inside. It's open only between May and October, every Tuesday to Sunday from 10am to 5pm, and completely closed the rest of the year. Guided tours, mostly in German, depart at 30-minute intervals throughout opening hours, and are priced at 4€ for adults, 3€ for children 6 to 17, free for children 5 and under.

North of the 80-hectare (198-acre) park, the **Cecilienhof Palace ★**, Im Neuer Garten (© **0331/969-42-00;** www.spsg.de; tram: 92 or 95, and then bus no. 692), was built in the style of an English country house by Kaiser Wilhelm II between 1913 and 1917. The 176-room mansion became the new residence of Crown Prince Wilhelm of Hohenzollern. It was occupied as a royal residence until March 1945, when the crown prince and his family fled to the West, taking many of their possessions. Cecilienhof was the headquarters of the 1945 Potsdam Conference. It's open year-round, Tuesday through Sunday, as follows: April through October from 9am to 5pm; November through March from 9am to 4pm. Between November and March visitors can see the palace interior only as part of a guided tour; adults pay 4€, and children 6 and under and students pay 3€. Between April and October guided tours are 6€ for adults, 5€ for children 6 and under and students; during this period (Apr–Oct), if visitors opt not to participate in the guided tour, they're free to visit the palace on their own for 4€ for adults and 3€ for students.

MUNICH ★★★ & THE BAVARIAN ALPS ★★

Sprawling Munich, home of some 1.5 million people and such industrial giants as Siemens and BMW, is the pulsating capital and cultural center of Bavaria. One of Germany's most festive cities, Munich exudes a hearty Bavarian *Gemütlichkeit* (cheer).

Longtime resident Thomas Mann wrote, "Munich sparkles." Although the city he described was swept away by some of the most severe bombing of World War II, Munich continues to sparkle, as it introduces itself to thousands of new visitors annually.

The Munich cliché as a beer-drinking town of folkloric charm is marketed by the city itself. Despite a roaring gross national product, Munich likes to present itself as a large, agrarian village peopled by jolly beer drinkers who cling to rustic origins despite the omnipresence of symbols of the computer age, high-tech industries, a sophisticated business scene, a good deal of Hollywood-style glamour, and fairly hip night action. Bavarians themselves are a minority in Munich—more than two-thirds of the population comes from other parts of the country or from outside Germany—but everybody buys into the folkloric charm and schmaltz.

Essentials

Getting There

BY PLANE The **Munich International Airport** (✆ **089/97-52-13-13;** www.munich-airport.de) lies 27km (17 miles) northeast of central Munich at Erdinger Moos.

S-Bahn (✆ **089/41-42-43-44**) trains connect the airport with the Hauptbahnhof (main railroad station) in downtown Munich, with departures every 20 minutes for the 40-minute trip. The fare is 10€; Eurailpass holders ride free. A taxi into the center costs about 50€ to 60€. You can also take the Lufthansa Airport Bus, which runs directly into the heart of Munich, with just one stop in Schwabing. The trip takes 35 to 50 minutes, depending on traffic, and costs 10€ to 15€ round-trip.

BY TRAIN Munich's main rail station, the **Hauptbahnhof,** on Bahnhofplatz, is one of Europe's largest. Near the city center, it contains a hotel, restaurants, shops, a parking garage, and banking facilities. All major German cities are connected to this station, most with service every hour. For information about long-distance trains, call ✆ **0800/150-70-90.**

BY BUS Munich is one of the biggest metropolitan areas in Europe, and as such, receives dozens of buses that congregate here from other parts of Europe. A few of them, including the bus that services central Munich from the airport, stop in the town center, at the **Zentraler BusBahnhof,** immediately adjacent (on the western end) of the city's main railway station (Hauptbahnhof München), with an entrance on the Arnulfstrasse. Note, however, that the majority of long-distance buses pulling into Munich arrive in the city's northern suburbs, at the **Fröttmanning Bus Terminal,** about 7km (about 4⅓ miles) north of the Marienplatz, beside the highway running between Munich and Nürnberg. (From central Munich, take U-Bahn line 6 for a 15-min. ride to reach it.) For information about most bus services coming into Munich from other parts of Germany and the rest of Europe, call **Touring** at ✆ **069/7903-501;** www.touring.de.

VISITOR INFORMATION **Tourist Offices** There are three tourist offices in Munich: Sendlinger Strasse 1 (✆ **089/233-03-00**), open Monday to Friday 8am to 8pm, Saturday 9am to 8pm, and Sunday 10am to 6pm; Bahnhofplatz 2, Monday to Saturday 9am to 8pm, Sunday 10am to 6pm; and Marienplatz in Neuen Rathaus, Monday to Friday 10am to 8pm, Saturday 10am to 4pm. For information call ✆ **089/233-96-500;** www.discover-munich.info.

Munich

ATTRACTIONS ●

Alte Pinakothek **2**
Altes Rathaus **29**
Amalienburg **20**
Antikensammlungen **24**
Asamkirche **14**
Bayerisches Nationalmuseum **22**
Deutsches Museum **34**
Frauenkirche **27**
Glyptothek **5**
Marstallmuseum **21**
Michaelskirche **10**
Museum Brandhorst **17**
Neue Pinakothek **1**
Neues Rathaus **28**
Peterskirche **30**
Pinakothek der Moderne **3**
Residenz **25**
Sammlung-Galerie **23**
Schloss Nymphenburg **19**
Staatsgalerie Moderner Kunst **4**

ACCOMMODATIONS ■

Advokat Hotel **35**
Am Markt **31**
An der Oper **26**
Anna Hotel **8**
Bayerischer Hof & Palais Montgelas **9**
Cortiina **32**
Creatif Hotel Elephant **6**
Eden-Hotel-Wolff **7**
Gästehaus Englischer Garten **18**
Hotel Exquisit **13**
Hotel Jedermann **11**
Hotel Mark **12**
Hotel Vier Jahreszeiten München **33**
La Maison **18**
Pension Westfalia **15**
Uhland Garni **16**

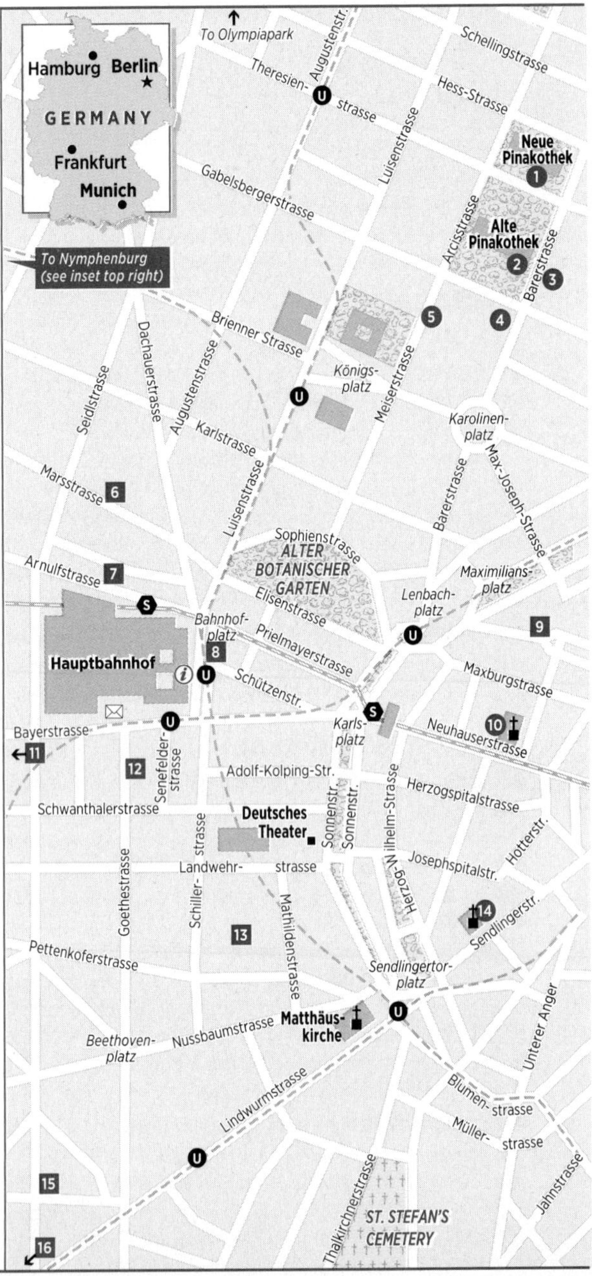

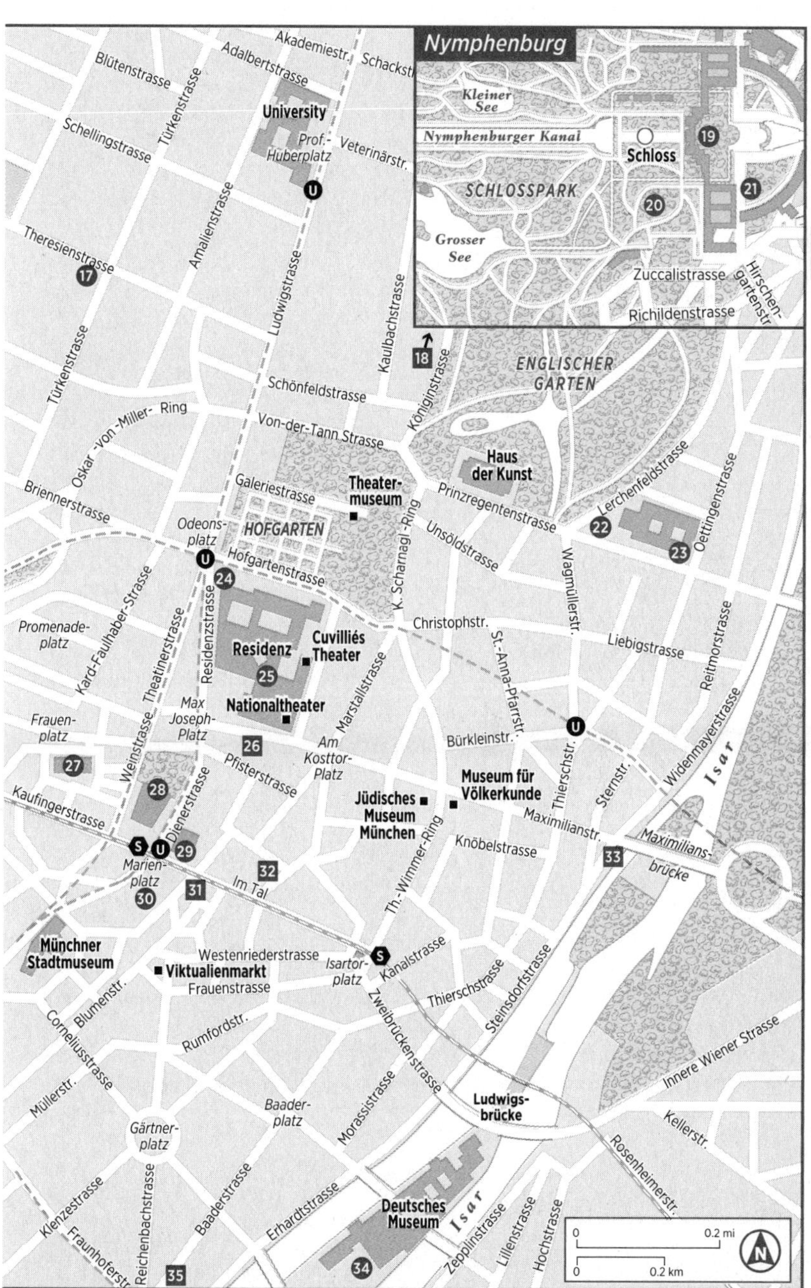

8 GERMANY | Munich & the Bavarian Alps

WEBSITES Updated for each year's Oktoberfest, **www.muenchen.de** from the Munich Tourist Office includes a program of events, a guide to various beer tents, and images from past festivals. Also included are descriptions of hotel packages and discount voucher packages. All things Bavarian are touched on at **www.bayern.by**, including Mad King Ludwig's castle, Oktoberfest beers, and a music raft ride down the river Isar.

A Money-Saving Tip

Munich's S-Bahn is covered by Eurail, so if you have a rail pass, don't buy a separate ticket.

CITY LAYOUT Munich's Hauptbahnhof lies just west of the town center and opens onto Bahnhofplatz. From the square, you can take Schützenstrasse to **Karlsplatz** (nicknamed Stachus), one of the major centers of Munich. Many tram lines converge on this square. From Karlsplatz, you can continue east along the pedestrians-only Neuhäuserstrasse and Kaufingerstrasse until you reach Marienplatz, where you'll be deep in the Altstadt (Old Town) of Munich.

From **Marienplatz,** the center and heart of the city, you can head north on Dienerstrasse, which will lead you to Residenzstrasse and finally to **Max-Joseph-Platz,** a landmark square, with the National Theater and the former royal palace, the Residenz. East of this square runs **Maximilianstrasse,** the most fashionable shopping and dining street of Munich. Between Marienplatz and the National Theater is the **Platzl** quarter, where you'll want to head for nighttime diversions, as it's the seat of some of the finest (and some of the worst) restaurants in Munich, along with the landmark Hofbräuhaus, the most famous beer hall in Europe.

North of the old town is **Schwabing,** the university and former bohemian section whose main street is Leopoldstrasse. The large, sprawling municipal park grounds, the Englischer Garten, are found due east of Schwabing.

GETTING AROUND **By Public Transportation** The city's efficient rapid-transit system is the **U-Bahn,** or Untergrundbahn, one of the most modern subway systems in Europe. The **S-Bahn** rapid-transit system, a 420km (260-mile) network of tracks, provides service to various city districts and outlying suburbs. The city is also served by a network of **trams** and **buses.** The same ticket entitles you to ride the U-Bahn, the S-Bahn, trams, and buses. For more information, call © **089/233-00** or go to www.muenchen.de.

A single-journey ticket for a ride within the city's central zone—a large area that few tourists ever leave—costs 2.30€. If you go to the outermost zones of the subway system, your ride could cost as much as 9.20€. One of the best things about Munich's transit system is that you can make as many free transfers between subways, buses, and trams as you need to reach your destination.

More economical than single-journey tickets is the ***Streifenkarte,*** a strip-ticket that contains 10 units, two of which are annulled for each zone of the system you travel through. A Streifencarte costs 11.50€. Children ages 6 to 14 can purchase a ***Kinderstreifenkarte*** for 11.50€. With this type of ticket, you can travel in one continuous direction during any 2-hour period with unlimited transfers. You can also use it for multiple passengers (for two people to ride two zones, simply stamp four units).

An even better deal may be the ***Tageskarte*** (day ticket), which for 5.20€ gives you unlimited access within the central zone for a full day. Double the price for access to all of Greater Munich—an 80km (50-mile) radius. For more information call ✆ **41-42-43-44;** www.mvv-muenchen.de.

BY TAXI Cabs are relatively expensive—you'll pay 2.70€ when you get inside, plus 1.60€ to 1.90€ per kilometer (⅔ mile); add 1€ if you call for pickup. In an emergency, call ✆ **089/2161-0** or 089/194-10 for a radio-dispatched taxi.

BY CAR Driving in the city, which has an excellent public transportation system, is not advised. The streets around Marienplatz in the Altstadt are pedestrian-only. If you are interested in renting a car locally, try **Sixt Autovermietung,** Einsteinstrasse 106 (✆ **1805/25-25-25;** www.sixt.de), or look under *Autovermietung* in the Munich Yellow Pages.

BY FOOT & BICYCLE Of course, the best way to explore Munich is by foot, as it has a vast pedestrian zone in the center. Many of its attractions can, in fact, be reached only by foot. Pick up a good map and set out.

The tourist office sells a pamphlet that outlines itineraries for touring Munich by bicycle called *Radl-Touren für unsere Gäste,* costing .40€. One of the most convenient places to rent a bike is **Radius Bikes** (✆ **089/59-61-13;** www.radiustours.com), at the far end of the Hauptbahnhof, near lockers opposite tracks 27 and 36. The charge is 14.50€ to 18€ for up to 4 hours, or else 17€ to 22€ from 10am to 6pm. Mountain bikes are rented for about 25% more. A deposit of 50€ is assessed; students and Eurailpass holders are granted a 10% discount. The store is open May to early October daily 10am to 6pm; it's closed November to April.

[Fast FACTS] MUNICH

Business Hours Most **banks** are open Monday to Friday 8:30am to 12:30pm and 1:30 to 3:30pm (many stay open until 5:30pm on Thurs). Most **businesses** and **stores** are open Monday to Friday 9am to 6pm and Saturday 9am to 2pm. On *langer Samstag* (first Sat of the month), stores remain open until 6pm. Many observe an 8 or 9pm closing on Thursday.

Consulates There's a **United States** consulate at Königinstrasse 5 (✆ **089/288-80;** U-Bahn: Universitäl); hours are Monday to Friday 8 to 11am. The consulate of **Canada** at Tal Strasse 29 (✆ **089/219-95-70;** U-Bahn: Marienplatz) is open Monday to Thursday 9am to noon and 2 to 5pm, Friday 9am to noon and 2 to 3:30pm. The Consulate General Office for the **United Kingdom** at Möhlstrasse 5 (✆ **089/21-10-90;** U-Bahn: Prinzregentenplatz) is open Monday to Friday 8:30am to noon and 1 to 3:30pm. The governments of Australia and New Zealand do not maintain offices in Munich.

Currency See "Fast Facts: Berlin," p. 369.

Currency Exchange You can get a better rate at a bank than at your hotel. On weekends or at night, you can exchange money at the Hauptbahnhof exchange, open daily from 6am to 11:30pm.

Dentists & Doctors For an English-speaking dentist, go to **Klinik und Poliklinik für Kieferchirurgie der Universität München,** Lindwurmstrasse 2A (✆ **089/51-60-00;** U-Bahn: Goetheplatz); it deals with emergency cases and is always open. The American, British, and Canadian consulates keep a list of recommended English-speaking physicians. For dental or medical emergencies, call **Notfallpraxis,** Elisenstrasse 3 (✆ **089/55-17-71;** bus: 69). It's open Monday, Tuesday, and Thursday from 7 to 11pm; Wednesday and Friday from 2 to 11pm; and Saturday, Sunday, and holidays from 8am to 11pm.

Drugstores For an international drugstore where English is spoken, go to **Bahnhof Apotheke,** Bahnhofplatz 2 (✆ **089/59-41-19;** U-Bahn/S-Bahn: Hauptbahnhof), open Monday to Friday from 8am to 6:30pm and Saturday from 8am to 2pm. If you need a prescription filled during off-hours, call ✆ **089/55-76-61** for information about what's open. The information is recorded and in German only, so you may need to get someone from your hotel staff to assist you.

Emergencies Call the police at ✆ **110.**

Internet Access You can send e-mails or check your messages at the **Easy Internet Café,** Bahnhofplatz 1; U-Bahn: Hauptbahnhof. It's open daily 7:30am to 11:45pm.

Post Office The most central post office is at Bahnhofplatz (U-Bahn/S-Bahn: Hauptbahnhof), opposite the main train-station exit. It's open Monday to Friday 7am to 8pm, and Saturday 9am to 4pm. You can have your mail sent here Poste Restante (general delivery), but include the postal code 80335. You'll need a passport to claim mail, and you can't call for information but have to show up in person.

Telephone The **country code** for Germany is **49.** The **city code** for Munich is **89.** Use this code when you're calling from outside Germany; if you're within Germany, use **089.**

Where to Stay

VERY EXPENSIVE

Bayerischer Hof & Palais Montgelas ★★★ A Bavarian version of New York's Waldorf-Astoria, this hotel is in a swank location, opening onto a little tree-filled square. Rooms range from medium to extremely spacious, each with plush duvets; many beds are four-posters. Decor ranges from Bavarian provincial to British country-house chintz. The large bathrooms have private phones and state-of-the-art luxuries.

Promenadeplatz 2–6, 80333 München. ✆ **089/2-12-00.** Fax 089/21-20-906. www.bayerischerhof.de. 350 units. 340€–490€ double; 550€–800€ junior suite; 1,600€–3,100€ suite. AE, DC, MC, V. Parking 28€. Tram: 19. **Amenities:** 4 restaurants; 5 bars; nightclub; babysitting; concierge; exercise room; pool (outdoor, rooftop); room service; sauna. *In room:* TV, hair dryer, minibar, Wi-Fi (26€ per day).

Hotel Vier Jahreszeiten München ★★★ This grand hotel, with a tradition dating from 1858, is the most elegant place to stay in Munich. Rooms range from medium to very spacious. Bedside controls, luxury furnishings, and Oriental rugs, plus spacious bathrooms with showers, will keep any guest comfortable. The restaurant is one of the most esteemed in Germany.

Maximilianstrasse 17, 80539 München. ✆ **800/426-3135** in the U.S., or 089/212-2799. Fax 089/21-25-20-00. www.kempinski.com/munich. 316 units. 255€–470€ double; 754€–1,021€ junior suite; from 1,218€ suite. AE, DC, MC, V. Parking 24€. Tram: 19. **Amenities:** Restaurant; 3 bars; bistro; babysitting; concierge; exercise room; indoor pool; room service; sauna. *In room:* A/C, TV, hair dryer, Wi-Fi (25€ per day).

EXPENSIVE

Advokat Hotel This hotel occupies a 1930s apartment house. Its streamlined interior borrows in discreet ways from Bauhaus and minimalist models. The rooms look as if Philippe Starck had gone on a shopping binge at Ikea. All come with neatly kept bathrooms. The result is an aggressively simple, clean-lined, and artfully spartan hotel with very few extras and facilities.

Baaderstrasse 1, 80469 München. ✆ **089/21-63-10.** Fax 089/21-63-190. www.hotel-advokat.de. 50 units. 165€–285€ double. Rates include breakfast. AE, DC, MC, V. Parking 12€. S-Bahn: Isartor. **Amenities:** Breakfast room. *In room:* TV, hair dryer, minibar, Wi-Fi (free).

An der Oper ★ Just off Maximilianstrasse, near Marienplatz, this is a superb base for sightseeing or shopping in the traffic-free malls, just steps from the Bavarian National Theater. Built in the 1970s, it's one of the best-run hotels in this price category. Recently renovated rooms, which range from small to medium, have such amenities as double-glazed windows, firm beds, a small sitting area, and a table for those who want breakfast in their rooms. Bathrooms are medium in size and beautifully maintained.

Falkenturmstrasse 11, 80331 München. ✆ **089/290-02-70.** Fax 089/290-02-729. www.hotelanderoper.com. 68 units. 180€–270€ double; 246€–390€ apt. Rates include buffet breakfast. AE, MC, V. Parking 15€ per day. Tram: 19. **Amenities:** Restaurant. *In room:* TV, fridge, Internet (5€ per day).

Anna Hotel In 1900 this building was a four-story office block, but in 2002 it was converted into a stylish and streamlined hotel. This clean, charming, well-managed hotel has a minimalist and stylish decor that's loaded with wood paneling and warm tones of ocher and russet, with touches of yellow and black marble in all the bathrooms. A collection of postmodern sculptures in the lobby are by Stephan Ester, a locally well-known artist. Many of the hotel clients are business travelers who appreciate the stylish and well-choreographed service and the comfortably secure bedrooms. Four of the suites are in a tower that affords exceptionally good views.

Schützenstrasse 1, 80335 München. ✆ **089/59-99-40.** Fax 089/55-99-43-33. www.annahotel.de. 73 units. 205€–275€ double; 270€–560€ tower rooms. Rates include breakfast and free access to nonalcoholic contents of minibar. MC, V. Parking 22€. U-Bahn: Karlsplatz or Hauptbahnhof. **Amenities:** Restaurant; bar; free access to health club and sauna at the Anna's sister hotel. *In room:* A/C, TV, hair dryer, minibar, Wi-Fi (free).

Cortiina ★ 🎁 Built in 2001, this hotel has quickly gained a foothold with a corps of loyal business clients. It rises five stories above a centrally located and historic neighborhood in the heart of Munich, in a cozy and warm design that evokes an alpine retreat. You'll find a sheathing of intricately crafted dark-stained oak and exposed flagstones in both the public areas and the bedrooms, and an allegiance throughout to the design principles of feng shui, wherein objects, windows, traffic patterns, and doors are balanced for a maximum of emotional and psychic harmony.

Lederstrasse 8, 80331 München. ✆ **089/242-24-90.** Fax 089/242249-100. www.cortiina.com. 30 units. 225€–390€ double; 245€–365€ studio; 275€–465€ suite. AE, DC, MC, V. Parking 15€–19€. S-Bahn: Marienplatz. **Amenities:** Breakfast room; honor bar; babysitting; room service. *In room:* TV/DVD, hair dryer, minibar, MP3 docking station, Wi-Fi (free).

Eden-Hotel-Wolff ★ If you must stay near the train station, this is your best bet, a hotel that lies directly across the street from the Munich terminus of the Lufthansa Airport Bus. With some exceptions, most rooms are spacious, their styles ranging from modern to rustic Bavarian. Rooms have luxurious appointments and double-glazed windows, and the large bathrooms have tub/shower combos. Some rooms are hypoallergenic with special beds and a private ventilation system.

Arnulfstrasse 4-8, 80335 München. ✆ **089/55-11-50.** Fax 089/551-15-555. www.eden-hotel-wolff-muenchen.de. 210 units. 158€–286€ double; 259€–346€ junior suite. 1 child up to age 6 stays free in parent's room. AE, DC, MC, V. Parking 17€. U-Bahn/S-Bahn: Hauptbahnhof. **Amenities:** Restaurant; bar; babysitting; concierge; room service. *In room:* TV, hair dryer, Wi-Fi (10€ per day).

MODERATE

Gästehaus Englischer Garten ★ This oasis of charm and tranquillity, close to the Englischer Garten, is one of our preferred stopovers. The decor of the rooms might be termed "Bavarian grandmother." Bathrooms are small and not one of the hotel's stronger features. In an annex across the street are 15 small apartments, each with a shower-only bathroom and a tiny kitchenette. Try for room no. 16, 23, 26, or especially 20; all are more spacious, are better furnished, and have better views. In fair weather, breakfast is served in a rear garden.

Liebergesellstrasse 8, 80802 München-Schwabing. ✆ **089/38-39-41-0.** Fax 089/38-39-41-33. www.hotelenglischergarten.de. 28 units, 22 with bathroom. 75€–109€ double without bathroom; 129€–169€ double with bathroom; 110€–163€ apt. AE, DC, MC, V. Parking 9€. U-Bahn: Münchner Freiheit. *In room:* TV, kitchenette (in some), minibar, Wi-Fi (12€ per day).

Hotel Exquisit ★ One of the most appealing hotels in the Sendlinger Tot neighborhood lies behind a wine-colored facade on a quiet residential street that seems far removed from the heavy traffic and bustle of the nearby theater district. Built in 1988, it has a paneled lobby whose focal point is a lounge that gets busy around 6 or 7pm. Staff is pleasant, offering a genuine welcome and ushering you up to rooms that are spacious and comfortably furnished. About half overlook an ivy-draped garden; others look over the street.

Pettenkoferstrasse 3, 80336 München. ✆ **089/55-19-900.** Fax 089/199-499. www.hotel-exquisit.com. 50 units. 145€–285€ double; 189€–315€ suite. Rates include breakfast. AE, DC, MC, V. Parking 22€. U-Bahn: Sendlinger Tor. **Amenities:** Restaurant; bar; Internet (free); room service. *In room:* TV, hair dryer, minibar.

Hotel Mark This hotel near the Hauptbahnhof's south exit is known for comfort and moderate prices. The rooms are functionally furnished, although a bit cramped, and furnishings were recently renewed, so you should sleep in peace. Bathrooms are small but tidily maintained, each with a shower unit. Breakfast is the only meal served.

Senefelderstrasse 12, 80336 München. ✆ **089/55-98-20.** Fax 089/559-82-2444. www.hotel-mark.de. 95 units. 82€–202€ double. Rates include buffet breakfast. AE, DC, MC, V. Parking 14€–17€. U-Bahn/S-Bahn: Hauptbahnhof. **Amenities:** Breakfast room. *In room:* TV, hair dryer, minibar, Wi-Fi (15€ per day).

La Maison ★ Many discriminating guests prefer to stay in the increasingly trendy Altschwabing district, with its chic cafes and nightclubs. Americans who stay here find that La Maison has a "California vibe." Everything seems designed to make a guest feel at home. The interiors of the midsize bedrooms mix modern design and charm and informal comfort. The cuisine at the La Maison bar and restaurant is recommended even if you're not an overnight guest. It's been defined as a California-lifestyle cuisine.

Occamstrasse 24, 80802 Muenchen. ✆ **089/330-35-55-0.** Fax 089/330-34-55-55. www.hotel-la-maison.com. 31 units. 180€–220€ double. AE, MC, V. Parking 15€. U-Bahn: Muenchener Freiheit. **Amenities:** Restaurant; bar; room service. *In room:* TV/DVD, hair dryer, minibar, Wi-Fi (free).

INEXPENSIVE

Am Markt This popular but basic Bavarian hotel stands in the heart of the older section. You're likely to find yourself surrounded by opera and concert artists who stay here to be close to where they perform. The rooms are trim, neat, and small—space to store your stuff is at a minimum. Private bathrooms are also small, and corridor bathrooms are kept quite fresh; all have shower units.

Heiliggeistrasse 6, 80331 München. © **089/22-50-14.** Fax 089/22-40-17. www.hotel-am-markt.eu. 32 units, 16 with bathroom (shower only). 74€–89€ double without bathroom; 99€–199€ double with bathroom. Rates include continental breakfast. MC, V. Parking 15€. U-Bahn/S-Bahn: Marienplatz. *In room:* TV, Wi-Fi (free).

Creatif Hotel Elephant Around the corner from the Bahnhof (the railroad station), this hotel offers one of the best deals in town, but reserve way in advance. The place is rather funky but up to date with a circus-inspired decor. All of its bedrooms, some quite small, have been restored and are well maintained. Bedrooms are spread across five floors, and there is an elevator. The buffet breakfast is of the all-you-can-eat variety. Most of the rooms are inexpensive, but there are a few that are superior and quite luxurious. Of course, you'll pay a high price for these (as evidenced by the wide range of rates below).

Lämmerstrasse 6, 80335 Muenchen. © **089/555-785.** Fax 089/550-1746. www.creatif-hotel-elephant.com. 40 units. 59€–299€ double. Extra bed 15€–99€. Rates include breakfast. AE, MC, V. Public parking nearby. U-Bahn: Hauptbahnhof. **Amenities:** Breakfast room; Internet (free). *In room:* TV.

Hotel Jedermann This pleasant spot's central location and value make it a good choice. It's especially good for families, as both cribs and cots are available. Rooms are generally small and old-fashioned, but are cozy and comfortable. Private bathrooms with shower stalls are also small. A generous breakfast buffet is served in a charming room.

Bayerstrasse 95, 80335 München. © **089/54-32-40.** Fax 089/54-32-41-11. www.hotel-jedermann.de. 55 units. 75€–189€ double. Rates include buffet breakfast. MC, V. Parking 8€. U-Bahn/S-Bahn: Hauptbahnhof. **Amenities:** Breakfast room; bar; Internet (free). *In room:* A/C (in some), hair dryer.

Pension Westfalia Facing the meadow where the annual Oktoberfest takes place, this 19th-century town house near Goetheplatz is one of Munich's top pensions. Rooms range from small to medium, but the owner takes great pride in seeing that they are well maintained and comfortable. Private bathrooms with shower stalls are small, and corridor bathrooms are well maintained and do the job just as well.

Mozartstrasse 23, 80336 München. © **089/53-03-77.** Fax 089/54-39-120. www.pension-westfalia.de. 19 units, 14 with bathroom (shower only). 50€–60€ double without bathroom; 68€–82€ double with bathroom. Rates include continental breakfast. AE, MC, V. Parking, when available, is free on the street. U-Bahn: Goetheplatz. Bus: 58. **Amenities:** Breakfast room. *In room:* TV, hair dryer, Wi-Fi (free).

Uhland Garni In a residential area, just a 10-minute walk from the Hauptbahnhof, the Uhland could easily become your home in Munich. It offers friendly, personal service. The stately town mansion, built in Art Nouveau style, stands in its own small garden. Its rooms are soundproof, traditional, and cozy. Only breakfast is served.

Uhlandstrasse 1, 80336 München. © **089/54-33-50.** Fax 089/54-33-52-50. www.hotel-uhland.de. 30 units. 76€–96€ double. Rates include buffet breakfast. AE, DC, MC, V. Free parking. U-Bahn/S-Bahn: Theresienwiese. Bus: 58. **Amenities:** Breakfast room. *In room:* TV, hair dryer, minibar, Wi-Fi (free).

Where to Dine

For beer halls serving plenty of low-priced food, see the box "What's Brewing at the Beer Halls?" on p. 417.

VERY EXPENSIVE

Restaurant Königshof ★★ INTERNATIONAL/FRENCH On the top floor of this deluxe hotel, this is Munich's best shot at hotel dining. You're rewarded not only with a fine cuisine, but also with a view of the city. Appetizers are sometimes pleasantly startling in their originality, as exemplified by the delicately diminutive rib and loin chops, liver, and rolled duck in a sweet-and-sour ice wine, the flavor enhanced by a pumpkin vinaigrette. Instead of the typical lasagna, you get a pasta layered with morels and crayfish, a real delicacy. The city's best veal dishes are served here; veal sweetbreads rest on a bed of fresh vegetables, including beets and green beans. The wine list is one of the finest in Germany, though it may take you a good hour just to read it.

In the Hotel Königshof, Karlsplatz 25 (Am Stachus). ✆ **089/55-13-60.** www.koenigshof-hotel.de. Reservations required. Main courses 42€–49€; fixed-price menus 90€–198€. AE, DC, MC, V. Tues–Sat noon–2:30pm and 6:30–10:30pm. S-Bahn: Karlsplatz. Tram: 19, 20, or 21.

Tantris ★★★ FRENCH/INTERNATIONAL Tantris serves Munich's finest cuisine. Hans Haas was voted the top chef in Germany in 1994, and, if anything, he has refined and sharpened his culinary technique since. Once inside, you're transported into an ultramodern atmosphere with fine service. You might begin with a terrine of smoked fish served with green cucumber sauce, and then follow with classic roast duck on mustard-seed sauce, or perhaps a delightful concoction of lobster medallions on black noodles. These dishes show a refinement and attention to detail that you find nowhere else in Munich. And just when you think you've had the perfect meal, the dessert arrives, and you're hungry again as you sample the gingerbread soufflé with chestnut sorbet.

Johann-Fichte-Strasse 7, Schwabing. ✆ **089/3-61-95-90.** www.tantris.de. Reservations required. Fixed-price 4-course lunch 115€; fixed-price dinner 165€–210€. AE, DC, MC, V. Tues–Sat noon–2pm and 6:30–1am. Closed public holidays and annual holidays in Jan and May. U-Bahn: Dietlindenstrasse.

EXPENSIVE

Alois Dallmayr ★ CONTINENTAL One of the city's most historic and famous dining spots was established in 1700 as a food shop. Today, you'll find one of the city's most prestigious delicatessens on the street level, and a rather grand restaurant upstairs, where you'll find a subtle German version of Continental cuisine that owes many of its inspirations to France. The food array is rich, varied, and sophisticated, including the best herring and sausages we've ever tasted, very fresh fish, meats, and game dishes. Partially thanks to its dual role as a delicatessen with products imported from around the world, you'll find such rare treats as vine-ripened tomatoes flown in from Morocco, splendid papayas from Brazil, and the famous French hens, *poulets de Bresse,* believed by many gourmets to be the world's finest.

Dienerstrasse 14–15. ✆ **089/213-51-00.** www.dallmayr.de. Reservations recommended. Main courses 40€–47€; set-price menus 95€–128€. AE, DC, MC, V. Mon–Fri 11:30am–7pm; Sat 9am–4pm. Tram: 19.

Boettner's ★ INTERNATIONAL This restaurant is housed in Orlandohaus, a Renaissance structure in the very heart of Munich. Culinary fans from yesterday will recognize its wood-paneled interior, which was dismantled from a previous site and moved here. The cookery is lighter and more refined, and seems better than ever. Try the lobster stew in a cream sauce and almost any dish with white truffles. Pike balls appear delectably in a Chablis herb sauce, and succulent lamb or venison appear enticingly in a woodsy morel sauce. Desserts are as sumptuous as ever. The French influence is very evident, as are many traditional Bavarian recipes.

Pfisterstrasse 9. ✆ **089/22-12-10.** www.boettners.de. Reservations required. Fixed-price lunch 36€; fixed-price dinner 86€. AE, DC, MC, V. Mon–Sat 11:30am–3pm and 6pm–midnight. U-Bahn/S-Bahn: Marienplatz.

Ederer ★★ MODERN INTERNATIONAL Noted as one of the most posh and immediately desirable addresses in Munich, and the culinary domain of celebrity chef Karl Ederer, this restaurant occupies an antique building with huge windows, very high ceilings, several blazing fireplaces, and an appealing collection of paintings. Inspiration for the menu items covers the gamut of cuisines from Bavaria, France, Italy, the New World, and the Pacific Rim. The menu changes with the seasons and the whim of the kitchen staff but might include such starters as marinated sweet-and-sour pumpkin served with shiitake mushrooms, parsley roots, and lukewarm chunks of octopus; and terrine of duckling foie gras with a very fresh brioche and a dollop of pumpkin jelly. Main courses might include a roasted breast of duckling with stuffing, glazed baby white cabbage, mashed potatoes, and gooseliver sauce; or pan-fried angler fish with a sauce made from olive oil, lemon grass, and thyme.

Kardinal Faulhaber Strasse 10. ✆ **089/24-23-13-10.** www.restaurant-ederer.de. Reservations recommended. Main courses 25€–38€; set-price 2-course lunch 29€; set-price 6-course dinner 150€. AE, DC, MC, V. Mon–Sat noon–2pm and 6:30–10pm. U-Bahn: Marienplatz or Odéonsplatz.

MODERATE

Bistro Terrine ★★ FRENCH The restaurant in Schwabing looks like an Art Nouveau French bistro, and its nouvelle cuisine is based on traditional recipes as authentic and savory as anything you'd find in Lyon or Paris. There's room for up to 50 diners at a time, but because of the way the dining room is arranged, with banquettes and wood and glass dividers, it seems bigger than it actually is. During clement weather, there's additional seating on an outdoor terrace.

Menu items are innovative, and might include tartar of herring with freshly made potato chips and salad, watercress salad with sweetbreads, cream of paprika soup, an autumn fantasy of nuggets of venison served with hazelnut-flavored gnocchi in port-wine sauce, zander baked in an herb-and-potato crust, or an alluring specialty salmon with a chanterelle-studded risotto.

Amalienstrasse 89. ✆ **089/28-17-80.** www.restaurant-terrine.de. Reservations recommended. Main courses 14€–32€; fixed-price lunch 14€–26€; fixed-price dinner 79€–89€. AE, MC, V. Tues–Fri noon–3pm; Mon–Sat 6:30pm–midnight. U-Bahn: U3 or U6 to Universität.

Buon Gusto (Talamonti) ★ ITALIAN Some of Munich's best Italian food is served here in the rustic-looking bistro, or in the more formal and more upscale-looking dining room. Menu items and prices are identical in both. Owned and managed by an extended family, the Talamontis, the restaurant emphasizes fresh ingredients, strong and savory flavors, and food items inspired by the Italian Marches and Tuscany. Stellar examples include ravioli stuffed with mushrooms and herbs, roasted lamb with potatoes, lots of scaloppine, and fresh fish that seems to taste best when served simply, with oil or butter and lemon. Especially appealing are the array of risottos whose ingredients change with the seasons. During Oktoberfest and trade fairs, the place is mobbed.

Hochbruckenstrasse 3. ✆ **089/296-383.** www.buon-gusto-talamonti.de. Reservations recommended. Main courses 12€–28€. AE, MC, V. Mon–Sat 11am–1am. Closed Dec 23–Jan 3. U-Bahn/S-Bahn: Marienplatz.

Hunsingers Pacific ★ SEAFOOD Despite the name, don't expect the menu to be devoted exclusively to Pacific Rim cuisine. Fish is the premier item here. Preparation is based on classic French-inspired methods, but the innovative flavors come from Malaysia (coconut milk), Japan (wasabi), Thailand (lemon grass), and India (curry). You could begin with a tuna carpaccio with sliced plum, fresh ginger, and lime. Main courses include a succulent version of bouillabaisse with aioli, which you might follow with cold melon soup garnished with a dollop of tarragon-flavored granita. Fried monkfish in the Malaysian style and turbot in chili-and-ginger sauce are evocative of Hawaii. Prices here are relatively low compared to those of its competitors.

Maximilianplatz 5 (entrance on Max-Joseph-Strasse). ✆ **089/5502-9741.** Reservations recommended. Main courses 18€–30€. AE, DC, MC, V. Mon–Fri 11:30am–3:30pm; Mon–Sat 6pm–1am. Closed Sun May–Sept. U-Bahn: Stachus/Odeonsplatz.

Pfistermühle BAVARIAN The country comes right into the heart of Munich at this authentic and old-fashioned place. A warm welcome and a refreshing cuisine await you here. Many of the dishes would be familiar to your Bavarian grandmother, and portions are generous and most satisfying. Come here for some of the most perfectly prepared roasts in the city. You can also opt for a fine array of fresh fish from the lakes and rivers of Bavaria, especially the delectable salmon trout or brown trout. Most fish dishes come with chive-flecked sour cream and a potato pancake. The fish is also simply prepared, such as pikeperch sautéed in butter. Finish with a pyramid of vanilla custard served with a fresh berry sauce, followed by a glass of wild cherry schnapps.

In the Platz Hotel, Pfistermühle 4. ✆ **089/2370-3865.** www.platzl.de. Reservations recommended. Main courses 16€–26€; set menus 35€–45€. AE, DC, MC, V. Mon–Sat 11:30am–midnight. U-Bahn: Marienplatz.

Ratskeller München BAVARIAN Go here for the old Bavarian ambience at one of the best town-hall cellars in the country. The decor is typical: lots of dark wood and carved chairs. The most interesting tables, the ones staked out by in-the-know locals, are the semiprivate dining nooks in the rear, under the vaulted painted ceilings. Bavarian music adds to the ambience. The menu, a showcase of regional fare, includes many vegetarian choices, which is unusual for a rathskeller. Some of the dishes are a little heavy and too porky, but you can find lighter fare if you search the menu.

Im Rathaus, Marienplatz 8. ✆ **089/219-98-90.** www.ratskeller.com. Reservations required. Main courses 8€–27€. AE, MC, V. Daily 10am–midnight. U-Bahn/S-Bahn: Marienplatz.

Spatenhaus ★ BAVARIAN/INTERNATIONAL One of Munich's best-known beer restaurants has wide windows overlooking the opera house on Max-Joseph-Platz. Of course, to be loyal, you should accompany your meal with the restaurant's own beer, Spaten-Franziskaner-Bier. You can sit in an intimate, semiprivate dining nook or at a big table. The Spatenhaus has old traditions, offers typical Bavarian food, and is known for generous portions and reasonable prices. If you want to know what all this fabled Bavarian gluttony is about, order the "Bavarian plate," which is loaded down with various meats, including lots of pork and sausages.

Residenzstrasse 12. ✆ **089/290-70-60.** www.kuffler-gastronomie.de. Reservations recommended. Main courses 11€–31€. AE, MC, V. Daily 9:30am–12:30pm. U-Bahn: Odeonsplatz or Marienplatz.

INEXPENSIVE

Andechser am Dom GERMAN/BAVARIAN Set on two floors of a postwar building erected adjacent to the back side of the Frauenkirche, this restaurant and beer hall serves copious amounts of a beer brewed in a monastery near Munich (Andechser) as well as generous portions of German food. Order a snack, a full meal, or just a beer, and enjoy the frothy fun of it all. Menu items include such dishes as veal schnitzels, steaks, turkey croquettes, roasted lamb, fish, and several kinds of sausages that taste best with tangy mustard. During clement weather, tables are set up on the building's roof and on the sidewalk in front, both of which overlook the back of one of the city's most evocative churches.

Weinstrasse 7A. ✆ **089/29-84-81.** www.andechser-am-dom.de. Reservations recommended. Main courses 8€–17€. AE, DC, MC, V. Daily 10am–1am. U-Bahn/S-Bahn: Marienplatz.

Donisl ★ BAVARIAN/INTERNATIONAL This is one of Munich's oldest beer halls, dating from 1715. The seating capacity of this relaxed and comfortable restaurant is about 550, and in summer you can enjoy the hum and bustle of Marienplatz while dining in the garden area out front. The standard menu offers traditional Bavarian food, as well as a weekly changing specials menu. The little white sausages, Weisswürst, are a decades-long tradition here.

Weinstrasse 1. ✆ **089/29-62-64.** www.bayerischer-donisl.de. Reservations recommended. Main courses 10€–15€. AE, DC, MC, V. Daily 9am–midnight. U-Bahn/S-Bahn: Marienplatz.

Nürnberger Bratwurst Glöckl Am Dom BAVARIAN In the coziest and warmest of Munich's local restaurants, the chairs look as if they were made by some Black Forest woodcarver, and the place is full of memorabilia—pictures, prints, pewter, and beer steins. Upstairs through a hidden stairway is a dining room decorated with reproductions of Dürer prints. The restaurant has a strict policy of shared tables, and service is on tin plates. The homesick Nürnberger comes here just for one dish: *Nürnberger Schweinwurstl mit Kraut* (little sausages with kraut). Last food orders go in at midnight. If you're with a party of between four and eight, consider ordering one of the house specialties, a *Pfanne* (large frying pan) that's loaded with a mixed grill of chops, wursts, and cutlets interspersed with potatoes and vegetables. Many groups of travelers opt for this, helping themselves to the contents as the pan is perched in the center of your table grouping. The cost per Pfanne is 56€ to 108€.

Frauenplatz 9. ✆ **089/29-19-450.** www.bratwurst-gloeckle.de. Reservations recommended. Main courses 8€–22€. MC, V. Mon–Sat 10am–1am; Sun 11am–11pm. U-Bahn/S-Bahn: Marienplatz.

Zum Alten Markt BAVARIAN/INTERNATIONAL Snug and cozy, Zum Alten Markt serves beautifully presented fresh cuisine. Located on a tiny square off Munich's large outdoor food market, the restaurant has a mellow charm and a welcoming host, Josef Lehner. The interior decor, with its intricately coffered wooden ceiling, came from a 400-year-old Tyrolean castle. In summer, tables are set up outside. Fish and fresh vegetables come from the nearby market. You may begin with a tasty homemade soup, such as cream of carrot or perhaps black-truffle tortellini in cream sauce with young onions and tomatoes. The chef makes a great *Tafelspitz* (boiled beef). You can also order classic dishes such as roast duck with applesauce or a savory roast suckling pig.

Am Viktualienmarkt, Dreifaltigkeitsplatz 3. ✆ **089/29-99-95.** www.zumaltenmarkt.de. Reservations recommended. Main courses 8€–20€. No credit cards. Mon–Sat noon–midnight. U-Bahn/S-Bahn: Marienplatz. Bus: 53.

Seeing the Sights

EXPLORING THE ALTSTADT (OLD TOWN)

Marienplatz, dedicated to the patron of the city whose statue stands on a huge column in the center of the square, is the heart of the Altstadt. On its north side is the **Neues Rathaus (New City Hall)** built in 19th-century Gothic style. Each day at 11am, and also at noon and 5pm in the summer, the **Glockenspiel** on the facade performs a miniature tournament, with enameled copper figures moving in and out of the archways. Because you're already at the Rathaus, you may wish to climb the 55 steps to the top of its tower (an elevator is available if you're conserving energy) for a good overall view of the city center. The **Altes Rathaus (Old City Hall),** with its plain Gothic tower, is to the right. It was reconstructed in the 15th century, after being destroyed by fire.

MUSEUMS & PALACES

Alte Pinakothek ★★★ This is one of the most significant art museums in Europe. The paintings represent the greatest European artists of the 14th through the 18th century. Begun as a small court collection by the royal Wittelsbach family in the early 1500s, the collection has grown and grown. There are two floors with exhibits, but the museum is immense. Albrecht Altdorfer, landscape painter par excellence of the Danube school, is represented by no fewer than six monumental works. Albrecht Dürer's works include his greatest—and final—*Self-Portrait* (1500). Here the artist has portrayed himself with almost Christlike solemnity. Also displayed is the last great painting by the artist, his two-paneled work called *The Four Apostles* (1526).

Barer Strasse 27. ✆ **089/238-052-16.** www.pinakothek.de/alte-pinakothek. Admission 13€ adults, 10.50€ students and seniors, free for children 15 and under, 7€ for all Sun. Tues 10am–8pm; Wed–Sun 10am–5pm. U-Bahn: Theresienstrasse. Tram: 27. Bus: 53.

Antikensammlungen (Museum of Antiquities) ★ This collection grew around the vase collection of Ludwig I, who had fantasies of transforming Munich into a second Athens. It was originally known as the Museum Antiker Kleinkunst (Museum of Small Works of Ancient Art). Many pieces displayed within are small in size but not in value or artistic significance. The museum's five main-floor halls house more than 650 Greek vases. The oldest, the pre-Mycenaean "goddess from Aegina" (3000 B.C.) carved from a mussel shell, is in room 1. The upper level of the Central Hall is devoted to large Greek vases discovered in Sicily and to Etruscan art. On the lower level is the collection of Greek, Roman, and Etruscan jewelry. (Note the similarities with today's designer fashions.) Also on this level are rooms devoted to ancient colored glass, Etruscan bronzes, and Greek terra cotta.

Königsplatz 1. ✆ **089/599888-30.** www.antike-am-koenigsplatz.mwn.de. Admission 3.50€ adults, 2.50€ students and seniors, free for children 15 and under. Joint ticket to the Museum of Antiquities and the Glyptothek 5.50€ students and seniors, free for children 15 and under. Tues–Sun 10am–5pm (Thurs to 8pm). U-Bahn: Königsplatz.

Bayerisches Nationalmuseum (Bavarian National Museum) ★★ Three vast floors of sculpture, painting, folk art, ceramics, furniture, textiles, and scientific instruments demonstrate Bavaria's artistic and historical riches. Entering the museum, turn to the right and go into the first large gallery, called the **Wessobrunn Room.** Devoted to early church art from the 5th to the 13th century, this room holds some of the oldest and most valuable works. The desk case contains ancient and medieval ivories, including the so-called Munich ivory, from about A.D. 400. The **Riemenschneider Room** is devoted to the works of the great sculptor Tilman Riemenschneider (ca. 1460–1531) and his contemporaries. The second floor contains a fine collection of stained and painted glass—an art in which medieval Germany excelled—baroque ivory carvings, Meissen porcelain, and ceramics.

Prinzregentenstrasse 3. ✆ **089/211-2401.** www.bayerisches-nationalmuseum.de. Admission 5€ adults, 4€ students and children, 1€ for all Sun. Tues–Sun 10am–5pm; Thurs 10am–8pm. U-Bahn: Lehel. Tram: 17. Bus: 53.

Deutsches Museum (German Museum of Masterpieces of Science and Technology) ★★★ On an island in the Isar River is the largest technological museum of its kind in the world. Its huge collection of priceless artifacts and historic originals includes the first electric dynamo (Siemens, 1866), the first automobile (Benz, 1886), the first diesel engine (1897), and the laboratory bench at which the atom was first split (Hahn, Strassmann, 1938). There are hundreds of buttons to push, levers to crank, and gears to turn, as well as a knowledgeable staff to answer questions and demonstrate how steam engines, pumps, or historical musical instruments work. Among the most popular displays are those on mining, with a series of model coal, salt, and iron mines, as well as the electrical power hall, with high-voltage displays that actually produce lightning. There are many other exhibits, covering the whole range of science and technology.

Museumsinsel 1. ✆ **089/2-17-91.** www.deutsches-museum.de. Admission 8.50€ adults, 7€ seniors, 3€ children 6–15, free for children 5 and under. Daily 9am–5pm. Closed major holidays. S-Bahn: Isartor. Tram: 18. U-Bahn: Fraunhoferstrasse.

Glyptothek ★ This museum has assembled a world-class collection of ancient Greek and Roman sculpture. Included are the famous pediments from the temple of Aegina, two marvelous statues of *kouroi* (youths) from the 6th century B.C., the colossal figure of a *Sleeping Satyr* from the Hellenistic period, and a splendid collection of Roman portraits.

Königsplatz 3. ✆ **089/28-61-00.** www.antike-am-koenigsplatz.mwn.de. Admission 3.50€ adults; 2.50€ students, seniors, and children. Joint ticket to the Glyptothek and the Museum of Antiquities 5.50€ students and seniors, free for children 15 and under. Tues–Sun 10am–5pm; Thurs 10am–8pm. U-Bahn: Königsplatz.

Museum Brandhorst ★ In the Museum Quarter, Udo and Anette Brandhorst have donated their collection of contemporary art, assembled over a lifetime, to this museum, which is unique in Munich. The building, using sustainable "green" features, is the most avant-garde in Munich. Perfectly lit, its exhibits are arranged according to the latest in 21st-century design. Paintings and sculptures range from Andy Warhol to a dozen original editions of books illustrated by Picasso—almost the whole of his *oeuvre* in this field.

The museum owns 60 works by Cy Twombly, an American artist celebrated for his calligraphic-style graffiti paintings. Damien Hirst, the British artist famous for his series of dead animals preserved in formaldehyde, has the most gruesome works on display. Other major works are by sigmar Polke and Gerhard Richter, the leaders of the "Capitalist Realism" school of painting, an anti-style of art inspired by advertising. Currently, the museum owns some 700 modern works of art, although not all of them are on a display at the same time.

Kunstareal, Theresienstrasse 35A. © **089/238-052-286.** www.museum-brandhorst.de. Admission 7€ adults, 5€ children ages 5–16, 1€ for all Sun. Tues–Sun 10am–6pm (Thurs to 8pm). U-Bahn: Königsplatz or Theresienstrasse. Bus: 100 or 154.

Neue Pinakothek ★★ This gallery is a showcase of Munich's most valuable 18th- and 19th-century art, an artistic period that was hardly the Renaissance but has its artistic devotees nonetheless. Across Theresienstrasse from the Alte Pinakothek, the museum has paintings by Gainsborough, Goya, David, Manet, van Gogh, and Monet. Among the more popular German artists represented are Wilhelm Leibl and Gustav Klimt. Note particularly the genre paintings by Carl Spitzweg.

Barer Strasse 29. © **089/23-80-51-95.** www.pinakothek.de/neue-pinakothek. Admission 7€ adults, 5€ students and seniors, free for children 15 and under, 1€ for all Sun. Thurs–Mon 10am–6pm; Wed 10am–8pm. U-Bahn: Theresienstrasse. Tram: 27. Bus: 53.

Pinakothek der Moderne ★★ In 2002, one of the world's largest museums devoted to the visual arts of the 19th and 20th centuries opened in Munich, just minutes from the Alte and Neue Pinakothek. Four major collections have been brought together under one roof, making this the most vast display of fine and applied arts in the country. It's Munich's version of the Tate Gallery in London or the Pompidou in Paris.

Wander where your interest dictates: the **Staatsgalerie Moderner Kunst (State Gallery of Modern Art) ★★★**, with paintings, sculpture, photography, and video; **Die Neue Sammlung,** which constitutes the national museum of applied art featuring design and craftwork; the **Architekturmuseum der Technischen Universität (University of Architecture Museum),** with architectural drawings, photographs, and models; and the **Staatliche Grapische Sammlung,** with its outstanding collection of prints and drawings.

Whenever we visit, we spend most of our time in the modern art collection, lost in a world of some of our favorite artists: Picasso, Magritte, Klee, Kandinsky, even Francis Bacon, de Kooning, and Warhol. The museum also owns 400,000 drawings and prints from Leonardo da Vinci to Cézanne up to contemporary artists. They are presented as alternating exhibits.

The architectural galleries hold the largest specialist collection of its kind in Germany, comprising some 350,000 drawings, 100,000 photographs, and 500 models. The applied arts section features more than 50,000 items. You go from the beginnings of the Industrial Revolution up to today's computer culture, with exhibitions of Art Nouveau and Bauhaus along the way.

Barerstrasse 40. © **089/23805-360.** www.pinakothek.de/pinakothek-der-moderne. Admission 10€ adults, 7€ students 15–25. Fri–Sun and Wed 10am–6pm; Thurs 10am–8pm. U-Bahn: Odeonsplatz.

Residenz ★ The official residence of Bavaria's rulers from 1385 to 1918, the complex is a conglomerate of various styles of art and architecture. Depending on how you approach the Residenz, you might first see a German Renaissance hall (the western facade), a Palladian palace (on the north), or a Florentine Renaissance palace (on the south facing Max-Joseph-Platz). The Residenz has been completely restored since its almost total destruction in World War II and now houses the Residenz Museum, a concert hall, the Cuvilliés Theater, and the Residenz Treasure House.

Residenzmuseum comprises the southwestern section of the palace, some 120 rooms of art and furnishings collected by centuries of Wittelsbachs. There are two guided tours, one in the morning and the other in the afternoon, or you may visit the rooms on your own.

If you have time to view only one item in the **Schatzkammer (Treasure House) ★★**, make it the 16th-century Renaissance statue of *St. George Slaying the Dragon*. The equestrian statue is made of gold, but you can barely see the precious metal for the thousands of diamonds, rubies, emeralds, sapphires, and semiprecious stones embedded in it.

From the Brunnenhof, you can visit the **Cuvilliés Theater ★**, whose rococo tiers of boxes are supported by seven bacchants. The huge box, where the family sat, is in the center. In summer, this theater is the scene of frequent concert and opera performances. Mozart's *Idomeneo* was first performed here in 1781.

Max-Joseph-Platz 3. ✆ **089/29-06-71.** www.residenz-muenchen.de. Admission 9€ adults, 8€ students and seniors, free for children 14 and under. Ticket for either Schatzkammer or Residenzmuseum 6€ adults, 5€ seniors and students, free for children 14 and under. Fri–Wed 9am–6pm; Thurs 10am–8pm. U-Bahn: Odeonsplatz.

Sammlung-Galerie To appreciate this florid and romantic overdose of sentimental German paintings of the 19th century, you've got to enjoy fauns and elves at play in picturesque, even magical, landscapes. Such art has its devotees. Obviously, if you're a Picasso cubist, you'd be better off going elsewhere. But this once-private collection adheres to the baroque tastes of Count Adolf Friedrich von Schack of Schwerin (1815–94), who spent a rich life acquiring works by the likes of Spitzweg, Schwind, Fuerbach, and others, many others, some of whom frankly should have been assigned to the dustbin of art history. Still, in all, we find a visit here fun, at least on a rainy, gray day. It's like wandering back to a lost world and getting absorbed in the taste of yesterday.

Prinzregentenstrasse 9. ✆ **089/23805-224.** www.sammlungschack.de. Admission 4€ adults, 3€ children 15 and under. Wed–Mon 10am–5pm. U-Bahn: U4 or U5 to Lehel.

Schloss Nymphenburg ★★ In summer, the Wittelsbachs would pack up their bags and head for their country house, Schloss Nymphenburg. A more complete, more sophisticated palace than the Residenz, it was begun in 1664 in Italian villa style and went through several architectural changes before completion.

The main building's great hall, decorated in rococo colors and stuccoes with frescoes by Zimmermann (1756), was used for both banquets and concerts. Concerts are still presented here in summer. From the main building, turn left and head for the arcaded gallery connecting the northern pavilions. The first room in the arcade is the Great Gallery of Beauties. More provocative, however, is Ludwig I's Gallery of Beauties in the south pavilion (the apartments of Queen Caroline). Ludwig commissioned no fewer than 36 portraits of the most beautiful women of his day. The paintings by J. Stieler include the *Schöne Münchnerin (Lovely Munich Girl)* and a portrait of Lola Montez, the dancer whose "friendship" with Ludwig I caused a scandal that factored into the revolution of 1848.

To the south of the palace buildings, in the rectangular block of low structures that once housed the court stables, is the **Marstallmuseum.** In the first hall, look for the glass coronation coach of Elector Karl Albrecht, built in Paris in 1740. From the same period comes the elaborate hunting sleigh of Electress Amalia, adorned with a statue of Diana, goddess of the hunt; even the sleigh's runners are decorated with shell work and hunting trophies. The coaches and sleighs of Ludwig II are displayed in the third hall.

One of Nymphenburg's greatest attractions is the **park** ★. Stretching for 200 hectares (494 acres) in front of the palace, it's divided into two sections by the canal that runs from the pool at the foot of the staircase to the cascade at the far end of the English-style gardens.

Within the park are a number of pavilions. The guided tour begins with **Amalienburg** ★★, whose plain exterior belies the rococo decoration inside. Built as a hunting lodge for Electress Amalia (in 1734), the pavilion carries the hunting theme through the first few rooms and then bursts into salons of flamboyant colors, rich carvings, and wall paintings. The most impressive room is the Hall of Mirrors, a symphony of silver ornaments on a faint blue background.

Other attractions include the **Porzellansammlung,** or museum of porcelain, which is above the stables of the Marstallmuseum. Some of the finest pieces of porcelain in the world, executed in the 18th century, are displayed here, along with an absolute gem—extraordinarily detailed miniature porcelain reproductions of some of the grand masterpieces in the Old Pinakothek, each commissioned by Ludwig I.

The **Botanischer Garten (Botanical Gardens)** ★★ is among the most richly planted in Europe. It's worth a spring trip to Munich for garden lovers to see this great mass of vegetation burst into bloom.

Schloss Nymphenburg 1. ✆ **089/17-908-668.** www.schloesser-bayern.de. Admission to all attractions 10€ adults, 8€ students and seniors, free for children 6 and under. Separate admission to Schloss Nymphenburg 5€ adults, 4€ seniors and students. Admission to either Marstallmuseum, Amalienburg, or Porzellansammlung 8€ adults, free for children 15 and under.

CHURCHES

When the smoke cleared from the 1945 bombings, only a fragile shell remained of Munich's largest church, the **Frauenkirche (Cathedral of Our Lady)** ★, Frauenplatz 1 (✆ **089/290-08-20;** U-Bahn/S-Bahn: Marienplatz). Workers and architects who restored the 15th-century Gothic cathedral used whatever remains they could find in the rubble, along with modern innovations. The overall effect of the rebuilt Frauenkirche is strikingly simple yet dignified. The twin towers, which remained intact, have been a city landmark since 1525. Instead of the typical flying buttresses, huge props on the inside that separate the side chapels support the edifice. The Gothic vaulting over the nave and chancel is borne by 22 simple octagonal pillars. Except for the tall chancel window, when you enter the main doors at the west end, you don't notice windows; they're hidden by the enormous pillars. According to legend, the devil laughed at the notion of hidden windows and stamped in glee at the stupidity of the architect—you can still see the strange footlike mark called "the devil's step" in the entrance hall.

Peterskirche (St. Peter's Church), Rindermarkt 1 (✆ **089/260-48-28;** U-Bahn/S-Bahn: Marienplatz), is Munich's oldest church (1180). Its tall steeple is worth the climb in clear weather for a view as far as the Alps. In its gilded baroque interior are murals by Johann Baptist Zimmermann. The **Asamkirche ★**, Sendlinger Strasse (U-Bahn/S-Bahn: Sendlingertor), is a remarkable example of rococo, designed by the Asam brothers, Cosmas Damian and Edgar Quirin, from 1733 to 1746. The **Michaelskirche,** Neuhauser Strasse 6 (U-Bahn/S-Bahn: Karlsplatz), has the distinction of being the largest Renaissance church north of the Alps. The lovely **Theatinerkirche,** Theatinerstrasse 22 (U-Bahn/S-Bahn: Odeonsplatz), with its graceful fluted columns and arched ceilings, is the work of the court architect, François Cuvilliés, and his son.

ORGANIZED TOURS

The easiest, and fastest, way to gain an overview of Munich is on a guided tour. One of the largest organizers of these is **Gray Line** (✆ **089/54-90-75-60;** www.grayline.com). At least a half-dozen touring options are available, ranging from a quickie 1-hour overview of the city to full-day excursions to such outlying sites as Berchtesgaden, Oberammergau, and Hohenschwangau, site of three of Bavaria's most stunning palaces. City tours encompass aspects of both modern and medieval Munich, and depart from the main railway station. Departures, depending on the season and the tour, occur between two and eight times a day, and tours are conducted in both German and English.

Depending on the tour, adults pay 11€ to 36€, and children 13 and under pay 6€ to 18€, for experiences that last between 1 and 2½ hours. Advance reservations for most city tours aren't required, and you can buy your ticket from the bus driver at the time you board. The company also offers a 4½-hour "Munich by Night" tour that costs 65€ per person and departs several nights a week at 7:30pm, and which hauls its participants in and out of a series of cabarets and beer halls for a lukewarm, and ultimately not particularly happy, encounter that has "I am a tourist" permeating almost every aspect of the experience.

If you want to participate in any tour that covers attractions outside the city limits, advance reservations are required, especially if you want the bus to pick you up at any of Munich's hotels. Travel agents in Munich, as well as the concierge or reception staff at your hotel, can book any of these tours.

Pedal pushers will want to try Mike Lasher's **Mike's Bike Tour** (✆ **089/255-43-988;** www.mikesbiketours.com). His bike rentals for 12€ to 18€ include maps and locks, child and infant seats, and helmets at no extra charge. English and bilingual tours of central Munich run from March to November, leaving daily at 10:30am (call to confirm). The 4-hour tour is 24€.

The Shopping Scene

The most interesting shops are concentrated on Munich's pedestrians-only streets between **Karlsplatz** and **Marienplatz.**

Handmade crafts can be found on the fourth floor of Munich's major department store, **Ludwig Beck am Rathauseck,** Am Marienplatz 11 (✆ **089/236-910;** U-Bahn/S-Bahn: Marienplatz). **Wallach,** Residenzstrasse 3 (✆ **089/22-08-72;** U-Bahn/S-Bahn: Odeonsplatz), is a fine place to obtain handicrafts and folk art, both new and antique. Shop here for a memorable object to remind you of your trip. You'll find antique churns, old hand-painted wooden boxes and trays, painted porcelain clocks, and many other items.

On the grounds of Schloss Nymphenburg at Nördliches Schlossrondell 8, you'll find **Nymphenburger Porzellan-manufaktur** (✆ **089/17-91-970;** U-Bahn: Rotkreuzplatz, and then tram no. 17 toward Amalienburgstrasse; bus: 41), one of Germany's most famous porcelain makers. You can visit the exhibition and sales rooms; shipments can be arranged if you make purchases. There's also a branch in Munich's center, at Odeonsplatz 1 (✆ **089/28-24-28;** U-Bahn/S-Bahn: Odeonsplatz).

Munich After Dark

To find out what's happening in the Bavarian capital, go to the tourist office and buy a copy of *Monatsprogramm* (2€). This monthly publication contains complete information about what's going on in Munich and how to purchase tickets.

THE PERFORMING ARTS

Nowhere else in Europe, other than London and Paris, will you find so many musical and theatrical performances. And the good news is the low cost of the seats—you'll get good tickets if you're willing to pay anywhere from 10€ to 65€.

A part of the Residenz (p. 413), **Altes Residenztheater (Cuvilliés Theater),** Residenzstrasse 1 (✆ **089/2185-19-40;** U-Bahn: Odeonsplatz), is a sightseeing attraction in its own right, and Germany's most outstanding example of a rococo tier-boxed theater. During World War II, the interior was dismantled and stored. You can tour it Tuesday to Friday from 2 to 4pm and Sunday from 11am to 5pm. **Bavarian State Opera** and the **Bayerisches Staatsschauspiel** (**State Theater Company;** ✆ **089/2185-1920**) perform smaller works here in keeping with the tiny theater's intimate character. Box office hours are Monday to Friday 10am to 6pm, plus 1 hour before performances; Saturday 10am to 1pm only. Opera tickets are 18€ to 175€; theater tickets, 15€ to 75€; building tours, 5€.

The regular season of the **Deutsches Theater,** Schwanthalerstrasse 13 (✆ **089/552-34-444;** www.deutsches-theater.de; U-Bahn: Karlsplatz/Stachus), lasts year-round. Musicals, operettas, ballets, and international shows are performed here. During carnival season (Jan–Feb), the theater becomes a ballroom for more than 2,000 guests. Tickets are 20€ to 84€, higher for special events.

Gasteig München GmbH, Rosenheimer Strasse 5 (✆ **089/48-09-80;** www.gasteig.de; S-Bahn: Rosenheimerplatz; tram: 18; bus: 51), is the home of the **Münchner Philharmoniker** (www.mphil.de), founded in 1893. Its present home opened in 1985 and shelters the Richard Strauss Conservatory and the Munich Municipal Library. The orchestra performs in Philharmonic Hall. Purchase tickets Monday to Friday 9am to 6pm, Saturday 9am to 2pm, for 10€ to 61€. The Philharmonic season runs mid-September to July.

Practically any night of the year, except from August to mid-September, you'll find a performance at the **Nationaltheater,** Max-Joseph-Platz 2 (✆ **089/21-85-1920;** www.bayerische.staatsoper.de; U-Bahn/S-Bahn: Marienplatz or Odeonsplatz), home of the **Bavarian State Opera,** one of the world's great opera companies. The productions are beautifully mounted and presented, and sung by famous singers. Hard-to-get tickets may be purchased Monday through Friday from 10am to 6pm, plus 1 hour before performance, Saturday from 10am to 1pm. The Nationaltheater is also home to the **Bavarian State Ballet.** Opera tickets are 15€ to 263€; ballet tickets, 8€ to 66€.

WHAT'S brewing AT THE BEER HALLS?

The world's most famous beer hall, **Hofbräuhaus am Platzl,** Am Platzl 9 (✆ **089/22-16-76;** www.hofbraeuhaus.de; U-Bahn/S-Bahn: Marienplatz), is a legend. Visitors with only 1 night in Munich usually target the Hofbräuhaus as their top nighttime destination. Owned by the state, the present Hofbräuhaus was built at the end of the 19th century, but the tradition of a beer house on this spot dates from 1589. In the 19th century it attracted artists, students, and civil servants and was known as the Blue Hall because of its dim lights and smoky atmosphere. When it became too small to contain everybody, architects designed another in 1897. This one was the 1920 setting for the notorious meeting of Hitler's newly launched German Workers Party. Today, 4,500 beer drinkers can crowd in on a given night. Several rooms are spread over three floors, including a top-floor room for dancing. The ground floor, with its brass band (which starts playing at 11am), is exactly what you'd expect of a beer hall—here it's eternal Oktoberfest. It's open daily from 10am to midnight.

In a century-old house northwest of Schwabing at the edge of Luitpold Park, **Bamberger Haus,** Brunnerstrasse 2 (✆ **089/308-89-66;** www.restaurant-la-villa.de; U-Bahn: Scheidplatz), is named after the city most noted for the quantity of beer its residents drink. Bavarian and international specialties served in the street-level restaurant include well-seasoned soups, grilled steak, veal, pork, and sausages. If you only want to drink, visit the rowdier and less expensive beer hall in the cellar, where a large beer is 2.70€ to 6.90€. The restaurant is open daily noon to midnight and the beer hall daily 5pm to 1am; in summer, weather permitting, a beer garden is open daily 11am to 11pm.

Englischer Garten, the park between the Isar River and Schwabing, is the biggest city-owned park in Europe. It has a main restaurant and several beer gardens, of which the **Biergärten Chinesischer Turm,** Englischer Garten 3 (✆ **089/38-38-73-27;** www.chinaturm.de; U-Bahn: Giselastrasse), is our favorite. It takes its name from its location at the foot of a pagoda-like tower. Plenty of beer and cheap Bavarian food are what you get here. A large glass or mug of beer (ask for *ein mass Bier*), enough to bathe in, costs 6€ to 8€. Homemade dumplings are a specialty, as are all kinds of tasty sausage. Oompah bands often play. It's open daily 10am to midnight (closed Jan 11–Feb 5).

On the principal pedestrian-only street of Munich, **Augustinerbrau,** Neuhäuserstrasse 27 (✆ **089/231-83-257;** www.augustiner-braeu.de; U-Bahn/S-Bahn: Stachus), offers generous helpings of food, good beer, and a mellow atmosphere. It's been around for a little less than a century, but beer was first brewed on this spot in 1328. The cuisine is not for dieters: It's hearty, heavy, and starchy, but it sure soaks up that beer. Hours are daily 9am to midnight. **Waldwirtschaft Grosshesslohe,** George-Kalb-Strasse 3 (✆ **089/74-99-4030;** tram: 7), is a popular summertime rendezvous seating some 2,000 drinkers. The gardens are open daily from 10am to 11pm (they have to close early because neighborhood residents complain). Music ranges from Dixieland to English jazz to Polish bands. Entrance is free and you bring your own food. It's above the Isar River in the vicinity of the zoo.

THE CLUB & MUSIC SCENE

You'll find some of Munich's most sophisticated entertainment at **Bayerischer Hof Night Club,** in the Hotel Bayerischer Hof, Promenadeplatz 2–6 (✆ **089/212-00;** www.bayerischerhof.de; tram: 19). Within one very large room is a piano bar where a musician plays melodies every night except Monday from 10am to 3am. The piano bar is free, but there's a nightclub cover charge of 5€ to 50€. Daily happy hour is from 7 to 8:30pm in the piano bar.

Jazzclub Unterfahrt, Einsteinstrasse 42 (✆ **089/448-27-94;** www.unterfahrt.de; U-Bahn/S-Bahn: Ostbahnhof), is Munich's leading jazz club, lying near the Ostbahnhof in the Haidhausen district. The club presents live music Tuesday to Sunday 8:30pm to 1am (it opens at 8pm). Wine, small snacks, beer, and drinks are sold as well. Sunday night there's a special jam session for improvisation. Cover Tuesday to Saturday is 10€ to 30€; Sunday jam session is 15€. Small, dark, and popular with blues and jazz aficionados, **Mister B's,** Herzog-Heinrichstrasse 38 (✆ **089/534901;** www.misterbs.de; U-Bahn: Goetheplatz), hosts a slightly older, mellower crowd than the rock and dance clubs. It's open Tuesday to Sunday 8pm to 3am. Blues, jazz, and rhythm-and-blues combos take the stage Thursday to Saturday. Cover is 5€ to 15€.

Parkcafé, Sophienstrasse 7 (✆ **089/51-61-79-80;** www.parkcafe089.de; U-Bahn: Lebachplatz), contains three distinct subdivisions, each catering to the food, beverage, and socializing needs of the young, the restless, and the occasionally cutting-edge residents of Munich. Come here for a drink, snack, or coffee at the **Parkcafé,** and perhaps extend the venue into a full meal at the immediately adjacent premises of the **Parkcafé Kitchen.** Both establishments are open daily 10am to midnight for food (until 1am for drinks). And if you're in the mood to dance, surrounded by nocturnal denizens of Munich who might be dressed in Teutonic punk or leather and perhaps heavily pierced, come here every night of the week from 11pm to 4am for access to the **Parkcafé Club,** where hipster music blares and entrance costs from 10€.

THE BAR & CAFE SCENE

Once a literary cafe, **Alter Simpl,** Türkenstrasse 57 (✆ **089/272-30-83;** www.eggerlokale.de; U-Bahn: University), attracts a diverse crowd of locals, including young people. The real fun begins after 11pm, when the iconoclastic artistic ferment becomes more reminiscent of Berlin than Bavaria. It's open Sunday to Thursday 11am to 3am, Friday and Saturday 11am to 4am.

Schumann's, Odeonsplatz 6–7 (✆ **089/22-90-60;** www.schumanns.de), doesn't waste any money on decor—it depends on the local beau monde to keep it looking chic. In warm weather the terrace spills onto the street. Schumann's is known as a "thinking man's bar." Charles Schumann, author of three bar books, wanted a bar that would be an artistic, literary, and communicative social focus of the metropolis. Popular with the film, advertising, and publishing worlds, his place is said to have contributed to a remarkable renaissance of bar culture in the city. It's open Sunday 6pm to 3am, Monday to Friday 9am to 3am; closed on Saturday.

GAY & LESBIAN CLUBS

Much of Munich's gay and lesbian scene takes place in the blocks between the Viktualienmarkt and Gärtnerplatz, particularly on Hans-Sachs-Strasse.

A virtual communications center of hip Munich, the **Stadtcafe,** St. Jakobsplatz 1 (✆ **089/266-949;** www.stadtcafe-muenchen.de; U-Bahn: Marienplatz), attracts creative people, often in the arts. By Munich nightlife standards, it closes relatively early; night owls drift on to other late-night venues. Expect lots of chitchat from table to table, and there's sure to be someone scribbling away at his or her unfinished story (or unfinished novel). It's open Monday to Saturday 11am to midnight, and Sunday 10:30am to midnight.

Day Trip from Munich

HERRENCHIEMSEE ★ & NEUES SCHLOSS ★★

Known as the "Bavarian Sea," Chiemsee is one of the Bavarian Alps' most beautiful lakes in a serene landscape. Its main attraction lies on the island of Herrenchiemsee, where "Mad" King Ludwig II built one of his fantastic castles.

Neues Schloss, begun in 1878, was never completed because of the king's death in 1886. The castle was to have been a replica of the grand palace of Versailles that Ludwig so admired. One of the architects was Julius Hofmann, whom the king had also employed for the construction of his alpine castle, Neuschwanstein. When work was halted in 1886, only the center of the enormous palace had been completed. The palace and its formal gardens remain one of the most fascinating of Ludwig's adventures, in spite of their unfinished state.

The splendid Great Hall of Mirrors most authentically replicates Versailles. The 17 door panels contain enormous mirrors reflecting the 33 crystal chandeliers and the 44 gilded candelabras. The vaulted ceiling is covered with 25 paintings depicting the life of Louis XIV. The dining room is a popular attraction because of "the little table that lays itself." A mechanism in the floor permitted the table to go down to the room below to be cleared and relaid between courses.

You can visit Herrenchiemsee at any time of the year. April to September, tours are given daily from 9am to 6pm; off season, daily 10am to 4:15pm. Admission—in addition to the boat fare—is 8€ adults, 7€ students, and free for ages 18 and under.

GETTING THERE Take the train to Prien am Chiemsee (trip time: 1 hr.). For information, call ✆ **08001/50-70-90.** There's also regional bus service offered by **RVO Regionalverkehr Oberbayern** (✆ **089/55-164-0;** www.rvo-bus.de). Access by car is via A-8 Autobahn.

From Prien, lake steamers make the trip to Herrenchiemsee. They are operated by **Chiemsee-Schifffahrt Ludwig Fessler** (✆ **08051/60-90;** www.chiemsee-schifffahrt.de). The round-trip fare is 7€. For visitor information, contact the **Kur und Verkehrsamt,** Alte Rathausstrasse 11, in Prien am Chiemsee (✆ **08051/69050**), open September to March Monday to Friday 8:30am to 5pm. April to August, the office is also open on Saturday 8:30am to 6pm.

Garmisch-Partenkirchen ★★★

In spite of its urban flair, Garmisch-Partenkirchen, Germany's top alpine resort, has maintained the charm of an ancient village. Even today, you occasionally see country folk in traditional costumes, and you may be held up in traffic while the cattle are led from their mountain grazing grounds down through the streets of town. Garmisch is about 88km (55 miles) southwest of Munich.

OUTDOORS IN THE bavarian alps

Hitting the Slopes & Other Winter Activities The winter **skiing** here is the best in Germany. A regular winter snowfall in January and February measures 30 to 50 centimeters (12–20 in.), which in practical terms means about 2m (6½ ft.) of snow in the areas served by ski lifts. The great **Zugspitzplatt** snowfield can be reached in spring or autumn by a rack railway. The Zugspitze, at 2,960m (9,710 ft.) above sea level, is the tallest mountain peak in Germany. Ski slopes begin at a height of 2,650m (8,700 ft.).

The second great ski district in the Alps is **Berchtesgadener Land,** with alpine skiing centered on Jenner, Rossfeld, Götschen, and Hochschwarzeck, and consistently good snow conditions until March. Here you'll find a cross-country skiing center and many miles of tracks kept in first-class condition, natural toboggan runs, one artificial ice run for toboggan and skibob runs, artificial ice-skating, and ice-curling rinks. Call the local "Snow-Telefon" at the Berchtesgaden Tourist Office ✆ **08652/9670** for current snow conditions.

From October to February, you can use the world-class **ice-skating** rink in Berchtesgaden (the Eisstadion). Less reliable, but more evocative of Bavaria's wild open spaces, it involves skating on the surface of the Hintersee Lake once it's sufficiently frozen. Rarer is an ice-skating experience on the Königsee, whose surface freezes to the degree that you can skate on average only once every 10 winters. A particularly cozy way to spend a winter's night is to huddle with a companion in the back of a **horse-drawn sled.** For a fee of 55€ to 85€ per hour, this can be arranged by calling ✆ **08652/1760.**

Hiking & Other Summer Activities In summer, **alpine hiking** is a major attraction—climbing mountains, enjoying nature, watching animals in the forest. Hikers are able at times to observe endangered species firsthand. One of the best areas for hiking is the 1,237m (4,058-ft.) **Eckbauer** lying on the southern fringe of Partenkirchen (the tourist office at Garmisch-Partenkirchen will supply maps and details). Many visitors come to the Alps in summer just to hike through the **Berchtesgaden National Park,** bordering the Austrian province of Salzburg. The 2,466m (8,091-ft.) Watzmann Mountain, the Königssee (Germany's cleanest, clearest lake), and parts of the Jenner—the pride of Berchtesgaden's four ski areas—are within the boundaries of the national park, which has well-mapped trails cut through protected areas, leading the hiker along spectacular flora and fauna. Information about hiking in the park is provided by the **Nationale Parkhaus,** Franciscanalplatz 7, 83471 Berchtesgaden (✆ **08652/64343**). It's open daily from 9am to 5pm.

From Garmisch-Partenkirchen, serious hikers can embark on full-day or, if they're more ambitious, overnight alpine treks, following clearly marked footpaths and staying in isolated mountain huts maintained by the German Alpine Association (Deutscher Alpenverein/DAV). Some huts are staffed and serve meals. For the truly remote unsupervised huts, you'll be provided with information on how to gain access and your responsibility in leaving them tidy after your visit. For information, inquire at the local tourist office or write to the **German Alpine Association,** Am Franciscanalplatz 7, 83471, Berchtesgaden (✆ **08652/64343**). At the same address and phone number, you'll also be routed to staff members of a privately owned tour operator, the **Summit Club,** an outfit devoted to the organization of high-altitude expeditions throughout Europe and the world.

If you're a true outdoors person, you'll briefly savor the somewhat touristy facilities of Garmisch-Partenkirchen, and then use it as a base for exploring the rugged **Berchtesgaden National Park,** which is within an easy commute of Garmisch. You can also stay at one of the inns in Mittenwald or Oberammergau and take advantage of a wide roster of sporting diversions within the wide-open spaces. Any of the outfitters below will provide directions and linkups with their sports programs from wherever you decide to stay. Street maps of Berchtesgaden and its environs are usually available free from the **Kurdirektion** (the local tourist office) at Berchtesgaden (✆ **08652/967-0**), and more intricately detailed maps of the surrounding alpine topography are available for a fee.

In addition to hill climbing and rock climbing, activities include **ballooning,** which, weather permitting, can be arranged through **Outdoor Club Berchtesgaden,** Am Gmundberg (✆ **08652/9776-0**), open Monday to Friday from 8am to 6pm. Local enthusiasts warn that ballooning is not a sport for the timid or anyone who suffers unduly in the cold: Warm thermal currents that prevail around Berchtesgaden in summer limit the sport to the cold-weather months. Consequently, the seasonal heyday for ballooning is from December to February. A local variation of **curling** *(Eisstock)* that makes use of wooden, rather than stone, instruments can usually be arranged even when ice and snows have melted on the surrounding slopes at the town's biggest ice rink, **Berchtesgaden Eisstadion,** An der Schiessstätte (✆ **08652/61405**). If you opted not to carry your ice skates in your luggage during your transatlantic flight, don't worry: A kiosk (✆ **08652/3384**) within the ice stadium rents a wide spectrum of ice skates in all sizes for around 5€ adults, 4€ children, per hour.

Cycling and **mountain biking,** available through the rental facilities of **Para-Taxi,** Maximilianstrasse 16 (✆ **08652/948450**), give outdoor enthusiasts an opportunity to enjoy the outdoors and exercise their leg muscles simultaneously. It's open Monday to Friday 9am to 12:30pm and 2 to 6pm, Saturday 9am to 12:30pm.

Anglers will find plenty of **fishing** opportunities (especially salmon, pikeperch, and trout) at Lake Hintersee and the rivers Ramsauer Ache and Königsseer Ache. To acquire a fishing permit, contact the Kurdirektion (tourist office) at Berchtesgaden, which will direct you to any of four authorities, based on where you want to fish. For fishing specifically within the Hintersee, contact officials at the **Kurverwaltung,** Im Tal 2 (✆ **08657/98-89-20**), at Ramsau, 12km (7½ miles) from Berchtesgaden.

Despite its obvious dangers, **hang gliding** or **paragliding** from the vertiginous slopes of Mount Jenner can be thrilling. To arrange it, contact **Para-Taxi,** Maximilianstrasse 15 (✆ **08652/948450**). The headquarters for a loosely allied group of parasailing enthusiasts, the **Berchtesgaden Gleitschirmflieger** (✆ **08652/23-63**), sometimes arranges communal paragliding excursions to which qualified newcomers are invited. Practice your **kayaking** or **white-water rafting** techniques on one of the many rivers in the area, such as the Ramsauer, Königisser, Bischofswiesener, and Berchtesgadener Aches. For information and options, contact the above-mentioned **Outdoor Club Berchtesgaden.**

ESSENTIALS

Getting There

BY TRAIN The **Garmisch-Partenkirchen Bahnhof** lies on the major Munich-Weilheim-Garmisch-Mittenwald-Innsbruck rail line with frequent connections in all directions. Twenty trains per day arrive from Munich (trip time: 1 hr. 22 min.). For rail information and schedules, call © **0800/1-50-70-90.**

BY BUS Both long-distance and regional buses through the Bavarian Alps are provided by **RVO Regionalverkehr Oberbayern** in Garmisch-Partenkirchen (© **08821/948-274** for information; www.rvo-bus.de).

BY CAR Access is via A-95 Autobahn from Munich; exit at Eschenlohe.

VISITOR INFORMATION For tourist information, contact the **Kurverwaltung und Verkehrsamt,** Richard-Strauss-Platz (© **08821/180-700**), open Monday to Saturday 8am to 6pm, Sunday 10am to noon.

GETTING AROUND An unnumbered municipal bus services the town, depositing passengers at Marienplatz or the Bahnhof, from where you can walk to all central hotels. This free bus runs every 15 minutes.

WHERE TO STAY

Atlas Grand Hotel ★ This is one of the town's most prestigious hotels. The U-shaped and handsomely furnished rooms are generally medium size. Duvets rest on comfortable beds, mostly doubles or twins. Bathrooms are handsomely maintained with deluxe toiletries. The balconies overlook a garden and offer a view of the Alps.

Ludwigstrasse 49, 82467 Garmisch-Partenkirchen. © **08821/9363-0.** Fax 08821/9363-2222. www.atlas-grandhotel.com. 59 units. 120€–170€ double; 180€ suite. Rates include buffet breakfast. AE, DC, MC, V. Free parking. **Amenities:** 2 restaurants; 4 dining rooms; bar. *In room:* TV, hair dryer, Wi-Fi (free).

Atlas Posthotel ★ This hotel in the heart of town was originally built in 1512 as a tavern and has retained its *gemütlich* antique charm. In the early 1990s, it was radically upgraded. Rooms range from rather small and cozy Bavarian nests to spacious retreats. The owners have installed comfortable furnishings, and bathrooms are beautifully kept.

Marienplatz 12, 82467 Garmisch-Partenkirchen. © **08821/7090.** Fax 08821/70-92-05. www.atlasposthotel.com. 44 units. 85€–135€ double. DC, MC, V. Free parking. **Amenities:** 2 restaurants; historic tavern; bar; room service. *In room:* TV, hair dryer, minibar, Wi-Fi (free).

Gästehaus Trenkler For a number of years, Frau Trenkler has made travelers feel well cared for in her quiet, centrally located guesthouse. She rents four doubles, each with shower and sink. Each duvet-covered bed is equipped with a good mattress. Rooms range from small to medium, and corridor bathrooms are adequate and tidily maintained.

Kreuzstrasse 20, 82467 Garmisch-Partenkirchen. © **08821/34-39.** Fax 08821/15-67. www.gaestehaus-trenkler.de. 4 units, all with shower. 70€ double. Rates include continental breakfast. No credit cards. Free parking. Bus: Eibsee no. 1. *In room:* No phone.

Reindl's Partenkirchner Hof ★★ This special Bavarian retreat maintains a high level of luxury and hospitality. The annexes have balconies, and the main building has wraparound verandas, giving each room an unobstructed view of the mountains and town. All rooms have a cozy charm. The best are suites opening onto panoramic views of mountains or the garden. Rustic pine furniture adds to the allure of this place. Bathrooms are spacious.

Bahnhofstrasse 15, 82467 Garmisch-Partenkirchen. ✆ **08821/943870.** Fax 08821/9438-7250. www.reindls.de. 63 units. 120€–150€ double; 180€–230€ suite. AE, DC, MC, V. Parking 10€. Closed Nov 15–Dec 15. **Amenities:** Restaurant (see "Where to Dine," below); 2 bars; exercise room; Jacuzzi; indoor pool; room service; sauna. *In room:* TV, hair dryer, minibar.

WHERE TO DINE

Flösserstuben INTERNATIONAL Regardless of the season, a bit of the Bavarian Alps always seems to flower amid the wood-trimmed nostalgia of this intimate restaurant close to the town center. You can select a seat at a colorful wooden table or on an ox yoke–inspired stool in front of the spliced saplings that decorate the bar. Moussaka and souvlakia, as well as sauerbraten and all kinds of Bavarian dishes, are abundantly available. You can also order Mexican tacos and tortillas or even *Tafelspitz* (boiled beef) from the Austrian kitchen. The menu isn't imaginative but is soul satisfying, especially on a cold night.

Schmiedstrasse 2. ✆ **08821/28-88.** Reservations recommended. Main courses 8€–18€. AE, MC, V. Daily 11:30am–2:30pm and 5–11pm. Town bus.

Joseph-Naus-Stub'n ★ GERMAN/CONTINENTAL One of the most charming dining spots in town lies on the lobby level of a prominent and very visible hotel, the Zugspitze, which, with its traditional alpine design, evokes a very large mountain chalet on steroids. Within a country-baroque decor that manages to be elegant and woodsy, but with a definite sense of almost ladylike grace, you can enjoy some of the most upscale and sophisticated cuisine in town. Menus change with the season, but the best examples include selections from an oft-changing array of oysters, crabs, North Sea sole and flounder, trout, and zander, each prepared in a different way every night or according to your specifications. During the autumn and winter, the focus is on game dishes, including filet of venison.

In the Zugspitze Hotel, Klammstrasse 19. ✆ **08821/9010.** Reservations recommended Fri–Sat nights. Main courses 11€–21€; fixed-price menus 29€ for 3 courses, 35€ for 4 courses, 59€ for 7 courses. AE, DC, MC, V. Mon–Sat 5:30–9pm; Sun noon–2pm.

Reindl's Restaurant ★ CONTINENTAL Reindl's is first class all the way. Chic, charming, cozy, and alpine, it's filled with Teutonic antiques and the scent of sophisticated, freshly cooked food. It has aquariums for both salt- and freshwater fish, for the storage of live lobsters, and for live freshwater alpine fish, including trout. Menu items change seasonally and to some extent daily, but enduring specialties include roasted rack of venison with forest mushrooms; zander with Riesling; and roasted saddle of lamb with garlic and herbs, and green beans and potatoes dauphinoise. About two-thirds of the 80-or-so seats are in an elegant main dining room; the remainder are within a richly paneled and very cozy room that evokes alpine and Bavarian *Gemütlichkeit.*

In the Partenkirchner Hof, Bahnhofstrasse 15. ✆ **08821/943-870.** www.reindls.de. Reservations required. Main courses 15€–30€; fixed-price menus 16€–45€. AE, DC, MC, V. Daily noon–2:30pm and 6:30–11pm. Closed Nov 10–Dec 15.

SEEING THE SIGHTS IN TOWN

The symbol of the city's growth and modernity is the **Olympic Ice Stadium,** Spiridon-Louis-Ring (✆ **089/30-67-21-50;** U-Bahn: 3 to Olympia-Zentrum), built for the 1936 Winter Olympics and capable of holding nearly 12,000 people. On the slopes at the edge of town is the much larger **Ski Stadium,** with two ski jumps and a slalom course. In 1936 more than 100,000 people watched the events in this stadium. Today it's still an integral part of winter life in Garmisch—the World Cup Ski Jump is held here every New Year.

Garmisch-Partenkirchen is a center for winter sports, summer hiking, and mountain climbing. In addition, the town environs offer some of the most panoramic views and colorful buildings in Bavaria. The **Philosopher's Walk** in the park surrounding the pink-and-silver 18th-century pilgrimage **Chapel of St. Anton** is a delightful spot to enjoy the views of the mountains around the low-lying town.

EXPLORING THE ENVIRONS

One of the most beautiful of the alpine regions around Garmisch is the **Alpspitz region,** which hikers and hill climbers consider uplifting and healing for both body and soul. Here, you'll find alpine meadows, masses of seasonal wildflowers, and a rocky and primordial geology whose savage panoramas might strike you as Wagnerian. Ranging in altitude from 1,200 to 1,800m (3,900–5,900 ft.) above sea level, the Alps around Garmisch-Partenkirchen are accessible via more than 30 ski lifts and funiculars, many of which run year-round.

The most appealing and panoramic of the lot includes the Alpspitz (Osterfelderkopf) cable car that runs uphill from the center of Garmisch to the top of the Osterfelderkopf peak, at a height of 1,980m (6,500 ft.). It makes its 9-minute ascent at least every hour, year-round, from 8am to 5pm. The round-trip cost for nonskiers is 47€ adults, 32.50€ persons ages 16 to 18, and 26€ children ages 6 to 15. After admiring the view at the top, you can either return directly to Garmisch or continue your journey into the mountains via other cable cars. If you opt to continue, take the Hochalm cable car across the high-altitude plateaus above Garmisch. At its terminus, you'll have two options, both across clearly marked alpine trails. The 20-minute trek will take you to the uppermost station of the Kreuzbergbahn, which will carry you back to Garmisch. The 75-minute trek will carry you to the upper terminus of the Hausbergbahn, which will also carry you back to Garmisch.

Another of the many cable-car options within Garmisch involves an eastward ascent from the center of Partenkirchen to the top of the 1,780m (5,840-ft.) Wank via the Wankbahn, for a round-trip price of 18€ adults, 13€ persons ages 16 to 18, and 10.50€ children. From here, you'll get a sweeping view of the plateau upon which the twin villages of Garmisch and Partenkirchen sit. With minor exceptions, the Wankbahn is open only between mid-April and early October. But during clement weather, the top of the Wank is a favorite with the patrons of Garmisch's spa facilities because the plentiful sunshine makes it ideal for the *Liegekur* (deck-chair cure).

If you plan on pursuing any of these options, it's to your advantage to invest in a day pass, the **Classic Garmisch Pass,** with which you'll be able to ride most of the cable cars in the region (including those to the above-recommended Alpspitz, Kreuzeck, and Wank, as well as several others that fan out over the Eckbauer and the Ausberg) as many times as you like within the same day. Available at any of the town's cable car stations, the pass costs 33€ for adults, 25.50€ ages 16 to 18, and 18.50€ ages 6 to 15. For information on all the cable car schedules and itineraries within the region, call © **08821/7970.**

Another option for exploring the environs of Garmisch involves an ascent to the top of the **Zugspitze,** at 2,960m (9,710 ft.) the tallest mountain in Germany, with a base set astride the Austrian frontier. Ski slopes begin at 2,650m (8,700 ft.). For a panoramic view over both the Bavarian and Tyrolean Alps, go to the summit. The first stage begins in the center of Garmisch by taking the cog railway to an intermediary alpine plateau (Zugspitzplatz). Trains depart hourly throughout the year from 7:39am to 2:15pm, although we recommend that you begin by 1:15pm (and preferably earlier) and not wait until the cog railway's final ascent from Garmisch. At Zugspitzplatz, you can continue uphill on the same cog railway to the debut of a high-speed, 4-minute ride aboard the Gletscherbahn cable car, the high-altitude conveyance you'll ride to the top of the Zugspitz peak. A ZugspitzCard, valid for 3 days, costs 44€ for adults or 25€ for ages 6 to 18. For more information, call ✆ **08821/720-688** or click on www.zugspitze.de.

Oberammergau ★

A visit to Oberammergau, 19km (12 miles) north of Garmisch-Partenkirchen, is ideal in summer or winter. It stands in a wide valley surrounded by forests and mountains, with sunny slopes and meadows. The world-famous **Passion Play** is presented here, usually every 10 years; the next one is scheduled for 2020. The area has also long been known for the skill of its woodcarvers. Here in this village right under the Kofel, farms are still intact, and tradition prevails.

ESSENTIALS

Getting There

By Train The Oberammergau Bahnhof is on the Murnau–Bad Kohlgrum–Oberammergau rail line, with frequent connections in all directions. Murnau has connections to all major German cities. Daily trains from Munich take 2 hours. For information, call ✆ **0800/1-50-70-90.**

BY BUS Regional bus service to nearby towns is offered by **RVO Regionalverkehr Oberbayern** in Garmisch-Partenkirchen (✆ **08821/948-274;** www.rvo-bus.de). An unnumbered bus travels between Oberammergau and Garmisch-Partenkirchen.

BY CAR Take A-95 Munich-Garmisch-Partenkirchen Autobahn and exit at Eschenlohe (trip time: 1½ hr.).

VISITOR INFORMATION Contact the **Oberammergau Tourist Information Office,** Eugen-Papst-Strasse 9A (✆ **08822/922740;** www.oberammergau.de), open Monday to Friday 9am to 6pm, Saturday 9am to 2pm, Sunday 10am to 1pm.

WHERE TO STAY & DINE

Alte Post This provincial inn in the village center with a wide overhanging roof, green-shuttered windows, and tables set on a sidewalk under a long awning is the village social hub. The interior has storybook charm, with a ceiling-high green ceramic stove, alpine chairs, and shelves of pewter plates. Most of the rustic rooms have views. Wide, comfortable beds with giant posts range in size from cozy to spacious. Bathrooms are medium size with a shower stall. Nonresidents are welcome to visit the thriving and excellent Bavarian restaurant.

Dorfstrasse 19, 82487 Oberammergau. ✆ **08822/91-00.** Fax 08822/910-100. www.ogau.de. 32 units. 72€–108€ double. Rates include buffet breakfast. AE, DC, MC, V. Free parking. **Amenities:** Restaurant; cafe. *In room:* TV, fridge, hair dryer, Wi-Fi (15€ for 10 hr.).

Hotel Café-Restaurant Friedenshöhe This 1906 villa enjoys a beautiful location and is among the town's best bargains. Well-maintained rooms range from rather small singles to spacious doubles. Corner rooms are bigger, but bathrooms tend to be small, each with a shower stall. Even nonresidents join the townspeople who head for one of the four dining rooms, which has both indoor and outdoor terraces opening onto panoramic views, and serves Bavarian favorites.

König-Ludwig-Strasse 31, 82487 Oberammergau. ✆ **08822/94484.** Fax 08822/43-45. www.friedenshoehe.com. 16 units. 67€–105€ double. Rates include buffet breakfast. AE, DC, MC, V. Free parking. Closed Nov–Dec 14. **Amenities:** Restaurant; bar. *In room:* TV on request.

Hotel Restaurant Böld A stone's throw from the river, this well-designed chalet hotel is one of the town's premier choices. Rooms in both the main building and the annex have equally good beds, usually doubles or twins. Most rooms open onto balconies. The spotless bathrooms are medium size with shower stalls. A tranquil atmosphere and attentive service await you here. The restaurant serves Bavarian and international fare.

König-Ludwig-Strasse 10, 82487 Oberammergau. ✆ **08822/91-22-00.** Fax 08822/71-02. www.hotel-boeld.de. 57 units. 87€–157€ double. Rates include continental breakfast. AE, MC, V. Free outside parking; 8€ in the garage. **Amenities:** Restaurant; bar; room service. *In room:* TV, hair dryer, minibar.

SEEING THE SIGHTS

Oberammergau's most respected citizens include an unusual group, the woodcarvers, many of whom have been trained in the village's woodcarver's school. In the **Pilatushaus,** Ludwigthomstrasse (✆ **08822/92310**), you can watch local artists at work, including woodcarvers, painters, sculptors, and potters. Hours are May to October, Monday to Friday 1 to 6pm. You'll see many examples of these art forms throughout the town, on the painted cottages and inns and in the churchyard. Also worth seeing when strolling through the village are the houses with 18th-century frescoes by Franz Zwink that are named after fairy-tale characters, such as "Hansel and Gretel House" and the "Little Red Riding Hood House."

Oberammergaumuseum, Dorfstrasse 8 (✆ **08822/94136**), has a notable collection of Christmas crèches, all hand-carved and painted, dating from the 18th century through the 20th century. It's open April to mid-October, Tuesday to Sunday 10am to 5pm. Admission is 3€ adults and 1€ children.

NEARBY ATTRACTIONS The Ammer Valley, with Oberammergau in the (almost) center, offers easy access to many nearby attractions. **Schloss Linderhof ★★** (✆ **08822/92-03-0;** www.linderhof.de), designed as a French rococo palace, the smallest of Ludwig II's constructions, is open year-round. This is in many ways the most successful of his palaces. The gardens and smaller buildings here are even more elaborate than the two-story main structure. Especially outstanding is a Hall of Mirrors, set in white and gold panels, decorated with gilded woodcarvings. The king's bedchamber overlooks a Fountain of Neptune and the cascades of the garden. The palace is open daily April to September 9am to 6pm, October to March 10am to 4pm. Admission is 7€ to 8€, free for children 16 and under. Buses arrive from Garmisch-Partenkirchen throughout the day. Motorists can leave Oberammergau following the road signs to Ettal, 5km (3 miles) away. From Ettal, follow the signs for another 5km (3 miles) to Draswang, at which point the road into Schloss Linderhof is signposted.

OUTDOOR ACTIVITIES

Numerous **hiking trails** lead through the mountains around Oberammergau to hikers' inns such as the **Kolbenalm** and the **Romanshohe.** You can, however, simply go up to the mountaintops on the Laber cable railway or the Kolben chairlift. Oberammergau also offers opportunities to tennis buffs, minigolf players, cyclists, swimmers, hang-gliding enthusiasts, and canoeists. The recreation center **Wellenberg,** with its large alpine swimming complex with open-air pools, hot water and fountains, sauna, solarium, and restaurant, is one of the Alps' most beautiful recreation centers.

THE ROMANTIC ROAD ★★

No area of Germany is more aptly named than the Romantische Strasse. Stretching 290km (180 miles) from Würzburg to Füssen in the foothills of the Bavarian Alps, it passes through untouched medieval villages and 2,000-year-old towns.

The best way to see the Romantic Road is by car, stopping whenever the mood strikes you and then driving on through vineyards and over streams until you arrive at the alpine passes in the south. Frankfurt and Munich are convenient gateways. Access is by A-7 Autobahn from north and south, or A-3 Autobahn from east and west; A-81 Autobahn has links from the southwest. You can also explore the Romantic Road by train or bus, or by organized tour.

Rothenburg ob der Tauber ★★★

This city was first mentioned in written records in 804 as Rotinbure, a settlement above *(ob)* the Tauber River that grew to be a free imperial city, reaching its apex of prosperity under a famous Burgermeister, Heinrich Toppler, in the 14th century.

The place is such a gem and so well known that its popularity is its chief disadvantage—tourist hordes march through here, especially in summer, and the concomitant souvenir peddlers hawk kitsch. Even so, if your time is limited and you can visit only one town on the Romantic Road, make it Rothenburg.

Contemporary life and industry have made an impact, and if you arrive at the railroad station, the first things you'll see are factories and office buildings. But don't be discouraged. Inside those undamaged 13th-century city walls is a completely preserved medieval town, relatively untouched by the passage of time.

ESSENTIALS

Getting There

BY TRAIN Rothenburg lies on the Steinach-Rothenburg rail line, with frequent connections to all major German cities, including Nürnberg and Stuttgart. Daily trains arrive from Frankfurt (trip time: 3 hr.), Hamburg (5½ hr.), or Berlin (7 hr.). For information, call ✆ **0800/1-50-70-90.**

BY BUS The bus that traverses the length of the Romantic Road is EB189 or EB189E, operated by **Deutsche Touring Frankfurt** (✆ **069/790-3521;** www.touring.de). Two buses operate along this route every day, but only from April to

October. Know in advance that although you'll see a lot of romantic color en route, travel time to Rothenburg from Frankfurt via these buses is 5 hours because of frequent stops en route. Any travel agent in Germany or abroad can book you a seat on any of these buses, each of which stops at Würzburg, Augsburg, Füssen, and Munich.

Regional bus service that's limited to towns and hamlets within the vicinity of Rothenburg and the rest of the Romantic Road is provided by **OVF Omnibusverkehr Franken GmbH,** Kopernikusplatz 5, 90459 Nürnberg (✆ **0911/43-90-60;** www.ovf.de).

VISITOR INFORMATION Contact **Stadt Verkehrsamt,** Marktplatz (✆ **09861/404800**), open Monday to Friday 9am to noon and 1 to 6pm, Saturday and Sunday 10am to 3pm (Nov–Mar it closes at 5pm weekdays).

WHERE TO STAY

Bayerischer Hof This little place, midway between the Bahnhof and the medieval walled city, doesn't even try to compete with the grand inns. And why should it? It's found a niche as a B&B, and although the outside looks rather sterile, many cozy, warm Bavarian touches grace the interior. Beds are comfortable, and rooms are small; bathrooms come with shower stalls. Housekeeping is excellent, and the staff is most hospitable.

Ansbacherstrasse 21, 91541 Rothenburg o.d.T. ✆ **09861/60-63.** Fax 09861/86-56-1. www.bayerischerhof.com. 9 units. 62€–105€ double. Rates include breakfast. MC, V. Free parking. Closed Jan. **Amenities:** Restaurant/bar. *In room:* TV.

Burg Hotel ★ This old-fashioned timbered house at the end of a cul-de-sac is out of the Brothers Grimm. Its Tauber Valley view, picket fences, and window boxes exude German charm. Rooms are spread across three floors (no elevator). Extras include spacious bathrooms with tub/shower combos and large mirrors. Any room is likely to please, but if you want a view, ask for no. 7, 12, or 25.

Klostergasse 1–3, 91541 Rothenburg o.d.T. ✆ **09861/94-89-0.** Fax 09861/94-89-40. www.burghotel.eu. 15 units. 95€–170€ double; from 180€ suite. Rates include buffet breakfast. MC, V. Parking 8€. **Amenities:** Breakfast room. *In room:* TV, hair dryer, Internet (free), minibar.

Eisenhut ★★★ The most celebrated inn on the Romantic Road, Eisenhut is also one of the finest small hotels in Germany. Four medieval patrician houses were joined to make this distinctive inn. Demand for rooms is great, and the staff appears forever overworked. No two rooms are alike—yours may contain hand-carved, monumental pieces or have a 1940s Hollywood touch with a tufted satin headboard. All are enhanced by comforters and pillows piled high on state-of-the-art German beds. Extras include bedside controls and spacious bathrooms outfitted with twin basins. The three-story galleried dining hall is one of the most distinctive in Germany, with a multitiered flagstone terrace on the Tauber.

Herrngasse 3–5, 91541 Rothenburg o.d.T. ✆ **09861/70-50.** Fax 09861/70-545. www.eisenhut-rothenburg.com. 79 units. 155€–205€ double; 280€–381€ suite. AE, DC, MC, V. Parking 9€. Closed Jan 3–Feb 28. **Amenities:** Restaurant; piano bar; Bavarian beer garden; room service. *In room:* TV, hair dryer, minibar, Wi-Fi (13€ per day).

Hotel Reichs-Küchenmeister ★ We consider this hotel, one of Rothenburg's oldest structures, near St. Jakobskirche, comparable with Tilman Riemenschneider. The owners take special care with the guests' comfort. Rooms are nicely furnished

The Romantic Road

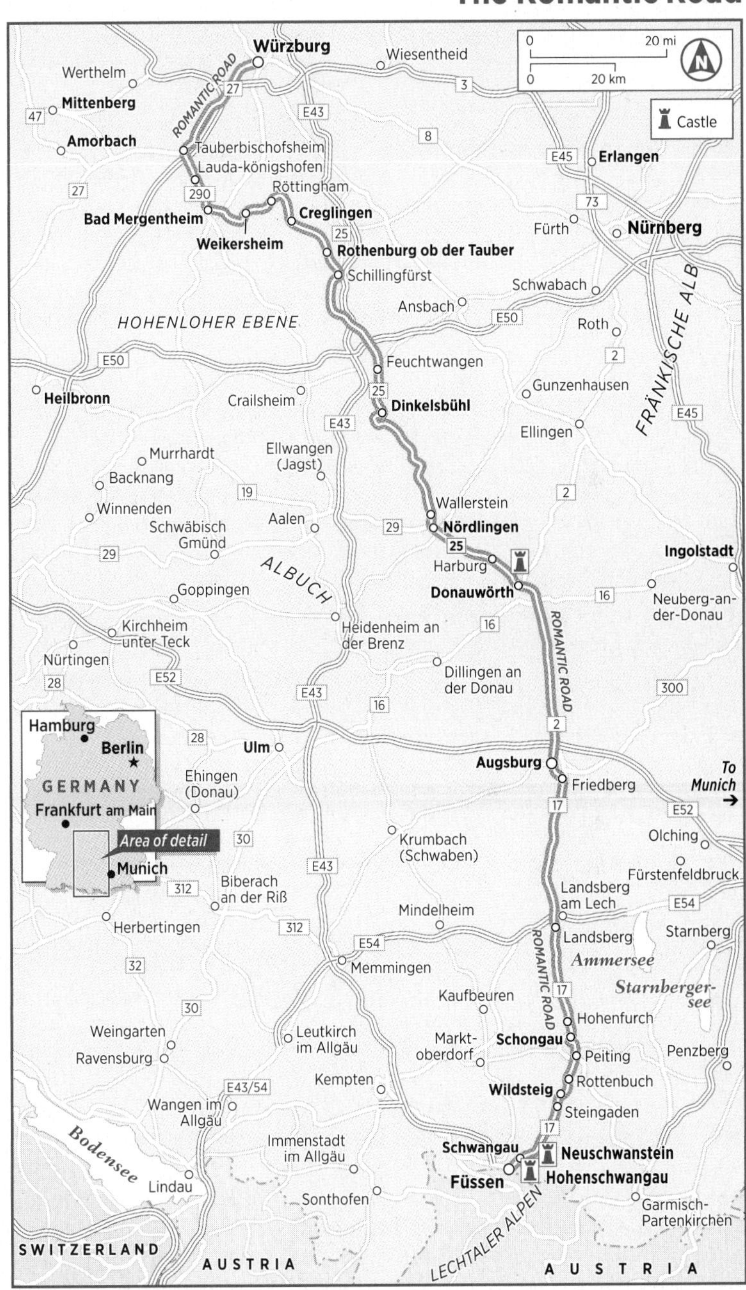

with painted wooden furniture. Bathrooms are a bit small, each with a shower stall. An extra 25 rooms are available in the duller annex across the street.

Kirchplatz 8, 91541 Rothenburg o.d.T. ✆ **09861/9700.** Fax 09861/970-409. www.reichskuechenmeister.com. 45 units. 75€–135€ double; 145€–170€ suite for 2; 150€–215€ suite for 5. Rates include buffet breakfast. AE, DC, MC, V. Parking 6.50€ in garage. **Amenities:** Restaurant (see "Where to Dine," below); wine bar; Internet (2€ per hour); sauna. *In room:* TV, hair dryer, minibar (in some).

Hotel Tilman Riemenschneider ★ This hotel's half-timbered facade rises directly above one of Rothenburg's busy historic streets. Its rear courtyard, adorned with geraniums, offers a cool and calm oasis from the heavy pedestrian traffic in front. Most rooms are medium size though a few are small. All have well-kept bathrooms.

Georgengasse 11–13, 91541 Rothenburg o.d.T. ✆ **09861/9790.** Fax 09861/29-79. www.romanticroad.com/tilman-riemenschneider. 60 units. 110€–235€ double; 160€–285€ triple. Rates include buffet breakfast. AE, DC, MC, V. Parking 6€. **Amenities:** Restaurant; lounge; exercise room; room service; sauna; Wi-Fi (free). *In room:* TV, hair dryer.

Ringhotel Glocke South of the town center off Wenggasse, this hotel does not have the charm and style of the premier inns, but it's a good choice for those who want plain, simple, affordable rooms; a family atmosphere; and good food. The small rooms, though a bit institutional, are nonetheless comfortable and a good value for pricey Rothenburg. Bathrooms are exceedingly small, each with a shower stall.

Am Plönlein 1, 91541 Rothenburg o.d.T. ✆ **09861/95899-0.** Fax 09861/95899-22. www.glocke-rothenburg.de. 24 units. 85€–108€ double. Rates include continental breakfast. AE, DC, MC, V. Parking 5€. Closed Dec 23–Jan 7. **Amenities:** Restaurant; smoke-free rooms. *In room:* TV, Internet (free).

Romantik Hotel Markusturm ★★ This is one of the charming nuggets of Rothenburg, without the facilities and physical plant of the Eisenhut, but a winner in its own right. When this hotel was constructed in 1264, one of Rothenburg's defensive walls was incorporated into the building. Some rooms have four-poster beds. Many guests request room no. 30, a cozy attic retreat. The hotel employs one of the most helpful staffs in town.

Rödergasse 1, 91541 Rothenburg o.d.T. ✆ **09861/9-42-80.** Fax 09861/9-42-81-13. www.markusturm.de. 25 units. 125€–190€ double. Rates include buffet breakfast. AE, DC, MC, V. Parking 3€–12€. **Amenities:** Restaurant; babysitting; room service. *In room:* TV, hair dryer, Internet (free).

WHERE TO DINE

Baumeisterhaus ★ FRANCONIAN Right off Marktplatz, the Baumeisterhaus is housed in an antique patrician residence, built in 1596. It has Rothenburg's most beautiful courtyard (which only guests can visit), with colorful murals, serenely draped by vines. Frankly, although the menu is good, the romantic setting is better. The food, for the most part, is rib-sticking fare beloved of Bavarians, including roast suckling pig with potato dumplings, and one of the chef's best dishes, sauerbraten, served with spaetzle.

Obere Schmiedgasse 3. ✆ **09861/94-700.** www.baumeisterhaus-rothenburg.de. Reservations required for courtyard tables. Main courses 8€–26€. AE, DC, MC, V. Wed–Mon 11am–7:30pm. Closed mid-Nov and mid-Mar.

Ratsstube FRANCONIAN This restaurant enjoys a position right on the market square, one of the most photographed spots in Germany. It's a bustling center of activity throughout the day—a day that begins when practically every Rothenburger stops by for coffee. Inside, a true tavern atmosphere prevails with hardwood chairs and tables, vaulted ceilings, and pierced copper lanterns. Downstairs you'll find a wine bar offering live music nightly. The a la carte menu of Franconian wines and dishes includes sauerbraten and venison, both served with fresh vegetables and potatoes. For dessert, you can order homemade Italian ice cream and espresso. This is a longtime favorite of those who prefer typical Franconian cookery without a lot of fuss and bother. If you arrive at 9am, the staff will serve you an American breakfast.

Marktplatz 6. ✆ **09861/55-11.** Reservations recommended. Main courses 10€–20€. MC, V. Mon–Sat 9am–10pm; Sun 9am–6pm.

Reichs-Küchenmeister FRANCONIAN The main dishes served here are the type Bavarians have loved for years, including sauerbraten, or pork tenderloin; white herring and broiled salmon are also available. The *Lebensknodel* (liver dumpling) or goulash soup is perfect for cold days. The chef makes one of the best Wiener schnitzels in town. The restaurant is near St. Jakobskirche and has a typical Weinstube decor, along with a garden terrace and a *Konditorei* (cake shop). Service is warm and efficient.

Kirchplatz 8. ✆ **09861/9700.** Reservations required. Main courses 8€–26€. AE, DC, MC, V. Daily 7:30am–10pm.

Ringhotel Glocke FRANCONIAN This traditional hotel and guesthouse serves good-tasting regional specialties along with a vast selection of local wine. Meals emphasize seasonal dishes and range from a simple vegetarian plate to lobster. If your expectations aren't too high, you'll probably enjoy this good regional cookery. Service is polite and attentive.

Am Plönlein 1. ✆ **09861/958-990.** Reservations recommended. Main courses 8€–24€. AE, DC, MC, V. Daily 11am–2pm; Mon–Sat 6–9:30pm. Closed Dec 24–Jan 6.

Tilman Riemenschneider FRANCONIAN This traditional old Weinstube is housed in one of Rothenburg's finest hotels. The old-fashioned cookery is served in generous portions. You might begin with air-dried beef or smoked filet of trout, and then follow it with poached eel, halibut steak, or loin of pork. Everything is served in generous portions with good results.

Georgengasse 11. ✆ **09861/9790.** Reservations recommended. Main courses 9.50€–25€; fixed-price menu 25€. AE, DC, MC, V. Daily 11:30am–2pm and 6–9pm.

EXPLORING THE MEDIEVAL TOWN

The **Rathaus (Town Hall)** ★ on the Marktplatz (✆ **09861/404-92**) and the Jakobskirche are the outstanding attractions, along with the medieval walls. The town hall consists of two sections; the older, Gothic section dates from 1240. From the 50m (164-ft.) tower of the Gothic hall, you get an overview of the town. The belfry has quite a history—in 1501, fire destroyed part of the building, and after that the belfry became a fire watchtower. Guards had to ring the bell every quarter-hour to prove they were awake and on the job. The newer Renaissance section, built in 1572, is decorated with intricate friezes, an oriel extending the building's full height, and a large stone portico opening onto the square. The octagonal tower at the center of the side facing the square contains a grand staircase leading to the upper hall. On the main floor is the large courtroom.

Admission to the tower is 1€ adults, .50€ children. The Rathaus is open Monday to Friday 8am to 6pm. The tower is open April to October, daily 9:30am to 12:30pm and 1 to 5pm; November to March, Saturday, Sunday, and holidays only, from noon to 3pm.

St. Jakobskirche (Church of St. James), Klostergasse 15 (© **09861/404-92**), contains the famous ***Altar of the Holy Blood*** ★★ (west gallery), a masterpiece of the Würzburg sculptor and woodcarver Tilman Riemenschneider (1460–1531). The Rothenburg Council commissioned the work in 1499 to provide a worthy setting for the *Reliquary of the Holy Blood.* The relic is contained in a rock-crystal capsule set in the reliquary cross in the center of the shrine, and beneath it the scene of *The Last Supper* makes an immediate impact on the viewer—Jesus is giving Judas the morsel of bread, marking him as the traitor. The altar wings show (left) the *Entry of Christ into Jerusalem* and (right) *Christ Praying in the Garden of Gethsemane.*

The vertical Gothic church has three naves. The choir, dating from 1336, is the oldest section and has fine late-Gothic painted-glass windows. To the left is the tabernacle (1390–1400), which was recognized as a "free place," a sanctuary for condemned criminals where they could not be touched. It's open April to October, Monday to Saturday 9am to 5:30pm, Sunday 11am to 5:30pm. In December, it's open daily 10am to 5pm. In November and January to March, it's open daily 10am to noon and 2 to 4pm. Admission costs 1.50€ adults, and .50€ children 5 and under and students of any age.

Also of interest is the **Reichsstadtmuseum** ★, Klosterhof 5 (© **09861/939-043;** www.rothenburg.de). This is Rothenburg's historical collection, housed in a 13th-century Dominican nunnery with well-preserved cloisters. You'll find on display here an enormous tankard that holds 3.5 liters, whose story has echoes all over the city. In 1631, during the Thirty Years' War, the Protestant city of Rothenburg was captured by General Tilly, commander of the armies of the Catholic League. He promised to spare the town from destruction if one of the town burghers would drink the huge tankard full of wine in one draft. Burgermeister Nusch accepted the challenge and succeeded, and so saved Rothenburg. There's a festival every spring at Whitsuntide to celebrate this event. Among the exhibits is the 1494 *Rothenburg Passion* series, 12 pictures by Martinus Schwartz, and works by English painter Arthur Wasse (1854–1930), whose pictures managed to capture in a romantic way the many moods of the city. Admission to the museum is 3.50€ adults, 2.50€ students, 2€ ages 6 to 18. The museum is open April to October daily 10am to 5pm, November to March daily 1 to 4pm.

Kriminal Museum, Burggasse 3 (© **09861/53-59**), is the only one of its kind in Europe. The museum's four floors display 10 centuries of legal history and provide insight into the life, laws, and punishments of medieval days. You'll see chastity belts, shame masks, a shame flute for bad musicians, and a cage for bakers who baked bread too small or too light. It's open daily April to October 9:30am to 6pm; November and January to February 2 to 4pm; and December and March 10am to 4pm. Admission is 4€ adults, 2.80€ students, 2.40€ children 6 and older.

Nördlingen ★

One of the most irresistible and perfectly preserved medieval towns along the Romantic Road, Nördlingen is still completely encircled by its well-preserved 14th- to 15th-century **city fortifications.** You can walk around the town on the covered parapet, which passes 11 towers and five fortified gates set into the walls.

Things are rather peaceful around Nördlingen today, and the city still employs sentries to sound the message *"So G'sell so"* ("All is well"), as they did in the Middle Ages. However, events around here weren't always so peaceful. The valley sits in a gigantic crater, the Ries. The Ries was once thought to be the crater of an extinct volcano; it is now known that a large meteorite was responsible. It hit the ground at more than 100,000 mph, the impact having the destructive force of 250,000 atomic bombs. Debris was hurled as far as Slovakia, and all plant and animal life within a radius of 160km (100 miles) was destroyed. This momentous event took place some 15 million years ago. Today it is the best-preserved and most scientifically researched meteorite crater on earth. The American Apollo 14 and 17 astronauts had their field training in the Ries in 1970.

ESSENTIALS

Getting There

BY TRAIN Nördlingen lies on the main Nördlingen-Aalen-Stuttgart line, with frequent connections in all directions (trip time: 2 hr. from Stuttgart and Nürnberg, 1 hr. from Augsburg). Call ✆ **0800/1-50-70-90** for information.

BY BUS The long-distance bus that operates along the Romantic Road includes Nördlingen; see "Rothenburg ob der Tauber," p. 427.

BY CAR Take B-25 south from Dinkelsbühl.

VISITOR INFORMATION Contact the **Verkehrsamt,** Marktplatz 2 (✆ **09081/84-116;** www.noerdlingen.de). The office is open Easter to October, Monday to Thursday 9am to 5pm and Friday 9am to 3:30pm. The rest of the year, hours are Monday to Thursday 9am to 6pm, Friday 9am to 4:30pm, and Saturday 9:30am to 1pm.

WHERE TO STAY

Kaiserhof Hotel Sonne ★ Next to the cathedral and the Rathaus is the Sonne, an inn since 1405. Among its guests have been Frederick III, Maximilian I, Charles V, and, in more recent times, the American Apollo astronauts. Many of the midsize rooms contain hand-painted four-posters to bring out the romantic in you. Others are regular doubles or twins. Goethe may have complained of the lack of comfort he found here, but you'll fare well. Bathrooms are fresh and immaculate.

Marktplatz 3, 86720 Nördlingen. ✆ **09081/50-67.** Fax 09081/23-999. www.kaiserhof-hotel-sonne.de. 43 units, 35 with bathroom. 70€ double without bathroom; 120€ double with bathroom. Rates include breakfast. AE, DC, MC, V. Free parking. **Amenities:** Restaurant; bar; babysitting; room service. *In room:* TV, hair dryer, minibar, Wi-Fi (free).

NH Klösterle Nördlingen ★ This is the best place to stay in town. In 1991, this 13th-century former monastery was renovated, a new wing added, and the entire complex transformed into the town's most luxurious hotel. Rated four stars by the government, it offers elevator access and a hardworking, polite staff. Rooms have excellent furnishings, lots of electronic extras, and large bathrooms with tub/shower combos and deluxe toiletries.

Am Klösterle 1, 86720 Nördlingen. ✆ **09081/81-870-80.** Fax 09081/870-8100. www.nh-hotels.com. 97 units. 120€–170€ double; 190€ suite. Rates include breakfast. AE, DC, MC, V. Parking 8€. **Amenities:** Restaurant; bar; exercise room; room service; sauna. *In room:* TV, hair dryer, minibar, Wi-Fi (free).

WHERE TO DINE

Meyer's Keller CONTINENTAL The conservative, modern decor here seems a suitable setting for the restrained *neue Küche* (new kitchen) of talented chef and owner Joachim Kaiser, adroit with both rustic and refined cuisine. The menu changes according to availability of ingredients and the chef's inspiration; typical selections are likely to include roulade of sea wolf and salmon with baby spinach and wild rice, or—a perfect delight—John Dory with champagne-flavored tomato sauce. The wine list is impressive, with many bottles quite reasonably priced.

Marienhöhe 8. ✆ **09081/44-93.** www.meyerskeller.de. Reservations required. Main courses 18€–28€; fixed-price meals 75€–119€. AE, MC, V. Wed–Sun 11am–2pm; Tues–Sun 6–10pm. Local bus to Marktplatz.

SEEING THE SIGHTS

At the center of the circular Altstadt within the walls is **Rübenmarkt.** If you stand in this square on market day, you'll be swept into a world of the past—the country people have preserved many traditional customs and costumes here, which, along with the ancient houses, create a living medieval city. Around the square stand a number of buildings, including the Gothic **Rathaus.** An antiquities collection is displayed in the **Stadtmuseum,** Vordere Gerbergasse 1 (✆ **09081/273-8230;** www.stadtmuseum-noerdlingen.de), open Tuesday to Sunday 1:30 to 4:30pm; closed November through February. Admission is 2.80€ adults and 1.75€ children.

The 15th-century Hallenkirche, the **Church of St. George,** on the square's northern side, is the town's most interesting sight and one of its oldest buildings. Plaques and epitaphs commemorating the town's more illustrious 16th- and 17th-century residents decorate the fan-vaulted interior. Although the original Gothic altarpiece by Friedrich Herlin (1470) is now in the Reichsstadt Museum, a portion of it, depicting the Crucifixion, remains in the church. Above the high altar today stands a more elaborate baroque altarpiece. The church's most prominent feature, however, is the 90m (295-ft.) French Gothic tower, called the "Daniel." At night, the town watchman calls out from the steeple, his voice ringing through the streets. The tower is open daily April to October 9am to 8pm. Admission is 2€ adults and 1€ children.

Rieskrater-Museum, Hintere Gerbergasse (✆ **09081/273-8220**), documents the impact of the stone meteorite that created the Ries. Examine fossils from Ries Lake deposits and learn about the fascinating evolution of this geological wonder. Hours are Tuesday through Sunday from 10am to noon and from 1:30 to 4:30pm. Admission is 3€ adults; 1.50€ students, seniors, and large groups. Tours of the crater are possible through the museum.

EN ROUTE TO AUGSBURG

After Nördlingen, B-25 heads south to Augsburg. After a 19km (12-mile) ride you can stop to visit **Schloss Harburg ★** (it's signposted), one of the best-preserved medieval castles in Germany. It once belonged to the Hohenstaufen emperors and contains treasures collected by the family over the centuries. It is open mid-March to October, Tuesday to Sunday 9am to 5pm; November, Tuesday to Sunday from 10am to 4pm. Admission is 5€ adults and 3€ children, including a guided tour. For information call ✆ **09080/96860.**

After exploring the castle, continue 11km (6¾ miles) south to the walled town of **Donauwörth ★**, where you can stop to walk through the oldest part of the town, on an island in the river, connected by a wooden bridge. Here the Danube is only a narrow, placid stream. The town's original walls overlook its second river, the Woernitz.

After a brief stopover, continue your southward trek for 48km (30 miles) to Augsburg, the largest city on the Romantic Road.

Augsburg ★★

Augsburg is near the center of the Romantic Road and the gateway to the Alps and the south. Founded 2,000 years ago by the Roman emperor Augustus, for whom it was named, it once was the richest city in Europe. Little remains from the early Roman period. However, the wealth of Renaissance art and architecture is staggering. Over the years, Augsburg has boasted an array of famous native sons, including painters Hans Holbein the Elder and Hans Holbein the Younger, and playwright Bertolt Brecht. It was here in 1518 that Martin Luther was summoned to recant his 95 theses before a papal emissary. Only 15% of the city was left standing after World War II, but there's still much here to intrigue. Today, Augsburg is an important industrial center on the Frankfurt-Salzburg Autobahn, and Bavaria's third-largest city after Munich and Nürnberg.

ESSENTIALS

Getting There

BY TRAIN About 90 Euro and InterCity trains arrive here daily from all major German cities. For information, call ✆ **0800/1-50-70-90.** There are 60 trains a day from Munich (trip time: 30–50 min.), and 35 from Frankfurt (3–4½ hr.).

BY BUS Long-distance buses (lines EB190 and 190A, plus line 189) service the Romantic Road. The buses are operated by **Deutsche Touring GmbH** at Am Römerhof in Frankfurt (✆ **069/790-350** for reservations and information).

VISITOR INFORMATION Contact **Tourist-Information,** Schiessgrabenstrasse (✆ **0821/50-20-70;** www.augsburg-tourismus.de), Monday to Friday 9am to 6pm, Saturday at Rathausplatz from 10am to 1pm; closed Sunday.

GETTING AROUND The public transportation system in Augsburg consists of 4 tram and 31 bus lines covering the inner city and reaching into the suburbs. Public transportation operates daily 5am to midnight.

WHERE TO STAY

Dom Hotel Although it may not have the decorative flair of the more expensive hotels such as Drei Mohren, the low rates and an indoor pool make this one of the most appealing choices in town. The hotel is a half-timbered structure, next to Augsburg's famous cathedral, and was built in the 15th century. Rooms on most floors are medium size and nicely appointed, although we prefer the smaller attic accommodations where you can rest under a beamed ceiling and enjoy a panoramic sweep of the rooftops of the city. Only breakfast is served, but it's a treat in a garden beside the town's medieval fortifications.

Frauentorstrasse 8, 86152 Augsburg. ✆ **0821/34-39-30.** Fax 0821/34-39-32-00. www.domhotel-augsburg.de. 52 units. 89€–135€ double; 115€–185€ suite. Rates include buffet breakfast. AE, DC, MC, V. Free street parking; 6€ garage. Tram: 2. **Amenities:** Indoor pool; sauna. *In room:* TV, hair dryer, minibar, Wi-Fi (free).

Hotel Am Rathaus Many repeat guests consider this hotel's location just behind the town hall to be its best asset. Built in a three-story contemporary format in 1986, it offers comfortable, midsize rooms but small bathrooms with well-maintained showers. The hotel serves a very generous breakfast buffet. It may be short on style but it's long on value.

Am Hinteren Perlachberg 1, 86150 Augsburg. ✆ **0821/34-64-90.** Fax 0821/346-49-99. www.hotel-am-rathaus-augsburg.de. 32 units. 105€–140€ double. Rates include breakfast. AE, DC, MC, V. Parking 9€. Tram: 1. **Amenities:** Bar. *In room:* TV, hair dryer, minibar.

Hotel Garni Weinberger One of the best budget accommodations in the area lies about 3km (1¾ miles) from the center along Augsburgerstrasse in the western sector. Rooms are small but well kept with good beds. The bathrooms are rather cramped with shower stalls, but housekeeping is excellent. The place is well patronized by bargain-hunting Germans.

Bismarckstrasse 55, 86391 Stadtbergen. ✆ **0821/24-39-10.** Fax 0821/43-88-31. www.cafe-weinberger.de. 31 units. 58€ double. Rates include buffet breakfast. AE, MC, V. Closed Aug 15–30. Tram: 3. **Amenities:** Cafe. *In room:* No phone.

Romantik Hotel Augsburger Hof ★★ Its main competitor, the Drei Mohren (below), has more flair, but this hotel enjoys a comfortable runner-up slot. Originally built in 1767 in a solid, thick-walled design with exposed beams and timbers, the hotel was carefully restored in 1988. In the town center, it's a favorite for its traditional atmosphere and excellent food. In spite of the Renaissance interior, the rooms are completely up to date and not as romantic as the name of the hotel suggests. They range from cozy to spacious, each with a fine bed. Those overlooking the calm inner courtyard are more expensive than ones facing the street. Some bathrooms are tiny, but each is beautifully maintained.

Auf dem Kreuz 2, 86152 Augsburg. ✆ **0821/34-64-90.** Fax 0821/346-4989. www.augsburger-hof.de. 36 units. 98€–125€ double. Rates include buffet breakfast. AE, DC, MC, V. Parking 8€. Tram: 2. **Amenities:** Restaurant; bar; room service; sauna. *In room:* TV, hair dryer, minibar, Wi-Fi (free).

Steigenberger Drei Mohren ★★ This is one of the premier choices for a stopover along the Romantic Road and one of the top inns if you didn't book into the Eisenhut at Rothenburg. The original hotel, dating from 1723, was renowned in Germany before its destruction in an air raid. In 1956, it was rebuilt in a modern style. Decorators worked hard to create a decor that was both comfortable and inviting, with thick carpets, subdued lighting, and double-glazing at the windows. Rooms vary in size and appointments, however, ranging from some economy specials that are a bit small with narrow twin beds and showers (no tubs) to spacious, luxurious rooms with full shower and tub.

Maximilianstrasse 40, 86150 Augsburg. ✆ **0821/5-03-60.** Fax 0821/15-78-64. www.steigenberger.com/en/Augsburg. 105 units. 110€–185€ double; 225€–600€ suite. AE, DC, MC, V. Parking 16€. Tram: 1. **Amenities:** Restaurant; bar; babysitting; golf by arrangement; room service; sauna (in suites). *In room:* TV, hair dryer, minibar, Wi-Fi (free).

WHERE TO DINE

Die Ecke ★ FRENCH/SWABIAN Dripping with atmosphere, this place seemingly dates from the Last Supper. Well, almost. At least it was founded in the year Columbus sighted the New World, and its guests have included Hans Holbein the Elder, Wolfgang Amadeus Mozart, and, in more contemporary times, Bertolt Brecht, whose sharp-tongued irreverence tended to irritate diners of more conservative political leanings. The Weinstube ambience belies the skilled cuisine of the chef, which wins us over year after year. Breast of duckling might be preceded by pâté, and the filet of sole in Riesling is deservedly a classic. Venison dishes in season are a specialty—the best in town.

Elias-Holl-Platz 2. ✆ **0821/51-06-00.** www.restaurant-die-ecke.de. Reservations required. Main courses 18€–44€; fixed-price dinner 50€ for 4 courses, 70€ for 6 courses. AE, DC, MC, V. Daily 11am–2pm and 5:30–10pm. Tram: 2.

Fuggerei Stube GERMAN/SWABIAN Not as atmospheric as Die Ecke, this is nonetheless a local and enduring favorite with good food and decent prices. The large dining room, suitable for 60 persons, has welcomed diners since 1946, with very little change in the menu, the decor, or the ambience. Expect generous portions of well-prepared food such as sauerbraten, roasted pork, and pork schnitzel; game dishes such as venison, pheasant, and rabbit; and fish such as filet of sole served with boiled potatoes and parsley. The beer foaming out of the taps here is Storchenbräu, and most visitors find that it goes wonderfully with the conservative German specialties.

Jakoberstrasse 26. ✆ **0821/3-08-70.** www.fuggerei-stube.de. Reservations recommended. Main courses 15€–22€; set-price menu 24€. AE, MC, V. Tues–Sun 12:30–2:30pm; Tues–Sat 5:30–11pm.

SEEING THE SIGHTS IN TOWN

Church of St. Ulrich and St. Afra ★ This is the most attractive church in Augsburg. It was constructed between 1476 and 1500 on the site of a Roman temple. The church stands immediately adjacent to St. Ulrich's Evangelical Lutheran Church, a tribute to the 1555 Peace of Augsburg, which recognized the two denominations, Roman Catholic and Lutheran. Many of the church's furnishings, including the three altars representing the birth and resurrection of Christ and the baptism of the church by the Holy Spirit, are baroque. In the crypt are the tombs of the Swabian saints, Ulrich and Afra.

Ulrichplatz 19. ✆ **0821/34-55-60.** Free admission. Daily 9am–5pm. Tram: 1.

Dom St. Maria The cathedral of Augsburg has the distinction of containing the oldest stained-glass windows in the world. Those in the south transept, dating from the 12th century, depict Old Testament prophets in a severe but colorful style. They are younger than the cathedral itself, which was begun in 944. You'll find the ruins of the original basilica in the crypt beneath the west chancel. Partially Gothicized in the 14th century, the church stands on the edge of the park, which also fronts the **Episcopal Palace,** where the basic Lutheran creed was presented at the Diet of Augsburg in 1530. The 11th-century bronze doors, leading into the three-aisle nave, are adorned with bas-reliefs of biblical and mythological characters. The cathedral's interior, restored in 1934, contains side altars with altarpieces by Hans Holbein the Elder and Christoph Amberger.

Hoher Weg. ✆ **0821/31-66-353.** Free admission. Mon–Sat 7am–5pm; Sun noon–5pm. Tram: 1.

Rathaus In 1805 and 1809, Napoleon visited the Rathaus, built by Elias Holl in 1620. Regrettably, it was also visited by an air raid in 1944, leaving a mere shell of the building that had once been a palatial eight-story monument to the glory of the Renaissance. Its celebrated "golden chamber" was left in shambles. Now, after costly restoration, the Rathaus is open to the public.

Am Rathausplatz 2. ✆ **0821/3249-2120.** Admission 2€ adults, 1€ children 7–14. Daily 10am–6pm. Tram: 1.

Schaezlerpalais Facing the Hercules Fountain is the Schaezlerpalais, home to the city's art galleries. Constructed as a 60-room mansion between 1765 and 1770, it was willed to Augsburg after World War II. Most of the paintings are Renaissance and baroque. One of the most famous is Dürer's portrait of Jakob Fugger the Rich, founder of the dynasty that was once powerful enough to influence the elections of the Holy Roman emperors. Other works are by local artists Hans Burgkmair and Hans Holbein the Elder; Rubens, Veronese, and Tiepolo are also represented.

Maximilianstrasse 46. ✆ **0821/324-4102.** Admission 8€ adults, 6€ children. Wed–Sun 10am–4pm. Tram: 1.

Neuschwanstein ★★★ & Hohenschwangau ★★: The Royal Castles

The 19th century saw a great classical revival in Germany, especially in Bavaria, mainly because of the enthusiasm of Bavarian kings for ancient art forms. Beginning with Ludwig I (1786–1868), who was responsible for many Greek Revival buildings in Munich, this royal house ran the gamut of ancient architecture in just 3 short decades. It culminated in the remarkable flights of fancy of "Mad" King Ludwig II, who died under mysterious circumstances in 1886. In spite of his rather lonely life and controversial alliances, both personal and political, he was a great patron of the arts.

Although the name "Royal Castles" is limited to Hohenschwangau (built by Ludwig's father, Maximilian II) and Neuschwanstein, the extravagant king was responsible for the creation of two other magnificent castles, Linderhof (near Oberammergau) and Herrenchiemsee (on an island in Chiemsee).

In 1868, after a visit to the great castle of Wartburg, Ludwig wrote to his good friend, composer Richard Wagner: "I have the intention to rebuild the ancient castle ruins of Hohenschwangau in the true style of the ancient German knight's castle." The following year, construction began on the first of a series of fantastic edifices, a series that stopped only with Ludwig's death in 1886, only 5 days after he was deposed because of alleged insanity.

The nearest towns to the castles are **Füssen,** 3km (1¾ miles) away at the very end of the Romantic Road, and **Schwangau,** where accommodations can be found.

ESSENTIALS

Getting There

BY TRAIN There are frequent trains from Munich (trip time: 2½ hr.) and Augsburg (3 hr.) to Füssen. For information, call ✆ **01805/99-66-33.** Frequent buses travel to the castles.

BY BUS Long-distance bus service into Füssen from other parts of the Romantic Road, including Würzburg, Augsburg, and Munich, is provided by the **Deutsche Touring GmbH** bus no. EB189 or EB190A. For information and reservations, call ✆ **069/790-268** in Frankfurt, or look on the Web at www.deutsche-touring.com. Regional service to villages around Füssen is provided by **RVA Regionalverkehr Allgau GmbH** in Füssen (✆ **08362/939-0505**). Its most important routing, at least for visitors to Füssen, includes about 14 orange, yellow, or white-sided buses that depart every day from Füssen's railway station for the village of Hohenschwangau, site of both Hohenschwangau Palace and Neuschwanstein Palace, a 10-minute ride. The cost of a one-way ticket to the village or to either of the two palaces is 2€. For more information, contact the Füssen tourist office, or Kurverwaltung (see below).

BY CAR Take B-17 south to Füssen; then head east from Füssen on B-17.

VISITOR INFORMATION For information about the castles and the region in general, contact the **Kurverwaltung,** Kaiser-Maximilian-Platz 1, Füssen (✆ **08362/938-50**), open in summer Monday to Friday 8:30am to 6:30pm, Saturday 9am to 2:30pm; winter hours are Monday to Friday 9am to 5pm, Saturday 10am to noon. Information is also available at the Kurverwaltung, Rathaus, Münchenerstrasse 2, Schwangau (✆ **08362/8-19-80;** www.schwangau.de). Hours vary so call ahead.

WHERE TO STAY

In Hohenschwangau

Hotel Müller Hohenschwangau As if the yellow walls, green shutters, and gabled alpine detailing of this hospitable inn weren't incentive enough, its location near the foundation of Neuschwanstein Castle makes it even more alluring. Midsize rooms are inviting and have a bit of Bavarian charm, each with a good bed. The shower-only bathrooms are spotless. Nature lovers usually enjoy hiking the short distance to nearby Hohenschwangau Castle. All rooms are nonsmoking.

Alpseestrasse 16, 87645 Hohenschwangau. ✆ **08362/8-19-90.** Fax 08362/81-99-13. www.hotel-mueller.de. 41 units. 98€–220€ double; 203€–270€ suite. Rates include buffet breakfast. AE, DC, MC, V. Free parking. Closed Jan–Feb. **Amenities:** 5 restaurants; bar; room service. *In room:* TV, hair dryer, minibar (in some).

Schlosshotel Lisl and Jägerhaus ★★ This graciously styled villa and its annex in a historic building across the street are among the better addresses in the area. Most rooms have a view of one or both castles. If you're assigned to the annex, never fear, as its rooms are just as fine as—or in some cases, even better than—those in the main building. Some of the bathrooms in the Jägerhaus are larger than some hotel rooms, and come complete with a large tub and shower. Both for charm and price, this one is a winner.

Neuschwansteinstrasse 1-3, 87645 Hohenschwangau. ✆ **08362/88-70.** Fax 08362/81-107. www.hohenschwangau.de. 47 units. 85€–115€ double; 95€–125€ suite. AE, DC, MC, V. Free parking. Closed Dec 21–26. **Amenities:** 2 restaurants; bar. *In room:* TV, minibar.

In or near Füssen

AlstadHotel Zum Hechten Family owners have maintained this impeccable guesthouse for generations—it's one of the oldest (and most comfortable) in town. In spring, you'll open your window to a flower box of geraniums, and feel like Gretel (or Hansel) getting ready to milk the cows. Rooms are small to medium size; the bathrooms are spotless but a bit cramped, containing shower stalls. Corridor bathrooms are adequate and well maintained.

Ritterstrasse 6, 87629 Füssen. ✆ **08362/91-600.** Fax 08362/91-6099. www.hotel-hechten.com. 35 units, 33 with bathroom. 94€–110€ double. Rates include buffet breakfast. AE, V. Free parking. **Amenities:** 2 restaurants. *In room:* TV.

Hotel Christine The Christine, 5 minutes by taxi from the train station in Füssen, is one of the best local choices for accommodations. The staff spends the winter months refurbishing the rooms so they'll be fresh and sparkling for spring visitors. A Bavarian charm pervades the hotel, and rooms are cozy, though hardly fit for King Ludwig. Each is well maintained and supplied with decent furnishings. The shower-only bathrooms are a bit cramped. Breakfast, the only meal offered, is served on beautiful regional china as classical music plays in the background.

Weidachstrasse 31, 87629 Füssen. ✆ **08362/72-29.** Fax 08362/94-05-54. www.hotel-christine-fuessen.de. 13 units. 95€–130€ double. Rates include breakfast. V. Free parking. Closed Jan 15–Feb 15. *In room:* TV, minibar.

Steig Mühle ★ Owners and hosts Gunter and Nedwig Buhmann like things to be cozy, and their chalet-like guesthouse is almost a cliché of Bavarian charm. The rooms open onto views of the lake or the mountains, and many have their own balconies. Each room has been outfitted with double or twin beds. Private bathrooms (shower only) are well kept. There aren't a lot of frills, but the place offers one of the most exceptional hotel values in the area.

Alte Steige 3, 87629 Weissensee-Oberkirch. ✆ **08362/91-76-0.** Fax 08362/31-48. www.steigmuehle.de. 24 units. 60€–66€ double. Rates include buffet breakfast. No credit cards. Free outside parking; 3€ in garage. From Füssen, take Rte. B310 north toward Kempten, a 5-min. drive. *In room:* TV.

WHERE TO DINE

Fischerhütte SEAFOOD In Hopfen am See, at the edge of the lake within sight of dramatic mountain scenery 5km (3 miles) northwest of Füssen, lie four old-fashioned dining rooms, plus a terrace in summer. As the name "Fisherman's Cottage" suggests, the establishment specializes in an array of international fish dishes: half an Alaskan salmon (for two); a garlicky version of French bouillabaisse; fresh alpine trout, pan-fried or with aromatic herbs in the style of Provence; North Atlantic lobster; and grilled halibut. A few meat dishes are also offered, as well as tempting desserts. The food is well prepared and top rate.

Uferstrasse 16, Hopfen am See. ✆ **08362/91-97-0.** www.fischerhuette-hopfen.de. Reservations recommended. Main courses 14€–46€. AE, DC, MC, V. Daily 10am–10:30pm.

Zum Schwanen SWABIAN/BAVARIAN This small, old-fashioned restaurant serves a conservative yet flavor-filled blend of Swabian and Bavarian specialties. Good-tasting and hearty specialties include homemade sausage, roast pork, lamb, and venison. Expect robust flavors and a crowd of cheery diners who don't believe in low-cal packaged dinners.

Brotmarkt 4, Füssen. ✆ **08362/61-74.** Reservations required. Main courses 6€–18€. MC, V. Tues–Sun 11:30am–2:30pm; Tues–Sat 5:30–9pm. Closed Nov plus 3 weeks in Mar and Sun in winter.

VISITING THE ROYAL CASTLES

There are often very long lines in summer, especially in August. With 25,000 people a day visiting, the wait in peak summer months can be as long as 4 or 5 hours for a 20-minute tour. For more information on Neuschwanstein, call ✆ **08362/9-39-88-0** or visit the website at **www.neuschwanstein.de**. For information on Hohenschwangau, call ✆ **08362/8-11-27** or visit the website at **www.hohenschwangau.de**.

Neuschwanstein ★★★

This is the fairy-tale castle of Ludwig II. Construction went on for 17 years, until the king's death, when all work stopped, leaving a part of the interior uncompleted. Ludwig lived here on and off for about 6 months from 1884 to 1886.

The doorway off the left side of the vestibule leads to the king's apartments. The study, like most of the rooms, is decorated with wall paintings showing scenes from the Nordic legends (which inspired Wagner's operas). The theme of the study is the Tannhäuser saga, painted by J. Aigner. The curtains and chair coverings are in hand-embroidered silk, designed with the Bavarian coat of arms.

From the vestibule, you enter the throne room through the doorway at the opposite end. This hall, designed in Byzantine style by J. Hofmann, was never completed. The floor, a mosaic design, depicts the animals of the world. The columns in the main hall are the deep copper red of porphyry.

The king's bedroom is the most richly carved and decorated in the entire castle—it took 4½ years to complete. Aside from the mural showing the legend of Tristan and Isolde, the walls are decorated with panels carved to look like Gothic windows. In the center is a large wooden pillar completely encircled with gilded brass sconces. The ornate bed is on a raised platform with an elaborately carved canopy.

The fourth floor of the castle is almost entirely given over to the **Singer's Hall,** the pride of Ludwig II and all of Bavaria. Modeled after the hall at Wartburg, where the legendary song contest of Tannhäuser supposedly took place, this hall is decorated with marble columns and elaborately painted designs interspersed with frescoes depicting the life of Parsifal.

The castle is open year-round, and in September, visitors have the additional treat of hearing Wagnerian concerts and other music in the Singer's Hall. For information and reservations, contact the tourist office in Schwangau, **Verkehrsamt,** at the Rathaus (✆ **08362/93-85-23**). The castle, which is seen by guided tour, is open daily April to September 9am to 6pm, October to March 10am to 4pm. Admission is 10€ adults, 8€ students and seniors over 65, free for children 13 and under.

Reaching Neuschwanstein involves a steep 1km (⅔-mile) climb from the parking lot of Hohenschwangau Castle—about a 25-minute walk for the energetic, an eternity for anybody else. To cut down on the climb, you can take a bus to Marienbrücke, a bridge that crosses over the Pollat Gorge at a height of 93m (305 ft.). From that vantage you, like Ludwig, can stand and meditate on the glories of the castle and its panoramic surroundings. If you want to photograph the castle, don't wait until you reach the top, where you'll be too close. It costs 2€ for the bus ride up to the bridge or 1€ if you'd like to take the bus back down the hill. From the Marienbrücke Bridge it's a 10-minute walk to Neuschwanstein over a very steep footpath that is not easy to negotiate for anyone who has trouble walking up or down precipitous hills.

The most colorful way to reach Neuschwanstein is by horse-drawn carriage, costing 5€ for the ascent, 2.50€ for the descent. However, some readers have objected to the rides, complaining that too many people are crowded in.

Hohenschwangau ★★

Not as glamorous or spectacular as Neuschwanstein, the neo-Gothic Hohenschwangau Castle nevertheless has a much richer history. The original structure dates from the 12th-century knights of Schwangau. When the knights faded away, the castle began to do so, too, helped along by the Napoleonic Wars. When Ludwig II's father, Crown Prince Maximilian (later Maximilian II), saw the castle in 1832, he purchased it and 4 years later had completely restored it. Ludwig II spent the first 17 years of his life here and later received Richard Wagner in its chambers, although Wagner never visited Neuschwanstein on the hill above.

The rooms of Hohenschwangau are styled and furnished in a much heavier Gothic mode than those in Ludwig's castle and are typical of the halls of medieval knights' castles. Also unlike Neuschwanstein, this castle has a comfortable look about it, as if it actually were a home, not just a museum. The small chapel, once a reception hall, still hosts Sunday Mass. The suits of armor and the Gothic arches set the stage. Among the most attractive chambers is the **Hall of the Swan Knight,** named for the wall paintings that tell the saga of Lohengrin.

Hohenschwangau is open April 1 to September from 8am to 5:30pm daily, off season from 9am to 3:30pm daily. Admission is 9€ adults, 8€ children 12 to 15 and seniors 66 and over, free for children 11 and under. Several parking lots nearby enable you to leave your car while visiting both castles. For ticket information for either castle, call © **08362/930-830.**

GREECE

by Sherry Marker

Today's Greece is a sophisticated, modern country—with, alas, the rising prices and economic turmoil to prove it. The days of absurdly cheap holidays are gone, but Greece now offers the dazzling glories of its fabled antiquity along with 21st-century pleasures and conveniences. Much of this combination stems from the 2004 Summer Olympic Games in Athens, which brought lasting changes throughout Greece. The pedestrianized walkways through Athens's "Archaeological Park" make strolling beneath the Acropolis and beside the Ancient Agora a traffic-free delight. And, in 2009, the spacious new Acropolis museum—originally planned to be finished in time for the Olympics—opened at the foot of the Acropolis. In addition, chic new boutique hotels (many with Wi-Fi and spa facilities) have opened in Athens and throughout Greece.

In addition to all that is new, the "glory that was Greece" continues to lure visitors, to attractions such as Olympia, where the games began; Delphi, with the magnificent temple of Apollo; Mycenae, where Agamemnon met his bloody death when he returned home from Troy; Epidaurus, with its astonishingly well-preserved ancient theater; and, of course, the best-known symbol of Greece: the Acropolis. But myths and monuments are only one aspect of the country's allure: Greece is also the quintessential vacationland of glorious beaches and towering mountain ranges. After sightseeing, you can laze the day away on a perfect beach—and then dance the night away in a cafe at the foot of the Acropolis or on one of the breathtakingly beautiful "isles of Greece." And no matter where you go, you can still experience the Greek *philoxenia*—the generous hospitality offered to strangers that leaves visitors determined to return as soon as possible.

ATHENS ★★★

Athens is the city that Greeks love to hate, complaining that it's too expensive, too polluted, and too crowded. More than five million people—some 40% of Greece's population—live in Athens, its port of Piraeus, and the surrounding suburbs. This is a city in constant flux, with most streets so congested that you'll suspect that everyone here has at least one car or motorcycle. That said, since 2004, the efficient and continuously expanding Metro (subway) has significantly diminished Athens's endemic gridlock and *nefos* (smog). Forever the city of a thousand contradictions, Athens is one of the few ancient cities in the world where the cutting edge, the hip, and the modern coexist harmoniously with the classical, and old and new complement each other to near perfection.

The almost 10 miles of pedestrianized streets and walkways that make up Athens's Archaeological Park link most major archaeological sites including Hadrian's Gate, the Acropolis, the Ancient Agora, and Kerameikos cemetery. Frequent exhibits are held along the walkways, and new cafes, restaurants, and galleries have sprung up nearby. Following the lead of Psirri and Thissio—two once down-at-the-heels ancient neighborhoods that are now the hippest downtown destinations—Gazi and Kerameikos have also risen from the ashes, going from gritty to urban chic.

Still, visitors momentarily overwhelmed by Athens's round-the-clock hustle and bustle (which sometimes includes motorcycles barreling along sidewalks) may be forgiven for sometimes wondering if Athens, even with all its recent updates and fabled glories, is the ideal holiday destination. Don't despair. You'll almost certainly develop your own love-hate relationship with the city, snarling at the traffic, gasping in wonder at the Acropolis, fuming at the taxi driver who tries to overcharge you, and marveling at the stranger who realizes that you're lost and walks several blocks out of his way to get you where you're going.

Essentials

GETTING THERE

BY PLANE **Athens International Airport Eleftherios Venizelos** (✆ **210/353-0000;** www.aia.gr), 27km (17 miles) northeast of Athens at Sparta, opened in 2001. Allow at least an hour for the journey from the airport to Athens (and vice versa). The Metro now runs all the way from the airport to central Athens (6€ one-way; 10€ round-trip). Trains run from 6am to midnight, though there is talk of initiating 24-hour service. If you don't have too much luggage, the Metro is now

Price Alert!

Greece is no longer a budget vacation destination. High season—once limited to summer months—now stretches from Easter to the end of October. Most hotels and restaurants took advantage of the 2004 Summer Olympics to hike their prices as high as possible, and many never lowered them. The weak dollar has also made everything here much pricier than only a few years ago. Another thing to keep in mind as you plan your visit: Greeks take so many year-round weekend jaunts to popular destinations such as Nafplion and the islands that many hotels double their rates on weekends.

Greece

a cheap and efficient option for reaching central Athens and the Piraeus, especially since buses run on erratic schedules and taxis can be costly. A taxi into central Athens usually costs from 20€ to 30€, depending on the time of day and traffic. Bus service to Syntagma Square or to Piraeus costs about 4€. Officially, there's one bus to Syntagma and one to Piraeus every 20 minutes. Bus and taxi stations are signposted at the airport. The airport's website and official publications cannot always be relied on for up-to-date information. Keep in mind that in 2009, the former Greek national airline, Olympic Airlines, became Olympic Air (www.olympicair.com), although both names continue to be used within Greece.

Tourist information, currency exchange, a post office, baggage storage (left luggage), and car rentals are available at the Arrivals level of the Main Terminal. ATMs, telephones, toilets, and luggage carts (1€) are available at the baggage-claim area. There are also several free phones from which you can call for a porter. ***Note:*** Porters' fees are highly negotiable.

There have been frequent complaints that adequate information on arrivals, departures, cancellations, delays, and gate changes is not always posted on the flight information screens. Nonetheless, it is important to check these screens and at the

Athens

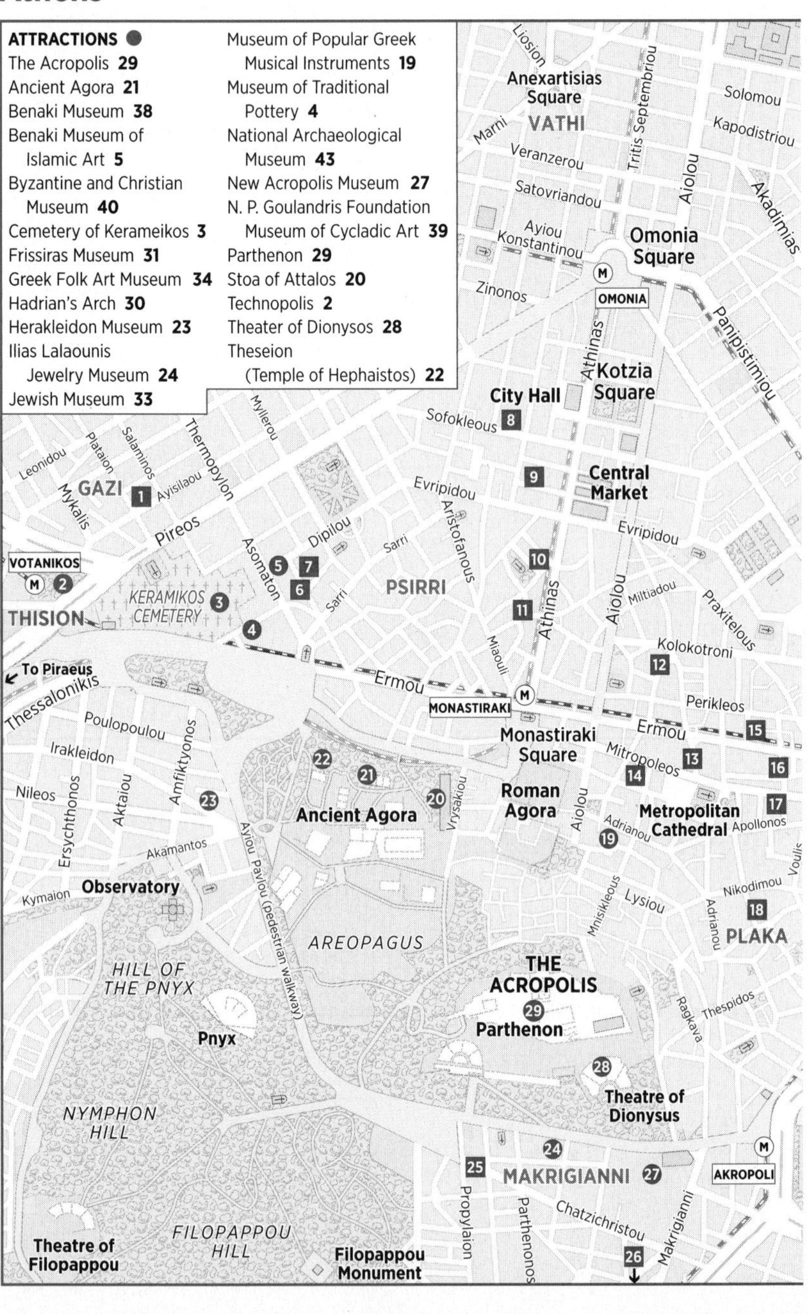
ATTRACTIONS
The Acropolis 29
Ancient Agora 21
Benaki Museum 38
Benaki Museum of Islamic Art 5
Byzantine and Christian Museum 40
Cemetery of Kerameikos 3
Frissiras Museum 31
Greek Folk Art Museum 34
Hadrian's Arch 30
Herakleidon Museum 23
Ilias Lalaounis Jewelry Museum 24
Jewish Museum 33
Museum of Popular Greek Musical Instruments 19
Museum of Traditional Pottery 4
National Archaeological Museum 43
New Acropolis Museum 27
N. P. Goulandris Foundation Museum of Cycladic Art 39
Parthenon 29
Stoa of Attalos 20
Technopolis 2
Theater of Dionysos 28
Theseion (Temple of Hephaistos) 22
Liosion
Anexartisias Square
VATHI
Marni
Veranzerou
Satovriandou
Ayiou Konstantinou
Zinonos
Tritis Septembriou
Aiolou
Solomou
Kapodistriou
Akadimias
Omonia Square
OMONIA
Panipistimiou
Athinas
Kotzia Square
City Hall
Sofokleous
Central Market
Evripidou
Aristofanous
Myllerou
Thermopylon
Salaminos
Plataion
Leonidou
GAZI
Ayisilaou
Mykalis
Pireos
Dipilou
Sarri
Asomaton
VOTANIKOS
THISION
KERAMIKOS CEMETERY
PSIRRI
Miltiadou
Praxitelous
Kolokotroni
Miaouli
To Piraeus
Thessalonikis
Ermou
MONASTIRAKI
Perikleos
Poulopoulou
Irakleidon
Nileos
Amfiktyonos
Monastiraki Square
Mitropoleos
Ersychthonos
Aktaiou
Vrysakiou
Roman Agora
Ancient Agora
Metropolitan Cathedral
Apollonos
Adrianou
Akamantos
Kymaion
Observatory
Ayiou Pavlou (pedestrian walkway)
Lysiou
Mnisikleous
Nikodimou
PLAKA
AREOPAGUS
HILL OF THE PNYX
THE ACROPOLIS
Parthenon
Ragkava
Thespidos
Pnyx
Theatre of Dionysus
NYMPHON HILL
MAKRIGIANNI
AKROPOLI
Propylaion
Parthenonos
Chatzichristou
Makrigianni
FILOPAPPOU HILL
Theatre of Filopappou
Filopappou Monument

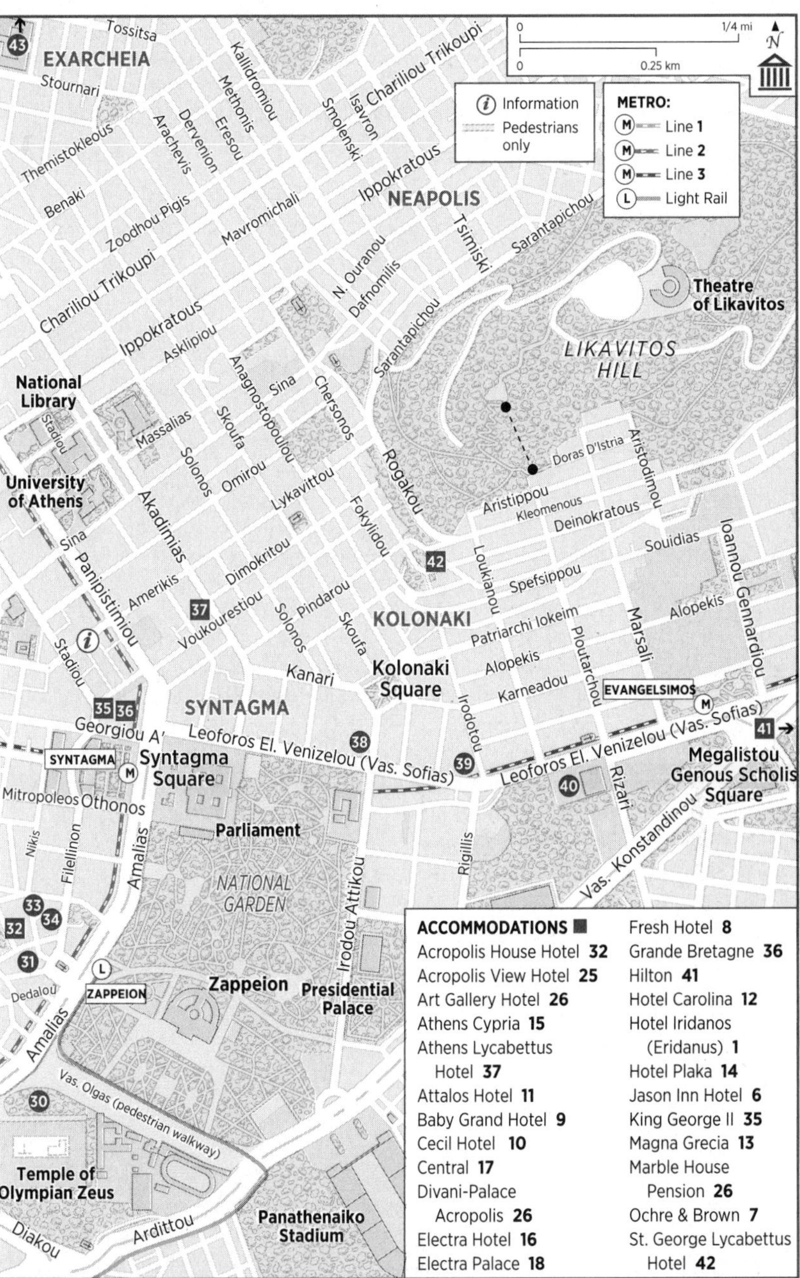
EXARCHEIA
NEAPOLIS
LIKAVITOS HILL
Theatre of Likavitos
National Library
University of Athens
KOLONAKI
Kolonaki Square
SYNTAGMA
Syntagma Square
Parliament
NATIONAL GARDEN
Zappeion
Presidential Palace
Temple of Olympian Zeus
Panathenaiko Stadium
Megalistou Genous Scholis Square
EVANGELSIMOS
SYNTAGMA
ZAPPEION
Tossitsa
Stournari
Themistokleous
Benaki
Zoodhou Pigis
Chariliou Trikoupi
Ippokratous
Asklipiou
Kallidromiou
Methonis
Eressou
Dervenion
Arachevis
Smolenski
Isavron
Mavromichali
N. Ouranou
Dafnomilis
Tsimiski
Sarantapichou
Massalias
Skoufa
Anagnostopoulou
Sina
Chersonos
Solonos
Omirou
Lykavittou
Rogakou
Fokylidou
Akadimias
Stadiou
Panipistimiou
Amerikis
Dimokritou
Voukourestiou
Pindarou
Kanari
Doras D'Istria
Aristodimou
Aristippou
Kleomenous
Deinokratous
Souidias
Ioannou Gennardiou
Loukianou
Spefsippou
Patriarchi Iokeim
Alopekis
Marsali
Ploutarchou
Karneadou
Irodotou
Georgiou A'
Leoforos El. Venizelou (Vas. Sofias)
Rizari
Vas. Konstandinou
Rigillis
Irodou Attikou
Mitropoleos
Othonos
Nikis
Filellinon
Amalias
Dedalou
Vas. Olgas (pedestrian walkway)
Diakou
Arditou
0 1/4 mi
0 0.25 km
N
Information
Pedestrians only
METRO:
Line 1
Line 2
Line 3
Light Rail
ACCOMMODATIONS
Acropolis House Hotel 32
Acropolis View Hotel 25
Art Gallery Hotel 26
Athens Cypria 15
Athens Lycabettus Hotel 37
Attalos Hotel 11
Baby Grand Hotel 9
Cecil Hotel 10
Central 17
Divani-Palace Acropolis 26
Electra Hotel 16
Electra Palace 18
Fresh Hotel 8
Grande Bretagne 36
Hilton 41
Hotel Carolina 12
Hotel Iridanos (Eridanus) 1
Hotel Plaka 14
Jason Inn Hotel 6
King George II 35
Magna Grecia 13
Marble House Pension 26
Ochre & Brown 7
St. George Lycabettus Hotel 42

Airport Taxi Savvy

If you decide to take a taxi, ask an airline official or a policeman what the fare should be, and let the taxi driver know you've been told the official rate before you begin your journey. If you're taking a taxi to the airport, try to have the desk clerk at your hotel order it for you well in advance of your departure. Many taxis refuse to go to the airport, fearing that they'll have a long wait before they get a return fare.

information desks, as there are currently **no** flight announcements. Arrive at your gate as early as possible; gates are sometimes changed at the last minute.

BY TRAIN Central Athens has two train stations, both about 1.5km (1 mile) northwest of Omonia Square. Trains from the west, including Eurail connections via Patra, arrive at the **Stathmos Peloponnissou (Peloponnese Station; ✆ 210/513-1601**). Trains from the north arrive 3 blocks north of (and on the opposite side of the tracks from) the Peloponnese Station at the **Stathmos Larissis (Larissa Station; ✆ 210/529-8837**). If you are making connections from one station to the other, allow 15 minutes for the walk. Both stations have currency-exchange offices usually open daily from 8am to 9:15pm, and luggage-storage offices charging 5€ per bag per day, open daily from 6:30am to 9:30pm. A **taxi** into the center of town should cost about 8€. You can purchase train tickets at the train station (running the risk that all seats may be sold); at the Omonia Square ticket office, 1 Karolou (**✆ 210/524-0647**); at 17 Filellinon, off Syntagma Square (**✆ 210/323-6747**); or from most travel agents. Information (in theory in English) on timetables is available at **✆ 145** or 147, and at www.ose.gr, the website of the **Greek Railroad Company (OSE).**

BY BOAT **Piraeus,** the main harbor of Athens's main seaport, 11km (6¾ miles) southwest of central Athens, is a 15-minute subway (Metro) ride from Monastiraki and Omonia squares. The subway runs from about 5am to midnight and costs 1€. The far-slower bus no. 040 runs from Piraeus to central Athens (with a stop at Filellinon off Syntagma Sq.) every 15 minutes between 5am and 1am and hourly from 1am to 5am, for .80€.

You might prefer to take a **taxi** to avoid what can be a long hike from your boat to the bus stop or subway terminal. Be prepared for some serious bargaining. The normal fare on the meter from Piraeus to Syntagma should be about 15€ to 20€, but many drivers simply offer a flat fare, which can easily be 30€. Pay it if you're desperate, or walk to a nearby street, hail another taxi, and insist that the meter be turned on.

If you travel to Piraeus by hydrofoil (*Flying Dolphin*), you'll probably arrive at the **Zea Marina** harbor, about a dozen blocks south across the peninsula from the main harbor. Getting a taxi from Zea Marina into Athens can involve a wait of an hour or more—and drivers usually drive a hard (and exorbitant) bargain. To avoid both the wait and the big fare, walk up the hill from the hydrofoil station and catch bus no. 905 for 1€; it connects Zea to the Piraeus subway station, where you can complete your journey into Athens. You must buy a ticket at the small ticket stand near the bus stop or at a newsstand before boarding the bus. ***Warning:*** If you arrive late at night, both the newsstand and the ticket stand may be closed.

VISITOR INFORMATION **Tourist Office** The **Greek National Tourism Organization** (**EOT** or **GNTO**) is located at 7 Tsochas St., Ambelokipi (✆ **210/870-0000;** www.gnto.gr and www.visitgreece.gr; Metro: Ambelokipi). The office is open Monday to Friday 8am to 3pm. The GNTO information desk office is at 26 Amalias (✆ **210/331-0392;** Metro: Syntagma; Mon–Fri 9am–7pm), across the street from the Gardens. There is also an information desk at the airport (✆ **210/345-0445**). Information about Athens, free city maps, transportation schedules, hotel lists, and other booklets on many regions of Greece are available at the office in Greek, English, French, and German—although all too often many publications are described as "all gone"—even when they are on display behind the counter just out of reach. The staff members often appear bored and irritated by questions; be persistent.

Available 24 hours a day, the **tourist police** (✆ **210/171**) speak English, as well as other languages, and will help you with problems or emergencies.

WEBSITES Helpful sites for Greece include the Ministry of Culture information site for archaeological sites, monuments, and museums (**www.culture.gr**), and the Greek National Tourist Office site (**www.gnto.gr** or **www.visitgreece.gr**). The Parliament also has its own website, **www.parliament.gr**. Two websites with a wealth of information and daily updates are **www.athensinfoguide.com** and **www.breathtakingathens.com**. Other helpful sites include **www.athensnews.gr** (*The Athens News,* Greece's English-language newspaper); **www.eKathimerini.com** (an insert of translations from the Greek press sold with the *International Herald Tribune*); **www.dilos.com** (travel information, including discounted hotel prices); **www.gtp.gr** (information on ferry service); **www.greekislands.gr** (information on the islands); **www.greektravel.com** (a helpful site run by American Matt Barrett); and **www.ancientgreece.com** and **www.perseus.tufts.edu** (excellent sources on ancient Greece).

CITY LAYOUT Think of central Athens as an almost perfect equilateral triangle, with its points at **Syntagma (Constitution) Square, Omonia (Harmony) Square,** and **Monastiraki (Little Monastery) Square,** near the **Acropolis.** Most Greeks consider Omonia Square the city center, but visitors usually get their bearings from Syntagma Square, where the House of Parliament stands beside the National Gardens. Omonia and Syngagma squares are connected by the parallel **Stadiou Street** and **Panepistimiou Street,** also called **Eleftheriou Venizelou.** West from Syntagma Square, ancient **Ermou Street** and broader **Mitropoleos Street** lead slightly downhill to **Monastiraki Square.** Fingers crossed that the current renovation of Monastiraki Square does not transform its bustling chaos into an Omonia-like concrete wasteland. Monastiraki is flanked by the **flea market,** the

Arriving in Greece

If you plan to travel by air in Greece or elsewhere in Europe, keep in mind that the luggage allowance for most flights within Greece and Europe is 20 kilos (44 lb.). This is almost certainly less than you would have been allowed if you have flown to Greece from the U.S. or Canada.

Ancient Agora (Market) below the Acropolis, and the **Plaka,** the oldest neighborhood, with a scattering of antiquities and many street names from antiquity, including its main drag, pedestrianized **Adrianou Street,** named for the emperor Hadrian. From Monastiraki Square, **Athinas Street** leads north to Omonia Square past the modern market (the Central Market); this is *the* place to buy everything from buttons and birdseed to herbs and sheeps' heads. Bustling with shoppers in the daytime, Athinas Street was once considerably less savory at night; the ongoing gentrification of the area means that prostitutes and drug dealers are now scarce. Between Athinas and Hermou streets the increasingly chic former industrial wasteland of **Psirri,** along with the neighboring **Gazi** district, is giving the longtime posh haven of **Kolonaki,** on the slopes of Mt. Lykabettus, a run for the money as the place to see and be seen. Still low-key by day, the nighttime scene in Gazi and Psirri's wall-to-wall art galleries, cafes, and restaurants makes Kolonaki seem sedate.

In general, finding your way around Athens is not too difficult, except in the Plaka, at the foot of the Acropolis. This labyrinth of narrow, winding streets can challenge even the best navigators. Don't panic: The area is small enough that you can't go far astray, and its side streets, with small houses and neighborhood churches, are so charming that you won't mind being lost. One excellent map may help: the Greek Archaeological Service's ***Historical Map of Athens,*** which includes the Plaka and the city center and shows the major archaeological sites. The map costs about 5€ and is sold at many bookstores, museums, ancient sites, and newspaper kiosks.

GETTING AROUND **By Public Transportation** In central Athens, keep an eye out for minibus nos. 60 and 150, which offer free service. As for other service, **blue-and-white buses** run regular routes in Athens and its suburbs every 15 minutes daily from 5am to midnight. The **orange electric trolley buses** serve areas in the city center daily from 5am to midnight. The **green buses** run between the city center and Piraeus every 20 minutes daily from 6am to midnight, and then hourly to 6am. Tickets cost .50€ and you must buy them in advance, usually in groups of 10, from any news kiosk or special bus ticket kiosks at the main stations. When you board, validate your ticket in the automatic machine. Hold onto it: Uniformed and plainclothes inspectors periodically check tickets and can levy a basic fine of 5€, or a more punitive fine of 20€, on the spot. ***Tip:*** The **Athens Urban Transport Organization** (www.oasa.gr) has lots of information on routes and timetables.

The major bus stations in Athens are **Suburban bus terminal** at Areos Park; **Long Distance Bus Terminal A,** 100 Kiffissou (reached by bus no. 051 from Zinonos and Menandrou sts., off Omonia Sq.); and **Long Distance Bus Terminal B,** 260 Liossion (reached by bus no. 024 from Amalias Ave., Syntagma Sq.).

Ride the Metro & View Artifacts & Antiquities

Allow a little extra time when you catch the Metro in central Athens. Several stations—notably **Syntagma Square** and **Acropolis**—display finds from the subway excavations. And, if you take the Metro to Piraeus, don't miss the spectacular view of the Acropolis as the metro comes aboveground by the Agora. For more on the Athens Metro, go to **www.ametro.gr.**

A Taxi Warning

Increasing numbers of unlicensed cabdrivers ply their trade in Athens and Piraeus. Usually, these pirate cabbies (many from eastern Europe) drive not the standard gray Athens taxi but a gray car you might mistake for an Athens cab. It's always a good idea to make sure your cabdriver has a meter and a photo ID. Many of the unlicensed cabdrivers are uninsured and unfamiliar with the metropolitan area.

The original **Metro** line links Piraeus, Athens's seaport; central Athens itself; and Kifissia, an upscale northern suburb. The new lines now crisscross central Athens and run as far out of town as the international airport to the east and Daphni to the southwest. Free maps of the entire metro system are often available at the information booths in metro stations. In the city center, the main stops are **Syntagma, Acropolis, Monastiraki, Omonia,** and **Viktorias (Victoria).** Trains run about every 5 to 15 minutes daily from 5am to midnight. Single-journey tickets cost .80€, and a day pass costs 3€. Validate your ticket in the machine as you enter the waiting platform, or risk a fine. Metro and bus tickets are not interchangeable, but it is usually possible to purchase a special 1€ ticket that is valid on all forms of public transportation for 90 minutes after purchase.

BY TAXI Supposedly there are 17,000 taxis in Athens, but finding one empty is rarely easy. Especially if you have travel connections to make, it's a good idea to pay the 2€ surcharge and reserve a radio taxi. The minimum fare in a taxi is 3€. Some radio taxi companies and phone numbers are **Athina** (✆ **210/921-7942**); **Express** (✆ **210/993-4812**); **Parthenon** (✆ **210/532-3300**); and **Piraeus** (✆ **210/418-2333**). Most hotels and restaurants will call a radio taxi for you without charge. ***Warning:*** Taxi-fare price hikes are in the works, but have not yet been announced.

When you get into a taxi, check to see that the meter is turned on and set on "1" rather than "2"; it should be set on "2" (double fare) only from midnight to 5am or if you take a taxi outside the city limits. (If you plan to take a cab out of town, it is best to negotiate a flat rate in advance.) Don't be surprised if your driver picks up other passengers en route; he'll work out everyone's share, and probably the worst that will happen is you'll get less of a break on the shared fare than you would if you spoke Greek. Most Greek passengers round out the fare to the nearest euro as a modest tip.

If you suspect you've been overcharged, ask for help at your hotel or other destination before you pay the fare. If you are taking a taxi from your hotel, a staff member can tell the driver your destination or write down the address for you to show to the driver. If you carry a business card from your hotel, you can show it to the driver when you return.

BY CAR Parking is so difficult and traffic so heavy in Athens that you should use a car only for trips outside the city. Keep in mind that on any day trip (to Sounion or Daphni, for example) you'll spend at least several hours leaving and reentering central Athens.

If you do decide on the spur of the moment to rent a car in Athens, you'll find many rental agencies south of Syntagma Square. Some of the better agencies include **Athens Cars,** 10 Filellinon (✆ 210/323-3783 or 210/324-8870); **Autorental,** 11 Leoforos Syngrou (✆ 210/923-2514); **Avis,** 46–48 Leoforos Amalias (✆ 210/322-4951 to -4957); **Budget Rent A Car,** 8 Leoforos Syngrou (✆ 210/921-4771 to -4773); **Eurodollar Rent a Car,** 29 Leoforos Syngrou (✆ 210/922-9672 or 210/923-0548); **Hellascars,** 148 Leoforos Syngrou (✆ 210/923-5353 to -5359); **Hertz,** 12 Leoforos Syngrou (✆ 210/922-0102 to -0104) and 71 Leoforos Vas. Sofias (✆ 210/724-7071 or 210/722-7391); **Interrent-Europcar/Batek SA,** 4 Leoforos Syngrou (✆ 210/921-5789); and **Thrifty Hellas Rent a Car,** 24 Leoforos Syngrou (✆ 210/922-1211 to -1213). Prices for rentals range from 50€ to 100€ per day. ***Warning:*** Be sure to take full insurance and ask if the price you are quoted includes everything—taxes, drop-off fee, gasoline charges, and other fees.

BY FOOT Most of what you probably want to see and do in Athens is in the city center, allowing you to sightsee mostly on foot. The pedestrian zones in sections of the Plaka, the commercial center, and Kolonaki make strolling, window-shopping, and sightseeing infinitely more pleasant than on other, traffic-clogged streets. Nonetheless, visitors should keep in mind that here, as in many busy cities, a red traffic light or stop sign is no guarantee that cars will stop for pedestrians.

[FastFACTS] ATHENS

Business Hours **Banks** are generally open Monday to Thursday 8am to 2pm and Friday 8am to 1:30pm. ***Warning:*** It is *not* a good idea to rely on exclusive use of **ATM**s in Greece, as the machines are often out of service when you need them most, particularly on holidays or during bank strikes.

In winter, **shops** are generally open Monday and Wednesday 9am to 5pm; Tuesday, Thursday, and Friday 10am to 7pm; and Saturday 8:30am to 3:30pm. In summer, shops are generally open Monday, Wednesday, and Saturday 8am to 3pm; and Tuesday, Thursday, and Friday 8am to 1:30pm and 5:30 to 10pm. Note that many shops geared to visitors stay open throughout the day. Most **food stores** and the **Central Market** are open Monday and Wednesday 9am to 4:30pm, Tuesday 9am to 6pm, Thursday 9:30am to 6:30pm, Friday 9:30am to 7pm, and Saturday 8:30am to 4:30pm. Many urban supermarkets are open 9am to 8pm, Monday to Saturday. Pastry shops are almost always open on Sundays.

Currency On January 1, 2002, the monetary unit in Greece became the euro €. At press time, 1€ = US$1.40.

Currency Exchange Most banks exchange currency using the rates set daily by the government, which are usually more favorable than those offered at unofficial exchange bureaus.

Dentists & Doctors If you need an English-speaking doctor or dentist, call your embassy (see below) for advice, or try **SOS Doctor** (✆ **1016** or 210/361-7089). There are two medical hot lines for foreigners: ✆ **210/721-2951** (day) and 210/729-4301 (night) for U.S. citizens; and ✆ **210/723-6211** (day) and 210/723-7727 (night) for British citizens. Most of the larger hotels can call a doctor for you in an emergency, and embassies will sometimes recommend local doctors. Some English-speaking physicians advertise in the daily *Athens News.*

Drugstores *Pharmakia,* identified by green crosses, are scattered throughout Athens. Hours are usually Monday to Friday 8am to 2pm. In the evenings and on weekends, most are closed, but each posts a notice listing the names and addresses of pharmacies that are open or will open in an emergency. Newspapers such as the *Athens News* list pharmacies open after hours.

Embassies & Consulates Locations are **Australia,** 37 Leoforos Dimitriou Soutsou (✆ 210/870-4000); **Canada,** 4 Ioannou Yenadiou (✆ 210/727-3400 or 210/725-4011); **Ireland,** 7 Vas. Konstantinou (✆ 210/723-2771); **New Zealand,** Xenias 24, Ambelokipi (✆ 210/771-0112); **South Africa,** 60 Kifissias, Maroussi (✆ 210/680-6645); **United Kingdom,** 1 Ploutarchou (✆ 210/723-6211); **United States,** 91 Leoforos Vas. Sofias (✆ 210/721-2951, or 210/729-4301 for emergencies). Phone ahead before you go to any embassy; most keep limited hours and are usually closed on both home and Greek holidays.

Emergencies In an emergency, dial ✆ **100** for the **police** and ✆ **171** for the **tourist police.** Dial ✆ **199** to report a **fire** and ✆ **166** for an **ambulance** and the **hospital.** Athens has a **24-hour** line for foreigners, the **Visitor Emergency Assistance** at ✆ **112** in English and French.

Hospitals Except for emergencies, hospital admittance is gained through a physician. See "Dentists & Doctors," above.

KAT, the emergency hospital in Kifissia (✆ **210/801-4411** to -4419), and **Asklepion Voulas,** the emergency hospital in Voula (✆ **210/895-3416** to -3418), both have emergency rooms open 24 hours a day. **Evangelismos,** a respected centrally located hospital below the Kolonaki district on 9 Vas. Sophias (✆ **210/722-0101**), usually has English-speaking staff on duty. If you need medical attention fast, don't waste time trying to call these hospitals: Just go. Their doors are open and they will see to you as soon as possible.

In addition, each major hospital takes its turn each day being on emergency duty. A recorded message in Greek at ✆ **210/106** tells which hospital is open for emergency services and gives the telephone number.

Internet Access Most midrange to top-end hotels have at least an "Internet corner," but for a current list of Athenian cybercafes, check out www.athensinfoguide.com. Also, keep in mind there are several **Wi-Fi hot spots** across the city, such as Syntagma Square, Kotzia Square, Flisvos marina, and the Thission; the airport and several cafes also offer free Wi-Fi.

Police In an **emergency,** dial ✆ **100.** For help dealing with a troublesome taxi driver, hotel staff, restaurant staff, or shop owner, stand your ground and call the **tourist police** at ✆ **171.**

Post Offices The main post offices in central Athens are at 100 Eolou, just south of Omonia Square; and in Syntagma Square, at the corner of 60 Mitropoleos. They are open Monday to Friday 7:30am to 8pm, Saturday 7:30am to 2pm, and Sunday 9am to 1pm. All post offices accept parcels, but the **Parcel Post Office** is at 4 Stadiou inside the arcade (✆ **210/322-8940**). It's open Monday to Friday 7:30am to 8pm. It usually sells twine and cardboard shipping boxes in four sizes. Parcels must remain open for possible inspection before you seal them at the post office.

Safety Athens is among the safest capitals in Europe, and there are few reports of violent crimes. **Pickpocketing,** however, is not uncommon, especially in the Plaka and Omonia Square areas, on the Metro and buses, and in Piraeus. Unfortunately, it is a good idea to be wary of Gypsy children. It's a good idea to avoid the side streets of Omonia and Piraeus at night. As always, leave your passport and valuables in a security box at the hotel. Carry a photocopy of your passport, not the original.

Taxes A VAT (value-added tax) of between 4% and 18% is added onto everything you buy. Some shops will attempt to cheat you by quoting one price and then, when you hand over your credit card, they will add on a hefty VAT charge. Be wary. In theory, if you are not a member of a Common Market/E.U. country, you can get a refund on major purchases at the Athens airport when you leave Greece. In reality, you have to arrive at the airport a day before your flight to navigate the line, do the paperwork, get a refund, and catch your flight!

Telephone The country code for Greece is **30.** The city code for Athens is **210.** To dial a number in Athens from outside Greece, dial 011-30 (Greece), plus 210 (Athens), and then the number. To dial Athens from within Greece, dial 201 plus the number. ***Remember:*** In Greece, you must use the area code even if you are phoning within the same area.

Many of the city's public phones now accept only phone cards, available at newsstands and the **Telecommunications Organization of Greece (OTE)** offices in several denominations, currently starting at 3€. Most OTE offices and **Germanos** stores (including in the airport) now sell cellphones and phone cards at reasonable prices; if you are in Greece for a month, you may find this a good option. Some kiosks still have metered phones; you pay what the meter records.

Tipping Athenian restaurants include a service charge in the bill, but many visitors add a 10% tip. Most Greeks do not give a percentage tip to taxi drivers, but often round up the fare; for example, round up a fare of 2.80€ to 3€.

Toilets Public restrooms are in the underground station beneath Omonia and Syntagma squares and beneath Kolonaki Square, but you'll probably prefer a hotel or restaurant restroom. (Toilet paper is often not available, so carry tissue with you. Do not flush paper down the commode; use the receptacle provided.)

Where to Stay

Although many guidebooks do, we don't recommend staying in any of the luxury hotels on Syngrou Avenue, which is ugly, noisy, and away from everything you want to see in Athens. The Gazi and Psirri areas are becoming popular locations for hotels—as are the side streets off busy Athinas Street between Omonia and Monastiraki squares. And Makrigianni, long a semipopular tourist destination due to its proximity to the sites and low-key residential ambience, is probably going to get much more popular due to the 2009 opening of the new Acropolis Museum.

A few suggestions: If shower and tub facilities are particularly important to you, be sure to have a look at the bathroom. Many Greek tubs are small by American standards, and the showers are hand-held. Don't assume that just because a hotel says it has air-conditioning, the air-conditioning is working—and check to see if the hotel has adequately functioning central heating in the winter. If you want Wi-Fi, double-check to see if the hotel you are interested in has it. Many Athenian hotels that did not have Wi-Fi at press time said that they would have it "soon."

Tip: Tourism in Greece slumped almost 10% in 2009, but if it rebounds, expect hotel prices to go up again. It never hurts to ask for the price of the least expensive room available. In addition, always ask for the discount usually given for stays of more than 3 nights and be sure to ask if the rates vary on different days of the week. Weekend hotel rates are sometimes cheaper in Athens, but usually *more* expensive out of Athens (especially in the islands). Winter rate reductions are not uncommon in many small Athenian hotels, while some well-known large downtown Athenian hotels offer reductions in August, when savvy travelers tend to avoid Athens and its heat. ***Warning:*** Whenever you go and wherever you stay, be sure to bring along a printout of your hotel reservation.

IN PLAKA

Expensive

Electra Palace ★★ The Electra, a few blocks southwest of Syntagma Square on a relatively quiet side street off busy Amalias Avenue, is the most relaxing Plaka hotel, thanks to its rooftop pool. The rooms on the 5th, 6th, and 7th floors are smaller than those on lower floors, but a top-floor room is where you want to be, both for the terrific view of the Acropolis and to escape traffic noise. Guest rooms here are comfortable, not elegant. The hotel restaurant has become one of the best and most sought-after restaurants in town with a view as sublime as the food. Note that the restaurant is closed Sunday.

18 Nikodimou, Plaka, 105 57 Athens. ✆ **210/324-1401** or 210/324-1407. Fax 210/324-1975. 106 units. www.electrahotels.gr. 180€ double. Rates include breakfast buffet. AE, DC, MC, V. Parking 12€ a day. Metro: Syntagma. **Amenities:** Restaurant; bar; exercise room; 2 pools (1 indoor, 1 rooftop); spa. *In room:* A/C, TV, hair dryer, minibar, Wi-Fi.

Moderate

Central ★★ Completely refurbished, this stylish, elegant hotel off Mitropoleos Square features wonderful sea-grass or wooden floors, marble bathrooms, and excellent soundproofing. Family and interconnecting rooms are also available, and the large roof has superb Acropolis views and a hot tub. If the Central is full, try the neighboring similarly priced Hermes (✆ **210/323-5514;** www.hermeshotel.gr) at 19 Apollonos.

21 Apollonos, 105 57 Athens. ✆ **210/323-4357.** www.centralhotel.gr. 84 units. 100€–135€ double. AE, DC, MC, V. Metro: Syntagma. **Amenities:** Bar; Jacuzzi. *In room:* A/C, TV, hair dryer, Internet.

Hotel Plaka ★★ This hotel is popular with Greeks, who prefer its modern conveniences to the old-fashioned charms of most other hotels in the Plaka area. It has fair prices and a terrific location near Mitropoleos Square just off Syntagma Square and the Plaka. Many rooms have balconies. Fifth- and sixth-floor rooms in the rear (where it's usually quieter) have views of the Plaka and the Acropolis, also splendidly visible from the roof-garden bar (open in summer). Friends who stayed here recently weren't charmed by the service but loved the Plaka's central and relatively quiet location. Rates here are usually considerably cheaper off season.

Mitropoleos and 7 Kapnikareas, 105 56 Athens. ✆ **210/322-2096.** Fax 210/322-2412. www.plakahotel.gr. 67 units, 38 with shower only. 145€–165€ double. Rates include breakfast. AE, MC, V. Metro: Syntagma. **Amenities:** Bar. *In room:* A/C, TV, hair dryer, minibar.

Magna Grecia ★★ In a hard-to-beat location (right on Mitropoleos Sq.), located inside a beautiful 19th-century neoclassical building with high ceilings, French doors, and hardwood floors, this is easily one of the best hotels in the Plaka. All front rooms have sweeping Acropolis views, and there is a pleasant and relaxing rooftop bar as well (also with Acropolis views) that has so far gone by rather unnoticed by glamour-seeking Athenians.

54 Mitropoleos, 105 63 Plaka. ✆ **210/324-0314.** Fax 210/324-0317. www.magnagreciahotel.com. 12 rooms. 150€–180€ double. AE, DC, MC, V. Metro: Syntagma. **Amenities:** Cafe/bar; room service. *In room:* A/C, TV/DVD, CD player, Internet.

Inexpensive

Acropolis House Hotel ★★ Location is the big plus in this venerable small hotel in the heart of Plaka, a 5-minute walk from Syntagma Square. Kodrou is a relatively quiet largely pedestrianized Plaka side street, although motorcycles can be a problem. Bedrooms are small, with minimalist furnishings, but the 150-year-old villa has been nicely renovated. Try to get room no. 401 or 402 for an Acropolis view. The newer wing (only 65 years old) isn't architecturally special, and the toilets (one for each room) are across the hall.

6–8 Kodrou, 105 58 Athens. ✆ **210/322-2344.** Fax 210/324-4143. www.acropolishouse.gr. 25 units, 15 with bathroom. 75€ double without bathroom, 85€ with bathroom. 10€ surcharge for A/C. Rates include continental breakfast. V. Metro: Syntagma. **Amenities:** Internet. *In room:* A/C, TV.

NEAR MONASTIRAKI SQUARE

Moderate

Attalos Hotel ★ The six-story Attalos is well situated for those wanting to take in the exuberant daytime street life of the nearby Central Market and the equally exuberant nighttime scene at the cafes and restaurants of the Psirri district. The rooms here are very plain, but 40 have balconies, 12 have Acropolis views, and a number will sleep three or four. The roof garden offers fine views of the city and the Acropolis. The Attalos—whose staff is usually very helpful—often gives a 10% discount to Frommer's readers.

29 Athinas, 105 54 Athens. ✆ **210/391-2801.** Fax 210/324-3124. www.attalos.gr. 80 units. 100€ double. Rates include buffet breakfast. AE, MC, V. Metro: Monastiraki. **Amenities:** Breakfast room; bar; Internet. *In room:* A/C, TV, hair dryer (in most).

Cecil Hotel ★ Another reasonably priced hotel on Athinas Street, the Cecil has 36 rooms in a beautifully restored neoclassical town house with great architectural details—the rooms might be small but they all have polished wood floors and high ceilings, and are soundproof. Full breakfast is served and there's also a welcoming roof garden restaurant.

39 Athinas, 105 54 Athens. ✆ **210/321-7079.** Fax 210/321-8005. www.cecil.gr. 115€ double. AE, MC, V. Metro: Monastiraki. **Amenities:** Roof garden restaurant/cafe; bar. *In room:* A/C, TV.

Jason Inn Hotel ★ If you don't mind walking a few extra blocks to most destinations, this is currently one of the best values in Athens, with a characteristically eager-to-help staff. On a dull street, but just a few blocks from the Agora, the Plaka, and the Psirri district, the Jason Inn has comfortable rooms (decent beds and reading lights) with double-paned windows for extra quiet.

12 Ayion Assomaton, 105 53 Athens. ✆ **210/325-1106.** Fax 210/523-4786. www.douros-hotels.com. 57 units. 100€ double. Rates include American buffet breakfast. AE, MC, V. Metro: Monastiraki. **Amenities:** Breakfast room; bar; Internet. *In room:* A/C, TV, hair dryer (most rooms), minibar.

PSIRRI

Expensive

Ochre & Brown ★★ This trendy, stylish, and small boutique hotel in the heart of Psirri opened in 2006 and has found its niche for fashion-conscious and experienced travelers looking for style, highly personalized service, high-tech comforts, and a chic urban experience. Some rooms have Thissio views but the finest room by far is the junior suite with Acropolis views from its terrace. Rooms have stylish furnishings, large work desks with Internet access, and marble bathrooms with custom-designed glass-enclosed showers. The hotel's lounge/bar and restaurant is one of the city's favorite haunts.

7 Leokoriou, 105 54 Athens. ✆ **210/331-2950.** Fax 210/331-2942. www.ochreandbrown.com. 11 units. 190€–220€ double. AE, MC, V. Metro: Monastiraki. **Amenities:** Restaurant; lounge bar. *In room:* A/C, TV, Wi-Fi.

GAZI/KERAMEIKOS

Expensive

Hotel Iridanos (Eridanus) ★★ This new boutique hotel in a neoclassical building is filled with original artwork. Many rooms have stunning Acropolis views, and the city's best fish restaurant, Varoulko, is just next door. The bedrooms have huge beds, enormous bathrooms, and large flatscreen TVs. This may not be the place to stay on your first trip to Athens, when you may wish to be closer to the center, but you are within a short walking distance of the city's best nightlife in Gazi, Thissio, and Psirri. The new line 3 (airport line) Metro stop at Kerameikos is practically next door to the hotel.

80 Piraeus, 105 51 Athens. ✆ **210/520-5360.** www.eridanus.gr. 38 units. 200€ double; 290€ double deluxe with Acropolis view. AE, MC, V. Metro: Kerameikos. **Amenities:** Restaurant; breakfast room; bar. *In room:* A/C, TV, Internet, minibar.

OMONIA

Moderate

Baby Grand Hotel ★★ Ten international artists from the fields of urban art, graffiti design, and illustration were handpicked to decorate the 57 "graffiti" rooms in this hotel, with themes ranging from Japanese and Byzantine art to comic book art. Check out the Spider-Man, Batman, and Smurfs rooms—although this may not be precisely what brought you to Athens! The nongrafitti rooms are also spacious, comfortable, and contemporary. The hotel's restaurant, **Meat Me,** is insanely popular with young Athenians and offers excellent and reasonably priced meat dishes.

65 Athinas and Lycourgou, 105 51 Athens. ✆ **210/325-0900.** www.classicalhotels.com. 120€–150€ double. Breakfast 10€. AE, DC, MC, V. Metro: Omonia. **Amenities:** Restaurant/bar; exercise room; indoor pool; smoke-free rooms; spa. *In room:* A/C, TV, hair dryer, minibar, Wi-Fi.

Fresh Hotel ★ A black vertical fireplace in the reception area sets the tone in one of the coolest and most stylish designer hotels in the city. The Magenta Restaurant offers many healthy options during the day; on the ninth floor the beautiful Air Lounge Bar with its wooden deck and swimming pool has great city panoramas and very good drinks, but the entire scene belongs almost exclusively to the very popular Orange Bar Restaurant that is busy and hopping well into the early-morning hours. The drawback of this place is its rather blah and somewhat out-of-the-way location.

26 Sofokleous and 2 Klisthenous, 105 64 Athens. ✆ **210/524-8511.** Fax 210/524-8517. www.freshhotel.gr. 133 units. 120€–170€ double. AE, DC, MC, V. Parking 12€ per day. Metro: Omonia. From Omonia Sq., head south along Athinas until you reach Sofokleus. From Monastiraki Sq., head north along Athinias until you reach Sofokleus. **Amenities:** Restaurant/bar; pool; minispa. *In room:* A/C, plasma TV, hair dryer, Wi-Fi.

ON & AROUND SYNTAGMA SQUARE

Very Expensive

Grande Bretagne ★★★ The legendary Grande Bretagne, one of Athens's most distinguished 19th-century buildings, had a 2-year, $70-million renovation for the Olympics and has had touch-ups since then. The major renovations preserved the exquisite Beaux Arts lobby, made dingy rooms grand once more, and added indoor and outdoor swimming pools. The Grande Bretagne prides itself on its service: From Winston Churchill to Sting, guests expect the highest level of attention—and get it, except, possibly, when a tour group is checking in. Ask for a room with a balcony overlooking Syntagma Square, the Parliament building, and the Acropolis.

Syntagma Sq., 105 64 Athens. ✆ **210/333-0000.** Fax 210/333-0160. www.grandebretagne.gr. 328 units. 277€–285€ double. AE, DC, MC, V. Metro: Syntagma. **Amenities:** 2 restaurants; 2 bars; free airport pickup; concierge; health club & spa w/Jacuzzi; 2 pools (indoor and outdoor); room service; smoke-free rooms. *In room:* A/C, TV, hair dryer, minibar, Wi-Fi.

King George II ★★★ Next door to the Grande Bretagne, the King George II is one of Athens's great historical hotels, opulent and classy, which fell into hard times and disrepair in the '80s, but reopened as a totally renovated boutique hotel in 2004. The rooms have lots of furniture with silk and satin upholstery, and spacious, gray marbled bathrooms with sunken tubs and glass-encased showers. The Tudor Bar on the rooftop has excellent views of the city and its landmarks, while the Greek-dining Tudor restaurant is sublime. The infamous ninth-floor penthouse suite—whose occupants have included Aristotle Onassis, Maria Callas, Grace Kelly and Prince Rainier, Marilyn Monroe, and Frank Sinatra, among others—is said to be spectacular, and at $10,000 a night it should be!

Vas Georgiou A2, Syntagma Sq., 105 64 Athens. ✆ **210/322-2210** or 210/728-0350. Fax 210/325-0564 or 210/728-0351. www.lux-hotels.com. 102 units. 220€–260€ double. AE, DC, MC, V. Metro: Syntagma. **Amenities:** Rooftop bar/restaurant; bar; health club; indoor swimming pool; smoke-free rooms; spa. *In room:* A/C, TV, Wi-Fi.

Expensive

Electra Hotel ★ If Ermou remains a pedestrian street, the Electra can boast a location that is quiet and central—steps from Syntagma Square. Most of the guest rooms have comfortable armchairs, large windows, and modern bathrooms with hair dryers. Take a look at your room before you accept it: Some are quite tiny. The front desk is sometimes understaffed but the service is generally acceptable.

5 Ermou, 105 63 Athens. ✆ **210/322-3223.** Fax 210/322-0310. electrahotels@ath.forthnet.gr. 110 units. 175€–200€ double. Rates include buffet breakfast. AE, DC, MC, V. Metro: Syntagma. **Amenities:** Restaurant; bar. *In room:* A/C, TV, hair dryer, Internet, minibar.

Moderate

Athens Cypria ★ In a marvelously convenient central location on a (usually) quiet street, the renovated and expanded Cypria has bright white halls and rooms, cheerful floral bedspreads and curtains, and freshly tiled bathrooms with new fixtures. Many rooms have balconies; some (10€ supplement) have Acropolis views. The hotel can be infuriatingly slow in responding to reservation requests.

5 Diomias, 105 62 Athens. ✆ **210/323-8034.** Fax 210/324-8792. www.athenscypria.com. 115 units. 125€–150€ double. Rates include buffet breakfast. AE, MC, V. Metro: Syntagma. **Amenities:** Breakfast room; bar; snack bar. *In room:* A/C, TV, hair dryer, minibar.

Inexpensive

Hotel Carolina ★★ ☺ The friendly, family-owned and -operated Carolina, on the outskirts of Plaka, is a brisk 5-minute walk from Syntagma and has always been popular with students. In the past few years, the Carolina has undertaken extensive remodeling and now attracts a wide range of frugal travelers. Double-glazed windows and air-conditioning make the guest rooms especially comfortable.

Many rooms have large balconies, and several (such as no. 308) with four or five beds are popular with families and students.

55 Kolokotroni, 105 60 Athens. ✆ **210/324-3551.** Fax 210/324-3350. www.hotelcarolina.gr. 31 units. 90€–100€ double. MC, V. Metro: Syntagma. **Amenities:** Breakfast room; bar. *In room:* A/C, TV.

IN KOLONAKI

Very Expensive

St. George Lycabettus Hotel ★★★ As yet, the distinctive, classy St. George does not get many tour groups, which contributes to its tranquil tone. The rooftop pool is a real plus, as are the two excellent restaurants. The Frame lounge in the lobby also attracts a seriously chic Athenian crowd. Most rooms look toward Mount Likavitos; some have views of the Acropolis; others overlook Dexamini Park or have interior views. The hotel is just steps from posh Kolonaki restaurants and shops. Something to keep in mind: This hotel is a serious walk from the nearest Metro stops (Syntagma and Evangelismos), and when you're returning, most of that walk is uphill.

2 Kleomenous, 106 75 Athens. ✆ **210/729-0711.** Fax 210/721-0439. www.sglycabettus.gr. 167 units. 170€–250€ double. Compulsory breakfast 20€. AE, DC, MC, V. Metro: Evangelismos. **Amenities:** 2 restaurants; 2 bars; concierge; rooftop pool; room service; smoke-free rooms. *In room:* A/C, TV, hair dryer, minibar, Wi-Fi.

Moderate

Athens Lycabettus Hotel ★ This little hotel is on Valeoritou, a chic pedestrian street between Syngagma and Kolonaki filled with stylish cafes, bars, restaurants, and lounges for the fashion-conscious crowd. Apart from its great location, this hotel has made a name for itself for its outstanding personal service. Rooms, though on the small side, are pleasant and bright with contemporary furnishings and nice-size marble bathrooms. The hotel also has a popular bar/cafe restaurant.

6 Valeoritou, at Voukourestiou, 106 71 Athens. ✆ **210360-0600.** www.athenslycabettus.gr. 25 units. 140€ double. MC, V. Metro: Syntagma. **Amenities:** Restaurant/bar; Wi-Fi. *In room:* A/C, TV, hair dryer, minibar.

IN THE EMBASSY DISTRICT

Very Expensive

Hilton ★★★ The guest rooms at this Hilton (looking toward either the hills outside Athens or the Acropolis) have large marble bathrooms and are decorated in the generic but comfortable international Hilton style, with some Greek touches. The Plaza Executive floor of rooms and suites offers a separate business center and a higher level of service. Small shops, a salon, and cafes and restaurants surround the glitzy glass-and-marble lobby. The Milos restaurant has superb seafood and the rooftop Galaxy bar has amazing views of just about everything there is to see for miles around (including drop-dead-elegant Athenians).

46 Leoforos Vas. Sofias, 115 28 Athens. ✆ **800/445-8667** in the U.S., or 210/728-1000. Fax 210/728-1111. www.hilton.com. 275€–400€ double. AE, DC, MC, V. Metro: Evangelismos. **Amenities:** 4 restaurants; 3 bars; airport transfers; babysitting; concierge; health club & spa w/Jacuzzi; 2 pools; room service; smoke-free rooms. *In room:* A/C, TV, hair dryer, minibar, Wi-Fi.

NEAR THE ACROPOLIS (MAKRIGIANNI & KOUKAKI DISTRICTS)

Expensive

Divani-Palace Acropolis ★★ Just 3 blocks south of the Acropolis, in a quiet—for Athens!—residential neighborhood, the Divani Palace Acropolis does a brisk tour business but also welcomes independent travelers. The blandly decorated guest rooms are large and comfortable, and some of the large bathrooms even have two wash basins. The cavernous marble-and-glass lobby contains copies of classical sculpture; a section of Athens's 5th-century-B.C. defense wall is preserved behind glass in the basement by the gift shop. The breakfast buffet is extensive.

19–25 Parthenonos, Makrigianni, 117 42 Athens. ✆ **210/922-2945.** Fax 210/921-4993. www.divaniacropolis.gr. 253 units. 180€ double; 300€ suite. Rates include breakfast buffet. AE, DC, MC, V. Metro: Akropolis. **Amenities:** 2 restaurants; 2 bars; concierge; outdoor pool; room service; smoke-free rooms. *In room:* A/C, TV, hair dryer, minibar, Wi-Fi.

Moderate

Acropolis View Hotel ★ This nicely maintained hotel is on a residential side street off Rovertou Galli, not far from the Herodes Atticus theater. The usually quiet neighborhood, at the base of Filopappos Hill (itself a pleasant area to explore) is a 10- to 15-minute walk from the heart of the Plaka. Many of the small guest rooms are freshly painted each year. All units have good bathrooms as well as balconies. Some, such as room no. 405, overlook Filopappos Hill, while others, such as room no. 407, face the Acropolis. A big plus is the rooftop garden with awesome Acropolis views.

Rovertou Galli and 10 Webster (Gouemster on some maps), 117 42 Athens. ✆ **210/921-7303.** Fax 210/923-0705. www.acropolisview.gr. 32 units. 125€ double. Rates include buffet breakfast. Substantial reductions Nov–Mar. AE, MC, V. Metro: Akropolis. **Amenities:** Breakfast room; bar; Internet. *In room:* A/C, TV, minibar.

Art Gallery Hotel ★ Once home to several artists, this small hotel in a half-century-old house maintains an artistic flair (and a nice old-fashioned cage elevator). Rooms are small and plain but comfortable, many with polished hardwood floors and ceiling fans. A nice Victorian-style breakfast room on the fourth floor is furnished with heavy marble-topped tables and old velvet-covered chairs.

5 Erechthiou, Koukaki, 117 42 Athens. ✆ **210/923-8376.** Fax 210/923-3025. www.artgalleryhotel.gr. 22 units. 100€ double. Rates include generous breakfast. Hotel sometimes closed Nov–Mar; when open then, prices reduced. AE, MC, V. Metro: Akropolis. *In room:* A/C, TV.

Inexpensive

Marble House Pension ★ Named for its marble facade, which is usually covered with bougainvillea, this small hotel, whose front rooms offer balconies overlooking quiet Zinni Street, is known among budget travelers (including many teachers) for its friendly staff. Over the past several years, the pension has been remodeled and redecorated, gaining new bathrooms and guest-room furniture (including small fridges). Two units have kitchenettes. If you're spending more than a few days in Athens and don't mind being outside the center (and a partly uphill 15- to 20-min. walk to the hotel from the Plaka), this is a homey base.

35 A. Zinni, Koukaki, 117 41 Athens. ✆ **210/923-4058.** Fax 210/922-6461. www.marblehouse.gr. 16 units, 12 with bathroom. 42€ double without bathroom, 48€ with bathroom. 9€ supplement for A/C. Monthly rates available off season. No credit cards. Metro: Akropolis. *In room:* A/C (9 units), TV, minibar.

THE COAST

Good beaches, excellent restaurants, and open-air clubs and bars, as well as excellent shops, make the coast very appealing during the summer and are a good choice if you don't have time to make it to the islands. You can get into Athens by the hotel shuttles, bus, tram, or taxi.

Very Expensive

Astir Palace Resort ★★ We're talking serious creature comfort here—as well as every activity from windsurfing to private Pilates instruction! Tranquil and beautiful, with incredible sea vistas and private pine-clad grounds, the Astir Palace is a series of secluded bungalows and three hotels with their own private beaches on 30 hectares (74 acres). Seven well-regarded restaurants, including **Matsuhisa Athens,** with the Omakase menu (90€), a seven-course repast with Nobu's signature dishes, are on-site. The Arion hotel sea-view rooms are arranged in such a way that even the bathtubs have prime water views; the Westin is run by Starwood Hotels, which manages New York's posh St. Regis; and the new W hotel (formerly Aphrodite) is supposed to open in 2012, following a long and extensive renovation. Everyone I know who has stayed at any of the Astir accommodations wants to go back, soon.

40 Apollonos, 166 71 Vouliagmeni. ✆ **210/890-2000.** Fax 210/896-2582. www.astir-palace.com. 526 units. Arion: 380€–460€ double. Westin: 340€–410€ double. AE, DC, MC, V. Free parking. Tram to Glyfada, then either taxi or bus 114. **Amenities:** 7 restaurants; 7 bars; 3 pools; 3 tennis courts w/flood lighting. *In room:* A/C, Internet TV, Wi-Fi.

Divani Apollon Palace & Spa ★★ In a prime location on Kavouri beach with towering palm trees, picturesque gardens, and two large swimming pools, this is as close to a secluded island experience as you are likely to get in any large city. With sea views from every room, large balconies and green marble bathrooms, and a private beach, this is perhaps the most romantic of Athens's hotels. Complementing the romantic ambience is the well-regarded on-site seafood restaurant, Mythos tis Thalassas (Legend of the Sea), with seafront tables.

10 Agiou Nikolaou and Iliou, 166 71 Vouliagmeni. ✆ **210/891-1100.** Fax 210/965-8010. www.divaniapollon.gr. 286 units. 220€ double; 340€ executive double; 1,600€ suite. AE, DC, MC, V. Free parking. Tram to Glyfada, then either taxi or bus 114. **Amenities:** 3 restaurants; bar; gym; 2 pools; spa; tennis court w/flood lighting. *In room:* A/C, TV, Wi-Fi.

Where to Dine

Athens has an astonishing number of restaurants and tavernas (and a growing number of fast-food joints, known locally as *Fastfooddadiko*) offering everything from good, cheap Greek food in bare-bones surroundings to fine Greek, French, Asian, and other international cuisines served in elegant dining rooms and a surprising number of neighborhood tavernas. In summer, when the heat soars, many Greeks have lunch inside (while tourists sit outside under the broiling sun) and dinner outside—seldom before 10pm, although you can get served most places from 8pm.

Most restaurants have menus in Greek and English, but many don't keep their printed (or handwritten) menus up to date. If a menu is not in English, there's almost always someone working at the restaurant who can either translate or rattle off suggestions for you in English. That may mean you'll be offered some fairly repetitive suggestions because restaurant staff members tend to suggest what most tourists request. In Athens, that means ***moussaka*** (baked eggplant casserole, usually with ground meat), ***souvlakia*** (chunks of beef, chicken, pork, or lamb grilled on a skewer), ***pastitsio*** (baked pasta, usually with ground meat and béchamel sauce), or ***dolmadakia*** (grape leaves, stuffed usually with rice and ground meat). Although all these dishes can be delicious, all too often restaurants catering to tourists serve profoundly dull moussaka and unpleasantly chewy souvlakia.

Don't Count on Credit Cards

One of my most humiliating travel moments happened a number of years ago when I was taking Athenian friends out to dinner—and planning to pay with a credit card. The restaurant took only cash, and my friends ended up having to take me to dinner. Much has changed in Athens since then, but many Athenian restaurants still do not accept credit cards. Consider yourself warned.

Mezedes (appetizers served with bread) are one of the great delights of Greek cuisine, and often can be enjoyed in lieu of a main course. Some perennial favorites include ***tzatziki*** (garlic, cucumber, dill, and yogurt dip), ***melitzanosalata*** (eggplant dip), ***skordalia*** (garlic sauce), ***taramosalata*** (fish roe dip), ***keftedes*** (crispy meatballs), ***kalamaria*** (squid), ***gigantes*** (large white beans in tomato sauce), ***loukanika*** (little sausages), and ***oktopodi*** (octopus).

If you're wondering what to drink, the best-known Greek table wine is **retsina.** It's usually white, although sometime rosé or red, and flavored with pine resin. In theory, the European Union now controls the amount of resin added, so you're less likely to come across the harsh retsina that some compare to turpentine. If you don't like the taste of retsina, try ***aretsinato*** (wine without resin).

To find out more about the wide range of excellent Greek wines, pick up a copy of Dimitri Hadjinicolaou's ***The A to Z Guide of Greek Wines*** (published by Oenos O Agapitos). This handy pocket-size Greek/English guide has illustrations of labels and information on vintages, and sells for about 10€.

When it comes time for dessert or a midafternoon infusion of sugar, Greeks usually head to a ***zaharoplastion*** (sweet shop). Consequently, most restaurants don't offer a wide variety of desserts. Almost all do serve fruit (stewed in winter, fresh in season), and, increasingly, many serve sweets such as ***baklava*** (pastry and ground nuts with honey), ***halva*** (sesame, chopped nuts, and honey), and ***kataifi*** (shredded wheat with chopped nuts and lots of honey). All these sweets are seriously sweet. If you want coffee with your dessert, keep in mind that for Greeks, regular coffee usually includes a mere teaspoon of sugar. Sweet coffee seems to be about a fifty-fifty mixture of coffee and sugar. Watch out for the grounds in the bottom of the cup—and try to get a Greek to show you how to tell your fortune from the grounds.

Greek **brandy** is a popular after-dinner drink (although—you guessed it—it's a bit sweet for non-Greek tastes), but the most popular Greek hard drink is **ouzo.** The anise-flavored liqueur is taken either straight or with water, which turns it cloudy white. You may see Greeks drinking quarter- and even half-bottles of ouzo with lunch; if you do the same, you'll find out why the after-lunch siesta is so popular. There are many cafes *(ouzeri)* where ouzo, wine, and a selection of mezedes are served from breakfast to bedtime.

In 2009, an E.U. nonsmoking law went into effect in restaurants, shops, and public buildings. At least initially, this law has shown signs of being honored more in the breach than in the observance. In any event, the law is unlikely to have much effect on the city's countless warm-season alfresco dining and drinking establishments.

IN THE PLAKA

Some of the most charming old restaurants in Athens are in the Plaka—as are some of the worst tourist traps. Here are a few things to keep in mind when you head off for a meal. First, Plaka is a bit of a maze: If you have trouble finding a particular restaurant—and you probably will—don't ask for directions at another restaurant—you may be told the place you want is closed and urged to sit right down and eat right there.

In general, it's a good idea to avoid places with floor shows; many charge outrageous amounts (and levy surcharges not always openly stated on menus) for drinks and food. If you get burned, and the proprietor is insistent, stand your ground, phone the **Tourist Police** (✆ **171**), and pay nothing before they arrive. Often the mere mention of the Tourist Police can miraculously cause a bill to be lowered.

Expensive

Daphne's ★★ ELEGANT GREEK Frescoes adorn the walls of this neoclassical 1830s former home, which includes a shady garden courtyard displaying bits of ancient marble found on-site. The courtyard makes this a real oasis in Athens, especially when summer nights are hot. The food here gives you all the old favorites with new distinction (try the zesty eggplant salad), and combines familiar ingredients in innovative ways (delicious hot pepper and feta cheese dip). I could cheerfully eat the hors d'oeuvres all night, although the *stifado* (stew) of rabbit in *mavrodaphne* (sweet-wine) sauce and the tasty prawns with toasted almonds are pretty irresistible. Many nights, there's live music (sometimes Greek, sometimes international). The staff is attentive, endearing, and beyond excellent.

4 Lysikratous (by the Monument of Lysikratous). ✆/fax **210/322-7971.** www.daphnesrestaurant.gr. Reservations recommended. Main courses 25€–40€, with some fish priced by the kilo. AE, DC, MC, V. Daily 8pm–1am. Closed Dec 20–Jan 15. Metro: Akropolis or Syntagma.

Moderate

Platanos Taverna ★★ TRADITIONAL GREEK This taverna on a quiet pedestrian square has tables outdoors in good weather beneath a spreading plane tree (*platanos* means plane tree). Inside, where locals usually congregate to escape the summer sun at midday and where tourists gather in the evening, you can enjoy the old paintings and photos on the walls. The Platanos has been serving good *spitiko fageto* (home cooking) since 1932 and has managed to keep steady customers happy while enchanting visitors. If artichokes or spinach with lamb are on the menu, you're

Eating Well

When you are at a restaurant that caters to tourists, tell your waiter you'd like to have a look at the food display case, often positioned just outside the kitchen, and then point to what you'd like to order. Many restaurants are perfectly happy to have you take a look in the kitchen itself, but it's not a good idea to do this without checking first. Not surprisingly, you'll get the best value and be able to avoid the ubiquitous favorites-for-foreigners dishes at establishments serving a predominantly Greek, rather than a transient tourist, clientele.

in luck: They're delicious. There's a wide choice of bottled wines from many regions of Greece, although the house wine is tasty. Plan to come here and relax, not rush, through a meal.

4 Diogenous. ✆ **210/322-0666.** Fax 210/322-8624. Main courses 8€–20€. No credit cards. Mon–Sat noon–4:30pm and 8pm–midnight; Sun in Mar–May and Sept–Oct noon–4:30pm. Metro: Syntagma.

Taverna Xinos ★ TRADITIONAL GREEK In summer, sit at tables in the courtyard; in winter, warm yourself by the coal-burning stove and admire the frescoes while dining on traditional Greek taverna food—often, as is traditional, served room temperature. While the strolling musicians may not be as good as the Three Tenors, they do sing wonderful Greek golden oldies, accompanying themselves on the guitar and bouzouki. (If you're serenaded, you may want to give the musicians a tip. If you want to hear the theme from *Never on Sunday,* ask for "Ena Zorbas.") Most evenings, tourists predominate until after 10pm, when locals begin to arrive—as they have since Xinos opened in 1935.

4 Geronta. ✆ **210/322-1065.** Main courses 8€–20€. No credit cards. Daily 8pm to any time from 11pm to 1am; sometimes closed Sun. Usually closed part of July and Aug. Metro: Syntagma.

Inexpensive

Damigos (The Bakaliarakia) ★★ GREEK/CODFISH This basement taverna just off Adrianou Street, with enormous wine barrels in the back room and an ancient column supporting the roof in the front room, has been serving delicious deep-fried codfish and eggplant, as well as chops and stews, since 1865. The wine comes from the family vineyards. There are few pleasures greater than sipping retsina—if you wish, you can buy a bottle to take away—while you watch the cook turn out unending meals in the absurdly small kitchen. Don't miss the delicious *skordalia* (garlic sauce), equally good with cod, eggplant, fresh tomatoes, bread—well, you get the idea.

41 Kidathineon. ✆ **210/322-5084.** Main courses 8€–12€. No credit cards. Daily 7pm to anytime from 11pm to 1am. Usually closed June–Sept. Metro: Syntagma or Akropolis.

Giouvetsakia ★ TRADITIONAL GREEK Run by the same family since 1950, this traditional taverna at the bustling junction of Adrianou and Thespidos is perfect for people-watching in a scenic environment while enjoying some delicious, traditional fare. Try the Giouvetsi pasta (still the house's specialty and its namesake) and be sure to leave room for the complimentary fruit dish topped with cinnamon.

144 Adrianou and Thespidos. ✆ **210/322-7033.** Main courses 6€–15€. MC, V. Daily 10am–2am. Metro: Syntagma.

NEAR MONASTIRAKI SQUARE

Moderate

Abyssinia Cafe ★ GREEK This small cafe in a ramshackle building across from the entrance to the Ancient Agora sports a nicely restored interior featuring lots of gleaming dark wood and polished copper. You can sit indoors or out with a coffee, but it's tempting to snack on Cheese Abyssinia (feta scrambled with spices and garlic), mussels and rice pilaf, or *keftedes* (meatballs). Everything is reasonably priced here, but it's easy to run up quite a tab, because everything is so good—especially the *mezedes* that are superior to the main courses. For a quieter experience, book a table on the mezzanine with its awesome views.

Plateia Abyssinia, Monastiraki. ✆ **210/321-7047.** Appetizers and main courses 8€–30€. No credit cards. Tues–Sun 10:30am–2pm (often open evenings as well). Usually closed for a week at Christmas and Easter; sometimes closed part of Jan and Feb and mid-July to mid-Aug. Metro: Monastiraki.

To Kouti ★★ CONTEMPORARY GREEK To Kouti (the Box) stands head and shoulders above its neighboring restaurants near the Ancient Agora that seem to rely too much on their location. The place looks like children decorated it with bright-colored crayons—even the menu is handwritten in brightly illustrated children's books. Beyond decor, To Kouti is great for people-watching and has an unusual but very tasty menu: Try the beef in garlic and honey or the shrimp in carrots, or opt for some of its exceptional vegetarian dishes. The homemade bread is served in (of course!) boxes.

23 Adrianou, Monastiraki. ✆ **210/321-3229.** Main courses 15€–30€. AE, MC, V. Daily 1pm–1am. Metro: Monastiraki.

Inexpensive

Diporto ★ GREEK This little place, sandwiched between olive shops, serves salads, stews, and delicious *revithia* (chickpeas) and *gigantes* (butter beans), both popular Greek winter dishes among stall owners, shoppers, and Athenians who make their way to the market for cheap and delicious food.

Central Market, Athinas. No phone. Main courses 8€–15€. No credit cards. Mon–Sat 6am–6pm. Metro: Monastiraki.

Papandreou ★ GREEK The butcher, the baker, and the office worker duck past the sides of beef hanging in the Meat Hall and head to this hole in the wall for zesty tripe dishes. Don't like tripe? Don't worry: Their menu offers choices that don't involve it. Papandreou has a virtually all-male clientele, but a woman alone need not hesitate to eat here.

Central Market, Athinas. ✆ **210/321-4970.** Main courses 8€–15€. No credit cards. Mon–Sat about 8am–5pm. Metro: Monastiraki.

Taverna Sigalas ★ GREEK This longtime Plaka taverna, housed in a vintage 1879 commercial building with a newer outdoor pavilion, boasts that it has been run by the same family for a century and is open 365 days a year. Huge old retsina kegs stand piled against the back walls; dozens of black-and-white photos of Greek movie stars are everywhere. After 8pm, Greek Muzak plays. At all hours, both Greeks and tourists wolf down large portions of stews, moussaka, grilled meatballs, baked tomatoes, and gyros, paired with the house red and white retsinas.

2 Plateia Monastiraki. ✆ **210/321-3036.** Main courses 8€–19€. No credit cards. Daily 7am–2am. Metro: Monastiraki.

Thanasis ★ GREEK/SOUVLAKI Just across from the Monastiraki Metro station, Thanasis serves terrific souvlaki and pita—and exceptionally good french fries—both to go and at its outdoor and indoor tables. As always, prices are higher if you sit down to eat. On weekends, it often takes the strength and determination of an Olympic athlete to get through the door and place an order here. It's worth the effort: This is both a great budget choice and a great place to take in the local scene.

69 Mitropoleos. ✆ **210/324-4705.** Main courses 6€–15€. No credit cards. Daily 9am–2am. Metro: Monastiraki.

Quick Bites in & Around Syntagma

In general, Syntagma Square is not known for good food, but the area has a number of places where you can grab a quick snack. **Apollonion Bakery,** 10 Nikis, and **Elleniki Gonia,** 10 Karayioryi Servias, make sandwiches to order and sell croissants, both stuffed and plain. **Ariston** is a small chain of *zaharoplastia* (confectioners) with a branch at the corner of Karayioryi Servias and Voulis (just off Syntagma Sq.); it sells snacks as well as pastries.

For the quintessentially Greek *loukoumades* (round doughnut center–like pastries that are deep-fried, then drenched with honey, and topped with powdered sugar and cinnamon), try **Doris ★**, 30 Praxitelous, a continuation of Lekka, a few blocks from Syntagma Square. If you're still hungry, Doris serves hearty stews and pasta dishes for absurdly low prices. If you're near Omonia Square when you feel the need for loukoumades or a soothing dish of rice pudding, try **Aigina ★**, 46 Panepistimiou. A short walk from Syntagma, the **Oraia Ellada (Beautiful Greece) ★★** cafe at the Center of Hellenic Tradition, opening onto both 36 Pandrossou and 59 Mitropoleos near the flea market, has a spectacular view of the Acropolis. You can revive yourself here with a cappuccino and pastries.

NEAR SYNTAGMA SQUARE

Expensive

Aegli/Cibus ★★ INTERNATIONAL For years, the bistro in the Zappeion Gardens was a popular meeting spot; when it closed in the 1970s, it was sorely missed. Now it's back, along with a cinema, a hip and highly recommended outdoor bar/club, and a fine restaurant. Once more, chic Athenian families head here, to the cool of the Zappeion Gardens, for the frequently changing menu. Some of the specialties include foie gras, oysters, tenderloin with ginger and coffee sauce, profiteroles, fresh sorbets, strawberry soup, and delicious yogurt crème brûlée. Tables indoors or outdoors by the trees offer places to relax with coffee. In the evening, take in a movie at the open-air cinema here before dinner, or have a drink and a snack at one of the nearby cafes.

Zappeion Gardens (adjacent to the National Gardens fronting Vas. Amalias Blvd.). © **210/336-9363.** Reservations recommended. Main courses 35€–55€. AE, DC, MC, V. Daily 10am–midnight. Sometimes closed in Aug. Metro: Syntagma.

Inexpensive

Neon ★ GREEK/INTERNATIONAL You'll find lots of tourists at the mostly self-service Neon, as well as Athenians in a rush to get a bite. This centrally located member of the chain is very convenient, although not as pleasant as the original on Omonia Square. You're sure to find something to your taste—maybe a Mexican omelet, spaghetti Bolognese, the salad bar, or sweets ranging from Black Forest cake to tiramisu. The Neon is a good spot for a cheap snack in pricey Kolonaki.

3 Mitropoleos (on the southwest corner of Syntagma Sq.). © **210/322-8155.** Snacks 5€–8€; sandwiches 5€–10€; main courses 8€–15€. No credit cards. Daily 9am–midnight. Metro: Syntagma.

IN KOLONAKI

Moderate

Filipou ★ TRADITIONAL GREEK This longtime Athenian favorite almost never disappoints. The traditional dishes such as stuffed cabbage, stuffed vine leaves, vegetable stews, and fresh salads are consistently good. In the heart of Kolonaki, this is a place to head when you want good home cooking in the company of the Greeks and resident expatriates who prize the food.

19 Xenokratous. ✆ **210/721-6390.** Main courses 8€–20€. No credit cards. Mon–Fri 8:30pm–midnight; Sat lunch. Metro: Evangelismos.

Rhodia ★ TRADITIONAL GREEK This respected taverna is located in a handsome old Kolonaki house. In good weather, tables are set up in its small garden—although the interior, with its tile floor and old prints, is equally charming. The Rhodia is a favorite of visiting archaeologists from the nearby British and American Schools of Classical Studies, as well as of Kolonaki residents. The octopus in mustard sauce is terrific, as are the veal and dolmades (stuffed grape leaves) in egg-lemon sauce. The house wine is excellent, as is the halva, which manages to be both creamy and crunchy.

44 Aristipou. ✆ **210/722-9883.** Main courses 8€–18€. No credit cards. Mon–Sat 8pm–2am. Metro: Evangelismos.

To Kafeneio ★★ GREEK/INTERNATIONAL This is hardly a typical *kafeneio* (coffee shop/cafe). Two can easily run up a tab of 60€ for lunch or dinner, but you can also just snack here. If you have something light, like the leeks in crème fraîche or onion pie, washed down with draft beer or the house wine, you can finish with profiteroles and not put too big a dent in your budget.

26 Loukianou. ✆ **210/722-9056.** Reservations recommended. Main courses 12€–25€. MC, V. Mon–Sat 11am–midnight or later. Closed most of Aug. Metro: Evangelismos.

To Ouzadiko ★★ GREEK/MEZEDES This lively ouzo bar in the rather grim Lermos Shopping Center offers at least 40 kinds of ouzo and as many mezedes, including fluffy *keftedes* (meatballs) that make all others taste leaden. To Ouzadiko is very popular with Athenians young and old (maybe too popular—service can be slow). A serious foodie friend of mine comes here especially for the wide variety of *horta* (greens), which she says are the best she's ever tasted.

25–29 Karneadou (in the Lemos International Shopping Center), Kolonaki. ✆ **210/729-5484.** Reservations recommended. Most mezedes and main courses 10€–20€. No credit cards. Tues–Sat 1pm–12:30am. Closed Aug. Metro: Evangelismos.

To Prytaneion ★ GREEK/INTERNATIONAL The trendy bare stone walls here are decorated with movie posters and illuminated by baby spotlights. Waiters serve customers tempting plates of some of Athens's most expensive and eclectic mezedes, including beef carpaccio, smoked salmon, bruschetta, and shrimp in fresh cream, as well as grilled veggies and that international favorite, the hamburger.

7 Milioni, Kolonaki. ✆ **01-364-3353.** Prytaniou@otenet.gr. Reservations recommended. Mezedes and snacks 10€–30€. No credit cards. Mon–Sat 10am–3am. Metro: Evangelismos.

RISING stars IN THE PSIRRI AND GAZI DISTRICTS

It's hard to keep up with the cafes, bars, restaurants, and galleries opening in the increasingly fashionable Psirri district, between Ermou and Athinas and extending toward the Thissio district and Gazi, the neighborhood beyond Kerameikos, where the old gas plants used to dominate the scene. All this began to change in 1984, when Athens bought the old gas factories and created the Technopolis Art City, with its museums, galleries, conference halls, and theaters—and, of course, the restaurants and cafes that sprang up around them. Only a few years ago Psirri and Gazi were largely noted for derelict warehouses and factories and tumbledown houses. Now, you'll see lots of places with bare brick walls, minimalist decor, and lots of wannabe beautiful people here, especially after dark. Here are some suggestions on where to eat, drink, and take in the scene. Gazi especially is still off the beaten tourist path, and it's easy to get confused here, especially at night. You may want to taxi to your destination and familiarize yourself with the neighborhood before exploring on foot.

At **Taki 13,** 13 Taki (✆ **210/325-4707**), the food is less the thing than the bar, the music, and the stylish young Athenians who gather here. **Zeidoron,** 10 Taki and Ayios Anaryiron (✆ **210/321-5368**), is basically a *mezedopoleio* (hors d'oeuvres place), although it also serves entrees. The mezedes are also delicious at **To Krasopoulio tou Kokkora,** Karaiskaki and 4 Aisopou (✆ **210/321-1565**), where you can dine indoors or out. **Elihrison,** 6 Agion Anargiton (✆ **210/321-5220**), has classic Greek dishes in a lovingly restored 19th-century former Turkish justice hall; there's both a roof garden and a courtyard for outdoor dining. **Oineas,** 9 Aisopou (✆ **210/321-5614**), has an early crowd of tourists and an all-night crowd of locals, all of whom enjoy the wide range of mezedes (try the fried feta in light honey). **Bar Guru Bar,** 10 Plateia Theatrou (✆ **210/324-6530**), usually closed mid-July to mid-August, is a fine Thai restaurant that also offers an infectious good time as a bar/club. Upstairs hosts live jazz, and downstairs is reserved for funky dance hits. Another restaurant/bar/club, the **Cubanita,** 28 Karaiskaki (✆ **210/331-4605**), may close in July and August, but hands down offers one of the most fun nights to be had in the city. At this place, Latin beats and excellent Cuban cuisine combine to make a great place to party until the early-morning hours. At **Soul Garden,** 65 Evripidou (✆ **210/331-0907**), the menu offers excellent Thai finger food and great Mohitos, served outdoors in the garden or inside at the bar. And if you want to watch a movie while

AROUND OMONIA SQUARE & THE NATIONAL ARCHAEOLOGICAL MUSEUM

Moderate

Archaion Gefsis (Ancient Flavors) ★ ANCIENT GREEK CUISINE More than a little on the kitsch side (columns, torches, and waitresses in togas), this is your one chance to dine like the ancients did. With recipes from ancient Greece (recorded by the poet Archestratos), offerings include cuttlefish in ink with pine nuts, wild-boar cutlets, goat leg with mashed vegetables, and pork with prunes and thyme, among other such delicious fare. Just remember: You may use a spoon and a knife, but no you eat on a summer night, head for **Couzina Cine-Psyrri,** 40 Sarri (✆ **210/321-5534**), which maintains Athens's long tradition of outdoor cinemas. Many of Psirri's galleries stay open late, which means that you can eat and browse—or browse and eat. **Epistrofi,** 6–8 Taki (✆ **210/321-8640**), is worth a visit just to see the handsomely restored early-19th-century town house it occupies; it sometimes hosts concerts as well as art exhibitions. **Stigma,** 20–22 Agios Anargyros (✆ **210/322-1675**), features frequent shows of local artists.

The line between the Psirri and Thissio districts can be a bit blurred, with partisans of both districts claiming some of the same territory. In that blurred area, near the Temple of Hephaestus (known locally as the "Thissio"), there's a terrific cluster of restaurants. **Kuzina,** 9 Adrianou (✆ **210/324-0133;** www.kuzina.gr), combines awesome views of the Temple of Hephaestus, the Agora, and the Acropolis from its roof garden; great contemporary Greek cuisine (such as delicious dumplings with feta cheese and pomegranate syrup); and a cutting-edge art gallery. **Pil-Poul,** 51 Apostolou Pavlou and Poulopoulou (✆ **210/342-3665**), has a Michelin star for its French/Mediterranean cuisine, and an amazing view of the Acropolis from the terrace outside the gorgeous 1920s neoclassical mansion the restaurant occupies. This place is not cheap; you may want to just have a drink in the cocktail lounge and enjoy the scene. At **Filistron,** 23 Apostolou Pavlou (✆ **210/346-7554;** www.filistron.com), a short walk away, you'll still have great views of the Acropolis and agora from the rooftop terrace and can have a wide range of reasonably priced *mezedes.*

When you tire of Psirri, strike out for neighboring **Gazi.** You're distinctly out of tourist territory here—but not, perhaps, for long, with Gazi's growing popularity. **Mamacas,** 41 Persephonous (✆ **210/346-4984;** www.mamacas.gr), an upmarket taverna that was one of the first of the new wave of restaurants here, is still one of the best; the spicy meatballs *(keftedakia)* take standard restaurant fare to a new and exuberant level. If it's sweet, not spicy you're after, head deeper into Gazi (probably by taxi) for **Prosopa,** 84 Konstantinoupoleos (✆ **210/341-3433;** www.prosopa.gr), famous for its "trio of death" complimentary dessert: cheesecake, chocolate brownie, and banana cream pie. And if it's seafood you want, try **Sardelles** (sardines), 15 Persefonis (✆ **210/347-8050**); if sardines are not your favorite treat, try the mixed seafood *mezedes.*

fork—ancient Greeks did not use them. Popular with tourists, this place also draws curious locals, foodies, and those in search of something truly different.

Plateia Karaiskaki, Metaxourgeio. ✆ **210/523-9661.** www.arxaion.gr. Main courses 20€–35€. MC, V. Mon–Sat 8pm–1am. Metro: Metaxourgeio.

Athinaikon ★★ GREEK/OUZERIE Not many tourists come to this favorite haunt of lawyers and businesspeople who work in the Omonia Square area. You can stick to appetizers or have a full meal. Appetizers include delicious *loukanika* (sausages) and *keftedes* (meatballs); pass up the more expensive grilled shrimp and the seafood paella. The adventurous can try *ameletita* (lamb's testicles). Whatever you have, you'll enjoy the old photos on the walls, the handsome tiled floor, the marble-topped tables and bentwood chairs, and the regular customers, who combine serious eating with animated conversation.

2 Themistokleous. ✆ **210/383-8485.** Appetizers and main courses 6€–20€. No credit cards. Mon–Sat 11am–midnight. Closed usually in Aug. Metro: Omonia.

Ideal ★ GREEK TRADITIONAL The oldest restaurant in the heart of Athens, today's Ideal has an Art Deco decor and lots of old favorites, from egg-lemon soup to stuffed peppers; from pork with celery to lamb with spinach. Ideal is a favorite of businesspeople, and the service is usually brisk, especially at lunchtime. Not the place for a quiet rendezvous, but definitely the place for good, hearty Greek cooking.

46 Panepistimiou. ✆ **210/330-3000.** Reservations recommended. Main courses 10€–20€. AE, DC, MC, V. Mon–Sat noon–midnight. Metro: Omonia.

Inexpensive

Taygetos ★ GREEK/SOUVLAKI This is a great place to stop for a quick meal on your way to/from the National Archaeological Museum. The service is swift and the souvlaki and fried potatoes are excellent, as are the chicken and the grilled lamb. The menu sometimes features delicious *kokoretsi* (grilled entrails).

4 Satovriandou. ✆ **210/523-5352.** Grilled lamb and chicken priced by the kilo. No credit cards. Mon–Sat 9am–1am. Metro: Omonia.

NEAR THE ACROPOLIS (KOUKAKI & MAKRIGIANNI)

Moderate

Strofi ★ GREEK The rooftop terrace here has a drop-dead view of the Acropolis and the Herodes Atticus theater. After performances, actors and members of the audience cross the street to Strofi to dine on grills, stews, good salads, and *horta* (greens). The cooking can be a bit rough-and-ready and the waiters a bit rushed, but the Acropolis view makes this place pretty irresistible.

25 Robertou Galli, Makrigianni (across from the Herodes Atticus theater). ✆ **210/921-4130.** Main courses 10€–20€. DC, MC, V. Mon–Sat 8pm–1am. Metro: Akropolis.

HERE & THERE

Expensive

Kalliste ★★ GREEK In a beautifully restored 19th-century house with polished wood floors and ornamental plaster ceilings, Kalliste is both cozy and elegant. The constantly changing menu usually includes traditional dishes with a distinctive flair, such as lentil soup with pomegranate, and chicken with hazelnuts and celery purée. Even that old standby, crème caramel, is enlivened by the addition of rose liqueur. This is a lovely refuge well away from the bustle of Athens.

137 Asklepiou, off Akadimias above the University of Athens. ✆ **210/645-3179.** Reservations recommended. Main courses 24€–30€. No credit cards. Mon–Sat noon–2pm and 8pm–midnight. Metro: Panepistimio.

Kostoyiannis ★★ TRADITIONAL GREEK Kostoyiannis has been doing everything right since the 1950s, serving a wide range of fresh seafood, grills, sweetbreads, and their signature *stifados* (rabbit or veal stews). Arriving here is a joy, as you walk past a display of the delicacies that can be whisked away and cooked to perfection for you.

Inside the bustling restaurant, contented diners tuck into their choices, many arriving as concerts and theater performances let out across Athens.

37 Zaimi, Pedion Areos, behind the National Archaeological Museum. ✆ **210/822-0624.** Reservations recommended. Main courses 15€–25€; fish and shellfish by the kilo. No credit cards. Mon–Sat 8pm–midnight. Closed late July to Aug. Metro: Victoria.

The Park ★★ ELEGANT GREEK The most remarkable thing about this place is that it has managed to remain a secret from tourists for so long. Tucked inside the Eleftherias Park, adjacent to the Athens Music/Concert Hall, the Park is one of the city's more charming places. During the day it functions as a lovely cafe set among the shady plane trees. At night it evolves into a romantic restaurant (with an always exceptional menu that changes daily). The adjoining bar/lounge heats up after 10pm with great music and clientele.

Eleftherias Park, Vassiliss Sofias. ✆ **210/722-3784.** Main courses 30€–45€. AE, DC, MC, V. Metro: Megaro Mousikis.

Spondi ★★★ INTERNATIONAL *Athinorama,* the weekly review of the Athenian scene, has chosen Spondi several years running as the best place in town. The menu features light dishes—the fresh fish, especially the salmon, is superb—as well as dishes that you will find either delightful or a bit cloying (roast pork with myzithra cheese and a fig-and-yogurt sauce). The setting, a handsome 19th-century town house with a courtyard, is lovely; the wine list, extensive; the service, excellent; and the desserts, divine. You'll probably want to take a cab here.

5 Pyrronos, Pangrati. ✆ **210/752-0658.** Reservations recommended. Main courses 45€–130€. No credit cards. Mon–Sat 8pm–1am. Pyrronos runs btw. Empedokleous and Dikearchou, behind the Olympic Stadium.

Varoulko ★★★ INTERNATIONAL/SEAFOOD After years in an unlikely location on a Piraeus side street, chef-owner Lefteris Lazarou has moved into the Thissio district of central Athens what many already considered the greater Athens area's finest seafood restaurant. I had one of the best meals of my life here—smoked eel; artichokes with fish roe; crayfish with sun-dried tomatoes; monkfish livers with soy sauce, honey, and balsamic vinegar—and the best sea bass and monkfish I have ever eaten. Sweetbreads, goat stew, and tripe soup have joined seafood on the menu—and you can't beat the view of the Acropolis.

80 Piraios, Athens. ✆ **210/522-8400.** www.varoulko.gr. Reservations required several days in advance. Dinner for 2 from about 120€; fish priced by the kilo. No credit cards. Mon–Sat about 8pm–midnight. Metro: Kerameikos.

Moderate

Chez Lucien ★★ FRENCH Off pedestrian Apostolou Pavlou and tucked away in one of many of Thissio's charming side streets you will find this very good and very popular French bistro with a small but excellent menu. There are no reservations so be prepared to wait and even share a table if need be. It's definitely worth it.

32 Troon, Thissio. ✆ **210/346-4236.** Main courses 20€–25€. No credit cards. Tues–Sat 8:30pm–1am. Metro: Thissio.

Meson el Mirador ★★ MEXICAN Finally! After years of pseudo-Mexican fare, here's a place serving genuine Mexican food. The restaurant occupies a beautifully restored mansion by the Kerameikos, Athens's ancient cemetery, which has given the surrounding neighborhood its name. This place is open for lunch, so you can treat yourself to a great meal after visiting the Kerameikos's monuments and excellent museum. Top-notch enchiladas, quesadillas, and pork chops with beans, plus a vegetarian menu, excellent sangria, and margaritas blow the would-be competitors out of the water. In summer there is a beautiful roof terrace with Acropolis views.

88 Agisilaou, corner Salaminas, Kerameikos. ✆ **210/342-0007.** www.el-mirador.gr. Main courses 20€–30€. Mon–Sat noon–2am. MC, V. Metro: Thissio/Kerameikos.

Vlassis ★★★ TRADITIONAL GREEK Greeks call this kind of food *paradosiako* (traditional), but paradisiacal is just as good a description. This very reasonably priced food is fit for the gods: delicious fluffy vegetable croquettes, a unique eggplant salad, and hauntingly tender lamb in egg-lemon sauce. A discreet sign announces Vlassis's presence in a small apartment building on hard-to-find Paster.

8 Paster (off Plateia Mavili). ✆ **210/646-3060.** Reservations recommended. Main courses 15€–23€. No credit cards. Mon–Sat 8pm–1am. Closed much of June–Sept. Metro: Megaro Mousikis. Across the street from Metro stop is Plateia Mavili; follow D. Tsoustou out of Plateia Mavili to Chatzikosta; Paster is the cul-de-sac on the left after you turn right onto Chatzikosta.

Seeing the Sights

THE TREASURES OF ANTIQUITY

The Acropolis ★★★ The monuments of the Acropolis began to undergo extensive renovation in honor of the 2004 Summer Olympics. These renovations continue and it is unclear when work will be finished. At press time, the Temple of Nike, which had been entirely dismantled for restoration, had been only partially reerected. The Propylaia and Parthenon were still encased in scaffolding. What follows is an attempt to describe what you should see when the renovations are completed.

If you do climb up the Acropolis—the heights above the city—you'll realize why people seem to have lived here as long ago as 5000 B.C. The sheer sides of the Acropolis make it a superb natural defense, just the place to avoid enemies and to be able to see invaders coming across the sea or the plains of Attica. And, of course, it helped that in antiquity there was a spring here, ensuring a steady supply of water.

In classical times, when Athens's population had grown to around 250,000, people lived on the slopes below the Acropolis, which had become the city's most important religious center. Athens's civic and business center, the Agora, and its cultural center, with several theaters and concert halls, bracketed the Acropolis; when you peer over the sides of the Acropolis at the houses in the Plaka and the

Museum Hours Update

If you visit Greece during the summer, check to see when sites and museums are open. According to the tourist office, most important places should be open from 8am to 7:30pm in summer and 8:30am to 3 or 5pm in winter, but some may close earlier in the day or even be closed 1 day a week. And remember that unexpected strikes and unpredicted closings are endemic in Greece.

The Acropolis & Ancient Agora

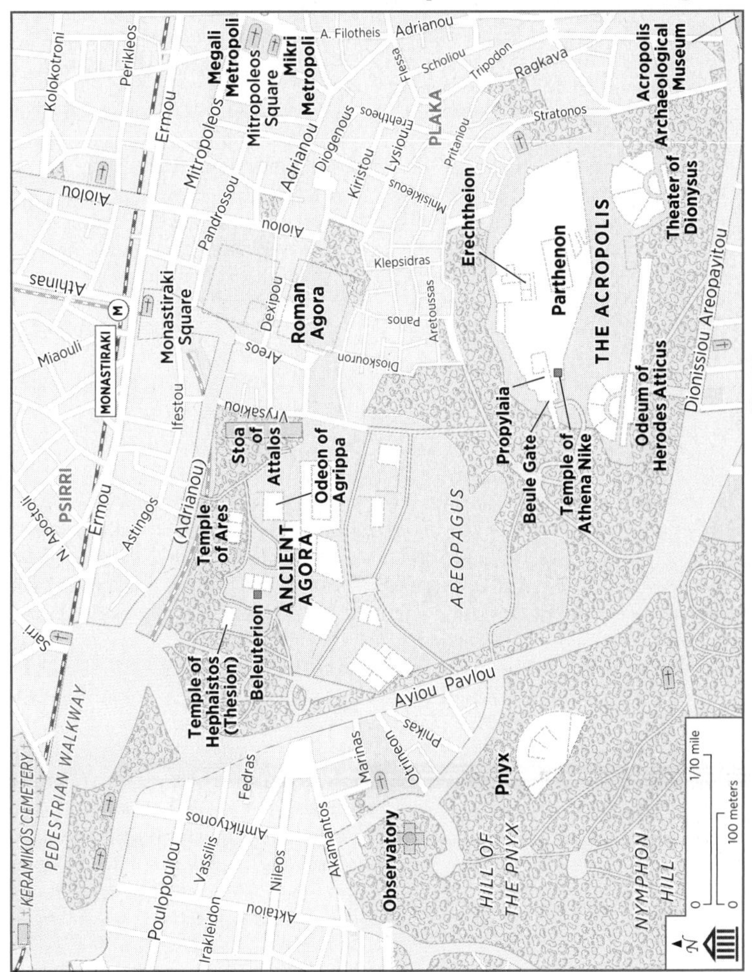

remains of the ancient **Agora** and the **Theater of Dionysos,** you'll see the layout of the ancient city. Syntagma and Omonia squares, the heart of today's Athens, were well out of the ancient city center.

Even the Acropolis's height couldn't protect it from the Persian invasion of 480 B.C., when most of its monuments were burned and destroyed. You may notice some immense column drums built into the Acropolis's walls. When the great Athenian statesman Pericles ordered the monuments rebuilt, he had the drums from the destroyed Parthenon built into the walls lest Athenians forget what had happened—and so they would remember that they had rebuilt what they had lost. Pericles'

Ticket Prices & Free Museum & Site Guides

The prices listed in this guide are based on the prices available at press time and "guesstimates" of forthcoming changes offered by some museums. As if that is not sufficiently confusing, keep in mind that virtually all the major attractions plan to raise their admission fees "soon." Because there is—surprise!—no fixed policy on cheaper tickets for students and seniors, be sure to ask about a discounted ticket if you are a senior or a student. Keep in mind that many discounts are valid only for Common Market citizens. The currently priced 12€ ticket that admits you to the Acropolis, Acropolis Museum, Ancient Agora, Theater of Dionysos, Karameikos Cemetery, Roman Forum, Tower of the Winds, and Temple of Olympian Zeus is one of the best buys in town (most individual admissions are 4€–6€). The ticket is usually available at the Acropolis. Also, ask for the handy free information brochure available at most sites and museums; ticket sellers do not always hand it over unless reminded.

rebuilding program began about 448 B.C.; the new Parthenon was dedicated 10 years later, but work on other monuments continued for a century.

The **Parthenon** ★★★—dedicated to Athena Parthenos (the Virgin), patron goddess of Athens—was the most important religious monument, but there were shrines to many other gods and goddesses on the Acropolis's broad summit. As you climb up, you pass first through the **Beule Gate,** built by the Romans and now known by the name of the French archaeologist who discovered it in 1852. Next comes the **Propylaia** ★, the monumental 5th-century-B.C. entryway. You'll notice the little **Temple of Athena Nike (Athena of Victory)** ★ perched above the Propylaia; the beautifully proportioned Ionic temple was built in 424 B.C. Off to the left of the Parthenon is the **Erechtheion** ★★, which the Athenians honored as the tomb of Erechtheus, a legendary king of Athens. A hole in the ceiling and floor of the northern porch indicates the spot where Poseidon's trident struck to make a spring (symbolizing control of the sea) gush forth during his contest with Athena to be the city's chief deity. Athena countered with an olive tree (symbolizing control of the rich Attic plain); the olive tree planted beside the Erechtheion reminds visitors of her victory. Give yourself a little time to enjoy the delicate carving on the Erechtheion, and be sure to see the original **caryatids** (the monumental female figures who served as columns on the Erechtheion's porch) in the new Acropolis Museum.

However charmed you are by these elegant little temples, you're probably still heading resolutely toward the **Parthenon,** and you may be disappointed to realize that visitors are not allowed inside, both to protect the monument and to allow any ongoing restoration work to proceed safely. If you find this frustrating, keep in mind that in antiquity only priests and honored visitors were allowed in to see the monumental 11m (36-ft.) statue of Athena designed by the great Phidias, who supervised Pericles' building program. Nothing of the huge gold-and-ivory statue remains, but there's a small Roman copy in the National Archaeological Museum—and horrific renditions on souvenirs ranging from T-shirts to ouzo bottles.

The Parthenon's entire roof and much of the interior were blown to smithereens in 1687, when a party of Venetians attempted to take the Acropolis from the Turks.

A shell fired from nearby Mouseion Hill struck the Parthenon—where the Turks were storing gunpowder and munitions—and caused appalling damage to the building and its sculptures. Most of the remaining sculptures were carted off to London by Lord Elgin in the first decade of the 19th century. Those surviving sculptures—known to much of the world as **Elgin Marbles,** but known here as the **Parthenon Marbles**—are on display in the British Museum, causing ongoing pain to generations of Greeks. Greece has undercut the British Museum's protests that Athens has no safe and suitable place to display the marbles by building the Acropolis Museum to house the marbles and the contents of the original Acropolis Archaeological Museum (see below).

The Parthenon originally had sculpture in both its pediments, as well as a frieze running around the entire temple. Alternating **triglyphs** (panels with three incised grooves) and **metopes** (sculptured panels) made up the frieze. The message of most of this sculpture was the triumph of knowledge and civilization (read: Athens) over the forces of darkness and barbarians. An interior frieze showed scenes from the Panathenaic Festival each August, when citizens walked in procession through the streets, bringing a new *peplos* (tunic) for the statue of Athena. Only a few fragments of any of the sculptures remain in place, and every visitor will have to decide whether it's a good or a bad thing that Lord Elgin removed so much before the smog spread over Athens and ate away at the remaining sculpture.

If you're lucky enough to visit the Acropolis on a smog-free and sunny day, you'll see the golden-and-cream tones of the Parthenon's handsome Pentelic marble at their most subtle. It may come as something of a shock to realize that the Parthenon, like most other monuments here, was painted in antiquity, with bright colors that have since faded, revealing the tones of the marble.

You'll probably want to spend half a day on the Acropolis.

Dionyssiou Areopagitou. ✆ **210/321-0219.** Admission 12€ adults, free on Sun. This ticket, valid for 1 week, includes admission to the Acropolis, Acropolis Museum, Ancient Agora, Theater of Dionysos, Karameikos Cemetery, Roman Forum, Tower of the Winds, and Temple of Olympian Zeus. The Acropolis is usually open summer daily 8am–7pm; winter daily 8:30am–3pm. The Acropolis Museum usually closes at least half an hour earlier than the Acropolis. The ticket booth, along with a small post office and a snack bar, are slightly below the Acropolis entrance. Metro: Acropolis.

Ancient Agora ★★ The Agora was Athens's commercial and civic center, with buildings used for a wide range of political, educational, philosophical, theatrical, and athletic purposes—which may be why what remains seems such a jumble. This is a nice place to wander and enjoy the views up toward the Acropolis; take in the herb garden and flowers planted around the 5th-century-B.C. **Theseion (Temple of Hephaistos);** peek into the heavily restored 11th-century church of **Ayii Apostoli (Holy Apostles);** and get a sense of what an entire ancient civic building looked

Explore Early and Often

Budget cuts and staff strikes make museums and ancient sites in Greece subject to unpredictable closures. What is open today may be unexpectedly closed tomorrow. It's always a good idea to visit the sites and museums that you want to see as soon as possible.

like from the 2nd-century-B.C. **Stoa of Attalos,** which was reconstructed in the 1950s.

The museum in the Stoa's ground floor has finds from 5,000 years of Athenian history, including sculpture and pottery, as well as a voting machine and a child's potty seat, all with labels in English. The museum (which, by the way, has excellent toilet facilities) closes 15 minutes before the site. You'll want to spend at least 2 hours here.

Below the Acropolis on the edge of Monastiraki (entrance on Adrianou, near Ayiou Philippou Sq., east of Monastiraki Sq. and on Ay. Apostoli, the road leading down into Plaka from the Acropolis). ✆ **210/321-0185.** Admission (includes museum) 6€, or free with purchase of 12€ Acropolis ticket. The Agora is usually open summer daily 8am–7pm; winter daily 8:30am–3pm. Metro: Monastiraki.

Cemetery of Kerameikos ★ This ancient cemetery, where **Pericles** gave his famous funeral oration during the Peloponnesian War, is a short walk from the Ancient Agora and not far from the presumed site of **Plato's Academy.** There are a number of well-preserved funerary monuments and the remains of the colossal **Dipylon Gate,** the main entrance to the ancient city of Athens. In 2002, the well-preserved marble figure of a *kouros* (youth) was found in excavations here, a hint of what treasures remain to be found. For now, you can see the substantial remains of the 5th-century-B.C. fortifications known as the "Long Walls" that ran from Athens to Piraeus. The Kerameikos is seldom crowded, which makes it a pleasant spot to sit and read. If you like cemeteries, be sure to take in Athens's enormous **First Cemetery,** near the Athens Stadium, where notables such as *Never on Sunday* actress Melina Mercouri are buried beneath elaborate monuments.

148 Ermou. ✆ **210/346-3553.** Admission 4€, or free with purchase of 12€ Acropolis ticket. Summer Tues–Sun 8:30am–6pm; winter Tues–Sun 8:30am–3pm. Walk west from Monastiraki Sq. on Ermou past Thisio Metro station; cemetery is on the right. Metro: Monastiraki or Thisio.

THE TOP MUSEUMS

The National Archaeological Museum ★★★ This is an enormous and enormously popular museum. Be sure to ask for the free pamphlet with a handy map of the galleries when you buy your ticket. The collection includes objects from the Neolithic to the Roman eras. Don't miss the stunning gold masks, cups, dishes, and jewelry unearthed from the site of Mycenae by Heinrich Schliemann in 1876; the elegant marble Cycladic figurines (ca. 2000 B.C.); and the famous marble and bronze statues. The museum—often listed as one of the 10 most important in the entire world—was largely closed during renovations from 2002 to 2005. The **Stathatos Gallery,** reopened in 2008, has stunning jewelry, vases, figurines, and objects from the middle Bronze Age to the post-Byzantine era. The **Egyptian Art Collection,** also reopened in 2008, is considered one of the world's finest. The enormous collection of Greek vases on the second floor is dazzling—and daunting! Try to visit more

Online Museum Updates

Information on most major museums and archaeological sites—and updates on any price hikes—should be available on www.athensinfoguide.com, www.visitgreece.gr, and www.culture.gr.

Planning Ahead

When you plan your sightseeing, keep in mind that three top museums—the Goulandris, the Benaki, and the Byzantine and Christian—are clustered near each other on or just off Vasilissis Sofias Avenue. If three major museums in one excursion seems like a lot, remember that the Benaki and Goulandris both have excellent cafes.

than once. Be sure not to miss the restored 3500-B.C. frescoes from the site of Akrotiri on the island of Santorini (Thira) also on view on the second floor; others are intended to be displayed on the island of Santorini itself. The museum shop has reproductions and books on aspects of the collection. You'll probably want to spend a minimum of 3 hours here—and wish you'd spent more.

The National Archaeological Museum celebrated its 120th anniversary in 2009 by inaugurating five new permanent exhibits housed next door in the former Numismatic Museum, now part of the National Archaeological Museum. The new displays feature Hellenistic ceramics and glass never before exhibited, including a wine cooler.

44 Patission (Patission appears as OKTOVRIOU/OCTOBER on some street signs). ✆ **210/821-7717.** Admission 6€, or 12€ with Acropolis entrance. Mon 12:30–5pm; Tues–Fri 8am–6pm; Sat–Sun and holidays 8:30am–3pm. Sometimes open until 7pm in summer. Metro: Omonia or Viktoria.

The New Acropolis Museum ★★★ This 21,000-sq.-m (226,000-sq.-ft.) glass-and-concrete museum is a stunning—some would say disconcertingly so—addition to Athens. The museum was built not merely to house the more than 4,000 treasures on display (10 times more than in the previous Acropolis museum) but to make a statement: Send the Parthenon marbles (aka the Elgin Marbles) in the British Museum back to Athens!

Metal ramps lead from the ongoing excavations in the museum's lower levels, where visitors can peer through glass panels at an ancient Athenian neighborhood (where houses, baths, shops, workshops, and roads have been thus far uncovered) and an early Christian settlement. The museum's first two floors display an astonishing number of artifacts, statues, sculptures, and free-standing objects that used to adorn the sacred rock (plus some little-known treasures from the Temple of Artemis Brauronia). The museum's top floor is the all-important Parthenon Gallery. The glass-walled gallery is rotated 23 degrees off its axis to mirror the layout of the Parthenon, which is splendidly visible throughout the gallery. On display within the gallery is all that remains in Greece of the original Parthenon sculptures and frieze—36 of the 115 original panels, alongside stark white plaster casts of the originals that are in London. The contrast is meant to bring home all that is missing, in the hopes that someday the Parthenon marbles will be reunited. Until then, the goddess Iris has her head in Athens, along with a plaster cast of her body, while the marble original of her body remains in London.

15 Dionisiou Aeropagitou. ✆ **210/900-0901.** www.theacropolismuseum.gr. Admission 5€. Tues–Sun 8am–8pm. Metro: Akropolis.

N. P. Goulandris Foundation Museum of Cycladic Art ★★★ This handsome museum just off Vasilissis Sofias Avenue houses the largest collection of

Cycladic art outside the National Archaeological Museum—and is a much more congenial, less crowded place to visit. See if you agree with those who have compared the faces of the Cycladic figurines to the works of the Italian painter Modigliani. Be sure to go through the courtyard into the elegant 19th-century Stathatos Mansion, which forms part of the museum. The mansion, which is used for special exhibits, has some of its original furnishings and provides a glimpse of how wealthy Athenians lived a hundred years ago. The museum shop has a wide variety of books and reproductions. You'll want to spend at least 3 hours here, perhaps with a break in the garden cafe.

4 Neophytou Douka. ✆ **210/722-8321.** www.cycladic-m.gr. Admission 6€. Mon and Wed–Fri 10am–4pm; Sat 10am–3pm. Metro: Syntagma.

Benaki Museum ★★★ This stunning private collection includes treasures from the Neolithic era to the 20th century. The folk-art collection (including magnificent costumes and icons) is superb, as are the two entire rooms from 18th-century northern Greek mansions, ancient Greek bronzes, gold cups, Fayum portraits, and rare early Christian textiles. A new wing doubles the exhibition space of the original 20th-century neoclassical town house that belonged to the wealthy Benaki family. Dine with a spectacular view over Athens at the excellent rooftop cafe, which offers a buffet supper (40€) Thursday evenings, when the museum remains open until midnight. This is a very pleasant place to spend several hours—or days. After you visit the Benaki, take in its new branch, Benaki Museum of Islamic Art (see the "Athens's New Museums" box, below).

1 Koumbari (at Leoforos Vasilissis Sofias, Kolonaki, 5 blocks east of Syntagma Sq.). ✆ **210/367-1000.** www.benaki.gr. Admission 6€, free on Thurs. Mon, Wed, and Fri–Sat 9am–5pm; Thurs 9am–midnight; Sun 9am–3pm. Metro: Syntagma or Evangelismos.

Byzantine and Christian Museum ★★ As its name makes clear, this museum, with two large new galleries flanking a 19th-century Florentine-style villa, is devoted to the art and history of the Byzantine era (roughly 4th–15th c. A.D.). If you love icons (paintings, usually of saints, usually on wood) or want to find out about them, this is the place to go. Exhibits include selections from Greece's most important collection of icons and religious art—along with sculptures, altars, mosaics, religious vestments, Bibles, and a small-scale reconstruction of an early Christian basilica. Allow at least an hour for your visit—two if a special exhibit is featured. And three is even better.

22 Vasilissis Sofias Ave. ✆ **210/723-1570** or 210/721-1027. Admission 4€. Tues–Sun 8:30am–3pm. Metro: Syntagma or Evangelismos.

Greek Folk Art Museum ★★ ☺ This endearing small museum has dazzling embroideries and costumes, carved wooden furniture and tools, and ceramic and copper utensils from all over the country, plus a small room with zany frescoes of gods and heroes done by eccentric artist Theofilos Hadjimichael, who painted in the early part of the 20th century. Lots of Greek schoolchildren visit here, and sometimes puppet shows are offered. I stop by here every time I'm in Athens, always finding something new, always looking forward to our next visit—and always glad I wasn't born a Greek woman 100 years ago, when (all thumbs) I would have spent endless hours embroidering, crocheting, and weaving. Much of what is on display was made by young women for their *proikas* (dowries) in the days when a bride was

ATHENS'S NEW museums

In addition to the new Acropolis Museum (see "The Top Museums," above), a number of terrific smaller museums have opened recently in Athens. The most impressive is **Benaki Museum of Islamic Art** (at Agio Asomaton and Dipylou, Psirri; ✆ **210/367-1000;** www.benaki.gr; admission 6€; Metro: Monastiraki or Thissio). The stunning collection, housed in a 19th-century town house, displays superb Islamic art (ceramics, carpets, woodcarvings, and other objects) that dates from the 14th century to the present. Labels are in Greek and English.

A block away, the **Museum of Traditional Pottery,** 4–6 Melidoni, Kerameikos (✆ **210/331-8491;** Mon–Fri 9am–3pm, Sun 10am–4pm; small cafe; free admission; Metro: Thissio), has a wide-ranging display of traditional and contemporary Greek pottery, labeled in Greek and English.

The **Herakleidon Museum,** 16 Iraklidon (✆ **210/346-1981;** www.herakleidon-art.gr; free admission; daily 1–9pm; closed mid-Aug; Metro: Thissio), housed in a beautiful neoclassical mansion on the busy cafe strip of Thissio, is an excellent private museum which holds one of the world's biggest collections of M. C. Escher and also hosts various temporary exhibitions.

In nearby Plaka, the **Frissiras Museum,** 3-7 Moni Asteriou (✆ **210/323-4678;** admission 6€; Wed–Thurs 11am–7pm, Fri–Sun 11am–5pm; Metro: Akropolis), has excellent special exhibits as well as a permanent collection of 20th-century and later European art, with labels in English.

The **Pierides Museum of Ancient Cypriot Art,** 34-35 Kastorias, Votanikos (✆ **210/348-0000;** www.athinais.com.gr; free admission; daily 10am–9pm; Metro: Kerameikos), does just what it says: It records the art—and politics—of Cyprus in the Athinais complex.

The stunning **Benaki Museum-Pireos Street Annexe,** 138 Pireos and Andronikou (✆ **210/345-3111;** www.benaki.gr), stages exhibitions, as does the huge multipurpose **Technopolis,** 100 Pireos (✆ **210/346-0981;** www.culture.gr).

The **Hellenic Cosmos** (also known as the **Foundation of the Hellenic World**), 254 Pireos, Tavris (✆ **210/483-5300;** www.fhw.gr; 10€ adults, 9€ children; hours in flux, check before visiting; Metro: Kalithea), is a child-friendly high-tech museum with interactive displays and virtual tours of Greece that allow visitors to call up and "see" moments in Greek history from ancient to modern times. Housed in a former factory, it also offers an Internet cafe and a museum shop. Call ahead to make sure an English-speaking guide is on duty.

supposed to arrive at the altar with enough embroidered linen, rugs, and blankets to last a lifetime.

17 Kidathineon, Plaka. ✆ **210/322-9031.** Admission 2€. Tues–Sun 10am–2pm. Metro: Syntagma or Acropolis.

Ilias Lalaounis Jewelry Museum ★★ The 3,000 pieces on display here are so spectacular that even those who don't care about jewelry will enjoy this small, sparkling museum, founded by one of Greece's most successful jewelry designers. Jewelry displayed includes pieces inspired by ancient, Byzantine, and Cycladic designs, as well as by flora and fauna. The museum also has frequent special exhibits, a cafe, a seductive boutique, and a small workshop. The jewelers in the shop can reproduce pieces in the museum, something to keep in mind if you want your own gold necklace inspired by insect vertebrae. Many of the exhibits here are small and detailed, so you may want to spend several hours here, with a break at the cafe.

12 Kalisperi (at Karyatidon). ✆ **210/922-1044.** www.lalaounis-jewelrymuseum.gr. Admission 4€. Mon and Thurs–Sat 9am–4pm; Wed 9am–9pm (free after 3pm); Sun 10am–4pm. Metro: Akropolis.

Jewish Museum ★★ Greece's Jewish community, a strong presence throughout the country and a dominant force in Thessaloniki, was essentially obliterated in the Holocaust. Perhaps the most impressive exhibit is the handsome reconstruction of part of the interior of the Patras synagogue. Articles of daily life and religious ceremony include children's toys and special Passover china. Most exhibits have English labels. If you contact museum curator Zanet Battinou in advance of your visit, she will try to have a staff member take you through the collection.

39 Nikis (discreetly marked on the left side of Nikis as you walk away from Syntagma Sq.). ✆ **210/322-5582.** Fax 210/323-1577. www.jewishmuseum.gr. Admission 5€. Mon–Fri 9am–2:30pm; Sun 10am–2pm. Metro: Syntagma.

Museum of Popular Greek Musical Instruments ★★ Photographs show the musicians, while recordings let you listen to the tambourines, Cretan lyres, lutes, pottery drums, and clarinets on display. In addition, this museum is just steps from the excellent Platanos taverna, so you can alternate the pleasures of food, drink, and music. On a recent visit, an elderly Greek gentleman listened to some music, transcribed it, stepped out into the courtyard, and played it on his own violin! The shop has a wide selection of CDs and cassettes, the garden has resident tortoises, and the wonderful Platanos restaurant (see "Where to Dine," earlier in this chapter) is just steps away. The museum sometimes hosts evening concerts; ask what's scheduled when you visit.

1–3 Dioyenous (around the corner from the Tower of the Winds). ✆ **01-325-0198.** Free admission. Tues and Thurs–Sun 10am–2pm; Wed noon–6pm. Metro: Acropolis or Monastiraki.

GALLERIES

One of the great (usually free) pleasures of visiting Athens is browsing in its small art galleries. Occasionally a gallery will have an admission fee for a special exhibit, but usually there is no charge. This is a wonderful way to get a sense of the contemporary Greek art scene and possibly buy something to take home. A good way to find out what's on is to pick up a free copy of the quarterlies ***Art and the City*** and the ***Athens Contemporary Art Map.*** Both are free, published in Greek and English, and usually available in hotels in galleries. Here are some galleries to keep an eye out for in central Athens. In trendy Psirri, **AD Gallery,** 3 Pallados (✆ **210/322-8785**), focuses on modern and conceptual Greek art; and **a.antonopoulou.art,** 20 Aristofanous (✆ **210/321-4994**), is one of the most stunning art spaces in the city concentrating on Greek contemporary artists. Also in Psirri, the **Epistrofi Gallery,** 6 Taki (✆ **210/321-8640**), has occasional concerts as well as shows.

Just off Athinas Street, the **Epikentro Gallery,** 10 Armodiou (✆ **210/331-2187**), stages frequent exhibits in its improbable location in the Athens Central Market. The **Rebecca Camhi Gallery,** 23 Sophokleous (✆ **210/321-0448;** www.rebeccacamhi.com), not far from the Central Market, is one of Athens's best-known galleries; in August, it's open by appointment only. **Bernier/Eliades Gallery,** 11 Eptachalkou, Theseion (✆ **210/341-3935;** www.bernier-eliades.gr), stages group exhibitions, as does **Kappatos,** 6 Agias Irenes (✆ **210/321-7931**).

There are also frequent shows at the **Melina Mercouri Cultural Center,** Iraklidon and 66 Thessalonikis (✆ **210/345-2150**), and at the **Melina Mercouri Foundation,** 9–11 Polygnotou (✆ **210/331-5601**), in the Plaka. Also in Plaka, the **Athens Gallery,** 14 Pandrossou St. (✆ **210/324-6942;** www.athensgallery.gr), occupies three floors in a beautiful old neoclassical home. In the fashionable Kolonaki district, **Astrolavos Art Life,** 11 Irodotou (✆ **210/722-1200;** www.astrolavos.gr), and **Medusa,** 7 Xenokratous (✆ **210/724-4552;** www.medusaartgallery.com), both feature cutting-edge contemporary Greek and international artists.

And keep in mind that the **National Museum of Contemporary Art** is scheduled to open in its new Syngrou-Fix location in 2010 in what appears to be yet another brilliant industrial-to-art conversion, but for now it is housed at the **Athens Conservatory,** 17–19 Vas. Georgiou (✆ **210/924-5200;** www.emst.gr). Until it's open, consider visiting the wonderful **Athens Municipal Art Gallery,** 51 Pireos, Plateia Koumoundourou, Gazi (✆ **210/324-3023**), with its rich collection of more than 2,300 works from leading 19th- and 20th-century Greek artists. One just-out-of-town suburban gallery that's well worth a visit (in part for its great cafe and shop) is the **Deste Foundation for Contemporary Art,** 8 Omirou, Nea Psychico (✆ **210/672-9460;** www.deste.gr), a 20-minute cab ride from Syntagma.

ORGANIZED TOURS

The **CitySightseeing bus** (www.city-sightseeing.com; 18€ adults, 8€ children) is an open-top double-decker red bus that begins and ends its journey at Syntagma Square. The ride through central Athens lasts 90 minutes, with stops at the Acropolis, Temple of Zeus, Plaka, the university, Omonia Square, Kerameikos, Monastiraki, Psirri, Thission, the Benaki Museum, the National Gallery, the Central Market, and the Panathenaiko Stadium. Prerecorded commentaries are available in English, Greek, Spanish, French, German, Italian, Russian, and Japanese. Tickets are valid for 24 hours and buses depart every half-hour from 7am to 6pm. Also, **Hop in Sightseeing** (✆ **210/428-5500;** www.hopin.com) allows you to get on and off the bus tour over 2 days and even does hotel pickups.

The best-known Athens-based tour groups are **CHAT Tours,** 4 Stadiou (✆ **210/323-0827;** www.chatours.gr), and **Key Tours,** 4 Kalliroïs (✆ **210/923-3166;** www.keytours.gr). Each offers half- and full-day tours of the city, "Athens by Night" tours, and day excursions from Athens. Expect to pay about 50€ for a half-day tour, 80€ for a full-day tour, and around 100€ for "Athens by Night" (including dinner and sometimes a folk-dance performance at the Dora Stratou Theater). To take any of these tours, you must book and pay in advance. At that time, you will be told when you will be picked up at your hotel, or where you should meet the tour.

Each company also offers excursions from Athens. A visit to the very popular **Temple of Poseidon at Sounion** costs about 60€ for a half-day trip, including swimming and a meal. A trip to **Delphi** usually costs about 110€ for a full day, which often includes stops at the Monastery of Osios Loukas and Arachova village. If you want to spend the night in Delphi (included are hotel, site, and museum admissions, as well as dinner, breakfast, and sometimes lunch), the price ranges from 50€ to 160€. Rates for excursions to the **Peloponnese,** taking in Corinth, Mycenae, and

Epidaurus, are similar to those for Delphi. If your time in Greece is limited, you may find one of these day trips considerably less stressful than renting a car for the day and driving yourself.

If you want to hire a private guide, speak to the concierge at your hotel or contact the **Panhellenic Guides Federation,** 9a Apollonas (✆ **210/322-9705**). Expect to pay 90€ for a 4-hour tour. Through **Athenian Days** (✆ **210/864-0415**) you will have classicist Andrew Farrington lead you through tailor-made cultural and historical tours of the city for up to six people. **Rania Vassiliadou** (✆ **210/940-3932;** www.raniavassiliadou.virtualave.net) does tours of Athens's archaeological sites and day trips for up to six people.

Pame Volta (Let's Go for a Ride), 20 Hadjichristou, Acropolis (✆ **210/922-1578;** www.pamevolta.gr; Wed–Fri 9am–5pm, Sat–Sun 11am–7pm), has taken advantage of post-Olympics pedestrian-friendly Athens and offers bicycles for rent and bicycle tours around the city. Much more expensive but also much more spectacular is the Helicopter Sightseeing Tour of Athens by **Hop In Zinon Tours,** 29 Zanni St., Piraeus (✆ **210/428-5500;** www.hopin.com). Seeing Athens from above, especially at night when all the monuments are lit, is an unforgettable (if pricey) experience.

The Shopping Scene

You may find a copy of the monthly magazines ***Athens Today*** and ***Now in Athens,*** both of which have a shopping section, in your hotel room. ***Note:*** Keep in mind that most of the restaurants and shops featured pay for the privilege.

You're in luck shopping in Athens, because almost everything you'll probably want to buy can be found in the central city, bounded by Omonia, Syntagma, and Monastiraki squares. This is where you'll find most of the shops frequented by Athenians, including a number of large **department stores.**

Monastiraki has its famous **flea market,** which is especially lively on Sundays. Although it has a vast amount of ticky-tacky stuff for sale here, it also has some real finds, including retro clothes and old copper. Many Athenians furnishing new homes head here to try to pick up old treasures.

The **Plaka** has pretty much cornered the market on souvenir shops, with enough T-shirts, reproductions of antiquities (including obscene playing cards, drink coasters, and more), fishermen's sweaters (increasingly made in the Far East), and jewelry (often not real gold) to circle the globe.

In the Plaka-Monastiraki area, several shops worth seeking out amid the endlessly repetitive souvenir shops include **Stavros Melissinos,** the Poet-Sandalmaker of Athens, relocated after 50 years on Pandrossou to his new location at 12 Agias Theklas (✆ 210/321-9247), where his son is now in charge; **Iphanta,** the weaving workshop, 6 Selleu (✆ 210/322-3628); **Emanuel Masmanidis' Gold Rose Jewelry Shop,** 85 Pandrossou (✆ 210/321-5662); the **Center of Hellenic Tradition,** 59 Mitropoleos and 36 Pandrossou (✆ 210/321-3023), which sells arts and crafts; and the **National Welfare Organization,** 6 Ipatias and Apollonos, Plaka (✆ 210/321-8272), where a portion of the proceeds from everything sold (including handsome woven and embroidered carpets) goes to the National Welfare Organization, which encourages traditional crafts.

Kolonaki, on the slopes of Mount Likavitos, is boutique heaven—but it's a better place to window-shop than to buy, as much of what you see is imported and heavily taxed. If you're here during the January or August sales, you may find some bargains.

If not, it's still a lot of fun to work your way up pedestrian Voukourestiou along Tsakalof and Anagnostopoulou (with perhaps the most expensive boutiques in Athens) before collapsing at a cafe on one of the pedestrian shopping streets (Milioni is a good choice) in Kolonaki Square. Then you can engage in the other really serious business of Kolonaki: people-watching. Give yourself about 15 minutes to discern the season's must-have accessory. If you want to make a small, traditional purchase, have a look at the "worry beads" at **Kombologadiko,** 6 Koumbari (✆ **210/362-4267**), or check out charms that ward off the evil eye at **To Fylakto Mou,** 20 Solonos (✆ **210/364-7610**).

Pedestrianized Ermou Street is the longtime main shopping drag in the city with more stores than you will have the time to visit, but if you want to do all your shopping in one take and not walk around outdoors, check out some of the 300 shops on the eight floors of the **Attica** department store in the CityLink Building at 9 Panepistimiou (✆ **210/180-2500;** www.atticadps.gr). If you're not in the mood to shop, you'll still be wowed by the window displays.

Athens After Dark

Greeks enjoy their nightlife so much that they take an afternoon nap to rest up for it. The evening often begins with a leisurely *volta* (stroll); you'll see it in most neighborhoods, including the Plaka and Kolonaki Square. Most Greeks don't think of dinner until at least 10pm. Around midnight the party may move on to a club—often out of central Athens—for the start of an evening of music and dancing. Feel free to try places on your own, although you may feel like the odd man out because Greeks seldom go anywhere alone. If you're a woman on your own and want to be left alone, you'll probably find hitting the bars and dance clubs uncongenial.

Ask the concierge or desk clerk at your hotel for nightlife recommendations. The listings in the weekly *Athinorama* (Greek) or in publications such as the English-language *Athens News,* the *Kathimerini* insert in the *Herald Tribune,* and hotel handouts such as *Best of Athens* and *Welcome to Athens* can also be very helpful.

Wherever you go, you're likely to face a cover charge of at least 20€. Thereafter, each drink will probably cost between 10€ and 20€. Many clubs plop a bottle on your table that's labeled (but doesn't necessarily contain) Johnny Walker Red or

Open in August

A great many popular after-dark spots close in August, when much of Athens flees the summer heat to the country. Some places that stay open include a number of bars, cafes, ouzeries, sweet shops, and tavernas on the pedestrian **Iraklion Walkway** at Thissio (Theseion). **Stavlos,** 10 Iraklidon (✆ **210/346-7206**), a restaurant, bar, and disco popular with all ages, remains open on August weekends. **Athinaion Politeia** (a cafe/bar/restaurant), 30 Apostolou Pavlou and 1 Akamanthos (✆ **210/341-3794**), has a great location with uninterrupted views of the Acropolis and passersby. And remember that some of the best lounges/bars in the city these days are found in hotels. Don't forget to have a drink at the top-floor **Galaxy** bar at the **Hilton** hotel for an amazing city view. For the most happening scene, stop by the hotel lounge/bars at the **St. George Lycabettus Hotel,** the **Fresh Hotel,** and **Ochre & Brown Hotel.**

Black, and then they try very hard to charge you at least 100€ whether you drink it or not.

If you hear music you like when you're out on the town, **Metropolis** (✆ **210/ 380-8549**) in Omonia Square has a wide choice of CDs and tapes of Greek music.

FESTIVALS

New festivals spring up every year in Athens and throughout Greece. You may want to check with the Greek National Tourist Office (www.visitgreece.gr) to see what's new at your destination. Additional information on the festivals below is available at www.greekfestival.gr, www.athensinfoguide.com, and www.greektourism.com.

HELLENIC FESTIVAL ★★★ Early June through September, the Hellenic Festival (also known as the **Athens** or **Greek Festival**) features famous Greek and foreign artists from Elton John to Placido Domingo performing on the slopes of the Acropolis. You may catch an opera, concert, drama, or ballet here—and see the Acropolis illuminated over your shoulder at the same time. Schedules and advance tickets are usually available at the **Hellenic Festival Office,** 39 Panepistimiou (in the arcade; ✆ **210/928-2900;** www.greekfestival.gr). You will have better luck if you come here in person rather than try to reach the office by phone. If available—and that's a big "if"—tickets (15€–50€) can be purchased at the Odeion of Herodes Atticus (✆ **210/323-2771** or 210/323-5582) several hours before the performance. Again, you will have better luck at the ticket office, although if your hotel has a concierge, he or she may be able to obtain tickets over the phone. Shows usually begin at 9pm.

EPIDAURUS FESTIVAL ★★★ From late June to late August, performances of ancient Greek tragedies and comedies (usually given in modern Greek translations) take place at Epidaurus, in Greece's most beautiful ancient theater. You can purchase bus service along with your ticket (about 2 hr. each way). Contact the **Greek National Tourism Organization,** the **Hellenic Festival Office** (see above), or the **Rex Theater** box office (✆ **210/330-1881**) on Panepistimiou just outside Spiromilios Arcade. You can sometimes get tickets at **Epidaurus** (✆ **27530/22-006**) just before a performance.

ATHENS INTERNATIONAL DANCE FESTIVAL Founded in 2003, this festival takes place during the first 2 weeks in July at the Technopolis arts complex, 100 Piraeus, Gazi. This is not the place to go for a traditional rendition of Swan Lake; groups performing here push the envelope of contemporary dance. Schedule and ticket information is at ✆ **210/346-1589** or 210/346-7322.

THE PERFORMING ARTS

The acoustically marvelous new **Megaron Mousikis Concert Hall ★★★**, 89 Leoforos Vas. Sofias (✆ **210/729-0391;** www.megaron.gr), hosts a wide range of classical music programs that includes everything from solo performances to operas. On performance nights, the box office is open Monday to Friday 10am to 6pm, Saturday 10am to 2pm, and Sunday 6 to 10:30pm. Tickets are also sold Monday to Friday 10am to 5pm in the Megaron's convenient downtown kiosk in the Spiromilios Arcade, 4 Stadiou. Ticket prices run from 5€ to more than 100€. The Megaron has a limited summer season but is in full swing the rest of the year.

The **Greek National Opera** performs at **Olympia Theater,** 59 Akadimias at Mavromihali (✆ **210/361-2461**). The summer months are usually off season.

Pallas Theater, 1 Voukourestiou (✆ **210/322-8275**), hosts many jazz and rock concerts, as well as some classical performances. Prices vary from performance to performance, but you can get a cheap ticket from about 10€.

Since 1953, **Dora Stratou Folk Dance Theater** ★ has been giving performances of traditional Greek folk dances on Filopappos Hill. At present, performances take place May through September, Tuesday through Sunday at 9:30pm, with additional performances at 8:15pm on Wednesday and Sunday. You can buy tickets at the **box office,** 8 Scholio, Plaka, from 8am to 2pm (✆ **210/924-4395,** or 210/921-4650 after 5:30pm; www.grdance.org). Prices range from 15€ to 25€. Tickets are also available at the theater before the performances.

Seen from Pnyx hill, **sound-and-light** shows illuminate (sorry) Athens's history by telling the story of the Acropolis. As lights pick out monuments on the Acropolis and the music swells, the narrator tells of the Persian attack, the Periclean days of glory, the invidious Turkish occupation—you get the idea. Shows are held April through October. The 45-minute performances in English are given at 9pm on Monday, Wednesday, Thursday, Saturday, and Sunday. Tickets (15€) can be purchased at the **Hellenic Festival Office,** 39 Panepistimiou (✆ **210/928-2900**), or at the entrance to the sound-and-light show (✆ **210/922-6210**). You'll hear the narrative best if you don't sit too close to the very loud public-address system.

LIVE-MUSIC CLUBS

Walk the streets of the Plaka on any night and you'll find lots of tavernas offering pseudo-traditional live music (usually at clip-joint prices) and a few offering the real thing. Don't bother to phone ahead to these places—the phone is almost never answered. **Taverna Mostrou,** 22 Mnissikleos (✆ **210/324-2441**), is one of the largest, oldest, and best known for traditional Greek music and dancing. Shows begin about 11pm and usually last to 2am. The cover charge (from about 30€) includes a fixed-price supper; a la carte fare is available but expensive. Nearby, **Palia Taverna Kritikou,** 24 Mnissikleos (✆ **210/322-2809**), is a lively open-air taverna with music and dancing.

Appealing tavernas offering low-key music along with good food include **Daphne's,** 4 Lysikratous (✆ 210/322-7971); **Nefeli,** 24 Panos (✆ 210/321-2475); **Dioyenis,** 4 Sellei (✆ 210/324-7933); **Stamatopoulou,** 26 Lissiou (✆ 210/322-8722); and longtime favorites **Klimataria,** 5 Klepsidrias (✆ 210/324-1809), and **Xinos,** 4 Agelou Geronta (✆ 210/322-1065).

Those interested in authentic *rembetika* (music of the urban poor and dispossessed) should consult their hotel receptionist or the current issue of *Athenscope* or *Athinorama* (in Greek) to find out which clubs are featuring the best performers. *Rembetika* performances usually don't start until nearly midnight, and though there's rarely a cover, drinks can cost as much as 20€. Many clubs close during the summer. One of the more central places for *rembetika* is **Stoa Athanaton,** 19 Sofokleous, in the Central Meat Market (✆ **210/321-4362**), which serves good food and has live music from 3 to 6pm and after midnight. It's closed Sunday. Open Wednesday through Monday, **Frangosyriani,** 57 Arachovis, Exarchia (✆ **210/360-0693**), specializes in the music of *rembetika* legend Markos Vamvakaris. The legendary Maryo I Thessaloniki (Maryo from Thessaloniki), described as the Bessie Smith of Greece, sometimes sings *rembetika* at **Perivoli t'Ouranou,** 19 Lysikratous (✆ **210/323-5517** or 210/322-2048), in Plaka.

A number of clubs and cafes specialize in jazz but also offer everything from Indian sitar music to rock and punk. The **Café Asante,** 78 Damareos in Pangrati (© **210/756-0102**), has music most nights from 11pm. As at most of these clubs and cafes, admission varies, but count on spending at least 35€ at the Café Asante if you have a couple of drinks. The very popular **Half Note Jazz Club,** 17 Trivonianou, Mets (© **210/921-3310**), offers up everything from medieval music to jazz nightly. Performance times vary from 8 to 11pm and later; admission is usually around 20€. At the **House of Art,** 4 Sahtouri and Sari (© **210/321-7678**), and at **Pinakothiki,** 5 Agias Theklas (© **210/324-7741**), both in increasingly fashionable Psyrri, you can often hear jazz from 11pm; admission is around 20€, including the first drink.

THE GAY & LESBIAN SCENE

You will not find a shortage of gay bars, cafes, and clubs in Athens, even though the gay male venues by far outnumber the lesbian ones. The legendary gay bars and clubs of the past remain in Makrigianni and are still popular, but the real scene is shifting to Gazi. The weekly publications *Athinorama* and *Time Out* often list gay bars, discos, and special events in the nightlife section. Get-togethers are sometimes advertised in the English-language press, such as the weekly *Athens News.* You can also look for the Greek publication ***Deon Magazine*** (© **210/953-6479;** www.deon.gr) or surf the Web at www.gaygreece.gr. **Gay Travel Greece,** at 377 Syngrou Ave. in central Athens (© **210/948-4385**), specializes, as its name proclaims, in travel for gay and lesbian visitors. Keep in mind that **Athens Pride** (www.athenspride.eu) takes place the third weekend in June.

A number of gay and lesbian favorites are in the increasingly popular Gazi district, including **Sodade,** 10 Triptopolemou, Gazi (© **210/346-8657;** www.sodade.gr; weeknights 10:30pm–4am, weekends 10:30pm–6am). Of late, **Noiz,** 41 Evmolpidon and Konstantinoupoleos, Gazi (© **210/342-4771;** www.noizclub.gr; weeknights 10:30pm–4am, weekends 10:30pm–6am), shows signs of becoming the most popular lesbian bar/club in town.

If you want to watch the trains and good-looking guys go by, head for **Blue Train,** 84 Konstantinoupoleos, Gazi (© **210/346-0677;** daily 8pm–4am), right by the railway tracks on the edge of Gazi. **Kazarma,** 1st floor, 84 Konstantinoupoleos, Gazi (© **210/346-0667;** Wed–Sun midnight–5am), above Blue Train, is one of the best gay clubs in the city. During summer the fun moves to the terrace. **Mayo,** 33 Persefonis, Gazi (© **210/342-3066;** daily 8pm–4am), a quiet bar with a great inner courtyard and a rooftop terrace with a killer view, is an excellent place to begin your evening with a couple of drinks on the balcony before hitting the more rowdy places. Just follow the crowd, and you may end up at **S'Cape,** Iera Odos and 139 Meg. Alexandrou, Gazi (© **210/345-2751;** weeknights 10:30pm–4am, weekends 10:30pm–6am). This large club, with army bunks, military-style motif, and a sexy crowd, is fun and very cruisy, but never takes itself too seriously. Monday is Karaoke night, Thursday is Greek night.

Gay and lesbian travelers will not encounter difficulties at any Athenian hotel, but one with a largely gay and lesbian clientele is the 41-room **Hotel Rio Athens** (www.hotel-rio.gr), at 13 Odysseos off Karaiskaki Square in a nicely restored neoclassical building.

THE NORTHERN PELOPONNESE & DELPHI ★★★

With the undeniable exception of the Acropolis in Athens, the most famous and beautiful ancient sites in Greece bracket the Gulf of Corinth that separates the mainland and the Peloponnese. On the mainland north of the wide Gulf, the sanctuary of Apollo's famous oracle at Delphi clings to mountain slopes; south of the Gulf in the northern Peloponnese are Agamemnon's palace at Mycenae, the Mycenaean fortress of Tiryns, the spectacular 4th-century-B.C. theater of Epidaurus, and Olympia, the birthplace of the Olympic Games. Some say that Delphi is the most spectacular ancient site in Greece; others give the laurels to Olympia. You decide—perhaps when you're relaxing at a taverna or on a beach after a day's sightseeing.

EXPLORING THE REGION BY CAR Thanks to the well-maintained highway that links Athens and the Peloponnese at Corinth, and the Rio-Antirio Bridge across the Gulf of Corinth (much speedier than the old ferry service), it's easy to combine a visit to Delphi with a tour of the most important ancient sites in the Peloponnese. Try to allow at least 4 days (spending 2 nights at Nafplion and 1 night each at Olympia and Delphi).

If traffic is light (and it almost never is), you can drive the 88km (55 miles) from Athens to Corinth on the National Road in an hour. After you take a look at the Corinth Canal and the sprawling site of ancient Corinth, an hour's drive through the farmland of Corinthia and Argolis will take you to Mycenae, 114km (71 miles) southwest of Athens. From Mycenae, less than an hour's drive will get you to Nafplion, 145km (90 miles) southwest of Athens. Generally considered the prettiest town in the Peloponnese, Nafplion is the perfect spot to visit for its own charms and to use as a base for seeing the northern Peloponnese.

Although it's only 32km (20 miles) from Nafplion to Epidaurus, the road is usually clogged with tour buses, especially when there are performances at the ancient theater; to be on the safe side, allow an hour for the drive. From Nafplion and Epidaurus, two main routes lead across the Peloponnese to Olympia. You can join the National Road at Argos and drive on good roads through the Arcadian mountains via Tripolis to Olympia, 320km (199 miles) west of Athens. If you don't like mountain

Driving Tips

Most Greek roads are quite good, but much of your journey to and around the Peloponnese will be on beautiful, but sometimes vertiginous, winding mountain roads and heavily trafficked coastal roads that make distances deceptive. Check for up-to-date information on road conditions with your rental-car agency in Athens when you pick up the car, or contact the **Greek Automobile Association (ELPA;** Athens Tower, 2–4 Mossogion, Athens 115 27; ✆ **210/779-1615**), which has a reciprocity arrangement with many foreign auto clubs. The ELPA emergency number is ✆ **104-00.** Remember that only Portugal has more traffic fatalities each year than Greece, so buckle up and be careful out there!

roads, you can return to Corinth and join the busy National Road, which runs as far as Patras, where you take the even busier coast road on to Olympia. (Although there are signs in Patras pointing you toward Olympia, the heavy traffic in Patras means that you can easily spend an hour getting across town.)

Either way, expect to spend at least 4 hours en route—and try to spend more so that you can enjoy the coastal scenery or the mountain villages of Arcadia. Then, to reach Delphi from Olympia, simply head to Rio, just north of Patras, and take the **Rio-Antirio Bridge** (13€–24€ 1-day round-trip ticket; www.gefyra.gr) across the Gulf. With a 2,252m (7,388-ft.) fully suspended continuous deck and 40km (25 miles) of cables, this is the longest cable-stayed bridge in the world, built to withstand both earthquakes and bombs. If you prefer—and if it has not been discontinued, as threatened—you can still take the Rio-AntiRio car ferry, which runs twice an hour from early morning until about 11pm (3€). From the north shore of the Gulf, a good road runs all the way to Delphi, 177km (110 miles) west of Athens. With a stop for a coffee break or two, the trip from Olympia to Delphi is about 5 hours; the Athens-to-Delphi journey takes about 3 hours, except on winter weekends, when skiers heading for Mt. Parnassus clog the road.

The Northern Peloponnese & the Classical Sites ★★★

One of the delights of visiting the northern Peloponnese during the summer high season (July–Aug) is that it's relatively uncrowded when many of the Cycladic islands in the Aegean are sagging under the weight of tourists. That doesn't mean you'll have famous spots like Mycenae, Epidaurus, and Olympia to yourself if you arrive at high noon in August. In fact, if you arrive at high noon in August, you'll find it hard to believe that anyone is visiting the islands! Still, if you arrive just as sites open or just before they close, you may have an hour under the pine trees at Olympia or Epidaurus virtually alone, and be able to stand in Mycenae's Treasury of Atreus with swallows as your only companions.

Because even the most avid tourists do not live by culture alone, it's good to know that one of the great delights of spending time in the northern Peloponnese comes from quiet hours spent watching shepherds minding their flocks and fishermen mending their nets. An hour in a seaside cafe watching the locals watching you watch them is the ideal way to unwind after a day's sightseeing. If you want to see even more of the countryside, check out http://en.agrotravel.gr, which has lots of information on agro-tourism—holidays that focus on rural tourism. In the Peloponnese alone, you could take in a cherry festival in Mantinea, an olive festival near Sparta, and a wine festival at Nemea.

CORINTH ★★

Today, as in antiquity, the cities of Corinth and Patras are the two major gateways to the Peloponnese. Corinth exported its pottery around the Mediterranean and dominated trade in Greece for much of the 8th century and 7th century B.C. It experienced a second golden age under the Romans in the 2nd century A.D. As you enter the Peloponnese, you'll want to leave the main highway (look for the turnoff for the Canal Tourist Area) to take a look at the Corinth Canal and visit ancient Corinth before heading deeper into the northern Peloponnese. If you are driving, keep an eye out for signs for ARCHAIA KORINTHOS/ANCIENT CORINTH and try to avoid the modern town of Corinth, which has neither antiquities nor modern charms.

ESSENTIALS

Getting There

BY TRAIN There are several trains a day from Athens's Stathmos Peloponnisou (train station for the Peloponnese) to the Corinth train station off Demokratias (✆ **27410/22-522** or 27410/22-523). These trains are almost invariably late, often taking 3 hours or more. For information on schedules and fares, call ✆ **210/529-8735** or 11100, or go to www.ose.gr.

BY BUS There are at least 15 buses a day, taking 2 to 2½ hours, from the Stathmos Leoforia Peloponnisou (bus station for the Peloponnese) in Athens, 100 Kifissou (✆ **210/512-4910;** www.ktel.org), to Corinth, where you can catch a bus for the short (15–20 min.) trip to Archaia Korinthos. For general information on Athens-Peloponnese schedules and fares, call ✆ **210/512-4910,** or check www.ktel.org. ***Warning:*** Buses from Athens to Corinth sometimes terminate at the canal; from there, another bus will run into Corinth itself. From Corinth, you can continue to Ancient Corinth.

Confusingly, at present buses for destinations in the Peloponnese leave Corinth from one of two badly signposted stations: one at the corner of Kolokotroni and Koilatsou (✆ **27410/24-444**) and the other at the corner of Ethnikis Konstantinou and Aratou (✆ **27410/24-403**). For most destinations in the Peloponnese beyond Tripolis, you'll change buses at Tripolis.

BY CAR The National Highway runs from Athens to Corinth. The highway, which has been widened over the past decade, still contains some nasty three-lane stretches. The highway now sweeps over the Corinth Canal; if you want to stop here, look for the signs indicating the Canal Tourist Area. Shortly after the canal, you'll see signs for Corinth (the modern town and ancient site), Isthmia (site of the Isthmian Games), and Patras. Allow about 1½ hours for the journey to the canal from Athens.

The Corinth Canal

The new highway rushes you over the **Corinth Canal** very quickly, and unless you're vigilant you can miss the turnoff to the **Canal Tourist Area.** Before the new road was completed in 1997, almost everyone stopped here for a coffee, a souvlaki, and a look at the ships squeezing through the narrow canal that separates the Peloponnese from the mainland. Now, traffic hurtles past, and the cafes, restaurants, and shops here are hurting. There's a small post office at the canal, along with a kiosk with postcards and English-language newspapers; most of the large souvlaki places have clean toilet facilities (but tough souvlaki). ***Warning:*** Be sure to lock your car door. This is a popular spot for thieves who prey on unwary tourists.

The French engineers who built the Corinth Canal between 1881 and 1893 used lots of dynamite, blasting through 87m (285 ft.) of sheer rock to make this 6km-long (3¾-mile), 27m-wide (89-ft.) passageway. The canal utterly revolutionized shipping in the Mediterranean; vessels that previously had spent days making their way around Cape Matapan, at the southern tip of the Peloponnese, could dart through the canal in hours. Although it took modern technology to build the canal, the Roman emperors Caligula and Nero had tried, and failed, to dig a canal with slave labor. Nero was obsessed with the project, going so far as to lift the first shovelful of earth with a dainty golden trowel. That done, he headed back to Rome and left the real work to the 6,000 Jewish slaves he had brought here from Judea.

Exploring Ancient Corinth

To reach Ancient Corinth, follow the signs after the Corinth Canal for Ancient and Old Corinth. It's about a 20-minute bus ride from the train or bus stations or 10 minutes by taxi. A number of small restaurants and cafes are adjacent to the ancient site; frankly, we have had bad or mediocre meals at most of them. The grandly named **Splendid** restaurant across from the site and the **Ancient Corinth** on the main square serve okay lunch and dinner (simple stews, chops, and salads) for around 15€. **Marinos Rooms** (✆ **27410/31-209**), a 5-minute walk from the excavations, has very simple rooms (around 50€) and good food. This place is usually taken over by visiting archaeologists in summer. If you are heading on to Nafplion, you will be able to get excellent accommodations and food there.

Ancient Corinth ★★ The site of Ancient Corinth is dominated by its spectacular 6th-century-B.C. temple. If you can, find a perch near the temple and look out over the sprawling site, which would have stretched from the temple to the sea. Much of what you are looking at is the extensive remains of the enormous **Roman Agora** (forum or marketplace). Although Corinth's greatest period of prosperity was between the 8th and 5th centuries B.C., most of the ancient remains here are from the Roman period. Razed and destroyed when the Romans conquered Greece in 146, Corinth was refounded by Julius Caesar in 44 B.C. and began a second period of wealth and prosperity. When Saint Paul visited here in A.D. 52, he found Corinth much too worldly, and chastised the Corinthians for their wanton ways.

By the 2nd century A.D., Corinth was much larger and more powerful than Athens, but during the next hundred years, a series of barbarian invasions and attacks undermined the city's prosperity. Historians concluded that Corinth lapsed into a long stagnant period as a provincial backwater with a glorious past. New evidence has turned up to make historians question that conclusion: Beginning in 1995, excavations have unearthed finds ranging from an extensive Roman villa of the 4th century A.D. to imported English china of the 19th century A.D.—important evidence that Corinth's prosperity lasted a very long time, indeed.

Ancient Corinth's main drag, the 12m-wide (39-ft.) marble-paved road that ran from the port of Lechaion into the heart of the marketplace, is clearly visible from the temple. Along the road, and throughout the Agora, are the foundations of hundreds of the stores that once stocked everything from spices imported from Asia Minor to jugs of wine made from Corinth's excellent grapes.

Two spots in the Agora are especially famous—the **Fountain of Peirene** and the **Bema.** The fountain honors the maternal devotion of Peirene, a woman who wept so hard when her son died that she dissolved into the spring that still flows here. In the 2nd century A.D., the famous Roman traveler, philhellene, benefactor, and compulsive builder Herodes Atticus is thought to have encased the modest Greek fountain in an elaborate two-story building with arches, arcades, and a 5-sq.-m (54-sq.-ft.) courtyard. Later benefactors further elaborated the fountain. As for the Bema (public platform), this was where Paul had to plead his case when the Corinthians, irritated by his constant criticisms, hauled him in front of the Roman governor Gallo in A.D. 52.

Old Corinth. ✆ **27410/31-207.** Admission to archaeological site and museum 6€. Summer daily 8am–8pm; winter daily 8am–3pm.

Archaeological Museum ★ As you'd expect, this museum just inside the site entrance has a particularly fine collection of the famous Corinthian pottery, which is often decorated with charming red-and-black figures of birds and animals. There are also a number of statues of Roman worthies and several mosaics, including one in which Pan is shown piping away to a clutch of cows. The museum courtyard is a shady spot in which to sit and read up on the ancient site, which has virtually no shade. When you visit, be sure to see the handsome sculpture and vases stolen from the museum in 1990; found hidden in a fish processing factory in Miami, Florida, in 1998; and officially handed over to Greece in 2001, some of which are again on display.

Insider tip: The Archaeological Museum has an extensive collection of finds from the Shrine of Asclepius; because many of these are graphic representations of intimate body parts, they are kept in a room that is usually locked. If you look solemn and express a scholarly interest, you may be able to persuade a guard to unlock the room.

Ancient Corinth, in the town of Old Corinth. ✆ **27410/31-207.** Admission to museum and archaeological site 6€. Summer daily 8am–7pm; winter daily 8am–3pm; sometimes closed Mon until noon.

Acrocorinth ★★ 📷 It's hard to say what's more impressive here: the massive fortifications or the spectacular view across the plain of Corinth to the Gulf and beyond into central Greece. A winding dirt road runs from the site of Ancient Corinth to the summit of this rugged limestone sugar loaf mountain topped by centuries of fortifications that dominates the plain of Corinth. A superb natural acropolis, Acrocorinth was fortified first by the Greeks and later by the Byzantines, Franks, Venetians, and Turks. Extensive remains of the centuries of walls, turrets, and towers built here still remain. After enjoying the seemingly endless view over the rich plain below, you can relax at the cafe just outside the site entrance. The walk up is tiring—allow at least an hour. Round-trip cab fare is around 25€, with a 30-minute wait on the summit; a cab only going up, if you can find a willing driver, is about 15€.

Old Corinth. ✆ **27410/31-966.** Admission 3€. Usually open daily 8:30am–7pm; winter daily 9am–3pm.

NAFPLION ★★★

Nafplion is far and away the most charming town in the Peloponnese, with stepped streets overhung with balconies dripping with bougainvillea, handsome neoclassical buildings, and enticing shops, restaurants, cafes, and, for that matter, two fine museums—and even a miniature castle (the Bourtzi) on a miniature island in the harbor! A good deal of Nafplion's appeal comes from the fact that for several years after the Greek War of Independence (1821–28), this was the country's first capital. Although the palace of Greece's young King Otto—a mail-order monarch from Bavaria—burned down in the 19th century, an impressive number of handsome neoclassical civic buildings and private houses have survived, as have a scattering of Turkish fountains and several mosques. You could spend several pleasant days here simply enjoying wandering the streets of this port town itself, but you'll probably want to use Nafplion as your home base for day trips to the ancient sites at Mycenae, Tiryns and Epidaurus, and—if you didn't see it on the way here—Corinth. Keep in mind that *lots* of Greeks come here year-round on weekends, so if you're visiting Nafplion on a weekend, reserve your hotel in advance. I've had trouble finding a parking place by the harbor even on a rainy February Sunday!

ESSENTIALS

Getting There

BY BUS There are at least a dozen buses a day to Nafplion from the Stathmos Leoforia Peloponnisou (bus station for the Peloponnese) in Athens, 100 Kifissou (✆ **210/512-4910;** www.ktel.org). The trip is a slow one (about 4 hr.) because the bus goes into both Corinth and Argos before reaching the Nafplion station on Syngrou Street (by Plateia Kapodistrias; ✆ **27520/28-555**). For general information on Athens-Peloponnese schedules and fares, call ✆ **210/512-4910** or go to www.ktel.org.

BY CAR From Athens, head south to the Corinth Canal. Take the Corinth-Tripolis national road to the Argos exit and follow signs into Argos and then for Nafplion. You'll almost certainly get lost at least once in Argos, which has an abysmal system of directional signs. Allow at least 3 hours for the drive from Athens to Nafplion, more, if you stop at Corinth, Mycenae, or Epidauros (all clearly signposted) en route. When you reach Nafplion, park in the large, free municipal lot by the harbor and be sure to lock your car.

VISITOR INFORMATION The **Municipal Tourist Office** is at 25 Martiou (✆ **27520/24-444**), diagonally across from the bus station. It's usually open Monday through Friday from 9am to 1pm and 5 to 8pm (but is often mysteriously closed during work hours). Ask for the useful brochure *Nafplion Day and Night*. The website www.nafplion.gr is helpful—when functioning. Information and tickets for special events, such as the concerts in the June **Nafplion Music Festival,** are sometimes available from the Town Hall (Demarkeion) in the old high-school building on Iatrou Square (✆ **27520/23-332**); you can also check at www.nafplionfestival.gr. There are a number of travel agencies in Nafplion, such as **Staikos Travel,** by the harbor (✆ **27520/27-950**), and **Yiannopoulos Travel,** on Plateia Syntagma (✆ **27520/28-054**), where you can get information on car rentals and day trips from Nafplion.

The **Odyssey,** Plateia Syntagma (✆ **27520/23-4300**), has maps, newspapers, magazines, and a wide range of books in English, including local guides. You can also pick up a copy of Timothy Gregory's *Nafplion* (Lycabettus Press); although published in 1980, it remains the best guide to the city's history and monuments.

Where to Stay

Remember, this town is so popular with both Greeks and tourists that reservations are strongly advised; every room in town is often taken on summer and holiday weekends. Be sure to bring a print copy with you confirming your reservation. And here's something to keep in mind when you make a reservation: At present, a surprising number of Nafplion's hotels do not take credit cards, but say that they plan to soon.

In addition to the hotels below, following are a few others to consider. Nafplion's 172-room **Amalia** (✆ **27520/24-400;** www.amalia.gr) had declined dreadfully in recent years, so it's good to say that it is spruced up after a total renovation in 2008. This is the place to stay if you don't mind being a mile or two out of Nafplion itself and want to relax in a big swimming pool. Like all Amalia Hotels, this one has extensive gardens; large, comfortable rooms; large bathrooms; efficient, attentive service—and lots of tour groups and wedding parties. Doubles start from 180€. If you feel like a serious splurge, check out the 42-unit **Amphitryon,** transformed from its down-at-the-heels days into a five-star member of the Leading Small Hotels of the World (✆ **27520/70-700;** www.amphitryon.gr or www.helioshotels.gr). The

Amphitryon has drop-dead-gorgeous flower arrangements, enormous bathrooms with fiendishly clever showers, and pool privileges up the hill at the Nafplia Palace Hotel, and promises "romantic moments in an ambience of privileged scenery." Doubles start at 350€. If, like me, you'd prefer the ambience of the pleasant residential neighborhood around Ayios Spiridon church, try the 21-unit **Pension Acronafplia** (www.pensionacronafplia.gr). The pension occupies four thoughtfully restored town houses whose very congenial accommodations range from simple (small room, no private bathroom) to quite elegant (large room, private bathroom and balcony with harbor view). Doubles range from 75€ to 130€.

Byron Hotel ★★ This was one of the first of the "boutique" hotels in Nafplion. The Byron is in a quiet, breezy location overlooking the Church of Agiou Spiridona, a short but steep hike from the main plateia. Sitting rooms and guest rooms contain nice bits of Victoriana, as well as modern conveniences. The cheapest rooms are quite small with no view; usually, for another 15€, you can get a view of Nafplion—and enough space that you won't feel the burden of togetherness with your roommate.

2 Platonos, Plateia Agiou Spiridona, 211 00 Nafplion. ✆ **27520/22-351.** Fax 27520/26-338. www.byronhotel.gr. 17 units. 90€–110€. AE, MC, V. **Amenities:** Breakfast room. *In room:* A/C, TV, hair dryer, minibar, Wi-Fi.

Hotel Ilion ★★ You'll have to decide whether you find the decor in this boutique hotel in a restored 19th-century town house on a stepped street above Plateia Syntagma engaging or overwhelming. Virtually every ceiling is painted (often with cupids), and wall frescoes with scenes from Greek mythology alternate with borders of fruit and flowers. Windows and beds alike are draped with filmy hangings. The mattresses are excellent. A friend who spent a happy week here reported that the service was top-notch, the neighborhood was quiet, and the breakfasts were delicious.

4 Efthimiopoulou and 6 Kapodistriou sts., 211 00 Nafplion. ✆ **27520/25-114.** Fax 27520/24-497. www.ilionhotel.gr. 15 units. 110€–125€ double; 140€–200€ suite. Breakfast 10€. No credit cards. **Amenities:** Bar/breakfast room. *In room:* A/C, TV, minibar, Wi-Fi.

Hotel Leto ★ Your effort in climbing up to the Leto, perched under Acronafplia, is rewarded with fine views over Nafplion. Guest units are simply furnished, with decent-size bathrooms; ask for a room with a balcony. The staff here has been praised as very helpful.

28 Zigomala, 211 00 Nafplion. ✆ **27520/28-098.** Fax 27520/29-588. 15 units. 75€–95€ double. No credit cards. *In room:* A/C, TV, minibar.

Hotel Nafsimedon ★ Another boutique hotel, this one is in a handsome mid-19th-century neoclassical house with a small garden with palm trees overlooking relatively quiet Kolokotronis Park. The guest rooms, many done in shades of apricot and peach, have handsome chandeliers, marble-topped tables, some old paintings—and good-size bathrooms and beds with firm mattresses. When the Nafsimedon is full, rooms are sometimes found at its younger sister hotel, the **Ippoliti** (www.ippoliti.gr), also a boutique hotel in a restored 19th-century town house at 9 Ilia Miniati and Aristidou just off the harbor (some rooms have harbor views) with a small outdoor pool (doubles 140€–190€).

Nafsimedon, 9 Sidiras Merarhias (on Kolokotronis Park), 211 00 Nafplion. ✆ **27520/25-060.** Fax 27520/26-913. www.nafsimedon.gr. 13 units. 100€–125€ double. No credit cards. **Amenities:** Bar/breakfast room. *In room:* A/C, TV.

King Otho I and II ★★ The King Otho I, a longtime favorite, was getting down at the heels before its completely successful renovation in 2000. In 2002, the owners bought and restored another wonderful town house a few blocks up the hill on Staikopoulou. Now, Nafplion has two small hotels that contend for the honor of the most breathtaking curved staircase in the Peloponnese. Both hotels have high ceilings (some with frescoes), wood floors, and period furniture, including marble-topped tables. The new Otho is more expensive, because every guest room has a view (of Nafplion, or of Nafplion and the harbor). Each hotel has a garden, a real plus for breakfast or a quiet hour's reading. Both sometimes close in winter.

King Otho II: 21 Staikopoulou, 211 00 Nafplion. ✆ **27520/97-790.** www.kingothon.gr. 10 units. 120€ double. Rates include continental breakfast. AE, MC, V. **Amenities:** Breakfast room. *In room:* A/C, TV, minibar, Wi-Fi.

Omorfi Poli Pension ★★ What a pleasant place! This small pension/hotel above the charming cafe by the same name (Greek for "beautiful city") has gone all out: The restoration of the building gives guests the sense that they are staying in a Nafplion home—but with privacy; when business is not brisk, you can sometimes get a suite at a double room price. The beds are good, the tile floors and prints on the walls are tasteful. Families will like the rooms with fridges and sleeping lofts for children as well as the breakfasts with freshly baked bread.

5 Sofroni, 211 00 Nafplion. ✆ **27520/21-565.** www.omorfipoli-pension.com. 9 units, all with shower only. 75€ double; 120€ family suite (for up to 5 persons). Rates include breakfast. No credit cards.

Where to Dine

Oddly enough, a number of the restaurants in and just off Nafplion's Syntagma Square are not the tourist traps you'd expect. Furthermore, you'll see a good number of Greeks at the big harborside cafes on Akti Miaoulis. In short, Nafplion has lots of good restaurants, and any number of ice-cream parlors selling elaborate gooey confections.

Antica Gelateria di Roma ★★★ SWEETS/ICE CREAM/COFFEE/DRINKS This is where I head first when I get to Nafplion and where I stop last before I leave. It's the best ice cream and ices in the Peloponnese—perhaps in Greece! You can have anything from a banana split to a tiny cup with just a taste. Don't miss the hazelnut, lemon, mango, strawberry, chocolate—well, you get the idea. If you tire of ice cream, you can try freshly made panini with tomato and mozzarella and finish off with espresso while keeping up with Italian soccer.

3 Pharmakopoulou and Komninou. ✆ **27520/23-520.** spyde@tri.forthnet.gr. Sweets and sandwiches 4€–12€. No credit cards. Daily about 10am–midnight.

Hellas Restaurant ★ ☺ GREEK Children who normally squirm in restaurants will enjoy the Hellas: Between courses, they can join the Greek kids kicking soccer balls and racing up and down Plateia Syntagma. Shady awnings make this a cool spot to eat outdoors. Locals tend to congregate in the indoor dining room year-round. Reliable dolmades with egg-lemon sauce are usually on the menu, as well as stuffed tomatoes and peppers in season. Just about everyone in town passes through Plateia Syntagma, so this is a great spot to watch the world go by.

Plateia Syntagma. ✆ **27520/27-278.** Main courses 7€–12€. AE, MC, V. Daily 9am–midnight.

Karamanlis ★ GREEK This simple harborfront taverna several blocks east of the cluster of cafes tends to get fewer tourists than most of the places in town. It serves up good grills and several kinds of meatballs (*keftedes, sousoutakia,* and *yiouvarlakia*). If you like the food here, you'll probably also enjoy **Arapakos, Kanares Taverna,** and **Hundalos Taverna,** also on Bouboulinas.

1 Bouboulinas. ✆ **27520/27-668.** Main courses 7€–15€; fresh fish priced by the kilo. AE, MC, V. Usually daily 11am–midnight.

Sokaki ★ COFFEE/DRINKS/SNACKS/BREAKFAST In the morning, tourists tuck into the full American breakfast here, while locals toy with tiny cups of Greek coffee. In the evening, young men lounge, some eyeing the women who pass by, others eyeing the men. In short, great people-watching and good margaritas.

8 Ethniki Antistaseos. ✆ **27520/26-032.** Drinks and snacks 5€–15€. No credit cards. Daily about 8am–8pm; summer daily 8am–midnight.

Ta Phanaria ★ GREEK A shaded table under Ta Phanaria's enormous scarlet bougainvillea makes for one of the prettiest places in the center of town for lunch or dinner. Ta Phanaria usually has several inventive vegetable dishes on the menu in addition to such standbys as moussaka. The stews and chops here are also good. In winter, hearty bean dishes are usually available. Like the Hellas, Ta Phanaria continues to attract steady customers, despite doing much of its business with tourists.

13 Staikopoulou. ✆ **27520/27-141.** Main courses 7€–15€. MC, V. Daily about noon–midnight.

Taverna Old Mansion (Paleo Archontiko) ★★ GREEK Sometimes when it's snowing in New England, where I spend part of the year, I dream of spending a cozy evening here, enjoying the good food and lively local scene. In summer, tables spill out along Siokou Street. The menu offers consistently good traditional Greek *spitiko* (home) cooking: stews, chops, and usually several vegetarian choices. When live music is featured in the evening, tables are at a premium.

7 Siokou. ✆ **27520/22-449.** Main courses 8€–15€. MC, V. Daily 7pm–midnight; summer weekends noon–4pm.

Exploring the Town

Nafplion is a stroller's delight, and one of the great pleasures here is simply walking through the parks, up and down the stepped side streets, and along the harbor. Don't make the mistake of stopping your harborside stroll when you come to the last of the large seaside cafes on the quay. If you continue, you can watch fishing boats putting in at the pier and explore several cliff-side chapels. Nafplion is so small that you can't get seriously lost, so have fun exploring. Here are some suggestions on how to take in the sights—and get in some shopping—after you've had your initial stroll.

ACRONAFPLIA & THE PALAMIDI ★★ Nafplion's two massive fortifications, the **Acronafplia** and the **Palamidi,** dominate the skyline and, as usual with fortresses, are most impressive when seen from afar. It's a very stiff climb to either fortress, and you may prefer to take a taxi up (around 6€) and walk back down. If you do walk up to Acronafplia, follow signs in the lower town to the **Church of Saint Spyridon,** one of whose walls has the mark left by one of the bullets that killed Ianni Kapodistria, the first governor of modern Greece.

From Saint Spyridon, follow the signs farther uphill to the **Catholic Church of the Metamorphosis.** This church is as good a symbol as any for Nafplion's vexed history. Built by the Venetians, it was converted into a mosque by the Turks and then reconsecrated as a church after the War of Independence. Inside, an ornamental doorway has an inscription listing philhellenes who died for Greece, including nephews of Lord Byron and George Washington. As you continue to climb to Acronafplia, keep an eye out for several carvings of the winged lion that was the symbol of Mark, the patron saint of Venice.

Similarly, if you're not in the mood to climb the 800-plus steps to the summit of the **Palamidi ★**, you can take a taxi up and then walk down. The Venetians spent 3 years building the Palamidi, only to have it conquered the next year (1715) by the Turks. You'll enter the fortress the way the Turkish attackers did, through the main gate to the east. Once inside, you can trace the course of the massive wall that encircled the entire summit and wander through the considerable remains of the five fortresses that failed to stop the Turkish attack. If you're in Nafplion during the June **Music Festival,** find out if any evening concerts are being held at the **Palamidi,** which is open in summer, Monday through Friday from 8am to 7pm, and Saturday and Sunday from 8am to 3pm; in winter, daily from 8am to 3pm. Admission is 3€.

THE BOURTZI ★★ Everyone's favorite fortress—and perhaps the only one to evoke squeals of "how cute" from tourists—the miniature **Bourtzi Fortress** was built by Venetians in the 15th century to guard the entrance to Nafplion's harbor. Since then, it's had a checkered career, serving as a home for retired executioners in the 19th century and as a small hotel in the 20th century. Small boats ply back and forth between the harbor and the Bourtzi (from 6€ round-trip); usually, you can stay as long as you wish, explore, and return with the same or a different boat. Take something to drink and a snack with you, as the small cafe here is often closed.

NAFPLION'S MUSEUMS Nafplion's museums are within easy walking distance of one another. Almost as soon as it opened in 1981, the **Folk Art Museum ★★**, also called the **Peloponnesian Folklore Foundation** (1 V. Alexandros; **✆ 27520/28-947;** www.pli.gr), with its superb collection of Greek costumes, won the European Museum of the Year Award. The museum occupies three full floors in an elegant 18th-century house with a shady courtyard. In 2005, the museum installed a new permanent exhibition focusing on urban Greece, particularly Nafplion in the 19th and 20th centuries. Dioramas show elegant town-house parlors stuffed with marble-topped furniture, Persian carpets, and ornate silver and china bibelots. There are often special exhibitions in a ground-floor gallery near the excellent shop. It's open Wednesday to Monday 9am to 3pm; closed Tuesday and the month of February. Admission is 4€.

About time! The **Nafplion Archaeological Museum ★**, Syntagma Square (**✆ 2750/27-502**), is once again open after 5 years of renovations. The museum now has large, bright rooms (no more dusty display cases) with exhibits themed to demonstrate life in the area from Neolothic to Christian times. An excellent video (with English text) shows and explains the sites where most objects were found. The collection, from sites in the area, includes pottery, jewelry, and some quite terrifying Mycenaean terra-cotta idols, as well as a handsome bronze Mycenaean suit of armor. The museum is in one of the best-looking buildings in town, the handsome 18th-century Venetian arsenal that dominates Plateia Syntagma. The thick walls make this a deliciously cool place to visit on even the hottest day. It's open Tuesday to Sunday from 8:30am to 1pm. Admission is 4€.

SHOPPING IN NAFPLION ★★ As you might expect of a town that has so many Greek visitors, Nafplion has some terrific shops. For a wide range of handsome handcrafted jewelry, try **Preludio,** 2 Vas. Konstantinou (✆ **27520/25-277**), just off Plateia Syntagma a few steps from the Hellas Restaurant. Staikopoulou Street, 1 block uphill from Plateia Syntagma, is great window-shopping territory. The **Komboloi Museum,** 25 Staikopoulou (✆/fax **27520/21-618;** www.komboloi.gr), is on the second floor of a shop selling *kombolo*—the round "worry beads" that many Greek men twirl. The beads sell for anything from a few to many thousand euros; museum admission is 2€. **To Enotion** (no phone) has museum-quality reproductions of characters from the Greek shadow theater—from country bumpkins to damsels in distress. The smallest of the colorful marionettes begins at about 20€. A few doors along, **Nafplio tou Nafpliou,** 56A Staikopoulou (no phone), sells icons showing virtually every saint in the Greek Orthodox church. Over on Siokou Street, **Konstantine Beselmes,** 7 Ath. Siokou (✆ **27520/25-842**), offers magical paintings of village scenes, sailing ships, and idyllic landscapes. Although new, the paintings are done on weathered boards, which gives each a pleasantly aged look. A few doors away, **Agynthes,** 10 Siokou (✆ **27520/21-704**), has hand-loomed fabrics that look and feel wonderful; some are fashioned into throws, bags, and scarves.

Nafplion has a number of art galleries, most of which sell what's on exhibit. Two of the best are the **Nafplion Art Gallery,** 5 Vassileos Alexandrou St. (✆ **27520/25-385**), which features the work of Greek and foreign artists, and the **Art Shop,** 14 Ipsilandou St. (✆ **27520/29-546**), featuring clothing, jewelry, toys, and books by Greek and foreign artists.

If you want Greek wine, try the **Wine Shop,** 5 Amalias (✆/fax **27520/24-446**); **Nektar and Ambrosia,** 6 Pharmakopoulou (✆ **27520/43-001**), is one of several new shops selling delicious herbs and organic honey products, including scented soaps.

A Day Trip from Nafplion: Tiryns

Tiryns ★★ is 5km (3 miles) outside Nafplion on the Argos road. If anything can out-do Mycenae's fortifications, it's Tiryns: From the moment you look up at these monumental dark stone walls, you'll understand why Homer called Tiryns's **citadel,** which may have been Mycenae's port, "well walled." Tiryns stands on a rocky outcropping 27m (89 ft.) high and about 302m (990 ft.) long, girdled by the massive walls that so impressed Homer—but that didn't keep Tiryns from being destroyed around 1200 B.C. Later Greeks thought that only the giants known as Cyclopes could have hefted the 14-ton red limestone blocks into place for the walls that archaeologists still call "Cyclopean." Even today, Tiryns's walls stand more than 9m (30 ft.) high; originally—and almost unimaginably—they were twice as tall and as much as 17m (56 ft.) thick. The citadel is crowned by the palace, whose **megaron** (great hall) has a well-preserved circular hearth and the base of a throne. This room would have been gaily decorated with frescoes (the surviving frescoes are now in the National Archaeological Museum in Athens).

The site is officially open Monday through Saturday, from 8am to 3pm; it is sometimes open later in summer. Admission is 4€. Visitors without cars can reach Tiryns from Nafplion by taxi (expect to pay about 30€ for the round-trip and an hour or so wait while you visit the site) or by the frequent (about every half-hour) Nafplion-Argos-Nafplion bus (about 2€; tell the driver you want to get off at Tiryns).

MYCENAE ★★★

Virtually every visitor to the Peloponnese comes to Mycenae, which can make for bumper-to-bumper tour buses on the narrow roads to the citadel and wall-to-wall

> **Insider Tip**
>
> If at all possible, visit Mycenae early in the morning (to avoid the midmorning and midday tour groups) or during the hour or two before closing (when crowds thin out). Wear a hat and sturdy shoes. There's no shade at the site (except in the cistern and the beehive tombs), and the rocks are very slippery. Bring a flashlight if you plan to explore the cistern. And, if you are staying here at full moon, be sure to walk up to see Mycenae's walls gleaming in the moonlight.

tourists inside the citadel itself. Why do they all come here? As the English philhellene Robert Liddell once wrote: "Mycenae is one of the most ancient and fabulous places in Europe. I think it should be visited first for the fable, next for the lovely landscape, and thirdly for the excavations."

First, the fable: Greek legend and the poet Homer tell us that King Agamemnon of Mycenae was the most powerful leader in Greece at the time of the Trojan War. In about 1250 B.C., Homer says, Agamemnon led the Greeks from Mycenae to Troy, where they fought for 10 years to re-claim fair Helen—who had eloped with the Trojan prince Paris—who just happened to be the wife of Agamemnon's brother Menelaus. Family honor was at stake, and the first of many wars between Greece and Turkey erupted. Centuries late, in 1874, the German archaeologist Heinrich Schliemann, who found and excavated Troy, began to dig at Mycenae, searching for evidence of Agamemnon's kingdom. Did Schliemann's excavations here prove that what Homer wrote was based on an actual event, not myth and legend? Scholars are suspicious, although most admit that Mycenae could be rebuilt from Homer's descriptions of its palace.

As to the landscape here, you will see how the steep hill that Mycenae occupies lords it over the fertile Argive plain. And as to the excavations, you will walk through a monumental gate topped by sculptured lions into one of Europe's first fortified palaces and see the astonishing tombs where its rulers were buried.

ESSENTIALS

Getting There

BY BUS Buses run frequently from Athens's **Stathmos Leoforia Peloponnisou,** 100 Kifissou (✆ **210/512-9233,** or 210/512-4910 for general information; www.ktel.org), to Corinth, Argos, and Nafplion. Allow 3 to 4 hours. From any of those places, allow an hour for the trip to Mycenae.

BY CAR From Corinth, take the new national highway toll road to the Nemea exit, where you will join the old Corinth-Argos highway, which has a clearly marked turnoff for Mycenae. If you prefer, you can take the old Corinth-Argos road to the Mycenae turnoff. This takes longer and you may get stuck behind a bus or truck, but you will have a better sense of the countryside than on the elevated highway. Either way, Mycenae is about 90km (56 miles) south of Corinth. From Nafplion, take the road out of town toward Argos. When you reach the Corinth-Argos highway, turn right and then, after about 16km (10 miles), turn right again at the sign for Mycenae. When you return from Mycenae to Nafplion, follow the signs for Nafplion.

Where to Stay & Dine

Most of the restaurants around Mycenae specialize in serving set-price meals to groups. If you eat at one of the big impersonal roadside restaurants, you're likely to be served a bland, lukewarm "European-style" meal of overcooked roast veal, underripe tomatoes, and, even in summer, canned vegetables. You'll have better luck at the smaller restaurants at the hotels listed below.

La Belle Helene ★ The real reason to stay here is to add your name to that of Schliemann and other luminaries in the guest book. Sentiment aside, this small hotel, one of the most famous in Greece, is usually quiet (although it does do a brisk business with tour groups in its large restaurant). The simple rooms are clean and comfortable. If you stay here, be sure to drive or walk up to the ancient site at night, especially if the moon is full.

Mycenae, 212 00 Argolis. ✆ **27510/76-225.** Fax 27510/76-179. 8 units, none with bathroom. 50€–65€ double, sometimes lower off season. Rates include breakfast. DC, V. **Amenities:** Restaurant.

La Petite Planete ★ This would be a nice place to stay even without its small swimming pool, which is irresistible after a hot day's trek around Mycenae. We've usually found it quieter here than at La Belle Helene, with very helpful owners, a decent restaurant, and fine views over the plain of Argos to the hills beyond (from the front rooms).

Mycenae, 212 00 Argolis. ✆ **27510/76-240.** 30 units. 70€ double. AE, V. Usually closed Jan–Feb. **Amenities:** Restaurant; bar; outdoor freshwater pool. *In room:* A/C, TV.

Exploring Ancient Mycenae

The Citadel & the Treasury of Atreus ★★★ As you walk uphill to Mycenae (passing the new Archaeological Museum; see below), you begin to get an idea of why people settled here as long ago as 5000 B.C. Mycenae straddles a low bluff between two protecting mountains and is a superb natural citadel overlooking one of the richest plains in Greece. By the time of the classical era, almost all memory of the Mycenaeans had been lost, and Greeks speculated that places like Mycenae and Tiryns had been built by the Cyclopes. Only such enormous giants, people reasoned, could have moved the huge rocks used to build the ancient citadels' defense walls.

You enter Mycenae through just such a wall, passing under the massive Lion Gate, whose two lions probably symbolized Mycenae's strength. The door itself (missing, like the lions' heads) probably was made of wood and covered with bronze for additional protection; cuttings for the doorjambs and pivots are clearly visible in the lintel. Soldiers stationed in the round **tower** on your right would have shot arrows down at any attackers who tried to storm the citadel.

One of the most famous spots at Mycenae is immediately ahead of the Lion Gate—the so-called **Grave Circle A,** where Schliemann found the gold jewelry now on display at the National Archaeological Museum in Athens. When archaeologist Heinrich Schliemann opened the tombs and found some 14 kilograms of gold here, including several solid-gold face masks, he concluded he had found the grave of Agamemnon himself. However, recent scholars have concluded that Schliemann was wrong, and that the kings buried here died long before Agamemnon was born.

From the grave circle, head uphill past the low remains of a number of houses. Mycenae was not merely a palace, but a small village, with administrative buildings and homes on the slopes below the **palace.** The palace had reception rooms, bedrooms, a throne room, and a large *megaron* (ceremonial hall). You can see the imprint of the four columns that held up the roof in the megaron, as well as the outline of a circular altar on the floor.

If you're not claustrophobic, head to the northeast corner of the citadel and climb down the flight of stairs to have a look at Mycenae's enormous **cistern.** (You may find someone selling candles, but it's a good idea to bring your own flashlight.) Along with Mycenae's great walls, this cistern, which held a water supply channeled from a spring 450m (1,476 ft.) away, helped make the citadel impregnable for several centuries.

There's one more thing to see before you leave Mycenae. The massive tomb known as the **Treasury of Atreus** is the largest of the tholos tombs (circular marble structures) found here. You'll see signs for the Treasury of Atreus on your right as you head down the modern road away from Mycenae. The Treasury of Atreus may have been built around 1300 B.C., at about the same time as the Lion Gate, in the last century of Mycenae's real greatness. The enormous tomb, with its 118-ton lintel, is 13m (43 ft.) high and 14m (46 ft.) wide. To build the tomb, workers first cut the 35m (115-ft.) passageway into the hill and faced it with stone blocks. Then the tholos chamber itself was built, by placing slightly overlapping courses of stone one on top of the other until a capstone could close the final course. As you look up toward the ceiling of the tomb, you'll see why these are called "beehive tombs." Once your eyes get accustomed to the poor light, you can make out the bronze nails that once held hundreds of bronze rosettes in place in the ceiling. This tomb was robbed even in antiquity, so we'll never know exactly what it contained, although the contents of Grave Circle A give an idea of what riches must have been here. If this was the family vault of Atreus, it's entirely possible that Agamemnon himself was buried here.

There's a good deal of up-and-down walking here, much on slippery terrain; give yourself at least 3 hours to absorb this magnificent and mysterious site.

✆ **27510/76-585.** Admission 8€ including Treasury of Atreus and museum. Summer daily 8am–7pm; winter daily 8am–3pm.

Archaeological Museum of Mycenae ★★ This long-awaited museum, on the slopes of the citadel, opened in 2004. The museum focuses on the story of the excavations here and of Mycenaean civilization in general. Unfortunately, because the museum's galleries are quite small, both the displays and the labels (in Greek and English) are hard to see when the museum is crowded, which it often is. Oddly, tickets to the museum (and the museum guidebook) are currently sold only at the main entrance to the site. Most displays are grouped with others found in the same area of the citadel in an attempt to show how people actually lived here. The so-called "Cult Center," for example, has striking pottery snakes and the wide-eyed figures they were found with. Still, it's an indication of how little is known of what went on at the Cult Center that it is not certain whether the figurines represent the deities who were worshiped or the mortals who worshiped them. Throughout the museum, exhibits are labeled in Greek and English, and there are very welcome toilet facilities.

✆ **27510/76-585.** Admission 4€, including admission to site; guidebook 5€. Summer daily 8am–7pm; winter shorter hours.

EPIDAURUS ★★★

Today, the Theater of Epidaurus is still one of the most impressive sights in all Greece, in one of the most famous places in ancient Greece. Greeks came to the shrine of Asclepios in antiquity as they go to the shrine of the Virgin on the Cycladic island of Tinos today, to give thanks for good health and in hopes of finding cures for their ailments. While at Epidaurus, patients and their families could "take the waters" at any one of a number of healing springs and in the superb baths. Visitors could also take in a performance in the theater, just as you can today. Probably built in the 4th century, the theater seats some 14,000 spectators and is astonishingly well preserved.

Warning: The village of Palea Epidaurus, a beach resort 10km (6¼ miles) from Epidaurus, is confusingly sometimes signposted ANCIENT EPIDAURUS; the theater and sanctuary are usually signposted ANCIENT THEATER.

To confuse things further, Palea Epidaurus has its own small theater and festival. If you want a swim, Palea Epidaurus is the nearest beach—but it is often quite crowded.

ESSENTIALS

Getting There

BY BUS Two buses a day run from the **Stathmos Leoforia Peloponnisou,** 100 Kifissou, Athens (✆ **210/512-9233,** or 210/512-4910 for general information; www.ktel.org). The trip takes about 3 hours. There are three buses a day to Epidaurus from the Nafplion bus station, off Plateia Kapodistrias (✆ **27520/28-555**), with extra buses when there are performances at the Theater of Epidaurus. The trip takes about an hour.

BY CAR Epidaurus is 63km (39 miles) south of Corinth and 32km (20 miles) east of Nafplion. If you're coming from Athens or Corinth, turn left at the sign for Epidaurus immediately after the Corinth Canal and take the coast road to the Theatro (ancient theater), not to Nea Epidaurus or Palaia Epidaurus. From Nafplion, follow the signs for Epidaurus. If you drive to Epidaurus from Nafplion for a performance, be alert; the road will be clogged with tour buses and other tourists.

THEATER PERFORMANCES **Classical performances** at the **ancient theater** are usually given Saturday and Sunday at around 9pm June through September. Many productions are staged by the **National Theater of Greece,** some by foreign companies. Ticket prices range from 20€ to 50€. For other information, contact the **Hellenic Festival Box Office,** 39 Panepistimiou, Athens (in the arcade; ✆ **210/928-2900;** www.greekfestival.gr); or the **Epidaurus Festival Box Office** (✆ **27530/22-006**). It's also possible to buy tickets at most of Nafplion's travel agencies and at the theater itself, starting at 5pm on the day of a performance.

Tip: If you're a theater buff, be sure to take in the **Epidaurus Festival Museum,** near the entrance to the site, with its displays of props, costumes, programs, and memorabilia from past performances. Free admission.

Where to Stay & Dine

You'll almost certainly want to stay in Nafplion when you visit Epidaurus. The small hotels closer to Epidaurus are usually booked by large tour groups well in advance of theater performances and are not sufficiently charming to recommend if you visit here when there is not a performance. As to food, several kiosks sell snacks and cold drinks near the ticket booth at Epidaurus. The only restaurant worth seeking out is **Leonidas** (© **27530/22-115**). This small restaurant with a garden on the main Epidaurus road is open for lunch and dinner year-round, has consistently good food, and attracts a post-theater crowd that often includes actors who relax here after performances.

Exploring the Ancient Site ★

The **excavation museum** at the entrance to the site helps put some flesh on the bones of the confusing remains of the Sanctuary of Asclepios. The museum has an extensive collection of architectural fragments from the sanctuary, including lovely acanthus flowers from the mysterious tholos, which you'll see when you visit the site. Also on view are an impressive number of votive offerings from pilgrims: The terra-cotta body parts show precisely what part of the anatomy was cured. The display of surgical implements will send you away grateful that you didn't have to go under the knife here, although hundreds of inscriptions record the gratitude of satisfied patients.

It's pleasant to wander through the shady **Sanctuary of Asclepios,** but it's not easy to decipher the scant remains. The Asclepion had accommodations for visitors, several large bathhouses, civic buildings, a stadium and gymnasium, and several temples and shrines. The remains are so meager that you might have to take this on faith. Try to find the round tholos, which you'll pass about halfway into the sanctuary. The famous 4th-century-B.C. architect Polykleitos, who built similar round buildings at Olympia and Delphi, was the designer. If you wonder why the inner foundations of the tholos are so convoluted and labyrinthine, you're in good company—scholars aren't sure what went on here; some suspect that Asclepios's healing serpents lived in the labyrinth.

The museum and archaeological site (© **27530/23-009**) are open in summer, weekdays from 8am to 7pm and Saturday and Sunday from 8:30am to 3:15pm; in winter, weekdays from 8am to 3pm and Saturday and Sunday from 8:30am to 3pm. Admission (also covering the theater; see below) is 6€.

The Theater ★★

If you found the remains of the ancient sanctuary a bit of a letdown, don't worry—the **Theater of Epidaurus** is one of the most impressive sights in Greece. Probably built in the 4th century B.C., possibly by Polykleitos, the architect of the tholos, the theater seats some 14,000 spectators. Unlike so many ancient buildings, and almost everything at the Sanctuary of Asclepios, the theater was not pillaged for building blocks in antiquity. As a result, it's astonishingly well preserved, and restorations have been minimal and tactful. It's always a magical moment when a performance begins, as the sun sinks behind the orchestra and the first actor steps onto the stage.

If you climb to the top of the theater, you can look down over the seats, divided into a lower section of 34 rows and an upper section with 21 rows. The upper seats were added when the original theater was enlarged in the 2nd century B.C. The acoustics are famous; you'll almost certainly see someone demonstrating that a whisper can be heard all the way from the orchestra to the topmost row of seats. Just as the stadium at Olympia brings out the sprinter in many visitors, the theater at Epidaurus tempts many to step center stage and recite poetry, declaim the opening of the Gettysburg Address, or burst into song. The 6€ admission to the museum and archaeological site (see above) includes the theater; they keep the same hours.

OLYMPIA ★★★

With its shady groves of pine, olive, and oak trees; the considerable remains of two temples; and the stadium where the first Olympic races were run in 776 B.C., Olympia is the most beautiful major site in the Peloponnese. It's wonderful to have more than just 1 day here, especially if your hotel has a swimming pool! The ancient site of Olympia is a 15-minute walk south of the modern village. Parking near the site is virtually nonexistent; you'll probably have to park in town and walk—with care: The road teems with tour buses, and the walk is less than relaxing.

The straggling modern village of Olympia (confusingly known as Ancient Olympia) is bisected by its one main street, Leoforos Kondili. The town has about 20 hotels and restaurants and the usual assortment of tourist shops. One pleasant exception to the T-shirt shops, the **Galerie Orphee,** Antonios Kosmopoulos's shop on the main street in Ancient Olympia (✆ **26240/23-555**), has a wide selection of books, an extensive range of cassettes and CDs of Greek music, and frequent displays of contemporary art.

ESSENTIALS

Getting There

BY TRAIN Several trains a day run from Athens to Pirgos, where you change to the train for Olympia. Information on schedules and fares is available from the **Stathmos Peloponnisou** (railroad station for the Peloponnese) in Athens (✆ **210/513-1601;** www.ose.gr).

BY BUS There are three buses a day to Olympia from the Stathmos Leoforia Peloponnisou (bus station for the Peloponnese) in Athens, 100 Kifissou (✆ **210/512-4910;** www.ktel.org). There are also frequent buses from Patras to Pirgos, with connecting service to Olympia. In Patras, KTEL buses leave from the intersection of Zaimi and Othonos (✆ **2610/273-694**). For general schedule information for Athens-Peloponnese service, try **210/512-4910** or www.ktel.org.

BY CAR Olympia, 320km (199 miles) from Athens, is a good 5- to 6-hour drive whether you take the coast road that links Athens to Corinth, Patras, and Olympia or head inland to Tripolis and Olympia on the Corinth-Tripolis road. Heavy traffic in Patras, 159km (99 miles) south, means that the drive from Patras to Olympia can easily take 2 hours.

VISITOR INFORMATION The tourist information office (the former **Greek National Tourist Organization [EOT]** office) is on the way to the ancient site near the south end of Leoforos Kondili, the main street (✆ **26240/22-262**). It's officially open daily, from 9am to 10pm in the summer and from 11am to 6pm in the winter. That said, on a number of occasions when I have been in Olympia out of high season, the office had an open sign in its window, but was closed.

Where to Stay

Olympia has more than 20 hotels, which means you can almost always find a room, although if you arrive without a reservation in July or August, you might not get your first choice. In the winter, many hotels are closed. If you're here in winter, check to see if the hotel you choose has functioning central heating.

Hotel Europa ★★★ The Europa is the best hotel in town—and one of the best in the Peloponnese. Part of the Best Western chain (but managed by a very helpful local family), it's a few minutes' drive just out of town on a hill overlooking both the modern village and the ancient site. Most units overlook the large pool and garden, and several have views of a bit of the ancient site. The rooms are large, with extra-firm mattresses and sliding glass doors opening onto generously sized balconies. The two very professional restaurants include a taverna in the garden, which serves tasty grills and stews; the indoor breakfast buffet is extensive.

27065 Ancient Olympia, Peloponnese. ✆ **800/528-1234** in the U.S., 26240/22-650 or 26240/22-700. Fax 26240/23-166. www.hoteleuropa.gr. 80 units. 70€–110€ double. Rates include breakfast. AE, DC, MC, V. **Amenities:** Restaurant; bar; Internet; pool. *In room:* A/C, fridge, hair dryer, minibar.

Hotel Olympia Palace Frankly, I had looked forward to staying here again after the renovations and I was disappointed. It's true that the Olympia Palace, which was completely remodeled for the 2004 Olympics, is an excellent choice if you want to be poised on the main street in order to investigate the village. The guest rooms have good beds, cheerful prints on the walls, and nice rag rugs on the floor; the bathrooms are modern and good size. However, street noise plagues the front rooms and a large parking lot flanks the side toward the ancient site; try for a rear room. Another problem: seriously ho-hum service.

2 Praxiteleous Kondili, 270 65 Ancient Olympia. ✆ **26240/23-101.** www.olympia-palace.gr. 58 units. 100€–130€ double. AE, MC, V. **Amenities:** Restaurant; bar. *In room:* A/C, TV, hair dryer, minibar.

Hotel Pelops ★★★ If you've heard how helpful Aussie expat Susanna Spiliopoulou and her family are, believe every word! Susanna, husband Theo, and the family make this one of the most welcoming hotels in Greece. Rooms are good size, cheerful, and very comfy, unlike all too many Greek hotels. Check out their website to learn about their 3- and 4-day cooking, writing, and painting classes, usually offered off season. An added bonus: Guests here can use the dishy pool at the Hotel Europa and order up a Pelops Platter (a wide variety of Greek *mezedes*) for dinner back at the Pelops. But the real bonus here is leaving the all-too-often anonymous world of hotels and entering a welcoming haven, in the center of town, but on a blissfully quiet street.

2 Varela, 270 65 Ancient Olympia. ✆ **26240/22-543.** www.hotelpelops.gr. 25 units. 70€ double. MC, V. **Amenities:** Breakfast room. *In room:* A/C, TV.

Where to Dine

There are almost as many restaurants as hotels in Olympia, but some of the best food in town is served at the **Hotel Europa** and the **Hotel Pelops** (see above). Do check to see whether the excellent **Kladeos Taverna** has reopened. On the main drag, **Tessera Epochi (Four Seasons), Zeus,** and the **Aegean** stand out from the many places that tend to have indifferent food and service. **Taverna Ambrosia,** by the railroad station, does a brisk business with tour groups, but also treats independent travelers well. Local cafes and bakeries are a good place to stop for a snack.

The Museums & the Ancient Site

Archaeological Museum ★★★ Even though you'll be eager to see the ancient site, it's a good idea to first visit the museum, which reopened after extensive renovations in 2004. The collection makes clear Olympia's astonishing wealth and importance in antiquity: Every victorious city and almost every victorious athlete dedicated a bronze or marble statue here, creating what was in effect one of the first outdoor museums of sculpture. Nothing but the best was good enough for Olympia, and many of these superb works of art are on view (with excellent labels in Greek, German, and English). Most of the exhibits are displayed in rooms to the right and left of the main entrance and follow an essentially chronological sequence, from severe Neolithic vases to baroque Roman imperial statues, neither of which will probably tempt you from heading straight ahead to see the museum's superstars. Still, don't miss the superb bronze heads of snarling griffins or the painted terra-cotta statue of a resolute Zeus abducting the youthful Ganymede.

The monumental **sculpture from the Temple of Zeus** is probably the finest surviving example of archaic Greek sculpture. The sculpture from the west pediment shows the battle of the Lapiths and Centaurs raging around the magisterial figure of Apollo, the god of reason. On the east pediment, Zeus oversees the chariot race between Oinomaos, the king of Pisa, and Pelops, the legendary figure who wooed and won Oinomaos's daughter by the unsporting expedient of loosening his opponent's chariot pins. Pelops not only won his bride but had the entire region named after him: the Peloponnese (Pelops's island). At either end of the room, sculptured metopes show scenes from the Labors of Hercules, including the one he performed at Olympia: cleansing the foul stables of King Augeus by diverting the Alfios River.

Just beyond the sculpture from the Temple of Zeus are the 5th-century-B.C. **Winged Victory,** created by the artist Paionios, and the 4th-century-B.C. figure of Hermes and the infant Dionysos, known as the **Hermes of Praxiteles.** The Hermes has a room to itself—or would, if tourists didn't make a beeline to admire Hermes smiling with amused tolerance at his chubby half-brother Dionysos. Many scholars think that this is not an original work by Praxiteles, but a Roman copy.

Directly across the street from the Ancient Site (see below). ✆/fax **26240/22-529.** www.culture.gr. Admission to site and museum 9€. Usually summer Mon-Fri 8:30am-7pm, Sat-Sun 8:30am-3pm; winter Mon-Fri 8am-5pm, Sat-Sun 8:30am-3pm.

Ancient Site ★★★ Olympia's setting is magical—pine trees shade the little valley, dominated by the conical Hill of Kronos that lies between the Alphios and Kladeos rivers. Reforestation of the hill of Kronos continues after the devastating fires of 2007 that ravaged the Peloponnese and threatened ancient Olympia itself. The 1980s excavations concentrated on Roman Olympia, especially in the southern area of the site. Although considerable progress has been made, neither the main entrance nor the route of the ceremonial way during Roman times is yet known. The handsome temples and the famous stadium are not at once apparent as you enter the site. Immediately to the left are the unimpressive low walls that are all that remain of the **Roman baths** where athletes and spectators could enjoy hot and cold plunge baths; some recently restored mosaics are on view. The considerably more impressive remains with the slender columns on your right mark the **gymnasium** and **palestra,** where athletes practiced their footracing and boxing skills. The enormous gymnasium had one roofed track where athletes could practice in bad weather. Also on the right are the fairly meager remains of a number of structures, including a swimming pool and the large square **Leonidaion,** which served as a hotel for visiting dignitaries until a Roman governor decided it would do nicely as his villa.

The religious sanctuary is dominated by two shrines: the good-size **Temple of Hera** and the massive **Temple of Zeus.** The Temple of Hera, with its three standing columns, is the older of the two, built around 600 B.C. If you look closely, you'll see that the temple's column capitals and drums are not uniform. That's because this temple was originally built with wooden columns, and as each column decayed, it was replaced; inevitably, each new column had slight variations. The Hermes of Praxiteles was found here, buried under the mud that covered Olympia for so long, caused by the repeated flooding of the rivers. The Temple of Zeus, which once had a veritable thicket of 34 stocky Doric columns, was built around 456 B.C. In 2004, one column was reerected in honor of the Athens Olympics. The entire temple—so austere and gray today—was anything but plain in antiquity. Gold, red, and blue paint was everywhere, and inside the temple stood an enormous gold-and-ivory statue of Zeus seated on an ivory-and-ebony throne. The statue was so ornate that it was considered one of the Seven Wonders of the Ancient World—and so large that people joked that if the Zeus stood up, his head would go through the temple's roof. In fact, the antiquarian Philo of Byzantium suggested that Zeus had created elephants simply so that the sculptor Phidias would have the ivory to make his statue.

Not only do we know that Phidias made the 13m (43-ft.) statue, but we know where he made it: The **Workshop of Phidias** was on the site of the well-preserved brick building clearly visible west of the temple outside the sanctuary. Between the Temples of Zeus and Hera you can make out the low foundations of a round building: This was all that remained of the **shrine** that Philip of Macedon, never modest, built here to pat himself on the back after conquering Greece in 338 B.C. until part of the facade was restored in 2004 in honor of the Athens Olympics.

Beyond the temples of Zeus and Hera, built up against the Hill of Kronos, are the curved remains of a once-elegant **Roman fountain** and the foundations of 11 **treasuries** where Greek cities stored votive offerings and money. In front of the treasuries are the low bases of a series of bronze statues of Zeus dedicated not by victorious athletes but by those caught cheating in the stadium. The statues would have been the last thing competitors saw before they entered the stadium.

✆/fax **26240/22-529.** www.culture.gr. Admission to site and museum 9€. Usually summer Mon–Fri 8:30am–7pm, Sat–Sun 8:30am–3pm; winter Mon–Fri 8am–5pm, Sat–Sun 8:30am–3pm.

The Museum of the History of the Olympic Games in Antiquity ★★ The museum, which opened in 2004, occupies the handsome neoclassical building that served as the site's original archaeological museum. The path to the museum is steep; it is sometimes possible to get permission to drive up and drop off passengers by the museum's entrance. The superb collection includes chariot wheels, musical instruments, statues of athletes, bronze dedications to Zeus, and all manner of athletic gear. A number of photos and drawings highlight the religious sanctuary. Each of the 12 galleries has a theme, including "The Beginning of the Games," "Zeus and His Cults," "The Events," and Games at other ancient sites (Nemea, Isthmia, Delphi). If you are an Olympics buff, also take in the small Museum of the Olympic Games, signposted in the village of Ancient Olympia; admission 2€; open Monday to Saturday from 8am to 3:30pm, Sunday and holidays 9am to 2:30pm.

✆ **26240/22-529.** Free admission (but a fee is planned). Summer Mon noon–7pm, Tues–Sun 8am–7pm; winter, usually closes by 5pm.

Delphi ★★★

Delphi, which the ancient Greeks believed was the center of the world, is the big enchilada of Greek sites. Even more than Olympia, Delphi has it all: a long and glorious history as the scene of Apollo's famous oracle and the Pythian games; a gravity-defying cliff-side location with the remains of treasuries, small temples, a stadium, and a theater; the massive temple of Apollo and a view over a plain of gnarled olive trees to the Gulf of Corinth. Look up and you see the cliffs and crags of Parnassus; look down at Greece's most beautiful plain of olive trees stretching as far as the eye can see toward the town of Itea on the Gulf of Corinth. The star of the Delphi museum is the famous bronze statue of the charioteer who raced his horses to victory in Delphi's stadium.

Many tour groups offer day trips to Delphi, stopping at the Byzantine monastery of Osios Loukas (see "Organized Tours," earlier in this chapter). In the summer, tour groups clog Delphi's few streets by day, but many head elsewhere for the night, which means that hotel rooms are usually available—although often all the cheap rooms are gone by midmorning. In the winter, thousands of Greeks head here each weekend, not for the archaeological site, but for the excellent skiing on Mount Parnassus. Getting a room in the once-sleepy nearby hamlet of Arachova is virtually impossible without a reservation on winter weekends, and Delphi itself is often full.

Every summer (usually in June), the European Cultural Center of Delphi sponsors the **Festival of Delphi,** featuring ancient Greek drama and works inspired by ancient pieces. Tickets and schedules are usually available at the Center's Athens office at 9 Frynihou, Plaka (✆ **210/331-2798**), and at the Center's Delphi office (✆ **22650/82-731**). ***Budget travelers take note:*** Tickets are sometimes substantially discounted or even free close to performance time.

ESSENTIALS

Getting There

BY BUS There are usually five buses daily to Delphi from the Athens bus station at 260 Liossion (✆ **210/831-7096,** 210/831-7179 in Athens, or 22650/82-317 in Delphi).

BY CAR Take the Athens-Corinth National Highway 74km (46 miles) west of Athens to the Thebes turnoff and continue 40km (25 miles) west to Levadia. If you want to stop at the monastery of Osios Loukas, take the Distomo turnoff for 9km (5⅔ miles). At the fork in the road in the village of Distomo, bear left, lest you follow a dead-end, but scenic, road to the sea. Return to Distomo and continue via Arachova for 26km (16 miles) to Delphi or via the seaside town of Itea for 64km (40 miles) to Delphi. The approach from Itea on a steeply climbing road with views back to the sea is well worth the time if you aren't in a hurry—and don't mind hairpin curves. As always near important sites in Greece, be prepared to encounter a tour bus at any turn in the road!

VISITOR INFORMATION The tourist information office (the former **Greek National Tourism Organization [GNTO]** office; ✆ **22650/82-900**) on the main street (Frederikis) is usually open from 8am to 3pm (sometimes later in summer)—and sometimes mysteriously closed.

GETTING AROUND The village of Delphi, with its two main one-way parallel streets connected by stepped side streets, is small enough that most visitors find it easiest to abandon their cars and explore on foot. If you have to drive to the site rather than make the 5- to 10-minute walk from town, be sure to set off early to get one of the few parking places. Whether you walk or drive, keep an eye out for the

> **The Delphi Tram**
>
> If you want to tour today's Delphi as well as the ancient sanctuaries, check out the free tram that leaves from the Hotel Vouzas and gives 30-minute rides around the village of Delphi daily in the summer.

enormous tour buses that barrel down the center of the road—and for the poorly marked one-way streets in the village.

WHERE TO STAY

There's no shortage of hotels in Delphi, and you can usually get a room even in July and August. Still, if you want a room in a specific price category or with a view, it's best to make a reservation. Finally, in summer (but not in winter when the skiers take over this hamlet), consider staying in nearby **Arachova,** where the hotels are usually less crowded. Be sure to check whether your hotel has good heating if you visit in the winter.

In addition to the following options, consider these three recently renovated hotels: The **Delphi Palace,** just out of the village, with pool and gardens; the **King Iniohos,** on one of the quiet upper streets; and the **Pythia Art Hotel,** on the non-view side of the main street, are jointly managed and share a reservations number and website (✆ **22650/82-151;** www.delphi-hotels.com). I no longer recommend the Hotel Vouzas, once *the* in-town hotel to stay at, because it has declined badly in recent years.

Tip: If you want a room with a view, be sure to ask for a room with a balcony that faces the Gulf of Corinth. You may not always see the water, but from your balcony you will almost always see the magnificent valley of olive trees that leads down to the Gulf—and avoid the traffic noise of the main street.

Hotel Acropole ★★★ One street below Delphi's main street, the 42-room Acropole has one of the quietest locations and best views in town over private houses, gardens, and the olive groves that stretch beneath Delphi to the sea. The Acropole stays open year-round and is owned and managed by the helpful and charming Kourelis family. If the Acropole is full, the staff can usually find you a room at one of their other Delphi hotels, both on the main street: the slightly more modest and less expensive **Parnassos** (✆ **22650/83-675;** www.delphi.com.gr) and the very appealing **Fedriades** (✆ **22650/82-370;** www.fedriades.com), which the Kourelis family purchased, renovated, and reopened in 2008. A 10% discount at all three is usually available to Frommer's readers. Check about special deals including a dinner plan at the excellent family-run Epikouros restaurant (see below).

13 Filellinon St., 330 54 Delphi. ✆ **22650-82-675.** www.delphi.com.gr. 42 units. From 80€ double. Rates include breakfast. AE, MC, V. **Amenities:** Breakfast room; lounge w/fireplace; Internet. *In room:* A/C, TV, fridge.

Hotel Varonos ★★★ This small hotel has to be the best buy in town, with Delphi's famous views over the olive plain from most rooms. Some 20 years ago, I once arrived here with an ailing gardenia plant, and the entire family pitched in to make sure it was well taken care of. In those days, the hotel was very simple, almost austere, but over the years, this has become one of the coziest and most comfortable small hotels in Greece. The guest rooms are very comfortable (terrific mattresses), painted in soothing pastels, and the lobby is anything but austere, with lots of plants and a fire when it's chilly (and free Internet service). The view is still fantastic, the Varonos family could not be more helpful, and the breakfast buffet in the cheerful breakfast room is unusually varied (four kinds of juice and at least as many baked goods, along with yogurt, fresh fruit, eggs, cheese, and ham). Check out the family-owned shop next door with local honey, herbs, preserves, and other goodies.

25 Vasileos Pavlou, 330 54 Delphi. ✆/fax **22650/82-345.** 12 units, 11 with shower (1 with tub/shower). 70€–100€ double. Rates include breakfast (room without breakfast sometimes possible). Inquire about a Frommer's 20% discount. MC, V. **Amenities:** Breakfast room; lounge w/fireplace; Internet. *In room:* A/C, TV, fridge.

WHERE TO DINE

You won't starve in Delphi, but restaurants here can sometimes be overwhelmed by tour groups; so if you are here anytime but winter, you may prefer to head to the village of Arachova, 10km (6¼ miles) to the north.

In Delphi, I strongly recommend the **Epikouros** Restaurant (✆ **22650/83-250**), at 33 Pavlou and Frederikis, owned and managed by the same helpful Kourelis family that runs the excellent Hotel Acropolis and Hotel Parnassos. This is a great place to make an entire meal of appetizers *(mezedes)*. The astonishingly wide and varied menu includes tasty vegetable fritters, the delicious local formaella cheese, lamb with fresh tomato sauce, and, in season, wild boar. The Epikouros also easily has the best view in town from a restaurant; entrees run from 9€ to 18€. **Taverna Skala,** also on Pavlou and Frederikis (✆ **22650/82-762**); **Taverna Vakchos,** 31 Apollonos (✆ **22650/83-186**); and **Taverna Lekaria,** 33 Apollonos (✆ **22650/82-776**), are reliable for simple taverna fare.

EXPLORING THE SITE

If possible, begin your visit when the site and museum open in the morning (both are sometimes relatively uncrowded in the hour before closing, too). If you begin your visit at the museum, you'll arrive at the site already familiar with many of the works of art that once decorated the sanctuary. As with Olympia, it's easy to spend a whole day here, taking in the site and museum, with a break for lunch. Unlike Olympia, the main site at Delphi—built on a slope of Mt. Parnassus—involves a great deal of climbing with almost no shade.

Delphi Archaeological Museum ★★★ This already-superb museum reopened in 2005 after extensive renovations and the addition of a new wing, shop, and cafe. Each of the museum's rooms has a specific focus: sculpture from the elegant Siphnian treasury in one room, finds from the Temple of Apollo in two rooms, discoveries from the Roman period (including the Parian marble statue of the epicene youth Antinous, the beloved of the emperor Hadrian) in another. Keep an eye out for the impressively large 4th-century-B.C. marble egg, a symbol of Delphi's position as the center of the world. According to legend, when Zeus wanted to determine the earth's center, he released two eagles from Mount Olympus. When the eagles met over Delphi, Zeus had his answer. (You can still see eagles in the sky above Delphi, but as often as not, the large birds circling overhead are the less distinguished Egyptian vultures.)

The star of the museum is the "must-see" 5th-century-B.C. **Charioteer of Delphi,** a larger-than-life bronze figure that was part of a group that originally included a four-horse chariot. It's an irresistible statue; the handsome youth's delicate eyelashes shade wide enamel and stone eyes, and realistic veins stand out in his hands and feet.

Although the charioteer is the star of the collection, he's in good company. Delphi was chockablock with superb works of art given by wealthy patrons, such as King Croesus of Lydia, who contributed the massive silver bull that's on display. Many of the finest exhibits are quite small, such as the elegant bronzes in the museum's last room, including one that shows Odysseus clinging to the belly of a ram. According to Homer, this is how the wily hero escaped from the cave of the ferocious (but nearsighted) monster Cyclops.

✆ **22650/82-312.** Admission 9€ includes admission to site; museum only, 6€. Summer Mon 11am–7pm, Tues–Fri 8am–7pm, Sat–Sun and holidays 8am–3pm; winter daily 8:30am–3pm. (Be sure to check these hours when you arrive in Delphi, as they can change without warning.)

Sanctuary of Apollo, Castalian Spring & Sanctuary of Athena Pronaia ★★★

As you enter the **Sanctuary of Apollo,** just past the museum, you'll be on the marble **Sacred Way,** following the route that visitors to Delphi have taken for thousands of years. The Sacred Way twists uphill past the remains of Roman **stoas** (porticoes) and a number of **Greek treasuries,** including the Siphnian and Athenian treasuries, whose sculpture is in the museum. The Athenian treasury is easy to spot, as it's the only one that has been restored. Take a close look at the Athenian treasury's walls: You'll see not only beautiful drywall masonry, but countless inscriptions. The ancient Greeks were never shy about using the walls of their buildings as bulletin boards. Alas, so many contemporary visitors have added their own names to the ancient inscriptions that the Greek Archaeological Service no longer allows visitors inside the massive 4th-century-B.C. **Temple of Apollo,** which was built here after several earlier temples were destroyed.

From the temple, it's a fairly steep uphill climb to the remarkably well preserved 4th-century-B.C. theater and the stadium, extensively remodeled by the Romans. In antiquity, contests in the Pythian festivals took place in both venues. Today the theater and stadium are used most summers for the Festival of Delphi—which, on occasion, has featured nonclassical pop music.

Keep your ticket as you leave the Sanctuary of Apollo and begin the 10-minute walk along the Arachova-Delphi road to the Sanctuary of Athena (also called the Marmaria, which refers to all the marble found here). En route, you'll pass the famous **Castalian Spring,** where Apollo planted the laurel from which later victory crowns were fashioned. Above are the rose-colored cliffs known as the Phaedriades (the Bright Ones), famous for the way they reflect the sun's rays. Drinking from the Castalian Spring has inspired legions of poets; however, the spring is currently off-limits to allow repairs to the Roman fountain facade.

A path descends from the main road to the **Sanctuary of Athena Pronaia,** goddess of wisdom, who shared the honors at Delphi with Apollo. The remains here are quite fragmentary, except for the large 4th-century-B.C. gymnasium, and you might choose simply to wander about and enjoy the site without trying too hard to figure out what's what. The round 4th-century-B.C. tholos with its three graceful standing

Doric columns is easy to spot—but no one knows why the building was constructed, why it was so lavishly decorated, or what went on inside. Again, the oracle is silent.

✆ **22650/82-313.** Admission (which includes the museum) 9€; site only, 6€. Summer Mon–Fri 7:30am–6:30pm, Sat–Sun and holidays 8:30am–3pm; winter usually daily 8:30am–3pm. (Be sure to check these hours when you arrive in Delphi, as they can change without warning.)

THE CYCLADES

When most people think of the "Isles of Greece," they're thinking of the Cyclades, the rugged (even barren) chain of Aegean islands whose villages of dazzling white houses look from a distance like so many sugar cubes. The Cyclades got their name from the ancient Greek word meaning "to circle," or surround, because the island chain encircles the sacred island of Delos. Today, especially in the summer, it's the visitors who circle these islands, taking advantage of the swift island boats and hydrofoils that link them. Visitors come to see the white villages, the blue-domed chapels, and the fiery sunsets over the cobalt blue sea. They also come to relax in chic boutique hotels, eat in varied and inventive restaurants, and to enjoy an ouzo—or a chocolate martini—in some of the best bars and cafes in Greece. In summer, only the fearless would come here without a hotel reservation! ***Tip:*** On many of these islands, the capital town has the name of the island itself. It's also sometimes called "Hora," or "Chora," a term meaning "the place" that's commonly used for the most important regional town.

Mykonos, with its maze of twisting lanes paved with stone and lined with dazzling white sugar-cube houses was the first of the islands to become popular in the 1960s. Although the Beautiful People may have moved on, Mykonos remains a "must see"—hence, expensive—island for virtually every visitor to Greece. The crescent of **Santorini (Thira),** with its black-sand beaches and blood-red cliffs, is all that remains of the island that was blown apart in antiquity by a volcano that still steams and hisses today. Santorini's exceptional physical beauty, dazzling relics, and elegant restaurants and boutiques make it contend with Mykonos for the title of the most popular Cycladic island. Both Santorini and Mykonos draw so many day-trippers from summer cruise ships that the islands almost sink under the weight of tourists. **Tinos,** whose hills are dotted with elaborate dovecotes, is the most important destination in all Greece for religious pilgrims, yet it remains one of the least commercialized islands of the Cyclades—and a joy to visit for that reason. Remember, however, that all these islands are seriously crowded between June and September. Prepare to be grateful for a tiny room with no view if you show up without a hotel reservation on summer weekends!

Tip: You can access a useful website for each of the Cyclades by entering "www.greeka.com/cyclades" and the name of the island (for example, www.greeka.com/cyclades/santorini).

Getting to the Cyclades

BY AIR **Olympic Air** (✆ **210/966-6666** or 210/936-9111; www.olympicair.com), the former Olympic Airlines, offers daily flights between Athens and the Santorini airport at Monolithos (which also receives European charters). There are connections with Mykonos five times per week, service three or four times per week to and from Rhodes, and service two or three times per week to and from Iraklion, Crete. **Aegean Airlines** (✆ **210/998-2888,** or 210/998-8300 in Athens), with an office at the Monolithos airport (✆ **22860/28-500**), also has service in summer between Athens and Santorini and Mykonos.

BY SEA **Ferries** leave daily from Athens's main port of Piraeus and from Rafina, the port east of Athens; confirm ferry schedules with the Athens **GNTO** (✆ **210/870-0000;** www.gnto.gr), the **Piraeus Port Authority** (✆ **210/451-1311** or 1440 or 1441; phone not always answered), or the Rafina Port Police (✆ **22940/22-300**). The speedy **Seajet** (✆ **210/414-1250**) catamaran service also departs from Rafina and zips between Andros, Syros, Tinos, Mykonos, Paros, Naxos, and Santorini (Thira).

It can take an hour for the 27km (17-mile) bus ride from Athens to Rafina (the most convenient port for Mykonos and Tinos), but you save about an hour of sailing time and usually about 20% on the fare. Buses leave every 30 minutes from 6am to 10pm from 29 Mavromateon (✆ **210/821-0872**), near Areos Park north of the National Archaeological Museum (indicated on most city maps).

In the summer there's regular ferry service to Iraklio, Crete, from Piraeus, the port of Athens. There are also ferry and hydrofoil connections several times a week between Mykonos and Kos and Rhodes; twice a week between Mykonos and Skyros, Skiathos, and Thessaloniki; daily between Tinos and Paros and Syros; and two or three times a week between Syros and the Dodecanese.

Remember: Almost all of the rural Greek National Tourist Offices (EOT) have been turned over to local authorities. In most cases, the office remains at the same address, with the same phone and work hours, but call in advance to make sure.

Getting Around the Cyclades

Although there is frequent ferry service among most of the islands, schedules can be erratic, and service diminishes suddenly at the end of the season. Changes in the line that serves an island can occur with little—or no—advance warning. To further complicate matters, a line will often authorize only one agent to sell tickets or limit the number of tickets available to an agency, giving other agents little incentive to tout its service. (For specifics, see "Getting There," under "Essentials," for each island.)

The Wind & the Sea

The winds frequently complicate sea travel on the Aegean. For this reason, plan to arrive back in Athens from the islands **at least** 24 hours before you have to make any critical air or sea connections. In July the strong winds known as the *meltemi* usually kick up, often playing havoc with hydrofoil schedules. The larger ferries still run, but if you're prone to seasickness, take precautions. In the winter the strong north winds *(vorias)* frequently make sea travel impossible for days at a time. This is still one of the best ways to travel and enjoy Greece—but, perhaps, as we say in Greece: *siga, siga* (slowly, slowly)—with all the more time to enjoy the moment.

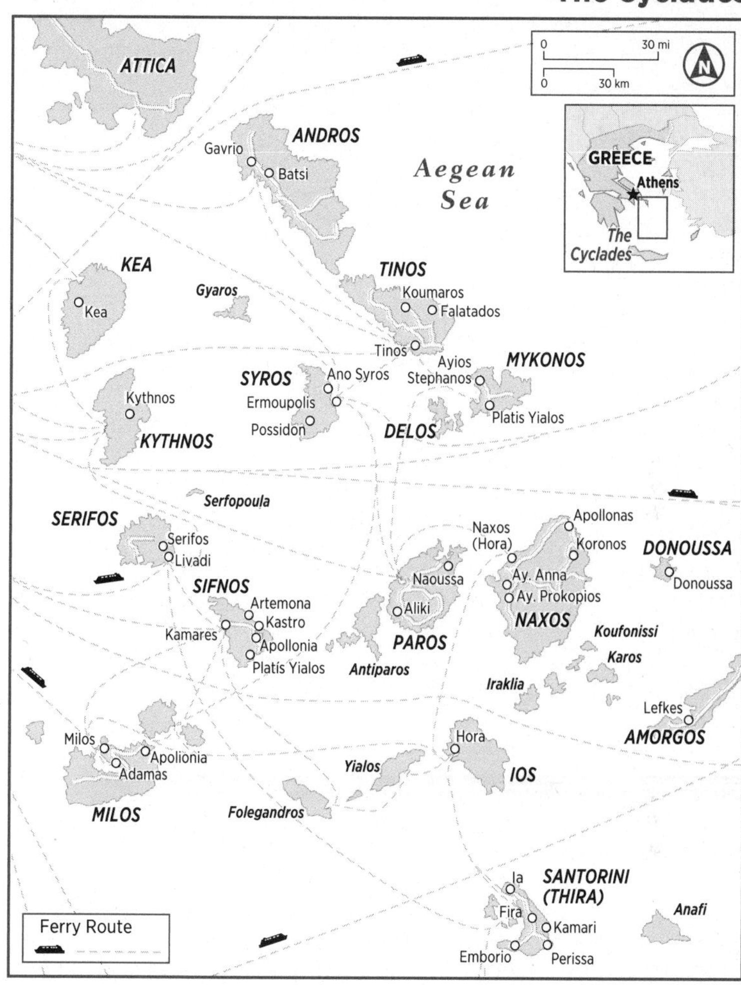

For information on cruises, contact the **Greek National Tourist Organization** (✆ **212/421-5777** in New York, 020/7734-5997 in London, or 210/331-0437 or 210/870-0000 in Athens; www.visitgreece.gr) or the **Greek Island Cruise Center** (✆ **800/342-3030** in the U.S.). **Sea Cloud Cruises** (✆ **888/732-2568** in the U.S.) uses a four-masted private yacht that takes up to 60 passengers on Aegean cruises.

Mykonos ★★★

What makes this small (about 16km/10 miles long), arid island so popular? At least initially, it was the exceptionally handsome Cycladic architecture—and the fact that many on the poor island were more than eager to rent their houses to visitors. First came the jet-setters, artists, and expatriates (including a number of sophisticated gay visitors), as well as the mainland Greeks who opened many of the chic shops and restaurants—all followed by a curious mixture of jet set wannabes and backpackers. Now, with cruise ships lined up in the harbor all summer and as many as 10 flights each day from Athens, it's easier to say who *doesn't* come to Mykonos than who does. That's why it's very important not to arrive here without reservations in July and August (when it can feel as if every one of the island's million annual visitors is here), unless you enjoy sleeping outdoors—and don't mind being moved from your sleeping spot by the police, who are not always charmed to find foreigners alfresco.

ESSENTIALS

Getting There

BY AIR Mykonos is served by Olympic Air (www.olympicair.com), the former Olympic Airlines, and Aegean Airlines (www.aegeanair.com). Although there may be as many as 10 flights from Athens to Mykonos a day in summer, it's usually impossible to get a last-minute seat, so book well in advance.

BY BOAT Mykonos now has two ports: the old port in Mykonos town, and the new port north of Mykonos town at Tourlos. Check before you travel to find out which port your boat will use. From Piraeus, the **Blue Star *Ithaki*** (www.ferries.gr) has departures once daily at 7:30am. The ***Pegasus*** has two weekly departures during summer at 7:30pm (Mon and Sat). The **High Speed** has two departures daily, at 7:15am and 4:45pm, and the ***Marina*** has three departures weekly at 11:50pm on Tuesday, and 5pm Thursday and Saturday. From Rafina, the **Super Ferry** has one departure at 8am daily; the **Super Jet 2** has two departures daily at 7:40am and 4pm. The ***Aqua Jewel*** has one departure daily at 5pm, while the ***Penelope*** leaves at 7:35pm daily. **High Speed** boats, lines **2** and **3,** have daily afternoon departures at 7:30pm and 4:30pm, respectively. Schedules can be checked with the **port police** (**© 22890/22-218**). There are daily ferry connections between Mykonos and Andros, Paros, Syros, and Tinos; five to seven trips a week to Ios; four a week to Iraklio, Crete; several a week to Kos and Rhodes; and two a week to Ikaria, Samos, Skiathos, Skyros, and Thessaloniki. **Hellas Flying Dolphins** offers service from **Piraeus** (**© 210/419-9100** or 210/419-9000; www.dolphins.gr) in summer. From the port of Lavrio, the Fly Cat 3 has an 11:15am departure daily to Mykonos.

On Mykonos, your best bet for getting up-to-date lists of sailings is to check at individual agencies. Or you can check with the **port authority** by National Bank (**© 22890/22-218**), **tourist police** at the north end of the harbor (**© 22890/22-482**), or **tourist office,** also on the harbor (**© 22890/23-990;** fax 22890/22-229).

Hydrofoil service to Crete, Ios, Paros, and Santorini is often irregular. For information, check at **Piraeus Port Authority** (**© 210/451-1311** or 210/422-6000; phone seldom answered); **Piraeus Port Police** (**© 210/451-1310**); **Rafina Port Police** (**© 22940/23-300**); or **Mykonos Port Police** (**© 22890/22-218**).

Warning: Check each travel agency's current schedule, because most ferry tickets are not interchangeable. Reputable agencies on the main square in Mykonos (Hora) town include **Sunspots Travel** (**© 22890/24-196;** fax 22890/23-790); **Delia Travel** (**© 22890/22-490;** fax 22890/24-440); **Sea & Sky Travel** (**© 22890/22-853;** fax 22890/24-753); and **Veronis Agency** (**© 22890/22-687;** fax 22890/23-763).

Finding an Address

Although some shops hand out maps of Mykonos town, you'll probably do better finding restaurants, hotels, and attractions by asking people to point you in the right direction—and saying *efcharisto* (thank you) when they do. Don't panic at how to pronounce *efcharisto;* think of it as a name and say "F. Harry Stowe." Most streets do not have their names posted. Also, maps leave off lots of small, twisting streets—and Mykonos has almost nothing but small, twisting streets! The map published by Stamatis Bozinakis, sold at most kiosks for 2€, is quite decent. The useful Mykonos Sky Map is free at some hotels and shops.

VISITOR INFORMATION **Mykonos Accommodations Center,** Enoplon Dhinameon and Malamatenias (✆ **22890/23-160;** www.mykonos-accommodation.com), helps visitors find accommodations. It also functions as a tourist information center. **Windmills Travel ★** (✆ **22890/23-877;** www.windmillstravel.com) has an office at Fabrica Square where you can get general information, book accommodations, arrange excursions, and rent a car or moped. Look for the free *Mykonos Summertime* magazine, available in cafes, shops, and hotels throughout the island.

TOWN LAYOUT Legend has it that the streets of Mykonos town—which locals call Hora—were designed to confuse pirates, so your own confusion is understandable. As you get off the ferry, you can see the main square south across the harbor beyond the small town beach and a cluster of buildings; we refer to it as **Taxi Square,** although it's officially called Plateia Manto Mavroyenous, after a local heroine. Here you'll find several travel agents, kiosks, snack bars, and, of course, the town's taxi stand.

The main street, **Matogianni,** leads south off Taxi Square behind the church; it's narrow, but you can hardly miss the bars, boutiques, and restaurants. Several "blocks" along it you'll find a "major" cross street, **Kaloyera,** and by turning right, you'll find several of the hotels and restaurants we recommend. If you get lost—and you will—remember that in Mykonos that's part of the fun.

GETTING AROUND **BY FOOT** One of Hora's greatest assets is the government decree that made the town an architectural landmark and prohibited motorized traffic on its streets. If you don't arrive with your donkey or bicycle, you can walk around town. Many of the town's large hotels ring the busy peripheral road, and a good bus system serves much of the rest of the island.

BY BUS Mykonos has one of the best bus systems in the Greek islands; the buses run frequently and on schedule. Depending on your destination, a ticket costs about .50€ to 4€. There are two bus stations in Hora: one near the archaeological museum and one near the Olympic Air office (follow the helpful blue signs). At the tourist office, find out from which station the bus you want leaves, or look for schedules in hotels. Bus information in English is sometimes available from the **KTEL** office (✆ **22890/23-360**).

BY BOAT Caiques to Super Paradise, Agrari, and Elia depart from Platis Yialos every morning, weather permitting; there is also service from Ornos in high season

(July–Aug) only. Caique service is highly seasonal, with almost continuous service in high season and no caiques October through May. Excursion boats to Delos depart Tuesday through Sunday between 8:30am and 1pm, from the west side of the harbor near the tourist office. (For more information, see a travel agent; guided tours are available.)

BY CAR & MOPED Rental cars are available from about 50€ per day, including insurance, in high season; most agencies are near one of the two bus stops in town. **Windmills Travel** (see "Visitor Information," above) can arrange a car rental for you and get good prices. The largest concentration of moped shops is just beyond the south bus station. Expect to pay about 15€ to 30€ per day, depending on the moped's engine size. Greek law now requires wearing a helmet; not all agents supply the helmet. Take great care when driving: Many drivers here are new to the island and unfamiliar with the roads.

Warning: If you park in town or in a no-parking area, the police will remove your license plates. You—not the rental office—will have to find the police station and pay a steep fine to get them back.

BY TAXI There are two types of taxis in Mykonos: standard **car taxis** for destinations outside town, and tiny, cart-towing **scooters** that buzz through the narrow streets of Hora. The latter are seen primarily at the port, where they wait to bring new arrivals to their lodgings in town—a good idea, as most in-town hotels are a challenge to find. Getting a car taxi in Hora is easy: Walk to Taxi (Mavro) Square, near the statue, and join the line. A notice board gives rates for various destinations. You can also call **Mykonos Radio Taxi** (✆ **22890/22-400**).

FAST FACTS **Commercial Bank** and **National Bank of Greece** are on the harbor a couple of blocks west of Taxi Square; both are open Monday through Friday from 8am to 2pm. ATMs are available throughout town. **Mykonos Health Center** (✆ **22890/23-994** or 22890/23-996) handles routine medical complaints; serious cases are usually airlifted to the mainland. The **tourist police** (✆ **22890/22-482**) are on the west side of the port near the ferries to Delos; the local **police** (✆ **22890/22-235**) are behind the grammar school, near Plateia Laka. The **post office** (✆ **22890/22-238**) is next to the police station; it's open Monday through Friday from 7:30am to 2pm. The **telephone office (OTE)** is on the north side of the harbor beyond the Hotel Leto (✆ **22890/22-499**), open Monday through Friday 7:30am to 3pm. **Internet access** is expensive here: Mykonos Cyber Cafe, 26 M. Axioti, on the road between the south bus station and the windmills (✆ **22890/27-684**), is open daily 9am to 10pm and charges 16€ per hour or 5€ for 15 minutes. Angelo's Internet Cafe, on the same road (✆ **22890/24-106**), may have lower rates.

WHERE TO STAY

In summer, reserve a room 1 to 3 months in advance (or more), if possible. Ferry arrivals are often met by a throng of people hawking rooms, some in small hotels, others in private homes. If you don't have a hotel reservation, one of these rooms may be very welcome. Many hotels are fully booked all summer by tour groups or regular patrons. Keep in mind that Mykonos is an easier, more pleasant place to visit in the late spring or early fall. Off-season hotel rates are sometimes half the quoted high-season rate. Also note that many small hotels, restaurants, and shops close in winter, especially if business is slow.

Mykonos Accommodations Center (MAC), 10 Enoplon Dinameon (✆ **22890/23-160** or 22890/23-408; fax 22890/24-137; www.mykonos-accommodation.com), is a very helpful service, especially if you are looking for hard-to-find inexpensive lodgings. The service is free when you book a hotel stay of 3 nights or longer. If you plan a shorter stay, ask about the fee, which is sometimes a percentage of the tab and sometimes a flat fee.

In & Around Hora

Andronikos Hotel ★★ Beautiful, elegant, and right in town, this impeccably designed hotel offers spacious verandas or terraces with incredible vistas of the sea and the town, a very good in-site restaurant, an edgy gallery, and a spa at affordable (for Mykonos) prices.

Hora 864 00, Mykonos. ✆ **22890/24-231.** Fax 22890/24-691. www.andronikoshotel.com. 53 units. 180€–230€ double without Jacuzzi, 240€–290€ with Jacuzzi. AE, DC, MC, V. **Amenities:** Restaurant; bar; exercise room; pool; spa. *In room:* A/C, TV, DVD player, hair dryer, Internet, Jacuzzi (in some rooms), minibar.

Apollon Hotel ★ No-nonsense, no-frills hotels in Mykonos are hard to come by. Rooms are basic yet comfortable and very well kept. But it's the price that is by far its biggest attraction.

Hora, 846 00 Mykonos. ✆ **22890/22-223.** Fax 22890/2437. 10 units. 50€–65€ single/double with shower. No credit cards. *In room:* A/C, TV.

Belvedere Hotel ★★ The all-white oasis of the Belvedere, in part occupying a handsomely restored 1850s town house on the main road into town, has stunning views over the town and harbor, a few minutes' walk away. Stay here if you want many of the creature comforts of Mykonos's beach resorts, but prefer to be within walking distance of Hora. Rooms are nicely, if not distinctively, furnished. The ultra-chic poolside scene buzzes all night and day, in part due to Nobu Matsuhisa's only open-air restaurant, the impeccable **Matsuhisha Mykonos** (see "Where to Dine," below), and the wonderful **CBar Lounge**—ideal for its sweeping sunset views.

Hora, 846 00 Mykonos. ✆ **22890/25-122.** Fax 22890/25-126. www.belvederehotel.com. 48 units. 230€–460€ double; 650€ suite. Rates include American buffet breakfast. Considerable off-season reductions. AE, DC, MC, V. **Amenities:** 2 restaurants; bar/lounge; fitness center; Jacuzzi; pool; sauna. *In room:* A/C, TV, hair dryer, Internet, minibar.

Cavo Tagoo ★★ This exceptional hotel set into a cliff with spectacular views over Mykonos town is hard to resist—and consistently makes it onto *Odyssey* magazine's list of 10 best Greek hotels. Hora's harbor is only a 15-minute walk away, although you may find it hard to budge: A saltwater pool and a good restaurant are right here. Cavo Tagoo's island-style architecture has won awards, and its gleaming marble floors, nicely crafted wooden furniture, queen- and king-size beds, and local-style weavings are a genuine pleasure. Elegantly minimalist with marble, spacious bathrooms, and large balconies with stunning sea vistas, Cavo Tagoo features suites with private pools, a Spa Center, a stunning lounge, and pool areas.

Hora, 846 00 Mykonos. ✆ **22890/23-692** to -695. Fax 22890/24-923. www.cavotagoo.gr. 69 units. 225€–420€ double. Rates include buffet breakfast. AE, DC, MC, V. Closed Nov–Mar. **Amenities:** Restaurant; bar; exercise room; saltwater pool; sauna. *In room:* A/C, TV, hair dryer, Internet, minibar.

Elysium ★★ The smartest gay hotel on the island is located on a steep hillside right in the old town; a walk down the steep hill will have you back in town in 3 minutes. Gardens, a pool, great views, a gym, a sauna, and a very relaxed atmosphere keep guests returning again and again.

Mykonos Old Town, 846 00 Mykonos. ✆ **22890/23-952.** Fax 22890/23-747. www.elysiumhotel.com. 42 units. 180€ double. AE, DC, MC, V. **Amenities:** Bar/cafe; exercise room; pool; sauna; spa. In *room:* A/C, TV, hair dryer, Internet.

Philippi Hotel ★ Each room in this homey little hotel in the heart of Mykonos town is different, so you might want to have a look at several before choosing yours. The owner tends the garden that often provides flowers for her son's restaurant, the Philippi (see "Where to Dine," below), which can be reached through the garden.

25 Kaloyera, Hora, 846 00 Mykonos. ✆ **22890/22-294.** Fax 22890/24-680. 13 units. 90€ double. No credit cards. **Amenities:** Restaurant; breakfast room.

Around the Island

Although most visitors prefer to stay in Hora and commute to the beaches, there are hotels near many of the more popular island beaches.

There are private studios and simple pensions at Paradise and Super Paradise beaches; but rooms are almost impossible to get, and prices more than double in July and August. Contact the **Mykonos Accommodations Center** (✆ **22890/23-160**)—or, for Super Paradise, **GATS Travel** (✆ **22890/22-404**)—for information on the properties they represent. The tavernas at each beach may also have suggestions.

AT KALAFATI The sprawling **Aphrodite Hotel** (✆ **22890/71-367**) has a large pool, two restaurants, and 150 rooms. It's a good value in May, June, and October, when a double costs from 100€. This place is popular with tour groups and Greek families.

AT ORNOS BAY ★★ Elegant **Kivotos Club Hotel ★★**, Ornos Bay, 846 00 Mykonos (✆ **22890/25-795;** fax 22890/22-844; www.kivotosclubhotel.gr), is a small, superb luxury hotel about 3km (1¾ miles) outside Mykonos town. Most of the 45 individually decorated units overlook the Bay of Ormos, but if you don't want to walk that far for a swim, head for the saltwater or freshwater pool, the Jacuzzi and sauna, or the pool with an underwater sound system piping in music! Kivotos is small enough to be intimate and tranquil; the service (including frozen towels for poolside guests on hot days) gets raves from guests. If you're ever tempted to leave, the hotel minibus will whisk you into town, but there are several restaurants on-site. The hotel even has its own traditional sailing ship, at the ready for spur-of-the moment sails. Doubles cost 290€ to 390€; suites are priced from 650€ to 1,000€.

The enormous **Santa Marina,** also at Ornos Bay (✆ **22890/23-200;** fax 22890/23-412), has 90 suites and villas on 8 landscaped hectares (20 acres) overlooking the bay. Like Kivotos, it has pools and spa facilities and its own restaurant; what it lacks is Kivotos's elegant intimacy. Doubles cost from 395€ to 600€; suites and villas, from 625€ to 2,400€; suites with private pool are available from 1,500€.

The more modest 25-unit **Best Western Dionysos Hotel** (✆ **22890/23-313**) is steps from the beach and has a pool, restaurant, bar, and air-conditioned rooms with fridges and TV; doubles cost from 200€. The even more modest 42-unit **Hotel Yiannaki** (✆ **22890/23-393**) is about 200m (656 ft.) away from the beach and has its own pool and restaurant; doubles begin at 125€. The nicest units have sea views and balconies.

Tips: Families traveling with children will find staying at one of the Ornos Bay hotels especially appealing. The beach is excellent and slopes into shallow, calm water. Furthermore, this is not one of Mykonos's all-night party beaches. If your hotel does not have watersports facilities, several of the local tavernas have surfboards and pedal boats to rent, as well as umbrellas. One minus: The beach is close to the airport, so you will hear planes come and go.

AT PLATI YIALOS The large and comfortable rooms of the 82-unit **Hotel Petassos Bay,** Plati Yialos, 846 00 Mykonos (✆ **22890/23-737;** fax 22890/24-101), all have air-conditioning and minibars. Doubles go for about 150€. Each has a balcony overlooking the relatively secluded beach, which is less than 36m (132 ft.) away. The hotel has a good-size pool, sun deck, Jacuzzi, gym, and sauna. It offers free round-trip transportation to and from the harbor or airport, safety-deposit boxes, and laundry service. The seaside restaurant has a great view and serves a big buffet breakfast (a smaller continental breakfast is included in the room rate).

AT AYIOS IOANNIS **Mykonos Grand** is a 100-room luxury resort a few kilometers out of Hora in Ayios Ioannis, 846 00 Mykonos (✆ **22890/25-555;** www.mykonosgrand.gr). With its own beach and many amenities—pools, tennis, squash, Jacuzzis, a spa—this is a very sybaritic place. The resort is popular with Greeks, Europeans, and Americans. Doubles start at 225€.

AT AYIOS STEPHANOS This popular resort, about 4km (2½ miles) north of Hora, has a number of hotels. Most close from November to March. The 38-unit boutique hotel beauty, **Mykonos Grace ★★**, Ayios Stefanos, 846 00 Mykonos (✆ **22890/26-690;** www.mykonosgrace.com), 230€ to 330€ double, 320€ to 420€ junior suite, was singled out by the *London Sunday Times* as one of the hippest new hotels of 2007 after its complete face-lift that year. Rooms range from standard to VIP suites, all with minimalistic design. Decor, food, privacy, pools, and Jacuzzis all get high marks—as do the prices, which are less extravagant than at some of Mykonos's other boutique hotels. It's only a 5-minute walk to town to boot. Other hotels here include the 38-unit **Princess of Mykonos,** Ayios Stephanos beach, 846 00 Mykonos (✆ **22890/23-806;** fax 22890/23-031), with bungalows, a gym, a pool, and an excellent beach; doubles cost from 200€. **Hotel Artemis,** Ayios Stephanos, 846 00 Mykonos (✆ **22890/22-345**), near the beach and bus stop, offers 23 units from 120€, breakfast included. Small but good-value **Hotel Mina,** Ayios Stephanos, 846 00 Mykonos (✆ **22890/23-024**), uphill behind the Artemis, has 15 doubles that go from 80€.

AT PSARROU BEACH **Grecotel Mykonos Blu ★★**, Psarrou Beach, 846 00 Mykonos (✆ **22890/27-900;** fax 22890/27-783; www.grecotel.gr), is another of the island's serious luxury hotels with award-winning Cyclades-inspired architecture. Like Cavo Tagoo and Kivotos, this place is popular with wealthy Greeks, honeymooners, and jet-setters. The private beach, large pool, and in-house Poets of the Aegean restaurant allow guests to be as lazy as they wish (although there is a fitness club and spa for the energetic). Doubles run from 250€ to 450€.

WHERE TO DINE

In addition to suggestions below on where to eat in Hora, here are some tips on where to eat when you are out on the island: On Psarou Beach, **N'Ammos** (✆ **22890/22-440**), with its casual elegance, varied menu (lobster-pumpkin risotto, anyone?), and beachfront setting, is one of the island's finest restaurants; entrees start at 25€. At Ayios Sostis Beach, **Kiki's Taverna** is reminiscent of the Greece that was: a small taverna (no phone, no sign, no electricity!) with a garden, where perfect grills and salads are served; entrees start at 8€. At Fokos Beach, the **Fokos** (✆ **22890/23-205**) has local meat and fish with fresh veggies flown in from the owners' garden on Crete; entrees start at 8€.

In Mykonos town**, Camares Cafe** (✆ **22890/28-570**), on Mavroyenous (Taxi) Square, has light meals and a fine view of the harbor from its terrace. It's open 24 hours and, for Mykonos, is very reasonably priced. Try the *striftopita* or crispy fried *xinotiro* (bitter cheese) and the thyme-scented grilled lamb chops. As is usual on the islands, most of the harborside tavernas are expensive and mediocre, although **Kounelas** on the harbor (no phone) is still a good value for fresh fish—as attested to by the presence of locals dining here. Dinner for two at either place from 50€.

Antonini's ★ GREEK Antonini's is one of the oldest of Mykonos's restaurants, and it serves consistently decent stews, chops, and mezedes. Locals still eat here, although in summer they tend to leave the place to tourists.

Plateia Manto, Hora. ✆ **22890/22-319.** Main courses 9€–20€. No credit cards. Summer daily noon–3pm and 7pm–1am. Usually closed Nov–Mar.

Edem Restaurant ★ GREEK/CONTINENTAL This is one of the oldest restaurants in Hora, with a reputation for good food built over 30 years. Tables are clustered around a courtyard pool—diners have been known to make a splash upon arrival with a preprandial swim—and the sunny courtyard is a pleasant place to enjoy a leisurely dinner even if you aren't dressed for the water. Edem is known especially for its variety of lamb dishes and fresh fish—but the eclectic menu includes steak, pasta, and a variety of traditional Greek and Continental dishes. The service is good and the produce as fresh as you'll see on Mykonos.

Above Panachra Church, Hora. ✆ **22890/23-355.** Reservations recommended July–Aug. Main courses 18€–40€. AE, DC, MC, V. Daily 6pm–1am; in off season, sometimes open for lunch.

Interni ★★ ASIAN FUSION With its avant-garde space and exceptional fusion cuisine, Interni is one of the island's most fashionable restaurants. A happening bar scene is popular with affluent young Athenians, but the attraction here is the cuisine. Consider the marinated salmon and stir-fried seafood noodles and you will see what all the fuss is about.

Hora, Matoyanni. ✆ **22890/26-333.** www.interni.gr. Main courses 18€–40€. DC, V. Daily 8pm–2am.

Mamakas Mykonos ★★ GREEK/MODERN This is a branch of the Mamakas that opened its second location in the down-at-the-heels area of Gazi in Athens in 1998 and helped transform the area from gritty to chic, and managed to start a new trend, traditional taverna fare with modern twists. This is where it all started, right by the Taxi Square, inside a lovely house built in 1845. You can dine in the courtyard (the terra-cotta planters were a gift from the Princess of Malta to the present owner's grandmother) or indoors. The meals are just as delicious and reasonably priced as ever. Check out the trays of cooked dishes *(magirefta)* and a range of dependable and delicious grills and appetizers—the spicy meatballs *(keftedakia)* are a must!

Hora, Mykonos. ✆ **22890/26-120.** Main courses 14€–30€. AE, MC, V. Daily 8pm–1:30am.

Matsuhisha Mykonos ★★ JAPANESE/SOUTH AMERICAN Nobu Matsuhisha has extended his sushi empire to this, his only open-air restaurant in the most happening hotel in town, the Belvedere. Right by the hotel's pool, with views of the sea and town, try the exceptional Japanese cuisine with Latin influences. Prices are very steep but the top-quality ingredients and sushi are flown in daily from Japan. Begin with a Sakepirnha, the famous Brazilian cocktail made with sake instead of cachaca, and then continue to pick your way through the chef's choice tasting menu.

At the Belvedere Hotel, Hora. ✆ **22890/25-122.** www.matsuhisamykonos.com. Reservations essential July–Sept. Main courses 68€–85€. AE, DC, MC, V. Daily 8pm–1am.

Philippi ★ GREEK/CONTINENTAL One of the island's most romantic dining experiences, Philippi is in a quiet garden. Old Greek favorites share space on the menu with French dishes and a more than usually impressive wine list. What this restaurant provides in abundance is atmosphere, and that's what has made it a perennial favorite.

Just off Matogianni and Kaloyera behind the eponymous hotel, Hora. ✆ **22890/22-294.** Reservations recommended July–Aug. Main courses 10€–25€. AE, MC, V. Daily 7pm–1am.

Sea Satin Market ★★ GREEK/SEAFOOD Below the windmills, beyond the small beach adjacent to Little Venice, the *paralia* (coastline) ends in a rocky headland facing the open sea. This is the remarkable location of one of Hora's most charming restaurants. Set apart from the clamor of the town, it's one of the quietest spots in the area despite the fact that the closing scene of *The Bourne Identity* was filmed here. On a still night just after sunset, the atmosphere is all you could hope for on a Greek island. At the front of the restaurant, the kitchen activity is on view along with the day's catch sizzling on the grill. You can make a modest meal on *mezedes* here, or let it rip with grilled bon filet.

Near the Mitropolis Cathedral, Hora. ✆ **22890/24-676.** Main courses 20€–45€. No credit cards. Daily 6:30pm–12:30am.

EXPLORING THE ISLAND

Even if you're here for the beaches or to visit the island of Delos, you'll probably want to spend some time exploring Hora, enjoying the twists and turns of the narrow streets, and admiring the harborfront's resident pelican. Try to remember to make haste slowly, and enjoy the unexpected sights you'll see when you (inevitably!) get lost in Hora's maze of narrow passageways. Keep in mind that the town is bounded on two sides by the bay, and on the other two by the busy vehicular District Road, and that all paths funnel eventually into one of the main squares: **Plateia Mantos Mavroyenous,** on the port (called **Taxi Square** because it's the main taxi stand); **Plateia Tria Pigadia;** and **Plateia Laka,** near the south bus station.

As you wander, you'll see Hora's small **Venetian Kastro** (fortress) and the island's most famous church, the **Panagia Paraportiani (Our Lady of the Postern Gate),** a thickly whitewashed asymmetrical edifice made up of four small chapels. Beyond the Panagia Paraportiani is the Alefkandra quarter, better known as **Little Venice ★★**, for its cluster of homes built overhanging the sea. This is the place to have that martini or margarita in one of the cheek-by-jowl edgy bars with drop-dead sunset views. Another place for sunset views and sundowners: the famous **Tria Pigadia (Three Wells) ★★**. Local legend says that if a virgin drinks from all three she is sure to find a husband; it's probably not a good idea to test this hypothesis by drinking the brackish well water. After you visit the Tria Pigadia, you may want to take in the famous **windmills** of **Kato Myli** and enjoy the views back toward Little Venice and out to sea.

Mykonos has a clutch of (largely neglected) small museums; visit almost any one and you may have it to yourself—and learn a lot about the island. Many of the museums keep somewhat irregular hours, but if one is closed, another is nearby. The **Nautical Museum of the Aegean** (✆ **22890/22-700**), across from the park on Enoplon Dinameon Street, has just what you'd expect, including some handsome ship models; usually open daily from 10:30am to 1pm and 7 to 9pm; admission is 3€. Also on Enoplon Dinameon Street, **Lena's House** (✆ **22890/22-591**) re-creates the home of a middle-class 19th-century Mykonos family; usually open daily Easter through October; free admission. The **Museum of Folklore** (✆ **22890/25-591**), in a 19th-century sea captain's mansion near the quay, has examples of local crafts and furnishings and a re-created 19th-century island kitchen; usually open Monday through Saturday from 4 to 8pm; admission is free. The **Archaeological Museum** (✆ **22890/22-325**), near the harbor, has finds from Delos; it's open Monday and Wednesday through Saturday from 9am to 3:30pm, Sunday and holidays from 10am to 3pm. Admission is 3€; free on Sunday.

THE SHOPS Mykonos has a lot of shops, many selling overpriced souvenirs, clothing, and jewelry to cruise ship day-trippers. That said, there are also a number of serious shops here, selling serious wares—at serious prices. **Soho-Soho,** 81 Matoyanni (✆ **22890/26-760**), is by far the most well-known clothing store on the island; pictures of its famous clientele (Tom Hanks, Sarah Jessica Parker, and so forth) carrying the store's bags have been in gossip publications around the world. Mykonos is also well known for its house-designed sandals in many colors and styles; perhaps no better selection can be found in the entire island than at **Eccentric by Design,** 11 Fiorou Zouganelis St. (✆ **22890/28-499**), where you can even find sandals encrusted with Swarvoski crystals. For more traditional sandals, check out **Kostas Rabias** on Matogianni Street (✆ **22890/22-010**). The finest jewelry shop on the island remains **LALAoUNIS ★**, 14 Polykandrioti (✆ **22890/22-444**), associated with the famous LALAoUNIS museum and shops in Athens. It has superb reproductions of ancient and Byzantine jewelry as well as original designs. If you can't afford LALAoUNIS, you might check out one of the island's oldest jewelry shops, the **Gold Store,** right on the waterfront (✆ **22890/22-397**). If you want to see some serious works of art, try the **Scala Gallery,** 48 Matoyianni (✆ **22890/23-407;** www.scalagallery.gr), which represents a wide range of contemporary Greek artists and frequently has exhibitions. Nearby on Panahrandou is **Scala II Gallery** (✆ **22890/26-993;** scala@otenet.gr), where the overflow from the Scala Gallery is sold at reduced prices. In addition, manager Dimitris Roussounelos of Scala Gallery manages a number of studios and apartments in Hora, so you might find lodgings as well as art at Scala!

There was a time when Mykonos was world-famous for its vegetable-dyed hand-loomed weavings, especially those of the legendary Kuria Vienoula. Today, **Nikoletta** (✆ **22890/27-503**) is one of the few shops where you can still see the island's traditional loomed goods. Eleni Kontiza's tiny shop **Hand Made** (✆ **22890/27-512**), on a lane between Plateia Tria Pigadia and Plateia Laka, has a good selection of hand-woven scarves, rugs, and tablecloths from around Greece.

Beach Notes

Activity on the beaches is highly seasonal, and all the information offered here pertains only to the months of June through September. The prevailing winds on Mykonos (and throughout the Cyclades) blow from the north, which is why the southern beaches are the most protected and calm. The exception to this rule is a southern wind that occurs periodically during the summer, making the northern beaches more desirable for sunning and swimming. In Mykonos town, this southern wind is heralded by particularly hot temperatures and perfect calm in the harbor. On such days, those in the know will avoid Paradise, Super Paradise, and Elia, heading instead to the northern beaches of Ayios Sostis and Panormos—or simply choose another activity for the day.

Works of culinary art can be found at **Skaropoulos** (✆ **22890/24-983**), 1.5km (1 mile) out of Hora on the road to Ano Mera, featuring the Mykonian specialties of Nikos and Frantzeska Koukas. Nikos's grandfather started making confections here in 1921, winning prizes and earning a personal commendation from Winston Churchill. Try their famed *amygdalota* (an almond sweet) or the almond biscuits (Churchill's favorite). You can also find Skaropoulos sweets at **Pantopoleion,** 24 Kaloyerou (✆ **22890/22-078**), along with Greek organic foods and natural cosmetics; the shop is in a beautifully restored 300-year-old Mykonian house. When you finish your shopping, treat yourself to yet another almond treat, from **Efthemios,** 4 Florou Zouganeli (✆ **22890/22-281**), off the harborfront.

THE BEACHES If you've come to Mykonos to find a secluded beach, you have made a serious mistake! People come to Mykonos to see and be seen, whether in their best togs at cafes or naked on nudist beaches. If you want to hit the "in" beaches, take a little time to ask around, because beaches go in and out of favor quickly. Then catch the bus or a caique to the beach of your choice. If you want a quick swim, the closest beach to Hora is **Megali Ammos (Big Sand),** about a 10-minute walk south of town, and usually very crowded.

Plati Yialos is another favorite. It's served by a bus that runs every 15 minutes from 8am to 8pm, and then every 30 minutes until midnight during the summer. If Plati Yialos is too crowded, you can catch a caique there for the more distant beaches of Paradise, Super Paradise, Agrari, and Elia. **Paradise,** the island's most famous nude beach, is popular with the gay crowd despite the wall-to-wall umbrellas.

Paradise is never a quiet experience but it is the premier party beach of the island and shows no signs of stopping. The **Tropicana Beach Bar** and the **Sunrise Bar** are both havens for the party crowd that goes all day, long after the sun has set. On top of the hill, the popular and internationally known **Cavo Paradiso Club** is a large, open-air nightclub with rotating international DJs and doors that do not open until after 2am. In fact, the "cool crowd" begins to arrive only after 5am. On the beach Paradise Club is the club destination from 6pm to midnight and then reopens again from 2 to 6am. One beach party on Paradise you shouldn't miss is the **Full Moon Party,** once a month. The only other party that compares to it is the **Closing Party** every September that has become an island institution. As in most of the island, the water here is breathtakingly beautiful, but hardly anybody comes to Paradise for the sea.

Elia, a 45-minute caique ride from Plati Yialos, is one of the island's best and largest beaches, attracting many nudists, gays, and—thanks to **Watermania,** a theme park with a water slide—families with children (open daily in season 9am–midnight; 12€ adults, 6€ children 11 and under).

The next major beach, **Kalo Livadi (Good Pasture),** a beautiful spot in an idyllic farming valley, is accessible by a scramble over the peninsula east from Elia and by bus from the north station in the summer. This is about as quiet a beach as you will find on Mykonos.

The last resort area on the southern coast accessible by bus from the north station is at **Kalafati,** a fishing village that was once the port for the ancient citadel of Mykonos. It's now dominated by the large Aphrodite Beach Hotel complex. Several miles farther east, accessible by a fairly good road from Kalafati, is **Lia,** which has fine sand, clear water, bamboo windbreaks, and a small taverna.

On the north coast, **Panormos** and **Ayios Sostis** are popular, but usually less crowded than beaches to the south. At press time, rental chairs and umbrellas were not available at these beaches, but there are several small tavernas.

Beaches to avoid on Mykonos because of pollution, noise, and crowds include **Tourlos** and **Korfos Bay.**

DIVING

The best established dive center is **Mykonos Diving Centre,** at Paradise Beach (✆/fax **22890/24-808**), which offers 5-day PADI certification courses in English from about 500€, including equipment. **Psarou Diving Center** in Mykonos town (✆ **22890/24-808**) has also been around for a long time. As always, before you sign up for lessons, be sure that all instructors are PADI certified. The **Union of Diving Centers in Athens** (✆ **210/411-8909**) usually has up-to-date information. In general, certified divers can join guided dives from 50€ per dive; beginners can take a 2-hour class and beach dive from 60€. There's a nearby wreck at a depth of 20 to 35m (65–114 ft.); wreck dives run from 60€.

MYKONOS AFTER DARK

Mykonos has the liveliest, most abundant (and expensive), and most chameleon-like nightlife—especially gay nightlife—in the Aegean. How much are you going to spend for one drink at a chic spot on Mykonos? As little as 10€—and after that, the sky really is the limit! By the way, don't think that you have to wait until after dark to party: There are plenty of virtually all-day beach parties here, especially at Psarrou, Paradise, and Super Paradise beaches. New places open and shut here every season. I'm not giving phone numbers for these bars and clubs—the official phones simply are not answered at these places, where staff carry and use private cellphones. At Super Paradise, two loud bar/clubs on opposite sides of the beach cater to gay and mixed crowds, respectively. At Paradise Beach's **Paradise Club,** all-day partying becomes all night around the gigantic swimming pool in the middle of the club, which steals the show with its nightly fireworks.

Back in town, things are less wild and more sophisticated around sunset. For over quarter of a century, **Caprice** has been the island's sunset institution, with chairs lined along its narrow porch overlooking Little Venice, the windmills, and the sea.

Other Little Venice hot spots include **Kastro,** near the Paraportiani Church; **Montparnasse; Veranda,** in an old mansion overlooking the water; and **Galeraki,** with its wide variety of exotic cocktails (and customers)—the in-house art gallery gives this popular spot its name, "Little Gallery."

The Mykonos scene really gets going well after dinner—some of these places are at their liveliest just before dawn. Right at the entrance of town from the old harbor, the Athenian hot spot Spanish restaurant/bar/club **El Pecado (the Sin)** moves to Mykonos in the summer and is famous for its sangria and the rum-based drinks combined with the Latin beats. Right on busy Matoyanni Street, in one of the finest people-watching locations, the **Aroma** bar goes day and night, as does **Astra. Uno,** a tiny bar also on Matoyanni, is a popular destination for Athenians—peek inside to see why or join in the fun. Also on Matoyanni, **Pierro's** is extremely popular with gay visitors and rocks all night long to American and European music. Adjacent **Icarus** is best known for its terrace and late-night drag shows. During the early-evening hours, both bars are so popular that sometimes just walking by is difficult. In Taxi Square, another popular gay club, **Ramrod,** has a terrace with a view over the harbor and live drag shows after midnight.

The **Anchor** plays blues, jazz, and classic rock for its 30-something clients, as do **Argo, Stavros Irish Bar, Celebrities Bar,** and **Scandinavian Bar-Disco.** They draw customers from Ireland, Scandinavia, and quite possibly as far away as Antarctica. If you'd like to sample Greek music and dancing, try **Thalami,** a small club underneath the town hall. For a more intense Greek night out, head to **Guzel**—at Gialos, by the waterfront and near the Taxi Square—the place to experience a supertrendy hangout populated mostly by trendy Athenians with Greek and international hits that drive the crowd into a frenzy, with people dancing on the tables and on the bars.

If having a quiet evening and catching a movie is more your speed, head for **Cinemanto** (**✆ 22890/27-190**), which shows films nightly around 9pm. Many films are American; most Greek films have English subtitles.

AN EXCURSION TO THE ISLAND OF DELOS ★★★

There is as much to see at **Delos** as at Olympia and Delphi, and there is absolutely no shade on this blindingly white marble island covered with shining marble monuments. Just 3km (1¾ miles) from Mykonos, little Delos was considered by the ancient Greeks to be one of the holiest of sanctuaries, the fixed point around which the other Cycladic islands circled. It was Poseidon who anchored Delos to make a sanctuary for Leto, impregnated by Zeus and pursued by Zeus's aggrieved wife Hera. Here, on Delos, Leto gave birth to Apollo and his sister Artemis; thereafter, Delos was sacred to both gods, although Apollo's sanctuary was the more important. For much of antiquity, people were not allowed to die or be born on this sacred island, but were bundled off to the nearby islet of Rinia.

Delos was not exclusively a religious sanctuary: For much of its history, the island was a thriving commercial port, especially under the Romans in the 3rd and 2nd centuries B.C. As many as 10,000 slaves a day were sold here on some days; the island's prosperity went into a steep decline after Mithridates of Pontus, an Asia Minor monarch at war with Rome, attacked Delos in 88 B.C., slaughtered its 20,000 inhabitants, and sailed home with as much booty as his ships could carry.

The easiest way to get to Delos is by caique from Mykonos; in summer, there are sometimes excursion boats here from Tinos and Paros. Try not to have a late night before you come here and catch the first boat of the day (usually around 8:30am). As the day goes on, the heat and crowds here can be overwhelming. On summer afternoons, when cruise ships disgorge their passengers, Delos can make the Acropolis look shady and deserted. Sturdy shoes are a good idea here; a hat, water, munchies, and sunscreen are a necessity. There is a cafe near the museum, but the prices are high, the quality is poor, and the service is even worse.

Carpe Diem

Heavy seas can suddenly prevent boats docking at Delos. Follow the advice of the Roman poet Horace and *carpe diem* (seize the day). Come here as soon as possible; if you decide to save your visit here for your last day in the area, rough seas may leave you stranded ashore.

GETTING THERE From Mykonos, organized guided and unguided excursions leave starting about 8:30am about four times a day Tuesday through Sunday at the harbor's west end. Every travel agency in town advertises its Delos excursions (some with guides). Individual caique owners also have signs stating their prices and schedules. The trip takes about 30 minutes and costs about 10€ round-trip; as long as you return with the boat that brought you, you can (space available) decide which return trip you want to take when you've had enough. The last boat for Mykonos usually leaves by 4pm. The site is **closed** on Mondays.

Exploring the Site

Joint entrance to the site and museum costs 6€, unless this was included in the price of your excursion. Signs throughout the site are in Greek and French (the French have excavated here since the late 19th c.).

The remains at Delos are scattered and not easy to decipher, but when you come ashore, you can head right toward the theater and residential area or left to the more public area of ancient Delos, the agora, the famous **Avenue of the Lions ★**, and the museum. If your time is limited, head left, toward the **Agora,** with scattered remains of the central market and civic area on ancient Delos. The agora mainly dates from the Roman period when Delos was more important as a port than as a religious sanctuary. To reach the earlier religious sanctuary, take the **Sacred Way** north from the agora toward the Sanctuary of Apollo. As at Delphi and Olympia, the sanctuary here on Delos would have been chockablock with temples, altars, statues, and votive offerings. You can see some of what remains in the **museum,** which has finds from the various excavations on the island. Beside the museum, the remains of the Sanctuary of Dionysos are usually identifiable by the crowd snapping shots of the display of marble phalluses, many on tall plinths.

North of the museum and the adjacent Tourist Pavilion is the **Sacred Lake,** where swans credited with powers of uttering oracles once swam. The lake is now little more than a dusty indentation most of the year, surrounded by a low wall. Beyond it is the famous **Avenue of the Lions ★**, made of Naxian marble and erected in the 7th century B.C. There were originally at least nine lions. One was taken away to Venice in the 17th century and now stands before the arsenal there. The whereabouts of the others lost in antiquity remain a mystery; five were carted off to the museum for restoration some years ago and replaced by replicas. Beyond the lake to the northeast is the large square courtyard of the gymnasium and the long narrow stadium, where the athletic competitions of the Delian Games were held.

If you stroll back along the Sacred Way to the harbor, you can head next to the **Maritime quarter,** a residential area with the remains of houses from the Hellenistic and Roman eras, when the island reached its peak in wealth and prestige. Several houses and magnificent villas contain brilliant **mosaics ★**, including Dionysos riding a panther in the **House of the Masks,** and a similar depiction in the **House of Dionysos.** Farther to the south is the massive **Theater,** which seated 5,500 people and was the site of choral competitions during the Delian Festivals, an event held every 4 years that included athletic competitions in addition to musical contests. If you visit here in spring, the wildflowers are especially beautiful, and the chorus of frogs that live in and around the ancient cisterns near the theater will be at its peak.

If you want to take in a great view of the site—and of the Cyclades—take the stepped path up **Mount Kinthos ★**, the highest point (112m/370 ft.) on the island. On many days, nearby Mykonos, Siros to the west, Tinos to the north, and Naxos and Paros to the south are easy to spot. On your way down, keep an eye out for the **Grotto of Hercules,** a small temple built into a natural crevice in the mountainside—the roof is formed of massive granite slabs held up by their own enormous weight.

Santorini (Thira) ★★★

This is one of the most spectacular islands in the world. Many Greeks joke, somewhat begrudgingly, that there are foreigners who know where Santorini is—but are confused about where Greece is! Especially if you arrive by sea, you won't confuse Santorini with any of the other Cyclades. What will confuse you is that the island is also known as Thira. While large ships to Santorini (pop. 7,000) dock at the port of Athinios, many small ships arrive in Skala, a spectacular harbor that's part of the enormous caldera (crater) formed when a volcano blew out the island's center sometime between 1600 and 1500 B.C. To this day, some scholars speculate that this destruction gave birth to the myth of the lost continent of Atlantis.

Your first choice upon disembarking at Skala will be to decide whether you want to ride the funicular (5€) or a donkey (5€) the 335m (1,100 ft.) up the sheer sides of the caldera to the island's capital, Fira. If you arrive on a large ship, you'll be spared this choice, as you'll dock at the new harbor at Athinios and grab a bus (2€) or cab (about 9€) into Fira. Once there, you may decide to reward yourself with a glass of the island's rosé wine before you explore the shops and restaurants of Fira, swim at the black volcanic beach of Kamari, or visit the dazzling site of Minoan Akrotiri, an Aegean Pompeii destroyed when the volcano erupted. (Don't worry—it's dormant now.)

Tip: The best advice we can offer is to avoid visiting here during the months of July and August. Santorini disappears under the weight of tourists during peak season, and crowds make strolling the streets of Fira and Oia next to impossible.

The real wonder is that Santorini exceeds all glossy picture-postcard expectations. Like an enormous crescent moon, Santorini encloses the pure blue waters of its caldera, the core of an ancient volcano. Its two principal towns, **Fira** and **Oia** (also transliterated as **Ia**), perch at the summit of the caldera; as you approach by ship, bending back as far as possible to look as far up the cliffs as possible, whitewashed houses look like a dusting of new snow on the mountaintop. Up close, you'll find that both towns' main streets have more shops (*lots* of jewelry shops), restaurants, and discos than private homes.

Akrotiri is Santorini's principal archaeological wonder: a town destroyed by the volcano eruption here, but miraculously preserved under layers of lava. As soon as you reach Santorini, check to see if Akrotiri is open; the site's protective roof collapsed in 2005 and the site has been totally, or partially, closed since then. If Akrotiri is closed, don't despair: If it weren't that Akrotiri steals its thunder, the site of **Ancient Thira** would be the island's must-see destination. Spectacularly situated atop a high promontory, overlooking a black lava beach, the remains of this Greek, Roman, and Byzantine city sprawl over acres of rugged terrain. Ancient Thira is reached after a vertiginous hike or drive up (and up) to the acropolis itself.

Arid Santorini isn't known for the profusion of its agricultural products, but the rocky island soil has long produced a plentiful grape harvest, and the local wines are among the finest in Greece. Be sure to visit one of the island **wineries** for a tasting. And keep an eye out for the tasty, tiny unique Santorini tomatoes and white eggplants—and the unusually large and zesty capers. Most important, allow yourself time to see at least one sunset over the caldera; the best views are from the ramparts of the kastro and from the footpath between Fira and Oia.

Tip: Some accommodations rates can be marked down by as much as 50% if you come off season. Virtually all accommodations are marked up by at least as much for desperate arrivals without reservations in July and August.

ESSENTIALS

Getting There

BY AIR **Olympic Air** (✆ **210/926-9111;** www.olympicair.com), the former Olympic Airlines, offers daily flights between Athens and the Santorini airport Monolithos (✆ **22860/31-525**), which also receives European charters. There are frequent connections with Mykonos and Rhodes, and service two or three times per week to and from Iraklion, Crete. **Aegean Airlines** (✆ **210/998-2888** or 210/998-8300 in Athens), with an office at the Monolithos airport (✆ **22860/28-500**), also has several flights daily between Athens and Santorini. A bus to Fira (3€) meets most flights; the schedule is posted at the bus stop, beside the airport entrance. A taxi to Fira costs about 12€.

BY SEA Ferry service runs to and from Piraeus at least twice daily; the trip takes 9 to 10 hours by car ferry on the Piraeus-Paros-Naxos-Ios-Santorini route, or 4 hours by catamaran if you go via Piraeus-Paros-Santorini. **Excursion boats** go to and from Iraklion, Crete, almost daily. All boats are notoriously late or early; your travel or ticket agent will give you an estimate of times involved in your journey. High-speed **hydrofoils** connect Santorini with Ios, Paros, Mykonos, and Iraklio, Crete, almost daily in the high season and three times weekly in the low season, if the winds aren't too strong. Information on all schedules is available from the Athens **GNTO** (✆ **210/870-0000;** www.gnto.gr), the **Piraeus Port Authority** (✆ **210/451-1311** or 1440 or 1441; phone not always answered), or the **Santorini Port Authority** (✆ **22860/22-239**).

VISITOR INFORMATION **Nomikos Travel** (✆ **22860/23-660;** www.nomikosvillas.gr), **Bellonias Tours** (✆ **22860/22-469**), and **Kamari Tours** (✆ **22860/31-390**) are well established on the island. Nomikos and Bellonias offer bus tours of the island, boat excursions around the caldera, and submarine tours beneath the caldera. Expect to pay about 40€ to join a bus tour to Akrotiri or Ancient Thira, about the same for a day-trip boat excursion to the caldera islands, and about twice that for the submarine excursion.

Getting Around

BY BUS Santorini has very good bus service. The island's central bus station is just south of the main square in Fira. Schedules and prices are posted on the wall of the office above it; most routes are serviced every half-hour from 7am to 11pm in the summer, less frequently in the off season.

BY CAR The travel agents listed above can help you rent a car. You might find that a local company such as **Zeus** (✆ **22860/24-013**) offers better prices than the big names, although the quality might be a bit lower. Be sure to take full insurance. Of the better-known agencies, try **Budget,** at the airport (✆ **22860/33-290**), or in Fira a block below the small square that the bus station is on (✆ **22860/22-900**); a small car should cost about 60€ a day, with unlimited mileage. If you reserve in advance through Budget in the U.S. (✆ **800/527-0700**), you should be able to beat that price.

Warning: Something to keep in mind if you rent a car: If you park in town or in a no-parking area, the police will remove your license plates and you, not the car-rental office, will have to find the police station and pay a steep fine to get them back. There's a free parking lot—often full—on the port's north side.

BY MOPED Many roads on the island are narrow and winding; add local drivers who take the roads at high speed, and visiting drivers who aren't sure where they're going, and you'll understand the island's high accident rate. If you're determined to use two-wheeled transportation, expect to pay about 25€ per day, less during off season. Greek law now requires wearing a helmet; not all agents supply the helmet.

BY TAXI The taxi station is just south of the main square. In high season, book ahead by phone (✆ **22860/22-555** or 22860/23-951) if you want a taxi for an excursion; be sure that you agree on the price before you set out. For most point-to-point trips (Fira to Oia, for example), the prices are fixed. If you call for a taxi outside Fira, you'll be charged a pickup fee of at least 2€; also, you're required to pay the driver's fare from Fira to your pickup point. Bus service shuts down at midnight, so book a taxi in advance if you'll need it late at night.

FAST FACTS The **National Bank** (Mon–Fri 8am–2pm), with an ATM, is a block south of the main square on the right near the taxi station. The **health clinic** (✆ **22860/22-237**) is on the southeast edge of town, near the bus station and Olympic Air office. There are a number of **Internet** cafes on the main square, including P.C. Club, in the Markozannes Tours office (✆ **22860/25-551**). There are several do-it-yourself launderettes in Fira; if you want your wash done for you, **Penguin Laundry** (✆ **22860/22-168**) is at the edge of Fira on the road to Oia, 200m (656 ft.) north of the main square. The **police** (✆ **22860/22-649**) are several blocks south of the main square, near the post office. For the **port police,** call ✆ **22860/22-239.** The **post office** (✆ **22860/22-238**), open Monday through Friday from 8am to 1pm, is south of the bus station. The **telephone office (OTE)** is off Ipapantis, up from the post office; hours are Monday through Saturday from 8am to 3pm.

WHERE TO STAY

Santorini is always packed in July and August—and increasingly crowded virtually year-round. If you plan a summer visit, make a reservation at least 2 months in advance. If you arrive without a reservation, try not to accept rooms offered (sight unseen) at the port—many are located in villages quite a distance from what you've come here to see. If you come between April and mid-June or in September or October, when the island is less crowded and far more pleasant, the rates can be less than the high-season rates we quote. Keep in mind that during the off season many of the hotels, restaurants, shops, and bars here close. Most of the hotels recommended below don't have air-conditioning, but with cool breezes blowing through, you won't need it; if you take a room here in the winter, make sure that it offers working central heat or a serviceable room heater. ***Note:*** Unless you're going to be participating in Fira's energetic nightlife, you may want to consider avoiding the hubbub by staying in one of the villages out on the island. We do suggest several hotels in Fira that are usually quiet.

In & Around Fira

Aigialos ★★ In a quiet caldera location, occupying 16 restored 18th- and 19th-century town houses, the Aigialos proclaims its intention to be a "Luxury Traditional Settlement." The oxymoron aside—rather few traditional settlements here or elsewhere have Jacuzzis, swimming pools, and counter swim exercise pools—this is a nifty place. As the price goes up, you get more space (two bathrooms, not just one) and more privacy (your own, not a shared terrace or your own balcony). There's an extensive breakfast buffet and a highly praised in-house, guests-only restaurant.

Fira, 847 00 Santorini. ✆ **22860/25-191.** www.aigialos.gr. 16 units. 400€–550€ double. Rates include breakfast. AE, DC, MC, V. Closed Nov–Mar. **Amenities:** Pool bar; pool; room service. *In room:* A/C, TV/DVD, CD player, fridge, Internet.

Hotel Aressana ★★ This hotel compensates for its lack of a caldera view with a large swimming pool and an excellent location, tucked away behind the Orthodox cathedral, in a relatively quiet location. Most rooms have balconies or terraces; many have the high barrel-vaulted ceilings typical of this island. Unusual in Greece are the nonsmoking rooms. The breakfast room opens onto the pool terrace, as do most of the guest rooms; the elaborate buffet breakfast includes numerous Santorinian specialties. The Aressana also maintains seven nearby apartments facing the caldera, starting at 250€, which includes use of the hotel pool.

Fira, 847 00 Santorini. ✆ **22860/23-900.** Fax 22860/23-902. www.aressana.gr. 50 units, 1 with shower. 250€–300€. Rates include full breakfast. AE, DC, MC, V. Closed mid-Nov to Feb. **Amenities:** Snack bar; bar; Internet; freshwater pool; room service. *In room:* A/C, TV, minibar.

Hotel Keti ★★ This simple little hotel offers one of the best bargains on the caldera. All of the (smallish) rooms have traditional vaulted ceilings and white walls and coverlets, and open onto a shared terrace overlooking the caldera. The bathrooms, at the back of the rooms, are carved into the cliff face. Clearly, the Keti is doing something right: Not many places this modest make it into Alastair Sawday's *Special Places*. One drawback if you have trouble walking: It's a steep 5- to 10-minute walk from the Keti's quiet cliff-side location to Fira itself.

Fira, 847 00 Santorini. ✆ **22860/22-324.** www.hotelketi.gr. 7 units. 100€–150€ double. No credit cards. Closed Nov to mid-Mar. **Amenities:** Breakfast room; bar. *In room:* A/C, TV, fridge, safe.

Pension George ★ With a small pool, simple wood furnishings, attractive and reasonably priced rooms, and helpful owners, the Pension offers good value if you're on a budget. To save even more money, opt for a room without a balcony. George and Helen Halaris will help you arrange car and boat rentals.

P.O. Box 324, Karterados, 847 00 Santorini. ✆ **22860/22-351.** www.pensiongeorge.com. 25 units. 60€–100€ double. Inquire about apts that sleep 2–5. No credit cards. **Amenities:** Breakfast on request; free transportation to airport or harbor. *In room:* A/C, TV (in some), fridge.

Around the Island

Astra Apartments ★★★ Perched on a cliff side, with spectacular views, this is one of the nicest places to stay in all of Greece. There are other places nearby which also have spectacular pools with spectacular views, but manager George Karayiannis is a large part of what makes Astra so special: He is always at the ready to arrange car rentals, recommend a wonderful beach or restaurant—or even help you plan your wedding and honeymoon here. The Astra Apartments look like a tiny, whitewashed village (with an elegant pool) set in the village of Imerovigli, which is still much less crowded than Fira or Oia. Nothing is flashy here; everything is just right. There are spa services (massage, sauna, and Jacuzzi) and a Greek-Mediterranean full-service restaurant that emphasizes local cuisine.

Imerovigli, 847 00 Santorini. ✆ **22860/23-641.** Fax 22860/24-765. www.astra-apartments.com. 16 apts, 12 suites. 200€–400€ apt; 500€–800€ suite. MC, V. **Amenities:** Restaurant; bar; pool; spa services. *In room:* A/C, TV/DVD, CD player, kitchenette, Wi-Fi.

Katikies ★★ If you find a more spectacular pool anywhere on the island, let us know: This one runs virtually to the side of the caldera so that you can paddle around and enjoy an endless view. (There's also a smaller pool intended for the use of guests staying in suites.) The hotel's island-style architecture incorporates twists and turns, secluded patios, beamed ceilings, and antiques. If the people in the next room like to sing in the shower, you might hear them—but most people who stay here treasure the tranquillity.

Oia, 847 02 Santorini. ✆ **22860/71-401.** Fax 22860/71-129. www.katikies.com. 22 units. 350€–420€ double. Rates include breakfast. MC, V. **Amenities:** 4 restaurants; bar; concierge; health club & spa; 4 pools; Wi-Fi. *In room:* A/C, TV, hair dryer, minibar.

Zannos Melathron ★★ Relatively uncrowded Pyrgos sits inland between Megalohori and Kamari. This 12-room boutique hotel, on one of the highest points on the island, occupies an 18th-century and a 19th-century building. The rooms mix antiques with modern pieces, the island views are lovely, the pool is welcoming. If you want nightlife, this is not the place for you; if you want a peaceful retreat and near-perfect service, this may be just the spot. If you want a cigar bar, look no further.

Pyrgos, 847 00 Santorini. ✆ **22860/28-220.** www.zannos.gr. 12 units. 250€–450€ double; 550€–1,000€ suite. MC, V (credit card required to make reservation, but cash usually expected for payment). **Amenities:** Restaurant; bar; airport pickup; concierge; pool; room service. *In room:* A/C, TV, minibar, Wi-Fi.

WHERE TO DINE

In Fira

Koukoumavlos ★★ GREEK The terrace at Koukoumavlos enjoys the famous caldera view, but unlike most caldera restaurants where a spectacular view compensates for mediocre food, here the view is a distraction from the inventive, even idiosyncratic, menu. One example: lobster and monkfish terrine with anchovy-caviar sour cream in a forest-fruit tea sauce. In short, you are likely to be either titillated or terrified by the combination of ingredients in most dishes. In either case, you are likely to be knocked over by the prices (salads at around 20€). Despite the pretentions of the cuisine, the staff is helpful and attentive.

Below the Hotel Atlantis, facing the caldera. ✆ **22860/23-807.** Reservations recommended for dinner. Main courses 20€ and up and up. AE, MC, V. Daily noon–3pm and 7:30pm–midnight.

Selene ★★★ GREEK The best restaurant on Santorini—and one of the best in Greece—Selene uses local produce to highlight what owner George Hatziyiannakis calls the "creative nature of Greek cuisine." The appetizers, including a delicious sea urchin salad on artichokes and fluffy fava balls with caper sauce, are deservedly famous. Entrees include *brodero* (seafood stew). The baked mackerel with caper leaves and tomato wrapped in a crepe of fava beans will convert even the most dedicated flesh eaters. The local lamb, quail, rabbit, and beef are all excellent. If you eat only one meal on Santorini, eat it here, in a truly distinguished restaurant with distinctive local architecture. In short, everything—location, ambience, view, service—comes together to form the perfect setting (never pretentious or coy, unlike some trendy spots) for the delicious, inventive food. The selection of cheeses from across the Cyclades is impressive. If you want to learn to make some of Selene's selections yourself, check out its cooking school at www.selene.gr.

Fira. ✆ **22860/22-249.** Fax 22860/24-395. www.selene.gr. Reservations recommended. Main courses 17€–30€. AE, MC, V. Mid-Apr to mid-Oct daily 7pm–midnight. Closed rest of year. In the passageway btw. the Atlantis and Aressana hotels.

Sphinx Restaurant ★ INTERNATIONAL Antiques, sculpture, and ceramics by local artists fill this restored mansion and large terrace with views of the caldera and the port at Skala Fira. You may not decide that you've come to Santorini to eat ostrich, but the fresh pasta is tasty, as is the seafood. Locals eat here—always a good sign.

Odos Mitropoleos. ✆ **22860/23-823.** Reservations recommended. Main courses 15€–25€; fish priced by the kilo. AE, DC, MC, V. Daily 11am–3pm and 7pm–1am. Near the Panagia Ypapantis Church.

Taverna Nikolas ★ GREEK This is another one of the few restaurants in Fira where locals queue up alongside throngs of travelers for a table—high praise for a place that has been here forever. There aren't any surprises; you'll get traditional Greek dishes prepared very well. The lamb with greens in egg-lemon sauce is particularly delicious. The dining room is always busy, so arrive early or plan to wait.

Just up from the main square in Fira. No phone. Main courses 12€–18€. No credit cards. Daily noon–midnight.

Around the Island

Restaurant-Bar 1800 ★★ CONTINENTAL For many years recognized as the best place in Oia for a formal dinner, the 1800 has a devoted following among visitors and locals. Many items are Greek dishes with a difference, such as the tender lamb chops with green applesauce and the cheese pie filled not just with feta, but with five cheeses. The restaurant, housed in a splendidly restored neoclassical captain's mansion, has undeniable romantic charm whether you eat indoors or on the rooftop terrace. After you eat, you can decide whether the owner (an architect and chef) deserves more praise for his skill with the decor or with the cuisine. "Each plate resembles a canvas," this restaurant proclaims.

Odos Nikolaos Nomikos, Oia. ✆ **22860/71-485.** www.oia-1800.com. Main courses 15€–30€. AE, DC, MC, V. Daily 8pm–midnight.

EXPLORING THE ISLAND

FIRA ★★ If you're staying overnight on Santorini, take advantage of the fact that almost all the day-trippers from cruise ships leave in the late afternoon, and explore the capital in the evening. As you stroll, you may be surprised to discover that Fira has a Roman Catholic cathedral and convent in addition to the predictable Greek Orthodox cathedral, a legacy from the days when the Venetians controlled much of the Aegean. The name Santorini, in fact, is a Latinate corruption of the Greek for "Saint Irene." The **Megaron Gyzi Museum** (✆ **22860/22-244;** Mon–Sat 10:30am–1pm and 5–8pm, Sun 10:30am–4:30pm; admission 3€), by the cathedral, has church and local memorabilia, including some before-and-after photographs of the island at the time of the devastating earthquake of 1956. The small **Archaeological Museum** (✆ **22860/22-217;** Tues–Sun 8:30am–3pm; admission 3€) has both Minoan and classical finds. You might find it almost deserted, as most visitors head directly for Thira's shops. Before you do the same, stop at the **Thera Foundation ★★** (✆ **22860/230-16;** Tues–Sun 8:30am–3pm; admission 4€), near the cable car station en route to Firostephani, to have a look at the spectacular reproductions and re-creations of the frescoes from Akrotiri. The **Museum of Prehistoric Thera** (✆ **22860/232-17;** Tues–Sun 8:30am–3pm; admission 3€) near the bus station has a small, but excellent, collection of finds (mainly from ancient Akrotiri).

VILLAGES ★★ Santorini's white villages, often cut out of the lava itself, are enchanting. Two beauties are **Pyrgos** (the name means "Tower"), the highest settlement on the island, and **Oia** (also spelled **Ia**). Oia is almost absurdly scenic, perched on a cliff above the caldera. Badly damaged in a massive earthquake in 1956, Oia was virtually a ghost town until it was rebuilt in the 1960s and 1970s and resettled. Now its chic shops (check out the **Art Gallery** and **Art Gallery Oia** on Oia's meandering main street) and gorgeous sunsets make it an increasingly popular place to stay or to visit—especially with those who find Fira too frenetic. The **Naval Museum** (✆ **22860/71-156;** open Wed–Mon 12:30–4pm and 5–8:30pm; admission 3€), in a restored neoclassical museum, showcases the island's long, intimate relationship with seafaring. If you travel to either village (local buses run here from Fira, or you can take a taxi), keep a lookout for some of the island's cave dwellings (homes hollowed out of Santorini's soft volcanic stone).

BEACHES Santorini's beaches may not be the best in the Cyclades, but the volcanic black and red sand here is unique in these isles—and gets very hot, very fast. **Kamari,** a little over halfway down the east coast, has the largest beach on the island. It's also the most developed, lined by hotels, restaurants, shops, and clubs. The natural setting is excellent, at the foot of cliffs rising precipitously toward Ancient Thira, but the black-pebbled beach becomes unpleasantly crowded in July and August. **Volcano Diving Center** (✆ **22860/33-177;** www.scubagreece.com), at Kamari, offers guided snorkel swims for around 25€ and scuba lessons from around 60€. **Perissa,** to the south, is another increasingly crowded beach resort, albeit one with beautiful black sand. **Red beach (Paralia Kokkini),** at the end of the road to Ancient Akrotiri, gets its name from its small red volcanic pebbles; it is—but for how long?—usually much less crowded than Kamari and Perissa. All three beaches have accommodations, cafes, and tavernas.

VINEYARDS For information on a number of winery tours on Santorini, check out www.santonet.gr/wineries. **Boutari** (✆ **22860/81-011;** www.boutari.gr) is the

Submerged Santorini

There's a great way to explore hidden Santorini: a 1-hour submarine ride under the surface of the caldera. Sink to 30m (100 ft.) below the surface and get a glimpse of the submerged volcanic crater. The trip costs 65€; information is available at ✆ 22860/28-900 or at most local travel agencies.

island's largest winery, and Greece's best-known wine exporter. A variety of tours are offered at their winery in Megalochiri on the road to Akrotiri, from a simple tasting of three wines (6€) to the "Libation to Santorini," with four wines, serious nibblies, and a multimedia show. This is a pleasant way to spend an hour or so (but never on Sun, when the winery, like most on Santorini, is closed). If you want to sample other local wines, stop by the underground **Volcan Wine Museum** (**✆ 22860/31-322; **www.volcanwines.gr), just outside Fira, on the mail road to Kamari. The museum, which occupies subterranean caves and tunnels, has an audio tour and reconstructions of the winemaking process; admission is 6€. Volcan's once-a-week Greek Night, featuring dinner and belly dancers, is popular with large tour groups.

ANCIENT THIRA & AKROTIRI ★★ Above Kamari beach on a rocky promontory are the ruins of **Ancient Thira** (**✆ 02860/22-217** or 02860/22-366), settled in the 9th century B.C., although most of the scattered remains date from the Hellenistic era. The site is usually open Tuesday though Sunday from 8:30am to 3pm, sometimes later in summer. Admission is 6€. A good but alarmingly narrow road runs almost to the summit, which can also be reached on foot or by donkey (for hire from some travel agents) on a path. The hilltop site is very fine, but if you have to choose between Ancient Thira and Akrotiri, and if Akrotiri is open, head there.

The excavations at **Akrotiri,** the Minoan settlement destroyed when the volcano erupted around 1450 B.C., have unearthed buildings three stories tall that were lavishly decorated with frescoes. ***Note:*** The site was closed to the public in 2005 when its protective roof collapsed, so check to see if it has reopened when you arrive on the island. If the entire site is closed when you want to visit, there's no point in coming here in the hopes of catching a glimpse of the remains: Unlike many sites, Akrotiri is *not* visible from the road.

If the site is open, it's breathtaking to walk down the streets and peek in the windows of houses in a town whose life was extinguished in a torrent of lava and ash so long ago. Most of the frescoes discovered were taken to the National Archaeological Museum in Athens, where a number are on display. In addition, you can see several frescoes from Akrotiri in the Museum of Prehistoric Thera in Fira. The **site** (**✆ 22860/81-366**) is open Tuesday through Sunday from 8:30am to 3pm; admission is 6€. Akrotiri can be reached by public bus, taxi, or one of the bus tours available from island travel agents.

SANTORINI AFTER DARK

Fira has all-night nightlife; as always on the islands, places that are hot one season are gone the next. I'm not listing phone numbers here because phones simply are not answered. If you want to kick off your evening with a drink on the caldera while watching the spectacular sunset, **Franco's, Tropical,** and **Palaia Kameni** are still

Santorini Swings

The height of the tourist season is also the height of the music season in Santorini: If you are here in July, you may want to take in the annual **Santorini Jazz Festival** (www.jazzfestival.gr), which has been bringing several dozen international jazz bands and artists here every summer since 1997. Many performances are on Kamari beach. In Fira every August and September, the **Santorini International Music Festival** (✆ **22860/23-166**), founded in 1978, features 2 weeks of mostly classical music.

the most famous and best places for this magic hour; be prepared to pay 15€ and up (and up) for a drink. If you are willing to forgo the caldera view, you'll find almost too many spots to sample along the main drag and around the main square, including the inevitable Irish pub, **Murphy's. Kirathira Bar** plays jazz at a level that permits conversation, and the nearby **Art Café** offers muted music.

Discos come and go, and you need only follow your ears to find them. **Koo Club** is the biggest, whereas **Enigma** is thronged most nights. **Tithora** is popular with a young, heavy-drinking crowd. There's usually no cover, but the cheapest drinks at most places are at least 15€.

Out on the island, in Oia, **Zorba's** is a popular cliff-side pub. The fine restaurant/bar **1800** (see above) is a quiet and sophisticated place to stop in for a drink—and certainly for a meal.

Kamari has lots of disco bars, including **Disco Dom, Mango's, Yellow Donkey,** and **Valentino's,** all popular with the youngish tour groupers who grope about here.

Remember: At virtually all of these places, be prepared to pay 15€ and way up for one drink.

Tinos ★★★

Unlike Santorini and Mykonos—where foreigners often outnumber locals—**Tinos** is one Cycladic island where you are likely to hear more Greek spoken than German or French. Tinos (161km/87 nautical miles southeast of Piraeus) is the most important destination in Greece for religious pilgrims, yet it remains one of the least commercialized islands of the Cyclades. That makes Tinos a real joy to visit—as do its lovely villages, uncrowded beaches, green hills crossed by stone walls and dotted with the elaborate ***peristerionades*** **(dovecotes)** for which the island is famous, and excellent restaurants that serve the thousands of year-round Greek pilgrims who come here to visit the **Panayia Evanyelistria** ("Our Lady of Good Tidings"), sometimes called the "Lourdes of Greece."

From well out to sea, the Panayia Evanyelistria—illuminated at night—is visible atop a hill overlooking Tinos town, which the inhabitants call "Hora." Like a number of the Cyclades, Tinos had a Venetian occupation, and a number of fine, old Venetian mansions (locally known as *pallada,* the name also used for the harborfront) still stand on the side streets off the harbor. **Megalocharis** is the long, steep street that leads from the harbor to the red-carpeted steps that are the final approach to the cathedral; some devout pilgrims make the entire journey on their knees. Running uphill parallel to Megalocharis, pedestrianized **Evangelistria** is a market street, as

When *Not* to Visit Tinos

Don't even think about arriving on Tinos without a reservation around **August 15,** when thousands of pilgrims travel here to celebrate the Feast of the Assumption of the Virgin. **March 25** (Feast of the Annunciation) is the second-most-important feast day here. Pilgrims also come here on **July 23** (the anniversary of St. Pelagia's vision of the icon) and **January 30** (the anniversary of the finding of the icon). In addition, it's not a good idea to show up here without a reservation on a weekend.

well as a pilgrimage route, with many shops selling candles and icons. There are also several jewelry and handicraft shops, one or two cafes, groceries, and old-fashioned dry-goods stores.

It's important to remember that Tinos *is* a pilgrimage place: It is considered disrespectful to wear shorts, short skirts, halters, or sleeveless shirts in the precincts of the Evanyelistria (or any other church, for that matter). And taking snapshots of the pilgrims, especially those approaching the shrine on hands and knees, is not appreciated.

The inland villages of Tinos are some of the most beautiful in the Cyclades. Many of the most picturesque are nestled into the slopes of **Exobourgo,** the rocky pinnacle visible from the port, connected by a network of walking paths that make this island a hiker's paradise. In these villages and dotting the countryside, you'll see the elaborately carved marble lintels, doorjambs, and fan windows on village houses, and ornately decorated medieval dovecotes. The island's beaches may not be the best in the Cyclades, but they are plentiful and uncrowded throughout the summer. All this may change if an airport is built here—all the more reason to visit Tinos now.

ESSENTIALS

GETTING THERE Several ferries travel to Tinos daily from Piraeus (5 hr.). Catamaran (1½ hr.) and ferry services (4 hr.) are available daily in summer from Rafina. Check schedules at the Athens **GNTO** (✆ **210/870-0000**); **Piraeus Port Authority** (✆ **210/459-3223** or 210/422-6000; phone seldom answered); or **Rafina Port Authority** (✆ **22940/22-300**). Several times a day, boats connect Tinos with nearby Mykonos and Siros (20–50 min.; there's usually daily service to Santorini Paros and Naxos in summer). Tinos has more winter connections than most Cycladic isles due to its religious tourism.

Be sure to find out from which pier your ship will depart—and be prepared for last-minute changes. Most ferries, and the small catamarans (Seajet, Flying Cat, and Jet One), as well as the excursion boat to Delos/Mykonos, dock at the old pier in the town center; some use the new pier to the north, on the side of town in the direction of Kionia. **Tinos Port Authority** (not guaranteed to be helpful) can be reached at ✆ **22830/22-348.**

VISITOR INFORMATION For information on accommodations, car rentals, island tours, and Tinos in general, head to **Windmills Travel** ★★★ (✆ **22830/23-398;** fax 22830/23-327; www.windmillstravel.com), in its new location just off the harbor on Kionion Street. Look for the windmills in the office's garden. Sharon Turner (sharon@thn.forthnet.gr) is the friendly, amazingly helpful and efficient manager, with unparalleled knowledge of Tinos and its neighboring islands. What's more, Turner can often get you substantial discounts on island accommodations, transportation, and tours.

GETTING AROUND

BY BUS The **bus station** (✆ **22830/22-440**) is on the harbor, by the National Bank of Greece. Schedules are usually posted or available here. There are frequent daily buses to most island villages.

BY CAR & MOPED Rental agencies in Tinos town include two just off the harbor on Trion Ierarchon, the street where taxis hang out: **Vidalis** (✆ **22830/23-995**) and **Dimitris Rental** (✆ **22830/23-585**). Expect to pay from 30€ per day for a car and half that for a moped. Greek law now requires wearing a helmet; not all agents supply the helmet.

BY TAXI Taxis hang out on Trion Ierarchon, which runs uphill from the harbor just before the Palamaris supermarket and the Hotel Tinion.

FAST FACTS There are several **banks** on the harbor, open Monday through Thursday from 8am to 2pm and Friday from 8am to 1:30pm; all have ATMs. The **first-aid center** can be reached at ✆ **22830/22-210.** There's a drop-off **laundry** service (✆ **22830/32-765**) behind the Lito Hotel—but be forewarned that it can be slow, up to 3 days in peak season. For **luggage storage,** try Windmills Travel (✆ **22830/23-398**). The **police** (✆ **22830/22-348**) are located just past the new pier, past Lito Hotel. The **post office** (✆ **22830/22-247**), open Monday through Friday from 7:30am to 2pm, is at the harbor's south end next to Tinion Hotel. The **telephone office (OTE),** open Monday through Friday from 7:30am to 12:30pm, is on the main street leading to the church of Panagia Evangelistria, about halfway up on the right (✆ **22830/22-399**). The harborside Cultural Foundation (✆ **22830/29-070**) has art exhibitions; admission sometimes charged.

WHERE TO STAY

Sharon Turner of **Windmills Travel** (see "Visitor Information," under "Essentials," above) can often get substantial discounts on island accommodations, transportation, and tours. In addition to hotel accommodations, Windmills has houses for rent in several villages.

Oceanis Hotel ★ This 10-year-old hotel is on the harbor but not where the boats dock, so it is quieter than other lodgings by the port. The balconies, with views of Siros in the distance, are a real plus. The hotel is often taken over by Greek groups visiting the island's religious shrines. As an independent traveler, you may feel a bit odd man out. The rooms are simply furnished, with good-size bathrooms. Don't bother with the restaurant. The Oceanis stays open all year and has reliable heat in the winter.

Akti G. Drossou, Hora, 842 00 Tinos. ✆ **22830/22-452.** Fax 22830/25-402. 47 units. From 90€ double. No credit cards. From the old harbor, walk south (right) along the paralia until you come to the Oceanis, whose large sign is clearly visible from the harbor. **Amenities:** Restaurant; bar. *In room:* A/C, TV.

Porto Tango ★ ✋ I am listing this place only because it was once thought to be the breakthrough fancy place on the island. Porto Tango does have all the frills—restaurant, sauna, spa, health club, pool, and so forth. But the management seriously overbooks rooms and puts many arrivals elsewhere and tries to charge the full price if guests use the hotel facilities. Did I mention that the beach is a 10-minute walk away, across a road? On the positive side, many rooms have balconies or terraces with sea views; some have both. In short, this is a place that has not got its act together, in either decor or service.

Porto, 842 00 Tinos. ✆ **22830/24-411.** Fax 22830/24-416. www.portotango.gr. 61 units. 150€ double; 450€ suite. Breakfast buffet included. AE, MC, V. **Amenities:** 2 restaurants; bar; health club; pool; spa. *In room:* A/C, TV, Internet, minibar.

Tinos Beach Hotel ★★ ☺ Despite a somewhat impersonal character, this is the best choice in a beachfront hotel. The decent-size rooms all have balconies, most with views of the sea and pool. The suites are especially pleasant—large sitting rooms open onto poolside balconies. The pool is the longest on the island, and there's a separate children's pool as well. No one seems to praise either the ambience or the service here, but if you want to be on Tinos, near Tinos town but on the beach, this is the place to be.

Kionia, 842 00 Tinos. ✆ **22830/22-626** or 22830/22-627. Fax 22830/23-153. www.tinosbeach.gr. 180 units. 80€–120€ double. Rates include breakfast. Children 7 and under stay free in parent's room. AE, DC, MC, V. Closed Nov–Mar. 4km (2½ miles) west of Tinos town on the coast road. **Amenities:** Restaurant; bar; saltwater pool; children's pool; tennis courts; watersports equipment rentals; Wi-Fi. *In room:* A/C, TV, minifridge.

WHERE TO DINE

As in many other Greek coastal towns, it's a good idea to avoid most harborfront joints, where the food is generally inferior and service rushed.

Metaxi Mas ★★ GREEK This is one of my two favorite restaurants on Tinos. The varied *mezedes* are irrestible, especially the vegetable croquettes, fried sun-dried tomatoes, piquant fried cheeses, and succulent octopus. The salads are crisp and the roasts are tender. There's a cozy interior dining room with a fireplace for when it's chilly, and tables outside in the pedestrianized lane for good weather.

Kontoyioryi, Paralia, Hora. ✆ **22830/24-857.** Main courses 8€–20€. No credit cards. Daily noon–midnight. Off the harbor, in the lane btw. the old and new harbors.

Palaia Pallada ★★ GREEK Palaia Pallada, next to Metaxi Mas, is a bit more down-home, a bit less inventive, but consistently good—and very good value. There are fewer ruffles and flourishes here, but the food (grills, stews, salads) in this family-run place is excellent, as is the local wine. You can eat indoors or outside in the lane.

Kontoyioryi, Paralia, Hora. ✆ **22830/23-516.** Main courses 7€–15€. No credit cards. Daily noon–midnight. Off the harbor, in the lane btw. the old and new harbors.

To Koutouki tis Eleni ★ GREEK Known in town simply as Koutouki, this excellent small taverna off Evangelistra Street doesn't usually have a menu. What it does have are good, basic ingredients cooked into simple meals that remind you how delightful Greek food can be. Local cheese and wine, fresh fish and meats, delicious vegetables—these are the staples that come together so well in this taverna, which demonstrates that you don't have to pay a fortune to experience good traditional home cooking.

Paralia, Hora. ✆ **22830/24-857.** Main courses 5€–15€. No credit cards. Daily noon–midnight.

EXPLORING THE ISLAND

TINOS TOWN The **Church of Panagia Evangelistria (Our Lady of Good Tidings) ★★★** and its museums are usually open from about 7am to 5pm in

A Swim, a Snack, an Ancient Site

If you're staying in Tinos town, the easiest place to take a dip is the beach at Kionia, about 3km (1¾ miles) west of Hora. Just across from the pebble and sand strand where you'll swim are the island's only excavated antiquities, the modest remains of the Temple of Poseidon and one of his many conquests, Amphitrite, a semidivine sea nymph (Tues–Sun 8:30am–3pm; admission 3€). When sheep or the custodians have trimmed the vegetation at the site, you can clearly make out the foundations of the 4th-century-B.C. temple, and a large altar and long stoa, both built in the 1st century B.C. As is inevitable with a site where Romans lived, there are the remains of a bath. Finds from the site are on display at the Tinos town Archaeological Museum (Tues–Sun 8:30am–3pm; admission 3€). When you head back to town, you can have a drink and a snack at either the Mistral or Tsambia taverna, both on the main road near the site. Closer to town, also on the main road, you can check your e-mail at the Para Pende cafe. You can do this excursion on foot, by public bus, or by taxi. If on foot, keep to the side of the road and don't expect the trucks and motorcycles to cut you any slack.

winter, later in summer. In 1822, a local nun, Pelagia, had a vision that a miraculous icon of the Virgin Mary would be found here; it was, and the church was erected to house the icon, which the faithful believe was painted by Saint Luke. The church is made of gleaming marble from Paros and Tinos, with handsome black-and-white pebble mosaics in the exterior courtyard. Inside, hundreds of gold and silver hanging lamps illuminate the icon, which is almost entirely hidden by the votive offerings of gold, silver, diamonds, and other precious jewels, dedicated by the faithful. Even those who do not make a lavish gift customarily make a small offering and light a candle. Beneath the church is the crypt with the chapel of the Zoodochos Pigi, where the icon was found, and several smaller chapels; the crypt is often crowded with Greek parents and children in white, waiting to be baptized with water from the font, or to fill vials with holy water from the spring.

Note: To enter the church, men must wear long pants and shirts with sleeves, and women must wear dresses or skirts and blouses with sleeves. Please remember that it's not appropriate to explore the church during a service. There are usually services in the early morning, in early evening, and periodically throughout the day.

Within the high walls that surround the church are various **museums and galleries,** each of which is worth a quick visit. The gallery of 14th- through 19th-century religious art has icons and church garments and vessels; the gallery of Tinian artists is just that; the picture gallery has the private collection of a local collector of Greek paintings of the 19th and 20th centuries; the sculpture museum has works by former and current island sculptors, many of whom studied with the help of the cathedral charitable foundation. Admission is sometimes charged at these collections, which keep irregular hours.

Exobourgo ★★, a knobbly mountain eminence crowned by the remains of a Venetian *kastro* (castle), is some 15km (9⅓ miles) outside of Hora, from which it is visible. The fortress is surrounded by sheer rock walls on three sides; the path to the summit starts behind a Catholic church at the base of the rock, on the road between

Affordable & Portable Tinian Folk Art

In a small hardware shop across from Pirgos's two museums, Nikolaos Panorios ★★★ makes and sells whimsical tin funnels, boxes, spoon holders, and dustpans, as well as dovecotes, windmills, and sailing ships. Each item is made of tin salvaged from containers like those that hold olive oil; each one is different, some with scenes of Pallas Athena, others with friezes of sunflowers, olive gatherers, or fruit and vegetables. All are delightful (from 20€). The shop (✆ 22830/32-263) is usually open from 9am to 1pm.

Mesi and Koumaros. As you make the ascent, you'll pass several lines of fortification—the whole hill is riddled with walls and hollow with chambers. As you might expect, the view over the Cyclades is superb from the summit (565m/1,854 ft.).

SHOPPING IN TINOS TOWN

Shops and stalls lining Evangelistria street sell a wide assortment of icons, incense, candles, medallions, and *tamata* (tin, silver, and gold votives)—as well as snow globes containing religious scenes. Many shops also sell the delicious local nougat, as well as *loukoumia* (Turkish delight) from Siros. There's also a fish market and a farmers' market weekdays in the square by the docks. Keep an eye out for the rather pink-plumed pelican that, reasonably enough, hangs out by the fish market.

There are two fine jewelry shops side by side on Evanyelistria: **Artemis,** 18 Evangelistria (**✆ 2830/23-781**), and **Harris Prassas Ostria-Tinos,** 20 Evangelistria (**✆ 22830/23-893**). Hand-painted icons (from around 200€) are for sale in the small shop of **Maria Vryoni,** the first left from the port off Leoforos Megaloharis, the second shop on the left. Cross over to 16 Megaloharis to the shop of the **local agricultural cooperative,** where you can buy pungent capers, creamy cheeses, olive oil, and the fiery local *tsiporo* liqueur (**✆ 22830/21-184**). Several shops along the harbor sell international newspapers and local guidebooks and maps.

VILLAGES

Most visitors to Tinos think that **Pirgos ★★**, at the western end of the island, is its most beautiful village. It has an enchanting small plateia with trees, a marble fountain, several cafes, and a couple of (overpriced) tavernas, usually open for lunch and dinner in summer, less regularly off season. Renowned for its school of fine arts, Pirgos is a center for marble sculpting, and many of the finest sculptors of Greece have trained here. In 2008, the superb **Museum of Marble Crafts** (**✆ 22830/31-290**) **★★★** opened just outside Pirgos. The museum takes visitors into the lives of the sculptors and artisans of Tinos, with the help of photos and videos. Displays include examples of the more than 100 kinds of Greek marble, glorious fanlight windows, doorway ornaments, and grave monuments done by Tinian artists—and a good selection of the tools used to make them. The museum has a cafe and an excellent small shop. The museum is open Wednesday to Monday 10am to 6pm in summer, 10am to 5pm off season (admission 3€). The **Dellatos Marble Sculpture School** (**✆ 22830/23-164;** www.tinosmarble.com), just outside the village by the police station, offers 1- and 2-week workshops for would-be marble workers. The **Museum of Yiannoulis Chalepas** and the **Museum of Panormian Artists** occupy adjacent houses, and give visitors a chance not only to see sculpture by local artists, but also to step into an island house. The museums are located near the bus station, on the main lane leading toward the village; both are open Tuesday through Sunday from 11am to 1:30pm and 5:30 to 6:30pm; admission 2€.

If you're interested in island crafts and excellent food, head for the villages of **Aetofolia** and **Volax,** north of Tinos town. The **Museum of Traditional Pottery** (admission 2€; open Apr–Sept Tues–Sun 10am–4pm; no phone or website at present), opened in 2009 in **Aetofolia,** one of the smallest and most charming Tinian villages. There are labels throughout in Greek and English and museum guide Lila Tsigkriki speaks excellent English. The museum showcases pottery made—or found—not only on Tinos, but on the neighboring island of Sifnos, as well as other Cyclades. The displays are delightful as is the traditional 19th-century island house that is now the museum, with its kitchen filled with locally made pottery. Don't miss the little pottery barbecue, called a "foufou" from the sound made when cooks blow on the coals! After touring the museum's well-stocked kitchen, you may be thinking of food, so head for the village of **Volax,** which is known for baskets of all sizes and shapes made by the local basket weavers. Just as you come into Volax, you'll see the tall trees that shade the excellent family-run **Taverna Volax** (✆ **22830/41-021**). Don't miss the local *loukanika* (sausages), best washed down with some Tinian wine. As you walk around the village, you may be startled to notice a stone amphitheater, which the villagers built from the massive round boulders that are found here. Sharon Turner at Windmills Travel (✆ **22830/23-398**) can let you know the schedule of theater performances (most occur in Aug). On your way back to Tinos town, perhaps stop at **Loutra,** which has a number of *stegasti,* the narrow tunnel-like lanes that run below the projecting second floors of village houses. Building a room out over the street below was a clever way for Tinians to have as much house as possible on a small amount of land.

BEACHES

Tinos is not best known for its beaches, but you'll find a decent fine-sand beach 3km (1¾ miles) west of Tinos town at **Kionia,** and another 2km (1¼ miles) east of town at busy **Ayios Fokas.** From Tinos, there's bus service on the south beach road (usually four times a day) to the resort of **Porto,** 8km (5 miles) to the east. Porto offers several long stretches of uncrowded sand, a few hotel complexes, and numerous tavernas, several at or near the beach. The beach at **Ayios Ioannis,** facing the town of Porto, is okay, but you'd be better off walking west across the small headland to a longer, less populous beach, extending from this headland to the church or Ayios Sostis at its western extremity; you can also get there by driving or taking the bus to Ayios Sostis. **Kolimbithres** has two beaches on the north side of the island, easily accessed by car, although protection from the *meltemi* winds can be a problem—the second is the best, with fine sand in a small rocky cove and two tavernas. Just beyond Pirgos, the beach at **Panormou** is in the throes of development as a holiday resort. Finally, a series of hairpin paved and unpaved roads leads down—and we mean "way down"—to beaches at **Ayiou Petrou, Kalivia,** and **Giannaki,** west of Tinos town.

TINOS AFTER DARK

There's less nightlife on Tinos than on many islands; as always on the islands, places that are hot one season are often gone the next. I'm not listing phone numbers here because phones simply are not answered. Two sweets shops, **Epilekto** and **Meskiles** (fantastic *loukoumades* with ice cream), both on the waterfront, stay open late. At the end of town near the largest quay, there is a clutch of bars with music, TV, and sometimes dancing, including **Koursaros, Kaktos, Volto,** and **Syvilla,** and, on the road toward Kiona, **Paradise.** If you want a late-night (or early-morning) coffee, try **Monopolio** on the harborfront; instead of a cup, this place brings you a delicious full pot of French filtered coffee.

HUNGARY

by Ryan James

Having joined the European Union in 2004, the tourism infrastructure has developed at a furious pace in Hungary. Poised between East and West, both geographically and culturally, it's at the center of the region's rebirth.

BUDAPEST

Budapest has a glorious history, having once rivaled its neighboring Vienna under the Austro-Hungarian monarchy. But don't let the city's rich past fool you: The Budapest of today buzzes with culture that is becoming more and more dynamically European. A vibrant young generation is proof of this. While the political elite continue to argue about the past, the youth are concentrating on the future. They're becoming multilingual; they're creating new film festivals and fashion shows. The scene they're developing is vibrant and fun—if a bit secretive and cliquish. While it might take some time to enter into their world, it's a pleasurable journey in the end. They are playing catch-up, living off the seat of their pants.

Essentials

GETTING THERE

BY PLANE Budapest is served by two adjacent airports, **Ferihegy 1** and **Ferihegy 2,** both located in the XVII district in southeastern Pest. Ferihegy 1 is the airport that all budget airlines use, while Ferihegy 2 (which has a **Terminal A** and a **Terminal B**) serves the flagship carriers and other traditional airlines. The distance between the Ferihegy 2 terminals is about 1 block, so there is no need to be concerned if you arrive at the airport for your flight and are at the wrong terminal, but there is some concern if you arrive at the wrong airport. With Hungary's entry into the Schengen zone, Terminal 2A is exclusively used for flights to Schengen countries, so you will pass through security, but not Passport Control. All other flights will depart from 2B and have Passport Control. There are several main information numbers: For airport information, call ✆ **1/296-9696;** and for general information, call ✆ **1/296-7000.** For ease of language, use the airport's English-version website at www.bud.hu/english for flight information.

The airport exclusively contracts with **Zóna Taxi** services (✆ **1/365-5555**), making this the official taxi service of both Budapest airports. The fares are fixed rates per cab, not per person, and adhere to predestined zones within the city. Fares run from zones 1 to 4 and cost from 3,500 Ft to 5,400 Ft. These taxis are also metered, so if the metered fare is less than the zone rate, you pay the reduced fare. By law, all taxis must give you a paper receipt for your fare.

Airport Shuttle (© **1/296-8555;** www.bud.hu/english) is a public service owned and operated by the Budapest Airport Authority. There is a clearly visible kiosk for the shuttle in each terminal. If you know you will use this service to return to the airport, a round-trip ticket is less expensive than two one-way tickets. A round-trip fare is 4,990 Ft per person and one-way is 2,990 Ft per person. For two traveling together, there is a discount: for one-way, it is 4,490 Ft for two and 8,490 Ft for a round-trip. The fares are the same for both airports. Depending on the number of people, you may find the taxi service to be less expensive. To arrange your return to the airport from where you are staying, call the number above 24 hours *in advance,* but not longer than 24 hours in advance and absolutely not less than 12 hours in advance. The shuttle office is open from 6am to 10pm, but be warned that you may have to wait on hold for some time and may possibly get disconnected in the process.

There are also two public transportation options with the trip taking about 1 hour total on either. Two buses leave the airport for the metro. From **Ferihegy 2,** you will take **bus no. 200E** to the last stop, Kőbánya-Kispest. From there, the Blue metro line runs to the Inner City of Pest. The cost is two transit tickets, which is 540 Ft for both; tickets can be bought from the automated vending machine at the bus stop (coins only and not recommended) or from any newsstand in the airport. From **Ferihegy 1,** take **bus no. 93 or 200E** to the same metro stop as above.

Trains stop at Ferihegy 1 only and go to Nyugati train station. After using the highway overpass, stand on the tracks and wait for the train. Take note that there is no station at the airport, but just a siding where the train stops. You must buy the 300 Ft ticket for a one-way journey at the airport. Purchasing a ticket on the train could result in a hefty fine. There are more than 30 trains daily. If you arrive at **Ferihegy 2,** take bus no. **200E** to **Ferihegy 1** in order to catch the train. Plans to extend the train tracks to the second airport remain in limbo.

BY TRAIN Trains arrive regularly from Vienna, Bratislava, and other European cities either as a destination or as a train passing through for somewhere else. It will depend on where your journey began as to which of the three stations you arrive at. In order to curb fare dodging, some tracks are barricaded by inspectors who will want to see your ticket when you're leaving a train as well as boarding it. Don't toss your tickets until you leave the station. For more information about Budapest train stations, see "Getting Around," below.

VISITOR INFORMATION You will find tourism-related information offices called **Tourinform** (© **1/438-8080** or 06/80-630-800; www.tourinform.hu), a branch of the Hungarian National Tourist Office, at V. Sütő u. 2, Budapest; open daily from 8am to 8pm. You'll also find a branch office in the heart of Budapest's Broadway, at Liszt Ferenc tér 11 (© **1/322-4098**), open daily from noon to 8pm. These offices can assist you with finding appropriate accommodations and restaurants, but outside of large cities, the amount of English decreases. The tourism authority, **Magyar Turizmus Rt** (© **1/488-8701;** www.hungarytourism.hu), also has offices throughout the world, and it is their mandate to promote Hungary as a destination for tourism.

For general country information and a variety of pamphlets and maps before you leave home, contact the government-sponsored **Hungarian National Tourist Office,** 350 Fifth Ave., New York, NY 10118 (✆ **212/695-1212;** www.gotohungary.com). In London, the **Hungarian National Tourist Office** is at 46 Eaton Place, London SW1X 8AL (✆ **020/7823-1032**). The Hungarian National Tourist Office's main website, a great source of information, is **www.gotohungary.co.uk**.

Other sites with lots of helpful current information including news, shopping, entertainment, and current venues for music, dance, and theatrical events for visitors and English-speaking locals are ***Funzine*** (www.funzine.hu), published every 2 weeks, and ***Where,*** published monthly, both free at Tourinform and many restaurants and hotels. ***Time Out,*** found in many major cities, is free from the Tourinform or 450 Ft at newsstands. The ***Budapest Times*** (www.budapesttimes.hu), both in print at newsstands and online, has news articles with an entertainment section. The Tourinform office puts out a monthly brochure called ***Budapest Panorama*** listing all of the scheduled events during the month. For news articles about Hungary, check out the Hungarian News Agency at **www.english.mti.hu**. It's updated daily.

CITY LAYOUT The city of Budapest came into being in 1873, making it relatively young in its present form. It is the result of a union of three separate cities: **Buda, Pest,** and **Óbuda** (literally meaning Old Buda) consisting of 23 self-governing municipal districts. Budapest is divided by the **River Danube (Duna)** with Pest, almost completely flat, on the eastern shore, making up almost two-thirds of the city. On the western bank is Buda and, farther yet, Óbuda, which has the hilly areas, these areas being much older settlements. If you look at a map of the city, you will see that the districts are numbered in a spiral pattern for the most part with

Budapest

ACCOMMODATIONS ■

- Burg Hotel **8**
- BudaBaB **26**
- City Ring Hotel **17**
- Domino Hostel **32**
- Four Seasons Hotel Gresham Palace **14**
- Hilton Budapest **5**
- Hotel Kulturinnov **7**
- Hotel Zara **33**
- Loft Hostel **31**
- Marco Polo Hostel **27**
- Medosz **23**
- NH Hotel **16**

ATTRACTIONS ●

- Budapesti Történeti Múzeum (Budapest History Museum) **10**
- Gellért Hegy (Gellért Hill) **12**
- Halászbástya (Fisherman's Bastion) **4**
- Hősök tere tere (Heroes' Square) **22**
- Király Baths **2**
- Magyar Állami Operaház (Hungarian State Opera House) **25**
- Margaret Island (Margit-sziget) **1**
- Mátyás Templom (Matthias Church) **6**
- Nemzeti Galéria (Hungarian National Gallery) **9**
- Nemzeti Múzeum (Hungarian National Museum) **34**
- Parliament **15**
- Rudas Baths **11**
- Széchenyi Baths **20**
- Szent István Bazilika (St. Stephen's Church) **28**
- Szépművészeti Múzeum (Museum of Fine Arts) **18**
- Vajdahunyad Castle **21**
- Vidám Park (Amusement Park) **19**

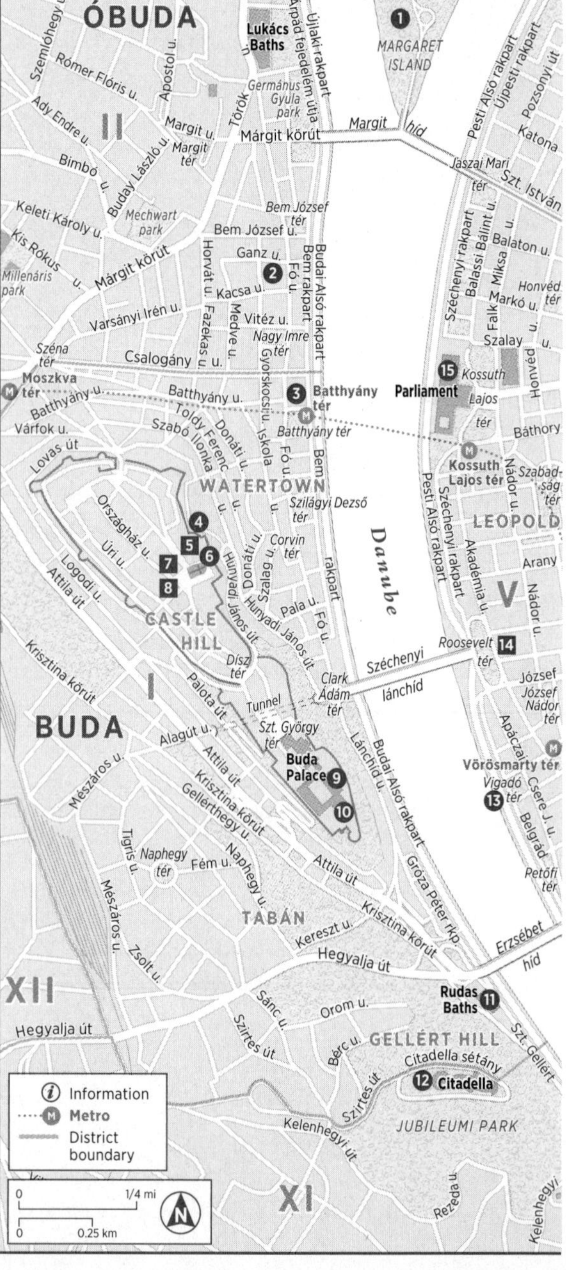

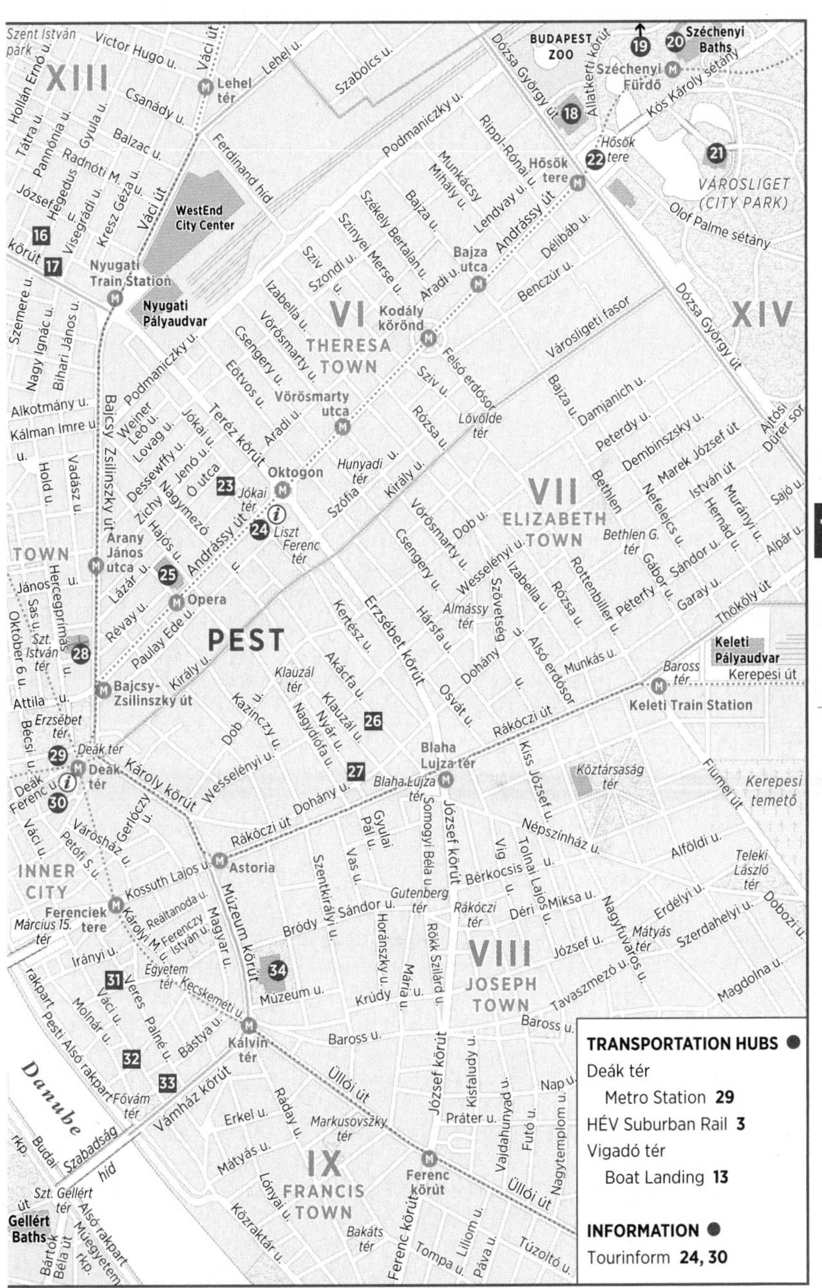
TRANSPORTATION HUBS
Deák tér
Metro Station 29
HÉV Suburban Rail 3
Vigadó tér
Boat Landing 13
INFORMATION
Tourinform 24, 30
XIII
VI
THERESA TOWN
VII
ELIZABETH TOWN
VIII
JOSEPH TOWN
IX
FRANCIS TOWN
XIV
PEST
INNER CITY
BUDAPEST ZOO
Széchenyi Baths
Széchenyi Fürdő
VÁROSLIGET (CITY PARK)
Hősök tere
WestEnd City Center
Nyugati Train Station
Nyugati Pályaudvar
Keleti Pályaudvar
Keleti Train Station
Kerepesi temető
Danube
Gellért Baths
Szent István park
Lehel tér
Kodály körönd
Bajza utca
Vörösmarty utca
Oktogon
Jókai tér
Liszt Ferenc tér
Arany János utca
Opera
Bajcsy-Zsilinszky út
Deák tér
Erzsébet tér
Szt. István tér
Blaha Lujza tér
Astoria
Ferenciek tere
Március 15. tér
Egyetem tér
Kálvin tér
Fővám tér
Ferenc körút
Köztársaság tér
Almássy tér
Klauzál tér
Lövölde tér
Hunyadi tér
Bethlen G. tér
Teleki László tér
Mátyás tér
Gutenberg tér
Rákóczi tér
Markusovszky tér
Bakáts tér
Szt. Gellért tér
Andrássy út
Váci út
Teréz körút
Erzsébet körút
József körút
Károly körút
Múzeum körút
Vámház körút
Rákóczi út
Üllői út
Thököly út
Kerepesi út
Dózsa György út
Városligeti fasor
Szabadság híd
Ferdinánd híd
Kós Károly sétány
Olof Palme sétány
Podmaniczky u.
Király u.
Dob u.
Wesselényi u.
Dohány u.
Kossuth Lajos u.
Baross u.
Népszínház u.
Fiumei út
16
17
18
19
20
21
22
23
24
25
26
27
28
29
30
31
32
33
34

districts I, II, and III on the Buda side and then IV starts the Pest side until XI, which again is the Buda side.

PEST Pest is as flat as a *palacsinta* (pancake), spread over a number of districts, taking in two-thirds of the city. Pest is the heartbeat with the commercial and administrative center of the capital and of all of Hungary. *Central Pest,* the term used in this chapter, is that part of the city between the Danube and the semicircular **Nagykörút (Outer Ring Boulevard),** where stretches of it are named after former Austro-Hungarian monarchs: Ferenc körút, József körút, Erzsébet körút, Teréz körút, and Szent István körút, changing names as the district changes. The Outer Ring begins at the Pest side of the Petőfi Bridge in the south and wraps itself around the center, ending at the Margit Bridge in the north. Several of Pest's busiest squares are along the Outer Ring, and Pest's major east-west avenues bisect the ring at these squares.

Central Pest is further defined by the **Kiskörút (Inner Ring),** which lies within the Outer Ring. It starts at Szabadság híd (Freedom Bridge) in the south and is alternately named Vámház körút, Múzeum körút, Károly körút, Bajcsy-Zsilinszky út, and József Attila utca, depending on the district, before ending at the Chain Bridge. Inside this ring is the **Belváros,** the actual city center and the historic Inner City of Pest. For the traveler, the Pest side is our recommended side for accommodations because this is where the lion's share of the action is and it is easy to walk to where you want to go.

Váci utca (distinct from Váci út) is a pedestrian-only, touristy shopping street between the Inner Ring and the Danube. It spills into **Vörösmarty tér,** one of the area's best-known squares. The **Dunakorzó (Danube Promenade),** a popular evening strolling spot, runs along the river in Pest between the Chain Bridge and the Erzsébet Bridge. The historic Jewish district of Pest is in the **Erzsébetváros (Elizabeth Town),** between the two ring boulevards.

BUDA & ÓBUDA On the left bank of the Danube is Buda; to its north, beyond the city center, lies Óbuda. Buda is as hilly as Pest is flat and is a good place for hiking. The two most advantageous vista points in the city are in central Buda on Castle Hill and the even higher Gellért Hill. Streets in Buda, particularly in the hills, are not as logically arranged as those in Pest.

Castle Hill is one of the most beautiful parts of Budapest with its magnificent view of Pest. Castle Hill is accessed by steep steps, walking paths, and small roads that are not open to general traffic. There are three less aerobic ways to access Castle Hill for those who want to conserve their energy for other adventures. From Clark Ádám tér (at the head of the Chain Bridge) you can take the funicular; from Várfok utca (near Moszkva tér) you can take the no. 10 bus; or from Deák take the no. 16 bus, all of which will take you to the top. Castle Hill consists of the royal palace itself, home to several museums. The previous castle was destroyed in World War II, but was rebuilt afterward and named the Royal Palace specifically to house museums. The Castle District has a long history going to pre-Celtic times, but what remains today are the medieval neighborhoods of small, winding streets, circling around Holy Trinity Square (Szentháromság tér), site of the Gothic Church of Our Lady or commonly referred to as St. Matthias Church.

Gellért Hill, to the south of Castle Hill, is named after the martyred Italian bishop who aided King István I (Stephen I) in his conversion of the Hungarian

Finding an Address

Budapest is divided into 23 districts, called *kerülets* (abbreviated as *ker.*). All addresses in Hungary start with a Roman numeral followed by a period signifying the *kerület;* for example, VII. Akácfa u. 18 is in the seventh *kerület.* Many street names are often used repeatedly in different districts, but are not all continuations of the same street. This makes it very important to know which *kerület* a certain address is in. You will also need to pay attention to the type of street: Is it utca, út, tér, or tere?

nation to Christianity in the 10th and 11th centuries. Below Castle Hill, along the Danube, is a long, narrow neighborhood and district known as **Víziváros (Watertown).** The main street of Watertown is Fő utca (Main St.). One of the original market places is off of Batthyány tér in this district. The famous Király thermal bath from Turkish times is right down the street.

Central Buda, the term used in this chapter, is a collection of mostly low-lying neighborhoods below Castle Hill. The main square of Central Buda is Moszkva tér, just north of Castle Hill, a hub for trams, buses, and the Red line metro; this area is in serious need of revitalizing. Beyond Central Buda, mainly to the east, are the Buda Hills.

Óbuda is on the left bank of the Danube, north of Buda. Although the greater part of Óbuda is lacking any architectural significance, reminding one of the Communist times, the area boasts a beautiful old city center and the impressive Roman ruins of Aquincum. Unfortunately, the road coming off the Árpád Bridge slices the old city center in half, destroying its integrity. The historic center of the old city is **Fő tér (Main Sq.),** a charming square dotted with small, yet impressive museums. **Óbudai-sziget (Óbuda Island)** is home to an enormous park that swells in size every August when it hosts Hungary's own annual Woodstock music festival, called the Sziget (Island) Festival.

GETTING AROUND Budapest has an extensive, efficient, and inexpensive public transportation system, but locals without global experiences disagree. If you have some patience and minimal skill with reading maps, you can easily learn the system. Public transportation, however, is not without its glitches, due to the construction of a fourth metro line that will continue for the next few years. There have been interruptions throughout parts of the city at various points in time, and this is likely to continue until 2013. The system is efficient enough, however, to provide buses to replace any tram or metro that has been disrupted by construction, but it can be confusing.

The biggest drawback to the system is that metro and tram routes shut down for the night at around 11:10 to 11:30pm, depending on the line. Some areas of the city, most notably the Buda Hills, are beyond the reach of some night bus services, making taxi drivers happy to provide those late-night journeys. Increased night bus service to overcome some of these problems has been dramatic, but it is still not perfect, with some long waits at dark and lonely bus stops. During rush hours, all forms of transport are crowded, making it best to plan your travel around these times. A disadvantage, mostly pertinent to travelers, is that Castle Hill can be reached in only three ways by public transportation and all of these modes of transportation are quite crowded in the high seasons. Most important, crowded public transport is the place where you are most likely to be targeted by Budapest's professional pickpockets. Just keep your hand on your wallet and purse.

FARES Fares generally increase in January and July. Transport passes provide unlimited transportation on **all forms of public transportation** (metro, bus, tram, trolleybus—an electric bus evident by the connection to wires above—some portions of the HÉV railway lines, and cogwheel railway) within Budapest city limits. If you are using individual tickets *(vonaljegy)*, which cost 300 Ft apiece (children 5 and under and E.U. citizens 65 and over travel free), you are required to validate the tickets as soon as you get on the transport. Each time you change lines, you have to validate a new ticket. You can buy single tickets at metro ticket windows, newspaper kiosks, and the occasional tobacco shop. There are also automated machines in most stations and at major transportation hubs, most of which have been recently modernized or installed and provide a somewhat reliable service, but I wouldn't depend on them. You can also buy a 10-ticket pack *(tizes csomag)* for 2,350 Ft.

I strongly recommend that you buy a transport pass, which does not require validation. They are available for 1 day *(napijegy)* for 1,550 Ft and are good for 24 hours from the day and time marked. The other pass options are 3 days *(turistajegy)* for 3,850 Ft, 7 days for 4,600 Ft, or, for longer stays, 14 days *(kéthétibérlet)* for 6,200 Ft. The 7- and 14-day passes need to be signed. If your plans are even longer, there is a 30-consecutive-day pass *(30 napos bérlet)* at 9,400 Ft, which requires a photo. If you are going to be here for 4 to 5 days, the 7-day *(hetijegy)* pass is still a saving over individual tickets. Passes are so much more convenient than having a handful of tickets that you have to worry about remembering to validate each time or replenishing your stock at odd hours. Honestly, these will save you money in the long run.

While the standard ticket is valid on the metro, there are other types of optional single-ride metro tickets introduced years ago, making ticket buying a bit more complicated for those who want the exactly appropriate ticket for their journey. Personally, I don't think any traveler should waste time caring about this, but I have met some who do. A metro section ticket *(metrószakaszjegy)*, at 250 Ft, is valid for a single metro trip stopping at three stations or fewer. A metro transfer ticket *(metróátszállójegy)*, at 470 Ft, allows you to transfer from one metro line to another on the same ticket, without any limit to the number of stations that the train stops at during your journey.

Transportation inspectors are those dreaded people who, like the secret police of yesteryear, whip out a hidden blue or red (the old color, but still sometimes used) armband when approaching you or stand guard at the top or bottom of an escalator at the metro stops, or hop on the tram or buses after the door has closed. Some are uniformed, so you know you are heading into the lion's den. However, many have become trickier and more covert over the years and are often in plainclothes. It is not until they materialize the dreaded armband and greet you that you realize you have had a false sense of security about having a peaceful ride. There were horror stories for years about how they treated people, screaming and yelling and causing a scene of hysterics when they caught someone without a ticket or an invalid one. Due to the hundreds of letters of complaints filling volumes, the system instituted mandatory customer service training meant to file down the teeth of these overly aggressive warriors of transportation justice. For some it has taken hold.

The **fines** for not having a validated ticket or pass are 6,000 Ft if paid on the spot or 10,000 Ft if paid later; this does not include the embarrassment of getting caught. An inspector has the right to ask for your passport (legally, you are required to carry it at all times) or ID and to call a police officer if the need arises. They do not have the authority to harm you or arrest you.

BY METRO The system is clean and efficient, with trains running every 3 to 5 minutes on weekdays and 6 to 8 minutes on weekends, from about 4:30am to about 11:10pm. The three lines are known by colors: Yellow, Red, and Blue. Officially, they have numbers as well (1, 2, and 3, respectively), which is what you will see on maps. All lines converge at **Deák tér,** the only point where any lines meet. Remember that if you change lines here, you need to validate a new ticket if you are not using a pass.

BY BUS With almost 175 different bus *(busz)* lines in greater Budapest, many parts of the city, most notably the Buda Hills, are best accessed by bus. With the exception of night buses, most lines are in service from about 4:30am to about 11:30pm. Some bus lines run far less frequently (or not at all) on weekends, while others run far more frequently (or only) on weekends.

Each time you change buses, you need a new, validated ticket. Black-numbered local buses constitute the majority of the city's lines. Buses with red numbers are express buses that follow the same routes as local buses with the same number, skipping minor stops along the way. If the red number on the bus is followed by an *E* (there are only five routes with an *E*), the bus makes very few stops between terminals and is best avoided.

It is common practice for the drivers to bypass stops when no one is waiting to get on and no one has signaled to get off. Chances are that the locals riding a given bus will know exactly where your stop is, and will kindly help you. You can also ask the driver to let you know when he has reached your stop.

BY TRAM You'll find Budapest's 32 bright-yellow tram lines *(villamos)* very useful, particularly nos. 4 and 6, which travel along the Outer Ring (Nagykörút). Tram no. 2, which travels along the Danube on the Pest side between Margit híd and Boráros tér, provides an incredible view of the Buda Hills, including the Castle District, and is far better than any sightseeing tour on a bus. We especially recommend this route at night when the castle is lit on the Buda side and Parliament is spotlighted on the Pest side. It is a romantic ride.

Tickets are self-validated onboard. As with buses, tickets are valid for one ride, not for the line itself. When a tram line is closed for maintenance, replacement buses are assigned the tram route. They go by the same number as the tram, with a *V* (for *villamos*) preceding the number.

BY TROLLEYBUS All of the 16 trolleybus lines are in Pest. Of particular interest to train travelers is no. 73, the fastest route between Keleti Station and within a block of Nyugati Station. All the information in the "By Bus" section above regarding boarding, ticket validation, and stops applies to trolleybuses as well.

BY COGWHEEL RAILWAY & FUNICULAR Budapest's **cogwheel railway** *(fogaskerekű)* runs from Városmajor, across the street from the Hotel Budapest on Szilágyi Erzsébet fasor in Buda, to Széchenyi-hegy, one terminus of the Children's Railway (Gyermek Vasút) and site of Hotel Panoráma in 20 minutes. The cogwheel railway runs from 5am to 11pm, and normal transportation tickets are used.

The **cable car** or **funicular** *(sikló)* connects Buda's Clark Ádám tér, at the head of the Széchenyi Chain Bridge, with Dísz tér, just outside the Buda Castle. The funicular is one of only two forms of public transportation serving the Castle District (bus no. 10 and bus no. 16 are the other possibilities). An extremely steep and short ride, but with a fun view, though like a solarium on sunny days, the funicular runs at frequent intervals from 7:30am to 10pm (closed on the second Mon of the month). Tickets cost 700 Ft to go up, and 1,300 Ft for a round-trip for adults, while children get a break at 400 Ft up and 750 Ft round-trip. After public protest, the funicular now goes slower than it originally did, as riders wanted to enjoy the scenery longer.

BY TAXI Budapest taxis fall into two general categories: legitimate and otherwise. All legal taxis must have a yellow license plate and a yellow taxi sign on the roof. The fare to be paid at the destination consists of three basic parts: the base fee; the kilometer fare, based on the distance traveled; and the waiting tariff, which is used if the taxi has had to stop or fails to move in traffic at a rate slower than 15kmph (9 mph). When you call for a taxi, the dispatcher will ask for the phone number you are calling from and they will get your address from this. They will also ask for a name. By law, the driver has to ask your name to ensure you are the one he is to pick up. Calling for a taxi is less expensive than getting one on the street, but if you cannot call, use the following companies only where their names are clearly displayed on the side. Make sure the driver starts the meter once you are in the taxi. By law, they must provide a written receipt. If you have a problem, write down the name of the driver from his license, his taxi number, and the company name and report it to the **Tourism Office of Budapest** at © **1/266-0479.**

I recommend **City Taxi** (© 1/211-1111). Other reliable fleets include **Volántaxi** (© 1/466-6666), **Rádió Taxi** (© 1/377-7777), **Fő Taxi** (© 1/222-2222), **Tele5** (© 1/355-5555), **6×6** (© 1/266-6666), and **Budataxi** (© 1/233-3333). You will seldom, if ever, wait more than 5 minutes for a fleet taxi unless you're in an extremely remote neighborhood (or in bad weather).

[Fast FACTS] BUDAPEST

American Express Budapest's only American Express office closed its doors in 2005.

Area Codes The country code for Hungary is **36.** All telephone numbers in this chapter are listed with the city code/telephone number. The area code for Budapest is **1.**

Business Hours Most **stores** are open Monday to Friday from 10am to 6pm and Saturday from 10am to 2pm with a few closing earlier at 1pm. The majority of stores are closed Sunday, except those in central tourist areas or malls. Very few shop owners and restaurateurs close for 2 weeks in August. On weekdays, food stores open early, at around 6 or 7am, and close around 6 or 7pm. Convenience stores, called "nonstops," are open 24 hours and just about every neighborhood has one. **Banks** in general are open Monday to Friday from 8am to 4pm. Some banks open a half-hour later on some days, but stay open an hour later that day too. There is no shortage of banking services or automated teller machines (ATMs) in the city.

Currency The basic unit of currency in Hungary is the **forint (Ft).** At press time, US$1 = 195 Ft.

Doctors & Dentists We recommend the **First Med Center,** I. Hattyu u. 14, 5th floor (✆ **1/224-9090;** www.firstmedcenters.com). Also recommended is the **Rózsakert Medical Center** (✆ **1/391-5903;** www.medical-center.hu), located in the Rózsakert Shopping Center, II. Gábor Áron u. 74–78/a **Pasarét Dental,** II. Pasaréti út. 8 (✆ **1/488-7919;** www.pasaretdental.hu), provides a wide range of services.

Embassies & Consulates The **Australian Embassy** is at XII. Királyhágó tér 8–9 (✆ **1/457-9777**). The **Canadian Embassy** is at II. Ganz u. 12–14 (✆ **1/392-3360**). The **Republic of Ireland Embassy** is at V. Szabadság tér 7 (✆ **1/301-4960**); the **United Kingdom Embassy** is at V. Harmincad u. 6 (✆ **1/266-2888**); and the **United States Embassy** is at V. Szabadság tér 12 (✆ **1/475-4400**). New Zealand does not have an embassy in Budapest, but the U.K. Embassy can handle matters for New Zealand citizens.

Emergencies The general emergency number in Europe is ✆ **112.** Dial ✆ **104** for an ambulance, ✆ **105** for the fire department, ✆ **107** for the police, and ✆ **188** for car breakdown service. ✆ **1/438-8080** is a 24-hour hot line in English for reporting crime.

Internet Access Most hotels now provide free Wi-Fi access. Outside of the hotel, you will find dozens of places where one drink will allow you to stay as long as you want to crawl the Web. Look for Wi-Fi signs on windows, doors, and standing signs outside doors of cafes, restaurants, and bookstores.

Mail The postal system is not the most efficient or honest, so take great care with sending or receiving packages. Even letters mailed "Registered with a Return Receipt Requested" card have not made it to their destination without issues. Most post offices are open Monday through Friday from 8am to 6pm; however, with the current state of the economy, many have shortened or will be shortening their hours on an office-by-office situation. Sending postcards to the U.K. or Ireland is 210 Ft, while Australia, Canada, New Zealand, or the U.S. is 230 Ft. Mailing a letter under 20 grams to the U.K. is 270 Ft, but Australia, Canada, New Zealand, and the U.S. are all 300 Ft. For packages, note there is a high percentage of mailings that never arrive at their destination, so I would avoid it at any cost. FedEx or UPS are prohibitively expensive for even sending a document. For example, sending a letter to the U.S. can cost over 5,000 Ft.

Police Dial ✆ **107** or for general emergency dial ✆ **112.**

Taxes Hungary has a value-added tax (VAT) on everything, but the rate depends on the service or product. Hotel VAT is now 18% and VAT on goods in shops is 20%. When you are shopping, the VAT is included in the posted price. However, some stores will break it down showing a *"netto"* and *"brutto"* price. You want to pay attention to the *brutto,* as this is what you will pay at the register.

Telephones Many convenience stores, kiosks, and Internet cafes sell **prepaid calling cards** in denominations up to 5,000 Ft; for international visitors these can be the least expensive way to call home. Many public pay phones are not properly serviced, but most require the use of a specific pay phone calling card also available as above.

Tipping In hotels, tip **bellhops** at least 500 Ft per bag (750–1,000 Ft if you have a lot of luggage) and tip the **chamber staff** 500 Ft per day (more if you've left a disaster area for him or her to clean up). Tip the **concierge** only if he or she has provided you with some specific service (for example, calling a cab for you or obtaining difficult-to-get theater tickets).

Tip the **valet-parking attendant** 500 Ft every time you get your car.

In restaurants, bars, and nightclubs, tip **service staff** and **bartenders** 10% to 15% of the check, and tip **valet-parking attendants** 500 Ft per vehicle.

Tip **cabdrivers** 10% of the fare.

Toilets In some areas, you will find public toilets on the streets. You will be required to pay the attendant to use the facility. Keep small change handy as it can cost from 50 Ft to 100 Ft. Because they are attended, safety is not a concern, but have extra paper with you—what they provide is minimal. If you think you can run into a fast-food restaurant, be prepared as they will charge unless you have ordered food. Your receipt is your admission ticket, but good for only one person. Split your order for more receipts. Other facilities are found in hotel lobbies if you hunt for them, bars, restaurants, museums, and railway and bus stations. Some full-menu restaurants, cafes, and bars reserve their restrooms for patrons.

Where to Stay

Lodging rates in Budapest have risen considerably, becoming more comparable to the rates of other European capitals. With that said, hotel occupancy has been decreasing over the past few years and dramatically in 2009. Reports have shown that many hotels are fewer than 50% occupancy during some peak periods, so deals can be had if you are a savvy Internet bargain hunter. After doing your research, compare the rates you have found with the hotel's website to look for specials. Don't stop until you try e-mailing the hotel directly to see if there are any unadvertised specials or discounts they are willing to offer.

The most-established accommodations agency is the former state-owned travel agent **Ibusz.** The main **Ibusz reservations office** is at V. Ferenciek tere 10 (**© 1/501-4911;** fax 1/501-4915; www.ibusz.hu), accessible by the Blue metro line. This office is open year-round Monday to Friday 9am to 6pm.

All hotels are required to charge a whopping 18% value-added tax (VAT), an increase instituted in July 2009. Most build the tax into their rates, while a few tack it on top of their rates. When booking a room, ask whether the VAT is included in the quoted price. Unless otherwise indicated, prices in this chapter include the VAT.

The majority of hotels and pensions in Budapest list their prices in euros (€), so the rates are listed in this chapter as the hotel designates. Listing rates in euros is not just intended as a means of transition to the E.U. currency (Hungary is not expected to join the euro zone until 2012 at the earliest and most likely later), it is also a hedge against forint inflation. (At press time, 1€ equaled approximately US$1.40.)

THE INNER CITY & CENTRAL PEST

Very Expensive

Four Seasons Hotel Gresham Palace ★★★ This Art Nouveau building, one of the most elegant and majestic properties in the city, stands as one of the finest in the world. With the Chain Bridge directly opposite the front doors, it has a picture-perfect view of the Buda Castle, making this the most picturesque location of any hotel in the city. As is Four Seasons tradition, guests are pampered in every way possible. While all rooms are beautifully decorated with mahogany furniture, the most expensive suites are equipped with bedroom sets made of mother-of-pearl and some have fireplaces. Every bathroom is fitted with Italian and Spanish marble with deep-soak bathtubs. No detail in design has been overlooked, and each room has been re-created in its original glory.

V. Roosevelt tér 5-6. ✆ **800/819-5053** in North America, or 1/268-6000. Fax 1/268-5000. www.fourseasons.com/budapest. 179 units. 300€-790€ double; 1,000€-5,000€ suite. Rates do not include VAT or tourist tax. Children stay free in parent's room. Breakfast 8,600 Ft. AE, DC, MC, V. Parking 12,000 Ft. Metro: Deák tér (all lines). **Amenities:** 2 restaurants; bar; concierge; exercise room; pool (luxurious heated indoor); room service; sauna; smoke-free rooms. *In room:* A/C, TV, fax machine (on request), hair dryer, Internet (for a fee), minibar.

Expensive

NH Hotel ★★★ Built from the ground up in 2003 directly behind the Vigszinház Theater, this hotel has taken a modern, minimalist approach oozing a warm welcome. The use of a variety of textiles in the room decor spanning shades of browns and tans with rich dark wood adds a cozy warmth to a spacious room. Add the mottled brown-and-tan marble used in the bathroom, and the feeling of quiet elegance is carried throughout. Sleep-inducing beds bring it all together for a perfect night's sleep. Although the exercise room on the eighth floor is limited, it contains the most modern exercise equipment, separate changing rooms for women and men, a solarium (for a fee), and a relaxation room with beautiful lounge chairs. It's eco-friendly to boot.

XIII. Vigszinház u. 3. ✆ **1/814-0000.** Fax 1/814-0100. www.nh-hotels.com. 160 units. 99€-196€ double. Rates include VAT. Breakfast 17€. AE, DC, MC, V. Secured parking 16€. Metro: Nyugati (Blue line) or tram 4 or 6. **Amenities:** Restaurant; bar; bikes; exercise room; room service. In room: A/C, TV, hair dryer, minibar, Wi-Fi (free).

Moderate

City Ring Hotel ★★★ This hotel is only a block away from Nyugati train station. Situated on the ring road, you have easy access to transportation, shopping, and restaurants. The rooms are a bit overwhelmed by the modern furniture, giving it a crowded feeling, but if you are out all day touring, they are more than adequate, impeccably clean, and the beds are comfy. We could have used thicker pillows, but they were sufficient. One caution is that the shower is on the small side, which may pose a challenge for larger people. Free Wi-Fi is available only in some rooms.

XIII. Szent István krt. 22. ✆ **1/340-5450.** Fax 1/340-4884. www.cityhotel.hu. 39 units. 51€-98€ double. Rates include full breakfast. AE, MC, V. Public parking nearby. Metro: Nyugati (Blue line) or tram 4 or 6. **Amenities:** Smoke-free rooms. *In room:* A/C, TV, fridge, hair dryer (on request), Wi-Fi (free; in some).

Hotel Zara ★★ Located on a small side street off of Váci utca, the pedestrian shopping street, this hotel, opened in 2006, is just 2 short blocks from the great market, a convenient location for shoppers. The decor is a beautifully executed mix of eclectic styles with Murano glass light coverings to Thai designs for the carpeting and drapery, created by Hungarian craftsman. Rooms seem small at 18 sq. m (194 sq. ft.), as most of them sport a queen-size bed, a rarity in less than a five-star hotel, but roomy enough to be comfortable. The furniture style is Asian modern with a soft pink and chocolate brown theme, while the bathrooms are tiled in browns and beiges, with showers only. Each corridor has only five rooms for an intimate feeling with designated smoking and nonsmoking floors. Excellent staff adds to the stay here.

V. Só u. 6. ✆ **1/577-0700.** Fax 1/577-0710. www.zarahotels.com. 74 units. 70€-120€ double. Rates include breakfast and city tax. Children 11 and under stay free in parent's room. AE, MC, V. Parking 18€. Metro: Kálvin tér (Blue line). **Amenities:** Restaurant; bar; room service; Wi-Fi in public areas. *In room:* A/C, TV, Internet, minibar.

Inexpensive

Medosz ★ This hotel, formerly a trade-union hotel for agricultural workers, retains its Communist utilitarian appearance with tread-worn carpeting and ugly halls. The rooms are simple, on the smallish side, and clean, but you can't beat the location. Jókai tér is less than a block from the bustling Oktogon and across from Liszt Ferenc tér with a dozen restaurants. Because of this, it can be noisy at night with the many restaurants and clubs in the area. Courtyard-view rooms are subject to neighbor noise, but not nearly as bad as the front of the hotel. The hotel remains a good value given its location. A reader in the past reported their bed had springs popping from the mattress; my advice is to check out the mattress immediately upon checking in and ask for a room change if needed. The entire hotel is nonsmoking.

VI. Jókai tér 9. ✆ **1/374-3001.** Fax 1/332-4316. www.medoszhotel.hu. 68 units. 49€–59€ double; 59€–69€ triple; 69€–79€ quad. Extra bed 10€ per night. Rates include breakfast and all taxes. DC, MC, V. Metered on-street parking; indoor garage nearby. Metro: Oktogon (Yellow line). **Amenities:** Restaurant; bar. *In room:* TV, no phone in most rooms.

THE CASTLE DISTRICT

Moderate

Burg Hotel ★★★ An overlooked treasure on Castle Hill, this hotel sits on a corner directly across from St. Matthias Church. The multilingual staff is as friendly as they are talented with languages. The rooms are spacious and beautifully decorated in muted greens, rose, and beige with modern comfortable furniture from their last remodel in 2007. The corner room is extra large, but any room would be comfortable. The blue-tiled bathrooms are simple, but sizable. All rooms have a view of Trinity Square. Breakfast is served in a large room with windows overlooking the square. There is no lift, but it is only three floors above the ground-floor entrance.

I. Szentháromság tér 7–8. ✆ **1/212-0269.** Fax 1/212-3970. www.burghotelbudapest.com. 26 units. High season 99€–175€ double; extra bed 29€–39€. Rates include breakfast and city tax. Children 13 and under stay free in parent's room. AE, MC, V. Parking 16€. Bus: 16A from Moszkva tér or 16 from Deák tér. **Amenities:** Bar. *In room:* A/C, TV, hair dryer, minibar, Wi-Fi (free).

Hilton Budapest ★★★ This Hilton has the most enviable piece of real estate in Budapest, sitting right next door to St. Matthias Church with part of the Fisherman's Bastion behind it. The hotel's award-winning design incorporates both the ruins of a 13th-century Dominican church (the church tower is alongside the hotel) and the baroque facade of a 17th-century Jesuit college, which makes up the hotel's main entrance. The hotel was renovated in 2007; the rooms are now a uniform rose, green, and beige color scheme. The corner suites are beautifully decorated with separate sitting areas, a dining area, and a bedroom with oversize windows for a spectacular view of the Bastion and Danube. The elegant Baroque Room is three levels and has a fully equipped kitchen. Two floors are nonsmoking.

I. Hess András tér 1–3. ✆ **1/899-6600.** Fax 1/899-6644. www.hilton.com. 322 units. 90€–230€ double. Rates do not include VAT or city tax. 1 child per adult stays free in parent's room. Breakfast 28€. AE, DC, MC, V. Parking 25€. Bus: 10 from Moszkva tér or 16 from Deák tér. **Amenities:** Restaurant; bar; babysitting; concierge; exercise room; room service. *In room:* A/C, TV, hair dryer, minibar, Wi-Fi (for a fee in standard room).

Hotel Kulturinnov ★ For those with cultural interests or a burning desire to stay on Castle Hill, this is a modest alternative. The actual hotel is located on the first floor in the building of the Hungarian Culture Foundation, built in the early

20th century. The building has an impressive entrance. Entering one long hall, the rooms are at the end. The rooms are small, impeccably clean, with very high ceilings. None of the rooms has an exceptional view, except perhaps no. 10, which overlooks the garden. However, for the location, the price is a bargain, but without luxury.

I. Szentháromság tér 6. ✆ **1/224-8100.** Fax 1/375-1886. www.mka.hu. 16 units. 19,000 Ft-24,000 Ft double; 22,000 Ft-30,000 Ft triple. Rates include breakfast and all taxes. Children 5 and under stay free in parent's room. MC, V. Parking 10€. Closed Dec 20–Jan 3. Bus: 16A from Moszkva tér or 16 from Deák tér. **Amenities:** Snack bar; Wi-Fi. *In room:* Hair dryer, minibar.

HOSTELS

Let me first state that not all hostels are created equal and should not be considered for young party people only. There are alternatives out there and I have listed a couple of good ones. There is intense competition in Budapest between the leading youth hostel companies and various privately run hostels as there are more than 85 hostels in the city.

Mellow Mood Ltd. operates a youth hostel placement office for their own hostels at Keleti Station (✆ **1/343-0748**), near the Baross Restaurant. This office is open daily 7am to 9pm. For other hostels, check out the website **www.hostelworld.com** for other offerings in the city. Run by Mellow Mood, **Domino Hostel,** V. Váci u. 77 (✆ **1/235-0492;** www.dominohostel.com), is on Váci utca, the ideal place for eating, drinking, and shopping, not to mention close to public transportation. The place is very clean, and the staff is friendly. Calling Mellow Mood's **Marco Polo Hostel,** VII. Nyár u. 6 (✆ **1/413-2555;** www.marcopolohostel.com), a youth hostel is a bit of a misnomer, as it closely resembles a hotel. The central location is ideal for hopping on a bus or catching the metro, and the rooms have clean and attractive linens.

The **Loft Hostel,** V. Veres Palne u. 19 IV/6 bell 44 (✆ **1/328-0916;** www.lofthostel.hu), is on the top floor of a building with dormer loft–type ceilings. The owners want to provide more for less, but they also want to keep their lease, so this is not a late-night party place. **BudaBaB,** VII. Akácfa u. 18 (✆ **1/267-5240;** www.budabab.com), is a homey B&B situated at the edge of the historic Jewish ghetto.

Where to Dine

Étterem is the most common Hungarian word for restaurant and is applied to everything from cafeteria-style eateries to first-class restaurants. A *vendéglő,* an inn or guesthouse, is a smaller, more intimate restaurant, often with a Hungarian folk motif; a *csárda* is a countryside *vendéglő* (often built on major motorways and frequently found around Lake Balaton and other holiday areas). An *önkiszolgáló* indicates a self-service cafeteria. *Büfés* (snack counters) are not to be confused with buffets in English. They are found all over the city, including transportation hubs. A *cukrászda* is a bakery for pastries and a coffee, while a *kávéház* is a coffeehouse that generally has a limited selection of pastries. Traditionally, many coffeehouses are places to sit for hours to meet with friends, read a book, or just sit and people-watch. Today, some establishments use the word *kávéház* in their name, but really are restaurants providing full meals.

The U.S. Embassy provides a list of restaurants that engage in unethical business practices, such as excessive billing, using physical intimidation to compel payment of excessive bills, and assaulting customers for nonpayment of excessive bills. Check the U.S. Embassy website for updated information: visit http://hungary.usembassy.gov/tourist_advisory.html.

THE INNER CITY & CENTRAL PEST

Expensive

Dió ★★★ HUNGARIAN MODERN Being frugal when eating out, I often bypass the more expensive eateries, but this one received such rave reviews from a reader, I could not miss out on the experience he described. Re-creating Hungarian folk art with oversize carved dark wooden panels on the walls interspersed with etched glass mirrors, the dining room has a cozy hearthlike warmth. Service was beyond reproach, but the food was a competitive shining star. I splurged by having the starter of three pieces of pumpkin and spinach pie. It was heavenly and I could have stopped there and been satiated, but I went forth with the duck breast served with sweet-potato soufflé with fig and thyme mousse. My dining companion decided on the Mangalitsa pork chops stuffed with goat cheese and chandelle mushrooms accompanied by a potato cake.

V. Sas u. 4. ✆ **1/328-0360.** www.diorestaurant.com. Reservations recommended. Main courses 2,880 Ft–4,680 Ft. AE, MC, V. Daily noon–midnight. Metro: Bajcsy-Zsilinszky út (Blue line) or Deák Ferenc tér (all lines).

Mátyás Pince ★★★ HUNGARIAN TRADITIONAL Art, history, or music buffs will love this restaurant established in 1904, named for King Mátyás; the myths and legends of his reign grace the walls in magnificent style. The frescoes and stained glass decorating the dining areas were registered as national monuments in 1973. Music is provided by the Sándor Déki Lakatos Gypsy music dynasty every night but Monday from 7pm until closing, creating an all-around romantic experience. I sampled the cold blackberry soup, rich in creamy fruit flavor. The main course was King Mátyás's favorite menu of sirloin of beef on a spit, leg of duck, gooseliver wrapped in bacon, roast sausage, onion potatoes, steamed cabbage, and letcho. The menu is extensive and the combination of an excellent meal and entertainment makes for an enjoyable evening out.

V. Március 15 tér 7–8. ✆ **1/266-8008.** www.cityhotels.hu. Main courses 3,500 Ft–10,900 Ft. AE, MC, V. Daily 11am–midnight. Metro: Ferenciek tere (Blue line).

Moderate

Alföldi Kisvendéglő ★★ HUNGARIAN TRADITIONAL Alföldi is named after Hungary's flat plain region and is paneled with horizontal brown wood-stripped walls with assorted old plates above, creating a homey country feel. The dining room offers wooden booths or tables with traditional country hand-embroidered tablecloths and place mats in folk designs. Each table has a basket of spicy homemade *pogácsas* (a type of biscuit), and you will be charged for each one eaten, but it's worth the nominal charge. The buttered veal scallops were ultratender with a light buttery sauce that was used for the potatoes and rice that came with it. The pork medallions were also splendid, served without any flare, in a down-home country manner.

V. Kecskeméti u. 4. ✆ **1/267-0224.** www.alfoldivendeglo.hu/hun. Reservations recommended. Main courses 1,440 Ft–5,140 Ft. MC, V. Daily 11am–midnight. Metro: Astoria (Red line) or tram 47 or 49 to Kálvin tér.

Blue Tomato Pub ★★★ HUNGARIAN MODERN Don't let the "Pub" in the name fool you; this is a serious place for treating your taste buds with tasty morsels.

I had the corn soup with bacon and almond slivers as a starter—thick, creamy, and with the chunks of bacon and lots of almonds, it was bowl-licking delicious. Quite embarrassing for my guest, actually. I tried the chicken served in the earthenware dish, which was layered chicken breast with sliced potatoes, tomato, onion, bacon of course, and a creamy cheese Dijon sauce over the entire dish. A fellow diner had chicken breast with green mascarpone sauce with forest mushrooms.

XIII. Pannónia u. 5–7. ✆ **1/339-8099.** www.bluetomato.hu. Reservations recommended. Main courses 1,390 Ft–3,900 Ft. MC, V. Mon–Sat noon–midnight; Sun noon–10pm. Tram: 4 or 6, Jászai Mari tér.

Café Eklektika ★★★ HUNGARIAN MODERN With tables and booths, a mellow mood is created by the soothing vocals with a cabaret feel serenading in the background, the monthly changing artwork on the walls, and the dependably excellent service. The chicken dish I loved on a previous visit was replaced with chicken breast stuffed with spinach served with a potato pie layered with cheese. It was good enough to make me forget the other dish I longed for. My dining guest had gnocchi with mozzarella balls and olives. He said the sauce was excellent. Outside seating is available in good weather, but inside you will be treated to unlimited Wi-Fi, for the price of a coffee.

V. Nagymező 30. ✆ **1/266-1226.** www.eklektika.hu. Reservations recommended. Main courses 1,490 Ft–2,390 Ft; pizza 1,290 Ft–1,890 Ft. No credit cards. Mon–Fri 10am–midnight; Sat–Sun noon–midnight. Metro: Opera (Yellow line).

Fészek ★★ HUNGARIAN TRADITIONAL Fészek, which means nest, is situated in the center of an old grand building that has seen better days. Once you traipse through a run-down lobby and enter the interior courtyard, you realize a restaurant is located here. The inner ring has tables both in a covered circular terrace area and in the exposed center courtyard, where 100-year-old chestnut trees canopy the tables. Service can sometimes be at a snail's pace so if you are in a hurry, avoid it. Choosing the veal paprikash with Hungarian noodles was a wise choice. Chunks of tender meat floated in a rich brown gravy alongside a field of freshly made noodles. Chicken coated in Parmesan was a flattened breast served with a heaping mound of mashed potatoes. Live music entertainment is offered each night, ranging from American show tunes to Gypsy fusion.

VII. Kertész u. 36 (corner of Dob u.). ✆ **1/322-6043.** www.feszeketterem.hu. Reservations recommended. Main courses 1,790 Ft–2,890 Ft. MC, V. Daily noon–midnight. Tram: 4 or 6, Király utca.

Firkász ★★★ HUNGARIAN MODERN The name means scribbler in English, referring to journalists who scribble their notes. The decor matches the name. Walls are covered with old newspapers from the early 20th century, accented with old typewriters; clocks; shadow boxes of old pens, erasers, and pencil sharpeners; and other memorabilia of yesteryear. I ordered the crispy pork with cabbage. The pork was crispy on the edges, but the tender meaty medallions were moist. A side of pan-fried potatoes was a delightfully large serving of mashed potatoes fried with onions. My fellow diner ordered the batter-dipped fried mushrooms with ewe cheese and leek sauce, which he was pleased with. A piano player plays from 7pm to midnight. This is one of the few restaurants of its class to add a 15% service charge to all tabs.

XIII. Tátra u. 18. ✆ **1/450-1118.** www.firkaszetterem.hu. Reservations recommended. Main courses 1,290 Ft–4,690 Ft. MC, V. Daily noon–midnight. Tram: 4 or 6, Jászai Mari tér.

Marquis de Salade ★★ AZERBAIJAN We discovered this restaurant on our first trip to Budapest in 1998 and loved it then. It is still going strong. The entrance is on the street level, but the restaurant is downstairs in a cavelike atmosphere, decorated with Asian rugs on the walls and ceiling. Our group of three started with the Marquis's salads, which is a sampler platter of six different salads. Along with the bread, this about constituted a diversely sumptuous meal, but we plunged forward with entrees: lamb shank with sweet red peppers, chicken with shrimp sauce and coconut, and steak topped with mushroom sauce. The last two received mixed reviews, so I would avoid them, but the salad is a meal for three without ordering more.

VI. Hajós u. 43. ✆ **1/302-4086.** www.marquisdesalade.hu. Reservations recommended. Main courses 2,600 Ft–3,900 Ft. No credit cards. Daily 11am–1am. Metro: Arany János (Blue line). Bus: 70 or 78 to Bajcsy-Zsilinszky út.

Inexpensive

Főzelékfalo Ételbar ★★ HUNGARIAN TRADITIONAL This tiny restaurant is so popular with Hungarians there is a line out the door at lunchtime. *Főzelék,* a cross between a soup and a stew, though it is puréed, is a national dish and treasure, so if you have not tried it, you have not officially been to Hungary. Inside there are only bar tables and stools, but if the weather is good, the sidewalk will be packed with tables. Take it to go if you have to. The blend comes in a number of varieties, but green pea and potato are the most popular. If you want something heartier, they sell fried chicken too.

VI. Nagymező 18. No phone. Reservations not accepted. Main courses 380 Ft–580 Ft; salads 180 Ft per kg. No credit cards. Mon–Fri 9am–10pm; Sat 10am–9pm; Sun 11am–6pm. Metro: Opera (Yellow line).

Kőleves Vendéglő (Stone Soup) ★★★ HUNGARIAN MODERN If you remember the story of *Stone Soup,* the playfulness of this establishment will charm you with light fixtures made of inverted glasses and cheese graters, the pieces of contemporary art that grace the walls, and the soup bowls adorning the bar. But the real delight comes with the food, made from preservative-free ingredients. I love the corn soup with chilies; it is thick and tangy. A recurring offering is chicken with Roquefort dressing, which is delightful. Some dishes are a la carte with a suggested side dish that is extra, at 360 Ft to 400 Ft, but others are complete meals.

VII. Kazinczy u. 35. ✆ **1/322-1011.** www.koleves.com. Reservations recommended. Main courses 1,350 Ft–3,560 Ft. AE, MC, V. Daily noon–midnight. Close to Dohány Synagogue on the corner of Kazinczy u. and Dob u.

CENTRAL BUDA

Expensive

Hemingway ★★★ HUNGARIAN MODERN You will feel as though you are escaping the city when visiting this restaurant next to a small lake with plenty of trees. The interior of the venue always makes us feel like we have joined Hemingway in one of his favorite Spanish getaways. The piano and bass duo adds to the relaxing Casablanca atmosphere with the Latin music. It may seem contradictory that the cuisine is Hungarian, but the fusion of food and atmosphere blend once you take your first bite. Try either of the indigenous Hungarian fares; the famous Mangalica pork is served as a crispy knuckle with cabbage noodles baked in freshly made strudel and fried onion strands. The most expensive menu item is the Hungarian Grey

Coffeehouses: Historic & Traditional

As part of the Austro-Hungarian empire, Budapest (just as in Vienna) developed a coffeehouse culture where people of like minds met to discuss politics, literature, or music. Each coffeehouse has its own story as to which literary movement or political circles favored their establishment. Of the old classics, we prefer **Centrál Kávéház,** V. Károlyi Mihály u. 9 (✆ **1/266-2110;** www.centralkavehaz.hu), in the Inner City; **Művész Kávéház,** VI. Andrássy út 29 (✆ **1/352-1337;** www.muveszkavehaz.hu), diagonally across Andrássy út from the Opera House; and **Rétesvar,** I. Balta köz 4 (no phone), in Castle Hill.

For a more modern take on coffee culture, find a spot at Aztek Choxolat Café, V. Karoly korut 22 or Semmelweiss u. 19 (✆ **1/266-7113**); Café Noé, VII. Wesselényi u. 13 (✆ 1/787-3842; www.torta.hu); or **Fröhlich Kóser Cukrászda,** VII. Holló u. 1 (✆ **1/267-2851**), all in Pest.

beef served as a chateaubriand with tomato-bacon steak potato. In fine weather, reserve a table outside on the terrace overlooking the water.

XI. Kosztolányi D. tér 2, Feneketlen tó. ✆ **1/381-0522.** www.hemingway-etterem.hu. Reservations recommended. Main courses 1,980 Ft–8,900 Ft. AE, DC, MC, V. Mon–Sat noon–midnight. Bus: 7 toward Buda from Ferenciek tér to Feneketlen tó, a small "lake." Tram: 19 or 49 to Kosztolányi Dezső tér.

Moderate

Angelika Kaveház és Étterem ★★ HUNGARIAN MODERN Angelika is housed in a historic building next to St. Anne's Church. Better known as a place for drinks and pastries on a summer's day, the multilevel terrace has perfect views of Parliament across the Danube. Inside you will find extra-large rooms where smokers and nonsmokers are truly segregated. The menu has expanded over time. I enjoyed the pork chops with cheese and beer sauce served with mashed potatoes and Roquefort salad; the pork with barbecue sauce was appealing, though the meat was mixed with a lot of bone. The vegetable soufflés served with it were a pleasant change of pace for a vegetable side dish.

I. Batthyány tér 7. ✆ **1/201-0668.** www.angelikacafe.hu. Main courses 1,090 Ft–3,990 Ft. MC, V. Daily 9am–midnight. Metro: Batthyány tér (Red line).

Inexpensive

Eden ★ 🎁 VEGETARIAN This historic building houses the first and only vegan restaurant in Buda. All ingredients are natural and fresh without any coloring, additives, or preservatives. After making your selection from the limited offerings, you have the choice of sitting in the charming country-cozy dining room or in the atrium garden. The food is quite tasty, and the selection of 12 juices freshly squeezed from fruit or vegetables will quench anyone's thirst. When you order, take note that the price for salad is by weight and the drinks are by volume.

I. Iskola utca 31, Batthyány tér. ✆ **06/20-337-7575** (mobile phone only). 590 Ft–890 Ft. No credit cards. Sun 11am–9pm; Mon–Thurs 7am–9pm; Fri 7am–6pm. Metro: Batthyány (Red line).

Seeing the Sights

Historic Budapest is smaller than people realize when they first arrive. Because this is an ideal walking city, many attractions listed in this chapter are easily reached on foot from the city center; if you would rather save some time, public transport will get you there too.

PEST

Nemzeti Múzeum (Hungarian National Museum) ★★ The Hungarian National Museum was founded in 1802 thanks to the numismatic, book, and document collections of Count Ferenc Szénchényi. This enormous neoclassical structure was finished in 1846. It was here that the poet Sándor Petőfi and others of like mind are said to have roused the emotions of the people of Pest to revolt against the Hapsburgs on March 15, 1848. The permanent exhibit holds more than one million pieces of Hungarian historical artifacts, including the main attraction, a replica of the so-called crown of King St. Stephen.

VIII. Múzeum krt. 14. ✆ **1/327-7700.** www.mnm.hu. Admission for permanent exhibits 1,040 Ft, 520 Ft children and seniors; temporary exhibits vary. Free admission Mar 15, Aug 20, and Oct 23. Photo 3,000 Ft; video 5,000 Ft. Tues–Sun 10am–6pm. Metro: Kálvin tér (Blue line).

Szépművészeti Múzeum (Museum of Fine Arts) ★★★ During the 1896 millennial celebration of the Magyars' settling and forming a nation in 896, the plans were proposed for the Museum of Fine Arts. Ten years later in the presence of Franz Josef, the king and emperor of Austria and Hungary, the Museum of Fine Arts was opened at the left side of Heroes' Square. This was the last great monument to be built during the most prosperous period of Hungary's history. Designed in the Beaux Arts style, the museum is the main repository of foreign art in Hungary and it houses one of central Europe's major collections of such works. The overall collection consists of more than 3,000 paintings, 10,000 drawings, and 100,000 prints. Trained docents offer a 1-hour guided tour, in English, free of charge. Stand by the cashier's desk close to the starting time and a docent will announce the tour. They are offered Tuesday through Friday at 11am and 2pm and Saturday at 11am.

XIV. Hősök tere. ✆ **1/469-7100.** www.szepmuveszeti.hu. Admission 1,400 Ft for permanent collection; temporary exhibits are in addition and vary. Photography permitted only in the permanent collection. Photo 300 Ft; video 1,500 Ft. Tues–Sun 10am–5pm (every 2nd Thurs on odd weeks until 10pm). Metro: Hősök tere (Yellow line).

BUDA

Budapesti Történeti Múzeum (Budapest History Museum) ★ This museum, also referred to as the Castle Museum, is easily overlooked since it is tucked in the back courtyard behind the palace. Once you approach it, there are no lavish signs advertising it either. If you are interested in the history of this great city as well as the whole Carpathian basin from medieval times, you will love this museum.

What you should not miss is the third-floor exhibit where you will find historic maps of battle plans and weapons used in the liberation from the Turkish occupation. At the back of the main floor, you will find a statue area that has an outstanding collection of Roman and medieval-era pieces. The highlight is the lowest level; it is actually part of the old palace and hidden back there is a chapel.

I. In Buda Palace, Wing E., on Castle Hill. ✆ **1/487-8887.** www.btm.hu. Admission 1,200 Ft adults, 600 Ft students and seniors. Photo 600 Ft; video 1,600 Ft. Audio-guided tours 850 Ft. Mar 20–Sept 15 daily 10am–6pm; Sept 16–Oct 31 Wed–Mon 10am–6pm; Nov 1–Mar 19 Wed–Mon 10am–4pm. Bus: 16A from Moszkva tér or 16 from Deák tér to Castle Hill. Funicular: From Clark Ádám tér to Castle Hill.

Nemzeti Galéria (Hungarian National Gallery) ★ With a collection of more than 10,000 art objects, this museum is not for the cultural faint of heart. I have yet to see the entire collection. Permanent exhibitions include medieval and Renaissance lapidariums, Gothic woodcarvings, Gothic winged altars, Renaissance and baroque art, and the Hungarian celebrities Mihály Munkácsy, László Paál, Károly Ferenczy, and Pál Szinyei Merse.

I. In Buda Palace, Wings B, C, and D, on Castle Hill. ✆ **1/375-5567.** Admission to permanent collection 700 Ft for everyone; temporary exhibits vary. Dome 400 Ft. Photo 1,600 Ft; video 2,100 Ft. Tues–Sun 10am–6pm. Bus: 16A from Moszkva tér or 16 from Deák tér to Castle Hill. Funicular: From Clark Ádám tér to Castle Hill.

CHURCHES

Mátyás Templom (Matthias Church) ★★★ Founded by King Béla IV in the 13th century, this church is officially named the Church of Our Lady and is a symbol of Buda's Castle District. It is popularly referred to as Matthias Church after the 15th-century king Matthias Corvinus, who added a royal oratory and was twice married here. Renovation has been an ongoing process as financial considerations allow, and it is currently half-covered with scaffolding. Regardless, it is a church not to be missed. Do not miss the museum upstairs; often overlooked by travelers who do not realize it is there, it has an interesting history of the royal crown and a wonderful view of the church.

I. Szentháromság tér 2. ✆ **1/355-5657.** www.matyas-templom.hu. Admission 750 Ft adults, 500 Ft students. Photos free. Mon–Fri 9am–5pm; Sat 9am–2:30pm, but depends on weddings; Sun 1–5pm. Metro: Moszkva tér, then bus 10; or Deák tér, then bus 16. Funicular: From Clark Ádám tér to Castle Hill.

Szent István Bazilika (St. Stephen's Church) ★★★ The country's largest church, this basilica took more than 50 years to build (the 1868 collapse of the dome caused significant delay) and was finally completed in 1906, which explains the differences in architectural designs. As you wander into the church and to the left in the back chapel, you can view St. Stephen's mummified hand or you can wait until August 20, his feast day, and see it free when it is paraded around the city. To get the box to light up to actually see it, you will have to spring for 100 Ft.

V. Szent István tér 33. ✆ **1/318-9159.** www.basilica.hu. Church free admission; treasury 400 Ft; panorama tower 500 Ft, 400 Ft students and seniors. Photos free. Tour 12,000 Ft. Church Mon–Fri 9am–5:15pm, Sat 9am–1pm, Sun 1–5pm. Services at 8am, 10am, noon, 6pm, 7:30pm; treasury daily 9am–5pm; Szent Jobb Chapel Mon–Sat 9am–5pm, Sun 1–5pm; panorama tower daily 10am–6pm. Metro: Arany János u. (Blue line) or Bajcsy-Zsilinszky út (Yellow line).

HISTORIC SQUARES & BUILDINGS

Hősök tere (Heroes' Square) ★★★ ☺ If you want a dramatic experience, come up from the Yellow metro station at Hősök tere from the city center at night. When Hősök tere is lit it is majestic in its splendor, not to say that it is not impressive during the day too. Located at the end of the grand World Heritage Boulevard, Andrássy út, the square is the entryway into the best-known park in the city, Városliget (City Park).

Two of Budapest's major museums, the Museum of Fine Arts and the Exhibition Hall, flank Heroes' Square.

Metro: To Hősök tere (Yellow line).

Magyar Állami Operaház (Hungarian State Opera House) ★★★ Built in a neo-Renaissance style, this is the most beautiful building of this style on Andrassy út. The architect was Miklós Ybl, the most successful and prolific architect of his time. He created what many agree is one of the most beautiful opera houses in Europe. It was completed in 1884. It is Budapest's and Hungary's most celebrated performance hall; the Opera House boasts a fantastically ornate interior featuring frescoes by two of the best-known Hungarian artists of the day, Bertalan Székely and Károly Lotz.

VI. Andrássy út 22. ✆ **1/332-8197.** www.opera.hu. Tour 2,800 Ft adults, 1,400 Ft students with international ID. Photo 500 Ft; video (with small camera) 500 Ft. Tours daily 3 and 4pm. Metro: Opera (Yellow line).

Parliament ★★★ Budapest's great Parliament, the second largest in Europe after London, is an eclectic design mixing the predominant Gothic revival style with a neo-Renaissance dome. Construction began in 1884, 16 years after Westminster, and was completed in 1902. Standing proudly on the Danube bank, visible from almost any riverside point, it has from the outset been one of Budapest's proud symbols, though until 1989 a democratically elected government had convened here only once (just after World War II, before the Communist takeover). As you walk up the imposing staircase, you are led under the dome along a 16-sided hallway with 16 statues of rulers. In the center floor under the dome is a glass case with the legendary jeweled crown and scepter of King St. Stephen. Historical records have shown that the crown is of two parts and from two different eras, neither from King St. Stephen's time, but Hungarians want to believe it was Stephen's. Nevertheless, it is one of the oldest royal crowns in history.

V. Kossuth tér. ✆ **1/441-4415.** Tourist.office@parliament.hu. Admission (by guided tour only) 50-min. tour in English 2,640 Ft adults, 1,320 Ft students, free admission for E.U. passport holders with passport. Photo free. Tickets available at gate X for individuals; prebooking for large groups mandatory by e-mail or phone ✆ **1/441-4904** or 1/441-4415. English-language tours year-round daily 10am, noon, and 2pm. Ticket office Mon–Fri 8am–6pm; Sat 8am–4pm; Sun 8am–2pm. Closed to tours when Parliament is in session, usually Mon and Thurs. Metro: Kossuth tér (Red line). Tram: 2 or 2A Szalay u.

PANORAMAS & PARKS

Gellért Hegy (Gellért Hill) ★★ towers 229m (750 ft.) above the Danube and offers the city's best panorama on a clear day (bus: 27 from Móricz Zsigmond körtér to Búsuló Juhász-Citadella). It's named for the Italian bishop Gellért, who assisted Hungary's first Christian king, Stephen I, in converting the Magyars to Catholicism. Gellért became a martyr when, according to legend, outraged vengeful pagans converted through the force and violent nature of Stephen's proselytism rolled Gellért in a nail-studded barrel to his death from the side of the hill. An enormous statue now stands on the hill to celebrate his memory. On top of Gellért Hill you'll find the **Liberation Monument,** built in 1947 to commemorate the Red Army's liberation of Budapest from Nazi occupation. Also atop the hill is the **Citadella,** built by the Austrians shortly after they crushed the Hungarian uprising from 1848 to 1849. Views of the city from both vistas are excellent, but the Citadella is spectacular. Don't bother paying the extra to traipse up to the upper part; the view is not that much higher, so don't waste your money.

Hlászbástya (Fisherman's Bastion) ★★, behind Matthias Church and the Hilton Hotel, has a spectacular panorama of the river and Pest beyond it. Built at the turn of the 20th century, it was included as part of the refurbishing of the church

A Cave Tour

You can tour the Pál-völgyi–Mátyás-hegyi cave system with **Barlangaszat ★★★** (✆ **06/20-928-4969** [mobile phone]; www.caving.hu). All the necessary equipment is provided with the tour: protective clothing, helmet, and headlamp. A changing room is available at the cave entrance. Crawling, scrambling, and hunkering down will be done many times during the tour, but no previous experience in caving is needed. Minimum age is 6 years, but no upper age limit. It is not recommended for those who are claustrophobic or unable to squeeze through tight places.

area. Local legend states that this stretch of medieval parapets was a protected area by the fishermen's guild, but the area was once a fish-market area, so either could be true. The local city council imposed a fee of 420 Ft to pass through the turnstile allowing you to climb to the top lookout points. If you happen to be in the area after 6 or 9pm in summer, it is no longer manned and you can go up free.

Popular **Margit-sziget (Margaret Island) ★★★** has an interesting royalty-related history going back to King Béla. He vowed that if he were successful in the Mongol invasion from 1242 to 1244, his daughter Margaret would be brought up as a nun. Well he was, so when she was 10, she was brought to the island to live a life of pious chastity. On the island, there are the ruins attesting to the religious who lived here. You can walk around what is left of the Dominican Convent, where you'll find signs mentioning St. Margaret, a 13th-century Franciscan church. The island was once called Rabbit Island since it seemed to be infested with them. No bunny was able to leave without a bridge connecting the island to shore at the time. The island has been open to the public since 1908, but visitors were charged a fee, double on Sunday. It was not until 1945 that it was declared free for all. The long, narrow island is a leisurely escape from the hectic city.

Városliget (City Park) ★★ sits behind Heroes' Square and is just as popular as Margaret Island for lazy walks, picnics in the grass, and the many attractions located in and around the park. The **Vajdahunyad Castle,** located by the lake, is magical when lit at night. The lake is used for small boat rides in the summer. Near the lake, an area is flooded to provide a frozen surface for ice-skating in winter. The park also embraces **Állatkerti körút (Animal Garden Boulevard),** where a zoo, a circus, and an amusement park are all found. You will also find Széchenyi Baths (p. 566) on one outer rim of the park. The nearby **Petőfi Csarnok** is the venue for a variety of popular cultural events, concerts, and the weekly flea market (Sat–Sun 7am–2pm). The Yellow metro line makes stops at Hősök tere (Heroes' Square), at the edge of the park, and at Széchenyi fürdő, in the middle of the park.

Vidám Park (Amusement Park) ★★ ☺ This is a must if you're traveling with kids or are a child at heart. Some rides in particular aren't to be missed. The 100-year-old **Merry-Go-Round** *(Körhinta),* constructed almost entirely of wood, has been restored to its original grandeur, though it still creaks mightily as it spins. The riders must actively pump to keep the horses rocking, which is a sight in itself, and authentic Würlitzer music plays. The **Roller Coaster,** operating since 1926, has a wooden frame and is listed as a historic monument. You rush over nine waves

BATHING IN HISTORY: BUDAPEST'S thermal BATHS

Thermal baths were popularized by the Turks, who started building them in 1565. Budapest and other parts of Hungary are built over hot springs, making this a natural way of acquiring the mineral-rich waters for bathing.

You are generally required to pay for the longest possible duration (4 hr. or more) when you enter the bathhouse. You are refunded on the basis of the actual time you spent on the premises when you exit. You are given a chip card upon entry; keep careful track of the card because if you lose it you are assumed to have stayed for the maximum time and will not receive a refund.

- **Király Baths ★★**, I. Fő u. 84 (✆ **1/202-3688;** metro: Batthyány tér, Red line), are some of the oldest baths in Hungary, dating from around 1563. The domed roof allows sunlight to filter through, giving the water a special glow. There is no longer a time restriction, so you can stay all day, though you're required to head to the lockers a half-hour before closing time. Bathing suits are required for both sexes, and take a towel with you. Women can use the baths on Monday and Wednesday from 8am to 7pm. Men are welcome on Tuesday, Thursday, Friday, and Saturday from 9am to 8pm. Sunday is a mixed day from 9am to 8pm.
- **Rudas Baths ★★**, I. Döbrentei tér 9 (✆ **1/356-1322;** bus: 7), near the Erzsébet Bridge in Buda, are the second oldest of Budapest's classic Turkish baths, built in the 16th century. The centerpiece is an octagonal pool under a domed roof with some stained-glass windows. On weekdays, these baths are for men only every day but Tuesday, when it's for women only. They're open for mixed use on weekends.
- **Széchenyi Baths ★★★**, XIV. Állatkerti út 11–14 (✆ **1/340-4505;** www.spasbudapest.com; metro: Széchenyi fürdő, Yellow line), are located in City Park, and are the most popular. From the outside, you'd never believe its enormity. Any tourist photo of older gentlemen playing chess on floating chess boards while half immersed in water is a photo of this bath.

before finishing the ride. The **Ikarus** will tickle your senses with its 30m (98-ft.) height and 30kmph (18-mph) speed making for a titillating 3-minute ride.

XIV. Állatkerti krt. 14–16. ✆ **1/343-9810.** www.vidampark.hu. Admission 15€ adults, 11€ children 100–140cm (39–55 in.) tall. Admission includes most rides with the wristband provided, but 5 are extra fees. Oct–Nov Mon–Fri noon–6pm; Mar weekends only noon–6pm; Apr–May weekdays 11am–6pm, Sat–Sun 10am–6pm; June–Sept daily 10am–8pm. Metro: Széchenyi fürdő.

ORGANIZED TOURS

What distinguishes the **Budapest Sightseeing Hop-on Hop-off Bus Tour** (✆ **1/317-7767;** www.programcentrum.hu/en) from the others, besides costing an extra 500 Ft to 1,000 Ft, is that you get two Danube riverboat rides. The boat tickets are good until the end of the year in which you buy your bus ticket, so don't feel obligated to cruise the same night of your bus tour. The added bonus is a discount booklet for different things within the city. The office is located at the Meridien Hotel, Program Centrum Travel Agency, I. Erzsébet tér 9–11. The first and earliest starting point is directly across the street.

The Shopping Scene

MAIN SHOPPING STREETS The hub of the tourist-packed capital is the first pedestrian shopping street in Budapest, **Váci utca.** It runs from the stately Vörösmarty tér in the center of Pest, across Kossuth Lajos utca, all the way to Vámház körút. The street is now largely occupied by Euro-fashion chain stores that flood every major city with their European-style prices. There are an overwhelming number of folklore/souvenir shops, which might be good for window-shopping, but unless we have recommended them below, you may be paying more than you should for that souvenir. This area is home to many cafes and bars, but it, like Castle Hill, is notorious for tourist traps. Another popular shopping area for travelers is the **Castle District** in Buda, with its abundance of overpriced folk-art boutiques and art galleries.

The **Központi Vásárcsarnok (Central Market Hall)**, IX. Vámház krt. 1–3 (✆ **1/217-6067;** metro: Kálvin tér on Blue line; tram: 47 or 49), is the largest and most spectacular market hall. Located on the Inner Ring (Kiskörút), just on the Pest side of the Szabadság Bridge, it was impeccably reconstructed in 1995. This bright, three-level market hall is a pleasure to visit. Fresh produce, meat, and cheese vendors dominate the space. Keep your eyes open for inexpensive saffron and dried mushrooms. We have had French guests who found truffles for less than 10€. The mezzanine level features folk-art booths, coffee and drink bars, and fast-food booths. The basement level houses fishmongers, pickled goods, a complete selection of spices, and Asian import foods, along with a large grocery store. Open Monday 6am to 5pm, Tuesday through Friday 6am to 6pm, and Saturday 6am to 2pm.

BEST BUYS

FOLKLORE Check out the second floor of the Central Market (see above) for a wide selection of popular handcrafted Hungarian gifts. Antiques shops, running along **Falk Miksa utca** in downtown Budapest, feature a broad selection of vintage furniture, ceramics, carpets, jewelry, and accessories, but over the years, it has become more expensive with less bargaining going on for tourists. One shop that has a wide selection and helpful staff is **Folkart Craftman's House** (✆ **1/318-5143**) on the side street, V. Régiposta u. 12, right off of Váci utca, and open daily 10am to 7pm. An outstanding private shop on Váci utca is **Vali Folklór,** in the courtyard of V. Váci u. 23 (✆ **1/337-6301**), open Monday to Saturday 10am to 8pm and Sunday noon to 8pm.

Ethnic Hungarians from Transylvania come to Budapest with bags full of handmade craftwork, selling their goods to Hungarians and tourists alike. Their prices are generally quite reasonable, and bargaining is customary. Keep your eyes open for these vendors, who sell on the street or in the metro plazas—they are unmistakable in their characteristic black boots and dark-red skirts, with red or white kerchiefs tied around their heads.

FOOD Hungarian salami is world famous. Connoisseurs generally agree that Pick Salami, produced in the southeastern city of Szeged, is the best brand. Herz Salami, produced locally in Budapest, is also a very popular product (though not as popular as Pick). You should be aware that some people have reported difficulty in clearing U.S. Customs with salami; take it home at your own risk. Another typical Hungarian food product is chestnut paste *(gesztenye pu[um]ré),* available in a tin or block wrapped in foil; it's used primarily as a pastry filling but can also top desserts and ice cream. Paprika paste *(pirosarany)* is another product that's tough to find outside Hungary. It usually comes in a bright-red tube. Three types are available: hot *(csípős),* deli-style *(csemege),* and sweet *(édes).* Powdered paprika also comes in the same three varieties as the paste. All of these items can be purchased at grocery stores *(élelmiszer),* delicatessens *(csemege),* and usually any convenience store. In the great market, you will find the powdered version in little decorated cloth bags, making it ready for gift giving.

PORCELAIN Another popular Hungarian item is porcelain, particularly from the country's two best-known producers, Herend and Zsolnay. Although both brands are available in the West, you'll find a better selection, but not lower prices, in Hungary. **Ajka Crystal,** V. József Attila u. 7 (✆ **1/317-8133**), is Hungary's renowned crystal producer from the Lake Balaton region. The Herend Shops are located at V. József nádor tér 11 (✆ **1/317-2622**), and I. Szentháromság u. 5 (✆ **1/225-1051**). An alternative to the classic Herend porcelain is **Herend Village Pottery,** II. Bem rakpart 37 (✆ **1/356-7899**), which is not associated with the Herend porcelain company. The *majolika* (village pottery) is a hand-painted folklore-inspired way of making pottery.

WINE The sweet white Tokaji Aszú, Tokaji Eszenzia, and Tokaji Szamorodni, and the mouth-tingling Egri Bikavér, Villányi Cuveé, Szekszárdi Bikavér, and Kékfrankos are the most representative of Hungarian wine. Stop at **La Boutique des Vins,** V. József Attila u. 12 (behind the Jaguar dealership) (✆ **1/317-5919** or 1/266-4397). Sophisticated, classy, and welcoming, this wine shop is a cut above the others. Not only does **Pántlika Borház,** V. Király Pál u. 10 (✆ **70/409-2569**), carry a vast selection of wines from all over Hungary, but the owner's knowledge of them is just as impressive.

Locals say that good palinka (a traditional form of brandy) should warm the stomach and not burn the throat. Visit the **House of Hungarian Pálinka,** VIII. Rákcozi u. 17 (✆ **1/338-4219;** www.magyarpalinkahaza.hu), for an initiation.

Budapest After Dark

For the most up-to-date information, go to www.jegymester.hu and click on the English link. This site includes information for the opera house as well as the major theaters in the city. A complete schedule of mainstream performing arts is found in the free bimonthly ***Koncert Kalendárium,*** available at any of the Tourinform offices, or you can check it online at **www.koncertkalendarium.hu**.

The **Cultur-Comfort Központi Jegyiroda (Cultur-Comfort Ticket Office),** VI. Paulay Ede u. 31 (✆ **1/322-0000**), is open Monday to Friday 9am to 6pm. They sell tickets to just about everything, from theater and operettas to sports events and rock concerts.

THE PERFORMING ARTS The **Budapesti Operettszínház (Budapest Operetta Theatre),** VI. Nagymező u. 17 (© **1/312-4866;** www.operettszinhaz.hu), is a highlight among Art Nouveau–style buildings. The off season is mid-July to mid-August. The box office is open Monday to Friday 10am to 2:30pm and 3 to 7pm and Saturday 1 to 7pm. Take the Metro to Opera or Oktogon (Yellow line). The season at the landmark **Magyar Állami Operaház (Hungarian State Opera House;** p. 564) runs from mid-September to mid-June. Summer visitors can take in approximately eight performances (both opera and ballet) during the Summer Operafest in July or August. The box office is open weekdays from 11am until the beginning of the performance, or to 5pm when there is no performance, and Sunday from 10am to 1pm and 4pm until the beginning of the performance. Take the Yellow line metro to Opera.

The main concert hall of the **Palace of Arts ★★**, IX. Komor Marcell u. 1 (© **1/555-3001;** www.mupa.hu), is the finest contemporary classical music venue in Budapest; it now hosts concerts from celebrated orchestras from around the world. To get there, take tram no. 2 from downtown toward the Lágymányos Bridge.

FOLK-DANCE Authentic folk-music workshops are held at least once a week at several locations around the city. The leading Hungarian folk band is **Muzsikás,** the name given to musicians playing traditional folk music in Hungarian villages. They have toured the U.S., playing to great acclaim, so may not always be available at a Budapest *táncház* (dance house). Every Thursday (Sept–May only) from 8pm to midnight for 700 Ft, there's music at the **Marczibányi tér Művelődési Ház (Marczibányi Square Cultural House),** II. Marczibányi tér 5/a (© **1/212-2820**). Take the Red line metro to Moszkva tér. Also try the **Fõvárosi Művelõdési Ház (Municipal Cultural House),** at XI. Fehérvári út 47 (© **1/203-3868**). At the **Kalamajka Dance House,** Belvárosi Ifjúsági Mûvelõdési Ház, V. Molnár u. 9 (© **1/371-5928**), reachable by M3 Ferenciek tere, is the biggest weekend dance, with dancing and instruction on the second floor, while jam sessions and serious palinka drinking take place on the fourth. The Kalamajka band is led by Béla Halmos, who started the dance-house movement in the 1970s. Usually, traditional villagers give guest performances. Open Saturday from 8pm to 1am for 700 Ft; you can dance until you drop.

An important heritage-preserving center, the **Almássy téri Művelődési Központ (Almássy Square Culture Center),** VII. Almássy tér 6 (© **1/352-1572**), hosts folk dances to the music of the electric Greeks Sirtos in the main hall from 6 to 10pm. Upstairs is a bit crazier with the small fanatic band of Magyar dancers who twirl to the Kalotaszeg sounds of the Berkó Band until midnight. A short walk from Blaha Lujza tér (Blue line or tram no. 4 or 6) gets you to this folk center. Entrance fees vary from 700 Ft to 1,500 Ft. In the City Park is **Petőfi Csarnok,** XIV. Zichy Mihály út 14 (© **1/363-3730;** www.pecsa.hu), an old-style no-frills hall whose stages are used for some of the best folk performances in the city.

DANCE CLUBS Budapest has a hot club scene, but what is offered at any given time is apt to change, often depending on the current trend. Try out **Barokko Club and Lounge,** VI. Liszt Ferenc tér 5 (© **1/322-0700;** www.barokko.hu), still one of the hot spots on Liszt Ferenc tér, where seeing and being seen is of the utmost importance.

Meeting Hungarian guys or the young fashionable ladies is not a problem at the huge and hedonistic **E-Klub,** X. Népligeti u. 2 (✆ **1/263-1614;** www.e-klub.hu). Touted as the biggest and most famous of the university pubs, **School Club Közgáz,** IX. Fővám tér 8 (✆ **1/215-4359**), is packed solid during weekends.

LIVE MUSIC The **A38 Boat ★★**, XI. Pázmány Péter sétány (✆ **1/464-3940;** www.a38.hu), is a former Ukrainian stone-carrying ship anchored at the Buda-side foot of the Petőfi Bridge. On the lower deck, you can get your fill of the city's best range of jazz, world, electronic, hip-hop, and rock music bands.

For the best jazz and blues in Hungary, head to **Old Man's Music Pub ★★**, V. Akácfa u. 13 (✆ **1/322-7645;** www.oldmans.hu), where Hobo and his blues band are regulars. See the list of current entertainment posted inside the door. In the back of **Spinoza Étterem ★★**, VII. Dob u. 15 ✆ **1/413-7488;** www.spinozahaz.hu), a small restaurant, is a small cabaret offering nightly music performances ranging from Klezmer to classical.

PUBS & CAFE BARS **Café Aloe,** VI. Zichy Jenő u. 37 (✆ **1/269-4536**), is a sizzling, comfortable cellar that offers powerful, yet remarkably cheap drinks prepared by attentive bar staff. For a lounge, cafe, restaurant, and bar all rolled into one, head to **Szilvuplé,** VI. Ó u. 33 (✆ **20/992–5115** [mobile phone]; www.szilvuple.hu). Talented DJs set the tone with rock and indie music; it also features karaoke nights and dance lessons during the week. For a cultural experience, you cannot pass up **Szimpla Kert ★★**, VII. Kertész u. 48 (✆ **1/321-9119;** www.szimpla.hu), a beer garden and alternative culture Mecca. Located in an abandoned apartment courtyard, Szimpla Kert mixes junkyard aesthetics with such modernisms as Wi-Fi, a daytime cafe, and evenings of live music and indie film screenings.

GAY & LESBIAN BARS Gay bars open and close in the blink of an eye. For reliable and up-to-date information, visit **www.budapestgaycity.net** or **www.gayguide.net**, or subscribe to the free Yahoo **Gay Budapest Information** group by sending an e-mail to gaybudapestinfo-subscribe@yahoogroups.com. **AlterEgo,** VI. Dessewffy u. 33 (✆ **06/70-345-4302** [mobile phone]), is a hip jumping club for the younger set, but older folks of both genders are welcome too for their different events. In the city center, **Árkádia,** V. Türr István u. 5 (✆ **06/20-496-5854**), is a small, intimate, sometimes packed bar with a popular backroom, the perfect place to meet, dance, or get cozy with an attractive stranger. **Habrolo Bisztro,** V. Szep u. 1/b (✆ **06/20-211-6701** [mobile phone]), is a small gay bar where locals hang out, so you can practice your Hungarian skills. Once known as the Mystery Bar, **Le Café M,** V. Nagysándor József u. 3 (✆ **1/312-1436;** www.lecafem.com), was the first gay bar in the city. It is a very tiny, but friendly place that draws a large foreign clientele, making it a great place to meet new people.

THE DANUBE BEND

The small but historic towns along the snaking Bend, in particular, Szentendre, Vác, Visegrád, and Esztergom, are easy day trips from Budapest as they're all within a half-hour to a couple of hours from the city. The natural beauty of the area, where forested hills loom over the river, makes it a welcome haven for those weary of the city. Travelers with more time in Budapest can easily make a long weekend out of a visit to the Bend, but I suggest a Budapest base with half-day or day trips.

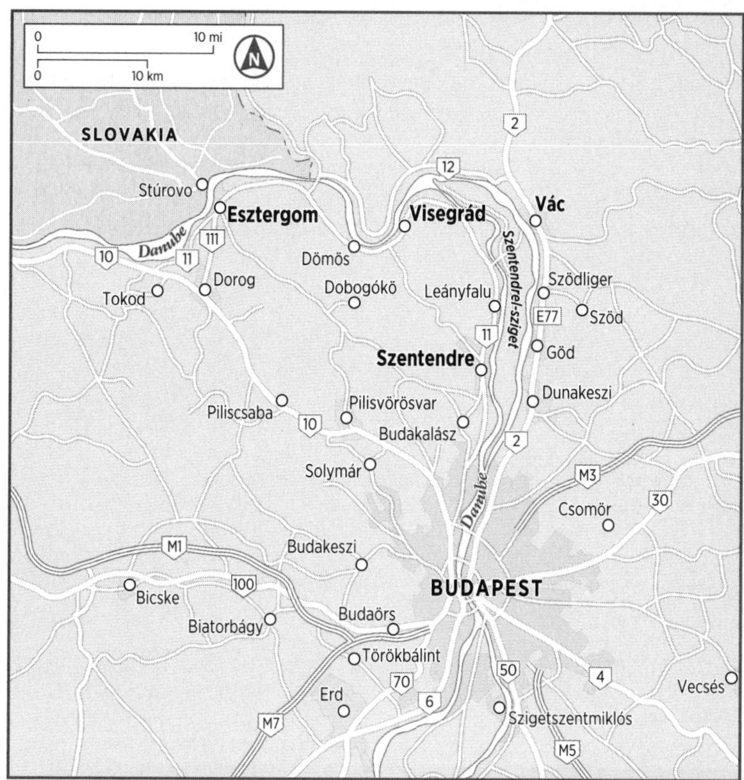

Getting There

BY BOAT From April to September, boats run between Budapest and the towns of the Danube Bend. A leisurely boat ride through the countryside is one of the highlights of a boat excursion. All boats depart from Budapest's Vigadó tér boat landing, which is located in Pest between Erzsébet Bridge and Szabadság Bridge, stopping to pick up passengers 5 minutes later at Buda's Batthyány tér landing, which is also a Red line metro stop, before it continues up the river.

Schedules and towns served are complicated and change sometimes due to water levels of the river, so contact **Mahart,** the state shipping company, at the Vigadó tér landing (✆ **1/318-1704;** www.mahartpassnave.hu; click on the British flag) for information. You can also get MAHART information from Tourinform.

One-way prices by riverboat are 1,490 Ft to Vác, 1,590 Ft to Visegrád, and 1,990 Ft to Esztergom. Trips to Szentendre cost 2,235 Ft round-trip. Children 5 and under ride free, children 15 and under receive a 50% discount, and students receive a 25% discount with the ISIC card.

The approximate travel time by boat from Budapest is 2 hours to Szentendre, 3½ hours to Visegrád, and 5 hours to Esztergom. If time is tight, consider the train or bus (both of which are also considerably cheaper).

BY TRAIN TO SZENTENDRE The HÉV suburban railroad connects Budapest's Batthyány tér Station with Szentendre. On the Pest side, you can catch the HÉV from the Margit Híd, Budai Híd Fő stop on tram no. 4 or 6. Trains leave daily, year-round, every 20 minutes or so from 4am to 11:30pm. The one-way fare is 600 Ft. If you have a valid Budapest public transportation pass, the supplemental ticket is 265 Ft each way. The trip is 45 minutes.

TO VISEGRÁD There's no direct train service to Visegrád. Instead you can take one of 28 daily trains departing from Nyugati Station for Nagymaros-Visegrád (trip time: 40 min.–1 hr.). From Nagymaros, take a ferry across the river to Visegrád. The ferry dock (RÉV; ✆ **26/398-344**) is a 5-minute walk from the train station. A ferry leaves every hour throughout the day. The train ticket to Nagymaros costs 955 Ft; the ferryboat ticket to Visegrád costs 250 Ft for adults and 125 Ft for students.

TO ESZTERGOM One train every hour makes the run daily between Budapest's Nyugati Station and Esztergom (trip time: 1½ hr.); InterCity trains are not available on this route. Train tickets cost 955 Ft each way.

BY BUS Approximately 30 buses travel the same route to Szentendre, Visegrád, and Esztergom, departing from Budapest's **Árpád híd bus station** (✆ **1/329-1450;** at the Blue line metro station of the same name). Some are only on specific days of the week, while others are daily. Buses charge by mileage ranges. Depending on the bus, the number of stops, and the day of the week, it could be a pleasant or excruciatingly long ride. The one-way fare to Szentendre is 475 Ft; the trip takes about 45 minutes. The fare to Visegrád is 750 Ft, and the trip takes anywhere from 1¼ to 3 hours. To Esztergom, take the bus that travels via a town called Dorog; it costs 1,050 Ft and takes from 1¼ hours to 2 hours depending on the day of the week or bus selected. Keep in mind, of course, that all travel by bus is subject to traffic delays, especially during rush hour.

Szentendre

Szentendre (pronounced *Sen*-ten-dreh, St. Andrew), 21km (13 miles) north of Budapest, has been populated since the Stone Age by Illyrians, the Celtic Eraviscus tribe, Romans, Lombards, Avars, and, naturally, Hungarians. Serbians settled here in the 17th century, embellishing the town with their unique characteristics. Szentendre counts half a dozen Serbian churches among its rich collection of historic buildings.

Since the turn of the 20th century, Szentendre has been home to an artists' colony, where today about 100 artists live and work, referred to as "The City of Artists."

The town is an extremely popular destination, with buses pouring tourists into the streets for a few hours of exploring. This is sometimes a turnoff for other visitors, but the town really is a treasure. To appreciate its rich flavor, we recommend you look beyond the touristy shops and wander the streets looking at the architecture, the galleries, and the churches, if only from the outside.

ESSENTIALS

One of Szentendre's information offices, **Tourinform,** is at Dumtsa Jenő u. 22 (✆ **26/317-965**), with maps of Szentendre (and the region), as well as concert and

BEST LÁNGOS ever

If you get a snack attack, you will find the best *lángos* in Hungary here in Szentendre at **Álom Lángos ★★★** at Fő tér 8 (✆ **06/20-970-7827** [mobile phone]), an unassuming little stand. Sometimes the long waiting lines are attesting to this fact, since most will be Hungarians in the know. *Lángos* is the Hungarian version of fried dough with toppings. In Fő tér, there are yellow signs near an alley with LÁNGOS written on them. Halfway up the alley is a gate for the small shed. This alone is worth a trip to Szentendre. The stand is open only March through November Tuesday through Saturday 10am to 6pm, and a *lángos* will cost you 300 Ft to 500 Ft.

exhibition schedules. The office can also provide hotel information. It is open April through August, Monday to Friday from 9am to 5:30pm, weekends 10am to 5:30pm. In September to November it's open Monday to Friday from 9:30am to 4:30pm, weekends 10am to 4pm. December through March, the hours are the same as autumn, but they open half an hour later weekdays. To get here, just follow the flow of pedestrian traffic into town on Kossuth Lajos utca. Like all things in this town, the office marches to the beat of its own drummer, not always keeping with the schedule it gives. If you arrive by boat, you may find the **Ibusz** office sooner, located on the corner of Bogdányi út and Gőzhajó utca (✆ **26/310-181**). This office is open April to October, Monday through Friday from 10am to 6pm and weekends 10am to 3pm. From November to March, it's open weekdays only, 10am to 5pm.

EXPLORING THE TOWN

The tiny **Blagovestenska Church ★** at Fő tér 4 dates from 1752 and was built on the site of a wooden church from the Serbian migration of 1690. It's open from Tuesday to Sunday, 10am to 5pm; admission is 300 Ft. The **Margit Kovács Museum ★★**, Vastagh György u. 1 (✆ **26/310-244**), features the work of Hungary's best-known ceramic artist, Margit Kovács. It's open from Tuesday to Sunday, 10am to 6pm. Admission is 1,000 Ft. The **Szabó Marzipan Museum ★★**, Dumsta Jeno u. 12 (✆ **26/311-931**), is the most widely known museum in this village. Who could pass up this chance to see the 1.5m-long (5-ft.) Hungarian Parliament made entirely in marzipan? The museum is open May to September daily from 10am to 7pm, and October to April daily 10am to 6pm. Admission is 400 Ft.

SHOPPING

Blue Land Folklor ★★★, Alkotmány u. 8 (✆ **26/313-610**), carries decorated eggs from 38 regions of Hungary, including some from the ethnic Hungarian areas prior to the Trianon Treaty's loss of land.

If you want to find a unique shop while in Hungary, come to **Handpets ★★★**, Dumsta Jeno u. 15 (✆ **30/954–2584** [mobile phone only]). Handpets are the most creative hand puppets I have ever seen. Designed by Kati Szili, they are handmade of high-quality material and are sure to delight children of all ages. This is the only exclusive shop where the entire collection is available, although limited designs and poor imitations are sold elsewhere.

WHERE TO STAY

Róz Panzió ★, located at Pannónia utca 6/b (✆ **26/311-737;** fax 26/310-979; www.hotelrozszentendre.hu), has 10 units and a garden overlooking the Danube where you can eat breakfast when weather permits. Rooms are 50€ to 55€ for a double; breakfast is included.

WHERE TO DINE

Aranysárkány Vendéglő (Golden Dragon Inn) ★, Alkotmány u. 1/a (✆ **26/301-479;** www.aranysarkany.hu), located just east of Fő tér on Hunyadi utca, is always filled to capacity. The crowd includes a large percentage of Hungarians, definitely a good sign in a heavily visited town like Szentendre. You can choose from such enticing offerings as alpine lamb, roast leg of goose, Székely-style stuffed cabbage (the Székely are a Hungarian ethnic group native to Transylvania), spinach cream, and venison steak. Vegetarians can order the vegetable plate, a respectable presentation of grilled and steamed vegetables in season. Set away from the bustle of the square, **Chez Nicolas ★★★**, Kígyó utca 10 (✆ **26/311-288**), is a charming restaurant with an outdoor terrace looking out to the river. We recommend the Pork Brasso with choice chunks of pork cooked in paprika, oil, and potatoes. If you walk directly south from Fő tér, you'll find **Régimódi ★★**, Futó u. 3 (✆ **26/311-105**). An elegant restaurant in a former private home, Régimódi is furnished with antique Hungarian carpets and chandeliers. The menu offers a wide range of Hungarian specialties, with an emphasis on game dishes. There are also numerous salad options, with specials each day on the board. Whatever you choose, the portions are hearty. The only drawback is that it does get crowded with tour groups.

Visegrád

Halfway between Szentendre and Esztergom, Visegrád (pronounced *Vee*-sheh-grod) is a sparsely populated, sleepy riverside village, which makes its history all the more fascinating and hard to believe. The Romans built a fort here, which was still standing when Slovak settlers gave the town its present name in the 9th or 10th century. It means "High Castle." After the Mongol invasion (1241–42), construction began on both the present ruined hilltop citadel and the former riverside palace. Eventually, Visegrád boasted one of the finest royal palaces ever built in Hungary.

ESSENTIALS

Visegrád Tours, RÉV u. 15 (✆ **26/398-160;** www.visegrad.org), is located across the road from the RÉV ferryboat landing. It is open daily 8am to 5:30pm from November to March, but they conduct business from the associated hotel next door. The lively time is summer, when there are historical re-creations, but other times of the year are fine for a sedate vacation experience.

EXPLORING THE PALACE & THE CITADEL

Once covering much of the area where the boat landing and Fő utca (Main St.) are now found are the excavated remnants and restoration of parts of the **King Matthias Museum ★★**, at Fő u. 27 (✆ **26/398-026;** www.visegradmuzeum.hu). The tower of the lower castle, known as **Solomon's Tower,** was built in the 13th century. Entrance to the palace is 1,040 Ft and 620 Ft for the tower. Both are open Tuesday to Sunday from 9am to 5pm, but the tower is closed from October 1 to April

30. The buried ruins of the palace, having achieved a near-mythical status, were not discovered until the 21st century.

The **Fellegvár (Cloud Castle) ★★★** (✆ **26/598-082**), a mountaintop citadel above Visegrád, affords one of the finest views you'll find over the Danube. Admission to the citadel is 900 Ft. It is open daily from 9:30am to 5:30pm from March 15 to October 14. The "City Bus," a van taxi that awaits passengers outside Visegrád Tours, takes people up the steep hill for a steep fare of 2,500 Ft apiece or 4,000 Ft for a round-trip, but to get the round-trip fare, you must stay at the top a maximum of 30 minutes; otherwise, it is again 2,500 Ft for the ride down. Note that it is not a casual walk to the citadel; consider it a day hike and pack accordingly with bottled water.

WHERE TO STAY

Good accommodations can be found at **Honti Panzió and Hotel,** Fő utca 66 (✆ **26/398-120**). Double rooms cost 50€ for the *panzio* and 65€ in the hotel, both with multinight packages. All rates include breakfast and VAT, but not the 300 Ft tax per person per night; parking is provided.

WHERE TO DINE

Set on a hilltop featuring one of the finest views of the Danube bend, **Nagyvillám Vadászcsárda (Big Lightning Hunter's Inn),** Fekete-hegy (✆ **26/398-070**), infuses a leafy, countryside dinner with an elegant and warm atmosphere. Although vegetarians may struggle with a menu consisting mainly of meat and game dishes, it is nevertheless an extensive menu combining Mediterranean influences with Hungarian recipes using 12 varieties of wild forest mushrooms.

Esztergom

Formerly a Roman settlement, **Esztergom** (pronounced *Ess*-tair-gome) was the seat of the Hungarian kingdom for 300 years. Hungary's first king, István I (Stephen I), renamed from Vajk by German priests, received the crown from the pope in A.D. 1000. He converted Hungary to Catholicism, and Esztergom became the country's center of the early church. Although its glory days are long gone due to invasions from the Mongols and later the Turks, it was rebuilt once again in the 18th and 19th centuries. This quiet town remains the seat of the archbishop primate, known as the "Hungarian Rome."

From Esztergom west all the way to the Austrian border, the Danube marks the border between Hungary and Slovakia, with an international ferry crossing at Esztergom. There's little to entice anyone to stay overnight here with Budapest so close, so I strongly recommend making this a day trip and returning to Budapest at the end of the day.

ESSENTIALS

The station is on the outskirts of town, while the tourist information center is in the city center. The primary reason to take the trip at all is the cathedral, so just take bus no. 1 or 6 to the Baszilika stop and walk up to the church. Buses depart from outside the train station, and you can buy your ticket on the bus. Bus no. 6 tickets cost 100 Ft, but on our return to the station, when we were much closer, the ticket on bus no. 1 was 165 Ft. We realized they are two different companies.

EXPLORING THE TOWN

The massive, neoclassical **Esztergom Cathedral ★★** (✆ **33/411-895**), on Szent István tér on Castle Hill, is the largest church in Hungary. Built in the last century, it was to replace the original cathedral ruined during the Turkish occupation. The crypt, built in old Egyptian style with a magnificent statue of an angel, is also the last resting place of bishops. The cathedral ***kincstár*** **(treasury) ★** contains a dazzling array of ecclesiastical jewels and gold works. If you brave the ascent of the cupola, you're rewarded with unparalleled views of Esztergom and the surrounding Hungarian and Slovakian countryside. Admission to the treasury is 700 Ft; admission to the cupola is 400 Ft. The cathedral is open daily in the summer, 8am to 7pm, and daily in winter 8am to 4pm; the treasury, crypt, and cupola are open daily in summer 9am to 4pm, and in winter, Tuesday to Sunday, noon to 4pm; the cupola is closed in winter. Take bus no. 6 from the train station and get off at the cathedral; in good weather, it is a nice walk. If you happen to be in town during the first week of August, don't miss out on one of the classical guitar concerts performed in the cathedral; the acoustics are said to be sublime. The concerts are part of Esztergom's annual **International Guitar Festival ★★**.

The **Keresztény Múzeum (Christian Museum),** Mindszenty József tér 2 (✆ **33/413-880;** www.keresztenymuzeum.hu), in the neoclassical former primate's palace, houses Hungary's largest collection of religious art and the largest collection of medieval art outside the National Gallery in Budapest. Admission is 600 Ft adults, 300 Ft children. The museum is open daily May to October 10am to 5pm, and November to April 11am to 3pm (closed Jan–Feb).

To get to the museum, leave the basilica by the museum downward path and follow it to the right. You will come to a souvenir shop. Turn right on that street, Mindszenty József u. When you get to the next church, the museum is beyond it to the right. Don't be fooled by the other building under renovation.

WHERE TO DINE

Creative specialties abound at **Padlizsán Étterem ★★★**, Pazmány Peter u. 21 (✆ **33/311-212**), a homey restaurant behind the basilica. In warm weather, enjoy the view of the basilica above the hill. Four of us dined here and each was impressed with our selection. At the time, the service was scattered, but most likely due to a wedding inside.

For a few other cafes and snack stops you can try the limited selections on the main square, **Széchenyi tér.**

IRELAND

by Christi Daugherty & Jack Jewers

Which Ireland do you want to visit? The old Emerald Isle of thatched cottages, craggy seascapes, and pubs that smell of polished mahogany and Guinness? Or do you imagine the hip, urban country of trendy bistros, sushi bars, and modern-art galleries? These days, both await you.

Old Ireland is still there to some extent, and the country remains a land of breathtaking beauty. But today's Ireland is not a poor cousin to other European nations. In the past few decades it's undergone a renaissance that has modernized it and brought it into the 21st century. After the mid-1990s, some "old Ireland" disappeared, replaced by designer shops, stomped by an army of Manolo Blahniks, and hidden behind a new forest of overpriced suburban McMansions.

Now, though, the boom is over. Ireland's economy took enough of a hammering in the global recession that it may be a while before you hear the phrase "Celtic Tiger" spoken in tones other than the nostalgic.

Still, although the country frets about tumbling house prices, prosperity and modernity are probably permanent residents now; they've just brought with them their unwelcome cousins—inflation and intolerance.

Inflation is the dark cloud behind the Irish economy's silver lining, as you'll discover when you book a hotel or dine in a restaurant. Forty-dollar entrees are the norm, rather than the exception. And a night in a no-frills hotel will set you back $150.

Intolerance has reared its head in terms of anti-immigration legislation designed to limit eastern European immigration, and ensure that Ireland stays "Irish."

Meanwhile, the peace agreement in the North is shakier than it's been in a decade. While residents fear the return of violence, most think it's unimaginable that the dangerous old days could return, after such massive progress was made.

It all means that this is a fascinating time to visit Ireland—whether you're rushing to see old Ireland before it goes, or hoping to visit trendy modern Ireland. Both await you, but keep your wallet at the ready. You're going to need it.

DUBLIN

"Seedy elegance" aptly described much, if not most, of Dublin until the mid-1990s, when the city's transformation from endearingly frumpy to cutting-edge cool began. Today's Dublin is a trendy place, where expensive restaurants and nightspots sprout up—and disappear—with startling speed. It is the emotional and political center of the country.

Essentials

GETTING THERE

BY PLANE **Dublin International Airport** (✆ **01/814-1111;** www.dublin airport.com) is 11km (6¾ miles) north of the city center. A Travel Information Desk in the Arrivals Concourse provides information on public bus and rail services throughout the country.

An excellent airport-to-city shuttle bus service called **AirCoach** operates 24 hours a day, making runs at 15-minute intervals. Its buses run direct from the airport to Dublin's city center and south side, stopping at O'Connell Street, St. Stephen's Green, Fitzwilliam Square, Merrion Square, Ballsbridge, and Donnybrook—that is, all the key hotel and business districts. The fare is €7 one-way or €12 round-trip (children 11 and under travel free); buy your ticket from the driver. Although Air-Coach is slightly more expensive than the Dublin Bus (see below), it makes fewer intermediary stops, so it is faster (the journey to the city center takes about 45 min.), and it brings you right into the hotel districts. To confirm AirCoach departures and arrivals, call ✆ **01/844-7118** or find it on the Web at **www.aircoach.ie**.

If you need to connect with the Irish bus or rail service, the **Airlink Express Coach** (✆ **01/844-4265;** www.dublinbus.ie) provides express coach services from the airport into central Dublin and beyond. Routes 747 and 748 go to the city's central bus station, **Busáras,** on Store Street, and on to **Connolly** railway station, and route 748 makes an additional stop at **Heuston** railway station. Service runs daily from 5:45am to 11:30pm (Sun 7:15am–11:30pm), with departures every 20 to 30 minutes. One-way fare is €6 for adults and €3 for children 11 and under.

Finally, **Dublin Bus** (✆ **01/872-0000;** www.dublinbus.ie) runs connections between the airport and the city center from 6am to 11:30pm. The one-way trip takes about 30 minutes, and the fare is €6. Nos. 16a, 41, 41b, 46x, 230, 746, 747, and 748 all serve the city center from Dublin Airport. Consult the Travel Information Desk in the Arrivals Concourse to figure out which bus will bring you closest to your hotel.

For speed and ease—especially if you have a lot of luggage—a **taxi** is the best way to get directly to your hotel or guesthouse. Depending on your destination in Dublin, fares average between €20 and €30. Surcharges include €.50 for each additional passenger and for each piece of luggage. Depending on traffic, a cab should take between 20 and 45 minutes to get into the city center. A 10% tip is standard. Taxis are lined up at a first-come, first-served taxi stand outside the arrivals terminal.

Major international and local car-rental companies operate desks at Dublin Airport.

BY FERRY Passenger and car ferries from Britain arrive at the **Dublin Ferryport** (✆ **01/855-2222**), on the eastern end of the North Docks, and at the **Dún Laoghaire Ferryport** (✆ **01/842-8864**). Call **Irish Ferries** (✆ **0818/300-400;**

Ireland

www.irishferries.co.uk), **P&O Irish Sea** (✆ **01/800-409-049;** www.poirishsea.com), or **Stena Line** (✆ **01/204-7777;** www.stenaline.com) for bookings and information. There is bus and taxi service from both ports.

BY TRAIN **Irish Rail** (✆ **01/850-366222;** www.irishrail.ie), also called Ianród Éireann, operates daily train service to Dublin from Belfast, Northern Ireland, and all major cities in the Irish Republic, including Cork, Galway, Limerick, Killarney, Sligo, Wexford, and Waterford. Trains from the south, west, and southwest arrive at **Heuston Station,** Kingsbridge, off St. John's Road; from the north and northwest at **Connolly Station,** Amiens Street; and from the southeast at **Pearse Station,** Westland Row, Tara Street.

BY BUS **Bus Éireann** (✆ **01/836-6111;** www.buseireann.ie) operates daily express coach and local bus service from all major cities and towns in Ireland into Dublin's central bus station, **Busáras,** Store Street.

BY CAR If you are arriving by car from other parts of Ireland or on a car ferry from Britain, all main roads lead into the heart of Dublin and are well signposted to An

Dublin

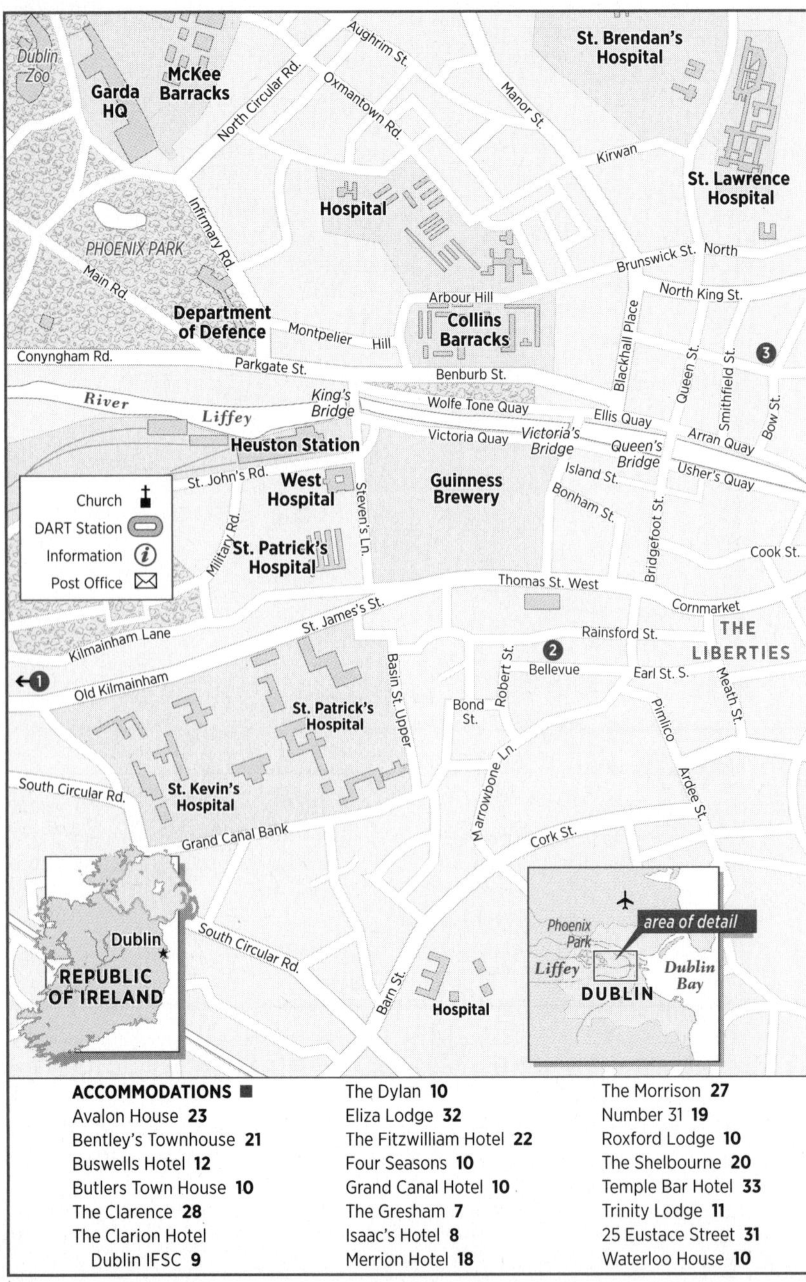
Dublin Zoo
Garda HQ
McKee Barracks
Aughrim St.
North Circular Rd.
Oxmantown Rd.
Manor St.
St. Brendan's Hospital
St. Lawrence Hospital
Kirwan
Hospital
Infirmary Rd.
PHOENIX PARK
Main Rd.
Brunswick St. North
North King St.
Arbour Hill
Collins Barracks
Department of Defence
Montpelier Hill
Conyngham Rd.
Parkgate St.
Benburb St.
Blackhall Place
Queen St.
Smithfield St.
Bow St.
River Liffey
King's Bridge
Wolfe Tone Quay
Ellis Quay
Arran Quay
Heuston Station
Victoria Quay
Victoria's Bridge
Queen's Bridge
Usher's Quay
Island St.
St. John's Rd.
West Hospital
Guinness Brewery
Bonham St.
Steven's Ln.
Military Rd.
St. Patrick's Hospital
Bridgefoot St.
Cook St.
Church
DART Station
Information
Post Office
Thomas St. West
Cornmarket
St. James's St.
Rainsford St.
THE LIBERTIES
Kilmainham Lane
Old Kilmainham
Basin St. Upper
Robert St.
Bellevue
Earl St. S.
Meath St.
Bond St.
Pimlico
St. Patrick's Hospital
South Circular Rd.
St. Kevin's Hospital
Marrowbone Ln.
Ardee St.
Grand Canal Bank
Cork St.
Dublin
REPUBLIC OF IRELAND
South Circular Rd.
Phoenix Park
area of detail
Liffey
DUBLIN
Dublin Bay
Barn St.
Hospital
ACCOMMODATIONS
Avalon House 23
Bentley's Townhouse 21
Buswells Hotel 12
Butlers Town House 10
The Clarence 28
The Clarion Hotel Dublin IFSC 9
The Dylan 10
Eliza Lodge 32
The Fitzwilliam Hotel 22
Four Seasons 10
Grand Canal Hotel 10
The Gresham 7
Isaac's Hotel 8
Merrion Hotel 18
The Morrison 27
Number 31 19
Roxford Lodge 10
The Shelbourne 20
Temple Bar Hotel 33
Trinity Lodge 11
25 Eustace Street 31
Waterloo House 10

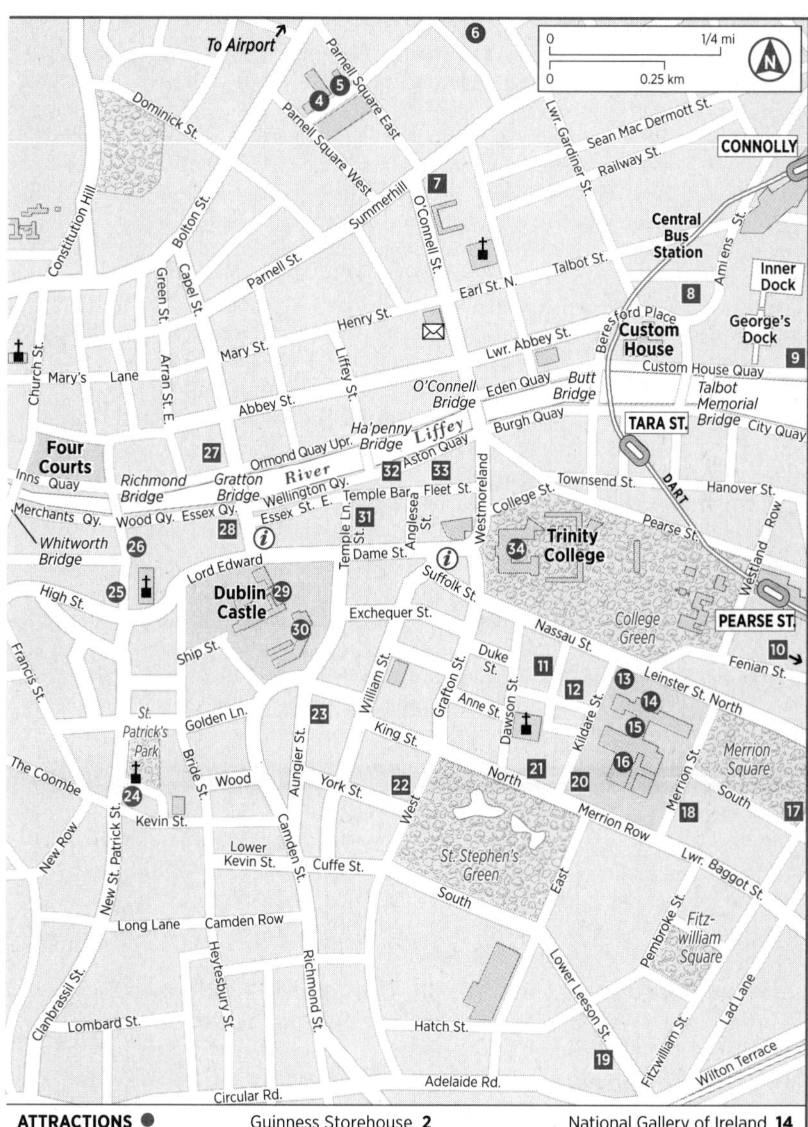

ATTRACTIONS ●

The Book of Kells **34**
Chester Beatty Library **30**
Christ Church Cathedral **26**
Dublin Castle **29**
Dublin Writers Museum **5**
Dublinia **25**
Guinness Storehouse **2**
Heraldic Museum/
Genealogical Office **13**
Hugh Lane Municipal
Gallery of Modern Art **4**
James Joyce Centre **6**
Kilmainham Gaol Historical Museum **1**
National Gallery of Ireland **14**
National Museum **16**
National Photographic
Archive **15**
Number Twenty Nine **17**
The Old Jameson Distillery **3**
St. Patrick's Cathedral **24**

Lar (City Centre). To bypass the city center, the East Link (toll bridge €1.90) and West Link are signposted, and M50 circuits the city on three sides.

VISITOR INFORMATION **Dublin Tourism** operates six walk-in visitor centers in greater Dublin that are open every day except Christmas. The principal center is on Suffolk Street, Dublin 2, open from June to August Monday to Saturday from 9am to 8:30pm, Sunday and bank holidays 10:30am to 3pm, and the rest of the year Monday to Saturday 9am to 5:30pm, Sunday and bank holidays 10:30am to 3pm. The Suffolk Street office has a currency exchange counter, a car-rental counter, an accommodations-reservations service, bus and rail information desks, a gift shop, and a cafe. For accommodations reservations throughout Ireland by credit card, contact Dublin Tourism at ✆ **01/605-7700** or www.visitdublin.com.

The five other centers are in the **Arrivals Hall** of Dublin Airport; **Upper O'Connell Street,** Dublin 1; **Baggot Street Bridge,** Baggot Street, Dublin 2; the **Square Towncentre,** Tallaght, Dublin 24; and the ferry terminal at **Dún Laoghaire Harbor** (all telephone inquiries should be directed to the number listed above, or ✆ **1850/230-330**). All centers are open year-round with at least the following hours: Monday to Friday 9am to 5:30pm and Saturday 9am to 5pm.

For information on Ireland outside of Dublin, call **Bord Fáilte** (✆ **1850/230330** in Ireland; www.discoverireland.com).

At any of these centers you can pick up the free ***Tourism News. In Dublin,*** a biweekly arts-and-entertainment magazine selling for €3, is available at most newsstands, or online at www.indublin.ie.

CITY LAYOUT The city is neatly divided down the middle by the curves of the River Liffey, which empties into the sea at the city's farthest edge. To the north and south, the city center is encircled by canals: The Royal Canal arcs across the north and the Grand Canal through the south. Traditionally, the area south of the river has been Dublin's buzzing, prosperous hub. It still holds most of the best hotels, restaurants, shops, and sights, but the Northside is on the upswing, with hip new bars and trendy hotels making it the new place to be. Both north and south, Dublin is compact and easily walked in an hour. In fact, a 45-minute walk from the bucolic peace of St. Stephen's Green, up Grafton Street, and across the Liffey to the top of O'Connell Street offers a good overview of the city's prosperous present and troubled past.

The most interesting suburban towns tend to be along Dublin Bay—these include (heading north along the bay) Drumcondra, Glasnevin, Howth, Clontarf, and Malahide; and (heading south along the bay) Ballsbridge, Blackrock, Dún Laoghaire, Dalkey, Killiney, Rathgar, and Rathmines.

GETTING AROUND **By Bus** **Dublin Bus** (✆ **01/873-4222;** www.dublinbus.ie) operates a fleet of green double-deckers and single-deckers, and minibuses (the latter charmingly called "imps"). Most originate on or near O'Connell Street, Abbey Street, and Eden Quay on the Northside, and at Aston Quay, College Street, and Fleet Street on the south side. Bus stops, which resemble big blue or green lollipops, are located every 2 or 3 blocks on main thoroughfares. To tell where the bus is going, look at the destination street and bus number above its front window; those heading for the city center indicate that with an odd mix of Gaelic and Latin: VIA AN LAR.

Bus service runs daily throughout the city, starting at 6am (10am on Sun), with the last bus at 11:30pm. On Thursday, Friday, and Saturday nights, **Nitelink** service runs from the city center to the suburbs from midnight to 3am. Buses operate every

10 to 15 minutes for most runs; schedules are posted on revolving notice boards at bus stops.

Inner-city fares are based on distances traveled. The minimum fare is €1.15; the maximum fare for journeys in the city center is €2.20, rising to €4.50 if you go as far as the outer suburbs. The Nitelink fare is a flat €5. Buy your tickets from the driver as you enter the bus; exact change is required, so have some change available. Following a rise in robberies of bus drivers in Dublin, all buses in the capital now operate an "Autofare" scheme. This means that fares must be paid with coins directly into a fare box next to the driver's cab, after which a ticket is issued. Notes are not accepted and no change is given. If you have to pay more than the cost of the ticket, the driver will issue you a refund ticket, which must be presented along with your travel ticket at the Dublin Bus office on Upper O'Connell Street to claim a refund for the difference. Inevitably this is rarely worth the effort, so be sure to have plenty of change handy if you're going to travel by bus, or buy a **bus pass.** Discounted 1-day, 3-day, and 5-day "rambler" passes are available in advance. The 1-day bus-only pass costs €6; the 3-day pass costs €13.50; and the 5-day pass goes for €20. Another option worth considering is the **freedom ticket.** Specially designed for tourists, it works like a standard 3-day bus pass, but also includes unlimited travel on the Airlink, Nitelink, and Dublin City Tour buses. The cost is €25 adults, €16 children 13 and under.

BY DART While Dublin has no subway in the strict sense, there is an electric rapid-transit train, known as the **DART** (Dublin Area Rapid Transit; ✆ **01/703-3592;** www.dart.ie). It travels mostly at ground level or on elevated tracks, linking the city-center stations at **Connolly Station, Tara Street,** and **Pearse Street** with suburbs and seaside communities as far as Malahide to the north and Greystones to the south. Service operates roughly every 10 to 20 minutes Monday to Saturday from around 6am to midnight and Sunday from 9:30am to 11pm. Typical adult fares cost around €1.60 for a single journey; combination rail and bus tickets, valid all day within the "short hop" zone of the city center, start from €9 adults. One-day, 3-day, and 10-trip passes, as well as student and family tickets, are available at reduced rates from ticket windows in stations.

BY TRAM The newest addition to Dublin's public transportation network, the sleek light-rail tram system known as **LUAS** (✆ **01/800-300-604;** www.luas.ie) opened in 2004. With trams traveling at a maximum speed of 70kmph (45 mph) and departing every 5 minutes in peak hours, LUAS has been popular enough to make at least a small impact on Dublin's appalling traffic congestion. Services run from 5:30am (6:30am Sat) to 12:30pm Monday to Saturday, and 7am to 11:30pm on Sundays. The lines link the city center at **Connolly Station** and **St. Stephen's Green** with the suburbs of Tallaght in the southwest and Dundrum and Sandyford to the south. For visitors, one of the handiest reasons to use the LUAS is to get between Connolly and Heuston stations. The one-way fare within the city center is €1.60 adults, €.90 children. One-day and multiple-day passes are also available.

ON FOOT Marvelously compact, Dublin is ideal for walking, as long as you remember to look right and then left (and in the direction opposite your instincts if you're from the U.S. or Canada) before crossing the street. Pedestrians have the right of way at specially marked, zebra-striped crossings (there are usually two flashing lights at these intersections). For some walking-tour suggestions, see "Seeing the Sights," later in this chapter.

BY TAXI It's very difficult to hail a taxi on the street; instead, they line up at taxi stands (called "ranks") outside major hotels, at bus and train stations, and on prime thoroughfares such as Upper O'Connell Street, College Green, and the Northside of St. Stephen's Green.

You can also phone for a taxi. Some of the companies that operate a 24-hour radio-call service are **Co-Op** (✆ **01/676-6666**), **NRC** (✆ **01/677-2222**), and **VIP/ACE Taxis** (✆ **01/478-3333**). If you need a wake-up call, VIP offers that service, along with especially courteous dependability.

Taxi rates are fixed by law and posted in each vehicle. The following are typical travel costs in the city center: The starting fare for the first kilometer (⅔ mile) is €4.10 by day and €4.45 at night. For the next 14km (8⅔ miles) the fare is €1.03 per kilometer by day, €1.35 by night, rising to a maximum of €1.77 per kilometer thereafter, day and night. You may instead be charged an equivalent price per minute (which runs a minimum €.36 during the day, up to a maximum of €.63 at night). It costs an extra €2 if you order a cab by phone, with €1 extra per passenger. ***Be warned:*** At some hotels, staff members will tack on as much as €5 for calling you a cab, although this practice violates city taxi regulations. Ask before you request a taxi whether you'll be charged.

BY BICYCLE The steady flow of Dublin traffic rushing down one-way streets may be a little intimidating for most cyclists, but there are many opportunities for more relaxed pedaling in residential areas and suburbs, along the seafront, and around Phoenix Park. The Dublin Tourism office can supply you with bicycle touring information and suggested routes. Bicycle rental averages around €20 per day, €70 per week, with a €65 deposit. In the center, bicycles can be rented from **Cycleways,** 185 Parnell St., Dublin 1 (✆ **01/873-4748;** www.raleigh.ie).

BY CAR Unless you plan to do a lot of driving from Dublin to neighboring counties, it's not practical or affordable to rent a car. If you must drive in Dublin, remember to keep to the *left-hand side of the road,* and don't drive in bus lanes. The most reliable and safest places to park are at surface parking lots or in multistory car parks in central locations, such as Kildare Street, Lower Abbey Street, Marlborough Street, and St. Stephen's Green West. The speed limit in the city is 50kmph (31 mph), although it's very unlikely you'll ever reach it, and seat belts must be worn at all times by drivers and passengers.

[Fast FACTS] DUBLIN

American Express There's an American Express office at 116 Grafton St. (✆ **01/677-2874**). It's open Monday to Friday from 9am to 5pm and on Saturday from 9am to noon. There's also an Amex desk at the **Dublin Tourism Centre** on Suffolk Street (✆ **01/605-7709**). After hours, you can call them at ✆ **01/872-1511,** 24 hours a day; this number connects you to the London office, but you pay the same as a call within Ireland.

Business Hours **Museums and sights** are generally open 10am to 5pm Tuesday to Saturday, and 2 to 5pm Sunday. **Shops** generally open 9am to

6pm Monday to Saturday, with late opening on Thursday. In the city center most department stores and many shops are open noon to 6pm on Sunday.

Currency The official currency of Ireland is the **euro** (€). At press time, the rate of exchange was €1 = US$1.40.

Currency Exchange Currency-exchange services, signposted as BUREAU DE CHANGE, are in most Dublin banks and at many branches of the Irish post office system, known as **An Post.** A bureau de change operates daily during flight arrival and departure times at Dublin airport; a foreign-currency note-exchanger machine is also available on a 24-hour basis in the main arrivals hall. Some hotels and travel agencies offer bureau de change services, although the best rate of exchange is usually with your bank card at an ATM.

Dentists For dental emergencies, contact the **Eastern Health Board Headquarters,** Parkgate St. Business Centre, Dublin 8 (✆ **01/635-2500**), or try **Molesworth Clinic,** 2 Molesworth Place, Dublin 2 (✆ **01/661-5544**). See also "Dental Surgeons" in the Golden Pages (Yellow Pages) of the telephone book. The American Embassy (see "Embassies & Consulates," below) can provide a list of dentists in the city. Expect to be charged upfront for services.

Doctors If you need to see a physician, most hotels and guesthouses will contact a house doctor for you. The **American Embassy** (see "Embassies & Consulates," below) can provide a list of doctors in the city and you should contact them first. Otherwise, you can call either the **Eastern Health Board Headquarters,** Parkgate St. Business Centre, Dublin 8 (✆ **01/635-2500**), or the **Irish Medical Organization** (a doctors' union) at 10 Fitzwilliam Place, Dublin 2 (✆ **01/676-7273**). Expect to pay for treatment upfront.

Drugstores Centrally located drugstores, known locally as pharmacies or chemist shops, include **City Pharmacy,** 14 Dame St., Dublin 2 (✆ **01/670-4523**). A late-night chemist shop is **Hamilton Long & Co.,** 5 Lower O'Connell St. (✆ **01/874-8456**), and its sister branch, **Hamilton Long Byrnes,** at 4 Merrion Rd., Dublin 4 (✆ **01/668-3287**). Both branches close at 9pm on weeknights and 6pm on Saturday.

Embassies & Consulates The **American Embassy** is at 42 Elgin Rd., Ballsbridge, Dublin 4 (✆ **01/668-8777**); the **Canadian Embassy,** at 7–8 Wilton Terrace, 3rd Floor, Dublin 2 (✆ **01/234-4000**); the **British Embassy,** at 29 Merrion Rd., Dublin 2 (✆ **01/205-3700**); and the **Australian Embassy,** at Fitzwilton House, Fitzwilton House, Wilton Terrace, 7th Floor, Dublin 2 (✆ **01/664-5300**). In addition, there is an **American Consulate** at 223 Stranmillis Rd., Belfast BT9 5GR (✆ **028/9038-6100**).

Emergencies For police, fire, or other emergencies, dial ✆ **999.**

Hospitals For emergency care, two of the most modern are **St. Vincent's University Hospital,** Elm Park (✆ **01/277-4000**), on the south side of the city, and **Beaumont Hospital,** Beaumont (✆ **01/837-7755**), on the Northside.

Internet Access Internet access is everywhere in Dublin; look for signs in cafes, pubs, shopping malls, hotels, and hostels. Like all of Dublin's public libraries, the **Central Library,** in the ILAC Centre, off Henry Street, Dublin 1 (✆ **01/873-4333**), has a bank of PCs with free Internet access. Centrally located cybercafes include the **Global Internet Café,** 8 O'Connell St., Dublin 2 (✆ **01/878-0295**), and the **Access Cyber Cafe,** 16b Parnell St., Dublin 1 (✆ **01/878-3403**), which also offers a left-luggage service. A half-hour online averages €4.

Post Office The Irish post office is best known by its Gaelic name, **An**

Post. The **General Post Office (GPO)** is located on O'Connell Street, Dublin 1 (✆ **01/705-7000;** www.anpost.ie). Hours are Monday to Saturday 8am to 8pm. Branch offices, identified by the sign OIFIG AN POST/POST OFFICE, are open Monday to Saturday only, 9am to 5pm.

Taxes Sales tax is called VAT (value-added tax) and is often already included in the price quoted to you or shown on price tags. VAT rates vary—for hotels, restaurants, and car rentals, it's 13.5%; for souvenirs and gifts, it's 21%. If you're not a citizen of an E.U. country, you're entitled to have this money refunded. You can get your money back through **Global Refund** (✆ **800/566-9828;** www.globalrefund.com), the world's largest private company offering VAT refunds. If a shop isn't part of the Global Refund network, get a full receipt at the time of purchase that shows the shop's name, address, and VAT paid. When you're ready to depart Ireland, go to the Customs office at the airport or ferry port and have your receipts stamped; then send the stamped receipts back to the store where you made your purchase, which will then mail you a VAT refund check.

Telephone The **country code** for the Republic of Ireland is **353.** The **city code** for Dublin is **01.** If you're calling from outside Ireland, drop the initial 0 (zero) from the city code. Thus, to call Dublin from the United States, you would dial ✆ 011-353-1, followed by the seven-digit local number. For direct-dial calls to the United States, dial the international access code (**00** from Ireland), and then the U.S. country code **(1),** followed by area code and number. To place a collect call to the United States from Ireland, dial ✆ **1-800/550-000** for USA Direct service. The toll-free international access codes are **AT&T,** ✆ **1-800-550-000; Sprint,** ✆ **1-800-552-001;** and **MCI,** ✆ **1-800-551-001.**

Local calls from a phone booth require a **Callcard,** a prepaid computerized card that you insert into the phone instead of coins. Callcards can be purchased in a range of denominations at phone-company offices, post offices, and many retail outlets (such as newsstands). There's a local and international phone center at the General Post Office on O'Connell Street. If you have difficulty reaching a party, the Irish toll-free number for **directory assistance** is ✆ **11811.**

Tipping Some hotels and guesthouses add a service charge to the bill, usually 12.5% to 15%, although some smaller places add only 10% or nothing at all. If you feel the service charge is sufficient, there is no need for more gratuities. If, however, staff members have provided exceptional service, by all means tip them extra. For taxi drivers, tip as you would at home, 10% to 15%. For restaurants, the policy is usually printed on the menu—either a gratuity of 10% to 15% is automatically added to your bill or it's left up to you (always ask if you are in doubt). As a rule, bartenders do not expect a tip, except when table service is provided.

Where to Stay

HISTORIC OLD CITY & TEMPLE BAR/ TRINITY COLLEGE AREA

Very Expensive

The Clarence ★★★ This has been the most famous hotel in Dublin since 1992, when U2's Bono and the Edge bought it. For some, knowing that a hotel is owned by rock stars might actually be a strike against the place, but don't be put off—this is one of the most sophisticated hotels in the city. The mid-19th-century,

Regency-style building was beautifully renovated, keeping the best of its antique charm, but adding layers of contemporary elegance. Rooms are designed with lush fabrics in neutral tones of oatmeal and chocolate, light Shaker-style oak furniture, and exceptionally comfortable, firm king-size beds. Suites and deluxe rooms have balconies, some with views over the Liffey. The elegant **Tea Room** restaurant (p. 593) is one of the best in town for contemporary Irish cuisine. The **Octagon Bar** has a good buzz, and the **Study,** which has the feel of an old-style gentlemen's club, is a relaxing place to read the papers and sip a glass of wine.

Room-Booking Savvy

Very good deals are available in the off season for those who book a month or more in advance. Discounts of 60% are not unusual in the winter and early spring, even at five-star hotels.

6-8 Wellington Quay, Dublin 2. ✆ **01/407-0800.** Fax 01/407-0820. www.theclarence.ie. 47 units. €390–€440 double; €780 1-bedroom suite; €980 2-bedroom suite. Full Irish breakfast €29. AE, DC, MC, V. Valet parking €25. Bus: 51B, 51C, 68, 69, or 79. **Amenities:** Restaurant; bar; babysitting; concierge; exercise room; room service; smoke-free rooms; spa. *In room:* A/C, TV/DVD, hair dryer, minibar.

Moderate

Buswells Hotel ★ This traditional hotel has a wonderful sense of class that saves it from feeling stuffy. The spacious, slightly masculine rooms are spread throughout three Georgian buildings. Its location near the Irish government buildings makes its bar and restaurant hotbeds of political intrigue, not to mention a prime spot for eavesdropping.

23–25 Molesworth St., Dublin 2. ✆ **01/614-6500.** Fax 01/676-2090. www.buswells.ie. 69 units. €90–€290 double. AE, DC, MC, V. Free parking nearby. DART: Pearse. Bus: 10, 11, 13, or 46A. **Amenities:** Restaurant; bar; babysitting; concierge; exercise room; room service; smoke-free rooms. *In room:* TV, hair dryer, Wi-Fi (free).

Eliza Lodge ★ This hotel lies right beside the Liffey and embodies all the exuberance and zest of Temple Bar. Guest rooms are simple and attractive, done up in neutral creams and blond woods, with big floor-to-ceiling windows—the better to take in the riverside vistas. At the top end, executive rooms have Jacuzzi tubs and bay windows looking out over the quay. But a better-value splurge is the smaller penthouse doubles that have balconies overlooking the river. Road noise here is a problem for some light sleepers.

23–24 Wellington Quay, Dublin 2. ✆ **01/671-8044.** Fax 01/671-8362. www.dublinlodge.com. 18 units. €115–€160 double; suites from €190. AE, MC, V. Bus: 51B, 51C, 68, 69, or 79. **Amenities:** Restaurant; bar; Internet; smoke-free rooms. *In room:* A/C, TV, hair dryer.

Temple Bar Hotel This five-story hotel was developed from a former bank building, and great care was taken to preserve the brick facade and Victorian mansard roof. Guest rooms are quite plain, if comfortable. The orthopedic beds are firm, although the smallish rooms are a bit cramped. **Buskers,** the hotel's nightclub, is very popular and *very* loud. Bear that in mind before you book—if you're looking for peace and quiet, this is probably not the place for you, at least on the weekend. Midweek, rooms are quieter and often cheaper.

Fleet St., Temple Bar, Dublin 2. ✆ **800/44-UTELL** (448-8355) in the U.S., or 01/612-9200. Fax 01/677-3088. www.templebarhotel.com. 129 units. €145–€200 double. Rates include full Irish breakfast. AE, MC,

A Parking Note

The majority of Dublin hotels do not offer parking; if you have a car, you'll have to find (and pay for) street parking. In this section, we've provided parking information only for the few hotels that do offer parking arrangements or discounts for guests.

V. DART: Tara St. Bus: 78A or 78B. **Amenities:** Restaurant; 2 bars; babysitting; concierge; room service. *In room:* TV, hair dryer, Wi-Fi (free).

Self-Catering

25 Eustace Street This wonderfully restored Georgian town house, dating from 1720, has an enviable location in the heart of Temple Bar. It is a showcase property for the Irish Landmark Trust (ILT), whose mission is to rescue neglected historic buildings and restore them. The three-story house has been faithfully restored, with a superb timber-paneled staircase, fireplaces in every room, mahogany furniture, and brass beds. There's a huge drawing room with a baby grand piano, full dining room, equipped galley kitchen, and three bedrooms. There are two bathrooms, one with a cast-iron claw-foot tub placed dead center. Bookshelves have been thoughtfully stocked with classics by Irish novelists. As with all ILT properties, there is no TV. All this, and Temple Bar at your doorstep. Some readers have reported that the house is a little too close for comfort to Temple Bar's party scene and the noise can be a bit much on weekends.

25 Eustace St., Dublin 2. Contact the Irish Landmark Trust, ✆ **01/670-4733.** www.irishlandmark.com. 1 apt. €2,100 per week during peak months. Weekly bookings only, July–Aug; rest of year 3- or 4-night stays. AE, MC, V. Bus: Any marked AN LAR. **Amenities:** Full kitchen. *In room:* No phone.

ST. STEPHEN'S GREEN/GRAFTON STREET AREA

Very Expensive

The Fitzwilliam Hotel ★★★ Take an unbeatable location with sweeping views over the Green, add a Michelin-starred restaurant, throw in contemporary design by Terence Conran, and you have a hit on your hands. Conran has a knack for easygoing sophistication, and in the Fitzwilliam he uses clean lines and only a few neutral colors (white, beige, gray) throughout the public rooms and guest rooms. Rooms are simply done in neutral tones with stripped-down furniture. **Thornton's,** the hotel restaurant, is very good.

109 St. Stephen's Green, Dublin 2. ✆ **01/478-7000.** Fax 01/478-7878. www.fitzwilliamhoteldublin.com. 130 units. €190–€375 double. Breakfast €22. AE, DC, MC, V. DART: Pearse. Bus: 10, 11A, 11B, 13, or 20B. **Amenities:** 2 restaurants; bar; babysitting; concierge; room service; smoke-free rooms. *In room:* A/C, TV, CD/MP3 player, hair dryer, Internet (free), minibar.

The Shelbourne ★★★ One of the city's true grande dame hotels, the Shelbourne has been a Dublin landmark since 1824. The hotel has played a significant role in Irish history—the Irish constitution was drafted here in 1922, in room no. 112—and it still attracts Irish politicians, especially to its bars and restaurants. Rooms are decorated in grand, traditional style, with soft yellows and pinks, and the hotel claims to have "Ireland's most luxurious beds," with 300-thread-count Egyptian cotton linens wrapped around feather mattresses. Rooms also have international power sockets, so your hair straightener shouldn't explode. The bars, restaurant, and lobby are still warmed by fireplaces and lighted by Waterford chandeliers, and the **Lord Mayor's Lounge** is still ideal for afternoon tea. Each evening guests are greeted with freshly made nibbles (fish cakes one day, brownies the next). The hotel even offers an in-house **genealogy butler,** who can help guests with Irish backrounds explore their family histories.

27 St. Stephen's Green, Dublin 2. ✆ **888/236-2427** in the U.S., or 01/663-4500. Fax 01/661-6006. www.theshelbourne.ie. 265 units. €250–€475 double. Breakfast €20–€26. AE, DC, MC, V. Limited free parking. DART: Pearse. Bus: 10, 11A, 11B, 13, or 20B. **Amenities:** 2 restaurants; 2 bars; babysitting; concierge; exercise room; room service. *In room:* A/C, TV, hair dryer, minibar, Wi-Fi.

Expensive

Number 31 A discreet plaque outside an elegant locked gate on a tiny side street is your only clue that what lies beyond is an award-winning guesthouse. It's actually two converted buildings—one a grand Georgian town house, the other a more modern coach house. In the main house, rooms are large and simply but classily decorated, while in the coach house rooms are elegant; some have their own patios. Handmade beds are enveloped in natural linens. Note that there's no restaurant, no bar, no room service, and no air-conditioning. Breakfast here is some consolation—cooked to order for you, with organic, seasonal ingredients, and choices ranging from mushroom frittatas to fresh-baked cranberry bread.

31 Leeson Close, Lower Leeson St., Dublin 2. ✆ **01/676-5011.** Fax 01/676-2929. www.number31.ie. 21 units. €150–€320 double. Rates include breakfast. AE, MC, V. Free parking. Bus: 11, 11A, 11B, 13, 13A, or 13B. **Amenities:** Lounge. *In room:* TV, hair dryer, Wi-Fi.

Moderate

Bentley's Townhouse Guest rooms at this elegantly renovated townhouse (four of which overlook St. Stephen's Green) are decorated in rich, modern tones that stay faithful to the building's Georgian heritage. Beds are large and comfortable. There's an excellent seafood restaurant—**Bentley's Oyster Bar and Grill**—run by Michelin-starred chef Richard Corrigan, although there are cheaper dining options nearby if you don't want to splurge.

22 St. Stephen's Green, Dublin 2. ✆ **01/638-3939.** Fax 01/638-3900. www.bentleysdublin.com. 10 units. €180–€200 double. Rates include breakfast. MC, V. DART: Pearse. Bus: 10, 11A, 11B, 13, or 20B. **Amenities:** Restaurant. *In room:* A/C, TV, hair dryer.

Trinity Lodge In an enormous Georgian town house, the Trinity is a classy option a few blocks off Grafton Street. The gray stone building dates to 1785, and its 10 large guest rooms are brightly decorated in keeping with that period, some with paintings by the respected Irish artist Graham Knuttel. The breakfast room downstairs is warmly designed in country-house style. There's a second building across the street where six large rooms have a more contemporary edge. These buildings are protected historical structures, so there's no elevator access to their four levels.

12 S. Frederick St., Dublin 2. ✆ **01/617-0900.** Fax 01/617-0999. www.trinitylodge.com. 16 units. €120–€130 double. Rates include breakfast. MC, V. Bus: All An Lar (cross-city) buses. **Amenities:** Restaurant; bar; room service; smoke-free rooms. *In room:* A/C (some), TV, Wi-Fi (free).

Inexpensive

Avalon House This warm and friendly hostel in a beautiful old red-brick building is well known among those who travel to Dublin on a budget. Its pine floors, high ceilings, and open fireplace make it a pleasant place in which to relax, and its cafe is a popular hangout for international travelers. Most beds are in dorms of varying sizes, with a few single and twin bedded rooms available, too. It's not exactly the Clarence, but it's got all you really need—clean, cheerful rooms in a safe location at a cheap price.

55 Aungier St., Dublin 2. ✆ **01/475-0001.** Fax 01/475-0303. www.avalon-house.ie. 12 units. €36–€45 per person double with private bathroom. Includes light continental breakfast. AE, MC, V. Bus: 16, 16A, 19, 22, or 155. No curfew but passes must be shown on entry after 9pm. **Amenities:** Cafe; Internet; smoke-free rooms.

FITZWILLIAM/MERRION SQUARE AREA

Very Expensive

Merrion Hotel ★ Housed in four restored Georgian houses, the Merrion is a traditionally elegant hotel. The lobby and lounges have formal furniture and fires glowing in hearths—the kinds of places where proper afternoon tea seems called for. The impressive contemporary art on the walls is part of one of the country's largest private collections. Service is discreetly omnipresent, and the spacious rooms overlook either the government buildings or the hotel's 18th-century-inspired gardens of acacia and lilac. Pamper yourself in the **Tethra Spa.** Stretch your credit card's limit at the Michelin-starred **Restaurant Patrick Guilbaud** or save a few pennies at the somewhat cheaper and more atmospheric **Cellar** restaurant.

Upper Merrion St., Dublin 2. ✆ **01/603-0600.** Fax 01/603-0700. www.merrionhotel.com. 142 units. €475–€595 double. Breakfast €24–€29. AE, DC, MC, V. Parking €20 per night. DART: Pearse. Bus: 10, 13, or 13A. **Amenities:** 2 restaurants; 2 bars; babysitting; concierge; health club & spa; indoor pool; room service. *In room:* A/C, TV/DVD, hair dryer, minibar, Wi-Fi.

O'CONNELL STREET AREA

Expensive

The Gresham ★★ Along with the Shelbourne, this is one of Dublin's two most historic hotels, and it has welcomed visitors for 200 years. With a row of flags out front and its grand, up-lighted facade, this hotel stands out, and the vast lobby is one of the best places in the city to have a cup of tea or a cocktail in elegant but relaxed surroundings. Rooms are generally small, but coolly decorated in neutral tones, with big, firm beds and huge windows. It has a friendly, modern bar, and a handy, slightly old-fashioned restaurant serving European cuisine. ***Tip:*** Take no notice of the (enormous) rack rates here. If you book far enough in advance, it's even possible to get a room for under €100.

23 Upper O'Connell St., Dublin 1. ✆ **01/878-6881.** Fax 01/878-7175. www.gresham-hotels.com. 288 units. €130–€500 double. Rates include breakfast. AE, DC, MC, V. Parking €15 per night. Bus: 11 or 13. **Amenities:** Restaurant; 2 bars; babysitting; concierge; room service; smoke-free rooms. *In room:* A/C, TV, fridge, hair dryer, Wi-Fi (free).

The Morrison ★★ This is really an oversize boutique hotel, with an ideal location just across the Liffey from Temple Bar. Fashion fans will surely have no trouble pegging the design as the work of design star John Rocha, who is responsible for everything from the crushed velvet bed throws in blood red to the Waterford crystal vases. Rocha uses a palette of neutral colors—cream, chocolate, and black—to achieve a kind of warm minimalism in the guest rooms, which have stereos, Egyptian-cotton linens, and cool Portuguese limestone in the bathrooms. The stylish atrium-style restaurant, **Halo,** is a favorite with celebrities.

Lower Ormond Quay, Dublin 1. ✆ **01/887-2400.** Fax 01/874-4031. www.morrisonhotel.ie. 138 units. €135–€505 double. AE, DC, MC, V. DART: Connolly. Bus: 70 or 80. **Amenities:** 2 restaurants; 2 bars; babysitting; concierge; room service. *In room:* A/C, CD/MP3 player, hair dryer, Internet (free), minibar.

Moderate

The Clarion Hotel Dublin IFSC ★ All smooth straight lines and extra touches, this relaxing, modern hotel is a good option for business travelers. The comfortable rooms are softened by Egyptian cotton bedding, and filled with the latest electronic gadgets, including PlayStation units. The stylish bar and restaurant are workaday but useful. This hotel's best offering is arguably its state-of-the-art health club, with its gorgeous low-lit pool that urges you to exercise. Happily, the sauna, steam room, and whirlpool require no physical exertion at all. Rooms at the front have a gorgeous view of the Liffey and Dublin skyline. ***Tip:*** It can be significantly cheaper to get a room-only rate here and grab breakfast somewhere else; good alternatives can be found nearby.

International Financial Services Centre, Dublin 1. ✆ **01/433-8800.** Fax 01/433-8811. www.clarionhotelifsc.com. 163 units. €110–€235 double. AE, DC, MC, V. Parking €12. Dart: Connolly. Bus: All An Lar (cross-city) buses. **Amenities:** Restaurant; bar; babysitting; concierge; health club; indoor pool; room service; smoke-free rooms; spa. *In room:* A/C, TV/DVD, hair dryer, Internet (free), minibar.

Isaac's Hotel This friendly guesthouse has had something of an upgrade recently; gone are the dormitories and kitchenettes, replaced by basic, cheap (by Irish standards) bedrooms and suites. Bedrooms are simply decorated but clean and comfortable, with polished pine furniture and large-screen TVs. Rooms in the Georgian wing are more elegantly designed, with fancier furnishings, and they cost a bit more. The supercentral location is handy (right by a bus and DART stop), but it can get quite noisy on weekends, and their attitude toward room amenities verges on the parsimonious. Want air-conditioning? That'll be an extra €15. How about a room with Wi-Fi? No problem, for €25, plus another charge to actually use it. Suddenly that bargain deal starts to look more mezzanine than basement. This is a good place to stay if you're on a budget and traveling at the last minute; otherwise, you might want to check for discounted rates at the more expensive places first.

2-5 Frenchman's Lane, Dublin 1. ✆ **01/855-6215.** Fax 01/855-6524. www.isaacs.ie. 54 units. €105–€190 double. Rates include breakfast. MC, V. DART: Connolly. All cross-city buses. **Amenities:** Restaurant; cafe/bar; exercise room. *In room:* A/C (extra fee), TV, Wi-Fi (in Georgian wing).

BALLSBRIDGE/EMBASSY ROW AREA

Situated south of the Grand Canal, this elegant part of town is known for its embassies, and leafy, tree-lined streets. If you're in Dublin for a conference at the RDS show grounds or a match at the Lansdowne Rugby Ground, this area is ideal. The downside is that it's a good 20- to 30-minute walk to the town center.

Very Expensive

The Dylan ★ This absurdly trendy hotel puts its cards on the table the moment you walk in the door—here, only two things matter: the size of your bank account, and how good you look. Chanel bag? Prada skirt? Some $500 shoes? Welcome to your new home! It's hallmarked by vivid colors: bright carpets and curtains, Murano glass chandeliers, studded leather wallpaper, and lime-green sofas. Guest rooms are quite small, and the decor is disco chic, albeit with Frette linens and 7th Heaven beds. Service here is excellent, but beauty's in the eye of the beholder, so this very hip, very adult hotel is certainly not for everyone. Families in particular might find its party-hearty atmosphere (it has a signature cocktail—vanilla vodka with crème de banana—as well as a thumping club soundtrack) a bit off-putting. But the young and single are lining up to spend hundreds of euros a night.

Eastmoreland Place, Ballsbridge, Dublin 4. ✆ **01/660-3000.** Fax 01/660-3005. www.dylan.ie. 44 units. €200–€390 double. Rates include full breakfast. AE, MC, V. Bus: 10, 46A, 46B, 63, or 84. **Amenities:** Restaurant; lounge; bar; nightclub; concierge; room service; smoke-free rooms. *In room:* TV/MP3, hair dryer, minibar, Wi-Fi (free).

Four Seasons ★★★ ☺ If money is no object, the Four Seasons lures you like a De Beers diamond. The beauty is in the details here: The indoor pool and whirlpool overlook a sunken garden; the lobby and guest rooms are equally smart and plush; the spa is outstanding and the restaurants are elegant. This is an excellent option for families, as there are complimentary cribs, childproof bedrooms, and a babysitting service. A menu of children's activities will keep the kids occupied while you have a romantic meal or just kick back for some quiet meditation (the better to prepare yourself for the bill). Always check the website's rates before booking; online discounts can be very good.

Simmonscourt Rd., Ballsbridge, Dublin 4. ✆ **800/819-5053** in the U.S., or 01/665-4000. Fax 01/665-4099. www.fourseasons.com/dublin. 259 units. €265–€465 double. Rates include full breakfast. AE, DC, MC, V. Free parking. DART: Sandymount (5-min. walk). Bus: 7, 7A, 7X, 8, or 45. **Amenities:** 2 restaurants; lobby lounge; bar; babysitting; children's programs; concierge; health club & spa; Jacuzzi; indoor pool; room service; smoke-free rooms. *In room:* TV/DVD/CD, hair dryer, Internet, minibar.

Expensive

Butlers Town House ★★ This beautifully restored Victorian town house feels like a gracious family home. The atmosphere is elegant, but comfortable; rooms are richly furnished with four-poster or half-tester beds, draped in luxurious fabrics in rich colors. The gem here, in our opinion, is the Glendalough Room, with a lovely bay window and small library; it requires booking well in advance. Free tea and coffee are offered all day, and breakfast and afternoon tea are served in the atrium dining room.

44 Lansdowne Rd., Ballsbridge, Dublin 4. ✆ **01/667-4022.** Fax 01/667-3960. www.butlers-hotel.com. 20 units. €240 double. Rates include full breakfast. AE, DC, MC, V. Secure free parking. Closed Dec 23–Jan 10. DART: Lansdowne Rd. Bus: 7, 7A, 8, or 45. **Amenities:** Breakfast room; babysitting; room service. *In room:* A/C, TV, hair dryer, Internet.

Moderate

Grand Canal Hotel ★ This modern hotel at the edge of Ballsbridge is a clean and pleasant alternative to bustling central Dublin. Its rooms are medium size, quiet, and comfortable with a bright, contemporary decor. The hotel's Gasworks Bar has a friendly pub atmosphere, and is popular with locals. As an added attraction, prices in the bar and the hotel's restaurant are noticeably lower than in comparable options a 20-minute walk away in the city center.

Grand Canal St., Ballsbridge, Dublin 4. ✆ **01/646-1000.** www.grandcanalhotel.com. 142 units. €90–€230 double. AE, MC, V. DART: Grand Canal. **Amenities:** Restaurant; bar; room service; smoke-free rooms. *In room:* TV, hair dryer, Wi-Fi (free).

Roxford Lodge ★ This lovely little hotel is slightly outside of central Dublin (Grafton Street is a 25-min. walk), but about as good as it gets anywhere in the city for the price. Rooms are simple and elegant, with little flourishes that incorporate elements of the original Victorian building, such as corniced ceilings and bay windows. Most bedrooms have their own whirlpool bathtubs and saunas, which sacrifices a little space but raises the luxury quotient. Service is personable and breakfasts are delicious. Guests can help themselves to free coffee all day in the lounge.

46 Northumberland Rd., Ballsbridge, Dublin 4. ✆ **01/668-8572.** Fax 01/668-8158. www.roxfordlodge.ie. €100–€180 double. Rates include breakfast. AE, MC, V. Bus: 11 or 13. **Amenities:** Lounge. *In room:* TV/CD, hair dryer, Wi-Fi (free).

Waterloo House ★ This classy guesthouse is charming in an old-world kind of way, with an elegant, high-ceilinged drawing room where you can linger over the morning papers or a good book. Guest rooms are large (some have two double beds), and most have fluffy white comforters and walls in lemony yellow. The varied breakfast menu offers more than the usual Irish fried eggs and bacon (French toast, waffles, croissants, for example). A quiet, peaceful alternative.

8–10 Waterloo Rd., Ballsbridge, Dublin 4. ✆ **01/660-1888.** www.waterloohouse.ie. 17 units. €130–€175 double. Rates include full breakfast. MC, V. Free parking. Closed Christmas week. DART: Lansdowne Rd. Bus: 5, 7, or 8. **Amenities:** Breakfast room. *In room:* TV, hair dryer, Wi-Fi.

Where to Dine

HISTORIC OLD CITY & TEMPLE BAR/ TRINITY COLLEGE AREA

Expensive

Eden ★★ INTERNATIONAL/MEDITERRANEAN This is one of Temple Bar's hippest restaurants, a cool minimalist space with an open-plan kitchen overlooking Meeting House Square. The food is influenced by the global village, with a special penchant for Mediterranean flavors and local meats and seafood, so Castletownbere scallops may be served with a side of pasta with tomato dressing and chieve beurre blanc, or filet of wild Irish venison alongside an *osso bucco,* rooster mash and braised red cabbage. ***Tip:*** The fixed-price lunch is a particularly good value.

Meeting House Sq. (entrance on Sycamore St.), Dublin 2. ✆ **01/670-5372.** www.edenrestaurant.ie. Main courses €18–€28; fixed-price lunch 2 courses €20, 3 courses €25. AE, DC, MC, V. Daily 12:30–3pm; Mon–Sat 6–10:30pm; Sun 6–10pm. Bus: 51B, 51C, 68, 69, or 79.

The Pig's Ear ★★ MODERN IRISH This stylish, modern restaurant is a great addition to the Dublin restaurant scene. Head chef Stephen McAllister (previously of the superb One Pico, below) is a TV chef in Ireland, although the clientele are usually far too cool to turn their heads if he puts in an appearance. The menu is an imaginative modern interpretation of traditional Irish cuisine; dishes such as shepherd's pie or grilled sea bass with walnut crust and spring cabbage are offset by the occasional ball out of left field; take the starter of house terrine with tea and prune chutney, for example, which seems innocuous enough until you get to the part about "crispy ears." The staff are lovely, and the view of Trinity College from the upstairs dining room is handsome. Best of all, the prices are reasonable.

4–5 Nassau St., Dublin 2. ✆ **01/670-3865.** www.thepigsear.ie. Reservations required. Main courses €17–€27; fixed-price early-bird menus €18–€22. AE, DC, MC, V. Mon–Sat 12:30–3pm and 5:30–10pm. DART: Pearse. Bus: 7, 8, 10, 11, or 46A.

The Tea Room ★★★ INTERNATIONAL This ultrasmart restaurant, ensconced in the U2-owned Clarence hotel, is guaranteed to deliver one of your most memorable meals in Ireland. This gorgeous room's soaring yet understated lines are the perfect backdrop for the complex but controlled cooking that takes form in dishes like filet of John Dory with wild mushroom and razor clams, or red leg partridge with juniper flavored *jus*. Chef Mathieu Melin's fixed-price "market dinner" menu, offering more straightforward, locally sourced fare, is available during all dinner hours Sunday through Thursday, and from 7 to 8pm on Friday and Saturday.

In the Clarence, 6–8 Wellington Quay, Dublin 2. ✆ **01/407-0813.** www.theclarence.ie. Reservations required. Main courses €14–€28; market menu 3-course fixed-price dinner €26. AE, MC, V. Mon–Fri 12:30–2pm; daily 6:30–9:45pm. Bus: 51B, 51C, 68, 69, or 79.

Moderate

Mermaid Café ★★ MODERN Owned by a chef and an artist, this popular eatery is a mixture of good restaurant and classy hangout. It's a lunchtime favorite of local professionals, and a good place to take a date in the evening. Dishes often found on the frequently changing menu range from slow-roasted pork belly to a rich seafood casserole. The popular weekend brunch can give you a taste of the menu at a less wallet-denting price than dinner.

69–70 Dame St., Dublin 2. ✆ **01/670-8236.** www.mermaid.ie. Reservations required. Main courses lunch €11–€16, dinner €18–€26; Sun brunch €11–€17. MC, V. Mon–Sat 12:30–2:30pm and 6–11pm; Sun noon–3:30pm (brunch) and 6–9pm. Bus: 50, 50A, 54, 56A, 77, 77A, or 77B.

Inexpensive

Juice ★ VEGETARIAN The best thing about Juice is that if nobody told you it was a vegetarian restaurant, you'd probably never notice, so interesting is the menu and so tasty is the food. The look of the place is lovely, with soaring 9m (30-ft.) ceilings softened by a suspended sailcloth and muted lighting. Brunch is classic here, with pancakes, huevos rancheros, and French toast topped with fresh fruit or organic maple syrup. The rest of the day, you can sample the homemade dips—hummus, baba ghanouj, tapenade, roasted carrot pâté—with crudités and pita-bread strips. True to its name, there are about 30 kinds of juices and smoothies on offer.

Castle House, 73–83 S. Great Georges St., Dublin 2. ✆ **01/475-7856.** www.juicerestaurant.ie. Reservations recommended Fri–Sat. Brunch €6–€15; dinner main courses €12–€16. AE, MC, V. Daily 11am–11pm. Bus: 50, 54, 56, or 77.

Leo Burdock's FISH AND CHIPS Established in 1913, this quintessential Irish take-away shop across from Christ Church Cathedral is a cherished Dublin institution. Cabinet ministers, university students, and Hollywood stars alike (Tom Cruise and Liam Neeson are both fans) can be found at the counter waiting for fish bought fresh that morning and good Irish potatoes, both cooked in "drippings" (none of that modern cooking oil!). There's no seating, but you can sit on a nearby bench or stroll down to the park at St. Patrick's Cathedral.

2 Werburgh St., Dublin 8. ✆ **01/454-0306.** www.leoburdocks.com. Main courses €6–€8. No credit cards. Mon–Sat noon–midnight; Sun 4pm–midnight. Bus: 21A, 50, 50A, 78, 78A, or 78B.

ST. STEPHEN'S GREEN/GRAFTON STREET AREA

Very Expensive

One Pico ★★★ MODERN EUROPEAN About a 5-minute walk from Stephen's Green, on a wee lane off Dawson Street, this is a sophisticated, grown-up, classy place, with excellent service and fantastic food. The food is a mixture of European influences in a menu that changes daily. If you're lucky, you might find the duck confit with red cabbage and beet chiffonade, or the roast pheasant with red-wine risotto. For dessert, a caramelized lemon tart is the end to a near-perfect meal. The fixed-price dinner menu is an excellent value for those who want to treat themselves without breaking the bank, although you must be finished by 8:45pm.

5-6 Molesworth Place, Schoolhouse Lane, Dublin 2. ✆ **01/676-0300.** www.onepico.com. Reservations required. Fixed-price menu lunch €20–€35, dinner €25–€39; dinner main courses €13–€17. AE, DC, MC, V. Mon–Sat 12:30–2:30pm and 6–11pm. DART: Pearse. Bus: 10, 11A, 11B, 13, or 20B.

Moderate

Café Mao ★ ASIAN This is where to go when you feel like some Asian cooking with an exhilarating attitude. The exposed kitchen lines one entire wall, and the rest of the space is wide open—great for people-watching. The menu reads like a Best of Asia list: Thai fish cakes, *nasi goreng,* chicken hoisin, salmon ramen. Everything is delicious—you can't go wrong. There are also branches in the Pavilion in Dún Laoghaire (✆ **01/214-8090**), and in Civic Square, Dundrum, Dublin 16 (✆ **01/296/2802**).

2 Chatham Row, Dublin 2. ✆ **01/670-4899.** www.cafemao.com. Reservations recommended. Main courses €10–€19. AE, MC, V. Mon–Wed noon–10:30pm; Thurs noon–11pm; Fri–Sat noon–11:30pm; Sun noon–10pm. DART: Pearse. Bus: 10, 11A, 11B, 13, or 20B.

Inexpensive

Cornucopia Wholefood Restaurant VEGETARIAN This little cafe just off Grafton Street is one of the best vegetarian restaurants in the city, and also serves wholesome meals for people on various restricted diets (vegan, nondairy, low sodium, low fat). Soups are particularly good here, as are the salads and the hot dishes such as roast squash and fennel with olive polenta and romescu sauce. This place is a delicious healthy alternative.

19 Wicklow St., Dublin 2. ✆ **01/677-7583.** www.cornucopia.ie. Main courses €11–€13. MC, V. Mon–Sat 8:30am–8pm; Sun noon–7pm. Bus: Any city-center bus.

Lemon ☺ PANCAKES The kids are bound to drag you to this one with its bright orange interior and fresh crepes with a dazzling array of fillings. Go sensible and have a savory filling for breakfast (mushrooms and eggs) or dive into chocolate and banana. In addition to pancakes there are waffles served with fruit, ice cream, and most things naughty, and there's good coffee as well.

60 Dawson St. ✆ **01/672-8898.** www.lemonco.com. Crepes €4–€10. No credit cards. Breakfast to early evening daily. DART: Pearse. Bus: 10, 11A, 11B, 13 or 20B.

FITZWILLIAM/MERRION SQUARE AREA

Very Expensive

L'Ecrivain ★★ FRENCH This is one of Dublin's truly exceptional restaurants, from start to finish. The atmosphere is relaxed, welcoming, and unpretentious, and chef Derry Clarke's food is extraordinary. Most dishes consist of Irish ingredients, prepared without dense sauces. You might find, on the constantly changing menu, seared wild Irish venison loin with caramelized pear, or seared Bere Island scallops with lobster strudel. Dinner prices are terrifying (and regularly raised), but the fixed-price lunch menus allow a chance to try the food here for slightly less.

109 Lower Baggot St., Dublin 2. ✆ **01/661-1919.** www.lecrivain.com. Reservations required. Fixed-price 3-course lunches €25–€45; dinner main courses €24–€45; fixed-price early-bird menu €50; fixed-price 7-course menu €65. AE, DC, MC, V. Mon–Fri 12:30–2pm; Mon–Sat 6:30–10:30pm. Bus: 10.

Restaurant Patrick Guilbaud ★★ FRENCH/IRISH Ireland's most award-winning restaurant (including two Michelin stars) holds court in elegant quarters at the equally elegant Merrion Hotel. The menu is lavish; roast loin of Wicklow lamb with eggplant caviar and black sole with creamed brown morels are two representative options. However, this is also one of the pricier restaurants in Dublin. A starter of potato salad with crispy pork and poached egg will set you back a startling €40, and an entree may cost you double that.

In the Merrion Hotel, 21 Upper Merrion St., Dublin 2. ✆ **01/676-4192.** www.restaurantpatrickguilbaud.ie. Reservations required. Fixed-price 2-course lunch €38; fixed-price 3-course lunch €50; dinner main courses €50–€80. Seasonal tasting menu around €85. AE, DC, MC, V. Tues–Sat 12:30–2:15pm and 7–10:15pm. DART: Westland Row. Bus: 10, 11A, 11B, 13, or 20B.

Expensive

Dobbins Wine Bistro ★ BISTRO Almost hidden in a lane between Upper and Lower Mount streets, this hip, friendly bistro is a haven for inventive Continental cuisine. A major refurbishment in 2008 replaced the once self-consciously kitsch decor with a sleek modern look—neutral fabrics and snazzy leather banquettes. The menu changes often, but usually includes such items as duckling with orange-and-port sauce; steamed *paupiette* of black sole with salmon, crab, and prawn filling; pan-fried veal kidneys in pastry; and filet of beef topped with crispy herb bread crumbs with shallot and Madeira sauce.

15 Stephen's Lane (off Upper Mount St.), Dublin 2. ✆ **01/661-9536.** Reservations recommended. Dinner main courses €15–€24. AE, DC, MC, V. Mon–Fri 12:30–2:30pm; Tues–Sat 7:30–10:30pm. DART: Pearse. Bus: 5, 7A, 8, 46, or 84.

Ely Winebar ★ ORGANIC IRISH This cosmopolitan, clever place does everything right. The owners get all the organic produce from their family farm in County Clare, so everything is as fresh as it possibly can be. The food is simple but expertly prepared versions of Irish favorites; the service, attentive and helpful. Think gourmet "bangers and mash" (wild boar sausages and mashed spuds), fresh Clare oysters, rich Irish stew, and a vast selection of artisan cheeses. Factor in a smashing wine list and you've got a winner. There are two other Ely venues in town: the **Ely Chq** brasserie in Customs House Quay (✆ **01/672-0010**) and the **Ely Hq** gastropub on Hanover Quay (✆ **01/633-9986**).

22 Ely Place (off Merrion Row), Dublin 2. ✆ **01/676-8986.** www.elywinebar.ie. Reservations recommended. Dinner main courses €15–€30. AE, DC, MC, V. Mon–Sat noon–3pm and 6–10:30pm. Bus: 7, 7A, 8, 10, 11, or 13.

Inexpensive

National Museum Café CAFETERIA This is a great place to step out of the rain, warm yourself, and then wander among the nation's treasures. The cafe is informal, but has a certain elegance, thanks to an elaborate mosaic floor, marble tabletops, and tall windows that look across a cobbled yard. Everything is made fresh: beef salad, chicken salad, quiche, an abundance of pastries. The soup of the day is often vegetarian, and quite good. Admission to the museum is free, so you can visit without worry.

National Museum of Ireland, Kildare St., Dublin 2. ✆ **01/677-7444.** Snacks and light meals €3–€5; lunch main courses around €8. MC, V. Tues–Sat 10am–5pm; Sun 2–5pm. Bus: 7, 7A, 8, 10, 11, or 13.

O'CONNELL STREET AREA

Very Expensive

Chapter One ★★ MODERN IRISH One of the city's most atmospheric restaurants, this remarkable eatery fills the vaulted basement space of the Dublin Writers Museum. Artfully lighted and tastefully decorated, it's a romantic location, although all that loveliness does not come cheap. Meals are prepared with local, organic ingredients, all cleverly used in remarkable dishes like the ravioli with Irish goat cheese and warm asparagus, and the Irish beef with shallot gratin.

18–19 Parnell Sq., Dublin 2. ✆ **01/873-2266.** www.chapteronerestaurant.com. Reservations recommended. Fixed-price lunches, 2 courses €30, 3 courses €38; dinner main courses €32–€40. AE, DC, MC, V. Tues–Fri 12:30–2:30pm and 6–11pm; Sat 6–11pm. Bus: 27A, 31A, 31B, 32A, 32B, 42B, 42C, 43, or 44A.

Moderate

101 Talbot ★ INTERNATIONAL This modest, second-floor eatery above a shop may be unassuming, but don't be fooled—it's actually a bright beacon of good cooking on the Northside. The menu features light, healthy food, with a strong emphasis on vegetarian dishes. Dishes change regularly, but mains might include linguine with homemade pork sausage, pan-fried sea trout with capers and cherry tomatoes, or a classic chargrilled Irish steak with mushroom and brandy sauce. The dining room is casually funky, with contemporary Irish art, big windows, and newspapers scattered about, if you should want one. The staff are endlessly friendly, making it a pleasure to visit.

101 Talbot St. (at Talbot Lane near Marlborough St.), Dublin 1. ✆ **01/874-5011.** www.101talbot.ie. Reservations recommended. 2-course early-bird menu €22; dinner main courses €15–€22. AE, MC, V. Tues–Sat 5–11pm. DART: Connolly. Bus: 27A, 31A, 31B, 32A, 32B, 42B, 42C, 43, or 44A.

Inexpensive

Epicurean Food Hall GOURMET FOOD COURT This wonderful food hall houses a wide variety of artisan produce, delicious local Irish meats, and regional specialties. Favorites include **Caviston's,** Dublin's premier deli, for smoked salmon and seafood; **Itsabagel,** for its delicious bagels, imported from H&H Bagels in New York City; **Crème de la Crème,** for its French-style pastries and cakes; **Missy and Mandy's,** for its American-style ice cream; **Nectar,** for its plethora of healthy juice drinks; **Christophe's Café,** for its delicious gourmet sandwiches, wraps, and panini; and **Layden's Fine Wines,** which sells wine by the bottle or glass, if you want to make your foraged meal just that little bit fancier. There is some seating in the hall, but this place gets jammed during lunchtime midweek, so visit at off-peak times if possible.

Middle Abbey St., Dublin 1. ✆ **01/878-7016.** All items around €3–€15. No credit cards. Mon–Sat 10am–6pm. Bus: 70 or 80.

Soup Dragon SOUPS This place is tiny, with fewer than a dozen stools alongside a bar, but it's big on drama: blue walls, black and red mirrors, orange slices and spice sticks flowing out of giant jugs. The menu changes daily, but usually features a few traditional choices (potato and leek, carrot and coriander) as well as the more exotic (Thai green chicken curry, for example). They also serve salads, bagels, sandwiches, and wraps. Breakfast is pretty good here too, with a nice balance of the healthy (banana bread, muesli, oatmeal/"porridge") and the hearty (such as the "dragon breakfast" with eggs and bacon, which will keep you going for hours).

168 Capel St., Dublin 1. ✆ **01/872-3277.** Breakfast €2–€7.50; soup €5.50–€13; other lunch items €4–€7. MC, V. Mon–Sat 9:30am–6pm; Sun 1–6pm. Bus: 70 or 80.

BALLSBRIDGE/EMBASSY ROW AREA

Expensive

Roly's Bistro IRISH/INTERNATIONAL This two-story, shop-front restaurant is a local institution, beloved for providing the kind of reliably good, tummy-warming food you never get tired of: roasted breast of chicken with orzo pasta and wild mushrooms or braised shank of lamb with root vegetable purée and rosemary *jus*, to name just two. The bright and airy main dining room can be noisy when the house is full, but there's also an enclave of booths for those who prefer a quiet tête-à-tête.

7 Ballsbridge Terrace, Dublin 4. ✆ **01/668-2611.** www.rolysbistro.ie. Reservations required. Main courses €20–€36; 3-course set-price dinner €42; 3-course set-price lunch €24; express lunch €16 Mon–Fri. AE, DC, MC, V. Daily noon–3pm and 6–9:45pm. DART: Lansdowne Rd. Station. Bus: 5, 6, 7, 8, 18, or 45.

Moderate

The French Paradox ★★★ WINE BAR This is a darling little bistro and wine bar that endears itself to everyone. The wine's the thing here, so relax with a bottle of bordeaux or Côte du Rhône and nibbles from the menu. Tapas is served between 3 and 7pm—typical dishes include superb Iberico hams from Spain and caviar d'aubergine with croutons—or come for the small evening menu, which offers bistro favorites such as Gravad Lax and blinis.

53 Shelbourne Rd., Dublin 4. ✆ **01/660-4068.** www.thefrenchparadox.com. Reservations recommended. Lunch main courses €9–€14; tapas €3–€13; main courses €13–€19. AE, MC, V. Mon–Fri noon–3pm and 6pm–midnight; Sat 3pm–midnight. DART: Lansdowne Rd. Bus: 5, 6, 7, 8, or 18.

Seeing the Sights

DUBLIN'S TOP ATTRACTIONS

Áras an Uachtaráin (The Irish President's House) Áras an Uachtaráin (Irish for "House of the President") was once the Viceregal Lodge, the summer retreat of the British viceroy, whose main digs were in Dublin Castle. From what were never humble beginnings, the original 1751 country house has been expanded several times, gradually accumulating more splendor. Sadly, you see only a bit of it. The house is open to the public only on Saturdays, and then only for guided tours. A bus brings you from the park's visitor center to the house, and the main focus of the 1-hour guided tour is the state reception rooms. Only 525 tickets are given out each Saturday morning on a first-come, first-served basis. No backpacks, strollers, cameras, or cellphones are allowed.

In Phoenix Park, Dublin 8. ✆ **01/677-0095.** www.president.ie. Free admission. Summer Sat 10am–5pm; winter Sat 10:30am–4pm. Closed Dec 24–26. Same-day tickets issued at Phoenix Park Visitor Centre (see later in this chapter). Bus: 10, 37, or 39.

The Book of Kells This extraordinary hand-drawn manuscript of the four gospels, dating from the year 800, is one of Ireland's jewels, and with elaborate scripting and colorful illumination, it is undeniably magnificent. It is displayed, along with another early Christian manuscript, at Trinity College's Old Library. Unfortunately, the need to protect the books for future generations means that there's little for you to actually see. The volumes are very small and displayed inside a wooden cabinet shielded by bulletproof glass. So all you really see here are the backs of a lot of tourists leaning over a small table trying to get a peek at two pages of the ancient books. It's quite anticlimactic, but the Library's Long Room goes some way toward making up for that, at least for bibliophiles. The grand, chained library holds many rare works on Irish history and has frequently changing displays of rare works. Still, it's hard to say that it's all worth the large admission fee. For a cheaper and more fulfilling alternative, try the Chester Beatty Library (below).

College Green, Dublin 2. ✆ **01/608-2320.** www.tcd.ie. Admission to Book of Kells €9 adults, €8 seniors and students, free for children 11 and under. Combination tickets for the Library and Dublin Experience also available. Mon–Sat 9:30am–5pm; Sun noon–4:30pm (opens at 9:30am June–Sept). Bus: Any cross-city bus marked AN LAR.

Chester Beatty Library ★★★ Sir Alfred Chester Beatty was an American of Irish heritage who made a fortune in the mining industry and collected rare manuscripts. In 1956, he bequeathed his extensive collection to Ireland, and this fascinating museum inside the grounds of Dublin Castle was the ultimate result of his largesse. The breathtaking array of early illuminated gospels and religious manuscripts outshines the Book of Kells, and there are endless surprises here: ancient editions of the Bible and other religious books, beautiful copies of the Koran, and endless icons from Western, Middle Eastern, and Far Eastern cultures. This is one of the best museums in Ireland, and it's free.

Clock Tower Bldg., Dublin Castle, Dublin 2. ✆ **01/407-0750.** www.cbl.ie. Free admission. Tues–Fri 10am–5pm (Mon–Fri May–Sept); Sat 11am–5pm; Sun 1–5pm. Free guided tours Wed and Sat 2:30pm. Closed Dec 24–26, Jan 1, and holidays. DART: Sandymount. Bus: 5, 6, 6A, 7A, 8, 10, 46, 46A, 46B, or 64.

Christ Church Cathedral ★ This magnificent cathedral is difficult to appreciate fully if you walk up the street that runs in front of it, as it is actually below street level. It was designed to be seen from the river, so walk to it from the river side in order to truly appreciate its size and the way it dominates the neighborhood. It dates from 1038, when Sitric, Danish king of Dublin, built the first wooden Christ Church here. In 1171, the original foundation was extended into a cruciform and rebuilt in stone by the Norman warrior Strongbow. However, the present structure dates mainly from 1871 to 1878, when a huge restoration took place that is controversial to this day, as much of the old detail was destroyed in the process. Still, magnificent stonework and graceful pointed arches survive. There's also a statue of Strongbow inside, and some believe his tomb is here as well, although historians are not convinced. Look out for a heart-shaped iron box in the southeast chapel, which is said to contain the heart of St. Laurence O'Toole. The best way to get a glimpse of what the original building must have been like is to visit the crypt, which is original to the 12th-century structure.

Christ Church Place, Dublin 8. ✆ **01/677-8099.** Admission €6 adults, €4 students and children 14 and under. June–Aug daily 9am–6pm; Sept–May daily 9:45am–5:30pm. Closed Dec 26. Bus: 21A, 50, 50A, 78, 78A, or 78B.

Dublin Castle This 13th-century structure was the center of British power in Ireland for more than 7 centuries, until the new Irish government took it over in 1922. You can walk the grounds for free, although this is largely municipal office space now and is disappointingly dominated by parking lots. Still, it's worth a wander. To see the inside you have to join a tour, although they're reasonably priced;

highlights include the 13th-century Record Tower; the State Apartments, once the residence of English viceroys; and the Chapel Royal, a 19th-century Gothic building with particularly fine plaster decoration and carved-oak gallery fronts and fittings. If they're open, check out the Undercroft, an excavated site on the grounds where an early Viking fortress stood, and the Treasury, built in the early 18th century. There are also a vaguely interesting on-site craft shop, heritage center, and restaurant.

Palace St. (off Dame St.), Dublin 2. ✆ **01/645-8813.** www.heritageireland.ie/en/Dublin/DublinCastle. Guided tours €4.50 adults, €3.50 seniors and students, €2 children 11 and under. €1 discount when State Apartments. aren't available (free for children). Mon-Fri 10am-4:45pm; Sat-Sun and holidays 2-4:45pm. Guided tours every 20–25 min. Bus: 50, 50A, 54, 56A, 77, 77A, or 77B.

Dublinia ☺ This museum aims to teach the little ones about the Viking and medieval history of Dublin through a series of interactive exhibits. With visual effects, background sounds (some on an annoying loop seem to follow you around repeating the same phrase over and over, until you can still hear it in your sleep weeks, even years later), and aromas ostensibly from that time, it's designed to stimulate, but will probably bore anybody over the age of 14. Still, you and the kids can dress up in medieval garb, be chained up as a Viking slave, and put yourselves in the town stocks. This seems to be one of those museums largely directed at kids on school field trips. If you plan to visit Dublinia and Christ Church Cathedral on the same day, keep hold of your ticket to claim reduced-price admission.

St. Michael's Hill, Christ Church, Dublin 8. ✆ **01/679-4611.** www.dublinia.ie. Admission €6.25 adults, €5.25 students, €5 seniors, €3.75 children, €17 families. Daily 10am–5pm (last admission 4:15pm, Oct-Mar last admission 4pm). Closed Dec 23–26 and Mar 17. Bus: 50, 78A, or 123.

Dublin Writers Museum ★★ This excellent little museum represents the best of what literary galleries can be, and lovers of Irish literature will find it hard to tear themselves away. The attraction is more than just seeing Joyce's typewriter or reading early playbills for the Abbey Theatre when Yeats helped to run it. The draw also comes from long letters from Brendan Behan to friends, talking about parties he was invited to with the Marx Brothers in Los Angeles after he hit the big time, and scrawled notes from Behan, Joyce, and Beckett about work, life, and love. This museum opens a window and lets light shine on Ireland's rich literary heritage, and it is wonderful to walk in that glow.

18-19 Parnell Sq. N., Dublin 1. ✆ **01/872-2077.** www.writersmuseum.com. Admission €7.50 adults, €6.30 seniors and students, €4.70 children, €20 families (2 adults and up to 3 children 11 and under). Combined ticket with either the Shaw Birthplace or Malahide Castle €11.50 adults, €9.50 seniors and students, €7.50 children, €31 families. Mon-Sat 10am-5pm (until 6pm June-Aug); Sun and holidays 11am-5pm. DART: Connolly Station. Bus: 11, 13, 16, 16A, 22, or 22A.

Hugh Lane Municipal Gallery of Modern Art ★ This outstanding little gallery has a strong collection of Impressionist works led by Degas's *Sur la Plage* and Manet's *La Musique aux Tuileries,* as well as sculptures by Rodin, a marvelous collection of Harry Clarke stained glass, and numerous works by modern Irish artists. One room holds the complete studio of the Irish painter Francis Bacon, which the gallery purchased and moved to Dublin piece by piece from London, and then reconstructed behind glass. Everything was moved, right down to the dust. It's an excellent, compact art museum, and a great place to spend an afternoon.

Parnell Sq. N., Dublin 1. ✆ **01/222-5550.** www.hughlane.ie. Free admission. Tues-Thurs 10am-6pm; Fri-Sat 10am-5pm; Sun 11am-5pm. DART: Connolly or Tara stations. Bus: 3, 10, 11, 13, 16, or 19.

Kilmainham Gaol Historical Museum ★★★ This is a key sight for anyone interested in Ireland's struggle for independence from British rule. Within these walls, Irish rebels became political prisoners from 1796 until 1924. The leaders of the 1916 Easter Uprising were all executed here, along with many others. The country's first *Taoiseach* (prime minister), Eamon de Valera, was the gaol's final prisoner. To walk along these corridors, through the grim exercise yard, or into the walled compound is a moving experience that lingers in your memory.

Kilmainham, Dublin 8. ✆ **01/453-5984.** www.heritageireland.ie. Guided tour €6 adults, €4 seniors, €2 children, €14 families. Apr–Sept daily 9:30am–6pm (last admission 5pm); Oct–Mar Mon–Sat 9:30am–5:30pm (last admission 4pm), Sun 10am–6pm (last admission 5pm). Bus: 51B, 78A, or 79.

National Gallery of Ireland ★ This museum houses Ireland's national art collection, as well as a collection of European art spanning the 14th to the 20th century. Every major European school of painting is represented, including selections by Italian Renaissance artists (especially Caravaggio's *The Taking of Christ*), French Impressionists, and Dutch 17th-century masters. The highlight of the Irish collection is the room dedicated to the mesmerizing works of Jack B. Yeats, brother of the poet W. B. Yeats. All public areas are wheelchair accessible. The museum has a shop and an excellent self-service **cafe.**

Merrion Sq. W., Dublin 2. ✆ **01/661-5133.** www.nationalgallery.ie. Free admission. Mon–Sat 9:30am–5:30pm (Thurs to 8:30pm); Sun noon–5:30pm. Closed Dec 24–26 and Good Friday. Free guided tours (meet in the Shaw Room) Sat 3pm, Sun 2, 3, and 4pm. DART: Pearse. Bus: 5, 6, 7, 7A, 8, 10, 44, 47, 47B, 48A, or 62.

National Museum ★★ This museum holds pieces of Ireland's heritage dating back as far as 2000 B.C. These include many of the country's greatest historical finds, including an extensive collection of glittering Irish Bronze Age gold, the Ardagh Chalice, the Tara Brooch, and the Cross of Cong. Other highlights include the artifacts from the Wood Quay excavations of the Old Dublin Settlements. The only place where it falls flat is on interactive exhibits, which are well thought out and *could* be excellent, but which have not been, on recent visits, well maintained.

Kildare St. and Merrion St., Dublin 2. ✆ **01/677-7444.** Free admission. Tues–Sat 10am–5pm; Sun 2–5pm. Closed Dec 25 and Good Friday. DART: Pearse. Bus: 7, 7A, 8, 10, 11, or 13.

St. Patrick's Cathedral ★ This is the largest church in Ireland, and one of the best-loved churches in the world. The present cathedral dates from 1190, but because of a fire and 14th-century rebuilding, not much of the original foundation remains. It is mainly early English in style, with a square medieval tower that houses the largest ringing peal bells in Ireland, with an 18th-century spire. The 90m-long (295-ft.) interior allows for sweeping perspectives of soaring vaulted ceilings and the vast nave. Consecrated by its namesake, it acts as a memorial to Irish war dead (represented in banners and flags throughout the building, some literally rotting away on their poles), and holds a memorial to the Irish soldiers who died fighting in the two world wars (although Ireland was neutral in World War II, at least 50,000 Irish volunteers died fighting with the British army in that war). St. Patrick's is closely associated with the writer Jonathan Swift, who was dean here from 1713 to 1745, and he is buried here alongside his longtime partner, Stella. St. Patrick's is the national cathedral of the Church of Ireland.

21-50 Patrick's Close, Patrick St., Dublin 8. ✆ **01/475-4817.** www.stpatrickscathedral.ie. Admission €5.50 adults, €4.70 students and seniors, €15 families. Year-round Mon–Fri 9am–6pm; Nov–Feb Sat 9am–5pm, Sun 10–11am and 12:45–3pm; Mar–Oct Sat 9am–6pm, Sun 9–11am, 12:45–3pm, and 4:15–6pm. Closed except for services Dec 24–26. Bus: 65, 65B, 50, 50A, 54, 54A, 56A, or 77.

MORE ATTRACTIONS

Guinness Storehouse ★ Founded in 1759, the Guinness Brewery is one of the world's largest breweries, producing a distinctive dark stout, famous for its thick, creamy head. You can explore the Guinness Hopstore, a converted 19th-century four-story building housing the World of Guinness Exhibition, and view a film showing how the stout is made; then move on to the Gilroy Gallery, dedicated to the graphic design work of John Gilroy; and last but not least, stop in at the breathtaking Gravity Bar, where you can sample a glass of the famous brew in the glass-enclosed bar 60m (197 ft.) above the ground, with 360-degree views of the city.

St. James's Gate, Dublin 8. ✆ **01/408-4800.** www.guinness-storehouse.com. Admission €15 adults, €11 seniors and students, €5 children 6–12, €34 families. Daily 9:30am–5pm. Guided tours every half-hour. Bus: 51B, 78A, or 123.

Heraldic Museum/Genealogical Office This museum is an excellent resource for families trying to track down their Irish heritage. Exhibits on display include shields, banners, coins, paintings, porcelain, and stamps depicting Irish coats of arms. The staff are very helpful in answering questions on how to research your family tree, and keep a list of recommended professional genealogists.

NATIVE behavior: THE ART OF POURING GUINNESS

No trip to Ireland is complete without sampling the national beverage, whether you call it Guinness or simply "the black stuff." Despite its thick-as-pitch color, don't be afraid of it; Guinness isn't a heavy beer, only 11 calories per ounce or about 150 calories per pint, about the same as domestic beer. Draft Guinness is actually lower in alcohol than Coors Light. To the Irish, it's a classic "session beer," one with low alcohol and a great taste that can be enjoyed without leaving you feeling bloated. There are plenty of hops thrown in to give it a robust taste, and the Irish will vouch for the old advertising slogan "Guinness is good for you."

Yet the Guinness ritual doesn't begin in the drinking; it starts in the pouring. And pouring the perfect pint is, as any respectable Irish barman will tell you, an art form known as the "two-shot pour." Watch as he quickly fills the pint glass three-quarters of the way with swirling stout, and then sets the glass on the counter for about a minute and a half so that the gas can break out. It's the 75% nitrogen to 25% carbon dioxide mix that builds the famous Guinness head. Next, the barman tops up the pint, and serves it while a sepia-colored storm brews inside. Patience, patience: No sipping until the pint has settled into a distinct line between the black stout and the honey-colored head. Classically, the head should stand "proud," just slightly above the rim of the glass and quite thick and moussey. And with a "Cheers!" or *"Slainte!"* (pronounced *slahn*-chuh, Irish for "To your health!") you're finally ready to enjoy your pint.

2 Kildare St., Dublin 2. ✆ **01/603-0200.** www.nli.ie. Free admission. Mon–Wed 10am–8:30pm; Thurs–Fri 10am–4:30pm; Sat 10am–12:30pm. DART: Pearse. Bus: 5, 7A, 8, 9, 10, 14, or 15.

James Joyce Centre Near Parnell Square and the Dublin Writers Museum, the Joyce center is in a restored 1784 Georgian town house, once the home of Denis J. Maginni, a dancing instructor who appears briefly in *Ulysses*. There are pros and cons to this place—there's not much in the way of real memorabilia related to Joyce, save for a writing table Joyce used in Paris when he was working on *Finnegan's Wake*, although there are early copies of his work. Overall, it's best to come here if an interesting speaker is scheduled. True Joyce fans, of course, will be in heaven. Call about James Joyce walking tours.

35 N. Great George's St., Dublin 1. ✆ **01/878-8547.** www.jamesjoyce.ie. Admission €5 adults; €4 seniors, students, and children 9 and under. Separate fees for walking tours and events. Tues–Sat 10am–5pm; Sun noon–5pm. Closed Dec 24–26. DART: Connolly. Bus: 3, 10, 11, 11A, 13, 16, 16A, 19, 19A, 22, or 22A.

National Photographic Archive The newest member of the Temple Bar cultural complex, this archive houses the extensive (with more than 300,000 items) photo collection of the National Library, and serves as its photo exhibition space. It's an excellent space, and photos are rotated out regularly, so there's always something new to see. In addition to the exhibition area, there are a library and a small gift shop.

Meeting House Sq., Temple Bar, Dublin 2. ✆ **01/603-0374.** www.nli.ie. Free admission. Mon–Fri 10am–5pm; Sat 10am–2pm. DART: Tara St. Bus: 21A, 46A, 46B, 51B, 51C, 68, 69, or 86.

Number Twenty Nine 🎁 ☺ This little museum in a typical town house on one of the fashionable Georgian streets on Dublin's south side re-creates the lifestyle of a middle-class family from 1790 to 1820. The exhibition is designed to be authentic all the way from the artifacts and artwork of the time to the carpets, curtains, plasterwork, and bell pulls. Tables are set with period dishes and the nursery is filled with toys from the time. It's both educational and particularly beautiful.

29 Lower Fitzwilliam St., Dublin 2. ✆ **01/702-6165.** www.esb.ie/numbertwentynine. Tours only, €6 adults, €3 seniors and students, free for children 15 and under. Tues–Sat 10am–5pm; Sun noon–5pm. Closed 2 weeks at Christmas. DART: Pearse. Bus: 7, 8, 10, or 45.

The Old Jameson Distillery This museum illustrates the history of Irish whiskey, known in Irish as *uisce beatha* (the water of life). Learn as much as you can bear from the film, whiskey-making exhibitions, and right-in-front-of-your-eyes demonstrations. At the conclusion of the tour, you can sip a little of the firewater and see what you think. A couple of lucky people on each tour are selected to sample different Irish, Scotch, and American whiskeys.

Bow St., Smithfield Village, Dublin 7. ✆ **01/807-2355.** www.whiskeytours.ie. Admission €13.50 adults; €10 seniors, students, and children; €30 families. Daily 9:30am–6pm (last tour at 5pm). Closed Good Friday and Christmas holidays. Bus: 67, 67A, 68, 69, 79, or 90.

PARKS & ZOOS

Phoenix Park The vast green expanses of Phoenix Park are Dublin's playground, and it's easy to see why. This is a well-designed, user-friendly park crisscrossed by a network of roads and quiet pedestrian walkways that make its 704 hectares (1,740 acres) easily accessible. It's a gorgeous place to spend a restful afternoon, but there's plenty to do here should you feel active. The homes of the Irish president and the U.S. ambassador are both in the park. Livestock graze peacefully on pasturelands, deer roam the forested areas, and horses romp on polo fields. The Phoenix Park Visitor Centre has background information on the park's history, for the particularly curious. The cafe/restaurant is open 10am to 5pm weekdays, 10am to 6pm weekends. Free car parking is adjacent to the center. The park is 3km (1¾ miles) west of the city center on the north bank of the River Liffey.

The **Dublin Zoo** (✆ **01/677-1425;** www.dublinzoo.ie), also located in the park, provides a naturally landscaped habitat for more than 235 species of wild animals and tropical birds. Highlights for youngsters include the Children's Pets' Corner and a train ride around the zoo. There are playgrounds interspersed throughout the zoo, as well as several restaurants, coffee shops, and gift shops.

Phoenix Park: Dublin 8. ✆ **01/677-0095.** www.heritageireland.ie. Free admission. Apr–Sept daily 10am–6pm; Nov–Mar daily 10am–5pm; Oct daily 10am–5:30pm. Zoo: ✆ **1800/924-848.** www.dublinzoo.ie. Admission €15 adults, €8.70 special-needs adults, €12 seniors, €12.50 students, €5.50 special-needs child, €10.50 children 3–16, free for children 2 and under, €44–€52 families, depending on number of children. Mar–Sept daily 9:30am–6pm; Oct daily 9:30am–5:30pm; Nov–Dec daily 9:30am–4pm; Jan daily 9:30am–4:30pm; Feb daily 9:30am–5pm. Last admission to zoo 1 hr. before closing; to African Plains half an hour before closing. Bus: 10, 25, or 26.

ORGANIZED TOURS

BUS TOURS The city bus company, **Dublin Bus** (✆ **01/873-4222;** www.dublinbus.ie), operates several tours of Dublin, all of which depart from the Dublin Bus office at 59 Upper O'Connell St., Dublin 1. You can buy your ticket from the bus driver or book in advance at the Dublin Bus office or at the Dublin Tourism ticket desk on Suffolk Street.

The 75-minute guided **Dublin City Tour** operates on a hop-on, hop-off basis, connecting 10 major points of interest, including museums, art galleries, churches and cathedrals, libraries, and historic sites. Rates are €15 for adults, €13 seniors and students, €6 for children 15 and under. Tours operate daily from 9:30am to 6:30pm.

The 2¼-hour **Dublin Ghost Bus** is a spooky evening tour run by Dublin Bus, departing Monday to Thursday at 8pm, Friday at 8 and 8:30pm, and Saturday and Sunday at 7 and 9:30pm. The tour addresses Dublin's history of felons, fiends, and phantoms. You'll see haunted houses, learn of Dracula's Dublin origins, and even get a crash course in body snatching. It's properly scary, though, and not recommended for children who do not have "teen" in their age. Fares are €25 for adults.

The 3-hour **Coast and Castle Tour** departs daily at 10am and 2pm, traveling up the north coast to Malahide and Howth. Fares are €25 for adults, €12 for children 13 and under. Visiting Malahide Castle will require an additional charge.

The 3¾-hour **South Coast Tour** departs daily at 11am and 2pm, traveling south through the seaside town of Dún Laoghaire, through the upscale "Irish Riviera" villages of Dalkey and Killiney, and farther south to visit the vast Powerscourt Estate. Fares are €25 for adults, €12 for children 13 and under.

Gray Line (✆ **01/605-7705;** www.irishcitytours.com) operates its own hop-on, hop-off city tour, covering all the same major sights as the Dublin Bus's "Dublin City Tour." The first tours leave at 9:30am from outside the Dublin Tourism office at 14 Upper O'Connell St., and run every 10 to 15 minutes thereafter. The last departures are at 5:30pm in summer, 4:30pm in winter. You can also join the tour at any of a number of pickup points along the route and buy your ticket from the driver. Gray Line's Dublin city tour costs €16 for adults, €13 for seniors and students, €7 for children, and €38 families. Gray Line also offers a range of full-day excursions from

Dublin to such nearby sights as Glendalough, Newgrange, and Powerscourt. Adult fares for their other tours range from about €20 to €40.

WALKING TOURS Small and compact, Dublin was made for walking. If you prefer to set off on your own, the **Dublin Tourism** office, St. Andrew's Church, Suffolk Street, Dublin 2, has maps for four tourist trails signposted throughout the city: Old City, Georgian Heritage, Cultural Heritage, and the "Rock 'n Stroll" music tour. However, if you'd like more guidance, historical background, or just some company, consider one of the following.

A walk with **Historical Walking Tours of Dublin** (✆ **01/878-0227;** www.historicalinsights.ie) is like a 2-hour primer on Dublin's historic landmarks, from medieval walls and Viking remains around Wood Quay, to the architectural splendors of Georgian Dublin, to highlights of Irish history. Guides are historians, and participants are encouraged to ask questions. Tours assemble just inside the front gate of Trinity College; no reservations are needed. Costs are €12 adults, €10 seniors and students, free for children 13 and under.

If you prefer an evening tour, there's the **Literary Pub Crawl** (✆ **01/670-5602;** www.dublinpubcrawl.com), a winner of the "Living Dublin Award." The tour follows in the footsteps of Joyce, Behan, Beckett, Shaw, Kavanagh, and other Irish literary greats to local pubs, with actors providing humorous performances and commentary between stops. Throughout the night, there is a Literary Quiz with prizes for the winners. No children allowed, for obvious reasons. The tour costs €12 adults, €10 students.

The creation of a local theater company, the **Walk Macabre** (✆ **087/677-1512**) is a 90-minute walk past the homes of famous writers around Merrion Square, St. Stephen's Green, and Merrion Row, while reconstructing scenes of past murders and intrigue. The tour includes reenactments from some of the darker pages of Yeats, Joyce, Bram Stoker, and Oscar Wilde. This one would be rated "R" for violent imagery, so it's not for children or the overly sensitive. Tours leave from the main gates of St. Stephen's Green; advance booking is essential. Cost is €15 adults, €12 students.

HORSE-DRAWN CARRIAGE TOURS If you don't mind being conspicuous, you can tour Dublin in style in a handsomely outfitted horse-drawn carriage while your driver points out the sights. To arrange a ride, consult with one of the drivers stationed with carriages on the Grafton Street side of St. Stephen's Green. Rides range from a short swing around the Green to an extensive half-hour Georgian tour or an hour-long Old City tour. Rides are available on a first-come, first-served basis from April to October (weather permitting) and cost anywhere from €20 to €60 for one to four passengers, depending on the duration of the ride.

LAND & WATER TOURS The immensely popular **Viking Splash Tour** (✆ **01/707-6000;** www.vikingsplash.ie) is an unusual way for kids to see Dublin. Aboard a reconditioned American World War II amphibious landing craft, or "duck," this tour starts on land (from Bull Alley St. beside St. Patrick's Cathedral) and eventually splashes into the Grand Canal. Passengers wear horned Viking helmets (a reference to the original settlers of the Dublin area) and are encouraged to issue war cries at appropriate moments. One of the ducks even has bullet holes as evidence of its military service. Tours depart roughly on the half-hour every day 9:30am to 5pm and last an hour and 15 minutes. It costs €20 for adults, €10 for children 12 and under, €18 seniors and students, and €60 for a family of five.

The Shopping Scene

In recent years, Dublin has surprised everyone by becoming a great shopping town. You'll find few bargains, but for your money you will get excellent craftsmanship in the form of hand-woven wool blankets and clothes in a vivid array of colors, big-name Irish crafts, and chic clothes from the seemingly limitless line of Dublin designers.

While the hub of mainstream shopping south of the Liffey is **Grafton Street,** crowned by the city's most fashionable department store, Brown Thomas (known as BT), and the jeweler Weirs, there's much better shopping on the smaller streets radiating from Grafton, like **Duke, Dawson, Nassau,** and **Wicklow.** On these streets proliferate the smaller, interesting shops that specialize in books, handicrafts, jewelry, gifts, and clothing. For clothes, look out for tiny **Cow Lane,** off Lord Edward Street—it is popular with those in the know for its excellent clothing boutiques selling the works of local designers.

Generally, Dublin shops are open from 9am to 6pm Monday to Saturday, and Thursday until 9pm. Many of the larger shops have Sunday hours from noon to 6pm.

Major department stores include, on the Northside, **Arnotts,** 12 Henry St., Dublin 1 (✆ **01/805-0400**), and the marvelously traditional **Clerys,** 18–27 Lower O'Connell St., Dublin 1 (✆ **01/878-6000;** www.clerys.com); and, on the south side, **Brown Thomas,** 15–20 Grafton St., Dublin 2 (✆ **01/605-6666**).

Dublin also has several clusters of shops in **multistory malls** or ground-level **arcades,** ideal for indoor shopping on rainy days. On the Northside, these include the **ILAC Centre,** off Henry Street, Dublin 1, and the **Jervis Shopping Centre,** off Henry Street, Dublin 1. On the south side, there's the **Royal Hibernian Way,** 49–50 Dawson St., Dublin 2; **St. Stephen's Green Centre,** at the top of Grafton Street, Dublin 2; and the **Powerscourt Townhouse Centre,** 59 William St. S., Dublin 2.

BOOKS This city of literary legends has quite a few good bookstores. The granddaddy of them all is **Hodges Figgis,** 57 Dawson St., Dublin 2 (✆ **01/677-4754**), an enormous place in which you could happily lose an afternoon browsing; for rare secondhand books and first editions, **Cathac Books,** 10 Duke St., Dublin 2 (✆ **01/671-8676**), is much beloved of serious bibliophiles; and the small but perfectly formed **Noble & Beggerman** at the Hugh Lane Gallery, Parnell Square North, Dublin 1 (✆ **01/874-9294;** www.nobleandbeggarmanbooks.com), is packed full of books on Irish art, architecture, and design. Finally, if all this inspires you to put pen to paper yourself, check out the lovely selection of stylish writing gear, arty cards, and notepaper at the **Pen Corner,** 12 College Green, Dublin 2 (✆ **01/679-3641**), which has been supplying pens and paper to the literati since 1927.

CRAFTS & GIFTS A wonderland of color fills **Avoca Handweavers,** 11–13 Suffolk St., Dublin 2 (✆ **01/677-4215;** www.avoca.ie), which offers soft, intricately woven fabrics, blankets, throws, light woolen sweaters, children's clothes, and toys, all in a delightful shopping environment spread over three floors near Trinity College. All the fabrics are woven using traditional methods in the Vale of Avoca in the Wicklow Mountains. The top-floor **cafe** is a great place for lunch. In a restored 18th-century town house, **Powerscourt Townhouse Centre,** 59 S. William St., Dublin 2 (✆ **01/671-7000;** www.powerscourtcentre.com), has more than 60 boutiques, as well as craft shops, art galleries, snack bars, wine bars, and restaurants. If you want to take home an antique but can't usually afford the price tag, check out the **Drawing Room,** 29 Westbury Mall, Dublin 2 (✆ **01/677-2083**). This unique place specializes in antique gifts, knickknacks, and furniture, all beautifully crafted, highly individual—and completely fake (they're replications).

FASHION **Alias Tom,** Duke House, Duke Street (✆ **01/671-5443**), is one of Dublin's best small men's designer shops. The emphasis is on Italian (Gucci, Prada, Armani) labels, but the range covers chic designers from the rest of Europe and America. **Claire Garvey,** 6 Cow's Lane (✆ **01/671-7287**), is a Dublin native with a talent for creating romantic, dramatic, and feminine clothing with Celtic flair. A favorite designer of Irish divas Enya and Sinead O'Connor, Garvey transforms hand-dyed velvet and silk into sumptuous garments that beg to be worn on special occasions. Her one-of-a-kind bijou handbags are a white-hot fashion accessory. **Jenny Vander,** 20 Market Arcade, South Great Georges Street, Dublin 2 (✆ **01/677-0406**), is where local actresses and models come to find extraordinary and stylish antique clothing. There are plenty of jeweled frocks, vintage day wear, and stunning costume jewelry filling the clothing racks and display cases.

KNITWEAR **Avoca,** mentioned above, is an excellent option for delicate knits, while **Blarney Woollen Mills,** 21–23 Nassau St. (✆ **01/671-0068;** www.blarney.ie), is known for its competitive prices, and stocks a wide range of woolen knitwear made at its home base in Blarney, as well as crystal, china, pottery, and souvenirs. **Dublin Woollen Mills,** 41 Lower Ormond Quay (✆ **01/677-0301**), is on the north side of the River Liffey next to the Ha'penny Bridge, a leading source of Aran hand-knit sweaters as well as vests, hats, jackets, and tweeds. For cashmere, go to **Monaghan's,** 4–5 Royal Hibernian Way, off Dawson Street ✆ **01/679-4451**), which has the best selection of colors, sizes, and styles for both men and women anywhere in Ireland.

Dublin After Dark

Nightlife in Dublin is a mixed bag of traditional old pubs, where the likes of Joyce and Behan once imbibed and where traditional Irish music is often reeling away, and cool modern bars, where the repetitive rhythms of techno now fill the air and the crowd knows more about Prada than the Pogues. There's little in the way of crossover, although there are a couple of quieter bars and a few with a rock music angle. Aside from the eternal elderly pubs, things change rapidly on the nightlife scene, so pick up a copy of *In Dublin* and the *Event Guide* at local cafes and shops for listings on the latest club scene.

The award-winning website of the ***Irish Times*** (**www.ireland.com**) offers a "what's on" daily guide to cinema, theater, music, and whatever else you're up for. The **Dublin Events Guide,** at www.dublinevents.com, also provides a comprehensive listing of the week's entertainment possibilities.

Advance bookings for most large concerts, plays, and so forth can be made through **Ticketmaster Ireland** (✆ **081/871-9300;** www.ticketmaster.ie), with ticket centers in most HMV stores, as well as at the Dublin Tourism Centre, Suffolk Street, Dublin 2.

THE PERFORMING ARTS

National Concert Hall, Earlsfort Terrace, Dublin 2 (✆ **01/417-0000;** www.nch.ie), is home to the National Symphony Orchestra and Concert Orchestra, and is host to an array of international orchestras and performing artists. In addition to classical music, there are Broadway-style musicals, opera, jazz, and recitals. The box office is open Monday to Friday from 10am to 3pm, and from 6pm on show nights; on weekends, it opens 1 hour before concerts. Tickets range from €10 to €45.

The **O2,** East Link Bridge, North Wall Quay (12–16 Andrews Lane, Dublin 2; ✆ **01/819-8888;** www.theo2.ie), is one of Dublin's most high-profile music venues. Major international acts and other high-profile events play here. All ticket sales are handled by **Ticketmaster** (✆ **081/871-9300**).

For more than 90 years, the **Abbey Theatre,** Lower Abbey Street, Dublin 1 (✆ **01/878-7222;** www.abbeytheatre.ie), has been the national theater of Ireland. The Abbey's artistic reputation within Ireland has risen and fallen over the years and is at present reasonably strong. The box office is open Monday through Saturday from 10:30am to 7pm; performances begin at 8 or 8:15pm. Tickets are €15 to €40.

Less well known than the Abbey, but just as distinguished, is the **Gate Theatre,** 1 Cavendish Row, Dublin 1 (✆ **01/874-4045;** www.gate-theatre.ie). This recently restored 370-seat theater was founded in 1928 by Irish actors Hilton Edwards and Michael MacLiammoir to provide a venue for a broad range of plays. That policy prevails today, with a program that includes a blend of modern works and the classics. Tickets run from €15 to €35.

THE PUB SCENE

Pubs for Conversation & Atmosphere

The brass-filled and lantern-lit **Brazen Head,** 20 Lower Bridge St. (✆ **01/679-5186**), has atmosphere in spades. It's a tad touristy, which isn't surprising when you consider that it's the city's oldest pub—licensed in 1661 and occupying the site of an earlier tavern dating from 1198. On the south bank of the River Liffey, it's at the end of a cobblestone courtyard and was once the meeting place of Irish freedom fighters such as Robert Emmet and Wolfe Tone.

Try for one of the comfy booths in the back of the **Mercantile,** Dame Street (✆ **01/679-0522**), an ultratrendy watering hole that draws a mixed crowd of locals and in-the-know out-of-towners. Despite being very big, it's always buzzing and tends to get overjammed on weekends, so midweek nights are the best. U2 members The Edge and Larry Mullen are regulars. Converted from an old merchant's warehouse, the **River Club,** in the Ha'penny Theatre, 48 Wellington Quay (✆ **01/677-2382**), is a wine bar–cum–supper club with soaring ceilings, an enviable position overlooking the river, and contemporary furnishings for an overall feeling of easygoing sophistication. It's a favorite of Ireland's film glitterati for a late drink, so don't be surprised to spy author-screenwriter Roddy Doyle, actor Pierce Brosnan, or director Jim Sheridan.

Referred to as a "moral pub" by James Joyce in *Ulysses,* **Davy Byrnes,** 21 Duke St., just off Grafton Street (✆ **01/677-5217**), has drawn poets, writers, and lovers of literature ever since. Davy Byrnes first opened the doors in 1873; he presided here for more than 50 years and visitors today can still see his likeness on one of the turn-of-the-20th-century murals hanging over the bar.

Flannery's Temple Bar, 47–48 Temple Bar (✆ **01/497-4766**), in the heart of the trendy Temple Bar district on the corner of Temple Lane, was established in 1840. The decor is an interesting mix of crackling fireplaces, globe ceiling lights, old pictures on the walls, and shelves filled with local memorabilia. Tucked into a busy commercial street, the **Long Hall,** 51 S. Great George's St. (✆ **01/475-1590**), is one of the city's most photographed pubs, with a beautiful Victorian decor of filigree-edged mirrors, polished dark woods, and traditional snugs (cozy little partitioned areas once reserved for women). The hand-carved bar is said to be the longest counter in the city.

Adjacent to the back door of the Gaiety Theatre, **Neary's,** 1 Chatham St., Dublin 2 (✆ **01/677-7371**), is a favorite with stage folk and theatergoers. Three generations of the Ryan family have contributed to the success of **J. W. Ryan,** 28 Parkgate St. (✆ **01/677-6097**), on the north side of the Liffey near Phoenix Park. The pub is a Victorian gem featuring a pressed-tin ceiling and domed skylight, etched glass, brass lamp holders, a mahogany bar, and four old-style snugs.

Pubs with Traditional & Folk Music

Tucked between St. Stephen's Green and Merrion Street, **O'Donoghue's,** 15 Merrion Row, Dublin 2 (✆ **01/660-7194**), is a much-touristed, smoke-filled kingpin of traditional music pubs, and impromptu music sessions happen almost every night.

In the heart of Temple Bar and named for one of Ireland's literary greats, **Oliver St. John Gogarty,** 57–58 Fleet St. (✆ **01/671-1822**), has an inviting old-world atmosphere, with shelves of empty bottles, stacks of dusty books, a horseshoe-shaped bar, and old barrels for seats. There are traditional music sessions every night from 9 to 11pm. A Saturday session is at 4:30pm, and a Sunday session from noon to 2pm.

Well worth the trip into the burbs, the **Merry Ploughboy,** Edmondstown Road, Rathfarnham, Dublin 16 (✆ **01/493-1495;** www.mpbpub.com), is a pub and restaurant owned and run by the musicians who play there. There's a show with live music and Irish dancing sessions every night at 8:30pm (Mar–Nov; €20 or €50 with dinner) and free, informal music sessions in the downstairs bar every Friday and Saturday at 9:30pm. Traditional Irish food is served in the restaurant, and the *craic* is lively.

THE CLUB & MUSIC SCENE

The club and music scene in Dublin is confoundingly complex and changeable. Jazz, blues, folk, country, traditional, rock, and comedy move from venue to venue, night by night. The first rule is to get the very latest listings and see what's on and where. Dozens of clubs and pubs all over town feature rock, folk, jazz, and traditional Irish music. This includes the so-called "late-night pubs"—pubs with an exemption allowing them to remain open past the usual closing time, mandated by law (11pm in winter, 11:30pm in summer). Check *In Dublin* magazine or the *Event Guide* (see above) for club schedules. One of the most popular rock clubs is **Whelan's,** 25 Wexford St., Dublin 2 (✆ **01/478-0766**); the second-oldest pub in Dublin is **Bleeding Horse,** 24–25 Camden St., Dublin 2 (✆ **01/475-2705**).

Dance clubs include **Lillie's Bordello** (Adam Court, Dublin 2), with its well-deserved reputation for posers and boy-band celebrities, and a callous door policy. More friendly is **Rí-Rá** (Dame Court, Dublin 2), which is both trendy and laid-back. **Spy Club** (Powerscourt Townhouse Centre, Dublin 2) is popular with fashionable 30-somethings who like the fact that the emphasis here is off dance and firmly on socializing.

The city's largest gay bar is the **George,** 89 S. Great George's St., Dublin 2 (✆ **01/478-2983**), a two-story venue where both the decor and the clientele tend toward camp. It's open daily from 12:30pm to 2:30am; check listings magazines for theme nights, which start around 10pm.

KERRY & THE DINGLE PENINSULA

With its softly rolling green fields; long, sweeping seascapes; and vibrant little towns, it's easy to see why so many visitors make a beeline for County Kerry. Charming villages like colorful Kenmare, and bustling historic towns like Killarney, seem as familiar as the Irish folk songs written about them. Craggy mountain ranges punctuated by peaceful green valleys are just what you hope for when you come to Ireland.

Kerry's tremendous popularity has been great for local businesses, but during the summer it can mean that the spectacular rural scenery fairly bursts at the seams with millions of tourists. In July and August, tour buses struggle to share narrow mountain roads with local traffic, and at the best vantage points, the view is often blocked by two or three of the behemoths.

Luckily, it's still easy to escape the crowds. If you're driving along a busy road and the crowds are getting to you, simply turn off onto a small country lane and you'll find yourself virtually alone and in the peaceful Irish wilderness within seconds. In the high season in Kerry, taking the road less traveled can be the best way to go.

Getting to County Kerry

BY TRAIN **Irish Rail** (✆ **01/836-6222;** www.irishrail.ie) operates daily train service from Dublin, Limerick, Cork, and Galway to the **Killarney Railway Station** (✆ **064/663-1067**) on Railway Road, off East Avenue Road.

BY BUS **Bus Eireann** (✆ **01-836-6111;** www.buseireann.ie) operates daily express coach and local bus services to Killarney from Dublin and other parts of Ireland. The bus depot (✆ **064/663-0011**) is adjacent to the train station at Railway Road, off East Avenue Road. Once you're there, there's also limited daily service from Killarney to Caherciveen, Waterville, Kenmare, and other towns on the Ring of Kerry. Some private, Killarney-based companies offer daily sightseeing tours of the Ring of Kerry by bus.

BY CAR Roads leading into Kerry include N6 from Dublin, N21 and N23 from Limerick, and N22 from Cork. The best way to do the Ring of Kerry (comprising the N70 and N71) is by car.

Killarney Town

Perhaps the busiest tourist hub in rural Ireland, Killarney's sidewalks are spacious enough in the winter, but in the summertime, they're packed, as the streets become one giant tour-bus traffic jam and horse-and-buggy drivers risk life and limb to push their way through. The locals are well practiced at dispensing a professional brand of Irish charm, even as they hike up the hotel and restaurant prices to capitalize on the hordes descending from the buses. It all feels a bit cynical, with a few too many cheesy gift shops for its own good. (There are actually road signs on the Ring of Kerry that say LEPRECHAUN CROSSING.) It's a bit much for some people, but luckily, it's easy enough to resist Killarney's gravitational pull and spend your time exploring the quieter countryside around it. You can always sneak into town from time to time for dinner or a night out in the pub with lots of people from your home nation.

Although Killarney is pleasant enough, the real attraction is the valley in which it nestles—a verdant landscape of lakes and mountains. Exploring its glories is certainly

County Kerry

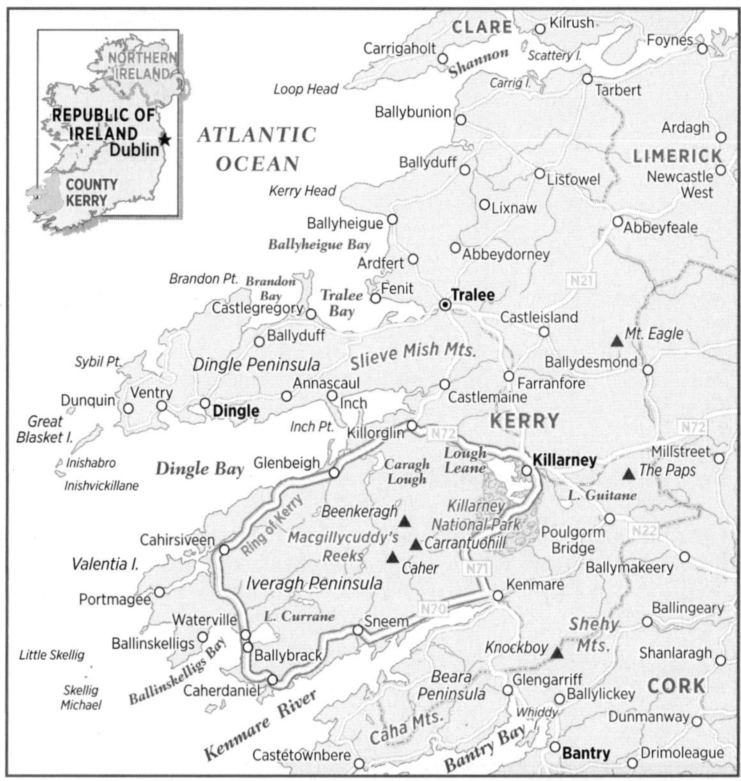

easy—just walk (or drive) from the town parking lot toward the cathedral and turn left. In a matter of minutes, you'll forget all that Killarney stress amid the quiet rural splendor of the 65-sq.-km (25-sq.-mile) **Killarney National Park.** Here the ground is a soft carpet of moss and the air is fragrant with wildflowers.

ESSENTIALS

VISITOR INFORMATION The **Killarney Tourist Office,** Aras Fáilte, is at the town center on Beech Road (✆ **064/663-1633**). It's open October to May, Monday to Saturday 9:15am to 5:15pm; June and September daily 9am to 6pm; July to August daily 9am to 8pm. During low season, the office occasionally closes for lunch from 1 to 2pm. It offers many helpful booklets and maps.

Useful local publications include ***Where: Killarney,*** a quarterly magazine distributed free at hotels and guesthouses. It is packed with current information on tours, activities, events, and entertainment.

GETTING AROUND Killarney Town is so small and compact that there is no local bus service; the best way to get around is on foot. For a quick and easy tour, follow the signposted "Tourist Trail" for the highlights of the main streets. It takes less than 2 hours to complete. A booklet outlining the sights along the trail is available at the tourist office.

Taxicabs line up at the stand on **College Square** (✆ **064/663-1331**). You can also phone for a taxi from **Killarney Cabs** (✆ **064/663-7444**), **Dave's Taxis** (✆ **087/679-8899**), or **Euro Taxis** (✆ **064/663-5624**).

There are a couple of large public parking lots near the town center, where parking costs €1 per hour. It's a good idea to leave your car in one of these unless you're heading out to Killarney National Park on the Muckross and Kenmare road (N71).

If you need to rent a car in Killarney, contact **Budget,** c/o International Hotel, Kenmare Place (✆ **064/663-4341**), and at Kerry Airport (✆ **066/976-3199;** www.budget.ie), or **Randles Bros.,** Muckross road (✆ **064/663-1237**). Alternatively, **Avis** also has a branch at Kerry Airport (✆ **01/605-7500;** www.avis.ie) and **Hertz** has branches at Cork Airport (✆ **021/496-5849;** www.hertz.ie) and Shannon Airport (✆ **061/471-369;** www.hertz.ie).

Horse-drawn **buggies,** called "jarveys," line up at Kenmare Place in Killarney Town. They offer rides to Killarney National Park sites and other scenic areas. Depending on the time and distance, prices range from around €15 to upwards of €50 per ride (up to four people).

KILLARNEY NATIONAL PARK ★★★

This is Killarney's centerpiece: a 10,000-hectare (25,000-acre) area of natural beauty. For many, the main attractions are the park's three lakes. The largest of these, the Lower Lake, is sometimes called Lough Leane or Lough Lein ("the lake of learning"). It's more than 6km (3¾ miles) long and is dotted with 30 small islands. Nearby is the Middle Lake or Muckross Lake, and the smallest of the three, the Upper Lake. The most noteworthy of Killarney's islands, **Innisfallen,** is on the Lower Lake; if you can get a boat and row yourself out (they're sometimes available for rent from Ross Castle, but we've found that often there's nobody around to actually rent you the boat), you'll find what's left of the monastery St. Fallen, which was founded in the 7th century and flourished for 1,000 years.

The park also contains a large variety of wildlife, including a rare herd of red deer. You can't drive through the park (parking lots are available, however, if you want to drive *to* it), so touring is best done by foot, bicycle, or horse-drawn jaunting car. The park offers four signposted walking and nature trails along the lakeshore. Access to the park is available from several points along the Kenmare road (N71), with the main entrance being at Muckross House. Admission is free, and the park is open year-round during daylight hours.

VIEWS & VISTAS The journey through the **Gap of Dunloe ★★** is gorgeous. The winding and rocky mountain pass sits amid rocky mountains and cool lakes about 10km (6¼ miles) west of Killarney. The route through the gap passes a kaleidoscope of sharp cliffs, meandering streams, and deep valleys. The route through the gap ends at Upper Lake. Horse fanciers may want to take one of the excursions offered by **Corcoran's Tours,** 8 College St. (✆ **064/663-6666;** www.corcorantours.com), or **Dero's Tours,** 22 Main St. (✆ **064/663-1251;** www.derostours.com).

Aghadoe Heights ★, on the Tralee Road (off N22), is a spectacular viewing point over the lakes and town. In the churchyard opposite are the evocative ruins of a stone church and round tower dating from 1027.

MORE ATTRACTIONS

Muckross House and Gardens ★★ This rambling ivy-covered Victorian mansion was built for a wealthy landowner in 1843 and donated to the state in the 1930s. It is now a museum of sorts, of life in the county, showcasing locally made furniture, prints, art, and needlework, although it mixes them with non-Irish items like Oriental screens, Chippendale chairs, and Turkish carpets. The gardens are lovely, and you can wander to the on-site restaurant and workshops, where local artisans demonstrate bookbinding, weaving, and pottery.

The ruin of the 15th-century **Muckross Abbey,** founded about 1448 and burned by Cromwell's troops in 1652, is also near the house. The abbey's central feature is a vaulted cloister around a courtyard that contains a huge yew tree, said to be as old as the abbey itself. W. M. Thackeray once called it "the prettiest little bijou of a ruined abbey ever seen."

Kenmare rd. (N71), Killarney, County Kerry. ✆ **064/667-0144.** www.muckross-house.ie. Admission to house only, €7 adults, €5.50 seniors, €3 students and children, €17.50 families. Joint ticket with Muckross Traditional Farms (below) €12 adults, €10 seniors, €6 students and children, €30 families. Daily 9am–5:30pm (9am–7pm July–Aug).

Muckross Traditional Farms ★ ☺ Not far from the Muckross House estate, these farms are designed to demonstrate what traditional farm life was like in previous centuries in County Kerry. It's cleverly done—the farmhouses and barns are so authentically detailed that you feel as if you've dropped in on real farms. Work really does go on here, so farmhands work the fields, while the blacksmith, carpenter, and wheelwright ply their trades. Women draw water from the wells and cook meals in historically accurate kitchens. Children get a kick out of the animals, and it's interesting enough to keep adults from getting bored as well.

Kenmare rd. (N71), Killarney, County Kerry. ✆ **064/663-1440.** www.muckross-house.ie. Admission €7.50 adults, €6 seniors, €4 students and children, €20 families. Joint ticket with Muckross House and Gardens (above) €12 adults, €10 seniors, €6 students and children, €30 families. Apr and Sept–Oct 1–6pm; May daily 1–6pm; June–Aug daily 10am–6pm.

Ross Castle This 15th-century restored fortress sits on the edge of the Lower Lake, 3km (1¾ miles) outside Killarney Town. Built by the O'Donoghue chieftains, this castle distinguished itself in 1652 as the last stronghold in Munster to surrender to Cromwell's forces. All that remains today is a tower house, surrounded by a fortified bawn (enclosure) with rounded turrets. The tower has been furnished in the style of the late 16th and early 17th centuries. While you can wander the grounds at will, you can see inside the castle only on a guided tour, and these tend to be a bit tedious, as the guides seem to scrounge around a bit for facts interesting enough to justify the ticket price. In good weather, the best way to reach it is via a lakeside walk (it's 3km/1¾ miles from Killarney to the castle). From the castle, you can take a boat tour of the lake, although these are not for those allergic to touristy things.

Ross Rd., off Kenmare rd. (N71), Killarney, County Kerry. ✆ **064/663-5851.** Admission €6 adults, €4 seniors, €2 students and children, €14 family. Apr–Oct daily 9:30am–5:45pm. Last admission 45 min. before closing. Closed Nov–Mar.

SIGHTSEEING TOURS

BUS TOURS **Dero's Tours,** 22 Main St. (✆ **064/663-1251;** www.derostours.com), offers a 3-hour tour showing off Killarney's lakes from the best vantage points, including Aghadoe, the Gap of Dunloe, Ross Castle, Muckross House, and the Torc

Waterfall. The tour is offered May through September daily at 10:30am; but schedules vary, so check in advance. They also run various coach/boat/pony-and-trap packages for between €30 and €50, and trips to the Gap of Dunloe and Dingle Peninsula.

Gap of Dunloe Tours, 7 High St., Killarney (✆ **064/663-0200;** www.gapofdunloetours.com), takes you on a tour through the spectacularly scenic countryside above Killarney. You then walk the 7 miles to Kate Kearney's Cottage (or go by jaunting car for an extra €20) and take a boat ride on the Killarney Lakes. The cost is €30.

In addition to Killarney's main sights, some bus tours also venture into the two prime scenic areas nearby: the Ring of Kerry and Dingle Peninsula. From May to September, tours are offered daily; prices average €18 to €25 per person. If that's the kind of tour for you, check out **Bus Eireann,** Bus Depot, Railway Road, off East Avenue Road (✆ **064/663-4777;** www.buseireann.ie), or **Corcoran's Tours,** 8 College St. (✆ **064/663-6666;** www.corcorantours.com).

JAUNTING-CAR TOURS If you prefer walking or bicycling, just say no to the numerous jaunting-car drivers who will inevitably offer their services as you make your way around the Killarney lakes. These quaint horse-driven buggies are one of the main features of the landscape here, and if at some point you decide to give one a try, keep in mind that jaunting-car rates are set and carefully monitored by the Killarney Urban District Council. Current rates (per person, based on four people to a jaunting cart) run roughly from €12 to €25, depending on where you go. The buggies are arguably the best way to get around the national park, as cars are not allowed. Destinations include Ross Castle, Muckross House and Gardens, Torc Waterfall, Muckross Abbey, Dinis Island, and Kate Kearney's Cottage, gateway to the Gap of Dunloe. You can hire a buggy at the park near Muckross House, or to arrange a tour in advance, contact **Tangney Tours,** 10B Muckross Close, Killarney (✆ **064/663-3358;** www.killarneyjauntingcars.com).

BOAT TOURS There is nothing quite like seeing the sights from a boat on the Lakes of Killarney. Two companies operate regular boating excursions, with full commentary. **MV *Pride of the Lakes* Tours,** Scotts Gardens, Killarney (✆ **087/236-4349**), sails daily in an enclosed boat from the pier at Ross Castle from April to October at 11am and 12:30, 2:30, 4, and 5pm. The trip lasts just over an hour, and reservations are suggested. The cost is €10 adults, €5 children. **MV *Lily of Killarney* Tours,** Old Weir Lodge, Killarney (✆ **064/663-1068**), sails from April to October daily at 10:30am, noon, and 1:45, 3:15, 4:30, and 5:45pm for €10 adults, €5 children, €25 family.

ENJOYING THE GREAT OUTDOORS

BICYCLING **Killarney National Park,** with its many lakeside and forest pathways, trails, and byways, is a paradise for bikers. Various vehicles are available for rent, from 21-speed touring bikes and mountain bikes to tandems. Rental charges average around €15 per day, €80 per week. Bicycles can be rented from **David O'Sullivan's Cycles,** Bishop Lane, New Street (✆ **064/663-1282;** www.killarneyrentabike.com). Most shops are open year-round daily 9am to 6pm, until 8 or 9pm in the summer.

FISHING Fishing for salmon and brown trout in Killarney's unpolluted lakes and rivers is a big attraction. Brown trout fishing is free on the lakes, but a permit is necessary for the rivers Flesk and Laune. A trout permit costs €8 to €15 per day.

Salmon fishing anywhere in Ireland requires a license; the cost is €36 per day, €50 for 21 days. Some rivers also require a salmon permit, which costs €10 to €15 per day. Permits and licenses can be obtained at the Fishery Office at the **Knockreer Estate Office,** New Street (✆ **064/663-1246**).

For fishing tackle, bait, rod rental, and other fishing gear, as well as permits and licenses, try **O'Neill's,** 6 Plunkett St. (✆ **064/663-1970**). The shop also arranges rentals of boats and *ghillies* (fishing guides) for around €80 per day on the Killarney Lakes, leaving from Ross Castle.

GOLF Visitors are always welcome at the twin 18-hole championship courses of the **Killarney Golf & Fishing Club,** Killorglin Road, Fossa (✆ **064/663-1034;** www.killarney-golf.com), 5km (3 miles) west of the town center. Widely praised as one of the most scenic golf settings in the world, these courses are surrounded by lake and mountain vistas. Greens fees are €70 to €130, depending on the course, and don't go up at weekends.

HORSEBACK RIDING Many trails in the Killarney area are suitable for horseback riding. Hiring a horse costs about €25 per hour at **Killarney Riding Stables,** N72, Ballydowney (✆ **064/663-1686**), and **Rocklands Stables,** Rockfield, Tralee Road (✆ **064/663-2592**). Lessons and weeklong trail rides can also be arranged.

WALKING There are four signposted nature trails in the **Killarney National Park.** The **Mossy Woods Nature Trail** starts near Muckross House, by Muckross Lake, and rambles 2.4km (1.5 miles) through yew woods along low cliffs. **Old Boat House Nature Trail** begins at the 19th-century boathouse below Muckross Gardens and leads half a mile around a small peninsula by Muckross Lake. **Arthur Young's Walk** (4.8km/3 miles) starts on the road to Dinis, traverses natural yew woods, and then follows a 200-year-old road on the Muckross Peninsula. The **Blue Pool Nature Trail** (2.4km/1.5 miles) goes from Muckross village through woodlands and past a small lake known as the Blue Pool. In addition, the **Cloghereen Nature Trail** is a small section of the Blue Pool trail that's designed to be fully accessible to blind visitors. A guide rope leads you along the route, which is lined by plants identified by scent and touch. An audio guide can be obtained from Muckross House, in addition to leaflets and maps for the other four trails.

THE SHOPPING SCENE

Shopping hours are normally Monday through Saturday from 9am to 6pm, but from May to September or October most shops stay open to 9 or 10pm. Although there are more souvenir and crafts shops in Killarney than you can shake a shillelagh at, here are a few of the best.

Christy's Irish Stores, 10 Main St., at the corner of Plunkett Street in the center of town (✆ **064/663-3222**), carries an array of reasonably priced wares ranging from cheesy leprechaun souvenirs to genuinely attractive hand-knit or hand-loomed sweaters, crystal, china, and pottery. **Quill's Woolen Market,** 1 High St. (✆ **064/663-2277**), is one of the best shops in town for hand-knit sweaters of all kinds, as well as tweeds, mohair, and sheepskins.

The Mucros Craft Centre, on the grounds of Muckross House (✆ **064-663-1440;** www.muckross-house.ie), is a studio and shop carrying on many County Kerry craft traditions; it features an on-premises weaver's workshop as well as a working pottery. There is also a wide selection of quality crafts from all over Ireland,

and a sky-lit cafeteria overlooking the walled garden area. In town, **Serendipity,** 15 College St. (✆ **064/663-1056**), offers a wide range of unusual crafts from local artisans, such as hand-thrown pottery from the likes of Nicholas Mosse and Stephen Pearce, Jerpoint glass, and handcrafted jewelry.

WHERE TO STAY

Expensive

Aghadoe Heights Hotel & Spa ★★ A few miles outside of town, and with spectacular views of the lake, Aghadoe Heights is a jarringly modern structure sitting rudely by an ancient ruined church, but inside it's a five-star oasis of luxury. Rooms are spacious and calming in neutral tones, with big, orthopedic beds. Many rooms have breathtaking views of the lake and surrounding hills through floor-to-ceiling, wall-to-wall windows. Nothing is impossible here, with 24-hour room service and the excellent **spa** available at the push of a button. Guests can book a relaxing hour in the steam rooms and saunas for €25. Breakfast is silver service, and the in-house **restaurant** specializes in modern Irish cuisine.

Lakes of Killarney, Killarney, County Kerry. ✆ **064/663-1766.** Fax 064/663-1345. www.aghadoeheights.com. 74 units. €240–€340 double. Rates include full breakfast. MC, V. Free parking. **Amenities:** Restaurant; bar; exercise room; Internet; indoor pool; full-service spa. *In room:* TV/DVD, hair dryer, minibar.

Randles Court ★ A former rectory dating from the early 20th century, this attractive yellow, gabled four-story house sits just outside Killarney Town on the road to Muckross House. With marble floors and chandeliers, and warmed by open fireplaces, the lounges and lobby are quite elegant. Rooms have traditional decor, including heavy armoires, antique desks, and vanities, and are tastefully decorated in bright colors.

Muckross rd. (N71), Killarney, County Kerry. ✆ **800/4-CHOICE** (424-6423) in the U.S., or 064/663-5333. Fax 064/663-5206. www.randlescourt.com. 55 units. €170–€260 double. Rates include service charge and full breakfast. AE, DC, MC, V. Free parking. **Amenities:** Restaurant; bar; babysitting; exercise room; indoor pool; room service. *In room:* TV.

Moderate

Earl's Court House A 5-minute walk from the town center, Earl's Court is the kind of genteel place where guests are greeted with tea and scones. The spacious guest rooms are tastefully furnished with Irish antiques, and have a distinct Victorian flair. Some have half-tester beds, others king-size beds and sitting areas, and nearly all have private balconies—the second-floor rooms have clear mountain views. The breakfast menu has a range of selections, from apple crepes to kippers and tomatoes.

Signposted off N71, Woodlawn Junction, Muckross rd., Killarney, County Kerry. ✆ **064/663-4009.** Fax 064/663-4366. www.killarney-earlscourt.ie. 24 units. €100–€145 double. Rates include service charge and full Irish breakfast. MC, V. Free parking. Closed Nov 6–Feb 5. **Amenities:** Room service; smoke-free rooms. *In room:* TV, hair dryer, Internet.

Fairview House ★ ☺ Somewhere between boutique hotel and upmarket guesthouse, Fairview House is an airy, modern kind of place in the center of town. Rooms are spacious and comfortable, with polished wood floors, subtle cream and red colors, and enormous beds. There are also good-size family rooms as well as wheelchair-accessible rooms. The restaurant earns good reviews, as its head chef came from the Cooperage, which, until its recent closure, was widely rated as one of the best restaurants in Killarney.

College St., Killarney. ✆ **064/663-4164.** www.fairviewkillarney.com. 29 units. €118–€165 double. MC, V. **Amenities:** Restaurant; room service. *In room:* TV, hair dryer, Internet.

Fuchsia House This modern house built in classic Victorian style is a darling guesthouse, beautifully run by Marie and Niel Burke. Bedrooms are bright and airy (although some might find the decor a little fussy), with firm, orthopedic beds. Families are welcome since most of the rooms are designed with space for both parents and children. Breakfast is served in a sunny conservatory, and the food is excellent.

Muckross rd., Killarney, County Kerry. ✆ **064/663-3743.** Fax 064/663-6588. www.fuchsiahouse.com. 9 units. €96–€110 double. Rates include full breakfast. MC, V. **Amenities:** Lounge; smoke-free rooms; Wi-Fi (free). *In room:* TV, hair dryer.

Gleann Fia Country House Although it's only 1.6km (1 mile) from town, this modern, Victorian-style guesthouse feels pleasantly secluded, with thick forests surrounding it like a blanket. Rooms are spacious and have firm, comfortable beds, but the main attraction is the great outdoors. You can enjoy nature walks through the woods, and peace and quiet to soothe your soul.

Deerpark, Killarney, County Kerry. ✆ **064/663-5035.** Fax 064/663-5000. www.gleannfia.com. 19 units. €90–€110 double. Rates include full breakfast. AE, MC, V. Free parking. **Amenities:** Lounge; smoke-free rooms. *In room:* TV.

WHERE TO DINE

Very Expensive

Gaby's Seafood Restaurant ★★ SEAFOOD The walls at Gaby's are filled with commendations and awards, which could be a bit tacky if the food weren't so good. Gaby's is known for its succulent lobster, served grilled or in a house sauce of cream, cognac, and spices. Other choices include turbot with glazed pastry, black sole meunière, and a giant Kerry shellfish platter—a veritable feast of prawns, scallops, mussels, lobster, and oysters.

27 High St., Killarney, County Kerry. ✆ **064/663-2519.** www.gabysireland.com. Reservations recommended. Main courses €25–€43. AE, DC, MC, V. Mon–Sat 6–10pm. Closed late Feb to mid-Mar and Christmas week.

Moderate

Bricín ★ TRADITIONAL IRISH Seafood dishes and old-time Kerry *boxty* (a traditional dish of potato pancakes filled with chicken, seafood, curried lamb, or vegetables) are the trademarks of this relaxed restaurant above a craft-and-book shop. Don't be put off by the fact that you enter through the shop—the building dates from the 1830s, and the dining room has a pleasant rustic feel, with wood-paneled walls, turf fireplaces, and wood floors. The seafood is excellent and the service is charming.

26 High St., Killarney, County Kerry. ✆ **064/663-4902.** Reservations recommended for dinner. Fixed-price 2-course dinner €24; dinner main courses €17–€28. AE, DC, MC, V. Year-round Tues–Sat 10am–4:30pm; Easter–Oct Mon–Sat 6–9:30pm.

Treyvaud's ★ IRISH When this place opened a couple of years back, it immediately became one of the most popular lunch spots in town. Owned by two Irish brothers, it offers a clever mix of traditional Irish favorites for lunch (stews, steak pie, and sandwiches). For dinner, it raises the ante, focusing on fresh local ingredients (lamb, salmon, sea bass) creatively prepared. It all works and the crowds keep coming.

62 High St., Killarney, County Kerry. ✆ **064/663-3062.** www.treyvaudsrestaurant.com. Reservations recommended. Dinner main courses €16–€25. MC, V. Tues–Sat noon–10:30pm.

Iveragh Peninsula/The Ring of Kerry

The Iveragh Peninsula is nearly 1,820 sq. km (700 sq. miles) of wild splendor, which you'll notice once you get off the tourist strip. Admittedly, almost everyone who gets this far feels compelled to "do" the Ring of Kerry; so, once it's done, why not take an unplanned turn, get truly lost, and let serendipity lead you to the unexpected and the unspoiled?

ESSENTIALS

Getting There

BY BUS **Bus Eireann** (✆ **064/663-0011**) provides limited daily service from Killarney to Caherciveen, Waterville, Kenmare, and other towns on the Ring of Kerry.

BY CAR This is by far the best way to get around the Ring. For the most part, the route follows N70.

VISITOR INFORMATION Stop in at the **Killarney Tourist Office,** Aras Fáilte, at the Town Centre Car Park, Beech Road, Killarney (✆ **064/663-1633**), before you explore the area. For hours, see "Visitor Information," under "Killarney Town," earlier in this chapter. The **Kenmare Tourist Office,** Market Square, Kenmare (✆ **064/41233**), is open daily Easter through September, 9:15am to 5:30pm, with extended hours in July and August. The rest of the year (Oct–Easter), it's open Monday to Saturday.

EXPLORING THE RING OF KERRY

Although it's possible to circle the peninsula in as little as 4 hours, the only way to get a feel for the area and the people is to leave the main road, get out of your car, and explore some of the inland and coastal towns. The ring is not short of good hotels and B&Bs, but most visitors chose to base themselves in **Killarney** for the convenience of having plentiful restaurants and shops. We prefer the gentler charms of **Kenmare.** Originally called *Neidin* (pronounced Nay-*deen,* meaning "little nest" in Irish), Kenmare is indeed a little nest of verdant foliage and colorful buildings nestled between the River Roughty and Kenmare Bay.

From Kenmare to busy **Killarney,** the Ring road takes you through a scenic mountain stretch known as **Moll's Gap.** Killarney is best known for its glorious surroundings, in particular the spectacular landscapes of **Killarney National Park** (see "Killarney Town," earlier in this chapter).

Departing Killarney, follow the signs for **Killorglin,** a smallish town that lights up in mid-August when it has a traditional horse, sheep, and cattle fair. Continue on the N70, and glimpses of Dingle Bay will soon appear on your right. **Carrantuohill,** at 1,041m (3,414 ft.) Ireland's tallest mountain, is to your left, and bleak views of open bog land constantly come into view.

Glenbeigh is next on the Ring, and it's a sweet little seafront town with streets lined with palm trees and a sandy beach. **Portmagee** is another lovely seaside town, connected by a bridge to **Valentia Island,** which houses the informative Skellig Heritage Centre.

The most memorable and magical site to visit on the Iveragh Peninsula is **Skellig Michael,** a rocky pinnacle towering over the sea, where medieval monks built their monastery in ascetic isolation. The crossing to the island can be rough, so you'll want to visit on a clear and calm day, if possible (the boat doesn't run in very bad weather).

Seabirds nest here in abundance, and more than 20,000 pairs of gannets inhabit neighboring Little Skellig during the summer nesting season.

Continuing on the N70, the next point of interest is **Derrynane,** at **Caherdaniel. Derrynane** is the former seat of the O'Connell clan and erstwhile home to Daniel O'Connell ("the Liberator" who freed Irish Catholics from the last of the English Penal Laws in the 19th c.). Watch for signs to **Staigue Fort,** about 3km (1¾ miles) off the main road. The well-preserved ancient circular fort is constructed of rough stones without mortar of any kind. The walls are 4m (13 ft.) thick at the base, and the diameter is about 27m (89 ft.). Experts think it dates from around 1000 B.C.

Sneem, the next village on the circuit, is a charming little place, where houses are painted in vibrant shades. The colors—blue, pink, yellow, and orange—burst out on a rainy day, like a little ray of sunshine.

WHERE TO STAY

Very Expensive

The Park Hotel Kenmare ★★★ Ensconced in a palm-tree-lined garden beside Kenmare Bay, this imposing 19th-century building is a grand, luxury hotel. In the high-ceilinged sitting rooms, fires crackle in the open fireplaces and original oil paintings decorate the walls. Guest rooms have exquisite Georgian and Victorian furnishings, and some have four-posters, all with firm mattresses, rich fabrics, and peaceful waterfront or mountain views. The hotel restaurant is acclaimed for its modern Irish cuisine. The hotel spa, **Sámas,** is famed in Ireland for its creative use of the gorgeous, bucolic setting.

Kenmare, County Kerry. ✆ **800/323-5463** in the U.S., or 064/664-1200. Fax 064/664-1402. www.parkkenmare.com. 46 units. €350–€550 double; €846 suite. AE, DC, MC, V. Closed Nov 30–Dec 22 and Jan 4–Feb 12. **Amenities:** Restaurant; bar; babysitting; concierge; 18-hole golf course; room service; smoke-free rooms; spa; tennis court. *In room:* TV/DVD, CD player, hair dryer, minibar.

Sheen Falls Lodge ★★★ Originally the 18th-century home of the earl of Kerry, this salubrious resort sits beside a natural waterfall amid vast, sprawling grounds. Reception staff members address guests by name, the bar feels like a drawing room, and the 1,000-volume library, with its green leather sofas and floor-to-ceiling bookshelves, is like an old-fashioned gentlemen's club. Guest rooms are spacious, decorated in rich, contemporary style; each overlooks the falls (stunning when floodlit at night) or the bay. There are self-catering cottages and villas available for those with deep pockets and a desire for privacy.

Kenmare, County Kerry. ✆ **800/537-8483** in the U.S., or 064/664-1600. Fax 064/664-1386. www.sheenfallslodge.ie. 66 units. €455–€600 double; €670–€1,870 suite. Full breakfast €17–€24. AE, DC, MC, V. Closed Jan 2–Feb 1. **Amenities:** 2 restaurants; bar; concierge; exercise room; Jacuzzi; indoor pool; room service; spa; tennis court. *In room:* A/C, TV/VCR, hair dryer, minibar.

Moderate

Iskeroon ★★ This is as good as it gets for this price. David and Geraldine Hare's charming B&B sits amid an arrestingly beautiful natural setting overlooking the sailboats of Derrynane Harbour and the Skelligs beyond. The Hares have renovated their villa in a fresh, Cape Cod style, with flagstone floors and a deep blue palette. There are extras, including iPod docking stations and DVD players with a vast library of films. Breakfasts are exceptional, with homemade bread and free-range eggs and bacon. They require a minimum 2-night stay and offer discounts if you stay longer. There's a charming self-catering cottage (€550 per week) for those who prefer to make their own breakfasts.

Bunavalla (near pier), Caherdaniel, County Kerry. ✆ **066/947-5119.** Fax 066/947-5488. www.iskeroon.com. 2 units, both with private bathroom. €150 double. Rates include service charge and full Irish breakfast. MC, V. Closed Oct–Apr. **Amenities:** Lounge. *In room:* TV.

Sallyport House ★★ This country-house B&B has many things going for it—a great location, a 2-minute walk into Kenmare, and its extensive manicured grounds. It's a handsome manor with a sophisticated, luxurious feel. The spacious guest rooms are furnished with well-chosen antiques and have grand bathrooms. The rooms have gorgeous views of the surrounding countryside.

Glengarriff Rd., Kenmare, County Kerry. ✆ **064/664-2066.** Fax 064/42067. www.sallyporthouse.com. 5 units. €100–€170 double. Rates include service charge and full breakfast. No children 11 and under. No credit cards. Closed Nov–Mar. **Amenities:** Lounge. *In room:* TV, hair dryer.

Shelburne Lodge ★★ This Georgian farmhouse has been transformed into one of the most original, stylish, and comfortable B&Bs in Killowen. Every room has polished wood parquet floors, quality antique furnishings, contemporary art, and a luxurious but homey feel. The guest rooms are all large and gorgeously appointed, and breakfasts are virtually decadent.

Killowen, Cork Rd., Kenmare, County Kerry. ✆ **064/664-1013.** Fax 064/664-2067. www.shelburnelodge.com. 9 units. €100–€170 double. Rates include service charge and full breakfast. MC, V. Closed Dec to mid-Mar. **Amenities:** Tennis court. *In room:* TV.

Tahilla Cove ★ This grand country house sprawls along the edge of the water in a secluded cove near Sneem. Owned by the same family for decades now, this is a house of great character. The vast wooded acreage around the building gives it a feeling of seclusion, and the friendly Waterhouse family runs the place with unpretentious affability. The spacious bedrooms are comfortably and simply furnished and have private balconies, some with great views of Beara Peninsula (ask for a room with a sea view). You can borrow one of the boats and row out into the water, or go for a walk with the family's energetic spaniels—bring your own dog! This is a dog-friendly hotel. **Dinners** here are like house parties, and are well worth staying for.

On the N70, follow signs, Sneem, County Kerry. ✆ **064/664-5204.** Fax 064/664-5104. www.tahillacove.com. 9 units. €80–€150 double. Discount for 5 nights. Rates include service charge and full breakfast. AE, MC, V. Closed Nov–Mar. **Amenities:** Lounge. *In room:* TV, hair dryer.

WHERE TO DINE

Expensive

Lime Tree ★★ MODERN IRISH Innovative cuisine is the focus at this Kenmare restaurant in an 1821 landmark renovated schoolhouse next to the Park Hotel. Paintings by local artists line the stone walls in the atmospheric dining room. The menu offers modern interpretations of classic Irish dishes and European cuisine; typical mains could include filet of beef with colcannon, sautéed onions and peppercorn *jus,* or hummus and blue cheese with orzo salad and beet salsa. Typical desserts include homemade praline ice cream and warm crepes with butterscotch sauce.

Shelbourne Rd., Kenmare, County Kerry. ✆ **064/664-1225.** www.limetreerestaurant.com. Reservations recommended. Main courses €19–€28. MC, V. Apr–Nov daily 6:30–10pm.

Moderate

The Blue Bull TRADITIONAL IRISH Sneem is so small that if you blink, you miss it. Yet it has several good pubs, and this one serves excellent food. There are three small rooms, each with an open fireplace, plus a sky-lit conservatory in the back. Traditional Irish fare, like smoked salmon and Irish stew, shares the menu with such dishes as salmon stuffed with spinach and Valencia scallops in brandy—all served to a backdrop of traditional Irish music on most nights. According to the pub's owners, the Blue Bull is composer Andrew Lloyd Webber's favorite place to eat in Ireland.

South Sq., Ring of Kerry rd. (N70), Sneem, County Kerry. ✆ **064/664-5382.** Reservations recommended. Main courses €10–€26. AE, MC, V. Bar food year-round daily 11am–8pm. Restaurant Mar–Oct daily 6–10pm.

Packie's MODERN IRISH If you're looking for a stylish place to have a great meal that won't break the bank, this is the place. There's always a buzz here, and the smart crowd fits in perfectly with the bistro look—colorful window boxes, slate floors, stone walls filled with contemporary art. Everyone comes for the food: tried-and-true favorites such as Irish lamb stew, crisp potato pancakes, seafood sausages, and crab claws in garlic butter. Desserts are terrific, too.

Henry St., Kenmare, County Kerry. ✆ **064/664-1508.** Reservations recommended. Main courses €15–€30. MC, V. Mid-Mar to Dec Tues–Sat 6–10pm (also Mon 6–10pm in summer). Closed Jan to mid-Mar.

Inexpensive

Prego ★ ITALIAN When you're craving a break from all that heavy Irish food, head here for fresh, tasty Italian cuisine. The pasta is all homemade, and served with a light touch on the sauce. Salads are big and crisp, and the thin-crust pizzas are all made from scratch to order. All the classics are here and are well made.

Henry St., Kenmare, County Kerry. ✆ **064/664-2350.** All items €7–€16. MC, V. Daily 9am–10:30pm.

Purple Heather ★ IRISH This lovely little eatery is *the* place to lunch in Kenmare. The food consists of tearoom classics with a gourmet twist—wild smoked salmon or prawn salad; smoked trout pâté; vegetarian omelets; Irish cheese platters; and fresh, homemade soups.

Henry St., Kenmare, County Kerry. ✆ **064/41016.** All items €6–€19. V. Mon–Sat 11am–5:30pm. Closed Sun and bank holidays.

SHOPPING IN KENMARE

At **De Barra Jewellery,** Main Street (✆ **064/664-1867**), talented jeweler Shane de Barra makes lovely freshwater pearl concoctions in silver and gold, and his restrained touch on gold rings and bangles marks this place as special. **Quills Woolen Market,** Main Street (✆ **064/664-1078**), is good for chunky, Aran hand knits, traditional Donegal tweed, delicate Irish linen, and Celtic jewelry. **Avoca Handweavers at Moll's Gap,** N71 (✆ **064/663-4720**), is a branch of the famous tweed makers of County Wicklow. This outlet is set on a high mountain pass between Killarney and Kenmare. The wares range from colorful hand-woven capes, jackets, throws, and knitwear to pottery and jewelry. It also has a great gourmet cafe.

The Dingle Peninsula

Like the Iveragh Peninsula, Dingle has a spectacularly scenic peripheral road, and a substantial tourist trade has blossomed along it. But as soon as you veer off the main roads, you'll discover extraordinary desolate beauty, seemingly worlds away from the tour buses. Dingle Town itself is smaller and less congested than Killarney, and the Dingle Peninsula is an ideal drive or bicycling tour.

Don't miss **Slea Head,** at the southwestern extremity of the peninsula, with its pristine beaches, great walks, and fascinating archaeological remains. The village of **Dunquin,** which sits between Slea Head and Clogher Head, is home to the useful Blasket Centre (admission €4).

Dunbeg Fort sits on a rocky promontory just south of Slea Head, its walls rising from the cliff edge. Although much of the fort has fallen into the sea, the place is well worth a visit at the bargain-basement rate of €3 per person. From Slea Head, the Dingle Way continues east to Dingle Town (24km/15 miles) or north along the coast toward Ballyferriter.

Just offshore from Dunquin are the seven **Blasket Islands;** a ferry (**✆ 066/915-6455**) connects Great Blasket with the mainland when the weather permits. Alternatively, you can take a 3-hour cruise around the islands with **Blasket Island Eco-Tour** (**✆ 066/915-6422**), leaving from Dunquin Pier. The islands were abandoned by the last permanent residents in 1953 and now are inhabited only by a few summer visitors who share the place with the seals and seabirds. A magnificent 13km (8-mile) walk goes to the west end of Great Blasket and back, passing sea cliffs and ivory beaches; you can stop along the way at the only cafe on the island.

Dingle Town (An Daingean)

Dingle *(An Daingean)* is a charming, brightly colored little town at the foot of steep hills and on the edge of a gorgeous stretch of coast. There's not much to do here, but it has plenty of hotels and restaurants and makes a good base for exploring the region.

EXPLORING THE TOWN

Despite the big-sounding name, **Dingle's Oceanworld Aquarium,** Dingle Harbour (**✆ 066/915-2111;** www.dingle-oceanworld.ie), is a relatively small aquarium with little to see to justify the ticket price: Admission costs €12 adults, €9 seniors, €7 children. Various sea critters swim behind glass in the aquarium's 29 tanks, and young staffers carry around live marine creatures and introduce them up close to visitors. It's open daily from 10am to 5pm.

Forget Flipper. In Dingle, the name to know is Fungie. Every day, **Fungie the Dolphin Tours ★★**, the Pier, Dingle (**✆ 066/915-2626**), ferries visitors out into the nearby waters to see the famous village mascot. Trips cost €16 for adults and €8 for children 11 and under. They last about 1 hour and depart regularly, roughly every 2 hours in the off season and as frequently as every half-hour in high season. Fungie swims up to the boat, and the boatmen stay out long enough for ample sightings—and long, wonderful eyefuls of the gorgeous bay. Wonderful though this tour can be, however, we do wonder how much longer Fungie will be drawing in the crowds, given that he's been at it for 25 years—and nobody quite knows how old he is. We understand he's as hale and hardy as ever—but perhaps it would be wise to call ahead first, especially before raising the hopes of dolphin-loving youngsters.

ENJOYING THE GREAT OUTDOORS

BEACHES The Dingle Peninsula is known for its dramatic beaches. The best known is **Inch Strand,** a 5km-long (3-mile) sandy stretch.

Kilmurray Bay at Minard is a Lilliputian dream come to life, as in the shadow of Minard Castle, giant sausage-shaped sandstone boulders form a beach unlike anything you've ever seen. Nearby, **Trabeg Beach** features exquisite wave-sculptured maroon sandstone statues, sheer rock cliffs, and sea caves lined with veins of crystalline quartz.

Castlegregory *(Caislean an Ghriare)* is a seaside village with two wide, sandy beaches. It's known for its good diving waters, and scuba divers and watersports fans flock to the place in summer. It's a bit bustling for isolationists, who are better off heading to tiny **Cloghane** *(An Clochán)* on the southern edge of Brandon Bay. With a population of 270 and a lovely beach, it's got much to offer.

BICYCLING Mountain bikes can be rented at **Foxy John Moriarty,** Main Street, Dingle (✆ **066/915-1316**). Alternatively, the staff at the **Mountain Man Outdoor Shop,** Strand Street, Dingle (✆ **066/915-2400;** www.themountainmanshop.com), can handle the arrangements for you. The cost is normally around €15 per day, or €55 per week. Foxy John's has the added advantage of also being a pub, although you might want to save your pints until after your bike ride.

DIVING On the North Dingle Peninsula, **Harbour House,** Scraggane Pier, Castlegregory, County Kerry (✆ **066/713-9292;** www.waterworld.ie), is a diving center that offers packages including diving, room, and board at good rates. Classes for beginners are available.

SAILING The **Dingle Sailing Centre,** the Marina, Dingle (✆ **066/915-6426;** www.saildingle.com), offers an array of courses taught by experienced, certified instructors. Summer courses run from about €130 to €200.

SEA ANGLING For sea-angling packages and day trips, contact Nicholas O'Connor at **Angler's Rest,** Ventry (✆ **066/915-9947**), or Seán O'Conchúir (✆ **066/915-5429**), representing the **Kerry Angling Association.**

WALKING The **Dingle Way** circles the peninsula, covering 153km (95 miles) of gorgeous mountain and coastal landscape. The most rugged section is along Brandon Head, where the trail passes between Mount Brandon and the ocean; the views are tremendous, but the walk is long (about 24km/15 miles or 9 hr.) and strenuous, and should be attempted only when the sky is clear. For more information, look for *The Dingle Way Map Guide,* available in local tourist offices and shops.

WHERE TO STAY

Expensive

Dingle Skellig Hotel ☺ This three-story hotel has an idyllic location next to Dingle Bay on the eastern edge of town. The look of the place is all polished pine and contemporary touches. Most guest rooms are done in neutral colors with floral touches, although some have slightly lurid color combinations. Many have gorgeous views. This is a family hotel in the classic sense—in the summer, there are evening cabaret performances and children's entertainment.

Annascaul Rd., Dingle, County Kerry. ✆ **066/915-1144.** Fax 066/915-1501. www.dingleskellig.com. 111 units. €118–€240 double; €170–€500 suite. Rates include full breakfast. AE, MC, V. Free parking. Closed Jan–Feb Mon–Thurs (open weekends). **Amenities:** Restaurant; bar; lounge; children's playroom; exercise room; Jacuzzi; indoor pool; room service; spa; steam room. *In room:* TV, hair dryer.

Moderate

Milltown House Tucked away near a tidal inlet just outside of Dingle, Milltown House is a simple, white-and-black 19th-century house, but it's a good guesthouse to know about. The spacious guest rooms have sitting areas and orthopedic beds.

Some have sea views and the others overlook the garden. Two rooms are wheelchair accessible. The nonsmoking sitting room—with easy chairs and an open fire—is comfortable, while the conservatory breakfast room (with a lavish breakfast menu) looks out on Dingle Bay. Film buffs might want to request room no. 2—it's where Robert Mitchum stayed while filming *Ryan's Daughter.*

Milltown (off Ventry Rd.), Dingle, County Kerry. ✆ **066/915-1372.** Fax 066/915-1095. www.milltownhousedingle.com. 10 units. €130–€170 double. Rates include full breakfast. MC, V. Closed mid-Nov to late Apr. **Amenities:** Lounge. *In room:* TV, hair dryer.

Pax Guest House ★ This former retirement home has been transformed into a comfortable B&B with homey touches. On a green hill overlooking Dingle Bay, Pax House's sunny balcony takes in sweeping views as far as Slea Head. The furniture is heavy pine (some four-poster beds), and the decor is bright and cheerful. This peaceful place is a real getaway.

Pax House is signposted on the N86, Dingle, County Kerry. ✆ **066/915-1518.** www.pax-house.com. 12 units. €120–€180 double. Rates include full breakfast. MC, V. Free parking. **Amenities:** Lounge. *In room:* TV, hair dryer.

Inexpensive

The Captain's House ★ Jim and Mary Milhench own and run this dapper little B&B in the middle of Dingle. The name is inspired by Jim's former career as a sea captain. It's a place we've long recommended, but recently we were sad to hear that the B&B side of things has had to be scaled back due to Jim's health. Accommodations now come mainly in the form of two holiday apartments (self-catering, although a continental breakfast is provided). The apartments are well equipped, with private patios that have views of the town and mountains. The patios also have a barbecue grill. The Captain's House remains a friendly, characterful place to stay, and we hope full service is resumed soon.

The Mall, Dingle, County Kerry. ✆ **066/915-1531.** Fax 066/915-1079. 2 units. €100–€110 suite. Rates include full breakfast. AE, MC, V. Closed Dec–Jan. **Amenities:** Sitting room. *In room:* TV.

WHERE TO DINE

Moderate

Ashe's Seafood Bar ★★ SEAFOOD Behind a distinctly nautical-looking old 19th-century pub facade lies an excellent seafood restaurant. Start with the popular seafood chowder then move on to a perfectly prepared tempura of cod, or seared scallops with caper and herb butter.

Main St., Dingle, County Kerry. ✆ **066/915-0989.** www.ashesseafoodbar.com. Reservations required. Dinner main courses €22–€30. MC, V. Mon–Sat noon–3pm and 6–9pm; Sun 6–9pm (July–Aug only).

The Chart House ★★ MODERN COUNTRY This popular restaurant (be sure to book ahead) has an inviting bistro atmosphere with lots of polished pine and warm, rose-colored walls. The cooking here is an ambitious blend of Irish dishes and outside influences. Main courses might include steak filet with black pudding mash, or pork with brandied apples. With unusual food and excellent service, it has carved out quite a reputation.

The Mall, Dingle, County Kerry. ✆ **066/915-2255.** www.charthousedingle.com. Reservations required. Main courses €15–€25. MC, V. Wed–Mon 6:30–10pm. Closed Jan 8–Feb 12.

Lord Bakers SEAFOOD/PUB GRUB The ages-old decor in this pub restaurant combines a stone fireplace and cozy alcoves with a more modern, sunlit conservatory and a few Art Deco touches. The menu offers standard bar food, but juices it up with things like crab claws in garlic butter, Kerry oysters, seafood Mornay, and steaks. Dinner specialties are more elegant, including sole stuffed with smoked salmon and spinach in cheese sauce, lobster, and rack of lamb.

Main St., Dingle, County Kerry. ✆ **066/915-1277.** www.lordbakers.ie. Reservations recommended for dinner. Bar food €10–€16; dinner main courses €16–€30. AE, MC, V. Fri–Wed 12:30–2pm and 6–9:30pm.

Inexpensive

An Cafe Liteartha CAFE/TEAROOM "The Literary Cafe" is a self-service cafe in an excellent bookstore. This is heaven for those interested in Irish history, literature, maps, and scones. The cafe sells fresh soups, sandwiches, salads, seafood, and scones and cakes. It's ideal for a quiet lunch or snack.

Dykegate St., Dingle, County Kerry. ✆ **066/915-2204.** All items €3–€6. No credit cards. Mon–Sat 9am–6pm (later in summer).

GALWAY CITY

For many travelers to Ireland, Galway is the farthest edge of their journey. It's just far enough from the madding crowds (3-hr. drive from Dublin) without pushing the limits of some people's comfort. If you've come this far, you've seen the land that drew the ancient settlers to Connemara and seduced the early Christian monks with its isolation. In fact, some went even farther—monastic remains have been found on 17 islands off the Galway coast.

These days, this region is bustling and affluent, its villages are brightly painted, and property prices are soaring. Galway City, the heart of the county, has an affluent, artsy population of 70,000, and is one of Ireland's most appealing cities. It is a busy workaday town, but it also has a lively art and music scene that has made it the unofficial arts capital of the country. The excellent Galway Arts Festival, held every summer, is an accessible, buzzing culture fest.

Essentials

GETTING THERE

BY PLANE **Aer Aran** flies from Dublin into Galway Airport (Carnmore, about 16km/10 miles east of the city; ✆ **091/755569;** www.galwayairport.com) four times daily. The airline also flies direct to Galway from London, Manchester, and Edinburgh in the U.K.

BY TRAIN **Irish Rail** trains from Dublin and other points arrive daily at **Ceannt Station** (✆ **091/561444;** www.irishrail.ie), off Eyre Square, Galway.

BY BUS Buses from all parts of Ireland arrive daily at **Bus Éireann Travel Centre,** Ceannt Station, Galway (✆ **091/562000;** www.buseireann.ie).

BY CAR As the gateway to west Ireland, Galway is the terminus for many national roads. They lead in from all parts of Ireland, including N84 and N17 from the north, N63 and N6 from the east, and N67 and N18 from the south.

VISITOR INFORMATION For information about Galway and the surrounding areas, contact or visit **Ireland West Tourism (Aras Fáilte),** Foster Street (✆ **091/537700;** www.irelandwest.ie). Hours are May, June, and September daily 9am to 5:45pm; July and August daily 9am to 7:45pm; and October to April Monday to Friday 9am to 5:45pm, Saturday 9am to 12:45pm. For further detailed information on events and news in Galway, consult **www.galway.net**.

GETTING AROUND Galway has excellent local bus service. Buses run from the **Bus Éireann Travel Centre** (✆ **091/562000**) or Eyre Square to various suburbs, including Salthill and the Galway Bay coastline. The fare starts at €1.50.

There are taxi stands at Eyre Square and all the major hotels in the city. If you need to call a cab, try **Abbey Cabs** (✆ **091/533333**), **Big-O Taxis** (✆ **091/585858**), or **Galway Taxis** (✆ **091/561111**).

A town of medieval arches, alleyways, and cobblestone lanes, Galway is best explored on foot (wear comfortable shoes). To see the highlights, follow the signposts on the Tourist Trail of Old Galway. A handy booklet, available at the tourist office and at most bookshops, provides historical and architectural details. If you must bring your car into the center of town, park it and then walk. There is free parking in front of Galway Cathedral, but most street parking uses a pay-to-park system. It costs upwards of €2 per hour. Multistory parking garages average €2.60 per hour or €22 per day.

Galway Airport has two main car-rental firms: **Avis** (✆ **091/786440;** www.avis.ie) and **Budget** (✆ **091/564570;** www.budget.ie).

Where to Stay

VERY EXPENSIVE

The G ★ 🎁 This trendy place was designed by the hat designer Philip Treacy and it shows. Wonderfully over-the-top, it looks like a cross between *Barbarella* and *My Fair Lady.* There are psychedelic touches (the Pink Salon is the color of Pepto-Bismol) and a clear love of disco chic (the otherwise subtle taupe-and-white grand salon has masses of huge glass baubles hanging overhead). Rooms are calmer, in soothing white with touches of coffee and cream, and luxuriant beds. Bathrooms are sensational, and many have showers built for two. The **ESPA spa** is oh-so-sophisticated, and it's all very Manhattan. It's about a 15-minute walk from central Galway. There is no place trendier on the Ireland's west coast.

Wellpark, Galway, County Galway. ✆ **091/865200.** Fax 091/865203. www.ghotel.ie. 101 units. €160–€240 double; €230–€360 suite. Rates include full breakfast. AE, MC, V. **Amenities:** Restaurant; bar; smoke-free rooms; spa. *In room:* TV, DVD/CD player, hair dryer, Wi-Fi.

Glenlo Abbey Hotel ★★ About 3km (1¾ miles) outside of Galway on the main Clifden road, this secluded, sprawling stone hotel overlooks Lough Corrib in a sylvan setting, surrounded by a 9-hole golf course. Dating from 1740, the building has retained its grandeur in the public areas, with hand-carved wood furnishings, ornate plasterwork, and an extensive collection of Irish art and antiques. The guest rooms, which have lovely views of Lough Corrib and the countryside, are luxuriously decorated with traditional furnishings.

Bushy Park, Galway, County Galway. ✆ **091/526666.** Fax 091/527800. www.glenlo.com. 46 units. €200–€400 double; €550–€980 suite. Breakfast €22. AE, DC, MC, V. Free parking. **Amenities:** 2 restaurants; 2 bars; concierge; 9-hole golf course; room service. *In room:* TV, hair dryer, Wi-Fi.

EXPENSIVE

The House Hotel ★★ This four-story stone building, in Galway's historic area next to the Spanish Arch, was formerly a warehouse, and is now a boutique loft hotel. From its low-key lobby with polished oak floors, columns, and big windows, to its subtle, contemporary rooms, it's a comfortable, modern alternative. Rooms are divided into categories like "comfy," "classy," and "swanky," and they pretty much do what it says on the label. The swanky rooms are definitely the swankiest. But all have comfortable beds, soft linens, lots of sunlight, high ceilings, and a refreshing urban feel. Its design has won accolades, and it prides itself on its service.

Lower Merchant's Rd., Galway, County Galway. ✆ **091/538900.** Fax 091/568262. www.thehousehotel.ie. 45 units. €130–€400 double. AE, DC, MC, V. **Amenities:** Restaurant; bar. *In room:* TV, hair dryer, Internet, minibar.

Park House Hotel ★ With a steady, old-fashioned approach to luxury, the Park House is a reliable option in central Galway. For 30 years, its warmly lit frontage has been welcoming travelers into the tastefully decorated lobby. Rooms are spacious and classically decorated with plaid bedspreads and colorful throw pillows. No two rooms directly face each other, ensuring peace and quiet for all guests. The **Park Room Restaurant** is an award-winning, luxurious operation.

Foster St., Eyre Sq., Galway, County Galway. ✆ **091/564924.** Fax 091/569219. www.parkhousehotel.ie. 84 units. €140–€350 double; €200–€500 suite. Rates include full breakfast. AE, MC, V. **Amenities:** Restaurant; bar; smoke-free rooms. *In room:* TV/DVD, CD player, hair dryer, Internet.

INEXPENSIVE

Barnacle's Quay Street House ★ This cheap and cheerful guesthouse is bright, attractive, and friendly—what more do you need? It's a 16th-century house, with marvelous fireplaces and lots of character. Bedrooms are done in sunny yellows, and there's a communal kitchen if you tire of restaurants. The clientele tends to be young, mostly college students filling the shared dorm rooms, but there are reasonably priced doubles, and the four-bed rooms are good for families traveling on a budget. All are welcome, and the location is central.

10 Quay St., Galway, County Galway. ✆ **091/568644.** www.barnacles.ie. 10 units. €10–€33 dorm; €95 double. Rates include continental breakfast. No credit cards. **Amenities:** Lounge; Internet; kitchen.

Devondell ★ You'd be hard-pressed to find a better B&B in Galway than Berna Kelly's much-lauded house in the Lower Salthill residential area, about 2km (1¼ miles) from Galway's city center and within walking distance of the seafront. It's a modern building, so guest rooms are spacious and done up with period furnishings and crisp Irish linens. Breakfasts are exceptional, with cereal, fresh fruit, yogurt, cheese, hash browns, kippers, eggs, and French toast.

47 Devon Park, Lower Salthill, County Galway. ✆ **091/528306.** www.devondell.com. 4 units. €80–€90 double. Rates include full breakfast. MC, V. Free parking. Closed Dec–Feb. **Amenities:** Lounge. *In room:* TV.

Where to Dine

VERY EXPENSIVE

Kirwan's Lane ★★ CONTINENTAL Chef-owner Michael O'Grady's stylish, inviting restaurant is widely acclaimed, and for good reason. The dining room is rustic chic, with pine furnishings and brightly-painted walls. It's particularly good value at lunchtime, when the constantly changing menu might include a starter of Irish brie crostini and marinated salmon roulade. The dinner menu features dishes with fresh local produce and seafood, all beautifully presented.

Kirwan's Lane. ✆ **091/568266.** Reservations recommended. Main courses €18–€30. AE, MC, V. Daily 12:30–2:30pm and 6–10:30pm. Closed Sun Sept–June.

The Malt House ★★ MODERN IRISH This long-established place on the High Street has developed something of a new lease on life since new owners came in a couple of years ago. Once rather starched and formal, it's now relaxed and cool. The dining room is bright and spacious, with chic contemporary art. The food is upmarket Irish bistro dishes with an international twist, and with an emphasis on locally sourced ingredients. Seafood is a specialty—the oysters are renowned for quality. Typical mains include king scallops in garlic butter, or roast rack of lamb with rosemary *jus.*

High St. ✆ **091/567866.** www.themalthouse.ie. Reservations recommended. 2- to 3-course early-bird dinner 6–7:30pm €25–€30; main courses €19–€30. AE, MC, V. Mon–Sat 12:30–3pm and 6–10:30pm.

MODERATE

Busker Browne's ★ CAFE/BAR A modern cafe in a medieval building, Busker Brown's is a favorite of locals and travelers for its funky decor that mixes ancient stonework with modern tables and art, as well as for its big breakfasts and homemade, inexpensive lunches and dinners. It offers everything from hamburgers and sandwiches to fresh stews and pasta. It also stays open late—one of a few Galway eateries to do so.

Upper Cross St. ✆ **091/563377.** www.buskerbrownes.com. Main courses €12–€23. MC, V. Mon–Sat 10:30am–11:30pm; Sun 12:30–11:30pm.

G.B.C. (Galway Bakery Company) ★ BISTRO With a distinctive Old Galway shop-front facade, this building is two eateries in one: a ground-level self-service coffee shop and a full-service bistro upstairs. The restaurant menu lists a variety of dishes, priced to suit every budget, from steaks and seafood dishes to chicken Kiev and *cordon bleu,* as well as quiches, omelets, salads, and stir-fried vegetable platters. Baked goods, particularly the homemade brown bread, are an added attraction. The coffee shop serves memorably good breakfasts and light lunches.

7 Williamsgate St. ✆ **091/563087.** www.gbcgalway.com. Coffee shop items under €8; fixed-price 3-course dinner €20; dinner main courses €13–€20. AE, DC, MC, V. Coffee shop daily 8am–10pm; restaurant daily noon–10pm.

Nimmo's ★★ WINE BAR/SEAFOOD This is one of Galway's trendy spots—a place to see and be seen that manages to serve fantastic food while constantly admiring itself. The menu changes according to season and tends to feature seafood in the summer and game during the winter. Start with the zesty fish soup or the smoked-salmon salad, and then move on to the delicious sea bream with olive crushed potatoes, rocket pesto and greens, or Syrian vegetable parcel with couscous and homemade harissa. Save room for dessert, which is brought in by Goya's, the best bakery in Galway. The wines are terrific, too.

Long Walk, Spanish Arch. ✆ **091/561114.** www.nimmos.ie. Reservations recommended. Main courses €14–€19. MC, V. Tues–Sun 12:30–3pm and 7–10pm.

INEXPENSIVE

Conlon SEAFOOD If you love seafood—you may be noticing a trend here—head for this place, as it is a local specialist, with 20 varieties of fresh fish and shellfish on the menu at any time. You're bound to find something to choose—the house specialties are wild salmon and oysters, so that's not a bad place to start. Entrees include grilled wild salmon, steamed Galway Bay mussels, and fishermen's platters with a bit of everything—smoked salmon, mussels, prawns, oysters, and crab claws. It's all so fresh that sometimes your order will literally just have been delivered by the fishermen.

Eglinton St. ✆ **091/562268.** Seafood bar items €4–€24; main courses €8–€27. DC, MC, V. Mon–Sat 11am–midnight; Sun 5pm–midnight.

McDonagh's FISH AND CHIPS/SEAFOOD For superfresh seafood, served up in an authentic maritime atmosphere, this is Galway's best choice. The place is divided into three parts: a traditional "chipper" for fish and chips, a smart restaurant in the back, and a fish market where you can buy raw seafood. The McDonaghs, fishmongers for more than four generations, buy direct from local fishermen every day, and it shows; crowds line up every night to get in. The menu includes salmon, trout, lemon or black sole (or both), turbot, and silver hake, all cooked to order. In the back restaurant, you can crack your own prawns' tails and crab claws in the shell, or tackle a whole lobster.

22 Quay St. ✆ **091/565809.** www.mcdonaghs.net. Reservations not accepted June–Aug. Main courses €13–€20 (seafood platter €35); fish and chips about €8. AE, MC, V. Restaurant Mon–Sat 5–10pm; fish and chip takeout Mon–Sat noon–11pm, Sun 4–10pm.

Exploring Galway City

Tucked between the Atlantic and the navy blue waters of Lough Corrib, Galway was founded by fishermen. Local legend has it that Christopher Columbus attended Mass at Galway's **St. Nicholas Collegiate Church** in 1477, before one of several attempts to circumnavigate the globe. Originally built in 1320, the church has been enlarged, rebuilt, and embellished over the years.

In the center of town, on Shop Street, is **Lynch's Castle,** dating from 1490 and renovated in the 19th century. It's the oldest Irish medieval town house used daily for commercial purposes (it's now a branch of the Allied Irish Bank). The stern exterior is watched over by a handful of amusing gargoyles.

In the 16th and 17th centuries, Galway was wealthy and cosmopolitan, with particularly strong trade links to Spain. Close to the city docks, you can still see the area where Spanish merchants unloaded cargo from their galleons. The **Spanish Arch** was one of four arches built in 1594, and the **Spanish Parade** is a small open square.

The hub of the city is a pedestrian park at **Eyre Square** (pronounced *Air Square*), officially called the John F. Kennedy Park in commemoration of his visit here in June 1963, a few months before his assassination. From here, it's a minute's walk to the **medieval quarter** with its festive, Left Bank atmosphere.

MORE ATTRACTIONS

Galway Irish Crystal Heritage Centre ★★ Visitors to this distinctive crystal manufacturer can watch the craftsmen at work—blowing, shaping, and hand-cutting glassware—and then go shop for the perfect pieces to take back home. Glassmaking demonstrations are continuous on weekdays. The shop and restaurant are open daily.

East of the city on the main Dublin road (N6), Merlin Park, Galway, County Galway. ✆ **091/757311.** Free admission. Mon–Fri 9am–5:30pm; Sat 10am–5:30pm; Sun 11am–5pm.

Nora Barnacle House ★ Just across from the St. Nicholas church clock tower, this restored 19th-century terrace house was once the home of Nora Barnacle, who later would become the wife of James Joyce. It contains letters, photographs, and other exhibits on the lives of the Joyces and their connections with Galway.

Bowling Green. ✆ **091/564743.** Admission €1.60. Mid-May to mid-Sept Mon–Sat 10am–5pm (closed for lunch), and by appointment.

CRUISES & TOURS

BUS TOURS In the summertime only, **Bus Éireann** (✆ **091/562000;** www.buseireann.ie) runs an 8-hour tour of Connemara that takes in Maam Cross, Recess, Roundstone, and Clifden, as well as Kylemore Abbey, Leenane, and Oughterard. The cost is €23 adults, €16 seniors and students, and €12 children.

BOAT TOURS The ***Corrib Princess*** (✆ **091/592447;** www.corribprincess.ie) is a 157-passenger, two-deck boat that cruises along the River Corrib, with commentary on points of interest. The trip lasts 90 minutes, passing castles, historical sites, and wildlife. There is a full bar and snack service. You can buy tickets at the dock or in the tourist office; fares are €15 adults, €13 seniors and students, €8 children.

ENJOYING THE GREAT OUTDOORS

BICYCLING To rent a bike, contact **Walsh Cycles,** Headford Road, Woodquay (✆ **091/565710**).

FISHING Set beside the River Corrib, Galway City and nearby Connemara are popular fishing centers for salmon and sea trout. For the latest information on requirements for licenses and local permits, check with the **Western Regional Fisheries Board (WRFB),** Weir Lodge, Earl's Island, Galway (✆ **091/563118;** www.wrfb.ie). For gear and equipment, try **Duffys Fishing,** 5 Main Guard St. (✆ **091/562367**), **Freeney Sport Shop,** 19 High St. (✆ **091/568794**), or **Great Outdoors Sports Centre,** Eglinton Street (✆ **091/562869**).

GOLF Less than 3km (1¾ miles) west of the city is the 18-hole, par-69 seaside course at **Galway Golf Club,** Blackrock, Galway (✆ **091/522033;** www.galwaygolf.com). Greens fees are €35.

HORSEBACK RIDING Riding enthusiasts head to **Aille Cross Equestrian Centre,** Aille Cross, Loughrea, County Galway (✆ **091/841216;** www.aille-cross.com), about 32km (20 miles) east of Galway City. For about €25 to €40 an hour, you can ride through nearby farmlands, woodlands, forest trails, and along beaches.

The Shopping Scene: Kerry Glass & More

Some of Galway's best shopping is in tiny malls of small shops clustered in historic buildings, such as the **Cornstore** on Middle Street, the **Grainstore** on Lower Abbeygate Street, and the **Bridge Mills,** a 430-year-old mill building beside the River Corrib. **Eyre Square Centre,** the downtown area's largest shopping mall, with 50 shops, incorporates a section of Galway's medieval town wall into its complex.

Mac Eocagain/Galway Woollen Market (21 High St.) is an excellent resource if you're shopping for traditional Aran hand knits and colorful hand-loomed sweaters and capes. Each item has two prices, one including value-added tax (VAT) and one tax-free for non–European Union (E.U.) residents.

P. Powell and Sons (the Four Corners, Williamsgate St.) is a family-run shop with a large supply of traditional Irish music, instruments, and recordings.

Also on Williamsgate Street, **Fallers of Galway** (www.fallers.com) is a prime source of Claddagh rings. Another option is nearby **Hartmann & Son Ltd.,** a traditional Galway jeweler.

For handicrafts, visit **Design Concourse** on Kirwan's Lane; filled with the work of dozens of talented Irish craftspeople.

ITALY

12

Italy is a feast for the senses and the intellect. Any mention of Italy calls up visions of Pompeii, the Renaissance, and Italy's rich treasury of art and architecture. But some of the country's best experiences can involve the simple act of living in the Italian style, eating the regional cuisines, and enjoying the countryside.

ROME ★★★

Rome is a city of images and sounds, all vivid and all unforgettable. You can see one of the most striking images at dawn—ideally from Gianicolo (Janiculum Hill)—when the Roman skyline, with its bell towers and cupolas, gradually comes into focus. As the sun rises, the Roman symphony begins. First come the peals of church bells calling the faithful to Mass. Then the streets fill with cars, taxis, tour buses, and Vespas, the drivers gunning their engines and blaring their horns. Next the sidewalks are overrun with office workers, chattering as they rush off to their desks, but not before ducking into a cafe for their first cappuccino. Shop owners loudly throw up the metal grilles protecting their stores; the fruit-and-vegetable stands are crowded with Romans out to buy the day's supply of fresh produce, haggling over prices and caviling over quality.

Around 10am, the visitors—you included, with your guidebook in hand—take to the streets, battling the crowds and traffic as they wend from Renaissance palaces and baroque buildings to ancient ruins like the Colosseum and the Forum. After you've spent a long day in the sun, marveling at the sights you've seen millions of times in photos and movies, you can pause to experience the charm of Rome at dusk.

Find a cafe at summer twilight, and watch the shades of pink and rose turn to gold and copper as night falls. That's when a new Rome awakens. The cafes and restaurants grow more animated, especially if you've found one in an ancient piazza or along a narrow alley deep in Trastevere. After dinner, you can stroll by the lighted fountains and monuments (the Trevi Fountain and the Colosseum look magical at night) or through Piazza Navona and have a gelato. The night is yours.

Essentials

GETTING THERE

BY PLANE Chances are, you'll arrive at Rome's **Leonardo da Vinci International Airport** (✆ **06-65951;** www.adr.it), popularly known as **Fiumicino,** 30km (19 miles) from the city center. (If you're flying by charter, you might land at Ciampino Airport; see below.) A tourist information office is at the airport's Terminal B, International arrival, open daily 8:15am to 7pm. A ***cambio*** (money exchange) operates daily 7:30am to 11pm, offering surprisingly good rates.

There's a **train station** in the airport. To get into the city, follow the signs marked TRENI for the 30-minute shuttle to Rome's main station, **Stazione Termini.** The shuttle (the Leonardo Express) runs from 6:37am to 11:37pm for 11€ one-way. On the way, you'll pass a machine dispensing tickets, or you can buy them in person near the tracks if you don't have small bills on you. When you arrive at Termini, get out of the train quickly and grab a baggage cart. (It's a long schlep from the track to the exit or to the other train connections, and baggage carts can be scarce.)

A **taxi** from da Vinci airport to the city costs 40€ and up for the 1-hour trip, depending on traffic. The expense might be worth it if you have a lot of luggage. Call **✆ 06-6645,** 06-3570, or 06-4994 for information.

If you arrive on a charter flight at **Ciampino Airport** (**✆ 06-65951**), you can take a Schiaffini bus (**✆ 06-570031**) to Stazione Termini. Trip time is about 45 minutes and costs 5€. A **taxi** from here to Rome costs the same as the one from the da Vinci airport (see above), but the trip is shorter (about 40 min.).

BY TRAIN OR BUS Trains and buses (including trains from the airport) arrive in the center of old Rome at the silver Stazione Termini, Piazza dei Cinquecento (✆ 892021). This is the train, bus, and subway transportation hub for all Rome, and it is surrounded by many hotels (especially cheaper ones).

If you're taking the **Metropolitana** (subway), follow the illuminated red-and-white M signs. To catch a bus, go straight through the outer hall and enter the sprawling bus lot of **Piazza dei Cinquecento.** You'll also find **taxis** there.

The station is filled with services. At a branch of the Banca San Paolo IMI (at tracks 1 and 24), you can exchange money. **Informazioni Ferroviarie** (in the outer hall) dispenses information on rail travel to other parts of Italy. There are also a **tourist information booth,** baggage services, newsstands, and snack bars.

BY CAR From the north, the main access route is the **Autostrada del Sole (A1).** The "Motorway of the Sun" links Milan with Naples via Bologna, Florence, and Rome. At 754km (469 miles), it is the longest Italian autostrada and is the "spinal cord" of Italy's road network. All the autostrade join with the **Grande Raccordo Anulare,** a ring road encircling Rome, channeling traffic into the congested city. Long before you reach this road, you should study a map carefully to see what part of Rome you plan to enter and mark your route accordingly. Route markings along the ring road tend to be confusing.

Warning: Return your rental car immediately, or at least get yourself to a hotel, park your car, and leave it there until you leave Rome. Don't even try to drive in Rome—the traffic is just too nightmarish.

VISITOR INFORMATION Information is available at Azienda Provinciale di Turismo (APT; **✆ 06-421381;** www.aptprovroma.it), Via XX Settembre 26. The headquarters is open Monday to Saturday 9am to 7pm.

More helpful, and stocking maps and brochures, are the offices maintained by the **Comune di Roma** at various sites around the city. They're staffed daily from 9:30am to 7pm, except the one at Termini (daily 8am–8:30pm). Other Comune di Roma offices are in Stazione Termini; at Piazza Pia near the Castel Sant'Angelo; on Via

Italy

FRANCE
SWITZERLAND
ALPS
AUSTRIA
SLOVENIA
CROATIA
BOSNIA
Courmayeur
Aosta
VALLE D'AOSTA
Lake Maggiore
Lake Como
Novara
Merano
TRENTINO-ALTO ADIGE
Bolzano
Como
LOMBARDY
Trent
DOLOMITES
Cortina d'Ampezzo
Turin
Vercelli
Asti
Bergamo
Lake Garda
Belluno
Brescia
Vicenza
FRIULI-VENEZIA GIULIA
PIEDMONT
Milan
Cremona
Verona
VENETO
Udine
Parma
Padua
Treviso
Cuneo
Mantua
Venice
Savona
Genoa
Ferrara
Trieste
LIGURIA
Modena
Gulf of Venice
San Remo
Gulf of Genoa
Rapallo
EMILIA-ROMAGNA
NORTHERN APPENNINES
La Spezia
Bologna
Ravenna
Lucca
Ligurian Sea
Pisa
SAN MARINO
Rimini
Florence
Livorno
Pesaro
TUSCANY
Gubbio
Siena
Ancona
Elba
Corsica (France)
Perugia
Assisi
MARCHES
Orvieto
Viterbo
UMBRIA
Spoleto
Terano
Civitavecchia
Terni
L'Aquila
Pescara
ROME
VATICAN CITY
Chieti
LAZIO
ABRUZZI
Campobasso
MOLISE
Caserta
Benevento
Foggia
Gulf of Gaeta
Naples
Mt. Vesuvius
APULIA
Ischia
Pompeii
Sorrento
Bari
Capri
Amalfi
Salerno
Paestum
Potenza
CAMPANIA
BASILICATA
Brindisi
Taranto
Tyrrhenian Sea
Gulf of Taranto
Lecce
Cosenza
SOUTHERN APPENNINES
CALABRIA
Trapani
Aeolian Islands
Catanzaro
Marsala
Palermo
Selinunte
Messina
Reggio di Calabria
Enna
Taormina
Ionian Sea
Agrigento
Mt. Etna
SICILY
Catania
Ragusa
Syracuse
MEDITERRANEAN SEA
Ólbia
Sassari
Nuoro
SARDINIA
Cagliari
0
100 Mi
0
100 Km

Nazionale 183, near the Palazzo delle Esposizioni; on Piazza Sonnino, in Trastevere; on Piazza Cinque Lune, near Piazza Navona; and on Via dell'Olmata, near Piazza Santa Maria Maggiore. All phone calls for Comune di Roma are directed through a centralized number: ✆ **06-0608.** Call daily 9am to 7pm.

Enjoy Rome, Via Marghera 8A (✆ **06-4451843;** www.enjoyrome.com), was begun by an English-speaking couple, Fulvia and Pierluigi. They dispense information about almost everything in Rome and are far more pleasant and organized than the Board of Tourism. They'll also help you find a hotel room, with no service charge (in anything from a hostel to a three-star hotel). Hours are Monday to Friday 8:30am to 5pm, and Saturday 8:30am to 2pm.

CITY LAYOUT Arm yourself with a detailed street map, not the general overview handed out free at tourist offices. Most hotels hand out a pretty good version at their front desks.

The bulk of ancient, Renaissance, and baroque Rome (as well as the train station) lies on the east side of the **Fiume Tevere (Tiber River),** which meanders through town. However, several important landmarks are on the other side: **St. Peter's Basilica** and the **Vatican,** the **Castel Sant'Angelo,** and the colorful **Trastevere** neighborhood.

The city's various quarters are linked by large boulevards (large, at least, in some places) that have mostly been laid out since the late 19th century. Starting from the **Vittorio Emanuele Monument,** a controversial pile of snow-white Brescian marble that's often compared to a wedding cake, there's a street running practically due north to **Piazza del Popolo** and the city wall. This is **Via del Corso,** one of the main streets of Rome—noisy, congested, crowded with buses and shoppers, and called simply "Il Corso." To its left (west) lie the Pantheon, Piazza Navona, Campo de' Fiori, and the Tiber. To its right (east) you'll find the Spanish Steps, the Trevi Fountain, the Borghese Gardens, and Via Veneto.

Back at the Vittorio Emanuele Monument, the major artery going west (and ultimately across the Tiber to St. Peter's) is **Corso Vittorio Emanuele.** Behind you to your right, heading toward the Colosseum, is **Via dei Fori Imperiali,** laid out in the 1930s by Mussolini to show off the ruins of the Imperial Forums he had excavated, which line it on either side. Yet another central conduit is **Via Nazionale,** running from **Piazza Venezia** (just in front of the Vittorio Emanuele Monument) east to **Piazza della Repubblica** (near Stazione Termini). The final lap of Via Nazionale is called **Via Quattro Novembre.**

GETTING AROUND Much of the inner core is traffic free, so you'll need to walk whether you like it or not. However, in many parts of the city it's hazardous and uncomfortable because of the crowds, heavy traffic, and narrow sidewalks.

BY SUBWAY The **Metropolitana,** or **Metro** for short, is the fastest means of transportation, operating daily 5:30am to 11:30pm, or until 12:30am on Saturday. A big red M indicates the entrance to the subway.

Tickets are 1€ and are available from *tabacchi* (tobacco shops), many newsstands, and vending machines at all stations. Some stations have managers, but they won't make change. Booklets of tickets are available at tabacchi and in some terminals. You can also buy a **tourist pass** on either a daily or a weekly basis (see "By Bus & Tram," below).

Building a subway system for Rome hasn't been easy because every time workers start digging, they discover an old temple or other archaeological treasure, and heavy earth moving has to cease for a while.

BY BUS & TRAM Roman buses and trams are operated by an organization known as **ATAC** (Agenzia del Trasporto Autoferrotranviario del Comune di Roma), Via Ostiense 131L (✆ **800-431784;** www.atac.roma.it).

For 1€ you can ride to most parts of Rome, although it can be slow going in all that traffic, and the buses are often very crowded. Your ticket is valid for 75 minutes, and you can get on many buses and trams during that time by using the same ticket. Ask where to buy bus tickets, or buy them in tabacchi or bus terminals. You must have your ticket before boarding because there are no ticket-issuing machines on the vehicles.

At Stazione Termini, you can buy a special **tourist pass,** which costs 4€ for a day or 16€ for a week. This pass allows you to ride on the ATAC network without bothering to buy individual tickets. The tourist pass is also valid on the subway—but never ride the trains when the Romans are going to or from work, or you'll be smashed flatter than fettuccine. On the first bus you board, you place your ticket in a small machine, which prints the day and hour you boarded, and then you withdraw it. You do the same on the last bus you take during the valid period of the ticket. One-day and weekly tickets are also available at tabacchi, many newsstands, and at vending machines at all stations.

Buses and trams stop at areas marked FERMATA. At most of these, a yellow sign will display the numbers of the buses that stop there and a list of all the stops along each bus's route in order so you can easily search out your destination. In general, they're in service daily from 6am to midnight. After that and until dawn, you can ride on special night buses (they have an N in front of their bus number), which run only on main routes. It's best to take a taxi in the wee hours—if you can find one.

At the **bus information booth** at Piazza dei Cinquecento, in front of the Stazione Termini, you can purchase a directory with maps of the routes.

Although routes change often, a few old reliable routes have remained valid for years, such as **no. 75** from Stazione Termini to the Colosseum, **H** from Stazione Termini to Trastevere, and **no. 40** from Stazione Termini to the Vatican. But if you're going somewhere and are dependent on the bus, be sure to carefully check where the bus stop is and exactly which bus goes there—don't assume that it'll be the same bus the next day.

BY TAXI If you're accustomed to hopping a cab in New York or London, then do so in Rome. But don't count on hailing a taxi on the street or even getting one at a stand. If you're going out, have your hotel call one. At a restaurant, ask the waiter or cashier to dial for you. If you want to phone for yourself, try one of these numbers: ✆ **06-6645,** 06-3570, or 06-4994.

The meter begins at 2.80€ for the first 3km (1¾ miles) and then rises .92€ per kilometer. Every suitcase costs 1€, and on Sunday a 4€ supplement is assessed. There's another 5.80€ supplement from 10pm to 7am. Avoid paying your fare with large bills; invariably, taxi drivers claim that they don't have change, hoping for a bigger tip (stick to your guns and give only about 15%).

BY CAR All roads might lead to Rome, but you don't want to drive once you get here. Because the reception desks of most Roman hotels have at least one English-speaking person, call ahead to find out the best route into Rome from wherever you're starting out. You're usually allowed to park in front of the hotel long enough to unload your luggage. You'll want to get rid of your rental car as soon as possible, or park in a garage.

You might want to rent a car to explore the countryside around Rome or drive to another city. You'll save the most money if you reserve before leaving home. But if you want to book a car here, know that **Hertz** is at Via Giovanni Giolitti 34 (✆ **06-4740389;** www.hertz.com; Metro: Termini), and **Avis** is at Stazione Termini (✆ **06-4814373;** www.avis.com; Metro: Termini). **Maggiore,** an Italian company, has an office at Stazione Termini (✆ **06-4883715;** www.maggiore.it; Metro: Termini). There are also branches of the major rental agencies at the airport.

BY BIKE Other than walking, the best way to get through the medieval alleys and small piazzas of Rome is perched on the seat of a bicycle. The heart of ancient Rome is riddled with bicycle lanes to get you through the murderous traffic. The most convenient place to rent bikes is **Bici & Baci,** Via del Viminale 5 (✆ **06-4828443;** www.bicibaci.com), lying 2 blocks west of Stazione Termini, the main rail station. Prices start at 4€ per hour or 11€ per day.

[Fast FACTS] ROME

American Express The Rome offices are at Piazza di Spagna 38 (✆ **06-67641;** Metro: Spagna). The travel service is open Monday to Friday 9am to 5:30pm. Hours for the financial and mail services are Monday to Friday 9am to 5pm. The tour desk is open during the same hours as those for travel services and also Saturday from 9am to 12:30pm (May–Oct).

Business Hours In general, **banks** are open Monday to Friday 8:30am to 1:30pm and 3 to 4pm. Some banks keep afternoon hours from 2:45 to 3:45pm. Regular business hours are generally Monday to Friday 9am (sometimes 9:30) to 1pm, and 3:30 (sometimes 4) to 7 or 7:30pm. The *riposo* (midafternoon closing) is often observed in Rome, Naples, and most southern cities. Most shops are closed, except for certain tourist-oriented stores that are now permitted to remain open on Sunday during the high season.

Currency Italy uses the **euro** (€). At press time, 1€ = US$1.40.

Currency Exchange There are exchange offices throughout the city. They're also at all major rail and air terminals, including Stazione Termini, where the cambio beside the rail information booth is open daily 8am to 8pm. At some exchange offices, you'll have to pay commissions, often 1½%. Likewise, banks often charge commissions.

Dentists For dental work, go to **American Dental Arts Rome,** Via del Governo Vecchio 73 (✆ **06-6832613;** www.adadentistsrome.com; bus: 41, 44, or 46B), which uses all the latest technology, including laser dental techniques. There is also a 24-hour **G. Eastman Dental Hospital** at Viale Regina Elena 287B (✆ **06-844831;** Metro: Policlinico).

Doctors Call the U.S. Embassy at ✆ **06-46741** for a list of doctors who speak English. All big hospitals have a 24-hour first-aid service (go to the emergency room, *pronto soccorso*). You'll find English-speaking doctors at the privately run **Salvator Mundi International Hospital,** Viale delle Mura Gianicolensi 67 (✆ **06-588961;** bus: 115A). For medical assistance, the **International Medical Center** is on 24-hour duty at Via Firenze 47 (✆ **06-4882371;** www.imc84.com; Metro: Piazza Repubblica). You could also contact the

Rome American Hospital, Via Emilio Longoni 69 (✆ **06-22551;** www.rah.it), with English-speaking doctors on duty 24 hours. A more personalized service is provided 24 hours by **MEDI-CALL,** Studio Medico, Via Cremera 8 (✆ **06-8840113;** www.medi-call.it; bus: 38). It can arrange for a qualified doctor to make a house call at your hotel or anywhere in Rome. In most cases, the doctor will be a general practitioner who can refer you to a specialist if needed. Fees begin at around 100€ per visit and can go higher if a specialist or specialized treatments are necessary.

Drugstores A reliable pharmacy is **Farmacia Internazionale,** Piazza Barberini 49 (✆ **06-4825456;** Metro: Barberini), open day and night. Most pharmacies are open from 8:30am to 1pm and 4 to 7:30pm. In general, pharmacies follow a rotation system, so several are always open on Sunday.

Embassies & Consulates The embassy of the **United States** is at Via Vittorio Veneto 121 (✆ **06-46-741;** http://rome.usembassy.gov). The embassy of **Canada** is at Via Salaria 243 (✆ **06-85444-2911;** www.canada.it). The embassy of the **United Kingdom** is at Via XX Settembre 80 (✆ **06-422-00001;** http://ukinitaly.fco.gov.uk/en). The embassy of **Australia** is at Via Antonio Bosio 5 (✆ **06-852-721;** www.italy.embassy.gov.au). The embassy of **New Zealand** is at Via Zara 28 (✆ **06-441-7171;** www.nzembassy.com/italy).

Emergencies To call the police, dial **113;** for an ambulance, **118;** for a fire emergency, **115.**

Internet Access In central Rome, **Internet Café,** Via dei Marrucini 12 (✆ **06-4454953;** www.internetcafe.it; bus: 3, 71, or 492), is open Monday to Friday 9:30am to 1am, Saturday 10am to 1am, and Sunday 2pm to midnight. A 30-minute visit costs 1.50€.

Mail It's easiest to buy stamps and mail letters and postcards at your hotel's front desk. Stamps *(francobolli)* can also be bought at tabacchi. You can buy special stamps at the **Vatican City Post Office,** adjacent to the information office in St. Peter's Square; it's open Monday to Friday 8:30am to 7pm and Saturday 8:30am to 6pm. Letters mailed from Vatican City often arrive far more quickly than mail sent from Rome for the same cost.

Police Dial ✆ **113.**

Safety Pickpocketing is the most common problem. Men should keep their wallets in their front pocket or inside jacket pocket. Purse snatching is also commonplace, with young men on Vespas who ride past you and grab your purse. To avoid trouble, stay away from the curb and keep your purse on the wall side of your body, and place the strap across your chest. Don't lay anything valuable on tables or chairs, where it can be grabbed up. Gypsy children have long been a particular menace, although the problem isn't as severe as in years past. If they completely surround you, you'll often literally have to fight them off. They might approach you with pieces of cardboard hiding their stealing hands. Just keep repeating a firm *no!*

Telephone The **country code** for Italy is **39.** The **city code** for Rome is **06;** use this code when calling from *anywhere* outside or inside Italy—you must add it within Rome itself (you must include the 0, even when calling from abroad).

Toilets Facilities are found near many of the major sights and often have attendants, as do those at bars, clubs, restaurants, cafes, and hotels, plus the airports and the rail station. (There are public restrooms near the Spanish Steps, or you can stop at the McDonald's there—it's one of the nicest branches of the Golden Arches you'll ever see!) The price for most public toilets is 1€. It's not a bad idea to carry some tissues in your pocket when you're out and about as well.

Where to Stay

NEAR STAZIONE TERMINI

Very Expensive

St. Regis Grand ★★★ This restored landmark is more plush and upscale than any hotel in the area; for comparable digs, you'll have to cross town to check into the Excelsior or Eden. And for sheer opulence, not even those hotels equal it. Its drawback is its location at the dreary Stazione Termini, but once you're inside its splendid shell, all thoughts of railway stations vanish.

When César Ritz founded this outrageously expensive hotel in 1894, it was the first to offer a private bathroom and two electric lights in every room. Restored to its former glory, it is a magnificent Roman *palazzo* (palace) combining Italian and French styles in decoration and furnishings. Guest rooms, most of which are exceedingly spacious, are luxuriously furnished. Hand-painted frescoes are installed above each headboard. For the best rooms and the finest service, ask to be booked on the St. Regis floor.

Via Vittorio Emanuele Orlando 3, 00185 Roma. ✆ **06-47091.** Fax 06-4747307. www.stregis.com/grandrome. 161 units. 343€–1,030€ double; from 1,133€ junior suite; from 2,255€ suite. AE, DC, MC, V. Parking 20€–30€. Metro: Repubblica. **Amenities:** Restaurant; bar; babysitting; concierge; exercise room; room service; spa. *In room:* A/C, TV, hair dryer, minibar.

Expensive

Residenza Cellini ★ This undiscovered small hotel from the '30s is run by the English-speaking De Paolis family, who welcome you with warm hospitality. In the heart of Rome, Cellini lies near the Termini, the rail station. Gaetano, Donato, and Barbara have only a few rooms and they lavished attention on them, making them comfortable and stylish. Bedrooms are spacious and traditionally furnished, with polished wood pieces and Oriental carpets on the hardwood floors. The king-size beds have hypoallergenic orthopedic mattresses, and the bathrooms come with hydrojet shower or Jacuzzi.

Via Modena 5, 00184 Roma. ✆ **06-47825204.** Fax 06-47881806. www.residenzacellini.it. 6 units. 145€–240€ double; 165€–280€ junior suite. Rates include buffet breakfast. AE, DC, MC, V. Parking 25€. Metro: Repubblica. **Amenities:** Bar; airport transfers (55€); room service. *In room:* A/C, TV, hair dryer, minibar, Wi-Fi (free).

Moderate

Royal Court ★ This winner lies in a restored Liberty-style palace a short walk from the Termini. The hotel evokes a tranquil, elegantly decorated private town house. Some of the superior rooms offer Jacuzzis in their bathrooms, but all units feature well-maintained and -designed bathrooms with tub/shower combinations. The superior rooms also come with small balconies opening onto cityscapes. Even the standard doubles are comfortable, but if you're willing to pay the price, you can stay in the deluxe doubles, which are like junior suites in most Rome hotels. Some of the bedrooms are large enough to sleep three or four guests comfortably.

Via Marghera 51, 00185 Roma. ✆ **06-44340364.** Fax 06-4469121. www.morganaroyalcourt.com. 24 units. 130€–250€ double. Rates include buffet breakfast. AE, DC, MC, V. Parking 24€. Metro: Termini. **Amenities:** Bar; babysitting; room service. *In room:* A/C, TV, hair dryer, minibar, Wi-Fi (free).

Inexpensive

Yes Hotel We definitely say yes to this hotel, which lies only 100m (328 ft.) from Stazione Termini. Opening in 2007, it was quickly discovered by frugally minded travelers who want a good bed and comfortable surroundings for the night. It's a two-story hotel housed in a restored 19th-century building with simple, well-chosen furnishings resting on tiled floors. There is a sleek, modern look to both the bedrooms and the public areas, and the staff is helpful but not effusive.

Via Magenta 15, 00185 Roma. ✆ **06-44363836.** Fax 06-44363829. www.yeshotelrome.com. 29 units. 82€–219€ double. DC, MC, V. Parking 17€. Metro: Termini. **Amenities:** Bar; babysitting; room service. *In room:* A/C, TV, hair dryer, Wi-Fi (5€ per 24 hr.).

NEAR VIA VENETO & PIAZZA BARBERINI

Very Expensive

Hotel Eden ★★★ The Eden is Rome's top choice for discerning travelers who like grand comfort but without all the ostentation. For several generations after its 1889 opening, this hotel, about a 10-minute walk east of the Spanish Steps, reigned over one of the world's most stylish shopping neighborhoods. Recent guests have included Pierce Brosnan, Tom Cruise, Emma Thompson, and Nicole Kidman. The Eden's hilltop position guarantees a panoramic city view from most guest rooms; all are spacious and elegantly appointed with a decor harking back to the late 19th century, plus marble-sheathed bathrooms. Try to get one of the front rooms with a balcony boasting views over Rome. The **La Terrazza** restaurant (p. 647) has a sweeping view of St. Peter's Basilica.

Via Ludovisi 49, 00187 Roma. ✆ **06-478121.** Fax 06-4821584. www.edenroma.com. 121 units. 314€–840€ double; from 1,340€ suite. AE, DC, DISC, MC, V. Parking 60€. Metro: Piazza Barberini. **Amenities:** Restaurant; bar; babysitting; concierge; exercise room; room service; Wi-Fi (23€ per 24 hr., in lobby). *In room:* A/C, TV/DVD, CD player, hair dryer, minibar.

Expensive

Hotel Alexandra ★ 🎁 This is one of your few chances to stay on Via Veneto without going broke (although it's not exactly cheap). Set behind the stone facade of what was a 19th-century mansion, the Alexandra offers immaculate and soundproof guest rooms. The rooms range from cramped to midsize, but each has been redecorated, filled with antiques or tasteful contemporary pieces. They have extras such as swing-mirror vanities and brass or wooden bedsteads. The breakfast room is appealing: Inspired by an Italian garden, it was designed by noted architect Paolo Portoghesi.

Via Vittorio Veneto 18, 00187 Roma. ✆ **06-4881943.** Fax 06-4871804. www.hotelalexandraroma.com. 60 units (some with shower only). 230€–290€ double; 360€–390€ suite. Rates include buffet breakfast. AE, DC, MC, V. Parking 26€–36€. Metro: Piazza Barberini. **Amenities:** Babysitting; room service; Wi-Fi (4€ per hour). *In room:* A/C, TV, hair dryer, minibar.

Moderate

La Residenza Hotel ★★ In a superb but congested location, this little hotel successfully combines intimacy and elegance. A bit old-fashioned and homey, the converted villa has an ivy-covered courtyard and a series of public rooms with Empire divans, oil portraits, and rattan chairs. Terraces are scattered throughout. The guest rooms are generally spacious, containing bentwood chairs and built-in furniture, including beds. The dozen or so junior suites boast balconies. The bathrooms have robes, and rooms even come equipped with ice machines.

Via Emilia 22–24, 00187 Roma. ✆ **06-4880789.** Fax 06-485721. www.hotel-la-residenza.com. 29 units. 250€–300€ double; 300€–330€ suite. Rates include buffet breakfast. AE, MC, V. Parking (limited) 20€. Metro: Piazza Barberini. **Amenities:** Bar; babysitting; room service. *In room:* A/C, TV, hair dryer, minibar.

Rome Accommodations

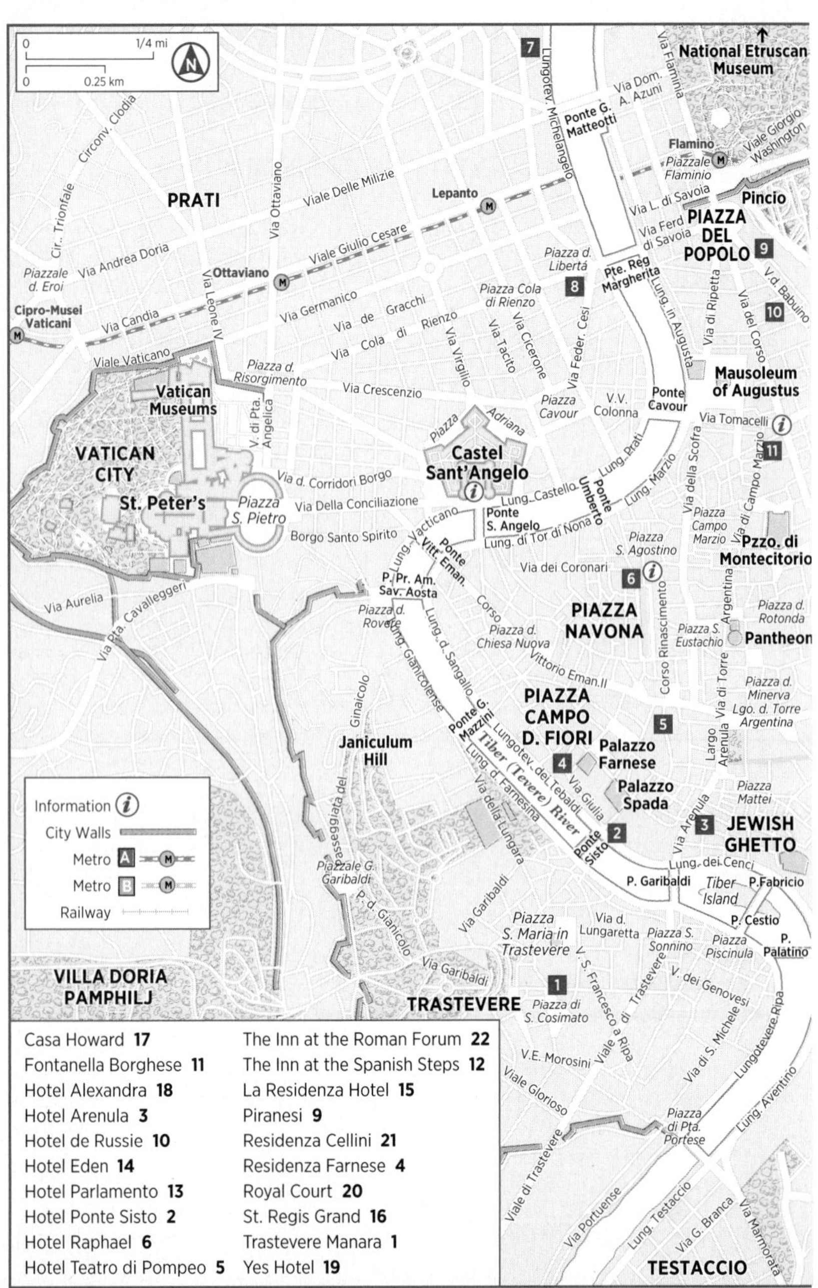

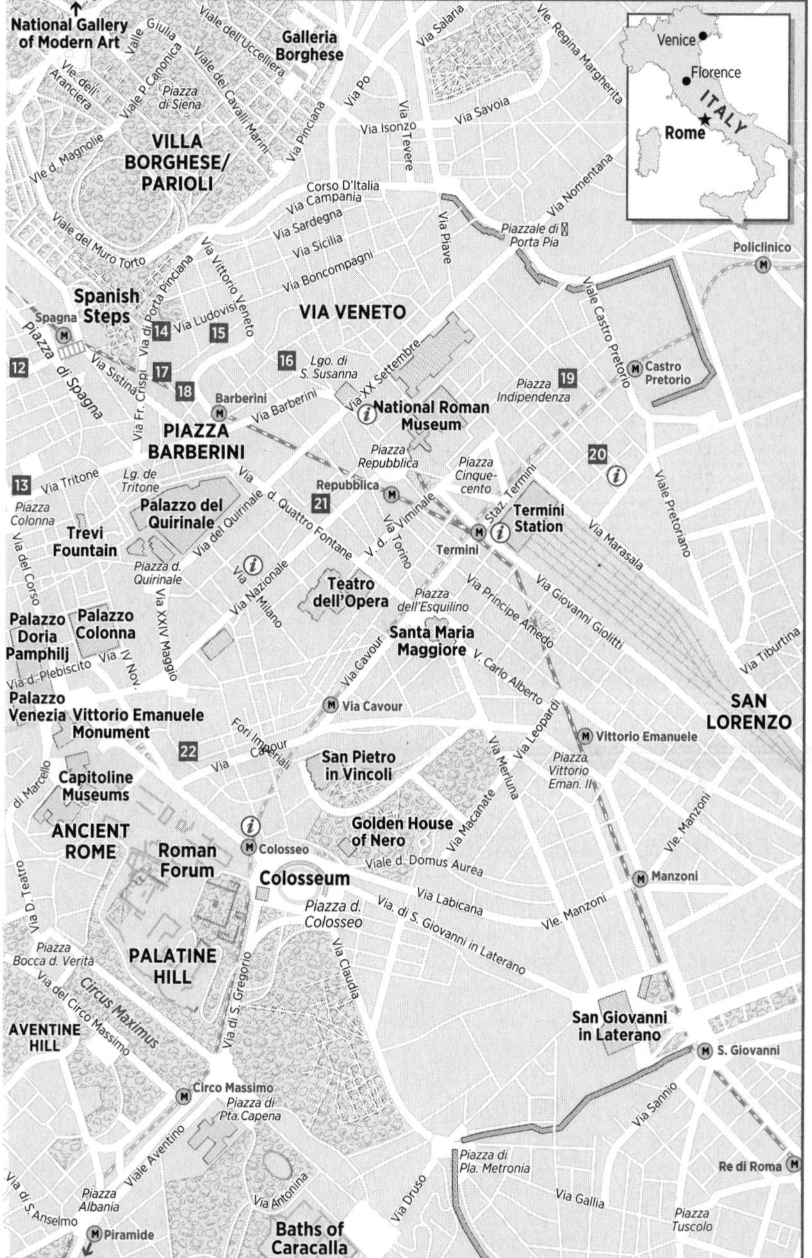

12

ITALY | Rome

NEAR ANCIENT ROME

Expensive

The Inn at the Roman Forum ★ 🎁 This is one of the secret discoveries of Rome, with the Roman Forum itself as a neighbor. A restored 15th-century building dripping with antiquity, the inn even has a small section of Trajan's Marketplace on-site. You enter the front doorway like a resident Roman, greeting your host in the living room. Sleek, classically styled bedrooms are spread across three upper floors, opening onto views of the heart of Rome. Three back bedrooms open onto a walled-in garden complete with fig and palm trees. The most elegant and expensive double has a private patio with a designer bathroom.

Via degli Ibernesi 30, 00184 Roma. ✆ **06-69190970.** Fax 06-45438802. www.theinnattheromanforum.com. 12 units. 166€–850€ double; from 990€ suite. Rates include buffet breakfast. AE, DC, MC, V. Parking 30€. Bus: 64 or 117. **Amenities:** Bar; airport transfers (55€); concierge; room service. *In room:* A/C, TV/DVD, hair dryer, minibar, MP3 docking station, Wi-Fi (10€ per day).

Inexpensive

Hotel Arenula ★ At last a hotel has opened in Rome's old Jewish ghetto, and it's a winner and quite affordable. It takes its name from Via Arenula, that timeworn street linking Largo Argentina to Ponte Garibaldi and the Trastevere area. The restored building is from the 19th century, and the Patta family turned it into this undiscovered and comfortable inn. Close at hand are such attractions as the Pantheon, the Colosseum, and the Piazza Navona. Rooms are furnished in a tasteful, traditional way. They are most inviting and comfortable, with pale-wood pieces and immaculate bathrooms. There's no elevator, so be prepared to climb some stairs.

Via Santa Maria de Calderari 47, 00186 Roma. ✆ **06-6879454.** Fax 06-6896188. www.hotelarenula.com. 50 units. 100€–133€ double. Rates include buffet breakfast. AE, DC, MC, V. Metro: Colosseo. Bus: 40. **Amenities:** Room service. *In room:* A/C, TV, hair dryer.

NEAR CAMPO DE' FIORI

Expensive

Residenza Farnese ★ Among the boutique hotels springing up around Campo de' Fiori, the new Farnese in a 15th-century mansion emerges near the top. Opt for one of the front rooms overlooking Palazzo Farnese, with Michelangelo's Renaissance cornice bathed in sunlight. Bedrooms are fresh and modernized, ranging in size from small to spacious, each with a freshly restored private bathroom with a shower. The location in the heart of ancient Rome puts you within walking distance of many of the major sights, particularly the Roman Forum or even St. Peter's. The owner, Signora Zema, is a gracious host who can provide much helpful advice. She has placed contemporary art throughout as a grace note, and she believes in a generous breakfast to fortify you for the day.

Via del Mascherone 59, 00186 Roma. ✆ **06-68210980.** Fax 06-80321049. www.residenzafarneseroma.it. 31 units. 250€–300€ double; 350€–500€ junior suite. Rates include buffet breakfast. MC, V. Bus: 64. **Amenities:** Bar; room service. *In room:* A/C, TV, hair dryer, minibar, Wi-Fi (.50€ per hour).

Moderate

Hotel Teatro di Pompeo ★★ 🎁 Built atop the ruins of the Theater of Pompey, this small charmer lies near the spot where Julius Caesar met his end on the Ides of March. Intimate and refined, it's on a quiet piazza near the Palazzo Farnese and Campo de' Fiori. The rooms are decorated in an old-fashioned Italian style with hand-painted tiles, and the beamed ceilings date from the days of Michelangelo.

The guest rooms range from small to medium in size, each with a tidy but cramped bathroom.

Largo del Pallaro 8, 00186 Roma. ✆ **06-68300170.** Fax 06-68805531. www.hotelteatrodipompeo.it. 13 units (shower only). 180€–210€ double; 240€–270€ triple. Rates include buffet breakfast. AE, DC, MC, V. Bus: 46, 62, or 64. **Amenities:** Bar; babysitting; room service; Wi-Fi (3€ per hour, in lobby). *In room:* A/C, TV, hair dryer, minibar.

NEAR PIAZZA NAVONA & THE PANTHEON

Very Expensive

Hotel Raphael ★★ With a glorious location adjacent to Piazza Navona, the Raphael is within easy walking distance of many sights. The ivy-covered facade invites you to enter the lobby, which is decorated with antiques that rival the cache in local museums (there's even a Picasso ceramics collection). The guest rooms (some quite small) were refurbished with a Florentine touch. Some of the suites have private terraces. The deluxe rooms, the executive units, and the junior suites were conceived by Richard Meier, the famous architect who has designed buildings all over the world. Each of them is lined with oak and equipped in a modern high-tech style that includes a digital sound system. The Raphael is often the top choice of Italian politicos in town for the opening of Parliament. We love its rooftop restaurant with views of all of the city's prominent landmarks.

Largo Febo 2, 00186 Roma. ✆ **06-682831.** Fax 06-6878993. www.raphaelhotel.com. 65 units. 250€–600€ double; 410€–900€ suite. AE, DC, MC, V. Parking 40€. Bus: 70, 81, 87, or 115. **Amenities:** Restaurant; bar; babysitting; concierge; exercise room; room service; sauna; Wi-Fi (free, in lobby). *In room:* A/C, TV, hair dryer, minibar.

NEAR PIAZZA DEL POPOLO & THE SPANISH STEPS

Very Expensive

Hotel de Russie ★★★ ☺ This government-rated five-star hotel has raised the bar for every other hotel in the city. For service, style, and modern luxuries, it beats out the Eden and the St. Regis Grand. Just off the Piazza del Popolo, it reopened in 2000 to media acclaim for its opulent furnishings and choice location. Public areas are glossy and contemporary. About 30% of the bedrooms are conservative, with traditional furniture, while the remaining 70% are more minimalist, with a stark and striking style.

Via del Babuino 9, 00187 Roma. ✆ **800/323-7500** in North America, or 06-328881. Fax 06-3288888. www.roccofortehotels.com. 125 units. 680€–955€ double; from 1,410€ suite. AE, DC, MC, V. Parking 55€. Metro: Flaminia. **Amenities:** Restaurant; bar; babysitting; children's programs; concierge; exercise room; room service; spa. *In room:* A/C, TV, hair dryer, minibar, Wi-Fi.

The Inn at the Spanish Steps ★★★ This intimate, upscale inn was the first new hotel to open in this location in years. The people who run Rome's most famous cafe, Caffè Greco, created it where Hans Christian Andersen once lived. Andersen praised the balcony roses and violets, and so can you. Every room is furnished in an authentic period decor, featuring antiques, elegant draperies, and parquet floors. The superior units come with fireplace, a frescoed or beamed ceiling, and a balcony. The hotel is completely modern, from its hypoallergenic mattresses to its generous wardrobe space.

Via dei Condotti 85, 00187 Roma. ✆ **06-69925657.** Fax 06-6786470. www.atspanishsteps.com. 24 units. 200€–720€ double; 1,200€ suite. Rates include buffet breakfast. AE, DC, MC, V. Metro: Piazza di Spagna. **Amenities:** Bar; airport transfers (68€); babysitting; concierge; room service. *In room:* A/C, TV, hair dryer, minibar.

Expensive

Piranesi ★★ Right off the Piazza del Popolo sits one of Rome's most select boutique hotels, boasting more affordable prices than at the Hotel de Russie, which fronts it. If you lodge here, you'll be staying in one of the most historic areas of Rome. Bedrooms are tranquil and decorated in a style evocative of the 18th-century Directoire. Bare pine-wood floors and cherrywood furniture are grace notes, as are the immaculate bathrooms. Don't miss the Piranesi's panoramic rooftop terrace.

Via del Babuino 196, 00187 Roma. ✆ **06-328041.** Fax 06-3610597. www.hotelpiranesi.com. 32 units. 220€–350€ double; 298€–420€ suite. Rates include buffet breakfast. AE, MC, V. Parking 35€. Metro: Flaminio. Bus: 117. **Amenities:** Bar; exercise room; room service; sauna. *In room:* A/C, TV, hair dryer, minibar.

Moderate

Casa Howard ★ It's rare to make a discovery in the tourist-trodden Piazza di Spagna area. That's why Casa Howard comes as a pleasant surprise. The B&B occupies about two-thirds of the second floor of a historic structure. The welcoming family owners maintain beautifully furnished guest rooms, each with its own private bathroom (although some bathrooms lie outside the bedrooms in the hallway). The Green Room is the most spacious, with its own en suite bathroom.

Via Capo le Case 18, 00187 Roma. ✆ **06-69924555.** Fax 06-6794644. www.casahoward.com. 5 units. 170€–250€ double. MC, V. Parking 25€. Metro: Piazza di Spagna. **Amenities:** Babysitting; room service; sauna. *In room:* A/C, TV, hair dryer, Wi-Fi (free).

Fontanella Borghese ★ Close to the Spanish Steps in the exact heart of Rome, this hotel surprisingly remains relatively undiscovered. Much renovated and improved, it has been installed on the 3rd and 4th floors of a palace dating from the end of the 18th century. The building once belonged to the princes of the Borghese family, and the little hotel looks out onto the Borghese Palace. It lies within walking distance of the Trevi Fountain, the Pantheon, and the Piazza Navona. The location is also close to Piazza Augusto and the Ara Pacis. In the midsize bedrooms, plain wooden furniture rests on parquet floors, and everything is in a classical tradition comfortably modernized for today's travelers.

Largo Fontanella Borghese 84, 00186 Roma. ✆ **06-68809-504.** Fax 06-6861295. www.fontanellaborghese.com. 29 units. 180€–230€ double; 210€–260€ triple. AE, DC, MC, V. Parking 25€ nearby. Metro: Spagna. **Amenities:** Room service. *In room:* A/C, TV, hair dryer, minibar.

Inexpensive

Hotel Parlamento The hard-to-find Parlamento has a two-star government rating and moderate prices. Expect a friendly *pensione*-style reception. The furnishings are antiques or reproductions, and carved wood or wrought-iron headboards back the firm beds. The bathrooms were recently redone with heated towel racks, phones, and (in a few) even marble sinks. Rooms are different in style; the best are no. 82, with its original 1800s furniture, and nos. 104, 106, and 107, which open onto the roof garden. You can enjoy the chandeliered and *trompe l'oeil* breakfast room, or carry your cappuccino up to the small roof terrace with its view of San Silvestro's bell tower.

Via delle Convertite 5 (at the intersection with Via del Corso), 00187 Roma. ✆/fax **06-69921000.** www.hotelparlamento.it. 23 units. 80€–195€ double; 98€–205€ triple. Rates include buffet breakfast. AE, DC, MC, V. Parking 30€. Metro: Spagna. **Amenities:** Bar; concierge; room service. *In room:* A/C, TV, hair dryer.

NEAR VATICAN CITY

Very Expensive

Visconti Palace Hotel ★★ Completely restructured and redesigned, this palatial hotel is graced with one of the most avant-garde contemporary designs in town. Stunningly modern, it uses color perhaps with more sophistication than any other hotel. The location is idyllic, lying in the Prati district between Piazza di Spagna and St. Peter's. The rooms and corridors are decorated with modern art; the bathrooms are in marble; and there are many floor-to-ceiling windows and private terraces. Taste and an understated elegance prevail in this bright, welcoming, yet functional atmosphere.

Via Federico Cesi 37, 00193 Roma. ✆ **06-3684.** Fax 06-3200551. www.viscontipalace.com. 242 units. 350€–380€ double; 450€ junior suite; 600€ suite. AE, DC, MC, V. Parking 35€. Metro: Ottaviano. Bus: 40, 62, or 74. **Amenities:** Bar; exercise room; room service; Wi-Fi (7€ per hour). *In room:* A/C, TV, hair dryer, minibar.

Moderate

Villa Laetitia ★★★ Anna Fendi, of the fashion dynasty, has opened this stylish and superchic haven of elegance along the Tiber. With its private gardens, this Art Nouveau mansion lies between the Piazza del Popolo and the Prati quarter. The bedrooms are virtual works of art and are decorated with antique tiles gathered by Fendi on her world travels along with other objets d'art. For the smart, trendy, and well-heeled traveler, this is a choice address. Many of the rooms contain well-equipped kitchenettes. Accommodations are like small studios with terraces or gardens. Each rental unit has a different design and personality. Artists and designers in particular are attracted to this intimate, personalized hotel.

Lungotevere delle Armi 22–23, 00195 Roma. ✆ **06-3226776.** Fax 06-3232720. www.villalaetitia.com. 15 units. 190€–220€ double; 270€–350€ suite. AE, DC, MC, V. Metro: Lepanto. **Amenities:** Bar; babysitting; room service; spa; Wi-Fi (free, in lobby). *In room:* A/C, TV/DVD, hair dryer, minibar.

IN TRASTEVERE

Expensive

Hotel Ponte Sisto ★ Steps from the River Tiber, this hotel lies on the most exclusive residential street in historic Rome at the gateway to Trastevere. The hotel is imbued with a bright, fresh look that contrasts with some of the timeworn buildings surrounding it. Windows look out on the core of Renaissance and baroque Rome. This 18th-century structure has been totally renovated with class and elegance. If you can live in the small bedrooms (the singles are really cramped), you'll enjoy this choice address with its cherrywood furnishings. Try for one of the upper-floor rooms for a better view; some come with their own terrace.

Via dei Pettinari 64, 00186 Roma. ✆ **06-6863100.** Fax 06-68301712. www.hotelpontesisto.it. 103 units. 200€–290€ double; 350€–550€ suite. Rates include buffet breakfast. AE, DC, MC, V. Parking 26€. Tram: 8. **Amenities:** Restaurant for guests only; room service. *In room:* A/C, TV, hair dryer, minibar.

Inexpensive

Trastevere Manara ★ Manara opened its restored doors in 1998 to meet the demand for accommodations in Trastevere. This little gem has fresh, bright bedrooms with immaculate tiles. All of the bathrooms have also been renovated and contain showers, although these bathrooms are small. The price is hard to beat for those who want to stay in one of the most atmospheric sections of Rome. Most of the rooms open onto the lively Piazza San Cosimato, and all of them have comfortable, albeit functional, furnishings. Breakfast is the only meal served, but many good restaurants lie just minutes away.

Via L. Manara 24–25, 00153 Roma. ✆ **06-5814713.** Fax 06-5881016. www.hoteltrastevere.net. 18 units. 103€–105€ double. Rates include buffet breakfast. AE, DC, MC, V. Bus: H. Tram: 8. **Amenities:** Airport transfers (52€–62€). *In room:* TV.

Where to Dine

NEAR STAZIONE TERMINI

Expensive

Agata e Romeo ★★ NEW ROMAN One of the most charming places near the Vittorio Emanuele Monument is this striking duplex restaurant done up in turn-of-the-20th-century Liberty style. You'll enjoy the creative cuisine of Romeo Caraccio (who manages the dining room) and his wife, Agata Parisella (who prepares her own version of sophisticated Roman food). The pasta specialty is *paccheri all'amatriciana* (large macaroni tubes with pancetta and a savory tomato sauce topped with pecorino cheese). The chef is equally adept at fish or meat dishes, including braised beef cheeks laid on chestnut purée or swordfish rolls scented with orange and fennel cream. The most luscious dessert is Agata's *millefoglie,* puff pastry stuffed with almonds. The wine cellar offers a wide choice of international and domestic wines.

Via Carlo Alberto 45. ✆ **06-4466115.** www.agataeromeo.it. Reservations recommended. All pastas 30€; meat and fish 45€. AE, DC, MC, V. Tues–Fri 1–2:30pm; Mon–Fri 8–10:30pm. Closed Aug 8–30. Metro: Vittorio Emanuele.

Inexpensive

Monte Arci ROMAN/SARDINIAN On a cobblestone street near Piazza Indipendenza, this restaurant is set behind a sienna-colored facade. It features Roman and Sardinian specialties such as *nialoreddus* (a regional form of *gnocchetti*); pasta with clams, lobster, or the musky-earthy notes of porcini mushrooms; and lamb sausage flavored with herbs and pecorino cheese. The best pasta dish we've sampled is *paglia e fieno al Monte Arci* (homemade pasta with pancetta, spinach, cream, and Parmesan). It's all home cooking, hearty but not that creative.

Via Castelfirdardo 33. ✆ **06-4941220.** www.ristorantemontearci.com. Reservations recommended. Main courses 8€–15€. AE, DC, MC, V. Mon–Fri 12:30–3pm; Mon–Sat 7–11:30pm. Closed Aug. Metro: Stazione Termini or Repubblica.

Trimani Wine Bar ★ CONTINENTAL Opened as a tasting center for French and Italian wines, spumantes, and liqueurs, this is an elegant wine bar with a stylish but informal decor and comfortable seating. More than 30 wines are available by the glass. To accompany them, you can choose from a bistro-style menu, with dishes such as salade niçoise, vegetarian pastas, herb-laden bean soups *(fagioli),* and quiche. Also available is a wider menu, including meat and fish courses. The specialty is the large range of little *bruschette* with cheese and radicchio—the chef orders every kind of prosciutto and cheese from all over Italy. The dishes are matched with the appropriate wines. The dessert specialty is cinnamon cake with apples and a flavor of fresh rosemary.

Via Cernaia 37B. ✆ **06-4469630.** www.trimani.com. Reservations recommended. Main courses 10€–18€; glass of wine (depending on vintage) 3€–18€. AE, DC, MC, V. Daily 11:30am–3pm and 5:30pm–12:30am. Closed 2 weeks in Aug. Metro: Repubblica or Castro Pretorio.

NEAR VIA VENETO & PIAZZA BARBERINI

Very Expensive

La Terrazza ★★★ ITALIAN/INTERNATIONAL La Terrazza serves some of the city's finest cuisine; you get the added bonus of a sweeping view over St. Peter's. The service is formal and flawless, yet not intimidating. Chef Adriano Cavagnini, the wizard behind about a dozen top-notch Italian restaurants around Europe, prepares a seasonally changing menu that's among the most polished in Rome. You might start with braised artichokes with scallops, salted cod purée, and a basil-scented mousse, or else delectable zucchini blossoms stuffed with ricotta and Taleggio cheese, black olives, and cherry tomatoes. The pasta specialty is penne filled with ricotta cheese, plus mortadella, walnuts, and pecorino cheese, which might be followed by such dishes as grilled swordfish with sweet-and-sour spinach and a tomato fondue, oven-baked whole baby chicken with wild mushrooms, or grilled filet of beef with smoked pancetta and fresh thyme.

In the Hotel Eden, Via Ludovisi 49. ✆ **06-478121.** Reservations recommended. Main courses 30€–65€. AE, DC, MC, V. Daily 12:30–2:30pm and 7:30–10:30pm. Metro: Barberini.

Moderate

Colline Emiliane ★★ 🎁 EMILIANA-ROMAGNOLA Serving the *classica cucina Bolognese,* Colline Emiliane is a small, family-run place—the owner is the cook and his wife makes the pasta (about the best you'll find in Rome). The house specialty is an inspired *tortellini alla panna* (with cream sauce and truffles), but the less-expensive pastas, including *maccheroni al funghetto* (with mushrooms) and *tagliatelle alla Bolognese* (in meat sauce), are excellent, too. As an opener, we suggest *culatello di Zibello,* a delicacy from a small town near Parma that's known for having the world's finest prosciutto. Main courses include *braciola di maiale* (boneless rolled pork cutlets stuffed with ham and cheese, breaded, and sautéed) and an impressive *giambonnetto* (roast veal Emilian-style with roast potatoes).

Via Avignonesi 22 (off Piazza Barberini). ✆ **06-4817538.** Reservations highly recommended. Main courses 12€–22€. MC, V. Tues–Sun 12:45–2:45pm; Tues–Sat 7:45–10:45pm. Closed Aug. Metro: Barberini.

NEAR ANCIENT ROME

Moderate

Crab ★ SEAFOOD This trattoria is ideal after a visit to the nearby Basilica of San Giovanni. As you enter, you are greeted with a display of freshly harvested crustaceans and mollusks, which are what you can expect to headline the menu. The signature dish is king crab legs (hardly from the Mediterranean). Fish is shipped in "from everywhere," including oysters from France, lobster from the Mediterranean and the Atlantic, and some catches from the Adriatic. The antipasti is practically a meal in itself, including a savory sauté of mussels and clams, an octopus salad, and scallops gratin, which might be followed by a succulent lobster ravioli in *salsa vergine* (a lobster-based sauce). Most of the main courses, except for some very expensive shellfish and lobster platters, are closer to the lower end of the price scale.

Via Capo d'Africa 2. ✆ **06-7720-3636.** Reservations required. Main courses 14€–85€. AE, DC, MC, V. Mon 7:45–11:30pm; Tues–Sat 1–3:30pm and 8–11:30pm. Closed Aug. Metro: Colosseo. Tram: 3.

Inexpensive

Hostaria Nerone ★ ROMAN/ITALIAN Built atop the ruins of the Golden House of Nero, this trattoria opened in 1929 at the edge of Colle Oppio Park. It contains two compact dining rooms and a flowering-shrub-lined terrace that offers a view over the Colosseum and the Bath of Trajan. The copious antipasti buffet offers the bounty of Italy's fields and seas. The pastas include savory spaghetti with clams and our favorite, *pasta e fagioli* (with beans). There are also grilled crayfish and swordfish, and Italian sausages with polenta. Roman-style tripe is a favorite, but maybe you'll skip it for the *osso buco* (veal shank) with mashed potatoes and seasonal mushrooms. The list of some of the best Italian wines is reasonably priced.

Via Terme di Tito 96. ✆ **06-4817952.** Reservations recommended. Main courses 12€-18€. AE, DC, MC, V. Mon-Sat noon-3pm and 7-11pm. Metro: Colosseo. Bus: 75, 85, 87, 117, or 175.

NEAR CAMPO DE' FIORI & THE JEWISH GHETTO

Moderate

Ristorante del Pallaro ★★ 🎁 ROMAN The cheerful woman in white who emerges with clouds of steam from the bustling kitchen is owner Paola Fazi, who runs two dining rooms where value-conscious Romans go for good food at bargain prices. (She also claims—though others dispute it—that Julius Caesar was assassinated on this site.) The fixed-price menu is the only choice and has made the place famous. Ms. Fazi prepares everything with love, as if she were feeding her extended family. As you sit down, your antipasto, the first of eight courses, appears. Then comes the pasta of the day, followed by such main dishes as roast veal with broad beans and homemade potato chips, or roast pork cutlets, tender and flavorful. For your final courses, you're served mozzarella, cake with custard, and fruit in season.

Largo del Pallaro 15. ✆ **06-68801488.** Reservations recommended. Fixed-price menu 25€. No credit cards. Tues-Sun noon-3:30pm and 7pm-12:30am. Closed Aug 12-25. Bus: 40, 46, 60, 62, or 64.

NEAR PIAZZA NAVONA & THE PANTHEON

Expensive

Il Convivio ★ ROMAN/INTERNATIONAL This is one of the most acclaimed restaurants in Rome, and one of the few to be granted a coveted Michelin star. Its 16th-century building is a classic setting in pristine white with accents of wood. The Troiano brothers turn out an inspired cuisine based on the best and freshest ingredients at the market. Their menu is seasonally adjusted to take advantage of what's good during any month. Start with a tantalizing fish and shellfish soup with green tomatoes and sweet peppers, and follow with such pastas as homemade lasagna with red prawns, coconut milk, pine nuts, artichokes, and mozzarella. More imaginative is the homemade duck ravioli in a red chicory sauce. A main dish might be oxtail served with spicy "smashed" potatoes and black truffles.

Vicolo dei Soldati 31. ✆ **06-6869432.** Reservations required. All main courses 27€-41€; fixed-price menu 98€. AE, DC, MC, V. Mon-Sat 8-11pm. Bus: 40 or 64. Metro: Piazza di Spagna.

Moderate

Osteria dell'Antiquario ★ 🎁 INTERNATIONAL/ROMAN This virtually undiscovered *osteria* enjoys a location a few blocks down the Via dei Coronari as you leave the Piazza Navona and head toward St. Peter's. In a stone-built stable from the 1500s, this restaurant has three dining rooms used in winter. In nice weather, try to get an outdoor table on the terrace; shaded by umbrellas, they face a view of the Palazzo Lancillotti. Begin with a delectable appetizer of sautéed shellfish (usually mussels and clams). Some of the more savory offerings include potato gnocchi with clams and wild mushrooms, stewed scorpion fish with tomato sauce, swordfish steak with a parsley-laced white-wine sauce, or veal escalope with ham and sage.

Piazzetta di S. Simeone 26-27, Via dei Coronari. ✆ **06-6879694.** www.osteriadellantiquario.it. Reservations recommended. Main courses 12€-25€. AE, DC, MC, V. Mon-Sat 7:30-11pm. Closed 15 days in mid-Aug, Christmas, and Jan 6-30. Bus: 70, 87, or 90.

Inexpensive

Osteria del Gallo ★ ROMAN You can escape the tourist traps of the Piazza Navona, such as Tre Scalini, by finding this place in a tiny alley off the west/northwest side of the fabled square. It's very small, with a lovely area for outdoor seating, and is definitely off the beaten track. The chef/owner comes out to take your order personally. He is justly proud of his homemade pastas such as gnocchi with mussels and arugula, linguine with seafood, and a typical Roman recipe for *tagliolini cacio e pepe* (with cheese and pepper). Menu items include a variety of fresh fish dishes roasted in a salt crust to retain their juice and flavor. Other favorites include filet of beef cooked with green pepper. All desserts are homemade, including one of the best tiramisu turned out in the area.

Vicolo di Montevecchio 27. ✆ **06-6873781.** www.osteriadelgalloroma.it. Reservations highly recommended. Main courses 8€-18€. AE, DC, MC, V. Wed-Mon 11:30am-3pm and 6:30-11:30pm. Metro: Piazza Navona.

NEAR PIAZZA DEL POPOLO & THE SPANISH STEPS

Expensive

El Toulà ★★ MEDITERRANEAN/VENETIAN Offering sophisticated haute cuisine, El Toulà is the glamorous flagship of an upscale chain that has gone international. The setting is elegant, with vaulted ceilings, large archways, and a charming bar. The impressive, always-changing menu has one section devoted to Venetian specialties in honor of the restaurant's origins. The chef will dazzle you with such offerings as sea bass filet with artichokes and clams; grilled tuna steak with fennel, oranges, and black olives; and tagliolini with pumpkin, fresh sage, pork cheeks, and smoked Provola cheese. Pure, authentic ingredients go into these dishes. Save room for the seasonal selection of sorbets and sherbets (the cantaloupe and fresh strawberry are celestial); you can request a mixed plate if you'd like to sample several. El Toulà usually isn't crowded at lunchtime. The wine list is extensive and varied, but hardly a bargain.

Via della Lupa 29B. ✆ **06-6873498.** www.toula.it. Reservations required for dinner. Main courses 21€-32€; 5-course tasting menu 78€; 4-course "flavor of Rome" 68€; 4-course vegetarian menu 50€. AE, DC, MC, V. Tues-Fri 1-3pm; Mon-Sat 8-11pm. Closed Aug. Bus: 70, 81, 87, 116, or 196.

Moderate

Dal Bolognese ★ BOLOGNESE This is one of those rare dining spots that's chic but actually lives up to the hype with noteworthy food. Young actors, models, artists from nearby Via Margutta, and even corporate types on expense accounts show up, trying to land one of the few sidewalk tables. To begin, we suggest *misto di pasta:* four pastas, each with a different sauce, arranged on the same plate. Another good choice is thin slices of savory Parma ham or the delectable prosciutto and vine-ripened melon. For your main course, specialties that win hearts year after year are *lasagne verdi* and *tagliatelle alla Bolognese.* The chefs also turn out the town's most recommendable veal cutlets Bolognese topped with cheese. They're not inventive, but they're simply superb.

You might want to cap your evening by dropping into the **Rosati** cafe next door (or the **Canova,** across the street) to enjoy one of the tempting pastries.

Piazza del Popolo 1-2. ✆ **06-3611426.** Reservations required. Main courses 19€-30€. AE, DC, MC, V. Tues-Sun 12:30-3pm and 7:30-11:30pm. Closed 3 weeks in Aug. Metro: Flaminio.

Inexpensive

Maccheroni ROMAN In a rustic tavern in the heart of Rome, you can savor food that you usually have to go to the countryside to enjoy. The decor is informal, with wood-paneled walls and pop art; and on a good night the place can seat 160 satisfied diners, both visitors and locals. The chef shops wisely for his bevy of regional dishes and backs up his menu with a well-chosen wine list that includes the house chianti. Pasta is the house specialty, and it's never better than in the spaghetti flavored with bacon and onion. You can also order fettuccini with black-truffle sauce or ravioli with pumpkin flowers. The menu features a traditional Roman cuisine, and everything is well prepared, including *maccheroni all'amatriciana* (either the red version with tomatoes and bacon along with pecorino cheese, or the white version without tomatoes). Tender, juicy beefsteaks are also served.

Piazza della Copelle 44. ✆ **06-68307895.** www.ristorantemaccheroni.com. Reservations recommended. Main courses 8€–19€. AE, MC, V. Daily 1–3pm and 8pm–midnight. Metro: Spagna. Bus: 64, 70, 75, or 116.

NEAR VATICAN CITY

Inexpensive

Hostaria dei Bastioni ROMAN/SEAFOOD This simple but well-managed restaurant is about a minute's walk from the entrance to the Vatican Museums and has been open since the 1960s. Although a warm-weather terrace doubles the size during summer, many diners prefer the inside room as an escape from the roaring traffic. The menu features the staples of Rome's culinary repertoire, including fisherman's risotto (a broth-simmered rice dish with fresh fish, usually shellfish), a vegetarian *fettuccine alla bastione* with orange-flavored creamy tomato sauce, and an array of grilled fresh fish. The food is first-rate—and a bargain at these prices.

Via Leone IV 29. ✆ **06-39723034.** Reservations recommended Fri–Sat. Main courses 8€–19€. AE, DC, MC, V. Mon–Sat noon–3pm and 7–11:30pm. Closed July 15–Aug 1. Metro: Ottaviano.

Siciliainbocca ★ SICILIAN The best Sicilian restaurant in Rome lies close to the Vatican, ideal for a lunch when visiting either St. Peter's or the papal museums. Natives of Sicily own and operate this place, and their specialties taste virtually the same as those encountered in Sicily itself. The menu features a large variety of delectable smoked fish, including salmon, swordfish, and tuna. The homemade pastas here are the best Sicilian versions in town, especially the classic *maccheroni alla Norma,* with ricotta, a savory tomato sauce, and sautéed eggplant. You might also opt for such dishes as linguine with sautéed scampi and cherry tomatoes; or a typical Palermitan pasta with sardines, wild fennel, and pine nuts. Other good-tasting and typical dishes include swordfish with capers, olives, tomatoes, and Parmesan cheese.

Via E. Faà di Bruno 26. ✆ **06-37358400.** Main courses 11€–22€. AE, DC, MC, V. Mon–Sat 1:30–3pm and 8–11:30pm. Closed 3 weeks in Aug. Metro: Ottaviano San Pietro.

IN TRASTEVERE

Expensive

Alberto Ciarla ★★ SEAFOOD The Ciarla, in an 1890 building in an obscure corner of an enormous square, is Trastevere's best restaurant and one of its most expensive. You'll be greeted with a cordial reception and a lavish display of seafood on ice. A dramatically modern decor plays light against shadow for a Renaissance chiaroscuro effect. The specialties include a handful of ancient recipes subtly improved by Signor Ciarla (such as the soup of pasta and beans with seafood).

Original dishes include a delectable fish in orange sauce, savory spaghetti with clams, and a full array of shellfish, including mixed fried seafood. The sea bass filet is prepared in at least three ways, including an award-winning version with almonds.

Piazza San Cosimato 40. ✆ **06-5818668.** www.albertociarla.com. Reservations required. Main courses 16€–32€; fixed-price menus 25€–68€. AE, DC, MC, V. Mon–Sat 1–3pm and 8:30pm–midnight. Closed 1 week in Jan and 1 week in Aug. Bus: 44, 75, 170, 280, or 718.

Moderate

Antico Arco ★ ITALIAN Named after one of the gates of early medieval Rome (Arco di San Pancrazio), which rises nearby, Antico Arco is on Janiculum Hill not far from Trastevere and the American Academy. It's a hip restaurant with a young, stylish clientele. Carefully crafted dishes with fresh ingredients include ravioli stuffed with beans in a seafood soup or green homemade tagliolini with red mullet and a saffron sauce. Other palate-pleasing dishes include crispy suckling pig in a sweet-and-sour sauce, with fennel and a citrus soufflé, or else crunchy shrimp with artichoke purée and an anise sauce. A white chocolate tiramisu is a heavenly concoction.

Piazzale Aurelio 7. ✆ **06-5815274.** www.anticoarco.it. Reservations recommended. Main courses 15€–28€; fixed-price menu 70€. AE, DC, MC, V. Daily 6pm–midnight. Bus: 115 or 870.

Exploring the Eternal City

Whether Rome's ancient monuments are time-blackened or still gleaming in the wake of the city's restoration efforts for the now-distant Jubilee Year in 2000, they are a constant reminder that Rome was one of the greatest centers of Western civilization. In the heyday of the empire, all roads led to Rome, with good reason. It was one of the first cosmopolitan cities, importing slaves, gladiators, great art, and even citizens from the far corners of the world. Despite its carnage and corruption, Rome left a legacy of law; a heritage of great art, architecture, and engineering; and an uncanny lesson in how to conquer enemies by absorbing their cultures.

But ancient Rome is only part of the spectacle. The Vatican has had a tremendous influence on making the city a tourism center. Although Vatican architects stripped down much of the city's glory, looting ancient ruins for their precious marble, they created great Renaissance treasures and even occasionally incorporated the old into the new—as Michelangelo did when turning the Baths of Diocletian into a church. And in the years that followed, Bernini adorned the city with the wonders of the baroque, especially his glorious fountains.

ST. PETER'S & THE VATICAN

St. Peter's Basilica ★★★ In ancient times, the Circus of Nero, where St. Peter is said to have been crucified, was slightly to the left of where the basilica is now located. Peter was allegedly buried here in A.D. 64 near the site of his execution, and in 324 Constantine commissioned a basilica to be built over Peter's tomb. That structure stood for more than 1,000 years, until it verged on collapse. The present basilica, mostly completed in the 1500s and 1600s, is predominantly High Renaissance and baroque. Inside, the massive scale is almost too much to absorb, showcasing some of Italy's greatest artists: Bramante, Raphael, Michelangelo, and Maderno. In a church of such grandeur—overwhelming in its detail of gilt, marble, and mosaic—you can't expect much subtlety. It's meant to be overpowering.

In the nave on the right (the first chapel) stands one of the Vatican's greatest treasures: Michelangelo's exquisite ***Pietà*** **★★★**, created while the master was still

Rome Attractions

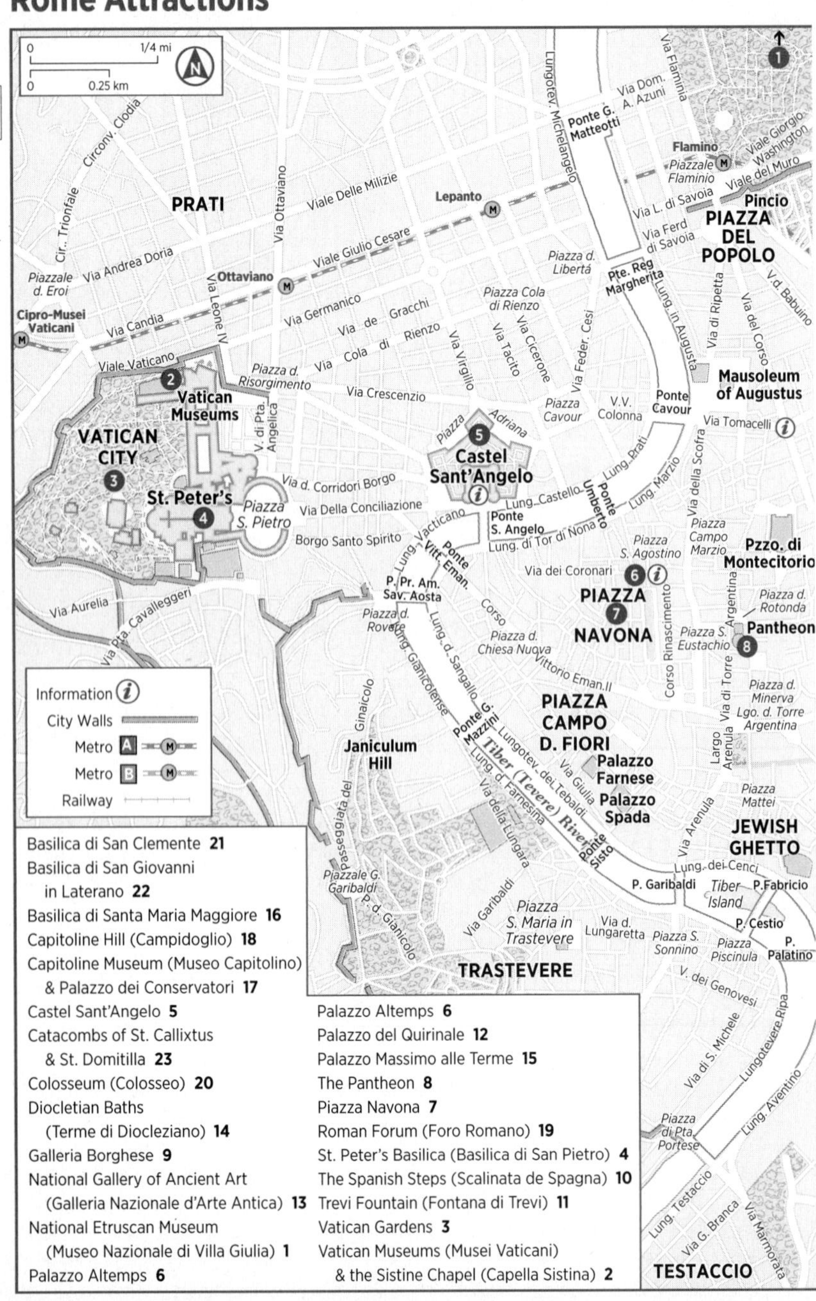

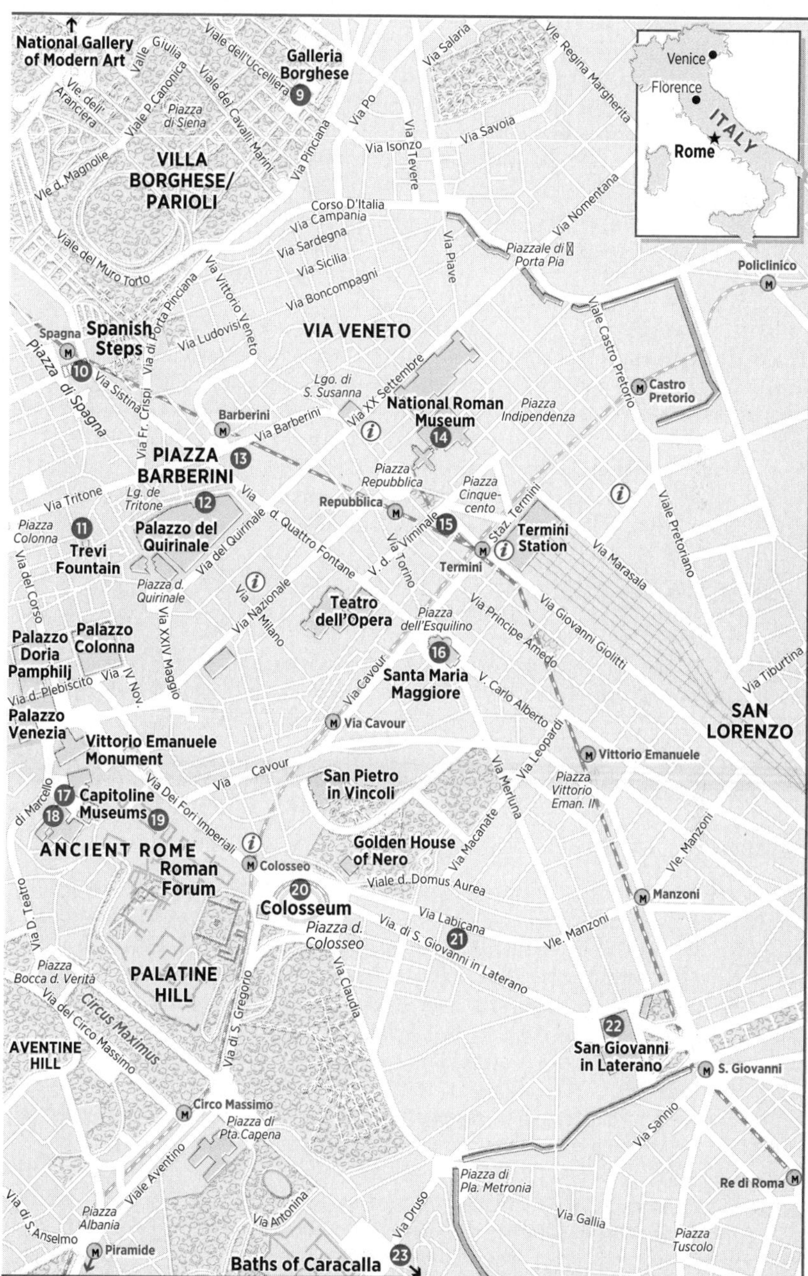

12 ITALY | Rome

in his 20s but clearly showing his genius for capturing the human form. (The sculpture has been kept behind reinforced glass since a madman's act of vandalism in the 1970s.) Note the lifelike folds of Mary's robes and her youthful features (although she would've been middle-aged at the time of the Crucifixion, Michelangelo portrayed her as a young woman to convey her purity).

Much farther on, in the right wing of the transept near the Chapel of St. Michael, rests Canova's neoclassical **sculpture of Pope Clement XIII ★★**. The truly devout stop to kiss the feet of the 13th-century **bronze of St. Peter ★**, attributed to Arnolfo di Cambio (at the far reaches of the nave, against a corner pillar on the right). Under Michelangelo's dome is the celebrated twisty-columned **baldacchino ★★** (1524), by Bernini, resting over the papal altar. The 29m-high (96-ft.) ultrafancy canopy was created in part, so it's said, from bronze stripped from the Pantheon, although that's up for debate.

To go even farther down, to the **Necropolis Vaticana ★★**, the area around St. Peter's tomb, you must send a fax 3 weeks beforehand to the **excavations office.** Apply in advance at the Ufficio Scavi (✆ **06-69885318;** fax 06-69873017), through the arch to the left of the stairs up the basilica. You specify your name, the number in your party, your language, and dates you'd like to visit. They'll notify you by phone of your admission date and time. For 10€, you'll take a guided tour of the tombs that were excavated in the 1940s, 7m (23 ft.) beneath the church floor. For details, check **www.vatican.va**. Children 14 and under are not admitted to the Necropolis Vaticana.

After you leave the grottoes, you'll find yourself in a courtyard and ticket line for the grandest sight: the climb to **Michelangelo's dome ★★★**, about 114m (375 ft.) high. You can walk up all the steps or take the elevator as far as it goes. The elevator saves you 171 steps, and you'll *still* have 320 to go after getting off. After you've made it to the top, you'll have an astounding view over the rooftops of Rome and even the Vatican Gardens and papal apartments—a photo op, if ever there was one.

Piazza San Pietro. ✆ **06-69881662.** Basilica (including grottoes) free admission. Guided tour of excavations around St. Peter's tomb 10€; children 14 and under not admitted. Stairs to the dome 5€; elevator to the dome 7€; Sacristy (with Historical Museum) free. Basilica (including the sacristy and treasury) daily 9am–6pm. Grottoes daily 8am–5pm. Dome Oct–Mar daily 8am–5pm; Apr–Sept daily 8am–6pm. Metro: Ottaviano/San Pietro, then a long stroll. Bus: 49.

Musei Vaticani (Vatican Museums) & Cappella Sistina (Sistine Chapel) ★★★

The Vatican Museums boast one of the world's greatest art collections. They are a gigantic repository of treasures from antiquity and the Renaissance, housed in a labyrinthine series of lavishly adorned palaces, apartments, and galleries leading you to the real gem: the Sistine Chapel. The Vatican Museums occupy a part of the papal palaces built from the 1200s on. From the former papal private apartments, the museums were created over a period of time to display the vast treasure-trove of art acquired by the Vatican.

You'll climb a magnificent spiral ramp to get to the ticket windows. After you're admitted, you can choose your route through the museum from **four color-coded itineraries** (A, B, C, D) according to the time you have (1½–5 hr.) and your interests. Choose from the picture gallery, which houses paintings and tapestries from the 11th to the 19th century, the Egyptian collection, the Etruscan museum, Greek and Roman sculpture, and several other museums. Don't miss the Stanze di Raphael, rooms decorated by Raphael when he was a young man. You determine your choice by consulting panels on the wall and then following the letter/color of your choice. All four itineraries culminate in the **Sistine Chapel.**

Michelangelo labored for 4 years (1508–12) over this epic project, which was so physically taxing that it permanently damaged his eyesight. Glorifying the human body as only a sculptor could, Michelangelo painted nine panels, taken from the pages of Genesis, and surrounded them with prophets and sibyls. The restoration of the Sistine Chapel in the 1990s touched off a worldwide debate among art historians. The chapel was on the verge of collapse, from both its age and the weather, and restoration took years, as restorers used advanced computer analyses in their painstaking and controversial work.

THE FORUM, THE COLOSSEUM & THE HIGHLIGHTS OF ANCIENT ROME

Foro Romano (Roman Forum), Palatino (Palatine Hill), and Museo Palatino (Palatine Museum) ★★★ The Forum was built in the marshy land between the Palatine and Capitoline hills, and flourished as the center of Roman life in the days of the republic, before it gradually lost prestige to the Imperial Forums. By day, the columns of now-vanished temples and the stones from which long-forgotten orators spoke are mere shells. But at night, when the Forum is silent in the moonlight, it isn't difficult to imagine Vestal Virgins still guarding the sacred temple fire.

If you want the stones to have some meaning, buy a detailed plan at the gate (the temples are hard to locate otherwise). The best of the ruins include the three Corinthian columns of the **Temple of the Dioscuri ★★★**, dedicated to the Gemini twins, Castor and Pollux. Forming one of the most celebrated sights of the Roman Forum, a trio of columns supports an architrave fragment. The founding of this temple dates from the 5th century B.C. The partially reconstructed **House of the Vestal Virgins ★★** (3rd–4th c. A.D.) was the home of the consecrated young women who tended the sacred flame in the Temple of Vesta. The overgrown rectangle of their gardens has lilied goldfish ponds and is lined with broken, heavily worn statues of senior Vestals on pedestals.

A long walk from the Roman Forum to the **Palatine Hill ★** (with the same hours as the Forum). The Palatine, tradition tells us, was the spot on which the first settlers built their huts under the direction of Romulus. In later years, the hill became a patrician residential district that attracted such citizens as Cicero. It's worth the climb for the panoramic view of both the Roman and the Imperial Forums, as well as the Capitoline Hill and the Colosseum.

The **Museo Palatino (Palatine Museum) ★** displays a good collection of Roman sculpture from the digs in the Palatine villas. In summer you can take guided tours in English daily at 11am, 11:45am, and 4:15pm for 4€; call in winter to see if they're still available. If you ask the custodian, he might take you to one of the nearby locked villas and let you in for a peek at surviving frescoes and stuccoes. The same ticket for the Palatine Hill and the Palatine Museum includes the visit to the Colosseum.

Largo Romolo e Remo. ✆ **06-39967700.** Forum free admission; Palatine Hill 9€. Oct 30–Dec and Jan 2–Feb 15 daily 8:30am–4:30pm; Feb 16–Mar 15 daily 8:30am–5pm; Mar 16–24 daily 8:30am–5:30pm; Mar 25–Aug daily 8:30am–7:15pm; Sept daily 8:30am–7pm; Oct 1–29 daily 8:30am–6:30pm. Last admission 1 hr. before closing. Guided tours are given daily at 11am, lasting 1 hr., costing 4€. Closed holidays. Metro: Colosseo. Bus: 75 or 84.

Colosseo (Colosseum) ★★★ Now a mere shell, the Colosseum still remains the greatest architectural legacy from ancient Rome. It was inaugurated by Titus in A.D. 80 with a bloody combat, lasting many weeks, between gladiators and wild beasts. At its peak, under the cruel Domitian, the Colosseum could seat 50,000. The Vestal Virgins from the temple screamed for blood, as exotic animals were shipped in from the far corners of the empire to satisfy jaded tastes (lion vs. bear, two humans vs. hippopotamus). Many historians now believe that one of the most enduring legends about the Colosseum—that Christians were fed to the lions—is unfounded.

Piazzale del Colosseo, Via dei Fori Imperiali. ✆ **06-39967700.** Admission 9€ all levels. Nov–Feb 15 daily 8:30am–4:30pm; Feb 16–Mar 15 daily 8:30am–5pm; Mar 16–27 daily 8:30am–5:30pm; Mar 28–Aug daily 8:30am–7:15pm; Sept daily 9am–7pm; Oct daily 8:30am–7pm. Guided tours in English Nov 1–Mar 15 daily at 9:45, 10:15, 11:15, and 11:45am, and 12:30, 1:45, and 3pm; Mar–Oct daily at 9:45, 10:15, 11:15, and 11:45am, and 12:30, 1:45, 3, 4:15, 4:45, 5:15, and 5:45pm. Tours 4€. Admission to Colosseo includes visits to Palatine Hill.

Museo Capitolino (Capitoline Museum) and Palazzo dei Conservatori ★★ Of Rome's seven hills, the **Campidoglio (Capitoline)** is the most sacred: Its origins stretch from antiquity, and an Etruscan temple to Jupiter once stood on this spot. The approach is dramatic as you climb the long, sloping steps by Michelangelo. At the top is a perfectly proportioned square, **Piazza del Campidoglio ★★**, also laid out by the Florentine artist.

One side of the piazza is open; the others are bounded by the **Senatorium (Town Council),** the statuary-filled **Palace of the Conservatori (Curators),** and the **Capitoline Museum.** These museums house some of the greatest pieces of classical sculpture in the world.

The **Capitoline Museum,** built in the 17th century, was based on an architectural sketch by Michelangelo. In the first room is ***The Dying Gaul*** **★★**, a work of majestic skill that's a copy of a Greek original dating from the 3rd century B.C. In a special gallery all her own is the ***Capitoline Venus*** **★★**, who demurely covers herself. This statue was the symbol of feminine beauty and charm down through the centuries (it's a Roman copy of a 3rd-c.-B.C. Greek original). The **equestrian statue of Marcus Aurelius ★★**, whose years in the piazza made it a victim of pollution, has been restored and is now kept in the museum for protection. This is the only such equestrian statue to have survived from ancient Rome, mainly because it was thought for centuries that the statue was that of Constantine the Great, and papal Rome respected the memory of the first Christian emperor.

Palace of the Conservatori ★★, across the way, was also based on a Michelangelo architectural plan and is rich in classical sculpture and paintings. One of the most notable bronzes, a Greek work of incomparable beauty dating from the 1st century B.C., is ***Lo Spinario*** **★★★** (a little boy picking a thorn from his foot). In addition, you'll find ***Capitoline Wolf (Lupa Capitolina)*** **★★★**, a rare Etruscan bronze that may date from the 5th century B.C. (Romulus and Remus, the legendary twins who were suckled by the wolf, were added at a later date.)

Piazza del Campidoglio 1. ✆ **06-82059127.** www.museicapitolini.org. Admission 6.50€. Tues–Sun 9am–8pm. Bus: 44, 81, 95, 160, 170, 715, or 780.

Castel Sant'Angelo ★ This overpowering castle on the Tiber was built in the 2nd century as a tomb for Emperor Hadrian; it continued as an imperial mausoleum until the time of Caracalla. If it looks like a fortress, it should—that was its function in the Middle Ages. In the 14th century, it became a papal residence. But its legend

The Colosseum, the Forum & Ancient Rome Attractions

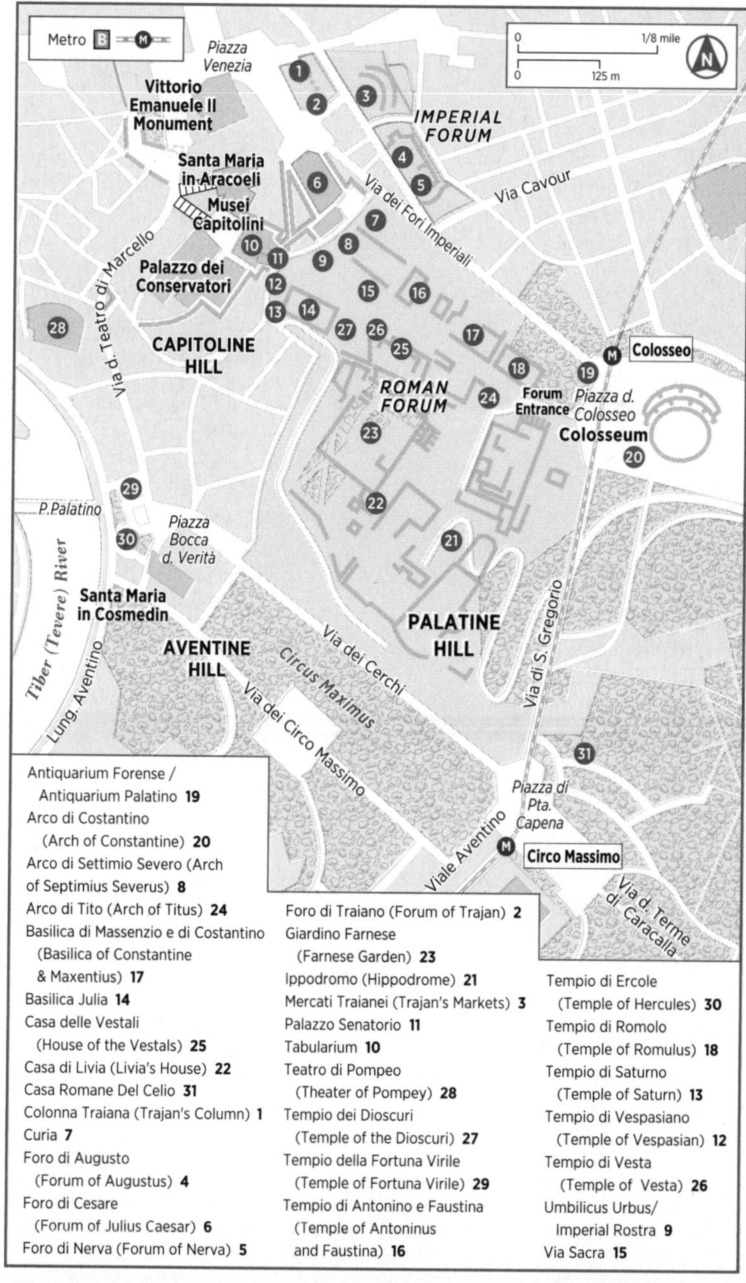

Antiquarium Forense / Antiquarium Palatino **19**
Arco di Costantino (Arch of Constantine) **20**
Arco di Settimio Severo (Arch of Septimius Severus) **8**
Arco di Tito (Arch of Titus) **24**
Basilica di Massenzio e di Costantino (Basilica of Constantine & Maxentius) **17**
Basilica Julia **14**
Casa delle Vestali (House of the Vestals) **25**
Casa di Livia (Livia's House) **22**
Casa Romane Del Celio **31**
Colonna Traiana (Trajan's Column) **1**
Curia **7**
Foro di Augusto (Forum of Augustus) **4**
Foro di Cesare (Forum of Julius Caesar) **6**
Foro di Nerva (Forum of Nerva) **5**
Foro di Traiano (Forum of Trajan) **2**
Giardino Farnese (Farnese Garden) **23**
Ippodromo (Hippodrome) **21**
Mercati Traianei (Trajan's Markets) **3**
Palazzo Senatorio **11**
Tabularium **10**
Teatro di Pompeo (Theater of Pompey) **28**
Tempio dei Dioscuri (Temple of the Dioscuri) **27**
Tempio della Fortuna Virile (Temple of Fortuna Virile) **29**
Tempio di Antonino e Faustina (Temple of Antoninus and Faustina) **16**
Tempio di Ercole (Temple of Hercules) **30**
Tempio di Romolo (Temple of Romulus) **18**
Tempio di Saturno (Temple of Saturn) **13**
Tempio di Vespasiano (Temple of Vespasian) **12**
Tempio di Vesta (Temple of Vesta) **26**
Umbilicus Urbus/ Imperial Rostra **9**
Via Sacra **15**

rests largely on its link with Pope Alexander VI, whose mistress bore him two children (those darlings of debauchery, Cesare and Lucrezia Borgia). Today the highlight here is a trip through the Renaissance apartments with their coffered ceilings and lush decoration. Their walls have witnessed some of the most diabolical plots and intrigues of the High Renaissance.

Lungotevere Castello 50. ✆ **06-39967600.** www.castelsantangelo.com. Admission 5€. Tues–Sun 9am–7pm. Metro: Ottaviano, then a long stroll. Bus: 23, 40, 46, 49, 62, 80, 87, 280, 492, or 910.

The Pantheon ★★★ Of all ancient Rome's great buildings, only the Pantheon ("All the Gods") remains intact. It was built in 27 B.C. by Marcus Agrippa and was reconstructed by Hadrian in the early 2nd century A.D. This remarkable building, 43m (142 ft.) wide and 43m (142 ft.) high (a perfect sphere resting in a cylinder) and once ringed with white marble statues of Roman gods in its niches, is among the architectural wonders of the world because of its dome and its concept of space. Hadrian himself is credited with the basic plan, an architectural design that was unique for the time. The once-gilded dome is merely show. A real dome, a perfect, massive hemisphere of cast concrete, is supported by a solid ring wall. Before the 20th century, the dome was the biggest pile of concrete ever constructed. The ribbed dome outside is a series of almost weightless cantilevered bricks. Animals were sacrificed and burned in the center, and the smoke escaped through the only means of light, the oculus, an opening at the top 5.5m (18 ft.) in diameter.

Michelangelo came here to study the dome before designing the cupola of St. Peter's (whose dome is .5m/2 ft. smaller than the Pantheon's).

Piazza della Rotonda. ✆ **06-68300230.** Free admission. Mon–Sat 9am–7:30pm; Sun 9am–1pm. Bus: 30, 40, 62, 64, 81, or 492 to Largo di Torre.

THE APPIAN WAY & THE CATACOMBS

Of all the roads that led to Rome, **Via Appia Antica** (built in 312 B.C.) was the most famous. It eventually stretched all the way from Rome to the seaport of Brindisi, through which trade with the colonies in Greece and the East was funneled. Along the Appian Way the patrician Romans built great monuments while early Christians buried their dead in the catacombs beneath. Of the catacombs open to the public, those of St. Callixtus and St. Domitilla are best.

Catacombe di San Callisto (Catacombs of St. Callixtus) ★★ "The most venerable and most renowned of Rome," said Pope John XXIII of these funerary tunnels. The founder of Christian archaeology, Giovanni Battista de Rossi (1822–94), called them "catacombs par excellence." These Catacombs are often packed with tour-bus groups, and they have perhaps the cheesiest tour, but the tunnels are simply phenomenal. They're the first cemetery of the Christian community of Rome, burial place of 16 popes in the 3rd century. The complex is a network of galleries stretching for nearly 19km (12 miles), structured in five levels and reaching a depth of about 20m (65 ft.). Paintings, sculptures, and epigraphs (with symbols such as the fish, anchor, and dove) provide invaluable material for the study of the life and customs of the ancient Christians and the story of their persecutions.

Via Appia Antica 110–126. ✆ **06-5130151.** Admission 8€ adults, 5€ children 6–15, free for children 5 and under. Thurs–Tues 9am–noon and 2–5pm. Bus: 118.

Catacombe di San Domitilla (Catacombs of St. Domitilla) ★★★ This oldest of the Catacombs is the hands-down winner for most enjoyable Catacomb experience. Groups are small, most guides are genuinely entertaining and personable, and, depending on the mood of the group and your guide, the visit may last anywhere from 20 minutes to over an hour. You enter through a sunken 4th-century church. There are fewer "sights" than in the other Catacombs—although the 2nd-century fresco of the Last Supper is impressive—but some of the guides actually hand you a few bones out of a tomb niche. (Incidentally, this is the only catacomb where you'll still see bones; the rest have emptied their tombs to rebury the remains in ossuaries on the inaccessible lower levels.)

Via d. Sette Chiese 280. ✆ **06-5110342.** Admission 5€ adults, 3€ children 6–14. Wed–Mon 9am–noon and 2–5pm. Closed Jan.

MORE ATTRACTIONS

Basilica di San Clemente ★ From the Colosseum, head up Via San Giovanni in Laterano to this basilica. It isn't just another Roman church—far from it. In this church-upon-a-church, centuries of history peel away. In the 4th century A.D., a church was built over a secular house from the 1st century, beside which stood a pagan temple dedicated to Mithras (god of the sun). The Normans destroyed the lower church, and a new one was built in the 12th century. In the eerie grottoes (which you can explore on your own), you'll discover well-preserved frescoes from the 9th to the 11th century.

Via San Giovanni in Laterano at Piazza San Clemente. ✆ **06-7740021.** www.basilicasanclemente.com. Basilica free admission; excavations 5€. Mon–Sat 9am–12:30pm and 3–6pm; Sun noon–6pm. Metro: Colosseo. Bus: 85, 87, or 850.

Basilica di San Giovanni in Laterano ★ This church (not St. Peter's) is the cathedral of the diocese of Rome, where the pope comes to celebrate Mass on certain holidays. Built in A.D. 314 by Constantine, it has suffered the vicissitudes of Rome, forcing it to be rebuilt many times. The present building is characterized by its 18th-century facade by Alessandro Galilei (statues of Christ and the Apostles ring the top). A 1993 terrorist bomb caused severe damage, especially to the facade.

Across the street is the **Santuario della Scala Santa (Palace of the Holy Steps),** Piazza San Giovanni in Laterano (✆ **06-7726641**). Allegedly, the 28 marble steps here (now covered with wood for preservation) were originally at Pontius Pilate's villa in Jerusalem, and Christ climbed them the day he was brought before Pilate. Today pilgrims from all over come here to climb the steps on their knees.

Piazza San Giovanni in Laterano 4. ✆ **06-69886452.** Basilica free admission; cloisters 2€. Summer daily 9am–6:45pm (off season to 6pm). Metro: San Giovanni. Bus: 16, 81, 85, 87, 186, 218, or 650.

Basilica di Santa Maria Maggiore ★ This great church, one of Rome's four major basilicas, was built by Pope Liberius in A.D. 358 and rebuilt by Pope Sixtus III from 432 to 440. Its 14th-century **campanile** is the city's loftiest. The basilica is noted for the 5th-century Roman mosaics in its nave, and for its coffered ceiling, said to have been gilded with gold brought from the New World. In the 16th century, Domenico Fontana built a now-restored "Sistine Chapel." The church also contains the **tomb of Bernini,** Italy's most important baroque sculptor and architect.

Piazza di Santa Maria Maggiore. ✆ **06-4465836.** Free admission. Daily 7am–7pm. Metro: Termini.

Fontana di Trevi (Trevi Fountain) ★★ As you elbow your way through the summertime crowds around the Trevi Fountain, you'll find it hard to believe that this little piazza was nearly always deserted before the 1954 film *Three Coins in the Fountain* brought renewed interest to this lovely spot. Supplied by water from the Acqua

Vergine aqueduct and a triumph of the baroque style, it was based on the design of Nicola Salvi (who's said to have died of illness contracted during his supervision of the project) and was completed in 1762. The design centers on the triumphant figure of Neptunus Rex, standing on a shell chariot drawn by winged steeds and led by a pair of tritons.

Galleria Borghese ★★★ This legendary art gallery includes such masterpieces as Bernini's *Apollo and Daphne,* Titian's *Sacred and Profane Love,* Raphael's *Deposition,* and Caravaggio's *Jerome.* One of the most popular pieces of sculpture in the gallery is Canova's sculpture of Pauline as *Venus Victorious.* ***Important information:*** No more than 360 visitors at a time are allowed on the ground floor, and no more than 90 are allowed on the upper floor. Reservations are essential, so call ✆ **06-32810** (Mon–Fri 9am–6pm; Sat 9am–1pm). However, the number always seems to be busy. If you'll be in Rome for a few days, try stopping by in person on your first day to reserve tickets for a later day. Better yet, before you leave home, contact **Select Italy** (✆ **800/877-1755;** www.selectitaly.com).

Piazza Scipione Borghese 5 (off Via Pinciano). ✆ **06-32810.** www.galleriaborghese.it. Admission 8.50€. Tues–Sun 9am–7pm. Bus: 5, 19, 52, 116, 204, 490, or 910.

Galleria Nazionale d'Arte Antica (National Gallery of Ancient Art) ★★ **Palazzo Barberini,** right off Piazza Barberini, is one of the most magnificent baroque palaces in Rome. It was begun by Carlo Maderno in 1627 and completed in 1633 by Bernini, whose lavishly decorated rococo apartments, the **Galleria d'Arte Decorativa (Gallery of Decorative Art),** are on view. This gallery is part of the **National Gallery of Ancient Art.** The splendid array of paintings from the 13th to the 16th century includes works by Simone Martini, Filippo Lippi, Andrea Solario, Francesco Francia, Il Sodoma, and Raphael. Many visitors come just to see the magnificent Caravaggios, including *Narcissus.*

Via delle Quattro Fontane 13. ✆ **06-4824184.** Admission 6€. Tues–Sun 8:30am–6:30pm. Metro: Barberini.

Museo Nazionale di Villa Giulia (National Etruscan Museum) ★★★ This 16th-century papal palace shelters a priceless collection of art and artifacts from the mysterious Etruscans, who predated the Romans. If you have time for only the masterpieces, head for room 7, with a remarkable 6th-century-B.C. *Apollo from Veio* (clothed, for a change). The other two widely acclaimed statues here are *Dea con Bambino (Goddess with a Baby)* and a greatly mutilated but still powerful *Hercules* with a stag. In room no. 8, you'll see the lions' sarcophagus from the mid–6th century B.C., which was excavated at Cerveteri, north of Rome. Finally, in room no. 9 is one of the world's most important Etruscan art treasures, a bride-and-bridegroom coffin from the 6th century B.C.

Piazzale di Villa Giulia 9. ✆ **06-3226571.** Admission 4€. Tues–Sun 8:30am–7:30pm. Metro: Flaminio.

Palazzo del Quirinale ★★ Despite its Renaissance origins (nearly every important architect in Italy worked on some aspect of its sprawling premises), this *palazzo* is rich in associations with ancient emperors and deities. The colossal statues of the Dioscuri Castor and Pollux, which now form part of the fountain in the piazza, were found in the nearby great Baths of Constantine; in 1793 Pius VI had the ancient Egyptian obelisk moved here from the Mausoleum of Augustus. The sweeping view of Rome from the piazza, which crowns the highest of the seven ancient hills of Rome, is itself worth the trip. This palace houses the president of the republic.

Piazza del Quirinale. No phone for visitor information. www.quirinale.it. 5€ admission. Sun 8:30am–noon. Closed late June to early Sept. Metro: Barberini.

Piazza Navona ★★★ One of the most beautifully baroque sites in all Rome, this ocher-colored gem is unspoiled by new buildings or traffic. Its shape results from the ruins of the Stadium of Domitian that lie beneath it. Chariot races were once held here, and in medieval times, the popes used to flood the piazza to stage mock naval encounters. Today the piazza is packed with vendors and street performers, and lined with pricey cafes where you can enjoy a cappuccino or gelato and indulge in unparalleled people-watching.

Besides the twin-towered facade of 17th-century Santa Agnes, the piazza boasts several baroque masterpieces. The best known, in the center, is Bernini's **Fontana dei Quattro Fiumi (Fountain of the Four Rivers) ★★★**, whose four stone personifications symbolize the world's greatest rivers: the Ganges, Danube, della Plata, and Nile. (***Hint:*** The figure with the shroud on its head is the Nile, so represented because the river's source was unknown at the time.)

The Spanish Steps ★★ Alive with azaleas and other flowers in spring, and bustling with flower vendors, jewelry dealers, and photographers snapping pictures of visitors year-round, the steps and the square (Piazza di Spagna) take their names from the Spanish Embassy, which used to be headquartered here. Designed by Italian architect Francesco de Sanctis and built from 1723 to 1725, they were funded almost entirely by the French as a preface to Trinità dei Monti at the top.

Piazza di Spagna. Metro: Spagna.

MUSEO NAZIONALE ROMANO

This museum is divided into four sections: Palazzo Massimo alle Terme; the Terme di Diocleziano (Diocletian Baths); the annex Octagonal Hall; and Palazzo Altemps.

Palazzo Altemps ★ This branch of the National Roman Museum is housed in a 15th-century palace that was restored and opened to the public in 1997. It is home to the fabled Ludovisi Collection of Greek and Roman sculpture. Among the masterpieces of the Roman Renaissance, you'll find the *Ares Ludovisi,* a Roman copy of the original dated 330 B.C. and restored by Bernini during the 17th century. In the Sala delle Storie di Mosè is *Ludovisi's Throne,* representing the birth of Venus. The Sala delle Feste (the Celebrations' Hall) is dominated by a sarcophagus depicting the Romans fighting against the Ostrogoth barbarians.

Piazza San Apollinare 48, near the Piazza Navona. ✆ **06-39967700.** Admission 10€. Tues–Sun 9am–7:45pm. Last admission 1 hr. before closing. Bus: 70, 81, 87, or 116.

Palazzo Massimo alle Terme ★ If you ever wanted to know what all those emperors from your history books looked like, this museum will make them live again, togas and all. In the central hall are works representing the political and social life of Rome at the time of Augustus. Other works include an altar from Ostia Antica, the ancient port of Rome, plus a statue of a wounded Niobid from 440 B.C. that is a masterwork of expression and character. Upstairs, stand in awe at all the traditional art from the 1st century B.C. to the Imperial Age. The most celebrated mosaic is of the *Four Charioteers.* In the basement are a rare numismatic collection and an extensive collection of Roman jewelry.

Largo di Villa Peretti 67. ✆ **06-39967700.** Admission 7€. Tues–Sun 9am–7:45pm. Last admission 1 hr. before closing. Admission includes entrance to Terme di Diocleziano (see below). Metro: Termini.

Terme di Diocleziano (Diocletian Baths) and Aula Ottagona (Octagonal Hall) ★ This museum occupies part of the 3rd-century-A.D. Baths of Diocletian and part of a convent that may have been designed by Michelangelo. The Diocletian Baths were the biggest thermal baths in the world. Nowadays they host a marvelous collection of funereal artworks, such as sarcophagi, and decorations dating from the Aurelian period. The **Octagonal Hall** occupies the southwest corner of the central building of the Diocletian Baths. Here you can see the *Lyceum Apollo*. Also worthy of a note is the *Aphrodite of Cyrene,* a copy dating from the second half of the 2nd century A.D. and discovered in Cyrene, Libya.

Viale E. di Nicola 79. ✆ **06-39967700.** Admission to the Baths 7€; Octagonal Hall free admission. Baths Tues–Sun 9am–7:45pm. Aula Ottagona Tues–Sat 9am–2pm; Sun 9am–1pm. Last admission 1 hr. before closing. Metro: Termini.

ORGANIZED TOURS

One of the leading tour operators is **American Express,** Piazza di Spagna 38 (✆ **06-67641;** Metro: Spagna). One popular tour is a 4-hour orientation to Rome and the Vatican, which departs most mornings at 9:30am or afternoons at 2:20pm and costs 70€ per person. Another 4-hour tour, which focuses on the Rome of antiquity (including visits to the Colosseum, the Roman Forum, the ruins of the Imperial Palace, and St. Peter in Chains), costs 70€. From April to October, a popular excursion outside Rome is a 5-hour bus tour to Tivoli, where tours are conducted of the Villa d'Este and its spectacular gardens and the ruins of the Villa Adriana, all for 60€ per person. The American Express Travel Office is open Monday to Friday 9am to 5:30pm and Saturday 9am to 12:30pm.

Context Rome, Via Baccina (✆ **888/467-1986** in the U.S., or 06-97625204; www.contexttravel.com), is a collaborative of scholars. Guides offer small-group tours, including visits to monuments, museums, and historic piazzas, as well as to neighborhood trattorie. Custom-designed tours are also available. Prices of the regular tours begin at 30€. There is also a special kids' program, including treasure hunts and other experiences that feature visits to museums of appeal to the younger set.

The Shopping Scene

The posh sopping streets **Via Borgognona** and **Via Condotti** begin near Piazza di Spagna, and both the rents and the merchandise are chic and ultraexpensive. **Via Frattina** runs parallel to Via Condotti, its more famous sibling. Not attempting the stratospheric image or prices of Via Condotti or Via Borgognona, **Via del Corso** boasts styles aimed at younger consumers. Some gems are scattered amid the shops selling jeans and sporting equipment. The most interesting are nearest the cafes of Piazza del Popolo.

Beginning at the top of the Spanish Steps, **Via Sistina** runs to Piazza Barberini. The shops are small, stylish, and based on the tastes of their owners. The pedestrian traffic is less dense than on other major streets. Most shoppers reach **Via Francesco Crispi** by following Via Sistina 1 long block from the top of the Spanish Steps. Near the intersection of these streets are several shops well suited for unusual and less expensive gifts. **Via Veneto** is filled these days with expensive hotels and cafes and an array of relatively expensive stores selling shoes, gloves, and leather goods.

Traffic-clogged **Via Nazionale** begins at Piazza della Repubblica and runs down almost to the 19th-century monuments of Piazza Venezia. You'll find an abundance of leather stores (more reasonable in price than those in many other parts of Rome) and a welcome handful of stylish boutiques.

Rome After Dark

Few evening occupations are quite as pleasurable as a stroll past the solemn pillars of old temples or the cascading torrents of Renaissance fountains glowing under the blue-black sky. The Fontana delle Naiadi (Fountain of the Naiads) on Piazza della Repubblica, the Fontana della Tartarughe (Fountain of the Tortoises) on Piazza Mattei, and the Trevi Fountain are particularly beautiful at night. The Campidoglio (Capitoline Hill) is magnificently lit after dark, with its measured Renaissance facades glowing like jewel boxes. The view of the Roman Forum seen from the rear of the trapezoidal Piazza del Campidoglio is the grandest in Rome, more so than even the Colosseum. Bus no. 84, 85, 87, 117, 175, 186, 271, 571, or 850 takes you here at night, or you can ask for a taxi. If you're across the Tiber, Piazza San Pietro (in front of St. Peter's) is impressive at night without the tour buses and crowds. And a combination of illuminated architecture, Renaissance fountains, and sidewalk shows and art expos enlivens Piazza Navona.

Even if you don't speak Italian, you can generally follow the listings of special events and evening entertainment featured in ***La Repubblica,*** a leading Italian newspaper. ***Wanted in Rome*** has listings of jazz, rock, and such and gives an interesting look at expatriate Rome. And ***Un Ospite a Roma,*** available free from the concierge desks of top hotels, is full of details on what's happening.

THE PERFORMING ARTS

If you're in the capital for the opera season, usually from late December to June, you might want to attend the historic **Teatro dell'Opera,** Piazza Beniamino Gigli 1, off Via Nazionale (✆ **06-481601;** www.operaroma.it; Metro: Repubblica). Nothing is presented in July and August; in summer, the venue usually switches elsewhere. Call ahead or ask your concierge before you go. Tickets are 11€ to 130€.

NIGHTCLUBS

Unless you're dead set on making the Roman nightclub circuit, try what might be a far livelier and less expensive scene—sitting late at night on **Via Veneto, Piazza della Rotonda, Piazza del Popolo,** or one of Rome's other piazzas, all for the cost of an espresso, a cappuccino, or a Campari.

In a high-tech, futuristic setting, **Alien,** Via Velletri 13–19 (✆ **06-8412212;** www.aliendisco.eu; bus: 38, 63, 80, or 92), provides a bizarre space-age dance floor, bathed in strobe lights and rocking to the sounds of house/techno music. The crowd is young. It's open Tuesday through Sunday from 11pm to 5am, with a cover of 16€ to 18€ that includes the first drink. It is closed from mid-June to early September.

Piper, Via Tagliamento 9 (✆ **06-8555398;** www.piperclub.it; bus: 63), opened in 1965 in a former cinema and became the first modern disco of its kind in Italy. Many dances such as "the shake" were first introduced to Italy at this club. No longer what it was in those *La Dolce Vita* years, the Piper is still going strong. Today it lures with fashion shows, screenings, some of the hottest parties in town, and various gigs, drawing a casual and mixed-age crowd. The pickup scene here is hot and heavy. The kind of music you'll hear depends on the night. It's open Monday to Saturday 11pm to 4am, charging a cover of 20€ to 26€, including one drink.

Gilda, Via Mario de' Fiori 97 (✆ **06-6797396;** Metro: Spagna), is an adventurous nightclub/disco/restaurant that attracts a post-35 set, most often couples. In the past, it has hosted Diana Ross and splashy Paris-type revues. Expect first-class shows, and disco music played between the live acts. The disco (midnight–4am) presents music of the 1960s plus more current tunes. The attractive piano bar, Swing, features Italian and Latin music. The cover is 30€ and includes the first drink. It's closed on Monday.

Don't be put off by the facade of **Locanda Atlantide,** Via dei Lucani 22B (✆ **06-44704540;** www.locandatlantide.it; Metro: Piazza Vittorio; bus: 71 or 492), thinking that you've arrived at a bunker for a Gestapo interrogation. This former warehouse in San Lorenzo is the setting of a nightclub, bar, concert hall, and theater. Every day there's something different—perhaps jazz on Tuesday, a play on Wednesday, or a concert on Thursday, giving way to dance-club action on Friday and Saturday with DJ music. The cover ranges from 3€ to 15€, depending on the evening; hours are Tuesday to Sunday from 8pm to 2am. It's closed June 15 to September 15.

L'Alibi, Via Monte Testaccio 44 (✆ **06-5743448;** www.lalibi.it; bus: 95), in Testaccio, is a year-round stop on many gay men's agendas. The crowd, however, tends to be mixed, both Roman and international, straight and gay, male and female. One room is devoted to dancing. It's open Wednesday through Sunday from 11pm to 4am, and the cover is 10€ to 15€.

Side Trips from Rome

TIVOLI

Tivoli, known as Tibur to the ancient Romans, was the playground of the emperors. Today its reputation continues unabated: It's the most popular half-day jaunt from Rome.

While the Villa d'Este ★★, a dank Renaissance structure with second-rate paintings, is not that noteworthy; its **spectacular gardens**—designed by Pirro Ligorio—dim the luster of Versailles. Visitors descend the cypress-studded slope to the bottom; on the way you're rewarded with everything from lilies to gargoyles spouting water, torrential streams, and waterfalls. The loveliest fountain is the Fontana dell Ovato (Ovato Fountain), by Ligorio. But nearby is the most spectacular achievement: the **Fontana dell'Organo Idraulico (Fountain of the Hydraulic Organ),** dazzling with its water jets in front of a baroque chapel, with four maidens who look tipsy. The best walk is along the promenade, with 100 spraying fountains. The garden is worth hours of exploration, but it's a lot of walking, with some steep climbs. Admission is 6.50€. The villa is open Tuesday to Sunday from 8:30am to 1 hour before sunset.

The Villa d'Este dazzles with artificial glamour, but the **Villa Gregoriana** relies more on nature. The gardens were built by Pope Gregory XVI in the 19th century. At one point on the circuitous walk carved along a slope, you can stand and look out onto the most panoramic waterfall (Aniene) at Tivoli. The trek to the bottom on the banks of the Anio is studded with grottoes and balconies that open onto the chasm. The only problem is that if you do make the full descent, you might need a helicopter to pull you up again (the climb back up is fierce). From one of the belvederes, there's a panoramic view of the Temple of Vesta on the hill. Following a $5.5-million restoration, the property has been much improved, and hikers can now explore the on-site grottoes. However, wear rubber-heeled shoes, and remember to duck your head. Admission is 5€. It's open April 1 to October 15 Tuesday to Sunday 10am to 6:30pm;

Rome & Environs

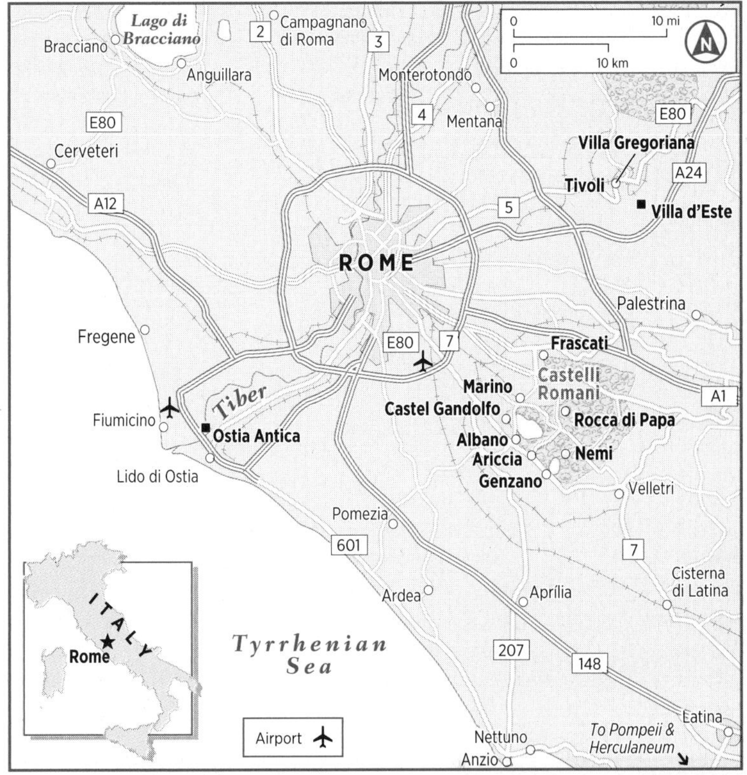

March and October 16 to November 30, Tuesday to Saturday 10am to 2:30pm, and Sunday 10am to 4pm.

Of all the Roman emperors dedicated to *la dolce vita,* the globe-trotting Hadrian spent the last 3 years of his life in the grandest style. Less than 6km (3¾ miles) from Tivoli, he built one of the greatest estates ever erected—**Villa Adriana (Hadrian's Villa) ★★★**, Via di Villa Adriana (✆ **0774-530203;** www.villa-adriana.net)—and he filled acre after acre with some of the architectural wonders he'd seen on his many travels. Hadrian directed the staggering feat of building much more than a villa: It was a self-contained world for a vast royal entourage and the hundreds of servants and guards they required to protect them, feed them, bathe them, and satisfy their libidos. Hadrian erected theaters, baths, temples, fountains, gardens, and canals bordered with statuary throughout his estate. He filled the palaces and temples with sculpture, some of which now rests in the museums of Rome. In later centuries, barbarians, popes, and cardinals, as well as anyone who needed a slab of marble, carted off much that made the villa so spectacular. But enough of the fragmented ruins remain for us to piece together the story. For a glimpse of what the villa used to be, see the plastic reconstruction at the entrance.

GETTING THERE Tivoli is 32km (20 miles) east of Rome on Via Tiburtina, about an hour's drive with traffic. If you don't have a car, take Metro Line B to the end of the line, the Rebibbia station. After exiting the station, board a COTRAL bus for the trip the rest of the way to Tivoli. Buses depart about every 20 minutes during the day.

OSTIA ANTICA'S RUINS ★★

Ostia Antica is one of the area's major attractions, particularly interesting to those who can't make it to Pompeii. At the mouth of the Tiber, Ostia was the port of ancient Rome, serving as the gateway for all the riches from the far corners of the empire. It was founded in the 4th century B.C. and flourished for about 8 centuries before it began to wither away.

A papal-sponsored commission launched a series of digs in the 19th century; however, the major work of unearthing was carried out under Mussolini's orders from 1938 to 1942 (the work had to stop because of the war). The city is only partially dug out today, but it's believed that all the chief monuments have been uncovered.

These principal monuments are clearly labeled. The most important spot is **Piazzale delle Corporazioni,** an early version of Wall Street. Near the theater, this square contained nearly 75 corporations, the nature of their businesses identified by the patterns of preserved mosaics.

Enter Ostia Antica on Viale dei Romagnoli 717 (✆ **06-56352830;** www.ostia antica.net). Admission is 6.50€. It's open November to February Tuesday to Sunday 8:30am to 4pm; March Tuesday to Sunday 8:30am to 5pm; April to October Tuesday to Sunday 8:30am to 6pm.

GETTING THERE Take the Metro Line B from Stazione Termini to the Magliana stop. Change here for the Lido train to Ostia Antica, about 26km (16 miles) from Rome. Departures are about every half-hour, and the trip takes only 20 minutes. The Metro lets you off across the highway that connects Rome with the coast. It's just a short walk to the excavations.

FLORENCE ★★

With the exception of Venice, no other European city lives off its past like Florence (Firenze). After all, it was the birthplace of the Renaissance, an amazing outburst of activity from the 14th to the 16th century that completely changed this Tuscan town and the world.

Florence might seem a bit foreboding at first glance. Architecturally, it's not a Gothic fantasy of lace like Venice. Many of its *palazzi* (palaces) look like severe fortresses, a characteristic of the Medici style—they were built to keep foreign enemies at bay. But these facades, however uninviting, mask treasures within, drawing thousands of visitors who overrun the narrow streets.

The city officials have been wise to keep the inner Renaissance core relatively free of modern architecture and polluting industry.

The locals bemoan the tourist crush but welcome the business it brings. May and September are the ideal times to visit. The worst times are the week before and including Easter, and from June to the first week of September—Florence is literally overrun during these times, and the streets weren't designed for mass tourism.

Essentials

GETTING THERE

BY PLANE From Rome, you can catch a short domestic flight to **Galileo Galilei Airport** at Pisa (✆ **050-849111;** www.pisa-airport.com), 93km (58 miles) west of Florence. **Alitalia** (✆ **06-2222;** www.alitalia.it) offers four flights a day from New York to Pisa with one stop in Rome. You can take an express train for the hour-long trip to Florence. There's also a small domestic airport, **Amerigo Vespucci,** on Via del Termine, near A-11 (✆ **055-3061300;** www.aeroporto.firenze.it), 5.5km (3½ miles) northwest of Florence, a 15-minute drive. From the airport, you can reach Florence by the "Vola in Bus" airport shuttle bus service operated by ATAF, which stops at the main Santa Maria Novella rail terminal. The airport shuttle bus costs 5€ one-way.

BY TRAIN If you're coming from Rome, count on a 2- to 3-hour trip, depending on your connection. **Santa Maria Novella rail station,** in Piazza della Stazione, adjoins Piazza Santa Maria Novella. For railway information, call ✆ **892021.** Some trains stop at the **Stazione Campo di Marte,** on the eastern side of Florence. A 24-hour bus service (no. 12) runs between the two rail terminals.

BY CAR Florence enjoys good autostrada connections with the rest of Italy, especially Rome and Bologna. A1 connects Florence with both the north and the south. Florence lies 277km (172 miles) north of Rome, 105km (65 miles) west of Bologna, and 298km (185 miles) south of Milan. Bologna is about an hour's drive away, and Rome is 3 hours away. The Tyrrhenian coast is only an hour from Florence on A11 heading west.

Use a car only to get *to* Florence, not to get around once you're there. Most of central Florence is closed to all vehicles except those of locals. If your hotel doesn't have parking, head for one of the city-run garages. Although you'll find a garage under the train station, a better deal is the **Parterre** parking lot under Piazza Libertà, north of Fortezza del Basso.

VISITOR INFORMATION Contact the **Azienda per il Turismo di Firenze (Florence Tourist Board),** which has several branches, including Via A. Manzoni 16 (✆ **055-23320;** www.firenzeturismo.it), open Monday through Friday from 9am to 1pm; and Via Cavour 1R (✆ **055-290832**), open year-round Monday to Saturday 8:30am to 6:30pm and Sunday 8:30am to 1:30pm. There are also information offices maintained by the **Comune di Firenze.** One is in Borgo Santa Croce 29R just south of Piazza Santa Croce (✆ **055-2340444**), open from March to October Monday to Saturday 9am to 7pm and Sunday 9am to 2pm. From November to February it's open Monday to Saturday 9am to 5pm and Sunday 9am to 2pm. A small **Ufficio Informazioni Turistiche** (also maintained by the Comune di Firenze) is outside the main train terminal, Piazza Stazione 4A (✆ **055-212245**); it's open Monday to Saturday 8:30am to 7pm and Sunday 8:30am to 2pm.

CITY LAYOUT Florence is a city designed for walking, with all the major sights in a compact area. The ***centro storico* (historic center)** is split by the **Arno River,** which usually is serene but can at times turn ferocious with floodwaters. The major part of Florence, certainly its historic core with most of the monuments, lies on the north (right) side of the river. But the "left" side isn't devoid of attractions, including some wonderful trattorie and some great shopping finds, not to mention the Pitti Palace and the Giardini di Boboli, a series of impressive formal gardens. In addition,

Florence

ATTRACTIONS ●

Basilica di San Lorenzo **18**
Basilica di Santa Croce **36**
Basilica di Santa Maria Novella **7**
Baptistery (Battistero San Giovanni) **20**
Bargello Museum (Museo Nazionale del Bargello) **28**
Boboli Gardens (Giardini di Boboli) **1**
Cappelle Medicee (Medici Chapels) **6**
Duomo Museum (Museo dell'Opera del Duomo) **23**
Galleria dell'Accademia **15**
Giotto's Bell Tower (Campanile di Giotto) **21**
Il Duomo (Cattedrale di Santa Maria del Fiore) **22**
Instituto e Museo di Storia della Scienza **35**
Loggia dei Lanzi **34**
Medici Laurentian Library **19**
Palazzo Medici-Riccardi **17**
Palazzo Pitti **2**
Palazzo Vecchio **32**
Piazza della Signoria **31**
Piazzale Michelangiolo **38**
St. Mark's Museum (Museo di San Marco) **14**
Uffizi Gallery (Galleria degli Uffizi) **33**

ACCOMMODATIONS ■

Carolus Hotel **13**
Grand Hotel Cavour **25**
Grand Hotel Villa Medici **8**
Hotel Albion **8**
Hotel Annabella **9**
Hotel Calzaiuoli **27**
Hotel Cellai **11**
Hotel Cimabue **40**
Hotel Vosari **10**
J.K. Place **5**
In Piazza della Signoria **29**
Montebello Splendid **8**
Pensione Maria Luisa de'Medici **26**
Piccolo Hotel **12**
Relais Uffizi **30**
Residenza dei Pucci **16**
Residenza Casanuova **24**
Ritz Hotel **37**
UNA Hotel Vittoria **3**
Villa La Vedetta **39**
Westin Excelsior **4**

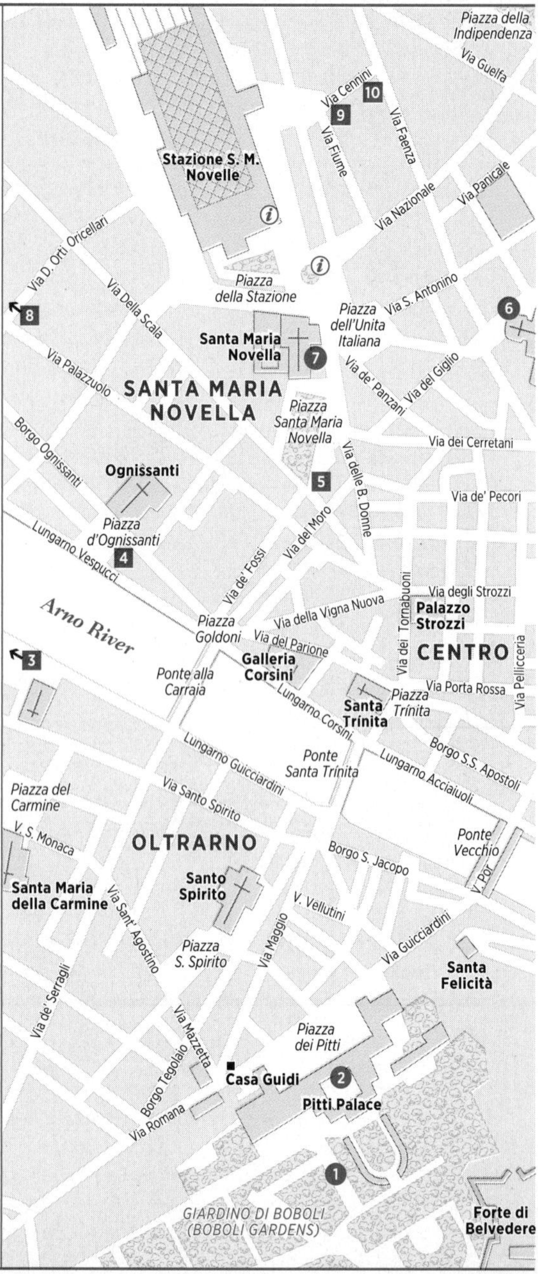

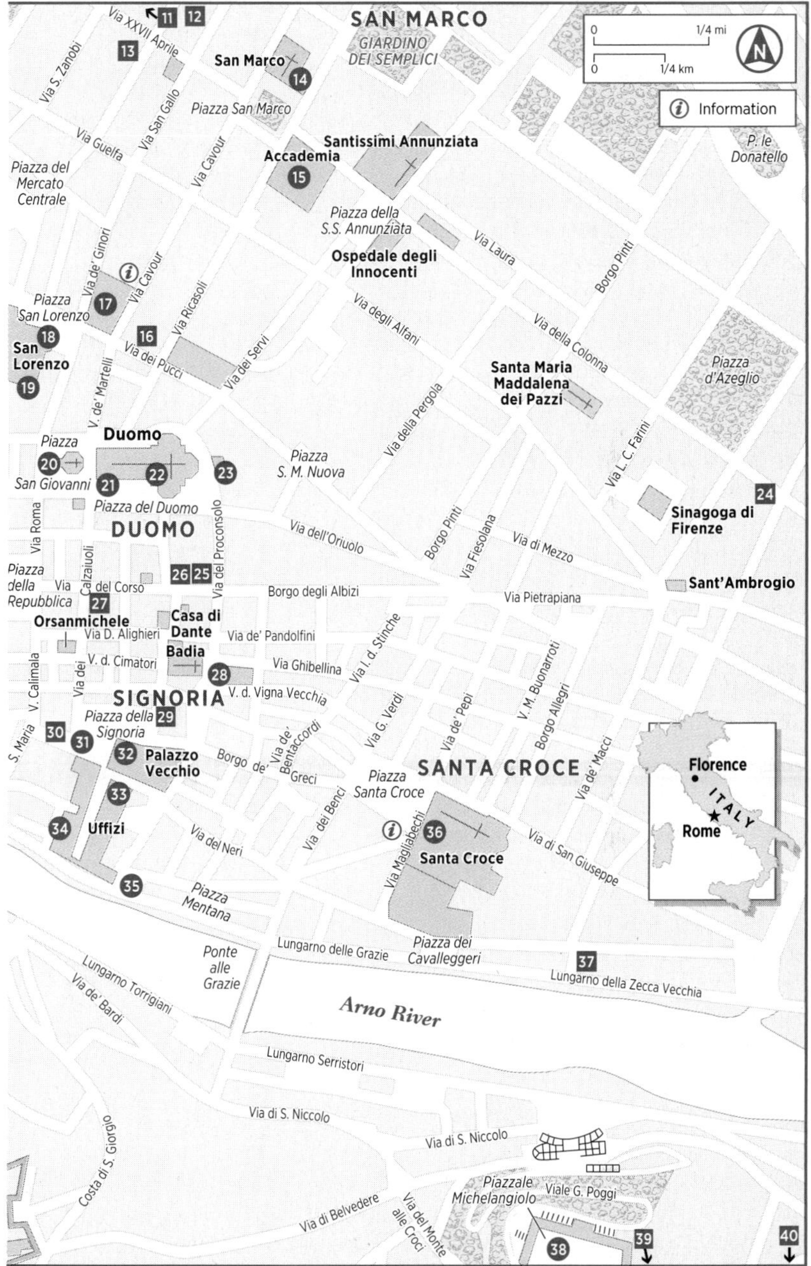
SAN MARCO
GIARDINO DEI SEMPLICI
0 1/4 mi
0 1/4 km
N
Information
Via XXVII Aprile
Via S. Zanobi
San Marco
Piazza San Marco
Via San Gallo
Via Guelfa
Via Cavour
Santissimi Annunziata
Accademia
Piazza del Mercato Centrale
Piazza della S.S. Annunziata
Via Laura
Ospedale degli Innocenti
P. le Donatello
Borgo Pinti
Via de' Ginori
Via Cavour
Piazza San Lorenzo
San Lorenzo
Via Ricasoli
Via dei Pucci
Via dei Servi
Via degli Alfani
Via della Colonna
Piazza d'Azeglio
Santa Maria Maddalena dei Pazzi
V. de' Martelli
Via della Pergola
Duomo
Piazza San Giovanni
Piazza del Duomo
Piazza S. M. Nuova
Via L. C. Farini
Sinagoga di Firenze
DUOMO
Via Roma
Via del Proconsolo
Via dell'Oriuolo
Borgo Pinti
Via Fiesolana
Via di Mezzo
Piazza della Repubblica
Via Calzaiuoli
Via del Corso
Borgo degli Albizi
Via Pietrapiana
Sant'Ambrogio
Orsanmichele
Via D. Alighieri
Casa di Dante
Via de' Pandolfini
Badia
Via Ghibellina
Via I. d. Stinche
V. d. Cimatori
V. Calimala
Via dei
SIGNORIA
V. d. Vigna Vecchia
Piazza della Signoria
V. M. Buonarroti
Borgo Allegri
Via de' Pepi
Via G. Verdi
Via de' Bentaccordi
S. Maria
Palazzo Vecchio
Borgo de' Greci
SANTA CROCE
Via de' Macci
Piazza Santa Croce
Uffizi
Via dei Benci
Santa Croce
Via Magliabechi
Via del Neri
Via di San Giuseppe
Florence
ITALY
Rome
Piazza Mentana
Piazza dei Cavalleggeri
Lungarno delle Grazie
Ponte alle Grazie
Lungarno della Zecca Vecchia
Lungarno Torrigiani
Via de' Bardi
Arno River
Lungarno Serristori
Via di S. Niccolo
Costa di S. Giorgio
Via di S. Niccolo
Piazzale Michelangiolo
Viale G. Poggi
Via di Belvedere
Via del Monte alle Croci
11 12 13 14 15 16 17 18 19 20 21 22 23 24 25 26 27 28 29 30 31 32 33 34 35 36 37 38 39 40

you'll want to cross over to check out the views of the city from Piazzale Michelangiolo—especially breathtaking at sunset.

The Arno is spanned by eight bridges, of which the **Ponte Vecchio (Old Bridge),** lined with overhanging jewelry stores, is the most celebrated and most central. Many of these bridges were ancient structures until the Nazis, in a hopeless last-ditch effort, senselessly destroyed them in their "defense" of Florence in 1944. With tenacity, Florence rebuilt its bridges, using pieces from the destroyed structures whenever possible. The **Ponte Santa Trínita** is the second-most-important bridge. It leads to **Via dei Tornabuoni,** the right bank's most important shopping street (don't look for bargains, however). At the Ponte Vecchio you can walk, again on the right bank of the Arno, along **Via per Santa Maria,** which becomes **Via Calimala.** This leads you into **Piazza della Repubblica,** a commercial district known for its cafes.

From here, you can take **Via Roma,** which leads directly into **Piazza di San Giovanni,** where you'll find the baptistery and its neighboring sibling, the larger **Piazza del Duomo,** with the world-famous cathedral and Giotto bell tower. From the far-western edge of Piazza del Duomo you can take **Via del Proconsolo** south to **Piazza della Signoria,** to see the landmark Palazzo Vecchio and its sculpture-filled Loggia della Signoria.

GETTING AROUND BY FOOT Because Florence is so compact, walking is the ideal way to get around—and, at times, the only way because of numerous pedestrian zones. In theory, at least, pedestrians have the right of way at uncontrolled zebra crossings, but don't count on that if you meet up with a speeding Vespa.

BY BUS If you plan to use public buses, buy your ticket before boarding. For 1.20€ you can ride on any public bus for a total of 90 minutes. A 24-hour ticket costs 5€. You can buy bus tickets at tabacchi (tobacconists) and newsstands. Once onboard, you must validate your ticket in the box near the rear door, or you stand to be fined 40€—no excuses accepted. The local **bus station** (which serves as the terminal for ATAF city buses) is at Piazza della Stazione (✆ **055-56501**), behind the train station.

Bus routes are posted at bus stops, but the numbers of routes can change overnight because of sudden repair work going on at one of the ancient streets—perhaps a water main broke overnight and caused flooding. We once found that a bus-route map printed only 1 week beforehand was already outdated. Therefore, if you're dependent on bus transport, you'll need to inquire that day for the exact number of the vehicle you want to board.

BY TAXI You can find taxis at stands at nearly all the major squares. The charge is .90€ per kilometer, with a 3.30€ minimum, 6.60€ between 10pm and 6am. If you need a **radio taxi,** call ✆ **055-4390** or 055-4798.

BY BICYCLE & MOTOR SCOOTER Bicycles and motor scooters, if you avoid the whizzing traffic, are two other practical ways of getting around. **Alinari,** near the rail station at Via S. Zanobi 38R (✆ **055-280500;** www.alinarirental.com), rents bikes for 2.50€ per hour, or 12€ to 18€ per day, depending on the model. Also available are small-engined, rather loud motor scooters. Rentals cost from 10€ to 15€ per hour or 30€ to 55€ per day. Renters must be 18 or over and must leave a passport, a driver's license, and the number of a valid credit card. Alinari is open year-round Monday to Saturday 9am to 1pm and 3 to 6pm, and also Sunday April to October 10am to 1pm and 3 to 7pm.

BY CAR Just forget it. Driving in Florence is hopeless—not only because of the snarled traffic and the maze of one-way streets, but also because much of what you've come to see is in a pedestrian-only zone. If you arrive by car, look for prominently posted blue signs with the letter P that will lead you to the nearest garage. Garage fees average 18€ to 25€ daily, depending on the size of your car, although vans or luxury cars might cost as much as 35€.

The most centrally located garages are the **International Garage,** Via Palazzuolo 29 (✆ **055-282386;** www.internationalgarage.com); **Garage La Stazione,** Piazzale Montelungo (✆ **055-284768**); **Autoparking,** Via Fiesolana 19 (✆ **055-2477871**); and **Garage Anglo-Americano,** Via dei Barbadori 5 (✆ **055-214418**). If these are full, you can almost always find a space at the **Garage Porte Nuove,** Via delle Portenuove 21 (✆ **055-333355**).

You will, however, need a car to explore the surrounding countryside. Car-rental agencies include **Avis,** Borgo Ognissanti 128R (✆ **055-213629;** www.avis.com); **Italy by Car,** Borgo Ognissanti 134R (✆ **055-287161**); and **Hertz,** Via del Termine 1 (✆ **055-307370;** www.hertz.com).

[FastFACTS] FLORENCE

American Express The office at Via Dante Alighieri 14R (✆ **055-50981**) is open Monday to Friday 9am to 5:30pm and Saturday 9am to 12:30pm.

Consulates The **U.S. Consulate** is at Lungarno Amerigo Vespucci 38 (✆ **055-266951**). The **U.K. Consulate** is at Lungarno Corsini 2 (✆ **055-284133**), near Piazza Santa Trinità. Citizens of other English-speaking countries, including **Canada, Australia,** and **New Zealand,** should contact their diplomatic representatives in Rome.

Currency Exchange Local banks have the best rates, and most are open Monday through Friday from 8:30am to 1:30pm and 2:45 to 3:45pm.

Dentists & Doctors For a list of English-speaking doctors or dentists, consult your consulate (above) or contact **Tourist Medical Service,** Via Lorenzo il Magnifico 59 (✆ **055-475411;** www.medicalservice.firenze.it). Visits without an appointment are possible only Monday to Friday 11am to noon and 5 to 6pm, and Saturday 11am to noon. After hours, an answering service gives names and phone numbers of dentists and doctors who are on duty.

Emergencies To report a fire, call ✆ **115;** for an ambulance, call ✆ **118;** for the police, call ✆ **113;** and for road service, call ✆ **803116.**

Hospitals Call the **General Hospital** of Santa Maria Nuova, Piazza Santa Maria Nuova 1 (✆ **055-27581**).

Internet Access You can check your messages or send e-mail at **Internet Train,** Via dell'Oriuolo 40R (✆ **055-2638968;** www.internettrain.it). Internet Train is open from Monday to Saturday 10am to 1pm, and Sunday 3 to 9pm.

Pharmacies The **Farmacia Molteni,** Via Calzaiuoli 7R (✆ **055-215472**), is open 24 hours.

Police Dial ✆ **113** in an emergency. English-speaking foreigners who want to see and talk to the police should go to the **Ufficio Stranieri station,** Via Zara 2 (✆ **055-4977587**), where English-speaking personnel are available Monday, Tuesday, Wednesday, and Friday 8:30am to noon, Thursday 8:30am to noon and 3 to 5pm.

Post Office The **Central Post Office,** at Via Pellicceria 3, off Piazza della Repubblica (✆ **055-2736481;** www.poste.it), is open Monday to Saturday 8:15am to 7pm. You can buy stamps and telephone cards at windows 21 and 22. A foreign exchange office is open Monday to Friday 8:15am to 6pm. If you want to send packages of up to 20 kilograms (44 lb.), go to the rear of the building and enter at Piazza Davantati 4.

Safety Violent crimes are rare in Florence; crime consists mainly of pickpockets who frequent crowded tourist centers, such as corridors in the Uffizi Galleries. Members of group tours who cluster together are often singled out as victims. Car thefts are relatively common: Don't leave your luggage in an unguarded car, even if it's locked in the trunk. Women should be especially careful in avoiding purse snatchers, some of whom grab a purse while whizzing by on a Vespa, often knocking the woman down. Documents such as passports and extra money are better stored in safes at your hotel, if available.

Telephone The **country code** for Italy is **39.** The **city code** for Florence is **055;** use this code when calling from *anywhere* outside or inside Italy—even within Florence (you must include the 0, even when calling from abroad).

Toilets Public toilets are found in most galleries, museums, bars and cafes, and restaurants, as well as bus, train, and air terminals. Usually they're designated as WC (water closet) or DONNE (women) and UOMINI (men). The most confusing designation is SIGNORI (gentlemen) and SIGNORE (ladies), so watch that final "i" and "e"!

Where to Stay

IN CENTRO

Inexpensive

Hotel Cellai ★★★ 🎁 In the heart of the historic zone, this 18th-century building is decorated in a 19th-century style. Small sofas and armchairs are placed here and there on the terra-cotta floors, creating the aura of a country manse. Most of the midsize to spacious bedrooms are in black-and-cream hues. Headboards are made of intertwined canes of black wood set in thick golden frames or padded and lined with a fabric in a black-and-white Kashmir floral pattern—or even padded in black with a shape evoking the black hats of the guards in pictures of Pinocchio's book for children.

Via 27 Aprile 14, 52R, 50129 Firenze. ✆ **055-489291.** Fax 055-470387. www.hotelcellai.it. 55 units. 89€–189€ double; 125€–250€ junior suite. Rates include buffet breakfast. AE, DC, MC, V. Parking nearby 23€. Bus: 7, 20, 32, or 33. **Amenities:** Babysitting; bikes; room service; smoke-free rooms. *In room:* A/C, TV, hair dryer, minibar.

NEAR PIAZZA DELLA SIGNORIA

Expensive

In Piazza della Signoria ★★ 🎁 This B&B is a rare find lying only a few steps from the landmark square of Florence in a four-story *palazzo* that dates from the 14th century. Restoration was carried out with meticulous care by Alessandro and Sonia, who cater to lovers of Florentine art and elegance. Each room is uniquely furnished with antiques, and they are spacious and well lit, the most desirable of which overlook the piazza itself. Accommodations are named for a famous personality associated with Florence—Machiavelli, Giotto, even Dante or Beatrice. The Michelangelo Room, for example, has the original 18th-century wall frescoes.

Via dei Magazzini 2, 50122 Firenze. ✆ **055-2399546.** Fax 055-2676616. www.inpiazzadellasignoria.com. 13 units. 160€–280€ double. Rates include buffet breakfast. AE, DC, MC, V. Parking 28€–30€. *In room:* A/C, TV, CD player, hair dryer, Wi-Fi (free).

Relais Uffizi ★ 🎁 Next door to the Uffizi, this appropriately named inn is a real find and an unbeatable value. The restored 15th-century villa is imbued with home-like comfort and old-fashioned style, with antiques used liberally throughout the hotel. Attractively furnished midsize to spacious bedrooms open onto the landmark Piazza della Signoria, and the entrance is through the charming little walking lane, Chiasso del Buco. Bedrooms all contain marble bathrooms, and the most preferred rooms contain canopied beds. Considering its location, it's amazing that the Relais Uffizi isn't better known.

Chiasso del Buco 16, 50122 Firenze. ✆ **055-2676239.** Fax 055-2657909. www.relaisuffizi.it. 10 units. 100€–220€ double; 180€–260€ suite. Rates include buffet breakfast. AE, DC, MC, V. Parking 30€. Bus: C1, C2, 23, or 71. **Amenities:** Bar; babysitting; room service. *In room:* A/C, TV, hair dryer, minibar, Wi-Fi (free).

NEAR PIAZZA DEL DUOMO

Expensive

Grand Hotel Cavour ★ Opposite the Bargello, this 13th-century palace stands on one of Florence's noisiest streets (even double-glazed windows can't quite block out the sounds). Check out the coved main lounge, with its frescoed ceiling and crystal chandelier, and the chapel now used as a dining room (the altar and confessional are still there). The guest rooms are traditional and comfortable but a little claustrophobic, though the bathrooms have more than enough shelf space. Every floor has a shared bathroom specially fitted for travelers with disabilities. At the front desk, the professional English-speaking staff can organize city tours upon request. The roof terrace, dubbed Michelangelo, offers incredible views.

Via del Proconsolo 3, 50122 Firenze. ✆ **055-266271.** Fax 055-218955. www.albergocavour.it. 105 units (some with shower only). 250€–400€ double; 450€ triple. Rates include buffet breakfast. AE, DC, MC, V. Valet parking 40€. Bus: 14, 23, or 71. **Amenities:** Restaurant; babysitting; exercise room; room service; spa. *In room:* A/C, TV, hair dryer, minibar, Wi-Fi (free).

Hotel Calzaiuoli ★ Midway between the Duomo and the Uffizi, this hotel enjoys a fabulous location. Although the building is old (it was a home in the 1800s) and the location is historic, the interior has been modernized in a minimalist contemporary style. Its *pietra serena* (sandstone) staircase remains, however. This four-story hotel has an elevator to bring guests to their soundproof rooms, which are medium size, with functional modern furnishings and good beds. Some rooms look out over the festive street scene (with its associated noise) or out back (either over the rooftops to the Bargello and Badia Towers or up to the Duomo's cupola). The recently renovated bathrooms are immaculately kept.

Via dei Calzaiuoli 6, 50123 Firenze. ✆ **055-212456.** Fax 055-268310. www.calzaiuoli.it. 45 units (half with shower only). 100€–350€ double. Rates include buffet breakfast. AE, DC, MC, V. Parking 30€ nearby. Bus: 22, 36, or 37. **Amenities:** Babysitting; room service. *In room:* A/C, TV, hair dryer, minibar, Wi-Fi (8€ per hour).

Inexpensive

Pensione Maria Luisa de' Medici ★ 🎁 This is an accommodations oddity with a lot of style and artistic flair, run by Angelo Sordi and his Welsh partner, Evelyn Morris. Charging some of the most affordable prices in Florence, they know how to take the bleakness out of a little *pensione*. The rooms are graced with frescoed portraits of the various Medici and filled with rare lamps, tables, and chairs, along with comfortable beds. The corridors are like a baroque museum of the 17th century, making for one of Florence's most unusual B&Bs. Bedrooms are most often spacious and can be shared with up to four guests. Reception is up three flights of stairs.

Via del Corso (btw. Via del Proconsolo and Via dei Calzaiuoli), 50122 Firenze. ✆ **055-280048.** 9 units, 2 with bathroom. 70€ double without bathroom, 80€ with bathroom. Rates include continental breakfast. No credit cards. Parking 28€ nearby. Bus: C1, C2, 14, or 23. **Amenities:** Room service. *In room:* Hair dryer, no phone.

Residenza dei Pucci ★★ You get a room with a view of the cathedral's dome here, though it takes a bit of neck craning to take it in. This elegantly restored 19th-century structure is a short walk from such attractions as the Uffizi and the Accademia. Large, high-ceilinged bedrooms are beautifully furnished with refined fabrics, and carpets are made of coconut fiber. The top-floor family suite is the most lavish accommodations, offering deluxe living in the heart of Florence. Each room is individually furnished, with lavish use made of French tapestries, four-poster beds, and marble bathrooms (only two have tubs; the rest have showers).

Via dei Pucci 9, 50122 Firenze. ✆ **055-281886.** Fax 055-264314. www.residenzadeipucci.com. 12 units. 80€-170€ double; 120€-250€ suite for 4. AE, DC, MC, V. Parking 25€. Bus: 1, 6, 14, or 17. **Amenities:** Room service. *In room:* A/C, TV, hair dryer.

NEAR PIAZZA SANTA MARIA NOVELLA & THE TRAIN STATION

Very Expensive

Grand Hotel Villa Medici ★★ This old-time favorite occupies an 18th-century Medici palace 2 blocks southwest of the train station. Of all the government-rated five-star hotels of Florence, it is the only one with its own pool and health club. Most rooms have twin beds. The most peaceful units front the garden, but during the day there's noise from the convent school next door. We prefer the sixth-floor accommodations because they open onto terraces. Out back is a private garden, not Florence's finest, but with one of the only swimming pools in town.

Via il Prato 42, 50123 Firenze. ✆ **055-277171.** Fax 055-2381336. www.villamedicihotel.com. 103 units. 200€-500€ double; 400€-600€ junior suite; from 600€ suite. AE, DC, MC, V. Parking 30€-50€. Bus: 1, 9, 14, 17, 23, 36, or 37. **Amenities:** Restaurant; babysitting; exercise room; outdoor pool; room service; sauna. *In room:* A/C, TV, hair dryer, minibar, Wi-Fi (3€ per hour).

J.K. Place ★★★ An artistic statement of refinement and taste, this hotel is unique in Florence—in fact, it calls itself "a museum of the soul, an archive of experiences." Close to the Piazza Santa Maria Novella, the Florentine house blends an elegant atmosphere of the past with modern conveniences. Statues, grace notes, and even fireplaces aglow in chilly weather help create a cozy, intimate ambience. Bedrooms are beautifully designed units containing the likes of four-poster beds and Louis XVI fireplaces, evoking the home of an aristocrat in Florence's past life. Breakfast is served in the courtyard covered with glass, and on the top floor is a terrace for relaxing.

Piazza Santa Maria Novella 7, 50123 Firenze. ✆ **055-264-5181.** Fax 055-265-8387. www.jkplace.com. 20 units. 350€-500€ double; 650€-1,000€ suite. Rates include buffet breakfast. AE, DC, MC, V. Parking 32€. Bus: 14 or 23. **Amenities:** Bar; babysitting; concierge; room service. *In room:* A/C, TV/DVD, hair dryer, minibar, Wi-Fi (free).

Westin Excelsior ★★★ ☺ This luxury address is one of the first choices for those who like glamour and glitz. The sumptuousness will bowl you over (if the high prices don't get you first). Near the Ponte Vecchio and the Uffizi, the hotel boasts the best service in town. Part of the hotel was once owned by Carolina Bonaparte, Napoleon's sister; the old *palazzi* were unified in 1927 and decorated with colored marbles, walnut furniture, Oriental rugs, and neoclassical frescoes. The opulent guest rooms have 19th-century Florentine antiques, sumptuous fabrics, "heavenly beds," and two-line phones. Accommodations come in a variety of configurations. The rooms on the top floor have balconies overlooking the Arno and the Ponte Vecchio.

Piazza Ognissanti 3, 50123 Firenze. ✆ **888/625-5144** in the U.S. and Canada, or 055-27151. Fax 055-210278. http://excelsior.hotelinfirenze.com. 171 units. 273€–993€ double; from 2,250€ junior suite. AE, DC, MC, V. Parking 50€. Bus: 6 or 17. **Amenities:** Restaurant; bar; babysitting; children's programs; concierge; exercise room; room service. *In room:* A/C, TV, hair dryer, minibar, Wi-Fi (16€ per 24 hr.).

Expensive

Montebello Splendid ★★ Full of charm and grace, this government-rated five-star boutique hotel is a hit. Enter a splendid garden in front of this restored palace, with a columned Tuscan-style *loggia,* and be ushered into a regal palace with Italian marble, stuccowork, and luminous niches. The decor provides a serene and harmonious setting, all in impeccably good taste. Each of the midsize to spacious bedrooms is individually decorated and soundproof—with a lavish use of parquet, marble, soft carpeting, and elegant fabrics—and deluxe beds and first-class bathrooms are clad in marble and equipped with hydromassages, among other features.

Via Garibaldi 14, 50123 Firenze. ✆ **055-27471.** Fax 055-2747700. www.montebellosplendid.com. 61 units. 159€–580€ double; 570€–920€ suite. Rates include buffet breakfast. AE, DC, MC, V. Parking 30€. Bus: 13. **Amenities:** Restaurant; bar; babysitting; concierge; exercise room; room service. *In room:* A/C, TV, hair dryer, Wi-Fi (10€ per 24 hr.).

Moderate

Hotel Vasari ★ This inn enjoys a rather literary history; for several years, it was the home of 19th-century French poet Alphonse de La Martine. Built in the 1840s as a home, it was a run-down hotel until 1993, when its owners poured money into its renovation and upgraded it. Its three stories are connected by elevator, and the rooms are comfortable, albeit somewhat spartan. Nonetheless, the beds are firm and the linen is crisp. The tiled bathrooms are small but immaculate. Some of the public areas retain their elaborate vaulting.

Via B. Cennini 9–11, 50123 Firenze. ✆ **055-212753.** Fax 055-294246. www.hotelvasari.com. 27 units (shower only). 155€ double; 210€ triple. Rates include buffet breakfast. AE, DC, MC, V. Parking 10€. Bus: 4, 7, 10, 13, 14, 23, or 71. **Amenities:** Bar; babysitting; room service. *In room:* A/C, TV, hair dryer, minibar.

Inexpensive

Hotel Albion ★★ A true gem. Housed in a lovely 19th-century English neoclassical *palazzo,* the family-owned Hotel Albion is the sort of place you'll come back to again and again. The rooms, some of which have balconies, are charmingly simple and spotless, and the hallways, reception area, and breakfast room are decorated with the family's eclectic art collection. The location, a short walk from the train station at Santa Maria Novella, the Duomo, and other major attractions, is ideal. But the big draw here is the service. Owner Massimo and his daughter Sara will happily reserve museum tickets for you long before you arrive and provide outstanding restaurant advice (and take care of the reservations).

Via il Prato 22R, 50123 Firenze. ✆ **055-214171.** www.hotelalbion.it. 85€–166€ double. Rates include continental breakfast. AE, MC, V. *In room:* A/C, TV, hair dryer, Wi-Fi (free).

Hotel Annabella ☺ Near the Santa Maria Novella rail station, within an easy walk of the Duomo, this is a well-run and relatively undiscovered family hotel. It's installed in a turn-of-the-20th-century palazzo. At the second-floor reception, Mrs. Vittoria and her son Simone welcome you to Florence and will house you well in this elevator building. There is nothing overly adorned here, but the rooms are nicely furnished, each one midsize with comfortable beds resting on tile floors and including such extras as writing desks. Each unit comes with a small bathroom with shower. Many of the rooms are large enough to house three or four guests, making them ideal for families.

Via Fiume 5, 50123 Firenze. ✆ **055-281877.** Fax 055-2396814. www.hotelannabella.it. 15 units. 75€–185€ double; 90€–225€ triple. AE, DC, MC, V. Parking 20€. Bus: 1, 6, 11, or 17. **Amenities:** Bar; babysitting; room service. *In room:* A/C, TV, hair dryer, Wi-Fi (3€ per 2 hr.).

NEAR PIAZZA SAN MARCO

Expensive

Carolus Hotel ★ This hotel lies inside an ancient neoclassical *palazzo*. Within easy reach of the city's major monuments and its best shops, the Carolus was recently renovated, its midsize and well-furnished bedrooms much improved with upgraded furniture. Accommodations open onto many of the best-known churches and monuments of Florence, with the hills of Fiesole on view in the background. Everything is decorated with sleek modern Italian styling.

Via XXVII Aprile 3, 50129 Firenze. ✆ **055-2645539.** Fax 055-2645550. www.carolushotel.com. 53 units. 83€–320€ double; 160€–390€ triple. Rates include buffet breakfast. AE, DC, MC, V. Parking 28€ in garage. Bus: 1, 7, or 25. **Amenities:** Bar; babysitting; room service. *In room:* A/C, TV, hair dryer, minibar, Wi-Fi (free).

Inexpensive

Hotel Cimabue ★ This hotel was built in 1904 as a Tuscan-style *palazzo,* and the most charming guest rooms are the six with original frescoed ceilings. Four of these are one floor above street level, and the other two are on the ground floor. Rooms have comfortable beds and range from small to medium in size. The bathrooms are not spacious but have adequate shelf space. The hotel was recently renovated and has turn-of-the-20th-century antiques that correspond to the building's age. Its Belgian-Italian management extends a warm multicultural welcome.

Via B. Lupi 7, 50129 Firenze. ✆ **055-471989.** Fax 055-4630906. www.hotelcimabue.it. 16 units (shower only). 79€–290€ double. Rates include buffet breakfast. AE, DC, MC, V. Parking 20€. Bus: 17. **Amenities:** Babysitting; room service. *In room:* A/C (in most units), TV, hair dryer, Wi-Fi (free).

Piccolo Hotel Conveniently located near the railway station and all the top sights, this town-house hotel offers an intimate atmosphere. You'll feel at home, thanks to Ms. Angeloni, the English-speaking manager, who's a fount of advice about the city. Rooms are medium in size; some have balconies, while all have simple, tasteful furniture and floral bed linens. Bathrooms are a little small but well organized and neat. The only meal served is the generous buffet breakfast, but the hotel is surrounded by good restaurants.

Via S. Gallo 51, 50129 Firenze. ✆ **055-475519.** Fax 055-474515. www.piccolohotelfirenze.com. 10 units (shower only). 85€–130€ double; 100€–155€ triple. Rates include buffet breakfast. AE, MC, V. Parking 15€ nearby. Bus: 1, 7, 11, or 17. **Amenities:** Bar; babysitting; room service. *In room:* A/C, TV, Wi-Fi (free).

NEAR PIAZZA SANTA CROCE

Moderate

Residenza Casanuova ★ A recently renovated mansion from 1871, this is one of the best B&Bs in Florence, enjoying a prime location near Piazza Santa Croce. It's filled with all the modern conveniences yet retains its original antique architectural style. English-speaking Beatrice and Massimiliano Gorgi are the young and hospitable owners, who will do much to make a stay memorable for one of their guests. The residence occupies the entire second floor of the building with a terrace open to views of the monuments and hills of Florence, on which guests often sit to enjoy the sunset and a glass of Tuscan wine. Rooms have lots of individual character and a warm decor.

Villa della Mattonaia 21, 50121 Firenze. ✆ **055-2343413.** Fax 338-5450758. www.residenzacasanuova.it. 5 units. 98€–169€. Rates include buffet breakfast. MC, V. Parking 26€ nearby. Bus: C2, 6, 14, or 23. *In room:* A/C, TV, fridge, hair dryer.

Ritz Hotel ★ Along the Arno, the Ritz of Florence has nothing to do with the pricey palaces of London or Paris. This Ritz is a family-run hotel that has been given a new lease on life by its owners, who have upgraded it and turned it into a reasonably priced alternative in a high-priced city. They have restored and redecorated, offering well-furnished, medium-size bedrooms, many with carpets, others with wood and marble. It's a short walk to the Ponte Vecchio or the Uffizi, and the Ritz enjoys a location right on the river, with nice views.

Lugarno Zecca Vecchia 24, 50122 Firenze. ✆ **055-2340650.** Fax 055-240863. www.hotelritz.net. 32 units (some with shower only). 88€–180€ double; 140€–280€ suite. Rates include buffet breakfast. AE, DC, MC, V. Parking 25€. Bus: 23. **Amenities:** Bar; babysitting; Internet (free, in lobby); room service. *In room:* A/C, TV, hair dryer, minibar.

ACROSS THE ARNO

Expensive

UNA Hotel Vittoria ★★ Is this a boutique hotel or a disco? You're not sure as you enter and are immediately sucked into the world of "wonder boy" designer Fabio Novembre. The modern, innovative modular design comes at you instantly in a series of swirls, rings, and spirals. A floor-to-ceiling floral mosaic encases the reception desk. The bedrooms are adorned with black-leather walls and fiber-optic lights. The sleek lines of the decor are so avant-garde that they appear to have been created deep into the 21st century. Depending on your concept of privacy, you'll either love or hate the bathrooms, which are located right by the doorway to each room and encased in crystal, so that all your charms can be displayed to an arriving room-service waiter.

Via Pisana 59, 50143 Firenze. ✆ **055-22771.** Fax 055-22772. www.unahotels.it. 84 units. 101€–502€ double. AE, DC, MC, V. Parking 20€. Bus: 6. **Amenities:** Restaurant; bar; babysitting; bikes; children's programs; concierge; room service; Wi-Fi (3€ per 30 min., in lobby). *In room:* A/C, TV, hair dryer, minibar.

NEAR PIAZZALE MICHELANGIOLO

Very Expensive

Villa La Vedetta ★★ This deluxe boutique hotel lies beside Piazzale Michelangiolo, with the most exceptional view of the Arno (and the monuments of Florence) of any hotel in town. A glamorous and sophisticated atmosphere prevails here, in a villa surrounded by gardens and reached by a tree-lined road. Behind its neoclassical facade, the hotel successfully blends contemporary and antique styles. Each individually decorated bedroom is luxurious, with parquet floors, fine marble bathrooms, and often a four-poster bed. A total of six units—two suites and four doubles—are housed in the equally distinguished annex. The hotel's Bellavista Suite is acclaimed as the largest in the hotel; it occupies two levels.

Viale Michelangelo Buonarroti 78, 50125 Firenze. ✆ **055-681631.** Fax 055-6582544. www.villalavedettahotel.com. 18 units. 349€–599€ double; from 699€ suite. AE, DC, MC, V. Free parking. Bus: 12. **Amenities:** Restaurant; bar; babysitting; exercise room; Jacuzzi; outdoor pool; room service; sauna; Wi-Fi (free, in lobby). *In room:* A/C, TV, hair dryer, minibar.

Where to Dine

IN CENTRO

Moderate

Cantinetta Antinori ★ FLORENTINE/TUSCAN Behind the severe stone facade of the 15th-century Palazzo Antinori is one of Florence's most popular restaurants and one of the city's few top-notch wine bars. It's no wonder the cellars are so well stocked: Antinori is the oldest (600 years), most distinguished wine company in Tuscany, Umbria, and Piedmont. You can sample these wines by the glass at the stand-up bar or by the bottle as an accompaniment to the meals served at wooden tables in the dining room, decorated with floor-to-ceiling racks of aged and dusty wine bottles. You can eat a meal or just snacks. The food is standard but satisfying, and many of the ingredients come directly from the Antinori farms. Especially good are two beef specialties—tender slices of beef with pecorino cheese from Castello della Sala or Tuscan entrecôte of beef grilled to perfection and served with roast potatoes. One of the best pasta specialties is with a wild boar ragout.

Piazza Antinori 3. ✆ **055-292234.** www.cantinetta-antinori.com. Reservations recommended. Main courses 12€–27€. AE, DC, MC, V. Mon–Fri 12:30–2:30pm and 7–10:30pm. Closed Aug and Dec 24–25. Bus: 6, 11, 14, 36, 37, or 68.

NEAR PIAZZA DEL DUOMO

Inexpensive

Le Mossacce FLORENTINE/TUSCAN The 35-seat Le Mossacce is midway between the Bargello and the Duomo. It opened in the early 1900s, and within its 300-year-old walls, hardworking waiters serve a wide range of excellent Florentine and Tuscan specialties, such as *ribollita* (a Tuscan bean soup), baked lasagna, and heavily seasoned baked pork. *Bistecca alla fiorentina* (local beefsteak) is a favorite—and you'll be hard-pressed to find it at a better price. Pasta buffs rightly claim that the cannelloni here is among Florence's finest—these baked pasta tubes are stuffed with spinach, a savory tomato sauce, and seasoned ground meat. For dessert, try the excellent *castagnaccio,* a cake baked with chestnut flour. Ask the waiters for advice and trust them; we had a great meal this way.

Via del Proconsolo 55R. ✆ **055-294361.** www.trattorialemossacce.it. Main courses 7€–18€. AE, DC, MC, V. Mon–Fri noon–2:30pm and 7–9:30pm. Closed Aug. Bus: 14.

NEAR PIAZZA DELLA SIGNORIA

Moderate

Paoli ★★ ITALIAN/TUSCAN This restaurant is one of the best located in Florence. Paoli, between the Duomo and Piazza della Signoria, was opened in 1824 by the Paoli brothers in a building dating in part from the 13th century. It has a wonderful medieval-tavern atmosphere, with arches and ceramics stuck into the fresco-adorned walls. The pastas are homemade, including a house specialty, green handmade gnocchi with Gorgonzola cheese. The chef does a superb chicken breast with curry and rice pilaf or else veal piccata with lemon zest. A recommended side dish is *piselli alla fiorentina* (garden peas). The ultrafresh vegetables are often served with olive oil, which your waiter will loudly proclaim as the world's finest.

Via dei Tavolini 12R. ✆ **055-216215.** Reservations required. Main courses 8€–20€. AE, DC, MC, V. Wed–Mon noon–3pm and 7–11pm. Closed 3 weeks in Aug. Bus: 16 or 17.

Inexpensive

Da Pennello FLORENTINE/ITALIAN This informal trattoria—also called Casa di Dante—offers many Florentine specialties on its a la carte menu and is known for its wide selection of antipasti; you can make a meal out of these delectable hors d'oeuvres. The ravioli is homemade, and one pasta specialty (loved by locals) is *spaghetti carrettiera,* with tomatoes and pepperoni. To follow that, you can have filet mignon in green-pepper sauce. Sometimes it's best to order the daily specials, which are made with food bought fresh that day at the market. A Florentine cake, *zuccotto,* rounds out the meal. Da Pennello is on a narrow street near Dante's house, about a 5-minute walk from the Duomo. Called "The Painter" in English, its walls are hung with art, and it used to attract such local guys as Cellini and Andrea del Sarto.

Via Dante Alighieri 4R. ✆ **055-294848.** Fax 055-21455. www.ristoranteilpennello.it. Main courses 7€–18€; fixed-price menus from 25€. AE, DC, MC, V. Tues–Sat noon–3pm and 7–10pm; Sun noon–3pm. Closed 1st 3 weeks in Aug and Dec 24–Jan 2. Bus: 14, 22, or 23.

Il Cavallino ITALIAN/TUSCAN A local favorite since the 1930s, Il Cavallino is on a tiny street (which probably won't even be on your map) leading off Piazza della Signoria at its northern end. Two of the three dining rooms have vaulted ceilings and peach-colored marble floors; the main room looks out over the piazza. Menu items are typical hearty Tuscan fare, including an assortment of boiled meats in green herb sauce, veal scaloppini with asparagus, chicken breast Medici style, and the inevitable Florentine spinach, which comes encased in a crepe with ricotta. The portions are large. Most diners prefer the house wine, but a limited selection of bottled wines is also available. The restaurant does not take phone reservations, which have to be made by faxing ✆ **055-214555.**

Via delle Farine 6R. ✆ **055-215818.** Reservations required (see above). Fixed-price menus 18€–22€. AE, DC, MC, V. Mar–Oct daily noon–3pm and 7–10pm; Nov–Feb Thurs–Tues noon–3pm, Thurs–Mon 7–10:30pm. Bus: C1 or C2.

NEAR PIAZZA SANTA MARIA NOVELLA & THE TRAIN STATION

Moderate/Inexpensive

Sostanza ★ FLORENTINE Sostanza, the city's oldest (opened in 1869) and most revered trattoria, is where working people go for excellent moderately priced food. In recent years, however, it has also begun attracting a more sophisticated set, despite its somewhat funky atmosphere. (Florentines call the place *Troia,* a word that means "trough" but also suggests a woman of easy virtue.) The small dining room has crowded family tables, but when you taste what comes out of the kitchen, you'll know that fancy decor would be superfluous. Specialties include breaded chicken breast, a succulent T-bone, and tripe Florentine style (cut into strips and then baked in a casserole with tomatoes, onions, and parmigiano).

Via del Porcellana 25R. ✆ **055-212691.** Reservations recommended. Main courses 11€–25€. No credit cards. June–July and Nov–Mar Mon–Fri 12:30–2pm and 7:30–9:45pm; Apr–May and Sept–Oct Mon–Sat 12:30–2pm and 7:30–9:45pm. Closed Aug and 2 weeks at Christmas. Bus: 12.

Trattoria Antellesi ★ TUSCAN Occupying a 15th-century historic monument just steps from the Medici Chapels and a 4-minute walk from the railway station, this place is devoted almost exclusively to well-prepared versions of time-tested Tuscan recipes. The restaurant changes its menu every 3 weeks, based on whatever is seasonal and fresh at the food market (Mercato San Lorenzo), which lies a short walk away. Dishes might include fresh fish (generally on Fri), and a superb *bistecca alla fiorentina.* Culinary creations are sometimes simple, sometimes complex, including such dishes as filet of salmon with a celery purée or *bottarga* (salted fish roe) with potatoes gratinée and zucchini. One of the best pastas is tagliolini with black truffles. Expect a wide selection of high-quality Italian wines, mostly Tuscan. A special dessert is *budino di castagna* (chestnut pudding).

Via Faenza 9R. ✆ **055-216990.** www.trattoriaantellesi.com. Reservations recommended. Main courses 8€–30€. AE, DC, MC, V. Daily noon–3pm and 7–10:30pm. Bus: 1, 6, 7, 11, 17, 33, 67, or 68.

ACROSS THE ARNO

Moderate

Mamma Gina ★ TUSCAN Mamma Gina is a rustic restaurant that prepares fine foods in the traditional manner. Although it's run by a corporation that operates other restaurants around Tuscany, this place is named after its founding matriarch, whose legend has continued despite her death in the 1980s. A few of the savory menu items are chicken breast with cognac and mushrooms, fresh rigatoni with a cream-cheese sauce, or risotto with angler fish and prawns. This is an ideal spot for lunch after visiting the Pitti Palace.

Borgo San Jacopo 37R. ✆ **055-2396009.** www.mammagina.it. Reservations required for dinner. Main courses 8€–19€. AE, DC, MC, V. Mon–Sat noon–2:30pm and 7–10:30pm. Closed 3 weeks in Aug. Bus: D.

Inexpensive

Fuori Porta ★ TUSCAN This is the city's best *enoteche* (wine tavern). As the name translates, it means "outside the gates," yet it's only a 15-minute taxi or bus ride from the landmark Piazza della Signoria, the historic core of Florence. The wine list ranks at the top in Florence, yet the prices are more than reasonable. Many of the finest selections are available by the glass. Discerning palates also appreciate the Tuscan fare, which is soul food to the Florentines. Two succulent pasta dishes include *taglierini* (flat noodles) with fresh mushrooms or linguine with an arugula pesto. We especially like the loaves of bread that arrive freshly baked from the oven and are most often served with mozzarella and vine-ripened tomatoes.

Via del Monte alle Croce 10R. ✆ **055-2342483.** www.fuoriporta.it. Reservations recommended. Main courses 7.50€–17€. AE, MC, V. Daily 12:30–3:30pm and 7pm–12:30am. Bus: 13 or 23.

Osteria Antica Mescita San Niccolò TUSCAN Across the Arno from the historic center, this much-frequented restaurant consistently turns on some of the most reasonably priced and flavorful dishes in town. Offered is a repertoire of mouthwatering dishes that are cooked fresh with the bounty of the Tuscan countryside. Florentines dig into the fabled *ribollita,* followed with Florentine-style tripe, an acquired taste for many eaters. You might opt instead for the beef stew with porcini mushrooms. Another savory dish is the rabbit with a Vernaccia wine sauce along with such familiar side dishes as white navy beans with garlic, tomato, and sage. Outdoor dining is possible in summer.

Via Niccolò 60R. ✆ **055-2342836.** Reservations recommended. Main courses 7€–18€. AE, MC, V. Mon–Sat 12:30–3pm and 7–11pm. Closed 3 weeks in Aug. Bus: C1 or 23.

AT ARTIMINO

Moderate

Da Delfina ★ TUSCAN Even on a short visit to Florence, give yourself a break and dip at least once into the countryside of Tuscany for a meal. Our candidate for an outing is this family-run restaurant in the medieval walled village of Artimino, a 15-minute train ride from the center of Florence. Based on the freshest of local ingredients, the food has a wonderful, earthy taste, and some of it comes from the nearby fields, including nettles, mushrooms, and wild herbs. If you arrive in fair weather, request a table on the terrace with its classic view of the Tuscan landscape. The chefs turn out some of the region's best homemade pasta dishes and delectable sausages. We'd visit just for a plate of the aged salami with its intense, meaty flavor. Raw fava beans appear with pecorino sheep's-milk cheese, and homemade pasta with wild mushrooms should win an award. Baby goat (*capretto*) is roasted to perfection in the oven.

Via della Chiesa 1, Artimino. ✆ **055-8718074.** www.dadelfina.it. Reservations recommended. Main courses 8€–20€. No credit cards. Wed–Sun 12:30–2:30pm; Tues–Sat 8–10:30pm. From Santa Maria Novella station in Florence take the Signa train. At Signa take a taxi for the 5-min. ride to Da Delfina.

Exploring the Renaissance City

Florence was the fountainhead of the Renaissance, the city of Dante and Boccaccio. For 3 centuries, the city was dominated by the Medici family, patrons of the arts, and masters of assassination. But it's chiefly through Florence's incomparable artists that we know of the apogee of the Renaissance: Ghiberti, Fra Angelico, Donatello, Brunelleschi, Botticelli, Leonardo da Vinci, and Michelangelo.

In Florence, you can trace the transition from medievalism to the age of "rebirth." For example, all modern painters owe a debt to an ugly, unkempt man named Masaccio (Vasari's "Slipshod Tom"), who died at 27. Modern painting began with his frescoes in the Brancacci Chapel in Santa Maria del Carmine, which you can see today. Years later, Michelangelo painted a more celebrated Adam and Eve in the Sistine Chapel, but even this great artist never realized the raw humanity of Masaccio's *Adam and Eve Expelled from Paradise.*

Group tourism has so overwhelmed this city that in 1996, officials demanded that organized tour groups book their visits in advance and pay an admission fee. No more than 150 tour buses are allowed into the center at one time (considering how small Florence is, even that's a stretch). Today there are more than seven tourists for each native Florentine, and that isn't counting the day-trippers, who rush off to Venice in the late afternoon. But despite all its traffic and inconveniences, Florence is still one of the world's greatest art cities.

TOP MUSEUMS

Galleria degli Uffizi (Uffizi Gallery) ★★★ When Anna Maria Ludovica, the last Medici grand duchess, died in 1737, she bequeathed to the people of Tuscany a wealth of Renaissance and even classical art. The paintings and sculptures had been accumulated by the powerful grand dukes during 3 centuries of rule that witnessed the height of the Renaissance. The collection is housed in an impressive *palazzo* commissioned by Duke Cosimo de' Medici in 1560 and initiated by Giorgio Vasari to house the Duchy of Tuscany's administrative offices (*uffizi* means offices).

After several renovations following a terrorist bomb in 1993, the Uffizi has a new look. A lobby has been added so that visitors don't have to wait in line outside; the galleries on the upper two floors are three times their previous size; the *trompe l'oeil* painting in the Loggiato sull'Arno has been restored to its original beauty; and walking down this hall, looking through the windows, you'll have enchanting views of Florence. There's also a bookstore.

You can buy tickets in advance through **Firenze Musei** (✆ **055-294-883;** www.polomuseale.firenze.it) and **www.selectitaly.com**, which has a full catalog of the museum's works on the Web. Any hotel in Florence that has a concierge can also make reservations for you, cutting down on the lines and hassle.

The Uffizi is nicely grouped into periods or schools to show the development and progress of Italian and European art.

Piazzale degli Uffizi 6. ✆ **055-2388651.** www.polomuseale.firenze.it. Admission 6.50€. Tues–Sun 8:15am–7pm (last entrance 45 min. before closing). Bus: C1, C2, 14, or 23.

Galleria dell'Accademia ★★ This museum boasts many paintings and sculptures, but they're completely overshadowed by one work: Michelangelo's colossal ***David*** **★★★**, unveiled in 1504 and now the world's most famed sculpture. It first stood in Piazza della Signoria but was moved to the Accademia in 1873 (a copy was substituted) and placed beneath the rotunda of a room built exclusively for its display. When he began work, Michelangelo was just 29. One of the most sensitive accounts we've ever read of how Michelangelo turned the 5m (17-ft.) "Duccio marble" into *Il Gigante* (the Giant) is related in Irving Stone's *The Agony and the Ecstasy.* Stone describes a Michelangelo "burning with marble fever," who set out to create a *David* who "would be Apollo, but considerably more; Hercules, but considerably more; Adam, but considerably more; the most fully realized man the world had yet seen, functioning in a rational and humane world." For his 500th birthday in 2004, David was given a bath to wash away the accumulated dirt and grime of centuries. The statue now has a bit more shine and polish.

David is so overpowering in his majesty that many visitors head here just to see him and leave immediately afterward. However, the hall leading up to him is lined with other Michelangelos, notably his quartet of celebrated ***Prisoners*** and ***Slaves*** **★★**. The statues are presumably unfinished, although art historians have found them more dramatic in their current state as they depict the struggles of figures to free themselves from stone. Michelangelo worked on these statues, originally intended for the tomb of Pope Julius II, for 40 years because he was never pleased with them. The gallery also displays Michelangelo's statue of St. Matthew, which he began carving in 1504.

The Accademia also owns a gallery of paintings, usually considered to be of minor importance (works by Santi di Tito, Granacci, and Albertinelli, for example). Yet there are masterpieces here as well, notably Lo Scheggia's 1440s *Cassone Adimari,* a panel from a wedding chest.

Warning: The wait to get in to see *David* can be up to an hour or more, so we highly recommend making reservations in advance (ask the concierge at your hotel or call ✆ 055/294-883). If you don't have a reservation, try getting there before the museum opens in the morning or an hour or two before closing time.

Via Ricasoli 60. ✆ **055-2388612.** www.polomuseale.firenze.it. Admission 6.50€. Tues–Sun 8:15am–7pm. Bus: C1, C2, D, or 12.

Istituto e Museo di Storia della Scienza ★ Since 1927, this museum has been a repository of ancient instruments and devices of historical and scientific interest, including Galileo's telescope. The most important exhibit is the **Medici Collection ★**, which displays scientific instruments owned by the Medicis, including the objective lens of the telescope with which Galileo discovered the satellites around Jupiter. Other exhibits include a planetary clock by Lorenzo della Volpaia, plus exhibits relating to 5 centuries of scientific collecting by the once-powerful Tuscan family of Lorraine. Dozens of other displays relate to instruments used in the early studies of mathematics, physics, meteorology, and electricity.

Piazza dei Giudici. ✆ **055-265311.** www.imss.fi.it. Admission 10€, free for children 5 and under. June–Sept Mon and Wed–Fri 9:30am–5pm, Tues and Sat 9:30am–1pm; Oct–May Mon and Wed–Sat 9:30am–5pm, Tues 9:30am–1pm. Bus: 13, 23, or 62.

Museo di San Marco (St. Mark's Museum) ★★ This state museum is a handsome Renaissance monastery whose cell walls are decorated with frescoes by the mystical **Fra Angelico.** In the days of Cosimo de' Medici, San Marco was built by Michelozzo as a Dominican convent. It contained bleak, bare cells, which Angelico and his students brightened considerably. Here you'll see one of his better-known paintings, ***The Last Judgment*** **★★** (1431). On the second floor visitors find the highlight of the museum: Fra Angelico's ***The Annunciation*** **★★★**.

Piazza San Marco 1. ✆ **055-2388608.** www.polomuseale.firenze.it. Admission 4€. Mon–Fri 8:30am–1:50pm; Sat 8:15am–6:50pm; Sun 8:15am–7pm. Ticket office closes 30 min. before the museum. Closed 2nd and 4th Mon and 1st, 3rd, and 5th Sun of the month; Jan 1; May 1; and Christmas. Bus: 7, 10, 11, 17, or 33.

Museo Nazionale del Bargello (Bargello Museum) ★★ A short walk from Piazza della Signoria, this is a 1255 fortress palace whose dark underground chambers resounded with the cries of the tortured when it served as the city's jail and town hall during the Renaissance. Today the Bargello is a vast repository of some of the most important Renaissance sculpture, including works by Michelangelo and Donatello.

Here you'll see **another Michelangelo *David*** (referred to in the past as *Apollo*), chiseled perhaps 25 to 30 years after the statuesque figure in the Accademia. Among the more significant sculptures is Giambologna's *Winged Mercury* (ca. 1564). The Bargello displays two versions of Donatello's ***John the Baptist*** **★**, one emaciated and the other a younger and much kinder-looking man.

Look for at least one more work: another *David,* this one by Andrea del Verrocchio, one of the finest of the 15th-century sculptors. The Bargello also contains a large number of terra cottas by the della Robbia clan.

Via del Proconsolo 4. ✆ **055-2388606.** www.polomuseale.firenze.it. Admission 4€. Daily 8:15am–1:50pm. Closed 2nd and 4th Mon and 1st, 3rd, and 5th Sun of each month; Jan 1; May 1; and Christmas. Bus: C1, C2, 14, or 23.

Palazzo Pitti & Giardini di Boboli (Boboli Gardens) ★★ The massive bulk of the **Palazzo Pitti** is one of Europe's greatest artistic treasure-troves, with the city's most extensive coterie of museums embracing a painting gallery second only to the Uffizi. It's a cavalcade of the works of Titian, Rubens, Raphael, and Andrea del Sarto. Built in the 16th century (Brunelleschi was probably the architect), this was once the residence of the powerful Medici family. Today there are several museums in this complex; the most important is the first-floor **Galleria Palatina (Palatine Gallery) ★★**, which houses one of Europe's great art collections and shows masterpieces hung one on top of the other as in the days of the Enlightenment. Other museums include the **Appartamenti Reali (Royal Apartments) ★**, which boast lavish reminders of when the Pitti was a private residence; the **Galleria d'Arte Moderna** (**Modern Art Gallery;** ✆ **055-2388616**); the **Galleria del Costume (Gallery of Costume);** and the **Museo degli Argenti** (**Museum of Silver) ★**, which displays the household wares of the Medicis.

Behind the Pitti Palace are the **Giardini di Boboli (Boboli Gardens) ★★**, Piazza Pitti 1 (✆ **055-2388786**), through which the Medicis romped. After a visit to the Boboli, wander over to the adjoining site, **Giardino Bardini,** a 14th-century garden spread over a 4-hectare (10-acre) site.

Piazza Pitti, across the Arno. ✆ **055-2388614.** www.polomuseale.firenze.it. Palatina and Modern Art Gallery 8.50€; 6€ for both Argenti and Boboli Gardens. Galleria Palatina, Appartamenti Reali, and Modern Art Gallery Tues–Sun 8:15am–6:45pm. Boboli Gardens and Museo degli Argenti June–Aug daily 8:15am–7:30pm; Apr–May and Sept–Oct daily 8:15am–6:30pm; Nov–Feb daily 8:15am–4:30pm; Mar daily 8:15am–5:30pm. Closed the 1st and last Mon of each month. Ticket office closes 1 hr. before the gardens. Bus: C1, C2, 11, 36, 37, or 68.

THE DUOMO, CAMPANILE & BAPTISTERY

Il Duomo (Cattedrale di Santa Maria del Fiore) ★★★ The Duomo, graced by Filippo Brunelleschi's red-tiled dome, is the crowning glory of Florence and the star of the skyline. Before entering, take time to view the exterior, with its geometrically patterned bands of white, pink, and green marble; this tricolor mosaic is an interesting contrast to the sienna-colored fortress-like *palazzi* around the city. The Duomo is one of the world's largest churches and represents the flowering of the "Florentine Gothic" style. Construction stretched over centuries: Begun in 1296, it was finally consecrated in 1436, although finishing touches on the facade were applied as late as the 19th century.

Volunteers offer **free tours** of the cathedral every day except Sunday from 10am to 12:30pm and 3 to 5pm. Most of them speak English; if there are many of you and you want to confirm the tours' availability, call ✆ **055-2710757** (Tues–Fri, mornings only). Looking rather professorial and kindly, they can be found sitting at a table along the right (south) wall as you enter the Duomo. They expect no payment, but a nominal donation to the church is always appreciated. They also organize tours of Santa Croce and Santa Maria Novella.

Brunelleschi's efforts to build the **dome ★★★** (1420–36) could be the subject of a Hollywood script. At one time before his plans were accepted, the architect was tossed out on his derrière and denounced as an idiot. He eventually won the commission by a clever "egg trick," as related in Giorgio Vasari's *Lives of the Painters,* written in the 16th century: The architect challenged his competitors to make an egg stand on a flat piece of marble. Each artist tried to make the egg stand, but each failed. When it was Brunelleschi's turn, he took the egg and cracked its bottom slightly on the marble and thus made it stand upright. Each of the other artists said he could've done the same thing, if he'd known he could crack the egg. Brunelleschi retorted that they also would've known how to vault the cupola if they had seen his model or plans.

His dome, a "monument for posterity," was erected without supports. When Michelangelo began to construct a dome over St. Peter's, he paid tribute to Brunelleschi's earlier cupola in Florence: "I am going to make its sister larger, yes, but not lovelier." You can climb 463 spiraling steps to the ribbed dome for a view that's well worth the trek (however, you can climb only 414 steps and get the same view from Giotto's campanile, below).

Inside, the overall effect of the cathedral is bleak. However, note the restored frescoes covering the inside of the cupola depicting the Last Judgment. Some of the stained-glass windows in the dome were based on designs by Donatello (Brunelleschi's friend) and Ghiberti (Brunelleschi's rival).

Piazza del Duomo. ✆ **055-2302885.** www.operaduomo.firenze.it. Cathedral free admission; excavations 3€; cupola 8€. Duomo Mon–Wed and Fri 10am–5pm; Thurs 10am–3:30pm; Sat 10am–4:45pm (1st Sat of each month 10am–3:30pm); Sun 1:30–4:45pm. Cupola Mon–Fri 8:30am–7pm; Sat 8:30am–5:30pm. Bus: C1 or C2.

Campanile di Giotto (Giotto's Bell Tower) ★★ Giotto left to posterity Europe's most beautiful campanile, rhythmic in line and form. That Giotto was given the position of *capomastro* (master builder) and grand architect (and pensioned for 100 gold florins for his service) is remarkable in itself because he's famous for freeing painting from the confinements of Byzantium. He designed the campanile in the last 2 or 3 years of his life and died before its completion.

The final work was carried out by Andrea Pisano, one of Italy's greatest Gothic sculptors (see his bronze doors on the baptistery). The "Tuscanized" Gothic tower, with bands of the same colored marble as the Duomo, stands 84m (274 ft.) high; you can climb 414 steps to the top for a panorama of the sienna-colored city. If you can make the tough climb up (and up and up) the cramped stairs, the **view ★★★** from the top of Giotto's bell tower is unforgettable, sweeping over the city, the surrounding hills, and Medici villas.

Piazza del Duomo. ✆ **055-2302885.** www.operaduomo.firenze.it. Admission 6€. Daily 8:30am–7:30pm. Last admission 40 min. before closing. Closed Jan 1, Easter, Sept 8, and Christmas. Bus: C1 or C2.

Battistero San Giovanni (Baptistery) ★★★ Named after the city's patron saint, Giovanni (John the Baptist), the octagonal baptistery dates from the 11th and 12th centuries. It's the oldest structure in Florence and is a highly original interpretation of the Romanesque style, with bands of pink, white, and green marble to match the Duomo and campanile. Visitors from all over the world come to gape at its three sets of **bronze doors ★★★**. The gilt-covered panels (representing scenes from the New Testament, including the Annunciation, the Adoration, and Christ debating the elders in the temple) make up a flowing narration in bronze. To protect them from the elements, the originals are now in the Duomo Museum (see later in this chapter), but the copies are works of art unto themselves.

Piazza San Giovanni. ✆ **055-2302885.** www.operaduomo.firenze.it. Admission 4€. Mon–Sat noon–7pm; Sun 8:30am–2pm. Last admission 30 min. before closing. Bus: C1 or C2.

OTHER CHURCHES

Basilica di San Lorenzo ★★ This is Brunelleschi's 1426 Renaissance church, where the Medicis attended services from their nearby palace on Via Larga, now Via Camillo Cavour. Most visitors flock to see Michelangelo's New Sacristy with his *Night* and *Day* (see the review for Cappelle Medicee, below), but Brunelleschi's handwork deserves some time, too.

Enter the **Biblioteca Medicea Laurenziana (Medici Laurentian Library) ★★** (✆ **055-210760**), at Piazza San Lorenzo 9. Designed by Michelangelo to shelter the expanding collection of the Medicis, the library showcases an extraordinary flight of stone steps. The library is filled with some of Italy's greatest manuscripts. ***Note:*** Call ahead before setting out because, at press time, the library was temporarily closed for restoration.

Piazza San Lorenzo. ✆ **055-216634.** Free admission. Mon–Sat 10am–5pm. Bus: 1, 6, 7, 11, 17, 33, 67, or 68.

Basilica di Santa Croce ★★ Think of this as Tuscany's Westminster Abbey. This church shelters the tombs of everyone from Michelangelo to Machiavelli, from

Dante (he was actually buried at Ravenna) to Galileo. Santa Croce, said to have been designed by Arnolfo di Cambio, was the church of the Franciscans.

In the right nave (the first tomb) is the Vasari-executed **monument to Michelangelo,** whose 89-year-old body was smuggled back to his native Florence from its original burial place in Rome. The **Trecento frescoes ★★** are reason enough for visiting Santa Croce—especially those by Giotto to the right of the main chapel.

Piazza Santa Croce 16. ✆ **055-2466105.** www.santacroce.firenze.it. Church free admission; cloisters and church museum 5€. Church Mon–Sat 9:30am–5:30pm; Sun 1–5:30pm. Museum and cloisters Mon-Sat 9:30am–5:30pm; Sun 1–5:30pm. Bus: C1, C2, 13, 23, or 71.

Basilica di Santa Maria Novella ★★ Near the rail station is one of Florence's most distinguished churches, begun in 1278 for the Dominicans. Its geometric facade, with bands of white and green marble, was designed in the late 15th century by Leon Battista Alberti. In the left nave as you enter, the third large painting is the great Masaccio's ***Trinità* ★**, a curious work that has the architectural form of a Renaissance stage setting but whose figures (in perfect perspective) are like actors in a Greek tragedy. If you view the church at dusk, you'll see the stained-glass windows in the fading light cast kaleidoscope fantasies on the opposite wall.

Piazza Santa Maria Novella. ✆ **055-282187.** Church free admission; Spanish Chapel and cloisters 2.75€. Church Mon–Thurs 9:30am–5pm. Spanish Chapel and cloisters Sat and Mon–Thurs 9am–5pm. Bus: C1, C2, 6, 9, 11, 36, 37, or 68.

Cappelle Medicee (Medici Chapels) ★★ The Medici tombs are adjacent to the Basilica of San Lorenzo (see above). You enter the tombs, housing the "blue-blooded" Medici, in back of the church by going around to Piazza Madonna degli Aldobrandini. The main reason to come here is to see the **Nuova Sacrestia (New Sacristy) ★★★**, designed by Michelangelo as a gloomy mausoleum. Working from 1521 to 1534, he created the Medici tombs in a style that foreshadowed the baroque. The two best-known figures within the sacristy are ***Night*** and ***Day* ★★★** at the feet of a sculpture of Giuliano, the duke of Nemours. *Night* is chiseled as a woman in troubled sleep, and *Day* is depicted as a man of strength awakening to a foreboding world.

Piazza Madonna degli Aldobrandini 6. ✆ **055-2388602.** www.polomuseale.firenze.it. Admission 4€. Daily 8:15am–1:50pm. Closed 2nd and 4th Sun, and 1st, 3rd, and 5th Mon of each month. Bus: 1, 6, 7, 11, 17, 33, 67, or 68.

PALACES

Palazzo Medici-Riccardi ★ This palace, a short walk from the Duomo, was the home of Cosimo de' Medici before he took his household to the Palazzo Vecchio. Art lovers visit today chiefly to see **Benozzo Gozzoli's mid-15th-century frescoes ★★** in the **Medici Chapel** (not to be confused with the Medici Chapels).

Via Camillo Cavour 1. ✆ **055-2760340.** www.palazzo-medici.it. Admission 7€. Thurs–Tues 9am–7pm. Bus: 1, 6, 11, or 17.

Palazzo Vecchio ★★ The secular "Old Palace" is Florence's most famous and imposing *palazzo*. It dates from the end of the 13th century. Its most remarkable architectural feature is the 94m (308-ft.) tower.

The 16th-century **Salone dei Cinquecento (Hall of the 500),** the most outstanding part of the palace, is filled with Vasari and company frescoes as well as sculpture. As you enter the hall, look for Michelangelo's ***Victory* ★**, depicting an insipid-looking young man treading on a bearded older man (it has been suggested that Michelangelo put his own face on that of the trampled man). You can also visit the private apartments of Eleanor of Toledo, the Spanish wife of Cosimo I, and a chapel begun in 1540 and frescoed by Bronzino.

Piazza della Signoria. ✆ **055-2768224.** Admission 6€. Mon–Wed and Fri–Sun 9am–7pm; Thurs 9am–2pm. Ticket office closes 1 hr. before palace. Bus: C1, C2, or 23.

The Shopping Scene

Skilled craftsmanship and traditional design unchanged since the days of the Medicis have made this a serious shopping destination. Florence is noted for its hand-tooled **leather goods** and various **straw merchandise,** as well as superbly crafted **gold jewelry.**

Florence isn't a city for bargain shopping, however. Most visitors interested in gold or silver jewelry head for the **Ponte Vecchio** and its tiny shops. It's difficult to tell one from another, but you really don't need to because the merchandise is similar. If you're looking for a charm or souvenir, these shops are fine. But the heyday of finding gold jewelry bargains on the Ponte Vecchio is long gone.

The street for antiques is **Via Maggio;** some of the furnishings and objets d'art here are from the 16th century. Another major area for antiques shopping is **Borgo Ognissanti.**

Florence's Fifth Avenue is **Via dei Tornabuoni,** the place to head for the best-quality leather goods, for the best clothing boutiques, and for stylish but costly shoes. Here you'll find everyone from Armani to Ferragamo.

The better shops are largely along Tornabuoni, but there are many on **Via Vigna Nuova, Via Porta Rossa,** and **Via degli Strozzi** as well. You might also stroll along the Arno. For some of the best buys in leather, check out **Via del Parione,** a short, narrow street off Tornabuoni.

FLORENCE'S FAMOUS MARKETS

Intrepid shoppers head for the **Mercato della Paglia ★★** or **Mercato Nuovo** (**Straw Market** or **New Market**), 2 blocks south of Piazza della Repubblica. It's called Il Porcellino by the Italians because of the bronze statue of a reclining wild boar, a copy of the one in the Uffizi; tourists pet its snout (which is well worn) for good luck. The market stands in the monumental heart of Florence, an easy stroll from the Palazzo Vecchio. It sells not only straw items but also leather goods (not the best quality), along with typical Florentine merchandise: frames, trays, hand embroidery, table linens, and hand-sprayed and -painted boxes in traditional designs. From mid-March to early November, this market is open daily 9am to 8pm; off-season hours are Tuesday to Sunday 9am to 7:30pm.

Even better bargains await those who make their way through the pushcarts to the stalls of the open-air **Mercato Centrale (Mercato San Lorenzo),** in and around Borgo San Lorenzo, near the rail station. If you don't mind bargaining, which is imperative, you'll find an array of merchandise such as raffia bags, Florentine leather purses, sweaters, gloves, salt-and-pepper shakers, straw handbags, and art reproductions. It's open Monday to Saturday from 9am to 6:30pm.

Florence After Dark

Evening entertainment in Florence isn't an exciting prospect, unless you simply like to walk through the narrow streets or head toward Fiesole for a truly spectacular view of the city at night. The typical Florentine begins an evening early at one of the cafes listed below.

THE PERFORMING ARTS

Teatro Comunale di Firenze/Maggio Musicale Fiorentino ★★★, Corso Italia 16 (✆ **055-27791;** www.maggiofiorentino.it), is Florence's main theater, with opera and ballet seasons presented September through December and a concert season January through April. This theater is also the venue for the Maggio Musicale, Italy's oldest and most prestigious festival.

Teatro della Pergola, Via della Pergola 18 (✆ **055-22641;** www.teatrodellapergola.com), is Florence's major legitimate theater, but you'll have to understand Italian to appreciate most of its plays. Plays are performed year-round except during the Maggio Musicale, when the theater becomes the setting for many of the festival events. Tickets cost 15€ to 29€. The box office is open from Monday to Friday 9:30am to 6:45pm, and Saturday 10am to 12:15pm.

LIVE-MUSIC CLUBS

If you want nonstop action and a freewheeling and fun-loving atmosphere, your best show in town is **Universale,** Via Pisana 77 (✆ **055-221122**), which attracts a diverse crowd ranging in age from 20 to 50. Entrance usually ranges from 13€ to 25€.

Red Garter, Via dei Benci 33R (✆ **055-2344904**), right off Piazza Santa Croce, has an American Prohibition–era theme and features everything from rock to bluegrass. Cover is 10€ to 15€.

CAFES

Café Rivoire ★, Piazza della Signoria 4R (✆ **055-214412;** www.rivoire.it), offers a classy and amusing old-world ambience with a direct view of the statues on one of our favorite squares in the world. There's a selection of small sandwiches, omelets, and ice creams, and the cafe is noted for its hot chocolate.

Procacci ★, Via de Tornabuoni 64R (✆ **055-211656**) has attracted the movers and shakers in Florentine couture. Ask for a glass of prosecco while surveying the food on the shelves, everything from Sicilian orange marmalade (which we consider Italy's finest) to the rarest of balsamic vinegars.

BARS & PUBS

La Dolce Vita, Piazza del Carmine 6R (✆ **055-284595;** www.dolcevitaflorence.com), draws the beautiful people. It's a see-and-be-seen type of place, lying south of the Arno and west of the historic core. You come here to drink, gossip, and look ever so chic. So you can see how you're doing, the owners have wisely covered the walls in mirrors.

The ritzy bar of Florence is the **ORVM,** in the Westin Excelsior, Piazza Ognissanti 3 (✆ **055-27151**). On the ground floor of the deluxe hotel, it can be entered through the lobby or through another door on the Arno River side. It has been completely redecorated in a tasteful Art Deco design with two impressive orange chandeliers casting a warm light over the brown leather and wood furnishings. The most popular time to visit is 7 to 9pm daily, when there is live background music.

A Side Trip to Fiesole

Fiesole, once an Etruscan settlement, is a virtual suburb of Florence and its most popular outing. Florentines often head for these hills when it's just too hot in the city. Bus no. 7, leaving from Piazza San Marco, will take you here in 25 minutes and give you a breathtaking view along the way. You'll pass fountains, statuary, and gardens strung out over the hills like a scrambled jigsaw puzzle.

When it comes to accommodations, consider the **Villa San Michele ★★★**, Via Doccia 4, Fiesole, 50014 Firenze (✆ **055-5678200;** fax 055-5678250; www.villasanmichele.com). This ancient monastery of unsurpassed beauty, in a memorable setting on a hill below Fiesole, is a 15-minute walk south of the center. It was built in the 15th century, damaged in World War II, and then restored. The facade and loggia were reportedly designed by Michelangelo. A curving driveway, lined with blossoming trees and flowers, leads to the entrance, and a 10-arch-covered loggia continues around the view side of the building to the Italian gardens at the rear. Double accommodations range from 860€ to 1,070€. It's closed from mid-November to early April.

In Fiesole you won't find anything as dazzling as the Renaissance treasures of Florence; the town's charms are more subtle. Fortunately, all major sights branch out within walking distance of the main square, **Piazza Mino da Fiesole,** beginning with the **Cattedrale di San Romolo (Duomo).** At first this cathedral might seem austere, with its concrete-gray Corinthian columns and Romanesque arches. But it has its own beauty. Dating from A.D. 1000, it was much altered during the Renaissance, and in the Salutati Chapel are important sculptural works by Mino da Fiesole. It's open daily from 7:30am to noon and 4 to 7pm.

The hardest task you'll have in Fiesole is to take the steep goat-climb up to the **Convent of San Francesco,** Via San Francesco 13 (✆ **055-59175**). You can visit the Gothic-style Franciscan church, built in the first years of the 1400s and consecrated in 1516. Inside are many paintings by well-known Florentine artists. In the basement of the church is the ethnological museum. Begun in 1906, the collection has a large section of Chinese artifacts, including ancient bronzes. An Etruscan-Roman section contains some 330 archaeological pieces, and an Egyptian section also has numerous objects.

The ecclesiastical **Museo Bandini (Bandini Museum),** Via Dupré 1 (✆ **055-5961293;** www.fiesolemusei.it), belongs to the Fiesole Cathedral Chapter, established in 1913. On the ground floor are della Robbia terra-cotta works, as well as art by Michelangelo and Pisano. On the top floors are paintings by the best Giotto students, reflecting ecclesiastical and worldly themes, most of them the work of Tuscan artists of the 14th century.

HIGHLIGHTS OF THE TUSCAN & UMBRIAN COUNTRYSIDE

The Tuscan landscapes look just like Renaissance paintings, with rolling plains of grass, cypress trees, and olive groves; ancient walled hill towns; and those fabled Chianti vineyards. **Tuscany** was where the Etruscans first appeared in Italy. The Romans followed, absorbing and conquering them. By the 11th century, the region had evolved into a collection of independent city-states, such as Florence and Siena, each trying to dominate the others. Many of the cities reached the apogee of their economic and political power in the 13th century. The Renaissance reached its apex in Florence, but was slow to come to Siena, which remains a gem of Gothic glory.

Tuscany might be known for its Renaissance artists, but the small region of **Umbria,** at the heart of the Italian peninsula, is associated mainly with saints. Christendom's most beloved saints were born here, including St. Francis of Assisi, founder of the Franciscans. Also born here were St. Valentine, a 3rd-century bishop of Terni, and St. Clare, founder of the Order of Poor Clares.

However, Umbrian painters also contributed to the glory of the Renaissance. Il Perugino, whose lyrical works you can see in the National Gallery of Umbria in Perugia, is one such example.

Umbria's countryside, also the subject of countless paintings, remains as lovely as ever today: You'll pass through a hilly terrain dotted with chestnut trees, interspersed with fertile plains of olive groves and vineyards.

Pisa ★★

Few buildings in the world have captured imaginations as much as the Leaning Tower of Pisa, the most instantly recognizable building in the Western World. But there's more to Pisa than just the tower. In addition to other historic sights, there are the modern busy streets surrounding the university and the market.

ESSENTIALS

GETTING THERE Both domestic and international flights arrive at Pisa's **Galileo Galilei Airport** (✆ **050-849111;** www.pisa-airport.com). From the airport, trains depart every 15 to 30 minutes, depending on the time of the day, for the 5-minute trip into Pisa. As an alternative, "LAM rossa," a bus, leaves the airport every 40 minutes for the city.

Trains link Pisa and Florence every 1½ hours for the 1-hour trip, costing 5.90€ one-way. Trains running along the seacoast link Pisa with Rome and require about 3 hours travel time. Depending on the time of day and the speed of the train, one-way fares are 17€ to 53€. In Pisa, trains arrive at the **Stazione Pisa Centrale,** Piazza Stazione (✆ **892021** for information in Italy), about a 30-minute walk from the Leaning Tower. Otherwise, you can take bus LAM rossa, which runs every 20 minutes, from the station to the heart of the city. A ticket costs 1€ and is valid for 60 minutes, 1.50€ if you buy it onboard.

If you're **driving,** leave Florence by taking the autostrada west (A11) to the intersection (A12) going south to Pisa. Travel time is about an hour each way.

VISITOR INFORMATION There is a **tourist office** at Piazza Vittorio Emanuele (✆ **050-42291;** www.pisaturismo.it), open Monday to Friday 9am to 7pm and Saturday 9am to 1:30pm.

WHERE TO STAY

Amalfitana ★ In the 15th century, this hotel—which stands in the historic center only 250m (820 ft.) from the Leaning Tower—was a monastery attached to the Church of San Leonardo. You can still see its facade with an ancient portal and tranquil cloister. The old building was converted into a hotel in 1992. The small to midsize bedrooms here are simply though comfortably furnished. The hotel has a little garden and a welcoming, inviting staff.

Via Roma 44, 56126 Pisa. ✆ **050-29000.** Fax 050-25218. www.hotelamalfitana.it. 21 units. 80€ double. Rates include continental breakfast. AE, MC, V. Free parking on street. Bus: 4. **Amenities:** Room service. *In room:* A/C, TV, hair dryer.

WHERE TO DINE

Antica Trattoria Da Bruno PISAN For around half a century, Da Bruno has flourished in this spot near the Leaning Tower. It's one of Pisa's finest restaurants, although it charges moderate tabs. It serves old-fashioned but market-fresh dishes of the Pisan kitchen, including hare with pappardelle, *zuppa alla pisana* (thick vegetable soup), and grilled salt cod with chickpeas. Other specialties include wild boar with olives and polenta.

Via Luigi Bianchi 12. ✆ **050-560818.** Reservations recommended for dinner. Main courses 12€–23€. AE, DC, MC, V. Mon noon–3pm; Wed–Sun noon–3pm and 7–10:30pm. Bus: 4.

EXPLORING THE CITY

Pisa's greatest legacy remains at **Piazza del Duomo,** where you'll find the top three attractions: the Duomo, the baptistery, and the campanile (that famous Leaning Tower).

A 6€ **combination ticket** (you can buy it at any of the included attractions) allows you to visit two of these three sights: the baptistery, the cemetery, and the Duomo

Museum. For 10€, you can visit the five major attractions: the baptistery, the Duomo, the cemetery, the Duomo Museum, and the Museum of Preliminary Frescoes.

Battistero (Baptistery) ★★★ Begun in 1153, the baptistery is like a Romanesque crown. Its most beautiful feature is the exterior, with its arches and columns, but you should visit the interior to see the hexagonal pulpit (1255–60) by Nicola Pisano. Supported by pillars resting on the backs of three marble lions, the pulpit contains bas-reliefs of the Crucifixion, the Adoration of the Magi, the presentation of the Christ Child at the temple, and the Last Judgment (many angels have lost their heads over the years). Column statues represent the Virtues. At the baptismal font is a contemporary John the Baptist by a local sculptor. The echo inside the baptistery shell has enthralled visitors for years.

Piazza del Duomo. ✆ **050-3872210.** www.opapisa.it. Admission 5€. Nov–Feb daily 10am–5pm; Mar and Oct daily 9am–7pm; Apr–Sept daily 8am–8pm. Bus: LAM rossa.

Il Duomo ★★ This cathedral was designed by Buscheto in 1063. In the 13th century Rainaldo erected the unusual facade with its four layers of open-air arches diminishing in size as they ascend. It's marked by three bronze doors, rhythmic in line, that replaced those destroyed in a disastrous 1595 fire. The most artistic is the original south Door of St. Ranieri, the only one to survive the fire; it was cast by Bonnano Pisano in 1180.

In the restored interior, the chief treasure is the polygonal pulpit by Giovanni Pisano, finished in 1310. It was damaged in the fire and finally rebuilt (with bits of the original) in 1926. It's held up by porphyry pillars and column statues symbolizing the Virtues, and the relief panels depict biblical scenes. The pulpit is similar to an earlier one by Giovanni's father, Nicola Pisano, in the baptistery across the way.

There are other treasures, too, including Galileo's lamp (which, according to tradition, the Pisa-born astronomer used to formulate his laws of the pendulum). At the entrance to the choir pier is a painting that appears to be the work of Leonardo. Actually *St. Agnes and Lamb* was done in the High Renaissance style by the great Andrea del Sarto. In the apse you can view a 13th-century mosaic, *Christ Pancrator,* finished in 1302 by Cimabue (it survived the great fire).

Piazza del Duomo 17. ✆ **050-3872210.** www.opapisa.it. Admission 2€; free Nov–Mar. Nov–Feb daily 10am–1pm and 2–5pm; Oct and Mar daily 10am–7pm; Apr–Sept daily 10am–8pm. Sightseeing visits are discouraged during Mass and religious rites. Bus: LAM rossa.

Leaning Tower of Pisa (Campanile) ★★★ ☺ In 1174, Bonnano began construction of this eight-story marble campanile, intended as a free-standing bell tower for the Duomo (see above). A persistent legend is that he deliberately intended the tower to lean. Another legend is that Galileo let objects of different weights fall from the tower, timing their descent to prove his theories of bodies in motion. The real story is that the tower began to tilt sometime after the completion of the first three stories; only then did its builders discover that the foundation wasn't rock solid, but water-soaked clay. Construction was suspended for a century and was eventually resumed, with completion in the late 14th century. The tower currently leans at least 4m (14 ft.) from perpendicular. If it stood straight, it would measure about 55m (180 ft.) tall.

From 1990 until 2001, the tower was closed because of dangerous conditions. Since that time, to stabilize its tilt, tons of soil were removed from under the foundation, and lead counterweights were placed at the monument's base.

Piazza del Duomo 17. ✆ **050-3872210.** Fax 050-560505. www.opapisa.it. Admission 15€. Only a group of 40 admitted at a time. Children 7 and under not admitted. Nov–Feb daily 10am–5pm; Oct and Mar daily 9am–7pm; Apr–June and Sept daily 8:30am–8:30pm; July–Aug daily 8:30am–11pm. Bus: LAM rossa.

Museo dell'Opera del Duomo (Duomo Museum) ★★ This museum exhibits works of art removed from the monumental buildings on the piazza. The heart of the collection, on the ground floor, consists of sculptures spanning the 11th to the 13th century. A notable treasure is an Islamic griffin from the 11th century, a bronze brought back from the Crusades as booty. For decades it adorned the cupola of the cathedral before being brought here for safekeeping. The most famous exhibit is the *Madonna and the Crucifix,* by Giovanni Pisano, carved from an ivory tusk in 1299.

Upstairs are paintings from the 15th to the 18th century. Some of the textiles and embroideries date from the 15th century; another section of the museum is devoted to Egyptian, Etruscan, and Roman works.

Piazza Arcivescovado. ✆ **050-3872210.** www.opapisa.it. Admission 5€. Nov–Feb daily 10am–5pm; Mar and Oct daily 9am–7pm; Apr–Sept daily 8am–8pm. Bus: LAM rossa.

San Gimignano ★★★

In its medieval heyday, **San Gimignano** had as many as 72 towers. Today, 13 towers remain. The city's fortress-like severity is softened by the subtlety of its harmonious squares. Many of its palaces and churches are enhanced by Renaissance frescoes. Stay overnight, if you can, so that you can enjoy the late afternoon or early evening and get a sense of the town without the crowds.

ESSENTIALS

GETTING THERE The **rail station** nearest to San Gimignano is at Poggibonsi, serviced by regular trains from Florence and Siena. At Poggibonsi, buses depart from the front of the rail station at frequent intervals, charging 2.50€ each way to the center of San Gimignano. For information, call ✆ **0577-204246.**

Buses operated by TRA-IN (✆ **0577-204111;** www.trainspa.it) service San Gimignano from Florence with a change at Poggibonsi (trip time: 85 min.); the one-way fare is 8.50€. TRA-IN also operates service from Siena; the one-way fare is 5.50€. In San Gimignano, buses stop at Piazzale Montemaggio, outside the Porta San Giovanni, the southern gate. You'll have to walk into the center because vehicles aren't allowed in most of the town's core.

If you have a **car,** leave Florence (1½ hr.) or Siena (1 hr. 10 min.) by the Firenze-Siena autostrada and drive to Poggibonsi, where you'll need to cut west along a secondary route (S324) to San Gimignano. There are parking lots outside the city walls.

VISITOR INFORMATION The **Associazione Pro Loco,** Piazza del Duomo 1 (✆ **0577-940008;** www.sangimignano.com), is open daily November through February from 9am to 1pm and 2 to 6pm, and March to October 9am to 1pm and 3 to 7pm.

WHERE TO STAY

Hotel Belsoggiorno This hotel, though no longer the town's best, is still a good, affordable alternative. Although the Gigli family has run it since 1886, there's not as much old-fashioned charm as you'd think. The medium-size rooms have cheap, functional furniture and beds verging on the oversoft, but the management is quite friendly. The best 10 rooms are those with private balconies. In summer, you'll be asked to take your meals at the hotel, which is no great hardship because the cuisine is excellent. The medieval-style **dining room** boasts murals depicting a wild-boar hunt (see "Where to Dine," below).

Via San Giovanni 91, 53037 San Gimignano. ✆ **0577-940375.** Fax 0577-907521. www.hotelbelsoggiorno.it. 22 units. 95€–120€ double; 120€–170€ suite. Rates include continental breakfast. AE, DC, MC, V. Parking 15€. Closed mid-Nov to Dec 27 and mid-Feb to mid-Mar. **Amenities:** Restaurant; bar. *In room:* A/C, TV, hair dryer, minibar (in some).

La Collegiata ★★★ Outside of town and surrounded by a park of Tuscan cypresses, this elegant, refined choice offers the finest accommodations in the San Gimignano area. The villa dates from 1587, when it housed Capuchin monks. You can walk to the building through a beautifully planted Italian garden. After checking in, you can go for a dip in an open-air swimming pool and enjoy the Tuscan landscape so beloved by painters. The cloister opens into the reception area, a wine bar, a coffee shop, sitting rooms, and a reading room. Bedrooms are beautifully furnished, often with such decorative touches as mullioned windows or small balconies. Most of those on the first floor open onto the inner courtyard.

Località Strada 27, 53037 San Gimignano. ✆ **800/735-2478** or 0577-943201. Fax 0577-940566. www.lacollegiata.it. 22 units. 230€–535€ double; from 500€ suite. AE, MC, V. Free parking. Closed Jan–Feb. **Amenities:** Restaurant; babysitting; exercise room; outdoor pool; Wi-Fi (free, in lobby). *In room:* A/C, TV, hair dryer, minibar.

WHERE TO DINE

Dorandò ★★ TUSCAN Between Piazza Duomo and Piazza Cisterna, this elegant restaurant in a 14th-century building in the heart of town is the supreme choice for dining. Three dining rooms with vaulted roofs and imposing stone walls form the backdrop, the walls decorated with original paintings from local artists. The inventive cuisine features the local products of Tuscany. The menu is seasonally adjusted to keep it market fresh. The dishes reflect the robust flavors of regional produce, including such appetizers as red-onion soup with toasted almonds and pecorino cheese or else a vegetable and mushroom soup served with a quail egg. Main-dish specialties include *pici* (a Tuscan spaghetti) served with guinea hen ragout or a filet of pork with a bittersweet apple purée.

Vicolo dell'Oro 2. ✆ **0577-941-862.** www.ristorantedorando.it. Reservations required. Main courses 8€–25€. MC, V. Daily noon–2:30pm and 7–9:30pm. Closed Mon Feb–Easter and Dec–Jan.

Ristorante Belsoggiorno TUSCAN Its windows and terrace overlook the countryside, and its kitchen uses only fresh ingredients from nearby farms. Two of the most appealing specialties (available only late summer to late winter) are roasted wild boar with red wine and mixed vegetables, and pappardelle pasta, garnished with a savory ragout of pheasant. Other pastas are pappardelle with roasted hare, and risotto with herbs and seasonal vegetables. The main courses stress vegetable garnishes and thin-sliced meats that are simply but flavorfully grilled over charcoal, and breads are homemade and baked on-site. Many dishes hearken back to medieval recipes.

In the Hotel Belsoggiorno, Via San Giovanni 91. ✆ **0577-940375.** Reservations recommended. Main courses 16€–18€; fixed-price menu 50€. AE, DC, MC, V. Thurs–Tues 12:30–2:30pm and 7:30–10pm. Closed mid-Nov to Dec 27 and mid-Feb to mid-Mar.

Ristorante Le Terrazze TUSCAN One of this restaurant's two dining rooms boasts stones laid in the 1300s, and the other offers lots of rustic accessories and large windows overlooking the old town and the Val d'Elsa. The food features an assortment of produce from nearby farms. The soups and pastas make fine beginnings, and specialties of the house include such delectable items as sliced filet of wild boar with polenta and chianti, goose breast with walnut sauce, *zuppa San Gimignanese* (a hearty minestrone), Florentine-style steaks, and *risotto con funghi porcini* (risotto with porcini mushrooms). A superb dessert wine is *vin santo,* accompanied by an almond cookie called a *cantucci*.

In La Cisterna, Piazza della Cisterna 24. ✆ **0577-940328.** Reservations required. Main courses 15€–20€. AE, DC, MC, V. Mar 11–Oct Wed 7:30–10pm, Thurs–Mon 12:30–2:30pm and 7:30–9:30pm; Nov–Jan 6 Mon and Wed–Sat 7:30–9:30pm. Closed Jan 7–Mar 10.

EXPLORING SAN GIMIGNANO

Connected with the irregularly shaped square is its satellite, **Piazza del Duomo ★★**, whose medieval architecture of towers and palaces is almost unchanged. It's the most beautiful spot in town. On the square, the **Palazzo del Popolo ★** was designed in the 13th century, and its **Torre Grossa,** built a few years later, is believed to have been the tallest "skyscraper" (about 53m/178 ft. high) in town (see Museo Civico [Civic Museum], below, for information on how to climb this tower).

Duomo Collegiata o Basilica di Santa Maria Assunta ★ Residents of San Gimignano still call this a Duomo (cathedral), even though it was demoted to a "Collegiata" after the town lost its bishop. Don't judge this book by its cover, though. The facade—dating from the 12th century—was never finished, which causes the building to look plain and austere on the outside, but it is richly decorated inside.

Once inside, head for the north aisle, where in the 1360s Bartolo di Fredi depicted scenes from the Old Testament. Seek out Bartolo's horrendous *Last Judgment,* one of the most perverse paintings in Italy. Abandoning briefly his rosy-cheeked Sienese Madonnas, he depicted distorted and suffering nudes, shocking at the time.

The chief attraction here is the **Cappella Santa Fina (Chapel of Santa Fina),** designed by Giuliano and Benedetto da Maiano. Michelangelo's fresco teacher, Domenico Ghirlandaio, frescoed it with scenes from the life of a local girl, Fina, who became the town's patron saint. According to accounts of the day, the little girl went to the well for water and accepted an orange from a young lad. When her mother scolded her for her wicked ways, she was so mortified that she prayed for the next 5 years until St. Anthony called her to heaven.

Piazza del Duomo. ✆ **0577-940316.** Church free admission; chapel 3.50€ adults, free for children 5 and under. Mar–Oct daily 9:30am–7pm; Nov–Feb Mon–Sat 9:30am–5pm, Sun 1–5pm.

Museo Civico (Civic Museum) ★ This museum is installed upstairs in the Palazzo del Popolo (town hall). Most notable is the **Sala di Dante (Dante Salon),** where the poet supporter of the White Guelph spoke out for his cause in 1300. Look for one of the masterpieces of San Gimignano: ***La Maestà*** (a Madonna enthroned), by Lippo Memmi (later touched up by Gozzoli). The first large room upstairs contains the other masterpiece: a ***Madonna in Glory,*** with SS. Gregory and Benedict, painted by Pinturicchio. On the other side of it are two depictions of the *Annunciation,* by Filippino Lippi. On the opposite wall, note the magnificent Byzantine Crucifix by Coppo di Marcovaldo.

Passing through the Museo Civico, you can scale the **Torre Grossa** and be rewarded with a bird's-eye view of this most remarkable town. The tower, the only one you can climb, is open during the same hours as the museum.

In the Palazzo del Popolo, Piazza del Duomo 1. ✆ **0577-990312.** Admission 5€ for adults, 4€ for students and children 17 and under. Mar–Oct daily 9:30am–7pm; Nov–Feb daily 10am–5:30pm.

Siena ★★★

Spread over three sienna-colored hills in Tuscany's center, Sena Vetus lies in Chianti country. Take your time enjoying this city of contemplation and profound exploration, characterized by Gothic palaces, almond-eyed Madonnas, aristocratic mansions, letter-writing St. Catherine (patron saint of Italy), narrow streets, and medieval gates, walls, and towers.

ESSENTIALS

GETTING THERE The **rail** link between Siena and Florence is sometimes inconvenient because you often have to change and wait at other stations, such as Empoli. But trains run every hour from Florence, costing 6.20€ one-way. You arrive at the station at Piazza Carlo Rosselli. This is an awkward half-hour climb uphill to the monumental heart of the city. However, bus no. 10 will take you to Piazza Gramsci near the center. For information and schedules, call ✆ **892021.**

TRA-IN, Piazza La Lizza (✆ **0577-204111;** www.trainspa.it), offers bus service from all of Tuscany in air-conditioned coaches. The one-way fare between Florence and Siena is 6.80€. The trip takes 1¼ hours (actually faster than taking the train, and you'll be let off in the city center). Ticket offices are open daily from 5:50am to 7:30pm.

If you have a **car,** head south from Florence along the Firenze-Siena autostrada, a superhighway linking the two cities, going through Poggibonsi. (It has no route number; just follow the green autostrada signs for Siena.)

Trying to drive into the one-way and pedestrian-zoned labyrinth that is the city center just isn't worth the headache. Siena's parking (✆ **0577-228711;** www.sienaparcheggi.com) is now coordinated, and all the lots charge 1.60€ per hour (although almost every hotel has a discount deal with the nearest lot wherein parking for hotel guests is either free or discounted by 40% or more). Lots are well signposted, just inside several of the city gates.

VISITOR INFORMATION The **tourist office** is at Piazza del Campo 56 (✆ **0577-280551;** www.terresiena.it). It's open daily 9am to 7pm. The office will give you a good free map.

WHERE TO STAY

Certosa di Maggiano ★★ This early-13th-century Certosinian monastery is now an intimate, plush retreat affiliated with Relais & Châteaux. The stylish public rooms fill the spaces in what used to be the ambulatory of the central courtyard, and the complex's medieval church still holds Mass on Sunday. The individually decorated guest rooms are spacious, with antiques, art objects, and sumptuous beds; one has a private walled garden. The hotel isn't easy to find; phone ahead for directions. The staff can help you arrange for guided tours, wine tastings, and many other outings. There's a shuttle into the historic center of town.

Siena

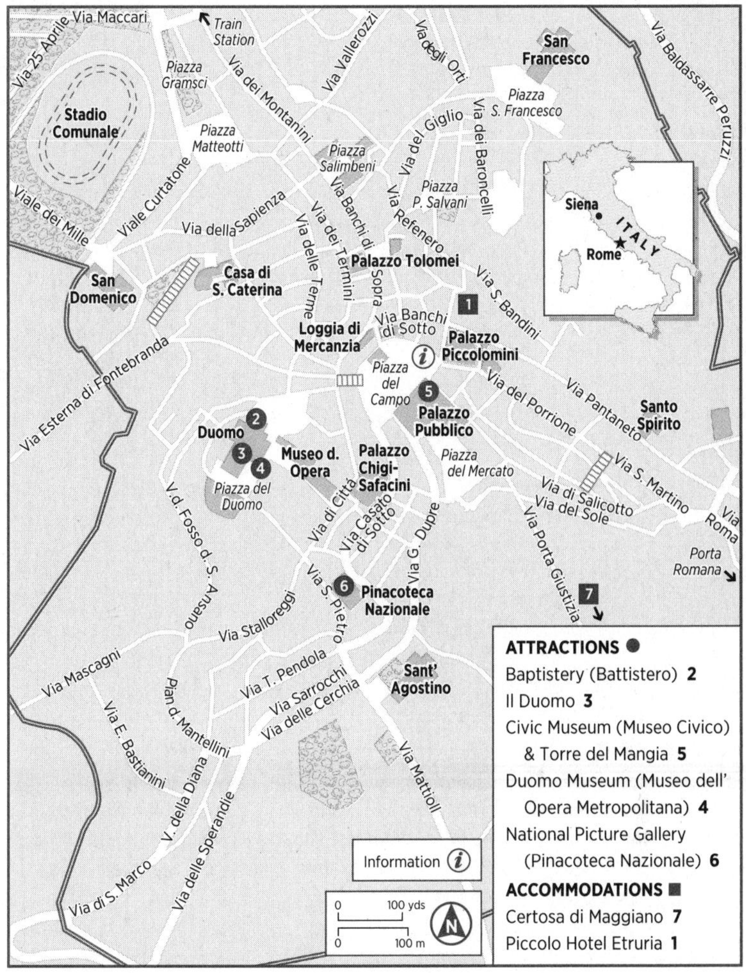

Strada di Certosa 82, 53100 Siena. ✆ **0577-288180.** Fax 0577-288189. www.certosadimaggiano.com. 17 units. 370€–660€ double; 750€–1,270€ suite. Rates include American buffet breakfast. AE, MC, V. Parking 30€. Closed Nov–Mar. Children 11 and under are not accepted. **Amenities:** Restaurant; bar; babysitting; exercise room; outdoor heated pool; room service; outdoor tennis court (lit). *In room:* A/C, TV, hair dryer, minibar.

Piccolo Hotel Etruria ★ This small family-run hotel could thumb its nose at the big corporate chains; it offers equally comfortable modern luxuries with twice the character at a fourth of the price. In both the main building and the annex across the street, the guest rooms have tiled floors, wood-toned built-in furnishings with stone-topped desks and end tables, leather strap chairs, and quite decent beds. The rooms aren't very spacious, but they aren't small either. The only real drawback is that the hotel closes from 1 to 7am.

Via Donzelle 3, 53100 Siena. ✆ **0577-288088.** Fax 0577-288461. www.hoteletruria.com. 13 units (shower only). 86€ double; 117€ triple. AE, MC, V. Closed Dec 17–27. Bus: 1, 2, 3, 9, or 10. **Amenities:** Room service. *In room:* A/C, TV, hair dryer.

WHERE TO DINE

Al Marsili SIENESE/ITALIAN This beautiful restaurant stands between the Duomo and Via di Città. You dine beneath crisscrossed ceiling vaults whose russet-colored brickwork was designed centuries ago. The antipasti offer some unusual treats, such as polenta with chicken-liver sauce; a medley of the best of Siena's cold cuts; and smoked venison, wild boar, and goose blended into a pâté. The wide selection of first courses ranges from the typical vegetable soup of Siena *(ribollita alla senese)* to a risotto with four cheeses. Pasta specialties include *pici all'aglione* (fresh Sienese pasta with a garlic and tomato sauce). For a main dish, you might try guinea hen cooked with pine nuts, almonds, and prunes.

Via del Castoro 3. ✆ **0577-47154.** www.ristorantealmarsili.it. Reservations recommended. Main courses 13€–20€. AE, DC, MC, V. Tues–Sun 12:30–2:30pm and 7:30–10:30pm. Bus: 1, 2, or 5.

Osteria Le Logge ★★ SIENESE/TUSCAN This popular trattoria is a bastion of superb cuisine in a refined and old-fashioned atmosphere. The menu, changed daily, overflows with freshness and flavor. Try the wild-boar stew with spicy tomato sauce or the delectable baked duck stuffed with fennel or grapes. In autumn, try the pappardelle with game sauce. The tender veal steaks are among the best in town, and you can also order taglierini pasta with black-truffle sauce. Save room for one of the desserts, which are made fresh each morning.

Via del Porrione 33. ✆ **0577-48013.** www.giannibrunelli.it. Reservations recommended. Main courses 10€–23€. AE, DC, MC, V. Mon–Sat noon–2:45pm and 7–10:30pm. Closed Jan 8–31.

EXPLORING SIENA

Start in the heart of Siena, the shell-shaped **Piazza del Campo ★★★**, described by Montaigne as "the finest of any city in the world." Pause to enjoy the **Fonte Gaia,** which locals sometimes call the Fountain of Joy. The square is truly stunning, designed like a sloping scallop shell; you'll want to linger in one of the cafes along its edge.

Battistero (Baptistery) ★ Although the lavish and intricate frescoes are a draw, the star of the place is a **baptismal font** (1417–30), one of the greatest in all Italy. The foremost sculptors of the early Renaissance from both Florence and Siena helped create this masterpiece. Jacopo della Quercia created *Annunciation to Zacharias,* Giovanni di Turino crafted *Preaching of the Baptist* and the *Baptism of Christ,* and Lorenzo Ghiberti worked with Giuliano di Ser Andrea on the masterful *Arrest of St. John.* Our favorite is Donatello's *Feast of Herod,* a work of profound beauty and perspective.

Piazza San Giovanni (behind the Duomo). ✆ **0577-283048.** www.operaduomo.siena.it. Admission 3€. Mar–May and Sept–Oct daily 9:30am–7pm; June–Aug daily 9:30am–8pm; Nov–Feb daily 10am–5pm. Closed Jan 1 and Dec 25. Bus: 1.

Il Duomo ★★★ With its colored bands of marble, the Sienese Duomo is an original and exciting building, erected in the Romanesque and Italian Gothic styles in the 12th century. The dramatic facade, designed in part by Giovanni Pisano, dates from the 13th century, as does the Romanesque campanile.

The zebra-like interior of black-and-white stripes is equally stunning. The floor consists of various inlaid works of art depicting both biblical and mythological subjects. In the chapel of the left transept (near the library) is a glass box containing an arm that tradition maintains is the one John the Baptist used to baptize Christ; the box also contains Donatello's bronze of John the Baptist.

Inside the Duomo is the **Piccolomini Library ★★**, renowned for its cycle of frescoes by the Umbrian master Pinturicchio.

Piazza del Duomo. ✆ **0577-283048.** www.operaduomo.siena.it. Duomo free admission; library 3€. Duomo Nov–Mar 15 daily 8am–1pm and 2:30–5pm (Mar 16–Oct to 7:30pm). Library Mar 15–Oct daily 9am–7:30pm; Nov–Mar 14 daily 10am–1pm and 2:30–5pm. Closed Sun mornings, Jan 1, and Dec 25. Bus: 1.

Museo Civico (Civic Museum) & Torre del Mangia ★★★ The Museo Civico, in the Palazzo Pubblico (1288–1309), is filled with important artworks by some of the leaders in the Sienese school of painting and sculpture.

In the **Sala del Mappomondo (Globe Room)** is Simone Martini's earliest-known work (ca. 1315) and his masterpiece, ***La Maestà*** **★★**, the Madonna enthroned with her Child, surrounded by angels and saints. The other remarkable Martini fresco (on the opposite wall) is the equestrian portrait of Guidoriccio da Fogliano, general of the Sienese Republic, in ceremonial dress.

The next room is the **Sala della Pace (Peace Room),** frescoed from 1337 to 1339 by Ambrogio Lorenzetti. The frescoes compose the **Allegory of Good and Bad Government and Their Effects on the Town and Countryside ★★★**. In this depiction, the most notable figure of the Virtues surrounding the king is La Pace (Peace). To the right of the king and the Virtues is a representation of Siena in peaceful times. On the left, Lorenzetti showed his opinion of "ward heelers," but some of the sting has inadvertently been taken out of the frescoes because the evil-government scene is badly damaged. These were propaganda frescoes in their day, commissioned by the party in power, but they're now viewed as among the most important of all secular frescoes to come down from the Middle Ages.

Accessible from the courtyard of the Palazzo Pubblico is the **Torre del Mangia,** the most prominent architectural landmark on the skyline of Siena. Dating from the 14th century, it soars to a height of 102m (335 ft.). The tower takes its name from a former bell ringer, a sleepy fellow called *mangiaguadagni* ("eat the profits"). Surprisingly, it has no subterranean foundations. The tower is open the same hours as the Civic Museum and charges 6€ for you to climb it.

In the Palazzo Pubblico, Piazza del Campo. ✆ **0577-226230.** Admission 7€. Museum mid-Mar to Oct daily 10am–7pm; Nov to mid-Mar daily 10am–6pm. Tower mid-Oct to Feb daily 10am–6pm; Mar to mid-Oct daily 10am–7pm. Bus: 1, 2, or 5.

Museo dell'Opera Metropolitana (Duomo Museum) ★★ This museum houses paintings and sculptures created for the Duomo. On the ground floor is much interesting sculpture, including works by Giovanni Pisano and his assistants. But the real draw hangs on the next floor: Duccio's fragmented ***La Maestà*** **★★** (1308–11), a Madonna enthroned, one of Europe's greatest late-medieval paintings. The majestic panel was an altarpiece by Duccio di Buoninsegna for the cathedral, filled with dramatic moments illustrating the story of Christ and the Madonna. A student of Cimabue, Duccio was the first great name in the school of Sienese painting. Upstairs are the collections of the treasury, and on the top floor is a display of paintings from the early Sienese school.

Piazza del Duomo 8. ✆ **0577-283048.** www.operaduomo.siena.it. Admission 6€. Mar–May and Sept–Oct daily 9:30am–7pm; June–Aug daily 9:30am–8pm; Nov–Feb daily 10am–5pm. Bus: 1.

Pinacoteca Nazionale (National Picture Gallery) ★★ Housed in a 14th-century *palazzo* near Piazza del Campo is the National Gallery's collection of the Sienese school of painting, which once rivaled that of Florence. Displayed are some of the giants of the pre-Renaissance, with most of the paintings covering the period from the late 12th century to the mid–16th century.

Of exceptional interest are the cartoons of Mannerist master Beccafumi, from which many of the panels in the cathedral floor were created.

In the Palazzo Buonsignori, Via San Pietro 29. ✆ **0577-281161.** Admission 4€. Mon 8:30am–1:30pm; Tues–Sat 8:30am–7pm; Sun 8:30am–1:30pm. Closed Jan 1, May 1, and Dec 25. Bus: A.

Assisi ★★★

Ideally placed on the rise to Mount Subasio, watched over by the medieval Rocco Maggiore, the purple-fringed Umbrian hill town of Assisi retains a mystical air. The site of many a pilgrimage, Assisi is forever linked in legend with its native son, St. Francis. But even without St. Francis, the hill town merits a visit for its sights and architecture. Tourists and pilgrims pack the town in summer, and at Easter or Christmas you're likely to be trampled underfoot. We've found it best and less crowded in spring or fall.

ESSENTIALS

GETTING THERE Although there's no rail station in Assisi, the city lies within a 30-minute bus or taxi ride from the rail station in nearby Santa Maria degli Angeli. From Santa Maria degli Angeli, buses depart at 15-minute intervals for Piazza Matteotti in the heart of Assisi. One-way fares are 1€. If you're coming to Assisi from Perugia by train, expect to pay around 2€ one-way. If you're coming from Rome, expect to pay 9.50€ to 25€ each way, depending on the train. Rail fares between Florence and Assisi are about 10€ each way. For more information call ✆ 892021.

Frequent **buses** connect Perugia with Assisi (run by APM; ✆ **075-5731707;** www.apmperugia.it). The trip takes 1 hour and costs 4€ one-way; a ticket costs 5€ if you buy it onboard. One bus a day arrives from Rome (run by SULGA; ✆ **800-099661** in Italy; www.sulga.it); it takes about 3 hours and costs 19€ one-way. Two buses pull in from Florence (also run by SULGA), taking 2½ hours and costing 12€ one-way.

If you have a **car,** you can make the trip from Perugia in 30 minutes by taking S3 southwest. At the junction of Route 147, just follow the signs toward Assisi. But you'll have to park outside the town's core because those neighborhoods are usually closed to traffic. (***Note:*** The police officer guarding the entrance to the old town will usually let motorists drop off luggage at a hotel in the historic zone, with the understanding that you'll eventually park in a lot on the outskirts of town.)

VISITOR INFORMATION The **tourist office** at Piazza del Comune 10 (✆ **075-812534;** www.umbria2000.it) is open Monday to Saturday 8am to 2pm and 3 to 6pm and Sunday 9am to 1pm.

WHERE TO STAY

Grand Hotel Assisi ★★ At last, Assisi—never known for its good hotels—has a front-ranking charmer. The Grand offers the most comfortable and best-furnished

Assisi

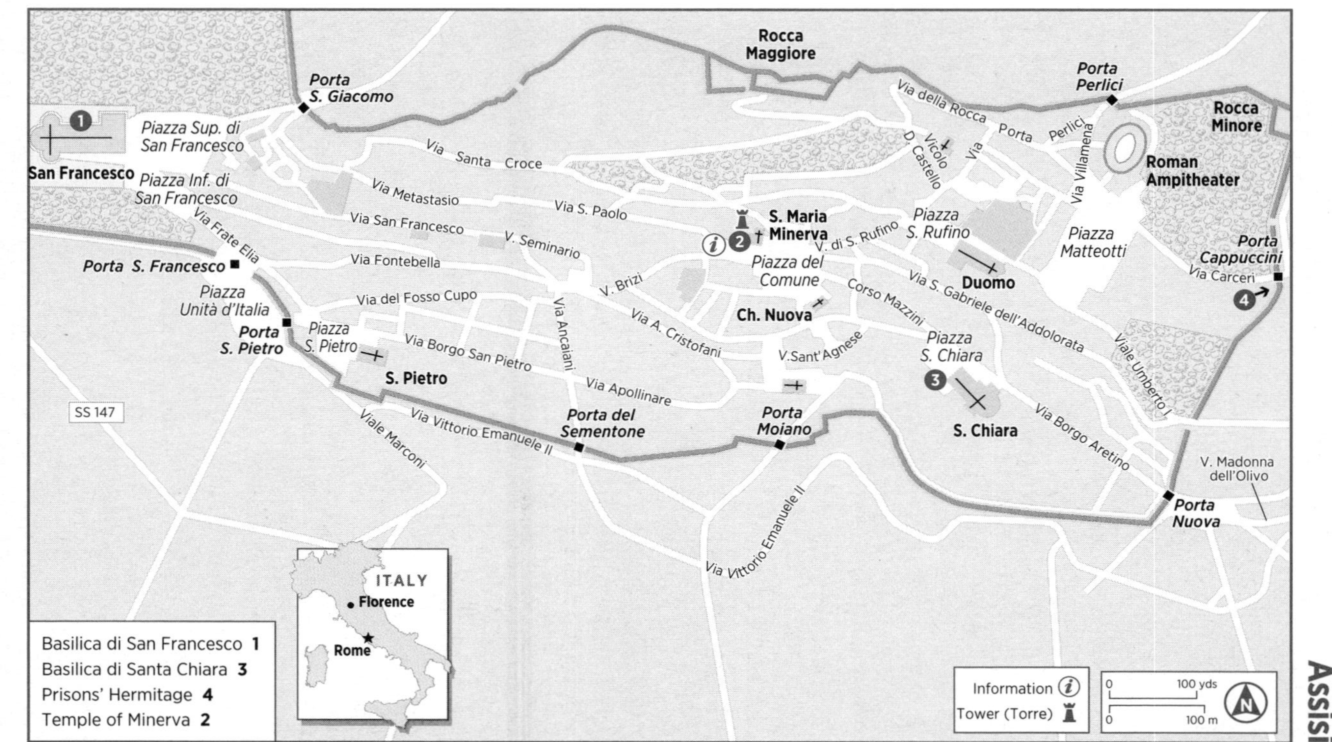
Rocca
Maggiore
Porta
S. Giacomo
Porta
Perlici
Rocca
Minore
Roman
Ampitheater
San Francesco
Piazza Sup. di
San Francesco
Piazza Inf. di
San Francesco
Via Santa Croce
Via Metastasio
Via San Francesco
Via S. Paolo
V. Seminario
Via Frate Elia
Porta S. Francesco
Via Fontebella
Piazza
Unità d'Italia
Porta
S. Pietro
Piazza
S. Pietro
S. Pietro
Via del Fosso Cupo
Via Borgo San Pietro
Via Ancaiani
V. Brizi
Via A. Cristofani
Via Apollinare
Via Vittorio Emanuele II
Viale Marconi
SS 147
Porta del
Sementone
Porta
Moiano
S. Maria
Minerva
Piazza del
Comune
Ch. Nuova
V.Sant'Agnese
V. di S. Rufino
Piazza
S. Rufino
Duomo
Corso Mazzini
Via S. Gabriele dell'Addolorata
Piazza
S. Chiara
S. Chiara
Via Borgo Aretino
Viale Umberto I
Via della Rocca
Vicolo
D. Castello
Via Porta Perlici
Via Villamena
Piazza
Matteotti
Porta
Cappuccini
Via Carceri
V. Madonna
dell'Olivo
Porta
Nuova
ITALY
Florence
Rome
Basilica di San Francesco 1
Basilica di Santa Chiara 3
Prisons' Hermitage 4
Temple of Minerva 2
Information
Tower (Torre)
0 100 yds
0 100 m
N

rooms in town. The suites come with a hydromassage tub and a balcony opening onto a panoramic view. The Grand's roof garden terrace is the hotel's most dramatic feature. The on-site restaurant Giotto & Leonardo is also one of the best in town, offering homemade pastas, delicious truffles, and other succulent ingredients, plus the finest wines from the Umbrian hills. Some visitors make the 40-minute walk into the center; others use the city bus.

Via Fratelli Canonichetti, 06081 Assisi. ✆ **075-81501.** Fax 075-8150777. www.grandhotelassisi.com. 156 units (some with tub only; some with shower only). 205€-240€ double; 280€-350€ suite. Rates include buffet breakfast. AE, DC, MC, V. Free parking. **Amenities:** 2 restaurants; 2 bars; babysitting; exercise room; indoor heated pool; room service; sauna. *In room:* A/C, TV, hair dryer, Jacuzzi (in some), minibar.

Hotel Sole For Umbrian hospitality and a general down-home feeling, the Sole is a winner. The severe beauty of rough stone walls and ceilings, terra-cotta floors, and marble staircases pays homage to the past, balanced by big-cushioned chairs in the TV lounge and contemporary wrought-iron beds and well-worn furnishings in the guest rooms. Some rooms are across the street in an annex. The hotel shows some wear and tear, but the price is right, the location is central, and the **restaurant** is a good choice even if you aren't a guest (you might want to take the meal plan if you are).

Corso Mazzini 35, 06081 Assisi. ✆ **075-812373.** Fax 075-813706. www.assisihotelsole.com. 38 units (shower only). 65€ double; 85€ triple. Half board (Apr–Nov) 53€ per person. AE, DC, MC, V. Parking 10€ nearby. **Amenities:** Restaurant (closed Dec–Mar); bar; room service. *In room:* TV, hair dryer (in some).

WHERE TO DINE

La Fortezza ★★ UMBRIAN Up a stepped alley from Piazza del Comune, this lovely restaurant has been family run for 40 years and is prized for its high quality and reasonable prices. An exposed ancient Roman wall to the right of the entrance establishes the antiquity of this *palazzo* with brick-vaulted ceilings; the rest dates from the 13th century. Truffles are an important ingredient in many dishes, such as a homemade pasta or else guinea fowl cooked in a truffle crust. The delicious homemade pastas are prepared with sauces that follow the season's fresh offerings, while the roster of meats skewered or roasted on the grill (*alla brace*) ranges from veal and lamb to duck. La Fortezza also rents seven rooms upstairs (54€–80€ double).

Via della Fortezza 2B. ✆ **075-812993.** Fax 075-8198035. www.lafortezzahotel.com. Reservations recommended. Main courses 8€-17€. AE, DC, MC, V. Tues and Sat–Sun 12:30–3pm; Mon–Wed and Fri–Sun 7-10:30pm. Closed Feb.

Ristorante Buca di San Francesco UMBRIAN/ITALIAN Evocative of the Middle Ages, this restaurant occupies a cave near the foundation of a 12th-century palace. Menu items change often, based on the availability of ingredients, but you're likely to find homemade tagliatelle with truffles; *umbricelli* (big noodles) with asparagus sauce; cannelloni with ricotta, spinach, and tomatoes; *carlaccia* (baked crepes) stuffed with cheese, prosciutto, and roasted veal; and *piccione alla sisana* (roasted pigeon with olive oil, capers, and aromatic herbs). There are about 100 seats in the dining room and another 60 in the garden overlooking Assisi's historic center.

Via Brizi 1. ✆ **075-812204.** Reservations recommended. Main courses 10€-20€. AE, DC, MC, V. Tues-Sun noon–2:30pm and 7–10pm. Closed July 1–15 and Jan 6–Feb 6.

EXPLORING ASSISI

Piazza del Comune, in the heart of Assisi, is a dream for lovers of architecture from the 12th to the 14th century. On the square is a pagan structure, with six Corinthian columns, called the **Tempio di Minerva (Temple of Minerva),** from the 1st century B.C. With Minerva-like wisdom, the people of Assisi turned the interior into a baroque church so as not to offend the devout. Adjoining the temple is the 13th-century **Torre (Tower)** built by Ghibelline supporters. The site is open daily from 7am to noon and 2:30pm to dusk.

Basilica di Santa Chiara (St. Clare) ★★ The basilica is dedicated to "the little plant of Blessed Francis," as St. Clare liked to describe herself. Born in 1193 into one of the noblest families of Assisi, Clare gave all her wealth to the poor and founded, together with St. Francis, the Order of the Poor Clares. Many of the frescoes that once adorned this basilica have deteriorated and fallen away as time has rolled by, but much remains that is worthy of note. Upon entering, your attention will be caught by the striking *Crucifix* behind the main altar, a painting on wood dating from the time of the church itself (ca. 1260).

Warning: The custodian turns away visitors in shorts, miniskirts, plunging necklines, and backless or sleeveless attire.

Piazza di Santa Chiara 1. ✆ **075-812282.** Free admission. Nov–Mar daily 6:30am–noon and 2–6:30pm; Apr–Oct daily 6:30am–noon and 2–7pm.

Basilica di San Francesco (St. Francis) ★★★ This basilica, with both an upper church (1230–53) and a lower church (1228–30), houses some of the most important **cycles of frescoes** in Italy, including works by such pre-Renaissance giants as Cimabue and Giotto. Reached by the entrance in Piazza Inferiore on the south side of the basilica, the **lower church** is dark and mystical and almost entirely covered with **frescoes ★★★** by the greatest pre-Renaissance painters of the 13th and 14th centuries. Under the lower church is the **crypt of St. Francis,** with some relics of the saint.

Piazza San Francesco. ✆ **075-819001.** www.sanfrancescoassisi.org. Free admission. Daily 8:30am–6:30pm.

Eremo delle Carceri (Prisons' Hermitage) ★★ This "prison," from the 14th and 15th centuries, is not a penal institution but a spiritual retreat. It's believed that St. Francis retired to this spot for meditation and prayer. One of the handful of friars who still inhabit the retreat will show you through. (In keeping with the Franciscan tradition, they're completely dependent on donations for their support.)

About 4km (2½ miles) east of Assisi, on Via Eremo delle Carceri. ✆ **075-812301.** www.eremocarceri.it. Free admission (donations accepted). Old refectory daily 9am–noon and 2:30–4:30pm. Tree of Birds Easter–Nov daily 6:30am–7:15pm; Dec–Apr daily 6:30am–sunset.

VENICE ★★★

Venice is a preposterous monument to both the folly and the obstinacy of humankind. It shouldn't exist, but it does, much to the delight of thousands of visitors, gondoliers, lace makers, hoteliers, restaurateurs, and glass blowers.

Centuries ago, in an effort to flee barbarians, Venetians left dry land and drifted out to a flotilla of "uninhabitable" islands in the lagoon, where they created the world's most beautiful city. To your children's children, however, Venice might be

Venice

ATTRACTIONS ●

- Academy Gallery **4**
- Bridge of Sighs **13**
- Ca' d'Oro **16**
- Ca' Rezzonico **3**
- Correr Civic Museum **9**
- Ducal Palace **12**
- The Grand Canal **2**
- Peggy Guggenheim Collection **5**
- Piazza San Marco **10**
- St. Mark's Basilica & Campanile **11**

ACCOMMODATIONS ■

- Albergo Marin **1**
- Boscolo Grand Hotel dei Dogi **17**
- Ca' Dei Dogi **14**
- Cipriani **8**
- DD724 **6**
- Gritti Palace **7**
- La Residenza **15**

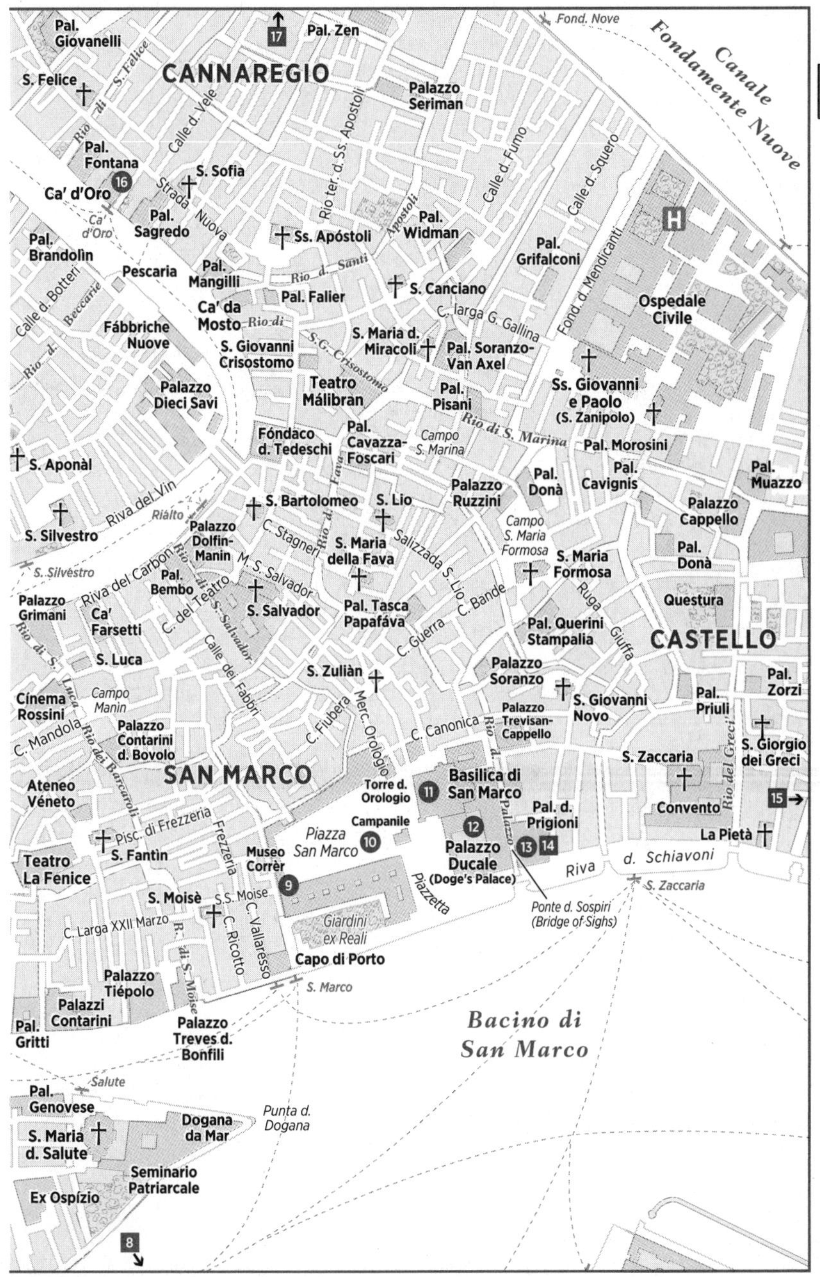
CANNAREGIO
SAN MARCO
CASTELLO
Canale Fondamente Nuove
Bacino di San Marco
Pal. Giovanelli
Pal. Zen
S. Felice
Palazzo Seriman
Pal. Fontana
Ca' d'Oro
S. Sofia
Pal. Sagredo
Pal. Brandolin
Ss. Apóstoli
Pal. Widman
Pal. Grifalconi
Ospedale Civile
Pescaria
Pal. Mangilli
Pal. Falier
S. Canciano
Ca' da Mosto
Fábbriche Nuove
S. Giovanni Crisostomo
S. Maria d. Miracoli
Pal. Soranzo-Van Axel
Teatro Málibran
Palazzo Dieci Savi
Pal. Pisani
Ss. Giovanni e Paolo (S. Zanipolo)
Fóndaco d. Tedeschi
Pal. Cavazza-Foscari
Pal. Morosini
S. Aponàl
Pal. Donà
Pal. Cavignis
Pal. Muazzo
S. Bartolomeo
S. Lio
Palazzo Ruzzini
Palazzo Cappello
S. Silvestro
Palazzo Dolfin-Manin
S. Maria della Fava
S. Maria Formosa
Pal. Donà
Pal. Bembo
Palazzo Grimani
Ca' Farsetti
S. Salvador
Pal. Tasca Papafáva
Questura
Pal. Querini Stampalia
S. Luca
S. Zuliàn
Palazzo Soranzo
Pal. Zorzi
Cínema Rossini
Palazzo Trevisan-Cappello
S. Giovanni Novo
Pal. Priuli
Palazzo Contarini d. Bovolo
S. Zaccaria
S. Giorgio dei Greci
Ateneo Véneto
Torre d. Orologio
Basilica di San Marco
Convento
Campanile
Pal. d. Prigioni
La Pietà
Piazza San Marco
Palazzo Ducale (Doge's Palace)
Teatro La Fenice
S. Fantìn
Museo Corrèr
Ponte d. Sospiri (Bridge of Sighs)
S. Moisè
Giardini ex Reali
Capo di Porto
Palazzo Tiépolo
Palazzi Contarini
Pal. Gritti
Palazzo Treves d. Bonfili
Pal. Genovese
Dogana da Mar
Punta d. Dogana
S. Maria d. Salute
Seminario Patriarcale
Ex Ospízio
Fond. Nove
Rialto
S. Silvestro
S. Zaccaria
S. Marco
Salute
Campo S. Marina
Campo S. Maria Formosa
Campo Manin
Riva d. Schiavoni
Piazzetta
Riva del Vin
Riva del Carbon
Strada Nuova
Calle d. Vele
Calle d. Fumo
Calle d. Squero
Fond. d. Mendicanti
C. larga G. Gallina
Rio di S. Marina
Salizzada S. Lio
Ruga Giuffa
C. Bande
C. Guerra
C. Canonica
C. Stagneri
M. S. Salvador
Calle dei Fabbri
Merc. Orologio
C. Fiubera
C. del Teatro
C. Mandola
Rio dei Barcaroli
Pisc. di Frezzeria
Frezzeria
C. Larga XXII Marzo
C. Ricotto
C. Vallaresso
Rio del Greci
Calle d. Botteri
16
17
11
12
10
9
13
14
15
8

nothing more than a legend. The city is sinking at an alarming rate of about 2½ inches per decade, and at the same time, the damp climate, mold, and pollution are contributing to the city's decay. Estimates are that, if no action is taken soon, one-third of the city's art will deteriorate within the next decade or so.

Although Venice is one of the world's most enchanting cities, you do pay a price, literally and figuratively, for all this beauty. Everyone leaves complaining about the outrageous prices, which can be double what they are elsewhere in the country. In the summer heat of the Adriatic, the canals become a smelly stew. Steamy and overcrowded July and August are the worst times to visit; May, June, September, and October are much better.

Essentials

ARRIVING The arrival scene at unattractive **Piazzale Roma** is filled with nervous expectation; even the most veteran traveler can become confused. Whether arriving by train, bus, car, or airport limo, everyone walks to the nearby docks (less than a 5-min. walk) to select a method of transport to his or her hotel. The cheapest way is by *vaporetto* (public motorboat); the more expensive is by gondola or motor launch (see the "Getting Around" section, below).

BY PLANE You can now fly nonstop from North America to Venice on Delta. You'll land at the **Aeroporto Marco Polo** (✆ **041-2606111;** www.veniceairport.it) at Mestre, north of the city on the mainland. The **Consorzio Motoscafi** (✆ **041-5222303;** www.motoscafivenezia.it) operates a *motoscafo* (shuttle boat) service that can deliver you from the airport directly to the center of Venice at Piazza San Marco in about 30 minutes. The boats wait just outside the main entrance, and the fare begins at 98€ for up to six passengers (if there are only two of you, find some fellow travelers to share the ride and split the fare with you). If you've got some extra euros to spend, you can arrange for a **private water taxi** by calling ✆ **041-5222303.** The cost of the ride to the heart of Venice is 98€.

Buses from the airport are less expensive, though they can take you only as far as Piazzale Roma; from there you will need to take a *vaporetto* to reach your hotel. The **Azienda Trasporti Veneto Orientale** (✆ **041-383672**) shuttle bus links the airport with Piazzale Roma for 3€. The trip takes about 20 minutes, and departures are about every 30 minutes daily 8:20am to 12:10am. Even cheaper is a local bus company, **ACTV** (✆ **041-2424**), whose bus no. 5 makes the run for 2€. The ACTV buses depart every half-hour and take about a half-hour to reach Piazzale Roma.

BY TRAIN Trains pull into the **Stazione di Santa Lucia,** at Piazzale Roma (✆ **041-892021** in Italy only). Travel time is about 5 hours from Rome, 3½ hours from Milan, 4 hours from Florence, and 2 hours from Bologna. The *vaporetto* departs near the station's main entrance. There's also a **tourist office** at the station (✆ **041-5298711**); open daily 8am to 6:30pm.

Anyone between the ages of 14 and 29 is eligible for a **Rolling Venice pass,** entitling you to discounts for museums, restaurants, stores, language courses, hotels, and bars. Valid for 1 year, it costs 4€ and can be picked up at any tourist office in Venice.

BY CAR The autostrada links Venice with the rest of Italy, with direct routes from such cities as Trieste (driving time: 1½ hr.), Milan (3 hr.), and Bologna (2 hr.). Bologna is 151km (94 miles) southwest of Venice, Milan is 266km (165 miles) west, Trieste is 156km (97 miles) east, and Rome is 526km (327 miles) southwest.

From the mainland, follow the signs leading to Venice, going to the Ponte della Libertà along S11, which links Venice to the mainland. The small island of Tronchetto appears on your right as the bridge comes to an end. Here you'll find the parking garages of Venice.

One of the most prominent garages is the **Garage San Marco,** Piazzale Roma (✆ **041-5232213**), near the *vaporetto,* gondola, and motor launch docks. The charge is 24€ for 12 hours or 30€ for 24 hours for any kind of car. From spring to fall, this municipal parking lot is nearly always filled. You can fax a reservation for a space to 041-5289969. You're more likely to find parking on **Isola del Tronchetto** (✆ **041-5207555**), which costs 21€ per day. From Tronchetto, take *vaporetto* no. 2 to Piazza San Marco. If you have heavy luggage, you'll need a water taxi. Parking is also available at Mestre.

VISITOR INFORMATION Visitor information is available at the **Azienda di Promozione Turistica,** San Marco 71/F (✆ **041-5298711;** www.turismovenezia.it). Year-round hours are daily 9am to 3:30pm. Posters around town with exhibit and concert schedules are more helpful. Ask for a schedule of the month's special events and an updated list of museum and church hours because these can change erratically and often. There is also another tourist office at the airport open daily from 9am to 9pm (✆ **041-5298711**).

CITY LAYOUT Venice lies 4km (2½ miles) from the Italian mainland (connected to Mestre by the Ponte della Libertà) and 2km (1¼ miles) from the open Adriatic. It's an archipelago of 118 islands. Most visitors, however, concern themselves only with **Piazza San Marco** and its vicinity. In fact, the entire city has only one piazza, which is San Marco (all the other squares are campos). Venice is divided into six districts *(sestieri)*: **San Marco, Santa Croce, San Polo, Castello, Cannaregio,** and **Dorsoduro.**

Many of Venice's so-called streets are actually canals *(rios)*—more than 150 in all, spanned by a total of 400 bridges. Venice's version of a main street is the **Canal Grande (Grand Canal),** which snakes through the city. Three bridges cross the Grand Canal: the white marble **Ponte Rialto,** the wooden **Ponte Accademia,** and the stone **Ponte degli Scalzi.** The Grand Canal splits Venice into two unequal parts.

South of Dorsoduro, which is south of the Grand Canal, is the **Canale della Guidecca,** a major channel separating Dorsoduro from the large island of La Guidecca. At the point where Canale della Guidecca meets the **Canale di San Marco,** you'll spot the little **Isola di San Giorgio Maggiore,** with a church by Palladio. The most visited islands in the lagoon, aside from the **Lido,** are **Murano, Burano,** and **Torcello.**

If you really want to tour Venice and experience that hidden, romantic trattoria on a nearly forgotten street, bring along a map that details every street and that has an index on the back.

A broad street running along a canal is a *fondamenta,* a narrower street running along a canal is a *calle,* and a paved road is a *salizzada, ruga,* or *calle larga.* A *rio terra* is a filled canal channel now used as a walkway, and a *sottoportego* is a passage beneath buildings. When you come to an open-air area, you'll often encounter the word *campo*—that's a reference to the fact that such a place was once grassy, and in days of yore cattle grazed there.

GETTING AROUND You can't hail a taxi—at least, not on land—so get ready to walk and walk and walk. Of course, you can break up your walks with *vaporetto* or boat rides, which are great respites from the packed (and we mean *packed*) streets in summer.

BY PUBLIC TRANSPORTATION Much to the chagrin of the once-ubiquitous gondoliers, Venice's **motorboats *(vaporetti)*** provide inexpensive and frequent, if not always fast, transportation in this canal city. The *vaporetti* are called "water buses," and they are indeed the "buses" of Venice because traveling by water is usually faster than traveling by land. The service is operated by **ACTV** (Azienda del Consorzio Trasporti Veneziano), Isola Nova del Tronchetto 32 (✆ **041-2424;** www.actv.it). An *accelerato* is a vessel that makes every stop; a *diretto* makes express stops. The average fare is 6.50€. Note that in summer, the *vaporetti* are often fiercely crowded. Pick up a map of the system at the tourist office. They run daily up and down the Grand Canal, with frequent service 7am to midnight and then hourly midnight to 7am.

The Grand Canal is long and snakelike and can be crossed via only three bridges, including the one at Rialto. If there's no bridge in sight, the trick in getting across is to use one of the ***traghetti* gondolas** strategically placed at key points. Look for them at the end of any passage called Calle del Traghetto. They're under government control, so the fare is only .60€.

BY MOTOR LAUNCH (WATER TAXI) Motor launches *(taxi acquei)* cost more than public *vaporetti,* but you won't be hassled as much when you arrive with your luggage if you hire one of the many private ones. You might or might not have the cabin of one of these sleek vessels to yourself because the captains fill their boats with as many passengers as the law allows before taking off. Your porter's uncanny radar will guide you to one of the inconspicuous piers where a water taxi waits.

The price of a transit by water taxi from Piazzale Roma (the road/rail terminus) to Piazza San Marco begins at 98€ for up to four passengers and 90€ for more than four. The captains adroitly deliver you, with luggage, to the canalside entrance of your hotel or on one of the smaller waterways within a short walking distance of your destination. You can also call for a water taxi; try the **Consorzio Motoscafi** at **✆ 041-5222303.**

BY GONDOLA You and your gondolier have two major agreements to reach: the price and the length of the ride. If you aren't careful, you're likely to be taken on both counts. It's a common sight to see a gondolier huffing and puffing to take his passengers on a "quickie," often reducing an hour to 15 minutes.

The average rate is 80€ for 40 minutes. The actual fare depends on how well you stand up to the gondolier. Many gondoliers offer rates beginning at 110€ for up to 50 minutes. Prices go up after 8pm. In fairness to them, we must say that their job is hard and has been overly romanticized: They row boatloads of tourists across hot, smelly canals with such endearments screamed at them as, "No sing, no pay!" And these fellows have to make plenty of euros while the sun shines because their work ends when the first cold winds blow in from the Adriatic. Speaking of winds, many visitors get very seasick in a gondola on the open water on a windy day.

Two major stations where you can hire gondolas are **Piazza San Marco** (✆ **041-5200685**) and **Ponte di Rialto** (✆ **041-5224904**).

[FastFACTS] VENICE

American Express The office at Calle San Moisè, San Marco 1471 (✆ **041-5200844**), a historic building a few steps from St. Mark's Square, is open Monday to Friday 9am to 5:30pm and Saturday and Sunday 9am to 12:30pm.

Currency Exchange There are many banks in Venice where you can exchange money. You might try the **Banca Intesa,** Calle Larga XXII Marzo, San Marco 2188 (✆ **041-5296811;** www.intesasanpaolo.com; *vaporetto:* San Marco), or Banco San Marco, Calle Larga San Marco, San Marco 383 (✆ **041-5293711;** www.bancosanmarco.it; *vaporetto:* San Marco). Hours are Monday to Friday 8:30am to 1:30pm and 2:45 to 4:15pm.

Dentists & Doctors Your best bet is to have your hotel set up an appointment with an English-speaking dentist or doctor. The American Express office and the British Consulate also have lists. Also see "Hospitals," below.

Drugstores If you need a pharmacist in the middle of the night, go to any drugstore, even a closed one. A list of after-hours pharmacies will be posted on the door. These drugstores operate on a rotational system of late nights. A well-recommended central one is **Antica Farmacia al Mondo,** Piscina Frezzeria, San Marco 1676 (✆ **041-5225813;** *vaporetto:* San Marco).

Emergencies Call ✆ **113** for the police, ✆ **118** for an ambulance, or ✆ **115** to report a fire.

Hospitals Get in touch with the **Ospedale Civile Santi Giovanni e Paolo,** Campo Santi Giovanni e Paolo in Castello (✆ **041-5294111;** *vaporetto:* San Toma), staffed with English-speaking doctors 24 hours.

Internet Access For laptop links or international calls, head for **Venetian Navigator,** Castello 5300 (✆ **041-2771056;** www.venetiannavigator.com; *vaporetto:* San Marco), which lies near Piazza San Marco in the heart of Venice. You can search the Web with an American-style keyboard, send a fax, download pictures from your digital camera, and even burn CDs and DVDs. You can purchase a card to use the facilities, costing 3€ for 15 minutes or 8€ for up to an hour.

Police See "Emergencies," above.

Safety The curse of Venice is the pickpocket. Violent crime is rare. But because of the overcrowding in *vaporetti* and on the narrow streets, it's easy to pick pockets. Purse snatchers are commonplace as well. They can dart out of nowhere, grab a purse, and disappear in seconds down some dark alley. Keep valuables locked in a safe in your hotel, if one is provided.

Telephone The **city code** for Venice is **041;** use this code for all calls—even within Venice itself (and you must now include the zero every time, even when calling from abroad).

Toilets These are available at Piazzale Roma and various other places, but they aren't as plentiful as they should be. A truly spotless one is at the foot of the Accademia Bridge. Often you'll have to rely on the restrooms in cafes, although you should buy something, perhaps a light coffee, because, in theory, the toilets are for customers only. Most museums and galleries have public toilets. You can also use the public toilets at the Albergo Diurno, Via Ascensione, just behind Piazza San Marco. Remember, *signori* means men and *signore* means women.

Where to Stay

NEAR PIAZZA SAN MARCO

Very Expensive

Gritti Palace ★★★ The Gritti, in a stately Grand Canal setting, is the renovated *palazzo* of 15th-century doge Andrea Gritti. Even after its takeover by ITT Sheraton, it's still a bit starchy and has a museum aura (some of the furnishings are roped off), but for sheer glamour and history, only the **Cipriani** tops it. (Stay at the Cipriani for quiet, isolation, and more recreational facilities, but stay here for a central location and service that's just as good.) The Gritti evokes a well-tailored, well-upholstered private home of a Venetian nobleman—discreet, tranquil, and horrendously upscale, providing a shelter for billionaires. The variety of guest rooms seems almost limitless, from elaborate suites to small singles. But throughout, the elegance is evident, as exemplified by the gilt mirrors, the antiques, and the hand-painted 18th-century-style furnishings.

Campo Santa Maria del Giglio, San Marco 2467, 30124 Venezia. ✆ **800/325-3535** in the U.S., or 041-794611. Fax 041-5200942. www.gritti.hotelinvenice.com. 91 units. 300€–1,390€ double; 1,400€ suite. Rates include buffet breakfast. AE, DC, MC, V. *Vaporetto:* Santa Maria del Giglio. **Amenities:** Restaurant; bar; babysitting; concierge; room service. *In room:* A/C, TV, hair dryer, minibar, Wi-Fi (15€ per 24 hr.).

Inexpensive

Ca' Dei Dogi ★★ 🎁 This small *albergo* (Italian hotel) in a tranquil pocket of Venice is reached down a maze of narrow alleyways, just a surprisingly short walk from the Bridge of Sighs and the Doge's Palace. At night you can sit out on the rooftop patio listening to the gondoliers singing beneath the bridge. This remarkable find combines luxury and value, two elements that rarely, if ever, come together in Venice. The most idyllic accommodations include a small alcove and overlook the ducal palace. Each of the midsize bedrooms is individually decorated, the details of the decor carefully chosen for both taste and comfort. Much altered over the years, the palace itself dates from the 15th century. Next door to the hotel, Taverna dei Dogi offers typically Venetian fare such as risotto with black cuttlefish flavored with orange. In summer, it offers outdoor dining in a garden.

Corte Santa Scolastica, Castello 4242, 30122 Venezia. ✆ **041-2413759.** Fax 041-5285403. www.cadeidogi.it. 6 units. 130€–250€ double. MC, V. *Vaporetto:* San Zaccaria. **Amenities:** Restaurant; bar; babysitting; room service. *In room:* A/C, TV, hair dryer, minibar.

CASTELLO/RIVA DEGLI SCHIAVONI

Moderate

La Residenza ★★ In a 14th-century building that looks a lot like a miniature Doge's Palace, this little hotel is on a residential square where children play soccer and older people feed the pigeons. You'll pass through a stone vestibule lined with ancient Roman columns before ringing another doorbell at the bottom of a flight of stairs. First an iron gate and then a door will open into an enormous salon filled with antiques, 300-year-old paintings, and some of the most marvelously preserved walls in Venice. The guest rooms are far less opulent, with contemporary pieces and good beds. The choice rooms are usually booked far in advance, especially for Carnevale.

Campo Bandiera e Moro, Castello 3608, 30122 Venezia. ✆ **041-5285315.** Fax 041-5238859. www.venicelaresidenza.com. 15 units (shower only). 80€–200€ double. Rates include continental breakfast. MC, V. *Vaporetto:* Arsenale. *In room:* A/C, TV, minibar, Wi-Fi (free).

IN CANNAREGIO

Expensive

Boscolo Grand Hotel dei Dogi ★★ 🎁 Once an embassy and later a convent, this is one of the hotel secrets of Venice, definitely a hidden gem. On the northern tier of Venice, Dei Dogi looks across the lagoon to the mainland. As you sit in the beautiful garden of rosebushes, you will think that you've arrived at a Venetian Shangri-La. The hotel lies just a short stroll down the canal from the Church of Madonna dell'Orto, where Tintoretto lies buried. Bedrooms are elegantly decorated in a palatial Venetian style, with gilt and polish. Some 18th-century frescoes often decorate the walls of the bedrooms, as do antique mirrors, swag draperies, and doors intricately inlaid with veneer.

Fondamenta Madonna dell'Orto 3500, 30121 Venezia. ✆ **041-2208111.** Fax 041-722278. www.boscolohotels.com. 76 units. 200€–390€ double; from 320€ junior suite. AE, DC, MC, V. *Vaporetto:* Madonna dell'Orto. **Amenities:** Restaurant; bar; babysitting; room service; spa. *In room:* A/C, TV, hair dryer, minibar.

SANTA CROCE

Inexpensive

Albergo Marin Since the 1930s this little gay-friendly hotel has been a "secret address" known to savvy travelers trying to escape the high prices of Venice. The place is a simple, no-frills hotel and not a haven for devotees of Venetian aesthetics. What it does it does very well: provides an affordable, decent, and comfortable bed for the night. It's more for travelers who like to explore Venice all day, returning to the hotel just to sleep in one of the midsize bedrooms. The location is a 5-minute walk from the train station at Santa Lucia.

Ramo delle Chioverete 670B, Santa Croce, 30135 Venezia. ✆ **041-718022.** Fax 041-721485. www.albergomarin.it. 60€–200€ double. Rates include breakfast. AE, DC, MC, V. *Vaporetto:* Ferrovia. **Amenities:** Wi-Fi (free, in lobby). *In room:* A/C, TV, hair dryer.

IN DORSODURO

Expensive

DD724 ★★ 🎁 Steps away from the Peggy Guggenheim Museum and the Accademia Gallery, this one-of-a-kind hotel is the brainchild of hotelier Chiara Bocchini. The odd name comes from the hotel's location in the Dorsoduro area. A house of charm and grace, it is a luxurious choice and is ideal for a romantic getaway. Abstract paintings by contemporary artists hang in the tiny lobby. Breakfast is cooked individually for each guest. Under wooden beamed ceilings, each bedroom is one of a kind with velvet armchairs and Signoria di Firenze linens. Every detail seems to have been taken care of, including careful attention to lighting design.

Dorsoduro 724, 30123 Venezia. ✆ **041-2770262.** Fax 041-2960633. www.dd724.it. 7 units. 155€–410€ double; 325€–580€ suite. Rates include buffet breakfast. AE, DC, MC, V. *Vaporetto:* Accademia. **Amenities:** Bar; babysitting; room service. *In room:* A/C, TV, hair dryer, minibar, Wi-Fi (free).

ON ISOLA DELLA GIUDECCA

Very Expensive

Cipriani ★★★ For old-world Venetian splendor, check into the Gritti or Danieli. But for chic, contemporary surroundings, flawless service, and refinement at every turn, the Cipriani is in a class by itself. Set in a 16th-century cloister on the island of Giudecca (reached by private hotel launch from St. Mark's Sq.), this pleasure palace was opened in 1958 by Giuseppe Cipriani, founder of Harry's Bar. The rooms range in design from tasteful contemporary to grand antique; all have splendid views and are sumptuous. We prefer the corner rooms, which are the most spacious and elaborately decorated.

Isola della Giudecca 10, 30133 Venezia. ✆ **041-5207744.** Fax 041-5203930. www.hotelcipriani.com. 110 units. 900€–1,320€ double; 1,680€–2,090€ junior suite; 2,420€–6,800€ suite. Rates include full American breakfast. AE, DC, MC, V. *Vaporetto:* Zitelle. Closed Nov 8–Apr 1. **Amenities:** 2 restaurants; 3 bars (including a piano bar); babysitting; concierge; exercise room; Olympic-size outdoor heated swimming pool; room service; sauna; spa; outdoor tennis court. *In room:* A/C, TV/DVD, hair dryer, minibar, Wi-Fi (15€ per day).

Where to Dine

NEAR PIAZZA SAN MARCO

Very Expensive

Quadri ★★★ VENETIAN/INTERNATIONAL One of Europe's most famous restaurants, Quadri's elegant premises open onto Piazza San Marco, where a full orchestra often adds to the magic. Many diners come just for the view and are often surprised by the high-quality cuisine and impeccable service (and the whopping tab). The skills of Quadri's chef are considerable. He's likely to tempt you with such appetizers as sea bass puff pastry or else smoked breast of goose with a pomegranate sauce. A pear salad is served with arugula and Parmesan cheese with a raspberry vinaigrette. For your main course, you can feast on filet of beef in a chestnut sauce with braised red chicory or grilled lamb cutlets with Venetian artichokes and a mint sauce. Filet of hake comes under an aromatic crust with anchovies and baby broccoli.

Piazza San Marco, San Marco 121. ✆ **041-5289299.** www.quadrivenice.com. Reservations required. Main courses 28€–35€. AE, DC, MC, V. Apr–Oct daily noon–2:30pm and 7–10:30pm; Nov–Mar Tues–Sun noon–2:30pm and 7–10:30pm. *Vaporetto:* San Marco.

Expensive

Antico Martini ★★★ VENETIAN/INTERNATIONAL Antico Martini elevates Venetian cuisine to its highest level (although we still give Harry's a slight edge). Elaborate chandeliers glitter and gilt-framed oil paintings adorn the paneled walls. The courtyard is splendid in summer. An excellent beginning is the smoked salmon with caviar. One of the best pasta dishes is black tagliolini with fresh zucchini, or the always-reliable smoked breast of wild duck. The chefs are better at regional dishes than international ones. Other menu items include pasta with scampi and mushrooms, scallops with basil and polenta, pappardelle with scampi and sweet peppers, and sea bass filet with wild fennel. The restaurant has one of the city's best wine lists, featuring more than 350 choices. The yellow Tocai is an interesting local wine and is especially good with fish dishes.

Campo San Fantin, San Marco 1983. ✆ **041-5224121.** www.anticomartini.com. Reservations required. Main courses 26€–65€; 4-course fixed-price menu 80€–85€; 6-course tasting menu 125€. AE, DC, MC, V. Wed 7–11:30pm; Thurs–Mon noon–2:30pm and 7–11:30pm. *Vaporetto:* San Marco or Santa Maria del Giglio.

Moderate

Osteria alle Testiere ★ VENETIAN/ITALIAN This little 24-seat restaurant has its priorities in order: good, fresh food at affordable prices. Nothing is spent on fancy white linen—the tables are covered in butcher paper. In such a tavern setting, you'll be tempted by an array of well-prepared dishes paired with a carefully selected wine list. Among menu temptations, tuna steak flavored with juniper berries is a delight, as is the potato gnocchi with calamari and a cinnamon flavor. Whitefish of the day is baked with aromatic fresh herbs, or else you can sample the heaven-sent scampi with freshly chopped tomatoes. Gnocchetti with baby squid turned out to be a savory and tasty dish, as was the whitefish of the day baked with aromatic fresh herbs. For another main course, the scampi was heaven sent, given extra flavor by a sprinkle of cinnamon, a dash of hot pepper, and freshly chopped tomatoes.

Castello 5801 (on Calle del Mondo Novo). ✆ **041-5227220.** www.osterialletestiere.it. Reservations recommended. Main courses 16€–24€. MC, V. Tues–Sat noon–2pm and 7–10pm. Closed Aug and Dec 20–Jan 15. *Vaporetto:* San Marco or Rialto.

Trattoria da Fiore ★ VENETIAN Don't confuse this trattoria with the well-known and much more expensive Osteria da Fiore. Start with the house specialty, *penne alla Fiore* (prepared with olive oil, garlic, and seven in-season vegetables), and you might be happy to call it a night. Or skip right to another popular specialty, *fritto misto,* comprising more than a dozen varieties of fresh fish and seafood. The *zuppa di pesce* is a soup stocked with mussels, crab, clams, shrimp, and chunks of fresh tuna. This is a great place for an afternoon snack or a light lunch at the Bar Fiore next door (daily 10:30am–10:30pm).

Calle delle Botteghe, San Marco 3461. ✆ **041-5235310.** www.dafiore.it. Reservations suggested. Pasta dishes 11€–18€; main courses 18€–29€. MC, V. Wed–Mon noon–3pm and 7–10pm. Closed Jan 15–30 and Aug 1–15. *Vaporetto:* Accademia.

CASTELLO/RIVA DEGLI SCHIAVONI

Expensive

Al Covo ★★ VENETIAN/SEAFOOD Al Covo has a special charm because of its atmospheric setting, sophisticated service, and the fine cooking of Cesare Benelli and his Texas-born wife, Diane. Look for a reinvention of a medieval version of fish soup, roast lamb chops with mint sauce and lentils, roast codfish with prunes and fresh rosemary, soft-shell crabs fried with potatoes and onion rings, and homemade potato gnocchi with baby calamari and spider crab roe. Al Covo prides itself on not having any freezers, guaranteeing that all food is fresh every day.

Campiello della Pescaria, Castello 3968. ✆ **041-5223812.** www.ristorantealcovo.com. Reservations recommended for dinner. Main courses 23€–35€; fixed-price menus 49€. MC, V. Fri–Tues 12:45–2:15pm and 7:30–10pm. *Vaporetto:* Arsenale.

Moderate/Inexpensive

Al Nuovo Galeon VENETIAN Sometimes it's a good idea to go where your waiter takes his family to eat on his day off. Such a choice might be this restaurant in the Castello neighborhood with a typical Venetian square outside. With its two dining rooms, it's decorated just like the interior of a 16th-century ship. The location is a 15-minute walk east of Piazza San Marco. The chef prepares good-value, wholesome food made with market-fresh ingredients. Specialties include scampi in *saorone* (fried scampi marinated in a sweet-and-sour sauce with lightly sautéed onions), or else a filet of turbot with curried vegetables. Our favorite is a large platter of seafood with such delights as spider crab, octopus, squid, sea bass, shrimp, and a couple of fish we don't recognize. You can also order linguine with clams, salt cod with polenta, or fried calamari. A lovely starter is either the salmon or sea bass carpaccio.

Via Garibaldi 1308, Castello. ✆ **041-5204656.** Reservations recommended. Main courses 16€–26€. AE, MC, V. Wed–Sun 12:30–2:30pm and 7:30–9:30pm. Closed Dec 9–Jan 22. *Vaporetto:* Ciardini.

Do Leoni ★★ VENETIAN/INTERNATIONAL This restaurant offers a view of a 19th-century equestrian statue ringed with heroic women taming (you guessed it) lions. The menu is something to savor. The chef isn't afraid to dip into Venice's culinary attic at times for inspiration—take the boneless sardines fried and left to marinate in onions before being served with fresh pine nuts and Cyprus sultanas. The risottos and pastas are delectable. Begin perhaps with the fried shrimp on polenta perfumed with garlic, or clams and mussels with croutons. Savor such main dishes as roast saddle of lamb with eggplant *(aubergine)*, filet of grouper with Swiss chard and an orange hollandaise mousse, or homemade tagliatelle with spider crab. If weather permits, you can dine out on the piazza.

In the Londra Palace, Riva degli Schiavoni, Castello 4171. ✆ **041-5200533.** Reservations required. Main courses 16€–38€. AE, DC, MC, V. Restaurant daily 12:30–2:30pm and 7:30–11pm. Bar daily 11am–12:30am. *Vaporetto:* San Zaccaria.

Nuova Rivetta SEAFOOD Nuova Rivetta is an old-fashioned trattoria where you get good food at a good price. The most popular dish is *frittura di pesce,* a mixed fish fry that includes squid or various other "sea creatures" from the day's market. Other specialties are gnocchi stuffed with spider crab, pasticcio of fish (a main course), and spaghetti flavored with squid ink. The most typical wine is sparkling prosecco, whose bouquet is refreshing and fruity with a slightly sharp flavor; it has long been one of the most celebrated wines of the Veneto.

Campo San Filippo, Castello 4625. ✆ **041-5287302.** Reservations required. Main courses 9.50€–25€. AE, MC, V. Tues–Sun noon–10pm. Closed July 20–Aug 20. *Vaporetto:* San Zaccaria.

NEAR THE PONTE DI RIALTO

Moderate

Fiaschetteria Toscana ★ VENETIAN The service at this hip restaurant might be uneven and the staff might be frantic, but lots of local foodies come here to celebrate special occasions or to soak in the see-and-be-seen ambience. The dining rooms are on two levels, the upstairs of which is somewhat more claustrophobic. In the evening, the downstairs is especially appealing with its romantic candlelit ambience. Menu items include *frittura della Serenissima* (a mixed platter of fried seafood with vegetables), a succulent ravioli filled with lobster and broccoli, and freshly caught fish from the North Adriatic along with tender and well-flavored Tuscan beefsteak.

Campo San Giovanni Crisostomo, Cannaregio 5719. ✆ **041-5285281.** www.fiaschetteriatoscana.it. Reservations required. Main courses 15€–35€; fixed-price menus 26€–50€. MC, V. Wed 7:30–10:30pm; Thurs–Mon 12:30–2:30pm and 7:30–10:30pm. Closed July 25–Aug 20. *Vaporetto:* Rialto.

L'Osteria di Santa Marina ★ VENETIAN/ITALIAN Near Ponte di Rialto, this discovery is the domain of Agostino Doria and Danilo Baldan, the latter a Cipriani alum. Together they have forged their own place with a combination of a rustic yet classic decor. In a warm, cozy setting, you feel right at home as you partake of their savory cuisine. Come here with a hearty appetite; it will be satisfied. The cuisine is light, full flavored, and impertinently inventive as evoked by the lasagna served crepe-style with fresh shrimp and purple radicchio. The ravioli with turbot and mussels in a crayfish sauce has subtly intermingled flavors. All the pasta is homemade. Another standout dish is the shrimp in *saor* (confit) with a smattering of chopped leeks and ginger, and the veal cheek braised with potatoes. Or else you might try the sautéed soft-shell crabs and artichokes, or the John Dory filet baked with vegetables au gratin.

Campo Santa Marina 5911. ✆ **041-5285239.** Reservations recommended. Main courses 14€–28€. AE, DC, MC, V. Mon 7:30–9:30pm; Tues–Sat 12:30–2:30pm and 7:30–9:30pm. Closed Jan 10–25 and 2 weeks in Aug. *Vaporetto:* Rialto.

IN DORSODURO

Expensive

Lineadombra ★★ INTERNATIONAL Venice doesn't look entirely as it did at the time of the doges. There is such a thing as Nouveau Venice, as exemplified by this modern restaurant with sleek contemporary lines. In Dorsoduro, it faces the Canale della Giudecca. In fair weather, you can sit out on the deck on cushy chairs. Here you will enjoy one of the most scenic spots in Venice behind the Church of the Salute. The chefs blend their creativity and imagination, turning out a mouthwatering range of freshly made dishes. The best of these include grilled scallops with a zucchini, yogurt, and a saffron sauce, or else tortelloni filled with spinach and ricotta. Baked turbot comes with a velvety sauce made with fresh asparagus. Every dish is a feast for the eye and palate, especially a *mille-feuille* of scampi with onions and green apples.

Ponte dell'Umilta, Dorsoduro 19. ✆ **041-2411881.** www.ristorantelineadombra.com. Reservations required. Main courses 25€–38€. AE, DC, MC, V. Thurs–Tues 12:30–3pm and 7:30–10pm. Closed Jan 1–Feb 10. *Vaporetto:* Salute.

ON ISOLA DELLA GUIDECCA

Very Expensive

Fortuny ★★★ ITALIAN The grandest of the hotel restaurants, Cipriani's Fortuny offers a sublime but relatively simple cuisine, with the freshest of ingredients used by one of the best-trained staffs along the Adriatic. This isn't the place to bring the kids—in fact, children 7 and under aren't allowed in the evening (a babysitter can be arranged). You can dine in the formal room with Murano chandeliers and Fortuny curtains when the weather is nippy, or on the terrace overlooking the lagoon. Freshly made pasta is a specialty, and it's among the finest we've sampled. Try the *taglierini verdi* with noodles and ham au gratin. Chef's specialties include mixed fried scampi and squid with tender vegetables, and sautéed veal filets with spring artichokes.

In the Hotel Cipriani, Isola della Giudecca 10. ✆ **041-5207744.** Reservations required. Jacket required for men, tie recommended. Main courses 25€–46€. AE, DC, MC, V. Daily 12:30–3pm and 8–10:30pm. Closed Nov 8–Mar 31. *Vaporetto:* Zitelle.

Exploring the Floating City

Venice appears to have been created specifically to entertain its legions of callers. Ever since the body of St. Mark was smuggled out of Alexandria and entombed in the basilica, the city has been host to a never-ending stream of visitors—famous, infamous, and otherwise. Venice has perpetually captured the imagination of poets and artists. Wordsworth, Byron, and Shelley addressed poems to the city, and it has been written about or used as a setting by many contemporary writers.

In the pages ahead, we'll explore the city's great art and architecture. But, unlike Florence, Venice would reward its guests with treasures even if they never ducked inside a museum or church. Take some time just to stroll and let yourself get lost in this gorgeous city.

THE CANAL GRANDE (GRAND CANAL) ★★★

Paris has its Champs-Elysées, and New York City has its Broadway—but Venice, for sheer uniqueness, tops them all with its Canal Grande. Lined with *palazzi* (many in the Venetian Gothic style), this great road of water is filled with *vaporetti,* motorboats, and gondolas. The boat moorings are like peppermint sticks. The canal begins at Piazzetta San Marco on one side and Longhena's La Salute church opposite. At midpoint, the Rialto Bridge spans it. Eventually, the canal winds its serpentine course to the rail station. We can guarantee that there's not a dull site en route.

THE BASILICA, DOGES' PALACE & CAMPANILE

Piazza San Marco was the heart of Venice in the heyday of its glory as a seafaring republic. If you have only 1 day for Venice, you need not leave the square: Some of the city's major attractions, such as St. Mark's Basilica and the Doge's Palace, are centered here or nearby.

Thanks to Napoleon, the square was unified architecturally. The emperor added the Fabbrica Nuova facing the basilica, thus bridging the Old and New Procuratie on either side. Flanked with medieval-looking palaces, Sansovino's Library, elegant shops, and colonnades, the square is now finished—unlike Piazza della Signoria in Florence.

If Piazza San Marco is Europe's drawing room, then the piazza's satellite, **Piazzetta San Marco ★**, is Europe's antechamber. Hedged in by the Doge's Palace, Sansovino's Library, and a side of St. Mark's, the tiny square faces the Grand Canal. Two tall granite columns grace the square. A winged lion, representing St. Mark, surmounts one. A statue of a man taming a dragon, supposedly the dethroned patron saint Theodore, tops the other. Both columns came from the East in the 12th century.

Basilica di San Marco (St. Mark's Basilica) ★★★ Dominating Piazza San Marco is the Chiesa d'Oro (Church of Gold), one of the world's greatest and most richly embellished churches, its cavernous candlelit interior gilded with mosaics added over some 7 centuries. In fact, it looks as if it had been moved intact from Istanbul. The basilica is a conglomeration of styles, although it's particularly indebted to Byzantium. Like Venice, St. Mark's is adorned with booty from every corner of the city's once-far-flung mercantile empire: capitals from Sicily, columns from Alexandria, porphyry from Syria, and sculpture from old Constantinople.

After touring the baptistery, proceed up the right nave to the doorway to the oft-looted **treasury *(tesoro)* ★**. Here you'll find the inevitable skulls and bones of some ecclesiastical authorities under glass, plus goblets, chalices, and Gothic candelabras. The entrance to the **presbytery** is nearby. In it, on the high altar, the alleged sarcophagus of St. Mark rests under a green marble blanket and is held by four Corinthian alabaster columns. Behind the altar is the rarest treasure at St. Mark's: the Byzantine-style **Pala d'Oro ★★★**, a golden altar screen measuring 3×1m (10×3¼ ft.). It's set with 300 emeralds, 300 sapphires, 400 garnets, 100 amethysts, and 1,300 pearls, plus rubies and topazes accompanying 157 enameled rondels and panels.

After leaving the basilica, head up the stairs in the atrium to the **Marciano Museum** and the **Loggia dei Cavalli.** The star of the museum is the world-famous ***Triumphal Quadriga* ★★**, four horses looted from Constantinople by Venetian crusaders during the sack of that city in 1204.

Piazza San Marco. ✆ **041-5225205.** www.basilicasanmarco.it. Basilica free admission; treasury 3€; presbytery 2€; Marciano Museum 4€. Basilica and presbytery Apr–Sept Mon–Sat 10am–5pm, Sun 2–5pm; Oct–Mar Mon–Sat 10am–4:30pm, Sun 2–4pm. Marciano Museum Apr–Oct Mon–Sat 10am–5pm, Sun 2–4pm; Nov–Mar Mon–Sat 10am–4pm, Sun 2–4pm. *Vaporetto:* San Marco.

Campanile di San Marco ★★ One summer night in 1902, the bell tower of St. Mark's, suffering from years of rheumatism in the damp Venetian climate, gave out a warning sound that sent the fashionable coffee drinkers in the piazza below scurrying for their lives. But the campanile gracefully waited until the next morning, July 14, before tumbling into the piazza. The Venetians rebuilt their belfry, and it's now safe to climb to the top. Unlike Italy's other bell towers, where you have to brave narrow, steep spiral staircases to reach the top, this one has an elevator so you can get a pigeon's view. It's a particularly good vantage point for viewing the cupolas of the basilica.

Piazza San Marco. ✆ **041-5224064.** www.basilicasanmarco.it. Admission 8€. Oct–Mar daily 9:30am–4pm; Apr–June daily 9am–7pm; July–Sept daily 9am–9pm. *Vaporetto:* San Marco.

Palazzo Ducale & Ponte dei Sospiri (Ducal Palace & Bridge of Sighs) ★★★ You enter the Palace of the Doges through the magnificent 15th-century **Porta della Carta ★★** at the piazzetta. This Venetian Gothic *palazzo* gleams in the tremulous light somewhat like a frosty birthday cake in pinkish-red marble and white Istrian stone. Italy's grandest civic structure, it dates to 1309, although a 1577 fire destroyed much of the original building.

After climbing the Sansovino stairway, you'll enter some get-acquainted rooms. Proceed to the **Sala di Anti-Collegio,** housing the palace's greatest works, notably Veronese's *Rape of Europa,* to the far left on the right wall. Tintoretto is well represented with his *Three Graces* and his *Bacchus and Ariadne.* Some critics consider the latter his supreme achievement.

The excitement continues downstairs. You can wander through the once-private apartments of the doges to the grand **Maggior Consiglio,** with Veronese's allegorical *Triumph of Venice* on the ceiling. The most outstanding feature, however, is over the Grand Council chamber: Tintoretto's *Paradise,* said to be the world's largest oil painting.

Reentering the Maggior Consiglio, follow the arrows on their trail across the **Ponte dei Sospiri (Bridge of Sighs) ★★**, linking the Doge's Palace with the Palazzo delle Prigioni. Here you'll see the cellblocks that once lodged the prisoners who felt the quick justice of the Terrible Ten. The Terrible Ten was a series of state inquisitors appointed by the city of Venice to dispense justice to the citizens. This often meant torture even for what could be viewed as a minor infraction.

If you're intrigued by the palace, you might want to check out the **"Secret Trails of the Palazzo Ducale" ("Itinerari Segreti del Palazzo Ducale").** These 16€ guided tours are so popular that they've recently been introduced in English (reserve in advance at the ticket-buyers' entrance or by calling ✆ **041-5209070**).

Piazzetta San Marco. ✆ **041-2715911.** Admission 12€ adults. Apr–Oct daily 9am–7pm; Nov–Mar daily 9am–6pm. Closed Dec 25 and Jan 1. *Vaporetto:* San Marco.

MUSEUMS & GALLERIES

Ca' d'Oro ★★★ Ca' d'Oro's architecture and decor compete with the works of art displayed here. It was built in the early 1400s, and its name translates as "House of Gold," although the gilding that once covered its facade eroded away long ago, leaving softly textured pink and white stone carved into lacy Gothic patterns. Historians compare its majesty to that of the Ducal Palace. The building was meticulously restored in the early 20th century by philanthropist Baron Franchetti, who attached it to a smaller nearby *palazzo* (Ca' Duodo), today part of the Ca' d'Oro complex. The interconnected buildings contain the baron's valuable private collection of paintings, sculpture, and furniture, all donated to the Italian government during World War I.

You enter into a stunning courtyard, 46m (150 ft.) from the *vaporetto* stop. The courtyard has a multicolored patterned marble floor and is filled with statuary. Proceed upstairs to the *palazzo.* One of the gallery's major paintings is Titian's voluptuous *Venus.* She coyly covers one breast, but what about the other?

In a niche reserved for the masterpiece of the Franchetti collection is Andrea Mantegna's icy-cold *St. Sebastian,* the central figure of which is riddled with what must be a record number of arrows.

Cannaregio 3931–3932. ✆ **041-5238790.** www.cadoro.org. Admission 5€. Mon 8:15am–2pm; Tues–Sun 8:15am–7:15pm. Closed Jan 1, May 1, and Dec 25. *Vaporetto:* Ca' d'Oro.

Ca' Rezzonico ★★ This 17th- and 18th-century palace along the Grand Canal is where Robert Browning set up his bachelor headquarters and eventually died in 1889. Pope Clement XIII also stayed here. It's a virtual treasure house, known for its baroque paintings and furniture. First you enter the **Grand Ballroom** with its allegorical ceiling, and then you proceed through lavishly embellished rooms with Venetian chandeliers, brocaded walls, portraits of patricians, tapestries, gilded furnishings, and touches of chinoiserie. At the end of the first walk is the **Throne Room,** with its allegorical ceilings by Giovanni Battista Tiepolo.

Upstairs is a survey of 18th-century Venetian art. Head for the **first salon** on your right (facing the canal), which contains the best works, paintings from the brush of Pietro Longhi. His most famous work, *The Lady and the Hairdresser,* is the first canvas to the right on the entrance wall. Others depict the life of the idle Venetian rich. On the rest of the floor are bedchambers, a chapel, and salons, some with badly damaged frescoes, including a romp of satyrs.

Fondamenta Rezzonico, Dorsoduro 3136. ✆ **041-2410100.** www.museiciviciveneziani.it. Admission 6.50€. Nov–Mar Wed–Mon 10am–5pm; Apr–Oct Wed–Mon 10am–6pm. Closed Jan 1, May 1, and Dec 25. *Vaporetto:* Ca' Rezzonico.

Collezione Peggy Guggenheim (Peggy Guggenheim Collection) ★★★ This is one of the most comprehensive and brilliant modern-art collections in the Western world, and it reveals both the foresight and the critical judgment of its founder. The collection is housed in an unfinished *palazzo,* the former Venetian home of Peggy Guggenheim, who died in 1979. In the tradition of her family, Peggy Guggenheim was a lifelong patron of contemporary painters and sculptors. In the 1940s, she founded the avant-garde Art of This Century Gallery in New York, impressing critics not only with the high quality of the artists she sponsored but also with her methods of displaying them. As her private collection increased, she decided to find a larger showcase and selected Venice. Today you can wander through the home and enjoy art in an informal and relaxed way.

Displayed here are works not only by Pollock and Ernst but also by Picasso (see his 1911 cubist *The Poet*), Duchamp, Chagall, Mondrian, Brancusi, Delvaux, and

Dalí, plus a garden of modern sculpture with Giacometti works (some of which he struggled to complete while resisting the amorous intentions of Marlene Dietrich). Temporary modern-art shows sometimes are presented during winter. Since Guggenheim's death, the collection has been administered by the Solomon R. Guggenheim Foundation, which also operates New York's Guggenheim Museum. In the new wing are a museum shop and a cafe, overlooking the sculpture garden.

In the Palazzo Venier dei Leoni, Calle Venier dei Leoni, Dorsoduro 701. © **041-2405411.** www.guggenheim-venice.it. Admission 12€ adults, 6.50€ children and students, free for children 11 and under. *Vaporetto:* Accademia.

Gallerie dell'Accademia (Academy Gallery) ★★★ The pomp and circumstance, the glory that was Venice, lives on in this remarkable collection of paintings spanning the 13th to the 18th century. The hallmark of the Venetian school is color and more color. From Giorgione to Veronese, from Titian to Tintoretto, with a Carpaccio cycle thrown in, the Accademia has samples of its most famous sons.

You'll first see works by such 14th-century artists as Paolo and Lorenzo Veneziano, who bridged the gap from Byzantine art to Gothic (see the latter's *Annunciation*). Next, you'll view Giovanni Bellini's *Madonna and Saint* and Carpaccio's fascinating yet gruesome work of mass crucifixion. Two of the most important works with secular themes are Mantegna's armored *St. George,* with the slain dragon at his feet, and Hans Memling's 15th-century portrait of a young man. Giorgione's *Tempest,* displayed here, is the single-most-famous painting at the Accademia.

Campo della Carità, Dorsoduro. © **041-5222247.** www.gallerieaccademia.org. Admission 8.50€. Mon 8:15am–2pm; Tues–Sun 8:15am–7:15pm. Closed Jan 1, May 1, and Dec 25. *Vaporetto:* Accademia.

Museo Civico Correr (Correr Civic Museum) ★★ This museum traces the development of Venetian painting from the 14th to the 16th century. On the second floor are the red-and-maroon robes once worn by the doges, plus some fabulous street lanterns and an illustrated copy of *Marco Polo in Tartaria.* You can see Cosmè Tura's *Pietà,* a miniature of renown from the genius in the Ferrara School. This is one of his more gruesome works, depicting a bony, gnarled Christ sprawled on the lap of the Madonna. Farther on, search out Schiavone's *Madonna and Child* (no. 545), our candidate for ugliest bambino ever depicted on canvas (no wonder his mother looks askance).

The star attraction of the Correr is the **Bellini salon,** which includes works by founding padre Jacopo and his son, Gentile. But the real master of the household was the other son, Giovanni.

In the Procuratie Nuove, Piazza San Marco. © **041-2405211.** www.museiciviciveneziani.it. Admission (including entrance to the Ducal Palace, above) 12€. Apr–Oct daily 10am–7pm; Nov–Mar daily 10am–5pm. Closed Dec 25 and Jan 1. *Vaporetto:* San Marco.

ORGANIZED TOURS

American Express, Calle San Moisè, San Marco 1471 (© **041-5200844**), which operates from a historic building a few steps from St. Mark's Square, offers an array of guided city tours. It's open for tours and travel arrangements Monday to Friday 9am to 5:30pm and Saturday and Sunday 9am to 12:30pm. Call ahead to ask about the current schedule and to make reservations. The offerings include a daily 2-hour guided tour of the city for 39€, and a tour of the islands of the Venetian lagoon for 25€.

The Shopping Scene

Venetian glass and lace are known throughout the world. However, selecting quality products in either craft requires a shrewd eye because there's much that's tawdry and shoddily crafted. Murano is the island famous for its handmade glass. However, you can find little glass-animal souvenirs in shops all over Venice. For lace, head out to Burano, where the latest of a long line of women put in painstaking hours to produce some of the finest lace in the world.

SHOPPING STROLLS

All the main shopping streets, even the side streets, are touristy and overrun. The greatest concentration of shops is around **Piazza San Marco** and the **Rialto Bridge.** Prices are much higher at San Marco, but the quality of merchandise is also higher. There are two major shopping strolls in Venice.

First, from **Piazza San Marco** you can stroll west toward spacious **Campo Morosini.** You just follow one shop-lined street all the way to its end (although the name will change several times). Begin at Salizzada San Moisè, which becomes Via 22 Marzo and then Calle delle Ostreghe before it opens onto Campo Santa Maria Zobenigo. The street then narrows and changes to Calle Zaguri before widening into Campo San Maurizio, finally becoming Calle Piovan before reaching Campo Morosini. The only deviation from this tour is a detour down Calle Vallaressa, between San Moisè and the Grand Canal, which is one of the major shopping arteries with some of the biggest designer names in the business.

The other great shopping stroll wanders from Piazza San Marco to the Rialto in a succession of streets collectively known as the **Mercerie.** It's virtually impossible to get lost because each street name is preceded by the word *merceria,* such as Merceria dell'Orologio, which begins near the clock tower in Piazza San Marco. Many commercial places, mainly shops, line the Mercerie before it reaches the Rialto, which then explodes into one vast shopping emporium.

SOME SHOPS WORTH A LOOK

Founded in 1913, **Valese Fonditore ★★**, Calle Fiubera, San Marco 793 (✆ **041-5227282;** www.valese.it), serves as a showcase for one of the most famous of the several foundries with headquarters in Venice. Some of the most appealing objects are the 50 or 60 replicas of the brass sea horses that grace the sides of many of the gondolas. A pair of medium-size ones, each about .3m (1 ft.) tall, begins at 150€.

The best place to buy Carnevale masks is **Mondonovo,** Rio Terrà Canal, Dorsoduro 3063 (✆ **041-5287344;** www.mondonovomaschere.it), where talented artisans labor to produce copies of both traditional and more modern masks, each of which is one of a kind. Prices range from 40€ for a fairly basic model to 1,830€ for something that you might display as a piece of art.

The art glass sold by **Venini ★★★**, Piazzetta Leoncini, San Marco 314 (✆ **041-5224045;** www.venini.com), has caught the attention of collectors from all over the world. Many of its pieces, including anything-but-ordinary lamps, bottles, and vases, are works of art representing the best of Venetian craftsmanship. Its best-known glass has a distinctive swirl pattern in several colors, called a *venature.* To visit the furnace, call ✆ **041-2737211.**

Venice After Dark

For such a fabled city, Venice's nightlife is pretty meager. Who wants to hit the nightclubs when strolling the city is more interesting than any spectacle staged inside? Ducking into a cafe or bar for a brief interlude, however, is a good way to break up your walk. Although Venice offers gambling and a few other diversions, it is pretty much an early-to-bed town. Most restaurants close at midnight.

The best guide to what's happening is ***Un Ospite di Venezia,*** a free pamphlet (part in English, part in Italian) distributed by the tourist office every 15 days. It lists any music and opera or theatrical presentation, along with art exhibits and local special events.

THE PERFORMING ARTS

Teatro La Fenice ★★★ (**✆ 041-786511;** www.teatrolafenice.it) reopened in 2004 after renovations in the wake of a 1996 fire. New seating gives the renovated hall a total of 1,076 seats, and the stage curtain was donated by Italian fashion designer Laura Biagiotti. Tickets and subscriptions can be purchased in person from the **Ve.La box offices** at **Piazzale Roma** and **Ferrovia Scalzi,** both of which are open daily 8:30am to 6:30pm. For further information call **Ve.La** (**✆ 041-2424**).

The **Teatro Goldoni ★**, Calle Goldoni, near Campo San Luca, San Marco 4650B (**✆ 041-2402011**), honors Carlo Goldoni (1707–93), the most prolific and one of the best of the Italian playwrights. The theater presents a changing repertoire of productions, often plays in Italian but musical presentations as well. The box office is open Monday to Saturday 10am to 1pm and 4:30 to 7pm, and tickets cost 15€ to 30€.

CAFES

All the cafes on Piazza San Marco offer a simply magical setting, several with full orchestras playing in the background. But you'll pay shockingly high prices (plus a hefty music charge) to enjoy a drink or a snack while you soak in the atmosphere. Prepare yourself for it, and splurge on a beer, a cappuccino, or an ice cream anyway. It'll be the most memorable 15€ to 20€ (that's *per person*) that you'll drop on your trip.

Venice's most famous spot is **Caffè Florian ★★★**, Piazza San Marco, San Marco 56–59 (**✆ 041-5205641;** www.caffeflorian.com), built in 1720 and elaborately decorated with red banquettes, elaborate murals under glass, and Art Nouveau lighting. The hippest cafe in Venice today is funky little **Cip's ★**, on Isola della Giudecca within the Cipriani Hotel (**✆ 041-5207744**).

BARS & DANCE CLUBS

Want more in the way of nightlife? All right, but be warned: The Venetian bar owners might sock it to you when they present the bill.

The most famous of all the watering holes of Ernest Hemingway is **Harry's Bar,** Calle Vallaresso, San Marco 1323 (**✆ 041-5285777;** www.cipriani.com). Harry's is known for inventing its own drinks and exporting them around the world, and it's said that carpaccio, the delicate raw-beef dish, was invented here.

Near the Accademia, **Il Piccolo Mondo,** Calle Contarini Corfu, Dorsoduro 1056A (**✆ 041-5200371;** www.piccolomondo.biz), is open during the day but comes alive with dance music at night. The crowd is often young. It's open daily 10pm to 4am, but the action actually doesn't begin until after midnight. Cover, including the first drink, is 10€ Thursday and Friday, and 15€ Saturday.

Day Trips from Venice

MURANO ★★ For centuries, glass blowers on the island of Murano have turned out those fantastic chandeliers that Victorian ladies used to prize so highly. They also produce heavily ornamented glasses so ruby red or so indigo blue that you can't tell whether you're drinking blackberry juice or pure-grain alcohol. Happily, the glass blowers are still plying their trade, although increasing competition (notably from Sweden) has compelled a greater degree of sophistication in design.

Murano remains the chief expedition from Venice, but it's not the most beautiful nearby island. (Burano and Torcello are far more attractive.)

You can combine a tour of Murano with a trip along the lagoon. To reach Murano, take ***vaporetto* no. 5 or 41** at Riva degli Schiavoni, a short walk from Piazzetta San Marco. The boat docks at the landing platform at Murano where the first furnace awaits conveniently. It's best to go Monday to Friday 10am to noon if you want to see some glass-blowing action.

BURANO ★★ Burano became world famous as a center of lace making, a craft that reached its pinnacle in the 18th century. The visitor who can spare a morning to visit this island will be rewarded with a charming fishing village far removed in spirit from the grandeur of Venice but only half an hour away by ferry. **Boats** leave from Fondamente Nuove, overlooking the Venetian graveyard (which is well worth the trip all on its own). To reach Fondamente Nuove, take ***vaporetto* no. 52** from Riva degli Schiavoni.

Once at Burano, you'll discover that the houses of the islanders come in varied colors: sienna, robin's egg or cobalt blue, barn red, butterscotch, and grass green.

Check out the **Scuola di Merletti di Burano,** Piazza Galuppi 187 (**✆ 041-730034**), in the center of the village at Piazza Baldassare Galuppi. From November to March, the museum is open Wednesday to Monday 10am to 4pm (to 5pm Apr–Oct). Admission is 4€ adults, 2.50€ seniors and children. The Burano School of Lace was founded in 1872 as part of a movement aimed at restoring the age-old craft that had earlier declined, giving way to such lace-making centers as Chantilly and Bruges. On the second floor you can see the lace makers, mostly young women, at their painstaking work, and you can purchase hand-embroidered or handmade lace items.

After visiting the lace school, walk across the square to the **Duomo** and its leaning **campanile** (inside, look for the *Crucifixion,* by Tiepolo). See it while you can, because the bell tower is leaning so precariously that it looks as if it might topple at any moment.

TORCELLO ★★ Of all the islands of the lagoon, Torcello, the so-called Mother of Venice, offers the most charm. If Burano is behind the times, Torcello is positively antediluvian. You can stroll across a grassy meadow, traverse an ancient stone bridge, and step back into that time when the Venetians first fled from invading barbarians to create a city of Neptune in the lagoon.

To reach Torcello, take ***vaporetto* LN** from Fondamenta Nuove. Fondamenta Nuove is in the Cannaregio district of Venice, it is not on Murano. The trip from Fondamenta Nuove to Torcello takes 1 hour.

Warning: If you go to Torcello on your own, don't listen to the gondoliers who hover at the ferry quay. They'll tell you that the cathedral is miles away. Actually, it's easily reached after a leisurely 12- to 15-minute stroll along the canal.

Cattedrale di Torcello, also called **Santa Maria Assunta Isola di Torcello ★** (**✆ 041-2960630**), was founded in A.D. 639 and subsequently rebuilt. It stands in a lonely grassy meadow beside an 11th-century campanile. The attractions here are its **Byzantine mosaics ★★**. Clutching her child, the weeping Madonna in the apse is a magnificent sight, and on the opposite wall is a powerful *Last Judgment.* Byzantine artisans, it seems, were at their best in portraying hell and damnation. In their *Inferno,* they've re-created a virtual human stew with the fires stirred by wicked demons. Reptiles slide in and out of the skulls of cannibalized sinners. The church is open daily: March to October 10:30am to 6pm (to 5pm Nov–Feb). Admission is 4€.

13

THE NETHERLANDS

by George McDonald

Like an Atlantis in reverse, Holland has emerged from the sea. Much of the country was once underwater. As the centuries rolled past, the land was recovered and stitched together through a combination of Dutch ingenuity and hard work. The result: a green-and-silver Mondrian of a country, with nearly half its land and two-thirds of its 16 million people below sea level.

The principal highlight of the Netherlands—the city of Amsterdam—happens also to be one of the highlights of the entire world. That's why it's as much a fixture on any well-conceived European tour as London, Paris, and Rome.

From Amsterdam you can make easy day trips to historic Haarlem and the old IJsselmeer lakeside villages of Volendam and Marken. In addition, make time for Delft, an ancient seat of Dutch royalty, hometown of Dutch master Vermeer, and famous for its blue-and-white porcelain.

AMSTERDAM

Easygoing and prosperous, Amsterdam is the natural focus of a visit to the Netherlands. The graceful waterways, bridges, and canal-houses in the Dutch capital recall Holland's 17th-century *gouden eeuw* (golden age) as the head of a vast trading network and colonial empire, a time when wealthy merchants constructed gabled residences along the city's laid-out canals.

A delicious irony is that some of the placid old structures now host brothels, smoke shops, and extravagant nightlife. The city's inhabitants, heirs to a live-and-let-live attitude, based on pragmatism as much as a long history of tolerance, aim to control what they cannot effectively outlaw. They permit licensed prostitution in the Rosse Buurt (Red-Light District) and the sale of hashish and marijuana in designated "coffee shops." Tolerance may have been a long-term tradition, but recent years have seen growing tensions between some Dutch and some members of ethnic minorities in Amsterdam, where, in 2010, migrants and their

The Netherlands

descendants and foreign residents for the first time outnumbered native locals. And both the coffee shops and the red-light haunts have been under pressure as the city works to improve its quality of life and reduce the negative values in its portfolio.

In any case, don't think Amsterdammers drift around town in a drug-induced haze. They are too busy zipping around on bikes, in-line skating through Vondelpark, consuming arrays of ethnic dishes, or simply watching the parade of street life from a sidewalk cafe. Small entrepreneurs have revitalized old neighborhoods like the Jordaan, turning distinctive houses into offbeat stores and bustling cafes and restaurants. Meantime, the city government and big entrepreneurs—along with some once-small ones that are now all grown-up—have been redeveloping the old harbor waterfront along the IJ (pronounced *Aye,* as in, "Aye aye, skipper") waterway in a shiny, modern style that's a long way from the spirit of Old Amsterdam.

Between dips into Amsterdam's artistic and historical treasures, be sure to take time out to absorb the freewheeling spirit of Europe's most vibrant city.

Amsterdam

ATTRACTIONS
Amsterdamse Bos 21
Amsterdams Historisch Museum 8
Anne Frankhuis 2
Artis 39
Begijnhof 9
Heineken Experience 23
Homomonument 4
Hortus Botanicus 38
Joods Historisch Museum 37
Koninklijk Paleis 6
Museum Het Rembrandthuis 30
Museum Van Loon 33
Museum Willet-Holthuysen 36
Nieuwe Kerk 5
Ons' Lieve Heer op Solder 27
Oude Kerk 28
Rijksmuseum 20
Stedelijk Museum 18
Tropenmuseum 40
Van Gogh Museum 19
Vondelpark 15
Westerkerk 3
ACCOMMODATIONS
Acacia 1
Agora 12
Ambassade 10
Amstel Botel 25
Amsterdam Wiechmann 11
Avenue Hotel 24
Bicycle Hotel Amsterdam 22
Bilderberg Hotel Jan Luyken 17
De Filosoof 14
Eden Amsterdam American 13
Estheréa 7
Hotel de l'Europe 31
Lloyd Hotel 26
NH Schiller Hotel 32
Piet Hein 16
Prinsenhof 35
Seven Bridges 34
Sofitel Amsterdam The Grand 29
Information
Metro Station
Post Office
Ferry route
Canal-boat tours
Railway
JORDAAN
GRACHTENGORDEL
MUSEUMBUURT
VONDELPARK
Nieuwe Kerk
Koninklijk Paleis
Madame Tussauds
Rijksmuseum
Concertgebouw
Leidse-plein
Koningsplein
Spui
Palmstraat
Brouwersgracht
Haarlemmerdijk
Lindengracht
Marnixstraat
Lijnbaansgracht
Westerstraat
Prinsengracht
Keizersgracht
Herengracht
Singel
Frederik Hendrikstraat
Nassaukade
Singelgracht
Egelantiersgracht
Leliegracht
Bloemgracht
Tweede Hugo de Grootstraat
Hugo de Grootgracht
Raadhuisstraat
Rozengracht
Rozenstraat
De Clerqstraat
Lauriergracht
Elandsstraat
Nieuwezijds Voorburgwal
Kalverstraat
Looiersgracht
Da Costa Gracht
Bilderdijk Gracht
Bilderdijkstraat
Jacob van Lennep kanaal
Leidsegracht
Leidsestraat
Nieuwe Spiegelstraat
Vijzelstraat
Eerste Constantijn Huygensstraat
Overtoom
Stadhouderskade
Weteringschans
Eerste Helmersstraat
Vondelstraat
Vossiusstraat
Pieter Cornelisz Hooftstraat
Hobbemastraat
Jan Luijkenstraat
Paulus Potterstraat
Van Baerlestraat
Willemsparkweg
Vijzelgracht
Van Breestraat
Gabriel Metsustraat
Vermeerstraat
Hobbemakade
Boerenwetering
Ferdinand Bolstraat
Albert Cuypstraat
De Lairessestraat

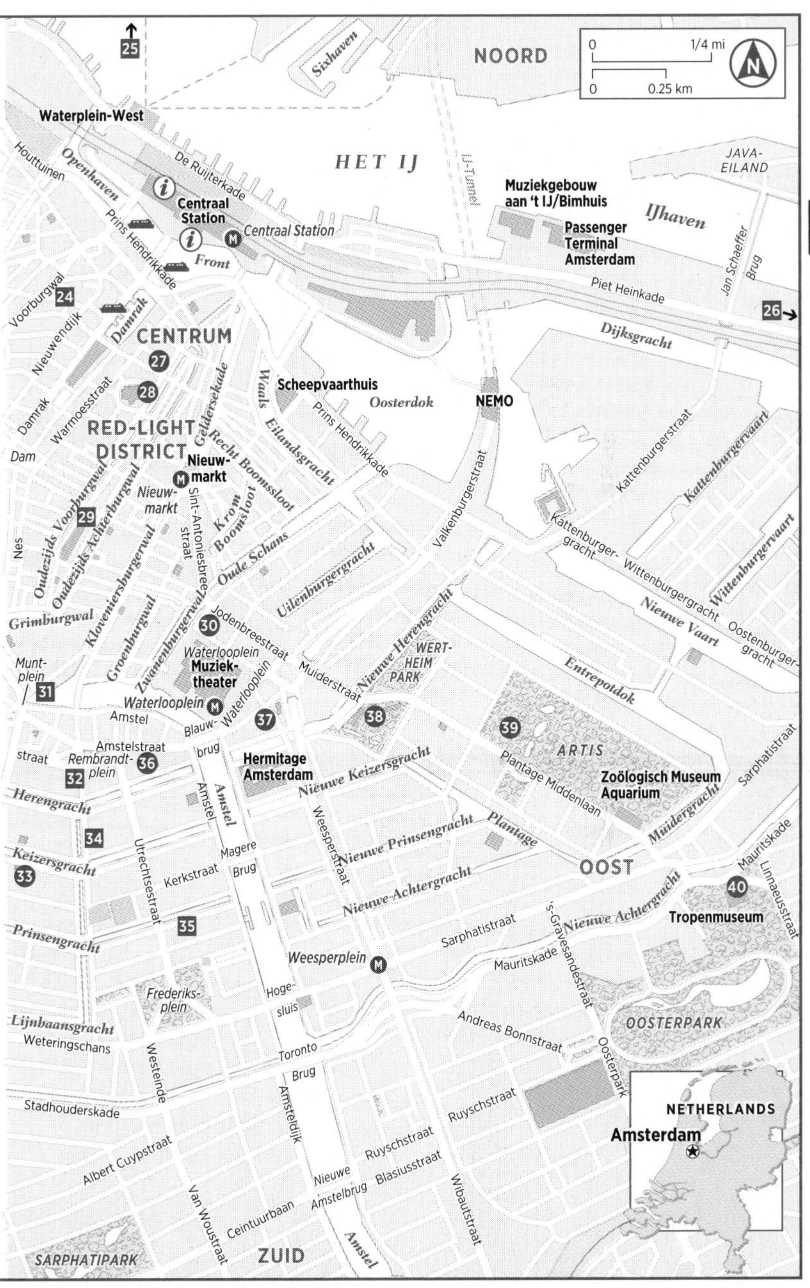

NOORD
HET IJ
Sixhaven
Waterplein-West
Centraal Station
Centraal Station
Front
Muziekgebouw aan 't IJ/Bimhuis
Passenger Terminal Amsterdam
IJhaven
JAVA-EILAND
CENTRUM
RED-LIGHT DISTRICT
Scheepvaarthuis
Oosterdok
NEMO
Nieuwmarkt
Muziektheater
Waterlooplein
Hermitage Amsterdam
WERTHEIM PARK
ARTIS
Zoölogisch Museum Aquarium
OOST
Tropenmuseum
Weesperplein
OOSTERPARK
SARPHATIPARK
ZUID
NETHERLANDS
Amsterdam
0 1/4 mi
0 0.25 km

Essentials

GETTING THERE

BY PLANE If you fly into Amsterdam, you arrive at the efficient, single-terminal **Amsterdam Airport Schiphol** (✆ **0900/0141** from inside Holland, or 31-20/794-0800 from outside Holland; www.schiphol.nl), 13km (8 miles) southwest of the center city. You exit from Customs into Schiphol Plaza, a combined arrivals hall and mall, where there are currency-exchange offices, ATMs, bars, restaurants, and stores. You can get questions answered and make last-minute hotel reservations at the **Holland Tourist Information** desk in Arrivals Hall 2, open daily from 7am to 10pm.

From Schiphol Station, a floor below Schiphol Plaza, **trains** connect the airport with Amsterdam's Centraal Station. Frequency ranges from six trains an hour at peak times to one an hour at night. The one-way fare is 3.80€ in second class and 6.50€ in first class, and the ride takes 15 to 20 minutes.

The **Connexxion Schiphol Hotel Shuttle** (✆ **038/339-4741;** www.schipholhotelshuttle.nl) runs daily every 10 to 30 minutes from 6am to 9pm, between the airport and about 100 Amsterdam hotels. Buy tickets from the Connexxion desk inside Schiphol Plaza or onboard from the driver. The fare is 15€ one-way and 24.50€ round-trip, 7.50€ and 12€, respectively, for children ages 4 to 14, and free for children 3 and under. It takes only 15 minutes to the Hilton from the airport, but almost an hour to the NH Barbizon Palace.

You find **taxi** stands in front of Schiphol Plaza. All taxis from the airport are metered. Expect to pay around 35€ to the center city.

BY TRAIN Whether you arrive by high-speed international train from Brussels, Paris, or Frankfurt, by ordinary international train, or by a train from elsewhere in the Netherlands, you'll likely find yourself deposited at **Centraal Station.** For information on trains (and other public transportation) in the Netherlands, call ✆ **0900/9292** or go to www.9292ov.nl. For international trains, call ✆ **0900/9296.** In addition to two tourist information desks, one inside and one outside (see below), you'll find 24-hour currency exchange, a host of restaurants and stores, and a rail information office where seat reservations can be made.

The station, an 1889 Dutch neo-Renaissance architectural monument, is more or less of a confusing construction site. A new Metro station, to be the hub of the Noord-Zuid (North-South) line, due to enter service in 2015, is being dug out and fitted out at the front; a new main entrance for the rail station and all-around improved passenger facilities are being tackled at the same time; and the waterfront zone at the rear is being completely revamped.

When you emerge at the front of the station, you will find a taxi stand; a bunch of stops for trams (streetcars) and buses; the entrance to the Metro station; and docks for tour boats, the Canal Bus, the Museum Boat, and the Water Taxi. At the rear of the station are docks for the ferryboats that shuttle passengers across the city's fast-developing waterfront.

BY BUS Buses from London, Paris, Brussels, and other cities, operated by **Eurolines** (✆ **020/560-8788;** www.eurolines.com), arrive at the bus station adjoining Amstel rail station (Metro: Amstel) in the south of the city.

BY CAR European expressways E19, E35, E231, and E22 converge on Amsterdam from France and Belgium to the south and from Germany to the north and east.

VISITOR INFORMATION **Tourist Office** The office of **VVV Amsterdam** (✆ **0900/400-4040,** or 31-20/551-2525 from outside the Netherlands; fax 020/625-2869; www.iamsterdam.nl; tram: 1, 2, 4, 5, 9, 13, 16, 17, 24, 25, or 26), on Platform 2B in Centraal Station, is open Tuesday to Saturday from 11am to 7pm. A second office, at Stationsplein 10 just in front of Centraal Station, is open daily from 9am to 6pm. Both offices provide maps, brochures, and details about the city; make last-minute hotel reservations; book tours; and sell theater and concert tickets.

WEBSITES In addition to VVV Amsterdam's site (see above), which lets you book a hotel online, and lays out the details on sightseeing, walking routes, wining and dining, shopping for antiques, and current events, the website of the **Netherlands Board of Tourism & Conventions** (**www.visitholland.com**) has useful advice for upcoming events, bicycling, and culture—and it even lets you know when the tulips bloom. One of the best virtual tours on the Net is **www.channels.nl**—the images are clear, you can direct your own tour, and you can chat with others about Amsterdam. Visitors provide their impressions of restaurants, hotels, museums, and hash houses. At **www.amsterdamhotspots.nl**, they really do mean "hot." Here are *the* places to fill your nights, from eating and drinking to where to toke, what the top gay bars are, and where to see those famous working girls on display behind picture windows. Good eating-out info is available from **www.dinnersite.nl**.

NATIVE behavior

- Look for someplace *gezellig,* and treasure it. *Gezelligheid* (the state of being *gezellig*) underlines everyday Dutch life. It's an imprecise, enigmatic, untranslatable-in-a-single-word concept that defines a mood and an attitude, the special *something* that makes a place comfortable, congenial, cozy, familiar, friendly, intimate, memorable, tolerant, warm, and welcoming. Dutch, in fact. You find it all over—in a "brown" cafe; in a candlelit restaurant with a view of a softly illuminated canal; even on board a packed-to-bursting tram where everyone sees the funny side of the situation.
- Not every local government in the Netherlands is as liberal-minded as Amsterdam when it comes to smoking pot—and Amsterdam is not so tolerant that you should just light up on the street, in cafes, and on trams and trains (though enough dopey people do).
- The bicycle might have been invented with Amsterdam in mind, and there are reckoned to be anywhere from 600,000 and up bikes in the city. To get close to the Amsterdam experience, you positively need to get into the saddle and ride. It can take a while to get used to pedaling smoothly and safely through the whirl of trams, cars, buses, trucks, fellow bikers, and pedestrians, particularly if you're on a typically ancient, one-speed, much-battered *stadfiets* (city bike), also known as an *omafiets* (grandmother bike)—the only kind that makes economic sense here, since anything fancier will attract a crowd of people wanting to steal it.

CITY LAYOUT Although Amsterdam center is small enough that residents think of it as a village, it can be one confusing village until you get the hang of it. A map like the handy Amsterdam City Map, available from VVV tourist offices for 2€, is essential.

When you step out of Centraal Station's main entrance, you're facing south toward the center. From here the **Old City** is laid out along five concentric semicircular canals: **Singel, Herengracht, Keizersgracht, Prinsengracht,** and **Singelgracht** (*gracht* means "canal"). Along this necklace of man-made waterways, wealthy 17th-century merchants built their elegant homes, most of which are still standing. Within these canals are many smaller canals and connecting streets, radiating from the center.

Damrak, a heavily touristed street, leads from Centraal Station to the **Dam,** once the location of the original dam on the Amstel River that gave the city its name and now a large open square on which stands the Royal Palace. To the left is the (in) famous **Red-Light District,** where government-licensed prostitutes sit in their windows, waiting for customers. A block to the right of Damrak is **Nieuwendijk** (which becomes **Kalverstraat** when it crosses the Dam), a pedestrianized shopping street. If you follow Kalverstraat to the end, you'll be at **Muntplein** (*plein* means "square"), identified by the old Mint Tower. Cross Singel and continue in the same direction to reach **Rembrandtplein,** one of the main nightlife areas. Beyond Rembrandtplein, **Waterlooplein** hosts the Muziektheater and a great flea market.

At the heart of another important nightlife zone is **Leidseplein,** on Singelgracht. Leidseplein is at the end of Leidsestraat, a pedestrians-only shopping street (but watch out for the trams). **Museumplein,** where you find Amsterdam's three most famous museums—the Rijksmuseum, Van Gogh Museum, and Stedelijk Museum—is a short walk along Singelgracht from Leidseplein (most of the Rijksmuseum is currently closed for refurbishment).

The **Jordaan,** an old neighborhood now speckled with inexpensive restaurants, unusual stores, and small galleries, lies between Prinsengracht, Brouwersgracht, Singelgracht, and Rozengracht. Turn right off Damrak at any point between Centraal Station and the Dam, and when you cross Prinsengracht, you're in the Jordaan.

Back at Centraal Station, at the rear and on both sides of the station, Amsterdam's **Waterfront** along the IJ channel has been opening up steadily in recent years and will continue to do so in future. New residential, business, cultural, nightlife, and entertainment assets have been developed, all of them marked either by the latest thing in modern architecture, or by old harbor installations that have been refurbished and put to new uses. Ferries, fast trams, and buses get you around these far-flung districts.

GETTING AROUND In looking at a map of Amsterdam, you might think the city is too large to explore by foot. This isn't true: It's possible to see almost every important sight in the Old City on a 4-hour walk.

BY TRAM, BUS & METRO Public transportation begins around 6am; regular service ends around midnight. After that, there are infrequent night buses. Riding the blue-gray **trams** (streetcars) is the most convenient means of getting around; they're fast, cheap, and fun, and provide a great view of the sights. Out of 16 tram routes in the city, 10 begin and end at Centraal Station (and another one passes through). An extensive **bus** network complements the trams and reaches to many points the trams don't cover.

The city's four **Metro** (subway) lines—50, 51, 53, and 54—don't serve most areas you'll likely want to visit. They're used mainly to get people to and from the suburbs, but from Centraal Station you can use Metro trains to reach both Nieuwmarkt and Waterlooplein in the central zone.

Maps showing the city's transit network are posted at most tram/bus shelters and all Metro stations. A free transit map is available from VVV tourist offices and from the **GVB Amsterdam Tickets & Info** office (✆ **0900/9292;** www.gvb.nl) on Stationsplein in front of Centraal Station. You can buy transit cards from this office, from sales points and ticket machines at Metro and train stations, and from some bus and tram drivers and conductors.

By the end of 2010, all public transportation in the Netherlands should be using a new electronic card called the **OV-chipkaart** in place of the old-style tickets. Three main types of OV-chipkaart are available: a reloadable "personal" card that can be used only by its pictured owner; a reloadable "anonymous" card that can be used by anyone; and nonreloadable "throwaway" cards. The personal and anonymous cards, both valid for 5 years, cost 7.50€ and can be loaded and reloaded with up to 30€. Throwaway cards cost 2.50€ for one ride and 4.80€ for two rides. A better bet for short-term visitors may be a 1-day or multiday card: 24 hours (7.50€), 48 hours (12€), 72 hours (15€), 96 hours (18€), 120 hours (23€), 144 hours (26€), 168 hours (29€). Reduced-rate cards are available for seniors and children. Electronic readers automatically deduct the correct fare; just hold your card up against the reader at both the start and the end of the ride.

Keep in mind that inspectors, sometimes undercover, may demand to see your card at any time. If you haven't paid the proper fare, you'll be fined 38€ on the spot plus the fare for the ride.

BY BICYCLE Follow the Dutch example and pedal. A bike is one of the best ways of getting around in this flat city where too many cars clog the narrow streets. You see children barely old enough to walk, their great-grandparents, and even businesswomen in high heels pedaling through the city in any kind of weather. Sunday, when the city is quiet, is a good day to pedal through the parks and to practice riding on cobblestones and dealing with trams before venturing into a rush-hour fracas.

Warning: Watch out for unpredictable car drivers and tourists who are unused to dealing with bicycles en masse, and always lock your bike and its front wheel to something fixed and solid—theft is common.

Rental rates typically begin around 9€ a day or 30€ a week, for a basic "city bike," and go up from there for fancier pair of wheels; add 50% for theft insurance; a deposit of 50€ is generally required. You can rent bikes from Centraal Station when you arrive, and from many rental stores, all of which have similar rates. **MacBike** (✆ **020/620-0985**) rents a range of bikes, including tandems and six-speed touring bikes; it has a branch at Centraal Station (tram: 1, 2, 4, 5, 9, 13, 16, 17, 24, 25, or 26); Mr. Visserplein 2 (tram: 4, 9, or 14), close to the Muziektheater; and Weteringschans 2 (tram: 1, 2, 5, 7, or 10), at Leidseplein. **Damstraat Rent-a-Bike** is at Damstraat 20–22 (✆ **020/625-5029;** tram: 4, 9, 14, 16, 24, or 25), close to the Dam.

BY TAXI Officially, you can't simply hail a cab from the street, but taxis will often stop if you do. You can get a taxi in front of any major hotel and at Centraal Station, the Dam, Leidseplein, Rembrandtplein, and other strategically located taxi stands sprinkled around town. To phone for a cab, call ✆ **020/777-7777.** Taxis are metered. Fares, which include a service charge, begin at 7.50€ when the meter starts and, after 2km, run up at 2.20€ a kilometer; after 25km at 1.75€ a kilometer; and after 50km at 1.45€ a kilometer.

BY BOAT The **Museum Line** (✆ **020/530-5412;** www.lovers.nl) operates Museumboat canal buses near virtually all Amsterdam's museums and attractions. The boats leave from in front of Centraal Station every 30 to 45 minutes daily from 10am to 5pm. Tickets are available from the Lovers Canal Cruises counter near the dock. A day ticket (valid for 24 hr.) is 20€ for adults, 10€ for children ages 4 to 12, and free for children 3 and under. Combination tickets are available that allow reduced admission to museums and attractions on the route.

The **Canal Bus** (✆ **020/623-9886;** www.canal.nl) boats operate daily from 10am to around 6:30pm on three fixed routes—Green, Red, and Blue—that connect important museums and shopping and entertainment districts, with two buses an hour at peak times. A day pass, valid until noon the next day and including discounted admission to some museums and attractions, is 20€ for adults and 15€ for children ages 4 to 12, and free for children 3 and under.

Yellow Cab Watertaxis (with minibar), for up to eight passengers, depart from a dock outside Centraal Station—you can board one here, wave one down as it sails by, or call to arrange a pickup point. Fares begin at 1.75€ per passenger. If you feel like a splurge, call **Watertaxi Amsterdam** (✆ **020/535-6363;** www.water-taxi.nl).

Note: Few Amsterdammers use these services. They are not designed as water transit for locals, but as a different way for visitors to get around.

BY CAR Don't drive in Amsterdam. The city is a jumble of one-way streets, narrow bridges, and trams and cyclists darting every which way. Tough measures are in place to make driving as difficult as possible. No-parking zones are rigorously enforced and the limited parking spaces are expensive. Break the parking rules and your car is sure to be clamped or towed, and can be recovered only with the loss of considerable time and money. As if all that isn't bad enough, car break-ins are common.

Outside the city, driving is a different story and you may want to rent a car for an excursion outside Amsterdam. All the top international firms have desks at Schiphol Airport and one or more rental locations in the city: **Avis** (✆ **0900/235-2847**); **Budget** (✆ **0900/1576**); **Europcar** (✆ **0900/0540**); and **Hertz** (✆ **020/201-3512**). Rates begin at around 50€ a day for a no-frills, subcompact auto with a stick shift and unlimited mileage.

Remember: You get the best deal if you arrange the rental before leaving home.

[FastFACTS] AMSTERDAM

American Express Amsterdam no longer has an American Express office that's open to the general public. For card services, call ✆ **020/504-8000.**

Business Hours **Banks** are open Monday to Friday from 9am to 4 or 5pm, and some to 7pm on Thursday. Regular **shopping** hours are Monday from 10 or 11am to 6pm; Tuesday, Wednesday, and Friday from 9am to 6pm; Thursday from 9am to 9pm; and Saturday from 9am to 5pm. Some stores are open Sunday from noon to 5pm.

Currency The Netherlands currency is the **euro** (€). At press time, 1€ = US$1.40.

Currency Exchange The best options for changing money are the VVV tourist offices, and banks. A fair-dealing *bureau de change* is **GWK Travelex** (✆ **0900/0566**), which has multiple exchanges in the city, including those at Centraal Station; Damrak 1–5 (tram: 4, 9, 14, 16, 24, 25, or 26); Dam 23–25 (tram: 4, 9, 14, 16, 24, or 25); and Leidseplein 31A (tram: 1, 2, 5, 7, or 10).

Some centrally located bank branches with **automated teller machines (ATMs)** are **ABN AMRO Bank,** Dam 2 (tram: 4, 9, 14, 16, 24, or 25), and at Leidsestraat 1 (tram: 1, 2, or 5); **Rabobank,** Dam 16 (tram: 4, 9, 14, 16, 24, or 25); and **Fortis Bank,** Singel 548 (tram: 4, 9, 14, 16, 24, or 25).

Doctors & Dentists Call the **Central Doctors Service** (✆ **020/592-3434**).

Drugstores & Pharmacies For both prescription and nonprescription medicines, go to an *apotheek* (pharmacy). Regular pharmacy hours are Monday to Saturday 9am to 5:30pm. Try **Dam Apotheek,** Damstraat 2 (✆ **020/624-4331;** tram: 4, 9, 14, 16, 24, or 25). All pharmacies post locations of nearby all-night and Sunday pharmacies on the door.

Embassies & Consulates **U.S. Consulate:** Museumplein 19 (✆ **020/575-5309;** http://netherlands.usembassy.gov; tram: 3, 5, 12, or 16), open for personal visits Monday to Friday from 8:30 to 11:30am, and for assistance by phone from 1:30 to 4:30pm; **U.K. Consulate:** Koningslaan 44 (✆ **020/676-4343;** www.britain.nl; tram: 2), open for passport inquiries Monday to Friday from 8:30am to 1:30pm, and for other business by appointment.

Several embassies are in The Hague (Den Haag), including the **U.S.** (Lange Voorhout 102; ✆ **070/310-2209;** http://netherlands.usembassy.gov); **Canada** (Sophialaan 7; ✆ **070/311-1600;** www.canada.nl); **U.K.** (Lange Voorhout 10; ✆ **070/427-0427;** www.britain.nl); **Ireland** (Dr. Kuyperstraat 9; ✆ **070/363-0993;** www.irishembassy.nl); **Australia** (Carnegielaan 4; ✆ **070/310-8200;** www.australian-embassy.nl); and **New Zealand** (Eisenhowerlaan 77N; ✆ **070/346-9324;** www.nzembassy.com/netherlands).

Emergencies For police assistance, an ambulance, or the fire department, call ✆ **112.**

Hospitals Two hospitals with emergency services are the **Onze-Lieve-Vrouwe Gasthuis,** Oosterpark 9 (✆ **020/599-9111;** www.olvg.nl; tram: 3, 7, or 10), in Amsterdam Oost; and the giant **Academisch Medisch Centrum (AMC),** Meibergdreef 9 (✆ **020/566-9111;** www.amc.uva.nl; Metro: Holendrecht), in Amsterdam Zuidoost.

Internet Access The **Mad Processor,** Kinkerstraat 11–13 (✆ **020/612-1818;** www.madprocessor.nl; tram: 7, 10, or 17), is open daily from noon to 1 or 2am.

Mail Most **TNT Post** offices are open Monday to Friday 9am to 5pm. The office at Singel 250, at the corner of Raadhuisstraat (tram: 13, 14, or 17), is open Monday to Friday 7:30am to 6:30pm, and Saturday 7:30 to 9:30am.

Police In an emergency, call the *politie* (police) at ✆ **112.** In nonurgent situations, visit a district police office; a centrally located one is at Lijnbaansgracht 219 (✆ **0900/8844;** tram: 1, 2, 5, 7, or 10), just off Leidseplein.

Safety Random violent crime is not common in Amsterdam, though it does happen. Nonviolent crimes like pickpocketing and theft from cars are common; tourists in particular are targets. Muggings are rarer, but you still need to watch out in some places and circumstances, like strolling through the Red-Light District or along a deserted canalside at night.

Taxes A **value-added tax (BTW)** of 6% is levied on hotel and restaurant bills (19% on beer, wine, and liquor), and 6% or 19% (the amount depends on the product) on purchases. For information on how to recover some of the 19% rate of tax on purchases, see "The Shopping Scene," later in this chapter.

Telephone The **country code** for the Netherlands is **31.** The **city code** for Amsterdam is **20;** use this code when you're calling from outside the Netherlands. If you're within the Netherlands but not in Amsterdam, use **020.** If you're calling within Amsterdam, simply leave off the code and dial only the regular seven-digit phone number.

You can use pay phones in booths with a KPN *telekaart* (phone card), selling for 5€, 10€, 20€, and 50€ from post offices, train ticket counters, and newsstands. Some pay phones take coins of .10€, .20€, .50€, and 1€.

For information inside the Netherlands, call ✆ **0900/8008;** for international information, call ✆ **0900/8418. For operator assistance:** To make an international collect call, dial ✆ **0800/0410.**

To charge a call to your calling card, dial **AT&T** (✆ 0800/022-9111); **MCI** (✆ 0800/022-9122); **Sprint** (✆ 0800/022-9119); **Canada Direct** (✆ 0800/022-9116); **British Telecom** (✆ 0800/022-9944); **Australia Direct** (✆ 0800/022-0061); or **Telecom New Zealand** (✆ 0800/022-4295).

Tipping A 15% service is included in the price of meals at almost all restaurants (if it isn't, it will generally say so on the menu), so it's not necessary to leave a tip. But waitstaff do appreciate tips, and if the service is good you may want to leave a small one by rounding up in cash, not on a credit card slip, to the nearest euro or the nearest 5€, depending on the price of the meal (in an expensive restaurant you may feel obliged to go up to the nearest 10€ or 10%). Taxi fares are high and include a service charge; drivers appreciate a tip, but it's not really necessary to give one unless you want to.

Where to Stay

Booking ahead is always advised. If you arrive in Amsterdam without a reservation, consult the **VVV tourist offices** (see "Visitor Information," earlier in this chapter). Or reserve through the VVV's **Amsterdam Reservation Center** (✆ **020/551-2525;** fax 020/625-2869; reservations@atcb.nl; www.amsterdamtourist.nl). There's a 15€ fee for reservations made by phone, fax, and e-mail; website reservations are free. In summer, it's imperative you look for a room early in the day—by late afternoon many hotels are already full.

Note: Many hotels have special offers, promotional rates, and on occasion just plain lower rates than the "regular" rates listed below. Be sure to check their website, or with reservations agencies, or phone direct to the hotel to see what's available.

THE OLD CENTER

Very Expensive

Hotel de l'Europe ★★ On a stretch of prime riverside real estate in the center city, this elegant old establishment's red-and-white facade, standing at the point where the Amstel River flows into the canal network, is an iconic city view. Built in 1896, the hotel has a grand style and a sense of ease, a smooth combination of aged dignity and modern comforts. Guest rooms and bathrooms are spacious and bright, furnished with classic good taste. Some rooms have small balconies overlooking the river, and all boast marble bathrooms. French restaurant **Excelsior** (p. 740) is among the toniest dining spots in town.

Nieuwe Doelenstraat 2-14 (facing Muntplein), 1012 CP Amsterdam. ✆ **800/223-6800** in the U.S. and Canada, or 020/531-1777. Fax 020/531-1778. www.leurope.nl. 100 units. 420€–510€ double; from 560€

suite; add 5% city tax. AE, DC, MC, V. Valet parking 53€. Tram: 4, 9, 14, 16, 24, or 25 to De Munt. **Amenities:** 2 restaurants; 2 bars; babysitting; concierge; health club; heated indoor pool; room service; sauna; smoke-free rooms. *In room:* A/C, TV, hair dryer, minibar, Wi-Fi (free).

Sofitel Amsterdam The Grand ★★ Set along an elegant stretch of Old Amsterdam canal, this 2010-renovated grande dame attracts a stately clientele. It occupies a building that housed a convent in the 15th century, a royal guesthouse in the 16th, the Amsterdam Admiralty in the 17th, and City Hall in the 19th. Beyond its courtyard with fountain, and brass-and-wood revolving door, the individually styled and furnished rooms reflect these different phases of the past, and have views on canals, the hotel garden, or the courtyard. A 1949 Karel Appel mural "diverts" diners in the Art Deco–inspired French restaurant **Bridges.**

Oudezijds Voorburgwal 197 (off Damstraat), 1012 EX Amsterdam. ✆ **800/515-5679** in the U.S. and Canada, or 020/555-3111. Fax 020/555-3222. www.thegrand.nl. 177 units. 550€–610€ double; from 850€ suite; add 5% city tax. AE, DC, MC, V. Valet parking 50€. Tram: 4, 9, 14, 16, 24, or 25 to Spui. **Amenities:** Restaurant; bar; babysitting; concierge; health club; Jacuzzi; heated indoor pool; room service; sauna; smoke-free rooms. *In room:* A/C, TV, hair dryer, minibar, Wi-Fi (20€ per 24 hr.).

Moderate

Avenue Hotel ★ Part of this hotel is a converted 17th-century warehouse that belonged to the V.O.C., the United East India Company. The rooms aren't huge, but they're bright and have clean furnishings and good-size bathrooms, some with a double sink. The location is pretty central and convenient for getting to and fro by tram—the downside is the clackety-clack of outside traffic. If this is likely to disturb you, ask for a room at the back. The Dutch buffet breakfast is more than decent, and the St. Jacobsstreet Café, around the corner on Sint-Jacobsstraat, takes care of dinner in reasonable style.

Nieuwezijds Voorburgwal 33 (near Centraal Station), 1012 RD Amsterdam. ✆ **020/530-9530.** Fax 020/530-9599. www.embhotels.nl. 80 units. 112€–160€ double; add 5% city tax. Rates include buffet breakfast. AE, DC, MC, V. Limited street parking. Tram: 1, 2, 5, 13, or 17 to Nieuwezijds Kolk. **Amenities:** Cafe/bar; room service; smoke-free rooms. *In room:* A/C (some rooms), TV, hair dryer, Wi-Fi (free).

THE WATERFONT

Expensive

Lloyd Hotel ★ Located at the redeveloped old steamship docks east of Centraal Station, the Lloyd was originally a hotel for emigrants when it opened in 1921. It has been thoroughly renovated, and reopened in 2004. Just about every room has a different shape, style, and modern decor, which accounts for the unusually large range of room rates. The most expensive rooms are the largest and have a view on the water, or a specially designed interior (or both). Beds are new and mattresses firm, but only a few rooms have king-size doubles.

Oostelijke Handelskade 34, 1019 BN Amsterdam (at IJhaven). ✆ **020/561-3636.** Fax 020/561-3600. www.lloydhotel.com. 117 units, 106 with bathroom. 140€–450€ double with bathroom; 95€ double without bathroom. AE, DC, MC, V. Parking 25€. Tram: 10 or 26 to Rietlandpark. **Amenities:** 2 restaurants; bar; babysitting; bikes; room service; smoke-free rooms. *In room:* TV, Wi-Fi (free).

Inexpensive

Amstel Botel ☺ Where better to experience a city on the water than on a boat? The Botel, moored permanently to a dock on the IJ waterway northwest of Centraal Station, is popular largely because of that extra thrill added by sleeping on the water—its modest (for Amsterdam) rates don't hurt either. This retired inland waterways cruise boat has cabins on four decks that are connected by an elevator. The bright, modern rooms are no-nonsense but comfortable, the showers small. Be sure to ask for a slightly more expensive room with a view on the water, to avoid the uninspiring quay.

NDSM-Werf 3 (Amsterdam-Noord), 1033 RG Amsterdam. ✆ **020/521-0350.** Fax 020/639-1952. www.amstelbotel.com. 175 units. 89€–94€ double. AE, DC, MC, V. Limited free parking on quay. Boat: NDSM ferry from Centraal Station. **Amenities:** Bar; bikes; Internet (20€ per minute, in bar); smoke-free rooms. *In room:* TV.

THE CANAL BELT

Expensive

Ambassade ★★ Perhaps more than any other hotel in Amsterdam, this one, in ten 17th- and 18th-century canal-houses on the Herengracht and Singel canals, re-creates the feeling of living in an elegant canal-house. The pastel-toned rooms are individually styled, their size and shape varying according to the character of each house. Anyone who lodges here is sure to enjoy the view each morning over breakfast in the bi-level, chandeliered breakfast room, or each evening in the adjoining parlor, with its Persian rugs and a stately grandfather clock ticking away.

Herengracht 341 (near Spui), 1016 AZ Amsterdam. ✆ **020/555-0222.** Fax 020/555-0277. www.ambassade-hotel.nl. 59 units. 195€–285€ double; 275€–375€ suite; add 5% city tax. AE, DC, MC, V. Limited street parking. Tram: 1, 2, or 5 to Spui. **Amenities:** Lounge; babysitting; bikes; room service; smoke-free rooms; access to nearby spa. *In room:* TV, hair dryer, Wi-Fi (free).

Estheréa ★★★ If you like to stay at elegant, not-too-big hotels, you'll be pleased by the Estheréa. It's been owned by the same family since its beginnings and, like so many hotels in Amsterdam, was built anew within the walls of a group of neighboring 17th-century canal-houses. The family touch shows in careful attention to detail and a breezy yet professional approach. While the hotel may look dated to some, the wood bedsteads and dresser-desks in fact lend warmth to renovated and upgraded rooms. The room sizes vary considerably according to their location in the canal-houses.

Singel 305 (near Spui), 1012 WJ Amsterdam. ✆ **800/223-9868** in the U.S. and Canada, or 020/624-5146. Fax 020/623-9001. www.estherea.nl. 92 units. 191€–314€ double; add 5% city tax. AE, DC, MC, V. Parking 55€. Tram: 1, 2, or 5 to Spui. **Amenities:** Bar; lounge; babysitting; smoke-free rooms. *In room:* TV, hair dryer, minibar, Wi-Fi (10€ per 24 hr.).

Moderate

Agora ★ Old-fashioned friendliness is the keynote at this efficiently run and well-maintained lodging. Though the hotel occupies a canal-house built in 1735, it's been fully restored in an eclectic style. Furniture from the 1930s and 1940s mixes with fine mahogany antiques. There's an abundance of overstuffed furniture; nearly every room has a puffy armchair you can sink into after a wearying day of sightseeing. Those rooms that don't have a canal view look out onto a pretty garden at the back. There's no elevator.

Singel 462 (at Koningsplein), 1017 AW Amsterdam. ✆ **020/627-2200.** Fax 020/627-2202. www.hotelagora.nl. 16 units. 75€–159€ double; add 5% city tax. Rates include buffet breakfast. AE, DC, MC, V. Limited street parking. Tram: 1, 2, or 5 to Koningsplein. **Amenities:** Smoke-free rooms. *In room:* TV, hair dryer, Wi-Fi (free).

Amsterdam Wiechmann ★ It takes only a moment to feel at home in the antiques-adorned Wiechmann, a classic, comfortable, casual kind of place. Besides, the location is one of the best you'll find in this or any price range. Most of the rooms

A Canal-House Warning

Be prepared to climb hard-to-navigate stairways if you want to save money on lodging in Amsterdam by staying in a canal-house. Narrow and as steep as ladders, these stairways were designed to conserve space in the narrow houses along the canals. If you have difficulty climbing stairs, ask for a room on a lower floor.

are standard, with good-size twin or double beds, and some have big bay windows. Furnishings are elegant. The higher-priced doubles, with a view on the canal, have antique furnishings. There's no elevator.

Prinsengracht 328–332 (at Looiersgracht), 1016 HX Amsterdam. ✆ **020/626-3321.** Fax 020/626-8962. www.hotelwiechmann.nl. 37 units. 90€–165€ double. Rates include continental breakfast. MC, V. Limited street parking. Tram: 1, 2, or 5 to Prinsengracht. **Amenities:** Lounge; bikes; smoke-free rooms. *In room:* TV, Wi-Fi (free).

Inexpensive

Prinsenhof A modernized canal-house near the Amstel River, this hotel offers rooms with beamed ceilings and basic yet reasonably comfortable beds. Front rooms look out onto the Prinsengracht, where colorful houseboats are moored. Breakfast is served in an attractive blue-and-white decorated dining room. There's no elevator, but a pulley hauls your luggage up and down the stairs.

Prinsengracht 810 (at Utrechtsestraat), 1017 JL Amsterdam. ✆ **020/623-1772.** Fax 020/638-3368. www.hotelprinsenhof.com. 11 units, 6 with bathroom. 89€ double with bathroom; 69€ double without bathroom. Rates include continental breakfast. AE, MC, V. Limited street parking. Tram: 4 to Prinsengracht. **Amenities:** Smoke-free rooms. *In room:* No phone.

THE JORDAAN

Inexpensive

Acacia ★ Not on one of the major canals, but in the Jordaan, facing a small canal just a block away from Prinsengracht, the Acacia is run by a friendly couple who are justifiably proud of their welcoming and well-kept hotel. Simple, clean, and comfortable, all rooms have canal views; the large front corner rooms are shaped like pie slices, sleep as many as five guests, and have windows on three sides. All rooms recently were outfitted with new beds, writing tables, and chairs. There's no elevator.

Lindengracht 251 (at Lijnbaansgracht), 1015 KH Amsterdam. ✆ **020/622-1460.** Fax 020/638-0748. www.hotelacacia.nl. 14 units. 80€–90€ double. Rates include continental breakfast. MC, V (5% charge). Limited street parking. Tram: 3 or 10 to Marnixplein. **Amenities:** Internet (in lobby); smoke-free rooms. *In room:* TV.

AROUND LEIDSEPLEIN

Expensive

Eden Amsterdam American ★★★ A fanciful, castle-like mix of Venetian Gothic and Art Nouveau, the American has been both a prominent landmark and a popular meeting place for Amsterdammers since 1900. While the exterior must always remain a protected architectural treasure of turrets, arches, and balconies, the interior (except that of the cafe, which is also protected) is modern and chic, though in places a tad gaudy. Rooms are subdued, refined, and superbly furnished.

Some have a view on Singelgracht; others overlook kaleidoscopic Leidseplein. The **Café Americain** (p. 743) is among Amsterdam's most elegant eateries.

Leidsekade 97 (at Leidseplein), 1017 PN Amsterdam. ✆ **020/556-3000.** Fax 020/556-3001. www.edenamsterdamamericanhotel.com. 175 units. 130€–290€ double; from 415€ suite; add 5% city tax. AE, DC, MC, V. No parking. Tram: 1, 2, 5, 7, or 10 to Leidseplein. **Amenities:** Restaurant; bar; concierge; exercise room; room service; sauna; smoke-free rooms. *In room:* A/C, TV, hair dryer, Internet (1€ per hour), minibar.

AROUND REMBRANDTPLEIN

Moderate

NH Schiller Hotel ★ An Amsterdam gem from 1912, fully restored, this hotel boasts a blend of Art Nouveau and Art Deco in its public spaces, a theme that is reflected in the tasteful furnishings in the rooms. Its sculpted facade, wrought-iron balconies, and stained-glass windows stand out on the often brash Rembrandtplein. **Brasserie Schiller** is a gracious, oak-paneled dining room, and **Café Schiller** is one of Amsterdam's few permanent sidewalk cafes.

Rembrandtplein 26–36, 1017 CV Amsterdam. ✆ **020/554-0700.** Fax 020/624-0098. www.nh-hotels.com. 92 units. 95€–203€ double; from 161€ suite. AE, DC, MC, V. Limited street parking. Tram: 4, 9, or 14 to Rembrandtplein. **Amenities:** Restaurant, 2 bars; babysitting; room service; smoke-free rooms. *In room:* TV, hair dryer, minibar, Wi-Fi (11€ per 24 hr.).

Seven Bridges ★★ One of Amsterdam's canal-house gems, not far from Rembrandtplein, gets its name from its view of seven arched bridges. There are antique furnishings, handmade Italian drapes, hand-painted tiles and wood-tiled floors, and Impressionist art posters. The biggest room, on the first landing, can accommodate up to four and has a huge bathroom with marble floor and double sinks. Attic rooms have sloped ceilings and exposed wood beams, and there are big, bright basement rooms done almost entirely in white. There's no elevator and no breakfast room; breakfast is served in the room in 8 out of the 11 rooms, and not at all in the remaining 3.

Reguliersgracht 31 (at Keizersgracht), 1017 LK Amsterdam. ✆ **020/623-1329.** Fax 020/624-7652. www.sevenbridgeshotel.nl. 11 units. 90€–250€ double. Rates include full breakfast (in 8 rooms only). AE, MC, V. Limited street parking. Tram: 4 to Keizersgracht. **Amenities:** Smoke-free rooms. *In room:* TV, hair dryer, Wi-Fi (free).

THE MUSEUM DISTRICT

Moderate

Bilderberg Hotel Jan Luyken ★ Close to the Rijksmuseum, this is a small hotel with some of the amenities and facilities of a large one—though without the large rooms. Everything here is done to maintain a balance between a sophisticated lineup of facilities and an intimate and personalized approach appropriate to a 19th-century residential neighborhood. That feel extends to the guest rooms, which look more like those in a well-designed home than a standard hotel room.

Jan Luijkenstraat 58 (near the Rijksmuseum), 1071 CS Amsterdam. ✆ **020/573-0730.** Fax 020/676-3841. www.janluyken.nl. 62 units. 99€–159€ double; from 500€ suite; add 5% city tax. AE, DC, MC, V. Limited street parking. Tram: 2 or 5 to Hobbemastraat. **Amenities:** Wine bar; concierge; room service; smoke-free rooms; small spa. *In room:* A/C, TV, hair dryer, minibar, Wi-Fi (17€ per 24 hr.).

De Filosoof ★ On a quiet street of brick houses near Vondelpark, this extraordinary, elegant hotel might be the very place if you fancy yourself as something of a philosopher. Each room is dedicated to a mental maestro or an important cultural figure—Aristotle, Plato, Goethe, Wittgenstein, Nietzsche, Marx, and Einstein are among those who get a look-in—or it is based on motifs like Eros, the Renaissance, and astrology. You can even consult your private bookshelf of philosophical works or join in a weekly philosophy debate. The rooms in an annex across the street are larger; some open onto a terrace.

Anna van den Vondelstraat 6 (off Overtoom, at Vondelpark), 1054 GZ Amsterdam. ✆ **020/683-3013.** Fax 020/685-3750. www.sandton.eu. 38 units. 105€–180€ double. Rates include buffet breakfast. AE, MC, V. Limited street parking. Tram: 1 to Jan Pieter Heijestraat. **Amenities:** Lounge; smoke-free rooms. *In room:* TV, hair dryer, Wi-Fi (free).

Inexpensive

Piet Hein Occupying a villa close to the city's most important museums, the Piet Hein is named after a Dutch folk hero, a 17th-century admiral who captured a Spanish silver shipment. Rooms are spacious and well furnished, and the staff friendly and professional. Half the rooms overlook the park; two second-floor doubles have semicircular balconies; and a honeymoon suite has a water bed. Lower-priced rooms are in an annex.

Vossiusstraat 52–53 (off Van Baerlestraat), 1071 AK Amsterdam. ✆ **020/662-7205.** Fax 020/662-1526. www.hotelpiethein.com. 65 units. 135€–250€ double. Rates include buffet breakfast. AE, DC, MC, V. Limited street parking. Tram: 3, 5, or 12 to Van Baerlestraat. **Amenities:** Bar; room service; smoke-free rooms. *In room:* TV, Wi-Fi (free).

AMSTERDAM SOUTH

Inexpensive

Bicycle Hotel Amsterdam ★ The proprietors of this establishment hit on an interesting idea: They cater to visitors who wish to explore Amsterdam on bikes and can help guests plan biking routes through and around the city. You can rent bikes for 7.50€ daily, no deposit, and stable your trusty steed indoors. The rooms have plain but comfortable modern furnishings; some have kitchenettes and small balconies, and there are large rooms for families. There's no elevator.

Van Ostadestraat 123 (off Ferdinand Bolstraat), 1072 SV Amsterdam. ✆ **020/679-3452.** Fax 020/671-5213. www.bicyclehotel.com. 16 units, 8 with bathroom. 60€–120€ double with bathroom; 40€–85€ double without bathroom. Rates include continental breakfast. AE, MC, V (4% charge). Parking 25€. Tram: 3, 12, or 25 to Ceintuurbaan-Ferdinand Bolstraat. **Amenities:** Lounge; bikes; Wi-Fi (free). *In room:* TV.

Where to Dine

As a trading and gateway city with a multiethnic population, Amsterdam has absorbed culinary influences from far and wide. You find dozens of ethnic eateries serving everything from Algerian to Vietnamese food—still waiting for W, X, Y, and Z!

Spice of Life

You haven't really eaten in Amsterdam until you've had an Indonesian *rijsttafel.* This traditional "rice table" banquet consists of as many as 20 succulent and spicy foods served in tiny bowls. Pick and choose from among the bowls and add your choice to the pile of rice on your plate. It's almost impossible to eat all the food set on your table, but give it a shot—it's a true taste of multicultural Amsterdam. For an abbreviated version served on one plate, try *nasi rames.* At lunch, the standard Indonesian fare is *nasi goreng* (fried rice with meat and vegetables) or *bami goreng* (fried noodles prepared in the same way).

Indonesian food is extremely popular, notably the *rijsttafel* (see "Spice of Life," above). Many of these ethnic places serve hearty and delicious meals at very reasonable prices. And you'll find plenty of traditional Dutch restaurants.

THE OLD CENTER

Very Expensive

Excelsior ★★ FRENCH/CONTINENTAL Located within the tony Hotel de l'Europe, one of Amsterdam's finest restaurants derives its reputation from French chef Jean-Jacques Menanteau's Michelin-star cuisine. It's more than a little formal—more than a lot by Amsterdam standards. Crystal chandeliers, elaborate moldings, crisp linens, fresh bouquets of flowers, and picture windows with great views on the Amstel River typify this classically grand establishment. A meal here is an exercise in refinement, aided by a diligent and discreet waitstaff. Respectable attire is required.

In the Hotel de l'Europe, Nieuwe Doelenstraat 2-14 (facing Muntplein). ✆ **020/531-1705.** Reservations recommended on weekends. Main courses 34€–38€; fixed-price menus 55€–95€. AE, DC, MC, V. Mon–Fri 12:30–2:30pm and 6–11pm; Sat–Sun 6–11pm. Tram: 4, 9, 14, 16, 24, or 25 to Muntplein.

Moderate

In de Waag ★ CONTINENTAL The castle-like 14th-century Sint-Antoniespoort Gate in the city walls, later a public weigh house, holds one of Amsterdam's most stylish cafe-restaurants, in an area that's becoming hipper by the day. It's indelibly romantic, with its long banquet-style tables lit by hundreds of candles in the evening. You can mix easily with other diners. The breast of Barbary duck with sesame-cracker and sherry dressing is pretty good, as is the vegetarian Kashmir bread with braised vegetables and coriander-yogurt sauce.

Nieuwmarkt 4. ✆ **020/422-7772.** Main courses 19€–25€; fixed-price menu 34€. AE, DC, MC, V. Daily 10am–1am. Metro: Nieuwmarkt.

THE WATERFRONT

Expensive

Fifteen Amsterdam ★ FUSION/ITALIAN British celeb-chef Jamie Oliver's hot spot in a refurbished spot in the harbor redevelopment zone east of Centraal Station has both a full-menu restaurant and a trattoria serving less-elaborate fare. Though Jamie doesn't often preside in person, you can try his eclectic-fun cooking concept in the vast main dining room. In the more intimate trattoria, where prices are more moderate, try risottos, pasta dishes, and other Italian fare. You can also dine outdoors on a waterside terrace.

Pakhuis Amsterdam, Jollemanhof 9 (at Oostelijke Handelskade). ✆ **0900/343-8336.** www.fifteen.nl. Reservations required for restaurant. Restaurant fixed-price menu 46€; trattoria main courses 23€–29€. AE, MC, V. Restaurant daily 6pm–1am (closed Sun July–Aug); trattoria Sun–Thurs 5:30pm–1am. Tram: 10 or 26 to Rietlandpark.

Moderate

Gare de l'Est ★ TRADITIONAL FRENCH/MEDITERRANEAN The detached, distinctive house, with a conservatory and a large sidewalk terrace, was built in 1901 as a coffeehouse for workers at the Oosterdok (Eastern Dock). Service is both relaxed and knowledgeable. The five-course formula (starter, salad, main course of meat or fish, cheese, and dessert) leaves no room for choice—except for the main course. How does this sound—*pulpo stofado* with *risotto nero* (octopus stew with black risotto) as a starter, and roast lamb with gazpacho sauce and farfalle pasta as a main course?

Cruquiusweg 9 (at Panamalaan). ✆ **020/463-0620.** Reservations recommended on weekends. Fixed-price menu 32€. No credit cards. Daily 6–11pm. Tram: 7 or 10 to Zeeburgerdijk.

Wilhelmina-Dok ★ CONTINENTAL Across the IJ waterway from Centraal Station, this great waterfront eatery more than justifies a short, free ferryboat ride followed by a 5-minute walk. Plain wood, candlelit tables, wood floors, and oak cabinets give the interior an old-fashioned maritime look, and large windows serve up views across the narrow, boat-speckled channel. The menu favors plain cooking and organic products. Tables on the outdoor terrace are sheltered from the wind in a glass-walled enclosure.

Nordwal 1 (at IJplein). ✆ **020/632-3701.** Reservations recommended on weekends. Main courses 18€–28€; buffet 18€–35€. AE, DC, MC, V. Daily 11am–midnight. Ferry: IJveer (IJ ferry) from Waterplein-West behind Centraal Station to the dock at IJplein; then walk east along the dike-top path.

THE CANAL BELT

Moderate

Bolhoed ★ VEGETARIAN Forget the dull, tofu-and-brown-rice image of vegetarian dining—Bolhoed adds a touch of spice to its health food formula with its Latin style, world music background, candlelight in the evenings, and fine views of the canal. Service is zestful and friendly. Try such veggie delights as the *ragoût croissant* (pastry filled with leeks, tofu, seaweed, and curry sauce) or *zarzuela* (tomato-based fish stew). If you want to go whole-hog, so to speak, and eat vegan, most dishes can be so prepared on request, and in any case most are made with organically grown produce. For outdoors dining in summer, there are a few canalside tables.

Prinsengracht 60–62 (near Noordermarkt). ✆ **020/626-1803.** Main courses 13€–17€; fixed-price menus 13€–19€. No credit cards. Sun–Fri noon–11pm; Sat 11am–11pm. Tram: 13, 14, or 17 to Westermarkt.

De Belhamel ★★ 🎁 CONTINENTAL Classical music complements Art Nouveau in a graceful setting overlooking the Herengracht and Brouwersgracht canals. The menu changes seasonally, and game is a specialty. You can expect such menu dishes as puffed pastries layered with salmon, shellfish, crayfish tails, and chervil beurre blanc to start; and beef tenderloin in Madeira sauce with zucchini rösti and puffed garlic for a main course. Vegetarian dishes are available.

Brouwersgracht 60 (at Herengracht). ✆ **020/622-1095.** Main courses 11€–27€; fixed-price menus 35€–45€. AE, MC, V. Sun–Thurs 6–10pm; Fri–Sat 6–10:30pm. Tram: 1, 2, 5, 13, or 17 to Martelaarsgracht.

Tempo Doeloe ★★ INDONESIAN For authentic Indonesian cuisine, from Java, Sumatra, and Bali—which doesn't leave out much—this place is hard to beat. Though its local reputation goes up and down with the tide, it's invariably busy. You dine in a batik ambience that's Indonesian but restrained, and a long way short of being kitsch. The attractive decor and the fine china are unexpected pluses. Try the many meat, fish, and vegetable dishes of the three rijsttafel options, from the 15-plate vegetarian rijsttafel *sayoeran* and the 15-plate rijsttafel *stimoelan* to the sumptuous 25-plate rijsttafel *istemewa*.

Utrechtsestraat 75 (btw. Prinsengracht and Keizersgracht). ✆ **020/625-6718.** Reservations required. Main courses 15€–26€; rijsttafel 28€–36€; fixed-price menu 28€–44€. AE, DC, MC, V. Mon–Sat 6–11:30pm. Tram: 4 to Keizersgracht.

Inexpensive

De Prins ★★ MODERN DUTCH/CONTINENTAL In a 17th-century canal-house, this companionable brown cafe/restaurant opposite the Anne Frankhuis serves the kind of food you'd expect from a much more expensive place. The clientele is loyal, so the relatively few tables fill up quickly. It's a quiet neighborhood restaurant—nothing fancy or trendy, but quite appealing, with the bar on a slightly lower level than the restaurant and a sidewalk terrace for drinks in summer.

Prinsengracht 124 (at Egelantiersgracht). ✆ **020/624-9382.** Main courses 11€–17€; lunch menu 12€. AE, DC, MC, V. Daily 10am–1 or 2am (kitchen to 10pm). Tram: 13, 14, or 17 to Westermarkt.

Golden Temple ★ VEGETARIAN In its fourth decade of tickling meat-shunning palates, this temple of taste is still one of the best vegetarian (and vegan) options in town. If anything, it's a tad too hallowed, an effect enhanced by a minimalist absence of decorative flourishes. The menu livens things up, however, with an unlikely roster of Indian, Middle Eastern, and Mexican dishes, and the multiple-choice platters are a good way to go.

Utrechtsestraat 126 (close to Frederiksplein). ✆ **020/626-8560.** Main courses 14€–16€; mixed platter 16€. MC, V. Daily 5–10pm. Tram: 4 to Prinsengracht.

AROUND SPUI

Expensive

D'Vijff Vlieghen ★ MODERN DUTCH Touristy? Yes, but the "Five Flies" is one of Amsterdam's most famous restaurants, and the food is authentic stick-to-the-ribs Dutch fare. The chef is passionate about an updated form of Dutch cuisine he calls "the new Dutch kitchen." If you're feeling adventurous, try the wild boar with sweet chestnuts and a sauce made with *jenever* (liquor flavored with juniper berries). The restaurant is a kind of Dutch theme park, within five canal-houses decorated with artifacts from Holland's golden age. Don't miss the four original Rembrandt etchings in the Rembrandt Room and the collection of handmade glass in the Glass Room.

Spuistraat 294–302 (at Spui; entrance at Vliegendesteeg 1). ✆ **020/530-4060.** Reservations recommended on weekends. Main courses 22€–39€; seasonal menu 26€–53€. AE, DC, MC, V. Daily 5:30–10pm. Tram: 1, 2, or 5 to Spui.

Moderate

Haesje Claes TRADITIONAL DUTCH If you're yearning for a cozy Old Dutch environment and hearty Dutch food at moderate prices, this is the place to go. It's inviting and intimate, with lots of nooks and crannies and with brocaded benches and traditional Dutch hanging lamps. The menu covers a lot of ground, ranging from canapés to caviar, but you'll likely be happiest with such Dutch stalwarts as tournedos, *hutspot* (stew), *stampot* (mashed potatoes and cabbage), or various fish stews, including those with IJsselmeer *paling* (eel).

Spuistraat 273–275 (at Spui). ✆ **020/624-9998.** Main courses 16€–26€; fixed-price menu 28€. AE, DC, MC, V. Daily noon–10pm. Tram: 1, 2, or 5 to Spui.

Kantjil & de Tijger ★ INDONESIAN Unlike Indonesian restaurants that wear their ethnic origins on their sleeve, the "Antelope and the Tiger" is modern and cool. Two bestsellers here are *nasi goreng Kantjil* (fried rice with pork kabobs, stewed beef, pickled cucumbers, and mixed vegetables) and the 20-item rijsttafel (rice with meat, seafood, and vegetables) for two. Other choices are stewed chicken in soy sauce, tofu omelet, shrimp with coconut dressing, Indonesian pumpkin, and mixed steamed vegetables with peanut-butter sauce. Finish with the cinnamon layer cake or the coffee with ginger liqueur and whipped cream.

Spuistraat 291–293 (beside Spui). ✆ **020/620-0994.** Reservations recommended on weekends. Main courses 11€–16€; rijsttafel 40€–50€ for 2. AE, DC, MC, V. Daily 4:30–11pm. Tram: 1, 2, or 5 to Spui.

Visrestaurant Lucius SEAFOOD Lucius, which means "pike" in Latin, has earned a reputation for fine seafood at fairly reasonable prices. Oysters and lobsters imported from Norway and Canada are the specialties. The three-course menu is also very popular. Among the six or so choices featured on the chalkboard menu, you might find fish soup to start, followed by grilled plaice, Dover sole, bass, or John Dory. The spectacular seafood plate includes six oysters, 10 mussels, clams, shrimp, and half a lobster. In summer, you can dine out on the sidewalk.

Spuistraat 247 (near Spui). ✆ **020/624-1831.** Main courses 19€–27€; fixed-price menu 38€. AE, DC, MC, V. Daily 5pm–midnight. Tram: 1, 2, or 5 to Spui.

AROUND LEIDSEPLEIN

Moderate

Café Americain ★ INTERNATIONAL This is a national monument of Dutch Jugendstil and Art Deco. Mata Hari held her wedding reception here in her pre-espionage days, and since its 1900 opening, this has been a haven for Dutch and international artists, writers, dancers, and actors. Leaded windows, newspaper-littered reading tables, bargello-patterned velvet upholstery, frosted-glass chandeliers from the 1920s, and tall, carved columns are all part of the dusky sit-and-chat setting. Menu dishes include monkfish, perch, rack of Irish lamb, and rosé breast of duck with creamed potatoes. Jazz lovers can dine to good music at a Sunday jazz brunch.

In the Eden Amsterdam American Hotel, Leidsekade 97 (at Leidseplein). ✆ **020/556-3000.** Main courses 16€–23€. AE, DC, MC, V. Mon–Fri 6:30am–11:30pm; Sat 7am–11:30pm. Tram: 1, 2, 5, 7, or 10 to Leidseplein.

THE JORDAAN

Expensive

Bordewijk ★★ FRENCH/FUSION This pleasantly located restaurant is often regarded as one of the best in the city. The decor is tasteful, with potted plants offsetting the severity of the white walls and metallic black tables. Service is relaxed yet attentive, and on mild summer evenings you can't beat dining alfresco on the canalside terrace. But the real treat is the food. An innovative chef accents French standards with Mediterranean and Asian flourishes to create an elegant fusion of flavors.

Noordermarkt 7 (at Prinsengracht). ✆ **020/624-3899.** Reservations required. Main courses 24€–29€; fixed-price menus 39€–72€. AE, MC, V. Tues–Sun 6:30–10:30pm. Tram: 1, 2, 5, 13, or 17 to Martelaarsgracht.

Moderate

Toscanini ★ SOUTH ITALIAN This small restaurant has a warm, welcoming ambience and excellent southern Italian food (at least that's the point of emphasis, but most regional Italian dishes are available—though not pizza). Popular with the artists and bohemians who inhabit the neighborhood, Toscanini has unembellished country-style decor and an open kitchen that speak of authenticity. Cooking is home-style and there's a long-as-your-arm list of Italian wines. Service is congenial and chatty but can be slow, though that doesn't deter loyal regulars.

Lindengracht 75 (off Brouwersgracht). ✆ **020/623-2813.** Main courses 17€–21€; fixed-price menu 45€. AE, DC, MC, V. Mon–Sat 6–10:30pm. Tram: 3 to Nieuwe Willemsstraat.

> **Sweet Talk**
>
> **If you have a sweet tooth, be sure to try some traditional Dutch desserts, such as *poffertjes* (miniature pancakes), *oliebollen* (like powdered sugar–covered doughnut holes), or pancakes. All these come with various fillings or toppings, many of which contain a liqueur of some sort. Traditional poffertje snack bars are garish affairs that look as though they're part of a circus.**

AMSTERDAM WEST

Moderate

Amsterdam ★★ CONTINENTAL Think of it as *Amsterdam: The Restaurant,* because it's quite a performance. Based in a century-old water-pumping station, complete with diesel-powered engine, this cafe-restaurant has taken this monument of Victorian industrial good taste and made of it a model of contemporary good eats. Service is friendly, and the food is good and moderately priced. If you're feeling flush, spring for a double starter of half a lobster with six Zeeland oysters. The Amsterdam is a little bit out from the center city, but is easily worth the tram ride. Watertorenplein 6 (off Haarlemmerweg). ✆ **020/682-2666.** Reservations recommended on weekends. Main courses 10€–18€. AE, DC, MC, V. Daily 11am–midnight. Tram: 10 to Van Hallstraat.

Seeing the Sights

Amsterdam has an almost bewildering embarrassment of riches. There are 160 canals to cruise, with a combined length of 76km (47 miles), spanned by 1,281 bridges; hundreds of narrow streets to wander; almost 8,000 historic buildings to see in the center city; more than 40 museums of all types to visit; diamond cutters and craftspeople to watch as they practice generations-old skills . . . the list is as long as every visitor's individual interests—and then some.

THREE KEY MUSEUMS

Anne Frankhuis ★★ A teenage Jewish girl, Anne Frank wrote her famous diary here while she and seven other Jewish refugees hid from the Nazis in a secret annex at the back of this large canal-house. Anne, the youngest Frank daughter, had been given a diary for her 13th birthday in 1942. With the eyes of a child and the writing skills of a girl who hoped one day to be a writer, she chronicled the almost silent life in hiding of the *onderduikers* ("divers," or hiders), the continued persecution of Jews by Hitler, the progress of the war, and her personal growth as a young woman. Anne achieved her dream of being a famous writer: Today more than 25 million copies of *The Diary of Anne Frank* have been sold in 50 languages.

The cramped, gloomy hiding place, where they were forced to maintain nearly total silence, kept them safe for more than 2 years until they were betrayed and pro-German Dutch police raided their refuge on August 4, 1944. Anne died of typhus in March 1945 at Bergen-Belsen, tragically close to the war's end; six of the others also died in concentration camps. Although the rooms contain no furniture and are as bare as they were when Anne's father, Otto, the only survivor, returned, the exhibits, including a year-by-year chronology of Anne's life, fill in the missing details. This lack of distraction allows you to project yourself into Anne's claustrophobic, fear-filled world.

Note: Lines here can be very long, especially in summer—try going on a weekday morning. An alternative strategy if you're in town from mid-March to mid-September, when the museum is open to 9 or 10pm, is to go in the evening. Or purchase your ticket online for a time of your choice. Once you're inside, an hour should do it, though many people linger.

Prinsengracht 263 (at Westermarkt). ✆ **020/556-7100,** or 020/556-7105 for recorded information. www.annefrank.org. Admission 8.50€ adults, 4€ children 10–17, free for children 9 and under. Mid-Mar to June and 1st 2 weeks of Sept Sun–Fri 9am–9pm, Sat 9am–10pm; July–Aug daily 9am–10pm; mid-Sept to mid-Mar daily 9am–7pm; Jan 1 noon–7pm; May 4 9am–7pm; Dec 21 and 31 9am–5pm; Dec 25 noon–5pm. Closed Yom Kippur. Tram: 13, 14, or 17 to Westermarkt.

Rijksmuseum ★★★ Most of Holland's premier museum, at Museumplein, is closed for renovations until 2013, which means that the majority of the museum's complete collection will be "invisible" to visitors until then. During this period, however, key paintings and other stellar works from the magnificent 17th-century Dutch golden age collections can be viewed in the museum's Philips Wing, under the head *The Masterpieces*. Other elements of the collection likely will be on view at other venues in the city.

The Rijksmuseum contains the world's largest collection of paintings by the Dutch masters, including the most famous of all, a single work that all but defines the golden age. The painting is *The Shooting Company of Captain Frans Banning Cocq and Lieutenant Willem van Ruytenburch,* 1642, better known as *The Night Watch,* by Rembrandt. In the scene it so dramatically depicts, gaily uniformed city militiamen are checking their weapons and accouterments before moving out on patrol. Works by Jacob van Ruisdael, Maarten van Heemskerck, Frans Hals, Paulus Potter, Jan Steen, Jan Vermeer, Pieter de Hooch, Gerard ter Borch, and Gerard Dou are also displayed. The range is impressive—individual portraits, guild paintings, landscapes, seascapes, domestic scenes, medieval religious subjects, allegories, and the incredible (and nearly photographic) Dutch still lifes.

Jan Luijkenstraat 1 (at Museumplein). ✆ **020/647-7000.** www.rijksmuseum.nl. Admission 13€ adults, free for children 18 and under. Sat–Thurs 9am–6pm; Fri 9am–8:30pm. Closed Jan 1. Tram: 2 or 5 to Hobbemastraat.

Van Gogh Museum ★★★ Anyone who has responded to van Gogh's vibrant colors and vivid landscapes should be moved when walking through the rooms of this rather stark contemporary building. The museum displays, in chronological order, more than 200 van Gogh paintings. As you move through the rooms, the canvases reflect the artist's changing environment and much of his inner life, so that gradually van Gogh himself becomes almost a tangible presence standing at your elbow. By the

Passport to Amsterdam

One of the best discounts in town is the I amsterdam Card, available at VVV tourist offices for 38€ for 1 day, 48€ for 2 days, and 58€ for 3 days. It affords free or discounted admission to around 40 museums and attractions (including the Rijksmuseum, Rembrandthuis, and Oude Kerk), a free canal cruise, and discounts on selected restaurants and stores. A free 1-, 2-, or 3-day public transportation card is included.

time you reach the vaguely threatening painting of a flock of black crows rising from a waving cornfield, you can almost feel the artist's mounting inner pain.

In addition to the paintings, nearly 600 drawings by van Gogh are on display in the museum's new wing, a free-standing, multistory, half-oval structure designed by the Japanese architect Kisho Kurokawa. It's constructed in a bold combination of titanium and gray-brown stone, and is connected to the main building by a subterranean walkway. ***Note:*** Lines at the museum can be very long, especially in summer—try going on a weekday morning. Allow 2 to 4 hours to get around once you're inside.

Paulus Potterstraat 7 (at Museumplein). ✆ **020/570-5200.** www.vangoghmuseum.nl. Admission 14€ adults, free for children 17 and under. Sat–Thurs 10am–6pm; Fri 10am–10pm. Closed Jan 1. Tram: 2, 3, 5, 12, 16, or 24 to Museumplein.

MORE TOP MUSEUMS & GALLERIES

Amsterdams Historisch Museum ★★ Set in a huge 17th-century former orphanage, now housing exhibits covering nearly 700 years of the city's history, the fascinating Amsterdam Historical Museum gives you a better understanding of everything you see as you explore the city. Gallery by gallery, century by century, you learn how a fishing village became a major world trading center. The main focus is on the city's 17th-century golden age, a period when Amsterdam was the richest city in the world, and some of the most interesting exhibits are of the trades that made it rich. You can also view many famous paintings by Dutch masters. Next to the museum is the **Schuttersgalerij (Civic Guard Gallery),** a narrow chamber bedecked with 17th-century group portraits of militiamen. The hours are the same as for the museum, and admission is free.

Nieuwezijds Voorburgwal 357 and Kalverstraat 92 (next to the Begijnhof). ✆ **020/523-1822.** www.ahm.nl. Admission 10€ adults, 7.50€ seniors, 5€ children 6–18, free for children 5 and under. Mon–Fri 10am–5pm; Sat–Sun and holidays 11am–5pm. Closed Jan 1, Apr 30, and Dec 25. Tram: 1, 2, 4, 5, 9, 14, 16, 24, or 25 to Spui.

Joods Historisch Museum ★ Housed in the four restored 17th- and 18th-century synagogues of the Ashkenazi Synagogue complex, the Jewish Historical Museum tells the intertwining stories of Jewish identity, religion, culture, and history of the Jewish Dutch community. Inside are objects, photographs, artworks, and interactive displays. Jewish religious artifacts are a major focus. An exhibit covers the persecution of Jews in the Netherlands and throughout Europe under Hitler. The synagogues stand at the heart of a neighborhood that was the Jewish quarter for 300 years until the Nazi occupation during World War II emptied the city of its Jewish population. The oldest of the four, built in 1670, is the oldest public synagogue in western Europe; the newest dates from 1752.

Nieuwe Amstelstraat 1 (at Waterlooplein). ✆ **020/531-0380.** www.jhm.nl. Admission 9€ adults, 6€ seniors and students, 4.50€ children 13–17, free for children 12 and under. Daily 11am–5pm. Closed Jewish New Year (2 days) and Yom Kippur. Metro: Waterlooplein. Tram: 9 or 14 to Waterlooplein.

Museum Het Rembrandthuis ★★ When Rembrandt van Rijn moved into this three-story house in 1639, he was already a well-established wealthy artist. However, the cost of buying and furnishing the house led to his financial downfall in 1656. The museum houses a nearly complete collection of Rembrandt's etchings, and the artist's printing press. Of the 300 prints he made, 250 are here, with around half hanging on the walls at any one time. Rembrandt's prints show amazing detail, and you can see his use of shadow and light for dramatic effect. Wizened patriarchs, emaciated beggars, children at play, Rembrandt himself in numerous self-portraits, and Dutch landscapes are the subjects you'll long remember after a visit here. Temporary exhibits are mounted in an adjacent house that belonged to Rembrandt's wife, Saskia.

Jodenbreestraat 4 (at Waterlooplein). ✆ **020/520-0400.** www.rembrandthuis.nl. Admission 9€ adults, 6€ students, 2.50€ children 6-17, free for children 5 and under. Daily 10am-5pm. Closed Jan 1. Metro: Waterlooplein. Tram: 9 or 14 to Waterlooplein.

Museum Van Loon This magnificent patrician house from 1672 was owned by the van Loon family from 1884 to 1945. On its walls hang more than 80 family portraits, including those of Willem van Loon, one of the founders of the Dutch United East India Company; Nicolaas Ruychaver, who liberated Amsterdam from the Spanish in 1578; and another Willem van Loon, who became mayor in 1686. A marble staircase with an ornately curlicued brass balustrade leads up through the house, connecting restored period rooms that are filled with richly decorated paneling, stuccowork, mirrors, fireplaces, furnishings, porcelain, chandeliers, rugs, and more. In the garden are carefully tended hedges and a coach house modeled on a Greek temple.

Keizersgracht 672 (near Vijzelstraat). ✆ **020/624-5255.** www.museumvanloon.nl. Admission 7€ adults, 5€ children 6-18, free for children 5 and under. Wed-Mon 11am-5pm. Tram: 16, 24, or 25 to Keizersgracht.

Museum Willet-Holthuysen For a glimpse of what life was like for Amsterdam's wealthy merchants during the 18th and 19th centuries, pay a visit to this elegant canal-house museum. Each room is furnished much as it would have been 200 years ago. In addition, there's an extensive collection of ceramics, china, glass, and silver. Of particular interest are the large old kitchen and the formal garden in back.

Herengracht 605 (at the Amstel). ✆ **020/523-1822.** www.willetholthuysen.nl. Admission 7€ adults, 5.25 seniors, 3.50€ children 6-18, free for children 5 and under. Mon-Fri 10am-5pm; Sat-Sun and holidays 11am-5pm. Closed Jan 1, Apr 30, and Dec 25. Tram: 4, 9, or 14 to Rembrandtplein.

Ons' Lieve Heer op Solder ★ Although Amsterdam has been known as a tolerant city for many centuries, just after the Protestant Reformation, Roman Catholics fell into disfavor. Forced to worship in secret, they devised ingenious ways of gathering for Sunday services. In an otherwise ordinary-looking 17th-century canal-house in the middle of the Red-Light District is "Our Lord in the Attic," the most amazing of these clandestine churches. Built in the 1660s by a wealthy Catholic merchant, the three houses making up this museum were designed specifically to house a church. Today they're furnished much as they would have been in the 18th century. Nothing prepares you for the minicathedral you come upon when you climb the last flight of stairs into the attic. A large baroque altar, religious statuary, pews to seat 150, and an 18th-century organ complete this miniature church.

Oudezijds Voorburgwal 40 (near the Oude Kerk). ✆ **020/624-6604.** www.opsolder.nl. Admission 7€ adults, 5€ students, 1€ children 5-18, free for children 4 and under. Mon-Sat 10am-5pm; Sun and holidays 1-5pm. Closed Jan 1 and Apr 30. Tram: 1, 2, 4, 5, 9, 13, 16, 17, 24, 25, or 26 to Centraal Station.

Stedelijk Museum ★ ***Note:*** Amsterdam's modern-art Municipal Museum is closed for renovation and expansion until at least the end of 2010, and likely later. The service information provided below is the latest available, and the admission is likely to increase when the museum reopens. This is the place to see works by such Dutch painters as Karel Appel, Willem de Kooning, and Piet Mondrian, alongside works by the French artists Chagall, Cézanne, Picasso, Renoir, Monet, and Manet and by the Americans Calder, Oldenburg, Rosenquist, and Warhol. The Stedelijk centers its collection around the De Stijl, Cobra, post-Cobra, Nouveau Réalisme, pop art, color-field painting, zero, minimalist, and conceptual schools of modern art.

Paulus Potterstraat (at Museumplein). ✆ **020/573-2911.** www.stedelijk.nl. Admission 9€ adults; 4.50€ seniors, students, and children 7–16; free for children 6 and under. Daily 10am–6pm. Closed Jan 1. Tram: 2, 3, 5, 12, 16, or 24 to Museumplein.

Tropenmuseum ★ ☺ Founded in the 19th century as a monument to the nation's colonial empire, in particular the Dutch East Indies, today's Indonesia, the Tropical Museum now focuses on contemporary culture and problems in tropical areas. On the three floors surrounding the spacious main hall are numerous life-size tableaux depicting life in tropical countries. There are displays of beautiful handicrafts and antiquities from these regions, but the main focus is the life of the people today. There are hovels from the ghettos of Calcutta and Bombay, and mud-walled houses from the villages of rural India. Bamboo huts from Indonesia and crowded little stores no bigger than closets show you how people live in such areas as Southeast Asia, Latin America, and Africa. Sound effects play over hidden speakers.

Linnaeusstraat 2 (at Mauritskade). ✆ **020/568-8200.** www.tropenmuseum.nl. Admission 9€ adults, 7.50€ seniors, 5€ students and children 6–17, free for children 5 and under. Daily 10am–5pm (to 3pm Dec 5, 24, and 31). Closed Jan 1, Apr 30, May 5, and Dec 25. Tram: 3, 7, or 9 to Wijttenbachstraat/Linnaeusstraat.

HISTORIC BUILDINGS & MONUMENTS

Just steps from busy shopping streets, the **Begijnhof** ★, at Spui (www.begijnhofamsterdam.nl; tram: 1, 2, or 5), is the city's most tranquil spot. Hidden behind a plain facade is a 14th-century courtyard with a central garden ringed with restored almshouses formerly occupied by *begijns,* pious laywomen of the order of the Beguines. Most of the tiny 17th- and 18th-century buildings house elderly widows, and you should respect their privacy. In the southwest corner of the cloister, at no. 34, stands **Het Houten Huys,** one of Amsterdam's pair of surviving timber houses, built around 1425. The complex includes a clandestine Roman Catholic church and the former Beguine church from 1419, donated by the city's Protestant rulers to Scottish Presbyterian exiles in 1607, and now misnamed slightly as the Engelse Kerk (English Church). You may visit the Begijnhof daily from 9am to 5pm. Admission is free.

Koninklijk Paleis The 17th-century neoclassical Royal Palace, built on top of 13,659 wooden pilings to prevent it from sinking into the soft Amsterdam soil, was Amsterdam's town hall for 153 years. It was first used as a palace during Napoleon's rule in the early 19th century, when from 1806 to 1810 the French emperor's brother Louis Bonaparte was king of the Netherlands. You can visit its high-ceilinged Citizens' Hall, Burgomasters' Chambers, and Council Room, as well as the Vierschaar—a marble tribunal where in the 17th century death sentences were pronounced.

Gay Remembrance

The *Homomonument,* Westermarkt (tram: 13, 14, or 17), a sculpture group of three pink granite triangles near the Anne Frankhuis, is dedicated to the memory of gays and lesbians killed during World War II, or as a result of oppression and persecution because of their sexuality. People also visit to remember those who have died of AIDS.

Although this is the monarch's official palace, Queen Beatrix rarely uses it for more than occasional receptions or official ceremonies.

Dam. ✆ **020/620-4060.** www.paleisamsterdam.nl. Admission 7.50€ adults; 6.50€ seniors, students, and children 5-16; free for children 4 and under. Generally July-Aug Tues-Sun 11am-5pm; Sept-June Tues-Sun noon-5pm (open days and hours vary; check before going). Closed during periods of royal residence and state receptions. Tram: 1, 2, 4, 5, 9, 13, 14, 16, 17, 24, or 25 to the Dam.

HISTORIC CHURCHES

Nieuwe Kerk This church across from the Royal Palace is the "New Church" in name only. Construction on this late-Gothic structure began about 1400, but much of the interior, including the organ, dates from the 17th century. Since 1815, all Dutch kings and queens have been crowned here. Today the church is used primarily as a cultural center where special art exhibits are held. Regular performances on the church's huge organ are held in summer.

Dam (next to the Royal Palace). ✆ **020/638-6909.** www.nieuwekerk.nl. Admission varies with different events; free when there's no exhibit. Daily 10am-6pm (Thurs to 10pm during exhibits). Tram: 1, 2, 4, 5, 9, 13, 14, 16, 17, 24, or 25 to the Dam.

Oude Kerk ★ The Gothic Old Church from the 13th century is the city's oldest. It stands in the middle of the Red-Light District, surrounded by old almshouses turned into prostitutes' rooms. Inside (the church, that is) are monumental tombs, including that of Rembrandt's wife, Saskia van Uylenburg, and handsome stained-glass windows. The organ, built in 1724, is played regularly in summer; many connoisseurs believe it has the best tone of any organ in the world. You can climb the 70m (230-ft.) tower for an excellent view of old Amsterdam. Just outside the Oude Kerk is what's claimed to be the world's first monument to prostitution. The bronze sculpture *Belle,* unveiled in 2007, depicts a hooker standing in a doorway and bears an inscription calling for "respect for sexworkers [sic] all over the world."

Oudekerksplein 23 (at Oudezijds Voorburgwal). ✆ **020/625-8284.** www.oudekerk.nl. Church admission 5€ adults, 4€ seniors and students, free for children 11 and under. Mon-Sat 11am-5pm; Sun 1-5pm. Tower admission 6€. Sat-Sun 1-5pm; tours every 30 min. Metro: Nieuwmarkt.

Westerkerk ★ Built between 1620 and 1630, the Western Church is a masterpiece of Dutch Renaissance style. At the top of the 84m (276-ft.) tower, the highest, most beautiful tower in Amsterdam, is a giant replica of the imperial crown of Maximilian of Austria. Somewhere in this church (no one knows where) is Rembrandt's grave. During summer, regular organ concerts are played on a 300-year-old instrument. You can climb the tower or go by elevator to the top for a great view.

Westermarkt. ✆ **020/624-7766.** www.westerkerk.nl. Church free admission. Apr-June and Sept Mon-Fri 11am-3pm; July-Aug Mon-Sat 11am-3pm. Tower admission 6€. Apr-Oct Mon-Sat 10am-5:30pm; tours every 30 min. Tram: 13, 14, or 17 to Westermarkt.

OTHER SIGHTS & ATTRACTIONS

Artis ★★ ☺ If you're at a loss for what to do with the kids, Artis is a safe bet—1.2 million visitors a year agree. Established in 1838, the oldest zoo in the Netherlands houses 6,000 animals from 1,400 species. Of course, you'll find the usual tigers, lions, giraffes, wolves, leopards, elephants, camels, monkeys, penguins, and peacocks no self-respecting zoo can do without. Yet Artis has much more, for no extra charge, like the excellent Planetarium (closed Mon morning), and a Geological and Zoological Museum. The refurbished Aquarium, built in 1882, is superbly presented, particularly

CHECKING OUT THE red-light DISTRICT

You might want to study the quaint gabled architecture along the narrow canals of De Wallen (the Walls), the oldest part of the city. And, oh yes, you might also notice certain ladies watching the world go by through their red-fringed windows.

A warren of streets east of the Dam, around Oudezijds Achterburgwal and Oudezijds Voorburgwal, is the Rosse Buurt (Red-Light District), one of the most famous features of Amsterdam sightseeing (Metro: Nieuwmarkt). It's extraordinary to see women of all nationalities dressed in exotic underwear and perched in windows waiting for customers. With iPod buds in their ears, they knit, brush their hair, or just slink enticingly in their seats.

The Red-Light District has become a major attraction, not only for customers of storefront sex but also for sightseers. If you do look around, you need to exercise some caution. Watch out for pickpockets. In a neighborhood where anything seems permissible, the one no-no is taking pictures. Violate this rule and your camera could be taken from you and broken.

In 2007, as part of a continuing effort to clean up the "unsavory" side of Amsterdam, the mayor forced the closure of a third of the red-light windows and bought up properties to be rented as fashion boutiques and other upscale small businesses.

the sections on the Amazon River, coral reefs, and Amsterdam's own canals with their fish populations and burden of wrecked cars, rusted bikes, and other urban detritus. In the children's farm kids can stroke and help tend to the needs of resident Dutch species. You can rest and have a snack or lunch at **Artis Restaurant.**

Plantage Kerklaan 38–40 (at Plantage Middenlaan). ✆ **020/523-3400.** www.artis.nl. Admission 18.50€ adults, 17€ seniors, 15€ children 3–9, free for children 2 and under. Apr–Oct daily 9am–6pm (Sat June–Aug to sunset); Nov–Mar daily 9am–5pm. Tram: 9 or 14 to Plantage Kerklaan.

Heineken Experience The experience unfolds inside the former Heineken brewing facilities, which date from 1867 to 1988. You "meet" Dr. Elion, the 19th-century chemist who isolated the renowned Heineken "A" yeast, which gives the beer its taste. In one amusing attraction, you stand on a moving floor, facing a large video screen, and get to see and feel what it's like to be a Heineken beer bottle—one of a half-million every hour—careening on a conveyor belt through a modern Heineken bottling plant. Best of all, in another touchy-feely presentation, you "sit" aboard an old brewery dray-wagon, "pulled" by a pair of big Shire horses on the video screen in front of you, that shakes, rattles, and rolls on a minitour of Amsterdam. The admission is steep, though, even if you do get two "free" glasses of Heineken beer.

Stadhouderskade 78 (at Ferdinand Bolstraat). ✆ **020/523-9222.** www.heinekenexperience.com. Admission 15€; children 17 and under must be accompanied by an adult. Daily 11am–7pm. Closed Jan 1 and Dec 25. Tram: 16, 24, or 25 to Stadhouderskade.

Hortus Botanicus ★ Established in 1682, Amsterdam's Botanical Garden is a medley of color and scent, containing 250,000 flowers and 115,000 plants and trees from 8,000 different varieties. It owes its origins to the treasure-trove of tropical plants the Dutch found in their colonies—Indonesia, Suriname, and the Antilles—and its popularity to the Dutch love affair with flowers. Among highlights are the **Semicircle,** which reconstructs part of the original design from 1682; the **Mexico-California Desert House; Palm House,** with one of the world's oldest palm trees; and the **Tri-Climate House,** which displays tropical, subtropical, and desert plants.

Plantage Middenlaan 2A (close to Artis Zoo). ✆ **020/625-9021.** www.dehortus.nl. Admission 7.50€ adults, 3.50€ seniors and children 5–14, free for children 4 and under. Feb–June and Sept–Nov Mon–Fri 9am–5pm, Sat–Sun 10am–5pm; July–Aug daily 9am–7pm; Dec–Jan Mon–Fri 9am–4pm, Sat–Sun 10am–4pm. Closed Jan 1 and Dec 25. Tram: 9 or 14 to Plantage Middenlaan.

THE JORDAAN ★★

Few traditional sights clutter the old Jordaan district that lies just west of the Canal Belt's northern reaches—though 800 of its buildings are protected monuments. But the area does provide an authentic taste of Old Amsterdam. The neighborhood of tightly packed houses and narrow streets and canals was built in the 17th century for craftsmen, tradesmen, and artists. Its name may have come from the French *jardin* (garden), from Protestant French Huguenot refugees who settled here in the late 17th century. Indeed, many streets and canals are named for flowers, trees, and plants. Some of today's streets used to be canals until they were filled in during the 19th century. The neighborhood's modest nature persists even though renewal and gentrification have brought in an influx of offbeat boutiques, quirky stores, cutting-edge art galleries, and trendy restaurants.

THE WATERFRONT ★

Amsterdam's waterfront along the narrow ship channel known as Het IJ hosts the city's biggest redevelopment project, touted as "a new life on the water." In the **Oosterdok (Eastern Harbor),** Java-Eiland, KNSM-Eiland, and other artificial islands have been cleared of most of their warehouses and other harbor installations. Modern housing and infrastructure take their place. A visit here is a good way to see how Amsterdam sees its future, away from its golden age heart.

A fast-tram service (line 26) connects Centraal Station with the Oosterdok. Among its stops are ones for the Muziekgebouw aan 't IJ and Bimhuis concert halls, the Passenger Terminal Amsterdam cruise-liner dock, and the Eastern Islands' new residential, shopping, and entertainment zones. The service goes out as far as the new IJburg suburb, constructed on an artificial island in the IJsselmeer's southern reaches.

In recent years, some of the redevelopment focus has switched to the **Westerdok (Western Harbor),** west of Centraal Station.

PARKS

When the sun shines in Amsterdam, people head for the parks. The most popular and conveniently located of Amsterdam's 30 parks is the 49-hectare (121-acre) **Vondelpark ★★** (tram: 1, 2, 3, 5, 7, 10, or 12), home to skateboarding, Frisbee flipping, in-line skating, model-boat sailing, soccer, softball, basketball, open-air concerts and theater, smooching in the undergrowth, parties, picnics, crafts stalls, topless sunbathing—you name it. Its lakes, ponds, and streams are surrounded by meadows, trees, and colorful flowers. Vondelpark lies generally southwest of Leidseplein and has entrances all around; the most popular is adjacent to Leidseplein, on Stadhouderskade. Beware the tasty-looking "gâteau" sold here, or you might find yourself floating above the trees: Drug-laced "space cake" is an acquired taste. This park, open daily from 8am to sunset, is extremely popular in summer with young people from all over the world; admission is free.

To enjoy scenery and fresh air, head out to the **Amsterdamse Bos** (bus: 170 or 172 from outside Centraal Station to the main entrance on Amstelveenseweg), in the Amstelveen southern suburb. Nature on the city's doorstep, this large park was laid out during the Depression years as a public works project. By now the trees, birds, insects, and small animals are firmly established. At the entrance on Amstelveenseweg, stop by the **Bezoekerscentrum,** Bosbaanweg 5 (**© 020/545-6100;** www.amsterdamsebos.nl), the park's visitor center, where you can trace the park's history, learn about its wildlife, and pick up a plan of the park. The center is open daily (except Dec 25–26) from noon to 5pm, and admission is free. Across the way is a bicycle rental shop (**© 020/644-5473;** www.amsterdamsebosfietsverhuur.nl) where bikes are available April to September, Tuesday to Saturday, for from 10€ a day. Then, follow the path to a long stretch of water called the **Bosbaan,** a 2km (1¼-mile) competition-rowing course. Beyond the course's western end is a big pond, the **Grote Vijver,** where you can rent boats, and the **Openluchttheater,** which often has open-air theater performances on summer evenings. The Amsterdamse Bos is open 24 hours; admission is free.

ORGANIZED TOURS

Although you could see most of Amsterdam's important sights in one long walking tour, it's best to break the city into shorter walks. Luckily, the **VVV Amsterdam** tourist office has done that. For 2€, you can buy a brochure outlining one of four walking tours: *Voyage of Discovery Through Amsterdam, A Walk Through Jewish Amsterdam, A Walk Through the Jordaan,* and *A Walk Through Maritime Amsterdam.*

A **canal-boat cruise** ★ is the best way to view the old houses and warehouses. This is a city built on the shipping trade, so it's only fitting you should see it from the water, just as the golden age merchants saw their city. There are several canal-boat jetties, all of which have signs stating the time of the next tour. The greatest concentration of canal-boat operators is along Damrak and Rokin from Centraal Station; another cluster is on Singelgracht, near Leidseplein. Most tours last 1 hour and are around 9€ for adults, 5€ for children ages 4 to 12, and free for children 3 and under (prices vary a bit from company to company). Because the tours are all basically the same, simply pick the one that's most convenient for you. Some cruises include snacks and drinks, with floating candlelit dinners extra.

You can take a self-guided, self-powered tour on a **water bike.** These small pedal boats (also know as *pedalos*) for two to four are available from three docks of **Canal Bike** (**© 020/626-5574;** www.canal.nl) at Leidseplein near the Rijksmuseum (tram: 1, 2, 5, 7, or 10), at Westerkerk (tram: 13, 14, or 17), and on Keizersgracht near Leidsestraat (tram: 1, 2, or 5). Canal bikes can be rented daily from 10am to 6pm in spring and autumn (to 9:30pm in summer). The hourly rate begins at 8€ a head for one or two people and 7€ a head for three or four. There's a 50€ refundable deposit. You can pick one up at one dock and drop it off at another.

A 2½-hour **bus tour** of the city is around 20€. Children 4 to 13 are usually charged half price, and children 3 and under ride free. Tour companies include the **Best of Holland,** Damrak 34 (**© 020/420-4000**); **Keytours Holland,** Paulus Potterstraat 8 (**© 020/305-5333**); and **Lindbergh Tour & Travel,** Damrak 26 (**© 020/622-2766**).

Ferry Tale

Free ferries across the IJ waterway connect the center city with Amsterdam-Noord (North). The short crossings for foot passengers and bikes on two of these ferries—the *Buiksloterwegveer* and the *IJpleinveer*—make ideal minicruises for the cash-strapped and provide a good view of the harbor. Ferries depart from the Waterplein-West dock behind Centraal Station on De Ruyterkade every 10 to 15 minutes round-the-clock to Buiksloterweg, and from around 6:30am to midnight to IJplein.

The Shopping Scene

Best buys in Amsterdam include special items produced by the Dutch to perfection, or produced to perfection in the past and that now retail as antiques—delftware, pewter, crystal, and old-fashioned clocks—or commodities in which they have significantly cornered a market, such as diamonds. If cost is an important consideration, remember the Dutch also produce inexpensive specialties such as cheese, flower bulbs, and chocolate.

For jewelry, trendy clothing, and athletic gear, try the department stores and specialized stores around the Dam. On the long, pedestrianized Nieuwendijk-Kalverstraat shopping street and on Leidsestraat, you find inexpensive clothing stores and souvenir stores. For designer boutiques and upscale fashion and accessories, shop on Pieter Cornelisz Hooftstraat and Van Baerlestraat. Pricey antiques and art dealers congregate on Nieuwe Spiegelstraat. For fashion boutiques and funky little specialty stores, or a good browse through a flea market or secondhand store, roam the streets of the Jordaan. The Red-Light District specializes in stores selling erotic clothing, sex aids and accessories, and pornographic books and magazines.

STORES WORTH A VISIT

The city's top department store, with the best selection of goods and a great cafe, is **De Bijenkorf,** Dam 1 (✆ **0900/0919;** tram: 4, 9, 14, 16, 24, or 25). For a cooler take, visit **Metz&Co** ★★, Leidsestraat 34–36 (✆ **020/520-7020;** tram: 1, 2, or 5), on the corner with Keizersgracht. You can find almost everything there is to buy in Amsterdam at **Magna Plaza** ★, Nieuwezijds Voorburgwal 182 (✆ **020/626-9199;** tram: 1, 2, 5, 13, 14, or 17), a splendid three-story mall in the old main post office building, behind the Dam.

For brand-name hand-painted pottery, head to opulent **Jorrit Heinen** ★★, Muntplein 12, at the medieval Munttoren (✆ **020/623-2271;** tram: 4, 9, 14, 16, 24, or 25), and Prinsengracht 440, off Leidsestraat (✆ **020/627-8299;** tram: 1, 2, or 5). Also recommendable is cluttered **Galleria d'Arte Rinascimento,** Prinsengracht 170 (✆ **020/622-7509;** tram: 13, 14, or 17).

Diamond showrooms offering free individual and small-group tours of their diamond-cutting and -polishing facilities include **Amsterdam Diamond Center,** Rokin 1–5 (✆ **020/624-5787;** tram: 4, 9, 14, 16, 24, or 25), just off the Dam; **Coster Diamonds,** Paulus Potterstraat 2–8 (✆ **020/305-5555;** tram: 2 or 5), across from the Rijksmuseum; and **Gassan Diamonds,** Nieuwe Uilenburgerstraat 173–175 (✆ **020/622-5333;** Metro: Waterlooplein), behind Waterlooplein.

Tax Saver

Watch for the TAX-FREE SHOPPING sign in some store windows. These stores provide refunds of **value-added tax (BTW)** to non-E.U. residents. This refund amounts to 13.75% of the total cost of purchases of more than 50€ per day in participating stores. When you're leaving by air, present the refund check to Customs, along with your purchases and receipts; they will stamp it and you can get an immediate refund from the ABN AMRO bank at Schiphol Airport.

A fine antiquarian since 1878, **Mathieu Hart,** Rokin 122 (✆ **020/623-1658;** tram: 4, 9, 14, 16, 24, or 25), at Spui, stocks color etchings of Dutch cities alongside rare old prints, 18th-century Delftware, and grandfather clocks. Jewelry and antique silver establishment **Premsela & Hamburger ★**, Rokin 98 (✆ **020/627-5454;** tram: 4, 9, 14, 16, 24, or 25), at Spui, purveyors to the Dutch royal court, opened in 1823.

For English-language books and magazines, the choice is large. Try the centrally located **American Book Center,** Spui 12 (✆ **020/625-5537;** tram: 1, 2, or 5), or the nearby branch of British chain **Waterstone's,** Kalverstraat 152 (✆ **020/638-3821;** tram: 1, 2, 4, 5, 14, 16, 24, or 25).

MARKETS

Buying flowers at the **Bloemenmarkt (Flower Market) ★★**, on a row of barges permanently moored along Singel between Muntplein and Leidsestraat (tram: 1, 2, 4, 5, 9, 14, 16, 24, or 25), is an Amsterdam ritual. The market is open Monday to Saturday 9am to 5:30pm, and Sunday from 11am to 5:30pm.

You can still find a few antiques and near-antiques at the **Waterlooplein flea market** (tram: 9 or 14), on the square around the Muziektheater, but most of what's for sale these days is used and cheap clothing. It's open Monday to Saturday from 10am to 5pm. The open-air **Albert Cuyp market,** Albert Cuypstraat (tram: 4, 16, 24, or 25), open Monday to Saturday 9am to 5pm, has more cheap clothing, plus fresh fish and flowers, Asian vegetables, textiles, electronics, cosmetics, and more. There's also a **flea market** on Noordermarkt in the Jordaan (tram: 1, 2, 5, 13, or 17) on Monday morning 8am until midday, and a market for **organic food** on Saturday from 10am to 4pm.

Spread through several old warehouses along the Jordaan canals, **Kunst & Antiek-centrum de Looier,** Elandsgracht 109 (✆ **020/624-9038;** tram: 7, 10, or 17), is a big art and antiques market. Individual dealers rent booths and corners to show their best wares in antique jewelry, prints, and engravings.

Amsterdam After Dark

Nightlife in the city centers on Leidseplein and Rembrandtplein, and you'll find dozens of bars, nightclubs, cafes, dance clubs, and movie theaters around these two squares. To reserve and purchase tickets for almost every venue in the city, stop by or contact the **Amsterdams Uitburo-AUB Ticketshop,** Leidseplein 26, on the corner of Marnixstraat (✆ **0900/0191;** www.aub.nl; tram: 1, 2, 5, 7, or 10), open Monday to Saturday from 10am to 7:30pm, and Sunday from noon to 7:30pm. Their free monthly magazine in Dutch, ***De Uitkrant,*** has a thorough listing of events (which should not be too hard for English speakers to follow) and is available from this office and from VVV offices, performance venues, and clubs.

THE PERFORMING ARTS

CLASSICAL MUSIC The renowned **Royal Concertgebouw Orchestra** is based at the **Concertgebouw ★★**, Concertgebouwplein 2–6 (✆ **020/671-8345;** www.concertgebouw.nl; tram: 2, 3, 5, 12, 16, or 24), which has some of the best acoustics of any hall in the world. Performances take place almost every night in the building's two halls. There are free half-hour rehearsal concerts on Wednesdays at 12:30pm. The box office is open daily from 10am to 7pm (to 8:15pm for same-day tickets), with tickets from 15€ to 75€.

The **Netherlands Philharmonic Orchestra** (the "NedPho") and the **Netherlands Chamber Orchestra** both perform at the impressive **Beurs van Berlage,** Damrak 213 (✆ **020/521-7500;** www.berlage.com; tram: 4, 9, 14, 16, 24, or 25), which was once the Amsterdam stock exchange and now houses two concert halls for symphonies and chamber music. The box office is open Tuesday to Friday from 12:30 to 6pm and Saturday from noon to 5pm; tickets are 8€ to 35€.

CONTEMPORARY MUSIC A spectacular piece of modern architecture, the **Muziekgebouw aan 't IJ ★**, Piet Heinkade 1 (✆ **020/788-2000;** www.muziekgebouw.nl; tram: 25 or 26 to Muziekgebouw), on the IJ waterfront just east of Centraal Station, is the city's home for avant-garde and experimental music. You can look for concerts of modern, old, jazz, electronic, and non-Western music, along with small-scale musical theater, opera, and dance. The box office is open Monday to Saturday from noon to 7pm; tickets are 10€ to 55€.

OPERA & DANCE The **Netherlands Opera** and the **National Ballet** both perform regularly at the modern **Muziektheater ★★★**, Waterlooplein (✆ **020/625-5455;** www.muziektheater.nl; tram: 9 or 14); the innovative **Netherlands Dance Theater** company from The Hague is a frequent visitor. The box office is open Monday to Saturday from 10am to 8pm, and Sunday and holidays from 11:30am to 6pm, with tickets from 22€ to 110€. Music and dance performances are occasionally held at the **Stadsschouwburg** (see "Theater," below).

THEATER The **Koninklijk Theater Carré,** Amstel 115–125 (✆ **0900/252-5255;** www.theatercarre.nl; Metro: Weesperplein), a huge old domed former circus-theater on the Amstel River near the Magere Brug (Skinny Bridge), occasionally presents touring shows from New York's Broadway or London's West End. The box office is open Monday to Saturday from 10am to 7pm and Sunday from 1 to 7pm, and tickets go for 12€ to 125€. At the Dutch Renaissance **Stadsschouwburg,** Leidseplein 26 (✆ **020/624-2311;** www.stadsschouwburgamsterdam.nl; tram: 1, 2, 5, 7, or 10), from 1894, performances include plays in Dutch and, occasionally, English, plus music and dance performances by international companies. The box office is open daily 10am to 6pm, with tickets at 15€ to 105€.

Compared by *Time* magazine to Chicago's famous Second City troupe, **Boom Chicago Theater ★**, Leidsepleintheater, Leidseplein 12 (✆ **020/423-0101;** www.boomchicago.nl; tram: 1, 2, 5, 7, or 10), puts on great improvisational comedy, and Dutch audiences have no problem with the English-language sketches. You can have dinner and a drink while enjoying the show at a candlelit table. It's open daily in summer, closed Sunday in winter. Dinner/theater packages vary from show to show, but begin from around 40€ per person.

THE LIVE-MUSIC SCENE

Amsterdam's biggest and most popular clubs book up-and-coming acts and always charge admission. Plenty of smaller clubs in cafes showcase local bands and charge no admission. A shiny metal box with windows that's an extension of the Muziekgebouw aan 't IJ (see above), on the waterfront east of Centraal Station, is home to the **Bimhuis ★**, Piet Heinkade 3 (✆ **020/788-2188;** www.bimhuis.nl; tram: 26 to Muziekgebouw), the city's premier jazz, blues, and improvisational club. Top local and international musicians are regularly featured.

A regular crowd frequents the small, intimate **Jazz Café Alto,** Korte Leidsedwarsstraat 115 (✆ **020/626-3249**), for nightly performances by both regular and guest combos. Check out also the funky **Bourbon Street,** Leidsekruisstraat 6–8 (✆ **020/623-3440**), for late-night blues and rock. Both bars are near Leidseplein, reached by tram no. 1, 2, 5, 7, or 10.

THE BAR SCENE

There are countless bars—or cafes, as they're called here—in the city, many around **Leidseplein** and **Rembrandtplein.** They usually open at noon and stay open all day. The most popular drink is draft Pilsener served in small glasses with two fingers of head on top. Also popular is *jenever* (Dutch gin) available in *jonge* (young) and *oude* (old) varieties—oude is stronger, more refined in taste, and higher in alcoholic content.

BROWN CAFES Particularly old and traditional bars often earn the appellation of ***bruine kroeg*** (brown cafe), a name said to have been derived as much from the preponderance of wood furnishings as from the browning of the walls from years of dense tobacco smoke. Some have been around since Rembrandt's time. At these warm and friendly cafes you can sit and sip a glass of beer or a mixed drink; at some you can even get a cheap meal.

Papeneiland, Prinsengracht 2, at the corner of Brouwersgracht (✆ **020/624-1989;** tram: 1, 2, 5, 13, or 17), is Amsterdam's oldest cafe: Since 1600 or thereabouts, folks have been dropping by for shots of jenever and glasses of beer. Originally a tasting house where people could try liqueurs distilled and aged on the premises, **De Drie Fleschjes,** Gravenstraat 18, between the Nieuwe Kerk and Nieuwendijk (✆ **020/624-8443;** tram: 1, 2, 4, 5, 9, 13, 14, 16, 17, 24, or 25), has been in business for more than 300 years. It's popular with businesspeople and journalists, who stop by to sample the wide variety of jenevers.

The dark walls, low ceilings, and old wooden furniture at **Hoppe,** Spui 18–20 (✆ **020/420-4420;** tram: 1, 2, or 5), one of Amsterdam's oldest and most popular brown cafes, have literally remained unchanged since the cafe opened in 1670. It has become a tourist attraction, but locals love it too, often stopping for a drink on their way home. There's usually standing room only.

Said to be where the builders of the Westerkerk were paid, **Café Chris,** Bloemstraat 42 (✆ **020/624-5942;** tram: 13, 14, or 17), opened in 1624 and has some curious old features, including a toilet that flushes from outside the bathroom door. In a medieval alley, wood-paneled **In de Wildeman,** Kolksteeg 3 (✆ **020/638-2348;** tram: 1, 2, 5, 13, or 17), serves more than 200 kinds of beer. The tile floor and rows of bottles and jars behind the counters are remnants from its early days as a distillery's retail store.

MODERN CAFES Amid subdued lighting, dark wood surfaces, and red tones, fancy **bubbles&wines ★**, Nes 37 (✆ **020/422-3318;** tram: 4, 9, 14, 16, 24, or 25), a few minutes' walk from the Dam, serves an extensive roster of champagne and wine labels, along with light snacks. Soft chairs, long banquettes, and chandeliers draw a hip, youthful crowd to **18twintig ★★**, Ferdinand Bolstraat 18–20 (✆ **020/470-0651;** tram: 16, 24, or 25), in the Pijp district, to sip mojitos and other cocktails, graze on plates of tempura, and dance to DJs on Friday and Saturday nights.

Other notable hangouts are **Café Dante,** Spuistraat 320 (✆ **020/638-8839;** tram: 1, 2, or 5), where a different modern-art exhibit is mounted every month; and **Café Schiller,** Rembrandtplein 26 (✆ **020/624-9846;** tram: 4, 9, or 14), which has a bright, glassed-in terrace on the square and a finely carved Art Deco interior; it's popular with artists and writers.

The concept of the Grand Cafe—combining drinks and food in elegant surroundings—has taken Amsterdam by storm. One of the best is **Café Luxembourg ★**, Spuistraat 24 (✆ **020/620-6264;** tram: 1, 2, or 5), a chic rendezvous that takes some of its menu dishes from top eateries around town. Whether you're in jeans or theater attire, you'll feel comfortable at **De Kroon,** Rembrandtplein 15 (✆ **020/625-2011;** tram: 4, 9, or 14), with fine views on the square through the big picture windows upstairs, amid a decor that's rigorously modern.

On summer evenings, trendies head to the terrace of **Café Vertigo,** Vondelpark 3 (✆ **020/612-3021;** tram: 2 or 5), in Vondelpark, for one of the liveliest scenes in town. The low, arched ceilings, subtle lighting, and unobtrusive music set a mood of casual sophistication.

DANCE CLUBS

Dozens of large and small clubs around **Leidseplein** and **Rembrandtplein** tend to rise and fall in popularity, so ask someone in a cafe what the current favorites are. Drinks can be expensive—a beer or Coke averages 5€, and a whiskey or cocktail 8€. Most dance clubs are open Thursday to Sunday 9 or 10pm to 2 or 3am.

Popular clubs include **Tonight,** at the Hotel Arena, Gravesandestraat 51 (✆ **020/850-2400;** tram: 7 or 10); **Escape,** Rembrandtplein 11 (✆ **020/622-1111;** tram: 4, 9, or 14); **Odeon,** Singel 460 (✆ **020/521-8555;** tram: 1, 2, or 5); **Paradiso,** Weteringschans 6–8 (✆ **020/626-4521;** tram: 1, 2, 5, 7, or 10); **Akhnaton,** Nieuwezijds Kolk 25 (✆ **020/624-3396;** tram: 1, 2, 5, 13, or 17); and **Melkweg ★**, Lijnbaansgracht 234A (✆ **020/531-8181;** tram: 1, 2, 5, 7, or 10). Cover and music varies.

THE GAY & LESBIAN SCENE

Amsterdam bills itself as the gay capital of Europe, proud of its open and generally tolerant attitude toward homosexuality. To find out more about the gay and lesbian scenes, stop by **COC,** Rozenstraat 14 (✆ **020/626-3087;** tram: 13, 14, or 17), 2 blocks off Westerkerk. You can also call the **Gay and Lesbian Switchboard** at ✆ **020/623-6565,** open daily from 10am to 10pm. ***Gay News,*** a monthly newspaper in English, is available free in gay establishments throughout Amsterdam.

Some of the more popular spots for men are **Arc,** Reguliersdwarsstraat 44 (✆ **020/638-5700;** tram: 1, 2, or 5), a sleek modern bar; **Cockring,** Warmoesstraat 96 (✆ **020/623-9604;** tram: 4, 9, 14, 16, 24, or 25), a heavy-duty dance club; **Argos,** Warmoesstraat 95 (✆ **020/622-6595;** tram: 4, 9, 14, 16, 24, or 25), Europe's oldest leather bar; and **Amstel FiftyFour,** Amstel 54 (✆ **020/623-4254;** tram: 4, 9, or 14), a late-night bar.

Vive la Vie, Amstelstraat 7 (✆ **020/624-0114;** tram: 4, 9, or 14), on the edge of Rembrandtplein, is the city's only lesbian bar; this convivial little corner spot on Rembrandtplein hosts periodic parties. **Saarein,** Elandsstraat 119 (✆ **020/623-4901;** tram: 7, 10, or 17), near Leidseplein, is a mixed-gender bar/cafe that has a large lesbian following.

"COFFEE SHOPS"

Amsterdam is a mecca for the marijuana smoker and seems likely to remain that way. Visitors often get confused about "smoking" coffee shops and how they differ from "nonsmoking" ones. Well, to begin with, "smoking" and "nonsmoking" don't refer to cigarettes—they refer to cannabis. "Smoking" coffee shops not only sell cannabis, most commonly in the form of hashish, but also provide somewhere patrons can sit and smoke it all day if they so choose. Generally, these smoking coffee shops are the only places in Amsterdam called "coffee shops"—regular cafes are called *cafes* or *eetcafes.*

Toker Talk

Don't buy on the street. You stand a fair chance of being ripped off, the quality is doubtful, and there may be unpleasant additives.

You are allowed to buy only 5 grams (1/5 oz.) of soft drugs at a time for personal use, but you're allowed to be in possession of 30 grams (1 oz.) for personal use.

Coffee shops are not allowed to sell alcohol, so they sell coffee, tea, and fruit juices. You won't be able to get any food, so don't expect to grab a quick bite. You're even allowed to smoke your own stuff in the coffee shop, as long as you buy a drink.

Some of the most notable smoking coffee shops are the **Rookies,** Korte Leidsedwarsstraat 145–147 (✆ **020/639-0978;** tram: 1, 2, 5, 7, or 10); **Sheeba,** Warmoesstraat 73 (✆ **020/624-0357**); and **Reefer,** Sint-Antoniesbreestraat 77 (✆ **020/623-3615;** Metro: Nieuwmarkt).

ENVIRONS OF AMSTERDAM

If Amsterdam is your only stop in the Netherlands, try to make at least one excursion into the countryside. Dikes, windmills, and some of Holland's quaintest villages await you just beyond the city limits.

Haarlem ★★

Just 18km (11 miles) west of Amsterdam, Haarlem is a graceful town of winding canals and medieval neighborhoods that also holds several fine museums. The best time to visit is Saturday, for the market on the Grote Markt, or in tulip season (Mar to mid-May), when the city explodes with flowers.

ESSENTIALS

GETTING THERE Haarlem is 15 minutes from Amsterdam by **train,** and two or three depart every hour from Centraal Station. A round-trip ticket is 12€ in first class, and 7€ in second class. The historic center is a 5- to 10-minute walk from

Haarlem's graceful 1908 Art Nouveau train station, which is decorated with painted tiles and has a fine station restaurant.

There are frequent **buses** from outside Amsterdam Centraal Station. By **car,** take N5 and then A5 west.

VISITOR INFORMATION **VVV Haarlem,** Verwulft 11, 2011 GJ Haarlem (✆ **0900/616-1600;** fax 023/534-0537; www.vvvzk.nl), at Grote Houlstraat. The office is open Monday to Friday from 9:30am to 5:30pm and Saturday from 10am to 5pm.

SEEING THE SIGHTS

Haarlem is where Frans Hals, Jacob van Ruysdael, and Pieter Saenredam were living and painting their famous portraits, landscapes, and church interiors while Rembrandt was living and working in Amsterdam.

Handel and Mozart made special visits just to play the magnificent organ of **Sint-Bavokerk (St. Bavo's Church),** also known as the **Grote Kerk ★**, Oude Groenmarkt 23 (✆ **023/553-2040;** www.bavo.nl). Look for the tombstone of painter Frans Hals (ca. 1580–1666) and for a cannonball that has been embedded in the church's wall ever since it came flying through a window during the 1572-to-1573 Spanish siege of Haarlem. And, of course, don't miss seeing the famous **Christian Müller Organ** (1738). It has 5,068 pipes and is nearly 30m (98 ft.) tall. The woodwork was done by Jan van Logteren. Mozart played the organ in 1766 when he was just 10 years old. St. Bavo's is open Monday to Saturday from 10am to 4pm. Admission is 2€ for adults, 1.25€ for children ages 12 to 16, and free for children 11 and under.

From St. Bavo's, it's a short walk to the **Frans Halsmuseum ★★**, Groot Heiligland 62 (✆ **023/511-5775;** www.franshalsmuseum.com), where the galleries are the halls and furnished chambers of a former pensioners' home, and famous paintings by the masters of the Haarlem school hang in settings that look like the 17th-century homes they were intended to adorn. The museum is open Tuesday to Saturday from 11am to 5pm, Sunday and holidays from noon to 5pm. Admission is 7.50€ for adults, 3.75€ for those ages 19 to 24, 2.50€ for children ages 13 to 18, and free for children 12 and under.

The oldest and perhaps the most unusual museum in the Netherlands, the **Teylers Museum,** Spaarne 16 (✆ **023/531-9010;** www.teylersmuseum.nl), contains a curious collection. There are drawings by Michelangelo, Raphael, and Rembrandt; fossils, minerals, and skeletons; instruments of physics; and an odd assortment of inventions, including a 19th-century radarscope. The museum is open Tuesday to Saturday from 10am to 5pm, and Sunday and holidays from noon to 5pm. Admission is 9€ for adults, 2€ for children ages 6 to 17, and free for children 5 and under.

An ideal way to tour the city is by **canal-boat cruise,** operated by **Post Verkade Cruises** (✆ **023/535-7723;** www.postverkadecruises.nl), from their Spaarne River dock at Gravenstenenbrug. Cruises run from April to October at 10:30am, noon, 1:30, 3, and 4:30pm (during some months the first and last tours are on request only), and are 9.50€ for adults, 4.50€ for children ages 3 to 10, and free for children 2 and under.

WHERE TO DINE

Jacobus Pieck ★ DUTCH/INTERNATIONAL This popular cafe-restaurant has a lovely shaded terrace in the garden for fine-weather days; inside, it's bustling and stylish. Outside or in, you get excellent food for reasonable prices and friendly, efficient service. Lunchtime features generous sandwiches and burgers, and salads that are particularly good. Main dinner courses range from pastas and Middle Eastern or Asian dishes to wholesome Dutch standards.

Warmoesstraat 18 (off Oude Groenmarkt). ✆ **023/532-6144.** www.jacobuspieck.nl. Main courses 16€–18€; *dagschotel* (daily special) 12€. AE, MC, V. Mon 11am–4pm; Tues–Sat 11am–4pm and 5:30–10pm.

Volendam & Marken

Volendam and Marken have long been combined on bus-tour itineraries from Amsterdam as a kind of "packaged Holland and costumes to go." Nonetheless, it's possible to have a delightful day in the bracing air of these two communities on the IJsselmeer lake, where a few residents (fewer with each passing year) may be seen going about their daily business in traditional dress.

There are separate, hourly **buses** to Volendam and Marken from outside Amsterdam's Centraal Station. The fare is around 7€ round-trip; the ride takes 30 minutes to Volendam and 40 minutes to Marken.

Geared to tourism, **Volendam,** 18km (11 miles) northeast of Amsterdam, has souvenir stores, boutiques, and restaurants. Its boat-filled harbor, tiny streets, and traditional houses have an undeniable charm. If you want a snapshot of yourself surrounded by fishermen wearing little caps and balloon-legged pants, Volendammers will gladly pose. They understand that the traditional costume is worth preserving, as is the economy of a small town that lost most of its fishing industry when the Zuiderzee enclosure dam cut it off from the North Sea. You can visit attractions like the fish auction, a diamond cutter, a clog maker, and a house with a room entirely wallpapered in cigar bands.

A causeway now connects the one-time island of **Marken ★**, 16km (10 miles) northeast of Amsterdam, with the mainland, but it remains as insular as ever. Quieter than Volendam, with a village of green-painted houses on stilts around a tiny harbor, it is also more rural. Clusters of farmhouses dot the *polders* (the reclaimed land from the sea that makes up two-thirds of the Netherlands), and a candy-striped lighthouse stands on the IJsselmeer shore.

Marken does not gush over tourists, but it will feed and water them, and let them wander around its pretty streets. Some villagers (fewer every year) wear traditional costume, as much to preserve the custom as to appease the tourists who arrive daily. The **Marker Museum,** Kerkbuurt 44–47 (✆ **0299/601-904;** www.markermuseum.nl), is a typical house open as a museum April to October, Monday to Saturday from 10am to 5pm (closed at 4pm in Oct) and Sunday from noon to 4pm. Admission is 2.50€ for adults, 1.25€ for children ages 5 to 12, and free for children 4 and under.

Delft ★

Yes, Delft, 54km (34 miles) southwest of Amsterdam, is the town of the famous blue-and-white porcelain. And, yes, you can visit the factory. But don't let delftware be your only reason to visit. Not only is this one of the prettiest small cities in the Netherlands, with linden trees bending over gracious canals, but Delft is also important as a cradle of the Dutch Republic and the traditional burial place of the royal family. Plus, it was the birthplace, and inspiration, of the 17th-century master of light and subtle emotion, painter Jan Vermeer.

ESSENTIALS

GETTING THERE There are several **trains** an hour from Amsterdam's Centraal Station to Delft Station, which is southwest of the center. The ride takes about 1 hour and is 37€ round-trip in first class, and 22€ in second. By **car,** take A4/E19 and then A13/E19 past Den Haag (The Hague) and watch for the Delft exit coming up.

VISITOR INFORMATION **Tourist Information Point Delft,** Hippolytusbuurt 4, 2611 HN Delft (✆ **0900/515-1555,** or 31-15/215-4051 from outside the Netherlands; www.delft.nl), is in the center of town. The office is open April to September, Sunday and Monday from 10am to 6pm, Tuesday to Friday from 9am to 6pm, and Saturday from 10am to 5pm; October to March, Sunday from 11am to 4pm, and Tuesday to Saturday from 10am to 4pm.

SEEING THE SIGHTS

Vermeer's house is long gone from Delft, as are his paintings. Instead, visit the **Oude Kerk ★**, Heilige Geestkerkhof (✆ **015/212-3015;** www.oudekerk-delft.nl), where he's buried. You might want to visit also the **Nieuwe Kerk ★★**, on Markt (✆ **015/212-3025;** www.nieuwekerk-delft.nl), where Prince William of Orange and other members of the House of Orange–Nassau are buried, and to climb its tower, which is 109m (358 ft.) high. Both churches are open mid-March to October, Monday to Saturday from 9am to 6pm; November to mid-March, Monday to Friday from 11am to 4pm, and Saturday from 10am to 5pm. Combined admission is 3.50€ for adults, 3€ for seniors, 1.50€ for children ages 6 to 12, and free for children 5 and under; separate admission to the Nieuwe Kerk tower is 3€ for adults, 2.50€ for seniors, 1.50€ for children ages 6 to 12, and free for children 5 and under.

The **Stedelijk Museum Het Prinsenhof ★**, Sint-Agathaplein 1 (✆ **015/260-2358;** www.prinsenhof-delft.nl), on the nearby Oude Delft canal, is where William I of Orange (William the Silent) lived and had his headquarters in the years during which he helped found the Dutch Republic. It's where he was assassinated in 1584, and you can still see the musket-ball holes in the stairwell. Today the Prinsenhof is a museum of paintings, tapestries, silverware, and pottery. It's open Tuesday to Sunday from 11am to 5pm. Admission is 7.50€ for adults, 4€ for students and children ages 12 to 16, and free for children 11 and under.

In the same neighborhood you can see a fine collection of old Delft tiles displayed in the wood-paneled setting of a 19th-century mansion museum, **Lambert van Meerten,** Oude Delft 199 (✆ **015/260-2358;** www.lambertvanmeerten-delft.nl). It's open Tuesday to Sunday from 11am to 5pm. Admission is 3.50€ for adults, 1.50€ for students and children ages 12 to 16, and free for children 11 and under.

To watch a demonstration of the traditional art of making and hand-painting delftware, visit the factory and showroom of **Koninklijke Porceleyne Fles (Royal Delft) ★**, Rotterdamseweg 196 (✆ **015/251-2030;** www.royaldelft.com; bus: 63, 121, or 129 to Jaffalaan), founded in 1653. It's open April to October, daily from 9am to 5pm; November to March, Monday to Saturday from 9am to 5pm. Admission is 6.50€, and free for children 12 and under.

WHERE TO DINE

Spijshuis de Dis ★ DUTCH Fine Dutch cooking that's traditional at heart but given a modern accent is served up at this atmospheric old restaurant. Among the top dishes are *bakke pot*—a stew made from beef, chicken, and rabbit; mussels prepared with garlic, ginger, and curry; and asparagus in season (May–June). The steaks and the pork and lamb filet dishes are great. Don't miss the homemade mushroom soup.

Beestenmarkt 36 (off Markt). ✆ **015/213-1782.** www.spijshuisdedis.com. Main courses 16€–25€. AE, DC, MC, V. Thurs–Tues 5–10:30pm.

Stadsherberg De Mol TRADITIONAL DUTCH Food is served here in the medieval manner—in wooden bowls from which you eat with your hands. Set menus include a starter (such as pâté in puff pastry), soup, a variety of meats (such as chicken, lamb, ham, and rabbit), salad, and baked potato. Prices are moderate and quantities copious, and there is fun, too, with live music and dancing.

Molslaan 104 (off Beestenmarkt). ✆ **015/212-1343.** www.stadsherbergdemol.nl. Main courses 12€–18€. MC, V. Tues–Sun 6–11pm.

NORWAY

by Darwin Porter & Danforth Prince

Norway is a land of tradition, as exemplified by its rustic stave churches—look for these mysterious, dark structures with steep gables surmounted by dragons' heads and pointed steeples—and folk dances stepped to the airs of a fiddler. But Norway is also modern, a technologically advanced nation that's rich in petroleum and hydroelectric energy. One of the world's last great natural frontiers, Norway is a land of astonishing beauty; its steep and jagged fjords, salmon-rich rivers, glaciers, mountains, and meadows invite exploration. In winter, the shimmering northern lights beckon; in summer, the midnight sun shines late and warm.

Long a poor cousin of Sweden, Norway today is one of the richest countries in the world, with prices to match. "When I was young, Swedes had whiter teeth, clearer skin, Abba, and Bjorn Borg. We had lots of fish," said Thomas Eriksen, a professor at the University of Oslo. "Today Swedes have been cut down to size, and are often in Norway working at menial jobs."

OSLO

After World War II, Oslo grew to 450 sq. km (174 sq. miles), making it one of the 10 largest capitals in the world in sheer area, if not in urban buildup. The city is one of the most heavily forested on earth, and fewer than half a million Norwegians live and work here.

One of the oldest Scandinavian capital cities, founded in the mid–11th century, Oslo has never been a mainstream tourist site. But the city is culturally rich with many diversions—enough to fill at least 3 or 4 busy days. It's also the center for many easy excursions along the Oslofjord or to towns and villages in its environs, both north and south.

In recent years Oslo has grown from what even the Scandinavians viewed as a Nordic backwater to one of Europe's happening cities. Restaurants, nightclubs, cafes, shopping complexes, and other venues keep on opening. A kind of Nordic *joie de vivre* permeates the city; the only drawback is that all this fun is going to cost you—Oslo ranks as one of Europe's most expensive cities.

Essentials

GETTING THERE

BY PLANE Flights from abroad arrive at **Oslo International Airport** (✆ **47-06-400;** www.osl.no), lying 50km (31 miles) east of the center of Oslo, about a 45-minute ride. All domestic and international flights coming into Oslo arrive through this much-upgraded airport, including aircraft belonging to SAS, British Airways, Continental, and Icelandair.

There's frequent bus service, departing every 20 minutes throughout the day, into the center of Oslo. It's maintained by both SAS (whose buses deliver passengers to the Central Railway station and to most of the SAS hotels within Oslo) and the **Norwegian Bus Express** (✆ **81-54-44-44;** www.nor-way.no), whose buses head for the main railway station. Both companies charge 135NOK to 230NOK per person, each way. There's also 20-minute high-speed railway service between Gardermoen and Oslo's main railway station, priced at 170NOK to 250NOK per person each way. If you want to take a taxi, be prepared for sticker shock: the trip will cost around 600NOK to 1,060NOK for up to four passengers plus their luggage. If you need a "maxi-taxi," a minivan that's suitable for between 5 and 15 passengers, plus their luggage, you'll pay from 800NOK.

BY TRAIN The first high-speed train between Oslo and Stockholm has reduced travel time to 4 hours and 50 minutes between these two Scandinavian capitals. There are two to three trains daily in each direction. Trains from the Continent, Sweden, and Denmark arrive at **Oslo Sentralstasjon (Central Station),** Jernbanetorget 1 (✆ **81-50-08-88;** www.nsb.no for train information). It's at the beginning of Karl Johans Gate, in the center of the city. The station is open daily 6am to 11:15pm. From the Central Station, trains leave for Bergen, Stavanger, Trondheim, Bodø, and all other rail links in Norway. You can also take trams to all major parts of Oslo.

BY CAR If you're driving from mainland Europe, the fastest way to reach Oslo is to take the car-ferry from Frederikshavn, Denmark (see below). You can also take a car-ferry from Copenhagen (see below) or drive from Copenhagen by crossing over to Helsingborg, Sweden, from Helsingør, Denmark. Once at Helsingborg, take E-6 north all the way to Stockholm. If you're driving from Stockholm to Oslo, follow E-18 west all the way (trip time: 7 hr.). Once you near the outskirts of Oslo from any direction, follow the signs into the SENTRUM, or city center.

BY FERRY Ferries from Europe arrive at the Oslo port, a 15-minute walk (or a short taxi ride) from the city center. From Denmark, Scandinavia's link with the Continent, ferries depart for Oslo from Copenhagen, Hirtshals, and Frederikshavn. From Strømstad, Sweden, in the summer, the daily crossing to Sandefjord, Norway, takes 2½ hours; from Sandefjord, it's an easy drive or train ride north to Oslo.

VISITOR INFORMATION Assistance and information for visitors are available at the **Tourist Information Office,** Fridtjof Nansens Plass 5, entrance on Roald Amundsen Street, Oslo (✆ **81-53-05-55;** bus: 27). Free maps, brochures, sightseeing tickets, and guide services are available. The office is open October to March, Monday to Friday 9am to 4pm; April to May and September, Monday to Saturday 9am to 5pm; June to August, daily 9am to 7pm.

There's also an Oslo-only **information office** at the Oslo Sentralstasjon (Central Station), Jernbanetorget 1, at the beginning of Karl Johans Gate (✆ **81-53-05-55**), open Monday to Friday 7am to 8pm, Saturday and Sunday 8am to 6pm. From May to September, weekend hours are extended to 8pm.

For information online, try the Norwegian Tourist Board (**www.visitnorway.com**) or Virtual Oslo (**www.visitoslo.com**).

CITY LAYOUT Oslo is at the mouth of the 95km (59-mile) Oslofjord. Opening onto the harbor is **Rådhusplassen (City Hall Square),** dominated by the modern City Hall, a major attraction. Guided bus tours leave from this square, and the launches that cruise the fjords depart from the pier facing the municipal building. (You can catch ferries to the Bygdøy Peninsula from the quay at Rådhusplassen.)

Oslo

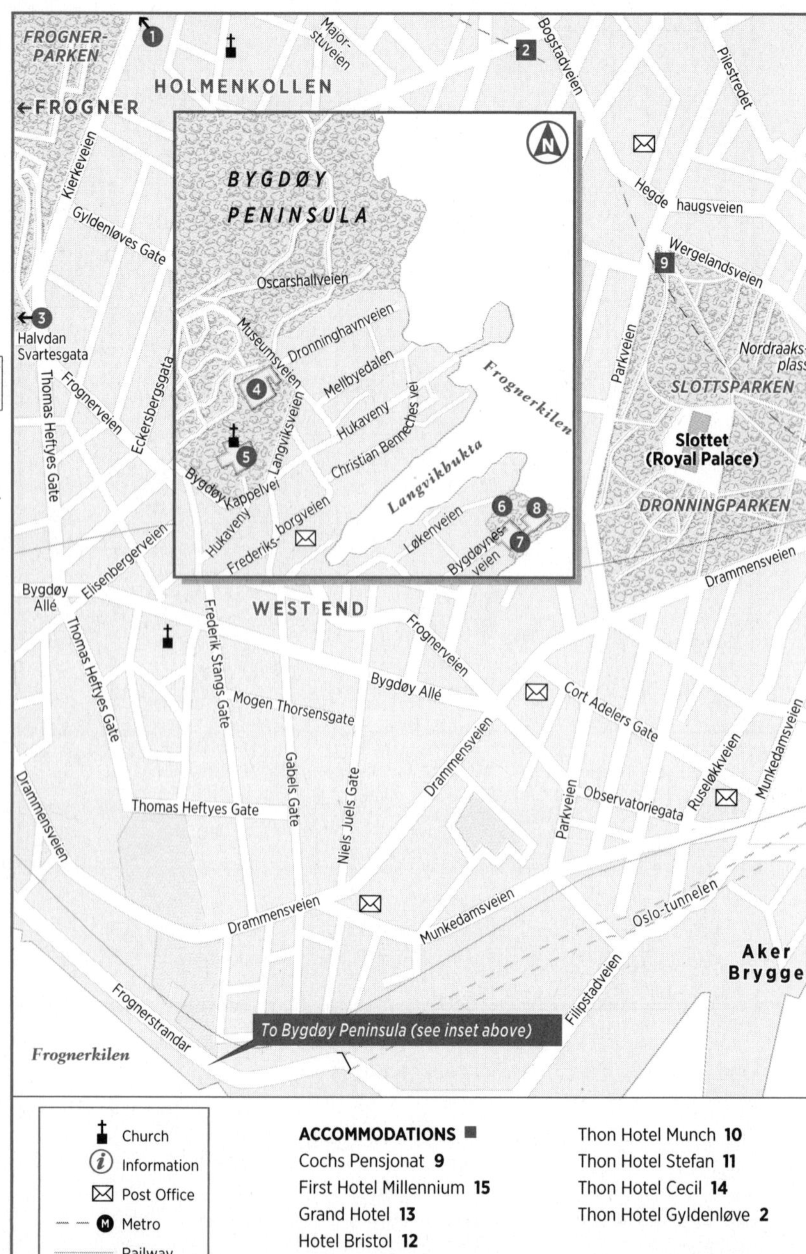
FROGNER-PARKEN
HOLMENKOLLEN
FROGNER
BYGDØY PENINSULA
Oscarshallveien
Museumsveien
Dronninghavnveien
Mellbyedalen
Hukaveny
Langviksveien
Christian Benneches vei
Bygdøy Kappelvei
Hukaveny
Frederiks- borgveien
Langvikbukta
Frognerkilen
Løkenveien
Bygdøynes-veien
Majorstuveien
Bogstadveien
Pilestredet
Hegdehaugsveien
Wergelandsveien
Parkveien
Nordraaks-plass
SLOTTSPARKEN
Slottet (Royal Palace)
DRONNINGPARKEN
Drammensveien
Kierkeveien
Gyldenløves Gate
Halvdan Svartesgata
Frognerveien
Eckersbergsgata
Thomas Heftyes Gate
Elisenbergerveien
Bygdøy Allé
WEST END
Frederik Stangs Gate
Frognerveien
Bygdøy Allé
Mogen Thorsensgate
Cort Adelers Gate
Drammensveien
Munkedamsveien
Ruseløkkveien
Observatoriegata
Parkveien
Gabels Gate
Niels Juels Gate
Thomas Heftyes Gate
Drammensveien
Munkedamsveien
Oslo-tunnelen
Aker Brygge
Filipstadveien
Frognerstrandar
To Bygdøy Peninsula (see inset above)
Frognerkilen
Church
Information
Post Office
Metro
Railway
ACCOMMODATIONS
Cochs Pensjonat 9
First Hotel Millennium 15
Grand Hotel 13
Hotel Bristol 12
Thon Hotel Munch 10
Thon Hotel Stefan 11
Thon Hotel Cecil 14
Thon Hotel Gyldenløve 2

0
1/4 mi
0
0.25 km
N
VÅR FRELSERS GRAVLUND
GRÜNERLØKKA
EASTERN OSLO
CENTRAL OSLO
GRØNLAND
GAMLEBYEN (OLD TOWN)
Sofies-gate
Stensberggata
Fredensborgveien
Gate
Thor Olsens
Osterhaus gate
Hausmannsgate
Møllergata
Torggata
Bernt Ankers Gate
Storgata
Norbygata
Pilestredet
Nordahl Brunsgate
St. Olavs plass
St Olavs Gate
Arne-Garborgs-plass
Henrik Ibsens Gate
Youngs gate
Lakkegata
Brugata
Grønland
Den Norske Opera
Ploensgate
Universitetsgata
Frederiks Gate
Kristian IV's Gate
Akersgata
Oslo Universitet
Grensen
Biskop Gunnerus Gate
Schwei-gaards Brua
Nationaltheatret
Karl Johans Gate
Stor-torvet
Stortingsgaten
Sentralstasjon
Fridtjof-Nansens-plass
Wessels plass
Slottsgate
Kongensgate
Kirkegata
Jernbane-torget
Nylandsveien
Haakon VII's Gate
Rosenkrantzgate
Havnegata
Prinsensgate
Dronningensgata
Tollbugata
Øvre
Bispe Brua
Oslo Konserthus
Rådhus-plassen (City Hall Square)
Rådhusgata
Vestbane-stasjonen
Dokkveien
Bank plassen
Myntgata
Bjørvika
Pier 4
Pier 3
Pier 2
Pier 1
Pipervika
Akershusstranda
Oslo-tunnelen
Skippergata
10
11
12
13
14
15
16
17
ATTRACTIONS
Akershus Castle 16
Frammuseet (Polar Ship Fram) 8
Kon-Tiki Museum 6
Munch Museum 17
Norsk Folkemuseum 4
Norsk Sjøfartsmuseum 7
Tryvannstårnet (Lookout Tower) 1
Vigelandsparken 3
Vikingskiphuset 5
OSLO
Area of detail
Bygdøy Peninsula

Out on a promontory to the east is the **Akershus Castle.** At **Bygdøy,** the much larger peninsula that juts out to the west, are four of Oslo's major attractions: the Viking ships, the Polar Ship *Fram* Museum, the *Kon-Tiki* Museum, and the Folk Museum.

Karl Johans Gate, Oslo's main street (especially for shopping and strolling), is north of City Hall Square. This boulevard begins at Oslo **Sentralstasjon (Central Station)** and stretches all the way to the 19th-century **Royal Palace** at the western end. A short walk from the palace is the famed **Student's Grove** (the University of Oslo is nearby), where everybody gathers on summer days to socialize. Dominating this area is the **National Theater.** South of the theater and near the harbor is **Stortingsgaten,** another shopping street.

The main city square is **Stortorvet,** although it's no longer the center of city life, which has now shifted to Karl Johans Gate.

At a subway stop near the National Theater, you can catch an electric train to **Tryvannstårnet,** the loftiest lookout in Scandinavia, and to the **Holmenkollen Ski Jump.**

GETTING AROUND The **Oslo Pass** (www.visitoslo.com) can help you become acquainted with the city at a fraction of the usual price. It allows free travel on public transportation, free admission to museums and other top sights, discounts on sightseeing buses and boats, a rebate on your car rental, and special treats in restaurants. You can buy the card at hotels, fine stores, and tourist offices; from travel agents; and in the branches of Sparebanken Oslo Akershus. Adults pay 230NOK for a 1-day card, 340NOK for 2 days, and 430NOK for 3 days. Children's cards cost 100NOK, 120NOK, and 160NOK.

BY BUS, TRAM & SUBWAY **Jernbanetorget,** in front of the Central Station, is the major bus and tram terminal in Oslo. Most buses and trams passing through the heart of town stop at Wessels Plass, next to the Stortinget (Parliament), or at Stortorvet, the main marketplace. Many also stop at the National Theater or University Square on Karl Johans Gate.

The **T-banen** (subway) has five main lines running to the east of Oslo and four lines running to the west. The most heavily traveled routes by tourists are the eastern lines. The western lines take in Holmenkollen and residential and recreational areas west and north of the city.

For schedule and fare information, call **Trafikanten** (✆ **81-50-01-76;** www.urbanrail.net/eu/osl/oslo.htm). Drivers sell single-trip tickets for 26NOK to 40NOK; children travel for half fare. Automated machines cancel tickets. An eight-coupon Maxi card costs 190NOK, half price for children. Maxi cards can be used for unlimited transfers for 1 hour from the time the ticket was stamped.

BY CAR Driving is not a practical way to get around Oslo because parking is limited. The efficient network of public transportation makes a private car unnecessary. You can reach even the most isolated areas by public transportation.

BY TAXI If you need a taxi, call ✆ **23-23-23-23,** 24 hours a day. Reserve at least an hour in advance. The approximate fare from Oslo International Airport to the center of Oslo is 600NOK to 1,060NOK. All taxis have meters, and Norwegian cabdrivers are generally honest. When a cab is available, a roof light goes on. Taxis can be hailed on the street, provided they're more than 90m (300 ft.) from a taxi stand. The worst times to hail a taxi are Monday through Friday from 8:30 to 10am and 3 to 5pm, and Saturday from 8:30 to 10am.

BY FERRY Beginning in mid-April, ferries depart for Bygdøy from Pier 3 in front of the Oslo Rådhuset. For schedules, call **Båtservice** (✆ **23-35-68-90**). The ferry or bus to Bygdøy is a good choice, because parking there is limited. Other ferries leave for various parts of the Oslofjord. Inquire at the **Tourist Information Office,** Roald Amundsen Street (✆ **81-53-05-55**).

BY BICYCLE City bikes (Oslo Bysykkel) are available from a large number of bike stations around Oslo. You need an electronic card costing 70NOK to use the bikes, and these cards can be purchased at the Tourist Information office at Oslo Central Station or behind City Hall. Call ✆ **22-02-34-43;** www.oslobysykkel.no for more information; bikes are rented April to November daily 6am to midnight.

[Fast FACTS] OSLO

Business Hours Most **banks** are open Monday to Friday 8:30am to 3:30pm (Thurs to 5pm). Most **businesses** are open Monday to Friday 9am to 4pm. **Stores** are generally open Monday to Friday 9am to 5pm (many stay open later on Thurs to 6 or 7pm) and Saturday 9am to 1 or 2pm.

Currency You'll pay your way in Norway with Norwegian kroner or crowns, which are universally abbreviated NOK. There are 100 øre in 1 krone. The exchange rate at presstime was US$1 = 6NOK (or 1NOK = approximately 16.6¢). Note that Norway is not a member of the European Union.

Currency Exchange **Banks** will exchange most foreign currencies or cash traveler's checks. Bring your passport for identification. If banks are closed, try automated machines at the Oslo Sentralstasjon to exchange currency. You can also exchange currency at the **Bureau de Change** at the main Oslo post office, Dronningensgaden 15 (✆ **23-14-90-00;** www.volvat.no).

Doctors & Dentists Some larger hotels have arrangements with doctors in case a guest becomes ill. You can also try the 24-hour **Oslo Kommunale Legevakten,** Storgata 40 (✆ **22-93-22-93**). A privately funded alternative is **Oslo Akutten,** Nedre Vollgate 8 (✆ **22-00-81-60**). For more routine medical assistance, you can contact the biggest hospital in Oslo, **Ullaval,** Kirkeveien 166 (✆ **22-11-80-80**). To consult a private doctor (nearly all of whom speak English), check the telephone directory or ask at your hotel for a recommendation.

For a dental emergency, contact the **Volvat Medisinke,** Borgen veien 2A, Majorstuen (✆ **22-95-75-00;** T-banen: Groønen), open daily Monday to Friday 8am to 10pm, Saturday and Sunday 10am to 10pm. For private dentists, look under *Tannleger* ("tooth doctors") in volume 1B of the telephone directory; there's rarely a language barrier.

Drugstores A 24-hour pharmacy is **Jernbanetorvets Apotek,** Jernbanetorget 4B (✆ **23-35-81-00;** T-banen: Jernbanetorget).

Embassies & Consulates The embassy of the **United States** is at Henrik Ibsens gate 48, N-0244 Oslo (✆ **21-30-85-40;** http://norway.usembassy.gov; T-banen: Sentrum). The embassy may move to new and better quarters, with greater security, during the life of this edition. Check before heading here. The embassy of the **United Kingdom** is at Thomas Heftyes Gate 8, N-0264 Oslo 2 (✆ **23-13-27-00;** http://ukinnorway.fco.gov.uk/en; T-banen: Nationaltheatret). The embassy of **Canada** is at Wergelandseien 7, N-0244 Oslo (✆ **22-99-53-00;**

www.canadainternational.gc.ca/Norway-norvege; T-banen: Nationaltheatret). Visitors from Ireland and New Zealand should contact the British embassy. Australians should contact the Canadian embassy. Call for hours.

Emergencies Dial the Oslo **police** at ✆ **112;** report a **fire** at ✆ **110;** call an **ambulance** at ✆ **113.**

Internet Access You can tap in free at the **Deichmanske Bibliotek (Oslo Public Library),** arne Garborgs Plass (✆ **23-43-29-00;** www.kulturetaten.oslo.kommune.no; T-Banen: Jernbang-Torget). Hours are May to September, Monday to Friday 10am to 7pm and Saturday 10am to 4pm; October to April, Monday to Friday 10am to 6pm and Saturday 11am to 2pm.

Post Office The **Oslo General Post Office** is at Dronningensgatan 15 (✆ **23-14-90-00** for information). Enter at the corner of Prinsensgate. It's open Monday to Friday 9am to 5pm, Saturday 9am to 2pm; closed Sunday and public holidays. You can arrange for mail to be sent to the main post office c/o General Delivery. The address is Poste Restante, P.O. Box 1181-Sentrum, Dronningensgatan 15, N-0101 Oslo, Norway. You must show your passport to collect mail.

Safety Of the four Scandinavian capitals, Oslo is widely considered the safest. However, don't be lulled into a false sense of security. Oslovians no longer leave their doors unlocked. Be careful, and don't carry your wallet visibly exposed or sling your purse over your shoulder.

Taxes Oslo has no special city taxes. Norway imposes a 19.35% value-added tax (VAT) on most goods and services, which is figured into your final bill. If you buy goods in any store bearing the tax-free sign, you're entitled to a cash refund of up to 18.5% on purchases costing over 310NOK. Ask the shop assistant for a tax-free shopping check, and show your passport to indicate that you're not a resident of Scandinavia. You may not use the articles purchased before leaving Norway, and they must be taken out of the country within 3 months of purchase. Complete the information requested on the back of the check you're given at the store; at your point of departure, report to an area marked by the tax-free sign, not at Customs. Your refund check will be exchanged there in *kroner* for the amount due you. Refunds are available at airports, ferry and cruise-ship terminals, borders, and train stations.

Telephone The country code for Norway is **47,** and the city code for Oslo is **22** (in some rare cases, **23**). For operator assistance in English, dial ✆ **115.**

Tipping Hotels add a 10% to 15% service charge to your bill, which is sufficient unless someone has performed a special service. Most bellhops get at least 10NOK per suitcase. Nearly all restaurants add a service charge of up to 15% to your bill. Barbers and hairdressers usually aren't tipped, but toilet attendants and hatcheck people expect at least 3NOK. Don't tip theater ushers. Taxi drivers don't expect tips unless they handle heavy luggage.

Where to Stay

VERY EXPENSIVE

Grand Hotel ★★★ Norway's leading hostelry is on the wide boulevard that leads to the Royal Palace. The stone-walled hotel with its mansard gables and copper tower has been an integral part of Oslo life since 1874. Famous guests have included Arctic explorer Roald Amundsen, Edvard Munch, Gen. Dwight Eisenhower, Charlie Chaplin, Henry Ford, and Henrik Ibsen. Frankly, although it's still the grande dame of Norway hotels, we feel the Grand's stuffiness has cost it its cutting edge. The guest rooms are in the 19th-century core and in one of the modern additions. Newer rooms contain plush facilities and electronic extras, but many guests prefer the old-fashioned accommodations in the older section, which have also been modernized. A special feature of the hotel is a series of 13 designer-created bedrooms especially for women, a whole floor set aside for them and dedicated to the country's most talented women.

Karl Johans Gate 31, N-0159 Oslo. ✆ **800/223-5652** in the U.S., or 23-21-20-00. Fax 23-21-21-00. www.grand.no. 290 units. 1,645NOK–2,910NOK double; from 3,635NOK suite. Rates include buffet breakfast. AE, DC, MC, V. Parking 330NOK. T-banen: Stortinget. **Amenities:** 3 restaurants; 3 bars; nightclub; health club; indoor unheated pool; room service; sauna. *In room:* A/C, TV, hair dryer, minibar, Wi-Fi (free).

EXPENSIVE

Hotel Bristol ★★★ Loaded with character, and the source of many entertaining anecdotes, this 1920s-era hotel competes aggressively and gracefully with other historic hotel "dragons" of Oslo, including the Grand (see above). The Bristol consistently emerges as the most liberal, the hippest, and the most accessible. Set in the commercial core of Oslo, a block north of Karl Johans Gate, it's warm, inviting, rich with tradition, and comfortable. It's becoming the preferred hotel of the media, arts, and showbiz communities, with a sense of playfulness that's unmatched by either of its more formal rivals. Guest rooms are comfortable, tasteful, and dignified. Lavish public areas evoke the Moorish-inspired Art Deco style in which they were built.

Kristian IV's Gate 7, N-0164 Oslo 1. ✆ **22-82-60-00.** Fax 22-82-60-01. www.thonhotels.no/Bristol. 251 units. 1,395NOK–2,895NOK double; 5,000NOK–6,000NOK suite. AE, DC, MC, V. Parking 300NOK. T-banen: Nationaltheater. Tram: 10, 11, 17, or 18. **Amenities:** Restaurant; 2 bars; nightclub; babysitting; small-scale exercise room and health club; room service. *In room:* TV, hair dryer, minibar, Wi-Fi (free).

MODERATE

First Hotel Millennium ★ 🎁 One of Oslo's large-scale hotels is housed in what was originally a 12-floor 1930s Art Deco office building. This is one of the "personality" hotels of Oslo, known for its atmosphere and character, and noted for a stylish kind of functional minimalism. It's within walking distance of virtually everything in central Oslo. Rooms are among the most spacious in town, with many Art Deco touches. The top floor offers a dozen rooms with their own large balconies. **Primo Ciaou-Ciaou** is one of Oslo's best restaurants.

Tollbugaten 25, N-0157 Oslo. ✆ **21-02-28-00.** Fax 21-02-28-30. www.firsthotels.com. 112 units. 1,295NOK–1,695NOK double; 1,595NOK–1,850NOK suite. AE, DC, MC, V. Nearby parking 230NOK. Metro: Stortingeg. Tram: 12, 15, or 19. **Amenities:** Restaurant; bar; babysitting; room service. *In room:* TV, hair dryer, minibar, Wi-Fi (free).

Thon Hotel Cecil ★ 🏷 This contemporary hotel enjoys a central location, with many restaurants, sights, and shops within a short walk of the main entrance of the hotel. Dating from 1989, it was constructed on the site of a previous hotel destroyed by fire. Most of its rooms are built to open onto a central atrium. Only four rooms on each of the eight floors overlook the street (the sometimes rowdy—at least, at night—Rosenkrantzgate). The well-maintained rooms are cozy and contain neatly kept bathrooms with tub/showers. Expect relatively simple styling with none of the trappings of more expensive nearby competitors—there's no health club, sauna, or full-fledged room service.

Stortingsgate 8 (entrance on Rosenkrantzgate), N-0130 Oslo. ✆ **23-31-48-00.** Fax 23-31-48-50. www.thonhotels.no. 111 units. 1,095NOK–1,545NOK double; 1,645NOK–1,845NOK family room. AE, DC, MC, V. Parking 225NOK. T-banen: Stortinget. **Amenities:** Breakfast room. *In room:* A/C, TV, hair dryer, minibar, Wi-Fi (50NOK per day).

Thon Hotel Gyldenløve "The Golden Lion" (its English name) was once a dowdy *hospits* (an inexpensive hotel, but better than a youth hostel). Lying only a 10-minute walk from the Royal Palace, it stands on a tree-lined street in the West End, a highly desirable neighborhood. In its latest reincarnation as part of the ever-growing Thon chain, it has become one of the city's most desirable addresses. Mid-size bedrooms are in a modernistic Nordic design, combining a light, airy feeling with Scandinavian pastels.

Bogstadveien 20, N-0355 Oslo. ✆ **23-33-23-00.** Fax 23-33-23-03. www.thonhotels.com. 164 units. 1,095NOK–2,2,95NOK double. Rates include breakfast. AE, DC, MC, V. Parking 150NOK. Tram: 11, 13, or 19. **Amenities:** Breakfast room; room service; smoke-free rooms. *In room:* TV, minibar, Wi-Fi (45NOK per day).

Thon Hotel Munch This hotel is somewhat like a bed-and-breakfast, and it's just 5 minutes north of Karl Johans Gate. Built in 1983, the solid, nine-floor hotel offers comfortably furnished, well-maintained guest rooms, decorated with reproductions of Edvard Munch's paintings. Although not overly large, the rooms are cozy and comfortable. If you don't plan to spend a lot of time in your room, this is an adequate choice, charging a fair price for what it offers.

Munchsgaten 5, N-0130 Oslo. ✆ **23-21-96-00.** Fax 23-21-96-01. www.thonhotels.no/munch. 180 units. 845NOK–1,045NOK double; 1,045NOK–1,245NOK triple. Rates include breakfast. AE, DC, MC, V. Parking 190NOK. T-banen: Stortinget. Tram: 8, 10, 11, or 17. Bus: 37. **Amenities:** Lounge. *In room:* TV, hair dryer, minibar, Wi-Fi (50NOK per day).

Thon Hotel Stefan In an excellent location in the center of the city, this hotel is comfortable and unpretentious. Built in 1952, it has been modernized and much improved. Rooms are traditional in style and well furnished and maintained. From May to August, weekend rates are granted only when reservations are made less than 48 hours before arrival. The restaurant is known for its Norwegian lunch buffets.

Rosenkrantzgate 1, N-0159 Oslo 1. ✆ **23-31-55-00.** Fax 23-31-55-55. www.thonhotels.no/stefan. 150 units. 845NOK–1,245NOK double. Rates include breakfast. AE, DC, MC, V. Parking 220NOK. Tram: 10, 11, 17, or 18. **Amenities:** Restaurant; bar; babysitting; room service. *In room:* TV, hair dryer, minibar, Wi-Fi (45NOK per day).

INEXPENSIVE

Cochs Pensjonat Built more than a century ago, with an ornate facade that curves around a bend in a boulevard that flanks the northern edge of the Royal Palace, this clean, well-conceived, inexpensive hotel represents excellent value. Major renovations added a postmodern gloss to many of the guest rooms. The result is a comfortable but simple lodging whose newer rooms have high ceilings and birch furniture, and a spartan but pleasant appearance. Expect very few, if any, amenities and services at this hotel, but because of the in-room kitchens and a nearby restaurant that offers hotel guests a 25% discount on meals, no one really seems to mind.

Parkveien 25, N-0350 Oslo. ✆ **23-33-24-00.** Fax 23-33-24-10. www.cochspensjonat.no. 88 units, 78 with bathroom and kitchenette. Rooms with bathroom and kitchenette 780NOK–840NOK double; 990NOK–1,050NOK triple; 1,220NOK quad. Rooms without kitchenette and without private bathroom 680NOK double; 870NOK triple; 1,060NOK quad. AE, DC, MC, V. No parking. Tram: 11 or 18. *In room:* TV, kitchenette (in some), no phone.

Where to Dine

Norwegians are as fond of smørbrød (smorgasbord) as the Danes (you'll see it offered everywhere for lunch). Basically, this is an open-faced sandwich that can be stacked with virtually anything, including ham with a peach slice resting on top or perhaps a mound of dill-flavored shrimp.

VERY EXPENSIVE

Restaurant Julius Fritzner ★★★ NORWEGIAN/CONTINENTAL This is one of the best and most impressive restaurants in Oslo. It's one floor above street level in Norway's most prestigious hotel. The venue is appropriately conservative, with a battalion of impeccably trained waiters who maintain their humor and personal touch despite the sophisticated setting. The dishes, all made with the finest Scandinavian ingredients, change with the season and the chef's inspiration. Examples include pan-fried turbot, lobster and caviar sauce, crispy fried cod with sautéed vegetables, poached halibut with vermouth sauce, filet of veal with crispy fried sweetbreads, and roast saddle of lamb with rosemary.

In the Grand Hotel, Karl Johans Gate 31. ✆ **23-21-20-00.** Reservations recommended. Main courses 345NOK–375NOK; 3-course fixed-price menu 595NOK; 5-course fixed-price menu 825NOK; 9-course fixed-price menu 1,095NOK. AE, DC, MC, V. Mon–Sat 5–10:30pm. Closed July–Aug 5. T-banen: Stortinget.

EXPENSIVE

Det Gamle Rådhus (Old Town Hall) ★ NORWEGIAN One of the oldest restaurants in Oslo, Det Gamle Rådhus is in Oslo's former Town Hall (1641). You'll dine within a network of baronial- or manorial-inspired rooms with dark wooden panels and Flemish, 16th-century-style wooden chairs. In the spacious dining room, a full array of open-faced sandwiches is served on weekdays only. A la carte dinner selections can be made from a varied menu that includes fresh fish, game, and Norwegian specialties. If you want to sample a dish that Ibsen might have enjoyed, check out the house specialty, lutefisk—but hold your nose. More to your liking might be smoked salmon (cured right on the premises), a parfait of chicken livers, freshwater pikeperch from nearby streams sautéed in a lime sauce, or Norwegian lamb coated with herbs and baked with a glaze.

Nedre Slottsgate 1. ✆ **22-42-01-07.** www.gamleraadhus.no. Reservations recommended. Lunch main courses 133NOK–225NOK; dinner main courses 248NOK–398NOK. AE, DC, MC, V. Mon–Fri 11am–3:30pm; Mon–Sat 5–10:30pm. Closed last 3 weeks in July. Bus: 27, 29, 30, 41, or 61.

MODERATE

Grand Café ★★ NORWEGIAN This traditional cafe is an Oslo legend. A large mural on one wall depicts Ibsen (a fan of whale steaks), Edvard Munch, and many other patrons. A postcard sold at the reception desk identifies the mural's subjects. You can order everything from a napoleon with coffee to a full meal with reindeer steaks. Sandwiches are available for 90NOK and up. The atmosphere and tradition here are sometimes more compelling than the cuisine. The menu, nonetheless, relies on Norwegian country traditions. (How many places still serve elk stew?) If you like solid, honest flavors, this is the place to visit.

In the Grand Hotel, Karl Johans Gate 31. ✆ **24-14-53-00.** Reservations recommended. Main courses 225NOK–355NOK; 3-course menu 420NOK; 4-course menu 580NOK. AE, DC, MC, V. Daily 11am–4pm and 6–11pm. T-banen: Stortinget.

Stortorvets Gjæstgiveri ★ NORWEGIAN Many legends surround this nostalgic dining room of yesterday. This is the oldest restaurant in Oslo. The present restaurant is composed of a trio of wood-framed buildings, the most antique of which dates from the 1700s. This restaurant changes throughout the course of an Oslovian day. Expect a cafe near the entrance, an old-fashioned and usually packed restaurant in back, and outside dining in good weather. Menu items are traditional, well prepared, and flavorful, and include steamed mussels in white wine and garlic, poached salmon in a butter sauce, or oven-baked halibut with a mussel velouté sauce. A specialty is roast reindeer in a red-wine sauce spiked with wild berries.

Grensen 1. ✆ **23-35-63-60.** Reservations recommended. Small platters and snacks 73NOK–130NOK; main courses 210NOK–335NOK. AE, DC, MC, V. Mon–Sat 11am–10:30pm. Tram: 12 or 17.

INEXPENSIVE

Brødre MEXICAN "Three Brothers" is named after the glove manufacturers who once occupied this building. The Mexican food here may have lost a bit of its punch traveling so far to the icy north, but this is a longtime favorite with locals. The fare is zesty and well prepared, and you'll get hearty portions at reasonable prices. Here you can pig out on all those fajitas you've been hungering for, including one version made with prawns, or dig into double-cheese enchiladas and burritos. The entire street level houses the bustling bar, while a piano bar resides upstairs. Lighter meals such as snacks and sandwiches are available on the outside dining terrace in the summer.

Øvre Slottsgate 14. ✆ **23-10-06-70.** Reservations recommended. Main courses 200NOK–250NOK. AE, DC, MC, V. Mon–Sat 2–10:30pm. Bus: 27, 29, or 30.

Engebret Café NORWEGIAN A favorite since 1857, this restaurant is directly north of Akershus Castle in two landmark buildings. It has good food in an old-fashioned atmosphere—it was formerly a bohemian literati haunt. During lunch, a tempting selection of open-faced sandwiches is available. The evening menu is more elaborate; you might begin with a terrine of game with blackberry port-wine sauce, or Engebret's fish soup. Main dishes include red wild boar with whortleberry sauce, Norwegian reindeer, salmon Christiania, or Engebret's big fish pot. For dessert, try the cloudberry parfait.

Bankplassen 1. ✆ **22-82-25-25.** www.engebret-cafe.no. Reservations recommended. Main courses 225NOK–305NOK. AE, MC, V. Mon–Fri 11:30am–11pm; Sat 5–11pm. Bus: 27, 29, or 30.

Mamma Rosa ☺ ITALIAN Established by two Tuscan brothers, this trattoria enjoys a popularity that's a good indication of Norwegians' changing tastes. The second-floor dining room is decorated in "reproduction rococo." You can order 15 kinds of pizza, fried scampi and squid, rigatoni, pasta Mamma Rosa (three kinds of pasta with three sauces), grilled steaks, and gelato. Frankly, some dishes are lacking in flavor, but Mamma Rosa is nonetheless a marvelous change of taste and texture.

Øvre Slottsgate 12. ✆ **22-42-01-30.** Main courses 75NOK–288NOK; pizzas from 100NOK. DC, MC, V. Sun–Fri 2–10pm; Sat 2–11pm. T-banen: Stortinget.

Seeing the Sights

IN THE BYGDØY PENINSULA

Frammuseet (Polar Ship Fram) A long walk from the Viking ships, the Frammuseet contains the sturdy polar exploration ship *Fram,* which Fridtjof Nansen sailed across the Arctic (1893–96). The vessel was later used by Norwegian explorer Roald Amundsen, the first man to reach the South Pole (1911).

Bygdøynesveien 36. ✆ **23-28-29-50.** http://fram.museum.no. Admission 60NOK adults, 25NOK children, 120NOK family ticket (2 adults, up to 3 children). Mar–Apr and Oct daily 10am–4pm; May and Sept daily 10am–5pm; June–Aug daily 9am–6pm; Nov–Dec daily 11am–3pm; Jan–Feb Mon–Fri 10am–3pm, Sat–Sun 10am–4pm. Ferry: From Pier 3 facing the Rådhuset (summer only). Bus: 30 from the National Theater.

Kon-Tiki Museum *Kon-Tiki* is the world-famed balsa-log raft in which the young Norwegian scientist Thor Heyerdahl and his five comrades sailed for 7,000km (4,350 miles) in 1947—all the way from Callao, Peru, to Raroia, Polynesia. Besides the raft, there are exhibits from Heyerdahl's subsequent visit to Easter Island, including an Easter Island family cave, with a collection of sacred lava figurines.

Bygdøynesveien 36. ✆ **23-08-67-67.** www.kon-tiki.no. Admission 60NOK adults, 40NOK students and seniors, 25NOK children. Jan–Feb and Nov–Dec daily 10:30am–3:30pm; Mar and Oct daily 10:30am–4pm; Apr–May and Sept daily 10am–5pm; June–Aug daily 9:30am–5:30pm. Closed Dec 24–25 and 31, Jan 1, and May 17. Ferry: From Pier 3 facing the Rådhuset (summer only). Bus: 30 from the National Theater.

Norsk Folkemuseum ★★ From all over Norway, 140 original buildings have been transported and reassembled on 14 hectares (35 acres) on the Bygdøy Peninsula. This open-air folk museum includes a number of medieval buildings, such as the Raulandstua, one of the oldest wooden dwellings still standing in Norway, and a stave church from about 1200. The rural buildings are grouped together by region of origin, while the urban houses have been laid out in the form of an old town.

Museumsveien 10. ✆ **22-12-37-00.** www.norskfolke.museum.no. Admission 75NOK–100NOK children 6–16, free for children 5 and under, 150NOK–200NOK family ticket. Jan to mid-May and mid-Sept to Dec Mon–Fri 11am–3pm, Sat–Sun 11am–4pm; mid-May to mid-Sept daily 10am–6pm. Ferry: From Pier 3 facing the Rådhuset (summer only). Bus: 30 from the National Theater.

Norsk Sjøfartsmuseum (Norwegian Maritime Museum) This museum, which contains a complete ship's deck with helm and chart house, and a three-deck-high section of the passenger steamer *Sandnaes,* chronicles the maritime history and culture of Norway. The Boat Hall features a fine collection of original small craft. The fully restored polar vessel *Gjoa,* used by Roald Amundsen in his search for America's Northwest Passage, is also on display. The three-masted 1916 schooner *Svanen* (*Swan*) now belongs to the museum and is used as a training vessel.

Bygdøynesveien 37. ✆ **24-11-41-50.** www.norsk-sjofartsmuseum.no. Admission to museum and boat hall 40NOK adults, 25NOK students and seniors, free for children 15 and under. Mid-May to Aug daily 10am–6pm; Sept to mid-May Mon–Wed and Fri–Sun 10:30am–4pm, Thurs 10:30am–6pm. Ferry: From Pier 3 facing the Rådhuset (summer only). Bus: 30 from the National Theater.

Vikingskiphuset (Viking Ship Museum) ★★★ Displayed here are three Viking burial vessels that were excavated on the shores of the Oslofjord and preserved in clay. The most spectacular find is the 9th-century ***Oseberg*** **★**, discovered near Norway's oldest town. This 20m (66-ft.) dragon ship features a wealth of ornaments and is the burial chamber of a Viking queen and her slave. The *Gokstad* find is an outstanding example of Viking vessels because it's so well preserved. The smaller *Tune* ship was never restored. Look for the *Oseberg* animal-head post, the elegantly carved sleigh used by Viking royalty, and the *Oseberg* four-wheeled cart.

Huk Aveny 35, Bygdøy. ✆ **22-13-52-80.** www.khm.uio.no/vikingskipshuset. Admission 60NOK adults, 30NOK children 8–16, 35NOK seniors and students, 140NOK famly ticket. Oct–Apr daily 10am–4pm; May–Sept daily 9am–6pm. Ferry: From Pier 3 facing the Rådhuset (summer only). Bus: 30 from the National Theater.

IN WESTERN OSLO

Vigeland Museet og Parken (Museum and Park) ★★ The lifetime work of Gustav Vigeland, Norway's greatest sculptor, is displayed inside the museum as well as throughout the nearby 80-hectare (198-acre) Frogner Park in western Oslo. Nearly 212 sculptures in granite, bronze, and iron can be admired. See in particular his four granite columns, symbolizing the fight between humanity and evil (a dragon, the embodiment of evil, embraces a woman). *The Angry Boy* is the most photographed statue in the park, but the really celebrated work is the 16m (52-ft.) monolith, composed of 121 figures of colossal size—all carved into a single piece of stone.

Frogner Park, Nobelsgate 32. ✆ **22-49-37-00.** www.vigeland.museum.no. Free admission to park. Museum 50NOK adults, 25NOK children 7–16 and seniors. Park daily 24 hr. Museum June–Aug Tues–Sun 10am–5pm; Sept–May Tues–Sun noon–4pm. Tram: 12 or 15. Bus: 20 or 45.

IN EASTERN OSLO

Munch Museum Devoted exclusively to the works of Edvard Munch (1863–1944), Scandinavia's leading painter, this exhibit (Munch's gift to the city) traces his work from early realism to his latter-day expressionism. The collection comprises 1,100 paintings, some 4,500 drawings, around 18,000 prints, numerous graphic plates, six sculptures, and important documentary material. Munch's *The Scream,* one of the world's most reproduced paintings, along with the artist's *Madonna,* were stolen in August 2004 in a daring daylight robbery (prompting a major security overhaul). The two paintings were recovered in good condition in 2006, so visitors can once again gaze upon these masterpieces.

Tøyengate 53. ✆ **23-49-35-00.** www.munch.museum.no. Admission 75NOK adults, 40NOK children, free for children 6 and under, free for all Oct–Mar. June–Aug daily 10am–6pm; Sept–May Tues–Fri 10am–4pm, Sat–Sun 11am–5pm. T-banen: Tøyen. Bus: 20.

IN THE CITY CENTER

Akershus Castle One of the oldest historical monuments in Oslo, Akershus Castle was built in 1300 by King Haakon V Magnusson. It was a fortress and a royal residence for several centuries. A fire in 1527 devastated the northern wing, and the castle was rebuilt and transformed into a Renaissance palace under the Danish-Norwegian king Christian IV. Now it's used for state occasions. A few rooms, including the chapel, are open to the public. In the rectangular court, markings show where the massive medieval keep used to stand. You can wander through two large halls (Olav's and Christian IV's), which occupy the top floor of the north and south wings, respectively. For many, the most interesting part is the dungeon, which includes an "escape-proof room" built for a prisoner, Ole Pedersewn Hoyland. After he was placed in the chamber and realized there was no way to escape, he killed himself.

Festnings-Plassen. ✆ **23-09-56-71.** Admission 65NOK adults, 25NOK children 6–18, 45NOK students and seniors, free for children 5 and under. May–Aug Mon–Sat 10am–4pm, Sun 12:30–4pm; Sept–Apr Thurs noon–2pm. Tram: 15 or 12. Bus: 60.

ATTRACTIONS NEARBY

Henie-Onstad Kunstsenter (Henie-Onstad Art Center) ★★ On a site beside the Oslofjord 11km (6¾ miles) west of Oslo, the former movie star and skating champion Sonja Henie and her husband, Niels Onstad, a shipping tycoon, opened a museum to display their art collection. This especially good 20th-century collection includes some 1,800 works by Munch, Picasso, Matisse, Léger, Bonnard, and Miró. Henie's Trophy Room is impressive, with 600 trophies and medals, including three Olympic gold medals—she was the star at the 1936 competition—and 10 world skating championships.

Sonja Henie vei 31, Høkvikodden, Baerum. ✆ **67-80-48-80.** www.hok.no. Admission 80NOK adults, 60NOK seniors, 50NOK students, 30NOK children 6–16, free for children 5 and under. Tues–Fri 11am–7pm; Sat–Sun 11am–5pm. Bus: 151.

Tryvannstårnet (Lookout Tower) This is the loftiest lookout tower in Scandinavia—the gallery is approximately 580m (1,900 ft.) above sea level and offers a view of the Oslofjord with Sweden to the east. A walk down the hill takes you to the famous restaurant Frognerseteren. You can take another 20-minute walk down the hill to the Holmenkollen ski jump, the site of the 1952 Olympic competitions, as well as the Holmenkollen Ski Festival, when skiers compete in downhill, slalom, giant slalom, cross-country ski races, and jumping.

Voksenkollen. ✆ **22-14-67-11.** Admission 60NOK adults, 30NOK children. May and Sept daily 10am–5pm; June–Aug 10am–7pm; Oct–Apr daily 10am–4pm. T-banen: Frognerseteren SST Line 1 from near the National Theater to Voksenkollen (30-min. ride), and then an uphill 15-min. walk.

ORGANIZED TOURS

H. M. Kristiansens Automobilbyrå, Hegdehaugsveien 4 (✆ **22-78-94-00;** www.hmk.no), has been showing visitors around Oslo for more than a century. Both of their bus tours are offered daily year-round. The 3-hour "Oslo Grand Highlights" tour is offered at 10am. It costs 300NOK for adults, 150NOK for children. The 2-hour "Oslo Panorama" tour costs 215NOK for adults, 105NOK for children. It departs at 10am. The starting point is in front of the National Theater, Vestbaneplassen 1; arrive 15 minutes before departure. Tours are conducted in English by trained guides.

The Shopping Scene

Near the marketplace and the Oslo Domkirche (cathedral), **Den Norske Husfliden,** Møllergata 4 (✆ **22-42-10-75;** www.dennorskehusfliden.no; T-banen: Stortinget; tram: 17)—or Husfliden, as it's called—is the display and retail center for the Norwegian Association of Home Arts and Crafts, founded in 1891. Today it's almost eight times larger than any of its competitors, with two floors displaying the very finest of Norwegian design in ceramics, glassware, furniture, and woodworking. You can also purchase souvenirs, gifts, textiles, rugs, knotted Rya rugs, embroidery, wrought iron, and fabrics by the yard. Goods are shipped all over the world.

Norway's largest department store, **Steen & Strøm,** Kongensgate 23 (✆ **22-00-40-01;** www.steenstrom.no; T-banen: Stortinget), is a treasure house with hundreds of Nordic items spread through 58 individual departments. Look for hand-knit sweaters and caps, hand-painted wooden dishes reflecting traditional Norwegian art, and pewter dinner plates made from old molds. **Heimen Husflid,** Rosenkrantzgate 8 (✆ **23-21-42-00;** T-banen: Nationaltheatret), about a block from Karl Johans Gate, carries folk costumes, antiques, and reproductions. Hand-knit sweaters in traditional Norwegian patterns are a special item, as are pewter and brass items.

William Schmidt, Fridtjof Nansens Plass 9 (✆ **22-42-02-88;** T-banen: Stortinget), established in 1853, is a leading purveyor of unique souvenirs, including pewter items (everything from Viking ships to beer goblets), Norwegian dolls in national costumes, woodcarvings (the troll collection is the most outstanding in Oslo), and sealskin moccasins. The shop specializes in hand-knit cardigans, pullovers, gloves, and caps; sweaters are made from mothproof 100% Norwegian wool.

Oslo After Dark

To find out what's happening when you're visiting, pick up ***What's On in Oslo,*** which details concerts and theaters and other useful information.

Theater, ballet, and opera tickets are sold at various box offices and also at **Billettsentralen,** Karl Johans Gate 35 (✆ **81-53-31-33;** www.billettservice.no; T-banen: Stortinget)—although this service costs quite a bit more than your typical box office. Tickets to sports and cultural events can now be purchased easily and more cheaply via computer linkup at any post office in the city, so when you buy a stamp you can also buy a voucher for a ticket to the ballet, theater, or hockey game.

THE PERFORMING ARTS

At long last Oslo has a **Norwegian National Opera & Ballet ★★★** house worthy of itself. Launched in 2008, the opera house lies in Bjørvika (✆ **21-42-21-21**), at the head of the Oslofjord. Sheathed in white marble, this futuristic opera house is one of the most architecturally avant-garde in Europe. The cultural complex consists of two companies—the National Opera and the National Ballet. Tickets, costing on the average 200NOK to 600NOK for most performances, are sold at the box office Monday to Friday 10am to 7pm and Saturday 11am to 5pm. From the Central Station in Oslo, walk over the pedestrian bridge to Bjørvika.

Home to the National Theater Company, the **National Theater,** Johanne Dybwads Plass 1 (✆ **81-50-08-11;** www.nationaltheatret.no; T-banen: Nationaltheatret), may be of interest to drama lovers who want to hear Ibsen and Bjørnson in the original. Avant-garde productions go on up at the **Amfiscenen,** in the same building. There are no performances in July and August. Guest companies often perform plays in English. Tickets range from 150NOK to 400NOK adults, 85NOK to 170NOK students and seniors.

Two blocks from the National Theater, **Oslo Konserthus,** Munkedamsveien 14 (✆ **23-11-31-11;** www.oslokonserthus.no; T-banen: Stortinget), is the home of the widely acclaimed Oslo Philharmonic. Performances are given from autumn to spring, on Thursday and Friday. Guest companies from around the world often appear on other nights. The hall is closed from June 20 to mid-August, except for occasional performances by folkloric groups. Tickets run from 200NOK to 850NOK.

Originally a movie theater, the 1931 building at Storgaten 23 was adapted for better acoustics and dedicated in 1959 to the **Den Norske Opera** (✆ **81-54-44-88;** www.operaen.no; T-banen: Jernbanetorget). It's also the leading venue for ballet—the companies alternate performances. About 10 different operas and operettas are staged every year. No performances are held from mid-June to August. Tickets are generally available to nonsubscribers; seats can be reserved in advance and paid for with a credit card. Tickets range from 100NOK to 375NOK except for galas.

Norwegian Folk Museum, Museumsveien 10, Bygdøy (✆ **22-12-37-00;** www.norskfolkemuseum.no), often presents folk dance performances by its own ensemble on summer Sunday afternoons at the museum's open-air theater. Admission to the museum includes admission to the dance performance; 70NOK to 120NOK adults, 50NOK to 85NOK students and seniors, 30NOK children.

THE CLUB & MUSIC SCENE

Smuget, Rosenkrantzgate 22 (✆ **22-42-52-62;** www.smuget.no; T-banen: Nationaltheatret), is the most talked-about nightlife hot spot in the city, and has the long lines (especially on weekends) to prove it. It's in a 19th-century building in back of the City Hall and has a restaurant, an active dance floor, and a stage where live bands perform. It's open Monday to Saturday from 7pm to 4am; the cover ranges from 75NOK to 100NOK.

Native Behavior

Although Norwegians love their beer, note that buying a round is virtually unheard of in a Norwegian pub. In this independent country, both men and women pay for their own libations. During the week, never ask someone you meet "out for a drink." He or she will think you're a drunk. On Friday or Saturday night, it's different. Anything goes. Beer taverns are wild and riotous, and few patrons are satisfied with a mere 10 beers.

Herr Nilsen ★, C.J. Hambros Place 5 (✆ **22-33-54-04;** http://herrnilsen.no; T-banen: Stortinget), is one of the most congenial spots in Oslo and it hosts some of the top jazz artists in Europe—and America, too. Overlooking the courthouse square, it's the perfect place to while away a snowy evening. The Dixieland music played here evokes New Orleans. Open Monday to Saturday 2pm to 3am, Sunday 3pm to 3am. The cover is 150NOK. **Muddy Waters,** Grensen 13 (✆ **22-40-33-70;** www.muddywaters.no), features live music almost nightly in its cavernous cellar pulsating to high-volume bands (often from the United States). The club also has what may be the longest bar in Norway. The cover ranges from 100NOK to 252NOK. Open Tuesday to Friday 4pm to 3am, Saturday 2pm to 3am, Sunday 8pm to 3am.

Day Trips from Oslo

The best 1-day excursion from Oslo includes visits to Fredrikstad and Tønsberg, which gives you a chance to explore the scenic highlights of the Oslofjord. A trip to Fredrikstad, in Østfold on the east bank of the Oslofjord, can easily be combined in 1 day with a visit to the port of Tønsberg on the west bank, by crossing over on the ferry from Moss to Horten and then heading south.

FREDRIKSTAD ★

In recent years Fredrikstad, 95km (59 miles) south of Oslo, has become a major tourist center, thanks to its Old Town and 17th-century fortress. Across the river on the west is a modern industrial section, and although a bridge links the two sections, the best way to reach Old Town is by ferry, which costs 10NOK. The departure point is about 4 blocks from the Fredrikstad railroad station—simply follow the crowd out the main door of the station, make an obvious left turn, and continue down to the shore of the river. It's also possible to travel between the two areas by bus no. 360 or 362, although most pedestrians opt for the ferry.

GETTING THERE To reach Fredrikstad, take E-6 south from Oslo toward Moss. Continue past Moss until you reach the junction of Route 110, which is signposted south of Fredrikstad. About six buses per day depart for the town from the Central Station in Oslo. Trains from Oslo's Central Station depart from Fredrikstad about every 2 hours during the day (trip time: 30 min.).

VISITOR INFORMATION **Fredrikstad Turistkontor** is on Toihusgata 41, Turistsenteret, Østre Brohode in Gamle Fredrikstad (✆ **69-30-46-00**). From June to September, it's open Monday to Friday 9am to 5pm and Saturday and Sunday 1am to 4pm; from October to May, it's open Monday to Friday 9am to 4:30pm.

Fredrikstad was founded in 1567 as a marketplace at the mouth of the River Glomma. **Gamlebyen (Old Town)** became a fortress in 1663 and continued in that role until 1903, boasting some 200 guns in its heyday. It still serves as a military camp. The main guardroom and old convict prison are now the **Fredrikstad Museum,** Mindre Alvsvei 5 (✆ **69-95-85-00**), open from May to September, Monday to Friday 10am to 4:30pm, Saturday and Sunday noon to 4:30pm. Admission is 50NOK adults and 25NOK children.

Outside the gates of Old Town is **Kongsten Fort,** on what was first called Gallows Hill, an execution site. When Fredrikstad Fortress was built, it was provisionally fortified in 1677, becoming known as Svenskeskremme (Swede Scarer). Present-day Kongsten Fort, with its 20 cannons, underground chambers, passages, and countermines, eventually replaced it.

Since Fredrikstad's heyday as a trading port and merchant base, Old Town has attracted craftspeople and artisans, many of whom create their products in the Old Town's historic houses and barns. Many of these glass blowers, ceramic artists, and silversmiths choose not to display or sell their products at their studios, preferring instead to leave the sales aspect to local shops.

TØNSBERG ★

Bordering the western bank of the Oslofjord, Tønsberg, 100km (62 miles) south of Oslo, is Norway's oldest town. It's divided into a historic area, filled with old clapboard-sided houses, and the commercial center, where the marketplace is located.

GETTING THERE You can drive back north from Fredrikstad to the town of Moss, where you can take a ferry to Horten. Once at Horten, signs will point the way south for the short drive to Tønsberg. Tønsberg is about 1½ hours from Oslo, with some 20 trains arriving daily.

VISITOR INFORMATION **Tourist Information** is at Nedre Langgate 36, N-3126 Tønsberg (✆ **33-35-45-20**). It's open June 19 to August 5 Monday to Saturday 9am to 7pm, Sunday 9am to 5pm; otherwise, Monday to Friday 9am to 2pm.

Tønsberg was founded a year before King Harald Fairhair united parts of the country in 872, and this Viking town became a royal coronation site. Svend Foyn, who invented modern whaling and seal hunting, was born here.

Slottsfjellet, a huge hill fortress directly ahead of the train station, is touted as "the Acropolis of Norway." But it has only some meager ruins, and people mostly come here for the view from the lookout tower. Built in 1888, the **Slottsfjelltårnet** (✆ **33-31-18-72**) is open May 15 to June 25 Monday through Friday from 10am to 3pm; June 26 to August 19 daily from 11am to 6pm; August 20 to September 15 Saturday and Sunday from noon to 5pm; and September 16 to September 29 Saturday and Sunday from noon to 3pm. Admission is 25NOK adults and 15NOK children.

Nordbyen is the old and scenic part of town, with well-preserved houses. **Haugar** cemetery, at Møllebakken, is right in the town center, with the Viking graves of King Harald's sons, Olav and Sigrød.

Sem Church, Hageveien 32 (✆ **33-37-96-80**), the oldest in Vestfold, was built of stone in the Romanesque style around 1100. It's open May to September, Tuesday to Friday from 9am to 2pm; ask at the vestry. Admission is free.

You should also see **Fjerdingen,** a street of charming restored houses. Tønsberg was also a Hanseatic town during the Middle Ages, and some houses have been redone in typical Hanseatic style.

In the **Vestfold Folk Museum ★**, Frammannsveien 30 (✆ **33-31-29-19**), you'll find many Viking and whaling treasures. One of the biggest thrills is the skeleton of a blue whale. A real Viking ship is displayed, the *Klastad* from Tjolling, built about A.D. 800. Admission is 50NOK adults, 15NOK children. It's open Monday to Friday 10am to 2pm.

BERGEN & THE FJORDS

In western Norway the landscape takes on an awesome beauty, with iridescent glaciers; deep fjords that slash into rugged, snowcapped mountains; roaring waterfalls; and secluded valleys that lie at the end of corkscrew-twisting roads. From Bergen the most beautiful fjords to visit are the **Hardanger** (best at blossom time, May and early June), to the south; the **Sogne,** Norway's longest fjord, immediately to the north; and the **Nordfjord,** north of that. A popular excursion on the Nordfjord takes visitors from Loen to Olden along rivers and lakes to the Brixdal Glacier.

If you have time, on the Hardangerfjord you can stop over at one of the fjord resorts, such as Ulvik or Lofthus. The Folgefonn Glacier, Norway's second-largest ice field, which spans more than 250 sq. km (100 sq. miles), can be seen from many vantage points.

Bergen, with its many sightseeing attractions, good hotels and restaurants, and excellent boat, rail, and coach connections, is the best center for touring the fjord district. This ancient city looms large in Viking sagas. Until the 14th century, it was the seat of the medieval kingdom of Norway. The Hanseatic merchants established a major trading post here, holding sway until the 18th century.

Bergen: Gateway to the Fjords

ESSENTIALS

Getting There

BY PLANE The **Bergen Airport** (✆ **47-67-03-15-55;** www.avinor.no/en/airport/bergen) at Flesland, 19km (12 miles) south of the city, offers frequent flights to Copenhagen and London, through which most international flights are routed. There is frequent airport bus service from the airport to the SAS Royal Hotel, Braathens airlines' office at the Hotel Norge, and the city bus station. Buses depart every 15 minutes from Monday to Friday and every 30 minutes Saturday and Sunday. The one-way fare is 85NOK. Taxis are readily available at the airport, or call ✆ **33-30-11-11.** A ride to the city center costs 450NOK to 500NOK.

BY TRAIN Day and night trains arrive from Oslo (trip time: 6–8½ hr.). For information, call the Bergen train station at ✆ **55-96-69-00.**

BY BUS Express buses travel to Bergen from Oslo in 11 hours. For long-distance bus information, call ✆ **55-55-90-70.**

BY CAR A toll is charged on all vehicles driven into the city center Monday to Friday 6am to 10pm. A single ticket costs 20NOK; a book of 20 tickets, 300NOK.

The trip from Oslo to Bergen is a mountainous drive filled with dramatic scenery. Because mountains split the country, there's no direct road. The southern route, E76, takes you through mountain passes until the junction with Route 47; then you head north to Kinsarvik and make the ferry crossing to E16 leading to Bergen. It's

The Bergen Card

The Bergen Card entitles you to free bus transportation and (usually) free museum entrance throughout Bergen, plus discounts on car rentals, parking, and some cultural activities. Ask for it at the tourist office (see "Visitor Information," below). A 24-hour card costs 190NOK for adults, 75NOK for children 3 to 15. A 48-hour card is 250NOK for adults, 100NOK for children 3 to 15. Children 2 and under generally travel or enter free.

quickest to take the northern route following E16 west. For the first time it's possible to make a ferry-free road connection to Bergen. In 2001 the world's longest tunnel opened, the 40km (25-mile) Laerdal Tunnel. It begins 300km (186 miles) northwest of Oslo and goes as deep as 1,470m (4,820 ft.) beneath one of Norway's most scenic mountain areas. It takes 20 minutes to go through the tunnel.

VISITOR INFORMATION **Tourist Information,** Vagsallmenningen 1 (✆ **55-55-20-00;** www.visitbergen.com), provides information, maps, and brochures about Bergen and the rest of the region. It's open June to August, daily from 8:30am to 10pm; May and September, daily 9am to 8pm; October to April, Monday to Saturday 9am to 4pm.

SPECIAL EVENTS The annual **Bergen Festival,** generally held the last 2 weeks in May, features performances by regional, national, and international orchestras, dance ensembles, and theater groups. The complete festival schedule is usually available by February of each year. For festival and ticket information, contact the **Bergen Festival Office** (✆ **55-21-06-30;** www.fib.no).

Getting Around

BY BUS The **Bystasjonen (Central Bus Station),** Strømgaten 8 (✆ **55-31-44-30**), is the terminal for all buses serving the Bergen and the Hardanger area, as well as the airport bus. Bergen is serviced by a network of buses; if you didn't purchase the Bergen Card (see above), the average fare within the city is 25NOK.

BY TAXI Sightseeing by taxi costs about 600NOK for the first hour and then 400NOK per hour after that (✆ **55-99-70-10**).

WHERE TO STAY

Expensive

Clarion Admiral Hotel ★ When it was built in 1906, this building was one of the largest warehouses in Bergen, with six sprawling floors peppered with massive trusses and beams. In 1987, it became a comfortable, tastefully appointed hotel, and in 1998, it was enlarged and renovated into the bustling establishment you'll see today. Rooms are a bit smaller than you might hope, but they are comfortable and have excellent beds. Many rooms lack water views, but the ones that open onto flower-bedecked balconies have the best harbor views in town.

Christian Sundts Gate 3, N-5004 Bergen. ✆ **55-23-64-00.** Fax 55-23-64-64. www.clarionadmiral.no. 211 units. Mon–Thurs 1,280NOK–2,495NOK double; Fri–Sun 1,080NOK–1,780NOK double, 3,000NOK suite. AE, DC, MC, V. Very limited parking 100NOK. Bus: 2, 4, or 11. **Amenities:** 2 restaurants; bar; room service. *In room:* TV, hair dryer, minibar, Wi-Fi (free).

First Hotel Marin ★★ In the heart of Bergen, this first-class hotel is one of Bergen's most modern and streamlined. The brown-brick building is set on a steep

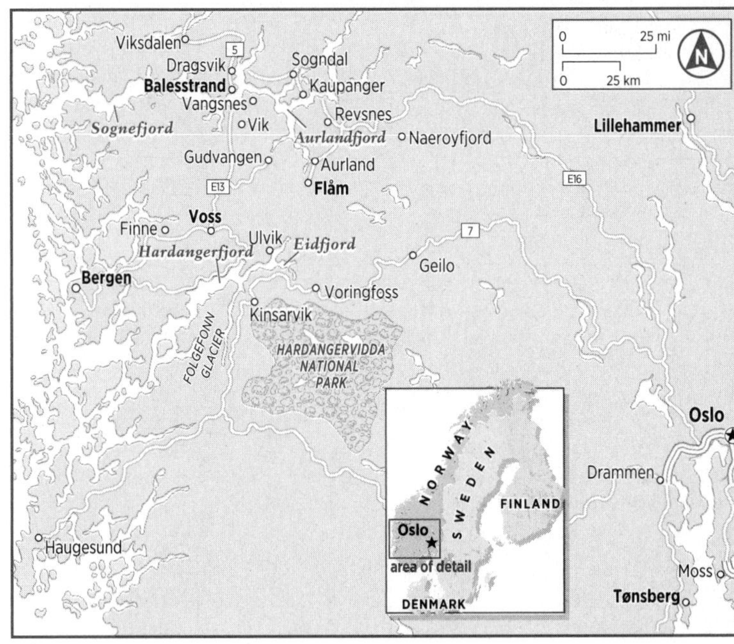

hillside. The bedrooms are moderate to spacious in size, and each is handsomely furnished in functional, stylish Nordic modern. For Bergen, the hotel offers a large number of suites—34 deluxe ones in all—the best of which are a trio of penthouse units with views so panoramic they encompass all seven mountains surrounding Bergen. The finest units are in front, overlooking the harbor.

Rosenkrantzgaten 8, N-5003 Bergen. ✆ **53-05-15-00.** Fax 53-05-15-01. www.firsthotels.com. 152 units. 1,295NOK–2,845NOK double; 1,945NOK–4,695NOK suite. AE, DC, MC, V. Parking 200NOK. Bus: 5, 6, 9, 30, or 90. **Amenities:** Restaurant; bar; exercise room; room service; sauna. *In room:* TV, hair dryer (in some), minibar, Wi-Fi (free).

Moderate

Augustin Hotel ★ The Augustin has one of the best locations in Bergen—right in the harbor's shopping district—with front rooms that have terrific harbor views. Constructed in 1909 in the Jugend or Art Nouveau style, Augustin has been in the same family for four generations. In 1995, it more than doubled in size by adding a new wing, with modern new rooms designed by award-winning Bergen architect Aud Hunskår. The hotel is decorated with lots of art, many pieces from well-known contemporary Norwegian artists.

Carl Sundts Gate 22, N-5004 Bergen. ✆ **55-30-40-00.** Fax 55-30-40-10. www.augustin.no. 109 units. July–Aug 1,390NOK–1,590NOK double, 1,790NOK suite; Sept–June 2,050NOK–2,250NOK double, 2,450NOK suite. AE, DC, MC, V. Parking 150NOK. Bus: 2. **Amenities:** Restaurant; bar. *In room:* TV, hair dryer, minibar, Wi-Fi (free).

Hotel Park ★ This converted 1890 town house is in an attractive university area near Grieghall and Nygård Park. The rooms are traditionally furnished, often with antiques. Accommodations vary in size but all have good beds. In the summer, a neighboring building (furnished in the same style) accommodates overflow guests. A delicious Norwegian breakfast is served in the dining room; later in the day, sandwiches, small hot dishes, and wine and beer are available there. In the summer, reserve well in advance. The Park is a 10-minute walk from the train and bus stations.

Harald Hårfagresgaten 35 and Allegaten 20, N-5007 Bergen. ✆ **55-54-44-00.** Fax 55-54-44-44. www.parkhotel.no. 33 units. 1,250NOK double. Rates include breakfast. AE, DC, MC, V. Parking 65NOK. Bus: 80 or 90. **Amenities:** Breakfast room. *In room:* TV, hair dryer, Wi-Fi (free).

Steens Hotel Owned and operated by the same family since 1950, this stylish 1890 town house offers great accommodations at most reasonable prices. The modern guest rooms are moderate in size and comfortable, and the bathrooms, though small, are beautifully maintained. The public rooms have plenty of atmosphere. The best rooms are in front and open onto a park. Within a short walk are the bus and railway stations and attractions in the center of town. Coffee and light meals are served.

22 Parkveien, N-5007 Bergen. ✆ **55-30-88-88.** Fax 55-30-88-89. www.steenshotel.no. 21 units. 1,340NOK double. Extra bed 250NOK. Rates include Norwegian breakfast. AE, MC, V. Free parking. Bus: 1 or 5. **Amenities:** Breakfast room. *In room:* TV.

WHERE TO DINE

Bryggeloftet and Stuene ★ NORWEGIAN The Bryggeloftet and Stuene is the best-established restaurant along the harbor. At street level, the Stuene has low-beamed ceilings, carved banquettes, and 19th-century murals of old Bergen, along with dozens of clipper-ship models. For a more formal meal, head upstairs to the Bryggeloftet, with its high ceilings and wood paneling. Dinner in either section might include fried *porbeagle* (a form of whitefish) served with shrimp, mussels, and white-wine sauce; roast reindeer with cream sauce; or pepper steak with a salad. Several different preparations of salmon and herring are featured, along with grilled filet of reindeer with a creamy wild game sauce. This is a quintessential Norwegian place—come here if you're seeking authentic flavors.

Bryggen 11. ✆ **55-30-20-70.** www.bryggeloftet.no. Reservations recommended. Main courses 200NOK–380NOK; lunch smørbrød 100NOK–180NOK. AE, DC, MC, V. Mon–Thurs 11am–11:30pm; Fri–Sat 11am–midnight; Sun 1–11:30pm. Bus: 1, 5, 9, 22, or 80.

Smauet Mat & Vinhus ★ CONTINENTAL/FRENCH/ITALIAN The romantic, cozy atmosphere and high-quality food continue to lure us here. Tempting smells and lots of energy emanate from the open kitchen of this candle-studded restaurant whose decor emulates the style of a 19th-century Norwegian farmhouse. Subtly intermingled flavors emerge in the rack of lamb with creamed artichokes and a shallot confit demi-glace or theme-marinated salmon with a spinach risotto. Other standouts include the monkfish studded with lardoons and served with braised Savoy cabbage; medallions of venison in a port-wine sauce; and the cinnamon-scented, pan-fried breast of chicken with pancetta.

Vaskerelvsmauet 1–3. ✆ **55-21-07-10.** Reservations recommended, especially on weekends. Main courses 275NOK–295NOK; 6-course menu 695NOK. Daily 5–10pm. AE, MC, V. Closed btw. Christmas and New Year's. Bus: 2, 3, or 4.

To Kokker ★ FRENCH/NORWEGIAN To Kokker ("Two Cooks") is a favorite with celebrities. Savvy local diners gravitate here for the chef's well-considered juxtaposition of flavors and textures. Menu items include such time-tested favorites as lobster soup; whitebait roe with chopped onions, sour cream, and fresh-baked bread; reindeer with lingonberry sauce; and filet of lamb with mustard sauce and *pommes* (potatoes) Provençal. The dining room, one floor above street level, has scarlet walls, old paintings, and a solid staff that works competently under pressure, albeit without a lot of flair.

Enhjørninggården. ✆ **55-30-69-55.** www.tokokker.no. Reservations required. Main courses 295NOK-330NOK; 4-course menu 595NOK; 5-course menu 695NOK; 7-course menu 795NOK. AE, DC, MC, V. Mon-Sat 5-10pm. Bus: 1, 5, 9, 70, or 80.

SEEING THE SIGHTS

In addition to the sights below, take a stroll around **Bryggen (the Quay) ★★★**. This row of Hanseatic timbered houses, rebuilt along the waterfront after the disastrous fire of 1702, is what remains of medieval Bergen. The northern half burned to the ground as recently as 1955. Bryggen is on UNESCO's World Heritage List as one of the world's most significant cultural and historical re-creations of a medieval settlement. It's a center for arts and crafts, where painters, weavers, and craftspeople have their workshops.

Bergen Art Museum ★★ In the center of the city, this vastly expanded art museum—one of the largest in Scandinavia—displays an impressive array of Norwegian and international artists. Overlooking Lille Lungegard Lake, the museum after massive rebuilding is now displaying its extensive collection of art, for the first time, including such renowned artists as Edvard Munch, Miró, and Picasso. Norwegian art from the 18th century to 1915 is also exhibited. The Steneresen collection offers one of Europe's finest assemblages of the work of Paul Klee.

Rasmus Meyer allee 3, 7, and 9. ✆ **55-56-80-00.** www.bergenartmuseum.no. Admission 60NOK adults, 40NOK students, free for children 16 and under. Daily 11am-5pm. Closed Mon Sept 15-May 14.

Det Hanseatiske Museum ★ In one of the best-preserved wooden buildings at Bryggen, this museum illustrates Bergen's commercial life on the wharf centuries ago. German merchants, representatives of the Hanseatic League centered in Lübeck, lived in these medieval houses built in long rows up from the harbor. The museum is furnished with authentic articles dating from 1704.

Finnegårdsgaten 1A, Bryggen. ✆ **55-54-46-90.** May-Sept admission 50NOK adults, Oct-Apr admission 30NOK adults; free for children 14 and under. May 15-Sept 15 daily 10am-5pm; Sept 16-May 14 Tues-Sat 11am-2pm, Sun 11am-4pm. Bus: 1, 5, or 9.

Fløibanen ★ A short walk from the fish market is the station where the funicular heads up to Fløien, the most famous of Bergen's seven hills, reached after an 8-minute ride. At 320m (1,050 ft.), the view of the city, the neighboring hills, and the harbor is worth every øre.

Vetrlidsalm 21. ✆ **55-33-68-00.** www.floibanen.com. Round-trip 70NOK adults, 35NOK children 4-16. Sept-Apr Mon-Thurs 7:30am-11pm, Fri 7:30am-11:30pm, Sat 8am-11:30pm, Sun 9am-11pm; May-Aug Mon-Fri 7:30am-midnight, Sat 8am-midnight, Sun 9am-midnight. Bus: 6.

Gamle Bergen ★ At Elsesro and Sandviken is a collection of houses from the 18th and 19th centuries set in a park. Old Town is complete with streets, an open square, and narrow alleyways. Some of the interiors are exceptional, including a merchant's living room in the typical style of the 1870s—padded sofas, heavy curtains, potted plants—a perfect setting for Ibsen's *A Doll's House*.

Elsesro and Sandviken. © **55-39-43-03.** Admission 70NOK adults, 35NOK children and students. Houses mid-May to Sept only, guided tours daily on the hour 10am–5pm. Park and restaurant daily noon–6pm. Bus: 9, 20, 21, 22, or 50.

Mariakirke (St. Mary's Church) ★ This Romanesque church is the oldest building in Bergen (its exact date is unknown, but perhaps from the mid–12th c.) and one of the most beautiful churches in Norway. Its altar is the oldest ornament in the church, and there's a baroque pulpit, donated by Hanseatic merchants, with carved figures depicting everything from Chastity to Naked Truth. Church-music concerts are given several nights a week from May to August.

Dreggen 15. © **55-31-59-60.** Admission 10NOK adults, free for children, free to all Sept 10–May 17. May–Sept Mon–Fri 11am–4pm; Oct–Apr Tues–Fri noon–1:30pm. Bus: 5, 9, 20, 21, or 22.

Troldhaugen (Troll's Hill) ★ This Victorian house, in beautiful rural surroundings at Hop, near Bergen, was the summer villa of composer Edvard Grieg. The house contains Grieg's own furniture, paintings, and mementos. His Steinway grand piano is frequently used at concerts given in the house during the annual Bergen festival, as well as at Troldhaugen's own summer concerts. Grieg and his wife, Nina, are buried in a cliff grotto on the estate.

Troldhaugveien 65, N-5232. © **55-92-29-92.** www.kunstmuseene.no. Admission 60NOK adults, 30NOK students, free for children. May–Sept daily 9am–6pm; Oct–Apr 10am–4pm. Closed Dec 19–Jan 4. Bus: To Hop from the Bergen bus station (platforms 18–20), exit, turn right, walk about 180m (600 ft.), turn left at Hopsvegen, and follow signs. Hop is about 5km (3 miles) from Bergen.

THE SHOPPING SCENE

Bargain hunters head to the **Torget (Marketplace).** Many local handicrafts from the western fjord district, including rugs and handmade tablecloths, are displayed. This is one of the few places in Norway where bargaining is welcomed. The market keeps no set hours, but is best visited between 8am and noon. Take bus no. 1, 5, or 9. You'll find the widest selection of national handicrafts in and around **Bryggen Brukskunst,** the restored Old Town near the wharf, where many craftspeople have taken over old houses and ply ancient Norwegian trades. Crafts boutiques often display Bergen souvenirs, many based on designs 300 to 1,500 years old. For example, we purchased a reproduction of a Romanesque-style cruciform pilgrim's badge. Other attractive items are likely to include sheepskin-lined booties and exquisitely styled hand-woven wool dresses. The leading outlet for glassware and ceramics, **Prydkunst-Hjertholm,** Olav Kyrres Gate 7 (© **55-31-70-27;** www.hjertholm.no), purchases much of its merchandise directly from the studios of Norwegian and other Scandinavian artisans who turn out quality goods not only in glass and ceramics, but also in pewter, brass, wood, and textiles.

BERGEN AFTER DARK

The modern **Grieghallen (Grieg Hall),** Edvard Grieg Plass 1 (© **55-21-61-00;** www.grieghallen.no), is Bergen's monumental showcase for music, drama, and a host of other cultural events. The **Bergen Symphony Orchestra,** founded in 1765, performs here from August to May on Thursday at 7:30pm and Saturday at 12:30pm.

Norway's oldest theater performs from September to June at **Den National Scene,** Engen 1 (✆ **55-54-97-00;** www.dns.no). Its repertoire consists of classical Norwegian and international drama and contemporary plays, as well as visiting productions of opera and ballet in conjunction with the annual Bergen Festival. Performances are held from Monday to Saturday.

In summer, the **Bergen Folklore dancing troupe** (✆ **55-55-20-00**) arranges a 1-hour folklore program at the Bryggens Museum on Tuesday and Thursday at 9pm. Tickets, which cost 100NOK, are sold at the tourist information center or at the door.

The most-frequented pub in the city center, **Kontoret Pub,** Ole Bulls Plass 8–10 (✆ **55-36-31-33**), lies adjacent to the Hotel Norge next to the Dickens restaurant/pub. Drinkers can wander freely between the two places, since they're connected. In the Kontoret you can order the same food served at Dickens, though most people seem to come here to drink. The pub is open Sunday to Thursday from 4pm to 12:30am, Friday 4pm to 2am, and Saturday from noon to 2am.

Exploring the Fjords

Norway's fjords can be explored from both Oslo and Bergen by ship and car or by a scenic train ride. Here are the details.

BY CAR FROM BERGEN

Bergen is the best departure point for trips to the fjords: To the south lies the famous **Hardangerfjord ★★** and to the north the **Sognefjord ★★★**, cutting 180km (112 miles) inland. We've outlined a driving tour of the fjords, starting in Bergen and heading east on Route 7 to Ulvik, a distance of 150km (93 miles).

Ulvik

Ulvik is that rarity: an unspoiled resort. It lies like a fist at the end of an arm of the Hardangerfjord that's surrounded in summer by misty peaks and fruit farms. The village's 1858 church is attractively decorated in the style of the region. It's open June through August, daily from 9am to 5pm, and presents concerts.

From Ulvik, you can explore the **Eidfjord** district, which is the northern tip of the Hardangerfjord, home to some 1,000 people and a paradise for hikers. Anglers are attracted to the area because of its mountain trout.

The district contains nearly one-quarter of **Hardangervidda National Park ★**, which is on Europe's largest high-mountain plateau. It's home to 20,000 wild reindeer. Well-marked hiking trails connect a series of 15 tourist huts.

Several canyons, including the renowned **Måbø Valley,** lead down from the plateau to the fjords. Here, you'll see the famous 170m (558-ft.) **Voringfoss ★** waterfall. The **Valurefoss** in **Hjømo Valley** has a free fall of almost 245m (800 ft.).

Part of the 1,000-year-old road across Norway, traversing the Måbø Valley, has been restored for hardy hikers.

EN ROUTE TO VOSS From Ulvik, take Hwy. 20 to Route 13. Follow Route 13 to Voss, 40km (25 miles) west of Ulvik and 100km (62 miles) east of Bergen.

Voss

Between the Sogne and Hardanger fjords, Voss is a famous year-round resort, also known for its folklore and as the birthplace of football hero Knute Rockne. Maybe the trolls don't strike fear into the hearts of farm children anymore, but they're still called out of hiding to give visitors a little fun.

Voss is a natural base for exploring the two largest fjords in Norway, the Sognefjord to the north and the Hardangerfjord to the south. In and around Voss are glaciers, mountains, fjords, waterfalls, orchards, rivers, and lakes.

A ride on the **Hangursbanen cable car** (✆ **56-53-02-20**) offers panoramic views of Voss and the environs. The hardy can take the cable car up, and then spend the rest of the afternoon strolling down the mountain. A round-trip ride costs 90NOK adults, 60NOK children 7 to 15, and is free for children 6 and under. The cable car entrance is on a hillside that's a 1-hour walk north of the town center. It operates June 2 to September 9 from 11am to 5pm.

Built in 1277, the **Vangskyrkje,** Vangsgata 3 (✆ **56-52-38-80**), with a timbered tower, contains a striking Renaissance pulpit, a stone altar and triptych, fine woodcarvings, and a painted ceiling. It's a 5-minute walk east of the railroad station. We recommend that you call in advance to reserve an English-speaking guide. Admission is free. The church is open only June to August Monday to Saturday 10am to 4pm, Sunday 1 to 4pm.

Voss Folkemuseum, Mølster (✆ **56-51-15-11;** www.vossfolkemuseum.no), is a collection of authentically furnished houses that shows what early farm life was like. Lying just north of Voss on a hillside overlooking the town, the museum consists of more than a dozen farmhouses and other buildings, ranging in age from the 1500s to around 1870. Admission is 50NOK adults, free for children. It's open mid-May to mid-September, daily from 10am to 5pm; and from mid-September to mid-May, Monday to Friday 10am to 3pm, Sunday noon to 3pm.

A little west of Voss in Finne, **Finnesloftet** (✆ **56-51-16-75**) is one of Norway's oldest timbered houses, dating from the mid–13th century. It's a 15-minute walk west of the railway station. Admission is 50NOK adults and 20NOK children. It's open June 15 to August 15, Tuesday to Sunday from 11am to 4pm.

Balestrand

Long known for its arts and crafts, Balestrand lies on the northern rim of the Sognefjord, at the junction of the Vetlefjord, the Esefjord, and the Fjaerlandsfjord.

Kaiser Wilhelm II, a frequent visitor to Balestrand, presented the district with two statues of old Norse heroes, King Bele and Fridtjof the Bold, which stand in the town center.

You can explore by setting out in nearly any direction, on scenic country lanes with little traffic, or a wide choice of marked trails and upland farm tracks. A touring map may be purchased at the **tourist office** in the town center (✆ **57-69-12-55** in summer, or 57-69-16-17 in winter). There's good sea fishing, as well as lake and river trout fishing. Fishing tackle, rowboats, and bicycles can all be rented in the area.

EN ROUTE TO FLÅM From Balestrand, follow Route 55 east along the Sognefjord, crossing the fjord via ferry at Dragsvik and by bridge at Sogndal. At Sogndal, drive east to Kaupanger, where you'll cross the Ardalsfjord by ferry, south to Revsnes. In Revsnes, pick up Route 11 heading southeast. Drive east until you connect with a secondary road heading southwest through Kvigno and Aurland. When you arrive in Aurland, take Route 601 southwest to the town of Flåm, 95km (59 miles) southeast of Balestrand and 165km (103 miles) east of Bergen.

Flåm ★

Flåm (pronounced *Flawm*) lies on the Aurlandsfjord, a tip of the more famous Sognefjord. In the village you can visit the old church dating from 1667, with painted walls done in typical Norwegian country style.

Flåm is an excellent starting point for excursions by car or boat to other well-known centers on the Sognefjord, Europe's longest and deepest fjord. Worth exploring are two of the wildest and most beautiful fingers of the Sognefjord: Nærøyfjord and Aurlandsfjord. Ask at the **tourist office,** near the rail station (✆ **57-63-21-06**), about a cruise from Flåm, from which you can experience the dramatic scenery of both of these fjords. From Flåm by boat, you can disembark in either Gudvangen or Aurland and continue the tour by coach. Alternatively, you can return to Flåm by train.

There are also a number of easy walks in the Flåm district. The tourist office has a map detailing these walks.

BY SHIP/TOUR FROM BERGEN

There are several ways to visit Sognefjord, Norway's longest fjord, from Bergen. One way is to cross the fjord on an express steamer that travels from Bergen to **Gudvangen.** From Gudvangen, passengers go to Myrdal, and from Myrdal a train runs back to Bergen. You can go by boat, bus, and then train for 1,150NOK round-trip. Details about this and other tours are available from **Bergen Visitor Information** in Bergen (✆ **55-55-20-00;** www.norwayinanutshell.com).

If you have more than a day to see the fjords in the environs of Bergen, you can take the grandest fjord cruise in the world, a **coastal steamer** going to the North Cape and beyond. The coastal steamers are elegantly appointed ships that cruise the western coast of Norway from Bergen to Kirkenes, carrying passengers and cargo to 34 ports along the Norwegian coast. Eleven ships in all make the journey year-round. The ships sail through Norway's more obscure fjords, providing panoramic scenery and numerous opportunities for adventure. Along the way, sightseeing excursions to the surrounding mountains and glaciers are offered, as well as sails on smaller vessels through some of the more obscure fjords.

One of the chief operators of these coastal cruisers is **Hurtigruten,** 5100 NW 33rd Ave., Ste. 255, Fort Lauderdale, FL 33309 (✆ **866/552-0371;** www.hurtigruten.us). Tours may be booked heading north from Bergen or south from Kirkenes. The 12-day northbound journey costs US$2,190 per person double occupancy, including meals, taxes, and port charges.

PORTUGAL

by Darwin Porter & Danforth Prince

Portugal, positioned at what was once thought to be the edge of the earth, has long been a seafaring nation. At the dawn of the Age of Exploration, mariners believed that two-headed, fork-tongued monsters as big as houses lurked across the Sea of Darkness, waiting to chew up a caravel and gulp its debris down their fire-lined throats.

15

There's a general feeling of optimism in Portugal; in spite of a world economic downturn, the Portuguese have high hopes for the new century. Lisbon's sidewalks are as crowded in the evening as Madrid's. Young Portuguese are much better tuned in to Europe than their parents were. The younger generation is as well versed in the electronic music coming out of London and Los Angeles as in fado repertoires, and more taken with French and Spanish films than with Portuguese lyric poetry. Still, as Portugal advances with determination deeper into the 21st century, its people retain pride in their historic culture.

LISBON & ENVIRONS

Lisbon, Europe's smallest capital, has blossomed into a cosmopolitan city. Sections along Avenida da Liberdade, the main street of Lisbon, at times evoke thoughts of Paris. As in Paris, sidewalk portrait painters will sketch your likeness, and artisans will offer you jewelry claiming that it's gold (when you both know it isn't). Handicrafts, from embroidery to leather work, are peddled right on the streets as they are in New York.

Lisbon is growing and evolving, and the city is considerably more sophisticated than it once was, no doubt due in part to Portugal's joining the European Union (E.U.). The smallest capital of Europe is no longer a backwater at the far corner of Iberia. Some 1.8 million people now live in Lisbon, and many of its citizens, having drifted in from the far corners of the world, don't even speak Portuguese.

Consider an off-season visit, especially in the spring or fall, when the city enjoys glorious weather. The city isn't overrun with visitors then, and you can wander about and take in its attractions without being trampled or broiled during the hot, humid weather of July and August.

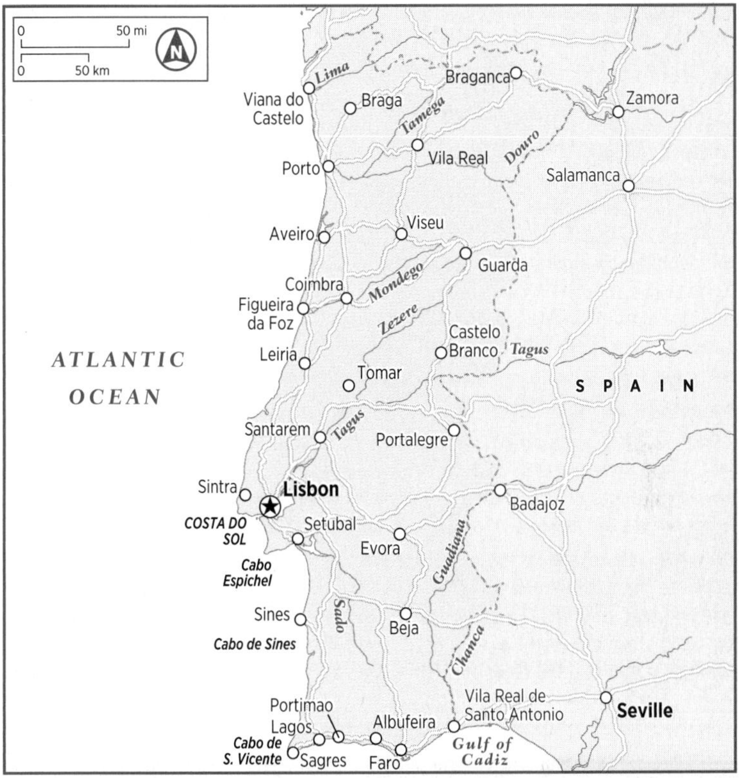

Portugal

Essentials

GETTING THERE

BY PLANE Foreign and domestic flights land at Lisbon's **Aeroporto de Lisboa** (✆ **21/841-35-00;** www.ana-aeroportos.pt), about 6.5km (4 miles) from the heart of the city. An AERO-BUS runs between the airport and the Cais do Sodré train station every 20 minutes from 7:45am to 8:15pm. The fare is 3.50€. It makes 10 intermediate stops, including Praça dos Restauradores and Praça do Comércio. There's no charge for luggage. Taxi passengers line up in a usually well-organized queue at the sidewalk in front of the airport, or you can call **Rádio Táxi** at ✆ **21/811-90-00.** The average taxi fare from the airport to central Lisbon is 12€. Each piece of luggage is 1.60€ extra.

For ticket sales, flight reservations, and information about the city and the country, you can get in touch with the Lisboa personnel of **TAP Air Portugal,** Loja Gare do Oriente, Edifício Estação do Oriente, Avenida de Berlim, 1998 Lisboa (✆ **70/720-57-00** for reservations; www.flytap.com).

BY TRAIN Most international rail passengers from Madrid and Paris arrive at the Estação da Santa Apolónia, Avenida Infante Dom Henrique, the major terminal. It's by the Tagus near the Alfama district. Two daily trains make the 10-hour run from Madrid to Lisbon. Rail lines from northern and eastern Portugal also arrive at this station. EXPO '98 brought a new, modern terminal to Lisbon. Connected to the Metro system and opened in 1998, Gare de Oriente at Expo Urbe is the hub for some long-distance and suburban trains, including service to such destinations as Porto, Sintra, the Beiras, Minho, and the Douro. At the Estação do Rossio, between Praça dos Restauradores and Praça de Dom Pedro IV, you can get trains to Sintra. The Estação do Cais do Sodré, just beyond the south end of Rua Alecrim, east of Praça do Comércio, handles trains to Cascais and Estoril on the Costa do Sol. Finally, you can catch a ferry at Sul e Sueste, next to the Praça do Comércio. It runs across the Tagus to the suburb of Barreiro; at the station there, Estação do Barreiro, you can catch a train for the Algarve and Alentejo. For all rail information, at any of the terminals above, call ✆ **80/820-82-08** (www.cp.pt) between 7am and 11pm daily.

BY BUS Buses from all over Portugal, including the Algarve, arrive at the **Rodoviária da Sete Rios** (✆ **21/358-14-81;** www.rede-expressos.pt). If your hotel is in Estoril or Cascais, you can take bus no. 1, which goes on to the Cais do Sodré. At least six buses a day leave for Lagos, a gateway to the Algarve, and nine buses head north every day to Porto. There are 14 daily buses to Coimbra, the university city to the north. One-way fare from Lagos to Lisbon is 18€.

BY CAR International motorists must arrive through Spain, the only nation connected to Portugal by road. You'll have to cross Spanish border points, which usually pose no great difficulty. The roads are moderately well maintained. From Madrid, if you head west, the main road (N620) from Tordesillas goes southwest by way of Salamanca and Ciudad Rodrigo and reaches the Portuguese frontier at Fuentes de Onoro. Most of the country's 15 border crossings are open daily from 7am to midnight. See "Getting Around" below for info on car-rental agencies in the city.

VISITOR INFORMATION The main **tourist office** in Lisbon is at the Palácio da Foz, Praça dos Restauradores (✆ **21/12-05-050;** www.visitportugal.com), at the Baixa end of Avenida da Liberdade. Open daily from 9am to 8pm (Metro: Restauradores), it sells the **Lisbon Card,** which provides free city transportation and entrance fees to museums and other attractions, plus discounts on admission to events. For adults, a 1-day pass costs 16€, a 2-day pass costs 27€, and a 3-day pass costs 34€. Children 5 to 11 pay 9.50€ for a 1-day pass, 14€ for a 2-day pass, and 17€ for a 3-day pass. Another tourist office is located across from the general post office in Lisbon on Rua do Arsenal 15, 1100-038 Lisbon (✆ **21/031-27-00;** www.visitlisboa.com). This tourist office is open daily from 9am to 7pm.

CITY LAYOUT **Main Streets & Squares** Lisbon is the westernmost capital of continental Europe. According to legend, it spreads across seven hills, like Rome. That statement has long been outdated—Lisbon now sprawls across more hills than that. Most of the city lies on the north bank of the Tagus.

No one ever claimed that getting around Lisbon was a breeze. Streets rise and fall across the hills, at times dwindling into mere alleyways. Exploring the city, however, is well worth the effort.

Lisbon

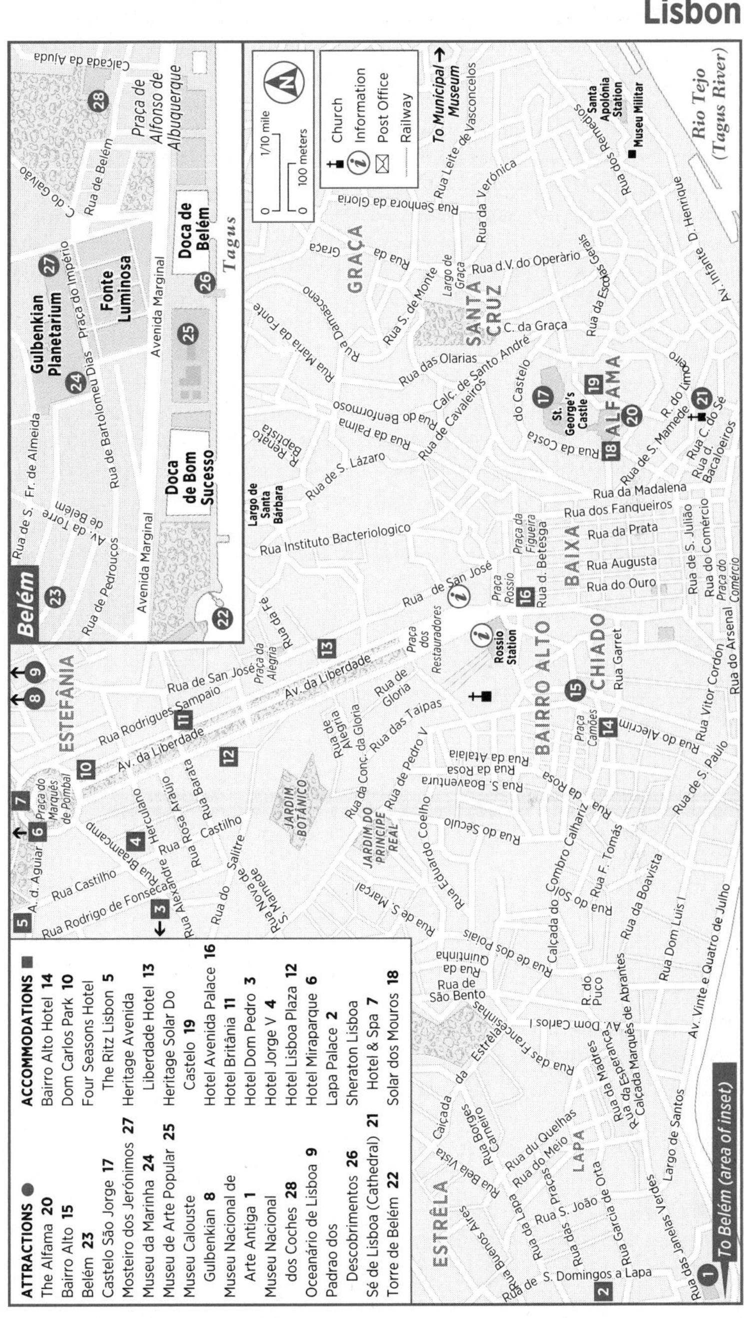
ATTRACTIONS ●
The Alfama 20
Bairro Alto 15
Belém 23
Castelo São Jorge 17
Mosteiro dos Jerónimos 27
Museu da Marinha 24
Museu de Arte Popular 25
Museu Calouste Gulbenkian 8
Museu Nacional de Arte Antiga 1
Museu Nacional dos Coches 28
Oceanário de Lisboa 9
Padrao dos Descobrimentos 26
Sé de Lisboa (Cathedral) 21
Torre de Belém 22
ACCOMMODATIONS ■
Bairro Alto Hotel 14
Dom Carlos Park 10
Four Seasons Hotel The Ritz Lisbon 5
Heritage Avenida Liberdade Hotel 13
Heritage Solar Do Castelo 19
Hotel Avenida Palace 16
Hotel Britânia 11
Hotel Dom Pedro 3
Hotel Jorge V 4
Hotel Lisboa Plaza 12
Hotel Miraparque 6
Lapa Palace 2
Sheraton Lisboa Hotel & Spa 7
Solar dos Mouros 18
Belém
Gulbenkian Planetarium
Fonte Luminosa
Doca de Bom Sucesso
Doca de Belém
Praça de Alfonso de Albuquerque
Tagus
Church
Information
Post Office
Railway
0 1/10 mile
0 100 meters
ESTEFÂNIA
GRAÇA
SANTA CRUZ
BAIRRO ALTO
BAIXA
CHIADO
ALFAMA
ESTRÊLA
LAPA
JARDIM BOTÂNICO
JARDIM DO PRINCIPE REAL
Rossio Station
St. George's Castle
Santa Apolónia Station
Museu Militar
To Municipal Museum →
To Belém (area of inset)
Rio Tejo (Tagus River)
Av. da Liberdade
Rua de San José
Rua Garret
Rua Augusta
Rua do Ouro
Rua da Prata
Rua dos Fanqueiros
Rua da Madalena
Av. Infante D. Henrique
Av. Vinte e Quatro de Julho

Lisbon is best approached through its gateway, **Praça do Comércio (Commerce Square),** bordering the Tagus. It's one of the most perfectly planned squares in Europe, rivaled only by the Piazza dell'Unità d'Italia in Trieste, Italy. Before the 1755 earthquake, Praça do Comércio was known as Terreiro do Paço, the Palace Grounds, because the king and his court lived in now-destroyed buildings on that site. To confuse matters further, English-speaking residents often refer to it as Black Horse Square because of its statue (actually a bronze-green color) of José I.

Today the square is the site of the Stock Exchange and various government ministries. Its center is used as a parking lot, which destroys some of its harmony. In 1908, Carlos I and his elder son, Luís Filipe, were fatally shot here by an assassin. The monarchy held on for another 2 years, but the House of Bragança effectively came to an end that day. Directly west of the square stands the City Hall, fronting Praça do Município. The building, erected in the late 19th century, was designed by the architect Domingos Parente.

Heading north from Black Horse or Commerce Square, you enter the hustle and bustle of **Praça de Dom Pedro IV,** popularly known as the Rossio. The "drunken" undulation of the sidewalks, with their arabesques of black and white, has led to the appellation "the dizzy praça." Here you can sit sipping strong unblended coffee from the former Portuguese provinces in Africa. The statue on the square is that of the Portuguese-born emperor of Brazil.

Opening onto the Rossio is the **Teatro Nacional de Dona Maria II,** a freestanding building whose facade has been preserved. From 1967 to 1970, workers gutted the interior to rebuild it completely. If you arrive by train, you'll enter the **Estação do Rossio,** whose exuberant Manueline architecture is worth seeing.

Separating the Rossio from Avenida da Liberdade is **Praça dos Restauradores,** named in honor of the Restoration, when the Portuguese chose their own king and freed themselves from 60 years of Spanish rule. An obelisk commemorates the event.

Lisbon's main avenue is **Avenida da Liberdade (Avenue of Liberty).** The handsomely laid-out street dates from 1880. Avenida da Liberdade is like a 1.5km-long (1-mile) park, with shade trees, gardens, and center walks for the promenading crowds. Flanking it are fine shops, the headquarters of many major airlines, travel agents, coffeehouses with sidewalk tables, and hotels.

At the top of the avenue is Praça do Marquês de Pombal, with a statue erected in honor of the 18th-century prime minister credited with Lisbon's reconstruction in the aftermath of the earthquake.

Proceeding north, you'll enter Parque Eduardo VII, named in honor of the son of Queen Victoria, who paid a state visit to Lisbon. In the park is the Estufa Fria, a greenhouse well worth a visit.

GETTING AROUND **CARRIS** (**✆ 21/361-30-00;** www.carris.pt) operates the network of funiculars, trains, subways, and buses in Lisbon. The company sells a *bilhete de assinatura turístico* (tourist ticket). A 1-day pass goes for 3.70€. Passes are sold in CARRIS booths, open from 8am to 8pm daily, in most Metro stations and network train stations. You must show a passport to buy a pass.

BY METRO Lisbon's Metro stations are designated by large M signs. A single ticket costs .80€, a day pass 3.70€. One of the most popular trips—and likely to be jampacked on *corrida* (bullfight) days—is from Avenida da República to Campo

Pequeno, the brick building away from the center of the city. Service runs daily from 6:30am to 1am. For more information, call © **21/350-01-15** (www.metrolisboa.pt).

BY BUS & TRAM Lisbon's buses and trams are among the cheapest in Europe. The *eléctricos* (trolley cars, or trams) make the steep run up to the Bairro Alto. The double-decker buses come from London and look as if they need Big Ben in the background to complete the picture. If you're trying to stand on the platform at the back of a jammed bus, you'll need both hands free to hold on.

The basic fare on a bus or eléctrico is 1.40€ if you buy the ticket from the driver (© **21/361-30-00;** www.carris.pt). The transportation system within the city limits is divided into zones ranging from one to five. The fare depends on how many zones you traverse. Buses and eléctricos run daily from 6am to 1am.

At the foot of the Santa Justa Elevator, on Rua Áurea, there's a stand with schedules pinpointing the zigzagging tram and bus routes. Your hotel concierge should have information.

BY ELECTRIC TRAIN A smooth-running, modern electric train system connects Lisbon to all the towns and villages along the Portuguese Riviera. There's only one class of seat, and the rides are cheap and generally comfortable. You can board the train at the waterfront Cais do Sodré Station in Lisbon and head up the coast all the way to Cascais.

The electric train does not run to Sintra. For Sintra, you must go to the Estação do Rossio station, opening onto Praça de Dom Pedro IV, or the Rossio, where frequent connections can be made. The one-way fare from Lisbon to Cascais, Estoril, or Sintra is 1.80€ to 4€ per person (© **21/261-30-00;** www.carris.pt).

BY FUNICULAR Lisbon has a trio of funiculars: the **Glória,** which goes from Praça dos Restauradores to Rua São Pedro de Alcântara; the **Bica,** from the Calçada do Combro to Rua da Boavista; and the **Lavra,** from the eastern side of Avenida da Liberdade to Campo Mártires da Pátria. A one-way ticket on any of these costs 1.40€ (© **21/261-30-00;** www.carris.pt).

BY TAXI Taxis in Lisbon tend to be inexpensive and are a popular means of transport for all but the most economy-minded tourists. They usually are diesel-engine Mercedes. The basic fare is 2.50€ for the first 153m (502 ft.), .10€ for each extra 162m (531 ft.), plus 20% from 10pm to 6am. The law allows drivers to tack on another 50% to your bill if your luggage weighs more than 30 kilograms (66 lbs.). Portuguese tip about 20% of the modest fare. For a Rádio Táxi, call © **21/811-90-00** (www.retalis.pt).

Many visitors stay at a Costa do Sol resort hotel, such as the Palácio in Estoril or the Cidadela in Cascais. If you stay there, you'll probably find taxi connections from Lisbon prohibitively expensive. Far preferable for Costa do Sol visitors is the electric train system (see above).

BY CAR In congested Lisbon, driving is extremely difficult and potentially dangerous—the city has an alarmingly high accident rate. It always feels like rush hour in Lisbon. Parking is seemingly impossible. Wait to rent a car until you're making excursions from the capital. If you drive into Lisbon from another town or city, call ahead and ask at your hotel for the nearest garage or other place to park. Leave your vehicle there until you're ready to depart. Car-rental kiosks at the airport and in the city center include **Avis,** Av. Praia da Vitória 12C (✆ **21/351-45-60;** www.avis.com); **Hertz,** Rua Castilho 72 (✆ **21/381-24-30;** www.hertz.com); and **Budget,** Rua Castillo 167B (✆ **21/386-05-16;** www.budget.com).

[FastFACTS] LISBON

American Express **Travel Store** represents American Express in Lisbon. Its offices are at Campo Grande 35-2A (✆ **21/356-53-00**) and at the Aeroporto de Lisboa (✆ **91/200-05-13**).

Business Hours **Banks** generally are open Monday to Friday 8:30am to 3pm. **Shops** are open, in general, Monday to Friday 9am to 1pm and 3 to 7pm, and Saturday 9am to 1pm.

Currency Portugal uses the **euro** (€). At press time, 1€ = US$1.40.

Currency Exchange Currency-exchange booths at Santa Apolónia station and at the airport are both open 24 hours a day. ATMs offer the best exchange rates. They pepper the streets of the central Baixa district and are also found less frequently in other parts of the city. The post office (see "Mail," below) will exchange money as well.

Doctors & Dentists In case of a medical emergency, ask at your hotel or call your embassy and ask the staff there to recommend an English-speaking physician. Or try the **British Hospital,** Rua Saraiva de Carvalho 49 (✆ **21/394-31-00**), where the telephone operator, staff, and doctors speak English.

The reception staff at most hotels maintains lists of local, usually English-speaking dentists who are available for dental emergencies. Some of them will contact a well-recommended dental clinic, **Clinica Medica e Dentaria da Praça d'Espanha,** Rua Dom Luís de Noronha 32 (✆ **21/796-74-57**). Some of the staff members speak English.

Drugstores **Farmácia Valmor,** Av. Visconde Valmor 60B (✆ **21/781-97-43**), is centrally located and well stocked.

Embassies The embassy of the **United States,** on Avenida das Forças Armadas (Sete Rios), 1600 Lisboa (✆ **21/727-33-00;** http://portugal.usembassy.gov), is open Monday to Friday 8am to 12:30pm and 1:30 to 5pm. The embassy of **Canada,** Av. da Liberdade 200, EDIT Victoria 4th Floor, 1269 Lisboa (✆ **21/316-46-00;** www.canadainternational.gc.ca/portugal), is open Monday to Friday 9am to noon and 2 to 4pm (to 1pm Fri July–Aug). The embassy of the **United Kingdom,** Rua São Bernardo 33, 1249 Lisboa (✆ **21/392-40-00;** http://ukinportugal.fco.gov.uk/en), is open Monday to Thursday 9:30 to 11:30am and 3 to 4:30pm, Friday 9am to 12:30pm. The embassy of the **Republic of Ireland,** Rua de Imprensa à Estrela 1, 1200 Lisboa (✆ **21/392-94-40;** www.embassyofireland.pt), is open Monday to Friday 9:30am to 12:30pm and 2:30 to 4:30pm. The embassy of **Australia,** Av. de Liberdade 200, 1250 Lisboa (✆ **21/310-15-00;** www.portugal.embassy.gov.au), is open Monday to Friday 9 to 11:30am and 3 to 4:30pm. **New Zealanders** should go to the British Embassy.

Emergencies To call the police or an ambulance, telephone ✆ **112.**

Internet Access You can check your e-mail at **Cyber.bica,** Duques de Bragança 7 (✆ **21/322-50-04;** www.cyberbica.com), in the Chiado district (Metro: Baixa-Chiado). It's open Monday to Friday 11am to midnight.

Mail While in Portugal, you can have your mail directed to your hotel (or hotels), to the American Express representative, or to Poste Restante (General Delivery) in Lisbon. You must present your passport to pick up mail. The main post office, Correio Geral, in Lisbon is at Praça do Restauradores, 1100 Lisboa (✆ **21/323-89-71**). It's open Monday to Friday 8am to 10pm, and Saturday and Sunday 9am to 6pm.

Police Call ✆ **112.**

Safety Lisbon used to be one of the safest capitals of Europe, but that hasn't been true for a long time. It's now quite dangerous to walk around at night. Many travelers report being held up at knifepoint. Some bandits operate in pairs or in trios. Not only do they take your money but they demand your ATM code. One of the robbers holds a victim captive while another withdraws money. (If the number proves to be fake, the robber might return and harm the victim.) During the day, pickpockets galore prey on tourists, aiming for wallets, purses, and cameras. Congested areas are particularly hazardous. Avoid walking at night, especially if you're alone.

Taxes Lisbon imposes no city taxes. However, the national value-added tax (VAT) applies to purchases and services. It ranges from 8% to 30%. Known in Portugal as the **IVA,** the amount is almost always written into the bottom line of the bill for any purchase. Hotel and restaurant bills are taxed at 18%. Car rentals are subject to an additional 18% tax. Deluxe goods such as jewelry, fur, and expensive imported liquors include a 30% built-in tax. To get a refund on purchases that qualify (ask the shopkeeper), present your passport to the salesperson and ask for the special stamped form. Present the form with your purchases at the booth marked for IVA tax refunds at the airport. You'll get your money refunded right at the booth. For VAT refunds, you can also apply at **Global Refund** (www.globalrefund.com).

Telephone The **country code** for Portugal is **351.** The **city code** for Lisbon is now **21;** use this code when calling from anywhere outside or inside Portugal—even within Lisbon itself.

You can make a local call in Lisbon in one of the many telephone booths. For most long-distance telephone calls, particularly transatlantic calls, go to the central post office (see "Mail," above). Give an assistant the number, and he or she will make the call for you, billing you at the end. Some phones are equipped for using calling cards, including American Express and Visa. You can also purchase phone cards. Lisbon's city code is ✆ 01.

Tipping Hotels add a service charge (known as *servio*), which is divided among the staff, but individual tipping is also the rule. Tip 1€ to the **bellhop** for running an errand, 1€ to the **doorman** who hails you a cab, 1€ to the **porter** for each piece of luggage carried, and 1.50€ to the **chambermaid.** Figure on tipping about 20% of your **taxi** fare for short runs. For longer treks, 15% is adequate.

Where to Stay

IN THE CENTER

Very Expensive

Four Seasons Hotel Ritz Lisbon ★★★ The 10-floor Ritz, built by the dictator Salazar in the late 1950s on one of Lisbon's seven hills, is now operated by Four Seasons. Its suites boast the finest decoration you'll see in any major Portuguese hotel: slender mahogany canopied beds with fringed swags, marquetry desks, satinwood dressing tables, and plush carpeting. Some of the soundproof, spacious, modern rooms have terraces opening onto Edward VII Park; each boasts a marble bathroom. The least desirable rooms are the even-numbered ones facing the street. The odd-numbered accommodations, opening onto views of the park, are the best. Some studios with double beds are rented as singles, attracting business travelers.

Rua Rodrigo de Fonseca 88, 1099-039 Lisboa. ✆ **800/819-5053** in the U.S., or 21/381-14-00. Fax 21/383-17-83. www.fourseasons.com. 282 units. 355€–600€ double; from 975€ suite. AE, DC, MC, V. Free parking. Metro: Marquês de Pombal. Bus: 1, 2, 9, or 32. **Amenities:** Restaurant; bar; babysitting; concierge; exercise room; indoor heated pool; room service; spa. *In room:* A/C, TV/DVD, CD player, hair dryer, minibar, Wi-Fi (20€ per 24 hr.).

Hotel Dom Pedro ★★ Rated five stars by the Portuguese government and associated with some of the most glamorous hotels of the Algarve and Madeira, this bastion of luxury is in the central Amoreiras district, across from one of the city's biggest shopping centers. A hypermodern sheathing of reflective glass covers its 21 stories. The interior is as conservative and rich-looking as the exterior is futuristic. The good-size guest rooms are richly furnished, usually with heraldic symbols or medallions woven subtly through the fabrics and wallpapers.

Av. Engenheiro Duarte Pacheco 24, 1070-109 Lisboa. ✆ **21/389-66-00.** Fax 21/389-66-01. www.dompedro.com. 263 units. 180€–395€ double; 330€–630€ suites. AE, DC, MC, V. Parking 17€. Metro: Marquês de Pombal. **Amenities:** 2 restaurants; 2 bars; airport transfers (35€); babysitting; concierge; room service; Wi-Fi (6€ per hour, in lobby). *In room:* A/C, TV, hair dryer, minibar.

Lapa Palace ★★★ ☺ In a palace built in 1870 for the count of Valença, this government-rated five-star hotel, purchased by Orient Express in 1998, is the most talked-about hotel in Lisbon. We never thought we'd see a hotel replace the Four Seasons Hotel Ritz Lisbon as the city's premier address, but Lapa has done just that. All but about 20 of the rooms are in a modern six-story wing. The spacious guest rooms in both sections contain amply proportioned marble surfaces, reproductions of French and English furniture, and a classic design inspired by a late-18th-century model. The marble bathrooms are among the city's most elegant, often adorned with bas-reliefs. Each unit opens onto a balcony. The older rooms have more charm and grace; many of the newer ones open onto panoramic vistas of Lisbon. The public areas have multicolored ceiling frescoes and richly patterned marble floors.

Rua do Pau da Bandeira 4, 1249-021 Lisboa. ✆ **21/394-94-94.** Fax 21/395-06-65. www.lapapalace.com. 109 units. 400€–725€ double; from 1,075€ suite. Rates include buffet breakfast. AE, DC, MC, V. Free parking. Bus: 13 or 27. **Amenities:** 2 restaurants; bar; babysitting; children's center; concierge; exercise room; 2 pools (1 heated indoors); room service; spa; Wi-Fi (15€ per 24 hr., in lobby). *In room:* A/C, TV, hair dryer, minibar.

Expensive

Heritage Avenida Liberdade Hotel ★ This sleekly modern hotel in a restored late-18th-century palace opened its doors in 2006. It's already considered one of Lisbon's best hotels, partly because the decor was created by famed architect Miguel Câncio Martins, known for such landmarks as the Buddha Bar in Paris. His designs combine traditional architectural features with the most modern of technology, a winning combination the way he does it. Though the 18th-century exterior was retained, the interior was virtually re-created to fit modern living standards. Rooms range from midsize to spacious, and are glamorously laid out. The six-floor hotel also boasts the sort of personalized service you'd expect from a small property.

Av. da Liberdade 28, 1250-145 Lisboa. ✆ **21/340-40-40.** Fax 21/340-40-44. www.heritage.pt. 42 units. 220€–320€ double; 253€–410€ triple. Children 11 and under stay free in parent's room. AE, DC, MC, V. Parking nearby 30€. Metro: Restauradores. **Amenities:** Bar; babysitting; exercise room; indoor heated pool; room service. *In room:* A/C, TV/DVD, CD player, hair dryer, minibar, Wi-Fi (free).

Hotel Avenida Palace ★★ Built in 1892, Hotel Avenida Palace is the grandest old-fashioned hotel in Lisbon, an antiques-filled link to the past. Its convenient location right at the Rossio is terribly noisy, but inside, it is another world entirely. Still the grand dame of Lisbon hotels, it retains its 19th-century aura and elegance, with a marble staircase, beautiful salons, and silk brocades. The Belle Epoque–style Palace offers all the modern comforts, especially in its restored guest rooms. They're soundproof and elegantly furnished, often in 17th- or 18th-century style.

Rua 1er Dezembro 123, 1200-359 Lisboa. ✆ **21/321-81-00.** Fax 21/342-28-84. www.hotel-avenida-palace.pt. 82 units. 176€–450€ double; 198€–550€ junior suite; from 234€ suite. Rates include buffet breakfast. AE, DC, MC, V. Free parking. Metro: Restauradores. Tram: 35. **Amenities:** Bar; babysitting; exercise room; room service. *In room:* A/C, TV, hair dryer, minibar, Wi-Fi (6€ per hour).

Hotel Lisboa Plaza ★★ In the heart of the city, this boutique hotel is a charmer. A family-owned and -operated government-rated four-star hotel, it has many appealing Art Nouveau touches, including the facade. The hotel was built in 1953 and has been frequently overhauled and modernized since. A well-known Portuguese designer, Graça Viterbo, decorated it in contemporary classic style. The midsize guest rooms—with well-stocked marble bathrooms and double-glazed windows—are well styled and comfortable. Try for a unit in the rear, looking out over the botanical gardens.

Travessa do Salitre 7, Av. da Liberdade, 1269-066 Lisboa. ✆ **21/321-82-18.** Fax 21/347-16-30. www.heritage.pt. 106 units. 99€–235€ double; 203€–450€ suite. Children 11 and under stay free in parent's room. AE, DC, MC, V. Parking nearby 10€. Metro: Avenida. Bus: 1, 2, 36, or 44. **Amenities:** Restaurant; bar; babysitting; exercise room; room service. *In room:* A/C, TV/DVD, CD player, hair dryer, minibar, Wi-Fi (free).

Sheraton Lisboa Hotel & Spa ★★ Built in 1972, and completely restored in 2007, this deluxe hotel is sheltered in a 25-floor skyscraper lying at a traffic-clogged intersection a bit removed from the center of the action, a few blocks north of Praça do Marquês de Pombal. The impressive pink-marble lobby features chandeliers and fancy carpeting. The guest rooms are small to midsize, but have been given a trendy look with all new furniture. The most desirable rooms are in the tower, opening onto views of the Vasco da Gama Bridge, the Tagus, or the city. There's also a private lounge and bar, as well as a bar on the 26th floor, with a panoramic view of Lisbon and dancing to live music nightly.

Rua Latino Coelho 1, 1069-025 Lisboa. ✆ **800/325-3535** in the U.S., or 21/312-00-00. Fax 21/354-71-64. www.sheratonlisboa.com. 366 units. 220€ double; from 415€ suite. AE, DC, MC, V. Parking 19€. Bus: 1, 36, 44, or 45. **Amenities:** Restaurant; 2 bars; babysitting; concierge; exercise room; outdoor pool; room service; spa. *In room:* A/C, TV, hair dryer, minibar, Wi-Fi (18€ per 24 hr.).

Moderate

Dom Carlos Park This central hotel lies just off Praça do Marquês de Pombal but it charges only a fraction of what its rivals in the neighborhood do. The curvy facade is all glass, lending an outdoorsy feeling reinforced by trees and beds of orange and red canna. The good-size guest rooms are paneled in reddish Portuguese wood; even so, they're rather uninspired and functional. An occasional hand-carved cherub softens the Nordic-inspired furnishings. The hotel faces a triangular park dedicated to Camilo Castelo Branco, a 19th-century poet. The lobby lounge is satisfactory; more inviting is the mezzanine salon, where sofas and chairs face the park.

Av. Duque de Loulé 121, 1050-089 Lisboa. ✆ **21/351-25-90.** Fax 21/352-07-28. www.domcarlospark.com. 76 units. 138€–170€ double; from 196€ junior suite. Rates include buffet breakfast. AE, DC, MC, V. Parking 11€. Metro: Marquês de Pombal. Bus: 1, 36, 44, or 45. **Amenities:** Restaurant; bar; babysitting; room service; Wi-Fi (free, in lobby). *In room:* A/C, TV, hair dryer, minibar.

Hotel Britânia ★ This boutique hotel is the only surviving original Art Deco inn in Lisbon. It was designed in 1942 by the well-known Portuguese architect Vassiano Branco. Located about a block from the Liberdade, it boasts a loyal clientele and much of its original decor, including murals in the bar and candelabras in the public lounge. The six-story hotel hasn't been renovated in quite a while, but there is yearly maintenance and upgrading on an as-needed basis. A former town house, it originally housed studio apartments, which explains why the bedrooms are much larger than those of most other competitors in Lisbon.

Rua Rodrigues Sampaio 17, 1150-278 Lisboa. ✆ **21/315-50-16.** Fax 21/315-50-21. www.heritage.pt. 32 units. 130€–245€ double. AE, DC, MC, V. Parking 15€. Metro: Avenida. Bus: 1, 2, 11, or 21. **Amenities:** Bar; room service. *In room:* A/C, TV/DVD, CD player, hair dryer, minibar, Wi-Fi (free).

Inexpensive

Hotel Jorge V The Jorge V is a neat little hotel with a 1960s design. It boasts a choice location a block off the noisy Avenida da Liberdade. Its facade contains rows of balconies roomy enough for guests to have breakfast or afternoon refreshments. A tiny elevator runs to a variety of aging rooms, which aren't generous in size but are comfortable; all have small tile bathrooms.

Rua Mouzinho da Silveira 3, 1250-165 Lisboa. ✆ **21/356-25-25.** Fax 21/315-03-19. www.hoteljorgev.com. 49 units. 79€–111€ double; 110€–135€ suite. Rates include continental breakfast. AE, DC, MC, V. Free parking. Metro: Avenida or Marquês de Pombal. **Amenities:** Bar; room service. *In room:* A/C, TV, hair dryer, minibar.

Hotel Miraparque Miraparque lies on a secluded, quiet street opposite Edward VII Park. The small guest rooms haven't been called modern since the 1960s, but are well maintained. The hotel is a little worn but still recommendable because of its central location and low prices. The wood-paneled lounges are furnished in simulated brown leather.

Av. Sidónio Pais 12, 1050-214 Lisboa. ✆ **21/352-42-86.** Fax 21/357-89-20. www.miraparque.com. 100 units. 65€–100€ double; 95€–125€ triple. Rates include buffet breakfast. AE, DC, MC, V. Parking (in nearby lot) 15€. Metro: Parque. Bus: 91. **Amenities:** Restaurant; bar; babysitting; room service. *In room:* A/C, TV, hair dryer, minibar, Wi-Fi (2€ per hour).

IN THE ALFAMA

Expensive

Heritage Solar Do Castelo ★★ 🎁 Lying inside the walls of the formidable 18th-century St. George's Castle (Lisbon's first royal palace), this hotel is reached only on foot because vehicles are off-limits. Some of the medieval architecture remains, such as an old cistern, part of the original palace. Although the building is antique, the bedrooms are in a high-quality contemporary design, mixing old elements such as original stone fortifications with contemporary fabrics and furnishings. Each room comes with a balcony overlooking a picture-perfect courtyard.

Rua das Cozinhas 2, 1100-181 Lisboa. ✆ **21/880-60-50.** Fax 21/887-09-07. www.heritage.pt. 14 units. 145€–340€ double. AE, DC, MC, V. Parking not available at the hotel. Metro: Rossio. Bus: 37. **Amenities:** Bar; babysitting; room service. *In room:* A/C, TV/DVD, CD player, hair dryer, Wi-Fi (free).

Moderate

Solar dos Mouros ★ 🎁 One of the most stylish small hotels in Lisbon occupies a tangerine-colored, steeply vertical antique building on a quiet street that runs parallel to the base of St. George's Castle. All of the rooms have a starkly modern minimalist decor that might remind you of a photo set from *Architectural Digest*. Rooms have hardwood floors, cutting-edge furniture, and lots of space; all of them open onto a starkly contemporary staircase. The location in the heart of the Alfama means you'll be amid some of the city's hippest and most avant-garde attractions.

Rua Milagre de Santo António 6, 1100-351 Lisboa. ✆ **21/885-49-40.** Fax 21/885-49-45. www.solardosmouros.com. 12 units. 119€–259€ double. AE, DC, MC, V. No parking. Tram: 28. **Amenities:** Bar; concierge; room service. *In room:* A/C, TV, CD player, minibar, Wi-Fi (free).

IN THE BAIRRO ALTO

Expensive

Bairro Alto Hotel ★★★ With a location that's unmatched for its association with literary, historic, and Romantic-era Portugal, this 2005 reincarnation of Lisbon's oldest hotel sits within an ocher-colored six-story baroque building within a few steps of the square (Praça Luís de Camões) that commemorates Portugal's most important literary patriarch. It originated in 1845 when it was rebuilt from the rubble of Lisbon's Great Earthquake less than a century before as the Hotel de l'Europe, then the capital's most visible hotel. Huge effort was taken to blend the historic with the cutting edge here, from the ample use of exotic hardwoods, to the presence of all the electronic accessories that the postmillennium generation would expect. Bedrooms and their furnishings are rich with antecedents to Portugal's imperial past, yet updated with a sense of upscale minimalism and with lots of postmodern amenities.

Praça Luís de Camões 8, 1200-243 Lisboa. ✆ **21/340-82-88.** Fax 21/340-82-00. www.bairroaltohotel.com. 55 units. 385€–475€ double; 530€–650€ suites. Rates include buffet breakfast. AE, DC, MC, V. Parking 15€. Metro: Baixa/Chiado. **Amenities:** Restaurant; bar; babysitting; concierge; exercise room; room service. *In room:* A/C, TV/DVD, hair dryer, minibar, Wi-Fi (5€ per hour).

Where to Dine

IN THE CENTER

Very Expensive

Casa da Comida ★★★ FRENCH/TRADITIONAL PORTUGUESE Local gourmets tout Casa da Comida as offering some of the finest food in Lisbon. The dining room is handsomely decorated, the bar is done in the French Empire style, and there's a charming walled garden. Specialties include lobster with vegetables, roast kid with herbs, a medley of shellfish, and *faisão à convento de Alcântara* (stewed pheasant marinated in port wine for a day). The cellar contains an excellent selection of wines. The food is often more imaginative here than at some of the other top-rated choices. The chef is extraordinarily attentive to the quality of his ingredients, and the menu never fails to deliver some delightful surprises.

Travessa de Amoreiras 1 (close to Jardim de Las Amoreiras). ✆ **21/388-53-76.** www.casadacomida.pt. Reservations required. Main courses 32€–65€. AE, DC, MC, V. Tues–Fri 1–3pm; Mon–Sat 8–11pm. Metro: Rato.

Clara Restaurante ★★ INTERNATIONAL/PORTUGUESE On a hillside amid decaying villas and city squares, this green-tile house owned by Célia Pimpista contains an elegant restaurant with a number of different seating areas. You can enjoy a drink under the ornate ceiling of the bar or grab a seat in the indoor dining room—perhaps near the large marble fireplace, in range of the soft music played during dinner; during lunch, you can sit near the garden terrace's plants and fountain. Specialties include tournedos Clara, stuffed rabbit with red-wine sauce, four kinds of pasta, codfish Clara, filet of sole with orange, pheasant with grapes, and Valencian paella. As in many of Lisbon's top-rated restaurants, these dishes aren't innovative in any way, but they're often prepared flawlessly.

Campo dos Mártires da Pátria 49. ✆ **21/885-30-53.** www.lisboa-clara.pt. Reservations required. Main courses 25€–45€. AE, DC, MC, V. Mon–Fri 12:30–3pm; Mon–Sat 7:30–11:30pm. Closed Aug 1–15. Metro: Avenida.

Expensive

António Clara ★★ INTERNATIONAL/PORTUGUESE Even if it weren't one of the capital's best restaurants, this exquisite turn-of-the-20th-century Art Nouveau villa would be famous as the former home of one of Portugal's most revered architects, Miguel Ventura Terra (1866–1918), whose photograph hangs amid polished antiques and gilded mirrors, dating from 1890. You might enjoy a before- or after-dinner drink in the 19th-century salon, where griffins snarl from the pink-shaded chandelier, or in the ground-floor bar, which contains an art gallery with frequent shows. The dining room itself is one of the loveliest in Lisbon, and the updated classic cooking served there is guaranteed to please. Most of the flavors are sublime. Meals include such specialties as paella for two, chateaubriand béarnaise, monkfish rice, codfish *Margarida da Praça* (baked with tomatoes and onions and served with deep-fried sweet potatoes), and beef Wellington. The dishes might be familiar, but only the highest-quality ingredients are used. Seafood dishes change often to reflect the best of market offerings.

Av. da República 38. ✆ **21/799-42-80.** Reservations recommended. Main courses 15€–36€. AE, DC, MC, V. Mon–Sat 12:30–3pm and 7:30–10:30pm. Metro: Saldanha.

Restaurante Lapa INTERNATIONAL/ITALIAN/PORTUGUESE This is the most upscale and most highly recommended restaurant in Lisbon's major government-rated five-star hotel, the Lapa Palace (see earlier in this chapter). The dignified, elegant dining room has a view of one of the most lavish gardens in this exclusive neighborhood. A la carte items available at lunch and dinner vary with the season. They might include fresh salmon fried with sage, lamb chops with mint sauce, a succulent version of a traditional Portuguese *feijoada* (meat stew), and perfectly prepared duck breast baked with pears.

In the Lapa Palace Hotel, Rua do Pau de Bandeira 4. ✆ **21/394-94-01.** Reservations recommended. Main courses 25€–37€. AE, DC, MC, V. Daily 12:30–3pm and 7:30–10:30pm. Closed for lunch in summer. Tram: 15.

Moderate

Bachus ★★ INTERNATIONAL/PORTUGUESE Amusing murals cover the wood-paneled facade of this deluxe restaurant; inside, the decor is elaborate and sophisticated. The ambience is a mixture of a private salon in a Russian palace, a turn-of-the-20th-century English club, and a stylized Manhattan bistro. A brass staircase winds around a column of illuminated glass to the dining room. Menu specialties change frequently, depending on what ingredients are available. Full meals might include mixed grill Bachus, chateaubriand with béarnaise, mountain goat, beef stroganoff, shrimp Bachus, or other daily specials.

Largo da Trindade 8–9. ✆ **21/342-28-28.** Reservations recommended. Main courses 17€–26€. AE, DC, MC, V. Tues–Fri noon–2pm and 7pm–midnight; Sat–Sun 6pm–2am. Metro: Chiado. Bus: 58.

Restaurant 33 ★ INTERNATIONAL Restaurant 33 is a treasure. Decorated in a style evocative of an English hunting lodge, it lies near many recommended hotels, including the Four Seasons Hotel Ritz Lisbon (p. 798). It specializes in succulent seafood dishes, including shellfish rice served in a crab shell, smoked salmon, and lobster Tour d'Argent; it also features tender, well-flavored pepper steak. One reader from New Rochelle, New York, found her meal here "flawless." A pianist performs during dinner. You can enjoy a glass of port in the small bar at the entrance or in the private garden.

Rua Alexandre Herculano 33A. ✆ **21/354-60-79.** Reservations recommended. Main courses 18€–32€. AE, DC, MC, V. Mon–Fri 12:30–3pm and 8–10:30pm; Sat 8–10:30pm. Metro: Marquês Do Pombal. Bus: 6 or 9.

Inexpensive

Cervejaria Brilhante PORTUGUESE/SEAFOOD Lisboans from every walk of life stop here for a stein of beer and *mariscos* (seafood). The tavern is decorated with stone arches, wood-paneled walls, and pictorial tiles of sea life. The front window is packed with an appetizing array of king crabs, oysters, lobsters, baby clams, shrimp, and even barnacles. The price changes every day, depending on the market, and you pay by the kilo. This is hearty, robust eating, although attracting a waiter's attention is a challenge.

Rua das Portas de Santo Antão 105 (opposite the Coliseu). ✆ **21/346-14-07.** Main courses 12€–22€. AE, DC, MC, V. Daily noon–midnight. Metro: Rossio or Restauradores. Bus: 1, 2, 36, 44, or 45.

Cervejaria Trindade PORTUGUESE This combination German beer hall and Portuguese tavern, in operation since 1836, is the oldest tavern in Lisbon, owned by the brewers of Sagres beer. It was built on the foundations of the 13th-century Convento dos Frades Tinos, which was destroyed by the 1755 earthquake. Surrounded by walls tiled with Portuguese scenes, you can order tasty little steaks and heaps of crisp french-fried potatoes. Many Portuguese diners prefer the *bife na frigideira* (steak with mustard sauce and a fried egg, served in a clay frying pan). But the tavern also features shellfish; the house specialties are *amêijoas* (clams) *à Trindade* and giant prawns. Meals are served in the inner courtyard on sunny days.

Rua Nova de Trindade 20C. ✆ **21/342-35-06.** www.cervejariatrindade.pt. Main courses 8€–33€. AE, DC, MC, V. Daily noon–2am. Metro: Chiado. Bus: 15, 20, 51, or 100.

Pastelaria Versailles ★ CAFE/PASTRIES This is the most famous teahouse in Lisbon, and it has been declared part of the "national patrimony." Some patrons reputedly have been coming here since it opened in 1932. In older days, the specialty was *licungo,* the famed black tea of Mozambique; you can still order it, but nowadays many drinkers enjoy English brands. (The Portuguese claim that they introduced the custom of tea drinking to the English court after Catherine of Bragança married Charles II in 1662.) The decor is rich, with chandeliers, gilt mirrors, stained-glass windows, tall stucco ceilings, and black-and-white marble floors. You can also order milkshakes, mineral water, fresh orange juice, beer, and liquor. Snacks include codfish balls and toasted ham-and-cheese sandwiches; platters of simple but wholesome Portuguese fare are on offer, too.

Av. da República 15A. ✆ **21/354-63-40.** www.pastelariaversailles.com. Sandwiches 3€; pastries 1€; *plats du jour* 9.50€–22€. AE, MC, V. Daily 7:30am–10pm. Metro: Saldanha.

IN THE BAIRRO ALTO

Expensive

Tasquinha d'Adelaide ★ 🎁 REGIONAL PORTUGUESE At the western edge of the Bairro Alto, about 2 blocks northeast of the Alcântara subway station and

2 blocks west of the Basilica da Estrela, this small restaurant is cramped and convivial. It's known for the culinary specialties of Trás-os-Montes, a rugged province in northeast Portugal, and for its homey, unpretentious warmth. Robust specialties include *alheiras fritas com arroz de grelos* (tripe with collard greens and rice) and *lulas grelhadas* (grilled squid served in a black clay casserole). To finish, try Dona Adelaide's *charcade de ovos* (a secret recipe made with egg yolks). Although we like this hearty cooking, the flavors might be too pungent for some palates.

Rua do Patrocínio 70–74. ✆ **21/396-22-39.** Reservations recommended. Main courses 13€–29€. AE, DC, MC, V. Mon–Sat 12:30–4pm and 8pm–2am. Metro: Rato. Tram: 25, 28, or 30. Bus: 9, 15, or 28.

Moderate

Comida de Santo 🎁 BRAZILIAN Opening in the early 1980s, this was the first all-Brazilian restaurant in Lisbon. At the edge of the Bairro Alto, in a century-old former private house, it contains only 12 tables. Recorded Brazilian music plays softly from the bar, lending a New World flavor, and a quintet of oversize panels depicts huge, idealized jungle scenes. The appropriate beginning of any meal is a deceptively potent *caipirinha* (aguardiente cocktail with limes and sugar). Main courses include spicy versions of *feijoada* (meat-and-bean stew), *picanha* (boiled Brazilian beef with salt), *vatapá* (peppery shrimp), and several versions of succulent grilled fish. The place is incredibly popular; reservations are very important.

Calçada Engenheiro Miguel Pais 39. ✆ **21/396-33-39.** www.comidadesanto.pt. Reservations recommended. Main courses 15€–18€; tasting menu 38€. AE, DC, MC, V. Daily 12:30–3:30pm and 7:30pm–1am. Metro: Rato. Bus: 58.

Consenso ★★ CONTINENTAL/PORTUGUESE Set within the cellar of the palace where the Marquês de Pombal (rebuilder of Lisbon after the earthquake of 1755) was born, this restaurant manages to be chic, historically conscious, and trendy all at the same time. It consists of four separate rooms, each with an individualized decor based on air (the bar), fire (*trompe l'oeil* flames adorn the ceiling, and an iron stove sends warmth into the room), earth, and water—check out their respective color schemes. Impeccably prepared menu items include marinated salmon with citrus pâté, bacon with dates, grilled monkfish and grouper served with shrimp-studded rice, and monkfish loin in a spicy cream sauce. Veal medallions "à la Consenso" are served with shellfish and shrimp.

Rua da Academia das Ciências 1-1A. ✆ **21/346-86-11.** www.restauranteconsenso.com. Reservations recommended. Main courses 13€–30€. AE, DC, MC, V. Mon–Sat 7:30–11:30pm. Closed holidays. Metro: Chiado. Bus: 28, 58, 92, or 100.

WEST OF THE CENTER

Moderate

Espalha Brasas 🎁 PORTUGUESE/TAPAS This is our favorite of the many shoulder-to-shoulder restaurants lined up at the Alcântara Docks, although part of your evening's entertainment will involve picking whichever of the 20 or so cheek-by-jowl restaurants you actually prefer. You'll enter a high-ceilinged room whose centerpiece is a weather-beaten wooden statue of a nude male beside stairs leading to an upstairs balcony with additional tables. The setting is comfortably cluttered and amiable, with candlelit tables and a display of whatever fresh seafood and meats can be grilled to your preference. The finest menu items include every imaginable kind of meat or fish, grilled the way you prefer, as well as daily specials that include rice studded with either turbot and prawns or marinated duck meat, baked haunch of pork, and codfish stuffed with prawns and spinach.

Doca de Santa Amaro, Armazém 12. Alcântara. ✆ **21/396-20-59.** www.espalhabrasas.eu. Reservations recommended for dinner Fri-Sat nights only. Main courses 11€-27€. AE, MC, V. Sept-July Mon-Sat noon-1am; Aug daily 7:30pm-1am. Bus: 57. Tram: 15 or 18.

Nariz de Vinho Tinto ★ PORTUGUESE This is one of our favorite restaurants in Lisbon—and known only to the most discerning of palates—so don't tell anyone about it. In the elegant Lapa district, the restaurant—"Red Wine Nose" in English—is owned by Antonio Ignacio. He gives equal attention to his wines as he does to his market-fresh produce. In two small dining rooms, decorated with cookbooks and wine bottles, he serves a cuisine that raises many dishes to gastronomic heights for Lisbon. His *pata negra* ham, for example, coming from the black-hoofed pig, is the single best platter of this dish we've ever tasted in Lisbon. Try his deeply smoky "game sausage" with its crackly skin and tantalizing filling, or else his cod roasted with ham fat (don't tell your doctor). Even the turnip tops cooked here are a savory treat and supergreen.

Rua do Conde 75. ✆ **21/395-30-35.** www.narizvinhotinto.com. Reservations required. Main courses 13€-30€. AE, DC, MC, V. Tues-Fri 12:30-3pm; Tues-Sun 7:45-11pm. Metro: Rato. Bus: 7 or 27.

Seeing the Sights

THE MAIN NEIGHBORHOODS

THE ALFAMA East of Praça do Comércio lies the oldest district, the Alfama. Saved only in part from the devastation of the 1755 earthquake, the Alfama was the Moorish section of the capital. Nowadays it's home in some parts to stevedores, fishermen, and *varinas* (fishwives). Overlooking the Alfama is **Castelo São Jorge,** or St. George's Castle, a Visigothic fortification that was later used by the Romans. On the way to the Alfama, on Rua dos Bacalhoeiros, stands another landmark, the **Casa dos Bicos (House of the Pointed Stones),** an early-16th-century town house whose facade is studded with diamond-shaped stones. Be careful of muggers in parts of the Alfama at night.

BAIRRO ALTO Continuing your ascent, you'll arrive at the Bairro Alto (Upper City). This sector, reached by trolley car, occupies one of the legendary seven hills of Lisbon. Many of its buildings were left fairly intact by the 1755 earthquake. Containing much of the charm and color of the Alfama, it's the location of some of the finest *fado* (meaning "fate" and describing a type of music) clubs in Lisbon, as well as excellent restaurants and bars. There are also antiques shops. Regrettably, many of the side streets at night are peopled with drug dealers and addicts, so be duly warned.

BELÉM In the west, on the coastal road to Estoril, is the suburb of Belém. It contains some of the finest monuments in Portugal, several built during the Age of Discovery, near the point where the caravels set out to conquer new worlds. (At Belém, the Tagus reaches the sea.) At one time, before the earthquake, Belém was an aristocratic sector filled with elegant town houses. Two of the country's principal attractions stand here: the **Mosteiro dos Jerónimos,** a Manueline structure erected in the 16th century, and the **Museu Nacional dos Coches,** the National Coach Museum, the finest of its kind in the world. Belém is Lisbon's land of museums—it also contains the Museu de Arte Popular and the Museu de Marinha.

THE TOP ATTRACTIONS

Castelo de São Jorge ★★ Locals speak of Saint George's Castle as the cradle of their city, and it might have been where the Portuguese capital began. Its occupation is believed to have predated the Romans—the hilltop was used as a fortress to guard the Tagus and its settlement below. Beginning in the 5th century A.D., the site was a Visigothic fortification; it fell to the Saracens in the early 8th century. Many of the existing walls were erected during the centuries of Moorish domination. The Moors held power until 1147, the year Afonso Henríques chased them out and extended his kingdom south. Even before Lisbon became the capital of the newly emerging nation, the site was used as a royal palace.

For the finest **view ★★** of the Tagus and the Alfama, walk the esplanades and climb the ramparts of the old castle. The castle's name commemorates an Anglo-Portuguese pact dating from as early as 1371. (George is the patron saint of England.) Portugal and England have been traditional allies.

Huddling close to the protection of the moated castle is a sector that appears almost medieval. At the entrance, visitors pause at the Castle Belvedere. The Portuguese refer to this spot as their "ancient window." It overlooks the Alfama, the mountains of Monsanto and Sintra, Ponte do 25 de Abril, Praça do Comércio, and the tile roofs of the Portuguese capital. In the square stands a heroic statue—sword in one hand, shield in the other—of the first king, Afonso Henríques.

Rua da Costa do Castelo. ✆ **21/880-06-20.** www.castelosaojorge.egeac.pt. Admission 5€ adults, free for children 9 and under. Mar–Oct daily 9am–9pm; Nov–Feb daily 9am–6pm. Bus: 37. Tram: 12 or 28.

Mosteiro dos Jerónimos ★★ In an expansive mood, Manuel I, the Fortunate, ordered this monastery built to commemorate Vasco da Gama's voyage to India and to give thanks to the Virgin Mary for its success. Manueline, the style of architecture that bears the king's name, combines flamboyant Gothic and Moorish influences with elements of the nascent Renaissance. Henry the Navigator originally built a small chapel dedicated to St. Mary on this spot. Today this former chapel is the Gothic and Renaissance **Igreja de Santa Maria ★★**, marked by a statue of Prince Henry the Navigator. The church is known for its deeply carved stonework depicting such scenes as the life of St. Jerome. The church's interior is rich in beautiful stonework, particularly evocative in its **network vaulting ★** over the nave and aisles.

The west door of the church leads to the **Cloisters ★★★**, which represent the apex of Manueline art. The stone sculpture here is fantastically intricate. The two-story cloisters have groined vaulting on their ground level. The recessed upper floor is not as exuberant but is more delicate and lacelike in character. The monastery was founded in 1502, partially financed by the spice trade that grew following the discovery of the route to India. The 1755 earthquake damaged but didn't destroy the monastery. It has undergone extensive restoration, some of it ill-conceived.

Many of the greatest figures in Portuguese history are said to be entombed at the monastery; the most famous is Vasco da Gama. The Portuguese also maintain that Luís Vaz de Camões, author of the epic *Os Lusíadas* (The Lusiads), in which he glorified the triumphs of his compatriots, is buried here. Both tombs rest on the backs of lions. The romantic poet Herculano (1800–54) is also buried at Jerónimos, as is the famed poet Fernando Pessoa.

Praça do Império. ✆ **21/362-00-34.** www.mosteirojeronimos.pt. Admission: Church free; cloisters 6€ adults 26 and older, 3€ ages 15–25, free for seniors 65 and over and children 14 and under. May–Sept Tues–Sun 10am–6pm; Oct–Apr Tues–Sun 10am–5pm.

Museu Calouste Gulbenkian ★★★ Opened in 1969, this museum, part of the Fundação Calouste Gulbenkian, houses what one critic called one of the world's finest private art collections. It belonged to the Armenian oil tycoon Calouste Gulbenkian, who died in 1955. The modern, multimillion-dollar center is in a former private estate that belonged to the count of Vilalva.

The collection covers Egyptian, Greek, and Roman antiquities; a remarkable assemblage of Islamic art, including ceramics and textiles from Turkey and Persia; Syrian glass, books, bindings, and miniatures; and Chinese vases, Japanese prints, and lacquerware. The European displays include **medieval illuminated manuscripts and ivories ★**, 15th- to 19th-century paintings and sculpture, Renaissance tapestries and medals, important collections of 18th-century French decorative works, French Impressionist paintings, René Lalique jewelry, and glassware.

In a move requiring great skill in negotiation, Gulbenkian managed to buy art from the Hermitage in St. Petersburg. Among his most notable acquisitions are two Rembrandts: *Portrait of an Old Man* and *Alexander the Great.* Two other well-known paintings are *Portrait of Hélène Fourment,* by Peter Paul Rubens, and *Portrait of Madame Claude Monet,* by Pierre-Auguste Renoir.

Av. de Berna 45. ✆ **21/782-30-00.** www.museu.gulbenkian.pt. Admission 4€; free for seniors 65 and over, students, and teachers; free for all Sun. Tues–Sun 10am–5:45pm. Metro: Sebastião or Praça de Espanha. Bus: 16, 26, 31, 41, 46, or 56.

Museu Nacional dos Coches (National Coach Museum) ★★ The most visited attraction in Lisbon, the National Coach Museum is the finest of its type in the world. Founded by Amélia, wife of Carlos I, it's housed in a former 18th-century riding academy connected to the Belém Royal Palace. The coaches stand in a former horse ring; most date from the 17th to the 19th century. Drawing the most interest is a trio of opulently gilded baroque carriages used by the Portuguese ambassador to the Vatican at the time of Pope Clement XI (1716). Also on display is a 17th-century coach in which the Spanish Hapsburg king, Phillip II, journeyed from Madrid to Lisbon to see his new possession.

Praça de Afonso de Albuquerque. ✆ **21/361-08-50.** Admission 4€, 1.60€ ages 14–25, free for children 13 and under. Tues–Sun 10am–6pm; closed holidays.

Museu Nacional de Arte Antiga ★★★ The National Museum of Ancient Art houses the country's greatest collection of paintings. It occupies two connected buildings—a 17th-century palace and an added edifice that was built on the site of the old Carmelite Convent of Santo Alberto. The convent's chapel was preserved and is a good example of the integration of ornamental arts, with gilded carved wood, glazed tiles, and sculpture of the 17th and 18th centuries.

The museum has many notable paintings, including the **polyptych ★★★** from St. Vincent's monastery attributed to Nuno Gonçalves between 1460 and 1470. There are 60 portraits of leading figures of Portuguese history. Other outstanding works are Hieronymus Bosch's triptych ***The Temptation of St. Anthony*** **★★★**, Hans Memling's *Mother and Child,* Albrecht Dürer's *St. Jerome,* and paintings by Velázquez, Poussin, and Courbet. Especially noteworthy is the *12 Apostles,* by Zurbarán. Paintings from the 15th through the 19th century trace the development of Portuguese art.

The museum also exhibits a remarkable collection of gold- and silversmiths' works, both Portuguese and foreign. Among these is the cross from Alcobaça and the monstrance of Belém, constructed with the first gold brought from India by Vasco da Gama. Another exceptional example is the 18th-century French silver tableware ordered by José I.

Rua das Janelas Verdes 95. ✆ **21/391-28-00.** www.mnarteantiga-ipmuseus.pt. Admission 4€ adults, 2€ students, free for children 13 and under. Tues 2-6pm; Wed-Sun 10am-6pm. Tram: 15 or 18. Bus: 27, 49, 51, or 60.

Oceanário de Lisboa ★★ This world-class aquarium is the most enduring and impressive achievement of EXPO '98. Marketed as the second-biggest aquarium in the world (the largest is in Osaka, Japan), it's in a stone-and-glass building whose centerpiece is a 5-million-liter holding tank. Its waters consist of four distinct ecosystems that replicate the Atlantic, Pacific, Indian, and Antarctic oceans. Each is supplemented with aboveground portions on which birds, amphibians, and reptiles flourish. Look for otters in the Pacific waters; penguins in the Antarctic section; trees and flowers that might remind you of Polynesia in the Indian Ocean division; and puffins, terns, and sea gulls in the Atlantic subdivision. Don't underestimate the national pride associated with this huge facility: Most Portuguese view it as a latter-day reminder of their former mastery of the seas.

Esplanada Dom Carlos I. ✆ **21/891-70-02.** www.oceanario.pt. Admission 11€ adults, 5.50€ students and children 12 and under. Summer daily 10am-8pm; winter daily 10am-7pm. Metro: Estação do Oriente. Pedestrians should turn right after leaving the Metro station and go along Av. Dom João II, where you'll see a signpost directing you left and to the water for the attraction itself.

ELSEWHERE IN LISBON

Museu de Marinha (Maritime Museum) ★★ The Maritime Museum, one of the best in Europe, evokes the glory that characterized Portugal's domination of the high seas. Appropriately, it's installed in the west wing of the Mosteiro dos Jerónimos. These royal galleys re-create an age of opulence that never shied away from excess. Dragons' heads drip with gilt; sea monsters coil with abandon. Assembling a large crew was no problem for kings and queens in those days. Queen Maria I ordered a magnificent galley built for the 1785 marriage of her son and successor, Crown Prince João, to the Spanish Princess Carlota Joaquina Bourbon. Eighty dummy oarsmen, elaborately attired in scarlet-and-mustard-colored waistcoats, represent the crew.

The museum contains hundreds of models of 15th- to 19th-century sailing ships, 20th-century warships, merchant marine vessels, fishing boats, river craft, and pleasure boats. In a section devoted to the East is a pearl-inlaid replica of a dragon boat used in maritime and fluvial corteges. A full range of Portuguese naval uniforms is on display, from one worn at a Mozambique military outpost in 1896 to a uniform worn as recently as 1961. In a special room is a model of the queen's stateroom on the royal yacht of Carlos I, the Bragança king who was assassinated at Praça do Comércio in 1908. It was on this craft that his son, Manuel II; his wife; and the queen mother, Amélia, escaped to Gibraltar following the collapse of the Portuguese monarchy in 1910. The Maritime Museum also honors some early Portuguese aviators.

Praça do Império. ✆ **21/362-00-19.** www.museumarinha.pt. Admission 4€ adults, 2€ students and children 6-17, free for seniors 65 and over and children 5 and under. Apr-Sept Tues-Sun 10am-6pm; Oct-Mar Tues-Sun 10am-5pm; closed holidays.

Padrão dos Descobrimentos ★ Like the prow of a caravel from the Age of Discovery, the Memorial to the Discoveries stands on the Tagus, looking ready to strike out across the Sea of Darkness. Notable explorers, chiefly Vasco da Gama, are immortalized in stone along the ramps.

At the point where the two ramps meet is a representation of Henry the Navigator, whose genius opened up new worlds. The memorial was unveiled in 1960, and one of the stone figures is that of a kneeling Philippa of Lancaster, Henry's English mother. Other figures in the frieze symbolize the crusaders (represented by a man holding a flag with a cross), navigators, monks, cartographers, and cosmographers. At the top of the prow is the coat of arms of Portugal at the time of Manuel the Fortunate. On the floor in front of the memorial lies a map of the world in multicolored marble, with the dates of the discoveries set in metal.

Praça da Boa Esperança, Av. de Brasília. ✆ **21/303-19-50.** www.padraodescobrimentos.egeac.pt. Admission 2.50€. May–Sept Tues–Sun 10am–7pm; Oct–Apr Tues–Sun 10am–6pm.

Sé de Lisboa ★ Even official tourist brochures admit that this cathedral is not very rich. Characterized by twin towers flanking its entrance, it represents an architectural wedding of Romanesque and Gothic style. The facade is severe enough to resemble a medieval fortress. At one point, the Saracens reportedly used the site of the present Sé as a mosque. When the city was captured early in the 12th century by Christian crusaders, led by Portugal's first king, Afonso Henríques, the structure was rebuilt. The Sé then became the first church in Lisbon. The earthquakes of 1344 and 1755 damaged the structure.

A visit to the sacristy and cloister requires a guide. The cloister, built in the 14th century by King Dinis, is of ogival construction, with garlands, a **Romanesque wrought-iron grill ★**, and tombs with inscription stones. In the sacristy are marbles, relics, valuable images, and pieces of ecclesiastical treasure from the 15th and 16th centuries. In the morning, the stained-glass reflections on the floor evoke a Monet painting.

Largo da Sé. ✆ **21/886-67-52.** Cathedral free admission; cloister 2.50€. Daily 9am–7pm; holidays 9am–5pm. Tram: 28 (Graça). Bus: 37.

Torre de Belém ★★ The quadrangular Tower of Belém is a monument to Portugal's Age of Discovery. Erected between 1515 and 1520, the Manueline-style tower is Portugal's classic landmark and often serves as a symbol of the country; the tower stands on or near the spot where the caravels once set out across the sea.

Its architect, Francisco de Arruda, blended Gothic and Moorish elements, using such architectural details as twisting ropes carved of stone. The coat of arms of Manuel I rests above the loggia, and balconies grace three sides of the monument. Along the balustrade of the loggias, stone crosses represent the Portuguese crusaders.

Praça do Império, Av. de Brasília. ✆ **21/362-00-34.** www.mosteirojeronimos.pt. Admission 4€ adults, 1.60€ ages 15–25, free for children 14 and under and for seniors 65 and over, free for all Sun until 2pm. Oct–Apr Tues–Sun 10am–5pm; May–Sept Tues–Sun 10am–6pm.

ORGANIZED TOURS

The best tours of Lisbon are offered by **Lisboasightseeing,** Rua Pascoal de Melo 3 (✆ **21/967-08-65-36;** www.lisboasightseeing.com). The half-day tour of Lisbon, costing 34€, is the most popular, taking in the highlights of the Alfama and visiting the major monuments, including Jerónimos Monastery and other attractions of Belém. It even goes over the bridge spanning the Tagus, for a panoramic view. Both morning and afternoon tours leave daily throughout the year.

The most recommended tour of the environs of Lisbon is a daily full-day tour costing 82€ and taking in all the highlights, concentrating on Sintra, Cascais, and Estoril. There's also a full-day (and jampacked) tour offered daily of the highlights north of Lisbon—Fátima, Batalha, Nazaré, and Óbidos. This tour costs 86€.

If you want a more personalized tour, check out the offerings of **Inside Lisbon Tours,** Av. Forças Armadas 95 (✆ **96/841-26-12;** www.insidelisbon.com). Patrons are transported around in small vans and then taken on different walking tours through the most colorful and historical zones of Lisbon. A popular summer addition is a twice-weekly pub-crawl. The tours are given in English and enough free time is provided to explore in some depth. Only eight people at a time are taken on a tour. The labyrinths of the Alfama are the most desirable and intriguing of the tours.

The Shopping Scene

Portuguese handicrafts often exhibit exotic influences, in large part because of the **Baixa,** a grid of streets dating from the 18th-century restoration of central Lisbon that is a major shopping area between the Rossio and the River Tejo. **Rua Aurea** (**Street of Gold,** the location of the major jewelry shops), **Rua da Prata (Street of Silver),** and **Rua Augusta** are Lisbon's three principal shopping streets. Another major upscale shopping artery is **Rua Garrett,** in Chiado, the district on the hill due west of Baixa. Antiques lovers gravitate to **Rua de São José** in the Graça District. **Rua Dom Pedro V,** in the Bairro Alto, is another street lined with antiques shops.

At the **Feira da Ladra,** an open-air flea market, vendors peddle their wares on Tuesday and Saturday; haggling is expected. Portable stalls and dropcloth displays are lined up in Campo de Santa Clara behind the Igreja São Vicente. Take bus no. 12 from the Santa Apolónia station.

Pottery is one of the best buys in Portugal, and pottery covered with brightly colored roosters from Barcelos is legendary, as is the ubiquitous blue-and-white pottery made in Coimbra. From Caldas da Rainha come yellow-and-green dishes in the shapes of vegetables, fruit, and animals. Vila Real is known for its black pottery, polychrome pieces come from Aceiro, and the red-clay pots from the Alentejo region are based on designs that go back to the Etruscans.

Another good buy in Portugal is gold. Gold is strictly regulated by the government, which requires jewelers to put a minimum of 19¼ karats in the jewelry they sell. Filigree jewelry, made of fine gold or silver wire, is an art that dates from ancient times. **W. A. Sarmento,** Rua Áurea 251 (✆ **21/347-07-83** or 21/342-67-74; Metro: Chiado), is the most distinguished silver- and goldsmith in Portugal, specializing in lacy filigree jewelry, including charm bracelets.

MORE SELECT SHOPS & GALLERIES In the same building as the Hotel Avenida Palace, **Casa Bordados da Madeira,** Rua do 1 de Dezembro 137 (✆ **21/342-14-47**), offers handmade embroideries from Madeira and Viana. If you wish to place an order, the staff will mail it to you. **Madeira House,** Rua Augusta 131–133 (✆ **21/342-68-13;** www.madeira-house.com; Metro: Chiado), specializes in high-quality regional cottons, linens, and gift items.

Galeria 111, Campo Grande 113 (✆ **21/797-74-18;** Metro: Entre Campus), features wide-ranging exhibitions of sculpture, painting, and graphics, including work by leading contemporary Portuguese artists.

Lisbon After Dark

If you have only 1 night in Lisbon, spend it at a fado club. The nostalgic sounds of fado, Portuguese "songs of sorrow," are at their best in Lisbon—the capital attracts the greatest *fadistas* (fado singers) in the world (see the box "Fado: The Music of Longing," below). Fado is high art in Portugal, so don't plan to carry on a private conversation during a show—it's bad form. Most of the authentic fado clubs are clustered in the Bairro Alto and in the Alfama, between St. George's Castle and the docks. You can "fado hop" between the two quarters.

For more information about nighttime attractions, go to the tourist office (see "Visitor Information," earlier in this chapter), which maintains a list of events. Another helpful source is the **Agência de Bilhetes para Espectáculos Públicos,** in Praça dos Restauradores (✆ **21/347-58-24**). It's open daily from 9am to 9:30pm; go in person instead of trying to call. The agency sells tickets to most theaters and cinemas.

Also check out copies of *What's On in Lisbon,* available at most newsstands; *Sete,* a weekly magazine with entertainment listings; or the free monthly guides *Agenda Cultural* and *LISBOaem.* Your hotel concierge is a good bet for information, too, because one of his or her duties is reserving seats. Note that the local newspaper, *Diário de Notícias,* carries all cultural listings, but in Portuguese only.

By North American standards, "the party" in Lisbon begins late. Many bars don't even open until 10 or 11pm, and very few savvy young Portuguese would set foot in a club before 1am. The Bairro Alto, with some 150 restaurants and bars, is the most happening place after dark.

FADO: THE MUSIC OF LONGING

The *saudade* (Portuguese for "longing" or "nostalgia") that infuses the country's literature is most evident in fado. The traditional songs express Portugal's sad, romantic mood. The traditional performers are women *(fadistas),* often accompanied by a guitar and a viola. Experiencing the nostalgic sounds of fado is essential to apprehending the Portuguese soul. Fado is Portugal's most vivid art form; no visit to the country is complete without at least 1 night spent in a local tavern listening to this traditional folk music.

A rough translation of *fado* is "fate," from the Latin *fatum* (prophecy). Fado songs usually tell of unrequited love, jealousy, or a longing for days gone by. The music, as is often said, evokes a "life commanded by the Oracle, which nothing can change."

Fado became famous in the 19th century when Maria Severa, the beautiful daughter of a Gypsy, took Lisbon by storm. She sang her way into the hearts of the people of Lisbon—especially the count of Vimioso, an outstanding bullfighter. Present-day fadistas wear a black-fringed shawl in her memory.

The most famous 20th-century exponent of fado was Amália Rodriguez, who was introduced to American audiences in the 1950s at the New York club La Vie en Rose. Born into a simple Lisbon family, she was discovered while walking barefoot and selling flowers on the Lisbon docks near the Alfama. For many, she is the most famous Portuguese figure since Vasco da Gama. Swathed in black, sparing of gestures and excess ornamentation, Rodriguez almost single-handedly executed the transformation of fado into an international form of poetic expression.

THE PERFORMING ARTS

Teatro Nacional de São Carlos ★★, Rua Serpa Pinto 9 (✆ **21/325-30-45;** www.saocarlos.pt; Metro: Baixa-Chiado), attracts opera and ballet aficionados from all over Europe, and top companies from around the world perform at the 18th-century theater. The season begins in mid-September and extends through July. The box office is open Monday to Friday 1 to 7pm, and Saturday, Sunday, and holidays from 1pm to 30 minutes after a show begins.

A full menu of jazz, dance, light opera, and chamber concerts is presented at the **Centro Cultural de Belém ★★**, Praça do Império (✆ **21/361-24-44;** www.ccb.pt; tram: 15). You can check the local newspapers upon your arrival in Lisbon to see if a featured presentation interests you.

From October to June, concerts, recitals, and occasionally ballet performances take place at **Museu Calouste Gulbenkian ★**, Av. de Berna 45 (✆ **21/782-30-00;** www.museu.gulbenkian.pt; Metro: Sebastião). Ticket prices vary widely.

Teatro Nacional D. Maria II ★, Praça de Dom Pedro IV (✆ **21/325-08-00,** or 21/325-08-35 for reservations; www.teatro-dmaria.pt; Metro: Rossio), the most famous theater in Portugal, presents a repertoire of both Portuguese and foreign plays, with performances strictly in Portuguese. Tickets range from 7.50€ to 16€, and are half price for students up to 25 years old and ages 65 and older with valid ID.

BARS

Bachus, Largo da Trindade 8–9 (✆ **21/342-28-28;** bus: 58 or 100), is both a restaurant and a convivial watering spot. Surrounded by Oriental carpets, bronze statues, intimate lighting, and polite uniformed waiters, you can hobnob with some of the most glamorous people in Lisbon. It's open Monday to Saturday noon to 3:30am.

A longtime favorite of journalists, politicians, and foreign actors, the once-innovative **Bar Procópio ★**, Alto de São Francisco 21 (✆ **21/385-28-51;** www.barprocopio.com; Metro: Rato), has become a tried-and-true staple among Lisbon's watering holes. Procópio might easily become your favorite bar, if you can find it. It lies just off Rua de João Penha, which is off the landmark Praça das Amoreiras. It's open Monday to Saturday 6pm to 3am.

CINCO Lounge ★★, Rua Ruben A. Leitão 17A (✆ **21/342-40-33;** www.cincolounge.com; Metro: Rato), is the hottest, chicest bar in all of Lisbon. Lying above the Bairro Alto section, it features an array of dazzling cocktails—some 100 in all—using only the most expensive of liquors and the freshest of fruit. The setting is elegant, with floor-to-ceiling windows, glass-topped tables, and the most flattering lighting in Lisbon. It's open daily from 5pm to 2am.

Pavilhão Chines, Rua Dom Pedro V 89 (✆ **21/342-47-29;** Metro: Rato), the mother of all flea market bars, is a mostly heterosexual watering hole in the Bairro Alto that contains a collection of kitsch that alone is worth the trek here. Replicas of everyone from Buddha to Popeye decorate the joint, along with bronze cupids, Toby tankards, baubles and beads, and enough Victoriana to fill half the attics of London. It's a lively venue open Monday to Friday 5pm to 2am, and Saturday 6pm to 2am.

FADO CLUBS

Opened in 1937, **Adega Machado,** Rua do Norte 91 (✆ **21/322-46-40;** bus: 58 or 100), is still one of Portugal's favored fado clubs. Alternating with fadistas are folk dancers in costume, whirling, clapping, and singing native songs. Dinner is a la carte, and the cuisine is mostly Portuguese. Expect to spend 25€ to 30€ for a complete meal. The dinner hour starts at 8pm, music begins at 9:15pm, and the doors don't close until 3am. It's open Tuesday to Sunday.

A Severa, Rua das Gáveas 51 (✆ **21/346-12-04;** bus: 20 or 24), is not quite as good as Adega Machado, but good food and the careful selection of fadistas make it a perennial favorite. Every night, top singers appear, accompanied by guitar and viola music, alternating with folk dancers. After midnight, tourists seem to recede a bit in favor of loyal habitués, who request and sometimes join in on their favorite fado number. The kitchen turns out regional dishes. Expect to spend at least 36€ per person for a meal with wine. It's open daily from 9pm to 2am.

Every fadista worth her shawl seems to have sung at **Parreirinha da Alfama,** Beco do Espírito Santo 1 (✆ **21/886-82-09;** bus: 9, 39, or 46), an old-time cafe that's just a minute's walk from the docks of the Alfama. It's fado only here, no folk dancing, and the place has survived more or less unchanged since its establishment in the early 1950s. In the first part of the program, fadistas get the popular songs out of the way and then settle into their more classic favorites. It's open daily from 8pm to 1am. Cover (credited toward drinks) is 15€.

DANCE CLUBS

Lux Frágil, Avenida Infante Don Henrique, Armazém (Warehouse) A, Cais da Pedra a Santa Apolónia (✆ **21/882-08-90;** www.luxfragil.com; bus: 9, 39, or 46), contains a labyrinth of interconnected spaces, each of which is likely to feature a radically different scene from the one in the room that's immediately adjacent. It attracts and amuses counterculture hipsters, with theatrical lighting, deep sofas, cutting-edge music, and some highly unusual accessories—one of them is an enormous chandelier composed entirely of steel wire and tampons. The upstairs bar, where a DJ spins records, is open daily from 10pm to 6am. The more manic, street-level dance floor is open Thursday to Saturday 1 to 7am. Entrance to both areas is free before midnight; after that, a 15€ cover applies.

If we had a date for a night in Lisbon with Madonna, we'd take her to **Silk ★★,** Rua da Misericórdia 14 (✆ **91/300-91-93;** www.silk-club.com), which is all black and fuchsia with a sexy sultriness. What you see going on in its deep plush couches would bring a blush to aging party boy Jack Nicholson. The visit here would be worthy if just for the incredible vista from the floor-to-ceiling windows. You can also perch on a candlelit outdoor deck on the sixth floor. The DJ spins the tunes as chic young things sip Moët & Chandon, or whatever. Open Tuesday to Saturday 10pm to 4am.

GAY & LESBIAN BARS & CLUBS

Finalmente Club, Rua da Palmeira 38 (✆ **21/347-99-23;** bus: 100), is the dance club that many gay men in Lisbon end up at after an evening of drinking and talking in other bars around the Bairro Alto. There's a hardworking, hard-drinking bar area; a crowded dance floor; and lots of bodies of all shapes and sizes. A stringent security system requires that you ring a bell before an attendant will let you in. It's open daily from 1am to between 3 and 6am, depending on business.

A short walk from Finalmente, you'll find **Bar 106,** Rua de São Marçal 106 (✆ **21/342-73-73;** www.bar106.com; bus: 100), a popular rendezvous point for gay men, most of whom arrive here after around 10pm. Expect a simple, restrained decor, a busy bar area, and enough space to allow subgroups and cliques of like-minded friends to form quickly and easily. It's open nightly from 9pm until 2am.

Don't expect a sign that indicates the location of **Frágil,** Rua da Atalaia 126–128 (© **21/346-95-78;** www.fragil.com.pt; Metro: Chiado). All you'll see are some blue neon lights and a vigilant doorman. Frágil devotes itself to counterculture music, gay men and women, and a scattering of heterosexuals who appreciate the cutting-edge music and permissive atmosphere. Technically, the place opens Tuesday to Saturday at 11:30pm, but don't expect a crowd until at least midnight—and a mob by around 2am. Closing is around 4am the following morning.

The Portuguese Riviera: Excursions Along the Costa do Sol

Lured by Guincho (near the westernmost point in continental Europe), the Boca do Inferno (Mouth of Hell), and Lord Byron's "glorious Eden" at Sintra, many travelers spend much of their time in the area around Lisbon. You could spend a day drinking in the wonders of the library at the monastery-palace of Mafra (Portugal's El Escorial), dining in the pretty pink rococo palace at Queluz, or enjoying seafood at the Atlantic beach resort of Ericeira.

However, the main draw in the area is the Costa do Sol. The string of beach resorts, including Estoril and Cascais, forms the Portuguese Riviera on the northern bank of the mouth of the Tagus. If you arrive in Lisbon when the sun is shining and the air is balmy, consider heading straight for the shore. Estoril is so near to Lisbon that darting in and out of the capital to see the sights or visit the fado clubs is easy. An inexpensive electric train leaves from the Cais do Sodré station in Lisbon frequently throughout the day and evening; its run ends in Cascais.

Take a ride out on the train, even if you don't plan to stay here. You'll pass pastel-washed houses with red-tile roofs and facades of antique blue-and-white tiles; miles of modern apartment dwellings; rows of canna, pine, mimosa, and eucalyptus; swimming pools; and, in the background, green hills studded with villas, chalets, and new homes. The sun coast is sometimes known as A Costa dos Reis, the Coast of Kings, because it's a magnet for deposed royalty—exiled kings, pretenders, marquesses from Italy, princesses from Russia, and baronesses from Germany.

ESTORIL ★

The first stop is 24km (15 miles) west of Lisbon. This once-chic resort has long basked in its reputation as a playground for monarchs. **Parque Estoril,** in the center of town, is a well-manicured landscape. At night, when it's floodlit, you can stroll amid the subtropical vegetation. The palm trees studding the grounds have prompted many to call it "a corner of Africa." At the top of the park sits the **casino,** which offers gambling, international floor shows, dancing, and movies.

Across the railroad tracks is the **beach,** where some of the most fashionable people in Europe sun themselves on peppermint-striped canvas chairs along the Praia Estoril Tamariz. The beach is sandy, unlike the pebbly strand at Nice. Although it is a lovely stretch of sand, we don't recommend going into the water, which is almost too polluted for swimming. You can enjoy the sands and the beach scene, but for actual swimming, head to one of the many hotel pools in the area.

CASCAIS ★

Just 6km (3¾ miles) west of Estoril and 61km (38 miles) west of Lisbon, Cascais was a tiny fishing village that attracted artists and writers to its little cottages. To say

Cascais is growing would be an understatement: It's exploding! Apartment houses, new hotels, and the finest restaurants along the Costa do Sol draw a never-ending stream of visitors every year.

However, the life of the simple fisher folk goes on. Auctions, called *lotas,* of the latest catch still take place on the main square. In the small harbor, rainbow-colored fishing boats share space with pleasure craft owned by an international set that flocks to Cascais from early spring to autumn.

The most popular excursion outside Cascais is to **Boca do Inferno (Mouth of Hell) ★**. Thundering waves sweep in with such power that they've carved a wide hole resembling a mouth, or *boca,* into the cliffs. However, if you should arrive when the sea is calm, you'll wonder why it's called a cauldron. The Mouth of Hell can be a wind-swept roar if you don't stumble over too many souvenir hawkers.

QUELUZ ★★

From the Estação do Rossio in Lisbon, take the Sintra line to Queluz. Departures during the day are every 15 minutes. The trip takes 30 minutes. There are two train stations in town. Get off at Queluz-Massamá, as it is closer to the palace. A one-way ticket costs 1.20€. Call ✆ **808/208-208** for schedules. At Queluz, turn left and follow the signs for less than 1km (⅔ mile) to the **Palácio Nacional de Queluz ★★**, Largo do Palácio, 2745-191 Queluz (✆ **21/434-38-60;** www.ippar.pt/monumentos/palacio_queluz.html), a brilliant example of the rococo in Portugal. Pedro III ordered its construction in 1747, and the work dragged on until 1787. What you'll see today is not what the palace was like in the 18th century; during the French invasions, almost all of its belongings were transported to Brazil with the royal family. A 1934 fire destroyed a great deal of Queluz, but tasteful and sensitive reconstruction restored the lighthearted aura of the 18th century. Inside you can wander through the queen's dressing room, lined with painted panels depicting a children's romp; the Don Quixote Chamber (Dom Pedro was born here and returned from Brazil to die in the same bed); the Music Room, complete with a French *grande pianoforte* and an 18th-century English harpsichord; and the mirrored throne room adorned with crystal chandeliers. The palace is open Wednesday to Monday 9am to 5pm. It's closed on holidays. Admission is 5€, free for children 13 and under.

SINTRA ★★★

Sintra, 29km (18 miles) northwest of Lisbon, is a 45-minute ride from the Estação do Rossio at the Rossio in Lisbon. Lord Byron called it "glorious Eden," and so it remains. Visitors flock here not only to absorb the town's beauty and scenic setting but also to visit two major sights.

Opening onto the central town square, the **Palácio Nacional de Sintra ★★★**, Largo da Rainha Dona Amélia (✆ **21/910-68-40;** www.ippar.pt/monumentos/palacio_sintra.html), was a royal palace until 1910. Much of the palace was constructed in the days of the first Manuel, the Fortunate. The palace's two conical chimney towers form the most distinctive landmark on the Sintra skyline. The Swan Room was a favorite of João I, one of the founding kings of Portugal, father of Henry the Navigator and husband of Philippa of Lancaster. The Room of the Sirens or Mermaids is one of the most elegant in the palace. The Heraldic or Stag Room holds coats of arms of aristocratic Portuguese families, and hunting scenes. The palace is rich in paintings and Iberian and Flemish tapestries, but perhaps it's simply worth a visit for its good views; in most of the rooms, wide windows look out onto attractive views of the Sintra mountain range. Admission is 5€ adults, 3€ ages 15 to 25, and free for children 14 and under; free admission for all on Sunday and some holidays. It's open Thursday to Tuesday 10am to 1pm and 2 to 5pm.

Towering over Sintra, the **Palácio Nacional da Pena ★★**, Estrada de Pena (✆ **21/910-53-40;** www.parquesdesintra.pt), sits on a plateau about 450m (1,476 ft.) above sea level. Part of the fun of visiting the castle is the ride up the verdant, winding road through the Parque das Merendas. At the top, the castle is a soaring agglomeration of towers, cupolas, and battlements. Crossing a drawbridge, you'll enter the palace proper, whose last royal occupant was Queen Amélia in 1910. Pena has remained much as Amélia left it, which is part of its fascination; it emerges as a rare record of European royal life before World War I. Admission is 11€, 9€ children 6 to 17, 9€ seniors, free for children 5 and under. It's open October to May Tuesday to Sunday 10am to 4:30pm; and June to September Tuesday to Sunday 10am to 6:30pm.

THE ALGARVE

The maritime province of the Algarve, often called the Garden of Portugal, is the southwesternmost part of Europe. Its coastline stretches 160km (99 miles) from Henry the Navigator's Cape St. Vincent to the border town of Vila Real de Santo António, fronting once-hostile Spain. The varied coastline contains sluggish estuaries, sheltered lagoons, low-lying areas where clucking marsh hens nest, long sandy spits, and promontories jutting out into the white-capped aquamarine foam.

Called Al-Gharb by the Moors, the land south of the *serras* (mountains) of Monchique and Caldeirão remains a spectacular anomaly that seems more like a transplanted section of the North African coastline. The countryside abounds in vegetation: almonds, lemons, oranges, carobs, pomegranates, and figs.

Even though most of the towns and villages of the Algarve are more than 240km (149 miles) from Lisbon, the great 1755 earthquake shook this area. Entire communities were wiped out; however, many Moorish and even Roman ruins remain. In the fret-cut chimneys, mosquelike cupolas, and cubist houses, a distinct Oriental flavor prevails. Phoenicians, Greeks, Romans, Visigoths, Moors, and Christians all touched this land.

Much of the historic flavor is gone forever, however, swallowed by a sea of dreary high-rise apartment blocks surrounding most towns. Years ago, Portuguese officials, looking in horror at what happened to Spain's Costa del Sol, promised more limited and controlled development so that they wouldn't make "Spain's mistake." That promise, in our opinion, has not been kept.

Many former fishing villages—now summer resorts—dot the Algarvian coast: Carvoeiro, Albufeira, Olhão, Portimão. The sea is the source of life, as it always has been. The village marketplaces sell esparto mats, copper, pottery, and almond and fig sweets, sometimes shaped like birds and fish.

Lagos and Faro make logical home bases, with ample lodging choices, railroad and air connections with Lisbon, and an easy driving range to all the likely destinations along the coast.

The Algarve

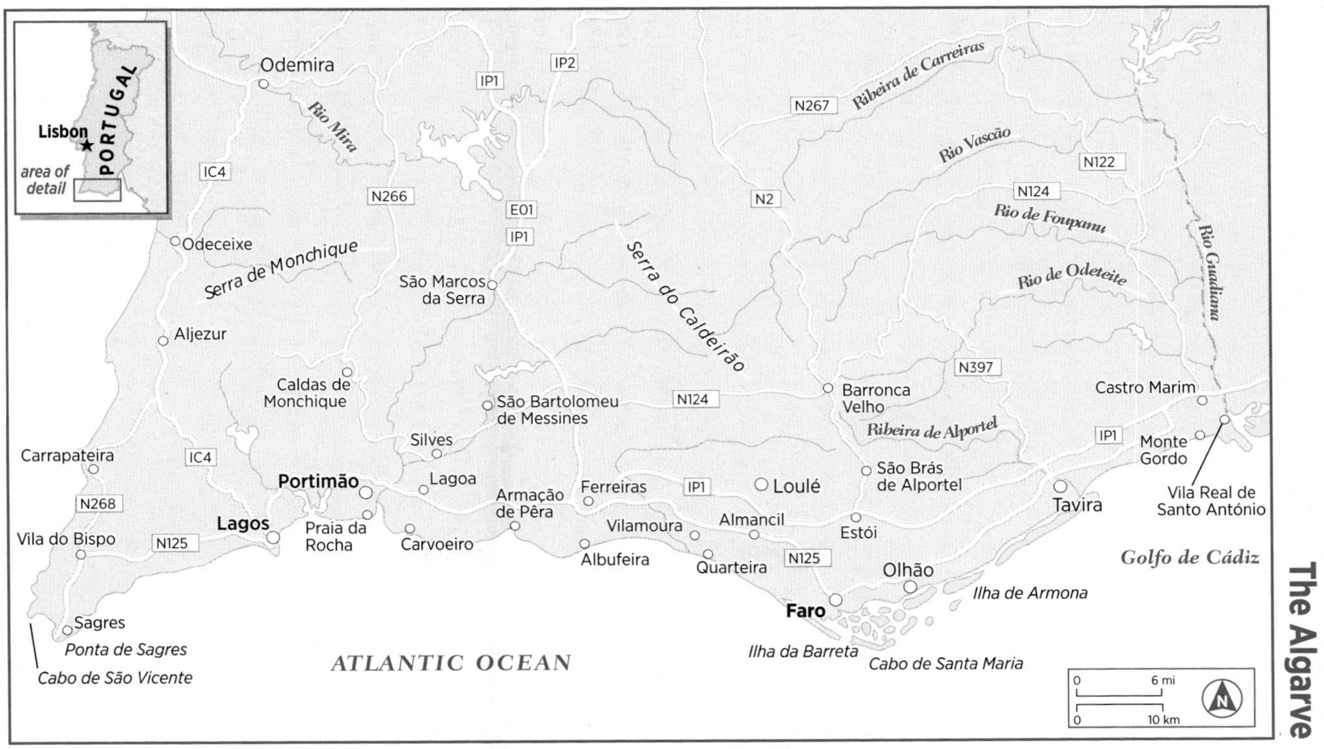

PORTUGAL
Lisbon
area of detail
Odemira
IP1
IP2
Rio Mira
N267
Ribeira de Carreiras
Rio Vascão
IC4
N266
N122
N2
N124
E01
Rio de Foupanu
Odeceixe
IP1
Serra de Monchique
São Marcos da Serra
Serra do Caldeirão
Rio de Odeteite
Rio Guadiana
Aljezur
N397
Caldas de Monchique
N124
Barronca Velho
Castro Marim
São Bartolomeu de Messines
Ribeira de Alportel
Silves
IP1
Monte Gordo
Carrapateira
IC4
São Brás de Alportel
Portimão
Lagoa
Ferreiras
IP1
Loulé
Tavira
Vila Real de Santo António
N268
Armação de Pêra
Lagos
Praia da Rocha
Almancil
Vila do Bispo
N125
Carvoeiro
Vilamoura
Estói
Albufeira
Quarteira
N125
Olhão
Golfo de Cádiz
Ilha de Armona
Faro
Sagres
Ponta de Sagres
Cabo de São Vicente
ATLANTIC OCEAN
Ilha da Barreta
Cabo de Santa Maria
0
6 mi
0
10 km
N

Lagos ★

Known to the Lusitanians and Romans as Lacobriga and to the Moors as Zawaia, Lagos became a shipyard of caravels during the time of Henry the Navigator. Edged by the Costa do Ouro (Golden Coast), the Bay of Sagres was at one point in its epic history big enough to allow 407 warships to maneuver with ease.

An ancient port city (one historian traced its origins to the Carthaginians, 3 centuries before the birth of Christ), Lagos was well known by the sailors of Admiral Nelson's fleet. From Liverpool to Manchester to Plymouth, the sailors spoke wistfully of the beautiful green-eyed, olive-skinned women of the Algarve. Eagerly they sailed into port, looking forward to carousing and drinking.

Not much has changed since Nelson's day. Few go to Lagos wanting to know its history; rather, the mission is to drink deeply of the pleasures of table and beach. In winter, the almond blossoms match the whitecaps on the water, and the weather is often warm enough for sunbathing. In town, a flea market sprawls through the narrow streets. Less than 2km (1¼ miles) down the coast, the hustle and bustle of market day is forgotten as the rocky headland of the **Ponta da Piedade (Point of Piety) ★★** appears. This spot is the most beautiful on the entire coast. Amid the colorful cliffs and secret grottoes carved by the waves are the most flamboyant examples of Manueline architecture.

ESSENTIALS

Getting There

BY FERRY & TRAIN From Lisbon, take an Algarve-bound train to the junction at Tunes, where a change of trains will take you south all the way to Lagos. Five trains a day arrive from Lisbon. The trip takes 5½ hours and costs at least 18€ one-way. For more information and schedules, call ✆ **808/208-208.**

BY BUS Six buses a day make the run between Lisbon and Lagos. The trip takes 4 hours and costs 19€ each way. Call ✆ **28/276-29-44** for schedules.

BY CAR If you're coming from Lisbon, after leaving Sines, take Route 120 southeast toward Lagos and follow the signs into the city. From Sagres, take N268 northeast to the junction with N125, which will lead you east to Lagos.

VISITOR INFORMATION The **Lagos Tourist Office,** Rua Belchior Moreira de Barbudo, Sítio de São João, Lagos (✆ **28/276-30-31;** www.visitalgarve.pt), is open daily 9:30am to 1pm and 2 to 5:30pm.

WHERE TO STAY

Casa da Moura ★ The "House of Moors" was built originally in 1892 for a rich Lagos family. It has been updated with a pool and a rooftop terrace overlooking the Atlantic Ocean. Lying inside the ramparts, a 5-minute walk from the center, the Casa imported much of its raw material from Morocco. The manor house is filled with wood-lined ceilings, stone and wooden floors, and wide corridors. For rent are two attractively furnished studios and six apartments. All accommodations have a different decoration and color scheme. Breakfast is served on an open-air terrace.

Rua Cardeal Neto 10, 8600-645. ✆ **28/277-07-30.** Fax 28/278-05-89. www.casadamoura.com. 8 units. 82€–100€ double. AE, MC, V. **Amenities:** Breakfast room; outdoor pool. *In room:* A/C, TV, hair dryer, Internet (free).

Romantik Hotel Vivenda Miranda ★★★ A real discovery, this small, Moorish-style hotel towers on a cliff overlooking the coast, 2.8km (1¾ miles) south of Lagos near the beach of Praia do Porto de Mos. Surrounded by exotic gardens and terraces, the inn opens onto the most panoramic views of any hotel in the area. Midsize to spacious bedrooms are stylish and exceedingly comfortable, with first-class tiled bathrooms. This is the kind of hotel that would be ideal for a honeymoon or romantic getaway. The restaurant offers a gourmet dinner with organic produce along with an excellent selection of regional wines.

Porto de Mós, 8600-282 Lagos. ✆ **28/276-32-22.** Fax 28/276-03-42. www.vivendamiranda.com. 28 units. 130€–200€ double; 140€–390€ suite. Rates include buffet breakfast. AE, MC, V. **Amenities:** Restaurant; bar; babysitting; outdoor freshwater pool; room service; spa; Wi-Fi (free, in lobby). *In room:* TV, hair dryer, minibar.

WHERE TO DINE

Restaurante D. Sebastião ★ REGIONAL PORTUGUESE This rustically decorated tavern on the main pedestrian street is one of the finest dining choices in Lagos. Portuguese-owned and -operated, it offers a varied menu of local specialties. Options include lip-smacking pork chops with figs, succulent shellfish dishes like clams and shrimp cooked with savory spices, and grills. Live lobsters are kept on the premises. One of the best selections of Portuguese vintage wines in town accompanies the filling, tasty meals. In summer, outdoor dining is available.

Rua do 25 de Abril 20–22. ✆ **28/278-04-80.** www.restaurantedonsebastiao.com. Reservations recommended. Main courses 8€–25€. AE, MC, V. Daily noon–10pm. Closed Dec 24–26 and Dec 31–Jan 2.

Rouxinol ★ PORTUGUESE Motorists can seek out this restaurant lying 42km (26 miles) from Lagos near the little town of Monchique. Discerning palates know they'll be served some of the best regional cuisine in the area. The first-class restaurant is installed in an old hunting lodge that has been restored by its owner/chef Stefhan. The chef has operated restaurants in West Africa, Morocco, the Canary Islands, and the Caribbean, and has brought the flavors of those exotic destinations with him to his Rouxinol (nightingale, in English). Food is served on an open-air terrace on balmy summer nights. Most guests order the freshly caught fish of the day, although the shellfish stew is the chef's signature dish. We can't wait to sample once again the grilled lamb from the Alentejo, followed by a warm raspberry pie with ice cream.

Estrada de Monchique. ✆ **28/291-39-75.** Reservations required. Main courses 12€–25€. AE, MC, V. Tues–Sun noon–9:30pm (to 10pm in summer). Closed Dec–Jan.

SEEING THE SIGHTS

Antigo Mercado de Escravos The Old Customs House stands as a painful reminder of the Age of Exploration. The arcaded slave market, the only one of its kind in Europe, looks peaceful today, but under its four Romanesque arches, captives were once sold to the highest bidders. The house opens onto the tranquil main square dominated by a statue of Henry the Navigator.

Praça do Infante Dom Henríques. Free admission. Daily 24 hr.

Igreja de Santo António ★ The 18th-century Church of St. Anthony sits just off the waterfront. The altar is decorated with some of Portugal's most notable baroque **gilt carvings ★**, created with gold imported from Brazil. Begun in the 17th century, they were damaged in the earthquake but subsequently restored. What you see today represents the work of many artisans—each, at times, pursuing a different theme.

Rua General Alberto Carlos Silveira. © **28/276-23-01.** Admission 2€ adults, 1€ students and seniors 65 and older, free for children 11 and under. Tues–Sun 9:30am–12:30pm and 2–5pm.

Museu Municipal Dr. José Formosinho The Municipal Museum contains replicas of the fret-cut chimneys of the Algarve, three-dimensional cork carvings, 16th-century vestments, ceramics, 17th-century embroidery, ecclesiastical sculpture, a painting gallery, weapons, minerals, and a numismatic collection. There's also a believe-it-or-not section displaying, among other things, an eight-legged calf. In the archaeological wing are Neolithic artifacts, Roman mosaics found at Boca do Rio near Budens, fragments of statuary and columns, and other remains of antiquity from excavations along the Algarve.

Rua General Alberto Carlos Silveira. © **28/276-23-01.** Admission 3€ for adults, 2€ children 12–14. Tues–Sun 9:30am–12:30pm and 2–5pm. Closed holidays.

GOLFING

Palmares Golf, Meia Praia, 8600 Lagos (© **28/279-05-00;** www.palmaresgolf.com), was designed by Frank Pennink in 1975 on land with many differences in altitude. Some fairways require driving a ball across railroad tracks, over small ravines, or around palm groves. Its landscaping suggests North Africa, partly because of its hundreds of palms and almond trees. The view from the 17th green is exceptionally dramatic. Par is 71. Greens fees are 63€ to 95€, depending on the season. The course lies on the eastern outskirts of Lagos, less than 1km (⅔ mile) from the center. To reach it from the heart of town, follow signs toward Meia Praia.

Another course is **Parque da Floresta,** Budens, Vale do Poço, 8650 Vila do Bispo (© **28/269-00-54**). One of the few important Algarvian courses west of Lagos, it's just inland from the fishing hamlet of Salema. Designed by the Spanish architect Pepe Gancedo and built as the centerpiece of a complex of holiday villas completed in 1987, the par-72 course offers sweeping views; we find it to be more scenic and more challenging than the Palmares course. Some shots must be driven over vineyards, and others over ravines, creeks, and gardens. Critics of the course have cited its rough grading and rocky terrain. Greens fees are 25€ to 50€ for 9 holes, and 43€ to 80€ for 18. To reach the course from the center of Lagos, drive about 15km (9⅓ miles) west, following road signs toward Sagres and Parque da Floresta.

Sagres ★★: "The End of the World"

At the extreme southwestern corner of Europe—once called *o fim do mundo* (the end of the world)—Sagres is a rocky escarpment jutting into the Atlantic Ocean. From here, Henry the Navigator, the Infante of Sagres, launched Portugal and the rest of Europe on the seas of exploration. Here he established his school of navigation, where Magellan, Diaz, Cabral, and Vasco da Gama apprenticed. A virtual ascetic, Henry brought together the best navigators, cartographers, geographers, scholars, sailors, and builders; infused them with his rigorous devotion; and methodically set Portuguese caravels upon the Sea of Darkness.

ESSENTIALS

Getting There

BY FERRY & TRAIN From Lisbon, take an Algarve-bound train to the junction at Tunes, where a change of trains will take you south all the way to Lagos. The rest of the distance is by bus (see below). For information and schedules, call ✆ **808/208-208** (www.cp.pt). From Lagos, buses go to Sagres.

BY BUS Ten EVA buses (✆ **28/276-29-44;** www.eva-bus.com) in Lagos run hourly from Lagos to Sagres each day. The trip time is 1 hour, and a one-way ticket costs 3.40€.

BY CAR From Lagos, drive west on Route 125 to Vila do Bispo, and then head south along Route 268 to Sagres.

WHERE TO STAY

Memmo Baleeira Hotel In a ship's-bow position, Memmo Baleeira Hotel is designed like a first-class *baleeira* (whaleboat) and spread out above the fishing port, lying 50m (164 ft.) from a pleasant beach. The largest hotel on this land projection, it offers guest rooms with sea-view balconies and a private beach. The number of its rooms has nearly doubled in recent years; the older ones are quite small, and some have linoleum floors.

Sítio da Baleeira, Sagres, 8650 Vila do Bispo. ✆ **28/262-42-12.** Fax 28/262-44-25. www.memmohotels.com. 144 units. 95€–190€ double; from 207€ suite. Rates include buffet breakfast. AE, DC, MC, V. **Amenities:** Restaurant; bar; babysitting; bikes; children's center; exercise room; 2 freshwater pools (1 heated indoor); room service; spa; outdoor tennis court (lit); limited watersports equipment/rentals; Wi-Fi (free, in lobby). *In room:* A/C, TV, DVD player (in some), kitchenette (in some), minibar.

Pousada do Infante ★★ Pousada do Infante, the best address in Sagres, seems like a monastery built by ascetic monks who wanted to commune with nature. You'll be charmed by the rugged beauty of the rocky cliffs, the pounding surf, and the sense of the ocean's infinity. The glistening white government-owned tourist inn spreads along the edge of a cliff that projects daringly over the sea. It boasts a long colonnade of arches with an extended stone terrace set with garden furniture, plus a second floor of accommodations with private balconies. Each midsize guest room is furnished with traditional pieces. Room nos. 1 to 12 are the most desirable. The public rooms are generously proportioned, gleaming with marble and decorated with fine tapestries depicting the exploits of Henry the Navigator. Large velvet couches flank the fireplace.

Ponta da Atalaia, 8650-385 Sagres. ✆ **28/262-02-40.** Fax 28/262-42-25. www.pousadas.pt. 39 units. 110€–190€ double; 165€–257€ suite. Rates include buffet breakfast. AE, DC, MC, V. **Amenities:** Restaurant; bar; babysitting; outdoor freshwater pool; room service.

WHERE TO DINE

Restaurante O Telheiro do Infante ★ SEAFOOD This two-floor restaurant is the best place for dining in the area, especially if you like your food fresh from the sea. There may be a bit of a wait, as all dishes are prepared to order. Originally, the location was a small farm, which grew and changed into its present role as tourism to the area increased. Raw ingredients are prepared with succulent simplicity. We always like to begin with the fresh oysters or the shrimp cocktail. Our favorite salad is the one made with fresh asparagus. Your best seafood selection is always the *peixe do dia,* or fresh catch of the day. It can be grilled to your specifications, or the fish can also be sautéed and served in a butter sauce with fresh vegetables. An array of pork and beef dishes from the Portuguese plains north of here should satisfy any meat eater. (The pork is very sweet because the pigs are often fed a diet of acorns.) Some tables are placed outside so that you can enjoy the view of the ocean.

Praia da Mareta. ✆ **28/262-41-79.** www.telheirodoinfante.com. Reservations recommended in summer. Main courses 12€–27€. AE, DC, MC, V. Wed–Mon 10am–10pm.

Restaurante Vila Velha ★★ INTERNATIONAL In a rustic setting in a villa, this first-class restaurant with its covered terrace in summer is elegant. The cuisine is going great guns, with pleasure exploding on the palate as you sample such dishes as stuffed quail in wine sauce; prawn curry; small pork filets with mango sauce; hake filets with scallops and hollandaise sauce; or tagliatelle with prawns and monkfish. Desserts are sumptuous, especially the homemade walnut ice cream with flambé bananas and a chocolate sauce.

Rua Patrão António Faustino. ✆ **28/262-47-88.** www.vilavelha-sagres.com. Reservations required. Main courses 28€–38€. MC, V. Tues–Sun 6:30–10pm (to 10:30pm July 15–Sept 15).

EXPLORING THE AREA

The cape and Sagres offer a view of the sunset. In the ancient world, the cape was the last explored point, although in time the Phoenicians pushed beyond it. Many mariners thought that when the sun sank beyond the cape, it plunged over the edge of the world.

Today, at the reconstructed site of Henry's wind-swept fortress on Europe's Land's End (named after the narrowing westernmost tip of Cornwall, England), you can see a huge stone compass dial. Henry supposedly used the Venta de Rosa in his naval studies at Sagres. Housed in the **Fortaleza de Sagres,** Ponta de Sagres, is a small museum of minor interest that documents some of the area's history. It's open May to September daily 9:30am to 8pm, October to April daily 9:30am to 5:30pm. Admission is 3€ for adults, 1.50€ for ages 15 to 25, and free for children 14 and under.

About 5km (3 miles) away is the promontory of **Cabo de São Vicente ★★**. It got its name because, according to legend, the body of St. Vincent arrived mysteriously here on a boat guided by ravens. (Others claim that the body of the patron saint, murdered at Valencia, Spain, washed up on Lisbon's shore.) A lighthouse, the second most powerful in Europe, beams illumination 100km (62 miles) across the ocean. To reach the cape, you can take a bus Monday through Friday leaving from Rua Comandante Matos near the tourist office. Trip time is 10 minutes, and departures are at 11:15am, 12:30pm, and 6pm; a one-way ticket costs 2€.

HITTING THE BEACH & OTHER OUTDOOR ACTIVITIES

BEACHES Many beaches fringe the peninsula; some attract nude bathers. Mareta, at the bottom of the road leading from the center of town toward the water, is the best and most popular. East of town is Tonel, also a good sandy beach. The beaches west of town, Praia da Baleeira and Praia do Martinhal, are better for windsurfing than for swimming.

BICYCLING If you'd like to rent a bike to explore the cape, go to **Posto de Turismo,** Rua Comandante Matoso, Sagres (✆ **28/262-48-73**). The charge is 8€ for 4 hours and 12€ for a full day.

FISHING Between October and January, you'll be assured of a prolific catch; and at times, you can walk down to almost any beach and hire a local fisherman to take you out for a half-day. Just about every large-scale hotel along the Algarve will arrange a fishing trip for you.

Praia da Rocha

En route to Praia da Rocha, off N-125 between Lagos and Portimão, 18km (11 miles) away, you'll find several good beaches and rocky coves, particularly at **Praia dos Três Irmãos** and **Alvor.** But the most popular seaside resort on the Algarve is the creamy yellow beach of Praia da Rocha. At the outbreak of World War II there were only two small hotels on the Red Coast, but nowadays, Praia da Rocha is booming. At the end of the mussel-encrusted cliff, where the Arcade flows into the sea, lie the ruins of the **Fortress of Santa Catarina.** The location offers views of Portimão's satellite, Ferragudo, and of the bay.

To reach Praia da Rocha from Portimão, you can catch a bus for the 2.5km (1½-mile) trip south. Service is frequent. Algarve buses aren't numbered but are marked by their final destination, such as PRAIA DA ROCHA.

WHERE TO STAY

Hotel Algarve Casino ★★★ The Algarve, the leading hotel in this area, is strictly for those who love glitter and glamour and don't object to the prices. With a vast staff at your beck and call, you'll be well provided for in this elongated block of rooms poised securely on the top ledge of a cliff. The midsize to spacious guest rooms have white walls, colored ceilings, intricate tile floors, mirrored entryways, indirect lighting, balconies with garden furniture, and bathrooms with separate tub/shower combinations. Many are vaguely Moorish in design, and have terraces opening onto the sea.

Av. Tomás Cabreira, Praia da Rocha, 8500-802 Portimão. ✆ **28/240-20-00.** Fax 28/240-20-99. www.solverde.pt. 208 units. 117€–264€ double; 173€–471€ suite. Rates include buffet breakfast. AE, DC, MC, V. **Amenities:** 2 restaurants; 2 bars; babysitting; children's center; exercise room; Jacuzzi; 2 freshwater pools (1 heated indoor); room service; sauna; 2 outdoor tennis courts (lit); limited watersports equipment/rentals. *In room:* A/C, TV, hair dryer, minibar, Wi-Fi (free; in some).

Hotel Bela Vista ★ This old Moorish-style mansion was built in 1916 as a wealthy family's summer home. It has a minaret-type tower at one end and a statue of the Virgin set into one of the building's corners. Since 1934, it has been a special kind of hotel, ideal for those who respond to the architecture of the past; you'll need to make a reservation far in advance. Guest rooms facing the sea, the former master bedrooms, are the most desirable. Decorations vary from crystal sconces to an inset tile shrine to the Virgin Mary. The hotel is on the ocean, atop its own palisade, with access to a sandy cove where you can swim. The villa is white with a terra-cotta tile roof, a landmark for fishermen bringing in their boats at sundown. It's flanked by the owner's home and a simple cliff-edge annex shaded by palm trees.

The attractive structure and its decorations have been preserved—the entry hallway has a winding staircase and an abundance of 19th-century blue-and-white tiles depicting allegorical scenes from Portuguese history—but that's partly counteracted by the plastic furniture in the public lounges.

Av. Tomás Cabreira, Praia da Rocha, 8500-802 Portimão. ✆ **28/245-04-80.** Fax 28/241-53-69. www.hotelbelavista.net. 14 units. 75€–140€ double; 105€–190€ junior suite. Rates include breakfast. AE, DC, MC, V. **Amenities:** Breakfast room; bar; room service. *In room:* TV, minibar.

WHERE TO DINE

Restaurante Titanic ★★★ INTERNATIONAL Complete with gilt and crystal, the 100-seat air-conditioned Titanic is the most elegant restaurant in town. Its open kitchen serves the best food in Praia da Rocha, including shellfish and flambé dishes. Despite the name, it's not on—or in, thank goodness—the water, but in a modern residential complex. You can dine very well here on such appealing dishes as the fish of the day, pork filet with mushrooms, prawns *a la plancha* (grilled on a plank of wood), Chinese fondue, or excellent sole Algarve. Service stands among the best in town.

In the Edifício Colúmbia, Rua Eng. Francisco Bivar. ✆ **28/242-23-71.** www.titanic.com.pt. Reservations recommended, especially in summer. Main courses 12€–32€. AE, DC, MC, V. Daily 7pm–midnight. Closed Nov 27–Dec 27.

GOLFING

Amid tawny-colored rocks and arid hillocks, **Vale de Pinta** (✆ **28/234-09-00**), Praia do Carvoeiro, sends players through groves of twisted olive, almond, carob, and fig trees. Views from the fairways, designed in 1992 by Californian Ronald Fream, sweep over the low masses of the Monchique mountains, close to the beach resort of Carvoeiro. Experts say it offers some of the most varied challenges in Portuguese golf. Clusters of "voracious" bunkers, barrier walls of beige-colored rocks assembled without mortar, and abrupt changes in elevation complicate the course. Par is 72. Greens fees are 60€ to 95€. From Portimão, drive 14km (8⅔ miles) east on N125, following signs to Lagoa and Vale de Pinta/Pestana Golf.

Praia dos Três Irmãos & Alvor ★★

Although **Praia dos Três Irmãos** is one of Portugal's more expensive areas, you may want to visit its beach, 5km (3 miles) southwest of Portimão. From Portimão's center, you can take one of the public buses; they run frequently throughout the day. The bus is marked PRAIA DOS TRÊS IRMÃOS. Departures are from the main bus terminal in Portimão, at Largo do Duque (✆ **28/241-81-20**).

Praia dos Três Irmãos has 15km (9⅓ miles) of burnished golden sand, interrupted only by an occasional crag riddled with arched passageways. This beach has been discovered by skin divers who explore its undersea grottoes and caves.

Nearby is the whitewashed fishing village of **Alvor,** where Portuguese and Moorish arts and traditions have mingled since the Arab occupation ended. Alvor was a favorite coastal haunt of João II, and now summer hordes descend on the long strip of sandy beach. It's not the best in the area, but at least you'll have plenty of space.

WHERE TO STAY

Le Méridien Penina Golf & Resort ★★★ This was the first deluxe hotel to be built on the Algarve. Located between Portimão and Lagos, it's now a Le Méridien property and has serious competition from the other luxury hotels. Fans of golf (see below) remain loyal to the Penina, however. It's a big sporting mecca and stands next to the Algarve's major casino. Besides the golf courses, the hotel has a private beach with its own snack bar and changing cabins, reached by a shuttle bus.

Most of the guest rooms contain picture windows and honeycomb balconies with views of the course and pool, or vistas of the Monchique hills. The standard rooms are furnished pleasantly, combining traditional pieces with Portuguese provincial spool beds. All rooms are spacious, with neatly kept bathrooms and good-size beds. The so-called attic rooms have the most charm, with French doors opening onto terraces. On the fourth floor are some duplexes, often preferred by families.

Estrada Nacional 125, 8501-952 Portimão. ✆ **800/225-5843** in the U.S., or 28/242-02-00. Fax 28/242-03-00. www.starwoodhotels.com. 196 units. 132€–280€ double; 354€–550€ junior suite; 645€–980€ suite. Rates include buffet breakfast. AE, DC, MC, V. **Amenities:** 5 restaurants; 3 bars; babysitting; bikes; children's programs; 3 golf courses; outdoor freshwater pool; room service; sauna; 6 outdoor tennis courts (lit); extensive watersports equipment/rentals; Wi-Fi (5€ per hour, in lobby). *In room:* A/C, TV, hair dryer, minibar.

Pestana Alvor Praia ★★★ "You'll feel as if you're loved the moment you walk in the door," said a visitor from the Midwest of the Pestana Alvor Praia. This citadel of hedonism has more *joie de vivre* than any other hotel on the Algarve. Its location, good-size guest rooms, decor, service, and food are ideal. Poised regally on a landscaped crest, many of the guest and public rooms face the ocean, the gardens, and the free-form Olympic-size pool. Gentle walks and an elevator lead down the palisade to the sandy beach and the rugged rocks that rise out of the water. Accommodations vary from a cowhide-decorated room evoking Arizona's Valley of the Sun to typical Portuguese-style rooms with rustic furnishings. Most contain oversize beds, plenty of storage space, long desk-and-chest combinations, and well-designed bathrooms.

Praia dos Três Irmãos, Alvor, 8501-904 Portimão. ✆ **28/240-09-00.** Fax 28/240-09-75. www.pestana.com. 195 units. 200€–300€ double; 330€–460€ suite. Rates include buffet breakfast. AE, DC, MC, V. **Amenities:** 2 restaurants; 2 bars; babysitting; bikes; health club; 3 saltwater pools (1 heated indoor); room service; sauna; 7 outdoor tennis courts (lit); Wi-Fi (18€ per 24 hr., in lobby). *In room:* A/C, TV, hair dryer, minibar.

WHERE TO DINE

Restaurante Búzio ★ INTERNATIONAL Restaurante Búzio stands at the end of a road encircling a resort development dotted with private condos and exotic shrubbery. In summer, so many cars line the narrow road that you'll probably need to park near the resort's entrance and then walk downhill to the restaurant.

Dinner is served in a room whose blue curtains reflect the shimmering ocean at the bottom of the cliffs. Your meal might include excellent fish soup, refreshing gazpacho, or *carré de borrego Serra de Estrela* (gratinée of roast rack of lamb with garlic, butter, and mustard). Other good choices are Italian pasta dishes, boiled or grilled fish of the day, flavorful pepper steak, and lamb kabobs with saffron-flavored rice. The restaurant maintains an extensive wine cellar.

Aldeamento da Prainha, Praia dos Três Irmãos. ✆ **28/245-87-72.** www.restaurantebuzio.com. Reservations recommended. Main courses 10€–30€. AE, DC, MC, V. Daily 7–10:30pm. Closed Dec 15–Jan 7.

GOLFING

Penina (✆ **28/242-02-00**) is 5km (3 miles) west of the center of Portimão, farther west than many of the other great golf courses. Completed in 1966, it was one of the first courses in the Algarve and the universally acknowledged masterpiece of the British designer Sir Henry Cotton. It replaced a network of marshy rice paddies on level terrain that critics said was unsuited for anything except wetlands. The solution involved planting groves of eucalyptus (350,000 trees in all), which grew quickly in the muddy soil. Eventually they dried it out enough for the designer to bulldoze dozens of water traps and a labyrinth of fairways and greens. The course wraps around a luxury hotel (Le Méridien Penina Golf & Resort). You can play the main championship course (18 holes, par 73), and two 9-hole satellite courses, Academy and Resort. Greens fees for the 18-hole course are 80€ to 120€; for either of the 9-hole courses, they're 50€ to 65€. To reach it from the center of Portimão, follow signs to Lagos, turning off at the signpost for Le Méridien Penina Golf & Resort.

Albufeira ★

This cliff-side town, formerly a fishing village, is the St. Tropez of the Algarve. The lazy life, sunshine, and beaches make it a haven for young people and artists, although the old-timers still regard the invasion that began in the late 1960s with some ambivalence. That development turned Albufeira into the largest resort in the region. Some residents open the doors of their cottages to those seeking a place to stay. Travelers with less money often sleep in tents.

With steep streets and villas staggered up and down the hillside, Albufeira resembles a North African seaside community. The big, bustling resort town rises above a sickle-shape beach that shines in the bright sunlight. A rocky, grottoed bluff separates the strip used by sunbathers from the working beach, where brightly painted fishing boats are drawn up on the sand. Access to the beach is through a tunneled rock passageway.

ESSENTIALS

Getting There

BY TRAIN Trains run between Albufeira and Faro (see "Faro," below), which has good connections to Lisbon. For schedule information, call © **808/208-208.** The train station lies 6.5km (4 miles) from the town's center. Buses from the station to the resort run every 30 minutes; the fare is 3€ one-way.

BY BUS Buses run between Albufeira and Faro every hour. Trip time is 1 hour, and a one-way ticket costs 4.20€. Twenty-three buses per day make the 1-hour trip from Portimão to Albufeira. It costs 4.05€ one-way. For information and schedules, call © **28/958-97-55.**

BY CAR From east or west, take the main coastal route, N125. Albufeira also lies near the point where the express highway from the north, N264, feeds into the Algarve. The town is well signposted in all directions. Take Route 595 to reach Albufeira and the water.

VISITOR INFORMATION The **Tourist Information Office** is at Rua do 5 de Outubro (© **28/958-52-79**). From July to September, hours are daily from 9:30am to 7pm; October to June, they're from 10am to 5:30pm.

WHERE TO STAY

Club Med da Balaïa ★ On 16 hectares (40 acres) of sun-drenched scrubland about 6.5km (4 miles) east of Albufeira, this all-inclusive high-rise resort is one of the most stable in the Club Med empire. Favored by vacationers from northern Europe, it encompasses a shoreline of rugged rock formations indented with a private beach and a series of coves for surf swimming. The small accommodations have twin beds, two safes, and piped-in music. They're decorated in understated, uncluttered style, with private balconies or terraces. Many vacationers here appreciate the nearby golf course; others opt to participate in semiorganized sports. Meals are usually consumed at communal tables; there are many lunchtime buffets and copious amounts of local wine.

Praia Maria Luisa, 8200-854 Albufeira. ✆ **800/CLUB-MED** (258-2633) in the U.S., or 28/951-05-00. www.clubmed.com. Fax 28/958-71-79. 372 units. 261€–550€ double. Rates include full board and use of most sports facilities. Children 4–12 20% discount in parent's room. AE, DC, MC, V. Free parking. **Amenities:** 3 restaurants; 3 bars; children's center; exercise room; 9-hole golf course; outdoor freshwater pool; room service; spa; 7 outdoor tennis courts (lit). *In room:* A/C, TV, hair dryer, minibar.

Estalagem do Cerro ★ Estalagem do Cerro, built in 1964, captures Algarvian charm without neglecting modern amenities. This Inn of the Craggy Hill is at the top of a hill overlooking Albufeira's bay, about a 10-minute walk from the beach. A similar Moorish style unites an older, regional-style building and a more modern structure. The tastefully furnished midsize guest rooms have verandas overlooking the sea, pool, or garden. Ten units are large enough for families.

Rua Samora Barros, Cerro da Piedade, 8200-320 Albufeira. ✆ **28/959-80-84.** Fax 28/959-80-01. www.pin.estalagemdocerro.pt. 95 units. 70€–150€ double; 190€ suite. AE, DC, MC, V. Limited free parking on street. **Amenities:** 2 restaurants; 2 bars; babysitting; bike rentals; children's playground; exercise room; Jacuzzi; 2 freshwater pools (1 heated indoor); room service; sauna; Wi-Fi (free, in lobby). *In room:* A/C, TV, hair dryer, minibar.

WHERE TO DINE

O Cabaz da Praia (The Beach Basket) FRENCH/PORTUGUESE The Beach Basket, near the Hotel Sol e Mar, sits on a colorful little square near the Church of São Sebastião. In a former fishermen's cottage, the restaurant boasts a large, sheltered terrace with a view over the main Albufeira beach. The food's good, too. Main courses, including such justifiable favorites as cassoulet of seafood, salade océane, monkfish with mango sauce, and beef filet with garlic and white-wine sauce, are served with a selection of fresh vegetables.

Praça Miguel Bombarda 7. ✆ **28/951-21-37.** Reservations recommended. Main courses 22€–26€. AE, MC, V. Fri–Wed noon–3pm and 7:30–11pm.

Vale do Lobo ★ & Quinta do Lago

Almancil, 13km (8 miles) west of Faro and 24km (15 miles) east along N-25 from Albufeira, is a small market town of little tourist interest, but it's a center for two of the most exclusive tourist developments along the Algarve. **Vale do Lobo** lies 6.5km (4 miles) southeast of Almancil, and **Quinta do Lago** is less than 10km (6¼ miles) southeast of town. Both are golfers' paradises.

WHERE TO STAY

Dona Filipa Hotel ★★★ A citadel of ostentatious living, Dona Filipa is a deluxe golf hotel with such touches as gold-painted palms holding up the ceiling. The grounds are impressive, embracing 180 hectares (445 acres) of rugged coastline with steep cliffs, inlets, and sandy bays. The hotel's exterior is comparatively uninspired, but the interior features such lavish touches as green silk banquettes, marble fireplaces, Portuguese ceramic lamps, and old prints over baroque-style love seats. The midsize to spacious guest rooms are handsomely decorated with antiques, rustic accessories, and handmade rugs. Most have balconies and twin beds.

Vale do Lobo, 8135-901 Almancil. ✆ **28/935-72-00.** Fax 28/935-72-01. www.donafilipahotel.com. 154 units. 245€–414€ double; 455€–626€ junior suite; 575€–930€ deluxe suite. Rates include buffet breakfast. AE, DC, MC, V. **Amenities:** 2 restaurants; bar; babysitting; bikes; children's playground; concierge; outdoor heated pool; room service; 3 outdoor tennis courts (lit); Wi-Fi (15€ per 24 hr., in lobby). *In room:* A/C, TV, hair dryer, minibar.

Hotel Quinta do Lago ★★★ A pocket of the high life since 1986, Hotel Quinta do Lago is a sprawling 800-hectare (1,977-acre) estate that contains some private plots beside the Ria Formosa estuary. Its riding center and 27-hole golf course are among the best in Europe. The estate's contemporary Mediterranean-style buildings rise three to six floors. The luxurious hotel rooms overlook a saltwater lake and feature modern comforts. Decorated with thick carpeting and pastel fabrics, the guest rooms are generally spacious, with tile or marble bathrooms. Rooms are decorated with contemporary art and light-wood furniture, and balconies have views of the estuary.

Quinta do Lago, 8135-024 Almancil. ✆ **800/223-6800** in the U.S., or 28/935-03-50. Fax 28/939-49-05. www.quintadolagohotel.com. 141 units. 207€–552€ double; 300€–520€ junior suite; 552€–2,650€ suite. Rates include buffet breakfast. AE, DC, MC, V. **Amenities:** 2 restaurants; bar; babysitting; bike rentals; exercise room; 2 freshwater heated pools (1 indoor); room service; spa; 2 outdoor tennis courts (lit). *In room:* A/C, TV, hair dryer, minibar, Wi-Fi (7€ per 24 hr.).

WHERE TO DINE

Casa Velha ★★★ FRENCH Casa Velha, an excellent dining choice, is not part of the nearby Quinta do Lago resort. Yet on a hillside behind its massive neighbor, it overlooks the resort's lake from the premises of a century-old farmhouse that has functioned as a restaurant since the early 1960s. The cuisine is mainly French, with a scattering of Portuguese and international dishes. Start with foie gras or marinated lobster salad. Specialties include a salad of chicken livers and gizzards with leeks and vinaigrette, and lobster salad flavored with an infusion of vanilla. Other good choices are carefully flavored preparations of sea bass, filet of sole, and breast of duck.

Quinta do Lago. ✆ **28/939-49-83.** www.restaurante-casavelha.com. Reservations recommended. Main courses 18€–30€. AE, MC, V. Mon–Sat 7–10:30pm.

São Gabriel ★★★ CONTINENTAL/SWISS A classic, elegant restaurant, this deluxe choice lies directly southeast of the center of Almancil. Gourmets drive for miles to sample the food and wine in the refined dining room, which also features a summer terrace. The actual dishes served depend on the time of the year and the mood of the chef. You might encounter lamb perfectly roasted in an old oven, tender duck flavored with port wine, or roasted veal cutlets with Swiss-style hash browns. The cuisine is remarkably well crafted, though not daringly original. You are, however, assured of the freshest of ingredients and a changing array of tempting desserts.

Estrada Vale do Lobo. ✆ **28/939-45-21.** www.sao-gabriel.com. Reservations required. Main courses 22€–40€. AE, MC, V. Tues–Sun 7–10:30pm. Closed Nov–Mar 2.

GOLFING

One of the most deceptive golf courses on the Algarve, **Pinheiros Altos,** Quinta do Lago, 8135 Almancil (✆ **28/935-99-10;** www.pinheirosaltos.com), has contours that even professionals say are far more difficult than they appear at first glance. American architect Ronald Fream designed the 100 hectares (247 acres), which abut the wetland refuge of the Rio Formosa National Park. Umbrella pines and dozens of small lakes dot the course. Par is 72. Greens fees are 45€ to 60€ for 9 holes and 80€ to 120€ for 18 holes. Pinheiros Altos lies about 5km (3 miles) south of Almancil. From Almancil, follow the signs to Quinta do Lago and Pinheiros Altos.

The namesake course of the massive development, **Quinta do Lago,** Quinta do Lago, 8135 Almancil (✆ **28/939-07-00;** www.quintadolagogolf.com), consists of two 18-hole golf courses, Quinta do Lago and Rio Formosa. Together they cover more than 240 hectares (593 acres) of sandy terrain that abuts the Rio Formosa Wildlife Sanctuary. Very few long drives here are over open water; instead, the fairways undulate through cork forests and groves of pine trees, sometimes with abrupt changes in elevation. Greens fees are 150€ for 18 holes. The courses are 6km (3¾ miles) south of Almancil. From Almancil, follow signs to Quinta do Lago.

Of the four golf courses at the massive Quinta do Lago development, the par-72 **São Lourenço (San Lorenzo)** course, Quinta do Lago, Almancil, 8100 Loulé (✆ **28/939-65-22**), is the most interesting and challenging. San Lorenzo opened in 1988 at the edge of the grassy wetlands of the Rio Formosa Nature Reserve. American golf designers William (Rocky) Roquemore and Joe Lee created it. The most panoramic hole is the 6th; the most frustrating is the 8th. Many long drives, especially those aimed at the 17th and 18th holes, soar over a saltwater lagoon. Greens fees are 75€ for 9 holes and 150€ for 18 holes. From Almancil, drive 8km (5 miles) south, following signs to Quinta do Lago.

The **Vale do Lobo** course, Vale do Lobo, 8135 Almancil (✆ **28/935-34-65**), technically isn't part of the Quinta do Lago complex. Because it was established in 1968, before any of its nearby competitors, it played an important role in launching southern Portugal's image as a golfer's mecca. Designed by the British golfer Henry Cotton, it contains four distinct 9-hole segments. All four include runs that stretch over rocks and arid hills, often within view of olive and almond groves, the Atlantic, and the high-rise hotels of nearby Vilamoura and Quarteira. Some long shots require driving golf balls over two ravines, where variable winds and bunkers make things particularly difficult. Greens fees, depending on the day of the week and other factors, range from 84€ to 94€ for 9 holes to 140€ to 155€ for 18 holes. From Almancil, drive 4km (2½ miles) south of town, following signs to Vale do Lobo.

Faro ★

Once loved by the Romans and later by the Moors, Faro is the provincial capital of the Algarve. In this bustling little city of some 30,000 permanent residents, you can sit at a cafe, sample the wine, and watch yesterday and today collide as old men leading donkeys brush past German backpackers in shorts. Faro is a hodgepodge of life and activity: It has been rumbled, sacked, and "quaked" by everybody from Mother Nature to the Earl of Essex (Elizabeth I's favorite).

Since Afonso III drove out the Moors for the last time in 1266, Faro has been Portuguese. On its outskirts, an international airport brings in thousands of visitors every summer. The airport has done more than anything else to increase tourism not only to Faro, but also to the entire Algarve.

ESSENTIALS

Getting There

BY PLANE Jet service makes it possible to reach Faro from Lisbon in 30 minutes. For flight information, call the **Faro airport** (✆ **28/980-08-00**). You can take bus no. 14 or 16 from the airport to the railway station in Faro for 2.70€. The bus operates every 35 minutes daily from 7:20am to 10:15pm.

BY TRAIN Trains arrive from Lisbon five times a day. The trip takes 4¾ hours and costs 18€. The train station is at Largo da Estação (✆ **808/208-208**). This is the most strategic railway junction in the south of Portugal, thanks to its position astride lines that connect it to the north-south lines leading from Lisbon.

BY BUS Buses arrive every 5 hours from Lisbon. The journey takes 3½ hours. The bus station is on Av. da República 5 (✆ **28/989-97-60**); a one-way fare is 19€.

BY CAR From the west, Route 125 runs into Faro and beyond. From the Spanish border, pick up N125 west.

VISITOR INFORMATION At the **tourist offices** at Rua da Misericórdia 8–12 (✆ **28/980-36-04**) or at the airport (✆ **28/981-85-82**), you can pick up a copy of *The Algarve Guide to Walks,* which will direct you on nature trails in the area. It's open daily 9:30am to 5:30pm September to May, and 9:30am to 7pm June to August.

WHERE TO STAY

Eva Hotel ★ Eva dominates the harbor like a fortress. It's a modern, eight-story hotel that occupies an entire side of the yacht-clogged harbor. Most of the midsize, albeit austere guest rooms offer direct sea views. The better rooms have large balconies and open onto the water. Three rooms are available for those with limited mobility. Eva's best features are its penthouse restaurant and rooftop pool, supported on 16 posts, with sun terraces and a bar.

Av. da República, 8000-078 Faro. ✆ **28/900-10-00.** Fax 28/900-10-02. www.tdhotels.pt. 148 units. 102€–165€ double; 145€–225€ suite. Rates include buffet breakfast. AE, DC, MC, V. Limited free parking available on street. **Amenities:** 2 restaurants; 3 bars; babysitting; exercise room; outdoor freshwater pool; room service; spa. *In room:* A/C, TV, hair dryer, minibar, Wi-Fi (4€ per hour).

WHERE TO DINE

Adega Nortenha PORTUGUESE It's hardly a deluxe choice, but if you gravitate to simple yet well-prepared regional food, this little restaurant does the job. It's also one of the best value spots in town, which is probably why locals swear by it. Fresh tuna steak is a delicious choice, as is the roast lamb, which is herb-flavored and perfumed with garlic. The service is friendly and efficient, and the restaurant is done up in typical Algarvian style. A balcony is great for people-watching on the street below.

Praça Ferreira de Almeida 25. ✆ **28/982-27-09.** www.adeganortenha.pt. Main courses 7.50€–13€. AE, DC, MC, V. Daily noon–3pm and 7–10pm.

Dois Irmãos PORTUGUESE This popular bistro, founded in 1925, offers a no-nonsense atmosphere and has many devotees. The menu is as modest as the establishment and its prices, but you get a good choice of fresh grilled fish and shellfish dishes. Ignore the paper napkins and concentrate on the fine kettle of fish before you. Clams in savory sauce are a justifiable favorite, and sole is regularly featured—but, of course, everything depends on the catch of the day. Service is slow but amiable.

Largo do Terreiro do Bispo 20. ✆ **28/982-33-37.** Reservations recommended. Main courses 10€–25€. AE, DC, MC, V. Daily noon–4pm and 6–11pm.

SEEING THE SIGHTS

The most bizarre attraction in Faro is the **Capela dos Ossos (Chapel of Bones).** Enter through a courtyard from the rear of the **Igreja de Nossa Senhora do Monte do Carmo do Faro,** Largo do Carmo (✆ **28/982-44-90**). Erected in the 19th century, the chapel is completely lined with human skulls (an estimated 1,245) and bones. It's open daily 10am to 2pm and 3 to 5:30pm. Entrance is free to the church and 1€ to the chapel.

The church, built in 1713, contains a gilded baroque altar. Its facade is also baroque, with a bell tower rising from each side. Topping the belfries are gilded, mosquelike cupolas connected by a balustraded railing. The upper-level windows are latticed and framed with gold; statues stand in niches on either side of the main portal.

Other religious monuments include the old **Sé** (cathedral), on Largo da Sé (✆ **28/989-83-00**). Built in the Gothic and Renaissance styles, it stands on a site originally occupied by a mosque. Although the cathedral has a Gothic tower, it's better known for its tiles, which date from the 17th and 18th centuries. The highlight is the Capela do Rosário, on the right. It contains the oldest and most beautiful tiles, along with sculptures of two Nubians bearing lamps and a red chinoiserie organ. Admission is free. The beautiful cloisters are the most idyllic spot in Faro. The cathedral is open daily from 10am to 5:30pm. Admission is 2€.

Igreja de São Francisco, Largo de São Francisco (✆ **28/987-08-70**), is the other church of note. Its facade doesn't even begin to hint at the baroque richness inside. Panels of glazed earthenware tiles in milk-white and Dutch blue depict the life of the patron saint, St. Francis. One chapel is richly gilded. Open hours are Monday through Friday from 8 to 9:30am and 5:30 to 7pm (but in the sleepy Algarve, you might sometimes find it closed).

But most visitors don't come to Faro to look at churches or museums, regardless of how interesting they are. Bus no. 16, leaving from the terminal, runs to **Praia de Faro;** the one-way fare is 1€. A bridge also connects the mainland and the beach, about 6km (3¾ miles) from the town center. At the shore, you can water-ski, fish, or just rent a deck chair and umbrella and lounge in the sun.

DAY TRIPS FROM FARO

OLHÃO This is the Algarve's famous cubist town, long beloved by painters. In its heart, white blocks stacked one upon the other, with flat red-tile roofs and exterior stairways on the stark walls, evoke the casbahs of North Africa. The cubist buildings are found only at the core. The rest of Olhão has almost disappeared under the onslaught of modern commercialism.

While you're here, try to attend the fish market near the waterfront when a *lota,* or auction, is underway. Olhão is also known for its "bullfights of the sea," in which fishers wrestle with struggling tuna trapped in nets en route to the smelly warehouses along the harbor.

If you're here at lunchtime, go to one of the inexpensive markets along the waterfront. At **Casa de Pasto O Bote,** Av. do 5 de Outubro 122 (✆ **28/972-11-83**), you can select your food from trays of fresh fish. Your choice is then grilled to your specifications. Meal prices start at 10€. It's open Monday to Saturday noon to 3pm and 7 to 10pm.

For the best view, climb **Cabeça Hill,** with grottoes punctured by stalagmites and stalactites, or St. Michael's Mount, offering a panorama of the casbah-like Baretta. Finally, to reach one of the most idyllic beaches on the Algarve, take a 10-minute motorboat ride to the Ilha da Armona, a nautical mile away. Ferries run hourly in summer; the round-trip fare is 5€. Olhão is 8km (5 miles) east of Faro.

SÃO BRÁS DE ALPORTEL Traveling north from Faro, you'll pass through groves of figs, almonds, and oranges, and through pine woods where resin collects in wooden cups on the tree trunks. After 20km (12 miles) you'll come upon isolated São Brás de Alportel, one of the most charming and least-known spots on the Algarve. Far from the crowded beaches, this town attracts those in search of pure air, peace, and quiet. It's a bucolic setting filled with flowers pushing through nutmeg-colored soil.

Northeast of Loulé, the whitewashed, tile-roofed town livens up only on market days. Like its neighbor, Faro, it's noted for its perforated plaster chimneys. The area at the foot of the Serra do Caldeirão has been described as one vast garden.

Pousada de São Brás de Alportel ★, Estrada de Lisboa (N2), 8150-054 São Brás de Alportel (✆ **28/984-23-05;** www.pousadas.pt), is a change of pace from seaside accommodations. The government-owned hilltop villa has fret-cut limestone chimneys and a crow's-nest view of the surrounding countryside. It's approached through a fig orchard. Many visitors come to the pousada just for lunch or dinner (served daily 1–3pm and 7:30–10pm), returning to the coastline at night, but a knowing few remain for the evening. In the dining room, rustic mountain-tavern chairs and tables rest on hand-woven rugs. The 28€ table d'hôte dinner offers soup, a fish course, a meat dish, vegetables, and dessert. The cuisine is plain but good. After dinner, you might want to retire to the sitting room to watch the embers of the evening's fire die down. The 33 guest rooms contain private bathrooms and phones. Doubles cost from 90€ to 189€, including breakfast. Amenities include an outdoor swimming pool, laundry service, and room service (until 10pm).

SCOTLAND

16

by Darwin Porter & Danforth Prince

Whether you go to Scotland to seek out your ancestral roots, explore ancient castles, drive the Malt Whisky Trail, or partake in the internationally acclaimed Edinburgh Festival, you'll find a country rich in history, legend, and romance. If it's the outdoors you love, Scotland offers great salmon fishing, peaceful walks in heather-covered Highland hills, and some of the best (and oldest) golf courses.

EDINBURGH & ENVIRONS

Called one of Europe's fairest cities, the "Athens of the North" is the second-most-visited city in Britain after London. In contrast to industrialized bastions like Aberdeen and Glasgow, it's a white-collar city. Home of the Royal Mile, Princes Street, and the popular Edinburgh Festival, with its action-packed list of cultural events, Edinburgh is both hip and historic. John Knox; Mary, Queen of Scots; Robert Louis Stevenson; Sir Arthur Conan Doyle; Alexander Graham Bell; Sir Walter Scott; Bonnie Prince Charlie; and Deacon Brodie are all part of the city's past. You can walk in their footsteps and explore sights associated with them.

Essentials

GETTING THERE

BY PLANE Edinburgh is about an hour's flying time from London, 633km (393 miles) south. **Edinburgh Airport** (© **0844/481-8989;** www.edinburghairport.com) is 10km (6¼ miles) west of the center, receiving flights from within the British Isles and the rest of Europe. Before heading into town, you might want to stop at the **information and accommodation desk** (© **0131/344-3295**); it's open Monday to Saturday 8am to 9pm and Sunday 9am to 4:30pm. A double-decker Airlink bus makes the trip from the airport to the city center every 10 minutes, letting you off near Waverley Bridge, between the Old Town and the New Town; the fare is £3.50 one-way or £6 round-trip, and the trip takes about 25 minutes. For more information, search www.flybybus.com. A **taxi** (© **0131/344-3344**) into the city will cost £20 or more, depending on traffic, and the ride will be about 25 minutes.

BY TRAIN InterCity trains link London with Edinburgh and are fast and efficient, providing both restaurant and bar service as well as air-conditioning. Trains from London's Kings Cross Station arrive in Edinburgh at **Waverley Station,** at the east end of Princes Street (✆ **08457/48-49-50;** www.nationalrail.com in London for rail info). Trains depart London every hour or so, taking about 4½ hours and costing £25 to £189 one-way. Overnight trains have a sleeper berth, which you can rent for an extra £45. Taxis and buses are right outside the station in Edinburgh.

BY BUS The least expensive way to go from London to Edinburgh is by bus, but it's an 8-hour journey. Nevertheless, it'll get you there for only about £15 one-way or £24 round-trip. Coaches depart from London's Victoria Coach Station, delivering you to Edinburgh's **St. Andrew Square Bus Station,** St. Andrew Square (✆ **08705/50-50-50** in London, or 0181/663-9233 in Edinburgh). Service across both countries is provided by **National Express** (✆ **08717/81-81-81;** www.nationalexpress.com) or **Megabus** (✆ **08705/50-50-50;** www.megabus.com).

BY CAR Edinburgh is 74km (46 miles) east of Glasgow and 169km (105 miles) north of Newcastle-upon-Tyne in England. No express motorway links London and Edinburgh. The M1 from London takes you part of the way north, but you'll have to come into Edinburgh along secondary roads: A68 or A7 from the southeast, A1 from the east, or A702 from the north. The A71 or A8 comes in from the west, A8 connecting with M8 just west of Edinburgh; A90 comes down from the north over the Forth Road Bridge. Allow 8 hours or more for the drive north from London.

VISITOR INFORMATION **Tourist Offices** **Edinburgh & Scotland Information Centre,** 3 Princes Mall, at the corner of Princes Street and Waverley Bridge (✆ **0845/225-5121;** www.edinburgh.org; bus: 3, 31, or 69), can give you sightseeing information and also help find lodgings. The center sells bus tours, theater tickets, and souvenirs. It's open year-round, Monday to Saturday 9am to 5pm. There's also an information and accommodations desk (✆ **0131/344-3295**) at Edinburgh Airport.

WEBSITES The official site of the **Scottish Tourist Board** (✆ **0871/789-6200;** www.scotland.org.uk) is an excellent source for events, lodging, getting around, and outdoor activities. However, the "Special Offers" section requires a lot of clicks for little payoff. The **Edinburgh and Lothians Tourist Board** (**www.edinburgh.org**) discusses what's new, travel tips, and events and festivals for city, coast, and country; they include a page about what to do with kids, written *by* kids.

Scotland Holiday Net (**www.aboutscotland.co.uk**) combines information on dining, lodging, and sightseeing with personal accounts. Curious about Scotland's top 20 free attractions? Interested in restaurant reviews from other diners? Try **www.scotland.org.uk**. Listing locations and greens fees, **www.uk-golfguide.com** will help you find a course wherever you plan to be.

CITY LAYOUT Edinburgh is divided into an **Old Town** and a **New Town.** Chances are, you'll find lodgings in New Town and visit Old Town for dining, drinking, shopping, and sightseeing.

New Town, with its world-famous **Princes Street,** came about in the 18th century in the "Golden Age" of Edinburgh. The first building went up in New Town in 1767, and by the end of the century, classical squares, streets, and town houses had been added. Princes Street runs straight for about a mile; it's known for its shopping and its beauty, as it opens onto the **Princes Street Gardens** with stunning views of Old Town.

Scotland

North of Princes Street, and running parallel to it, is the second great street of New Town, **George Street.** It begins at Charlotte Square and runs east to St. Andrew Square. Directly north of George Street is another impressive thoroughfare, **Queen Street,** opening onto Queen Street Gardens on its north side.

You'll also hear a lot about **Rose Street,** directly north of Princes Street. It has more pubs per square block than any other place in Scotland, and is also filled with shops and restaurants.

Everyone seems to have heard of the **Royal Mile,** the main thoroughfare of Old Town, beginning at Edinburgh Castle and running all the way to the Palace of Holyroodhouse. A famous street to the south of the castle (you have to descend to it) is **Grassmarket,** where convicted criminals were hanged on the dreaded gallows that once stood here.

GETTING AROUND **Walking** is the best way to explore Edinburgh, particularly Old Town, with its narrow lanes, wynds, and closes. Most attractions are along the Royal Mile, along Princes Street, or on one of the major streets of New Town.

Edinburgh

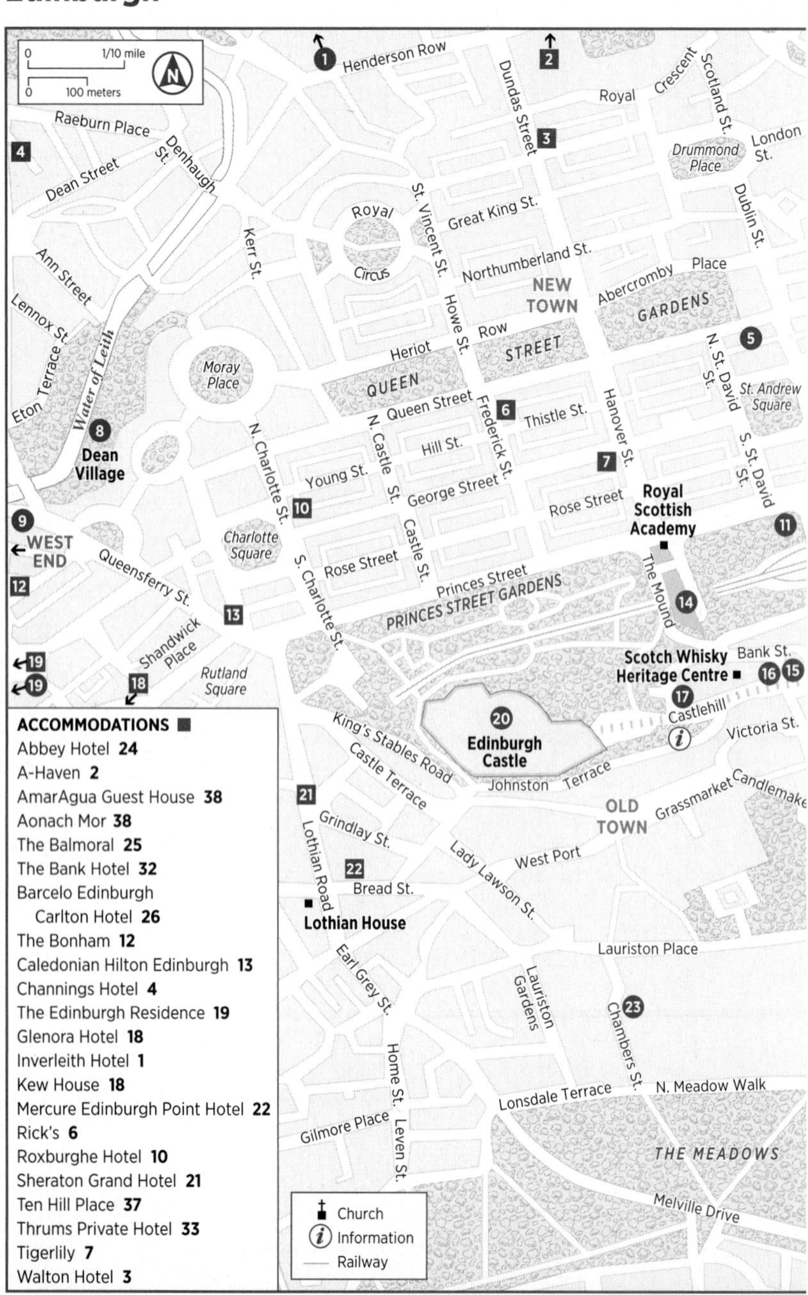
0 1/10 mile
0 100 meters
N
Henderson Row
Royal Crescent
Scotland St.
Dundas Street
Drummond Place
London St.
Dublin St.
Raeburn Place
Denhaugh St.
Dean Street
Royal Circus
St. Vincent St.
Great King St.
Northumberland St.
Kerr St.
NEW TOWN
Abercromby Place
GARDENS
Ann Street
Lennox St.
Eton Terrace
Water of Leith
Moray Place
Howe St.
Heriot Row
QUEEN STREET
N. St. David St.
St. Andrew Square
Dean Village
Queen Street
Frederick St.
Thistle St.
Hanover St.
N. Charlotte St.
N. Castle St.
Hill St.
Young St.
George Street
S. St. David St.
Rose Street
Royal Scottish Academy
WEST END
Charlotte Square
Queensferry St.
S. Charlotte St.
Castle St.
Princes Street
PRINCES STREET GARDENS
The Mound
Shandwick Place
Rutland Square
Scotch Whisky Heritage Centre
Bank St.
Castlehill
Edinburgh Castle
King's Stables Road
Castle Terrace
Johnston Terrace
Victoria St.
Candlemaker
Grassmarket
OLD TOWN
Grindlay St.
Lothian Road
Lady Lawson St.
West Port
Bread St.
Lothian House
Earl Grey St.
Lauriston Place
Lauriston Gardens
Chambers St.
Home St.
Leven St.
Lonsdale Terrace
N. Meadow Walk
Gilmore Place
THE MEADOWS
Melville Drive
Church
Information
Railway
ACCOMMODATIONS
Abbey Hotel 24
A-Haven 2
AmarAgua Guest House 38
Aonach Mor 38
The Balmoral 25
The Bank Hotel 32
Barcelo Edinburgh Carlton Hotel 26
The Bonham 12
Caledonian Hilton Edinburgh 13
Channings Hotel 4
The Edinburgh Residence 19
Glenora Hotel 18
Inverleith Hotel 1
Kew House 18
Mercure Edinburgh Point Hotel 22
Rick's 6
Roxburghe Hotel 10
Sheraton Grand Hotel 21
Ten Hill Place 37
Thrums Private Hotel 33
Tigerlily 7
Walton Hotel 3

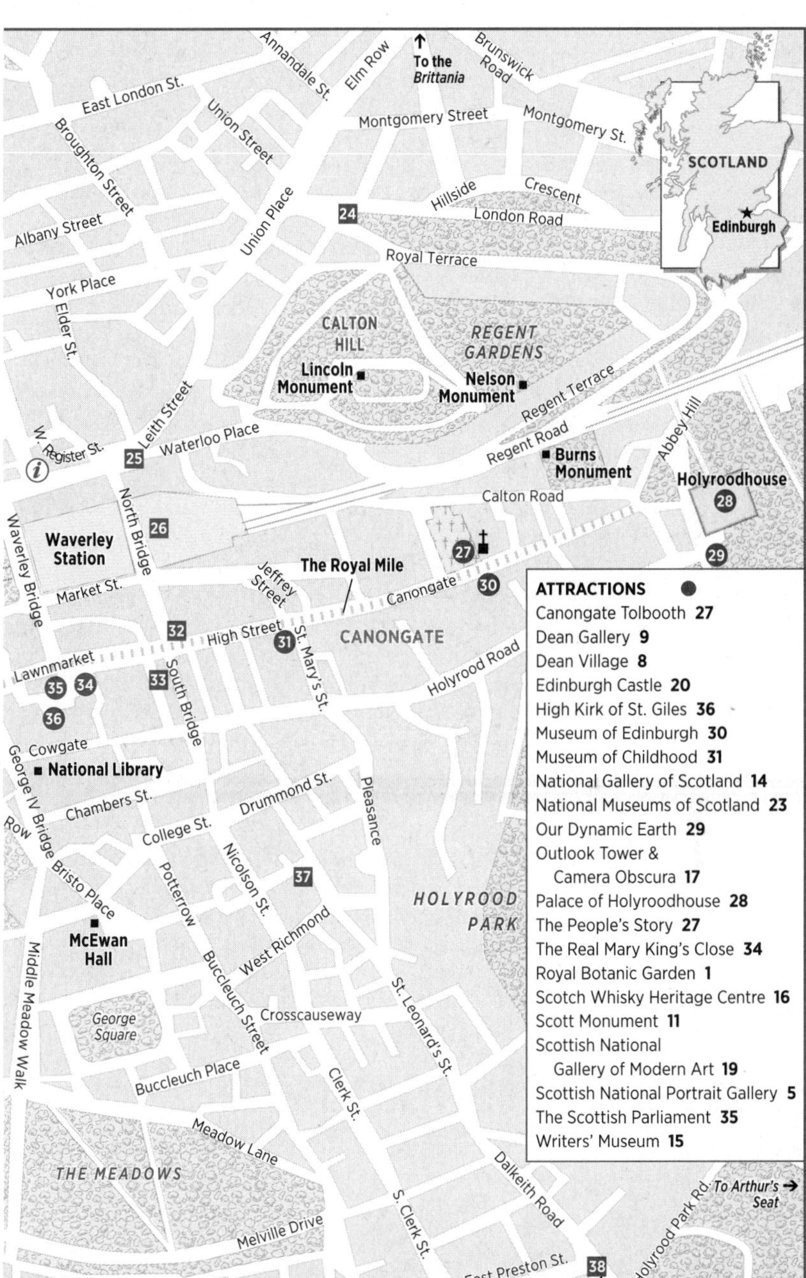
Annandale St.
Elm Row
To the Brittania
Brunswick Road
East London St.
Union Street
Montgomery Street
Montgomery St.
Broughton Street
SCOTLAND
Edinburgh
Hillside
Crescent
24
London Road
Albany Street
Union Place
Royal Terrace
York Place
Elder St.
CALTON HILL
REGENT GARDENS
Lincoln Monument
Nelson Monument
Leith Street
Regent Terrace
W. Register St.
Waterloo Place
25
Regent Road
Burns Monument
Abbey Hill
Holyroodhouse
28
Calton Road
Waverley Station
North Bridge
26
Waverley Bridge
27
29
The Royal Mile
Jeffrey Street
Canongate
30
Market St.
32
High Street
31
St. Mary's St.
CANONGATE
Lawnmarket
35
34
33
South Bridge
Holyrood Road
36
Cowgate
National Library
George IV Bridge
Chambers St.
Drummond St.
Pleasance
Row
College St.
Nicolson St.
37
Bristo Place
Potterrow
HOLYROOD PARK
McEwan Hall
West Richmond
Buccleuch Street
Middle Meadow Walk
George Square
Crosscauseway
St. Leonard's St.
Buccleuch Place
Clerk St.
Meadow Lane
THE MEADOWS
Dalkeith Road
To Arthur's Seat
Holyrood Park Rd.
S. Clerk St.
Melville Drive
East Preston St.
38
ATTRACTIONS
Canongate Tolbooth 27
Dean Gallery 9
Dean Village 8
Edinburgh Castle 20
High Kirk of St. Giles 36
Museum of Edinburgh 30
Museum of Childhood 31
National Gallery of Scotland 14
National Museums of Scotland 23
Our Dynamic Earth 29
Outlook Tower & Camera Obscura 17
Palace of Holyroodhouse 28
The People's Story 27
The Real Mary King's Close 34
Royal Botanic Garden 1
Scotch Whisky Heritage Centre 16
Scott Monument 11
Scottish National Gallery of Modern Art 19
Scottish National Portrait Gallery 5
The Scottish Parliament 35
Writers' Museum 15

BY BUS The bus will probably be your chief method of transport. The fare is £1.20 for one journey, any distance. Children ages 5 to 15 are charged a flat rate of 70p, but teenagers ages 16 to 18 must carry a **teen card** (available where bus tickets are sold—see below) as proof of age and their fare is 70p; children 4 and under ride free. Exact change is required if you're paying your fare on the bus.

The **Edinburgh Day Saver Ticket** allows 1 day of unlimited travel on city buses at a cost of £3 adults and £2 children.

For daily commuters or die-hard Scottish enthusiasts, a **RidaCard** (http://lothianbuses.com/ridacard.php) season ticket allows unlimited travel on all buses. For adults, the price is £15 for 1 week and £45 for 4 weeks; tickets for children cost £10 for 1 week and £30 for 4 weeks. Travel must begin on Sunday.

You can get these tickets and further information in the city center at the **Waverley Bridge Transport Office,** Waverley Bridge (✆ **0131/554-4494;** bus: 3 or 31), open Monday to Saturday 8:30am to 5pm and Sunday 9:30am to 5pm; or at the Hanover Street office (bus: 3 or 31), open Monday to Saturday 8:30am to 6pm. For details on timetables, call ✆ **0131/555-6363.**

BY TAXI You can hail a taxi or pick one up at a taxi stand. Meters start at £1.60 and a typical fare across town might cost £7. Taxi stands are at Hanover Street, North St. Andrew Street, Waverley Station, Haymarket Station, and Lauriston Place. Fares are displayed in the front of the taxi and charges posted, including extra charges for night drivers or destinations outside the city limits; a call-out is charged at 60p. You can also call a taxi. Try **City Cabs** at ✆ **0131/228-1211** (www.citycabs.co.uk) or **Central Radio Taxis** at ✆ **0131/229-2468** (www.taxis-edinburgh.co.uk and www.fastblacks.com).

BY CAR Car rentals are relatively expensive, and driving in Edinburgh is a tricky business. The city is a warren of one-way streets, with parking spots at a premium. A car is convenient, however, and sometimes a must, for touring the countryside. Most companies will accept your U.S. or Canadian driver's license, provided you have held it for more than a year and are 21 and over. At the Edinburgh airport, try **Avis** (✆ **0870/608-6335**), **Hertz** (✆ **0131/333-1019**), or **Europcar** (✆ **0131/333-2588**).

BY BICYCLE Biking isn't a good idea for most because the city is constructed on a series of high ridges and terraces. You may, however, want to rent a bike for exploring the flatter countryside around the city. **Bike Trax,** 13 Lochrin Place (✆ **0131/228-6333;** bus: 10), off Home Street in Tollcross, near the Cameo Cinema, charges around £16 to £20 per day (plus a £100 deposit). The shop is open June to September, Monday to Saturday 9:30am to 6pm and Sunday noon to 7pm, and October to May, Monday to Saturday 10am to 5:30pm.

[Fast FACTS] EDINBURGH

Business Hours In Edinburgh, banks are usually open Monday to Wednesday 9:30am to 3:45pm and Thursday and Friday 9:30am to 5 or 5:30pm. Shops are generally open Monday to Saturday 10am to 5:30 or 6pm; on Thursday, stores stay open to 8pm.

Currency The basic unit of currency is the **pound sterling** (£), which is divided into 100 **pence** (p). The exchange rate at press time is £1 = $1.60. Note that though the United Kingdom is part of the E.U., it does not plan to switch to the euro at this time.

Currency Exchange There's a **Bureau de Change** of the Clydesdale Bank at 20 Hanover St. (✆ **0131/4564560**).

Dentists & Doctors For a dental emergency, go to the **Edinburgh Dental Institute,** 39 Lauriston Place (✆ **0131/536-4970**), open Monday to Friday 9am to 3pm. In a medical emergency, you can seek help from the **Edinburgh Royal Infirmary,** 51 Royal Infirmary, Old Dalkeitl Rd. (✆ **0131/536-1000**). Medical attention is available 24 hours.

Drugstores There are no 24-hour drugstores ("chemists" or "pharmacies") in Edinburgh. The major drugstore is **Boots,** 48 Shandwick Place (✆ **0131/225-6757;** bus: 3 or 31), open Monday to Friday 8am to 8pm, Saturday 8am to 6pm, and Sunday 10am to 4pm.

Embassies & Consulates The consulate of the **United States** is at 3 Regent Terrace (✆ **0131/556-8315;** www.usembassy.org.uk/scotland/index.htm; bus: 26, 85, or 86), which is an extension of Princes Street beyond Nelson's Monument. All the other embassies are in London (see chapter 6).

Emergencies Call ✆ **999** in an emergency to summon the police, an ambulance, or firefighters.

Hospital The best and most convenient is the **Edinburgh Royal Infirmary,** 1 Lauriston Place (✆ **0131/536-1000;** bus: 23 or 41).

Internet Access At the **International Telecom Centre,** 52 High St. (✆ **0131/559-7114;** bus: 1 or 6), along the Royal Mile, the rate is £1 for 15 minutes. The center is open daily from 9am to 10pm.

Post Office The Edinburgh Branch Post Office, St. James's Centre, is open Monday to Friday 9am to 5:30pm and Saturday 8:30am to noon. For postal information and customer service, call ✆ **0845/222-3344.**

Telephones The United Kingdom's **country code** is **44.** The city code for **Edinburgh** is **0131.** If you're calling from inside the United Kingdom but outside the city code area, dial the complete area code; if you're calling from outside the United Kingdom, drop the zero. If you're calling from inside the code area, dial just the seven-digit number.

Public phones cost 40p (80¢) for the first 20 minutes and accept coins of various denominations. You can also buy a phone card for use in special phones at post offices and newsstands.

Tipping In most restaurants, tax and service charge are included, so it's unnecessary to leave a tip. If a service charge hasn't been included in the bill, the standard tip is 10%. Taxi drivers also expect a 10% tip.

Where to Stay

IN THE CENTER

Very Expensive

The Balmoral ★★★ This legendary establishment was opened in 1902 as the largest, grandest, and most impressive hotel in the north of Britain. Its soaring clock tower is a city landmark. Rooms are distinguished, conservative, and large, a graceful reminder of Edwardian sprawl with a contemporary twist. Many benefit from rounded or oversize windows and the various Victorian/Edwardian quirks that were originally designed as part of its charm.

1 Princes St., Edinburgh EH2 2EQ. ✆ **888/667-9477** or 0131/556-2414. Fax 0131/557-3747. www.thebalmoralhotel.com. 188 units. £360–£535 double; from £670 suite. AE, DC, MC, V. Valet parking £25. Bus: 3, 8, 22, 25, or 30. **Amenities:** 3 restaurants; 2 bars; babysitting; concierge; health club; indoor pool; room service; sauna; spa. *In room:* A/C, TV, hair dryer, minibar, Wi-Fi (£15 per day).

Caledonian Hilton Edinburgh ★★★ "The Caley," built in 1903, is Edinburgh's most visible hotel, with commanding views over Edinburgh Castle and the Princes Street Gardens. The pastel-colored public areas are reminiscent of Edwardian splendor. Rooms are conservatively but individually styled, and are often exceptionally spacious. Fifth-floor rooms are the smallest. Although the accommodations are comparable to those of other first-class hotels in Edinburgh, the Caledonian lacks the leisure facilities of its major competitor, the Balmoral.

Princes St., Edinburgh EH1 2AB. ✆ **0131/222-8888.** Fax 0131/222-8889. www.caledonian.hilton.com. 249 units. £139–£239 double; £614–£639 suite. Children 15 and under stay free in parent's room. AE, DC, MC, V. Parking £9.50. Bus: 12, 25, or 33. **Amenities:** 3 restaurants; bar; babysitting; concierge; exercise room; indoor pool; room service. *In room:* TV, hair dryer, minibar, Wi-Fi (£12 per day).

Sheraton Grand Hotel ★★ This elegant hotel, in a postmodern complex on a former railway siding a short walk from Princes Street, is the most appealing modern hotel in the capital. If you seek Victorian grandeur, make it the Caledonian. But if you'd like to be situated in the "new Edinburgh" (a financial center called the Exchange), then make it the Sheraton Grand. Rooms may lack character, but they are exceedingly comfortable. The best units are called "Castle View," and they are on the top three floors.

1 Festival Sq., Edinburgh, Lothian EH3 9SR. ✆ **800/325-3535** in the U.S. and Canada, or 0131/229-9131. Fax 0131/228-4510. www.starwoodhotels.com. 260 units. £259–£342 double; £359–£442 suite. AE, DC, MC, V. Parking £20. Bus: 10, 22, or 30. **Amenities:** 4 restaurants; 2 bars; babysitting; concierge; exercise room; 2 pools (indoor and outdoor); room service; sauna; spa. *In room:* A/C, TV, hair dryer, minibar, Wi-Fi (£15 per day).

Expensive

Barcelo Edinburgh Carlton Hotel ★★ The Victorian turrets, Flemish gables, and severe gray stonework rise imposingly from a street corner on the Royal Mile, a few steps from Waverley Station. The former department store has been converted into a bright and airy milieu full of modern conveniences. Rooms have a kind of Scandinavian simplicity. Bathrooms tend to be small. Although the hotel doesn't have the style and grandeur of the Caledonian, it has more facilities.

19 North Bridge, Edinburgh, Lothian EH1 1SD. ✆ **0131/472-3000.** Fax 0131/556-2691. www.barcelo-hotels.co.uk. 189 units. £120–£224 executive double. Children 14 and under stay free in parent's room. AE, DC, MC, V. Parking £20. Bus: 3, 8, 14, or 29. **Amenities:** Restaurant; bar; babysitting; concierge; health club; indoor pool; room service; sauna. *In room:* TV, hair dryer, minibar, Wi-Fi (free).

The Bonham ★★ One of Edinburgh's most stylish hotels occupies a trio of Regency town houses. Rooms are outfitted in an urban and very hip blend of old and new. The decor combines ancient vases, Art Nouveau objects, marble busts, contemporary art—an eclectic but tasteful mix. Each unit has a TV with a keyboard hooked up to the Internet, the first setup of its kind in Scotland.

35 Drumsheugh Gardens, Edinburgh EH3 7RN. ✆ **0131/226-6050.** Fax 0131/226-6080. www.townhousecompany.com/thebonham. 48 units. £100–£280 small double; £155–£320 superior double; £220–£400 suite. Rates include continental breakfast. AE, DC, MC, V. Free parking. Bus: 19 or 37. **Amenities:** Restaurant; room service. *In room:* TV, hair dryer, Internet (free), minibar.

Channings Hotel ★★ Five Edwardian terrace houses were combined to create this hotel 7 blocks north of Dean Village in a tranquil residential area. It maintains the atmosphere of a Scottish country house. Rooms are outfitted in a modern yet elegant style. Front units have views of a cobblestone street. Back rooms are quieter, and standard accommodations are a bit cheaper but are much smaller. The most desirable rooms are labeled "Executive," and have bay windows and wingback chairs.

15 S. Learmonth Gardens, Edinburgh EH4 1EZ. ✆ **0131/315-2226.** Fax 0131/332-9631. www.townhousecompany.com/channings. 46 units. £115–£300 double; £190–£390 suite. Rates include breakfast. Children 14 and under £30 extra. AE, DC, MC, V. No parking. Bus: 37. **Amenities:** 2 restaurants. *In room:* TV, hair dryer, Internet (free).

The Edinburgh Residence ★★★ If Robert Burns, who liked his luxuries, were checking into a hotel in Edinburgh today, he no doubt would be booked in here. It's one of the finest luxury hotels in Scotland, a series of elegant town-house suites installed in a trio of architecturally beautiful and sensitively restored Georgian buildings. As you enter, grand staircases and classic wood paneling greet you. A stay here is like finding lodging in an elegant town house from long ago, albeit with all the modern conveniences. Accommodations are the ultimate in local comfort. A trio of classic suites have private entrances. All units are spacious—even the smallest is the size of a tennis court—and all are nonsmoking.

7 Rothesay Terrace, Edinburgh EH3 7RY. ✆ **0131/226-3380.** Fax 0131/274-7405. www.townhousecompany.com/theedinburghresidence. 29 units. £125–£400 suite; £295–£500 apt. Rates include continental breakfast. AE, MC, V. Free parking. Bus: 13. **Amenities:** Bar; room service. *In room:* TV, hair dryer, Internet (free), minibar.

Mercure Edinburgh Point Hotel ★ With one of the most dramatic contemporary interiors of any hotel in Edinburgh, this stylish place is in the shadow of Edinburgh Castle. The decor has appeared in a book detailing the 50 premier hotel designs in the world, with a great emphasis on color and innovation, including a black stone floor at the front that's marked by "dusty footprints." In one area, an optical fantasy is created when blue walls are brilliantly lighted by red neon. For a dramatic minimalist effect, a lone armchair and sofa occupy 93 sq. m (1,000 sq. ft.) of space. Standard rooms are a bit small, the premium rooms more comfortable and spacious. Most of the guest rooms open onto views of the castle; however, those in the rear do not. If you like stainless steel, laser projections, and chrome instead of Scottish antiques, this might be an address for you.

34 Bread St., Edinburgh EH3 9AF. ✆ **0131/221-5555.** Fax 0131/221-9929. www.accorhotels.com. 139 units. £120–£180 double; £185–£250 suite. AE, DC, MC, V. No parking. Bus: 2 or 28. **Amenities:** Restaurant; bar; room service. *In room:* TV, hair dryer, Wi-Fi (£15 per day).

Roxburghe Hotel ★ Originally a stately Robert Adam town house, the hotel stands on a tree-filled square a short walk from Princes Street. In 1999, it opened another wing, more than doubling the original size of the hotel. The old wing maintains a traditional atmosphere with ornate ceilings and woodwork, antique furnishings, and tall, arched windows. The more modern wing offers government-rated four-star hotel comfort, completely contemporary styling, and up-to-date furnishings.

38 Charlotte Sq. (at George St.), Edinburgh EH2 4HQ. ✆ **0844/879-9063.** Fax 0131/240-5555. www.macdonaldhotels.co.uk/roxburghe. 198 units. £133–£191 double; £539–£619 suite. Rates include breakfast. AE, DC, MC, V. Parking £20. Bus: 100. **Amenities:** Restaurant; bar; babysitting; concierge; health club; indoor pool; room service; sauna. *In room:* TV, hair dryer, minibar, Wi-Fi (£13 per day).

Tigerlily ★ This boutique hotel address is a good choice for those seeking a hip alternative to a traditional Edinburgh B&B. It's even popular with locals who crowd its bars and stylish lounge areas every evening. From its minisuites to its Georgian-style rooms, the hotel is the latest word in modernity. Thoughtful extras abound—iPods are regularly updated with the latest tunes, an umbrella is in the stand for rainy days, and a dressing gown and slippers await you after a hard day of sightseeing. There is access to a gym and pool at the Roxburghe across the street, and the personal service here is the best in town.

125 George St., Edinburgh EH2 4JN. ✆ **0131/225-5005.** Fax 0131/225-7046. www.tigerlilyedinburgh.co.uk. 33 rooms. £195–£235 double; from £255 suite. Rates include breakfast. AE, DC, MC, V. Bus: 3, 8, 22, 25, 30. **Amenities:** Restaurant; bar; babysitting; room service. *In room:* TV, hair dryer, minibar, Wi-Fi (free).

Moderate

The Bank Hotel This modest hotel in a 1923 building offers better value than many of its competitors in this congested neighborhood beside the Royal Mile. Until around 1990 it was a branch of the Royal Bank of Scotland, and the past is still evident in its bulky, no-nonsense design. Upstairs, high ceilings, simple furnishings, and king-size beds provide comfort in the clean guest rooms.

Royal Mile at 1 S. Bridge St., Edinburgh EH1 1LL. ✆ **0131/556-9940.** Fax 0131/558-1362. www.festival-inns.co.uk. 9 units. £116–£172 double. Rates include breakfast. AE, MC, V. Nearby parking £5. Bus: 4, 15, 31, or 100. **Amenities:** Restaurant; bar; Wi-Fi (free). *In room:* TV, hair dryer.

Glenora Hotel Only a 10-minute walk from Princes Street and the city center is this refurbished bed-and-breakfast. Its convenient location and comfortable rooms make this a favorite among visitors and business clients alike. Everywhere you look there are Victorian touches, such as brass servant's bells and speaking tubes. The rooms—all nonsmoking—are nothing special, just clean and cozy. Each unit has a small bathroom with a shower. The kitchen serves a vegetarian breakfast, plus a traditional Scottish breakfast.

14 Rosebury Crescent, Edinburgh EH12 5JY. ✆ **0845/180-0045.** Fax 0131/337-1119. www.glenorahotel.co.uk. 11 units. £85–£145 double; £109–£156 triple. Rates include Scottish breakfast. MC, V. No parking. Bus: 12, 26, or 31. **Amenities:** Dining room. *In room:* TV, hair dryer, Wi-Fi (free).

Inverleith Hotel Across from the Royal Botantic Gardens, on the street that Robert Louis Stevenson once called home, is a charming, family-run bed-and-breakfast. Steve and Adriene Case, the hotel owners, are congenial and helpful people who run the place with great care. The small to midsize rooms are comfortable, with basic British decor and direct-dial telephones. A large Scottish breakfast is served. There is a lounge that specializes in malt whisky.

5 Inverleith Terrace, Edinburgh EH3 4NS. ✆ **0131/556-2745.** Fax 0845/644-2076. www.inverleithhotel.co.uk. 10 units. £59–£129 double; £89–£159 apt. Rates include Scottish breakfast. AE, MC, V. Free parking. Bus: 8, 23, or 27. **Amenities:** Dining room; room service.

Kew House ★ ☺ One of New Town's most successful Victorian restorations, this complex near the Murrayfield Rugby Stadium lies 1.6km (1 mile) west of Princes Street and is easily reached by public transportation, a 10-minute walk from Haymarket rail station. Each bedroom has been furnished in an individual style, with much comfort, including private bathrooms with shower. Thoughtful touches abound, including the gift of chocolates and sherry upon your arrival. There are six bedrooms here, plus two well-furnished apartments that lie a 5-minute walk from the main house. The apartments, ideal for families, also contain full kitchens and sitting rooms.

1 Kew Terrace, Murrayfield, Edinburgh EH12 5JE. ✆ **0131/313-0700.** Fax 0131/313-0747. www.kewhouse.com. 7 units. July–Aug £120–£165 double, £190 apt; off season £89–£120 double, £140 apt. Rates include breakfast. MC, V. Free parking. Bus: 12, 26, or 31. **Amenities:** Lounge. *In room:* TV, fridge (in some), hair dryer, kitchen (in some), Wi-Fi (free).

Rick's ★ A cool, sleek choice, Rick's name may have been inspired by Bogie's famous bar in the movie *Casablanca*. It is a boutique hotel of charm and informality. Bedrooms are custom designed, from the elegant walnut headboards on the beds to the Angora and lamb's-wool blankets. From dawn to dusk, Scottish meals are served in the contemporary restaurant, featuring fresh produce from local suppliers. Alfresco dining is offered on the covered terrace.

55A Frederick St., Edinburgh EH2 1HL. ✆ **0131/622-7800.** www.ricksedinburgh.co.uk. 10 units. £85–£130 double. DC, MC, V. Bus: 24 or 29. **Amenities:** Restaurant; bar; room service. *In room:* TV/DVD, CD player, hair dryer, Wi-Fi (free).

Ten Hill Place ★ This chic new address was created by merging a modern building with a traditional Georgian stone terrace house. Many of its elegant bedrooms open onto views of the landmark Arthur's Seat with the Firth of Forth in the distance. The rooms are spacious and furnished with a velvety decor, and the bathrooms are large and luxurious. Although you wouldn't know it, the hotel is actually owned by a charitable institution set up by the Royal College of Surgeons. It lies about a 10-minute walk from Edinburgh Castle and in the heart of Old Town.

10 Hill Place, Edinburgh EH8 9DS. ✆ **0131/662-2080.** Fax 0131/662-2082. www.tenhillplace.com. 78 units. £68–£188 double. Rates include breakfast. AE, DC, MC, V. Bus: 47. **Amenities:** Restaurant; bar; room service. *In room:* TV, hair dryer, Wi-Fi (free).

Inexpensive

Abbey Hotel This 1820 Georgian house is furnished with antiques to give it the right spirit. There are singles, doubles, twins, and three family rooms, all centrally heated and all with private bathrooms with showers. Rooms open onto views of a

NATIVE behavior

The quickest way to brand yourself a tourist is to ask a kilt-wearing Scotsman what he wears underneath the kilt. A true Scotsman—and, of course, many a Scottish lass—already knows the answer to that one (nothing). A guard at Edinburgh Castle told us, "I must get asked that question at least 10 times a day."

It takes more than the swirl of tartan to make you blend in with the Scots. It also helps to perk up your ears at the skirl of pipes and to claim membership in a clan, the more ancient the better. If you're a big man, the ability to toss a giant caber (tree trunk) will get you a free round of brew at the local pub.

When talking with Scots, it helps if you express a firm belief in the existence of the Loch Ness monster and refer to her as "Nessie." If you really want to show your familiarity with the creature, call her "Beastie," as do the locals who actually live on the loch. To report an actual sighting endears you even more to the Scots.

If you're invited to a Scottish home, you'll immediately be offered tea no matter what time of day. As a local told us, "It's always teatime in Scotland." In the Lowlands it's called "a fly cup"—that is, a quick cup between meals. In the Highlands, it's called "a wee strupach," which means the same thing.

And finally, on the subject of drink, it's wise to drink only Scottish whisky (spelled without the "e") and to express your loathing of such "hogwash" as American, Canadian, or Irish whiskey with an "e."

private garden or the Firth of Forth and are so large that 10 of them contain a double bed and two singles.

9 Royal Terrace, Edinburgh EH7 5AB. ✆/fax **0131/557-0022.** www.abbeyhoteledinburgh.co.uk. 16 units. £40–£150 double. Rates include breakfast. AE, MC, V. No parking. Bus: 1, 4, 5, or 15. **Amenities:** Bar. *In room:* TV, hair dryer, Wi-Fi (free).

A-Haven This semidetached 1862 Victorian house is a 15-minute walk or 5-minute bus ride north of the rail station. Rooms are of various sizes, with the biggest on the second floor, although most rooms are much smaller and less expensive. Some in back overlook the Firth of Forth, and those in the front open onto views of Arthur's Seat. David Kay extends a Scottish welcome in this family-type place, and often advises guests about sightseeing.

180 Ferry Rd., Edinburgh EH6 4NS. ✆ **0131/554-6559.** Fax 0131/554-5252. www.a-haven.co.uk. 16 units. £70–£130 double. Rates include breakfast. AE, MC, V. Free parking. Bus: 7, 11, 14, or 21. **Amenities:** Bar; children's playground. *In room:* TV, hair dryer, Wi-Fi (free).

AmarAgua Guest House This bed-and-breakfast, a favorite of the Scottish Tourist board, is located in an 1880s Victorian residential 1.6km (1 mile) from Princes Street. The quaint rooms are not for those who seek modern accommodations, but are well kept. After a good night's sleep in the small to midsize rooms, visitors can head downstairs for breakfast in the light-flooded dining room. Guest choose their meals "a la carte" style, a rarity for a small bed-and-breakfast.

10 Kilmaurs Terrace, Edinburgh EH16 5DR. ✆ **0131/667-6775.** Fax 0131/667-7687. www.amaragua.co.uk. 7 units. £70–£125 double. Rates include breakfast. MC, V. Free parking. Bus: 30 or 33. **Amenities:** Dining room. *In room:* TV, hair dryer, Wi-Fi (free).

Aonach Mor ★ 🎁 In the Newington district of the city, 1.6km (1 mile) from the center, this small, family-run guesthouse is a restored Victorian terraced building. It is an informal, friendly home that is comfortable, and it offers one of the best home-cooked breakfasts in town. Rooms, each with private bathroom, open onto views of either Arthur's Seat or walled gardens. Each room is individually decorated and refurbished, the most spectacular—and obviously the most expensive—being a luxurious Jacobean-style double with an elegant four-poster bed.

14 Kilmaurs Terrace, Newington, Edinburgh EH16 5DR. ✆ **0131/667-8694.** www.aonachmor.com. 8 units. £35–£90 double. Rates include breakfast. Children 4 and under are not accepted. MC, V. Free parking. Bus: 13 or 33. **Amenities:** Dining room/lounge. *In room:* TV, hair dryer, Wi-Fi (free).

Walton Hotel ★ 🎁 This little hotel lies right in the heart of Edinburgh in a restored 200-year-old town house. A complete refurbishment and renovation have maintained the essential Georgian character and elegant features, but have revitalized and modernized the entire hotel. Guest rooms are midsize, cozy, comfortable, and tranquil. The location is only a few minutes' walk to Princes Street. Don't expect much here in the way of service.

79 Dundas St., Edinburgh EH3 6SD. ✆ **0131/556-1137.** Fax 0131/557-8367. www.waltonhotel.com. 10 units. Summer £139–£149 double; off season £85–£130 double. Rates include breakfast. MC, V. Free parking. Bus: 23 or 27. *In room:* TV, hair dryer, Wi-Fi (free).

SOUTH OF THE CENTER

Thrums Private Hotel Situated 1.6km (1 mile) south of Princes Street, Thrums is a pair of connected antique buildings, one a two-story 1820 Georgian and the other a small inn from around 1900. The hotel contains recently refurbished high-ceilinged rooms with contemporary furnishings (in the inn) or reproduction antique furnishings (in the Georgian). Each unit comes with a tidy midsize private bathroom with shower. The bistro-inspired Thrums restaurant serves set-price menus of British food, and there's also a bar and a peaceful garden.

14-15 Minto St., Edinburgh EH9 1RQ. ✆ **0131/667-5545.** Fax 0131/667-8707. www.thrumshotel.com. 5 units. £55–£110 double; £180–£230 family room. Rates include breakfast. MC, V. Free parking. Bus: 3, 7, 8, 31, 81, or 87. **Amenities:** Restaurant; bar; Internet (free). *In room:* TV, hair dryer.

Where to Dine

IN THE CENTER—NEW TOWN

Expensive

The Atrium ★ MODERN SCOTTISH/INTERNATIONAL Since 1993, this has been one of the most emulated restaurants in Edinburgh. No more than 60 diners can be accommodated in the "deliberately moody" atmosphere that's a fusion of Argentine hacienda and stylish Beverly Hills bistro. Flickering oil lamps create shadows on the dark-colored walls while patrons enjoy dishes prepared with taste and flair. Although offerings vary according to the inspiration of the chef, our favorites include grilled salmon and roasted sea bass, the latter with Dauphinois potatoes, baby spinach, charcoal-grilled eggplant, and baby fennel. The desserts are equally superb, especially the lemon tart with berry soulis and crème fraîche.

10 Cambridge St. (beneath Saltire Court in City Center, a 10-min. walk from Waverly Train Station). ✆ **0131/228-8882.** www.atriumrestaurant.co.uk. Reservations recommended. Fixed-price lunch menu £10–£20; fixed-price dinner menu £55; main courses £18–£22. AE, DC, MC, V. Mon–Fri noon–2pm and 6–10pm; Sat 6–10pm. Closed for 1 week at Christmas. Bus: 11 or 15.

No. 1 ★ SCOTTISH/CONTINENTAL This intimate, crimson-colored enclave is the premier restaurant in the Balmoral Hotel. The walls are studded with Scottish memorabilia in formal yet sporting patterns. You can sample the likes of pan-seared Isle of Skye monkfish with saffron mussel broth; roulade of Dover sole with langoustine, oyster, and scallop garnish; or grilled filet of Scottish beef served with bourguignon sauce. For dessert you can have a variety of sorbets or British cheeses, or something more exotic such as mulled wine parfait with a cinnamon sauce. The restaurant has a vegetarian menu and a wide-ranging wine list with celestial tariffs.

In the Balmoral Hotel, 1 Princes St. ✆ **0131/556-2414.** Reservations recommended. 3 courses £58; tasting menu £62. AE, DC, MC, V. Daily 6:30–10pm.

Moderate

Café Saint-Honoré FRENCH/SCOTTISH Between Frederick and Hanover streets, this is a French-inspired bistro with a dinner format that's much more formal and expensive than its deliberately rapid lunchtime venue. An upbeat and usually enthusiastic staff serves a combination of Scottish and French cuisine that includes venison with juniper berries and wild mushrooms, local pheasant in wine and garlic sauce, and lamb kidneys with broad beans. The fish is very fresh.

34 NW Thistle St. Lane. ✆ **0131/226-2211.** www.cafesthonore.com. Reservations recommended. £9.50–£13; main courses £17–£20; fixed-price dinner £15–£20; fixed-price pre-theater meal £15 for 2 courses. AE, DC, MC, V. Mon–Fri noon–2:15pm and 5–10pm (pre-theater meal 5–7pm); Sat 6–10pm. Bus: 3, 16, 17, 23, 27, or 31.

Haldanes Restaurant ★ SCOTTISH Set in the cellar of the Albany Hotel building, within a pair of royal blue and gold-tinted dining rooms, Haldanes features the cuisine of George Kelso. During clement weather, the venue moves out to the building's verdant garden. Our recent party of Scottish friends dug into such delights as braised shank of Scottish lamb with Puy lentils; pan-fried breast of guinea fowl stuffed with a leek mousse; and baked filet of Scottish salmon topped with a chive crème fraîche. If you want to go truly local, order the Highland venison with black pudding and beets in a rosemary sauce.

39A Albany St. ✆ **0131/556-8407.** Reservations required. Main courses £16–£23. DC, MC, V. Tues–Fri noon–1:45pm; Sun–Thurs 5:30–9pm; Fri–Sat 5:30–9:30pm. Bus: 15.

Hewat's ★ SCOTTISH/INTERNATIONAL Hewat's is ideally located for the theater and offers reasonably priced pre- and post-theater dinners. Owned by Lara Kearney, John Rutter, and Glyn Stevens, all formerly of the Atrium (reviewed above), this is a fast-growing, popular place. The bold yellow walls and black-and-white floor give this converted antiques shop a unique, contemporary look. The cuisine is ambitious and seductive. Main courses include sea bass roasted in olive oil, chargrilled tuna, and chicken and foie gras terrine with onion jam. The rhubarb crumble with tamarind ice cream is a great way to end an enjoyable meal.

19–21 Causewayside. ✆ **0131/466-6660.** Reservations recommended. Main courses £12–£18; set-price 3-course lunch £17; pre- and post-theater 3-course dinner £18. AE, MC, V. Mon–Sat noon–2pm; Mon–Wed 6–9:30pm; Thurs–Sat 6–10:30pm. Bus: 42.

9 Cellars Restaurant & Bar ★★ INDIAN In 2007, Chef Thakur was named best Indian chef of the year in Scotland. Today, his unique menu is just as good as ever, perhaps even better. Instead of countless curries, Thakur features a more concise selection that represents various regions of the subcontinent. Our favorite dishes include his North Indian chili garlic chicken (hot and spicy), and lamb cooked with fresh vegetables and flavored with Indian rum. The freshly made breads are reason enough to go here. Thakur told us, "This is not an Indian restaurant but a restaurant specializing in Indian food." We agree.

1–3 York Place. ✆ **0131/557-9899.** www.9cellars.co.uk. Reservations required. Main courses £8.50–£11. MC, V. Mon–Sat noon–2:30pm; daily 5:30–11:30pm. Bus: 4, 8, or 16.

Olorosa ★★★ MODERN BRITISH At the end of Princes Street, this citadel of fine food sits atop the landmark Basil Spencer Building, opening onto a roof terrace, with views to Edinburgh Castle and Fife in the distance. The restaurant is a high-fashion setting that would be at home in Los Angeles instead of Edinburgh. Chef Tony Singh doesn't follow trends—so "expect the unexpected," as the staff says.

Creative cookery with quality ingredients characterizes this hyperüber restaurant. Expect the best of Highland beef, venison, and freshly caught salmon. The meat, including all forms of steak, comes with a wide choice of accompaniments, ranging from anchovy butter to red-wine *jus*. The selection of starters is the capital's finest. We love the mozzarella-and-herb croissants and the smoked haddock and chive cakes. For dessert, you can hardly go wrong with passion fruit parfait with sambuca sabayon or the banana tart tatin with coconut ice cream and rum and raisin sauce.

33 Castle St. ✆ **0131/226-7614.** Reservations required. Fixed-price lunch £19 for 2 courses, £24 for 3 courses; fixed-price dinner £33 for 2 courses, £39 for 3 courses. AE, MC, V. Daily noon–2:30pm and 6:45–10pm. Bus: 26 or 44.

The Tower ★★ SEAFOOD/MODERN BRITISH This is a hot dining ticket set at the top of the Museum of Scotland. The inventive kitchen will regale you with hearty portions of some of the finest steaks and roast beef, along with excellent and freshly caught seafood. Dig into an array of oysters or lobsters, or try a platter of mixed seafood. We still remember fondly the smoked haddock risotto with a poached egg and shavings of Parmesan cheese. Sea bass is perfectly seasoned and grilled, and there's even sushi on the menu. Scottish loin of lamb is given a modern twist with a side dish of minted couscous.

In the Museum of Scotland, Chambers St. ✆ **0131/225-3003.** Reservations required. 2-course lunch £14; dinner main courses £32; fixed-price dinner £30. AE, DC, MC, V. Daily noon–11pm. Bus: 2, 41, or 42.

Inexpensive

Henderson's Salad Table ★ VEGETARIAN This is a Shangri-La for health food lovers. Hot dishes such as peppers stuffed with rice and pimiento are served on request, and a vegetarian twist on the national dish of Scotland, haggis, is usually available. Other well-prepared dishes filled with flavor include cheese and onion potato croquette, vegetable lasagna, and a broccoli-and-cheese crumble. The homemade desserts include a fresh fruit salad and a cake with double-whipped cream and chocolate sauce. The wine cellar offers 30 wines. Live music, ranging from classical to jazz to folk, is played every evening.

94 Hanover St. ✆ **0131/225-2131.** Main courses £6–£9; fixed-price lunch £9; fixed-price dinner £12. AE, MC, V. Daily noon–9:30pm. Bus: 13, 23, or 27.

Tony's Table ★ ITALIAN In the heart of Edinburgh, this two-level restaurant welcomes you with courtesy and efficiency and serves good, home-style Italian cookery for those who have had too much haggis. Starters tempt with crispy quail with a spicy glaze or crab broth with crab won tons. Justifiably favorite dishes include pigeon pie with Puy lentils and puffy pastry or John Dory with Mediterranean vegetables. The lunch menu is different, with duck pie, fish pie, chili pig pie, or even a mug of leek-and-potato soup with "Ugly" bread. The cakes are good and freshly baked, including a warm orange polenta cake with ice cream, or you can order dessert from "Tony's Trolley," where the chef comes around and prepares your dessert at the table.

58A N. Castle St. ✆ **0131/226-6743.** www.tonystable.com. Reservations recommended. Main courses lunch £4.95–£9.95; fixed-price dinners £18 for 2 courses or £20 for 3 courses. MC, V. Tues–Sat noon–2:30pm and 6:30–10pm. Bus: 31 or 33.

IN THE CENTER—OLD TOWN

Moderate

Gusto ★ ITALIAN A shining culinary star on Edinburgh's Restaurant Row, this restaurant offers some of the best Italian food in the city. It's a marvelous change of pace from traditional Scottish fare. The location is in the very heart of town along George Street, near St. Andrew Square and Charlotte Square. Chefs are highly skilled, using market-fresh ingredients to turn out such delights as salt-baked sea bass with orange and fennel or slow-braised lamb shoulder with polenta. The kitchen is open to view, and you can watch as the cooks toss pizzas, rather theatrically we might add. Both contemporary and traditional Italian dishes appear on the menu.

135 George St. ✆ **0131/225-2555.** Reservations required. Main courses £11–£30; pizzas £5.95–£10. AE, DC, MC, V. Mon–Thurs noon–10:30pm; Fri–Sat noon–11pm. Bus: 3, 8, 22, 25, or 30.

Inexpensive

Baked Potato Shop VEGETARIAN/WHOLE FOOD This is the least expensive restaurant in a very glamorous neighborhood, and it attracts mobs of office workers every day. Many carry their food away. Only free-range eggs, whole foods, and vegetarian cheeses are used. Vegan cakes are a specialty.

56 Cockburn St. ✆ **0131/225-7572.** Reservations not accepted. Food items £1.30–£5. No credit cards. Daily 9am–9pm (to 10pm in summer). Bus: 5.

LEITH

In the northern regions of Edinburgh, Leith is the old port town, opening onto the Firth of Forth. Once it was a city in its own right until it was slowly absorbed into Edinburgh.

Expensive

Martin Wishart ★★★ MODERN FRENCH Several gourmet associations rate this as one of the finest restaurants in all of Scotland. The owner-chef Martin Wishart takes it all in stride and continues to improve the quality of his cuisine in a fashionable part of the Leith docklands. With white walls and modern art, the decor is minimalist. The menu is short but sweet and ever changing. Many dishes are simply prepared, the natural flavors coming through. Others show a touch of elegance and fantasy, including partridge breast with black truffle and foie gras, and lobster ravioli with a light shellfish cream. After you eat the glazed lemon tart with praline ice cream on which white raspberry coulis has been dribbled, the day is yours.

54 The Shore, Leith. ✆ **0131/553-3557.** Reservations required. Set lunch menu £25 for 3 courses; tasting menu £65. MC, V. Tues–Sat noon–2pm and 7–10pm. Bus: 7 or 10.

Moderate

Vintner's Room ★ 🎁 FRENCH/SCOTTISH Join locals and visitors down by the waterfront in Leith. Chances are they are heading to this restaurant. Near the entrance, beneath a venerable ceiling of oaken beams, a wine bar serves platters and drinks beside a large stone fireplace. Most diners, however, head for the small but elegant dining room, illuminated by flickering candles. Fresh ingredients are used in a vast array of specialties. You might begin with such appetizers as pear-and-watercress soup or pigeon-and-juniper terrine. The baked halibut with lobster bisque makes a tasty main course, as does the saddle of hare with brandy and grapes. Game delights are the thyme-flavored roast partridge with Marsala or the noisettes of venison with heather honey and red currants. Finish off with grilled apricots flavored with amaretto and served with a basil-flavored ice.

The Vaults, 87 Giles St., Leith. ✆ **0131/554-6767.** www.thevintnersrooms.com. Reservations recommended. Main courses £17–£20 lunch, £15–£30 dinner. AE, MC, V. Tues–Sat noon–2pm and 7–10:30pm. Closed 2 weeks at Christmas. Bus: 22 or 34.

Seeing the Sights

THE ROYAL MILE ★★

The Royal Mile (bus: 23, 27, 35, 36, 41, 42, or 46) stretches from Edinburgh Castle all the way to the Palace of Holyroodhouse. Walking along it, you'll see some of the most interesting old structures in Edinburgh, with turrets, gables, and towering chimneys.

High Kirk of St. Giles Built in 1120, a short walk downhill from Edinburgh Castle, this church is one of the most important architectural landmarks along the Royal Mile. It combines a dark and brooding stone exterior with surprisingly graceful and delicate flying buttresses. One of its outstanding features is its **Thistle Chapel,** housing beautiful stalls and notable heraldic stained-glass windows. Cathedral guides are available at all times to conduct tours.

High St. ✆ **0131/225-9442.** www.stgilescathedral.org.uk. Free admission, but £3 donation suggested. May–Sept Mon–Fri 9am–7pm, Sat 9am–5pm, Sun 1–5pm; Oct–Apr Mon–Sat 9am–5pm, Sun 1–5pm. Sun services at 8, 10, and 11:30am and 6 and 8pm. Bus: 23 or 27.

Museum of Childhood ☺ The world's first museum devoted solely to the history of childhood stands just opposite John Knox's House. Contents of its four floors range from antique toys to games to exhibits on health, education, and costumes, plus video presentations and an activity area. Because of the youthful crowd it naturally attracts, it ranks as the noisiest museum in town.

42 High St. ✆ **0131/529-4142.** www.cac.org.uk. Free admission. Mon–Sat 10am–5pm; during the Edinburgh Festival, also Sun noon–5pm. Bus: 28, 35, 41, or 42.

Museum of Edinburgh Across from the Canongate Tolbooth is this fine example of a restored 16th-century mansion, whose builders preferred a bulky, relatively simple design that suited its role as a secular, rather than an ecclesiastical, building. Today, it functions as Edinburgh's principal museum of local history. Inside are faithfully crafted reproductions of rooms inspired by the city's traditional industries, including glassmaking, pottery, wool processing, and cabinetry.

142 Canongate. ✆ **0131/529-4143.** www.cac.org.uk. Free admission. June–Sept Mon–Sat 10am–6pm (Aug also open Sun noon–5pm); Oct–May Mon–Sat 10am–5pm. Bus: 35 or 36.

The People's Story Continue downhill along Canongate toward Holyroodhouse, and you'll see one of the handsomest buildings on the Royal Mile. Built in 1591, the **Canongate Tolbooth** was once the courthouse, prison, and center of municipal affairs for the burgh of Canongate. Now it contains a museum celebrating the social history of the inhabitants of Edinburgh from the late 18th century to the present, with lots of emphasis on the cultural displacements of the Industrial Revolution.

163 Canongate. ✆ **0131/529-4057.** www.cac.org.uk. Free admission. June–Sept Mon–Sat 10am–6pm; Oct–May Mon–Sat 10am–5pm. Bus: 35 or 36.

The Real Mary King's Close Beneath the City Chambers on the Royal Mile lies Old Town's deepest secret, a warren of hidden streets where people lived and worked for centuries. This attraction allows you to go back into the turbulent days of plague-ridden Edinburgh in the 17th century. Today's visitors can see a number of underground "closes," originally very narrow walkways with houses on either side, some dating back centuries. When the Royal Exchange (now the City Chambers) was constructed in 1753, the top floors of the buildings of the close were torn down, although the lower sections were used as the foundations of the new building, leaving a number of dark and mysterious passages intact. In April 2003, guided parties were allowed to visit these dwellings for the first time. Subtle lighting and audio effects add to the experience. You can visit everything from a gravedigger's family stricken with the plague to a grand 16th-century town house. The haunted **Shrine Room** is the best surviving 17th-century house in Scotland.

2 Warriston's Close, off the Royal Mile. ✆ **0870/243-0160.** www.realmarykingsclose.com. Admission £11 adults, £10 students and seniors, £6 children. Nov–Mar daily 10am–5pm; Apr–Oct daily 10am–9pm. Closed Dec 25. Bus: 1 or 6.

Scotch Whisky Heritage Centre This center is privately funded by a conglomeration of Scotland's biggest distillers. It highlights the economic effect of whisky on both Scotland and the world, and illuminates the centuries-old traditions associated with whisky making. You get to see a 7-minute audiovisual show and ride an electric car past 13 sets showing historic moments in the whisky industry. A tour entitling you to sample four whiskies costs £20 per person.

354 Castlehill (10-min. walk from Waverley Train Station). ✆ **0131/220-0441.** www.whisky-heritage.co.uk. Admission £11.50 adults, £8.95 seniors and students with ID, £5.95 children 6–17, free for children 5 and under. Sept–May daily 10am–6pm; June–Aug daily 9:30am–6:30pm. Closed Dec 25.

The Scottish Parliament Modern architecture has come to Edinburgh thanks to the late Spanish architect Enric Miralles, who died in 2000 and never got to see his vision completely materialize. After years of delay the first Scottish parliament in nearly 300 years was opened to much controversy over the high price and the design. Some called it a "granite monstrosity," whereas others felt it that is was just what Scotland needed to shed the stereotype of tartan and bagpipes. The London *Times* and *Guardian* newspapers called the building a masterpiece, but some traditionalists have likened it to a "collection of coffins, bananas, and boomerangs." There is one thing that everyone can agree on, however: It is unique. That feature is what has made the buildings one of Edinburgh's top attractions. Guided tours are the best way to go here, and you get colorful anecdotes along the way. If you can go when Parliament is in session, you'll often hear heated debates about Scotland's relationship with England.

Cannongate and Holyrood Rd. ✆ **0131/348-5200.** www.scottish.parliament.uk. Free admission. Tues–Thurs 9am–6:30pm; Mon and Fri (and weekdays when Parliament not in season) 10am–5:30pm (to 4pm Nov–Mar); Sat–Sun 11am–5:30pm. Bus: 35 or 36.

Writers' Museum This 1622 house takes its name, Lady Stair's House, from a former owner, Elizabeth, the dowager countess of Stair. Today it's a treasure-trove of portraits, relics, and manuscripts relating to three of Scotland's greatest men of letters. The Robert Burns collection includes his writing desk, rare manuscripts, portraits, and many other items. Also on display are some of Sir Walter Scott's possessions, including his pipe, chess set, and original manuscripts. The museum holds one of the most significant Robert Louis Stevenson collections anywhere, including personal belongings, paintings, photographs, and early editions.

In Lady Stair's House, off Lawnmarket. ✆ **0131/529-4901.** www.cac.org.uk. Free admission. Mon–Sat 10am–5pm; Sun noon–5pm Aug only. Bus: 23, 27, 41, or 45.

HISTORIC SITES

Edinburgh Castle ★★ Although its early history is vague, it's believed that Edinburgh was built on the dead volcano Castle Rock. It's known that in the 11th century Malcolm III (Canmore) and his Saxon queen, later venerated as St. Margaret, founded a castle on this same spot. The only fragment left of their original castle—in fact the oldest structure in Edinburgh—is **St. Margaret's Chapel.** Built in the Norman style, the oblong structure dates principally from the 12th century.

Inside the castle you can visit the **State Apartments,** particularly Queen Mary's bedroom, where Mary, Queen of Scots, gave birth to James VI of Scotland (later James I of England). The highlight is the Crown Chamber, which houses the Honours of Scotland (Scottish Crown Jewels), used at the coronation of James VI, along with the scepter and the sword of state of Scotland.

For Mr. Hyde Fans

Near Gladstone's Land, a 17th-century mansion still standing on the Royal Mile near Edinburgh Castle, is Brodie's Close, a stone-floored alleyway. You can wander into the alley for a view of old stone houses that'll make you think you've stepped into a scene from a BBC production of a Dickens novel. It was named in honor of the notorious Deacon Brodie, a respectable councilor by day and a thief by night (he was the inspiration for Robert Louis Stevenson's *The Strange Case of Dr. Jekyll and Mr. Hyde,* though Stevenson set his story in foggy London town, not in Edinburgh). Brodie was hanged in 1788, and the mechanism used for the hangman's scaffolding had previously been improved by Brodie himself—for use on others, of course. Across the street is the most famous pub along the Royal Mile: Deacon Brodie's Tavern (see later in this chapter).

You can also view the **Stone of Scone,** or "Stone of Destiny," on which Scottish kings had been crowned since time immemorial. Edward I of England carried the stone off to Westminster Abbey in 1296, where it rested under the British coronation chair. It was finally returned to its rightful home in Scotland in November 1996, where it was welcomed with much pomp and circumstance.

Castlehill. ✆ **0131/225-9846.** www.edinburghcastle.gov.uk. Admission £12 adults, £10 seniors, £6 children 6–15 and under, free for children 5 and under. Apr–Sept daily 9:30am–6pm; Oct–Mar daily 9:30am–5pm. Bus: 23, 27, 41, or 45.

Palace of Holyroodhouse ★★ This palace was built adjacent to an Augustinian abbey established by David I in the 12th century. The nave, now in ruins, remains today. James IV founded the palace nearby in the early part of the 16th century, but only the north tower is left. Much of what you see today was ordered built by Charles II. The most dramatic incident in the history of Holyroodhouse occurred in the old wing when Mary, Queen of Scots, was in residence. Her Italian secretary, David Rizzio, was murdered (with 56 stab wounds) in the audience chamber by Mary's husband, Lord Darnley, and his accomplices. The palace suffered long periods of neglect, although it basked in glory at the ball thrown by Bonnie Prince Charlie in the mid–18th century. The present queen and Prince Philip live at Holyroodhouse when they visit Edinburgh. When they're not in residence, the palace is open to visitors.

Canongate, at the eastern end of the Royal Mile. ✆ **0131/556-5100.** www.royal.gov.uk. Admission £10 adults, £9.30 seniors and students, £6.20 children 6–17, free for children 5 and under. Nov–Mar daily 9:30am–4:30pm; Apr–Oct daily 9:30am–6pm. Closed 2 weeks in May and 3 weeks in late June and early July (dates vary). Bus: 35 or 36.

MORE ATTRACTIONS

Dean Gallery ★ Across from the Scottish National Gallery of Modern Art, Dean Gallery houses the Modern Art's extensive collections of dada and surrealism. For those of us who are fascinated by these art movements, there's nothing better in Scotland. All of our favorite artists—and maybe yours too—are here, from Max Ernst to Joan Miró and, of course, Salvador Dalí. The major exhibit here consists of a large part of the works of Sir Eduardo Paolozzi, a hip modern Scottish sculptor. The

BRITANNIA: THE PEOPLE'S yacht

In case the queen never invited you for a sail on her 125m (410-ft.) yacht, there's still a chance to go aboard this world-famous vessel. Launched on April 16, 1953, the luxury yacht was decommissioned December 11, 1997. Today, the yacht—technically a Royal Navy ship—which has sailed more than a million miles, rests at anchor in the port of Leith, 3km (1¾ miles) from the center of Edinburgh. The gangplank is now lowered for the public, whereas it once was lowered for such world leaders as Tony Blair and Nelson Mandela.

British taxpayers spent £160 million maintaining the yacht throughout most of the 1990s. Even a major refit would have prolonged the vessel's life for only a few more years. Because of budgetary constraints, a decision was made to put it in dry dock. The public reaches the vessel by going through a visitor center designed by Sir Terence Conran. At its centerpiece is the yacht's 12m (39-ft.) tender floating in a pool.

Once onboard, you're guided around all five decks by an audio tour. You can also visit the drawing room and the Royal Apartments, once occupied by the likes of not only the queen, but Prince Philip and princes William, Harry, Edward, and Andrew, as well as princesses Anne and Margaret. Even the engine room, the galleys, and the captain's cabin can be visited.

All tickets should be booked as far in advance as possible by calling ✆ **0131/555-5566** or logging onto www.royalyachtbritannia.co.uk. The yacht is open daily except Christmas, with the first tour beginning at 10am, the last tour at 3:30pm. Lasting 90 to 120 minutes, each tour is self-guided with the use of a headset lent to participants. Adults pay £10.50, seniors and children ages 5 to 17 £6.75; those age 5 and under visit free. A family ticket, good for two adults and up to 3 children, is £31. From Waverley Bridge, take city bus (Lothian Transport) 1, 11, 22, 34, or 35, or else the Guide Friday tour bus, which is marked all over its sides with the words BRITANNIA.

collection of prints, drawings, plaster maquettes (models), molds, and contents of his studio are housed in the gallery.

73 Belford Rd. ✆ **0131/624-6200.** www.nationalgalleries.org. Free admission to permanent collection; variable prices to special exhibitions. Daily 10am–5pm. Closed Dec 25–26. Bus: 13.

National Gallery of Scotland ★★★ This museum is located in the center of Princes Street Gardens. The gallery is rather small, but the collection was chosen with great care. The duke of Sutherland has lent the museum some paintings, including two Raphaels, Titian's two Diana canvases and his *Venus Rising from the Sea,* and the *Seven Sacraments,* a work of the great 17th-century Frenchman Nicolas Poussin. The Spanish masters are represented as well. You can also see excellent examples of English painting: Gainsborough's *The Hon. Mrs. Graham* and Constable's *Dedham Vale,* along with works by Turner, Reynolds, and Hogarth. Naturally, the work of Scottish painters is prominent, including Alexander Naysmith and Henry Raeburn, whose most famous work, *The Reverend Walker,* can be seen here.

2 The Mound. ✆ **0131/624-6200.** www.nationalgalleries.org. Free admission. Daily 10am–5pm (to 7pm Thurs; extended hours daily during the festival). Closed Dec 25–26. Bus: 23, 27, 41, 42, or 45.

National Museums of Scotland (NMS) ★★★ In 1998, two long-established museums, the Royal Museum of Scotland and the National Museum of Antiquities, were united into this single institution 2 blocks south of the Royal Mile. The museum showcases exhibits in the decorative arts, ethnography, natural history, geology, archaeology, technology, and science. Six modern galleries distill billions of years of Scottish history, a total of 12,000 items ranging from rocks found on the island of South Uist dating back 2.9 billion years to a Hillman Imp, one of the last 500 cars manufactured at the Linwood plant near Glasgow before it closed in 1981. One gallery is devoted to Scotland's role as an independent nation before it merged with the United Kingdom in 1707. Another gallery, devoted to industry and empire from 1707 to 1914, includes exhibits on shipbuilding, whisky distilling, the railways, and such textiles as the tartan and paisley.

Chambers St. ✆ **0131/225-7534.** www.nms.ac.uk. Free admission. Daily 10am–5pm. Walk south from Waverley Station for 10 min. to reach Chambers St. or take bus 2, 7, 23, 31, or 35.

Our Dynamic Earth ★ ☺ The Millennium Dome at Greenwich outside London may have been a bust, but the millennium museum for Scotland is still packing in the crowds. Not far from the Palace of Holyroodhouse, Our Dynamic Earth tells the story of earth in all its diversity. You can push buttons to simulate earthquakes, meteor showers, and views of outer space. You can see replicas of the slimy green primordial soup where life began. Time capsules wind their way back through the eons, and a series of specialized aquariums re-create primordial life forms. That's not all; there is so much more, ranging from simulated terrains of polar ice caps to tropical rainforests with plenty of creepy-crawlies. All 11 galleries have stunning special effects.

Holyrood Rd. (10-min. walk from Waverley Train Station). ✆ **0131/550-7800.** www.dynamicearth.co.uk. Admission £9.50 adults, £7.50 students and seniors, £5.95 ages 3–15. Nov–Mar Wed–Sun 10am–5pm; Apr–June and Sept–Oct daily 10am–5pm; July–Aug daily 10am–6pm. Bus: 35 or 36.

Outlook Tower & Camera Obscura ☺ The 1853 periscope is at the top of the Outlook Tower, from which you can view a panorama of the surrounding city. Trained guides point out the landmarks and talk about Edinburgh's fascinating history. In addition, there are several entertaining exhibits, all with an optical theme, and a well-stocked shop selling books, crafts, and compact discs.

Castlehill. ✆ **0131/226-3709.** www.camera-obscura.co.uk. Admission £8.95 adults, £7.15 seniors and students, £6.10 students and children 5–15. Apr–June daily 9:30am–7pm; July–Aug daily 9:30am–7:30pm; Sept–Oct daily 9:30am–6pm; Nov–Mar daily 10am–5pm. Bus: 23, 27, 41, or 45.

Scottish National Gallery of Modern Art ★★ Scotland's national collection of 20th-century art is set on 5.5 hectares (14 acres) of grounds, just a 15-minute walk from the west end of Princes Street. The collection is international in scope and high in quality despite its modest size. Major sculptures outside the building include pieces by Henry Moore and Barbara Hepworth. Inside, the collection ranges from a fauve Derain and cubist Braque and Picasso to recent works by Paolozzi. There's a strong representation of English and Scottish artists—William Turner, John Constable, Henry Raeburn, and David Wilkie, to name a few. Works by Matisse, Miró, Kirchner, Kokoschka, Ernst, Ben Nicholson, Nevelson, Balthus, Lichtenstein, Kitaj, and Hockney are also on view.

75 Belford Rd. ✆ **0131/556-8921.** www.nationalgalleries.org. Free admission, except for some temporary exhibits. Daily 10am–5pm. Bus: 13 stops by the gallery but is infrequent; 18, 20, and 41 pass along Queensferry Rd., a 5-min. walk up Queensferry Terrace and Belford Rd. from the gallery.

Scottish National Portrait Gallery ★ Housed in a red stone Victorian Gothic building by Rowand Anderson, this portrait gallery gives you a chance to see what the famous people of Scottish history looked like. The portraits, several by Ramsay and Raeburn, include everybody from Mary, Queen of Scots, to Sean Connery, and from Flora Macdonald to Irvine Welsh. The gallery is slated to reopen late in 2011.

1 Queen St. ✆ **0131/624-6200.** www.nationalgalleries.org. Free admission, except for some temporary exhibits. Fri–Wed 10am–5pm; Thurs 10am–7pm. Closed Dec 25–26. Bus: 4, 10, 12, 16, or 26.

Scott Monument ★ Completed in the mid–19th century, the Gothic-inspired Scott Monument is the most famous landmark of Edinburgh. Sir Walter Scott's heroes are carved as small figures in the monument, and you can climb to the top. You can also see the first-ever **floral clock,** which was constructed in 1904, in the West Princes Street Gardens.

In the E. Princes St. Gardens. ✆ **0131/529-4068.** www.edinburgh.gov.uk. Admission £3. Apr–Sept Mon–Sat 9am–6pm, Sun 10am–7pm; Oct–Mar Mon–Sat 9am–3pm, Sun 10am–3pm. Bus: 3, 10, 12, 17, 25, 29, 33, 41, or 45.

A GARDEN

Gardeners and nature lovers will be attracted to the **Royal Botanic Garden,** Inverleith Row (✆ **0131/552-7171**). Main areas of interest are the Exhibition Hall, Alpine House, Demonstration Garden, annual and herbaceous borders (summer only), copse, Woodland Garden, Wild Garden, Arboretum, Peat Garden, Rock Garden, Heath Garden, and pond. Admission is £4.50 adults, £3.50 students and seniors, £1.20 ages 5 to 15. It is open daily November to February 10am to 4pm, March and October 10am to 6pm, and April to September 10am to 7pm.

ORGANIZED TOURS

For a quick introduction to the principal attractions in and around Edinburgh, consider the tours offered from April to late October by **Lothian Region Transport,** 14 Queen St. (✆ **0131/555-6363**). You can see most of the major sights of Edinburgh, including the Royal Mile, the Palace of Holyroodhouse, Princes Street, and Edinburgh Castle, by double-deck motorcoach for £12 for adults, £11 for seniors and students, and £5 for children. This ticket is valid all day on any **LRT Edinburgh Classic Tour bus,** which allows passengers to get on and off at any of the

A Step Back in Time at Historic Dean Village

The village is one of the most photographed sights in the city. Set in a valley about 30m (100 ft.) below the level of the rest of Edinburgh, it's full of nostalgic charm. The settlement dates from the 12th century, and for many centuries it was a grain-milling center. The current residents worked hard to restore the old buildings—many of which were converted into flats and houses—and managed to maintain all of the original Brigadoon-like charm. A few minutes from the West End, it's located at the end of Bell's Brae, off Queensferry Street, on the Water of Leith. You can enjoy a celebrated view by looking downstream under the high arches of Dean Bridge, designed by Telford in 1833. The most scenic walk is along the water in the direction of St. Bernard's Well.

15 stops along its routes. Buses start from Waverley Bridge every day beginning at 9:40am, departing every 15 minutes in summer and about every 30 minutes in winter, and then embark on a circuit of Edinburgh, which if you remain on the bus without ever getting off will take about 1 hour. Commentary is offered along the way.

Tickets for any of these tours can be bought at LRT offices at Waverley Bridge or at the tourist information center in Waverley Market. Advance reservations are a good idea. For more information, call ✆ **0131/220-0770** daily 9am to 5pm.

McEwan's Literary Pub Tour (✆ **0131/226-6665;** www.edinburghliterarypubtour.com) follows in the footsteps of such literary greats as Robert Burns, Robert Louis Stevenson, and Sir Walter Scott. The *Edinburgh Evening News* has hailed this tour (and we concur) as "vivid, erudite, and entertaining." The tour goes into the city's famous or infamous taverns and *howffs* (Scottish pubs), highlighting such literary events as tales of Dr. Jekyll and Mr. Hyde or the erotic love poetry of Burns. Tours depart from the Beehive Pub on Grassmarket in the Old Town, going along the Royal Mile. The 2-hour tour costs £10 for adults or £9 for children. From June to September tours leave nightly at 7:30pm; March, April, May, October, and November, Thursday to Sunday at 7:30pm; and December to February, Friday at 7:30pm. Reservations are recommended.

The **Witchery Tours** (✆ **0131/225-6745;** www.witcherytours.com) are filled with ghosts, gore, and witchcraft, enlivened by "jumper-outers"—actors who jump out to scare you. Two tours—Ghost & Gore, and Murder & Mystery—are a bit similar and overlap in parts. Scenes of many horrific tortures, murders, and supernatural happenings in the historic Old Town are visited, all under the cloak of darkness. The ghost tour departs May to September daily at 7 and 7:30pm, with the murder tour leaving daily at 9 and again at 10pm year-round. Tours last 1 hour and 15 minutes, costing £7.50 or £5 for children. Departures are from outside the Witchery Restaurant on Castlehill. Reserve early for the tour.

Mercat Tours (✆ **0131/557-6464;** www.mercattours.com) conducts the best walking tours of Edinburgh, covering a wide range of interests from "Secrets of the Royal Mile" to a "Haunted Underground Experience." Tours meet outside the Tourist Office on Princes Street. The Secrets of the Royal Mile Tour leaves daily at 10:30am with a Grand Tour departing at 10am daily. The Hidden Vaults Tour runs hourly from May to September noon to 4pm, off season daily at 2 and 4pm. The cost of these tours begins at £8.50 for adults, £7.50 seniors and students, or £5 for children. Reservations are recommended for these 1½-hour tours.

Guide Friday (✆ **0131/556-2244**) is good for a quick overview. You can later follow up with more in-depth visits. You're taken around the city in one of the company's fleet of open-top, double-decker buses, with informed and often amusing running commentaries. Highlights include the Royal Mile, Princes Street, Holyrood Palace, and Edinburgh Castle, as well as the New Town. Tours run between 9:20am and dusk, costing £12 for adults, £11 for seniors and students, or £5 for kids ages 5 to 15. Reservations are recommended. Departures are from Waverly Bridge, with tours lasting 1 hour.

The Shopping Scene

The best buys are tartans and woolens, along with bone china and Scottish crystal. Princes Street, George Street, and the Royal Mile are the major shopping arteries. Here are a few suggestions.

Looking for a knitted memento? Moira-Anne Leask, owner of the **Shetland Connection,** 491 Lawnmarket (✆ **0131/225-3525;** bus: 28), promotes the skills of the Shetland knitter, and her shop is packed with sweaters, hats, and gloves in colorful Fair Isle designs. She also offers hand-knitted mohair, Aran, and Icelandic sweaters. Items range from fine-ply cobweb shawls to chunky ski sweaters hand-crafted by skilled knitters in top-quality wool.

If you've ever suspected that you might be Scottish, **Tartan Gift Shops,** 54 High St. (✆ **0131/558-3187;** bus: 1), has a chart indicating the place of origin, in Scotland, of your family name. You'll then be faced with a bewildering array of hunt-and-dress tartans. The high-quality wool is sold by the yard as well as in the form of kilts for both men and women.

Clan Tartan Centre, 70–74 Bangor Rd., Leith (✆ **0131/553-5161;** bus: 7 or 10), is one of the leading tartan specialists in Edinburgh, regardless of which clan you claim as your own. If you want help in identifying a particular tartan, the staff at this shop will assist you. At the same location is the **James Pringle Woollen Mill** (✆ **0131/553-5161**), which produces a large variety of top-quality wool items, including a range of Scottish knitwear—cashmere sweaters, tartan and tweed ties, travel rugs, tweed hats, and tam-o'-shanters. In addition, the mill has the only Clan Tartan Centre in Scotland, where more than 2,500 sets and trade designs are accessible through their research facilities.

The two best department stores in Edinburgh are **Debenhams,** 109–112 Princes St. (✆ **08445/61-61-61;** www.debenhams.com; bus: 22 or 26), and **Jenners,** 48 Princes St. (✆ **0131/225-2442;** www.jenners.com; bus: 22 or 26). Both stock Scottish and international merchandise.

Established in 1866, **Hamilton & Inches,** 87 George St. (✆ **0131/225-4898;** bus: 41 or 42), is a gold- and silversmith with both modern and antique designs. It has a stunning late-Georgian interior as well.

Edinburgh After Dark

For a thorough list of entertainment options during your stay, pick up a copy of ***The List,*** a biweekly entertainment paper available free at the Edinburgh & Scotland Information Centre.

FESTIVALS

The highlight of Edinburgh's year—some would say the only time the real Edinburgh emerges—comes in the last weeks of August during the **Edinburgh International Festival.** Since 1947, the festival has attracted artists and companies of the highest international standard in all fields of the arts, including music, opera, dance, theater, exhibition, poetry, and prose, and "Auld Reekie" takes on a cosmopolitan air.

During the festival, one of the most exciting spectacles is the Military Tattoo on the floodlit esplanade in front of Edinburgh Castle, high on its rock above the city. Vast audiences watch the precision marching of Scottish regiments and military units from all parts of the world, and of course the skirl of the bagpipes and the swirl of the kilt.

Less predictable in quality but greater in quantity is the **Edinburgh Festival Fringe** (180 High St., Edinburgh EH1 IQS; ✆ **0131/226-0026;** www.edfringe.com), an opportunity for anybody—professional or nonprofessional, an individual, a group of friends, or a whole company of performers—to put on a show wherever they can find an empty stage or street corner. Late-night reviews, outrageous and irreverent contemporary drama, university theater presentations, maybe even a full-length opera—Edinburgh gives them all free rein. A **Film Festival, Jazz Festival, Television Festival,** and **Book Festival** (every second year) overlap in August.

Ticket prices vary from £5 to £10. You can get information from **Edinburgh International Festival,** The Hub, Castle Hill, Edinburgh EH1 7ND (✆ **0131/473-2000;** fax 0131/473-2002), open Monday to Friday from 9:30am to 5:30pm. Other sources of information are the **Edinburgh Festival Fringe,** 180 High St., Edinburgh EH1 IQ5 (✆ **0131/226-0026**); **Edinburgh Book Festival,** 5A Charlotte Sq., Edinburgh EH2 4DR (✆ **0131/718-5666;** www.edbookfest.co.uk); and **Edinburgh Film Festival,** 88 Lothian Rd., Edinburgh EH3 9BZ (✆ **0131/228-4051**).

THEATER

Edinburgh has a lively theater scene. In 1994, the **Festival Theatre,** 13–29 Nicolson St. (✆ **0131/662-1112** for administration, 0131/529-6000 for tickets during festival times with an additional phone line, 0131/473-2000, that's operational during the Aug festival; bus: 3, 31, or 33), opened in time for some aspects of the Edinburgh Festival. Set on the eastern edge of Edinburgh, near the old campus of the University of Edinburgh, it has since been called "Britain's de facto Dance House" because of its sprung floor, its enormous stage (the largest in Britain), and its suitability for opera presentations of all kinds. Tickets are £9 to £90.

Another major theater is the **King's Theatre,** 2 Leven St. (✆ **0131/529-6000;** bus: 10 or 11), a 1,600-seat Victorian venue offering a wide repertoire of classical entertainment, including ballet, opera, and West End productions. The **Scottish Storytelling Centre and Netherbow Theatre,** 43 High St. (✆ **0131/556-9579;** bus: 1), has been called "informal," and productions here are often experimental and delightful—new Scottish theater at its best.

The resident company of **Royal Lyceum Theatre,** Grindlay Street (✆ **0131/248-4848;** bus: 11 or 15), also has an enviable reputation; its presentations range from the works of Shakespeare to new Scottish playwrights. The **Traverse Theatre,** Cambridge Street (✆ **0131/228-1404;** bus: 11 or 15), is one of the few theaters in Britain funded solely to present new plays by British writers and first translations into English of international works. In a modern location, it now offers two theaters under one roof: Traverse 1 seats 250 and Traverse 2 seats 100.

BALLET, OPERA & CLASSICAL MUSIC

The **Scottish Ballet** and the **Scottish Opera** perform at the **Playhouse Theatre,** 18–22 Greenside Place (✆ **0844/847-1660;** bus: 7 or 14), which, with 3,100 seats, is the town's largest theater. The **Scottish Chamber Orchestra** makes its home at the **Queen's Hall,** 85–89 Clerk St. (✆ **0131/668-2019;** bus: 3, 33, or 31), also a major venue for the Edinburgh International Festival.

FOLK MUSIC & CEILIDHS

Folk music is presented in many clubs and pubs in Edinburgh, but these strolling players tend to be somewhat erratic or irregular in their appearances. It's best to read notices in pubs and talk to the tourist office to see where the ceilidhs will be on the night of your visit.

Some hotels feature regularly scheduled presentations of traditional Scottish music. The **Tempest Bar** in the George Hotel, 19–21 George St. (✆ **0131/225-1251;**

A Wee Dram for Fans of Malt Whisky

It requires a bit of an effort to reach it (take bus no. 10A, 16, or 17 from Princes St. to Leith), but for fans of malt whisky, the **Scotch Malt Whisky Society** has been called "The Top of the Whisky Pyramid" by distillery-industry magazines in Britain. It's on the second floor of a 16th-century warehouse at 87 Giles St., Leith (✆ **0131/554-3451**), and was originally designed to store bordeaux and port wines from France and Portugal. All you can order are single-malt whiskies, served neat, usually in a dram (unless you want yours watered down with branch water), and selected from a staggering choice of whiskies from more than 100 distilleries throughout Scotland. Hours are Monday and Tuesday 10am to 5pm, Thursday to Saturday 10am to 11pm, and Sunday 11am to 10pm.

bus: 86), offers it every Sunday afternoon from 3 to 6pm, although the time and day, we were warned, might change during the lifetime of this edition. Between April and October, daily at 7pm, there's a somewhat more elaborate event known as **Jamie's Scottish Evening,** wherein a four-course dinner with wine accompanies a show that features everything old-fashioned, Celtic, Scottish, and musical. The venue is at the **King James Hotel** on Leith Street (✆ **0131/556-0111** for reservations; bus: 22). The all-inclusive price, per person, is £55.

PUBS & BARS

Edinburgh's most famous pub, **Café Royal Circle Bar,** 17 W. Register St. (✆ **0131/556-4124;** bus: 22, 25, or 44), is a long-enduring favorite. Part of it is now occupied by the Oyster Bar of the Café Royal, but life in the Circle Bar continues at its old pace. The opulent trappings of the Victorian era are still to be seen. Go up to the serving counter, which stands like an island in a sea of drinkers, and place your order.

The **Abbotsford,** 3 Rose St. (✆ **0131/225-5276;** bus: 3, 31, or 33), is near the eastern end of Rose Street, a short walk from Princes Street. This pub has served stiff drinks and oceans of beer since it was founded in 1887. Inside, the gaslight era is alive and thriving, thanks to a careful preservation of the original dark paneling, long battered tables, and ornate plaster ceiling. The inventories of beer on tap change about once a week, supplementing a roster of single-malt Scotches. Established in 1806, **Deacon Brodie's Tavern,** 435 Lawnmarket (✆ **0131/225-6531;** bus: 25 or 35), is the neighborhood pub along the Royal Mile. It perpetuates the memory of Deacon Brodie, good citizen by day, robber by night (see the box "For Mr. Hyde Fans," p. 851). The tavern and wine cellars contain a restaurant and lounge bar.

Day Trips from Edinburgh

LINLITHGOW

In this royal burgh, a county town in West Lothian, 29km (18 miles) west of Edinburgh, Mary, Queen of Scots, was born in 1542. Her birthplace, the roofless Linlithgow Palace (✆ **01506/842-896**), can still be explored today, even if it's but a shell of its former self. The queen's suite was in the north quarter but was rebuilt for the homecoming of James VI (James I of England) in 1620. The palace burned to the ground in 1746. The Great Hall is on the first floor, and a small display shows some of the more interesting architectural relics. The ruined palace is 1km (⅔ mile) from Linlithgow Station. Admission is £5.20 adults, £4.20 seniors, £2.60 children 5 to 15. It is open April to September, daily 9:30am to 5:30pm; October to March, daily 9:30am to 4:30pm.

South of the palace stands the medieval kirk of **St. Michael's Parish Church** (✆ **01506/842-188**), open May to September daily from 10:30am to 4pm (closes at 1pm off season). Many a Scottish monarch has worshiped here since its consecration in 1242. Despite being ravaged by the disciples of John Knox and transformed into a stable by Cromwell, it's one of Scotland's best examples of a parish church.

In the midst of beautifully landscaped grounds, laid out along the lines of Versailles, sits **Hopetoun House** (✆ **0131/331-2451**), 16km (10 miles) from Edinburgh. This is Scotland's greatest Adam mansion, and a fine example of 18th-century architecture. The splendid reception rooms are filled with 18th-century furniture, paintings, statuary, and other artworks. From a rooftop platform you see a panoramic view of the Firth of Forth. You can take the nature trail, explore the deer parks, investigate the Stables Museum, or stroll through the formal gardens, all on the grounds. The house is 3km (1¾ miles) from the Forth Road Bridge near South Queensferry, off A-904. If you don't have a car, take a cab from the rail station in Dalmeny for £5. Admission is £8 adults, £7 seniors and students, £4.25 children, £22 family (up to six). Hours are from 10:30am to 5pm (last admission 4pm) daily Easter weekend to last weekend in September.

GETTING THERE From Edinburgh, direct **trains** (✆ **0345/484950**) run every 15 minutes during the day to Linlithgow (trip time: 20 min.). Round-trip fare is £10 adults, £5 children 5 to 15. **Motorists** can take A902 to Corstorphine, and then A8 to M9, getting off at the signposted junction (no. 3) to Linlithgow.

DIRLETON

This little town, a preservation village, vies for the title of "prettiest village in Scotland." The town plan, drafted in the early 16th century, is essentially unchanged today. Dirleton has two greens shaped like triangles, with a pub opposite Dirleton Castle, placed at right angles to a group of cottages.

A rose-tinted 13th-century castle with surrounding gardens, once the seat of the wealthy Anglo-Norman de Vaux family, **Dirleton Castle** (✆ **01620/850-330**) looks like a fairy-tale fortification, with its towers, arched entries, and oak ramp. Ruins of the Great Hall and kitchen can be seen, as well as what's left of the lord's chamber where the de Vaux family lived. The 16th-century main gate has a hole through which boiling tar or water could be poured to discourage unwanted visitors. The castle's country garden and bowling green are still in use. Admission is £4.70 adults, £3.80 seniors and students, £2.80 ages 5 to 15. You can tour the castle April to September, daily 9:30am to 6:30pm; October to March, Monday to Saturday 9:30am to 4:30pm, Sunday 2:30 to 4:30pm.

GETTING THERE Dirleton is on the Edinburgh–North Berwick road (A198); North Berwick is 8km (5 miles) east and Edinburgh 31km (19 miles) west. There's no train service. Buses, including nos. 124 and 125, depart from the St. Andrews Square station in Edinburgh (✆ **0800/015-4212** for information). They take 25 minutes and cost £5 one-way. If you're driving, take A1 in the direction marked THE SOUTH and DUNBAR; then turn onto A198, following the signs to Dirleton.

GLASGOW ★★★

Glasgow is just 65km (40 miles) west of Edinburgh, but the contrast between the two cities is striking. Scotland's economic powerhouse and its largest city (Britain's third-largest), Glasgow is now the country's cultural capital and home to half its population. It has long been famous for ironworks and steelworks; the local shipbuilding industry produced the *Queen Mary,* the *Queen Elizabeth,* and other ocean liners.

Once polluted by industry and plagued with some of the worst slums in Europe, Glasgow has been transformed. Urban development and the decision to locate the Scottish Exhibition and Conference Centre here have brought great changes: Industrial grime is being sandblasted away, overcrowding has been reduced, and more open space and less traffic congestion mean cleaner air. Glasgow also boasts a vibrant and even edgy arts scene; it's now one of the cultural capitals of Europe.

In the process, the splendor of the city has reemerged. The planners of the 19th century thought on a grand scale when they designed the terraces and villas west and south of the center, and John Betjeman and other critics have hailed Glasgow as "the greatest surviving example of a Victorian city."

Glasgow's origins are ancient, making Edinburgh, for all its wealth of history, seem comparatively young. The village that grew up beside a fjord 32km (20 miles) from the mouth of the River Clyde as a medieval ecclesiastical center began its commercial prosperity in the 17th century. As it grew, the city engulfed the smaller medieval towns of Ardrie, Renfrew, Rutherglen, and Paisley.

Essentials

GETTING THERE

BY PLANE The **Glasgow Airport** is at Abbotsinch (✆ **0870/40008;** www.glasgowairport.com), 16km (10 miles) west of the city via M8. To reach the center of Glasgow, take the **Flyer Airport Express;** a single fare costs £4.50. Service during the day is every 10 minutes (trip time: 15 min.), and the Flyer calls at all major city hotels, ending up at the Buchanan Bus Station.

Monday to Friday, British Airways (www.ba.com) runs almost hourly shuttle service from London's Heathrow Airport to Glasgow. Service is reduced on weekends, depending on volume. For flight schedules and fares, call British Airways in London at ✆ **0844/4930-787,** or go to www.ba.com.

British Midland (✆ **800/788-0555;** www.flybmi.com) flies from Heathrow to Glasgow. **Aer Lingus** (✆ **800/474-7424,** or 0818/365-00 in Ireland; www.aerlingus.ie) flies daily from Dublin to Glasgow. Most visitors fly first to London on one of the major airlines such as **American** (✆ **800/433-7300;** www.aa.com), then take a shuttle flight into Glasgow or Edinburgh to begin their Scotland adventure.

BY TRAIN Headquarters for British Rail is at Glasgow's Central Station and Queen Street Station. For **National Rail Enquiries,** call ✆ **08457/484-950,** or go to www.nationalrail.co.uk. The **Queen Street Station** serves the north and east of Scotland, with trains arriving from Edinburgh every 30 minutes during the day; the one-way trip between the two cities costs £11 and takes 50 minutes. You'll also be able to travel to such Highland destinations as Inverness and Fort William from here.

The **Central Station** serves southern Scotland, England, and Wales, with trains arriving from London's Euston and King's Cross Stations (call ✆ **08457/484-950** in London for schedules) frequently throughout the day (trip time is about 4½ hr.). The trains leave Euston Monday to Saturday from 5:30am to 7:30pm, and then the night train departs at 11:50pm, getting into Glasgow at 7:16am. From Glasgow, trains leave for London every hour from 4:20am to 6:40pm. The night train leaves at 11:40pm. Try to avoid Sunday travel—the frequency of trains is considerably reduced and the duration of the trip lengthened to at least 7 hours because of more stopovers en route.

BY BUS The **Buchanan Street Bus Station** is 2 blocks north of the Queen Street Station on Killermont Street (✆ **0141/333-3708**). **National Express** runs daily coaches from London's Victoria Coach Station to Buchanan frequently throughout the day. Buses from London take approximately 8½ hours to reach Glasgow, though trip time varies depending on the number of stops en route. Scottish CityLink (✆ **08705/505-050**) also has frequent bus service to and from Edinburgh, with a one-way ticket costing £6.50.

Contact National Express Enquiries at ✆ **0990/808-080** for more information.

BY CAR Glasgow is 65km (40 miles) west of Edinburgh, 356km (221 miles) north of Manchester, and 625km (388 miles) north of London. From England in the south, Glasgow is reached by M74, a continuation of M8 that goes right into the city, making an S curve. Call your hotel and find out what exit you should take. M8, another express motorway, links Glasgow and Edinburgh.

Other major routes into the city are A77 northeast from Prestwick and Ayr and A8 from the west (this becomes M8 around the port of Glasgow). A82 comes in from the northwest (the Highlands) on the north bank of the Clyde, and A80 also goes into the city. (This route is the southwestern section of M80 and M9 from Stirling.)

VISITOR INFORMATION The **Visit Scotland Tourist Information Office,** 11 George Sq. (✆ **0141/5204-4400;** Underground: Buchanan St.), is the country's most helpful office. October to May, it's open Monday to Saturday 9am to 5pm; June, July, and September hours are daily 9am to 6pm; August, daily 9am to 8pm. Every Thursday throughout the year, the office delays its morning opening till 9:30am.

GETTING AROUND The best way to explore Glasgow is on foot. The center is laid out on a grid system, which makes map reading relatively easy. However, many of the major attractions, such as the Burrell Collection, are in the surrounding environs, and for those you'll need to rely on public transportation. ***Remember:*** Cars drive on the left, so when you cross streets make certain to look both ways.

BY BUS Glasgow is serviced by **First Glasgow Bus Company** (✆ **0141/423-6600**). Most of the buses are white, although a few of the older models might still

A Bargain Ticket for First-Day Touring

For only £1.60, you can buy a Discovery Ticket allowing you to hop on and off buses and to be granted discounts for such select attractions as the House for an Art Lover. A pocket-size city map is also provided. The ticket is valid daily from 9:30am to midnight. It's available at tourist information centers, Underground or bus stations, and certain attractions. For more information, check www.seeglasgow.com.

be painted in tones of blue and yellow. Bus service is frequent throughout the day, but after 11pm service is greatly curtailed. The major bus station is the **Buchanan Street Bus Station,** Killermont Street (call Traveline at ✆ **0871/200-2233,** or go to www.travelinescotland.com, for schedules and information on any mode of public transportation throughout Scotland), 2 blocks north of the Queen Street Station. Depending on the distance you'll travel, one-way fares range between £1 and £3 (this last one for transit to Glasgow's most far-flung suburbs), which you'll pay directly to the driver, but you must have exact change. A special "day fare," valid for adult, all-day transport on any bus line in Glasgow, costs £3.50.

BY UNDERGROUND Called the "Clockwork Orange" (from the vivid orange of the trains) by Glaswegians, a 15-stop subway services the city. Most Underground trains operate from these stops every 5 minutes, with longer intervals between trains on Sunday and at night. The fare is £1.20. Service is Monday to Saturday 6:30am to 11:30pm and Sunday 10am to 6pm. For more information, call ✆ **0871/200-2233.**

The **Travel Centre,** within the Buchanan Street Bus Station (✆ **0141/333-3708**), is open Monday to Saturday 6:30am to 10:30pm and Sunday 7am to 10:30pm. Here you can buy tickets on any of the buses heading from central Glasgow to far-flung points within the region, as well as tube (subway) tickets in bulk. A package with 10 subway tickets costs £10; 20 tickets cost £19; and a ticket valid for 7 unrestricted consecutive days of tube rides costs £13. You can also buy a £3.50 **discovery ticket,** covering unlimited rides for 1 day. For details, call ✆ **0141/332-7133.**

BY TAXI Taxis are the same excellent ones found in Edinburgh or London. You can hail them on the street or call Glasgow Taxis (aka **TOA Taxis**) at ✆ **0141/429-7070.** Fares are displayed on a meter next to the driver. When a taxi is available on the street, a taxi sign on the roof is lit a bright yellow. Most taxi trips within the city cost £6 to £9.50. The taxi meter starts at £2 and increases by 25p every 61m (200 ft.), with an extra 15p assessed for each additional passenger after the first two. A £1.50 surcharge is imposed midnight to 6am.

BY CAR Driving around Glasgow is a tricky business, even for locals. You're better off with public transportation. The city is a warren of one-way streets, and parking is expensive and difficult to find. Metered parking is available, but you'll need 20p coins, entitling you to only 20 minutes. Be on the lookout for zealous traffic wardens issuing tickets. Some zones are marked PERMIT HOLDERS ONLY—your vehicle will be towed if you have no permit. A yellow line along the curb indicates no parking. Multistory parking lots (car parks), open 24 hours a day, are found at Anderston Cross and Cambridge, George, Mitchell, Oswald, and Waterloo streets.

If you want to rent a car to explore the countryside, it's best to arrange the rental before leaving home. But if you want to rent a car locally, most companies will accept your American or Canadian driver's license. All the major rental agencies are represented at the airport. Try **Avis Rent-a-Car** at 64–80 Lancefield St. (✆ **870/608-6339;** bus: 6 or 6A), or **Europcar** at Kingston Bridge (✆ **0141/418-0040;** bus: 38, 45, 48, or 57).

BY BICYCLE Parts of Glasgow are fine for biking, or you might want to rent a bike and explore the surrounding countryside. For what the Scots call cycle hire, go to a well-recommended shop about a kilometer (⅔ mile) west of the town center, just off Great Western Road: **West End Cycles,** 16–18 Chancellor St., in the Hillhead district (✆ **0141/357-1344;** Underground: Kelvin Bridge or Hillhead). It rents 21-speed trail and mountain bikes that conform well to the hilly terrain of Glasgow and its surroundings. The cost of £15 per day must be accompanied by a cash deposit of £100 or the imprint of a valid credit card. You can also rent weekly for £55.

[FastFACTS] GLASGOW

Business Hours Most **offices** are open Monday to Friday 9am to 5 or 5:30pm. Most **banks** are open Monday to Wednesday and Friday 9:30am to 4pm, Thursday 9:30am to 5:30pm, and Saturday 10am to 7pm. Opening times can vary slightly from bank to bank. **Shops** are generally open Monday to Saturday 10am to 5:30 or 6pm. On Thursday, stores remain open until 7pm.

Currency Exchange The tourist office will exchange most major foreign currencies, or else you can do so at the Post Office on St. Vincent Street (✆ **0141/204-3689**). City center banks also operate a *bureau de change.*

Dentists If you have an emergency, go to the Accident and Emergency Department of **Glasgow Dental Hospital & School NHS Trust,** 378 Sauchiehall St. (✆ **0141/211-9600;** bus: 57). Its hours are Monday to Friday 9:15am to 3:15pm and Sunday and public holidays 10:30am to noon.

Doctors The major hospital is the **Royal Infirmary,** 82–86 Castle St. (✆ **0141/211-4000;** bus: 2 or 2A).

Emergencies Call ✆ **999** in an emergency to summon the police, an ambulance, or firefighters.

Internet Access At **Yeeha Internet Café,** 48 W. George St. (✆ **0141/332-6543**), the cost is £2.30 per hour.

Pharmacies The best is **Boots,** 200 Sauchiehall St. (✆ **0141/332-1925;** bus: 57), open Monday to Saturday 8:30am to 6pm, and Sunday 11am to 5pm.

Post Office The main branch is at 47 St. Vincent St. (✆ **0845/722-3344;** Underground: Buchanan St.; bus: 6, 8, or 16). It's open Monday to Friday 8:30am to 5:45pm and Saturday 9am to 5pm.

Where to Stay

It's important to reserve your room well in advance (say, 2 months beforehand), especially in late July and August. Glasgow's rates are generally higher than those in Edinburgh, but many business hotels offer bargains on weekends. The airport and the downtown branches of Glasgow's tourist office offer an **Advance Reservations Service**—with 2 weeks' notice, you can book your hotel by calling ✆ **0845/225-5121** (www.visitscotland.com). The cost for this service is £4.

CENTRAL GLASGOW

Expensive

The ArtHouse (ABode Hotel Glasgow) ★★ 🎁 Acclaimed for its contemporary interior, this 1911 Edwardian building, 6 blocks northwest of Central Station, originally housed school board offices. Today, its conversion to a hotel is one of the most striking in Glasgow, with dramatic colors and textures blending in perfectly with the structure's older features. Commissioned art and period pieces evoke some of the original Edwardian splendor, although everything has been given a modern overlay with rich, bold tones. Sleek furniture and state-of-the-art bathrooms with a combination tub/shower are grace notes. **Michael Caines Restaurant** is one of the city's finest.

129 Bath St., Glasgow G2 2SY. ✆ **0141/221-6789.** Fax 0141/221-6777. www.abodehotels.co.uk. 59 units. £100–£200 double. AE, MC, V. Underground: St. Enoch. **Amenities:** Restaurant; cafe; bar; room service; Wi-Fi (free). *In room:* TV, hair dryer.

Hilton Glasgow Hotel ★★★ ☺ Glasgow's only government-rated five-star hotel occupies Scotland's tallest building (20 floors). Dignified and modern, it rises in the heart of the city's business district, near the northern end of Argyle Street and exit 18 (Charing Cross) of M8. The good-size guest rooms—plush and conservative, popular with both vacationers and business travelers—offer fine views as far as the Clyde dockyards. The executive floors enjoy the enhanced facilities of a semiprivate club. The youthful staff is alert and helpful.

1 William St., Glasgow G3 8HT. ✆ **800/445-8667** in the U.S. and Canada, or 0141/204-5555. Fax 0141/204-5004. www.hilton.co.uk/glasgow. 331 units. £115–£165 double; £300 suite. AE, DC, MC, V. Parking £10. Bus: 62. **Amenities:** 3 restaurants; bar; babysitting; concierge; exercise room; indoor heated pool; room service; sauna. *In room:* A/C, TV, hair dryer, minibar, Wi-Fi (£15 per day).

Malmaison ★★ This place beats out all competitors in having the best contemporary interior. The hip Malmaison opened in 1994 in a historically important building constructed in the 1830s as a Greek Orthodox church. In 1997, an annex with additional bedrooms was added, designed to preserve the architectural character of the church's exterior. Inside, few of the original details remain—the decor is sleek and ultramodern. Bedrooms vary in size from smallish to average but are chic and appointed with extras like CD players, specially commissioned art, and top-of-the-line toiletries.

278 W. George St., Glasgow G2 4LL. ✆ **0141/572-1000.** Fax 0141/572-1002. www.malmaison.com. 72 units. £115–£170 double; from £195 suite. AE, DC, MC, V. Parking nearby £10. Bus: 11. **Amenities:** Restaurant; 2 bars; babysitting; exercise room; indoor heated pool; room service. *In room:* A/C, TV, hair dryer, Wi-Fi (£10 per day).

Millennium Hotel Glasgow ★★★ Following a $5-million upgrade, this striking landmark, the original Copthorne from 1810, is now better than ever. It stands near Queen Street Station where trains depart for the north of Scotland. When its high-ceilinged public rooms were renovated, designers searched out antiques and glistening marble panels to give it the aura of the Victorian era. The building has been completely modernized with all the amenities and services you'd expect of such a highly rated hotel. The decor is lighter and more comfortable than ever before. Bedrooms are among the finest in Glasgow, with tasteful furnishings and first-class bathrooms. The best accommodations are at the front of the building facing George Square; the less desirable ones are those in the rear with no view.

George Sq., Glasgow G2 1DS. ✆ **0141/332-6711.** Fax 0141/332-4264. www.millenniumhotels.com. 117 units. £80–£160 double. AE, DC, MC, V. Underground: Buchanan St. **Amenities:** Restaurant; 2 bars; babysitting; concierge; room service; Wi-Fi (free). *In room:* A/C, TV, hair dryer, minibar.

Park Inn ★ If you're looking for Victorian Glasgow, head elsewhere—nothing here is evocative of the city in any way. But if you gravitate to a minimalist Japanese style, check in at this trendy and exceedingly contemporary hotel close to the Buchanan Galleries Shopping Mall and the Glasgow Royal Concert Hall. A diverse medley of bedrooms in various shapes, sizes, and configurations awaits you, each with a certain flair. Nothing is overly adorned here, yet comfort and style, along with a mix of colors and textures, make every unit a winner. The smallest are the studios, but you can also rent a duplex, a theme suite, or a very large suite. Beautifully kept bathrooms contain such extras as power showers with body jets, with flowing and curving interiors. To emphasize the Asian theme all the more, Japanese body treatments are offered in the on-site **Oshi Spa.** Of the two on-site restaurants, one serves Mediterranean cuisine, the other an array of light fusion foods, including sushi.

2 Port Dundas Place, Glasgow G2 3LD. ✆ **0141/333-1500.** Fax 0141/333-5700. www.parkinn.com. 100 units. £89–£129 double; £159 suite. AE, MC, V. Underground: Queen St. Station. **Amenities:** Restaurant; bar; exercise room; room service; sauna; spa. *In room:* TV, hair dryer, minibar, Wi-Fi (£14 per day).

Moderate

Brunswick Hotel ★ In the Merchant City area, this structure stands in dramatic contrast between two old warehouses, each 5 centuries old. A trendy, minimalist design prevails, from the leather-walled restaurant to the sleek-looking bedrooms. The rooms are soothing and inviting with neutral tones, comfortable furnishings, and tiny but adequate bathrooms. The most stunning of the accommodations is a three-bedroom penthouse nesting under a copper curved roof.

106–108 Brunswick St., Glasgow G1 1TF. ✆ **0141/552-0001.** Fax 0141/552-1551. www.brunswickhotel.co.uk. 18 units. £60–£100 double. Rates include continental breakfast. AE, MC, V. Underground: Central or Queen St. **Amenities:** Restaurant; bar; room service. *In room:* TV, hair dryer, Wi-Fi (free).

The Kelvingrove Hotel This family-run hotel gives off a certain air of sophistication. All of their midsize rooms are well kept and decorated in an urbane fashion. Clean white is the color scheme for rooms, while the reception area is a little more adventurous with leather couches and hanging paintings. Being close to the city center, guests can easily get to top attractions like Kelvingrove Park and the Glasgow Museum of Transport. Staff members here are especially helpful when it comes to giving directions and will arrange for a taxi to take you wherever you're going.

944 Sauchiehall St., Glasgow G3 7TH. ✆ **0141/339-5011.** Fax 0141/339-6566. www.kelvingrove-hotel.co.uk. 22 units. £60–£80 double; £75–£90 triple; £85–£100 quad. Rates include breakfast. MC, V. Free parking. Underground: Queen St. Station. **Amenities:** Dining room; Internet (free). *In room:* TV, hair dryer.

Inexpensive

Babbity Bowster In Merchant City, this small but delightful Robert Adam–designed hotel doubles as an art gallery. The guest rooms vary in size but are all attractive, with Victorian reproductions and white-lace bedding (some with shower only). The hotel attracts students and faculty from Strathclyde University and displays the work of Glaswegian artists (most are for sale). In summer, there's an outdoor barbecue area.

16–18 Blackfriars St., Glasgow G1 1PE. ✆ **0141/552-5055.** Fax 0141/552-7774. www.pubutopia.com. 5 units. £60–£85 double. Rates include Scottish breakfast. AE, MC, V. Free parking. Underground: Buchanan St. Bus: 40. **Amenities:** Restaurant; bar; room service. *In room:* TV, hair dryer, no phone.

Kirkland House On a quiet street about a 10-minute walk from the Glasgow Art Gallery and Museum, the university, and the Scottish Exhibition Centre, the Kirkland is an impeccably maintained 1832 Victorian crescent house. A mix of antiques and reproductions is used in the large guest rooms, each equipped with a shower bathroom. The owners are keen admirers of American swing music and display a collection of 78 rpm gramophone records, old photographs, and pictures. All rooms are nonsmoking.

42 St. Vincent Crescent, Glasgow G3 8NG. ✆ **0141/248-3458.** Fax 0141/221-5174. www.kirkland.net43.co.uk. 5 units. £50–£65 double. Rates include continental breakfast. No credit cards. Free parking. Underground: Exhibition Centre. *In room:* TV, hair dryer, no phone.

The Premier Inn Hotel Location, location, location is what sells this property. Two blocks west of the central rail depot, this contemporary seven-story hotel is surrounded by dreary commercial buildings but is a viable option in the center of Glasgow. Upstairs, the rooms are inviting—although they are small. Massively renovated, it is better than ever.

377 Argyle St. (opposite Cadogan Sq.), Glasgow G2 8LL. ✆ **0870/850-6358.** www.premierinn.com. 121 units. £112–£118 double. AE, DC, MC, V. No parking. Underground: Buchanan St. **Amenities:** Restaurant; bar; room service. *In room:* TV, hair dryer, Wi-Fi (£10 per day).

MERCHANT CITY

Very Expensive

Blythswood Square ★★★ Opening in the autumn of 2009, this luxury hotel, operated by the Town House Group, quickly became the number one choice in Glasgow for an upmarket clientele. The hoteliers took over the former Royal Scottish Automobile Club in the center of the city, a building dating from 1823, and restored it to its former glory. Its deluxe hotel rooms and state-of-the-art bathrooms are elegant, supremely comfortable, and the epitome of good taste.

The hotel's leisure club and spa is the city's finest. The structure has some of the greatest architectural features (added in the early 20th c.) of all the buildings in Glasgow: wood paneling, grand staircases, marble floors, and many elegant Art Deco fittings and fixtures. The restaurant and bar is Edwardian in inspiration, with a high ceiling and grand dimensions. The famous Rally Bar is named after the Monte Carlo Rally, which once started from Blythswood Square.

Blythswood Sq., 11 Blythswood Sq., Glasgow G2 4AD. ✆ **0131/274-7450.** www.townhousecompany.com. 88 units. £120–£245 double; £315–£400 junior suite; £865–£1,500 suite. AE, DC, MC, V. Parking £15. **Amenities:** Restaurant; bar; concierge; health club & spa; 2 pools (indoor); room service. *In room:* A/C, TV/DVD, CD player, hair dryer, minibar, Wi-Fi (free).

THE WEST END

Very Expensive

Hotel du Vin ★★★ This hotel tops even perfection, beating out all others as the most glamorous, most elegant, and most tranquil hotel in Scotland. It also boasts a restaurant, the **Bistro** (p. 869), that serves a finer cuisine than that found in any other major Glasgow restaurant. In the Hyndland district just west of the center, the house at no. 1 was built in 1880 and is now even more elegant than it was in its heyday. At the ring of the doorbell, a pair of Edwardian chambermaids with frilly aprons and dust bonnets appear to welcome you. Each of the eight guest rooms in this building is furnished in period style, with lots of luxurious accessories. The success of no. 1 led to the acquisition of building nos. 2 and 3. The newer rooms have the same elegant touches and high price tags.

1 Devonshire Gardens, Glasgow G12 0UX. ✆ **0141/339-2001.** Fax 0141/337-1663. www.hotelduvin.com. 38 units. £150–£325 double; from £410 suite. AE, DC, MC, V. Free parking. Underground: Hillhead. **Amenities:** 2 restaurants; bar; exercise room; room service. *In room:* TV, hair dryer, minibar, Wi-Fi (£10 per day).

Moderate

Manor Park Hotel This impressive West End town house was a private home when built in 1895, near the end of Victoria's reign. In 1947 it was converted into a hotel, and it has been much improved and upgraded since that time. Owners Angus and Catherine MacDonald—true Scots to the core, both of whom speak Gaelic—offer grand Scottish hospitality. Naturally, they freely use the tartan when decorating.

Their home is a blend of modern and traditional furnishings, including beechwood pieces set against a background of floral wallpaper. Each guest room comes with a neat little bathroom with either tub or shower.

28 Balshagray Dr., Glasgow G11 7DD. ✆ **0141/339-2143.** Fax 0141/339-5842. www.manorparkhotel.com. 10 units. £60 double; £75 family room. Rates include full breakfast. AE, MC, V. Free parking. Underground: Patrick Station. **Amenities:** Wi-Fi (free). *In room:* TV, hair dryer.

Inexpensive

Albion Hotel This unpretentious hotel was formed by connecting two nearly identical beige-sandstone row houses in the heart of Glasgow's West End. It offers high-ceilinged guest rooms with modern furniture, some with both tub and shower. If your hotel needs are simple, you'll likely be happy here.

405 N. Woodside Rd., Glasgow G20 6NN. ✆ **0141/339-8620.** Fax 0141/334-8159. www.glasgowhotelsandapartments.co.uk. 20 units. £50–£75 double without breakfast, £60–£85 double with breakfast; £84 triple without breakfast, £100 triple with breakfast; £104 quad without breakfast, £115 quad with breakfast. AE, DC, MC, V. Free parking. Underground: Kelvin Bridge. **Amenities:** Bar. *In room:* TV, fridge, hair dryer, Wi-Fi (free).

Ambassador Hotel ★ Across from the Botanic Garden, this small hotel in an Edwardian town house (ca. 1900) is one of the better B&Bs in Glasgow. The good-size guest rooms are furnished with modern pieces, each with a combination tub/shower. The hotel is well situated for exploring the West End, with several galleries and many good local restaurants nearby.

7 Kelvin Dr., Glasgow G20 8QJ. ✆ **0141/946-1018.** Fax 01419/455377. www.glasgowhotelsandapartments.co.uk. 16 units. £50–£75 double without breakfast, £60–£85 double with breakfast; £85 triple without breakfast, £100 triple with breakfast; £95 quad without breakfast, £115 quad with breakfast. AE, DC, MC, V. Free parking. Underground: Hillhead. **Amenities:** Bar. *In room:* TV, hair dryer, Wi-Fi (free).

Where to Dine

CENTRAL GLASGOW

Expensive

Brian Maule at Chardon d'Or ★★★ FRENCH/SCOTTISH Ayr-born Brian Maule is hailed as one of the finest chefs in Scotland. He's earned that praise, having been elevated to head chef at the age of 24 at Le Gavroche, still hailed as London's best restaurant. Returning to his native roots north of the border, he brought all the skill and finesse that has earned him fame in his homeland. In Glasgow he prepares his cuisine with a passionate commitment, searching everywhere to find the best possible regional ingredients. Each dish is a creation of his own original style, beginning with such starters as pressed chicken, ham, and foie gras terrine with roast beet and a shallot salsa, or warm wood pigeon salad with celeriac and apple rémoulade with a Madeira-laced dressing. We are dazzled by his light, full-flavored, and impertinently inventive mains, especially his roast filet of duck with a cabbage-and-potato cake or his chump of Scottish lamb with asparagus tips, and Puy green lentils flavored with sherry vinegar.

176 W. Regent St. ✆ **0141/248-3801.** Reservations required. Main courses £22–£27. Fixed-price lunch £17 for 2 courses or £20 for 3 courses; fixed-price dinner £55 for 6 courses. AE, MC, V. Mon–Fri noon–2:30pm; Mon–Sat 6–10pm. Underground: Buchanan St.

Cameron's ★★ MODERN SCOTTISH This is one of the most glamorous restaurants in Glasgow's best hotels, outfitted like a baronial hunting lodge in the wilds of the Highlands. The chef's conservative menu holds few surprises but is a deftly prepared celebration of market-fresh ingredients. Small slip-ups sometimes mar the effect of a dish or two, but we have always come away pleased. Your best bet when ordering is to stay Scottish. Go with whisky-cured Isle of Arran salmon, confit of Highland duck, or Firth of Lorne sea scallops—and that's only the appetizers. For a main course, try rack of Scottish lamb with a crust of whisky-steeped oatmeal and Arran mustard.

In the Glasgow Hilton Hotel, 1 William St. ✆ **0141/204-5511.** Reservations recommended. Lunch main courses £16–£20; dinner main courses £28–£33. AE, DC, MC, V. Mon–Fri noon–10pm; Sat 6–10pm. Bus: 6A, 16, or 62.

Rogano ★★ SEAFOOD Rogano boasts a perfectly preserved Art Deco interior from 1935, when Messrs. Rogers and Anderson combined their talents and names to create a restaurant that has hosted virtually every star of the British film industry. You can enjoy dinner amid lapis lazuli clocks, etched mirrors, ceiling fans, semicircular banquettes, and potted palms. The menu always emphasizes seafood, such as halibut in champagne-and-oyster sauce and lobster grilled or thermidor. A less expensive menu is offered downstairs in the **Cafe Rogano,** where main courses begin at £9.50.

11 Exchange Place. ✆ **0141/248-4055.** www.roganoglasgow.com. Reservations recommended. Main courses £23–£32; fixed-price lunch £17–£25. AE, DC, MC, V. Restaurant daily noon–2:30pm and 6–10:30pm; cafe daily noon–11pm. Underground: Buchanan St.

Two Fat Ladies at the Buttery ★ SCOTTISH/FRENCH The pews, pulpits, and stained glass that adorn this place are from a church in northern England. It's the only restaurant in Glasgow where you can contemplate Christ in Majesty while you enjoy a pint of ale. The kitchen produces daily specials like steak pie with roast potatoes; roast rack of lamb with rosemary, thyme, and caramelized shallots; and the Belfry mussel bowl with shallots. The cook is well known for making clever use of fresh Scottish produce. In the basement you can dine at **Shandon Belles,** on cuisine that's also fresh and good, except main courses here are less expensive, ranging from £8.50 to £15. Hours are Wednesday to Saturday noon to 10pm.

In the basement of the Buttery, 652 Argyle St. ✆ **0141/221-8188.** www.twofatladiesrestaurant.com. Reservations recommended. Main courses £15–£24. AE, MC, V. Daily noon–3pm and 5:30–10pm. Underground: St. Enoch.

Moderate

City Merchant SCOTTISH/INTERNATIONAL This cozy restaurant in the heart of the city offers friendly service and an extensive menu, and serves throughout the day. The cuisine is more reliable than stunning, but it delivers quite an array of well-prepared fresh food at a good price. Try the roast breast of duck, rack of lamb, or escalope of venison. Also tempting are the fast-seared scallops and classic smoked haddock. Some of the desserts evoke old-time Scotland, such as the clootie dumpling, made with flour, spices, and fried fruit and served with home-churned butter.

97–99 Candlebiggs. ✆ **0141/553-1577.** Reservations recommended. Main courses £17–£35. AE, DC, MC, V. Mon–Sat noon–10:30pm; Sun 1–9pm. Underground: St. Enoch.

Ho Wong Restaurant ★ CANTONESE Jimmy Ho and David Wong opened this remote outpost of their Hong Kong establishment 2 blocks from the Central Station. It's now one of the city's finest Chinese restaurants. The menu features at least eight duck dishes, along with four types of fresh lobster and some sizzling platters.

82 York St. ✆ **0141/221-3550.** Reservations required. Main courses £12–£20; fixed-price 2-course lunch £11. AE, DC, MC, V. Mon–Sat noon–2pm and 6–11:30pm; Sun 5–10:30pm. Underground: St. Enoch.

Two Fat Ladies ★ MODERN SCOTTISH/SEAFOOD This ranks high on the list of everybody's favorite restaurants, especially for irreverent diners who appreciate the unexpected. The "Two Fat Ladies" are its street number—a nickname for the number 88 in Scotland's church-sponsored bingo games. The restaurant packs in crowds for specialties like pan-fried squid salad with coriander-flavored yogurt sauce, grilled chicken salad with apple chutney, and charcoal-grilled king scallops with tomato-basil sauce. The best dessert is the Pavlova (a chewy meringue) with summer berries and Drambuie sauce.

88 Dumbarton Rd. ✆ **0141/339-1944.** www.twofatladiesrestaurant.com. Reservations recommended. Fixed-price lunch £13 for 3 courses; fixed-price pre-theater supper (6–7pm) £13–£15; main courses £12–£18. AE, MC, V. Daily 5:30–10pm. Bus: 16, 42, or 57.

Inexpensive

Cafe Gandolfi SCOTTISH/FRENCH Many students and young professionals will tell you this popular place in Merchant City is their favorite "caff" (British slang for a small cafe)—you may sometimes have to wait for a table. A remake of a Victorian pub, it boasts rustic wooden floors, benches, and stools. If you don't fill up on soups and salads, try smoked venison with gratin dauphinois or smoked pheasant with an onion tartlet in winter. Vegetarians will also find solace here.

64 Albion St. ✆ **0141/552-6813.** www.cafegandolfi.com. Reservations recommended on weekends. Main courses £7–£14. MC, V. Daily 9–11:30am. Underground: St. Enoch/Cannon St.

Sloans SCOTTISH The city's oldest bar and restaurant, just off Argyll and Buchanan streets, reopened for business in 2007 after a complete restoration. The new four-story landmark building contains a bistro downstairs and a more formal restaurant upstairs. Launched as a coffeehouse in 1797, Sloans became famous for its courtyard cockfights. Many architectural details remain from its past, including rare acid-etched glass or ceilings decorated with plaster moldings. The bistro is ideal for lunch, serving good pub grub such as lemon and thyme roast chicken or smoked penne with chicken and roast pine nuts. Steak burgers and fish and chips are always featured. The more formal restaurant features roast rump of lamb with butternut squash or confit of duck leg with parsnip purée. Some of the dishes would be familiar to Mary, Queen of Scots.

62 Argyle Arcade, 108 Argyle St. ✆ **0141/221-8886.** www.sloansglasgow.com. Reservations not needed. Restaurant main courses £8–£18; bistro main courses £6–£10. AE, MC, V. Daily noon–10pm for food; daily noon–midnight for drinks. Underground: St. Enoch.

THE WEST END

Expensive

The Bistro ★★ SCOTTISH/FRENCH This restaurant has a menu that changes daily, but it's a delight on any day you show up. The talented chefs take quality produce, often regional in origin, and cook it simply, without destroying its natural flavor. You peruse the menu in an intimate, oak-paneled setting that's most atmospheric. True foodies wanting regional flavors may select a starter such as a ravioli of John Dory with smoked eel and black pudding. Wonderfully delicate mains include roast filet of roe deer and a *boudin* of guinea fowl. One of our favorites is the butter-roasted loin of lamb from the Borders served with an anchovy beignet. For an original dessert, opt for the tonka bean crème brûlée with eucalyptus ice cream.

In the Hotel du Vin, 1 Devonshire Gardens. ✆ **0141/339-2001.** Reservations required. Main courses £22–£26. AE, MC, V. Daily 7–9:30pm. Underground: Hillhead.

Moderate

Stravaigin ★★ GLOBAL We've never seen any restaurant like this in Glasgow. The chef-owner truly roams the globe for inspiration. Although some of his ideas might come from as far away as China or the Caribbean, he also knows how to use the finest of the regional bounty of Scotland. Expect concoctions such as marinated venison filet, served with butter-bean and parsley mash, roast baby eggplant, and pomegranate sauce. Rabbit is perfectly cooked and served with tomato essence, while mullet is roasted and served with crisp Parmesan polenta, caponata, and roast pimento sauce. Many locals finish with a selection of Scottish cheeses with red-grape and hazelnut chutney.

28 Gibson St., Hillhead. ✆ **0141/334-2665.** www.stravaigin.com. Reservations required. Fixed-price menus £24–£30; main courses £9.50–£23. AE, DC, MC, V. Daily 11am–midnight. Underground: Kelvinbridge.

Inexpensive

Ashoka West End ★ INDIAN/PUNJABI This is a culinary landmark in Glasgow, serving the finest cuisine of the subcontinent. Many generations of Glaswegians learned to "eat Indian" at this very restaurant. The eclectic decor features rugs, brass objects, murals, and greenery. The dishes are full of flavor and arrive at your table with fragrant and most pleasing aromas. You might launch your repast with *pakora,* deep-fried chicken, mushrooms, or fish fritters. From here you can order *jalandhri,* a potent fusion of ginger, garlic, onions, peppers, coconut cream, and fresh herbs that can be served with a choice of chicken, lamb, or mixed vegetables. Most dishes are priced at the lower end of the scale.

1284 Argyle St. ✆ **0141/389-3371.** www.ashokarestaurants.com. Reservations required. Main courses £8–£15. AE, DC, MC, V. Sun–Thurs 5pm–midnight; Fri 5pm–1am. Underground: Kelvin Hall.

Seeing the Sights

Burrell Collection ★★★ This museum houses the mind-boggling treasures left to Glasgow by Sir William Burrell, a wealthy ship owner who had a lifelong passion for art. Burrell started collecting when he was 14, his passion continuing until 1958, when he died at the age of 96. His tastes were eclectic: Chinese ceramics, French paintings from the 1800s, tapestries, stained-glass windows from churches, even stone doorways from the Middle Ages. It is said that the collector "liked about everything," including one of the very few original bronze casts of Rodin's *Thinker.* He did find some art to his distaste, including avant-garde works ("Monet was just too impressionistic"). You can see a vast aggregation of furniture, textiles, ceramics, stained glass, silver, art objects, and pictures in the dining room, hall, and drawing room reconstructed from Sir William's home, Hutton Castle at Berwick-upon-Tweed. Ancient artifacts, Asian art, and European decorative arts and paintings are featured. There is a restaurant on-site, and you can roam through the surrounding park, 5km (3 miles) south of Glasgow Bridge.

Pollok Country Park, 2060 Pollokshaws Rd. ✆ **0141/287-2550.** www.glasgowmuseums.com. Free admission. Mon–Thurs and Sat 10am–5pm; Fri and Sun 11am–5pm. Bus: 45, 47, 48, or 57.

Cathedral of St. Kentigern ★★★ Also known as St. Mungo's, this cathedral was consecrated in 1136, burned down in 1192, and was rebuilt soon after; the Laigh Kirk (lower church), whose vaulted crypt is said to be the finest in Europe, remains to this day. Visit the tomb of St. Mungo in the crypt, where a light always burns. The edifice is mainland Scotland's only complete medieval cathedral from the 12th and 13th centuries. It was once a place of pilgrimage, but 16th-century zeal purged it of all monuments of idolatry.

Highlights of the interior include the 1400s nave, with a stone screen (unique in Scotland) showing the seven deadly sins. Both the choir and the lower church are in the mid-1200s First Pointed style. The church, though a bit austere, is filled with intricate details left by long-ago craftspeople—note the tinctured bosses of the ambulatory vaulting in the back of the main altar. The lower church, reached via a set of steps north of the pulpit, is where Gothic reigns supreme, with an array of pointed arches and piers. Seek out, in particular, the **Chapel of the Knights,** with its intricate net vaulting and bosses carved with fine detailing. The **Blacader Aisle** projecting from the south transept was the latest addition, a two-story extension of which only the lower part was completed in the late Gothic style.

For the best view of the cathedral, cross the Bridge of Sighs into the **Glasgow Necropolis** (✆ **0141/552-3145;** bus: 2 or 27), the graveyard containing almost every type of architecture in the world. Built on a rocky hill and dominated by a statue of John Knox, this fascinating graveyard was opened in 1832. It is open daily from 7am to 4:30pm.

Cathedral Sq., Castle St. ✆ **0141/552-6891.** Free admission. Apr–Sept Mon–Sat 9:30am–6pm, Sun 1–5pm; Oct–Mar Mon–Sat 9:30am–4pm, Sun 1–4pm. Sun services at 11am and 6:30pm. Underground: High St. Station.

Glasgow Science Centre ★★★ ☺ Opened in 2001, this is Britain's most successful millennium project. It lies in the heart of the city, on the banks of the River Clyde and opposite the Scottish Exhibition and Conference Centre. It's the focal point of Glasgow's drive to become one of Europe's major high-tech locales. Situated in three landmark buildings, the center features the first titanium-clad structures in the United Kingdom, including Scotland's only Space Theatre. Other features include innovative laboratories, multimedia and science theaters, interactive exhibits, and a 360-degree rotating tower. The overall theme is that of the challenges facing Scotland in the 21st century. The center is also a showcase depicting Glasgow's contribution to science and technology in the past, present, and future.

Children will love the hands-on activities. They'll be able to make their own soundtrack and animation, do a 3-D head scan and rearrange their own features, or star in their own digital video. At special shows and workshops, you'll see a glass smashed by sound, "catch" shadows, experience a million volts of indoor lighting, see liquid nitrogen, view bacteria that lurk on you, and build a lie detector.

50 P50 Pacific Quay. ✆ **0141/420-5000.** www.gsc.org.uk. Admission £8.25 adults, £6.25 students and seniors. Nov–Mar Tues–Sun 10am–6pm (open on some Mon; check the website); Apr–Oct daily 10am–6pm. Underground: Buchan St. Station to Cessnock, from which there's a 10-min. walk.

Hunterian Art Gallery ★★ This gallery owns the artistic estate of James McNeill Whistler, with some 60 of his paintings bestowed by his sister-in-law. It also boasts a Charles Rennie Mackintosh collection, including the architect's home (with his own furniture) on three levels, decorated in the original style. The main gallery exhibits 17th- and 18th-century paintings (Rembrandt to Rubens) and 19th- and 20th-century Scottish works. Temporary exhibits, selected from Scotland's largest collection of prints, are presented in the print gallery, which also houses a permanent display of printmaking techniques.

University of Glasgow, 22 Hillhead St. ✆ **0141/330-5431.** www.hunterian.gla.ac.uk. Free admission. Mon–Sat 9:30am–5pm (Mackintosh House closed 12:30–1:30pm). Closed Jan 1, July 21, Sept 29, and Dec 25. Underground: Hillhead.

Kelvingrove Art Gallery and Museum ★★★ Neil MacGregor, director of London's National Gallery, hailed this Glasgow landmark "one of the greatest civic collections in Europe." Long closed for restoration, the galleries traditionally attract one million visitors annually, making it the most visited museum in the United Kingdom outside London. You can view a wide range of exhibits, not only fine and decorative arts but 300-million-year-old fossils of marine life as well as one of the world's greatest collections of arms and armor.

The museum displays such important works as Salvador Dalí's controversial painting *Christ of St. John of the Cross.* Also on view is a superb collection of Dutch and Italian Old Masters and French 19th-century paintings, including Giorgione's *Adultress Brought Before Christ,* Rembrandt's *Man in Armor,* Millet's *Going to Work,* and Derain's *Blackfriars.* Scottish painting is well represented from the 17th century to the present. One of the gallery's major paintings is *Whistler's Arrangement in Grey and Black no. 2: Portrait of Thomas Carlyle,* the first Whistler to be hung in a British gallery. The artist took great pride in his Scottish background. The James McNeill Whistler collection includes the contents of his studio.

The museum also displays outstanding ethnography collections featuring artifacts of the Eskimo and North Indian Americans, Africa, and Oceania, as well as a large section devoted to natural history. Furniture and other decorative items created by Charles Rennie Mackintosh are also on display.

Argyle St. and Byros Rd. ✆ **0141/276-9599.** www.glasgowmuseums.com. Free admission. Mon–Thurs and Sat 10am–5pm; Fri–Sun 11am–5pm. Underground: Kelvin Hall.

Museum of Transport ★★ This museum contains a fascinating collection of all forms of transportation and related technology. Displays include a simulated 1938 Glasgow street with period shop fronts, appropriate vehicles, and a reconstruction of one of the Glasgow Underground stations. The superb and varied ship models in the Clyde Room reflect the significance of Glasgow and the River Clyde as one of the world's foremost areas of shipbuilding and engineering.

1 Bunhouse Rd., Kelvin Hall. ✆ **0141/287-2720.** www.glasgowmuseums.com. Free admission. Mon–Thurs and Sat 10am–5pm; Sun and Fri 11am–5pm. Closed Jan 1 and Dec 25. Underground: Kelvin Hall.

St. Mungo Museum of Religious Life and Art ★ Opened in 1993, this eclectic and often controversial museum lies close to the Cathedral of St. Kentigern. It embraces a collection that spans the centuries and highlights various religious groups that have lived in Glasgow and the surrounding area over the years. The museum is hailed as unique in the world in that Buddha, Ganesha, Shiva, and all the "gang" are represented. Also on display is the Chinese robe worn in the film *The Last Emperor,* by Bernardo Bertolucci. In back of the museum is the U.K.'s only Japanese Zen garden.

2 Castle St. ✆ **141/553-2557.** Free admission. Mon–Thurs and Sat 10am–5pm; Fri and Sun 11am–5pm. Bus: 11, 36, 37, 38, 42, 89, or 138.

The Tall Ship at Glasgow Harbour Here's a rare chance to explore one of the last remaining Clyde-built tall ships, the SV *Glenlee,* built in 1896, a vessel that circumnavigated Cape Horn 15 times. Restored in 1999, *Glenlee* is one of only five

Clyde-built sailing ships that remain afloat. You can explore the ship and take in an onboard exhibition detailing the vessel's cargo-trading history. On the dock, the **Victorian Pumphouse Centre** contains a restaurant and a nautical gift shop along with exhibition galleries.

100 Stobcross Rd. ✆ **0141/222-2513.** www.thetallship.com. Admission £5.95 adults; £4.65 seniors, students, and children; 1 free child admission with paying adult. Mar–Oct daily 10am–5pm; Nov–Feb daily 10am–4pm. Take the low-level train from Glasgow Central to Finnieston/SECC.

ORGANIZED TOURS

The ***Waverley*** is the world's last seagoing paddle steamer, and from the last week of June to the end of August (depending on weather conditions), the Paddle Steamer Preservation Society conducts 1-day trips from Anderston Quay in Glasgow to historic and scenic places beyond the Firth of Clyde. As you sail along, you can take in what were once vast shipyards, turning out more than half the earth's tonnage of oceangoing liners. You're welcome to bring your own sandwiches for a picnic aboard, or you can enjoy lunch in the Waverley Restaurant. Boat tours cost £18 to £38. Kids are charged half price. For details, contact **Waverley Excursions,** Waverley Terminal, Anderston Quay, Broomielaw (✆ **0141/243-2224;** www.waverleyexcursions.co.uk).

There's also regular ferry service run by **Caledonian MacBrayne** (✆ **0870/565-0000;** www.calmac.co.uk) in Gourock on the banks of the Clyde. The ferry stands close to the station in Gourock, connected to Glasgow Central Station by trains that leave every hour and take 30 to 45 minutes. The ferry service, which can take cars, runs every hour to the attractive seaside resort of Dunoon at the mouth of the Clyde. The journey takes about 20 minutes, and ferries run from 6:20am to 10:20pm, April to October 16; in winter the service is less frequent and visitors are advised to check beforehand as it's liable to change. The round-trip costs £7.20 per person.

The best Glasgow tours are run by **Scotguide Tourist Services (City Sightseeing Glasgow),** operated from 153 Queen St. at George Square, opposite the City Chambers (✆ **0141/204-0444;** Underground: Buchanan St.). July and August, departures are every 15 minutes from 9:30am to 6:30pm (Nov 1–Mar 31 every 30 min.). The price is £10 adults, £8 students and seniors, and £4 children ages 5 to 14, free for children 4 and under.

If you prefer to stay on terra firma, **Mercat Walks** (✆ **0141/586-5378**) focus on a ghostly, ghoulish Glasgow. Historians re-create macabre Glasgow—a parade of goons like hangmen, ghosts, murderers, and body snatchers. Tours cost £8 for adults, £7 for seniors, students, and kids. The tours take 1½ hours.

The Shopping Scene

A warren of tiny shops stands in a slightly claustrophobic cluster called **Victorian Village,** 93 W. Regent St. (✆ **0141/332-9808;** bus: 23, 38, 45, 48, or 57). Much of the merchandise isn't particularly noteworthy, but you can find many exceptional pieces if you're willing to go hunting. Several of the owners stock reasonably priced 19th-century articles; others sell old jewelry and clothing, a helter-skelter of artifacts.

The work of some of the finest craftspeople in Scotland is highlighted at **Scottish Craft Centre ★★**, Princes Square Mall, 48 Buchanan St. (✆ **0141/248-2885;** Underground: St. Enoch; bus: 9, 12, 44, 66, or 75). Most of the items are exquisitely crafted in porcelain, metal, glass, and wood. You can select from such items as metal candleholders, hand-carved wooden boxes, exquisite glasses and china, porcelain vases, and other choice items.

Frasers department store, Buchanan Street (✆ **0141/204-3182;** Underground: St. Enoch), is Glasgow's version of Harrods. A soaring Victorian-era glass arcade rises four stories, and inside you'll find everything from clothing to Oriental rugs, crystal to handmade local artifacts of all kinds.

The tiny **Mackintosh Shop** ★★★, 167 Renfrew St. (✆ **0141/353-4500;** Underground: Queen St.), prides itself on its stock of books, cards, stationery, coffee and beer mugs, glassware, and sterling-and-enamel jewelry created from the original designs of Mackintosh. The Mackintosh Shop is in the foyer of the Glasgow School of Art.

Drop in the **National Trust for Scotland Shop** ★, Hutcheson's Hall, 158 Ingram St. (✆ **0141/552-8391;** Underground: Buchanan St.), for maps, calendars, postcards, pictures, dish towels, and kitchenware. Some of the crockery is in Mackintosh-design styles.

Glasgow After Dark

OPERA & CLASSICAL MUSIC

The **Theatre Royal,** Hope Street and Cowcaddens Road (✆ **0141/332-9000;** Underground: Cowcaddens; bus: 23, 48, or 57), is the home of the **Scottish Opera** (✆ **0141/248-4567**), as well as the **Scottish Ballet** (✆ **0141/331-2931**). The theater also hosts visiting companies from around the world. Called "the most beautiful opera theatre in the kingdom" by the *Daily Telegraph,* it offers splendid Victorian Italian Renaissance plasterwork, glittering chandeliers, and 1,547 comfortable seats, plus spacious bars and buffets on all four levels. However, it's not the decor but the ambitious repertoire that attracts operagoers. Ballet tickets run £7 to £34 and opera tickets cost £17 to £46. On performance days, the box office is open Monday to Saturday 10am to 8pm; on nonperformance days, hours are Monday to Saturday 10am to 6pm.

In winter, the **Royal Scottish National Orchestra** (✆ **0141/2263-8681;** www.rsno.org.uk) offers Saturday-evening concerts at the **Glasgow Royal Concert Hall,** 2 Sauchiehall St. (box office ✆ **0141/353-8000;** Underground: Buchanan St.). The **BBC Scottish Symphony Orchestra** presents concerts at the **BBC Broadcasting House,** Queen Margaret Drive (Underground: St. Enoch), or at **City Halls,** Albion Street (Underground: St. Enoch). In summer, the Scottish National Orchestra has a short Promenade season (dates and venues are announced in the papers). Tickets can be purchased only at individual venues.

THEATER

Although hardly competition for London, Glasgow's theater scene is certainly the equal of Edinburgh's. Young Scottish playwrights often make their debuts here, and you're likely to see anything from Steinbeck's *The Grapes of Wrath* to Wilde's *Salome* to *Romeo and Juliet* done in Edwardian dress.

The prime symbol of Glasgow's verve remains the **Citizens Theatre,** Gorbals and Ballater streets (✆ **0141/429-0022;** www.citz.co.uk; bus: 12 or 66), founded after World War II by James Bridie, a famous Glaswegian whose plays are still produced on occasion there. It's home to a repertory company, with tickets at £4 to £17. The box office hours are Monday 10am to 6pm and Tuesday to Saturday 10am to 9pm. The company is usually closed June to the first week in August.

THE CLUB & MUSIC SCENE

Barrowland, Gallowgate 244 (✆ **0141/552-4601;** Underground: St. Enoch; bus: 61 or 62), seats 2,000 and is open only on nights when shows are booked. July and August are the quiet months, as most shows are geared toward a student audience. The cover runs highest when the hall hosts popular bands like the Proclaimers or the Black Rebel Motorcycle Club, and ranges from £6 to £25.

The **13th Note,** 50–60 King St. (✆ **0141/553-1638;** bus: 21, 23, or 38), has moved away from jazz in the past couple of years and now books mainly heavy rock bands on Wednesday and Thursday nights, country on Monday. On Friday, Saturday, and Sunday, the night is dedicated to ambient and alternative music. Open Sunday and Wednesday to Thursday from 11pm to 3am, Friday and Saturday from 9pm to 3am. Cover charge ranges from £5 to £18.

Most of the crowd at **Fury Murry's,** 96 Maxwell St. (✆ **0141/221-6511;** Underground: St. Enoch), is made up of students looking for nothing more complicated than a good, sometimes rowdy, time listening to disco music that's upbeat but not ultratrendy. It's situated in a cellar, a 2-minute walk from the very central St. Enoch Shopping Centre. It has a very busy bar, a dance floor, and ample opportunities to meet the best and brightest in Scotland's university system. Jeans and T-shirts are the right garb. It's open Thursday to Sunday from 11pm to 3am. Thursday and Friday feature live bands, and other nights are strictly for dancing or can be reserved for private parties. Cover charges range from £5 to £10.

FAVORITE PUBS

The amiably battered **Bon Accord,** 153 North St. (✆ **0141/248-4427;** bus: 6, 8, or 16), is a longtime favorite. It has an array of hand pumps—a dozen devoted to real British ales, the rest to beers and stouts from the Czech Republic, Belgium, Germany, Ireland, and Holland. The pub is likely to satisfy your taste in malt whisky as well, and offers affordable bar snacks. It's open Monday to Saturday from noon to midnight, Sunday from noon to 11pm.

The **Cask and Still,** 154 Hope St. (✆ **0141/333-0980;** bus: 21, 23, or 38), is the best place for sampling malt whisky. You can taste from a selection of more than 350 single malts, at a variety of strengths (perhaps not on the same night) and maturities. Many prefer the malt whisky that has been aged in a sherry cask. There's good bar food at lunch, including cold-meat salads and sandwiches. It's open Monday to Thursday noon to 11pm, Friday and Saturday noon to midnight.

TAYSIDE & GRAMPIAN

Tayside and Grampian, two history-rich sections in northeast Scotland, offer a vast array of sightseeing in what are relatively small areas. Tayside, for example, is about 137km (85 miles) east to west, and some 97km (60 miles) south to north. The two regions share the North Sea coast between the Firth of Tay in the south and the Firth of Moray farther north. The so-called Highland Line separating the Lowlands in the south from the Highlands in the north crosses both regions. The Grampians, the highest mountain range in Scotland, are to the west of this line.

Carved out of the old counties of Perth and Angus, **Tayside** is named for its major river, the 190km (118-mile) Tay. The region is easy to explore, and its tributaries and dozens of lochs and Highland streams are among the best salmon and trout waters in Europe. One of the loveliest regions of Scotland, Tayside is filled with heather-clad Highland hills, long blue lochs under tree-lined banks, and miles and miles of walking trails. Tayside provided the backdrop for many novels by Sir Walter Scott, including *The Fair Maid of Perth, Waverley,* and *The Abbot*. Its golf courses are world famous, especially the trio of 18-hole courses at Gleneagles.

The **Grampian** region has Braemar, site of the most famous of the Highland gatherings. The queen herself comes here to holiday at Balmoral Castle, her private residence, a tradition dating back to the days of Queen Victoria and her consort, Prince Albert. As you journey on the scenic roads of Scotland's northeast, you'll pass heather-covered moorland and peaty lochs, wood glens and salmon-filled rivers, granite-stone villages and ancient castles, and fishing harbors as well as North Sea beach resorts.

Gleneagles

This famous golfing center and sports complex is on a moor between Strathearn and Strath Allan. Gleneagles has three **18-hole golf courses:** King's Course, the longest one; Queen's Course, next in length; and the PGA Centenary Course, the newest of the trio. They're among the best in Scotland, and the sports complex is one of the best equipped in Europe.

ESSENTIALS

Getting There

BY TRAIN The 15-minute ride from Perth costs £5.40. The trip from Edinburgh takes 1 hour and 20 minutes and costs £12. For information, call ✆ **08457/484-950,** or visit www.nationalrail.co.uk.

BY BUS Frequent buses arrive from both Glasgow, costing £22 to £25 round-trip, and Edinburgh, costing £21 to £26 round-trip. There are also frequent arrivals from Inverness, a round-trip costing £11 to £15. For bus schedules in Aberdeen, call ✆ **01224/212-266.**

BY CAR Gleneagles is on A-9, about halfway between Perth and Stirling, a short distance from the village of Auchterarder. It lies 88km (55 miles) from Edinburgh and 72km (45 miles) from Glasgow.

VISITOR INFORMATION The **Aberdeen Tourist Information Centre** is at 24–28 Exchange St., Aberdeen, Aberdeenshire AB11 6PH (✆ **01224/288-800;** www.agtb.org). July and August, it's open Monday to Friday 9am to 7pm, Saturday 9am to 5pm, and Sunday 10am to 4pm; September to June, hours are Monday to Friday 9am to 5pm and Saturday 10am to 2pm.

WHERE TO STAY & DINE

Gleneagles Hotel ★★★ Britain's greatest golf hotel stands on its own 344-hectare (850-acre) estate. When it was built in isolated grandeur in 1924, it was Scotland's only five-star hotel. It's a true resort and has tried to keep ahead of the times by offering spa treatments. Rooms vary greatly in size. The best and most spacious choices are in the 60- to 90-block series; these have recently been refurbished. The less desirable rooms, called courtyard units, are a bit small and equipped with shower-only bathrooms. A more modern building has been added, with 54 more rooms. As for cuisine, the golfers rarely complain, but no one dines here to collect recipes.

Tayside & Grampian

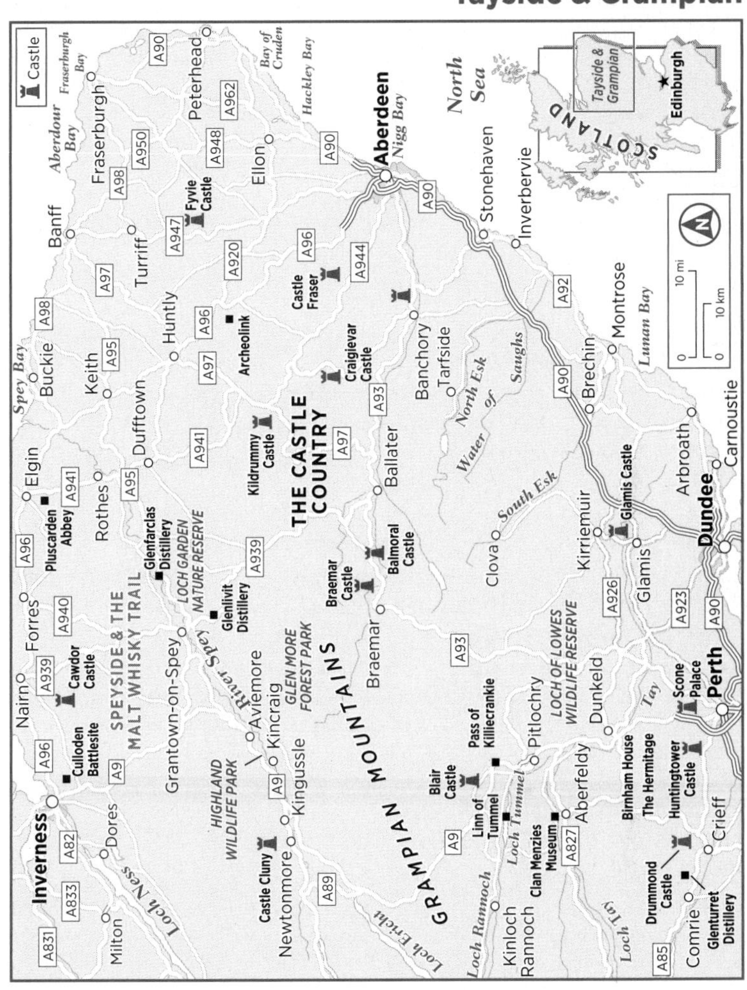

Auchterarder PH3 1NF. ✆ **1-866-881-9525** in the U.S., or 01764/662-231. Fax 01764/662-134. www.gleneagles.com. 269 units. £299–£399 double; from £660 suite. Rates include Scottish breakfast. AE, DC, MC, V. Free parking. Take A9 2.5km (1½ miles) southwest of Auchterarder. **Amenities:** 4 restaurants; 4 bars; babysitting; 3 golf courses; health club; 3 pools (1 indoor heated, 1 outdoor heated, 1 lap); room service; spa; tennis court. *In room:* TV, hair dryer, minibar, Wi-Fi (free).

Crieff

From Perth, 70km (43 miles) north of Edinburgh, head west on A-85 for 29km (18 miles) to Crieff. At the edge of the Perthshire Highlands, with good fishing and golf, Crieff makes a pleasant stopover. This small burgh was the seat of the court of the earls of Strathearn until 1747, and the gallows in its marketplace was once used to execute Highland cattle rustlers.

You can take a "day trail" into **Strathearn,** the valley of the River Earn, the very center of Scotland. Here Highland mountains meet gentle Lowland slopes, and moorland mingles with rich green pastures. North of Crieff, the road to Aberfeldy passes through the narrow pass of the **Sma' Glen,** a famous spot of beauty, with hills rising on either side to 600m (1,970 ft.).

ESSENTIALS

Getting There

BY TRAIN There's no direct service. The nearest rail stations are at Gleneagles, 14km (8⅔ miles) away, and at Perth, 29km (18 miles) away. Call ✆ **08457/484-950** for information and schedules.

BY BUS Once you arrive in Perth, you'll find regular connecting bus service hourly during the day. For information and schedules, call **Stagecoach** at ✆ **01738/629-339.** The bus service from Gleneagles is too poor to recommend.

BY TAXI A taxi from Gleneagles will cost from £15 to £20.

VISITOR INFORMATION The year-round **tourist information office** is in the Town Hall on High Street (✆ **01764/652-578**). It's open November to March, Monday to Friday 10am to 4pm; April to June, Monday to Saturday 9:30am to 5:30pm, Sunday 10am to 4pm; July and August, Monday to Saturday 9:30am to 6:30pm, Sunday 11am to 6pm; and September and October, Monday to Saturday 9:30am to 5pm, Sunday 10am to 4pm.

SEEING THE SIGHTS

Drummond Castle Gardens ★ The gardens of Drummond Castle, first laid out in the early 17th century by John Drummond, second earl of Perth, are among the finest formal gardens in Europe. There's a panoramic view from the upper terrace, overlooking an example of an early Victorian parterre in the form of St. Andrew's Cross. The multifaceted sundial by John Mylne, master mason to Charles I, has been the centerpiece since 1630.

Grimsthorpe, Crieff. ✆ **01764/681-433.** www.drummondcastlegardens.co.uk. Admission £5 adults, £4 seniors, £2 children. May–Oct daily 1–6pm. Closed Nov–Apr. Take A822 for 5km (3 miles) south of Crieff.

Glenturret Distillery Ltd Scotland's oldest distillery, Glenturret was established in 1775 on the banks of the River Turret. Visitors can see the milling of malt, mashing, fermentation, distillation, and cask filling, followed by a free "wee dram" dispensed at the end of the tour. Guided tours take about 50 minutes and leave at frequent intervals—sometimes as often as every 10 minutes when there's a demand for it. The tour can be followed or preceded by a 20-minute video, *The Water of Life,* presented adjacent to a small museum devoted to the implements of the whisky trade.

The Hosh, Hwy. A85, Glenturret. ✆ **01764/656-565.** www.scotchwhisky.net. Guided tours £8.50 adults, £6.95 seniors and children 12–17, free for children 11 and under. Jan Mon–Fri 11:30am–4pm; Feb Mon–Sat 11:30am–4pm, Sun noon–4pm; Mar–Dec Mon–Sat 9:30am–6pm, Sun noon–6pm. Take A85 toward Comrie; 1.2km (¾ mile) from Crieff, turn right at the crossroads; the distillery is .5km (⅓ mile) up the road.

GOLFING

Crieff Golf Club (✆ **01764/652909;** www.crieffgolf.co.uk) has two courses—both with panoramic views and excellent facilities. The most challenging is the

18-hole Fern Tower, a par-71 course with three par-5 holes. The Dornock is a 64-par, 9-hole course with three par-3 holes. It's not quite as difficult as the Fern Tower, but a test nonetheless. Greens fees for the Fern Tower are £28 to £36 Monday to Friday, and £36 to £42 weekends. Greens fees for the Dornock are £12 for 9 holes and £16 for 18 holes. April to October, the golf club is open from 8am to 7:30pm; November to March, it's open daily from 9am to 5pm.

Dundee & Glamis Castle ★★

This royal burgh and old seaport is an industrial city on the north shore of the Firth of Tay. When steamers took over the whaling industry from sailing vessels, Dundee became the leading home port for ships from the 1860s until World War I. Long known for its jute and flax operations, we think today of the Dundee fruitcakes, marmalades, and jams. This was also the home of the man who invented stick-on postage stamps, James Chalmers. Dundee has a raffish charm and serves well as a base for a trip to Glamis Castle.

Spanning the Firth of Tay is the **Tay Railway Bridge,** opened in 1888. Constructed over the tidal estuary, the bridge is some 3km (1¾ miles) long, one of the longest in Europe. There's also a road bridge 2km (1¼ miles) long, with four traffic lanes and a walkway in the center.

ESSENTIALS

Getting There

BY TRAIN ScotRail offers frequent service between Perth, Dundee, and Aberdeen. One-way fare from Perth to Dundee is £6; from Aberdeen, £24. Phone ✆ **08457/484-950** for schedules and departure times.

BY BUS CityLink buses offer frequent bus service from Edinburgh and Glasgow. Call ✆ **0990/505-050** for information.

BY CAR The fastest way to reach Dundee is to cut south back to Perth along A9 and link up with A972 going east.

VISITOR INFORMATION The **tourist information office** is at 21 Castle St. (✆ **01382/527-527;** www.angusanddundee.co.uk). Hours are usually Monday to Saturday 10am to 5pm, Sunday 11am to 4pm.

WHERE TO STAY

Hilton Dundee ★ This chain hotel helps rejuvenate the once-seedy waterfront of Dundee. Built in a severe modern style, the five-story block takes its name from a famous English tea, which most often accompanies marmalade and Dundee fruitcakes, the city's two most famous products. Some of the well-furnished rooms overlook the Firth, the river, or the Tay Bridge. Both the business and the leisure traveler will find solace here in rooms with bright floral upholstery and draperies, blond wood furnishings, and small bathrooms.

Earl Grey Place, Dundee DD1 4DE. ✆ **01382/229-271.** Fax 01382/200-072. www.dundee.hilton.com. 129 units. £104–£148 double. AE, DC, MC, V. Parking £3. Bus: 1A, 1B, or 20. From the south, the hotel is on the left-hand side as you come over the Tay Rd. Bridge into town. **Amenities:** Restaurant; bar; health club; indoor pool; room service. *In room:* TV, hair dryer, Wi-Fi (in some; free).

Invercarse Hotel In landscaped gardens overlooking the River Tay, this privately owned hotel lies 5km (3 miles) west of the heart of Dundee. Many prefer it for its fresh air, tranquil location, and Victorian country-house aura. Well-maintained rooms come in a variety of sizes and open onto views across the Tay to the hills of the Kingdom of Fife.

371 Perth Rd., Dundee DD2 1PG. ✆ **800/528-1234** in the U.S., or 01382/669-231. Fax 01382/644-112. www.bw-invercarsehotel.co.uk. 44 units. £75–£110 double; £140 suite. Rates include Scottish breakfast. AE, DC, MC, V. Free parking. Drive 5km (3 miles) west of Dundee on the Perth Rd. The hotel is clearly signposted. **Amenities:** Restaurant; bar; access to nearby health club; room service. *In room:* TV, hair dryer, Wi-Fi (free).

WHERE TO DINE

Jahangir Tandoori INDIAN Built around an indoor fishpond in a dining room draped with the soft folds of an embroidered tent, this is one of the most exotic restaurants in the region. Meals are prepared with fresh ingredients and cover the gamut of recipes from both north and south India. Some preparations are slow-cooked in clay pots (tandoori) and seasoned to the degree of spiciness you prefer. Both meat and meatless dishes are available.

1 Sessions St. (at the corner of Hawk Hill). ✆ **01382/202-022.** Reservations recommended. Main courses £12–£20; lunch buffet £5.95. AE, DC, MC, V. Mon–Fri noon–4pm; daily 5pm–midnight.

SEEING THE SIGHTS

For a panoramic view of Dundee, the Tay bridges across to Fife, and mountains to the north, go to **Dundee Law,** a 175m (574-ft.) hill just north of the city. The hill is an ancient volcanic plug.

Broughty Castle This 15th-century estuary fort lies about 6km (3¾ miles) east of the city center on the seafront, at Broughty Ferry, a little fishing hamlet and once the terminus for ferries crossing the Firth of Tay before the bridges were built. Besieged by the English in the 16th century, and attacked by Cromwell's army under General Monk in the 17th century, it was eventually restored as part of Britain's coastal defenses in 1861. Its gun battery was dismantled in 1956, and it's now a museum with displays on local history, arms and armor, and Dundee's whaling story. The observation area at the top of the castle provides fine views of the Tay estuary and northeast Fife.

Castle Green, Broughty Ferry. ✆ **01382/436-916.** Free admission. Apr–Sept Mon–Sat 10am–4pm, Sun 12:30–4pm; Oct–Mar Tues–Sat 10am–4pm, Sun 12:30–4pm. Bus: 75 or 76.

HM Frigate Unicorn ★ ☺ This 46-gun wooden ship of war commissioned in 1824 by the Royal Navy, now the oldest British-built ship afloat, has been restored and visitors can explore all four decks: the quarterdeck with 32-pound cannonades, the gun deck with its battery of 18-pound cannons and the captain's quarters, the berth deck with officers' cabins and crews' hammocks, and the orlop deck and hold. Displays portraying life in the sailing navy and the history of the *Unicorn* make this a rewarding visit.

Victoria Dock. ✆ **01382/200-900.** www.frigateunicorn.org. Admission £4 adults, £3 seniors and children, £9–£11 family ticket. Easter–Oct daily 10am–4pm; Nov–Mar Wed–Sun noon–4pm. Bus: 6, 23, or 78.

GOLFING

Caird Park Golf Club at Dundee (✆ **01382/453-606**) is an 18-hole, par-69 course that presents most golfers with an average challenge. The course is quite flat, but there are more than a few bunkers to navigate. There's also a restaurant and bar on the premises. Greens fees are £22 for 18 holes, or £28 for a day ticket. No carts of any sort are allowed on the course, and there's no particular dress code. The park is open April to October daily 7:30am to 8pm.

PLAYING THE WORLD'S OLDEST course

At **St. Andrew's,** 23km (14 miles) southeast of Dundee and 82km (51 miles) northeast of Edinburgh, the rules of golf in Britain and the world were codified and arbitrated. Golf was played for the first time in the 1400s, probably on the site of St. Andrew's Old Course, and enjoyed by Mary, Queen of Scots, there in 1567. All six of St. Andrew's golf courses are open to the public on a more-or-less democratic basis—ballots are polled 1 day in advance. To participate in the balloting, you first must be staying in St. Andrews for a minimum of 2 days, and you must be able to present a current handicap certificate issued by the governing golf body of your home country. If you meet those requirements, you can enter the ballot in person at the golf course, or by phone at ✆ **01334/466-666,** before 1:45pm on the day before the one on which you wish to play. At 2pm each day, the balloting is drawn, and the following day's players are announced at 4pm. Bear in mind that your wait to play will most likely be from 4 to 6 days; however, some lucky players get on the course the next day. Players who call the golf course several weeks in advance to make reservations can often circumvent the balloting system, depending on demand.

The **Old Course,** St. Andrews, Golf Place, St. Andrew's, Fife (✆ **01334/466-666**), is a 6,000m (6,562-yd.) 18-hole course billed as "the Home of Golf." Greens fees are £130 per round from April to September or £64 to £91 otherwise. A caddy will cost £40 plus tip. Golf clubs rent for £35 per round. Electric carts are not allowed, and you can rent a cart only on afternoons from April to October for £4. The course is a par 72.

To reach St. Andrews from Edinburgh, travel along the A90 north to Dunfermline. From there, continue northeast along A910, which becomes A915 at Leven. From Leven, drive northeast on A915 directly to St. Andrews (trip time: 1 hr.).

A DAY TRIP TO GLAMIS

The little village of Glamis (pronounced without the "i") grew up around **Glamis Castle ★★**, Castle Office (✆ **01307/840393;** www.glamis-castle.co.uk). Next to Balmoral Castle, visitors to Scotland most want to see Glamis Castle for its link with the crown. For 6 centuries it has been connected to members of the British royal family. The queen mother was brought up here; and Princess Margaret was born here, becoming the first royal princess born in Scotland in 3 centuries. The present owner is the queen's great-nephew. The castle contains Duncan's Hall—the Victorians claimed this was where Macbeth murdered King Duncan, but in the play, the murder takes place at Macbeth's castle near Inverness. In fact, Shakespeare was erroneous as well—he had Macbeth named Thane of Glamis, but Glamis wasn't made a thaneship (a sphere of influence in medieval Scotland) until years after the play takes place.

The present Glamis Castle dates from the early 15th century, but there are records of a castle having been in existence in the 11th century. Glamis Castle has been in the possession of the Lyon family since 1372, and it contains some fine plaster ceilings, furniture, and paintings.

The castle is open to the public, with access to the Royal Apartments and many other rooms, as well as the fine gardens, the end of March to October, daily 10:30am to 4:30pm. Admission to the castle and gardens is £8.75 adults, £6 children, £25 family ticket. If you wish to visit the grounds only, the charge is £4.50 adults, £3.50 children. Buses run between Dundee and Glamis. The 55-minute ride costs £5 one-way. ***Note:*** Buses don't stop in front of the castle, which lies 1km (⅔ mile) from the bus stop.

Where to Dine

Strathmore Arms CONTINENTAL/SCOTTISH Try this place near the castle for one of the best lunches in the area. You might begin with the freshly made soup of the day or the fresh prawns. Some of the dishes regularly featured might include steak pie or venison. For something a little more exotic, go for the Indian chicken breast marinated in yogurt and spices; for vegetarians, phyllo parcels stuffed with asparagus and cauliflower.

The Square, Glamis. ✆ **01307/840-248.** Reservations recommended. Main courses £9–£22. AE, MC, V. Daily noon–9pm.

Braemar

In the heart of some of Grampian's most beautiful scenery, Braemar not only is known for its own castle, but makes a good center from which to explore Balmoral Castle (see "Ballater & Balmoral Castle," below). In this Highland village, set against a massive backdrop of hills covered with heather in summer, Clunie Water joins the River Dee. The massive **Cairn Toul** towers over Braemar, reaching a height of 1,293m (4,242 ft.).

ESSENTIALS

Getting There

BY TRAIN Take the train to Aberdeen, and then continue the rest of the way by bus. For information and schedules, call ✆ **08457/484-950.**

BY BUS Buses run daily from Aberdeen to Braemar six times a day (trip time: 2 hr.). One-way fare is £10. The bus and train stations in Aberdeen are next to each other on Guild Street (✆ **01224/212-266** for information about schedules).

BY CAR To reach Braemar from Dundee, return west toward Perth, and then head north along A93, following the signs into Braemar. The 113km (70-mile) drive will take 70 to 90 minutes.

VISITOR INFORMATION The year-round **Braemar Tourist Office** is in The Mews, Mar Road (✆ **01339/741-600**). Hours are as follows: January to May and November and December Monday to Saturday 10:30am to 1:30pm and 2 to 5pm, Sunday 1 to 4pm; June, July, September, and October daily 9am to 5pm; August daily 9am to 6pm.

SPECIAL EVENTS The spectacular **Royal Highland Gathering** takes place annually in late August or early September in the Princess Royal and Duke of Fife Memorial Park. The queen herself often attends the gathering. These ancient games are thought to have been originated by King Malcolm Canmore, a chieftain who ruled much of Scotland at the time of the Norman conquest of England. He selected his hardiest warriors from all the clans for a "keen and fair contest."

Call the tourist office (see "Visitor Information," above) for more information. Braemar is overrun with visitors during the gathering—anyone thinking of attending would be wise to reserve accommodations anywhere within a 32km (20-mile) radius of Braemar no later than early April.

WHERE TO STAY & DINE

Braemar Lodge Hotel ☺ This hotel, popular with skiers who frequent the nearby Glenshee slopes, is set on 1 hectare (2½ acres) of grounds at the head of Glen Clunie. Units vary in shape and size, but each is comfortable and well equipped, containing a well-maintained bathroom with tub and shower. Rooms are bright and airy, with soothing color schemes. Two rooms are large enough for families. On cool evenings, you're greeted by log fires. The hotel is on the road to the Glenshee ski slopes near the cottage where Robert Louis Stevenson wrote *Treasure Island*. On the grounds, three log cabins have been recently built. Fully equipped with all modern conveniences, they can sleep up to six persons.

6 Glenshee Rd., Braemar AB35 5YQ. ✆/fax **01339/741-627.** www.braemarlodge.co.uk. 7 units. £70–£120 double; £295–£395 log cabin per week. Rates include Scottish breakfast. MC, V. Free parking. Closed Nov. Lies a 2-min. walk south from the bus station. **Amenities:** Restaurant; bar. *In room:* TV, hair dryer.

Invercauld Arms Thistle Hotel ★ This is the leading inn of the town, with superior amenities and greater comfort than Braemar Lodge. The oldest part of this old granite building dates from the 18th century. In cool weather there's a roaring log fire on the hearth. You can go hill walking and see deer, golden eagles, and other wildlife. Fishing and winter skiing are other pursuits in the nearby area. Rooms are comfortably furnished. Although they lack any style or glamour, they serve their purpose well, and come in a wide range of sizes. In the pub close by, you'll meet the "ghillies" and "stalkers" (hunting and fishing guides).

Invercauld Rd., Braemar AB35 5YR. ✆ **01339/741-605.** Fax 01339/741-428. 68 units. £85 double. Rates include Scottish breakfast. AE, DC, MC, V. Free parking. Bus: 201. **Amenities:** Restaurant; bar. *In room:* TV, hair dryer.

SEEING THE SIGHTS

If you're a royal-family watcher, you might be able to spot members of the family, even the queen, at **Crathie Church,** 14km (8⅔ miles) east of Braemar on A93 (✆ **01339/742-208**), where they attend Sunday services when in residence. Services are at 11:30am; otherwise, the church is open to view April to October, Monday to Saturday 9:30am to 5:30pm and on Sunday 2 to 5:30pm.

Nature lovers may want to drive to the **Linn of Dee,** 10km (6¼ miles) west of Braemar, a narrow chasm on the River Dee, which is a local beauty spot. Other beauty spots include Glen Muick, Loch Muick, and Lochnagar. A **Scottish Wildlife Trust Visitor Centre,** reached by a minor road, is located in this Highland glen, off the South Deeside road. An access road joins B976 at a point 26km (16 miles) east of Braemar. The tourist office (see above) will give you a map pinpointing these beauty spots.

Braemar Castle ★ This romantic 17th-century castle is a fully furnished private residence with architectural grace, scenic charm, and historical interest. The castle has barrel-vaulted ceilings and an underground prison and is known for its remarkable star-shaped defensive curtain wall.

On the Aberdeen-Ballater-Perth Rd. (A93). ✆ **01337/41600.** Admission £5 adults; £4 seniors, students, and children 5–15; free for children 4 and under. Sat–Sun 11am–4pm; also Wed July–Aug (call ✆ 013397/41600 for times). Closed Nov–Easter. Take A93 .8km (½ mile) northeast of Braemar.

GOLFING

Braemar Golf Club, at Braemar (✆ **01339/741-618**), is the highest golf course in the country. The second-hole green is 380m (1,247 ft.) above sea level—this is the trickiest hole on the course. Pro golf commentator Peter Alliss has deemed it "the hardest par 4 in all of Scotland." Set on a plateau, the hole is bordered on the right by the River Clunie and lined on the left by rough. Greens fees are as follows: Monday to Friday £25 for 18 holes and £30 for a day ticket; Saturday and Sunday £25 for 18 holes and £30 for a day ticket. Pull-carts can be rented for £5 per day, and sets of clubs can be borrowed for £9 per day. The only dress code is "be reasonable." The course is open only April to October daily (call in advance as hours can vary).

Ballater & Balmoral Castle ★★

Ballater is a vacation resort center on the Dee River, with the Grampian Mountains in the background. The town is still centered around its Station Square, where the Royal Family used to be photographed as they arrived to spend vacations. The railway is now closed.

ESSENTIALS

Getting There

BY TRAIN Go to Aberdeen and continue the rest of the way by connecting bus. For rail schedules and information, call ✆ **08457/484-950.**

BY BUS Buses run hourly from Aberdeen to Ballater. The bus and train stations in Aberdeen are next to each other on Guild Street (✆ **01224/212-266** for information). Bus no. 201 from Braemar runs to Ballater (trip time: 1¼ hr.). The fare is £5.

BY CAR From Braemar, go east along A93.

VISITOR INFORMATION The **tourist information office** is at Station Square (✆ **01339/755-306**). Hours are January 4 to June 25 and September 4 to December daily 10am to 5pm, June 26 to September 3 daily 9am to 6pm.

WHERE TO STAY

Darroch Learg Hotel ★ 🎁 Built in 1888 as an elegant country home, this pink granite hotel stands in 2 hectares (5 acres) of lush woodlands opening onto views of the Dee Valley toward the Grampian Mountains. Constructed at the peak of the golden age of the Royal Deeside area (given the "Royal" designation due to the presence of Balmoral Castle, Queen Victoria's summer home), the hotel is imbued with a relaxing charm. The individually decorated bedrooms are divided between the main house and Oakhall, a baronial mansion on the same grounds. Some units have four-poster beds and private terraces.

Darroch Learg, Braemar Rd. (on A93 at the west end of Ballater), Ballater AB35 5UX. ✆ **01339/755-443.** Fax 01339/755-252. www.darrochlearg.co.uk. 17 units. £65–£115 double. Rates include breakfast. MC, V. Free parking. Closed Christmas and last 3 weeks in Jan. **Amenities:** Restaurant; Internet (free); room service. *In room:* TV, hair dryer.

Hilton Craigendarroch Hotel ★ This hotel, built in the Scottish baronial style, is set amid old trees on a 13-hectare (32-acre) estate. Modern comforts have been added, but the owners have tried to maintain a 19th-century aura. The public rooms include a regal oaken staircase and a large sitting room. The fair-size rooms open onto views of the village of Ballater and the River Dee. Each is furnished in individual style, with private bathrooms (showers only). Public facilities are luxurious, especially the oak-paneled study with a log fire and book-lined shelves.

Braemar Rd., Ballater AB35 5XA. ✆ **01339/755-858.** Fax 01339/755-447. www.hilton.co.uk/craigendarroch. 45 units. £109–£129 double; £170 suite. Rates include Scottish breakfast and dinner. AE, DC, MC, V. Free parking. Signposted directly west of town on the road to Braemar. **Amenities:** 3 restaurants; 2 bars; babysitting; children's playground; health club; indoor pool; sauna; steam room; tennis court; Wi-Fi (£10 per day). *In room:* TV, hair dryer.

WHERE TO DINE

Green Inn SCOTTISH In the heart of town, once a former temperance hotel, this is now one of the finest dining rooms in town, especially for traditional Scottish dishes. The chef places emphasis on local produce, including homegrown vegetables when available. In season, loin of venison is served with a bramble sauce, and you can always count on fresh salmon and the best of Angus beef with Loch fine scallops.

Three simply furnished double rooms, with shower-only bathroom, TV, and half board, go for £70 to £90 per person.

9 Victoria Rd., Ballater. ✆/fax **01339/755-701.** Reservations required. Fixed-price menu £34 for 2 courses, £41 for 3 courses. AE, DC, MC, V. Easter–Dec Tues–Sat 7–9pm; Jan–Easter Wed–Sat 7–9pm.

Oaks Restaurant BRITISH The most glamorous restaurant in the region, the Oaks is in the century-old mansion that was originally built by the "marmalade kings" of Britain, the Keiller family. (The company's marmalade is still a household word throughout the United Kingdom.) This is the most upscale of the three restaurants in a resort complex that includes hotel rooms, timeshare villas, and access to a nearby golf course. To start, try the venison and duck terrine flavored with orange and brandy and served with a warm black conch vinaigrette. Other main courses are roast rack of lamb, breast of Grampian chicken, loin of venison, and filet of Aberdeen Angus beef.

In the Hilton Craigendarroch Hotel, Braemar Rd. ✆ **01339/755-858.** Reservations strongly recommended. Fixed-price 4-course dinner £36. AE, DC, MC, V. Thurs–Sun 6:30–9:15pm.

THE CASTLE

Balmoral Castle "This dear paradise" is how Queen Victoria described Balmoral Castle, rebuilt in the Scottish baronial style by her "beloved" Albert and completed in 1855. Today Balmoral, 13km (8 miles) west of Ballater, is still a private residence of the British sovereign. Its principal feature is a 30m (100-ft.) tower. Of the actual castle, only the ballroom is open to the public; it houses an exhibit of pictures, porcelain, and works of art. On the grounds are many memorials to the royal family, along with gardens, country walks, souvenir shops, a refreshment room, and pony trekking for £35 for a 2-hour ride (available to adults and children 13 and over, daily 10am–noon or 2–4pm).

Balmoral, Ballater. ✆ **01339/742-534.** www.balmoralcastle.com. Admission £8.50 adults, £7.50 students and seniors, £4.50 children 5–16, free for children 4 and under. Apr–July daily 10am–5pm. Closed Aug–Mar. Crathie bus from Aberdeen.

Speyside ★ & the Malt Whisky Trail ★

Much of the Speyside region covered in this section is in the Moray district, on the southern shore of the Moray Firth, a great inlet cutting into the northeastern coast of Scotland. The district stretches in a triangular shape south from the coast to the

SPOTTING nessie

Sir Peter Scott's *Nessitera rhombopteryx* continues to elude her pursuers. "Nessie," as she's more familiarly known, has captured the imagination of the world, drawing thousands of visitors yearly to Loch Ness. The Loch Ness monster has been described as one of the world's greatest mysteries. Half a century ago, A82 was built alongside the western banks of the loch. Since that time, many more sightings have been recorded.

All types of high-tech underwater contraptions have searched for the Loch Ness monster, but no one can find her. Dr. Robert Rines and his associates at the Academy of Applied Science in Massachusetts maintain a year-round watch with sonar-triggered cameras and strobe lights suspended from a raft in Urquhart Bay.

The loch is 39km (24 miles) long, 1.6km (1 mile) wide, and some 230m (755 ft.) deep. Even if the monster doesn't put in an appearance, you can enjoy the loch seascape. In summer, you can take boat cruises across Loch Ness from both Fort Augustus and Inverness.

Buses from either Fort Augustus or Inverness traverse A82, taking you to Drumnadrochit. Call ✆ **08705/808-080** for schedules and more information. The bucolic hamlet of Drumnadrochit lies 1.6km (1 mile) from Loch Ness at the entrance to Glen Urquhart. It's the nearest village to the part of the loch from which sightings of the monster have been reported most frequently.

From Grantown-on-Spey, take A938 west until you merge with northwest-bound E15/A9, which leads to Inverness, on the north tip of Loch Ness. From Inverness, travel on the A82 south, which runs the length of the western shoreline. The eastern shoreline can be traveled by following signposted rural roads from Inverness.

wild heart of the Cairngorm Mountains near Aviemore. It's a land steeped in history, as its many castles, battle sites, and ancient monuments testify. It's also a good place to fish and, of course, play golf. Golfers can purchase a 5-day ticket from tourist information centers that will allow you to play at more than 11 courses in the area.

One of the best of these courses is **Boat of Garten,** Speyside (✆ **01479/831282**). Relatively difficult, the almost 5,500m (6,000-yd.) course is dotted with many bunkers and wooded areas. April to October greens fees are £45 Monday to Friday and hours are from 9:30am to 11pm. Saturday greens fees are £50, and hours are from 10am to 4pm. In winter, call to see if the course is open. Greens fees are then reduced to £18. Pull-carts can be rented for £2.50, and electric carts are available for £20. Dress reasonably; bluejeans are not acceptable.

The valley of the second-largest river in Scotland, the Spey, lies north and south of Aviemore. It's a land of great natural beauty. The Spey is born in the Highlands above Loch Laggan, which lies 64km (40 miles) south of Inverness. Little more than a creek at its inception, it gains in force, fed by the many "burns" that drain water from the surrounding hills. One of Scotland's great rivers for salmon fishing, it runs between the towering Cairngorms on the east and the Monadhliath Mountains on the west. Its major center is Grantown-on-Spey.

The major tourist attraction in the area is the **Malt Whisky Trail,** 113km (70 miles) long, running through the glens of Speyside. Here distilleries, many of which can be visited, are known for their production of *uisge beatha,* or "water of life." "Whisky" is its more familiar name.

Half the malt distilleries in the country lie along the River Spey and its tributaries. Here peat smoke and Highland water are used to turn out single-malt (unblended) whisky. The five malt distilleries in the area are **Glenlivet, Glenfiddich, Glenfarclas, Strathisla,** and **Tamdhu.** Allow about an hour each to visit them.

The best way to reach Speyside from Aberdeen is to take A-96 northwest, signposted ELGIN. If you're traveling north on the A-9 road from Perth and Pitlochry, your first stop might be Dalwhinnie, which has the highest whisky distillery in the world at 575m (1,886 ft.). It's not in the Spey Valley but is at the northeastern end of Loch Ericht, with views of lochs and forests.

KEITH

Keith, 18km (11 miles) northwest of Huntly, grew up because of its strategic location, where the main road and rail routes between Inverness and Aberdeen cross the River Isla. It has an ancient history, but owes its present look to the "town planning" of the late 18th and early 19th centuries. Today it's a major stopover along the Malt Whisky Trail.

The oldest operating distillery in the Scottish Highlands, the **Strathisla Distillery,** on Seafield Avenue (✆ **01542/783-044**), was established in 1786. From April 6 to October, hours are Monday to Saturday 9:30am to 4pm, Sunday 2 to 4pm. Admission is £5 for adults, free for children age 8 to 18; children age 7 and under are not admitted. The admission fee includes a £3 voucher redeemable in the distillery shop against a 70cl bottle of whisky. Be warned that tours of this distillery are self-guided.

DUFFTOWN

James Duff, the fourth earl of Fife, founded this town in 1817. The four main streets of town converge at the battlemented **clock tower,** which is also the tourist information center. A center of the whisky-distilling industry, Dufftown is surrounded by seven malt distilleries. The family-owned **Glenfiddich Distillery** is on A941, 1km (⅔ mile) north (✆ **01340/820-373**). It's open Monday to Friday from 9:30am to 4:30pm (also Easter to mid-Oct, Sat 9:30am–4:30pm and Sun noon–4:30pm). Guides in kilts show you around the plant and explain the process of distilling. A film of the history of distilling is also shown. At the finish of the tour, you're given a dram of malt whisky to sample. The tour is free, but there's a souvenir shop where the owners hope you'll spend a few pounds.

Other sights include **Balvenie Castle,** along A941 (✆ **01340/820-121**), the ruins of a moated 14th-century stronghold that lie on the south side of the Glenfiddich Distillery. During her northern campaign against the earl of Huntly, Mary, Queen of Scots spent 2 nights here. April to September, it's open daily from 9:30am to 6:30pm. Admission is £3.50 for adults, £2.25 for seniors, and £1 for children.

Mortlach Parish Church in Dufftown is one of the oldest places of Christian worship in the country. It's reputed to have been founded in 566 by St. Moluag. A Pictish cross stands in the graveyard. The present church was reconstructed in 1931 and incorporates portions of an older building.

Where to Dine

Taste of Speyside ★ SCOTTISH True to its name, this restaurant in the town center, just off the main square, avidly promotes a Speyside cuisine as well as malt whiskies. In the bar you can buy the product of each of Speyside's 46 distilleries. A platter including a slice of smoked salmon, smoked venison, smoked trout, pâté flavored with malt whisky, locally made cheese (cow or goat), salads, and homemade oat cakes is offered at noon and at night. Nourishing soup is made fresh daily and is served with homemade bread. There's also a choice of meat pies, including venison with red wine and herbs, or rabbit. For dessert, try Scotch Mist, which contains fresh cream, malt whisky, and crumbled meringue.

10 Balvenie St. ✆ **01340/820-860.** Reservations recommended for dinner. Main courses £15–£20; fixed-price lunch £13; fixed-price dinner £24. AE, MC, V. Mon–Sat noon–9pm. Closed Jan.

GLENLIVET

As you leave Grantown-on-Spey and head east along A95, drive to the junction with B9008; go south and you won't miss the **Glenlivet Distillery.** The location of the **Glenlivet Reception Centre** (✆ **01340/821-720**) is 16km (10 miles) north of the nearest town, Tomintoul. Near the River Livet, a Spey tributary, this distillery is one of the most famous in Scotland. It's open mid-March to June, and September to October, Monday to Saturday from 10am to 4pm, and Sunday from 12:30 to 4pm; July and August, Monday to Saturday from 10am to 4pm and Sunday from 12:30 to 4pm. Admission is free.

Back on A95, you can visit the **Glenfarclas Distillery** at Ballindalloch (✆ **01807/500-209;** www.glenfarclas.co.uk), one of the few malt whisky distilleries that's still independent of the giants. Founded in 1836, Glenfarclas is managed by the fifth generation of the Grant family. There's a small craft shop, and each visitor is offered a dram of Glenfarclas Malt Whisky. Admission is free and visits are possible April 6 to October Monday to Saturday 9:30am to 4pm, Sunday 12:30 to 4pm. Kids 7 and under aren't permitted for safety reasons.

SPAIN

by Darwin Porter & Danforth Prince

17

For a nation with such a rich, storied past, Spain has a remarkable verve for the present. This land of sun-washed beaches, terraced vineyards, tranquil hill towns, and dazzling Moorish palaces has grown into a new-found prosperity after more than 2 decades of working to catch up with the rest of Europe. Cultural innovations, high-tech ventures, and contemporary art abound in the new Spain, and even the millenniums-old siesta is no longer sacred. This mix of old and new, of "castles in Spain" and cutting-edge cuisine, is making Spain a place that can hold its national head high in the 21st century.

MADRID ★★★

Madrid was built to rule, established on a broad, flat plateau in the geographical center of the Iberian peninsula to bring Spain's many fractious regions together. It's no wonder, then, that Madrid is Spain's melting pot. Native Madrileños are joined here not only by Basques, Galicians, Catalonians, and Andalusians, but by immigrants from Africa and South America. Far from the sea and lacking the multimillennial history of Barcelona or Seville, Madrid can still claim more than its fair share of world-class attractions: its impressive royal palace, handsome parks, wealth of art museums, and passionate and diverse population. Madrileños work hard and party even harder, dining at midnight and dancing until dawn in throbbing, multilevel nightclubs or whiling away the evening in smoky, atmospheric tapas bars.

Renovation and reconstruction are everywhere in Madrid, whether invisible in the lifted gloom of the Chueca neighborhood, once a dangerous, crime-ridden area and now the city's hottest nightlife district, or thrillingly obvious in the modern wings of the Prado, Thyssen, and Reina Sofia museums, three of Spain's greatest temples of art. The result of all this work is a city of comfortable, well-lighted plazas and winding yet approachable streets, and a population that looks to the future with power and pride.

Essentials

GETTING THERE

BY PLANE **Aeropuerto Madrid Barajas** (✆ **91-240-47-04;** www.aena.es), Madrid's international airport, is 14km (8⅔ miles) east of the city center and has three terminals. Most international flights arrive at Terminal 1. The cheapest ride (3€) into town is on **Metro line no. 8.** Its disadvantages are that the station is near Terminal 3, a long trek on moving walkways from Terminal 1, where most international flights arrive, and you have to make at least one line change at Nuevos Ministerios, with more walking. It's a speedy trip, though: Expect to be in the center about half an hour after you enter the system. For 2.45€, the no. 89 **airport bus** runs daily from 4:45am to 1:30am (departures every 10–15 min. 6am–10pm, less often at other times) between the airport and Plaza de Colón in the center of town. A **taxi** costs about 25€ plus tip and supplemental charges, and the ride takes 30 to 45 minutes, although during rush hours it can take up to an hour. Avoid unmetered limousines.

BY TRAIN Madrid has three major railway stations: **Atocha,** Avenida Ciudad de Barcelona (Metro: Atocha RENFE), for trains to and from Lisbon, Toledo, Andalusia, and Extremadura; **Chamartín,** in the northern suburbs at Augustín de Foxá (Metro: Chamartín), for trains to Barcelona, Asturias, Cantabria, Castilla y León, the Basque country, Aragón, Catalonia, Levante (Valencia), Murcia, and the French border; and **Estación Príncipe Pío** or Norte, Paseo del Rey 30 (Metro: Principe Pío), for trains to northwest Spain (Salamanca and Galicia). Many trains to Atocha run through to Chamartín and vice versa—good to know because the old part of town is much closer to Atocha than to Chamartín.

For information about connections from any of these stations, contact **RENFE,** the Spanish railway company (✆ **90-224-02-02** daily 5am–11:45pm; www.renfe.es). For tickets, go to the principal office of RENFE, Alcalá 44 (Metro: Banco de España), open Monday to Friday 9:30am to 8pm; or go to any of the three main stations listed above.

In the United States, **Rail Europe** sells a variety of **rail passes** valid for use throughout Europe or in one or more specific countries, including Spain. For details, call ✆ **888/382-7245** or visit **www.raileurope.com**.

BY BUS Madrid has at least eight major bus terminals, including the large **Estación Sur de Autobuses,** Calle Méndez Alvaro 83 (✆ **91-468-42-00;** Metro: Alvaro). Most buses pass through or arrive at this station.

BY CAR The following are the major highways into Madrid, with driving distances to the city: Route NI from Irún, 507km (315 miles); NII from Barcelona, 626km (389 miles); NIII from Valencia, 349km (217 miles); NIV from Cádiz, 624km (388 miles); NV from Badajoz, 409km (254 miles); and NVI from Galicia, 602km (374 miles).

VISITOR INFORMATION

TOURIST OFFICE The **regional government's tourist office** is at Duque de Medinaceli 2 (✆ **91-429-4951;** www.turismomadrid.es; Metro: Antón Martín). Open Monday to Saturday 9am to 7pm, Sunday and holidays 9am to 3pm. The city information office is at Plaza Mayor 27 (✆ **01-588-16-36;** www.munimadrid.es; Metro: Sol or Opera). Open daily 9:30am to 8:30pm. This office is primarily a distribution center for brochures and maps, although attendants can answer questions.

WEBSITES The Tourist Office of Spain (**www.okspain.org**) can help you plan your trip with listings of lodging options, attractions, tour operators, and packages, plus handy tips on getting around. For the viewpoints of individual travelers, check **www.tripadvisor.com** and **www.virtualtourist.com**. The highly personal **www.madridman.com** has a home page that looks frivolous but provides a surprising amount of info, especially on cheap hostels.

CITY LAYOUT The old city of Madrid sits like a small, dense walnut in the middle of Madrid's vast sprawl. The **Gran Vía** is the major east-west artery of the old town, beginning at **Plaza de España,** with one of Europe's tallest skyscrapers, Edificio España. Large numbers of shops, hotels, restaurants, and cinemas are concentrated on this principal avenue. Gran Vía ends at Calle de Alcalá, and at this juncture lies **Plaza de la Cibeles,** with its fountain to Cybele, "the mother of the gods," and what has become known as "the cathedral of post offices." From Cibeles northward, the wide **Paseo de Recoletos** begins a short run to **Plaza de Colón.** From this latter square, the majestic **Paseo de la Castellana** heads north through new Madrid, flanked by expensive shops, apartment buildings, luxury hotels, and foreign embassies. Parallel to the Paseo de la Castellana, **Calle de Serrano** is a prominent shopping street that forms the spine of the prosperous Salamanca neighborhood.

Heading south from Cibeles is **Paseo del Prado,** home to the eponymous **Museo del Prado,** as well as the **Jardín Botánica (Botanical Garden).** The paseo continues on to the Atocha Station, at the southern border of the old town. To

Travel Discounts Galore

The Madrid Card grants access to dozens of museums, discounts on public transport, and reductions at many restaurants. Available at local tourist offices, the card costs 47€, 60€, and 74€ for 1, 2, or 3 days of use, respectively. The card also acts as a pass for 5 or 10 days of trips on the city's subway and buses. Even some participating nightclubs offer free drinks or discounts on their cover charges.

the east of the Prado lies the **Parque del Retiro,** once reserved for royalty, with restaurants, nightclubs, a rose garden, and two lakes.

South of Gran Vía is the central **Puerta del Sol,** a half-moon-shaped plaza. All road distances in Spain are measured from here, and it is an important hub for buses and the Metro. Here, **Calle de Alcalá** begins and runs east for 4km (2½ miles).

A couple of blocks west is the **Plaza Mayor,** the heart of Old Madrid, and an attraction in itself with its mix of French and Georgian architecture.

GETTING AROUND The tourist office (see above) provides a street map that includes a schematic of the public transit system. The bus and expanding Metro networks are efficient and extensive, and taxis are abundant. Because traffic is nearly always heavy, though, plan to cover distances under 10 blocks by walking.

BY METRO (SUBWAY) The **Metro** (✆ **90-244-44-03;** www.metromadrid.es) is complex, but clean, speedy, and convenient—often more convenient than navigating the tangle of streets in the old town. A **single ticket** *(una sencilla)* is 1€ and a **10-trip pass** *(metrobús)* a more economical 7.40€. Ticket machines in the stations accept coins, bills, and credit cards. The subway runs daily from 6am to 2am.

BY BUS Madrid's bus system can be perplexing, as buses travel on circuitous routes. Prices and tickets are the same as on the Metro. Route information is available from the **E.M.T. kiosks** in Plaza de Callao, Puerta del Sol, Plaza de Cibeles, and Atocha (open Mon–Fri 8am–8:15pm) or on the Web at www.emtmadrid.es. At **Empresa Municipal de Transportes,** Alcántara 24 (✆ **91-406-88-00**), you can purchase a guide to bus routes daily 8am to 2pm. Regular buses run 6am to 11:30pm. A limited night service runs every half-hour 12:30am to 2am, and then every hour to 6am.

BY TAXI When you flag down a taxi, the meter should read 2.05€ and increase by a rate varying from 1€ to 1.15€ per kilometer, with the higher rates applying on weekends and late at night. There's a long list of authorized supplements for trips to and from the bullfighting ring, airport, and bus or rail stations. It's customary to tip about 10% of the fare. To call a taxi, dial ✆ **90-250-11-30.**

BY CAR Driving is nightmarish and potentially dangerous in very congested Madrid—it always feels like rush hour. It's not a good idea to maintain a rental car while staying in the city. It's nearly impossible to park, and rental cars are the frequent targets of thieves.

Should you want to rent a car to tour the environs, however, you have several choices. Save money before leaving for Spain by making arrangements with **Auto Europe** (✆ **888/223-5555;** www.autoeurope.com), which brokers economical rates with established firms abroad, including some of the companies mentioned below. The major in-city firms are **Hertz,** Barajas Airport (✆ **91-393-72-28;** www.hertz.com; Metro: Plaza de España); and **Avis,** Gran Vía 60 (✆ **91-547-20-48;** www.avis.com; Metro: Gran Vía). **Europcar** is also at Barajas Airport (✆ **91-393-72-35;** www.europcar.com).

Note: You'll need only your state or provincial driver's license to rent a car, but if you're in an accident or stopped on the road by police, a recent regulation stipulates you must produce an **International Drivers Permit.** These are available at AAA offices in the States for $10 to $15. Know too that stiff fines are collected when drivers are caught speaking on a hand-held cellphone while driving.

[Fast FACTS] MADRID

Business Hours Banks are open Monday to Friday 9:30am to 2pm and Saturday 9:30am to 1pm. Major stores are open Monday to Saturday from 9:30am to 8pm; smaller establishments, however, often take a siesta, doing business 9:30am to 1:30pm and 4:30 to 8pm. Hours can vary from store to store.

Currency The Spanish peseta gave way to the **euro** on March 1, 2002. At press time, 1€ = $1.40.

Dentists & Doctors For an English-speaking dentist or doctor, contact the U.S. Embassy, Calle Serrano 75 (✆ **91-587-22-40;** www.embusa.es), which maintains a list of dentists and doctors who have offered their services to Americans abroad. Also, hotel concierges *(conserjes)* usually have lists of available doctors and dentists. For dental services, also consult **Unidad Médica Anglo-Americana,** Conde de Arandá 1 (✆ **91-435-18-23;** www.unidadmedica.com), Monday to Friday 9am to 8pm and Saturday 10am to 1pm. There's a 24-hour answering service.

Drugstores For a late-night pharmacy, dial ✆ **098** or look in the daily newspaper under *"Farmacias de Guardia"* to learn what drugstores are open after 8pm. Another way to find an open pharmacy is to go to any pharmacy, even if it's closed—it will have posted a list of nearby pharmacies that are open late. Madrid has hundreds of pharmacies but one of the most central is **Farmacia de la Paloma,** Calle de Toledo 46 (✆ **91-365-34-58;** Metro: Puerta del Sol or La Latina).

Embassies The **United States Embassy,** Calle de Serrano 75 (✆ **91-587-22-00;** http://madrid.usembassy.gov; Metro: Núñez de Balboa), is open Monday to Friday 9am to 6pm. The **Canadian Embassy,** Núñez de Balboa 35 (✆ **91-423-32-50;** www.espana.gc.ca; Metro: Velázquez), is open Monday to Thursday 8:30am to 5:30pm, and Friday 8:30am to 2:30pm. The **British Embassy,** Calle Fernando el Santo 16 (✆ **91-700-82-00;** http://ukinspain.fco.gov.uk/en; Metro: Colón), is open Monday to Friday 9am to 1:30pm and 3 to 6pm. The **Republic of Ireland** has an embassy at Paseo de la Castellana 46 (✆ **91-436-40-93;** www.irlanda.es; Metro: Serrano); it's open Monday to Friday 9am to 2pm. The **Australian Embassy,** Torre Espacio, Paseo de la Castellana 259D (✆ **91-353-66-00;** www.spain.embassy.gov.au; Metro: Begoña), is open Monday to Thursday 8:30am to 5pm and Friday 8:30am to 2:15pm. Citizens of **New Zealand** have an embassy at Pinar 7, 3rd Floor (✆ **91-523-02-26;** www.nzembassy.com/spain; Metro: Gregorio Marañón); it's open Monday to Friday 9am to 2pm and 3 to 5:30pm.

Emergencies In an emergency, call ✆ **112** to report a **fire,** to reach the **police,** or to request an **ambulance.**

Hospitals & Clinics **Unidad Médica Anglo-Americana,** Conde de Arandá 1 (✆ **91-435-18-23;** www.unidadmedica.com; Metro: Retiro), is a private outpatient clinic offering specialized services. This is not an emergency clinic, although someone on the staff is always available. The daily hours are from 9am to 8pm. In a real medical emergency, call ✆ **112** for an ambulance.

Internet Access Internet cafes have sprung up all over the city. Typical of these is **La Casa de Internet,** Calle Luchana 20, corner of Calle de Francisco Rojas (✆ **91-446-80-41** or 91-594-42-00; Metro: Bilbao; bus: 147 or 40). It costs 1.80€ per hour, and is open daily 8am to 1am.

Post Office If you don't want to receive your mail at your hotel, direct it to *Lista de Correos* at the central post office in Madrid. To pick up mail, go to the window marked LISTA, where you'll be asked to show your passport. Madrid's central office is the **Palacio de Comunicaciones** at Plaza de Cibeles (✆ **91-536-01-11;** Metro: Banco de España). An airmail letter or postcard to the United States is .75€.

Safety Leave valuables in a hotel safe or other secure place when going out. You may need your passport, however, as the police sometimes stop foreigners for identification checks. Carry only enough cash for the day's needs. Pickpockets and purse snatchers work major tourist sites, trains, restaurants, and ATMs. Criminals often work in pairs, grabbing purses from pedestrians, cyclists, even cars. Several scams are meant to divert the victim's attention, such as spilling something on his or her clothing, or thrusting maps or newspapers into his or her face.

Taxes The internal sales tax (known in Spain as IVA) ranges between 7% and 33%, depending on the commodity being sold. Food, wine, and basic necessities are taxed at 7%; most goods and services (including car rentals) at 13%; luxury items (jewelry, all tobacco, imported liquors) at 33%; and hotels at 7%.

If you are not a European Union resident and make purchases in Spain worth more than 90€, you can get a tax refund. To get the refund, you must complete three copies of a form that the store will give you, detailing the nature of your purchase and its value. Citizens of non-E.U. countries show the purchase and the form to the Spanish Customs Office. The shop is then supposed to refund the amount due to you. Discuss in what currency your refund will arrive.

Telephone The country code for Spain is **34** and the city code for Madrid is **91.** All numbers in Spain are now nine digits, starting with the two- or three-digit city code. You must dial all nine digits, no matter where you're calling from or to. Telephone centers are called *locutorios.* The minimum charge for **local telephone calls** is .25€. Many pay phones accept major credit cards as well as phone cards you can buy at tobacconists' and post offices.

Tipping Customary tips are somewhat less than you'd see in the U.S. or the U.K. In restaurants, tip 5% to 10%, depending on the quality of the service. Tip the hotel porter 1€ for carrying your bags, the doorman .90€ if he's truly helpful, and the hotel maid 1€ per day. Tip cabdrivers 10% of the fare.

Where to Stay

ALONG THE PASEO DE LA CASTELLANA

Very Expensive

Ritz Madrid ★★★ At the heart of Madrid near the Prado, this remains Madrid's most prestigious address, a bastion of glamour and an enduring relic of the Edwardian Age. Its grand public areas, with their soaring ceilings and graceful columns, were built in 1908 at the request of Alfonso XIII, who was embarrassed that his capital didn't have suitable accommodations for visiting royals. Rooms are spacious, elegantly furnished, and filled with fresh flowers. Each is equipped with a well-accessorized bathroom. The restaurant, which receives good reviews, has tables that spill onto a garden terrace in warm months.

Plaza de la Lealtad 5, 28014 Madrid. ✆ **800/237-1236** in the U.S. and Canada, or 91-701-67-67. Fax 91-701-67-76. www.ritzmadrid.com. 167 units. 572€–690€ double; from 1,177€ junior suite; from 2,621€ suite. AE, DC, MC, V. Parking 35€. Metro: Banco de España. **Amenities:** Restaurant; bar; airport transfers (120€); concierge; exercise room; room service; sauna; spa. *In room:* A/C, TV, hair dryer, minibar, Wi-Fi (22€ per day).

The Westin Palace ★★★ An ornate 1912 structure that captures the pre–World War I grand hotel style, the Palace faces the Prado and Neptune Fountain. When it first opened, it was the largest hotel in Europe. Everyone from Dalí to Picasso, from Sarah Bernhardt to Sophia Loren, has spent the night here. Nevertheless, the Westin Palace hasn't achieved the cachet of its sibling, the Ritz, across the Paseo de Castellana, perhaps because the Westin is so much larger. Rooms are traditional, with plenty of space, containing large marble bathrooms. Do have a drink under the great stained-glass dome at the back of the main floor.

Plaza de las Cortes 7, 28014 Madrid. ✆ **888/625-4988** in the U.S., or 91-360-80-00. Fax 91-360-81-00. www.westinpalacemadrid.com. 468 units. 198€–558€ double; from 475€ junior suite. AE, DC, MC, V. Valet parking 35€. Metro: Banco de España. **Amenities:** 2 restaurants; bar; airport transfers (100€); babysitting; concierge; exercise room; room service; sauna. *In room:* A/C, TV, hair dryer, minibar, Wi-Fi (19€ per day).

Inexpensive

Mora ★ Long one of Madrid's top budget choices, even with rate jumps, the Mora is still an excellent choice. The spacious lobby with chandeliers sets the tone. The narrow but bright halls lead to rooms of varied configuration, but all are sufficiently furnished in muted tones, with carpeting. English is spoken by the helpful people at the front desk. The adjacent restaurant, **Bango** (separate management), attracts a polished crowd for low-cost meals.

Paseo del Prado 32, 28014 Madrid. ✆ **91-420-15-69.** Fax 91-420-05-64. www.hotelmora.com. 62 units. 83€ double; 101€ triple. AE, DC, MC, V. Parking nearby 21€. Metro: Atocha. **Amenities:** Restaurant; bar. *In room:* A/C, TV.

NEAR PLAZA ESPAÑA

Moderate

Casón del Tormes This attractive hotel is around the corner from the Royal Palace and Plaza de España. Behind a four-story red-brick facade with stone-trimmed windows, it overlooks a quiet one-way street. A long, narrow lobby floored with marble opens onto a public room. Guest rooms are generally roomy and comfortable, with color-coordinated fabrics and dark wood, including mahogany headboards. Motorists appreciate the public parking lot near the hotel.

Calle del Río 7, 28013 Madrid. ✆ **91-541-97-46.** Fax 91-541-18-52. www.hotelcasondeltormes.com. 63 units. 60€–121€ double; 156€ triple. AE, DC, MC, V. Nearby parking 23€. Metro: Plaza de España. **Amenities:** Restaurant; bar; babysitting; room service. *In room:* A/C, TV, hair dryer, Wi-Fi (5€ per day).

Santo Domingo ★ This stylish, carefully decorated hotel adjacent to the Gran Vía is a 2-minute walk from Plaza de España. It was inaugurated in 1994, after an older building was gutted and reconfigured into the comfortable modern structure

Madrid

FRANCE
Madrid
SPAIN
PORTUGAL

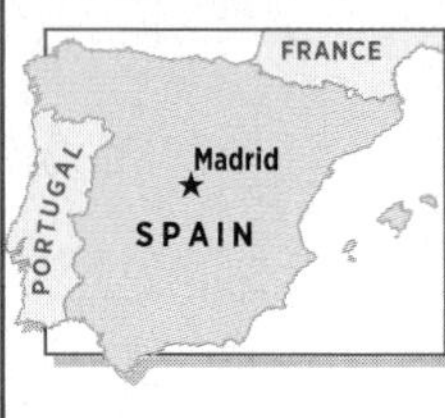

ATTRACTIONS ●

Casa de Campo **9**
Monastario de las Descalzas Reales **5**
Museo Arqueológico Nacional **12**
Museo del Prado **27**
Museo Lázaro Galdiano **11**
Museo Nacional Centro de Arte Reina Sofía **31**
Museo Thyssen-Bornemisza **24**
Palacio Real **8**
Parque del Retiro **26**
Real Academia de Bellas Artes de San Fernando **18**
Real Jardín Botánico **29**

ACCOMMODATIONS ■

AC Palacio del Retiro **19**
Anaco **16**
Casa de Madrid **6**
Casón del Tormes **1**
De Las Letras **15**
Hotel A. Gaudí **14**
Hotel Meninas **4**
Hotel Preciados **3**
Hotel Urban **21**
Inglés **22**
Jardin de Recoletos **13**
Laura **7**
Liabeny **17**
ME Madrid **28**
Mora **30**
Plaza Mayor **10**
Quo Puerta del Sol **20**
Ritz Madrid **25**
Santo Domingo **2**
The Westin Palace **23**

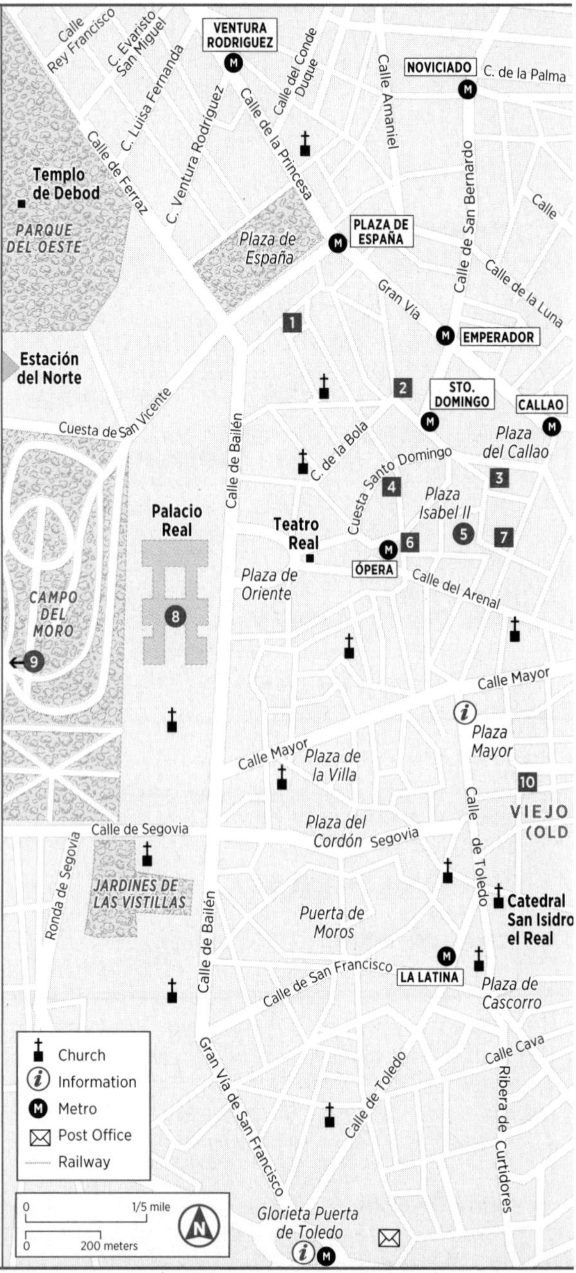
Calle Rey Francisco
C. Evaristo San Miguel
C. Luisa Fernanda
VENTURA RODRIGUEZ
Calle del Conde Duque
Calle Amaniel
NOVICIADO
C. de la Palma
Calle de Ferraz
C. Ventura Rodriguez
Calle de la Princesa
Templo de Debod
PARQUE DEL OESTE
Plaza de España
PLAZA DE ESPAÑA
Calle de San Bernardo
Calle
Calle de la Luna
Gran Vía
EMPERADOR
Estación del Norte
STO. DOMINGO
CALLAO
Cuesta de San Vicente
Calle de Bailén
C. de la Bola
Cuesta Santo Domingo
Plaza del Callao
Plaza Isabel II
Palacio Real
Teatro Real
ÓPERA
Plaza de Oriente
Calle del Arenal
CAMPO DEL MORO
Calle Mayor
Plaza Mayor
Plaza de la Villa
VIEJO (OLD
Calle de Segovia
Plaza del Cordón
Segovia
Ronda de Segovia
JARDINES DE LAS VISTILLAS
Calle de Toledo
Catedral San Isidro el Real
Puerta de Moros
Calle de San Francisco
LA LATINA
Plaza de Cascorro
Calle Cava
Gran Vía de San Francisco
Calle de Toledo
Ribera de Curtidores
Church
Information
Metro
Post Office
Railway
0
1/5 mile
0
200 meters
N
Glorieta Puerta de Toledo

Wax Museum
Calle de Genova
Paseo de la Castellana
Calle de Goya
SERRANO
Plaza de la Villa
Plaza de Colón
COLÓN
JARDINES DEL DESCUBRIMIENTO
Calle de la Palma
Calle de Fuencarral
Calle Fernando VI
Calle Bárbara de Braganza
C. de El Escorial
del Pez
Corredera Baja de San Pablo
Calle de Valverde
Calle de Fuencarral
Calle de Augusto
Hortaleza
Gravina
CHUECA
Figueroa
San Marcos
Calle de Prim
Paseo de Recoletos
Calle de Serrano
BARRIO DE SALAMANCA
Infantas
Calle de Barquillo
GRAN VÍA
Red. de San Luis
Gran Vía
Plaza de la Cibeles
Calle de Alcalá
Plaza de la Independencia
BANCO DE ESPAÑA
SEVILLA
Calle de Montalbán
Naval Museum
Palacio de Villahermosa
C. del Carmen
C. de Preciados
Calle Montera
Calle de Alcalá
Paseo del Prado
Plaza de la Lealtad
Calle A. Maura
Calle de Alfonso XII
Puerta del Sol
SOL
Carrera de San Jerónimo
Plaza C. del Castillo
Plaza de las Cortes
Calle de la Cruz
Calle del Prado
Calle de Cervantes
Army Museum
Plaza Jacinto Benavente
MADRID MADRID)
Calle Atocha
Calle de las Huertas
Museo del Prado
Paseo del Prado
PARQUE DEL BUEN RETIRO
Calle de Espalter
TIRSO DE MOLINA
Calle de la Magdalena
ANTÓN MARTÍN
Calle de la Cabeza
Calle de Gobernador
REAL JARDIN BOTANICO
Calle de Santa Isabel
Calle Atocha
Calle Jesús y María Levapiés
Calle del Amparo
Baja
Calle Mesón de Paredes
Calle de Embajadores
Reina Sofía
Plaza Lavapies
LAVAPIES
ATOCHA
Paseo de la Infanta Isabel
Sta. María de la Cabeza
Estación de Atocha
C. Miguel Servet
Ronda de Atocha
11 12 13 14 15 16 17 18 19 20 21 22 23 24 25 26 27 28 29 30 31

you see today. The soundproof units are decorated individually, each a wee bit differently from its neighbor, in pastel-derived shades. Some contain gold damask wallcoverings, faux tortoiseshell desks, and striped satin bedspreads. The best units are the fifth-floor doubles, especially those with furnished balconies and views over the tile roofs of Old Madrid.

Plaza Santo Domingo 13, 28013 Madrid. ✆ **91-547-98-00.** Fax 91-547-59-95. www.hotelsantodomingo.net. 120 units. 75€–180€ double; 195€–305€ suite. AE, DC, MC, V. Parking 27€. Metro: Santo Domingo. **Amenities:** Restaurant; bar; babysitting; room service; Wi-Fi (free). *In room:* A/C, TV, hair dryer, minibar.

ON OR NEAR THE GRAN VÍA

Expensive

De Las Letras ★ This hotel with its youthful vibe was inspired by literature. A member of the stylish chain, Epoque Hotels, it stands in the heart of the Gran Vía, "the main street of Madrid." Inscriptions by notable Spanish writers adorn walls in the public areas, with stone carvings and original, hand-painted tiles. The wood-and-iron elevator remains from the original 1917 building. The contemporary bedrooms are painted in vivid colors such as ocher or burgundy, and most of them rest on wooden floors under high ceilings. Bathrooms are the latest in modern design, and each suite opens onto a terrace with a whirlpool bath.

Gran Vía 11, 28013 Madrid. ✆ **91-523-79-80.** Fax 91-523-79-81. www.hoteldelasletras.com. 103 units. 180€–250€ double; 270€–310€ suite. AE, DC, MC, V. Metro: Sevilla or Gran Vía. **Amenities:** Restaurant; bar; exercise room; room service; spa. *In room:* A/C, TV, hair dryer, minibar, Wi-Fi (free).

Hotel Urban ★★★ With a postage-stamp swimming pool open to the sky, a moonlit restaurant, and a spectacular patio, Urban is the latest word in city chic. Opposite the lower house of the Spanish Parliament, Urban evokes an office building atrium, but its grace notes are the towering sculptures from Papua, New Guinea. Rooms are luxurious and modern with dark-wood furnishings and lots of dark leather. Elegant Madrileños flood the sleek Europa Deco restaurant at night to savor its Mediterranean fusion cuisine. Just below the lobby is a Museum of Egyptian Art with sculptures from the heyday of the Pharaohs.

Carrera de San Jerónimo, 28014 Madrid. ✆ **91-787-77-70.** Fax 91-787-77-99. www.derbyhotels.es. 102 units. 175€–313€ double; 210€–373€ junior suite; 550€ suite. AE, DC, MC, V. Parking 26€. Metro: Sevilla. **Amenities:** Restaurant; bar; airport transfers (90€); exercise room; outdoor heated pool. *In room:* A/C, TV, minibar, Wi-Fi (20€ per day).

Moderate

Hotel A. Gaudí ★ A majestic early-1900s building at the end of the Gran Vía was gutted to be transformed into this near-luxury hotel. Plaza Mayor and the Prado and Thyssen museums are within walking distance. A siesta-time retreat to these quiet teak-lined quarters is restorative. The guest rooms come in a number of sizes, each comfortably furnished and well maintained. If Barcelona is not on your itinerary, you may want to sample the Catalán cuisine in the stylish on-site restaurant, Pedrera.

Gran Vía 9, 28013 Madrid. ✆ **91-531-22-22.** Fax 91-531-54-69. www.hoteles-catalonia.es. 185 units. 80€–197€ double; from 300€ suite. AE, DC, MC, V. Nearby parking 30€. Metro: Gran Vía. **Amenities:** Restaurant; bar; babysitting; exercise room w/sauna and whirlpool; room service. *In room:* A/C, TV, hair dryer, minibar, Wi-Fi (free).

Hotel Preciados ★★ ☺ A beautiful mingling of old and new has resulted in this gorgeous hotel in an 1861 building. The original architecture remains, but the rooms are sparkling and well kept, with spacious bathrooms. Light wood furnishings give the rooms a clean, airy feel; hardwood and marble floors recall its classic past. The hotel staff is welcoming to kids. One floor is nonsmoking, and another is for women only. The **Varela** restaurant downstairs serves innovative Spanish cuisine.

Preciados 37, 28013 Madrid. ✆ **91-454-44-00.** Fax 91-454-44-01. www.preciadoshotel.com. 73 units. 90€–203€ double; 208€–350€ suite. MC, V. Parking 20€. Metro: Puerta del Sol or Santo Domingo/Callao. **Amenities:** Restaurant; bar; airport transfers (70€); babysitting; concierge; room service. *In room:* A/C, TV, hair dryer, minibar, Wi-Fi (free).

Liabeny This hotel, named after the original owner (pronounced, more or less, Ya-*bay*-nee) is on a busy plaza midway between the Gran Vía and the Puerta del Sol—the pedestrian shopping district containing the main branch of El Corte Inglés is down a short hill. The contemporary-styled rooms have been redecorated. Personalized attention from the staff adds to the comfort of your stay. The hotel has its own secure garage. Prices jumped a bit after the latest renovations, but in its category, this hotel is still a solid value.

Salud 3, 28013 Madrid. ✆ **91-531-90-00.** Fax 91-532-74-21. www.liabeny.com. 220 units. 123€–150€ double; 161€ triple. AE, MC, V. Parking 17€. Metro: Puerta del Sol, Callao, or Gran Vía. **Amenities:** Restaurant; bar; babysitting; exercise room; room service. *In room:* A/C, TV, hair dryer, minibar, Wi-Fi (free).

Inexpensive

Anaco It may not quite sparkle, but the Anaco is a fine place to stay. The first five floors of this popular hotel have been renovated with witty alternating red-and-green color schemes, right down to the towels. Double-glazed windows provide blessed silence. Off the lobby, the busy cafeteria offers an inexpensive *menú del día* and stays open from 7:30am to 2am every day.

Tres Cruces 3 (at Plaza del Carmen), 28013 Madrid. ✆ **91-522-46-04.** Fax 91-531-64-84. www.anacohotel.com. 39 units. 60€–120€ double; 80€–150€ triple. AE, DC, MC, V. Parking 30€. Metro: Gran Vía or Puerta del Sol. **Amenities:** Restaurant; bar; babysitting; room service. *In room:* A/C, TV, hair dryer, Wi-Fi (free).

NEAR THE PUERTA DEL SOL

Expensive

Casa de Madrid ★★★ This small, elegant B&B lies across the street from the Royal Opera. Doña Maria Medina's enclave lies on the second floor of an 18th-century mansion. She has exquisitely decorated each bedroom with antiques, including Persian rugs. Each of the accommodations has a different theme. The simplest chamber is called the Zen room (a single). Among the most elegant units are the Spanish Room, the Indian Room, the Greek Room, and the Blue Room; the grandest is the Damascus Suite. The house is filled with valuable objets d'art.

Calle Arrieta 2, 28013 Madrid. ✆ **91-559-57-91.** Fax 91-540-11-00. www.casademadrid.com. 17 units. 250€–285€ double; 400€ suite. Rates include continental breakfast. AE, DC, MC, V. Nearby parking 15€. Metro: Opera. **Amenities:** Airport transfers (55€). *In room:* A/C, TV, minibar, Wi-Fi (free).

ME Madrid ★ In the Huertas district, this hotel began life as a palace in 1923, lying behind an ornate stone facade, which is protected today by National Heritage. It may be old on the outside, but the interior has been brought completely up to date, with all the latest state-of-the-art technology. Substance and style go hand in hand in the contemporary, well-maintained, and comfortable bedrooms, most of them small to midsize, although some are spacious. You can stay here in a standard double, a self-contained studio, or else some of the most glamorous suites in Madrid. Ernest Hemingway preferred to lodge in the Tower Suite.

Plaza Santa Ana 14, 28012 Madrid. ✆ **91-701-60-00.** Fax 91-522-03-07. www.memadrid.com. 191 units. 189€–283€ standard double; 334€–358€ studio; from 434€ suite. AE, DC, MC, V. Metro: Tirso de Molina or Sol. **Amenities:** Restaurant; 2 bars; babysitting; concierge; exercise room; room service. *In room:* A/C, TV/DVD, hair dryer, minibar, MP3 docking station, Wi-Fi (free).

Quo Puerta del Sol ★ One of Spain's most famous interior decorators played a large part in transforming this early-20th-century building into a first-rate hotel with a sleek interior of modern design, one of the best of its type in Madrid. The location is among the most convenient, lying between Plaza Santa Ana and Puerta del Sol. Try for one of the top-floor rooms, each with a private patio overlooking Calle Mayor. The traditional facade conceals the high-tech amenities of the interior. Bedrooms are medium in size and furnished with contemporary pieces that offer both style and comfort.

Calle de Sevilla 4, 28014 Madrid. ✆ **91-532-90-49.** Fax 91-531-28-34. www.epoquehotels.com. 61 units. 150€–248€ double; 275€ suite. AE, DC, MC, V. Parking 28€. Metro: Sol. **Amenities:** Restaurant; bar; airport transfers (30€); babysitting; concierge; room service. *In room:* A/C, TV, hair dryer, minibar, Wi-Fi (free).

Moderate

Hotel Meninas ★ In the very center of Madrid, this little hotel was created out of a 19th-century building that was transformed into one of the better bargains in the area. The antique structure features many modern improvements. The midsize and soundproof bedrooms come in a range of sizes and styles, going from singles to suites, even some triples. The hotel, of course, takes its name from *Las Meninas,* the most famous painting in the Prado, the creation of the incomparable Diego Velázquez.

Calle Campomanes 7, 28013 Madrid. ✆ **91-541-28-05.** Fax 91-541-28-06. www.hotelmeninas.com. 37 units. 109€–185€ double; 189€ triple; 210€ suite. AE, MC, V. Parking nearby 30€. Metro: Opera. **Amenities:** Breakfast room; bar; Wi-Fi (free). *In room:* A/C, TV/DVD, hair dryer, minibar.

Inexpensive

Inglés ★ A large ship model in the front window alerts you to this popular little hotel. Enter the lobby, with its comfy sofas and armchairs, and you'll find that little has changed in recent years, including the room rates and the too-often dour gents at the front desk. Just beyond the TV lounge is the bar/cafeteria where breakfast is served. Many rooms have sitting areas. Nearby Plaza Santa Ana and Calle de las Huertas are brimming with tapas and music bars. A parking garage has 25 spaces for guests. Note that only about half of the hotel is air-conditioned, so ask for an air-conditioned room in summer.

Calle Echegaray 8, 28014 Madrid. ✆ **91-429-65-51.** Fax 91-420-24-23. www.hotel-ingles.net. 58 units. 118€ double; 128€ suite. AE, DC, MC, V. Parking 13€. Metro: Sol. **Amenities:** Cafeteria; bar; concierge; exercise room. *In room:* TV, hair dryer.

Laura ★ This is a hotel of fairly recent construction—2006—although it follows the pure design of the 1800s. The interior designer created a spacious lobby and avant-garde decoration. Some guests have likened Laura to a modern hotel in New York, and the location is one of the best in town, a 2-minute walk from the heartbeat Plaza Mayor or a 4-minute walk from the Puerta del Sol (the Times Square of Madrid). Bedrooms are loftlike or else duplexes, each beautifully decorated and comfortable, even elegantly furnished, if your tastes are minimalist. We are impressed with the hotel's room amenities and the fact that the maid leaves a fresh apple on the nightstand. Each of the accommodations also comes with a minikitchen.

Travesia de Trujillos 3, 28013 Madrid. ✆ **91-701-16-70.** Fax 91-521-76-55. www.room-matehotels.com. 34 units. 117€ standard double; 139€ duplex; 170€ suite. AE, DC, MC, V. Metro: Puerta del Sol. Parking 19€. **Amenities:** Babysitting; concierge. *In room:* A/C, TV/DVD, hair dryer, kitchenette, minibar, Wi-Fi (free).

Plaza Mayor ★ A crisp hotel in the shell of a 19th-century church, this is a welcome addition to Madrid's often dreary budget lodgings. Despite its name, the brick-red building wedges into Plaza Santa Cruz, slightly east of Plaza Mayor. An entrance has been carved out of the ground-floor *taberna* (bar). The bright, contemporary (though often oddly shaped) rooms are of sufficient size, with double-thick windows sealing off traffic noise; four have double beds. The corner rooms offer light and extra space.

Calle Atocha 2, 28012 Madrid. ✆ **91-360-06-06.** Fax 91-360-06-10. www.h-plazamayor.com. 34 units. 85€-100€ double; 115€ suite. Rates include breakfast. AE, MC, V. Parking 18€. Metro: Sol or La Latina. **Amenities:** Coffee shop; bar. *In room:* A/C, TV, hair dryer, Wi-Fi (free).

NEAR RETIRO/SALAMANCA

Expensive

AC Palacio del Retiro ★★ Perhaps the best located hotel in Madrid, this well-run oasis across from Retiro Park sits close to the cultural triangle formed by the Thyssen, Prado, and Reina Sofia museums. The restored building dates from the early 20th century and is a protected National Heritage monument. Its interior has been completely restored to modern tastes. Much of its elegant past can be seen in the stained-glass windows shipped in from Paris, the ceramics handmade in Talavera, the marble floors, and Grecian columns. The midsize bedrooms are both stylish and comfortable, with state-of-the-art bathrooms. Most bedrooms open onto panoramic views of Retiro Park.

Alfonso XII 14, 28014 Madrid. ✆ **91-523-74-60.** Fax 91-523-74-61. www.ac-hotels.com. 50 units. 240€-640€ double; from 820€ suite. AE, DC, MC, V. Parking 8€. Metro: Banco de España. **Amenities:** Restaurant; bar; babysitting; concierge; exercise room; room service. *In room:* A/C, TV, hair dryer, minibar, Wi-Fi (free).

Moderate

Jardín de Recoletos ★ Built in 1999, this contemporary apartment hotel welcomes its guests to the chic Salamanca district of Madrid. It is close to both the financial district and the best shops, on a quiet street close to the Plaza Colón. The inviting lobby has sleek marble floors and a stained-glass ceiling; adjacent is a combined cafe and restaurant. Most of the rooms are spacious and attractively decorated in a traditional style, with small sitting and dining areas. The accommodations come with well-equipped kitchenettes—unusual for Madrid. If you want to pay extra, you can book either a unit rated "superior" or a suite that offers a hydromassage bathroom and a big terrace.

Gil de Santivañes 6, 28001 Madrid. ✆ **91-781-16-40.** Fax 91-781-16-41. www.vphoteles.com. 43 units. 148€-209€ double; 200€-268€ suite. Rates include buffet breakfast. AE, DC, MC, V. Parking 18€. Metro: Serrano. **Amenities:** Restaurant; cafe; room service. *In room:* A/C, TV, kitchenette, hair dryer, minibar, Wi-Fi (free).

Where to Dine

NEAR PLAZA DE LA CIBELES

Moderate

El Mirador del Museo ★★ CONTINENTAL The Museo Thyssen-Bornemisza has converted its rooftop into a summer terrace dining event. You are not only rewarded with panoramic views but also presented with one of the most finely honed cuisines in the area. Gigantic umbrellas protect you at lunch from the sun, but at night you dine under the stars. The chef displays a rare talent, a union of traditional and imaginative dishes, each platter filled with market-fresh ingredients rendered with skill. We still remember our veal sirloin with cardamom-flavored vanilla pasta. You might begin with a refreshing vichyssoise with couscous. Fresh fish always appears on the menu—perhaps sea urchins for a bit of exotica. All dishes are well balanced in flavors, and the cellar is awash in fine Spanish vintages.

Paseo Prado 8. ✆ **91-429-27-32.** Reservations required. Main courses 25€–36€. AE, DC, MC, V. May–Oct Wed–Mon 8pm–1am. Closed Nov–Apr. Metro: Banco de España.

Inexpensive

Tocororo CUBAN This is Madrid's finest Cuban restaurant. The nostalgia is evident in the pictures of Old Havana. The waitstaff is as lively as the pop Cuban music playing on the stereo. The dishes are typical Caribbean dishes, such as *ropa vieja* (shredded meat served with black beans and rice) or lobster enchilada. If you prefer a simpler repast, try a selection of *empanadas y tamales* (fried potato pastries and plantain dough filled with onions and ground meat). Special house cocktails include *mojitos* (rum, lime juice, mint, and a hint of sugar) and daiquiris. Winter brings live Cuban music. Discreet but pleasant, this restaurant is located in the zone of La Letras. (Many of Madrid's bars and discos are in this area.)

Calle del Prado 3 (at the corner of Echegaray). ✆ **91-369-40-00.** www.el-tocororo.com. Reservations required Thurs–Sat. Main courses 16€–22€; fixed-price menu 10€. AE, DC, MC, V. Tues–Sun 1:30–5pm and 8:30pm–midnight. Closed last 2 weeks Feb and last 2 weeks Sept. Metro: Sevilla.

NEAR THE PLAZA DE LAS CORTES

Expensive

Restaurante Europa Deco ★★ MEDITERRANEAN Tucked away in the Urban, one of the chicest hotels in Spain, this elegant enclave of good food attracts celebrities, politicians, and soccer stars. The setting is stunning, with Papuan totems, golden Venetian mosaic columns, and black Brazilian granite floors. The *pijos* (the smart set) shows up here in hordes, and serious foodies are drawn to the smashing champagne cocktails and such delights as some of Madrid's best sushi. When ordering, we gravitate to the deboned pork or the sautéed scallops, among the chef's specialties. Joaquin de Felipe is rightly hailed as one of the city's most accomplished chefs. Perhaps you'll agree after sampling his "New Wave" gazpacho made with fava beans and Kamone-tomato purée. His skirt steak of Iberian pig is reason enough to come back. End with one of his daily changing but always sumptuous desserts.

In the Urban Hotel, Carrera de San Jerónimo 34. ✆ **91-787-77-80.** Reservations required. Main courses 27€–40€. AE, DC, MC, V. Daily 8pm–midnight. Metro: Sevilla.

Moderate

Errota-Zar BASQUE Next to the House of Deputies and the Zarzuela Theater, Errota-Zar means "old mill," a nostalgic reference to the Basque country, home of the Olano family, owners of the restaurant. A small bar at the entrance displays a collection of fine cigars and wines, and the blue-painted walls are adorned with paintings of Basque landscapes. The restaurant has only about two dozen tables, which can easily fill up. Many Basques begin their meal with a *tortilla de bacalao* (salt-cod omelet). For main dishes, sample the delights of *chuletón de buey* (oxtail with grilled vegetables), or *kokotxas de merluza en aceite* (cheeks of hake cooked in

TAPA TO tapa TO TAPA

No need to go hungry waiting around for the traditional Madrid dinner hour—10pm or later. Throughout the city you'll find bars—variously known as *mesónes, tascas,* and *tabernas*—that set out platters of tempting hot and cold appetizers known as *tapas:* mushrooms, salads, baby eels, shrimp, lobster, mussels, sausages, ham, and, in one establishment at least, bull testicles. Described below are some favorite tapas bars out of hundreds. ***Tip:*** You can often save money by eating at the bar rather than occupying a table.

Casa Mingo, Paseo de la Florida 24 (✆ **91-547-79-18;** www.casamingo.es; Metro: Norte), has been known for decades for its cider, both still and bubbly. The perfect accompanying tidbit is a piece of Asturian *cabrales* (goat cheese), but the roast chicken is the specialty of the house. Patrons share big tables under the vaulted ceiling of the dining room; in summer, the staff sets tables out on the sidewalk.

Hemingway and the bullfighter Luís Miguel Dominguín used to frequent the casual **Cervecería Alemania,** Plaza de Santa Ana 6 (✆ **91-429-70-33;** Metro: Alonso Martín or Tirso de Molina), which earned its name because of its long-ago German clients. Opening onto one of the liveliest plazas in Madrid, it clings to its early-1900s traditions. To accompany your *caña* (a short beer), try the fried sardines or a wedge of *tortilla,* a firm potato-and-egg omelet served at room temperature.

Unique in Madrid, the **Cervecería Santa Bárbara,** Plaza de Santa Bárbara 8 (✆ **91-319-04-49;** www.cerveceria santabarbara.com; Metro: Alonzo Martínez; bus: 3, 7, or 21), is an outlet for a beer factory, and the management has spent a lot to make it modern and inviting. Globe lights and spinning ceiling fans hang above the black-and-white marble floor. You come here for beer, of course: *cerveza negra* (black beer) or *cerveza dorada* (golden beer). Brews are best accompanied by the very pricey shrimp, the lobster, or the ugly but tasty goose barnacles called *percebes.* It's open daily from 11:30am to midnight. Many Madrileños begin their nightly *tapeo* at **Toscana,** Manuel Fernandez y Gonzales 10 (✆ **91-429-60-31;** www.tabernatoscana.com; Metro: Puerta del Sol or Sevilla). They sit on crude stools, under sausages, peppers, and sheaves of golden wheat hung from the dark beams, as a man behind the bar ladles out bowls of the nightly specials—kidneys in sherry sauce, perhaps, or veal stew.

virgin olive oil). Hake cheeks may not sound appetizing, but Spaniards and many foreigners praise this fish dish. You might opt for *foie al Pedro Jiménez* (duck liver grilled and served with a sweet wine sauce).

Jovellanos 3, 1st floor. ✆ **91-531-25-64.** www.errota-zar.com. Reservations recommended. Main courses 22€–58€. AE, DC, MC, V. Mon–Sat 1–4pm and 9pm–midnight. Closed Aug 15–30 and Easter. Metro: Banco España or Sevilla.

ON OR NEAR THE GRAN VÍA

Moderate

El Mentidero de la Villa ★ MEDITERRANEAN The Mentidero ("Gossip Shop," in English) is a truly multicultural experience. The owner describes the cuisine as "modern Spanish with Japanese influence and a French cooking technique." That may sound confusing, but the result is an achievement; each ingredient manages to retain its distinctive flavor. The kitchen plays with such adventuresome combinations as fried duck liver with caramelized eggplant; lasagna with mushrooms and duck liver; noisettes of veal with tarragon; filet steak with a sauce of mustard and brown sugar; and medallions of venison with purée of chestnut and celery. The postmodern decor includes *trompe l'oeil* ceilings, exposed wine racks, ornate columns with unusual lighting, and a handful of antique carved merry-go-round horses.

Santo Tomé 6, Plaza de las Salesas. ✆ **91-308-12-85.** www.mentiderodelavilla.es. Reservations required. Main courses 18€–30€; fixed-price menus 60€–75€. AE, DC, MC, V. Mon–Fri 1:30–4:30pm; Mon–Sat 9pm–midnight. Closed Aug. Metro: Alonso Martínez or Chueca. Bus: 37.

NEAR THE PUERTA DEL SOL

Expensive

Lhardy SPANISH/INTERNATIONAL A Madrileño legend since it opened in 1839, this restaurant's street-level room contains what might be the most elegant snack bar in town. Cups of steaming consommé are self-dispensed from silver samovars into delicate porcelain cups, accompaniments to tasty tapas that run along the lines of creamy-centered croquettes. Early evening is the fashionable time for a stop here. Some of the city's older literati and politicians gather in the formal restaurant upstairs.

Carrera de San Jerónimo 8 (east of Puerta del Sol). ✆ **91-521-33-85.** www.lhardy.com. Reservations recommended in the upstairs dining room. Main courses 32€–39€. AE, DC, MC, V. Daily 1–3:30pm and 8:30–11pm. Closed Aug. Metro: Puerta del Sol or Sevilla.

Moderate

Taberna del Alabardero BASQUE/SPANISH In proximity to the Royal Palace, this little Spanish classic is known for its selection of tasty tapas, ranging from squid cooked in wine to fried potatoes dipped in hot sauce. Photographs of famous former patrons, including Nelson Rockefeller and the race-car driver Jackie Stewart, line the walls. The restaurant in the rear is said to be another of the city's best-kept secrets. Decorated in typical tavern style, it serves a savory Spanish and Basque cuisine made with market-fresh ingredients.

Felipe V no. 6. ✆ **91-547-25-77.** www.alabardero.eu. Reservations required for restaurant only. Bar tapas 3€–12€; glass of house wine 4€. Restaurant main courses 17€–25€; *menú degustación* 51€. AE, DC, MC, V. Daily 1–4pm and 9pm–midnight. Metro: Opera.

Inexpensive

La Biotika ★ 🎁 VEGETARIAN Vegetarian cuisine doesn't get a lot of attention in most Madrid restaurants, but this discovery is a rare exception. Opening east of the landmark Plaza Santa Ana, it is intimate and charming. It serves the capital's best macrobiotic vegetarian cuisine, and does so exceedingly well. We always begin with one of the homemade soups, which are made fresh daily, then have one of the large, crisp salads. The bread is also made fresh daily. A specialty is the "meatball without meat"—made with vegetables, shaped like a meatball. Tofu with zucchini and many other offerings appear daily.

Amor de Dios 3. ✆ **91-429-07-80.** www.labiotika.es. *Menú del día* 9.90€. MC, V. Mon–Sat 10am–11:30pm; Sun 10am–5pm. Metro: Antón Martín.

CHUECA

Expensive

Asiana ★★★ 🎁 FRENCH/ASIAN Our temptation is to dine here every night—it's that special. Jaime Renedo had to persuade his mother to allow him to open this hidden-away restaurant inside her store devoted to Asian antiques in the increasingly gentrified Chueca district. After ringing the bell, you'll be shown to one of seven candlelit tables in a cellar space filled with gilt Buddhas and Ming vases. Walk-ins are not accepted, and a major credit card is needed to reserve a table at what is the most private public restaurant in town.

There is no menu. Renedo and his Japanese partner dream up multicourse feasts every night, using first-rate ingredients to concoct a daily tasting menu that is simply sublime. Fresh and tender squid is shipped in from Galicia and mated with porcini petals and a macadamia oil aioli. Two of the best specialties are ravioli stuffed with fish and potato mousse, and melon gazpacho with lobster.

Traversia de San Mateo 4. ✆ **91-310-09-65.** Reservations required—no exceptions. Tasting menu 90€. AE, DC, MC, V. Daily 9:30–11pm. Closed Aug. Metro: Alonzo Martínez.

Moderate

Casa Salvador SPANISH/MADRILENA This is a robust, macho enclave of Madrid. The owner of this bustling restaurant configured it as a minimuseum to his hobby and passion, the Spanish art of bullfighting. Inside, near a bar that stocks an impressive collection of sherries and whiskeys, you'll find the memorabilia of years of bull watching, including photographs of great matadors beginning in the 1920s, and agrarian artifacts used in the raising and development of fighting bulls. The menu is as robust as the decor, featuring macho-size platters of oxtail in red-wine sauce; different preparations of hake (one of which is baked delectably in a salt crust); stuffed pepper, fried calamari, and shrimp entrees; and, for dessert, the local version of *arroz con leche.*

Calle Barbieri 12. ✆ **91-521-45-24.** Reservations recommended. Main courses 12€–28€. AE, DC, MC, V. Mon–Sat 1:30–4pm and 9–11:30pm. Closed 2 weeks July–Aug. Metro: Chueca.

NEAR THE ROYAL PALACE

Inexpensive

La Bola REGIONAL SPANISH Easily spotted by its crimson exterior, La Bola has been on the scene since 1870. Hemingway and Ava Gardner were patrons, as attested to by photos above the carved wainscoting. Ask about the restaurant's history and you'll get a leaflet. The big menu item is *cocido madrileño,* the traditional Castilian Sunday boiled dinner: Several kinds of meat and vegetables are slow-cooked together for hours, and the rich broth is then strained off and tiny noodles are dropped in as a first course. This course is followed by the vegetables (potatoes, chickpeas, cabbage) and the meats (usually chicken, chorizo, beef, and pork). Fish dishes are well suited to smaller appetites.

Bola 5 (2 blocks north of the Teatro Real). ✆ **91-547-69-30.** www.labola.es. Main courses 18€–36€. No credit cards. Daily 1:30–4pm; Mon–Sat 8:30–11pm. Metro: Santo Domingo.

NEAR RETIRO & SALAMANCA

Expensive

El Amparo ★★ BASQUE This superior gastronomic enclave hides with four other restaurants behind a curtain of vines at the end of an alley. The multitiered space is defined by rough-hewn beams, and is illuminated by sunlight through the long skylight. The innovative offerings have included cod cheeks in a red-pepper purée, and ravioli with crayfish. A battalion of correct, unobtrusive waiters bring two different *aperitivos* to stoke the appetite, and then serve such main courses as cold marinated salmon with tomato sorbet, *lubina* (sea bass), bisque of shellfish with Armagnac, pigs' feet stuffed with morels, and platters of steamed fish of the day.

Callejón de Puígcerdá 8 (at the corner of Jorge Juan). ✆ **91-431-64-56.** Reservations required. Main courses 25€–40€. AE, MC, V. Mon–Fri 1:30–3:30pm and 9–11:30pm; Sat 9–11:30pm. Closed the week before Easter and 1 week in Aug. Metro: Goya. Bus: 21 or 53.

Horcher ★★ GERMAN/INTERNATIONAL Berlin was the first home of this legendary luxury restaurant, which opened in 1904. Prompted by a tip from a high-ranking officer that Germany was losing World War II, Herr Horcher moved his restaurant to neutral Madrid in 1943. Ever since, the restaurant has continued its grand European traditions, including service by knowledgeable waiters and uniformed doormen. Among the tempting possibilities are shrimp tartare and a distinctive warm hake salad. The venison stew in green pepper with orange peel, and the crayfish with parsley and cucumber, are examples of the elegant fare, served with impeccable style. The kitchen does well with wild boar, veal, and sea bass as well. Alfonso XII 6 (near Valenzuela). ✆ **91-532-35-96.** www.restaurantehorcher.com. Reservations required. Jackets and ties required for men. Main courses 25€–40€. AE, DC, MC, V. Mon–Fri 1:30–4pm and 8:30pm–midnight; Sat 8:30pm–midnight. Metro: Retiro.

Pan de Lujo ★★ MEDITERRANEAN/ASIAN Artful and elegant, with a battery of lights that, as they change, are almost breathtaking, this big-windowed restaurant near Parque del Retiro has earned rave reviews both for its interior design and for its cuisine. Some areas of the floor are also lit from beneath, creating the illusion that diners and staff are bathed in patterns of light that subtly change throughout the course of a meal. Alberto Chicote, one of the city's most famous chefs, mixes Asian and Mediterranean ideas in ways that have pleased late-night Madrileños. Some of the finest of Spain's regional produce goes into the imaginative, creative dishes served here. Begin perhaps with an appetizer of paper-thin eggplant in delicate virgin olive oil resting on hummus, followed by poached red snapper with crisp baby vegetables. Calle Jorge Juan 20. ✆ **91-436-11-00.** www.pandelujo.es. Reservations required. Main courses 18€–42€. AE, DC, MC, V. Daily 1:30–4pm and 9pm–midnight. Metro: Serrano or Retiro.

Viridiana ★ INTERNATIONAL Long praised as one of Madrid's most notable restaurants, Viridiana is named after the 1961 Luís Buñuel film classic. As soon as patrons are settled, the captain launches into a lengthy recitation of the day's specials, from salads to desserts. Among these are contemporary takes on traditional recipes, often with Asian touches. Some fine examples include tuna tartare, salads of exotic greens with smoked fish, steak filet with truffles, guinea fowl stuffed with herbs and wild mushrooms, baby squid with curry on a bed of lentils, and roast lamb in puff pastry with fresh basil. While rarely as brilliant as it was perceived to be 2 decades ago, the food here is never predictable—you'll find an exciting twist or two in every dish. Juan de Mena 14 (west of Alfonso XII). ✆ **91-523-44-78.** www.restauranteviridiana.com. Reservations recommended. Main courses 30€–37€. V. Mon–Sat 1:30–4pm and 9pm–midnight. Closed Aug and 1 week at Easter. Metro: Retiro Bancode España.

Moderate

El Borbollón BASQUE/FRENCH The welcoming Castro family presides over this little charmer lying between Calle de Serrano and Paseo de Recoletos, near both Plaza Cibeles and Plaza Colón. Since 1984 they have welcomed some of Madrid's more discerning palates. Eduardo Castro, the chef, is a local personality and a whiz in the kitchen. He is known for such dishes as a perfectly grilled *rape* (monkfish). Steak is cooked with savory green peppers, and a chateaubriand appears enticingly drenched in whiskey. Fresh turbot and hake appear regularly on the menu, and rich game dishes such as partridge are featured in the autumn. Choice cutlets of Segovian lamb are awakened with garlic cloves. Fresh flowers and bucolic art make for a soothing decor.

Calle Recoletos 7. ✆ **91-431-41-34.** www.elborbollon.es. Main courses 20€–47€; *menú completo* 55€–60€. AE, DC, MC, V. Mon–Fri 1–4pm; Mon–Sat 9pm–midnight. Metro: Retiro or Plaza Colón.

La Gamella ★★ INTERNATIONAL This restaurant occupies the 19th-century building where the Spanish philosopher Ortega y Gasset was born. The prestigious Horcher, one of the capital's legendary restaurants (see above), is just across the street, but the food at La Gamella is better. The russet-colored, high-ceilinged design invites customers to relax. The founder has prepared his delicate and light-textured specialties for the king and queen of Spain, as well as for Madrid's most talked-about artists and merchants, many of whom he knows and greets personally between sessions in his kitchen.

Typical menu items include a seviche of Mediterranean fish, sliced duck liver in truffle sauce, a dollop of goat cheese served over caramelized endive, and duck breast with peppers. An array of well-prepared desserts includes an all-American cheesecake. Traditional Spanish dishes such as chicken with garlic have been added to the menu, plus what has been called "the only edible hamburger in Madrid."

Alfonso XII no. 4. ✆ **91-532-45-09.** www.lagamella.com. Reservations required. Main courses 17€–25€; *menú degustación* 36€. AE, DC, MC, V. Mon–Fri 1:30–4pm and 9pm–midnight; Sat 9pm–midnight. Closed 4 days around Easter. Metro: Retiro. Bus: 19.

CHAMBERI

Very Expensive

La Manduca de Azagra ★★ NAVARRE/SPANISH A table here at night is one of the most sought after in Madrid. Fashionistas show up, blending in with French sophisticates, bourgeois Madrileños, and even young gay professionals. It's on the see-and-be-seen circuit. Fortunately, the cuisine is also very worthy. On the night of our last visit, cross-dressers looking like extras in a Pedro Almodóvar film shared the next table—they raved about the food, we're happy to report. We agreed with their appraisals. Incidentally, their table went for *rabo de toro,* the bull's tail; our table preferred the tender, succulently sweet roast suckling pig, prepared in the style of Segovia, and the *lomo de lubina salvaje* (wild sea bass). One of our favorite offerings here is the fried white asparagus and fresh artichokes. Each dish is a delight, carefully crafted from market-fresh ingredients. The menu bursts with freshness and originality, and the service is both polite and efficient. The wine carte is also worthy, too, but a bit expensive.

Sagasta 14. ✆ **91-591-01-12.** www.lamanducadeazagra.com. Reservations required. Main courses 36€–60€. AE, DC, MC, V. Mon–Sat 1:30–4pm and 9pm–midnight. Closed Aug. Metro: Alonso Martínez.

Expensive

Jockey ★★★ INTERNATIONAL Into its sixth decade, this was Madrid's premier restaurant during the Franco era. The food here is more classic than adventurous, but it remains a favorite of international celebrities and executives. The chef prides himself on coming up with creative twists on old-fashioned dishes featuring ingredients that justify the steep prices, such as lobster ragout with fresh pasta showered with grated truffle. The cold melon soup with shrimp is soothing on a hot day, especially when followed by roasted pigeon from Talavera cooked in its own juice or monkfish en papillote with Mantua sauce. Dress up for your meal.

Amador de los Ríos 6. ✆ **91-310-04-11.** www.restaurantejockey.net. Reservations required. Main courses 29€–40€. AE, DC, MC, V. Daily 1:45–4pm and 9pm–midnight. Closed Aug. Metro: Colón.

NEAR PLAZA MAYOR

Moderate

Casa Lucio CASTILIAN Set on a historic street whose edges once marked the perimeter of Old Madrid, this is a venerable tasca with all the requisite antique accessories. Dozens of cured hams hang from hand-hewn beams above the well-oiled bar. Among the clientele is a stable of sometimes surprisingly well-known public figures—perhaps even the king of Spain. The two dining rooms, each on a different floor, have whitewashed walls, tile floors, and exposed brick. A well-trained staff offers classic Castilian food, which might include Jabugo ham with broad beans, shrimp in garlic sauce, hake with green sauce, several types of roasted lamb, and a thick steak served sizzling hot on a heated platter (called *churrasco de la casa*).

Cava Baja 35. ✆ **91-365-32-52.** www.casalucio.es. Reservations required. Main courses 15€–28€. AE, DC, MC, V. Sun–Fri 1–4pm; daily 9–11:30pm. Closed Aug. Metro: La Latina.

El Schotis ★ SPANISH El Schotis was established in 1962 on one of Madrid's oldest and most historic streets. A series of large and pleasingly old-fashioned dining rooms is the setting for an animated crowd of Madrileños and foreign visitors, who receive ample portions of conservative, well-prepared vegetables, salads, soups, fish, and, above all, meat. Specialties of the house include roast baby lamb, grilled steaks and veal chops, shrimp with garlic, and fried hake in green sauce. Traditional desserts are served as well. There's a bar near the entrance for tapas and before- or after-dinner drinks.

Cava Baja 11. ✆ **91-365-32-30.** Reservations recommended. Main courses 20€–28€. AE, DC, MC, V. Mon–Sat 1–4pm and 8:30pm–midnight; Sun 1–4pm. Closed Aug 15–Sept 7. Metro: Puerta del Sol or La Latina.

Sobrino de Botín ★★ SPANISH According to the *Guinness Book of World Records,* this is the oldest continually operating restaurant in the world. It opened in 1725, and Goya supposedly worked here before becoming a painter. About 100 years later, Ernest Hemingway helped make this place famous when he had Jake Barnes invite Lady Brett here for dinner. They had the house specialty, roast suckling pig, washed down with Rioja. You'll see an open kitchen with a charcoal hearth, hanging copper pots, an 18th-century tile oven for roasting suckling pig, and a big pot of regional soup whose aroma drifts across the room. Roast lamb is also good. Yes, it's packed with tourists, but don't let that stop you.

Calle de Cuchilleros 17 (off southwest corner of Plaza Mayor). ✆ **91-366-42-17.** www.botin.es. Reservations required. Main courses 14€–29€; *menú del día* 40€. AE, DC, MC, V. Daily 1–4pm and 8pm–midnight. Closed Christmas. Metro: Puerta del Sol or Tirso de Molina.

CHAMARTÍN

Very Expensive

Zalacaín ★★★ INTERNATIONAL Outstanding in food, decor, and service, Zalacaín occupies the apex of Madrid's gastronomical pyramid, although younger challengers are crowding it. When it opened in 1973, it introduced nouvelle cuisine to Madrid. The menu features dishes of French and Basque origin subjected to a great deal of experimentation. The chefs might offer a superb sole in a green sauce, but they also know the glory of grilled pigs' feet. Among other recommendable dishes are roast duck with peppers and cherries, crepes stuffed with smoked fish, and bouillabaisse. One quibble is the restaurant's inclination to stick with one set of menu items for too long, not justifiable at these prices.

Alvarez de Baena 4 (north of María de Molina). ✆ **91-561-48-40.** Reservations required. Jacket and tie required for men. Main courses 29€–48€. AE, DC, MC, V. Mon–Fri 1:15–4pm; Mon–Sat 9pm–12:20am. Closed Holy Week and Aug. Metro: Rubén Darío.

Seeing the Sights

Madrid has something to amuse and enlighten everyone. As the capital of Spain since the 16th century, Madrid is where kings and conquistadors deposited the booty and brilliance of a globe-girdling empire. The city has more than 50 museums and one of the world's grandest palaces. Elegant public parks have been developed from imperial hunting grounds.

THE TOP SIGHTS

Museo del Prado ★★★ With more than 20,000 paintings and other artworks, the Prado is one of the most important repositories of art in the world. The Prado has no equal when it comes to paintings from the Spanish school, so if it's your first visit, concentrate on the Spanish masters. You'll find a treasure-trove of works by El Greco, the Crete-born artist who lived much of his life in Toledo. Look for *Las Meninas,* the museum's most famous painting, and other works by the incomparable Diego Velázquez. The Francisco de Goya collection includes the artist's unflattering portraits of his patron, Charles IV, and his family, as well as the *Clothed Maja,* the *Naked Maja,* and pictures from his black period. There are also paintings by Zurbarán and Murillo, and be sure to search out Flemish genius Hieronymus Bosch's best-known work, *The Garden of Earthly Delights.* (Confusingly, the Spanish call Bosch "El Bosco.") In 2005 the Prado launched a $92-million expansion, much of it underground. Floor space doubled, and there are new attractions such as children's workshops. The main structure, from 1785, is now linked underground to a modern annex. Several adjacent buildings have been incorporated, and many modern galleries for temporary exhibits have opened.

Paseo del Prado s/n. ✆ **91-330-28-00.** http://museoprado.mcu.es. Admission 8€ adults, 4€ students, free for seniors and for children 17 and under. Free entry days: Sun (9am–7pm), Oct 12, Dec 6, May 2, and May 18. Tues–Sat 9am–8pm. Metro: Atocha or Banco de España. Bus: 9, 10, 14, 19, 27, 34, 37, or 45.

Museo Nacional Centro de Arte Reina Sofía ★ This museum is a great repository of modern art, including both the 20th and the 21st centuries. After a $95-million expansion, it is better than ever. The core is a former 18th-century hospital, once called "the ugliest building in Spain." Its most celebrated work is Picasso's *Guernica* (some critics call it his masterpiece), depicting the horrors of war during the Franco era. Works by other Spanish artists, including Dalí, Miró, Gris, and Solana, supplement Picasso's masterwork. The collection of the Sofia is ever growing. Its curators hope that one day soon it will rival the Centre Pompidou in Paris. Two mammoth galleries are set aside for large-scale, temporary exhibitions.

Santa Isabel 52 (at the corner of Atocha). ✆ **91-774-10-00.** www.museoreinasofia.es. Admission 6€ adults, 3€ students and children 17 and under, free for all Sat after 2:30pm, free for seniors and children Sun. Mon–Sat 10am–9pm; Sun 10am–2:30pm. Metro: Atocha.

Museo Thyssen-Bornemisza ★★★ On display in the late-18th-century Palacio de Villahermosa and an extension that opened in 2004 are the works gathered by three generations of the Thyssen-Bornemisza family (pronounced *Tees*-ahn Bore-noh-*mees*-uh). In all, 16 new galleries have opened up, allowing 200 more paintings to be displayed. Viewing the quirky collection of paintings is like taking a class in art history, with an image or two covering practically every major style and period from the late 13th century to the present. The collection of 19th- and 20th-century paintings is especially strong—certainly the strongest of any Madrid museum. The nucleus of the collection consists of 700 world-class paintings, including works by El Greco, Velázquez, Dürer, and Rembrandt, as well as art from the Impressionist period. Works from the American abstract expressionist movement and related movements are also featured.

Paseo del Prado 8. ✆ **91-369-01-51.** www.museothyssen.org. Admission to permanent collection 8€ adults, 5.50€ seniors and students, free for children 11 and under. Tues–Sun 10am–7pm. Metro: Banco de España. Bus: 1, 2, 5, 9, 10, 14, 15, 20, 27, 34, 45, 51, 52, 53, 74, 146, or 150.

Palacio Real (Royal Palace) ★★ This opulent palace was begun in 1738 for Felipe V on the site of the Alcázar, a fortified castle that burned in 1734. The decor is a mix of baroque and neoclassical styles. Some of the palace's 2,800 rooms are open to the public, while others are still used for state business. The multilingual guided tour includes the reception room, the state apartments, the royal pharmacy, and the stunning state dining room. The rooms are filled with art treasures and antiques—salon after salon of monumental grandeur, with no apologies for the damask, mosaics, stucco, Tiepolo ceilings, gilt and bronze, chandeliers, and paintings. In the Armory, a collection of weaponry features bizarre scaled-down suits of armor for the royal toddlers.

Plaza de Oriente, Calle de Bailén 2. ✆ **91-454-88-00.** www.patrimonionacional.es. Admission 10€ adults; 3.50€ seniors, students, and children 16 and under. Oct–Mar Mon–Sat 9:30am–5pm, Sun 9am–2pm; Apr–Sept Mon–Sat 9am–4pm, Sun 9am–3pm. Metro: Opera. Bus: 3, 25, 39, or 148.

MORE ATTRACTIONS

Monasterio de las Descalzas Reales ★★ In the heart of old Madrid, near the Puerta del Sol, this richly endowed royal convent was founded in the mid–16th century in the palace where Juana of Austria, Felipe II's sister, was born. She used it as a retreat and brought the Poor Clare nuns here. For many years, the convent sheltered only royal women. Typically, the daughters of aristocrats were sequestered here until they were old enough for arranged marriages. The girls didn't live a spartan existence, though, judging from the wealth of religious artwork that surrounded them, including tapestries, sculptures, and paintings by **Rubens, Brueghel the Elder,** and **Titian.** The main staircase features *trompe l'oeil* paintings and frescoes, and you can view 16 of the 32 lavishly decorated chapels. Compulsory tours for groups of 25 or fewer are conducted in Spanish by guides who hasten visitors from canvas to tapestry to chapel. Try to slow their pace, for there's much to savor. There are frequent alterations to the visiting hours noted below.

Plaza de las Descalzas 3. ✆ **91-454-88-00.** www.patrimonionacional.es. Admission 5€ adults; 2.50€ seniors, students, and children 12 and under; free to all Wed. Tues–Thurs and Sat 10:30am–12:45pm and 4–5:45pm; Fri 10:30am–12:45pm; Sun and holidays 11am–1:45pm. From Plaza del Callao, off Gran Vía, walk down Postigo de San Martín to Plaza de las Descalzas Reales; the convent is on the left. Metro: Opera.

Museo Arqueológico Nacional ★★ This underrated museum is in the same vast building as the National Library (which has a separate entrance on Paseo de Recoletos). It houses antiquities from prehistory to the Middle Ages. Most of the artifacts are related specifically to the development of the Iberian Peninsula, although there are some Egyptian and Greek objects. Most illuminating are the rooms devoted to the Iberian period, before Christ and the waves of sequential conquerors, and those rooms containing relics of the Visigoths, who left relatively little behind, rendering these objects of even greater interest. A particular treasure is the ***Dama de Elche*** ★★, a resplendent example of 4th-century-B.C. Iberian sculpture, easily equal to the better-known works produced in Greece at the same time.

Serrano 13 (facing Calle Serrano). ✆ **91-577-79-12.** http://man.mcu.es. Free admission. Tues–Sat 9:30am–8pm; Sun 9:30am–2:30pm. Metro: Serrano or Retiro.

Museo Lázaro Galdiano Madrid was the beneficiary of financier/author José Lázaro Galdiano's largesse, for when he died, he left the city his 30-room, early-1900s mansion and a substantial private art collection. There are paintings from Spain's golden age, including works by Spaniards El Greco, Zurbarán, Murillo, and Goya; works by Renaissance Italians Tiepolo and Leonardo da Vinci; and canvases by Englishmen Gainsborough and Constable. However, the museum is most admired for its comprehensive array of enamels, ivories, and works in gold and silver, much of it created during the Middle Ages.

Serrano 122. ✆ **91-561-60-84.** www.flg.es. Admission 4€ adults, 3€ students, free for seniors and children 11 and under, free for all Wed. Wed–Mon 10am–4:30pm. Metro: Rubén Dario or Gregorio Marañón.

Real Academia de Bellas Artes de San Fernando (San Fernando Royal Fine Arts Academy) ★ An easy stroll from the Puerta del Sol, this museum is located in the restored and remodeled 17th-century baroque palace of Juan de Goyeneche. The collection—more than 1,500 paintings and 570 sculptures, ranging from the 16th century to the present—was started in 1752 during the reign of Fernando VI (1746–59). It emphasizes works by Spanish, Flemish, and Italian artists. Masterpieces by El Greco, Rubens, Velázquez, Zurbarán, Ribera, Cano, Coello, Murillo, and Sorolla are here. The Goya collection in itself is worth a visit. Goya was a member of the academy from 1780, and the museum houses two of his self-portraits, along with a full-size portrait of the actress La Tirana, and a portrait of the royal favorite Manuel Godoy. Goya's carnival scene, *Burial of the Sardine,* and eight more of his oils are also on view.

Alcalá 13. ✆ **91-524-08-64.** http://rabasf.insde.es. Admission 3€ adults, 1.50€ students, free for seniors and children 17 and under, free for all Wed. Tues–Fri 9am–7pm; Sat–Mon and holidays 9am–2:30pm. Metro: Puerta del Sol or Sevilla.

PARKS & GARDENS

Casa de Campo (Metro: Batán), the former royal hunting grounds, is composed of miles of parkland west of the Royal Palace across the Manzanares River. You can see the gate through which the kings rode out of the palace grounds—either on horseback or in carriages—on their way to the park. Casa de Campo has a zoo, many trees, and a lake that's usually filled with rowers. You can have refreshments around the lake or go swimming in a municipally operated pool. The park can be visited daily 24 hours.

Parque del Retiro ★★ (Metro: Retiro), originally a playground for the Spanish monarchs and their guests, is now a park of more than 120 hectares (297 acres). The huge palaces that once stood here were destroyed in the early 19th century, and only the former dance hall, Casón del Buen Retiro (housing some of the Prado's modern works), remains. The park has many fountains and statues, plus a large lake in front of an extravagant monument to Alfonso XII. Along the promenade beside the lake are rows of tarot card readers, puppeteers, musicians, and other street performers. There are also two exposition centers: the Velázquez and the Crystal palaces. In summer, the rose gardens are worth a visit. The park is open daily 24 hours, but it's safest, as most public parks are, during daylight hours.

Immediately south of the Prado Museum is the **Real Jardín Botánico (Royal Botanical Garden),** Plaza de Murillo 2 (✆ **91-420-30-17;** www.rjb.csic.es; Metro: Atocha). Founded in the 18th century, the garden contains more than 100 species of trees and 3,000 types of plants. Hours are daily as follows: October and March 10am to 7pm; April and September 10am to 8pm; May to August 10am to 9pm; November to February 10am to 6pm. Admission is 2€ for adults, 1€ for students, free for children 10 and under.

ORGANIZED TOURS

Many of the city's hotel concierges, and all of the city's travel agents, will book anyone who asks for a guided tour of Madrid or its environs with one of Spain's largest tour operators, **Pullmantur,** Plaza de Oriente 8 (✆ **91-541-18-07;** www.pullmantur cruises.com). Regardless of destination and trip duration, virtually every tour departs from the Pullmantur terminal at that address. The Madrid Sightseeing Tour goes for 21€.

Toledo is the most popular full-day excursion outside the city limits. Trips cost 67€. These tours (including lunch) depart daily at 9:45am, last all day, and include ample opportunities for wandering at will through Toledo's narrow streets. You can, if you wish, take an abbreviated morning tour of Toledo, without stopping for lunch, for 55€. Tour times are at 9am and 3pm.

The Shopping Scene

THE MAIN SHOPPING AREAS

The sheer diversity of Madrid's shops is staggering. One of the greatest concentrations of stores lies immediately north of **Puerta del Sol,** along the pedestrian streets of Calle del Carmen and Calle Preciados.

Conceived, designed, and built in the 1910s and 1920s as a showcase for the city's best shops, hotels, and restaurants, the **Gran Vía** has since been eclipsed by other shopping districts, although fragments of its Art Nouveau and Art Deco glamour still survive. The book and music shops along here are among the best in the city, as are the outlets for fashion, shoes, jewelry, and handicrafts from all regions of Spain.

Spain's Biggest Flea Market

Foremost among Madrid's flea markets is **El Rastro,** Plaza Cascorro and Ribera de Curtidores (Metro: La Latina; bus: 3 or 17), which occupies a roughly triangular area of streets and plazas that are a few minutes' walk south of Plaza Mayor. This market will delight anyone attracted to sometimes-intriguing kitsch. Goods are sold from open stalls arranged in front of stores selling antiques and paintings. ***Note:*** Thieves are rampant here, so secure your purse and wallet, be alert, and proceed with caution. The market is open Saturday and Sunday only, from 9am to 2pm and (to a lesser extent) from 5 to 8pm.

The **Salamanca** district is the quintessential upscale shopping neighborhood. Here, you'll find exclusive furniture, fur, fashion, and jewelry stores, plus rug and art galleries. The main shopping streets here are Serrano and Velázquez. This district lies northeast of the center of Madrid, a few blocks north of Retiro Park. Its most central Metro stops are Serrano and Veláquez.

SOME NOTEWORTHY SHOPS

El Corte Inglés ★★, Preciados 3 (✆ **91-379-80-00;** www.elcorteingles.es; Metro: Puerta del Sol), is Spain's number-one department store chain. The store sells Spanish handicrafts along with glamorous fashion articles, such as Pierre Balmain designs, often at lower prices than you'll find in most European capitals.

For unique craft items, **El Arco de los Cuchilleros Artesania de Hoy,** Plaza Mayor 9 (basement; ✆ **91-365-26-80;** Metro: Puerta del Sol or Opera), may be a mouthful of a name to remember, but it has an unparalleled array of pottery, leather, textiles, glassware, and jewelry produced by individual artisans throughout Spain. It's open daily 11am to 9pm, even during siesta.

La Maison de la Lanterne Rouge, Corredera Baja de San Pablo 45 (✆ **91-310-79-61;** www.lamaison.es; Metro: Gran Vía), is an avant-garde showcase of cutting-edge fashion housed within a former brothel. Clothing is artistically arranged against a backdrop of Shanghai-inspired accents.

Just outside the walls of Plaza Mayor, **Mercado de San Miguel ★★**, Plaza de San Miguel (✆ **91-542-49-39;** www.mercadodesanmiguel.es; Metro: Opéra), has reopened after years of laying dormant. Its hype is that it is a traditional market for the 21st-century shopper. With its dazzling display of foodstuff, you can go "grazing" here for an offbeat luncheon stopover.

Since 1846, **Loewe ★★★**, Calle Serrano 26 and 34 (✆ **91-577-60-56;** www.loewe.com; Metro: Banco de España), has been Spain's most elegant leather store. Its designers keep abreast of changing tastes and styles, but the inventory retains a timeless chic. The store sells luggage, handbags, and jackets for men and women (in leather or suede). At **Casa de Diego,** Puerta del Sol 12 (✆ **91-522-66-43;** www.casadediego.net; Metro: Puerta del Sol), you'll find a wide inventory of fans, ranging from plain to fancy, from plastic to exotic hardwood, from cost-conscious to lavish.

Madrid After Dark

From May to September, the municipal government sponsors a series of plays, concerts, and films, and the city has the atmosphere of a free arts festival. Pick up a copy of ***Guía del Ocio*** (available at most newsstands) for listings of these events. This guide also provides information about occasional discounts for commercial events, such as the concerts given in Madrid's parks. The guide is in Spanish, but it's not difficult to make out the times, locations, and prices for various events.

With some exceptions, flamenco in Madrid is geared primarily to tourists, and nightclubs are expensive. But since Madrid is a city of song and dance, you can often be entertained at very little cost—for the price of a glass of wine or beer, in fact—if you sit at a bar with live entertainment.

Tickets to dramatic and musical events can cost anywhere from 8€ to 200€, with discounts of up to 50% granted on certain days (usually Wed and early performances on Sun). In the event that your choice is sold out, you may be able to get tickets (with a reasonable markup) at **Localidades Galicia,** Plaza del Carmen 1 (✆ **91-531-27-32;**

www.bullfightticketsmadrid.com; Metro: Puerta del Sol). It's open Tuesday to Sunday 10am to 1pm and 4:30 to 7:30pm. Telephone ticket sales are also provided by **Corté Ingles** (✆ **90-240-02-22;** www.elcorteingles.es/entradas).

THE PERFORMING ARTS

Ballet Nacional de España (✆ **91-517-99-99;** http://balletnacional.mcu.es) is devoted exclusively to dances created by Spanish choreographers. Its performances are always well attended. Also look for performances by choreographer Nacho Duato's **Compañía Nacional de Danza** (✆ **91-354-50-53;** http://cndanza.mcu.es).

World-renowned flamenco sensation António Canales and his troupe, **Ballet Flamenco António Canales,** offer high-energy, spirited performances. Productions are centered around Canales's impassioned *Torero*—his interpretation of the physical and emotional struggles of a bullfighter.

CLASSICAL MUSIC

Madrid's opera company is the **Teatro de la Opera,** and its symphony orchestra is the outstanding **Orquesta Sinfónica de Madrid** (at Teatro Real; see below).

Teatro Real, Plaza Isabel II (✆ **90-516-06-60;** www.teatro-real.com; Metro: Opera), is one of the world's finest stage and acoustic settings for opera. Guided tours of the grand hall are available every day except Tuesday from 11am to 1:30pm at a cost of 5€. Today, the building is home to the Compañía del Teatro Real and the Teatro de la Opera, and is the major venue for classical music and opera. Tickets are 8€ to 115€.

Auditorio Nacional de Música, Príncipe de Vergara 146 (✆ **91-337-01-39;** www.auditorionacional.mcu.es; Metro: Cruz del Rayo), is the ultramodern home of both the **National Orchestra of Spain,** which pays particular attention to the music of Spanish composers, and the **National Chorus of Spain.** Just north of Madrid's Salamanca district, the concert hall ranks as a major addition to the classical music circuit in Europe. Tickets are 6€ to 100€.

FLAMENCO

At Madrid's flamenco *tablaos,* doors usually open at 9 or 9:30pm, and the show starts at about 10:45pm and ends at 12:30am or even later. To save money, go after dinner, when the still-hefty admission at least includes a drink. The later performances are usually better anyway, after the tour groups leave and the performers are warmed up. These stages feature large troupes with several dancers, two or three guitarists, and one or two singers, all in costume. Among the established tablaos are **Las Tablas ★**, Plaza de España 9 (✆ **91-542-05-20;** www.lastablasmadrid.com; Metro: Callao); **Corral de la Morería,** Morería 17 (✆ **91-365-84-46;** www.corraldelamoreria.com; Metro: Opera); and **Café de Chinitas ★**, Torija 7 (✆ **91-547-15-02;** Metro: Santa Domingo).

For a flamenco club that doesn't cater primarily to tourists, try **Casa Patas ★**, Cañizares 10 (✆ **91-369-04-96;** www.casapatas.com; Metro: Antón Martín). In front, it's a restaurant, with a long bar, a high ceiling held up by cast-iron pillars, and three rows of tables with checked tablecloths. A potbellied stove in the middle provides heat, and photos of matadors and flamenco performers cover the walls. That's not where the shows are, though. Go to the closed door in back. Shortly before showtime, a shuttered window opens, your money is taken, and you are allowed to enter. You are then seated at tiny tables around the open stage. The music will be powerful, the dancing fiery and gripping. Monday to Thursday, shows are at 8pm, and Friday and Saturday, shows are at 7:30pm and 1am. Call ahead to reserve a table. The cover is 28€ to 40€ per person. It's worth the cost and effort, for this is modern flamenco at its best.

LIVE MUSIC

Off Plaza de Santa Ana, **Café Central ★**, Plaza del Angel 10 (✆ **91-369-41-43;** www.cafecentralmadrid.com; Metro: Antón Martín), is *the* place for live jazz. Black bench seating, marble-topped tables, and glistening brass set the scene, and the place is usually packed with students, visitors, and Madrid's night beauties. Performances are usually at 10pm and midnight. While jazz is the main course, the cafe also hosts folkies, blues belters, and performers of related music. Calle de las Huertas runs through this plaza, so a visit to the cafe could be the start or the end of an extended pub-crawl. It's open daily 1:30pm to 2 or 3am, with a cover that varies from 7€ to 15€.

Not far from the Central is **Café Jazz Populart ★**, Calle Huertas 22 (✆ **91-429-84-07;** www.populart.es; Metro: Antón Martín), a showcase for American blues, Latin salsa, and Caribbean reggae as well as many varieties of jazz. The large space allows for a little elbowroom, and the atmosphere is laid-back. You can relax at the marble-topped bar or the tables ringing the stage. Admission is often free, but the drink prices tend to jump sharply when music is playing. Still, it's cheaper than Central. Open Monday to Thursday 6pm to 2:30am, Friday and Saturday 6pm to 3:30am; the music usually starts around 11pm.

With dozens of small tables and a huge bar in its dark and smoky interior, **Clamores ★**, Albuquerque 14 (✆ **91-445-79-38;** www.salaclamores.com; Metro: Bilbao), is the largest and one of the most popular jazz clubs in Madrid. It has thrived because of the noted American and Spanish jazz bands that appear here. Clamores is open daily from 7pm to 3am or so, but jazz is presented only from Tuesday to Saturday. From Tuesday to Thursday, performances are at 11pm and 1am; Saturday they're at 11:30pm and 1:30am. There are no live performances Sunday or Monday. Cover from Tuesday to Saturday is 7€ to 27€, depending on the act.

DANCE CLUBS

Madrid's most popular dance clubs operate with a selective entrance policy, so dress stylishly and try to look as young, gorgeous, celebrated, and/or rich as possible. The clubs are usually open nightly until 5am or later, with nothing much happening before 2am. (***Tip:*** It's easier to get past the unsmiling gents at the door if you arrive before then.) Some clubs have a matinee, usually 7 to 9 or 10pm, attended primarily by teenagers. After closing for an hour or two to clear out the youngsters, they reopen to older patrons.

The most multicultural, multifarious, and multimusical disco in Madrid, **Kapital,** Atocha 125 (✆ **91-420-29-06;** www.grupo-kapital.com; Metro: Atocha), has seven floors, with the main dance floor at street level, a terrace up top, and more bars and dance floors (with different kinds of music) in between. Laser shows, karaoke, a movie room, and what used to be called go-go dancers are added attractions. Throngs of kids show up for the "afternoon" session from 6 to 11pm. Grown-ups arrive after midnight and stay until 6am. The cover is 12€ to 15€.

Pachá, Barceló 11 (✆ **91-447-01-28;** www.pacha-madrid.com; Metro: Tribunal), is a late-night club, attracting the 20- to 40-year-old age group to a setting that in the 1930s was a movie theater. By the 1980s it had become a "dance cathedral."

Loud music and hard drinking rule the night. Cover ranges from 12€ to 15€, including the first drink.

Both homegrown and foreign bands appear at **Nasti,** Vicente Ferrer 33 (✆ **91-521-76-05;** www.nasti.es; Metro: Tribunal), attracting grimy hipsters. Garage bands or punk rockers appear before stoned audiences. Cover is 10€.

PUBS & BARS

Hemingway and his journalist buddies suffered the Civil War siege of Madrid at **Museo Chicote,** Gran Vía 12 (✆ **91-532-67-37;** Metro: Gran Vía). Photos on the walls to the left and right of the entrance document the patronage of Coop, Ty, Orson, and Ava. A superior martini is still available, and they've added breakfast and light meals. **Bar Cock,** Reina 16 (✆ **91-532-28-26;** www.barcock.com; Metro: Gran Vía), a dark, cavernous room on a narrow street parallel to Gran Vía, is another old-timer, where Madrid's artistic and showbiz elite routinely assault their livers. It was given renewed cachet by the presence of internationally known film director Pedro Almodóvar.

If you want to witness a supremely assured professional mixologist in action, head up the same street a few doors. **Del Diego,** Reina 12 (✆ **91-523-31-06;** Metro: Gran Vía), is a stylish, contemporary watering hole that attracts exactly the upmarket crowd it seeks, including government ministers and upper-echelon executives. The maestro twirling the swizzle sticks is the eponymous head man, never losing his composure as he shakes and stirs everything from pure martinis to Long Island iced teas and Madrid's drink of the moment, the *mojito* (rum, lime juice, mint, and a hint of sugar).

Pop in for at least a quick drink to admire the variety of pictorial ceramic tiles covering the walls of the five rooms of **Los Gabrieles,** Echegaray 17 (✆ **91-369-07-57;** Metro: Sol or Sevilla), a century-old tavern. Live music, mostly flamenco, is presented Tuesday nights (no cover). Students and 20-something singles have given the 1890 tavern **Viva Madrid,** Manuel Fernández González 7 (✆ **91-429-36-40;** Metro: Sol or Antón Martín), new life as a trendy meeting place. Both the facade and the interior are resplendent with intricately patterned tiles, and mythical creatures hold up carved ceilings. Light meals and tapas are served in the room behind the bar.

GAY & LESBIAN CLUBS & CAFES

The Plaza Chueca area (Metro: Chueca) is now Spain's number-one hot spot for gays and bohemian straights, with more than 60 gay-friendly bars, cafes, and discos.

Black and White, Libertad 34 (✆ **91-531-11-41;** www.discoblack-white.net), remains the major gay bar of Madrid, but draws a mixed crowd on weekends. There's a disco in the basement. The turn-of-the-20th-century **Café Figueroa,** Augusto Figueroa 17 (✆ **91-521-16-73**), attracts a diverse clientele including a large number of gays and lesbians.

Cruising, Perez Galdos 5 (✆ **91-524-51-43;** Metro: Chueca), is one of the landmark gay bars of Madrid. There are virtually no women inside, but count on meeting a hustler looking for a tourist john. After all, the place is named Cruising.

Day Trips from Madrid

TOLEDO ★★★

Once the capital of Visigothic Spain, Toledo—69km (43 miles) southwest of Madrid—bristles with steeples and towers spread over an unlikely hill that's almost completely moated by the River Tajo. Toledo is one of the most photogenic cities on the peninsula, its streets tilting and twisting past buildings representing more than 1,500 years of construction. Here is history . . . deep, palpable, warming the stones. Those familiar with the painting of the city by El Greco, who lived most of his creative life here, will be struck by how closely his 16th-century canvas, *View of Toledo,* conforms to the present view, in overall impression if not in detail.

The streets are clogged all year with tour buses and their occupants and crammed with shops hung with Toledo cutlery, fake armor, Lladró figurines, and every kind of gaudy souvenir. If possible, stay overnight to get a less feverish picture of the city when it's briefly returned to its citizens.

GETTING THERE You can reach Toledo by **train** (six trips daily from Madrid's Atocha Station) or by **bus** (from Madrid's Estación Sur de Autobuses). The one-way trip takes about an hour and 15 minutes by either method. The train fare is 9.50€, while the bus (www.alsa.es) costs 4.70€. Taxis are available at the charming neo-Mudéjar train station in Toledo, but not in great numbers and not always when you want them. We don't recommend driving to Toledo, but if you want to, take Route 401 for 69km (43 miles) south of Madrid.

VISITOR INFORMATION The **tourist office** is at Puerta de Bisagra (✆ **92-525-40-30;** www.diputoledo.es), open Monday to Friday 9am to 6pm, Saturday 9am to 7pm, and Sunday 9am to 3pm.

EXPLORING TOLEDO Although ranked among the greatest of Gothic structures, the **Cathedral ★★★**, Cardenal Cisneros (✆ **92-522-22-41;** www.architoledo.org/cathedral/default.htm), actually reflects a variety of styles because of the more than 2½ centuries that passed during its construction, from 1226 to 1493. Among its art treasures, the *transparente* stands out—a wall of marble and florid baroque alabaster sculpture overlooked for years because of the cathedral's poor lighting. The sculptor Narcisco Tomé cut a hole in the ceiling, much to the consternation of Toledans, and now light touches the high-rising angels, a *Last Supper* in alabaster, and a Virgin in ascension. The Treasure Room has a 225-kilogram (496-lb.) 15th-century gilded monstrance (receptacle of the Host)—allegedly made with gold brought back from the New World by Columbus—that's still carried through the streets of Toledo during the feast of Corpus Christi. Admission to the cathedral is free; admission to the Treasure Room is 7€. Both are open Monday to Saturday 10:30am to 6:30pm, and Sunday 2 to 6pm.

The **Alcázar,** Cuesta de Carlos V, near Plaza de Zocodover (✆ **92-523-88-00**), at the eastern edge of the old city, dominates the Toledo skyline. It was damaged frequently over its centuries as a fortress and royal residence and leveled during a siege of the Spanish Civil War. The existing structure is essentially a replica but is built over the old cellars and foundations. Today it has been turned into an army museum, housing such exhibits as a plastic model of what the fortress looked like after the civil war, electronic equipment used during the siege, and photographs taken during the height of the battle. At press time, the Alcázar remained closed for renovations, but hopefully will reopen during the lifetime of this edition—check locally.

Queen Isabel had a hand in arranging the construction of the 16th-century building housing the **Museo Santa Cruz,** Cervantes 3 (✆ **92-522-14-02**), with its impressive Plateresque facade. The paintings within are mostly from the 16th century and 17th century, with yet another by El Greco. Find the museum immediately east of Plaza de Zocodover. Admission is free. Hours are Monday to Saturday 10am to 6pm, and Sunday 10am to 2pm.

EL ESCORIAL PALACE ★★

The second-most-important excursion from Madrid is a 55km (34-mile) trip to the Royal Monastery in the village of San Lorenzo de El Escorial. Felipe II commissioned Juan Bautista de Toledo and his assistant, Juan de Herrera, to build this gloomy Xanadu in the Sierra de Guadarrama, northwest of Madrid. Its purported intent was to commemorate an important victory over the French in Flanders, but the likely real reason was that the ascetic Felipe was unnerved by the stress of overseeing an empire bridging four continents and this retreat insulated him from the intrigues of the Madrid court. He ruled his troubled empire from the rooms here for the last 14 years of his life, and it was from here that he ordered his doomed "Invincible Armada" to set sail.

GETTING THERE More than two dozen **trains** depart daily from Madrid's Atocha and Chamartín stations (trip time: 60–80 min.), costing 3.30€ one-way. For schedules and information, contact **RENFE** (✆ **90-224-02-02;** www.renfe.es).

Buses, however, are preferable. Use line nos. 661 and 664, run by **Empresa Herranz,** Calle Del Rey 27 (✆ **91-890-19-15**), and which cost 5€ for the 55-minute trip one-way; they drop you closer to Felipe's royal retreat than do the trains.

If you're **driving,** take N-IV northwest from Madrid; after about 48km (30 miles), exit south on M-505 about 10km (6¼ miles) to El Escorial.

VISITOR INFORMATION The **tourist office** at Calle Grimaldi 2 in El Escorial can be reached at ✆ **91-890-53-13;** www.sanlorenzoturismo.org.

EXPLORING THE MONASTERY The huge monastery/palace/mausoleum that is the **Real Monasterio de San Lorenzo de El Escorial ★★★**, San Lorenzo de El Escorial 1 (✆ **91-890-59-03;** www.patrimonionacional.es), is typically praised for its massive, brooding simplicity. That impression is allayed inside, as the wealth of sumptuous detail, the hundreds of rooms, and the 24km (15 miles) of corridors are revealed. An extraordinary library reflects the scholarly king's intellectual interests, with tens of thousands of volumes and rare manuscripts in many languages, representative of the three primary religions that had existed in Spain. Also in the building is a sizable church with a frescoed dome more than 90m (300 ft.) high. The main altar is four stories high with gold sculptures and paintings framed in jasper. Beneath the basilica is a royal pantheon with sarcophagi containing the remains of most of Spain's monarchs since Carlos V. Galleries and royal apartments contain canvases by El Greco, Titian, Ribera, Tintoretto, Rubens, and Velázquez, among others. Throughout the building, you'll see copies of a gridlike symbol that echoes the layout of the palace itself. These symbols represent St. Lawrence, who was roasted alive on a grill by the Romans. April to September, El Escorial is open Tuesday to Sunday and holidays 10am to 7pm (to 5pm in winter). An all-inclusive ticket is 8€ adults and 4€ seniors and students, and guided tours are 10€. Free on Wednesday.

SEGOVIA ★★★

Less commercial than Toledo, Segovia, 87km (54 miles) northwest of Madrid, typifies the glory of Old Castile. Wherever you look, you'll see reminders of a golden era—whether it's the spectacular Alcázar or the well-preserved Roman aqueduct.

Segovia lies on the slope of the Guadarrama Mountains, where the Eresma and Clamores rivers converge. Isabel was proclaimed queen of Castile here in 1474.

GETTING THERE **Buses** are preferable to trains for price and speed, if not comfort. Between Madrid and Segovia, the bus takes 75 to 90 minutes and the train 2 hours.

Buses arrive at and depart from **Estacionamiento Municipal de Autobuses,** Paseo de Ezequiel González 10 (✆ **92-142-77-06**), near the corner of Avenida Fernández Ladreda and the steeply sloping Paseo Conde de Sepúveda. There are 20 to 35 buses a day to and from Madrid (which depart from Paseo de la Florida 11; Metro: Norte), and about four a day traveling between Avila and Segovia. One-way tickets from Madrid cost 8€.

Trains depart from Madrid's Atocha, Nuevos Ministerios, and Chamartín stations every 2 hours from 6am to 8pm, costing 7€ each way. The train station is a 20-minute walk from the town center, so take local bus no. 3 instead; it leaves every 15 minutes for the Plaza Mayor.

If you're **driving,** take NVI northwest out of Madrid; after about 98km (61 miles), exit north on Route 603. It's 55km (34 miles) from there to Segovia.

VISITOR INFORMATION The **tourist office** is at Plaza del Azoguejo 1 (✆ **92-146-67-21;** www.turismodesegovia.com), open daily 10am to 8pm.

EXPLORING SEGOVIA The town is quite walkable. Its narrow medieval streets suffer less from the ravages of mass tourism (except on weekends and holidays) than other destinations in Madrid's orbit and reveal much about what life must have been like here 500 years ago.

Located here is what might be the most recognizable structure in Spain—an intact **Roman Aqueduct ★★**, Plaza de Azoguejo. A spectacular engineering feat even if it were contemplated today, the double-tiered Roman aqueduct cuts across the city to the snow-fed waters of the nearby mountains. Almost 730m (2,400 ft.) long and nearly 30m (98 ft.) at its highest point at the east end of town, it contains more than 160 arches fashioned of stone cut so precisely that no mortar was needed in the construction. Probably completed in the 2nd century A.D. (although some sources date it as many as 3 centuries earlier), it has survived war and partial dismantling by the Moors. Amazingly, it carried water until only a few decades ago.

Constructed between 1515 and 1558, the **Catedral de Segovia ★★**, Plaza de la Catedral, Marqués del Arco (✆ **92-146-22-05**), was the last Gothic cathedral built in Spain. Fronting the Plaza Mayor, it stands on the spot where Isabel I was proclaimed queen of Castile. It contains numerous treasures, such as a chapel created by the flamboyant Churriguera, elaborately carved choir stalls, and 16th- and 17th-century paintings. More interesting, if only for historical reasons, is the attached 15th-century **cloister ★**. After rebels razed the earlier cathedral, its cloister was moved here stone by stone and reassembled. The cloister contains a small museum. To reach the cathedral, walk west along Calle de Cervantes, which becomes Calle Bravo. Admission to the cathedral is free, but the cloister and museum cost 3€. It's open April to October daily 9am to 6:30pm, November to March daily 9:30am to 5:30pm.

Continue west on Calle de Daolz, where the prow of the old town rears above the confluence of the Clamores and Eresma rivers. **El Alcázar ★**, Plaza de la Reina Victoria Eugenia (✆ **92-146-07-59;** www.alcazardesegovia.com), a fortified castle almost as familiar a symbol of Castilla (Castile) as the aqueduct, occupies this dramatic location. Though it satisfies our "castles in Spain" fantasies, at least from the outside, note that it's essentially a late-19th-century replica of the medieval fortress that stood here before a devastating fire in 1868. Admission is 4€ adults; 3€ seniors, students, and children; and free for children 5 and under. It's open April to September daily 10am to 7pm, October to May daily 10am to 6pm.

BARCELONA ★★★

With an unforgettable visual style, passionate life force, and continuous churn of old and new, the capital of the autonomous region of Catalonia (don't call it Spanish!) is easily Spain's most enjoyable city, a place where people play with gusto but still manage to get things done. Catalonians consider themselves a distinct nationality, speaking a language that owes as much to French as it does to Spanish. It says something that Catalonia's favorite sons have been four artists known for their brilliant eccentricity: Gaudí, Miró, Picasso, and Dalí.

Since the 19th century, the Catalán metropolis has always been at the forefront of modernity. Barcelona was the nation's first industrial center, expanding from its ancient settlement into the surrounding hills by the 1920s. The end of the 20th century brought another burst of expansion: first for the 1992 Olympics, and in 2004 for Expo 2004, a 6-month festival that gave rise to the construction of an entirely new neighborhood on the waterfront.

A visual expression of Barcelona's quirky personality and willingness to take risks is some of Europe's most amazing architecture, from the Gothic cathedral to the parade of modernist masterpieces along the Passeig de Gràcia. The region has given birth to some of history's most visionary artists, among them the 21st-century chefs who have put themselves on the world map creating a brilliant, almost surrealist cuisine. Joyously joining the Europe of the millennium, Barcelona has everything going for it—good looks, a sharp business sense, an appreciation for all forms of culture, and an unerring eye for style.

Essentials

GETTING THERE

BY PLANE **El Prat Airport** (**✆ 90-240-47-04;** www.aena.es) lies 13km (8 miles) southwest of the city. A **train** runs between the airport and the Estació Sants rail station every 30 minutes from 6:25am to 11:05pm, continuing to the more central Plaça de Catalunya; it costs 3.50€. **Aerobuses** (**✆ 93-415-60-20**) run among the three terminals at the airport and to Plaça de Catalunya (with intermediate stops) Monday to Friday every 12 minutes 6am to 1am. The trip takes 25 to 40 minutes and costs 4.05€. A **taxi** into town costs from 20€ to 27€, plus tip and supplements for luggage.

BY TRAIN A high-speed train called Trenhotel runs between Paris and Barcelona in just 12 hours. National and international trains arrive at the **Estació Sants** or the **Estació de França,** both situated slightly outside the city center but linked to the municipal Metro network. Many trains also stop at the Metro station at **Plaça de Catalunya.** For schedules and prices, call **RENFE** (**✆ 90-224-02-02;** www.renfe.es).

BY BUS Bus travel to Barcelona is possible but not popular—it's pretty slow. Barcelona's Estació del Nord is the arrival and departure point for **Alsa** (✆ **90-242-22-42;** www.alsa.es) buses to and from southern France and Italy. Alsa also operates 24 buses per day to and from Madrid (trip time: 7½ hr.). A one-way ticket from Madrid costs 27€ to 47€. **Linebús** (✆ **90-233-55-33;** www.linebus.com) offers six trips a week to and from Paris. **Eurolines Viagens,** Carrer Viriato (✆ **90-240-50-40;** www.eurolines.es), operates seven buses a week to and from Frankfurt and another five per week to and from Marseille.

BY CAR From France, the major access route is at the eastern end of the Pyrenees, with the choice of the express highway (E-15) or the more scenic coastal road. From France, it's possible to approach Barcelona via Toulouse. Cross the border into Spain at Puigcerdá (frontier stations are there), near the principality of Andorra. From here, take N-152 to Barcelona. From Madrid, take N-2 to Zaragoza, and then A-2 to El Vendrell, followed by A-7 to Barcelona.

VISITOR INFORMATION

TOURIST OFFICE A conveniently located tourist office is the subterranean **Centre d'Informació,** at the southeast corner of Plaça Catalunya (✆ **93-285-38-34;** www.barcelonaturismo.com; Metro: Catalunya), open daily 9am to 9pm.

WEBSITES A good place to start is **www.okspain.org**, where you can find up-to-date information and book hotels, restaurants, and tours. The excellent municipal website, **www.bcn.es**, features a terrific interactive map. Additional sources are **www.barcelonaturisme.com** and **www.bcn-guide.com**.

CITY LAYOUT Old Barcelona sits just north of the Mediterranean, bisected by the Rambla promenade. The **Barri Gótic,** the Gothic Quarter and the oldest part of town, lies east of the Rambla; south of the Barri Gótic is the **Ribera** district, also known as **El Born,** developed during the 13th and 14th centuries and home to the Picasso Museum.

The old-town areas west of the Rambla are grittier; the residential **Raval** district, home to many of Barcelona's Muslim residents, is currently balancing on the knife edge between marginally unsafe and breathtakingly hip. The **Barri Xinés,** south of Nou de la Rambla, is a once-rough area that's still best avoided at night.

Southeast of the Old City, right on the water, is **Barceloneta,** originally home to the city's fishermen and now known for its seafood restaurants. Farther east along the coast are the **Vila Olímpica** and **Diagonal Mar** neighborhoods, areas developed for the 1992 Olympics and 2004 Forum, respectively.

West of the Old City is the brooding **Montjuïc,** a towering hill that's home to the Miró Museum and a large park.

Plaça de Catalunya marks the northern edge of the old city, leading out onto the **Passeig de Gràcia,** Barcelona's proudest boulevard. The Passeig de Gràcia cuts north across the **Eixample,** a grid of wide streets and modernist buildings that was the product of Barcelona's growing prosperity in the late 19th century. North of the Eixample are **Gràcia,** an area of small squares and lively bars and restaurants that's known as "Barcelona's Greenwich Village"; **Sarría,** a quiet residential area; and **Tibidabo,** Barcelona's tallest mountain.

GETTING AROUND The best deal for getting around Barcelona is the T10 10-ride **Metro/bus pass,** which costs 7.70€ and can be shared by multiple people.

Barcelona

FRANCE
Barcelona
Madrid
PORTUGAL
SPAIN

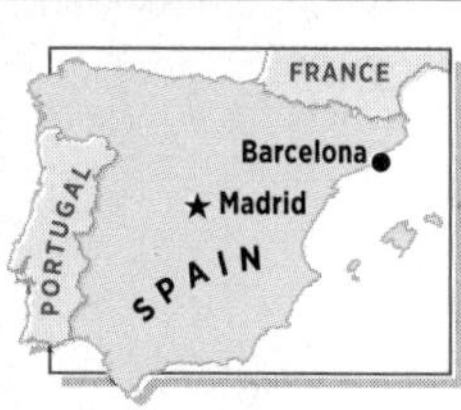

ATTRACTIONS ●
- Casa Batlló **15**
- Fundació Antoni Tàpies **14**
- Fundació Joan Miró **4**
- La Pedrera **10**
- L'Aquàrium **31**
- La Sagrada Família **11**
- Montjuïc **5**
- Museu Barbier-Mueller **29**
- Museu d'Art Contemporàni **20**
- Museu d'Art Modern **34**
- Museu d'Historia de la Ciutat **27**
- Museu Frederic Marés **26**
- Museu Marítim **30**
- Museu Nacional d'Art de Catalunya **3**
- Museu Picasso **28**
- Parc Güell **7**
- Passeig de Gràcia **13**
- Poble Espanyol **2**
- Tibidabo Amusement Park **1**
- Tibidabo Mountain **6**

ACCOMMODATIONS ■
- Astoria **8**
- Axel **17**
- Claris **12**
- Colón **24**
- Cram **16**
- Duques de Bergara **18**
- Eurostar Grand Marina Hotel **32**
- Fashion House B&B **19**
- Gallery Hotel **9**
- Grand Hotel Central **25**
- Hotel Arts **35**
- Hotel España **22**
- Hotel 54 **33**
- Le Meridien Barcelona **21**
- Neri **23**
- Pulitzer **18**

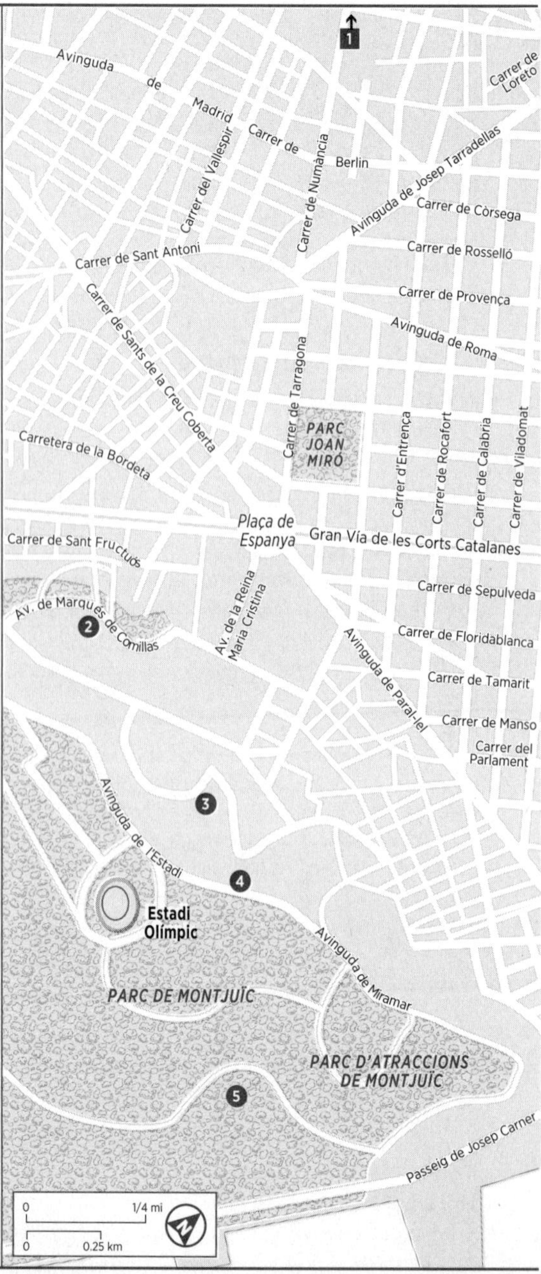
1
Avinguda de Madrid
Carrer de Loreto
Carrer de Berlin
Avinguda de Josep Tarradellas
Carrer del Vallespir
Carrer de Numància
Carrer de Còrsega
Carrer de Sant Antoni
Carrer de Rosselló
Carrer de Provença
Carrer de Sants de la Creu Coberta
Avinguda de Roma
Carrer de Tarragona
PARC JOAN MIRÓ
Carrer d'Entrença
Carrer de Rocafort
Carrer de Calabria
Carrer de Viladomat
Carretera de la Bordeta
Plaça de Espanya
Gran Vía de les Corts Catalanes
Carrer de Sant Fructuós
Carrer de Sepulveda
Av. de Marqués de Comillas
2
Av. de la Reina Maria Cristina
Avinguda de Paral-lel
Carrer de Floridablanca
Carrer de Tamarit
Carrer de Manso
Carrer del Parlament
3
Avinguda de l'Estadi
4
Estadi Olímpic
Avinguda de Miramar
PARC DE MONTJUÏC
PARC D'ATRACCIONS DE MONTJUÏC
5
Passeig de Josep Carner
0
1/4 mi
0
0.25 km
N

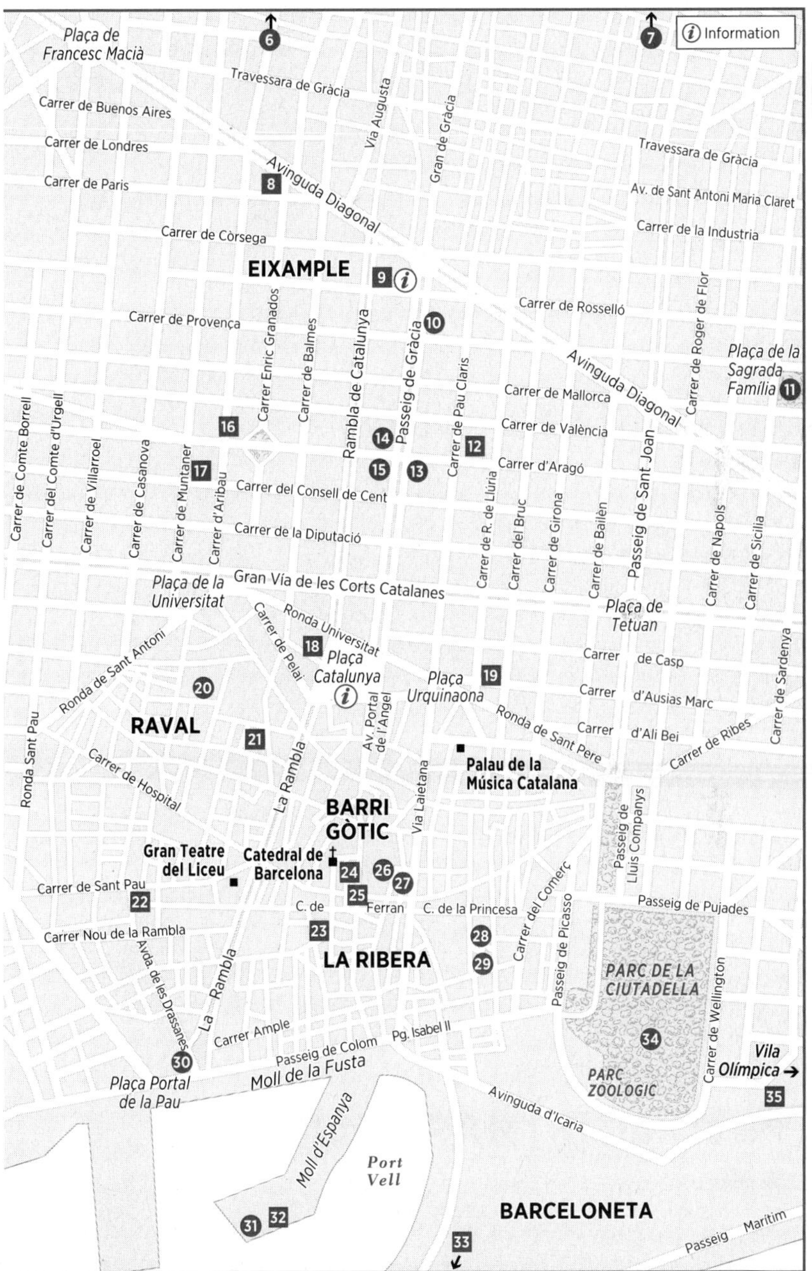
Plaça de Francesc Macià
6
7
Information
Travessara de Gràcia
Via Augusta
Gran de Gràcia
Carrer de Buenos Aires
Carrer de Londres
Carrer de Paris
8
Avinguda Diagonal
Travessara de Gràcia
Av. de Sant Antoni Maria Claret
Carrer de la Industria
Carrer de Còrsega
EIXAMPLE
9
Carrer de Rosselló
Carrer de Provença
Carrer Enric Granados
Carrer de Balmes
Rambla de Catalunya
Passeig de Gràcia
10
Carrer de Pau Claris
Carrer de Roger de Flor
Plaça de la Sagrada Família
11
Avinguda Diagonal
Carrer de Mallorca
Carrer de València
Carrer d'Aragó
16
14
12
15
13
17
Carrer de Comte Borrell
Carrer del Comte d'Urgell
Carrer de Villarroel
Carrer de Casanova
Carrer de Muntaner
Carrer d'Aribau
Carrer del Consell de Cent
Carrer de la Diputació
Carrer de R. de Llúria
Carrer del Bruc
Carrer de Girona
Carrer de Bailèn
Passeig de Sant Joan
Carrer de Napols
Carrer de Sicilia
Plaça de la Universitat
Gran Vía de les Corts Catalanes
Plaça de Tetuan
Carrer de Pelai
Ronda Universitat
18
Plaça Catalunya
Plaça Urquinaona
19
Carrer de Casp
Carrer d'Ausias Marc
Carrer d'Ali Bei
Carrer de Sardenya
Ronda de Sant Antoni
20
RAVAL
21
Av. Portal de l'Angel
Ronda de Sant Pere
Carrer de Ribes
Ronda Sant Pau
Carrer de Hospital
La Rambla
Palau de la Música Catalana
BARRI GÒTIC
Via Laietana
Passeig de Lluís Companys
Gran Teatre del Liceu
Catedral de Barcelona
24
26
27
25
Carrer de Sant Pau
22
C. de Ferran
C. de la Princesa
Carrer del Comerç
Passeig de Pujades
Carrer Nou de la Rambla
23
28
LA RIBERA
29
Passeig de Picasso
PARC DE LA CIUTADELLA
Carrer de Wellington
Avda. de les Drassanes
La Rambla
Carrer Ample
Pg. Isabel II
34
Vila Olímpica
30
Passeig de Colom
Moll de la Fusta
PARC ZOOLOGIC
35
Plaça Portal de la Pau
Avinguda d'Icaria
Moll d'Espanya
Port Vell
BARCELONETA
31
32
Passeig Marítim
33

This pass is available at most Metro stations, tourist offices, many newsstands and lottery shops, and the office of the local transportation agency **TMB** (© **93-138-70-74** for information; www.tmb.net).

BY METRO (SUBWAY) The Metro and integrated commuter train lines (called FGC) operate Monday to Thursday 5am to midnight, Friday and Saturday 5am to 2am, and Sunday and holidays 6am to midnight. The lines you'll want to use within the city are numbered L1 through L8; other lines starting with L, R, and S serve various suburbs. The one-way fare is 1.30€.

BY BUS TMB runs Barcelona's bus system, which has dozens of complicated, frequent, and useful lines. Board at the front to pay your fare, or get your pass punched in one of the machines just inside the bus. For schedules and route information, visit one of the service offices mentioned above, call © **93-318-70-74,** or visit TMB's website at **www.tmb.net**. The single fare is 1.30€, same as the Metro.

BY TAXI Taxis are black and yellow. When available, they display a sign reading LIBRE (Spanish) or LLIURE (Catalán) and/or an illuminated green roof light. The fare starts at 2€ and increases by .85€ per kilometer. You can hail a taxi on the street or call one at © **93-303-30-33;** www.radiotaxi033.com.

BY CAR Driving is a headache in congested Barcelona, but a car is ideal for touring the environs. Car-rental firms are found at the airport and at downtown offices. Check with **Avis,** at Calle Corcega 293–295 (© **90-218-08-54**).

BY FUNICULAR & TELEFERIC At some point in your journey, you may want to visit Tibidabo or Montjuïc (or both). A train called **Tramvía Blau (Blue Streetcar)** goes from Plaça Kennedy to the bottom of the funicular to Tibidabo. It operates every 15 to 20 minutes from 10am to 6pm on weekends only. The fare is 2.70€ one-way, 4.10€ round-trip. During the week, buses run from the Plaça Kennedy to the bottom of the funicular approximately 10am to 6pm daily. The bus costs 1.35€ one-way.

At the end of the run, you can go the rest of the way by funicular to the top, at 503m (1,650 ft.), for a stunning panoramic view of Barcelona. The funicular operates only when the Fun Fair at Tibidabo is open. Opening times vary according to the time of year and the weather conditions. As a rule, the funicular starts operating 20 minutes before the Fun Fair opens and then every half-hour. During peak visiting hours, it runs every 15 minutes. The cost is 2€ one-way, 3€ round-trip.

The **Tibibus** (© **93-211-79-42**) goes from the Plaça de Catalunya (in the city center) to Tibidabo from June 24 to September 15 on Saturday and Sunday. It runs every 30 minutes from 11am to 6:30pm and sometimes 8:30pm, depending on when the park closes. The one-way fare is 2.50€. To reach Montjuïc, the site of the 1992 Olympics, take the **Montjuïc funicular** (© **93-318-70-74**). It links with subway lines 2 and 3 at Paral.lel. The funicular runs daily 10am to 7pm in April, May, and October; 10am to 9pm June to September; and 10am to 6pm November to March.

[Fast FACTS] BARCELONA

Consulates For information on embassies, see "Fast Facts: Madrid," earlier in this chapter. The **U.S. Consulate,** Reina Elisenda 23 (© **93-280-22-27;** train: Reina Elisenda), is open Monday to Friday 9am to 1pm. The **Canadian Consulate,** Plaça de Catalunya 9 (© **93-412-72-36;** Metro: Plaça de Catalunya), is open Monday to Friday 9am to 12:30pm. The **U.K. Consulate,** Av. Diagonal 477 (✆ **93-366-62-00;** Metro: Hospital Clínic), is open Monday to Friday 8:30am to 1:30pm. The **Australian Consulate** is at Plaza gal-al Placídia 1–3, 1st Floor (✆ **93-490-90-13;** bus: 22 or 24), and is open Monday to Friday 10am to noon.

Dentists Call **Clinica Dental Beonadex,** Paseo Bona Nova 69, 3rd Floor (✆ **93-418-44-33;** bus: 22), for an appointment. It's open Monday 3 to 9pm and Tuesday to Friday 8am to 3pm.

Drugstores After hours, various pharmacies take turns staying open at night. All pharmacies that are not open post the names and addresses of the pharmacies that are open all night in the area.

Emergencies To report a **fire,** dial ✆ **080;** to call an ambulance, ✆ **061;** the police, ✆ **091.**

Hospitals Barcelona has many hospitals and clinics, including **Hospital Clínic,** Casanova 143 (✆ **93-227-54-00;** Metro: Hospital Clinic), and **Hospital de la Santa Creu i Sant Pau,** at the intersection of Carrer Cartagena and Carrer Sant Antoni Maria Claret (✆ **93-291-90-00;** Metro: Hospital de Sant Pau).

Post Office The main post office is at Plaça d'Antoni López (✆ **93-486-80-50;** www.correos.es; Metro: Jaume I). It's open Monday to Friday 8am to 9pm and Saturday 8am to 2pm.

Safety Be particularly careful with cameras, purses, and wallets, all favorite targets of thieves and pickpockets in Barcelona—especially on La Rambla, in the Gothic Quarter, in the streets around the Picasso Museum, and in the parts of the old town near the waterfront. Avoid those sections at night or travel them by taxi. Muggings, increasingly violent, are reportedly on the upswing. New lighting on side streets is intended to alleviate the problem, but urban caution is still in order.

Telephone The **country code** for Spain is **34.** The **city code** for Barcelona is **93.** To make an **international call,** dial **07,** wait for the tone, and dial the country code, the area code, and the number. Note that an international call from a public phone booth requires stacks of coins. As an alternative, purchase a **phone card** from a tobacco shop *(estanco),* the post office, or another authorized dealer.

Where to Stay

CIUTAT VELLA (OLD CITY)

Very Expensive

Le Meridien Barcelona ★★★ This is the finest hotel in the old town, thanks in large part to a major refurbishment. A fave with CEOs and celebs—Madonna stayed here—it's far superior in both amenities and comfort to any competitor in the old town. It's a genteel retreat in the middle of the area's action. Have a cocktail in the calming piano bar after a long day of sightseeing. Rooms are spacious and comfortable, with double-glazed windows, extra-large beds, and bathrooms with heated floors.

Las Ramblas 111, 08002 Barcelona. ✆ **800/543-4300** in the U.S., or 93-318-62-00. Fax 93-301-77-76. www.meridienbarcelona.com. 233 units. 253€–395€ double; 480€–2,100€ suite. AE, DC, MC, V. Parking 37€. Metro: Liceu or Plaça de Catalunya. **Amenities:** Restaurant; bar; babysitting; concierge; room service; Wi-Fi (free, in lobby). *In room:* A/C, TV, hair dryer, minibar.

Neri ★★★ This worthy hotel in the Gothic barrio is a real charmer—a hidden gem buried deep within a labyrinth of streets. Lying at the Plaça Felip Neri close to the cathedral, the palace housing the Neri dates from the 17th century. It's a romantic and fashionable address. Stone floors and walls set off crystal chandeliers and velvet couches, a contrast in textures. The plush bedrooms are inviting, with silk draperies, rough-stone bathroom walls, rustic wooden tables, shot-silk pillowcases, and throw rugs. A rooftop garden is rich with jasmine and creepers. The on-site restaurant serves a savory Catalan cuisine, including delights such as loin of venison with chopped figs and pomegranates.

Sant Sever 5, Barri Gòtic, 08002 Barcelona. ✆ **93-304-06-55.** Fax 93-304-03-37. www.hotelneri.com. 22 units. 195€–360€ double; 235€–395€ junior suite. AE, DC, MC, V. Public parking nearby 25€. Metro: Jaume or Liceu. **Amenities:** Restaurant; airport transfer (65€); babysitting; concierge; room service. *In room:* A/C, TV/DVD, CD player, hair dryer, minibar, Wi-Fi (free).

Expensive

Grand Hotel Central ★★ This hip hotel in the heart of El Born was created out of a 1920s office building. Boasting one of the most helpful staffs in Barcelona, it offers as a special feature a small rooftop terrace with a plunge pool. The bedrooms are a bit Zen, with limed oak furniture and taupe-painted walls. The rooms have a sophisticated color scheme of tobacco, chocolate, and pewter. The location is between the Santa Caterina market and the 13th-century cathedral. Opt for one of the sixth-floor doubles that don't face traffic-clogged Via Laietana.

Vía Laietana 30, 08003 Barcelona. ✆ **93-295-79-00.** Fax 93-268-12-15. www.grandhotelcentral.com. 147 units. 165€–290€ double; 208€–765€ suite. AE, MC, V. Parking 30€. Metro: Barceloneta. **Amenities:** Restaurant; bar; airport transfers (90€); babysitting; concierge; exercise room; rooftop heated pool; room service; Wi-Fi (14€ per 24 hr., in lobby). *In room:* A/C, TV/DVD, CD player, hair dryer, minibar.

Moderate

Colón ★★ This immensely popular hotel is blessed with one of the most dramatic locations in Barcelona, opposite the cathedral. Inside you'll find conservative and slightly old-fashioned public areas and a helpful staff. Rooms are filled with cushy furniture and (despite continuing renovations) an appealingly dowdy kind of charm. Though lacking views, those in back are quieter, especially when celebrations and rock concerts take place in front of the cathedral. Sixth-floor rooms have terraces overlooking the square, and are the most desirable and hardest to reserve. Some lower rooms are dark.

Av. de la Catedral 7, 08002 Barcelona. ✆ **93-301-14-04.** Fax 93-317-29-15. www.hotelcolon.es. 145 units. 110€–245€ double; from 245€–280€ suite. AE, DC, MC, V. Metro: Catalunya or Jaume I. **Amenities:** Restaurant; bar; babysitting; concierge; room service; Wi-Fi (11€ per day). *In room:* A/C, TV/DVD, hair dryer, minibar.

Duques de Bergara ★ Here, guests can enjoy a striking 1898 mansion that underwent an expansion to triple the number of rooms. Some *modernista* details have been retained, including the magnificent carved wood and marble entry, although most everything else is sleekly contemporary. The halls were constructed to allow for relatively spacious rooms, many of which have separate seating and desk areas. The desk staff is multilingual.

Bergara 11, 08002 Barcelona. ✆ **93-301-51-51.** Fax 93-317-34-42. www.hoteles-catalonia.com. 151 units. 109€–245€ double; 146€–295€ triple. AE, DC, MC, V. Public parking nearby 40€. Metro: Plaça de Catalunya. **Amenities:** Restaurant; bar; babysitting; concierge; outdoor heated pool; room service. *In room:* A/C, TV, hair dryer, minibar, Wi-Fi (free).

Inexpensive

Hotel España Although the rooms at this cost-conscious hotel have none of the architectural grandeur of Barcelona's modernist age, they're well scrubbed, comfortably sized, and outfitted with functional furniture. The building itself is a relic of the city's turn-of-the-20th-century splendor, as it was constructed in 1902 by fabled architect Domènech i Montaner, designer and architect of the Palau de la Música. It was once patronized by the likes of Salvador Dalí. There's an elevator for the building's four floors, a facade that still evokes the past, and a hardworking staff that's comfortable with non-Spanish-speaking visitors.

Carrer Sant Pau 9, 08001 Barcelona. ✆ **93-318-17-58.** Fax 93-317-11-34. www.hotelespanya.com. 80 units. 110€ double; 135€ triple. AE, DC, MC, V. No parking. Metro: Liceu. **Amenities:** 3 restaurants; public computer w/Internet (3€ per 30 min., in lobby). *In room:* A/C, TV, hair dryer.

EIXAMPLE

Very Expensive

Claris ★★ An 1882 aristocratic residence was converted into one of only two officially designated *gran lujo* (grand luxury) hotels in the city center. The hotel opened in 1992, in time for the Olympics, and has a small pool and garden on its roof, as well as a gallery of Egyptian antiquities on its second floor. Rooms with clean-lined contemporary furnishings incorporate pieces of ancient Egyptian art, both real and copies, and all the high-end electronic accessories you could wish for.

Carrer de Pau Claris 150, 08009 Barcelona. ✆ **800/888-4747** in the U.S., or 93-487-62-62. Fax 93-215-79-70. www.hotelclaris.es. 124 units. 170€–481€ double; 280€–1,210€ suite. AE, DC, MC, V. Parking 25€. Metro: Passeig de Gràcia. **Amenities:** 2 restaurants; 2 bars; babysitting; concierge; exercise room; outdoor heated pool; room service; sauna. *In room:* A/C, TV, hair dryer, minibar, Wi-Fi (17€ per day).

Expensive

Cram ★ 🎁 Don't judge this hotel by its name. A hip crowd of guests, most of whom are in their 30s and 40s, seek out this hot address, with its textured red-leather walls, glossy black surfaces, and whimsical touches like UFO-shaped chairs. This gem is housed in a restored and architecturally beautiful building from the 19th century. The team of architects respected the facade but turned the interior into a modern palace of convenience and comfort. The bedrooms are high quality with mirrored walls, amber-wood floors, and sophisticated color schemes such as mustard yellow and saffron. The location is good, too, right in the center of Barcelona, just 4 blocks from the Passeig de Gràcia.

Aribau 54, 08011 Barcelona. ✆ **93-216-77-00.** Fax 93-216-77-07. www.hotelcram.com. 67 units. 143€–278€ double; 200€–430€ executive and privilege units; 286€–515€ suite. Rates include buffet breakfast. AE, MC, V. Parking 15€. Metro: Universitat. **Amenities:** Restaurant; bar; concierge; outdoor pool; room service; spa. *In room:* A/C, TV/DVD, movie library, hair dryer, Wi-Fi (free).

Pulitzer ★★ 🎁 With its high-concept modern design, attractive guest rooms, and immensely welcoming sense of comfort, this fashionable boutique hotel is our favorite hotel in an area that is too often marred by stark commercial lodging. Pulitzer, located right off the heartbeat Plaça Catalunya, boasts a rooftop bar that opens onto panoramic views of Las Ramblas and the Gothic Quarter. The bedrooms are decorated in tones of charcoal gray, squid-ink black, and stark white, and some of them are a bit cramped. But even the humblest abode here has a bit of flair, with leather, silk, and glamorous fabrics.

Bergata 8, 08002 Barcelona. ✆ **93-481-67-67.** Fax 93-481-64-64. www.hotelpulitzer.es. 91 units. 109€–250€ standard double; 139€–275€ superior double. AE, DC, MC, V. Parking 25€. Metro: Plaça de Catalunya. **Amenities:** Restaurant; bar; airport transfers (80€); babysitting; concierge; exercise room; access to nearby health club & spa; room service. *In room:* A/C, TV, hair dryer, minibar, Wi-Fi (free).

Moderate

Axel ★ You don't have to be young and gay to check in here, but it certainly helps. Cutting-edge architectural designs and a liberal, cosmopolitan atmosphere prevail at this chic bastion of comfort and charm. *outTraveler* magazine awarded it "Best Hotel" in 2005, and that award-winning standard of hospitality still prevails today. Hotel-savvy travelers, and not just gay ones, view Axel as a cherished, unique address. You might meet Mr. Right at the rooftop pool and sun deck, or perhaps in the hip cocktail bar or lobby restaurant. The designers of the hotel weren't afraid to use splashes of scarlet against a mellow background of whites and neutrals. Bedrooms are midsize and soundproof, with king-size beds.

Aribau 33, 08011 Barcelona. ✆ **93-323-93-93.** Fax 93-323-93-94. www.axelhotels.com. 66 units. 96€–234€ double; 115€–269€ superior double; 261€–353€ suite. AE, DC, MC, V. Parking 20€. Metro: Universitat. **Amenities:** Restaurant; 2 bars; exercise room; Jacuzzi; outdoor heated pool; room service; sauna. *In room:* A/C, TV, hair dryer, Wi-Fi (6€).

Inexpensive

Astoria Another property from the growing Derby chain, the 1954 Astoria has a between-the-wars facade that makes it appear older than it is. The high ceilings, geometric designs, and brass-studded detailings in the gracious public areas hint of Moorish Andalusia. Rooms are soundproof and feature the warmth of exposed cedar as well as elegant modern accessories.

París 203, 08036 Barcelona. ✆ **93-209-83-11.** Fax 93-202-30-08. www.derbyhotels.es. 117 units. 90€–140€ double; 215€–265€ suite. AE, DC, MC, V. Nearby parking 25€. Metro: Diagonal. **Amenities:** Restaurant; bar; exercise room; outdoor pool; room service; sauna. *In room:* A/C, TV, hair dryer, minibar, Wi-Fi (free).

Fashion House B&B ★ B&B is not a typical concept for staying in Barcelona, but this boutique hotel may be a trendsetter. The gay-friendly house is situated in the heart of the Eixample, a few minutes' walk from La Pedrera and only 3 blocks off Plaça Catalunya. In a restored 19th-century building, Fashion House has been converted to receive and house guests in comfort. Decorated with stucco and friezes, the B&B evokes a homelike aura. Bedrooms are attractively furnished, each cheerily decorated with pastels, and the finest units open onto little verandas.

Bruc 13 Principal, 08010 Barcelona. ✆ **63-790-40-44.** Fax 93-165-15-60. www.bcn-fashionhouse.com. 8 units. 55€–102€ double; 75€–122€ triple; 95€–140€ suite. MC, V. Parking 25€. Metro: Urquinaona. *In room:* A/C, TV (in suite only), kitchenette (in suite only).

NORTH DIAGONAL

Expensive

Gallery Hotel ★★ Perched at the top of the Passeig de Gràcia, this superstylish, ultramodern hotel is a perfect base for attacking the shops of both the Eixample and Gràcia. The spare, spacious rooms have an almost Asian feel to them, with furnishings in red and black, firm beds, and big bathtubs. Service is impeccable.

Calle Rosello 249, 08008 Barcelona. ✆ **93-415-99-11.** Fax 93-415-91-84. www.galleryhotel.com. 115 units. 165€–280€ double; 251€–406€ suite. AE, DC, MC, V. Parking 25€. Metro: Diagonal. **Amenities:** Restaurant; bar; babysitting; exercise room; room service; sauna. *In room:* A/C, TV, fax, hair dryer, minibar, Wi-Fi (free).

VILA OLIMPICA

Very Expensive

Hotel Arts ★★★ This deluxe hotel is the only lodging in Barcelona that gives the Palace serious competition. The hotel occupies part of a postmodern tower marked by a huge Frank Gehry sculpture of a fish above the terrace facing the sea. The location is about 2.5km (1½ miles) east of Barcelona's historic core, adjacent to the sea and the Olympic Port. The decor is contemporary and elegant, and both the public and private areas are filled with contemporary art. Views from the rooms sweep the skyline and the Mediterranean. The multinozzle showers are a truly uplifting experience.

Carrer de la Marina 19–21, 08005 Barcelona. ✆ **800/241-3333** in the U.S., or 93-221-10-00. Fax 93-221-10-70. www.ritzcarlton.com. 483 units. 221€–605€ double; 370€–2,600€ suite. AE, DC, MC, V. Parking 35€. Metro: Ciutadella–Vila Olímpica. **Amenities:** 5 restaurants; 2 bars; children's programs; concierge; exercise room; outdoor heated pool; room service; spa. *In room:* A/C, TV, hair dryer, minibar, Wi-Fi (free).

MOLL DE BARCELONA

Expensive

Eurostar Grand Marina Hotel ★★ No, it's not New York's iconic Guggenheim Museum, although its circular, upside-down wedding-cake design evokes that famous building. Next to Barcelona's World Trade Center, the hotel naturally attracts businesspeople, bankers, and conventioneers, although it's equally suitable as a holiday hotel. It lies at the end of a long pier that juts into the Barcelona harbor. Some of the most panoramic views of water and cityscape can be seen from the hotel's windows. The eight-floor hotel offers spacious, well-furnished guest rooms, with private terraces in some units.

Moll de Barcelona s/n, 08039 Barcelona. ✆ **93-603-90-00.** Fax 93-603-90-90. www.grandmarinahotel.com. 278 units. 150€–280€ double; 240€–350€ junior suite; from 290€ suite. AE, DC, MC, V. Parking 25€. Metro: Drassanes. **Amenities:** Restaurant; bar; babysitting; concierge; exercise room; Jacuzzi; small outdoor heated pool; room service; sauna; Wi-Fi (free, in lobby). *In room:* A/C, TV, hair dryer, minibar.

Moderate

Hotel 54 ★ In the increasingly fashionable fishing quarter of Barceloneta, this boutique hotel has been installed in an old building of the Association of Fishermen, offering panoramic views of the harbor and skyline. It stands in front of Port Vell, close to Playa San Sebastián and within an easy walk of Las Ramblas. After a major restoration, the hotel is elegantly modern. There are such trendy decorative touches as neon mood lighting and green-glass sinks in the bathrooms. Bedrooms have a lighting system allowing you to "personalize" your choice of color.

Passeig Joan de Borbó 54, 08003 Barcelona. ✆ **93-225-00-54.** Fax 93-225-00-80. www.hotel54barceloneta.com. 28 units. 135€–150€ double. MC, V. Nearby parking 20€. Metro: Barceloneta. **Amenities:** Bar; room service. *In room:* A/C, TV, hair dryer, minibar, Wi-Fi (free).

Where to Dine

CIUTAT VELLA (OLD CITY)

Expensive

Casa Leopoldo ★ 🎁 SEAFOOD This surprisingly sophisticated restaurant in the somewhat seedy Barri Xinés has thrived since 1929. It offers some of the freshest seafood in town, and caters to a loyal clientele. Pictographic tiles and bullfighting paraphernalia constitute much of the traditional decor. There's a thriving tapas bar in front, plus two dining rooms, one slightly more formal than the other. Specialties include stuffed oxtail, roast *merluza* (hake) and *rape* (monkfish) with a *sofrito* of garlic and shrimp, and baby eels boiled in oil—a pricey delicacy. An enduring specialty is the enormous platter of fish and shellfish, prepared only for two.

Sant Rafael 24 (near Carrer de la Riereta). ✆ **93-441-30-14.** www.casaleopoldo.com. Reservations recommended. Main courses 45€–70€; tasting menu 50€ dinner. AE, DC, MC, V. Tues–Sat 1:30–4pm and 9–11pm; Sun 1:30–4pm. Closed Aug 4–Sept 4. Metro: Liceu.

Espai Sucre ★★ DESSERTS Espai Sucre (literally, "Sugar Space") is Barcelona's most unusual dining room, with a minimalist decor and seating for 30. For the dessert lover, it is like entering a heaven created by the sugar fairy. The desserts here are original creations. "Salad" is likely to be small cubes of spicy milk pudding resting on matchsticks of green apple with baby arugula leaves, peppery caramel, dabs of lime kefir and lemon curd, and toffee. A tiny phyllo pyramid, no bigger than a pencil eraser, conceals a filling of lemon and rosemary marmalade. Ever had a soup of litchi, celery, apple, and eucalyptus? If some of the concoctions frighten your palate, you'll find comfort in the more familiar—vanilla cream with coffee sorbet and caramelized banana. Every dessert comes with a recommendation for the appropriate wine to accompany it.

Princesa 53. ✆ **93-268-16-30.** www.espaisucre.com. Reservations required. Tasting menus 45€–50€; 3-dessert platter 30€; 5-dessert platter 40€. DC, MC, V. Tues–Thurs 9–11:30pm; Fri–Sat 8:30–11:30pm. Closed Dec 24 to 1st week of Jan. Metro: Arco de Triompho or Jaume I.

Moderate

Comerç 24 ★ CATALAN/ASIAN/ITALIAN View a dining visit here as an opportunity to experience the culinary vision of a rare aesthete and artist. The chef and owner is Carles Abellan, who has given his imaginative, distinctive interpretation to all the longtime favorite dishes of Catalonia. With his avant-garde and minimalist design, he offers a soothing backdrop for his cuisine. The restaurant lies close to the waterfront along Barceloneta, the Parc de la Ciutadella, and the old Gothic barrio. The chef uses fresh seasonal ingredients, balanced sauces, and bold but never outrageous combinations, and he believes in split-second timing. Perhaps you'll sample his fresh salmon "perfumed" with vanilla and served with yogurt. Other vibrant, earthy dishes include a veal entrecôte with wasabi sauce or ravioli with cuttlefish and fresh morels.

Carrer Comerç 24, La Ribera. ✆ **93-319-21-02.** www.comerc24.com. Reservations required. Main courses 12€–36€; tasting menu 62€. MC, V. Tues–Sat 1:30–3:30pm and 8:30–11:30pm. Closed 10 days in Aug and 10 days in Dec. Metro: Arco de Triompho or Estación de Francia.

Els Quatre Gats CATALAN This has been a Barcelona legend since 1897. The "Four Cats" (in Catalán slang, "just a few people") was a favorite of Picasso, Rusiñol, and other artists, who once hung their works on its walls. On a narrow cobblestone street in the Barri Gòtic near the cathedral, the *fin de siècle* cafe was the setting for piano concerts by Isaac Albéniz and Ernie Granados, and murals by Ramón Casas. It was a base for members of the modernismo movement and figured in the city's intellectual and bohemian life.

Today the restored bar is a popular meeting place. The fixed-price meal is one of the better bargains in town, considering the locale. The unpretentious Catalán cooking here is called *cucina de mercat* (based on whatever looks fresh at the market). The constantly changing menu reflects the seasons.

Montsió 3. ✆ **93-302-41-40.** www.4gats.com. Reservations required Sat–Sun. Main courses 12€–20€; fixed-price menu (Mon–Fri) 13€. AE, DC, MC, V. Daily 10am–1am. Metro: Plaça de Catalunya.

Quo Vadis ★ SPANISH/CATALAN/CONTINENTAL Elegant and impeccable, this is one of the finest restaurants in Barcelona. In a century-old building near the open stalls of the Boqueria food market, it was established in 1948 and has been a discreet but thriving business ever since. The three paneled dining rooms exude conservative charm. Culinary creations include roast suckling pig, fried gooseliver with prunes, filet of *toro* (bull) with wine sauce, and a variety of grilled or flambéed fish. There's a wide choice of desserts made with seasonal fruit imported from all over Spain.

Carme 7. ✆ **93-302-40-72.** www.restaurantquovadis.com. Reservations recommended. Main courses 21€-35€. AE, MC, V. Mon-Sat 1:15-4pm and 8:30-11:30pm. Metro: Liceu or Plaça de Catalunya.

Inexpensive

Café de L'Academia ★ CATALAN/MEDITERRANEAN In the center of Barri Gòtic a short walk from Plaça Sant Jaume, this 15-table (20–25 in summer) restaurant looks expensive but is really one of the most affordable as well as the best in the medieval city. The building dates from the 15th century, but the restaurant was founded in 1987. At a small bar you can peruse the menu and study the wines. Dishes of this quality usually cost three times as much in Barcelona. The chef is proud of his "kitchen of the market," suggesting that only the freshest ingredients from the day's shopping are featured. Try such delights as *lassanye de butifarra i ceps* (lasagna with Catalán sausage and flap mushrooms), or *bacalla gratinado i musselina de carofes* (salt cod gratinée with an artichoke mousse).

Carrer Lledó 1 (Barri Gòtic), Plaça Sant Just. ✆ **93-319-82-53.** Reservations required. Main courses 10€-18€; fixed-price menu (lunch only) 14€. AE, MC, V. Mon-Fri 1:30-5pm and 8:30pm-1am. Closed last 2 weeks Aug. Metro: Jaume I.

Cuines Santa Caterina ★ ASIAN/MEDITERRANEAN/ITALIAN In the Santa Caterina market, this soaring space with an open kitchen has a tapas bar. With its different types of kitchens, ranging from Asia to Italy, this fusion cuisine is served against a backdrop that includes columns of light; ficus trees planted in between tables; and one wall composed of shelves stacked with wine, olive oil, and various vinegars. The food comes directly from the market, so it's very fresh. Many dishes are suitable for vegetarians, especially those fresh green asparagus emerging from the grill or the delicious salads made, say, of melted cheese, nuts, and dates. The sushi tastes fresh and is prepared in the best tradition of Japan.

Mercado de Santa Caterina, Avinguda Francesc Cambó 17, La Ribera. ✆ **93-319-82-53.** www.cuines-santacaterina.com. Reservations not required. Main courses 8€-22€. MC, V. Daily 1-4pm and 8-11:30pm. Metro: Jaume I.

Garduña CATALAN This is the most famous restaurant in Barcelona's covered food market, La Boquería. Battered, somewhat ramshackle, and a bit claustrophobic, it's fashionable with an artistic set that might have been designated as bohemian in an earlier era. It's near the back of the market, so you'll pass endless rows of fresh produce, cheese, and meats before you reach it. You can dine downstairs near a crowded bar, or a bit more formally upstairs. Food is ultrafresh—the chefs certainly don't have to travel far for the ingredients. You might try "hors d'oeuvres of the sea," cannelloni Rossini, or grilled hake with herbs.

Jerusalén 18. ✆ **93-302-43-23.** Reservations recommended. Main courses 13€-30€; fixed-price lunch 15€; fixed-price dinner 22€. AE, DC, MC, V. Mon-Sat noon-5pm and 8pm-midnight. Metro: Liceu.

Los Caracoles CATALAN "The Snails" was founded back in 1835 in the heart of the Gothic Quarter near the Rambles, and the tantalizing aroma of roasting chicken still wafts through this seedy street after all these years. Even though Los Caracoles hasn't been acclaimed the best restaurant in Barcelona since the time of the American Civil War, it remains a bastion of local culture and a favorite of old-time locals. The food on the menu at this old favorite—which was featured in the inaugural edition of *Spain on $5 a Day* and recommended for many years—has never been altered.

Escudellers 14. ✆ **93-301-20-41.** www.loscaracoles.es. Reservations recommended. Main courses 8€–30€. AE, DC, MC, V. Daily 1:15pm–midnight. Metro: Drassanes.

Pla de la Garsa ★ MEDITERRANEAN/CATALAN In Barrio Ribera close to the cathedral, this historic building is fully renovated but retains some 19th-century fittings. The restaurant boasts one of the city's best wine lists, and features a daily array of traditional Catalán and Mediterranean favorites. Begin with one of the pâtés, especially the goose, or a confit of duck thighs. You can also order meat and fish pâtés. One surprise is a terrine with black olives and anchovies.

Assaonadors 13. ✆ **93-315-24-13.** Reservations recommended for weekends. Main courses 7€–16€; fixed-price menu 25€. AE, MC, V. Daily 8pm–1am. Metro: Jaume I.

DIAGONAL & ABOVE

Very Expensive

Botafumeiro ★★ SEAFOOD Widely regarded as Barcelona's best seafood restaurant, this is where the king of Spain comes for his fish. The menu is stacked with dozens of preparations of fish, mussels, clams, lobster, scallops, and other sea life. Whether grilled, fried, or served in paella, the fish is always fresh and often heartbreakingly simple, showcasing the beauty of Galician seafood. The *Mariscos Botafumeiro* specialty is a grand parade of all the shellfish owner Moncho Neira can get his hands on. Don't come here if you intend to eat anything other than fish, though a few meat dishes do lurk at the edges of the menu. White-jacketed waiters, always snapping to attention, make you feel like royalty. If the prices here are too high, Neira owns several other restaurants in town; grilled seafood is the specialty at **Moncho's Barcelona,** Travessera de Gràcia 44–46 (✆ **93-414-66-22**).

Gran de Gràcia 81. ✆ **93-218-42-30.** www.botafumeiro.es. Reservations recommended. Main courses 26€–60€. AE, DC, MC, V. Daily 1pm–1am. Metro: Fontana.

Drolma ★★★ FRENCH/SPANISH The setting here meets the high expectations fostered by the glowing reviews this trendsetter has garnered since the day it opened. A squad of scrupulously trained male and female servers tends to your needs. They'll wheel over a cart of wines and offer any of them as an aperitif. Following that, they bring not one but two *aperitivos*—Spanish for *amuse-bouche*—an airy little dumpling, maybe, or a shot glass of crabmeat in basil oil. That's only a hint of what's to come. There's the salad with four quail eggs and four chunks of grilled foie gras, the potato soup with mushrooms and slivered truffles, the glazed goat, the lamb—some dishes even come with second helpings. The restaurant has a faint aura of corporate calm, but the bravura display of skill and largesse is not soon forgotten by serious diners.

In the Hotel Majestic, Passeig de Gràcia 68. ✆ **93-496-77-10.** www.drolmarestaurant.cat. Reservations required. Main courses 42€. AE, DC, MC, V. Mon–Sat 1–3:30pm and 8:30–11pm. Closed in Aug at lunch. Metro: Passeig de Gràcia.

Moderate

Cata 181 ★★ 🎁 CATALAN/TAPAS All dishes here are tapas size, and how innovative they seem until you learn that many of the recipes are based on time-tested favorites from Grandmother Catalonia's cupboard. Take the pig trotters with walnuts and fresh figs, accompanied by a scoop of honey ice cream. Sweetened pig's-foot flan in some variation has been served in Catalonia for centuries. Another startling but flavor-filled dish is squid stuffed with minced pork and served with an almond-flavored chocolate sauce. A savory rice dish is served with fresh asparagus and black truffles, and ravioli come stuffed with codfish and minced smoked ham. A Catalán favorite, cannelloni, is presented in a truffle-studded béchamel sauce.

Calle Valencia 181. ✆ **93-323-68-18.** www.cata181.com. Reservations required. Tasting menu 34€ for 9 dishes, 45€ for 11 dishes; tapas 8€–11€. AE, DC, MC, V. Sun–Fri 1pm–midnight; Sat 8pm–12:30am. Closed 3 weeks in Aug. Metro: Passeig de Gràcia or Hospital Clínic.

Gresca ★★ 🎁 CATALAN/INTERNATIONAL This small restaurant, a real discovery, is the creation of Chef Rafael Peña, who finely tuned his culinary skills under Ferran Adrià, hailed as the world's greatest chef. In this modern setting, a chic crowd of foodies is lured to taste the offerings of this highly talented and imaginative chef. Food-smart Catalán s can be seen ordering some of the more experimental dishes—fresh calves' liver with plantains and licorice, for example. The octopus carpaccio was a surefire winner, and so was the black butifarra (a regional sausage popular in Catalonia). Here it's served with fried potatoes.

Carrer Provenza 230. ✆ **93-451-61-93.** Reservations required. Main courses 15€–30€; fixed-price menu 45€. MC, V. Daily 1:30–3:30pm; Mon–Sat 8:30–11pm. Metro: Catalunya or Hospital Clinic.

L'Olive ★ CATALAN/MEDITERRANEAN You assume that this two-floor restaurant is named for the olive that figures so prominently into its cuisine, but actually it's named for the owner, Josep Olive. The building is designed in modern Catalán style. The tables are topped in marble, the floors impeccably polished. There are sections on both floors where it's possible to have some privacy, and overall the feeling is one of elegance with a touch of intimacy. You won't be disappointed by anything on the menu, especially *bacalla llauna* (raw salt cod) or *filet de vedella al vi negre al forn* (baked veal filets in a red-wine sauce), and *salsa maigret* of duck with strawberry sauce.

Calle Balmes 47 (corner of Concéjo de Ciento). ✆ **93-452-19-90.** www.rte-olive.com. Reservations recommended. Main courses 15€–29€. AE, DC, MC, V. Daily 1–4pm; Mon–Sat 8:30pm–midnight. Metro: Passeig de Gràcia.

LA RIBERA & BARCELONETA

Expensive

Can Costa ★ SEAFOOD This is one of the oldest seafood restaurants in this seafaring town. Established in the late 1930s, it has two busy dining rooms, a practiced staff, and an outdoor terrace, although a warehouse blocks the view of the harbor. Fresh seafood prepared according to traditional recipes rules the menu. It includes the best baby squid in town—sautéed in a flash so that it has a nearly grilled flavor, almost never overcooked or rubbery. A long-standing chef's specialty is *fideuá de peix,* a relative of the classic Valencian shellfish paella, with noodles instead of rice. Desserts are made fresh daily.

Passeig Don Joan de Borbò 70. ✆ **93-221-59-03.** www.cancosta.com. Reservations recommended. Main courses 11€–41€. MC, V. Daily 12:30–4:30pm; Thurs–Tues 8–11:30pm. Metro: Barceloneta.

7 Portes ★ CATALAN In business since 1836, these "Seven Doors" open into a food emporium that is a lunchtime favorite for businesspeople (the Stock Exchange is across the way) and an evening favorite for anyone who enjoys the peachy glow of the hanging lamps and the ministrations of the piano player. Known for its paellas, changed daily, there are also regional dishes that include grilled rabbit, fresh herring with onions and potatoes, a wide selection of superfresh fish and oysters, and an herb-laden stew of black beans with pork. Portions are enormous.

Passeig Isabel II 14. ✆ **93-319-30-33.** www.7portes.com. Reservations required weekends. Main courses 16€–30€. AE, DC, MC, V. Daily 1pm–1am. Metro: Barceloneta.

Moderate

Cal Pep ★ SPANISH This fine little tapas bar just south of the Picasso Museum is popular with both locals and visitors. There are 20 seats at the long marble bar and a tiny sit-down back room. While you'll probably get a seat if you arrive at 1:30pm during the week, expect a wait after 2pm and on weekends. (If it *is* full, there are two other cafes on the same square.) There's no menu—the manager will tell you what's available and use his lapel mic to relay your order to the kitchen when it gets busy. What comes forth from the kitchen doesn't stray far from the traditional repertoire, but it's so much better prepared. This is the way *pescados fritos* (fried fish), *almejas con jamón* (steamed clams with ham), and *pan con tomate* (Catalán tomato bread) should taste.

Plaça de les Olles 8. ✆ **93-310-79-61.** www.calpep.com. Reservations required for dining room. Main courses 15€–28€. AE, DC, MC, V. Tues–Sat 1:15–4pm and 8–11:30pm; Mon 8–11:30pm. Closed Aug. Metro: Jaume I.

Seeing the Sights

Spain's second-largest city is also its most cosmopolitan. Barcelona is more European and internationalist than Madrid. The city is filled with landmark buildings and world-class museums, including Antoni Gaudí's Sagrada Família, Museu Picasso, the Gothic cathedral, and La Rambla, the famous tree-lined promenade cutting through the heart of the old city from Plaça de Catalunya to the harbor.

THE TOP ATTRACTIONS

Catedral de Barcelona (La Seu) ★★★ Begun in the late 13th century and completed in the mid–15th century (except for the main facade, which dates from the late 19th c.), this Gothic cathedral attests to the splendor of medieval Barcelona. Its main points of interest are the central choir, the 14th-century alabaster crypt of Santa Eulàlia, and the *Cristo de Lepanto,* whose twisted torso allegedly dodged a bullet during the naval battle of the same name. Do see the adjoining **cloister ★**, with access down on the right from the front entrance. It encloses palm and magnolia trees, flowering medlars, a fountain erupting from a moss-covered rock, and a gaggle of live geese, said to be reminders of the Roman occupation (or of the Apostles or the virtuous St. Eulàlia, depending on the various convictions of writers and guides). On the steps at noon on Sunday, a band with ancient instruments plays the eerily haunting *sardana,* the music of the hallowed Catalán folk dance.

Plaça de la Seu. ✆ **93-315-15-54.** www.catedralbcn.org. Cathedral free admission. Global ticket to museum, choir, rooftop terraces, and towers 5€. Cathedral daily 8am–12:45pm and 5:15–7:30pm. Museum Mon–Sat 10am–12:45pm and 5–6:45pm; Sun 10am–1:15pm and 5–6:45pm. Metro: Jaume I. Bus: 17, 19, 40, or 45.

Fundació Joan Miró ★★ A tribute to the Catalán lyrical surrealist Joan Miró, this contemporary museum follows his work from 1914 to 1978 and includes many of his sculptures, paintings, and multimedia tapestries. Even the roof displays his whimsical sculptures as well as bestows impressive city vistas. There's also a gallery of "Miró's contemporaries"—"minor" artists like Henry Moore. Temporary exhibits of other contemporary artists are held on a regular basis. From the top of the Montjuïc funicular, turn left and walk down to the museum.

Parc de Montjuïc. ✆ **93-443-94-70.** www.bcn.fjmiro.es. Admission 8€ adults, 6€ students, free for children 14 and under. July–Sept Tues–Sat 10am–8pm (Thurs to 9:30pm), Sun and holidays 10am–2:30pm; Oct–June Tues–Sat 10am–7pm, Sun and holidays 10am–2:30pm. Funicular: Montjuïc. Bus: 50 or 55 from Plaça de Espanya.

La Sagrada Família ★★ If you see but one monument in Barcelona, make it this one. Looking like something halfway between a fever dream and a giant sand castle, this *modernista* cathedral will be Europe's largest, with a 158m (518-ft.) central dome—*if* it's ever finished. In 1884, architect Antoni Gaudí i Cornet took over the then-2-year-old project and turned it into the ultimate statement of his flamboyant, surrealist vision. At the pinnacles of the completed towers, for example, are vivid mosaic sunbursts of gold and crimson, and much of the east facade appears to have melted under the blast of a giant blowtorch. Unfortunately, Gaudí died in 1926 after being run over by a tram and he left no detailed plans. Construction has continued off and on, with different additions reflecting different eras, sometimes quite dissonantly (such as the aggressively cubist sculptures on the west facade). As art critic Robert Hughes has written, Gaudí "is not someone with whom one can collaborate posthumously." One of the towers has an elevator that takes you up to a magnificent view. The crypt's **Museu del Temple** chronicles the cathedral's structural evolution.

Mallorca 401. ✆ **93-207-30-31.** www.sagradafamilia.org. Admission 11€. Elevator 3€. Apr–Sept daily 9am–8pm; Oct–Mar daily 9am–6pm. Metro: Sagrada Família. Bus: 19, 33, 34, 43, 44, 50, or 51.

Museu Picasso ★★★ Barcelona's most popular single attraction, this museum reveals much about the artist whose long, prolific career extended well beyond cubism. The paintings, drawings, engravings, and ceramics go all the way back to the artist's juvenilia, but the museum is light on his most famous later paintings—except for the series based on Velázquez' *Las Meninas,* on display here. The galleries in the original three Renaissance mansions have been expanded into two more adjoining palaces.

Montcada 15–19. ✆ **93-256-30-00.** www.museupicasso.bcn.es. Admission to permanent exhibits 9€ adults, 6€ students and ages 16–25, free for children 15 and under. Tues–Sun 10am–8pm. Metro: Jaume I (line 4).

MORE ATTRACTIONS

Casa Batlló As part of the 2002 citywide celebration of Gaudí, this, the architect's second-most-important commission on the Passeig de Gràcia, was opened to public visits for the first time. Unlike La Pedrera (see below), Gaudí didn't design this building from the ground up. Instead, he transformed an existing structure with a facade of shimmering tiles and a free-form roofline that evokes the scaly back of a dragon. The interior is just as striking. Inquire ahead to be certain it is still open.

Passeig de Gràcia 43 (corner of Aragó). ✆ **93-216-03-06.** www.casabatllo.es. Admission 16€ adults, 13€ children 5–16 and students, free for children 4 and under. Daily 9am–8pm. Metro: Passeig de Gràcia.

La Pedrera ★★ Formally the Casa Milà, the popular name of this apartment/office block means the "Stone Quarry." Antoni Gaudí didn't restrain himself here: The undulating exterior of carved stone gives the building the aspect of the lair of a mythical dragon, its balconies enclosed by free-form wrought iron. The top floor and an apartment are open to visitors. Don't miss the roof terrace, populated with highly sculptural chimneys and vents that might have been imagined by H. G. Wells.

Provença 261–265 (at the corner of Passeig de Gràcia). ✆ **93/484-59-00.** Admission to attic, terrace, and apartment. 9.30€ adults, 6€ seniors and students, free for children 11 and under. Daily 10am–8pm; guided tours daily at 4pm. Metro: Diagonal.

L'Aquàrium ★ ☺ This carefully conceived aquarium is one of the largest in Europe. It exhibits more than 8,000 marine creatures of 450 species in 21 tanks. A highlight is the clear tunnel where you glide on a moving walkway through a tank stocked with prowling sharks and gliding rays. The admission fee is shockingly high.

Port Vell, on the Moll d'Espanya, in the harbor. ✆ **93-221-74-74.** www.aquariumbcn.com. Admission 17.50€ adults, 14.80€ seniors, 12.50€ children 4–12, free for children 3 and under. July–Aug daily 9:30am–11pm; June and Sept daily 9:30am–9:30pm; Oct–May daily 9:30am–9pm. Metro: Drassanes or Barceloneta. Bus: 14, 17, 19, 36, 38, 40, 45, 57, 59, 64, 91, or 100.

Poble Espanyol ★ ☺ This "village," executed for the 1929 World's Fair, houses examples of architectural styles found throughout Spain. After renovations and changes in operational philosophy, the once-stuffy open-air museum has become almost a village in its own right, with working artisans, dozens of crafts shops, restaurants, and assorted nightclubs and bars. Some visitors judge it a slightly kitschy theme park, but, in fact, the buildings are accurate full-size replicas of specific structures in the various regional styles of Spain. Nightclubs, discos, and restaurants take over in the evening; most stay open well into the early hours.

Marqués de Comillas, Montjuïc. ✆ **93-508-63-30.** www.poble-espanyol.com. Admission 8.90€ adults, 6.50€ seniors and students, 5.50€ children 4–12, free for children 3 and under, 20€ family ticket. Mar–Oct Mon 9am–8pm, Tues–Thurs 9am–2am, Fri–Sat 9am–4pm, Sun 9am–midnight; Nov–Feb Mon–Thurs 9am–8pm, Fri–Sun 9am–4pm. Metro: Plaça de Espanya, and then bus 61 or the free double-decker Poble Espanyol shuttle bus (on the half-hour).

MORE MUSEUMS

Fundació Antoni Tàpies ★ Housed in a *modernista* building designed by Lluís Domènech i Muntaner and refurbished by his great-grandson in 1989, this museum continues the Barcelona tradition of honoring prominent native artists. Tàpies is thought by many to be the living heir to Miró and Picasso, and this exhibit space rotates examples of his work and that of younger Catalán artists. The tangle of tubing atop the building is a Tàpies sculpture called *Chair and Cloud*—it makes more sense if you keep the title in mind as you look at it.

Aragó 255. ✆ **93-487-03-15.** www.fundaciotapies.org. Admission 6€ adults, 4€ seniors and students, free for children 15 and under. Tues–Sun 10am–8pm. Metro: Passeig de Gràcia.

Museu Barbier-Mueller ★ Dedicated by Queen Sofia in 1997, this collection highlights 6,000 pieces of pre-Columbian sculpture. It contains religious, funerary, and ornamental objects of considerable variety, in stone and ceramics and, in some cases, jade. Richest are the exhibits relating to Mayan culture, originating in 1000 B.C. Descriptions are in English.

Montcada 12-14. © **93-310-45-16.** www.barbier-mueller.ch. Admission 3€ adults, 1.50€ seniors and students, free for children 15 and under. Tues-Sat 10am-6pm; Sun and holidays 10am-3pm. Metro: Jaume I. Bus: 17, 39, 40, 45, or 51.

Museu d'Art Contemporàni (MACBA) ★ Much excitement attended the 1995 opening of this light-filled building by American architect Richard Meier. Standing in stark contrast to the 16th-century convent opposite and the surrounding tenements with laundry drying on their balconies, this museum generated a renewal of the El Raval neighborhood. The permanent collection comprises about 1,300 paintings and sculptures from the late 1940s, including works by many Catalán and Spanish artists and a few by non-Spaniards such as Calder and Dubuffet. To get here, walk 5 blocks west from the upper Rambla along Carrer Bonsucces, which changes to Elisabets.

Plaça de les Angels 1. © **93-412-08-10.** www.macba.es. General admission 3€ adults, 2€ students, free for children 13 and under. Mon-Fri 11am-7:30pm; Sat 10am-8pm; Sun and holidays 10am-3pm. Metro: Catalunya or Universitat.

Museu d'Historia de la Ciutat (Museum of the History of the City) ★ Housed in a 15th-century mansion that was moved here stone by stone from Carrer Mercaders, several blocks away, this museum features **excavations ★** of Roman and Visigothic remains below ground. On the upper floors are jumbled assortments of sculptures, weapons, ceramics, household implements, and more—a sort of municipal attic.

Plaça del Rei. © **93-315-11-11.** www.museuhistoria.bcn.es. Admission 6€ adults, free for children 16 and under. Free to all 1st Sat afternoon of the month. June-Sept Tues-Sat 10am-8pm, Sun and holidays 10am-3pm (the rest of the year closes 2-4pm). Metro: Jaume I.

Museu Frederic Marés ★★ This repository of medieval sculpture is located just behind the cathedral, with a pleasant shaded courtyard in front. Housed in an ancient palace that's impressive in its own right, it displays hundreds of polychrome ecclesiastical sculptures.

Plaça de Santa Iú 5-6. © **93-256-35-00.** www.museumares.bcn.es. Admission 4.20€ adults, 2.40€ students, free for children 15 and under, free for all 1st Sun of the month. Tues-Sat 10am-7pm; Sun 10am-3pm. Metro: Jaume I. Bus: 17, 19, or 45.

Museu Marítim (Maritime Museum) ★ Located in the Drassanes, the 14th-century Gothic royal shipyards, this museum's superb collection of maritime vessels and artifacts is distinguished by a full-size replica of Don Juan of Austria's galleon. The baroque flagship of the Spanish and Italian fleet defeated a naval force of the

An Ancient Neighborhood to Explore

The **Barri Gótic ★★** is Barcelona's old aristocratic quarter, parts of which have survived from the Middle Ages, and fragments of which have lasted from Roman times. To explore the Gothic Quarter's narrow streets and squares, start walking up Carrer del Carme, east of La Rambla. The buildings, for the most part, are austere and sober, and the cathedral is the crowning achievement. Roman ruins and the vestiges of 3rd-century walls add further interest. This area is packed full of details and attractions that are easy to miss, so take your time. A nighttime stroll adds drama, but exercise caution.

Ottoman Empire in the 1571 Battle of Lepanto. There are also humbler fishing boats, intricate ship models, and a map owned by Amerigo Vespucci.

Av. de les Drassanes 1. ✆ **93-342-99-20.** www.diba.es/mmaritim. Admission 6.50€ adults, 5.20€ ages 11–25 and seniors, 3.25€ children 6–10. Free for all 1st Sat of the month 3–6pm. Daily 10am–8pm. Metro: Drassanes.

Museu Nacional d'Art de Catalunya (MNAC) ★★★ In this building—built for the 1929 World's Fair and redesigned inside by controversial Italian architect Gae Aulenti in the 1990s—is a collection of Catalán art from the Romanesque and Gothic periods as well as the 16th century to the 18th century, along with works by high-caliber non-Catalán artists like El Greco, Velázquez, Zurbarán, and Tintoretto. Pride of place goes to the sculptures and frescoes removed from the Romanesque churches strung across Catalunya's northern tier. The view of the city from the front steps is a bonus.

In the Palau Nacional, Parc de Montjuïc. ✆ **93-622-03-76.** www.mnac.es. Admission to permanent collection 8.50€ adults, 6€ ages 15–20, free for children 14 and under. Tues–Sat 10am–7pm; Sun and holidays 10am–2:30pm. Metro: Espanya.

PARKS & GARDENS

Parc Güell ★, a fanciful park on the northern edge of Barcelona's inner core, is much more than green space. Begun by Antoni Gaudí as an upper-crust real-estate venture for his wealthy patron, Count Eusebi Güell, it was never completed. Only two houses were constructed, but Gaudí's whimsical creativity, seen in soaring columns that impersonate trees and splendid winding benches of broken mosaics, is on abundant display. The city took over the property in 1926 and turned it into a public park. Don't miss the ceramic mosaic lizard at the park's entrance stairway, the Hall of a Hundred Columns, and the panoramic views from the plaza above.

Parc de la Ciutadella ★ occupies the former site of a detested 18th-century citadel, some remnants of which remain. Here, you'll find the Museu d'Art Modern, the Museu de Zoología, the Museu de Geología, the regional Parliament, the zoo, and an ornate fountain that's in small part the work of the young Gaudí.

Another attraction, **Tibidabo ★**, offers the best panoramic view of Barcelona. A funicular takes you up 490m (1,600 ft.) to the summit. A retro amusement park—with Ferris wheels and airplanes that spin over Barcelona—has been there since the '30s. There's also a church in this carnival-like setting called Santa Creu (Sacred Heart), plus bars and restaurants. Take the funicular uphill from Plaça John Kennedy.

ORGANIZED TOURS

Pullmantur, Gran Vía de les Corts Catalanes 645 (✆ **93-317-47-08;** www.pullmanturcruises.com; Metro: Plaça de Catalunya), offers a number of tours and excursions with English-speaking guides. For a preview of the city, you can take a morning tour. They depart daily from the company's terminal at 9:30am and take in the cathedral, the Gothic Quarter, the monument to Columbus, the Spanish Village, and the Olympic Stadium. Tickets cost 60€. A daily afternoon tour leaves at 3:30pm and visits some of the most outstanding architecture in the Eixample, including Gaudí's La Sagrada Família. The tour includes Parc Güell and a stop at the Picasso Museum. The cost is 60€.

Pullmantur also offers several excursions outside Barcelona. The daily tour of the monastery of Montserrat includes a visit to the Royal Basilica to view the famous sculpture of the Black Virgin. This tour, which costs 74€, departs at 9:30am and returns at 2:30pm to the company's terminal. A full-day Girona-Figueres tour includes a visit to Girona's cathedral and its Jewish Quarter, plus a trip to the Dalí museum. This excursion, which costs 153€, leaves Barcelona at 8:30am and returns at approximately 6:30pm (June–Sept Tues and Thurs). Call ahead—a minimum number of participants is required.

The Shopping Scene

THE BEST SHOPPING STREETS

Barcelona's most beautiful shopping street is **Passeig de Gràcia.** Stroll this street from the Avinguda Diagonal (also called Avenida Diagonal) to the Plaça de Catalunya, and you'll pass some of Barcelona's most elegant boutiques. You'll also find interesting shops nearby in the Eixample on Avinguda Diagonal and Carrer de Balmes, and farther north in Gràcia on the Travessera de Gràcia and Carrer Verdi.

In the **old quarter,** the principal shopping streets are La Rambla, Carrer del Pi, Carrer de la Palla, and Avinguda Portal de l'Angel. Moving north in the Eixample are Passeig de Catalunya, Passeig de Gràcia, and Rambla de Catalunya.

THE BEST BUYS

El Corte Inglés ★ is Spain's most prominent department store. Its main Barcelona emporium is at Plaça de Catalunya 14 (✆ **93-306-38-00;** www.elcorteingles.es; Metro: Catalunya), with a large branch a block away on Portal de l'Angel. It stays open through the siesta period and has a full-size supermarket in the basement and a cafeteria/restaurant on the ninth floor. Up in the Eixample, the **Centre Comercial Barcelona Glòries,** Av. Diagonal 208 (✆ **93-486-04-04;** www.lesglories.com; Metro: Glories), is a three-story emporium, the largest shopping center in the heart of Barcelona. It's based on the California model with more than 100 shops, some posh, others much less so.

For designer housewares and the best in Spanish contemporary furnishings, a good bet is **Vincón ★★**, Passeig de Gràcia 96 (✆ **93-215-60-50;** www.vincon.com), housed in the former home of artist Ramón Casas. Various high-end shops on the Passeig de Gràcia and Avinguda Diagonal showcase men's and women's fashions. You'll find cutting-edge boutiques (and few tourists) on **Carrer Verdí** in the Gràcia neighborhood, from the Plaça Revolució stretching about 6 blocks north and onto side streets. Pick up a shopping map from any of the Verdi boutiques.

In the city of Miró, Tàpies, and Picasso, art is a major business. There are dozens of galleries, especially in the Barri Gótic and around the Picasso Museum. In business since 1840, **Sala Parés ★★**, Petritxol 5 (www.salapares.com; Metro: Plaça de Catalunya), displays paintings in a two-story amphitheater; exhibitions change about once a month. At **Art Picasso,** Tapinería (✆ **93-268-32-40;** Metro: Jaume I), you can purchase good lithographic reproductions of the works of not only Picasso but Miró and Dalí as well.

For antiques, drop by **El Bulevard des Antiquarius ★★**, Passeig de Gràcia 55 (✆ **93-215-44-99;** Metro: Passeig de Gràcia). This 70-unit complex, just off the city's most aristocratic avenues, has a huge collection of art and antiques assembled in a series of boutiques. Seekers after antiques should enjoy the open-air **Mercat Gòtic de Antigüedades** by the cathedral (Metro: Jaume I), held every Thursday 9am to 8pm (except Aug), and more often during holiday periods.

Seeking out small specialty shops is a particular treat. A number of shops offer authentic ceramics from various regions of the country that are known for their pottery. One worthwhile stop is **Itaca,** Carrer Ferrán (✆ **93-301-30-44;** Metro: Jaume I), near Plaça Sant Jaume.

La Manual Alpargatera, Carrer Avinyó 7 (✆ **93-301-01-72;** www.lamanual.net; Metro: Jaume I), is the best shop for the handmade espadrilles seen on dancers of the sardana. It offers many styles and also sells hats and folk art.

Angel Jobal, Princesa 38 (✆ **93-319-78-02;** Metro: Jaume I), offers a variety of teas and spices, along with especially good prices on thread saffron, the world's costliest spice. Find it a block past the turn for the Picasso Museum. **La Boquería,** La Rambla 91–101 (✆ **93-318-25-84;** www.boqueria.info), officially the Mercat de Sant Josep, is Spain's most extensive, most fascinating market, purveying glistening-fresh produce, meats, cheeses, fish, and every imaginable edible daily. An open market of artisan food items, including cheeses, honey, vinegars, pâtés, fruit preserves, and quince pastes, is held on **Plaça del Pi** (Metro: Liceu) on Friday, Saturday, and Sunday.

Barcelona After Dark

Barcelona's nightlife runs from the campy burlesque of El Molino to the bizarre opulence of the Palau de la Música Catalana. For the latest information on concerts and other musical events, call the **Amics de la Música de Barcelona** at ✆ **93-302-68-70,** Monday to Friday from 10am to 1pm and 3 to 8pm.

For a comprehensive list of evening activities, pick up a copy of the weekly ***Guía del Ocio*** or the entertainment guide offered with the Thursday edition of ***El País.***

THE PERFORMING ARTS

The **Gran Teatre del Liceu ★★★**, La Rambla 51–54 (✆ **93-485-99-13;** www.liceubarcelona.com; Metro: Liceu), is the traditional home to opera and ballet. It suffered a devastating fire in 1994 but has reopened after extensive renovations. The result is glorious, especially considering that only the walls were left standing after the fire. The decision was made to replicate the neobaroque interior, with lashings of gilt, intricate carvings, and swaths of brocade and velvet. Music lovers and balletgoers will find more comfortable seats and better sightlines. The theater presents 8 to 12 operas every season and strives to make them accessible to a wide audience. You can book tickets with credit cards from outside the country daily 10am to 10pm Barcelona time at ✆ **93-274-64-11.** In Barcelona, call ✆ **90/253-33-53** any time up to 3 hours before the performance desired.

A magnificent *modernista* concert hall, the **Palau de la Música Catalana ★★★**, Sant Francese de Paulo 2 (✆ **93-295-72-00;** www.palaumusica.org; Metro: Urquinaona), is the work of Catalán architect Lluís Domènech i Montaner, a rival of Antoni Gaudí. Its distinctive facade is a tour de force of brick, mosaic, and glass. Inside, the interplay of ceramic mosaics, stained glass, and a central skylight build to the stunning crescendo of massive carvings framing the stage. Many of the seats have limited sightlines, but this hall is devoted to music, not opera and dance, and even the cheapest corners enjoy superb sound. The Palau is home to the Orquestra Simfònica de Barcelona, one of whose directors is American Lawrence Foster, and hosts a variety of classical and jazz concerts and recitals. The box office is open Monday to Saturday 10am to 9pm.

Symphonic and chamber music is presented at **L'Auditori ★★**, Lepant 150 (✆ **93-247-93-00;** www.auditori.org; Metro: Glòries), with both large and small performance spaces. The Barcelona Symphony Orchestra, traveling groups, the Joven Orquestra de España (Young Orchestra of Spain), and string quartets all perform here.

LIVE-MUSIC CLUBS

The most popular jazz club, **Jamboree ★★**, Plaça Reial 17 (✆ **93-319-17-89;** www.masimas.com; Metro: Liceu), is on a raucously diverse plaza off the lower Rambla. The cover charge can be anywhere from 10€ to 12€, depending on who's playing; you descend to a vaulted brick cellar filled with young to middle-aged natives and visitors. Most shows start at 11pm. Arrive around 9:30pm and you'll probably get in free and might also catch the rehearsal.

A popular old-timer is the **Harlem Jazz Club ★**, Comtessa de Sobradiel 8 (✆ **93-310-07-55**), with live jazz nightly in all its permutations—flamenco fusion, Brazilian salsa, Afro-Caribbean, blues. Admission is free during the week, but costs 8€ on Friday, Saturday, and holidays.

For the best Latino and jazz on weekends, head for **Luz de Gas,** Carrer de Muntaner 246 (✆ **93-209-77-11;** www.luzdegas.com; Metro: Diagonal), which has cabaret on other nights. The lower two levels open onto a stage floor and stage. Call to see what the lineup is on any given night—jazz, pop, soul, rhythm and blues, whatever. Open daily from 11pm until 4 or 5am. Cover 15€.

Flamenco is best seen in Seville or Madrid, but if you aren't getting to those cities on your trip, **El Tablao de Carmen ★**, Arcs 9 in Poble Espanyol (✆ **93-325-68-95;** www.tablaodecarmen.com), is the best place in Barcelona to see the passionate dance and music of Andalusia. Admission is 69€ to 94€ for dinner and the first show, or 35€ for the first show and a drink. Dinner begins at 9pm; the first show is at 9:30pm, the second at 11:55pm. Closed Monday.

DANCE CLUBS

La Paloma, Tigre 27 (✆ **93-301-68-97;** Metro: Universitat), is a retreat for those with a sense of nostalgia—remember the fox trot? The mambo? Live orchestras provide the music in this old-time dance hall, the most famous in Barcelona. Cover is 8€.

Mojito Club, Carrrer Rossellón 217 (✆ **93-237-65-28;** www.mojitobcn.com), rocks with a Latin beat, as its name suggests. An international crowd keeps the place festive; cover is 10€.

Razzmatazz, Carrer Pamplona 88 (✆ **93-272-09-10;** Metro: Bogatell), lies in a converted warehouse, five clubs in one. Each club within the club presents its own music. One entrance fee, ranging from 12€ to 15€, includes admission to each club.

It's almost impossible to miss ads for multilevel superclub **Otto Zutz ★★**, Lincoln 15 (✆ **93-238-07-22;** www.ottozutz.com; Metro: Plaça Molina). Go early to avoid the restrictive entrance policy, or pick up one of the little cards at shops around town that give you "guaranteed" entry. There are eight bars, there's dancing everywhere, and there's live rock on Wednesday night. The club is open Tuesday to Saturday midnight to 5am or later, with a 15€ cover that includes a drink.

BARS & COCTELERIAS

Over in **Poble Nou,** near the Parc de la Ciutadella, the two skyscrapers marking the location of the former Olympic Port also point the way to the site of a frenetic bar scene. The artificial harbor that was the launch point for the Olympic sailing competition is now lined on three sides with more than *200* bars and cafes that pound on until dawn. This is one of the safest nightlife districts.

Betty Ford, Carrer de Joaquin Costa 56 (✆ **93-304-13-68;** Metro: Universitat), named for the former U.S. First Lady, has a simple but elegant decor. You get the feeling you're entering a sophisticated cocktail lounge with risqué conversation. Try the mojitos, the bartender's special.

Established in 1933, **Cocktail Bar Boadas,** Tallers 1 (✆ **93-318-88-26;** Metro: Placa de Catalunya), lies near the top of Las Ramblas. The bar stocks a wide range of Caribbean rums, Russian vodkas, and English gins.

GAY & LESBIAN BARS

Gays have a number of beguiling bars and dance clubs to choose from, but lesbians have relatively few. For the latest on the scene, log on to **www.gaybarcelona.net**. It's in Spanish, but it's not too difficult to decipher. Ads and listings in such weekly guides as ***Guía del Ocio*** referring to *el ambiente* nearly always mean places with a mostly or totally gay clientele.

Metro, Sepulveda 185 (✆ **93-323-52-27;** www.metrodiscobcn.com; Metro: Universitat), still reigns as one of the most popular gay discos, attracting everyone from startlingly thin male models to beefy macho men. There are two dance floors playing everything from Spanish pop to contemporary house. The gay press called the backroom "a notorious, lascivious labyrinth of lust." Cover is 10€.

Going strong since the dawn of the millennium, **Salvation,** Ronda de Sant Pere 19–21 (✆ **93-318-06-86;** Metro: Urquinaona), also remains a leading gay dance club. The waiters are the hottest hunks in town. The 13€-to-15€ cover includes the first drink.

Women should check in at **Aire-Sala Diana,** Valencia 236 (✆ **93-451-58-12;** www.arenadisco.com; Metro: Passeig de Gràcia), the hub of the city's lesbian scene. Patrons and staff can offer advice on what else is happening in town. You'll find a large dance floor and bustling bar packed with Barcelona hotties.

Day Trips from Barcelona

SITGES ★

The most frequented resort of the Costa Dorada, Sitges is packed in summer, mostly with affluent young northern Europeans, many of them gay. For years, the resort, 40km (25 miles) south of Barcelona, was patronized largely by middle-class industrialists from Barcelona, but those rather staid days have gone. Sitges is as lively today as Benidorm and Torremolinos in the south, but it's nowhere near as tacky. By mid-October it goes into hibernation, but its scenic charms and museums may be motive enough for a winter visit. Things pick up with Carnaval in February, a riotously turbulent event with costumed revelers partying for days.

Long known as a city of culture, thanks in part to resident artist/playwright/bohemian mystic Santiago Rusinyol, this was the birthplace of the 19th-century *modernista* movement. The town remained a scene of artistic encounters and demonstrations long after *modernisme,* the Catalán form of Art Nouveau, waned. Salvador Dalí and the poet Federico García Lorca were regular visitors.

GETTING THERE RENFE's (✆ **90-224-02-02;** www.renfe.es) Line C2 commuter trains run from Barcelona-Sants or Passeig de Gràcia to Sitges. From 5:45am to 10pm daily, there's a train at the rate of one every 10 to 15 minutes (trip time:

40 min.). A one-way round-trip fare is 3.50€, with variations depending upon day of the week and other factors.

Sitges is a 45-minute drive from Barcelona along C-246, a coastal road. An express highway, A-7, is faster but less scenic.

VISITOR INFORMATION The **tourist information office** is at Carrer Sínia Morera 1 (✆ **93-894-50-04;** www.sitges.com). It's open June to September 15, daily 9am to 9pm; September 16 to May, Monday to Friday 9am to 2pm and 4 to 6:30pm, and Saturday 10am to 1pm.

EXPLORING SITGES The **beaches** attract most visitors. They have showers and changing facilities, and kiosks rent such items as motorboats and floating air cushions. Beaches on the eastern end and those inside the town center are the most peaceful, including **Aiguadoiç** and **Els Balomins. Playa San Sebastián, Fragata Beach,** and **"Beach of the Boats"** (under the church and next to the yacht club) are the area's family beaches. Most young people go to the **Playa de la Ribera,** in the west. The main gay beach is the **Playa del Mort.**

Beaches aside, Sitges has a couple of good museums. **Museu Cau Ferrat,** Fonollar 8 (✆ **93-894-03-64**), is the legacy of wealthy Catalán painter Santiago Rusinyol, a leading light of Belle Epoque Barcelona. His 19th-century house, fashioned of two 16th-century fishermen's homes, contains not only a collection of his works, but also several pieces by Picasso and El Greco, much ornate wrought iron (a Catalán specialty), folk art, and archaeological finds.

Next door is **Museu Maricel de Mar,** Fonollar s/n (✆ **93-894-67-02**), the legacy of Dr. Pérez Rosales, whose impressive accumulation of furniture, porcelain, and tapestries draws largely from the medieval, Renaissance, and baroque periods. Both museums are open Tuesday to Sunday between June 15 and September 30 from 10am to 2pm and 5 to 9pm. During the rest of the year, they're open Tuesday to Friday 10am to 1:30pm and 3 to 6:30pm, Saturday 10am to 7pm, and Sunday 10am to 3pm. Admission to each is 3.50€ adults, 1.75€ students, free for kids 11 and under.

MONTSERRAT ★

The vast **Montserrat Monastery** complex (www.abadiamontserrat.net), 52km (32 miles) northwest of Barcelona, contains a basilica with a venerated Black Virgin, an art museum, hotels, restaurants, and an excess of souvenir shops and food stalls. One of the most important pilgrimage spots in Spain, it's a good place to avoid on weekends.

The best and most exciting way to get to Montserrat is via the Catalan railway, **Ferrocarrils de la Generalitat de Catalunya** (Manresa line), with 12 trains a day leaving from the Plaça d'Espanya in Barcelona. The central office is at Plaça de Catalunya 1 (✆ **93-205-15-15;** www.fgc.es). The train connects with an aerial cableway (Aeri de Montserrat), which is included in the fare of 18€ round-trip.

The train, with its funicular tie-in, has taken over as the preferred means of transport. However, a long-distance **bus** service is provided by **Autocars Julià** in Barcelona. Daily service from Barcelona to Montserrat is generally available, with departures near the Estacio Central de Barcelona-Santa on Plaça de Països Catalanes. One bus makes the trip at 9:15am, returning at 5pm (6pm July–Aug); the round-trip ticket costs 12€. On Saturday and Sunday the round-trip fare is 13€. Contact Autocars Julià at Santa Eulàlia 236 (✆ **93-402-69-00;** www.autocaresjulia.es).

GETTING THERE Motorists can take N-2 southwest of Barcelona toward Tarragona, turning west at the junction with N-11. The signposts and exit to Montserrat will be on your right. From the main road, it's 14km (8⅔ miles) to the monastery through dramatic scenery with eerie rock formations.

VISITOR INFORMATION The **tourist office** is at Plaça de la Creu (✆ **93-877-77-01;** www.montserratvisita.com), open daily 8:50am to 7:30pm.

EXPLORING MONTSERRAT The monastery—a 19th-century structure that replaced a former monastery leveled by Napoleon's army in 1812—is 730m (2,400 ft.) up Montserrat. Its name, Montserrat, refers to the serrated peaks of the mountain, bulbous elongated formations that provided shelter for 11th-century Benedictine monks. One of the noted institutions of the monastery is the 50-voice **Escolanía ★★** or Boys' Choir, begun in the 13th century. The boys sing at 1 and 6:45pm. Their performances are thrilling to the faithful and curious alike and are the best reason for a visit. Admission is free.

The subterranean **Museu de Montserrat** (✆ **93-877-77-77**), near the entrance to the basilica, brings together artworks that were once scattered around the complex. You'll see gold and silver liturgical objects, archaeological artifacts from the Holy Land, and paintings from both the Renaissance and the 20th century. Numerous funiculars and paths lead to **hermitages** and **shrines** higher up the mountain.

Thousands travel here every year to see and touch the 12th-century statue of **La Moreneta (the Black Virgin) ★**, the patron saint of Catalunya at the Benedictine monastery of La Moreneta. To view the statue, enter the church through a side door to the right. The church is open Monday to Friday 9:30am to 6pm, Saturday and Sunday 9:30am to 6:30pm. Admission is 6.50€ adults, 5.50€ seniors, free for children 17 and under.

ANDALUSIA & THE COSTA DEL SOL

Andalusia is the Spain of legend, where Moorish princes held court and veiled maidens danced flamenco under fragrant orange trees. The eight provinces of Spain's southernmost region were held, at least in part, by Muslim rulers for 700 years before Ferdinand and Isabella united Spain in 1492. They left a rich heritage of architectural treasures, including Seville's Giralda, Córdoba's Mezquita, and the unforgettable Alhambra in Granada.

This is also the land of the famed *pueblos blancos* ("white villages") and undulating olive groves that roll over tawny hillsides to the skirts of impressive mountain ranges. Give Andalusia a week and you'll still have only skimmed the surface of its many offerings.

Andalusia also embraces the Costa del Sol (Sun Coast), Spain's most noted and visited—inundated—strip of beach resorts. (Málaga, Marbella, and Torremolinos are covered here.) Go to the Costa del Sol for golf, tennis, watersports, after-dark partying, and relaxation, but save some days for the folklore, history, and architectural wonders of the major Andalusian cities.

The mild winter climate and almost-guaranteed sunshine in summer have made the Costa del Sol a year-round attraction. It begins at the western frontier harbor city

Andalusia & the Costa del Sol

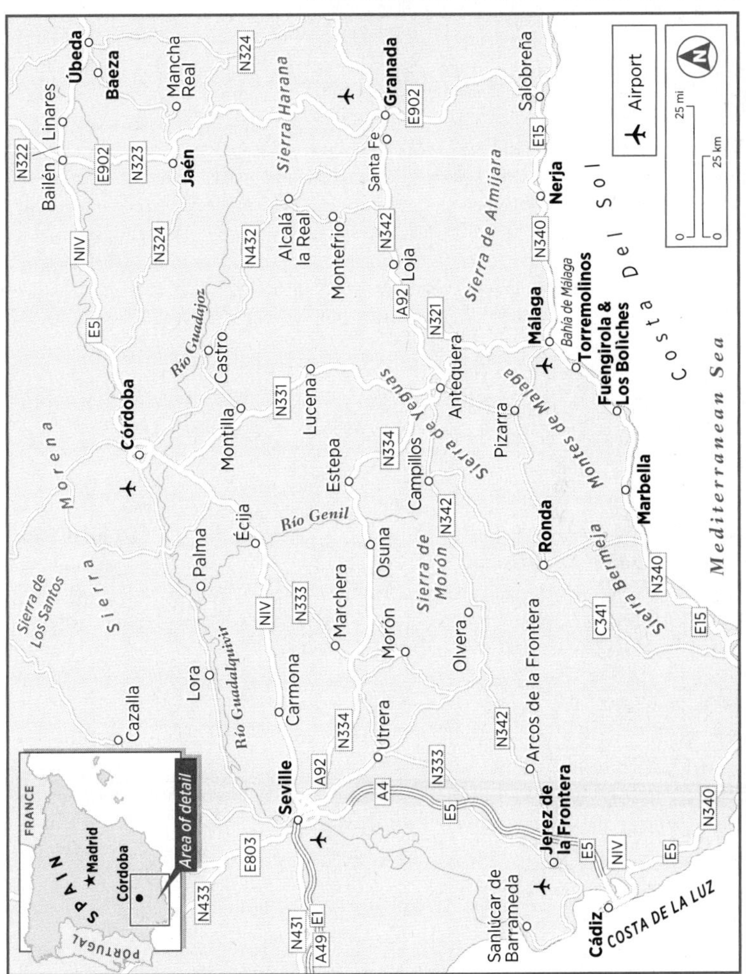

of Algeciras and stretches east to the port city of Almería. Sandwiched between these points is a rugged coastline backed by the Sierra Nevada. The beaches are no better than poor to fair, it should be said, but there are sandy coves, whitewashed houses, olive and almond trees, phalanxes of new apartment houses, fishing boats, a couple of dozen world-class golf courses, souvenir stands, fast-food outlets catering to the tastes of every national group, and widely varied flora and fauna—both human and vegetable. From June to October the coast is mobbed, so make sure that you've nailed down a reservation.

Seville ★★★

Seville, Andalusia's capital, is a city of operatic passion and romance. It is 550km (342 miles) southwest of Madrid and 217km (135 miles) northwest of Málaga. Mozart's Don Juan, Bizet's Carmen, and Rossini's Figaro all made their homes in the winding streets of Spain's third-largest city, and it's where Christopher Columbus landed and told his queen of a new world beyond the Atlantic. For decades after, the treasure galleons from the New World emptied their cargos here.

Unlike most Spanish cities, it has fared well under most of its conquerors—the Romans, Arabs, and Christians—in part because its people chose to embrace rather than fight them. Much of the pleasure of strolling Seville—as with all of Andalusia—isn't necessarily in visiting specific museums or sites, but rather in kicking back over a *very* long lunch and embracing the city's beauty on your own time and pace.

ESSENTIALS

Getting There

BY PLANE **Iberia** flies several times a day from Madrid and Barcelona to the **Aeropuerto San Pablo** (✆ **95-444-90-00;** www.aena.es), about 13km (8 miles) east of downtown on the Seville-Carmona road. A **taxi** (about 18€) is the easiest way into town, but the Route EA **bus** (✆ **90-221-03-17**) goes to Puerta de Jerez for only 3€ roughly on the hour daily 6:30am to 10:30pm.

BY TRAIN Train service into Seville is now centralized at the **Estación Santa Justa,** Avenida Kansas City (✆ **95-224-02-02;** www.renfe.es for information and reservations). Frequent buses marked CI connect the train station to the city center. The high-speed AVE train between Madrid and Seville charges 78€ each way, subject to frequent change and depending on class and the days and hours of travel (trip time: 2½ hr.). It makes up to 20 runs a day, with a stop in Córdoba. Between Seville and Córdoba, the AVE train takes 40 minutes, costing 29€.

BY BUS Buses from other Andalusian towns arrive and depart from the city's largest **bus terminal,** on the southeast edge of the old city, at Prado de San Sebastián, Calle José María Osborne 11 (✆ **95-441-71-18**). Long-distance lines pick up and discharge passengers at the **Plaza de Armas terminal** (✆ **95-490-80-40**) at the east end of the Chapina Bridge. Many lines also converge on Plaza de la Encarnación, on Plaza Nueva, in front of the cathedral on Avenida Constitución, and at Plaza de Armas (across the street from the old train station, Estación de Córdoba). From here, buses from several companies make frequent runs to and from Córdoba (trip time: 2½ hr.). One prominent bus company is **T. Alsina Graells Sur** (✆ **90-441-88-11**).

VISITOR INFORMATION The **Oficina de Información del Turismo,** at Av. de la Constitución 21B (✆ **95-478-75-78;** www.andalucia.org), is open Monday to Saturday 9am to 7pm and Sunday and holidays 10am to 2pm.

WHERE TO STAY

Seville hotels have three distinct pricing periods: lowest in winter, middling in summer, and highest during the adjacent celebratory weeks of Semana Santa (Holy Week) and the Fería de Abril (April Fair). During these last events, room rates are doubled or even tripled.

Seville

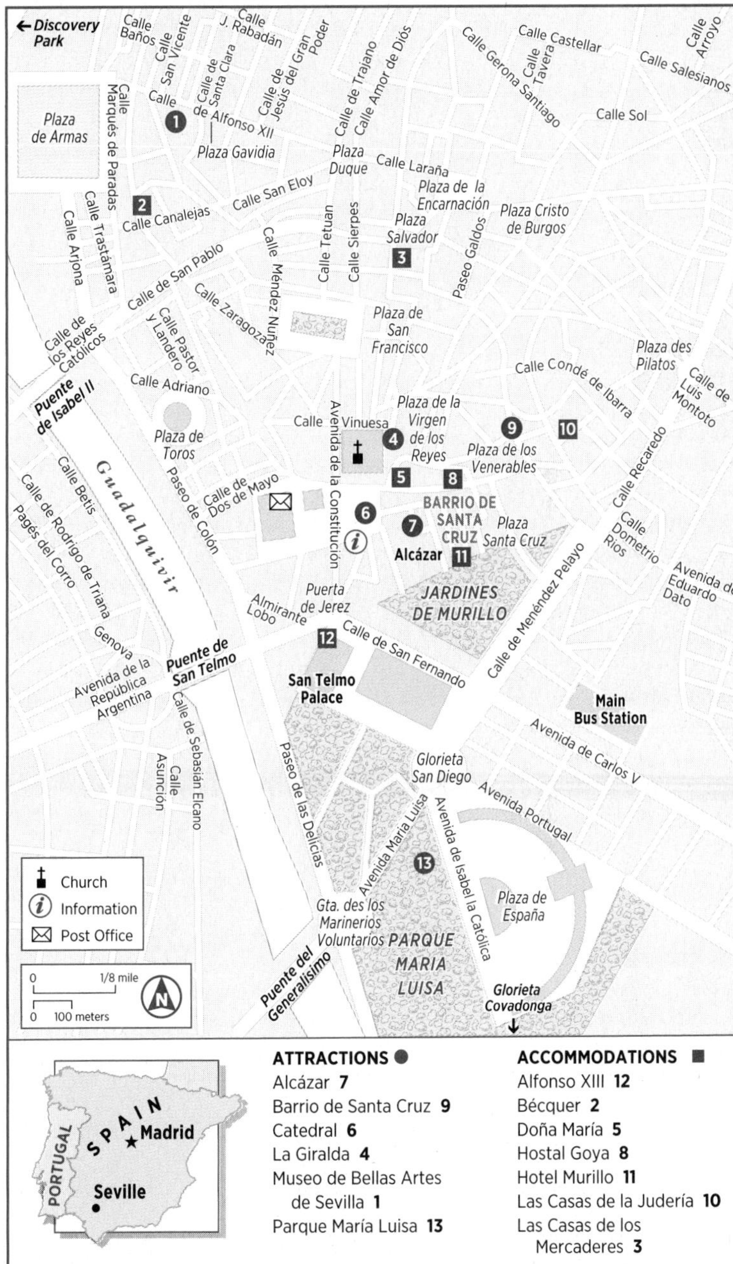

ATTRACTIONS ●

- Alcázar **7**
- Barrio de Santa Cruz **9**
- Catedral **6**
- La Giralda **4**
- Museo de Bellas Artes de Sevilla **1**
- Parque María Luisa **13**

ACCOMMODATIONS ■

- Alfonso XIII **12**
- Bécquer **2**
- Doña María **5**
- Hostal Goya **8**
- Hotel Murillo **11**
- Las Casas de la Judería **10**
- Las Casas de los Mercaderes **3**

Very Expensive

Alfonso XIII ★★★ At the southwestern corner of the gardens surrounding the Alcázar, this is a near-legendary hotel, Seville's *gran lujo* (grand luxury) address and one of Spain's most expensive lodgings. Run by the U.S. chain Starwood, it reigns supreme as a bastion of glamour and privilege, the site of royal receptions and corporate celebrations. The lobby fountain is the cocktail-hour rallying point for the local Establishment. Built in 1929, the building simulates a Mudéjar palace, its halls lined with lustrous hand-painted tiles, acres of marble and mahogany, and antique furniture embellished with intricately embossed leather. Even if you can't afford to stay here, splurge for a drink in the bar and feel like a head of state.

San Fernando 2, 41004 Sevilla. ✆ **800/221-23-40** in the U.S. and Canada, or 95-491-70-00. Fax 95-491-70-99. www.starwoodhotels.com. 147 units. 350€–650€ double; from 700€ suite. AE, DC, MC, V. Parking 17€. **Amenities:** 2 restaurants; 3 bars; airport transfers 75€; babysitting; concierge; exercise room; outdoor saltwater pool; room service; tennis court (lit). *In room:* A/C, TV, hair dryer, minibar, Wi-Fi (3€ per hour).

Moderate/Expensive

Bécquer A short walk from the action of the Seville bullring and only 2 blocks from the river, Bécquer is on a street full of cafes where you can order tapas and enjoy Andalusian wine. The Museo Provincial de Bellas Artes is also nearby. Built in the 1970s, the hotel was enlarged and much renovated since then. It occupies the site of a former mansion and retains many objets d'art rescued before that building was demolished. You are shown to one of the functionally furnished rooms—a good value in a pricey city, as most units are at the lower end of the price scale.

Calle Reyes Católicos 4, 41001 Seville. ✆ **95-422-89-00.** Fax 95-421-44-00. www.hotelbecquer.com. 141 units. 105€–210€ double; 250€–324€ suite. AE, DC, MC, V. Parking 15€. Bus: C1, C2, or C4. **Amenities:** Restaurant; 2 bars; babysitting; outdoor rooftop pool; room service; spa. *In room:* A/C, TV, hair dryer, minibar, Wi-Fi (free).

Doña María ★ Its location around the corner from the cathedral, Giralda, and the Alcázar creates a dramatic view from the rooftop terrace (where the postage-stamp-size pool is located). Originally built in 1969, this compact hotel has undergone needed upgrading. None of the rooms looks exactly like any other, but the decor favors elaborate headboards and some four-poster beds combined with provincial furniture and flowered patterns. Some units are rather small.

Don Remondo 19, 41004 Sevilla. ✆ **95-422-49-90.** Fax 95-421-95-46. www.hdmaria.com. 64 units. 96€–294€ double. AE, DC, MC, V. Parking 20€. **Amenities:** 2 bars; outdoor pool; room service. *In room:* A/C, TV, hair dryer, minibar, Wi-Fi (free).

Las Casas de la Judería ★★ Long on charm, short on modernity, this is Old Seville with a vengeance. Expect neither voice mail nor Internet connections. The hotel is constituted of a connected row of noble 16th-century residences, and the exteriors, up a cobblestone lane from a discreet archway, hint at Seville's Moorish past, as do the interior patios and splashing fountains. Some suites have saunas and whirlpools. The genteel staff, many of whom speak English, provides alert but understated attention. A restaurant has been added, and a piano is now played during the evenings in the lounge. Except during the holidays, you should be able to haggle a rate reduction.

Callejón de Dos Hermanas 7 (off Plaza Santa María la Blanca), 41004 Sevilla. ✆ **95-441-51-50.** Fax 95-442-21-70. www.casasypalacios.com. 118 units. 128€–265€ double; 360€–385€ junior suite. AE, DC, MC, V. Parking 15€. **Amenities:** Restaurant; bar; babysitting; concierge; outdoor pool; room service; Wi-Fi (free). *In room:* A/C, TV, hair dryer, minibar.

Las Casas de los Mercaderes ★ 🎁 Under the same ownership as Las Casas de la Judería (see above) and demonstrating a similar sensibility, this converted mansion has a far better location than its older sibling. It's right in the middle of things, with many of the best shops and department stores within 2 or 3 blocks and every major sight within walking distance. The grand lobby leads to an 18th-century inner court with a stained-glass skylight. Rooms are larger than usual, with carpeting, a small desk, and an easy chair or two.

Calle Alvarez Quintero 9–13 (1 block south of Plaza del Salvador), 41004 Sevilla. ✆ **95-422-58-58.** Fax 95-422-98-84. www.casasypalacios.com. 47 units. 91€–128€ double. AE, DC, MC, V. Parking 18€. **Amenities:** 2 bars; babysitting; room service. *In room:* A/C, TV, hair dryer, minibar.

Inexpensive

Hotel Goya Its location, in a narrow-fronted town house in the oldest part of the barrio, is one of the Goya's strongest virtues, but the building's gold-and-white facade, ornate iron railings, and picture-postcard demeanor are all noteworthy. The rooms are cozy and simple. Guests congregate in the marble-floored ground-level salon, where a skylight floods the couches and comfortable chairs with sunlight. No meals are served. Reserve well in advance. Parking is often available along the street.

Mateus Gago 31, 41004 Seville. ✆ **95-421-11-70.** Fax 95-456-29-88. www.hostalgoyasevilla.com. 19 units. 55€–95€ double. MC, V. Parking 15€ nearby. Bus: 10, 12, 41, or 42. *In room:* A/C, TV.

Hotel Murillo Tucked away on a narrow street in the heart of Santa Cruz, the Residencia Murillo (named after the artist who used to live in this district) is very close to the gardens of the Alcázar. Inside, the lounges harbor some fine architectural characteristics and antique reproductions. The guest rooms feature a modern, warm-toned Sevilian decor with hand-carved wooden furniture and marble floors. You can reach this *residencia* from the Menéndez y Pelayo, a wide avenue west of the Parque María Luisa, where a sign leads you through the **Murillo Gardens** on the left.

Calle Lope de Rueda 7–9, 41004 Seville. ✆ **95-421-60-95.** Fax 95-421-96-16. www.hotelmurillo.com. 57 units. 75€–100€ double; 93€–125€ triple. AE, DC, MC, V. Parking 15€ nearby. Bus: 21 or 23. **Amenities:** Wi-Fi (free). *In room:* A/C, TV, hair dryer.

WHERE TO DINE

Expensive

Egaña Oriza ★★★ BASQUE/INTERNATIONAL Seville's most stylish restaurant is within the conservatory of a restored mansion adjacent to the Murillo Gardens. Its reputation stems in large part from a game-heavy menu in a region otherwise devoted to seafood. The restaurant was opened by Basque-born owner/chef José Mari Egaña, who combines his passion for hunting with his flair for cooking. Many of the ingredients have been trapped or shot within Andalusia. Specialties depend on the season but might include ostrich carpaccio, casserole of wild boar with cherries and raisins, duck *quenelles* in a potato nest with apple purée, and woodcock flamed in Spanish brandy. The wine list provides an ample supply of hearty Spanish reds.

San Fernando 41. ✆ **95-422-72-11.** www.restauranteoriza.com. Reservations required. Main courses 22€–56€. AE, DC, MC, V. Mon–Fri 1:30–3:30pm and 8:30–11:30pm; Sat 8:30–11:30pm. Closed Aug. Bus: 21 or 23.

Enrique Becerra ★ ANDALUSIAN Off Plaza Nueva near the cathedral, this restaurant has flourished since 1979 and just might provide one of your best meals in Seville. A popular tapas bar occupies the front, with a daily menu of more than

25 possibilities, most of them notches above the usual renditions. The dining rooms upstairs and at the ground level are intimate settings made warmer by the friendly welcome. It's as good a place as any for your first taste of gazpacho and icy sangria. Specialties include roast lamb stuffed with spinach, honey, and pine nuts; rockfish cooked in Amontillado sherry; and oxtail braised in red wine. Many vegetarian dishes are also featured.

Gamazo 2 (2 blocks south of Plaza Nueva). ✆ **95-421-30-49.** Main courses 22€–38€; fixed-price menus 22€–38€. AE, DC, MC, V. Mon–Sat 1–5pm and 8pm–midnight.

Moderate

Barbiana ★★ ANDALUSIAN/SEAFOOD Close to the Plaza Nueva in the heart of Seville, this is one of the city's best fish restaurants. Chefs endeavor to secure the freshest seafood, even though Seville is inland. In the classic Andalusian architectural tradition, a tapas bar is up front. In the rear is a cluster of rustically decorated dining rooms. If you visit for lunch, you can try the chef's specialty, seafood with rice (not available in the evening). We've sampled many items on the menu, none better than *ortiguilla,* a sea anemone quick-fried in oil, and the *tortillitas de camarones,* chickpea fritters with bits of chopped shrimp and fresh scallions. If you're going to order shellfish, the specialty here, get it *a la plancha* (fresh from the grill).

Calle Albareda 11. ✆ **95-422-44-02.** www.restaurantebarbiana.com. Reservations recommended. Main courses 12€–21€. AE, DC, MC, V. Mon–Sat noon–5pm and 8pm–midnight; Sun 8pm–midnight. Bus: 21, 25, 30, or 40.

Taberna del Alabardero ★★ ANDALUSIAN One of Seville's most prestigious restaurants occupies a 19th-century town house 3 blocks from the cathedral. Famous as the dining choice of nearly every politician and diplomat who visits Seville, it has hosted the king and queen of Spain, and the Spanish president. Amid a collection of European antiques and oil paintings, you'll dine in any of two main rooms, and perhaps precede your meal with a drink or tapas on the flowering patio. Tantalizing menu items include spicy peppers stuffed with pulverized thigh of bull, Andalusian fish (*urta*) on a compote of aromatic tomatoes with coriander, cod filet with essence of red peppers, and Iberian beefsteak with foie gras and green peppers.

Calle Zaragoza 20, 41001 Seville. ✆ **95-450-27-21.** Reservations recommended. Main courses 20€–30€. AE, DC, MC, V. Daily 1–4pm and 8pm–midnight. Closed Aug. Bus: 21, 25, 30, or 43.

EXPLORING SEVILLE

Alcázar ★★★ This magnificent 14th-century Mudéjar palace was built by Pedro the Cruel after the reconquest of the city from the Moors. From the Dolls' Court to the Maidens' Court through the domed Ambassadors' Room, it contains some of the finest work of Sevillian artisans, most of them descendants of the former occupants of the palace. In many ways, it evokes the Alhambra at Granada. Isabel and Fernando, who at one time lived in the Alcázar, welcomed Columbus here on his return from America. On the top floor, the Oratory of the Catholic Monarchs has a fine altar in polychrome tiles made by Pisano in 1504.

Plaza del Triunfo. ✆ **95-450-23-23.** www.patronato-alcazarsevilla.es. Entrance is north of the cathedral. Admission 7.50€ adults; free for seniors, students, and children 12 and under. Apr–Sept Tues–Sat 9:30am–7pm, Sun 9:30am–1:30pm; Oct–Mar Tues–Sat 9:30am–5pm, Sun 9:30am–1:30pm.

Catedral ★★★ Alleged to be the largest Gothic building in the world, Seville's cathedral was designed by builders with a stated goal—that "those who come after us

SPLENDID strolls

What was once a ghetto for Spanish Jews, who were forced out of Spain in the 15th century in the wake of the Inquisition, the **Barrio de Santa Cruz ★★★** today is Seville's most colorful district. Near the old walls of the Alcázar, winding medieval streets with names like Vida (Life) and Muerte (Death) open onto pocket plazas. Balconies with draping bougainvillea and potted geraniums jut out over this labyrinth, and through numerous wrought-iron gates, you can glimpse tile-lined patios filled with fountains and plants. To enter the Barrio Santa Cruz, turn right after leaving the Patio de Banderas exit of the Alcázar. Turn right again at Plaza de la Alianza and go down Calle Rodrigo Caro to Plaza de Doña Elvira. Use caution when strolling through the area, particularly at night.

About a 7-minute walk northeast of the cathedral on the northern edge of the Barrio de Santa Cruz is the **Casa de Pilatos ★★**, Plaza Pilatos 1 (✆ **95-422-52-98**). This 16th-century palace of the dukes of Medinaceli recaptures the splendors of the past, combining Gothic, Mudéjar, and Plateresque styles in its courtyards, fountains, and salons. Don't miss the two old carriages or the rooms filled with Greek and Roman statues. Admission to the museum upstairs is 8€. The museum and gardens are open daily 9am to 6:30pm.

Parque María Luisa ★★, dedicated to María Luisa, sister of Isabel II, was once the grounds of the Palacio de San Telmo, Avenida de Roma. The former private royal park later became the site of the 1929 Ibero-Americana exposition, for which the vast Plaza de España was created. Running south along the Guadalquivir River, the park attracts those who want to take boat rides, walk along paths bordered by flowers, jog, or go bicycling. The most romantic way to traverse it is by rented horse and carriage, but this can be expensive, depending on your negotiation with the driver. Exercise caution while walking through this otherwise delightful park, as many muggings have been reported.

will take us for madmen." Construction began in the late 1400s and took centuries to complete. Built on the site of an ancient mosque, the cathedral claims to contain the remains of Columbus, with his tomb mounted on four statues. That claim is in doubt, but it's fairly certain his son Fernando is buried here. Works of art abound, most immediately evident in the side chapels, the 75 stained-glass windows, and the elaborate choir stalls, and also including paintings by Murillo, Goya, and Zurbarán. On the north side you'll find the fresh citrus scents and chirping birds of the Patio of Orange Trees, a relic of the original mosque, as is La Giralda (see below).

Plaza del Triunfo, Av. de la Constitución. ✆ **95-421-49-71.** www.catedraldesevilla.es. Admission including La Giralda 8€ adults, 2€ seniors and students 25 and under, free for children 12 and under. Free for all Sun. Mon–Sat 11am–5pm; Sun 2:30–6pm.

La Giralda ★★★ Just as Big Ben symbolizes London, La Giralda evokes Seville. This square-sided, 98m (322-ft.) bell tower, next to the cathedral, is the city's most famous monument. It began as a minaret for the mosque, progressing from the austere stonework of the fundamentalist Almohad Dynasty to the decorative brick patterns and pointed arches of their less rigid successors, and culminating in the florid

Renaissance-influenced upper floors added by the Catholic bishops. Determined visitors can take the 35 ramps inside up to a **viewing platform ★★★** at the 70m (230-ft.) level. Make it to the top and you'll have an unsurpassed vista of the city.

Plaza Virgen de los Reyes. Entrance through the cathedral (admission is included with cathedral).

Museo de Bellas Artes de Sevilla ★★ A lovely old convent off Calle de Alfonso XII, this museum houses an important Spanish art collection. Some art experts claim that after the two leading art museums of Madrid, this is the most valuable and significant repository of art in Spain. A whole gallery is devoted to two paintings by El Greco, and works by Zurbarán are also exhibited; however, the devoutly religious paintings of the Seville-born Murillo outnumber all the others. An entire wing is given over to macabre paintings by the 17th-century artist Valdés-Leál. The top floor, which displays modern paintings, is less interesting.

Plaza del Museo 9. ✆ **95-478-65-00.** www.museosdeandalucia.es. Admission 1.50€. Tues 2:30–8pm; Wed–Sat 9am–8pm; Sun 9am–2pm. Bus: C3 or C4.

SHOPPING

Seville's major shopping street is the pedestrianized **Calle Sierpes,** which runs from Plaza Magdalena Campaña to the top of Plaza San Francisco. For handmade ceramics, you should also prowl **Calle Alfareria** across the Isabel II bridge from the old town. On Sunday mornings, once the Saturday-night drunks have been cleared away, a huge flea market is held on the **Alameda de Hercules** plaza in the Macarena neighborhood. Close to Seville's town hall, **Ceramics Martian,** Sierpes 74 (✆ **95-421-34-13**), sells a wide array of painted tiles and ceramics, all made in or near Seville. Many pieces reproduce traditional patterns of Andalusia. Near the cathedral, **El Postigo,** Arfe s/n (✆ **95-456-00-13**), sells a wide selection of Andalucian ceramics. Some of the pieces are much too big to fit into your suitcase—others, especially the hand-painted tiles—make memorable souvenirs that can be easily transported.

Past the north end of Sierpes, over to the left, is the local branch of the preeminent national department store, **El Corte Inglés,** Plaza del Duque de la Victoria 10 (✆ **95-459-70-00;** www.elcorteingles.es).

SEVILLE AFTER DARK

In the 1990s, Seville finally got its own opera house, **Teatro de la Maestranza,** Núñez de Balboa (✆ **95/422-33-44;** www.teatromaestranza.com), which quickly became a premier venue for world-class operatic performances. Jazz, classical music, and the quintessentially Spanish *zarzuelas* (operettas) are also performed here. The opera house can't be visited except during performances. The box office is open daily from 10am to 2pm and 5:30 to 8:30pm. Tickets vary in cost depending on the performance.

If you're under 35 (or just feel that way), join Seville's youth at the **Alameda de Hercules** just north of the city center, where more than a dozen bars and two dance clubs attract hundreds of college students and a smaller crowd of revelers in their 20s and 30s to chat, drink, flirt, and show off.

A showcase for Spanish folk song and dance, **El Patio Sevillano,** Paseo de Cristóbal Colón 11 (✆ **95-421-41-20;** www.elpatiosevillano.com), presents the most widely varied flamenco program in town. Sometimes classical music is inserted, including works by Falla and Chueca. Three shows at 7:30, 10, and 11:45pm are presented nightly March to October. Off season there are two shows nightly at 9 and 11:30pm. The cover of 30€ includes your first drink.

A less touristy and more authentic flamenco is presented at **Tablao Los Gallos ★**, Plaza de Santa Cruz 11 (✆ **95-421-69-81;** www.tablaolosgallos.com), lying 2 blocks south of Ximénez de Enciso along Santa Teresa. The club lies deep in the heart of Barrio Santa Cruz. Shows are presented nightly at 8pm and 10:30am, costing a cover of 30€, including your first drink.

Córdoba ★★★

Ten centuries ago, Córdoba was one of the world's greatest cities. The capital of Muslim Spain, it was Europe's largest city (with a reported population of 900,000) and a prominent cultural and intellectual center. This seat of the Western Caliphate flourished, constructing public baths, mosques, a great library, and palaces. But greedy hordes descended on the city, sacking ancient buildings and carting off art treasures. Despite these assaults, Córdoba retains traces of its former glory—enough to rival Seville and Granada in attraction.

A visit to Andalusia can easily begin in Córdoba, 418km (260 miles) southwest of Madrid. The city lies astride NIV (E-5) connecting Madrid with Seville and is one of the few stops made by the high-speed AVE train, only 1¾ hours out of Madrid. Today, this provincial capital is known chiefly for its great mosque, but it is filled with other artistic and architectural riches, especially its domestic dwellings. The old Arab and Jewish quarters are famous for their narrow streets lined with whitewashed homes and flower-filled patios and balconies; it's perfectly acceptable to walk along gazing into the courtyards.

ESSENTIALS

Getting There

BY TRAIN Córdoba is a railway junction for routes to the rest of Andalusia and Spain. The main rail station is on the town's northern periphery, at Avenida de América 130, near the corner of Avenida de Cervantes. For information about services in Córdoba, contact **RENFE** (✆ **95-747-58-84;** www.renfe.es). There are about 22 Talgo and AVE trains daily between Córdoba and Madrid (trip time: 1½–2 hr.). Other trains take 5 to 8 hours for the same trip. There are also 25 trains from Seville every day (45 min. by AVE).

BY BUS Several bus companies maintain separate terminals. The town's major bus terminal is at Calle Torrito 10, 1 block south of Avenida Medina Azahara (✆ **95-740-40-40;** www.alsa.es), on the western outskirts of town (just west of the gardens beside Paseo de la Victoria). There are at least 10 buses per day to Seville (trip time: 2 hr.).

VISITOR INFORMATION The **tourist office,** Calle Torrijos 10 (✆ **95-735-51-79;** www.andalucia.org), is open Monday to Friday 9am to 7:30pm, Saturday 10am to 2pm and 5 to 7pm, and Sunday and holidays 10am to 2pm.

WHERE TO STAY

Expensive

Parador de Córdoba ★★ About 4km (2½ miles) outside of town, in the suburb of El Brillante, this hotel from around 1960 (named after an Arab word meaning "palm grove") offers the conveniences and facilities of a resort hotel at reasonable rates. Built atop the foundations of a former caliphate palace, with panoramic views, the spacious rooms within have been furnished with fine dark-wood pieces; some have balconies.

Avenida de la Arruzafa s/n, 14012 Córdoba. ✆ **95-727-59-00.** Fax 95-728-04-09. www.parador.es. 94 units. 143€–179€ double; 229€–248€ suite. AE, DC, MC, V. Free parking. **Amenities:** Restaurant; bar; babysitting; heated outdoor pool; room service; tennis court; Wi-Fi (free). *In room:* A/C, TV, hair dryer, minibar, Wi-Fi (free).

Moderate

El Conquistador ★ Benefiting from one of the most evocative locations in Córdoba, this hotel lies just across a narrow street from one side of the Mezquita. It opened in 1986 within the renovated premises of a connected pair of 19th-century villas. The marble-and-granite lobby opens onto an interior courtyard filled with seasonal flowers, a pair of splashing fountains, and a symmetrical stone arcade. The quality, size, and comfort of the rooms have earned the hotel four stars in the government rating system.

Magistral González Francés 15, 14003 Córdoba. ✆ **95-748-11-02.** Fax 95-747-46-77. www.hotelconquistadorcordoba.com. 132 units. 109€–169€ double. AE, MC, V. Garage parking 15€. Bus: 12. **Amenities:** Cafe; bar; babysitting; room service. *In room:* A/C, TV, hair dryer, minibar, Wi-Fi (8€ per hour).

Inexpensive

Hotel Marisa In front of the Mezquita, this modest hotel is one of the most centrally located in Córdoba, not to mention one of the city's best values. Completed in the early 1970s, ongoing renovations have kept it in good shape. Most recent improvements have been to the bathrooms with showers, where the plumbing was renewed. The rooms are small but cozily comfortable—ask for one with a balcony overlooking either the statue of the Virgin of Rosales or the Patio de los Naranjos. The architecture and furnishings are in a vague Andalusian style.

Cardenal Herrero 6, 14003 Córdoba. ✆ **95-747-31-42.** Fax 95-747-41-44. www.hotelmarisacordoba.com. 28 units. 55€–75€ double. AE, DC, MC, V. Parking 15€. Bus: 3 or 16. **Amenities:** Cafeteria; room service. *In room:* A/C.

Mezquita ★ The owners have incorporated ancient columns, arches, and genuinely old paintings for a downright grand effect. Many of the guest rooms carry through with that theme. Opposite the east entrance to the Mezquita, the intriguing parts of the Judería are a mere stroll away. Prices go up during Holy Week and the Feria de Abril.

Plaza Santa Catalina 1, 14003 Córdoba. ✆ **95-747-55-85.** Fax 95-747-62-19. 31 units. 52€–74€ double. AE, DC, MC, V. Parking nearby 15€. *In room:* A/C, TV, hair dryer.

WHERE TO DINE

Moderate

El Caballo Rojo ★ SPANISH Córdoba's best-known restaurant is up an alley opposite the Mezquita's Puerta del Perdón. Hugely popular with both locals and visitors, the place has the noise level you'd expect, but the skilled waiters cope smoothly with all the demands. As soon as you order, they bring a dish of fritters and pour a complimentary aperitif. There are three floors, and enough room to get away from smokers if you wish. In addition to regional dishes, the chef offers centuries-old Sephardic and Mozarabic recipes, an example of the latter being monkfish with pine nuts, currants, carrots, and cream. *Rabo de toro* (oxtail stew) is among the favorites on the long menu.

Cardinal Herrero 28, Plaza de la Hoguera. ✆ **95-747-53-75.** www.elcaballorojo.com. Reservations required. Main courses 12€–25€; fixed-price menu 25€. AE, DC, MC, V. Daily 1–4:30pm and 8pm–midnight. Bus: 12.

La Almudaina ★★★ SPANISH/FRENCH Fronting the river in the former Judería—the Jewish Quarter—La Almudaina is widely regarded as the city's top restaurant. That's a reach, in truth, but it's an attractive place, with dining in the central courtyard, with its stained-glass roof, or in one of the lace-curtained salons to the side. In cool weather, braziers under the table warm your feet. Specialties include salmon crepes, *merluza* (hake) with baby clams and shrimp, and spring lamb and pork loin in wine sauce. Meats are the best options, because fish is too often cooked to mushiness.

Plaza de los Santos Mártires 1. ✆ **95-747-43-42.** www.restaurantealmudaina.com. Reservations required. Main courses 16€–20€; fixed-price menu 35€. AE, DC, MC, V. Mon–Sat 12:30–4pm and 8:30pm–midnight; Sun 12:30–4pm. Closed Sun mid-June to Aug. Bus: 12.

EXPLORING CÓRDOBA

Alcázar de los Reyes Cristianos ★ Commissioned in 1328 by Alfonso XI (the "Just"), the Alcázar de los Reyes Cristianos (Fortress of the Christian Kings) is a fine example of military architecture. Fernando and Isabel governed Castile from this fortress on the river as they prepared their assault on Granada, the last Moorish stronghold in Spain. Columbus journeyed here to fill Isabel's ears with his plans for exploration. Two blocks southwest of the mosque, this quadrangular building is notable for mighty walls and a trio of towers: the Tower of the Lions, the Tower of Allegiance, and the Tower of the River. The Tower of the Lions contains intricately decorated ogival ceilings that are the most notable example of Gothic architecture in Andalusia. The beautiful gardens (illuminated May–Sept Tues–Sat 10pm–1am) and the Moorish bathrooms are celebrated attractions. The Patio Morisco is a lovely spot, its pavement decorated with the arms of León and Castile.

Caballerizas Reales. ✆ **95-742-01-51.** Admission 4€ adults, free for children 17 and under. May–Sept Tues–Sat 8:30am–2pm and 6–8pm, Sun 10am–2pm; Oct–Apr Tues–Sat 10am–2pm and 4:30–6:30pm, Sun 9:30am–2:30pm. Bus: 3 or 12.

Mezquita-Catedral ★★★ Dating from the 8th century, this mosque was the crowning Muslim architectural achievement in the West, rivaled only by the architecture at Mecca. Córdoba's mosque boasts a fantastic labyrinth of red-and-white-striped pillars, more than 850 of them, topped with double arches, some of them with scalloped edges. They are made from marble, onyx, granite, limestone, even wood. Of different heights and thickness, many were scavenged from Roman, Carthaginian, and Visigothic sites. They support a flat roof covering almost 3 hectares (7⅓ acres).

Dropped into this graceful space is a Gothic-baroque cathedral that the bishops of the Church Triumphant ordered built after the reconquest of the city. While it squats awkwardly in the middle of the mosque, it would be impressive in its own right if it stood alone, somewhere else. The mosque's most intriguing feature is the *mihrab,* a domed shrine lined with golden, glittering mosaics. The mihrab once housed a Koran. After exploring the interior, stroll through the Courtyard of the Orange Trees with its beautiful fountain.

Calle Cardenal Herrero. ✆ **95-822-52-45.** Admission 8€ adults and students 14 and up, 4€ children 10–13, free for children 9 and under. Mar–Sept daily 10am–7pm; Oct–Feb daily 10am–6pm. Bus: 3 or 12.

Museo de Bellas Artes Housed in an old hospital, the Fine Arts Museum contains medieval Andalusian paintings, examples of Spanish baroque art, and works by many of Spain's important 19th- and 20th-century painters, including Goya. The museum is east of the Mezquita, about a block south of the San Francisco (Church of St. Francis).

Plaza del Potro 1. ✆ **95-835-55-50.** Admission 1.60€, free for children 11 and under. June 15–Sept 15 Tues 3–8pm, Wed–Sat 9am–8pm, Sun 9am–3pm (shorter hours during the rest of the year). Bus: 3, 4, or 7.

Museo de Julio Romero de Torres Across the patio from the Museo de Bellas Artes, this museum honors Julio Romero de Torres, a Córdoba-born artist (1874–1930) who was known for his sensual portraits of women. He caused the greatest scandal with his "hyper-realistic nudes," and in 1906 the National Exhibition of Fine Arts banned his *Vivadoras del amor.* On display here is his celebrated *Oranges and Lemons,* and other notable works such as *The Little Girl Who Sells Fuel, Sin,* and *A Dedication to the Art of the Bullfight.* A corner of Romero's Madrid studio has been reproduced in one of the rooms, displaying the paintings left unfinished at his death.

Plaza del Potro 1. ✆ **95-749-19-09.** www.museojulioromero.org. Admission 4€. Sept 16–June 15 Tues–Fri 8:30am–7:30pm, Sat 9:30am–4:30pm, Sun 9:30am–2:30pm; June 16–Sept 15 Tues–Sat 8:30am–2:30pm, Sun 9:30am–2:30pm.

THE SHOPPING SCENE

The largest and most comprehensive association of craftspeople in Córdoba is **Arte Zoco,** Calle de los Júdios s/n (✆ **95-729-05-75**). Opened in the Jewish quarter as a business cooperative in the mid-1980s, it assembles the creative output of about a half-dozen artisans, whose mediums include leather, wood, silver, crystal, terra cotta, and iron. Some of the artisans maintain on-premises studios, which you can visit to check out the techniques and tools they use to pursue their crafts. The center is open Monday to Friday 9:30am to 7pm and Saturday and Sunday 9:30am to 2pm. The workshops and studios of the various artisans open and close according to the whims of their occupants, but are usually open Monday to Friday 10am to 2pm and 5:30 to 8pm.

At taller **Meryan,** Calleja de las Flores 2 (✆ **95-747-59-02**), artisans make leather objects in a 250-year-old building. Most items must be custom ordered, but there are some ready-made pieces for sale, including cigarette boxes, jewel cases, attaché cases, book and folio covers, and ottoman covers. Meryan is open Monday to Friday 9am to 8pm and Saturday 9am to 2pm.

Granada ★★★

Granada, 122km (76 miles) northeast of Málaga, is 670m (2,200 ft.) above sea level. The last stronghold of Moorish Spain, it was finally captured in 1492 by the Catholic monarchs Ferdinand and Isabella. Granada is best known for the castle complex of the **Alhambra ★★★** (www.alhambra-patronato.es), one of the world's grandest and most elegant monuments, ranking up there with the Acropolis and the Taj Mahal. Author/diplomat Washington Irving lived in a former royal apartment on the grounds before he wrote his *Tales of the Alhambra.*

But Granada itself has much more to offer. The winding, hilly streets of the formerly Jewish Albayzín quarter and the gracious plazas of the 19th-century city below come together into a supremely civilized city, one that rewards wandering.

ESSENTIALS

Getting There

BY PLANE **Iberia** flies to Granada's small airport once or twice daily from both Barcelona and Madrid. Granada's airport (✆ **90-240-47-04**) is 16km (10 miles) west of the city center. Airline ticketing problems and information are more easily handled at the **Iberia ticketing office** in the city center, at Plaza Isabel la Católica 2 (✆ **90-240-05-00**). A shuttle bus makes runs several times a day between the airport and the city center, at hours that are timed to coincide with the arrivals and departures of flights. The buses meander through the city center before heading out to the airport, but the most convenient and central place to catch one is on the Gran Vía de Colón, immediately in front of the city's cathedral. It costs 7€ each way.

BY TRAIN Two trains daily connect Granada with Madrid's Atocha Station (trip time: 6–8 hr.), and there are four trains daily between Seville and Granada (3 hr.). Granada's railway station is on Calle Dr. Jaime García Royo (✆ **90-243-23-43;** www.renfe.es), at the end of Avenida Andaluces.

BY BUS Granada is served by far more **buses** than trains. It has links to virtually all the major towns and cities in Andalusia, even to Madrid. The main bus terminal is **Estación de Autobuses de Granada,** Carretera de Jaén s/n (✆ **95-818-54-80**). One of the most heavily used bus routes is the one between Seville and Granada. Ten buses run per day, costing 34€ for a one-way ticket. The trip is 3 hours. You can also reach Granada in 3 hours on one of nine daily buses from Córdoba; cost is 14€ for a one-way ticket. If you're on the Costa del Sol, the run is just 2 hours, costing 12€ per one-way ticket. This is a very popular routing with 19 buses going back and forth between Granada and the coast per day. For bus information call **Alsina Graells** at ✆ **95-818-54-80** (www.alsa.es).

VISITOR INFORMATION The **tourist information office** is at Plaza de Mariana Pineda 10 (✆ **95-824-71-46;** www.turismodegranada.org), open Monday to Saturday 9am to 7pm and Sunday 10am to 2pm.

WHERE TO STAY

Casa del Capitel Nazari ★ The least expensive of a quartet of historic Albayzín hotels brings together charm and affordability in a way no other Granada hotel quite pulls it off. Built in 1503 by workers who remembered the last Moorish rulers of Granada, it was a private home for centuries before being converted to a hotel in 2001. The rooms, on three floors, cluster around an open-air patio. Yes, that means it rains *inside* the hotel sometimes; the patio has its own drainage system. Rooms are decorated with tapestries and old rugs, with tiny but sparkling bathrooms (shower only, no bathtub). Top-floor rooms have gorgeous wood-beam ceilings, and a few rooms have views of the Alhambra. The staff speaks a bit of English.

Cuesta Aceituneros 6, 18010 Granada. ✆ **95-821-52-60.** Fax 95-821-58-06. www.hotelcasacapitel.com. 17 units. 68€–110€ double. MC, V. Parking 20€ nearby. **Amenities:** Breakfast room. *In room:* A/C, TV, hair dryer, minibar.

Parador de San Francisco ★★★ The most famous hotel of Spain's "Parador" lodging chain (a distinguished chain of Spanish government-owned hotels, normally set in notable historical buildings) is housed in a 15th-century structure with a modern annex, set within the grounds of the Alhambra. A decidedly Andalusian ambience informs the decor, which is respectful of the rich history of its surroundings. Part of the building is a former convent founded by the Catholic monarchs immediately after they conquered the city in 1492. They were interred in one of its enclosed courts until the cathedral was built downtown. From the hotel's terrace, outside the dining room, there are views of the Alhambra gardens and Albayzín hill. Rooms are generally spacious and comfortable, if not extravagant. The hotel cannot begin to meet demand, though, and reservations must be made months in advance. (In the confusing manner of the Parador chain, this is also known as the "Parador de Granada.")

Real de la Alhambra, 18009 Granada. ✆ **95-822-14-40.** Fax 95-822-22-64. www.parador.es. 249€-349€ double; 601€ suite. AE, DC, MC, V. Free parking. Bus: 30. **Amenities:** Restaurant; bar; room service. *In room:* A/C, TV, hair dryer, minibar, safe.

Room Mate Migueletes ★★ One of the best known of Granada's historic hotels was built in the 17th century as a slew of houses around a central courtyard; over the years, it became the headquarters for the local police and then a set of slum dwellings, before finally being left in ruins in 1995.

The Migueletes is full of high-tech conveniences, including a rollback roof over the central courtyard and even an electrically heated courtyard floor. The varied rooms come with certifiably antique furniture and well-maintained bathrooms; a few have views of the Alhambra. A 24-hour, ground-floor wine cellar serves as the world's largest minibar. Feel like having some fresh ham and a bottle of *vino tinto*? Just ask. The Migueletes's greatest asset, though, is its staff. All frontline staff speak fluent English and are helpful when it comes to recommending restaurants and attractions, providing the intangible smoothness that creates a luxury experience.

Calle Benelua 11, 18010 Granada. ✆ **95-821-07-00.** Fax 95-821-07-02. www.casamigueletes.com. 25 units. 96€-199€ double; 154€-229€ junior suite; 221€-349€ suite. AE, DC, MC, V. Parking 15€. Bus: 30, 31, or 32. *In room:* A/C, TV, hair dryer, minibar, Wi-Fi (free).

WHERE TO DINE

Carmen de San Miguel ANDALUSIAN Located on the hill leading up to the Alhambra, this likable restaurant offers spectacular views over the city center. Meals are served in a glassed-in dining room and patio-style terrace, where the banks of flowers are changed seasonally. Specialties include grilled hake, a pâté of partridge with a vinaigrette sauce, Iberian ham with Manchego cheese, and a casserole of monkfish and fresh clams. The food, although good, doesn't quite match the view. The wines are from throughout the country, with a strong selection of Riojas.

Plaza de Torres Bermejas 3. ✆ **95-822-67-23.** www.carmensanmiguel.com. Reservations recommended. Main courses 10€-24€; 4-course *menú degustación* 55€. AE, DC, MC, V. Mon-Sat 1:30-4pm and 8:30-11:30pm; winter Sun 1:30-4pm. Bus: 30 or 32.

Las Tinajas ★ ANDALUSIAN This restaurant, a short walk from the cathedral, is named for the huge amphorae depicted on its facade. For more than 3 decades it has been the culinary showcase of José Alvarez. The decor is classical Andalusian, with wood walls adorned with ceramic tiles and pictures of Old Granada. Diners are surrounded by antique ornaments interspersed with modern elements and fixtures. To start, try the cold zucchini-and-almond cream soup or the white beet stuffed with ham and cheese. Follow with a delectable monkfish cooked with local herbs, or the peppered sirloin steak.

Martínez Campos 17. ✆ **95-825-43-93.** www.restaurantelastinajas.com. Reservations recommended. Main courses 12€-25€. AE, DC, MC, V. Daily noon-5pm and 8pm-midnight. Closed July 15-Aug 15. Bus: 4 or 6.

EXPLORING GRANADA

Alhambra ★★★ A fortress-palace of grand ambition, built over centuries for the governing caliphs during the long Moorish occupation, the Alhambra was a royal city surrounded by walls. The heart of the Alhambra, the **Palacios Nazaríes (Nasrid Palaces),** is a series of three connected palaces. Here, sultans and emirs conducted state business, concocted conspiracies, raised their families, and were entertained by their harems.

The first structure you'll enter is the **Casa Real,** built between 1335 and 1410. Signs direct visitors through rooms with reliefs of Arabic script and floral motifs carved in the plaster walls. This pathway leads into one of the Alhambra's most-photographed spaces, the **Patio de Comares (Court of the Myrtles),** a long, flat band of water bordered by rows of sculptured myrtle. At one end is the splendid **Salón de Embajadores (Hall of the Ambassadors),** one of the palace's loveliest rooms, with a high vaulted ceiling of carved cedar and walls of lustrous tiles and carved script. Exiting, you soon arrive in the **Patio de los Leones (Court of Lions),** named after its fountain, a basin resting on the haunches of 12 stylized stone lions standing in a circle. This was the heart of the palace, the most private section. Opening onto the court are the Hall of the Two Sisters, where the "favorite" of the moment was kept, and the Gossip Room, a factory of intrigue. In the dancing room in the Hall of Kings, entertainment was provided nightly to amuse the sultan's party. You can see the room where Washington Irving lived (in the chambers of Carlos V).

Carlos V may have been horrified when he saw the cathedral placed in the middle of the great mosque at Córdoba, but he's responsible for his own architectural meddling here, building a ponderous Renaissance palace in the middle of the Alhambra. Today, it houses the **Museo de la Bellas Artes en la Alhambra** (✆ **95-822-14-49**), a site devoted to painting and sculpture from the 16th to the 19th century; and the **Museo de la Alhambra** (✆ **95-822-75-27**), which focuses on the region's traditions of Hispanic-Muslim art and architecture. Both museums are open Monday to Saturday 9am to 2pm.

Palacio de Carlos V. ✆ **90-244-12-21.** www.alhambra-patronato.es. Comprehensive ticket, including Alhambra and Generalife (see below), 12€ adults, free for children 7 and under. Mar–Oct daily 8:30am–8pm, floodlit visits Tues–Sat 10–11:30pm; Nov–Feb daily 8:30am–6pm, floodlit visits Fri–Sat 8–9:30pm. Take bus 30 from the Plaza Nueva.

Reserving for the Alhambra

Because of the overwhelming crowds, the government limits the number of people who can enter the Alhambra. Go as early as possible, but even if you get there at 10am you may not be admitted until 1:30pm. If you arrive after 4pm, it's unlikely you'll get in at all. There's a way to avoid these long lines. Tickets can be acquired on the Internet (www.alhambra-tickets.es) or by calling ✆ 90-288-80001. You can find complete information about ticket sales by searching www.alhambra-patronato.es. Tickets carry a 1€ surcharge. Tickets bought on the Internet or by phone can be picked up in the automatic machines of La Caixa at the entrance to the Alhambra. Of course, you have to use the credit card you used for booking the tickets. These automatic machines are in the Access Pavilion at the Alhambra. The ticket is valid only for the day you specified.

Generalife ★ The sultans used to spend their summers in this palace (pronounced, roughly, Hay-nay-rahl-*ee*-fay) with their wives, consorts, and extended families. Built in the 13th century to overlook the Alhambra, the Generalife's glory is in its gardens and courtyards. Don't expect an Alhambra in miniature: There are no major buildings—the Generalife is a place of fragrances and fountains, a retreat even from the splendors of the Alhambra.

Alhambra, Cerro de Sol. For tickets and hours, see the Alhambra, above.

Catedral & Capilla Real ★ This Renaissance-baroque cathedral, with its spectacular altar, is one of the country's architectural highlights, acclaimed for its beautiful facade and gold-and-white decor. It was begun in 1521 and completed in 1714. Behind the cathedral (entered separately) is the Flamboyant Gothic **Capilla Real (Royal Chapel),** where the remains of Isabel and Fernando lie. It was their wish to be buried in recaptured Granada, not their home regions of Castile or Aragón. The coffins are remarkably tiny—a reminder of how short they must have been. Accenting the tombs is a wrought-iron grill masterpiece. In much larger tombs are the remains of their daughter, Joanna the Mad, and her husband, Philip the Handsome. The Capilla Real abuts the cathedral's eastern edge.

Plaza de la Lonja, Gran Vía de Colón 5. ✆ **95-822-29-59.** www.capillarealgranada.com. Admission to cathedral 3.50€, to the chapel 3.50€. Daily 10:30am–1:30pm and 3:30–6:30pm (4–8pm in summer).

ALBAYZÍN ★

This old Arab quarter (also spelled "Albaicín") occupies one of the two main hills of Granada, but it doesn't belong to the city of 19th-century buildings and wide boulevards beneath it. The district once flourished as the residential section of the Moors, even after the city's reconquest, but it fell into decline when the Christians eventually drove the Moors out. A labyrinth of steep, crooked streets, it escaped the fate of much of Granada, which was torn down in the name of progress. Fortunately, it has been preserved, as have its plazas, whitewashed houses, villas, and the decaying remnants of the old city gate. Here and there, you can catch a glimpse of a private patio filled with fountains and plants—these are home to a traditional and graceful way of life that flourishes today. Car traffic is allowed only 6 hours a day, so walk or take bus no. 31 from the Plaza Nueva deep into the quarter. Many bars and restaurants cluster around the Plaza Larga. You can always get out by walking downhill until you hit the Gran Vía or the river.

THE GYPSY CAVES OF SACROMONTE

Next to Albayzín are the Gypsy caves of Sacromonte. They are tawdry tourist traps, and wouldn't even be mentioned here if so many visitors didn't get conned into going, despite warnings. A few of the caves serve as troglodyte nightclubs. Strung with colored lights and furnished with stubby little tables and chairs, they function as flamenco tablaos. They aren't remotely romantic. With few exceptions, the performances of the singers, guitarists, and dancers are execrable. Patrons are hounded to buy vile sherry, shoddy trinkets, and cassettes, and to tip everyone in sight. You will be encouraged by leaflets scattered around the city and in every hotel lobby to join a "Granada by Night" tour. ***Don't!***

THE SHOPPING SCENE

The **Alcaicería,** once the Moorish silk market, is next to the cathedral in the lower city. The narrow streets of this rebuilt village of shops are filled with vendors selling the arts and crafts of the province. The Alcaicería offers you one of Spain's most diverse assortments of tiles, castanets, and wire figures of Don Quixote chasing windmills. The jewelry found here compares favorably with the finest Toledan work. For the window-shopper in particular, it makes a pleasant stroll.

Málaga

Málaga is a bustling commercial and residential center whose economy doesn't depend exclusively on tourism. Its chief attraction is the mild off-season climate—summer can be sticky. Málaga's most famous native son is Pablo Picasso, born in 1881 at Plaza de la Merced, in the center of the city.

ESSENTIALS

GETTING THERE **Iberia** (✆ **800/772-4642** in the U.S.) has flights every 2 hours into Málaga from Madrid. There are at least five trains a day from Madrid (trip time: 4½ hr.). For rail information in Málaga, contact **RENFE** (✆ **90-224-02-02;** www.renfe.es). Buses from all over Spain arrive at the terminal on Paseo de los Tilos, behind the RENFE office. Málaga is linked by bus to all the major cities of Spain. Call ✆ **90-242-22-42** in Málaga for **bus information** or go to **www.alsa.es**.

VISITOR INFORMATION The **tourist information office** at Plaza de la Marina 11 (✆ **95-221-20-20;** www.malagaturismo.com) is open Monday to Friday 9am to 7pm and Saturday and Sunday 10am to 2pm.

WHERE TO STAY

Parador de Málaga-Gibralfaro ★★ Originally established in 1948, this member of the Parador chain is immediately adjacent to the foundations of a medieval castle. The lodging occupies the steep hill that dominates the city center, providing a vista that takes in the harbor, the bullring, mountains, and beaches. Rooms have sitting areas and wide glass doors opening onto terraces with garden furniture. They're tastefully decorated with modern furnishings and reproductions of Spanish antiques.

Monte Gibralfaro, 29016 Málaga. ✆ **95-222-19-02.** Fax 95-222-19-04. www.parador.es. 38 units. 160€–223€ double. AE, DC, MC, V. Free parking. **Amenities:** Restaurant; bar; rooftop outdoor pool; room service. *In room:* A/C, TV, hair dryer, minibar, Wi-Fi (free).

WHERE TO DINE

Café de Paris ★★ FRENCH/SPANISH Málaga's best restaurant is in La Malagueta, the district surrounding the Plaza de Toros (bullring). Much of the menu is French cuisine adapted to the Spanish palate, but classic Spanish recipes are also featured. Try crepes gratinées (filled with *angulas*—baby eels) or *lubina* or *dorada a la sal*—fish baked in a hard crust of salt and cracked open at the table; the fish proves to be exceptionally moist and not at all salty. Beef stroganoff is made here, but with *rabo de toro*—oxtail. Other specialties include artichokes stuffed with foie gras and a version of hake wrapped around pulverized shellfish and served with a tomato sauce.

Vélez Málaga 8. ✆ **95-222-50-43.** www.rcafedeparis.com. Reservations required. Main courses 18€–28€; *menú del día* 45€. AE, DC, MC, V. Tues–Sat 1–4pm and 8:30–11pm. Closed Holy Week and last 2 weeks of July. Bus: 13.

EXPLORING MÁLAGA

The remains of the Moorish **Alcazaba ★**, Plaza de la Aduana, Alcazabilla (✆ **95-212-20-20;** bus: 4, 18, 19, or 24), are within easy distance of the city center, off Paseo del Parque (plenty of signs point the way up the hill). The fortress was erected in the 10th or 11th century, though there have been later additions and reconstructions. Fernando and Isabel stayed here when they reconquered the city. The Alcazaba has extensive gardens and houses a small archaeological museum, with artifacts from cultures ranging from Greek to Phoenician to Carthaginian. Admission is 2€; it's open Tuesday to Sunday from 9:30am to 7pm in the summer and 8:30am to 6pm during the winter.

The 16th-century Renaissance **cathedral,** Plaza Obispo (✆ **95-221-59-17;** bus: 14, 18, 19, or 24), in Málaga's center, was built on the site of a great mosque. It suffered damage during the Civil War, but it remains vast and impressive, reflecting changing styles of interior architecture. Its most notable attributes are its richly ornamented choir stalls by Ortiz, Mena, and Michael. Admission is 3.50€. It's open Monday to Friday 10am to 6pm, 10am to 5pm on Saturday.

In the Old Quarter, **Museo Picasso Málaga ★★★**, San Augustin 8 (✆ **95-212-76-00;** www.museopicassomalaga.org), displays some of his most important works.

Many of the artworks are virtual family heirlooms, including paintings depicting one of the artist's wives, such as *Olga Kokhlova with Mantilla,* or one of his lovers, *Jacqueline Seated.* Basically this is the art Picasso gave to his family or else the art he wanted to keep for himself—in all, more than 200 paintings, drawings, sculpture, ceramics, and graphics. Some other notable works on display—many of them never on public view before—include *Bust of a Woman with Arms Crossed Behind Her Head, Woman in an Armchair,* and *The Eyes of the Artist.* There is also a memorable painting of Picasso's son, done in 1923. A combined ticket for the permanent collection and exhibitions costs 8€; half price for seniors, students, and children 11 to 16; free for kids 10 and under. Hours are Tuesday to Thursday and Sunday 10am to 8pm, Friday and Saturday 10am to 9pm.

Marbella

Though packed with visitors, ranking just behind Torremolinos in numbers, Marbella is still the most exclusive resort along the Costa del Sol—with such bastions of posh as the Hotel Puente Romano. Despite the hordes, Marbella persists as a large, busy, but still mostly pleasant town at the foot of the Sierra Blanca, 80km (50 miles) east of Gibraltar and 76km (47 miles) east of Algeciras, or 600km (373 miles) south of Madrid.

Traces of the recent and distant past are found in Marbella's palatial town hall, its medieval ruins, and fragments of its Moorish walls. The most attractive area is the **old quarter,** with its narrow cobblestone streets and clustered houses, centering around Plaza de los Naranjos, which is planted with palms, trumpet vines, and orange trees. Seek out the Plaza de la Iglesia and the streets around it, with a church on one side and a rampart of an old fortress on the other.

The biggest attractions in Marbella are **El Fuerte** and **La Fontanilla,** the two main beaches. There are other, more secluded beaches, but you'll need your own transportation to get to them.

ESSENTIALS

GETTING THERE At least 14 buses run between Málaga and Marbella daily. Four buses come in from Madrid and another three come from Barcelona.

VISITOR INFORMATION The **tourist office,** on Glorieta de la Fontanilla (✆ **95-277-14-42;** www.marbella.es), is open April to October, Monday to Friday 9:30am to 9pm and Saturday 10am to 2pm. Another tourist office is on Plaza Naranjos (✆ **95-282-35-50**), keeping the same hours.

WHERE TO STAY

El Castillo This small 1960s *hostal* is at the foot of the castle in the narrow streets of the old town. The spartan rooms are scrubbed clean and look out onto a small, covered courtyard. No meals are served, but many cafes, suitable for breakfast, are nearby. A tiny bit of English is spoken.

Plaza San Bernabé 2, 29601 Marbella. ✆ **95-277-17-39.** Fax 95-282-11-98. www.hotelcastillo.com. 26 units. 38€–52€ double. MC, V. No parking. *In room:* No phone.

El Fuerte ★★ ☺ This is the largest and most recommendable hotel in the center of Marbella. An underground tunnel leads beneath an all-pedestrian, traffic-free promenade to the sands of the beach. Built in 1957, it caters to a sedate clientele of conservative northern Europeans. There's a palm-fringed pool across the street from a sheltered lagoon and a wide-open beach. The hotel offers a handful of terraces, some shaded by flowering arbors.

Av. del Fuerte, 29600 Marbella. ✆ **800/448-8355** in the U.S., or 95-286-15-00. Fax 95-282-44-11. www.fuertehoteles.com. 263 units. 101€–342€ double; from 220€ suite. AE, DC, MC, V. Parking 10€. **Amenities:** 2 restaurants; bar; babysitting; health club; 2 freshwater pools (1 heated indoor); room service; sauna; outdoor tennis court (lit). *In room:* A/C, TV, hair dryer, minibar, Wi-Fi (in some; 12€ per 24 hr.).

Marbella Club ★★★ The first luxury hotel on the coast, this exclusive enclave was established in 1954 and has been renovated and refreshed many times since to keep up with newer competitors. It sprawls over a generously landscaped property that slopes from a roadside reception area down to the beach, incorporating small clusters of garden pavilions, bungalows, and small-scale annexes. Elegantly furnished rooms have private balconies or terraces. Golf can be arranged nearby, and tennis courts are within a 2-minute walk.

Bulevar Príncipe Alfonso von Hohenlohe, 29600 Marbella. ✆ **800/448-8355** in the U.S., or 95-282-22-11. Fax 95-282-98-84. www.marbellaclub.com. 121 units. 290€–920€ double; from 410€ suite. AE, DC, MC, V. Free parking. **Amenities:** 2 restaurants; bar; babysitting; bikes; concierge; 18-hole golf course; 3 pools (1 indoor); room service; state-of-the-art spa. *In room:* A/C, TV, hair dryer, minibar, Wi-Fi (free).

Puente Romano ★★★ This hotel began life as a condo annex of the older Marbella Club, down the road, but it soon surpassed its sibling in luxe and panache. There is no finer resort on the Costa. Like many of its fellows, the exterior style is mock Andalusian pueblo. A set of 27 small buildings encloses luxuriant gardens, with a brook spanned at one point by the Roman bridge that inspired the hotel's name. The always-stylish international clientele is afforded a beach club, twice-daily maid service, and reassuring security patrols. Rooms are vast and airy, with ground-floor units opening onto the gardens. Service excels: Order breakfast as you step into the shower and it arrives before you've reached for the towel.

Carretera de Cádiz, Km 177, 29600 Marbella. ✆ **95-282-09-00.** Fax 95-277-57-66. www.puenteromano.com. 285 units. 227€–426€ double; from 406€ suite. AE, DC, MC, V. Limited free parking. **Amenities:** 3 restaurants; 2 bars; babysitting; children's center; concierge; 18-hole golf course (nearby); state-of-the-art health club; 3 outdoor freshwater pools; room service; sauna; 10 outdoor tennis courts (lit); extensive watersports equipment/rentals. *In room:* A/C, TV, TV/DVD player (in some), CD player (in some), hair dryer, minibar, Wi-Fi (19€ per 24 hr.).

WHERE TO DINE

Calima ★★★ ANDALUSIAN/INTERNATIONAL Dani García is the most exciting and innovative chef in Marbella. As an example of his inventiveness, he injects liquid nitrogen into olives. When they explode, they become popcorn-like morsels, which he then serves with fresh lobster salad. Or he'll take wild baby shrimp and lay them on a slate heated to 300°F (148°C), which he garnishes with an olive-oil emulsion and fennel dust. But, for the most part, he is not some mad scientist in a lab. Instead he keeps his menu local, relying on the famous products of the region, not only the regional olive oil but such delights as Andalusian *jamón* (ham) and sherry from Jerez. Meals are enjoyed on a large terrace overlooking the ocean.

In the Gran Meliá Don Pepe hotel. Calle José Meliá. ✆ **95-276-42-52.** Reservations required. Main courses 22€–38€. AE, DC, MC, V. Tues–Sat 1:30–3:30pm and 8:30–10:30pm.

Casa de la Era ★ 🎁 ANDALUSIAN This little discovery outside Marbella is in a rustic house, very much in the style of an old hacienda with internal patios decorated with plants, trees, and flowers. Wooden furniture only adds to the old-fashioned look, as do hanging hams and ceramics used for decoration. In addition, the restaurant offers a beautiful terrace. Some of the best of the chef's specialties include noodles with angler fish and baby clams, as well as baby goat from the mountains above Málaga. Codfish is a savory dish here when cooked in a spicy fresh tomato sauce. Other delectable delights include free-range chicken stewed with Montilla wine and fresh garlic or else rabbit pan-cooked with fresh thyme and served with an almond sauce.

Finca El Chorraero-Carretera de Ojén, Km 0.5. ✆ **95-277-06-25.** www.casadelaera.com. Reservations recommended. Main courses 12€–24€. AE, DC, MC, V. Sept–June Mon–Sat 1–4pm and 8–11pm; July–Aug daily 8–11pm.

La Hacienda ★ MEDITERRANEAN La Hacienda, 13km (8 miles) east of Marbella, has long enjoyed a reputation for serving some of the best food along the Costa del Sol. In cooler months, dine in the rustic tavern before an open fireplace; in fair weather, meals are served on a patio. The chef may offer foie gras with leeks, Serrano ham with green gazpacho, and saddle of hare with mushrooms and juniper, but the menu changes frequently. The expert kitchen knows how to heighten the flavors of the fresh ingredients, and the food presentation is stylish. Several items—guinea fowl, roast lamb, wild duck—are for two persons. Although the food is admirable, the service is sometimes lacking.

Urbanización Hacienda Las Chapas, Carretera de Cádiz, Km 193. ✆ **95-283-12-67.** www.restaurantelahacienda.com. Reservations recommended. Main courses 20€–30€; *menú degustación* 50€–60€. AE, DC, MC, V. Sept–June Wed–Sun 7:30–11pm, Sun 1:30–3:30pm; July Tues–Sun 8:30pm–midnight; Aug daily 8:30pm–midnight. Closed Nov 12–Dec 7.

La Meridiana ★★★ ITALIAN/INTERNATIONAL If it's not the most sophisticated restaurant along the Costa del Sol, La Meridiana certainly is the most romantic—with its garden terrace—and arguably serves the best cuisine as well. A sweep of a glass-enclosed porch has been added to the original restaurant. The menu of Italian and Andalusian specialties changes four times yearly. Some of the most tantalizing items likely to be featured on the menu include wild sea bass seasoned with thyme and served with a prawn sauce, or else roast monkfish with a red-pepper preserve on a bed of onion purée. You might also order the house specialty, roast duck flambé in Calvados with truffles, fried onions, dates, and dried figs.

Camino de la Cruz s/n. ✆ **95-277-61-90.** www.lameridiana.es. Reservations required. Main courses 14€–28€. AE, DC, MC, V. Daily 8pm–midnight.

MARBELLA AFTER DARK

Near Puerto Banús, **Casino Nueva Andalucía Marbella,** Urbanización Nueva Andalucía (✆ **95-281-40-00;** www.casinomarbella.com), is on the lobby level of the Andalucía Plaza Hotel. It stands in an upscale development surrounded by foreign-owned condos and lush golf courses, 7km (4⅓ miles) from Marbella's center beside the road leading to Cádiz. Gambling includes individual games such as French and American roulette, blackjack, punto y banco, craps, and chemin de fer. Entrance to the casino is 5€, and you'll have to present a valid passport. You can dine in the Casino Restaurant before or after gambling. The casino is open daily from 8pm to 4 or 5am.

Torremolinos

This is the most famous—which isn't to say the finest—Mediterranean beach resort in Spain. It's a gathering place for international visitors, a stew of northern Europeans and North and South Americans. The once tranquil fishing village of Torremolinos has been engulfed in concrete-walled resort hotels. Some travelers relax here after whirlwind tours of Spain—the living is easy, the people are in a party mood, and there are no historic monuments to visit. Torremolinos is often a cacophonous refuge for people with nothing more elevated in mind than an all-over tan by Sunday. The sands along the beachfront tend to be gritty and grayish. The best beaches are **El Bajondillo** and **La Carihuela,** the latter bordering an old fishing village. All beaches here are public, but don't expect changing facilities. Many women go topless on the beaches. ***Note:*** If for some reason you find yourself here in December, January, or February, expect many restaurants, hotels, and casinos to be closed.

ESSENTIALS

GETTING THERE Torremolinos is served by the nearby Málaga airport, 14km (8⅔ miles) west. There are frequent rail departures from the terminal at Málaga; for information, contact **RENFE** (✆ **90-224-02-02;** www.renfe.es). Buses run frequently between Málaga and Torremolinos; for information, call ✆ **90-214-31-44.**

VISITOR INFORMATION The **tourist information office** is at Plaza Independencia (✆ **95-237-42-31**). It's open daily 8am to 3pm (in winter Mon–Fri 9:30am–2:30pm).

WHERE TO STAY

Hotel Cervantes ★ The government-rated four-star Cervantes, located in a shopping center, is a 7-minute walk from the beach. It has a garden and is adjacent to a maze of patios and narrow streets of boutiques and open-air cafes. Rooms have modern furniture and spacious terraces; many have balconies with sea views. In midsummer this hotel is likely to be booked with tour groups from northern Europe, many of whom can be seen sunning themselves on the hotel's rooftop terrace. A special feature in summer is the luncheon buffet and barbecue by the pool.

Calle las Mercedes s/n, 29620 Torremolinos. ✆ **95-238-40-33.** Fax 95-238-48-57. www.hotasacervantes.com. 397 units. 52€–175€ double. Rates include buffet breakfast. AE, DC, MC, V. Parking 15€. **Amenities:** Restaurant; 2 bars; babysitting; exercise room; 2 freshwater pools (1 heated indoor); room service; sauna. *In room:* A/C, TV, hair dryer, Wi-Fi (10€ per 24 hr.).

Hotel Tropicana & Beach Club ★ This government-rated four-star hotel stands right on a beach at the beginning of the La Carihuela coastal strip. Boasting its own beach club, Tropicana is desirable mainly because it's removed from the summer hysteria in the heart of Torremolinos. In honor of its namesake, a tropical motif dominates. Some decorators tried to give a little flair to the comfortably furnished and midsize bedrooms. Most of the rooms open onto private balconies with sea views. Many seafood restaurants are only a 5-minute stroll from the hotel's door, or else you can patronize the Tropicana's **Restaurante Mango,** with its terrace facing the sea.

Trópico 6, 29620 Torremolinos. ✆ **95-238-66-00.** Fax 95-238-05-68. www.hoteltropicana.es. 84 units. 50€–210€ double. Rates include continental breakfast. AE, DC, MC, V. Free parking. **Amenities:** Restaurant; bar; babysitting; outdoor freshwater pool; room service; Wi-Fi (free, in lobby). *In room:* A/C, TV, fridge, hair dryer.

Meliá Costa del Sol Admittedly nothing memorable, this massive chain hotel provides most everything expected of it. The beach is just across the street, and the attached Centro de Talasoterapia purveys that nontiring, nondietary route to robust health so dear to Europeans: water therapy. The facility offers massages, a mud bath, a whirlpool, a sauna, a pool, and a Turkish bath. Forgive the management the stunningly unattractive sand-colored stucco exterior—it's better inside.

Paseo Marítimo 11, 29620 Torremolinos. ✆ **95-238-66-77.** Fax 95-238-64-17. www.meliacostadelsol.solmelia.com. 540 units. 78€–225€ double; 138€–299€ junior suite; 298€–530€ suite. Rates include buffet breakfast. AE, MC, V. Free parking. **Amenities:** 2 restaurants; 2 bars; babysitting; bikes; concierge; health club & spa; outdoor freshwater pool; room service. *In room:* A/C, TV, hair dryer, minibar, Wi-Fi (free).

Parador de Málaga Golf ★★ Also known as the Parador de Torremolinos and other variations thereof, this resort hotel was created by the Spanish government. The hacienda-style hotel is flanked by a golf course on one side and the Mediterranean on another. It's 3km (1¾ miles) from the airport, 10km (6¼ miles) from Málaga, and 4km (2½ miles) from Torremolinos. Rooms have balconies with a view of the golfing greens, the circular pool, or the water; some are equipped with Jacuzzis. Long tiled corridors lead to the air-conditioned public areas and graciously furnished lounges.

Carretera de Málaga, Torremolinos, 29080 Apartado 324, Málaga. ✆ **95-238-12-55.** Fax 95-238-89-63. www.parador.es. 60 units. 160€–209€ double; 240€–273€ suite. AE, DC, MC, V. Free parking. **Amenities:** Restaurant; bar; babysitting; 18-hole golf course; outdoor pool; room service; spa; outdoor tennis court (lit); Wi-Fi (free, in lobby). *In room:* A/C, TV, hair dryer, minibar.

WHERE TO DINE

Casa Juan ★ SEAFOOD Nautical decor, such as boat models and brass-bordered windows, not to mention a lavish display of lobsters and company near the door, makes clear the objectives of this restaurant. With that in mind, you have some difficult choices to make. *Gazpachuelo,* a warm, creamy chowder crowded with fish and vegetables, is a splendid way to begin. Then, perhaps, the *fritura mixta*—lightly fried fish, squid, and other creatures—or paella, or *zarzuela,* a tomato-based fish stew. The restaurant is in a modern building in the old-fashioned satellite hamlet of La Carihuela, west of Torremolinos center. Whenever it gets busy (which is frequently), the staff is inclined to impatience. There are outdoor tables.

San Ginés 20, La Carihuela. ✆ **95-237-35-12.** Reservations recommended. Main courses 12€–42€. AE, DC, MC, V. Tues–Sun 1–4:30pm and 7pm–midnight. Closed Dec 11–Jan 11.

Figón de Montemar ★ SPANISH/ANDALUSIAN One of the better restaurants in the area, Figón de Montemar lies near the beach, and like so many others it's decorated with glass, tiles, and various nautical paraphernalia. Its chefs call its cuisine *cocina de mercado,* which means its menus are based on what was good and fresh at the market that day, including the daily seafood catch. From the mountains in the distance comes lamb that is perfectly roasted and seasoned with garlic and spices and served with a mint sauce. *Merluza* (hake) is baked with fresh spices, and fresh codfish is prepared in a delightful red sauce. Want something more adventurous? You can also order oxtail, a local specialty.

Av. Espada 101. ✆ **95-237-26-88.** Reservations recommended. Main courses 14€–24€; set menus 15€–25€. AE, DC, MC, V. Mon noon–1:30pm; Tues–Sat noon–1:30pm and 5:30–8pm. Closed Jan 10–Feb 10.

TORREMOLINOS AFTER DARK

One of the major casinos along the Costa del Sol, **Casino Torrequebrada,** Avenida del Sol s/n, Benalmádena Costa (✆ **95-244-60-00;** www.casinotorrequebrada.net), is on the lobby level of the Hotel Torrequebrada. The Torrequebrada combines a nightclub/cabaret, a restaurant, and an array of tables devoted to blackjack, chemin de fer, punto y banco, and two kinds of roulette. The nightclub presents a flamenco show from Tuesday to Saturday at 10:30pm. Many visitors prefer to just attend the show, paying 35€, including the first drink. Dinner is served Wednesday to Saturday at 9pm and costs 65€, which includes admission to the show. The casino is especially lively in midsummer. The casino, its facilities, and its gaming tables are open daily 9pm to 5am. The entrance fee to the gaming rooms is 4€. You need a passport to enter.

SWEDEN

by Darwin Porter & Danforth Prince

18

Although it was founded 7 centuries ago, Stockholm didn't become Sweden's capital until the mid–17th century. Today it's the capital of a modern welfare state with a strong focus on leisure activities and access to nature only a few minutes away.

Stockholm is the most regal, elegant, and intriguing city in Scandinavia, although don't tell our Danish and Norwegian friends that we said that. Stockholm presides over a country the size of California without the massive population of that state.

Because of Sweden's neutrality in World War II, it was spared from aerial bombardment, so much of what you see today is antique, especially the historical heart, Gamla Stan (Old Town). In contrast, Stockholm is one of the world's leading exponents of modern architecture.

STOCKHOLM & ENVIRONS

Stockholm is built on 14 islands in Lake Mälaren, marking the beginning of an archipelago of 24,000 islands, skerries, and islets that stretches all the way to the Baltic Sea. It's a city of bridges and islands, towers and steeples, cobblestone squares and broad boulevards, Renaissance splendor and steel-and-glass skyscrapers. The medieval walls of Gamla Stan (Old Town) no longer stand, but the winding streets have been preserved. You can even go fishing in downtown waterways, thanks to a long-ago decree from Queen Christina.

Once an ethnically homogeneous society, Stockholm has experienced a vast wave of immigration in the past several years. More than 10% of Sweden's residents are immigrants or children of immigrant parents, with most coming from other Scandinavian countries. Because of Sweden's strong stance on human rights, the country has also become a major destination for political and social refugees from Africa, the Middle East, and the former Yugoslavia as well.

An important aspect of Stockholm today is a growing interest in cultural activities. Over the past quarter of a century, attendance at live concerts has grown, book sales are up, and more and more people are visiting museums.

Sweden

Essentials

GETTING THERE

BY PLANE You'll arrive at **Stockholm Arlanda Airport** (✆ **08/797-60-00;** www.lfv.se), about 45km (28 miles) north of Stockholm on the E-4 highway. **SAS** (✆ **800/221-2350;** www.flysas.com) is the most common carrier. The fastest and cheapest way to go from the airport to the Central Station in Stockholm is on the **Arlanda Express** (www.arlandaexpress.com) train, which takes only 20 minutes and is covered by the Eurailpass. This high-speed link is the finest option for the rail traveler. Trains run every 15 minutes daily from 5am to midnight (six times an hour during rush hour Mon–Fri). If you don't have a rail pass, the cost of a one-way ticket is 240SEK for adults and 120SEK for seniors and students (kids 7 and under ride free). For more information, call ✆ **020/22-22-24.** A **bus** (✆ **08/588-22-828;**

www.flygbussarna.se), called **Flygbussarna,** outside the terminal building also goes to the City Terminal, Klarabergsviadukten, in the city center every 10 to 15 minutes (trip time: 40 min.), for 119SEK. A taxi to or from the airport is expensive, costing 450SEK to 550SEK or more. ***Travelers beware:*** Smaller taxi companies may charge up to 700SEK for the same ride. Be sure to ask in advance what the price is to your destination. **Taxi Stockholm** (✆ **08/15-00-00**) is a large, reputable company.

BY TRAIN The first high-speed train between Stockholm and Oslo has reduced travel time to 4 hours and 50 minutes between these two once remotely linked Scandinavian capitals. Depending on the day, there are two to three trains daily in each direction. This high-speed train now competes directly with air travel. Trains arrive at Stockholm's **Centralstationen (Central Station)** on Vasagatan 14, in the city center (✆ **07/717-57-575**). There you can make connections to Stockholm's subway, the T-bana. Follow the TUNNELBANA sign.

BY BUS Buses arrive at the **Centralstationen** on Vasagatan, and from here you can catch the T-bana (subway) to your Stockholm destination. For information in the Stockholm area, call ✆ **08/440-85-70.** Ticket office hours are Sunday to Friday 9am to 6pm; Saturday 9am to 4pm.

BY CAR Getting into Stockholm by car is relatively easy because the major national expressway from the south, E-4, joins with the national express highway, E-18, coming in from the west and leads right into the heart of the city. Stay on the highway until you see the turnoff for Central Stockholm or Centrum.

VISITOR INFORMATION

TOURIST OFFICES The **Tourist Centre** is at Sweden House, Hamngatan 27, off Kungsträdgården (Box 7542), S-103 93 Stockholm (✆ **08/508-31-508;** http://beta.stockholmtown.com). It's open Monday to Friday 9am to 7pm, Saturday 10am to 5pm, and Sunday 10am to 4pm. Closed December 24 and 25, and January 1. Maps and other free materials are available.

Kulturhuset, Sergels Torg 3 (✆ **08/508-314-00;** http://kulturhuset.stockholm.se), distributes information about cultural activities and organizations throughout Sweden and Europe. The largest organization of its kind in Sweden, it was built in 1974 by the city of Stockholm as a showcase for Swedish and international art and theater. There are no permanent exhibits; display spaces hold a changing array of paintings, sculpture, photographs, and live performance groups. Inside are a snack bar, a library (which has newspapers in several languages), a reading room, and a collection of recordings. Admission is 50SEK for adults, 25SEK for children 12 to 18, free for children 11 and under. It's open Tuesday to Friday 11am to 6pm, and Saturday and Sunday 11am to 5pm.

WEBSITES Go to the Scandinavian Tourism Board website at **www.goscandinavia.com** for maps, sightseeing information, ferry schedules, and other advice. Other useful sites are **http://beta.stockholmtown.com**, for updated events listings and advice on dining, lodging, and museums, and **www.visitsweden.com**.

CITY LAYOUT On the island of Normalm north of the Old Town are Stockholm's major streets, such as **Kungsgatan** (the main shopping street), **Birger Jarlsgatan,** and **Strandvägen** (leading to the Djurgården—home of many of the city's top sights). **Stureplan,** at the junction of the major avenues Kungsgatan and Birger Jarlsgatan, is the city's commercial hub.

The Stockholm Card

Stockholmskortet (Stockholm Card) is a discount card that allows unlimited travel by bus (except airport buses), subway, and local trains throughout the city and county of Stockholm. Admission to 75 attractions is included in the package. You can also take a sightseeing tour with City Sightseeing, getting on and off as often as you please. Tours are available daily from mid-June to mid-August. The card is good for a 50% discount on a boat trip to the Royal Palace of Drottningholm.

You can buy the card at several places in the city, including the Tourist Centre in Sweden House, Hotell-Centralen, the Central Station, the tourist information desk in many hotels, City Hall (summer only), the Kaknäs TV tower, SL-Center Sergels Torg (subway entrance level), and Pressbyrån newsstands. The cards are stamped with the date and time at the first use. A 24-hour card costs 395SEK for adults, 195SEK for children 7 to 17. Other cards are good for 48 hours, costing adults 525SEK or children 225SEK. Yet another card, valid for 72 hours, goes for 625SEK for adults, 245SEK for children. The card is a bargain if you plan to make a lot of use of it, running around all over the city, with an action-filled agenda. Of course, if you're more of a leisurely touring type, it would be much less of a bargain.

About 4 blocks west of the Stureplan rises **Hötorget City,** a landmark of modern urban planning. Its main traffic-free artery is the **Sergelgatan,** a 3-block shoppers' promenade that eventually leads to the modern sculptures in the center of the **Sergels Torg.** About 9 blocks south of the Stureplan, at **Gustav Adolfs Torg,** are the Royal Dramatic Theater and the Royal Opera House. A block east of the flaming torches of the Royal Opera House is the verdant north-south stretch of **Kungsträdgården,** part avenue, part public park, which serves as a popular gathering place for students and as a resting perch for shoppers. Three blocks southeast, on a famous promontory, lie the landmark Grand Hotel and the National Museum.

Kungsholmen, King's Island, is across a narrow canal from the rest of the city, a short walk west of the Central Station. It's visited chiefly by those wanting to tour Stockholm's elegant Stadshuset (City Hall). South of the island where **Gamla Stan (Old Town)** is located—and separated from it by a narrow but much-navigated stretch of water—is **Södermalm,** the southern district of Stockholm. Quieter than its northern counterpart, it's an important residential area with a distinctive flavor of its own.

To the east of Gamla Stan, on a large and forested island completely surrounded by the complicated waterways of Stockholm, is **Djurgården (Deer Park).** The rustically unpopulated summer pleasure ground of Stockholm, it's the site of many of the city's most popular attractions: the open-air museums of Skansen, the *Vasa* man-of-war, Gröna Lund's Tivoli, the Waldemarsudde estate of the "painting prince" Eugen, and the Nordic Museum.

GETTING AROUND Walking is the best way to get to know the city. In any case, you have to explore Gamla Stan on foot, as cars are banned from most of the streets. Djurgården and Skeppsholmen are other popular haunts for strolling.

BY PUBLIC TRANSPORTATION You can travel throughout Stockholm county by bus, local train, subway (T-bana), and tram, going from Singö in the north to Nynäshamn in the south. The routes are divided into zones, and one ticket is valid for all types of public transportation in the same zone within 1 hour of being stamped.

REGULAR FARES The basic fare for public transportation (subway, tram, streetcar, or bus) is 25SEK. Purchase a ticket for a tram or streetcar at the tollbooth on the subway platform. On buses you pay the driver. To travel in most of Stockholm, all the way to the borders of the inner city, requires two tickets. The maximum ride, to the outermost suburbs, requires five tickets. You can transfer free (or double back and return to your starting point) within 1 hour of your departure. Day passes can be purchased at the SL Center.

SPECIAL DISCOUNT TICKETS Your best transportation bet is a **tourist season ticket.** A 1-day card costs 100SEK and is valid for 24 hours of unlimited travel by T-bana (subway), bus, and commuter train within Stockholm. It also includes passage on the ferry to Djurgården. Most visitors will probably prefer the 3-day card for 200SEK, valid for 72 hours in Stockholm and the adjacent county. The 3-day card is also valid for admission to the Kaknäs tower and to Gröna Lund Tivoli, and a 50% discount to the Skansen museum. A day card for a child 7 to 17 costs 60SEK; kids 6 and under travel free with an adult. Tickets are available at tourist information offices, in subway stations, and from most news vendors. Call ✆ **08/689-10-00** for more information.

You can also opt for the **Stockholm Card;** see the box above for full details.

BY T-BANA (SUBWAY) Subway entrances are marked with a blue T on a white background. Tickets are bought on the platform. For information about schedules, routes, and fares, phone ✆ **08/600-10-00.**

BY BUS Where the subway line ends, the bus begins. If the subway doesn't reach an area, a bus will. Many visitors ride the bus to Djurgården (although you can walk), where the T-bana doesn't go. If you're staying long enough to warrant it, you can buy the *SL Stockholmskartan* booklet for 100SEK at the Tourist Centre at Sweden House, Hamngatan 27, off Kungsträdgården (✆ **08/789-24-95** for a list of bus routes).

BY FERRY Ferries from Skeppsbron on Gamla Stan (near the bridge to Södermalm) can take you to Djurgården if you don't want to walk or go by bus. They leave every 20 minutes Monday to Saturday, and about every 15 minutes on Sunday, from 9am to 6pm. The fare is 30SEK for adults, 25SEK for seniors and children 7 to 12, free for children 6 and under.

BY TAXI Taxi fares in Stockholm are the most expensive in the world and vary with different taxi companies. In Stockholm, even a short ride can cost 100SEK. You can hail those that display the sign LEDIG, or you can request one by phone. **Taxi Stockholm** (✆ **08/15-00-00**) is a large, reputable company.

BY CAR In general, you can park in marked spaces Monday through Friday from 8am to 6pm, but these spaces are hard to come by. Consider leaving your car in a parking garage—there are several in the city center and on the outskirts—and using public transportation. Parking exceptions or rules for specific areas are indicated on signs in the area. At Djurgården, parking is always prohibited, and from April to mid-September, it's closed to traffic Friday to Sunday.

Avis (✆ **07/70-82-00-62**) and **Hertz** (✆ **08/797-99-00**) maintain offices at Arlanda Airport. Hertz's downtown office is at Vasagatan 26 (✆ **08/454-62-50**); Avis's central office is at Vasagatan 10B (✆ **08/20-20-60**). Rentals at both organizations are usually cheaper if you reserve them by phone before leaving home.

[FastFACTS] STOCKHOLM

Currency You'll pay your way in Sweden with Swedish krone (singular, krona), or crowns, which is universally abbreviated SEK. These are divided into 100 øre. The exchange rate used throughout this chapter was $1 = 7SEK. Note that although Sweden is a member of the E.U., in 2002 it opted not to adopt the euro as its national currency.

Dentists In an emergency, go to **Sct. Eriks Hospital,** Fleminggatan 22 (✆ **08/654-11-17**), open daily from 8am to 5pm.

Doctors For 24-hour emergency medical care, check with **Medical Care Information** (✆ **08/672-10-00**). There's also a private clinic, **City Akuten,** Apelberg Sq. 481, 4th Floor (✆ **08/412-29-61**).

Drugstores One 24-hour pharmacy is **C. W. Scheele,** Klarabergsgatan 64 (✆ **08/454-81-00;** T-bana: Centralen).

Embassies & Consulates The embassy of the **United States** is at Daghammarskjölds väg 31, S-115 89 Stockholm (✆ **08/783-53-00;** T-bana: Östermalmstorg); the embassy of the **United Kingdom** (✆ **08/671-30-00**) is at Skarpügatan 6–8 (mailing address: P.O. Box 27819, S-115 93 Stockholm); the embassy of **Canada** is at Tegelbacken 4, S-103 23 Stockholm (✆ **08/453-30-00;** T-bana: Centralen); the embassy of **Ireland** (✆ **08/661-80-05;** T-bana: Östermalmstorg) is at Östermalmsgatan 97 (mailing address: P.O. Box 10326, S-100 55 Stockholm); the embassy of **Australia** (✆ **08/613-29-00;** T-bana: Hötorget) is at Sergels Torg 12 (mailing address: P.O. Box 7003, S-103 86 Stockholm); the embassy of **South Africa** is at Linnégaten 76, S-115 00 Stockholm (✆ **08/24-39-50;** T-bana: Östermalmstorg); and the General Consulate of **New Zealand** is at Stureplan 2, S-102 27 (✆ **08-506-32-00;** T-bana: Östermalmstorg). Call for hours.

Emergencies Call ✆ **211** or 90-000 for the police, ambulance service, or the fire department.

Internet One of the best places for receiving e-mail or checking messages is **Matrix Web World,** Hötorget X (✆ **08/200-293;** T-bana: Hötorget). It charges only 1SEK per minute, and is open Monday to Thursday daily from 10am to midnight, Friday and Saturday 10am to 3am.

Post Office The main post office is at Sveavagen 31 (✆ **08/411-61-17**), open Monday to Friday 9am to 6pm and Saturday 9am to noon.

Taxes Sweden imposes a "value-added tax," called *moms,* on most goods and services. Visitors from North America can beat the tax, however, by shopping in stores with the yellow-and-blue tax-free shopping sign. There are more than 15,000 of these stores in Sweden. To get a refund, your total purchase must cost a minimum of 200SEK. Tax refunds range from 14% to 18%, depending on the amount purchased. Moms begins at 12% on food items, but is 25% for most goods and services. The tax is part of the purchase price, but you can get a tax-refund voucher before you leave the store. When you leave Sweden, take the voucher to a tax-free Customs desk at the airport or train station you're leaving from. They will give you your moms refund (minus a small service charge) before you wing off to your next non-Swedish destination. Two requirements: You cannot use your purchase in Sweden (it should be sealed in its original packaging), and it must be taken out of the country within 1 month after purchase. For more information, call **Global Refund** at ✆ **20/741741;** or go to www.globalrefund.com.

Telephone The **country code** for Sweden is **46.** The **city code** for Stockholm is **8;** use this code when you're calling from outside Sweden. If you're within Sweden but not in Stockholm, use **08.** If you're calling within Stockholm, simply leave off the code and dial the regular phone number.

Instructions in English are posted in **public phone boxes,** which can be found on street corners. Very few phones in Sweden are coin-operated; most require the purchase of a phone card (called a **Telekort**). You can obtain phone cards at most newspaper stands and tobacco shops.

You can make international calls from the **Tele-Center Office** on the Central Station's ground floor (✆ **08/789-24-56**), open daily from 8am to 9pm, except major holidays. Long-distance rates are posted.

For directory listings or other information for Stockholm or other parts of Sweden only, dial ✆ **118118;** for other parts of Europe, dial ✆ **118119.**

Tipping Hotels include a 15% service charge in your bill. Restaurants, depending on their class, add 13% to 15% to your tab. Taxi drivers are entitled to 8% of the fare, and cloakroom attendants usually get 8SEK.

Where to Stay

By the standards of many North American cities, hotels in Stockholm are very expensive. If the prices make you want to cancel your trip, read on. Dozens of hotels offer reduced rates on weekends all year and daily from around mid-June to mid-August. For further information, inquire at a travel agency or the tourist office (see "Visitor Information," above). In the summer, it's best to make reservations in advance just to be on the safe side.

Most medium-priced hotels are in Norrmalm, north of the Old Town, and many of the least expensive lodgings are near the Central Station. There are comparably priced inexpensive accommodations within 10 to 20 minutes of the city, easily reached by subway, streetcar, or bus. We'll suggest a few hotels in the Old Town, but they're limited and more expensive.

Note: In most cases a service charge ranging from 10% to 15% is added to the bill, plus the inevitable 25% moms. Unless otherwise indicated, all our recommended accommodations come with a private bathroom.

IN THE CITY CENTER

Very Expensive

Grand Hotel ★★★ Opposite the Royal Palace, this hotel—a bastion of elite hospitality since 1874 and a member of the Leading Hotels of the World—is the finest in Sweden. The most recent restoration was in 2006, which retained the grand and conservatively modern styling of the lobby, but added 72 new rooms and made major changes to the bar and to the grander of the two hotel restaurants. Guest rooms come in all shapes and sizes, all elegantly appointed with traditional styling. The priciest rooms overlook the water. The hotel's ballroom is an exact copy of Louis XIV's Hall of Mirrors at Versailles.

Södra Blasieholmshamnen 8, S-103 27 Stockholm. ✆ **800/745-8883** in the U.S. and Canada, or 08/679-35-60. Fax 08/679-35-61. www.grandhotel.se. 368 units. 3,900SEK–6,800SEK double; from

7,500SEK suite. AE, DC, MC, V. Parking 395SEK. T-bana: Kungsträdgården. Bus: 46, 55, 62, or 76. **Amenities:** 2 restaurants; bar; babysitting; concierge; exercise room; room service; sauna. *In room:* A/C (in some), hair dryer, minibar, Wi-Fi (free).

Expensive

Berns Hotel ★★ During its 19th-century heyday, this was the most elegant hotel in Sweden, with an ornate Gilded Age interior that was the setting for many a legendary rendezvous. In 1989, following years of neglect, it was rebuilt in the original style, and the restaurant facilities were upgraded. Although the dining and drinking areas are usually crowded with club kids and bar patrons, the guest rooms are soundproof and comfortably isolated from the activities downstairs. Each room has a bathroom sheathed in Italian marble; the bathrooms are small but have neatly maintained shower units. The **Red Room** is the setting and namesake of Strindberg's novel *Röda Rummet.*

Näckströmsgatan 8, S-111 47 Stockholm. ✆ **08/566-322-22.** Fax 08/566-322-01. www.berns.se. 82 units. 2,800SEK–4,100SEK double; 4,800SEK–6,500SEK suite. Rates include breakfast. AE, DC, MC, V. Parking 375SEK. T-bana: Östermalmstorg. **Amenities:** Restaurant; 2 bars; babysitting; concierge; exercise room; room service; sauna. *In room:* TV, hair dryer, minibar, Wi-Fi (free).

Nordic Hotel ★★ There's nothing in Scandinavia quite like this hotel, named "The World's Sexiest Hotel" by *Elle UK* magazine. It's sort of a split personality—its astrological sign is definitely Gemini. You're given a choice of a room of "watery calm" in the 367-room Nordic Sea or "postminimalist luminescence" in the 175-room Nordic Light. Each hotel has its own individual design. Nordic Sea, of course, turns to the ocean for its inspiration and features a 530-liter aquarium. Nordic Light is filled with sun-shaped projections that guarantee a bright light even on the darkest winter days. The suggestive light patterns projecting from the walls re-create the ever-changing patterns of the lights of the north. This hotel is not just about gimmicks, however—it offers real comfort. Nordic Light guest rooms have the best sound insulation in town. Wood, steel, and glass create both clublike and maritime auras in Nordic Sea rooms.

4-7 Vasaplan. ✆ **800/337-4685** in the U.S., or 08/50-56-30-00. Fax 08/50-56-30-40. www.nordicseahotel.se. 367 units in Nordic Sea, 175 units in Nordic Light. 1,400SEK–4,000SEK double; June 20–Aug 17 and during selected Fri–Sun nights throughout the winter, rates are reduced. AE, DC, MC, V. T-bana: Centralen. **Amenities:** Restaurant; 2 bars; babysitting; concierge; exercise room; room service; sauna; spa; steam bath; Wi-Fi (120SEK per day). *In room:* TV, hair dryer, minibar.

Native Behavior

Although not as common as it once was, partaking in a Swedish smörgåsbord is the most typical of Swedish culinary delights. Some restaurants and hotels still stage this lavish banquet. The secret of surviving it is to go gracefully to the table that's groaning with heaping platters of food and not overload your plate. You can always return for more of the *gravad lax* (thinly sliced salmon cured in dill) or Swedish meatballs.

And when you've had too much smörgåsbord or other Swedish food delicacies, and joined in too many toasts fueled by the lethal aquavit, you can also always do as the Swedes do and retire to the nearest sauna bath to revitalize yourself for yet more revelry in the evening to come.

Stockholm

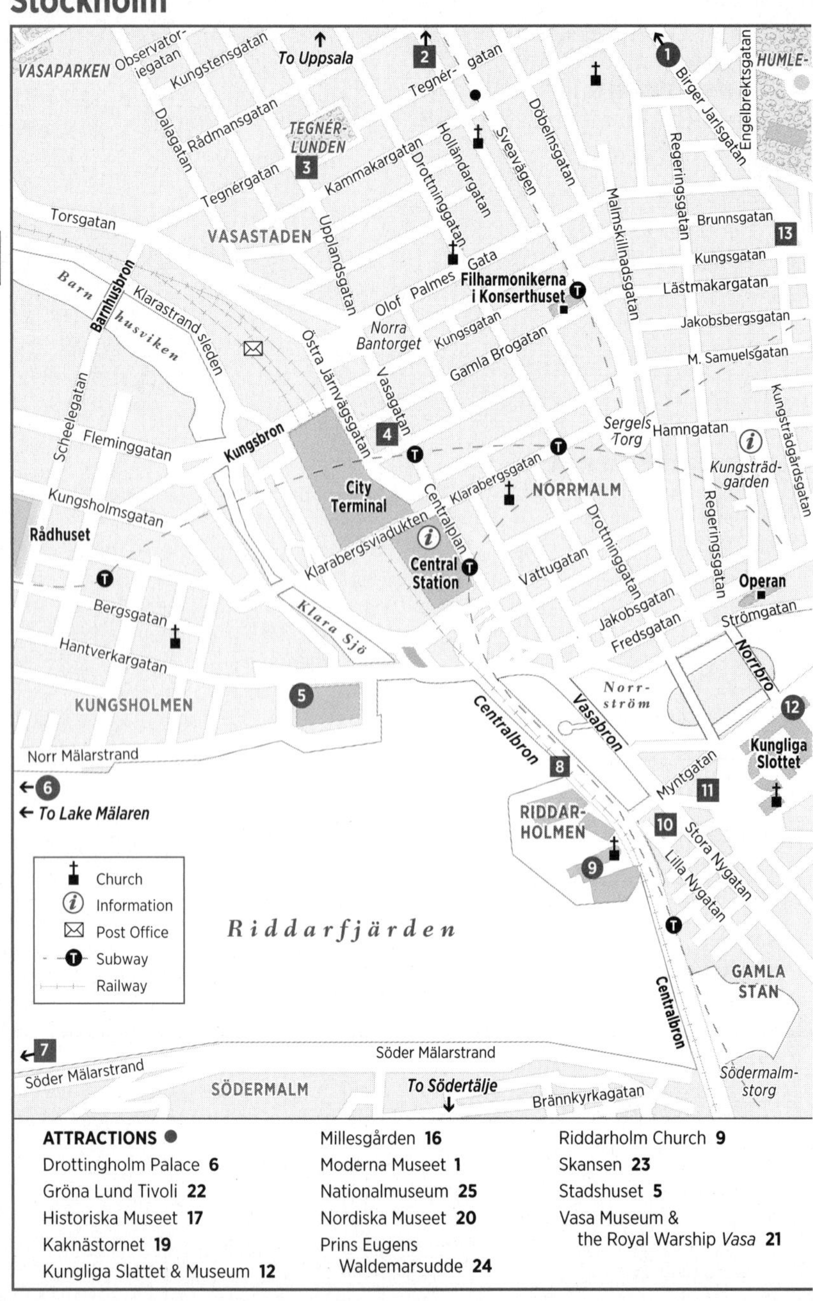
To Uppsala
VASAPARKEN
Observatoriegatan
Kungstensgatan
Dalagatan
Rådmansgatan
TEGNÉRLUNDEN
Tegnérgatan
Kammakargatan
Drottninggatan
Holländargatan
Sveavägen
Döbelnsgatan
Birger Jarlsgatan
Engelbrektsgatan
HUMLE-
Regeringsgatan
Malmskillnadsgatan
Brunnsgatan
Kungsgatan
Lästmakargatan
Jakobsbergsgatan
M. Samuelsgatan
Torsgatan
VASASTADEN
Upplandsgatan
Olof Palmes Gata
Filharmonikerna i Konserthuset
Barnhusbron
Barnhusviken
Klarastrand sleden
Östra Järnvägsgatan
Norra Bantorget
Kungsgatan
Gamla Brogatan
Vasagatan
Sergels Torg
Hamngatan
Kungsträdgårdsgatan
Kungsträdgarden
Scheelegatan
Fleminggatan
Kungsbron
City Terminal
Centralplan
Klarabergsgatan
NORRMALM
Kungsholmsgatan
Rådhuset
Klarabergsviadukten
Central Station
Drottninggatan
Vattugatan
Regeringsgatan
Operan
Strömgatan
Bergsgatan
Hantverkargatan
Klara Sjö
Jakobsgatan
Fredsgatan
Norrbro
KUNGSHOLMEN
Norrström
Centralbron
Vasabron
Kungliga Slottet
Norr Mälarstrand
To Lake Mälaren
RIDDARHOLMEN
Myntgatan
Stora Nygatan
Lilla Nygatan
Church
Information
Post Office
Subway
Railway
Riddarfjärden
GAMLA STAN
Centralbron
Söder Mälarstrand
Söder Mälarstrand
SÖDERMALM
To Södertälje
Brännkyrkagatan
Södermalmstorg
ATTRACTIONS
Drottingholm Palace 6
Gröna Lund Tivoli 22
Historiska Museet 17
Kaknästornet 19
Kungliga Slattet & Museum 12
Millesgården 16
Moderna Museet 1
Nationalmuseum 25
Nordiska Museet 20
Prins Eugens Waldemarsudde 24
Riddarholm Church 9
Skansen 23
Stadshuset 5
Vasa Museum & the Royal Warship Vasa 21

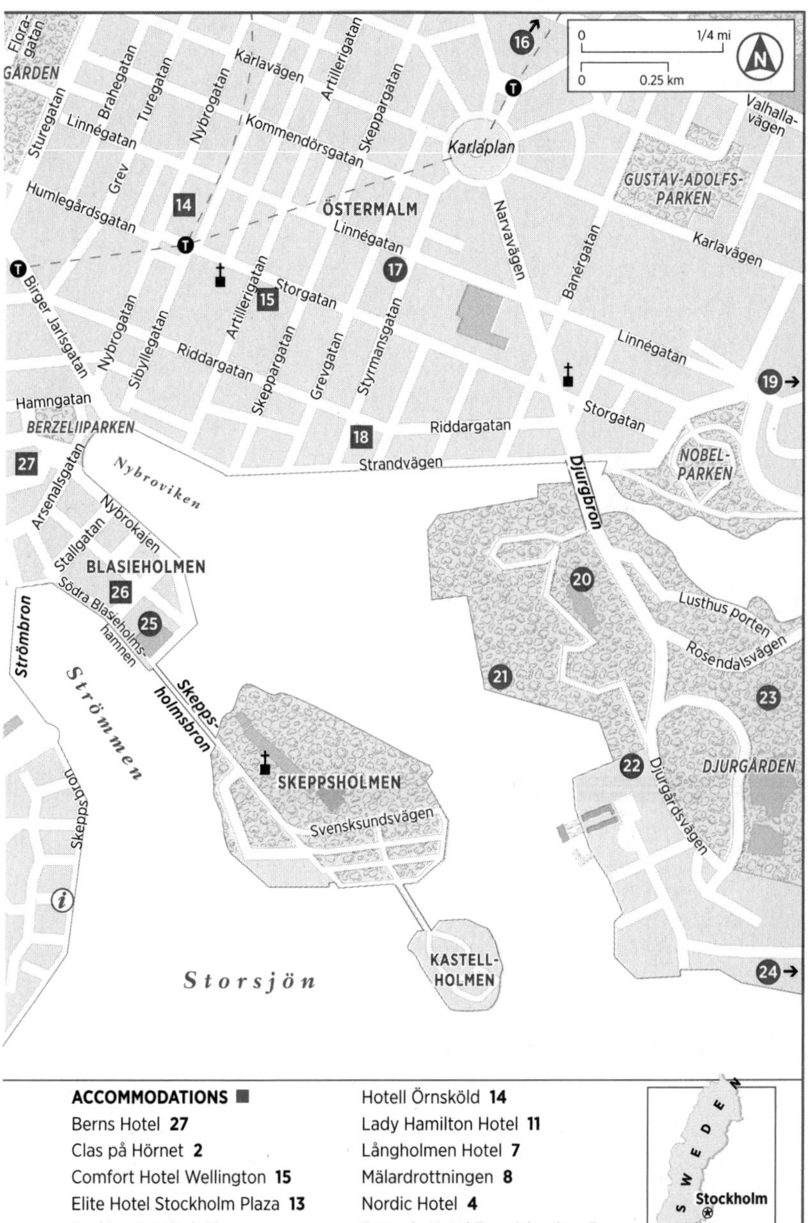
0 1/4 mi
0 0.25 km
N
Flora-gatan
GÄRDEN
Sturegatan
Brahegatan
Turegatan
Nybrogatan
Karlavägen
Artillerigatan
Skeppargatan
Linnégatan
Grev
Kommendörsgatan
Karlaplan
Valhalla-vägen
GUSTAV-ADOLFS-PARKEN
Humlegårdsgatan
14
ÖSTERMALM
Narvavägen
Banérgatan
Karlavägen
16
17
15
Birger Jarlsgatan
Storgatan
Sibyllegatan
Riddargatan
Grevgatan
Styrmansgatan
Linnégatan
19
Hamngatan
BERZELIIPARKEN
18
Riddargatan
Strandvägen
Storgatan
NOBEL-PARKEN
27
Arsenalsgatan
Nybroviken
Djurgbron
Nybrokajen
Stallgatan
BLASIEHOLMEN
26
Södra Blasieholms-hamnen
25
20
Lusthus porten
Rosendalsvägen
Strömbron
Strömmen
Skepps-holmsbron
21
23
Skeppsbron
SKEPPSHOLMEN
22
Djurgårdsvägen
DJURGÅRDEN
Svensksundsvägen
KASTELL-HOLMEN
Storsjön
24
ACCOMMODATIONS
Berns Hotel 27
Clas på Hörnet 2
Comfort Hotel Wellington 15
Elite Hotel Stockholm Plaza 13
Esplanade Hotel 18
Grand Hotel 26
Hotell Örnsköld 14
Lady Hamilton Hotel 11
Långholmen Hotel 7
Mälardrottningen 8
Nordic Hotel 4
Ramada Hotel Tegnérlunden 3
Victory Hotel 10
SWEDEN
Stockholm

Moderate

Clas på Hörnet ★★ 🎁 Built in the 1730s as a private house, this small, upscale, and charming inn is less than a kilometer (½ mile) north of the commercial heart of Stockholm. Its attention to period detail—whose installation was supervised by the curators of the Stockholm City Museum—lends a distinctive country-inn ambience that's enhanced with bedrooms outfitted in the late-18th-century style of Gustavus III. Each of the bedrooms is outfitted in a different color scheme and motif, and wide floorboards and antiques. Many have four-poster beds.

Surbrunnsgatan 20, S-113 48 Stockholm. ✆ **08/16-51-36.** Fax 08/612-53-15. www.claspahornet.se. 10 units. Sun–Thurs 1,695SEK double, Fri–Sat 1,395SEK double; Sun–Thurs 2,395SEK double suite, Fri–Sat 1,595SEK double suite. Rates include breakfast. AE, DC, MC, V. Parking 220SEK. Bus: 46 or 53. **Amenities:** Breakfast room; lounge. *In room:* TV, minibar, Wi-Fi (free).

Comfort Hotel Wellington ★ This is a good, safe address—the type of place your great-aunt wants you to stay in. The nine-story Wellington sounds like something you'd find in London. Built in the late 1950s, it maintains some English decorative touches and lies in a convenient neighborhood. The public rooms are filled with engravings of English hunting scenes and leather-covered chairs. Some of the small but stylish guest rooms overlook a flower-filled courtyard, and units on higher floors have panoramic views.

Storgatan 6, S-11451 Stockholm. ✆ **08/667-09-10.** Fax 08/667-12-54. www.wellington.se. 60 units. 1,950SEK–3,295SEK double. Rates include breakfast. AE, DC, MC, V. Parking 250SEK. T-bana: Östermalmstorg. **Amenities:** Breakfast room; bar; sauna. *In room:* TV, hair dryer, Wi-Fi (free).

Elite Hotel Stockholm Plaza ★ Built on a triangular lot that might remind some visitors of New York's Flatiron Building, this first-class hotel is a well-run and inviting choice in the city center. From the time of its construction in 1903, the building had many uses—a run-down rooming house, private apartments, and offices. The light, fresh guest rooms have firm beds and tiled bathrooms.

Birger Jarlsgatan 29, S-103 95 Stockholm. ✆ **08/566-220-00.** Fax 08/566-220-20. www.elite.se. 143 units. 1,550SEK–2,700SEK double; 2,650SEK–5,200SEK suite. Rates include breakfast. AE, DC, MC, V. Parking 280SEK. T-bana: Hötorget or Östermalmstorg. **Amenities:** Restaurant; bar; dance club; room service; sauna. *In room:* TV, hair dryer, minibar, Wi-Fi (free).

Esplanade Hotel ★ This informal hotel, next to the more expensive Diplomat, attracts representatives from the nearby embassies and others who like its comfortable charm and traditional atmosphere. Constructed in 1910, it became a family-style hotel in 1954. Many of the rooms, furnished in old-fashioned style, have minibars. Single rooms are minuscule. Most doubles have double-glazed windows and extra-long beds. Four rooms open onto a water view, and the English lounge features a balcony with a view of Djurgården. Only breakfast is served.

Strandvägen 7A, S-114 56 Stockholm. ✆ **08/663-07-40.** Fax 08/662-59-92. www.hotelesplanade.se. 34 units. Mon–Thurs 2,395SEK–2,595SEK double; Fri–Sun 1,795SEK double. Rates include breakfast. AE, DC, MC, V. Parking nearby 250SEK. T-bana: Östermalmstorg. Bus: 47 or 69. **Amenities:** Lounge; sauna. *In room:* TV, hair dryer, minibar, Wi-Fi (free).

Hotell Örnsköld The five-story building that contains this hotel was built in 1910, and today the nearby Royal Dramatic Theater uses most of it for prop storage and staff housing. The hotel is situated on the second floor. High-ceilinged rooms have simple, contemporary furnishings, and more expensive units are big enough to hold extra beds if necessary.

Nybrogatan 6, S-114 43 Stockholm. ✆ **08/667-02-85.** Fax 08/667-69-91. www.hotelornskold.se. 27 units. 1,495SEK–2,195SEK double. Rates include breakfast. AE, MC, V. T-bana: Östermalmstorg. **Amenities:** Lounge. *In room:* TV, hair dryer, minibar, Wi-Fi (free).

Ramada Hotel Tegnérlunden ★ ☺ In a 19th-century building at the edge of a city park, this hotel has a few public rooms, a lobby, and a bar. The best feature is the tasteful, functionally furnished rooms, many suitable for families. They're blissfully quiet, especially those opening onto the rear. The rooms vary in size and shape, and those we inspected were well maintained. The hotel offers comfort but not a lot of style. The bathrooms equipped with shower units are small but beautifully kept.

Tegnérlunden 8, S-113 59 Stockholm. ✆ **08/545-455-50.** Fax 08/545-455-51. www.hoteltegnerlunden.se. 102 units. 1,090SEK–2,690SEK double; 1,690SEK–3,290SEK junior suite. Rates include breakfast. AE, DC, MC, V. Parking 250SEK in nearby garage. Bus: 47, 53, or 69. **Amenities:** Bar; sauna. *In room:* TV, hair dryer, Wi-Fi (free).

IN GAMLA STAN (OLD TOWN)

Expensive

Lady Hamilton Hotel ★ 🎁 This hotel consists of three connected buildings, and stands on a quiet street surrounded by antiques shops and restaurants—a very desirable location indeed. Dozens of antiques are scattered among the well-furnished guest rooms. Most rooms have beamed ceilings. The beds (queen-size or double) are of high quality. Top-floor rooms have skylights and memorable views over the Old Town. You'll get a sense of the 1470 origins of this hotel when you use the luxurious sauna, which encompasses the stone-rimmed well that formerly supplied the building's water. The ornate staircase wraps around a large model of a clipper ship suspended from the ceiling.

Storkyrkobrinken 5, S-111 28 Stockholm. ✆ **08/506-401-00.** Fax 08/506-401-10. www.lady-hamilton.se. 34 units. 1,290SEK–3,690SEK double. AE, DC, MC, V. Parking 395SEK. T-bana: Gamla Stan. Bus: 48. **Amenities:** Bistro; room service; sauna. *In room:* TV, hair dryer, Wi-Fi (120SEK per day; 1st 6 hr. free).

Victory Hotel ★★ A small but stylish hotel, the Victory offers warm, inviting rooms, each named after a prominent sea captain. They sport a pleasing combination of exposed wood, antiques, and 19th-century memorabilia. Many rooms are smoke free, and the beds are comfortable. The hotel rests on the foundations of a 1382 fortified tower. In the 1700s the building's owners buried a massive silver treasure under the basement floor—you can see it in the Stockholm City Museum. From the stairs you'll see one of Sweden's largest collections of 18th-century nautical needlepoint, much of it created by the sailors during their long voyages.

Lilla Nygatan 3–5, S-111 28 Stockholm. ✆ **08/506-400-00.** Fax 08/506-400-10. www.victory-hotel.se. 45 units. 1,390SEK–3,690SEK double; 2,690SEK–5,090SEK suite. AE, DC, MC, V. Parking 395SEK. T-bana: Gamla Stan. Bus: 48. **Amenities:** Restaurant; bar; babysitting; small indoor pool; room service. *In room:* TV, hair dryer, minibar, Wi-Fi (free).

Moderate

Mälardrottningen ★ 🎁 During its heyday, this was the most famous motor yacht in the world, the subject of gossip columns everywhere, thanks to the complicated friendships that developed among the passengers and, in some cases, the crew. Built in 1924 by millionaire C. K. G. Billings, it was the largest (72m/236 ft.) motor yacht in the world, and was later acquired by the Woolworth heiress, Barbara Hutton. The below-deck space originally contained only seven suites. The yacht was converted into a hotel in the early 1980s, and was permanently moored beside a satellite island of Stockholm's Old Town. The cabins are now cramped and somewhat claustrophobic. Most have bunk-style twin beds. Considering the hotel's conversation-piece status, and its location close to everything in the Old Town, it might be worth an overnight stay.

Riddarholmen, S-111 28 Stockholm. ✆ **08/545-187-80.** Fax 08/24-36-76. www.malardrottningen.se. 60 units. Sun–Thurs 1,340SEK–2,420SEK double; Fri–Sat 1,110SEK–2,400SEK double. Rates include breakfast. AE, DC, MC, V. Parking 220SEK per 24 hr. T-bana: Gamla Stan. **Amenities:** Restaurant; bar; sauna. *In room:* TV, hair dryer, Wi-Fi (free).

ON LÅNGHOLMEN

Långholmen Hotel Beginning in 1724, on the little island of Långholmen, this structure was a state penitentiary for women charged with "loose living." The last prisoner was released in 1972, and today it's a newly restored and reasonably priced hotel that, in addition to comfortable but small rooms, also houses a museum of Sweden's prison history and one of the best restaurants in the country. Instead of a prison induction area, you get the hotel's reception area and a 24-hour snack bar. Accommodations were carved from some 200 cells, creating cramped but serviceable rooms. Eighty-nine of the rooms are rented only to solo travelers, making this one of the best hotels in Stockholm for the single visitor on a budget. Just 13 rooms are large enough to accommodate two persons.

Långholm, S-102 72 Stockholm. ✆ **08/720-85-00.** Fax 08/720-85-75. www.langholmen.com. 102 units. Sun–Thurs 1,540SEK single, 1,890SEK double; Fri–Sat 1,090SEK single, 1,950SEK double. Extra bed 250SEK per person. Rates include breakfast. AE, DC, MC, V. T-bana: Hornstul. Bus: 4, 40, or 66. **Amenities:** Restaurant; bar. *In room:* TV, hair dryer, Wi-Fi (free).

IN SÖDERMALM

Rival Hotel ★★ 🎁 Stockholm's first boutique hotel is a little charmer, and it's also home to a restaurant, bar, and bistro, and even a cinema, cocktail lounge, cafe, and bakery. A partnership with Sony allowed the hotel to get 32-inch plasma TVs and DVD players in all of its rooms and to install a wireless communication system that runs throughout the building. The Art Deco designs and film theme combine harmoniously. The hotel's owner, Benny Anderson, wanted to re-create the aura of the Aston Hotel, which opened on this site in the 1930s. Some of the bedrooms are small, others much larger, and some have a French-style balcony. Movie scenes can be seen above the bed in each room.

Mariatorget 3, S-118 91 Stockholm. ✆ **08/545-78900.** Fax 08/545-78924. www.rival.se. 99 units. Sun–Thurs 2,495SEK–2,955SEK double; Fri–Sat 1,595SEK–2,195SEK double. AE, DC, MC, V. T-bana: Mariatorget. **Amenities:** Restaurant; bistro; cafe; bar. *In room:* A/C, TV/DVD, hair dryer, minibar, Wi-Fi (free).

Where to Dine

IN THE CITY CENTER

Very Expensive

If you're into gourmet and ethnic foods, stop at **Hötorgshallen** (www.hotorgshallen.se; T-bana: Hötorget), an indoor market that contains 32 cafes and stores. Food specialties from all over the world are sold here, including delectable lamb, bitter orange marmalade, fresh shellfish, rare jams (some from Nordic climes), cheeses, and all kinds of meats. The market dates from the 13th century, although the present building is more recent. It's an ideal place to grab something to eat and take in the cultural diffusion of Sweden.

Mathias Dahlgren ★★★ SWEDISH/INTERNATIONAL At this exclusive restaurant, two different dining experiences complement each other: the *Matsalen* ("Dining Room") and *Matbaren* ("Food Bar"). The chef, for whom the restaurant is named, has been chosen as chef of the year in Sweden twice since 2000. He is known for his surprising combinations of taste, his contrasting textures, and his highly evolved sauces. Meals start with a marble-size ball of bread that was a staple of his childhood. Main courses can be simple and regional, as evoked by Dahlgren's pig's cheek paired with sausage, Jerusalem artichokes, and black trumpet mushrooms. Or they can be grand, with more elaborate dishes such as a six-course tasting menu, saddle of roe deer, or a fusion of cauliflower and lobster. Desserts can be daringly modern, such as pumpkin vanilla licorice. Guests pass through a sea-blue bar on their way to the Food Bar, which has local Swedish dishes, such as brisket of lamb with potatoes and truffles, salmon tartare with apples and horseradish cream, or the classic raw and smoked reindeer with whitefish roe.

In the Grand Hotel, Södra Blasieholmshamnen 8. ✆ **08/679-35-84.** Reservations required. Main courses 345SEK–495SEK; tasting menu 1,400SEK; *Matbaren* meal 1,500SEK. AE, DC, MC, V. *Matsalen* Tues–Sat 7pm–midnight; *Matbaren* Mon–Fri noon–2pm, Mon–Sat 6pm–midnight. Bus: 45, 55, 62, or 76.

Operakällaren (The Opera House) ★★★ FRENCH/SWEDISH Opposite the Royal Palace, this is the most famous and unashamedly luxurious restaurant in Sweden. Its elegant decor and style are reminiscent of a royal court banquet. The service and house specialties are impeccable. Many come here for the elaborate fixed-price menus; others prefer the classic Swedish dishes or the modern French ones. A house specialty that's worth the trip is the platter of northern delicacies, with everything from smoked eel to smoked reindeer, along with Swedish red caviar. Salmon and game, including grouse from the northern forests, are prepared in various ways. There's a cigar room, too.

Operahuset, Kungsträdgården. ✆ **08/676-58-01** or 08/676-58-00. Reservations required. Main courses 320SEK–515SEK; 4-course fixed-price menu 860SEK; 9-course *menu dégustation* with wine 1,240SEK. AE, DC, MC, V. Tues–Sat 6pm–midnight. Closed July. T-bana: Kungsträdgården.

Expensive

Franska Matsalen (French Dining Room) ★★ FRENCH Widely acclaimed as one of the greatest restaurants in Stockholm, this elegant establishment is on the street level of the city's finest hotel. The dining room is appointed with polished mahogany, ormolu, and gilt accents under an ornate plaster ceiling. Tables on the enclosed veranda overlook the Royal Palace and the Old Town. Begin with a cannelloni of foie gras with crepes, or perhaps mousseline of scallops with sevruga caviar. Main dishes include seared sweetbreads served with artichokes; *langoustines* (prawns) and frogs' legs with broad beans; and veal tartare with caviar. Fresh Swedish salmon is also featured. The chefs—highly trained professionals working with the finest ingredients—have pleased some of Europe's more demanding palates.

In the Grand Hotel, Södra Blasieholmshamnen 8. ✆ **08/679-35-84.** Reservations required. 5-course menu 1,250SEK; 8-course menu 1,500SEK. AE, DC, MC, V. Tues–Sat 7–11pm. T-bana: Kungsträdgården. Bus: 46, 55, 62, or 76.

Wedholms Fisk ★★★ SWEDISH/FRENCH This is one of the classic—and one of the best—restaurants in Stockholm. It has no curtains in the windows and no carpets, but the display of modern paintings by Swedish artists is riveting. You might begin with marinated herring with garlic and bleak roe, or tartare of salmon with salmon roe. The chef has reason to be proud of such dishes as perch poached with clams and saffron sauce, prawns marinated in herbs and served with Dijon hollandaise, and grilled filet of sole with Beaujolais sauce. The cuisine is both innovative and traditional—for example, chèvre mousse accompanies simple tomato salad, but the menu also features homey, comforting cream-stewed potatoes.

Nybrokajen 17. ✆ **08/611-78-74.** Reservations required. Main courses 200SEK-255SEK lunch, 265SEK-595SEK dinner. AE, DC, MC, V. Mon-Fri 11:30am-11pm; Sat 5-11pm. In July, open only for dinner. T-bana: Östermalmstorg.

Moderate

Bakfickan ★ SWEDISH Tucked away behind the Operakällaren, the "Back Pocket" is a chic place to eat for a moderate price. It shares a kitchen with its glamorous neighbor Operakällaren (see above), but its prices are more bearable. Main dishes may include salmon in several varieties, including boiled with hollandaise and salmon roe. You might also try beef Rydberg (thinly sliced tenderloin). In season you can order reindeer and elk. In the summer, nothing's finer than the rich ice cream with a sauce of arctic cloudberries. Many patrons like to dine at the horseshoe-shaped bar.

Jakobs Torg 12. ✆ **08/676-58-09.** Reservations not accepted. Main courses 149SEK-299SEK. AE, DC, MC, V. Daily 11:30am-11pm. T-bana: Kungsträdgården.

Eriks Bakfica SWEDISH Although other restaurants in Stockholm bear the name Eriks, this one is relatively inexpensive and offers particularly good value. Established in 1979, it features a handful of Swedish dishes from the tradition of *husmanskost* (wholesome home cooking). A favorite opener is toast Skagen, with shrimp, dill-flavored mayonnaise, spices, and bleak roe. There's also a daily choice of herring appetizers. Try the tantalizing "archipelago stew," a ragout of fish prepared with tomatoes and served with garlic mayonnaise. Marinated salmon is served with hollandaise sauce. You might also try Eriks's cheeseburger with the special secret sauce, but you have to ask for it—you won't find it on the menu.

Fredrikshovsgatan 4. ✆ **08/660-15-99.** Reservations recommended. Main courses 250SEK-300SEK. AE, DC, MC, V. Mon-Fri 11:30am-midnight; Sat-Sun 5-11pm. Bus: 47.

KB Restaurant SWEDISH/CONTINENTAL A traditional artists' rendezvous in the center of town, KB Restaurant features good Swedish food as well as Continental dishes. Fish dishes are especially recommended. You might begin with salmon trout roe and Russian caviar, followed by boiled turbot or lamb roast with stuffed zucchini in thyme-flavored bouillon. Dishes usually come with aromatic, freshly baked sourdough bread. Desserts include sorbets with fresh fruit and berries, and a heavenly lime soufflé with orange-blossom honey. There's also a relaxed and informal bar.

Smålandsgatan 7. ✆ **08/679-60-32.** Reservations recommended. Main courses 155SEK-325SEK lunch, 200SEK-400SEK dinner. AE, DC, MC, V. Mon-Fri 11:30am-11:30pm; Sat 5-11pm. Closed June 23-Aug 7. T-bana: Östermalmstorg.

Lisa Elmquist ★ ☺ SEAFOOD Under a soaring roof, amid the food stalls of Stockholm's produce market (the Östermalms Saluhall), you'll find this likable cafe and oyster bar. Because of its good, affordable food, this is the most popular choice for Stockholm families visiting the market. It's owned by one of the city's largest fish distributors, so its menu varies with the catch. Some patrons come here just for shrimp with bread and butter. Typical dishes include fish soup, salmon cutlets, and sautéed filet of lemon sole. It's not the most refined cuisine in town—it's an authentic "taste of Sweden," done exceedingly well.

Östermalms Saluhall, Nybrogatan 31. ✆ **08/553-404-10.** Reservations recommended. Main courses 129SEK-345SEK. AE, DC, MC, V. Mon-Fri 11:30am-midnight; Sat-Sun 1-10pm. T-bana: Östermalmstorg.

Prinsens SWEDISH A 2-minute walk from Stureplan, this artists' haunt has become increasingly popular with foreign visitors. It has been serving people since 1897. You can dine outdoors in summer. The fresh, flavorful cuisine is basically Swedish food prepared in a conservative French style. It includes such traditional Swedish dishes as veal patty with homemade lingonberry preserves, sautéed fjord salmon, and roulades of beef. For dessert, try the homemade vanilla ice cream. Later in the evening, the restaurant becomes something of a drinking club.

Mäster Samuelsgatan 4. ✆ **08/611-13-31.** www.restaurangprinsen.com. Reservations recommended. Main courses 189SEK-379SEK. AE, DC, MC, V. Mon-Fri 11:30am-11:30pm; Sat 1-11:30pm; Sun 5-10pm. T-bana: Östermalmstorg.

Sturehof ★ SWEDISH This is the most classic French-style brasserie in all of Stockholm, and it's been going strong since the day it opened in 1897. It remains the best spot in central Stockholm for dining at almost any time of the day or night. In summer you can sit out on the terrace and watch Stockholmers pass by. Or else you can chill out in the Upper lounge, with the sweet young things. The dining room is more formal and elegant, with uniformed waiters and stiffly pressed white linen tablecloths.

Seafood and shellfish have been a century-long tradition here, and so it continues to this day. Expect a daily changing menu of husmanskost. Or else try the locally famous *sotare* (small grilled Baltic herring). This is also one of the few places around still serving boiled salt veal tongue, a local delicacy.

Stureplan 2. ✆ **08-440-57-30.** www.sturehof.com. Main courses 125SEK-455SEK. AE, DC, MC, V. Mon-Fri 11am-2am; Sat noon-2am; Sun 1pm-2am. T-bana: Östermalmstorg.

IN GAMLA STAN (OLD TOWN)

Expensive

Den Gyldene Freden ★ SWEDISH "Golden Peace" is said to be Stockholm's oldest tavern. The restaurant opened in 1722 in a structure built the year before. The Swedish Academy owns the building, and members frequent the place every Thursday night. The cozy dining rooms are named for Swedish historical figures who were patrons. Today it's popular with artists, lawyers, and poets. You get good traditional Swedish cooking, especially fresh Baltic fish and game from the forests. Herring is a favorite appetizer. More imaginative appetizers include a pan-seared foie gras with red-wine glazed chicory and brown sugar–fried pear, and smoked salmon with bleak roe, corn cream, and horseradish dressing. Notable main courses are grilled pikeperch with crayfish bouillabaisse, and loin of reindeer with a bean and bacon casserole. A particular delight is homemade duck sausage with three kinds of mushrooms in black-pepper sauce. Want something different for dessert? How about cloudberry soup with caramelized crouton and vanilla ice cream?

Österlånggatan 51. ✆ **08/24-97-60.** www.gyldenefreden.se. Reservations recommended. Main courses 185SEK-400SEK. AE, DC, MC, V. Mon-Fri 11:30am-2:30pm; Mon-Thurs 5-10pm; Fri 5-11pm; Sat 1-11pm. Closed Dec 26-Jan 2. T-bana: Gamla Stan.

Inexpensive

Cattelin Restaurant SWEDISH This restaurant on a historic street opened in 1897 and continues to serve fish and meat in a boisterous, convivial setting. Don't expect genteel service—the clattering of china can sometimes be almost deafening, but few of the regular patrons seem to mind. First-rate menu choices include various preparations of beef, salmon, trout, veal, and chicken, which frequently make up the daily specials often preferred by lunch patrons. This restaurant has survived wars, disasters, and changing food tastes, so it must be doing something right. It remains a sentimental favorite—and not just for the memories. In a city where people have been known to faint when presented with their dining tabs, it has always been a good, reasonably priced choice.

Storkyrkobrinken 9. ✆ **08/20-18-18.** www.cattelin.com. Reservations recommended. Main courses 128SEK–295SEK. AE, DC, MC, V. Mon–Fri 10am–9pm; Sat 11am–9pm. T-bana: Gamla Stan.

IN DJURGÅRDEN

Moderate

Ulla Winbladh ★ SWEDISH Since it opened in 1994, this restaurant has enjoyed an explosion of publicity, which has impressed even the most jaded of Stockholm's restaurant aficionados. It's in a white stone structure, built as part of Stockholm's International Exposition of 1897. There's a large dining room decorated with works by Swedish artists, and a summer-only outdoor terrace laced with flowering plants. The menu focuses on conservative Swedish cuisine, all impeccably prepared. In 1996 the king presented a medal to chef Emel Ahalen for his proficiency in preparing Swedish cuisine. Menu choices include fried venison with scorzonova, and fried pigeon with apples. Fish selections might be platters of poached halibut with Parmesan cheese sauce; divine turbot with bordelaise; salmon with scampi and pumpkin, avocado, and cabbage salad; and others that vary with the season.

Rosendalsvägen 8. ✆ **08/534-89-701.** www.ullawinbladh.se. Reservations required. Main courses 135SEK–335SEK; 2-course business lunch 355SEK. AE, DC, MC, V. Mon 11:30am–10pm; Tues–Fri 11:30am–11pm; Sat 12:30–11pm; Sun 12:30–10pm. Bus: 47 or 69.

Seeing the Sights

Everything from the *Vasa* Ship Museum to the changing of the guard at the Royal Palace to the Gröna Lund Tivoli amusement park will keep you intrigued. Even just window-shopping for well-designed Swedish crafts can be a great way to spend an afternoon.

THE TOP ATTRACTIONS

At Djurgården

Nordiska Museet (Nordic Museum) ★★ This museum houses an impressive collection of implements, costumes, and furnishings of Swedish life from the 1500s to the present. The highlights are the period costumes ranging from matching garters and ties for men to purple flowerpot hats from the 1890s. In the basement is an extensive exhibit of the tools of the Swedish fishing trade, plus relics from nomadic Lapps.

Djurgårdsvägen 6–16, Djurgården. ✆ **08/519-546-00** or 08/457-06-60. www.nordiskamuseet.se. Admission 80SEK adults, free for ages 18 and under. Mon–Fri 10am–4pm; Sat–Sun 11am–5pm. Bus: 44 or 47.

The Changing of the Royal Guard

It may not have the pomp of a similar show in London, but the **Changing of the Royal Guard** in Stockholm at least provides a photo op. In summer you can watch the parade of the military guard daily. In winter it takes place less frequently; on days when there's no parade, you can still see the changing of the guard. For information on the time of the march, ask at the Tourist Centre in Sweden House. The changing of the guard takes place May to August, Monday to Saturday 12:15pm, Sunday 1:15pm; April, September, and October, Wednesday and Saturday 12:15pm, Sunday 1:15pm; November to March, Wednesday and Saturday noon, Sunday 1pm, in front of the Royal Palace.

Prins Eugens Waldemarsudde ★★ This once-royal residence is today an art gallery and a memorial to one of the most famous royal artists in recent history, Prince Eugen (1865–1947). The youngest of King Oscar II's four children, he is credited with making innovative contributions to the techniques of Swedish landscape paintings, specializing in depictions of his favorite regions in central Sweden. Among his most visible works are the murals on the inner walls of the Stadshuset.

Prins Eugens Väg 6. ✆ **08/545-837-00.** www.waldemarsudde.se. Admission 95SEK adults, 75SEK seniors and students, free for ages 18 and under. Tues–Sun 11am–5pm (to 8pm Thurs). Bus: 47 to the end of the line.

Skansen ★★★ Often called "Old Sweden in a Nutshell," this 35-hectare (86-acre) open-air museum and zoological park, near Gröna Lund's Tivoli, contains more than 150 dwellings, most from the 18th and 19th centuries. Exhibits range from a windmill to a manor house to a complete town quarter. Browsers can explore the old workshops and see where the early book publishers, silversmiths, and pharmacists plied their trade. Handicrafts (glass blowing, for example) are demonstrated here, along with peasant crafts like weaving and churning. Folk dancing and open-air symphonic concerts are also featured.

Djurgården 49–51. ✆ **08/442-80-00.** www.skansen.se. Depending on time of day, day of the week, and season, admission is 70SEK–140SEK adults, 30SEK–50SEK children 6–15, free for children 5 and under. Historic buildings Jan–Apr daily 10am–4pm; May and Sept daily 10am–8pm; June–Aug daily 10am–10pm; Oct–Dec daily 10am–3pm (to 4pm Sat–Sun). Bus: 47 from central Stockholm. Ferry from Slussen.

Vasa Museum & the Royal Warship Vasa ★★★ This 17th-century man-of-war is the number one attraction in Scandinavia—and for good reason. Housed in a museum specially constructed for it at Djurgården near Skansen, the *Vasa* is the world's oldest identified and complete ship. In 1628, on its maiden voyage and in front of thousands of horrified onlookers, the ship capsized and sank to the bottom of Stockholm harbor. When it was salvaged in 1961, more than 4,000 coins, carpenters' tools, and other items of archaeological interest were found onboard. Best of all, 97% of the ship's 700 original sculptures were retrieved. Carefully restored and preserved, they're back aboard the ship, which looks stunning now that it once again carries grotesque faces, lion masks, fish-shaped bodies, and other carvings, some with their original paint and gilt.

Galärvarvsvägen, Djurgården. ✆ **08/519-548-00.** www.vasamuseet.se. Admission 110SEK adults, 80SEK seniors and students, free for children 17 and under, Wed 5–8pm 80SEK. June–Aug daily 8:30am–6pm; Sept–May Wed 10am–8pm, Thurs–Tues 10am–5pm. Closed Jan 1 and Dec 23–25. Bus: 44, 47, or 69. Ferry from Slussen year-round, from Nybroplan in summer only.

On Gamla Stan & Neighboring Islands

Kungliga Slottet (Royal Palace) & Museum ★★ Severely dignified, even cold looking on the outside, this palace has a lavish interior designed in the Italian baroque style. Kungliga Slottet is one of the few official residences of a European monarch that's open to the public. Although the Swedish king and queen prefer to live at Drottningholm, this massive 608-room showcase, built between 1691 and 1754, remains their official address. The most popular rooms are the **State Apartments ★★**; look for at least three magnificent baroque ceiling frescoes and fine tapestries. In the building's cellar is the **Stattkammaren (Treasury) ★★**, the repository for Sweden's crown jewels. Most intriguing to any student of war and warfare is the **Royal Armoury,** whose entrance is on the castle's rear side, at Slottsbacken 3. Gustavus III's collection of sculpture from the days of the Roman Empire can be viewed in the **Antikmuseum (Museum of Antiquities).**

Kungliga Husgerådskammaren. ✆ **08/402-60-00.** www.royalcourt.se. Royal Apartments 100SEK adults, 50SEK seniors and students, free for children 6 and under; Museum of Antiquities 100SEK adults, 50SEK seniors and students, free for ages 18 and under; Treasury 100SEK adults, 50SEK seniors and students, free for children 6 and under. Combination ticket to all parts of palace 140SEK adults; 70SEK seniors, students, and children. Apartments and Treasury Sept–May Tues–Sun noon–3pm (closed in Jan); June–Aug daily 10am–5pm; closed during government receptions. Royal Armoury Sept–May Tues–Sun 11am–4pm (closes at 8pm on Thurs); June–Aug daily 10am–5pm. Museum of Antiquities May 15–31 and Sept 1–14 daily 10am–4pm; June–Aug daily 10am–5pm. T-bana: Gamla Stan. Bus: 43, 46, 59, or 76.

Riddarholm Church ★ The second-oldest church in Stockholm is on the tiny island of Riddarholmen, next to Gamla Stan. It was founded in the 13th century as a Franciscan monastery. Almost all the royal heads of state are entombed here, except for Christina, who is buried in Rome. There are three principal royal chapels, including one, the Bernadotte wing, that belongs to the present ruling family.

Riddarholmen. ✆ **08/402-61-30.** Admission 80SEK adults, 35SEK students, free for children 6 and under. May 15–Sept 14 daily 10am–4pm (to 5pm in July); Sept 15–May 14 Tues–Sun noon–3pm. T-bana: Gamla Stan.

In the City Center

Historiska Museet (Museum of National Antiquities) ★★ If you're interested in Swedish history, especially the Viking era, here you'll find the nation's finest repository of relics left by those legendary conquerors who once terrorized Europe. Many relics have been unearthed from ancient burial sites. The collection of artifacts ranges from prehistoric to medieval times, including Viking stone inscriptions and 10th-century coins, silver and gold jewelry, large ornate charms, elaborate bracelet designs found nowhere else in the world, and a unique neck collar from Färjestaden.

Narvavägen 13–17. ✆ **08/519-556-00.** www.historiska.se. Free admission. May–Sept daily 10am–5pm; Oct–Apr daily 11am–5pm (to 8pm on Thurs). T-bana: Karlaplan or Östermalmstorg. Bus: 44, 47, 56, 69, or 76.

Moderna Museet (Museum of Modern Art) ★ Renovated in 2004, this museum focuses on contemporary works by Swedish and international artists, including kinetic sculptures. Highlights are a small but good collection of cubist art by Picasso, Braque, and Léger; Matisse's *Apollo* decoupage; the famous *Enigma of William Tell,* by Salvador Dalí; and works by Brancusi, Max Ernst, Giacometti, and Arp, among others.

Klarabergsviadukten 61. ✆ **08/5195-5200.** www.modernamuseet.se. Admission 80SEK adults, free for ages 18 and under. Tues 10am–8pm; Wed–Sun 10am–6pm. T-bana: Kungsträdgården. Bus: 65.

Nationalmuseum (National Museum of Art) ★★ At the tip of a peninsula, a short walk from the Royal Opera House and the Grand Hotel, is Sweden's state treasure house of paintings and sculpture, one of the oldest museums in the world. The first floor is devoted to applied arts (silverware, handicrafts, porcelain, furnishings), but first-time visitors may want to head directly to the second floor to the painting collection with works by Rembrandt and Rubens, Lucas Cranach's most amusing *Venus and Cupid,* and a rare collection of mid-16th-century Russian icons. The most important room in the gallery has one whole wall devoted to Rembrandt, and features his *Portrait of an Old Man, Portrait of an Old Woman,* and *Kitchen Maid.*

Södra Blasieholmshamnen. ✆ **08/519-543-00.** www.nationalmuseum.se. Admission 100SEK adults, 80SEK students and seniors, free for ages 19 and under. Additional fees for special exhibitions. Tues and Thurs 11am–8pm; Wed and Fri–Sun 11am–5pm. T-bana: Kungsträdgården. Bus: 46, 62, 65, or 76.

Stadshuset (Stockholm City Hall) ★★ Built in what is called the "National Romantic Style," the Stockholm City Hall, on the island of Kungsholmen, is one of Europe's finest examples of modern architecture. Designed by Ragnar Ostberg, the red-brick structure is dominated by a lofty square tower, topped by three gilt crowns and the national coat of arms. The Nobel prize banquet is held annually in the Blue Hall. About 18 million pieces of gold and colored mosaics made of special glass cover the walls, and the southern gallery contains murals by Prince Eugen, the painter prince.

Hantverksgatan 1. ✆ **08/508-290-58.** www.stockholm.se/cityhall. Admission 80SEK adults, 60SEK students and seniors, 40SEK children 12–18, free for children 11 and under. Tower additional 20SEK. May–Sept daily 10am–4pm. City Hall tours (subject to change) Sept–May at 10am, noon, and 2pm; several times a day in summer (call or check the website for details). T-bana: Centralen or Rådhuset. Bus: 3 or 62.

JUST OUTSIDE STOCKHOLM

Drottningholm Palace ★★★ Conceived as the centerpiece of Sweden's royal court, this regal complex of stately buildings sits on an island in Lake Mälaren. Dubbed the "Versailles of Sweden," Drottningholm (Queen's Island) lies about 11km (6¾ miles) west of Stockholm. The palace, loaded with courtly art and furnishings, sits amid fountains and parks, and functions as one of the royal family's official residences.

On the grounds is one of the most perfectly preserved 18th-century theaters in the world, **Drottningholm Court Theater** (✆ **08/759-04-06;** www.dtm.se). Between June and August, 30 performances are staged. Devoted almost exclusively to 18th-century opera, it seats only 450 for one of the most unusual entertainment experiences in Sweden. Many performances sell out far in advance to season-ticket holders. The theater can be visited only as part of a guided tour, which focuses on the original sets and stage mechanisms. For tickets to the evening performances, which range in cost from 170SEK to 650SEK, call ✆ **08/660-82-25.**

Ekerö, Drottningholm. ✆ **08/402-62-80.** Palace 100SEK adults, 50SEK students and ages 25 and under, free for children 6 and under; theater guided tour 70SEK adults, 50SEK students, free for children 16 and under. Palace Oct–Apr Sat–Sun noon–3pm; May–Aug daily 10am–5pm; Sept daily 11am–3:30pm.

Theater guided tours May daily noon-4:30pm; June-Aug daily 11am-4:30pm; Sept daily 1-3:30pm; Oct-Apr Sat-Sun noon, 1pm, and 2pm. T-bana: Brommaplan, and then bus 301 or 323 to Drottningholm or 177 or 178. Ferry from the dock near City Hall.

Millesgården ★★ On the island of Lidingö, northeast of Stockholm, is Carl Milles's former villa and sculpture garden beside the sea, now a museum. Many of his best-known works are displayed here (some are copies), as are works of other artists. Milles (1875–1955), who relied heavily on mythological themes, was Sweden's most famous sculptor.

Carl Milles Väg 2, Lidingö. ✆ **08/446-75-80.** www.millesgarden.se. Admission 90SEK adults, 65SEK seniors and students, free for ages 19 and under. May 15-Sept 30 daily 11am-5pm (Thurs closes at 8pm); Oct 1-May 14 Tues-Sun noon-5pm (Thurs closes at 8pm). T-bana: Ropsten, and then bus to Torsviks Torg or train to Norsvik.

A VIEW ON HIGH

Kaknästornet (Kaknäs Television Tower) Situated in the northern district of Djurgården is the tallest constructed structure in Scandinavia—a radio and television tower that stands 155m (509 ft.) high. Two elevators take visitors to an observation platform, where you can see everything from the cobblestone streets of Gamla Stan (Old Town) to the city's modern concrete-and-glass structures and the archipelago beyond.

Mörkakroken. ✆ **08/667-21-05.** www.kaknastornet.se. Admission 40SEK adults, 20SEK children 7-15, free for children 6 and under. Mon-Sat 10am-9pm; Sun 10am-6pm. Closed Jan 1 and Dec 24-25. Bus: 69.

AN AMUSEMENT PARK

Gröna Lund Tivoli ☺ For those who like Coney Island–type thrills, this is a good nighttime adventure. Unlike its Copenhagen namesake, this is an amusement park, not a fantasyland. You'll find everything here from bumper cars to the Tunnel of Love to the Hall of Mirrors. The Blue Train takes you on a classic horror trip.

Lilla Allmänna Gränd 9. ✆ **08/587-501-00.** www.gronalund.com. Admission 80SEK; free for children 6 and under. All-day ride pass 289SEK. Late Apr to Sept daily noon-midnight (hours subject to weekly variation). Bus: 44 or 47. Djurgården ferry from Nybroplan.

ORGANIZED TOURS

The quickest and most convenient way to see the highlights of Stockholm is to take one of the bus tours that leave from Karl XII Torg, near the Kungsträdgården. **City Sightseeing** (✆ **08/587-140-20**) operates a 24-hour Hop-on, Hop-off Sightseeing Tour of the city, including the Nybro Ferry. The tour costs 260SEK adults, 50SEK ages 6 to 11, free for kids 5 and under. The bus takes you to the highlights of Stockholm, and you can get off, see what you want, and then continue on the next bus.

Stockholm Sightseeing, Skeppsbron 22 (✆ **08/1200-4000**), offers a variety of tours, mostly in the summer. The most popular is the 1-hour "royal Canal Tour," for 150SEK. It leaves daily 10:30am to 3:30pm year-round from the shady canal of Djurgården. "Under the Bridges" takes 2 hours and goes through two locks and two bodies of water. Departures are from Stromkajen (near the Grand Hotel), daily from June 4 to mid-September. The cost is 190SEK. The 45-minute "Sightseeing Anno 1935" explores the Stockholm harbor in an open-topped wooden boat, with a captain in period uniform. The tour costs 140SEK. Daily departures, from June 28 to mid-August, are from the statue of Gustavus III by the Royal Palace.

The Shopping Scene

A whopping 25% goods tax makes shopping in Sweden expensive, and you can get most items at home for less money. On the positive side, Swedish stores usually stock items of the highest quality. Swedish glass is world famous. The wooden items are outstanding, and many people love the functional furniture in blond pine or birch. Other items to look for include children's playsuits, silver necklaces, reindeer gloves, hand-woven neckties and skirts, sweaters and mittens in Nordic patterns, clogs, and colorful handicrafts from the provinces. The most famous souvenir is the Dala horse from Dalarna.

For details on **tax rebates** on local goods, go to the "Fast Facts: Stockholm" section, earlier in this chapter.

For the best shopping and window-shopping, explore the many boutiques, art galleries, and jewelry stores along the streets of **Gamla Stan** (especially **Västerlånggatan**). Attractive shops and galleries can also be found along the **Hornsgats-Puckeln** (the Hornsgatan-Hunchback, a reference to the shape of the street), on **Södermalm.** Other good browsing streets are **Hamngatan, Birger Jarlsgatan, Biblioteksgatan,** and **Kungsgatan,** all in **Norrmalm.**

In the center of Stockholm, the largest department store in Sweden is **Åhlesns City,** Klarabergsgatan 50 (✆ **08/676-60-00;** www.ahlens.se; T-bana: T-Centralen), with a gift shop, a restaurant, and a famous food department. Also seek out the fine collection of home textiles and Orrefors and Kosta crystal ware. **Nordiska Kompanient (NK),** Hamngatan 18–20 (✆ **08/762-80-00;** T-bana: Kungsträdgården), is another high-quality department store. Most of the big names in Swedish glass are displayed at NK. Swedish handcrafted items are in the basement.

At **Loppmarknaden i Skärholmen (Skärholmen Shopping Center),** Skärholmsvagen, Skärholmen (✆ **08/710-00-60;** T-bana: 13 or 23 to Skärholmen), the biggest flea market in northern Europe, you might find *anything*. Try to go on Saturday or Sunday (the earlier the better) when the market is at its peak. The location is 10km (6¼ miles) southwest of the center in the suburb of Skärholmen. Hours are Monday to Friday 11am to 6pm, when admission is free; Saturday 9am to 3pm, costing 20SEK; and Sunday, 10am to 3pm, with the entrance going for 15SEK.

Stockholm After Dark

Pick up a copy of ***Stockholm This Week,*** distributed at the Tourist Centre in the Sweden House (see "Visitor Information," earlier in this chapter), to see what's on.

THE PERFORMING ARTS

All the major opera, theater, and concert seasons begin in autumn, except for special summer festival performances. Fortunately, most of the major opera and theatrical performances are funded by the state, which keeps the ticket price reasonable.

Founded by Gustavus III in 1766, the **Drottningholm Court Theater,** Drottningholm (✆ **08/759-04-06;** www.dtm.se; T-bana: Brommaplan, then bus no. 301 or 323; boat from the City Hall in Stockholm), is on an island in Lake Mälaren, 11km (6¾ miles) from Stockholm. It stages operas and ballets with full 18th-century regalia, period costumes, and wigs. Its machinery and 30 or more complete theater sets are intact and in use. The theater, a short walk from the royal residence, seats only 450, which makes it difficult to get tickets. Eighteenth-century music performed on antique instruments is a perennial favorite. The season is from

May to September. Most performances begin at 8pm and last 2½ to 4 hours. You can order tickets in advance by phone with an American Express card. Tickets cost 275SEK to 895SEK.

Filharmonikerna I Konserthuset (Concert Hall), Hötorget 8 (✆ **08/50-66-77-88;** www.konserthuset.se; T-bana: Hötorget), home of the **Stockholm Philharmonic Orchestra,** is the principal place to hear classical music in Sweden. (The Nobel prizes are also awarded here.) Box office hours are Monday to Friday noon to 6pm, Saturday 11am to 3pm. Tickets are 100SEK to 650SEK.

Founded in 1773 by Gustavus III (who was later assassinated here at a masked ball), the **Operahuset (Royal Opera House),** Gustav Adolfs Torg (✆ **08/24-82-40;** T-bana: Kungsträdgården; www.operan.se), is the home of the Royal Swedish Opera and the Royal Swedish Ballet. The building dates from 1898. Performances are usually Monday to Saturday at 7:30pm (closed mid-June to Aug). The box office is open Monday to Friday 10am to 6pm (until 7:30pm on performance nights), Saturday noon to 3pm (✆ **08/24-82-40**). Tickets cost from 80SEK to 550SEK; ask about the 10%-to-30% senior and student discounts.

NIGHTCLUBS

Café Opera, Operahuset, Kungsträdgården (✆ **08/676-58-07;** www.cafeopera.se; T-bana: Kungsträdgården)—Swedish Beaux Arts at its best—functions as a brasserie-style restaurant during dinner hours and one of the most popular nightclubs in Stockholm late at night. Near the entrance of the cafe is a stairway leading to one of the Opera House's most beautiful corners, the clublike Operabaren (Opera Bar). Café Opera is open Wednesday to Sunday 10pm to 3am.

Göta Källare, in the Medborgplatsen subway station, Södermalm (✆ **08/642-08-28;** T-bana: Medborgplatsen), is the largest and most successful supper-club-style dance hall in Stockholm. Large, echoing, and paneled with lots of wood in a *faux-Español* style, it has a large terrace that surrounds an enormous tree, and a restaurant. Expect a crowd of people ages 45 and older, and music from a live orchestra (a DJ on Fri and Sat nights). The place is usually open every night from 8pm. Cover is 100SEK after 11pm only.

ROCK & JAZZ CLUBS

Some of Sweden's and the world's best-known jazz musicians regularly play **Fasching,** Kungsgatan 63 (✆ **08/534-829-60;** T-bana: T-Centralen). Small, cozy, and well known among jazz fans throughout Scandinavia, this is one of the most visible of the jazz clubs of Stockholm, with artists appearing from North America, Europe, and around the world. Cramped to the point of claustrophobia, it gives you the feeling that you're very, very close to the men and women producing the music. The venue varies according to the night of the week and the availability of the artists performing, but after the end of most live acts, there's likely to be dancing to salsa, soul, and perhaps R & B. With many exceptions, varying with the acts being presented, the club is usually open Monday to Saturday from 8pm to at least midnight. Cover costs vary from 120SEK to 170SEK (if there is a big star, the price can reach 400SEK).

Pub Engelen and **Nightclub Kolingen,** Kornhamnstorg 59B (✆ **08/20-10-92;** T-bana: Gamla Stan), share a single address. The restaurant, which serves some of the best steaks in town, is open Sunday to Thursday 5 to 11:30pm, Friday and Saturday 5pm to 1:30am. Prices for platters of bar food run from 150SEK to 250SEK. Live performances, usually soul, funk, and rock by Swedish groups, take over the pub daily from 8:30pm to midnight. The pub is open daily from 4pm to 3am. Beer begins at 45SEK, and items on the bar menu cost 29SEK to 150SEK. The Nightclub Kolingen is a dance club nightly from 10pm to about 3am. It charges the same food and drink prices as the pub, and you must be at least 23 to enter. Cover runs from 50SEK to 100SEK after 8pm.

BARS

One of the most talked-about bars in Stockholm, **Blue Moon Bar,** 18 Kungsgatan (✆ **08/20-14-11;** www.bluemoonbar.se; T-bana: Östermalmstorg), attracts a bevy of supermodels and TV actors. The street level has black leather upholstery and an atmosphere of postmodern cool. The clean, modern decor of the basement-level bar draws an equally chic crowd. On both levels, everybody's favorite drink seems to be the Russian-inspired *caprinoshka,* concocted from vodka and limes. You might hear anything from recorded dance hits (Fri–Sat at midnight) to live salsa and merengue (Wed 9pm–5am). The place is open Monday to Saturday 7pm to 3am. Incidentally, no one will object if you light up a cigar. Cover is 130SEK.

Cadierbaren (Cadier Bar), Södra Blasieholmshamnen 8 (✆ **08/679-35-85;** T-bana: Kungsträdgården), is one of the most sophisticated places in Stockholm. From the bar, which is situated in the Grand Hotel—one of the most famous hotels in Europe—you'll have a view of the harbor and the Royal Palace. Light meals—open-faced sandwiches and smoked salmon—are served all day in the extension overlooking the waterfront. Drinks run 98SEK to 200SEK. It's open Monday to Saturday 7pm to 2am, Sunday 7pm to 1am; a piano player performs Wednesday to Saturday 9:30pm to 1:30am.

GAY & LESBIAN STOCKHOLM

Looking for a nonconfrontational bar peopled with regular guys who happen to be gay? Consider a round or two at **Sidetrack,** Wollmar Yxkullsgatan 7 (✆ **08/641-16-88;** T-bana: Mariatorget). Small and committed to shunning trendiness, it's named after the founder's favorite gay bar in Chicago. It's open Wednesday to Saturday night from 6pm to 1am. Other nights are fine, too—Sidetrack is something like a Swedish version of a bar and lounge at the local bowling alley where everyone happens to be into same-sex encounters.

Many gays and lesbians gather at **Torget,** Mälartorget 13 (✆ **08/20-55-60;** T-bana: Gamla Stan), a cozy, Victorian-era cafe and bar in the Old City (Gamla Stan) that's open for food every afternoon and for drinks around 5pm until around midnight. A gay place with a greater emphasis on food, but with a busy and crowded bar area and a particularly helpful and informative staff, is **Babs Kök n bar,** Birger Jarlsgatan 37 (✆ **08-23-61-01;** T-bana Östermalmstorg). It's open daily 5pm to 1am.

For an online version of the online gay and lesbian magazine *QX,* which is available in hard copy in newsstands, go to www.qx.se.

DAY TRIPS FROM STOCKHOLM

Skokloster Castle ★★

Skokloster, S-746 96 Skokloster (✆ **018/38-60-77**), is a splendid 17th-century castle and one of the most interesting baroque museums in Europe. It's next to Lake Mälaren, 64km (40 miles) west of Stockholm and 40km (25 miles) south of Uppsala.

Original interiors aside, the castle is noted for its rich collections of paintings, furniture, applied art, tapestries, arms, and books. Admission is 70SEK, free for ages 18 and under. Guided tours are conducted from May to August daily every hour from 12:15 to 3:15pm. In September the guided tours are given from Tuesday to Friday at 3pm; Saturday and Sunday every hour from 12:15 to 3:15pm. The site is closed from November 5 to April 30.

Skokloster Motor Museum (✆ **018/38-61-00**), on the palace grounds, contains the largest collection of vintage automobiles and motorcycles in the country. One of the most notable cars is a 1905 eight-horsepower De Dion Bouton. Admission costs 50SEK adults, 25SEK children 7 to 14, free for children 6 and under. It's open from May to August, daily from noon to 4pm.

GETTING THERE From Stockholm take a **train** to the hamlet of Bålsta, which lies 19km (12 miles) from the castle. At the village train station, you can either take **bus** no. 894 directly to Skokloster, or call for a **taxi** from a direct telephone line that's prominently positioned just outside the railway station.

Uppsala ★★

The major university city of Sweden, Uppsala, 68km (42 miles) northwest of Stockholm, is the most popular destination for day-trippers from Stockholm, and for good reason. Uppsala has not only a great university, but also a celebrated 15th-century cathedral. Even in the time of the Vikings, this was a religious center, the scene of animal and human sacrifices in honor of the old Norse gods. And it was once the center of royalty as well; Queen Christina occasionally held court here. The church is still the seat of the Swedish archbishop, and the first Swedish university was founded here in 1477.

GETTING THERE The **train** from Stockholm's Central Station takes about 40 minutes. Trains leave about every hour during peak daylight hours. Some visitors spend the day in Uppsala and return to Stockholm on the commuter train in the late afternoon. Eurailpass holders ride free. **Boats** between Uppsala and Skokloster depart Uppsala Tuesday through Sunday at 11:30am, returning to Uppsala at 5:15pm. Round-trip passage costs 165SEK. For details, check with the tourist office in any of the towns.

VISITOR INFORMATION The **Tourist Information Office** is at Fyris Torg 8 (✆ **018/727-48-00;** www.uppsala.se), open Monday to Friday 10am to 6pm and Saturday from 10am to 3pm.

EXPLORING UPPSALA At the end of Drottninggatan is the **Carolina Rediviva (University Library)** ★ (✆ **018/471-39-00;** bus: 6, 7, 9, 18, 20, or 22), with its more than five million volumes and 40,000 manuscripts, among them many rare works from the Middle Ages. But the manuscript that really draws visitors is the *Codex Argenteus* (Silver Bible), translated into the old Gothic language in the middle of the 3rd century and copied in about A.D. 525. It's the only book extant in the old Gothic script. Also worth seeing is the original woodblock engraving of the *Carta Marina,* the first printed map of the Nordic countries (1539), a fairly accurate rendering of Sweden and its neighboring countries. Admission is 25SEK, free for children 11 and under. The library's exhibition room is open June 13 to August 14, Monday to Friday 9am to 5pm, Saturday 10am to 5pm; August 15 to June 12, Sunday 11am to 4pm.

Linnaeus Garden & Museum, Svartbäcksgatan 27 (✆ **018/471-28-38** for the museum, or 018/471-25-76 for the garden; walk straight from the rail station to Kungsgatan, and proceed for about 10 min. to Svartbäcksgatan), is the former home of Swedish botanist Carl von Linné, also known as Carolus Linnaeus, who developed a classification system for the world's plants and flowers. This museum is on the spot where he restored Uppsala University's botanical garden, which resembles a miniature baroque garden. His detailed sketches and descriptions of the garden have been faithfully followed. Admission to the museum is 60SEK adults, free for ages 15 and under. A donation is suggested for admission to the gardens. The museum is open from May to September 1, Tuesday to Sunday 11 to 5pm. The gardens are open from May to September daily from 11am to 8pm.

The largest cathedral in Scandinavia at nearly 120m (395 ft.) tall, the twin-spired Gothic **Uppsala Domkyrka** ★, Domkyrkoplan 5 (✆ **018/18-71-53;** www.uppsala domkyrka.se; bus: 1 or 2), was founded in the 13th century. It was severely damaged in 1702 in a disastrous fire that swept over Uppsala, and then was restored near the turn of the 20th century. Among the regal figures buried in the crypt is Gustavus Vasa. The remains of St. Erik, patron saint of Sweden, are entombed in a silver shrine. Botanist Linnaeus and philosopher-theologian Emanuel Swedenborg are also buried here. A small museum displays ecclesiastical relics of Uppsala. Admission to the cathedral is free; museum admission is 30SEK adults, 15SEK seniors and students, free for children 15 and under. Open daily 8am to 6pm. The gift shop and Treasure Chamber Museum are open May to September Monday to Saturday 10am to 5pm, Sunday 12:30 to 5pm; October to April Monday to Saturday from 10am to 4pm and Sunday from 12:30 to 4pm. During church services, movement around the church may be limited.

Gripsholm Castle ★★

On an island in Lake Mälaren, Gripsholm Slottsfervaltning (Gripsholm Castle), P.O. Box 14, 64721 Mariefred (✆ **0159/101-94**)—the fortress built by Gustavus Vasa in the late 1530s—is one of the best-preserved castles in Sweden. It lies near Mariefred, an idyllic small town known for its vintage narrow-gauge railroad.

Even though Gripsholm was last occupied by royalty (Charles XV) in 1864, it's still a royal castle. Its outstanding features include a large collection of portrait paintings depicting obscure branches of the Swedish monarchy, its brooding architecture, and its 18th-century theater built for the amusement of the 18th-century actor-king Gustavus III. It's open September 16 to May 14 Saturday and Sunday noon to 3pm; May 15 to September 15 daily 10am to 4pm. Admission is 80SEK adults, 40SEK children 7 to 15, free for ages 6 and under.

GETTING THERE Gripsholm Castle is 68km (42 miles) southwest of Stockholm. By **car,** follow E20 south; you can drive directly to the castle parking lot. The Eskilstuna **bus** runs to the center of Mariefred, as do the boats. **Boats** leave from mid-May to September at 10am from Klara Mälarstrand Pier. The castle is a 10-minute walk from the center of Mariefred.

SWITZERLAND

by Darwin Porter & Danforth Prince

Switzerland evokes images of towering peaks, mountain lakes, lofty pastures, and alpine villages, but it also offers a rich cultural life, with many fine museums, theaters, and world-renowned orchestras, in cities such as sophisticated Geneva and perfectly preserved medieval Bern.

19

GENEVA

Many patriotic French feel this French-speaking city of elegance and charm should belong in France. And though it does indeed sit on the doorstep of France, Geneva in some respects is international, belonging to the world with its 250 international organizations based here, the most important being the European headquarters for the United Nations, the World Health Organization, and the International Red Cross.

It's the most orderly and serene of all major European cities (or most sterile, in the view of those who'd like more local color, nightlife, and excitement).

Because of its ideological and geographic isolation from Switzerland, Geneva almost feels like one of those old European "city-states." Locals here used to burn books by Rousseau until Voltaire arrived and set them straight. Those romantics Shelley and Byron came here seeking inspiration from the surrounding mountains, but Lenin failed to convert anyone to communism.

As one local and very wealthy lady told us, "Geneva is one of the few places on the planet I can walk around in my white sable without fear I'll be hit by a rotten tomato by an animal-rights fanatic, or else have it stolen from me by some poor wretched down and out." She actually said that.

Essentials

GETTING THERE

BY PLANE The **Geneva-Cointrin Airport** (✆ **022/717-71-11;** www.gva.ch), although busy, is quite compact and easily negotiated. **Swiss International Air Lines** (✆ **877/359-7947** from the U.S.; www.swiss.com) serves Geneva more frequently than any other airline and offers the best local connections, connecting Geneva with Lugano, Zurich, and Bern, plus flying in from several European capitals. Other international airlines flying into Geneva include **Air France** (✆ **800/237-2747** from the U.S.; www.airfrance.com), with 10 flights daily from

Paris; and **British Airways** (✆ **800/217-9297;** www.britishairways.com), with 8 daily flights from London.

To get into the center of Geneva, there's a train station linked to the air terminal with trains leaving about every 8 to 20 minutes from 5:25am to 12:25am for the 7-minute trip; the one-way fare is 13F in first class and 10F in second class. A taxi into town will cost between 30F and 40F, or you can take bus no. 10 for 12F.

BY TRAIN Geneva's CFF (Chemins de Fer Fédéraux) train station in the town center is **Gare Cornavin,** place Cornavin (✆ **0900/300-300** for ticket information). A small tourist-office branch is at the train station.

Note: When the Lausanne-Geneva railroad line was extended to Cointrin Airport, a second "main" railroad station was built here with both long-distance and intercity trains. To avoid having to make the trip back to the center from the airport, be sure you get off the train at the Cornavin station.

BY CAR From Lausanne, head southwest on N1 to the very end of southwestern Switzerland.

BY LAKE STEAMER There are frequent daily arrivals by Swiss lake steamer year-round from Montreux, Vevey, and Lausanne (you can use your Eurailpass for the trip). If you're staying in the Left Bank (Old Town), get off at the Jardin Anglais stop in Geneva; Mont Blanc and Pâquis are the two Right Bank stops. For more information, call ✆ **0848/811-848** or visit www.cgn.ch.

VISITOR INFORMATION Geneva's tourist office, the **Office du Tourisme de Genève,** is located at 18, rue du Mont-Blanc (✆ **022/909-70-00;** www.geneve-tourisme.ch), and is open daily year-round from 9am to 6pm. The staff provides

Geneva

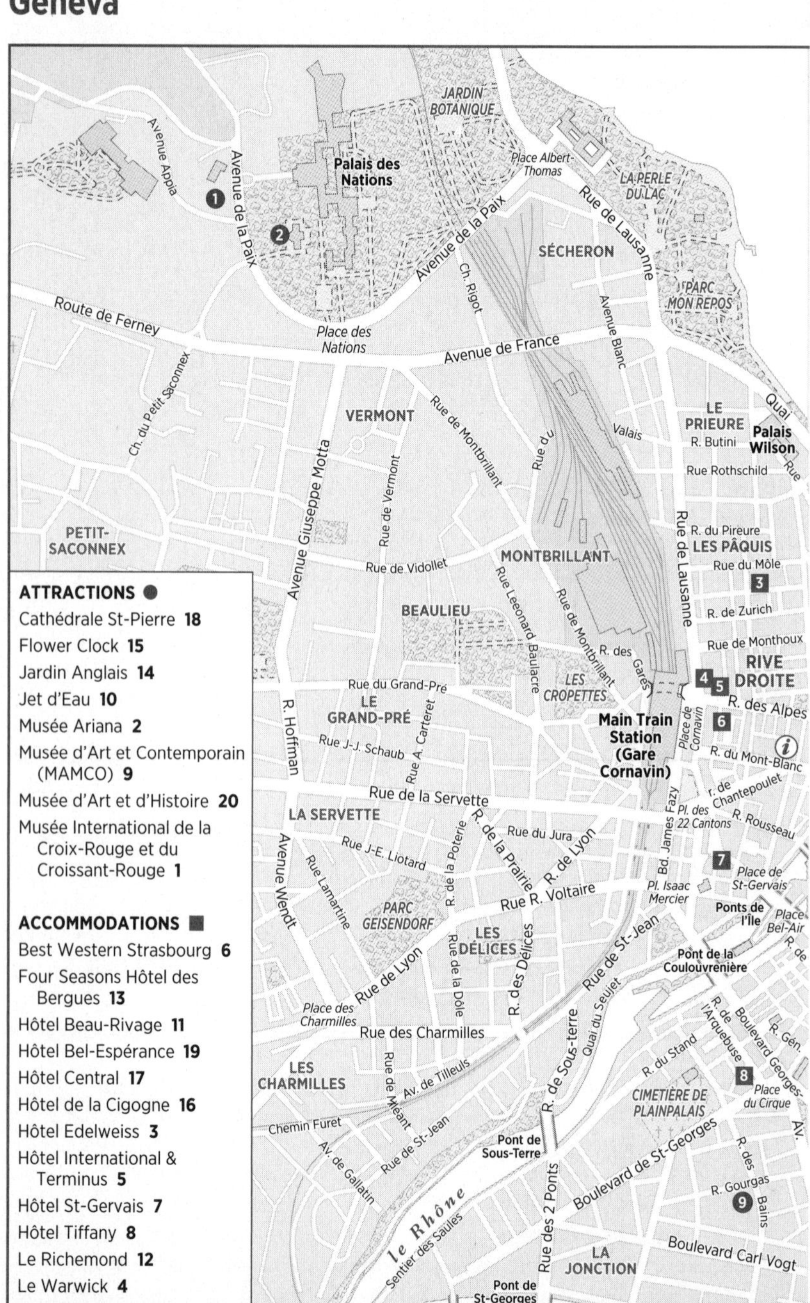
ATTRACTIONS ●
Cathédrale St-Pierre 18
Flower Clock 15
Jardin Anglais 14
Jet d'Eau 10
Musée Ariana 2
Musée d'Art et Contemporain (MAMCO) 9
Musée d'Art et d'Histoire 20
Musée International de la Croix-Rouge et du Croissant-Rouge 1
ACCOMMODATIONS ■
Best Western Strasbourg 6
Four Seasons Hôtel des Bergues 13
Hôtel Beau-Rivage 11
Hôtel Bel-Espérance 19
Hôtel Central 17
Hôtel de la Cigogne 16
Hôtel Edelweiss 3
Hôtel International & Terminus 5
Hôtel St-Gervais 7
Hôtel Tiffany 8
Le Richemond 12
Le Warwick 4
JARDIN BOTANIQUE
Avenue Appia
Avenue de la Paix
Palais des Nations
Place Albert-Thomas
LA PERLE DU LAC
Rue de Lausanne
SÉCHERON
PARC MON REPOS
Ch. Rigot
Avenue Blanc
Route de Ferney
Place des Nations
Avenue de France
Ch. du Petit Saconnex
VERMONT
Rue de Montbrillant
Rue du Valais
LE PRIEURE
Palais Wilson
R. Butini
Rue Rothschild
Quai
Avenue Giuseppe Motta
Rue de Vermont
PETIT-SACONNEX
R. du Pireure
LES PÂQUIS
Rue du Môle
MONTBRILLANT
Rue de Vidollet
BEAULIEU
Rue Leeonard Baulacre
R. de Zurich
Rue de Monthoux
R. des Gares
RIVE DROITE
LES CROPETTES
Rue du Grand-Pré
LE GRAND-PRÉ
R. Hoffman
Main Train Station (Gare Cornavin)
Place de Cornavin
R. des Alpes
R. du Mont-Blanc
Rue J-J. Schaub
Rue A. Carteret
r. de Chantepoulet
Rue de la Servette
LA SERVETTE
Bd. James Fazy
Pl. des 22 Cantons
R. Rousseau
Rue du Jura
R. de la Prairie
R. de Lyon
Rue J-E. Liotard
Avenue Wendt
Rue Lamartine
R. de la Poterie
Pl. Isaac Mercier
Place de St-Gervais
Rue R. Voltaire
PARC GEISENDORF
LES DÉLICES
Ponts de l'Île
Place Bel-Air
Rue de la Dôle
R. des Délices
Rue de St-Jean
Pont de la Coulouvrenière
Rue de Lyon
Place des Charmilles
Quai du Seujet
Rue des Charmilles
R. de l'Arquebuse
Boulevard Georges-
R. Gén.
R. du Stand
LES CHARMILLES
Rue de Miléant
Av. de Tilleuls
R. de Sous-terre
CIMETIÈRE DE PLAINPALAIS
Place du Cirque
Av.
Chemin Furet
Av. de Gallatin
Rue de St-Jean
Pont de Sous-Terre
Boulevard de St-Georges
R. des Bains
R. Gourgas
le Rhône
Sentier des Saules
Rue des 2 Ponts
Boulevard Carl Vogt
LA JONCTION
Pont de St-Georges

Information
Railway
Basel
Zurich
SWITZERLAND
Bern
Geneva
0
1/5 mile
0
200 meters
N
Lac Léman
Rade de Genève
Jet d'Eau
Quai Cologny
Rampe de Cologny
Route de Vandœuvres
Place de Traînant
FRONTENEX
PARC DES EAUX-VIVES
Quai Gustave Ador
Plateau de Frontenex
Route de Frontenex
PARC LA GRANGE
Chemin Frank Thomas
Av. Rosemont
Avenue W. Favre
MONTCHOISY
Rue des Eaux-Vives
Rue de Montchoisy
Rue des Vollandes
rue du 31 Décembre
Gare des Eaux-Vives
Route de Chêne
LES EAUX-VIVES
R. de la Miarie
Ch. de la Petite Boissière
Av. de l'Amandolier
Promenade Martin
Av. Pictet De Rochemont
Rue Agasse
R. F-Versonnex
Place des Eaux-Vives
RIVE GAUCHE
Rue de la Terassière
Cours de Rive
rd.-pt de Rive
R. Lachenal
Woodrow Wilson
Jacquet
Rue Plantamour
Quai du Mont-Blanc
Square du Mont-Blanc
Pont du-Mont-Blanc
JARDIN ANGLAIS
ILE ROUSSEAU
Pont des Bergues
Quai Général Guisan
Place du Rhône
Rue du Rhône
RUES BASSES
R. de la Croix-d'Or
R. De Rive
Rue de la Confédération
R. du Marché
R. la Fontaine
VIELLE VILLE (OLD TOWN)
Grand Rue
R. de l'Hôtel-de-Ville
Place du Bourg-de-Four
La Corraterie
Hôtel de Ville
R. de la Croix Rouge
Place Neuve
Promenade des Bastions
Université
Dufour
Favon
R. de Candolle
Rue St. Leger
Rue Hodler
Pl. Em. Guyenot
Route de Malagnou
Chemin Rieu
Bd. Jacques Dalcroze
Bd. Helvetique
Ch. Galland
Bd. des Tranchées
FLORISSANT
Route de Florissant
Rue de l'Athenée
Cours des Bastions
Place Ed. Claparède
Rue de l'Athenée
Avenue Bertrand
PARC A. BERTRAND
PLAINE DE PLAINPALAIS
Rd-pt. de Plainpalais
Bd. des Philosophes
Avenue Peschier
Av. Henri Dunant
du Mail
Rue A. Lombard
Bd. de la Cluse
Avenue de Champel
CHAMPEL
Avenue de Miremont
Avenue Louis Aubert
R. de Carouge
Boulevard du Pont d'Arve
R. Prévost-Martin
LA CLUSE
10
11
12
13
14
15
16
17
18
19
20

information about the city, and can also arrange hotel reservations both in Geneva and throughout Switzerland, and refer you to other establishments specializing in car and motorcycle rentals and excursion bookings. They can also give you details about audio-guided visits to the Old Town.

CITY LAYOUT Geneva is a perfect city to explore on foot. It's divided by Lac Léman (Lake Geneva) and the Rhône River into two sections: the Right Bank and the Left Bank. You may rent an audio-guided tour in English from the tourist office (see above) for 10F. This tour covers more than two dozen highlights in the Old Town, and comes complete with cassette, player, and map. Its estimated duration is 2 hours. A 50F deposit is collected prior to your receipt of a cassette player.

RIVE GAUCHE (LEFT, OR SOUTH BANK) This compact and colorful area is the oldest section of the city. Here you'll find Old Town, some major shopping streets, the famous Flower Clock, the university, and several important museums.

Grand-Rue is the well-preserved main street of Old Town. It's flanked by many houses dating from the 15th and 18th centuries. The street winds uphill from the ponts de l'Ile; at place Bel-Air it becomes rue de la Cité, then Grand-Rue, and finally rue de l'Hôtel-de-Ville. (Rousseau was born in a simple house at no. 40 Grand-Rue.) Eventually it reaches **place du Bourg-de-Four**—one of the most historic squares of Geneva. South of this street is **promenade des Bastions,** a greenbelt area overlooking the Arve River, with a monument to the Reformation. Directly to the west, in the northern corner of promenade des Bastions, is **place Neuve,** which is the finest square in Geneva.

From place Neuve, you can take rue de la Corraterie, which was once surrounded by the city wall, to the Rhône and the **ponts de l'Ile.** On this bridge is the **Tour-de-l'Ile,** what's left of the 13th-century bishops' castle.

On the shore of Lake Geneva is the **Jardin Anglais (English Garden)** with its Flower Clock and, farther out, the **Parc La Grange** and the **Parc des Eaux-Vives.**

RIVE DROITE (RIGHT, OR NORTH BANK) You can cross to the other side of the Rhône on any of several bridges, including pont du Mont-Blanc, pont de la Machine, pont des Bergues, and ponts de l'Ile. The Right Bank is home to Gare Cornavin, the major international organizations, and several attractive parks.

Place St-Gervais is in the St-Gervais district; this has been the area for jewelers and watchmakers since the 18th century.

Along the northern shore of Lake Geneva is **quai du Président-Wilson,** named for the U.S. president who helped found the League of Nations.

The Right Bank is surrounded by parks, from the tree-shaded promenades along the Rhône to the **Parc de la Perle du Lac, Parc Barton,** and on the city outskirts, **Parc Mon-Repos.**

RUES BASSES Rues Basses (translated either as "low streets" or figuratively as "lower town") is found between Old Town and the south bank of the Rhône. It's the major commercial and shopping district of Geneva. Its major street is rue du Rhône, although rue de la Confédération and rue du Marché are also important arteries.

VIEILLE VILLE (OLD TOWN) At an altitude of 398m (1,305 ft.), Old Town is the most history-rich section of Geneva. This is Left Bank Geneva, with its narrow streets, flower-bedecked fountains, and architectural blends of Gothic, Renaissance, and 18th-century features. The twin towers of the Cathedral of St. Pierre dominate Old Town, whose geographical and spiritual center is place du Bourg-de-Four.

THE PROMENADES OF GENEVA These streets almost constitute a "neighborhood" in themselves. This section of quays along both Lake Geneva and the Rhône is best experienced by walking. One of the most scenic walks is from the Parc des Eaux-Vives on the Left Bank to the Parc de Mon-Repos on the Right Bank. Along the way is a clear view of Geneva's most famous and visible monument, the Jet d'Eau. Set a few inches above the surface of the lake, this fountain spurts a plume of shimmering water that rises to heights, depending on the wind on the day it's being measured, of between 140m and 145m (459–476 ft.). Except for a 2-week maintenance regime conducted every midwinter, Jet d'Eau operates year-round, except when winds blow hard down from the Alps, during which period it's shut off to avoid drenching the passersby on the nearby quais.

GETTING AROUND Walking, of course, is the most practical form of transportation in Geneva. It's also the most advantageous from a tourist's point of view. Tree-shaded promenades line the edges of the lake, and you can browse many chic shops walking at a moderate pace along streets that include rue du Rhône. Savor the measured tempo of life here that makes this city particularly alluring to the foreign visitor.

BY PUBLIC TRANSPORTATION Most of Geneva's public tram and bus lines begin either at the very central place Cornavin in front of the main railroad station, or on the opposite bank of the river, at the place du Bel Air. Local buses and trams operate daily from 5am to midnight, and you can purchase a ticket from a vending machine before you board. Instructions are also given in English. **Transport Publics Genevois** (✆ **0900/022-021;** www.tpg.ch), next to the tourist office in Gare Cornavin, offers free maps of local bus routings. Trips that stay within zone 10, enveloping most of Geneva, cost 3F, and unlimited use of all zones costs 10F for 1 day.

Guests who have proof that they are booked into a hotel, B&B, or hostel are granted free rides on public transportation. Ask at your hotel for a public transportation ticket.

BY TAXI The meter on whatever cab you take in Geneva will automatically begin calculating your fare at 7F, and then add between 3F and 3.50F for every kilometer you travel, depending on the time of day or night. The fare from the airport to the center of town ranges from 30F to 40F. No tipping is required, but extra baggage may cost 1.50F. To call for a **taxi,** call ✆ **022/331-41-33** or 022/320-20-20.

BY CAR Driving is not recommended; parking is difficult and the many one-way streets make navigation complicated. However, should you wish to rent a car and tour Lake Geneva, you'll find many car-rental companies represented in the arrivals hall of the airport and in the center of the city. Major car-rental companies in Geneva include **Avis,** 44, rue de Lausanne (✆ **022/731-90-00,** or at the airport 022/929-03-30; www.avis.com); **Budget,** at the airport (✆ **022/717-86-75;** www.budget.com); **Hertz,** at the airport (✆ **022/717-80-80;** www.hertz.com); and **Europcar,** 37, rue de Lausanne (✆ **022/909-69-90;** www.europcar.com). If you absolutely insist on driving a car, and if your hotel doesn't offer parking facilities and valet parking, the best bet for parking within the city limits tends to be within any of the many underground parking garages, whose presence is indicated with large blue-and-white signs designated with a letter *P.* Rates for underground parking average between 1.50F and 2F per hour.

BY BIKE Touring the city by bicycle isn't particularly practical because of the steep cobblestone streets, speeding cars, and general congestion. However, you might want to consider renting a bike for touring the countryside around Geneva. The major rental outlet is at the baggage desk at **Gare Cornavin** (✆ **022/791-02-50**), where city bikes cost 33F. Another major outlet, charging from 24F to 34F per day, depending on the degree of sophistication of the bicycle, is **Genève Roule,** 17, place Montbrillant (✆ **022/740-13-43;** www.geneveroule.ch).

[Fast FACTS] GENEVA

Business Hours Most banks are open Monday to Friday 8:30am to 4:30pm (until 5:30pm Wed). Most offices are open Monday to Friday 8:30am to 5:30pm, although this can vary. It's always best to call first.

Consulates If you lose your passport or have other business with your home government, go to your nation's consulate: **United States,** 7, rue Versonnex (✆ **022/840-51-60**); **Australia,** 2, chemin des Fins (✆ **022/799-91-00**); **Canada,** 5, av. de L'Ariana (✆ **022/919-92-00**); **New Zealand,** 2, chemin des Fins (✆ **022/929-03-50**); the **United Kingdom,** 58, av. Louis Casaï, Cointrin (✆ **022/918-24-00**).

Currency The basic unit of Swiss currency is the Swiss franc (F), which is made up of 100 centimes. At press time, 1F equals about 94¢ (US).

Currency Exchange In a city devoted to banking and the exchange of international currencies, you'll find dozens of places to exchange money in Geneva. Three of the most visible outlets, however, are run by **UBS-SA,** one of the country's largest banking conglomerates. You'll find a branch at the **Gare Cornavin,** 12, place Cornavin (✆ **022/748-27-11**), that's open Monday to Friday from 8:30am to 4:30pm; a branch at the **Cointrin Airport** (✆ **022/306-14-88**) that's open Monday to Friday from 8:30am to 4:30pm; and a downtown branch at 75, rue du Rhône (✆ **022/375-75-75**), that's open Monday to Friday from 8am to 4pm. The branches in the airport and in the railway station also house "money-automats"—you receive an equivalent amount of Swiss francs for every $20, $50, or $100 bill you insert into the machine.

Dentists & Doctors English-speaking dentists are available at one of the ***cliniques dentaires*** at 5, chemin de Malombré (✆ **022/346-64-44;** www.malodent.ch), open daily from 8am to 7pm. If you become ill and want to consult a doctor, including one who will travel to your hotel, call ✆ **022/322-20-20;** or arrange an appointment with an English-speaking doctor at the **Hôpital Cantonal,** 22, rue Micheli-du-Crest (✆ **022/372-33-11**).

Drugstores Each night a different set of four drugstores stays open to either 9 or 11pm. Call ✆ **144** or 111 to find out which drugstore will be open. One of the world's biggest drugstores, **Pharmacie Principale,** in Confédération-Centre, 8, rue de la Confédération (✆ **022/318-66-60**), sells everything from medicine to clothing, perfumes, optical equipment, cameras, and photo supplies. It's open daily from 9am to 9pm.

Emergencies In an emergency, dial ✆ **117** for the police, ✆ **144** for an ambulance, or ✆ **118** to report a fire.

Hospitals A prime choice for medical aid is the **Geneva University Hospital,** 24, rue Micheli-du-Crest (✆ **022/372-60-19;** www.hug-ge.ch). Most physicians speak English and German.

Police In an emergency, call ✆ **117.** For nonemergency matters, call ✆ **022/327-41-11.**

Post Office There's a limited **Office de Poste** at Gare Cornavin, 16, rue des Gares (✆ **0848/888-888**), open Monday to Friday from 6am to 10:45pm, Saturday from 6am to 8pm, and Sunday from noon to 8pm. A better bet is the city's main post office, **Bureau de Poste Montbrillant,** rue des Gares (✆ **022/739-23-58**), which offers a full range of telephone, telegraph, and mail-related services Monday to Friday from 8am to 10:45pm, Saturday 8am to 10pm, and Sunday noon to 8pm.

Safety Geneva is one of the safest cities in the world, but that doesn't mean you shouldn't take the usual precautions when traveling anywhere. Protect your valuables. Car thefts have been on the rise. High-class prostitutes and confidence swindlers proliferate in Geneva to prey on the well-heeled.

Taxes There is no special city tax, other than the 7.6% value-added tax (VAT) attached to most goods and services throughout Switzerland.

Telephone The country code for Switzerland is **41** and the city code for Geneva is **22.** To make a local call within Switzerland, dial directly after you hear the dial tone (no area code needed); for other places within Switzerland, dial the area code and then the number.

Tipping Most restaurants and hotels, even taxis, add a service charge of between 10% and 15% to your bill, so, strictly speaking, no further tipping is necessary. Tipping rituals have evolved recently within Geneva to reflect practices within neighboring France, so today, many diners leave a few coins—we established guidelines of around 2F for each member of a dining party, as a sign of respect for your waitstaff, but only if the service was adequate.

Toilets You'll find public facilities at all rail and air terminals and on main squares. Otherwise, you can patronize those in cafes and other commercial establishments such as department stores.

Where to Stay

ON THE RIGHT BANK

Very Expensive

Four Seasons Hôtel des Bergues ★★★ This elegant, four-story hotel—designated a historic monument by the Swiss—once catered to the monarchs of Europe. After being conglomerated into a Four Seasons, the hotel underwent a massive renovation, downsizing from 122 rooms to 103 more spacious rooms. It is now the most ostentatiously elegant hotel in Geneva.

Stratospherically expensive, with an armada of uniformed, polite staff members, the Four Seasons is a favorite with the haute international business community, diplomats, and members of European society. Grandly memorable from its centrally located position at the edge of the Rhône, the hotel also hosted many meetings of the League of Nations.

The hotel's public rooms are among the most lavish in Switzerland. The bedrooms have Directoire and Louis Philippe furnishings. Accommodations ranked "superior" on the Bel Etage floor are the finest choices here, although all units are beautifully appointed. Lakeview rooms are more expensive.

33, quai des Bergues, CH-1211 Genève. ✆ **022/908-70-00.** Fax 022/908-74-00. www.hoteldesbergues.com. 103 units. 810F–1,040F double; from 2,250F suite. AE, DC, MC, V. Parking 40F. Bus: 1. **Amenities:** Restaurant; bar; airport transfers (110F); babysitting; children's programs; concierge; exercise room; room service; spa. *In room:* A/C, TV/DVD, CD player, hair dryer, minibar, Wi-Fi (30F per 24 hr.).

Hôtel Beau-Rivage ★★★ This grand old landmark 1865 hotel receives our highest recommendation for its traditional Victorian charm and impeccable service. The most tragic event in its history was the assassination of Empress Elisabeth ("Sissi") of Austria, who was stabbed on the nearby quays in 1898 by the anarchist Luigi Lucheni, and then carried back to her lodgings in the Beau-Rivage to die a few hours later. To this day, history buffs rent the pale-blue Empress Suite.

Its most striking feature is the open, five-story lobby. The hotel also became the first in Europe to install elevators. The rooms are individually furnished and frequently redecorated. All front rooms have views of the lake. Accommodations are categorized by size, with "romantic" rooms being more spacious and "classical" rooms being medium in size. Some of the romantic units contain ceiling frescoes teeming with cherubs and mythical heroes.

13, quai du Mont-Blanc, CH-1201 Genève. ✆ **022/716-66-66.** Fax 022/716-60-60. www.beau-rivage.ch. 94 units. 900F–1,400F double; from 1,900F suite. AE, DC, MC, V. Parking 40F. Bus: 1. **Amenities:** 2 restaurants; bar; babysitting; concierge; exercise room; room service. *In room:* A/C, TV/DVD, CD player, fax, hair dryer, minibar, Wi-Fi (free).

Le Richemond ★★★ Le Richemond has for years been identified as the greatest hotel in Geneva. Erected in 1875, the neoclassical, travertine building has wrought-iron balustrades, each emblazoned with the letter *R,* and is situated across the quay-side boulevard from the lake, across from a small park. In the 19th century it was an unpretentious guesthouse. But its acquisition by the Rocco Forte chain catalyzed a radical reexamination of its decor. Accommodations range from the most spacious in the city to medium in size; nearly half of the units here are suites, attracting all of Europe, plus international CEOs. This is true Grand Hotel living, with elegant fabrics, tasteful upholstery, and luxurious beds, plus spacious marble bathrooms with robes and a basket of expensive toiletries.

Jardin Brunswick, CH-1201 Genève. ✆ **022/715-70-00.** Fax 022/715-70-01. www.lerichemond.com. 98 units. 720F–1,300F double; from 1,600F suite. AE, DC, MC, V. Parking 50F. Bus: 1. **Amenities:** Restaurant; bar; babysitting; concierge; exercise room; room service; spa; Wi-Fi (free, in lobby). *In room:* A/C, TV, DVD (in some), hair dryer, minibar, MP3 docking station (in some).

Expensive

Le Warwick ★ ☺ This contemporary and solidly reliable hotel, located across from the train station, was built during the 1970s. The abstractly modern lobby contains sweeping staircases, loggias, balconies, marble floors, and Oriental rugs. On hand is a large but somewhat depersonalized and anonymous-looking staff in the kind of smart, upscale uniforms that evoke a hotel a bit grander than it really is. The refurbished, soundproof bedrooms are often sunny, boldly patterned, and comfortable, with marble bathrooms. Its brasserie is open for light meals and snacks all day long.

14, rue de Lausanne, CH-1201 Genève. ✆ **800/203-3232** in the U.S. and Canada, or 022/716-80-00. Fax 022/716-80-01. www.warwickgeneva.com. 167 units. 700F–850F double; from 1,500F suite. Children 12 and under stay free in parent's room. AE, DC, MC, V. Parking 18F. **Amenities:** Restaurant; bar; babysitting; concierge; room service. *In room:* A/C, TV, hair dryer, minibar, Wi-Fi (free in suites and business rooms; 30F per 24 hr. in other units).

Moderate

Best Western Strasbourg ★ Set close to the railway station on a tranquil dead-end street, this building was originally constructed around 1900 by a nostalgic entrepreneur originally from Strasbourg. Over the years many different renovations, both inside and out, have kept it looking fresh and new, albeit bland and uncontroversial. Some of the bedrooms have wooden surfaces and pastel colors; others are comfortably and traditionally conservative. The bedrooms, as befits a turn-of-the-20th-century hotel, range from spacious (usually on the lower floors) to a bit cramped. Each bedroom has fine linens, plus compact bathrooms with tile and decent plumbing.

10, rue Pradier, CH-1201 Genève. ✆ **800/528-1234** in the U.S., or 022/906-58-00. Fax 022/906-58-14. www.bestwestern.com. 51 units. 250F–270F double; 400F–500F suite. Rates include continental breakfast. AE, DC, MC, V. Bus: 1, 2, 3, 4, 8, 12, 13, or 44. **Amenities:** Concierge; room service. *In room:* TV, hair dryer, minibar, Wi-Fi (10F per hour).

Hôtel Edelweiss This brown-and-white, eight-story hotel towers above its neighbors within the bustling, working-class Pâquis neighborhood, a short walk from the hyperexpensive quai du Président-Wilson. Inside, it has a rustic decor that contrasts with its modern exterior. The bedrooms are cozy and furnished with pine-wood furniture crafted in a country-Swiss style. Even though it's in the heart of Geneva, you get provincial comfort here and a sense of high-alpine Switzerland far from the moneyed, urban gloss of modern-day Geneva. (Fans praise it as a short-term substitute for a trip to Switzerland's mountainous interior.) Bedrooms are medium in size with sitting areas and desk space. Bathrooms, although small and plain, are neatly kept. Built in the early 1960s, the hotel is frequently spruced up.

2, place de la Navigation, CH-1201 Genève. ✆ **022/544-51-51.** Fax 022/544-51-99. www.manotel.com/edelweiss. 42 units. 210F–400F double. Rates include buffet breakfast. AE, DC, MC, V. Bus: 1. **Amenities:** Restaurant; bar; room service. *In room:* A/C, TV, minibar, Wi-Fi (free).

Inexpensive

Hôtel Bel'Espérance Appealingly located at the gateway to Old Town, close to the lake, this is a decent, completely unpretentious budget hotel managed by the Salvation Army. It's not bare-bones, though: It has well-furnished, good-size bedrooms, accompanied by private bathrooms. Many rooms are suitable for up to four people, and the most desirable units open onto a private balcony with a view of the Cathédrale de St. Pierre. A homey, warm atmosphere prevails.

1, rue de la Vallée, CH-1204 Genève. ✆ **022/818-37-37.** Fax 022/818-37-73. www.hotel-bel-esperance.ch. 40 units. 154F–190F double; 186F–228F triple. Rates include breakfast. AE, DC, MC, V. Bus: 8. *In room:* TV, Wi-Fi (free).

Hôtel International & Terminus ☺ This hotel lies across the street from the main entrance of Geneva's railway station and has been directed by three generations of the Cottier family. Originally built in 1900, it has been radically upgraded, with pairs of smaller rooms reconfigured into larger units especially good for families. Rated three stars by the local tourist board, the hotel offers exceedingly good value. The small to spacious bedrooms are fitted with first-rate furnishings, and the maintenance level is high. Bathrooms seem to have been added as an afterthought in areas not designed for them, and are a bit cramped with shower stalls. The restaurant, La Veranda, serves some of the most reasonable meals in Geneva, and keeps the pizza ovens caldron-hot.

20, rue des Alpes, CH-1201 Genève. ✆ **022/906-97-77.** Fax 022/906-97-78. www.international-terminus.ch. 60 units. 170F–290F double. Rates include buffet breakfast. AE, DC, MC, V. **Amenities:** Restaurant. *In room:* TV, hair dryer, minibar, Wi-Fi (free).

Hôtel St-Gervais One of the simplest hotels we recommend in this guide, the St-Gervais is inside an old-fashioned, vaguely nondescript building in Geneva's medieval core, a 3-minute walk from Gare Cornavin. Although it has quirky idiosyncrasies that appeal to architects and historic renovators, some guests have expressed annoyance at having to navigate their way to the upper floors with a lot of luggage. Fortunately, there's a cramped elevator on-site. The place is minimalist but comfortable, with an emphasis on durable, functionalist furniture. You get routine rooms here, and well-worn but still-comfortable beds. As for plumbing, you most often have to settle for just a sink, although the hotel maintains an adequate number of hallway bathrooms, which are kept very tidy.

20, rue des Corps-Saints, CH-1201 Genève. ✆ **022/732-45-72.** Fax 022/731-42-90. www.stgervais-geneva.ch. 24 units, 3 with bathroom. 119F double without bathroom; 145F double with bathroom. Rates include breakfast. AE, DC, MC, V. **Amenities:** Bar; Wi-Fi (20F per 24 hr.).

ON THE LEFT BANK

Expensive

Hôtel de la Cigogne ★★★ Personalized and charming, this is our favorite Left Bank hotel, a chic, glamorous retreat for the discerning. This deluxe hotel was rebuilt after years of dilapidation and turned into an offbeat Relais & Châteaux that showcases designer and decorator talent. Combined with an adjoining building, the old hotel and its mate have the renovated facades of the original 18th- and 19th-century structures. With three sheltered courtyards overlooking a flowering plaza, this is one of the most tranquil hotels in Geneva. The bedrooms contain handmade mattresses, luxurious bathrooms, and bed linens embroidered with the hotel's coat of arms. Each bedroom is furnished differently, ranging from 1930s movie-mogul style to the "baron and baroness at their country place." Some units have working fireplaces.

17, place Longemalle, CH-1204 Genève. ✆ **022/818-40-40.** Fax 022/818-40-50. www.cigogne.ch. 52 units. 495F–620F double; 870F–970F suite. Rates include continental breakfast. AE, DC, MC, V. Parking 27F. **Amenities:** Restaurant; babysitting; room service. *In room:* A/C, TV, hair dryer, minibar, Wi-Fi (free).

Hôtel Tiffany ★ This little charming five-story Belle Epoque boutique hotel lies on a Left Bank street 3 blocks south of the river and about a 12-minute stroll from the center and the lake. Although it can hardly match the style and glamour of the lakeside palaces, it's attractive in its own modest way, featuring touches like stained glass, Art Nouveau bed frames, leather-clad armchairs, and a summertime sidewalk cafe. In its category, it offers some of the most reasonable prices in Geneva, especially considering its style. Bedrooms are midsize with lots of extras, including soundproofing and spacious bathrooms. We prefer the rooms in the "attic," with their beams, rooftop vistas, and sloping walls.

1, rue des Marbriers, CH-1204 Genève. ✆ **022/708-16-16.** Fax 022/708-16-17. www.hotel-tiffany.ch. 46 units. 430F–480F double; from 650F suite. AE, DC, MC, V. Parking nearby 34F. **Amenities:** Restaurant; bar; exercise room; room service. *In room:* A/C, TV, DVD and CD player (in suites), hair dryer, minibar, Wi-Fi (10F per hour).

Inexpensive

Hôtel Central Confusingly located on the 5th, 6th, and 7th floors of a prominent building erected in 1924, this hotel has been a haven for cost-conscious visitors to Geneva since 1928. You'll find a very modern format, with a minimalist interior, on a street lined with banks and upscale shops. You'll register in the sixth-floor reception area, containing carved antiques from Bali. (The establishment's Danish-born owner used to manage a five-star hotel there.) Know in advance that the smallest rooms have two-tiered bunk beds, toilets in alcoves off the hallway, and very little space. The more expensive rooms are bigger and more comfortable. Be alert that the reception staff is available only from 7am to 9pm, so if you're planning on a late-night check-in, make prior arrangements. Breakfast is served in the bedrooms.

2, rue de la Rôtisserie, CH-1204 Genéve. © **022/818-81-00.** Fax 022/818-81-01. www.hotelcentral.ch. 32 units, 28 with private toilet. 95F double without toilet, 115F–165F with toilet; 215F suite. Rates include continental breakfast. AE, DC, MC, V. Bus: 12. **Amenities:** Room service. *In room:* TV, Wi-Fi (free).

Where to Dine

ON THE RIGHT BANK

Very Expensive

Le Chat-Botté ★★★ FRENCH This grand restaurant is in one of the fanciest hotels in Geneva. Suitably decorated with tapestries, sculpture, and rich upholstery, with a polite and correct staff, it serves some of the best food in the city. There are some critics who consider it among the best restaurants of Europe. If the weather is right, you can dine on the flower-bedecked terrace, overlooking the Jet d'Eau. The cuisine, although inspired by French classics, is definitely contemporary. Typical starters include delectable zucchini flowers stuffed with vegetables and essence of tomato; and lobster salad with eggplant "caviar," olive oil, and fresh herbs. Some of the most enticing items on the menu include carpaccio with black olives and Parmesan cheese, poached wing of skate in an herb-flavored sauce, and oven-roasted Sisteron lamb with stuffed vegetables. The chef's best-known dish is a delicate filet of perch from Lake Geneva, which is sautéed until it's golden.

In the Hôtel Beau-Rivage, 13, quai du Mont-Blanc. © **022/716-69-20.** Reservations required. Main courses 60F–90F; fixed-price menus 185F–220F. AE, DC, MC, V. Daily noon–2pm and 7–9:45pm. Bus: 1.

Spices ★★ INTERNATIONAL There's something yummy and mellow-looking about the tawny decor of this restaurant, positioned off the sprawling lobby of the Hôtel Président Wilson. It's the best-decorated and most exciting hotel restaurant in Geneva, with big windows overlooking the lake. Menu items change with the season and the inspiration of the chef, but are likely to include warm marinated salmon with sage and a wasabi-flavored pistou; a sweet-and-sour combination of freshwater crayfish with Maine lobster; Chinese-style raviolis stuffed with foie gras of duckling with a ginger-flavored cream sauce; line-caught sea bass fried with Sicilian artichokes; and a superb version of breast of Bresse chicken in which, on one platter, you'll find versions braised with teriyaki and stuffed with foie gras.

In the Hôtel Président Wilson, 47, quai Wilson. © **022/906-65-52.** Reservations recommended. Main courses 75F–110F. AE, DC, MC, V. Mon–Fri noon–2pm; Mon–Sat 7:30–10pm.

Windows ★ CONTINENTAL Flooded with sunlight from large panoramic windows, and permeated with an undeniably upscale but discreet and rather clubby sense of old-fashioned exclusivity, it attracts a clientele of French-Swiss politicians, film-industry personnel, writers, and the merely rich. Menu items change with the seasons, but are likely to include orange-marinated chicken cutlets with a yogurt-flavored avocado sauce and bulgur wheat; zucchini flowers stuffed with eggplant "caviar" and Provençal herbs; asparagus and Roquefort soup; roasted omble chevalier, a whitefish from the nearby lake, served with a reduction of carrot juice and a passion fruit–flavored butter sauce; and pan-fried veal cutlets served with a demi-glace of veal drippings and green asparagus. And if you happen to be walking along the quais between 3 and 5pm, consider dropping into this place for high tea (30F per person), which includes finger sandwiches and pastries.

In the Hôtel d'Angleterre, 17, quai du Mont-Blanc. ✆ **022/906-55-55.** Reservations recommended. Main courses 49F–74F; fixed-price lunch 54F, dinner 70F–190F. AE, DC, MC, V. Daily noon–2pm and 7–10:30pm. Bus: 1.

Expensive

Chez Jacky ★ SWISS This provincial bistro should be better known, although it already attracts everyone from grandmothers to young skiers en route to Verbier. It's the domain of Jacky Gruber, an exceptional chef from the Valais. There's subtlety in Monsieur Gruber's cooking that suggests the influence of his mentor, Frédy Giradet, hailed as Switzerland's greatest chef before his recent retirement. The chef tirelessly seeks the most select produce for his imaginative and innovative dishes, and he continues to dazzle his regular clients year after year, winning new converts as well. You may begin with Chinese cabbage and mussels and continue with filet of turbot roasted with thyme, or perhaps beautifully prepared pink duck on a bed of spinach with a confit of onions. Be prepared to wait for each course, though.

11, rue Jacques-Necker. ✆ **022/732-86-80.** www.chezjacky.ch. Reservations recommended. Main courses 43F–46F; fixed-price lunch 28F–48F, dinner 67F–93F. AE, DC, MC, V. Mon–Fri 11:30am–2pm and 7–10pm. Closed 1st week of Jan and mid-July to mid-Aug. Bus: 5, 10, or 44.

Moderate

Jeck's Place ★ THAI/SINGAPOREAN Near the Gare Cornavin, this place is a delight. It's like taking a culinary trip to Southeast Asia, with stopovers in such places as China, Malaysia, Thailand, and India. Escaping from the traffic outside, you enter a warm and friendly enclave, where Jeck Tan of Singapore will greet you. The cuisine of Asian specialties provides temptation with every order, and the trays of delicacies are brought out by waitresses in sarongs. The specials of the day will be seasoned with delicate blends of spices, notably lemon grass and curry, but also chili and ganlaga (from the ginger family). It's not the dull beef sauté, for example, but a medley of delight in a sauce flavored with cloves, curry, cinnamon, coconut milk, and lemon grass. We often make a meal of the appetizers alone, including homemade steamed dumplings stuffed with a blend of pork and vegetables flavored with coriander. The house specialty, and our favorite dish, is Jeck's chicken in green curry.

14, rue de Neuchâtel. ✆ **022/731-33-03.** Reservations recommended. Main courses 22F–36F; special lunch platter 14F. AE, DC, MC, V. Mon–Fri 11:30am–2pm; daily 6:30–10:30pm. Bus: 4, 5, or 9.

Le Boeuf Rouge LYONNAIS Few other restaurants in Geneva's center work so hard to bring you an authentic version of the brasserie-style cuisine of Lyon, and although the place isn't as famous or as much talked about as it was during its 1980s heyday, it's still a viable dining choice. You'll find such dishes as Lyonnais sausage with scalloped potatoes, chateaubriand in red-wine sauce, blood sausage, and quenelles of pikeperch—any of which might be preceded by a delectable version of onion soup or green salad with croutons and bacon. The staff here is brusque but kind.

17, rue Alfred-Vincent (corner of rue Pâquis). ✆ **022/732-75-37.** www.boeufrouge.ch. Reservations recommended. Main courses 17F–46F; fixed-price menus 44F–48F. AE, DC, MC, V. Mon–Fri noon–2pm and 7–10:30pm; Sat 7–10pm. Bus: 1.

ON THE LEFT BANK

Expensive

Brasserie de l'Hôtel de Ville ★ SWISS This is one of the most deliberately archaic-looking restaurants in Geneva, with a reputation that dates from 1764 and a clientele that prefers that absolutely nothing changes in either its old-fashioned decor or its choice of dishes. In spite of its look, it's rather hip and popular with the Genevois. Be aware that this place doesn't have a lot of patience with diners who aren't familiar with dining rituals as practiced in an upscale brasserie, and the staff can be brusque. Nonetheless, we continue to recommend it as we would a time capsule to another era. The menu is more sophisticated and better than ever. Try the filets of freshwater lake perch meunière. Sometimes the prized fish of Lake Geneva, omble chevalier, is also served in a butter sauce. One old-fashioned dish remains on the menu: *Longeole du val d'Arve* (traditional Geneva-style sausages flavored with cumin). You can also order such delights as rack of lamb flavored with herbs of Provence.

19, Grand-Rue. ✆ **022/311-70-30.** www.hdvglozu.ch. Reservations recommended. Main courses 27F–45F; fixed-price menu 47F–67F. AE, DC, MC, V. Daily 11:30am–11:30pm. Bus: 36.

Brasserie Lipp SWISS Located on the ground floor of a modern shopping complex, this bustling restaurant is named after the famous Parisian brasserie, and when you enter, especially at lunch, you'll think you've been transported to Paris. Waiters in black jackets with long white aprons are constantly rushing about with platters of food. The menu contains a sampling of French bistro dishes. Like its Parisian namesake, the Geneva Lipp specializes in several versions of charcuterie. You can also order three kinds of *pot-au-feu* and such classic dishes as a Toulousian cassoulet with *confit de canard* (duckling). The fresh oysters are among the best in the city. These dishes will not dazzle you with subtle nuances, and service is a bit frantic, but the restaurant appeals to all lovers of the old-fashioned French brasserie.

In Confédération-Centre, 8, rue de la Confédération. ✆ **022/318-80-30.** www.brasserie-lipp.com. Reservations recommended. Main courses 31F–50F; *plats du jour* 19F–37F lunch only; fixed-price menus 67F–83F. AE, DC, MC, V. Mon–Sat 7am–2am; Sun 9am–2am. Bus: 12.

La Coupole SWISS This is a true brasserie—far more elegant than its Parisian namesake. The place is more popular at noon, especially with shoppers and office workers, than it is at night. Fanciful and fun, it's dotted with grandfather clocks, a bronze Venus, Edwardian palms, and comfortable banquettes. The menu is limited but well selected; the *cuisine du marché* (fare with local and seasonal ingredients) is a delight, although many patrons stick to the standard old red-meat bistro specials such as the inevitable entrecôte.

116, rue du Rhône. ✆ **022/787-50-10.** www.lacoupole.ch. Reservations recommended. Main courses 32F–46F; fixed-price menu 49F. AE, DC, MC, V. Mon–Sat 11:30am–2:30pm and 7–11pm. Bus: 2, 9, or 22. Tram: 12.

La Favola ★ TUSCAN/ITALIAN It's the best Italian restaurant in Geneva, and its most devoted habitués hail it as the best restaurant in Geneva—period. Set a few steps from the Cathédrale de St. Pierre, it contains only two cramped dining rooms. The menu is small but choice, varying with the availability of ingredients and the seasons. Look for such delightful dishes as carpaccio of beef; *vitello tonnato* (paper-thin veal with a tuna sauce); lobster salad; potato salad with cèpe mushrooms; such pastas as fresh ravioli with either eggplant or bolete mushrooms; and a luscious version of tortellini stuffed with ricotta, meat juices, red wine, and herbs. Meat and fish vary daily. Don't even think of coming here on weekends, as the place is locked tight.

15, rue Calvin. ✆ **022/311-74-37.** www.lafavola.com. Reservations required. Main courses 31F–60F. No credit cards. Mon–Fri noon–2pm and 7:15–10pm. Closed 2 weeks in July–Aug and 1 week at Christmas. Tram: 12.

Moderate

Au Pied de Cochon ★ LYONNAIS/SWISS Named after a restaurant at Les Halles in Paris, this is the best place to go in Geneva for hearty Lyonnais fare, if you don't mind the smoke and the noise. The setting is *fin de siècle,* with a staff dressed entirely in black and white. The bistro maintains its Lyonnais antecedents, which every Francophile knows are the most illustrious for fine brasserie-style food. A lot of young people, artists, and local workers dine here, as well as lawyers from the Palais de Justice across the way. The cooking is as grandmother used to prepare it, provided she came from the Lyon area. Naturally, the namesake *pieds de cochon* (pigs' feet) is included on the menu, along with tender alpine lamb, grilled anguillettes, and tripe.

4, place du Bourg-de-Four. ✆ **022/310-47-97.** www.pied-de-cochon.ch. Reservations recommended. Main courses 26F–38F. AE, DC, MC, V. Daily 7:30am–2:30pm and 6:30pm–midnight. Closed Sun June–Aug. Bus: 2 or 7. Tram: 12.

Café du Centre SWISS/CONTINENTAL This cafe is usually hysterically busy, and permeated with a kind of brusque anonymity. But despite its drawbacks, this remains very much an Old Geneva institution, established in 1871. Despite the thousands of cups of coffee and glasses of beer served here, it's more akin to a restaurant that serves drinks than a cafe that offers food. During nice weather, most of the business takes place outdoors on a terrace opening onto the square, while the rest of the year, business moves inside into a pair of street-level rooms whose nostalgic decor may remind you of an old-fashioned brasserie in Lyon. A thick, multilingual menu offers food items such as excellent versions of fresh fish, as well as Wiener schnitzel, a savory version of onglet of beef, and pepper steak.

5, place du Molard. ✆ **022/311-85-86.** www.cafeducentre.ch. Reservations recommended. Main courses 27F–44F; fixed-price *assiette du jour* 19F at lunch Mon–Fri only. AE, DC, MC, V. Mon 6am–midnight; Tues–Sat 9am–1am; Sun 9am–midnight. Tram: 12.

Inexpensive

L'Aïoli FRENCH Named after the famous garlic sauce of Provence, this popular neighborhood restaurant stands opposite Le Corbusier's Maison de Verre. Something of a local secret, it offers personalized service and some of the finest Provençal cooking in town. Among the featured dishes are lamb gigot, frogs' legs Provençal, scampi Provençal, and a delectable *pot-au-feu* of beef. Look for the daily specials, such as a savory, Provence-derived lamb stew called *gardiane camarguaise.*

6, rue Adrien-Lachenal. ✆ **022/736-79-71.** Reservations not required. Main courses 16F–36F; fixed-price dinner 33F–35F. AE, DC, MC, V. Mon–Sat 6:30pm–2am. Closed Aug. Bus: 1 or 6. Tram: 12.

Nologo ★ MEDITERRANEAN/ITALIAN Surrounded by a gaggle of less creative restaurants, this is the most sophisticated, most upscale, and most "design-conscious" restaurant in the burgeoning Pâquis district, a bustling and irreverent working-class neighborhood immediately downhill from the railway station. It features the kind of high-style black and stainless steel decor you might have expected in Milan, and some of the most sophisticated and creative food in the neighborhood.

Examples include veal cutlets with pesto-mint sauce, served with rosemary-roasted potatoes; sea bass with ratatouille and caponata; beefsteak with rocket and exotic mushrooms; and wide-noodle pappardelle with fresh tuna, roasted eggplant, fresh tomatoes, and mint.

11, rue de Fribourg. ✆ **022/901-0333.** www.nologo.ch. Reservations recommended Fri–Sat nights. Main courses 15F–41F. AE, DC, MC, V. Mon–Fri noon–2:30pm; Mon–Sat 7–10:30pm. Bus: 1.

Nô Sushi JAPANESE Popular, hip, and mobbed every day at lunchtime, this is a large, high-ceilinged space devoted to a labyrinth of countertops that merge into the most bemusing and whimsical Japanese restaurant in town. This is the only automated sushi bar in Switzerland, and as such, adds an eccentric and trend-conscious flair to a neighborhood that's better known for its relative conservatism. You'll know how much something costs by the color of the platter that contains it. You can pluck everything except the miso soup, which is carried to your seat by a waitress, directly from the moving conveyer belt. Hot foods remain hot thanks to a candle flickering beneath. Sushi (with rice) and sashimi (without rice) choices include mullet, calamari, octopus, salmon, and tuna. There are also teriyaki dishes, tempura, and a medley of rice and noodle dishes, any of which you can combine into a full meal.

Confédération Centre, 8, rue de la Confédération. ✆ **022/810-39-73.** Reservations not necessary. Sushi, sashimi, rolls, and small platters 22F–43F. AE, MC, V. Mon–Sat 11:30am–11pm. Bus: 12.

Sam-Lor Thai ("The Tricycle") THAI This restaurant is unpretentious and something of an insiders' secret, and hip, cost-conscious Genevois have been coming here for years. It was the first Thai restaurant in the bustling Pâquis district. Inside, there's a medley of Thai and Indonesian art objects that might be appropriate in a temple, including representations of Buddha, and a pair of teak-wood opium beds that were each artfully transformed into platforms for dining tables. Menu items include at least four kinds of both chicken and pork (including versions with either red or green curry, with ginger, or with white pepper and garlic); monkfish with tamarind sauce; noodles sautéed with tofu and garlic; duck meat with red curry and coconut; and vermicelli with shrimp, brought to the table in an iron pot that's continually heated with a burning candle.

17, rue de Monthoux. ✆ **022/738-80-55.** Reservations recommended Fri–Sat nights. Main courses 14F–29F. AE, DC, MC, V. Mon–Thurs noon–2pm and 7–10:30pm; Fri noon–2pm and 7:30–11pm; Sat 7:30–11pm; Sun 7–10pm. Bus: 1.

Seeing the Sights

THE TOP ATTRACTIONS

In addition to the sites listed below, Geneva's other top attractions—all premier sights—are the **Jet d'Eau,** the famous fountain that has virtually become the city's symbol; the **Flower Clock,** in the Jardin Anglais, with 6,500 flowers (it was the world's first when it was inaugurated in the 1950s; today, it's less of a showstopper); and **Old Town,** the oldest part of the city.

Musée Ariana ★★ Located to the west of the Palais des Nations, this Italian Renaissance building was constructed by Gustave Revilliod, the 19th-century Genevese patron who began the collection. Today it's one of the top porcelain, glass, and pottery museums in Europe. You'll see Sèvres, Delft faience, and Meissen porcelain, as well as pieces from Japan and China. It's also the headquarters of the International Academy of Ceramics.

10, av. de la Paix. © **022/418-54-50.** www.ville-ge.ch. Free admission to the permanent collection; temporary exhibitions 5F adults, 3F students, free for children 17 and under. Wed–Mon 10am–5pm. Bus: 8 or F.

Musée d'Art et Contemporain (MAMCO) ★ Some 20 years in the making, Geneva's first modern-art museum opened in 1994 in a former factory building, and immediately evoked comparisons to some of the excellent collections of modern art in Paris. This prestigious showcase displays a vast collection of European and American art covering the past 4 decades. Out of some 1,000 works of art owned by the museum, only 300 are permanently on display. This space is packed with all the big names—Frankenthaler, Stela, Segal, and others. Some 150 sq. m (1,600 sq. ft.) of space is set aside for exhibitions that change three times a year.

10, rue des Vieux-Grenadiers. © **022/320-61-22.** www.mamco.ch. Admission 8F adults, 6F students, free for children 17 and under. Tues–Fri noon–6pm; Sat–Sun 11am–6pm. Bus: 1 or 32.

Musée d'Art et d'Histoire ★★ At Geneva's most important museum, displays include prehistoric relics, Greek vases, medieval stained glass, 12th-century armor, Swiss timepieces, Flemish and Italian paintings, and Switzerland's largest collection of Egyptian art. The Etruscan pottery and medieval furniture are both impressive. A 1444 altarpiece by Konrad Witz depicts the "miraculous" draft of fishes. Many galleries also contain works by such artists as Rodin, Renoir, Hodler, Vallotton, Le Corbusier, Picasso, Chagall, Corot, Monet, and Pissarro. There's a well-managed restaurant on the premises of this place.

2, rue Charles-Galland (btw. bd. Jacques-Dalcroze and bd. Helvétique). © **022/418-26-00.** www.centre.ch. Free admission. Temporary exhibitions 5F adults, 2F children. Tues–Sun 10am–5pm. Bus: 1, 3, 5, 8, or 17.

Musée International de la Croix-Rouge et du Croissant-Rouge (International Red Cross and Red Crescent Museum) ★ Here you can experience the legendary past of the Red Cross in the city where it started; it's across from the visitors' entrance to the European headquarters of the United Nations. The dramatic story from 1863 to the present is revealed through displays of rare documents and photographs, films, multiscreen slide shows, and cycloramas. You're taken from the battlefields of Europe to the plains of Africa to see the Red Cross in action. When Henry Dunant founded the Red Cross in Geneva in 1863, he needed a recognizable symbol to suggest neutrality. The Swiss flag (a white cross on a red field), with the colors reversed, ended up providing the perfect symbol for one of the world's greatest humanitarian movements.

17, av. de la Paix. © **022/748-95-25.** www.micr.org. Admission 10F adults; 5F students, seniors, and children 12–16; free for children 11 and under. Wed–Mon 10am–5pm. Bus: 8, F, V, or Z.

ORGANIZED TOURS

If you're new in Geneva and want an easy-to-digest breakdown of the way the city is divided into various neighborhoods and districts, consider a trolley car tour. Departing from the south bank's Place du Rhône (Mar–Dec only), red-painted, open-sided trolley cars meander through neighborhoods that include the city's medieval center, the glossy shopping districts, and the hotel- and museum-studded precincts of the river's north bank. Trams depart at 45-minute intervals every day between 10:45am and 6:45pm, last about 45 minutes, and cost 9.90F for adults and 6.90F for children. For more information, contact **STT Trains Tours S.A.,** 36, bd. St-Georges (✆ **022/781-04-04;** www.sttr.ch).

A 2-hour City Tour is operated daily all year by **Key Tours S.A.,** 7, rue des Alpes, square du Mont-Blanc (✆ **022/731-41-40;** www.keytours.ch). The tour starts from the Gare Routière, the bus station at place Dorcière, near the Key Tours office. From November to March the tour is offered only once a day at 1:30pm, but from April to October two tours leave daily at 10:30am and 1:30pm.

A bus will drive you through the city to see the monuments, landmarks, and lake promenades. In the Old Town you can take a walk down to the Bastions Park and the Reformation Wall. After a tour through the International Center, where you'll be shown the headquarters of the International Red Cross, the bus returns to its starting place. Adults pay 23F and children 4 to 12 accompanied by an adult are charged 12F, while children 3 and under go free.

Additionally, two separate companies offer cruises along the lake. The smaller of the two, **Mouettes Genevoises Navigation,** 8, quai du Mont-Blanc (✆ **022/732-47-47;** www.swissboat.com), specializes in small-scale boats carrying only about 100 passengers at a time. Each features some kind of prerecorded commentary, in French and English, throughout. An easy promenade that features the landscapes and bird life along the uppermost regions of the river Rhône draining the lake is the company's 2¾-hour **Tour du Rhône (Rhône River Tour).** The trip originates at quai des Moulins, adjacent to Geneva's Pont de l'Ile, and travels downstream for about 14km (8⅔ miles) to the Barrage de Verbois (Verbois Dam) and back. From April to October, departures are Wednesday, Saturday, and Sunday at 2:15pm. It costs 17F for adults and 12F for children 4 to 12; it's free for children 3 and under.

Mouettes Genevoises Navigation's largest competitor, **CGN** (Compagnie Générale de Navigation), quai du Mont-Blanc (✆ **0848/811-848;** www.cgn.ch), offers roughly equivalent tours, in this case between May and September, that last an hour, departing six to seven times a day (depending on the season) from the company's piers along quai du Mont-Blanc. Known as Les Belles Rives Genevoises, the tours cost 16F for adults and 9F for children 6 to 16; children 5 and under ride free. Tours include prerecorded commentaries and are, frankly, about as long in duration as many short-term visitors to the city really want.

The Shopping Scene

From boutiques to department stores, Geneva is a shopper's dream come true. The city, of course, is known for its watches and jewelry, but it's also a good place to buy embroidered blouses, music boxes from the Jura region, cuckoo clocks from German Switzerland, cigars from Havana (not allowed into the United States), chocolate, Swiss Army knives, and many other items.

Geneva practically invented the wristwatch. In fact, watchmaking in the city dates from the 16th century. Be sure to avoid purchasing a Swiss watch in one of the souvenir stores. If jewelers are legitimate, they'll display a symbol of the Geneva Association of Watchmakers and Jewelers. Here, more than in any other Swiss city, you should be able to find all the best brands, including Vacheron & Constantin, Longines, Omega, and Blancpain, to name just a few. Sometimes there are discounts on such items as cameras. Most salespeople you'll encounter speak English and are very helpful.

A shopping spree may begin at **place du Molard,** once the harbor of Geneva before the water receded. Merchants from all over Europe used to bring their wares to trade fairs here in the days before merchants migrated to the richer markets in Lyon.

If you walk along rue du Rhône and are put off by the prices, go 1 block south to rue du Marché, which in various sections becomes rue de la Croix-d'Or and rue de Rive, and is sometimes referred to by locals as "la rue du Tram" because of the many trolleys that run along its length. Don't be afraid to comparison-shop in Geneva—many stores jack up prices for visitors.

Store hours vary in Geneva. Most stores are open Monday to Friday 8am to 6:30pm and Saturday from 8am to 5pm.

SELECT SHOPS

The **Antiquorum ★★★**, 2, rue du Mont-Blanc (✆ **022/909-28-50;** www.antiquorum.com), is the largest repository of antique timepieces in the world, with a reputation that's known to connoisseurs throughout the world. Virtually all of its inventory consists of antique jewelry and antique watches. Almost everything is sold at auction, rather than over-the-counter. The array of watches includes some of the most historically important watches in the world.

The aroma from **Confiserie Rohr,** 3, place du Molard (✆ **022/311-63-03;** www.chocolats-rohr.ch), practically pulls you in off the street. Among other specialties, you'll find chocolate-covered truffles, "gold" bars with hazelnuts, and *poubelles au chocolat* (chocolate "garbage pails"). Another store is at 42, rue du Rhône.

Located opposite the Mont Blanc Bridge, **Bucherer ★**, 45, rue du Rhône (✆ **022/319-62-66;** www.bucherer.com), sells deluxe watches and diamonds. The store offers such name brands as Rolex, Piaget, Ebel, Baume & Mercier, Omega, Tissot, Rado, and Swatch. The carpeted third floor is filled with relatively inexpensive watches. You'll also find a large selection of cuckoo clocks, music boxes, embroideries, and souvenirs, as well as porcelain pillboxes and other gift items.

Geneva After Dark

For a listing of nightlife and cultural activities, free copies of the bilingual monthly *Genève Le Guide* (www.le-guide.ch) are distributed at hotel desks and tourist information centers.

THE PERFORMING ARTS

Geneva has always attracted the culturally sophisticated, including Byron, Jean-Baptiste Camille Corot, Victor Hugo, Balzac, George Sand, and Franz Liszt. Ernst Ansermet founded Geneva's great **Orchestre de la Suisse Romande,** whose frequent concerts entertain music lovers at **Victoria Hall.** For opera there's the 1,500-seat **Grand Théâtre,** which welcomes Béjart, the Bolshoi, and other ballet companies, in addition to having a company of its own.

For a preview of events at the time of your visit, pick up a copy of the monthly "List of Events" issued by the tourist office.

THE BAR SCENE

Most bars in Geneva close at 1:30 or 2am.

If you want to experience life in the very posh fast lane of what's probably the most consistently expensive hotel in Geneva, the suave and silky bar staff at **Le Bar des Bergues ★★★**, in the Four Seasons (p. 1001), is ready, willing, and able to welcome you—especially if you're fetchingly dressed and nubile—into the inner sanctums of this elegant and very upscale wood-paneled bar. If you're not actually staying at the hotel at the time of your appearance, you won't be alone: At least half the clients of this bar aren't residents of the hotel.

The Fashionable **Le Francis Bar,** 8, bd. Helvétique (✆ **022/346-32-52;** www.lefrancis.ch), which, during headier days, attracted *le tout Genève* or "cream of the crop" of Geneva, still manages to transform itself into an attractive piano bar on some evenings.

On the other end of the spectrum, **Scandale,** 24, rue de Lausanne (✆ **022/731-83-73;** www.lescandale.ch), attracts the young, the restless, and the rebellious 20- and 30-somethings of Geneva to a wholesale rejection of the glittering sense of posh that prevails within more upscale neighborhoods beside the city's lakefront. Furnishings include artfully battered, hand-me-down sofas, an elongated bar where you're likely to meet hipsters from all over Europe and the Middle East, and a blend of house and electro-jazz music that keeps everybody hopping. Don't even ask about the gender preferences of the clientele here—everyone seems way beyond even attempting an easy and pat self-definition.

BERN & THE BERNESE OBERLAND

Bern is a popular starting point for many excursions, especially to the lakes and peaks of the Bernese Oberland, a vast recreational area only minutes from the capital.

Bern

As the Swiss capital, Bern, with a relatively small population of only 130,000, is an important city of diplomats and the site of many international organizations and meetings. It's one of the oldest and loveliest cities in Europe, with origins going back to the 12th century. Since much of its medieval architecture remains today, Bern evokes the feeling of a large provincial town rather than a city. In 1983 the United Nations declared it a World Heritage Site.

The modern mingles harmoniously with the old in this charming city, and in recent years residents have discreetly added contemporary-style homes and structures to the historic environment. Such coexistence between the old and new is also evident in Bern's university, known equally for traditional studies and pioneering scientific research.

ESSENTIALS

Getting There

BY PLANE The **Bern-Belp Airport** (✆ **031/960-21-11;** www.alpar.ch) is 9.6km (6 miles) south of the city in the area of Belpmoos. International flights arrive from Munich, Rome, and London, but transatlantic jets are not able to land here. Fortunately, it's a short hop to Bern from the international airports in Zurich and Geneva.

A taxi from the airport to the city center costs about 35F to 50F, so it's better to take the shuttle bus that runs between the airport and the Bahnhof (train station)—it costs 16F one-way.

BY TRAIN Bern has direct connections to the Continental rail network that includes France, Italy, Germany, the Benelux countries, and even Scandinavia and Spain. The TGV high-speed train connects Paris with Bern in just 4½ hours. Bern also lies on major Swiss rail links, particularly those connecting Geneva (90 min.) and Zurich (58 min.). For **rail information** and schedules, call ✆ **0900/300-300.**

The **Bahnhof** rail station, on Bahnhofplatz, is right in the center of town near all the major hotels. If your luggage is light, you can walk to your hotel; otherwise, take one of the taxis waiting outside the station.

BY CAR Bern lies at a major expressway junction, with A1 coming in east from Zurich, A2 heading south from Basel, and A12 running north from Lake Geneva.

VISITOR INFORMATION **Bern Tourist Center,** in the Bern Bahnhof, on Bahnhofplatz (✆ **031/328-12-12;** www.berninfo.com), is open June to September daily 9am to 8:30pm, and October to May Monday to Saturday 9am to 6:30pm and Sunday from 10am to 5pm. If you need help finding a hotel room, the tourist center can make a reservation for you in the price range you select. You can also find good local maps here.

CITY LAYOUT **Main Arteries & Streets** The geography of the city is neatly pressed into a relatively small area, so getting about is quite easy. You can walk to most of the major sights. **Altstadt,** or Old Town, lies on a high rocky plateau that juts out into a "loop" of the Aare River. A majority of the major hotels and attractions lie in this loop.

Most arrivals are at the Bahnhof on Bahnhofplatz, in the center of town. From here you can walk along the major arteries of Bern: **Spitalgasse, Marktgasse, Kramgasse,** and **Gerechtigkeitsgasse.** The town's major squares include **Theaterplatz,** with its famed Zytgloggeturm (Clock Tower); **Kornhausplatz** and its much-photographed Ogre Fountain; and **Rathausplatz,** on which stands the old Rathaus (town hall), seat of the cantonal government.

The three major bridges crossing the Aare into this historic loop are **Kirchenfeldbrücke, Kornhausbrücke,** and **Lorrainebrücke.**

Only two of Bern's many neighborhoods are of particular interest to tourists:

ALTSTADT This is the heart of Bern, lying inside a bend of the Aare River. Filled with flower-decked fountains, it encompasses some 6km (3¾ miles) of arcades and medieval streets, many reserved for pedestrians only. Its main street is Kramgasse, filled with luxury shops and 17th- and 18th-century houses.

SOUTH OF THE AARE You can reach this sprawling district by crossing the Kirchenfeldbrücke. The neighborhood has four major museums: Swiss Alpine Museum, Bern Historical Museum, Natural History Museum, and Museum of Communication.

Getting Around

ON FOOT This is the only practical means of exploring Altstadt and its many attractions. You can see what there is to see here in about 2½ hours.

Don't overlook the possibility of walks in Greater Bern, including Bern's own mountain, **Gurten,** a popular day-trip destination reached in 25 minutes by tram no. 9 and rack railway. Once here, you'll find walks in many directions and can enjoy a panorama over the Alps. There's also a children's playground.

Bern

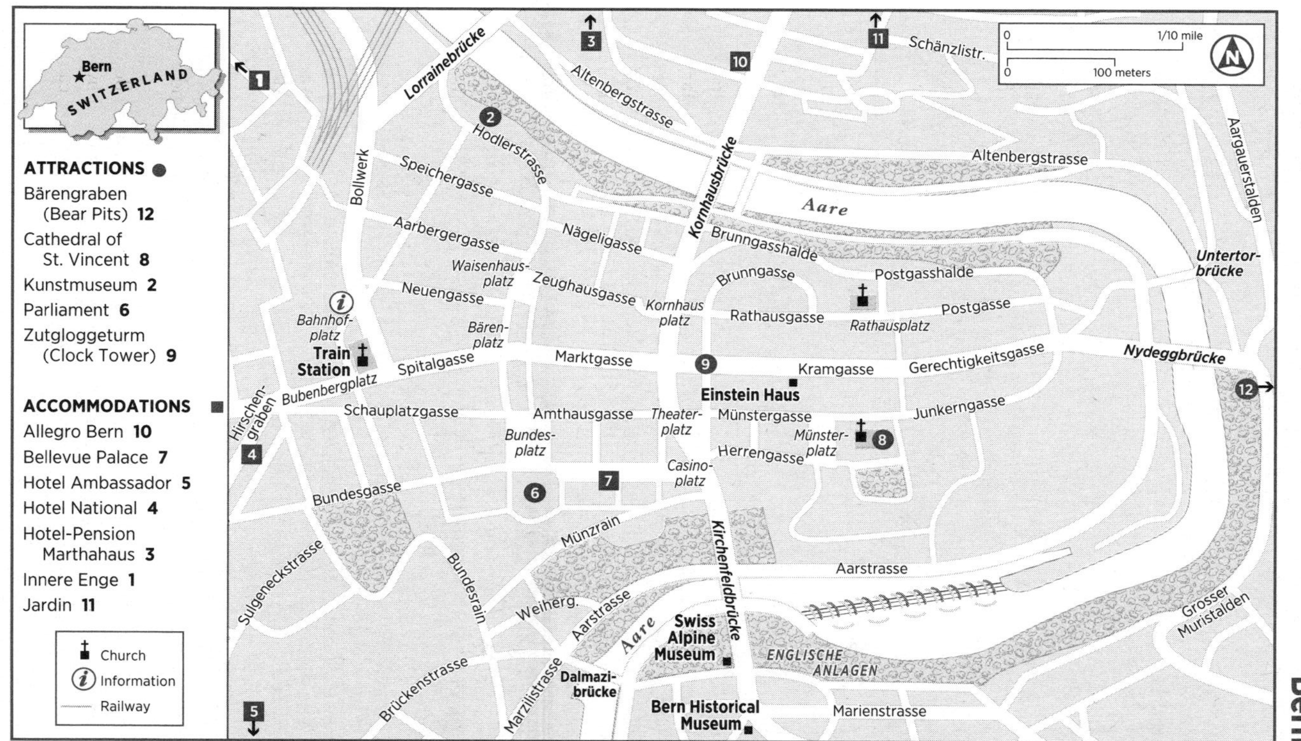

Bern
SWITZERLAND
ATTRACTIONS
Bärengraben (Bear Pits) 12
Cathedral of St. Vincent 8
Kunstmuseum 2
Parliament 6
Zutgloggeturm (Clock Tower) 9
ACCOMMODATIONS
Allegro Bern 10
Bellevue Palace 7
Hotel Ambassador 5
Hotel National 4
Hotel-Pension Marthahaus 3
Innere Enge 1
Jardin 11
Church
Information
Railway
0 1/10 mile
0 100 meters
Schänzlistr.
Lorrainebrücke
Altenbergstrasse
Hodlerstrasse
Kornhausbrücke
Altenbergstrasse
Aargauerstalden
Bollwerk
Speichergasse
Aare
Aarbergergasse
Nägeligasse
Brunngasshalde
Untertorbrücke
Waisenhausplatz
Zeughausgasse
Brunngasse
Postgasshalde
Neuengasse
Kornhausplatz
Rathausgasse
Rathausplatz
Postgasse
Bahnhofplatz
Bärenplatz
Train Station
Spitalgasse
Marktgasse
Kramgasse
Gerechtigkeitsgasse
Nydeggbrücke
Bubenbergplatz
Einstein Haus
Hirschengraben
Schauplatzgasse
Amthausgasse
Theaterplatz
Münstergasse
Junkerngasse
Bundesplatz
Münsterplatz
Herrengasse
Casinoplatz
Bundesgasse
Münzrain
Kirchenfeldbrücke
Aarstrasse
Sulgeneckstrasse
Bundesrain
Weiherg.
Aarstrasse
Aare
Swiss Alpine Museum
Grosser Muristalden
ENGLISCHE ANLAGEN
Brückenstrasse
Marzilistrasse
Dalmazibrücke
Bern Historical Museum
Marienstrasse

Walks in and around Bern include 250km (155 miles) of **marked rambling paths.** One of the most scenic walks is along the banks of the Aare through the English gardens, the Dählhölzli Zoological Gardens, Elfenau Park, and the Bremgarten woods.

For **jogging and running,** the best spots are the Aare River Run—Dalmaziquai, stretching 4km (2.5 miles), or the Aare River Run—Bear Pits, which is 5km (3 miles) long.

BY BUS & TRAM The public transportation system, the **Bernmobil,** is a reliable, 77km (48-mile) network of buses and trams. Before you board, purchase a ticket from one of the automatic machines (you'll find one at each stop) because conductors don't sell tickets. If you're caught traveling without one, you'll be fined 80F in addition to the fare for the ride. A short-range ride (within six stations) costs 2F; a normal ticket, valid for 60 minutes one-way, goes for 3.80F.

To save time and money, you might purchase a Bern Card (see the box "Saving Francs with the Bern Card," below), which, among other benefits, entitles you to unlimited travel on the city's bus and tram lines. Just get the ticket stamped at the automatic machine before beginning your first trip. Tickets are available at Rail City, Tourist Center, the Bear Pits Center, and in some hotels and museums.

BY TAXI You can catch a taxi at the public cab ranks, or call a dispatcher. **Nova Taxi** is at ✆ **031/331-33-13, Bären Taxi** at ✆ **031/371-11-11.** The basic rate is 6.80F, plus 3.80F per kilometer.

BY CAR Seeing Bern by car is very impractical due to traffic congestion in Old Town, its confusing layout of one-way streets, and a lack of on-street parking. If you have a car, it's best to park in a public garage and explore the city on foot; its miles of arcades were designed to protect pedestrians from rain, snow, and traffic.

If you want to rent a car to explore the environs, arrangements can be made at **Europcar,** Laupenstrasse 22 (✆ **031/381-75-55;** www.europcar.com); **Hertz,** Kasinoplatz at Kochergasse 1 (✆ **031/318-21-60;** www.hertz.com); or **Avis,** Wabernstrasse 41 (✆ **031/378-15-15;** www.avis.com).

Saving Francs with the Bern Card

This is one of those touristic grace notes which, while not essential, can certainly enrich a stopover in Bern and render it more economical. Sold at any branch of the Bern Tourist Office, the card entitles its holder to free admission to the permanent exhibitions within the city's museums; unlimited free use of the city's bus and tram lines; and a 25% discount on guided walking tours of the old town, the Clock Tower tour, and rental of any audio guide. Cards come in validation periods of between 24 and 72 hours and are priced as follows: cards valid for 24 hours cost 20F for adults and 16F for children 6 to 16 years old; cards valid for 48 hours cost 31F for adults and 26F for children; cards valid 72 hours cost 38F for adults and 31F for children. For information and sales, contact any branch of the Bern Tourist Office or call ✆ **031/328-12-12.**

BY BICYCLE Altstadt is compressed into such a small area that it's better to cover the historic district on foot than on a bike (bicycles aren't allowed on many pedestrian-only streets, anyway). However, in Greater Bern and its environs, there are 400km (248 miles) of cycling paths, which are marked on a special cycling map available at the tourist center (see above). The narrow yellow lanes throughout the road network are reserved for bikers. The point of departure for most official routes is Bundesplatz in Parliament Square. Special red signs will guide you through a wide variety of landscapes. Bikes can be checked out free at the **Zeughausgasse** (✆ **079/277-28-57**).

[FastFACTS] BERN

Business Hours Banks are open Monday to Friday 8am to 4:30pm (on Thurs until 6pm). Most offices are open Monday to Friday 9am to 5pm, and on Saturday 9am to noon.

Currency Exchange This is available on the lower level of the Bahnhof, on Bahnhofplatz, open Monday to Friday 7am to 8pm, Saturday 7am to 7pm, and Sunday 9am to 7pm.

Doctors & Dentists Call ✆ **0900/576-747** for a referral to an English-speaking doctor.

Drugstores Try **Central-Apotheke Volz & Co.,** Zytgloggelaube 2 (✆ **031/311-10-94;** www.central-apotheke-volz.ch). It's near the Clock Tower in Old Town. The staff speaks English and can suggest over-the-counter substitutes for foreign drugs that can't be found in Europe. It's open on Monday 9am to 6:30pm, Tuesday to Friday 7:45am to 6:30pm, and on Saturday 7:45am to 4pm. **Bahnhof Apotheke,** at the Bahnhofplatz (✆ **031/329-25-25**), is open daily 6am to 10pm.

Embassies & Consulates The **U.S. Embassy** is at Jubiläumsstrasse 93 (✆ **031/357-70-11**). Other embassy addresses are **Canada,** Kirchenfeldstrasse 88 (✆ **031/357-32-00**), and **United Kingdom,** Thunstrasse 50 (✆ **031/359-77-00**). **New Zealand** citizens should call their consulate-general in Geneva (✆ **022/929-03-50**).

Emergencies Call ✆ **117** for the police, ✆ **144** for an ambulance, ✆ **118** to report a fire, or ✆ **140** for the road patrol, but only for an emergency.

Hospital The city's largest is **Insel Hospital,** Freiburgstrasse (✆ **031/632-21-11**), the clinic affiliated with the University of Bern.

Internet Access Internet access is available at **Internetcafé,** Aarbergergasse 46 (✆ **031/311-98-50;** www.internetcafe-bern.com).

Police The police station is at Waisenhausplatz 32 (✆ **031/321-21-21**).

Post Office The main post office (Schanzenpost), at Schanzenstrasse 4 (✆ **031/386-61-11**), is open Monday to Friday from 7:30am to 9pm, on Saturday from 8am to 4pm, and Sunday 4 to 9pm.

Safety Bern is Europe's safest capital. Nevertheless, you should take the usual precautions; protect your valuables. It's generally safe to walk the streets at night, and crimes against women are rare.

Taxes A 7.6% value-added tax (VAT) is included in the price of all goods and services rendered, including hotel and restaurant bills. There are no other special taxes.

Toilets You'll find public facilities in the Bahnhof and in some squares in Old Town.

WHERE TO STAY

Very Expensive

Bellevue Palace ★★★ Built in 1913 and located next to the Bundeshaus (the seat of the Swiss government), this grand old dame of Bern reopened in 2003 after massive renovations and improvements. It's the most lavish and opulent choice in town, with carved Corinthian columns and ornate details, and one of its grand salons is covered with a stained-glass ceiling. The setting is definitely old world, and the service is impeccable. The spacious and beautifully furnished bedrooms open onto views of the Jungfrau and the Bernese Alps. The trappings of the Belle Epoque era have been combined with a state-of-the-art infrastructure that still pays homage to its architectural heritage. The market-fresh cuisine is some of the most sophisticated in town—a parade of gourmet delicacies. Dining on the renowned Bellevue Terrace is one of the reasons to come to Bern.

Kochergasse 3-5, 3001 Bern. ✆ **031/320-45-45.** Fax 031/320-46-46. www.bellevue-palace.ch. 130 units. 495F–590F double; from 715F suite. Rates include buffet breakfast. AE, DC, MC, V. Parking 28F. Tram: 3, 9, or 12. **Amenities:** 2 restaurants; bar; babysitting; concierge; room service. *In room:* A/C, TV, hair dryer, minibar, Wi-Fi (25F per 24 hr.).

Expensive

Allegro Bern ★★★ This is the hippest, most savvy, and most sophisticated hotel in town, with a charming, well-trained, and hardworking staff and a flair for elegance. Guests appreciate the panoramic view of the medieval town center of Bern and the Swiss Alps. That's reason enough to check in—that and the fact that this is the best-rated hotel in town for comfort and a sense of grace. Set just across the river from the town's historic core, the hotel runs as efficiently as a Swiss clock. There is grand comfort everywhere, especially in the midsize to spacious bedrooms, which are well furnished, immaculately kept, and equipped with well-accessorized bathrooms. The best accommodations are in the Panorama Club at the front of the hotel. These are especially sought out for their view of the Bernese Alps.

Kornhausstrasse 3, CH-3000 Bern. ✆ **031/339-55-00.** Fax 031/339-55-10. www.allegro-hotel.ch. 171 units. 219F–410F double; 499F–900F suite. AE, DC, MC, V. Parking 24F. **Amenities:** 3 restaurants; 2 bars; babysitting; concierge; exercise room; Jacuzzi; room service; sauna. *In room:* A/C, TV, hair dryer, minibar, Wi-Fi (30F per 24 hr.).

Innere Enge ★★★ 🎁 When you tire of Bern's impersonal bandbox hotels, head for this inn that occupies a building from the 1700s. This small but choice hotel, a 20-minute walk from the center of town, has windows that open onto views of the Bernese Oberland; a tranquil setting within a verdant park; and a pervasive, and sometimes just a bit cloying, jazz theme—both its melodies and its history. The well-kept and individually designed bedrooms are often spacious and filled with sunshine. Furnishings are traditional, and maintenance meets the high standards set by the manager. The most romantic units are on the top floor, resting under the eaves with sloped ceilings. The Louis Armstrong Bar, also called Marians Jazzroom (p. 1025), is linked to the hotel, offering drinks, food, and traditional jazz performances February to June and September to December.

Engestrasse 54, CH-3012 Bern. ✆ **031/309-61-11.** Fax 301/309-61-12. www.zghotels.ch. 26 units. 330F–370F double; from 370F suite. AE, DC, MC, V. Free parking. Bus: 21. **Amenities:** Restaurant; bar; babysitting; room service. *In room:* A/C (in some), TV, hair dryer, minibar, Wi-Fi (36F per 24 hr.).

Moderate

Hotel Ambassador ★ This restored nine-story hotel is the tallest building in a neighborhood of old houses with red-tile roofs, approximately 3km (1¾ miles) west of the center of Bern's Old Town. The guest rooms come with refrigerators, and many have a view of the federal palace, the Bundeshaus. They tend to be smallish and furnished in a minimalist style, but they are well maintained, with firm beds and neat bathrooms. Since the hotel caters to business travelers, its rooms offer fax and computer hookups. It's located about a mile from the train station and easily reached by tram. Dining choices include the Japanese Teppan Restaurant, surrounded by a Japanese garden. It's also the only hotel in Bern with an on-site spa.

Seftigenstrasse 99, CH-3007 Bern. ✆ **031/370-99-99.** Fax 031/371-41-17. www.fhotels.ch. 99 units. 235F–360F double. AE, DC, MC, V. Free parking. Tram: 9. **Amenities:** 2 restaurants; babysitting; indoor heated pool; room service; spa. *In room:* A/C, TV, hair dryer, minibar, Wi-Fi (free).

Inexpensive

Hotel National Originally built in 1908 as a brewery and later transformed into a textile factory, this simple but dignified government-rated two-star hotel enjoys a consistently high occupancy and many compliments based on its good value and well-scrubbed interior. It's run by two sisters, members of the Grünewald family, who maintain its very high ceilings and its confusing layout with verve and a kind of charm. The reception area lies one floor above street level, and to reach it, you'll either take the stairs or a "historically significant" elevator that might remind you of a rather quaint bird cage. Accommodations are sober but reliable, utterly devoid of any contemporary fashion statements or accessories, and occupied by a value-conscious clientele from throughout Europe and the world. Of particular note are the bedrooms on the uppermost floor, where a recent renovation exposed some of the massive timber trusses that form the exterior's mansard roof. The hotel's restaurant is recommended separately (p. 1021).

Hirschengraben 24, CH-3011 Bern. ✆ **031/381-19-88.** Fax 031/381-68-78. www.nationalbern.ch. 46 units, 32 with private bathroom. Double with shared bathroom 130F, with private bathroom 150F–170F. AE, MC, V. Tram: 3, 5, or 9. **Amenities:** Restaurant. *In room:* TV, no phone (in some), Wi-Fi (35F per 24 hr.).

Hotel-Pension Marthahaus Set within a verdant suburb about a 12-minute walk to the city center, this five-story hotel was originally built around 1900 and has comfortably battered, semiantique bedrooms, each with a different floor layout (it may remind some visitors of a slightly dowdy college dormitory). There's a tiny elevator to carry guests upstairs, and a simple but respectable and clean format that symbolizes good value in an otherwise expensive town. Present management—an organization that directs a pension and retirement fund for women—has been in place here since the 1970s. The better rooms contain small private bathrooms.

Wyttenbachstrasse 22A, CH-3013 Bern. ✆ **031/332-41-35.** Fax 031/333-33-86. www.marthahaus.ch. 40 units, 6 with bathroom. 99F–110F double without bathroom, 140F–160F with bathroom. Rates include buffet breakfast. MC, V. Parking 10F. Bus: 20. **Amenities:** Bikes; Wi-Fi (free, in lobby). *In room:* TV.

Jardin Set less than a kilometer (½ mile) north of Bern's center, Jardin lies within a leafy residential suburb with lots of parking. This establishment functioned as a restaurant and apartment building between the year it was built (ca. 1900) and 1985. Then its apartments were transformed into modern, warmly appealing hotel rooms that are larger than virtually anything else within their price category. All rooms are equipped with private bathrooms. Your hosts are identical twins Andreas and Daniel Balz. Joggers and nature enthusiasts will appreciate the large verdant spaces (part of a military academy) across the street from this russet brown, four-story hotel.

Militärstrasse 38, CH-3014 Bern. ✆ **031/333-01-17.** Fax 031/333-09-43. www.hotel-jardin.ch. 18 units. 160F double; 220F triple. Rates include buffet breakfast. AE, DC, MC, V. Free parking. Tram: 9 to Breitenrainplatz. **Amenities:** Restaurant. *In room:* TV, hair dryer.

WHERE TO DINE

Very Expensive

Wein & Sein ★★★ INTERNATIONAL In terms of underground, word-of-mouth chic, this is the most fashionable and hip restaurant in Bern today. Set within the cellar of a historic building in the city's medieval core, it's accessible via a steep staircase that leads you past an open kitchen where a view of the staff composes part of the allure. Chef and owner Beat Blum, a celebrity whose fame derives from his former administration of a more expensive restaurant near Lucerne, is the impresario who directs the show here. Within a severely spartan-looking dining room, you can order a la carte, but many locals prefer the market-fresh fixed-price menu, which is written on a blackboard. The menu might consist of such heavenly concoctions as braised tuna and free-range chicken served with braised pepperoni in a sweet-and-sour sauce; terrine of melon; beef filet with a vegetable purée; and a quark (white cheese) mousse served with pineapple and homemade ice cream. You'll select your wine from racks at one end of the dining room, a system that affords lots of interplay with the staff over whatever it is that you propose drinking with your meal.

Münstergasse 50. ✆ **031/311-98-44.** www.weinundsein.ch. Reservations required. Main courses 37F–45F; fixed-price menu 95F. MC, V. Tues–Sat 6pm–midnight. Closed 3 weeks in July–Aug. Bus: 10 or 12. Tram: 3, 5, or 9.

Expensive

Jack's Brasserie (Stadt Restaurant) ★★ FRENCH/CONTINENTAL Although the once-imperial-looking white elephant of a hotel (the Schweizerhof) that contained this restaurant has closed, Jack's continues to flourish, and it's a congenial spot for a fine meal or even a celebratory dinner. Decorated in a style that might remind you of a Lyonnais bistro, replete with paneling, banquettes, and etched glass, it bustles in a way that's chic, friendly, and matter-of-fact, all at the same time. Menu items include fish soup; the kind of Wiener schnitzels that hang over the sides of the plate; succulent versions of sole meunière and sea bass; veal head vinaigrette for real regional flavor; and smaller platters piled high with salads, risottos, and pastas.

Bahnhofplatz 11. ✆ **031/326-80-80.** www.schweizerhof-bern.ch. Reservations recommended. Main courses 29F–60F; fixed-price menu 88F. AE, DC, MC, V. Daily 11:45am–10:45pm (limited menu 1:45–6:15pm). Tram: 3, 9, or 12.

Zum Zähringer ★ CONTINENTAL No restaurant in Bern projects such a high mountain atmosphere. It occupies a weathered chalet that sits across a quiet street from the surging waters of the Aare, at the bottom of the steep cliff whose top contains the cathedral and the rest of medieval Bern. Many aspects, particularly its riverfront terrace, evoke a country inn that's far removed from the politics of the Swiss capital, but with a menu that's much more modern than you might have expected. Menu items are creative and filled with flair. They include asparagus mousse served with a tartare of salmon; veal shank in wine sauce; house-made terrine with green peppercorn and chutney; braised chicken livers with arugula; pikeperch with chive-flavored cream sauce; an artfully composed "hamburger" of goose meat with Asian vegetables and basmati rice; and scallops with spring vegetables served with olive-studded mashed potatoes.

Badgasse 1 (corner of Aarbergergasse). ✆ **031/312-08-88.** www.restaurant-zaehringer.ch. Reservations recommended. Main courses lunch 16F–58F, dinner 28F–58F. MC, V. Tues–Fri 11am–2:30pm; Mon–Sat 6–11:30pm.

Moderate

Kirchenfeld ★ INTERNATIONAL A 10-minute walk southeast of Bern's railway station delivers you to this Swiss-style bistro, the domain of Charlotte and Maurice Rota. They've hired a hardworking team of chefs to tempt your palate with a number of delights. Their impressive repertoire of dishes includes such starters as a Thai-style lemon-grass soup flavored with red curry, tartare of veal flavored with olive oil and lemon zest, or medallions of sole with a lemon risotto. The same fine craftsmanship extends to their main dishes, especially the breast of chicken flavored with a port-wine sauce or the rack of New Zealand lamb with a parsley sauce, a tapenade of olives, and roast potatoes. Their desserts are made fresh daily, many of them rich and creamy. In summer, they open their garden for dining.

Thunstrasse 5. ✆ **031/351-0278.** Reservations recommended. Fixed-price lunch 20F–30F, dinner 68F; main courses 25F–43F. AE, DC, MC, V. Tues–Sat 8am–11:30pm.

Mille Sens ★ EUROPEAN FUSION This old factory building converted into a restaurant by Urs Messerli is an intimate choice and one of the leading restaurants of Bern. The open kitchen and accessible wine cellar add to the warm ambience of this sophisticated eatery. Light menu items include a chicken club sandwich with curried mayonnaise, tomatoes, and pickles, and a vegetable-stuffed crepe with a sweet-and-sour-sauce topping. If you want a more substantial meal, we recommend you start with the seasonal green salad with melon and summer herbs, or cured Parma ham slices in a roulade with walnut-oil vinaigrette. For your main course, enticing dishes include sautéed breast of cornfed chicken with strips of cured ham and saffron-flavored risotto, and filet of Angus beef in a red-wine sauce along with strips of Mediterranean polenta.

Markethalle, Bubenbergplatz 9. ✆ **031/329-29-29.** www.millesens.ch. Reservations recommended. Main courses 28F–45F; business lunch 68F. AE, DC, MC, V. Mon–Thurs 11am–11:30pm; Fri 11am–1:30am; Sat 4pm–12:30am.

Restaurant National CONTINENTAL Few other restaurants in Bern convey as effectively a sense of difficult-to-influence, unhurried, old-fashioned Switzerland of the 1930s. It occupies a sprawling, high-ceilinged dining room on the street level of the also-recommended Hotel National, a stately looking building behind the railway station. The focus here is on "slow-cooked food," a low-key rebellion against anything edible that carries even a whiff of America-inspired modernity. Stews and ragouts here each tend to have been slow-simmered for hours, and vegetables and salads are very fresh and prepared simply, with a maximum of the original nutrients still intact. Examples include a daily variation of vegetable soup; a ragout of beef with summer vegetables and polenta; stewed vegetables within a "ring" of couscous; braised filets of salmon with herbs and onions; ricotta-stuffed tortellini with spinach and a tomato-enriched cream sauce; and calves' liver with Madeira sauce.

In the Hotel National, Hirschengraben 24. ✆ **031/381-19-88.** Reservations not needed. Main courses 21F–37F. AE, MC, V. Mon–Fri 11am–2pm; Mon–Sat 5:30–10pm. Tram: 3, 5, or 9.

SEEING THE SIGHTS

Before you rush off to sample the sightseeing attractions of the capital of Switzerland, stop in at the **Brasserie zum Bärengraben,** Muristalden 1 (© **031/331-42-18**), immediately across the street from the Bear Pits, the town's major attraction (see below). At a table here you can enjoy a slice of local life better than anywhere else. Many habitués settle down to read the morning news, ordering their favorite coffee, a beer, or a glass of wine.

The Top Attractions

Bärengraben (Bear Pits) ★ is a deep, half-moon-shaped den where the bears, Bern's mascots, have been kept since 1480. According to legend, when the duke of Zähringen established the town in 1191, he sent his hunters out into the surrounding woods, which were full of wild game. The duke promised to name the city after the first animal slain, which was a *Bär* (bear). Since then, the town has been known as Bärn (Bern). Today the bears are beloved, pampered, and fed by both residents and visitors (carrots are most appreciated). The Bear Pits lie on the opposite side of the **Nydeggbrücke (Nydegg Bridge)** from the rest of Old Town. The bridge was built over one of the gorges of the Aare River; its central stone arch has a span of 54m (177 ft.) and affords a sweeping view of the city. Below the Bear Pits, you can visit the **Rosengarten (Rose Gardens),** with its much-photographed view of the medieval sector of the city.

Zytgloggeturm (Clock Tower) ★ (*Zeitglocketurm* in standard German), on Kramgasse, was built in the 12th century and restored in the 16th century. Four minutes before every hour, crowds gather for the world's oldest and biggest horological puppet show. Mechanical bears, jesters, and emperors put on an animated performance. Staged since 1530, it's one of the longest-running acts in show business.

Cathedral of St. Vincent ★★ The *Münster* is one of the "newer" Gothic churches in Switzerland, dating from 1421. The belfry, however, was completed in 1893. The most exceptional feature of this three-aisle, pillared basilica is the tympanum over the main portal, which depicts the Last Judgment and contains more than 200 figures. You'll see mammoth 15th-century stained-glass windows in the chancel, but the most remarkable window, the *Dance of Death,* can be found in the Matter Chapel. The cathedral's 90m (295-ft.) belfry dominates Bern and offers a panoramic sweep of the Bernese Alps; to reach the viewing platform, you must climb 270 steps. The vista also includes the old town, its bridges, and the Aare River. Outside the basilica on Münsterplatz is the Moses Fountain, built in 1545.

Münsterplatz. © **031/312-04-62.** Free admission to cathedral; viewing platform 4F adults, 2F children. Easter–Oct Tues–Sat 10am–5pm, Sun 11:30am–5pm; Nov–Easter Tues–Fri 10am–noon and 2–4pm, Sat 10am–noon and 2–5pm, Sun 11:30am–2pm. Viewing platform closes 30 min. before cathedral. Bus: 12.

Kunstmuseum (Fine Arts Museum) ★ The focus of this museum is on a worthy collection of paintings, sculptures, and art objects crafted and created up until the end of the 19th century. There's a collection of Italian 14th-century primitives, including Fra Angelico's *Virgin and Child.* Swiss primitives include some from the "Masters of the Carnation." Hodler, the romantic artist, is represented by allegorical paintings depicting day and night. Impressionists include Monet, Manet, Sisley, and Cézanne, along with Delacroix and Bonnard. Surrealistic painters represented here include Dalí, Seligman, Oppenheim, and Tschumi. You'll also see works by Kandinsky, Modigliani, Matisse, Kirchner, Soutine, and Picasso, as well as contemporary Swiss artists.

Hodlerstrasse 12. ✆ **031/328-09-44.** www.kunstmuseumbern.ch. Permanent collection 7F adults, 5F seniors; special exhibitions 14F–18F extra. Tues 10am–9pm; Wed–Sun 10am–5pm. Bus: 20.

Zentrum Paul Klee (Paul Klee Collection) ★★★ Until around 2004, most of the artworks within this museum were contained within an overcrowded series of rooms within the also-recommended Kunstmuseum. That was before they were moved into a museum created expressly for them by Renzo Piano, one of the most celebrated architects of Italy. Today, in a location about 5km (3 miles) east of Bern's Altstadt, more than 4,000 works by the artist Paul Klee are proudly displayed as a kind of homage to Bern's "local son who made good." The painter was born in Switzerland in 1879. The local collection of his works includes 40 oils, 2,000 drawings, and many gouaches and watercolors. Klee had a style characterized by fantasy forms in line and light colors. There's a gift shop and a restaurant on the premises, serving platters of food Tuesday to Sunday 11:30am to 11:30pm.

Monument in Fruchtland 3. ✆ **031/359-01-01.** www.paulkleezentrum.ch. Admission 18F adults, 8F children 6–16, free for children 5 and under. Tues–Sun 10am–5pm (Thurs to 9pm). Bus: 12. Tram: 5.

Organized Tours

The tourist office conducts **walking tours** of Bern May to October. The daily meeting point is either at the tourist office at 11am or at Zytgloggeturm at 11am. The cost is 12F for adults, 6F for children 6 to 16, and free for children 5 and under. Depending on demand, this guided walking tour may or may not be offered by the time of your visit, since the focus of the tourist office's walking tours is to an increasing degree trained upon iPod-style audio guides that play a prerecorded 2-hour walking tour of Bern that can be started and stopped at any point, depending on the pace you want to maintain. Interspersed with descriptions of the Bernese monuments en route are anecdotes, folk songs, cheerful music, and far more than you might have initially thought of. These audio guides rent for 18F per day (14F per day for anyone who opts to buy a Bern Card), with a 50F deposit. For more information about how and where to acquire these audio guides, contact the Bern city tourist office.

THE SHOPPING SCENE

With a few exceptions, stores in the city center are open on Monday 9am to 7pm; on Tuesday, Wednesday, and Friday 8:15am to 6:30pm; on Thursday 8:15am to 9pm; and on Saturday 9am to 5pm.

With 6km (3¾ miles) of arcades, stores of all types are sheltered in Bern. The main shopping streets are **Spitalgasse, Kramgasse, Postgasse, Marktgasse,** and **Gerechtigkeitsgasse.**

BERN AFTER DARK

Most Bern residents get up early on weekday mornings, so they usually limit their evening entertainment to a drink or two at a historic cellar such as the Kornhauskeller or the Klötzlikeller. Nevertheless, the city offers several late-night clubs, with dancing and cabaret, for the nocturnally active international crowd. ***Bern Guide,*** distributed free by the tourist office, keeps a current list of cultural events.

The Performing Arts

The **Bern Symphony Orchestra** is one of the finest orchestras in Switzerland. Concerts by the orchestra are usually performed at the concert facilities in the **Bern Kursaal,** Herrengasse 25 (✆ **031/328-02-28;** www.kursaal-bern.ch). Except for a summer vacation, usually lasting from July to mid-August, the box office is open Monday to Friday noon to 6:30pm, Saturday 10am to 2pm. Tickets range from 20F to 55F.

Concerts with fewer musicians, especially chamber music, are often performed in any of four or five churches; in the auditorium at the **Konservatorium für Musik,** Kramgasse 36 (✆ **031/326-53-53;** www.konsibern.ch); or in the concert and recording facilities of **Radio Studio Bern,** Schwarztorstrasse 21 (✆ **031/388-91-11**).

Major opera and ballet performances are usually staged in what is generally acknowledged as Bern's most beautiful theater, the century-old **Stadttheater,** Kornhausplatz 20 (✆ **031/329-51-11;** www.stadttheaterbern.ch). Performances are often in German, and to a lesser degree in French, but even if you don't understand those languages, you might want to attend a performance. Other plays and dance programs, including ballet and cabaret, are presented in the **Theater am Käfigturm,** Spitalgasse 4 (✆ **031/311-61-00;** www.theater-am-kaefigturm.ch).

The Club & Bar Scene

The best gay bar in Bern, **Bar aux Petits Fours,** Kramgasse 67 (✆ **031/312-73-74**), attracts a multilingual, attractive, and international group of gay people, mostly men. There's no dance floor and no restaurant on the premises, but what you get is a low-key bar, filled with regular clients, where a newcomer can usually break the glacial freeze of Swiss reserve with a bit of effort.

Some people in Bern consider **Cesary Bar,** Kornhausplatz 11 (✆ **031/318-93-83**), the most stylish and intriguing bar in the Swiss capital, with an ongoing stream of some of its most beautiful people. Set on one of the showcase squares of the Old Town (behind a terrace that opens during clement weather for an additional 30 seats), it evokes the kind of stylish Milanese modernity you might have expected far to the south, beyond the mountains. There's a sampling of simple platters, especially sandwiches, priced at 10F to 15F each, many kinds of cocktails for the drink-a-holic set, and whiskeys with soda priced at around 14F each.

The **Come Back Bar,** Rathausgasse 42 (✆ **031/311-77-13**), is a tavern that's cosmopolitan and tolerant, and likely to attract lots of genuinely cool artists and hipsters. It occupies the cellar vaults below the medieval buildings of the Rathausgasse. Inside, blinking lights frame a discreet dance floor, and a long bar functions as a local hangout for many of the gay and gay-friendly residents of the Old Town. It's especially crowded on weekends, with a calmer, more low-key approach to things during weeknights.

Klötzlikeller, Gerechtigkeitsgasse 62 (✆ **031/311-74-56;** www.kloetzlikeller.ch), the oldest wine tavern in Bern, is near the Gerechtigkeitsbrunnen (Fountain of Justice), the first fountain you see on your walk from the Bärengraben (Bear Pits) to the Zytgloggeturm (Clock Tower). Watch for the lantern outside an angled cellar door. The well-known tavern dates from 1635 and is leased by the city to an independent operator. Some 20 different wines are sold by the glass, with prices starting at 8.50F.

Marians Jazzroom, in the Innere Enge Hotel, Engestrasse 54 (✆ **031/309-61-11;** www.mariansjazzroom.ch), serves up not only food and drink, but the finest traditional jazz performed live by top artists from around the world. Two concerts are presented each day, Tuesday to Saturday, starting at 7:30 and 10pm. On some Sundays there is a jazz brunch from 10am to 1:30pm.

Gambling

Grand Casino Kursaal Bern, on the fifth floor of the Allegro Hotel Bern, Kornhausstrasse 3 (✆ **031/339-55-55;** www.kursaal-bern.ch), is the only place in town to gamble. Indeed, it's a great spot for novices to learn because the size of bets is limited, and consequently, serious money rarely changes hands here. It's open daily noon to 2am, and admission is 10F. Drinks cost 10F to 15F. Within the immediate vicinity, and managed by the Allegro Hotel Bern, are three restaurants and two bars, plus a dance hall that charges a 10F cover. It's open Friday and Saturday 9pm to 3:30am, and Sunday 3 to 10pm.

The Bernese Oberland

The Bernese Oberland is one of the greatest tourist attractions in the world, mainly because it's one of the best areas for winter sports. The region sprawls between the Reuss River and Lake Geneva, with the Rhône forming its southern border. The area contains two lakes, the Thun and the Brienz, and takes in a portion of the Alps (culminating in the Finsteraarhorn at 4,207m/13,799 ft.). The canton of Bern, which encompasses most of the area, is the second largest in Switzerland and contains about 160 sq. km (62 sq. miles) of glaciers.

EXPLORING THE BERNESE OBERLAND

To compensate for the region's almost impossible geography, Swiss engineers have crisscrossed the Oberland with cogwheel railways (some of them still driven by steam), aerial cableways, and sinuous mountain roads. Though often a confusing experience, getting to a particular resort can be part of the fun. The region's busiest railroad junction, and the point where most travelers change trains for local railways, is **Interlaken.**

You can buy a **transportation pass** for the Bernese Oberland from the Swiss Rail System. The train ticket is valid for 7 days and costs 230F in second class and 279F in first class. Another pass, valid for 15 days, costs 277F in second class and 332F in first class. With the 7-day pass, you'll travel free for 3 days and pay a reduced fare for the final 4 days. With a 15-day pass, you'll travel free for 5 days and pay reduced fares for the rest of the time. Children travel at half price. The pass is valid on most railroads; all mountain trains, cable cars, chairlifts, and steamers on Lakes Thun and Brienz; and most postal-bus lines in the area. The ticket also qualifies you for a 25% reduction on the Kleine Scheidegg-Eigergletscher-Jungfraujoch railway, the Mürren-Schilthorn aerial cable line, and the bus to Grosse Scheidegg and Bussalp. You must purchase the pass at least 1 week before you arrive. For information about the pass, call ✆ **058/327-32-71.**

Because Interlaken is the focal point of one of the most complicated networks of ski lifts in the world, most visitors opt to buy a comprehensive pass that allows unlimited access to the cog railways, buses, cable cars, chairlifts, and gondolas (incorporating every mechanical lift in and around Interlaken, Wengen, Grindelwald, and

Mürren). Sold at the Interlaken tourist office (see "Interlaken," below) and tourist offices at the other leading resorts, it's called the **Jungfrau Top Ski Region Pass.** You can buy the 2-day pass for 126F, the 5-day pass for 265F, or the 7-day pass for 334F. Discounts of 10% are offered to seniors 62 and older, discounts of 20% to youths ages 16 to 20, and discounts of 50% to children 6 to 15. Kids 5 and under travel for only 10% of the above rates. This pass incorporates access to 44 ski lifts, 204km (127 miles) of well-groomed downhill runs, 99km (62 miles) of prepared walking and cross-country ski paths, and 50km (31 miles) of tobogganing runs. It covers the region around Grindelwald, Wengen, and Mürren.

BY MOUNTAIN BIKE Hundreds of miles of cycling paths riddle the Bernese Oberland, and most of them begin in Interlaken. Separate from the network of hiking paths, the bike routes are signposted and marked on rental maps distributed at bike-rental agencies; it's the law to use only specially signposted routes and not destroy plant and animal life or ride across private fields. Hikers, incidentally, are given the right of way over bikers. To make arrangements to rent a bike, call ✆ **033/823-15-34.** Rates usually begin at 45F per day, going up.

ON FOOT The Bernese Oberland is ideal for walkers and hikers. The natural terrain here will satisfy everyone from the most ambitious mountain hiker to the casual stroller.

Trails designed for walkers branch out from almost every junction. Most are paved and signposted, showing distances and estimated walking times. Tourist offices can suggest itineraries for walkers.

For the more athletic, itineraries include long hikes far afield in the mountains, with suggestions for overnight accommodations en route.

INTERLAKEN ★★★

Interlaken is the tourist capital of the Bernese Oberland. Cableways and cog railways designed for steeply inclined mountains connect it with most of the region's villages and dazzling sights, including the snowy heights of the Jungfrau, which rises a short distance to the south. Excursion possibilities from Interlaken are both numerous and dazzling.

This "town between the lakes" (Thun and Brienz) has been a vacation resort for over 300 years. Although it began as a summer resort, it developed into a year-round playground, altering its allure as the seasons change. During the winter skiers take advantage of the town's low prices. Interlaken charges low-season prices in January and February, when smaller resorts at higher altitudes are charging their highest rates of the year. The most expensive time to visit Interlaken is during midsummer, when high-altitude and snowless ski resorts often charge their lowest rates.

Essentials

GETTING THERE There are several trains daily between Zurich and Interlaken (2 hr.) and between Bern and Interlaken (40 min.). Frequent train service also connects Geneva with Interlaken (2½ hr.). For additional **rail information,** call ✆ **0900/300-300.**

Note: Although the town has two different railway stations, Interlaken East and Interlaken West, West is more convenient to the city's center.

If you're **driving** from Bern, head south on N6 to Spiez, then continue east on N8 to Interlaken.

The Bernese Oberland

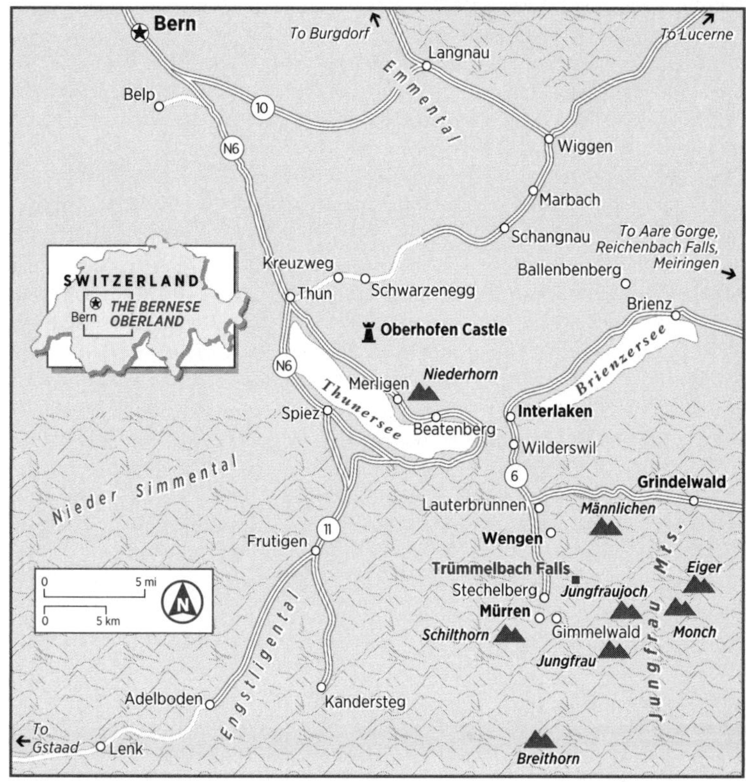

VISITOR INFORMATION The **Tourism Organization Interlaken** is in the Hotel Metropole at Höheweg 37 (✆ **033/826-53-00;** www.interlaken.ch). It's open July to mid-September Monday to Friday 8am to 7pm, Saturday 8am to 5pm, and Sunday 10am to noon and 5 to 7pm. From mid-September to October, hours are Monday to Friday 8am to 6pm and Saturday 9am to 1pm. Hours November to April are Monday to Friday 8am to noon and 1:30 to 6pm, and Saturday 9am to noon. May to June the office is open Monday to Friday 8am to 6pm and Saturday 8am to 4pm.

A **visitor's card** is granted to persons registered at local hotels and confers certain discounts to some of the local attractions.

GETTING AROUND **Train** arrivals are at either Interlaken East or Interlaken West. If you're loaded with luggage, you'll want to grab a taxi. However, after you've been deposited at one of the local hotels (nearly all of which are in the city center), you'll rarely need a taxi—the town is closely knit and best explored on foot. Buses are convenient for connections to the satellite towns and villages or heading to the outskirts. The **bus station** is at Areckstrasse 6 (✆ **033/828-88-28**).

Where to Stay

Hotel Interlaken ★ This is the resort's oldest hotel, receiving overnight guests since 1323, first as a hospital, later as a cloister, and, beginning in the early 1400s, as a tavern and inn. Guests have included Byron and Felix Mendelssohn. The hotel, directly east of the casino, has been gutted and rebuilt since, with a salmon-colored facade sporting baroque touches. The most expensive rooms have a few 19th-century antiques; the rest have conservative, modern furnishings with excellent beds and well-maintained bathrooms.

Höheweg 74, CH-3800 Interlaken. ✆ **033/826-68-68.** Fax 033/826-68-69. www.interlakenhotel.ch. 60 units. 220F–330F double. Rates include buffet breakfast. Half board 45F per person. AE, DC, MC, V. Free parking. **Amenities:** Restaurant; bar; room service; sauna. *In room:* TV, hair dryer, minibar, Wi-Fi (30F per 24 hr.).

Hotel Metropole ★★ Americans often prefer this sleek, modern hotel in the city center (the only skyscraper in the Bernese Oberland) to the aging palaces of Interlaken. The 18-story building was built in 1976 and has since been stylishly renovated. It's the most up-to-date and best-managed hotel in town. The small, standardized rooms have plush carpeting, modern furniture, and balconies. All units have neatly kept bathrooms. Those facing south have a panoramic view of Interlaken and the towering mountains. Try to steer clear of the 18 units in the annex, as they are a bit lackluster and have no views.

Höheweg 37, CH-3800 Interlaken. ✆ **800/223-5652** in the U.S., or 033/828-66-66. Fax 033/828-66-33. www.metropole-interlaken.ch. 95 units. 142F–363F double; 386F–593F suite. Half board 55F per person. AE, DC, MC, V. Parking 8F outside, 14F in garage. **Amenities:** 2 restaurants; bar; babysitting; indoor heated pool; room service; sauna. *In room:* TV, hair dryer, minibar, Wi-Fi (29F per 24 hr.).

Park-Hotel Mattenhof ★ This large, old-fashioned, government-rated four-star hotel is in a secluded area at the edge of a forest 2km (1¼ miles) south of the town center; you can reach it by heading away from the center toward Wilderswil. The exterior looks like a private castle, with its high, pointed roof, tower, loggias, and balconies. It was originally built as a simple and sedate pension in 1897, but adopted most of its mock-medieval form after a massive enlargement in 1906. During World War II it functioned as a hospital for injured soldiers, but for the past 30 years it has been managed by Peter Bühler and his family. They offer a calm retreat with terraces, manicured lawns, and panoramic views of the Alps. The salons are warmly decorated and sunny, and some of the small, well-furnished bedrooms have a view of the Jungfrau and the Niederhorn. All have well-kept bathrooms, and several also are equipped with a balcony.

Hauptstrasse, Matten, CH-3800 Interlaken. ✆ **033/828-12-81.** Fax 033/822-28-88. www.park-mattenhof.ch. 76 units. May–Sept 200F–260F double; off season 140F–170F double. AE, DC, MC, V. Free parking. **Amenities:** 2 restaurants; 2 bars; outdoor pool. *In room:* TV, hair dryer, minibar.

Royal St. Georges ★ Built in 1907, this oft-restored hotel is a historical landmark structure. In spite of several renovations, it has retained its traditional character. In contrast to the old-style architecture, the bedrooms are as up to date as tomorrow, ranging in size from small to exceedingly spacious. Some of the suites are in the Victorian style. Bathrooms are generous in size and often stylized, such as a special Art Nouveau bathroom. The hotel is divided into two parts, the Royal Wing and the St. Georges Wing, both linked to each other through a gangway. Unlike most peas-in-a-pod hotel rooms, this government-rated four-star choice offers individualized bedrooms—you'd be hard-pressed to find two rooms that are identical.

Höheweg 139, CH-3800 Interlaken. ✆ **033/822-75-75.** Fax 033/823-30-75. www.royal-stgeorges.ch. 95 units. 230F–330F double; 300F–430F suite. Rates include buffet breakfast. AE, DC, MC, V. **Amenities:** Restaurant; bar; Jacuzzi; room service; sauna. *In room:* TV, hair dryer, minibar, Wi-Fi (30F per 24 hr.).

The Swiss Inn This small Edwardian inn with balconies and gables offers good value. Mrs. Vreny Müller Lohner rents tasteful, simply decorated one- to three-room apartments equipped with comfortable beds and well-kept bathrooms. They accommodate two to six guests, and children's beds or cots are available. The inn has a lounge, a sitting area with a fireplace, and a grill for barbecues in the garden.

Général Guisanstrasse 23, CH-3800 Interlaken. ✆ **033/822-36-26.** Fax 033/823-23-03. www.swiss-inn.com. 9 units. 100F–160F double; 140F–200F apt for 2; 230F–250F apt for 4. AE, MC, V. Free parking. *In room:* TV, kitchenette (in some).

Where to Dine

Il Bellini ★★ INTERNATIONAL This is one of the finest restaurants in the Bernese Oberland. Established in 1994, it sits one floor above the lobby in the tallest hotel in Interlaken, the Metropole, and is outfitted in a graceful 19th-century rendition of pale pinks and greens. The fresh, good-tasting food is served with a discreet panache you might have expected in Italy, and includes an assortment of antipasti. You can order individual selections of hors d'oeuvres, including prosciutto with melon or smoked salmon and carpaccio. The soups, especially the homemade minestrone, are tasty, and the main courses include such delectable specialties as tender beefsteak Florentine, saltimbocca, and chicken breast grilled with tomatoes and mozzarella. The fish selections are limited but well chosen.

In the Hotel Metropole, Höheweg 37. ✆ **033/828-66-66.** www.metropole-interlaken.ch. Reservations recommended Fri–Sun. Main courses 22F–49F. AE, DC, MC, V. Daily 6:30–11pm.

Schuh SWISS/CHINESE/THAI This attractive restaurant and tearoom in the center of town has been known for its pastries since 1885. They are still the town's finest. The alpine building has a thick roof arched over the fourth-floor windows and, in back, a sunny terrace with a view of the Jungfrau and a well-kept lawn. The dining room has large windows and a Viennese ambience. A pianist provides music. The menu changes with the season, but Swiss regional dishes are a feature, along with several Asian dishes, notably from Thailand and China.

Höheweg 56. ✆ **033/888-80-50.** www.schuh-interlaken.ch. Main courses 15F–46F. AE, DC, MC, V. Apr–Sept Sun–Thurs 9am–11:30pm, Fri–Sat 9am–12:30am; Oct–Mar Sun–Thurs 9am–10pm, Fri–Sat 9am–11pm.

Spice India ★ INDIAN The Mathur family waited a long time for a restaurant of their own, and when they got it, they didn't disappoint. Ideally located in between the Hotel Metropole and the Chalet Hotel Oberland, this is a place where anyone who likes Indian food can enjoy a good meal served by people who are passionate about their restaurant. Among the top menu options are the Barrah kabobs (oven-grilled lamb marinated in yogurt with garlic and ginger paste), fish curry, filets of chicken, and basmati rice. There is also a vegetarian section on the menu, and from that we recommend the *baingan ka bharta* (chargrilled eggplant with yogurt and cheese) and the *aloo ghobi,* a potato-and-cauliflower dish. The decor is a little bland for an exotic restaurant, but the food makes up for it.

Postgasse 6. ✆ **033/821-00-91.** www.spice-india.net. Reservations required for large groups only. Main courses 22F–38F. AE, DC, MC, V. Tues–Sun noon–2:30pm; daily 6–10:30pm.

Exploring the Area

It's very simple: The best way to see everything in Interlaken is to walk. You can either randomly stroll around, enjoying the panoramic views in all directions, or follow a more structured walking tour. If you'd like some guidance, go to the tourist office (see above) and ask for a copy of *What a Wonderful World,* providing maps and listing hotels and local attractions.

The **Höheweg ★★** covers 14 hectares (35 acres) in the middle of town between the two train stations. Once the property of Augustinian monks, it was acquired in the mid–19th century by the hotel keepers of Interlaken, who turned it into a park. As you stroll along Höhenpromenade, admire the famous view of the Jungfrau mountain. Another beautiful sight is the flower clock at the Casino Kursaal. You're also sure to see some *fiacres* (horse-drawn cabs). The promenade is lined with hotels, cafes, and gardens.

Cross over the Aare River to **Unterseen,** built in 1280 by Berthold von Eschenbach. Here you can visit the parish church, with its late-Gothic tower dating from 1471. This is one of the most photographed sights in the Bernese Oberland. The Mönch appears to the left of the tower, the Jungfrau on the right.

Back in Interlaken, visit the **Touristik-Museum der Jungfrau-Region,** am Stadthausplatz, Obere Gasse 26 (✆ **033/822-98-39**), the first regional tourism museum in the country. Exhibitions show the growth of tourism in the region throughout the past 2 centuries. The museum is open from May to mid-October Tuesday to Sunday from 2 to 5pm. Admission is 5F, or 4F with a visitor's card. Children are charged 3F.

To see the sights of Interlaken, Matten, and Unterseen by **fiacre,** line up at the Interlaken West train station. The half-hour round-trip tour costs 40F for one or two, plus 12F for each additional person; children 7 to 16 are charged half fare, and those 6 and under ride free.

MÜRREN ★★

This village has a stunning location, high above the Lauterbrunnen Valley. At 1,624m (5,327 ft.), Mürren is the highest year-round inhabited village in the Bernese Oberland. It's an exciting excursion from Interlaken in the summer and a major ski resort in the winter. Downhill and slalom skiing were developed here in the 1920s. Mürren is also the birthplace of modern alpine racing.

Essentials

GETTING THERE Take the mountain **railway** from the Interlaken East rail station to Lauterbrunnen (trip time: 1 hr.). Once at Lauterbrunnen, you can take a cogwheel train the rest of the way to Mürren. Departures from Lauterbrunnen are every half-hour from 6:30am to 8:30pm daily, costing 10F one-way.

A regular **postal-bus** service goes once an hour from Lauterbrunnen to Stechelberg; the rest of the way you must travel by cable car, costing 8F round-trip. Departures are every half-hour, and the trip takes about 10 minutes.

Mürren is not accessible to traffic. You can **drive** as far as Stechelberg, the last town on the Lauterbrunnen Valley road, and switch to the cable car discussed above.

VISITOR INFORMATION The **Mürren Tourist Information Bureau** is at the Sportzentrum (✆ **033/856-86-86**). There is no street plan—follow the clearly indicated signs to the various hotels and commercial establishments. The office is open Monday to Friday 9am to noon and 2 to 7pm, Saturday and Sunday 2 to 6:30pm.

Where to Stay

Hotel Alpenruh Set in the most congested yet charming section of the village, the Alpenruh possesses an interior that's plusher than its chalet-style facade implies. The old building was upgraded in 1986 to government-rated three-star status without sacrificing any of its charm. The small rooms have pine paneling and a mix of antique and contemporary furniture, and most of them open onto a view of the Jungfrau. The hotel is owned by the company that operates the aerial cable cars to the Schilthorn's Piz Gloria, and you can get a voucher to have breakfast there. The hotel contains one of the finest restaurants in Mürren, offering a large and varied French-inspired menu.

CH-3825 Mürren. ✆ **033/856-88-00.** Fax 033/856-88-88. www.alpenruh-muerren.ch. 26 units. 160F–270F double. Rates include buffet breakfast. Half board 40F per person. AE, DC, MC, V. **Amenities:** Restaurant; bar; sauna. *In room:* TV, hair dryer, minibar.

Hotel Eiger ★ Founded in the 1920s, this chalet is the longest-established hotel in Mürren. The public rooms are warmly decorated, and many of the windows have panoramic views. The bedrooms are small, cozy, and comfortable and decorated in a typical alpine style. The hotel, managed by the Stähli family, lies across the street from the terminus of the cable car from Lauterbrunnen. The cuisine at the hotel's Eiger Stübli restaurant includes fondue and an international range of hearty and well-prepared specialties well suited to the alpine heights and chill.

Bahnhofplatz CH-3825 Mürren. ✆ **033/856-54-54.** Fax 033/856-54-56. www.hoteleiger.com. 44 units. 275F–335F double; 400F–530F suite. Rates include buffet breakfast. AE, DC, MC, V. Closed Easter to early June and mid-Sept to mid-Dec. **Amenities:** Restaurant; bar; babysitting; Jacuzzi; indoor heated pool; room service; sauna. *In room:* TV, hair dryer.

Hotel Jungfrau/Haus Mönch This government-rated three-star, 19th-century building, located a 3-minute walk from the Mürrenbahn, lies under gables behind green shutters, stucco, and brick walls. A comfortable annex was constructed in 1965; both buildings have an inviting, modern decor with open fireplaces, clusters of armchairs, and a shared dining room. The small bedrooms are bright and appealing. Twenty of the rooms are in the Hotel Jungfrau and 29 are across the street in the lodge. Units are equal in comfort.

Im Gruebi, CH-3825 Mürren. ✆ **033/856-64-64.** Fax 033/856-64-65. www.hoteljungfrau.ch. 49 units. 220F–240F double. Rates include buffet breakfast. AE, DC, MC, V. Closed mid-Apr to late May and mid-Oct to mid-Dec. **Amenities:** Restaurant; bar. *In room:* TV, Wi-Fi (free).

Where to Dine

Restaurant Piz Gloria ★ 🎁 SWISS Piz Gloria is the most dramatically located restaurant in Europe, with a setting so inhospitable and an architecture so futuristic that it was used as the setting for the James Bond film *On Her Majesty's Secret Service*. Designed like a big-windowed flying saucer and anchored solidly to the alpine bedrock, it was built at staggering expense in one of Switzerland's highest locations, the Schilthorn. Closed during blizzards, the restaurant has a terrace where newcomers should beware of becoming seriously sunburned by the rays of the high-altitude, unfiltered sunlight. You'll dine inside at long wooden tables, each with a wraparound view. The menu includes hearty dishes suited to the climate. There are both weekly and daily specials, ranging from chicken *cordon bleu* to filet of codfish with rice and vegetables. One spaghetti dish is named for James Bond; it's made with peppers, mushrooms, bacon, and Italian veal sausages. Another dish often served is puff pastry filled with veal and served with a white sauce. The 007 dessert is a bowl of five different scoops of ice cream topped with fruit.

Schilthorn. ✆ **033/856-21-40.** Main courses 20F–42F. AE, DC, MC, V. Daily from the 1st cable car's arrival until the last cable car's afternoon departure. The 1st departure from Stechelberg is at 7:25am in summer and at 7:55am in winter. The cable car's last departure from Schilthorn's summit is at 6pm in summer and 5pm in winter. Closed mid-Nov to early Dec and 1 week after Easter. The only access is via the Schilthorn cable car, which departs from the relatively low-lying town of Stechelberg and stops at 3 way stations, the most prominent of which is Mürren. Round-trip fare from Stechelberg 92F, round-trip fare from Mürren 71F.

Outdoor Activities

There are miles of downhill runs in the area. Mürren, one of the finest ski resorts of Switzerland, provides access to the Schilthorn at 2,923m (9,587 ft.), the start of a 15km (9⅓-mile) run that drops all the way to Lauterbrunnen. It also has one funicular railway, seven lifts, and two cable cars. A 1-day ski pass that includes the area around Schilthorn costs 59F, while a 6-day pass goes for 256F. For cross-country skiers, there's a 12km (7½-mile) track in the Lauterbrunnen Valley, 10 minutes by railway from Mürren.

The alpine **Sportzentrum (Sports Center),** in the middle of Mürren (✆ **033/856-86-86**), is one of the finest in the Bernese Oberland. The modern building has an indoor pool, a lounge, a snack bar, an outdoor skating rink, a tourist information office, and a children's playroom and library. There are facilities for squash, tennis, and curling. Hotel owners subsidize the operation, tacking the charges onto your hotel bill. Supplemental charges include 33F to 39F per hour for tennis, 25F per 45-minute session for squash, 19F per 2 hours' use of the sauna. The facility is usually open Monday to Friday from 9am to noon and 1 to 6:45pm, and from Christmas to April and July to mid-September also on Saturday from 1 to 6:30pm and Sunday from 1 to 5:30pm; but check locally as these times can vary.

WENGEN ★★★

The Mönch, Jungfrau, and Eiger loom above this sunny resort town built on a sheltered terrace high above the Lauterbrunnen Valley, at about 1,250m (4,100 ft.). Wengen (pronounced *Ven*-ghen) is one of the more chic and better-equipped ski and mountain resorts in the Bernese Oberland. It has 30 hotels in all price categories, as well as 500 apartments and chalets for rent.

In the 1830s, the International Lauberhorn Ski Race was established here. At that time Wengen was a farm community. The British were the first to popularize the resort, after World War I. Today parts of the area retain their rural charm. The main street, however, is filled with cafes, shops, and restaurants welcoming tourists. Robert Redford is a frequent visitor. No cars are allowed in Wengen, but the streets are still bustling with service vehicles and electric luggage carts.

Essentials

GETTING THERE Take the train from Interlaken West to Wengen with a change of train at Lauterbrunnen. Departures are every 45 minutes from 6:30am to 11pm, costing 16F one-way. After a stopover at Wengen, the train goes on to Kleine Scheidegg and Jungfraujoch. For **rail information,** call ✆ **0900/300-300.**

If you're driving, head south from Interlaken toward Wilderswil, following the minor signposted road to Lauterbrunnen, where you'll find garages and open-air spaces for parking. You cannot drive to Wengen—you must take the train. You can park in one of the garages at Lauterbrunnen for 12F to 18F a day. Trains from Lauterbrunnen to Wengen leave at the rate of one every 15 minutes from 6am to midnight, costing 8F one-way.

VISITOR INFORMATION There are no street names; hotels, restaurants, and other major establishments are signposted with directional signs, which make them relatively easy to find. The **Wengen Tourist Information Office** (✆ **033/855-14-14;** www.mywengen.ch) is in the center of the resort. It's open mid-June to mid-September and mid-December to Easter only, Monday to Saturday 9am to noon and 2 to 5pm.

Exploring the Area

The **ski area** around Wengen is highly developed, with ski trails carved into the sides of Männlichen, Kleine Scheidegg, Lauberhorn, and Eigergletscher. A triumph of alpine engineering, the town and its region contain three mountain railways, two aerial cableways, one gondola, 31 lifts, and 250km (155 miles) of downhill runs. You'll also find a branch of the Swiss Ski School, more than 11km (7 miles) of trails for cross-country skiing, an indoor and outdoor skating rink, a curling hall, an indoor swimming pool, and a day nursery.

During the summer the district attracts hill climbers from all over Europe. The **hiking trails** are well maintained and carefully marked, with dozens of unusual detours to hidden lakes and panoramas. Wengen also has five public tennis courts available through the tourist office (see above), a natural skating rink (*natureisbahn*), and a partially sheltered indoor rink (*kunsteisbahn*). The hours these rinks keep are subject to change, so check with the tourist office for details.

Nearby Attractions

From Wengen and Grindelwald, a number of excursions take you up and down the Lauterbrunnen Valley. You can visit **Trümmelbach Falls ★★★**, which plunges in five powerful cascades through a gorge. You can take an elevator built through the rock to a series of galleries (bring a raincoat). The last stop is at a wall where the upper fall descends. The falls can be visited from the end of May to June and in September and October daily from 9am to 5pm; in July and August daily from 8:30am to 6pm. They're closed during other months. Admission is 11F for adults, 4F for children 6 to 16, and free for children 5 and under. It takes about 45 minutes to reach the falls on foot. For information, call ✆ **033/855-32-32.** A postal bus from Lauterbrunnen (only 15 min. from Wengen by train) stops at Trümmelbach Falls. It costs only 4F for adults, 3F for children, and departs once an hour from Lauterbrunnen. For information, call ✆ **033/828-70-38.**

You might also want to visit the base of the **Staubbach Waterfall ★★**, which plunges nearly 300m (984 ft.) in a sheer drop over a rock wall in the valley above Lauterbrunnen. Lord Byron compared this waterfall to the "tail of the pale horse ridden by Death in the Apocalypse." Staubbach can be reached from the resort village of Lauterbrunnen, which lies only 15 minutes from Wengen by train (see "Essentials," above). From the center of Lauterbrunnen, follow the signposts along a walkway running along a creek and then be prepared for some steep stairs to reach the viewing point for the falls.

Where to Stay

All the hotels in Wengen are mobbed most of the winter, so make reservations well in advance if you plan to arrive during ski season.

Hotel Alpenrose ★★ A longtime favorite of ours, this hotel is invitingly traditional, with a family atmosphere. Most of the cozy, well-furnished bedrooms have views over the Lauterbrunnen Valley, lots of light, and plenty of pine paneling. Accommodations facing south are more desirable because they get more sunlight and so they're slightly higher in price. The hotel is efficiently run and filled with cozy public rooms and a large formal dining area where, if you've been gathering wildflowers that day, you'll probably find them in a vase at your supper. In ski season, fans of this hotel, all sports lovers, fill up the rooms. Staying on-site for your meals is hardly a hardship, as the food is well prepared with fresh ingredients whenever possible. Old favorites pepper the menu, including fondue bourguignon, trout with almonds, and terrine maison.

CH-3823 Wengen. ✆ **033/855-32-16.** Fax 033/855-15-18. www.alpenrose.ch. 50 units. Winter 272F–424F double; summer 232F–368F double. Rates include half board. AE, DC, MC, V. **Amenities:** Restaurant; bar. *In room:* TV.

Hotel Regina ★★ Wengen's most time-honored hotel lies in an embellished Victorian elephant of a building with balconies and lots of charm. Guido Meyer has been known to arrange unusual concerts for his guests (once, during our stay, a group of Oklahoma high-school students gave a concert on the front lawn). One of the public rooms has a baronial carved-stone fireplace. The midsize to spacious bedrooms are comfortable and cozy, each well furnished and immaculately maintained. Maintenance is high, as is the level of service.

CH-3823 Wengen. ✆ **033/856-58-58.** Fax 033/856-58-50. www.hotelregina.ch. 90 units. Winter 300F–460F double, 400F–500F junior suite; summer 260F–360F double, 340F–400F junior suite. Rates include half board. AE, DC, MC, V. Closed mid-Oct to mid-Dec. **Amenities:** 2 restaurants; bar; babysitting; exercise room; room service; sauna. *In room:* TV, hair dryer, minibar, Wi-Fi (free).

Where to Dine

Arvenstube SWISS This is a local favorite, with pine-wood panels and a polite crew ready to serve you. The well-prepared menu may include smoked trout with horseradish, air-dried alpine beef, smoked breast of goose, Bernese-style beef with mushrooms, filet of fera (a lake fish), and veal steak Alfredo and morels. Three kinds of fondue are also offered. The fondue bourguignon is particularly stunning with 40 garnitures—you must order it a day in advance. The Valais-style braserade of beef cooks over a small flame at your table.

In the Hotel Eiger. ✆ **033/856-05-05.** Reservations recommended. Main courses 20F–56F. AE, DC, MC, V. Daily 11am–2pm and 6–9:30pm (all day in winter). Closed May.

Hotel Hirschen Restaurant 🎁 SWISS This quiet retreat at the foot of the slopes has true alpine flavor. The rear dining room is decorated with hunting trophies, pewter, and wine racks. Johannes Abplanalp and his family offer a dinner special called Galgenspiess—filet of beef, veal, and pork flambéed at your table. Other dishes include filet of breaded pork, rump steak Café de Paris, and fondue Bacchus (in white-wine sauce), *bourguignon* (hot oil), or *chinoise* (hot bouillon). A hearty lunch is *Winzerrösti,* consisting of country ham, cheese, and a fried egg with homemade *rösti.*

CH-3823 Wengen. ✆ **033/855-15-44.** Reservations recommended. Main courses 14F–47F. MC, V. Fri–Mon 6–11pm. Closed mid-Apr to May and late Sept to mid-Dec.

GRINDELWALD ★★★

The "glacier village" of Grindelwald, at 1,033m (3,388 ft.), is set against a backdrop of the Wetterhorn and the towering north face of the Eiger. It's both a winter and a summer resort.

Unlike Wengen and Mürren, it's the only major resort in the Jungfrau region that can be reached by car. Because of its accessibility, Grindelwald is often crowded with visitors, many of whom come just for the day.

Grindelwald is surrounded by folkloric hamlets, swift streams, and as much alpine beauty as you're likely to find anywhere in Switzerland. Although at first the hiking options and cable car networks might seem baffling, the tourist office will provide maps of the local peaks and valleys and help clear up any confusion.

Essentials

GETTING THERE The **Bernese Oberland Railway (BOB)** leaves from the Interlaken East station. The trip takes 35 minutes. Call ✆ **0900/300-300** for information.

If you're **driving,** take the Wilderswil road south from Interlaken and follow the signs all the way to Grindelwald.

VISITOR INFORMATION The resort doesn't use street names or numbers; instead of street names, hotel direction signs are used to locate places. If you're booked into a hotel or tourist home in Grindelwald, request a pass at your hotel that will entitle you to many discounts, especially on mountain rides.

The tourist office is at the **Sportzentrum,** on Hauptstrasse (✆ **033/854-12-12**). It's open Monday to Friday 8am to noon and 1:30 to 6pm, and Saturday and Sunday 8am to noon and 1:30 to 5pm.

Where to Stay

Grand Hotel Regina ★★★ Across from the Grindelwald train station, this hotel is part rustic and part urban slick and dates from the turn of the 20th century. It became a hotel in 1953 and still evokes the glamour of that era. The facade of the oldest part has an imposing set of turrets with red-tile roofs. One of the salons has Victorian chairs clustered around bridge tables, with sculpture in wall niches. The collection of art includes etchings, gouaches, and oil paintings. The large bedrooms, done in various styles, are comfortable and contain well-maintained bathrooms. These elegantly furnished rooms are your finest choice for a vacation here in either summer or winter. Most bedrooms enjoy panoramic views.

CH-3818 Grindelwald. ✆ **800/223-6800** in the U.S., or 033/854-86-00. Fax 033/854-86-88. www.grandregina.ch. 90 units. 630F–740F double; 760F–2,690F suite. AE, DC, MC, V. Free parking outside, 20F in garage. Closed mid-Oct to mid-Dec. **Amenities:** 2 restaurants; 2 bars; babysitting; exercise room; 2 pools (1 heated indoor); room service; spa. *In room:* TV, minibar, Wi-Fi (5F per 30 min.).

Hotel Eiger This hotel looks like a collection of interconnected balconies from the outside, each on a different plane and built of contrasting shades of white stucco and natural wood. The interior is attractive, simple, and unpretentious, with lots of warmly tinted wood, hanging lamps, and contrasting lights. The small to midsize bedrooms are comfortable, well furnished, and alpine cozy. Maintenance is high, and the hotel staff is extremely inviting and hospitable.

CH-3818 Grindelwald. ✆ **033/854-31-31.** Fax 033/854-31-30. www.eiger-grindelwald.ch. 50 units. Winter 124F–194F double, 154F–269F per person suite; summer 154F–184F per person double, 179F–264F per person suite. Rates include buffet breakfast. Half board 35F per person. AE, DC, MC, V. Free parking outdoors, 6F–12F in garage. **Amenities:** 2 restaurants; 2 bars; babysitting; exercise room; spa; Wi-Fi (free). *In room:* TV, hair dryer, minibar.

Romantik Hotel Schweizerhof ★★ Originally built in 1912 on the former site of an ironmonger's and blacksmith's shop, this spacious and gracious hotel sits on the main street of Grindelwald, close to the railway station, behind a facade of very dark wood that resembles an oft-expanded chalet. The public areas are comfortably outfitted with deep upholstered wing chairs and sofas, and bedrooms have tile-sheathed bathrooms, carved-pine panels, comfortable furniture, and lots of folkloric charm. Staff is helpful and friendly.

CH-3818 Grindelwald. ✆ **033/854-58-58.** Fax 033/854-58-59. www.hotel-schweizerhof.com. 52 units. 400F–550F double; 570F–1,142F suite. Rates include half board. AE, DC, V. Closed Oct to mid-Dec and Apr 6 to late May. **Amenities:** 2 restaurants; bar; babysitting; exercise room; indoor heated pool; room service; spa; Wi-Fi (free, in lobby). *In room:* A/C, TV, hair dryer, minibar.

Where to Dine

Il Mercato ITALIAN/SWISS The decor is elegant and alpine, with Italian touches you might expect in the Ticino. The dining room's visual centerpiece is a large window with a sweeping view over the mountains. During warm weather, tables are set out on a flower-dotted terrace. Menu items include virtually everything from the Italian repertoire, with an emphasis on cold-weather dishes from the Val d'Aosta (northern Italy's milk and cheese district). There's a tempting array of salads, pizzas, pastas, risottos, and grilled veal, beef, and chicken dishes, always with fresh ingredients.

In the Hotel Spinne. ✆ **033/854-88-88.** www.spinne.ch. Reservations recommended. Main courses 18F–54F. AE, DC, MC, V. Daily noon–2pm and 6–9:30pm. Closed Oct to mid-Dec.

Restaurant Français ★★ INTERNATIONAL This is the best restaurant in Grindelwald. The owner, Urs Hauser, is always in the dining room during meal hours to aid and advise diners. Special buffets are a feature of the restaurant. As you listen to the soothing sounds of a live pianist, you can study the menu, which changes frequently. Just to give you an idea, you may be served an appetizer of game terrine, Grindelwald air-dried meat, or thinly sliced lamb carpaccio. Fish dishes may include poached filet of turbot served on zucchini and potato rounds with a yellow-red pepper sauce, or fried filet of salmon with a truffle-butter sauce. Main dishes are likely to include lamb entrecôte in a coating of peppercorns, or breast of guinea fowl with red wine and prunes. The cuisine intelligently blends flavors with imagination and zest. The cooks in the kitchen really know their stuff, and the wine list is among the finest in the area.

In the Hotel Belvedere. ✆ **033/854-54-54.** Reservations recommended. Main courses 36F–41F; 6-course gourmet menu 69F. AE, DC, MC, V. Daily noon–1pm and 6:45–9pm.

Outdoor Activities

For details about the tours below, including seasonal changes, consult the tourist office (see above).

If you've come to Switzerland to see the Alps, Grindelwald and its surroundings offer dozens of challenging paths and mountain trails that are well marked and carefully maintained. Outdoor adventures range from an exhilarating ramble across the gentle incline of an alpine valley to a dangerous trek with ropes and pitons along the north face of Mount Eiger. The choice depends on your inclination and your skills. A map showing the region's paths and trails is available at the town's tourist office.

If you're adventurous enough to be tempted by peaks 3,900m (12,792 ft.) high or higher, or if you'd like to learn the proper way to climb rocks and ice, contact the **Bergsteigerzentrum** (✆ **033/854-12-90**), which lies adjacent to the Sunstar Hotel in Grindelwald. The Bergsteigerzentrum can also provide information on a modest 1-day hiking tour suitable for anyone capable of hiking in boots for 2 or 3 hours.

In winter Grindelwald is one of the major ski resorts of Europe, perfect as a base for skiing in the Jungfrau ski region. It has 22 lifts, eight funiculars, a trio of cable cars, and more than 160km (100 miles) of downhill runs. Snowboarders and novice skiers are also welcome. It's a ski circus for all ages and various skills.

In the winter skiers take the cableway to **Männlichen,** at 2,200m (7,216 ft.), which opens onto a panoramic vista of the treacherous Eiger. From here there is no direct run back to Wengen; however, skiers can enjoy an uninterrupted ski trail stretching 7.2km (4½ miles) to Grindelwald. The cost of the Männlichen cable car (Grindelwald-Grund to Männlichen) is 35F each way, or 58F round-trip. For information, call the departure point for the **Männlichen Bahn** in Grindelwald (✆ **033/854-80-80**).

GSTAAD ★★

Against a backdrop of glaciers and mountain lakes, Gstaad is a haven for the rich and famous. Frequent visitors include King Juan Carlos II of Spain, Elizabeth Taylor, and Julie Andrews.

Built at the junction of four quiet valleys near the southern tip of the Bernese Oberland, Gstaad was once only a place to change horses during the grueling voyage through the Oberland. But as the railroad lines developed, it grew into a resort. After the opening of the deluxe Alpina Grand Hotel, wealthy Russian and Hungarian families started coming, bringing their entourages of valets, nannies, and translators. In 1912, 2 years before the outbreak of World War I, a hotel that was to become one of the most legendary in Switzerland, the Palace, opened, promising the ultimate in luxury. In 1916 Le Rosey school (listed in the *Guinness Book of World Records* as "the most expensive prep school in the world") opened its doors in the satellite town of Tolle. The school contributed to the fame of Gstaad, as prestigious visitors, including King Leopold of Belgium, came to see their children.

The town, by far the most chic in the Bernese Oberland, retains much of its turn-of-the-20th-century charm. Some first-time visitors, however, say that the resort is a bore if you can't afford to stay at the Gstaad Palace or mingle with the stars in their private chalets. Yet the town has many moderately priced hotels, taverns, and guesthouses with an allure of their own. Many of the bistros and cafes close from late April to mid-June and from October to mid-December.

Essentials

GETTING THERE Gstaad is on the local train line connecting Interlaken with Montreux and several smaller towns in central-southwest Switzerland. About a dozen trains come into Gstaad every day from both of those cities, each of which is a railway junction with good connections to the rest of Switzerland. Travel time from Montreux can be as little as an hour and 20 minutes; from Interlaken, about 30 minutes, sometimes with a change of train at the hamlet of Zweisimmen. Call ✆ **0900/300-300** for **rail schedules** and information.

If you're **driving** from Spiez, head southwest on Route 11; from Bulle, head south and then east on Route 11.

VISITOR INFORMATION Some streets have names; others are placed outside street plans, but there are directional signs to lead you to hotels and restaurants. The **Gstaad-Saanenland Tourist Association,** CH-3780 Gstaad (✆ **033/748-81-81;** www.gstaad.ch), is a useful source of information, open July and August Monday to Friday from 8:30am to 6:30pm, Saturday 9am to 6pm, and Sunday 10am to 5pm; September to June, hours are Monday to Friday 8:30am to noon and 1:30 to 6pm, and Saturday 10am to noon and 1:30 to 5pm.

Where to Stay

Grand Hotel Park ★★★ This landmark hotel lives again. In 1990 one of the Oberland's most venerable hotels was demolished and rebuilt in a style that reflects the 1910 original. Associated with, and partially owned by, investors in the Palace Hotel, it sits astride a hill overlooking the center of the town and across from the Palace. Its design, including the bedrooms, evokes a mixture of the Edwardian age with a posh ski resort you might find in Vail, Colorado. Standard rooms measure a generous 35 sq. m (377 sq. ft.), and the more expensive rooms facing south open onto views of the Wispile, Eggli, and Glacier des Diablerets. Each room comes with an immaculately kept bathroom. Although some of the original turn-of-the-20th-century furniture was incorporated into the new design, much of the interior is sleekly modern and richly accessorized with decorative and structural bands of chiseled granite, polished marble, and burnished pine. It's also home to the first Louis Vuitton boutique in a European hotel.

Wispilenstrasse CH-3780 Gstaad. ✆ **033/748-98-00.** Fax 033/748-98-08. www.grandhotelpark.ch. 99 units. Winter 690F–990F double, from 1,540F suite; summer 395F–920F double, from 1,200F suite. Rates include buffet breakfast. AE, DC, MC, V. Parking 20F in winter, free in summer. Closed mid-Mar to mid-June and mid-Sept to mid-Dec. **Amenities:** 5 restaurants; 3 bars; babysitting; concierge; exercise room; 2 pools (1 indoor heated saltwater); room service; spa. *In room:* TV/DVD, hair dryer, minibar, Wi-Fi (25F per 24 hr.).

Hostellerie Alpenrose ★★★ For those who seek the charm of a small inn, this is the preferred choice in the area—it's the only Relais & Châteaux listing within 48km (30 miles). The pine-paneled rooms are exquisitely decorated with rustic furnishings, and the small bedrooms are comfortable and tastefully appointed. Its kindly host, Michel von Siebenthal, is a memorable fellow, setting the fashionable tone of the chalet, which is famous for its restaurant. Its varied menu, offering regional cuisine, changes every 3 weeks. Lobster is almost always on the menu, but look for marinated salmon, which remains a delectable house specialty.

Saanenmöserstrasse, CH-3778 Schönried-Gstaad. ✆ **033/748-91-91.** Fax 033/748-91-92. www.hotelalpenrose.ch. 19 units. 390F–630F double; 420F–830F suite. Rates include half board. AE, DC, MC, V. Free parking. Closed mid-Oct to mid-Dec. **Amenities:** 2 restaurants; 2 bars; bikes; Jacuzzi; room service; sauna. *In room:* TV, minibar, Wi-Fi (free).

Hotel Olden ★★ This is one of the most low-key and gracefully unpretentious hotels in Gstaad, a sort of Victorian country inn set amid a sometimes chillingly glamorous landscape—or at least a chillingly expensive landscape. The Olden has a facade painted with regional floral designs and pithy bits of folk wisdom. Embellishments are carved or painted into the stone lintels around many of the doors. The small to midsize rooms are generally furnished in a typical alpine style, although the bathrooms have been modernized. Some guests are housed in the adjacent chalet wing (the comfort level and amenities are the same).

Hauptstrasse, CH-3780 Gstaad. ✆ **033/748-49-50.** Fax 033/748-49-59. www.hotelolden.ch. 16 units. Winter 500F–680F double, 680F–850F junior suite, 780F–1,680F suite; summer 350F–550F double, 550F–690F junior suite, 650F–1,500F suite. Rates include continental breakfast. AE, DC, MC, V. Parking 20F. Closed late Apr to late May. **Amenities:** Restaurant; bar; room service. *In room:* TV, minibar, Wi-Fi (free).

Palace Hotel Gstaad ★★★ This other landmark hotel on a wooded hill overlooks the center of Gstaad. Opened in 1912, the Palace has mock-fortified corner towers and a neomedieval facade. The designer, Valentino, called the architecture a "brutal Sleeping Beauty castle." It's one of the most sought-after luxury hideaways in the world, attracting corporation heads, movie stars, and fashionable aristocrats, many of whom return every winter and stay a long time, earning the Palace the reputation as "Switzerland's largest family boardinghouse." Owner and manager Ernst Scherz's motto is "Every king is a client, and every client is a king." It's true—if you can afford it.

The nerve center of this chic citadel is an elegantly paneled main salon, with an "eternal flame" burning in the baronial stone fireplace (though this flame isn't so eternal—it burns only in winter). Radiating hallways lead to superb restaurants, bars, discos, and sports facilities. The plush, spacious rooms are tastefully furnished and very distinguished.

Palacestrasse 1, CH-3780 Gstaad. ✆ **800/223-6800** in the U.S., or 033/748-50-00. Fax 033/748-50-01. www.palace.ch. 104 units. Winter 720F–1,890F double, 1,350F–2,390F junior suite, 2,350F–6,100F suite; summer 650F–1,210F double, 1,130F–1,480F junior suite, 2,050F–4,600F suite. Rates include half board. AE, DC, MC, V. Free parking outside, 20F in garage. Closed end of Mar to mid-June and late Sept to shortly before Christmas (dates vary). **Amenities:** 5 restaurants; 2 bars; babysitting; children's center; concierge; exercise room; health club & spa; 2 pools (1 heated indoor); room service; 4 outdoor tennis courts (lit). *In room:* TV, hair dryer, minibar, Wi-Fi (25F per 24 hr.).

Where to Dine

Olden Restaurant ★★ MEDITERRANEAN/FRENCH This is the most formal restaurant of the several dining choices available in the Hotel Olden. On the street level, it attracts the latest visiting celebrity with its country charm. Meals are formally served in the pine-paneled dining room. The always-tempting menu might include smoked salmon, fresh gooseliver terrine, shrimp bisque with green peppercorns, house-style tagliatelle, raclette, veal cutlet Milanese, Scottish lamb, or sea bass with olives, potatoes, tomatoes, and onions. Although there are grander restaurants in Gstaad, as well as dining rooms serving a more haute cuisine, the Olden remains our most satisfying choice year after year.

In the Hotel Olden, Hauptstrasse. ✆ **033/744-34-44.** Reservations recommended. Main courses 27F–73F. AE, DC, MC, V. Tues–Sun noon–2:30pm and 6:30–10:30pm. Closed mid-Apr to mid-May and 2 weeks in Nov.

Restaurant Chesery ★★★ FRENCH/SWISS At an elevation of 1,097m (3,598 ft.), this is one of the 10 best restaurants in Switzerland. The floors are pink marble and the walls are polished pine. The menu changes daily, based on the freshest ingredients available. The chef is a perfectionist and shops far and wide for only the finest of produce with which to dazzle his clients—grouse from Scotland, Charolais beef from France, truffles from Umbria. You may sample his salt-crusted sea bass with wild rice, chicken Houban (a very special breed from France), Scottish lamb with a crust of fresh herbs, or rack of venison with whortleberries. In the basement bar,

Casino, a piano player entertains nightly, and the bar is open from 6pm to 3am, when the last ski bunny departs.

Lauenenstrasse. ✆ **033/744-24-51.** www.chesery.ch. Reservations required. Main courses 37F–68F; fixed-price lunch 78F–82F, dinner 168F. AE, DC, MC, V. Tues–Sun 11:30am–2:30pm and 7pm–midnight. Closed mid-Oct to mid-Dec, Easter to mid-June, and in winter (Tues–Fri) for lunch.

Outdoor Activities

Gstaad is a resort rich in entertainment and sports facilities. Many skiers stay in Gstaad by night and venture to one of the nearby ski resorts during the day. Cable cars take passengers to altitudes of 1,500m and 3,000m (4,920 ft. and 9,840 ft.)—at the higher altitudes there's skiing even in the summer. Other facilities include tennis courts, heated indoor and outdoor swimming pools, and about 320km (200 miles) of hiking trails. Many of these scenic trails are possible to walk or hike year-round (the tourist office will advise). The **Gstaad International Tennis Tournament,** beginning the first Saturday in July, is the most important tennis event in Switzerland.

Skiers setting off from Gstaad have access to 70 lifts, mountain railroads, and gondolas. The altitude of Gstaad's highest skiable mountain is 1,965m (6,445 ft.), with a vertical drop of 1,066m (3,496 ft.). Most beginner and intermediate runs are east of the village in Eggli, a ski area reached by cable car. Eggli has a sunny, southern exposure. Wispellan-Sanetch is favored for afternoon skiing, with lots of runs down to the village. At its summit is the Glacier des Diablerets, at a height of 2,970m (9,741 ft.). Wasserngrat, reached from the south side of the resort, is yet another skiing area. Advanced skiers prize Wasserngrat for its powder skiing on steep slopes.

Index

A

B

C

E

G

H

J

K

L

N

O

Q

R

S

NOTES